GAINSBOROUGH
STALLIONS

In England	CADEA ...
	Standin... ...shire

FANTASTIC LIGHT by Rahy - ...
Standing at Dalham Hall Stud, Newmarket, Suffolk

GREEN DESERT by Danzig - Foreign Courier
Standing at Shadwell Stud, Thetford, Norfolk

ROYAL APPLAUSE by Waajib - Flying Melody
Standing at The Royal Studs, Sandringham, Norfolk

STORMING HOME by Machiavellian - Try To Catch Me
Standing at Shadwell Stud, Thetford, Norfolk

ZILZAL by Nureyev - French Charmer
Standing at Lanwades Stud, Newmarket, Suffolk

In Ireland

DILSHAAN by Darshaan - Avila
Standing at Tara Stud, Tara, Co. Meath

KEY OF LUCK by Chief's Crown - Balbonella
Standing at Tara Stud, Tara, Co. Meath

KRIS KIN by Kris S - Angel In My Heart
Standing at Derrinstown Stud, Maynooth, Co. Kildare

TOUCH OF THE BLUES by Cadeaux Genereux - Silabteni
Standing at The Irish National Stud, Co. Kildare

In USA

ELUSIVE QUALITY by Gone West - Touch of Greatness
Standing at Gainsborough Farm, Versailles, Kentucky

QUIET AMERICAN by Fappiano - Demure
Standing at Gainsborough Farm, Versailles, Kentucky

RAHY by Blushing Groom - Glorious Song
Standing at Three Chimneys Farm, Lexington, Kentucky

SHADEED by Nijinsky - Continual
Standing at Gainsborough Farm, Versailles, Kentucky

In Canada

ASCOT KNIGHT by Danzig - Bambee T.T.
Standing at Windfields Farm, Oshawa, Ontario

Enq to: M.H. Goodbody, **Gainsborough Stud**, Woolton Hill, Newbury, Berkshire RG20 9TE
Tel: +44 (0) 1635 253273   Fax: +44 (0) 1635 254690
E: office@gainsborough-stud.com   W: www.gainsborough-equine.com

AGE, WEIGHT & DISTANCE TABLE
Timeform's scale of weight-for-age for the flat

Dist	Age	Jan 1-16	Jan 17-31	Feb 1-16	Feb 17-28	Mar 1-16	Mar 17-31	Apr 1-16	Apr 17-30	May 1-16	May 17-31	June 1-16	June 17-30
5f	4	10–0	10–0	10–0	10–0	10–0	10–0	10–0	10–0	10–0	10–0	10–0	10–0
	3	9—5	9—5	9—6	9—7	9—7	9—8	9—8	9—9	9—9	9-10	9-10	9-11
	2						8—0	8—1	8—3	8—4	8—5	8—6	8—7
6f	4	10–0	10–0	10–0	10–0	10–0	10–0	10–0	10–0	10–0	10–0	10–0	10–0
	3	9—2	9—3	9—4	9—5	9—5	9—6	9—7	9—7	9—8	9—8	9—9	9—9
	2									8—0	8—2	8—3	8—4
7f	4	9-13	9-13	10–0	10–0	10–0	10–0	10–0	10–0	10–0	10–0	10–0	10–0
	3	9—0	9—1	9—2	9—3	9—4	9—4	9—5	9—6	9—6	9—7	9—8	9—8
	2											7-13	8—1
1m	4	9-13	9-13	9-13	9-13	10–0	10–0	10–0	10–0	10–0	10–0	10–0	10–0
	3	8-12	8-13	9—0	9—1	9—2	9—2	9—3	9—4	9—5	9—5	9—6	9—7
	2												
9f	4	9-12	9-12	9-12	9-13	9-13	9-13	9-13	10–0	10–0	10–0	10–0	10–0
	3	8-10	8-11	8-12	8-13	9—0	9—1	9—2	9—2	9—3	9—4	9—5	9—5
	2												
1¼m	4	9-11	9-12	9-12	9-12	9-13	9-13	9-13	9-13	9-13	10–0	10–0	10–0
	3	8—8	8—9	8-10	8-11	8-12	8-13	9—0	9—1	9—2	9—2	9—3	9—4
	2												
11f	4	9-10	9-11	9-11	9-12	9-12	9-12	9-13	9-13	9-13	9-13	9-13	10–0
	3	8—6	8—7	8—8	8—9	8-10	8-11	8-12	8-13	9—0	9—1	9—2	9—2
1½m	4	9-10	9-10	9-10	9-11	9-11	9-12	9-12	9-12	9-13	9-13	9-13	9-13
	3	8—4	8—5	8—6	8—7	8—8	8—9	8-10	8-11	8-12	8-13	9—0	9—1
13f	4	9—9	9—9	9-10	9-10	9-11	9-11	9-11	9-12	9-12	9-12	9-13	9-13
	3	8—2	8—3	8—4	8—5	8—7	8—8	8—9	8-10	8-11	8-12	8-13	9—0
1¾m	4	9—8	9—8	9—9	9—9	9-10	9-10	9-11	9-11	9-12	9-12	9-12	9-13
	3	8—0	8—2	8—3	8—4	8—5	8—6	8—7	8—8	8—9	8-10	8-11	8-12
15f	4	9—7	9—8	9—8	9—9	9—9	9-10	9-10	9-11	9-11	9-11	9-12	9-12
	3	7-13	8—0	8—1	8—2	8—4	8—5	8—6	8—7	8—8	8—9	8-10	8-11
2m	4	9—6	9—7	9—7	9—8	9—9	9—9	9-10	9-10	9-11	9-11	9-11	9-12
	3	7-11	7-12	7-13	8—1	8—2	8—3	8—4	8—5	8—6	8—7	8—8	8—9
2¼m	4	9—5	9—5	9—6	9—7	9—7	9—8	9—9	9—9	9-10	9-10	9-10	9-11
	3	7—8	7—9	7-11	7-12	7-13	8—0	8—2	8—3	8—4	8—5	8—6	8—7
2½m	4	9—3	9—4	9—5	9—6	9—6	9—7	9—7	9—8	9—9	9—9	9-10	9-10
	3	7—5	7—7	7—8	7—9	7-11	7-12	7-13	8—1	8—2	8—3	8—4	8—5

For 5-y-o's and older, use 10-0 in all cases
Race distances in the above tables are shown only at 1 furlong intervals.
For races over odd distances, the nearest distance shown in the table should be used:
thus for races of 1m to 1m 109 yards, use the table weights for 1m;
for 1m 110 yards to 1m 219 yards use the 9f table

**The age, weight and distance table covering July to December
appears on the end paper at the back of the book**

RACEHORSES
OF 2004

Price £70.00

A TIMEFORM PUBLICATION

CONTENTS

The age, weight and distance tables, for use in applying the ratings in races involving horses of different ages, appear on the end papers at the front and back of the book

Compiled and produced by

G. Greetham (Director), C. S. Williams (Managing Editor & Handicapper), J. Ingles (Essays & Editor for pedigrees & 'Top Horses Abroad'), E. K. Wilkinson (Essays & Editor), M. J. Dwyer (Short Commentaries & Editor), S. D. Rowlands (Handicapper & Short Commentaries), G. J. McGibbon, G. J. North (Handicappers), J. Early, P. Morrell (Essays), R. J. O'Brien, J. A. Todd (Short Commentaries), M. S. Rigg (Short Commentaries & Additional Essays), D. Johnson (Additional Essays), S. Wright (pedigrees, database updates), G. Crowther, G. Johnstone (proof checking), M. Hall, D. Holdsworth, W. Muncaster, A-M. Stevens, R. Todd, C. Wright (Production)

© **Portway Press Limited 2005**   ISBN 1 901570 48 7

Racehorses of 2004

Introduction

'I'm reminded of Mrs Beeton's famous first line in her recipe for jugged hare—"First, catch your hare."' The observation of John Brown, the former chairman of William Hill, pointedly summed up his reaction to a shock verdict delivered by the European Court of Justice in November. The highly complex judgement, which is set to be reviewed by the Court of Appeal, affects the funding of British racing and came at the end of a drawn-out legal process in which the British Horseracing Board initially brought an action against William Hill for listing runners and riders on its internet betting site. The BHB claimed that fixture lists and race cards—pre-race data—formed a database for which it could charge, a view accepted by the High Court and by the Court of Appeal, which, however, referred certain points to the European Court of Justice. Meanwhile, the BHB pressed on with plans to negotiate commercial contracts with betting organisations and others, based on the sale of data, a blueprint devised by the then BHB chairman Peter Savill. In 2002, the BHB entered into commercial licencing agreements, providing data in return for 10% of bookmakers' gross profits and estimated to be worth around £100m a year. The agreements were due to run until 2007 and were set to replace payments made by bookmakers to the statutory Levy Board.

The BHB campaigned vigorously in the Savill years for an end to the independent Levy Board, which Savill decried because the BHB was not in control of the spending. With a new BHB chairman, Martin Broughton, installed

The new BHB chairman Martin Broughton presents the trophy for the Juddmonte International to Sheikh Mohammed after the success of Sulamani, whose victory at York also clinched the BHB's Middle Distance Championship; the BHB scheme, which also promoted a 'Summer Triple Crown', was one of the casualties in cutbacks of £8.7m announced in December after a ruling on data rights by the European Court of Justice

in the middle of the year, an extension of the Levy Board's life became the focus of contingency plans in the light of the ruling of the European Court of Justice. Revenue from the levy—which has been offset since 2002 against payments due to the BHB under commercial agreements—has been buoyant because of the boom in off-course turnover (up from £7bn to over £30bn on all betting) since the abolition of betting tax in 2001. It was embarrassing for the BHB to find itself doing a U-turn on the Levy Board, especially as Parliament had just voted to abolish it. The Minister for Sport, Richard

Caborn, did, however, throw the BHB a lifeline by intimating that the Government might delay the closure of the Levy Board (due to be wound up in September 2006) if racing could recommend—by March 2005—an agreed way of securing the bookmakers' continued 'contribution to racing.' The BHB set up an independent four-man body chaired by Lord Donoughue to come up with a 'long-standing solution' after consultation with bodies within racing and with the major bookmakers—who have paid 15% of their gross profits to the Government since the abolition of the old betting tax. The Government also has powers over the use of lucrative fixed-odds betting terminals in the betting shops and the minister was confident the big bookmakers would co-operate in the review. The minister made clear that extending the life of the Levy Board—which could prompt a European Commission challenge on state aid—was only an interim

Richard Caborn, Minister for Sport, a key figure in the search for a long-term solution for the funding of racing

option. 'The racing and betting industries should continue to plan for deciding future financial arrangements between themselves,' he warned.

The BHB relies for something like a third of its own £30m income at present on the revenue received from bookmakers outside Britain—mainly Irish—and this is not covered by the levy. In the uncertainty, the BHB invoked emergency powers in December to impose cutbacks of £8.7m in its expenditure on prize money incentive schemes, owners' premiums and in other areas 'with immediate effect', the Levy Board agreeing at the same time to subsidise the low-grade, regional fixtures which were due to be funded by the BHB in 2005. Another consequence of the decision of the European Court of Justice was the suspension of some of the BHB's plans to implement *The Modernisation of British Racing*, a document outlining changes after a settlement was finally reached—expedited at a tricky stage by the Minister for Sport—with the Office of Fair Trading over an investigation into anti-competitive practices. Plans involved an overall increase in the number of meetings to 1,496 by 2006, virtually all the expansion accounted for by a growth of just under a third in the number of Flat fixtures, with field sizes restricted to twelve or fourteen depending on the time of year. There was criticism that this would end sixteen-runner handicaps, a type of race in which the general terms of each-way betting slightly favour the punters. Reaction to the changes, which apply to bread-and-butter handicaps and not to so-called heritage handicaps, is enlarged upon in the essay on Stewards' Cup winner **Pivotal Point**. The Minister for

Sport, whose cajoling of racing's bickering factions has been impressive, made it clear that the expansion of the fixture list and other changes, such as the transfer of regulatory powers from the Jockey Club to a new independent body (which is also reliant on guaranteed funding), must remain urgent priorities. The agreement with the OFT, he said, would lead to 'a freer, more competitive future for racing and betting.' One of the important concessions made by the OFT was to relax its objections to the centralised sale of data. By this time, the unviable ten-year £307m media rights deal with attheraces, the dedicated horseracing channel, was already doomed. Two separately-operated channels, a revamped At The Races and the subscription-based Racing UK (owned by around thirty of the racecourses) had been launched by the middle of the year, amid unresolved legal questions still hanging over the old attheraces contracts.

Peter Savill saw the commercial agreements on data and media rights as the most important legacy of his six-year chairmanship of the BHB, which ostensibly left British racing in a far healthier position. When Savill took over, the levy was yielding £55m a year; in 2003 it produced almost £110m, though the growth arose mainly out of the bookmakers' successful campaign—led by John Brown—to abolish betting tax. Prize money rose from £60m to £94m in the Savill era, touching £100m for the first time in 2004, when racecourse attendances again topped 6m. Another of Savill's aims had been to see the Tote brought under BHB control, and thereby increase its contribution to racing (£11.7m in the year ending March 31st 2004, half of its net profit). The Government's policy of ending direct state involvement in racing has seen plans drawn up to sell the Tote (now trading off-course as totesport) to racing, but to a racing trust rather than the BHB. Proposing and supporting the sale of the Tote may, arguably, eventually prove to have been a strategic mistake. The European Commission has already questioned—under state aid rules—the arrangement whereby a racing trust would pay the Government, which effectively nationalised the Tote in 2003 so it could be sold off, half of an agreed 'fair price', whatever that might be. The Tote is Britain's fifth largest bookmaker and, using the prices it has paid for betting shops in the last two years or so as a guide, the value of its four hundred and fifty high street retail outlets alone must be in the region of £250m. The betting shop division

Europe's richest handicap the totesport Ebor is one of the portfolio of races supported by the sport's biggest sponsor; promoting the sale of the Tote may turn out to have been a strategic mistake by the BHB

contributes over two-thirds of the Tote's turnover. The big bookmakers contend that the Tote should be sold to the highest bidder and they have made representations to Brussels in the hope of blocking 'a cosy deal with racing'. If a racing trust buys the Tote, the money will have to come from future profits that would otherwise—at least in part—have gone to racing anyway. Why pay millions for something from which racing already receives considerable benefit? The Government will be the winner, getting paid for something it did not own and had never invested a penny in.

The BHB's commercial deal with the big bookmakers, based on a share of their gross profits from British racing, gave the BHB an incentive to work with the bookmakers. The BHB had crossed swords with the bookmakers during the Savill era, as it had with many other groups in racing, including the Race-course Association, the Levy Board and the Tote. The emergence of person-to-person on-line betting exchanges gave the BHB and the bookmakers a common cause to fight. Savill himself, presenting his final annual report, said the exchanges provided 'unlimited opportunity for skulduggery' and were 'a honeypot for the Pooh Bears of the underworld.' The odds available on the exchanges, which allow punters to bypass bookmakers and place bets with each other, frequently offer better value, but the speed of their growth has still surprised many. The exchanges suffered the loss of one of their number when Sporting Options collapsed in November, but the biggest exchange Betfair went a long way to bailing out the customers of Sporting Options with a rescue package. Chris Bell, head of Ladbrokes, has alleged that 'at least one race a day, if not more, is being corrupted by the availability of laying horses to lose on betting exchanges,' and the chief executive of William Hill, David Harding, has said that exchanges offer 'carte blanche for skulduggery.' All of which has led to an unfortunate culture of suspicion growing up around the exchanges, which has done racing no good at all. Ironically, the big bookmakers themselves were facing an investigation at the end of the year by the National Criminal Intelligence Service, ordered by the Treasury after a request from the Minister for Sport, into whether criminals and terrorist organisations might be using bookmakers, who accept large, anonymous cash wagers, for money-laundering. The bookmakers' reaction to this 'outrageous slur' was ironic given their attempts to discredit the exchanges, which do not accept cash bets and make a virtue of their regulated environment, often flaunting the fact that they report unusual or suspicious betting patterns to the Jockey Club security team, in a way which traditional bookmakers, who value client confidentiality, do not.

Information passed on by exchanges was central to the launching of a series of investigations in 2004 into races in which there were suspicions that horses

The trading room at Betfair, which was matching £60m a week on horseracing by the end of 2004 and is thought to have more than an 80% share of the exchange betting market in Britain

had been prevented from running on their merits. Racing became mired by allegations of corruption and conspiracy as City of London police took on what a spokesperson described as a 'huge investigation' into criminal activity involving so-called 'fixing' of races. 'Cops probe 80 races', 'Racing In The Gutter', 'Queen's jockey in fixing quiz' were just some of the headlines following a series of arrests in the autumn. One of those arrested was champion jockey Kieren Fallon, fuller details given in the introduction to the essay on **Gamut**. The Jockey Club warned off the founder of Platinum Racing, Miles Rodgers, for two years in March after he was found to have laid horses owned by his club to lose on the exchanges (against Jockey Club rules). Investigations reportedly revealed that he had laid other horses whose running had stirred controversy, among them a jumper called Ice Saint and a two-year-old Hillside Girl. Ice Saint's little-known rider Sean Fox was subsequently cleared by the Jockey Club of deliberately jumping off his mount; the case involving the pulling up of Hillside Girl at Carlisle in June 2003 virtually collapsed, a Jockey Club inquiry in September unable to establish guilt on the main charges. Three of the four men involved in the Hillside Girl case, trainer Alan Berry, jockey Paul Bradley and blacksmith Steve O'Sullivan were later arrested by City of London police in connection with their own on-going investigation, bringing the total number arrested to twenty-five by early-December. Jockeys Darren Williams, Fergal Lynch and trainer Karl Burke, as well as Rodgers, were among earlier arrests, while Robert Winston became the fifth jockey arrested in early-February, 2005. The bail on all those arrested—no charges have been brought—was extended until the spring of 2005 as the police said they needed 'more time and resources to fully investigate.' Officers were said to have listed over 1,000 exhibits, and to be analysing telephone records and computers seized during its raids. The investigation is thought to centre on the laying, on betting exchanges, of horses that were prevented from winning.

In a separate case, former champion apprentice Gary Carter, who left Britain in the second half of the year to continue his career in Spain and Dubai, faced a Jockey Club inquiry regarding the running of eight horses he rode in August and September 2003. The inquiry will also look into his association with punter Christopher Coleman, who was banned for two years in January 2003 after being found guilty of seeking to gain betting advantage by accessing privileged information from former jump jockey Barrie Wright. Coleman successfully refuted charges that he had had links with the fugitive drug baron Brian Wright (no relation to Barrie Wright) who was 'warned off' indefinitely in December 2002 after being found to be at the centre of a long-running investigation into doping and race-fixing. Among those who had connections with Brian Wright was bloodstock agent and former jump jockey Graham Bradley who lost his appeal to the High Court against a five-year Jockey Club ban for passing on information for reward and other offences, when a jockey. Bradley's ban from the racecourse, and from dealing in any capacity with racehorses, began in October. In another pending Jockey Club case, trainer Shaun Keightley and jockey Pat McCabe face a hearing over the running of Red Lancer at Wolverhampton in October 2003. Leading apprentice Robert Miles, who won the Chester Vase on Red Lancer in 2004, was another jockey in trouble, banned until the middle of 2005 for cocaine use after a hearing at the Jockey Club's new Shaftesbury Avenue headquarters.

The race for the jockeys' title between Kieren Fallon and Frankie Dettori was one of the features of the season. Dettori's triumph in the turf season championship recognised by the Jockeys' Association earned the lion's share of the publicity and was a boost for the sport's public relations, but Fallon was the rightful champion—for the seventh time—by virtue of riding most winners

Frankie Dettori rode his 2,000th winner in Britain on Nightfall on King George day at Ascot;
Kieren Fallon won his third Derby on North Light

in the calendar year, two hundred in all (his fifth double century). There is more on the championship in the essay on Hong Kong Mile winner **Firebreak**, one of eleven Group/Grade 1 winners—in six different countries—for Godolphin in 2004. The Godolphin stable in Britain was expanded from its usual sixty horses to around two hundred and forty, undoubtedly a factor in stable-jockey Dettori's resurgence. Saeed bin Suroor celebrated his tenth year as the licence holder for the Godolphin operation with a fifth British trainers' championship, gaining his fifth King George victory with Timeform Horse of the Year **Doyen**, who had earlier put up a top-class performance in the Hardwicke, also over Ascot's mile-and-a-half course. Doyen, whose essay provides, among other things, an update on sectional timing analysis (see also **Iceman**), was one of six Godolphin winners at the Royal meeting—to be held at York in 2005 because of redevelopment—which included Group 1 victories for subsequent Coral-Eclipse winner **Refuse To Bend** in the Queen Anne and for **Papineau** who became the stable's fourth Gold Cup winner when beating France's top stayer **Westerner**. Among the other domestic highlights for Godolphin were the St Leger victory of **Rule of Law** and the Juddmonte International win of **Sulamani**, who went on to add the Canadian International, a leg of the World Series whose future is discussed.

Godolphin's radical change to running its two-year-olds 'in house' is aired on **Librettist**, though the stable's best two-year-old was **Dubawi** who won the National Stakes at the Curragh to provide the most important success so far from Dubai Millennium's only crop. Godolphin strengthened its hand for the 2005 classics with the now-expected end-of-season spending spree, purchases including National Stakes runner-up **Berenson**. Also wearing the Godolphin colours will be the likes of **Henrik**—third behind the impressive **Motivator** in the Racing Post Trophy—**Layman**, and the Johnston-trained **Shamardal**, the last-named, diagnosed as a 'wobbler' as a foal, proving himself the best two-year-old in Europe. Godolphin also had a change of approach in the latest season towards the Dubai World Cup meeting, as set out in the write-up on the fourth North American-trained winner of the world's most valuable race, **Pleasantly Perfect**. Saeed bin Suroor was the leading British-based trainer for the seventh year in a row in terms of foreign earnings, with prize money overseas of £1,416,776, according to figures produced by the International

Racing Bureau, to add to record first-three prize money earnings of £4,146,844 in Britain. The stable sent out 115 winners in Britain, only four fewer than the leading trainer by number of winners, Mark Johnston, who completed an eleventh consecutive century, now two ahead of the previous record held by Henry Cecil. Richard Hannon, achieving a seventh successive century, was the only other trainer to complete a century of domestic winners in 2004, the stable's two-year-olds playing a significant part including **Galeota**, whose entry examines the burgeoning career of jockey Ryan Moore.

British-based trainers earned £10,699,943 abroad in 2004 (according to the IRB statistics), though they won only eighty-seven races, the lowest since 1991. There were ninety-three British runners—who earned £911,596—at the newly-instituted, nine-week Dubai International Carnival in early spring, without which the figures for overseas earnings would have been relatively disappointing (it was the sixth time since 1996 that earnings topped the £10m mark). Sir Mark Prescott was the most successful British trainer by number of winners on foreign soil, sending out ten from twenty-four runners, the highlight a Group 1 hat-trick in Germany for **Albanova**. Prescott's domestic season is touched on in the entry on **Masafi**, who won seven races in a row in eighteen days in July, while **Intrigued** and **Cupid's Glory** encourage hopes of a belated first classic runner in Britain for the stable in 2005. Prescott's stable-jockey Seb Sanders finished third in the jockeys' championship with one hundred and sixty-five winners, his other big race winners including **Bachelor Duke**, whose owner the Duke of Devonshire did not live to see him victorious in the Irish Two Thousand Guineas, and Nunthorpe winner **Bahamian Pirate**, owned by the Lucayan Stud whose boss Edward St George also died in the latest season. St George took over his family's racing interests after the death of his brother Charles in 1992. Bahamian Pirate's first Group 1 victory, at the age of nine, was one of the highlights on the sprinting scene, in which he was not the only

Saeed bin Suroor (left), champion trainer in Britain for the third time, returns with Doyen,
led in by Sheikh Mohammed, after victory in the King George VI and Queen Elizabeth Diamond Stakes

*Derby winner North Light (nearside) and Oaks winner Ouija Board
canter back together after the Arc*

Yorkshire-trained winner at the highest level. **Fayr Jag** won the Golden Jubilee
at Royal Ascot while stable-companion **Somnus**, whose essay outlines some
notable successes in 2004 for sprinters bought on a shoestring, was beaten
narrowly by **Tante Rose** in the Stanleybet Sprint Cup at Haydock. Somnus
won two Group 1s in France where British-trained sprinters had a particularly
lucrative time, as enlarged upon in the entry on **The Trader**. Ex-American
Var's victory in the Prix de l'Abbaye was a notable achievement by veteran
trainer Clive Brittain who also enjoyed overseas success with Coronation Cup
winner **Warrsan** and finished second behind Suroor in the overseas earnings
table with £787,769.

Ireland provided the richest foreign pickings for British trainers who won
three of the Irish classics, the fillies **Attraction** and **Ouija Board** following
up classic successes at home. Their victories, along with those of Bachelor
Duke and of **North Light** at Epsom, put the dukes and lords of British racing
back into the spotlight. The essay on **Ouija Board**, who went on to record one of
two Breeders' Cup successes for Britain (the seemingly-exposed two-year-old
Wilko was the other), looks at the influence on racing of some of the ancestors
of the present Lord Derby, particularly of the 17th Earl, a theme highlighted
also in the essay on **Whipper**. North Light's Derby success, in the silks made
famous first by Sir Michael Sobell and then by Lord Weinstock, is the subject
of a wide-ranging essay in which the standing of Europe's richest race, whose
French counterpart is being reduced in distance (see **Blue Canari**), is examined
from a number of different angles. **Grey Swallow** beat North Light in the Irish
Derby, his stable-companion **Vinnie Roe** won the Irish St Leger (for the fourth
time) and **Azamour** also kept the big prize for the Irish Champion Stakes in
Ireland. Most unusually for a top three-year-old owned by the Aga Khan,
Azamour is to be kept in training, a point developed in his essay. The Aga

Khan was thought to be negotiating for the racing and breeding empire of the late Jean-Luc Lagardère whose family sold Arc runner-up **Cherry Mix** to Godolphin at the end of the season. The Niarchos colours were carried to their first Arc victory by **Bago** and the family also had the unbeaten two-year-old filly **Divine Proportions**, the best of her age and sex in Europe. She looked like being challenged for that title by Irish-trained **Damson** until that filly met with defeat in the Cheveley Park, won by 40/1-shot **Magical Romance** whose stablemate **Rebuttal** went close to giving trainer Brian Meehan a double in the Middle Park, beaten three quarters of a length by **Ad Valorem**.

Until Ad Valorem's victory, Ballydoyle had had little to shout about in a disappointing season by its traditionally high standards. It had picked up only one Group 1 victory, in the Tattersalls Gold Cup with **Powerscourt** (also disqualified from first in the Arlington Million, the essay discussing a difficult year for jockey Jamie Spencer who quit his job at Ballydoyle). **One Cool Cat**, whose extended entry contains an interesting insight into Aidan O'Brien, had not lived up to the highest expectations held for him, and another big hope **Yeats** had been sidelined by injury since before the Derby. Two days after the Middle Park, **Oratorio** added a second Group 1 for the Ballydoyle two-year-olds when getting home in a nail-biting finish from **Early March** and Layman to the Prix Jean-Luc Lagardère. The commentaries on Ad Valorem and Layman include details of the remarkable stud careers of Danzig and Japanese-based Sunday Silence, while details about Sadler's Wells, who made it a record-breaking fourteenth British and Irish sires' championship, are included in the essay on Doyen. Early March represented the same connections associated with the previous year's Jean-Luc Lagardère winner **American Post**, whose fortunate victory in the Poule d'Essai des Poulains completed a full set of British and French classic victories for owner-breeder Khalid Abdulla, though

The greatest sire in European bloodstock history Sadler's Wells won his fourteenth British and Irish sires' championship, surpassing the record set by Highflyer in 1798

his Juddmonte operation still had the cloud of the so-called 'Endless Summer affair' hanging over it at the end of the year (a topic discussed on American Post). Abdulla, leading owner in Britain in 2003, was pushed down to fifth, behind Godolphin, Hamdan Al Maktoum (whose **Haafhd** won a strong Two Thousand Guineas—those behind went on to win five Group 1s—and the Champion Stakes), Cheveley Park Stud (who enjoyed a tremendous year with its top fillies, **Russian Rhythm**, **Chic** and **Chorist**), and Ballymacoll Stud (North Light). Fillies and mares made a bigger impact than usual on the season. Russian Rhythm, Chic, Tante Rose, **Frizzante** (the July Cup winner whose essay exposes some myths about the influence of the draw), **Soviet Song**, **Alexander Goldrun** and **Grey Lilas** (whose write-up covers the latest European adventures of American jockey Gary Stevens) were among those who successfully took on the colts in big races, while **Quiff** came second in the St Leger and Chorist second in the Champion. The upgraded programme for older fillies is a topic for the extended entry on **Soviet Song**, who held on narrowly from **Nayyir** in the Sussex Stakes and twice got the better during the season of Attraction, the top three-year-old filly at a mile. The first World Thoroughbred Racehorse Rankings puzzlingly put Attraction—who won four Group 1s—on a 1 lb lower mark than was allotted to her at two in the now-defunct International Classifications. Timeform rates her 7 lb higher than the year before, the level of Timeform's two-year-old ratings over the years one of the topics covered in Attraction's essay.

The year had its share of equine 'characters' at the top level, headed by the volatile **Rakti** who won two Group 1s in tremendous style, the Prince of Wales's Stakes and the Queen Elizabeth II Stakes, both at Ascot, but let himself down as often as he did himself justice. **Norse Dancer**, **Antonius Pius** (who threw away the Poule d'Essai des Poulains and tried to duck left when beaten in the Breeders' Cup Mile) and **Salselon**, who has been returned to Italy, were others on the receiving end of plenty of criticism. Italy has struggled to keep hold of its best horses in recent years, Falbrav and Rakti among them, and **Electrocutionist** is another Italian performer who may well make his mark on the international stage. The same remark applies to German-trained **Shirocco**.

The racing world mourned the death, at the age of sixty-seven, of leading owner/breeder Robert Sangster who, in partnership with stud owner John

Soviet Song (left) gets the better of Attraction in the Matron Stakes at Leopardstown, one of a series of upgraded races for fillies and mares

Robert Sangster, the dominant owner in European racing in the late-'seventies and early-'eighties, died in April; veteran jockey George Duffield, who has ridden 2,547 winners, was out of action in the second half of the season, putting his future in the saddle in doubt

Magnier and trainer Vincent O'Brien, dominated European racing for nearly a decade up to the mid-'eighties, buying the best-bred American yearlings, racing them successfully and then establishing them as stallions at Coolmore which was turned into one of the world's most powerful breeding operations. The entry on **Playful Act** has more on Robert Sangster. Along with the Duke of Devonshire and Edward St George, both mentioned earlier, Sir Stanley Clarke, founder and chairman of Northern Racing, and Newmarket trainer Alec Stewart were also among the sad losses for racing. There was, understandably, less coverage of the death of Dick Whitford who compiled the first universal handicap, published in a prototype Timeform annual in 1948. Timeform's founder Phil Bull (time), already a successful punter and publisher, and Whitford (form) combined to produce the innovative 'Timeform Supplement', covering 1947. Nearly all ratings systems since have used the Timeform model. Derby-winning jockey Willie Ryan and trainers Ben Hanbury, Peter Harris, who handed over to son-in-law Walter Swinburn, Toby Balding, who transferred his dual purpose licence to his assistant Jonathan Geake, and Bryan McMahon, turning over his string to son Eddie after forty years as a trainer, announced their retirement, while another Derby-winning jockey Alan Munro announced he is to return to race-riding in Britain in 2005. Veteran jockey George Duffield was facing the prospect of his career being over; he suffered a badly damaged shoulder after a horse reared over on him at his wife's stable.

Racing is a global sport nowadays and Timeform ratings are used around the world. The 'Top Horses Abroad' section provides Timeform ratings for practically all the world's best thoroughbreds not featured in the A to Z. As usual, the horses highlighted in bold in this introduction are among those with essays—written to entertain as well as to inform—in this edition of *Racehorses*.

February 2005

2004 STATISTICS

The following tables show the leading owners, trainers, jockeys, sires of winners and horses on the Flat in Britain during 2004 (Jan 1–Dec 31). The prize money statistics, compiled by *Timeform*, relate to first-three prize money and win money. Win money was traditionally used to decide the trainers' championship until, in 1994, the BHB and the National Trainers' Federation established a championship decided by total prize money as determined by *Racing Post*. The jockeys' championship has traditionally been decided by the number of winners ridden during the year, though since 1997 the Jockeys' Association has recognised a championship that runs for the turf season (Mar–Nov).

	OWNERS (1,2,3 earnings)	Horses	Indiv'l Wnrs	Races Won	Runs	%	Stakes £
1	Godolphin	172	84	115	455	25.2	4,146,844
2	Mr Hamdan Al Maktoum	148	55	73	464	15.7	1,621,073
3	Cheveley Park Stud	68	37	58	218	26.6	1,091,994
4	Ballymacoll Stud	11	6	8	27	29.6	913,912
5	Mr K. Abdulla	121	41	54	328	16.4	821,133
6	Maktoum Al Maktoum	66	27	33	235	14.0	721,672
7	Sheikh Mohammed	118	43	52	312	16.6	624,568
8	Elite Racing Club	13	8	16	64	25.0	544,452
9	Duke of Roxburghe	2	1	3	5	60.0	487,018
10	Sheikh Ahmed Al Maktoum	66	31	36	266	13.5	464,569
11	H.H. Aga Khan	16	8	11	42	26.1	447,785
12	Mr L. Neil Jones	4	2	4	13	30.7	378,699

	OWNERS (win money, £½m+)	Horses	Indiv'l Wnrs	Races Won	Runs	%	Stakes £
1	Godolphin	172	84	115	455	25.2	3,057,927
2	Mr Hamdan Al Maktoum	148	55	73	464	15.7	1,179,559
3	Ballymacoll Stud	11	6	8	27	29.6	908,581
4	Cheveley Park Stud	68	37	58	218	26.6	713,696
5	Maktoum Al Maktoum	66	27	33	235	14.0	567,880
6	Mr K. Abdulla	121	41	54	328	16.4	523,384

	TRAINERS (1,2,3 earnings)	Horses	Indiv'l Wnrs	Races Won	Runs	%	Stakes £
1	Saeed bin Suroor	172	84	115	455	25.2	4,146,844
2	Sir Michael Stoute	148	68	87	400	21.7	2,776,052
3	M. Johnston	182	79	119	799	14.8	2,323,100
4	M. R. Channon	166	70	98	1039	9.4	1,579,066
5	B. W. Hills	160	57	82	636	12.8	1,468,788
6	R. Hannon	208	87	113	1201	9.4	1,331,156
7	M. A. Jarvis	85	45	65	371	17.5	1,218,323
8	J. H. M. Gosden	150	53	66	458	14.4	1,134,772
9	J. R. Fanshawe	78	32	44	294	14.9	1,134,753
10	J. L. Dunlop	135	42	55	513	10.7	1,113,473
11	L. M. Cumani	67	29	42	293	14.3	1,024,319
12	T. D. Easterby	131	43	62	738	8.4	867,455

TRAINERS (win money, £1m+)	Horses	Indiv'l Wnrs	Races Won	Runs	%	Stakes £
1 Saeed bin Suroor	172	84	115	455	25.2	3,057,927
2 Sir Michael Stoute	148	68	87	400	21.7	2,301,038
3 M. Johnston	182	79	119	799	14.8	1,726,942
4 B. W. Hills	160	57	82	636	12.8	1,099,339

TRAINERS (with 100+ winners)	Horses	Indiv'l Wnrs	Races Won	2nd	3rd	Runs	%
1 M. Johnston	182	79	119	111	77	799	14.8
2 Saeed bin Suroor	172	84	115	75	43	455	25.2
3 R. Hannon	208	87	113	123	127	1201	9.4

JOCKEYS (by winners)	1st	2nd	3rd	Unpl	Total Mts	%
1 K. Fallon	200	166	136	607	1109	18.0
2 L. Dettori	195	132	89	434	850	22.9
3 S. Sanders	165	119	87	631	1002	16.5
4 D. Holland	152	137	137	752	1178	12.9
5 R. L. Moore	132	125	107	644	1008	13.1
6 N. Callan	126	117	103	684	1030	12.2
7 R. Winston	114	105	114	675	1008	11.3
8 A. Culhane	111	104	108	725	1048	10.5
9 E. Ahern	111	99	108	698	1016	10.9
10 P. Hanagan	101	70	100	558	829	12.1
11 S. Drowne	99	93	103	819	1114	8.8
12 J. Fanning	97	72	70	546	785	12.3

Note: L. Dettori was leading jockey in the turf season with 192 winners

JOCKEYS (1,2,3 earnings)	Races Won	Rides	%	Stakes £
1 K. Fallon	200	1109	18.0	4,711,187
2 L. Dettori	195	850	22.9	4,479,997
3 D. Holland	152	1178	12.9	2,219,546
4 S. Sanders	165	1002	16.5	1,766,807
5 J. Murtagh	77	574	13.4	1,764,842
6 K. Darley	85	822	10.3	1,637,530
7 R. Hills	66	454	14.5	1,517,314
8 R. L. Moore	132	1008	13.1	1,410,392
9 P. Robinson	67	552	12.1	1,350,573
10 K. McEvoy	44	322	13.6	1,260,794
11 J. Fortune	72	615	11.7	1,236,346
12 T. Quinn	76	689	11.0	1,200,450

JOCKEYS (win money, £1m+)	Races Won	Rides	%	Stakes £
1 L. Dettori	195	850	22.9	3,564,364
2 K. Fallon	200	1109	18.0	3,486,754
3 S. Sanders	165	1002	16.5	1,345,922
4 D. Holland	152	1178	12.9	1,280,041
5 J. Murtagh	77	574	13.4	1,265,206
6 K. Darley	85	822	10.3	1,197,335
7 R. Hills	66	454	14.5	1,110,997

Total

APPRENTICES (by winners)	1st	2nd	3rd	Unpl	Mts	%
1 T. P. Queally...............................	66	65	52	565	748	8.8
2 N. Mackay..................................	52	40	35	259	386	13.4
3 T. Eaves......................................	45	31	40	490	606	7.4
4 P. Makin	42	30	36	315	423	9.9

SIRES OF WINNERS (1,2,3 earnings)	Races Won	Runs	%	Stakes £
1 Sadler's Wells (by Northern Dancer)	58	464	12.5	2,587,850
2 Danehill (by Danzig)	75	469	15.9	1,880,457
3 Pivotal (by Polar Falcon)	85	516	16.4	1,250,959
4 Efisio (by Formidable)	60	505	11.8	1,108,246
5 Kingmambo (by Mr Prospector)	30	190	15.7	1,069,973
6 Barathea (by Sadler's Wells)	60	531	11.2	1,001,591
7 Selkirk (by Sharpen Up)	61	464	13.1	943,547
8 Machiavellian (by Mr Prospector)	61	424	14.3	930,562
9 Polar Falcon (by Nureyev)	60	439	13.6	816,659
10 Cape Cross (by Green Desert)	49	307	15.9	809,821
11 Polish Precedent (by Danzig)	17	240	7.0	737,436
12 Indian Ridge (by Ahonoora)	47	490	9.5	732,552

SIRES OF WINNERS (win money)	Horses	Indiv'l Wnrs	Races Won	Stakes £
1 Sadler's Wells (by Northern Dancer)	121	44	58	1,708,191
2 Danehill (by Danzig)	106	47	75	1,526,597
3 Pivotal (by Polar Falcon)	89	51	85	901,324
4 Efisio (by Formidable)	78	39	60	891,010
5 Barathea (by Sadler's Wells)	89	34	60	777,728
6 Selkirk (by Sharpen Up)	87	39	61	730,607
7 Kingmambo (by Mr Prospector)	52	21	30	669,818
8 Alhaarth (by Unfuwain)	52	18	28	663,467
9 Machiavellian (by Mr Prospector)	87	34	61	661,467
10 Cape Cross (by Green Desert)	66	33	49	602,042
11 Polish Precedent (by Danzig)	55	11	17	584,955
12 Marju (by Last Tycoon)	56	27	44	563,557

LEADING HORSES (1,2,3 earnings)	Races Won	Runs	Stakes £
1 North Light 3 b.c. Danehill – Sought Out	2	2	872,320
2 Rule of Law 3 b.c. Kingmambo – Crystal Crossing	2	4	649,180
3 Doyen 4 b.c. Sadler's Wells – Moon Cactus	2	4	571,200
4 Attraction 3 b.f. Efisio – Flirtation	3	4	487,018
5 Haafhd 3 ch.c. Alhaarth – Al Bahathri	3	5	418,814
6 Refuse To Bend 4 b.c. Sadler's Wells – Market Slide	2	6	409,720
7 Sulamani 5 b.h. Hernando – Soul Dream	1	4	371,300
8 Soviet Song 4 b.f. Marju – Kalinka	2	6	362,600
9 Rakti 5 b.h. Polish Precedent – Ragera	2	3	348,000
10 Quiff 3 b.f. Sadler's Wells – Wince	2	4	256,851
11 Warrsan 6 b.h. Caerleon – Lucayan Princess	1	4	245,980
12 Caesar Beware 2 b.g. Daggers Drawn – Red Shareef	3	4	232,726

TIMEFORM CHAMPIONS IN EUROPE 2004

HORSE OF THE YEAR
BEST MIDDLE DISTANCE HORSE
BEST OLDER MALE RATED AT 132

DOYEN

BEST TWO-YEAR-OLD FILLY RATED AT 119

DIVINE PROPORTIONS

BEST TWO-YEAR-OLD COLT RATED AT 126p

SHAMARDAL

BEST THREE-YEAR-OLD FILLIES RATED AT 125

ATTRACTION

OUIJA BOARD

BEST THREE-YEAR-OLD COLT RATED AT 130

BAGO

BEST OLDER FEMALES RATED AT 126

SOVIET SONG

TANTE ROSE

BEST SPRINTERS RATED AT 126

SOMNUS

TANTE ROSE

BEST MILERS RATED AT 129

HAAFHD

RAKTI

BEST STAYER RATED AT 128

VINNIE ROE

BEST PERFORMANCE IN A HANDICAP IN BRITAIN

POLAR WAY

ran to 120
when second in totesport International Stakes at Ascot

BEST PERFORMANCES ON ALL-WEATHER IN BRITAIN

JACK SULLIVAN

ran to 115
when winning betdirect.co.uk Handicap at Lingfield

COMPTON BOLTER

ran to 115
when winning Bet Direct On 0800 32 93 93 Handicap at Wolverhampton

THE TIMEFORM 'TOP HUNDRED'

Here are listed the 'Top 100' two-year-olds, three-year-olds and older horses in the annual. Fillies and mares are denoted by (f).

2 YEAR OLDS

126p	Shamardal
123p	Dubawi
122p	Motivator
121p	Ad Valorem
119	Divine Proportions (f)
119	Etlaala
119	Oratorio
118	Early March
118	Helios Quercus
118	Montgomery's Arch
118	Rebuttal
118	Wilko
117	Iceman
117	Layman
116	Cupid's Glory
115p	Manduro
114p	Berenson
114p	Footstepsinthesand
114p	Henrik
114p	Librettist
114	Andronikos
114	Musketier
114	Satchem
114	Southern Africa
114	Walk In The Park
113p	Albert Hall
113p	Playful Act (f)
113	Damson (f)
112p	Merger
112	Caesar Beware
112	Centifolia (f)
112	Dubai Surprise (f)
112	Perfectperformance
112	Russian Blue
111	Galeota
111	Maids Causeway (f)
110p	Comic Strip
110p	Windsor Knot
110	Captain Hurricane
110	Magical Romance (f)
110	Moth Ball
110	Soar (f)
110	Tony James
110	Tremar
109p	Birthstone (f)
109p	Dash To The Top (f)
109	Blue Dakota
109	Capable Guest
109	Cougar Cat
109	Council Member
109	Dark Cheetah
109	Democratic Deficit
109	Gaff
109	Queen of Poland (f)
109	Suez (f)

108p	Jazz Princess (f)
108p	Last Rhapsody (f)
108p	Paita (f)
108p	Yehudi
108	Chateau Istana
108	Indesatchel
108	Mona Lisa (f)
108	Mystical Land
108	Scandinavia
108	Silk And Scarlet (f)
107p	Afrashad
107p	Fraloga (f)
107	Don Pele
107	Golden Legacy (f)
107	Jewel In The Sand (f)
107	Titian Time (f)
106p	Ayam Zaman (f)
106p	Konigstiger
106p	Storm Silk
106	Elliots World
106	Salsa Brava (f)
106	Slip Dance (f)
105p	Diktatorial
105p	Intrigued (f)
105p	Oude
105p	Whazzat (f)
105	Abraxas Antelope
105	Distinctly Game
105	Johnny Jumpup
105	Penkenna Princess (f)
105	Portrayal (f)
105	Prince Charming
105	Skywards
105	Something Exciting (f)
105	Songerie (f)
105	Sumora (f)
104	Castelletto (f)
104	Chelsea Rose (f)
104	Cornus
104	Crimson Sun
104	Dance Night
104	Embossed
104	Hearthstead Wings
104	Josh
104	Mister Genepi
104	Obe Gold
104	Tournedos
104	Turnkey

3 YEAR OLDS

134	Smarty Jones
130	Bago
129	Cherry Mix
129	Haafhd
128	Azamour
128	Lucky Story

127	Grey Swallow
126	North Light
125	Attraction (f)
125	Electrocutionist
125	Ouija Board (f)
125	Rule of Law
125	Shirocco
125	Whipper
124+	Snow Ridge
124	Acropolis
124	Egerton
124	Quiff (f)
123	Mister Monet
123	One Cool Cat
123	Pastoral Pursuits
123	Tycoon
123§	Antonius Pius
122	Bachelor Duke
122	Let The Lion Roar
121	Alexander Goldrun (f)
121	American Post
121	Diamond Green
121	Latice (f)
121	Maraahel
121	Mikado
121	Percussionist
120	Crocodile Dundee
120	Grey Lilas (f)
120	Intendant
119p	Cacique
119p	Into The Dark
119	Bull Run
119	Denebola (f)
119	Madid
119	Millemix
119	Millionaia (f)
119	Voix du Nord
118p	Ecomium
118	Ace
118	Blue Canari
118	Darsalam
118	Go For Gold
118	Moss Vale
118	Peak To Creek
118	Prospect Park
118	Salford City
118	Valixir
117	Byron
117	Groom Tesse
117	Mac Love
117	Three Valleys
117	Torrestrella (f)
117	Yeats
116p	Sleeping Indian
116	Always First
116	Day Flight

116	Kheleyf	
116	Lune d'Or (f)	
116	Pepperstorm	
116	Punctilious (f)	
116	Silverskaya (f)	
115	African Dream	
115	Gatwick	
115	Illustrious Miss (f)	
115	Jack Sullivan	
115	Necklace (f)	
115	Sundrop (f)	
115	Two Miles West	

116 Kheleyf
116 Lune d'Or (f)
116 Pepperstorm
116 Punctilious (f)
116 Silverskaya (f)
115 African Dream
115 Gatwick
115 Illustrious Miss (f)
115 Jack Sullivan
115 Necklace (f)
115 Sundrop (f)
115 Two Miles West
114p Eleusis (f)
114 Balmont
114 Benbaun
114 Boogie Street
114 Book of Kings
114 Fokine
114 Leitrim House
114 Red Bloom (f)
113p Eisteddfod
113 All Too Beautiful (f)
113 Brunel
113 Caradak
113 Castleton
113 Fong's Thong
113 Hathrah (f)
113 Hazarista (f)
113 Majestic Desert (f)
113 Peter Paul Rubens
113 Ruby Rocket (f)
113 Rum Shot
113 Take A Bow
113 Troubadour
113 Zosima (f)
112p Pukka
112p Remaadd
112 Baqah (f)
112 Coy (f)
112 Hamairi
112 Hazyview
112 Majestic Missile
112 Milk It Mick
112 Relaxed Gesture
112 Tahreeb
112d Top Seed

OLDER HORSES
137 Ghostzapper
132 Doyen
131 Roses In May
130 Pleasantly Perfect
129 Rakti
128 Refuse To Bend
128 Silent Witness
128 Sulamani
128 Vinnie Roe
127 Hard Buck
127 Warrsan
126 Exceed And Excel
126 Nayyir
126 Somnus

126 Soviet Song (f)
126 Tante Rose (f)
126 Zenno Rob Roy
125 Firebreak
125 Makybe Diva (f)
125 Tap Dance City
125§ Norse Dancer
124 Bandari
124 Gamut
124 Magistretti
124 National Currency
124 Papineau
124 Powerscourt
124 Var
124§ Salselon
123 Arakan
123 Chic (f)
123 Ikhtyar
123 Patavellian
123 Royal Millennium
123 The Tatling
123 The Trader
123 Westerner
122 Altieri
122 Ashdown Express
122 Epalo
122 High Accolade
122 Ingrandire
122 Mubtaker
122 Prince Kirk
122 Russian Rhythm (f)
122 Touch of Land
121 Alkaadhem
121 Execute
121 Fair Mix
121 Frizzante (f)
121 Le Vie dei Colori
121 Millenary
121 Pivotal Point
121 Senex
121 Simonas
120 Autumn Glory
120 Barolo
120 Brian Boru
120 Chorist (f)
120 Favourable Terms (f)
120 Kalaman
120 Monsieur Bond
120 Muqbil
120 Osterhase
120 Phoenix Reach
120 Polar Way
120 Polish Summer
120 Silence Is Golden (f)
120 Six Perfections (f)
120 Vallee Enchantee (f)
120 Victory Moon
119 Albanova (f)
119 Ancient World
119 Eagle Rise
119 First Charter
119 Martillo

119 My Risk
119 Nebraska Tornado (f)
119 Passing Glance
119 Persian Majesty
119 Policy Maker
119 Scott's View
119 Sights On Gold
119 Soldier Hollow
119 Star Valley
119 Tillerman
119 Vangelis
119 Vespone
118 Alcazar
118 Bahamian Pirate
118 Crimson Palace (f)
118 Distinction
118 Feet So Fast
118 Gateman
118 Hurricane Alan
118 Imperial Dancer
118 Keltos
118 Maktub
118 Mamool
118 Mr Dinos
118 Nysaean
118 Orientor
118 Paolini
118 Polar Ben
118 Right Approach
118 Smokin Beau
118 Systematic
118 Whortleberry (f)
118? Risk Seeker

EXPLANATORY NOTES

'Racehorses of 2004' deals individually, in alphabetical sequence, with every horse that ran on the Flat in Britain in 2004, plus numerous overseas-trained horses not seen in Britain. For each of these horses is given (1) its age, colour and sex, (2) its breeding, and, where this information has not been given in a previous Racehorses Annual, a family outline, (3) a form summary giving its Timeform rating at the end of the previous year, followed by the details of all its performances during the past year, (4) a Timeform rating, or ratings, of its merit in 2004 (which appears in the margin), (5) a Timeform commentary on its racing or general characteristics as a racehorse, with some suggestions, perhaps, regarding its prospects for 2005, and (6) the name of the trainer in whose charge it was on the last occasion it ran. For each two-year-old the foaling date is also given.

TIMEFORM RATINGS

The Timeform Rating of a horse is a measure of the *best* form it displayed in the season under review, expressed in pounds and arrived at by the use of handicapping techniques which include careful examination of a horse's running against other horses. Without going into complexities, the scale used for Timeform ratings represents around 3 lb a length at five furlongs, 2 lb a length at a mile and a quarter and 1 lb at two miles. Timeform maintains a 'running' handicap of all horses in training throughout the season, the in-season ratings usually reflecting Timeform's interpretation of a horse's *current* form, as opposed to its *best* form, where the two may be different.

THE LEVEL OF THE RATINGS

The attention of buyers of British bloodstock and others who may be concerned with Timeform ratings as a measure of absolute racing merit is drawn to the fact that at the close of each season the ratings of all the horses that have raced are re-examined. If necessary, the general level of the handicap is adjusted so that all the ratings are kept at the same standard level from year to year. Some of the ratings may, therefore, be different from those in the final issue of the 2004 Timeform Black Book series. The 'Racehorses Annual' figure is the definitive Timeform Rating.

RATINGS AND WEIGHT-FOR-AGE

The reader has, in the ratings in this book, a universal handicap embracing all the horses in training it is possible to weigh up, ranging from tip-top performers, with ratings from 130 to 145, through categories such as high-class, very smart, smart, useful, fairly useful, fair and modest, down to the poorest, rated around the 20 mark. All the ratings are at weight-for-age, so that equal ratings mean horses of equal merit: perhaps it would be clearer if we said that the universal rating handicap is really not a single handicap, but four handicaps side by side: one for two-year-olds, one for three-year-olds, one for four-year-olds and one for older horses. Thus, a three-year-old rated, for argument's sake, at 117 is deemed to be identical in point of 'merit' with a four-year-old also rated at 117: but for them to have equal chances in, say, a mile race in May, the three-year-old would need to be receiving 9 lb from the four-year-old, which is the weight difference specified by the Age, Weight and Distance Tables on the end papers at the front and back of the book.

USING THE RATINGS

A. Horses of the Same Age

If the horses all carry the same weight there are no adjustments to be made, and the horses with the highest ratings have the best chances. If the horses carry different weights, jot down their ratings, and to the rating of each horse add one point for every pound the horse is set to carry less than 10 st, or subtract one point for every pound it has to carry more than 10 st.

B. Horses of Different Ages

Consult the Age, Weight and Distance Tables printed on the end papers at the front and back of the book. Treat each horse separately, and compare the weight it has to carry with the weight prescribed for it in the tables, according to the age of the horse, the distance of the race and the time of the year. Then, add one point to the rating for each pound the horse has to carry less than the weight given in the tables: or, subtract one point from the rating for every pound it has to carry more than the weight prescribed by the tables.

Example (1½ miles on June 30th)

(Table Weights: 5-y-o+ 10-0; 4-y-o 9-13; 3-y-o 9-1)

6 Bay Pearl (10-2)	....	Rating 115	....	subtract 2	....	113
4 Elshabeeba (9-9)	....	Rating 114	....	add 4	....	118
5 Regal Charge (9-5)	....	Rating 115	....	add 9	....	124
3 Inclination (9-2)	....	Rating 120	....	subtract 1	....	119

Regal Charge (124) has the best chance at the weights,
with 5 lb in hand of Inclination

TURF AND ARTIFICIAL-SURFACE RATINGS

When a horse has raced on turf and on an artificial surface and its form on one is significantly different from the other, the two ratings are given, the one for artificial surfaces set out below the turf preceded by 'a'. Where there is only one rating, that is to be used for races on both turf and artificial surfaces.

NOTE ON RIDERS' ALLOWANCES

For the purposes of rating calculations it should, in general, be assumed that the allowance a rider is able to claim is nullified by his or her inexperience. Therefore, the weight adjustments to the ratings should be calculated on the weight allotted by the handicapper, or determined by the race conditions.

WEIGHING UP A RACE

The ratings tell you which horses in a race are most favoured by the weights; but complete analysis demands that the racing character of each horse, as set out in its commentary, is also studied carefully to see if there is any reason why the horse might be expected not to run up to its rating or indeed, with a lightly raced or inexperienced horse, might improve on it. It counts for little that a horse is thrown in at the weights if it has no pretensions to staying the distance, is unable to act on the prevailing going, or to accommodate itself to the conformation of the track.

There are other factors to consider too. For example, the matter of pace versus stamina: as between two stayers of equal merit, racing over a distance suitable to both. Firm going, or a small field with the prospect of a slowly-run race, would favour the one with the better pace and acceleration, whereas good to soft or softer going, or a big field with the prospect of a strong gallop, would favour the sounder stayer. There is also the matter of the horse's temperament; nobody should be in a hurry to take a short price about a horse which might not put its best foot forward. The quality of jockeyship is also an important factor when deciding between horses with similar chances.

Incidentally, in setting out the various characteristics, requirements and peculiarities of each horse in its commentary, we have expressed ourselves in as critical a manner as possible, endeavouring to say just as much, and no more, than the facts seem to warrant. Where there are clear indications, and conclusions can be drawn with fair certainty, we have drawn them; if it is a matter of probability or possibility we have put it that way, being careful not to say the one when we mean the other; and where real conclusions are not to be drawn, we have been content to state the facts. Furthermore, when we say that a horse *may* not be suited by firm going, we do not expect it to be treated as though we had said the horse *is not* suited by firm going. In short, both in our thinking and in the setting out of our views we have aimed at precision.

THE FORM SUMMARIES

The form summary enclosed in the brackets lists each horse's performances on the Flat during the past year in chronological sequence, showing, for each race, the distance, the state of the going and the horse's placing at the finish.

The distance of each race is given in furlongs, fractional distances being expressed in the decimal notation to the nearest tenth of a furlong. The prefix 'a' signifies a race on an artificial surface (except for 'f' for fibresand at Wolverhampton until June and Southwell, and 'p' for polytrack at Wolverhampton from October, and Lingfield).

The going is symbolised as follows: f=firm (turf) or fast (artificial surface); m=good to firm, or standard to fast (artificial surface); g=good (turf) or standard (artificial surface); d=good to soft/dead, or standard to slow (artificial surface); s=soft (turf) or slow, sloppy, muddy or wet (artificial surface); v=heavy.

Placings are indicated, up to sixth place, by the use of superior figures, an asterisk being used to denote a win.

Thus [2004 81: 10s* 12f³ 11.7g f11g² Sep 7] signifies that the horse was rated 81 the previous year (if there is no rating it indicates that the horse did not appear in 'Racehorses' for that year). In 2004 it ran four times, winning over 10 furlongs on soft going first time out, then finishing third over 12 furlongs on firm going, then out of the first six over 11.7 furlongs on good going, then second over 11 furlongs on standard going on a fibresand track. The date of its last run was September 7.

Included in the pedigree details are the highest Timeform Annual ratings during their racing careers of the sires, dams and sires of dams of all horses, where the information is available.

Where sale prices are considered relevant F denotes the price as a foal, Y the price as a yearling, 2-y-o as a two-year-old, and so on. These are given in guineas unless prefixed by IR (Irish guineas), $ (American dollars), € (euros) or accompanied by francs (French francs). Other currencies are converted approximately into guineas or pounds sterling at the prevailing exchange rate. Significant sales after the horse's final outing are mentioned towards the end of the commentaries.

THE RATING SYMBOLS

The following may be attached to, or appear instead of, a rating:-

p   likely to improve.

P   capable of *much* better form.

+   the horse may be better than we have rated it.

d   the horse appears to have deteriorated, and might no longer be capable of running to the rating given.

§   unreliable (for temperamental or other reasons).

§§   so temperamentally unsatisfactory as not to be worth a rating.

?   the horse's rating is suspect. If used without a rating the symbol implies that the horse can't be assessed with confidence, or, if used in the in-season Timeform publications, that the horse is out of form.

RACEHORSES OF 2004

Horse	Commentary	Rating

AAHGOWANGOWAN (IRE) 5 b.m. Tagula (IRE) 116 – Cabcharge Princess (IRE) **69**
64 (Rambo Dancer (CAN) 107) [2004 66: 5g 5v 5m⁵ 5g² 5g* 5g⁵ 5g 5d⁵ 5d² 5d 5g Oct 8]
sturdy mare: poor mover: fair handicapper: won at Hamilton in June: probably best at 5f:
acts on any going: tried visored, not since 2002: tongue tied: races prominently. *M. Dods*

AASTRAL MAGIC 2 b.f. (Apr 19) Magic Ring (IRE) 115 – Robanna (USA) 127) [2004 6g* 6f* 6m⁴ 5.7d⁶ Aug 27] first foal: dam, maiden who stayed 1¾m, **80**
half-sister to Jersey Stakes winner Lots of Magic (by Magic Ring): fairly useful perform-
er: won maiden at Kempton in May and minor event at Windsor in June: below form in
minor events after: will probably stay 7f: races up with pace. *R. Hannon*

ABBAJABBA 8 b.g. Barrys Gamble 102 – Bo' Babbity 75 (Strong Gale 116) [2004 **73**
95: f6s 6g 6g 6v 6d² 6s 7f⁵ 7.1d 6s⁶ p7.1d Nov 4] quite good-topped gelding: has a round
action: fair performer: best around 6f: acts on firm ground, all wins on good or softer:
usually waited with. *C. W. Fairhurst*

ABBEYGATE 3 b.g. Unfuwain (USA) 131 – Ayunli 81 (Chief Singer 131) [2004 62: **49**
10d 9.9d p12g 12g 13.8v p16g p13.9g p10m Dec 21] strong gelding: poor maiden: should
stay 1½m: tried tongue tied/blinkered/in cheekpieces. *T. Keddy*

ABBIEJO (IRE) 7 b.m. Blues Traveller (IRE) 119 – Chesham Lady (IRE) (Fayruz **35**
116) [2004 –: f5g⁶ f7g⁵ f8g⁶ f7m⁶ 6.1g 10.2s p9.5g Dec 13] poor maiden: stays 7f: acts on
fibresand: tried in cheekpieces. *G. Fierro*

A BEETOO (IRE) 4 b.f. Bahhare (USA) 122 – Sonya's Pearl (IRE) (Conquering Hero **–**
(USA) 116) [2004 63: p10g Jan 28] modest maiden: best form at 7f/1m: raced only on
all-weather: sometimes slowly away. *J. R. Best*

ABELARD (IRE) 3 b.g. Fasliyev (USA) 120 – Half-Hitch (USA) 88 (Diesis 133) **67**
[2004 66: 5d⁶ 5m⁵ 6g 6m⁵ 5m 5m² p6g p5.1g³ f5g³ Nov 9] smallish gelding: fair maiden: **a56**
should stay 6f: acts on polytrack, yet to race on extremes of going on turf: tried visored/in
cheekpieces. *R. A. Fahey*

ABERDEEN (IRE) 2 b.c. (Mar 30) Xaar 132 – Olivia Jane (IRE) (Ela-Mana-Mou **80**
132) [2004 p7g⁶ 6m² 8.5g⁴ Oct 2] €30,000Y, 52,000 2-y-o: eighth foal: half-brother to 7f
(at 2 yrs) to 1¼m winner King O' The Mana (by Turtle Island) and 1¾m seller winner
Ziggy's Viola (by Roi Danzig): dam unraced: fairly useful form in frame in maiden at
Goodwood and minor event at Epsom: should stay 1¼m: joined D. Oughton in Hong
Kong. *P. Mitchell*

ABERDEEN PARK 2 gr.f. (May 12) Environment Friend 128 – Michelee 58 (Merdon **70**
Melody 98) [2004 5.1s⁵ 6m 5g 5.7f⁴ 7.1d⁵ 6g² 7m² 7d 6v³ p6g Nov 13] workmanlike
filly: second foal: dam 2-y-o 6f seller winner: fair maiden: placed in nurseries: effective at
6f/7f: acts on any turf going: sometimes slowly away: tends to edge left. *Mrs H. Sweeting*

ABERDOVEY 2 b.f. (Feb 3) Mister Baileys 123 – Annapurna (IRE) 101 (Brief Truce **77**
(USA) 126) [2004 6m⁵ 6f* 6m³ 6.5m³ 7g Oct 2] 50,000Y: first foal: dam,
2-y-o 7f winner, half-sister to Rockfel winner Name of Love: fair performer: won maiden
at Redcar in June: ran creditably in nurseries next 2 starts: should stay 1m. *M. L. W. Bell*

ABIDE (FR) 2 ch.f. (Mar 30) Pivotal 124 – Ariadne (GER) (Kings Lake (USA) 133) **85**
[2004 7g⁶ 7g² 7g⁶ Oct 11] 30,000Y: tall filly: fifth foal: half-sister to 3 winners abroad:
dam, German 1m winner, out of sister to dam of King's Best and Urban Sea: best effort
in maidens when eased 6 lengths second to Fen Shui at Kempton: badly hampered final
start: should stay 1m. *R. Hannon*

A BID IN TIME (IRE) 3 b.f. Danetime (IRE) 121 – Bidni (IRE) (Maelstrom Lake **53**
118) [2004 54: p5g f5g 5s² 5.1g 5d⁶ 5d⁶ 6s⁶ 6m Jul 7] leggy, good-topped filly: modest
performer: best at 5f: acts on soft and good to firm ground: sometimes slowly away/
unruly in stall. *D. Shaw*

ABIGAIL ADAMS 3 ch.f. Kris 135 – Rose Vibert (Caerleon (USA) 132) [2004 8.1d **–**
10m Sep 7] fourth foal: half-sister to 4-y-o Serbelloni and 6-y-o Sky Quest: dam unraced

daughter of smart 7f performer Premier Rose: well held in maidens at Sandown and Leicester. *P. W. Harris*

ABINGTON ANGEL   3 ch.f. Machiavellian (USA) 123 – Band (USA) (Northern **78** Dancer) [2004 78: 7m 8.2m 9s p12g* 12g Sep 22] close-coupled, good-quartered filly: has a quick action: fair performer: won maiden at Lingfield in September by 8 lengths: looked most reluctant final appearance: stays 1½m: acts on polytrack and good to firm going: tried tongue tied, wore hood/blinkers last 3 outings. *B. J. Meehan*

A BIT OF FUN   3 ch.g. Unfuwain (USA) 131 – Horseshoe Reef 88 (Mill Reef (USA) **44** 141) [2004 –: f8.5g⁵ f9.4s² p8g f9.4g* 8.5m 8.5g Jul 13] useful-looking gelding: poor performer: won banded race at Wolverhampton in May: stays 9.4f: acts on fibresand, raced only on good/good to firm ground on turf: has looked difficult ride. *J. J. Quinn*

ABLAJ (IRE)   3 ch.g. Horse Chestnut (SAF) 119 – Passe Passe (USA) 78 (Lear Fan **54** (USA) 130) [2004 66: 8d 7m⁴ 7f⁴ p12d⁵ Jun 26] sturdy gelding: modest maiden: stays easy 1½m: acts on polytrack and good to firm going: tried visored. *E. A. L. Dunlop*

ABLE BAKER CHARLIE (IRE)   5 b.g. Sri Pekan (USA) 117 – Lavezzola (IRE) **101** (Salmon Leap (USA) 131) [2004 100p: 8g⁴ 8f² 8m 9g Oct 2] useful-looking gelding: useful performer: very good head second of 31 to Mine in Hunt Cup at Royal Ascot: below par after, mid-field in Cambridgeshire at Newmarket final one: effective at 1m/1¼m: acts on polytrack, firm and good to soft ground: has worn crossed noseband: has edged right: usually waited with. *J. R. Fanshawe*

ABLE CHARLIE (GER)   2 ch.g. (Feb 19) Lomitas 129 – Alula (GER) (Monsun **76** (GER) 124) [2004 6g² 7d⁶ 6g Sep 14] €28,000Y: close-coupled gelding: good mover: first foal: dam German 2-y-o 6.5f winner: best effort in maidens when second at Doncaster: needs to settle to stay beyond 6f: reluctant final start: refused to enter stall following month. *Mrs J. R. Ramsden*

ABLE MIND   4 b.g. Mind Games 121 – Chlo-Jo 65 (Belmez (USA) 131) [2004 79: 6m **65** 10.1s 7.1d⁶ 7.9g³ 7.2s³ Oct 12] rather leggy, lengthy gelding: fair maiden: stays 1m: acts on soft and good to firm ground: carries head awkwardly. *A. C. Whillans*

ABOUSTAR   4 b.g. Abou Zouz (USA) 109 – Three Star Rated (IRE) 79 (Pips Pride **46** 117) [2004 –: f8g⁵ f7s f6s⁵ 5g⁵ Sep 6] tall, leggy gelding: poor maiden: stays 1m: acts on fibresand: tried in cheekpieces. *M. Brittain*

ABOVE BOARD   9 b.g. Night Shift (USA) – Bundled Up (USA) (Sharpen Up 127) **–** [2004 –: f6g⁵ f6g f6g² f6g f6g³ f6s f6g* f5g f6g⁶ 6.1s 6v May 10] smallish, robust gelding: **a52** modest performer: won banded race at Southwell in March: stays 6f: acts on fibresand, no form on turf since 2 yrs: occasionally wears cheekpieces/blinkers: usually tongue tied: inconsistent. *R. F. Marvin*

ABRACADABJAR   6 b.g. Royal Abjar (USA) 121 – Celt Song (IRE) (Unfuwain **–** (USA) 131) [2004 –: f11g Jan 6] short-backed gelding: of little account. *Miss Z. C. Davison*

ABRAXAS   6 b.g. Emperor Jones (USA) 119 – Snipe Hall 93 (Crofthall 110) [2004 45, **44 §** a61: f5s⁵ p5g f5s 5s 5s 5v May 10] unreliable maiden: effective at 5f/6f: acts on all- **a55 §** weather and good to firm going: tried blinkered, wears cheekpieces. *J. Akehurst*

ABRAXAS ANTELOPE (IRE)   2 b.c. (Mar 25) Imperial Ballet (IRE) 110 – Lyph- **105** arden (IRE) (Lyphard's Special (USA) 122) [2004 6m* 6d* 6s³ 6d² Aug 30] €15,500F, €10,000Y, 50,000 2-y-o: close-coupled colt: half-brother to several winners in Italy/Spain: dam, poor Irish maiden, out of half-sister to Irish 1000 Guineas and Yorkshire Oaks winner Sarah Siddons: useful performer: won maiden at Hamilton in June and minor event at Doncaster in July: placed in Gimcrack Stakes (1¾ lengths third to Tony James) at York and listed race (bit below best) at Ripon: will stay 1m: sold to race in Hong Kong. *J. Howard Johnson*

ABROGATE (IRE)   3 b.g. Revoque (IRE) 122 – Czarina's Sister (Soviet Lad (USA)) **51** [2004 51: p8g f8g² f8g⁴ 8m⁵ 8m Jul 23] good-topped gelding: modest maiden handicapper: stays 1m: acts on fibresand, good to firm and good to soft going: wore cheekpieces final start. *P. C. Haslam*

ABSENT FRIENDS   7 b.g. Rock City 120 – Green Supreme (Primo Dominie 121) **89** [2004 108: 5v 5m⁶ 5m 5d⁶ 5d 5d 5g 5m 5.2g⁴ 5m 5s Sep 25] strong, lengthy gelding: just fairly useful in 2004: best at 5f: acts on firm and good to soft going, not on soft/heavy: sometimes early to post: often forces pace. *J. Balding*

ABSINTHER   7 b.g. Presidium 124 – Heavenly Queen (Scottish Reel 123) [2004 56: **54** 12m 12f² 11.9f* 11.6f⁴ 11.9f³ 11.6g³ 10s 12f Sep 4] good-bodied gelding: modest handicapper: won at Brighton in June: stays 1½m: acts on fibresand, firm and soft ground: visored once earlier in career: has run well sweating: sometimes slowly away: held up. *M. R. Bosley*

ABSOLUT EDGE 2 ch.g. (Apr 23) Atraf 116 – Sparkling Edge 56 (Beveled (USA)) – [2004 5m f5g⁶ Jul 9] slowly away, last in maiden/seller. *J. A. Pickering*

ABSOLUTELY FAB (IRE) 3 ch.f. Entrepreneur 123 – Hamama (USA) (Majestic Light (USA)) [2004 –: 7f p12d f8g Jul 9] lengthy, good-bodied filly: no form. *Mrs C. A. Dunnett*

ABSOLUTELY PERHAPS (IRE) 2 b.f. (Mar 20) Daylami (IRE) 138 – Dream **47** Lover (Pursuit of Love 124) [2004 p10g⁶ Nov 27] €15,000Y: third foal: dam unraced half-sister to dual Gold Cup winner Royal Rebel: 50/1, sixth in maiden at Lingfield: will be suited by 1½m+. *D. Morris*

ABSOLUTELY SOAKED (IRE) 3 b.f. Alhaarth (IRE) 126 – Vasilopoula (IRE) **62 d** (Kenmare (FR) 125) [2004 62: 10d⁵ 10s⁶ 11.6s 10.1m 10.1g 7g² 6d Nov 5] smallish filly: modest maiden at best: may prove best around 1m: acts on soft and good to firm ground: refused to settle fourth outing: blinkered last 2 starts. *Dr J. D. Scargill*

ABSOLUTELYTHEBEST (IRE) 3 b.c. Anabaa (USA) 130 – Recherchee (Rain- **84** bow Quest (USA) 134) [2004 64p: p10g* 12.3g² 11.9d² 12g⁶ 14.1m⁴ 11.6g⁵ 14d 11g Sep 22] good-topped colt: has scope: fairly useful performer: won maiden at Lingfield in January: ran poorly last 2 outings: stays 1½m, possibly not 1¾m: acts on polytrack, unraced on extremes of going on turf: tried visored: sold 35,000 gns. *E. A. L. Dunlop*

ABSOLUTE UTOPIA (USA) 11 b.g. Mr Prospector (USA) – Magic Gleam (USA) **68** 122 (Danzig (USA)) [2004 63, a69: p10g p10g² p10g² p10g³ p10g⁴ p10g* 10.2g* 10.2f May 21] tall gelding: hobdayed/had soft palate operation early in career: fair performer: won claimer at Lingfield in March and seller at Bath in April: pulled up final start: best at 1¼m/1½m: acted on polytrack, firm and good to soft going: tried blinkered: held up: dead. *J. L. Spearing*

ABSTRACT FOLLY (IRE) 2 b.g. (Apr 7) Rossini (USA) 118 – Cochiti 35 (Kris **58** 135) [2004 7m⁴ 7m⁴ Sep 29] leggy gelding: good mover: modest form in maidens at Thirsk and Newcastle: will stay 1m. *J. D. Bethell*

ABUELOS 5 b.g. Sabrehill (USA) 120 – Miss Oasis 54 (Green Desert (USA) 127) **47** [2004 –: p7g³ p8g⁴ p6g p7g 15.8m⁵ 8.3d 9.2d⁶ 8m⁶ 9.3m⁵ Sep 11] smallish, well-made gelding: poor performer nowadays: left S. Dow after third outing, T. McGovern after fourth (reluctant to race): stays 1m: acts on polytrack, probably on any turf going: tried in cheekpieces: often slowly away. *D. W. Thompson*

ABUNAWWAS (IRE) 4 b.c. In The Wings 128 – Copper Creek 78 (Habitat 134) **112** [2004 110: 7s 6d* 8g* 7f 7.5v 7v⁵ Oct 31] sturdy colt: smart performer: won listed races at Naas (beat Millybaa short head) in May and Leopardstown (by neck from Napper Tandy) in June: well below form last 3 starts: effective at 6f to 1m: acts on soft going: sold 48,000 gns. *K. Prendergast, Ireland*

ACADEMY (IRE) 9 ch.g. Archway (IRE) 115 – Dream Academy (Town And **61** Country 124) [2004 68, a50: 16.1m² 17.1f 16m 16.2m² 15.8m Sep 18] close-coupled **a–** gelding: modest handicapper on turf nowadays, poor on all-weather: effective at 1¾m to 19f: acted on firm going and fibresand: held up: dead. *Andrew Turnell*

ACCA LARENTIA (IRE) 3 gr.f. Titus Livius (FR) 115 – Daisy Grey 46 (Nordance **52 ?** (USA)) [2004 60: 10m 8f 7d³ 7.5g 8g 7g⁶ 10f⁵ 10g⁶ p9.5d Oct 23] leggy, close-coupled filly: fluent mover: maiden: probably stays 1¼m: acts on firm and good to soft going. *R. M. Whitaker*

ACCELERATION (IRE) 4 b.g. Groom Dancer (USA) 128 – Overdrive 99 (Shirley **69 §** Heights 130) [2004 69§: 16.1v* 16g⁶ 12.1g 16d Nov 3] big gelding: fair handicapper: won at Newcastle in March: best at 2m+: acts on heavy and good to firm ground: wore headgear last 6 outings: ungenuine. *R. Allan*

ACCENDERE 3 b.g. Machiavellian (USA) 123 – Littlewick (IRE) 49 (Green Desert **66** (USA) 127) [2004 p7g p7g 7.1d⁵ 8.1s 7m* 7m 7.1m³ p8.6g² p8.6g Dec 17] 7,000Y, 11,500 2-y-o: brother to 1m winner Alnasreya, closely related to French 1m to 11f winner Renshaw (by Woodman) and half-brother to Chilean Grade 1 11f winner Fontanella Borghese (by Roy): dam lightly-raced half-sister to dam of very smart 7f/1m performer Rebecca Sharp (by Machiavellian): fair performer: won handicap at Salisbury in June: stays easy 8.6f: acts on polytrack and good to firm ground: tried tongue tied. *R. M. Beckett*

ACCEPTING   7 b.g. Mtoto 134 – D'Azy 91 (Persian Bold 123) [2004 62§: 18v⁵ 21.6v   **58 §**
19.1f² 16m⁴ 17.1g Oct 4] close-coupled gelding: modest handicapper: stays 19f: acts on
firm and good to soft going (well held on soft/heavy): tried in cheekpieces, blinkered in
2004: sometimes hangs: unreliable. *J. Mackie*

ACE CLUB   3 ch.g. Indian Rocket 115 – Presently 48 (Cadeaux Genereux 131) [2004   **70 d**
74p: 6.1d⁵ 6m p6g 6f⁴ 5.3s² 6m 6m 6d f6g p6g p5.1g Dec 31] angular gelding: fair
performer: left W. Haggas prior to below form last 3 starts: likely to prove best at 5f/6f:
acts on soft ground, probably on firm. *J. Hetherton*

ACE COMING   3 b.g. First Trump 118 – Tarry 65 (Salse (USA) 128) [2004 68d: 10.3g   **72 d**
8s³ 8s* 9.2d* 8.3d 9.2f 8.1g 9.2d 8m 10s Nov 1] sparely-made gelding: fair handicapper:
won at Newcastle in April and Hamilton in May: lost form after: stays 9f: acts on firm and
soft going: usually blinkered: sold 12,000 gns. *D. Eddy*

ACE IN THE HOLE   4 br.f. So Factual (USA) 120 – Timely Raise (USA) (Raise A   **–**
Man (USA)) [2004 –: 10.9d 8.2m May 25] maiden: no form since 2002, including in
cheekpieces. *F. Jordan*

ACE (IRE)   3 b.c. Danehill (USA) 126 – Tea House 107 (Sassafras (FR) 135) [2004   **118**
8g* 8m* 8m* 8m⁵ Sep 25] €300,000Y: close-coupled colt: brother to very smart 1m
winner Hawkeye (stayed 1¼m) and US Grade 1 9f winner Danish, and closely related/
half-brother to numerous winners: dam Irish 6f and 1m winner: smart performer, lightly
raced: easy winner of first 3 starts, maiden at Navan in June, 4-runner minor event at
Leopardstown in July and 5-runner Desmond Stakes at Leopardstown (by 2 lengths from
Hamairi) in August: not discredited when 8¼ lengths fifth to Rakti in Queen Elizabeth II
Stakes at Ascot final outing, edging right: should stay 1¼m: raced only on good/good to
firm ground. *A. P. O'Brien, Ireland*

ACE-MA-VAHRA   6 b.m. Savahra Sound 111 – Asmarina 50 (Ascendant 96) [2004   **50**
f8g⁶ f8s f7g⁶ f8g* f11g⁶ f8g 6.1s 5m f7m⁵ 5d 6m³ 5g f6g⁶ f6m³ f8m³ 6m⁵ 8d f6s⁵ 8f   **a52**
p7.1d² p8.6g f7g⁴ f7g Dec 12] leggy mare: modest performer: won apprentice maiden
handicap at Southwell in February: effective at 6f to 1m: acts on all-weather and good
to firm ground, below form on softer than good: tried in cheekpieces, often blinkered:
inconsistent. *S. R. Bowring*

ACE OF HEARTS   5 b.g. Magic Ring (IRE) 115 – Lonely Heart 101 (Midyan (USA)   **98**
124) [2004 94: 8g 8.3d⁵ 8.1d 8.5g² 8f* 8m* 8m* 8.1d 8d 8g³ 8d 8d Oct 30] short-
backed gelding: useful performer: won minor event at Newmarket in May and handicaps
at Doncaster and Pontefract (beat Calcutta by ½ length) in June: best form around 1m:
acts on fibresand, firm and soft going: free-going sort. *C. F. Wall*

ACHILLES RAINBOW   5 ch.g. Deploy 131 – Naughty Pistol (USA) 69 (Big Pistol   **45**
(USA)) [2004 39: p10g⁴ p8g p10g⁶ p10g Mar 2] angular gelding: poor maiden: broke
leg at Lingfield: seemed to stay 1¼m: acted on polytrack, firm and soft going: dead.
K. R. Burke

ACOLA (FR)   4 ch.f. Acatenango (GER) 127 – Wardara 107 (Sharpo 132) [2004 a7.5g   **59**
9.9s p10g 10.1f 8m Jul 22] second foal: half-sister to 5-y-o Dark Charm: dam 5f/6f
winner: modest maiden at best: left F. Bellenger in France after reappearance: usually
wore headgear: covered by Kyllachy. *R. M. H. Cowell*

ACOMB   4 b.g. Shaamit (IRE) 127 – Aurora Bay (IRE) (Night Shift (USA)) [2004 74:   **85**
7g 7s⁶ 8.1g 8m* 8.1d* 8.3m 10.1g 8.1g⁶ 7m f8g Dec 11] good-bodied gelding: fairly useful handicapper: won at Thirsk in May and Sandown in June: below form subsequently,
leaving M. Easterby after ninth start: best efforts around 1m: acts on good to firm and
good to soft ground: sometimes carries head awkwardly/finds little. *N. Wilson*

ACORAZADO (IRE)   5 b.g. Petorius 117 – Jaldi (IRE) 75 (Nordico (USA)) [2004   **53**
70: p7g p7g² p7g p8g* p8g⁶ p8g² 7m f7g⁴ 8.2v⁶ p7g p7m² p7g Dec 30] quite good-topped   **a73**
gelding: fair handicapper on all-weather, modest on turf: won at Lingfield in February:
stays easy 1m: acts on all-weather and soft going: often blinkered/visored. *G. L. Moore*

ACROPOLIS (IRE)   3 b.c. Sadler's Wells (USA) 132 – Dedicated Lady (IRE)   **124**
101 (Pennine Walk 120) [2004 101: 10m* 12m⁴ Oct 3]
Lot 421 in the catalogue for the Autumn Horses In Training Sales in
late-October didn't turn up at Newmarket. The sale-ring would have been buzzing
had it done so. At the time the entry for the three-year-old colt Acropolis was sub-
mitted he must have been considered surplus to requirements at Ballydoyle, but it
wouldn't have been long before connections did an about-turn. Recovered from
various problems which had kept him on the sidelines during the first eight months

O₂ Kilternan Stakes, Leopardstown—Acropolis overcomes an absence of over ten months to reel in the front-running Lord Admiral (No.5); Trefflich (left) is third

of the year, Acropolis made a successful return in a listed event and followed that with fourth in the Prix de l'Arc de Triomphe. Far from being surplus to requirements, Acropolis showed himself to be at least the equal of any other horse in the O'Brien stable.

Acropolis hadn't been one of Ballydoyle's top two-year-olds in 2003; following his victory in a maiden at Galway, he'd finished last of six to American Post in the Prix Jean-Luc Lagardere at Longchamp, then ten lengths third to Bago in the Criterium International at Saint-Cloud. With a step up to a mile and a quarter or more looking sure to suit him, it was on the cards that Acropolis would prove himself a better three-year-old. Further improvement duly came when Acropolis tackled a mile and a quarter in the O₂ Kilternan Stakes at Leopardstown on his reappearance in September. Up against five useful performers, Acropolis was sent off favourite, despite looking in need of the run, and managed to justify the support, hanging as he made ground under pressure to reel in front-running Lord Admiral close home. The entry made for Acropolis in the Arc seemed optimistic, and in a nineteen-runner field only Imperial Dancer started at longer odds. With the step up to a mile and a half proving very much in his favour, however, Acropolis, looking in great shape, excelled himself at Longchamp. Soon behind after a tardy start, he was poorly placed running down the hill but, racing towards the rail, galloped on strongly in the straight, passing several tiring rivals to snatch fourth on the line, just three and a half lengths behind Bago. There is a chance that Acropolis might have been flattered to some degree, but for now he has been given full credit for his performance.

		Sadler's Wells (USA) (b 1981)	Northern Dancer (b 1961)	Nearctic
				Natalma
Acropolis (IRE) (b.c. 2001)			Fairy Bridge (b 1975)	Bold Reason
				Special
		Dedicated Lady (IRE) (b 1989)	Pennine Walk (b 1982)	Persian Bold
				Tifrums
			Salabella (b 1979)	Grey Sovereign
				Supreme Lady

Acropolis is closely related to three winners, notably the smart performers Fairy Queen (by Fairy King) and Tashawak (by Night Shift), the former successful at up to an extended mile and a half, including in the Prix de Royallieu, and the latter at up to a mile, including in the Falmouth Stakes. Their dam Dedicated Lady won three times in Ireland at two over five and six furlongs. A half-sister to the

27

useful 1986 two-year-old six-furlong winner Rockfella and the useful winner at up to a mile Silk Petal, Dedicated Lady (bought for 145,000 guineas at the 1999 December Sales when in foal to Entrepreneur) is a daughter of a maiden half-sister to the Irish St Leger winner M-Lolshan and is from the family of Vinnie Roe. Acropolis himself fetched 550,000 guineas when he went through the sale-ring at Newmarket three years after his dam. A strong sort who acts on soft and good to firm ground, Acropolis is a good walker but has a short, unimpressive action in his faster paces, and seemed not to be striding out freely in the early stages of the Arc. Acropolis is a very smart colt judged on his Arc performance, though as yet not quite so good as his namesake who in 1955 finished third in the Derby, for which he started favourite, and second, beaten a head, in the King George VI and Queen Elizabeth Stakes. The previous Acropolis was expected by many to carry all before him as a four-year-old, but after winning the John Porter Stakes on his reappearance he failed to land the odds on his next two starts and was retired to stud. Expectations won't be quite so high for the present-day Acropolis. *A. P. O'Brien, Ireland*

ACTION FIGHTER (GER) 4 ch.g. Big Shuffle (USA) 122 – Action Art (IRE)   **90**
(Bustino 136) [2004 98: f8.5g³ f7g Jan 15] fairly useful performer: easily better effort in 2004 when third in minor event at Wolverhampton on reappearance: stays 1m: acts on fibresand, raced only on good/good to soft ground on turf: tried blinkered/in cheekpieces: gelded after final start. *N. P. Littmoden*

ACTIVE ACCOUNT (USA) 7 b. or br.g. Unaccounted For (USA) 124 – Ameritop   **75 d**
(USA) (Topsider (USA)) [2004 77: f8.5s² f8.5g² f8.5g⁵ 8.1g⁶ 7.9f⁶ 10s³ 10.5d 10m 10m 10f⁶ p9.5g Dec 13] fair handicapper: on the downgrade: has reportedly had a wind operation: effective at 1m, barely at 11f: acts on all-weather, firm and soft ground: wandered for only win (at Wolverhampton): tried blinkered. *Mrs H. Dalton*

ACTIVE ASSET (IRE) 2 ch.c. (Mar 1) Sinndar (IRE) 134 – Sacristy 54 (Godswalk   **89**
(USA) 130) [2004 6g² 7m* 7.1m² 10d Oct 30] €30,000Y: good-topped colt: half-brother to several winners, including fairly useful 2002 2-y-o 5f winner Bravo Ragasso (by Primo Dominie) and useful 7f (at 2 yrs) and 9f winner Holtye (by Danehill): dam maiden half-sister to Park Appeal, Desirable and Alydaress: won maiden at Yarmouth in July: good second of 4 to Kamakiri in minor event at Sandown, much better effort after: needs to settle to stay 1¼m. *M. R. Channon*

ACT OF THE PACE (IRE) 4 b.f. King's Theatre (IRE) 128 – Lady In Pace (Burslem   **86**
123) [2004 51: 11.1g⁴ 12.3m* 11.9g² 13f⁶ 14.8d³ Aug 27] leggy, unfurnished filly: fairly useful performer: won maiden at Ripon in June: good efforts when placed in handicaps after: stays 15f: acts on good to firm and good to soft going. *M. Johnston*

ACTRICE (IRE) 4 b.f. Danehill (USA) 126 – Ange Bleu (USA) (Alleged (USA)   **114**
138) [2004 109: 10g* 10d⁶ 10.5g⁵ 8f⁴ 8g 10m⁵ Oct 3] big, leggy, lengthy filly: second foal: half-sister to useful French 11.5f to 12.5f winner Arlesienne (by Alzao): dam, third at 1¼m in France, half-sister to Breeders' Cup Classic winner Arcangues and to dams of Cape Verdi and Aquarelliste: smart performer: won listed race at Longchamp in April and Prix Corrida at Saint-Cloud (beat Visorama 1½ lengths) in May: below best last 3 starts, including when fourth to Favourable Terms in Windsor Forest Stakes at Royal Ascot and fifth to Alexander Goldrun in Prix de l'Opera at Longchamp (wandered): best form around 1¼m: acts on good to soft ground: held up. *E. Lellouche, France*

ACUZIO 3 b.c. Mon Tresor 113 – Veni Vici (IRE) (Namaqualand (USA)) [2004 10.5g⁶   **61**
8.1m⁶ 8.1d 7.2g⁴ 8.1d 7m 8.1s⁵ 10.2s Sep 20] second foal: brother to 2002 2-y-o 8.5f seller winner Fortuna Mea: dam ran once in Ireland: modest maiden: stays 1m. *W. M. Brisbourne*

ADAIKALI (IRE) 3 b.c. Green Desert (USA) 127 – Adaiyka (IRE) 110 (Doyoun   **98**
124) [2004 67p: 7d 8.1m² 10f* 10m² 10f 10f⁴ 7.9g² Oct 8] smallish, deep-bodied colt: has a quick action: useful handicapper: won at Pontefract in June: very good second to Nashaab at York final start: stays 1¼m: acts on firm going: sold 90,000 gns, joined S. Woods in Hong Kong. *Sir Michael Stoute*

ADALAR (IRE) 4 br.g. Grand Lodge (USA) 125 – Adalya (IRE) (Darshaan 133)   **76 d**
[2004 –: p12g p10g p10g p10g⁶ 10d 10m 12.3g 10.1m⁴ 8g 8.1m² 8m² 8.1g p8.6g² p8.6g p9.5g⁴ p9.5g⁶ Dec 20] fair handicapper: on downgrade: stays 1¼m: acts on polytrack, good to firm and good to soft going: tried visored/in cheekpieces. *P. D. Evans*

ADALPOUR (IRE) 6 b.g. Kahyasi 130 – Adalya (IRE) (Darshaan 133) [2004 60:   **–**
f16.2g f12g Jan 23] modest handicapper: stays 2m: acts on all-weather, raced mainly on

good ground or softer on turf: sometimes slowly away: tried tongue tied earlier in career. *D. Burchell*

ADANTINO   5 b.g. Glory of Dancer 121 – Sweet Whisper 63 (Petong 126) [2004 64: p6g⁶ f7g³ f9.4g⁴ p7g* p7g³ p7g³ 7m⁶ 6f³ 6m* 6m⁶ 5.7m p7g⁶ p7g⁶ p6g* p7m³ p6m⁴ p7g Dec 30] smallish, compact gelding: fair performer: won maiden in February, handicap in July and minor event in November, all at Lingfield: effective at 6f/easy 7f: acts on all-weather, firm and good to soft going: usually blinkered: sometimes looks none too keen, but is consistent. *B. R. Millman*   **67**

ADAPTABLE   3 b.f. Groom Dancer (USA) 128 – Adeptation (USA) (Exceller (USA) 129) [2004 75p: 8.3g 10.2g Jun 3] smallish, good-topped filly: fair form in 2 maidens at 2 yrs: well held in 2004: should stay 1¼m. *H. Candy*   **–**

ADEEBA (IRE)   3 b.f. Alhaarth (IRE) 126 – Nedaarah 83 (Reference Point 139) [2004 55: f9.4g⁶ p10g May 29] rather leggy filly: maiden: well held in 2004. *E. A. L. Dunlop*   **–**

ADEES DANCER   3 b.f. Danehill Dancer (IRE) 117 – Note (GER) (Reliance II 137) [2004 65p: 8.5s 9.9g 9.9g⁵ 16.2g 12m Jul 30] leggy filly: modest maiden: should stay 1½m+. *B. Smart*   **51**

ADIEMUS   6 b.g. Green Desert (USA) 127 – Anodyne 100 (Dominion 123) [2004 108, a115: a9f⁴ a9f³ 10m* 12m Mar 11] useful-looking gelding: smart performer: won handicap at Nad Al Sheba in February by 3 lengths from Swift Tango: broke knee and cannon bone there following month: best form at 9f/1¼m: acted on polytrack and probably any turf going: usually held up: blinkered/visored last 6 starts, tried in cheekpieces: dead. *J. Noseda*   **110**

ADJAWAR (IRE)   6 b.g. Ashkalani (IRE) 128 – Adjriyna 82 (Top Ville 129) [2004 91: 10m 10.5s 12v Oct 16] good-topped gelding: fairly useful at 5 yrs: tailed off in 2004: visored twice at 3 yrs: tried in cheekpieces/tongue tie. *J. J. Quinn*   **–**

ADJIRAM (IRE)   8 b.g. Be My Guest (USA) 126 – Adjriyna 82 (Top Ville 129) [2004 p10g³ p12g⁵ f9.4s⁴ 8g* p12g² 12f Jun 25] well-made gelding: modest on all-weather, poor on turf: won banded race at Brighton in May: effective at 1m to easy 1½m: acts on polytrack, probably on good to firm going: visored last 4 starts. *A. W. Carroll*   **38 a50**

ADMIRAL COMPTON   3 ch.c. Compton Place 125 – Sunfleet 59 (Red Sunset 120) [2004 60p: 8g² 7.1m² 8.2m³ p8m* p7g p8m⁴ Dec 21] lengthy colt: fairly useful performer: trained by A. Stewart until after second start: won maiden at Lingfield in October (left E. Vaughan after): not sure to stay much beyond 1m: acts on polytrack, raced only on good/good to firm ground on turf: visored fourth/fifth starts: reliable. *J. R. Boyle*   **82 +**

ADMIRAL (IRE)   3 b.c. Alhaarth (IRE) 126 – Coast Is Clear (IRE) 60 (Rainbow Quest (USA) 134) [2004 77p: 8g 12g* 11.9d³ 12m* 12g Jul 28] rangy, good sort: fluent   **91**

King George V Stakes (Handicap), Royal Ascot—
a 1,2 for Sir Michael Stoute as Admiral (dark cap) holds top weight Maraahel (blaze);
unlucky-in-running Etmaam (left) and Le Tiss (right) also make the frame ahead of Golden Quest (stars)

mover: fairly useful performer: won handicaps at Goodwood in May and Royal Ascot (King George V Stakes, by a neck from Maraahel): below form at Goodwood final start: effective at 1¼m/1½m: unraced on extremes of going: sold 60,000 gns in October. *Sir Michael Stoute*

ADMITTANCE (USA)   2 b. or br.f. (Feb 12) Red Ransom (USA) – Quittance (USA)   **49** (Riverman (USA) 131) [2004 6g 6g 6s 7d 7.5m Sep 15] €24,000Y: tall, leggy filly: second foal: dam useful French 7f and 9f winner: poor maiden: should stay 1m: best effort on good going. *Mrs J. R. Ramsden*

ADOBE   9 b.g. Green Desert (USA) 127 – Shamshir 116 (Kris 135) [2004 79, a–: 8.1s   **72** 8m 8.3m³ 8.1f⁴ 8f⁴ 8g² 8g 8.2g 8m⁴ 8m 8m⁵ 7.9m 8g 8.1d 8.2g p8.6d* p8.6d⁵ p8.6g⁶   **a62** p8.6g⁶ p8.6g Dec 17] small, stocky gelding: fair performer: won banded race at Wolverhampton in October: best around 1m: acts on all-weather, firm and good to soft going: tongue tied earlier in career: usually claimer ridden: held up: tough. *W. M. Brisbourne*

ADOPTED HERO (IRE)   4 b.g. Sadler's Wells (USA) 132 – Lady Liberty (NZ)   **105** (Noble Bijou (USA)) [2004 105: a12g* May 16] useful performer: won Mijas Cup in May (by 7½ lengths from demoted Oceaninternational) on only Flat outing in 2004: will stay 2m: acts on polytrack/sand and soft going, ran creditably but gave impression uneasy on good to firm: races prominently. *G. L. Moore*

ADORATA (GER)   3 b.f. Tannenkonig (IRE) 111 – Adora (GER) (Danehill (USA)   **71** 126) [2004 f6g p6g 6.1s 6m³ 7f² 7g 6.9g² f6g³ 8.5g 8d² f8g* 7.9g 10g 8.2v 8s⁶ Oct 29] rather sparely-made filly: first foal: dam German 1m winner: fair performer: won maiden at Southwell in August: seems to stay 1¼m: acts on fibresand, firm and soft going. *J. Jay*

ADORATION   2 b.g. (Apr 1) Royal Applause 124 – Unconditional Love (IRE) 104   **74** (Polish Patriot (USA) 128) [2004 5s³ 6m² 6m⁵ 7g 8.1g 6v Oct 23] good-topped gelding: fourth foal: half-brother to 3-y-o First Order and 5-y-o Beamish Prince: dam 5f (at 2 yrs) and 1¼m winner: fair maiden: should stay 7f: acts on soft and good to firm ground: gelded after final start. *M. Johnston*

A DOUBLE EWE BEE   3 b.f. Kingsinger (IRE) 94 – Some Dream 53 (Vitiges (FR)   **–** 132) [2004 p8.6g 8d f7s f7g Dec 12] half-sister to 2000 2-y-o 5f seller winner Some Dust (by King's Signet): dam, maiden on Flat who stayed 1m, winning hurdler: well held in claimers/seller. *W. G. M. Turner*

ADRIATIC ADVENTURE (IRE)   3 ch.f. Foxhound (USA) 103 – Theda 61   **–** (Mummy's Pet 125) [2004 –: f6g p8g Feb 3] small, close-coupled filly: well held, including in claimers. *J. L. Spearing*

AD VALOREM (USA)   2 b.c. (Apr 27) Danzig (USA) – Classy Women (USA)   **121 p** (Relaunch (USA)) [2004 6m* 6g* 6g* Oct 1]

Twenty-seven-year-old Danzig's retirement from active service at Claiborne Stud in Kentucky in July marked the end of a remarkable stud career that started in 1981. Unbeaten in three non-stakes races at around seven furlongs but difficult to train because of knee problems, Danzig has sired more than forty Group/Grade 1 winners from just over a thousand foals of racing age for total earnings of nearly a hundred million dollars. In Europe his Group 1 winners have included Anabaa (Timeform 130), Danehill (126), Dayjur (137), Green Desert (127), Maroof (126), Polish Patriot (128) and Polish Precedent (131), with no fewer than six winners of the July Cup on the score sheet. Though never champion sire in Britain, Danzig has occupied that position three times in the States, with such as Breeders' Cup winners Chief's Crown, Lure and Dance Smartly, the last-named Horse of the Year in Canada in 1991. Predictably, Danzig's progeny were always in demand at the sales, with his three hundred and fifty or so auction yearlings averaging 475,000 dollars and including the top-priced colts sold at Keeneland in 1995 and 2003. The story is not over yet, either at the sales or on the course, since Danzig had twenty-five foals in 2003, thirty-two foals in 2004 and got twenty-five mares in foal in his final season at a private fee believed to be between 200,000 dollars and 250,000 dollars. Moreover, his two-year-olds of 2004 from a crop of thirty-eight include two leading lights in Europe, Dewhurst Stakes fifth Librettist and Ad Valorem. The latter put up one of the best performances of the season by a two-year-old in the Shadwell Stud Middle Park Stakes, thereby achieving what Antonius Pius should have done several months earlier by providing Danzig with his first Group 1 success since 2001. As can be gathered from the European horses

Shadwell Stud Middle Park Stakes, Newmarket—
Ad Valorem defies his inexperience and establishes himself as one of the top two-year-olds;
Rebuttal (right) is second with favourite Iceman going on strongly in third;
chasing them home are (from left to right) Satchem, Russian Blue and Josh

named above, speed rather than stamina has always been the hallmark of runners by Danzig, the average distance of races won by his three-year-olds and up in Britain and the States being just under a mile. Judged on his Middle Park victory, Ad Valorem may well be another in the same mould, and those who have backed him at 16/1 for the Two Thousand Guineas are taking it on trust that he will be effective at the mile trip.

Ad Valorem arrived at Newmarket much less highly tried than either of Aidan O'Brien's previous winners of the race, Minardi in 2000 and Johannesburg in 2001, since both those colts had already notched Group 1 victories. Despite not having contested a pattern event, Ad Valorem went off joint-second favourite, doubtless because he was his trainer's selected—a major consideration even in a year when O'Brien's two-year-olds had not hit the heights collectively—and he was unbeaten in two starts. The races involved, both at the Curragh in September, were a twenty-three-runner maiden, which Ad Valorem won readily as favourite, and the listed St Bernard Blenheim Stakes, for which he started joint-favourite with Indesatchel and beat him pushed out by a length after being close up throughout. Both times Ad Valorem showed plenty of speed without displaying any headstrong tendencies. Ad Valorem's eight rivals in the Middle Park included the favourite Iceman, successful in the Coventry Stakes and runner-up to Etlaala in the Champagne Stakes when giving him weight. There were two other pattern winners in the field, Chateau Istana (Flying Childers Stakes) and Satchem (Sirenia Stakes), plus listed winner Prince Charming, Mill Reef Stakes third Rebuttal, National Stakes third Russian Blue (also trained by O'Brien) and two minor winners. In a race run at a less than searching gallop, Ad Valorem quickened ahead two furlongs out, galloped on resolutely to fend off a dangerous-looking challenge from Rebuttal and won going away by three quarters of a length. Iceman was two and a half lengths further back. On his Middle Park showing, Ad Valorem will not be found wanting in courage at three and his form bears close inspection too, since it places him above all the two-year-olds in Europe with the exception of Shamardal, Dubawi and Motivator. Given the shape of the sprint pattern in Europe, with no Group 1 races before June and the most important championship events, the July Cup and Nunthorpe Stakes, in July and August respectively, the advantages of giving Ad Valorem a crack at the Guineas almost certainly outweigh the disadvantages. This is especially so because O'Brien has already shown with Stravinsky and Mozart that he is fully capable of bringing a colt back from seven furlongs or a mile to land a sprint championship. It has to be said, though, that at this stage of his career Ad Valorem looks more of a natural sprinter than either Stravinsky or Mozart did at the same stage.

31

Mrs John Magnier's "Ad Valorem"

Ad Valorem (USA) (b.c. Apr 27, 2002)	Danzig (USA) (b 1977)	Northern Dancer (b 1961)	Nearctic
			Natalma
		Pas de Nom (b or br 1968)	Admiral's Voyage
			Petitioner
	Classy Women (USA) (b 1988)	Relaunch (gr 1976)	In Reality
			Foggy Note
		Aironlass (b 1979)	Proud Clarion
			Classic Perfection

Ad Valorem, a medium-sized, good-topped colt who has raced only on good or good to firm going, fetched a price just below his sire's overall average when sold as a yearling at Saratoga, 450,000 dollars, which looks a bargain now. The distaff family is a bit short of Grade 1 performers. Ad Valorem is the fifth foal out of Classy Women to win; the best of the rest was his brother Designer, third in the Middle Park Stakes in 1997 but not a great success thereafter. Another sibling, Curragh Stakes third Petite Princess (by Dayjur), foaled a winner of the Canadian Derby, which despite the grand title is a Grade 3 race. Classy Women won a Grade 3 over eight and a half furlongs but she also set a track record for five furlongs on turf at Hollywood Park and was out of a precocious filly in Aironlass, a stakes winner and stakes-placed at two. *A. P. O'Brien, Ireland*

AEGEAN MIST   4 ch.f. Prince Sabo 123 – Dizzydaisy 57 (Sharpo 132) [2004 –: 6g⁴ Sep 25] poor maiden: probably stays 6f: acts on good to firm going. *M. Mullineaux*   **48 ?**

AESCULUS (USA)   3 b. or br.f. Horse Chestnut (SAF) 119 – Crafty Buzz (USA) (Crafty Prospector (USA)) [2004 71p: 8d 7g⁵ 5.7f³ 7m 9.9g³ 8m² 8f* Aug 4] tall, lengthy   **76**

filly: fluent mover: fair handicapper: won at Brighton in August: stays 1¼m: acts on polytrack and firm ground: sent to USA. *L. M. Cumani*

AETHELING (USA) 3 b.f. Swain (IRE) 134 – Etheldreda (USA) 64 (Diesis 133) –
[2004 p12g Sep 1] half-sister to several winners, notably very smart 1m (at 2 yrs) to 10.5f (Prix Lupin) winner Flemensfirth (by Alleged): dam, placed at 1m at 3 yrs, half-sister to US 2-y-o Grade 1 1m winner Bundler: started very slowly when tailed off in maiden at Lingfield: sent to USA. *Mrs A. J. Perrett*

AFADAN (IRE) 6 br.g. Royal Academy (USA) 130 – Afasara (IRE) (Shardari 134) 82
[2004 87: p12.2g² Dec 14] rangy gelding: fairly useful handicapper: creditable second at Wolverhampton only run in 2004: should stay 2m: acts on polytrack, raced mainly on good ground or softer on turf: sometimes tongue tied: has started slowly. *J. R. Jenkins*

AFRASHAD (USA) 2 ch.c. (Apr 4) Smoke Glacken (USA) 120 – Flo White (USA) 107 p
(Whitesburg (USA)) [2004 p6g* Jul 14] $15,500Y, $500,000 2-y-o: sixth foal: half-brother to winner in USA by Just A Cat: dam 5.5f winner in USA: 2/1-on, won 7-runner maiden at Lingfield by 5 lengths from Wazir, setting very strong pace and soon clear (recorded fast time): suffered ligament problem after: likely to prove best at 5f/6f: should make his mark in better company. *Saeed bin Suroor*

AFRICAN BREEZE 2 b.f. (Feb 21) Atraf 116 – Luanshya 78 (First Trump 118) 79
[2004 5m 5m⁴ 5g* 6g⁴ 5m⁵ 6.5m 6d Sep 17] smallish, strong filly: first foal: dam 6f winner: fair performer: won maiden at Redcar in June: creditable efforts next 2 starts: effective at 5f/6f: acts on good to firm going. *R. M. Whitaker*

AFRICAN DAWN 6 b.g. Spectrum (IRE) 126 – Lamu Lady (IRE) 70 (Lomond (USA) 55 d
128) [2004 72: 12m⁶ 12f 12.6g f16g⁴ Jul 23] leggy gelding: modest performer: on the downgrade: stays 1¾m: acts on all-weather and firm going: tongue tied: wore cheek-pieces final start. *L. G. Cottrell*

AFRICAN DREAM 3 b.g. Mark of Esteem (IRE) 137 – Fleet Hill (IRE) 99 (Warrs- 115
han (USA) 117) [2004 p8g³ p8g* 9s* 8g* 10d* 10.3d* 10d 10d⁴ 8d Aug 12] 34,000F: rather leggy, good-topped gelding: third foal: half-brother to fairly useful Irish 9f winner Fenella's Link (by Linamix) and winner in USA by Miner's Mark: dam, 2-y-o 6f/7f winner, later stayed 1¼m and successful in USA: smart performer: won claimer at Lingfield (left P. Cole £20,000), minor event at Kempton, handicap at Newbury (by 2 lengths from Red Lancer), Betfred Classic Trial at Sandown (beat Privy Seal by 3½ lengths, despite jinking left) and Jardine Lloyd Thompson Dee Stakes at Chester (landed odds comfortably by ¾ length from Putra Sas in 3-runner event) between February and May: below form in Coral-Eclipse Stakes at Sandown and Prix Eugene Adam at Maisons-Laffitte next 2 starts: respectable seventh to Norse Dancer in Sovereign Stakes at Salisbury final outing: stays 10.3f: acts on polytrack and soft going, unraced on firmer than good. *P. W. Chapple-Hyam*

Jardine Lloyd Thompson Dee Stakes, Chester—
the gelding African Dream completes a five-timer and lands his second recognised Derby trial;
Putra Sas chases him home, and Mutawassel completes the field

AFRICAN EMPEROR (FR) 2 gr.g. (Apr 26) Highest Honor (FR) 124 – Land of **36**
Ivory (USA) 109 (The Minstrel (CAN) 135) [2004 6m⁶ p8g p6g Oct 7] poor form in
maidens/claimer: slowly away first 2 outings. *W. Jarvis*

AFRICAN GIFT 2 b.f. (Mar 19) Cadeaux Genereux 131 – African Light 65§ (Kala- **59**
glow 132) [2004 6d³ 6g 7m⁶ 5g 6d Oct 11] tall filly: half-sister to several winners,
including fairly useful 9f winners Reciprocal (by Night Shift) and Orpailleur (in Ireland,
by Mon Tresor): dam maiden who stayed 1¼m: modest maiden: stays 7f: acts on good to
firm and good to soft ground: hung left third start. *J. G. Given*

AFRICAN SAHARA (USA) 5 br.h. El Gran Senor (USA) 136 – Able Money **92**
(USA) (Distinctive (USA)) [2004 90: f9.4g⁶ p10g* p10g p8g* p8g⁶ 8g 8.3d⁶ 10g 8.1d
8m⁶ 8m 8d³ 8m⁴ 8m³ 8m* 8.1d⁴ 8.3d² 8.1g² p10g p9.5g⁴ p10m Dec 22] close-coupled,
good-topped horse: fairly useful performer: won handicap in February and minor event
in March, both at Lingfield, and handicap at Redcar in August: effective at 1m/easy
1¼m: acts on all-weather, firm and good to soft going: tongue tied: tough and reliable.
Miss D. Mountain

AFRICAN SPUR (IRE) 4 b.g. Flying Spur (AUS) – African Bloom (African Sky **73 d**
124) [2004 84, a74: f6g f5g f6g² f5s² 6s 7s 6v 6s 7.1d 6d 5m 6f⁶ 7.1f⁵ f6g 8m p10g 5m 6f⁴
6m⁶ 6m Aug 7] deep-girthed gelding: fair performer, on the downgrade: left P. Blockley
after third start, S. Keightley after fourth: stays easy 7f: below form on heavy going, acts
on any other turf and fibresand: tried tongue tied/in headgear: unreliable. *D. Carroll*

AFRICAN STAR 3 b.c. Mtoto 134 – Pass The Rose (IRE) (Thatching 131) [2004 58: **54**
p7g⁶ 10.9f⁵ 11.5m⁶ p10g⁴ 9.9s 10m Sep 23] workmanlike colt: modest maiden: seems to
stay 11f: wore cheekpieces last 2 starts. *Mrs A. J. Perrett*

AFRICAN STORM (IRE) 2 b.g. (Feb 11) Fasliyev (USA) 120 – Out of Africa (IRE) **70**
98 (Common Grounds 118) [2004 5m⁵ 5m² 5g² 6g 5s⁶ 5.1s Oct 19] €110,000Y: first foal:
dam, 2-y-o 6f/7f winner, half-sister to very smart sprinter Pipalong: fair maiden: second
at Lingfield and Kempton: will probably prove best at 5f/easy 6f: acts on good to firm
ground: gelded after final start. *S. Kirk*

AFRICAN SUNSET (IRE) 4 b.g. Danehill Dancer (IRE) 117 – Nizamiya (Darshaan **–**
133) [2004 10m³ 10.4m⁵ Jun 11] in rear in maiden at Naas in 2002 for A. O'Brien: little
form in maiden at Ayr and claimer at York when next seen on Flat. *J. Howard Johnson*

AFTER ALL (IRE) 3 gr.f. Desert Story (IRE) 115 – All Ashore (Nureyev (USA) 131) **51 §**
[2004 64: p5g³ p6g⁵ Feb 23] modest maiden: stays 6f: raced only on polytrack and good/
good to firm going: temperamental: sold €13,000 in June, sent to USA. *G. A. Butler*

AFTER LENT (IRE) 3 b.g. Desert Style (IRE) 121 – Yashville (Top Ville 129) [2004 **57 +**
8m 9.2f⁶ 7v p9.5g Dec 6] smallish gelding: modest maiden: not knocked about final start:
stays 9.5f: acts on polytrack and good to firm going. *P. A. Blockley*

AFTER THE SHOW 3 b.c. Royal Applause 124 – Tango Teaser (Shareef Dancer **73**
(USA) 135) [2004 71: 6d⁶ 5.1g 6g⁶ 5m 6g² 5m 6d 7s Oct 27] useful-looking colt: fair
handicapper: effective at 5f/6f: acts on polytrack, soft and good to firm going: tends to
hang left: usually races prominently. *J. R. Jenkins*

AFTER THE SNOW (IRE) 2 b.f. (Mar 4) Danetime (IRE) 121 – State (Dominion **40**
123) [2004 6m 7d⁵ p8.6g Nov 12] small filly: half-sister to an Italian winner up to 7f by
Seattle Dancer: dam unraced: poor form in claimers. *I. A. Wood*

AGAIN JANE 4 ch.f. Then Again 126 – Janie-O 62 (Hittite Glory 125) [2004 f12g **–**
Feb 19] eighth foal: dam, best at 7f/1m on Flat, winning selling hurdler: well beaten in
bumpers, and in claimer at Southwell. *J. M. Jefferson*

AGENT KENSINGTON 2 b.f. (Mar 11) Mujahid (USA) 125 – Monawara (IRE) 73 **65**
(Namaqualand (USA)) [2004 5g² 5s² 6m⁵ 6.1s³ 5m² 5.1m⁴ 5.7m² 5.1f 6.5g 5.1g Oct 10]
2,500Y: close-coupled filly: first foal: dam, ran twice, third at 5f at 2 yrs: fair maiden:
below form last 3 starts: stays 5.7f: acts on good to firm ground, probably on soft.
R. Hannon

AGE OF KINGS (USA) 2 b.g. (Jan 17) Kingmambo (USA) 125 – Everhope (USA) **85**
(Danzig (USA)) [2004 5g³ 5f⁶ Jun 15] $280,000Y: smallish, attractive gelding: fourth
foal: dam, minor stakes winner in USA, half-sister to very smart US performer up to 1½m
Parade Ground (by Kingmambo): favourite but green, fairly useful form in maiden at
Salisbury and listed event (sixth to Chateau Istana) at Royal Ascot (gelded after): bred to
stay at least 1m. *J. H. M. Gosden*

AGGI MAC 3 b.f. Defacto (USA) – Giffoine 79 (Timeless Times (USA) 99) [2004 43: **47**
f7g⁵ 6m f8f 7.9m 7m 8.1s f7g f12g⁶ Dec 28] close-coupled, good-topped filly: poor

maiden: left N. Bycroft after second start: stays 6f: acts on polytrack and good to firm ground: tried in eyeshields, blinkered last 2 outings. *Andrew Turnell*

AGGRAVATION   2 b.g. (Apr 24) Sure Blade (USA) 130 – Confection (Formidable   **66** (USA) 125) [2004 p7m p6g 7s p7.1d p7g³ p6g* Dec 29] 3,500Y, resold 6,000Y: half-brother to several winners, including 1995 2-y-o 5f/6f winner (stayed 1¼m) Anthelia and 1m to 1¼m winner Athenian, both useful performers by Distant Relative: dam ran twice: fair performer: won maiden at Lingfield: effective at 6f/7f: acts on polytrack. *Andrew Reid*

AGILETE   2 b.g. (May 8) Piccolo 121 – Ingerence (FR) (Akarad (FR) 130) [2004 5.1s   **68** 5.7f³ 5f³ 5g⁵ 6.1m Sep 6] 22,000Y: fourth foal: brother to smart performer up to 7f Pan Jammer, 5f/6f winner at 2 yrs, and half-brother to 1¼m winner Kiss Me Kate (by Aragon): dam French maiden: fair maiden: should stay 6f: acts on firm going. *L. G. Cottrell*

AGILIS (IRE)   4 b.g. Titus Livius (FR) 115 – Green Life 63 (Green Desert (USA) 127)   **71 d** [2004 88: p8g p8g⁶ p7g p8g p8g p8g 8m 8g 7m 7f⁶ May 28] smallish gelding: fair performer: below form after second start: best at 7f/1m: acts on polytrack, probably on good to firm going: usually blinkered/visored nowadays. *Jamie Poulton*

AGOUTI   3 b.f. Pennekamp (USA) 130 – La Dama Bonita (USA) 87 (El Gran Senor   **–** (USA) 136) [2004 8.3g 10m Jun 14] well-made filly: half-sister to 3 winners, notably smart 5f to 1m winner in UAE Conflict (by Warning), earlier successful up to 10.5f in Britain: dam, 5f (at 2 yrs) and 7f winner, closely related to high-class French 6f to 1m performer Polar Falcon: well held in maidens at Windsor: sold 10,000 gns in July. *D. W. P. Arbuthnot*

AGREAT DAYOUTWITHU   2 ch.f. (Mar 9) Defacto (USA) – Lonely Lass 53   **–** (Headin' Up) [2004 6m 5d 5g Sep 25] 500Y: sixth foal: dam, maiden, stayed 6f: well beaten in maidens. *P. T. Midgley*

AGUILA LOCO (IRE)   5 ch.g. Eagle Eyed (USA) 111 – Go Likecrazy 51 (Dowsing   **61** (USA) 124) [2004 43: f6g³ f6g² f5g⁶ f6s² f8g⁵ f6s³ f7s* p7g⁴ p7g p6g⁶ f7g² 6d f6g³ f7g 7g³ 6g⁶ p6g 7f 7f f6m⁴ p7.1g⁴ Dec 22] smallish, good-topped gelding: modest handicapper: left M. Chapman after fifth start: won at Wolverhampton in February: stays easy 7f: acts on all-weather, firm and good to soft going: tried blinkered (raced freely)/wears cheekpieces nowadays: usually races prominently. *Mrs Stef Liddiard*

AGUILERA   3 ch.f. Wolfhound (USA) 126 – Mockingbird 64 (Sharpo 132) [2004 –:   **–** 5s 6m 7.1m 5g⁴ 6m 5.9m 5s 5g Sep 6] lengthy filly: poor maiden: should be suited by 6f+: tried in cheekpieces. *M. Dods*

AHAZ   2 b.g. (Feb 17) Zaha (CAN) 106 – Classic Faster (IRE) (Running Steps (USA)   **47** 79) [2004 5.1g 6d⁶ 7g 6f⁵ 6m⁴ 7g⁶ 6m Sep 1] poor maiden: should stay 7f: best effort on good to firm going: blinkered/in cheekpieces last 4 starts: sometimes looks none too keen. *I. A. Wood*

AHDAAF (USA)   2 b.f. (Feb 23) Bahri (USA) 125 – Ashraakat (USA) 105 (Danzig   **68** (USA)) [2004 6g³ 6.1g³ 6g⁴ Oct 2] third foal: half-sister to 3-y-o Hezaam: dam, 6f/7f (latter at 2 yrs) winner, sister to high-class sprinter Elnadim and closely related to very smart 1m/1¼m performer Mehthaaf: fair form in maidens at Newmarket and Nottingham: should stay 1m. *J. L. Dunlop*

AIMEE'S DELIGHT   4 b.f. Robellino (USA) 127 – Lloc 79 (Absalom 128) [2004   **68 ?** 85: 8.3d 8m 8g⁶ 8g 8m 8f 8.2s 8m Jul 6] strong filly: just a fair handicapper nowadays: stays 1m: acts on fibresand and good to firm ground, seemingly not on softer than good: blinkered (ran badly) seventh start. *J. G. Given*

AINTNECESSARILYSO   6 ch.g. So Factual (USA) 120 – Ovideo 58 (Domynsky   **62** 110) [2004 51: f7g⁵ p7g² f6s* f6g⁴ p6g³ f5g⁶ p6g³ f6g³ 5.1d³ 5.3g² 5g² p6g² 6f³ 6g⁶ 6g* 6m* 6m⁵ 5.7g³ 5m⁶ 6m 6g Aug 7] workmanlike gelding: has a quick action: modest handicapper: won at Southwell (dead-heat) in January, and Goodwood and Doncaster in June: effective at 5f/6f: yet to race on heavy ground, acts on any other turf and all-weather: tried in blinkers/cheekpieces (only once in 2004): tough and consistent. *N. E. Berry*

AIREDALE LAD (IRE)   3 b.g. Charnwood Forest (IRE) 125 – Tamarsiya (USA)   **–** (Shahrastani (USA) 135) [2004 –: f8s⁶ f7g⁴ f8m⁵ 8.5g 11.8g Oct 12] of no account. *J. R. Norton*

AIRE DE MOUGINS (IRE)   2 b.g. (Mar 15) Pennekamp (USA) 130 – Colouring   **75** (IRE) 79 (Catrail (USA) 123) [2004 6s 6m⁴ 7d⁴ 7m⁴ 8.3d² Sep 27] €12,500F, 26,000Y: close-coupled gelding: first foal: dam 8.5f winner in Ireland: fair maiden: second at

Hamilton: stays 1m: acts on soft and good to firm ground: free-going sort: sold 13,000 gns. *P. C. Haslam*

AIRGUSTA (IRE)   3 b.g. Danehill Dancer (IRE) 117 – Ministerial Model (IRE) 94   **53**
(Shalford (IRE) 124§) [2004 66: p7g 8.2s 11.6s 10d p12g f8g p16g Nov 30] close-coupled gelding: modest maiden: left C. Egerton after third start: stays easy 1½m. *C. P. Morlock*

AIR MAIL   7 b.g. Night Shift (USA) – Wizardry 83 (Shirley Heights 130) [2004 –,   **–**
a93: f9.4g⁴ f7g f8.5s f7s f7g⁴ f8.5g⁶ f8.5g f8g⁶ f7f⁴ f7s* f8g³ f7g² Dec 16] leggy gelding: **a85 d**
fairly useful on all-weather, modest on turf: below form after reappearance, though still won seller at Southwell (left Mrs N. Macauley) in November: stays 9.4f: acts on fibresand (below form on polytrack) and any turf going: tried in headgear. *N. Wilson*

AIR OF ESTEEM   8 b.g. Forzando 122 – Shadow Bird 70 (Martinmas 128) [2004   **48**
59: f8.5g⁵ f8.5g⁵ f9.4s⁶ f8s f8g² f7m⁴ f7d⁵ f8m f8g² Dec 12] smallish gelding: poor performer: best at 7f/1m: acts on fibresand, good to firm and good to soft going: tried visored/in cheekpieces. *Ian Emmerson*

AIR OF SUPREMACY (IRE)   3 gr.c. Royal Applause 124 – Lap of Luxury 107   **72**
(Sharrood (USA) 124) [2004 p7g p8g⁶ 8g p10g Dec 30] 16,000F, €105,000Y: has a quick   **a55**
action: second foal: dam 1m winner: easily best effort in maidens when seventh at Doncaster penultimate start: off 9 months after: stays 1m. *J. Noseda*

AIRWAVE   4 b.f. Air Express (IRE) 125 – Kangra Valley 56 (Indian Ridge 123) [2004   **112**
120: 6s⁶ 6f⁶ 6g 5m* 5s⁶ 6g 5.2g³ 6f² Sep 25] rangy, good sort: very smart at best: won Cheveley Park Stakes at 2 yrs and Temple Stakes at 3 yrs: smart form in 2004, winning listed race at Ayr in July by 1¼ lengths from Forever Phoenix: creditable efforts after,

Mr Henry Candy & Partners' "Airwave"

including 1½ lengths third to The Tatling in World Trophy at Newbury and 3 lengths second to Pivotal Point in Diadem Stakes at Ascot last 2 starts: effective at 5f/6f: acts on firm and good to soft going: usually blanketed for stall entry: has won when sweating: usually held up: sold 550,000 gns, joined A. O'Brien in Ireland. *H. Candy*

AITANA   4 b.f. Slip Anchor 136 – Tsungani 64 (Cure The Blues (USA)) [2004 61:   –
p12g⁶ f12g⁴ f9.4g Feb 13] has a round action: maiden: soundly beaten in 2004: should be suited by 1¼m+: tried blinkered. *S. C. Williams*

AJEEL (IRE)   5 b.g. Green Desert (USA) 127 – Samheh (USA) 62 (Private Account   –
(USA)) [2004 7m Jun 18] big, strong, rangy gelding: fluent mover: fairly useful winning handicapper in 2002: not at best in UAE for P. Rudkin in 2003: off 15 months and back with former trainer, well held only run in 2004: stays 1m: acts on soft and good to firm going: effective blinkered or not. *J. L. Dunlop*

AKASH (IRE)   4 b.g. Dr Devious (IRE) 127 – Akilara (IRE) 87 (Kahyasi 130) [2004   **97 d**
95: 10v* 11.5g² 10g 12g 10g 10.5s Sep 24] well-made ex-Irish gelding: useful performer: left J. Oxx 55,000 gns after final 3-y-o start: won minor event at Pontefract in April: well held in handicaps last 4 starts: stays 1½m: acts on any going: blinkered last 2 starts at 2 yrs: races up with pace. *M. Johnston*

AKIMBO (USA)   3 b.c. Kingmambo (USA) 125 – All At Sea (USA) 124 (Riverman   **90**
(USA) 131) [2004 96p: 8g³ Apr 17] medium-sized, quite attractive colt: placed in maidens at Newbury at 2 yrs (coltish and green) and on only run in 2004 (again odds on, 3¼ lengths third to Mudawin): will probably stay 1¼m. *H. R. A. Cecil*

AKIRAMENAI (USA)   4 b. or br.f. Salt Lake (USA) – Bold Wench (USA) (Bold   **?**
Forbes (USA)) [2004 p5g 6v⁴ 7m 6g⁶ 5d 6m 6g p10g Sep 18] $45,000Y, 5,500 3-y-o: half-sister to several winners in USA/Japan: dam US Grade 3 9.5f winner: signs of a little ability: tried blinkered. *Mrs L. Stubbs*

AKRAAN   2 ch.f. (Mar 29) Erhaab (USA) 127 – Nafhaat (USA) 91 (Roberto (USA)   **69**
131) [2004 7m 7g 8.5s⁵ 8d² Nov 5] workmanlike filly: half-sister to numerous winners, including 3-y-o Deraasaat and smart 1¼m to 14.6f winner Ranin (by Unfuwain): dam, 1½m winner, out of sister to US Grade 1 1¼m winner Sisterhood: fair maiden: second of 20 in nursery at Yarmouth: should stay at least 1¼m: best effort on good to soft going. *E. A. L. Dunlop*

AKRITAS   3 b.c. Polish Precedent (USA) 131 – Dazzling Heights 99 (Shirley Heights   **92**
130) [2004 83: 12.3d⁴ 12g⁴ 11.9d⁵ 16.2m³ Jul 23] quite good-topped colt: fairly useful handicapper: ran creditably in 2004: likely to prove best at 1¾m/2m: acts on good to firm going: hung badly left second start at 2 yrs. *P. F. I. Cole*

AKSHAR (IRE)   5 b.h. Danehill (USA) 126 – Akilara (IRE) 87 (Kahyasi 130) [2004   **103**
113: 10d 10g³ 10m 12f Jun 27] good-bodied horse: carries plenty of condition: smart performer at 4 yrs for Sir Michael Stoute: only raced in 2004, easily best effort when third to Nysaean in Mooresbridge Stakes at the Curragh on second start: effective at 1m to 10.5f: acts on firm ground: blinkered last 3 outings: ran in snatches (at Royal Ascot) third start. *D. K. Weld, Ireland*

ALAARED (USA)   4 b.g. King of Kings (IRE) 125 – Celtic Loot (USA) (Irish River   –
(FR) 131) [2004 87: 11.9m³ Aug 16] useful-looking gelding: has no off eye: fairly useful in 2003: well below form only run on Flat in 2004: tends to wander/carry head awkwardly. *M. R. Channon*

ALAFDAL (USA)   4 b. or br.g. Gone West (USA) – Aqaarid (USA) 116 (Nashwan   –
(USA) 135) [2004 70: 13.1f May 22] leggy gelding: maiden: has run as if amiss last 4 starts. *R. Allan*

ALAFZAR (IRE)   6 b.g. Green Desert (USA) 127 – Alasana (IRE) (Darshaan 133)   **69**
[2004 69: p7g⁴ p7g p8g* p8g³ p7g* 7m³ 7m 7f⁴ 7.1m 8f⁴ p7d⁴ 8s 8.1m* p8m 8d p8.6g Nov 11] lengthy gelding: fair handicapper: won twice at Lingfield in February, and seller at Chepstow in September: stays 1m: acts on polytrack, firm and good to soft going: usually visored/blinkered/tongue tied. *P. D. Evans*

ALAGON (IRE)   4 b.g. Alzao (USA) 117 – Forest Lair (Habitat 134) [2004 f12g Nov   –
22] fair maiden: left C. Laffon-Parias in France and off 17 months, well held in maiden at Southwell on British debut: stays 1½m. *Ian Williams*

ALAIPOUR (IRE)   5 b.g. Kahyasi 130 – Alaiyda (USA) 84 (Shahrastani (USA) 135)   **64 d**
[2004 13m³ 16g 13d⁵ 16s p12.2d p16g Nov 30] maiden: well held after reappearance: stays 13f: form only on good/good to firm going: tried in cheekpieces. *Lindsay Woods, Ireland*

ALALOOF (USA) 3 b.f. Swain (IRE) 134 – Alattrah (USA) (Shadeed (USA) 135) **70**
[2004 68: 10.2g⁶ 12.3g⁶ 11.5g Jun 30] smallish, well-made filly: fair maiden: should stay
at least 1½m: raced only on good ground or firmer: has looked difficult ride (very slowly
away on reappearance). *J. L. Dunlop*

ALAMIYAN (IRE) 2 b.c. (Apr 8) King's Best (USA) 132 – Alasana (IRE) (Darshaan **53 p**
133) [2004 8s⁶ Oct 19] sixth living foal: half-brother to several winners, including smart
7f (at 2 yrs) and 1m winner Alasha (by Barathea) and 6-y-o Alafzar: dam, French 1m/9f
winner, half-sister to high-class French 1½m performer Altayan: 6/1 and green, sixth in
maiden at Bath, weakening: should improve. *Sir Michael Stoute*

ALAM (USA) 5 b.g. Silver Hawk (USA) 123 – Ghashtah (USA) (Nijinsky (CAN) 138) **68**
[2004 –: 17.5d⁶ 13d 15s⁵ Oct 11] fair maiden, lightly raced: barely stays 15f: raced only
on going softer than good. *P. Monteith*

ALANI (IRE) 2 b.f. (Mar 5) Benny The Dip (USA) 127 – Toi Toi (IRE) 82 (In The **61**
Wings 128) [2004 7s² 8.3d⁵ 7.9g Oct 9] 7,500Y: third foal: half-sister to Italian 9f (at
2 yrs) to 11f winner by Kahyasi: dam, 1¾m winner, out of sister to very smart stayer
Assessor: modest form in maidens: second at Newcastle: should stay at least 1½m.
Jedd O'Keeffe

ALASTAIR SMELLIE 8 ch.g. Sabrehill (USA) 120 – Reel Foyle (USA) 77 (Irish **52 §**
River (FR) 131) [2004 55§, a–§: f5g f7s 6v² f6m² p6g* f6g f6g f6m 5s f5g p5m³ Dec 15]
good-topped gelding: modest performer: won banded race at Lingfield in April: effective
at 5f to 7f: acts on polytrack and any turf going: usually visored: sometimes slowly away
(refused to race once): flashes tail/looks awkward ride: unreliable. *S. L. Keightley*

AL AZHAR 10 b.g. Alzao (USA) 117 – Upend 120 (Main Reef 126) [2004 79: f11d⁶ **44**
12.1g³ 12m³ Jul 14] well-made gelding: has reportedly had knee trouble: only poor in
2004: stays 1½m: acts on fibresand, heavy and good to firm going: sometimes starts
slowly: usually patiently ridden. *M. Dods*

ALBADI 3 b.g. Green Desert (USA) 127 – Lyrist 77 (Cozzene (USA)) [2004 –: 7s 7m **52 §**
8m 7f* 7m 7m 8m Sep 25] sturdy gelding: form only when winning handicap at Brighton
in June: stays 7f: acts on firm going: blinkered last 5 starts: gelded. *C. E. Brittain*

ALBANOVA 5 gr.m. Alzao (USA) 117 – Alouette 105 (Darshaan 133) [2004 113: **119**
12d* 12g* 12s* Sep 26]
    Alborada's full sister Albanova returned better than ever at the age of five
and was unbeaten in three races, all of them Group 1 events in Germany. She is the
first horse since Lomitas in 1991 to win three Group 1s in that country in a calendar
year, Monsun, Tiger Hill and Ungaro having taken two seasons to do so and the
Clive Brittain-trained Luso three, while Lando won four between 1993 and 1995.
Albanova's trainer Sir Mark Prescott is second to none when it comes to placing his
horses in Britain, and he clearly knows his way around the foreign programme
book, too. In the latest season he also won listed races in France, Germany and
Ireland with the appropriately-named Foreign Affairs, who also just failed to
land the Stockholm Cup International at Taby; the Prescott-trained Hypnotic was
successful in the French Provinces, as was No Refuge in Germany.
    Albanova has raced more times abroad than she has in Britain, and her last
appearance on home soil came in the 2003 Coronation Cup, in which she finished
seventh. It was her first and only defeat in Britain, having won a maiden at Haydock
on her only start at two, a minor event at Pontefract and a listed race at Chepstow at
three, and a listed contest at Haydock on her reappearance at four. Albanova had to
wait until the latest season before she opened her account abroad, though. In three
previous sorties she had acquitted herself well when fifth in the Prix Vermeille and
second in the Preis von Europa, but had pulled hard and run some way below form
when tried in blinkers and stepped up to almost two miles in the Prix Royal-Oak.
All her races in 2004 were over a mile and a half, which seems her optimum trip, and
took place in a period of just two months. First up was the WestLB Deutschlandpreis at Dusseldorf in July, for which Albanova was the outsider of seven, the
only other overseas challenger Brian Boru the clear favourite. Having won first
time out in each of her previous seasons, Albanova defied a nine-month absence to
maintain that record, racing prominently and leading well inside the final furlong to
beat the Italian Derby runner-up Dayano by a neck.

Rheinland-Pokal der Stadtsparkasse Koln, Cologne—Albanova overhauls High Accolade (visor) to complete the middle leg of her hat-trick in German Group 1s; Deutsches Derby runner-up Malinas (dark sleeves) does best of the home-trained contingent

Albanova returned to Germany three weeks later for the Rheinland-Pokal der Stadtsparkasse at Cologne. She was again one of two overseas runners taking on five home-trained horses, High Accolade being the other visitor. The pair dominated the finish, Albanova leading close home to win by three quarters of a length after having to be switched twice inside the last two furlongs. Cologne was also the venue for Albanova's final appearance, in the IVG-Preis von Europa. The race suffers because of its proximity to the Arc, but it attracted a field of nine, of which two apart from Albanova were from outside Germany, the more interesting of that pair the Slovak-trained Darsalam who had finished a good sixth in the St Leger on his previous outing. Once again Albanova had to show her battling qualities to gain the upper hand in the closing stages—her rider received a two-day ban for excessive use of the whip—and this time she had half a length to spare over the three-year-old filly Saldentigerin, who in turn finished three quarters of a length in front of third-placed Darsalam. In becoming the first of her sex to win this prestigious event, Albanova had completed a notable hat-trick and produced the perfect finale to a career in which she won seven races worth nigh on £250,000.

Albanova (gr.m. 1999)	Alzao (USA) (b 1980)	Lyphard (b 1969)	Northern Dancer Goofed
		Lady Rebecca (b 1971)	Sir Ivor Pocahontas II
	Alouette (gr 1990)	Darshaan (br 1981)	Shirley Heights Delsy
		Alruccaba (gr 1983)	Crystal Palace Allara

Albanova is almost as good as the dual Champion Stakes winner Alborada, whose overall record for the same owner and trainer read six wins and three placings for earnings of almost £600,000. Alborada, who didn't race beyond a mile and a quarter, was also a grey, as are all the mares on the bottom line of the pedigree. Their dam Alouette has bred three other winners: Alakananda (by Hernando) and Alba Stella (by Nashwan) both showed fairly useful form over a mile and a half, while her three-year-old colt Albinus (by Selkirk) made into a useful performer at around that distance in the latest season. The winner of three races herself at a mile to a mile and a half in Ireland, as well as finishing second in the Galtres Stakes, Alouette now has a yearling filly and a colt foal, both by Sadler's Wells. The next dam Alruccaba, who raced only as a two-year-old and won a six-furlong maiden at Brighton, is responsible for numerous other winners, notably the Nassau Stakes and Sun Chariot Stakes winner Last Second, by Albanova's sire Alzao, and the

Miss K. Rausing's "Albanova"

Doncaster Cup winner Alleluia. One of Alruccaba's produce, Jude, failed to win, but she has more than made up for that at stud, producing the Irish One Thousand Guineas winner Yesterday and the Moyglare Stud Stakes winner Quarter Moon, the latter also runner-up in the Irish One Thousand Guineas, Oaks and Irish Oaks. Albanova's great grandam Allara won at seven furlongs in the French Provinces and is a half-sister to the dams of Aliysa and Nishapour. This is an excellent family. The tall Albanova acted on heavy and good to firm going. She was thoroughly genuine. *Sir Mark Prescott*

ALBANOV (IRE)   4 b.g. Sadler's Wells (USA) 132 – Love For Ever (IRE) (Darshaan **100** 133) [2004 104: 21g 16.2g 13.4s⁴ 14g 12f 13d² 12s Nov 6] quite good-topped gelding: useful handicapper: creditable efforts in 2004 only when in frame at Chester (listed rated stakes) and Hamilton (short-headed by Zeitgeist): stays 15.5f: raced mainly on good going or softer (acts on heavy): effective blinkered or not: usually races prominently. *M. Johnston*

ALBASHOOSH   6 b.g. Cadeaux Genereux 131 – Annona (USA) 72 (Diesis 133) [2004 **79 +** 91d: 6d⁶ 7.2f⁵ 7.1m⁶ 6f* 5.9f 6g³ 6m⁴ 6g³ 6d² 7.2s Sep 18] quite good-topped gelding: fair handicapper: won at Pontefract in June: best at 6f: acts on firm and soft going: tried blinkered/visored, not in 2004: free-going sort: usually waited with. *D. Nicholls*

ALBAVILLA   4 b.f. Spectrum (IRE) 126 – Lydia Maria 70 (Dancing Brave (USA) **82** 140) [2004 70: 11.7g³ 11.8m² 12g⁵ 12g 11.6d³ p13.9g* 14.1s Oct 27] rangy, good sort: fairly useful performer: won handicap at Wolverhampton on all-weather debut in October: stays 1¾m: acts on polytrack, soft and good to firm ground. *P. W. Harris*

AL BEEDAA (USA)   3 ch.f. Swain (IRE) 134 – Histoire (FR) (Riverman (USA) 131) **77** [2004 75: 12s⁴ 14.6g³ 11.9m³ 14g Jun 11] strong, short-backed filly: fair maiden: stays

14.6f: unraced on heavy going, seems to act on any other turf: visored final start: possibly temperamental: sold 90,000 gns in December, sent to USA. *J. L. Dunlop*

ALBEE (IRE) 4 b.g. Grand Lodge (USA) 125 – Wolf Cleugh (IRE) 65 (Last Tycoon 131) [2004 f9.4g⁶ f9.4g⁶ f9.4g⁴ 12d 8.2v f8s³ f12g f8d Dec 21] modest maiden: stays 9.4f: acts on fibresand: tried in cheekpieces/visor: inconsistent. *Miss Gay Kelleway* **55**

ALBERT HALL 2 b.c. (Apr 18) Danehill (USA) 126 – Al Theraab (USA) 81 (Roberto (USA) 131) [2004 7g² 8d* 8s² Oct 23] 510,000F: strong, angular colt: has scope: brother to French 6f winner (including at 2 yrs) Barsine and French 6f/7f winner Algallarens (both useful), closely related to 2 winners, including useful 7f (at 2 yrs) to 8.5f winner Flighty Fellow (by Flying Spur), and half-brother to useful French 1m winner Ebdaa (by Nashwan): dam, 1m winner, best at 1½m: won 5-runner Juddmonte Beresford Stakes at the Curragh in October by ½ length from Merger (pair clear), making running: good 2½ lengths second of 8 to Motivator in Racing Post Trophy at Doncaster final start, staying on having been held up: will be suited by 1¼m/1½m: acts on soft ground: tends to wander/carry head awkwardly: should progress and win more races as 3-y-o. *A. P. O'Brien, Ireland* **113 p**

ALBERTINE 4 b.f. Bahhare (USA) 122 – Rosa Royale 61 (Arazi (USA) 135) [2004 –: 6g 8m p8g f12g f6g Dec 28] little form: tried tongue tied. *C. A. Dwyer* **–**

ALBINUS 3 gr.c. Selkirk (USA) 129 – Alouette 105 (Darshaan 133) [2004 69p: 8g 10.2m² 12.3m* 12d* 11.9s³ 11m⁵ Sep 17] big, good sort: useful performer: won handicaps at Ripon in May and Salisbury in June: much improved last 2 starts, close third to Frank Sonata in listed race at Haydock (made most) and 4 lengths fifth to Sights On Gold in Arc Trial at Newbury (hung markedly right): will stay 1¾m: acts on soft and good to firm going: blinkered last 5 starts. *A. M. Balding* **109**

ALBURY HEATH 4 b.g. Mistertopogigo (IRE) 118 – Walsham Witch 61 (Music Maestro 119) [2004 –: p6g p8g Feb 23] good-bodied gelding: little form: tried visored. *T. M. Jones* **–**

Juddmonte Beresford Stakes, the Curragh—
Albert Hall and Merger (noseband) come together, the former getting the better of the tussle
to provide Aidan O'Brien with his seventh win in the race in nine years

totesport Rated Stakes (Handicap), Newmarket—
the progressive Alderney Race quickens well and holds off Mahmoom (No.17) and Valjarv;
third-placed Two Step Kid (No.7) leads home those nearest the camera

ALCAIDESA 3 b.g. Charnwood Forest (IRE) 125 – Calachuchi 74 (Martinmas 128) **63 ?**
[2004 8v⁴ 7g May 3] heavy-topped gelding: seventh foal: half-brother to several winners,
including 1½m and 2m winner Quezon City (by Keen): dam prolific winner from 7.5f
to 12.4f: better effort in maidens when fourth at Newcastle: will stay at least 1¼m.
Miss J. A. Camacho

ALCAZAR (IRE) 9 b.g. Alzao (USA) 117 – Sahara Breeze 85 (Ela-Mana-Mou 132) **118**
[2004 117: 14.1g* 13.9d² 20m 14g⁵ 15.5s³ 16d* Nov 3] workmanlike gelding: smart
performer: missed 1999/2000 (reportedly due to broken pelvis and injured tendon) and
2002: won listed races at Nottingham (for second year running) in April and Musselburgh
(beat Winged d'Argent by 5 lengths) in November: good efforts in between when 3
lengths second to Millenary in Yorkshire Cup at York, fifth to Vinnie Roe in Irish St Leger
at the Curragh and third to Westerner in Prix Royal-Oak at Longchamp: stays 2m (well
beaten over 2½m in last 2 Gold Cups, bled from nose in 2004): best recent efforts on good
ground or softer (acts on soft): has run well when sweating: has been bandaged: usually
tracks leaders. *H. Morrison*

ALCHARINGA (IRE) 2 b.g. (Apr 24) Ashkalani (IRE) 128 – Bird In Blue (IRE) 57 **64**
(Bluebird (USA) 125) [2004 5m⁵ 5m 5g⁴ Jun 17] €11,000Y: strong gelding: fifth foal:
half-brother to 3 winners abroad, including Italian 9f/1¼m winner by Alhaarth: dam,
maiden, sister to smart 7f/1m performer Bluegrass Prince: modest form in maidens/minor
event: bred to stay at least 1m. *T. J. Etherington*

ALCHEMIST MASTER 5 b.g. Machiavellian (USA) 123 – Gussy Marlowe 118 **80**
(Final Straw 127) [2004 55, a85+: 8m⁶ 7.5d² 7f² 8g² 7m* 8g* 7.9d⁴ 7m⁶ 8m³ 8d p7g
7.5m³ 7.1g Sep 26] leggy, quite good-topped gelding: fairly useful handicapper: won at
Catterick in June and Ripon in July: effective at 7f/1m: acts on all-weather, firm and good
to soft ground: wears cheekpieces nowadays: reportedly distressed when pulled up final
outing: sold 5,500 gns. *R. M. Whitaker*

ALCHERA 3 b.g. Mind Games 121 – Kind of Shy 61 (Kind of Hush 118) [2004 77: 6d **68**
6s 5g⁶ 5.1g⁴ 5g⁴ 5g 7m⁴ 8.3d 8m 8m⁵ 8d Oct 18] quite attractive gelding: shows a quick
action: fair performer: stays 7f: acts on good to firm going, probably on good to soft:
effective blinkered or not: sold 3,000 gns. *R. F. Johnson Houghton*

ALCOTT (FR) 2 ch.g. (Apr 9) Medaaly 114 – Louisa May (IRE) (Royal Abjar (USA) **–**
121) [2004 p8.6g Dec 31] first foal: dam unraced: 50/1, well held in seller at Wolverhampton. *J. Jay*

ALDENTE 2 b.f. (Apr 26) Green Desert (USA) 127 – Alruccaba 83 (Crystal Palace **77** (FR) 132) [2004 7m² 7s Aug 21] leggy, quite good-topped filly: half-sister to numerous winners, including very smart 1¼m performer Last Second (by Alzao), 6f/7f winner at 2 yrs, and dam of 5-y-o Albanova: dam 2-y-o 6f winner: second to Dubai Surprise in maiden at Redcar: pulled up at Chester: dead. *Sir Mark Prescott*

ALDERNEY RACE (USA) 3 ch.c. Seeking The Gold (USA) – Oyster Catcher **109** (IRE) 105 (Bluebird (USA) 125) [2004 89p: p6g⁵ 6s² 6m* 6m⁴ 6m* 6g² 6g* Aug 14] tall colt: useful performer: progressed well in 2004, winning maiden in May and handicaps at Newmarket in July and August, beating Mahmoom on last 2 occasions, by a neck on final one: stays 6f: acts on good to firm going. *R. Charlton*

ALEKHINE (IRE) 3 b.g. Soviet Star (USA) 128 – Alriyaah 73 (Shareef Dancer **89** (USA) 135) [2004 86p: 8m² 8m³ 10.1m 8.1g 10g⁶ 10.3g 8f⁵ 10.3s Oct 22] strong, lengthy gelding: fairly useful handicapper: effective at 1m/1¼m: acts on firm ground: sweated/moved short to post third start: sold 20,000gns. *P.W. Harris*

ALENUSHKA 3 b.f. Soviet Star (USA) 128 – National Portrait (IRE) (Royal Academy **73** (USA) 130) [2004 10m 8.3f⁶ 8.3f⁴ 8.1m² Aug 11] lengthy filly: second foal: dam, placed at 1m in France, out of high-class French 6f/7f performer Proskona: best effort in maidens when second at Sandown: stays 1m. *H. Candy*

ALERON (IRE) 6 b.g. Sadler's Wells (USA) 132 – High Hawk 124 (Shirley Heights **79** 130) [2004 85, a68: 12.3d² 10.1s* 10m² 11.9g 9d⁴ 10.3g³ 12.3d⁵ 12.3m² 12d Aug 15] quite good-topped gelding: fair performer: won minor event at Newcastle in May: effective at 1¼m, barely stays 2m: acts on dirt/fibresand, soft and good to firm ground: tried visored/in cheekpieces: tried tongue tied: has hung/found little. *J. J. Quinn*

ALESHANEE 2 b.f. (Apr 4) Bold Edge 123 – Nesyred (IRE) 75 (Paris House 123) **–** [2004 5g 5g 6g 6m Sep 7] £15,000Y: leggy filly: first foal: dam 6f winner: last in maidens. *J. R. Best*

ALESSANO 2 ch.c. (May 15) Hernando (FR) 127 – Alessandra 101 (Generous (IRE) **79 p** 139) [2004 p8m* Dec 21] fourth foal: half-brother to 3-y-o Kryssa: dam, 1½m winner, closely related to Park Hill winner Casey and to dam of 4-y-o Avonbridge and 6-y-o Patavellian: 9/2, won 11-runner maiden at Lingfield by length from In The Know, leading close home: will be suited by 1¼m/1½m: should improve. *G. L. Moore*

ALETHEA GEE 6 b.m. Sure Blade (USA) 130 – Star Flower (Star Appeal 133) [2004 **–** –: 8g 6.9f 10g⁶ Aug 2] little sign of ability. *Mrs M. Reveley*

ALEUTIAN 4 gr.g. Zafonic (USA) 130 – Baked Alaska 93 (Green Desert (USA) 127) **106** [2004 p6g* p7g* f7s* p7g⁶ 7d 6g Sep 1] tall gelding: useful performer: reportedly had foot problem in 2003: won first 3 starts, namely maiden and minor event at Lingfield, and minor event (beat Cardinal Venture by short head) at Wolverhampton: well held in listed event at Leicester and handicap at York last 2 starts 4 months apart: stays 7f: acts on all-weather: has worn crossed noseband: withdrawn after going down in stall intended debut: sold 26,000 gns in October, sent to UAE. *D. R. Loder*

ALEXANDER AMBITION (IRE) 3 b.f. Entrepreneur 123 – Lady Alexander (IRE) **69** 112 (Night Shift (USA)) [2004 75: p10g⁴ f8f³ p7g⁴ p8g² p7g* Mar 23] first foal: dam Irish 2-y-o 5f/6f winner: fair performer: trained by D. Weld in Ireland at 2 yrs: won handicap at Lingfield in March: stays 1m: acts on all-weather, raced only on firm/good ground on turf: tried tongue tied. *S. Kirk*

ALEXANDER CAPETOWN (IRE) 2 b.f. (Feb 25) Fasliyev (USA) 120 – Hawas **68** 93 (Mujtahid (USA) 118) [2004 5s² 5d⁵ 6m⁶ 6g⁴ 6.1m⁴ 6g 6v Oct 23] €180,000Y: lengthy filly: third foal: half-sister to useful 7f (at 2 yrs in France) to 1¼m (in Ireland) winner Power Elite (by Linamix): dam, Irish 1m winner, sister to smart Irish 1½m winner Mutakarrim out of half-sister to 3-y-o Haafhd: fair maiden: should stay 7f: acts on soft and good to firm ground. *B. W. Hills*

ALEXANDER DUCHESS (IRE) 3 b.f. Desert Prince (IRE) 130 – Lionne (Dar- **103** shaan 133) [2004 99: 7s⁶ 11.4d 7m² 8m⁶ 8.5m 7.5s Aug 19] 40,000F: good-topped filly: second foal: half-sister to fairly useful Irish 2002 2-y-o 7f winner Great Idea (by Lion Cavern) who stays 11f: dam unraced daughter of smart but untrustworthy filly up to 1½m Percy's Lass: useful performer: successful at 2 yrs in maiden at Fairyhouse and nursery at Leopardstown: creditable effort in 2004 only when second to Sugarhoneybaby in handicap at the Curragh in June: should stay at least 1m (well held in 11f listed race at Chester second outing): acts on good to firm ground: wore cheekpieces final outing. *James G. Burns, Ireland*

ALEXANDER GOLDRUN (IRE)   3 b.f. Gold Away (IRE) 125 – Renashaan **121**
(FR) (Darshaan 133) [2004 100: 8v* 7d* 8m² 10.5g⁴ 10m² 10m* 10m* Dec 12]

Owner Mrs Miriam O'Callaghan's practice of prefacing her horses' names
with 'Alexander' regardless of sex may seem idiosyncratic and likely to cause
occasional confusion among racegoers, but she has no cause for complaint over
the results achieved. Four of the seven Alexanders who ran in her colours on the
Flat in Britain or Ireland in the season under review—all seven were fillies—were
successful, increasing Mrs O'Callaghan's overall tally to eleven winners. The 2003
Park Hill Stakes winner Alexander Three D was smart, but the leader of the group
is Alexander Goldrun, who proved herself one of the toughest, most consistent and
best of her age and sex with a seven-race campaign culminating in victories in the
Prix de l'Opera Casino Barriere d'Enghien Les Bains at Longchamp and the Cathay
Pacific Hong Kong Cup at Sha Tin. These wins took her earnings above the million-
pound mark—not bad for a filly which cost IR 40,000 guineas as a foal and who spent
most of her two-year-old campaign contesting nurseries.

By the time of the Irish One Thousand Guineas at the Curragh in May,
Alexander Goldrun had run ten times, beginning in March 2003. She had shown
progressive form as a juvenile, winning the listed Silken Glider Stakes at the
Curragh on her final start, her only substandard display coming at Galway in the
summer when her stall failed to open and she had to force her way out, hitting her
head in the process. The experience seemed to colour Alexander Goldrun's attitude
towards the stalls, and who can blame her for that? Significantly, the event helped
accelerate a decision by the Irish authorities to replace the portable New Zealand-
type stalls, which had been used on most Irish tracks for nearly twenty years. New,
Italian-made stalls were introduced in May and promptly failed to function
efficiently at Cork, Limerick and Bellewstown, resulting in a withdrawal from use
for extensive checks and the temporary reintroduction of the old stalls. A cynic
might observe that this fitted perfectly with what has become known as Hutber's
Law: 'Progress means deterioration'. Alexander Goldrun swiftly put two more
races on her scoresheet in the spring, the listed Irish Stallion Farms EBF Park
Express Stakes at the Curragh by a length from Blue Reema, and the Derrinstown
Stud One Thousand Guineas Trial at Leopardstown, where she won by a short head
from Misty Heights, overcoming trouble in running to lead close home. Alexander
Goldrun started favourite in only one of her ten races before the Irish Guineas and,
up against a strong British raiding party headed by Attraction, she looked to have
little hope of adding a classic to her total. She was, though, the shortest-priced of
the home-trained contingent and ran a smashing race to go down by a length to
the front-running favourite, chasing hard from the outset and sticking to her task
valiantly.

Talk of running Alexander Goldrun in the Oaks, for which she would have
had to be supplemented, came to nothing but she stayed on the classic trail in the
Prix de Diane at Chantilly, making good progress in the closing stages, after being
none too well away, to finish two lengths fourth to Latice. Alexander Goldrun again
battled on stoutly when favourite and a half-length second to Chorist in the Audi
Pretty Polly Stakes at the Curragh at the end of June but, after four hard races in the

Prix de l'Opera Casino Barriere d'Enghien Les Bains, Longchamp—Alexander Goldrun returns from a
break better than ever to land the spoils from the Andre Fabre-trained pair Grey Lilas (left) and Walkamia;
Yesterday (blaze), Actrice (noseband) and Whortleberry (blinkers) are in the next group

Cathay Pacific Hong Kong Cup, Sha Tin—Alexander Goldrun (far side) rounds off her campaign with a second Group 1, narrowly holding the strong-finishing Bullish Luck, with Touch of Land third

space of seven weeks, she was put by until the autumn. With Chorist a late withdrawal and Ouija Board going for the Arc, the Prix de l'Opera was not so strongly contested as it might have been—Alexander Goldrun started third favourite behind Prix du Moulin winner Grey Lilas at odds on and the four-year-old Yesterday, trying to recapture her good form of the previous season. The seven other runners included Actrice (Prix Corrida), Shapira (Henkel-Rennen), Menhoubah (Oaks d'Italia), Vallera (fourth in the Prix Vermeille) and dual Group 2 winner Whortleberry. Held up after once again missing the break, Alexander Goldrun galloped on in the last half mile to catch doubtful stayer Grey Lilas, bumping her slightly, and win by a length.

This was Alexander Goldrun's best performance up to that time, and a similar display enabled her to take the Hong Kong Cup by the skin of her teeth. The competition was pretty hot, though there is never any guarantee for a race run in December that every European runner will be in top form. The thirteen other runners included five Group 1 winners from Europe in the current season—Ancient World, Latice, Powerscourt, Rakti and Soldier Hollow—plus dual Group 2 scorer Touch of Land. There were also contenders from Australia and Japan. Alexander Goldrun was held up as usual and had most of the field to pass in the straight. She produced a typically strong run to lead with half a furlong to go and battled on stoutly to hold the late challenge of Hong Kong-trained Bullish Luck by a short head. Touch of Land was three quarters of a length away third, with Powerscourt fourth and Ancient World fifth. Rakti pulled too hard and failed to reproduce his best in seventh. Once again Alexander Goldrun was not the punters' choice, hardly surprising given the quality of the opposition, but her odds of 21.5/1 contrasted with her 10/1 industry starting price in Britain, providing confirmation that for punters wishing to bet on European horses running abroad, especially on another continent, the sensible route is to back at racecourse odds. Local racegoers the world over show a pretty consistent ignorance and/or obstinacy regarding the chances of the 'foreigners'.

Alexander Goldrun, a medium-sized, sturdy filly who impressed with her well-being at Longchamp, will continue her career as a four-year-old. Given the increasing opportunities for older fillies and mares, and the fact that Alexander Goldrun is not beholden to the state of the going, she can be expected to pay her way at a mile and a quarter, which trip evidently suits her. There are no guarantees that she will be fully effective over further since her pedigree contains more speed

Mrs N. O'Callaghan's "Alexander Goldrun"

				Nureyev
		Goldneyev		Nureyev
	Gold Away (IRE)	(b or br 1986)		Gold River
	(ch 1995)	Blushing Away		Blushing Groom
Alexander Goldrun (IRE)		(ch 1987)		Sweet Revenge
(b.f. 2001)		Darshaan		Shirley Heights
	Renashaan (FR)	(br 1981)		Delsy
	(b 1989)	Gerbera		Lyphard
		(ch 1984)		Greenway

than stamina. She is from the first crop of her sire Gold Away, a specialist miler and a good one, finishing in the first three in all his fourteen starts, notably winning the Prix du Muguet and finishing runner-up in four Group 1s, including the Prix du Moulin twice. Gold Away's initial fee was 20,000 francs, then €3,000, upped to €5,000 for 2005, so he is hardly at the top end of the market. The dam Renashaan was sold carrying Alexander Goldrun for 30,000 guineas at the 2000 Newmarket December Sales, a far cry from the 640,000 guineas she fetched at the same venue two months after the Prix de l'Opera, in foal to Pivotal. Renashaan showed useful form in winning over a mile at two and nine furlongs at three—the latter a listed race—and all her five runners have won. The best before Alexander Goldrun was the 1999 foal Medecis (by Machiavellian), a smart miler who finished second in the Poule d'Essai des Poulains and Prix de la Foret. The two-year-old Rio (by Namid) is unraced and there is a foal brother to Medecis. Renashaan's dam Gerbera was a minor winner out of a very smart filly in Greenway, a five-furlong specialist who is grandam of temperamental Gold Cup winner Royal Rebel. This is also the family of Prix de l'Arc de Triomphe winner Gold River, a half-sister to Greenway's dam Gracious; Gold River, who also won the Prix Royal-Oak and Prix du Cadran, appears in the top half of the pedigree as the dam of Gold Away's sire. *J. S. Bolger, Ireland*

ALEXANDER SAPPHIRE (IRE) 3 gr.f. Pennekamp (USA) 130 – Beautiful France **61**
(IRE) (Sadler's Wells (USA) 132) [2004 –: 8d 10m 7d 8g f12g³ Nov 22] IR 31,000F,
€60,000Y: half-sister to several winners, including useful Irish 1996 2-y-o 7f winner
Beautiful Fire (by Selkirk), later successful in Hong Kong, and fairly useful Irish 1m
winner French Smile (by Indian Ridge): dam Irish 9f winner on only start: modest
maiden: left C. O'Brien in Ireland after fourth start: should stay 1¾m: acts on fibresand.
P. W. Chapple-Hyam

ALEXEI 3 ch.g. Ashkalani (IRE) 128 – Sherkova (USA) (State Dinner (USA)) [2004 –
8.1s p12g² p13g⁵ 11.9s Oct 15] 28,000Y: workmanlike gelding: eighth foal: half-brother **a61**
to several winners, including 1m winner Russian Party (by Lycius) and 2m winner
Norma's Lady (by Unfuwain): dam unraced half-sister to Prix de Diane winner Lady In
Silver: modest maiden: stays 13f: acts on polytrack: sold 11,000 gns. *J. R. Fanshawe*

ALEXIA ROSE (IRE) 2 b.f. (Mar 4) Mujadil (USA) 119 – Meursault (IRE) (Salt **80**
Dome (USA)) [2004 6m⁶ 5g 5d⁴ 5g³ 5f² 6s* 5d² 6s Oct 29] €16,000F, 15,000Y: leggy,
lengthy filly: third foal: dam, third in Irish bumper only start, out of Champion New
Zealand filly La Mer: fairly useful performer: won maiden at Haydock in September:
creditable second in minor event at Musselburgh next time: effective at 5f/6f: acts on firm
and soft ground: usually races prominently: tends to wander/flash tail. *A. Berry*

ALEYAH 2 ch.f. (Mar 23) Bachir (IRE) 118 – Silver Peak (FR) (Sillery (USA) 122) –
[2004 6g Sep 3] 3,500Y: good-bodied filly: fourth foal: half-sister to French 1¼m and
13f winner Blue Peak (by Bluebird): dam, French 9f winner, half-sister to dam of 3-y-o
Alexander Goldrun: 50/1 and burly, last of 13 in maiden at Kempton. *C. F. Wall*

ALFELMA (IRE) 4 ch.f. Case Law 113 – Billie Grey 72 (Chilibang 120) [2004 57: –
6m 6.1m 5d Jun 9] of little account. *P. R. Wood*

ALFHALA (IRE) 3 b.f. Acatenango (GER) 127 – Maid of Kashmir (IRE) 94 (Dancing –
Brave (USA) 140) [2004 8g Jul 16] fifth foal: half-sister to useful 1¼m winner Bezzaaf
(by Machiavellian) and UAE 1m to 2m winner Shaalayn (by In The Wings): dam Irish
1¼m winner who stayed 1½m: 100/1 and backward, always behind in maiden at
Newmarket. *A. C. Stewart*

ALFIE LEE (IRE) 7 ch.g. Case Law 113 – Nordic Living (IRE) 53 (Nordico (USA)) **45**
[2004 50: 5f 5f⁴ 5d Oct 17] compact, well-made gelding: unimpressive mover: poor
performer: raced mainly at 5f: acts on fibresand and firm going: tried in blinkers/cheek-
pieces: tongue tied. *D. A. Nolan*

ALFIE NOAKES 2 b.c. (Apr 25) Groom Dancer (USA) 128 – Crimson Rosella 54 **83**
(Polar Falcon (USA) 126) [2004 7g³ 8g⁵ p8g³ Oct 25] 36,000Y: brother to fairly useful
8.5f/1¼m winner Crimson Dancer and half-brother to 2 winners, including fairly useful
6f (at 2 yrs)/7f winner Sabo Rose (by Prince Sabo): dam, maiden who probably stayed
1½m, half-sister to high-class sprinter Mr Brooks: third in maidens at Newbury (best
effort) and Lingfield (not clear run, probably unlucky): hung right in between: should
stay 1¼m: slowly away first 2 outings. *Mrs A. J. Perrett*

ALFONSO 3 ch.g. Efisio 120 – Winnebago 63 (Kris 135) [2004 71p: f7g* 8g 8m 7g² **92**
8d⁴ 8s² 7d* Oct 30] good-bodied gelding: has a round action: fairly useful performer:
won maiden at Wolverhampton in February and handicap at Newmarket in October:
effective at 7f/1m: acts on fibresand and soft going. *B. W. Hills*

ALFRED THE GREAT (IRE) 2 b.c. (Apr 22) King's Best (USA) 132 – Aigue 96 –
(High Top 131) [2004 8g Oct 10] half-brother to 3 winners, including 7f (at 2 yrs) and
1¼m winner Mezzogiorno (by Unfuwain), also third in Oaks and dam of 5-y-o Monturani, and winner around 1¼m Rainbow Top (by Rainbow Quest), both useful: dam, 1m
winner, sister to smart 1¼m/13f winner Torchon: 12/1, slowly away and always rear in
maiden at Bath. *M. Johnston*

ALFRIDINI 3 ch.g. Selkirk (USA) 129 – Vivre En Paix (Nureyev (USA) 131) [2004 **80**
p8g p7g p7g² p7g² p10g* p8g⁴ 11.6s 8m* 9.9d³ 8d⁵ 9.7m⁵ Jul 22] well-made gelding:
brother to 1999 2-y-o 6f winner Alfini and half-brother to 3 winners, including fairly
useful 1m/1¼m winner Treaty of Peace (by Alleged): dam French 1m winner: fairly useful handicapper: won at Lingfield (ran in snatches) in March and Salisbury (apprentices)
in June: may prove best around 1m: acts on polytrack and good to firm going: blinkered
on debut: gelded. *D. R. C. Elsworth*

AL GARHOUD BRIDGE 2 b.c. (Feb 3) Josr Algarhoud (IRE) 118 – Pluck 80 **91**
(Never So Bold 135) [2004 6m⁵ 6.1g 7m* 7m⁴ Jul 31] €40,000Y: big colt: has a quick
action: sixth living foal: half-brother to 3 winners, including 5-y-o Balakiref and 3-y-o
Cotton Easter: dam, 6f winner (including at 2 yrs), out of half-sister to very smart sprinter
Piccolo: fairly useful performer: won maiden at Catterick in June: respectable fourth in
nursery at Goodwood: stays 7f: sometimes edges left: sold 16,000 gns. *M. R. Channon*

47

ALGHAAZY (IRE) 3 b.g. Mark of Esteem (IRE) 137 – Kentmere (FR) (Galetto (FR) — 118) [2004 8.1s 10.2g Oct 10] strong, close-coupled gelding: well held in maidens at Haydock and Bath: sold 5,000 gns. *L. M. Cumani*

ALGORITHM 2 b.f. (Mar 4) Danehill Dancer (IRE) 117 – Dominelle 74 (Domynsky **59** 110) [2004 5d 6m⁶ 5m⁵ 7f⁶ 7m² 7m³ 8g⁴ 7g 8s Nov 1] stocky filly: unimpressive mover: first foal: dam 5f and (including at 2 yrs) 6f winner: modest maiden: should stay 1m: acts on firm and good to soft ground. *T. D. Easterby*

ALHAADH (USA) 2 b.f. (Mar 8) Diesis 133 – Wishah (USA) 85 (Red Ransom (USA)) **57 P** [2004 6g Oct 2] good-topped filly: first living foal: dam 2-y-o 7f winner on only start: favourite, ninth of 13 to Loyal Love in maiden at Newmarket, slowly away and travelling strongly long way: likely to do considerably better. *J. H. M. Gosden*

ALIABAD (IRE) 9 b. or br.g. Doyoun 124 – Alannya (FR) (Relko 136) [2004 –: — f16.2g⁵ Jan 14] of little account nowadays. *J. G. M. O'Shea*

ALIANNA (FR) 3 b.f. Anabaa (USA) 130 – Ambassadrice (FR) (Be My Guest (USA) — 126) [2004 p7g p8g 9.7s 10d p12d p9.5d⁵ Nov 5] €90,000Y: second living foal: half-sister to French 1½m to 15f winner Coming Home (by Exit To Nowhere): dam French 9f to 1½m and hurdles winner: no form. *S. Dow*

ALIBA (IRE) 3 ch.g. Ali-Royal (IRE) 127 – Kiba (IRE) (Tirol 127) [2004 62: f7g⁴ 7m **62** f7d f7s² 8m p7.1g Oct 19] modest maiden: should stay 1m: acts on fibresand, unraced on extremes of going on turf: none too reliable. *B. Smart*

ALIBONGO (CZE) 3 ch.g. Dara Monarch 128 – Alvilde 70 (Alzao (USA) 117) — [2004 43: f6g f7g Feb 12] close-coupled gelding: poor maiden: stays 6f: acts on good to soft ground. *P. A. Blockley*

ALI BRUCE 4 b.g. Cadeaux Genereux 131 – Actualite (Polish Precedent (USA) 131) **86** [2004 10m⁵ 8g² f7g* p7d³ 8.1d⁴ p8g⁴ p7g² f8g* p7m* Dec 21] big gelding: fairly useful performer: won apprentice claimer at Southwell (left D. Cantillon) in June, and minor events at Southwell and Lingfield in December: effective at 7f/1m: acts on all-weather and good to soft going: front runner. *G. L. Moore*

ALICE BLACKTHORN 3 b.f. Forzando 122 – Owdbetts (IRE) 69 (High Estate **62** 127) [2004 70: 6.1g 6d 6.9f⁵ 7m 7.1f 7d f7g* Nov 8] leggy, rather unfurnished filly: modest performer: won banded race at Southwell in November: stays 7f: acts on fibre-sand and good to firm ground: often sweats away: sold 18,000 gns. *B. Smart*

ALICE KING (IRE) 2 b.f. (Mar 24) Key of Luck (USA) 126 – Java Jive 63 (Hotfoot **46** 126) [2004 5s⁴ 5s⁴ 5g p5g² 6f⁵ p6g Aug 6] €2,000Y: close-coupled filly: half-sister to fairly useful Irish 1996 2-y-o 6f winner Bob The Broker (by Bob Back) and 1½m winner Miss Foxtrot (by Bustino): dam 5f winner: poor maiden: best effort at 5f on polytrack. *W. G. M. Turner*

ALI DEO 3 ch.g. Ali-Royal (IRE) 127 – Lady In Colour (IRE) 71 (Cadeaux Genereux **71** 131) [2004 79: 7.5g* 8.1g³ 8s 10m⁶ 7m 8g p8.6g p10g⁴ p9.5g⁴ p9.5g Dec 13] good-topped gelding: fair performer: won maiden at Beverley in May: left W. Haggas after ninth start: stays 1¼m: acts on polytrack and good to firm going: tried in cheekpieces: looked tricky ride fourth outing. *V. Smith*

ALIMISTE (IRE) 4 b.f. Ali-Royal (IRE) 127 – Miss Senate (IRE) (Alzao (USA) — 117) [2004 p10g p10g p10g p12g p13g 10.2d Apr 23] first foal: dam unraced sister to smart performer up to 1½m Suplizi: little form. *I. A. Wood*

ALINDA (IRE) 3 b.f. Revoque (IRE) 122 – Gratclo 65 (Belfort (FR) 89) [2004 69p: **86** 7m* 7.1m* Jul 23] rather leggy, lengthy filly: fairly useful form in only 4 runs: won minor events at Leicester and Chepstow (jarred a knee) in July: will probably stay 1m: won on fibresand at 2 yrs, unraced on extremes of going on turf. *P. W. Harris*

ALI PASHA 5 b.g. Ali-Royal (IRE) 127 – Edge of Darkness 62 (Vaigly Great 127) — [2004 45d: f9.4m⁶ Apr 19] poor maiden. *W. M. Brisbourne*

ALISA (IRE) 4 b.f. Slip Anchor 136 – Ariadne (GER) (Kings Lake (USA) 133) [2004 p8g p12g³ p12g⁵ p12g⁵ p10g⁶ 11.6m May 24] third foal: half-sister to middle-distance **a62** winners abroad by Vettori and Ezzoud: dam, German 1m/8.5f winner, out of sister to dam of King's Best and Urban Sea: modest maiden: should stay beyond 1½m: acts on polytrack: sometimes tongue tied. *B. I. Case*

A LITTLE BIT YARIE 3 b.g. Paris House 123 – Slipperose 72 (Persepolis (FR) **78 d** 127) [2004 81: 5s³ 5d 5g⁴ 6d 5.1d 5s p6g f5g f5f Dec 28] tall gelding: fair performer: below form after reappearance: likely to prove best at 5f/6f: acts on soft and good to firm ground: tried visored: tends to hang/has carried head awkwardly. *K. R. Burke*

ALIZAR (IRE) 3 b.f. Rahy (USA) 115 – Capua (USA) (Private Terms (USA)) [2004 **62** 58, a61: p7g p5g^2 f6g^3 p6g* f5g^4 p5g^2 p6g^3 5.3m^6 5.3m 6.1g^6 6m 6f* 5.3f p6g 6f 6g 6m 5g Sep 15] unfurnished filly: modest performer: won seller at Lingfield (left M. Polglase) in January and handicap at Brighton in June: effective at 5f to 7f: acts on all-weather, raced only on good ground or firmer on turf: tried in cheekpieces at 2 yrs: edgy sort. *S. Dow*

ALJAAREH (USA) 3 b. or br.c. Storm Cat (USA) – Muhbubh (USA) 108 (Blushing **58** Groom (FR) 131) [2004 8m May 15] attractive, good-bodied colt: half-brother to several winners, including useful 1995 2-y-o 5f/6f winner Amaniy (by Dayjur) and smart 6f (at 2 yrs) and 7f (including US Grade 2) winner Kayrawan (by Mr Prospector): dam won Princess Margaret Stakes: 8/1, burly, green and moved poorly to post when twelfth to Madid in maiden at Newbury, niggled along some way out: sold 10,000 gns in July. *M. P. Tregoning*

ALJAFLIYAH 3 ch.f. Halling (USA) 133 – Arruhan (IRE) 87 (Mujtahid (USA) 118) **–** [2004 8m 7g 7g 7d 8g Aug 28] tall, leggy filly: second foal: dam 5f (at 2 yrs) and 7f winner: little sign of ability in maidens, unseating rider leaving stall on debut, very slowly away next 3 outings: apprentice ridden. *L. M. Cumani*

ALJOMAR 5 b.g. College Chapel 122 – Running For You (FR) (Pampabird 124) **34** [2004 44: f7g f11g^6 f8g f8.5s Mar 1] leggy gelding: poor maiden: stays 8.5f: acts on fibresand and firm ground: sometimes wears cheekpieces: none too consistent. *R. E. Barr*

ALKAADHEM 4 b.c. Green Desert (USA) 127 – Balalaika 108 (Sadler's Wells (USA) **121** 132) [2004 106p: 8g^5 8g^4 9.9g* 8f 10d^4 12m^3 9.9m* 9.9g* Sep 22] strong colt: improved into a very smart performer: successful 3 times at Goodwood in 2004, in listed race in May and Select Racing UK On Sky 432 Stakes (by 2½ lengths from Battle Chant, despite edging left) and listed event (beat Privy Seal by 3½ lengths with something in hand, quickening clear 1f out), both in September: will prove best up to 1¼m: acts on good to firm going, seemed ill at ease on good to soft fifth start: blinkered last 2 outings. *M. P. Tregoning*

Mr Hamdan Al Maktoum's "Alkaadhem"

bet365 Old Newton Cup (Handicap), Haydock—Alkaased runs away with this well-contested race; Crow Wood (noseband) and Grampian (star on cap) finish well, with Hambleden (dark cap) fourth

ALKAASED (USA)   4 b.c. Kingmambo (USA) 125 – Chesa Plana (Niniski (USA)   **117**
125) [2004 103: 12m² 11.9g* 12m* 12m² Sep 4] big, strong, good-bodied colt: unimpressive mover: smart performer, lightly raced: left Sir Michael Stoute at 3 yrs: much
improved in 2004, winning bet365 Old Newton Cup (Handicap) at Haydock (by 4 lengths
from Crow Wood) and listed race at Goodwood (beat First Charter a neck), both in July:
very good ½-length second of 4 to Mamool in September Stakes at Kempton final outing:
at least as effective at 1½m as 1¾m: raced only on good/good to firm ground: has worn
crossed noseband: edgy last 2 starts. *L. M. Cumani*

ALL A DREAM   2 br.f. (Jan 29) Desert Story (IRE) 115 – Alioli (Nishapour (FR) 125)   **78**
[2004 f5m⁶ f5g p7g³ p6g p7.1g³ p7.1g* p7.1g⁵ f8g⁴ Dec 28] fourth foal: half-sister to
winner in Greece by Zilzal: dam, no form, out of half-sister to very smart 1¼m performer
Last Second: fair performer: left R. Guest after fourth start: won nursery at Wolverhampton in November: should stay 1¼m: acts on all-weather. *Mrs L. Williamson*

ALL BLEEVABLE   7 b.g. Presidium 124 – Eve's Treasure (Bustino 136) [2004 12m⁶   **53**
12.3g⁶ 12g f14g² Nov 22] modest maiden, lightly raced: stays 1¾m: acts on fibresand.
Mrs S. Lamyman

ALL BLUE (IRE)   3 b.g. Green Desert (USA) 127 – Talented 112 (Bustino 136) [2004   **74 d**
8.2d⁴ 10g⁴ 14d 10v Oct 20] tall, lengthy gelding: sixth foal: brother to 2002 2-y-o 5f
winner Secret Pride and half-brother to 2001 2-y-o 7f winner Zaeema (by Zafonic), both
fairly useful: dam 1¼m (including Sun Chariot Stakes) winner who stayed 1½m: fair
maiden at best: regressed after debut: probably stays 1¼m: visored final outing: tongue
tied: temperament under suspicion: left Godolphin 12,000 gns. *Saeed bin Suroor*

ALLEGRETTO (FR)   2 b.c. (Feb 23) Anabaa (USA) 130 – Aimores (IRE) (Persian   **74 p**
Heights 129) [2004 6.1v² Nov 4] €94,000F, €45,000Y, 24,000 2-y-o: lengthy, good-
topped colt: fourth foal: half-brother to fairly useful 1999 2-y-o 1m winner Lonely Place
(by Lake Coniston) and French 1½m winner Agent Special (by Grand Lodge): dam,
Italian 7.5f winner, half-sister to Oaks winner Shahtoush: 20/1, 6 lengths second of 14 to
Starchy in maiden at Nottingham, late headway: likely to stay 1m: will improve. *S. Kirk*

ALLERTON BOY   5 ch.g. Beveled (USA) – Darakah 78 (Doulab (USA) 115) [2004   **42**
64d: f5g⁴ f6g f5g⁶ p5g Feb 16] poor maiden: should stay 6f: acts on fibresand and firm
ground: blinkered final 4-y-o start: has pulled hard. *R. J. Hodges*

ALLEZ MOUSSON   6 b.g. Hernando (FR) 127 – Rynechra 102 (Blakeney 126) [2004   **–**
67: 18g 18v 16.2s 16.1d 17.1d Aug 15] tall, leggy gelding: handicapper, little form in
2004: tried blinkered/in cheekpieces. *A. Bailey*

ALL FOR LAURA   2 ch.f. (Mar 5) Cadeaux Genereux 131 – Lighthouse 92 (Warning   **92**
136) [2004 6m⁴ 5.1g* 5.2g⁵ 6g⁵ 7g 6s⁴ Oct 29] leggy filly: second foal: sister to 3-y-o
Kehaar, 1m winner from 3 starts, half-sister to Middle Park winner First Trump out
of half-sister to high-class sprinter Mr Brooks: fairly useful performer: won maiden at
Nottingham in July: respectable efforts in listed races after, fourth to Bahia Breeze at
Newmarket: stays 6f, seemingly not quite 7f: acts on soft going. *D. R. Loder*

ALLIED CAUSE   2 ch.f. (Feb 2) Giant's Causeway (USA) 132 – Alligram (USA) 61   **73 p**
(Alysheba (USA)) [2004 7g 7g⁵ p7g* Oct 28] tall, angular filly: good mover: seventh
foal: half-sister to very smart 1m/1¼m winner Kissogram (by Caerleon) and 7-y-o Bucks:
dam, lightly-raced maiden, out of top-class miler Milligram: progressed in maidens,
winning at Lingfield by neck from Celtique, leading 1f out: will stay at least 1m: has
scope to do better as 3-y-o. *L. M. Cumani*

ALLIED VICTORY (USA)   4 b.c. Red Ransom (USA) – Coral Dance (FR) 111   **76**
(Green Dancer (USA) 132) [2004 81: f8g⁴ f8.5g f11g 10.5g² 10.5d 9.2d³ 12.1s 11.9g⁴   **a71**
Sep 3] useful-looking colt: fair performer: won maiden at Southwell in January: stays
1½m: acts on fibresand, firm and soft going: tongue tied (ran at least creditably) last 2
starts. *E. J. Alston*

50

ALLIZAM 2 b.c. (Feb 23) Tragic Role (USA) – Mazilla 59 (Mazilier (USA) 107) [2004 **55**
6s 6m⁴ 5d 8.2v Nov 4] quite good-topped colt: modest maiden: will be suited by 1¼m/
1½m: best effort on heavy going. *B. A. McMahon*

ALL NIGHT DANCER (IRE) 2 b.f. (Apr 4) Danehill Dancer (IRE) 117 – Nocturnal **83**
(FR) 71 (Night Shift (USA)) [2004 5m* 6m⁵ 6g² 6d 7m 7d 6.3g² 6d Oct 10] leggy, quite
good-topped filly: second foal: half-sister to fairly useful Irish 6f winner (including at 2
yrs) Lady Portia (by College Chapel): dam, Irish maiden, out of half-sister to smart
French winner up to 1m Orangerie: fairly useful form: won maiden at Navan in May:
second in minor event at Haydock and valuable contest at the Curragh (beaten 2 lengths
by Slip Dance): probably best at 5f/6f: acts on good to firm going. *D. Wachman, Ireland*

ALLODARLIN (IRE) 3 b.f. Cape Cross (IRE) 129 – Sharp Circle (IRE) 83 (Sure **–**
Blade (USA) 130) [2004 60: 10m 11.5f 8m Aug 16] leggy, quite good-topped filly:
maiden: no form in 2004: sent to Saudi Arabia. *P. F. I. Cole*

ALL ON MY OWN (USA) 9 ch.g. Unbridled (USA) 128 – Some For All (USA) **41 §**
(One For All (USA)) [2004 44: f14.8g f9.4g⁴ f8.5g² p10g⁴ f8.5s p8g f8.5m⁵ 8.1g³ 10v⁴
8.5m May 24] close-coupled, workmanlike gelding: poor maiden: effective at 1m to easy
2m: acts on heavy and good to firm going: usually blinkered, tried in visor/cheekpieces:
unreliable. *I. W. McInnes*

ALL QUIET 3 b.f. Piccolo 121 – War Shanty 66 (Warrshan (USA) 117) [2004 70: 6m³ **72 d**
7g² 8f³ 7m⁵ 6d⁵ 7m⁵ 6m Sep 27] leggy filly: fair maiden: below form after second outing:
stays 1m: acts on firm and good to soft ground. *R. Hannon*

ALLSTAR PRINCESS 2 b.f. (Jan 27) Environment Friend 128 – Turf Moor (IRE) **46**
53 (Mac's Imp (USA) 116) [2004 5.9g 6g 7g 7d Aug 27] 1,800Y: strong filly: second
foal: half-sister to 3-y-o Turf Princess: dam, maiden, stayed 7f: poor maiden: possibly
temperamental. *R. A. Fahey*

ALL TOO BEAUTIFUL (IRE) 3 b.f. Sadler's Wells (USA) 132 – Urban Sea (USA) **113**
126 (Miswaki (USA) 124) [2004 10d* 10d* 12m² 12f⁴ 10g³ Sep 19] 1,100,000F: rangy,

Mr M. Tabor & Mrs John Magnier's "All Too Beautiful"

rather unfurnished filly: has a powerful, round action: sister to Derby winner Galileo and very smart 1¼m/1½m winner Black Sam Bellamy and half-sister to 1¼m winner Melikah (by Lammtarra) and 1m (at 2 yrs) to 1½m winner Urban Ocean (by Bering), both smart: dam, 1m (at 2 yrs) to 1½m (Arc) winner, closely related to 2000 Guineas winner King's Best: smart performer: won maiden at Leopardstown in March and listed race at Navan (by 2½ lengths from Queen Astrid) in April: in frame in Oaks at Epsom (favourite, 7 lengths second to Ouija Board), Irish Oaks at the Curragh (led early when below-form fourth to same filly)'and Blandford Stakes at the Curragh (running-on ½-length third to Monturani): effective at 1¼m/1½m: acts on good to firm and good to soft going: sometimes carries head awkwardly. *A. P. O'Brien, Ireland*

ALLY MAKBUL 4 b.f. Makbul 104 – Clarice Orsini (Common Grounds 118) [2004 61: f8.5g* f8.5g* f12g⁴ f8.5g f8.5s* Feb 17] modest performer: won claimers at Wolverhampton in January and February: best form at 6f to 8.5f nowadays: acts on all-weather, raced only on good/good to firm ground on turf. *J. R. Best* **62**

AL MABROOK (IRE) 9 b.g. Rainbows For Life (CAN) – Sky Lover (Ela-Mana-Mou 132) [2004 f14g Jun 16] leggy gelding: poor handicapper: sometimes blinkered. *N. G. Richards* **–**

ALMAH (SAF) 6 b.m. Al Mufti (USA) 112 – Jazz Champion (SAF) (Dancing Champ (USA)) [2004 16.2g 14g 16.2g⁶ 14g 16.2m Sep 25] big ex-South African mare: third foal: dam unraced: winner of 5 of 24 starts in native country, including Group 2 handicap at Kenilworth in 2003: off 11 months before reappearance in July: best effort in Britain when sixth in handicap at Ascot: stays 2m: blinkered (looked tricky ride) last outing: fairly useful hurdler. *Miss Venetia Williams* **92**

ALMANAC (IRE) 3 b.c. Desert Style (IRE) 121 – Share The Vision (Vision (USA)) [2004 –: f8g p8g f8g 8.1m Sep 6] well held in maidens: dead. *B. P. J. Baugh* **–**

ALMANSHOOD (USA) 2 b. or br.c. (Jan 24) Bahri (USA) 125 – Lahan 117 (Unfuwain (USA) 131) [2004 7.1d⁵ 8d³ Aug 20] big, good sort: fluent mover: first foal: dam 7f (at 2 yrs) and 1m (1000 Guineas) winner: better effort in maidens (green and burly on debut) when third to Bayeux de Moi at Salisbury: should stay 1¼m: type to do better at 3 yrs. *J. H. M. Gosden* **70 p**

ALMANSOORA (USA) 2 b.f. (Mar 13) Bahri (USA) 125 – Bashayer (USA) 103 (Mr Prospector (USA)) [2004 6g² 7g* Sep 2] tall, leggy filly: half-sister to several winners, including useful 1m winner Mosayter (by Storm Cat) and 3-y-o Thaminah: dam, 1m winner (including at 2 yrs) who stayed 11.4f, closely related to Nayef and half-sister to Nashwan and Unfuwain: confirmed debut promise when winning 16-runner maiden at Salisbury by short head from Elizabethan Age, getting up close home: will stay 1m: useful prospect. *Saeed bin Suroor* **78 p**

ALMARA 4 b.f. Wolfhound (USA) 126 – Alacrity 62 (Alzao (USA) 117) [2004 –: p7g f5g⁴ f6g p6g⁵ Apr 27] bad maiden. *Miss K. B. Boutflower* **–**

ALMATY EXPRESS 2 b.g. (Apr 27) Almaty (IRE) 113§ – Express Girl 75 (Sylvan Express 117) [2004 5v³ 6s 5f 5f³ 5g⁴ 5m* Jul 7] smallish gelding: modest performer: won seller at Catterick: should stay 6f: probably acts on any turf going. *M. Todhunter* **58**

ALMAVIVA (IRE) 4 b.f. Grand Lodge (USA) 125 – Kafayef (USA) 46 (Secreto (USA) 128) [2004 93: 8d 10g May 1] leggy, lengthy filly: fairly useful performer at best, very lightly raced: well held in listed race and handicap in 2004. *J. Noseda* **–**

ALMENDRADOS (IRE) 2 b.f. (Feb 9) Desert Prince (IRE) 130 – Sevi's Choice (USA) (Sir Ivor (USA) 135) [2004 6m³ Jun 5] 150,000F, 260,000Y: second foal: half-sister to 2003 2-y-o 5f winner Dontstopthemusic (by Night Shift): dam German 1¼m winner: 8/1, 2 lengths third of 9 to Park Romance in maiden at Newmarket, not knocked about: should do better if all is well. *J. Noseda* **78 p**

ALMIGHTY (USA) 2 b.c. (Apr 21) Sadler's Wells (USA) 132 – Saganeca (USA) 120 (Sagace (FR) 135) [2004 7f⁶ 8s* Oct 20] half-brother to several winners, notably 1½m winner (including Arc) Sagamix (by Linamix) and 2000 2-y-o 9f/1¼m winner who stayed 1½m Sagacity (by Highest Honor), both high class in France: dam won 12.5f Prix de Royallieu: better effort in maidens when landing odds in 18-runner event at Navan in October by 3 lengths from Maria Luisa, always prominent: will be suited by at least 1½m: sure to progress. *A. P. O'Brien, Ireland* **98 p**

ALMIZAN (IRE) 4 b.g. Darshaan 133 – Bint Albaadiya (USA) 108 (Woodman (USA) 126) [2004 96: 18.7d 14g 18g⁴ 20f 21g⁴ 15.9s³ 16m 18s 16d⁵ Nov 3] leggy, angular gelding: fairly useful handicapper: stays 21f: acts on firm and soft going: visored fifth to eighth starts. *M. R. Channon* **89**

ALMNADIA (IRE)   5 b.m. Alhaarth (IRE) 126 – Mnaafa (IRE) 70 (Darshaan 133)   **51**
[2004 16.1v 16.1m⁵ 14.1m⁶ May 31] well-made mare: modest performer: should stay
2m: acts on polytrack and good to firm going: wore cheekpieces last 2 starts: held up: fair
hurdler. *S. Gollings*

ALMOND BEACH   4 ch.g. Hector Protector (USA) 124 – Dancing Spirit (IRE) 72   –
(Ahonoora 122) [2004 –: f7g p8g Jan 7] lengthy gelding: of little account nowadays.
B. J. Meehan

ALMOND WILLOW (IRE)   3 b.f. Alhaarth (IRE) 126 – Miss Willow Bend (USA)   **77**
(Willow Hour (USA)) [2004 69: 10m 8.1d² 8.1s 7.9g⁶ p8.6g² p10g³ Oct 13] good-topped
filly: fluent mover: fair performer: stays 1¼m: acts on all-weather, soft and good to firm
ground: flashes tail: sold 15,000 gns, sent to Saudi Arabia. *J. Noseda*

ALMOST PERFECT (IRE)   2 ch.f. (Feb 12) Priolo (USA) 127 – Talbiya (IRE)   **57**
(Mujtahid (USA) 118) [2004 f5d⁶ 6g³ Jun 3] €5,000Y: first foal: dam, well beaten only
start, out of half-sister to Dante winner Torjoun: better effort in maidens when third at
Hamilton: bred to stay at least 1m. *T. D. Barron*

ALMOST WELCOME   3 b.g. First Trump 118 – Choral Sundown 81 (Night Shift   **58**
(USA)) [2004 55?: p7g p8g p10g³ p10g⁵ 11.1g 11.7f p10g Aug 21] good-bodied gelding:
modest maiden: stays 1¼m: acts on polytrack, raced only on good ground or firmer
on turf: gelded. *S. Dow*

ALMURAAD (IRE)   3 b.c. Machiavellian (USA) 123 – Wellspring (IRE) 88 (Caerleon   **106**
(USA) 132) [2004 100p: 8m* 9s Oct 16] angular, good-bodied colt: useful performer,
lightly raced: won minor event at Newmarket in May by ½ length from Mukafeh:
below-par tenth in Darley Stakes there 5 months later: should stay 9f: acts on firm ground.
Sir Michael Stoute

ALNAJA (USA)   5 b.g. Woodman (USA) 126 – Cursory Look (USA) (Nijinsky (CAN)   –
138) [2004 82p: 12.4v 15.4s Apr 20] fairly useful handicapper at best, lightly raced:
ran as though amiss in 2004: visored/tongue tied last start: one to treat with caution.
W. J. Haggas

ALONG CAME MOLLY   2 ch.f. (Feb 24) Dr Fong (USA) 128 – Torrid Tango (USA)   –
(Green Dancer (USA) 132) [2004 8v p8.6g Dec 3] 30,000F: half-sister to several winners,
including 7-y-o Torrid Kentavr and Irish 2-y-o 1m winner/US Grade 2 7f winner Dancing
(by Spectrum): dam lightly-raced half-sister to dam of Suave Dancer: well held in
maidens at Newbury (slowly away) and Wolverhampton (blinkered). *B. J. Meehan*

ALONG THE NILE   2 b.g. (Feb 12) Desert Prince (IRE) 130 – Golden Fortune 102   **69 §**
(Forzando 122) [2004 6g 6g³ 6s⁶ 6d 7f 7m⁴ 8s⁶ 7s Nov 6] 40,000Y: strong, lengthy
gelding: third foal: brother to 3-y-o Fortune's Princess and half-brother to 4-y-o Fortunes
Favourite: dam 6f (at 2 yrs) to 7.5f winner: fair maiden: probably stay 1m: acts on soft and
good to firm going: all but refused to race fifth outing: not one to trust. *Mrs J. R. Ramsden*

ALPAGA LE JOMAGE (IRE)   2 b.c. (Feb 12) Orpen (USA) 116 – Miss Bagatelle   **88 §**
70 (Mummy's Pet 125) [2004 5g³ 5s³ 5.1d² 5f⁴ 5g⁵ 5f 5.2m⁵ 5g* 5.2m⁴ 6m f6s² f5g Dec
7] €13,000Y, resold 24,000Y: lengthy, quite good-topped colt: brother to French/Spanish
1m winner Renedo and half-brother to several winners abroad: dam, Irish 6f winner,
half-sister to Gold Cup winner Arcadian Heights: fairly useful performer: won maiden at
Musselburgh in July: below form last 3 starts, leaving B. Meehan after second of them:
will prove best at 5f/easy 6f: acts on firm and soft ground: blinkered (below form) once:
tends to hang/carry head high: not one to trust. *M. J. Polglase*

ALPH   7 b.g. Alflora (IRE) 120 – Royal Birthday (St Paddy 133) [2004 p12g⁴ Aug 21]   **70**
signs of ability in 2 starts over hurdles: 100/1, 6 lengths fourth to Red Damson in maiden
at Lingfield: refused to enter stall intended next outing: will stay 1¾m. *R. Ingram*

ALPHA ECHO (USA)   5 b. or br.g. Spinning World (USA) 130 – Add (USA) (Spec-   –
tacular Bid (USA)) [2004 –: f9.4g Mar 27] quite good-topped ex-Irish gelding: fifth in
Newmarket maiden on debut in 2002 (only run for A. O'Brien, very slowly away): well
beaten both starts since. *M. F. Harris*

ALPHA JULIET (IRE)   3 b.f. Victory Note (USA) 120 – Zara's Birthday (IRE) 71   **45**
(Waajib 121) [2004 7d⁶ 9m⁶ 12.3d⁶ Aug 30] €10,000Y: leggy filly: fourth foal: half-sister
to 3 winners, including 1¾m/2m winner Blair (by Persian Bold): dam Irish maiden who
stayed 1½m: poor form in maidens: should stay 1½m. *G. M. Moore*

ALPHA ZETA   3 b.g. Primo Dominie 121 – Preening 62 (Persian Bold 123) [2004 –:   –
6g 6d 5d 8m 7.9f 10f Sep 13] stocky gelding: no sign of ability. *C. W. Thornton*

ALPHECCA (USA) 3 b.c. Kingmambo (USA) 125 – Limbo (USA) (A P Indy (USA) **102**
131) [2004 –p: 10g* 10m³ 10.1g⁶ Aug 30] close-coupled, quite good-topped colt: useful
form: won maiden at Lingfield in June: much better effort in minor events after when 2
lengths third to Wunderwood at Ascot: will probably stay 1½m: raced only on good/good
to firm ground: sold 24,000 gns. *Sir Michael Stoute*

ALPHONSINA 2 b.f. (Mar 6) Josr Algarhoud (IRE) 118 – Club Elite 57 (Salse (USA) **–**
128) [2004 p8.6g p7.1g Dec 31] third foal: dam staying maiden: well held in maidens at
Wolverhampton. *Mrs L. Williamson*

ALPHUN (IRE) 2 b.g. (May 3) Orpen (USA) 116 – Fakhira (IRE) 83 (Jareer (USA) **61**
115) [2004 p6g⁶ p6g² Dec 29] €24,000F, €20,000Y: sixth foal: half-brother to 2001 2-y-o
7f and 8.5f winner Offa's Dyke and 7f winner Akhira (both fairly useful, by Emperor
Jones): dam, Irish 2-y-o 5f winner, half-sister to smart 6f/7f performer Danehill Dancer:
modest form in maidens at Lingfield, second to Aggravation: should stay 7f. *B. J. Meehan*

ALPINE GOLD (IRE) 2 b.f. (May 3) Montjeu (IRE) 137 – Ski For Gold 76 (Shirley **82**
Heights 130) [2004 7m 7g 8.1s* 8s* 8d Oct 30] well-made filly: fifth foal: closely related
to 2001 2-y-o 1m winner (stayed 1½m) Ski For Me (by Barathea): dam, 2-y-o 7f winner
who might have proved best around 1¾m, half-sister to US Grade 1 1¼m winner
Bequest: fairly useful performer: won maiden at Chepstow in August and nursery at
Doncaster in October: seemed to run creditably in listed race at Newmarket final start:
should stay at least 1½m: acts on soft ground. *J. L. Dunlop*

ALPINE HIDEAWAY (IRE) 11 b.g. Tirol 127 – Arbour (USA) 76 (Graustark) **51**
[2004 51: 7m 7.5g⁶ 8d 8.5d* 8f 9.9m Sep 21] good-topped gelding: modest performer:
won claimer at Beverley (third success in race) in August: effective at 1m/1¼m: acts on
fibresand and any turf going: tried blinkered/visored, often in cheekpieces nowadays:
inconsistent. *J. S. Wainwright*

ALPINE SPECIAL (IRE) 3 gr.g. Orpen (USA) 116 – Halomix (Linamix (FR) 127) **74**
[2004 71: 7g⁶ 10f f12m⁴ 10.5s² 12.1s² 14g p12.2g Oct 2] good-topped gelding: fair
handicapper: stays 1½m: acts on fibresand, dirt and good to firm ground. *P. C. Haslam*

ALPINO CHILENO (ARG) 5 gr.h. Alpino Fitz (ARG) – Fairyland (ARG) (Lode **108**
(USA)) [2004 107: a12g* a14g* 12g* 11d⁵ 12m⁶ 9s⁴ 12g⁴ 12m Sep 26] Argentinian-bred
horse: useful performer: joined current stable after second start in 2003 (formerly trained
in Chile where twice a winner): won minor events at Ovrevoll and Taby and handicap at
Ovrevoll in May/June: good 3 lengths fourth to Collier Hill in Stockholm Cup International at Taby penultimate start: stiff task and not discredited in Cumberland Lodge
Stakes at Ascot final outing: stays 1¾m: acts on dirt, soft and good to firm ground:
blinkered nowadays. *R. Haugen, Norway*

ALQAAHIR (USA) 2 b.c. (Apr 2) Swain (IRE) 134 – Crafty Example (USA) (Crafty **76 p**
Prospector (USA)) [2004 7g³ Sep 15] rangy colt: half-brother to several winners, includ-
ing top-class miler Intikhab (6f winner at 2 yrs) and fairly useful French 1¼m winner
Jadarah (both by Red Ransom): dam, ran once, out of sister to top-class miler Polish
Precedent: 9/2, 3¼ lengths third to Home Affairs in maiden at Yarmouth, quickening well
from rear and not unduly knocked about: will stay at least 1m: sure to improve. *Saeed bin
Suroor*

ALQAAYID 3 b.g. Machiavellian (USA) 123 – One So Wonderful 121 (Nashwan **– §**
(USA) 135) [2004 71§: p9.5g f8g Dec 7] sturdy, useful-looking gelding: fluent mover:
lightly-raced maiden: tailed off in 2004: tried blinkered: probably ungenuine. *P. W. Hiatt*

AL QUDRA (IRE) 2 b.c. (Mar 8) Cape Cross (IRE) 129 – Alvilda (IRE) (Caerleon **91**
(USA) 132) [2004 5.1g⁵ f6g* 7g 6m⁵ 6m² 7m 6g Oct 8] 17,000F, 16,000Y: leggy colt:
first foal: dam unraced out of half-sister to very smart miler/Champion Hurdle
winner Alderbrook: fairly useful performer: won maiden at Southwell in June: good 6
lengths second of 6 to Caesar Beware in minor event at Windsor: should stay 7f: acts on
fibresand and good to firm going: blinkered (last in nursery) final start: sent to UAE.
B. J. Meehan

ALQWAH (IRE) 3 b.f. Danehill (USA) 126 – Delage (Bellypha 130) [2004 7d* Jun **85**
23] €150,000Y: tall, leggy filly: fourth foal: half-sister to 2 winners, including 1¼m/11.6f
winner Mystic Mile (by Sadler's Wells): dam unraced half-sister to very smart performer
up to 7f College Chapel: 5/1 and tongue tied, won maiden at Salisbury readily by 2
lengths from Red Top, quickening from front 2f out: will stay 1m: left Godolphin. *Saeed
bin Suroor*

ALRAFIDAIN (IRE) 2 b.c. (Jan 25) Monsun (GER) 124 – Demeter (USA) 79 (Diesis **84**
133) [2004 8g⁴ 7.2s² Oct 12] 110,000Y: strong, useful-looking colt: has a powerful, round

action: first foal: dam, third at 1m at 2 yrs on only start, daughter of Irish 1000 Guineas winner Nicer: in frame in maidens at Newmarket and Ayr (dictated pace when beaten length by Kames Park): should be suited by 1¼m/1½m. *M. Johnston*

ALRAFID (IRE)   5 ch.g. Halling (USA) 133 – Ginger Tree (USA) 86 (Dayjur (USA)   **93** 137) [2004 93: 10g 10g⁵ 8g⁶ 8.5m² 8d 9.9g 9m⁶ 8m Sep 26] fairly useful handicapper: stays 1¼m: acts on polytrack, soft and good to firm going: has been slowly away: usually held up: fair hurdler. *G. L. Moore*

ALRIDA (IRE)   5 b.g. Ali-Royal (IRE) 127 – Ride Bold (USA) (J O Tobin (USA)   **73 +** 130) [2004 86d: 16.1v⁴ 21g* Jul 28] leggy gelding: fair handicapper: won at Goodwood in July: stays 21f: acts on any going: tried in cheekpieces: held up. *R. A. Fahey*

ALRIGHT MY SON (IRE)   2 b.c. (Mar 5) Pennekamp (USA) 130 – Pink Stone (FR)   **89** (Bigstone (IRE) 126) [2004 5.1s 5s² 6f⁴ 7m⁵ 7m² 8d⁴ 8m 8m² 8.3g* 8s⁶ Oct 22] €16,000F, €28,000Y: rather leggy colt: first foal: dam, French maiden who stayed 10.5f, half-sister to very smart French 1m/1¼m winner Pink: fairly useful performer: won nursery at Windsor in October: should stay 1¼m: acts on soft going, probably on firm: sometimes sweats/looks none too keen. *R. Hannon*

AL'S GLENNMAY   2 b.f. (May 1) High Estate 127 – Payvashooz 78 (Ballacashtal (CAN)) [2004 7s Oct 21] eighth foal: half-sister to fairly useful 5f/6f winner (including at 2 yrs and in France) Socks For Glenn (by Factual) and 7-y-o Strensall: dam 5f (at 2 yrs) to 7f winner: 66/1, tailed off in maiden at Brighton. *M. S. Saunders*

ALSHARQ (IRE)   2 b.f. (Apr 10) Machiavellian (USA) 123 – Balaabel (USA) 83   **65 p** (Sadler's Wells (USA) 132) [2004 7g 7d Oct 30] rather leggy filly: seventh foal: sister to 4-y-o Maksad and half-sister to 2 winners, including useful 2000 2-y-o 7f (Rockfel Stakes) winner Sayedeh (by Darshaan): dam, 1m winner, half-sister to US Grade 2 7f winner Kayrawan: fair form in maidens at Leicester and Newmarket (went well long way): will stay 1m: should improve. *M. P. Tregoning*

ALSHAWAMEQ (IRE)   3 b.g. Green Desert (USA) 127 – Azdihaar (USA) 81 (Mr   **95** Prospector (USA)) [2004 81: 8m³ 8m* 8m 8g⁵ 8g³ 8d² a7f a8g² Dec 10] tall, leggy gelding: useful handicapper: won at Newmarket in June: good placed efforts after on same course (met trouble), Pontefract (slowly away) and, having left J. Dunlop after sixth outing, Jebel Ali: should prove as effective at 7f as 1m: acts on dirt, good to firm and good to soft going: blinkered (looked less than straightforward) last 2 starts in 2003: has run well when sweating. *D. Watson, UAE*

AL SHUUA   3 b.f. Lomitas 129 – Sephala (USA) (Mr Prospector (USA)) [2004 67: 9g²   **76 d** 10f 10f⁴ 10d 10.2g Sep 27] leggy filly: fair maiden at best: should stay at least 1¼m: sold 4,000 gns. *C. E. Brittain*

AL SIFAAT   3 ch.f. Unfuwain (USA) 131 – Almurooj 54 (Zafonic (USA) 130) [2004   **73** 88p: 9.9g 8m⁴ Jun 18] lengthy, rather dipped-backed filly: fairly useful winner at 2 yrs: well held in 2004: headstrong, and likely to have proved best up to 1m: raced only on good/good to firm going: tongue tied in 2004: visits Cape Cross. *Saeed bin Suroor*

ALSU (IRE)   2 b.f. (Apr 17) Fasliyev (USA) 120 – Pourquoi Pas (IRE) 109 (Nordico   **72** (USA)) [2004 5.1g³ 6d* 6.3g 6g⁶ 5f³ 5g³ 5d⁶ a6.5f a8.5s⁵ Dec 31] €35,000Y: compact filly: second foal: half-sister to an Italian winner around 1m by Royal Academy: dam Italian Group 2 1¼m winner: fair performer: won maiden at Hamilton in May: third in nurseries after: left A. Balding before penultimate outing: effective at 5f/6f: acts on firm and good to soft going. *R. R. Root, USA*

ALTA PETENS   2 b.f. (Apr 5) Mujadil (USA) 119 – Be Exciting (IRE) 88 (Be My   **86** Guest (USA) 126) [2004 5v⁴ 6g* 6m 5.2m 7f⁴ 8m⁵ 6.5g⁶ 7g 6d⁵ Oct 14] tall, lengthy filly: sixth foal: half-sister to a winner in Greece by Second Empire: dam, 1m (at 2 yrs) and 1½m winner, closely related to very smart 1m/1¼m performer Almushtarak: fairly useful performer: won maiden at Yarmouth in May: creditable efforts in listed races/sales events last 4 starts: effective at 6f to 1m: probably acts on any turf going: sold 20,000 gns. *M. L. W. Bell*

ALTARES   3 b.c. Alhaarth (IRE) 126 – Reach The Wind (USA) (Relaunch (USA))   **–** [2004 –: p10g p8g f8.5g 11g 11.6g Jul 12] small colt: of little account. *P. Howling*

ALTAY   7 b.g. Erins Isle 121 – Aliuska (IRE) 70 (Fijar Tango (FR) 127) [2004 86: 10.4g   **84 +** 12d³ Nov 3] tall gelding: has a round action: fairly useful handicapper: effective at 1¼m to 13f: acts on polytrack, firm and soft going: usually races prominently: fairly useful hurdler. *R. A. Fahey*

ALTIERI 6 ch.h. Selkirk (USA) 129 – Minya (USA) (Blushing Groom (FR) 131) [2004 **122**
117: 10d* 10s* 10g* 12m⁴ 10d Nov 7] very smart performer: won minor event at Rome
in March, and listed race at Milan and Premio Presidente della Repubblica at Rome
(career-best effort, beat Vespone 3 lengths) in May: reportedly finished lame in Gran
Premio di Milano following month and ran poorly after absence in Premio Roma final
start: best at 1m/1¼m: acts on heavy and good to firm ground. *V. Caruso, Italy*

ALTITUDE DANCER (IRE) 4 b.g. Sadler's Wells (USA) 132 – Height of Passion **58**
(Shirley Heights 130) [2004 67: f16g³ f16s² f16g* f16s⁴ 18g 16.1v p16.5g f16g⁵ Dec 14] **a70**
smallish gelding: fair handicapper: won at Southwell in February: should stay beyond
2m: acts on fibresand, good to firm and good to soft going: blinkered once at 2 yrs.
P. A. Blockley

ALULA 2 ch.f. (Mar 31) In The Wings 128 – Aryaf (CAN) (Vice Regent (CAN)) [2004 **54**
6d 8m 8.2m Sep 28] sturdy filly: half-sister to several winners, notably very smart 5f
winner (including at 2 yrs) Mind Games (by Puissance): dam lightly-raced maiden:
modest form in maidens: will probably stay 1¼m. *R. Hannon*

ALVARINHO LADY 2 b.f. (Mar 8) Royal Applause 124 – Jugendliebe (IRE) (Persian **72**
Bold 123) [2004 5.1g* 5s⁵ 6g⁴ 6g⁴ 6.1g 6.5m Sep 8] 10,000F, €21,000Y, resold 13,000Y:
smallish filly: sixth foal: sister to useful 2002 2-y-o 6f winner All Nines (later won at
1¼m in Hong Kong as Pacific Alliance) and half-sister to 2m winner Lago (by Maelstrom
Lake): dam German 1¼m winner: fair performer: won maiden at Nottingham in March:
ran poorly in nurseries last 2 starts: barely stays 6f. *D. Haydn Jones*

ALWAYS BELIEVE (USA) 8 b.g. Carr de Naskra (USA) – Wonder Mar (USA) (Fire –
Dancer (USA)) [2004 –, a56: f7g f9.4s Mar 8] of little account nowadays. *Mrs P. Ford*

ALWAYS DARING 5 b.m. Atraf 116 – Steamy Windows § (Dominion 123) [2004 –: –
7.1f f7m 5.9f Jul 29] no longer of much account. *C. J. Teague*

ALWAYS ESTEEMED (IRE) 4 b.g. Mark of Esteem (IRE) 137 – Always Far **104**
(USA) (Alydar (USA)) [2004 104d: 8.1d² 10.4d 10m 8m⁴ p8g* 8f⁴ 7.9s 8f 7d Oct 15] big,
lengthy gelding: useful performer: won minor event at Lingfield in July by 1½ lengths
from Fiveoclock Express: poor efforts in handicaps last 3 starts: probably best around
1m: acts on polytrack, firm and good to soft ground: blinkered twice: none too consistent,
and sometimes looks difficult ride: sold 43,000 gns. *G. Wragg*

ALWAYS FIRST 3 b.c. Barathea (IRE) 127 – Pink Cristal 113 (Dilum (USA) 115) **116**
[2004 102P: 8.3m 9.2g² 12g³ 11.9d⁴ 11m Sep 17] rangy, good-topped colt: smart performer: improved form when 1½ lengths third to Cutting Crew in handicap at Goodwood
and 5¼ lengths fourth to Rule of Law in Great Voltigeur Stakes at York: ran as though
amiss in Arc Trial at Newbury subsequent outing: will be suited by more of a test at 1½m,
and will stay 1¾m: yet to race on extremes of going: sent to USA. *Sir Michael Stoute*

ALWAYS FLYING (USA) 3 ch.g. Fly So Free (USA) 122 – Dubiously (USA) (Jolie **73 d**
Jo (USA)) [2004 70: f9.4g* p10g⁵ 10.3g² 9.2d⁶ 10m⁶ 9g 9m² 7.5g 8.5m 8m 10s⁴ f12g²
Nov 9] leggy, quite good-topped gelding: fair performer at best: made all in maiden at
Wolverhampton in January: claimed from M. Johnston £8,000 seventh start: stays 1¼m:
acts on fibresand, good to firm and good to soft ground: blinkered (ran poorly) once in
2003: races prominently. *N. Wilson*

ALWAYS MINE 2 ch.f. (Mar 21) Daylami (IRE) 138 – Mamoura (IRE) 97 (Lomond **83**
(USA) 128) [2004 7g⁵ 8d⁶ Oct 30] leggy filly: half-sister to several winners, including
smart Irish 1½m (including Prix de Royallieu) winner Mouramara (by Kahyasi): dam
Irish 1¼m/1½m winner: green, fifth in maiden at Leicester and sixth to Squaw Dance
in listed race at Newmarket, better effort in latter: should be suited by 1¼m/1½m.
Mrs A. J. Perrett

ALWAYS RAINBOWS (IRE) 6 b. or br.g. Rainbows For Life (CAN) – Maura's –
Guest (IRE) (Be My Guest (USA) 126) [2004 16d 12.3d May 7] fairly useful handicapper
at 4 yrs: well held both runs on Flat since: tried in headgear. *B. S. Rothwell*

ALWAYS WAINING (IRE) 3 b.c. Unfuwain (USA) 131 – Glenarff (USA) (Irish **101**
River (FR) 131) [2004 9g³ 10.5m³ 12.1g* 11.9g⁵ 12g³ 12m* 12g⁶ 13.9s 11.9g⁴ 12d* 12s
Nov 6] 9,000Y: good-bodied colt: half-brother to several winners, including smart 6f (at
2 yrs) and 1m winner Mastermind (by Dolphin Street) and smart performer in Britain/
Hong Kong up to 1½m Housemaster (by Rudimentary), 6f winner at 2 yrs: dam French
1m winner: useful performer: won maiden at Chepstow in May, handicap at Ascot (beat
Fort by 5 lengths) in July and claimer at Newmarket (left M. Johnston £30,000) in
October: ran as if amiss subsequent start: should stay 1¾m: acts on good to firm and good
to soft ground: races up with pace. *P. L. Clinton*

ALYOUSUFEYA (IRE)   3 ch.f. Kingmambo (USA) 125 – Musicale (USA) 109 (The   **51**
Minstrel (CAN) 135) [2004 75: 8g⁴ Apr 8] close-coupled filly: fair form in 2 maidens at 2
yrs: well below form only run in 2004: likely to prove best at 1m. *J. L. Dunlop*

ALZARMA   2 b.g. (Feb 7) Alzao (USA) 117 – Skimra 91 (Hernando (FR) 127) [2004   **55**
6.1g 6g³ 5g 6m⁶ 6m p7.1g⁶ Oct 18] smallish, lightly-made gelding: modest maiden: best
efforts on second (then left Mrs L. Williamson) and fourth starts: should stay at least 7f.
A. Bailey

AMALFI COAST   5 b.g. Emperor Jones (USA) 119 – Legend's Daughter (USA)   **–**
(Alleged (USA) 138) [2004 53?: 9.9d 12g 9.9m 15.8g Oct 5] tall gelding: maiden handicapper: well held in 2004. *W. S. Cunningham*

AMALGAM (IRE)   2 ch.f. (Feb 24) Namid 128 – Carhue Gold (IRE) 82 (Bob Back   **47 ?**
(USA) 124) [2004 5.1s 6g 7.1g 5m⁵ f7d 5.7g Sep 27] €5,000F, €7,500Y: first foal: dam,
Irish maiden who stayed 1m, half-sister to useful Irish sprinter Carhue Lass: poor maiden:
seemingly best effort at 5.7f. *Mrs P. N. Dutfield*

AMALIE (IRE)   2 b.f. (Apr 16) Fasliyev (USA) 120 – Princess Amalie (USA) (Rahy   **89 p**
(USA) 115) [2004 7g 6f* Sep 13] 12,000Y: sturdy filly: third foal: dam, lightly raced in
USA, half-sister to William Hill Futurity winner Al Hareb: clearly better effort in
maidens when winning at Redcar comfortably by 3 lengths from May Morning, leading
1f out: should stay 7f: useful prospect. *C. E. Brittain*

AMANDA'S LAD (IRE)   4 b.g. Danetime (IRE) 121 – Art Duo 86 (Artaius (USA)   **60**
129) [2004 52§: f8g⁶ f6g³ f6g⁴ f5g f6g⁶ f8g⁴ f5g⁶ f6s⁶ 6g³ 6s⁵ 7g⁵ 5m 6m⁴ 7m² 6m 6m³   **a50**
5g⁵ 5m⁴ 5d⁵ 5m⁶ 5m³ 6m³ 5m 6g⁴ f5g f6s⁶ f5g⁴ f6g Dec 12] tall gelding: modest maiden:
effective at 5f to 7f: acts on all-weather, firm and good to soft going: tried blinkered: often
races prominently. *M. C. Chapman*

AMANDERICA (IRE)   2 b.f. (Feb 26) Indian Lodge (IRE) 127 – Striking Gold   **–**
(USA) (Strike The Gold (USA) 123) [2004 5m 7.5g 7.5d 8f f8d Dec 21] 5,000Y, 4,000
2-y-o: small filly: first foal: dam unraced: seems of little account. *M. C. Chapman*

AMANDUS (USA)   4 b.g. Danehill (USA) 126 – Affection Affirmed (USA) (Affirmed   **103**
(USA)) [2004 100: 10v 8.1d 8g² 8f⁴ 7g 8m Jul 30] close-coupled, good-topped gelding:
useful handicapper: good efforts in frame at Goodwood and Royal Ascot (very close
fourth to Mine in Hunt Cup): effective at 1m/9f: acts on all-weather, firm and soft going:
usually visored prior to 2004: reliable. *D. R. Loder*

AMANKILA (IRE)   3 b.f. Revoque (IRE) 122 – Steel Habit (Habitat 134) [2004 10d   **62**
10s³ 9.7s* f12g² 8.3m⁴ 8s Jun 26] compact filly: closely related to fairly useful 1997 Irish
2-y-o 6f winner Family Crest (by Fairy King) and half-sister to several winners, notably
very smart 1¼m performer Batshoof (by Sadler's Wells): dam, Italian 7f/1m winner,
sister to dam of King of Kings: modest performer: landed odds in maiden at Folkestone
in May: stays 1¼m: acts on soft and good to firm ground. *M. L. W. Bell*

AMANPURI (GER)   6 br.g. Fairy King (USA) – Aratika (FR) (Zino 127) [2004 –:   **46**
p7g f9.4s⁴ f9.4s f9.4s⁶ 15g² 13.1g f14g Dec 11] poor performer: left Gay Kelleway after
fourth start: stays 15f: acts on soft going: tried blinkered. *P. A. Blockley*

AMAR (CZE)   3 ch.g. Beccari (USA) 112 – Autumn (FR) 55 (Rainbow Quest (USA)   **–**
134) [2004 –: f7g f11g 13.8m Sep 18] good-topped, rather leggy gelding: no form.
P. A. Blockley

AMARETTE (GER)   3 b.f. Monsun (GER) 124 – Avocette (GER) (Kings Lake (USA)   **107**
133) [2004 11g* 11g* Jun 6] second foal: half-sister to German 1¼m/11f winner Anavera
(by Acatenango): dam German 9f listed winner: unbeaten in maiden at Dusseldorf at 2
yrs, Schwarzgold-Rennen at Cologne (by 1¾ lengths from Saldentigerin) in May and
pferdewetten.de Preis der Diana at Hamburg (by head from La Ina) in June: stayed 11f:
visits Tiger Hill. *A. Schutz, Germany*

AMARETTO EXPRESS (IRE)   5 b.g. Blues Traveller (IRE) 119 – Cappuchino   **– §**
(IRE) 59 (Roi Danzig (USA)) [2004 –§: 10f Sep 13] useful-looking gelding: temperamental maiden. *R. E. Barr*

AMAZIN   2 b.c. (Mar 27) Primo Dominie 121 – Aegean Blue (Warning 136) [2004 6m²   **94**
6g* 5.1g² 6m⁵ 5f⁴ 6m 5s Oct 16] 25,000F: tall colt: has scope: third foal: half-brother to
3-y-o Hawaajes: dam unraced: fairly useful performer: won minor event at Kempton in
June: good 3¾ lengths fourth to Chateau Istana in Flying Childers Stakes at Doncaster:
well below form last 2 starts: effective at 5f/6f: acts on firm going: tends to be slowly
away. *R. Hannon*

AMAZING GRACE MARY   2 b.f. (Apr 27) Dancing Spree (USA) – Frisky Miss   **32**
(IRE) 70 (Fayruz 116) [2004 5m 6.1m p5.1g f7g Dec 12] fifth foal: dam won at 5f/6f:
poor maiden: tried blinkered/visored: hung markedly left on debut. *S. R. Bowring*

AMAZING VALOUR (IRE)   2 b.c. (May 6) Sinndar (IRE) 134 – Flabbergasted   **68**
(IRE) (Sadler's Wells (USA) 132) [2004 8f² 10g 10v Oct 20] 40,000Y: good-bodied colt:
ninth foal: half-brother to 3 winners in France, notably smart 1¼m/1m/11f performer Without
Connexion (by Rainbow Quest), also successful in Italy: dam, French 10.5f winner, sister
to Dewhurst winner Scenic: fair maiden: second at Pontefract: slowly away/looked no
easy ride after: should stay at least 1½m: sold 15,000 gns. *M. Johnston*

AMAZONIC   3 b.f. First Trump 118 – Mystic Beauty (IRE) (Alzao (USA) 117) [2004   –
p10g May 29] 3,000F, 1,000Y: second foal: half-sister to fairly useful 1m (at 2 yrs) to
1¾m winner Mystic Fox (by Charnwood Forest): dam unraced: 100/1, tailed off in
maiden at Lingfield. *T. T. Clement*

AMBER FOX (IRE)   3 b.f. Foxhound (USA) 103 – Paradable (IRE) 82 (Elbio 125)   **51**
[2004 57: 6f⁵ 5g⁶ 6m⁵ 8m 7.1s³ 7m f7g⁶ p10m f7g Dec 12] modest maiden: left A. Berry   **a44**
after third start: stays 7f, at least as effective at 6f: acts on soft and good to firm ground:
tried in cheekpieces. *P. D. Evans*

AMBER LEGEND   3 b.f. Fraam 114 – Abstone Queen 66 (Presidium 124) [2004 58:   –
f5s p6d f5g Dec 1] leggy filly: poor nowadays: stays 6f: acts on all-weather, probably on
firm going: ran badly in blinkers once at 2 yrs: none too consistent. *Ms Deborah J. Evans*

AMBERLINA (IRE)   2 b.f. (Feb 26) Monashee Mountain (USA) 115 – Try My Rosie   **56**
93 (Try My Best (USA) 130) [2004 5f³ p8.6g² p9.5g⁵ Nov 15] €3,500F, €1,900Y: half-
sister to 3 winners, including fairly useful Irish 1995 2-y-o 5f winner Zebra Stripes (by
Tirol) and 4-y-o Burnt Copper: dam, Irish 2-y-o 6f winner, best at 1m: modest maiden:
best effort when second in claimer at Wolverhampton: stays 8.6f: acts on polytrack.
P. Morris, Ireland

AMBERSONG   6 ch.g. Hernando (FR) 127 – Stygian (USA) 73 (Irish River (FR) 131)   **58**
[2004 59: p13g³ f12g³ p16g f14g⁶ f12g⁴ 12m³ 14.1m³ 11.7g 11.6f* 10.2m⁴ 11.5d³ 10.9m⁶
12m p13.9g Nov 29] strong, angular gelding: modest performer: won seller at Windsor in
July: stays 14.8f: acts on all-weather and firm ground: tried visored: sometimes slowly
away. *A. W. Carroll*

AMBUSHED (IRE)   8 b.g. Indian Ridge 123 – Surprise Move (IRE) (Simply Great   **47**
(FR) 122) [2004 70: 8d⁶ 9m⁴ 10g 9g Sep 13] poor performer nowadays: stays 1¼m: acts
on fibresand and any turf going: tried blinkered earlier in career: held up. *P. Monteith*

AMEEQ (USA)   2 b. or br.c. (May 11) Silver Hawk (USA) 123 – Haniya (IRE) 92   **85**
(Caerleon (USA) 132) [2004 7g³ 8g³ 8g Sep 20] quite good-topped colt: sixth foal:
half-brother to 3 winners, including useful 7.6f (at 2 yrs) to 1¼m winner Zulfaa (by
Bahri) and 7f winner Musawah (by Gulch): dam, 1½m winner, half-sister to very smart
performer up to 1½m Volochine: third in maidens at Newbury and Kempton: ran as if
amiss final start, hanging left: will be suited by 1¼m/1½m. *M. P. Tregoning*

AMELIA (IRE)   6 b.m. General Monash (USA) 107 – Rose Tint (IRE) (Salse (USA)   **66**
128) [2004 57: f6g⁵ f6g² f6s⁵ p6g⁵ f5g⁵ p7g³ f6g 6.1s* 5.7s³ 6m² 6m⁵ 5.5g³ 6m³ 5f Jul 31]
neat mare: has a short action: fair handicapper: won at Nottingham in April: ran as if
amiss final outing: best around 6f: unraced on heavy going, acts on any other turf and on
all-weather: edgy sort: sometimes hangs under pressure. *W. M. Brisbourne*

AMERICAN COUSIN   9 b.g. Distant Relative 128 – Zelda (USA) (Sharpen Up 127)   **70 d**
[2004 65: 6s⁵ 6v 5m* 6m 5g² 5m⁵ 6d 5f 5m⁶ 5f⁶ 6g⁵ 5s Aug 13] sturdy gelding: fair
performer: won claimer at Newcastle in March and seller at Musselburgh in May: below
form after: best at 5f/6f: acts on fibresand and any turf going: tried blinkered, not since
1999: sometimes slowly away: often held up: inconsistent. *D. Nicholls*

AMERICAN DUKE (USA)   3 b.g. Cryptoclearance (USA) – Prologue (USA)   **81**
(Theatrical 128) [2004 73: 7m 10d 10m² 10m 10.5g⁵ 9.9g* 9s Oct 22] leggy,
useful-looking gelding: fairly useful handicapper: won apprentice race at Salisbury in
September: stays 1¼m: acts on good to firm and good to soft going. *B. J. Meehan*

AMERICAN EMBASSY (USA)   4 b.c. Quiet American (USA) – Foreign Courier   **57**
(USA) (Sir Ivor (USA) 135) [2004 46: f7g⁶ p7m⁵ p8.6g² Dec 22] good-bodied colt:
modest maiden: stays 8.6f: acts on polytrack: tried tongue tied. *V. Smith*

AMERICAN POST   3 br.c. Bering 136 – Wells Fargo (Sadler's Wells (USA)   **121**
132) [2004 118p: 8g* 8g* 8g* 12m⁶ 8g Sep 5]
    American Post's win in the Gainsborough Poule d'Essai des Poulains left
his trainer with a sense of disappointment and prompted bookmakers to push out
American Post's odds for the Derby. Those are hardly the usual reactions from

either quarter to a winner of the French Guineas, but then the circumstances of American Post's victory were unusual to say the least. Prominent throughout, American Post still held every chance in the straight at Longchamp but his winning opportunity looked to have gone when Antonius Pius burst through a gap on his inner to go a length up inside the final furlong. Keeping on down the outside with the rest of the field still in close touch, American Post looked set for second at best when Antonius Pius suddenly veered to his right around fifty yards out, hitting the rail and losing all momentum as he struggled to keep his footing. His closest pursuers swept past, American Post best placed among them to take the race by half a length. Diamond Green, the worst sufferer from the leader's antics, was next, a neck ahead of Byron, who had led for much of the straight. The strong-finishing outsider Ershaad also managed to pass Antonius Pius in the closing stages, with the latter only fifth in the end, beating just his pacemaker Newton and the winner's stable-companion Sunday Doubt. There was no doubt in anyone's mind that the result would have been different had Antonius Pius kept straight once in front, hence Criquette Head-Maarek's reaction to American Post's performance, 'I was disappointed because he would have been second and he was beat.' Whether Diamond Green would have been the main beneficiary instead was less certain, though his rider Gary Stevens felt that the interference cost him the race.

However fortunate he was, American Post now had a sequence of six wins to his name. His only defeat had come when beaten narrowly over six furlongs on his debut as a two-year-old. Later that season, Group 1 successes in the Prix Jean-Luc Lagardere at Longchamp and the Racing Post Trophy at Doncaster established American Post as one of the best of his generation in Europe. He made his reappearance with a smooth four-length win over four opponents in a listed race at Saint-Cloud at the end of March and then accounted for just three rivals, notably Antonius Pius and Diamond Green, in the main trial for the Poule d'Essai des Poulains, the Prix de Fontainebleau at Longchamp. It was to provide a foretaste of the drama to come in the big race three weeks later. American Post won entirely on merit, however, and did so from the front, avoiding the trouble which saw Diamond Green on the receiving end of interference from Antonius Pius, who was demoted from second place.

The Poule d'Essai des Poulains was a good prize in its own right but the Derby had long been American Post's main objective. He had been at single-figure odds with at least one firm ever since the Racing Post Trophy and his odds had been trimmed further after his reappearance, even though neither the standard of his rivals (whom he was meeting on level terms) in that listed race nor the steadily-run mile, were in any way a test of his credentials for Epsom. American Post's stamina beyond a mile remained unproven right up until Derby Day itself. On pedigree, American Post looked a near certainty to stay a mile and a half, but more importantly the doubts expressed about American Post's stamina at the end of his two-year-old campaign—because of his free-going nature—had not been dispelled by three wins over a mile in the spring. For connections, though, the ground at Epsom was a bigger worry than the trip, his trainer feeling that American Post had

Gainsborough Poule d'Essai des Poulains, Longchamp—American Post (No.1) is fortunate to extend his winning sequence to six, whilst Diamond Green (rail), Byron and Ershaad also pass Antonius Pius, who looks to have the race in safe keeping until colliding with the rail

not been striding out properly at Longchamp on ground considered to be on the firm side, though by our reckoning it was no firmer than good.

American Post was sent off third favourite at Epsom but went far too freely in the early stages to give himself a chance of seeing out the trip. He was poised at Tattenham Corner and was second entering the final furlong, though clearly struggling by that stage, tending to carry his head high and wandering under pressure, and managed only sixth, some six lengths behind the winner North Light. American Post was seen out only once more after Epsom. Three months later and back at a mile, he beat only one home in the Prix du Moulin at Longchamp where his old rivals Diamond Green and Antonius Pius filled the places. In November it was reported that American Post had a problem with a hind hock and soon afterwards he was retired to stand at the Haras d'Etreham at a fee of €7,000 (October 1st and special live foal terms).

American Post's sire Bering was also trained by Criquette Head, and he, rather than American Post, could easily have been the trainer's first Derby runner some eighteen years earlier. However, the top-class Bering ran in, and won, the Prix du Jockey Club instead and finished his career in a memorable Arc when second to Dancing Brave. Although Bering was suited by a mile and a half, American Post is by no means alone among his best offspring in not needing a test of stamina. American Post's career is not that dissimilar to another French-trained son of Bering, Pennekamp. He too was a leading two-year-old who went on to classic success over a mile at three before failing in the Derby, though injury played a part in his Epsom flop. Even if Bering was not going to be an obvious influence for stamina, it could have been expected that the bottom half of American Post's pedigree would more than make up for that. His dam Wells Fargo never ran, but she can safely be described as stoutly bred, being a Sadler's Wells half-sister to the St Leger runner-up High And Low and the Chester Cup third Corradini. Grandam Cruising Height was second in the Lancashire Oaks and a half-sister to the Park Hill winner Trampship, out of a half-sister to the top-class Prix Vermeille winner Paulista. American Post turned out to be his dam's only foal.

American Post's Poule d'Essai des Poulains win was one of the highlights of the season in Europe for Khalid Abdulla, that race completing a full set of both British and French classics for the owner/breeder. On the other hand, Khalid Abdulla's Juddmonte operation had a cloud hanging over it for much of the year as a result of what came to be known as the 'Endless Summer affair'. Evidence came to light that the Juddmonte-bred Endless Summer, who had enjoyed a particularly successful juvenile campaign in 2000 for Khalid Abdulla and John Gosden, winning the Richmond Stakes and finishing second in the Prix Morny and Middle Park Stakes, had in fact been foaled on December 26th 1997, making him, as the *Rules of Racing* stand, a three-year-old at the time of his juvenile campaign. Endless Summer had apparently been falsely and deliberately registered with Weatherbys as having been foaled on January 2nd 1998 to make him eligible to compete as a two-year-old in 2000. No suspicions were aroused at the time, though just how early a foal he was must have been known only to a few, his trainer and owner among those kept in the dark. Rule 30 of the *Rules of Racing* states simply and categorically that 'the age of a horse shall be reckoned as beginning on January 1st in the year in which he was foaled.' That a rule had been broken was in no doubt, though it was interesting to see the range of reactions the case provoked.

Outside those connected with the breeding industry, the affair was seen as nothing short of a scandal, the general view being that 'rules are rules'. Within the industry, there was widespread backing and sympathy for Juddmonte Farms' manager Philip Mitchell, the individual who took the responsibility for falsifying Endless Summer's foaling date. That might be interpreted as the bloodstock world closing ranks, but the affair did at least bring into the open an issue which is evidently a genuine problem for breeders, and one that had been little discussed hitherto. Breeders who find themselves with a foal born on the 'wrong' side of January 1st are faced with the foal being ineligible to race against others of its own generation, whilst being at a huge disadvantage in terms of maturity compared with those foals born during the spring in the same calendar year. One solution is to race the horse in the southern hemisphere where a December foal would be at less of a disadvantage given that the official birthday of horses there is August 1st. That option was taken by Cheveley Park Stud, whose mare Fearless Revival foaled a colt on Christmas Day 1993, just eleven months after producing Pivotal earlier the same year; he was sent to race in New Zealand.

The option of 'hushing up' the early foaling date, falsifying the paperwork and hoping that nobody will be any the wiser will almost certainly have been taken many times before. For practical reasons, the existing system has to function largely on trust, with Weatherbys stating, 'We've no powers to check foaling dates. Our job is to record accurately the information breeders send to us.' An idea that has wide support in the northern hemisphere—not just in Britain from the likes of Chris Richardson (Cheveley Park Stud) and the Duchess of Bedford (Bloomsbury Stud)—but also from Dan Rosenberg, President of Three Chimneys Farm in Kentucky, is to determine age by the date a mare is covered rather than when the foal is born, based on the fact that the former is controllable whereas the latter is not. This system has been adopted in recent years in Australia, New Zealand and South Africa, resulting in any foal born prior to August 1st not being deemed a year older than those foaled after that date, as long as the mare was covered at the normal time (after September 1st in the southern hemisphere). There are some telling statistics from Australia resulting from the change in the rule legitimising pre-August 1st foals. Under the old system in 2000, only one foal was officially registered as having been born in July, whereas in 2001, the year the new rule took effect, that number leapt to forty-six. Was there really a forty-six-fold increase in the number of July foals from one year to the next? According to Philip Freedman of the Thoroughbred Breeders' Association, adopting the Australian system in Britain and Ireland (and by necessity, the rest of Europe too, a lengthy and complex process) would create too great an upheaval which the very small number of pre-January 1st foals would not justify. 'Both the age of a horse and the dates of a covering season would need to be the subject of legislation. That would represent quite a change for the breeding world, given that it hardly features under the *Rules of Racing*. Consideration would also have to be given as to whether imposing a strict period of covering would constitute a restraint of trade.' The Thoroughbred Breeders' Association favours instead having instances of foals born prior to January 1st being considered by a panel on a case-by-case basis, with 'the presumption that the foal should not become a yearling on that day should all be in order.'

At the time of writing, the Endless Summer affair had not reached its conclusion. The Jockey Club's Disciplinary Panel had charged Philip Mitchell under a rule covering 'corrupt or fraudulent practice in relation to racing' though a planned hearing of the case in October was postponed. As for Endless Summer, he had a spell in the States after his 'juvenile' campaign and even earned a place at stud back in Britain on the back of his achievements in 2000. He failed as a stallion however and resumed his racing career, winning a couple of handicaps for Tony Carroll in the latest season. Weatherbys have amended his date of birth, making Endless Summer a seven-year-old in 2004, and he looks set to be disqualified from all the races he contested as a two-year-old.

American Post (br.c. 2001)			
	Bering (ch 1983)	Arctic Tern (ch 1973)	Sea Bird II
			Bubbling Beauty
		Beaune (ch 1974)	Lyphard
			Barbra
	Wells Fargo (b 1996)	Sadler's Wells (b 1981)	Northern Dancer
			Fairy Bridge
		Cruising Height (b 1987)	Shirley Heights
			Nomadic Pleasure

Back to American Post. He is a strong, good-topped colt who took the eye in appearance on Derby Day. He acted on soft and good to firm ground and, while a mile and a half proved beyond him, he should have stayed a mile and a quarter. His exuberant nature was not just in evidence during his races. He seemed to get a bit agitated on the way to the start at Epsom, though once at the stalls, where he was attended by expert handler Steve Dyble, he gave no undue cause for concern. In that respect, his behaviour improved a good deal from his antics at the start of the Prix Jean-Luc Lagardère the previous autumn when he reared repeatedly. Loaded first from then on, a carrot (rather than the stick) was apparently the secret to tempting him into the stalls. *Mme C. Head-Maarek, France*

AMETHYST ROCK 6 b.g. Rock Hopper 124 – Kind Lady 56 (Kind of Hush 118) **45**
[2004 41: p12g f9.4m³ f8m* f8m⁶ f8.5m² 12m f8m Jul 26] smallish, strong gelding:
poor performer: won banded race at Southwell in April: stays 1¼m, not 1½m: acts on
fibresand: raced only on going firmer than good on turf. *P. L. Gilligan*

AMEYRAH (IRE) 3 b. or b.f. In The Wings 128 – Alfaaselah (GER) 97 (Dancing **–**
Brave (USA) 140) [2004 59: p10g 11.8d 10s Apr 20] quite good-topped filly: maiden,
well beaten in 2004: sold 3,200 gns, sent to Belgium. *M. R. Channon*

AMICA 2 b.f. (Mar 12) Averti (IRE) 117 – Friend For Life 64 (Lahib (USA) 129) [2004 **77**
6m² 5.1s² 6g* 6.1g⁵ Sep 29] second foal: sister to 3-y-o Averami: dam, fourth at 1m,
out of useful half-sister to Shirley Heights: fair performer: won maiden at Epsom in
September: possibly amiss final start: will probably stay 7f: acts on soft and good to firm
ground. *G. L. Moore*

AMID THE CHAOS (IRE) 4 ch.g. Nashwan (USA) 135 – Celebrity Style (USA) **89**
96 (Seeking The Gold (USA)) [2004 95: 10m 20f 14g* 12f⁵ Jul 18] strong gelding: fairly
useful performer: won amateur event at Bellewstown in July: seems to stay 2m: acts on
firm ground: visored/tongue tied (well held in Ascot Stakes) second outing: blinkered last
2 starts: fair hurdler. *D. K. Weld, Ireland*

AMIGRA (IRE) 2 b.f. (Feb 27) Grand Lodge (USA) 125 – Beaming 93 (Mtoto 134) **58**
[2004 6g 6m p8g⁴ p7g p7m Dec 21] 2,000Y: seventh foal: half-sister to 3-y-o Little Eye
and French 10.5f/1½m winner Tunnel Topics (by Sri Pekan): dam, 6f (at 2 yrs) and 1m
winner, out of smart 2-y-o sprinter Glancing: modest maiden: should stay 1¼m: acts on
polytrack: blinkered (best efforts) third/fourth starts. *Miss Jacqueline S. Doyle*

AMIR ZAMAN 6 ch.g. Salse (USA) 128 – Colorvista (Shirley Heights 130) [2004 **–**
67, a82: f12g* f11s⁶ p16.5g f11g f14g Dec 7] big, strong, lengthy gelding: fairly useful **a85 d**
handicapper: won at Southwell (apprentices) in January: well below form after: effective
at 1½m to 2m: acts on all-weather, firm and good to soft ground. *J. R. Jenkins*

AMMENAYR (IRE) 4 b.g. Entrepreneur 123 – Katiyfa (Auction Ring (USA) 123) **82**
[2004 85: p8g 7s 7d³ 7d⁵ 7g³ 7d⁶ 7m p7g⁵ p6g⁶ Oct 19] medium-sized, lengthy gelding:
fairly useful performer: should stay 1m: acts on polytrack, good to firm and good to soft
going: visored sixth start: temperament under suspicion: sold 7,000 gns. *T. G. Mills*

AMMIRARE 2 b.f. (Mar 10) Diktat 126 – Mathaayl (USA) 79 (Shadeed (USA) 135) **47**
[2004 5g 7.1d Nov 3] leggy, unfurnished filly: sixth living foal: half-sister to 3 winners,
including 3-y-o Sahool: dam 6f and 1¼m winner: green and slowly away, poor form in
maidens at Catterick and Musselburgh: will stay 1m. *C. W. Thornton*

AMNESTY 5 ch.g. Salse (USA) 128 – Amaranthus (Shirley Heights 130) [2004 74: **68**
p12g p10g⁴ p13g⁵ p10g p10g p8g⁶ 8.3d* 9.7s* 8.3g⁵ 8s² 8g 8.2v 10v Nov 4] lengthy **a61**
gelding: fair on turf, modest on all-weather: won seller at Windsor and handicap at Folkestone in April: stays 9.7f: acts on polytrack, soft and good to firm going: wears blinkers
nowadays: sometimes races freely. *G. L. Moore*

AMONG DREAMS 3 ch.f. Among Men (USA) 124 – Russell Creek 80 (Sandy Creek **–**
123) [2004 67: p7g 7.1s 8.3m p8.6g Nov 11] big, workmanlike filly: fair performer at 2
yrs: no form in 2004, leaving J. Osborne after reappearance. *A. G. Newcombe*

AMONG EQUALS 7 b.g. Sadler's Wells (USA) 132 – Epicure's Garden (USA) 102 **– §**
(Affirmed (USA)) [2004 10.2g Apr 8] fairly useful in 2000/2001: virtually refused to race
when tailed off only Flat run since (has refused to race over hurdles): blinkered last 2
starts at 3 yrs. *C. M. Meade*

AMONG FRIENDS (IRE) 4 b.g. Among Men (USA) 124 – Anita's Contessa (IRE) **56**
68 (Anita's Prince 126) [2004 75: 7d⁶ 6.1s 5m 6.1m 8.2s 10.2g 5.7s Oct 19] leggy,
good-topped gelding: modest nowadays: effective at 5f/6f: acts on good to firm ground:
tried blinkered: very slowly away last start. *B. Palling*

A MONK SWIMMING (IRE) 3 br.g. Among Men (USA) 124 – Sea Magic (IRE) **40**
85 (Distinctly North (USA) 115) [2004 –: 8f⁴ 12m³ 11.5f Aug 5] tall, workmanlike gelding: poor maiden: stays 1½m: acts on good to firm going: found little final start. *John
Berry*

AMPELIO (IRE) 2 ch.c. (Feb 11) Grand Lodge (USA) 125 – Bordighera (USA) **61 p**
(Alysheba (USA)) [2004 8g 8g Oct 12] 800,000Y: big, lengthy, good-topped colt: has
plenty of scope: fifth foal: brother to high-class but quirky 7f (at 2 yrs) to 11f winner
Grandera and half-brother to French 1¼m winner Fifty Five (by Lake Coniston): dam
useful French 13f winner: better effort in maidens (very green on debut) when eighth at
Leicester: should do better at 1¼m/1½m. *Sir Michael Stoute*

AMPHITHEATRE (IRE)   2 b.g. (Apr 26) Titus Livius (FR) 115 – Crimson Ring   **66**
(Persian Bold 123) [2004 5m⁵ 6.1g 6m³ 7g f6d³ 7m³ f7g 7m* a8g* Dec 28] close-coupled
gelding: half-brother to 3 winners, including 1m winner Fistful of Bucks (by Lochnager):
dam lightly-raced maiden: fair performer: won selling nursery at Leicester (final outing
for F. J. Houghton) in September and minor event at Taby (by 5 lengths) in December:
stays 1m: acts on dirt/fibresand and good to firm going: sometimes edgy. *C. Bjorling, Sweden*

AMSTERDAM (IRE)   2 b.c. (Mar 29) Danehill (USA) 126 – Dathiyna (IRE) (Kris   **99**
135) [2004 6s⁵ 6g* 7m³ Jul 24] quite attractive colt: fourth foal: half-brother to 4-y-o Let
Me Try Again, 1¼m winner Sadlers Law and fairly useful French 1¾m winner New
Sadlers (all by Sadler's Wells): dam, unraced, out of very smart 6f/7f winner Dafayna,
herself half-sister to 2000 Guineas winner Doyoun: ran at York on debut: won maiden at
Leopardstown in June: useful form when length third to Elusive Double in listed race at
Leopardstown, making most: should stay 1m: sent to Hong Kong. *A. P. O'Brien, Ireland*

AMUSEMENT   8 ch.g. Mystiko (USA) 124 – Jolies Eaux 73 (Shirley Heights 130)   **48**
[2004 f14.8g⁴ p12g⁶ p10g f16g³ f14g p12.2g⁵ f11g Dec 12] poor maiden: stays 2m: raced
only on all-weather. *D. G. Bridgwater*

AMWELL BRAVE   3 b.g. Pyramus (USA) 78 – Passage Creeping (IRE) 75 (Persian   **75**
Bold 123) [2004 71: p10g² p10g² p10g³ p10g³ p10g⁵ 8g 10s⁵ 8.2s 8.3s f12g 10d⁶ 10.2s
p8.6d p12g p12g* f12g Dec 28] rather leggy gelding: fair performer: won maiden at
Lingfield in November: stays 1½m: acts on all-weather and soft ground: tried visored,
tongue tied last 2 starts: sometimes races freely. *J. R. Jenkins*

ANACAPRI   4 b.f. Barathea (IRE) 127 – Dancerette (Groom Dancer (USA) 128) [2004   **–**
–: f8f f7s⁶ f11g 10g Apr 29] of little account. *W. S. Cunningham*

ANAK PEKAN   4 ch.g. In The Wings 128 – Trefoil (FR) (Blakeney 126) [2004 94p: **111**
16d* 18.7d⁶ 16.1s³ 16m 20m 16s Oct 16] stocky gelding: smart performer: heavily
backed, won handicaps at Kempton in April and Chester (totesport Chester Cup, beat
Misternando by 5 lengths) in May: very good length third to Mirjan in Northumberland
Plate at Newcastle next start: below form after in Goodwood Cup, Prix du Cadran at
Longchamp (unimpressive to post) and Jockey Club Cup at Newmarket: stays 18.7f: best
efforts on ground softer than good: reportedly had breathing problem third 3-y-o start:
usually races prominently. *M. A. Jarvis*

*totesport Chester Cup (Handicap), Chester—the heavily-backed favourite Anak Pekan storms clear;
Misternando (rail) is second, while Mana d'Argent (white cap) loses third and fourth places late on
to Big Moment (partially obscured by Mana d'Argent) and Distant Prospect (noseband)*

ANALYZE (FR)   6 b.g. Anabaa (USA) 130 – Bramosia (Forzando 122) [2004 82: 8m² **79**
8g³ 8.1f⁵ 9.9g⁴ 10.1g p8m* p8g² p8g⁴ p8g* p8.6g p10g p8g* p10m³ p8g⁴ Dec 30] smal- **a88**
lish, workmanlike gelding: fairly useful performer: won seller in October, handicap in
November and claimer in December, all at Lingfield: effective at 1m to 1¼m: acts on
polytrack, firm and good to soft ground: often held up: tough. *B. G. Powell*

ANANI (USA)   4 b.c. Miswaki (USA) 124 – Mystery Rays (USA) 122 (Nijinsky (CAN) **110**
138) [2004 110: a9f 10m³ a10f⁴ p10g² 12g 9.9g⁶ 10m 9.9g⁴ 7.9s a10g 8g a10f² Dec 24]
sturdy colt: smart performer: several creditable efforts in 2004, including when neck
second to Caluki in listed Winter Derby at Lingfield in March, fourth for Coat of Honour
in handicap at Goodwood in July, and, having left E. Dunlop after ninth outing, ¾-length
second to El Hurano in listed race at Jebel Ali in December: effective at 1¼m/1½m:
acts on polytrack, dirt, firm and soft going: blinkered and tongue tied tenth outing.
M. Al Kurdi, UAE

ANATOLIAN QUEEN (USA)   3 b.f. Woodman (USA) 126 – Imia (USA) (Riverman **77**
(USA) 131) [2004 8v³ 8.3d⁴ 7g* Jul 10] $75,000Y: third foal: dam, second over 6f at 2
yrs in France on only start, half-sister to Craven Stakes winner King of Happiness out of
very smart French winner up to 1½m Mystery Rays: fair form in maidens, winning at
York in July: will stay 9f: sent to USA. *J. M. P. Eustace*

ANATOM   3 ch.f. Komaite (USA) – Zamarra 59 (Clantime 101) [2004 –: f5s p6g⁵ 6v⁴   **–**
f6m May 17] little form: tongue tied last 3 starts, also visored final one. *P. S. McEntee*

ANCHOR DATE   2 b.c. (Apr 7) Zafonic (USA) 130 – Fame At Last (USA) 98 (Quest **80**
For Fame 127) [2004 6s² 6d Oct 4] angular colt: first foal: dam, lightly-raced 2-y-o 7f
winner (stayed 11.4f), out of half-sister to smart 1¼m winner Rambushka: much better
effort in maidens when promising second at Salisbury under considerate ride: odds on,
slowly away when only seventh at Windsor: should stay 1m. *B. W. Hills*

ANCIENT EGYPT   2 b.c. (May 2) Singspiel (IRE) 133 – Nekhbet 74 (Artaius (USA)   **– p**
129) [2004 8g Oct 10] 140,000F: brother to 3-y-o On Every Street, closely related to
very smart 1m/1¼m performer Right Wing (by In The Wings) and half-brother to several
winners, including useful 6f/7f performer Cim Bom Bom (by Dowsing): dam, maiden,
half-sister to Irish St Leger winner M-Lolshan: 14/1, not knocked about when well held
in maiden at Bath: should do better at 1¼m/1½m. *J. H. M. Gosden*

ANCIENT WORLD (USA)   4 br.g. Spinning World (USA) 130 – Headline **119**
(Machiavellian (USA) 123) [2004 112p: 8.3s² 8.2g² 8m* 8d 10d* 8m* 10m⁵
Dec 12]
    Ancient World became the first gelding to win a Group 1 for Godolphin
when he won the Premio Vittorio di Capua at Milan in October, a fairly remarkable
statistic considering that the Godolphin stable has won one hundred and fifteen
Group 1 races worldwide since its inception in 1994. Ancient World produced a
smart performance when making most to beat Majestic Desert and Hurricane Alan
by a length and a quarter and a length and a half. It was Godolphin's fourth win in
the event in six years, following Muhtathir's win in 1999 and Slickly's in 2001 and
2002. Like Slickly, Ancient World had started off his career in France with Andre
Fabre before being transferred at the end of his three-year-old career, along with

William Hill Mile (Handicap), Goodwood—top weight Ancient World is in control;
Impeller, Tuning Fork (rail) and El Coto (No.4) make the frame

Premio Vittorio di Capua, Milan—Ancient World makes most to provide Saeed bin Suroor and Frankie Dettori with their fourth win in the race in six years; Majestic Desert (striped sleeves) and Hurricane Alan (out of picture) make it a clean sweep of the places for British-trained runners

Doyen and Papineau, to Saeed bin Suroor. Fabre's loss turned out to be Godolphin's gain as all three were successful in Group 1 company in 2004.

Still an entire at the start of the latest season, Ancient World was gelded after just respectable efforts on his first two starts and, after missing Royal Ascot, lined up at Goodwood in July for the William Hill Mile (Handicap) in a renewal that was not so competitive as it has been in recent years. Ancient World, despite top weight of 9-10, ran off a BHB handicap mark of 103, whereas the previous year's top weights Heretic and Smirk had run off 110. Available at 13/2 on the morning of the race, Ancient World was the 9/2 favourite at the off. Ridden to take advantage of a good draw in this twenty-one runner contest, Ancient World raced close up, travelling strongly, quickened to the front around a furlong out and went on to win by a length and a quarter from Impeller, having something to spare. He thus became the first favourite to win the event, and the first horse since Waajib, successful in the inaugural running in 1987, to carry top weight to victory in it. Afterwards his rider Frankie Dettori said of Ancient World, 'He's a completely different horse physically and mentally (since being gelded).' Ancient World went on to win the Stan James Winter Hill Stakes at Windsor in August, gaining his first victory in pattern company when beating Gateman by a length and a quarter and—kept in training after the Premio Vittorio di Capua—was also a creditable fifth to Alexander Goldrun in the Hong Kong Cup at Sha Tin in December.

		Nureyev	Northern Dancer
	Spinning World (USA)	(b 1977)	Special
	(ch 1993)	Imperfect Circle	Riverman
Ancient World (USA)		(b 1988)	Aviance
(br.g. 2000)		Machiavellian	Mr Prospector
	Headline	(b 1987)	Coup de Folie
	(b 1993)	Priceless Fame	Irish Castle
		(b or br 1975)	Comely Nell

Ancient World is the third foal out of Headline, an unraced half-sister to the North American two-year-old Grade 1 mile winner Saratoga Six and to the high-class two-year-old seven-furlong and mile (William Hill Futurity) winner Dunbeath. Ancient World is a half-brother to the smart filly Jilbab (by A P Indy), winner of the Coaching Club American Oaks over a mile and a half for Godolphin, and the fair two-year-old maiden World Music (by Dixieland Band) while the dam has also produced Dubai Moon (by Seattle Slew), a modest maiden in the UAE.

Godolphin's "Ancient World"

The strong, useful-looking Ancient World, who was tongue tied on his reappearance, may need to improve to add to his Group 1 tally. Still relatively lightly raced after just eleven career starts, it is a possibility that he will do so. Races like the Lockinge and Queen Anne are likely to be on his agenda in the first part of 2005. Ancient World is effective at a mile to a mile and a quarter, and acts on soft and good to firm ground. *Saeed bin Suroor*

ANDAAD   4 b.f. Alzao (USA) 117 – Ghazwat (USA) (Riverman (USA) 131) [2004 **46** p10g⁵ f12s⁴ p10g 11g 8.5s 10.3g⁵ 11g²ᵈ 11g² 11d⁵ 12d 10.5f⁵ 10g⁴ 10.5g 14.5s a9.5g Nov 14] poor maiden: left D. Daly after third outing: stays 11f: best efforts on good ground. *J. H. Smith, Holland*

ANDALUZA (IRE)   3 b.f. Mujadil (USA) 119 – Hierarchy 91 (Sabrehill (USA) 120) **74** [2004 p6g⁴ f7g* 7m³ 7.1f May 31] 5,000F, 16,500Y: workmanlike filly: first foal: dam Irish 7f winner out of sister to Poule d'Essai des Poulains runner-up Noble Minstrel: fair performer: won maiden at Wolverhampton in April: should be suited by 1m: sweating and unimpressive to post final start. *P. D. Cundell*

ANDEAN   3 b.c. Singspiel (IRE) 133 – Anna Matrushka (Mill Reef (USA) 141) [2004 **105** 82p: 8m* 10.4s⁵ May 12] quite attractive colt: useful form: impressive winner of maiden at Yarmouth in April by 7 lengths from Maclean, dictating pace: 10 lengths fifth to North Light in Dante Stakes at York following month, racing freely (wore crossed noseband) and no extra final 2f: bred to stay at least 1½m: joined Godolphin, but wasn't seen out again (suffered suspensory problem). *D. R. Loder*

ANDREYEV (IRE)   10 ch.g. Presidium 124 – Missish (Mummy's Pet 125) [2004 –:   **–** 6g⁶ 6d 6v 7.2m 8d⁵ 8s Oct 30] tall gelding: no longer of much account: tried in headgear. *J. S. Goldie*

ANDRONIKOS   2 ch.c. (Mar 27) Dr Fong (USA) 128 – Arctic Air 79 (Polar Falcon **114** (USA) 126) [2004 5f* 6s² 6g 6s* 6s* Nov 16] 57,000Y: lengthy colt: has scope: second living foal: dam, 2-y-o 7f winner, half-sister to smart performers Barrow Creek (effective at 6f to 1m) and Last Resort (7f) out of smart 6f/7f winner Breadcrumb: smart performer: won maiden at Hamilton in July and listed races at Doncaster (tongue tied, beat Harvest Warrior by 2 lengths) in October and Saint-Cloud (by 2½ lengths from Starpix) in November: also ran well when 1¼ lengths second to Tony James in Gimcrack Stakes at York second start: should stay 7f: acts on firm and soft ground: free-going sort, sometimes wanders/carries head awkwardly: has run well when sweating. *P. F. I. Cole*

AND TOTO TOO 4 br.f. Averti (IRE) 117 – Divina Mia 66 (Dowsing (USA) 124) **77**
[2004 79: p8g p7g⁶ p6g² p7g⁴ p7g⁴ 7g² 7m⁴ 8m 7m² 7.6g 7m⁴ 7m⁴ 7m² 7g* 7g⁴ 8m 6.1g⁶ p8g p8.6g p8.6g Nov 13] neat filly: fair performer: won handicap at Salisbury in July: effective at 6f to easy 8.5f: acts on all-weather, firm and soft going: blinkered/visored: sometimes slowly away/looks none too keen: tough: sold 32,000 gns. *P. D. Evans*

ANDURIL 3 ch.c. Kris 135 – Attribute 69 (Warning 136) [2004 70: p8g⁶ 7.5d 8m³ 8.3s⁶ **68**
10m⁴ 10m 10m 8.1s⁴ 10d 11.9s p8.6g* p8.6g² p7.1g⁵ Dec 4] workmanlike colt: fair performer: won seller at Wolverhampton in November (left J. Eustace): trained by P. McEntee on next start only: races freely, but seems to stay 1¼m: acts on polytrack, good to firm and good to soft ground: tried in cheekpieces/blinkers: difficult ride. *P. A. Blockley*

ANDY MAL 2 b.f. (Apr 12) Mark of Esteem (IRE) 137 – Sunflower Seed 70 (Mummy's **44**
Pet 125) [2004 7d 7d⁶ 7m Sep 4] 5,000F, €7,500Y: strong, close-coupled filly: half-sister to 3 winners, including fairly useful 7f/1m winner Strathmore Clear (by Batshoof) and 1½m winner Redouble (by First Trump): dam maiden who stayed 1½m: poor form in maidens: will stay at least 1m. *R. A. Fahey*

ANFIELD DREAM 2 b.c. (Mar 6) Lujain (USA) 119 – Fifth Emerald 54 (Formidable **73**
(USA) 125) [2004 5g⁶ 5m³ 5.1g p5g⁵ p6g⁵ p6g³ Dec 10] third foal: half-brother to 4-y-o Goodbye Mr Bond: dam, 1m winner, out of close relation to smart middle-distance filly Valley of Gold: fair maiden: stays 6f: acts on polytrack and good to firm going. *J. R. Jenkins*

ANGELA'S GIRL 2 gr.f. (Mar 16) Baryshnikov (AUS) – Filly Bergere (IRE) (Sadler's **–**
Wells (USA) 132) [2004 5.3f 5.1m 6d Aug 24] 3,000Y: first foal: dam, useful French 11f winner, out of half-sister to Prix Saint-Alary winner Muncie and Prix Royal-Oak winner Mersey: well held in maidens/seller, slowly away. *J. M. Bradley*

ANGELICA GARNETT 4 ch.f. Desert Story (IRE) 115 – Vanessa Bell (IRE) (Lahib **55**
(USA) 129) [2004 –: p7g p8g⁶ p8g p8g p12g* 12d 11.7s May 4] rather leggy filly: fluent mover: modest performer: won banded race at Lingfield in March: ran as if amiss last 2 starts: stays 1½m: acts on polytrack: tried in cheekpieces/blinkers: races freely. *T. E. Powell*

ANGEL ISA (IRE) 4 b.f. Fayruz 116 – Isa (Dance In Time (CAN)) [2004 58: 5.9f 6m **48**
7m 7.2g 5.9f³ 6m³ 6d Oct 16] quite attractive filly: poor performer: stays 7f: acts on fibresand and firm going, below form on good to soft: visored last 2 starts. *R. A. Fahey*

ANGEL MAID 3 b.f. Forzando 122 – Esilam 62 (Frimley Park 109) [2004 –: 5m Aug **–**
4] sturdy filly: well held in maidens. *G. B. Balding*

ANGELOFTHENORTH 2 b.f. (Mar 31) Tomba 119 – Dark Kristal (IRE) 66 **66**
(Gorytus (USA) 132) [2004 5d³ 5f⁴ 5m³ 6f³ 6s³ 5.1g 5g* 6d Oct 14] 2,300F: leggy filly: half-sister to 3 winners, including 3-y-o Sachin and fairly useful 2001 2-y-o 6f winner Saphir Indien (by Bijou d'Inde): dam 6f winner: fair performer: won maiden at Ripon in September, making most: stays 6f: acts on soft going: tends to wander. *J. D. Bethell*

ANGELO'S PRIDE 3 ch.g. Young Ern 120 – Considerable Charm 51 (Charmer 123) **58**
[2004 55: f9.4g³ f7g f9.4s² f8g³ f8s³ f7g³ f9.4g* f12d⁵ p8.6g Dec 27] modest performer: won handicap at Wolverhampton in April: stays 9.4f: raced mainly on fibresand: possibly none too genuine. *J. A. Osborne*

ANGEL RAYS 2 ch.f. (Jan 27) Unfuwain (USA) 131 – Success Story 60 (Sharrood **68**
(USA) 124) [2004 p7m⁴ p7g⁵ Oct 28] sister to useful 1¼m/1½m winner Film Script and half-sister to 2 winners, including fairly useful 2001 2-y-o 6f/7f winner National Park (by Common Grounds): dam, 1¼m winner, out of smart 1¼m performer Starlet: fair form in maidens at Lingfield, taking strong hold: bred to stay at least 1m. *G. A. Butler*

ANGEL RIVER 2 ch.f. (Apr 3) Bold Edge 123 – Riviere Rouge (Forzando 122) **50**
[2004 7s 6d p6g⁶ Nov 16] 2,600F: fifth foal: half-sister to 3-y-o Crewes Miss Isle and winner in Italy by Weldnaas: dam no form: modest form in maidens: stays 6f: acts on polytrack. *M. J. Ryan*

ANGEL SPRINTS 2 b.f. (Feb 25) Piccolo 121 – Runs In The Family 69 (Distant **83**
Relative 128) [2004 5g³ 5.1f³ 5d⁶ 6f* 6d* 6g⁴ Sep 29] 16,000Y: good sort: third foal:
half-sister to an Italian 2003 2-y-o 5f winner by Daggers Drawn: dam 5f and (at 2 yrs) 6f
winner: fairly useful performer: made all in maiden in July and minor event in August,
both at Windsor: creditable fourth to Yajbill in minor event at Salisbury: should prove
best at 5f/6f: acts on firm and good to soft going. *L. G. Cottrell*

ANGELS VENTURE 8 ch.g. Unfuwain (USA) 131 – City of Angels (Woodman –
(USA) 126) [2004 59: p13g Feb 28] close-coupled gelding: modest handicapper: stays
1½m: acts on polytrack, soft and good to firm going: tried visored: often tongue tied
earlier in career: sometimes hangs left. *J. R. Jenkins*

ANGIOLINI (USA) 7 ch.g. Woodman (USA) 126 – Danse Royale (IRE) 112 (Caer- –
leon (USA) 132) [2004 f12s Feb 17] strong, sturdy ex-Irish gelding: poor maiden: stays
2m: acts on heavy and good to firm going: has been tongue tied. *A. E. Jones*

ANGLO SAXON (USA) 4 br.c. Seeking The Gold (USA) – Anna Palariva (IRE) 108 **79**
(Caerleon (USA) 132) [2004 89p: 8.3d 10g 10.2g³ 10g⁶ 8.5f⁴ 8.5d* Nov 28] useful-
looking colt: just fair performer in 2004: left D. Loder 17,000 gns after fourth outing: won
optional claimer at Golden Gate Fields in November: stays 1¼m: acts on good to firm
and good to soft going: reportedly had breathing problem in 2003. *S. Shulman, USA*

ANGRY BARK (USA) 3 ch.f. Woodman (USA) 126 – Polemic (USA) 114 (Roberto **62**
(USA) 131) [2004 10.5v⁴ 9g² 10.2g⁴ p8m 10.2s Oct 19] small filly: half-sister to several
winners, including smart French/US performer up to 1¼m Cyrillic (by Irish River): dam
6.5f winner in France at 2 yrs and later smart around 1¼m in USA: in frame first 2 starts
in France for P. Bary: sold 75,000 gns in July: modest form when fourth in maiden at
Bath, easily best effort in Britain: should prove as effective at 1m as 1¼m. *H. S. Howe*

ANICAFLASH 3 b.f. Cayman Kai (IRE) 114 – Sharp Top 62 (Sharpo 132) [2004 –: –
7s 8g Apr 15] leggy, lengthy filly: well held in maidens: has looked wayward. *M. Dods*

ANISETTE 3 b.f. Abou Zouz (USA) 109 – Natural Gold (USA) (Gold Meridian **50**
(USA) 112) [2004 57: f6g³ f7g f6g⁶ 6g f8.5g⁶ 11.5f⁴ 10m p8g 10m⁶ 8m³ 8s⁶ 9.7f⁵ 10d³
10g Oct 11] modest maiden: stays 1¼m: acts on fibresand, firm and good to soft ground:
tried visored: sometimes slowly away. *Julian Poulton*

ANISSATI 2 ch.f. (Apr 4) Machiavellian (USA) 123 – Inchacooley (IRE) 99 (Rhoman –
Rule (USA)) [2004 8s Oct 22] 100,000Y: first foal: dam 1m/1¼m winner in Ireland/USA:
25/1, well beaten in maiden at Doncaster. *C. E. Brittain*

ANNA GAYLE 3 ch.f. Dr Fong (USA) 128 – Urban Dancer (IRE) 89 (Generous (IRE) –
139) [2004 10g 8.3f 11.7m⁵ 9.7f p10g p12g Nov 27] second foal: dam, Irish 1m winner
from 2 starts, out of half-sister to high-class miler Chalon: no solid form: left Mrs
A. Perrett after fifth start. *R. Rowe*

ANNAKITA 4 b.f. Unfuwain (USA) 131 – Cuban Reef 54 (Dowsing (USA) 124) **50**
[2004 –: 12v p16g 14.1m 14.1m⁴ 16m* 14.1d² 14.1d³ Oct 16] leggy, sparely-made filly:
modest performer: won handicap at Yarmouth in July: stays easy 2m: acts on good to firm
and good to soft going. *W. J. Musson*

ANNALS 2 b.f. (Feb 19) Lujain (USA) 119 – Anna of Brunswick 78 (Rainbow Quest **74 +**
(USA) 134) [2004 6s* 7g⁴ Sep 17] quite good-topped filly: fifth foal: half-sister to 3-y-o
Goslar and a German 1m/9f winner by Salse: dam, 1¼m winner who stayed 1¾m, half-
sister to dams of very smart performers up to 1½m Annaba and Annus Mirabilis: won
maiden at Goodwood in August: last of 4 to Shanghai Lily in minor event at Newbury:
should stay at least 1m. *H. Candy*

ANNAMBO 4 ch.g. In The Wings 128 – Anna Matrushka (Mill Reef (USA) 141) **80**
[2004 93: 12g 12m May 24] useful-looking gelding: unimpressive mover: fairly useful
performer: probably stays 1¾m: acts on firm and good to soft ground: visored last 6
outings: has carried head awkwardly/flashed tail: sold 20,000 gns, joined D. Morris and
gelded. *D. R. Loder*

ANNA PALLIDA 3 b.f. Sadler's Wells (USA) 132 – Masskana (IRE) (Darshaan 133) **90**
[2004 8g 9.9g² 10m² 11.9d³ 10g* 10g² 10.3s 8f³ 8.9g⁶ Oct 19] 300,000Y: strong, good-
bodied filly: sixth foal: closely related to 9f winner Twilight World (by Night Shift) and
half-sister to smart miler Wallace (by Royal Academy) and smart performer up to 15.5f
Sulk (by Selkirk), 7f/1m (Prix Marcel Boussac) winner at 2 yrs: dam French 9f/1¼m
winner out of Poule d'Essai des Pouliches winner Masarika: fairly useful performer: won
maiden at Kempton in July: stays 1¼m: acts on firm ground, poor effort on soft: visored
(not discredited) final outing. *P. W. Harris*

ANNA PANNA 3 b.f. Piccolo 121 – Miss Laetitia (IRE) (Entitled 126) [2004 55p: 7d⁶ **73**
6.1m² 6g⁵ 8.3m⁵ 8.1d² 8.3d Aug 28] quite good-topped filly: fair maiden: stays 1m: acts
on good to firm and good to soft going. *H. Candy*

ANNATALIA 2 ch.f. (Feb 15) Pivotal 124 – See You Later 98 (Emarati (USA) 74) **82**
[2004 5m⁴ 6.3g⁶ 5.1f* 5.2m 5g 5g p5.1g p7g⁴ p7.1g p7.1g² Nov 26] €50,000Y: tall filly: **a70**
first foal: dam, 5f winner (including at 2 yrs), half-sister to 3-y-o Peak To Creek: fairly
useful on turf, fair on all-weather: landed odds in maiden at Bath in July by 6 lengths,
making all: blinkered, creditable second in nursery at Wolverhampton: stays easy 7f: acts
on polytrack and firm going: sold 18,000 gns. *B. J. Meehan*

ANNA WALHAAN (IRE) 5 b.g. Green Desert (USA) 127 – Queen's Music (USA) **76**
66 (Dixieland Band (USA)) [2004 88: 8.1s 8g 8.1d² 10m⁵ 8.1d Sep 18] close-coupled,
deep-bodied gelding: only fair at best nowadays: stays 8.5f: acts on firm and good to soft
going: tried visored earlier in career. *Ian Williams*

ANNIBALE CARO 2 b.c. (Apr 22) Mtoto 134 – Isabella Gonzaga 75 (Rock Hopper **59 p**
124) [2004 p6g p7g⁵ p7.1d Nov 3] second foal: dam, 1¼m/1½m winner, granddaughter
of high-class French middle-distance performer Dunette: modest form, slowly away and
not knocked about, in maidens: likely to do fair bit better at 1¼m+. *Sir Mark Prescott*

ANNIE HARVEY 3 ch.f. Fleetwood (IRE) 107 – Resemblance (State Diplomacy **72**
(USA)) [2004 75: 6.1g 7v f8g² 8.5d⁵ Jul 3] close-coupled, good-topped filly: fair handicapper: stays 1m: acts on fibresand, good to firm and good to soft going. *B. Smart*

ANNIE MILLER (IRE) 3 b.f. Night Shift (USA) – Lost Dream (Niniski (USA) 125) **52**
[2004 67: 6m 7f Aug 5] rather leggy filly: lightly-raced maiden: below form in 2004:
likely to prove best at 5f/6f: raced only on ground firmer than good on turf. *M. J. Wallace*

ANNIJAZ 7 b.m. Alhijaz 122 – Figment 75 (Posse (USA) 130) [2004 64: 5.7s² 7v² **62 d**
7m⁴ 5.7f 7g 7g⁴ 7m⁶ 7m 7.1g 7.1m 8.1m 8m 7.1g Sep 3] sparely-made mare: modest
handicapper: below form after third outing: acts at 5.7f to 1m: acts on fibresand and
any turf going: held up: wore cheekpieces final start. *J. M. Bradley*

ANNISHIRANI 4 b.f. Shaamit (IRE) 127 – Silent Miracle (IRE) 80 (Night Shift **77**
(USA)) [2004 82: p8g p7g⁶ Jan 24] fair performer: effective at 7f to 1¼m: acts on polytrack, raced only on good going or firmer on turf: free-going sort: difficult at stall and
found little second 3-y-o start. *G. A. Butler*

ANNIVERSARY GUEST (IRE) 5 b. or br.m. Desert King (IRE) 129 – Polynesian **43**
Goddess (IRE) (Salmon Leap (USA) 131) [2004 42: p16g p12g³ 15g⁴ p16g³ p13g 13.1m **a48**
14.1m⁵ 12m Jun 4] close-coupled mare: poor maiden: stays 2¼m: acts on polytrack and
firm going: sometimes slowly away/races freely: ran creditably in cheekpieces fourth
start. *Mrs Lucinda Featherstone*

ANNUS IUCUNDUS (IRE) 3 b.f. Desert King (IRE) 129 – Mezzanine (Sadler's **64**
Wells (USA) 132) [2004 10d 10s 10v⁶ f8g⁶ Dec 16] second foal: closely related to 4-y-o
The Kiddykid: dam unraced out of close relation to Prix du Jockey Club winner Natroun:
modest maiden: left D. Barry in Ireland after third start: stays 1¼m. *E. J. O'Neill*

ANOTHER BOTTLE (IRE) 3 b.g. Cape Cross (IRE) 129 – Aster Aweke (IRE) 87 **93**
(Alzao (USA) 117) [2004 74: 7g 9.1f* 8m* 8g³ 8d* Aug 30] round-barrelled gelding:
type to carry condition: fairly useful performer: won maiden at Ayr in May and handicaps
at Newbury in July and Ripon in August: should stay 1¼m: acts on firm and good to soft
ground: consistent. *T. P. Tate*

ANOTHER CHOICE (IRE) 3 ch.g. Be My Guest (USA) 126 – Gipsy Rose Lee **89**
(IRE) 100 (Marju (IRE) 127) [2004 66: 8.2g³ 9.9s* 10.2g* 11m 12g 10g 10d⁴ 10.1d*
10g⁶ 10d² 10.3s² 12s Nov 6] big, workmanlike gelding: fairly useful performer: won
handicaps at Beverley and Bath in April and minor event at Yarmouth in August: stays
10.3f: goes well on good ground or softer: tongue tied: gelded after final start.
N. P. Littmoden

ANOTHER CON (IRE) 3 b.f. Lake Coniston (IRE) 131 – Sweet Unison (USA) **–**
(One For All (USA)) [2004 55: p10g⁴ p10g* p10g⁴ p12g⁵ 10.9d 10.2g p12g² 11.6m **a70**
p12d⁵ p10g 10m p16g p12.2d* p12.2g p12.2g p13.9g Dec 13] fair handicapper: won at
Lingfield in February (left Mrs P. Dutfield after seventh start) and Wolverhampton in
November: stays easy 1½m: acts on polytrack, no form on turf: tried in cheekpieces/
visor: races up with pace. *P. Howling*

ANOTHER DEAL (FR) 5 ch.g. Barathea (IRE) 127 – Mill Rainbow (FR) (Rainbow **–**
Quest (USA) 134) [2004 71?: 7m 8.1d 10.2s Aug 30] workmanlike gelding: maiden, well
held in 2004. *R. J. Hodges*

ANO

ANOTHER EXPLETIVE 3 b.f. Wizard King 122 – French Project (IRE) 84 (Project — Manager 111) [2004 43: f7g p8g⁶ Feb 16] poor maiden: stays 7f: raced only on all-weather and good/good to firm ground. *J. White*

ANOTHER FAUX PAS (IRE) 3 b.f. Slip Anchor 136 – Pirie (USA) (Green Dancer 73 (USA) 132) [2004 –: 7g* 8.1d Jun 1] sturdy filly: fair form: easily best effort from 3 runs when winning maiden at Goodwood in May (100/1): should stay 1m. *R. Hannon*

ANOTHER GLIMPSE 6 b.g. Rudimentary (USA) 118 – Running Glimpse (IRE) 79 84 (Runnett 125) [2004 75, a80: p5g⁴ p6g* p6g 5s 6s² 5s³ f6m² 6m p7g p6g⁴ p5.1d³ a84 p5g p7g p6m Dec 21] strong, close-coupled gelding: fairly useful handicapper: won at Lingfield in March: stays easy 7f: acts on all-weather, firm and soft ground: tongue tied: sometimes races freely/wanders. *Miss B. Sanders*

ANOTHER MISK 2 ch.g. (Mar 5) Storm Boot (USA) – Pure Misk 55 (Rainbow 52 p Quest (USA) 134) [2004 p9.5g⁵ Dec 20] 17,000F, 32,000Y: fifth living foal: half-brother to 3 winners, including 6-y-o Certain Justice and useful 7f (at 2 yrs) to 10.5f winner Shfoug (by Sheikh Albadou): dam, ran twice, half-sister to useful 1993 2-y-o 6f winner Fast Eddy: 25/1, fifth in maiden at Wolverhampton, racing freely up with pace: should do better. *S. C. Williams*

ANOTHER PLAN (IRE) 2 b.g. (Mar 28) Entrepreneur 123 – Tammany Hall (IRE) — 66 (Petorius 117) [2004 7.9g p8g Oct 31] €10,000Y: workmanlike gelding: first foal: dam, Irish maiden who probably stayed 9.5f, half-sister to Coventry Stakes winner CD Europe: well held in maidens at York and Lingfield. *M. G. Quinlan*

ANOTHER SECRET 6 b.m. Efisio 120 – Secrets of Honour (Belmez (USA) 131) 56 [2004 55: p10g³ p10g⁵ p10g⁴ Feb 28] sturdy mare: modest handicapper: stays easy 1¼m: acts on polytrack, soft and good to firm ground: tried in cheekpieces/blinkers/eyeshields. *G. L. Moore*

ANOTHER VICTIM 10 ch.g. Beveled (USA) – Ragtime Rose (Ragstone 128) [2004 40 53: 5m⁶ 5g Jul 12] leggy gelding: poor handicapper, lightly raced nowadays. *M. R. Bosley*

ANOUSA (IRE) 3 b.c. Intikhab (USA) 135 – Annaletta 89 (Belmez (USA) 131) [2004 100 81: 9g 9v* 11.9d 10d 12m 12.3d³ 14.8m* 11.9s 14m⁴ 14.8d 14g Sep 30] strong, stocky colt: useful performer: won handicap at Kempton in May and 4-runner listed race at Newmarket (beat Top Seed 3½ lengths) in July: good fourth to Lochbuie in handicap at Goodwood, but ran as if amiss last 2 starts: stays 15f: acts on heavy and good to firm going: effective visored or not: usually waited with. *P. Howling*

ANSELLS LEGACY (IRE) 2 b.g. (Apr 3) Charnwood Forest (IRE) 125 – Hanzala 51 (FR) (Akarad (FR) 130) [2004 7.1m 7s 7.1g⁶ 7.2s Oct 12] modest maiden: will stay 1m: tends to start slowly. *A. Berry*

ANSWER DO 4 b.f. Groom Dancer (USA) 128 – Be My Lass (IRE) (Be My Guest — (USA) 126) [2004 6f⁶ May 22] 4,800 2-y-o: sixth foal: half-sister to several winners, including useful 7f winner Qazween (by Primo Dominie) and fairly useful 1½m winner My Lass (by Elmaamul): dam, French 11f winner, half-sister to smart middle-distance performers Bonne Ile and Ile de Nisky: 25/1 and green, well beaten in maiden at Ayr, starting slowly and flashing tail throughout. *M. J. Polglase*

ANSWERED PROMISE (FR) 5 g.g. Highest Honor (FR) 124 – Answered Prayer 61 (Green Desert (USA) 127) [2004 61: p8g f9.4g p10g⁶ p10g² 8.1f³ 8m³ 8g Jul 11] strong, short-backed gelding: has a quick action: modest performer: left A. Carroll after fourth start: effective at 1m/1¼m: acts on all-weather, soft and firm ground. *I. A. Wood*

ANTEDILUVIAN 3 b.f. Air Express (IRE) 125 – Divina Mia 66 (Dowsing (USA) 106 p 124) [2004 91p: 8.3g* 8.1d* Jul 3] big, well-made filly: has scope: unbeaten in 3 starts, namely maiden at Redcar for J. Given at 2 yrs (subsequently sold 150,000 gns), minor event at Hamilton (by 1½ lengths from Celtic Heroine) in June and listed race at Sandown (by ¾ length from Snow Goose) in July: should stay 1¼m: acts on good to firm and good to soft going: joined B. Cecil in USA: already useful, and seems open to further improvement. *Sir Michael Stoute*

ANTHEMION (IRE) 7 ch.g. Night Shift (USA) – New Sensitive (Wattlefield 117) 67 [2004 70: 7.1g 8.3g² 8.3d 8g 8d 9.2d 8g⁵ 8.3g³ 9.2f* 8g³ 9.2f² 9.2d 8g 7.2d 8g 8m Oct 2] good-topped gelding: fair handicapper: won at Hamilton in July: effective at 1m/9f: acts on fibresand, firm and good to soft going: usually races prominently. *Mrs J. C. McGregor*

ANTHOS (GER) 3 b.f. Big Shuffle (USA) 122 – Anemoni (GER) (Motley (USA) 123) — [2004 91: 6m⁵ 6g Jul 16] rather leggy, lengthy filly: fairly useful performer: reportedly

70

sustained hairline fracture of a cannon bone final 2-y-o start: below form in 2004: will need to settle to stay beyond 6f: acts on firm going. *J. R. Fanshawe*

ANTICIPATING   4 b.g. Polish Precedent (USA) 131 – D'Azy 91 (Persian Bold 123)   **93**
[2004 93: p13g 12m⁴ 12f 11.6f² 14g 12d 12g 11g Sep 17] lengthy, good-topped gelding: fairly useful performer: effective at 1¼m given test, and should stay beyond 14.6f (saddle slipped at 2m): acts on firm and good to soft going: very slowly away final outing: sold 30,000 gns. *A. M. Balding*

ANTIGIOTTO (IRE)   3 ch.g. Desert Story (IRE) 115 – Rofool (IRE) (Fools Holme   **79**
(USA)) [2004 p8g 7d 10s 9.7m⁴ 9.9d² 10m² 11.9f 10g 9.2d³ Sep 27] €23,000Y: good-bodied gelding: third foal: half-brother to 7.5f/1m winner in Italy by Eagle Eyed: dam Italian 5f to 9f winner: fair maiden: stays 1¼m: acts on good to firm and good to soft going: blinkered/visored last 2 starts: sold 22,000 gns. *L. M. Cumani*

ANTIGUA BAY (IRE)   3 b.f. Turtle Island (IRE) – Vilanika (FR) 81 (Top Ville   **66**
129) [2004 7g 8m 6g² f7s⁶ 6g³ 7g⁴ p8g Oct 25] close-coupled filly: sixth foal: half-sister to 3 winners, including smart 5f (at 2 yrs) to 1½m winner Largesse (by Cadeaux Gene-reux): dam 7f/1m winner: fair maiden: should stay 1m: raced only on good/good to firm ground on turf: sold 7,000 gns. *J. A. R. Toller*

ANTLEY COURT (IRE)   2 ch.g. (Feb 27) Tagula (IRE) 116 – Changed Around   **–**
(IRE) (Doulab (USA) 115) [2004 5f May 24] slowly away and tailed off in maiden at Carlisle. *A. Berry*

ANTOINETTE (USA)   2 b.f. (Apr 2) Silver Hawk (USA) 123 – Excellentadventure   **70 p**
(USA) (Slew City Slew (USA)) [2004 7d⁶ Oct 30] $200,000Y: big, lengthy filly: has scope: second foal: half-sister to US 2003 2-y-o 6f minor stakes winner Excellent Band (by Dixieland Band): dam, won in USA, sister to US Grade 2 2-y-o 1m winner Evansville Slew: 14/1 and backward, 2½ lengths sixth of 19 to Read Federica in maiden at New-market, prominent long way: will stay at least 1m: sure to do better. *Sir Michael Stoute*

ANTONIO CANOVA   8 ch.g. Komaite (USA) – Joan's Venture (Beldale Flutter   **82**
(USA) 130) [2004 –: 6s 6v 6.1s* 6m 6m 7g⁵ 6g 6g Aug 28] stocky gelding: just fairly useful nowadays: easily best effort in 2004 when winning minor event at Nottingham in May: best at 5f/6f: acts on firm and soft going: visored penultimate start. *Bob Jones*

ANTONIO STRADIVARI (IRE)   2 b. or br.c. (Mar 18) Stravinsky (USA) 133 –   **64**
Dearest (USA) (Riverman (USA) 131) [2004 6m p7g 6g⁵ a5.5f a8s³ Dec 31] €75,000Y: strong colt: third foal: dam, US maiden, half-sister to Kentucky Derby winner Sea Hero and to dam of Mozart: modest form in maidens/minor event, leaving A. Balding after third start: probably stays 1m: acts on dirt: visored/blinkered last 3 outings. *R. R. Root, USA*

ANTONIUS PIUS (USA)   3 b.c. Danzig (USA) – Catchascatchcan 122 (Pursuit   **123 §**
of Love 124) [2004 105: 8g²ᵈ 8g⁵ 8f³ 6g 8g⁵ 8g³ 8m 8d² Dec 12]
            A tendency to hang failed to prevent Catchascatchcan going unbeaten through a four-race career which culminated with success in the Yorkshire Oaks, but for her first foal, Antonius Pius, the same quirk cast a shadow over his three-year-old campaign, costing him certain victory in a classic, and possibly success in the Breeders' Cup Mile, too. Catchascatchcan's racing career was ended by a hairline fracture of her near-fore knee sustained in winning the Yorkshire Oaks, and Antonius Pius was fortunate not to cause himself serious injury through his meandering in the Poule d'Essai des Poulains at Longchamp in May. Antonius Pius burst between Byron and favourite American Post to take up the running just inside the final furlong, going a length up, but he suddenly veered right once in front and collided with the rail around fifty yards out, losing his footing and momentum. Antonius Pius was passed by four rivals, including the winner American Post, though beaten around a length and a half in the end. Antonius Pius' behaviour was hardly a bolt from the blue. He kicked Sunday Doubt's rider Olivier Peslier on the arm prior to the Poulains and had also hung right in the Prix de Fontainebleau over the same course and distance on his reappearance the previous month, flashing his tail for good measure, after briefly looking a threat to all-the-way winner American Post, Antonius Pius demoted to last after crossing the line second. Jamie Spencer received suspensions of four days after the Fontainebleau, and six days after the Poulains, the stewards deeming he had not done enough to keep his mount straight in the latter, though Spencer had his whip in the correct hand. Spencer could perhaps have done a little more to keep Antonius Pius running in a true line in the

Mr M. Tabor & Mrs John Magnier's "Antonius Pius"

Breeders' Cup Mile at Lone Star Park in October, though whether his decision not to pull his whip through to his left hand in the closing stages cost Antonius Pius the half length he was beaten into second by Singletary is arguable. Antonius Pius quickened through from towards the rear but had to be straightened out twice after trying to duck left away from Spencer's whip.

Antonius Pius managed to keep straight in the St James's Palace Stakes at Royal Ascot on his third outing, but his finishing effort was not completely convincing there either. Antonius Pius was on the bridle longer than any of his rivals, eased to the outside of winner Azamour a furlong out, but he did not look keen when shaken up and was beaten a length into third. Dropped in trip to contest the July Cup on his next start, Antonius Pius couldn't follow in the footsteps of the most recent Ballydoyle winners Stravinsky and Mozart, though not discredited in finishing seventh behind Frizzante after missing the break slightly, being pushed along by halfway and fading after coming through to challenge for a place in the final furlong. Antonius Pius was visored for the Sussex Stakes at Goodwood the following month but didn't enjoy the run of the race, still going well as the field bunched around him over two furlongs out and left with too much to do once in the clear. Spencer was in Ireland when Antonius Pius was returned to Longchamp in September for the Prix du Moulin, in which he did little wrong under Johnny Murtagh, though still found Grey Lilas and Diamond Green too good. A first poor effort came in the Queen Elizabeth II Stakes at Ascot later in September, Antonius Pius taking a long time to settle under Kieren Fallon and managing only ninth, four places behind stablemate Ace, the preferred mount of Spencer. Antonius Pius made no impression in the Hong Kong Mile at Sha Tin on his final appearance.

Antonius Pius (USA) (b.c. 2001)	Danzig (USA) (b 1977)	Northern Dancer (b 1961)	Nearctic
			Natalma
		Pas de Nom (b or br 1968)	Admiral's Voyage
			Petitioner
	Catchascatchcan (b 1995)	Pursuit of Love (b 1989)	Groom Dancer
			Dance Quest
		Catawba (b 1985)	Mill Reef
			Catalpa

Catchascatchcan's racing career spanned little more than two months during the summer of her three-year-old season. She was raced exclusively at around a mile and a half and shaped as if she would have stayed further, even though she was by Pursuit of Love, who never raced beyond a mile and put up his best performances over six and seven furlongs. Grandam Catawba was a useful winner over an extended mile and a quarter, while the next two dams on the bottom line of the pedigree, Catalpa and Ostrya, both won the Ribblesdale Stakes, as did Catawba's half-sister Strigida. Catchascatchcan has a two-year-old filly by A P Indy, and a yearling colt by Storm Cat who went through the Keeneland September Sales unsold at 1,200,000 dollars. Antonius Pius, bred by Ryanair founder Dr Tony Ryan, was purchased at the same sale in 2002 for 1,500,000 dollars. The close-coupled Antonius Pius is by the now-retired Danzig, who is an influence for speed. Antonius Pius is unlikely to stay beyond a mile and should prove fully effective back at seven furlongs, over which trip he made a successful debut in a maiden at Gowran as a juvenile, before winning the Railway Stakes at the Curragh on his next outing. He sometimes wore a tongue strap as a three-year-old and is proven on all going apart from soft and heavy, on which he has yet to race. He reportedly stays in training in 2005, when it is to be hoped he can make headlines for the right reasons. He clearly has the ability to win in top company. *A. P. O'Brien, Ireland*

ANTONY EBENEEZER 5 ch.h. Hurricane Sky (AUS) – Captivating (IRE) 63 **41** (Wolfhound (USA) 126) [2004 49: f11g[5] f12f[3] f14g p13g f12s* p12g[5] p13g 10g f12m[2] 10f[6] Sep 13] leggy horse: poor handicapper: won apprentice event at Southwell in March: effective at 11f to 2m: acts on all-weather and firm going, seemingly not on ground softer than good: often tongue tied: sometimes carries head awkwardly: none too consistent. *C. R. Dore*

ANUVASTEEL 3 gr.g. Vettori (IRE) 119 – Mrs Gray 61 (Red Sunset 120) [2004 84: **79** 9s[6] 8m 7g 7.1g[6] 7g p8g[6] p6g f8g p9.5g[2] Dec 27] leggy, quite good-topped gelding: fair performer: stays 9.5f: acts on polytrack, good to firm and good to soft going. *N. A. Callaghan*

ANYHOW (IRE) 7 b.m. Distant Relative 128 – Fast Chick 93 (Henbit (USA) 130) **71** [2004 71: p10g p12g p12g[2] p12g* p10g[4] p12g[5] 11.7g[4] p10g[2] 13.1m* 12.1g[5] 12m[3] 12m[2] 13.3g* p12g 11.6f[5] 12g[5] 12.2g p12.2g[2] p10g p12.2g[6] p12.2g[4] p12.2g Nov 29] angular mare: fair handicapper: won at Lingfield in March, Bath in May and Newbury in June: effective at 1¼m to 13f: acts on all-weather, firm and soft going: usually held up: sometimes wanders. *Miss K. M. George*

ANY NEWS 7 ch.g. Karinga Bay 116 – D'Egliere (FR) (Port Etienne (FR)) [2004 **–** p8.6g Oct 9] fair maiden for W. Mullins in Ireland in 2002: tongue tied, last in handicap at Wolverhampton on British debut. *Miss M. E. Rowland*

A ONE (IRE) 5 b.g. Alzao (USA) 117 – Anita's Contessa (IRE) 68 (Anita's Prince 126) **88** [2004 60, a–: p7g[4] 7m[3] 7.1m* 8.3f* 10f* 7.1g 10m* 10f* 8.3m[5] 11.7m 10d 10g p5.1g **a–** Nov 6] rather leggy gelding: fairly useful on turf, little form on all-weather: won claimer at Chepstow (left B. Palling) and handicaps at Windsor (3) and Sandown in June/July: stays 1¼m: acts on any turf going: sometimes early to post: front runner. *H. J. Manners*

AONINCH 4 ch.f. Inchinor 119 – Willowbank 66 (Gay Fandango (USA) 132) [2004 **67** 72: p12g[6] 14.4s 12d[5] 13.1m 10f[6] 12m 12d[2] 11.8f[6] 12g[2] 12s[6] 12.6g 14.1g[5] p12g Oct 28] lengthy filly: fair handicapper: stays easy 1¾m: acts on polytrack, firm and soft ground: free-going sort: has hung/found little: usually dropped out. *Mrs P. N. Dutfield*

APACHE POINT (IRE) 7 ch.g. Indian Ridge 123 – Ausherra (USA) 106 (Diesis **60** 133) [2004 73: 8v 8v 10d[5] 9f[4] 8g[5] 8.1g[5] 9.2g[2] 10g[3] 8.1g[5] 9.2d[5] 9v[5] 6.9g[5] 8.5m 8m[5] 9d[5] Oct 15] rather leggy gelding: modest handicapper: effective at 1m/1¼m: acts on any ground: sometimes races freely: usually waited with. *N. Tinkler*

APERITIF 3 ch.g. Pivotal 124 – Art Deco Lady 51 (Master Willie 129) [2004 74p: **96** 7.9d 8.1m[4] 8g[3] 6.9f[3] 8.1s* 8.1g 10d[3] 8.3d* 8d 8s[4] Oct 19] strong, good sort: useful performer: won maiden at Haydock in August and handicap at Hamilton (beat Strong Hand by 5 lengths) in September: likely to prove best around 1m: acts on soft and good to firm ground· usually early to post: sometimes awkward leaving stall: sold 50,000 gns. *W. J. Haggas*

APETITE 2 ch.g. (Mar 28) Timeless Times (USA) 99 – Petite Elite 47 (Anfield 117) **60** [2004 5m 6m 5d 7d² 6d* 7m 8s 6g 6m Oct 10] close-coupled gelding: modest performer: won seller at Ripon in August: below form in nurseries after: stays 7f: acts on good to soft ground: sometimes slowly away. *N. Bycroft*

APEX 3 ch.g. Efisio 120 – Royal Loft 105 (Homing 130) [2004 74: 7.1s* 8m⁵ 8m 8d³ **94** 7m² 6d* 6g 6.5f 7d Oct 15] leggy, angular gelding: has a short, round action: fairly useful handicapper: won at Warwick in May and Newbury in August: below form last 3 starts: effective at 6f to 1m: acts on soft and good to firm going: sometimes finds little: gelded after final start. *E. A. L. Dunlop*

APOLLO GEE (IRE) 3 b.g. Spectrum (IRE) 126 – Suspiria (IRE) 87 (Glenstal (USA) **–** 118) [2004 68: f8g f7g Apr 17] lightly-raced maiden: well held both starts within 3 days in 2004, in seller (blinkered) final one: will probably stay 7f. *B. J. Meehan*

APOLOGIES 2 b.c. (Feb 17) Robellino (USA) 127 – Mistook (USA) (Phone Trick **74** (USA)) [2004 5g 5s* 5g⁴ 7g 5s⁶ 5g 5s³ 5g⁶ 6.1d³ p6g³ Oct 7] 5,000Y: sturdy, close-coupled colt: fourth foal: dam unraced: fair performer: won maiden at Haydock in April: creditable efforts when in frame, including in nurseries/claimer, after: stays 6f: acts on polytrack and soft going: blinkered last 4 starts: sold 13,500 gns. *B. A. McMahon*

APPALACHIAN TRAIL (IRE) 3 b.g. Indian Ridge 123 – Karinski (USA) (Palace **97** Music (USA) 129) [2004 78: 8g³ 8g* 8.1d² 7.6d 8.1m⁴ 8m* 7.1d⁶ 8g⁶ 7m⁵ 8g⁵ p8.6g* Dec 10] sturdy, lengthy gelding: useful performer: won maiden at Ripon in April, minor event at Newmarket in June and handicap at Wolverhampton in December: stays 8.6f: acts on polytrack, good to firm and good to soft ground: tried visored: sweating/on edge eighth start. *I. Semple*

APPETINA 3 b.f. Perugino (USA) 84 – Tina Heights 79 (Shirley Heights 130) [2004 **65 d** 76: 9g⁵ 9.7m⁵ 7f⁴ 10.3d⁴ 12s 8d 6g p9.5g Dec 15] tall, quite good-topped filly: has a fluent, round action: fair maiden: ran poorly last 4 starts, leaving J. Given before final one: bred to stay at least 1¼m: acts on good to firm and good to soft ground: blinkered penultimate outing. *J. Parkes*

APPLE OF MY EYE 2 b.f. (Apr 15) Fraam 114 – Fresh Fruit Daily 92 (Reprimand **70** 122) [2004 5g 6f⁴ 6m* 6d 6.5m Sep 8] strong filly: sister to 3-y-o Pick of The Crop and half-sister to 5-y-o Fruit of Glory: dam 1¼m/1½m winner: fair performer: won maiden at Windsor in August: well beaten in nurseries after: should stay 7f: acts on good to firm going. *J. R. Jenkins*

APPOLONIOUS 3 b.g. Case Law 113 – Supreme Thought 68 (Emarati (USA) 74) **58 ?** [2004 p8g p8g 6m 7m 6m⁶ 5.7s Oct 19] tall gelding: modest maiden at best: tried tongue tied. *D. R. C. Elsworth*

APRIL ACE 8 ch.g. First Trump 118 – Champ d'Avril 89 (Northfields (USA)) [2004 **–** p12g Jan 15] big, lengthy gelding: modest handicapper at 3 yrs: lightly raced and little form since: tried visored. *R. J. Baker*

APRIL SHANNON 2 b.f. (Mar 27) Tipsy Creek (USA) 115 – Westering 54 (Auction **–** Ring (USA) 123) [2004 6m 7g p7g p7g Dec 20] fourth foal: half-sister to 7-y-o Inchinnan: dam maiden: no sign of ability. *J. E. Long*

APRON (IRE) 3 b.f. Grand Lodge (USA) 125 – Sultana 86 (Unfuwain (USA) 131) **58 d** [2004 10g 9.9g 8m 10v 11.5d p13.9g Nov 29] rather leggy filly: first foal: dam 7f winner who stayed 1¼m: modest maiden at best: left R. Charlton after third start. *M. J. Ryan*

APSARA 3 br.f. Groom Dancer (USA) 128 – Ayodhya (IRE) (Astronef 116) [2004 **84** 10d² 10m* 10f⁴ Aug 1] leggy filly: half-sister to several winners, including useful 5f/6f winner Ambitious (by Ardkinglass) and fairly useful 11.8f winner Amalianburg (by Hector Protector): dam French 2-y-o 6f/7f winner: fairly useful form: well-backed favourite, did well when fourth to Portmanteau in handicap at Newbury next time, losing 10 lengths after being reluctant to leave stall then staying on well: should have stayed 1½m: acted on firm ground: visored: looked quirky: stud. *H. R. A. Cecil*

AQRIBAA (IRE) 6 b. or br.g. Pennekamp (USA) 130 – Karayb (IRE) 93 (Last Tycoon **– §** 131) [2004 57§: 8.5m 9.9m Sep 21] lengthy, angular gelding: inconsistent handicapper: tried blinkered. *A. J. Lockwood*

AQUALUNG 3 b.c. Desert King (IRE) 129 – Aquarelle (Kenmare (FR) 125) [2004 **85**
78p: 10.2g 9g* 10.4m 8f Sep 11] tall, good-topped colt: fairly useful performer: best
effort when winning maiden at Ripon in May: stays 9f: too headstrong penultimate start:
sold 4,000 gns. *B. W. Hills*

AQUA PURA (GER) 5 b.g. Acatenango (GER) 127 – Actraphane (Shareef Dancer **–**
(USA) 135) [2004 –: f16g Feb 12] well held in Britain: tried blinkered. *B. J. Curley*

A QUI LE TOUR 2 b.g. (Apr 26) Pyramus (USA) 78 – Dolphin Beech (IRE) (Dolphin **40**
Street (FR) 125) [2004 5g p5d 7.1d p8g Nov 20] poor maiden. *M. R. Hoad*

ARABIAN ANA (IRE) 2 b.c. (Apr 20) Night Shift (USA) – Al Shaqrah (USA) 76 (Sir **71**
Ivor (USA) 135) [2004 6g⁶ 7g* 7s⁴ 8s⁴ Aug 30] €12,000Y, 17,000 2-y-o: tall colt: half-
brother to winners abroad by Elmaamul and Common Grounds: dam staying maiden: fair
performer: won maiden at Newcastle in July: fourth in claimer at Chester and nursery
(weakened) at Newcastle: barely stays testing 1m. *B. Smart*

ARABIAN DANCER 2 b.f. (Feb 12) Dansili 127 – Hymne (FR) (Saumarez 132) **85**
[2004 6f² 6m⁶ 6m⁵ 8f³ 6.1d⁵ 5.1f* 6.5g² 6d⁴ Oct 14] 3,000Y: leggy filly: first foal: dam,
French 9f winner, half-sister to useful French 2000 2-y-o 1m winner Hope Town: fairly
useful performer: won maiden at Bath in September: good efforts in sales events at
Newbury (short-headed by Salamanca) and Newmarket after: bred to stay 1m: acts on
firm and good to soft ground. *M. R. Channon*

ARABIAN KNIGHT (IRE) 4 ch.g. Fayruz 116 – Cheerful Knight (IRE) (Mac's **45 §**
Imp (USA) 116) [2004 64§: p6g f5g 5.7g 6s 6s 5.7m 7.1m Sep 9] close-coupled gelding:
poor nowadays: stays 5.7f: acts on all-weather, soft and good to firm going: effective
blinkered/visored or not: lazy, and ungenuine. *R. J. Hodges*

ARABIAN MOON (IRE) 8 ch.g. Barathea (IRE) 127 – Excellent Alibi (USA) **74 d**
(Exceller (USA) 129) [2004 –: 11.9m* 12s 15.9g p12.2g f12g⁴ p16.5g f12d Dec 21]
leggy, quite good-topped gelding: easy mover: fair performer: won claimer at Brighton in
August: effective at 1½m to 21f: acts on polytrack, best turf efforts on good going or
firmer: tried blinkered/visored: usually held up: often finds little. *R. Brotherton*

ARABIE 6 b.g. Polish Precedent (USA) 131 – Always Friendly 111 (High Line 125) **65 +**
[2004 95: 12m a10f 10m 10d 7g⁴ f8d Jul 23] lengthy, angular gelding: one-time smart
performer: left M. Johnston after fourth start: form in 2004 only when fourth in claimer at
Epsom: best around 1¼m: yet to race on heavy going, acts on any other: free going sort:
blinkered third outing. *Ian Williams*

ARAGON DANCER 3 b.g. Aragon 118 – Jambo 68 (Rambo Dancer (CAN) 107) **–**
[2004 –: p6g Jan 6] well beaten in maidens/claimer. *T. M. Jones*

ARAGON'S BOY 4 ch.g. Aragon 118 – Fancier Bit (Lion Cavern (USA) 117) [2004 **73**
75: 10g 7.5d 8f* 8g 8.2g⁴ 8f 7g 8m p9.5g Dec 6] fair performer: won maiden at Brighton
in June: left H. Candy after sixth start: stays 1m: acts on firm ground: has carried head
awkwardly: usually races prominently. *T. D. Easterby*

ARAKAN (USA) 4 br.c. Nureyev (USA) 131 – Far Across (Common Grounds **123**
118) [2004 119: 6g* 6s³ 6m² 8f 7m* Jun 26]
  Arakan progressed again as a four-year-old when he proved himself a very
smart performer on his day, and might have proved himself better still had he not
picked up an unspecified injury that kept him off the track after the end of June.
Arakan had endured a nightmare passage when runner-up to Nayyir in the Lennox
Stakes as a three-year-old after which *Timeform Perspective* commented that he
was 'a pattern race winner waiting to happen', though few would have anticipated
that he would have to wait eleven months—until the Bango Criterion Stakes at
Newmarket in June.
  Arakan reappeared in the listed Abernant Stakes, over six furlongs at Newmarket's Craven meeting, producing a career-best performance to beat Frizzante
and Ashdown Express by half a length and a length and a half, with Bahamian
Pirate a further four lengths back in fourth. Arakan's connections could have been
forgiven for wondering what might have been as Arakan nursed a season-ending
injury whilst Frizzante gained a narrow victory over Ashdown Express in the July
Cup and Bahamian Pirate won the Nunthorpe. But Arakan's campaign wasn't without its hiccups between the Abernant and the Criterion. Arakan could not reproduce
his Abernant form in the Duke of York Stakes at York, always pushed along on the
soft ground before running on for a respectable third to Monsieur Bond and Steen-

NGK Spark Plugs Abernant Stakes, Newmarket—
Arakan holds off Frizzante and Ashdown Express, first and second in the July Cup later in the season,
with subsequent Nunthorpe winner Bahamian Pirate (noseband) back in fourth

berg. Arakan again failed to travel with much fluency when second in the Greenlands Stakes at the Curragh to The Kiddykid and faced his stiffest task over a mile in the Queen Anne Stakes. Recording his only poor effort of the season, he was never able to get into the race at Royal Ascot after being held up to get the trip.

Then came the Criterion Stakes. Arakan travelled very strongly and took up the running a furlong out, quickening past the 2003 winner Trade Fair before being eased inside the last fifty yards, value at the finish for further than the winning margin of three quarters of a length over Desert Destiny; Trade Fair finished a further two lengths away in third. Arakan's form was not far behind that of the best sprinters and he wouldn't have looked out of things had he managed to make the July Cup line-up.

Arakan's best form at three had come at seven furlongs, and perhaps a short-age of opportunities at the trip was the reasoning behind Arakan's being tried as a sprinter, and then as a miler, in the first half of the 2004 season. The only Group 1 over seven furlongs in Europe that Arakan could have contested in 2004 was the Prix de la Foret at Longchamp in October; the British calendar provides just six pattern events at this trip open to four-year-olds and upwards colts and geldings, the most important of them, Goodwood's Lennox Stakes in July—which would almost certainly have been a target again for Arakan had injury not intervened—Doncaster's Park Stakes in September and Newmarket's Challenge Stakes in October, all Group 2 events.

		Northern Dancer (b 1961)	Nearctic
			Natalma
	Nureyev (USA) (b 1977)	Special (b 1969)	Forli
			Thong
Arakan (USA) (br.c. 2000)		Common Grounds (b 1985)	Kris
			Sweetly
	Far Across (b 1996)	City Ex (ch 1986)	Ardross
			Rythmique

Arakan is a good-topped, attractive colt who has shown his best form at up to seven furlongs and is effective held up or ridden prominently. Below form when sweating on his sixth start as a three-year-old, he has raced mainly on good ground or firmer and remains the sort to run well in pattern events provided he makes a full recovery. Arakan is the first foal of Far Across, an unraced half-sister to the French seven-furlong and mile performer Donkey Engine and the French and North American mile- to a mile-and-a-quarter performer Petit Poucet, both of whom are smart. *Sir Michael Stoute*

ARAMAT 2 b.f. (Apr 1) Cigar 68 – Winze Kible (Baldhu Cavalier) [2004 5g p7m p7g   –
Oct 13] first foal: dam unraced: no form in maidens. *J. R. Boyle*

ARAWAN (IRE) 4 b.g. Entrepreneur 123 – Asmara (USA) 109 (Lear Fan (USA) 130)   **52**
[2004 91: 10.5d 10.3g 10g 9f 10m 8.5g 8g 9d f11g Nov 8] sturdy gelding: fairly useful
performer at 3 yrs for J. Oxx in Ireland: just modest form in 2004: stays 1m: acts on firm
going: tried blinkered. *M. W. Easterby*

ARBELLA 2 ch.f. (Apr 23) Primo Dominie 121 – Kristal Bridge 75 (Kris 135) [2004   **94**
7g² 7m⁴ 7f⁴ 7m³ Sep 7] leggy, useful-looking filly: third foal: half-sister to fairly useful

1½m winner Palamedes (by Sadler's Wells): dam, maiden best around 1¼m, out of Nassau Stakes and Yorkshire Oaks winner Connaught Bridge: 2 lengths fourth to Maids Causeway in Sweet Solera Stakes at Newmarket penultimate start: just fair form in maidens otherwise: will stay at least 1m: best effort on firm going. *P. W. Harris*

ARBORS LITTLE GIRL 2 b.f. (Feb 4) Paris House 123 – Arbor Ealis (IRE) 62 (Woods of Windsor (USA)) [2004 5.1m* 5.7g* 6.1d⁵ 6m³ p7g p7g⁶ f8g³ Nov 23] smallish, leggy filly: first foal: dam 2-y-o 5f seller winner: fair on turf, modest on all-weather: won seller (landed gamble) in August and nursery in September, both at Bath: stays easy 1m: acts on all-weather, good to firm and good to soft going: wore cheekpieces last 2 starts. *B. R. Millman*   **66 a56**

ARCALIS 4 gr.g. Lear Fan (USA) 130 – Aristocratique 71 (Cadeaux Genereux 131) [2004 100p: 10m* 10.4g* Jul 10] tall, quite good-topped gelding: smart handicapper: progressed again in 2004, winning at Ayr (easily by 2 lengths from Oldenway) in May and York (John Smith's Cup, beat Promotion by head) in July: effective at 1¼m/1½m: acts on firm and good to soft ground: usually waited with: tough and consistent: useful form over hurdles in December. *J. Howard Johnson*   **112 +**

ARC EL CIEL (ARG) 6 b.g. Fitzcarraldo (ARG) – Ardoise (USA) (Diamond Prospect (USA) 126) [2004 –, a84: f7g⁸ f8.5g³ f8.5g⁵ p8g f8.5s f8.5s³ p8g f7s⁶ p7.1g p8.6g Dec 27] fairly useful handicapper: won at Wolverhampton (sixth course success) in January: effective at 6f (given test) to 8.5f: acts on fibresand, probably on polytrack: usually visored: game. *Mrs Stef Liddiard*   **– a86**

ARC EN CIEL 6 b.g. Rainbow Quest (USA) 134 – Nadia Nerina (CAN) 82 (Northern Dancer) [2004 –: p16g⁴ p13g Jan 31] useful-looking gelding: fairly useful handicapper at 3 yrs: lightly raced and modest at best since: tried visored/tongue tied. *G. L. Moore*   **54 ?**

ARCHDUKE FERDINAND (FR) 6 ch.g. Dernier Empereur (USA) 125 – Lady Norcliffe (USA) (Norcliffe (CAN)) [2004 97: 18.7d 14g² 16.2d Jun 5] strong, close-coupled gelding: useful handicapper: form in 2004 only when second at Goodwood: best form at 2m+: well held only run on heavy going, acts on any other: has worn cheekpieces: often races freely: none too consistent. *P. F. I. Cole*   **95**

John Smith's Cup (Handicap), York—Arcalis, whose jockey Robert Winston has lost his whip, nails Promotion close home; Starry Lodge and Red Fort (checked sleeves) are third and fourth

ARCHENKO   4 b.g. Weldnaas (USA) 112 – Silverdale Rose (Nomination 125) [2004   –
12g 11.1g 12.1g[6] 9.9m[5] May 24] no form. *A. Berry*

ARCHEOLOGY (USA)   2 b. or br.f. (Feb 22) Seeking The Gold (USA) – Caress   **80**
(USA) (Storm Cat (USA)) [2004 6g[5] 6d p7g[2] Oct 28] leggy filly: fifth foal: closely related
to winner in USA by Gulch and half-sister to smart US 2002 Grade 1 2-y-o 7f winner Sky
Mesa (by Pulpit) who stayed 9f: dam, US Grade 3 winner up to 9f, sister to smart Irish
performer up to 7f Bernstein and half-sister to smart Irish performer up to 1½m Della
Francesca: best effort in maidens when second to Royal Jelly (pair clear) at Lingfield:
should stay 1m: ran as if amiss on good to soft going. *Saeed bin Suroor*

ARCHERFIELD (IRE)   3 ch.f. Docksider (USA) 124 – Willow River (CAN) 66 (Vice   **73 d**
Regent (CAN)) [2004 64: p8g[2] p8g[2] p8g[3] 8g 7g 8f[2] 8.5g[3] 8.5g[3] 8.5f[4] 8.1g[4] 8m Sep 23]
close-coupled filly: fair maiden at best: stays 8.5f: acts on polytrack and firm ground:
tongue tied 5 of last 6 starts: sold 8,000 gns. *J. W. Hills*

ARCH FOLLY   2 b.g. (Apr 28) Silver Patriarch (IRE) 125 – Folly Fox (Alhijaz 122)   **61**
[2004 8.3m 8.1g[6] 8d Oct 16] 1,600F, 3,000Y: first foal: dam unraced: modest form in
maidens: will stay at least 1½m: best effort on good going. *J. G. Portman*

ARCHIAS (GER)   5 b.g. Darshaan 133 – Arionette (Lombard (GER) 126) [2004   **62**
16.1g Sep 6] won 11f maiden and 1½m handicap in Germany in 2002: left P. Schiergen
after only 4-y-o outing: modest but headstrong winning hurdler for R. C. Guest: last in
handicap at Newcastle on return to Flat: acts on soft going. *J. J. Quinn*

ARCHIE BABE (IRE)   8 ch.g. Archway (IRE) 115 – Frensham Manor (Le Johnstan   **74 d**
123) [2004 74: 12g 12.4v* 12v[5] 10d 11.9g 11.9s 11.9g 13.8s Nov 2] workmanlike gelding: fair handicapper: won at Newcastle in April: below form after: should stay 1¾m:
below form on firm going, acts on any other turf and fibresand: usually held up: sometimes looks ungenuine. *J. J. Quinn*

ARCHIE CLARKE (GER)   4 b.g. Taishan (GER) – Anthela (GER) (Orfano (GER))   –
[2004 p9.5d f7s Nov 17] last in maiden at Wolverhampton and seller at Southwell.
J. Gallagher

ARCHIE GLENN   2 b.c. (May 25) Lake Coniston (IRE) 131 – La Ballerine 62   **79**
(Lafontaine (USA) 117) [2004 5m 6m 6m[4] 6.1s[2] 6g Oct 11] fourth foal: half-brother to
6-y-o Sunny Glenn: dam 9f and 15f winner: fair maiden: left Mrs P. N. Dutfield after
second start: second at Chepstow: will stay 7f: acts on soft and good to firm going.
M. S. Saunders

ARCHIE WRIGHT   2 ch.c. (Mar 6) Lake Coniston (IRE) 131 – Roisin Clover 73   **47**
(Faustus (USA) 118) [2004 7d 7.1g 8.5g[4] 6d Oct 18] strong colt: poor maiden: best effort
at 7f on good ground. *R. Hannon*

ARCHIRONDEL   6 b.g. Bin Ajwaad (IRE) 119 – Penang Rose (NZ) (Kingdom Bay   **63**
(NZ)) [2004 70: p10g[6] p10g 12g 12.4v 9.9d 8v[2] 9f* 8m 12f[2] 12m* 11.1g[5] 12.3g[5] Aug 2]
smallish gelding: modest handicapper: won at Redcar and Musselburgh in June: stays
1½m: acts on polytrack and any turf going: sometimes races freely/finishes weakly:
usually held up. *M. D. Hammond*

ARC OF LIGHT (IRE)   2 b.c. (May 17) Spectrum (IRE) 126 – Siwaayib 97 (Green   **64**
Desert (USA) 127) [2004 6m[5] 6g 7m Aug 8] rather leggy colt: seventh foal: closely
related to smart 1½m/1¾m winner Rainbow Ways and 1½m winner Storm Seeker (both
by Rainbow Quest): dam 6f (including at 2 yrs) winner: modest form in maidens, not
knocked about: should stay at least 1m. *B. W. Hills*

ARCTIC BLUE   4 b.g. Polar Prince (IRE) 117 – Miss Sarajane 74 (Skyliner 117)   –
[2004 –: 11.5m p16g Jul 24] maiden: tried in cheekpieces. *M. J. Gingell*

ARCTIC BURST (USA)   4 b.g. Royal Academy (USA) 130 – Polar Bird 111 (Thatch-   **45**
ing 131) [2004 85: 5d 6v 6g p6g 5g 7m 5.1m 5m 5d p5m[4] f5g[5] f6d[4] Dec 21] strong,
lengthy gelding: has a quick, fluent action: only poor nowadays: effective at 6f/7f: acts on
polytrack and good to firm ground: tried tongue tied/blinkered, usually visored: often
slowly away. *D. Shaw*

ARCTIC COVE   3 b.g. Vettori (IRE) 119 – Sundae Girl (USA) 75 (Green Dancer   –
(USA) 132) [2004 8g Aug 28] last in maiden at Newmarket. *J. Nicol*

ARCTIC DESERT   4 b.g. Desert Prince (IRE) 130 – Thamud (IRE) (Lahib (USA)   **86**
129) [2004 100: p7g 7d 7m 6m 7.1g 7m p7d[6] 7g* 8.3d[6] 7m[2] 7m 7g 7d[2] Oct 30] big,
good-topped gelding: impresses in appearance: just fairly useful in 2004, winning minor
event at Folkestone in August: free-going sort, but stays 7f: acts on polytrack, firm and
good to soft going: tried tongue tied/visored (not when successful). *A. M. Balding*

ARCTIC SILK 3 ch.f. Selkirk (USA) 129 – Cape Verdi (IRE) 126 (Caerleon (USA) **80**
132) [2004 10d 8g³ 8m² 9d Aug 12] useful-looking filly: first foal: dam, won 1000
Guineas (also 6f winner at 2 yrs), out of sister to Breeders' Cup Classic winner Arcangues: fairly useful maiden: best effort when ¾-length second to Tarfah at Ascot on
penultimate start: ran badly final outing: may prove best around 1m: acts on good to firm
ground: tongue tied after debut: left Godolphin. *Saeed bin Suroor*

ARDASNAILS (IRE) 2 b.g. (Apr 27) Spectrum (IRE) 126 – Fey Lady (IRE) (Fairy **–**
King (USA)) [2004 7f 7g Aug 11] 100/1, well held in maiden/claimer. *P. Burgoyne*

ARDERE (USA) 3 ch.f. El Prado (IRE) 119 – Flaming Torch 92 (Rousillon (USA) **–**
133) [2004 10g Sep 10] fifth living foal: half-sister to 1m winner Flame Cutter (by
Miswaki) and 1996 2-y-o 7f winner Flaming West (by Gone West), later 6.5f to 8.5f
winner in USA: dam 1m (in France at 2 yrs) to 11f (US Grade 3) winner: 12/1, well held
in maiden at Sandown (saddle reportedly slipped). *H. R. A. Cecil*

ARDKEEL LASS (IRE) 3 ch.f. Fumo di Londra (IRE) 108 – Wot-A-Noise (IRE) **58**
(Petorius 117) [2004 67: 5.1g 5g 5f² 5.1g⁴ 5.3s⁵ 5.7f 5.1m⁶ f6g³ Nov 23] modest
performer: left D. Ivory after third start: effective at 5f/6f: acts on fibresand, firm and
good to soft going: often races prominently. *D. Haydn Jones*

ARE YOU THERE 3 b.f. Presidium 124 – Scoffera 63 (Scottish Reel 123) [2004 **39**
64d: f7f p6g⁶ f7g⁴ p8g Feb 21] rather leggy, workmanlike filly: poor performer: left
T. D. Barron after reappearance: should stay 6f: acts on all-weather and good to firm
going: tried blinkered/visored. *P. S. McEntee*

ARFINNIT (IRE) 3 b.g. College Chapel 122 – Tidal Reach (USA) 68 (Kris S (USA)) **61**
[2004 84: 7g 6d³ 7.1s 7g⁶ 5.7f⁵ 6m* 7m⁶ 6g⁶ 6g* 6.1m⁶ 5.3g⁴ 5.1g 6m 6g 5.7m² 5.3s⁴ 5s⁶
5.7g 5d⁴ Oct 17] good-topped gelding: has a quick action: modest performer: won
claimers at Ripon in May and Ayr in June: effective at 5f/6f: acts on firm and soft going:
usually visored nowadays: sold 8,000 gns. *M. R. Channon*

ARGAMIA (GER) 8 b.m. Orfano (GER) – Arkona (GER) 108 (Aspros (GER)) [2004 **–**
55: p13.9g Dec 22] tall, angular mare: modest performer: effective at 1½m (given test) to
2m: acts on fibresand, heavy and good to firm going: blinkered 3 times at 4 yrs: usually
held up. *P. J. McBride*

ARGENT 3 b.g. Barathea (IRE) 127 – Red Tiara (USA) 60 (Mr Prospector (USA)) **50**
[2004 55: f12g 12g 9.9v² 8m 8g 8g 9.2f² 9.2d³ Aug 23] sturdy gelding: modest maiden:
left D. Carroll after third start: stays 1¼m: acts on fibresand and any turf going: wore
cheekpieces last 4 starts: tongue tied last 2 starts in 2003. *Miss L. A. Perratt*

ARGENTUM 3 b.g. Sillery (USA) 122 – Frustration 108 (Salse (USA) 128) [2004 –: **65**
8.3d 7g⁵ 10g* 12.1m² 14.1g Sep 29] big, plain gelding: fair performer: won handicap
at Nottingham (slowly away) in August: stays 1½m: acts on good to firm going. *Lady
Herries*

ARGONAUT 4 ch.g. Rainbow Quest (USA) 134 – Chief Bee 89 (Chief's Crown **96**
(USA)) [2004 86p: 10v⁶ 12m³ 12f 14.8d⁴ p12.2g⁶ Dec 17] smallish, quite good-topped
gelding: useful performer, lightly raced: left Sir Michael Stoute after fourth start: stays
15f: acts on firm and good to soft going, well held on polytrack: usually held up. *Ian
Williams*

ARIAN 2 b.f. (May 5) Josr Algarhoud (IRE) 118 – Hope Chest 70 (Kris 135) [2004 7g⁵ **69**
Oct 11] quite good-topped filly: fourth foal: half-sister to 5-y-o Liberty Royal and 2003
2-y-o 5f/6f winner Lotto (by Nicolotte): dam lightly-raced maiden: 66/1 and green, 4
lengths fifth of 19 to Corcoran in maiden at Leicester: likely to stay 1m. *C. G. Cox*

ARIANE STAR (IRE) 2 b.f. (Mar 1) Marju (IRE) 127 – Northgate Raver (Absalom **49**
128) [2004 6m 6.1s 5.2m⁵ 7m Aug 6] €20,000Y: fourth foal: half-sister to 3 winners
abroad, including French 2000 2-y-o 1m winner Catch A Cab (by Eagle Eyed): dam of
little account: poor maiden: should stay 7f. *M. A. Jarvis*

ARIAN'S LAD 3 b.g. Prince Sabo 123 – Arian Da 81 (Superlative 118) [2004 5.1m **50 ?**
5.1g f7d 7.1d³ Aug 19] leggy gelding: modest maiden: stays 7f. *B. Palling*

ARICIA (IRE) 3 b.f. Nashwan (USA) 135 – Rahaam (USA) 91 (Secreto (USA) 128) **88**
[2004 7g 7f* 8m 8d p8g⁶ Oct 31] strong, useful-looking filly: half-sister to several
winners, notably sharp sprinter (also won at 7f) Cassandra Go (by Indian Ridge) and
1996 2-y-o 6f (Coventry Stakes) winner Verglas (by Highest Honor) who stayed 1m,
later successful in USA: dam 7f winner who stayed 1¼m: fairly useful performer: won
maiden at Newmarket in May by 5 lengths: creditable sixth to Miss George in listed

race at Lingfield (after 3-month break): stays 1m: acts on polytrack and firm going. *J. H. M. Gosden*

ARIESANNE (IRE)   3 ch.f. Primo Dominie 121 – Living Legend (ITY) (Archway   **– p**
(IRE) 115) [2004 5s³ 5d 6m⁶ Sep 4] €5,500Y: lengthy, workmanlike filly: third foal: dam
unraced half-sister to very smart miler Missed Flight: well held in maidens, ridden by
inexperienced claimer final start: type to do better. *R. A. Fahey*

ARIES (GER)   4 ch.f. Big Shuffle (USA) 122 – Auenlust (GER) (Surumu (GER))   **–**
[2004 76: 8m p10d Jun 12] lengthy, workmanlike filly: fair handicapper: well held in
2004: stays 7f: acts on firm and soft going: tried visored. *M. J. Wallace*

ARIODANTE   2 b.g. (Jan 20) Groom Dancer (USA) 128 – Maestrale (Top Ville 129)   **78**
[2004 6m³ 6m⁶ 7m⁴ 7s Aug 19] 9,000Y: smallish gelding: half-brother to several winners, including useful 1m winner Ebony Heights (by Polar Falcon) and 7f to 1¼m winner
Birthday Venture (by Soviet Star): dam unraced half-sister to high-class middle-distance
performer Head For Heights: fair performer: won maiden at Lingfield in July: respectable
fourth in minor event at Ascot, better effort after: needs to settle to stay beyond 7f.
J. M. P. Eustace

ARJAY   6 b.g. Shaamit (IRE) 127 – Jenny's Call (Petong 126) [2004 65: p10g 8d f9.4m³   **52**
f9.4m⁵ 9f³ f12d 10.5s Jul 17] tall, rather leggy gelding: modest nowadays: effective at 7f
to 1¼m: acts on any turf going: tried blinkered: none too reliable. *Andrew Turnell*

ARK ADMIRAL   5 b.g. Inchinor 119 – Kelimutu 58 (Top Ville 129) [2004 68d: 9g   **60 ?**
6d 8.1m Aug 5] good-bodied gelding: just modest in 2004: tried blinkered/tongue tied:
free-going type. *C. L. Tizzard*

ARKHOLME   3 b.g. Robellino (USA) 127 – Free Spirit (IRE) (Caerleon (USA) 132)   **92**
[2004 81p: 9.9s⁴ 11.9d 8m² 8g* 8m² 10m 8.3g³ 8g* 8g⁴ 8g⁴ Sep 30] useful-looking
gelding: fairly useful performer: won maiden at Ascot (left W. Haggas £22,000) in July
and apprentice handicap at Kempton in September: should stay at least 1¼m: acts on soft
and good to firm going: seems best in blinkers. *P. Winkworth*

ARMAGNAC   6 b.g. Young Ern 120 – Arianna Aldini (Habitat 134) [2004 89: 6g 6g   **91**
6g 6g³ 6m⁶ 6m 6m 6.5g² 6m³ 6g² 7f³ 7g 6m 7.1g* 7m 7g⁵ Oct 9] tall, good-topped
gelding: unimpressive mover: fairly useful handicapper: won at Sandown in September:
effective at 6f/7f: yet to race on heavy going, acts on any other: tried in cheekpieces at 5
yrs: occasionally slowly away/pulls hard: held up. *M. A. Buckley*

ARMATORE (USA)   4 b.g. Gone West (USA) – Awesome Account (USA) (Lyphard   **64**
(USA) 132) [2004 11.5g 10.3g p9.5g⁵ p9.5g⁴ p8.6g² Dec 27] maiden: left F. Rohaut in
France 11,000 gns after final 3-y-o outing: only modest form in Britain: stays 9.5f: acts
on polytrack and heavy going: tried blinkered/in cheekpieces. *E. R. Oertel*

ARMENTIERES   3 b.f. Robellino (USA) 127 – Perfect Poppy 73 (Shareef Dancer   **60 §**
(USA) 135) [2004 59§, a55§: p10g⁶ 11.9m 9.9d 10g⁶ 8s² 7.1g³ 7.1m⁴ 8g 7g* 8.2v f8g   **a45 §**
p8m⁶ p8.6g Dec 22] deep-girthed filly: modest performer: won selling handicap at
Leicester in October: best at 7f/1m: acts on all-weather, firm and soft going: usually
blinkered, tried in cheekpieces: temperamental. *J. L. Spearing*

ARMS ACROSSTHESEA   5 b.g. Namaqualand (USA) – Zolica 60 (Beveled (USA))   **66**
[2004 –: 12d² 11m* f9.4m* 10g⁴ 12.6f f8g 10.1m⁶ 10.1g⁶ 10m 10d Sep 17] leggy
gelding: fair performer: won claimer at Redcar (left A. Whillans) and handicap at Wolverhampton in May, and claimer at Yarmouth in August: stays 11f: unraced on heavy going,
probably acts on any other turf and fibresand: tried in headgear. *J. Balding*

ARMY OF ANGELS (IRE)   2 ch.c. (Apr 24) King's Best (USA) 132 – Angelic   **103 p**
Sounds (IRE) (The Noble Player (USA) 126) [2004 6m² 6m* 6g² Sep 16] €250,000F:
big, strong colt: half-brother to several winners, including Irish 5f winner Alegranza (by
Lake Coniston), 1999 2-y-o 5f winner Seraphina (by Pips Pride), both useful, and 3-y-o
Zameyla: dam, Irish 2-y-o 5f winner, half-sister to very smart 6f/7f performer Mount
Abu: odds on, won maiden at Leicester in July by 8 lengths: creditable neck second of 4
to Josh in minor event at Yarmouth, briefly short of room: should stay at least 7f: tongue
tied: type to train on well as 3-y-o. *Saeed bin Suroor*

ARNIE DE BURGH   2 br.c. (Mar 16) Amfortas (IRE) 115 – Align 69 (Petong 126)   **68**
[2004 p7.1g³ p7g* Dec 20] 1,000F: first foal: dam, 1m winner who deteriorated, half-
sister to 1¼m performer Arriving: fair form: won maiden at Lingfield by neck
from Dudley Docker: should stay 1m. *D. J. Daly*

AROGANT PRINCE   7 ch.g. Aragon 118 – Versaillesprincess (Legend of France   **66 d**
(USA) 124) [2004 73d: f7g⁴ f6g⁴ f6g f7g⁶ f6s³ f5g* f6s f5s* f6s 5s f5g 6s* f5d 5g 6f⁶ 7m
p7g p6d f6g f5g Dec 21] smallish gelding: fair performer at best: left I. Semple after

second start: won seller and handicap at Wolverhampton in February and (having left A. Carroll) apprentice handicap at Folkestone in April: below form after: probably best at 5f/6f: acts on fibresand and any turf going: usually wears headgear: often leads. *C. R. Dore*

AROUS (FR) 2 br.f. (Apr 20) Desert King (IRE) 129 – Moneefa 73 (Darshaan 133) [2004 6.1m Sep 28] small filly: fifth foal: half-sister to 6-y-o Dandoun and useful 1m/9f winner Zyzania (by Zafonic): dam 1¼m winner: 12/1, seventh in maiden at Nottingham, not knocked about: will stay at least 1m: should do better. *J. L. Dunlop* **54 p**

ARRAN 4 ch.g. Selkirk (USA) 129 – Humble Pie 92 (Known Fact (USA) 135) [2004 –: 7f 8m³ 7g f8g² f8m* p7d 8.2g⁵ 7.1g 7g Oct 11] sturdy gelding: fair handicapper: won at Southwell in July: best at 1m: raced only on all-weather and good ground or firmer. *V. Smith* **60 a67**

ARRAN SCOUT (IRE) 3 b.g. Piccolo 121 – Evie Hone (IRE) 69 (Royal Academy (USA) 130) [2004 74: 8d³ 7.9m 10s 7s² p8.6g³ f8g² Dec 7] big, strong gelding: fair maiden, lightly raced: left Mrs L. Stubbs after second start: should stay 1¼m: acts on all-weather and soft ground: blinkered (well held after absence) third outing. *K. A. Ryan* **73**

ARRESTING 4 b.g. Hector Protector (USA) 124 – Misbelief 107 (Shirley Heights 130) [2004 86+: 11.8d* 14.4v 12m⁶ 14.8m⁵ 11.8g Oct 12] leggy, useful-looking gelding: fairly useful performer: landed odds in maiden at Leicester in April: stays 1½m: acts on good to firm and good to soft ground: sold 15,000 gns, joined B. Galvin in Ireland. *J. R. Fanshawe* **92**

ARRGATT (IRE) 3 gr.c. Intikhab (USA) 135 – Nuit Chaud (USA) (Woodman (USA) 126) [2004 –p: 8m³ 10m² 11g² 8.3f* 10m⁴ a10f Dec 4] lengthy colt: fairly useful performer: won maiden at Hamilton in July: left M. Jarvis after next start: stays 11f: raced only on good ground or firmer on turf. *D. J. Selvaratnam, UAE* **86**

ARRIVATO 2 b.f. (Feb 13) Efisio 120 – Beloved Visitor (USA) 83 (Miswaki (USA) 124) [2004 p7g Oct 28] half-sister to 3 winners, notably very smart 6f winner (including at 2 yrs) Captain Rio (by Pivotal): dam Irish 2-y-o 6f winner: 28/1, ninth of 14 to Allied Cause in maiden at Lingfield, slowly away and hampered: should do better. *A. M. Balding* **61 p**

ARRJOOK 3 b.c. Intikhab (USA) 135 – Chief Ornament (USA) 88 (Chief's Crown (USA)) [2004 8m⁴ Jun 19] good-topped colt: sixth living foal: half-brother to 3 winners abroad, including UAE 7f winner Takteek (by Machiavellian): dam, 8.5f/1¼m winner, out of half-sister to champion US filly Althea and to dam of Green Desert: 33/1 and coltish, 4¾ lengths fourth to Namroc in maiden at Newmarket, keeping on from mid-field despite edging left: joined D. Selvaratnam in UAE. *A. C. Stewart* **70**

ARROW 5 b.g. Pivotal 124 – Cremets 94 (Mummy's Pet 125) [2004 –: p10g Mar 4] big gelding: lightly-raced maiden: should stay 1m: blinkered final 4-y-o start. *Mrs L. B. Normile* **45**

ARRY DASH 4 b.g. Fraam 114 – Miletrian Cares (IRE) 67 (Hamas (IRE) 125§) [2004 92: p10g⁴ 8g 10.5s² 10.1s 10m 8m³ 10g 10.1g⁶ 10g 8.2g⁶ 9d² 8s³ 9.9s² 10m³ 10.1m² 10g⁵ 8g 10g 10s* p10g Dec 18] small gelding: fairly useful performer: won minor event at Brighton in October (final run for M. Channon): effective at 1m/1¼m: acts on all-weather, soft and good to firm ground: tried visored. *C. A. Dwyer* **94**

ARTADI 2 b.f. (Apr 22) Bien Bien (USA) 125 – Gibaltarik (IRE) 68 (Jareer (USA) 115) [2004 5s 5s³ 5.3m⁵ 7m⁶ f5s⁵ 6m⁴ 7m⁶ 8g⁶ Sep 16] 7,000F, 8,000Y: small, leggy filly: sixth foal: half-sister to three 2-y-o winners: dam 2-y-o 5f winner: poor maiden: probably stayed 1m: blinkered last 4 starts: sometimes slowly away: dead. *P. M. Phelan* **48**

ARTE ET LABORE (IRE) 4 b.f. Raphane (USA) 102 – Bouffant (High Top 131) [2004 46§, a–§: f9.4s Feb 2] lengthy filly: temperamental maiden. *K. A. Ryan* **– §**

ART ELEGANT 2 b.c. (Apr 11) Desert Prince (IRE) 130 – Elegant (IRE) (Marju (IRE) 127) [2004 7m 8g⁵ 8g Sep 22] 50,000F, 58,000Y: useful-looking colt: second foal: half-brother to winner in Italy by Intikhab: dam, little form, out of half-sister to Desirable, Park Appeal, Alydaress and the dam of Russian Rhythm: fair form in maidens, fading late on last 2 starts: not sure to stay much beyond 1m: likely to do better in handicaps as 3-y-o. *B. W. Hills* **73 p**

ART EXPERT (FR) 6 b.g. Pursuit of Love 124 – Celtic Wing (Midyan (USA) 124) [2004 –§: f12g Jun 25] sturdy gelding: temperamental maiden. *Mrs N. Macauley* **– §**

ART EYES (USA) 2 ch.f. (Jan 11) Halling (USA) 133 – Careyes (IRE) (Sadler's Wells (USA) 132) [2004 7g³ Oct 11] 48,000Y: first foal: dam unraced out of half-sister to dam of High Chaparral: 8/1, 3½ lengths third of 19 to Saywaan in maiden at Leicester, **75 p**

slowly away and finishing strongly: likely to be suited by 1¼m/1½m: sure to do better. *D. R. C. Elsworth*

ARTHURS DREAM (IRE) 2 b.c. (Apr 13) Desert Prince (IRE) 130 – Blueprint **54** (USA) (Shadeed (USA) 135) [2004 6.1m 8d Nov 3] €37,000F, 60,000 2-y-o: third foal: half-brother to useful French 11f winner Toujours Amour (by Croco Rouge): dam unraced half-sister to smart performer up to 1½m Glamis: modest form in maidens, very slowly away on debut: will probably stay 1¼m. *J. G. M. O'Shea*

ARTHUR WARDLE (USA) 2 b.g. (May 12) Stravinsky (USA) 133 – Avanti Sassa **67** (GER) (Sassafras (FR) 135) [2004 6m² 6g⁵ 6f 6m⁶ 7m Sep 7] 30,000 2-y-o: half-brother to several winners in USA, including smart performer up to 11f Just Listen (by Local Talent): dam winner in USA: fair maiden: should stay 7f: visored final start: possibly none too genuine. *M. L. W. Bell*

ARTIC FOX 2 b.g. (Feb 18) Robellino (USA) 127 – Lets Be Fair 94 (Efisio 120) [2004 **58** 6s⁵ 6g 6s 7.9g 8m 7m⁵ 7s⁵ Nov 2] leggy, good-topped gelding: modest maiden: seems to stay 1m: acts on soft and good to firm going: blinkered last 3 starts: probably ungenuine. *T. D. Easterby*

ARTICULATION 3 b.c. Machiavellian (USA) 123 – Stiletta (Dancing Brave (USA) **88** 140) [2004 10m⁴ 12m² 10.5g* Aug 5] close-coupled, good-topped colt: fifth live foal: dam unraced sister to Derby winner Commander In Chief and half-sister to Warning, Deploy and Dushyantor: fairly useful form in maidens, justifying favouritism at Haydock in August by head from Countrywide Luck: stays 1½m: raced only on good/good to firm going: sold 18,000 gns. *H. R. A. Cecil*

ARTIE 5 b.g. Whittingham (IRE) 104 – Calamanco 71 (Clantime 101) [2004 88: 6g 6s **92** 5d² 5v* 5s 5d 5d* 6m 5g 6s 6d 5d 6g⁴ 5s⁵ 6s⁵ Nov 1] big, good-topped gelding: fairly useful handicapper: won at Beverley in May and York in July: creditable efforts last 3 starts: effective at 5f/6f: acts on any going: often races up with pace. *T. D. Easterby*

ARTIE'S LAD (IRE) 3 ch.g. Danehill Dancer (IRE) 117 – Bold Avril (IRE) (Persian **63** Bold 123) [2004 6s⁵ Apr 20] IR 12,500F, €26,000Y: half-brother to 3 winners, including 1¼m winner Field Master (by Foxhound): dam unraced half-sister to useful sprinter Mary Hinge: 33/1, fifth to Primo Way in maiden at Southwell, slowly away, soon close up taking good hold, and not knocked about once held. *D. Nicholls*

ARTISTICIMPRESSION (IRE) 3 b.c. Rainbow Quest (USA) 134 – Entice (FR) **–** 111 (Selkirk (USA) 129) [2004 70: p8g 10s Apr 12] good-bodied colt: maiden, well beaten in 2004: bred to be suited by 1¼m/1½m: sold 7,000 gns in July. *E. A. L. Dunlop*

ARTISTIC LAD 4 ch.c. Peintre Celebre (USA) 137 – Maid For The Hills 101 (Indian **–** Ridge 123) [2004 –: 10.3f⁵ Sep 10] lengthy colt: won maiden at Leicester on only run at 2 yrs: well held both runs since: should stay 1¼m: sold 7,500 gns. *Sir Michael Stoute*

ARTISTIC STYLE 4 b.c. Anabaa (USA) 130 – Fine Detail (IRE) 93 (Shirley Heights **98** 130) [2004 84?: 6s 8d⁶ 8.2d 8m 8m* 9m³ 10g* 9v* 10.9s* 11.9s² 10s* 12s⁶ Nov 6] rather leggy ex-French colt: useful performer: much improved in 2004, winning seller at Musselburgh in July and handicaps at Nottingham (apprentices) and Newcastle in August and Ayr in September and October (beat Reem One by 9 lengths): stays 1½m: has won on good to firm going, best efforts on softer than good. *B. Ellison*

ARTIST RIFLE (IRE) 3 b.g. Orpen (USA) 116 – Rosy Scintilla (IRE) (Thatching **–** 131) [2004 8m Jun 19] deep-girthed gelding: 12/1, not knocked about when well held in maiden at Newmarket: sold 1,000 gns in October. *J. L. Dunlop*

ARTISTRY 4 b.f. Night Shift (USA) – Arriving 105 (Most Welcome 131) [2004 64: **61** p7g* 8m⁵ 7s 7g 7m⁵ p7d² p6g p7.1g⁶ Nov 27] sturdy, lengthy filly: fair handicapper: won **a69** at Lingfield in April: races freely, and probably best around 7f: acts on polytrack and firm going, probably on soft. *B. J. Meehan*

ARTISTS RETREAT 5 ch.m. Halling (USA) 133 – Jumairah Sunset 67 (Be My **–** Guest (USA) 126) [2004 10.2m 9.9s Aug 29] tall, leggy mare: of little account nowadays. *B. D. Leavy*

ART LEGEND 2 b.g. (Mar 1) Indian Ridge 123 – Solo Performance (IRE) 72 **41** (Sadler's Wells (USA) 132) [2004 5d⁴ 6m 8.1d p8g p8m Dec 8] poor maiden: stays 1m. *D. R. C. Elsworth*

ART ROYAL (USA) 2 b.c. (Apr 19) Royal Academy (USA) 130 – Chelsea Green **73** (USA) (Key To The Mint (USA)) [2004 7m⁵ 7g Oct 1] $62,000F, €64,000Y: well-made colt: fourth foal: dam, 6f to 9f winner in USA, half-sister to dam of US Grade 1 1¼m winner Chelsey Flower: much better effort in maidens when fifth at Leicester: should stay 1m. *Mrs A. J. Perrett*

ART TRADER (USA) 3 b.c. Arch (USA) 127 – Math (USA) (Devil's Bag (USA)) **109**
[2004 95p: 10g² 9.9m* Jul 29] big, good-topped colt: has a quick action: useful form:
justified strong support in ladbrokes.com Stakes (Handicap) at Goodwood in July by 1¼
lengths from Fine Silver, travelling well and quickening to lead final 2f: stays 1¼m: acts
on good to firm going, below form on good to soft: reportedly sold, and joined J. Moore
in Hong Kong. *Mrs A. J. Perrett*

ARTURIUS (IRE) 2 b.c. (Apr 2) Anabaa (USA) 130 – Steeple (Selkirk (USA) 129) **62 p**
[2004 7s⁶ Oct 27] 230,000Y: third foal: half-brother to French 1m/9f winner Royal Puck'r
(by Bering): dam, French 9f winner, closely related to smart performers around 1m
Soprano and Enharmonic: 7/1, sixth of 14 to Plea Bargain in maiden at Yarmouth, slowly
away, green and not knocked about: should stay 1m: sure to do better. *Sir Michael Stoute*

ARTZOLA (IRE) 4 b.f. Alzao (USA) 117 – Polistatic 53 (Free State 125) [2004 –: **44**
p8g p10d p7g 10m Sep 25] good-bodied filly: poor maiden: should prove best around
1¼m: acts on polytrack and good to firm going. *C. A. Horgan*

ASAATEEL (IRE) 2 br.c. (Apr 11) Unfuwain (USA) 131 – Alabaq (USA) 111 (River- **61**
man (USA) 131) [2004 7m 8.1d 8.1s⁴ 7.1d Sep 18] modest maiden: stays 1m: acts on soft
going, probably on good to firm. *J. L. Dunlop*

ASADARA 2 ch.f. (Apr 14) Timeless Times (USA) 99 – Julie's Gift (Presidium 124) **53 ?**
[2004 5m⁶ Jul 25] first foal: dam, ran twice, out of half-sister to Irish 2000 Guineas
winner Dara Monarch: 100/1, sixth in maiden at Pontefract, slowly away. *N. Bycroft*

ASALEEB 3 b.f. Alhaarth (IRE) 126 – Gharam (USA) 108 (Green Dancer (USA) 132) **86**
[2004 79p: 10m² 11.5m* 12g² 12m Sep 4] lengthy, good-topped filly: fairly useful
performer, lightly raced: won 3-runner maiden at Yarmouth (final start for A. Stewart) in
July and handicap at Salisbury in August: likely to stay beyond 1½m: raced only on good/
good to firm going. *E. F. Vaughan*

ASAWER (IRE) 2 b.f. (Apr 7) Darshaan 133 – Sassy Bird (USA) (Storm Bird (CAN) **82 p**
134) [2004 8s³ Oct 22] 600,000Y: sixth foal: half-sister to 3 winners abroad, including
smart French 6f/7f performer Chercheuse (by Seeking The Gold) and French 15f winner
Taste The Stars (by Benny The Dip): dam, lightly raced in USA, sister to high-class 7f/
1m performer Mukaddamah: 13/2, 3 lengths third of 11 to Her Own Kind in maiden at
Doncaster, slowly away and green: will be suited by 1¼m/1½m: should do better.
Sir Michael Stoute

ASBO 4 b.f. Abou Zouz (USA) 109 – Star 83 (Most Welcome 131) [2004 54: 6m⁵ 6m⁴ **66**
6s³ 6.1d⁵ 6g⁶ p6g³ p7g⁴ p7.1g* Nov 20] leggy, workmanlike filly: fair maiden: effective
at 6f/7f: acts on polytrack, soft and good to firm going. *Dr J. D. Scargill*

ASCENMOOR 4 b.g. Mistertopogigo (IRE) 118 – Asmarina 50 (Ascendant 96) [2004 **–**
f7g Dec 12] well held in claimer at Southwell. *S. R. Bowring*

ASCERTAIN (IRE) 3 ch.g. Intikhab (USA) 135 – Self Assured (IRE) 97 (Ahonoora **108**
122) [2004 79: p10g* p10g² p8g* a9f⁵ a8.5s⁶ a8.5f⁶ a9f⁵ Aug 21] useful performer:
successful at Lingfield in handicap in January and minor event in February: good head
second to Skidmark in handicap there in between: respectable 6 lengths fifth to Lundy's
Liability in UAE Derby at Nad Al Sheba fourth start, then left N. Littmoden: well held in
varied company in US: effective at 1m/1¼m: acts on polytrack/dirt. *N. M. O'Callaghan,*
USA

AS HANDSOME DOES 2 ch.g. (Jun 2) Handsome Ridge 121 – Fast To Light (Pharly **59**
(FR) 130) [2004 6g² 6g 6d 7f Sep 2] sparely-made gelding: modest maiden: form on first
and final starts only: should stay 1m: tongue tied. *N. Tinkler*

ASHARON 2 b.c. (Jan 23) Efisio 120 – Arriving 105 (Most Welcome 131) [2004 8.2g **75**
8s⁶ 8m⁶ 8m 5.2s⁵ 7s p7g² p7.1g² Nov 20] 25,000Y: sturdy colt: third foal: half-brother to
3-y-o Attune and 4-y-o Artistry: dam 1¼m/11f winner: fair maiden: second in nurseries
at Lingfield and Wolverhampton: stays 1m: acts on polytrack, soft and good to firm
going: ran as if amiss fourth/sixth outings. *C. E. Brittain*

ASH BOLD (IRE) 7 ch.g. Persian Bold 123 – Pasadena Lady (Captain James 123) **47**
[2004 8.5d⁴ 8s² 9.1s p8.6g³ f8g f7g⁵ Dec 16] poor maiden: stays 1m: acts on all-weather
and soft ground: tried blinkered/in cheekpieces. *B. Ellison*

ASHDOWN EXPRESS (IRE) 5 ch.g. Ashkalani (IRE) 128 – Indian Express 61 **122**
(Indian Ridge 123) [2004 117: 6g³ 6s 6m² 6f 6g² 6.5g⁴ 6g 6v 6d Oct 15] sturdy, lengthy
gelding: very smart performer: 100/1, best effort when neck second to Frizzante in July
Cup at Newmarket fifth start: creditable ¾-length fourth to Somnus in Prix Maurice de
Gheest at Deauville month later: badly short of room 1f out and couldn't recover when

Mr W. J. P. Jackson's "Ashdown Express"

behind in Sprinters Stakes at Nakayama penultimate start: below form in Bentinck Stakes at Newmarket final outing: races freely, and better around 6f than 7f: acts on firm and good to soft going, well held on soft/heavy: blinkered (below form) once: often sweats: oftens wears crossed noseband/goes early to post: held up. *C. F. Wall*

ASHES (IRE) 2 b.f. (Feb 6) General Monash (USA) 107 – Wakayi 87 (Persian Bold 123) [2004 5g 6s⁵ 5m⁴ 5g 6d⁵ 5.1v⁶ p5.1g³ p6g³ p5.1g* Dec 13] €8,000Y: good-topped filly: half-sister to several winners, including 5-y-o Royal Storm: dam, 2-y-o 5f winner, half-sister to smart sprinter Reesh: modest performer: won maiden at Wolverhampton in December: barely stays 6f: acts on polytrack, heavy and good to firm ground: blinkered (well beaten) fourth start. *K. R. Burke*   **56 a62**

ASH HAB (USA) 6 b.g. A P Indy (USA) 131 – Histoire (FR) (Riverman (USA) 131) [2004 14.1g p16g p16g Sep 18] no longer of any account. *A. B. Haynes*   **–**

ASHKAL WAY (IRE) 2 ch.c. (Jan 31) Ashkalani (IRE) 128 – Golden Way (IRE) 94 (Cadeaux Genereux 131) [2004 8g⁵ Sep 20] compact colt: first foal: dam 1¼m winner: 25/1 and in need of race, close fifth to Australian in maiden at Kempton, leading briefly 1f out: should stay 1¼m: sold 20,000 gns: likely to improve. *E. A. L. Dunlop*   **77 p**

ASH LADDIE (IRE) 4 ch.g. Ashkalani (IRE) 128 – Lady Ellen 67 (Horage 124) [2004 60: 7g 9f 8.1m f8m 7.9m Sep 11] lengthy, useful-looking gelding: poor maiden: left E. Alston after fourth outing: wore cheekpieces/blinkers last 3 starts. *J. S. Wainwright*   **–**

ASHSTANZA 3 gr.g. Ashkalani (IRE) 128 – Poetry In Motion (IRE) 76 (Ballad Rock 122) [2004 60: p8g⁴ f11g³ f12g⁴ 10d 8.1d 6f p7g Oct 31] smallish, well-made gelding: modest maiden: left M. Jarvis and off 4½ months before tailed off final start: stays 11f: acts on all-weather (no form on turf): tried in cheekpieces/blinkers: found little second/ third outings. *Mrs L. Richards*   **– a63**

ASHTAROUTE (USA)   4 b.f. Holy Bull (USA) 134 – Beating The Buzz (IRE) 96   –
(Bluebird (USA) 125) [2004 60?: f16g⁶ 12m 16.2d⁵ Jul 3] little solid form: tends to
wander/carry head awkwardly. *M. C. Chapman*

ASHTREE BELLE   5 b.m. Up And At 'em 109 – Paris Babe 94 (Teenoso (USA) 135)   **87**
[2004 84: f7g² Jan 2] fairly useful handicapper: good second at Wolverhampton only
outing in 2004: best at 7f: acts on all-weather, good to firm and good to soft going:
sometimes slowly away/races freely: consistent. *D. Haydn Jones*

ASHWAAQ (USA)   3 b.f. Gone West (USA) – Wasnah (USA) 96 (Nijinsky (CAN)   **74**
138) [2004 81p: 8g² 7d 8g Oct 4] big, good-topped filly: has scope: fair performer: won
maiden at Ripon in April: stays 1m: raced only on good/good to soft going: visits
Noverre. *J. L. Dunlop*

ASIAN HEIGHTS   6 b.h. Hernando (FR) 127 – Miss Rinjani 83 (Shirley Heights 130)   –
[2004 123: 12v Oct 23] leggy, quite attractive horse: has a quick action: very smart
performer at best: reported in May to have thrown a splint, and virtually pulled up in St
Simon Stakes at Newbury on belated return: stays 13.4f: acts on good to firm going,
probably on heavy: has awkward head carriage but seems genuine: held up. *G. Wragg*

ASIAN TIGER (IRE)   2 b.c. (Apr 12) Rossini (USA) 118 – Dry Lightning 63   **82**
(Shareef Dancer (USA) 135) [2004 5s² 5g² 5m⁵ 6g³ 7g⁵ p7g 6m* Aug 16] 32,000Y: good
sort: third foal: half-brother to winners around 7f in Italy by Victory Note and Russian
Revival: dam 1¼m winner: fairly useful performer: made hard work of winning maiden
at Brighton: likely to prove best at 6f/7f: acts on soft ground: sold 9,500 gns, sent to
Austria. *R. Hannon*

ASIATIC   3 ch.c. Lomitas 129 – Potri Pe (ARG) (Potrillazo (ARG)) [2004 81p: 12.3d²   **92**
11.9d 12m 11.6f⁴ Jul 5] lengthy, angular colt: fairly useful performer: best effort when
second in handicap at Chester: stays 1½m: acts on good to firm and good to soft going:
sold 27,000 gns, sent to UAE. *M. Johnston*

ASIA WINDS (IRE)   3 ch.f. Machiavellian (USA) 123 – Ascot Cyclone (USA) 93   **90**
(Rahy (USA) 115) [2004 95: 10.4s⁵ 8.1m 7g 7g Oct 1] close-coupled filly: fairly useful
performer: off over 3 months after second outing: stays 1m: acts on firm and good to soft
ground. *B. W. Hills*

ASK FOR RAIN   2 gr.f. (Apr 4) Green Desert (USA) 127 – Requesting (Rainbow   **66 p**
Quest (USA) 134) [2004 7g 6g³ Sep 17] rather leggy filly: second foal: dam unraced
half-sister to very smart 1¼m filly Last Second and to dams of Alborada, Albanova,
Quarter Moon and 4-y-o Yesterday: better effort in maidens when third to Newsround at
Newbury: should stay 1m: likely to improve. *B. W. Hills*

ASK FOR THE MOON (FR)   3 ch.f. Dr Fong (USA) 128 – Lune Rouge (IRE)   **110**
(Unfuwain (USA) 131) [2004 10d* 10.5d* 10.5g* 10g* 10.5g Jun 13] €110,000Y: first

Prix Saint-Alary, Longchamp—
Ask For The Moon provides 2004's French champion jockey Ioritz Mendizabal with his
only Group 1 success of the year; Asti (second left) takes the runner-up spot ahead of Agata (right)

foal: dam useful French 1¼m winner: smart performer: won minor events at Lyon Parilly in 2003, Salon-de-Provence in February and Saint-Cloud in March, Prix Penelope at Saint-Cloud (by 2 lengths from Super Lina) in April and Prix Saint-Alary at Longchamp in May: beat Asti by a neck in last-named event, leading ½f out despite carrying head awkwardly and idling: respectable seventh to Latice in Prix de Diane at Chantilly after: stays 10.5f: raced only on good ground or softer: sent to USA. *J-C. Rouget, France*

ASK THE CLERK (IRE) 3 b.g. Turtle Island (IRE) 123 – Some Fun (Wolverlife   **86**
115) [2004 74: p7g f6g³ p5g⁵ f5g 6s* 6d 6s² 6.1s 6f³ 6m⁴ 7m⁶ 6m⁴ 7g³ 6f³ 6g 6d⁵ 6m⁴ 7g² 7d 8.5g 7g³ 7s³ 7s* Oct 27] close-coupled gelding: fairly useful handicapper: left H. Collingridge after fourth start: won at Folkestone in March and Yarmouth in October: best at 6f/7f: acts on any turf going: tried in cheekpieces/blinkers, not after reappearance. *V. Smith*

ASK THE DRIVER 3 b.g. Ashkalani (IRE) 128 – Tithcar 67 (Cadeaux Genereux   **58**
131) [2004 51: 8.2g² 8s⁴ p10g³ 8g³ 10g p10g 8g⁵ Sep 27] lengthy gelding: modest maiden: stays easy 1¼m: blinkered (not discredited) final start: sometimes slowly away. *D. J. S. ffrench Davis*

ASKWITH (IRE) 2 b.g. (Apr 7) Marju (IRE) 127 – Hayward 81 (Indian Ridge 123)   **63**
[2004 7g⁵ 7d³ 7.5m Sep 15] 15,000Y: workmanlike gelding: third foal: dam Irish 9.6f winner: modest form in maidens: should stay at least 1¼m: well below best on good to firm going. *J. D. Bethell*

ASPEN RIDGE (IRE) 2 ch.f. (Mar 3) Namid 128 – Longueville Lady (IRE) (Hamas   **58**
(IRE) 125§) [2004 5g 5g p6d 6.1d 6g⁵ f6g Nov 9] €20,000Y: neat filly: first foal: dam 1m winner in Scandinavia: modest maiden: will probably stay 7f. *C. Tinkler*

ASPIRED (IRE) 3 b.f. Mark of Esteem (IRE) 137 – Dreams 88 (Rainbow Quest (USA)   **57**
134) [2004 10f 9.9d Aug 11] fourth foal: half-sister to useful winner around 1¼m First Fantasy (by Be My Chief): dam, untrustworthy 1¼m winner, half-sister to Melbourne Cup winner Jeune and smart winner up to 1½m Beneficial: modest form in maiden at Windsor on debut: hung left and virtually unrideable subsequent outing, eventually pulled up. *J. R. Fanshawe*

ASSOON 5 b.g. Ezzoud (IRE) 126 – Handy Dancer 87 (Green God 128) [2004 64: 7m   **65**
18d³ Aug 19] fair maiden: stays 2¼m: acts on firm and good to soft going: wore cheek-pieces (ran well, though looked difficult ride) final start: fair hurdler. *G. L. Moore*

ASSURED (IRE) 2 ch.f. (Mar 14) Shinko Forest (IRE) – Errazuriz (IRE) 94 (Classic   **–**
Music (USA)) [2004 7m 6g 8.2m p7.1g Oct 18] 8,000F: workmanlike filly: fourth foal: half-sister to an Italian 1m winner by Mukaddamah and 4-y-o Evangelist: dam Irish 2-y-o 1m winner: well held in maidens/seller: tried in cheekpieces/blinkers. *P. W. D'Arcy*

ASTEEM 2 b.g. (Apr 30) Mark of Esteem (IRE) 137 – Amidst 86 (Midyan (USA) 124)   **53**
[2004 6m 6d⁵ 6.1d 7.1m 6m Sep 23] modest maiden: should stay 1m: best efforts on good to soft going. *R. F. Johnson Houghton*

ASTON LAD 3 b.c. Bijou d'Inde 127 – Fishki 36 (Niniski (USA) 125) [2004 10.1m⁴   **55**
10m⁶ 13.8m⁶ 9d² 9.9d⁵ 14.1g 9.2d⁵ 10s Oct 30] half-brother to 2 winners, including 4-y-o Green 'n' Gold: dam, 11.5f to 15f winner, also won over jumps: modest maiden: should stay 1½m (seemed not to stay 1¾m): form only on good to soft going. *M. D. Hammond*

ASTRAC (IRE) 13 b.g. Nordico (USA) – Shirleen (Daring Display (USA) 129) [2004   **56**
58: 5d⁵ f6g 6.1s 7.1m² 6g⁴ 7m 6m 5.7f 5m⁴ 6d Oct 2] sturdy gelding: one-time smart performer, winner of 17 of his 122 starts: just modest in later years: said to have finished lame final outing and reportedly retired: effective at 5f to 7.5f: acted on fibresand, firm and soft going: blinkered once: thought to be the first horse to have run at every Flat course in Britain. *Mrs A. L. M. King*

ASTRAL PRINCE 6 ch.g. Efisio 120 – Val d'Erica 119 (Ashmore (FR) 125) [2004   **45 §**
53§: 8s⁵ 12d⁶ May 4] strong gelding: poor performer on Flat in 2004 (won over fences in May): stays 1¼m: acts on fibresand and good to firm going, probably on soft: sometimes blinkered: tried tongue tied: has taken good hold: not one to trust. *Mrs K. Walton*

ASTROCHARM (IRE) 5 b.m. Charnwood Forest (IRE) 125 – Charm The Stars   **105**
(Roi Danzig (USA)) [2004 85: 8g⁵ 12m* 12m 10m⁵ 11.9g* 12g² 12m* 14m* 14.6m 12f⁵ Sep 24] leggy mare: has a round action: useful performer: won handicaps at Newmarket and Haydock, minor event at Pontefract and Vodafone Fillies' Stakes (Lillie Langtry) at Goodwood (beat Pongee by ¾ length) between May and July: not discredited in Park Hill Stakes at Doncaster penultimate start: stays 1¾m: acts on firm and good to soft ground: tried blinkered, better form when not: usually held up. *M. H. Tompkins*

ASTROMANCER (USA) 4 b. or br.f. Silver Hawk (USA) 123 – Colour Dance (Rain-   **55**
bow Quest (USA) 134) [2004 62: p12g p16g⁴ 14.1g⁵ 16d 13.1f 13.9m³ 14.1g* 14.1m
16.2g³ 15.8g p13.9g⁵ p16g⁴ p16.5g Dec 4] rather leggy filly: modest handicapper: won at
Redcar in June: stays easy 2m: acts on polytrack, good to firm and good to soft ground:
tried blinkered. *M. H. Tompkins*

ASTRONOMIC 4 b.g. Zafonic (USA) 130 – Sky Love (USA) 93 (Nijinsky (CAN)   **–**
138) [2004 106: 11.9d Jul 9] useful performer: won handicap at Maisons-Laffitte in 2003:
left A. Fabre in France 190,000 gns and off nearly 9 months, well held in handicap at York
only run in 2004: stays 1¼m: raced only on good/good to soft ground: fairly useful
hurdler. *J. Howard Johnson*

ASTRONOMICAL (IRE) 2 b.c. (Apr 13) Mister Baileys 123 – Charm The Stars (Roi   **74 p**
Danzig (USA)) [2004 7s³ 8g Sep 30] 14,000Y: strong, close-coupled colt: has a quick
action: fourth foal: half-brother to 5-y-o Astrocharm and 3-y-o Sand And Stars: dam, ran
twice, out of half-sister to Breeders' Cup Turf winner Northern Spur and high-class stayer
Kneller: fair form in maidens at Salisbury (close third to Brecon) and Newmarket: will
stay at least 1¼m: open to improvement. *B. W. Hills*

ASTYANAX (IRE) 4 b.c. Hector Protector (USA) 124 – Craigmill 85 (Slip Anchor   **90**
136) [2004 81: 14.1d 16.2g⁵ 16.2m 14.1m* 15.9s 16g² 16g* 18s Oct 16] lengthy colt:
fairly useful handicapper: won at Yarmouth (ladies event, for second successive year) in
August and Musselburgh in September: stays 2m: acts on fibresand and good to firm
going, well held on softer than good: often races prominently: sold 75,000 gns, joined
N. Henderson. *Sir Mark Prescott*

ASWAN (IRE) 6 ch.g. Ashkalani (IRE) 128 – Ghariba 112 (Final Straw 127) [2004 78:   **69**
10m⁵ 8.5g³ 8.5g 7.1d 8g 7m p9.5g⁶ p9.5g* p7.1g Dec 20] sturdy gelding: fair handicapper: won at Wolverhampton in December: effective at 1m/1¼m: acts on polytrack and
firm going, no form on softer than good: tried blinkered: usually tongue tied: often races
freely and has carried head high/found little. *S. R. Bowring*

ATACAMA STAR 2 ch.g. (Apr 9) Desert King (IRE) 129 – Aunty (FR) 114 (Riverman   **77**
(USA) 131) [2004 7g 6m² 7g Oct 12] 10,000 2-y-o: close-coupled, workmanlike gelding:
half-brother to several winners, including Irish 1988 2-y-o 5f/6f winner Kyra (by Sadler's
Wells) and 5f (at 2 yrs) and 6f winner Dame Laura (by Royal Academy), both useful:
dam, French 1¼m winner, half-sister to Ebor winner Crazy: best effort when second in
claimer at Lingfield: slowly away final outing: should stay 7f. *B. G. Powell*

ATAHUELPA 4 b.g. Hernando (FR) 127 – Certain Story (Known Fact (USA) 135)   **80**
[2004 90: a13f 8d p8g 8g³ 11.5m³ Aug 6] compact gelding: fairly useful performer: left
M. Harris after third start: stays 11.5f: acts on fibresand, soft and good to firm ground:
races prominently: fairly useful hurdler. *A. King*

ATAVUS 7 b.h. Distant Relative 128 – Elysian 94 (Northfields (USA)) [2004 104: 7.9s   **97**
7m⁶ 7m 7.1m⁵ 7g 7f 6g² 6m⁶ 7g Sep 30] sturdy horse: poor mover: useful performer: won
9 of his 55 races: creditable efforts in 2004 in Victoria Cup at Ascot (sixth to Mine) on
second outing and ½-length second to Prince Aaron in listed race at Newmarket: effective
at 6f to 1m: acted on firm and good to soft going: blinkered (well held) once: sometimes
slowly away/edged right: usually made running: none too consistent: reportedly retired.
G. G. Margarson

A TEEN 6 ch.h. Presidium 124 – Very Good (Noalto 120) [2004 73, a58: p6g⁵ p6g² p6g   **59**
p6g* p6g⁶ 6s⁶ 6g 6g 6m⁶ 6f 6m 6g 6d⁵ 5d⁶ 6.1g 6g 5.7s p7.1d⁶ p6g³ p7m f5g³ f6g p6g⁶
Dec 20] modest handicapper: won at Lingfield in February: effective at 5f, barely at 7f:
acts on all-weather, firm and good to soft ground, probably on soft: tried blinkered earlier
in career: has carried head high. *P. Howling*

ATHBOY 3 ch.g. Entrepreneur 123 – Glorious (Nashwan (USA) 135) [2004 55: p10g   **74**
p8g* p7g* p8g p8g 8.1s Sep 20] fair performer: won 2 handicaps at Lingfield in February:
effective at 7f/1m: acts on polytrack, tailed off on turf debut final start: visored last 5
outings. *M. J. Wallace*

ATHBOY NIGHTS (IRE) 2 b.f. (May 2) Night Shift (USA) – Missing Love (IRE)   **62**
(Thatching 131) [2004 6g 6.1v p6g³ p5.1g³ p5.1g³ p6g⁴ Dec 30] 42,000Y: sturdy filly:
half-sister to several winners, including fairly useful Irish 6f (at 2 yrs)/7f winner Anthem
of Love (by Silver Hawk), later successful in USA, and Irish 1m to 1½m winner Rumours
Abound (by With Approval): dam Irish 6f winner: modest maiden: stays easy 6f: acts on
polytrack. *M. J. Wallace*

ATHOLLBROSE (USA) 3 b.g. Mister Baileys 123 – Knightly Cut Up (USA) (Gold   **55**
Crest (USA) 120) [2004 57: 10s⁴ 9.9s² 12.6s⁴ 9.9g⁵ 8.5m⁴ 8g 8.5g 10f³ Sep 13] useful-

looking gelding: unimpressive mover: modest maiden: stays 1½m: acts on fibresand, firm and soft going: blinkered last 2 starts: sold 4,100 gns. *T. D. Easterby*

ATLANTIC ACE   7 b.g. First Trump 118 – Risalah (Marju (IRE) 127) [2004 95: 8g 8d 8m 8m⁶ 8.5g 8d 8g 8g 7.5m 8m p8.6g² p8.6g² f8g Dec 16] good-topped gelding: just fair performer nowadays: effective at 7f to 9f: acts on all-weather, best turf form on good ground or firmer: sometimes wears cheekpieces: sometimes slowly away: usually held up. *B. Smart*   **71**

ATLANTIC BREEZE   3 br.f. Deploy 131 – Atlantic Air (Air Trooper 115) [2004 65: f9.4g f11g f7g 10d 10s f12d³ 10s May 7] quite good-topped filly: poor handicapper: probably stays 1½m: acts on fibresand and soft going: visored on reappearance, wore cheekpieces (found little) final outing: unreliable. *Mrs N. Macauley*   **46 §**

ATLANTIC CITY   3 ch.g. First Trump 118 – Pleasuring 68 (Good Times (ITY)) [2004 71: 10.1m² 10m⁵ p12g p10g⁴ p12g² p12m³ Dec 22] quite good-topped, attractive gelding: fair maiden: left W. Haggas after second start: stays 1½m: raced only on polytrack/good to firm ground: has worn cheekpieces: sometimes looks none too keen. *Mrs L. Richards*   **73**

ATLANTIC QUEST (USA)   5 b. or br.g. Woodman (USA) 126 – Pleasant Pat (USA) (Pleasant Colony (USA)) [2004 90: 7g 7d⁵ 10.3g 7m 7m* 8m⁵ 8m 7.2g 8.5m 8m⁴ p7.1g* p8.6g⁶ p8m p7.1g³ Dec 31] rather leggy, close-coupled gelding: fairly useful performer: won minor event at Thirsk in May and (having left G. Harker) handicap at Wolver-hampton in November: effective at 7f to 9f: acts on polytrack, firm and good to soft going: often visored/in cheekpieces (including for last 5 wins): tends to wander/carry head high. *K. R. Burke*   **88**

ATLANTIC STORY (USA)   2 b. or br.c. (Apr 22) Stormy Atlantic (USA) – Story Book Girl (USA) (Siberian Express (USA) 125) [2004 7d 7g* 8d² Oct 14] $300,000 2-y-o: angular, good-topped colt: has scope: has a short, quick action: second foal: dam unraced: won maiden at Epsom in August: improved again when head second to Danehill Willy in nursery at Newmarket, travelling smoothly in front until tiring late on: likely to prove best up to 1m: should make a useful handicapper at least at 3 yrs. *Saeed bin Suroor*   **94 p**

ATLANTIC TERN   3 b.c. Atraf 116 – Great Tern 59 (Simply Great (FR) 122) [2004 –: p10g⁶ p10g 10.3g Mar 26] big, close-coupled colt: little form. *N. M. Babbage*   **–**

ATLANTIC VIKING (IRE)   9 b.g. Danehill (USA) 126 – Hi Bettina 96 (Henbit (USA) 130) [2004 103: 5m 5m 5m⁴ 5d 5m 5.7m* 6m⁴ 5g* 5.6m Sep 8] well-made gelding: useful performer: won claimer at Bath and handicap at Epsom (beat Texas Gold by ½ length) in August: best at 5f/easy 6f: has form on soft ground, best recent efforts on good or firmer: tried blinkered/visored, not in 2004: sometimes wanders: none too consistent. *D. Nicholls*   **99**

ATLANTIC WALTZ   4 b.g. Singspiel (IRE) 133 – Fascination Waltz 83 (Shy Groom (USA)) [2004 10d Apr 24] 100/1 and tongue tied, tailed off in maiden at Leicester. *J. J. Sheehan*   **–**

ATRIFFIC STORY   2 ch.g. (May 16) Atraf 116 – Composition 82 (Wolfhound (USA) 126) [2004 6s Nov 6] 10,500Y: strong gelding: second foal: half-brother to 4-y-o Ephesus: dam, 2-y-o 6f winner, out of sister to smart sprinter Jester: 33/1 and green, slightly hampered when tenth of 21 to Bow Wave in maiden at Doncaster: should do better. *Miss Gay Kelleway*   **61 p**

ATSOS (IRE)   2 b.g. (May 6) Imperial Ballet (IRE) 110 – Victim of Love 75 (Damister (USA) 123) [2004 5v⁶ 5g⁶ 6m 5.1m⁵ 5.7g⁶ 7m Sep 22] close-coupled gelding: third foal: half-brother to 2002 2-y-o 5f seller winner G I Bride (by General Monash): dam 7f winner, including at 2 yrs: modest maiden: stays 5.7f: acts on good to firm going: sold 6,500 gns, sent to Belgium. *R. Hannon*   **61**

ATTACCA   3 b.g. Piccolo 121 – Jubilee Place (IRE) 76 (Prince Sabo 123) [2004 78: 8g⁶ 6g 6d 8m 6d 6g Sep 25] tall, quite good-topped gelding: just modest handicapper nowadays: best form at 6f: acts on good to firm ground: usually wears cheekpieces/blinkers. *J. R. Weymes*   **56**

ATTACK MINDED   3 ch.g. Timeless Times (USA) 99 – French Ginger 66 (Most Welcome 131) [2004 –: 8g Sep 14] well held in 2 maidens: looked difficult ride on debut. *L. R. James*   **–**

ATTILA THE HUN   5 b.g. Piccolo 121 – Katya (IRE) 93 (Dancing Dissident (USA) 119) [2004 –: 5s⁴ 5m⁶ 5m 5g⁵ Jun 3] poor maiden: best at 5f: acts on fibresand: tried visored/in cheekpieces. *F. Watson*   **33**

ATTISHOE   2 b.f. (May 4) Atraf 116 – Royal Shoe (Hotfoot 126) [2004 5g 6m Sep 7] half-sister to winner around 1½m Princess Moodyshoe (by Jalmood): dam winning jumper: poor form in maidens at Windsor and Lingfield. *Miss B. Sanders*   **40**

ATTORNEY 6 ch.g. Wolfhound (USA) 126 – Princess Sadie 86 (Shavian 125) [2004 **56**
62d: f6g³ f6g f6g* p6g f6s f6s⁴ f5s f6s f5s⁶ f6s⁵ p6g³ f6g p6g f5g* p6g* 5.1d² f5d 5.7m³ **a60**
6g⁶ 6d⁶ 6g⁵ 6.1g f5g f6m 6d⁶ 5d 6m f5g f5g² Dec 21] tall gelding: modest performer:
won banded events at Wolverhampton in January and Southwell/Lingfield in April: left
D. Shaw before final start: effective at 5f/6f: acts on all-weather, soft and good to firm
going: tried blinkered, usually visored nowadays: often gets behind. *R. A. Harris*

ATTRACTION 3 b.f. Efisio 120 – Flirtation (Pursuit of Love 124) [2004 118: **125**
8m* 8m* 8m* 8m² 8d 8m² 8g* Oct 2]
　　　　There wasn't a three-year-old filly in Europe to touch Attraction at a mile in
the latest season, when she completed the unique treble of One Thousand Guineas,
Irish One Thousand Guineas and Coronation Stakes. Victory in the last-named
cemented her position as one of the most popular fillies for years and crowned a
remarkable story. The Coronation Stakes extended an unbeaten run which stretched
back to Attraction's very first racecourse appearance in April 2003 in a lowly
median auction event at Nottingham. The imperfect conformation of Attraction's
forelegs (particularly her off-fore)—a subject well-nigh done to death in the media
as she rose through the ranks—meant that her owner/breeder did not consider
submitting her at any of the yearling sales. After John Hills—charged 'to win a little
race'—was unable to find an owner or a syndicate to lease her, Attraction was taken
back and sent instead to race in her owner/breeder's colours with Mark Johnston,
who was given the more ambitious brief of 'winning a race and then getting black
type.' Attraction's achievements rightly saw the racing public take her to their
hearts, but also resulted in her place in racing history being exaggerated for years.
One senior writer, harking back to Sceptre and Pretty Polly early in the twentieth
century, claimed after Royal Ascot that 'Attraction deserves comparison with the
great fillies of all time,' while another ranked her 'among the very best fillies of
modern times.' Even someone with long experience could perhaps be forgiven for
being guilty of over-enthusiasm immediately after Attraction's striking victory, but
the praise came with some misplaced criticism for 'those applying the slide-rule'
and using 'cold, soulless mathematics' to assess the 'wonder filly'. Such remarks
were heard less often once Attraction met her first defeat.
　　　　Having achieved his first task with Attraction on her racecourse debut,
Mark Johnston went on to achieve the second—Attraction adding a victory at
Thirsk in the interim—in the listed Hilary Needler Trophy at Beverley. Even better
was to come when Attraction was stepped up to pattern company at two, first at
Royal Ascot, then at the Newmarket July meeting. She produced the best performance seen in the Queen Mary Stakes for some time and recorded an even more
crushing victory in the Cherry Hinton, her Timeform rating of 118 after the latter
placing her among the most highly-rated two-year-old fillies seen out by the end of
July in over twenty years. Only Ma Biche, rated 120 in 1982 after a victory over the
colts in the Prix Robert Papin, and Circus Ring, rated 122 following a runaway win
in the 1981 Princess Margaret Stakes, had been rated more highly in fairly recent
times. However, nothing went right for Attraction after the Cherry Hinton and she
wasn't seen again that season. Her training was interrupted by various problems
including an overreach (suffered whilst swimming) and then, towards the end of
September, a cracked pedal bone in her near-hind foot put paid to plans for the
Cheveley Park.
　　　　Attraction's rating in *Racehorses of 2003* prompted a question about the
fall in the number of two-year-olds rated 120 or more in the Timeform annuals,
compared to twenty years or so ago. The nature of two-year-old racing—starting
with a crop of immature, unraced horses—has always dictated that form builds up
through the season as the better horses mature and other good animals begin to
appear. Attraction's form to the end of July still ranked her head and shoulders
above the other two-year-old fillies seen out by the end of the season, but it was
possible that, had she stayed sound and thrashed her rivals in similar style in the big
races in the autumn, her rating in *Racehorses of 2003* would have been higher. On
the general issue, the fall in the numbers of highly-rated two-year-olds is linked to a
change in emphasis, which began during the 'eighties and has continued since, on
having thoroughbreds at their peak more as three- and four-year-olds than as two-
and three-year-olds. This has been the result of a shift in priorities among many of

the top owners and trainers, some of whom regard a high level of success by a horse as a juvenile as less important nowadays. The increased globalisation of racing has probably had something to do with the change, most of the relatively newly-created big international events being for three-year-olds and older horses.

With Timeform ratings for two-year-olds, it has always been a question of putting them into the context of the juvenile population as a whole. If a two-year-old is rated too highly at the end of its juvenile campaign, it becomes apparent when it runs the following season. It became clear in the 'eighties that some of the leading two-year-olds weren't training on so well as previously. The level of the three-year-old ratings—and thereby indirectly the ratings of the two-year-olds—was also lowered as a consequence of the Timeform weight-for-age scale being amended in favour of the older horses in 1990. There hasn't been much fluctuation since in the overall level of Timeform ratings and there were actually more horses rated 120+ in the six editions of *Racehorses* from 1998 to 2003 than there were in the six editions between 1990 and 1995. The most marked change has been between three-year-olds and older horses. In *Racehorses of 1990*, for example, there were thirty-seven three-year-olds rated 120+ and twenty-five older horses (total sixty-two); in *Racehorses of 2003* there were only twenty-seven three-year-olds at 120+, but no fewer than fifty-two older horses (total seventy-nine). There has been a marked knock-on effect on the number of highly-rated two-year-olds, the relative weakness of two-year-old racing evidenced, for example, by the fact that Aidan O'Brien, one trainer who campaigns his top horses in line with the 'traditional' programme, managed to win nine of the ten Group 1 races in Europe for juvenile colts in 2001.

Attraction's rating of 118 gave her a good chance on the form-book of winning the One Thousand Guineas (a reproduction of her Cherry Hinton form would, on the face of it, have been enough to win nine of the twelve previous renewals). But there were question marks over a filly who was returning from a ten-month absence in the Guineas. Had she trained on? Was she over her training troubles, in the course of which precautionary x-rays had also shown up bony changes in her knees? The owner revealed after the Guineas that veterinary advice had been received after the Cherry Hinton to retire Attraction, but in the winter and in the run-up to Newmarket the filly's preparation was reportedly straightforward. The stable issued an upbeat assessment towards the end of March, saying that Attraction was well forward and had pulled up sound after her first full-scale gallop. But perhaps the biggest imponderable was whether Attraction would be the same force stepped up to a mile. She had shown speed in abundance as a two-year-old and the majority—ourselves included—harboured doubts about her staying a mile. *Racehorses of 2003* concluded that, on pedigree, Attraction 'should stay a mile, but her style of racing suggests otherwise . . . her best prospects of adding a Group 1 race to her tally appear to lie, not in the classics, but in the top sprints.'

With the finishing touches put to her preparation in a gallop over six furlongs at Ripon racecourse, Attraction started second favourite to the Fillies' Mile winner Red Bloom in an open-looking but not particularly strong One Thousand Guineas, sponsored by UltimateBet.com. The Fillies' Mile runner-up Sundrop represented Godolphin, along with the Cheveley Park winner Carry On Katie (who like Attraction had not performed as a two-year-old as if she would prove suited by a mile) and Cairns, winner—from Sundrop and Punctilious—of the Godolphin trial staged at Nad Al Sheba. The Moyglare Stud Stakes winner Necklace, the only runner trained outside Britain, represented Ballydoyle. All of those mentioned were making their seasonal reappearance in the Guineas. Others that had contested the recognised three-year-old trials in Britain included the Cheveley Park runner-up Majestic Desert, successful in the Fred Darling, the May Hill runner-up Hathrah, winner of the Masaka Stakes by a wide margin, and the first two in the Nell Gwyn, Silca's Gift (who was supplemented) and Incheni.

The sight of a leading contender out in front, in full flow, in championship events at a mile and upwards is not commonplace in Europe. Being in front, or handily placed, is, however, an everyday occurrence with horses trained at Kingsley House and it came as no surprise, even with doubts about her stamina, to see Attraction sent off to try to make all at Newmarket. Very few got into contention as she made nonsense of the theory that she would prove best at sprint distances. A very well-judged ride by Kevin Darley saw Attraction last home by half a length

*UltimateBet.com 1000 Guineas Stakes, Newmarket—Attraction makes all under
a well-judged ride by Kevin Darley and just holds the strong-finishing Sundrop (right);
Hathrah (striped cap) is third, with favourite Red Bloom (sash) fourth*

and the same from the strong-finishing Sundrop and Hathrah, with Red Bloom a
further length and a quarter back in fourth. Attraction edged left and began to
tire after she met the rising ground but kept on gamely for a thoroughly deserved
victory, one which gave her trainer a second classic victory, following the success
of always-prominent Mister Baileys in the 1994 Two Thousand Guineas. Mister
Baileys and Attraction—along with the Malton-trained 2002 St Leger winner
Bollin Eric—are the only classic winners trained north of the Trent since the 1977
One Thousand Guineas winner Mrs McArdy and the only ones trained at Middleham since Dante won the Derby in 1945. The triumph of Mister Baileys coincided
with Mark Johnston's saddling a hundred winners in a season for the first time,
something he has achieved every year since, his feat establishing a new record of
eleven consecutive centuries, now two ahead of that once held by Henry Cecil.

Attraction's performance at Newmarket was reminiscent of that of another
natural front-runner, Al Bahathri, runner-up in the 1985 renewal. Al Bahathri, dam
of the latest Two Thousand Guineas winner Haafhd, appeared likely to get home
narrowly from Bella Colora before Oh So Sharp came along to pip the pair in a
finish of short heads. The outstanding Oh So Sharp was raced over longer distances
afterwards, completing the fillies' triple crown, winning the Oaks by six lengths
(with Bella Colora among those behind) and beating the colts in the St Leger.
Al Bahathri went on to win both the Irish One Thousand and the Coronation and
came closest of any before Attraction to winning all three races. The following year
Sonic Lady won at the Curragh and Royal Ascot after finishing third at Newmarket,
while Kooyonga (1991) and Marling (1992) both won the Irish version and the
Coronation after finishing runner-up in the One Thousand Guineas, Marling
unluckily beaten a head after meeting trouble in running. Numerous other fillies
have contested all three races and reached a place in at least two of them in the
period under review: Milligram, second in 1987 at Newmarket and the Curragh
before winning at Royal Ascot; Heart of Joy, placed in all three races in 1990; Las
Meninas (won at Newmarket, second at the Curragh before coming fifth at Ascot)
and Mehthaaf (fourth at Newmarket before winning at the Curragh and coming
third at Royal Ascot), both in 1994; Harayir, who won at Newmarket, came fifth in
Ireland and third at Ascot in 1995; Golden Silca, runner-up at the Curragh and
Royal Ascot after finishing seventh at Newmarket in 1999; Princess Ellen, second,
fifth and second in the three races in 2000; and Crystal Music (fourth, second and
second) and Toroca (third, third and sixth), both in 2001. Gossamer started
favourite for all three races in 2002, flopping at Newmarket and Royal Ascot but
winning in Ireland, but no filly contested all three races in 2003, the two best British
three-year-olds of their sex at a mile, Russian Rhythm and Soviet Song, first and
fourth and first and second respectively in the One Thousand and the Coronation,
both bypassing the Curragh.

The Irish One Thousand Guineas comes mid-way between Newmarket and
Royal Ascot, three weeks after the Guineas and just over three before the Coronation, the only other Group 1 over a mile in Britain restricted to three-year-old fillies.

Boylesports Irish 1000 Guineas, the Curragh—
Attraction (right) becomes the first filly to win both the British and Irish 1000 Guineas;
Alexander Goldrun chases her home and Illustrious Miss (star on cap) battles on for third

Even more surprising perhaps than the fact that no filly had won all three was the fact that the Guineas double had never been completed either. Wince had been the most recent—and the first since Harayir—to attempt it, managing only fifth when a hot favourite at the Curragh after success at Newmarket in 1999. The connections of Attraction paid €40,000 to supplement her for the Boylesports Irish One Thousand Guineas, which attracted a field of fifteen, nine of whom had been successful at listed or pattern level, or both. Judged on paddock inspection at Newmarket, Attraction was fully wound up for the One Thousand Guineas and it would not have been a surprise to have seen some of those who took her on again at the Curragh finish a little closer to her. Among them was Secret Charm, who had shaped well at Newmarket, finishing strongly in fifth after being hampered, and who was reported by her trainer to have pleased in her work since. Attraction started favourite at the Curragh ahead of Secret Charm and the supplemented Illustrious Miss, who had won the Chartwell Fillies' Stakes at Lingfield after missing the Guineas. Alexander Goldrun, narrow winner of the One Thousand Guineas Trial at Leopardstown, was the only other runner to start at shorter than 12/1 and—along with 16/1-shot Necklace (one of five saddled by O'Brien)—the only home-trained runner at shorter than 20/1. The Curragh mile is slightly stiffer than the one at Newmarket but conditions—good to firm as at Newmarket—placed the emphasis on speed and, on a very hot day, Attraction again proved wrong those who still harboured reservations about her stamina. She was soon out in front and never looked in danger of defeat, sticking to her task to hold off Alexander Goldrun, who chased her throughout, by a length, with Illustrious Miss a further two lengths away third, followed by the May Hill winner Kinnaird, who had missed Newmarket through a setback, Secret Charm, Necklace and Majestic Desert.

The form of the Irish One Thousand Guineas looked marginally better than that of the English version (Secret Charm and Majestic Desert both being beaten further by Attraction, for example). But it was impossible to assess Attraction on racecourse evidence as an outstanding Guineas winner. What was now needed was for her to be measured against the colts or against older fillies such as Russian Rhythm (who had beaten the colts in the Lockinge at Newbury) or Soviet Song (runaway winner of the Ridgewood Pearl Stakes at the Curragh the day before the Irish Guineas). Royal Ascot was next on the agenda for Attraction, Russian Rhythm and Soviet Song, the Queen Anne reportedly Russian Rhythm's target and the new Windsor Forest Stakes looking ideal for Soviet Song. In the event, the Lockinge turned out to be Russian Rhythm's final race and Soviet Song was set the stiffer task of tackling the colts in the Queen Anne, a race which also attracted the very smart French-trained four-year-old fillies Six Perfections (who started favourite) and Nebraska Tornado. Soviet Song finished a very good second to the previous year's Two Thousand Guineas winner Refuse to Bend, with Nebraska Tornado and Six Perfections fourth and sixth, form which at the end of Royal Ascot looked only a little inferior to that shown by the thriving Attraction, who made it eight out of eight in the Coronation Stakes.

Pre-race fears at Royal Ascot centred around whether Attraction might have been exposed to a coughing virus that had hit some of the inmates at Kingsley House. Connections need not have worried. Attraction was soon into her customary rhythm at the head of affairs and put up her best display of the season, readily settling matters when quickening two furlongs out—flashing her tail when given a backhander—and winning comfortably by two and a half lengths (value four) from Majestic Desert, with Red Bloom a head away third, and the rest strung out. Attraction finished the stiff Ascot mile with her jockey sitting up, wagging a finger at the crowd, but her time was only three hundredths of a second outside the record for the course and distance. A fast time is of little significance in itself; a number of other factors—including the prevailing conditions—have to be taken into account, quantified and their effects compensated for. The actual value of Attraction's time performance—as evidenced by her Timeform computer timefigure—was a very good 0.86 fast, by some way the best recorded in Britain by any filly or mare at a mile during the latest season. The timefigure translated to a timerating of 122, providing confirmation of the value of the bare form of the Coronation Stakes (3 lb added to Attraction's Timeform rating to take account of the amount she had in hand).

'Annual records and a place in history is what we are shooting for now,' said Mark Johnston after the Coronation Stakes, describing Attraction as 'the most phenomenal racehorse I have trained by a long way.' Attraction had now won three Group 1 events in as many starts as a three-year-old, but the prestige of those races, and her unbeaten status, blinded some to the fact that her string of sterling displays had been recorded against fillies of her own age. Immediately after the Irish

Coronation Stakes, Royal Ascot—more clear cut this time for Attraction; Majestic Desert (striped sleeves) edges Red Bloom (rail) out of second, with Moon Dazzle (right) back in fourth

Guineas, Attraction's trainer had posed the question of whether it might be better to return her to six furlongs for the July Cup, rather than continue running her at a mile after the Coronation Stakes. In the end, she was kept at a mile. There was a record first-day crowd of 12,900 at the Newmarket July meeting when Attraction started odds on against Soviet Song in the Falmouth Stakes, one of a number of races for fillies and mares promoted to Group 1 status in the latest season. The form of the Queen Anne at Royal Ascot had been made to look all the better by Refuse To Bend's subsequent victory in the Eclipse and it seemed unlikely that Attraction would be able to brush aside Soviet Song as easily as she had a Coronation field consisting of fillies she had largely seen off before. That Attraction was actually beaten in the Falmouth, however, came as a surprise at the time, attention focussed on whether the early gallop had been strong enough to bring out the best in her. The front-running Attraction had no response to Soviet Song's turn of foot, going down by two and a half lengths, though she beat the five other runners decisively, the smart French three-year-old Baqah finishing third with Illustrious Miss back in fifth, beaten over three times as far by Attraction as she had been in the Irish Guineas. Attraction's trainer was one of those who thought that Attraction had gone too steadily in the first part of the race. To Attraction's regular rider, Kevin Darley, however, the explanation for the defeat lay with the filly herself whom he thought was 'a bit below par'. Attraction was afterwards found to be in season.

Attraction took on the colts for the only time in her career so far in the Prix Jacques le Marois at Deauville in mid-August when she encountered going softer than good for the first time. Under pressure soon after halfway and eased down once her chance had gone, Attraction trailed home last, causing her trainer to regret running her (withdrawal had reportedly been under consideration at one time). Attraction had now suffered two successive defeats, but, like another British sporting heroine with a previously unblemished reputation, Paula Radcliffe, who capitulated in both the Olympic marathon and 10,000 metres in August, Attraction returned to the track to end her campaign on a high note. While Radcliffe's failures—which she put behind her when winning the New York marathon—were supposedly accounted for by a stomach upset caused by high doses of anti-inflammatories to tackle a leg injury, Attraction's Jacques le Marois performance merely convinced her connections not to risk her again on softish going.

The going was good to firm when Attraction had a rematch with Soviet Song in the Matron Stakes—also run for the first time as a Group 1—at Leopardstown on Irish Champion Stakes day. Soviet Song was odds on this time, having gone on to win the Sussex Stakes after the Falmouth, becoming the first of her sex to win the Goodwood championship event since Sayyedati in 1995. Attraction took the eye before the Matron, but she was overhauled late on, after Soviet Song had been left with around eight lengths to make up in the final straight, the margin of victory being half a length. The smart Phantom Wind, a late withdrawal from the One Thousand Guineas with a high temperature and winner of the Oak Tree Stakes at Goodwood, was five lengths behind Attraction in third. As at Royal Ascot, Attraction flashed her tail under the whip but kept on well.

Attraction's defection later in the month from the Queen Elizabeth II Stakes—which would, among other things, have produced a third meeting with Soviet Song—was controversial. Attraction's trainer announced early in the week his 'shock' that Ascot was planning to water and, when the Ascot executive went ahead, Attraction was taken out at the forty-eight-hour declaration stage. The going on the day was good to firm but the result—Rakti won from Attraction's stablemate Lucky Story, the pair clear of Refuse To Bend with Soviet Song sixth—suggested that Attraction would have been in the shake-up. Rerouted to Newmarket in early-October, Attraction tackled the upgraded Kingdom of Bahrain Sun Chariot Stakes, gaining a first victory over fillies outside her own age group and her fourth Group 1 of the season, more than any other performer in Europe. The going was good—good to soft in a few places—and connections gave the final go-ahead for Attraction to run only on the day of the race after the trainer and jockey had walked the course. Still looking in good condition, Attraction started third favourite behind two of the season's leading older milers, the Hungerford and Celebration Mile winner Chic, and Nebraska Tornado, a close third when short-priced favourite for the Prix d'Astarte at Deauville on her only start since Royal Ascot. Also in a

Kingdom of Bahrain Sun Chariot Stakes, Newmarket—Attraction gets the better of Chic in a stirring finish; Nebraska Tornado is unable to sustain her challenge in third, with Majestic Desert finishing fourth

five-strong line-up was Majestic Desert, in the frame in the Brownstown Stakes at Leopardstown, the Prix d'Astarte and the Jacques le Marois since the Coronation Stakes. Attraction made the running as usual and, after seeing off Nebraska Tornado, the first to try to challenge over two furlongs out, Attraction rallied up the hill to hold off Chic by a neck, despite changing her legs a number of times as she had to call on all her reserves in the last hundred yards. It was a memorable finish, Attraction emerging with particular credit as Chic, who did nothing wrong herself, looked the likely winner when drawing upsides entering the final furlong. Nebraska Tornado was a length and a half behind Chic in third with a further five back to a below-par Majestic Desert in fourth.

The quite good-topped Attraction may be an unimpressive mover with an ungainly action, but her trainer is right when he says that, judged on conformation, 'there are a lot worse horses than her.' Johnston does things his way and is less influenced by some conformation faults than the vast majority of trainers and agents who do the rounds at the yearling sales. 'There are too many idiots out there who try to break it down—it toes in or toes out, it's back at the knee or over at the knee. You can't do that,' he told *Thoroughbred Owner & Breeder* in the latest season. 'When you're looking at a Ferrari, are you looking at the wheels, at the hubcaps, at the headlamps? You're looking at the whole machine.' 'Every single year there are surprises,' added Johnston who said his own surprises hadn't 'come any bigger' than Double Trigger and Attraction, while he said of Bijou d'Inde that 'of twenty yearlings that year, if I could have given one back it would have been him.' Attraction's owner-breeder the Duke of Roxburghe, whose Floors Stud in Scotland houses around twenty mares, describes the filly as a product of 'the cheapest mare, using the cheapest stallion we used that year.' In his interview, Johnston revealed that he regards pedigree as paramount, though 'if anyone seriously believes that a horse in the eighth generation can have any influence, then I'm Bonny Prince Charlie. It flies in the face of Darwin.'

95

The deeper reaches of Attraction's pedigree might not concern her trainer, but they are of academic interest nonetheless. Attraction is from the famous Verdict family, as it is known, a family that was finally admitted to the *General Stud Book* only in 1969, through the mare Lavant and her half-sisters, after a welter of evidence had built up over half a century. The first good horses descended from the 'non-thoroughbred' Coronation Cup and Cambridgeshire winner Verdict were her daughters Quashed, who won the Oaks and the Gold Cup, and Versicle, winner of the Ribblesdale. Even after the achievements of Lavant's offspring the top sprinters Lucasland (Attraction's fourth dam) and her half-brother So Blessed in the mid- to late-'sixties, Weatherbys still reportedly at first turned down an application to admit the family because 'the line lacks the necessary eight or nine crosses of pure blood', though Lucasland's and So Blessed's female line could be traced back for eleven generations, most of the evidence provided by *Prior's Half-Bred Stud Book*. Admission to the *General Stud Book* was at the sole discretion of Weatherbys, though nowadays admission is governed by an agreement reached in 1985 between the international stud book authorities, which now number fifty-seven. Eight recorded crosses are still required, along with 'performances . . . as to warrant assimilation'. Versicle, incidentally, was the great grandam of Lucasland and So Blessed, while Lucasland herself is the great grandam of Sonic Lady who, after her victories in the Irish One Thousand Guineas and Coronation Stakes, went on to beat the colts in both the Sussex Stakes and the Prix du Moulin. Attraction's Timeform rating is 4 lb below that achieved by Sonic Lady.

Attraction (b.f. 2001)	Efisio (b 1982)	Formidable (b 1975)	Forli
			Native Partner
		Eldoret (b 1976)	High Top
			Bamburi
	Flirtation (b 1994)	Pursuit of Love (b 1989)	Groom Dancer
			Dance Quest
		Eastern Shore (ch 1979)	Sun Prince
			Land Ho

Duke of Roxburghe's "Attraction"

It must be debatable whether either Sonic Lady or Attraction would have been bred at all if the authorities had not relented. None of the first three dams on the bottom line of Attraction's tabulated pedigree won a race. Attraction is the second foal of the once-raced Flirtation, following the fairly useful two-year-old five-furlong winner Aunty Mary (by Common Grounds) who did not train on. Attraction's grandam Eastern Shore was bought, in foal to Ile de Bourbon, by Floors Stud for 155,000 guineas at the 1983 December Sales. Quite a modest maiden who stayed a mile and a half, she has had four winners, the best of them the French mile-and-a-half listed winner Carmita. Attraction's great grandam Land Ho is also the great grandam of Prix de la Salamandre winner Lord of Men and his half-sister the Prix de Diane runner-up Her Ladyship. Attraction's sire the very smart miler Efisio, who won in pattern company each year from two to five, started his stallion career at a fee of £2,000 and didn't command five figures until the latest season. After the successes of Attraction and July Cup winner Frizzante in the latest season, his fee for 2005 has been raised to £12,000. Efisio has built up an admirable record at stud, despite being unfashionable for most of his career and not having anything like the numbers of mares of most latter-day leading sires (his crops averaging around forty). Attraction stays a mile and probably would not be inconvenienced by a return to six furlongs as a four-year-old. However, in the light of her owner's reported explanation for Attraction's missing the Sussex Stakes—'Why race against the whole horse population when you can race against fifty per cent of it?'—it could be that Attraction will be kept mainly to Group 1 races restricted to fillies and mares, of which there is much more choice at a mile than over shorter. All being well, and unless there is a wet summer, the decision to keep Attraction in training should be handsomely rewarded. It would certainly be worth giving her another chance against the colts, perhaps in the Lockinge in early-May, before finalising a target at the Royal meeting. She acts on firm going and seems unlikely to be risked again on going softer than good. Although she has flashed her tail under pressure, Attraction is game, genuine and consistent, as well as being tough (she kept her form admirably through a long season for a classic filly). A natural front-runner, she is a pleasure to watch. *M. Johnston*

ATTUNE 3 ch.f. Singspiel (IRE) 133 – Arriving 105 (Most Welcome 131) [2004 64p: **102** 7g[4] 8s 8m* 8.1d 8.2g 7f* 7g* 7m* 8g Oct 1] lengthy filly: useful performer: won minor event at Thirsk, handicaps at Newmarket (blinkered) and Salisbury and listed event at Doncaster (beat Gonfilia by length) between May and September: effective at 7f/1m: acts on firm going: races prominently. *B. J. Meehan*

AT YOUR REQUEST 3 gr.g. Bering 136 – Requesting (Rainbow Quest (USA) 134) **76** [2004 10v[3] 12.1s[3] 12.1m[3] p12g Nov 10] compact gelding: first foal: dam unraced half-sister to Nassau Stakes winner Last Second and to dams of Alborada, Albanova, Yesterday and Quarter Moon: fair maiden: left E. Dunlop 32,000 gns after third start: stays 1½m: acts on heavy and good to firm ground. *Ian Williams*

AUDIENCE 4 b.g. Zilzal (USA) 137 – Only Yours 113 (Aragon 118) [2004 103: 8g 7d **108** 8v 7m 8f 8m[2] 8m[4] 8m[6] 7.9s* 8.1g[3] 9g 8d Oct 30] big, good-topped gelding: useful performer: edgy, won handicap at York in August by ½ length from Take A Bow: easily best effort after when good 2¼ lengths third to With Reason in listed event at Haydock: stays 1m: acts on firm and soft ground: blinkered last 4 outings at 3 yrs, wears cheek-pieces nowadays: sometimes takes good hold. *J. Akehurst*

AUDITORIUM 3 b.c. Royal Applause 124 – Degree 81 (Warning 136) [2004 114: 7m[4] **102** 7f 8m Jul 31] sturdy, useful-looking colt: smart performer at 2 yrs: well below that level in 2004, including when fourth to Fokine in listed race at Newmarket: looked none too keen final start: should be suited by 1m+: raced only on good ground or firmer: has been coltish in preliminaries, including on last 2 starts: usually soon off bridle. *Sir Michael Stoute*

AUENTRAUM (GER) 4 br.c. Big Shuffle (USA) 122 – Auenglocke (GER) (Surumu **?** (GER)) [2004 6d[3] 5m p6g p6g p7g Dec 4] ex-German colt: brother to 2 winners in Germany, including smart sprinter Auenklang and half-brother to a winner there by Shirley Heights: dam German 7f/1m winner: won maiden at Mulheim and handicap at Frankfurt in 2003: left U. Ostmann after reappearance, then well held in Britain: stays 6.5f: acts on good to soft going: tried blinkered: very slowly away penultimate outing. *D. Flood*

AUGUSTINE 3 b.g. Machiavellian (USA) 123 – Crown of Light 112 (Mtoto 134) **50 +** [2004 72: p7g[4] Dec 29] close-coupled gelding: fifth in maiden at Newmarket only run at

2 yrs: left D. Loder 6,200 gns and off 19 months, shaped quite well when fourth in similar event at Lingfield, slowly away and not knocked out: bred to be suited by 1¼m/1½m. *P. W. Hiatt*

AUNT DORIS 7 b.m. Distant Relative 128 – Nevis 61 (Connaught 130) [2004 –: f6g f8g Jan 12] poor handicapper: tried in visor/cheekpieces. *Paul Johnson* –

AUNT JULIA 2 b.f. (Feb 3) In The Wings 128 – Original (Caerleon (USA) 132) [2004 7g³ Sep 20] 21,000Y: good-topped filly: first foal: dam unraced half-sister to smart 1½m winner Xtra: 50/1, 2¾ lengths third of 14 to Quickfire in maiden at Kempton, no extra late on: should be suited by 1¼m/1½m: likely to do better. *R. Hannon* **73 p**

AUNTY EURO (IRE) 2 br.f. (Mar 9) Cape Cross (IRE) 129 – Alexander Goddess (IRE) (Alzao (USA) 117) [2004 p5g⁴ 5s³ 6m³ 7m f7m⁶ Jul 26] €25,000Y: fourth foal: half-sister to 3-y-o Great Blasket: dam unraced out of half-sister to US Grade 1 1¼m winner Ida Delia and to dam of very smart US 1m/1¼m performer Victory Speech: modest maiden: barely stays 7f: acts on fibresand, soft and good to firm going. *E. J. O'Neill* **59**

AURELIA 3 b.f. Rainbow Quest (USA) 134 – Fern 100 (Shirley Heights 130) [2004 78: 11.9m³ 16m Sep 11] sturdy filly: fairly useful handicapper: stays 1½m: raced only on going firmer than good: often slowly away: sometimes finds little: tail swisher. *Sir Mark Prescott* **80**

AUROVILLE 3 b.c. Cadeaux Genereux 131 – Silent Tribute (IRE) 104 (Lion Cavern (USA) 117) [2004 66: 7.5d 8.2s⁴ 8m 8.5m⁵ 10m 10d 12m⁶ 10.1g² p10g 11.5g⁵ 10g⁶ Oct 11] leggy, lengthy colt: fair maiden: best form up to 8.2f: acts on soft and good to firm ground: tried visored: sold 4,000 gns, sent to Belgium. *M. L. W. Bell* **66**

AUSTRALIAN 2 b.c. (Feb 8) Danzero (AUS) – Auspicious 103 (Shirley Heights 130) [2004 8g* Sep 20] 58,000F, 125,000Y: rather leggy, useful-looking colt: second foal: half-brother to 3-y-o Doctrine: dam, 1¼m winner, sister to smart middle-distance stayer Sacrament and half-sister to dam of 5-y-o Chorist: 8/1, won 10-runner maiden at Kempton by neck from Kerashan, leading 2f out: likely to stay 1¼m: should improve. *J. H. M. Gosden* **80 p**

AUTHENTICATE 2 b.f. (Apr 29) Dansili 127 – Exact Replica (Darshaan 133) [2004 6.1d⁴ 8.2g⁶ 7g 6.5g Sep 18] 24,000Y: tall filly: second living foal: half-sister to French 1m winner Greenfly (by Green Desert): dam unraced sister to smart performer up to 9f Darnay: fair maiden: stays 1m: acts on good to soft going. *B. A. McMahon* **65**

AUTHORITY (IRE) 4 b.g. Bluebird (USA) 125 – Persian Tapestry 70 (Tap On Wood 130) [2004 75: p8m⁵ p7g p10g* Dec 4] rangy, good sort: fair performer: won maiden at Lingfield in December: should stay 1½m: acts on polytrack and good to firm going. *Lady Herries* **65 +**

AUTUMN DAZE 2 b.f. (Mar 4) Danzig Connection (USA) – Autumn Stone (IRE) (Bigstone (IRE) 126) [2004 p6d p6g p7.1g 6d p5.1g Nov 12] 800Y: first foal: dam unraced: soundly beaten in maidens. *M. J. Ryan* –

AUTUMN FANTASY (USA) 5 b. or br.h. Lear Fan (USA) 130 – Autumn Glory (USA) (Graustark) [2004 –: 14g⁴ 16d 16.1m 16m May 26] good-topped horse: little form since 2002. *B. Ellison* –

AUTUMN FLYER (IRE) 3 ch.g. Salse (USA) 128 – Autumn Fall (USA) (Sangla-more (USA) 126) [2004 66: 10.2m 10m 10m 11.7m⁵ 11.9m Sep 23] modest maiden: stays 11.7f: raced only on polytrack and good to firm ground. *C. G. Cox* **55**

AUTUMN GLORY (IRE) 4 b.c. Charnwood Forest (IRE) 125 – Archipova (IRE) (Ela-Mana-Mou 132) [2004 89: 8g* 7.9s* 8f 7m 8d⁶ 8v* 7d⁵ 9s* Oct 16] good-topped, rather lengthy colt: impresses in appearance: very smart performer: much improved in 2004, winning handicaps at Doncaster (Spring Mile, impressively by 1½ lengths from St Petersburg) in March and York (beat Duck Row by 2 lengths) in May, Prix Quincey Fouquet's Barriere at Deauville (gamely, by short neck from Keltos) in August and Rolls-Royce Motor Cars London Darley Stakes at Newmarket (made all to beat Sights On Gold 2 lengths) in October: stays 9f: acts on heavy ground, possibly not on firmer than good. *G. Wragg* **120**

AUTUMN MELODY (FR) 2 b.f. (Mar 23) Kingmambo (USA) 125 – Dance of Leaves (Sadler's Wells (USA) 132) [2004 7g⁵ 7m⁶ 7m⁵ Aug 7] sturdy filly: half-sister to several winners, including high-class 7f/1m winner Charnwood Forest (by Warning) and smart 1996 2-y-o 7f/1m (latter Racing Post Trophy) winner Medaaly (by Highest Honor): dam unraced out of US 2-y-o Grade 1 7f winner and outstanding broodmare Fall Aspen: fair form in maidens: should stay 1m: tongue tied: left Godolphin. *Saeed bin Suroor* **67**

AUTUMN PEARL   3 b.f. Orpen (USA) 116 – Cyclone Flyer 67 (College Chapel 122) **102**
[2004 82p: 6v* 5m² 5m³ 5m⁶ 5m 5d² 6s Oct 29] lengthy, rather unfurnished filly: unimpressive mover: useful performer: won minor event at Kempton in May: good efforts
when 1¼ lengths second to Night Prospector in Temple Stakes at Epsom and close third
to Green Manalishi in handicap at Newmarket second/third starts: effective at 5f/6f: acts
on polytrack, heavy and good to firm going: usually races prominently. *M. A. Jarvis*

AUTUMN WEALTH (IRE)   3 ch.f. Cadeaux Genereux 131 – Prickwillow (USA) **93**
75 (Nureyev (USA) 131) [2004 10g² 10g² 9.9s* 11.7s* 10.3s³ Nov 6] €170,000Y: fourth
foal: half-sister to useful 2002 2-y-o 7f winner Wilful (by Bering): dam, 1¼m winner,
out of smart performer around 1¼m Braiswick: fairly useful performer: won maiden at
Beverley (hung badly left) in August and handicap at Bath in October: good third to
Mango Mischief in listed race at Doncaster final start: stays 11.7f. *Mrs A. J. Perrett*

AUWITESWEETHEART   2 b.f. (Apr 24) Josr Algarhoud (IRE) 118 – Miss Kirsty **70**
(USA) 82 (Miswaki (USA) 124) [2004 6g⁵ 5.1d⁵ 6s⁵ 5.1g³ 5.1s² Oct 19] leggy, lengthy
filly: first foal: dam, 1m winner, out of US Grade 1 1¼m winner Spit Curl: fair maiden:
placed at Bath, including in nursery: should stay 6f: tongue tied second start: hangs left.
B. R. Millman

AVEIRO (IRE)   8 b.g. Darshaan 133 – Avila 76 (Ajdal (USA) 130) [2004 41, a48: **38**
f12g² f11g* f12g³ f12g³ f16.2s³ p12g² f16.2g* f12g² 21.6v 14.4v 11.8m f14.8g⁵ 13m Jun **a66**
16] big gelding: fair on all-weather, poor on turf: won banded event at Southwell in
January and (having left B. Powell after fourth start) handicap at Wolverhampton in
March: effective at 11f to easy 2m: acts on all-weather, firm and soft ground: effective
with or without blinkers/visor: races prominently. *Miss Gay Kelleway*

AVENING   4 br.g. Averti (IRE) 117 – Dependable (Formidable (USA) 125) [2004 91d: **88**
5g* 7s² 7g 6d 6d* 6g 5s⁴ 6m² 6g Sep 29] useful-looking gelding: fairly useful performer:
left R. Hannon after final 3-y-o start: won minor event at Moulins in April (originally
demoted but reinstated on appeal) and handicap at Chantilly in July: well beaten in
handicap at Salisbury final start: subsequently gelded: best at 5f/6f: acts on firm going,
probably on heavy: has had tongue tied: blinkered last 5 starts. *J. E. Hammond, France*

AVENTURA (IRE)   4 b.g. Sri Pekan (USA) 117 – La Belle Katherine (USA) (Lyphard **85 d**
(USA) 132) [2004 95?: p10g f8.5s p8g⁴ 8g 10.5s 6g 7.1s 7m 7v p7.1d f11g Nov 23]
sturdy, close-coupled gelding: fairly useful performer: below form after third start (left
M. Polglase after eighth outing): effective at 6f to easy 9f: acts on polytrack, good to
firm and good to soft going: sometimes starts slowly/races freely: none too reliable.
S. R. Bowring

Rolls-Royce Motor Cars London Darley Stakes, Newmarket—the much improved Autumn Glory
stretches away again late on from Sights On Gold, one of the few able to get in a challenge

Prix du Gros-Chene, Chantilly—Porlezza (noseband) is foiled in her bid to win the race for the third year in succession by Avonbridge, who makes all; The Trader (blinkers) finishes best of all but too late

AVERAMI 3 b.f. Averti (IRE) 117 – Friend For Life 64 (Lahib (USA) 129) [2004 68: p7g p7g⁵ 6s 7m p5g⁶ 6m 6g p7g⁶ p5m p7m* p7m² Dec 15] leggy filly: modest performer: won banded race at Lingfield in December: stays 7f: acts on polytrack: usually visored/blinkered. *A. M. Balding* **59**

AVERLLINE 3 b.f. Averti (IRE) 117 – Spring Sunrise 59 (Robellino (USA) 127) [2004 74: 6f 6g 7f 6g Aug 21] modest nowadays: barely stays 7f: acts on good to firm and good to soft going. *B. De Haan* **56**

AVERSHAM 4 b.c. Averti (IRE) 117 – Vavona 60 (Ballad Rock 122) [2004 101: 6.5f a6f 6f 6m³ 6g⁵ p6g⁴ p7g Nov 16] strong, close-coupled colt: fairly useful performer: no form in UAE for E. Charpy first 3 starts: mostly creditable efforts in handicaps after: effective at 6f/7f: acts on polytrack, firm and soft going: tried blinkered. *R. Charlton* **92**

AVERTAINE 3 b.f. Averti (IRE) 117 – Roufontaine 85 (Rousillon (USA) 133) [2004 p7g p7g 9.7s⁵ 10s² 12.1g p10g⁶ 8f⁵ 8.1g Jul 9] second foal: dam 1¼m/1½m and bumper winner: modest maiden: stays 1¼m: acts on soft going: blinkered last 2 starts. *G. L. Moore* **55**

AVERTIGO 2 b.c. (May 12) Averti (IRE) 117 – Green Run (USA) (Green Dancer (USA) 132) [2004 6m⁵ 6m³ 6m² 6d 6m² 6d⁴ 6d Oct 14] 5,000Y: leggy, close-coupled colt: first foal: dam, French 7f/1m winner, half-sister to useful French performer up to 13.5f Turn To Black: fair maiden: likely to stay 7f: acts on good to firm ground: blinkered final start: sold 17,000 gns, sent to Germany. *W. R. Muir* **68**

AVERTING 2 br.c. (Mar 7) Averti (IRE) 117 – Sweet Compliance 71 (Safawan 118) [2004 5.1f⁵ 6m² 6g 6.1m 6.1d 5m Sep 27] smallish, leggy colt: modest maiden: likely to stay 7f: acts on good to firm going: ran badly in blinkers last 2 starts. *R. F. Johnson Houghton* **53**

AVESOMEOFTHAT (IRE) 3 b.g. Lahib (USA) 129 – Lacinia 107 (Groom Dancer (USA) 128) [2004 74: 10.2m⁶ 12g Jun 2] maiden, well held on Flat in 2004. *Mrs P. N. Dutfield* **–**

AVESSIA 3 b.f. Averti (IRE) 117 – Alessia 91 (Caerleon (USA) 132) [2004 –p: 6g⁴ Jul 24] leggy filly: better effort in maidens 9 months apart (trained by R. Charlton on debut) when 1½ lengths fourth to Kostar at Salisbury. *G. L. Moore* **65**

AVIATION 2 b.g. (Apr 11) Averti (IRE) 117 – Roufontaine 85 (Rousillon (USA) 133) [2004 6s 6g³ 6m⁵ 7g⁵ 6g Oct 11] quite good-topped gelding: third foal: dam 1¼m/1½m and bumper winner: fair maiden: best efforts on second and fourth starts: should stay 1m: gelded after final outing. *R. Hannon* **78**

AVIT (IRE) 4 ch.f. General Monash (USA) 107 – Breakfast Boogie 59 (Sizzling Melody 117) [2004 52: p5g p6g p5g² p5g³ 5.3g f5m⁶ f6g 5.3f* 5g⁴ 5.1m⁵ 5m 5.1m² 5g 6m 6d⁶ p7.1g Nov 15] compact filly: poor handicapper: won at Brighton in June: best at 5f/6f: acts on polytrack, firm and good to soft ground: tried blinkered. *P. L. Gilligan* **43**

AVIZANDUM (IRE) 2 b.g. (May 6) Daggers Drawn (USA) 114 – Miss Dilletante **59** (Primo Dominie 121) [2004 6g 7.9g p7.1g Dec 10] strong gelding: form in maidens only at Wolverhampton (raced very wide off home turn) final start. *T. J. Etherington*

AVONBRIDGE 4 b.c. Averti (IRE) 117 – Alessia 91 (Caerleon (USA) 132) [2004 **117** 116: 5g² 5g* 6f⁵ 5m⁴ 5s⁴ 5m⁵ Oct 3] strong, angular, good-topped colt: smart performer: short-headed by Frizzante in Palace House Stakes at Newmarket on reappearance: made all in Prix du Gros-Chene at Chantilly (beat Porlezza ½ length) in June: at least respectable efforts last 3 starts when fourth to Ringmoor Down in King George Stakes at Goodwood and to Bahamian Pirate in Nunthorpe Stakes at York, and fifth to Var in Prix de l'Abbaye at Longchamp: very best efforts at 5f: acts on firm and soft going: blinkered last 2 starts: races up with pace: consistent. *R. Charlton*

AWAASER (USA) 2 ch.f. (Feb 24) Diesis 133 – Forest Storm (USA) (Woodman **63 p** (USA) 126) [2004 6g⁴ Sep 17] €300,000Y: tall filly: fourth foal: dam unraced half-sister to May Hill and Musidora Stakes winner Marillette and US Grade 1 1¼m winner Storm Trooper (both by Diesis): 6/1, 8¼ lengths fourth of 10 to Newsround in maiden at Newbury, outpaced final 2f: should stay 1m: likely to do better. *M. P. Tregoning*

AWAKE 7 ch.g. First Trump 118 – Pluvial 90 (Habat 127) [2004 88: 5g 6v⁶ 5s⁵ 5v 5.1g* **90** 5g⁶ 5m² 5g 5g* 5g 5s 5d Oct 18] smallish, strong gelding: fairly useful handicapper: won at Chester in June and Newcastle in July: effective at 5f/easy 6f: acts on heavy and good to firm going: visored twice: sometimes early to post. *D. Nicholls*

AWAKEN 3 b.f. Zafonic (USA) 130 – Dawna 106 (Polish Precedent (USA) 131) [2004 **–** 10.1m 12d Oct 17] 4,000 3-y-o: fourth foal: dam, 1m winner, half-sister to smart French middle-distance performer Ordinance: signs of ability only in maiden at Newcastle (failed to settle) on debut. *G. A. Swinbank*

AWARDING 4 ch.g. Mark of Esteem (IRE) 137 – Monaiya (Shareef Dancer (USA) **74 d** 135) [2004 84: f6g⁵ p5g p6g 6m 10.2g 8g 6d Aug 12] good-topped gelding: fair performer: left F. J. Houghton after third start: ended season out of sorts: best at 5f/6f: acts on polytrack and firm going: tried blinkered: sometimes tongue tied: sometimes slowly away: tends to carry head high. *Dr J. R. J. Naylor*

AWESOME LOVE (USA) 3 br.c. Awesome Again (CAN) 133 – Circus Toons **76** (USA) (Wild Again (USA)) [2004 75p: 7m³ 8m² 7.5d² 8.5g² 10m⁶ 8g 11.1s⁵ Aug 17] fair maiden: stays 8.5f: acts on good to firm ground: tried blinkered: sold 13,000 gns. *M. Johnston*

A WOMAN IN LOVE 5 gr.m. Muhtarram (USA) 125 – Ma Lumiere (FR) (Niniski **87** (USA) 125) [2004 68: p7g⁶ 7m* 7f* 8f* 7.6g* 7g⁴ 8m 8f Aug 4] angular mare: fairly useful handicapper: won 3 times at Brighton and once at Lingfield in May/June: effective at 6f to 1m: acts on polytrack, raced only on good ground or firmer on turf: sometimes slowly away: free-going sort, usually held up. *Miss B. Sanders*

AWWAL MARRA (USA) 4 ch.f. King of Kings (IRE) 125 – Secretariat Lass (USA) **–** (Secretariat (USA)) [2004 12m 8.3f³ 9.9m 9.9d 12g Sep 14] second in maiden for M. Johnston only run at 2 yrs: well held in 2004. *E. W. Tuer*

AXFORD LORD 4 gr.g. Petong 126 – Bellypha (Bellypha 130) [2004 10.1g⁶ 6d **–** 7.2s 9.1d Sep 16] seems of little account nowadays. *A. C. Whillans*

AYAM ZAMAN (IRE) 2 b.f. (Feb 8) Montjeu (IRE) 137 – Kardashina (FR) (Darshaan **106 p** 133) [2004 8m⁵ 10g* 10d* Oct 30] €95,000Y: neat filly: third foal: closely related to Irish 1½m winner Russian Tsar (by King of Kings) and half-sister to 4-y-o Rudood: dam, French 11f/1½m winner, half-sister to smart French pair Karmifira and Karmousil: easy winner of maiden at Pontefract and listed race at Newmarket in October, useful form when beating Fantasy Ride by 5 lengths in latter, leading 2f out and quickly clear: will stay at least 1½m: open to progress, should win more races. *M. A. Jarvis*

AYLMER ROAD (IRE) 2 b.c. (Feb 8) Groom Dancer (USA) 128 – Pekan's Pride 84 **78** (Sri Pekan (USA) 117) [2004 7.9g² 10v⁴ Oct 20] rather leggy colt: first foal: dam, 2-y-o 7f winner on only start, out of useful 1m winner London Pride: much better effort in maidens when strong-finishing second to Maidanni at York: should stay 1¼m. *P. F. I. Cole*

AYNSLEY 2 ch.f. (Apr 15) Tomba 119 – Eggy (Risk Me (FR) 127) [2004 5g⁴ 5f⁵ p5.1g **53** Oct 2] 6,500Y: sturdy filly: first foal: dam unraced out of half-sister to very smart sprinter Devon Ditty: fourth in maiden at Haydock, best effort: ran in seller final start: sold 800 gns, sent to Holland. *M. A. Jarvis*

AZAHARA   2 b.f. (Feb 17) Vettori (IRE) 119 – Branston Express (Bay Express 132)   **68**
[2004 6d 7g 7m* 8s Nov 1] 11,000Y: sturdy filly: sister to 1m and (in USA) 9.5f winner
National Pride and half-sister to several winners, including 5f winner Keramic (by
Efisio): dam unraced half-sister to dam of smart pair Branston Abby and Desert Deer: fair
performer: 100/1, won maiden at Newcastle in October, getting up close home: no other
form: should stay 1m. *K. G. Reveley*

AZAMOUR (IRE)   3 b.c. Night Shift (USA) – Asmara (USA) 109 (Lear Fan   **128**
(USA) 130) [2004 108p: 8g³ 8m² 8f* 10m* 10s³ Oct 16]
      The Aga Khan, like his grandfather, does not make a habit of keeping
his top three-year-old colts in training, for reasons he expressed succinctly in an
interview three years ago: 'Stallions are the economic driver for the rest of the
operation.' The operation is on a massive scale, with around one hundred and
seventy mares and well over one hundred horses in training each year. The Aga
Khan III retired all his five Derby winners at the end of their classic season and the
present Aga Khan has done exactly the same with his five Derby and/or Irish Derby
winners (Shergar, Shahrastani, Kahyasi, Sinndar and Alamshar), his six Prix du
Jockey Club winners (Charlottesville, Top Ville, Darshaan, Mouktar, Natroun and
Dalakhani), his Two Thousand Guineas winner Doyoun and five of his seven Poule
d'Essai des Poulains winners (Zeddaan, Kalamoun, Blushing Groom, Nishapour
and Ashkalani). In fact, out of twenty-nine three-year-old Group 1-winning colts
from 1960 to 2003, only five raced for the Aga Khan at four—Daylami also carried
on, but for Godolphin. The quintet was Jour Et Nuit III (Prix d'Ispahan), Vayrann
(Champion Stakes), Lashkari (Breeders' Cup Turf), Valanour (Grand Prix de Paris)
and Sendawar (Poule d'Essai des Poulains, St James's Palace Stakes and Prix du
Moulin). Jour Et Nuit III was rated 123, Vayrann 133, Lashkari 128, Valanour 122
and Sendawar 129. The latest addition to the list, Azamour, fits in at the top end of
this scale and looks one to follow at four.
      Azamour's victory in the Baileys Irish Champion Stakes at Leopardstown
in September was his second in Group 1 company and one of the best by any colt of
his age all year. The Irish Champion Stakes is rarely contested by a large field—the
tally has reached double figures only once since 1987—but the roll of honour is
impressive, especially from 1999, when the race was included in the World Series.
Winning that title used to mean more to the Maktoum family than seemingly it
means now, and Swain, Daylami, Fantastic Light and Grandera all landed the race
for them, while Giant's Causeway and High Chaparral won for Ballydoyle in the
two other years. Even if the World Series is no longer so relevant as formerly, the
prize money for the Irish Champion Stakes is exceptional, the £393,878 on offer to
the winner in the latest season placing it second only to the Irish Derby among Irish
Group 1 events. Indeed, it was worth nearly fifty per cent more than the next
most valuable ten-furlong Group 1 in Europe, the Juddmonte International at York.
Understandably, Godolphin and Ballydoyle sent their best horses in the shape of

St James's Palace Stakes, Royal Ascot—Azamour edges past Diamond Green;
Antonius Pius and Haafhd (No.8) are next home, with 66/1-shot Castleton close up in fifth

*Baileys Irish Champion Stakes, Leopardstown—Azamour comes from last to first
to win going away from Norse Dancer (second right); next are Powerscourt (blinkers),
Grey Swallow (noseband) and Rakti, while odds-on Doyen (left) beats only his pacemaker*

Doyen, having his first start since winning the King George comfortably, and
Powerscourt, first past the post in the Tattersalls Gold Cup and Arlington Million.
Doyen was odds on ahead of another colt dropping back in trip, Irish Derby winner
Grey Swallow, and Prince of Wales's Stakes winner Rakti, who had blotted his
copybook with a headstrong display in the Coral-Eclipse. Then came Azamour (at
8/1), Powerscourt and Juddmonte International runner-up Norse Dancer. The
eight-runner field was completed by Imperial Dancer and Doyen's pacemaker
Millstreet. With Rakti pulling too hard for his own good again and Doyen running
way below his best, the Irish Champion took less winning than expected but
Azamour, having his first try at a mile and a quarter, was still most impressive. Held
up in last, he was switched outside in the straight and produced a sustained surge,
forging past all his rivals and catching Norse Dancer and Powerscourt in the final
furlong to beat the former by half a length going away. Grey Swallow and Rakti
were next to finish and the first five were covered by around two lengths; after
being prominent turning for home, Doyen dropped right out to finish last but one.
    Undoubtedly this was an improved display and a visually impressive one—
Azamour made up five lengths on the leaders in the final furlong—though
Azamour had hardly been hiding his light under a bushel. After winning both his
starts at two, notably the Beresford Stakes, Azamour was placed in two classics and
won the St James's Palace Stakes at Royal Ascot. His form in these races was much
of a muchness. In the Two Thousand Guineas, following a setback in the spring, he
finished strongly after being held up and was beaten less than three lengths into
third behind Haafhd. With Haafhd missing, Azamour then failed to justify
favouritism in the Irish equivalent at the Curragh, unable to match Bachelor Duke's
turn of foot and going down by a length. Azamour went one better at Royal Ascot,
reversing form with those who had beaten him in the two classics. He started
second favourite behind Haafhd, ahead of Bachelor Duke and Antonius Pius, who
should have won the Poule d'Essai des Poulains on his last start, and Diamond
Green, runner-up in the latter race. Kept in closer touch than previously, Azamour
responded well to firm handling to get his nose in front in the last fifty yards,
beating Diamond Green by a neck. Antonius Pius came next, followed by a
below-form Haafhd; Bachelor Duke was seventh. Azamour was due to make his
next start in the Juddmonte International but connections bypassed that race owing
to the soft going, which trainer John Oxx believed would not suit the colt so well as
some of his rivals. However, he did encounter soft on his final start, in the Emirates
Airline Champion Stakes at Newmarket, and he also encountered Haafhd in top

form again. Never far off the pace, Azamour was unable to respond when Haafhd quickened but stuck to his task gamely and lost second place only by a length to Chorist, with Haafhd a further two and a half lengths ahead. Azamour was six lengths clear of the remainder.

		Northern Dancer	Nearctic
	Night Shift (USA)	(b 1961)	Natalma
	(b 1980)	Ciboulette	Chop Chop
Azamour (IRE)		(b 1961)	Windy Answer
(b.c. 2001)		Lear Fan	Roberto
	Asmara (USA)	(b 1981)	Wac
	(b 1993)	Anaza	Darshaan
		(b 1986)	Azaarika

Oddly, only one of the Aga Khan's Group 1 winners mentioned above who stayed in training added to his reputation—Valanour, successful in the Prix d'Harcourt and Prix Ganay. Sendawar at least won a Group 1, the Prix d'Ispahan, but Jour et Nuit III ran unplaced in the Prix Ganay, Vayrann was unplaced in two starts and Lashkari won just a minor event. The genuine Azamour should buck the trend, if five horses over forty years can set a trend. Points in Azamour's favour are that he is lightly raced, and that he made great physical progress through the year, filling out into a tall, good sort who invariably impressed in appearance. He can be expected to develop into a fine-looking four-year-old. His ideal trip seems to be a mile and a quarter, and the Tattersalls Gold Cup and Prince of Wales's Stakes have been mentioned as targets by his trainer for the first half of the season prior to a challenge for the King George VI and Queen Elizabeth Stakes. Azamour may stay a mile and a half but, as noted in *Racehorses of 2003*, his pedigree is not that of a horse who will be suited by the trip. There is little to add to those details, apart from

H.H. Aga Khan's "Azamour"

the facts that Asmara's half-brother Ansar won the Galway Plate in August and that she has produced three foals since Azamour—the unraced two-year-old colt Arafan (by Barathea), a yearling colt by Sinndar and a colt foal by Selkirk. Additionally, the sire Night Shift merits a word or two. He is getting on in years and has never exactly been one of Coolmore's 'star-spangled' sires. Equally, he has produced his share of big winners—Azamour is his ninth in Group 1 company, though the first colt to score at this level in Britain, Ireland or France. For the record, Azamour is also a good mover and, while he clearly acts on soft, it will be no surprise if connections try to campaign him principally on firm, which suited him admirably at both Ascot and Leopardstown. *J. Oxx, Ireland*

AZAROLE (IRE) 3 b.g. Alzao (USA) 117 – Cashew 80 (Sharrood (USA) 124) [2004 **106** 109: 7g⁵ 8m⁴ 7g⁴ Sep 17] strong gelding: useful performer: reportedly underwent treatment for a soft palate problem after second start: good 1½ lengths fourth to Royal Storm in listed event at Newbury subsequent outing: gelded after: probably stays 1m: raced only on good/good to firm ground. *J. R. Fanshawe*

AZA WISH (IRE) 2 b.f. (Mar 25) Mujadil (USA) 119 – Kilcsem Eile (IRE) (Comman- **52** che Run 133) [2004 5g 5.1d⁵ 6g 6f 7m⁶ 7m⁵ 9d⁵ 8s Oct 22] €8,000Y: rather unfurnished filly: fifth foal: half-sister to useful Irish 1¼m to 2m winner Al Eile (by Alzao): dam Irish maiden out of half-sister to Oaks winner Shahtoush: modest maiden: barely stays 9f: acts on firm and good to soft going: sometimes slowly away. *Ms Deborah J. Evans*

AZEEZAH 2 ch.f. (Mar 11) Hernando (FR) 127 – Brave Vanessa (USA) 62 (Private **64 p** Account (USA)) [2004 p7.1g⁵ Dec 10] seventh foal: half-sister to 1¼m winner Simiola (by Shaamit): dam, 6f winner who stayed 1m, sister to US Grade 2 winner around 1m Topicount: 12/1, 2½ lengths fifth of 12 to Croon in maiden at Wolverhampton: should be suited by 1¼m/1½m: likely to improve. *B. A. McMahon*

AZIZAM 2 ch.f. (Mar 10) Singspiel (IRE) 133 – Perdicula (IRE) (Persian Heights 129) **67 p** [2004 8d Oct 15] smallish, sturdy filly: fourth foal: half-sister to fairly useful 6f (at 2 yrs) and 1m winner Zandicular (by Forzando), later successful up to 9.5f in Italy: dam, German winner around 1¼m, half-sister to Derby winner High-Rise and to grandam of 2-y-o Dubawi: 66/1, seventh of 21 to Proclamation in maiden at Newmarket, tiring late on: should be suited by 1¼m/1½m: sure to improve. *P. W. Chapple-Hyam*

AZREME 4 ch.c. Unfuwain (USA) 131 – Mariette 35 (Blushing Scribe (USA) 107) **85** [2004 75, a68: 7.1v* 8.2d⁵ 7m f7g⁴ f6d⁵ 8.3m⁴ 7g³ 7m 7s² 7g 7.2s* 7.1d² 7d 7s Nov 2] **a61** well-made colt: fairly useful performer on turf, modest on all-weather: won minor event at Warwick in May and handicap at Ayr in September: barely stays 1m: acts on all-weather and good to firm ground, goes well on softer than good: successful in visor at 3 yrs: usually waited with. *D. K. Ivory*

AZUREE (IRE) 2 b.f. (Mar 4) Almutawakel 126 – Cappella (IRE) 75 (College **70** Chapel 122) [2004 5s² 6s⁶ 6m³ 5d 6g⁴ 7f³ 5g 7g⁵ 6g⁴ 6v p6g² p7.1g⁶ p8m p6g⁴ p6g* p6g³ **a61** Dec 18] €45,000Y: leggy filly: second foal: half-sister to 3-y-o Red Birr: dam 2-y-o 5f winner: fair on turf, modest on all-weather: won seller at R. Hannon after eleventh start: barely stays 7f: acts on polytrack, soft and good to firm going: usually blinkered: tongue tied last 2 starts: no easy ride. *P. S. McEntee*

B

BAAWRAH 3 ch.g. Cadeaux Genereux 131 – Kronengold (USA) (Golden Act (USA)) **66** [2004 76: p10g² p10g* p10g⁴ 10.3g 10d⁶ 12g Oct 5] strong, workmanlike gelding: fair **a76** performer: awarded maiden at Lingfield (wandered) in January: left M. Channon, gelded and off 3 months prior to final outing: likely to prove best at 1m/1¼m: acts on all-weather and good to soft going: usually races prominently. *M. Todhunter*

BABA (IRE) 3 ch.g. Indian Ridge 123 – Theory of Law (Generous (IRE) 139) [2004 **–** 7s 7g 5s Nov 2] lengthy, well-made gelding: poor maiden. *T. P. Tate*

BABE MACCOOL (IRE) 2 ch.c. (May 23) Giant's Causeway (USA) 132 – Kotama **65 p** (USA) 96 (Shahrastani (USA) 135) [2004 6d⁶ 6g⁶ Oct 11] 50,000Y: seventh foal: half-brother to winner in Norway by Woodman: dam, Irish 7f and 9f winner, half-sister to dam of High Chaparral: fair form in maidens at Windsor, not knocked about behind Nota Bene on second occasion: will stay at least 1m: capable of better. *B. W. Hills*

Freephone Stanleybet Lincoln (Handicap), Doncaster—
Babodana puts up a smart performance to defy top weight; Quito (blinkers), Dark Charm (No.24)
and Wing Commander chase him home as the group on the stand side dominate

BABODANA   4 ch.c. Bahamian Bounty 116 – Daanat Nawal (Machiavellian (USA)   **115**
123) [2004 105: 8g* 8.1d⁶ 7.1g³ 8.3m⁵ 8g⁵ 7g⁴ 7s⁶ 8.9g⁴ 9s³ 8d² Oct 30] good-topped
colt: smart performer: first past post in Freephone Stanleybet Lincoln (Handicap) at
Doncaster in March (top weight, beat Quito by ¾ length) and, for second successive year,
listed race at Newmarket in October (beat Sleeping Indian by short head but demoted to
second after edging right and causing interference final 1f): stays easy 9f: acts on heavy
and good to firm going: blinkered eighth start. *M. H. Tompkins*

BABOOSH (IRE)   3 b.f. Marju (IRE) 127 – Slipper 94 (Suave Dancer (USA) 136)   **79**
[2004 78p: 8d² 8.2m* 10.3s Nov 6] leggy filly: fair performer: won maiden at Nottingham in September: well beaten in listed race at Doncaster final start: should stay 1¼m:
acts on good to firm ground: sold 32,000 gns. *J. R. Fanshawe*

BABOUSHKA (IRE)   3 b.f. Soviet Star (USA) 128 – Kabayil 75 (Dancing Brave   **–**
(USA) 140) [2004 62p: 8v 9.9s Apr 22] workmanlike filly: maiden: well beaten in 2004.
Miss J. A. Camacho

BABY BARRY   7 b.g. Komaite (USA) – Malcesine (IRE) 46 (Auction Ring (USA)   **59 §**
123) [2004 65§: 6m 5.9f f8g 7.6g³ 7.1m 7m² 7s 7.9m² 8g* p8.6g Oct 7] good-topped
gelding: modest handicapper: won claiming event at Goodwood in September: stays
1m: acts on all-weather and firm going: often used to wear blinkers/visor (not last 7
starts). *Mrs G. S. Rees*

BACHELOR AFFAIR   2 b.c. (Mar 18) Bachir (IRE) 118 – Profit Alert (IRE) 97   **– p**
(Alzao (USA) 117) [2004 7g 7d Oct 30] 20,000Y: angular, good-topped colt: second foal:
dam, Irish 7f and 11f winner, half-sister to useful 1¼m/1½m performer Razana, out of
half-sister to Irish St Leger second Rayseka: behind in maidens at Newmarket, prominent
long way on second occasion: likely to do better. *W. Jarvis*

BACHELOR DUKE (USA)   3 b.c. Miswaki (USA) 124 – Gossamer (USA)   **122**
(Seattle Slew (USA)) [2004 115p: 8g 8m* 8f Jun 15]
     'Rudeness sets you back for a whole week. We talk about the environment,
but I think good manners would make a difference to people's lives.' Sentiments of
the 'old school' articulated by the Duke of Devonshire, who famously made a
gesture to the booing and jeering crowd at Longchamp when Park Top returned
after being beaten at long odds on in the Prix de Royallieu, the final race of her
splendid career. The Duke's own attitude to disappointments in racing—of which
he had more than a few—was always one of unfailing politeness and sportsman-
ship. Owning the best mare (at the time) to race over a mile and a half in Britain
since Petite Étoile gave him some of his best moments, her thirteen wins including
the 1969 King George VI and Queen Elizabeth Stakes and Coronation Cup, and
also gave him some of his worst, since she should have won an Eclipse and an Arc
as well, managing to find her way blocked in a seven-runner race at Sandown and
finishing spectacularly fast after another very poor run at Longchamp. In more
recent times the Duke of Devonshire won the July Cup with 50/1-shot Compton
Place, but he did not live to see Bachelor Duke give him what would have been a
first classic winner. The Duke, who has been succeeded by his son Lord Hartington
the founding chairman of the British Horseracing Board, died aged eighty-four two

days after the Two Thousand Guineas in which Bachelor Duke finished a respectable seventh on his seasonal reappearance.

Bachelor Duke was highly tried after finishing a promising third in a maiden at Yarmouth on his racecourse debut in September 2003. His two subsequent appearances as a two-year-old came in pattern company, finishing in the frame in the Somerville Tattersall Stakes and in the Dewhurst, both times starting at 25/1. After his run in the Guineas, in which he travelled as well as anything for six furlongs, Bachelor Duke lined up still a maiden for the Boylesports Irish Two Thousand Guineas at the Curragh later in May. In a weakened eight-runner field lacking Guineas winner Haafhd, the betting was dominated by the Newmarket third and fourth Azamour and Grey Swallow, both trained in Ireland. The only British challenge came from Bachelor Duke and Leitrim House, who had beaten the Dewhurst winner Milk It Mick at Lingfield in April and followed up in the Tetrarch Stakes at the Curragh; the pair were third and fourth favourite, 12/1-shot Bachelor Duke, who took the eye more than he had at Newmarket, starting at more than twice the odds of his compatriot. It is not unheard of for Guineas form to be turned on its head in the Irish equivalent for which the going, for one thing, is sometimes different. Indian Haven reversed Newmarket placings at the Curragh the previous year with the Guineas runner-up, fourth, fifth and eighth; the Newmarket eighth Yesterday also turned the tables in the fillies' equivalent on One Thousand Guineas runner-up Six Perfections.

Bachelor Duke followed in the footsteps of Indian Haven to provide a second successive Irish Two Thousand Guineas victory for a relatively small Newmarket stable. The early pace was only fair—the winning time was slower than the two other races over a mile on the same card—but a change to waiting tactics still worked well on Bachelor Duke. He took a little time to respond when the race began in earnest around three furlongs out, but stormed home to catch Azamour and Grey Swallow near the finish, beating them by a length and a half a length, with Leitrim House fourth. Bachelor Duke wandered a little under a robust ride from Seb Sanders who is seldom found wanting when strength in a finish is needed. Sanders rides principally for Sir Mark Prescott, whose stable had a splendid season after making a very late start, and he finished third in the jockeys' championship after a particularly fruitful July in which he rode forty-five winners. Despite his reliability, however, Sanders hasn't so far had much of a look-in when it has come to the big races and Bachelor Duke was his first classic winner, as well as being the first for James Toller who also trained Compton Place.

Though limited experience was not a factor that had to be taken into account when assessing Bachelor Duke's chance, he was the first maiden successful in the Irish Two Thousand Guineas since Ballymore won in 1972 on his racecourse debut. Maidens rarely win classics, the last to do so in Britain, Ireland or France being Snurge in the 1990 St Leger, although he had been first past the post in the Criterium de Saint-Cloud (demoted to second) the previous year. Pearl Bracelet had been third in her only race before gaining a 50/1 success in the 1989 Poule d'Essai

Boylesports Irish 2000 Guineas, the Curragh—Bachelor Duke reverses Newmarket placings with Azamour (rail) and Grey Swallow (noseband); Leitrim House is a creditable fourth

des Pouliches. The winner of the same race in 1996, Ta Rib, gained her first success in a maiden just nine days beforehand. The fillies' classics have featured more successes by maidens than the colts' equivalents, Lady Capulet (no previous racecourse experience) and Olwyn winning the Irish Guineas and Irish Oaks respectively in 1977, eleven years after the maidens Valoris and Merry Mate had completed the same double. Madam Gay was a maiden when she won the 1981 Prix de Diane, while the last filly to win a British classic as a maiden was Sun Princess who routed her field in the 1983 Oaks. Sun Princess was the first maiden successful in a classic in Britain since another Oaks winner, Asmena, thirty-three years earlier.

Bachelor Duke (USA) (b.c. 2001)	Miswaki (USA) (ch 1978)	Mr Prospector (b 1970)	Raise A Native Gold Digger
		Hopespringseternal (ch 1971)	Buckpasser Rose Bower
	Gossamer (USA) (b 1991)	Seattle Slew (b or br 1974)	Bold Reasoning My Charmer
		Lisaleen (ch 1982)	Northern Dancer Lisadell

The good-topped Bachelor Duke looked the type to prove better at three than two but his campaign after the Curragh was an anticlimax. He managed only seventh to Azamour in the St James's Palace Stakes at Royal Ascot, fighting for his head under restraint for a long way after becoming stirred up in the preliminaries. The Juddmonte International and the Queen Elizabeth II Stakes were both said to be on the agenda, but he missed York after some in his trainer's string were hit by a virus and, after being a late withdrawal at Ascot through lameness, he was packed off to stud. Bachelor Duke's retirement—he will stand at the Ballylinch Stud in Ire-

Exors of the late Duke of Devonshire's "Bachelor Duke"

land at a fee of €12,500 in 2005—coincided with the death of his American-based sire Miswaki at the age of twenty-six. Miswaki, who had been retired in August because of declining fertility (he reportedly covered only six mares in 2004, none of whom got in foal), won the Prix de la Salamandre over seven furlongs and none of his four victories as a three-year-old in the States was achieved at much beyond a mile. His stud career was marked by a Horse of the Year in North America, the Breeders' Cup Classic winner Black Tie Affair, and his offspring did particularly well on turf in Europe where the average distance of races won by them at three and above was around a mile, though Miswaki also had the distinction of being represented by winners of both the Arc (Urban Sea) and the Prix de l'Abbaye (Kistena). Bachelor Duke's Irish Two Thousand Guineas victory was the fortieth European pattern win by the progeny of Miswaki. With the likes of Galileo, Hernando and the half-brothers Daylami and Dalakhani among the produce of his daughters, Miswaki will have a lasting influence. Bachelor Duke is closely related to a useful winner trained in Germany called Translucid (by another son of Mr Prospector, Woodman) who stayed a mile and a half on the Flat and has also been successful over hurdles and fences. Another older half-brother Allover (by Spinning World) was tailed off in a Warwick maiden as a three-year-old on his only start in Britain but won twice in minor company as a four-year-old in North America, at up to eight and a half furlongs. The American-raced dam Gossamer is not to be confused with the Irish One Thousand Guineas winner of the same name; this Gossamer finally managed a couple of wins at around a mile as a four-year-old, after failing to win at two or three. Gossamer does, though, come from an excellent family, her dam Lisaleen, a useful winner at seven furlongs and a mile in Ireland, being closely related to the Irish Two Thousand Guineas runner-up Fatherland and the smart sprinter of the late-'seventies Yeats (a successful sire in Australia). Bachelor Duke's great grandam the Coronation Stakes winner Lisadell was a sister to the top-class sprinter/miler Thatch as well as to Special, the dam of Nureyev and the grandam of Sadler's Wells and Fairy King. Bachelor Duke, who never raced beyond a mile but would probably have stayed a mile and a quarter, raced only on good going or firmer. *J. A. R. Toller*

BACK AT DE FRONT (IRE)   3 b.f. Cape Cross (IRE) 129 – Bold Fashion (FR)   **62 d**
(Nashwan (USA) 135) [2004 70: f6g* f6g⁵ f5g⁵ p6g⁴ f5s⁵ f6s⁶ p7g 6.1g 6m f6g f6g⁶ Jun 16] lengthy filly: modest performer: won handicap at Wolverhampton in January: should stay 7f: acts on firm ground and all-weather. *N. E. Berry*

BACKGAMMON   3 b.g. Sadler's Wells (USA) 132 – Game Plan 118 (Darshaan 133)   **83**
[2004 10s² 9.2d³ 8g* 8g⁴ 8s Oct 19] compact gelding: closely related to fairly useful 1m/ 1¼m winner Night Vigil (by Night Shift) and half-brother to several winners, including very smart Irish 1m (at 2 yrs)/1¼m winner Strategic (by Caerleon) and smart French 1¼m winner Sobieski (by Polish Precedent): dam, 1¼m winner and second in Oaks, half-sister to Oaks winner Shahtoush: fairly useful performer: won maiden at Newcastle in September: respectable fourth at Pontefract, better effort in handicaps: should stay 1½m: acts on soft going: sold 20,000 gns, joined K. Reveley, then gelded. *D. R. Loder*

BACK IN ACTION   4 b.g. Hector Protector (USA) 124 – Lucca (Sure Blade (USA)   **63 ?**
130) [2004 –: 8.3m 12g Jul 8] leggy gelding: just modest maiden in 2004: tried blinkered: tongue tied. *M. A. Magnusson*

BACK IN FASHION   3 b.f. Puissance 110 – Spring Collection (Tina's Pet 121) [2004   **–**
–: 7g Jun 24] no sign of ability in sellers. *J. Mackie*

BACK IN SPIRIT   4 ch.g. Primo Dominie 121 – Pusey Street Girl 87 (Gildoran 123)   **44 §**
[2004 –: f6g f6s f5m f6g 6.1d² f5g⁴ 7.1s f6g f6d⁶ Dec 21] well-grown gelding: poor performer: stays 6f: acts on fibresand and good to soft going: tongue tied: inconsistent. *B. A. McMahon*

BACKLASH   3 b.f. Fraam 114 – Mezza Luna (Distant Relative 128) [2004 –: p6g p6g   **52**
f6s 7.1s⁵ p8g⁵ 8.1d* p10m⁵ p9.5g⁶ Dec 22] modest performer: won banded event at Warwick in October: stays 1m: acts on soft going. *A. W. Carroll*

BACKSTREET LAD   2 b.c. (Mar 1) Fraam 114 – Forest Fantasy 61 (Rambo Dancer   **53 ?**
(CAN) 107) [2004 7d 7s 8g p8.6g Oct 16] compact colt: seemingly modest form in maidens: best effort at 7f on soft going. *B. R. Millman*

BACK TO REALITY   2 ch.g. (Apr 12) Magic Ring (IRE) 115 – Arian Da 81 (Super-   **56**
lative 118) [2004 7.1m 10.2g 8.2v Nov 4] big, close-coupled gelding: best effort in
maidens when eighth at Nottingham on final start: not bred to stay beyond 1m. *B. Palling*

BA CLUBMAN (IRE)   4 b.g. Royal Abjar (USA) 121 – Ah Ya Zein (Artaius (USA)   **54 +**
129) [2004 10d 9.7s⁵ 11.9m p6g⁴ Dec 14] IR 7,000Y, 38,000 2-y-o: half-brother to several
winners, including smart 1m (at 2 yrs) and 1¼m winner Moutahddee (by Alzao) and
useful 7.6f (at 2 yrs) and 1¼m winner Najm Mubeen (by Last Tycoon): dam French 1¼m
winner: modest maiden: form only at Wolverhampton on first start for 7 months: should
stay 7f: blinkered on debut, wore cheekpieces third outing. *S. C. Williams*

BADDAM   2 b.c. (Mar 26) Mujahid (USA) 125 – Aude La Belle (FR) 81 (Ela-Mana-   **69**
Mou 132) [2004 6.1g⁴ 7m 7.1g⁶ 8d³ Nov 5] 15,000Y: rather leggy, quite good-topped
colt: sixth foal: half-brother to 2 winners in Germany, including 1¼m and 15f winner
Anastacia (by Bahamian Bounty): dam, 1¾m/2m winner, out of half-sister to Acatenan-
go: fair maiden: staying-on third in nursery at Yarmouth: will be suited by 1¼m/1½m.
J. L. Dunlop

BAD INTENTIONS (IRE)   4 b.f. Victory Note (USA) 120 – Fallacy (Selkirk (USA)   **–**
129) [2004 76: 5.7f⁶ 6m 5.5g 7f⁶ 7d Aug 29] tall, leggy filly: well held in 2004. *Miss
D. Mountain*

BADMINTON   3 b.f. Zieten (USA) 118 – Badawi (USA) 103 (Diesis 133) [2004   **106**
103p: 7m* 7s Oct 16] quite lightly-made filly: useful performer: won listed race at Ascot
in September by 3 lengths from Pearl Grey, leading over 1f out: well beaten in Challenge
Stakes at Newmarket 3 weeks later: should stay 1m: acts on good to firm going: tongue
tied in 2004. *Saeed bin Suroor*

BADOU   4 b.g. Averti (IRE) 117 – Bint Albadou (IRE) 91 (Green Desert (USA) 127)   **50**
[2004 55, a59: p8g⁶ f7g* p8g⁴ p6g* p6g p7g p6g² 5v⁴ 7f 6g 7m 6m p7m Dec 15]
good-topped gelding: modest performer: won banded events at Wolverhampton and
Lingfield in February: stays easy 1m: acts on all-weather, heavy and good to firm going:
sometimes visored, blinkered final start. *L. Montague Hall*

BADR (USA)   3 b.c. Theatrical 128 – Bejat (USA) (Mr Prospector (USA)) [2004 67p: **61**
9g⁶ 9.9g 11m⁵ 10g 9.2g Jul 10] rangy, good sort: modest maiden: should stay 1½m: sold
5,500 gns. *M. Johnston*

BAFFLE   3 b.f. Selkirk (USA) 129 – Elude (Slip Anchor 136) [2004 76: 8.1s* 9v⁵ 8.1g   **78**
8.1g⁶ 8.1g Sep 3] sturdy, workmanlike filly: poor mover: fair performer: won maiden at
Haydock in April: should stay 1¼m: acts on heavy and good to firm going: looked none
too keen third start: races prominently: sold 8,000 gns. *J. L. Dunlop*

BAGAN (FR)   5 b.h. Rainbow Quest (USA) 134 – Maid of Erin (USA) (Irish River   **92**
(FR) 131) [2004 96: 12g⁴ 12g⁴ 10.4d⁴ 11.9d 12f⁴ 12g Oct 1] big, good-topped, attractive
horse: fairly useful handicapper: mostly at least respectable efforts in 2004: effective at
1¼m/1½m: acts on firm and good to soft going: held up: sold 26,000 gns, joined C. Mann.
H. R. A. Cecil

BAGO (FR)   3 b. or br.c. Nashwan (USA) 135 – Moonlight's Box (USA) (Nureyev   **130**
(USA) 131) [2004 121p: 9g* 10g* 10.4d³ 12d³ 12m* Oct 3]
    If Attraction was popularly regarded by midsummer as a 'wonder filly',
then French-trained Bago was her counterpart in Europe at the time among the
colts. An unbeaten record and a towering reputation often result in a classic colt
being given the 'superstar' mantle by modern-day commentators, most of whom
seem more concerned with passing on or mirroring the views of 'professionals'
than with rational appreciation. After Bago had stretched his unbeaten run to six in
the Prix Jean Prat and the Juddmonte Grand Prix de Paris, his trainer—who has
handled Breeders' Cup winners Spinning World and Tikkanen—called him 'the
best I have trained by a long way', while top American jockey Gary Stevens, who
partnered Cacique to be second to Bago at both Chantilly and Longchamp, said
'Bago is as good as any horse I have seen in my career—and I have seen a good few
horses.' When an animal is the subject of such extravagant promotion it is hard for
it not to disappoint, but Bago fared pretty well in the circumstances.
    Bago lost his aura of invincibility when a beaten favourite in both the Inter-
national Stakes at York and the Prix Niel, but he ended the season with the best
performance of his career so far by winning the Prix de l'Arc de Triomphe, one
of the events that counts most in the European racing year. Bago won a slightly
below-average renewal of the Arc and, taken overall, his achievements probably

fell a little short of the very high expectations that attended him at the end of his two-year-old career. However, he remains in training so there will be another opportunity to put his career into historical perspective. For the moment it is fairest to judge and celebrate Bago on what he has achieved, rather than damn him for what he has not. He proved himself a top-class three-year-old, the best in training over a mile and a half in Europe, and, at the very least, will provide a strong challenge for the rising generation of classic colts in any of the big, open-aged events that he contests. With the likes of Doyen, Azamour, Grey Swallow, North Light and Cherry Mix also staying in training, the leaders of the next classic crop look as if they may have their work cut out against the older horses.

Among the other good horses handled by Bago's trainer was the Prix du Jockey Club runner-up Act One, winner of the first running of the Criterium International at Saint-Cloud, which replaced the Grand Criterium in 2001 as France's Group 1 event over a mile for two-year-old colts. Dalakhani won the second running and Bago followed in his footsteps. Bago won by six lengths, making it four wins from four starts as a two-year-old and ending the season rated more highly than either Act One or Dalakhani at the same stage. In a year when no two-year-old colt stood out clearly, Bago was rated the best of his age by Timeform and his prospects at three looked excellent. However, while Act One and Dalakhani both had pedigrees which pointed to their taking a traditional route to the Prix du Jockey Club, Bago looked much more likely to contest the Poule d'Essai des Poulains or Two Thousand Guineas before any decision was made about tackling further.

In fact, Bago missed the classics altogether, an infection putting him out of his planned Guineas trial in the Prix de Fontainebleau in late-April and also out of the Poule d'Essai des Poulains three weeks later. He made an impressive return in early-June, not in the Prix du Jockey Club (he also held a Derby entry) but in another Group 1 on the same day at Chantilly, the Prix Jean Prat over nine furlongs. Bago's pacemaker was taken on for the lead by the only British challenger, Pearl of Love, which ensured a strongly-run race. Held up fourth of the eight runners, Bago moved smoothly into the lead a furlong and a half out and won readily by three lengths from Cacique. The choice for his next race seemed to be between the St James's Palace Stakes over a mile at Royal Ascot and the Grand Prix de Paris over a mile and a quarter, a tilt at the Irish Derby quickly being ruled out. The Grand Prix de Paris always seemed the more likely choice. Millkom and Vespone had completed the Jean Prat/Grand Prix de Paris double in the previous ten years, while Peintre Celebre had followed up in the Grand Prix de Paris after winning the Prix du Jockey Club. Bago was opposed by only three, one of whom was his pacemaker, in the smallest field in the history of the Grand Prix de Paris which was first run in 1863 and was one of the world's great races for over a century (run over a mile and seven) until being allowed to decline by the French authorities. Subsequent Arc winners Saumarez, Subotica and Peintre Celebre have won the race since its distance was reduced in 1987 (it will be a mile and a half from 2005), but there have been some eminently forgettable renewals and Longchamp must have been grateful for the presence of Bago in the latest edition. He again accounted for Cacique, though not so impressively this time, having to be ridden to get on top by half a length in a rather muddling race, the steady early pace probably not in his favour.

Prix Jean Prat, Chantilly—Bago belatedly carries on where he had left off as a two-year-old with an authoritative success; Cacique and Ershaad (striped cap) are second and third

BAG

Bago had his first race outside France, and his first outside his own age group, in another Juddmonte-sponsored major event, the International at York in August. Bago, Cacique and the Irish Derby third Tycoon were the only three-year-olds in a nine-strong line-up and Bago came out best of the trio. However, starting a short-priced favourite, he found the King George VI and Queen Elizabeth third Sulamani and the Eclipse and Sussex Stakes fourth Norse Dancer too good for him on the day, closing on them but being beaten three quarters of a length and the same. Bago's end-of-season objective had been announced as the Breeders' Cup Classic over a mile and a quarter on dirt, but his style of racing, and the fact that he looked to have more left than most at the end of the International, encouraged connections to regard races at a mile and a half as a feasible option for the autumn. The Niarchos colours had never been carried to victory in an Arc—Northern Trick, Hernando and Sulamani (afterwards purchased by Godolphin) had finished second—but Bago's performance in the Prix Niel on Longchamp's 'day of Arc trials' was none too convincing.

Contesting the Niel has become a well-trodden route to the Arc for top French three-year-old colts returning from a summer break. Six of the ten previous Niel winners had gone on to win the big race—Carnegie, Helissio, Sagamix, Montjeu, Sinndar and Dalakhani—while Sulamani and Golan had also won the Niel in the same period and finished in the frame in the Arc. Defeat in the Niel doesn't always rule out victory in the Arc—unlucky-in-running Peintre Celebre was beaten in the 1997 Niel—but Bago managed only third to Valixir and Prospect Park, who had filled the places, in reverse order, in the Prix du Jockey Club. Bago didn't move with the same fluency that characterised his summer performances—there seemed a possibility that he was not quite right on the day—and a final decision on his participation in the Arc was not taken until the week of the race, the announcement that he would run coming as something of a welcome surprise at the time.

The line-up for the Prix de l'Arc de Triomphe Lucien Barriere was the biggest since Carnegie beat nineteen rivals in 1994, when the size of the field was first reduced to a maximum of twenty, a number which suits the French betting system. Places in the oversubscribed field in Carnegie's year were decided on earnings, but, in the latest renewal, the first to be oversubscribed since, the order of elimination was drawn up by the French handicappers. The Prix Niel sixth Mister Farmer was eliminated to get the field down to twenty at the final stage (Irish-trained Acropolis would have been the next to go) but the late withdrawal of the Deutsches Derby winner Shirocco (fears about the firmish going) resulted in nineteen going to post. Shirocco's presence would have given the Arc field a sixth classic winner from the current crop, joining North Light (Derby), Grey Swallow (Irish Derby), Blue Canari (Prix du Jockey Club)—the two last-named both supplemented—Ouija Board (Oaks and Irish Oaks) and Latice (Prix de Diane).

Juddmonte Grand Prix de Paris, Longchamp—in the smallest field ever for this historic race, Bago gets the better of Cacique (rail) again; Alnitak and Privy Seal (right) chase them home

Prix de l'Arc de Triomphe Lucien Barriere, Longchamp—with 100 metres to go, Bago is about to reel in Cherry Mix (rail); Ouija Board (black colours) passes North Light to get up for third, while Acropolis (behind North Light) snatches fourth in a finish dominated by three-year-olds

If the classic generation was well represented—Prospect Park (who started a surprising favourite at 5/1 on the pari-mutuel after being widely tipped in the French press) and Valixir were also there—the same could hardly be said of the older horses. Outnumbered by the three-year-olds and lacking some of the biggest names, the older-horse challenge looked modest by the Arc's own very high standards. Godolphin had won two of the three previous runnings but had to rely on the five-year-old Mamool in the absence of Sulamani and the King George winner Doyen, whose surprise defeat in the Irish Champion had thrown the ante-post market on the Arc into confusion. Seven-year-old Execute hadn't run since May when winning the Prix Ganay, a race in which he had been runner-up the two previous years; six-year-old Warrsan had won the Coronation Cup (for the second successive year) and the Grosser Preis von Baden but, along with the four-year-old filly Vallee Enchantee, had failed to make the frame in 'Britain's Arc', the King George; and while seven-year-old Tap Dance City, successful in the 2003 Japan Cup and winner of both his starts in Japan in 2004, looked an interesting contender, he nearly missed the race, alternative travel arrangements from Japan having to be hastily drawn up at the eleventh hour. With free-going Tap Dance City vying with the enterprisingly-ridden North Light for the lead from a long way out, the latest Arc was strongly run, the winning time surpassing that in Sinndar's year to become the second fastest—2m 25.0sec—in the history of the race, behind only the 2m 24.6sec recorded by Peintre Celebre.

The Arc unfolded more or less perfectly for Bago whose rider Thierry Gillet gave a fine exhibition of riding a waiting race, having Bago well away—he was among the leaders in the first furlong—before gently restraining him in the middle of the race. In tenth place rounding the home turn, where North Light and Tap Dance City were going at it hammer and tongs out in front, Bago enjoyed an uninterrupted passage in the home straight, his rider never having to move far from the inside where he had been all the way. The more prominently-ridden Cherry Mix looked all over the winner when looming up alongside North Light over two furlongs out and he briefly showed clear entering the final furlong. But Bago was now in full cry and he kept on strongly to collar Cherry Mix close home. The winning margin was half a length, with strong-finishing Ouija Board a length further away third after being involved in a little scrimmaging around and after the home turn and having to be switched to the outside. The 84/1-shot Acropolis, poorly placed approaching the home turn after a tardy start and sticking to the rail, just caught North Light to finish fourth, with sixth-placed Vallee Enchantee the first of the older generation across the line. Warrsan (ninth) and Execute (eleventh) were the only other older horses in the first twelve. Tap Dance City weakened quickly in the straight and had only the obviously amiss Grey Swallow and another of the early leaders Policy Maker (the only member of the 2003 field in the line-up) behind him. Bago's near-record time was a reflection of the prevailing conditions— the going was on the firm side—and of the way the race was run, rather than evidence of exceptional merit in the winner. Just over nine lengths separated Bago from Prospect Park in sixteenth. Of the last fifteen winners, only Urban Sea, Carnegie,

Sagamix and Marienbard have recorded a lower Timeform rating in the Arc than Bago. Three-year-old colts, incidentally, have now won nine of the last eleven runnings.

The Arc was Bago's final race as a three-year-old, though there was continued talk immediately after Longchamp of his being sent to the Breeders' Cup, with the Classic still the target. In the end, it was considered better for the big, leggy Bago's prospects as a four-year-old if he missed the Breeders' Cup. He tended to sweat and become a shade edgy before his races as a three-year-old, a trait that it is to be hoped will become less evident with maturity. Bago is second only to dual King George VI and Queen Elizabeth winner Swain among the offspring of the now-deceased Nashwan, who won the Two Thousand Guineas, the Derby, the Eclipse and the King George before being beaten in the Prix Niel at 5/1-on, after which he was retired. Remarkably, Swain and Bago are the only sons of Nashwan that have won more than once in pattern company.

Bago is the first foal of the unraced Moonlight's Box, an impeccably-bred mare by Nureyev out of the Prix Morny and Prix de la Salamandre winner Coup de Genie, who finished third in the One Thousand Guineas. Coup de Genie is a sister to the first-rate sire Machiavellian, who, coincidentally, also won the Morny and Salamandre before finishing second in the Two Thousand Guineas. Machiavellian, one of the mainstays of the Darley stallion operation, had to be put down in the latest season after suffering from laminitis (a similar fate also befell another Darley stalwart In The Wings). Coup de Folie, the dam of Coup de Genie and Machiavellian, was so named because Stavros Niarchos ended up paying much more for her as a yearling—825,000 dollars—than he had intended. Coup de Folie was out of a half-sister to Northern Dancer and, after winning four races at up to a mile and a quarter including the Group 3 Prix d'Aumale as a two-year-old, she enjoyed a

Niarchos Family's "Bago"

stud career that now makes her look a bargain. As well as Coup de Genie and Machiavellian, Coup de Folie also produced their full brother Ocean of Wisdom, winner of the Prix La Rochette; the very smart miler Exit To Nowhere and the Poule d'Essai des Pouliches runner-up Hydro Calido were also out of Coup de Folie. It may not be long before Coup de Genie's own success at stud begins to rival that of Coup de Folie. All Coup de Genie's offspring to reach the racecourse so far have won. Loving Kindness (by Seattle Slew) and Denebola (by Storm Cat) both followed in the footsteps of their dam by winning the Prix de Cabourg, Denebola going on to win the Prix Marcel Boussac to establish herself, like her dam, as the best two-year-old filly of her year in France. Denebola was placed in the Prix du Moulin and the Prix de la Foret as a three-year-old. Coup de Genie has also produced two stakes winners in North America, both by A P Indy: Snake Mountain won three Grade 3 events at around nine furlongs and Glia, after being transferred from France where she won the Prix Imprudence, also won at nine furlongs and was runner-up in the Grade 2 Mrs Revere Stakes over eight and a half furlongs.

		Blushing Groom	Red God
	Nashwan (USA)	(ch 1974)	Runaway Bride
	(ch 1986)	Height of Fashion	Bustino
Bago (FR)		(b 1979)	Highclere
(b. or br.c. 2001)		Nureyev	Northern Dancer
	Moonlight's Box (USA)	(b 1977)	Special
	(b 1996)	Coup de Genie	Mr Prospector
		(b 1991)	Coup de Folie

Bago's useful two-year-old half-sister Million Wishes (by Darshaan) made it two winning foals out of two to reach the racecourse for Moonlight's Box when she was successful at six and seven furlongs, though she proved unable to maintain the family's tradition in the Prix de Cabourg in which she was the unplaced favourite. Moonlight's Box has a yearling colt by Hernando and a filly foal by Selkirk. Most of the family's more illustrious members have been milers but Bago stays a mile and a half well. Usually waited with and suited by a strongly-run race, he acts on soft and good to firm going. Bago takes his name from a town in Burma, famous as the home of the country's tallest pagoda, and follows a recent habit with some of the Niarchos horses, Sulamani being one of the country's most important temples. Both are appropriately named, since Bago in Phrygian, an ancient language of Western Asia, means 'the good', and Sulamani means 'crowning jewel'. *J. E. Pease, France*

BAHAMA BELLE 3 b.f. Bahamian Bounty 116 – Barque Bleue (USA) (Steinlen 127) **55** [2004 63: 6g 7m⁴ 6m 5.1m p7g p7.1d p7m⁴ p8m³ p6g* Dec 22] workmanlike filly: modest performer: left H. Howe after fifth start: won banded race at Wolverhampton in December: stays easy 1m: acts on polytrack and good to firm going: tried blinkered. *Mrs L. C. Jewell*

BAHAMA REEF (IRE) 3 b.g. Sri Pekan (USA) 117 – Caribbean Dancer 71 (Shareef **59** Dancer (USA) 135) [2004 72: p7g 8g p6g⁵ 7f² 8g 7m³ 7m³ 7.6f³ 7m Sep 7] angular gelding: modest maiden: barely stays 1m: acts on polytrack, raced only on good going or firmer on turf: has run badly in visor/cheekpieces. *B. Gubby*

BAHAMIAN BAY 2 b.f. (Feb 13) Bahamian Bounty 116 – Moly 64 (Inchinor 119) **37** [2004 7d 6f 5g Sep 25] 2,000Y: quite good-topped filly: second foal: dam ran 3 times: poor form in maidens. *M. Brittain*

BAHAMIAN BELLE 4 b.f. Bahamian Bounty 116 – Marjorie's Memory (IRE) 76 **56 d** (Fairy King (USA)) [2004 61, a52: p6g⁶ p6g 5g⁴ 5.7s 5.1d 5g 5m 5.3f 5.3f 5g⁵ 6m 6m 7d⁴ f7g p7m p5.1g Dec 20] good-topped filly: modest maiden: tried tongue tied/blinkered/in cheekpieces. *P. S. McEntee*

BAHAMIAN BREEZE 3 b.g. Piccolo 121 – Norgabie 94 (Northfields (USA)) [2004 **–** 78: 6g 5g May 17] robust gelding: below form both starts in 2004: visored final outing: sold 1,800 gns. *J. Noseda*

BAHAMIAN MAGIC 2 b.c. (Mar 14) Royal Applause 124 – Out Like Magic 82 **80** (Magic Ring (IRE) 115) [2004 6g⁴ p5d³ 5.7g* 6g p6m² Oct 6] 28,000F, 65,000Y: quite **a87** attractive colt: first living foal: dam 2-y-o 5f winner who barely stayed 1m: fairly useful performer: won maiden at Bath in September by ½ length from Lighted Way: good second in nursery at Lingfield: stays 6f: best efforts on polytrack: sold 25,000 gns, sent to USA. *D. R. Loder*

Victor Chandler Nunthorpe Stakes, York—Bahamian Pirate (noseband) becomes the oldest winner of a Group 1 race in Britain; The Tatling (third left) is runner-up for a second successive year, ahead of One Cool Cat (second left) and Avonbridge (blinkered)

BAHAMIAN PIRATE (USA) 9 ch.g. Housebuster (USA) – Shining Through (USA) (Deputy Minister (CAN)) [2004 113: 5.1g* 6g⁴ 7d⁴ 6g² 5v* 6s 5f 6f 6d 6g 5m* 5m⁶ 5s* 6g 5m Oct 3] **118**

Athlete Justin Gatlin streaked to gold aged twenty-two in the men's hundred metres in the Olympics at Athens in August, but success didn't come overnight for Bahamian Pirate before his win in one of racing's premier tests of speed, the Nunthorpe Stakes at York in the same month. The gelding Bahamian Pirate achieved his first victory at the top level as a nine-year-old at York, taking advantage of a substandard renewal of Britain's only Group 1 event at five furlongs to become the oldest Group 1 winner in Britain since the pattern began in 1971. Opinions vary on the relationship between horses and humans in terms of age but, according to one recently published chart, horses in theory age at six and a half times the rate of humans for the first three years of life, whereafter the rate slows to two and a half times per year, suggesting Bahamian Pirate was going on thirty-five in human terms at York. Regular activity and a healthy lifestyle can help slow the ageing process for racehorses as well as for humans and Yavana's Pace was ten when winning the Group 1 Credit Suisse Pokal over a mile and a half in Germany in 2002. Other sprinters have also made a mark of late in pattern races at the veteran stage—Tedburrow was also ten when winning the Group 3 Chipchase Stakes at Newcastle in 2002, the same age as Repertory was when he won the Group 3 Prix du Petit Couvert at Longchamp in 2003, while My Best Valentine won the Prix de l'Abbaye as an eight-year-old entire in 1998. Bahamian Pirate's success was all the more remarkable in that he suffered illness and injury as a young horse and at the start of 2004 his best days seemed behind him.

Bahamian Pirate came close to Group 1 success when runner-up in the Prix de l'Abbaye at Longchamp back in 2001 and when second to his stable-companion Continent in the following season's July Cup at Newmarket, but, continuing to do the rounds, he arrived at York not having reached a place in pattern company since being runner-up in the Palace House Stakes at Newmarket on his first outing in 2003. He gained his three successes in 2004 in minor events at Nottingham in March, Beverley in May and Newmarket in July, putting up his best effort for some time when edging out July Cup third Balmont in a small field at Newmarket. The three-year-old Balmont took him on again at York, going off at 13/2. Favourite at 3/1 in a field of twelve was One Cool Cat, another three-year-old fresh from success in the Group 3 Phoenix Sprint Stakes over six furlongs at the Curragh after flopping as Guineas favourite at Newmarket. Among those already successful in a pattern race at the minimum trip earlier in the season, Orientor, winner of the Champagne Laurent-Perrier Sprint at Sandown, was at 9/2, King's Stand winner The Tatling was at 13/2 and Prix du Gros-Chene winner Avonbridge at 8/1. Airwave at 6/1 and Moss Vale at 14/1 were also preferred in the betting to Bahamian Pirate, who started at 16/1, despite an upbeat bulletin from his trainer, who reported him to be 'in tremendous form, absolutely bouncing.' Bahamian Pirate had been taken off his feet when only sixth in the King George Stakes on good to firm ground at Goodwood on his one outing since Newmarket, finishing three places behind The Tatling even in receipt of 8 lb, but it was a different story at York, where the ground was the softest it had been for the race in many years. Partnered for the first time by Seb Sanders, Bahamian Pirate raced in mid-division as the runners swarmed up the centre. Ridden along as his stable-companion Fire Up The Band, along with Avonbridge, tried to stretch the field two furlongs out, Bahamian Pirate responded so well on the outside that he had gone a length up on the pack inside the final furlong, getting first run on some of the market leaders, and, though tired, he held on by a neck. Those that ran him closest probably weren't quite at their best. Runner-up The Tatling had his effort delayed slightly longer, and One Cool Cat, who had been left with a lot to do after being switched from the stalls, finished well to be a length further behind. Avonbridge was fourth and Orientor a close fifth after meeting trouble.

Despite the conditions at York, little over three lengths covered the first nine home, and the form was probably as weak as it had been for the Nunthorpe since Ya Malak gave David Nicholls his one previous success in the race when dead-heating with Coastal Bluff in 1997. All the same, the race added another proud chapter in the Nunthorpe story for Nicholls, who was runner-up in the race on Soba as a jockey, and whose wife Alex Greaves partnered Ya Malak, while it was another well-deserved Group 1 win for Sanders, who pressed Dettori and Fallon hard in the jockeys' championship before ending the season third. Bahamian Pirate had two more races in pattern company, finishing unplaced each time. Remarkably for a Group 1 winner on his latest outing, he started at 40/1 in the Sprint Cup at Haydock, coming home twelfth of nineteen to Tante Rose after being hampered over a furlong out. He finished ninth of fifteen behind Var, who had been missing at York, in the

Lucayan Stud's "Bahamian Pirate"

Prix de l'Abbaye at Longchamp on his final outing, never a threat but not disgraced in being beaten around five lengths, back at the minimum trip on firmish ground.

Bahamian Pirate (USA) (ch.g. 1995)	Housebuster (USA) (br 1987)	Mt Livermore (ch 1981)	Blushing Groom
			Flama Ardiente
		Big Dreams (b or br 1980)	Great Above
			Dolphins Dream
	Shining Through (USA) (b 1989)	Deputy Minister (b or br 1979)	Vice Regent
			Mint Copy
		Solar (ch 1976)	Halo
			Sex Appeal

Bahamian Pirate would have had a career at stud a long time ago had he still been an entire. By Housebuster, champion sprinter in the States at three and four, he is from the family of El Gran Senor and Try My Best. Two subsequent foals of his dam, the unraced Shining Through, each fetched over a million dollars as yearlings, one of them Strong Hope (by Grand Slam) going on to win two Grade 2 events as a three-year-old in 2003, the Dwyer Stakes over eight and a half furlongs at Belmont and the Jim Dandy Stakes over nine furlongs at Saratoga, as well as being placed in three Grade 1 races before being retired to stud at the end of the latest season. As it is, Bahamian Pirate will presumably have an easier time of things once retired from racing, though that might not be for a while. 'He doesn't look nine,' his trainer said after York. A sturdy gelding, with a distinctive mane and white blaze and socks, he was trained in Ireland at three, and looked a typical sprinter physically the first time we saw him as a four-year-old—on the all-weather at Southwell. He had a bone chip removed from a knee before breaking his duck on his final outing that season and was operated on for a slipped spleen before winning the Ayr Gold Cup at five, but he has raced regularly each season since. A tough sort, he acts on any going and is effective at five furlongs and six, though he possibly needs a good test at the minimum trip nowadays. He is sometimes slowly away and takes time to warm up, but has never been tried in headgear. *D. Nicholls*

BAHAMIAN SPRING (IRE)   2 b.g. (Mar 25) Danehill Dancer (IRE) 117 – Siana   –
Springs (IRE) 59 (Emarati (USA) 74) [2004 7d Aug 27] €42,000F, €110,000Y: good-
bodied gelding: second foal: dam, 2-y-o 5f seller winner, out of half-sister to Lockinge
winner Prismatic and smart 1¼m performer Perpendicular: 14/1, possibly amiss when
last in maiden at Newmarket (gelded after). *D. R. Loder*

BAHIA BREEZE   2 b.f. (Mar 23) Mister Baileys 123 – Ring of Love 77 (Magic Ring   **100**
(IRE) 115) [2004 6s⁴ 6m* 6m 6s* Oct 29] 3,200F, 5,000Y: compact filly: second foal:
dam 5f winner (including at 2 yrs): useful performer: won maiden at Folkestone (made
all, by 7 lengths) in September and listed race at Newmarket (led 1f out to beat Nanabanana by head) in October: will probably stay 7f. *R. Guest*

BAHIANO (IRE)   3 ch.c. Barathea (IRE) 127 – Trystero (Shareef Dancer (USA) 135)   **108 ?**
[2004 73p: f8.5g2 p7g* p8g² p7g³ 7g⁶ 7s 8.1m 7f⁴ 7m 8m 7g 7m Sep 25] compact colt:
useful performer: won maiden at Lingfield in February: best efforts after when fourth in
Jersey Stakes at Royal Ascot (possibly flattered when beaten 2½ lengths by Kheleyf)
eighth start and eighth to Kehaar in valuable handicap at same course final one: barely
stays 8.5f: acts on all-weather and firm going. *C. E. Brittain*

B A HIGHFLYER   4 b.g. Compton Place 125 – Primulette 82 (Mummy's Pet 125)   **67**
[2004 71: p6g 7s⁵ 8s 6g 7f 6m⁵ 6d⁴ 5.7m Aug 15] good-bodied gelding: fair handicapper:
broke a shoulder at Bath in August: best at 6f/7f: acted on all-weather, firm and soft
going: tried visored: dead. *M. R. Channon*

BAHJA (USA)   2 ch.f. (Mar 29) Seeking The Gold (USA) – Valentine Waltz (IRE) 116   **76**
(Be My Guest (USA) 126) [2004 7g⁴ 7g³ Sep 2] 500,000Y: quite attractive filly: second
foal: dam, 7f (including at 2 yrs) and 1m (Poule d'Essai des Pouliches) winner, out of
half-sister to top-class sprinter/miler Last Tycoon: fair form in maidens at Newmarket
and Salisbury (third to Almansoora): will stay 1m. *J. H. M. Gosden*

BAILAMOS (GER)   4 b.c. Lomitas 129 – Bandeira (GER) (Law Society (USA) 130)   **113**
[2004 15.5s⁵ 14.8s³ 16g² 16g* 14m⁴ 15.9d 15s⁵ 17s³ Oct 31] strong colt: first foal: dam
German 11f/1½m winner: smart performer: won 3 races at 3 yrs, notably listed race at
Mulheim: good 1½ lengths second to Darasim in Betty Barclay-Rennen at Baden-Baden
before winning listed race at Hamburg in June: below best afterwards (including in
Lonsdale Cup at York sixth start), though ran respectably in listed events at Cologne and
Mulheim last 2 outings: stays 17f: acts on soft ground. *P. Schiergen, Germany*

BAILANDA (GER) 2 b.f. (May 16) Mondrian (GER) 125 – Brasilia (GER) (Esclavo –
(FR)) [2004 p7.1g Dec 31] sixth foal: half-sister to 2 winners in Germany, including 7.5f
winner Buffalo Bill (by Highland Chieftain): dam German 10.5f winner: 40/1, last in
maiden at Wolverhampton. *J. Jay*

BAILAORA (IRE) 3 b.g. Shinko Forest (IRE) – Tart (FR) 76 (Warning 136) [2004 71
81: 8v⁶ 8m 7m⁶ 10s³ 9.7m 10g⁵ 11.7m 9.7g⁴ Aug 22] good-bodied gelding: fair maiden:
stays 1¼m: acts on firm and soft going: tried tongue tied: usually blinkered: gelded after
final start. *B. W. Duke*

BAILEY GATE 2 b.f. (Apr 4) Mister Baileys 123 – Floppie (FR) (Law Society (USA) 85 p
130) [2004 6d 6g 6s* Oct 22] quite good-topped filly: half-sister to several winners,
notably 5-y-o Ringmoor Down: dam, French 1m winner, half-sister to useful 1¼m to
1¾m winner Raise A Prince: easily best effort in maidens when winning at Newbury by
3½ lengths from Westland: likely to stay 7f: should progress. *R. Hannon*

BAILEYS APPLAUSE 2 b.f. (Feb 14) Royal Applause 124 – Thicket 87 (Wolfhound 59
(USA) 126) [2004 5g⁵ f5m³ 6m⁶ 5m 6g 5g⁶ 5.3m⁴ p6g³ p6g⁶ p5.1g⁴ Dec 20] 8,500F,
12,000Y: leggy filly: second foal: dam, 5f winner, ran only at 2 yrs: modest maiden: stays
6f: acts on all-weather and good to firm going: usually wears cheekpieces/blinkers.
C. A. Dwyer

BAILEYS DANCER 3 b.f. Groom Dancer (USA) 128 – Darshay (FR) 87 (Darshaan 82
133) [2004 90: 8.1d 8.2s⁴ 10m 8.2m 10m² 12.3d 11.9m* 12d 12g Sep 13] sparely-made
filly: has a quick action: fairly useful handicapper: won at Carlisle in August: stays 1½m:
acts on good to firm going: blinkered (folded tamely) sixth start. *M. Johnston*

BAILEYS HONOUR 2 b.f. (Mar 6) Mark of Esteem (IRE) 137 – Kanz (USA) 115 56
(The Minstrel (CAN) 135) [2004 6f 7.9g p8g p10g⁴ p9.5g p8.6g³ Dec 31] 7,500Y:
good-bodied filly: closely related to 1m (including at 2 yrs)/9f winner in Ireland/UAE
Treasurer (by Darshaan) and half-sister to 3 winners, including useful 10.5f to 2m winner
Kansk (by Top Ville): dam 1m winner (including at 2 yrs) who stayed 1½m: modest
maiden: claimed £6,000 after final start: should stay 1½m: acts on polytrack. *M. Johnston*

BAILIEBOROUGH (IRE) 5 b.g. Charnwood Forest (IRE) 125 – Sherannda (USA) 75
(Trempolino (USA) 135) [2004 75§: 7g 7s⁶ 8s 7.1d³ 8.3d⁴ 8m 8m* 7.5d³ f8d 9m* 10g⁶
7g⁵ 8f* 7.2g* 9.2d³ 9g² 7.9m Sep 5] quite good-topped gelding: fair performer: won
claimers at Pontefract in May, Musselburgh in June and July and Ayr in August: effective
at 7f to easy 9f: acts on firm and good to soft going: visored after sixth start: often slowly
away. *D. Nicholls*

BAKER OF OZ 3 b.c. Pursuit of Love 124 – Moorish Idol 90 (Aragon 118) [2004 75: 77 d
p8g² f8.5s⁶ 7d⁴ 8.3m* 7m 9m 8d 7.1d Sep 18] strong, close-coupled colt: fair performer:
won minor event at Windsor in June: well below form after: stays 1m: acts on polytrack,
good to firm and good to soft going: sold 5,500 gns. *R. Hannon*

BAKHTYAR 3 gr.g. Daylami (IRE) 138 – Gentilesse 81 (Generous (IRE) 139) [2004 62
64p: 11.6s 11.6s 11.6d⁴ p16g⁵ 18d⁴ p16g Oct 13] leggy, quite good-topped gelding:
modest maiden handicapper: stays 2¼m: acts on polytrack, soft and good to firm going:
blinkered last 4 outings: sold 20,000 gns. *R. Charlton*

BAKIRI (IRE) 6 b.g. Doyoun 124 – Bakiya (USA) 94 (Trempolino (USA) 135) [2004 65
8.3d 15.4s⁴ 12.3d 14.1d⁵ 12.4g² 12m³ 12f² 12.6f⁴ 11m 11.6f 11.6g* Aug 9] leggy gelding:
fair handicapper: collapsed after winning at Windsor in August: barely stayed 15.4f:
acted on firm and soft going: sometimes found little: dead. *Andrew Reid*

BAKKE 2 b.g. (May 5) Danehill (USA) 126 – Valagalore 91 (Generous (IRE) 139) 60
[2004 6m 7m Jul 1] tall, rather leggy gelding: third foal: half-brother to 4-y-o The Varlet:
dam, 1¾m winner, half-sister to Mozart (by Danehill): modest form, pulling hard, in
maidens at Newbury: subsequently gelded. *M. P. Tregoning*

BALAKIREF 5 b.g. Royal Applause 124 – Pluck 80 (Never So Bold 135) [2004 73d: 83 +
6d* 6s 7s² 6g² 7.1v² 7m 7.2d* 6d 7g 7g 6s⁵ 6s* 6g³ 6d⁴ Sep 17] quite attractive gelding:
fairly useful handicapper: won at Southwell in April and Ayr in June and August: good
efforts in frame last 2 starts: effective at 6f/7f: acts on fibresand and any turf going: tried
visored: sometimes slowly away: usually held up, and has turn of foot. *M. Dods*

BALALAIKA TUNE (IRE) 5 b.m. Lure (USA) 131 – Bohemienne (USA) (Polish 39
Navy (USA)) [2004 38: f7g f8g f11g f11s⁶ 10.1v 13.1g⁴ 16d 12.3m 16f⁴ 14.1g⁶ 17.2g
12m³ 12m² 12m⁶ p8.6g⁵ Dec 27] leggy mare: poor maiden: left W. Storey after penultimate start: stays 2m: acts on all-weather and firm going: tried tongue tied. *B. R. Foster*

BALASHOVA 2 b.f. (Feb 25) Imperial Ballet (IRE) 110 – Almasi (IRE) 96 (Petorius – 117) [2004 5d⁵ 5s Apr 26] 800Y: rather leggy filly: first foal: dam 6f winner (including at 2 yrs): last/unseated in minor event/claimer. *K. R. Burke*

BALAVISTA (USA) 3 b. or br.c. Distant View (USA) 126 – Balabina (USA) 110 **85** (Nijinsky (CAN) 138) [2004 8.1g* 8.1g Aug 5] rangy colt: closely related to 5-y-o Balerno and half-brother to numerous winners, including 7f (at 2 yrs) and 1¼m winner Bal Harbour (by Shirley Heights) and 1½m winner Bequeath (by Rainbow Quest), both smart: dam 1½m winner: won maiden at Haydock in July: disappointed in handicap on same course: should stay 1¼m. *R. Charlton*

BALEARIC STAR (IRE) 3 b.g. Night Shift (USA) – La Menorquina (USA) 65 **78** (Woodman (USA) 126) [2004 73: 8.2g⁶ 9v 8.3m* 9m 10d 8g⁶ 8.2g* Aug 18] strong, close-coupled gelding: fair handicapper: won at Windsor in May and Nottingham in August: should stay 1¼m: acts on good to firm going: gelded after final start. *B. R. Millman*

BALERNO 5 b.g. Machiavellian (USA) 123 – Balabina (USA) 110 (Nijinsky (CAN) **69** 138) [2004 58: p8g* p8g³ p8g p8g⁴ p8g⁵ p7g p7g⁵ 7m² 7.1g³ 8f 7g⁴ 8.1f 7m² 7g* 7m² 8m⁵ 7s 7m⁶ Sep 9] close-coupled gelding: fair performer: won banded stakes at Lingfield in January and handicap at Kempton in July: effective at 7f, barely at 1¼m: acts on all-weather, good to firm and good to soft going: tried in headgear/tongue strap at 3/4 yrs. *R. Ingram*

BALGARTH (USA) 2 b.g. (Feb 18) Zamindar (USA) 116 – Vaguely Regal (IRE) **– p** (Sadler's Wells (USA) 132) [2004 6d Aug 4] $22,000F, $20,000Y: close-coupled gelding: fifth foal: half-brother to winners in USA by Gold Fever and Unbridled's Song: dam unraced out of very smart performer up to 1¼m in France/USA Reine Mathilde: 20/1, behind in maiden at Newcastle, travelling comfortably long way and not knocked about: should do better. *T. D. Barron*

BALIMAYA (IRE) 3 b.f. Barathea (IRE) 127 – Banque Privee (USA) 78 (Private **87** Account (USA)) [2004 8g 10.3d⁶ 8d* a7.5g² 9.5g⁶ 8g Oct 8] leggy, close-coupled filly: sister to smart French/US performer around 1¼m Blue Steller and half-sister to 3 winners in Ireland around 1½m, including fairly useful Banariya (by Lear Fan): dam, 1½m winner, half-sister to Rothmans International winner River Memories: fairly useful performer: trained by J. Noseda first 2 starts: better form subsequently in minor events for new stable, winning at Longchamp in June: stays 9.5f: acts on good to soft going, and on all-weather at Deauville. *E. Libaud, France*

BALI ROYAL 6 b.m. King's Signet (USA) 110 – Baligay 84 (Balidar 133) [2004 111: **97 d** 5m⁶ 6m⁴ 5d 5d 5m 6g Aug 7] strong, good-quartered mare: smart at 5 yrs: only useful in 2004, comfortably best efforts when sixth and eighth in listed races at Kempton and Chantilly first and third starts: best at 5f: acts on fibresand, firm and soft going: has been early to post/mounted on track (upset in stall, got loose and withdrawn on intended reappearance): front runner: sold 21,000 gns in November. *M. S. Saunders*

BALI-STAR 9 b.g. Alnasr Alwasheek 117 – Baligay 84 (Balidar 133) [2004 53: f5g **52** f5g² p5g⁴ p5g 5d p5g⁴ 5.1d* 6.1s 5.7m May 17] modest performer: won banded stakes at Chepstow in April: effective at 5f/easy 6f: acts on all-weather, firm and good to soft going: tried blinkered: none too consistent. *R. J. Hodges*

BALKAN KNIGHT 4 b.c. Selkirk (USA) 129 – Crown of Light 112 (Mtoto 134) **90** [2004 88: 10g⁶ 11.9s* 11.9g 14.8g³ Jul 17] fairly useful handicapper: won at York in May: creditable third to Bendarshaan at Newmarket final outing: stays 14.8f: acts on soft and good to firm going: visored: ran as if amiss penultimate start: sold 28,000 gns. *D. R. Loder*

BALKAN LEADER (USA) 2 b.c. (May 6) Stravinsky (USA) 133 – Baydon Belle **74** (USA) 64 (Al Nasr (FR) 126) [2004 6m⁴ p7m² Oct 6] seventh foal: half-brother to smart US 2003 2-y-o Grade 2 9f winner Read The Footnotes (by Smoke Glacken): dam, fourth at 1m, from family of Stravinsky: much better effort in maidens (odds on, slowly away and flashed tail on debut) when 2½ lengths second to Qadar at Lingfield, dictating pace: will probably stay 1m. *Saeed bin Suroor*

BALLARE (IRE) 5 b.g. Barathea (IRE) 127 – Raindancing (IRE) 94 (Tirol 127) **58** [2004 56: p10g p8g³ p8g⁴ p7g⁶ p8g* 7m 7s⁴ 8f 7.1m 9.7f p7g² 8.1d* p8.6d p7m⁵ p8m Dec 8] good-topped gelding: modest performer: won banded races at Lingfield in April and Warwick in October: effective at 7f to 1¼m: acts on polytrack, soft and good to firm going: tried in cheekpieces, usually visored. *Bob Jones*

BALL BOY 2 b.g. (Jan 19) Xaar 132 – Tanz (IRE) 79 (Sadler's Wells (USA) 132) [2004 **73** 7m 7g⁵ 7.5m² 8.3d⁵ Aug 11] big gelding: half-brother to several winners, including useful 7f winner (stayed 11.4f) Tanzilla (by Warning) and fairly useful 1½m/

1¾m winner Tarxien (by Kendor): dam, Irish 1½m winner, sister to smart 1½m/1¾m filly Spring and closely related to Pentire: fair maiden: second at Beverley: likely to be suited by 1¼m/1½m: gelded after final start. *M. R. Channon*

BALLERINA SUPREMA (IRE) 4 b.f. Sadler's Wells (USA) 132 – Gravieres (FR) **87** (Saint Estephe (FR) 123) [2004 10m⁵ 14m Jul 31] quite good-topped filly: fairly useful form: missed 2003: creditable fifth in handicap at Windsor on reappearance: ran as if amiss at Goodwood following month: should stay beyond 1¼m: raced only on good/good to firm going. *C. R. Egerton*

BALLET BALLON (USA) 2 b.f. (Apr 15) Rahy (USA) 115 – Bella Ballerina 90 **– p** (Sadler's Wells (USA) 132) [2004 7g Sep 20] well-made filly: fifth foal: half-sister to useful 1¼m winner Design Perfection (by Diesis): dam, 9f winner, sister to high-class 1¼m performer Stagecraft from family of Opera House and Kayf Tara: 25/1 and backward, always rear in maiden at Kempton, swishing tail: should do better. *M. A. Jarvis*

BALLETOMAINE (IRE) 2 b.f. (Apr 21) Sadler's Wells (USA) 132 – Ivy (USA) **56** (Sir Ivor (USA) 135) [2004 7m 7.5d p7g Sep 7] sister to 3 winners, including 2-y-o 7f winners Ivrea (in 1989) and Iviza (in 1992, probably ungenuine), both later useful at 1¼m/1½m, and half-sister to 3 winners, notably Oaks d'Italia winner Ivyanna (by Reference Point): dam maiden in USA: modest form in maidens: tailed off final start, racing freely: should be suited by 1¼m/1½m. *B. W. Hills*

BALLET RUSE 3 ch.f. Rainbow Quest (USA) 134 – El Opera (IRE) 100 (Sadler's **–** Wells (USA) 132) [2004 –p: 8.3f 8m 16.2s Aug 30] leggy, quite good-topped filly: no sign of ability. *Sir Mark Prescott*

BALLETTO 2 b.f. (Feb 22) Robellino (USA) 127 – Denial (Sadler's Wells (USA) **59** 132) [2004 6m³ 6m Jul 23] 27,000Y: lengthy filly: first foal: dam, French 11f winner, half-sister to smart French miler Battle Dore out of very smart French performer up to 1¼m Nashmeel: modest form in maidens at Pontefract and Ascot (raced too freely): bred to stay at least 1m. *K. R. Burke*

BALLINGER EXPRESS 4 ch.f. Air Express (IRE) 125 – Branston Ridge (Indian **68** Ridge 123) [2004 p8g p8g⁵ p8g³ 7m² 6m 6.1d 6f² 5m 5.1m 6.1d 6m³ Sep 27] good-topped filly: second foal: half-sister to 5-y-o Ballinger Ridge: dam unraced: fair maiden: effective from 6f to 1m: acts on polytrack and firm going: blinkered after third start: sometimes slowly away, including final outing (blindfold removed late): sold 8,000 gns, sent to Holland. *A. M. Balding*

BALLINGER RIDGE 5 b.g. Sabrehill (USA) 120 – Branston Ridge (Indian Ridge **71** 123) [2004 79: p8g² p7g³ p8g² p8g² p10g* p8g⁶ 8f² 10g 8g 7m 8.5m⁵ Jul 28] good-topped gelding: fair performer: won maiden at Lingfield in March: short-headed in similar event at same course previous outing, caught close home after jockey had stopped pushing him out briefly: left A. Balding after sixth start: stays easy 1¼m: acts on polytrack and firm going: wore headgear after second start. *T. G. McCourt, Ireland*

BALLIN ROUGE 3 ch.f. Dr Fong (USA) 128 – Bogus John (CAN) (Blushing John **–** (USA) 120) [2004 –: 7.5g 10g 7.9m⁶ Sep 11] strong filly: little form: tongue tied last 2 starts. *T. J. Fitzgerald*

BALLINTENI 2 b.c. (Mar 21) Machiavellian (USA) 123 – Silabteni (USA) (Nureyev **88 p** (USA) 131) [2004 7s* Oct 22] leggy colt: sixth foal: half-brother to 3 winners, notably high-class French/US 7f/1m performer Touch of The Blues (by Cadeaux Genereux): dam unraced close relation to Indian Skimmer: 5/1 and green, tongue tied when winning 13-runner maiden at Doncaster by 2½ lengths from Full of Zest, switched and quickening to lead final 1f: will stay 1m: useful prospect at least, and should win more races. *Saeed bin Suroor*

BALLYBORO (IRE) 3 b.f. Entrepreneur 123 – Tathkara (USA) (Alydar (USA)) [2004 **–** 57p: 7d⁵ 7m 11.5f Jun 10] close-coupled filly: reportedly broke pelvis after only 2-y-o start: well held in 2004: visored (reportedly made a noise) final outing. *M. J. Wallace*

BALLYBUNION (IRE) 5 ch.g. Entrepreneur 123 – Clarentia 111 (Ballad Rock 122) **63** [2004 76: 6g 5m 5m 6m 5g⁵ 5g³ 5g 6g 5g 5d 6m⁵ 5m* 6m 5.7m³ 6g² 5d 5f⁴ 5m⁴ Sep 29] strong gelding: modest handicapper: won at Pontefract in July: effective at 5f/6f: acts on polytrack and firm going: tried visored/tongue tied at 4 yrs: sometimes slowly away. *D. Nicholls*

BALLYCROY GIRL (IRE) 2 ch.f. (Apr 2) Pennekamp (USA) 130 – Hulm (IRE) **68** 79 (Mujtahid (USA) 118) [2004 6m⁶ 7.2d² 7d⁵ 7.2m* 7m 7m⁶ 8s Sep 18] 15,000Y: good-topped filly: fifth foal: half-sister to 4-y-o Blonde En Blonde: dam 7f winner: fair performer: won maiden at Ayr in July: hung left when running creditably in nursery next time: stays 7f: acts on good to firm and good to soft going. *A. Bailey*

Hong Kong Jockey Club Sprint (Handicap), Ascot—Baltic King collars Pivotal Point (left) late on, with Forever Phoenix (noseband) first home in the other group

BALLYGRIFFIN KID 4 gr.g. Komaite (USA) – Ballygriffin Belle (Another Realm 118) [2004 50: p7g p6g³ f5g⁴ p7g* 8.2m p5m³ p6g p7m* p7.1g* Dec 22] modest performer: won banded events at Lingfield in May (apprentices) and, having left T. McGovern after fifth start, at Lingfield and Wolverhampton in December: stays 7f: acts on polytrack and firm going: tried visored. *Miss Gay Kelleway* **62**

BALLY HALL (IRE) 4 b.g. Saddlers' Hall (IRE) 126 – Sally Rose 92 (Sallust 134) [2004 81: p10g Feb 18] strong, close-coupled gelding: fair handicapper: not discredited (slowly away) only outing in 2004: stays 1¾m: acts on firm and soft going: usually tongue tied at 3 yrs. *G. A. Butler* **73**

BALLYHURRY (USA) 7 b.g. Rubiano (USA) – Balakhna (FR) (Tyrant (USA)) [2004 83: 7.1g 7.2f⁶ 7.1m⁴ 7.2d⁶ 8m 7.1g⁴ 7m⁴ p7.1d⁵ Nov 4] angular gelding: fair handicapper: effective at 7f/1m: acts on firm and soft going: successful in blinkers earlier in career: usually held up. *J. S. Goldie* **74**

BALLYLIFFIN (IRE) 3 b.g. Daggers Drawn (USA) 114 – Blues Quartet (Cure The Blues (USA)) [2004 10.2g 9.7s² May 6] better effort in maidens when 11 lengths second at Folkestone. *S. Kirk* **49**

BALLYRUSH (IRE) 4 ch.g. Titus Livius (FR) 115 – Mandoline (IRE) (Suave Dancer (USA) 136) [2004 72?: f9.4g f8.5s⁵ f8.5s⁴ f11g⁵ 8.3d⁶ 10d⁵ f9.4g² f8g* 8.2m May 25] fair maiden at 2/3 yrs in Ireland for M. Halford: just modest in 2004, winning banded race at Southwell in May: stays 9.4f: acts on fibresand and soft going: wore cheekpieces/blinkers last 4 outings. *K. R. Burke* **52**

BALMACARA 5 b.m. Lake Coniston (IRE) 131 – Diabaig 76 (Precocious 126) [2004 57: p8g p8g 8.1m⁶ 8m 8m⁵ 7m p7.1d Oct 23] lengthy, angular mare: poor maiden: stays 1m: acts on polytrack and firm going: tried blinkered/in cheekpieces. *Miss K. B. Boutflower* **45**

BALMONT (USA) 3 b.c. Stravinsky (USA) 133 – Aldebaran Light (USA) (Seattle Slew (USA)) [2004 117: 6g³ 5m² 5s 7s⁵ Oct 16] tall, quite good-topped colt: smart performer: awarded Middle Park Stakes at Newmarket at 2 yrs: edgy, creditable 2¼ lengths third to Frizzante in July Cup on same course on reappearance: respectable efforts behind Bahamian Pirate next 2 starts, beaten a neck in minor event there and 2½ lengths when seventh in Nunthorpe Stakes at York: travels strongly, and likely to prove best at 5f/6f: acts on soft and good to firm going. *J. Noseda* **114**

BALTHASAR 2 b.c. (Jan 31) Lujain (USA) 119 – Anatase (Danehill (USA) 126) [2004 5m 8.3d⁶ 6d 6d⁶ Aug 30] compact colt: modest maiden: ran badly in seller final start: should stay 1m. *P. A. Blockley* **56**

BALTIC BLAZER (IRE) 4 b.g. Polish Precedent (USA) 131 – Pine Needle 89 (Kris 135) [2004 78p: 10.5d⁵ 10.1g 10.4g Oct 8] sturdy gelding: fair performer: stays 10.6f: raced only on good/good to soft going: visored (found little) final start: sold 5,000 gns. *P. W. Harris* **72**

BALTIC DIP (IRE) 2 b.f. (Feb 18) Benny The Dip (USA) 127 – Drei (USA) 67 (Lyphard (USA) 132) [2004 6g* 6m⁴ 6.5g 7g⁴ Oct 2] 38,000Y: big, good-topped filly: half-sister to several winners, including 9f winner Trois (by Efisio) and 1¼m winner **95**

Triple Sharp (by Selkirk), both fairly useful: dam once-raced daughter of smart performer up to 1¼m Triple Tipple: useful performer: won maiden at Goodwood in May: creditable fourth in listed races won by Slip Dance and Penkenna Princess at Newmarket: should stay at least 1m: very slowly away penultimate outing. *R. Hannon*

BALTIC KING 4 b.c. Danetime (IRE) 121 – Lindfield Belle (IRE) 78 (Fairy King (USA)) [2004 112: 5g⁶ 6m 5m* 5d³ 5m⁶ 5m* 5g³ 6d⁵ Oct 15] lengthy colt: smart performer: won valuable handicap at Ascot (by neck from Pivotal Point) in July and minor event at Beverley (beat If Paradise 3½ lengths) in September: effective at 5f/6f: acts on firm and good to soft going: tongue tied: has worn crossed noseband/been bandaged behind: waited with: none too reliable. *H. Morrison* **112**

BALTIC WAVE 3 b.g. Polish Precedent (USA) 131 – Flourish (Selkirk (USA) 129) [2004 93: 7m⁶ 7d⁴ 6m Jul 6] good-topped gelding: fairly useful handicapper: best effort in 2004 when fourth to Mrs Moh at Chester: stays 7f: acts on good to firm and good to soft going: sent to Hong Kong, where renamed Come Ho Choi. *T. D. Barron* **92**

BALWEARIE (IRE) 3 b.g. Sesaro (USA) 81 – Eight Mile Rock 76 (Dominion 123) [2004 64: 5g⁶ 8m 6m⁶ May 31] sturdy gelding: little form in 2004: tried in cheekpieces. *Miss L. A. Perratt* **–**

BAMBOOZLED 2 b.f. (Apr 22) Mujadil (USA) 119 – Tintinara (Selkirk (USA) 129) [2004 p5g⁶ 5v p5g 5m⁵ Jun 7] 4,000Y: fifth foal: dam unraced: poor maiden: visored/blinkered last 2 starts. *P. D. Evans* **41**

BAMFORD CASTLE (IRE) 9 b.g. Scenic 128 – Allorette 100 (Ballymore 123) [2004 p16g Jan 21] missed 2003: well held in seller (wore cheekpieces) only start in 2004. *R. Ford* **–**

BAMZOOKI 2 b.f. (Feb 16) Zilzal (USA) 137 – Cavernista 75 (Lion Cavern (USA) 117) [2004 6m⁴ 6g⁵ Aug 21] second foal: half-sister to 3-y-o Capetown Girl: dam, lightly-raced maiden, half-sister to smart stayer Give Notice: modest form in maidens at Lingfield: should stay 1m. *J. R. Fanshawe* **60**

BANANA GROVE (IRE) 3 b.g. Sesaro (USA) 81 – Megan's Dream (IRE) 56 (Fayruz 116) [2004 9.2g³ 8m 8.1g 9m* 9.2d⁴ 8g 9.2s⁶ 8s³ Oct 11] €8,000Y: close-coupled gelding: second living foal: dam, Irish maiden, best at 5f: fair performer: won maiden at Redcar in August: stays 9f: acts on good to firm and good to soft ground: saddle slipped third start. *A. Berry* **71**

BANCHIERI 2 b.c. (Feb 6) Dubai Millennium 140 – Belle Et Deluree (USA) (The Minstrel (CAN) 135) [2004 7m³ 7g³ 8.2d² Sep 17] close-coupled colt: half-brother to several winners, including smart 5f (at 2 yrs) to 7f winner Dazzle (by Gone West) and useful 1999 2-y-o 7f winner Hypnotize (by Machiavellian): dam French 1m (at 2 yrs) and 1¼m winner: fairly useful form in maidens: neck second to Catch A Star at Nottingham: likely to stay 1¼m: soon off bridle last 2 starts. *Saeed bin Suroor* **83**

BAND 4 b.g. Band On The Run 102 – Little Tich (Great Nephew 126) [2004 82d: 8s 8.1m f8d 10m 10.5d⁴ 10.5s 10.5g⁵ 8m* 7.9g 8.2v⁶ 10v⁴ Nov 4] strong, close-coupled gelding: modest handicapper: won at Yarmouth in August: stays 10.6f: acts on any going. *B. A. McMahon* **63**

BANDARI (IRE) 5 b.h. Alhaarth (IRE) 126 – Miss Audimar (USA) (Mr Leader (USA)) [2004 118: 12g 10g* 10.3d* 10d* 10f 12m* 12m 12m³ 12m³ 12d Oct 17] **124**
Bandari's career appeared on the slide in 2003, when a truncated four-race campaign failed to produce a win, but an operation to remove a chip from a hind fetlock after his final four-year-old outing clearly worked wonders. Bandari returned to his best in the latest season, winning four races and running more regularly than in previous years. The highlight was his success in the Princess of Wales's cantorodds.com Stakes at Newmarket in July, the field for which compared favourably with those of other recent renewals, featuring a Group 1 winner in Sulamani, as well as The Great Gatsby, High Accolade and Magistretti, runner-up in the previous season's Derby, St Leger and Juddmonte International respectively. That quartet were among five ahead of 12/1-shot Bandari in the betting, Sulamani, conceding 5 lb all round, sent off favourite at 11/8. Usually sweating and on edge before his races, Bandari was uncharacteristically relaxed in the preliminaries, the ear plugs he was reportedly fitted with a couple of hours earlier almost certainly a factor. In accordance with the rules, the ear plugs were removed before the start and, once under way, Bandari was patiently ridden until High Accolade took up the

Princess of Wales's cantorodds.com Stakes, Newmarket—
Bandari (striped cap) holds off Sulamani; High Accolade finishes third

running two furlongs out. Bandari quickened through a gap to lead soon after and, with the benefit of the rail, was able to hold off Sulamani, who didn't keep so straight, by half a length, with two and a half lengths back to High Accolade. Bandari had earlier completed a hat-trick, winning a listed race, held up, at Chester in May, in between making most in a minor event at Newmarket earlier that month and in the betfair.com Brigadier Gerard Stakes at Sandown at the start of June. Bandari's performance in the last-named was on a par with any in his career, as he rallied tenaciously to get the better of Ikhtyar by a neck, with Sunstrach seven lengths back in third. Ear plugs were again employed when Bandari finished a creditable seventh in the King George VI and Queen Elizabeth Stakes at Ascot in July, but he performed poorly on his other attempts at Group 1 level, becoming stirred up before the Prince of Wales's Stakes at Royal Ascot, and trailing in last in the Gran Premio del Jockey Club Italiano at Milan on his final outing. Bandari ran well conceding 5 lb all round when third in both the September Stakes at Kempton, where he was calm beforehand even without ear plugs, and in the Cumberland Lodge Stakes back at Ascot, in which he was beaten only a length by High Accolade.

Bandari (IRE) (b.h. 1999)	Alhaarth (IRE) (b 1993)	Unfuwain (b 1985)	Northern Dancer
			Height of Fashion
		Irish Valley (ch 1982)	Irish River
			Green Valley
	Miss Audimar (USA) (b 1981)	Mr Leader (b 1966)	Hail To Reason
			Jolie Deja
		Quick Selection (ch 1972)	Viceregal
			Lachine

According to his trainer, Bandari had been in need of his leg operation since his third in the 2002 St Leger, for which he went off favourite following successes in the Derby Trial at Lingfield, the Gordon Stakes at Goodwood and the Great Voltigeur Stakes at York, though he had proved a disappointment in the Derby on his first start for Sheikh Hamdan. Bandari seemed barely to stay the extended mile and three quarters of the St Leger, and has raced exclusively at a mile and a quarter and a mile and a half at four and five, proving equally effective at both distances. Bandari's pedigree has been covered in earlier editions of *Racehorses*. The only thing which needs to be added is that his ageing dam, Miss Audimar, a winner at up to eleven furlongs in America, is also responsible for the two-year-old Given A Choice (by Trans Island), who showed fair form in maidens in 2004. The lengthy, angular Bandari acts on soft and good to firm going, and, though he has hung right on occasions, is far more genuine when racing than his pre-race demeanour sometimes might suggest. *M. Johnston*

BANDBOX (IRE) 9 ch.g. Imperial Frontier (USA) 112 – Dublah (USA) (Private **31** Account (USA)) [2004 42: f7g f7d⁵ f7g 6f³ Aug 5] small, strong gelding: poor handicapper: stays 7f: acts on fibresand, firm and soft going: tried tongue tied/in headgear. *M. Salaman*

BANDIT QUEEN   4 b.f. Desert Prince (IRE) 130 – Wildwood Flower 107 (Distant   **89** Relative 128) [2004 88: 6g³ 6f⁴ 7g² 6.5g Jul 9] leggy filly: fairly useful handicapper: placed at Ripon and Chester: stays 7f: acts on firm and good to soft ground, last (in blinkers) only run on polytrack: raced freely/carried head awkwardly second outing. *W. Jarvis*

BANDOS   4 ch.g. Cayman Kai (IRE) 114 – Lekuti (Le Coq d'Or 101) [2004 84: 7f³   **78** 7.2d 7s 7.2s⁴ 7m⁵ p7.1g³ p6g p7.1g Dec 20] lengthy gelding: fair performer: barely stays 1m: acts on polytrack, firm and soft going: tongue tied: usually races prominently. *I. Semple*

BANJO BAY (IRE)   6 b.g. Common Grounds 118 – Thirlmere (Cadeaux Genereux   **82 d** 131) [2004 95: 7.6d 6m 6m³ 6m 7m 5g⁶ 6g 7m 5.3d 7m 6f⁵ 6g Sep 25] close-coupled gelding: fair handicapper: below form after third start: should prove as effective at 5f as 6f/7f: acts on firm and soft going: sometimes gets worked up/slowly away: none too reliable. *D. Nicholls*

BANJO PATTERSON   2 b.c. (Apr 10) Green Desert (USA) 127 – Rumpipumpy 80   **– p** (Shirley Heights 130) [2004 6d Oct 14] 115,000Y: second foal: half-brother to 2002 2-y-o 7f winner Persian Jasmine (by Dynaformer): dam, maiden in Britain, later Grade 2 9f winner in USA, half-sister to Irish 1000 Guineas winner Classic Park: 20/1, behind in maiden at Newmarket, travelling strongly long way and not unduly punished: will do better. *G. A. Huffer*

BANK GAMES   3 b.g. Mind Games 121 – Piggy Bank 71 (Emarati (USA) 74) [2004   **–** 6m f6g f6g⁶ 5g⁵ 7.5s 6d Oct 16] little form: blinkered final start: dead. *M. W. Easterby*

BANKNOTE   2 b.c. (Apr 6) Zafonic (USA) 130 – Brand (Shareef Dancer (USA) 135)   **75** [2004 6m⁴ 5.9g⁴ 7.5m* 8m Sep 9] smallish, quite good-topped colt: eighth foal: half-brother to 3 fairly useful winners, including 2002 2-y-o 6f/7f winner Captain Ginger (by Muhtarram) and 3-y-o Royal Warrant: dam unraced half-sister to useful performer up to 1½m Clever Cliche, from family of Unfuwain, Nashwan and Nayef: fair performer: won maiden at Beverley in July: ran poorly in nursery final start: should stay at least 1m. *A. M. Balding*

BANK ON HIM   9 b.g. Elmaamul (USA) 125 – Feather Flower 74 (Relkino 131)   **64** [2004 –, a64: p10g* p10g⁶ p10g* p8g² p10g² p10g² p10g² f8.5g⁵ 10m* p12g³ 9g⁴ p10d³   **a72** p12.2g² p9.5g p10g³ p10g Dec 29] fair performer: won seller and handicap at Lingfield in January and, having left C. Weedon after sixth start, apprentice handicap at Brighton in May: effective at 1m to easy 1½m: acts on all-weather and good to firm ground: free-going sort: usually races prominently. *G. L. Moore*

BANNERS FLYING (IRE)   4 ch.g. Zafonic (USA) 130 – Banafsajee (USA) 107   **–** (Pleasant Colony (USA)) [2004 78: f7g f8.5m f12g⁴ 8g f12m⁴ f12m 16s 14.1f 10f p12.2g Oct 9] big gelding: maiden: showed little in 2004: blinkered final start. *D. W. Chapman*

BANNINGHAM BLAZE   4 b.f. Averti (IRE) 117 – Ma Pavlova (USA) 102 (Irish   **57** River (FR) 131) [2004 67: f11g 13.8g 11.9m⁴ 11.9m* 11.8m² 11.9f² 12.6f³ 11.9f⁶ 11.8m⁵ 11.9m³ 14.1g* 11.9f³ 11.9f² 11.9m² 12.1g² 16.2m³ 12.6d² 12m⁵ 15.8g⁴ 14.1d* p12.2d Nov 3] close-coupled, good-topped filly: modest performer: won seller at Brighton (left C. Dore) in May, selling handicap at Nottingham in July and banded event at Yarmouth in October: stays easy 2m: acts on polytrack, firm and good to soft going: effective blinkered/visored or not: held up: tough and consistent. *A. W. Carroll*

BANNISTER   6 ch.g. Inchinor 119 – Shall We Run 59 (Hotfoot 126) [2004 66: p6g³   **66** f6s 7s³ 8.3g Apr 26] useful-looking gelding: has a quick action: fair handicapper: left D. Nicholls after reappearance: stays 7f: acts on polytrack, firm and soft going: tried blinkered/visored/tongue tied. *Mrs Stef Liddiard*

BANSHA BRU (IRE)   4 b.g. Fumo di Londra (IRE) 108 – Pride of Duneane (IRE)   **59** (Anita's Prince 126) [2004 f8.5g³ 9.7s May 6] third in maiden at Wolverhampton: collapsed in similar event at Folkestone: dead. *Miss E. C. Lavelle*

BAQAH (IRE)   3 ch.f. Bahhare (USA) 122 – Filfilah 99 (Cadeaux Genereux 131)   **112** [2004 6s³ 5.5d* 6s² 7g* 8g* 8m³ 8d 8m Oct 2] lengthy filly: first foal: dam, 6f (including at 2 yrs)/7f winner, granddaughter of Breeders' Cup Juvenile Fillies winner Brave Raj: smart performer: won minor event at Maisons-Laffitte in March and listed race in May and Prix de Sandringham (by ½ length from Miss Mambo) in June, both at Chantilly: creditable 5 lengths third to Soviet Song in Falmouth Stakes at Newmarket next time: below form last 2 starts in Prix Jacques le Marois at Deauville and Prix Daniel Wildenstein at Longchamp: stayed 1m: acted on soft and good to firm going: blinkered final 2-y-o start: had had tongue tied: visits Green Desert. *F. Head, France*

BARABELLA (IRE)   3 gr.f. Barathea (IRE) 127 – Thatchabella (IRE) (Thatching   **60 d**
131) [2004 65: 8g 5.1g⁵ 5.7s 5.7f⁴ 6d⁵ 6.1d 6.1g 7.1s p9.5g⁶ p13.9g p10g
Dec 20] modest maiden: below form after fifth start, leaving R. Hodges after eleventh: probably stays 9.5f: acts on polytrack and firm going: tried in cheekpieces: ungenuine. *B. A. Pearce*

BARADORE (IRE)   2 ch.f. (Mar 29) Baratea (IRE) 127 – High Flying Adored (IRE)   **82 p**
85 (In The Wings 128) [2004 7g² 8f* Aug 5] close-coupled, useful-looking filly: sixth foal: half-sister to 4-y-o Eva Peron and Italian winner around 9f by Emperor Jones: dam 1½m winner: fairly useful form in maidens at Newmarket and Yarmouth, beating Silver Highlight by 1½ lengths on latter course (led halfway): should be suited by 1¼m/1½m: sent to USA. *M. G. Quinlan*

BARAKA (IRE)   3 b.f. Danehill (USA) 126 – Cocotte 111 (Troy 137) [2004 75P: 11.5s*   **106**
10g Sep 19] sister to smart Japanese performer (Group 1 winner up to 11f) Fine Motion, closely related to top-class 1¼m/1½m winner Pilsudski (by Polish Precedent), and half-sister to several winners: dam, 1¼m winner, granddaughter of Irish 1000 Guineas winner Gaily: useful form: ninth in minor event at the Curragh only 2-y-o start: won listed race at Lingfield in May readily by 6 lengths from Bowstring: missed Prix de Diane in June reportedly due to foot abscess: only ninth in Blandford Stakes at the Curragh when next seen out: stays 11.5f: acts on soft going: sent to USA. *A. P. O'Brien, Ireland*

BARAKANA (IRE)   6 b.g. Baratea (IRE) 127 – Safkana (IRE) 78 (Doyoun 124)   **–**
[2004 p10g Mar 29] good-topped gelding: won twice in Spain in 2001 and 2002: well held in banded race only 6-y-o start: tried blinkered. *C. Tinkler*

BARANOOK (IRE)   3 b.c. Baratea (IRE) 127 – Gull Nook 120 (Mill Reef (USA)   **73**
141) [2004 10m 10g 10.5g⁵ p12m³ Oct 6] 35,000Y: strong colt: brother to useful 1¼m winner Kittiwake, closely related to 2 winners by Sadler's Wells, including smart 1½m/1¾m winner Spring, and half-brother to several winners, notably top-class 6f (at 2 yrs) to 1½m winner Pentire (by Be My Guest): dam French 10.5f/1½m winner: fair maiden: stays easy 1½m: acts on polytrack: sold 42,000 gns. *P. W. Harris*

BARATHEA BLUE   3 ch.c. Baratea (IRE) 127 – Empty Purse (Pennine Walk 120)   **79**
[2004 10g⁵ 10g² 10g* p12g Oct 25] 52,000Y: strong, compact colt: brother to useful 7f (at 2 yrs) to 15f winner Barathea Blazer, and half-brother to 3 winners, including 1½m winner Three White Sox (by Most Welcome): dam unraced: fair form: second to Maraakeb in maiden at Sandown prior to winning similar event at Nottingham later in September by ¾ length from Skibereen: should stay 1½m. *P. W. Harris*

BARATHEA DREAMS (IRE)   3 b.c. Baratea (IRE) 127 – Deyaajeer (USA) 64   **87**
(Dayjur (USA) 137) [2004 p10g* p10g* p12g⁴ 8.1d* 7.9d³ 10m 8m 8.1g⁵ 8f 7s⁵ p10g   **a79**
p10m Dec 22] 5,500Y: strong, lengthy colt: fifth foal: half-brother to useful 7f (including at 2 yrs) to 9f (in UAE) winner Al Mohallab (by Marju): dam, ran once, half-sister to Nashwan, Unfuwain and Nayef: fairly useful performer: won maiden in February and minor event in March, both at Lingfield, and handicap at Sandown in April: below form after sixth outing: stays easy 1¼m: acts on polytrack and good to soft going: front runner. *J. S. Moore*

BARATI (IRE)   3 b.c. Sadler's Wells (USA) 132 – Oriane 109 (Nashwan (USA) 135)   **104**
[2004 8s* 10d⁴ 10m³ 12m³ 10d⁵ Jul 14] stocky, good-bodied colt: impresses in appearance: third foal: half-brother to fairly useful 2001 2-y-o 7f winner Cassirer (by Zafonic): dam, Irish 1m winner, half-sister to smart miler Killer Instinct out of smart half-sister to Irish Oaks winner Colorspin, herself dam of Opera House and Kayf Tara: useful performer: won maiden at the Curragh in April: in frame in Derrinstown Stud Derby Trial at Leopardstown, Gallinule Stakes at the Curragh (1¾ lengths third to Meath) and King Edward VII Stakes at Royal Ascot (7 lengths third to Five Dynasties): will stay 1¾m: acts on soft and good to firm going: joined M. O'Brien. *J. Oxx, Ireland*

BARBAJUAN (IRE)   3 b.c. Danehill Dancer (IRE) 117 – Courtier (Saddlers' Hall   **93 ?**
(IRE) 126) [2004 109: 8d⁵ 8g 10.4s 8m 6m 8g 7m 10g⁵ 8d Oct 15] good-topped colt: has a round action: fairly useful performer: mostly well beaten in 2004, including in 2000 Guineas at Newmarket and Dante Stakes at York: stays 1¼m: acts on firm and good to soft going: blinkered fifth to seventh starts: sent to Macau. *N. A. Callaghan*

BARBARY COAST (FR)   2 b.c. (Apr 14) Anabaa (USA) 130 – Viking's Cove (USA)   **84**
(Miswaki (USA) 124) [2004 7g⁶ 7g 8g² 8s p7g³ p7g⁶ Nov 27] €105,000Y: neat colt: fourth foal: dam unraced half-sister to very smart French performers Vetheuil (miler)

and Verveine (up to 1½m), latter dam of 4-y-o Vallee Enchantee: fairly useful maiden: easily best efforts when placed at Leicester and Lingfield: stays 1m: acts on polytrack. *W. R. Muir*

BARBILYRIFLE (IRE)   3 b.g. Indian Rocket 115 – Age of Elegance (Troy 137)   **64 §**
[2004 73§: p5g f6s 6d³ 5.7s May 4] good-topped gelding: modest performer: stays 6f: acts on firm and good to soft ground: tried blinkered, usually wears cheekpieces: unreliable: sold £2,400. *H. Morrison*

BARBIROLLI   2 b.c. (Apr 2) Machiavellian (USA) 123 – Blushing Barada (USA) 53   –
(Blushing Groom (FR) 131) [2004 8g Sep 29] half-brother to several winners, including 4-y-o Blythe Knight and fairly useful 12.5f to 2m winner Bid Me Welcome (by Alzao): dam maiden half-sister to Irish St Leger winner Authaal: 12/1 and tongue tied, always rear in maiden at Salisbury. *J. H. M. Gosden*

BARCARDERO (USA)   2 b.c. (Apr 4) Danzig (USA) – Very Confidential (USA)   **63 p**
(Fappiano (USA)) [2004 7s Oct 27] $100,000Y: sixth foal: closely related to fairly useful 1¾m winner High Tension (by Sadler's Wells) and half-brother to 2 winners abroad: dam, US maiden, half-sister to US Grade 1 9f/1¼m winner Awe Inspiring: 14/1 and green, 8¾ lengths eighth of 14 to Zalongo in maiden at Yarmouth: should improve. *M. Johnston*

BARCELONA   7 b.g. Barathea (IRE) 127 – Pipitina 91 (Bustino 136) [2004 12.1g Jul   –
9] sturdy gelding: fairly useful at best: blinkered, well held only 7-y-o start: usually tongue tied. *G. L. Moore*

BARGAIN HUNT (IRE)   3 b.g. Foxhound (USA) 103 – Atisayin (USA) (Al Nasr   **47**
(FR) 126) [2004 54: 10s 9.2g² 12.3g 10f 7.9g³ 9m⁶ 6m 7.2g 8m⁴ 7.9m³ Sep 11] smallish gelding: poor maiden: stays 9f: acts on good to firm going: tried in cheekpieces, sometimes visored: free-going sort: often races prominently. *W. Storey*

BARHOLM CHARLIE   3 b.g. Atraf 116 – Lady-H (Never So Bold 135) [2004 6m   –
5.1g 10.9g Jul 8] big, lengthy gelding: no form in maidens/seller. *M. A. Buckley*

BARKING MAD (USA)   6 b. or br.g. Dayjur (USA) 137 – Avian Assembly (USA)   **87**
(General Assembly (USA)) [2004 92: 10g⁶ 10m⁴ 10m³ 10m² 10.3g* 10g⁶ 10g² 10m⁶ 10g* 9g² 10m 10.1s Oct 27] sturdy, lengthy gelding: fairly useful performer: won minor event at Chester in July and claimer at Windsor in August: stays 10.3f: acts on firm and good to soft going: sometimes races freely: usually makes running. *M. L. W. Bell*

BARMAN (USA)   5 ch.g. Atticus (USA) 121 – Blue Tip (FR) 117 (Tip Moss (FR))   **90**
[2004 89: 12g 11.7m 13.9m* Sep 5] big, quite good-topped gelding: fairly useful handicapper: won at York in September by 1¾ lengths from Valance: stays 1¾m: acts on polytrack, firm and soft ground: tried blinkered/in cheekpieces: usually tongue tied (has reportedly had breathing problems): free-going sort: none too resolute: sold 21,000 gns. *P. F. I. Cole*

BARNBROOK EMPIRE (IRE)   2 b.f. (Mar 1) Second Empire (IRE) 124 – Home   **62**
Comforts (Most Welcome 131) [2004 6.1g 7.5g⁵ 6.1m³ 5.7m Aug 10] €8,500Y: third foal: closely related/half-sister to winners around 7f in Italy by Victory Note and Orpen: dam, ran twice in Ireland, half-sister to smart winner up to 10.5f Glowing With Pride: modest maiden: easily best effort at 6f on good to firm going. *I. A. Wood*

BAR OF SILVER (IRE)   4 ch.g. Bahhare (USA) 122 – Shaping Up (USA) 89 (Storm   **46**
Bird (CAN) 134) [2004 61: f9.4g p8g⁵ f6s p7g⁵ Apr 21] poor maiden: stays 1m: acts on all-weather and good to firm going: tried in cheekpieces: visored last 3 starts. *R. Brotherton*

BAROLO   5 b.g. Danehill (USA) 126 – Lydia Maria 70 (Dancing Brave (USA) 140)   **120**
[2004 106: 12g 14g* 16.1s 14d* 14.1g* Sep 2] strong, close-coupled gelding: very smart performer: much improved in 2004, winning handicap at Goodwood (by 5 lengths from Archduke Ferdinand) in May, listed race at Leopardstown (made all, beat Two Miles West 1½ lengths) in July and minor event at Salisbury (by neck from Grampian, leading 1½f out) in September: sent to contest Melbourne Cup, but reportedly off his food and was scratched from race: should stay 2m: acts on firm and good to soft going: game. *P. W. Harris*

BARON RHODES   3 b.f. Presidium 124 – Superstream (Superpower 113) [2004 68:   **88**
5s² 5g² 5m² 5d³ 5m* 5d³ 6m 5d⁵ 5f* 5d³ 5s 5d 5d 5s 5d³ 6s³ 5d Nov 3] compact filly: fairly useful handicapper: won at Sandown in June and Hamilton in July: stays 6f: acts on firm and soft going: ran poorly in cheekpieces final start. *J. S. Wainwright*

BARON'S PIT   4 gr.c. Night Shift (USA) – Incendio (Siberian Express (USA) 125)   **104 +**
[2004 119: 6g* Apr 12] big, well-made colt: type to carry condition: smart at 3 yrs: useful

form when winning minor event at Kempton only outing in 2004, leading over 1f out and beating Smokin Beau 2 lengths: had suspensory problem after: better at 6f than 7f: raced only on good going or firmer. *R. Hannon*

BARONS SPY (IRE) 3 b.c. Danzero (AUS) – Princess Accord (USA) 115 (D'Accord (USA)) [2004 66: 7f⁴ 7.1m² 8m 8g³ 7g² Oct 11] lengthy colt: fair maiden: stays 1m: acts on good to firm and good to soft going: tongue tied both starts at 2 yrs: flashed tail final outing. *A. W. Carroll* **74**

BAROQUE 3 b.c. Merdon Melody 98 – Dubitable 59 (Formidable (USA) 125) [2004 f8s 11.8d 10g 9.9v⁶ 14.1m 12m Jun 28] close-coupled colt: no form, including in seller: blinkered final start. *C. Smith* **–**

BARRANTES 7 b.m. Distant Relative 128 – Try The Duchess 99 (Try My Best (USA) 130) [2004 90: 6m 8.3m 6g 11.7m 8g Sep 3] well held in 2004. *Miss S. West* **–**

BARRAS (IRE) 3 b.g. Raphane (USA) 102 – Lady Fleetsin (IRE) (Double Schwartz 128) [2004 57: f6g f5g f6s³ f6g⁵ f5s⁴ f5g 7m 8g³ Aug 2] modest handicapper: best at 5f/ 6f: acts on fibresand, good to firm and good to soft going: wears headgear. *Miss Gay Kelleway* **55**

BARRISSIMO (IRE) 4 b.g. Night Shift (USA) – Belle de Cadix (IRE) 82 (Law Society (USA) 130) [2004 97?: 10g 10.4d May 13] strong, good-bodied gelding: sweated/raced freely when well held in handicaps in 2004. *W. J. Musson* **–**

BARRY ISLAND 5 b.g. Turtle Island (IRE) 123 – Pine Ridge 80 (High Top 131) [2004 85: p10g* p12g⁵ p12g² p10g⁴ p10g⁴ 10g 10g 12g³ 10f 12g⁶ 10m⁴ 10f* 10d p10g* p10g p10m Dec 22] good-topped gelding: type to carry condition: fairly useful performer: won claimer at Lingfield in January and handicaps at Newmarket in July and Lingfield (apprentices) in November: effective at 1¼m/1½m: acts on polytrack and firm going: sometimes slowly away. *D. R. C. Elsworth* **84**

BARTON FLOWER 3 br.f. Danzero (AUS) – Iota 83 (Niniski (USA) 125) [2004 –p: 8v 8v 9.9g 12m 16.2g 14.1g Aug 28] leggy filly: poor maiden: probably stays 1¾m: blinkered final start. *M. W. Easterby* **35**

BARTON SANDS (IRE) 7 b.g. Tenby 125 – Hetty Green (Bay Express 132) [2004 70: 10.9g* 10.1g* 11.5d² 9m⁴ 10m⁴ p10m⁴ Dec 22] neat gelding: fair performer: won seller at Warwick (for M. Pipe) in April and minor event at Yarmouth in August: left J. Jay after third start: barely stays 1½m: acts on firm and good to soft going, shaped quite well on polytrack final start: tried blinkered/visored: often tongue tied. *Andrew Reid* **73**

BARZAK (IRE) 4 b.g. Barathea (IRE) 127 – Zakuska 96 (Zafonic (USA) 130) [2004 74: f7g f8f⁵ f6g³ 7d 8d 7.1m 7.5d p7.1g p9.5g p9.5g⁶ p8.6g³ Dec 17] sturdy gelding: fair handicapper on all-weather, modest on turf: effective at 6f to 8.6f: acts on all-weather and good to soft going: tried in headgear: often tongue tied. *S. R. Bowring* **54 a65**

BASIC SYSTEM (USA) 2 b.c. (Apr 11) Belong To Me (USA) – Foible (USA) (Riverman (USA) 131) [2004 6g 7f⁵ Jul 29] stocky colt: second foal: dam, French 1m (at 2 yrs) and 1½m winner, half-sister to US 1984 Grade 1 2-y-o 1m winner Contredance and to dam of 1000 Guineas winner Wince: modest form in maidens at Newmarket and Epsom: will stay 1m: sold 6,000 gns. *Sir Michael Stoute* **62**

BASINET 6 b.g. Alzao (USA) 117 – Valiancy 87 (Grundy 137) [2004 72: 8d 8.3d 9f 8d⁴ 8g 9.2f⁶ 8.1d⁴ 10m 8.5m Sep 15] strong gelding: modest handicapper: stays 9f: acts on all-weather, firm and soft going: sometimes wears cheekpieces: often slowly away/races freely: held up. *J. J. Quinn* **60**

BASSERAH (IRE) 2 b.f. (Feb 16) Unfuwain (USA) 131 – Blueberry Walk (Green Desert (USA) 127) [2004 8m 8d Oct 15] 45,000F: sturdy filly: sixth foal: half-sister to 3 fairly useful winners, including French 1m (at 2 yrs) and 1¼m winner Jungle Rumbler (by Charnwood Forest): dam unraced sister to useful stayer Hawait Al Barr: better effort in maidens at Newmarket when seventh: travelled strongly long way following month: should be suited by 1¼m/1½m. *B. W. Hills* **76**

BATCHWORTH BEAU 3 ch.g. Bluegrass Prince (IRE) 110 – Batchworth Belle 100 (Interrex (CAN)) [2004 6s 8m 6m 5.2m Jun 22] workmanlike gelding: well held in maidens. *E. A. Wheeler* **–**

BATCHWORTH BREEZE 6 ch.m. Beveled (USA) – Batchworth Dancer 67 (Ballacashtal (CAN)) [2004 –: f6g Jan 8] of little account. *E. A. Wheeler* **–**

BATHWICK BILL (USA) 3 ch.g. Stravinsky (USA) 133 – Special Park (USA) (Trempolino (USA) 135) [2004 85: 6d 6s⁶ 5.1f² 6m³ 6g 6g 6g 5d Oct 18] workmanlike **85**

gelding: fairly useful performer: creditable efforts in 2004 only when placed: effective at 5f/6f: acts on firm going: blinkered final 2-y-o start. *B. R. Millman*

BATHWICK BRUCE (IRE) 6 b.g. College Chapel 122 – Naivity (IRE) 72 (Auction 67 Ring (USA) 123) [2004 77: 8.1s 8.1d p8.6g p10m⁴ Dec 21] good-topped gelding: fair handicapper: stays 1¼m: acts on polytrack, soft and good to firm going: tongue tied final start. *B. R. Millman*

BATHWICK DREAM 7 b.m. Tragic Role (USA) – Trina 37 (Malaspina 118) [2004 – –: p13g Feb 3] well beaten both starts since 2001. *B. R. Millman*

BATHWICK FINESSE (IRE) 2 b.f. (Apr 3) Namid 128 – Lace Flower (Old Vic 79 136) [2004 6.1d 8.1g* 8s⁴ 8s Oct 22] €19,500F, 12,000Y: leggy filly: third foal: half-sister to Italian 11f winner by Spectrum: dam, French 9f (at 2 yrs) to 13f winner, out of half-sister to very smart French middle-distance stayer Light The Lights: fair performer: made all in maiden at Chepstow in September: fourth at Salisbury, better effort in nurseries after: stays 1m: acts on soft going. *B. R. Millman*

BATIK (IRE) 3 gr.f. Peintre Celebre (USA) 137 – Dali's Grey (Linamix (FR) 127) 79 p [2004 8.1m³ 10.2g* 12s⁵ Oct 29] good-bodied filly: first foal: dam, French 11f winner, sister to smart French 10.5f winner Diamonixa and half-sister to 3-y-o Diamond Green: fair form: won maiden at Bath in September, leading close home: some improvement when close fifth behind Into The Shadows in handicap at Newmarket: will stay at least 1¾m: acts on soft and good to firm going: should continue to progress. *L. M. Cumani*

BATTLE BACK (BEL) 3 b.f. Pursuit of Love 124 – Batalya (BEL) (Boulou) [2004 – –: p7g f9.4g Jan 14] well-made filly: well beaten in maidens/banded event: blinkered final start. *S. C. Williams*

BATTLE CHANT (USA) 4 b.g. Coronado's Quest (USA) 130 – Appointed One 115 (USA) (Danzig (USA)) [2004 105: 8m³ 8m 10.1g² 9.9m² 9.9g³ 9s⁵ Oct 16] rangy gelding: smart performer: best efforts when 1½ lengths third to Everest in handicap at Newbury and 2½ lengths second to Alkaadhem in Select Stakes at Goodwood first/fourth starts: stays easy 1¼m: acts on good to firm going, probably on soft: sometimes reluctant to go to start (got loose before Select Stakes): tried tongue tied. *Mrs A. J. Perrett*

BATTLEDRESS (IRE) 2 b.g. (Mar 4) In The Wings 128 – Chaturanga (Night Shift 80 (USA)) [2004 7d 8g³ 10.2g⁴ Sep 27] close-coupled, quite good-topped gelding: fourth foal: half-brother to 9.4f winner Folaann (by Pennekamp) and Irish 6f/7f (latter at 2 yrs) winner Cocorica (by Croco Rouge): dam unraced half-sister to very smart 1¼m performer Strategic out of Oaks second Game Plan, herself half-sister to Oaks winner Shahtoush: best effort in maidens when third at Bath: should be suited by 1¼m/1½m: raced freely final start, then gelded. *M. P. Tregoning*

BAYADERE (GER) 4 b.f. Laviroc (GER) 125 – Brangane (IRE) (Anita's Prince 126) – [2004 93: 9.9g 10.1s 12s Nov 6] leggy, lengthy filly: soundly beaten in 2004, in visor final start. *V. Smith*

BAYARD (USA) 2 gr.c. (Apr 10) Lord Avie (USA) – Mersey 123 (Crystal Palace (FR) 74 132) [2004 8v⁴ 8d p8m Dec 21] half-brother to 2 winners, including useful French 1m (at 2 yrs) and 12.5f winner Martien (by Private Account): dam, won Prix Royal-Oak, half-sister to Prix Saint-Alary winner Muncie: easily best effort in maidens when staying-on fourth at Newbury: will stay at least 1½m. *D. R. C. Elsworth*

BAYBERRY (UAE) 4 ch.f. Bering 136 – Baya (USA) 116 (Nureyev (USA) 131) 109 ? [2004 9.9g⁵ 8.1d² 10.3f³ Sep 10] rangy filly: fifth foal: half-sister to 7f winner Kafhanee (by Seeking The Gold) and French 2001 2-y-o 1m winner Quelea (by Gone West): dam French 1m winner and second in Prix de Diane out of sister to Triptych: useful performer: trained by A. Fabre at 3 yrs, winning maiden at Bordeaux: sold €230,000 after last 3-y-o start: apparently much improved when length third to Big Bad Bob in minor event at Doncaster final outing: stays 1¼m: acts on firm and good to soft ground. *H. R. A. Cecil*

BAYCHEVELLE (IRE) 3 ch.f. Bahamian Bounty 116 – Phantom Ring 62 (Magic – Ring (IRE) 115) [2004 55: 6.1s Apr 30] workmanlike filly: better effort in 6f maidens at Nottingham when ninth at 2 yrs. *Mrs H. Dalton*

BAYEUX DE MOI (IRE) 2 b.c. (Feb 19) Barathea (IRE) 127 – Rivana 79 (Green 91 p Desert (USA) 127) [2004 7m⁴ 8d* 10g² Oct 11] heavy-topped colt: second foal: half-brother to 6f winner in Hong Kong by Selkirk: dam, Irish maiden (stayed 9f), half-sister to Irish Oaks winner Winona: won maiden at Salisbury in August: best effort when ½-length second to Sunday Symphony in minor event at Leicester: will stay 1½m: should make a useful 3-y-o handicapper. *Mrs A. J. Perrett*

BAYEUX (USA) 3 b.g. Red Ransom (USA) – Elizabeth Bay (USA) 116 (Mr Prospector **102**
(USA)) [2004 116: 10g⁵ 8m³ 10.3g 8f 7d³ Oct 15] big, lengthy, attractive gelding: just
useful performer in 2004, best effort when tenth to Calcutta in handicap at Doncaster
penultimate start: visored, shaped better than result when 7½ lengths third to Stream
of Gold in similar event at Newmarket final outing: gelded after: stays 1m: acts on firm
going, probably on good to soft: has worn crossed noseband: usually tongue tied (reportedly had breathing problem second 2-y-o start). *Saeed bin Suroor*

BAY HAWK 2 b.c. (Jan 30) Alhaarth (IRE) 126 – Fleeting Vision (IRE) 79 (Vision **75 p**
(USA)) [2004 7d³ Jul 10] 3,000Y: fourth foal: half-brother to 4-y-o Killing Joke: dam,
Irish 1½m to 2¼m winner, out of half-sister to St Leger winner Snurge: green, third in
maiden at Salisbury: will stay at least 1½m: likely to do better. *A. M. Balding*

BAYHIRR 3 b.c. Selkirk (USA) 129 – Pass The Peace 116 (Alzao (USA) 117) [2004 **92**
–p: 10d³ 10d* 10.4s⁵ 8.3f² 8g Jul 17] big, strong, rangy colt: fairly useful performer: won
maiden at Leicester in April: best effort when second to A One in handicap at Windsor
penultimate start: effective at 1m, barely at 10.4f: acts on firm and soft ground: free-going
sort: joined D. Selvaratnam in UAE. *M. A. Jarvis*

BAYLAW STAR 3 b.g. Case Law 113 – Caisson 67 (Shaadi (USA) 126) [2004 78: 5s⁶ **73**
5g³ 6g 5d⁴ 5m 5d 5d⁶ 6d 5m 6s⁶ p7.1g³ f6g³ Dec 7] sturdy, close-coupled gelding: fair
handicapper: left J. Balding after sixth start: barely stays 7f: acts on all-weather, firm and
soft going: tried in headgear: usually races up with pace. *K. A. Ryan*

BAYMIST 2 b.f. (Jan 20) Mind Games 121 – Milliscent 49 (Primo Dominie 121) [2004 **68**
5g⁵ 5g⁶ 5g* 6f⁴ 5g* 5s⁶ 5g Sep 25] 5,200Y: leggy, quite good-topped filly: second foal:
dam, maiden who stayed 1m, half-sister to useful sprinter Amber Mill: fair performer:
won claimer at Beverley in July and nursery at Haydock in August: should stay 6f: best
efforts on good ground: tended to hang final start. *M. W. Easterby*

BAYONET 8 b.m. Then Again 126 – Lambay 88 (Lorenzaccio 130) [2004 45: 7g 6g **–**
Aug 21] deep-girthed mare: well held in 2004: tried blinkered/in cheekpieces. *Jane
Southcombe*

BAYOU PRINCESS 3 ch.f. Bluegrass Prince (IRE) 110 – Josifina (Master Willie **59**
129) [2004 9.7s 12.1g 10m⁵ 12.1s³ 16s⁶ Aug 28] second living foal: dam refused to enter
stall only intended Flat outing, later winner over hurdles: modest maiden: stays 1¼m:
acts on good to firm ground. *B. De Haan*

BAYREUTH 2 ch.f. (Mar 9) Halling (USA) 133 – South Shore 102 (Caerleon (USA) **–**
132) [2004 8.2g Aug 18] half-sister to several winners, including useful 7f/1m winner
South Rock (by Rock City) and fairly useful 1m winner Leonica (by Lion Cavern): dam,
1¼m/1½m winner, half-sister to very smart 7f/1m performer Soviet Line: 40/1, well held
in maiden at Nottingham. *J. G. Given*

BAY SOLITAIRE 3 b.g. Charnwood Forest (IRE) 125 – Golden Wings (USA) (Devil's **–**
Bag (USA)) [2004 –: 10m⁶ 12m 14.1g Aug 28] tall, angular gelding: well held in
maidens/handicaps. *T. D. Easterby*

BAYTOWN FLYER 4 ch.f. Whittingham (IRE) 104 – The Fernhill Flyer (IRE) 71 **52**
(Red Sunset 120) [2004 –: f7g² p8g² f6s p7g* f6m* p7g* f7g² 6.1g* p7g* p6g² f6g 6g
p6d p7.1g⁵ f7g f7g p7m⁵ p6g⁴ Dec 20] smallish filly: modest performer: won banded
races at Lingfield (3, including amateur event), Wolverhampton and Warwick, all in
April: best at 6f/7f: acts on all-weather, firm and good to soft going: tried blinkered/in
cheekpieces: races prominently. *P. S. McEntee*

BAY TREE (IRE) 3 b.f. Daylami (IRE) 138 – My Branch 111 (Distant Relative 128) **94**
[2004 100: 7g⁶ 10.4s³ 8f 10d 8.5f⁵ 8.5d Oct 23] small, quite attractive filly: just fairly
useful performer in 2004: respectable 7¾ lengths third to Punctilious in Musidora Stakes
at York: left D. Loder after fourth outing: stays 10.4f: acts on soft and good to firm going.
H. G. Motion, USA

BAZELLE 2 ch.f. (Mar 29) Ashkalani (IRE) 128 – Dona Royale (IRE) 86 (Darshaan **82**
133) [2004 6m 7g⁴ 8m² 8m⁶ Sep 21] €35,000Y: sturdy filly: third foal: sister to fairly
useful 2003 2-y-o 7f winner Old Malt: dam, second at 1m/1¼m in Ireland all 3 starts,
half-sister to very smart performers Foresee (up to 1¾m) and Royal Touch (up to 9f):
fairly useful maiden: ½-length second to Dash To The Top at Leicester: respectable sixth
at Newmarket: will be suited by 1¼m/1½m. *P. W. D'Arcy*

BEACH PARTY (IRE) 3 b.f. Danzero (AUS) – Shore Lark (USA) (Storm Bird **60**
(CAN) 134) [2004 58: p8g³ f8.5g f8.5g Apr 24] sturdy filly: modest maiden: barely stays 1m:
acts on polytrack, raced only on good/good to firm ground on turf: free-going sort.
M. L. W. Bell

BEACON BLUE (IRE) 3 ch.f. Peintre Celebre (USA) 137 – Catch The Blues (IRE) **56 +**
115 (Bluebird (USA) 125) [2004 68: 12.1d⁶ 8m 12d Nov 3] leggy, lengthy filly: maiden
handicapper: should stay 1½m (ran as if amiss when tried both times): acts on soft and
good to firm going. *M. Johnston*

BEACON STAR (USA) 2 ch.g. (Feb 27) Stravinsky (USA) 133 – Careless Kitten **52**
(USA) (Caro 133) [2004 5s 7s p7g f8g⁶ Dec 11] quite good-topped gelding: modest
maiden: best effort at 7f on polytrack: gelded after final start. *M. Johnston*

BEADY (IRE) 5 b.g. Eagle Eyed (USA) 111 – Tales of Wisdom 70 (Rousillon (USA) **51**
133) [2004 73: 10g⁶ f12g⁶ f14g⁴ f14g⁵ p13.9g Dec 22] good-topped gelding: modest
performer: stays easy 1¾m: acts on fibresand, soft and good to firm going. *B. Smart*

BEAMISH PRINCE 5 ch.g. Bijou d'Inde 127 – Unconditional Love (IRE) 104 **59 §**
(Polish Patriot (USA) 128) [2004 66§: 10.1d 8g Sep 13] close-coupled gelding: modest
performer: stays 1¼m: acts on good to firm going, probably on dirt: blinkered last 3 starts
at 5 yrs: ungenuine: fair hurdler. *G. M. Moore*

BEAMSLEY BEACON 3 ch.g. Wolfhound (USA) 126 – Petindia 65 (Petong 126) **44**
[2004 62: 10s 8s 5.9f⁴ 7m f6g⁶ f6g⁴ f8g⁴ 7.5s 7m⁵ Sep 18] sturdy gelding: poor maiden:
left G. M. Moore after sixth start: stays 7f: acts on fibresand and firm going: tried in headgear. *Ian Emmerson*

BEAT THE HEAT (IRE) 6 b.g. Salse (USA) 128 – Summer Trysting (USA) 83 **84**
(Alleged (USA) 138) [2004 89: 10.4g² Oct 8] lengthy gelding: fairly useful handicapper:
creditable second to Go Tech at York only outing in 2004: stays 1½m: acts on fibresand
and any turf going: blinkered 4 times in 2001. *Jedd O'Keeffe*

BEAUCHAMP PILOT 6 ch.g. Inchinor 119 – Beauchamp Image 79 (Midyan **107 +**
(USA) 124) [2004 117: 8.5m⁶ 8f 8.3m⁴ Jun 26] big, rather leggy gelding: just useful form
in 2004: sixth to Passing Glance in Diomed Stakes at Epsom and fourth to Gateman in
listed event at Windsor (ran as if amiss in Queen Anne Stakes at Royal Ascot in between):
effective at 1m to 1¼m: acts on polytrack, dirt, firm and good to soft going: has worn
crossed noseband/been bandaged in front: usually waited with. *G. A. Butler*

BEAUCHAMP RIBBON 4 b.f. Vettori (IRE) 119 – Beauchamp Kate 61 (Petoski **– §**
135) [2004 75§: 11.6m 12.1m 10.1f Jul 29] smallish, sturdy filly: tailed off in handicaps in 2004: tried tongue tied/in cheekpieces, usually blinkered: temperamental.
A. J. Chamberlain

BEAUCHAMP STAR 3 ch.f. Pharly (FR) 130 – Beauchamp Cactus 86 (Niniski **75**
(USA) 125) [2004 7d 7.1d³ 8.1s² 9g 10.3m⁴ 10.9f² p8.6g p7.1g² Nov 29] half-sister to 1m **a60**
winner in Italy by Northern Park: dam, 17.6f winner, half-sister to very smart 1½m
winner Beauchamp Hero: fair maiden on turf, modest on all-weather: should stay 1½m:
acts on polytrack, firm and soft going: blinkered last 3 starts, raced freely last 2.
G. A. Butler

BEAUCHAMP TRUMP 2 b.g. (Mar 24) Pharly (FR) 130 – Beauchamp Kate 61 **66**
(Petoski 135) [2004 p6g 7g 7m⁴ Sep 9] fourth foal: half-brother to 4-y-o Beauchamp
Ribbon: dam disappointing maiden half-sister to useful 1½m winner Beauchamp Jade:
best effort in maidens when fourth of 6 at Epsom: will stay at least 1½m. *G. A. Butler*

BEAUCHAMP TURBO 2 ch.g. (Mar 4) Pharly (FR) 130 – Compton Astoria (USA) **62**
(Lion Cavern (USA) 117) [2004 p6g⁵ 6m⁵ 7v⁶ 7s p7.1g⁵ Nov 12] modest maiden: should
stay 1m: acts on polytrack and good to firm going: blinkered (below form) final start.
G. A. Butler

BEAUCHAMP TWIST 2 b.f. (Apr 1) Pharly (FR) 130 – Beauchamp Cactus 86 **58**
(Niniski (USA) 125) [2004 5.2m 5m p7g 7.6m⁶ 7.1d⁴ Oct 17] smallish filly: half-sister to
1m winner in Italy by Northern Park: dam, 17.6f winner, half-sister to very smart 1½m
winner Beauchamp Hero: modest maiden: should be suited by at least 1¼m: blinkered
last 2 starts (best effort on first occasion). *G. A. Butler*

BEAU JAZZ 3 br.c. Merdon Melody 98 – Ichor 52 (Primo Dominie 121) [2004 61: **65 d**
p5g⁵ p5g³ p5g 6d⁵ 5.7g 5.1g 5.1m p5.1g p8g Dec 20] strong colt: disappointing
maiden: tried in cheekpieces. *W. de Best-Turner*

BEAU MARCHE 2 b.g. (May 9) My Best Valentine 122 – Beau Dada (IRE) 66 (Pine **69**
Circle (USA)) [2004 6m⁵ 5.1m 6g 6m² 8m 6d* 6.1v p6g⁶ p7g² p6g⁵ p7m⁶ p6g² Dec 30]
£3,200Y: half-brother to 3 winners, including 7-y-o Smokin Beau and 3-y-o Smokin Joe:
dam 6f (at 2 yrs) to 1m winner: fair performer: won maiden at Brighton in October:
effective at 6f/easy 7f: acts on polytrack, good to firm and good to soft going: wore cheekpieces fifth start. *I. A. Wood*

Tattersalls Ireland Sale Stakes, the Curragh—
Beaver Patrol gives Fulke Johnson Houghton his second win in this race in three years,
following Tout Seul's success in 2002; Indesatchel is eased when held in second

BEAUMONT GIRL (IRE) 2 ch.f. (Mar 15) Trans Island 119 – Persian Danser **56**
(IRE) 69 (Persian Bold 123) [2004 5s 7d* 8g 7m Sep 18] €5,000F, €5,000Y: leggy filly:
third foal: half-sister to 6-y-o Sheer Focus: dam Irish 9f winner: modest performer: form
only when winning seller at Thirsk in August: ran as if amiss last 2 starts (breathing
problem on first occasion): should stay 1m. *G. A. Swinbank*

BEAUNE 2 b.c. (Feb 5) Desert Prince (IRE) 130 – Tipsy 95 (Kris 135) [2004 5g³ 6.1d⁶ **68**
p6g Oct 7] smallish, well-made colt: first living foal: dam, 8.5f to 1½m winner, half-
sister to 5-y-o Salselon out of half-sister to top-class miler Markofdistinction: best effort
when third in maiden at Haydock: needs to settle to stay beyond 5f: sold 5,000 gns.
W. J. Haggas

BEAUTEOUS (IRE) 5 ch.g. Tagula (IRE) 116 – Beauty Appeal (USA) (Shadeed **71**
(USA) 135) [2004 74, a–: f7g f9.4g f7s⁶ 7.1g⁴ p7g⁴ f6g* f8.5m* p8g* f7g* 8.3g⁴ May 2]
tall gelding: fair performer: left A. Berry after third start: won banded races at Southwell,
Wolverhampton and Lingfield within 7 days in April: angular, useful-looking filly:
all-weather, firm and good to soft ground: races prominently. *M. J. Polglase*

BEAUTIFUL MARIA (IRE) 2 b.f. (Jan 19) Sri Pekan (USA) 117 – Puteri Went- **–**
worth 88 (Sadler's Wells (USA) 132) [2004 5g Apr 14] angular, useful-looking filly:
second foal: sister to 3-y-o Putra Sas: dam, 1½m to 2½m winner, half-sister to smart
sprinter Watching: very green, well held in maiden at Newmarket. *P. F. I. Cole*

BEAUTIFUL MOVER (USA) 2 ch.f. (Mar 30) Spinning World (USA) 130 – **72**
Dancer's Glamour (USA) (Danzig Connection (USA)) [2004 6m² 6f³ 5m p6g⁴ 5m Sep
27] $32,000Y: sturdy filly: sixth foal: half-sister to 3 winners in North America: dam,
won in USA, out of half-sister to US Grade 1 9f winner Beau's Eagle: fair maiden: form
only at 6f: acts on polytrack and firm going. *J. W. Hills*

BEAUTIFUL NOISE 3 b.f. Piccolo 121 – Mrs Moonlight (Ajdal (USA) 130) [2004 **65**
67p: 8.2s 7m⁶ 7m⁵ 7m⁵ 7f⁵ 6g⁵ 8.2d⁵ 8m² 8g p7g Nov 27] tall filly: fair maiden: stays 1m:
acts on soft and good to firm going: blinkered last 5 starts: has been slowly away/raced
freely: sometimes finds little: sold 6,800 gns. *D. Morris*

BEAUTY OF DREAMS 3 b.f. Russian Revival (USA) 125 – Giggleswick Girl 67 **66**
(Full Extent (USA) 113) [2004 70: 8.1g 6s 7f 7m⁵ 8m³ 7s 7.5s⁶ 8g 8m⁴ 8s³ p8.6g p8g
p8.6d⁴ p7m p8m* p8.6g* p7g* Dec 30] leggy, close-coupled filly: fair performer: won
banded races at Lingfield and Wolverhampton and handicap at former track, all in Dec-

ember: stays 8.6f: acts on polytrack, soft and good to firm going: tried visored: sometimes slowly away. *M. R. Channon*

BEAUVRAI   4 b.g. Bahamian Bounty 116 – Lets Be Fair 94 (Efisio 120) [2004 84: f6g **84** p5g 6g 5g 5m⁵ 6m³ 5m 5g 6m² 5.3f³ 6s* 6g* 5.1g³ 5s f6g Nov 9] close-coupled gelding: fairly useful performer: left J. J. Quinn after second start: won claimers at Yarmouth (left V. Smith) and Epsom (left D. Flood) in August: stays 6f: acts on all-weather, best turf efforts on good/good to firm going: wore cheekpieces/blinkers last 8 outings: has been very slowly away: reportedly broke blood vessel tenth appearance. *G. C. H. Chung*

BEAVER DIVA   3 b.f. Bishop of Cashel 122 – Beaver Skin Hunter (Ballacashtal **39** (CAN)) [2004 –: 10.1v⁴ 9.2g f7g 6g² 5m² 6d 6.9m 6m Sep 25] workmanlike filly: poor maiden: stays 6f: acts on good to firm going: has shown signs of temperament. *W. M. Brisbourne*

BEAVER PATROL (IRE)   2 ch.c. (Apr 18) Tagula (IRE) 116 – Erne Project (IRE) **102** 80 (Project Manager 111) [2004 5s⁵ 5.1d³ 5g² 6m* 6f 6m⁶ 7g² 6m* 6m⁵ 8s⁵ Oct 23] €8,000F, €18,000Y: well-made colt: third foal: brother to Golden Tagula, winner up to 1m in Italy: dam won at 13f in Ireland: useful performer: won maiden at Windsor in April, minor event at Kempton in May and Tattersalls Ireland Sale Stakes at the Curragh (by length from Indesatchel) in August: below-form fifth in listed race at Redcar and Racing Post Trophy at Doncaster: stays 7f, not testing 1m: acts on soft and good to firm ground. *R. F. Johnson Houghton*

BE BOP   2 ch.g. (Apr 12) Groom Dancer (USA) 128 – Norpella 95 (Northfields (USA)) **48** [2004 8m 9f 8d Oct 15] strong, close-coupled gelding: poor form in maidens. *N. Tinkler*

BE BOP ALOHA   2 b.f. (Apr 3) Most Welcome 131 – Just Julia (Natroun (FR) 128) **50** [2004 5g 6g⁶ f7g³ 7g⁵ 7m 8.3m 7m 7.5m Sep 15] 3,200Y: tall filly: seventh foal: sister to 4-y-o Welcome Stranger and half-sister to fairly useful 1996 2-y-o 5f/6f winner Just Visiting (by Superlative): dam no form: modest maiden: best efforts at 7f: acts on fibresand: wore cheekpieces sixth start. *I. A. Wood*

BEBOPSKIDDLY   3 b.g. Robellino (USA) 127 – Adarama (IRE) (Persian Bold 123) [2004 63: p8m 11.5d⁶ Nov 5] maiden: well held in 2004, including in seller. *B. G. Powell*

BECKERMET (IRE)   2 b.g. (May 3) Second Empire (IRE) 124 – Razida (IRE) 106 **102** (Last Tycoon 131) [2004 5g³ 5m* 5m* 5m² 5.1d* 5.1g* 5g 5s⁴ 5f 5d⁵ Sep 17] €12,500Y: close-coupled, rather leggy gelding: half-brother to winner in Switzerland by Perugino: dam Irish 2-y-o 7f winner: useful performer: won maiden at Haydock in May and minor events at Thirsk and Chester (2, beating Amazin by 2½ lengths on second occasion) in June/July: respectable fourth in listed race at York, best effort after: should stay 6f: acts on good to firm and good to soft going. *R. F. Fisher*

Nexus GSA Conditions Stakes, Chester—
a fourth win for Beckermet, who draws clear of Amazin (left) and Oh Dara

Godolphin's "Belenus"

BEDTIME BLUES 2 b.f. (Mar 22) Cyrano de Bergerac 120 – Boomerang Blade 100 **43**
(Sure Blade (USA) 130) [2004 5g 5d Apr 14] 15,000Y: strong filly: first foal: dam 6f
winner (including at 2 yrs): poor form in maidens. *J. A. Glover*

BEECHES THEATRE (IRE) 2 b.f. (Apr 9) King's Theatre (IRE) 128 – Sandpiper **25**
(Green Desert (USA) 127) [2004 5.1g 5g p5.1g f5f Dec 28] compact filly: fifth foal:
half-sister to Italian 5f winner by Victory Note: dam lightly-raced maiden: bad maiden.
R. Brotherton

BEECHY BANK (IRE) 6 b.m. Shareef Dancer (USA) 135 – Neptunalia 70 (Slip **70**
Anchor 136) [2004 78: p13g 13.1m 13.3g^5 16.2g^3 16.2m^5 16g Sep 3] leggy mare: fair **a63**
handicapper: stays 2m: acts on good to firm and good to soft going: blinkered twice early
in career. *Mrs Mary Hambro*

BEE DEES LEGACY 3 b.g. Atraf 116 – Bee Dee Dancer (Ballacashtal (CAN)) [2004 **–**
–: p10g p12d 9g 12g Jul 8] no form: looked wayward in blinkers final start. *G. L. Moore*

BEEJAY 3 b.f. Piccolo 121 – Letluce 92 (Aragon 118) [2004 66: 6.1g* 7m 6.1g 6d 5g^6 **77**
p6g p6d Oct 30] fair handicapper: won at Nottingham in April: ran creditably after only
when sixth at Sandown: will probably stay 7f: acts on polytrack, probably on good to soft
going. *P. F. I. Cole*

BEEKEEPER 6 b.h. Rainbow Quest (USA) 134 – Chief Bee 89 (Chief's Crown **–**
(USA)) [2004 10g May 1] tall, close-coupled horse: smart performer at 3 and 4 yrs: well
held both subsequent outings: stayed 2m: acted on firm going: often tongue tied: dead.
D. R. Loder

BEE MINOR 3 b.f. Barathea (IRE) 127 – Bee Off (IRE) 59 (Wolfhound (USA) 126) **74 §**
[2004 73: 7m 6m^2 7m 6m 6g^2 6d^4 p6g Dec 11] workmanlike filly: fair maiden: left
R. Hannon after seventh start: effective at 6f/7f: acts on good to firm and good to soft
going: unreliable. *Ms Deborah J. Evans*

BEENABOUTABIT 6 b.m. Komaite (USA) – Tassagh Bridge (IRE) (Double Schwartz –
128) [2004 –: p6g p7g 5.3f⁵ 5g Jun 24] angular mare: poor maiden: tried visored/in
cheekpieces: sometimes tongue tied. *Mrs L. C. Jewell*

BEE SHARP 2 ch.f. (Jun 7) Twice As Sharp 99 – Bee Gee 42 (Beveled (USA)) [2004 –
p7.1g Dec 10] first foal: dam 1½m seller winner: 33/1, well held in maiden at Wolverhampton. *J. Jay*

BEE STINGER 2 b.c. (May 6) Almaty (IRE) 113§ – Nest Egg (Prince Sabo 123) [2004   **70**
6m 7g³ 6m² 7g² 6g⁴ Aug 5] £4,000Y: second foal: dam unraced: fair maiden: second at
Lingfield and Newcastle: effective at 6f/7f. *I. A. Wood*

BEFITTING 2 b.g. (Apr 15) Inchinor 119 – Ellebana 69 (Tina's Pet 121) [2004 5.1s   **53**
p5g p5g p5.1g Nov 27] modest maiden: best effort on debut. *J. A. Osborne*

BEFORE THE DAWN 2 b.f. (Feb 3) Lugana Beach 116 – Chayanee's Arena (IRE)   **45**
(High Estate 127) [2004 6.1s 6.1m 6g 6m 5.1g Oct 10] 1,200Y: first foal: dam seemed
of little account: poor maiden: should stay 7f: acts on soft and good to firm ground.
A. G. Newcombe

BEFRIEND (USA) 4 ch.f. Allied Forces (USA) 123 – Approcheer (USA) (With   **53**
Approval (CAN)) [2004 p8.6g⁴ p7.1g Dec 4] missed 2003: just modest form at 4 yrs:
stays 8.6f: acts on polytrack and firm going. *P. A. Blockley*

BEHAN 5 ch.g. Rainbows For Life (CAN) – With Finesse (Be My Guest (USA) 126)   –
[2004 44: f12g f12g⁵ f16.2g Feb 6] smallish, sturdy gelding: no longer of much account:
usually blinkered/visored. *A. Crook*

BEHKARA (IRE) 4 b.f. Kris 135 – Behera 129 (Mill Reef (USA) 141) [2004 115: 15s⁶   **116**
12.5m³ 15.5s² 12.5v* 12s² Dec 5] smart performer: off 10 months before reappearance,
right back to best when 2½ lengths second to Westerner in Prix Royal-Oak at Longchamp
in October: won listed race at Maisons-Laffitte (by neck from Maia Eria) in November:
below best when 2 lengths second to Ostankino in similar event at Toulouse: stays 15f
well: acts on good to firm ground but goes particularly well on soft/heavy. *A. de Royer
Dupre, France*

BELENUS (IRE) 2 ch.c. (Mar 22) Dubai Millennium 140 – Ajhiba (IRE) 110 (Bara-   **103 p**
thea (IRE) 127) [2004 7m* Jul 6] big, strong, good sort: good mover: second foal: dam,
1m/1¼m winner from 3 starts, half-sister to Second Empire out of half-sister to Flame of
Tara (dam of Salsabil and Marju): favourite, won maiden at Newmarket easily by 1½
lengths from Frith, leading well over 1f out: suffered ligament problem after: will be
suited to 1m/1¼m: should make his mark in stronger company. *Saeed bin Suroor*

BELISCO (USA) 3 b.g. Royal Academy (USA) 130 – A Mean Fit (USA) (Fit To Fight   **67**
(USA)) [2004 70: 10.2g 10g 8g⁶ p10g* 10f p10g p10g p10m Dec 22] lengthy, useful-
looking gelding: fair performer: won claimer at Lingfield (left Mrs A. Perrett) in August:
stays 1¼m: acts on polytrack and good to firm going: sometimes tongue tied/blinkered/
visored. *C. A. Dwyer*

BELLA BEGUINE 5 b.m. Komaite (USA) – On The Record 72 (Record Token 128)   **52**
[2004 65, a78: f6g⁵ p6g f7g² 7.1m 7.2g⁴ 5g⁴ 5m⁵ 7s 5d Aug 15] workmanlike mare:
modest performer: effective at 5f to 7f: acts on fibresand, soft and good to firm going:
usually blinkered/visored: none too consistent. *A. Bailey*

BELLA BOY ZEE (IRE) 3 b.f. Anita's Prince 126 – Waikiki (GER) (Zampano   **61**
(GER)) [2004 62: f5g³ f6s² f5s⁵ 5g* 6m 5d Aug 9] workmanlike filly: modest handicapper: won at Doncaster in July: effective at 5f/6f: acts on fibresand, good to firm and
good to soft going: visored final 2-y-o start. *P. A. Blockley*

BELLALOU 2 b.f. (Apr 19) Vettori (IRE) 119 – Spinning Mouse 65 (Bustino 136)   **54**
[2004 6m 7f 6m³ p7d f8g p8g* Nov 20] 10,000Y: third foal: half-sister to 1½m winner
Bunkum (by Robellino): dam, 1¾m winner, half-sister to smart sprinter/miler May Ball:
modest performer: won seller at Lingfield: should be suited by 1¼m/1½m: acts on polytrack and firm going. *N. A. Callaghan*

BELLA MIRANDA 2 ch.f. (Apr 17) Sinndar (IRE) 134 – Bella Lambada 87 (Lamm-   –
tarra (USA) 134) [2004 p7g Oct 28] 100,000Y: first foal: dam, 10.4f winner from 2 starts,
half-sister to high-class 1¼m performer Stagecraft out of smart winner up to 1¼m Bella
Colora: 10/1, well held in maiden at Lingfield. *D. R. Loder*

BELLA PAVLINA 6 ch.m. Sure Blade (USA) 130 – Pab's Choice 61 (Telsmoss 91)   **77**
[2004 34: f9.4g* f12f² f12s* f12g* f12s⁴ f12g* f12s⁵ f12g* 12g p12g³ p9.5g⁶ f12g⁴ Dec
28] smallish mare: fair performer: progressed well in early-2004, winning apprentice
banded races at Wolverhampton in January and February, banded race and claimer at

Southwell in February, and handicap at latter course in March: stays 1½m: acts on all-weather, probably on firm and soft going. *W. M. Brisbourne*

BELLA PLUNKETT (IRE) 2 ch.f. (Feb 20) Daggers Drawn (USA) 114 – Amazona **49** (IRE) (Tirol 127) [2004 6g 6.1g 7.1g 8g⁶ 7d² f6g Nov 8] 1,500Y: second foal: dam unraced half-sister to smart Italian colt around 1¼m Nonno Carlo: poor maiden: stays 7f: acts on good to soft going: no easy ride. *W. M. Brisbourne*

BELLA TUTRICE (IRE) 3 b.f. Woodborough (USA) 112 – Institutrice (IRE) 87 **72 d** (College Chapel 122) [2004 78: 5m 6m³ 5m⁴ p6g p6g³ 6m 6g 6m p6m 5.7g p5.1g f5f⁵ Dec 28] small, good-bodied filly: fair performer: creditable efforts in 2004 only when in frame in handicaps, leaving I. Wood after tenth start: effective on polytrack, good to firm and good to soft going: tried in cheekpieces. *M. J. Attwater*

BELLE CHANSON 2 b.f. (May 16) Kingsinger (IRE) 94 – Tallulah Belle 92 (Crown- **50** ing Honors (CAN)) [2004 6s 6g p7g Oct 13] leggy filly: first foal: dam 9f to 1½m winner: modest form in maidens: best effort on soft going. *J. R. Boyle*

BELLE LARGESSE 2 b.f. (Mar 9) Largesse 112 – Palmstead Belle (IRE) 79 (Wolf- **33** hound (USA) 126) [2004 5s⁵ 5.1m p6g Oct 19] smallish filly: first foal: dam 2-y-o 5f winner: poor maiden. *C. B. B. Booth*

BELLE ROUGE 6 b.m. Celtic Swing 138 – Gunner's Belle 69 (Gunner B 126) [2004 **86** p12g² 14.4s² 12d* 16m² p16g* 16.4m² 13.1d* 16g² 12g* 11.6d* 14.6s³ Oct 22] work-manlike mare: missed 2003: progressed into a fairly useful performer on return, winning handicaps at Folkestone in April, Lingfield in July and Bath in August, and minor events at Goodwood in September and Windsor in October: effective at 1½m to 2m: acts on all-weather, heavy and good to firm going: tough, game and consistent. *C. A. Horgan*

BELLS BEACH (IRE) 6 ch.m. General Monash (USA) 107 – Clifton Beach (Auction **54** Ring (USA) 123) [2004 55, a43: f6g⁶ f6s² f6g p6g* p6g p6g* p6g⁵ p6g⁶ p6g* 6s f6d⁴ 6g⁴ **a59** p6g* 5m⁵ 6.1s p7g f6g 6g Aug 21] strong, close-coupled mare: modest performer: won 3 sellers (second a handicap) and claimer in first half of 2004, all at Lingfield: effective at 5f/6f: acts on all-weather, good to firm and good to soft going. *P. Howling*

BELLS BOY'S 5 b.g. Mind Games 121 – Millie's Lady (IRE) (Common Grounds **42** 118) [2004 43: f5g³ f6g³ f6s⁵ f6s f6g⁴ f6s f5m³ 6.1m³ 6m 6m 6m Jul 31] workmanlike gelding: poor maiden: stays 6f: acts on fibresand and firm going: wears cheekpieces/blinkers. *K. A. Ryan*

BELLY DANCER (IRE) 2 gr.f. (Apr 21) Danehill Dancer (IRE) 117 – Persian Mist- **81** ress (IRE) (Persian Bold 123) [2004 5m⁶ f5g⁴ 7.1d² 7g⁶ p7.1g² p6g³ p7g³ p6g² Dec 4] €10,000F, 20,000Y: rangy filly: half-sister to Irish 6.5f winner Pip'n Judy (by Pips Pride): dam unraced half-sister to high-class sprinter Hallgate: fairly useful maiden: best effort sixth start: found little final one: stays easy 7f: acts on polytrack (promise on fibresand) and good to soft going. *P. F. I. Cole*

BELSHAZZAR (USA) 3 b.g. King of Kings (IRE) 125 – Bayou Bidder (USA) (Prem- **70** iership (USA)) [2004 9g 10m⁴ 8.5g 8.1d⁵ 10.5g Aug 5] $42,000Y: good-bodied gelding: fifth foal: half-brother to winner in USA by Chief's Crown: dam minor 6f stakes winner in USA: fair maiden: stays 1m: acts on good to soft going: sold 11,500 gns, then gelded. *T. P. Tate*

BELTANE 6 b.g. Magic Ring (IRE) 115 – Sally's Trust (IRE) 51 (Classic Secret (USA) **46 §** 91) [2004 –: p10g p10g p8g* p8g² 7m 8.3m 8m 8m⁵ 8.1g 8d 8d Oct 16] modest **a57 §** performer: won amateur banded stakes at Lingfield in February: stays 1m: acts on poly-track and good to firm going: unreliable. *W. de Best-Turner*

BELTON 2 b.g. (Mar 9) Lujain (USA) 119 – Efficacious (IRE) 49 (Efisio 120) [2004 **59** 6m 6m 7s 8v 7m 7.5m* f8g Dec 28] rather leggy, angular gelding: modest performer: won selling nursery at Beverley in September (gelded after): should stay 1m. *Ronald Thompson*

BE MY ALIBI (IRE) 3 ch.f. Daggers Drawn (USA) 114 – Join The Party (Be My **–** Guest (USA) 126) [2004 56d: 7s f6m⁵ 5g 7.1m 6s Oct 30] quite good-topped filly: poor maiden: stays 6f: acts on fibresand and good to soft going. *W. M. Brisbourne*

BEN BACCHUS (IRE) 2 b.g. (Mar 16) Bahhare (USA) 122 – Bodfaridistinction **59** (IRE) 77 (Distinctly North (USA) 115) [2004 7d p7.1g⁵ p7g Dec 20] €9,000F, €12,000Y: third foal: half-brother to 6f winner Blandys (by Dolphin Street): dam 2-y-o 5f winner: easily best effort in maidens when fifth at Wolverhampton: not sure to stay much beyond 7f. *M. H. Tompkins*

BENBAUN (IRE) 3 b.g. Stravinsky (USA) 133 – Escape To Victory (Salse (USA) **114**
128) [2004 85: 6g* 6.1d 5m* 5m² 5m* 5m³ 5m² Sep 5] useful-looking gelding: quickly
progressed into a smart performer at 3 yrs, winning handicaps at Haydock and Thirsk in
May and minor event at Sandown in June: also ran well in listed race at Naas (short-
headed by Osterhase), Premio Citta di Napoli at Naples (close third to T E Lawrence) and
Flying Five at the Curragh (beaten head by Ringmoor Down): effective at 5f/6f: acts
on firm and good to soft going: effective blinkered/visored or not: races prominently:
sometimes soon off bridle. *M. J. Wallace*

BENBYAS 7 b.g. Rambo Dancer (CAN) 107 – Light The Way 72 (Nicholas Bill 125) **79**
[2004 12g⁶ 12v* 14s* 10.1v⁵ Apr 26] sturdy, lengthy gelding: fair handicapper: won at
Pontefract (apprentices) and Haydock in April: visored, well held final start: has suffered
from knee trouble and reportedly laminitis: stays 1¾m: has form on good to firm ground,
all 5 wins on softer than good (acts on heavy): sometimes visored/blinkered earlier in
career: front runner: useful hurdler. *D. Carroll*

BEN CASEY 2 b.c. (Feb 20) Whittingham (IRE) 104 – Hot Ice (IRE) 53 (Petardia **64**
113) [2004 5m 5.1g⁶ 5f³ 5m³ 5g⁵ Oct 5] small, sturdy colt: modest maiden: likely to prove
best at 5f/easy 6f: acts on firm going. *B. Smart*

BENDARSHAAN 4 b.c. Darshaan 133 – Calypso Run (Lycius (USA) 124) [2004 **90**
84: a10f a9f 11g 12m⁴ 12m* 14.8g* 12m² 14g 13.3d⁵ 14g 14s⁵ 12d 12s³ 12s³ Nov 6]
close-coupled colt: fairly useful performer: well held for D. Watson in UAE first 3 starts
in 2004: won maiden at Pontefract and handicap at Newmarket in July: creditable third
in handicaps at Doncaster last 2 starts, blinkered in latter: stays 14.8f: acts on soft and
good to firm going: looked temperamental when well held tenth to twelfth outings.
M. Johnston

BENEDICT 2 b.c. (Apr 5) Benny The Dip (USA) 127 – Abbey Strand (USA) 78 **– p**
(Shadeed (USA) 135) [2004 6m 7g Aug 30] half-brother to several winners, including
5-y-o Right Approach and useful 9f/1¼m winner New Assembly (by Machiavellian):
dam 1m winner: green, well held in maidens at Windsor and Epsom: sold 18,000gns:
should do better at 1¼m/1½m. *Sir Michael Stoute*

BENEDICT BAY 2 b.c. (Mar 26) In The Wings 128 – Persia (IRE) (Persian Bold 123) **58**
[2004 7g⁶ 7d 7m 8s 7d Oct 10] sturdy colt: modest maiden: should stay 1m: visored final
start. *G. B. Balding*

BENEKING 4 b. or br.g. Wizard King 122 – Gagajulu 75 (Al Hareb (USA) 123) [2004 **59**
80d: 8.1v 7m³ 7.1m 6.1g⁶ 7.6g 9.9m⁵ 9.9d 10.4m 9.9m 12g Oct 4] rather leggy gelding:
modest maiden handicapper: barely stays 1¼m: acts on polytrack and good to firm going:
tried blinkered/in cheekpieces: none too consistent. *R. Hollinshead*

BENEVENTA 4 b.f. Most Welcome 131 – Dara Dee 87 (Dara Monarch 128) [2004 **110**
100: 8d* 9m* 10.4s² 8f 12g** 12.5d 12f Sep 24] tall, leggy filly: smart performer: won
listed race at Kempton in April, Letheby & Christopher Dahlia Stakes at Newmarket
(by 2½ lengths from Silence Is Golden) in May and listed race at Newmarket (by 3½
lengths from Selebela) in July: also ran well when ¾-length second to Crimson Palace in
Middleton Stakes at York third start: effective at 1m to 1½m: acts on firm and soft going:
usually races prominently: game: sold 250,000 gns. *J. L. Dunlop*

BEN HUR 5 b.g. Zafonic (USA) 130 – Gayane 125 (Nureyev (USA) 131) [2004 72: **79**
9.9d 8m* 7.5d 7.9f² 8d* 10.3d* 8.5g⁵ 10.3g⁴ 12.3m⁵ 8d* 9.1d p8.6g⁶ p9.5g p9.5g **a67**
p12.2g⁵ Dec 27] lengthy gelding: fair performer: won claimer at Leicester in May and
seller at Ayr and claimer at Chester in June: effective at 1m to 1½m: acts on all-weather,
firm and soft going: tried in cheekpieces: sometimes hangs right: usually races prominently. *W. M. Brisbourne*

BENJAMIN (IRE) 6 b.g. Night Shift (USA) – Best Academy (USA) (Roberto (USA) **48 d**
131) [2004 48+: p8g² p8g² p8g⁵ 8.2m 8.1m 11.7g 7f⁵ Aug 3] poor maiden: stays 1m: acts
on polytrack and firm going: tongue tied: usually blinkered. *Jane Southcombe*

BEN KENOBI 6 ch.g. Accondy (IRE) 79 – Nour El Sahar (USA) (Sagace (FR) 135) **45 §**
[2004 55§: f7g⁵ f7g² f9.4m² 10.9m 12.6m² 12.1g p12.2d Oct 23] well-made gelding: poor
performer: stays 12.6f: acts on fibresand and firm going: unreliable. *Mrs P. Ford*

BEN LOMAND 4 ch.g. Inchinor 119 – Benjarong 50 (Sharpo 132) [2004 82: 6s 6g **57**
6d³ 7s 6.1g 7s p6g⁶ p6g⁵ Dec 1] good-bodied gelding: modest handicapper: best at 6f:
acts on polytrack, good to firm and good to soft going. *B. W. Duke*

BENNANABAA 5 b.g. Anabaa (USA) 130 – Arc Empress Jane (IRE) (Rainbow Quest **–**
(USA) 134) [2004 p10g p8g⁵ p7g 8g f8g 7.1m 5.1f 5.1m⁵ 5.7m 6d 6v 5g Sep 2] poor
maiden: tongue tied: blinkered final start. *S. C. Burrough*

BENNY BATHWICK (IRE) 3 b.g. Midyan (USA) 124 – Sweet Pavlova (USA) 71 – (Zilzal (USA) 137) [2004 7m 8.3d Jun 21] better effort in maidens when seventh at Salisbury on debut. *B. R. Millman*

BENNY THE BALL (USA) 3 b. or br.g. Benny The Dip (USA) 127 – Heloise (USA) – (Forty Niner (USA)) [2004 86p: 7g 8.1m 6g p7g p9.5g Oct 18] big, good-bodied gelding: disappointed and well held in 2004. *N. P. Littmoden*

BENNY THE BUS 2 b.g. (May 21) Komaite (USA) – Amy Leigh (IRE) 78 (Imperial **70** Frontier (USA) 112) [2004 7m 5g 6d 5g² p7.1g p5.1g⁶ Nov 19] strong gelding: second living foal: brother to 5-y-o Katy O'Hara: dam 5f (including at 2 yrs)/6f winner: fair maiden: will prove best at 5f/6f: acts on polytrack. *Mrs G. S. Rees*

BENS GEORGIE (IRE) 2 ch.f. (Apr 12) Opening Verse (USA) 126 – Peperonata **54** (IRE) 91 (Cyrano de Bergerac 120) [2004 p7g⁶ Dec 20] fifth reported foal: half-sister to Italian 2001 2-y-o 7f/1m winner by Polar Falcon: dam, 2-y-o 5f winner (became one to treat with caution), sister to very smart middle-distance performer Millkom: 22/1, sixth in maiden at Lingfield. *D. K. Ivory*

BEN'S REVENGE 4 b.g. Emperor Jones (USA) 119 – Bumble Boogie (IRE) (Blue- – bird (USA) 125) [2004 11.8m⁶ 10.5g 12.1s⁵ p12.2d⁶ p9.5g p10m Dec 15] little form: wore cheekpieces last 2 starts. *M. Wellings*

BENTLEY BROOK (IRE) 2 ch.c. (May 27) Singspiel (IRE) 133 – Gay Bentley **71** (USA) (Riverman (USA) 131) [2004 p6g² p6g² p7.1g⁵ Dec 31] €20,000Y, 19,000 2-y-o: closely related to 2 winners by In The Wings, including Irish 1½m winner Vintage Port and half-brother to several winners, including useful Italian sprinter Gentle Fan (by Lear Fan): dam maiden in USA: fair form in maidens at Wolverhampton: will stay at least 1m. *P. A. Blockley*

BENTLEY'S BALL (USA) 3 b. or br.g. Stravinsky (USA) 133 – Slide By 83 (Aragon **93** 118) [2004 93: 6d⁶ 8m 7.1d 7.1m³ 6g⁴ 6.5f⁴ Sep 24] rather leggy, quite good-topped gelding: fairly useful handicapper: good efforts last 3 starts, fourth to Khabfair at Ascot final one: stays 7f: acts on firm ground: sometimes slowly away: carried head awkwardly third/fourth outings: sold 42,000 gns, joined M. Al Kurdi in UAE. *R. Hannon*

BENTLEY'S BUSH (IRE) 2 ch.f. (Apr 5) Barathea (IRE) 127 – Veiled Threat (IRE) **96** 105 (Be My Guest (USA) 126) [2004 5.2g⁵ 6m² 6g* 6g³ 7.1m³ Jul 22] 45,000Y: lengthy filly: fourth foal: sister to French 10.5f winner The Veil and half-sister to French 5.5f (at 2 yrs) to 1m winner Desert Threat (by Desert Prince): dam, French 1m/1¼m performer, out of sister to dam of Pentire: useful performer: won maiden at Goodwood in June: third in nursery at Ascot and listed race at Sandown (much improved when beaten 3½ lengths by Queen of Poland): will stay 1m. *R. Hannon*

BENVOLIO 7 br.g. Cidrax (FR) – Miss Capulet (Commanche Run 133) [2004 –: – 12.1m Sep 21] small gelding: no sign of ability. *I. W. McInnes*

BERENSON (IRE) 2 b.c. (Mar 17) Entrepreneur 123 – On Air (FR) 93 (Chief **114 p** Singer 131) [2004 7m* 7g² Sep 19]
It isn't likely that the first two in the National Stakes at the Curragh in September will clash again, as both are now in the same ownership. Berenson, second to the hot favourite Dubawi when carrying the colours of the wife of his trainer Tommy Stack, was subsequently sold privately and in 2005 will be racing in the royal blue of Godolphin. Berenson's new owners have acquired a colt who has shown himself smart after two runs and looks sure to improve a fair bit more, particularly when given the opportunity to tackle longer distances. Both of Berenson's runs took place at seven furlongs, the first of them a maiden at the Curragh in August in which he justified favouritism by a length and a half from another newcomer Sanserif. The Group 1 National Stakes represented a big step up in class but Berenson, without the tongue tie he had worn on his debut, showed he was well worth his place in the field with a cracking effort. After tracking Dubawi, Berenson was unable to quicken when that colt took command inside the two-furlong marker and also showed his inexperience by wandering under pressure, but to his credit he kept on well to finish three lengths second.
The fifth living foal of On Air, Berenson is a full brother to the four-year-old filly Swiss Roll, who has shown fairly useful form at up to two miles for Stack, winning twice. On Air, a daughter of a French mile-and-a-quarter winner, was a useful winner herself at that distance, both in France and Britain, and she stayed a

		Entrepreneur (b 1994)	Sadler's Wells (b 1981)	Northern Dancer
Berenson (IRE) (b.c. Mar 17, 2002)				Fairy Bridge
			Exclusive Order (ch 1979)	Exclusive Native
				Bonavista
		On Air (FR) (b 1988)	Chief Singer (br 1981)	Ballad Rock
				Principia
			Green Light (b 1982)	Green Dancer
				Ranimer

mile and a half. On Air's half-sister, the smart Another Dancer, won the Prix de Malleret at the latter trip, while her grandam Ranimer was second in the same race and the Hardwicke Stakes, as well as successful in the Sun Chariot. On Air also ran in three two-mile novice hurdles in Britain, winning one of them. It is worth underlining how well suited Berenson will be by a step up in trip. He is likely to stay at least a mile and a quarter. *T. Stack, Ireland*

BERESFORD BOY 3 b.g. Easycall 115 – Devils Dirge 68 (Song 132) [2004 53: 5.7f **63** 6m p6g² Oct 18] close-coupled gelding: modest maiden: easily best effort when second at Wolverhampton final start: stays 6f: acts on polytrack. *D. K. Ivory*

BERGAMO 8 b.g. Robellino (USA) 127 – Pretty Thing 83 (Star Appeal 133) [2004 **–** 54: f16g f14s Mar 14] small, compact gelding: well held on Flat in 2004: wears headgear. *B. Ellison*

BERHAM MALDU (IRE) 2 b.f. (Apr 15) Fraam 114 – Corniche Quest (IRE) 74 **–** (Salt Dome (USA)) [2004 5g 5.1g 8.3g Oct 11] lightly-made filly: fourth foal: half-sister to 3 winning sprinters, including 4-y-o Blakeshall Quest: dam 5f to 1m winner: well held, including in seller. *M. J. Wallace*

BERKELEY HEIGHTS 4 b.f. Hector Protector (USA) 124 – Dancing Heights (IRE) **48** 80 (High Estate 127) [2004 –: f12g⁴ f11g f14s⁶ f16s² f16.2m³ f14m⁴ f14g* 19.1f 16m Jul

5] sturdy filly: poor performer: left B. Smart after second start: won banded race at Southwell in May: stays easy 2m: acts on fibresand and good to soft ground: tried blinkered/visored: often soon off bridle. *Mrs J. Candlish*

BERKHAMSTED (IRE) 2 b.c. (Mar 30) Desert Sun 120 – Accounting (Sillery **102** (USA) 122) [2004 5d* 6f⁶ 7g² 7g⁵ 8v* 8f 8d⁵ 8s⁶ Oct 23] €27,000F, €50,000Y: strong, good-topped colt: good mover: first foal: dam, maiden in France/Britain who stayed 12.5f, out of half-sister to very smart US 8.5f/9f winner Joyeux Danseur and dam of Arazi: useful performer: won maiden at Leicester in April and listed race at Deauville (by head from Glazed Frost) in August: creditable fifth to Konigstiger in Gran Criterium at Milan, best effort after: should stay 1¼m: acts on heavy ground, probably on firm. *J. A. Osborne*

BERRY RACER (IRE) 3 ch.f. Titus Livius (FR) 115 – Opening Day (Day Is Done – **–** 115) [2004 53?: 6.1m Jun 14] maiden: well held in handicap only start in 2004. *N. P. Littmoden*

BERRYWHITE (IRE) 6 ch.g. Barathea (IRE) 127 – Berryville (USA) (Hatchet Man **48** (USA)) [2004 f12s 10.1v 14.4v³ 16.1m³ 16f⁵ Jun 8] ex-German gelding: successful at 1¼m/11f at 4 yrs, and placed 4 times in 2003 for U. Stoltefuss: poor form in Britain: barely stays 2m: acts on any going: sent to Denmark. *C. Grant*

BERTOCELLI 3 ch.c. Vettori (IRE) 119 – Dame Jude 76 (Dilum (USA) 115) [2004 **70 d** 76: 6g 7m 7m³ 8.2g⁴ 7m 8m 7m⁶ 8g 10f 8g 10m⁴ 10g⁴ p10m p7m² p7m Dec 15] compact colt: fair performer at best: probably stays 1¼m: acts on polytrack and firm going. *G. G. Margarson*

BERTROSE 2 ch.c. (Mar 2) Machiavellian (USA) 123 – Tularosa (In The Wings 128) **75** [2004 7g⁴ 8g⁵ 8g³ 8.3g Oct 11] smallish, close-coupled colt: third living foal: half-brother to fairly useful 1¼m/1½m winner Ambrosine (by Nashwan) and 3-y-o Camrose: dam, French 11f winner, half-sister to Most Welcome: fair maiden: soon off bridle when running poorly in nursery final start: will be suited by 1¼m/1½m. *J. L. Dunlop*

BESEEKA RUNNIN FOX 3 b.f. Hi Nod 106 – Windsor Fox (IRE) (Mandalus 110) **–** [2004 12m Jun 20] smallish filly: second foal: dam poor hurdler: 100/1, showed nothing in maiden at Pontefract. *Mrs L. Williamson*

BESPOKE 2 ch.g. (Feb 23) Pivotal 124 – Immaculate (Mark of Esteem (IRE) 137) **44** [2004 6g⁵ 6g⁶ 6g 8s a8g⁴ Dec 12] sparely-made gelding: poor maiden: left Sir Mark Prescott 3,500 gns before final start: probably stays 1m: usually slowly away. *S. Hernandez, Spain*

BESSEMER (JPN) 3 b.g. Carnegie (IRE) 129 – Chalna (IRE) 83 (Darshaan 133) **90** [2004 92: 7.1g⁵ 8m³ 7.1m⁶ 10g* 10.3s⁴ 10d 8.3s³ 12s Nov 6] rangy gelding: fairly useful performer: left M. Johnston after third start: won 4-runner minor event at Ayr in August: stays 1¼m: acts on soft and good to firm ground: tongue tied final outing: sometimes slowly away: has shown signs of waywardness. *I. Semple*

BEST ABOUT 2 ch.f. (Feb 23) King's Best (USA) 132 – Up And About 77 (Barathea **67 p** (IRE) 127) [2004 7g Sep 20] 54,000Y: close-coupled filly: second foal: half-sister to 3-y-o Tamarillo: dam 15f winner out of very smart 1¼m/1½m winner Upend: 11/1 and tongue tied, seventh in maiden at Kempton, slowly away: will stay at least 1m: should do better. *D. R. Loder*

BEST BEFORE (IRE) 4 b.g. Mujadil (USA) 119 – Miss Margate (IRE) 60 (Don't **86** Forget Me 127) [2004 70§: p6g p8g p8g* 8.3g² 8.1s² 8g 9g² 8.3m* 8g³ 8m³ 9g³ 8g* 8m⁶ 8.3g 8.9g 8v 7s Nov 6] workmanlike gelding: fairly useful handicapper: won at Lingfield in February, Windsor in June and Newmarket in July: should stay 1¼m: acts on polytrack, soft and good to firm going: tried blinkered at 3 yrs. *P. D. Evans*

BEST BE GOING (IRE) 4 b.g. Danehill (USA) 126 – Bye Bold Aileen (IRE) (Warn- **84** ing 136) [2004 88p: 10g 10f 9g⁵ 11.8f⁴ 11.9d 10m 10g* Oct 11] sturdy, close-coupled gelding: fairly useful handicapper: visored, won at Windsor in October: barely stays 1½m: acts on firm going. *P. W. Harris*

BESTBYFAR (IRE) 2 b.c. (Apr 11) King's Best (USA) 132 – Pippas Song 75 (Refer- **– p** ence Point 139) [2004 7.2d Sep 17] 50,000Y: good-topped colt: seventh foal: half-brother to 3 winners, including useful 5f to 7f winner Nightbird (by Night Shift) and 3-y-o Night Air: dam, 1½m winner, half-sister to smart 11.4f winner Rockerlong: 16/1 and green, well held in maiden at Ayr, not knocked about: should do better. *J. G. Given*

BEST DESERT (IRE) 3 b.g. Desert Style (IRE) 121 – La Alla Wa Asa (IRE) 60 **66** (Alzao (USA) 117) [2004 65: 7g⁴ 7m² 7g 8d 7m⁵ 6.9m* 8g⁵ 8d 6s 8m⁶ p7.1g³ p8g⁴ p9.5d **a63** p9.5g p7g Dec 30] good-bodied gelding: fair performer: won minor event at Carlisle

in August: stays 1m: acts on polytrack and good to firm going: found little third start.
J. R. Best

BEST FLIGHT   4 gr.g. Sheikh Albadou 128 – Bustling Nelly 94 (Bustino 136) [2004   **70**
78p: 10.3g 10g 10f⁴ 16.2m 12g 12.6g Aug 30] workmanlike gelding: fair handicapper:
stays 1¼m: acts on fibresand and firm going: slowly away penultimate outing: sold
16,500 gns. *B. W. Hills*

BEST FORCE   3 b.f. Compton Place 125 – Bestemor 60 (Selkirk (USA) 129) [2004   **55**
–p: 5.1g⁴ 6s May 6] neat filly: modest maiden: stays 6f: acts on good to firm going: edged
left on reappearance. *G. A. Butler*

BEST GAME   2 b.g. (Mar 29) Mister Baileys 123 – Bestemor 60 (Selkirk (USA) 129)   **60**
[2004 6m 7s 8s⁶ 8s p8g³ Nov 20] quite good-topped gelding: modest maiden: blinkered, third in seller at Lingfield: stays 1m: acts on soft going, probably on polytrack.
G. A. Butler

BEST LEAD   5 b.g. Distant Relative 128 – Bestemor 60 (Selkirk (USA) 129) [2004   **58**
58: f5g* f5s f6g⁴ f5s⁴ f5g³ 5d⁴ 5m³ 5g³ 5m³ 6d³ 6g p5.1g* p5.1g⁶ p5.1g³ Dec 31] leggy   **a70**
gelding: fair on all-weather, modest on turf: won claimer in January and handicap in
November, both at Wolverhampton: best at 5f/easy 6f: acts on all-weather, firm and soft
going: tried visored, blinkered nowadays. *Ian Emmerson*

BEST PORT (IRE)   8 b.g. Be My Guest (USA) 126 – Portree 82 (Slip Anchor 136)   **70**
[2004 63: 13.8g 14.1g* f16g 14.1m³ 16.1v⁶ 16m* 13.9m 14.1f⁴ 14.1m³ 18d⁵ p16.5g²   **a60**
Nov 6] lightly-made gelding: fair handicapper on turf, modest on all-weather: won at
Nottingham in April, Redcar in May and Thirsk in July: best form at 1¾m/2m: acts on
polytrack, firm and good to soft going: held up. *J. Parkes*

BESTSELLER   4 ch.f. Selkirk (USA) 129 – Top Shop 75 (Nashwan (USA) 135) [2004   **47**
–: f12g⁴ f12g³ f12s⁵ Feb 20] angular, good-topped filly: poor maiden: stays 1½m.
J. G. M. O'Shea

BETFRED   3 b.g. Pursuit of Love 124 – Shamaka 53 (Kris 135) [2004 9.2f Jul 31] 33/1,   –
tailed off in maiden at Hamilton. *A. Berry*

BETHANYS BOY (IRE)   3 ch.g. Docksider (USA) 124 – Daymoon (USA) (Dayjur   –
(USA) 137) [2004 81: 10.3g 8g 8.2d May 15] close-coupled gelding: fairly useful at 2
yrs: no form in 2004. *B. Ellison*

BETTALATETHANNEVER (IRE)   3 ch.g. Titus Livius (FR) 115 – Shambodia   **102**
(IRE) (Petardia 113) [2004 85: p7g* p7g⁴ 7g 7m 8m² p8g⁶ 7m 7.1m 7g* Oct 21] lengthy
gelding: useful performer: won handicap at Lingfield in January and minor event at
Epsom (best effort, beat Manaar 6 lengths) in October: stays easy 1m: raced only on polytrack and good/good to firm going: sometimes edges left: found little penultimate start:
held up: sold 110,000 gns, joined M. Al Kurdi in UAE. *S. Dow*

BETTER OFF   6 ch.g. Bettergeton 97 – Miami Pride 48 (Miami Springs 121) [2004 –,   –
a85d: f7g⁵ f7g f7g⁶ f9.4g f8.5g⁵ May 11] strong gelding: poor mover: little form at 6 yrs:
tried visored, usually wears cheekpieces. *Mrs N. Macauley*

BETTER PAL   5 ch.g. Prince Sabo 123 – Rattle Along 80 (Tap On Wood 130) [2004   –
64d: f8g Jan 8] good-bodied gelding: maiden: blinkered once. *P. R. Wood*

BETTERTHEDEVILUNO   5 b.g. Hector Protector (USA) 124 – Aquaglow 84   –
(Caerleon (USA) 132) [2004 f8g Mar 23] third of 5 in claimer in 2001: tailed off in
amateur claimer at Southwell only start on Flat since. *D. McCain*

BETTERWARE BOY   4 ch.g. Barathea (IRE) 127 – Crystal Drop 101 (Cadeaux   –
Genereux 131) [2004 68: p16g 11.6m Aug 21] maiden: well beaten in handicaps in 2004.
P. M. Phelan

BETTY'S PRIDE   5 b.m. Lion Cavern (USA) 117 – Final Verdict (IRE) (Law Society   **64**
(USA) 130) [2004 62§: 5m 5m⁴ 6m 5m⁶ 5.5g⁶ 5f 5f* 5f 5m⁶ 5m* 5m Sep 29] leggy, quite
good-topped mare: modest performer: won seller at Musselburgh in July and handicap at
Lingfield in September: best at 5f: acts on firm going: often slowly away. *M. Dods*

BETTY STOGS (IRE)   3 b.f. Perugino (USA) 84 – Marabela (IRE) 79 (Shernazar   –
131) [2004 81: 8d 8d⁵ 7g 7g Sep 30] sturdy filly: fairly useful at 2 yrs: last in listed race/
handicaps in 2004, leaving D. Elsworth prior to final start. *C. G. Cox*

BETTYS VALENTINE   4 b.f. My Best Valentine 122 – Fairy Ballerina (Fairy King   –
(USA)) [2004 f11s⁴ 8v 8g 7.5m 5m 6d Jun 25] of little account. *D. W. Barker*

BEVELLER   5 ch.g. Beveled (USA) – Klairover 50 (Smackover 107) [2004 61: p6g   **57**
f6g⁵ Dec 28] rangy gelding: modest maiden: free-going sort, effective at 6f/7f: acts on
fibresand and good to firm going: has been slowly away. *W. M. Brisbourne*

BEVERLEY BEAU   2 b.g. (Apr 29) Inchinor 119 – Oriel Girl 65 (Beveled (USA))   **67**
[2004 5g⁵ 5g⁵ 5m⁴ 6g⁴ 5m⁴ 5g⁵ p5.1d⁶ Oct 23] 3,000Y: leggy gelding: second foal: dam
5f (at 2 yrs) to 7f winner: fair maiden: best effort at Beverley on fifth start: likely to prove
best at 5f/6f: sometimes sweating/coltish: gelded after final outing. *Mrs L. Stubbs*

BEVIER   10 b.g. Nashwan (USA) 135 – Bevel (USA) (Mr Prospector (USA)) [2004   **50**
53: f9.4s⁵ f12s³ f9.4s⁴ f9.4s² 12v f12g⁴ f9.4g 10.2s 9.3m Sep 11] leggy gelding: modest
performer: effective at 9.4f to 1½m: acts on fibresand and firm going: blinkered (raced
freely) once. *T. Wall*

BE WISE GIRL   3 ch.f. Fleetwood (IRE) 107 – Zabelina (USA) 57 (Diesis 133) [2004   **58**
49: f8s³ 10g* 10.9d p9.5g Oct 2] workmanlike filly: modest handicapper: won at
Nottingham in April: stays 1¼m: acts on fibresand: free-going front runner: tail flasher.
J. G. Given

BEYOND CALCULATION (USA)   10 ch.g. Geiger Counter (USA) – Placer Queen   **60**
(Habitat 134) [2004 83, a–: 5d 5.1d 5m 5.3f 6g⁴ 6d 6.1s¹⁴ 6.1d⁴ 5m⁵ 6m 6g Aug 30] sturdy   **a–**
gelding: modest performer: effective at 5f/6f: acts on all-weather, firm and soft going:
wore cheekpieces/blinkers last 8 starts: none too consistent. *J. M. Bradley*

BEYOND THE CLOUDS (IRE)   8 b.g. Midhish 109 – Tongabezi (IRE) 75 (Sher-   **83**
nazar 131) [2004 97: 5g 5d 5m 5g² 5d 5d 5g³ 5d 5g 5d⁶ 5f² 5g 5m 5d Oct 18] big gelding:
just fairly useful handicapper in 2004: best at 5f (all wins)/easy 6f: acts on firm and good
to soft going: tried visored, wore cheekpieces last 5 starts: sometimes slowly away: none
too consistent. *J. S. Wainwright*

BEYOND THE POLE (USA)   6 b.g. Ghazi (USA) – North of Sunset (USA) (North-   **65**
ern Baby (CAN) 127) [2004 71: p13g* p12g p12g* p16g Nov 30] fair performer: won
claimer and handicap at Lingfield in February: stays easy 2m: acts on polytrack, firm and
soft going: tried blinkered at 4 yrs. *B. R. Johnson*

BHUTAN (IRE)   9 b.g. Polish Patriot (USA) 128 – Bustinetta 89 (Bustino 136) [2004   **51**
70: 12m 10m² 11.6m Aug 2] lengthy gelding: just modest form in 2004: effective at 1¼m
to 17.5f: acts on all-weather/any turf going: visored once: held up, and often finds little.
G. B. Balding

BIASCA   2 ch.f. (Mar 25) Erhaab (USA) 127 – Beacon (High Top 131) [2004 p10g Nov   **–**
27] 40,000Y: closely related to useful performer up to 1½m Indian Light (by Be My
Chief), 7f/1m winner at 2 yrs, and half-sister to 3 winners, including useful 1¼m and
1¾m winner Maycocks Bay (by Muhtarram): dam unraced half-sister to smart performer
up to 2½m Compton Ace out of Irish St Leger winner Mountain Lodge: 12/1, well held in
maiden at Lingfield. *J. H. M. Gosden*

BIBI HELEN   2 b.f. (Apr 19) Robellino (USA) 127 – Tarry 65 (Salse (USA) 128) [2004   **– §**
6m⁶ 7m 8d f8g Nov 9] 2,500F: sturdy filly: fourth foal: half-sister to 3-y-o Ace Coming:
dam, 7f (at 2 yrs) and 1¾m winner, also won over hurdles: temperamental maiden (twice
bolted to post). *N. A. Callaghan*

BIBURY FLYER   2 br.f. (Feb 12) Zafonic (USA) 130 – Affair of State (IRE) 99 (Tate   **98**
Gallery (USA) 117) [2004 5s² 5v² 5m³ 5.1f³ 5d⁵ 5m² 5d² 5.2m⁶ 5g* 6m² 6m 6d 5s³ 5.1s³
6.5m³ 7g² 6.5g⁴ 7d⁵ 6d* 7s⁴ 7v* 6s Oct 29] 35,000Y: good-topped filly: sister to useful
1¼m/1½m winner Mojalid and half-sister to several winners, including 4-y-o Gun
Salute: dam 2-y-o 5f/6f winner: useful performer: won nursery at Doncaster in July and
listed races at the Curragh and Newbury (beat Wedding Party by 2 lengths) in October:
left M. Channon 75,000 gns, rare poor effort final start: effective at 6f/7f: acts on any turf
going: edgy sort: held up/carries head high/idles in front, but is tough and consistent.
J. Noseda

BID FOR FAME (USA)   7 b. or br.g. Quest For Fame 127 – Shroud (USA) (Vaguely   **81**
Noble 140) [2004 97: 16d 16g 13.9s 14.1f 16s p16.5g Nov 8] leggy, lengthy gelding: has
a quick, rather round action: just useful handicapper in 2004: stays 16.5f: acts on all-
weather, best turf efforts on good going or firmer: tried blinkered/in cheekpieces.
C. G. Cox

BID SPOTTER (IRE)   5 b.g. Eagle Eyed (USA) 111 – Bebe Auction (IRE) (Auction   **–**
Ring (USA) 123) [2004 –: f12g⁴ f14g 11.5m Jul 1] poor performer: stays 1½m: tried   **a44**
visored/in cheekpieces. *Mrs Lucinda Featherstone*

BIEN GOOD   3 b.f. Bien Bien (USA) 125 – Southern Sky 89 (Comedy Star (USA) 121)   **–**
[2004 –: 13.8m³ 9d⁵ 15.8g 10s Nov 1] rangy filly: little form. *K. G. Reveley*

BIENHEUREUX 3 b.g. Bien Bien (USA) 125 – Rochea 67 (Rock City 120) [2004 **69 +** 48+: f8g f8g p7g 8m 12m² 12m* 16g⁵ p12.2g⁴ p13m* p12.2g* p12.2g* Dec 20] workmanlike gelding: fair performer: left W. Musson after fifth start: won handicap at Folkestone in July, banded race at Lingfield in November, and minor event and handicap at Wolverhampton in December: should stay 1¾m: acts on polytrack and good to firm going. *Miss Gay Kelleway*

BIENVENUE 3 ch.f. Bien Bien (USA) 125 – Mossy Rose 78 (King of Spain 121) [2004 **76** 67p: 10m⁴ 11.6f* 11.6g² 14m⁶ 11.7m 12g⁶ Sep 8] fair performer: won maiden at Windsor (idled/hung right) in June: stays 11.6f: acts on polytrack and firm going: sometimes races freely. *M. P. Tregoning*

BIGALOS BANDIT 2 ch.c. (Mar 9) Compton Place 125 – Move Darling (Rock City **95** 120) [2004 5s* 5g² 5m⁴ 5.1g 5g⁴ 5s³ 5d³ 6m 5d* Oct 17] 13,500Y: big, useful-looking colt: good walker: fifth foal: half-brother to 4-y-o Clann A Cougar and a 2-y-o 6f winner in Italy by Sabrehill: dam ran twice: useful performer: won maiden at Redcar in April and minor event at Musselburgh in October: good fourth in Molecomb Stakes at Goodwood and third in listed race at York fifth/sixth starts: best at 5f: acts on soft ground. *J. J. Quinn*

BIG BAD BOB (IRE) 4 br.c. Bob Back (USA) 124 – Fantasy Girl (IRE) 55 (Marju **116** (IRE) 127) [2004 118: 9.9g³ 10g⁴ 10m⁵ 10.3f* Sep 10] rather leggy colt: smart performer: won minor event at Doncaster in September by ¾ length from Red Fort: also ran well when in frame in listed race at Goodwood (third to Alkaadhem) and La Coupe at Longchamp (fourth to Aubonne): best around 1¼m: raced only on good going or firmer (acts on firm): free-going front runner (often establishes big lead): somewhat quirky. *J. L. Dunlop*

BIG BAD BURT 3 ch.g. Efisio 120 – Mountain Bluebird (USA) 79 (Clever Trick **66** (USA)) [2004 61p: p8g⁴ p7g² p6g² p7g³ 8.1v 8.2d³ 7m⁴ 8.3m⁶ f8m 10.1m 10.1m⁴ 12.3s 10s⁴ Aug 24] fair maiden: left M. Wallace after fourth start, Gay Kelleway after eighth: stays easy 1¼m: acts on polytrack, good to firm and good to soft going: tried visored/in cheekpieces/tongue tied. *G. C. H. Chung*

BIG BAMBO (IRE) 2 ch.c. (Feb 18) Monashee Mountain (USA) 115 – Bamboo (IRE) **–** (Thatching 131) [2004 5d 6g May 22] well held in maidens. *Mrs P. N. Dutfield*

BIG BERTHA 6 ch.m. Dancing Spree (USA) – Bertrade 75 (Homeboy 114) [2004 75: **73** p13g⁴ f12g² p12g 10m 12s⁴ Oct 29] strong mare: fair handicapper: stays easy 13f: acts on all-weather and soft going: held up. *John Berry*

BIG BRADFORD 3 b.g. Tamure (IRE) 125 – Heather Honey (Insan (USA) 119) [2004 **93 d** 89: 6m² 6m 6m 7g p7g⁶ 6g 6g Sep 29] sturdy gelding: has a quick, fluent action: fairly useful handicapper: easily best effort in 2004 when second to Buy On The Red at Newmarket in May: barely stays 7f: acts on polytrack, firm and good to soft going: blinkered/visored: often races prominently. *P. G. Murphy*

BIG HASSLE (IRE) 2 b.c. (Apr 9) Namid 128 – Night After Night (Night Shift **92 p** (USA)) [2004 5g⁵ 5g² 5g* 6s Aug 18] €16,000Y, resold €15,000Y: big, strong colt: second living foal: dam unraced close relative to very smart 1¼m performer Batshoof out of sister to dam of 2000 Guineas winner King of Kings: won maiden at Beverley in July by 3½ lengths from Breaking Shadow, making all: well beaten in Gimcrack Stakes at York: should stay 6f: likely to make a useful handicapper if all is well. *T. D. Easterby*

BIG HOO HAH 2 ch.f. (Mar 14) Halling (USA) 133 – Gentilesse 81 (Generous (IRE) **64** 139) [2004 7g 7g⁶ 8.1s⁴ 8g Sep 16] 6,500Y: lightly-made filly: fourth foal: half-sister to fairly useful Irish 1m winner Signora Rossa (by Groom Dancer): dam won at 1¼m only outing: modest maiden: should stay 1¼m. *C. A. Cyzer*

BIG HURRY (USA) 3 b.f. Red Ransom (USA) – Call Me Fleet (USA) (Afleet **–** (CAN)) [2004 9f Aug 1] $260,000Y: fifth foal: sister to fairly useful Irish 1¼m winner Rapid Ransom and half-sister to 2 winners, including smart Irish sprinter Warrior Queen (by Quiet American): dam unraced half-sister to dam of high-class French 1m/1¼m winner Green Tune and Cheveley Park winner Pas de Reponse out of half-sister to Storm Bird: 12/1, raced freely when eleventh of 14 in maiden at Newbury. *R. Charlton*

BIG MOMENT 6 ch.g. Be My Guest (USA) 126 – Petralona (USA) (Alleged (USA) **106** 138) [2004 102: 18.7d³ 22.2f⁵ 14g⁶ 14s² 12d² 12s* Nov 6] leggy, good-topped gelding: has a short, round action: useful performer: won listed race at Doncaster in November easily by 5 lengths from Foreign Affairs: good efforts otherwise when placed in handicaps at Chester (5¾ lengths third to Anak Pekan in Chester Cup), Haydock (found less than seemed likely when ¾-length second to Regal Setting) and Newmarket (head second to Flamboyant Lad): effective at 1½m to 18.7f (below form in 2¾m Queen Alexandra

Stakes second start): acts on firm and soft going: held up, and travels strongly: consistent. *Mrs A. J. Perrett*

BIG MYSTERY (IRE) 3 b.f. Grand Lodge (USA) 125 – Mysterious Plans (IRE) (Last Tycoon 131) [2004 p5.1g f5g p7.1g f8g p7g Dec 20] sixth foal: half-sister to 3 winners, including French 1m/1¼m winner Ti For Too (by Exit To Nowhere): dam, French 10.5f winner, sister to smart French sprinter Monde Bleue and half-sister to high-class sprinter Sayf El Arab: little form in maidens/banded race. *J. R. Best* –

BIG SMOKE (IRE) 4 gr.g. Perugino (USA) 84 – Lightning Bug (Prince Bee 128) [2004 84: 8.3m f11d⁴ f12g⁵ 11.9f³ p12.2g⁶ Dec 20] rather leggy gelding: modest performer: left J. H. Johnson after fourth start: stays easy 1½m: acts on all-weather, firm and good to soft going: tried blinkered/in cheekpieces: none too genuine. *J. C. Tuck* 61

BIG TOM (IRE) 3 ch.c. Cadeaux Genereux 131 – Zilayah (USA) 79 (Zilzal (USA) 137) [2004 67: 8s⁵ 6d 6d 8.1g f5f 5d 6g 8.1d Oct 9] sturdy colt: disappointing maiden: left D. O'Connell in Ireland after third start and rejoined former trainer. *D. Carroll* –

BIJAN (IRE) 6 b.m. Mukaddamah (USA) 125 – Alkariyh (USA) 79 (Alydar (USA)) [2004 44: f6g f7g⁴ f7g Jan 12] leggy mare: poor performer: stays easy 7f: acts on fibresand, good to firm and good to soft going: tried visored/in cheekpieces. *R. Hollinshead* 39

BIJOU DAN 3 ch.g. Bijou d'Inde 127 – Cal Norma's Lady (IRE) 87 (Lyphard's Special (USA) 122) [2004 8.3f⁴ 10m⁶ 9.2d 10s⁵ 12s p8.6g⁴ p9.5g² f8g³ p9.5g⁵ p8.6g* Dec 27] angular, close-coupled gelding: half-brother to several winners, including 1997 2-y-o 6f winner Magical (by Magic Ring), later Grade 3 1m winner in USA: dam 2-y-o 6f/7f winner who stayed 1¼m: modest performer: won maiden at Wolverhampton in December, edging right: stays 9.5f: acts on all-weather: wore cheekpieces last 5 starts. *I. Semple* 63

BIJOU DANCER 4 ch.g. Bijou d'Inde 127 – Dancing Diana 82 (Raga Navarro (ITY) 119) [2004 55: 8.3g 8m f7d⁶ 10.2g f6g f6d Dec 21] medium-sized gelding: maiden: well held in 2004: tried in headgear. *M. R. Bosley* –

BILL BENNETT (FR) 3 b.g. Bishop of Cashel 122 – Concert (Polar Falcon (USA) 126) [2004 70, a74: p10g⁶ f9.4g f12g⁶ 12g⁵ 10.9d* 12.6s* 14.1s² 12g⁵ 14d 11.6d* 12.1d⁴ 14g 16s³ 16s p12g p16.5g f14g⁵ Dec 7] fairly useful handicapper on turf, fair on all-weather: won at Warwick in April and May and at Windsor in June: stays 2m: acts on fibresand and soft going, probably on firm: tried blinkered/tongue tied at 2 yrs: usually held up. *J. Jay* 87 a68

BILLY BATHWICK (IRE) 7 ch.g. Fayruz 116 – Cut It Fine (USA) (Big Spruce (USA)) [2004 68, a–: 10g 10.2f 10.2m³ 10.2m³ 10.1m* 10.2g 10.2g⁵ 9m 11.5g 9.9g p12m 11.7g Oct 10] smallish, close-coupled gelding: fair handicapper: won at Yarmouth in July: stays easy 1½m: acts on firm and soft going: tried blinkered/in cheekpieces. *J. M. Bradley* 65 a–

BILLY ONE PUNCH 2 b.c. (Mar 11) Mark of Esteem (IRE) 137 – Polytess (IRE) (Polish Patriot (USA) 128) [2004 7d Aug 27] good-bodied colt: fourth foal: half-brother to fairly useful 2000 2-y-o 6f winner Norcroft Lady (by Mujtahid) and to 1m seller winner Our Lady (by Primo Dominie): dam, second at 1¼m in France, out of close relation to smart French 9f to 11f winner Lichine: 10/1, seventh to The Coires in maiden at Newmarket: should stay 1m: likely to do better. *P. W. Chapple-Hyam* 65 p

BILLY TWO RIVERS (IRE) 5 ch.g. Woodborough (USA) 112 – Good Visibility (IRE) (Electric 126) [2004 16m⁵ Jul 5] stocky gelding: lightly raced and little form. *D. R. MacLeod* –

BILLY WHISTLER 3 ch.c. Dancing Spree (USA) – Polar Refrain 59 (Polar Falcon (USA) 126) [2004 –: f8s Mar 14] tailed off in maidens at Redcar and Southwell (blinkered). *J. Balding* –

BINANTI 4 b.g. Bin Ajwaad (IRE) 119 – Princess Rosananti (IRE) (Shareef Dancer (USA) 135) [2004 95: 8.1f 7.1m⁶ 7.1m⁶ p8g 7m 7.1d⁵ p7g⁵ 7.1g³ 8g p7g² p8.6g* p8m² p8g* Dec 30] smallish, useful-looking gelding: fairly useful performer: won handicap at Wolverhampton and minor event at Lingfield in December: stays 8.6f: acts on all-weather, firm and good to soft going: sometimes visored. *P. R. Chamings* 94

BINARY VISION (USA) 3 ch.c. Distant View (USA) 126 – Binary 109 (Rainbow Quest (USA) 134) [2004 7.9m* 8.3m⁶ Jun 26] strong, compact colt: fourth foal: half-brother to smart 7f to 9f winner Binary File (by Nureyev) and 9f winner Hawksbill (by Silver Hawk): dam, 9f/1¼m winner in France/USA, sister to smart 1½m winner Bequeath: favourite, won maiden at York by 7 lengths from Sharaab, missing break and running green but quickening well: 3 lengths sixth to Gateman in listed race at Windsor 14 days later, keeping on strongly not knocked about: not sure to stay much beyond 1m: 107

wore crossed noseband/heavily bandaged hind-joints at York: looked a smart prospect. *J. H. M. Gosden*

BINNION BAY (IRE) 3 b.g. Fasliyev (USA) 120 – Literary 79 (Woodman (USA) – 126) [2004 84: 6g 8m 8g 7m⁶ 8m p6m p7g Dec 30] tall gelding: little form in 2004: left R. Hannon after fifth start: stays 1m: raced only on polytrack and good/good to firm going. *J. J. Bridger*

BINT IL SULTAN (IRE) 2 b.f. (Feb 2) Xaar 132 – Knight's Place (IRE) 72 (Hamas **60** (IRE) 125§) [2004 6g³ 7g 6g p7d Aug 9] 45,000F, 115,000Y: first foal: dam, Irish maiden who stayed 1m, half-sister to useful stayer El Conquistador and to dam of Prix Vermeille winner Pearly Shells: clearly best effort on debut: should stay at least 1m: tends to be slowly away: sold 4,000 gns. *E. A. L. Dunlop*

BINT ROYAL (IRE) 6 ch.m. Royal Abjar (USA) 121 – Living Legend (USA) **65** (Septieme Ciel (USA) 123) [2004 69, a76: f6g⁵ 6m⁵ 7m 6f³ 7f⁴ 6m 6m⁴ 7g³ 6m 7m 7.1d⁵ 7d 8m 7m 7.1f² 6.9f* 7.1m 7m* 6g⁵ 6g⁵ f6g f6g f7g f7g⁶ Dec 14] close-coupled, workmanlike mare: modest handicapper: won at Carlisle in July and Catterick in September: effective at 6f to 1m: acts on all-weather, firm and good to soft going: tried in headgear: none too reliable. *Miss V. Haigh*

BINTY 2 b.f. (Apr 14) Prince Sabo 123 – Mistral's Dancer (Shareef Dancer (USA) 135) **43** [2004 6s 6d Nov 5] 8,500Y: close-coupled filly: sister to 6f (at 2 yrs)/7f winner Cruise and 1m winner Brocketeer and half-sister to 2 winners by Risk Me, including fairly useful 5f (at 2 yrs) to 11.6f winner Queen's Pageant: dam, maiden, best at 7f: poor form in maidens at Newmarket (backward) and Yarmouth. *J. L. Spearing*

BI POLAR 4 b.g. Polar Falcon (USA) 126 – Doctor Bid (USA) (Spectacular Bid **80** (USA)) [2004 89: 6g 7g 7m² 7g² 7m 7s³ 7m⁶ 7g³ Sep 30] close-coupled, workmanlike gelding: fairly useful performer: raced mainly at 7f: acts on soft and good to firm going: sold 12,500 gns. *D. R. C. Elsworth*

BIRCHALL (IRE) 5 b.g. Priolo (USA) 127 – Ballycuirke (Taufan (USA) 119) [2004 **57** 62: 12v 12d 8v² 10m 10g Jul 16] ex-Irish gelding: modest handicapper: won at Roscommon in 2003: left F. Flood prior to final 5-y-o start: effective at 1m to 1½m: acts on heavy going. *Ian Williams*

BIRD KEY 3 b.f. Cadeaux Genereux 131 – Portelet 91 (Night Shift (USA)) [2004 6f – Aug 7] third foal: half-sister to 2-y-o Etlaala, 5-y-o Selective and useful 6f (at 2 yrs) to 7.5f (in Italy) winner Overspect (by Spectrum): dam 5f winner out of half-sister to smart middle-distance stayer Braashee: 14/1, extremely green when last in maiden at Newmarket: sold 75,000 gns in November. *R. Guest*

BIRD OVER 2 b.f. (May 4) Bold Edge 123 – High Bird (IRE) (Polar Falcon (USA) **61 p** 126) [2004 p7g⁴ p7.1g* Oct 25] £900Y: first foal: dam unraced: favourite, won maiden at Wolverhampton by 2 lengths from Fullandby, taking good hold and leading over 1f out: will probably stay 1m: should progress. *R. M. Beckett*

BIRIKINA 3 b.f. Atraf 116 – Fizzy Fiona (Efisio 120) [2004 75d: f6g⁶ f6g Jan 16] – close-coupled filly: no form since ninth 2-y-o start: tried in cheekpieces: sent to Israel. *A. Berry*

BIRIYANI (IRE) 2 b.f. (Mar 27) Danehill (USA) 126 – Breyani 101 (Commanche **71 p** Run 133) [2004 6g⁴ Sep 3] €180,000Y: rather leggy, attractive filly: half-sister to several winners, including 3-y-o Mister Monet and Moyglare Stud Stakes/Irish 1000 Guineas winner Tarascon (by Tirol): dam Irish 11f and 2m winner: 20/1, 4 lengths fourth to Halle Bop in maiden at Kempton, not knocked about: will stay 1m: sure to improve. *P. W. Harris*

BIRTHDAY STAR (IRE) 2 b.c. (Feb 28) Desert King (IRE) 129 – White Paper (IRE) – (Marignan (USA) 117) [2004 6m Sep 5] 17,500F, 12,000Y: close-coupled colt: third reported foal: half-brother to 2001 2-y-o 6f winner Funksoulborough (by Woodborough): dam unraced: 66/1 and better for race, well held in maiden at York, slowly away. *W. J. Musson*

BIRTHDAY SUIT (IRE) 3 ch.f. Daylami (IRE) 138 – Wanton 106 (Kris 135) [2004 **82 ?** 94: 6g³ 8g³ May 3] strong filly: fairly useful performer: reportedly suffered fractured cannon bone final 2-y-o start: below best in 2004, seemingly easily better effort when 2½ lengths third to Bonne de Fleur in listed race at Ripon in April: should have stayed 7f: raced only on good/good to firm going: stud. *T. D. Easterby*

BIRTH OF THE BLUES 8 ch.g. Efisio 120 – Great Steps 88 (Vaigly Great 127) **48** [2004 48: p10g p13g f12s⁶ p12g³ p13g* p12g⁴ 11.9m⁶ 11.9m⁶ May 12] lengthy, angular gelding: poor performer: won banded stakes at Lingfield in April: stays easy 13f: acts on polytrack and any turf going: tried visored/blinkered at 4 yrs. *A. Charlton*

BIRTHSTONE 2 ch.f. Machiavellian (USA) 123 – Baya (USA) 116 (Nureyev (USA) **109 p**
131) [2004 8s* 8g* Sep 13] sixth foal: closely related to 7f winner Kafhanee (by Seeking
The Gold) and French 2001 2-y-o 1m winner Quelea (by Gone West) and half-sister to
4-y-o Bayberry: dam French 1m winner and second in Prix de Diane out of sister to
Triptych: won minor event at Deauville in August and Prix d'Aumale at Chantilly
(comfortably by 1½ lengths from Portrayal, leading over 1f out) in September: will stay
1¼m: joined Godolphin: potentially smart, and should win more races. *H-A. Pantall,
France*

BISCAR TWO (IRE) 3 b.g. Daggers Drawn (USA) 114 – Thoughtful Kate 64 (Rock **56**
Hopper 124) [2004 –: f8g⁴ f11g⁶ 8s² 8s² 8.2s² 10m 10g* 10g Aug 18] leggy gelding:
modest performer: won seller at Ripon in July: stays 1¼m: acts on fibresand and soft
going: visored/blinkered 3 of last 4 starts: often slowly away/races lazily. *R. M. Whitaker*

BISH BASH BOSH (IRE) 3 b.f. Bien Bien (USA) 125 – Eurolink Virago (Charmer **–**
123) [2004 36: f6g f7g Feb 12] close-coupled filly: maiden: well held in claimer/seller
(blinkered) in 2004. *M. F. Harris*

BISHOPRIC 4 b.g. Bishop of Cashel 122 – Nisha (Nishapour (FR) 125) [2004 81+: **100**
10.3g 8.1d* 8.1g 10.4s Aug 18] lengthy gelding: useful handicapper, lightly raced: won
at Haydock in June by 1½ lengths from Prizeman, racing in small group on inside rail:
ran as if amiss otherwise in 2004: stays 1m: raced only on good going or softer: visored
penultimate start. *H. Candy*

BISHOPS BOUNCE 3 b.g. Bishop of Cashel 122 – Heights of Love 51 (Persian **–**
Heights 129) [2004 73d: 8g 5.9f Jul 29] small, plain gelding: maiden: well held in
claimers in 2004. *T. A. K. Cuthbert*

BISHOPS COURT 10 ch.g. Clantime 101 – Indigo 86 (Primo Dominie 121) [2004 **114 d**
112: 5.2g* 5v² 5s 5m³ 5d³ 5.1g 5m 5.1g² 5d⁵ 5g⁶ 5m⁵ 5s 5d 5s⁶ Oct 23] big, good-
quartered gelding: impresses in appearance: smart performer: just about as good as ever
first 2 starts in 2004, winning handicap at Newbury (by short head from Peruvian Chief)
in April and head second to Bahamian Pirate in minor event at Beverley following month:
just useful form after, including when third in Temple Stakes at Epsom and listed race at
Chantilly in June: best at 5f: acts on any going: tongue tied in 2000: usually bandaged
nowadays: reportedly bled 3 times at 10 yrs: usually held up. *Mrs J. R. Ramsden*

BISHOPS FINGER 4 b.g. Bishop of Cashel 122 – Bit of A Tart (Distant Relative **54**
128) [2004 52, a68: p10g⁶ Dec 30] just modest form only 4-y-o start: stays 1¼m: acts on
all-weather, unraced on extremes of going on turf: blinkered/visored: sometimes slowly
away: has looked none too keen: not one to trust implicitly. *Jamie Poulton*

BISHOPSTONE MAN 7 b.g. Piccolo 121 – Auntie Gladys 49 (Great Nephew 126) **77**
[2004 83, a–: 8.3d 8.1d 8m⁴ 8f 8g⁶ 7.1m² Jul 23] well-made gelding: fair handicapper: **a–**
best at 7f/1m: acts on fibresand, firm and soft going: effective visored or not: sometimes
hangs. *H. Candy*

BISHOP TO ACTRESS 3 ch.f. Paris House 123 – Chess Mistress (USA) 59 (Run **–**
The Gantlet (USA)) [2004 54: f6g f5g Feb 24] leggy filly: maiden: well held in 2004.
M. J. Polglase

BJORLING 3 ch.c. Opening Verse (USA) 126 – Pola Star (IRE) (Un Desperado (FR) **–**
125) [2004 p10g Dec 30] 66/1 and tongue tied, well held in maiden at Lingfield.
I. A. Wood

BLACKBURN MEADOWS 7 b.m. Flying Tyke 90 – Hatshepsut (Ardross 134) **–**
[2004 7d Jun 24] sixth foal: dam of little account: 80/1, showed nothing in maiden at
Thirsk. *P. R. Wood*

BLACKCHURCH MIST (IRE) 7 b.m. Erins Isle 121 – Diandra (Shardari 134) **–**
[2004 22.2f Jun 19] lengthy mare: fifth foal: half-sister to Irish 1m to 1½m winner Celtic
Project (by Project Manager): dam ran once: 100/1 and tongue tied, tailed off in Queen
Alexandra Stakes at Royal Ascot: winning jumper. *B. W. Duke*

BLACK COMBE LADY (IRE) 2 b.f. (Apr 22) Indian Danehill (IRE) 124 – Flor- **–**
inda (CAN) (Vice Regent (CAN)) [2004 5f 6m 7.1m 7m f7d Jul 23] €5,000F, €8,500Y:
half-sister to several winners, including useful 1997 2-y-o 5f winner Diligence (by
Dilum) and Irish 11f winner Little Rort (by Ali-Royal): dam unraced: seems of little
account. *A. Berry*

BLACKCOMB MOUNTAIN (USA) 2 b. or br.f. (Apr 8) Royal Anthem (USA) **65**
135 – Ski Racer (FR) (Ski Chief (USA) 115) [2004 7.1g⁵ 7.5g³ 7.1f⁴ p7d⁴ 7s 8g³ 8f⁶ 9d⁶ **a70**
Oct 17] 4,000 2-y-o: leggy filly: second foal: dam French 13f winner, half-sister to smart

French performer up to 9f Bouccaneer: fair maiden: should stay 1¼m: acts on polytrack and firm going: hung markedly left third start. *M. F. Harris*

BLACK DRAFT   2 b. or br.g. (Apr 8) Josr Algarhoud (IRE) 118 – Tilia 56 (Primo Dominie 121) [2004 5g 5m May 25] rather leggy gelding: modest form in maidens. *Jean-Rene Auvray* **53**

BLACK FALCON (IRE)   4 ch.g. In The Wings 128 – Muwasim (USA) (Meadowlake (USA)) [2004 97§: p16.5g p9.5g* p9.5g p9.5g⁴ Dec 31] rather leggy gelding: fairly useful handicapper: won at Wolverhampton (awarded race after bumped and short-headed by Nashaab) in November: should stay 1½m: acts on polytrack and firm going: well beaten only try in visor: formerly ungenuine. *Ian Williams* **94**

BLACKHEATH (IRE)   8 ch.g. Common Grounds 118 – Queen Caroline (USA) 67 (Chief's Crown (USA)) [2004 91: 6g 5s⁴ 6g⁴ 6m 6m⁶ 6m² 6g² 5d⁶ 5d⁴ 6f* 6m⁴ 5m⁵ 6m 5g 6d Sep 17] barrel-shaped gelding: type to carry condition: fluent mover: fairly useful handicapper: made all at Hamilton in July: best at 5f/6f: acts on firm going, probably on soft: tried blinkered/tongue tied: often early to post: sometimes reluctant stall: usually travels strongly. *D. Nicholls* **98**

BLACK LEGEND (IRE)   5 b.g. Marju (IRE) 127 – Lamping (Warning 136) [2004 –: 10.2s² f14g⁴ 10.2s 12.1g⁵ 12.6d⁶ Oct 9] poor maiden: best form at 1¼m: acts on fibresand and heavy going: tried blinkered/tongue tied. *R. Lee* **46**

BLACKMAIL (USA)   6 b.g. Twining (USA) 120 – Black Penny (USA) (Private Account (USA)) [2004 68, a87: p7g 12g p8g p12g⁵ p10g p12g⁴ p10g³ Dec 29] sturdy gelding: fair handicapper: stays easy 1½m: acts on polytrack and good to firm going: tried tongue tied/visored, blinkered nowadays. *Miss B. Sanders* **– a71**

BLACKNYELLO BONNET (USA)   2 b. or br.f. (Mar 7) Seeking The Gold (USA) – Salt It (USA) (Salt Lake (USA)) [2004 6d 7m 7s p8.6g Dec 3] $30,000Y: good-bodied filly: second foal: dam US Grade 2 9f winner: poor maiden. *M. Johnston* **43**

BLACK OVAL   3 b.f. Royal Applause 124 – Corniche Quest (IRE) 74 (Salt Dome (USA)) [2004 78d: p7g⁴ 5g⁴ 5.1g⁵ 6.1g 5s³ 6m 7g 5.3f⁵ 6d 6f 6f 5g p6g Dec 20] quite good-topped filly: modest performer: below form after fourth start, leaving M. Channon after fifth: stays easy 7f: acts on polytrack and firm going: tried visored: sometimes slowly away: ungenuine. *S. Dow* **61 d**

BLACKPOOL JACK   3 b.g. Mtoto 134 – Endearing Val 33 (Entitled 126) [2004 6.9m 9.1s 7.2s Oct 30] tailed off in claimers/seller. *F. P. Murtagh* **–**

BLACK SABBETH   3 br.g. Desert Story (IRE) 115 – Black Orchid (IRE) (Persian Bold 123) [2004 8v 7m 7.1m 6g⁶ 5m⁴ 6m 5.7g p7.1g f6s* f6g f7g Dec 11] 3,500Y: stocky gelding: third foal: dam unraced out of half-sister to very smart sprinter Indian Ridge: modest performer: 50/1-winner of maiden at Southwell in November, first start after leaving P. Makin: stays 6f: acts on fibresand: tried visored: temperamental. *Miss A. Stokell* **58 §**

BLACK SWAN (IRE)   4 b.g. Nashwan (USA) 135 – Sea Spray (IRE) 101 (Royal Academy (USA) 130) [2004 –: 12.1m 14m⁵ 18d 16.2m Sep 6] lengthy gelding: little form. *G. A. Ham* **–**

BLACKTHORN   5 ch.g. Deploy 131 – Balliasta (USA) (Lyphard (USA) 132) [2004 74: 12g⁴ 14.1s 12m³ 12.4g³ 16m⁶ Jul 31] strong, compact gelding: modest performer: stays 12.4f: acts on firm and soft going: tried in cheekpieces: no easy ride: sold 10,000 gns. *Mrs J. R. Ramsden* **64**

BLACK VELVET   2 br.g. (Feb 24) Inchinor 119 – Three Owls (IRE) 79 (Warning 136) [2004 5g* 6m² 7g Jul 28] 40,000F, 165,000Y: useful-looking gelding: first foal: dam, 1m winner (from 3 starts), half-sister to smart French performer up to around 1¼m Thames and granddaughter of top-class middle-distance filly Three Troikas: won maiden at Salisbury in May: useful form when 2 lengths second to Don Pele in listed race at Newbury: blinkered/on toes, respectable eighth in Vintage Stakes at Goodwood, fading (gelded after): should stay at least 7f: sent to Australia. *M. P. Tregoning* **100**

BLADE OF GOLD (IRE)   2 ch.f. (Apr 8) Daggers Drawn (USA) 114 – Be Prepared (IRE) (Be My Guest (USA) 126) [2004 6.1m Sep 6] 11,000Y: sturdy filly: fifth foal: half-sister to 4-y-o Countess Elton and fairly useful 7f (at 2 yrs) to 2m winner Look First (by Namaqualand): dam unraced: 22/1 and backward, never dangerous in maiden at Warwick, not knocked about: should do better. *J. A. Osborne* **– p**

BLADE RUNNER (IRE)   2 ch.f. (Apr 11) Daggers Drawn (USA) 114 – Leitrim Lodge (IRE) 64 (Classic Music (USA)) [2004 5d 6.1d 5.7g p7.1g p6g Dec 13] €8,500F, 15,000Y: fourth foal: half-sister to 4-y-o Tango Step and winners abroad up to around 9f by Royal Abjar and Danehill Dancer: dam 2-y-o 5f seller winner: seems of little account. *D. Haydn Jones*

BLADES BOY   2 ch.g. (Mar 13) Paris House 123 – Banningham Blade 94 (Sure Blade   **70** (USA) 130) [2004 6g 6g 5g* p5.1g⁵ f5g* p5.1g² Dec 20] tall gelding: third foal: dam best at 2 yrs when 5f winner: fair performer: won maiden at Musselburgh (made most/ wandered) in September and nursery at Southwell in December: should prove best at 5f/ easy 6f: acts on all-weather. *K. A. Ryan*

BLADE'S DAUGHTER   3 gr.f. Paris House 123 – Banningham Blade 94 (Sure Blade   – (USA) 130) [2004 –: 6v⁶ f6g 5g f6g⁶ May 11] leggy filly: little form: tried blinkered/in cheekpieces. *K. A. Ryan*

BLADE'S EDGE   3 b.c. Daggers Drawn (USA) 114 – Hayhurst (Sandhurst Prince   **57 d** 128) [2004 73: p7g p6g⁵ 6g³ 5g 7.2g 6.1s 7.6g 7.2g 6m 7f 7.2s³ f8g Dec 12] leggy, close-coupled colt: modest maiden: well below form after third start: probably stays 7f: acts on polytrack and firm going: tried blinkered/visored: sometimes slowly away. *A. Bailey*

BLAEBERRY   3 b.f. Kirkwall 118 – Top Berry 87 (High Top 131) [2004 61: 8g 10g   **69** 8m⁵ 8f⁵ 10m⁴ 7m* 7f⁵ 7m* 8m² 7m 8m Oct 2] lengthy, good-topped filly: fair handi- capper: won twice at Lingfield in July: best form at 7f/1m: acts on good to firm and good to soft going: blinkered last 6 outings: sometimes hangs left. *P. L. Gilligan*

BLAINA   4 ch.f. Compton Place 125 – Miss Silca Key 102 (Welsh Saint 126) [2004   **74 §** 76§: 8.1g⁵ 7m Jun 9] big, lengthy filly: fair maiden: stays 1m: acts on firm and soft going: temperamental. *D. R. C. Elsworth*

BLAISE CASTLE (USA)   4 b.f. Irish River (FR) 131 – Castellina (USA) (Danzig   **97** Connection (USA)) [2004 95: 7s⁴ 7m² 6d 8d³ 7d 8s Nov 23] strong filly: useful performer: best effort when ¾-length third to Kamanda Laugh in handicap at Newmarket in October: effective at 7f/1m: acts on soft and good to firm going: blinkered (folded) third start: has been heavily bandaged fore joints: usually races prominently. *G. A. Butler*

BLAISE HOLLOW (USA)   2 b.g. (Apr 22) Woodman (USA) 126 – Castellina (USA)   **87** (Danzig Connection (USA)) [2004 6g 7m⁵ 8.3m* 8.2g⁵ Aug 16] well-made gelding: fifth foal: half-brother to 4-y-o Blaise Castle and fairly useful 1¼m winner Castle River (by Irish River): dam, US 8.5f winner, half-sister to smart US Grade 1 1¼m winner Chelsey Flower: fairly useful performer: won maiden at Windsor in August comfortably by 3 lengths from Lithos: possibly amiss final start (gelded after): should stay 1¼m. *R. Charlton*

BLAISE WOOD (USA)   3 b.g. Woodman (USA) 126 – Castellina (USA) (Danzig   **52 ?** Connection (USA)) [2004 61: 8g 10g⁶ 7f 8f² 6m 7f p10d Aug 9] good-topped gelding: seemingly modest maiden on Flat: stays 1¼m: raced only on polytrack and good going or firmer on turf: tried in cheekpieces/blinkers: successful over hurdles in November. *G. L. Moore*

BLAKE HALL LAD (IRE)   3 b.g. Cape Cross (IRE) 129 – Queen of Art (IRE) 74   **60** (Royal Academy (USA) 130) [2004 7d 7s 7d⁵ 8g* p8g⁶ 8s Oct 29] 5,500 2-y-o: lengthy gelding: first foal: dam Irish 7f winner: modest performer: won apprentice maiden handicap at Bath in September, edging left: stays 1m. *Miss J. Feilden*

BLAKESET   9 ch.g. Midyan (USA) 124 – Penset (Red Sunset 120) [2004 67, a79+:   – f7g* f7g f6g* f7s* f6g² p7g³ f7s f6g⁵ f6g³ f6d² Apr 29] sturdy gelding: fairly useful   **a87 d** performer: won handicap at Wolverhampton and 2 claimers at Southwell in winter: below form after, including in seller: effective at 6f/7f: acts on fibresand/dirt, good to firm and good to soft going: tried tongue tied: effective with/without blinkers: usually visored nowadays: sometimes runs as if amiss. *T. D. Barron*

BLAKESEVEN   4 b.g. Forzando 122 – Up And Going (FR) (Never So Bold 135)   **55** [2004 60: f8g³ f7g² f8g² p7g³ p7g 7g 7d 8d⁶ Oct 16] leggy gelding: modest maiden: stays 1m: acts on all-weather and good to firm going: wore blinkers/cheekpieces last 2 outings: sold 7,000 gns. *W. J. Musson*

BLAKESHALL GIRL   4 ch.f. Piccolo 121 – Giggleswick Girl 67 (Full Extent (USA)   – 113) [2004 64d: f6g f8.5s Feb 14] workmanlike filly: maiden: well held in seller/claimer (blinkered) in 2004. *J. L. Spearing*

BLAKESHALL HOPE   2 ch.g. (Mar 13) Piccolo 121 – Elite Hope (USA) 84   **56** (Moment of Hope (USA)) [2004 6.1g³ f6m 5.1m 5.1m⁴ Aug 10] smallish, workmanlike gelding: modest maiden: visored (below form) final start. *P. D. Evans*

BLAKESHALL QUEST   4 b.f. Piccolo 121 – Corniche Quest (IRE) 74 (Salt Dome   **57 ?** (USA)) [2004 63, a78: f6s f6g⁴ f6g⁴ f6g⁴ f7s⁵ f5g* 5d f6g* 6.1s f6m 6g p6g p6d f6g f6g   **a75**

p5.1g⁵ Dec 31] compact filly: fair handicapper on all-weather, modest on turf: won at Wolverhampton in March and April (amateurs): stays easy 7f: acts on fibresand and good to soft going: visored after reappearance. *R. Brotherton*

BLA SHAK (IRE) 2 b.c. (Feb 16) Alhaarth (IRE) 126 – Really Gifted (IRE) (Cadeaux Genereux 131) [2004 6m May 15] €30,000F, 75,000Y: sturdy, lengthy colt: first foal: dam unraced half-sister to useful performer up to 1m Misterah: favourite, dismounted in maiden at Newbury, having broken bone in hind leg. *M. P. Tregoning* —

BLATANT 5 ch.g. Machiavellian (USA) 123 – Negligent 118 (Ahonoora 122) [2004 117: a8f a9f⁵ a10f⁶ 8m Sep 25] lengthy gelding: smart performer at best: just useful form on dirt at Nad Al Sheba first 3 outings in 2004: left I. Mohammed and rejoined former trainer, acted as pacemaker when last in Queen Elizabeth II Stakes at Ascot final appearance (gelded after): stays 1m: acts on firm and good to soft going: usually tongue tied, often visored. *Saeed bin Suroor* **102**

BLAU GRAU (GER) 7 b.g. Neshad (USA) 108 – Belle Orfana (GER) (Orfano (GER)) [2004 50: 17.2g 10d Oct 2] ex-German gelding: well held in 2004: tried blinkered. *N. E. Berry* —

BLAZE OF COLOUR 3 ch.f. Rainbow Quest (USA) 134 – Hawait Al Barr 100 (Green Desert (USA) 127) [2004 –p: 10s³ 12.1g⁴ 11.6d² 11.6m³ 11.9m* 11.9f⁴ 12g² 12d⁴ 10.5s p12.2g* Dec 14] strong, good-bodied filly: fairly useful handicapper: won at Brighton in July, and having left Sir Michael Stoute after eighth start, Wolverhampton in December: stays 1½m: acts on polytrack, firm and good to soft going: visored fifth to eighth outings. *P. F. I. Cole* **87**

BLAZE THE TRAIL 3 b.f. Classic Cliche (IRE) 128 – Explorer (Krisinsky (USA)) [2004 8.3d 12m⁶ 10f 10.2s Oct 19] good-topped filly: third foal: dam unraced half-sister to dam of smart 1½m/13f winner Phantom Gold: no form in maidens: blinkered final start. *Jean-Rene Auvray* —

BLAZING BAILEY 2 b.g. (Feb 15) Mister Baileys 123 – Wannaplantatree 72 (Niniski (USA) 125) [2004 p6g p7m Dec 22] third foal: half-brother to fairly useful 11f/1½m winner Aker Wood (by Bin Ajwaad) and 2002 2-y-o 7f winner Armada Grove (by Fleetwood): dam 1¾m/2m winner: seemingly better effort in maidens at Lingfield final start: slowly away both outings. *S. C. Williams* **52 ?**

BLAZING SADDLES (IRE) 5 b.g. Sadler's Wells (USA) 132 – Dalawara (IRE) (Top Ville 129) [2004 –: f14g⁶ Feb 15] rather leggy, workmanlike gelding: disappointing maiden: tried visored/in cheekpieces. *Mrs J. Candlish* —

BLAZING THE TRAIL (IRE) 4 ch.g. Indian Ridge 123 – Divine Pursuit 69 (Kris 135) [2004 73: p10g⁴ p10g p10g² p10g⁵ p10g* 9.7d³ 10s² 10g³ 10f 10m⁶ 11.5g⁶ 9.9g 10g⁴ Oct 12] fair performer: won minor event at Lingfield in March: stays 1½m: acts on polytrack and soft going: below form both starts in blinkers: carries head high: held up: sold 18,000 gns. *J. W. Hills* **71**

BLAZING VIEW (USA) 2 b.f. (Mar 30) Bahri (USA) 125 – Dixie Eyes Blazing (USA) 56 (Gone West (USA)) [2004 6f⁵ 6m 6g Sep 3] 75,000Y: tall filly: fifth foal: half-sister to 1m winner Johnny Reb (by Danehill) and winners in Japan and Italy by Barathea and Kris: dam, ran twice, out of sister to dam of Zafonic: best effort in maidens at Windsor on debut: should stay 1m: sold 4,000 gns. *E. A. L. Dunlop* **60**

BLESSED PLACE 4 ch.g. Compton Place 125 – Cathedra (So Blessed 130) [2004 69: p5g f5s p6g 5s f5g 8.1m 5f³ 6.1g³ 5g⁵ 5.1f⁴ 5g* 5m⁵ 5g 5m 5.7m⁶ f5g Nov 8] leggy gelding: modest handicapper: left Jean-Rene Auvray after third start: won at Windsor in July: stays 6f: acts on all-weather, firm and soft going: tried in cheekpieces/blinkers (raced too freely): usually tongue tied: races prominently. *D. J. S. ffrench Davis* **56**

BLESSINGINDISGUISE 11 b.g. Kala Shikari 125 – Blowing Bubbles 72 (Native Admiral (USA)) [2004 57: 6m 5g 5g Jul 3] strong gelding: well held in 2004: blinkered. *M. W. Easterby* —

BLISSPHILLY 2 b.f. (Mar 25) Primo Dominie 121 – Majalis 79 (Mujadil (USA) 119) [2004 5m 6m⁶ 7.1g Aug 26] 3,500F, 15,500Y: leggy, quite good-topped filly: second foal: dam 5f winner who stayed 1m: poor form in maiden/sellers. *R. A. Fahey* **32**

BLOFELD 3 b.g. Royal Applause 124 – Bliss (IRE) 75 (Statoblest 120) [2004 70: f6g* f6g⁶ 9f 8.5f a9f 6.5f⁵ 5.5f² 5.5f⁴ a6.5s Dec 29] good-bodied gelding: fair performer: won handicap at Southwell in January: sold 30,000 gns after next start: in frame in 2 claimers in US in November: stays 6f: acts on all-weather, raced only on firm/good to firm going on turf: blinkered last 4 outings. *J. M. Cassidy, USA* **73**

BLONDE EN BLONDE (IRE)　4 ch.f. Hamas (IRE) 125§ – Hulm (IRE) 79 (Muj- **57 §** tahid (USA) 118) [2004 57, a74: f7g⁶ f7g⁶ p7g p7g* f7g² p7g p6g³ p7g³ p8g 6m 7.2g³ **a76 §** 5.5g 6.9f⁵ 7f⁶ p7d p8g p7g³ Oct 13] good-bodied filly: fair on all-weather, modest on turf: won handicap at Lingfield in January: stays 7f: acts on all-weather, firm and soft going: usually blinkered: sometimes slowly away: ungenuine. *N. P. Littmoden*

BLONDE STREAK (USA)　4 ch.f. Dumaani (USA) 115 – Katiba (USA) 99 (Gulch **85** (USA)) [2004 87: 8m⁴ 8m⁴ 7.9g 7.9d* 8.3d⁶ 8.9g p8.6g⁶ Nov 6] tall, close-coupled filly: fairly useful handicapper: won at York in July by neck from Tedsdale Mac, making most: probably stays 8.6f: acts on polytrack, good to firm and good to soft going. *T. D. Barron*

BLOOD MONEY　2 b.g. (Feb 25) Dracula (AUS) 115 – Guinea (Sillery (USA) 122) **– p** [2004 7d Oct 30] 15,000Y: leggy gelding: first foal: dam unraced out of half-sister to Grand Lodge: 20/1, always behind in maiden at Newmarket: likely to do better. *N. A. Callaghan*

BLOOM OF TARA (IRE)　6 ch.m. Midhish 109 – No Diplomacy (IRE) 58 (Fayruz **44** 116) [2004 25, a38: 16s 10m⁵ 8.5d 7f⁵ 8d 10g a6g* f7g Nov 8] second foal: dam, Irish maiden, stayed 1m: poor performer: won handicap at Laytown in September, last start for G. Keane: well held in banded race at Southwell final outing: stays 7f: acts on sand and firm going. *S. J. Mahon, Ireland*

BLUE AZURE (USA)　2 b. or br.f. (Feb 19) American Chance (USA) 117 – Kibitzing **67** (USA) (Wild Again (USA)) [2004 p7.1d⁵ p8g⁵ Nov 13] third foal: half-sister to winner in USA by Smoke Glacken: dam 6f to 8.5f winner in Canada: green, not given hard time when fifth in maidens at Wolverhampton and Lingfield: should stay 1¼m. *G. A. Butler*

BLUE BAJAN (IRE)　2 b.g. (Feb 22) Montjeu (IRE) 137 – Gentle Thoughts 73 (Dar- **66** shaan 133) [2004 8m⁶ 7.2s p8.6g p9.5g* Dec 20] quite good-topped gelding: second foal: dam, lightly raced in Ireland, sister to useful 1½m winner Firecrest: fair performer: improved to win maiden at Wolverhampton, coming from rear: should stay at least 1½m. *Andrew Turnell*

BLUEBERRY JIM　3 ch.g. First Trump 118 – Short And Sharp 88 (Sharpen Up 127) **–** [2004 –: 10.3d 8.1g Jul 1] small gelding: little form. *T. H. Caldwell*

BLUEBERRY RHYME　5 b.g. Alhijaz 122 – Irenic 64 (Mummy's Pet 125) [2004 **68 §** 73§: f5s² p5g² f5s* f5g f5g* 6d⁵ 5f 5m 6g 5d* p6g p5.1g f6g³ Dec 7] good-topped geld- ing: fair performer: won maiden at Southwell in February, seller at Wolverhampton in March (then left P. Makin) and handicap at Ayr (26-runner event, made all) in September: effective at 5f/easy 6f: acts on all-weather, firm and soft going: visored: ungenuine. *P. A. Blockley*

BLUEBERRY TART (IRE)　2 b.f. (Feb 16) Bluebird (USA) 125 – Tart (FR) 76 **72** (Warning 136) [2004 6d⁵ 7d⁴ 7g p7.1g Oct 19] 16,000Y: sturdy filly: fourth foal: half- sister to German winner around 11f Twingo (by Bigstone): dam 1¼m and 11.5f winner: fair maiden: fourth at Newmarket, best effort: should stay at least 1m. *B. J. Meehan*

BLUE BIJOU　4 b.g. Bijou d'Inde 127 – Jucea 77 (Bluebird (USA) 125) [2004 –: f7g **–** f11s⁵ 8g Apr 29] tailed off in maidens/sellers. *T. T. Clement*

BLUEBOK　3 ch.c. Indian Ridge 123 – Blue Sirocco (Bluebird (USA) 125) [2004 68: **67** 7.1g² 6g³ p7.1g Oct 9] compact colt: fair maiden: should stay 1m: tongue tied final start: sold 17,000 gns. *D. R. Loder*

BLUE CANARI (FR)　3 ch.c. Acatenango (GER) 127 – Delicieuse Lady (Trempo- **118** lino (USA) 135) [2004 10.5g³ 10.5g⁴ 12g³ 12g* 12d⁵ 12m Oct 3]
　　　　The French authorities take a pragmatic approach to their racing prog- ramme and are not prone to letting tradition get in the way of what they see as progress. If, in their view, the structure needs changing, they change it. In 2001, the two-year-old programme was overhauled, with the Prix de la Salamandre scrapped, the old Grand Criterium (now the Prix Jean-Luc Lagardere) shortened in trip and the Criterium International inaugurated. In 2004, it was the turn of the three-year- old programme to come under scrutiny, a more controversial shake-up which moved quickly—too quickly for some—with the proposed changes made public in a surprise announcement in early-September. By the end of the following month, the changes were as good as ratified, and were due to take effect as early as 2005.
　　　　The main changes are as follows: the Prix du Jockey Club will be cut from twelve furlongs to ten and a half and will have its prize money boosted; the Grand Prix de Paris will go up from ten furlongs to a mile and a half and be moved from

the last Sunday in June to the French national holiday of July 14th; the Grand Prix de Saint-Cloud will be closed to three-year-olds and moved from the first Sunday in July to the last Sunday in June; and the Prix Jean Prat will be reduced from nine furlongs to a mile and will be run on the first Sunday in July instead of the first Sunday in June, with its prize money doubled. In addition, the Prix Lupin, now rendered obsolete by the shorter Prix du Jockey Club for which it had served as the main trial, will be scrapped. Proposals to move the Grand Prix de Saint-Cloud to Longchamp (with a change of name) and the Grand Prix de Paris from Longchamp to Saint-Cloud were shelved.

Inevitably, it was the shortening of the distance of the Prix du Jockey Club, the French Derby, which was the most controversial, even provoking reaction from the British side of the Channel from those who feared the Epsom Derby might be in line for the same treatment. The instigators of the plan, headed by new France Galop president Edouard de Rothschild, put forward arguments for the changes but, where the Prix du Jockey Club was concerned, none was very convincing. It was said that the Prix du Jockey Club was struggling to keep its prestige and was being overshadowed by the Derby, which is now run just a day before the Chantilly race. However, although Epsom boasts a much bigger prize, there is no evidence of French trainers deserting Chantilly for Epsom; in the latest season, American Post became the first French horse to run in the Derby for five years. If prestige is measured instead by quality of winner, the Prix du Jockey Club has no reason for an inferiority complex. Recent top-class winners at Chantilly such as Peintre Celebre, Montjeu, Sulamani and Dalakhani compare well with the best that the Derby has produced in the same period. The fact that the 2004 renewal of the Prix du Jockey Club was substandard is not evidence of long-term loss of quality.

Objections that a Derby must, by definition, be run over a mile and a half—as every major Derby is in Europe—were countered by the scheme's supporters who pointed to the Kentucky Derby, run over ten furlongs. That was hardly comparing like with like, and did little to appease those who saw the move as a step towards the 'Americanisation' of French racing. The most absurd claim by proponents of the plan was that the ratings of recent winners of the Prix de Diane (run over an extended ten furlongs) were superior to those of Prix du Jockey Club winners, pointing to the latter race's decline. Although the latest Prix de Diane winner Latice achieved a higher rating than Prix du Jockey Club winner Blue Canari, that is only the second time in the last fifteen runnings of the two races that the Diane winner has achieved a higher rating in her race—at least on Timeform figures.

If the Prix du Jockey Club in its existing form seemed in no need of change, the same could not be said for the Grand Prix de Paris. The arguments for changes to this race, which has long been in a less than healthy state, look a lot stronger. It was not stated explicitly, but it would be no surprise if reviving the fortunes of this event was just as important to those behind the changes to the three-year-old programme. The Grand Prix de Paris was inaugurated in 1863 with the aim of bringing together the best horses from both Britain and France. Indeed, for much of the nineteenth century it was the only race in France open to non French-breds. Six Epsom Derby winners have won the race, the last of them Phil Drake in 1955. Before 1965, the Grand Prix de Paris was actually worth more than the Prix du Jockey Club but, as staying races lost their appeal, the value of the fifteen-furlong event declined sharply. '1986 witnessed the last rites of what was once one of the world's great races,' lamented *Racehorses* that year when the winner was the maiden Swink over a field 'which would hardly have done justice to an Italian Group 3 race.' The following year, the distance of the Grand Prix de Paris was cut to ten furlongs in an attempt to improve the quality of the race. That may have happened, but single-figure fields have become the norm in recent seasons and the Epsom and Chantilly Derby winners these days are much more likely to meet at the Curragh in the Irish Derby. Bago's defeat of just three rivals (one of those his own pacemaker!), in the smallest field in the race's history, must have made up the minds of the French authorities to think again about the race's future.

Making the Grand Prix de Paris a mile and a half will give the French three-year-old colts a Group 1 opportunity at that trip to compensate for the loss of such an opportunity in the Prix du Jockey Club, though the authorities should have been a lot more even-handed when it came to sharing out the prize money for the

*Prix du Jockey Club, Chantilly—Blue Canari (right) finishes strongly to spring a surprise,
providing trainer Pascal Bary with his fifth winner in the last eleven runnings of the race;
Prospect Park (third right), Valixir and Day Flight (rail) are second, third and fourth*

two races. In 2005, the Prix du Jockey Club is scheduled to be worth €1,500,000,
three times the value of the Grand Prix de Paris, leaving the latter once again much
the poorer relation. A more equitable split would have made the latest incarnation
of the Grand Prix de Paris more attractive, particularly as it is now vulnerably
sandwiched in the European calendar between the Irish Derby in late-June and the
King George VI and Queen Elizabeth Stakes in late-July. As such, the Grand Prix
de Paris could miss out, with the top mile-and-a-half horses being aimed at one or
both of those races instead.

The strongest argument in favour of the amended classic programme is that,
with the Prix du Jockey Club now at an intermediate trip, it creates a logical
progression, from the Poule d'Essai des Poulains at a mile to the Grand Prix de
Paris at a mile and a half. One of the criticisms of the existing programme for
three-year-old colts was that it kept apart the milers and the middle-distance
performers right from the beginning of their three-year-old careers. Whilst fillies
who contest the Poule d'Essai des Pouliches regularly tackle the Prix de Diane, and
whilst in Britain some Derby contenders run first in the Two Thousand Guineas, it
was very rare for a French colt to attempt a classic double in the Poulains and
Jockey Club. Opinions on the reforms split French racing down the middle. Andre
Fabre, Criquette Head-Maarek and Alec Wildenstein were among those in support,
while the likes of the Aga Khan, Alain de Royer-Dupre and Olivier Peslier were
reported to have signed a petition against it. Others were unhappy with certain
elements of the scheme, or with the manner in which it had been rushed through.

Trainer Pascal Bary, surprisingly, was one of those who reportedly had no
objections to the shortening of the Prix du Jockey Club. 'Surprisingly' because he
has enjoyed such success in the race in its traditional form. Except for a break in the
sequence in 2000, Bary has trained the Prix du Jockey Club winner every other
year, starting with Celtic Arms in 1994 and continuing with Ragmar, Dream Well,
Sulamani and, in the latest season, Blue Canari. Like the first two winners, Blue
Canari carried the dark green and pink colours of Jean-Louis Bouchard (who also
owned a half-share in Dream Well), having bought the horse as a birthday present
for his wife. None of Bary's first four Jockey Club winners had started at shorter
than 5/1 on the pari-mutuel (Sulamani had started at almost 20/1) and Blue Canari
was the longest-priced of the lot at around 33/1. Confidence in Blue Canari's
chance beforehand was hard to find anywhere. Connections decided it would be
'fun' to have a runner in the race again, reportedly with the possibility that he might
finish fifth if they were lucky, his trainer having seriously been considering a listed
race for him instead a few days later. The French media virtually ignored Blue
Canari; just one of the thirty-six tipsters listed in *Paris-Turf* believed he'd finish in
the first eight, the only one who did placing him seventh!

Blue Canari's form warranted the scepticism beforehand, not least because he had already been beaten by several in the Jockey Club field. He had won a minor event at Maisons-Laffitte on his second and final outing at two but had met with defeat at Longchamp on all three of his starts prior to the Jockey Club at three. Third place in two listed races, won by Prospect Park and then Reefscape (the pair who shared favouritism with two others at Chantilly), came either side of a run in the Prix Greffulhe in which he had been promoted to fourth behind the ill-fated Millemix. Narrowly beaten subsequently by Voix du Nord in the Prix Lupin, Millemix broke a leg in a work-out prior to the Jockey Club. Voix du Nord, who would have started favourite for the Jockey Club, was another leading contender ruled out by injury, suffering a serious leg injury on the eve of the race after being declared a runner. That left an open and substandard-looking field of fifteen. Besides Prospect Park and Reefscape, the unbeaten Prix Hocquart winner Lord du Sud, the Prix La Force winner Delfos and the Lupin third Valixir were among the other leading French-trained runners. Britain was represented by the wide-margin Glasgow Stakes winner Day Flight (who shared favouritism), the Dante fourth Top Seed (whose York conquerors had dominated again at Epsom the day before), and Manyana who had won the Predominate Stakes at Goodwood.

One thing is certain. Blue Canari would not have won a Prix du Jockey Club run over a furlong and a half shorter; one even a couple of yards short of a mile and a half would not have seen him first past the post. Instructed to give Blue Canari the same sort of ride that he had given Sulamani two years earlier, Thierry Thulliez settled Blue Canari well in rear. Improving initially up the rail in the straight as Day Flight was sent for home, Blue Canari was gradually manoeuvred wide from behind a wall of horses snapping at the leader's heels and finally saw daylight ahead of him a furlong out. After at first looking as though he was going to hang in behind Prospect Park, who had now taken over in front, Blue Canari was pulled out a second time and Thulliez conjured a storming run out of him in the last fifty yards to nail Prospect Park on the line by a head. Inside them, and just half a length back, Valixir kept on to deprive Day Flight of third place by three quarters of a length, with a gap of two and a half lengths after the first four.

If Blue Canari had risen from obscurity for the Prix du Jockey Club, that was effectively where he returned after it. He had no other Group 1 entries, so had to be supplemented for the Prix de l'Arc de Triomphe, with a preparatory run first in the Prix Niel, in which he was beaten over seven lengths into fifth behind three of the colts he had defeated at Chantilly—Valixir, Prospect Park and Lord du Sud—and also behind Bago who was third. Three weeks later, Blue Canari actually ran right up to his Chantilly form in the Arc behind Bago, but it was good enough to see him finish only twelfth (with Valixir tenth and Prospect Park sixteenth), admittedly after being hampered in the early stages. Their performances were hardly a compliment to the standard of the latest Prix du Jockey Club.

Blue Canari is by Acatenango, a Derby winner himself in his native Germany and already responsible for two other Deutsches Derby winners in Lando and Borgia. Acatenango was retired from stud duties early in the year due to failing fertility. The Prix du Jockey Club featured in the careers of a couple of sires close up on the dam's side of Blue Canari's pedigree. His dam's sire Trempolino was runner-up in 1987 and his grandam's sire Caerleon won the race three years before that. Blue Canari cost €135,000 as a yearling at Deauville and is the first foal of his dam Delicieuse Lady. Her second, the two-year-old Crabapple (by Unfuwain), has finished third in his two starts to date in France for the Marquesa de Moratalla, showing fairly useful form. Delicieuse Lady did all her racing in Scandinavia, where she won four races at up to nine furlongs and finished third in the Swedish version of the One Thousand Guineas. Her dam, Savoureuse Lady, was a smart middle-distance performer in France for Andre Fabre, winning the Prix Fille de l'Air. Savoureuse Lady is a daughter of the remarkable broodmare Amazer, who produced fifteen winners from sixteen foals. The top-class Mtoto stands out among them, but her descendants have not surprisingly been both many and varied. They include the very smart middle-distance horse Mutamam and his half-brother Lafi, the Wokingham winner from the latest season. They are out of a full sister to Savoureuse Lady. This is also the family of The Tatling, who, like Blue Canari, has Amazer as his great grandam.

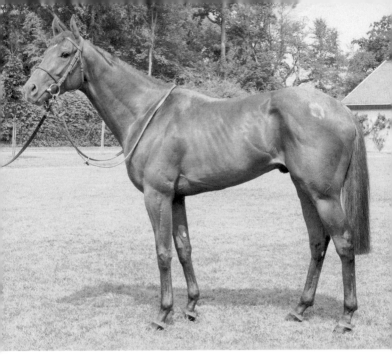

Ecurie Jean-Louis Bouchard's "Blue Canari"

Blue Canari (FR) (ch.c. 2001)	Acatenango (GER) (ch 1982)	Surumu (ch 1974)	Literat
			Surama
		Aggravate (b 1966)	Aggressor
			Raven Locks
	Delicieuse Lady (ch 1995)	Trempolino (ch 1984)	Sharpen Up
			Trephine
		Savoureuse Lady (ch 1987)	Caerleon
			Amazer

The leggy, short-backed Blue Canari, who reportedly takes his name from a cocktail, has a markedly round action. That might be taken by some to mean he will be suited by soft ground (his two-year-old win came on soft), though he did not encounter such conditions in the latest season and his run in the Arc showed he is effective on good to firm. Blue Canari will not be remembered as one of the best winners of the Prix du Jockey Club, but he will go down as the last one to win the race over a mile and a half. *P. Bary, France*

BLUE CIRCLE 4 b.c. Whittingham (IRE) 104 – Reshift 94 (Night Shift (USA)) [2004 –: f6g f6g Jan 12] smallish, heavy-topped colt: of little account. *M. Mullineaux*   –

BLUE CRUSH (IRE) 3 ch.f. Entrepreneur 123 – Prosaic Star (IRE) 81 (Common Grounds 118) [2004 101: 5d 6m 5m 5m 5s 5g 5m⁶ 5m p5g Nov 13] €21,000Y: close-coupled filly: fourth foal: half-sister to 3 winners, including useful 5f (including at 2 yrs) winner Lupine (by Lake Coniston) and fairly useful 1999 2-y-o 5f winner Barringer (by Nicolotte), later 6f winner in Sweden: dam Irish 2-y-o 1m winner: useful at 2 yrs, winning minor event and nursery at Tipperary: just fairly useful form in 2004, leaving E. Lynam in Ireland after third start: best at 5f: raced mainly on good going or firmer: tried tongue tied/in blinkers. *K. R. Burke*   **82**

BLUE DAKOTA (IRE) 2 b.c. (Apr 7) Namid 128 – Touraya (Tap On Wood 130) **109**
[2004 5g* 5s* 5g* 5m* 6m⁶ Jul 30] €62,000Y: big, strong, good sort: has a quick action:
closely related to useful 7f winner Modern British, later 1m/9f winner in Hong Kong
where known as Good Record, and fairly useful 2001 2-y-o 6f winner Helen Bradley
(both by Indian Ridge), and half-brother to 2 winners by Dominion, including Irish 1000
Guineas third Tarwiya (5f and 7f winner at 2 yrs): dam French 1m winner: useful performer: won maiden at Newmarket in April, minor events at Windsor in May and Norfolk
Stakes at Royal Ascot (favourite, hung on by neck from Mystical Land) in June: raced
much too freely in Richmond Stakes at Goodwood (suffered injury): will prove best at 5f/
easy 6f: acts on soft and good to firm ground: races prominently: attended by expert in
stall entry at Royal Ascot. *J. Noseda*

BLUE DAZE 3 b.f. Danzero (AUS) – Sparkling (Kris 135) [2004 75: 7m 7m 9m⁵ **52**
8.1g⁵ 8.1g⁵ 7f 9s 7s 7g⁶ Sep 20] lengthy filly: fair performer: below form after third start,
including in seller: barely stays 9f: acts on good to firm going: blinkered (raced freely)
fifth outing. *R. Hannon*

BLUE DREAM (IRE) 4 b.f. Cadeaux Genereux 131 – Hawait Al Barr 100 (Green **100**
Desert (USA) 127) [2004 7m 6m² 6m⁴ 5m³ 7.5s⁴ 6.1g² 7m 6d Oct 10] fifth foal: half-
sister to useful 1m (at 2 yrs)/9f winner Equity Princess (by Warning): dam 1½m to 2m
winner: useful performer: trained by A. Fabre in France at 3 yrs, winning minor event at
Saint-Cloud: left D. Selvaratnam in Ireland after fifth outing in 2004: good ½-length
second to Simianna in listed race at Chester next time: well held in similar events after:
effective at 5f to 7.5f: acts on soft and good to firm going: wore cheekpieces last 3 starts,
tongue tied final one: sold 100,000 gns. *T. Hogan, Ireland*

BLUE EMPEROR (IRE) 3 b.g. Groom Dancer (USA) 128 – Bague Bleue (IRE) **–**
(Last Tycoon 131) [2004 64: f6g 6d f7g⁵ f7g 6m 8d 8m Jun 26] leggy, quite good-topped
gelding: maiden: no form in 2004, leaving P. Blockley after fourth start: tried blinkered/
tongue tied. *P. T. Midgley*

BLUE EMPIRE (IRE) 3 b.g. Second Empire (IRE) 124 – Paleria (USA) 77 (Zilzal **?**
(USA) 137) [2004 76: p8g⁴ p7g⁵ f7g* p10g⁴ p8g² f7g⁶ 9g 8.5m p7.1g² p7.1g⁵ Dec 20] **a79**
leggy gelding: fair on all-weather, modest at best on turf: won claimer at Wolverhampton (left P. Haslam) in February: best at 7f/1m: acts on all-weather: twice slowly
away. *P. A. Blockley*

BLUEFIELD (IRE) 3 b.c. Second Empire (IRE) 124 – Imco Reverie (IRE) (Grand **58**
Lodge (USA) 125) [2004 7p: 8.3g⁴ Oct 11] tall, leggy colt: better effort in maidens at 2
yrs when third at Newbury: well below that form when fourth in similar event at Windsor
11½ months later: should stay at least 1¼m. *R. F. Johnson Houghton*

BLUEGRASS BOY 4 b.g. Bluegrass Prince (IRE) 110 – Honey Mill 67 (Milford **68**
119) [2004 73: 10.2g³ 10g 10m 11m 10m³ 9.9g* 10m 9.9g⁵ 10d Oct 18] angular gelding:
fair handicapper: won at Salisbury in August: should stay 1½m: acts on polytrack and
good to firm going: held up. *G. B. Balding*

BLUE HEDGES 2 b.c. (Mar 12) Polish Precedent (USA) 131 – Palagene (Generous **67**
(IRE) 139) [2004 p7m 8d p8g⁴ p8.6g⁶ Nov 29] €55,000Y, 20,000 2-y-o: big, workmanlike colt: fourth foal: half-brother to 2 winners in France, including 10.5f and 1½m winner
Preziosilla (by Mark of Esteem): dam, French 14.5f winner, half-sister to 5-y-o Vortex:
fair maiden: barely stays 8.6f. *H. J. Collingridge*

BLUE HILLS 3 br.g. Vettori (IRE) 119 – Slow Jazz (USA) 106 (Chief's Crown **66**
(USA)) [2004 74: 11.6s 12.1g⁵ 14d 16s 14.1g p12.2g⁴ p13.9g⁵ p13g⁶ Dec 29] tall gelding:
modest maiden: left M. Johnston after third start: stays 1¾m: acts on polytrack and good
to soft going. *P. W. Hiatt*

BLUE JAVA 3 ch.g. Bluegrass Prince (IRE) 110 – Java Bay (Statoblest 120) [2004 66: **65**
7m 7g 8.5g 7m² f8g⁵ p8g² p8.6g Oct 19] smallish gelding: fair maiden: stays 8.6f: acts on
all-weather, raced only on good/good to firm going on turf. *H. Morrison*

BLUE KANDORA (IRE) 2 b.c. (Apr 26) Cape Cross (IRE) 129 – Party Dress (Lahib **70**
(USA) [2004 5s⁴ 7m Jun 19] 75,000Y: leggy, useful-looking colt: first foal: dam
French maiden who stayed 11.5f: much better effort in maidens when fourth at York: bred
to stay at least 7f: sold 4,500 gns. *M. A. Jarvis*

BLUE KNIGHT (IRE) 5 ch.g. Bluebird (USA) 125 – Fer de Lance (IRE) (Diesis **81 d**
133) [2004 78: f5g² f6s⁴ p6g 5s⁶ 5g² 6g 6f⁴ p6g p7.1d p7.1d p8g p8.6g p7.1g⁶ p8.6g⁶
p5.1g* Dec 31] big, lengthy gelding: fairly useful performer at best: left A. Jarvis after
seventh start: dropped long way in weights before winning handicap at Wolverhampton
in December: effective at 5f to 7f: acts on all-weather and good to firm going, probably
on soft: tried in cheekpieces. *P. Howling*

BLUE LEADER (IRE) 5 b.g. Cadeaux Genereux 131 – Blue Duster (USA) 118 – (Danzig (USA)) [2004 78?: p12g Jan 24] rangy gelding: well held only 5-y-o outing: wore cheekpieces last 3 starts. *G. Brown*

BLUE LINE 2 gr.f. (Apr 5) Bluegrass Prince (IRE) 110 – Out Line 98 (Beveled (USA)) [2004 5g 5.3f⁵ 7f Aug 5] second foal: dam 6f/7f winner: form in maidens only on second start: should stay 7f. *M. Madgwick* — 58

BLUE MAEVE 4 b.g. Blue Ocean (USA) 87 – Louisville Belle (IRE) 71 (Ahonoora 122) [2004 45: f7g⁴ f8.5g f7s⁴ f8g 5f 5m⁵ 5d² 5d⁴ 5m² 5m* 5d⁵ 5.1s 6f 5f* 5m³ 5g Oct 8] leggy gelding: fair handicapper: won at Catterick in August and Pontefract in September: speedy, and best at 5f: acts on fibresand, firm and good to soft going: tried blinkered: races up with pace. *J. Hetherton* — 72

BLUE MARBLE 2 b.g. (Mar 14) Fraam 114 – Fizzy Fiona (Efisio 120) [2004 5g⁴ 6m⁶ 6m 5.1s* 5g 6m Jul 31] 14,000Y, 25,000 2-y-o: leggy, close-coupled gelding: fourth foal: half-brother to 4-y-o Frascati and 3-y-o Birikina: dam unraced: fair performer: won maiden at Nottingham in July: ran poorly in nurseries after, then gelded: likely to prove best at 5f/6f: acts on soft ground: joined S. Seemar in UAE. *C. E. Brittain* — 70

BLUE MARINER 4 b.g. Marju (IRE) 127 – Mazarine Blue 65 (Bellypha 130) [2004 –: 8d 7m³ 10m² 9.9g² 9g 8.2g 8.2g p8.6g* p8g p7g p7.1g Dec 11] sturdy gelding: fair handicapper: won maiden event at Wolverhampton in October, final start for P. Harris: stays easy 1¼m: acts on polytrack and good to firm going. *W. R. Swinburn* — 75

BLUE MOON HITMAN (IRE) 3 ch.g. Blue Ocean (USA) 87 – Miss Kookaburra (IRE) 44 (Namaqualand (USA)) [2004 56: 5.1f³ 6.1m 5f³ 5m³ 5m 6.1d f5g p6g Dec 22] small gelding: modest maiden: best at 5f: acts on fibresand, firm and good to soft going: tried in cheekpieces/blinkers. *R. Brotherton* — 61

BLUE NUN 3 b.f. Bishop of Cashel 122 – Matisse 65 (Shareef Dancer (USA) 135) [2004 10.1v⁵ 9g 8m 10g⁵ 9d 7.5s 8m Sep 4] 1,400Y: close-coupled filly: fourth foal: half-sister to 3 winners abroad, including useful German 1m to 11f winner Grantley (by Deploy): dam maiden who stayed 1m: of little account. *Mrs A. Duffield* — –

BLUE OASIS (IRE) 3 b.f. Sadler's Wells (USA) 132 – Humble Eight (USA) (Seattle Battle (USA)) [2004 8d* 8.5m⁵ 10.1s² 9.5d 10m 10d⁵ 10.3s Nov 6] quite good-topped filly: fourth foal: sister to useful Irish 2001 2-y-o 1m winner Stage Call (later successful in USA) and useful Irish 1¼m winner Humilis: dam, US Grade 3 8.5f winner, out of half-sister to top-class 1½m filly Balanchine: fairly useful performer: won maiden at Thirsk in May: ran creditably after in listed races at Newcastle (neck second to Ice Palace) and Longchamp (ninth behind Flip Flop) fifth start: should stay 1½m: acts on soft and good to firm going. *R. Guest* — 94

BLUE OPAL 2 b.f. (Mar 15) Bold Edge 123 – Second Affair (IRE) 85 (Pursuit of Love 124) [2004 7s³ p9.5g Dec 20] first foal: dam, 1½m winner, out of smart performer up to 14.6f Startino: better effort in maidens when third to Game Lad at Redcar: needs to settle to stay beyond 7f. *Miss S. E. Hall* — 64

BLUE OTIS (IRE) 2 ch.f. (Mar 3) Docksider (USA) 124 – Minstrel's Gift 92 (The Minstrel (CAN) 135) [2004 p7.1d f7g Nov 23] fifth foal: half-sister to fairly useful Italian 9f to 11f winner by Darshaan: dam 6f winner: well held in maidens. *Mrs H. Sweeting* — –

BLUE PATRICK 4 gr.g. Wizard King 122 – Great Intent (Aragon 118) [2004 92: p12g 10.3d 8m 6f² 6m 7m⁶ 7s⁵ 8g 8s⁵ 7m p6g f8g⁶ f8g⁴ Dec 28] rather leggy gelding: fluent mover: fairly useful performer: below form after sixth start, leaving J. Eustace after tenth: effective at 6f to 1m: acts on firm going: sometimes wears cheekpieces: sometimes slowly away: inconsistent. *K. A. Ryan* — 82 d

BLUE POWER (IRE) 3 b.g. Zieten (USA) 118 – La Miserable (USA) (Miswaki (USA) 124) [2004 67: f5g p5g f5g³ 5s⁵ 5f³ 5g* 5d 5d² 5s f5f² 5d 5d f5g⁶ f5f Dec 28] well-made gelding: fair handicapper on all-weather, modest on turf: won at Southwell in June: best at 5f: acts on fibresand and good to soft going. *K. R. Burke* — 63 a70

BLUE PRINCE (USA) 2 ch.c. (Mar 15) Dixieland Band (USA) – Tussle (USA) (Kris S (USA)) [2004 7.5g² Jul 19] $135,000Y: well-made colt: first foal: dam, maiden in USA, out of sister to champion US 2-y-o (later Grade 1 9f/1¼m winner) Forty Niner: 10/1, 6 lengths second to Where With All in minor event at Beverley: will stay 1¼m: sold 85,000 gns, sent to USA: should do better. *R. Charlton* — 74 p

BLUE QUIVER (IRE) 4 b.g. Bluebird (USA) 125 – Paradise Forum 78 (Prince Sabo 123) [2004 57: p10g⁶ p8g² 7.1g 10.2s 8g Sep 22] modest maiden: stays 1m: form only on polytrack. *C. A. Horgan* — 63

BLUE RONDO (IRE)   4 b.g. Hernando (FR) 127 – Blueberry Walk (Green Desert   –
(USA) 127) [2004 64: p13g Mar 2] maiden: visored, well beaten in claimer only start in
2004: tried blinkered. *Ian Williams*

BLUES AND ROYALS (USA)   2 b.c. (Apr 20) Honour And Glory (USA) 122 –   **98**
Dixieland Blues (USA) (Dixieland Band (USA)) [2004 6m* 7m² 7.1m⁴ Aug 11]
$400,000Y: angular, good-topped colt: has quick action: third foal: half-brother to smart
US performer up to 1¼m Limehouse (by Grand Slam), fourth in Kentucky Derby: dam,
ran once, out of US 2-y-o Grade 2 6f winner Blue Jean Baby: won maiden at York in June:
much better effort in minor events after when neck second to Grand Marque at Newbury,
though found little: should stay 1m. *Saeed bin Suroor*

BLUE SAVANNA   4 ch.g. Bluegrass Prince (IRE) 110 – Dusk In Daytona 64 (Beveled   **52**
(USA)) [2004 55: p16g⁶ f8.5g⁴ p10g² p12g* 12d 11.6m⁵ p12d⁶ 11.6g⁴ 11.6f⁴ 11.9f² p12d⁶
Aug 9] modest performer: won seller at Lingfield in March: found little final start: stays
1½m: acts on all-weather and firm going: wears cheekpieces/blinkers. *J. G. Portman*

BLUE SKY THINKING (IRE)   5 b.g. Danehill Dancer (IRE) 117 – Lauretta Blue   **102**
(IRE) (Bluebird (USA) 125) [2004 104+: p10g* p10g⁵ p10g⁶ 8g 10m³ 7.9d⁴ 7.9s⁶ 8d²   **a108**
10.3f p10g Nov 30] tall, rather leggy gelding: useful performer: won handicap at Lingfield in January by 1¾ lengths from Northside Lodge: some creditable efforts after:
effective at 1m (given a test), should stay 1½m: acts on polytrack, good to firm and good
to soft going: has been bandaged in front: often hangs left: held up. *K. R. Burke*

BLUES OVER (IRE)   3 b.f. Sri Pekan (USA) 117 – Crystal Blue (IRE) (Bluebird   –
(USA) 125) [2004 –: p10g Jan 3] well held in sellers/claimer. *W. J. Musson*

BLUE SPECTRUM (IRE)   2 b.g. (Apr 18) Spectrum (IRE) 126 – Storm River   –
(USA) 81 (Riverman (USA) 131) [2004 7m 7.6m 7m 8p p8m Dec 8] tall gelding: little
form, including in seller: wore cheekpieces final start. *J. S. Moore*

BLUE SPINNAKER (IRE)   5 b.g. Bluebird (USA) 125 – Suedoise (Kris 135) [2004   **112**
97+: 8g 8d* 7.9s⁴ 10m* 10.4g 10.4s⁴ 8f⁶ 10d³ 9g⁴ Oct 2] sturdy gelding: smart handicapper: won at Thirsk and Redcar (beat James Caird by neck in totesport Zetland Gold
Cup, strong run to lead on line) in May: good efforts when third to Spuradich in John

*totesport Zetland Gold Cup (Handicap), Redcar—Blue Spinnaker overcomes trouble in running
to snatch the spoils close home, beating James Caird and Crow Wood (near side)*

Smith's Stakes at Newbury and 1¾ lengths fourth of 32 to Spanish Don in Cambridgeshire at Newmarket (first home in centre) last 2 starts: stays 10.4f: acts on firm and soft going: held up: game and consistent. *M. W. Easterby*

BLUES PRINCESS   4 b.f. Bluebird (USA) 125 – Queen Shirley (IRE) (Fairy King (USA)) [2004 66: 5m 5d 5g 6m Jul 31] smallish, sturdy filly: no form in handicaps in 2004: tried blinkered. *R. A. Fahey*

BLUE STREAK (IRE)   7 ch.g. Bluebird (USA) 125 – Fleet Amour (USA) (Afleet (CAN)) [2004 56: p10g 11.9f⁵ 11.5d⁵ Aug 26] tall, rangy gelding: poor performer: stays easy 1½m: acts on polytrack, firm and good to soft going: tried in headgear/tongue tied: modest hurdler. *G. L. Moore*

BLUE TOMATO   3 b.c. Orpen (USA) 116 – Ocean Grove (IRE) 84 (Fairy King (USA)) [2004 105: 7g Apr 14] lengthy colt: useful at 2 yrs: ran poorly in listed Free Handicap at Newmarket only start in 2004. *P. F. I. Cole*

BLUETORIA   3 b.f. Vettori (IRE) 119 – Blue Birds Fly 78 (Rainbow Quest (USA) 134)   **73 §**
[2004 –: 8m⁴ 8.2g 10f⁵ 10m Sep 7] good-topped filly: fair maiden: stays 1¼m: acts on firm going: raced freely last 2 starts: gave plenty of trouble at stalls in 2004 (refused to enter twice), and banned from Flat races started from stalls until March 15 2005. *J. A. Glover*

BLUE TORPEDO (USA)   2 ch.g. (Apr 13) Rahy (USA) 115 – Societe Royale   **82 p**
(Milford 119) [2004 7.1d p7m* p7g³ p8g³ Nov 16] $50,000Y: half-brother to several winners, including 6f/7f performer Coconut Creek (by Danehill) and 7f/1m winner Royale (by Royal Academy), both useful in Ireland: dam unraced half-sister to top-class sprinter Double Form and Lupe Stakes winner Scimitarra: won maiden at Lingfield in October by ¾ length from Optimus: not run of race when third in nurseries there: stays 1m: should progress. *Mrs A. J. Perrett*

BLUE TRACK (IRE)   3 b.c. Woodborough (USA) 112 – Aryaah 51 (Green Desert   **–**
(USA) 127) [2004 10m 12m p10d Aug 7] well beaten in maidens. *M. J. Attwater*

BLUE TRAIN (IRE)   2 b.c. (Apr 2) Sadler's Wells (USA) 132 – Igreja (ARG) 101   **78 P**
(Southern Halo (USA)) [2004 7.9g⁴ Oct 9] 500,000Y: third foal: dam, third in South Africa (including Group 1 event), ran 3 times in Britain: 6/1, 6¼ lengths fourth to Daring Ransom in maiden at York, green and never nearer, not knocked about: has scope to do good deal better as 3-y-o, and should win races. *Sir Michael Stoute*

BLUE TROJAN (IRE)   4 b.g. Inzar (USA) 112 – Roman Heights (IRE) (Head For   **97**
Heights 125) [2004 88, a76: p10g² p10g² 8s 8g 8.1m* 8.1f⁴ 8.5m 7m 8m⁴ 7.1g² 8m 7.1d   **a76**
8.3g 7m² 8g* 9g Oct 2] neat gelding: useful handicapper on turf, fair on all-weather: successful at Haydock in May and Kempton (beat Just Fly 1¼ lengths) in September: should also have won at Newbury fourteenth start, eased prematurely by 7-lb claimer and short-headed by Chateau Nicol: very best form at 7f/1m: acts on all-weather, firm and good to soft going: sometimes edges left. *S. Kirk*

BLUE VENTURE (IRE)   4 ch.g. Alhaarth (IRE) 126 – September Tide (IRE) 58   **50**
(Thatching 131) [2004 59: f8g 9.9v 7.9f 12.3m⁴ 12m 17.2g 12m³ Jul 21] good-bodied gelding: modest maiden: stays 1½m: acts on fibresand and firm going: tried in cheekpieces: sold 5,000 gns. *P. C. Haslam*

BLUE VIKING (IRE)   3 b.g. Danetime (IRE) 121 – Jenny Spinner (IRE) 58 (Blue-   **50 ?**
bird (USA) 125) [2004 –: 10m f8g⁵ f12g p9.5g Oct 2] modest form only on second outing. *J. R. Weymes*

BLUE WATER   4 b.f. Shaamit (IRE) 127 – November Song (Scorpio (FR) 127) [2004   **–**
45: f12s Mar 1] quite good-topped filly: maiden: tailed off only start in 2004: wears cheekpieces. *M. Mullineaux*

BLUFF   2 b.g. (Feb 19) Bluebird (USA) 125 – Show Off 56 (Efisio 120) [2004 p7.1g⁶   **66**
p7m² p7.1g⁴ Dec 31] 34,000Y: second foal: dam, sprint maiden (ran only at 2 yrs), half-sister to smart sprinter Easy Option: fair form in maidens at Wolverhampton and Lingfield: should stay 1m: slowly away and looked difficult ride final outing. *W. J. Haggas*

BLUNHAM   4 b.g. Danzig Connection (USA) – Relatively Sharp 86 (Sharpen Up 127)   **49**
[2004 61, a–: f5g⁴ f6g⁵ f6g 7g 7.5g⁶ 8g² 7m 8d 7g Oct 12] tall, rather leggy gelding: **a40**
poor performer nowadays: stays 1m: acts on good to firm going: tried blinkered. *M. C. Chapman*

BLUSHING PRINCE (IRE)   6 b.g. Priolo (USA) 127 – Eliade (IRE) 82 (Flash of   **– §**
Steel 120) [2004 51§, a71§: f9.4g⁵ Mar 17] ran poorly in claimer only start in 2004: tongue tied. *Mrs L. Stubbs*

BLUSHING RUSSIAN (IRE) 2 b.g. (Mar 8) Fasliyev (USA) 120 – Ange Rouge **59**
(Priolo (USA) 127) [2004 6f 5.1g 7m³ 8s Oct 12] useful-looking gelding: modest maiden:
stays 7f: acts on good to firm going: possibly none too genuine. *P. C. Haslam*

BLYTHE KNIGHT (IRE) 4 ch.c. Selkirk (USA) 129 – Blushing Barada (USA) 53 **110**
(Blushing Groom (FR) 131) [2004 108: 10d⁴ 10.1s* 10g⁴ 10.1m⁶ 10m³ 10.4g 9.9g 10.4s
9g⁶ 10v⁵ Oct 23] quite good-topped colt: has a round action: smart handicapper: won at
Epsom (beat Bonecrusher a short head) in April: creditable efforts after, particularly
when sixth to Spanish Don in Cambridgeshire at Newmarket penultimate start: effective
at 9f to 1½m: acts on soft and good to firm going: wore cheekpieces last 2 starts: held up,
and travels strongly. *E. A. L. Dunlop*

BLYTHE SPIRIT 5 b.g. Bahamian Bounty 116 – Lithe Spirit (IRE) 74 (Dancing **87**
Dissident (USA) 119) [2004 88: 6m⁵ 6m 6g 6m 7.1f⁶ 7m⁶ 6g* 6g* 6g* 6g³ 6g² 6g
6g² 6g⁴ Dec 13] lengthy gelding: fairly useful performer: won handicaps at Ripon and
Wolverhampton (2) in autumn: left R. Fahey after eleventh start: effective at 6f to 1m:
acts on polytrack, firm and soft going: tried blinkered, effective with or without cheekpieces: sometimes edges left. *C. R. Dore*

BOANERGES (IRE) 7 br.g. Caerleon (USA) 132 – Sea Siren 68 (Slip Anchor 136) **63 d**
[2004 74d: 5d 5v⁵ 5m⁶ 6f² 5m⁴ 5g 5g 5.3g⁵ 5.1f 5d 6m 5d 6g p5m Nov 22] smallish,
strong gelding: modest handicapper: below form after fifth start: effective at 5f/easy 6f:
acts on firm and good to soft going: tried in headgear. *J. M. Bradley*

BOAVISTA (IRE) 4 b.f. Fayruz 116 – Florissa (FR) (Persepolis (FR) 127) [2004 61: **68**
p6g f7s³ f6g² p7g⁴ p5g⁵ f6s³ 6d⁴ 5d⁴ f6g² 5.1m² 5.7f* 5m 6m 6.1m 5.5g² 5.1g² 5m 5m³
5.1g³ 5.1m⁶ Aug 10] small, angular filly: fair handicapper: won at Bath in May: best at
5f/6f: acts on all-weather, firm and good to soft going: tried tongue tied: edgy sort (has
been early to post): usually races prominently. *P. D. Evans*

BOB BAILEYS 2 b.g. (Mar 13) Mister Baileys 123 – Bob's Princess 69 (Bob's Return **62**
(IRE) 123) [2004 p6d⁴ 7.1g Aug 30] 4,000Y: second foal: dam 2-y-o 7f winner who
stayed 1½m: much better effort in maidens when fourth at Lingfield: slowly away and
still green at Warwick: should stay at least 1m. *P. R. Chamings*

BOBBIE LOVE 2 ch.g. (Apr 9) Fraam 114 – Enlisted (IRE) 83 (Sadler's Wells (USA) **49**
132) [2004 7m⁶ 7g Jul 1] sturdy gelding: poor form in maidens at Newmarket and Epsom.
M. R. Channon

BOBBY CHARLES 3 ch.g. Polish Precedent (USA) 131 – Dina Line (USA) 60 **70**
(Diesis 133) [2004 8.2d f8g⁴ p10g³ Dec 30] good-topped gelding: fair form in maidens:
slowly away first 2 outings. *Dr J. D. Scargill*

BOBERING 4 b.g. Bob's Return (IRE) 123 – Ring The Rafters (Batshoof 122) [2004 **–**
–: 9.3g p7.1g f12g p9.5g Dec 13] strong gelding: little form in maidens/claimers.
B. P. J. Baugh

BOB'S BUZZ 4 ch.g. Zilzal (USA) 137 – Aethra (USA) 89 (Trempolino (USA) 135) **75**
[2004 77: 6d 6m⁵ 7m³ 7m⁵ p7d² 7m 7m⁵ p6g² p6g⁶ 7g² p6g Oct 19] strong, close-coupled **a84**
gelding: fairly useful handicapper on all-weather, fair on turf: effective at 6f/7f: acts
on polytrack and firm going: sometimes slowly away: usually held up: sold 14,000 gns.
S. C. Williams

BOB'S FLYER 2 br.f. (Jan 29) Lujain (USA) 119 – Gymcrak Flyer 73 (Aragon 118) **67**
[2004 6g 5d⁴ 5.1f 5g² 5g⁴ 5g⁴ p5.1g* p6g⁶ Nov 19] leggy filly: first foal: dam 6f to 1m
winner: fair performer: won seller at Wolverhampton in October, final start for D. Given:
likely to prove best at 5f: acts on polytrack, best turf effort on good going. *J. G. M. O'Shea*

BOBSLEIGH 5 b.g. Robellino (USA) 127 – Do Run Run 75 (Commanche Run 133) **75**
[2004 88: 18g⁶ 16d 14.8g⁴ 21g⁶ 14.1m³ Aug 4] leggy, useful-looking gelding: fair
handicapper: stays 21f: acts on firm and good to soft going. *Mrs A. J. Perrett*

BODDEN BAY 2 b.g. (Apr 22) Cayman Kai (IRE) 114 – Badger Bay (IRE) 67 (Salt **52**
Dome (USA)) [2004 8m 6.9m 6m p6g p7g p7.1g Nov 26] modest maiden: stays 7f: wore
cheekpieces (best effort) penultimate start, visor (ran as if amiss) final one. *C. A. Dwyer*

BODFARI DREAM 3 ch.f. Environment Friend 128 – Al Reet (IRE) 92 (Alzao **–**
(USA) 117) [2004 8.1s 10s Oct 12] close-coupled filly: second foal: dam 6f (in Ireland)
to 7f winner: no show in maidens at Haydock (slowly away) and Ayr. *M. Mullineaux*

BODHI TREE (USA) 2 b.f. (Mar 10) Southern Halo (USA) – Dharma (USA) (Zilzal **67 p**
(USA) 137) [2004 p7g³ Oct 13] third foal: dam, ran 3 times in France, half-sister to very
smart German performer up to 1m Royal Abjar: 7/1, 1¼ lengths third to Meditation in

maiden at Lingfield, soon prominent after slow start: should stay 1m: likely to improve.
J. H. M. Gosden

BOGAZ (IRE)   2 b.c. (Feb 21) Rossini (USA) 118 – Fastnet (Forzando 122) [2004 5s² **68**
5m p6d 6m p5.1g f6g³ p8g⁵ f7g* p7.1g f8g* Dec 28] 17,000Y: smallish, robust colt: third
living foal: dam well beaten only start: fair performer: left R. Beckett after fourth start
(visored, ran as if amiss): won seller in November and nursery in December, both at
Southwell: stays easy 1m: acts on all-weather and probably on soft going: sometimes
looks bit wayward. *P. A. Blockley*

BOHOLA FLYER (IRE)   3 b.f. Barathea (IRE) 127 – Sharp Catch (IRE) 98 (Com- **84**
mon Grounds 118) [2004 75: p6g* 6d⁴ 6s⁶ 6s⁴ 6m* 6m* 6g⁴ 6f 5g⁵ 6g⁶ Sep 20]
neat filly: fairly useful performer: won maiden at Lingfield in April and 2 handicaps at
Windsor in June: stays 6f: acts on polytrack, firm and soft going. *R. Hannon*

BOING BOING (IRE)   4 b.g. King's Theatre (IRE) 128 – Limerick Princess (IRE) **53**
68 (Polish Patriot (USA) 128) [2004 63: 7m 12.6g⁶ 10.5g⁵ Sep 3] modest performer: stays
1m: acts on polytrack and firm going: tried visored. *Miss S. J. Wilton*

BOISDALE (IRE)   6 b.g. Common Grounds 118 – Alstomeria 61 (Petoski 135) [2004 **53**
64d: f6g⁶ f6m* p6g⁶ f5g⁵ 5g* f6m 7s³ 5.2d⁵ p6g Oct 18] workmanlike gelding: **a64**
modest performer: won banded event in May and handicap in June, both at Southwell:
effective at 6f/7f: acts on fibresand, soft and good to firm going: tried tongue tied: none
too consistent. *S. L. Keightley*

BOJANGLES (IRE)   5 b.g. Danehill (USA) 126 – Itching (IRE) (Thatching 131) **65**
[2004 –: f12s 10.9s 8.1d* 8.1v³ 8.1m 8.1f³ f8g⁴ 9g⁵ 12.6g³ 12.1m⁴ 10d* 10.2s² 16.2m⁵
10.9d* 12g⁵ p16.5g Nov 6] deep-girthed gelding: fair performer: won banded race at
Chepstow in April and handicaps at Newbury (ladies event) in August and Warwick in
September: stays 12.6f: acts on fibresand, firm and soft going: tried in cheekpieces.
R. Brotherton

BOLD BLADE   3 b.g. Sure Blade (USA) 130 – Golden Ciel (USA) (Septieme Ciel **75 d**
(USA) 123) [2004 71: f9.4g² f8.5g⁵ 7.5d 8d f12m* 12.3d f8g 15.8m² 12.1d⁴ 14g 16.2g
13.8g 13.8m⁶ 13.9g Oct 9] good-bodied gelding: fair performer: left B. Smart after fourth
outing: won claimer at Wolverhampton in May: below form subsequently: effective at
9.4f to easy 2m: acts on fibresand, good to firm and good to soft going: tried blinkered,
including first 7 outings in 2004: races prominently. *M. J. Polglase*

BOLD BUNNY   3 b.f. Piccolo 121 – Bold And Beautiful 105 (Bold Lad (IRE) 133) **54**
[2004 6m³ 6m³ 6s f6g Dec 28] closely related to 1m to 1¼m winner Bold Faith and
smart French performer up to 15f Warbler (both by Warning), and half-sister to 3 winners:
dam best at 1m: modest maiden: should stay 7f: form only on good to firm going.
S. C. Williams

BOLD CHEVERAK   2 b.g. (Feb 10) Bold Edge 123 – Curlew Calling (IRE) 51 (Pen- **70**
nine Walk 120) [2004 f7g⁵ p6g f7g* p7g² Dec 29] 13,000F, €36,000Y: fifth foal: dam, ran
once, half-sister to 3-y-o Snow Goose and smart 1¼m performer Merry Merlin: fair
maiden: second in nursery at Lingfield in December: stays easy 7f: acts on all-weather. *M. R. Channon*

BOLD COUNSEL (IRE)   2 b.c. (Apr 29) Titus Livius (FR) 115 – Daisy Dobson **68**
(Gorytus (USA) 132) [2004 7f⁵ 7m² p7g⁶ 8m* Sep 25] 5,000Y: close-coupled, quite
attractive colt: half-brother to Irish 2m winner Daisy Gold (by Goldmark): dam unraced
half-sister to Yorkshire Oaks winners Sally Brown and Untold: fair performer: won
maiden at Kempton, rallying well: likely to stay 1¼m: best efforts on good to firm going:
blinkered third start: sold 17,000 gns. *B. J. Meehan*

BOLD DIKTATOR   2 b.c. (Mar 18) Diktat 126 – Madam Bold (Never So Bold 135) **60**
[2004 7g 7m⁶ p7g⁶ Oct 13] 8,500F: strong colt: half-brother to several winners, including
1994 2-y-o 5f winner Rigsby (by Fools Holme) and 1997 2-y-o 6f winner Miss Vivien
(by Puissance): dam unraced out of sister to top-class sprinter Sigy: modest form in
maidens: will probably stay 1m: best effort on polytrack. *W. R. Muir*

BOLD EAGLE (IRE)   2 ch.c. (Feb 5) Rainbow Quest (USA) 134 – Britannia (GER) **– p**
(Tarim) [2004 8d Oct 15] tall, lengthy, rather leggy colt: has a fluent, round action: half-
brother to 3 winners abroad, notably Deutsches Derby winners Borgia (by Acatenango)
and Boreal (by Java Gold), latter also successful in Coronation Cup: dam won up to 2m
in Germany, including Deutsches St Leger: 7/1 and green, slowly away and never
dangerous in maiden at Newmarket: should do better at 1¼m+. *Sir Michael Stoute*

BOLD EFFORT (FR)   12 b.g. Bold Arrangement 127 – Malham Tarn (Riverman **– §**
(USA) 131) [2004 –§: f7g f6s Mar 8] good-quartered, dipped-backed gelding: one-time

useful performer: no form after 2001: usually wore headgear: dead. *K. O. Cunningham-Brown*

BOLD HAZE   2 ch.g. (Apr 23) Bold Edge 123 – Melody Park 104 (Music Boy 124)   **58**
[2004 6s³ 6m 7s⁴ Nov 2] big gelding: modest form in maidens: stays 7f: form only on soft ground: slowly away final outing. *Miss S. E. Hall*

BOLDINI (USA)   3 ch.g. Atticus (USA) 121 – Bold Bold (IRE) (Sadler's Wells (USA)   **75 d**
132) [2004 7s 10.5d³ p9.5d f8g⁶ p9.5g⁶ p12.2g Dec 27] fourth foal: half-brother to 1¼m winner True Wooman (by Capote) and 1¼m winner Ambobo (by Kingmambo), both fairly useful in France: dam, French 1¼m winner, sister to smart middle-distance performer Sabadilla: better effort in France when close third in claimer at Maisons-Laffitte in June: left Mme C. Head-Maarek, then showed modest form in 3 starts over hurdles for M. Pipe: poor form on all-weather after: stays 10.5f: acts on good to soft going: tried tongue tied. *Mrs Stef Liddiard*

BOLD MAGGIE   2 ch.f. (Feb 19) Bold Edge 123 – Vera's First (IRE) 69 (Exodal   **50**
(USA)) [2004 5m⁶ p7g p6g⁵ Dec 29] fourth foal: half-sister to 4-y-o Lucky Valentine: dam 2-y-o 7f seller winner: modest form in maidens at Sandown (very slowly away) and Lingfield: not sure to stay beyond 7f. *G. L. Moore*

BOLD MARC (IRE)   2 b.g. (Apr 2) Bold Fact (USA) 116 – Zara's Birthday (IRE) 71   **83**
(Waajib 121) [2004 5s⁴ 5g* 5d² 5m* 5f 6m⁶ 5m⁴ 6g⁶ p6g³ p6g⁵ Nov 8] €21,000F, 11,500Y: leggy, good-topped gelding: half-brother to 3 winners, including 1¾m/2m winner Blair (by Persian Bold) and 1½m winner Maunsell's Road (by Desert Style): dam Irish maiden who stayed 1½m: fairly useful performer: won maiden at Musselburgh in April and minor event at Redcar in May: creditable efforts in frame in minor events after: barely stays easy 6f: acts on polytrack and good to firm going. *K. R. Burke*

BOLD MINSTREL (IRE)   2 br.c. (Apr 21) Bold Fact (USA) 116 – Ponda Rosa   **82**
(IRE) 66 (Case Law 113) [2004 5m 5.1f³ 5m² 5.1g* 5.1m² 5.1g⁴ 5.7d² 6m⁵ 5m⁵ 5m⁶   **a88**
p5.1g² Oct 7] €7,000Y: good-bodied colt: first foal: dam Irish 6f winner: fairly useful performer: won maiden at Chester in July: good second in minor events after: barely stays 5.7f: acts on polytrack, good to firm and good to soft going: races up with pace: consistent. *M. Quinn*

BOLD PHOENIX (IRE)   3 b.c. Dr Fong (USA) 128 – Subya 107 (Night Shift (USA))   –
[2004 8m 10m 10m⁶ 8s 8.1d 10v Nov 4] sturdy colt: fifth foal: half-brother to smart 1¼m/1½m winner Villa Carlotta (by Rainbow Quest) and 4-y-o Seeyaj: dam 5f (at 2 yrs) to 1¼m winner: little form, trained by A. Stewart/E. Vaughan until before final outing. *B. J. Curley*

BOLD PURSUIT (IRE)   2 br.c. (Mar 1) Bold Fact (USA) 116 – Lyphard Belle (Noble   **43**
Patriarch 115) [2004 7.1d p7.1g⁶ p6g Nov 27] poor form in maidens. *Mrs A. Duffield*

BOLD RIDGE (IRE)   4 b.g. Indian Ridge 123 – Cutting Ground (IRE) 85 (Common   –
Grounds 118) [2004 57?: 8g 6m 10f p8.6g⁶ Oct 25] poor maiden: left S. Kirk before final start: blinkered last 2 outings. *B. G. Powell*

BOLD TRUMP   3 b.g. First Trump 118 – Blue Nile (IRE) 70 (Bluebird (USA) 125)   **49**
[2004 –: p7g⁴ 6s 7.1s 5.7f Sep 6] leggy gelding: poor maiden: stays 7f: acts on polytrack: visored final start. *Jean-Rene Auvray*

BOLD WOLF   3 b.g. Wolfhound (USA) 126 – Rambold 72 (Rambo Dancer (CAN)   **52**
107) [2004 52: p6g⁴ 7.1s⁴ f6g⁴ 6m 6.1m 6m 6f f6s⁴ p7g 6d f6g³ f6g Dec 12] modest maiden: effective at 6f/7f: acts on all-weather, firm and soft going: tried tongue tied/in cheekpieces. *J. L. Spearing*

BOLEYN CASTLE (USA)   7 ch.g. River Special (USA) – Dance Skirt (CAN) (Cau-   **90 d**
casus (USA) 127) [2004 103: 5m 6f 5m 6m⁴ 6g 5m 6g⁶ 5m p5g p6g p6g p6m p5.1g Dec 31] strong, compact gelding: just a fairly useful performer nowadays: easily best effort in 2004 on fourth start: stays 6f: acts on firm and soft going: tried in headgear: tongue tied (well held) last 3 starts: races prominently: none too consistent. *P. S. McEntee*

BOLLIN ANNABEL   3 b.f. King's Theatre (IRE) 128 – Bollin Magdalene 55 (Teen-   **61**
oso (USA) 135) [2004 –p: 12s² 10s⁵ 12.1g 14.1m⁴ 14g 16.2g Jul 19] close-coupled, rather unfurnished filly: modest maiden: stays 1¾m: acts on soft and good to firm going: won juvenile hurdle in November. *T. D. Easterby*

BOLLIN ARCHIE   3 b.c. First Trump 118 – Bollin Joanne 118 (Damister (USA) 123)   **53**
[2004 6g⁵ 6s 6s⁴ Apr 28] strong, lengthy colt: poor form in maidens. *T. D. Easterby*

BOLLIN EDWARD   5 b.g. Timeless Times (USA) 99 – Bollin Harriet (Lochnager   **72**
132) [2004 81d: 6m⁶ 6f⁵ 7f³ 6m² 6m 7m² 7m 6g² 7m 7.2d⁴ Sep 16] good-bodied gelding:

fair handicapper: stays easy 7f: acts on firm and good to soft going: effective blinkered/visored or not. *T. D. Easterby*

BOLLIN JANET 4 b.f. Sheikh Albadou 128 – Bollin Emily 82 (Lochnager 132) [2004   –
83: 6v 6g 5m 6g 5.1d Jul 10] strong, well-made filly: handicapper: little form in 2004:
tried blinkered. *T. D. Easterby*

BOLLIN RUTH 2 gr.f. (Feb 6) Silver Patriarch (IRE) 125 – Bollin Roberta 75 (Bob's   – p
Return (IRE) 123) [2004 7f Jun 15] sturdy filly: first foal: dam 7f and 8.5f winner:
25/1 and green, always behind in maiden at Thirsk: should do better at 1¼m/1½m.
T. D. Easterby

BOLLIN THOMAS 6 b.g. Alhijaz 122 – Bollin Magdalene 55 (Teenoso (USA) 135)   –
[2004 89: 14s Sep 25] close-coupled, workmanlike gelding: handicapper: carrying condition, tailed off only start in 2004. *T. D. Easterby*

BOLODENKA (IRE) 2 b.c. (Mar 21) Soviet Star (USA) 128 – My-Lorraine (IRE) 77   75 p
(Mac's Imp (USA) 116) [2004 6g p6g² 6s³ Oct 29] €35,000Y: useful-looking colt: third
living foal: half-brother to 5-y-o Izmail: dam, Irish 5f/6.5f winner, half-sister to smart
Irish sprinter Catch The Blues: fair form in maidens: placed at Lingfield and Newmarket
(went well long way): likely to prove best at 5f/6f: should progress. *W. J. Musson*

BOLSHEVIK (IRE) 3 b.g. Fasliyev (USA) 120 – Cheviot Amble (IRE) 105 (Pennine   –
Walk 120) [2004 –p: 6s 7.9f 7m Jun 4] lengthy, good-topped gelding: maiden: well held
in 2004. *T. D. Easterby*

BOLSHOI BALLET 6 b.g. Dancing Spree (USA) – Broom Isle 74 (Damister (USA)   –
123) [2004 76: 13.8g 14.6m⁶ Jun 26] quite good-topped gelding: handicapper: blinkered,
ran poorly in 2004: fair hurdler. *J. Mackie*

BOLTON HALL (IRE) 2 b.g. (Feb 6) Imperial Ballet (IRE) 110 – Muneera (USA)   78
67 (Green Dancer (USA) 132) [2004 5m* 7f⁶ 6d⁵ 6g⁶ 7g⁵ 5g 6g Oct 8] 22,000Y: strong,
angular gelding: second foal: brother to 7f and 1¼m winner in Denmark: dam, ran twice,
sister to useful German miler Huambo out of half-sister to Irish St Leger winner Mashaal-
lah: fair performer: won minor event at Beverley in June, hanging left: some creditable
efforts after: not knocked about in nurseries last 2 starts: probably stays 7f: acts on firm
going: edgy sort: sometimes races freely. *R. A. Fahey*

BO MCGINTY (IRE) 3 ch.g. Fayruz 116 – Georges Park Lady (IRE) (Tirol 127)   93
[2004 83: 6.1d 6d* 6m² 6m 6f 6g⁴ 5g⁵ 5g* 6s⁵ Sep 25] good-topped gelding: fairly useful
handicapper: won at Hamilton in May and Sandown in September: hampered final start:
effective at 5f/6f: acts on good to firm going, probably on soft. *R. A. Fahey*

BOND BABE 2 b.f. (Mar 10) Forzando 122 – Lindfield Belle (IRE) 78 (Fairy King   59
(USA)) [2004 5f⁴ 5m² 5d³ 5d⁵ 6g Oct 19] 14,000Y: quite good-topped filly:
half-sister to several winners, notably 4-y-o Baltic King: dam 2-y-o 5f winner: modest
maiden: will probably prove best at 5f: acts on good to firm and good to soft going,
promise on polytrack. *B. Smart*

BOND BOY 7 b.g. Piccolo 121 – Arabellajill 97 (Aragon 118) [2004 102: f6g⁴ f6g f6g   96
f6s⁴ 5g 5d⁶ 6m 5d³ 6g 6s 6s 5g⁴ 6s 5s 5s⁴ 5d⁴ Nov 3] sturdy gelding: useful handicapper:
creditable fourth at Doncaster and Musselburgh (behind Harrison's Flyer) last 2 starts:
effective at 5f/6f: acts on fibresand and any turf going: usually held up: none too consistent. *B. Smart*

BOND CAT (IRE) 2 ch.f. (Feb 9) Raise A Grand (IRE) 114 – Merrily 73 (Sharrood   51 p
(USA) 124) [2004 7v⁴ 8d⁶ Nov 3] €50,000Y: second foal: half-sister to 4-y-o Vigorous:
dam, disappointing sprint maiden, half-sister to useful sprinter Deep Finesse: modest
form in maidens at Catterick and Musselburgh (led long way): will prove best up to 1m:
capable of better. *B. Smart*

BOND CITY (IRE) 2 b.g. (Apr 10) Trans Island 119 – Where's Charlotte 53 (Sure   99
Blade (USA) 130) [2004 6m 5g* 5g³ 5.2m³ 5s⁵ 5d² 5f⁵ 6m p5.1g* 5s² p5g* Oct 28]
€16,000F, 16,000Y: neat gelding: second foal: dam sprint maiden: useful performer: won
maiden at Carlisle in June and minor events at Wolverhampton and Lingfield (beat
Cyclical by 1¼ lengths) in October: should stay easy 6f: acts on polytrack, firm and soft
going: tough and reliable. *B. Smart*

BOND DOMINGO 5 b.g. Mind Games 121 – Antonia's Folly 64 (Music Boy 124)   – §
[2004 ?, a50§: f6s f5g f5s³ f6g⁶ f5g⁴ Apr 22] strong, well-made gelding: poor performer: a39 §
best at 5f: acts on fibresand and heavy going: blinkered/visored: unreliable. *B. Smart*

BOND FINESSE (IRE) 2 b.f. (Apr 25) Danehill Dancer (IRE) 117 – Funny Cut (IRE)   57
(Sure Blade (USA) 130) [2004 5g⁴ 5v⁴ p6g 7d⁴ f6g³ p7.1g f7g Dec 14] €4,000Y: tall,

leggy filly: half-sister to 4-y-o Landing Strip and winner in Sweden by Malvernico: dam Swedish 1m/1¼m winner: modest maiden: stays 7f: acts on fibresand and heavy going: tends to be slowly away. *B. Smart*

BOND MAY DAY　4 b.f. Among Men (USA) 124 – State Romance 67 (Free State 125) [2004 79: 10g 12f 12.6m⁴ 9.9d⁴ 10.2m 12m Sep 18] angular filly: fair handicapper: stays 12.6f: acts on fibresand and firm going: very slowly away final outing: usually races prominently. *B. Smart*　**67**

BOND MILLENNIUM　6 ch.g. Piccolo 121 – Farmer's Pet 90 (Sharrood (USA) 124) [2004 69, a71: f8s 10.1g 8g² 8m 10.1m p8.6g⁴ p9.5d f8g² f8s Nov 17] sturdy gelding: fair performer: effective at 1m/1¼m: acts on all-weather, firm and soft going: reportedly lost action final start: waited with: none too consistent. *B. Smart*　**73**

BOND MOONLIGHT　3 ch.g. Danehill Dancer (IRE) 117 – Interregnum (Interrex (CAN)) [2004 68: f8g² f12s² f8.5s³ f12g² 10s 10v f12g⁵ Dec 11] good-topped gelding: fair maiden: stays easy 1½m: acts on fibresand, no form on turf: wore cheekpieces penultimate start. *B. Smart*　**–**
a65

BOND PLAYBOY　4 b.g. Piccolo 121 – Highest Ever (FR) (Highest Honor (FR) 124) [2004 –, a97: f6g⁵ f5g⁶ f6g f6s⁶ 5s 6s 6v 7m 7.5g 7d³ 6d* 6d 7v³ Oct 16] good-bodied gelding: fairly useful on all-weather, fair on turf: won handicap at Hamilton and minor event at Redcar in August: best at 5f/6f: acts on fibresand, good to firm and good to soft going: tried blinkered at 2 yrs: usually races prominently. *B. Smart*　**74**
a94

BOND PUCCINI　2 b.g. (Feb 27) Piccolo 121 – Baileys By Name 66 (Nomination 125) [2004 5g 5d² 5g 6g Oct 4] good-bodied gelding: modest maiden: second at Ripon: should stay 6f. *B. Smart*　**60**

BOND ROMEO (IRE)　3 ch.g. Titus Livius (FR) 115 – At Amal (IRE) (Astronef 116) [2004 75: 5d 5s⁵ p5.1g Nov 6] lengthy gelding: maiden: well below form in 2004. *B. Smart*　**–**

BOND ROYALE　4 ch.f. Piccolo 121 – Passiflora 75 (Night Shift (USA)) [2004 88: f6g² f6g f6s Feb 20] strong, close-coupled filly: fairly useful handicapper: easily best effort of season when creditable second at Southwell on reappearance: stayed 6f: acted on fibresand and good to firm going: stud. *B. Smart*　**85**

BOND SHAKIRA　3 ch.f. Daggers Drawn (USA) 114 – Cinnamon Lady 77 (Emarati (USA) 74) [2004 –: 5s³ 6s 5d⁴ f5g 5g f5m⁴ f6m⁵ 5s Aug 13] well-made filly: modest maiden: below form after third outing: should prove best at 5f: raced only on fibresand and good ground or softer on turf: sometimes hangs left. *B. Smart*　**54 d**

BONECRUSHER　5 b.g. Revoque (IRE) 122 – Eurolink Mischief 84 (Be My Chief (USA) 122) [2004 109: 9f⁶ p10g⁴ f8.5s 10d⁵ 10.1s² 12.1d 10m⁵ 10.1d⁵ 9.9g³ 10.5g⁶ 10.3f⁴ 10.9s³ 9s 10s³ Oct 29] strong gelding: smart performer: several creditable efforts in 2004, 1¾ lengths third to Spanish Don in listed race at Newmarket final outing: stays 11f: acts on polytrack, firm and soft going: effective visored or not: has worn crossed noseband: edgy sort: held up: ungenuine: joined M. Al Muhairi in UAE. *D. R. Loder*　**112 §**

BONFIRE　2 b.c. (Feb 3) Machiavellian (USA) 123 – Forest Express (AUS) (Kaaptive Edition (NZ)) [2004 7f⁴ 7d Oct 30] 140,000Y: good-topped colt: first foal: dam, Australian Group 3 7f winner, out of half-sister to Phoenix Champion Stakes winner Park Express: better effort in maidens when fourth of 5 at Ascot, going in snatches: should stay at least 1m. *M. Johnston*　**71**

BONGOALI　2 b.f. (Mar 19) Fraam 114 – Stride Home 78 (Absalom 128) [2004 7m⁴ 7f⁵ 8v² 8f⁵ 8g 10m 8d p8.6g² f8g⁴ p9.5g⁶ Dec 20] leggy, close-coupled filly: eighth foal: sister to fairly useful 1¼m/1½m winner Pedro Pete and half-sister to 2 winners, including 1m seller winner Senor Pedro (by Piccolo): dam 5f (at 2 yrs) to 1¼m winner: modest maiden: left M. Channon after ninth start: should stay 1¼m: acts on all-weather and any turf going. *Mrs C. A. Dunnett*　**62**
a51

BONJOUR BOND (IRE)　3 ro.g. Portrait Gallery (IRE) 110 – Musical Essence 65 (Song 132) [2004 63: f8s⁴ 10s 12.6s 9.9v³ 12.1g 10g³ 8.5g 12.1m⁵ 8.3d 13.8m⁵ Sep 18] leggy gelding: poor maiden: stays 1½m: acts on heavy and good to firm going: wore headgear last 7 starts. *B. Smart*　**49**

BONNABEE (IRE)　2 b.f. (Feb 19) Benny The Dip (USA) 127 – Samhat Mtoto 64 (Mtoto 134) [2004 7g p7g 8m⁶ Sep 25] 2,400Y: fourth foal: half-sister to 3-y-o Cape Vincent: dam, won at 11f in Spain, half-sister to dam of 1000 Guineas winner Ameerat: modest form in maidens: should be suited by 1¼m/1½m: best effort on good to firm going. *C. F. Wall*　**53**

BONNE DE FLEUR 3 b.f. Whittingham (IRE) 104 – L'Estable Fleurie (IRE) 76 **90 d**
(Common Grounds 118) [2004 80: 6g* 6m 6g 6g⁵ 5s 6g Sep 3] small, strong filly: fairly
useful performer: won listed event at Ripon in April, making all to beat Petite Rose
½ length: below form after, reportedly lame final start: will probably stay 7f: acts on firm
ground. *B. Smart*

BONNETTS (IRE) 3 ch.f. Night Shift (USA) – Brief Lullaby (IRE) (Brief Truce **–**
(USA) 124) [2004 7g 8g 7d 8g Aug 28] €80,000Y: strong, lengthy filly: second foal:
half-sister to winner in Japan by Desert Prince: dam unraced half-sister to US Grade 2 9f
winner Wait Till Monday and smart Irish performer up to 1½m Token Gesture: little form
in maidens: has shown signs of temperament. *H. Candy*

BON NUIT (IRE) 2 b.f. (Feb 26) Night Shift (USA) – Pray (IRE) (Priolo (USA) 127) **81 p**
[2004 6.1m* Sep 28] €65,000Y: good-topped filly: fourth foal: half-sister to useful 6f
(at 2 yrs) to 1¼m winner In A Silent Way and winner in Belgium (both by Desert Prince):
dam unraced half-sister to smart performer up to 9f Anshan: 25/1, green and better for
race, won maiden at Nottingham by 1¾ lengths from Nan Jan, slowly away and behind
but leading final 1f: should stay 7f: will improve. *G. Wragg*

BONSAI (IRE) 3 b.f. Woodman (USA) 126 – Karakia (IRE) 101 (Sadler's Wells (USA) **66 d**
132) [2004 –: 8.3g 10d 9f 8.1d 8m p13.9g Dec 13] good-topped filly: disappointing
maiden: tried tongue tied. *R. T. Phillips*

BONTADINI 5 b.g. Emarati (USA) 74 – Kintail 76 (Kris 135) [2004 –, a70d: p10g⁵ **56 §**
p10g f9.4s 10f³ 10f 10d p9.5g p10m⁴ Dec 15] good-topped gelding: modest performer: **a52 §**
stays 1¼m: acts on all-weather and firm going: sometimes visored, blinkered final start:
unreliable. *D. Morris*

BONUS (IRE) 4 b.g. Cadeaux Genereux 131 – Khamseh 85 (Thatching 131) [2004 110: **99**
6g⁶ 6s 6m 6m 5m⁵ 6g⁵ Oct 9] big, strong, angular gelding: just useful form in 2004,
leaving R. Hannon after fourth start: effective at 5f/6f: acts on firm going: tried tongue
tied: often lethargic in preliminaries: races up with pace: gelded after last outing.
W. J. Haggas

BONUS POINTS (IRE) 3 b.c. Ali-Royal (IRE) 127 – Asta Madera (IRE) 67 (Toca **62**
Madera 111) [2004 f8g p10g⁶ p10g 10m³ Sep 27] 37,000 2-y-o: fifth foal: half-brother to
5f winner On The Fairway (by Danehill Dancer): dam Irish 5f winner: modest maiden:
stays 1¼m: blinkered third start: slowly away first 2 outings. *B. J. Meehan*

BOO 2 b.g. (Mar 24) Namaqualand (USA) – Violet (IRE) 77 (Mukaddamah (USA) 125) **65**
[2004 6s⁴ 6m⁶ 8.3d⁴ 7s Oct 16] 5,000F, 24,000 2-y-o: quite good-topped gelding: first
foal: dam, 6f and 8.5f winner, half-sister to smart performer up to 1½m Sobriety (by Namaqualand): fair maiden: probably stays 7f: acts on soft and good to firm going: gelded
after final start. *K. R. Burke*

BOOGIE MAGIC 4 b.f. Wizard King 122 – Dalby Dancer 71 (Bustiki) [2004 65: 7f **52**
11.5m² 11.6g³ 10.1m p12d⁴ Aug 9] good-topped filly: modest maiden: trained by
C. Allen until before final start: stays 11.6f: acts on soft and good to firm going: tried in
cheekpieces. *G. A. Huffer*

BOOGIE STREET 3 b.c. Compton Place 125 – Tart And A Half 83 (Distant Relative **114**
128) [2004 108p: 5g³ 6m² 5m* 5f⁵ 5d⁴ 5m² 5.2g Sep 18] big, lengthy, good-topped colt:
smart performer: won listed race at Kempton in May by length from Lochridge: raced in
pattern company after, best effort when head second to Ringmoor Down in King George
Stakes at Goodwood: best at 5f: acts on firm going: often tongue tied: races up with pace.
R. Hannon

BOOKIESINDEXDOTCOM 3 b.f. Great Dane (IRE) 122 – Fifth Emerald 54 **46 §**
(Formidable (USA) 125) [2004 63: f7g f7g³ p6g f6g⁶ f7s⁶ 8.1s f7g⁵ f6g⁵ 7m⁶ 7d Oct
16] poor maiden: stays 7f: acts on all-weather and good to firm going: wears headgear:
ungenuine. *J. R. Jenkins*

BOOK MATCHED 3 b.g. Efisio 120 – Princess Latifa 63 (Wolfhound (USA) 126) **–**
[2004 69p: f8.5s³ f8.5s* f8g⁴ 8.2g f8d⁶ 9g f8d* f8g³ 7.9g 7g f8g f8g Dec 11] leggy **a74**
gelding: fair performer: won maiden at Wolverhampton in February and claimer at Southwell in July: stays 8.5f: acts on fibresand, little form on turf. *B. Smart*

BOOK OF KINGS (USA) 3 b.c. Kingmambo (USA) 125 – Honfleur (IRE) 100 **114**
(Sadler's Wells (USA) 132) [2004 8s* 12f⁶ Jun 27] $450,000Y: fourth foal: closely
related to useful Irish 2001 2-y-o 7f winner Creekview (by Gone West) and fairly useful
1m winner Argentan (by Gulch) and half-brother to a winner in USA by Thunder Gulch:
dam, 1¼m and 13.5f winner, sister to Arc winner Carnegie and daughter of Arc winner
Detroit: won 27-runner maiden at the Curragh in April by a head: smart form when

6¼ lengths sixth to Grey Swallow in Irish Derby there nearly 3 months later, keeping on without threatening: stays 1½m: joined M. Al Kurdi in UAE. *A. P. O'Brien, Ireland*

BOOM OR BUST (IRE) 5 ch.g. Entrepreneur 123 – Classic Affair (USA) 66 (Trempolino (USA) 135) [2004 54: p10g p12g p10g Jul 7] well held in 2004: wears headgear. *Miss K. M. George* —

BOOT 'N TOOT 3 b.f. Mtoto 134 – Raspberry Sauce 65 (Niniski (USA) 125) [2004 9.7s 10m* 10g 10.1g⁶ Sep 15] rangy, rather sparely-made filly: first foal: dam 1m to 11.6f winner: fairly useful form: won maiden at Windsor in August: best effort when 8 lengths sixth to Polar Jem in listed event at Yarmouth: bred to stay 1½m. *C. A. Cyzer* **83**

BOOZY DOUZ 4 ch.f. Abou Zouz (USA) 109 – Ackcontent (USA) (Key To Content (USA)) [2004 –: 8.5s f7g⁶ 10m May 25] bad maiden: tried in cheekpieces. *H. S. Howe* —

BOPPYS BABE 3 ch.f. Clan of Roses – Joara (FR) (Radetzky 123) [2004 –: 9.9d 7d Oct 16] leggy filly: little form. *R. A. Fahey* —

BOPPYS DREAM 2 ch.f. (May 1) Clan of Roses – Laurel Queen (IRE) 76 (Viking (USA)) [2004 5m⁶ 5g 6d⁵ Oct 18] 1,200Y: small, strong filly: fifth foal: half-sister to 3-y-o Boppys Princess: dam prolific 6f to 8.5f winner: poor form in maidens. *R. A. Fahey* **36**

BOPPYS PRINCESS 3 b.f. Wizard King 122 – Laurel Queen (IRE) 76 (Viking (USA)) [2004 38: 8.5g* 7.9f² 8.1s* 8s* 8.5m⁵ p9.5g* 8.2v* Nov 4] quite good-topped filly: fair handicapper: progressed well at 3 yrs, winning at Beverley (apprentices) in July, Haydock and Ayr in August, Wolverhampton in October and Nottingham in November: stays 9.5f: acts on polytrack and any turf going: visored final 2-y-o start: effective held up or ridden from front. *R. A. Fahey* **77**

Hippodrome Racing's "Boogie Street"

BORACAY BEAUTY 2 b.f. (Mar 17) Tipsy Creek (USA) 115 – Grandads Dream **24** (Never So Bold 135) [2004 5s 5d 6m 5f Jun 21] sturdy filly: first foal: dam unraced: bad maiden. *J. R. Weymes*

BORACAY DREAM (IRE) 2 ch.c. (May 6) Grand Lodge (USA) 125 – Mild Intrigue **63** (USA) 91 (Sir Ivor (USA) 135) [2004 7d p8g Dec 18] €50,000Y: leggy, quite good-topped colt: half-brother to several winners, including Irish 1m (at 2 yrs) to 1½m (Irish Oaks) winner Margarula (by Doyoun) and useful Irish 1998 2-y-o 1m/9f winner Wild Heaven (by Darshaan): dam 1¼m winner: better effort (bit reportedly slipped on debut) when last of 8 in minor event at Lingfield: should stay 1¼m. *P. W. Chapple-Hyam*

BORDER ARTIST 5 ch.g. Selkirk (USA) 129 – Aunt Tate (Tate Gallery (USA) 117) **71** [2004 74, a54: 6s 8s 7.1m* 8m 8.3m 7f⁴ 7.5g³ 8g⁴ 6.9f⁵ 6f⁵ Jul 24] well-made gelding: **a–** fair performer: won handicap at Musselburgh in May: stays 1m: acts on all-weather, firm and good to soft going: blinkered once as 3-y-o: usually held up. *D. Nicholls*

BORDER CASTLE 3 b.c. Grand Lodge (USA) 125 – Tempting Prospect 95 (Shirley **94** Heights 130) [2004 82p: 10g* 10f Sep 24] deep-girthed colt: fairly useful performer: won handicap at Newmarket in August by 2 lengths from Zero Tolerance: respectable seventh to Destination Dubai in minor event at Ascot following month: should stay 1½m: raced only on good going or firmer. *Sir Michael Stoute*

BORDER EDGE 6 b.g. Beveled (USA) – Seymour Ann (Krayyan 117) [2004 95: p7g **77** p7g 8.3g 8g 7m 7g 10g p8g p7g³ p10g* Dec 18] fair handicapper: made all at Lingfield in December: stays easy 1¼m: acts on all-weather, firm and good to soft going: tried blinkered, usually visored. *J. J. Bridger*

BORDERLESCOTT 2 b.c. (Apr 21) Compton Place 125 – Jeewan 82 (Touching **71** Wood (USA) 127) [2004 5m⁶ 5g 5g³ 6f* Jul 31] 13,000Y: half-brother to several winners, including 5-y-o Woodbury and 7f to 1¼m winner Harry Browne (by Al Hareb): dam 1½m winner: fair performer: improved to win nursery at Hamilton: stays 6f. *R. Bastiman*

BORDER MUSIC 3 b.g. Selkirk (USA) 129 – Mara River 86 (Efisio 120) [2004 83p: **90** p7g 8g 8.1g³ 8g² 8g² 10g³ 8f⁴ 8d Oct 10] big gelding: fairly useful handicapper: good efforts at 3 yrs when in frame, unlucky fourth to Granston at Ascot penultimate start, persistently short of room when full of running in straight: will prove at least as effective at 7f as 1¼m: acts on polytrack and firm going: waited with, and travels strongly: well up to winning handicaps in 2005. *A. M. Balding*

BORDER SAINT 3 b.g. Selkirk (USA) 129 – Caramba 114 (Belmez (USA) 131) **83** [2004 p12g³ f12g 12d⁴ 11.9d May 13] angular, workmanlike gelding: fourth foal: brother to 7f winner Carafe and half-brother to 1m winner Coyote (by Indian Ridge), both fairly useful: dam, 1m (Falmouth Stakes) and 1¼m (Nassau Stakes) winner, half-sister to smart performer up to 1m Lemon Souffle: fairly useful maiden: best effort when fourth to Percussionist at Newmarket: twice ran as if amiss, including final start: sold only 800 gns, joined N. Rossiter. *M. L. W. Bell*

BORDER SUBJECT 7 b.g. Selkirk (USA) 129 – Topicality (USA) (Topsider (USA)) **94 ?** [2004 117: 6m⁶ 5m 6f Jul 24] big, strong gelding: reportedly suffered from breathing problem and broken blood vessels: one-time smart performer, winner of 6 races: well below form in 2004, including in listed event (blinkered): sometimes tongue tied earlier in career: retired. *R. Charlton*

BORDER TALE 4 b.g. Selkirk (USA) 129 – Likely Story (IRE) 94 (Night Shift (USA)) **89** [2004 87: p12g f12s* f12s Mar 5] strong gelding: fairly useful handicapper: won at Wolverhampton in February: stays 1½m: acts on all-weather, soft and good to firm going: tried visored/tongue tied at 2 yrs. *C. Weedon*

BORDER TERRIER (IRE) 6 b.g. Balnibarbi 95 – Ring Side (IRE) (Alzao (USA) **44** 117) [2004 65: 10.1v 12m 10.5d 10.9d³ 12m 10.9g⁴ 14.1g⁴ 11.9g Sep 2] workmanlike gelding: poor handicapper: stayed 1¾m: acted on soft and good to firm going: blinkered/visored last 5 outings: dead. *M. D. Hammond*

BORIS THE SPIDER 3 b.g. Makbul 104 – Try Vickers (USA) 72 (Fuzzbuster (USA)) **62** [2004 64?: 6s² 6d 5.9f 7m⁵ 8g⁵ 8.5g⁴ 10d⁶ 13.1s* p12.2g f14g* f14g Dec 11] big gelding: modest performer: won banded event at Ayr in October and handicap at Southwell in November: stays 1¾m: acts on all-weather, soft and good to firm going. *M. D. Hammond*

BORN FOR DANCING (IRE) 2 b.f. (Mar 8) Fasliyev (USA) 120 – Fancy Boots **73** (IRE) 62 (Salt Dome (USA)) [2004 5m² 5.1f⁵ 5m² 5s³ Oct 16] €37,000F, €45,000Y: fifth foal: half-sister to fairly useful Irish 5f/6f winner After Shock (by Grand Lodge): dam, Irish maiden, half-sister to dams of dual Breeders' Cup Mile winner Da Hoss and Prix Morny winner Tagula: fair maiden: second at Warwick and Lingfield, best efforts: needs to settle to stay beyond 5f: acts on good to firm going: blinkered second start: sold 2,200 gns. *B. W. Hills*

BORN FOR DIAMONDS (IRE)   2 b.f. (Mar 3) Night Shift (USA) – Kirri (IRE)   **54**
(Lycius (USA) 124) [2004 6m 6.1m⁵ 7s f6g⁶ Nov 9] €12,000F, €65,000Y: well-made
filly: first foal: dam, ran once in Ireland, out of half-sister to Washington International
winner Providential and Prix Marcel Boussac winner Play It Safe: modest maiden: ran in
seller final start: should stay 1m: best efforts on good to firm going. *B. W. Hills*

BORODINSKY   3 b.g. Magic Ring (IRE) 115 – Valldemosa 81 (Music Boy 124) [2004   **54**
–: 6m⁵ 7f 6s⁴ 6.9g 7m² 9m⁴ 7v 7f² Sep 13] heavy-topped gelding: modest maiden: stays
9f: acts on firm and soft going. *R. E. Barr*

BORREGO (IRE)   4 b.c. Green Desert (USA) 127 – Pripet (USA) 86 (Alleged (USA)   **83**
138) [2004 85p: 7m² 7.1m 8m⁶ 8.1g 8f 7f⁴ 7m* 8g 7m Sep 29] good-bodied colt: fairly
useful performer: won handicap at Doncaster in September: effective at 7f/1m: raced only
on good going or firmer: blinkered last 4 starts: none too consistent: joined S. Seemar in
UAE. *C. E. Brittain*

BORTHWICK GIRL (IRE)   2 b.f. (Feb 23) Cape Cross (IRE) 129 – Shannon Dore   **96**
(IRE) 81 (Turtle Island (IRE) 123) [2004 6m* 7.1m⁴ 7m 7g³ 8d³ Oct 30] 35,000Y: quite
good-topped filly: first foal: dam 2-y-o 6f winner: useful performer: won maiden at
Newmarket in June: third in listed races on same course won by Penkenna Princess and
Squaw Dance, weakening late on when bit below form in latter: best form at 7f: acts on
good to firm ground, probably on good to soft. *B. J. Meehan*

BORZOI MAESTRO   3 ch.g. Wolfhound (USA) 126 – Ashkernazy (IRE) 60 (Salt   **78**
Dome (USA) [2004 81: 5.7s² 5g³ 6f* 5f 5m⁴ 6g³ 5m 5m⁵ 6d 5m⁶ 6g 5g⁵ 5g⁵ p6g⁵ p6g
Oct 16] small gelding: fair performer: won minor event at Brighton in May: effective
at 5f/easy 6f: acts on all-weather and firm going: effective with or without cheekpieces:
races prominently. *J. L. Spearing*

BOSCHETTE   2 b.f. (Mar 9) Dansili 127 – Secret Dance (Sadler's Wells (USA) 132)   **–**
[2004 7.9g⁵ 7m Oct 10] 7,500Y, resold 13,000Y: leggy filly: half-sister to 3 winners, including 4-y-o Secluded and 6f to 10.5f winner Silver Secret (by Absalom): dam unraced:
well held in maidens at York (signs of a little ability) and Newcastle. *J. D. Bethell*

BOSCO (IRE)   3 br.g. Petardia 113 – Classic Goddess (IRE) (Classic Secret (USA)   **57**
91) [2004 65: 11.6s 11.6g 10g 10f* 10m⁶ 11.6g 10g Jul 16] modest performer: won seller
at Brighton (left R. Hannon) in June: tongue tied, below form after: stays 1¼m: acts on
firm: tried blinkered: gelded after final start. *P. S. McEntee*

BOSPHORUS   5 b.g. Polish Precedent (USA) 131 – Ancara 109 (Dancing Brave (USA)   **48**
140) [2004 66: p12g³ f12g* Apr 22] strong gelding: poor performer: won banded event at
Wolverhampton in April: stays easy 2m: acts on fibresand, raced only on going firmer
than good on turf: visored. *D. G. Bridgwater*

BOSTON LODGE   4 ch.g. Grand Lodge (USA) 125 – Ffestiniog (IRE) 96 (Efisio   **104**
120) [2004 98: 8m³ 6.5f² 6.5m³ 6.5m² 5m⁴ 5m 6f 8.1d 7m³ 7m² 7m Sep 25] lengthy,
close-coupled gelding: useful performer: several good efforts in 2004, 1¾ lengths second
to Ettrick Water in handicap at Goodwood penultimate start: effective at 5f to 9f: acts
on polytrack and firm going: blinkered/visored 7 of last 8 starts: has worn crossed noseband: has run well when sweating: usually waited with: consistent. *G. A. Butler*

BOTANICAL (USA)   3 b.c. Seeking The Gold (USA) – Satin Flower (USA) 115   **98**
(Shadeed (USA) 135) [2004 97: 6g⁵ 7m 6g Aug 14] well-made colt: good walker: has a
quick action: useful performer: creditable 2½ lengths fifth to So Will I in listed race at
Newbury in May: stiff tasks in handicaps after: should stay 7f: raced on good going or
firmer: visored final 2-y-o start, tongue tied in 2004. *Saeed bin Suroor*

BOTTOMLESS WALLET   3 ch.f. Titus Livius (FR) 115 – Furry Dance (USA)   **55**
(Nureyev (USA) 131) [2004 10.1m⁶ 10s⁴ Nov 1] 1,700Y: half-sister to 6f winner Elegant
Dance (by Statoblest) and 1¼m winner Nuvellino (by Robellino): dam ran once: better
effort in maidens when sixth in slowly-run event at Newcastle. *F. Watson*

BOUGHT DIRECT   5 b.g. Muhtarram (USA) 125 – Muhybh (USA) 80 (Dayjur   **57**
(USA) 137) [2004 66: f9.4g f8s f8g⁶ f9.4g⁵ f8.5g⁴ 7.1g⁶ 8.1g Jul 3] workmanlike gelding:
handicapper: won at Listowel and Leopardstown in 2003 when trained by J. Gorman in
Ireland: just modest form in 2004: stays 9.5f: acts on fibresand, good to firm and good to
soft going: often blinkered/tongue tied at 3 yrs: very slowly away on reappearance: sent
to Spain. *R. J. Smith*

BOULE D'OR (IRE) 3 b.c. Croco Rouge (IRE) 126 – Saffron Crocus 83 (Shareef **99**
Dancer (USA) 135) [2004 84: 7m⁴ 9g* 12m⁴ 10d² 8g 10m* 10.1g⁴ 10f⁴ 10g³ 8d² p10g
Nov 20] tall, quite good-topped colt: good walker: useful performer: won handicap at
Goodwood in May and minor event at Newmarket in August: mostly creditable efforts
otherwise, neck second to Kamanda Laugh in handicap at Newmarket penultimate
start: stays 1¼m: acts on firm and good to soft going: usually waited with: consistent.
R. Ingram

BOUMAHOU (IRE) 4 b.c. Desert Story (IRE) 115 – Kilbride Lass (IRE) (Lahib **59**
(USA) 129) [2004 66: p16g³ p13g³ p13g³ p16g* 14.4s Mar 27] sturdy colt: fairly useful on **a81**
all-weather, modest on turf: won handicap at Lingfield in February: stayed easy 2m: acted
on polytrack: dead. *A. P. Jarvis*

BOUNDLESS PROSPECT (USA) 5 b.g. Boundary (USA) 117 – Cape (USA) (Mr **84**
Prospector (USA)) [2004 82: p8g p8g 8g 8m 7g² 7m³ 7m* 8m⁶ 7g 8g p6g p7g Dec 4] **a75**
good-bodied gelding: fairly useful handicapper: best effort in 2004 when winning at
Newbury in July: left J. Hills after tenth start: effective at 7f/easy 1m: acts on polytrack,
firm and good to soft going: tried visored: often slowly away: held up. *D. Flood*

BOUND TO PLEASE 9 b.g. Warrshan (USA) 117 – Hong Kong Girl 94 (Petong **–**
126) [2004 6.1g f6d⁶ f8.5g May 11] fair at best: missed 2003: no form at 9 yrs: visored.
Miss A. Stokell

BOUNTIFUL 2 gr.f. (Jan 14) Pivotal 124 – Kinsaile 56 (Robellino (USA) 127) [2004 **56**
6m Jul 16] smallish, leggy filly: first foal: dam lightly-raced half-sister to 6-y-o The
Trader: seventh in maiden at Newbury. *M. Blanshard*

BOUNTY QUEST 2 b.c. (Apr 2) Fasliyev (USA) 120 – Just Dreams 85 (Salse (USA) **73**
128) [2004 5.2m³ 6g⁴ 7f³ Jul 29] €60,000Y, 25,000 2-y-o: sturdy colt: first living foal:
dam, lightly-raced winner, sister to St Leger/Gold Cup winner Classic Cliche and
half-sister to Prix Vermeille winner My Emma: fair form in maidens: third at Newbury
and Epsom: should stay 1m: joined D. Watson in UAE. *R. Hannon*

BOURGAINVILLE 6 b.g. Pivotal 124 – Petonica (IRE) 77 (Petoski 135) [2004 114: **108 d**
p10g p10g⁴ 10d⁵ 10.3d⁵ 12g 10m 10.4g 10m 10v Oct 23] tall, close-coupled gelding:
usually looks well: has a long, rather round stride: useful performer: creditable efforts
in 2004 only when fourth to Caluki in listed race at Lingfield and fifth to Chancellor in
Gordon Richards Stakes at Sandown second/third starts: stays 1¼m: acts on polytrack,
firm and soft going: tried in cheekpieces: refused to go to start (visored) intended seventh
outing. *A. M. Balding*

BOURGEOIS 7 ch.g. Sanglamore (USA) 126 – Bourbon Girl 116 (Ile de Bourbon **105**
(USA) 133) [2004 107: 10v² 12.1d³ 12m* 11.9g 13.9g 10.4s 14.6f Sep 10] strong, deep-
girthed gelding: useful handicapper: won at Thirsk (beat Highland Games a neck) in
May: well below form after next start: effective at 1¼m (given good test) to easy 19f: acts
on any going: tried blinkered/visored: probably best held up. *T. D. Easterby*

BOWING 4 b.g. Desert Prince (IRE) 130 – Introducing 78 (Mtoto 134) [2004 89§: **– §**
f8.5g p12g⁵ p10g 11.6d 10.2f f12g Jun 25] leggy, lengthy gelding: ungenuine maiden:
well held in 2004: tried in cheekpieces. *P. G. Murphy*

BOWLAND BRIDE (IRE) 2 b.f. (Apr 5) Raise A Grand (IRE) 114 – Red Riding **49 d**
Hood (FR) 62 (Mummy's Pet 125) [2004 5s⁵ 5d 6g⁴ 6f⁴ 6m* 6g f7g 5m⁵ f7d Jul 23]
€2,000F, €1,200Y: close-coupled filly: half-sister to 2 winners abroad, including French
7f (at 2 yrs) and 1¼m winner Sizzling Rage (by Sizzling Melody): dam ran 4 times at 2
yrs: poor performer: easily best effort when winning seller at Thirsk in May: stays 6f: acts
on good to firm ground: blinkered last 2 starts. *A. Berry*

BOWLED OUT (GER) 2 b.f. (May 3) Dansili 127 – Braissim (Dancing Brave (USA) **68**
140) [2004 7d⁴ 6m 7g 8d* Nov 5] 2,000Y: close-coupled filly: third living foal: half-sister
to Italian winner up to 8.5f by Lion Cavern: dam unraced half-sister to smart performers
White Heart (7f to 1¼m) and Kind Regards (1¼m/1½m): fair performer: won 20-runner
nursery at Yarmouth by 1¼ lengths from Akraan, leading over 1f out: should stay 1¼m:
form only on good to soft going. *P. J. McBride*

BOWLEGS BILLY 4 gr.g. Raphane (USA) 102 – Swallow Bay 54 (Penmarric (USA) **38**
111) [2004 61: 5.5g 5d 7m 8m f7g f8g Dec 12] leggy gelding: poor maiden: may prove best
at 5f: acts on good to firm and good to soft going: tried in cheekpieces. *J. Balding*

BOWLING ALONG 3 b.f. The West (USA) 107 – Bystrouska (Gorytus (USA) 132) **66**
[2004 59: 6.1s⁵ 6m 6m 6m 7m⁴ 6m³ 5.9m² 6m 7.1g 6f* 6g⁶ 6.1m 8d Oct 18] leggy, rather
unfurnished filly: fair handicapper: won apprentice event at Redcar in September: best at

6f: acts on firm and soft going: visored once in 2003: refused to enter stall sixth intended outing: sometimes slowly away. *M. E. Sowersby*

BOWMAN'S CROSSING (IRE)   5 b.g. Dolphin Street (FR) 125 – Biraya (Valiyar   **117**
129) [2004 121: 8d³ 10m³ 8m⁵ 10m⁴ 10g³ 8f 8g⁶ 7m³ 8m² 10m² 10m Dec 12] good-topped gelding: smart performer: trained in Ireland at 2 yrs by D. Wachman, winning maiden at Leopardstown: winner 3 times since at Sha Tin in Hong Kong: ran well when fourth to River Dancer in Queen Elizabeth II Cup at Sha Tin fourth outing in 2004: ran at Ascot sixth/seventh starts, better effort (visored) when creditable seventh behind Refuse To Bend in Queen Anne Stakes on first occasion: second to Ain't Here in Group 3/2 events back at Sha Tin in autumn, but last of 14 in Hong Kong Cup there final outing: effective at 1m/1¼m: acts on firm ground: usually held up. *D. Oughton, Hong Kong*

BOW SPRIT   4 ch.g. Fleetwood (IRE) 107 – Longwood Lady 56 (Rudimentary (USA)   **–**
118) [2004 54: p12g Jan 6] workmanlike gelding: maiden: tailed off only start in 2004. *B. G. Powell*

BOW STRADA   7 ch.g. Rainbow Quest (USA) 134 – La Strada (Niniski (USA) 125)   **75**
[2004 16m³ Jul 14] leggy, quite attractive gelding: fair handicapper: will stay beyond 2m: acts on good to firm and good to soft going: useful chaser. *P. J. Hobbs*

BOWSTRING (IRE)   3 b.f. Sadler's Wells (USA) 132 – Cantanta 74 (Top Ville 129)   **105 §**
[2004 –p: 9.7s* 10.1s² 11.5s² 10.1s³ 14.6m³ 14.1s³ 10.3s Nov 6] lengthy, sturdy filly: useful performer: won maiden at Folkestone in March: best efforts when third in handicap at Newbury (beaten 2 lengths by Posteritas) and Park Hill Stakes at Doncaster (beaten 1½ lengths by Echoes In Eternity) fourth/fifth starts: stays 14.6f: acts on soft and good to firm going: races prominently: irresolute. *J. H. M. Gosden*

BOW WAVE   2 b.c. (Feb 18) Danzero (AUS) – Moxby (Efisio 120) [2004 6s* Nov 6]   **81 p**
9,000F, 18,000Y: good-topped colt: first foal: dam unraced sister to useful 7f performer Abbey's Gal: 11/1, green and bandaged hind-joints, won 21-runner maiden at Doncaster by 1¾ lengths from Westlake Bond, slowly away and leading final 1f: will stay 7f: sure to improve. *H. Candy*

BOX BUILDER   7 ch.g. Fraam 114 – Ena Olley (Le Moss 135) [2004 f16g* f14g² Feb   **72**
19] close-coupled, good-topped gelding: has reportedly had wind operation: fair handicapper: won at Southwell in February: should stay beyond 2m: acts on all-weather, soft and good to firm going: tried blinkered: tongue tied in 2002. *H. Morrison*

BOXGROVE (FR)   3 gr.g. Trempolino (USA) 135 – Little Emily 48 (Zafonic (USA)   **67**
130) [2004 75: p8g f8.5g⁶ a12g⁶ 14.5s⁵ 11.8d* Sep 26] fair performer at best: ran as if amiss first 2 starts in 2004, then left C. Brittain: blinkered, won 4-runner apprentice minor event at Le Pin Au Haras in September: stays 11.8f: acts on polytrack and good to soft ground. *J. E. Pease, France*

BOXHALL (IRE)   2 b.c. (Feb 22) Grand Lodge (USA) 125 – March Hare 60 (Groom   **69 p**
Dancer (USA) 128) [2004 7d⁶ 7g Sep 15] €140,000Y: rangy, unfurnished colt: second foal: half-brother to useful 1¼m winner (including at 2 yrs) Toy Show (by Danehill): dam, maiden who stayed 1½m, half-sister to smart 1m/1¼m performer Inglenook out of smart middle-distance stayer Spring, herself half-sister to Pentire: fair form in maidens at Newmarket (green) and Yarmouth (green): likely to do better at 1¼m/1½m. *P. W. Harris*

BRACE OF DOVES   2 b.g. (Apr 7) Bahamian Bounty 116 – Overcome (Belmez   **69**
(USA) 131) [2004 5d f6d⁵ 6s² 6m³ 7m³ 7.1f² 7d³ 8g 7m 8d Oct 18] 5,600Y, resold 7,500Y: quite good-topped gelding: first foal: dam, German 1¼m winner, out of half-sister to German Derby winners Orofino and Ordos: fair maiden: placed 5 times, including in nurseries: stays 7f: acts on firm and soft going (some promise on fibresand). *T. D. Barron*

BRADS HOUSE (IRE)   2 b.c. (Mar 8) Rossini (USA) 118 – Gold Stamp (Golden Act   **–**
(USA)) [2004 7.1d Nov 3] €15,000F, 13,000Y: seventh foal: half-brother to 3 winners, including 1m (at 2yrs) to 1¼m winner Philatelic Lady (by Pips Pride) and Irish 7f winner Woodstamp (by Woodborough), both fairly useful: dam unraced: 66/1 and green, always behind in maiden at Musselburgh. *J. G. M. O'Shea*

BRAGADINO   5 b.g. Zilzal (USA) 137 – Graecia Magna 109 (Private Account   **85 d**
(USA)) [2004 97: 9v 7.2s 6m 7m 8g⁶ 7m 8d a7g⁶ p6d p5.1d p8.6g⁴ Dec 27] close-coupled, quite good-topped gelding: useful at best: trained by P. Prendergast at 4 yrs: mostly well held in 2004: ran respectably in handicap at Wolverhampton final start: stays 9f: acts on polytrack, firm and soft going: tried in blinkers/visor/tongue tie. *Lindsay Woods, Ireland*

BRAG (IRE)   2 b.f. (Mar 26) Mujadil (USA) 119 – Boast 99 (Most Welcome 131) [2004   **81**
5g² 5.1f⁴ 5d 5f* 5m³ 5g Aug 14] rather leggy filly: first foal: dam 5f (at 2 yrs)/6f winner:

fairly useful performer: won nursery at Leicester in July: creditable third at Thirsk (despite not clear run), much better effort in nurseries after: will prove best at 5f/easy 6f: acts on firm going: sold 35,000 gns, sent to USA. *R. Charlton*

BRAHMINY KITE (USA) 2 b.c. (Apr 22) Silver Hawk (USA) 123 – Cope's Light (USA) (Copelan (USA)) [2004 7.5d² 8.1d* Aug 20] $300,000Y: closely related to US Grade 3 winners Zillah The Hun (1m at 2 yrs) and Political Attack 8.5/9f (both by Hawk Attack) and half-brother to 3 winners: dam sprint winner in USA: still green, confirmed promise when winning 3-runner minor event at Sandown by 2 lengths from Destinate, getting on top final 1f despite edging right: likely to stay at least 1¼m: open to progress. *M. Johnston* — **99 p**

BRAIN WASHED 3 b.f. Mind Games 121 – Bollin Dorothy 73 (Rambo Dancer (CAN) 107) [2004 6g 6g⁴ 6d² 7m⁵ 5d³ 6g³ 6g⁶ Oct 5] tall, lengthy filly: third foal: sister to 4-y-o Certa Cito: dam 7f winner: modest maiden: should stay 7f: acts on good to soft ground: seemed ill at ease both starts at Catterick. *T. D. Easterby* — **62**

BRAMANTINO (IRE) 4 b.g. Perugino (USA) 84 – Headrest (Habitat 134) [2004 –: f8s⁵ f9.4s³ f11s* p12g 12.4v² 14m⁵ 12m 14d⁵ 12s⁵ 12.1s* 11.9g* 10m³ 11.9s⁵ Sep 24] strong, lengthy gelding: fair handicapper: won at Southwell in February, Beverley in August and York (amateurs) in September: stays 12.4f: acts on fibresand, heavy and good to firm going: wears headgear. *R. A. Fahey* — **67**

BRAMASOLE (USA) 2 b.f. (Apr 20) Thunder Gulch (USA) 129 – Smooth As Silk (USA) (Deputy Minister (CAN)) [2004 p8.6g p8m⁶ Dec 21] first foal: dam, 1m/9f winner in USA, out of US Grade 3-winning sprinter Sacque: green, modest form in maidens at Wolverhampton (slowly away) and Lingfield: should stay 1¼m. *J. H. M. Gosden* — **54**

BRANDEXE (IRE) 2 b.f. (May 15) Xaar 132 – Tintara (IRE) 72 (Caerleon (USA) 132) [2004 7g 7.1m⁵ 7.2d⁴ 7s Oct 16] €24,000Y: fifth foal: half-sister to Italian 9f/1¼m winner by Namaqualand: dam 1½m winner: best effort in maidens when fourth at Ayr: ran as if amiss final start: will stay at least 1m. *B. W. Hills* — **65**

BRANDY COVE 7 b.g. Lugana Beach 116 – Tender Moment (IRE) 78 (Caerleon (USA) 132) [2004 –, a74: f8g⁴ f8g f8d⁵ f8g⁵ f8g⁵ Jul 23] tall gelding: fair handicapper: best at 1m: acts on fibresand, little form on turf: slowly away last 3 outings. *B. Smart* — **– a65**

BRANDYWINE BAY (IRE) 4 b.f. Mujadil (USA) 119 – Ned's Contessa (IRE) 48 (Persian Heights 129) [2004 49: p8g p8g⁴ 7f* 6g⁵ 7m 8d Oct 16] poor performer: won apprentice handicap at Brighton in August: reportedly finished lame final start: stays 1m: acts on all-weather and firm going: tried blinkered/tongue tied, wears cheekpieces nowadays. *A. P. Jones* — **45**

BRANSTON LILY 2 ch.f. (Apr 8) Cadeaux Genereux 131 – Indefinite Article (IRE) (Indian Ridge 123) [2004 6g³ 6f⁴ 6m 7d Oct 15] fourth foal: half-sister to 5f/6f winner (including at 2 yrs) Branston Pickle (by Piccolo) and 5-y-o Branston Nell: dam unraced sister to very smart Irish performer up to 1½m Definite Article: modest maiden: form only on first 2 starts, then left G. A. Swinbank: should stay 7f: sold 15,000 gns. *Mrs J. R. Ramsden* — **45**

BRANSTON NELL 5 b.m. Classic Cliche (IRE) 128 – Indefinite Article (IRE) (Indian Ridge 123) [2004 63d: f12s p13g⁵ Mar 2] smallish mare: well held in 2004: tried visored/blinkered. *C. R. Dore* — **–**

BRANSTON PENNY 2 ch.f. (Mar 2) Pennekamp (USA) 130 – Branston Jewel (IRE) 95 (Prince Sabo 123) [2004 6m p7.1g² p6g f8g Nov 23] quite good-topped filly: fourth foal: half-sister to useful 5f/6f (including at 2 yrs) winner Falcon Hill (by Polar Falcon): dam, 2-y-o 5f winner, half-sister to Branston Abby (smart at 6f/7f) and 6-y-o Desert Deer: poor maiden: second in seller at Wolverhampton, final start for J. Given: should stay 1m: acts on polytrack. *P. D. Evans* — **45**

BRANSTON TIGER 5 b.g. Mark of Esteem (IRE) 137 – Tuxford Hideaway 102 (Cawston's Clown 113) [2004 85: f7s⁵ 6g 6s 6d 6g⁶ 7m⁵ 7m 7.1d f6m* 6g⁴ 6.1g³ 7.2d 6d³ 6g p6d f7s² f6g* Dec 7] rangy gelding: fair performer: won claimer (left J. Given) in July and handicap (first start since leaving P. D. Evans) in December, both at Southwell: effective at 6f/7f: acts on all-weather, firm and soft going: usually blinkered/visored. *Ian Emmerson* — **74**

BRANTWOOD (IRE) 4 b.g. Lake Coniston (IRE) 131 – Angelic Sounds (IRE) (The Noble Player (USA)) [2004 89d: 5.7g 5d 5v 5.1d⁴ 6m³ f6d² 6g³ 7m 6m⁶ 6g 5d⁵ 5d Sep 16] angular, quite good-topped gelding: fair handicapper: probably best at 5f/6f: acts on fibresand, heavy and good to firm going: tried in blinkers (bolted before start)/cheekpieces, usually tongue tied: sold 500 gns. *B. A. McMahon* — **67**

BRAVE BURT (IRE) 7 ch.g. Pips Pride 117 – Friendly Song 48 (Song 132) [2004 **89 d**
91: 5m 5.1d 5m 5.2g² 6d 5.1s 5g 5d 5d p5.1g Nov 6] good-topped gelding: fairly useful
performer: easily best effort in 2004 when neck second to Strawberry Patch in handicap
at Newbury: best at 5f: acts on firm and good to soft going: usually leads. *D. Nicholls*

BRAVE CHIEF 3 ch.c. Komaite (USA) – Victoria Sioux 54 (Ron's Victory (USA) 129) **49**
[2004 55: f6g 5.7m f6g⁵ f5g⁶ f5g f5m⁵ f5g⁶ f7g³ Dec 12] strong, lengthy colt: modest
maiden: stays 7f: raced only on fibresand/good to firm going: sometimes slowly away.
J. A. Pickering

BRAVE DANE (IRE) 6 b.g. Danehill (USA) 126 – Nuriva (USA) 100 (Woodman **81**
(USA) 126) [2004 62: p10g* p10g* p10g⁵ p10g⁶ 10.3g* p8g² p10d 7m 7f² 10m Aug
16] lengthy, angular gelding: fairly useful performer: won handicaps at Lingfield (2) in
February and Doncaster (ladies race) in March: probably best at 7f to 1¼m: acts on polytrack and any turf going: tried blinkered: carries head high: held up. *A. W. Carroll*

BRAVE KNIGHT 7 b.g. Presidium 124 – Agnes Jane (Sweet Monday 122) [2004 –: **–**
12.1d Aug 11] big, lengthy gelding: maiden: well held only start in 2004: tried blinkered.
N. Bycroft

BRAVELY DOES IT (USA) 4 gr.g. Holy Bull (USA) 134 – Vigors Destiny (USA) **61**
(Vigors (USA)) [2004 11.9d 10.3m 10m⁶ 14.1f² 15.9s 12g p12.2g⁵ p16.5g⁵ p13.9g⁴
p12.2g* p12.2g* p12.2g p12.2g⁴ Dec 20] big, strong gelding: modest performer: won
banded race and handicap at Wolverhampton in November: barely stays 16.5f: acts on
polytrack and firm going. *W. M. Brisbourne*

BRAVEMORE (USA) 2 b.c. (Mar 24) Diesis 133 – Private Indy (USA) (A P Indy **72**
(USA) 131) [2004 7g⁶ p7.1g⁴ p10g³ Nov 27] well-made colt: first foal: dam unraced
daughter of US Grade 2 1m winner Topicount: fair form in maidens: close third at Lingfield: should stay 1½m. *B. J. Meehan*

BRAVE TARA (IRE) 2 b.f. (Jan 21) Brave Act 119 – Gone With The Wind (IRE) **–**
(Common Grounds 118) [2004 7d 6.9m 5g f7g Dec 16] 6,500Y: smallish filly: first foal:
dam, no form, sister to smart sprinter Flanders: no form in maidens, leaving T. Easterby
after third start. *J. Balding*

BRAVO MAESTRO (USA) 3 b.g. Stravinsky (USA) 133 – Amaranthus (USA) **92**
(Kingmambo (USA) 125) [2004 95p: p7g⁶ p8g 7g⁵ 6.5f 8g Oct 1] tall, leggy gelding: **a98**
useful performer: creditable efforts in listed races first 2 starts: off over 4 months after
next outing, ran as if amiss final one (gelded after): barely stays 1m: acts on polytrack,
raced only on good ground or firmer on turf. *D. W. P. Arbuthnot*

BRAZILIAN TERRACE 4 ch.f. Zilzal (USA) 137 – Elaine's Honor (USA) (Chief's **82**
Crown (USA)) [2004 84: p8g³ p8g⁴ 8m 8.2d* 8f* 8f³ p8g 8.2g² 8m² 8.3d 8g³ Sep 15] **a79 ?**
sparely-made filly: fairly useful performer: won minor event at Nottingham in May
and handicap at Bath in June: stays 1m: acts on polytrack, firm and good to soft going.
M. L. W. Bell

BRAZIL NUT 3 b.g. Deploy 131 – Garota de Ipanema (FR) (Al Nasr (FR) 126) [2004 **–**
16.2m Jul 23] 40/1, tailed off in claimer at Chepstow. *Miss K. Marks*

BREAD OF HEAVEN 3 b.f. Machiavellian (USA) 123 – Khubza 86 (Green Desert **– §**
(USA) 127) [2004 79p: 6v 7.1m⁶ Jul 23] strong, heavy-topped filly: well below form both
starts in 2004: tried blinkered: probably temperamental. *Mrs A. J. Perrett*

BREAKING SHADOW (IRE) 2 br.g. (May 24) Danehill Dancer (IRE) 117 – Crim- **82**
bourne 83 (Mummy's Pet 125) [2004 5g² 5m³ 5.1g³ 6d* 6f 6g⁶ 7s 8s 7s* Nov 6]
€15,000F, 12,000Y: close-coupled gelding: half-brother to several winners, including
1¼m/11f winner Gone For A Burton (by Bustino) and 1997 2-y-o 5f/6f winner Monte
Lemos (by Mukaddamah), later successful up to 7.5f in Italy, both useful: dam maiden
best at 7f: fairly useful performer: won nurseries at Ripon in August and Doncaster (wore
cheekpieces, beat Royal Orissa by ½ length in 20-runner race) in November: stays 7f:
acts on soft ground. *R. A. Fahey*

BREAKING THE RULE (IRE) 3 ch.f. King of Kings (IRE) 125 – Thirtysomething **–**
(USA) (Thirty Six Red (USA)) [2004 p10g 11.7f⁶ 10g⁵ 10g 10m Sep 23] IR 35,000F:
first foal: dam, winner in USA, out of half-sister to dam of Entrepreneur: little form.
P. R. Webber

BREAMORE 2 b.c. (Apr 1) Dansili 127 – Maze Garden (USA) (Riverman (USA) 131) **60 p**
[2004 8s Oct 27] fourth foal: half-brother to 4-y-o Roman Maze and 10.5f and 15f winner
Crossed Wire (by Lycius): dam useful French 1m winner: 25/1, green and better for race,

eighth to Very Wise in maiden at Yarmouth, not unduly punished: should improve. *Mrs A. J. Perrett*

BREATHING FIRE 2 b.c. (Apr 20) Pivotal 124 – Pearl Venture 92 (Salse (USA) **74 p** 128) [2004 6g⁵ 6s³ Sep 24] 50,000Y: big, useful-looking colt: fourth living foal: dam 5f (at 2 yrs) to 2m winner: fair form in maidens at Newmarket (slowly away, shaped well) and Haydock: will stay at least 1m: type to do better as 3-y-o. *W. J. Musson*

BREATHING SUN (IRE) 3 b.g. Bahhare (USA) 122 – Zapata (IRE) 77 (Thatching **82** 131) [2004 79: 10g 7.9d 10d 10m³ 10d Aug 21] tall gelding: fairly useful handicapper: creditable effort in 2004 only when third at Windsor: stays 1¼m: acts on good to firm and good to soft going: usually tongue tied: often slowly away: sold 7,500 gns. *W. J. Musson*

BRECON 2 ch.f. (Feb 27) Unfuwain (USA) 131 – Welsh Valley (USA) 64 (Irish River **89** (FR) 131) [2004 7s* 7v⁴ 10d⁴ Oct 30] leggy, lengthy filly: first foal: dam, maiden (second at 6f), half-sister to Gimcrack winner Chilly Billy: won maiden at Salisbury in September: raced freely when fourth in listed races won by Bibury Flyer at Newbury and Ayam Zaman at Newmarket: stays 1¼m. *D. R. C. Elsworth*

BRECON BEACON 2 b.c. (Mar 3) Spectrum (IRE) 126 – Ffestiniog (IRE) 96 (Efisio **101** 120) [2004 5s* 6m* 7f² 7m* 7d⁴ 7s⁴ Oct 22] good-topped colt: has a quick action: third foal: half-brother to 4-y-o Boston Lodge and 3-y-o Eisteddfod: dam 6f (at 2 yrs) to 1m winner: useful performer: won maiden at York in May and minor events at Brighton in May and Newmarket (beat Perfectperformance by ¾ length) in July: reportedly finished lame when second in listed race at Royal Ascot: respectable fourth at Newbury in listed race and Horris Hill Stakes (beaten 8½ lengths by Cupid's Glory): stays 7f: winner on soft ground, best efforts on firmer than good: usually ridden up with pace prior to final start. *P. F. I. Cole*

BREEDER'S FOLLY 2 b.f. (Feb 11) Mujahid (USA) 125 – Wynona (IRE) 89 **36** (Cyrano de Bergerac 120) [2004 5g 7s p8.6g Nov 26] 1,800Y, resold 15,000Y: fifth foal: half-sister to winners abroad by Dilum and Bluebird: dam 2-y-o 7f winner who stayed 1¼m: poor form in maidens. *T. J. Fitzgerald*

BREEZER 4 b.g. Forzando 122 – Lady Lacey 66 (Kampala 120) [2004 65: 10.2g 8d **34** 11.7d³ Aug 27] maiden: only poor form in 2004. *G. B. Balding*

BREEZIT (USA) 3 b.f. Stravinsky (USA) 133 – Sharka 97 (Shareef Dancer (USA) **56** 135) [2004 61: 8.2g⁴ 8m⁴ 6.1m⁵ 8.2g p6d³ p8.6d⁵ f8g³ f8g Dec 1] angular filly: has a quick action: modest performer: stays 8.6f: acts on all-weather and firm going: tried in cheekpieces/blinkers at 2 yrs. *S. R. Bowring*

BREGAGLIA 2 ch.f. (Mar 24) Zaha (CAN) 106 – Strath Kitten 36 (Scottish Reel 123) **40** [2004 7f 7m 7g f5s³ 6m p8g f7g⁵ Nov 22] smallish, strong filly: fifth foal: half sister to winner in Turkey by Dancing Spree: dam, maiden, stayed 1¼m: poor maiden: form only on fibresand: wore visor/cheekpieces last 4 starts. *R. M. H. Cowell*

BREGO (IRE) 2 b.g. (May 6) Monashee Mountain (USA) 115 – White-Wash 94 (Final **50** Straw 127) [2004 8g 8.1m 7.1s 8s Oct 15] stocky gelding: modest maiden: form only at 1m on good to firm going: blinkered last 2 starts. *J. H. M. Gosden*

BRENDAN'S SURPRISE 2 b.g. (Jun 19) Faustus (USA) 118 – Primrose Way 59 **59 p** (Young Generation 129) [2004 p7m Dec 22] 4,800 2-y-o: half-brother to 9.4f winner Sweet Amoret (by Forzando) and 9.5f and 12.5f winner in Holland by Emarati: dam middle-distance maiden: 33/1, 3½ lengths seventh of 13 to Resplendent Prince in maiden at Lingfield, late headway having run green: should do better. *I. A. Wood*

BRESSBEE (USA) 6 ch.g. Twining (USA) 120 – Bressay (USA) (Nureyev (USA) **a76** 131) [2004 60, a84: f8.5g f11g² f11s⁴ p12g f9.4g* p8g 9.7d Apr 7] close-coupled gelding: fair performer on all-weather, modest on turf: won claimer at Wolverhampton (left J. Unett) in March: pulled up (reportedly lame) final start: stays 11f: acts on fibresand and any turf going: visored/blinkered: often races up with pace: none too reliable. *N. P. Littmoden*

BRETTON 3 b.g. Polar Prince (IRE) 117 – Understudy 60 (In The Wings 128) [2004 **54** 48: f9.4s² f9.4g⁶ f8.5g⁶ 12v⁴ f8d⁴ 9.9v⁴ f12g³ f8g p10g² 10m⁵ p10g 9.7f p16g p12.2d² f12g f11g² p10m Dec 15] stocky, close-coupled gelding: modest maiden: left R. Hollinshead after eighth start: stays 1½m: acts on all-weather and any turf going: often wears cheekpieces/blinkers: none too consistent. *B. A. Pearce*

BREVITY 9 b.g. Tenby 125 – Rive (USA) (Riverman (USA) 131) [2004 85d: 5m 8.1g **–** Jul 9] big, strong gelding: useful sprinter at best: has regressed considerably: tongue tied earlier in career: tried in headgear. *J. G. M. O'Shea*

BRIAN BORU   4 b.c. Sadler's Wells (USA) 132 – Eva Luna (USA) 114 (Alleged   **120**
(USA) 138) [2004 124: 10d⁵ 10g⁵ 12m⁵ 20m⁵ 12d⁵ 15s² 14g² 12g³ 12m Dec 12] angular,
good-topped colt: very smart performer: won Racing Post Trophy at Doncaster at 2 yrs
and St Leger on same course in 2003: landed odds in listed race at Leopardstown (edged
left) in March but failed to recapture best 3-y-o form in 2004: creditable efforts nonetheless in Coronation Cup at Epsom (fifth to Warrsan), Prix Kergorlay at Deauville (didn't
have much room when 1½ lengths second to Gold Medallist), Irish St Leger at the
Curragh (2½ lengths second to Vinnie Roe) and Canadian International at Woodbine (3½
lengths third to Sulamani): ideally suited by further than 1½m and probably stayed 2½m
(respectable fifth to Papineau in Gold Cup at Royal Ascot): acted on soft and good to firm
going: usually tongue tied: sometimes wore crossed noseband/had 2 handlers/swished
tail in paddock: often sweated up: carried head awkwardly: held up: to stand at The
Beeches Stud, Glencairn, Co Waterford, Ireland fee €3,500. *A. P. O'Brien, Ireland*

BRIANNIE (IRE)   2 b.f. (Feb 3) Xaar 132 – Annieirwin (IRE) 94 (Perugino (USA)   **53**
84) [2004 6g⁶ 7.1d⁶ 6d Oct 4] €32,000Y: first foal: dam Irish 1m/9f winner: modest form
in maidens: should stay 1m. *J. R. Boyle*

BRIANNSTA (IRE)   2 b.g. (Apr 19) Bluebird (USA) 125 – Nacote (IRE) (Mtoto 134)   **78**
[2004 6g⁶ 8.3m⁵ 7g² 7.1g* 8s 7d p7g* Nov 10] €5,000F, 10,000Y: quite attractive gelding: fifth foal: half-brother to 3 winners, including 3-y-o Desert Light and Irish 2002
2-y-o 6f winner Sineogron (by Lycius): dam unraced: fair performer: won maiden at
Warwick in August and nursery at Lingfield in November (gelded after): stays 7f: acts on
polytrack: often races prominently. *M. R. Channon*

BRIAR (CZE)   5 b.g. House Rules (USA) – Bright Angel (AUT) (Antuco (GER)) [2004   –
–: f8g⁶ Jan 6] winning hurdler for current stable: showed little in 2 maidens at Southwell,
looking none too keen in cheekpieces only 5-y-o outing. *M. Pitman*

BRIAREUS   4 ch.g. Halling (USA) 133 – Lower The Tone (IRE) 74 (Phone Trick   **85**
(USA)) [2004 85: p12g p12g 10g 10.3g² 10g 10.5d³ 12f⁶ 12g 11m⁶ Jul 16] big, rather
leggy gelding: fairly useful handicapper: some creditable efforts in 2004: dropped
away tamely final start: effective at 1¼m to 1½m: acts on polytrack, firm and good to soft
going: races prominently. *A. M. Balding*

BRIAR GHYLL   2 ch.f. (Mar 21) Zaha (CAN) 106 – Charlotte Penny (High Kicker   –
(USA)) [2004 8.2v p8.6g p8m Dec 21] fifth foal: dam of little account: little form in
maidens. *I. A. Wood*

BRIDEGROOM   2 b.c. (Mar 17) Groom Dancer (USA) 128 – La Piaf (FR) (Fabulous   **73 p**
Dancer (USA) 124) [2004 p8.6d⁵ p8.6g* Nov 26] seventh foal: brother to 3-y-o Show No
Fear and half-brother to 3 winners, including 4-y-o Merlin's Dancer and useful 7f/1m
winner Gilded Dancer (by Bishop of Cashel): dam, French 2-y-o 7.5f winner (later
winner in USA), half-sister to very smart US 9f/1¼m performer Golden Apples: better
effort in maidens at Wolverhampton in November when making all to beat Suivez Moi
1¼ lengths: likely to stay 1¼m: should improve. *E. A. L. Dunlop*

BRIDEWELL (USA)   5 b.g. Woodman (USA) 126 – La Alleged (USA) (Alleged   –
(USA) 138) [2004 –: f11s 14g 10g⁶ p12g May 13] neat gelding: no form since 2002: tried
in visor/cheekpieces. *F. Watson*

BRIDGE PAL   4 ch.f. First Trump 118 – White Domino 67 (Sharpen Up 127) [2004   –
67: 12.1f⁶ 14g Sep 11] sturdy, close-coupled filly: maiden handicapper: tailed off both
starts in 2004. *P. Monteith*

BRIDGE PLACE   2 b.c. (Feb 23) Polar Falcon (USA) 126 – Dark Eyed Lady (IRE)   **83**
82 (Exhibitioner 111) [2004 5s 6m³ 6m² 7.5g* 8d 8f² Oct 24] 27,000Y: half-brother to
several winners, including fairly useful 2002 2-y-o 6f winner Vision of Dreams (by
Efisio): dam 5f/6f winner, including at 2 yrs: fairly useful performer: won maiden at
Beverley in June (left B. Meehan after): beaten a neck in optional claimer at Louisiana
Downs final start: stays 1m: acts on firm going: blinkered last 4 outings: tends to hang
left. *W. B. Calhoun, USA*

BRIDGE T'THE STARS   2 b.f. (Feb 15) Josr Algarhoud (IRE) 118 – Petra's Star 61   **70**
(Rock City 120) [2004 5.7g⁴ 6g⁵ 7g⁴ 8g Aug 26] smallish, quite good-topped filly: sixth
foal: half-sister to winner in Spain by Aragon: dam ran 3 times: fair performer: won
maiden at Bath in July: well below form in nursery final start: stays 6f. *R. F. Johnson
Houghton*

BRIDGEWATER BOYS   3 b.g. Atraf 116 – Dunloe (IRE) 54 (Shaadi (USA) 126)   **83**
[2004 58, a69: f6g⁴ f7g* f7g³ 6g⁴ 6m⁴ 6m² 6m⁴ 6g⁵ 6d p7g p6g⁶ p6d³ p7.1d f7g⁴ Dec 14]   **a75**
lengthy gelding: fairly useful handicapper on turf, fair on all-weather: won at Wolver-

hampton in January, Salisbury and Haydock in May and Ripon in June: effective at 6f/7f: acts on all-weather and firm going: wears headgear: tough. *K. A. Ryan*

BRIEF GOODBYE 4 b.g. Slip Anchor 136 – Queen of Silk (IRE) 93 (Brief Truce (USA) 126) [2004 80: 8g* 10.3g⁴ 8m 8m* 8g⁴ 8.1g 7g⁶ 7.1d Oct 17] fairly useful performer: won handicap at Musselburgh in April and minor event at Newbury (dictated pace, possibly flattered) in June: below form after: effective at 1m/1¼m: acts on firm and good to soft going: sometimes finds little. *John Berry* **88 ?**

BRIERY MEC 9 b.g. Ron's Victory (USA) 129 – Briery Fille 81 (Sayyaf 121) [2004 –: f11g p12g⁶ 10m Jul 13] tall gelding: no longer of much account. *H. J. Collingridge* **–**

BRIGADIER MONTY (IRE) 6 b.g. College Chapel 122 – Miss St Cyr 86 (Brigadier Gerard 144) [2004 72: 7d 5v⁶ 6m 5g 5m² 5d⁵ 5g⁵ 5m 6g 5s f5m⁴ Nov 22] ex-Irish gelding: fair handicapper for J. A. Flynn in 2003, winning at Navan: modest form in Britain: stays 6f: acts on fibresand, soft and good to firm going: tried tongue tied/blinkered. *Mrs S. Lamyman* **57**

BRIGADORE 5 b.g. Magic Ring (IRE) 115 – Music Mistress (IRE) 55 (Classic Music (USA)) [2004 81: 5d⁵ 5m³ 5f⁶ 5m May 29] small, good-quartered gelding: fair handicapper: barely stays 6f: acts on firm and good to soft going: races prominently. *J. R. Weymes* **69**

BRIGHT FIRE (IRE) 3 b.f. Daggers Drawn (USA) 114 – Jarmar Moon (Unfuwain (USA) 131) [2004 52: f6s⁵ 8m⁴ 10m⁶ 10g² Aug 18] modest maiden: stays 1¼m: acts on good to firm going. *W. J. Musson* **57**

BRIGHT MIST 5 b.m. Anita's Prince 126 – Out On Her Own (Superlative 118) [2004 5.1d f5m⁴ f7d f6g Jun 28] poor maiden: stays easy 7f: acts on fibresand: visored once. *B. Palling* **34**

BRIGHT MOLL 2 b.f. (Mar 11) Mind Games 121 – Molly Brown 95 (Rudimentary (USA) 118) [2004 5s* 5.1s² 5m² 5f⁵ 6g* Jul 1] 37,000Y: tall, rather unfurnished filly: first foal: dam, 5f (at 2 yrs)/6f winner, half-sister to useful Italian 7f/1m winner Stato King: fairly useful performer: won maiden at Folkestone in March and minor event at Haydock in July: good fifth in Queen Mary Stakes at Royal Ascot: stays 6f: acts on firm and soft going. *M. L. W. Bell* **88**

BRIGHT MORNING 2 b.f. (Mar 19) Dubai Millennium 140 – Sabaah (USA) 65 (Nureyev (USA) 131) [2004 8g³ a6.5g* Oct 20] half-sister to several winners, notably high-class Irish 2000 Guineas/Irish Derby winner Desert King, 7f/1m winner at 2 yrs, and smart 6f (at 2 yrs) 1¼m winner Chianti (both by Danehill): dam, lightly-raced maiden, closely related to Queen Elizabeth II Stakes winner Maroof: better effort when winning 7-runner minor event at Deauville by 1½ lengths from Norwegian Pride, leading 1f out: joined Godolphin: sure to improve. *A. Fabre, France* **95 p**

BRIGHT SKY (IRE) 5 ch.m. Wolfhound (USA) 126 – Bright Moon (USA) 123 (Alysheba (USA)) [2004 120: 10d² 8.9m Mar 27] medium-sized, lengthy mare: had a quick action: very smart performer: won Prix de Diane at Chantilly and Prix de l'Opera at Longchamp at 3 yrs and Prix d'Astarte at Deauville in 2003: creditable short-head second to Polish Summer in Prix Exbury at Saint-Cloud on reappearance: never a threat when keeping-on seventh to Paolini and Right Approach in Dubai Duty Free at Nad Al Sheba final outing: best at 1m/1¼m: acted on good to firm and good to soft going, also won on heavy at 2 yrs: held up: visited Fasliyev. *E. Lellouche, France* **117**

BRIGHT SUN (IRE) 3 b.c. Desert Sun 120 – Kealbra Lady (Petong 126) [2004 88: 6d 7.6d 7s 6.1g⁴ 6g³ 6g 8g³ 7f⁴ 8d* 7g 8d⁶ 8.5g 10.3s Oct 22] useful-looking colt: fair performer: won minor event at Newmarket in August: raced freely when below form last 3 starts, tongue tied final one: stays 1m: acts on firm and good to soft going. *N. Tinkler* **77**

BRILLIANT RED 11 b.g. Royal Academy (USA) 130 – Red Comes Up (USA) (Blushing Groom (FR) 131) [2004 92, a101: p12g p10g p16g⁶ p12g⁴ p13g p10g⁵ 12g May 1] tall, lengthy gelding: has a long stride: fairly useful performer: creditable efforts in 2004 on fourth/fifth starts only: stays easy 13f: acts on polytrack, firm and soft going: tried visored: tongue tied: sometimes slowly away: tends to carry head awkwardly/race lazily. *Jamie Poulton* **83**

BRILLIANTRIO 6 ch.m. Selkirk (USA) 129 – Loucoum (FR) 93 (Iron Duke (FR) 122) [2004 65, a49: f7g² f7g⁴ f8g f7g⁶ f7g f7s³ f6s⁶ 8f² 8f* Jun 8] big, workmanlike mare: fair on turf, poor on all-weather: won handicap at Redcar in June: acts on fibresand, firm and good to soft going: tried visored/blinkered/tongue tied: sometimes rears as stalls open (unseated rider fifth start): ungenuine: sold £10,500 after final start, resold €20,000 in November. *M. C. Chapman* **66 §** **a48 §**

BRILLIANT WATERS   4 ch.g. Mark of Esteem (IRE) 137 – Faraway Waters 102 – (Pharly (FR) 130) [2004 55: p7g Mar 24] maiden: reportedly broke blood vessel final 3-y-o start and when tailed off only outing in 2004. *D. W. P. Arbuthnot*

BRILLYANT DANCER   6 b.m. Environment Friend 128 – Brillyant Glen (IRE) – (Glenstal (USA) 118) [2004 –: f7g⁶ f7s Feb 29] of little account. *Mrs A. Duffield*

BRINDISI   3 b.f. Dr Fong (USA) 128 – Genoa 96 (Zafonic (USA) 130) [2004 75p: 8g³   99 10m⁴ 8.1m* 8f⁴ 8.1d⁴ 8m⁶ 8m* 8m 9s Oct 16] quite attractive filly: useful performer: won maiden at Haydock in May and listed event at Bath (beat Moon Dazzle 1½ lengths) in August: ran poorly in Darley Stakes at Newmarket final start: should prove at least as effective at 7f as 1m/1¼m: acts on firm going: edgy sort: reluctant to enter stall on reappearance: sometimes races freely/edges left: joined D. Selvaratnam in UAE. *B. W. Hills*

BRIOS BOY   4 ch.g. My Best Valentine 122 – Rose Elegance 83 (Bairn (USA) 126) – [2004 –: p12.2d f7g⁵ Dec 12] poor maiden, lightly raced: stays 7f: acts on fibresand: tried in cheekpieces. *K. R. Burke*

BRIOSO (IRE)   4 b.g. Victory Note (USA) 120 – Presently 48 (Cadeaux Genereux 131) – [2004 –, a62: f6s Jan 29] compact gelding: handicapper: well below form only start in 2004: tried blinkered: sold 4,700 gns in February, sent to Spain. *J. M. P. Eustace*

BROADWAY SCORE (USA)   6 b.g. Theatrical 128 – Brocaro (USA) (Mr Prospector – (USA)) [2004 105§: 8v 10.5d 10.3g 10g 9.9d 10g 8.5g 10d Jul 17] good-bodied gelding: has reportedly been treated for a vertebra problem: useful handicapper at best: well held in 2004, in blinkers final start. *M. W. Easterby*

BRONWEN (IRE)   2 b.f. (May 6) King's Best (USA) 132 – Tegwen (USA) 79 (Nijin- – p sky (CAN) 138) [2004 7d⁶ Aug 27] tall, shallow-girthed filly: half-sister to several winners, including 1999 2-y-o 6f and 1m (including Fillies' Mile) winner (stayed 1½m) Teggiano (by Mujtahid) and 3-y-o Rio de Jumeirah: dam 11.5f winner who stayed 1¾m well: 20/1, never dangerous in maiden at Newmarket, hanging left: should do better. *J. Noseda*

BRONX BOMBER   6 ch.g. Prince Sabo 123 – Super Yankee (IRE) (Superlative 118)   ? [2004 43: p6g* f7g* f7g 6m f6g⁴ Dec 7] leggy gelding: modest performer: won banded   a58 races at Lingfield and Southwell in May: best at 6f/7f: acts on all-weather, little form on turf: tried tongue tied: usually blinkered. *Dr J. D. Scargill*

BRONZE DANCER (IRE)   2 b.g. (Mar 7) Entrepreneur 123 – Scrimshaw (Selkirk   67 (USA) 129) [2004 7.1g 8m 7g 7m* 8s Oct 12] €10,000F, 2,500Y: lengthy gelding: fourth foal: half-brother to 3-y-o Messe de Minuit: dam unraced granddaughter of Arc winner Ivanjica: fair performer: won maiden at Newcastle in September: should stay 1m: acts on good to firm going: carries head awkwardly: hung left final start. *G. A. Swinbank*

BROOKLANDS LODGE (USA)   3 ch.f. Grand Lodge (USA) 125 – Princess Dixie-   58 land (USA) (Dixieland Band (USA)) [2004 67p: 8m⁶ 8.2s 10g 11.5m 10m 11.5g p12.2g³ p12.2g² p12.2d p16.5g p12m Dec 15] strong filly: modest maiden: stays 1½m: acts on polytrack and good to firm going: tried in cheekpieces/visor. *M. J. Attwater*

BROOKLANDS TIME (IRE)   3 b.f. Danetime (IRE) 121 – Lute And Lyre (IRE) – 96 (The Noble Player (USA) 126) [2004 63: f6g f6s f6s p7g 7g Mar 31] rather leggy filly: maiden: little form in 2004. *I. W. McInnes*

BROOKLIME (IRE)   2 b.c. (Jan 25) Namid 128 – Wildflower 84 (Namaqualand   80 (USA)) [2004 p6d⁶ 6m⁴ 6.1d* 6g 6d⁵ 7.1d² 7m⁶ 7d 7s⁶ 6v Oct 23] €50,000Y: quite attrac- tive colt: first foal: dam 7f winner: fairly useful performer: won maiden at Chepstow in August: creditable efforts in nurseries after until final start: stays 7f: acts on soft and good to firm ground, promise on polytrack: sold 40,000 gns. *J. A. Osborne*

BROOKLYN'S GOLD (USA)   9 b.g. Seeking The Gold (USA) – Brooklyn's Dance   82 (FR) 119 (Shirley Heights 130) [2004 84: p10g⁶ 10.5s 10g Oct 11] good-topped gelding: fairly useful handicapper on Flat (lightly raced) and over hurdles: stays 10.5f: acts on polytrack, heavy and good to firm going. *Ian Williams*

BROTHER CADFAEL   3 ch.g. So Factual (USA) 120 – High Habit 79 (Slip Anchor   50 136) [2004 47: f8.5g³ f8g f8g³ 7d² 8.2g⁶ 7.1g⁶ 7g⁶ 8.2s f8g 8f 9.7f 10g Oct 11] strong gelding: modest maiden: stays 8.5f: acts on fibresand and good to soft going: tried tongue tied/in cheekpieces. *John A. Harris*

BROUGH SUPREME   3 b.g. Sayaarr (USA) – Loriner's Lady (Saddlers' Hall (IRE)   66 126) [2004 61p: 10g⁵ 14.1s⁴ 10.9m⁶ 14.1d p10d³ Aug 7] rangy, good sort: fair maiden: barely stays 1¾m: acts on polytrack, soft and good to firm going: found little second and third (pulled hard) outings at 3 yrs. *H. Morrison*

BROUGHTON BOUNTY 3 b.f. Bahamian Bounty 116 – Sleave Silk (IRE) 58 –
(Unfuwain (USA) 131) [2004 68: 8m Jul 23] good-topped filly: maiden: well held only
start in 2004. *W. J. Musson*

BROUGHTON KNOWS 7 b.g. Most Welcome 131 – Broughtons Pet (IRE) (Cyrano **56**
de Bergerac 120) [2004 46§: f12g* p12g* f14g* f11g* f12s² f14g⁴ 14.4v⁶ 12g⁴ p12g* **a75**
11.9g p13.9g² f16s⁴ p13.9g³ p12.2g* f11g⁵ p12m p13.9g Dec 31] tall gelding: fair on
all-weather, modest on turf: won handicap at Southwell then banded events at Lingfield
and Southwell (2) in January/February (left W. Musson after seventh start), minor event
at Lingfield in October and claimer at Wolverhampton in December: effective at 11f to
2m: acts on all-weather and soft going: effective with or without blinkers: often slowly
away: held up: somewhat wayward. *Miss Gay Kelleway*

BROUGHTON MELODY 5 ch.m. Alhijaz 122 – Broughton Singer (IRE) 61 **43**
(Common Grounds 118) [2004 –: f14g³ f14g f16.2s⁴ f14g⁴ f14m⁵ Jul 12] poor maiden:
stays 1¾m: acts on fibresand. *W. J. Musson*

BROUGHTONS FLUSH 6 b.g. First Trump 118 – Glowing Reference (Reference **51**
Point 139) [2004 p16g f14g f14m⁵ f14g* 16v Oct 25] modest performer: missed 2003:
won handicap at Southwell in June, then left W. Musson: stays 2m: acts on all-weather:
often visored, blinkered final start: held up. *Paul John Gilligan, Ireland*

BROUGHTONS MILL 9 gr.g. Ron's Victory (USA) 129 – Sandra's Desire (Grey **38**
Desire 115) [2004 –: p10g⁵ p12g⁶ p10g⁶ f8.5s p12g⁶ Apr 21] poor maiden: stays 12.4f:
acts on polytrack, soft and good to firm going: tried blinkered/in cheekpieces. *J. A. Supple*

BROWN DRAGON 3 ch.g. Primo Dominie 121 – Cole Slaw (Absalom 128) [2004 **63**
–: f6g⁶ f6s² f6g² 6s 6m f6g⁶ p7.1g f6g² Dec 28] workmanlike gelding: modest maiden:
stays 6f: form only on fibresand. *D. Haydn Jones*

BROWN FOX (FR) 3 b.f. Polar Falcon (USA) 126 – Garmeria (FR) (Kadrou (FR) **73**
126) [2004 8v³ 7g 8g⁴ 8g 8d a7.5s* a7.5g 8s p6m Dec 21] first foal: dam, French 1¼m/
11f winner, half-sister to smart French performer up to 15f Trait de Genie: winner of 2
races in France, including claimer at Deauville in August: left T. Clout after eighth
start: fair form when eighth in handicap at Lingfield final outing: stays 1m: acts on dirt,
polytrack and heavy going. *G. L. Moore*

BRUMAIRE (IRE) 2 b.c. (Mar 11) Second Empire (IRE) 124 – Ar Hyd Y Knos 36 –
(Alzao (USA) 117) [2004 7.1d 7s Oct 21] well held in maidens. *J. L. Dunlop*

BRUNEL (IRE) 3 b.c. Marju (IRE) 127 – Castlerahan (IRE) (Thatching 131) [2004 **113**
105: 7g* 8g* 8f⁵ 6.5g 8s⁶ Aug 28] big, angular, good-topped colt: smart performer: made
all in listed Free Handicap at Newmarket (beat Moonlight Man 5 lengths) in April and
Mehl-Mulhens-Rennen at Cologne (beat Lazio ½ length) in May: creditable 2¾ lengths

*Mehl-Mulhens-Rennen, Cologne—Brunel makes all to give William Haggas his second winner,
following Dupont's success in 2002, in the German version of the 2000 Guineas*

fifth to Azamour in St James's Palace Stakes at Royal Ascot: not discredited when eleventh to Somnus in Prix Maurice de Gheest at Deauville, but below form in Celebration Mile at Goodwood (edgy) final outing: stays 1m: acts on firm going: usually races prominently/makes running. *W. J. Haggas*

BRUT 2 b.g. (Mar 19) Mind Games 121 – Champenoise 64 (Forzando 122) [2004 5g 5g⁶ 5g² 6s 5s⁵ 5f⁵ p5.1g⁶ Dec 13] lengthy, good-topped gelding: modest maiden: will prove best at 5f/easy 6f: acts on firm going. *D. W. Barker* **59**

BRUT FORCE (IRE) 2 b.g. (Feb 24) Desert Style (IRE) 121 – La Foscarina (Rudimentary (USA) 118) [2004 7s p8.6g⁶ p8.6g f8g Nov 23] poor maiden. *Miss V. Haigh* **47**

BRUZELLA 5 b.m. Hernando (FR) 127 – Hills' Presidium (Presidium 124) [2004 p10g p12g Mar 8] fourth foal: half-sister to useful 1¼m winner (stays 15.5f) Saltrio (by Slip Anchor) and fairly useful 1m winner Barabaschi (by Elmaamul): dam Italian 5f (at 2 yrs) to 1m winner: last in maiden and claimer (slowly away) at Lingfield. *A. J. Lidderdale* **–**

BUBBLING FUN 3 b.f. Marju (IRE) 127 – Blushing Barada (USA) 53 (Blushing Groom (FR) 131) [2004 ?: 10d⁴ 9.9g 10f⁴ 10m³ 11.5g³ 11.9m² 10m⁶ 9.2d² 10.1m² p9.5g* p9.5g Dec 14] leggy, quite good-topped filly: fair performer: won maiden at Wolverhampton in November, first start after leaving E. Dunlop: effective at 9f to 1½m: acts on polytrack, firm and good to soft going. *T. Wall* **72**

BUCHANAN STREET (IRE) 3 b.c. Barathea (IRE) 127 – Please Believe Me 93 (Try My Best (USA) 130) [2004 ?: 8f 8f⁶ 8f⁶ 10g² 16.2m⁵ 12.1d 10g Sep 29] strong, close-coupled colt: poor maiden: left N. Callaghan after fourth start: should prove best short of 2m: acts on firm going: tried blinkered/tongue tied. *J. G. M. O'Shea* **47**

BUCKENHAM STONE 5 ch.m. Wing Park 104 – Walk That Walk 61 (Hadeer 118) [2004 –: 7s 10m f8g p10g 10.1m p12d Aug 9] leggy mare: little form. *J. Pearce* **–**

BUCKEYE WONDER (USA) 3 b.c. Silver Hawk (USA) 123 – Ameriflora (USA) (Danzig (USA)) [2004 94: 10d² 10g* 10m Jun 17] close-coupled colt: has round action: useful performer: won maiden at Sandown in June: good 5 lengths second to Ecomium in similar event at Newmarket on reappearance: close second when stumbling badly over 3f out in listed race won by Moscow Ballet at Royal Ascot (reportedly pulled muscles) final start: likely to stay 1½m: acts on good to firm and good to soft going. *M. A. Jarvis* **96**

BUCKS 7 b.g. Slip Anchor 136 – Alligram (USA) 61 (Alysheba (USA)) [2004 81: p12g 11.6d³ 12s 14.1s² 14.1d* 12m* 11.9g² 14.4g⁵ 12m 10g² 11.7m² 12.3s⁵ 14.1d⁶ 12f Sep 24] quite good-topped gelding: fairly useful handicapper: won at Nottingham in May and Newmarket (amateurs) in June: mostly creditable efforts after: effective at 1¼m to easy 2m: acts on all-weather, firm and soft going: waited with. *D. K. Ivory* **87**

BUDDY BROWN 2 b.c. (Mar 17) Lujain (USA) 119 – Rose Bay 64 (Shareef Dancer (USA) 135) [2004 7.2d* 6d² 8m 7s Oct 23] 13,000F, 13,000Y, 76,000 2-y-o: smallish, close-coupled colt: second foal: dam, maiden, who should have proved best at 1½m, out of half-sister to top-class 1m/1¼m winner Cormorant Wood, herself dam of Rock Hopper: fairly useful performer: won maiden at Ayr in June: good second in minor event at Hamilton, only other form: should stay 1m: acts on good to soft going. *J. Howard Johnson* **81**

BUDE 5 gr.g. Environment Friend 128 – Gay Da Cheen (IRE) (Tenby 125) [2004 –: p13.9g Nov 12] small gelding: maiden: tried blinkered. *S. A. Brookshaw* **–**

BUGLE CALL 4 b.g. Zamindar (USA) 116 – Petillante 101 (Petong 126) [2004 58, a–: f12g p7g f8.5s f8.5s Mar 8] tall gelding: temperamental maiden: tried blinkered/tongue tied: dead. *K. O. Cunningham-Brown* **–**

BUKIT FRASER (IRE) 3 b.g. Sri Pekan (USA) 117 – London Pride (USA) 106 (Lear Fan (USA) 130) [2004 79p: 11.1m* 11m⁴ 12g 12d 14m 14.4m⁵ 14.8d 12g Sep 22] leggy, quite good-topped gelding: fairly useful performer: won maiden at Kempton in April: best effort after when 6¼ lengths fourth to Pukka in handicap at Newbury following month: barely stays 14.4f: acts on good to firm going: tried tongue tied: often soon off bridle. *P. F. I. Cole* **89**

BULAWAYO 7 b.g. Prince Sabo 123 – Ra Ra Girl 77 (Shack (USA) 118) [2004 66: f7g⁵ f7g³ f7g f8.5s³ f8.5s f8s⁶ f7g* f6g 7m⁶ f7g⁴ f7d² f8m* f8m f8m⁴ f8f⁴ p7.1g f8g p8.6g p8g³ Dec 20] strong gelding: modest performer: won handicaps at Wolverhampton in March and Southwell (seller) in July: stays easy 8.5f: acts on all-weather, good to firm and good to soft going: tried visored, usually blinkered. *Andrew Reid* **57**

Sheikh Mohammed's "Bull Run"

BULBERRY HILL   3 b.g. Makbul 104 – Hurtleberry (IRE) 87 (Tirol 127) [2004 f8.5s **53**
f8s⁵ 7g⁵ 7g 10g p10m³ p8.6g⁵ Dec 22] modest maiden: stays easy 1¼m: acts on polytrack.
M. G. Quinlan

BULGARIA MOON   4 ch.g. Groom Dancer (USA) 128 – Gai Bulga 110 (Kris 135)   **–**
[2004 –: 14.4v 13.9m 16f 17.2g Jul 3] big gelding: little form: tried tongue tied. *C. Grant*

BULL RUN (IRE)   3 ro.c. Daylami (IRE) 138 – Bulaxie 110 (Bustino 136) [2004 10d* **119**
10.1s* Apr 21] 180,000Y: fifth foal: half-brother to smart 1m/1¼m winner Claxon (by
Caerleon) and 1¼m winner Brazen (by Singspiel): dam, won Fred Darling and Lupe
Stakes (also 7f winner at 2 yrs), half-sister to smart/very smart middle-distance performers Dust Dancer and Zimzalabim: won maiden at Windsor (by 9 lengths) and minor
event at Epsom in April: smart form when beating Bowstring most impressively by 15
lengths in 4-runner race in latter, leading 2f out and coasting clear: should stay 1½m:
looked an exciting prospect, and joined Godolphin, but reportedly injured a foreleg in
May: stays in training. *D. R. Loder*

BULLSEYE   2 b.c. (Apr 11) Polish Precedent (USA) 131 – Native Flair 87 (Be My   **–**
Native (USA) 122) [2004 7d Oct 30] robust colt: half-brother to several winners, including 1m/1¼m winner Holy Smoke (by Statoblest) and 1m (at 2 yrs) to 1¾m winner Nosey
Native (by Cyrano de Bergerac), both fairly useful: dam 1¼m/1½m winner: 50/1, well
beaten in maiden at Newmarket. *P. W. D'Arcy*

BULWARK (IRE)   2 b.c. (Mar 30) Montjeu (IRE) 137 – Bulaxie 110 (Bustino 136)   **74**
[2004 7g 8g⁴ 8v⁵ Oct 23] good-bodied colt: sixth foal: half-brother to 3 winners, including 3-y-o Bull Run and smart 1m/1¼m winner Claxon (by Caerleon): dam, won Fred
Darling and Lupe Stakes (also 7f winner at 2 yrs), half-sister to smart/very smart middle-
distance performers Dust Dancer and Zimzalabim: fair form in maidens: should be suited
by 1¼m/1½m: carried head awkwardly second start. *Mrs A. J. Perrett*

BUMPTIOUS   3 b.c. Mister Baileys 123 – Gleam of Light (IRE) 81 (Danehill (USA)   **90**
126) [2004 73: 10d³ 12.3g³ 12.1g* 14d⁴ 16.2m⁴ 14.8m³ 14.8d Aug 27] strong, close-
coupled colt: fairly useful performer: won maiden at Hamilton in May: best efforts when

fourth to Duke of Venice in Queen's Vase at Royal Ascot and third of 4 to Anousa in listed race at Newmarket fifth/sixth starts: stays 2m: acts on good to firm and good to soft going: blinkered last 3 starts. *M. H. Tompkins*

BUNDABERG 4 b.g. Komaite (USA) – Lizzy Cantle 52 (Homing 130) [2004 –: f8s4 – f7g2 f7g2 f7g3 p8.6g 8.2v f8s3 p9.5g f11g* f12g Dec 28] modest performer: won maiden **a64** at Southwell in December: stays easy 11f: form only on all-weather. *P. W. Hiatt*

BUNDITTEN (IRE) 2 gr.f. (Feb 6) Soviet Star (USA) 128 – Felicita (IRE) 97 (Cat- **92** rail (USA) 123) [2004 p5g* 5f3 5f4 5d4 5f 5s 6s6 Oct 29] 36,000Y: small, sturdy filly: second foal: dam, French 2-y-o 5.5f to 7f winner, granddaughter of 1000 Guineas winner Caergwrle: fairly useful performer: won minor event at Lingfield in March: in frame in listed races at Sandown (below form on second occasion) and Queen Mary Stakes at Royal Ascot (fourth to Damson): best at 5f: acts on polytrack and firm going: usually bandaged/early to post: often front runner: sometimes hangs right: sold 50,000 gns. *Andrew Reid*

BUNDY 8 b.g. Ezzoud (IRE) 126 – Sanctuary Cove (Habitat 134) [2004 74: 7s 6s 7.1v **71** 6m2 6m2 6g3 6g2 6m 6g4 6g4 7.2d 6d Sep 27] smallish, leggy gelding: fair performer: effective at 6f/7f: acts on heavy and good to firm going: blinkered once at 3 yrs: held up. *M. Dods*

BUNINO VEN 3 gr.g. Silver Patriarch (IRE) 125 – Plaything 69 (High Top 131) [2004 – –: p10g 10.1m4 12v 11.9g5 f12g4 May 11] good-bodied gelding: little form: tried blink- ered/visored. *S. C. Williams*

BUNKHOUSE 4 ch.g. Wolfhound (USA) 126 – Maid Welcome 81 (Mummy's Pet **49 ?** 125) [2004 6g 6g 7.1m p8g 7f 10.2s f5g f6s p6g5 p5.1g4 Dec 20] leggy gelding: poor maiden: left Miss E. Lavelle after fourth start, W. G. M. Turner after sixth: stays 6f: acts on all-weather: tried in headgear. *Mrs N. Macauley*

BUNNY RABBIT (USA) 2 b.c. (Feb 24) Cherokee Run (USA) 122 – Jane's The **97** Name (USA) (Trempolino (USA) 135) [2004 6m3 7m5 p7g4 8m 8m* Sep 21] $150,000Y: quite good-topped colt: first foal: dam unraced half-sister to US Grade 1 9f winner Joyeux Danseur and to dam of Arazi and Noverre: useful performer: improved to win nursery at Newmarket by head from Alright My Son, leading close home: stays 1m. *B. J. Meehan*

BUNYAH (IRE) 3 ch.f. Distant View (USA) 126 – Miss Mistletoes (IRE) 89 (The – Minstrel (CAN) 135) [2004 6p: p7g Mar 24] quite attractive filly: better effort in maidens when tenth at Doncaster at 2 yrs: sold 20,000 gns. *E. A. L. Dunlop*

BUREAUCRAT 2 b.g. (Mar 2) Machiavellian (USA) 123 – Lajna 88 (Be My Guest **83 p** (USA) 126) [2004 8g4 8s6 Oct 27] closely related to smart US 6f/7f performer Gold Land (earlier successful in Britain, by Gone West) and half-brother to several winners, including useful 1m/1¼m winner Ninia (by Affirmed): dam, ran twice, half-sister to very smart miler Soviet Line: better effort in maidens when promising fourth at Salisbury after slow start: favourite, went well long way at Yarmouth: not sure to stay much beyond 1m: should progress. *J. H. M. Gosden*

BURGUNDIAN (USA) 2 b.c. (Apr 10) Red Ransom (USA) – Prospectora (USA) **76** (Mr Prospector (USA)) [2004 7g4 a6g5 a7f* Dec 30] $350,000Y: well-made colt: fourth foal: closely related to useful performer up to 9f in USA Settlement (by Kris S): dam un- raced close relative to smart 6f to 1m performer Mutakddim out of half-sister to Breeders' Cup Juvenile winner Rhythm: fourth in maiden at Yarmouth (then left J. Noseda): won similar event at Nad Al Sheba in December by ¾ length from Clasp: will stay 1m: acts on dirt: blinkered second outing. *M. Al Kurdi, UAE*

BURGUNDY 7 b.g. Lycius (USA) 124 – Decant 68 (Rousillon (USA) 133) [2004 79§: **71** p10g6 p8g3 p8g4 p10g2 10.9d 10m 10m 10.1f3 10m6 8.5g* p10g* p10g* 10.1f2 8m* 10m2 10.1g5 8m4 12g6 Oct 2] smallish gelding: fair performer: won claimer at Epsom and 2 sellers at Lingfield in July and apprentice handicap at Kempton in August: effective at 1m/1¼m: acts on polytrack, firm and soft ground: usually wears headgear: usually slowly away: often hangs: held up. *P. Mitchell*

BURKEES GRAW (IRE) 3 ch.g. Fayruz 116 – Dancing Willma (IRE) (Dancing **49 §** Dissident (USA) 119) [2004 67d: f7g f5g f5g 7m 5m2 5g 5g2 f5f Aug 20] sturdy gelding: **a– §** poor handicapper: effective at 5f/6f: acts on firm going: tried visored/blinkered at 2 yrs: unreliable. *Mrs S. Lamyman*

BURLEY FIREBRAND 4 b.g. Bahamian Bounty 116 – Vallauris 94 (Faustus 118) **55** [2004 67: 10.9d 10d 10.9d Jun 18] quite good-topped gelding: modest handicapper: stays 1½m: acts on good to firm going and fibresand: visored/blinkered last 2 starts: sold 5,500 gns. *J. G. Given*

BURLEY FLAME   3 b.g. Marju (IRE) 127 – Tarsa 81 (Ballad Rock 122) [2004 60p: **88**
7.1d[4] 7d[3] 8m[3] 7.5m* 8m 8m[3] 7.5g* 8.2g[6] 7.1m 7g 8.5g p6g* 6s Nov 1] sturdy, angular
gelding: fairly useful handicapper: won at Beverley in June and July and Wolverhampton
in October: effective at 6f to 1m: acts on polytrack, good to firm and good to soft going.
J. G. Given

BURLINGTON PLACE   3 b.g. Compton Place 125 – Wandering Stranger 69 (Petong   **63**
126) [2004 68: 7g p6g 8m[2] 8f 8.1g Sep 3] leggy gelding: fair maiden: ran as if amiss last
2 starts: barely stays 1m: acts on polytrack and good to firm going. *S. Kirk*

BURN   3 ch.f. Selkirk (USA) 129 – River Cara (USA) 86 (Irish River (FR) 131) [2004   **63**
10m 9.2g[3] 8.3f 8.3f Jul 19] third foal: half-sister to 2001 2-y-o 9.4f winner Araglin (by
Sadler's Wells) and 2002 2-y-o 1m winner Ciel (by Rainbow Quest): dam French 2-y-o
1m winner: modest maiden: best effort on debut: tailed off final start: stays 1¼m: sold
5,000 gns. *M. L. W. Bell*

BURNING MOON   3 b.c. Bering 136 – Triple Green 69 (Green Desert (USA) 127)   **92**
[2004 75p: 8.1s[5] 10.1v* 12g 9.9d 10d 10g[3] Oct 11] leggy, useful-looking colt: fairly
useful performer: won minor event at Newcastle in June by 5 lengths: respectable effort
in handicaps after only when third at Windsor, edging right: should stay 1½m: acts on
heavy going: visored last 2 starts: sold 14,000 gns. *J. Noseda*

BURNING TRUTH (USA)   10 ch.g. Known Fact (USA) 135 – Galega (Sure Blade   **–**
(USA) 130) [2004 14.1g Jul 24] angular gelding: fairly useful at best: well beaten only
start since 2002: fair jumper. *M. Sheppard*

BURNLEY AL (IRE)   2 ch.g. (Apr 30) Desert King (IRE) 129 – Bold Meadows 80   **64**
(Persian Bold 123) [2004 6s[5] 6m Sep 5] 6,000Y: close-coupled gelding: half-brother to
several winners, including useful Irish performer up to 1¾m Judicial Field (by Law
Society) and fairly useful 5f (at 2 yrs) to 13f winner Field of Vision (by Vision): dam Irish
7f (at 2 yrs) and 1½m winner: green, better effort in maidens at York when fifth: should
be suited by 1¼m/1½m. *R. A. Fahey*

BURNT COPPER (IRE)   4 b.g. College Chapel 122 – Try My Rosie 93 (Try My   **60**
Best (USA) 130) [2004 65: 12f 10m* 11.7g 12.1m 9.7m p8.6d p9.5g p12.2g p12m Dec 8]   **a47**
leggy, quite good-topped gelding: modest on turf, poor on all-weather: won ladies handicap at Pontefract in July: stays 1½m: acts on polytrack, raced only on good going or
firmer on turf: tried in cheekpieces/visor: often slowly away: none too consistent.
J. R. Best

BURTON ASH   2 b. or br.f. (Apr 19) Diktat 126 – Incendio (Siberian Express (USA)   **68**
125) [2004 5d 6f[4] 6.1d[3] 7m[4] 7f 8f Sep 23] angular filly: sixth foal: half-sister to 4-y-o
Baron's Pit and winner abroad by Be My Chief: dam winning sprinter in Italy: fair
maiden: stays 7f: acts on good to firm and good to soft going. *J. G. Given*

BUSACO   2 b.c. (Apr 5) Mister Baileys 123 – War Shanty 66 (Warrshan (USA) 117)   **61**
[2004 6m 7f[4] p8g[6] Oct 31] 10,000Y: third foal: dam lightly-raced half-sister to very smart
sprinter Bold Edge: modest form in maidens: stays 1m. *J. L. Dunlop*

BUSCADOR (USA)   5 ch.g. Crafty Prospector (USA) – Fairway Flag (USA) (Fairway   **42**
Phantom (USA)) [2004 58, a78: f9.4g 10s 10d 9f 9.1d 10.3g p9.5g* p9.5g Dec 27] fair   **a78**
handicapper on all-weather, poor on turf: form in 2004 only when winning at Wolverhampton (first start for 5 months) in December: stays 1¼m: acts on all-weather, soft and
good to firm going: races prominently. *W. M. Brisbourne*

BUSHIDO (IRE)   5 br.g. Brief Truce (USA) 126 – Pheopotstown (Henbit (USA) 130)   **57**
[2004 14d[6] 12s 15.8m[2] 17.1g Oct 4] stocky gelding: fair maiden when trained by D. Weld
in Ireland at 2/3 yrs: modest form in handicaps in 2004: stays 15.8f: acts on good to firm
and good to soft going: blinkered at 3 yrs: fairly useful hurdler. *Mrs S. J. Smith*

BUSINESS MATTERS (IRE)   4 b.f. Desert Style (IRE) 121 – Hear Me (Simply   **56 ?**
Great (FR) 122) [2004 63?: p12g 10.1v 8v 8d[3] 9f[5] 9.1d Sep 16] smallish filly: modest
maiden: left H. Alexander after third start. *Miss R. Bowden, Ireland*

BUSINESS TRAVELLER (IRE)   4 ch.g. Titus Livius (FR) 115 – Dancing Venus   **–**
61 (Pursuit of Love 124) [2004 47: 16.2g Aug 30] strong, close-coupled gelding: maiden
handicapper: tailed off only start in 2004. *R. J. Price*

BUSTAN (IRE)   5 b.g. Darshaan 133 – Dazzlingly Radiant 81 (Try My Best (USA)   **110**
130) [2004 110: p10g[3] 10g[2] 10d 10.1d[4] p10g[6] Nov 20] strong, compact gelding: smart
performer: best effort in 2004 when 3 lengths second to Scott's View in listed race at
Kempton in April: effective at 1¼m/1½m: acts on polytrack and firm going: blinkered
(raced freely) third start: gelded after final outing. *M. P. Tregoning*

BUSTER HYVONEN (IRE)   2 b.c. (Apr 5) Dansili 127 – Serotina (IRE) 73 (Mtoto   **74 p**
134) [2004 f7g² Nov 23] 13,000F, 25,000Y: half-brother to several winners, including
useful 1¼m winner Serotonin (by Barathea) and fairly useful 1997 2-y-o 6f/7f winner
Alconleigh (by Pursuit of Love): dam, 9f winner, half-sister to dam of 6-y-o Keltos: 14/1,
head second to Party Boss in maiden at Southwell, green early and finishing strongly:
should stay at least 1m: sure to improve. *J. R. Fanshawe*

BUST (IRE)   2 b.c. (Mar 6) Fraam 114 – Purse 78 (Pursuit of Love 124) [2004 5m 7.1m⁶   **45**
Jun 28] €7,000F, 5,500Y: quite good-topped colt: second foal: dam, maiden who stayed
1m, out of half-sister to Grand Lodge. poor form in maidens. *T. D. Easterby*

BUSTLING RIO (IRE)   8 b.g. Up And At 'em 109 – Une Venitienne (FR) (Green   **74**
Dancer (USA) 132) [2004 72: f16.2g⁴ p16g f16s* 18v Apr 6] big, good-topped gelding:
fair handicapper: won amateur event at Southwell in February: stays 2¼m well: acts on
fibresand and firm going: tried in cheekpieces: held up, and tends to idle/hang in front.
P. C. Haslam

BUTHAINA (IRE)   4 b.f. Bahhare (USA) 122 – Haddeyah (USA) 68 (Dayjur (USA)   **–**
137) [2004 71: 8.1g 7v 8m 8.1d 10.3d 8.1g 6g Aug 6] leggy filly: little form in 2004.
T. H. Caldwell

BUYING A DREAM (IRE)   7 ch.g. Prince of Birds (USA) 121 – Cartagena Lady   **46**
(IRE) (Prince Rupert (FR) 121) [2004 f12s⁵ f11s p12g* f11m³ p12g* May 13] lengthy,
quite good-topped gelding: poor performer: won banded races at Lingfield in April and
May: stays easy 1½m: acts on all-weather, good to firm and good to soft going: sometimes blinkered. *Andrew Turnell*

BUY ON THE RED   3 b.c. Komaite (USA) – Red Rosein 97 (Red Sunset 120) [2004   **103**
71: p6g² 5s² 6m* 6m* 6g 5m² 5m 6.1g p7g* p6g² p6g⁴ p7g Dec 29] tall, quite good-
topped colt: useful performer: won maiden at Brighton and handicap at Newmarket in
May (edged right both times) and handicap at Lingfield in November: best effort when
short-head second to Chateau Nicol in handicap on last-named course next time: stays
easy 7f: acts on polytrack and good to firm going: often races prominently. *W. R. Muir*

BUZ KIRI (USA)   6 b.g. Gulch (USA) – White Corners (USA) (Caro 133) [2004 42:   **54**
p12g³ p13g² f12g* f11g² f14g² f12s* f16.2s² f12g² f12g⁶ 10.2d² 11.9g* May 4] smallish,
sturdy gelding: modest performer: won banded races at Wolverhampton in February and
March, and at Brighton in May: stays easy 2m: acts on all-weather, firm and good to soft
going: tried blinkered/visored/tongue tied. *A. W. Carroll*

BUZZ BUZZ   3 b.f. Mtoto 134 – Abuzz 101 (Absalom 128) [2004 67: 8f 10d 7s Oct   **–**
27] lengthy filly: maiden: well held in handicaps at 3 yrs. *C. E. Brittain*

BUZZ MAITE   2 b.g. (May 17) Komaite (USA) – Scotland Bay 66 (Then Again 126)   **–**
[2004 6g⁵ Jun 4] 50/1, last in maiden at Goodwood. *P. Butler*

BY DEFINITION (IRE)   6 gr. or b.m. Definite Article 121 – Miss Goodbody (Castle   **–**
Keep 121) [2004 –: f9.4g f8g p8g Feb 29] rather sparely-made mare: of little account.
J. C. Tuck

BYGONE DAYS   3 ch.g. Desert King (IRE) 129 – May Light 62 (Midyan (USA) 124)   **95**
[2004 74p: 6s* 7s³ 6m⁴ 6d⁵ 6g* 5s³ Aug 18] quite attractive gelding: useful performer:
won maiden at Kempton in March and handicap at Ripon (set strong pace and held
Inter Vision by short head) in August: respectable third to Enchantment in handicap at
York final start: will prove best at 5f/easy 6f: acts on soft and good to firm going: races
prominently. *W. J. Haggas*

BYINCHKA   4 br.g. Inchinor 119 – Bystrouska (Gorytus (USA) 132) [2004 52: f8g   **–**
Jan 8] close-coupled gelding: maiden: visored, well beaten only start in 2004: tried
blinkered. *S. L. Keightley*

BYO (IRE)   6 gr.g. Paris House 123 – Navan Royal (IRE) 61 (Dominion Royale 112)   **78**
[2004 75: p5g 5s⁶ 5s² 5s 5m* 5.3f 5.7f⁶ 6.1f⁶ 5.7f 5.7g 5.1m* 5.3f³ 5.7m⁴ 5g 5g⁴ 5g³
p5.1d² p5.1g² Nov 19] smallish, workmanlike gelding: fair performer: won apprentice
handicap at Haydock in May and claimer at Bath in July: best at 5f/easy 6f: acts on all-
weather, probably on any turf going: visored (below form) once: usually races prominently. *M. Quinn*

BYRD ISLAND   3 b.f. Turtle Island (IRE) 123 – Arusha (IRE) 84 (Dance of Life   **–**
(USA)) [2004 8g 8m 10.1g May 14] lengthy, angular filly: seventh foal: dam, 2-y-o 1m
winner, half-sister to 2000 Guineas winner Don't Forget Me: well beaten in maiden/
seller. *D. Morris*

Betfair Cup (Lennox), Goodwood—Byron has enough in hand to hold off Suggestive (blinkers) and his stable's first string Kheleyf (centre), with Naahy (rail) fourth

BYRON   3 b.c. Green Desert (USA) 127 – Gay Gallanta (USA) 112 (Woodman (USA) 126) [2004 111: 8g³ 8f 7g* 8d Aug 15] strong, medium-sized colt: good mover: smart performer: won Betfair Cup (Lennox) at Goodwood in July by ¾ length from Suggestive, quickening clear over 1f out: creditable ¾-length third to American Post in Poule d'Essai des Poulains at Longchamp on reappearance: below form in St James's Palace Stakes at Royal Ascot and Prix Jacques le Marois at Deauville: likely to prove best at 6f/7f: acts on good to firm going: has worn tongue tie/crossed noseband/had 2 handlers. *Saeed bin Suroor*   **117**

BYRON BAY   2 b.c. (Apr 16) My Best Valentine 122 – Candarela 41 (Damister (USA) 123) [2004 6g 8g 7s⁵ 7m 8s³ 7s p7g Nov 10] tall, leggy colt: modest maiden: ran poorly last 2 starts: stays 1m: best efforts on soft going. *J. J. Bridger*   **59**

C

CABIN FEVER   2 b.f. (Feb 27) Averti (IRE) 117 – Julietta Mia (USA) 72 (Woodman (USA) 126) [2004 6m 5.7m⁵ 6g 6m 8m³ Sep 25] 6,000F, €5,000Y: leggy filly: third foal: half-sister to 4-y-o Ivory Venture: dam 2-y-o 7f winner: modest maiden: looked none too keen when good third at Kempton: stays 1m. *J. C. Fox*   **61**

CABOPINO LAD (USA)   2 b.g. (May 10) Comic Strip (USA) 115 – Roxanne (USA) (Woodman (USA) 126) [2004 9f Sep 13] slowly away and always rear in maiden at Redcar. *Mrs L. Stubbs*   **–**

CACIQUE (IRE)   3 b.c. Danehill (USA) 126 – Hasili (IRE) (Kahyasi 130) [2004 7d* 8g* 9g² 10g² 9g* 10.4d⁴ 8m* Oct 2] big, good-topped colt: fifth foal: brother to high-class 1m/1¼m performer Banks Hill, high-class miler Dansili and very smart performer up to 1m Intercontinental and closely related to very smart 1m/1¼m performer Heat Haze (by Green Desert): dam French 2-y-o 5f to 8.5f winner: smart performer: won newcomers   **119 p**

Prix Daniel Wildenstein Casino Barriere La Rochelle, Longchamp—Cacique gains his second pattern-race win, holding on well from Hurricane Alan (rail) and Mister Sacha (No.8)

race at Saint-Cloud in April, minor event at Longchamp in May, Prix Daphnis at Chantilly (made all, beat Ershaad easily by 1½ lengths) in July and Prix Daniel Wildenstein Casino Barriere La Rochelle at Longchamp (beat Hurricane Alan ½ length) in October: also second to Bago in Prix Jean Prat at Chantilly and Grand Prix de Paris at Longchamp, and ran respectably when fourth of 9 to Sulamani in International Stakes at York, hanging left: stays 1¼m, at least as effective at 1m: very best form on good/good to firm ground: type to win more good races in 2005. *A. Fabre, France*

CADEAUX ROUGE (IRE)   3 ch.f. Croco Rouge (IRE) 126 – Gift of Glory (FR)   **56**
(Niniski (USA) 125) [2004 63: 11.6s⁴ 14.1s 11.8g 9.9m Jul 27] leggy filly: modest maiden handicapper: well beaten after reappearance: stays 1½m: acts on firm and soft ground. *Mrs P. N. Dutfield*

CADOGEN SQUARE   2 ch.f. (Mar 26) Takhlid (USA) 91 – Mount Park (IRE) 73   **45**
(Colonel Collins (USA) 122) [2004 5g 6d 6.1g 6m⁴ 5g 5f 7.5m f5g f5f⁵ Dec 28] smallish, strong filly: first foal: dam unreliable 5f winner: poor maiden: barely stays 7.5f: acts on good to firm going: blinkered final outing. *D. W. Chapman*

CA'D'ORO   11 ch.g. Cadeaux Genereux 131 – Palace Street (USA) 103 (Secreto (USA)   **–**
128) [2004 8.1d 8.2v⁵ Nov 4] small gelding: fair handicapper in 2000: well held both starts since. *G. B. Balding*

CADWALLADER (USA)   4 ch.g. Kingmambo (USA) 125 – Light On Your Feet   **–**
(USA) (Nijinsky (CAN) 138) [2004 49: f12g⁴ p12g⁶ p12g⁵ p16g 16m 14.1m May 25] good-topped gelding: maiden: no form in 2004: tried tongue tied/in cheekpieces. *P. Burgoyne*

CAERPHILLY GAL   4 b.f. Averti (IRE) 117 – Noble Lustre (USA) 71 (Lyphard's   **59**
Wish (FR) 124) [2004 63: 6g 7.1g 7m 7.1m 8m* 8d² 7.1d³ 8d* p8.6d 8.2v p8g Dec 20]   **a46**
modest performer: won banded races at Kempton in September and Yarmouth in October: stays 1m: acts on firm and good to soft ground: free-going sort: usually races prominently. *P. L. Gilligan*

CAESAR BEWARE (IRE)   2 b.g. (Feb 8) Daggers Drawn (USA) 114 – Red Shareef   **112**
(Marju (IRE) 127) [2004 6.1g* 6m* 6m* 6m² Oct 2] 12,000F: strong, useful-looking gelding: fluent mover: first foal: dam Italian 1m to 11f winner, including at 9f at 2 yrs: smart performer: won maiden at Chepstow in June, minor event at Windsor in August and £200000 St Leger Yearling Stakes at Doncaster (beat Distinctly Game by 2 lengths in 22-runner event) in September: reportedly had slightly sore shins after last-named: not discredited when length second to Obe Gold in listed event at Redcar: will stay 7f, probably 1m: joined M. Al Kurdi in UAE. *H. Candy*

CAFE AMERICANO   4 b.g. Labeeb 124 – Coffee Ice 92 (Primo Dominie 121) [2004   **59**
56: 7m 6.1g⁵ 7m 6m² 7.1d² 6s 8g Sep 22] modest maiden: stays 1m: acts on polytrack, firm and good to soft going: tried visored: free-going sort (has been early to post): sold 5,000 gns. *D. W. P. Arbuthnot*

CAIRNS (UAE)   3 b.f. Cadeaux Genereux 131 – Tanami 111 (Green Desert (USA) 127)   **107**
[2004 106p: 8m 8g⁶ 8m 7s⁵ Oct 23] leggy, attractive filly: useful performer: good sixth to Torrestrella in Poule d'Essai des Pouliches at Longchamp in May: off 4 months, respectable fifth to Meshaheer in minor event at Doncaster final start: stays 1m: acts on soft and good to firm going: left Godolphin. *Saeed bin Suroor*

£200000 St Leger Yearling Stakes, Doncaster—
Caesar Beware makes it a third successive win as he sprints clear of Distinctly Game,
who finishes ahead of Moscow Music and German raider Omasheriff (blinkers)

CAITLIN (IRE) 2 ch.f. (Mar 18) Intikhab (USA) 135 – Esteraad (IRE) 90 (Cadeaux **77** Genereux 131) [2004 5s⁶ f6d² f6m⁴ f7m* f7g³ 7f* 7m² 8g³ 7g Oct 2] €28,000Y: quite good-topped filly: second foal: half sister to 3-y-o Noora: dam 2-y-o 6f winner who stayed 1¼m: fair performer: won nurseries at Southwell in July and Redcar in September: stayed 1m: acted on fibresand and firm going: dead. *B. Smart*

CAKE IT EASY (IRE) 4 ch.f. Kendor (FR) 122 – Diese Memory (USA) (Diesis 133) – [2004 71: 13.1s Oct 12] leggy, quite good-topped filly: fair winner at 3 yrs: tailed off only start in 2004. *K. G. Reveley*

CALA FONS (IRE) 2 b.f. (Apr 17) Alhaarth (IRE) 126 – Lemon Tree (USA) (Zilzal **37** (USA) 137) [2004 6g 7d 8.1g 7m Oct 10] 12,000Y: leggy filly: second foal: dam 2-y-o winner in Italy: poor maiden. *N. Tinkler*

CALAMARI (IRE) 2 ch.f. (Apr 3) Desert King (IRE) 129 – Mrs Fisher (IRE) 94 **60** (Salmon Leap (USA) 131) [2004 6m 7.5d⁴ 8.2m Sep 28] heavy-topped filly: sister to 3-y-o Masafi and half-sister to 2 winners, including 6-y-o Grandma Lily: dam 7f winner, including at 2 yrs: best effort in maidens when fourth at Beverley: should stay at least 1m. *Mrs A. Duffield*

CALAMINTHA 4 b.f. Mtoto 134 – Calendula 75 (Be My Guest (USA) 126) [2004 **70** 66: 14.1s² 13.1m⁶ 18g* 16g³ 16.2g⁵ Aug 30] fair performer: made all in handicap at Chepstow in June: will stay 2½m: acts on soft and good to firm ground: races up with pace. *M. C. Pipe*

CALARA HILLS 3 ch.f. Bluegrass Prince (IRE) 110 – Atlantic Line (Capricorn Line **52** 111) [2004 51: 10g 12.6s³ 12.1g May 18] leggy filly: modest maiden: should stay 1¾m: acts on fibresand and soft ground. *W. M. Brisbourne*

CALATAGAN (IRE) 5 ch.g. Danzig Connection (USA) – Calachuchi 74 (Martinmas **73** 128) [2004 13.8g³ 9.9d* 12.1g⁵ 10d⁵ 11.9g² 10.9s 11.9g⁵ Oct 8] short-backed gelding: fair handicapper: won at Beverley in April: best at 1¼m/1½m: acts on good to firm and good to soft going, below form on soft: races freely/prominently. *J. M. Jefferson*

CALCAR (IRE) 4 b.g. Flying Spur (AUS) – Poscimur (IRE) (Prince Rupert (FR) – 121) [2004 54: f12g 12s f7g 8g Dec 12] tall gelding: well held in 2004: tried visored. *Mrs S. Lamyman*

CALCULAITE 3 b.g. Komaite (USA) – Miss Calculate 67 (Mummy's Game 120) **62** [2004 51?: 8.1m 6m⁶ 6g⁶ 6g⁴ 6d⁵ f6s 7.9m* p7g³ p9.5g⁴ 9d⁶ p8.6d³ Nov 3] modest performer: won banded event at Carlisle in September: effective at 6f to 8.6f: acts on polytrack, good to firm and good to soft ground: usually races prominently. *Mrs G. S. Rees*

CALCUTTA 8 b.h. Indian Ridge 123 – Echoing 93 (Formidable (USA) 125) [2004 **108** 109: 7d 7.9s 7m 8.1f 8f 8m² 8.1d 8m³ 8g 8.9m* 8f* 7.9g Oct 8] smallish, sturdy horse: carries condition: useful performer: won claimer at York and handicap at Doncaster (for third time) in September, beating Funfair a neck in latter: stays easy 9f: acts on dirt, firm and good to soft going: tried blinkered, not in 2004: sometimes swishes tail/looks less than keen, and usually produced late: tough. *B. W. Hills*

CALDY DANCER (IRE) 3 ch.f. Soviet Star (USA) 128 – Smile Awhile (USA) – (Woodman (USA) 126) [2004 97: 9f 8m Aug 15] useful-looking filly: has a quick action: useful performer at 2 yrs (reportedly chipped a bone in a knee final outing): well beaten in listed races in 2004: stays 7f: acts on firm going. *M. R. Channon*

CALEDONIAN (IRE) 3 b.g. Soviet Star (USA) 128 – Supercal 106 (Environment **95** Friend (IRE)) [2004 78: 7m 8g p10g² p10m⁵ Dec 22] quite good-topped gelding: useful performer, lightly raced: good efforts in handicaps at Lingfield last 2 starts: stays 1¼m: acts on polytrack. *D. R. C. Elsworth*

CALENDAR GIRL (IRE) 4 b.f. Revoque (IRE) 122 – March Fourteenth (USA) 61 – (Tricky Creek (USA)) [2004 55: f5g p5g⁶ Feb 16] maiden: well held in 2004, including in blinkers. *P. J. Makin*

CALFRAZ 2 b. or br.g. (May 12) Tamure (IRE) 125 – Pas de Chat (Relko 136) [2004 **49** 6.9m 7s Nov 1] poor form in maidens. *M. D. Hammond*

CALIBAN (IRE) 6 ch.g. Rainbows For Life (CAN) – Amour Toujours (IRE) (Law **52** Society (USA) 130) [2004 60: f14.8m 14.1m 19.1f³ 16.2g 12.6d Sep 18] lengthy gelding: modest handicapper: stays 19f: acts on fibresand and firm going: visored earlier in career: races freely: inconsistent. *Ian Williams*

CALIBRE (USA) 4 b.c. Lear Fan (USA) 130 – Carya (USA) (Northern Dancer) **96 ?** [2004 103?: 12m⁶ 13.9g Jul 10] big, strong, well-made colt: useful performer, very lightly raced: stayed 1½m: raced only on good/good to firm going: sometimes blanketed for stall entry: free-going sort: looked ungenuine: retired. *J. H. M. Gosden*

CALLED UP 3 b.g. Easycall 115 – Clued Up 63§ (Beveled (USA)) [2004 6.1s⁴ 6m 7m 6m⁵ p7g 6m⁴ 5.7g³ Oct 10] 3,500Y: lengthy, rather sparely-made gelding: first foal: dam, 1m to 1½m winner who stayed 2m, not one to trust: fair maiden: best efforts around 6f: acts on soft and good to firm going: sold 4,000 gns. *H. Candy* **66**

CALL ME MAX 2 b.g. (Mar 3) Vettori (IRE) 119 – Always Vigilant (USA) 85 (Lear Fan (USA) 130) [2004 7m⁴ 8.3m³ 7g⁵ 8.1g³ Sep 3] 20,000Y: quite attractive gelding: first foal: dam 1m winner: fair maiden: third at Windsor and Haydock: should stay 1¼m. *E. A. L. Dunlop* **79**

CALL ME SUNSHINE 4 b.f. Robellino (USA) 127 – Kirana (Niniski (USA) 125) [2004 71, a?: f9.4g* f12s f12s⁵ 12v 12m³ 14.1m May 31] compact filly: fair performer: won maiden at Wolverhampton in February: stays 1½m: acts on all-weather and good to firm going: ran well in cheekpieces final 3-y-o start: inconsistent. *P. C. Haslam* **67**

CALL OF THE WILD 4 ch.g. Wolfhound (USA) 126 – Biba (IRE) (Superlative 118) [2004 62: f1g f9.4s³ f8s³ f9.4g³ 10.9s⁶ f9.4m⁴ f8g⁴ f9.4m² 7.9f f8g Jun 28] lengthy gelding: modest maiden handicapper: stays 9.4f: acts on fibresand, firm and soft ground: often wears headgear. *R. A. Fahey* **57**

CAL MAC 5 b.g. Botanic (USA) – Shifting Mist 76 (Night Shift (USA)) [2004 92§: 8g f8.5m 8f 10f² 10.1d p10g Jul 17] smallish, quite good-topped gelding: modest performer: stays 1¼m: acts on fibresand and firm going: tried visored/in cheekpieces: usually held up: ungenuine: sold 1,600 gns, sent to Sweden. *R. M. H. Cowell* **54 §**

CALOMERIA 3 b.f. Groom Dancer (USA) 128 – Calendula 75 (Be My Guest (USA) 126) [2004 –p: 10d 10g 12.3g 12d⁴ 14.1d 16.2s³ 16.1d 18d 13.8m³ 12.6d³ Oct 9] close-coupled filly: fair maiden on Flat: stays 2m: acts on soft ground: sometimes blinkered: has run in snatches: flashes tail: joined D. McCain, fair winning form over hurdles. *R. M. Beckett* **66**

CALONNOG (IRE) 4 ch.f. Peintre Celebre (USA) 137 – Meadow Spirit (USA) (Chief's Crown (USA)) [2004 68p: 12d² 9.9g May 18] lengthy filly: very lightly-raced maiden: just modest form in 2004: will stay 1¾m. *H. R. A. Cecil* **61**

CALUKI 7 b.h. Kris 135 – Chevisaunce 75 (Fabulous Dancer (USA) 124) [2004 109: a10g* a9.5g⁴ p10g* a10.5g² a8.7f 8m 8g 8g 9.5d³ 8d⁴ Nov 23] half-brother to several winners in Italy, including 8.5f to 1½m winner Cholas (by Shirley Heights): dam, maiden, **109**

Littlewoods Bet Direct Winter Derby, Lingfield—Frankie Dettori partners Italian raider Caluki (left), who gets the better of front-running Anani and Bustan (far side)

seemed to stay 1½m: useful performer: won listed races at Cagnes-sur-Mer (by 2 lengths from Night Bokbel) in February and Lingfield (Littlewoods Bet Direct Winter Derby, by neck from Anani) in March: well below form last 6 starts: stays 10.5f: acts on polytrack/dirt, soft and good to firm going. *F. & L. Camici, Italy*

CALUSA LADY (IRE)   4 ch.f. Titus Livius (FR) 115 – Solas Abu (IRE) 82 (Red **57** Sunset 120) [2004 66: 5.7s⁵ 7m 6d² 6g 7g³ 5.7s⁴ f6g p7.1g⁴ p6g Dec 30] smallish, lengthy **a52** filly: modest maiden: effective at 6f/7f: acts on polytrack, firm and soft going: tried tongue tied/visored, not in 2004. *J. A. Geake*

CALVADOS (USA)   5 b.g. Seattle Slew (USA) – A Votre Sante (USA) 109 (Irish River **66** (FR) 131) [2004 f12s² 12v 13m May 14] lengthy, attractive gelding: fair maiden: missed 2003: blinkered, second at Wolverhampton on reappearance: stays 1½m: acts on fibresand and heavy ground: tried tongue tied. *John A. Quinn, Ireland*

CALY DANCER (IRE)   2 ch.g. (Feb 17) Entrepreneur 123 – Mountain Dancer (IRE) **87** 71 (Rainbow Quest (USA) 134) [2004 5s 5g⁵ 5g³ 6m³ 7f³ 6d* 8d⁵ Oct 14] 18,000Y: well-made gelding: has a quick action: first foal: dam, 1½m winner, out of half-sister to smart 1¼m filly Optimistic Lass: fairly useful performer: won nursery at Salisbury in August: should stay 1m: acts on firm and good to soft ground. *D. R. C. Elsworth*

CALYPSO DANCER (FR)   4 b.f. Celtic Swing 138 – Calypso Grant (IRE) 98 (Dane- **61** hill (USA) 126) [2004 6d 6g⁴ 5f² 4.5g⁴ 5s 5f 5f 5g p7g⁶ f7g p7.1g Nov 20] first foal: dam, 1m (including at 2 yrs) winner who stayed 1¼m, sister to 4-y-o Leporello: won handicap at Vichy in 2003: left R. Pritchard-Gordon in France after fifth 4-y-o start: only moderate form in Britain: seems to stay 7f: acts on polytrack, firm and soft going: tried visored: sold 8,500 gns. *T. D. Barron*

CAMACHO   2 b.c. (Feb 4) Danehill (USA) 126 – Arabesque 100 (Zafonic (USA) 130) **92 p** [2004 6g* 7m³ Sep 8] good-bodied colt: good walker: has a short, quick action: first foal: dam, 6f winner, out of Cheveley Park winner Prophecy: won maiden at Newmarket in July, always up with pace: better form when 5 lengths third of 5 to Librettist in minor event at Doncaster, not knocked about when held: will probably stay 1m: useful prospect. *H. R. A. Cecil*

CAMBERLEY (IRE)   7 b.g. Sri Pekan (USA) 117 – Nsx 74 (Roi Danzig (USA)) [2004 **98** 98: 7s² 7d⁵ 6g May 1] rangy gelding: good mover: useful handicapper: good second to Zilch at Kempton on reappearance: best at 7f: acts on firm and soft going: tried blinkered in 2001: free-going sort: sometimes finds little. *P. F. I. Cole*

CAMBERWELL   3 b.g. Royal Applause 124 – Into Orbit 63 (Safawan 118) [2004 7m* **83** 7d⁵ 7.1m 7.1m 8g 7d Oct 30] €30,000Y: first foal: dam, ran once at 2 yrs, granddaughter of smart 6f/7f winner Rocket Alert: fairly useful performer: won maiden at Salisbury in June: below form after next outing: stays 7f: acts on good to firm ground, probably on good to soft. *T. G. Mills*

CAMBO (FR)   3 b. or br.g. Mansonnien (FR) 122 – Royal Lie (FR) (Garde Royale **60** 120) [2004 10.5v 10s⁶ 12g p16g⁴ 17.2s⁵ f16s Nov 17] modest maiden: claimed from A. Hosselet in France €16,500 second start: stays 2m: acts on polytrack and soft ground. *R. Ford*

CAMERON ORCHID (IRE)   2 b.f. (Apr 27) Sri Pekan (USA) 117 – London Pride **67 p** (USA) 106 (Lear Fan (USA) 130) [2004 7d Oct 30] strong, good sort: sister to 1999 2-y-o 7f winner Pekan's Pride and 3-y-o Bukit Fraser and half-sister to German 1m winner by Shadeed: dam 1m winner and third in Fred Darling Stakes on only starts in Britain: 10/1 from 20/1, 3½ lengths ninth of 19 to Read Federica in maiden at Newmarket, leading on stand side long way then green: should stay 1m: sure to do better. *M. A. Jarvis*

CAMILLE PISSARRO (USA)   4 b.g. Red Ransom (USA) – Serenity 98 (Selkirk **–** (USA) 129) [2004 99: 8.1s 9g 10g 8v 10v Nov 4] big, strong, lengthy gelding: useful in 2003: well held at 4 yrs: tried blinkered. *D. J. Wintle*

CAMMIES FUTURE   2 gr.c. (Mar 28) Efisio 120 – Impulsive Decision (IRE) 71 **95** (Nomination 125) [2004 5s³ 6g* 5v² 6m⁶ Sep 8] 22,000Y: small, close-coupled colt: third foal: half-brother to 3-y-o Ermine Grey: dam 6f (at 2 yrs) and 1m winner: useful performer: won maiden at Doncaster in July: good efforts in listed event at Deauville (beaten ½ length by Beautifix) and sales race at Doncaster after: stays 6f: acts on heavy and good to firm going: sold 50,000 gns, sent to USA. *P. W. Chapple-Hyam*

CAMPBELLS LAD   3 b.c. Mind Games 121 – T O O Mamma's (IRE) 50 (Classic **56** Secret (USA) 91) [2004 –: f5g⁵ f7g⁴ 8.1d 8g 7.9g⁵ 12.1m³ 9.9d 9.3m² 10s⁴ p9.5d³ 8s² Oct 30] big colt: modest maiden: effective at 1m to 1½m: acts on all-weather, soft and good to firm going. *A. Berry*

CAMPBELL'S TALE (IRE) 5 gr.g. Lake Coniston (IRE) 131 – Fair Tale (USA) – (Groovy (USA)) [2004 f8f f6s Feb 2] well beaten in maiden/claimer: tried tongue tied: dead. *T. J. Fitzgerald*

CAMP COMMANDER (IRE) 5 gr.h. Pennekamp (USA) 130 – Khalatara (IRE) **104** (Kalaglow 132) [2004 110, a102: 7s 7m⁴ 8f⁵ 8.1d 8m 8g 7s 10d p7.1g* p8.6g Nov 8] **a87** rather leggy horse: fluent mover: useful on turf, fairly useful on all-weather: good efforts in Victoria Cup (won race in 2003) and Hunt Cup at Ascot second/third starts: below form after, including when winning claimer at Wolverhampton (claimed from C. Brittain £11,000) in October: effective at 7f to 9f: acts on polytrack, best turf form on good going or firmer (acts on firm): usually tongue tied: sometimes slowly away: held up. *C. R. Dore*

CAMPEON (IRE) 2 b.g. (Feb 17) Monashee Mountain (USA) 115 – Arctic Lead **69** (USA) (Arctic Tern (USA) 126) [2004 5g 5d⁵ 5g 5m⁵ 7g² 6m⁴ 6f³ 5g⁵ 6m² f6s⁴ 5d² Aug 28] €25,000Y: good-bodied gelding: sixth foal: half-brother to fairly useful Irish 2002 2-y-o 7f winner Macedonian King (by King of Kings) and French 1¼m winner Wind Draft (by Lear Fan): dam unraced: fair maiden: effective at 5f to easy 7f: acts on firm and good to soft going: visored (below form in claimer/seller) last 2 starts: sometimes races freely/wanders. *M. J. Wallace*

CAMROSE 3 ch.c. Zafonic (USA) 130 – Tularosa (In The Wings 128) [2004 89: 10d⁴ **99** 11g³ 9.9m² 11.6m⁵ 10.1g² 12g⁸ 11.8g Oct 11] good-bodied colt: useful performer: won minor event at Kempton in September by short head from Elmustanser: stays 1½m: unraced on extremes of going: carries head high. *J. L. Dunlop*

CANADIAN DANEHILL (IRE) 2 b.c. (Apr 13) Indian Danehill (IRE) 124 – San **58** Jovita (CAN) 71 (St Jovite (USA) 135) [2004 p7g p8.6d p6g p6g³ Dec 29] modest maiden: easily best effort when third at Lingfield: bred to stay at least 7f. *R. M. H. Cowell*

CANADIAN STORM 3 gr.c. With Approval (CAN) – Sheer Gold (USA) (Cutlass **69** (USA)) [2004 70: 7.1d⁵ 7g 11.8g⁴ 10f⁵ 10m* Jul 3] close-coupled colt: fair performer: made all in claimer at Leicester (claimed to join Venetia Williams £10,000) in July: stays 1¼m: acts on good to firm and good to soft going: sometimes finds little/hangs. *M. H. Tompkins*

CANARY DANCER 2 b.f. (Apr 28) Groom Dancer (USA) 128 – Bird of Time (IRE) **54 d** 75 (Persian Bold 123) [2004 6m 5g⁴ 6f² 7m 7s 7d f7g f7g Dec 14] 12,000Y: strong, lengthy filly: sixth foal: half-sister to winner in USA by Conte di Savoya: dam 7f/1m winner: modest maiden: below form after second at Pontefract: should stay 7f: acts on firm ground. *P. C. Haslam*

CANARY ISLAND (IRE) 2 b.g. (May 18) Polar Falcon (USA) 126 – Yellow Trum- **81 +** pet 75 (Petong 126) [2004 p5g* p6g Dec 30] €26,000F, €30,000Y: first foal: dam, 2-y-o 5f winner, sister to useful sprinter Petula and half-sister to 4-y-o Naahy: won maiden at Lingfield in November impressively by 1¾ lengths from Latin Express, held up pulling hard and quickening smartly: slowly away and ran wide when only seventh in nursery there: likely to prove best at 5f/6f. *D. R. C. Elsworth*

CANATRICE (IRE) 4 gr.f. Brief Truce (USA) 126 – Cantata (IRE) (Saddlers' Hall – (IRE) 126) [2004 57: 11.7s May 4] well beaten only start in 2004: often wears visor/cheekpieces. *T. D. McCarthy*

CAN CAN FLYER (IRE) 3 ch.c. In The Wings 128 – Can Can Lady 82 (Anshan **73** 119) [2004 62: 9.9d* 12.1s² 13.8g² 11.9s 12g Oct 5] tall colt: fair handicapper: won at Beverley in August: will stay 2m: raced only on fibresand and good ground or softer: sold 26,000 gns. *M. Johnston*

CANDLERIGGS (IRE) 8 ch.g. Indian Ridge 123 – Ridge Pool (IRE) 74 (Bluebird **58** (USA) 125) [2004 81: 5v 5m 5.9f 5m Jul 21] smallish, sturdy gelding: modest handicapper: best at stiff 5f/6f: acts on firm and good to soft ground. *D. Nicholls*

CANDY ANCHOR (FR) 5 b.m. Slip Anchor 136 – Kandavu 87 (Safawan 118) [2004 **47** 38: p10g² p10g f8g Jul 9] lengthy mare: poor maiden: stays 1½m: acts on polytrack, firm and good to soft going: often blinkered: tried tongue tied: none too consistent. *R. E. Peacock*

CANLIS 5 b.g. Halling (USA) 133 – Fajjoura (IRE) 84 (Fairy King (USA)) [2004 42: **53 d** 7m 8m² 7.5g 8f 12m 8d⁵ 11.9g 8m 10f 7.2s⁶ Oct 30] modest maiden: below form after second start: stays 1m: acts on good to firm going: tried blinkered/in cheekpieces: none too consistent. *D. W. Thompson*

CANNI THINKAAR (IRE) 3 b.g. Alhaarth (IRE) 126 – Cannikin (IRE) 82 (Lahib **61** (USA) 129) [2004 72: 10m⁶ 12.3g 14.1f 10d⁴ 10g p10g³ 9m Sep 12] angular gelding: modest maiden handicapper: left P. Harris after sixth start: stays 1¼m: acts on polytrack, good to firm going and good to soft ground: tried in cheekpieces. *P. Butler*

£100000 Tattersalls Autumn Auction Stakes, Newmarket—Cape Columbine makes a big impression in beating Obe Gold (No.1), Gifted Gamble (far side, noseband), Arabian Dancer (striped sleeves), Alta Petens (No.18), Diamonds And Dust (No.6) and Mary Read (hooped cap)

CANTARNA (IRE) 3 ch.f. Ashkalani (IRE) 128 – Lancea (IRE) (Generous (IRE) 139) **76** [2004 80: 8.1d² 8.1m³ 10m⁵ 8.2d* 8g⁶ 8s Oct 29] €10,500 2-y-o: rather sparely-made filly: third foal: dam unraced half-sister to very smart performer up to 1½m Riyadian out of Irish Oaks winner Knight's Baroness: fair performer: trained in 2003 by M. Halford in Ireland: well backed, won maiden at Nottingham in September: should stay 1¼m: acts on good to firm and good to soft going. *J. Mackie*

CANTEMERLE (IRE) 4 b.f. Bluebird (USA) 125 – Legally Delicious 67 (Law **58 d** Society (USA) 130) [2004 67d: 12.4s² 11.8m 12d 11.9g⁶ 16.2s 11.9g Sep 2] strong filly: modest maiden handicapper: below form after reappearance: stays 1½m: acts on soft ground: usually blinkered: none too genuine. *W. M. Brisbourne*

CANTERLOUPE (IRE) 6 b.m. Wolfhound (USA) 126 – Missed Again 84 (High **82 d** Top 131) [2004 89: f6g 6m 6g 6m 6g* 6s 6g p5.1g⁵ f6g p6g⁴ p6g⁶ p6g⁵ Dec 30] quite good-topped mare: fairly useful performer: won handicap at Goodwood in August: below form subsequently: left P. Makin 7,000 gns after seventh start: should stay 7f: acts on all-weather, good to firm and good to soft ground: tried tongue tied: sometimes steadily to post/slowly away. *C. A. Dwyer*

CANTON (IRE) 2 b.c. (Feb 1) Desert Style (IRE) 121 – Thirlmere (Cadeaux Genereux **91** 131) [2004 5s⁶ p5g* 5.1d⁴ 6g⁴ 5.2m⁵ p5g³ 5g³ 6d³ 6m Sep 8] 30,000Y: sturdy colt: fourth foal: half-brother to 2 winners, including 6-y-o Banjo Bay: dam unraced half-sister to useful 5f performer Power Lake: fairly useful performer: won maiden at Lingfield in April: third in minor events/nursery: probably stays 6f: acts on polytrack and good to firm going: reportedly found to be lame on off fore after penultimate start: sold 9,000 gns. *R. Hannon*

CANTORIS 4 b.g. Unfuwain (USA) 131 – Choir Mistress (Chief Singer 131) [2004 **–** 65: 17.2f Jun 12] strong gelding: maiden: blinkered (well held) only start in 2004. *C. L. Popham*

CANTRIP 4 b.f. Celtic Swing 138 – Circe 73 (Main Reef 126) [2004 74, a?: p16g p12g **58** 11.9m 11.6m 12m* 14m³ 14.4m p16d 12f⁵ p16g 16g⁵ Sep 30] sparely-made filly: modest performer: won handicap at Folkestone in June: stays 1¾m: acts on good to firm ground, well held on polytrack: tried blinkered/tongue tied: often makes running: none too consistent. *Miss B. Sanders*

CAONA (USA) 2 b.f. (Mar 6) Miswaki (USA) 124 – Hawzah (Green Desert (USA) **69** 127) [2004 6m 6m⁵ 6d p7g p7.1g* Dec 15] 170,000Y: strong, lengthy filly: fourth foal: half-sister to minor winner in USA by Devil's Bag: dam unraced sister to smart performer

188

up to 1½m Fahim: fair performer: wearing cheekpieces, made all in nursery at Wolverhampton, best effort: stays 7f: acts on polytrack. *J. Noseda*

CAPABLE GUEST (IRE) 2 b. or br.c. (Mar 25) Cape Cross (IRE) 129 – Alexander **109**
Confranc (IRE) 73 (Magical Wonder (USA) 125) [2004 6s³ 6m³ 6f³ 7m² 7m* 7d⁴ 8m³
8d⁴ Sep 18] 130,000Y: rather leggy, attractive colt: second foal: half-brother to 3-y-o
Petardias Magic: dam Irish 2-y-o 7f winner: useful performer: third in Coventry Stakes
at Royal Ascot: won maiden at Leicester in August: very good close fourth to Helios
Quercus in Prix des Chenes at Longchamp final start: stays 1m: acts on firm and soft
ground. *M. R. Channon*

CAPE CANAVERAL (IRE) 5 b.g. Sadler's Wells (USA) 132 – Emmaline (USA) **–**
(Affirmed (USA)) [2004 p12g Feb 18] fairly useful form when second in maiden at
Leopardstown at 3 yrs for A. O'Brien: well beaten only Flat outing since: winning hurdler
in between. *G. L. Moore*

CAPE COLUMBINE 2 b.f. (Jan 31) Diktat 126 – Cape Merino 103 (Clantime 101) **99 P**
[2004 6g² 6d* Oct 14] 11,000Y, resold 33,000Y: big, lengthy filly: has scope: third foal:
half-sister to 6-y-o Cape of Good Hope and 4-y-o Cape St Vincent: dam 5f/6f winner,
including at 2 yrs: promising second in maiden at Goodwood: joint favourite and bandaged behind, won 29-runner £100000 Tattersalls Autumn Auction Stakes at Newmarket
impressively by 2 lengths from Obe Gold, storming through from poor position to lead
over 1f out: will stay 7f, probably 1m: potentially smart, and should win more races.
D. R. C. Elsworth

Mrs R. F. Lowe's "Cape Columbine"

CAPE ENTERPRISE (USA)   2 b.c. (Apr 22) Cape Canaveral (USA) 115 – Princip-   **70**
essa (USA) (Alydeed (CAN) 120) [2004 p7g p7.1d³ p7.1g³ Nov 27] $35,000F, $60,000Y:
second foal: dam unraced half-sister to US Grade 2 1m winner She Can: fair form when
third in maidens at Wolverhampton: should stay 1m. *J. W. Hills*

CAPE FEAR   3 b.c. Cape Cross (IRE) 129 – Only In Dreams 78 (Polar Falcon (USA)   **103**
126) [2004 110: 7s 8d 6s⁵ Nov 6] lengthy colt: useful performer: creditable efforts last 2
starts, including when fifth to Quito in listed race at Doncaster: stays 7f: acts on soft and
good to firm going. *B. J. Meehan*

CAPE GREKO   2 ro. or gr.c. (Apr 22) Loup Sauvage (USA) 125 – Onefortheditch   **102**
(USA) 79 (With Approval (CAN)) [2004 7g² 7g* Jul 10] 5,000F, 35,000Y: tall colt: has
scope: third foal: half-brother to 4-y-o Morning After and 3-y-o Royal Prince: dam 1m/
1¼m winner: neck second to Perfectperformance in maiden at Salisbury: won minor
event at Ascot by ¾ length from Berkhamsted: fractured a knee after: will stay at least
1m: useful. *A. M. Balding*

CAPE OF GOOD HOPE   6 ch.g. Inchinor 119 – Cape Merino 103 (Clantime 101)   **116**
[2004 121: 7m⁶ 5m³ 5m² 6m² 5f² 6f³ 6g⁴ 6s³ 5m⁴ 5m² Dec 12] big, strong, lengthy
gelding: trained by D. Elsworth at 3 yrs: has made into a smart performer in Hong Kong,
successful 4 times in 2002, but hasn't won since: several good placed efforts behind Silent
Witness at Sha Tin in 2004, including when beaten easy 1¾ lengths in Hong Kong Sprint
final start: also ran well all 4 starts outside Hong Kong when 1½ lengths second to The
Tatling in King's Stand Stakes, 2 heads third to Fayr Jag in Golden Jubilee Stakes (got
behind after stumbling leaving stall), both at Royal Ascot, 2½ lengths fourth to Frizzante
in July Cup at Newmarket and 4¼ lengths third to Calstone Light O in Sprinters Stakes at
Nakayama fifth to eighth outings: best at 5f/6f: acts on any ground: visored/tongue tied:
held up: tough. *D. Oughton, Hong Kong*

CAPE QUEST   2 b.c. (Mar 10) Piccolo 121 – Belle Vue 78 (Petong 126) [2004 7m 6f³   **85**
6g* 7f Sep 11] 28,000Y, 35,000 2-y-o: useful-looking colt: third living foal: half-brother
to 6f/7f winner (including at 2 yrs) It Was Meant To Be (by Distant Relative): dam 6f
winner from 2 starts at 2 yrs: fairly useful performer: easily best effort when winning
maiden at Salisbury in August by ¾ length from Nota Bene, making all: likely to prove
best at 5f/6f: joined D. Watson in UAE. *R. Hannon*

CAPER   4 b.g. Salse (USA) 128 – Spinning Mouse 65 (Bustino 136) [2004 51: 14.1f   **–**
f14g 11.9g 15.8m p12.2d Oct 23] smallish, good-topped gelding: maiden: well beaten in
2004. *R. Hollinshead*

CAPE ROYAL   4 b.g. Prince Sabo 123 – Indigo 86 (Primo Dominie 121) [2004 90: 5g   **96**
5g⁶ 5s* 5.1d 5s⁶ 5m 5.1d² 5d 5g³ 5.2f² 5g Aug 7] good-bodied gelding: useful handicapper: won at Epsom in May: good efforts after when placed: best at bare 5f: acts on firm
and soft ground: sometimes slowly away, and usually held up: unseated rider to post fifth
start: sold 21,000 gns. *Mrs J. R. Ramsden*

CAPESTAR (IRE)   3 b.f. Cape Cross (IRE) 129 – Sedulous 107 (Tap On Wood 130)   **78**
[2004 7g⁶ 7s² 8m* 7m⁴ Jun 26] €110,000Y: sturdy, close-coupled filly: half-sister to
several winners, including useful 6f/7f winner Indaba (by Indian Ridge) and useful 1m
winner So Sedulous (by The Minstrel), latter dam of 3-y-o Shirocco: dam, Irish 2-y-o 5f
to 1m winner, later successful in USA: fair performer: won maiden at Kempton in
May: found little final start: effective at 7f/1m: acts on soft and good to firm ground.
B. G. Powell

CAPE ST VINCENT   4 gr.g. Paris House 123 – Cape Merino 103 (Clantime 101)   **83**
[2004 78p: 6.1s f6m* 5.5m² 6g 6m p6g² p6g⁴ p7.1g³ Dec 20] fairly useful handicapper:
won at Wolverhampton in May: effective at 5.5f to easy 7f: acts on all-weather and firm
going, well held on soft: visored last 7 starts: sometimes slowly away. *H. Morrison*

CAPETOWN GIRL   3 b.f. Danzero (AUS) – Cavernista 75 (Lion Cavern (USA)   **68 d**
117) [2004 71: 6v* 8.1d 7m 7.2g 6.9g 6m 7.2s 7g Sep 20] lengthy filly: fair performer:
well below form after winning maiden at Pontefract in April: stays 7f: acts on good to
firm and heavy going: tried in cheekpieces/visor. *K. R. Burke*

CAPE UNKNOWN (USA)   2 b. or br.g. (Mar 14) Cape Canaveral (USA) 115 –   **59 p**
Danyross (IRE) 99 (Danehill (USA) 126) [2004 p7m⁶ Dec 22] $5,000F, €55,000Y: third
foal: half-brother to 3-y-o Inescapable: dam, Irish 2-y-o 5f winner, later successful in
USA: 7/2, 3¼ lengths sixth of 13 to Resplendent Prince in maiden at Lingfield, very
green, refusing to settle and hanging in straight: should do better. *G. A. Butler*

CAPE VINCENT   3 b.c. Cape Cross (IRE) 129 – Samhat Mtoto 64 (Mtoto 134) [2004   **90**
92p: 7d* 9s⁵ Aug 27] strong, lengthy colt: fairly useful performer: off 11 months, landed

odds in maiden at Salisbury in August by 4 lengths from Patterdale: well-backed favourite, ran as if amiss in handicap at Goodwood next time: stays 1m: raced only on ground softer than good. *J. H. M. Gosden*

CAPITOLE (IRE)   3 b.g. Imperial Ballet (IRE) 110 – Blue Glass 58 (Ardkinglass   **65**
114) [2004 8m 10m⁴ 8d⁵ 8g⁴ 8.5m 13.8v³ Oct 16] IR 25,000F, €100,000Y: first foal: dam, 2-y-o 8.5f seller winner, half-sister to useful 7f to 1¼m winner K-Battery: fair maiden: trained by A. Stewart first 2 starts: stays 1¾m: acts on good to firm and heavy going: tried visored: sold 15,000 gns. *E. F. Vaughan*

CAPPED FOR VICTORY (USA)   3 b.c. Red Ransom (USA) – Nazoo (IRE) 99   **89**
(Nijinsky (CAN) 138) [2004 102: 8d² 8.1m 7m Jul 24] good-topped colt: fairly useful maiden: best 3-y-o effort when seventh to Gatwick in valuable handicap at Haydock second start: unraced on extremes of going: races prominently/freely: sold 23,000 gns in October, resold 16,000 gns in November. *Sir Michael Stoute*

CAPRICHO (IRE)   7 gr.g. Lake Coniston (IRE) 131 – Star Spectacle (Spectacular   **103**
Bid (USA)) [2004 116: 6g 6g⁴ 7m 7f 7s 6g 6s 6f⁶ 6d Oct 15] tall, useful-looking gelding: just useful form in 2004: effective at 6f/7f: acts on firm and soft going: has been bandaged hind joints: sometimes finds little. *J. Akehurst*

CAPTAIN CLIPPER   4 b.g. Royal Applause 124 – Collide 102 (High Line 125) [2004   **83**
79: 10.1v³ 12s* 11.9s May 11] good-bodied gelding: fairly useful performer: won minor event at Thirsk in April: stays 1½m: acts on heavy and good to firm going: usually held up. *D. Nicholls*

CAPTAIN CLOUDY   4 b.g. Whittingham (IRE) 104 – Money Supply (Brigadier   **58**
Gerard 144) [2004 69: p7g⁵ p8g⁶ p7g⁶ 5.3m 5.1m 7f³ 8m 6.1g⁴ 7.1m 8g⁴ p7m Nov 22] leggy, good-topped gelding: modest maiden: stays 1m: acts on polytrack, soft and good to firm ground: tried visored, not in 2004. *M. Madgwick*

CAPTAIN CRUSOE   6 b.g. Selkirk (USA) 129 – Desert Girl (Green Desert (USA)   **63**
127) [2004 f11g³ p12g Mar 24] strong gelding: maiden: missed 2003: just modest in 2004, finishing lame final start: stays 1½m: acts on all-weather and good to firm ground: tongue tied (well held) once. *P. Howling*

CAPTAIN DARLING (IRE)   4 b.g. Pennekamp (USA) 130 – Gale Warning (IRE)   **70**
(Last Tycoon 131) [2004 72: f7s⁶ p10g 7d² 8s 8m 7m⁵ 6f p7g f7s⁶ p8.6g⁵ f8g f7g p8.6g³ f8g p7g² Dec 30] big gelding: fair performer: stays 8.6f: acts on all-weather, firm and good to soft ground: often wears headgear: tried tongue tied: often slowly away: none too consistent. *R. M. H. Cowell*

CAPTAIN FEARLESS   3 ch.g. Defacto (USA) – Madam Poppy (Risk Me (FR) 127)   **–**
[2004 f8g p10g 10.1m⁶ Apr 12] no sign of ability. *Mrs C. A. Dunnett*

CAPTAIN HURRICANE   2 b.c. (Feb 11) Desert Style (IRE) 121 – Ravine 81 (Indian   **110**
Ridge 123) [2004 6f² 6g² 6m* 6s⁴ 6m Sep 8] 21,000Y: leggy colt: first foal: dam, 6f/7f winner, half-sister to 1000 Guineas second Niche: smart performer: much improved to

TNT July Stakes, Newmarket—Captain Hurricane (nearest camera) leads close home to beat Royal Ascot runners-up Council Member and Mystical Land

win TNT July Stakes at Newmarket in July by short head from Council Member, quickening to lead near finish despite edging left: respectable fourth to Divine Proportions in Prix Morny at Deauville, better effort after: reportedly finished sore final start: will probably stay 7f: acts on good to firm going: sometimes races freely: held up. *P. W. Chapple-Hyam*

CAPTAIN JOHNNO (IRE)   2 b.g. (Feb 3) Tagula (IRE) 116 – Thornby Park 94   **78** (Unfuwain (USA) 131) [2004 7d 6d³ 5m³ p6g* Oct 19] 8,500F, 20,000Y: big, lengthy gelding: first foal: dam 1¾m winner: fair performer: won maiden at Wolverhampton by 2½ lengths from Mambazo: needs to settle to stay beyond 6f: acts on polytrack, good to firm and good to soft ground: blinkered/visored after debut. *D. R. Loder*

CAPTAIN MARGARET   2 b.f. (Apr 20) Royal Applause 124 – Go For Red (IRE)   **62** (Thatching 131) [2004 6g 7m⁵ 7.1g 8g 7m³ 8d Nov 5] 13,000Y: well-made filly: seventh foal: half-sister to useful 1m (at 2 yrs) winner Primary Colours and 1¼m winner Pinot Noir (both by Saddlers' Hall): dam unraced: modest maiden: should stay 1m: best efforts on good to firm going: tongue tied after debut, also wore cheekpieces fourth start. *J. Pearce*

CAPTAIN MARRYAT   3 ch.g. Inchinor 119 – Finlaggan 83 (Be My Chief (USA) 122)   **67** [2004 –p: 8g² 8v 8m² 8.2g² 8.3m³ 10.5g² 10.2m³ p12.2g² p12.2g⁴ Nov 11] useful-looking gelding: fair maiden: left P. Harris 25,000 gns after eighth start: stays 1m: acts on polytrack and good to firm going, well held on heavy: difficult ride. *J. Akehurst*

CAPTAIN MILLER   8 b.g. Batshoof 122 – Miller's Gait 74§ (Mill Reef (USA) 141)   **77** [2004 13.9s² 12g² 14.8d Aug 27] leggy gelding: fair handicapper, very lightly raced: stays 2m: acts on any going: tongue tied (raced freely, well held) final outing. *N. J. Henderson*

CAPTAIN SAIF   4 b.c. Compton Place 125 – Bahawir Pour (USA) (Green Dancer   **65** (USA) 132) [2004 95: 8g 7m 8d 8.5g⁴ 7g³ 7.5m 10s Nov 1] tall, leggy colt: just fair performer in 2004: left R. Hannon after fifth start: stays 1m: acts on good to firm ground: tried blinkered/tongue tied: carries head high. *N. Wilson*

CARA BELLA   3 ch.f. Seeking The Gold (USA) – Cherokee Rose (IRE) 122 (Dancing   **80** Brave (USA) 140) [2004 7s: 7g 8.1s⁵ 7m³ 7m⁶ Jul 1] close-coupled filly: fairly useful maiden: reportedly fractured pelvis after debut at 2 yrs: good third in handicap at Newmarket: should stay 1m: acts on good to firm ground, well held on soft: sent to Australia. *D. R. Loder*

CARACARA (IRE)   3 ch.f. Nashwan (USA) 135 – Vivid Imagination (USA) (Raise   **–** A Man (USA)) [2004 88p: 10.4s May 11] tall, angular filly: easy mover with a round action: fairly useful winner at 2 yrs: tailed off in handicap at York only 3-y-o start: should stay at least 1m: acts on good to firm going: sold 15,000 gns, sent to USA. *M. Johnston*

CARADAK (IRE)   3 b.c. Desert Style (IRE) 121 – Caraiyma (IRE) 84 (Shahrastani   **113** (USA) 135) [2004 8d⁴ 7m* 8f* 8g³ 7s⁶ Oct 16] useful-looking colt: fourth foal: half-brother to useful Irish 6f winner Carallia (by Common Grounds): dam, Irish 9f winner, sister to smart Irish middle-distance performer Cajarian: smart performer: won maiden at Galway in July and listed race at Cork (by 1½ lengths from One More Round) in August: not knocked about after showing up well long way when sixth of 12 to Firebreak in Challenge Stakes at Newmarket final start: stays 1m: acts on firm going. *J. Oxx, Ireland*

CARA DILIS (USA)   3 b.f. El Prado (IRE) 119 – Runexample (USA) (Runaway   **–** Groom (CAN)) [2004 8m 7g 10m 8g 9.6d 10g f16s Nov 17] first foal: dam unraced half-sister to Intikhab: little form: left M. Gunn in Ireland after sixth start: will prove best short of 2m: tried blinkered. *P. A. Blockley*

CARA FANTASY (IRE)   4 b.f. Sadler's Wells (USA) 132 – Gay Fantasy (Troy 137)   **84** [2004 81: 14s⁴ 14g 14.8g² Jul 17] rather leggy, lengthy filly: fairly useful handicapper: stays 14.8f: acts on firm and soft ground: sent to USA. *J. L. Dunlop*

CARA SPOSA (IRE)   2 b.c. (Apr 28) Lend A Hand 124 – Charlton Spring (IRE) 70   **–** (Masterclass (USA) 116) [2004 6s Oct 29] €6,000Y: lightly-made colt: second foal: dam, 6f (at 2 yrs) to 8.5f (in Ireland) winner, out of half-sister to smart sprinter Perion: 40/1, tailed off in maiden at Newmarket, very green and slowly away. *Mrs Stef Liddiard*

CARDINAL VENTURE (IRE)   6 b.g. Bishop of Cashel 122 – Phoenix Venture   **98** (IRE) 69 (Thatching 131) [2004 96, a103: f7s² 8g 7d 7.6d 6d* 6f 6s 6g 7d⁴ p7g Nov 20] big, strong, close-coupled gelding: useful handicapper: easy winner at Haydock in June: probably best at 6f/7f nowadays: acts on fibresand, firm and good to soft going: tried in cheekpieces/blinkers, not in 2004: often makes running. *K. A. Ryan*

Vodafone 'Dash' Stakes (Handicap), Epsom—just over a length
separates the first eight home as Caribbean Coral (No.5) arrives fast and late for victory;
Plateau (diamonds on body) also finishes strongly for second ahead of Tychy (No.7), Texas Gold (epaulets),
Watching (centre), Corridor Creeper (spots on cap), Whitbarrow (far side) and Talbot Avenue (spots)

CARGO   5 b.g. Emarati (USA) 74 – Portvasco 90 (Sharpo 132) [2004 63: p6g p6g⁴ **59** p6g² p6g p7g² f6m³ 7m² 8.1f 6.1s 7m² 6f² 8m 6m 6d² p5.1g* f5g* f5g Dec 1] angular gelding: modest performer: left H. Collingridge after second start, D. Flood after fourth: won banded races at Wolverhampton in October and Southwell in November: effective at 5f to easy 7f: acts on all-weather, firm and soft ground: usually wears headgear/tongue strap: sometimes races freely/finds little. *B. A. Pearce*

CARIBBEAN BLUE   3 b.f. First Trump 118 – Something Blue (Petong 126) [2004 **–** 61: 6m⁵ 7m 6s 6m 6g 6d Oct 16] rather leggy filly: little form in 2004: visored/blinkered last 2 starts. *R. M. Whitaker*

CARIBBEAN CORAL   5 ch.g. Brief Truce (USA) 126 – Caribbean Star 81 (Soviet **106** Star (USA) 128) [2004 96: 5g 5d² 5m* 5d* 6m 5d 5m³ 5.2g 5m⁴ 5d⁴ 5s Oct 23] strong, good sort: useful performer: won handicaps at Epsom (Vodafone 'Dash', by short head from Plateau) and Newcastle (Northern Rock Gosforth Park Cup, by ¾ length from Corridor Creeper) in June: in frame after in listed race at Doncaster (third to Celtic Mill) and handicaps at Epsom and Newmarket: best at 5f: acts on firm and good to soft ground, well held on soft: waited with. *J. J. Quinn*

CARIBBEAN DANCER (USA)   2 b.f. (Feb 10) Theatrical 128 – Enticed (USA) **70** (Stage Door Johnny (USA)) [2004 7.5d 8f 9d² 8d Nov 5] $55,000Y: good-topped filly: half-sister to several winners in USA, including minor stakes winners by Vice Regent and Lord At War: dam minor stakes winner in USA up to 8.5f: fair maiden: second at Musselburgh: will be suited by 1¼m/1½m: acts on good to soft going. *M. Johnston*

CARIBBEAN DIAMOND (IRE)   2 b.f. (Feb 14) Imperial Ballet (IRE) 110 – Bebe **–** Auction (IRE) (Auction Ring (USA) 123) [2004 8f Aug 5] €5,500F, €5,000Y: sixth foal: half-sister to 2 winners, including 5-y-o Bid Spotter: dam unraced: 66/1, well held in maiden at Yarmouth. *I. A. Wood*

CARIBE (FR)   5 b.g. Octagonal (NZ) 126 – Caring Society 65 (Caerleon (USA) 132) **–** [2004 8s⁶ 7.2f 6m f6d f7m Jul 12] leggy, good-topped gelding: winner of 4 races in Spain, including handicap at Mijas in 2003 for P. Haley: well held all starts in Britain. *A. Berry*

CARINI   3 b.f. Vettori (IRE) 119 – Secret Waters 100 (Pharly (FR) 130) [2004 97p: **94** 9.9g³ 12g⁶ 10m³ 10.1s 12d⁵ Oct 10] smallish, sparely-made filly: fairly useful performer:

third in listed race at Goodwood (beaten 6¼ lengths by Halicardia) and minor event at Newmarket (2½ lengths behind Corriolanus): stays 1½m: acts on good to firm ground, below form on softer than good: sold 40,000 gns, sent to USA. *H. Candy*

CARK 6 b.g. Farfelu 103 – Precious Girl 76 (Precious Metal 106) [2004 56§, a47§: f5g⁶ f5g* p5g² f5s f5s f5g 5v May 4] sturdy gelding: modest performer: won seller at Southwell in January: trained by J. Jay fourth and fifth starts only: best at 5f: acts on fibresand and any turf going: tried visored (pulled too hard): often wears cheekpieces: races prominently: sometimes idles/wanders: unreliable. *J. Balding*   **54 §**

CARLA MOON 3 b.f. Desert Prince (IRE) 130 – Khambani (IRE) 80 (Royal Academy (USA) 130) [2004 68?: 7g 6m 10.1m 7f Aug 5] well-made filly: little form in 2004: sent to Italy. *C. F. Wall*   **–**

CARLBURG (IRE) 3 b.g. Barathea (IRE) 127 – Ichnusa 83 (Bay Express 132) [2004 75: 11g 7g 7m p8g p8.6g Oct 9] smallish, close-coupled gelding: maiden: little form in 2004: tried blinkered. *C. E. Brittain*   **–**

CARLTON (IRE) 10 ch.g. Thatching 131 – Hooray Lady 92 (Ahonoora 122) [2004 76, a69: p7g p6g⁴ f7s⁴ p6g 6d² 7m⁴ f7g⁵ 6v² 6s² 6.1v² 7s f7g 7.5g⁵ 7d 6d 7.5d Aug 28] sturdy gelding: fair handicapper: effective at 6f/7f: acts on all-weather and any turf going: usually blinkered before 2000, visored once. *C. R. Dore*   **65 a63**

CARLYS QUEST 10 ch.g. Primo Dominie 121 – Tuppy (USA) (Sharpen Up 127) [2004 20f Jun 15] leggy gelding: very lightly raced on Flat since 2001, well beaten in Ascot Stakes only 10-y-o start: usually wears blinkers/visor/tongue strap. *Ferdy Murphy*   **–**

CARMANIA (IRE) 2 b.g. (Mar 30) Desert Sun 120 – Scatter Brain (Risk Me (FR) 127) [2004 6g 5.1g⁵ 5s 5g 5f p5.1g f8d³ Dec 21] compact gelding: poor maiden: seems to stay 1m: acts on fibresand. *R. P. Elliott*   **48**

CARMARTHEN BELLE 4 b.f. Merdon Melody 98 – Woodland Steps 86 (Bold Owl 101) [2004 6d 8d p7.1g⁶ Dec 11] leggy filly: fourth foal: sister to 3 winners, including 3-y-o Platinum Pirate: dam 2-y-o 7f winner: well held in maidens/claimer. *Miss L. C. Siddall*   **–**

CARNIVORE 2 ch.c. (May 20) Zafonic (USA) 130 – Ermine (IRE) 86 (Cadeaux Genereux 131) [2004 5m² Jul 31] 58,000Y: second foal: half-brother to 3-y-o Hoh Bleu Dee: dam, 1m winner, half-sister to very smart 1¼m/1½m winner Border Arrow: 11/2, 2½ lengths second to Turnaround in maiden at Thirsk, late headway not knocked about: should stay 1m: will do better. *T. D. Barron*   **67 p**

CARNT SPELL 3 b.g. Wizard King 122 – Forever Shineing 62 (Glint of Gold 128) [2004 –: 8.1s Sep 24] well-made gelding: no form. *Ms Deborah J. Evans*   **–**

CAROLS CHOICE 7 ch.m. Emarati (USA) 74 – Lucky Song 91 (Lucky Wednesday 124) [2004 –, a56d: f6g⁶ f5g⁵ f5g Jan 12] poor performer: best at 5f: acts on fibresand, firm and good to soft ground: tried in headgear, not in 2004. *A. Sadik*   **– a39**

CARONTE (IRE) 4 b.g. Sesaro (USA) 81 – Go Likecrazy 51 (Dowsing (USA) 124) [2004 54: f7g f5g f6s f7g p7g f5g* f6g f5m 5m May 17] sturdy gelding: poor performer: won banded race at Southwell in March: effective at 5f to 1m: acts on fibresand, firm and good to soft going: wears blinkers/cheekpieces: tried tongue tied, not in 2004: inconsistent. *S. R. Bowring*   **41 §**

CAROUBIER (IRE) 4 ch.g. Woodborough (USA) 112 – Patsy Grimes 95 (Beveled (USA)) [2004 75, a84: f9.4g⁵ f9.4g² f8g* f8.5s² p8g 8.3d* 10g 8g 10m 7.9g f12m⁶ 12.6g 10m p8.6g p9.5g⁴ p9.5g⁴ Dec 27] close-coupled gelding: fairly useful performer: won claimer at Southwell (claimed from T. D. Barron) in February and handicap at Windsor in April: below form after: effective at 1m to 11f: acts on all-weather, firm and good to soft going: tried blinkered/visored: often slowly away, and usually held up: none too consistent. *J. Gallagher*   **84 d**

CARRIACOU 3 b.f. Mark of Esteem (IRE) 137 – Cockatoo Island 99 (High Top 131) [2004 85, a69: 9g⁶ f8.5g⁴ 7s⁵ 8g 7g⁵ 10.1m³ 10.1g 9s⁴ 10d 11.7g³ p12.2g 12s⁶ f12g Nov 22] rather leggy, useful-looking filly: fair maiden: ran poorly last 3 starts: stays 11.7f: acts on fibresand, soft and good to firm going: often races freely: held up. *P. W. D'Arcy*   **73 a68**

CARRIZO CREEK (IRE) 3 b.c. Charnwood Forest (IRE) 125 – Violet Spring (IRE) 32 (Exactly Sharp (USA) 121) [2004 106: 7g 7g Aug 14] useful-looking colt: useful performer: much better effort in 2004 when seventh to Chic in Hungerford Stakes at Newbury second start: free-going sort, likely to prove better at 6f than 7f: best efforts on good ground: sent to Hong Kong. *B. J. Meehan*   **104**

Enter The £1 Million totetentofollow November Stakes (Handicap), Doncaster—
Kieren Fallon may have lost the Jockeys' Association championship, but he wins the last big race of
the turf season on Carte Diamond ahead of main rival Frankie Dettori on Distant Prospect (noseband)
with Bendarshaan and Jeepstar third and fourth

CARROWDORE (IRE) 4 b.c. Danehill (USA) 126 – Euromill (Shirley Heights 130) **77**
[2004 85: p12g² 12m⁴ 13.3m³ 14.8m⁴ 10.1m² 11.5m² 10m⁴ 11.5g³ 12g⁴ Oct 2] small,
strong, well-made colt: fair performer: left R. Hannon after reappearance: trained next 4
starts by C. Allen: effective at 1¼m and stays 14.8f: acts on firm ground and polytrack:
effective with or without cheekpieces: consistent. *G. A. Huffer*

CARRY ON DOC 3 b.c. Dr Devious (IRE) 127 – Florentynna Bay 61 (Aragon 118) **86**
[2004 74: f7g³ 8f⁶ 8g* 7f⁵ 7f³ 8.5g* 8.5g 8.5g Oct 2] compact colt: fairly useful performer: won maiden at Brighton in July and handicap at Epsom in August, best effort when
beating Compton Drake by 1¾ lengths in latter: stays 8.5f: raced only on fibresand/good
going or firmer: free-going sort. *J. W. Hills*

CARRY ON KATIE (USA) 3 br.f. Fasliyev (USA) 120 – Dinka Raja (USA) (Wood- **108**
man (USA) 126) [2004 109p: 8m⁶ 8g May 16] good-topped filly: useful performer: won
Lowther Stakes at York and Cheveley Park Stakes at Newmarket at 2 yrs for J. Noseda:
creditable 3 lengths sixth to Attraction in 1000 Guineas at Newmarket: only ninth to
Torrestrella in Poule d'Essai des Pouliches at Longchamp next time: stays 1m: raced only
on good/good to firm ground: nervy sort: wears crossed noseband: taken separately to
post: left Godolphin. *Saeed bin Suroor*

CARTE DIAMOND (USA) 3 ch.c. Theatrical 128 – Liteup My Life (USA) (Green **111**
Dancer (USA) 132) [2004 11g* 11.9d* 14g² 11.8g³ 12s* Nov 6] $25,000Y: tall colt: fifth
foal: half-brother to a winner in USA by Storm Cat: dam, won in USA, half-sister to
top-class 1¼m/1½m performer Royal Anthem and high-class US Grade 1 1m/9f winner
Sharp Cat: smart performer, lightly raced: won maiden at Redcar in June and handicap
at York in July: left M. Johnston 105,000 gns, best effort when beating Distant Prospect
2½ lengths in Enter The £1 Million totetentofollow November Stakes (Handicap) at
Doncaster final start: effective at 1½m/1¾m: raced only on good going or softer: races
prominently: won over hurdles in November. *B. Ellison*

CARTE NOIRE 3 b.f. Revoque (IRE) 122 – Coffee Cream 87 (Common Grounds **55**
118) [2004 65: 8g⁵ 7m* f7g 8.3f 7m 8m Sep 23] workmanlike filly: modest performer:
won maiden at Thirsk in June: stays 1m: acts on good to firm ground: tried in cheekpieces. *J. G. Portman*

CARTE ROYALE 2 ch.g. (Feb 10) Loup Sauvage (USA) 125 – Noble One 107 **89**
(Primo Dominie 121) [2004 5f* 5.1f² 6g⁶ Jun 24] 22,000Y: quite good-topped gelding:
second foal: half-brother to 3-y-o Peeress: dam 5f winner, including at 2 yrs: won maiden
at Carlisle in May: second of 4 at Bath, much better effort in minor events: should stay 6f:
gelded, then sold 6,500 gns. *M. Johnston*

CARTE SAUVAGE (USA) 3 gr. or ro.c. Kris S (USA) – See You (USA) (Gulch **104**
(USA)) [2004 98: a8f⁶ 10v 10s⁴ p10g Nov 20] close-coupled, good-topped colt: has a
quick action: useful performer: sixth to Little Jim in UAE 2000 Guineas at Nad Al Sheba
in February (off 8½ months after): good 4¼ lengths fourth of 6 to Spanish Don in listed
race at Newmarket third start: will stay 1½m: acts on polytrack/dirt, soft and good to firm
ground: races prominently. *M. Johnston*

CARTOGRAPHY (IRE) 3 b.c. Zafonic (USA) 130 – Sans Escale (USA) (Diesis 133) **110**
[2004 103: 7m³ 7f³ 6m² 6g 6d² Sep 27] useful-looking colt: smart performer: good efforts

when placed in listed race at Newmarket (length third to Fokine), Jersey Stakes at Royal Ascot (2¼ lengths third to Kheleyf) and listed event at Newbury (head second to Pastoral Pursuits): below form in Sprint Cup at Haydock and minor event at Hamilton after: effective at 6f/7f: acts on firm and good to soft ground: tongue tied last 4 starts: has worn crossed noseband. *Saeed bin Suroor*

CARTRONAGEERAGHLAD (IRE) 3 b.g. Mujadil (USA) 119 – Night Scent (IRE) 85 (Scenic 128) [2004 83: 7g 6d 7.1s 8g 9g² 10m⁴ 9m⁴ 10d⁵ 10m⁴ 10m 9s 8d³ p9.5g⁶ Oct 18] sturdy gelding: fairly useful handicapper: stays 1¼m: acts on all-weather, soft and good to firm ground: effective blinkered or not: usually held up: sold 22,000 gns. *J. A. Osborne* **83**

CASALESE 2 ch.g. (May 10) Wolfhound (USA) 126 – Little Redwing 37 (Be My Chief (USA) 122) [2004 6.9m 8.3d 8s Oct 30] well beaten in maidens. *M. D. Hammond* **–**

CASANTELLA 3 b.f. Atraf 116 – Ramajana (USA) (Shadeed (USA) 135) [2004 47: f8g f7g⁴ f8f⁵ f8g f8s⁵ f8g p7g p10g Mar 14] workmanlike filly: poor maiden: stays 1m: raced only on all-weather and good/good to firm ground: tried blinkered/visored. *M. J. Polglase* **38**

CASCADE LAKES 2 ch.f. (Apr 22) Fraam 114 – Spring Flyer (IRE) 66 (Waajib 121) [2004 7s p8.6g p8.6g p7.1g Dec 31] seventh foal: dam, 7f (at 2 yrs) to 9.4f winner, half-sister to smart sprinter A Prayer For Wings: no promise in maiden. *W. M. Brisbourne* **40**

CASEY'S HOUSE 4 gr.f. Paris House 123 – Case Dismissed (IRE) (Case Law 113) [2004 7.1g 5s 6g f6g Aug 19] first foal: dam unraced: no sign of ability. *F. Watson* **–**

CASH 6 b.g. Bishop of Cashel 122 – Ballad Island 83 (Ballad Rock 122) [2004 –, a75: f6g f5s* f5s³ f5g⁵ 5g 5v 6s 5d* 5m 5s f5m⁴ Nov 22] angular gelding: fair handicapper: won at Wolverhampton in February and Musselburgh in May: effective at 5f/easy 6f: acts on fibresand and good to soft ground: usually wears visor/cheekpieces: unreliable. *Paul Johnson* **70 §**

CASHBAR 3 b.f. Bishop of Cashel 122 – Barford Sovereign 72 (Unfuwain (USA) 131) [2004 p8g² 8.2g* 8g Aug 14] first foal: dam, maiden on Flat (stayed 2m) but winning hurdler/chaser, half-sister to smart 7f performer Warningford and 6-y-o Heretic: fairly useful form: won maiden at Nottingham in July by 3 lengths from Marsh Orchid: ran as if amiss in handicap at Newmarket next time: stays 1m. *J. R. Fanshawe* **81**

CASHEL HOUSE (IRE) 2 b.c. (Apr 18) Bishop of Cashel 122 – Forest Treasure (USA) (Green Forest (USA) 134) [2004 5f² 5m³ 6.5d 5g⁵ p5g⁴ Oct 28] €8,500F, €21,000Y: half-brother to several winners, including fairly useful 1996 2-y-o 6f winner Open Credit (by Magical Wonder): dam unraced: fair maiden: fourth in minor event at Lingfield: form only at 5f: acts on polytrack and firm going. *D. Loughnane, Ireland* **67**

CASHEL MEAD 4 b.f. Bishop of Cashel 122 – Island Mead 86 (Pharly (FR) 130) [2004 88: p6g⁵ f6g p7g 6s⁶ 6d 6.1s p7.1g p6d p6g⁴ f6g⁴ p6g² f5f* Dec 28] leggy filly: fairly useful performer: below form after reappearance, though won claimer at Southwell in December: stays 6f: acts on all-weather, raced only on good ground or softer on turf: blinkered last 4 starts: sometimes slowly away. *J. L. Spearing* **85**

CASHEL QUEEN (USA) 3 b.f. Kingmambo (USA) 125 – Caerlina (IRE) 120 (Caerleon (USA) 132) [2004 8m³ 10m⁴ 9.6d⁵ 10d 8d p10g p9.5g³ p10m Dec 21] half-sister to useful 1997 2-y-o 7f winner who stayed 1m La Nuit Rose (by Rainbow Quest) and to 3 winners in Japan: dam won Prix de Diane: maiden: fair form first 2 outings only: left J. Bolger in Ireland after fifth start: stays 1¼m: acts on good to firm ground: tried in cheekpieces/blinkers/tongue tie. *J. Noseda* **69 d**

CASHEMA (IRE) 3 b.f. Cape Cross (IRE) 129 – Miss Shema (USA) 81 (Gulch (USA)) [2004 –: 8.3s 10s 8g 11.6d Jun 21] leggy, lengthy filly: little form: tried in cheek-pieces. *Mrs P. N. Dutfield* **–**

CASHIER 2 gr.c. (Feb 14) Alhaarth (IRE) 126 – Cashew 80 (Sharrood (USA) 124) [2004 7s³ Oct 22] 360,000Y: rather unfurnished colt: half-brother to several winners, including smart 1m (including at 2 yrs)/1¼m winner Macadamia (by Classic Cliche), smart Scandinavian sprinter Pistachio (by Unblest) and 3-y-o Azarole: dam 1m winner: 6/1, no extra final 1f when 5 lengths third of 13 to Ballinteni in maiden at Doncaster: should stay 1m: sure to improve. *J. H. M. Gosden* **76 p**

CASHNEEM (IRE) 6 b.g. Case Law 113 – Haanem 64 (Mtoto 134) [2004 67: 7.1v⁴ 7m⁶ 7f* 7m⁴ 8g 8d 7.1g 8m 7m Oct 10] strong gelding: fair handicapper: won amateur event at Yarmouth in June: stays 1m: acts on firm ground: free-going sort: none too consistent. *W. M. Brisbourne* **68**

CASH ON (IRE) 2 ch.c. (May 11) Spectrum (IRE) 126 – Lady Lucre (IRE) 73 (Last **58** Tycoon 131) [2004 8d p8g Oct 25] €28,000Y: good-topped colt: third foal: half-brother to useful 1¼m/1½m winner Prompt Payment (by In The Wings): dam, ran once, from family of Golan and Gamut (both by Spectrum): green, modest form in maidens at Newmarket and Lingfield. *M. P. Tregoning*

CASH TIME 2 ch.f. (May 13) Timeless Times (USA) 99 – Cashmirie 53 (Domynsky **41** 110) [2004 6g6 6g 5m4 7s Aug 13] quite good-topped filly: second foal: dam 1¼m winner: poor maiden: form only at 5f. *J. O'Reilly*

CASINO (IRE) 2 b.g. (Feb 16) Desert Sun 120 – Go Indigo (IRE) 67 (Cyrano de **66** Bergerac 120) [2004 p7.1g5 p7.1g Dec 10] fifth foal: half-brother to fairly useful Irish 7f (at 2 yrs) and 1¾m winner Estival Park (by Elbio) and 4-y-o Curragh Gold: dam Irish 5f winner: much better effort in maidens at Wolverhampton when fifth: favourite, never going well final start. *V. Smith*

CASPIAN DUSK 3 b.g. Up And At 'em 109 – Caspian Morn 63 (Lugana Beach 116) **70** [2004 42: f8s2 p10g3 f8s* f8d2 f11g* f12m3 f11d p10g p13.9g5 p12.2g2 f11g* Dec 11] fair performer: won maiden at Southwell in March and claimers on same course in May and December: barely stays 1¾m: acts on all-weather: below form only try in cheekpieces. *W. G. M. Turner*

CASPIAN LAKE (IRE) 3 ch.g. Lake Coniston (IRE) 131 – Hardtimes (IRE) (Dist- **–** inctly North (USA) 115) [2004 8.3g p9.5d p7.1g f8g Nov 23] poor maiden. *Mrs L. C. Jewell*

CASSANOS (IRE) 3 b.g. Ali-Royal (IRE) 127 – I'm Your Girl (Shavian 125) [2004 **56** 56: f9.4s3 f8g6 p12.2g6 f12g Dec 11] rather leggy gelding: modest maiden: left Gay Kelleway and off 10 months after second start: stays 1½m: raced only on all-weather/good to firm ground: tried in cheekpieces. *D. G. Bridgwater*

CASSYDORA 2 b.f. (Feb 28) Darshaan 133 – Claxon (Caerleon (USA) 132) **99** [2004 7m6 7g* 8m4 Sep 9] leggy, useful-looking filly: good mover: first foal: dam, 1m (including at 2 yrs) and 1¼m (including Premio Lydia Tesio) winner, half-sister to 3-y-o Bull Run: won maiden at Newmarket in August by 2½ lengths from Playful Act, making all: led until 2f out when 5¾ lengths fourth to same filly in May Hill Stakes at Doncaster: bred to be suited by 1¼m/1½m: useful. *J. L. Dunlop*

CASTAGNA (USA) 3 ch.f. Horse Chestnut (SAF) 119 – Thrilling Day 112 (Groom **87** Dancer (USA) 128) [2004 –p: 10g4 10g* 11.9s 12f Sep 24] smallish, sparely-made filly: fairly useful performer: best effort when winning maiden at Nottingham in July by 8 lengths from Autumn Wealth: highly tried last 2 starts: stays 1¼m: sent to New Zealand. *H. R. A. Cecil*

CASTAIGNE (FR) 5 ch.m. Pivotal 124 – Storm Warning 117 (Tumble Wind) [2004 **55 §** 70§: p10g p10g 10g6 10.2f 10.9m4 9.7g4 10m Jul 13] workmanlike mare: modest maiden handicapper: stays easy 11f: acts on polytrack, firm and good to soft ground: tried tongue tied/blinkered in cheekpieces: often slowly away: ungenuine. *B. W. Duke*

CASTANET 5 b.m. Pennekamp (USA) 130 – Addaya (IRE) (Persian Bold 123) [2004 **44** 16s5 12.1g May 31] rangy, angular mare: poor maiden: stays 2m: acts on fibresand: tried visored. *A. E. Price*

CASTANZA 2 b.f. (Feb 8) Bachir (IRE) 118 – Sylhall (Sharpo 132) [2004 p7.1g2 **67 p** Dec 31] 40,000Y: fourth foal: half-sister to 3 winners, including 4-y-o Crimson Silk and 2001 2-y-o 5f winner Dearest Daisy (by Forzando): dam unraced: 25/1, 1¾ lengths second of 12 to Sir Nod in maiden at Wolverhampton, soon prominent: should improve. *H. Morrison*

CASTAWAY QUEEN (IRE) 5 ch.m. Selkirk (USA) 129 – Surfing 71 (Grundy 137) **65** [2004 70: 10.2g2 p10g 10g 8f3 10.2g Jul 9] strong, close-coupled mare: fair maiden: stays 1¼m: acts on firm and good to soft going, well below form on all-weather: tried in cheekpieces/blinkers. *W. R. Muir*

CASTELLETTO 2 b.f. (Apr 14) Komaite (USA) – Malcesine (IRE) 46 (Auction Ring **104** (USA) 123) [2004 5.1s3 5.1g2 5f 5m2 5g* 5.2g2 6s5 6g2 6s3 5s* Oct 16] 15,500Y: good sort: sister to several winners, including 3-y-o Lake Garda and 7-y-o Baby Barry: dam 1m seller winner: useful performer: won maiden at Ripon in July and Cornwallis Stakes at Newmarket (by ¾ length from Cornus) in October: second past post in listed races at Newbury and Salisbury and Firth of Clyde Stakes at Ayr (beaten ¾ length by Golden Legacy, but hung left and demoted a place) in between: barely stays 6f: acts on soft going, probably on good to firm: on toes/mounted on track at Newmarket: usually races close up: sold 85,000 gns, joined S. Seemar in UAE. *B. A. McMahon*

CASTEROSSA 2 ch.f. (Feb 11) Rossini (USA) 118 – First Musical 107 (First Trump **67**
118) [2004 6g⁶ 6.1g⁴ 6m⁴ 6.1g⁶ 6.5g Sep 18] 52,000Y: first foal: dam 2-y-o 5f/6f winner:
fair maiden: should stay 7f. *D. Haydn Jones*

CASTLESHANE (IRE) 7 b.g. Kris 135 – Ahbab (IRE) 81 (Ajdal (USA) 130) [2004 **–**
100: 10m May 31] big, strong gelding: useful handicapper: well held only start in 2004:
stays 1½m: acts on any going: blinkered (raced freely) twice: usually forces pace: useful
hurdler. *S. Gollings*

CASTLETON 3 b.c. Cape Cross (IRE) 129 – Craigmill 85 (Slip Anchor 136) [2004 **113**
99: 7s² 10m³ 8m* 8f⁶ 8m Dec 18] leggy, close-coupled colt: smart performer: landed
odds in maiden at Newmarket in June: 66/1, 2½ lengths sixth to Azamour in St James's
Palace Stakes at Royal Ascot next time, leading most of way but held when slightly
hampered near finish: left H. Cyzer, off 6 months and renamed Able Knight, well held
final start at Sha Tin: effective at 1m/1¼m: acts on firm and good to soft ground.
J. Moore, Hong Kong

CASUAL GLANCE 2 b.f. (Apr 11) Sinndar (IRE) 134 – Spurned (USA) 91 (Robel- **– p**
lino (USA) 127) [2004 7m 8d Aug 20] half-sister to several winners, including 7f and (at
2 yrs) 1m winner Hidden Meadow, 7f (at 2 yrs) to 1½m winner Scorned (both smart and
by Selkirk) and 5-y-o Passing Glance: dam 2-y-o 7f winner who stayed 1¼m: backward,
signs of a little ability in maidens at Goodwood and Salisbury: will be suited by 1¼m/
1½m: should do better. *A. M. Balding*

CATALINI 3 ch.g. Seeking The Gold (USA) – Calando (USA) 110 (Storm Cat (USA)) **67**
[2004 84: p8g² p8g⁵ 7f⁵ 8.3d⁶ Jun 29] small, quite attractive gelding: fair maiden: should
stay 1¼m: acts on polytrack, firm and soft going: sold 6,000 gns. *M. R. Channon*

CATCHABIRD (IRE) 6 ch.m. Flying Spur (AUS) – Magic Bird (IRE) (Bluebird **–**
(USA) 125) [2004 7m 8.5d 13f 7d 5s f6d Dec 21] 3,000F: second foal: dam maiden: poor
maiden: left Mrs A. Naughton (Ireland) after fifth start: stays 7f: acts on good to soft
going: tried tongue tied. *K. G. Wingrove*

CATCH A STAR 2 ch.f. (Apr 6) Giant's Causeway (USA) 132 – Amy Hunter (USA) **82**
(Jade Hunter (USA)) [2004 6m³ 6m⁵ 7m 6g³ 8.2d⁷ 7g³ 8.3g⁶ Oct 11] 65,000F, 180,000Y:
tall filly: second foal: half-sister to 3-y-o Cobalt Blue: dam 6f winner in USA: fairly
useful performer: caught eye third start (rider banned): won at Nottingham in
September: good third at Newmarket, better effort in nurseries after: stays 1m: acts on
good to soft going. *N. A. Callaghan*

CATCHTHEBATCH 8 b.g. Beveled (USA) – Batchworth Dancer 67 (Ballacashtal **53 d**
(CAN)) [2004 55: p5g⁴ f5g³ f5g 5g f5g 5m 6m 5g p5m Dec 15] lengthy, sparely-made
gelding: modest performer: well held after second start: effective at 5f/easy 6f: acts
on all-weather and good to firm going: tried blinkered: sometimes slowly away.
E. A. Wheeler

CATCH THE CAT (IRE) 5 b.g. Catrail (USA) 123 – Tongabezi (IRE) 75 (Shernazar **81**
131) [2004 74, a54: 5g³ 6s 5v² 5.1d 5m* 5m⁶ 6m⁵ 5d 5d 5g 5f* 5g 5.1g 5g 5m Oct 2] **a–**
well-made gelding: fairly useful handicapper on turf, modest when last seen on all-
weather: won at Musselburgh in May and July: reluctant to race final outing: best at 5f:
acts on fibresand and any turf going: wears headgear: sometimes slowly away: often
races prominently. *J. S. Wainwright*

CATCH THE FOX 4 b.g. Fraam 114 – Versaillesprincess (Legend of France (USA) **57**
124) [2004 48?: 7g 8.1d² 7v 10g 9g⁴ 9g 8m 10d 8s⁴ p8g 7d³ 8.3g³ 9s Oct 22] leggy,
workmanlike gelding: modest maiden: stays 9f: best efforts on good going or softer:
difficult ride: none too consistent. *J. J. Bridger*

CATCH THE WIND 3 b.f. Bahamian Bounty 116 – Tinkerbird 76 (Music Boy 124) **87**
[2004 81: 6.1d 5.1f⁵ p6g⁵ 5d⁶ 5.1m* 5.1g² 5d² 5d p5g Nov 13] sturdy filly: fairly useful **a75**
handicapper on turf, fair on all-weather: won at Bath in July: best form at 5f: acts on
polytrack, firm and good to soft ground: wore cheekpieces 5 starts. *I. A. Wood*

CATERHAM COMMON 5 b.g. Common Grounds 118 – Pennine Pink (IRE) 72 **31**
(Pennine Walk 120) [2004 –: f8f f7g⁶ f8g f8.5s f7g⁵ Mar 23] smallish, sturdy gelding:
poor performer: should stay 1¼m: acts on all-weather and firm going: tried blinkered.
D. W. Chapman

CATHERINE HOWARD 3 b.f. Kingmambo (USA) 125 – Darling Flame (USA) **73**
101 (Capote (USA)) [2004 74: 8g⁴ 8m 8.2m⁴ 8.5g⁵ Jun 17] rather leggy filly: fair performer: stays 1m: raced only on good/good to firm ground: sent to Australia. *M. R. Channon*

CATHERINE WHEEL   3 b.f. Primo Dominie 121 – Prancing 98 (Prince Sabo 123)   **83**
[2004 6s² 5m* 6m* p6g* Jul 14] strong, good-topped filly: fourth foal: sister to 6-y-o
Firework: dam, 2-y-o 5f winner who stayed 1m, half-sister to Middle Park winner First
Trump (by Primo Dominie): fairly useful performer: won maiden at Doncaster in May
then handicaps at Newbury (idled) in June and Lingfield in July, quickening well to beat
Eccentric by ½ length in last-named: effective at 5f/6f: acted on polytrack, soft and good
to firm going: stud. *J. R. Fanshawe*

CATSTAR (USA)   3 br.f. Storm Cat (USA) – Advancing Star (USA) 115 (Soviet Star   **104 ?**
(USA) 128) [2004 105: a8f* 7.1g⁵ 7.1f⁵ Jun 19] lengthy filly: useful performer: won UAE
1000 Guineas at Nad Al Sheba in February by 1¼ lengths from Menhoubah, dictating
pace: well below that form in listed races back in Britain: stays 1m: acts on dirt, raced
only on good ground or firmer on turf: tongue tied in 2004: left Godolphin, and sent to
USA. *Saeed bin Suroor*

CAT'S WHISKERS   5 b.g. Catrail (USA) 123 – Haut Volee (Top Ville 129) [2004   **86**
98: 10.5s 8d³ 8m⁴ 10.3g 8g² 10g 9.1d⁵ Sep 16] leggy gelding: fairly useful handicapper:
effective at 1m/1¼m: acts on soft and good to firm going: has been early to post/blanketed
for stall entry. *M. W. Easterby*

CATWALK CLERIC (IRE)   2 b.c. (Apr 27) Orpen (USA) 116 – Ministerial Model   **85**
(IRE) 94 (Shalford (IRE) 124§) [2004 5s⁴ 5.1d* 5.5g² 6f 6.1g⁴ 8s⁴ 6d Oct 11] €16,000F,
26,000Y: sturdy, useful-looking colt: has a quick action: third foal: dam, Irish 7f/1m
winner, also won over hurdles: fairly useful performer: won maiden at Chester in May:
good efforts after when in frame in listed race at Rome and nurseries at Warwick and
Ayr: barely stays testing 1m: acts on soft going: edgy sort: sold 27,000 gns, sent to Macau.
M. J. Wallace

CAUSE CELEBRE (IRE)   3 gr.f. Peintre Celebre (USA) 137 – Madame Belga (USA)   **80**
(Al Nasr (FR) 126) [2004 79: 10.2m* 11.9d 10.9m* 10m* 10m⁶ 11g 10m p10g Nov 10] leggy
filly: has a quick action: fairly useful performer: won maiden at Bath in May and
handicap at Warwick in June: should stay 1½m: acts on firm ground: well beaten on good
to soft and polytrack. *B. W. Hills*

CAUSEWAY GIRL (IRE)   2 br.f. (Feb 22) Giant's Causeway (USA) 132 – Darbela   **–**
(IRE) 102 (Doyoun 124) [2004 7g 7d Oct 30] leggy, close-coupled filly: second foal:
dam, Irish 1½m and 2m winner (also successful over hurdles), half-sister to Prix de Diane
and Prix Vermeille winner Daryaba: well held in maidens at Newmarket. *D. M. Simcock*

CAUSTIC WIT (IRE)   6 b.g. Cadeaux Genereux 131 – Baldemosa (FR) (Lead On   **93**
Time (USA) 123) [2004 58d: f6g* f6g 6s* 6m* 6m* 6m* 6m² 6m² 6m 6g 5s⁴ 6g⁶ 6g⁶ Sep
29] leggy, quite good-topped gelding: fairly useful handicapper: back to form in 2004,
winning at Wolverhampton in January, Folkestone and Leicester in May and at Salisbury
and Windsor in June: effective at 5f/6f: acts on fibresand, soft and good to firm ground:
usually wears cheekpieces: tough. *M. S. Saunders*

CAUTIOUSLY (USA)   3 b.f. Distant View (USA) 126 – Curiously 91 (Warning 136)   **77 ?**
[2004 8m 7f* p8g p8g p6g Dec 30] second foal: half-sister to fairly useful Irish 1¼m to
1¾m winner Serjeant At Arms (by Bluebird): dam Irish 7f and 1¼m winner who stayed
1½m: fair performer: won maiden at Down Royal in July: left J. Oxx in Ireland 6,500 gns
and off 5 months afterwards: claimed from D. Flood £12,000 next time: stays 1m: acts on
polytrack and firm ground. *J. A. R. Toller*

CAVA BIEN   2 b.g. (Feb 7) Bien Bien (USA) 125 – Bebe de Cham 75 (Tragic Role   **70**
(USA)) [2004 7f 7.1m³ 7.1f³ 7.9g 10m⁵ 8d* Oct 16] 2,000Y: angular gelding: first foal:
dam, 5f (at 2 yrs) and 6f winner, probably ungenuine: fair performer: won maiden at Yarmouth, making most: stays 1¼m: acts on firm and good to soft going: hung persistently
right penultimate start. *J. G. Given*

CAVALARRA   2 b.c.s (Jan 20) Green Desert (USA) 127 – Ya Tarra 74 (Unbridled (USA)   **61 p**
128) [2004 5g 6.1d⁵ Sep 17] strong colt: first foal: dam, placed at 1¼m both starts,
half-sister to Lammtarra out of Oaks winner Snow Bride: better effort in maidens when
fifth to The Abbess at Nottingham, no extra late on: should stay 1m: joined E. Charpy in
UAE: likely to do better again. *B. W. Hills*

CAVAN GAEL (FR)   2 b.c. (Apr 29) Dansili 127 – Time Will Show (FR) (Exit To   **68**
Nowhere (USA) 122) [2004 8g 7s⁶ 6s 6f8g² p7.1g² Dec 31] 21,000F: leggy colt: first
foal: dam, French maiden, half-sister to useful French 1¼m winner Wedding Night: fair
maiden: second at Southwell and Wolverhampton: stays easy 1m: acts on all-weather and
soft going: free-going sort. *P. Howling*

CAVARADOSSI 2 gr.c. (Mar 18) Lake Coniston (IRE) 131 – Floria Tosca § (Petong –
126) [2004 6f 6m Aug 16] pulled up/well held in maidens at Windsor. *B. J. Meehan*

CAVE OF THE GIANT (IRE) 2 b.c. (Apr 18) Giant's Causeway (USA) 132 – Mar- **73**
oussie (FR) 115 (Saumarez 132) [2004 8.1g⁵ 8g Oct 12] 25,000Y: leggy, close-coupled
colt: third foal: half-brother to useful 7f to 9f winner Mamounia (by Green Desert) and
3-y-o Clipperdown: dam French 1¼m (including Prix Fille de l'Air) winner: much better
effort in maidens when fifth at Sandown, slowly away: finished lame at Leicester: gave
trouble and withdrawn in November: should be suited by 1¼m/1½m. *T. D. McCarthy*

CAVERAL 3 ch.f. Ashkalani (IRE) 128 – Melting Gold (USA) 108 (Cadeaux Genereux **103**
131) [2004 82p: 8s 7g 6m* 6d 6g³ 7g 7m⁶ 7m Sep 26] tall, leggy filly: useful performer:
best effort when winning minor event at Windsor in May by 3 lengths from Fruit of Glory:
effective at 6f/7f: acts on good to firm ground: has folded tamely: none too consistent.
R. Hannon

CAVORTING 2 ch.g. (Mar 30) Polar Falcon (USA) 126 – Prancing 98 (Prince Sabo **77**
123) [2004 5g⁴ 5g Oct 5] useful-looking gelding: fifth foal: half-brother to 6-y-o Firework and 3-y-o Catherine Wheel: dam, 2-y-o 5f winner who stayed 1m, half-sister to
Middle Park winner First Trump: much better effort in maidens 6 months apart when
fourth at Newmarket (gelded after): likely to prove best at 5f/6f: sold 9,000 gns, sent to
Sweden. *D. R. Loder*

CAYENNE (GER) 2 ch.f. (Mar 7) Efisio 120 – Carola Rouge (Arazi (USA) 135) **53**
[2004 5g⁵ 7m⁵ Sep 4] 18,000Y: first foal: dam German 7f winner: burly, modest form in
maidens: should stay 1m. *D. M. Simcock*

CAYMAN BREEZE 4 b.g. Danzig (USA) – Lady Thynn (FR) (Crystal Glitters (USA) **57**
127) [2004 74: p7g f7g⁵ p6g⁴ p7g* 7m 5.7m⁵ 8.1m 5.7g 7g⁴ p7.1d p7m Nov 22] smallish,
sturdy gelding: modest performer: won claimer at Lingfield (left from S. Dow) in
February: stays 7f: acts on all-weather, raced mainly on good ground or firmer on turf:
tried in visor/cheekpieces. *J. M. Bradley*

CAYMAN CALYPSO (IRE) 3 ro.g. Danehill Dancer (IRE) 117 – Warthill Whispers **65**
59 (Grey Desire 115) [2004 8m 7m 7.1m⁶ 10m 8m⁶ 8.1g² 8.5d² 10d 8.5m 8.2g 10g f8g
f8g Dec 16] 26,000 2-y-o: tall gelding: third foal: dam, sprint maiden, one to treat with
caution: fair maiden: runner-up in claimers: left M. Jarvis after seventh start: well held for
new stable: stays 1m: acts on good to firm and good to soft going: tried visored/blinkered.
J. M. Jefferson

CAYMAN KING 2 b.g. (Apr 28) Cayman Kai (IRE) 114 – Distinctly Laura (IRE) –
(Distinctly North (USA) 115) [2004 6m Sep 29] 100/1, last in maiden at Newcastle.
R. Craggs

CAYMAN MISCHIEF 4 b.f. Cayman Kai (IRE) 114 – Tribal Mischief 61 (Be My –
Chief (USA) 122) [2004 –: f9.4g 6d 5.9f⁶ 5s Aug 13] no sign of ability. *James Moffatt*

CAYMANS GIFT 4 ch.g. Cayman Kai (IRE) 114 – Gymcrak Cyrano (IRE) 61 (Cyrano **65**
de Bergerac 120) [2004 12.1g⁴ 9.2d⁵ 8m⁶ 13.1d³ 12m Jun 28] fair maiden: ran as if amiss
final start: stays 13f: acts on good to soft going. *A. C. Whillans*

CAYMAN SUNRISE (IRE) 4 gr.f. Peintre Celebre (USA) 137 – Sum (USA) (Spec- **56**
tacular Bid (USA)) [2004 68: f9.4g Jan 16] leggy filly: modest maiden: stays 1¼m: acts
on polytrack, good to firm and good to soft ground. *E. A. L. Dunlop*

CAYUSE 2 b.f. (Feb 14) Double Trigger (IRE) 123 – Suile Mor 65 (Satin Wood 117) –
[2004 7d 7d Oct 30] 800Y: close-coupled filly: third foal: half-sister to 2001 2-y-o 7f
seller winner Last Gesture (by Jester): dam, 2-y-o 7f winner who stayed 11f, showed
temperament: well beaten in maidens at Newmarket. *T. T. Clement*

CAZENOVE 3 b.g. Royal Applause 124 – Celestina (IRE) (Priolo (USA) 127) [2004 **60 ?**
9g 7g⁴ 7g⁶ 7.1m 7m Aug 16] modest maiden: form seemingly only on third start: tried in
cheekpieces. *M. G. Quinlan*

CAZISA STAR (USA) 3 ch.f. Mister Baileys 123 – Placer Queen (Habitat 134) –
[2004 63: 10m 10.1m 12m Jul 22] rather leggy, close-coupled filly: maiden: well held in
2004. *P. W. Harris*

CD EUROPE (IRE) 6 ch.g. Royal Academy (USA) 130 – Woodland Orchid (IRE) **96**
64 (Woodman (USA) 126) [2004 100: 6m 6f 6d 7g 6f⁶ 6m 6s 6m² 6d² Sep 17] lengthy
gelding: carries little condition: has reportedly had sinus problems: useful handicapper:
left K. Ryan after seventh outing: second at Goodwood and Ayr (beaten ¾ length by Eisteddfod in Silver Cup): best at 6f: acts on firm and soft going: often wears cheekpieces/
blinkers: held up. *J. J. Quinn*

CD FLYER (IRE)   7 ch.g. Grand Lodge (USA) 125 – Pretext (Polish Precedent (USA) **94**
131) [2004 94: 6g⁵ 6v² 6g 6d 6d⁴ 6g* 6d 7g⁴ 6m³ 6s⁵ 6s⁶ 6d 7g² 6s 7s Nov 6] lengthy,
angular gelding: good walker: fairly useful handicapper: won at Redcar in June: effective
at 6f/7f: acts on polytrack and any turf going: held up: tough. *B. Ellison*

CEASAR (IRE)   3 b.g. Orpen (USA) 116 – Fen Princess (IRE) 72 (Trojan Fen 118) **60**
[2004 63d: f8g² f11g* f12g 12v* 12.1g³ 14.1f Jun 10] workmanlike gelding: modest
performer: won handicap at Southwell in February and seller at Pontefract (left P. Haslam
9,000 gns) in April: stayed 1½m: acted on fibresand, heavy and good to firm going: sometimes wore cheekpieces: dead. *P. A. Blockley*

CEDAR MASTER (IRE)   7 b.g. Soviet Lad (USA) – Samriah (IRE) (Wassl 125) **62**
[2004 82: 14m 16m Jul 14] quite attractive gelding: modest handicapper: stays 2m: acts
on polytrack, firm and good to soft going: usually visored/blinkered: tongue tied last 2
starts: tends to hang: none too consistent. *J. R. Boyle*

CEDRIC COVERWELL   4 ch.g. Charmer 123 – Marsara (Never So Bold 135) [2004 **43**
p6g⁴ 7g 6s 5.1g 5.3f 6.1s 5m⁵ 6f Aug 7] compact gelding: poor maiden: stays 6f: tried
blinkered. *D. K. Ivory*

CEFIRA (USA)   3 b.f. Distant View (USA) 126 – Bold Jessie (Never So Bold 135) **66**
[2004 63: 6v³ 6g 6f* 6.1d 6d p8g Nov 10] useful-looking filly: fair performer: won
maiden at Ayr in May: stays 6f, not 1m: acts on polytrack, firm and good to soft ground.
M. H. Tompkins

CEIRIOG VALLEY   2 b.f. (Feb 14) In The Wings 128 – Bodfari Quarry 92 (Efisio **86**
120) [2004 7m 7s* 8.1g Sep 4] close-coupled filly: second foal: half-sister to Swiss 1m
winner by Dr Devious: dam, 5f (at 2 yrs) to 1½m winner, out of half-sister to top-class
1¼m performer Cormorant Wood: won maiden at Chester in August by 8 lengths: last in
nursery at Haydock final start: should be suited by 1¼m/1½m: easily best effort on soft
going. *B. W. Hills*

CELADON (IRE)   3 b.g. Fasliyev (USA) 120 – Dancing Drop 103 (Green Desert **55**
(USA) 127) [2004 70: p5g² Feb 14] fair maiden at 2 yrs: below best only outing in 2004:
should be suited by 6f+: often slowly away. *N. P. Littmoden*

CELEBRE CITATION (IRE)   3 ch.g. Peintre Celebre (USA) 137 – Kotama (USA) **–**
96 (Shahrastani (USA) 135) [2004 8m 10m⁵ 8g 11.9s Sep 24] €35,000Y: sixth foal: half-
brother to a winner in Norway by Woodman: dam, Irish 7f/9f winner, half-sister to dam
of High Chaparral: little form: tongue tied last 3 outings. *J. R. Fanshawe*

CELESTIAL ARC (USA)   2 b.c. (Feb 26) Southern Halo (USA) – Perfect Arc **65**
(USA) 120 (Brown Arc (USA)) [2004 7g³ 7d 6g 8m 10m Sep 24] big, lengthy colt: third
foal: half-brother to useful 6f (at 2 yrs) to 1½m winner Kepler (by Spinning World): dam
US Grade 1 9f winner: fair maiden: stays 1¼m: acts on good to firm going: sent to USA.
P. F. I. Cole

CELLARMASTER (IRE)   3 ch.g. Alhaarth (IRE) 126 – Cheeky Weeky (Cadeaux **86**
Genereux 131) [2004 73p: 11.6d³ 10d* 10m⁴ 11g³ 10.3s Oct 22] angular, useful-looking
gelding: has a quick action: fairly useful handicapper: won at Nottingham (final outing
for A. Stewart) in July: good third to Solo Flight at Newbury fourth start: effective at
1¼m to 11.6f: acts on fibresand, good to firm and good to soft ground, well held on soft:
sold 18,000 gns. *E. F. Vaughan*

CELLINO   3 b.f. Robellino (USA) 127 – Celandine 80 (Warning 136) [2004 56: f5g **45**
5m⁴ 5m 6m 6.1d 7.9m 7d Oct 16] smallish filly: poor maiden. *Andrew Turnell*

CELLO   3 gr.c. Pivotal 124 – Raffelina (USA) (Carson City (USA)) [2004 78: 7.1d² **93**
8.5s* 7.6d⁶ 7m 8m 9d⁴ 9s² 8f³ 8s* Oct 19] big, good-topped colt: fairly useful performer:
won maiden at Epsom in April and handicap at Bath in October, best effort when beating Alfonso by 2 lengths in latter: stays 9f: acts on firm and soft going: tongue tied last 4
outings: carries head awkwardly. *R. Hannon*

CELTIC BLAZE (IRE)   5 b.m. Charente River (IRE) 67 – Firdaunt (Tanfirion 110) **61**
[2004 67: 16.2g³ 16m 16g 16.1g⁵ Sep 6] close-coupled mare: modest handicapper: stays
2m: acts on firm ground and fibresand: wore cheekpieces/tongue tie in 2004: none too
consistent. *B. S. Rothwell*

CELTIC CARISMA   2 b.f. (Apr 2) Celtic Swing 138 – Kathryn's Pet 92 (Blakeney **–**
126) [2004 6d 7s Nov 1] first foal: dam, 1½m/1¾m winner, also fairly useful hurdler:
well held in maidens at Redcar. *K. G. Reveley*

Sandringham Rated Stakes (Handicap), Royal Ascot—Celtic Heroine gives trainer Michael Jarvis a double following Rakti's success earlier in the day in the Prince of Wales's Stakes; Coy (rail) and Zosima (noseband) fill the places

CELTIC HEROINE (IRE) 3 ch.f. Hernando (FR) 127 – Celtic Fling 77 (Lion Cavern (USA) 117) [2004 83: 9g² 8.3d* 8f² 8f* 8.3g² 10m⁵ 8m² 8s⁶ Aug 19] sturdy filly: smart performer: won handicaps at Hamilton in May and Royal Ascot (listed rated stakes, by ½ length from Coy) in June: best effort when neck second to Coy in listed race at Ascot penultimate start: best around 1m: acts on all-weather, firm and good to soft ground: genuine. *M. A. Jarvis* **111**

CELTIC MILL 6 b.g. Celtic Swing 138 – Madam Millie 99 (Milford 119) [2004 98: f6g⁴ f6g⁴ 6g 6m* 6m* 6d 5m 6g⁶ 5m* 5.2g 6f⁴ p6g⁴ Nov 29] tall, leggy gelding: smart performer on turf, useful on all-weather: won handicaps at Wolverhampton in January and Thirsk in May and listed races at Windsor (beat Ashdown Express by 1¼ lengths) in May and Doncaster (beat Talbot Avenue ½ length) in September: creditable fourth to Pivotal Point in Diadem Stakes at Ascot penultimate start: effective at 5f/6f: acts on all-weather, firm and good to soft going: wore cheekpieces last 4 starts: front runner: tough. *D. W. Barker* **111 a99 +**

CELTIC PROMISE (IRE) 2 b.f. (Apr 6) Celtic Swing 138 – Tainted Halo (USA) (Halo (USA)) [2004 p7m 10v⁶ 10.1d⁵ Nov 5] 10,000F, €12,000Y: third foal: dam unraced: best effort in maidens when fifth to Quizzene at Yarmouth: will stay at least 1½m. *Mrs A. J. Perrett* **66**

CELTIC ROMANCE 5 b.m. Celtic Swing 138 – Southern Sky 89 (Comedy Star (USA) 121) [2004 –: 8v 7s 8.1d 7v⁵ 8f 7.2g⁶ 7.5g 12m⁴ Jul 14] sparely-made mare: poor performer: stays 1m: acts on good to firm and heavy ground: tried in cheekpieces: often slowly away nowadays. *Mrs M. Reveley* **43**

CELTIC SOLITUDE (IRE) 3 b.f. Celtic Swing 138 – Smart 'n Noble (USA) (Smarten (USA)) [2004 –: 9g 14.1m Jun 1] strong, close-coupled filly: no form: sold 25,000 gns in July, joined R. Bouresly in UAE. *Mrs M. Reveley* **–**

CELTIC SPA (IRE) 2 gr.f. (Feb 18) Celtic Swing 138 – Allegorica (IRE) (Alzao (USA) 117) [2004 5g 5.1s* 5f 5f⁵ 5f³ 5.2m 6m⁴ 6s 6v p6g p8g Nov 30] €10,000Y: leggy, close-coupled filly: second foal: dam Italian 5f (at 2 yrs) and 7f winner: fairly useful performer: won minor event at Nottingham in May: creditable efforts in listed events/sales race next 2 and seventh starts: barely stays 6f: acts on firm and soft ground. *Mrs P. N. Dutfield* **81**

CELTIC STAR (IRE) 6 b.g. Celtic Swing 138 – Recherchee (Rainbow Quest (USA) 134) [2004 67: 12.6f 10.2f⁶ 10f Jul 26] tall gelding: modest handicapper: stays 1m: acts on good to soft ground: tried in headgear: winning hurdler/chaser. *Miss K. M. George* **56**

CELTIC TANNER (IRE) 5 b.g. Royal Abjar (USA) 121 – Mills Pride (IRE) (Posen (USA)) [2004 p9.5d p6g p7.1g Nov 29] little form. *D. J. Wintle* **–**

CELTIC THATCHER 6 b.g. Celtic Swing 138 – Native Thatch (IRE) 47 (Thatching 131) [2004 –: f8.5m² May 28] modest performer, lightly raced: second in seller at Wolverhampton only 6-y-o start: best at 1m/9f: acts on all-weather: tried in cheekpieces, usually visored. *N. P. Littmoden* **55**

CELTIC THUNDER 3 b.g. Mind Games 121 – Lake Mistassiu 86 (Tina's Pet 121) [2004 86p: 5g² 5m 5f⁵ 5m 6d² 6g 6g⁴ 6m⁴ 6m 5g⁵ 5d p7g p6g⁵ Nov 26] good-topped gelding: fairly useful handicapper: effective at 5f/6f: acts on polytrack, firm and good to soft going: often races prominently. *T. J. Etherington* **88**

Earth Mortgages Scarbrough Stakes, Doncaster—
Celtic Mill wins his second listed race of the season under a fine front-running ride by Frankie Dettori;
he is chased home by Talbot Avenue and Caribbean Coral

CELTIC VISION (IRE)   8 b.g. Be My Native (USA) 122 – Dream Run (Deep Run – 119) [2004 14.1g⁶ 12.4v⁶ 7.1d 16d 16d⁴ f14.8m⁶ 10.9f⁵ Jun 20] no form on Flat: tried tongue tied/in cheekpieces. *M. Appleby*

CELTIQUE   2 b.f. (Apr 4) Celtic Swing 138 – Heart's Harmony (Blushing Groom 77 (FR) 131) [2004 7d² 8m³ p7g² Oct 28] leggy, good-topped filly: half-sister to several winners, including smart 1¼m winner National Anthem (by Royal Academy) and useful 6f (at 2 yrs) and 1¼m winner Tug of Love (by Halling): dam won at 1m from 2 starts in France: fair form in maidens: second at Newmarket and Lingfield: should be suited by 1¼m/1½m: edged left first 2 starts. *Sir Michael Stoute*

CEMGRAFT   3 b.f. In The Wings 128 – Soviet Maid (IRE) (Soviet Star (USA) 128) 63 ? [2004 11.5g⁵ 12f 8s⁶ p12m Oct 6] 35,000F. big, strong, lengthy filly: fifth foal: half-sister to 3 winners, including 2000 2-y-o 7f winner Ridgeway Dawn (by Mujtahid): dam unraced half-sister to very smart 1½m/1¾m performer Air Marshall: modest form when fifth to Light of Morn in maiden at Lingfield: well held after: should stay 1¾m. *Miss E. C. Lavelle*

CENTAURUS   2 br.c. (Jan 26) Daylami (IRE) 138 – Dandanna (IRE) 97 (Linamix (FR) 97 p 127) [2004 7d* Oct 30] angular colt: first foal: dam, 2-y-o 6f winner (only start), half-sister to very smart middle-distance performer Courteous out of sister to Darshaan: 3/1 and green, won 19-runner maiden at Newmarket by 1¼ lengths from Master of The Race, racing prominently before getting on top final 1f: will be suited by 1¼m/1½m: should make his mark in stronger company. *Saeed bin Suroor*

CENTIFOLIA (FR)   2 gr.f. (Mar 15) Kendor (FR) 122 – Djayapura (FR) (Fabulous 112 Dancer (USA) 124) [2004 6d* 6g 6g* 5s* 6s* Oct 29] €42,000Y: second foal: dam French 12.5f winner: smart performer: trained first 2 starts by D. Soubagne: won newcomers race at Maisons-Laffitte in July, minor event at Chantilly in September and listed race at Maisons-Laffitte (by 4 lengths) and Criterium de Maisons-Laffitte (by 2 lengths) in October, beating stable-companion Salut Thomas for last 2 wins: likely to prove best at 5f/6f: acts on soft ground. *R. Collet, France*

CEREBUS   2 b.f. (Feb 28) Wolfhound (USA) 126 – Bring On The Choir 87 (Chief 74 Singer 131) [2004 6g⁶ 6m⁴ 6m² 7f³ 7f³ 6g⁶ 7g Oct 2] 3,500F: strong, close-coupled filly: fourth foal: half-sister to 2000 2-y-o 7f winner Meriden Mist (by Distinctly North): dam, 2-y-o 5f winner, later stayed 1m: fair maiden: stays 7f: acts on firm going. *N. P. Littmoden*

CERTA CITO   4 b.f. Mind Games 121 – Bollin Dorothy 73 (Rambo Dancer (CAN) 62 107) [2004 64, a–: 6s 6s 6m⁵ 6m 5g 5m⁴ 7g Oct 12] big, good-topped filly: modest a– handicapper: left T. Easterby after fifth start: effective at 5f/6f: acts on good to firm ground, well held on fibreand: tried blinkered. *D. Flood*

CERTAIN JUSTICE (USA)   6 gr.g. Lit de Justice (USA) 125 – Pure Misk 55 (Rain- 69 bow Quest (USA) 134) [2004 95: 8.1d 7.1s⁶ 8.1g⁵ p8g 7g⁵ f8d Jul 23] rather leggy gelding: just fair performer in 2004: stays 1m: acts on soft and good to firm going: tried blinkered and in cheekpieces. *P. F. I. Cole*

CERTIFIABLE   3 b.g. Deploy 131 – Gentle Irony 65 (Mazilier (USA) 107) [2004 70 f9.4s⁴ p8g* p8g* 8.1d⁵ 7.9d 10.3m⁵ p8g p7.1d p8g² p8g⁴ p7.1g* p8.6g Dec 27] brother to a82 6f to 8.5f (including 7f at 2 yrs) winner Violent and half-brother to 5f winner Shorts (by Primo Dominie): dam, 7f (including at 2 yrs) to 11f winner, out of half-sister to very smart performer up to 8.5f Forzando: fairly useful performer on all-weather, fair on turf: won maiden at Lingfield in February, minor event there in March and claimer at Wolverhampton (left A. Reid) in December: effective at 7f/1m: acts on polytrack and good to soft ground: withdrawn after refusing to enter stall intended debut: often races up with pace. *Miss S. J. Wilton*

CERULEAN ROSE   5 ch.m. Bluegrass Prince (IRE) 110 – Elegant Rose 72 (Noalto   **76** 120) [2004 77: 5s⁴ 5g 5m² 6m 5.1m³ 5g 5.1g² 5d⁴ 6d 5g Oct 8] workmanlike mare: fair handicapper: best at 5f: acts on firm and soft going: tried blinkered/tongue tied at 3 yrs. *A. W. Carroll*

CESARE   3 b.g. Machiavellian (USA) 123 – Tromond 94 (Lomond (USA) 128) [2004   **77 +** 8.1s² 8.5s* 8.9g Oct 9] deep-girthed gelding: sixth foal: closely related to very smart 1m (at 2 yrs) to 1½m winner Nowhere To Exit (by Exit To Nowhere) and half-brother to 2 useful winners, including 1m winner (including at 2 yrs) Embraced (by Pursuit of Love): dam, 9f winner who stayed 1½m, out of half-sister to Yorkshire Oaks winner and St Leger second Hellenic: fair form: easily landed odds in maiden at Beverley in April: ran as if needing race in handicap at York 5½ months later: should be suited by 9f+. *J. R. Fanshawe*

CESAR MANRIQUE (IRE)   2 ch.c. (Mar 2) Vettori (IRE) 119 – Norbella (Nordico   **82** (USA)) [2004 5g 5g⁵ 5f⁴ 5.1s* Oct 19] leggy colt: fifth foal: half-brother to 3 winners, including useful 5f (at 2 yrs) to 1m winner Achilles Star (by Deploy) and fairly useful 6f winner in France Cabeza de Vaca (by Lahib): dam unraced: fairly useful performer: won maiden at Bath by 1½ lengths from Auwitesweetheart, leading over 1f out: should stay at least 6f: acts on firm and soft ground. *B. W. Hills*

CEYLON ROUND (FR)   3 b.f. Royal Applause 124 – Tea Colony (USA) (Pleasant   **–** Colony (USA)) [2004 8g 8.3f 10m⁶ p8.6g p7.1g p7m Dec 8] 350,000 francs F, 30,000Y: fourth foal: half-sister to winners abroad by Celtic Swing and Elmaamul: dam unraced: little form. *M. J. Wallace*

CEZZARO (IRE)   6 ch.g. Ashkalani (IRE) 128 – Sept Roses (USA) (Septieme Ciel   **43** (USA) 123) [2004 51, a–: f8g⁵ f8m⁶ 12.1m 10g² 12.1g² 8d 12m f12m 12m⁵ 8s Oct 30]   **a–** compact gelding: poor performer: left S. R. Bowring after ninth start: stays 12.6f: acts on any turf ground, little form on all-weather: tried visored/in cheekpieces: tongue tied (well held) once: usually races prominently. *T. A. K. Cuthbert*

CHAIN OF HOPE (IRE)   3 ch.g. Shinko Forest (IRE) – Fleeting Smile (IRE) (Blue   **47** bird (USA) 125) [2004 57: 6.1d 6g 8.3g p12.2g p12m Dec 8] lengthy gelding: poor maiden: seems to stay 1½m. *D. E. Cantillon*

CHAIRMAN BOBBY   6 ch.g. Clantime 101 – Formidable Liz 66 (Formidable (USA)   **78 d** 125) [2004 76: 5g⁵ 5d 6d 5d³ 6m² 6m 5m² 6m⁵ 5m 6m 5m 5d 6f p6g p7g p6g f6g⁶ Dec 7] smallish, sturdy gelding: fair handicapper: below form after seventh start: left D. Barker after fourteenth: best at 5f/6f: acts on fibresand, firm and soft going: tried in cheekpieces: carries head awkwardly: often races prominently. *B. A. McMahon*

CHAIRMAN RICK (IRE)   2 b.c. (Mar 28) Danehill Dancer (IRE) 117 – Come   **61** Together 68 (Mtoto 134) [2004 7g p6g⁶ 5.2m⁴ 6m 5.9g Sep 2] €40,000F, 68,000Y: second foal: dam 11f winner: modest maiden: should stay at least 6f: visored fourth start (ran poorly), then left D. Loder. *D. Nicholls*

CHAKRA   10 gr.g. Mystiko (USA) 124 – Maracuja (USA) (Riverman (USA) 131) [2004   **–** p6g⁶ 10.2g⁵ 8g³ f7g 10.2f May 21] big gelding: little form on Flat since 2001 (missed 2003): tried blinkered. *C. J. Gray*

CHALISON (IRE)   2 b.c. (Feb 22) Anabaa (USA) 130 – Raincloud (Rainbow Quest   **86** (USA) 134) [2004 5s² 6g³ 7g⁵ Jul 10] 42,000Y: sturdy, close-coupled colt: second foal: closely related to 4-y-o Low Cloud: dam, lightly-raced French 1½m winner, sister to smart performer up to 1¾m Tuning: fairly useful form in maidens/minor event: jarred up after: should stay 1m. *R. Hannon*

CHAMBRAY (IRE)   3 b.f. Barathea (IRE) 127 – Spurned (USA) 91 (Robellino (USA)   **56** 127) [2004 –p: 8g 8.1g 11.6m⁵ Jun 28] modest maiden: should stay 1½m. *A. M. Balding*

CHAMPAGNE BRANDY (IRE)   2 ch.f. (Mar 10) Spectrum (IRE) 126 – Petite Liq   **–** ueuerelle (IRE) (Shernazar 131) [2004 5g 6.1g 6m p8.6g p8.6g Dec 11] €8,000Y: small, plain filly: sister to 3-y-o Revenir and half-sister to several winners, including useful 5f (at 2 yrs) to 1m winner Caviar Royale (by Royal Academy) and 1½m winner Typhoon Todd (by Entrepreneur): dam unraced: little sign of ability in maidens/claimers: unruly and withdrawn once. *P. D. Evans*

CHAMPAGNE CRACKER 3 ch.f. Up And At 'em 109 – Kiveton Komet 71 **67** (Precocious 126) [2004 65: 6v 6f³ 5d* 5d⁵ 6m 5f 6s⁶ 5d Sep 16] big, strong filly: fair handicapper: below form after winning at Haydock in June: best efforts at 5f: acts on good to firm and good to soft going. *Miss L. A. Perratt*

CHAMPAGNE IN PARIS 2 gr.f. (Mar 2) Paris House 123 – Ashleen (Chilibang 120) – [2004 5d Apr 12] first foal: dam lightly-raced maiden: tailed off in maiden at Warwick. *J. A. Glover*

CHAMPAGNE LUJAIN 2 b.g. (Jan 20) Lujain (USA) 119 – Brief Glimpse (IRE) **47** 108 (Taufan (USA) 119) [2004 6m 7v⁵ 7s Nov 1] tall gelding: poor form in maidens. *M. W. Easterby*

CHAMPAGNE RIDER 8 b.g. Presidium 124 – Petitesse 55 (Petong 126) [2004 –, – a53d: f7g³ f7g⁵ f6g* Jan 20] leggy, angular gelding: poor performer: won banded race at **a46** Southwell: effective at 6f to 1¼m: acts on fibresand, heavy and good to firm ground: tried blinkered/visored: sometimes looks none too keen. *D. Shaw*

CHAMPAGNE ROSSINI (IRE) 2 b.g. (Apr 7) Rossini (USA) 118 – Alpencrocus **53** (IRE) (Waajib 121) [2004 5g 8f⁵ f6s⁶ 8g f6g⁶ f6s Nov 17] workmanlike gelding: modest maiden: likely to prove best at 5f/6f: best efforts on fibresand. *M. C. Chapman*

CHAMPAGNE SHADOW (IRE) 3 b.c. Kahyasi 130 – Moet (IRE) 72 (Mac's Imp **73** (USA) 116) [2004 67: p8g p10g⁴ p10g p12g² 11.6g p12d² p10d³ p12g² 16g p12g p12g³ p12g Nov 16] €24,000Y: first foal: dam, 6f winner, out of half-sister to smart miler Patriach and very smart Belmont Stakes runner-up My Memoirs: fair maiden: trained by A. Mullins in Ireland at 2 yrs: should stay 1¾m: acts on polytrack, raced only on good ground or firmer on turf: usually blinkered. *G. L. Moore*

CHAMPAIN SANDS (IRE) 5 b.g. Green Desert (USA) 127 – Grecian Bride (IRE) **61** (Groom Dancer (USA) 128) [2004 70d: f9.4g³ 10d⁴ 10f² 9.2g⁵ 10g 10d 10.4m 8.5m⁶ Sep 15] smallish gelding: modest handicapper: stays 11.5f: acts on all-weather, firm and good to soft ground: tried visored/blinkered/tongue tied, not in 2004: none too reliable. *W. M. Brisbourne*

CHAMPION LION (IRE) 5 b.g. Sadler's Wells (USA) 132 – Honey Bun 51 (Unfu- **74** wain (USA) 131) [2004 88: 12g 14s 12s⁵ 12g 12.3d⁶ 10d³ 10.9s³ 10m⁵ 11.7g Oct 10] strong, close-coupled gelding: fluent mover: fair handicapper: barely stays 1¾m: acts on soft and good to firm going: sometimes slowly away: usually waited with. *M. R. Channon*

CHAMPOLUC (IRE) 3 ch.f. Indian Ridge 123 – Just Ice 90 (Polar Falcon (USA) **64** 126) [2004 81: 7d 6s 8v 10d p8g p7.1g² p7g² Dec 29] 55,000Y: fifth foal: half-sister to useful sprinter Jezebel (by Owington) and German 9f to 1½m winner Franchetto (by Pursuit of Love): dam, 5f/6f winner, ran only at 2 yrs: fairly useful maiden at 2 yrs: just fair form in 2004, leaving Miss I. Oakes in Ireland after fourth start: best efforts at 7f: acts on polytrack and good to soft going: tried in cheekpieces/tongue strap. *W. R. Swinburn*

CHANCE FOR ROMANCE 3 ch.f. Entrepreneur 123 – My First Romance 61 **81** (Danehill (USA) 126) [2004 75+: 6g² 6d⁶ 6f⁵ 6f 6g Aug 14] strong filly: fairly useful performer: below form on reappearance: stays 6f: acts on firm going: tried in cheekpieces/visor: races up with pace. *W. R. Muir*

CHANCELLOR (IRE) 6 ch.h. Halling (USA) 133 – Isticanna (USA) 96 (Far North **116 d** (CAN) 120) [2004 114: 10g 10d* 10.5d 10d 10d 10.5g⁶ p10g p12.2g Dec 17] strong, lengthy horse: smart performer: showed little after winning Betfred Gordon Richards Stakes at Sandown (beat Nysaean a neck) in April: left J. Dunlop after sixth outing: tongue tied, refused to race final one: beat around 1¼m: below form on firm going, acts on any other: tried in cheekpieces: one to avoid. *G. A. Butler*

CHANDELIER 4 ch.g. Sabrehill (USA) 120 – La Noisette (Rock Hopper 124) [2004 **54 §** 60: f7g⁵ p8g³ p8g⁶ p8g f7g³ f7m² 8f 8.1g* 7m⁶ 8.1m 8.1s 8.1s⁶ 8f p8m³ 7g Oct 12] fair on **a66 §** all-weather, modest on turf: won selling handicap at Chepstow in July: effective at 7f/1m: acts on all-weather and good to firm ground: tried blinkered/in cheekpieces: sometimes slowly away: refused to race thirteenth outing: one to treat with caution. *M. S. Saunders*

CHANFRON 3 ch.g. Double Trigger (IRE) 123 – Mhargaidh Nua (Thowra (FR)) [2004 **62** 64: 11.8g 11.6d⁵ 16.2g² 12.1m p12g Oct 1] lengthy gelding: modest maiden: reportedly badly struck into final start: stays 1½m: acts on good to soft ground: races prominently. *B. R. Millman*

CHANGARI (USA) 3 b.f. Gulch (USA) – Danzari 111 (Arazi (USA) 135) [2004 90: – 5m⁵ Jun 12] leggy filly: fairly useful 5f/6f performer at 2 yrs: well held only outing in 2004: sold 30,000 gns in December. *R. Charlton*

CHANTACO (USA) 2 b.c. (Mar 5) Bahri (USA) 125 – Dominant Dancer 97 (Primo **78** Dominie 121) [2004 7f⁵ 7f² 7m* Sep 4] 5,000Y, 12,000 2-y-o: close-coupled colt: first foal: dam, 2-y-o 6f winner, granddaughter of top-class miler Milligram: best effort in maidens when making all at Thirsk: will probably stay 1m: races up with pace. *A. M. Balding*

CHANTELLE (IRE) 4 b.f. Lake Coniston (IRE) 131 – Kristabelle (IRE) 78 (Elbio **61 d** 125) [2004 60: 5d 5d* 6m 5f 5g⁵ 6f 5g 5m 7.1d⁴ p7.1g f7g³ f5g⁴ Dec 1] first foal: dam, Irish 2-y-o 5f winner, half-sister to useful Irish sprinter Ingabelle: modest handicapper on turf, poor on all-weather: won apprentice race at Navan in April: left T. Lacy in Ireland after sixth start: effective at 5f/6f: acts on fibresand, firm and good to soft ground: often blinkered. *S. Kirk*

CHANTELLE'S DREAM 2 ch.f. (Apr 13) Compton Place 125 – Polar Peak 41 – (Polar Falcon (USA) 126) [2004 p5g 5g⁶ Aug 13] £3,500Y: third foal: dam ran 4 times at 2yrs: well beaten in minor event/maiden, slowly away. *I. A. Wood*

CHANTELOUP 3 ch.f. Grand Lodge (USA) 125 – Nibbs Point (IRE) 107 (Sure Blade **84** (USA) 130) [2004 8.5s² 10.4s⁴ 10m⁴ 10.5g³ 11.9g⁵ p13g Oct 1] lengthy filly: half-sister to several winners, including smart but untrustworthy 1¼m/1½m performer Border Arrow (by Selkirk) and fairly useful 9.4f to 1½m winner Shingles (by Desert Prince): dam 1¼m/1½m winner who stayed 2m: fairly useful maiden: flattered when fourth of 6 to Punctilious in Musidora Stakes at York on second start: stays 1½m: acts on soft going, below form on good to firm and polytrack: sold 45,000 gns. *J. R. Fanshawe*

CHANTERELLE (IRE) 3 ch.f. Indian Ridge 123 – Chantereine (USA) (Trempolino **88 ?** (USA) 135) [2004 86p: 6g⁶ 7d⁶ 7d Sep 18] lengthy filly: fairly useful performer: best form at 6f, should stay further: unraced on extremes of going. *J. L. Dunlop*

CHANTEUSE 4 b.f. Rudimentary (USA) 118 – Enchanting Melody 71 (Chief Singer – 131) [2004 60d: f6g f6g⁶ f7g Feb 2] big, good-topped filly: maiden: no form in 2004: tried visored/blinkered. *D. W. Chapman*

CHANTILLY BEAUTY (FR) 2 b.f. (Mar 10) Josr Algarhoud (IRE) 118 – Lysa- **95** belle (FR) (Lesotho (USA) 118) [2004 5s 5.5m* 6m 7.5d⁶ 8s 6m³ 6g⁴ 6g² 6g* Oct 24] €26,000Y: big filly: second foal: dam French 11f/1½m winner: useful performer: won maiden at Le Mans in May and listed race at Rome (by 1½ lengths from Kuaicoss) in October: several creditable efforts in between, though not at Royal Ascot third start (in cheekpieces/carried head awkwardly): probably stays 7.5f: acts on good to firm and good to soft ground: blinkered 4 of last 5 starts. *R. Pritchard-Gordon, France*

CHANTILLY GOLD (USA) 5 ch.m. Mutakddim (USA) 112 – Bouffant (USA) – (Alydar (USA)) [2004 –: f7g f6g⁵ f8g Jan 12] little form: tried in cheekpieces/blinkers. *J. M. Bradley*

CHANTILLY SUNSET (IRE) 3 b.f. General Monash (USA) 107 – Alpine Sunset – (Auction Ring (USA) 123) [2004 –: 6m 7g Sep 14] no sign of ability. *J. Balding*

CHANTRESS 4 b.f. Peintre Celebre (USA) 137 – Up Anchor (IRE) 114 (Slip Anchor **93** 136) [2004 99: 9m 11.9m³ 11.9g Jul 3] leggy, lengthy filly: fairly useful performer, lightly raced: wearing cheekpieces, creditable third to Pongee in listed race at Haydock in May: well beaten in Lancashire Oaks there next time: stays 1½m: raced only on good ground or firmer: often races prominently: sent to USA. *Mrs J. R. Ramsden*

CHANTRY FALLS (IRE) 4 br.g. Mukaddamah (USA) 125 – Woodie Dancer (USA) **48** (Green Dancer (USA) 132) [2004 52: f7g f9.4m⁶ 6m 7g f7g p9.5g⁶ Dec 22] tall gelding: modest maiden: stays 9.5f: acts on polytrack and firm going: tried tongue tied/blinkered. *J. G. Given*

CHAPELCO 3 b.g. Robellino (USA) 127 – Lady Kris (IRE) (Kris 135) [2004 10m⁶ – 12m 12.1s Aug 12] big, plain gelding: no form in maidens, pulled up final start: sold 3,000 gns. *J. L. Dunlop*

CHAPEL ROYALE (IRE) 7 gr.g. College Chapel 122 – Merci Royale (Fairy King – (USA)) [2004 68, a–: f9.4g⁶ f12g⁵ Feb 13] tall gelding: well held in 2004: tried in cheek-pieces: usually tongue tied. *Mrs N. S. Sharpe*

CHAPLIN 3 b.c. Groom Dancer (USA) 128 – Princess Borghese (USA) 82 (Nijinsky **89 ?** (CAN) 138) [2004 –p: 12d² 11.9d 11.9s⁴ Oct 15] big, rangy colt: clearly best effort in maidens when 1½ lengths second to Percussionist at Newmarket: stays 1½m: acts on good to soft ground: tried in cheekpieces: possibly temperamental: sold 27,000 gns. *B. W. Hills*

CHAPPEL CRESENT (IRE)   4 ch.g. College Chapel 122 – Inshad 81 (Indian King   97
(USA) 128) [2004 91?: f8.5g f6g 6g 7v⁵ 7d² 8d⁵ 7.6d* 6d⁵ 7s 6d 8s 6s Oct 23] strong,
angular gelding: useful performer: trained at 2 yrs (6f winner)/3 yrs by G. Keane in
Ireland: made all in handicap at Chester in May: left D. Nicholls before final outing: stays
7.6f: acts on heavy and good to firm ground, well held on fibresand: tried in tongue tie/
cheekpieces: races up with pace: none too consistent. *Ms J. Morgan, Ireland*

CHAPTER HOUSE (USA)   5 b.g. Pulpit (USA) 117 – Lilian Bayliss (IRE) 100   71
(Sadler's Wells (USA) 132) [2004 –: f8g⁶ 12.6m 12s 10.5g Sep 23] tall gelding: fair handicapper: no form after reappearance: stays 1¼m: acts on fibresand, best turf efforts on
good ground: tried visored/blinkered. *M. W. Easterby*

CHAPTER (IRE)   2 ch.c. (Mar 12) Sinndar (IRE) 134 – Web of Intrigue 66 (Machia-   75
vellian (USA) 123) [2004 7.1m² 7g² 8.1d 8f³ 8g⁵ Sep 22] 55,000F, 100,000Y: rather
leggy, useful-looking colt: fourth foal: half-brother to 4-y-o Dubonai: dam lightly-raced
half-sister to Yorkshire Oaks winner Catchascatchcan, herself dam of 3-y-o Antonius
Pius: fair maiden: likely to be suited by 1¼m/1½m: acts on firm ground. *R. Hannon*

CHARA   3 ch.f. Deploy 131 – Subtle One (IRE) (Polish Patriot (USA) 128) [2004 65:   72
9.7s³ 12.1d* 11.6g 11.5s⁵ 10g⁵ 12f⁵ 14d 12.1m p12.2d Nov 4] close-coupled filly: fair
handicapper: won at Beverley in April: well below form last 3 starts: should stay 1¾m:
acts on polytrack, firm and soft going. *J. R. Jenkins*

CHARING CROSS (IRE)   3 ch.c. Peintre Celebre (USA) 137 – Charlotte Corday 105   76 d
(Kris 135) [2004 11d⁵ p12g p12g 12s 9.9g⁶ 11.9s p10g Dec 20] well-made colt: 2¾ leng-
ths fifth of 10 in newcomers event at Longchamp in May on only start for J. Hammond in
France: well held in Britain, including in blinkers/tongue strap. *G. L. Moore*

CHARIOT (IRE)   3 ch.g. Titus Livius (FR) 115 – Battle Queen 85 (Kind of Hush 118)   –
[2004 64: f8s 8s p8.6g f8g Nov 23] sturdy gelding: maiden: well held in 2004: tried
visored. *M. R. Bosley*

CHARLATAN (IRE)   6 b.g. Charnwood Forest (IRE) 125 – Taajreh (IRE) 89 (Mtoto   –
134) [2004 6m Jun 1] good-topped, workmanlike gelding: no form. *Mrs C. A. Dunnett*

CHARLESTON   3 ch.g. Pursuit of Love 124 – Discomatic (USA) (Roberto (USA)   75
131) [2004 8v² 10.2m² 10.2g² p12d⁴ 11.6f p12g p13g Dec 4] sturdy gelding: half-brother
to 3 winners, notably smart 1¾m winner Tuning (by Rainbow Quest): dam, French 9f
winner, half-sister to 1987 Phoenix Stakes winner Digamist: fair maiden: left J. Gosden
after fifth start: stays 1½m: acts on polytrack, heavy and good to firm ground: ran poorly
only try in blinkers. *R. Rowe*

CHARLIE BEAR   3 ch.c. Bahamian Bounty 116 – Abi 84 (Chief's Crown (USA))   75
[2004 70p: 10.9d 8m² 8.3m p7.1g³ Oct 9] tall colt: fair maiden handicapper: effective at
7f/1m: acts on good to firm going and polytrack: sold 25,000 gns. *E. A. L. Dunlop*

CHARLIE GEORGE   3 ch.g. Idris (IRE) 118 – Faithful Beauty (IRE) (Last Tycoon   –
131) [2004 8g 10.5g⁶ 9.2d⁵ Aug 11] sparely-made gelding: little form. *P. Monteith*

CHARLIEISMYDARLING   3 b.g. Mind Games 121 – Blessed Lass (HOL) (Good   41
Times (ITY)) [2004 58: 6m⁴ 7m 8f Jun 23] poor maiden: seems to stay 7f: acts on good to
firm ground and all-weather. *J. A. Osborne*

CHARLIE KENNET   6 b.g. Pyramus (USA) 78 – Evaporate 51 (Insan (USA) 119)   61
[2004 p12g p10g³ Dec 4] better effort in maidens (modest form) when third at Lingfield.
Mrs H. Sweeting

CHARLIE MASTERS   3 b.g. Polar Falcon (USA) 126 – Bowden Rose 100 (Dashing   70
Blade 117) [2004 7m 10m p8m p8.6g² p8.6g³ p8.6g³ p8.6g⁴ Dec 10] second foal: dam 5f
and (including at 2 yrs) 6f winner: fair maiden: left P. Howling after fifth start: stays 8.6f:
acts on polytrack. *W. J. Musson*

CHARLIE PARKES   6 ch.g. Pursuit of Love 124 – Lucky Parkes 108 (Full Extent   –
(USA) 113) [2004 95: 5m 5m May 22] strong, lengthy gelding: one-time useful 5f
performer: well held in handicaps in 2004. *E. J. Alston*

CHARLIESLASTCHANCE   2 b.f. (May 5) Sure Blade (USA) 130 – Sea Mist (IRE)   –
53 (Shalford (IRE) 124§) [2004 8m 8.3g Oct 11] £400Y: fourth foal: dam maiden who
stayed 7f: last in maiden/seller. *J. J. Bridger*

CHARLIES PROFIT   3 ch.f. Deploy 131 – Care And Comfort 64 (Most Welcome   –
131) [2004 p10g Jan 10] £300Y: third foal: half-sister to German 7f and 1¼m winner
Gudaut (by Elmaamul): dam 1m winner: always behind in maiden at Lingfield.
J. J. Bridger

Polypipe Flying Childers Stakes, Doncaster—Chateau Istana (left) puts up his best performance, beating Tournedos (centre) and Kissing Lights (quartered cap)

CHARLIE TANGO (IRE) 3 b.g. Desert Prince (IRE) 130 – Precedence (IRE) 88 **74** (Polish Precedent (USA) 131) [2004 72: p10g³ 10d 8.5v 10.2m 9.1f³ 10d 8m⁴ 9g* 10f³ 10g⁴ 9f³ 10.9g⁵ 10g 7.9g 8g 8.5m⁴ p8.6g 10s² 8s⁴ f8g Dec 16] leggy gelding: fair handicapper: won at Redcar in June: left M. Channon after tenth start: effective at 1m to 11f: acts on polytrack and firm ground, probably on soft: tried blinkered/visored/tongue tied. *N. Tinkler*

CHARLOTTEBUTTERFLY 4 b.f. Millkom 124 – Tee Gee Jay 63 (Northern Temp- **63** est (USA) 120) [2004 63: 5.7s 6m⁴ 6m 7g 6g³ 7g 6m⁴ p7.1d* p7.1g Nov 20] good-topped filly: modest performer: won minor event at Wolverhampton in November: stays 7f: acts on all-weather and good to firm going. *T. T. Clement*

CHARLOTTE VALE 3 ch.f. Pivotal 124 – Drying Grass Moon 66 (Be My Chief **78** (USA) 122) [2004 60: 7.9d⁶ 8.1d⁵ 9.1g² 12d* 11d³ 12g* 11.9m² 12.1d³ 13.1s⁶ Oct 12] leggy, plain filly: fair handicapper: won at Thirsk in June and Pontefract in July: stays 1½m: acts on good to firm and good to soft going: sometimes hangs left: consistent. *M. D. Hammond*

CHARLOTTINE (IRE) 3 b.f. Spectrum (IRE) 126 – Lady Dulcinea (ARG) (General **58** (FR)) [2004 72: 7.5v⁵ 8m 8f⁵ 8f³ 8g⁵ 7m 10.2s³ Sep 20] half-sister to several winners, including 1m to 1¼m winner It's Our Secret (by Be My Guest): dam won in Peru: modest maiden handicapper: effective at 1m/1¼m: acts on any ground: wore cheekpieces/ blinkers last 4 starts. *M. P. Sunderland, Ireland*

CHARMATIC (IRE) 3 br.f. Charnwood Forest (IRE) 125 – Instamatic 97 (Night Shift **70** (USA)) [2004 –p: 8v⁵ 8v² 8.2s² 8.5v* 8.2m⁵ 10f⁴ 10g⁵ 9.9s 8.5m⁶ 11.9g p9.5d² p9.5g² p9.5g Nov 13] strong, lengthy filly: fair handicapper: won at Beverley in May: effective at 1m/1¼m: acts on polytrack and any turf going: tried tongue tied, not in 2004: has worn crossed noseband. *J. A. Glover*

CHARMED BY FIRE (USA) 3 b.c. Silver Charm (USA) 132 – Mama Dean (USA) **70** (Woodman (USA) 126) [2004 10g 9f 10d⁵ 10g Aug 23] $120,000Y: third foal: dam, winner in USA and second in Grade 3 1m event, half-sister to very smart US performer up to 9f Vicar: fair maiden: should prove as effective at 1m as 1¼m: acts on firm and good to soft going: tongue tied (ran poorly) final start: sold 13,000 gns. *Mrs A. J. Perrett*

CHARMING ADMIRAL (IRE) 11 b.g. Shareef Dancer (USA) 135 – Lilac Charm **56** 87 (Bustino 136) [2004 –: 18v⁶ 21.6v² Apr 19] workmanlike gelding: carries plenty of condition: modest handicapper: stays 21.6f: seems best on ground softer than good: usually visored/blinkered. *Mrs A. Duffield*

CHARM OFFENSIVE 6 b.m. Zieten (USA) 118 – Shoag (USA) (Affirmed (USA)) **–** [2004 f16g Dec 14] well beaten only Flat outing since 2002. *C. J. Gray*

CHARNOCK BATES ONE (IRE) 3 b.f. Desert Sun 120 – Fleetwood Fancy **79** (Taufan (USA) 119) [2004 64: 7.5d⁴ 8.2s⁶ 8s 8.5d⁴ 8g² 8g² 10s² 10.5s³ 10s⁶ 10.3s Oct 22] angular filly: has a quick action: fair handicapper: won at Beverley in July: stays 1¼m: acts on soft and good to firm going: sometimes slowly away: consistent. *T. D. Easterby*

CHARNWOOD PRIDE (IRE) 3 gr.g. Charnwood Forest (IRE) 125 – Pride of **–** Pendle 80 (Grey Desire 115) [2004 10m 10g 12m Jul 6] tongue tied, well beaten in maidens. *P. W. Harris*

CHARNWOOD STREET (IRE)   5 b.g. Charnwood Forest (IRE) 125 – La Vigie   –
(King of Clubs 124) [2004 56d: f14g⁵ f14g⁵ Jan 20] leggy gelding: well held both starts
in 2004: usually wears visor. *D. Shaw*

CHASE THE RAINBOW   3 gr.f. Danzig Connection (USA) – Delta Tempo (IRE)   –
(Bluebird (USA) 125) [2004 57: f8.5g⁶ 9.2g⁶ 8m 7g⁶ 7m 8f Jun 23] compact filly: poor
performer: left A. Berry after fourth start: stays 7f: acts on fibresand and good to firm
going. *Miss K. M. George*

CHASING THE DREAM (IRE)   3 b.f. Desert Sun 120 – Dream of Jenny 73   **68**
(Caerleon (USA) 132) [2004 p8g* p10g² 9.9s⁶ 9g 8.3m³ 8g⁴ Jun 24] €14,500Y: seventh
foal: half-sister to several winners, including 7-y-o Jack Dawson: dam placed around 1m
at 2 yrs (only season to race): fair performer: won maiden at Lingfield in January: stays
1¼m: acts on polytrack and good to firm going. *A. M. Balding*

CHASM   2 b.c. (Feb 19) Gulch (USA) – Subito 94 (Darshaan 133) [2004 7m³ 8m⁵ Sep   **66 p**
29] tall colt: first foal: dam, 7f winner (ran only at 2yrs), should have stayed at least 1¼m:
green, fair form in maidens at Epsom and Newcastle: likely to stay 1¼m: sold 32,000 gns,
sent to USA: open to improvement. *M. Johnston*

CHATEAU ISTANA   2 ch.c. (Apr 26) Grand Lodge (USA) 125 – Miss Queen (USA)   **108**
(Miswaki (USA) 124) [2004 5s⁶ 5m* 5f* 6m 5f* 6g Oct 1] €85,000Y: strong colt: third
foal: half-brother to 3-y-o Mandobi: dam, US 6f winner, half-sister to useful 6f/7f winner
Tajannub: useful performer: won maiden at Leicester in May, listed race at Royal Ascot
in June and Polypipe Flying Childers Stakes at Doncaster (by 2 lengths) in September,

Mr Ivan Allan's "Chateau Istana"

last 2 from Tournedos: needs to settle to stay 6f: acts on firm ground: tongue tied last 2 outings: reportedly sold, and joined C. S. Shum in Hong Kong. *N. P. Littmoden*

CHATEAU NICOL   5 b.g. Distant Relative 128 – Glensara (Petoski 135) [2004 79: p6g* p6g³ p7g p7g* p7g⁴ 7d* 6v³ 7.1s³ 7g³ 7g⁴ 7d* 6m⁵ 7g⁶ 6m⁶ 7m 7m* p7.1g⁴ 6s³ 7d p6g* p6g² p7g² Dec 29] well-made gelding: useful performer: won handicaps at Lingfield in January and February, minor event at Folkestone in April and handicaps at Kempton in June, Newbury (by short head from Blue Trojan, whose rider stopped riding close home) in September and Lingfield (by short head from Buy On The Red) in December: effective at 6f/7f: acts on all-weather, heavy and good to firm going: effective visored/blinkered: sometimes hangs: consistent. *B. G. Powell*   **97**

CHATER FLAIR   7 b.g. Efisio 120 – Native Flair 87 (Be My Native (USA) 122) [2004 f12g Jan 26] rather leggy gelding: lightly raced and no form on Flat since 2001: often blinkered/visored. *D. Burchell*   **–**

CHATSHOW (USA)   3 br.g. Distant View (USA) 126 – Galanty Show 76 (Danehill (USA) 126) [2004 6m 8.1g 6m⁴ 6m f8g⁵ 6m 6f 7.1s 6d³ 5d 5.7s* p5.1g² 6d² p6g⁴ f5g* f6g f5f⁴ p5.1g⁴ Dec 31] first foal: dam, 6f winner, out of half-sister to Desirable and Park Appeal: modest performer: trained by P. Bary in France only 2-y-o start: left L. Dace after eighth outing: won apprentice handicap at Bath in October and banded race at Southwell in December: effective at 5f/6f: acts on all-weather and soft going: tried tongue tied. *A. W. Carroll*   **62**

CHECKIT (IRE)   4 br.c. Mukaddamah (USA) 125 – Collected (IRE) (Taufan (USA) 119) [2004 117: 8.9m⁴ 8.9m³ 8m³ 8.9m⁶ 8.1d 8m 9.3g³ 8.5m⁴ 8f 8g³ 10m⁴ 8g 10.5g³ 9s⁶ 8s² 9d² 8g Oct 1] well-made colt: has a quick, fluent action: smart performer: put up numerous creditable efforts in good company in 2004, including close sixth to Paolini and Right Approach in Dubai Duty Free at Nad Al Sheba fourth outing, 3 lengths third to Prince Kirk in Prix d'Ispahan at Longchamp on seventh and 2 lengths second to Pepperstorm in Darley Oettingen-Rennen at Baden-Baden on fifteenth: effective at 1m/1¼m: acts on firm and soft ground: visored (ran creditably) once: held up: tough and consistent: sold 75,000 gns, joined R. Bouresly in UAE. *M. R. Channon*   **114**

CHEEKY CHI (IRE)   3 b.f. Desert Style (IRE) 121 – Grey Patience (IRE) (Common Grounds 118) [2004 p7g⁴ p7g⁴ p6g³ 5s* f6d⁴ 5.1d 5.3m 5g 5.3m 5.3s⁶ p6g 6d p6g f5g p7m Dec 8] IR4,000F, €6,500Y: small filly: third foal: half-sister to fairly useful Irish 2002 2-y-o 6f winner Vanilla Sky (by Flying Spur): dam unraced half-sister to smart 7f/1m performer Cape Town: fair performer: mostly well below form after winning maiden at Redcar in April: effective at 5f to easy 7f: acts on soft ground and polytrack: tried in cheekpieces. *P. S. McEntee*   **61 d**

Moyglare Stud Stakes, the Curragh—with the first two in the betting below par,
Chelsea Rose takes advantage; Pictavia is second ahead of Saoire, Umniya and Belle Artiste (No.1)

CHEENEY BASIN (IRE) 6 ch.g. King's Signet (USA) 110 – Gratclo 65 (Belfort – (FR) 89) [2004 f6g f5s f7g Dec 14] leggy gelding: off nearly 2 years, well held in handicaps at Southwell. *M. C. Chapman*

CHEESE 'N BISCUITS 4 b.f. Spectrum (IRE) 126 – Bint Shihama (USA) 78 **74** (Cadeaux Genereux 131) [2004 94: 8m 6g 7.6s² 8m 7g 7.1g p7d 7d⁵ 7g⁴ p7g 7s 6d p7g p8g p8g² p7.1g* Dec 14] fair performer: won claimer at Wolverhampton in December: stays 1m: acts on polytrack, heavy and good to firm going: often wears cheekpieces. *G. L. Moore*

CHEHALIS MIST (IRE) 2 b.c. (Apr 23) Orpen (USA) 116 – Classic Heights **60 p** (Shirley Heights 130) [2004 p8.6g⁴ Dec 17] €30,000Y: ninth foal: brother to Italian 5f (at 2 yrs) to 7.5f winner Queen Duck and half-brother to winner abroad by Saddlers' Hall: dam unraced sister to high-class 1½m performer Head For Heights: 8/1, 4¼ lengths fourth to Swift Oscar in maiden at Wolverhampton: should improve. *M. J. Wallace*

CHEK OI 2 b.c. (Feb 13) Dr Fong (USA) 128 – Silver Sun 83 (Green Desert (USA) **56** 127) [2004 5g 7g p6g 6m⁶ p7.1g Oct 18] modest maiden: best effort at 6f on good to firm going: blinkered, broke leg final start: dead. *W. R. Muir*

CHELSEA ROSE (IRE) 2 ch.f. (Feb 11) Desert King (IRE) 129 – Cinnamon Rose **104** (USA) 96 (Trempolino (USA) 135) [2004 7m* 7m³ 7m* Sep 5] 38,000Y: third foal: half-sister to useful Irish 1m winner European (by Great Commotion), later 9f winner in USA, and French/Spanish 1¼m to 15f winner Ruente (by Persian Bold): dam, Irish 1¼m winner, half-sister to smart French 1¼m performer River Warden: won maiden at Leopardstown in June and Moyglare Stud Stakes at the Curragh (by ¾ length from Pictavia, leading 2f out) in September: 2½ lengths third to Silk And Scarlet in Debutante Stakes at the Curragh in between: should be suited by 1¼m/1½m: useful. *C. Collins, Ireland*

Mrs A. J. Donnelly's "Chelsea Rose"

CHELSEA'S DIAMOND 4 b.f. Man Among Men (IRE) – Sharp Thistle 87 (Sharpo   –
132) [2004 11.7f⁵ 11.5g 7f Jul 29] sister to 1m winner Sharp Monkey and half-sister to a
winner abroad by Kalaglow: dam 7f winner who stayed 1½m: no form: tried blinkered
and in cheekpieces. *J. Akehurst*

CHEM'S LEGACY (IRE) 4 b.g. Victory Note (USA) 120 – Merlannah (IRE) (Shy   **44**
Groom (USA)) [2004 6g 8.1m⁴ 7m Jul 24] poor form in maidens. *W. R. Muir*

CHERISHED NUMBER 5 b.g. King's Signet (USA) 110 – Pretty Average 40 (Sky-   **83**
liner 117) [2004 92, a64: 8v 8d⁴ 8.1m 8m⁶ 8.3m³ 10g³ 7.9g 8.2d⁴ 8m⁴ 9.2f 8m⁵ 9.2d³ 8.3d   **a69**
8.9m⁴ 9.1d³ 8.3d³ 7.2s⁴ p8.6g³ p9.5g⁵ p8.6g* Dec 17] workmanlike gelding: fairly useful
performer on turf, fair on all-weather: won handicap at Wolverhampton in December:
effective at 7f to 1¼m: acts on all-weather and any turf going: often wears headgear.
I. Semple

CHEROKEE BAY 4 b.f. Primo Dominie 121 – Me Cherokee 48 (Persian Bold 123)   **49**
[2004 70d: p10g⁴ p8g³ p8g p10g Feb 23] good-topped filly: poor performer: stays 1¼m:
acts on polytrack, soft and good to firm ground: fair hurdler. *G. L. Moore*

CHEROKEE NATION 3 br.c. Emperor Jones (USA) 119 – Me Cherokee 48 (Persian   **82**
Bold 123) [2004 52: 10g⁴ f9.4g⁴ 6m* 6m 6m² 6m* 6g* 6m 6g³ 6m⁵ f6f 6g p6g² p6d⁴
p5.1g* p6g* p6g p6m Dec 21] tall colt: fairly useful handicapper: won at Lingfield in
May, Yarmouth in June, Ripon in July and at Wolverhampton and Lingfield in November:
stays 6f: raced only on all-weather and good/good to firm ground: usually waited with.
P. W. D'Arcy

CHEROKEE (USA) 2 b.f. (Mar 26) Storm Cat (USA) – Totemic (USA) (Vanlanding-   **102 p**
ham (USA)) [2004 6m⁶ 7s⁵ Oct 16] big, close-coupled filly: seventh foal: half-sister to 2
winners in USA by Pine Bluff, notably very smart Grade 2 8.5f winner Lil's Lad: dam US
Grade 3 8.5f winner: won Go And Go Round Tower Stakes at the Curragh in September
by short head from Lock And Key, quickening well from unpromising position: possibly
unsuited by soft going when only fifth to Maids Causeway in Rockfel Stakes at Newmarket: likely to stay 1m: potentially smart as 3-y-o. *A. P. O'Brien, Ireland*

CHERRY MIX (FR) 3 gr.c. Linamix (FR) 127 – Cherry Moon (USA) (Quiet   **129**
American (USA)) [2004 10.5d³ 11g² 12d³ 10.5d² 12s* 12.5v* 12m² Oct 3]
    The racing and breeding empire built up by prominent industrialist and
chairman of France Galop Jean-Luc Lagardere now looks set for dispersal, partly
to meet death duties. The family has continued to manage operations—involving
around two hundred horses in all—since Lagardere's death in March 2003 but
representatives of the Aga Khan confirmed in December that 'discussions have
taken place' about purchasing the Lagardere interests lock, stock and barrel. Other
prospective buyers were also thought to be interested. If the Aga Khan's Irish and
French studs pursue their interest, it will be in anticipation that adding the Lagardere bloodstock interests—second in the owners' table in France in 2004 and easily
the top breeder (tenth title)—proves as successful as the purchases of the studs of
Mme Francois Dupre and Marcel Boussac in the late-'seventies. Acquiring quality
mares from the Dupre and Boussac studs offered a greater prospect of success, in
the judgement of the Aga Khan, than picking out fillies from sales catalogues. He
was proved right, mares descended from the Boussac families, for example, now
being the second biggest group—behind descendants of mares bred by his grand-
father and father—in his unmatched breeding operation. A few of the Lagardere
fillies in training were offered at the December Sales and a colt that the Aga Khan
won't be getting his hands on—if a deal is done—will be the Prix de l'Arc de
Triomphe runner-up Cherry Mix, who was acquired privately by Godolphin after
Longchamp. Godolphin enjoyed plenty of success on the international scene with
the 2002 Arc runner-up Sulamani, purchased from the Niarchos Family, and Cherry
Mix looks a ready-made replacement for that horse, who is now at stud. Cherry Mix
is to start off his 2005 campaign in the Dubai Sheema Classic at Nad Al Sheba, the
race in which Sulamani made a successful debut in the Godolphin colours as a four-
year-old.
    The progress made by Cherry Mix in the second half of his three-year-old
season was striking. He showed only fairly useful form at two—winning an apprentice maiden at Fontainebleau on the first of two starts—and was demonstrably
below classic standard in the first part of his latest campaign. A beaten favourite in
listed company at Saint-Cloud in March on his reappearance, Cherry Mix then went

Grand Prix de Deauville Lucien Barriere, Deauville—a 1,2,3 for trainer Andre Fabre as Cherry Mix gains a four-length success from older horses Martaline (grey), Bailador (rail) and Swing Wing

down in two recognised Prix du Jockey Club trials at Longchamp, beaten three lengths by Voix du Nord in the Prix Noailles in April and three quarters of a length and three lengths by Lord du Sud and Prospect Park in the Prix Hocquart in May. These looked creditable efforts at the time, though, none too surprisingly, they didn't earn Cherry Mix a place in the line-up at Chantilly, third-placed Valixir doing best of his stable's three Prix du Jockey Club runners (the Hocquart principals Prospect Park and Lord du Sud were second and sixth, while Voix du Nord didn't make it to Chantilly because of injury).

It was back to the Provinces in the summer for Cherry Mix, who gained his first victory of the campaign in a listed event at Vichy in July before returning to the principal tracks in August. Cherry Mix was back in pattern company for the Grand Prix de Deauville Lucien Barriere, in which he was one of three Fabre runners and the only three-year-old in a seven-strong line-up. Cherry Mix showed himself much improved since the Prix du Jockey Club trials, running out a convincing four-length winner on heavy ground after coming from the back of a tightly-grouped field to forge clear in the final furlong. His in-form stablemates Martaline and Bailador, successful respectively in listed and pattern company on their previous starts, made it a one, two, three for the stable. The Grand Prix de Deauville is won more often by one of the older generation, its place in the calendar slightly too soon for a top French three-year-old returning from a traditional summer break. Cherry Mix's trainer is among those to have won the race with three-year-olds, however, most notably with Swain, who went on to finish third to Lammtarra in the Arc. Cherry Mix put up an even better performance at Longchamp than Swain had done, almost giving Andre Fabre—champion in France for the eighteenth successive year—his sixth training success in the race. Cherry Mix moved supremely well from the start, kept to the inside and never far off the leaders, and looked all over the winner when bursting past front-running North Light in the home straight and briefly showing clear over a furlong out. Bago needed nearly the whole of the final furlong to peg him back, Cherry Mix going down by half a length. On firmish going—conditions contrasting sharply with Deauville—Cherry Mix's form continued its upward curve and he put up an excellent performance, one that augurs well for his prospects as a four-year-old.

The small, quite attractive Cherry Mix is by France's champion sire Linamix, winner of the Poule d'Essai des Poulains in the grey silks of Jean-Luc Lagardere, whose home-breds by Linamix have included numerous other pattern winners with the distinctive 'mix' suffix, among them an Arc winner in Sagamix, a Prix Jacques le Marois winner in Miss Satamixa, a Poule d'Essai des Poulains and Jacques le Marois winner (both on disqualifications) in Vahorimix, a Grand Prix de

Famille Lagardere's "Cherry Mix"

Cherry Mix (FR) (gr.c. 2001)	Linamix (FR) (gr 1987)	Mendez (gr 1981)	Bellypha Miss Carina
		Lunadix (gr 1972)	Breton Lutine
	Cherry Moon (USA) (b 1995)	Quiet American (b 1986)	Fappiano Demure
		Datsdawayitis (b 1989)	Known Fact Baton Twirler

Saint-Cloud winner in Fragrant Mix, a Prix Ganay winner in Fair Mix (after he was bought out of a claimer from Lagardere for the French racing magazine *Week-End*) and a Criterium de Saint-Cloud winner in Goldamix. Linamix has also sired two other Group 1 winners in Slickly (Grand Prix de Paris, Prix du Moulin and twice winner of the Premio Vittorio di Capua) and Amilynx (Prix Royal-Oak twice). The Lagardere mares have made a notable contribution to the success of Linamix, who would probably be included in any dispersal package, along with the Haras du Val Henry where he stands and the Haras d'Ouilly, which was purchased from the Dupre family in 1986, as well as the 'grey, pink cap' livery formerly carried with distinction by Dupre horses such as Reliance and Relko. Cherry Mix is the first foal of Cherry Moon, a winner four times in North America at up to eight and a half furlongs, including in a listed handicap. Cherry Mix stays twelve and a half furlongs and, on his Arc showing, won't be inconvenienced by a return to distances around a mile and a quarter. He acts on heavy and good to firm going. *A. Fabre, France*

CHERTSEY (IRE) 3 ch.f. Medaaly 114 – Cerisette (IRE) 94 (Polar Falcon (USA) **63**
126) [2004 7f³ 8f³ 6.1m⁵ 8m 7f⁵ 6g⁶ f7s⁵ Aug 23] smallish filly: second foal: half-sister
to a winner in Greece by Lion Cavern: dam, 7f winner at 2 yrs on only outing, half-sister
to very smart 1m/1¼m performer Crimplene: modest maiden: stays 7f: acts on firm
going: free-going sort: sold 2,800 gns, joined M. Hourigan in Ireland. *C. E. Brittain*

CHERUBIM (JPN) 3 ch.f. Sunday Silence (USA) – Curly Angel (JPN) (Judge **79**
Angelucci (USA)) [2004 79: 10g⁵ 8.1m⁵ 10f* p10g² 12g 16g p9.5g Oct 18] rather leggy,
lengthy filly: fair performer: won maiden at Brighton in June: stays 1¼m: acts on
polytrack, raced only on good ground or firmer on turf: races prominently: none too
consistent. *D. R. Loder*

CHESNUT RIPPLE 5 ch.m. Cosmonaut – Shaft of Sunlight 58 (Sparkler 130) [2004 **46**
71d: f8g4 Jan 6] strong mare: maiden: just poor form only outing in 2004: barely stays
1½m: acts on fibresand, good to firm and soft ground: tried visored: sometimes gives
trouble at stall/takes strong hold. *D. Shaw*

CHESTALL 3 b.g. Polar Prince (IRE) 117 – Maradata (IRE) 68 (Shardari 134) [2004 **64**
12.1g⁴ 12g⁴ 11.8g⁵ f11g² Dec 16] big, close-coupled gelding: modest maiden: stays 1½m:
acts on fibresand. *R. Hollinshead*

CHESTMINSTER GIRL 2 ch.f. (Jan 30) Tomba 119 – Nannie Annie 60 (Persian **–**
Bold 123) [2004 8.1m p7.1g 8.2v Nov 4] plain filly: half-sister to several winners,
including 1m winner New Diamond (by Bijou d'Inde): dam ran 3 times at 2 yrs: no form
in maidens/seller: in cheekpieces last 2 starts. *A. P. Jones*

CHEVERAK FOREST (IRE) 3 ch.g. Shinko Forest (IRE) – Meranie Girl (IRE) 52 **59**
(Mujadil (USA) 119) [2004 70: 7.5d 10g 8s 7.9g 8g 7d⁴ f8s f8g Dec 1] smallish gelding:
modest performer: should stay 1m: acts on fibresand, good to firm and good to soft going:
tried visored/tongue tied. *Don Enrico Incisa*

CHEVIN 5 ch.m. Danzig Connection (USA) – Starr Danias (USA) (Sensitive Prince **52**
(USA)) [2004 55: 12m⁵ 12m 13.8m* 14.1f 12g 12m Sep 25] sparely-made mare: modest
handicapper: won at Catterick in August: effective at 11f to 2m: acts on firm ground:
free-going sort. *R. A. Fahey*

CHEVRONNE 4 b.g. Compton Place 125 – Maria Isabella (FR) (Young Generation **65**
129) [2004 75: 10s 7m 7.1m² 9g 7.1g Jul 9] compact gelding: fair maiden: effective at 7f
to easy 1½m: acts on polytrack and good to firm ground: tried blinkered/in cheekpieces:
winning hurdler. *L. G. Cottrell*

CHIC 4 ch.f. Machiavellian (USA) 123 – Exclusive 115 (Polar Falcon (USA) 126) **123**
[2004 104: 8g⁶ 8f 7m³ 7g* 8s* 8g² Oct 2]

As one very smart four-year-old chestnut filly owned by the Cheveley Park
Stud and trained by Sir Michael Stoute bowed out, another, somewhat unexpect-
edly, came along to take her place. Chic, one of the extras while Russian Rhythm
took centre stage during their two- and three-year-old careers, was given the chance
to play the lead when injury ended the latter's racing career, and she proved something of a star. At the time that Russian Rhythm was making her final appearance
and winning her fourth Group 1 event in the Lockinge Stakes in May, Chic hadn't
even contested a pattern race. The closest she had come to doing so was when
considered as a possible pacemaker for Russian Rhythm in the previous season's
Queen Elizabeth II Stakes! Twelve months later Chic was on the verge of being
supplemented for the same race until meeting with a setback—a good indication of
the marked progress she had made in the interim.

Chic ran twice at two and developed into a useful filly at three, when she
won a maiden at Chester, a handicap at Kempton and, on her final start, a listed
event at Ascot. Defeats on her first three outings in the latest season might have
suggested that Chic's limitations had been exposed. However, she was in need of
the race first time up, all but came down when clipping the heels of a rival just over
two furlongs out in the Windsor Forest Stakes at Ascot on her next start and was set
too much to do when third to Phantom Wind in the Oak Tree Stakes at Goodwood.
The Stan James Online Hungerford Stakes in August was the stage for Chic's fourth
appearance, and she took the race by storm. One of thirteen in a good renewal of
this Group 3 contest, run over seven furlongs at Newbury, Chic settled matters
when quickening to lead over a furlong out, and she ran on strongly, despite drifting

totesport Celebration Mile, Goodwood—
Chic cuts down Nayyir (right) close home; Hurricane Alan is third

left, to win by a length and three quarters. Suggestive finished well to take second without threatening the winner. Two weeks later Chic lined up for a Group 2 run over a furlong further and on ground much more testing than that which she had encountered at Newbury. The totesport Celebration Mile at Goodwood attracted just six other runners, but they included Nayyir, who, over the same course and distance on his previous start, had put up a high-class performance when finishing runner-up to Soviet Song in the Sussex Stakes. Nayyir was sent off favourite at 5/4 with Chic second favourite at 4/1, and the pair dominated the finish. Chic was in rear and off the bridle as Passing Glance and Naahy pressed for home much too early, the pair ignored by the rest of the field until the straight where the runners came across to the stand rail. Initially, Chic could make no headway, whereas Nayyir moved through to lead two furlongs out and looked sure to win when quickening clear soon after. The picture changed dramatically inside the final furlong. Nayyir began to tire, Chic, switched off the rail, was now in full cry and stormed through to catch him close home, finishing so strongly that there was a length and a quarter between them at the line. Chic was clearly worth her place in Group 1 company now and, having made a quick recovery from the setback (kicked by another horse) which put her out of the reckoning for the Queen Elizabeth II, she was sent off favourite for the Sun Chariot Stakes at Newmarket. Chic didn't look quite so well as she had done in the summer but matched her Celebration Mile form in going down gamely by a neck to Attraction, finding the front-running winner pulling out extra after Chic had managed to get upsides a furlong out. Both fillies seem set to stay in training, so they could be providing more memorable finishes in 2005.

Chic is from the ninth crop of Machiavellian, who suffered from laminitis and was put down in June. Machiavellian was the top two-year-old of his year in France and went on to finish second in the Two Thousand Guineas, though he only just got a mile. He proved most versatile, as well as highly successful, at stud, siring plenty of horses who stayed better than he did, his Group 1 winners scoring at distances ranging from five furlongs (the Prix de l'Abbaye winner Patavellian) to two and a half miles (the Prix du Cadran winner Invermark). Others include the

Dubai World Cup winners Almutawakel and Street Cry, the Champion Stakes winner Storming Home and the Poule d'Essai des Poulains winner Vettori, as well as Medicean, who won the Lockinge and Eclipse in the colours of the Cheveley Park Stud and took up stallion duties there in 2002. Chic is the first foal of Exclusive, who also raced for Cheveley Park, winning a minor event at Kempton and finishing third in the Fillies' Mile on her only starts at two years, and from four outings in the following season winning the Coronation Stakes and finishing third in the One Thousand Guineas. On her final outing Exclusive showed herself effective at a mile and a quarter when sixth in the International at York, beaten just over three lengths despite meeting trouble in the final furlong. Chic's grandam Exclusive Order, a very smart winner in France at six to seven furlongs, has produced a host of other winners, notably the 1997 Two Thousand Guineas winner Entrepreneur, the 1995 Cheshire Oaks winner and Oaks runner-up Dance A Dream, and the smart middle-distance performer Sadler's Image. Exclusive's second

Chic (ch.f. 2000)	Machiavellian (USA) (b 1987)	Mr Prospector (b 1970)	Raise A Native Gold Digger
		Coup de Folie (b 1982)	Halo Raise The Standard
	Exclusive (ch 1995)	Polar Falcon (b 1987)	Nureyev Marie d'Argonne
		Exclusive Order (ch 1979)	Exclusive Native Bonavista

Cheveley Park Stud's "Chic"

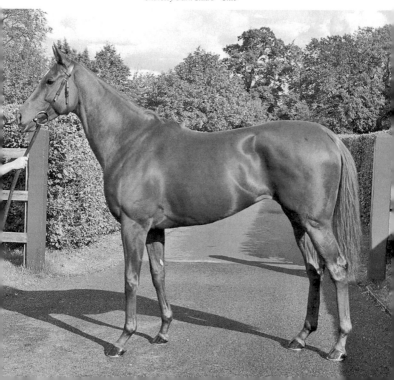

produce Echoes (by Rainbow Quest) never raced and was sold in foal to Where Or When in July. Her third, Echelon (by Danehill), made a very promising start when winning a maiden at Newmarket in August, and again showed useful form, despite not getting the run of things, when seventh in the Fillies' Mile the following month. The tall, lengthy Chic is effective at seven furlongs and a mile, and she acts on soft and good to firm going. *Sir Michael Stoute*

CHICAGO BOND (USA) 3 b.f. Real Quiet (USA) 131 – Shariyfa (FR) (Zayyani 119) [2004 64: 7d 9.9g 9d⁶ 8m Aug 8] leggy, rather sparely-made filly: maiden: well held in 2004. *B. Smart*   –

CHICAGO NIGHTS (IRE) 2 ch.f. (Feb 11) Night Shift (USA) – Enclave (USA) (Woodman (USA) 126) [2004 5d⁴ 5m 6g f6d⁵ 6s² 7m 6m f5f Dec 28] €8,000Y, resold 10,000Y: good-bodied filly: first foal: dam, ran twice in France, half-sister to 5-y-o Comfy: modest maiden on turf, poor on all-weather: left P. Haslam prior to final outing: stays 6f: acts on soft going: in cheekpieces sixth start. *Ronald Thompson*   **51**

CHICA (IRE) 3 gr.f. Spectrum (IRE) 126 – Wild Rose of York 64 (Unfuwain (USA) 131) [2004 –: p7g Jan 3] leggy filly: little sign of ability. *J. A. Osborne*   –

CHICA ROCA (USA) 3 ch.f. Woodman (USA) 126 – Amenixa (FR) 73 (Linamix (FR) 127) [2004 8m 7g 6m⁶ 6m p8g Sep 1] €400,000Y: rather leggy, close-coupled filly: has a quick action: second foal: half-sister to smart French 2002 2-y-o sprinter Zinziberine (by Zieten): dam, 1m winner, sister to high-class French stayer Amilynx: fairly useful form in minor events in France in 2003 for A. Fabre: well held in Britain: tried blinkered/tongue tied. *B. J. Meehan*   **49**

CHICKADO (IRE) 3 b.f. Mujadil (USA) 119 – Arcevia (IRE) 85 (Archway (IRE) 115) [2004 69: f6g³ 6d⁶ 6m 6d⁶ p6d² Nov 5] angular filly: fair performer: stays 6f: acts on all-weather, firm and good to soft going: races prominently. *D. Haydn Jones*   **59 a65**

CHICKASAW TRAIL 6 ch.m. Be My Chief (USA) 122 – Maraschino 53 (Lycius (USA) 124) [2004 39, a–: f9.4g f9.4s f8.5s f9.4g⁶ 8.1g⁵ 8g* 10v 8.2m⁵ 7.1m 8.1m Jun 14] small mare: poor performer: won banded race at Brighton in May: stays 1m: acts on fibresand, firm and soft going: tried in cheekpieces/visor: unreliable. *R. Hollinshead*   **47 § a– §**

CHICKEN SOUP 2 br.c. (Mar 1) Dansili 127 – Radiancy (IRE) 77 (Mujtahid (USA) 118) [2004 6g⁶ p6g³ 7g 7m 7s³ Oct 16] 8,000Y, 32,000 2-y-o: leggy colt: fourth foal: half-brother to 4-y-o Radiant Bride and a winner in Italy by Emperor Jones: dam, ran twice (second at 7f), half-sister to useful stayer Upper Strata: should stay 1m: acts at Lingfield and Catterick: should stay 1m: acts on polytrack and soft going. *J. A. Osborne*   **73**

CHICKS BABE 2 br.f. (Apr 19) Chickawicka (IRE) 97 – Ballasilla 59 (Puissance 110) [2004 p7.1g Oct 18] first foal: dam maiden sprinter: well held in seller at Wolverhampton, slowly away. *B. Palling*   –

CHICO GUAPO (IRE) 4 b.g. Sesaro (USA) 81 – Summer Queen 80 (Robellino (USA) 127) [2004 82: p5g p5g⁵ 5g 5s 5d* 5s 5m⁵ 5m 5.1g 5f 5m 5d 5g 5.1g 5f Sep 23] compact gelding: fairly useful handicapper: mostly well below form after winning at Thirsk in May: speedy, and best at bare 5f: acts on all-weather, good to firm and good to soft going, probably not on soft: sometimes wears cheekpieces/blinkers: free-going front runner: inconsistent: sold 6,000 gns. *J. A. Glover*   **82 d**

CHIEF DIPPER 2 b.c. (Apr 8) Benny The Dip (USA) 127 – Cuban Reef 54 (Dowsing (USA) 124) [2004 8m p6g⁴ p6g⁴ p6g f8g Dec 28] smallish, stocky colt: third foal: half-brother to 4-y-o Annakita: dam 7f and 1¼m winner: fair maiden: well beaten in nurseries last 2 starts: should stay 1m. *P. J. McBride*   **65**

CHIEF EXEC 2 b.g. (Feb 17) Zafonic (USA) 130 – Shot At Love (IRE) 79 (Last Tycoon 131) [2004 6d p7g² p7g* p7.1g² Dec 14] leggy gelding: fifth foal: half-brother to 7f winner (including at 2 yrs) Silence And Rage (by Green Desert): dam 1m winner: fairly useful performer: made all in minor event at Lingfield in November: creditable effort in similar event at Wolverhampton final start: likely to stay 1m: acts on polytrack. *C. A. Cyzer*   **83**

CHIEF SCOUT 2 br.c. (Mar 15) Tomba 119 – Princess Zara (Reprimand 122) [2004 6s 7d⁴ 7d* 7g Sep 30] big colt: second foal: dam unraced: fairly useful performer: best effort when winning maiden at Newmarket in August, making most: well held in Somerville Tattersall Stakes on same course final start: should stay 1m. *B. J. Meehan*   **87**

CHIGORIN 3 b.g. Pivotal 124 – Belle Vue 78 (Petong 126) [2004 70p: 8m 8.1m[6] 8s **72** 8m 7.9g[3] p10g p10g[5] Nov 16] big, leggy gelding: fair maiden: stays 1¼m: acts on poly-track and good to firm ground. *J. M. P. Eustace*

CHILALI (IRE) 2 b.f. (Apr 20) Monashee Mountain (USA) 115 – Pam Story (Sallust **54** 134) [2004 5g[5] f5m 5m[3] 5g[3] 5g 5.1g[3] 5g[6] 5m[4] 5.1g f5s[2] f5g f5f[4] Dec 28] €6,000Y: half-sister to several winners, including 1992 2-y-o 6f winner Stroika (by Shy Groom): dam placed in Ireland/France: modest maiden: will prove best at 5f/easy 6f: acts on fibre-sand and good to firm going: usually races up with pace. *A. Berry*

CHILLIN OUT 2 ch.c. (Feb 2) Bahamian Bounty 116 – Steppin Out 63 (First Trump **–** 118) [2004 6d p6g Nov 16] first foal: dam 6f winner: well held in maidens. *W. Jarvis*

CHILLY CRACKER 2 ch.f. (Mar 4) Largesse 112 – Polar Storm (IRE) 76 (Law **71** Society (USA) 130) [2004 5d[2] 5.1d[6] f5g* 6m 5g 5g[3] 5.1g* 5.1v f5g Dec 7] 5,000Y: sixth foal: half-sister to 6-y-o Run On and Irish 9f winner Lawnett (by Runnett): dam, 6f (at 2 yrs) to 1m winner, half-sister to smart sprinter Polar Bird: fair performer: won maiden at Southwell in June and nursery at Bath in October: likely to prove best at 5f: acts on fibresand and good to soft going: sometimes early to post: usually races up with pace. *R. Hollinshead*

CHIMALI (IRE) 3 b.g. Foxhound (USA) 103 – Mari-Ela (IRE) 60 (River Falls 113) **83 +** [2004 69p: 5d* 5d[4] p6g[3] 6m* 6g[3] p5g[4] p6g[3] p6g* p5g[4] Dec 18] sturdy gelding: fairly useful performer: left J. Noseda after fifth start: won maiden at Beverley in July and handicaps at Lingfield in September and December: effective at 5f/6f: acts on polytrack, good to firm and good to soft going: visored last 6 starts. *J. R. Boyle*

CHIMES AT MIDNIGHT (USA) 7 b.h. Danzig (USA) – Surely Georgies (USA) **– §** (Alleged (USA) 138) [2004 20f 20m 12f 14d 10m 16m 14g 10d 10s Oct 23] well-made horse: formerly smart but inconsistent performer: missed 2003: no sign of retaining abil-ity in 2004, running at Royal Ascot first 2 starts: usually blinkered. *Luke Comer, Ireland*

CHIMES EIGHT 3 b.f. Octagonal (NZ) 126 – Bell Toll 87 (High Line 125) [2004 40: **–** f9.4g Jan 19] poor maiden. *R. A. Fahey*

CHINALEA (IRE) 2 b.c. (Apr 23) Danetime (IRE) 121 – Raise-A-Secret (IRE) **72** (Classic Secret (USA) 91) [2004 5.7g[5] 5.7g[5] 6s[4] Nov 6] €21,000F, €26,000Y, 20,000 2-y-o: fifth foal: brother to Italian 7.5f winner and half-brother to 2 winners abroad: dam unraced: fair form in maidens: hung left when fourth at Doncaster: will probably prove best at 5f/6f. *C. G. Cox*

CHIN DANCER 2 ch.f. (Apr 29) Inchinor 119 – Red Hot Dancer (USA) (Seattle **33** Dancer (USA) 119) [2004 7g 7.1g f7d[6] 7g Aug 11] £2,500Y: sixth foal: half-sister to winner in USA by Technology: dam, placed in USA, half-sister to winner of Poule d'Essai des Pouliches winner Ta Rib: poor maiden: blinkered/tongue tied last 2 starts. *B. R. Millman*

CHINESE PUZZLE 2 b.c. (Mar 13) Dr Fong (USA) 128 – Verbose (USA) 97 (Storm **74** Bird (CAN) 134) [2004 7d[6] 7.5m[6] 7m 8m[3] 9f[3] Sep 13] first foal: dam, 1m winner, out of half-sister to dam of Poule d'Essai des Pouliches winner Matiara: fair maiden: third at Thirsk and Redcar: likely to stay 1½m: acts on firm going: tongue tied: sold 8,500 gns. *H. R. A. Cecil*

CHINKARA 4 ch.g. Desert Prince (IRE) 130 – You Make Me Real (USA) (Give Me **95** Strength (USA)) [2004 96: 8g 8.1f 8f 9f[4] 9.9g 9m[3] 9g Oct 2] strong, good-bodied gelding: type to carry condition: useful handicapper: good efforts in frame at Kempton and Goodwood: stays easy 1¼m: acts on polytrack, raced only on good ground or firmer on turf: sometimes early to post: races freely: sold 48,000 gns, sent to UAE. *B. J. Meehan*

CHIQITITA (IRE) 3 b.f. Saddlers' Hall (IRE) 126 – Funny Cut (IRE) (Sure Blade **39** (USA) 130) [2004 59: p7g p6g 6.1g 6s f8g 7m 7m[6] 9.7f 7.9m[5] 10g Oct 11] smallish filly: poor maiden: left T. Clement after fresh start: should stay at least 1m: acts on firm ground: tried blinkered. *Miss M. E. Rowland*

CHIRACAHUA (IRE) 2 ch.g. (Mar 7) Desert Prince (IRE) 130 – Irish Celebrity **–** (USA) (Irish River (FR) 131) [2004 7g p6g p7g Oct 28] strong gelding: well beaten in maidens. *B. J. Meehan*

CHISEL 3 ch.g. Hector Protector (USA) 124 – Not Before Time (IRE) (Polish Precedent **–** (USA) 131) [2004 7.5g 8m 7.5d[6] 9.2d 9.9g 10m 9.2d[5] 8s Aug 30] lengthy gelding: little form. *M. Johnston*

CHISELLED (IRE) 2 b.g. (Feb 26) Rossini (USA) 118 – Con Dancer (Shareef Dancer **78** (USA) 135) [2004 5s[4] 5g[2] 5m[2] 5.2m 5d[4] 5g[2] Sep 2] 20,000Y: deep-girthed gelding: third foal: dam placed in Belgium: fair maiden: likely to prove best at 5f: acts on good to firm going: tongue tied final start (gelded after). *K. R. Burke*

CHIVALRY   5 b.g. Mark of Esteem (IRE) 137 – Gai Bulga 110 (Kris 135) [2004 102p: **?**
8g Mar 27] big, lengthy gelding: useful handicapper: won Cambridgeshire at Newmarket on only 4-y-o start: left Sir Mark Prescott and successful over hurdles prior to well held in Lincoln at Doncaster only 5-y-o start: stays 1¼m: acts on firm and soft ground: has raced freely/carried head awkwardly. *J. Howard Johnson*

CHIVITE (IRE)   5 b.g. Alhaarth (IRE) 126 – Laura Margaret (Persian Bold 123)   **63**
[2004 68: 13.3m 11.7g Oct 10] well-made gelding: modest maiden: stays 1¾m: acts on soft going: tried visored: fairly useful hurdler. *P. J. Hobbs*

CHOCOLATE BOY (IRE)   5 b.g. Dolphin Street (FR) 125 – Kawther (Tap On   **63**
Wood 130) [2004 43: p8g⁵ p8g² p10g⁴ p12g⁴ p12g* p13g 11.9m² 11.9f⁵ 10f⁶ p12g p12g⁶ Nov 13] modest handicapper: won at Lingfield in March: stays 1½m: acts on good to firm going and polytrack: tried in cheekpieces, usually wears eyeshields/blinkers. *G. L. Moore*

CHOCOLATE CARAMEL (USA)   2 b.c. (Mar 28) Storm Creek (USA) – Sandhill   **73**
(BRZ) (Baynoun 128) [2004 p8g⁵ p9.5g² p10g* Nov 27] $85,000Y: fourth foal: half-brother to winner in Japan by Grand Slam: dam, Brazilian Grade 3 1m winner, sister to high-class US 1¼m/1½m performer Sandpit: fair form: won maiden at Lingfield by short head from The Geezer, dictating pace: will probably stay 1½m. *Mrs A. J. Perrett*

CHOIR LEADER   3 b.g. Sadler's Wells (USA) 132 – Choir Mistress (Chief Singer   **93 p**
131) [2004 10d 8m* 8d³ Aug 15] big, good-topped gelding: seventh foal: closely related to useful 1998 2-y-o 7f winner Choirgirl (by Unfuwain) and half-brother to 3 winners, notably 5-y-o Chorist: dam unraced half-sister to smart middle-distance stayer Sacrament: fairly useful form: won maiden at Pontefract in July by 9 lengths from Killmorey: good 3¼ lengths third to Double Vodka in handicap on same course, still looking green: gelded after: should stay 1¼m: open to further improvement, and type to win more races at 4 yrs. *W. J. Haggas*

CHOOKIE HEITON (IRE)   6 br.g. Fumo di Londra (IRE) 108 – Royal Wolff (Prince   **110**
Tenderfoot (USA) 126) [2004 112: 6g⁴ 6m⁵ 7g 6f 5d* 6s Sep 18] strong, lengthy gelding: smart performer: 40/1, back to near best when winning listed event at Beverley in August by 1¼ lengths from Simianna, leading close home: best at 5f/6f: acts on firm and good to soft going, below form on soft: has been bandaged in front: reportedly lame second start. *I. Semple*

CHOREOGRAPHIC (IRE)   2 b.c. (Apr 24) Komaite (USA) – Lambast 70 (Relkino   **56**
131) [2004 5g 6m³ 6g 5.9g Sep 2] rather leggy colt: modest maiden: third at Catterick: should stay 7f: best effort on good to firm going. *R. A. Fahey*

CHORIST   5 ch.m. Pivotal 124 – Choir Mistress (Chief Singer 131) [2004 114+:   **120**
8f* 10m* 9.9m³ 10s³ 10s² Oct 16]
   The 2004 season was yet another memorable one for the Cheveley Park Stud. For the second successive year its runners topped the million-pound mark in total prize money won, while the horses racing for the stud surpassed their previous best in terms of number of races won, with thirty-seven individual winners picking up sixty races between them. Two of those races took place outside Britain, the now very well known red, white and blue colours carried to victory by Chorist in the Audi Pretty Polly Stakes at the Curragh, a race upgraded to Group 1 in 2004, and by Hypnotic in a listed event at Craon in the French Provinces.
   Chorist was better than ever at the age of five. Well held in a maiden at Redcar on her only start at two, she made into a useful filly at three, gaining the last of her four wins in a listed race at Salisbury, and a smart performer at four, when successful in a listed event at Newcastle and two Group 3 contests, the Golden Daffodil Stakes at Chepstow and the Blandford Stakes at the Curragh. A listed race at Pontefract in June provided Chorist with a fine opportunity to make a successful return in the latest season, and she gave those who laid the odds on her little cause for concern, making most and comfortably holding off her only serious challenger Ice Palace, who is also owned by Cheveley Park Stud. Alexander Goldrun, second in the Irish One Thousand Guineas and fourth in the Prix de Diane on her previous two starts, just shaded Chorist in the betting in the six-runner Audi Pretty Polly Stakes later in June, and this pair also dominated the finish. Chorist made the running again and drifted left off the rail when pressed strongly by Alexander

Audi Pretty Polly Stakes, the Curragh—Chorist (left) and Alexander Goldrun pull clear of Ivowen and Soldera (right) in a race upgraded to Group 1 status

Goldrun in the closing stages, but she proved as game as ever when the chips were down and held on by half a length. It was a particularly notable victory for the Cheveley Park Stud, as it was the first Group 1 won with the offspring of a home-bred sire and a home-bred mare. Chorist failed to win again, but she might well have done so had she been able to contest the Prix de l'Opera on Arc day. A creditable third to Favourable Terms in the Nassau Stakes at Goodwood and to Whortleberry in the Prix Jean Romanet at Deauville, her two races after the Pretty Polly, Chorist was being loaded onto a plane to take her to France for the Prix de l'Opera when she played up and banged her head, resulting in her withdrawal from a race which was won by Alexander Goldrun. Any regrets connections had about Chorist missing a good opportunity to win another Group 1 would have been temp-ered by her performance when she reappeared later in October, in the Champion Stakes at Newmarket. The only one of her sex in the eleven-runner field, Chorist produced a career-best effort in finishing second, beaten two and a half lengths by the Two Thousand Guineas winner Haafhd, collared by the winner approaching the final furlong having gone a couple of lengths clear soon after halfway. Thoughts of keeping Chorist in training for another season were entertained, but in late-October came the announcement that she had been retired and would visit King's Best.

		Polar Falcon	Nureyev
	Pivotal	(b or br 1987)	Marie d'Argonne
	(ch 1993)	Fearless Revival	Cozzene
Chorist		(ch 1987)	Stufida
(ch.m. 1999)		Chief Singer	Ballad Rock
	Choir Mistress	(br 1981)	Principia
	(b 1990)	Blessed Event	Kings Lake
		(b 1984)	Friedrichsruh

Chorist is the fifth foal of Choir Mistress, an unraced half-sister to the smart middle-distance performer Sacrament and daughter of the smart mile-and-a-quarter winner and Yorkshire Oaks second Blessed Event. The next dam on the bottom line

Cheveley Park Stud's "Chorist"

of the pedigree, Friedrichsruh, won the German Oaks. Choir Mistress is responsible for four winners apart from Chorist, the pick of them the useful Choirgirl (by Unfuwain), who stayed a mile and a quarter, and the fairly useful Choir Leader (by Sadler's Wells), successful over a mile in the latest season. Chorist, a big, angular mare, stayed a mile and a quarter and acted on firm and soft going. Notably tough and game, she was a credit to her trainer, winning nine races and finishing out of the first three on only four occasions in twenty-one starts. *W. J. Haggas*

CHORISTAR   3 ch.g. Inchinor 119 – Star Tulip 99 (Night Shift (USA)) [2004 60: 7m⁶ 7m² 6m⁵ 7.6m³ Jul 24] modest maiden: should stay 1m: raced only on good/good to firm ground. *W. R. Muir*   **62**

CHORUS   7 b.m. Bandmaster (USA) 97 – Name That Tune 40 (Fayruz 116) [2004 63§: f7g f6g³ 8s 6.1g 5d p6d² f7g* p6g f6g p6g⁵ Dec 27] neat mare: modest performer: won banded race at Southwell in November: effective at 6f/7f: acts on all-weather, firm and soft ground: often wears headgear: has reared badly leaving stall/veered under pressure: untrustworthy. *B. R. Millman*   **58 §**

CHORUS BEAUTY   3 b.f. Royal Applause 124 – Happy Lady (FR) 72 (Cadeaux Genereux 131) [2004 64p: 6.1g 8.1v 7m p8d³ f7m* p8g Nov 30] fair performer: won minor event at Southwell in July: stays 1m: acts on all-weather: sold 1,600 gns. *G. Wragg*   **67**

CHRISTINA'S DREAM   3 b.f. Spectrum (IRE) 126 – Christine Daae 74 (Sadler's Wells (USA) 132) [2004 74p: 7m⁵ p7g Jul 21] well-made filly: fair maiden: should stay at least 1m. *P. W. Harris*   **71**

CHRISTMAS TRUCE (IRE)   5 b.g. Brief Truce (USA) 126 – Superflash (Superlative 118) [2004 78d: f11g f16.2g Jan 9] good-topped gelding: well held in 2004: tried visored/in cheekpieces. *Ian Williams*   **–**

222

CHRISTOM 2 b.g. (Apr 2) Groom Dancer (USA) 128 – Throw Away Line (USA) **55** (Assert 134) [2004 8v p8g 7.1d 10.1d Nov 5] useful-looking gelding: modest maiden: probably stays 1¼m: flashed tail final start (gelded after). *G. A. Butler*

CHUBBES 3 b.g. Kris 135 – St Radegund 85 (Green Desert (USA) 127) [2004 79: 8m **54** 10m 7g⁴ 7.9g⁴ 8m 6.9m* 10s 8f Sep 6] modest performer: left M. Pipe after second start: won claimer at Carlisle in August on final start for M. Hammond: effective at 7f/1m: acts on polytrack, good to firm and good to soft going: usually wears headgear: none too consistent. *B. J. Llewellyn*

CHUTNEY MARY (IRE) 2 b. or br.f. (Jan 24) Indian Danehill (IRE) 124 – Grade **68** A Star (IRE) (Alzao (USA) 117) [2004 5g 5f⁶ 7.5g² f7m² f7m⁵ 7f² 6d⁵ 7m 6g³ 7g⁶ p7.1g⁵ Oct 19] €23,000Y: useful-looking filly: sixth living foal: half-sister to useful 6f (including at 2 yrs) winner March Star (by Mac's Imp) and fairly useful 1¼m winner Jimmy Swift (by Petardia): dam Irish 2-y-o 1m winner: fair maiden: stays 7.5f: acts on fibresand and firm going: races prominently: sold 10,000 gns, sent to Austria. *J. G. Portman*

CIACOLE 3 b.f. Primo Dominie 121 – Dance On A Cloud (USA) 76 (Capote (USA)) **47** [2004 68: p7g f8s⁴ 12.1d 12v³ 9.9v* 12.1g 12m 10g⁵ Jul 5] leggy filly: poor performer: left S. Williams after second start: won seller at Beverley in May: stays 1½m: acts on good to firm and heavy ground. *Ronald Thompson*

CICATRICE 3 ch.g. Wolfhound (USA) 126 – Capricious Lady (IRE) (Capricorn Line **63 ?** 111) [2004 –: p10g p10g p10g⁶ Dec 30] seemingly modest maiden, lightly raced: stays easy 1¼m: raced only on polytrack. *I. A. Wood*

CIEL BLEU 2 ch.f. (Mar 14) Septieme Ciel (USA) 123 – Valthea (FR) (Antheus (USA) **–** 122) [2004 7d Oct 30] 80,000Y: sturdy, close-coupled filly: sister to useful French 7f winner Vert Val, also 6f to 9f winner at 2 yrs, and half-sister to French 1997 2-y-o 1m winner Prospectheus (by Gone West), later successful in USA: dam, French 11f winner, half-sister to Green Dancer: 20/1, well held in maiden at Newmarket. *B. W. Hills*

CIENDRA GIRL (IRE) 2 ch.f. (May 1) Rossini (USA) 118 – Simply Special (IRE) **–** (Petit Loup (USA) 123) [2004 7.1m 8g 6d Oct 4] second foal: half-sister to 4-y-o Star Lad: dam ran once: well beaten in maidens. *R. Brotherton*

CILLA'S SMILE 2 b.f. (Mar 25) Lake Coniston (IRE) 131 – Tinkerbird 76 (Music **49** Boy 124) [2004 5g 5g⁶ 6m 5s⁶ Oct 16] lengthy, good-topped filly: half-sister to several winners, including 3-y-o Catch The Wind and 5f/6f winner Bataleur (by Midyan): dam 5f/6f winner: poor maiden: should stay 6f. *M. A. Buckley*

CILS 3 b.f. Zilzal (USA) 137 – My Valentina 84 (Royal Academy (USA) 130) [2004 **68** 8d⁶ 9v² 8d 8f² 10m³ 12g⁴ 10d 8s p10g Dec 30] 22,000Y: third foal: dam, 2-y-o 7f winner who stayed 1¼m, half-sister to smart sprinter Averti: fair maiden: poor efforts last 2 starts, at Lingfield final one: best effort at 9f on heavy ground. *E. Tyrrell, Ireland*

CIMYLA (IRE) 3 b.c. Lomitas 129 – Coyaima (GER) 100 (Night Shift (USA)) [2004 **97** 78p: 9s³ 10g 8.2s* 8m 9m* Jun 12] good-topped colt: useful performer: won minor event at Nottingham in May and handicap at Sandown in June, best effort when beating Lets Roll by 2 lengths in latter: reportedly fractured a pastern after: should stay 1¼m: acts on soft and good to firm going: reportedly lost action at Newmarket second/fourth starts: waited with. *C. F. Wall*

CINNAMON RIDGE (IRE) 3 b.g. Indian Ridge 123 – Savoury 67 (Salse (USA) **–** 128) [2004 –p: 5s 6m 5.1f May 21] big, good-bodied gelding: little form: blinkered last 2 starts: headstrong. *B. J. Meehan*

CIRCASSIAN (IRE) 3 b.g. Groom Dancer (USA) 128 – Daraliya (IRE) (Kahyasi **85** 130) [2004 –p: 10m 12d² 11.5g* 12m* 11.9s⁴ 13.1s² p12g⁵ Oct 25] big, lengthy gelding: fairly useful handicapper: won at Yarmouth and Catterick in September: good length second to Winged d'Argent at Ayr penultimate start, edging markedly left: will be suited by 1¾m+: acts on soft and good to firm going: often soon off bridle. *Sir Mark Prescott*

CIRCLE OF WOLVES 6 ch.g. Wolfhound (USA) 126 – Misty Halo 93 (High Top **–** 131) [2004 12.6d Oct 9] lightly raced and little form on Flat since 2000. *H. J. Manners*

CIRCUIT DANCER (IRE) 4 b.g. Mujadil (USA) 119 – Trysinger (IRE) (Try My **101** Best (USA) 130) [2004 92: 6s³ 6g⁴ 6d 6m* 6f 6g⁵ 6m 7s⁴ 6g 6s 6d⁴ 6s Nov 1] tall gelding: useful performer: won handicap at York in June by short head from Marsad: respectable efforts at best after: stays 6f: acts on firm and soft going: often slowly away. *A. Berry*

CIRCUMSPECT (IRE) 2 b.g. (Mar 23) Spectrum (IRE) 126 – Newala 61 (Royal **70** Academy (USA) 130) [2004 6f² p7.1g² p9.5g⁴ Dec 20] 11,000Y: third foal: closely related to 3-y-o Red Skelton: dam second at 7f/1m: fair form when runner-up in maidens at Pontefract and Wolverhampton: should stay at least 1m. *P. C. Haslam*

CIRCUS MAXIMUS (USA)   7 b.g. Pleasant Colony (USA) – Crockadore (USA)   **61 §**
102 (Nijinsky (CAN) 138) [2004 65§: 14m 14.1g⁴ 16.4g 17.2g² 16m³ p16g 17.2g Sep 27]
strong gelding: modest handicapper: stays 17f: acts on polytrack, firm and soft ground:
usually wears blinkers/cheekpieces: ungenuine. *Ian Williams*

CIRRIOUS   3 gr.f. Cloudings (IRE) 112 – Westfield Mist (Scallywag 127) [2004 8.2d   **54 ?**
8.2m⁶ 10.2s⁵ Oct 19] close-coupled filly: first foal: dam poor bumper winner: seemingly
modest maiden: stays 1¼m: acts on soft and good to firm ground. *B. Palling*

CITRINE SPIRIT (IRE)   3 gr.f. Soviet Star (USA) 128 – Casessa (USA) (Caro 133)   **76**
[2004 –p: 10d⁶ 8.2s* 8m³ 8.2m 8.1g 7s Oct 23] sturdy filly: fair performer: won maiden
at Nottingham in May: below form last 3 starts: stays 1m: acts on soft and good to firm
ground. *J. H. M. Gosden*

CITRUS MAGIC   7 b.g. Cosmonaut – Up All Night 56 (Green Desert (USA) 127)   **46 §**
[2004 46§: f14.8g* f14g² f12f Jan 22] poor performer: won banded race at Wolverhampton in January: stays 2m: acts on fibresand, soft and good to firm going: usually
wears headgear: carries head awkwardly: unreliable. *K. Bell*

CITY AFFAIR   3 b.g. Inchinor 119 – Aldevonie 75 (Green Desert (USA) 127) [2004   **55**
63: p5g f6g p7g⁴ 7g May 13] modest maiden: stays 7f: acts on polytrack and good to firm
ground: often wears blinkers/cheekpieces. *Mrs L. C. Jewell*

CITY GENERAL (IRE)   3 ch.g. General Monash (USA) 107 – Astra (IRE) (Glenstal   **54**
(USA) 118) [2004 62: 7g³ 7d³ 7g⁴ 7m³ 8m⁵ 7m 7m² 7g 8f⁵ 8f* 7.1s 10m⁵ 8d⁶ 8f 8m 8d
Oct 16] workmanlike gelding: modest handicapper: won seller at Yarmouth in August:
stays 1¼m: acts on all-weather, firm and good to soft going: wears cheekpieces: often
races prominently. *J. S. Moore*

CITY LASS   4 b.f. Rock City 120 – Kilkenny Lass (IRE) (Fayruz 116) [2004 8d Aug 15]   **–**
workmanlike filly: third foal: dam unraced: 100/1, well beaten in maiden at Pontefract.
M. E. Sowersby

CITY PALACE   3 ch.g. Grand Lodge (USA) 125 – Ajuga (USA) 102 (The Minstrel   **81**
(CAN) 135) [2004 74p: 8.1s* 10.4s May 11] strong gelding: fair form: won maiden at
Warwick in April: well beaten in handicap at York next time: should be suited by 1¼m+:
sold 25,000 gns in August, joined S. Gollings and gelded. *B. W. Hills*

CITY TORQUE (USA)   2 ch.f. (Feb 23) Marquetry (USA) 121 – Citiscape (USA)   **53**
(Citidancer (USA)) [2004 5g⁶ 5g Jun 3] $25,000Y, resold $5,500Y: first foal: dam
unraced half-sister to smart performer up to 1½m Santillana: better effort when sixth in
maiden at Musselburgh: slowly away final outing. *T. D. Barron*

CITY TRADER   2 ch.c. (Mar 28) Entrepreneur 123 – Kameez (IRE) 72 (Arazi (USA)   **–**
135) [2004 7m 8v 10.1d Nov 5] sturdy colt: last in maidens: blinkered final start: sold
1,200 gns, sent to Denmark. *C. E. Brittain*

CITY ZONE (IRE)   2 gr.f. (May 27) Zafonic (USA) 130 – City Fortress (Troy 137)   **64 p**
[2004 p7.1g* Dec 10] half-sister to several winners, notably smart performer up to 1½m
Desert Boy (by Green Desert), later Hong Kong Horse of the Year as Oriental Express,
and high-class US 1m/9f performer Fastness (by Rousillon): dam French 1¼m and 12.5f
winner: 8/1, won maiden at Wolverhampton by head from Davenport, hampered halfway
but leading close home: will stay at least 1m: sure to improve. *B. J. Meehan*

CLANN A COUGAR   4 ch.g. Bahamian Bounty 116 – Move Darling (Rock City   **57**
120) [2004 78: f8.5g f7g 8s⁶ 8.3d 7m⁶ 7.5g 11.7g Jul 11] leggy gelding: has a quick
action: modest handicapper: stays 11.7f: acts on soft and good to firm going: usually
wears blinkers/cheekpieces. *I. A. Wood*

CLAPTRAP   4 b.c. Royal Applause 124 – Stardyn (Star Appeal 133) [2004 55, a65:   **57**
f12s² f12g⁵ f16.2g⁶ Feb 6] modest performer: stays 15f: acts on fibresand, raced only on
ground firmer than good on turf. *R. Brotherton*

CLARA BOW (IRE)   2 b.f. (Mar 26) Sadler's Wells (USA) 132 – Brigid (USA) (Irish   **67 p**
River (FR) 131) [2004 7g⁶ 7v Oct 23] 750,000Y: rangy filly: fifth living foal: sister to
2000 Moyglare Stud Stakes winner Sequoyah (later smart up to 1½m) and half-sister to
useful Irish 6f winner Oyster Catcher (by Bluebird): dam, French 1m winner, sister to
dam of Irish 2000 Guineas winner Saffron Walden (by Sadler's Wells) and high-class
sprinter/miler Dolphin Street: shaped well when sixth to Quickfire in maiden at Kempton:
last in listed event at Newbury: will stay at least 1m: should do better. *B. W. Hills*

CLARADOTNET 4 b.f. Sri Pekan (USA) 117 – Lypharitissima (FR) (Lightning (FR) **71** 129) [2004 82: 11.6d 11.7g 12g 14m⁶ 11.1g³ 14.1f 14.1g³ 16m² 14g 17.2g 13.9g 18d⁶ Oct 18] angular filly: fair handicapper: stays 2m: acts on firm going, probably on good to soft: none too genuine: sold 5,500 gns. *M. R. Channon*

CLARANETE PRINCESS (IRE) 3 b.f. Princely Heir (IRE) 111 – Sheryl Lynn **47** (Miller's Mate 116) [2004 p7g⁶ 8d p10g p10m Dec 15] €4,900Y: fifth foal: half-sister to useful 1m (at 2 yrs) and 1½m winner Borders Belle (by Pursuit of Love) and a winner in Italy by Be My Guest: dam German 1m winner: poor maiden: reportedly fractured knee on debut (off 9½ months after). *M. J. Wallace*

CLARE GALWAY 3 b.f. Compton Place 125 – Oublier L'Ennui (FR) 79 (Bellman **64** (FR) 123) [2004 p6g p8g⁵ p10g 11.5m p10g⁴ p10d 8s* p7.1g p9.5g⁵ p8g² Dec 20] eighth foal: sister to a winner in Greece and half-sister to 8.5f winner Arctic High and 6f winner (including at 2 yrs) Shudder (both by Distant Relative): dam, maiden on Flat who probably stayed 1½m, winning hurdler/chaser: modest performer: left T. McCarthy and off 3½ months before winning handicap at Brighton in October: stays easy 1¼m: acts on polytrack and soft ground. *S. Kirk*

CLARET AND AMBER 2 b.g. (Feb 19) Forzando 122 – Artistic Licence (High Top **95** 131) [2004 5g³ 6g⁵ 6f⁵ 6m* 7s* 6m⁵ 6g² 8d⁶ Oct 18] 13,000Y: sturdy gelding: has a quick action: brother to 4-y-o Riska King and half-brother to several winners, including 3-y-o Little Jimbob: dam maiden who stayed 1¼m: useful performer: won nurseries at Redcar and Chester (by 6 lengths) in August: creditable efforts in sales race at Doncaster and minor event at Salisbury (beaten neck by Yajbill) next 2 starts: stays 7f: acts on soft and good to firm ground: tends to take time to warm to task. *R. A. Fahey*

CLARINCH CLAYMORE 8 b.g. Sabrehill (USA) 120 – Salu 65 (Ardross 134) **80** [2004 80: 14.1d² 14m 16.2d⁵ 14.6m³ 16.2g* 16.2d⁵ Aug 11] smallish, good-bodied gelding: fairly useful handicapper: won at Beverley (for second year running) in July: effective at 13f to 2m: acts on heavy going, good to firm and fibresand: sometimes races freely: held up. *J. M. Jefferson*

CLASP 2 ch.c. (Mar 12) Singspiel (IRE) 133 – Embrace Me (Nashwan (USA) 135) **84** [2004 7g 8g² a6g⁶ a7f² Dec 30] 25,000E, 75,000 2-y-o: lengthy, quite attractive colt: first foal: dam, well beaten only start, out of half-sister to smart French stayer Molesnes: runner-up in maidens at Yarmouth (best effort, then left M. Bell) and Nad Al Sheba: should be well suited by 1¼m/1½m: blinkered last 2 starts, also tongue tied final one. *M. Al Kurdi, UAE*

CLASSICAL DANCER 3 ch.f. Dr Fong (USA) 128 – Gorgeous Dancer (IRE) (Nord- **98** ico (USA)) [2004 86p: 8.3s* 8g² 10m³ 10.2g Jul 9] workmanlike filly: useful performer: won maiden at Windsor in April: good length third of 6 to Incheni in listed race at Newbury on third start: well held in Golden Daffodil Stakes at Chepstow final outing: stays 1¼m: acts on soft and good to firm ground: carries head awkwardly. *H. Candy*

CLASSICAL WALTZ (IRE) 6 ch.m. In The Wings 128 – Fascination Waltz 83 **34** (Shy Groom (USA)) [2004 –: f9.4g⁴ f9.4m³ 10m 12m Jun 7] poor maiden. *J. J. Sheehan*

CLASSIC EVENT (IRE) 3 ch.g. Croco Rouge (IRE) 126 – Delta Town (USA) **64** (Sanglamore (USA) 126) [2004 62: 12g 12.3g 12m² 12s³ Nov 12] tall, close-coupled gelding: unimpressive mover: modest maiden: stays 1½m: acts on soft and good to firm ground: often slowly away, markedly so final outing. *T. D. Easterby*

CLASSIC EXPRESSION 3 ch.f. Classic Cliche (IRE) 128 – Breezy Day 85 (Day Is **–** Done 115) [2004 f6g⁶ 6f f8g 8.1s Sep 24] 1,800Y: sturdy filly: sixth foal: half-sister to 2 winning sprinters, including fairly useful 6f winner Positive Air (by Puissance): dam 5f/ 6f winner: well held in maidens. *B. A. McMahon*

CLASSIC GUEST 2 b.f. (Mar 25) Xaar 132 – My Lass 91 (Elmaamul (USA) 125) **59 d** [2004 6g⁴ 5.2m⁶ 7g 6m Sep 21] 100,000Y: angular filly: second foal: half-sister to 3-y-o Mac Love: dam 1½m winner: modest maiden: ran as if amiss after debut: should stay 7f. *M. R. Channon*

CLASSICISM (USA) 2 b. or br.f. (Apr 4) A P Indy (USA) 131 – Colour Chart (USA) **82 p** 122 (Mr Prospector (USA)) [2004 7g⁵ Sep 2] quite good-topped filly: sister to very smart US 2001 2-y-o 5.5f to 8.5f (Breeders' Cup Juvenile Fillies) winner Tempera, and half-sister to several winners, including smart French 7.5f (at 2 yrs) to 1¼m winner Equerry (by St Jovite): dam French 1m (at 2 yrs) to 1¼m winner: 9/2, 5 lengths fifth of 15 to Donyana in maiden at Salisbury, upsides winner when going lame final 1f and eased (suffered condylar fracture to off-fore): should stay 1m: will do better if all is well. *Saeed bin Suroor*

CLASSIC LEASE 3 b.g. Cyrano de Bergerac 120 – Vado Via 56 (Ardross 134) [2004 **54** 8.1g 7m⁵ 8.1s³ 10.5g Sep 4] tall, leggy gelding: modest maiden: should stay 1¼m: acts on soft and good to firm ground. *R. Hollinshead*

CLASSIC LIN (FR) 4 gr.f. Linamix (FR) 127 – Classic Storm 73 (Belfort (FR) 89) **–** [2004 f12s Mar 5] fourth foal: dam 2-y-o 5f/6f winner: tailed off in maiden at Wolverhampton. *A. Berry*

CLASSIC MILLENNIUM 6 b.m. Midyan (USA) 124 – Classic Colleen (IRE) 79 **62** (Sadler's Wells (USA) 132) [2004 72, a?: p13g f12g² f12g² 13.1m⁵ 13.3m 13.3g⁴ Jun **a54** 22] small, lightly-made mare: modest handicapper: stays 14.4f: acts on all-weather, firm and soft going: tried blinkered earlier in career: sometimes slowly away: held up. *W. J. Musson*

CLASSIC ROLE 5 b.g. Tragic Role (USA) – Clare Island 108 (Connaught 130) **86** [2004 84, a79: p12g⁴ p12g p12g³ p12g⁴ p12g* 11.6d² 10.9d² 10.1s 10g 10m p10g p12m p13g² Dec 29] sparely-made gelding: fairly useful handicapper: won at Lingfield in March: unlucky at same track final outing: effective at 1¼m to 13f: acts on polytrack, soft and good to firm going: visored last 9 starts: takes good hold/carries head awkwardly. *R. Ingram*

CLASSIC STYLE (IRE) 2 b.f. (Apr 17) Desert Style (IRE) 121 – Classic Ring **62** (IRE) 50 (Auction Ring (USA) 123) [2004 f5g⁵ 6s f7m 7g⁵ Jul 24] €24,000Y: half-sister to several winners, including 7-y-o Seven No Trumps and 5-y-o Waterside: dam 2-y-o 7f winner: modest maiden: easily best effort at 7f on good going. *T. D. Easterby*

CLASSIC VISION 4 b.f. Classic Cliche (IRE) 128 – Orient 106 (Bay Express 132) **59** [2004 57: f6g* f6f p6g p6g⁴ 7d⁵ 8f 8m* 8m 8.3m⁶ 8g 8g 8m Jul 22] leggy filly: modest performer: won maiden at Southwell in January and handicap at Leicester in June: stays 1m: acts on all-weather, good to firm and good to soft going: wore cheekpieces/blinkers last 7 starts. *W. J. Haggas*

CLEAR IMPRESSION (IRE) 2 b.f. (Jan 7) Danehill (USA) 126 – Shining Hour **87 P** (USA) 104 (Red Ransom (USA)) [2004 6g² Jul 28] smallish, well-made filly: first foal: dam 5f (Queen Mary Stakes)/5.7f winner, ran only at 2 yrs: favourite, 2½ lengths second to Suez in maiden at Goodwood, smooth headway to challenge 2f out and not knocked about: coughing after: sure to do good deal better. *P. W. Chapple-Hyam*

CLEARING SKY (IRE) 3 gr.f. Exploit (USA) 117 – Litchfield Hills (USA) (Re- **59** launch (USA)) [2004 56: 6m⁶ 5.7s p7m* p8g⁶ p7g³ Dec 30] modest performer: won banded race at Lingfield in November: stays 7f: acts on polytrack. *J. R. Boyle*

CLEAVER 3 ch.g. Kris 135 – Much Too Risky 87 (Bustino 136) [2004 –p: 11.1g⁵ 11.5g **61** May 14] leggy, quite good-topped gelding: modest maiden: sold 6,500 gns. *W. Jarvis*

CLEO COLLINS (IRE) 2 b.f. (Apr 8) General Monash (USA) 107 – Madrina 70 **–** (Waajib 121) [2004 5.1s May 4] €6,000F, €12,000Y: fifth foal: half-sister to 6-y-o Laurel Dawn, 5-y-o Joyce's Choice and 4-y-o Telepathic: dam, 6f winner, out of half-sister to very smart sprinter Bolshoi: 12/1, slowly away and always rear in maiden at Bath. *S. Kirk*

CLEVELAND WAY 4 b.g. Forzando 122 – Fallal (IRE) 47 (Fayruz 116) [2004 55: **53 d** f6g* f7g² f6g⁶ f6s⁵ f6g⁶ f5s⁴ f5g⁵ 6d f6g² f6m² f7m⁶ f5m² f6g* 6f 5m 6m f5g Dec 1] good-topped gelding: modest performer: won banded races at Wolverhampton in January and Southwell in May: left D. Carroll after fourteenth start: no form after: effective at 5f to 7f: acts on firm going and fibresand: usually visored/blinkered: usually races prominently. *J. O'Reilly*

CLIFFIE (IRE) 2 ch.g. (Apr 25) Timeless Times (USA) 99 – Suppression (Kind of **–** Hush 118) [2004 6f 8d 7s Nov 1] small, close-coupled gelding: no form in maidens. *J. Hetherton*

CLIMATE CHANGE (USA) 2 ch.c. (Jun 9) Langfuhr (CAN) 124 – Summer Mist **– p** (USA) 75 (Miswaki (USA) 124) [2004 8v Oct 23] strong, lengthy colt: second foal: dam, 8.5f winner in USA, half-sister to dam of Poule d'Essai des Pouliches winner Matiara: 10/1, well held in maiden at Newbury: slowly away and green: likely to do better. *J. H. M. Gosden*

CLIMATE (IRE) 5 ch.g. Catrail (USA) 123 – Burishki 49 (Chilibang 120) [2004 93§: **84 §** p8g⁵ 8.3d⁴ 8s 8g² p8g* 7.6g⁶ 8.3m³ 6m 7s f8g p8.6g² Dec 6] strong, compact gelding: fairly useful handicapper: won at Lingfield in May: left J. Boyle after seventh start: stays easy 1¼m: acts on polytrack, soft and firm going: effective blinkered/visored or not: ungenuine. *K. A. Ryan*

CLO

CLINET (IRE) 2 b.f. (Apr 5) Docksider (USA) 124 – Oiche Mhaith 74 (Night Shift **73** (USA)) [2004 5g 6g⁵ 5g² 6.1s 6g⁵ 7m p7g 8f* 10m³ Sep 28] €4,000F, €8,000Y: leggy filly: half-sister to winners in Italy up to 7.5f by Catrail and Thatching: dam Irish 6f winner: fair performer: won nursery at Bath in September: good third in similar event at Nottingham, finishing strongly from poor position: stays 1¼m: acts on firm ground: often slowly away. *P. M. Phelan*

CLIPPERDOWN (IRE) 3 b.g. Green Desert (USA) 127 – Maroussie (FR) 115 (Sau- **76** marez 132) [2004 8.1g³ 8g 8g* 10g⁶ Sep 29] 70,000Y: strong, well-made gelding: second foal: brother to useful 7f to 9f winner Mamounia: dam French 1¼m (including Prix Fille de l'Air) winner: fair performer: won maiden at Pontefract in August: good sixth in handicap at Nottingham: barely stays 1¼m: raced only on good going. *P. W. Harris*

CLIPPER HOY 2 ch.c. (Feb 13) Bahamian Bounty 116 – Indian Flag (IRE) 39 (Indian **63** Ridge 123) [2004 5v⁶ 6s p5g³ Nov 10] first foal: dam maiden who stayed 1¼m: form in maidens only when third to Music Teacher at Lingfield, making running: likely to prove best at 5f/6f. *Mrs H. Sweeting*

CLIQUEY 5 b.g. Muhtarram (USA) 125 – Meet Again (Lomond (USA) 128) [2004 **–** f9.4g f12g p12g Feb 24] missed 2003: well held on Flat in 2004: dead. *B. J. Llewellyn*

CLOANN (IRE) 2 b.f. (May 27) Danetime (IRE) 121 – Rustic Lawn (Rusticaro (FR) **53** 124) [2004 6g⁵ 5m 6m* p6g Dec 17] €7,000Y: quite good-topped filly: half-sister to fairly useful 1m/1¼m winner Silver Groom (by Shy Groom) and 2001 2-y-o 1m winner Capallin (by Desert Style): dam unraced: modest performer: won seller at Windsor for R. Hannon in June, making most: wearing cheekpieces, ran as if amiss final start: should stay 7f. *D. Shaw*

CLOONAVERY (IRE) 2 b.g. (Apr 1) Xaar 132 – Hero's Pride (FR) (Hero's Honor **83 p** (USA)) [2004 8.1m⁴ p8.6g* Oct 7] 28,000Y: third foal: half-brother to fairly useful Irish 1½m winner Cozzene's Honor (by Cozzene): dam, winner in France/USA including at 1¼m, also second in US Grade 2 event: still green, better effort in maidens when winning at Wolverhampton by ¾ length from Desperation: will stay 1¼m: should progress. *J. A. Osborne*

CLOUD CATCHER (IRE) 3 br.f. Charnwood Forest (IRE) 125 – Notley Park 71 **–** (Wolfhound (USA) 126) [2004 –: 7g f8.5m 10m 11.7m p8.6d Nov 5] no sign of ability: left I. Wood after second start: tried tongue tied. *M. Appleby*

CLOUD DANCER 5 b. or br.m. Bishop of Cashel 122 – Summer Pageant 81 (Chief's **91 +** Crown (USA)) [2004 84: p7g³ p7g f7s² f8.5s² 6m* 6m³ 6g⁵ 7m 6d⁴ 7m⁵ 7.1g⁶ p8.6g³ p8g⁶ f6g² f7g* Dec 14] leggy mare: fairly useful handicapper: won at York in June and Southwell (best effort, beat Kalani Star by 5 lengths) in December: effective at 6f to 8.6f: acts on all-weather and good to firm going, probably on good to soft: usually waited with: tough. *K. A. Ryan*

CLOUDINGSWELL 3 b.f. Cloudings (IRE) 112 – L'Ancressaan 67 (Dalsaan 125) **38** [2004 69: 10g 12.6s⁶ 8.3m⁶ 10m⁴ 10.9g⁴ 12.6d p8.6g Oct 25] close-coupled filly: poor maiden: stays 11f: acts on polytrack and good to firm going: visored (ran creditably) once: often races prominently. *D. L. Williams*

CLOUDLESS (USA) 4 b. or br.f. Lord Avie (USA) – Summer Retreat (USA) 78 **61 d** (Gone West (USA)) [2004 75: f6g f8.5s² f7g⁴ p7g f7g³ f5g³ 8.1d⁶ 5.7s⁶ 6g f7m 5g 6g 5.7s p5.1g f6g⁶ f5g Dec 21] modest performer: well below form after sixth start: stays easy 7f: acts on fibresand, raced only on good going or softer (acts on heavy) on turf: tried blinkered/tongue tied: none too consistent. *J. W. Unett*

CLOUDS OF GOLD (IRE) 3 b.f. Goldmark (USA) 113 – Tongabezi (IRE) 75 **45 ?** (Shernazar 131) [2004 7.1g 6s³ 9g 6m f7g f11g Dec 12] close-coupled filly: fifth foal: half-sister to 3 winners, including 5-y-o Catch The Cat: dam Irish 2-y-o 7f winner: poor maiden: well beaten last 4 starts: stays 1¼m: acts on soft ground. *J. S. Wainwright*

CLOUDY SKY (IRE) 8 b.g. Sadler's Wells (USA) 132 – Dancing Shadow 117 **–** (Dancer's Image (USA)) [2004 14.1s May 2] useful in 1999 for Sir Michael Stoute: well beaten only Flat outing after: won only start over hurdles (in May): dead. *Simon Earle*

CLOVE (USA) 2 b.f. (Mar 2) Distant View (USA) 126 – Nidd (USA) 112 (Known **80** Fact (USA) 135) [2004 5d⁴ 5f* 5f² 5m Sep 27] leggy filly: sixth foal: sister to US 5.5f winner Guise Cliff and half-sister to 3 winners, including 5-y-o Expected Bonus: dam, 5.5f to 7f (Prix de la Porte Maillot) winner in France/USA, closely related to Breeders' Cup Classic winner Skywalker: fairly useful performer: won maiden at Windsor in July: better effort in nurseries after when good second at Redcar: not run of race final start: should stay 6f: acts on firm going, promise on good to soft. *B. W. Hills*

227

Sterling Insurance Summer Stakes (Handicap), Goodwood—
the grey Coat of Honour denies Impeller (left), the fast-finishing Bonecrusher (visor, far right),
Anani (centre) and Spanish Don (breastgirth)

CLUELESS 2 b.c. (Feb 4) Royal Applause 124 – Pure (Slip Anchor 136) [2004 8g⁴ 8g³ Sep 30] 26,000Y: big, lengthy colt: fourth foal: half-brother to 7f winner Angel Annie (by Alzao): dam unraced sister to Oaks/St Leger winner User Friendly: fairly useful form in maidens at Yarmouth and Newmarket (mulish stall, staying-on third to Pevensey): will stay 1¼m: should progress. *W. J. Haggas*   **87 p**

COALITION 5 b.g. Polish Precedent (USA) 131 – Selection Board 75 (Welsh Pageant 132) [2004 12g 14.1g² 14m² 16.1f³ Aug 7] rather leggy, good-topped gelding: fairly useful handicapper: placed 3 times in 2004: will stay further than 2m: acts on all-weather, firm and good to soft going: sold 7,000 gns. *H. Candy*   **86**

COAT OF HONOUR (USA) 4 gr.g. Mark of Esteem (IRE) 137 – Ballymac Girl 63 (Niniski (USA) 125) [2004 101p: 10.4g 9.9g* 10.5g² 12.9f* Sep 4] lengthy gelding: useful performer: won handicap at Goodwood (by neck from Impeller) in July and minor event at Down Royal (beat Lord Admiral by 4 lengths) in September: good second to Dunaskin in valuable handicap at Haydock in between: stays 13f: acts on firm and good to soft going (yet to race on soft/heavy): effective blinkered or not: races prominently: tends to idle: sold privately, and joined J. Howard Johnson, fairly useful form over hurdles. *Sir Mark Prescott*   **106**

COBALT BLUE (IRE) 3 b.g. Bluebird (USA) 125 – Amy Hunter (USA) (Jade Hunter (USA)) [2004 58: 8m 8.1d⁶ 8f* 10d⁵ p10g⁵ 12g 10m³ 8d 10m² Sep 23] tall gelding: modest handicapper: made all at Musselburgh in June: effective at 1m/1¼m: acts on firm going: usually wears headgear: sold 10,000 gns, sent to Bahrain. *W. J. Haggas*   **59**

COBALT RUNNER (IRE) 3 b.g. Fayruz 116 – Bui-Doi (IRE) 58 (Dance of Life (USA)) [2004 p5g 5m Jun 5] well held in maidens: left G. Margarson after debut: gelded after final start. *Miss D. A. McHale*   **–**

COCONUT COOKIE 3 ch.f. Bahamian Bounty 116 – Spicy Manner (USA) (Crypto-clearance (USA)) [2004 68: 7m 8.2m 8f Jun 14] leggy filly: maiden: well held in 2004: sold 6,000 gns, sent to Belgium. *R. Hannon*   **–**

COCONUT MOON 2 b.f. (Feb 25) Bahamian Bounty 116 – Lunar Ridge (Indian Ridge 123) [2004 5d⁶ Aug 9] 4,500Y: small filly: third foal: half-sister to winner in USA by Alzao: dam unraced half-sister to US Grade 3 6.5f winner Wrekin Pilot: 20/1, sixth of 12 in maiden at Thirsk, short of room and not knocked about: should improve. *R. A. Fahey*   **64 p**

COCONUT PENANG (IRE) 4 b.c. Night Shift (USA) – Play With Fire (FR) (Priolo (USA) 127) [2004 103: 6g 5d 6f² 7g 6m 6g⁵ 6m Sep 11] deep-girthed colt: useful performer: left B. R. Millman before very good 1½ lengths second to Lafi in Wokingham at Royal Ascot third outing: effective at 5f/6f: acted on any going: tried blinkered: dead. *P. W. Chapple-Hyam*   **101**

COCONUT SQUEAK 2 b.f. (May 10) Bahamian Bounty 116 – Creeking 65 (Persian Bold 123) [2004 7g³ 7.2s⁶ 7d 7m 6m* 6s Oct 22] 7,000Y: lengthy filly: fifth foal: half-sister to 1m winner Yalla (by Groom Dancer) and 1½m winner in Sweden by Intikhab: dam, maiden, effective at 7f to 1¼m: fair performer: won claimer at Lingfield in October: **66**

228

left J. Given, respectable effort in sales race at Doncaster final start: stays 7f: acts on good to firm going. *Mrs Stef Liddiard*

COCO POINT BREEZE 3 b.f. Great Dane (IRE) 122 – Flying Colours (IRE) 61 (Fairy King (USA)) [2004 p8g 8m 8.1m 9.7g 9.3m Sep 11] first foal: dam 2m winner: no form: tried blinkered. *J. G. Given* —

COCO REEF 3 b.f. Kingsinger (IRE) 94 – Highland Blue 55 (Never So Bold 135) [2004 64: 7g6 f6m f6g5 5.7m f5g f5g f6g p5.1g p6g4 Dec 22] poor maiden: left B. Palling after seventh start: stays 6f: acts on fibresand: tried in cheekpieces. *M. Mullineaux* — **47**

CODE ORANGE 2 b.f. (Mar 24) Green Desert (USA) 127 – Warning Belle (Warning 136) [2004 6m2 6g2 Sep 3] 150,000Y: sturdy filly: fourth foal: half-sister to useful 2001 2-y-o 7f winner Desert Warning (by Mark of Esteem): dam unraced half-sister to high-class 1¼m performer Stagecraft from family of Opera House and Kayf Tara: ½-length second in maidens won by Satin Kiss at Leicester and Penkenna Princess at Kempton: will probably stay 1m: useful prospect, and should win a race or 2. *J. H. M. Gosden* — **91 p**

CODY 5 ch.g. Zilzal (USA) 137 – Ibtihaj (USA) 97 (Raja Baba (USA)) [2004 52: p16g3 17.2g Sep 27] good-topped gelding: poor maiden: stays 2m: acts on good to soft going and polytrack: tried visored/tongue tied. *G. A. Ham* — **48**

COEUR COURAGEUX (FR) 2 b.c. (Mar 29) Xaar 132 – Linoise (FR) 108 (Caerwent 123) [2004 7g Jul 31] €8,000Y, 23,000 2-y-o: third foal: dam French sprinter: 8/1, well held in maiden at Doncaster, very slowly away: likely to do better. *D. Flood* — **– p**

COIS NA TINE EILE 2 br.f. (Apr 29) Cois Na Tine (IRE) 101 – Water Pixie (IRE) (Dance of Life (USA)) [2004 6g3 f7g 7.5d3 8m 10g 9d f8g6 f8g5 p8.6g5 f8d6 Dec 21] 1,200Y: strong, close-coupled filly: sixth foal: half-sister to 1m winner Pix Me Up (by Up And At 'em) and 2003 2-y-o 6f and 1m winner (latter in Spain) Doctor Price (by Wolfhound): dam unraced: modest maiden: trained first 3 starts by K. Ryan: stays 8.6f: acts on polytrack and good to soft ground. *Ms Deborah J. Evans* — **52**

COLD CLIMATE 9 b.g. Pursuit of Love 124 – Sharpthorne (USA) 91 (Sharpen Up 127) [2004 64, a73: p7g p7g4 6m 7g5 6m2 6m2 6d 7m4 Sep 9] lengthy gelding: fair handicapper: stays 7f: acts on any turf going and polytrack: occasionally visored, not in 2004: usually comes from behind. *Bob Jones* — **64 a71**

COLD ENCOUNTER (IRE) 9 ch.g. Polar Falcon (USA) 126 – Scene Galante (FR) (Sicyos (USA) 126) [2004 p16g Sep 18] well held only Flat since since 2000: tried visored. *R. M. Stronge* —

COLD TURKEY 4 b.g. Polar Falcon (USA) 126 – South Rock 102 (Rock City 120) [2004 89: p12g* p12g* p12g3 p13g2 16d4 12s* 12m2 14g4 10.1g 12s p16.5g2 p12g p12.2g5 Dec 17] leggy gelding: useful handicapper: won at Lingfield (twice) in January and Epsom (by 3 lengths from General) in April: best at 1½m/1¾m: acts on polytrack, soft and firm ground: sometimes slowly away/edges right: free-going sort: usually dropped out in rear: tough. *G. L. Moore* — **95**

COLEMANSTOWN 4 b.g. Charnwood Forest (IRE) 125 – Arme Fatale (IRE) (Trempolino (USA) 135) [2004 81: 7v 7s 6m 6g 6m 7s 7g 7m 7.5d 8g3 7g f8g* p8.6g p6g2 Dec 27] lengthy, good-topped gelding: fair handicapper: won amateur event at Southwell in November: effective at 6f to 1m: acts on all-weather, firm and good to soft going. *B. Ellison* — **72**

COLEORTON DANCER 2 ch.g. (Apr 2) Danehill Dancer (IRE) 117 – Tayovullin (IRE) 65 (Shalford (IRE) 124§) [2004 5.1g 5d4 f5g4 5f4 5.1g 5d* 5.1g* 5.1g* 6g* 6g 6s Oct 22] quite good-topped gelding: second foal: dam, 7f winner, out of half-sister to Vintage Crop: fairly useful performer: won maiden at Thirsk and nurseries at Nottingham, Chester and Newmarket (by ½ length from Marching Song), all in August: blindfold left on too long final start: will probably stay 7f: acts on good to soft going. *K. A. Ryan* — **88**

COLEORTON DANE 2 gr.g. (May 24) Danehill Dancer (IRE) 117 – Cloudy Nine (Norton Challenger 111) [2004 6s6 7.1m3 7m2 7.1f* 6d3 8m Sep 9] leggy, lengthy gelding: second foal: dam unraced: fair performer: made all in maiden at Musselburgh in August: good third at Ripon, much better effort in nurseries after (moved poorly to post final start): effective at 6f/7f: acts on firm and soft ground: raced up with pace. *K. A. Ryan* — **79**

COLEORTON PRINCE (IRE) 3 b.g. Paris House 123 – Tayovullin (IRE) 65 (Shalford (IRE) 124§) [2004 37: p6g Feb 11] close-coupled gelding: poor maiden: well beaten only 3-y-o start: tried in cheekpieces. *K. A. Ryan* —

COLISAY 5 b.g. Entrepreneur 123 – La Sorrela (IRE) (Cadeaux Genereux 131) [2004 112: 7m3 8.1d6 8g4 10.3f* 9.9g4 9.5s Oct 13] sturdy gelding: useful performer: trained by — **108**

A. Stewart until after second start: won handicap at Doncaster in September by neck from Courageous Duke: creditable fourth to Alkaadhem in listed race at Goodwood next time: effective at 1m/1¼m: acts on firm and good to soft going: ran respectably only try in visor: sold 62,000 gns. *E. F. Vaughan*

COLLADA (IRE) 3 b.f. Desert Prince (IRE) 130 – Bright Spells (USA) (Alleged (USA) 138) [2004 8.3s 9g 7m⁶ 7.1s Aug 12] unfurnished filly: fourth foal: half-sister to 7f winners (including at 2 yrs) Blazing Thunder and Clearing (both by Zafonic), latter also second in Poule d'Essai des Poulains: dam fairly useful French 1½m winner: well held in maidens/handicap. *J. H. M. Gosden* —

COLLEGE DELINQUENT (IRE) 5 br.g. College Chapel 122 – St Cyr Aty (IRE) (Ela-Mana-Mou 132) [2004 60, a76: p8g³ p8g⁴ p8g⁶ p8g p8.6g p8.6g⁵ p9.5g p8.6g Dec 17] quite good-topped gelding: fair performer: stays 1m: acts on polytrack, firm and soft ground: often blinkered in 2002, tongue tied nowadays. *K. Bell* — a72

COLLEGE HIPPIE 5 b.m. Cosmonaut – Eccentric Dancer 47 (Rambo Dancer (CAN) 107) [2004 64, a49: 5d 5f 5g 5d Jul 15] plain, angular mare: well held in 2004, including in blinkers/cheekpieces. *J. F. Coupland* —

COLLEGE MAID (IRE) 7 b.m. College Chapel 122 – Maid of Mourne (Fairy King (USA)) [2004 66: 5g⁴ 5g 5d⁶ 5m 5f 6m² 6m⁴ 7.2g* 6g³ 5g⁵ 7m⁶ 6m⁶ 6m⁶ 7.1f⁶ 6g⁵ 6s³ 6f 5d 5m⁶ 6d Oct 12] sturdy mare: fair handicapper: won at Ayr in June: effective at 5f to 7f: acts on any going: usually wears headgear: sometimes mulish in paddock: effective held up or ridden prominently: none too consistent. *J. S. Goldie* 68

COLLEGE QUEEN 6 b.m. Lugana Beach 116 – Eccentric Dancer 47 (Rambo Dancer (CAN) 107) [2004 74: 6g 5m⁶ 6m⁵ 5m⁴ 6m⁵ 5g² 6m 5g 6f⁵ 5.1m³ 6.1d 5g p5g Dec 18] strong mare: fair handicapper: effective at 5f/6f: acts on fibresand, firm and good to soft going: tried tongue tied, often wears blinkers/cheekpieces: usually races up with pace. *S. Gollings* 69

COLLEGE STAR 6 b.g. Lugana Beach 116 – Alis Princess (Sayf El Arab (USA) 127) [2004 –, a32: f8g f7g Feb 5] no longer of any account. *J. F. Coupland* —

COLLETON RIVER (IRE) 3 gr.g. Croco Rouge (IRE) 126 – Midnight Angel (Machiavellian (USA) 123) [2004 p12.2g⁶ Dec 4] third foal: half-brother to winners abroad by Entrepreneur and Ashkalani: dam unraced out of useful sprinter Night At Sea: 11/2, 2½ lengths sixth of 12 to Flaming Eyes in maiden at Wolverhampton, held up and short of room: sure to improve. *W. J. Haggas* 69 p

COLLIER HILL 6 ch.g. Dr Devious (IRE) 127 – Polar Queen 76 (Polish Precedent (USA) 131) [2004 103: 18.7d 12.1d* 16.1s²¹ 13.9g³ 13.9s 12g* 12v⁵ Oct 23] strong gelding: good mover: smart performer: won listed rated stakes at Hamilton in May and Stockholm Cup International at Taby (beat Foreign Affairs by short head) in September: effective at 1½m to 2m: acts on soft going, lightly raced and below form on firmer than good: usually waited with. *G. A. Swinbank* 112

COLLOQUIAL 3 b.g. Classic Cliche (IRE) 128 – Celia Brady 62 (Last Tycoon 131) [2004 p12g⁵ Nov 27] fifth living foal: closely related to fairly useful 1¼m and 11.7f winner Clarisse (by Salse), later successful abroad, and half-sister to 1½m winner Stahr (by Liboi): dam 1m winner: 16/1, 2½ lengths fifth of 14 to Amwell Brave in maiden at Lingfield, staying on from rear: open to improvement. *H. Candy* 69 p

COLLOSEUM 3 b.g. Piccolo 121 – Trig Point (Rudimentary (USA) 118) [2004 60: 7.1g 8m⁴ 7f 10g 9.1g⁸ p8.6g p7m Dec 8] good-topped gelding: modest maiden: stays 1m: raced only on polytrack/good ground or firmer. *T. J. Etherington* 51

COLNE VALLEY AMY 7 b.m. Mizoram (USA) 105 – Panchellita (USA) 78 (Pancho Villa (USA)) [2004 –: p8g⁴ p10g² f8g p8g f8d Jul 23] tall mare: poor performer: left G. L. Moore after fourth start: stays 1¼m: acts on all-weather, firm and good to soft ground: sometimes blinkered: often races up with pace. *Mrs S. J. Smith* 47

COLONEL BILKO (IRE) 2 b.g. (Feb 11) General Monash (USA) 107 – Mari-Ela (IRE) 60 (River Falls 113) [2004 5s² 5.1g 6f⁶ 6m* 6m p6g Dec 10] 19,000Y: third foal: half-brother to 3-y-o Chimali: dam 2-y-o 7f seller winner: fair performer: won nursery at Leicester in July: stays 6f: acts on soft and good to firm going: blinkered (pulled hard) third start: tried tongue tied: tends to hang: unreliable. *B. R. Millman* 71 §

COLONEL COTTON (IRE) 5 b.g. Royal Applause 124 – Cutpurse Moll 76 (Green Desert (USA) 127) [2004 115: 5d⁶ 5g 5v⁶ 5m⁵ 5m⁵ 5f 5d³ 6m 5m⁶ 6m⁵ 6g³ 5m⁴ 5g 6d Oct 15] good-topped gelding: just useful in 2004: effective at 5f/6f: acts on firm and soft 101

going: effective blinkered/visored: has worn crossed noseband: sometimes slowly away: held up, and best in well-run race: none too consistent: sold 44,000 gns. *N. A. Callaghan*

COLONIAL GIRL (IRE)   2 b.f. (Apr 18) Desert Style (IRE) 121 – Telemania (IRE)   **65**
87 (Mujtahid (USA) 118) [2004 5m⁴ 5.1g³ f5g² 5g⁴ Jul 5] €5,000F, €21,000Y: sturdy filly: fourth foal: dam, 2-y-o 6f winner, stayed 1m: fair maiden: should stay 6f: acts on fibresand and good to firm going. *T. D. Easterby*

COLONNADE   5 b.m. Blushing Flame (USA) 109 – White Palace 80 (Shirley Heights   **–**
130) [2004 59?: f14g² f16g f14s³ 14.4v 11.9m 13.8v Oct 16] lengthy mare: modest   **a50**
maiden: left C. Grant after fourth start: stays 2m: acts on firm going and fibresand. *N. Wilson*

COLOPHONY (USA)   4 ch.g. Distant View (USA) 126 – Private Line (USA) 105   **76**
(Private Account (USA)) [2004 83: 10g 10m⁴ 11.9g 10m⁶ p10g Dec 18] big, strong gelding: just fair performer in 2004: stays 10.5f: raced only on good going or firmer: tongue tied since debut. *K. A. Morgan*

COLORADO FALLS (IRE)   6 b.g. Nashwan (USA) 135 – Ballet Shoes (IRE) 75   **86**
(Ela-Mana-Mou 132) [2004 13g* 12.1m⁵ 13.1d⁴ 13f 16.1d⁴ 13d³ 14.4s⁴ Aug 30] useful-looking gelding: fairly useful handicapper: first run on Flat since 2002 when winning at Hamilton in May: effective at 1½m to 2m: acts on good to firm and heavy ground: has edged left/carried head high. *P. Monteith*

COLOUR BLIND (IRE)   2 b.g. (May 13) Spectrum (IRE) 126 – Sarooh's Love   **34**
(USA) (Nureyev (USA) 131) [2004 8s 8.2v p8.6g Nov 26] well-made gelding: poor maiden. *M. L. W. Bell*

COLOUR CODE (IRE)   3 b.g. Spectrum (IRE) 126 – Viendra Nur (USA) (Nureyev   **–**
(USA) 131) [2004 72: 7g Apr 12] robust gelding: fair maiden, lightly raced: well beaten only 3-y-o start (gelded after). *M. P. Tregoning*

COLOURFUL LADY (USA)   4 b.f. Quest For Fame 127 – Special Park (USA)   **–**
(Trempolino (USA) 135) [2004 70: f12g⁵ Jan 12] compact filly: well held only 4-y-o start: tried in cheekpieces. *P. W. Harris*

COLOUR WHEEL   3 ch.c. Spectrum (IRE) 126 – Risanda (Kris 135) [2004 89p: **95**
8.1d⁶ 8.1m 7m² 7g 7.1m 7g Oct 1] good-bodied colt: useful handicapper: short-headed by Ettrick Water at Newmarket: should stay 1m: acts on good to firm ground: visored (not discredited) final start: usually tongue tied: sold 25,000 gns, joined M. Al Kurdi in UAE. *R. Charlton*

COLUMBIAN EMERALD (IRE)   3 ch.g. Among Men (USA) 124 – Sarabi 64   **–**
(Alzao (USA) 117) [2004 9g 10m⁴ 12.1g⁵ 10.9g p16g Sep 1] little form. *T. J. Etherington*

COLWAY RITZ   10 b.g. Rudimentary (USA) 118 – Million Heiress (Auction Ring   **69**
(USA) 123) [2004 73?: 12.1s 10.4m² 12m² 14.1m⁵ 10.1m⁵ 10d³ Oct 18] big, strong gelding: good mover: fair handicapper: effective at 1¼m to 13.8f: acts on firm and good to soft going: tried blinkered and in cheekpieces, not in 2004: usually held up. *W. Storey*

COMANCHE WOMAN   4 b.f. Distinctly North (USA) 115 – Possibility 59   **–**
(Robellino (USA) 127) [2004 –: f14.8g Jan 3] no sign of ability: tried tongue tied. *K. O. Cunningham-Brown*

COME AWAY WITH ME (IRE)   4 b.f. Machiavellian (USA) 123 – Vert Val (USA)   **65 +**
103 (Septieme Ciel (USA) 123) [2004 55p: 6g² 5.5g⁺ Jul 8] fair performer, lightly raced: won handicap at Warwick in July: will prove best at 5f/6f: acts on fibresand and firm going, unraced on softer than good. *M. A. Buckley*

COME GOOD   2 ch.g. (Mar 25) Piccolo 121 – The Frog Lady (IRE) 52 (Al Hareb   **73**
(USA) 123) [2004 5s⁵ 5.7f² 6m⁶ 6m³ 6.1d² 6d Aug 24] 30,000Y: close-coupled gelding: fifth foal: brother to useful 2000 2-y-o 6f winner Piccolo Player, later successful in USA, and half-brother to 2 winners, including 3-y-o Fizzy Lady: dam, maiden, best at 1¼m/1½m: fair maiden: will stay 7f: acts on firm and good to soft ground: hung left third start: sent to Macau. *R. Hannon*

COMEINTOTHESPACE (IRE)   2 b.c. (Apr 5) Tagula (IRE) 116 – Playa Del Sol   **61**
(IRE) (Alzao (USA) 117) [2004 6.5g 6.5d 7.5s 8v 8d⁶ 7d p8.6g⁶ p8m² Dec 8] €10,000Y: first foal: dam Italian 1¼m winner: modest maiden: left D. Weld after second start: runner-up in claimer at Lingfield: stays 1m: acts on polytrack and heavy going: blinkered first 2 starts. *P. Morris, Ireland*

COME ON   5 b.g. Aragon 118 – All On 68 (Dunbeath (USA) 127) [2004 6d⁵ p5.1g⁵   **54**
Nov 6] good-bodied gelding: modest form in maidens at Redcar and Wolverhampton, only outings: should stay 7f. *J. Hetherton*

Neil Greig – Osborne House's "Comic Strip"

COME ON JONNY (IRE) 2 b.c. (May 2) Desert King (IRE) 129 – Idle Fancy 79 **80**
(Mujtahid (USA) 118) [2004 6g 6d³ 6g⁴ 8.3d* 8.3g Oct 11] 20,000Y: close-coupled colt:
fourth foal: half-brother to 3 winners, including 3-y-o Crafty Fancy and 6-y-o Idle Power:
dam, Irish 1m winner, half-sister to dam of smart 1½m performer Ela Athena: fairly
useful performer: much improved to win nursery at Windsor in October: ran as if amiss
final start: stays 1m: best effort on good to soft going. *R. M. Beckett*

COMERAINCOMESHINE (IRE) 3 ch.f. Night Shift (USA) – Future Past (USA) **67**
(Super Concorde (USA) 128) [2004 61: p5g³ 5.1g⁶ 5m⁴ 6m² 6d 5.1m 5.7f* Sep 6] sturdy
filly: fair performer: won maiden at Bath in September: stays 6f: acts on polytrack and
firm going. *T. G. Mills*

COME TO DADDY (IRE) 2 ch.g. (Apr 20) Fayruz 116 – Forgren (IRE) (Thatching **45**
131) [2004 6g 6d⁵ 7s Oct 27] poor form in maidens/minor event: slowly away first 2
outings. *F. Jordan*

COME WHAT AUGUSTUS 2 b.g. (Feb 17) Mujahid (USA) 125 – Sky Red 75 **–**
(Night Shift (USA)) [2004 p8m Dec 21] 45,000F: third foal: dam, 5f winner, sister to
useful sprinter Night Haven: 10/1, last of 11 in maiden at Lingfield. *E. A. L. Dunlop*

COME WHAT JULY (IRE) 3 b.g. Indian Rocket 115 – Persian Sally (IRE) (Persian **69**
Bold 123) [2004 68: p10g* f9.4s² p10g⁵ 12g⁶ 10.1v⁶ 8m p12g³ 10.9g⁵ f8g* 9.9g 9.9m³ **a76**
9.9d⁶ f8g p10g p8.6g⁴ f8g p9.5g f8g p12.2g* Dec 27] compact gelding: fair performer:
won maiden at Lingfield in February, claimer at Southwell (claimed from R. Guest) in
July and seller at Wolverhampton in December: stays 1½m: acts on all-weather, good
to firm and good to soft going: usually blinkered/visored, not for final success. *Mrs
N. Macauley*

COMFY (USA) 5 b.h. Lear Fan (USA) 130 – Souplesse (USA) (Majestic Light (USA)) **113**
[2004 116: 10d⁵ 10f Jun 16] strong, good sort: good mover: smart performer, lightly raced

232

(missed 2002 due to leg injury): creditable seventh of 10 to Rakti in Prince of Wales's Stakes at Royal Ascot (sweating and edgy, last to post), much better effort in 2004: stays 1¼m: acts on firm and good to soft ground: sent to Australia. *Sir Michael Stoute*

COMICAL ERRORS (USA) 2 b.g. (Feb 25) Distorted Humor (USA) 117 – Falli-bility (USA) (Tom Rolfe) [2004 6g 7d⁴ 7d⁵ 10m f8g Nov 9] close-coupled gelding: modest maiden: should stay 1m: best effort on good to soft going. *P. C. Haslam* **62**

COMIC GENIUS 3 b.f. Comic Strip (USA) 115 – Itsy Bitsy Betsy (USA) (Beau Genius (CAN)) [2004 46: f8s³ f8.5g⁵ 10s 12.1d⁶ Apr 23] poor maiden: stays 1m: acts on fibresand and soft going: tried blinkered/visored. *D. Haydn Jones* **40**

COMIC STRIP 2 b.g. (May 7) Marju (IRE) 127 – Comic (IRE) 87 (Be My Chief (USA) 122) [2004 f6m* 7.5g⁴ 7g* 8s* 8.5g* 8d* Oct 18] 26,000Y: tall, quite good-topped gelding: second foal: dam, 1¼m/11.5f winner, half-sister to smart US 1m/1¼m performer Brave Act: won maiden at Southwell in July, nurseries at Chester and Ayr in September and minor event at Epsom and listed contest at Pontefract in October: improved again when accounting for Wise Dennis impressively by 3½ lengths in last-named, travelling strongly and quickening to lead over 1f out before duck-ing left and idling: likely to stay 1¼m: acts on fibresand and soft going: should progress and make his mark in pattern company. *Sir Mark Prescott* **110 p**

COMIC TALES 3 b.g. Mind Games 121 – Glorious Aragon 88 (Aragon 118) [2004 –: 6m⁶ 7m⁶ 7.1s 7f⁶ 6g⁵ p6g Dec 22] good-topped gelding: poor maiden: stays 7f: acts on polytrack and good to firm ground: tried in blinkers/cheekpieces: usually starts slowly. *M. Mullineaux* **44**

COMIC TIMES 4 b.f. Puissance 110 – Glorious Aragon 88 (Aragon 118) [2004 –: 5d Jun 9] of little account. *M. Mullineaux* **–**

COMING AGAIN (IRE) 3 b.g. Rainbow Quest (USA) 134 – Hagwah (USA) 109 (Dancing Brave (USA) 140) [2004 91p: 10d⁵ 10m² 12m Jun 5] quite good-topped gelding: fairly useful maiden: short-headed by Motive at Windsor second start: tailed off in Derby at Epsom final one: stays 1¼m: acts on good to firm and good to soft ground: sold 22,000 gns, joined D. McCain. *B. W. Hills* **85**

COMINTRUE (IRE) 2 ch.f. (Feb 16) Namid 128 – Gute (IRE) 77 (Petardia 113) [2004 p5g 5d 6g 5d² 5f 6m Sep 4] €8,000F, €7,000Y: first foal: dam Irish 2-y-o 5f winner: modest maiden: should stay 6f: best efforts on good to soft ground. *E. J. O'Neill* **50**

COMMANDER BOND 3 b.g. Piccolo 121 – Lonesome 60 (Night Shift (USA)) [2004 74p: 6d 7m f7g* 6.9g f6m 6g f7f 8g⁵ 7.1d p7.1g Oct 9] well-made gelding: fair performer: won handicap at Southwell in June: well below form after, including in claimers last 3 starts: stays 7f: acts on good to firm going and fibresand, probably on polytrack. *B. Smart* **74 d**

COMMANDER FLIP (IRE) 4 ch.g. In Command (IRE) 114 – Boldabsa 96 (Persian Bold 123) [2004 57: f12s⁴ 12v Apr 6] tall, leggy, close-coupled gelding: modest maiden at best: dead. *R. Hollinshead* **–**

COMMANDO SCOTT (IRE) 3 b.g. Danetime (IRE) 121 – Faye 79 (Monsanto (FR) 121) [2004 78: 6s* 6.1d 6m 6g² 7d² 6g² 7.5g⁶ 6s* 6g* 6g⁵ 6.1g 6s Sep 25] good-topped gelding: fairly useful performer: won maiden at Thirsk in April and handicaps at Hay-dock and Doncaster in July: best efforts at 6f: acts on soft and good to firm ground: usually races prominently. *A. Berry* **95**

COMMEMORATION DAY (IRE) 3 b.g. Daylami (IRE) 138 – Bequeath (USA) (Lyphard (USA) 132) [2004 66: 8d 12m⁶ f12g 10d Jul 10] strong, compact gelding: has a fluent, round action: modest maiden: stays 1½m: acts on good to firm ground. *J. G. Given* **59**

COMMENDABLE COUP (USA) 2 b. or br.c. (Mar 25) Commendable (USA) 122 – Bird Dance (USA) (Storm Bird (CAN) 134) [2004 6g⁵ 6g 8.1g⁶ Sep 3] $14,500Y: big, strong colt: sixth foal: half-brother to several winners, including 3-y-o Miss Ladybird: dam maiden in USA: best effort in maidens when fifth at Thirsk: on toes and took good hold final start: should stay 1m. *T. D. Barron* **65**

COMMITMENT LECTURE 4 b.f. Komaite (USA) – Hurtleberry (IRE) 87 (Tirol 127) [2004 64: 8v⁵ 8.1d* 8.1v⁴ 8g⁶ p8.6g⁵ 8.2v³ f8s Nov 17] smallish filly: modest handicapper: won at Haydock in April: stays 1m: acts on good to firm and heavy going, below form on all-weather: usually tongue tied: usually held up. *M. Dods* **64**

COMPASSION (IRE) 3 b.f. Alhaarth (IRE) 126 – Titania (Fairy King (USA)) [2004 62: f8.5g 6m 8g 8g⁴ 9.2g⁴ 12.1d⁵ 9m³ 7.2g⁶ 6.9m 7.2g³ 8.3d Aug 17] rather leggy filly: **48**

poor maiden: trained until after fourth start by G. Chung: stayed 9f: acted on good to firm going: often wore cheekpieces: dead. *Miss L. A. Perratt*

COMPETITOR 3 b.c. Danzero (AUS) – Ceanothus (IRE) 61 (Bluebird (USA) 125) **66** [2004 72: p10g2 8g 10m 9.9s5 10g 9.9g6 11.7g p10g5 p10g p10m6 Dec 22] fair handi- **a73** capper: stays 1¼m: acts on polytrack and good to firm ground: tried in cheekpieces: has reportedly had breathing problem (ran creditably in tongue tie final start). *J. Akehurst*

COMPLICATION 4 b.f. Compton Place 125 – Hard Task 82 (Formidable (USA) 125) **79** [2004 74: 6g 6f6 6m2 6m4 6m2 6m* 6f Sep 16] smallish, sturdy filly: fair handicapper: won at Pontefract in July: stays 6f: acts on firm ground: blinkered. *J. A. R. Toller*

COMPTON ARROW (IRE) 8 b.g. Petardia 113 – Impressive Lady 98 (Mr Fluoro- **–** carbon 126) [2004 71: 6.1v 7g 7m 7m 6m 7.1m p8m Dec 8] big, rangy gelding: well held in 2004: tried blinkered/visored/tongue tied earlier in career. *A. W. Carroll*

COMPTON AVIATOR 8 ch.g. First Trump 118 – Rifada 103 (Ela-Mana-Mou 132) **58** [2004 65: p10g6 11.7s p12g5 11.7g 11.5m6 10.9m5 8g Sep 22] lengthy gelding: modest handicapper: effective at 1¼m/easy 1½m: acts on polytrack, good to firm and good to soft going: tongue tied: tried in blinkers/cheekpieces: held up. *A. W. Carroll*

COMPTON BANKER (IRE) 7 br.g. Distinctly North (USA) 115 – Mary Hinge **72 d** 100 (Dowsing (USA) 124) [2004 91: f5g 7.1m6 6.1f5 5.3f2 6d 5.1m3 6g 5.7f p6g6 p7.1g3 Dec 14] small, strong gelding: fair performer: below form after fourth outing, claimed from G. Butler on sixth: effective at 5f to easy 7f: acts on firm going and polytrack: often wears headgear: tongue tied last 2 starts: sometimes rears stall/starts slowly: usually held up. *P. D. Evans*

COMPTON BAY 4 b.g. Compton Place 125 – Silver Sun 83 (Green Desert (USA) **–** 127) [2004 –: f7g f6s f6s f7g5 Apr 16] leggy, plain gelding: little form since 2 yrs: tried blinkered. *M. Brittain*

COMPTON BOLTER (IRE) 7 b.g. Red Sunset 120 – Milk And Honey 102 (So **115** Blessed 130) [2004 118: a10f4 12m 12m5 12m 13.4d3 9.9g2 10.1m5 10m 10d6 12m5 13.3g3 11.6d3 12f2 11m3 12m4 p10g2 p9.5g* Dec 31] smallish gelding: has a quick action: smart performer: in frame 9 times in 2004 (ran at Nad Al Sheba first 4 starts), winning handicap at Wolverhampton in December under top weight by length from Linning Wine: other good efforts when neck second to Alkaadhem in listed race at Goodwood sixth outing, 2½ lengths second to Mubtaker in Geoffrey Freer Stakes at Newbury on eleventh and 2 lengths third to Sights On Gold in Arc Trial at Newbury on fourteenth: effective at 1¼m to 13f: acts on dirt/polytrack, firm and good to soft going: tongue tied for first time since 2001 at Wolverhampton: occasionally visored/blinkered: tough. *G. A. Butler*

COMPTON CLASSIC 2 b.c. (Mar 12) Compton Place 125 – Ayr Classic 74 (Local **55** Suitor (USA) 128) [2004 6g 5g6 6d6 6d Oct 11] good-bodied colt: modest maiden: form only on penultimate start: likely to prove best at 5f/6f. *J. S. Goldie*

COMPTON COMMANDER 6 ch.g. Barathea (IRE) 127 – Triode (USA) 105 (Shar- **– §** pen Up 127) [2004 94§: p10g f12s Mar 5] useful-looking gelding: well held in 2004: tried blinkered/visored: ungenuine. *Ian Williams*

COMPTON DRAGON (USA) 5 ch.g. Woodman (USA) 126 – Vilikaia (USA) 125 **82** (Nureyev (USA) 131) [2004 106d: p7g 8g 10.3g5 10g 10.5m6 10.1g2 10.3g2 12f5 9.9d2 10.3g 9.3f6 10.3g 10s4 10g Aug 31] compact gelding: fairly useful handicapper: stays 1¼m: acts on polytrack and good to firm going, probably on soft: often wears headgear: edgy sort: often slowly away. *D. Nicholls*

COMPTON DRAKE 5 b.g. Mark of Esteem (IRE) 137 – Reprocolor 114 (Jimmy **89** Reppin 131) [2004 75: 8g 9.9g2 8.1d* 8.5g2 11g4 p10g* 8.9g p10g3 p8m6 p7.1g5 Dec 31] big, good-topped gelding: fairly useful performer: won handicap at Chepstow in August and minor event at Lingfield in September: effective at 1m to 1½m: acts on all-weather, good to firm and good to soft ground: tried blinkered/tongue tied: has raced freely, and usually patiently ridden. *G. A. Butler*

COMPTON EAGLE 4 b.g. Zafonic (USA) 130 – Gayane 125 (Nureyev (USA) 131) **–** [2004 60: 7d f7m6 May 10] rangy gelding: maiden: well held in 2004: joined J. Lambe in Ireland, and won selling hurdle in August. *G. A. Butler*

COMPTON ECLAIRE (IRE) 4 ch.f. Lycius (USA) 124 – Baylands Sunshine **67 §** (IRE) (Classic Secret (USA) 91) [2004 66, a61: f12g3 14g3 f14.8m2 13.1m4 12.1g6 12.6f* 11.9f2 11.8m4 p16g2 14.1d4 p16g Sep 1] good-topped filly: fair handicapper: won at Warwick in June: stays easy 2m: acts on all-weather and firm going: usually blinkered/visored: ungenuine. *G. A. Butler*

COMPTON MICKY 3 ch.g. Compton Place 125 – Nunthorpe 79 (Mystiko (USA) **64** 124) [2004 –: 7g 6s⁶ 6m 7m⁵ 7f⁶ 6g 8s⁵ 10g 7d p7.1g* p8.6d⁵ f7g² Dec 11] strong gelding: fair performer: 50/1-winner of banded race at Wolverhampton in October: barely stays 1m: acts on all-weather, firm and soft ground: usually wears cheekpieces: free-going sort: carries head high. *J. Balding*

COMPTON PLUME 4 ch.g. Compton Place 125 – Brockton Flame 72 (Emarati **72** (USA) 74) [2004 56: 6d 6m³ 6m*ᵈⁱˢ 6m³ 6g² 6m* 6m 5g 5d 5m* 6g Sep 25] strong, lengthy gelding: fair performer: passed post first in amateur maiden handicap at Redcar (disqualified after rider weighed in 2 lb light) and maiden at Catterick in June and handicap at Beverley in September: best at stiff 5f/6f: acts on firm ground: usually blinkered/visored at 3 yrs. *W. H. Tinning*

COMPTON PRINCESS 4 b.f. Compton Place 125 – Curlew Calling (IRE) 51 **43 ?** (Pennine Walk 120) [2004 49: 6v³ f6m⁶ 6g 7.5m 7m 6m Jun 17] workmanlike filly: poor maiden: stays 7f: acts on any going: tried visored/blinkered. *Mrs A. Duffield*

COMPTON QUAY 2 ch.c. (Mar 12) Compton Place 125 – Roonah Quay (IRE) (Soviet **75** Lad (USA)) [2004 7.1m⁶ 7g p7m⁶ p7.1g* p8g Nov 16] 16,000Y, 24,000 2-y-o: rather leggy colt: second foal: half-brother to fairly useful 2003 2-y-o 5f winner Makila King (by Wizard King): dam little form: fair performer: won nursery at Wolverhampton in November: should stay 1m: acts on polytrack, promise on turf. *A. King*

COMPTON'S ELEVEN 3 gr.g. Compton Place 125 – Princess Tara 85 (Prince Sabo **104** 123) [2004 92: 6d 6s 7g 8.1d 7m⁵ 7m² 6g* 7m² 6g² 6.1g² 6.5f² 6g Oct 9] good-topped gelding: progressed in second half of year into a useful performer: won minor event at Hamilton in July: best effort when head second to Khabfair in handicap at Ascot eleventh start: effective at 6f/7f: acts on firm ground: sometimes carries head high/edges left. *M. R. Channon*

COMPTON SPARK 2 ch.g. (May 14) Compton Place 125 – Rhinefield Beauty (IRE) **–** 52 (Shalford (IRE) 124§) [2004 p6d Oct 30] third foal: dam sprint maiden: 28/1, well beaten in maiden at Wolverhampton, slowly away. *J. S. Goldie*

COMPTON STAR 4 ch.g. Compton Place 125 – Darakah 78 (Doulab (USA) 115) **–** [2004 –: p10g Dec 30] little form. *R. J. Hodges*

COMTESSE LALANDE (USA) 2 ch.f. (Feb 10) King of Kings (IRE) 125 – Beyond **52** The Realm (USA) (Stop The Music (USA)) [2004 5m⁶ Jun 26] 57,000Y: second foal: dam lightly-raced sister to smart French 1994 2-y-o sprinter Doree: sixth of 7 in maiden at Lingfield. *M. L. W. Bell*

CONCER ETO 5 ch.g. Sabrehill (USA) 120 – Drudwen (Sayf El Arab (USA) 127) **85** [2004 82: p8g p7g p8g² p8g³ 8m⁴ 7m* 8m² 7g 7m 8g⁴ 7g² p8g³ Oct 13] fairly useful **a80** handicapper: won at Yarmouth in July despite carrying head high: effective at 7f/1m: acts on all-weather, firm and good to soft ground: usually wears cheekpieces, also tried blinkered/tongue tied: sold 16,000 gns, sent to Saudi Arabia. *S. C. Williams*

CONCERT HALL (USA) 3 b.f. Stravinsky (USA) 133 – Proflare (USA) 101 (Mr **–** Prospector (USA)) [2004 76: 9.7s⁴ 9.9d⁶ Jun 23] leggy filly: maiden: well held in 2004: stud. *Mrs A. J. Perrett*

CONCERT TIME 2 ch.f. (Mar 3) Timeless Times (USA) 99 – Thalya (Crofthall 110) **46** [2004 5g 5g³ 6m⁶ f7g⁵ 5m³ p6g³ 5.1g Oct 10] 1,700Y: sturdy filly: sixth foal: half-sister to 6-y-o Fairgame Man and 3-y-o Defana: dam unraced: poor maiden: left P. Midgley after second start: likely to prove best at 5f/easy 6f: acts on polytrack and good to firm going: often races up with pace. *C. R. Dore*

CONCHONITA 4 b.f. Bishop of Cashel 122 – Cactus Road (FR) (Iron Duke (FR) **–** 122) [2004 37, a49: f9.4g Jan 26] poor maiden: well held only 4-y-o start. *B. Palling*

CONCUBINE (IRE) 5 b.m. Danehill (USA) 126 – Bye Bold Aileen (IRE) (Warning **65** 136) [2004 74, a–: 7f³ 7f 7g² 6m⁴ 7g 7.6m 6g Aug 14] close-coupled mare: fair handi- **a–** capper: stays 7f: acts on good to firm and good to soft going: tried in cheekpieces/blinkers: none too consistent. *J. R. Boyle*

CONFUZED 4 b.g. Pivotal 124 – Times of Times (IRE) 78 (Distinctly North (USA) **52** 115) [2004 –: p6g p5g³ p7g⁶ p6g p5g p6g f5g 6m⁴ f6m 5.7m 7s³ 8f³ 10.1d f7g³ p10m p10g Dec 20] strong gelding: modest maiden: claimed from A. Reid £9,000 on reappearance: effective at 5f, and seems to stay easy 1¼m: acts on all-weather, good to firm and soft going: usually wears eyeshields/blinkers. *D. Flood*

CONGO MAN 11 b.g. Rainbow Quest (USA) 134 – African Dance (USA) (El Gran Senor (USA) 136) [2004 13m 16.2s Jul 17] well held in 2004, only outings on Flat after winning maiden at 3 yrs: dead. *D. W. Whillans* —

CONJUROR 3 b.g. Efisio 120 – Princess Athena 119 (Ahonoora 122) [2004 6g 6f* 6g Sep 3] 21,000Y, 16,000 2-y-o: half-brother to several winners, notably smart sprinter Acclamation (by Royal Applause) and useful 6f/7f winner Waypoint (by Cadeaux Genereux): dam 5f winner, including Queen Mary Stakes: seemingly fairly useful form when winning maiden at Newmarket in August by 1¼ lengths from Imtalkinggibberish: unseated rider shortly after start on debut: reportedly lame when tailed off final outing (gelded after). *A. M. Balding* **82 ?**

CONNECT 7 b.g. Petong 126 – Natchez Trace 52 (Commanche Run 133) [2004 95: 5m² 5m⁴ 5m 5d⁴ 5g* 5m⁴ 5.2f 5g 5.6m 6s 6g⁴ 5d⁶ Oct 17] strong, lengthy gelding: unimpressive mover: useful handicapper: won at Newmarket in July by neck from First Order: good fourth to Baltic King at Ascot next time: effective at 5f/easy 6f: acts on all-weather, firm and good to soft ground: tried visored, blinkered nowadays: sometimes hangs: usually held up. *M. H. Tompkins* **100**

CONNOTATION 2 b.f. (Feb 12) Mujahid (USA) 125 – Seven Wonders (USA) (Rahy (USA) 115) [2004 5.3f² p5g² 6f³ p7g 5f* 6m⁶ p5.1g³ p6g³ p8.6g³ Nov 29] €17,000Y: first foal: dam unraced half-sister to smart 1¼m US performer Boatman out of half-sister to Irish 1000 Guineas winner Al Bahathri, herself dam of 3-y-o Haafhd: fair performer: won nursery at Redcar in September: creditable efforts in minor event/nurseries after: stays 8.6f: acts on polytrack and firm going: visored/blinkered fifth to eighth outings. *P. W. D'Arcy* **73**

CONQUERING LOVE (IRE) 6 b.g. Pursuit of Love 124 – Susquehanna Days (USA) 68 (Chief's Crown (USA)) [2004 89: 11.9d 12m 12m Sep 4] quite good-topped gelding: no form in 2004, refusing to race last 2 starts (left B. Ellison before final one). *C. Grant* **§§**

CONSENSUS (IRE) 5 b.m. Common Grounds 118 – Kilbride Lass (IRE) (Lahib (USA) 129) [2004 89, a–: 6g⁴ 5v 6g 6m³ 6m 6m 5g⁴ 5d⁶ 5d 6f 5m Sep 29] leggy mare: unimpressive mover: fairly useful handicapper: below form last 4 starts: effective at 5f/6f: well held on heavy ground, acts on any other on turf: races up with pace: none too consistent. *M. Brittain* **83 d a–**

CONSIDER THIS 2 b.f. (Apr 21) Josr Algarhoud (IRE) 118 – River of Fortune (IRE) 68 (Lahib (USA) 129) [2004 6m² 6.1s⁵ 6m³ 6g² 6.5m 7.2d² 8s³ 7s⁴ 7.1d² Nov 3] 5,000Y: quite good-topped filly: fourth foal: dam 2-y-o 7f seller winner: fairly useful maiden: placed 6 times, including in nursery: stays 1m: acts on soft and good to firm going: edgy sort: sometimes finds little. *W. M. Brisbourne* **81**

CONSIDINE (USA) 3 b.c. Romanov (IRE) 119 – Libeccio (NZ) (Danzatore (CAN) 120) [2004 61: f8g 12s* 14d² 14.1f* 16.1v 14m² 14d⁶ 14.4m⁴ Sep 4] big, workmanlike colt: fair handicapper: won at Pontefract in April and Yarmouth in June: stays 13¾m, probably not 2m: acts on firm and soft ground: races up with pace: game. *J. M. P. Eustace* **76**

CONSIGNIA (IRE) 5 ch.m. Definite Article 121 – Coppelia (IRE) (Mac's Imp (USA) 116) [2004 55: f9.4g f9.4g f8.5g⁵ Jan 19] lengthy mare: well held in 2004: tried tongue tied: usually wears headgear. *D. Haydn Jones* —

CONSONANT (IRE) 7 ch.g. Barathea (IRE) 127 – Dinalina (FR) (Top Ville 129) [2004 f8.5g* f8.5g* f8.5s* p10g* 10.3d 8.1f⁶ 8.9m 8d² 8.1g³ 10.4g 7.9s 9m Sep 11] sturdy, lengthy gelding: useful performer: ran twice at 2 yrs for D. Loder, winning minor event at Chantilly: off over 4 years, won seller, amateur handicap and handicap at Wolverhampton and handicap at Lingfield in January/February: effective at 1m/easy 1¼m: acts on all-weather, firm and good to soft going, possibly not on soft: has edged right. *D. G. Bridgwater* **103**

CONSTABLE BURTON 3 b.g. Foxhound (USA) 103 – Actress 73 (Known Fact (USA) 135) [2004 –: 7.1g f7g* 7.2d p7.1d p7.1d⁴ f7s⁴ f8g* f7g⁶ Dec 14] big, workmanlike gelding: fair performer: won maiden at Southwell in April and seller on same course in November: effective at 7f/1m: acts on fibresand: blinkered/visored last 3 starts: inconsistent. *Mrs A. Duffield* **? a74**

CONSTANTINE 4 gr.g. Linamix (FR) 127 – Speremm (IRE) (Sadler's Wells (USA) 132) [2004 80: 12f Sep 24] leggy gelding: well held only 4-y-o start. *G. L. Moore* —

CONSTRUCTOR 3 b.g. So Factual (USA) 120 – Love And Kisses 70 (Salse (USA) 128) [2004 8.3f p12g p12g 8.2m Sep 28] well held in maidens. *C. A. Cyzer* —

totesport Cesarewitch (Handicap), Newmarket—Contact Dancer (No.15) holds off Mr Ed (cheekpieces) in a thrilling finish; High Point (stripes), Quedex (rail), Escayola and Mirjan are next

CONSULAR 2 br.c. (Apr 28) Singspiel (IRE) 133 – Language of Love 63 (Rock City 120) [2004 8.2v³ Nov 4] lengthy, useful-looking colt: second foal: half-brother to 3-y-o Tregarron: dam, maiden who stayed 7f, sister to smart 6f/7f performer Tomba and half-sister to Prix du Jockey Club winner Holding Court: 6/1, 1¾ lengths third of 15 to Tawqeet in maiden at Nottingham, switched several times before staying on: likely to be suited by 1¼m/1½m: sure to improve. *M. A. Jarvis* **75 p**

CONTACT DANCER (IRE) 5 b.g. Sadler's Wells (USA) 132 – Rain Queen (Rainbow Quest (USA) 134) [2004 96?: 16.2g⁶ 15.9s⁴ 18s* 16.5s³ Nov 6] leggy gelding: fairly useful handicapper: won 34-runner totesport Cesarewitch at Newmarket in October by ½ length from Mr Ed: respectable third to Sendintank at Doncaster: stays 2¼m: successful on good to firm going, best efforts on softer than good (acts on heavy). *M. Johnston* **91**

CONTENTED (IRE) 2 b.c. (Mar 6) Orpen (USA) 116 – Joyfullness (USA) (Dixieland Band (USA)) [2004 p7g⁵ p8g³ Oct 25] first foal: dam unraced daughter of US Grade 1 2-y-o 8.5f winner Arewehavingfunyet: modest form in maidens at Lingfield, finishing well on second occasion: will probably stay 1¼m: sold 6,500 gns. *E. A. L. Dunlop* **60**

CONTINENT 7 ch.g. Lake Coniston (IRE) 131 – Krisia (Kris 135) [2004 115§: 6g³ 6g 5.1g* 5d 5m⁵ 6s³ 5m Oct 3] angular gelding: smart performer: won minor event at Nottingham in August by 2 lengths from Bishops Court: good 4½ lengths third of 24 to stable-companion Funfair Wane in Ayr Gold Cup (Handicap) sixth outing: effective at 5f/6f: acts on firm and soft ground: often tongue tied prior to 2004: visored once at 6 yrs: has run well when sweating: often slowly away: held up: unreliable. *D. Nicholls* **113 §**

CONTINENTAL FLYER (IRE) 2 b.f. (Apr 2) Piccolo 121 – Sunshine Coast 86 (Posse (USA) 130) [2004 7d 7m Sep 29] 13,000Y: sparely-made filly: half-sister to several winners, including 6-y-o Inchdura and 3-y-o Vademecum: dam 7f winner: refused to race on debut: blinkered, well held in maiden. *M. Dods* **– §**

CONVENT GIRL (IRE) 4 b.f. Bishop of Cashel 122 – Right To The Top (Nashwan (USA) 135) [2004 107: 8g 7.9s 8.1f 8.5m 8f 8m 7g⁶ 8m 8s p8g Nov 20] big filly: poor walker: fairly useful performer: mostly well held in 2004: best at 1m/9f: acts on firm going: sometimes slowly away: waited with: inconsistent. *Mrs P. N. Dutfield* **93 d**

CONVICTION 3 b.g. Machiavellian (USA) 123 – Beldarian (IRE) 101 (Last Tycoon 131) [2004 10m⁵ 10.3m Jun 26] rather lengthy gelding: well held in maidens: sold 3,000 gns. *J. R. Fanshawe* **–**

CONVINCE (USA) 3 ch.g. Mt Livermore (USA) – Conical 63 (Zafonic (USA) 130) [2004 95: 6d 7s 8.1m 7d⁵ 7m⁶ 7m⁵ 10g p10g Sep 22] tall, close-coupled gelding: fair handicapper: acts on good to firm ground: tried in cheekpieces: free-going sort: carries head awkwardly. *M. A. Buckley* **78**

COODEN BEACH (IRE) 4 b.f. Peintre Celebre (USA) 137 – Joyful (IRE) 71 (Green Desert (USA) 127) [2004 56: f9.4g p10g⁴ p8g⁴ 8.2d⁴ 8f Jun 2] leggy filly: modest performer: stays 1¼m: acts on polytrack, firm and good to soft going: tried tongue tied, not in 2004. *M. L. W. Bell* **50**

COOL BART 4 ch.g. Cool Jazz 116 – Margaretrose Anna 58 (Handsome Sailor 125) [2004 –: f6g Jan 12] of no account. *B. P. J. Baugh* **–**

237

COOL BATHWICK (IRE) 5 b.g. Entrepreneur 123 – Tarafa 93 (Akarad (FR) 130) **48** [2004 –: f12g* f12g² f12g⁶ 10.9d 11.7s 10d 11.6m 14.1m 17.2g⁴ 14.1g⁵ Jul 24] useful- **a67** looking gelding: fair performer on all-weather, poor on turf: won maiden at Wolverhampton in January: stays 17f: acts on fibresand, firm and good to soft going: tried tongue tied: often wears headgear: none too consistent. *B. R. Millman*

COOL CLEAR WATER (USA) 3 b.f. Seeking The Gold (USA) – Miznah (IRE) **56** 102 (Sadler's Wells (USA) 132) [2004 p7g 10d 9g 10.2g⁶ Jun 3] strong filly: half-sister to several winners, notably high-class middle-distance performer Zindabad (by Shirley Heights) and useful 1¼m/11.6f winner Navado (by Rainbow Quest): dam, Irish 2-y-o 6f winner, closely related to dam of US champion turf mare Flawlessly: modest maiden: stays 1¼m. *B. J. Meehan*

COOL CRISTAL 2 ch.f. (Feb 25) Loup Sauvage (USA) 125 – Lyrical Bid (USA) 77 **–** (Lyphard (USA) 132) [2004 7g 5g 6g Sep 6] 2,700F: useful-looking filly: fourth foal: half-sister to winner in Spain by Primo Dominie: dam 2-y-o 7.5f winner on only start: slowly away when behind in maidens: trained on debut by R. Cowell. *M. W. Easterby*

COOLEYCALL STAR (IRE) 3 b.g. Foxhound (USA) 103 – Ozwood (IRE) (Royal **–** Academy (USA)) [2004 59?: 10g 10d 7m 9m 8v f8g p6g Dec 22] signs of only a little ability: left H. Rogers in Ireland after fifth start: tried in blinkers/tongue tie. *J. S. Moore*

COOLFORE JADE (IRE) 4 ch.f. Mukaddamah (USA) 125 – Cashel Princess (IRE) **58** 91 (Fayruz 116) [2004 69: p10g f12g* f9.4g⁴ f11g* f12g⁴ f12s³ f12s⁵ p12g p12g⁵ f12s f12g 10m 12m⁶ f12g³ p12d 10.2s 10s 12f⁶ 12.1m⁴ 10d p12.2g⁶ f11g³ f11d⁵ Dec 21] leggy filly: modest performer: won 2 sellers at Southwell in January: trained by N. Berry until before final start: stays 13f: acts on all-weather and firm ground: sometimes races freely. *R. A. Harris*

COOLING CASTLE (FR) 8 ch.g. Sanglamore (USA) 126 – Syphaly (USA) (Lyph- **–** ard (USA) 132) [2004 f12s Feb 17] of little account on Flat nowadays. *Ronald Thompson*

COOL PANIC (IRE) 2 b.c. (Mar 27) Brave Act 119 – Geht Schnell (Fairy King **81** (USA)) [2004 5f 6f² 6m⁵ 7g*⁷ 7s⁶ Oct 23] €26,000Y, 42,000 2-y-o: rather leggy, quite good-topped colt: half-brother to several winners, notably 3-y-o Ruby Rocket: dam Irish sprint maiden out of half-sister to high-class sprinter Anita's Prince: fairly useful performer: won minor event at Redcar in August: well held in nursery final start: stays 7f: best effort on good going: carried head high third start. *M. L. W. Bell*

COOL SANDS (IRE) 2 b.c. (Apr 17) Trans Island 119 – Shalerina (USA) (Shalford **55** (IRE) 124§) [2004 7g 6g p5.1g⁶ Oct 7] form only when sixth in minor event at Wolverhampton: should stay 6f. *D. Shaw*

COOL TEMPER 8 b.g. Magic Ring (IRE) 115 – Ovideo 58 (Domynsky 110) [2004 **69** 79, a85: 8g⁵ 8.5s³ 8.1g 10m 8m 8.1s² 8.1s Aug 30] sturdy gelding: fair handicapper: stays easy 1¼m: acts on fibresand and any turf going: tried in blinkers/cheekpieces: sometimes tongue tied: often held up. *P. F. I. Cole*

COOMBE CENTENARY 2 b.f. (Apr 6) Robellino (USA) 127 – Shining Dancer 71 **60** (Rainbow Quest (USA) 134) [2004 6m 6f 7g p7g p8m⁵ Dec 21] 5,800Y: second living foal: dam 1¼m to 2m winner: modest maiden: should stay 1½m: easily best effort on polytrack. *S. Dow*

COPPERFIELDS LASS 5 b.m. Millkom 124 – Salvezza (IRE) 97 (Superpower **–** 113) [2004 –: f7g f7s Feb 17] poor maiden: tried in headgear. *W. G. M. Turner*

COPPICE (IRE) 3 ch.g. Rainbow Quest (USA) 134 – Woodwin (IRE) 97 (Woodman **77** (USA) 126) [2004 8m⁶ 9f⁴ 9.7g⁵ 8.2d³ Sep 17] strong gelding: second foal: half-brother to fairly useful 2002 2-y-o 6f winner Sheriff Shift (by Night Shift), later successful in Hong Kong: dam, Irish 1m winner, out of half-sister to dam of Irish Oaks winner Wemyss Bight: fair maiden: will stay at least 1¼m: acts on firm and good to soft ground: hung left second outing, slowly away on third: gelded after final start. *L. M. Cumani*

COPPINGTON FLYER (IRE) 4 ch.f. Eagle Eyed (USA) 111 – Miss Flite (IRE) **54 d** (Law Society (USA) 130) [2004 75, a68: p7g⁴ p8g p8g⁴ p8g p8g⁴ 8.3m 7m 7m⁴ p7m Dec 15] smallish, strong filly: modest handicapper: below form after third start: barely stays 1m: acts on firm going and all-weather: tried blinkered/tongue tied: inconsistent. *B. W. Duke*

COPPLESTONE (IRE) 8 b.g. Second Set (IRE) 127 – Queen of The Brush (Averof **– §** 123) [2004 49§: f12g 13.1g⁶ 14.1g Jun 19] tall gelding: poor handicapper: well held in 2004: tried visored/tongue tied/in cheekpieces: ungenuine. *W. Storey*

COQUETERIA (USA) 3 b.f. Cozzene (USA) – Miss Waikiki (USA) (Miswaki (USA) **101**
124) [2004 83p: 8d² 8d³ 8g² p8g Oct 31] tall, leggy filly: useful performer: 9 lengths
second to Hathrah in listed race at Kempton on reappearance: best effort when 2½ lengths
third to Shapira in Henkel-Rennen at Dusseldorf: off 5 months, long way below form last
2 starts: stays 1m: acts on good to soft ground: free-going sort. *G. Wragg*

CORANGLAIS 4 ch.g. Piccolo 121 – Antonia's Folly 64 (Music Boy 124) [2004 82: **68 §**
7d 7g 6g 6m 6m 5.3f⁴ 5.1g* 5.1m 6m 6g⁵ 5.7m 5.7f 5.1m⁵ 5m 5d² 5.7s² p5.1g p6g²
p6m⁶ Dec 22] compact gelding: fair performer: won minor event at Bath in July: effective
at 5f to easy 7f: acts on polytrack, soft and good to firm ground: usually wears blinkers/
cheekpieces: unreliable. *J. M. Bradley*

CORBEL (USA) 4 b.f. Diesis 133 – Corsini 88 (Machiavellian (USA) 123) [2004 65: **–**
8g 7s p8.6g Nov 13] angular filly: maiden: well held in 2004. *Miss Gay Kelleway*

CORCORAN (USA) 2 b.f. (Mar 28) Lear Fan (USA) 130 – Corsini 88 (Machiavellian **81 p**
(USA) 123) [2004 7g* Oct 11] lengthy filly: has scope: third foal: sister to 3-y-o Corsican
Native: dam, 2-y-o 7f winner, out of close relative to dam of Zafonic: 16/1, won 19-
runner maiden at Leicester by neck from Kahira, slowly away but travelling strongly to
lead over 1f out: will stay at least 1m: should improve. *Mrs A. J. Perrett*

CORDAGE (IRE) 2 ch.c. (Apr 10) Dr Fong (USA) 128 – Flagship 84 (Rainbow **75**
Quest (USA) 134) [2004 6g⁵ 6d⁴ 6g⁴ 8d⁴ 10.1d² Nov 5] third foal: dam, 1¼m winner,
sister to smart 1992 2-y-o 7f winner Yawl out of Oaks winner Bireme: fair maiden: in
cheekpieces, second at Yarmouth, making running: stays 1¼m: seemed to get unbalanced
at Epsom third start. *G. A. Butler*

CORDIAL (IRE) 4 gr.g. Charnwood Forest (IRE) 125 – Moon Festival 74 (Be My **80**
Guest (USA) 126) [2004 80: p10g² f12s⁴ Nov 17] big, lengthy gelding: fairly useful
handicapper: off 16 months, short-headed by Barry Island in apprentice race at Lingfield,
better effort in 2004: should stay 1½m: acts on polytrack and good to firm ground. *Sir
Mark Prescott*

CORDIER 2 b.c. (Mar 8) Desert Style (IRE) 121 – Slipper 94 (Suave Dancer (USA) **– p**
136) [2004 7.6m Jul 31] 50,000Y: third foal: half-brother to 1m winner Baboosh (by
Marju) and French 1m (at 2 yrs) and 10.5f winner Cartier Opera (by Zilzal): dam 1½m
winner: 7/1, behind in maiden at Lingfield: likely to do better. *D. R. Loder*

CORKER 2 ch.g. (Feb 15) Grand Lodge (USA) 125 – Immortelle (Arazi (USA) 135) **63**
[2004 5.7f⁶ 6g⁵ p7.1g Nov 27] 88,000Y: second foal: dam unraced half-sister to Poule
d'Essai des Pouliches winner Danseuse du Soir: modest form in maidens: should stay 1m.
G. A. Butler

CORKY (IRE) 3 br.g. Intikhab (USA) 135 – Khamseh 85 (Thatching 131) [2004 7m⁴ **82**
6m³ 7g* 7.1m 7g³ 7m p8g Oct 25] 30,000Y: sturdy gelding: third foal: half-brother to
4-y-o Bonus: dam, 7f winner, half-sister to high-class performer up to 1½m Predappio:
fairly useful performer: won maiden at Folkestone in July: creditable third in handicap at
Lingfield after: should stay 1m. *R. Hannon*

CORMORANT WHARF (IRE) 4 b.g. Alzao (USA) 117 – Mercy Bien (IRE) 63 **82**
(Be My Guest (USA) 126) [2004 –: p6g p8g⁶ p7g⁵ p7g p8g p6g⁵ p6g 6m 6d⁶ p6g⁴ 8.1m³
9m² 9s² p10g⁴ p9.5g² p10g Dec 18] well-made gelding: fairly useful handicapper: stays
easy 1¼m: acts on polytrack, soft and good to firm ground: tried tongue tied and in
headgear: keen sort, usually held up. *T. E. Powell*

CORNELIUS 7 b.g. Barathea (IRE) 127 – Rainbow Mountain 71 (Rainbow Quest **89**
(USA) 134) [2004 108: f8.5s 8v 8d⁵ Jun 23] tall, good-topped gelding: has an unimpressive, round action: just fairly useful in 2004, form only on final outing: raced mainly at
1m: acts on heavy and good to firm going: usually races prominently: tends to carry head
high. *P. F. I. Cole*

CORNICHE DANCER 2 b.f. (Jan 1) Marju (IRE) 127 – Sellette (IRE) 88 (Selkirk **69**
(USA) 129) [2004 7m 6g 8.3m p6g² 6g* 6.5g 6m⁵ p6g² 7.1d 6v p7.1g⁵ p6g⁴ p5.1g³ p6g
Nov 20] 22,000Y: leggy filly: third foal: dam, 1m winner, half-sister to useful Irish performer up to 1m Dashing Colours: fair performer: won maiden at Catterick in September:
stays 6f, not quite 7f: acts on polytrack, best turf effort on good going: sometimes slowly
away: often races freely. *M. R. Channon*

CORNISH GOLD 3 b.f. Slip Anchor 136 – Sans Diablo (IRE) (Mac's Imp (USA) **68**
116) [2004 65: 10m 10.2g² 9s Oct 22] workmanlike filly: fair maiden handicapper: stays
1¼m: acts on good to soft going. *N. J. Henderson*

CORNUS 2 ch.c. (Apr 8) Inchinor 119 – Demerger (USA) (Distant View (USA) 126) **104** [2004 5d* 5d* 5s² 5s² 6s Oct 23] 16,000Y: smallish, attractive colt: first foal: dam unraced out of half-sister to smart performer up to around 1m in Britain/USA Tychonic: useful performer: won maiden at Windsor and minor event at Newmarket in April: second in minor event at Ascot and Cornwallis Stakes (best effort when beaten ¾ length by Castelletto) 6 months apart: ran no sort of race final start: likely to prove best at 5f/easy 6f. *R. Hannon*

CORNWALLIS 3 b.g. Forzando 122 – Up And Going (FR) (Never So Bold 135) **71** [2004 57: p6g 5.7s* 6g² 8.3f f6m Jul 26] fair performer: won claimer at Bath (claimed from R. Guest £5,000) in May: raced mainly at 6f: acts on soft ground. *J. S. King*

CORONADO FOREST (USA) 5 b.g. Spinning World (USA) 130 – Desert Jewel **66 d** (USA) (Caerleon (USA) 132) [2004 71: p10g² p10g⁴ p10g* p10g p10g 9.7s 10f⁶ p10g p10m p10g Dec 30] fair performer: well held after winning maiden at Lingfield in January: stays 1¼m: acts on all-weather and firm ground, below form on soft: tried blinkered: races prominently. *M. R. Hoad*

CORPS DE BALLET (IRE) 3 b.f. Fasliyev (USA) 120 – Dwell (USA) 96 (Habitat **92** 134) [2004 85: 5.1f 6.1g* 6m 6m 6m 5m⁵ 5d² p6g Oct 31] close-coupled filly: fairly useful handicapper: won at Nottingham in June: effective at 5f/6f: acts on good to firm and good to soft going: usually races prominently: none too consistent. *J. L. Dunlop*

CORRAN ARD (IRE) 3 b.g. Imperial Ballet (IRE) 110 – Beeper The Great (USA) **86** (Whadjathink (USA)) [2004 –: 10.5g⁴ 9g* 10m⁶ 10m³ Jun 13] €18,000Y: third foal: brother to fairly useful 11f winner Phamedic and half-brother to a winner in Italy by Red Ransom: dam unraced half-sister to Prix Marcel Boussac winner Tropicaro: fairly useful performer: fourth to Destination Dubai in maiden at Haydock (slowly away, carried head high) on reappearance: won handicap at Ballinrobe in May: stays 1¼m: acts on good to firm ground. *Mrs J. Harrington, Ireland*

CORRIB ECLIPSE 5 b.g. Double Eclipse (IRE) 122 – Last Night's Fun (IRE) (Law **106** Society (USA) 130) [2004 22.2f* 16.4d⁶ 15.9d⁶ 18m⁶ 18f⁶ 16.2m⁴ Sep 26] good-topped gelding: bumper winner: useful performer: won Queen Alexandra Stakes at Royal Ascot (Flat debut, beat Dancing Bay by 1½ lengths) in June and minor event at Pontefract (by 1¾ lengths from Pushkin) in September: stays 2¾m: acts on firm and good to soft going. *Jamie Poulton*

Queen Alexandra Stakes, Royal Ascot—
Corrib Eclipse makes a winning debut on the Flat to deny Dancing Bay (black cap);
Romany Prince (right) and Holy Orders (chevrons on sleeves) also make the frame

CORRIDOR CREEPER (FR)   7 ch.g. Polish Precedent (USA) 131 – Sonia Rose   **111**
(USA) (Superbity (USA)) [2004 102: 5.1d⁵ 5s⁴ 5g⁴ 5m² 5m⁶ 6f 5d² 5d³ 5m⁶ 6m 5g³
5g⁵ 5.6m 5s³ 5m² 5d* 5d² 5s⁵ Oct 23] smallish gelding: smart handicapper: won at
Newmarket in October by ½ length from If Paradise: very good 1¾ lengths second to
Malapropism at Musselburgh next time: best at 5f: acts on firm and soft ground: tried
blinkered/tongue tied, usually wears cheekpieces: races handily: splendidly tough and
consistent. *J. M. Bradley*

CORRINE (IRE)   5 gr.m. Spectrum (IRE) 126 – La Luna (USA) (Lyphard (USA)   **99**
132) [2004 12g* 12g* 11s 9.8d² 12s* 11s² 14.1s² Oct 27] IR 32,000Y: half-sister to
several winners, including smart performer up to 1½m Etoile (by Kris), 7f winner at 2
yrs: dam, French 9f winner, sister to top-class French miler Bellypha: useful performer:
successful at Ovrevoll in handicaps in May/June and listed race (by 1½ lengths from
Simsala) in August: very good 1½ lengths second of 12 to Modesta in listed race at
Yarmouth final start: stays 1¾m: acts on soft ground. *S. E. Lilja, Norway*

CORRIOLANUS (GER)   4 b.c. Zamindar (USA) 116 – Caesarea (GER) (Generous   **110**
(IRE) 139) [2004 108: p10g³ p10g 10g 10.1s 12g⁶ 10m 10m⁶ 10m* 9s 8f 9.9g
p12g² p10g* Nov 30] strong, close-coupled ex-German colt: second foal: half-brother to
German 1¼m to 1½m winner Carion (by Monsun): dam, German 11f/1½m winner, sister
to smart German 1½m performer Catella: smart performer: won maiden at Frankfurt in
2003 for A. Schutz: won minor event at Newmarket in August and handicap at Lingfield
(beat Caledonian by ½ length) in November: stays easy 1½m: acts on polytrack, firm and
good to soft going: effective blinkered or not: usually waited with. *P. Mitchell*

CORSICAN NATIVE (USA)   3 b.c. Lear Fan (USA) 130 – Corsini 88 (Machiavel-   **100**
lian (USA) 123) [2004 79p: 9.9m* 10g² 11.8g Oct 11] big, good-topped colt: useful
performer: won maiden at Goodwood in September: best effort when ½-length second to
Flamboyant Lad in handicap at Newmarket, finishing well: should stay 1½m: acts on soft
and good to firm ground: sold 70,000 gns. *Mrs A. J. Perrett*

CORTON DENHAM   3 ch.g. Wolfhound (USA) 126 – Wigit (Safawan 118) [2004 –:   **–**
p10g Jan 24] twice raced and no form. *G. P. Enright*

CORTON (IRE)   5 b. or gr.g. Definite Article 121 – Limpopo 49 (Green Desert (USA)   **88**
127) [2004 90: 16m³ 16.2m⁶ 12d 16d Nov 3] strong gelding: fairly useful handicapper:
tailed off last 2 starts, including in cheekpieces: effective at 1½m to 2m: acts on good to
firm going: often races prominently. *P. F. I. Cole*

COSI FAN TUTTE   6 b.g. Inchinor 119 – Bumpkin 108 (Free State 125) [2004 11.6m²   **72**
10m³ 11.9m 10f 10.2m² p12d² p12.2g Dec 3] strong, lengthy gelding: fair performer:
pulled up reportedly lame final outing: stays 1½m: acts on polytrack, soft and good to
firm going: usually blinkered/visored: tongue tied in 2004. *M. C. Pipe*

COSMIC CASE   9 b.m. Casteddu 119 – La Fontainova (IRE) (Lafontaine (USA) 117)   **54**
[2004 58: 13.1f* 13g 13m³ 13g⁵ 12m² 13g³ 13f 15g³ 13f* 12.1f² 14g⁵ 14g Sep 11]
angular mare: modest handicapper: won at Ayr (dead-heated) in May and Musselburgh
(apprentice race) in July: effective at 1½m/1¾m: acts on any going: tried visored earlier
in career: usually held up. *J. S. Goldie*

COSMIC DESTINY (IRE)   2 b.f. (Apr 16) Soviet Star (USA) 128 – Cruelle (USA)   **56 p**
(Irish River (FR) 131) [2004 6m Sep 5] 11,000Y: smallish filly: second foal: dam, placed
up to 7.5f in France, out of sister to smart sprinter King's Signet: 4/1, seventh of 20 to
Ridder in maiden at York, travelling strongly in front until weakening final 1f: should
progress. *E. F. Vaughan*

COSMIC RANGER   6 b.g. Magic Ring (IRE) 115 – Lismore 61 (Relkino 131) [2004   **–**
f12m Jul 12] leggy, useful-looking gelding: maiden: well held only 6-y-o start: tried
blinkered/visored/tongue tied. *H. Alexander*

COSTA DEL SOL (IRE)   3 ch.g. General Monash (USA) 107 – L'Harmonie (USA)   **35 §**
(Bering 136) [2004 55: p6g p7g p7g p8g⁴ 7m 9g 6m⁶ 7f 6g p10g Sep 18] good-topped
gelding: poor maiden: stays easy 1m: acts on all-weather and firm going: tried in headgear: ungenuine. *J. J. Bridger*

COST ANALYSIS (IRE)   2 ch.g. (Feb 20) Grand Lodge (USA) 125 – Flower Girl   **63**
108 (Pharly (FR) 130) [2004 7d 7m⁶ 8g⁵ 7s Oct 22] strong, lengthy gelding: half-brother
to several winners, including smart performer up to 14.6f Eco Friendly (by Sabrehill),
1m winner at 2 yrs: dam 6f winner, including at 2 yrs: modest maiden: best effort when
fifth at Bath: will stay 1¼m: usually races up with pace: sold 31,000 gns, then gelded.
M. A. Jarvis

COTE QUEST (USA) 4 b.f. Green Desert (USA) 127 – West Brooklyn (USA) (Gone **96**
West (USA)) [2004 8d⁴ 7d 7.9s 8g⁴ 8f⁴ 10.1s³ 10.2g⁶ 8m 8m Sep 25] big, leggy, good-
topped ex-French filly: third foal: half-sister to French 2001 2-y-o 7f winner Brooklyn's
Sky (by Septieme Ciel): dam, French 1m (at 2 yrs) and 1¼m winner, half-sister to 3-y-o
Prospect Park: useful performer: won minor event at Longchamp in 2003 for Mme
C. Head-Maarek: in frame in 4 listed races in 2004: stays 1¼m: acts on heavy and good to
firm ground. *S. C. Williams*

COTE SOLEIL 7 ch.g. Inchinor 119 – Sunshine Coast 86 (Posse (USA) 130) [2004 **–**
59: f12g 10d 8s Aug 27] smallish gelding: well held in 2004: tried blinkered/visored
earlier in career. *C. R. Egerton*

COTOSOL 3 b.g. Forzando 122 – Emerald Dream (IRE) 47 (Vision (USA)) [2004 77: **80**
7g 7s* 7.1s⁵ 7.9d f7g³ a6f⁶ a7.5g³ a9f³ a9f* Dec 30] strong, lengthy gelding: fairly useful
handicapper: won at Thirsk in April and, having left B. McMahon after fifth start, Nad Al
Sheba in December: stays 9f: acts on fibresand/dirt, soft and good to firm going: often
races prominently. *D. Watson, UAE*

COTTAM GRANGE 4 b.c. River Falls 113 – Karminski 70 (Pitskelly 122) [2004 **–**
47: f12g Jan 5] maiden: well held only 4-y-o start. *M. W. Easterby*

COTTAM KARMINSKI 3 b.f. River Falls 113 – Karminski 70 (Pitskelly 122) [2004 **–**
7.5m 7.5m 6m 5d⁶ 8.5g 8m Jul 23] half-sister to a winner in Norway by Blazing Saddles:
dam middle-distance stayer: little form. *J. S. Wainwright*

COTTINGHAM (IRE) 3 b.g. Perugino (USA) 84 – Stately Princess 70 (Robellino **65**
(USA) 127) [2004 70: f8g* 7d⁴ 8.5d⁶ 8g⁶ 7m 8s² 7.9g 10f⁶ 7g⁶ 10d⁶ 10f² 12g⁴ 8d f8g
Nov 9] workmanlike gelding: fair performer: won maiden at Southwell in January: barely
stays 1¼m: acts on fibresand, firm and soft going. *M. C. Chapman*

COTTON EASTER 3 b.f. Robellino (USA) 127 – Pluck 80 (Never So Bold 135) **62**
[2004 7g 8.1g 8.1m⁶ 8.3f 7.1m 10g 10.2s³ 11.9s⁶ p12.2g Nov 19] good-topped
filly: fifth living foal: half-sister to 5-y-o Balakiref (by Royal Applause) and Swedish
winner up to 1¼m Cup Chief (by Be My Chief): dam, 5.7f (at 2 yrs) and 6f winner, out of
half-sister to very smart sprinter Piccolo: modest handicapper: won at Chepstow
in September: stays 1¼m, not 1½m: acts on soft ground: sometimes slowly away.
Mrs A. J. Bowlby

COUGAR CAT (USA) 2 b.c. (Mar 22) Storm Cat (USA) – Excellent Meeting (USA) **109**
119 (General Meeting (USA)) [2004 5m* 5m⁴ 6.3f² Jul 18] quite attractive colt: first
foal: dam US Grade I 1m/8.5f winner (including at 2 yrs) and second in Breeders' Cup
Juvenile Fillies: landed odds in maiden at Tipperary in May: in frame in Norfolk Stakes
at Royal Ascot and Anglesey Stakes (best effort when beaten length by Oratorio, despite
having to wait for gap) at the Curragh: will stay 7f, probably 1m. *A. P. O'Brien, Ireland*

COULD SHE BE MAGIC (IRE) 3 b.f. Titus Livius (FR) 115 – Ponteilla (FR) **?**
(Arctic Tern (USA) 126) [2004 42, a58: f8g² f7g* f7g f7g² 7s 6m⁵ May 25] close- **a65**
coupled, workmanlike filly: modest performer on all-weather, poor on turf: won handicap
at Wolverhampton in February: races freely, and better form at 7f than 1m: acts on fibresand: tried blinkered: sold 4,000 gns. *T. D. Easterby*

COUNCELLOR (FR) 2 b.c. (Feb 21) Gilded Time (USA) – Sudden Storm Bird **84**
(USA) (Storm Bird (CAN) 134) [2004 6m³ 7m⁴ 6g⁴ 7m² Sep 21] €140,000Y: big, strong
colt: half-brother to 3 winners, including useful French 7f (at 2 yrs)/1m winner (stayed
1½m) Suborneuse (by Diesis): dam unraced sister to smart 1¼m/1½m performer
Knoosh: fairly useful maiden: 4 lengths second to Grosvenor Square at Newmarket:
should stay 1m: acts on good to firm going. *R. Hannon*

COUNCIL MEMBER (USA) 2 b.c. (Apr 3) Seattle Slew (USA) – Zoe Montana **109**
(USA) (Seeking The Gold (USA)) [2004 5g* 6f² 6m² 6s 6m² Sep 4] $800,000F: lengthy,
quite attractive colt: second foal: dam unraced half-sister to top-class miler Half A Year:
useful performer: won maiden at Newcastle in June: good second in Coventry Stakes at
Royal Ascot (beaten ½ length by Iceman), July Stakes at Newmarket (beaten short head
by Captain Hurricane) and Sirenia Stakes at Kempton (beaten 1½ lengths by Satchem):
will probably stay 7f: acts on firm ground, tailed off on soft: races prominently. *Saeed bin
Suroor*

COUNSEL'S OPINION (IRE) 7 ch.g. Rudimentary (USA) 118 – Fairy Fortune 78 **111**
(Rainbow Quest (USA) 134) [2004 111: 10d³ 10.1m⁴ 12f 11.9g 10m⁴ 12g² 10d Sep 18]
big gelding: smart performer: several creditable efforts in 2004, including when placed in
handicaps at Kempton (length third to Silence Is Golden in Rosebery Stakes) and Ascot
(neck second to Desert Quest): effective at 1¼m/1½m: acts on fibresand, soft and good

to firm going, well below form on firm: has worn crossed noseband: sometimes early to post/slowly away: takes strong hold, and usually held up: game and reliable. *C. F. Wall*

COUNT BORIS 3 b.g. Groom Dancer (USA) 128 – Bu Hagab (IRE) (Royal Academy **66** (USA) 130) [2004 8m 8.3m 10g 8.1m 9s³ 10.1d² Nov 5] 3,500F, 20,000Y: fourth foal: half-brother to winners up to 1¼m abroad by In The Wings and Robellino: dam unraced: fair maiden: will stay 1½m: acts on soft going: sometimes slowly away. *G. B. Balding*

COUNT COUGAR (USA) 4 b.g. Sir Cat (USA) 118 – Gold Script (USA) (Seeking **64** The Gold (USA)) [2004 73: f5s³ p5g 5m⁶ 5m 5m 5m f5m p5.1g f6g⁵ Dec 7] sturdy gelding: poor walker and mover: modest performer: best at 5f: acts on all-weather, firm and soft ground: tried blinkered/in cheekpieces. *S. P. Griffiths*

COUNTDOWN 2 ch.c. (Mar 2) Pivotal 124 – Quiz Time 90 (Efisio 120) [2004 5f³ **88** p5d² 5g* 5d* 5g² 5.5m p5.1g⁵ Oct 7] 170,000Y: close-coupled colt: fourth foal: closely related to useful 2002 2-y-o 5f/6f winner Cool Question (by Polar Falcon) and half-brother to winner in Spain by Pursuit of Love: dam 2-y-o 5f winner: fairly useful performer: won maiden at Haydock and nursery at Sandown in August: ran poorly final start: should prove best at 5f/6f: acts on polytrack, firm and good to soft going: blinkered (ran respectably in France) sixth start: sold 40,000 gns. *Sir Mark Prescott*

COUNT DRACULA 3 b.g. Dracula (AUS) 121 – Chipaya 116 (Northern Prospect **67** (USA)) [2004 74: p8g* 9g f8g⁶ 8m Aug 10] close-coupled gelding: fair performer: well held after winning maiden at Lingfield in March: left A. Balding after third outing: stays 1m: acts on polytrack: tried visored. *Jean-Rene Auvray*

COUNTESS ELTON (IRE) 4 ch.f. Mukaddamah (USA) 125 – Be Prepared (IRE) **– §** (Be My Guest (USA) 126) [2004 –§: f8g Jan 4] tall, leggy filly: no form since 2 yrs: temperamental. *R. E. Barr*

COUNTESS FOLEY 2 b.f. (Jun 8) Wizard King 122 – Princess Foley (IRE) 64 **40** (Forest Wind (USA) 111) [2004 p9.5g p7.1g Dec 10] second foal: half-sister to 3-y-o Foley Prince: dam sprint maiden: poor form in maidens. *D. Burchell*

Godolphin's "Council Member"

COUNT KRISTO   2 br.c. (Feb 22) Dr Fong (USA) 128 – Aryadne (Rainbow Quest   **79**
(USA) 134) [2004 7g² 7g Sep 18] 40,000F, €140,000Y: tall, leggy colt: first foal: dam
unraced sister to Derby winner Quest For Fame: much better effort in maidens at Newbury when second to Etlaala, slowly away/racing freely: should stay 1m. *C. G. Cox*

COUNT ON US   4 ch.g. Danehill Dancer (IRE) 117 – Capricious Lady (IRE) (Capri-   –
corn Line 111) [2004 –: p10g Mar 9] no form. *P. Burgoyne*

COUNTRY RAMBLER (USA)   2 b.c. (Feb 10) Red Ransom (USA) – Country   **102**
Garden 100 (Selkirk (USA) 129) [2004 6m 7.1f* 7g 7.6g³ 6g* Sep 25] $125,000F: strong,
good-topped colt: first foal: dam 2-y-o 7f winner, later Grade 2 9f winner in USA: useful
performer: won maiden at Warwick (by 5 lengths) in June and 2-runner minor event at
Ripon (beat eased Loaderfun 16 lengths in good time) in September: free-going sort,
likely to prove best at 6f/7f: acts on firm going: joined D. Watson in UAE. *B. W. Hills*

COUNTRY REEL (USA)   4 b.c. Danzig (USA) – Country Belle (USA) 108 (Seattle   **113 ?**
Slew (USA)) [2004 110: 6s 6m⁴ 6f⁴ 6g 7g 6g² 6f⁵ 6d⁴ Oct 15] strong, lengthy colt: fluent
mover: smart performer: good length fourth to Fayr Jag in Golden Jubilee Stakes at
Royal Ascot third outing: respectable fourth to Royal Millennium in Bentinck Stakes at
Newmarket final one: best form at 6f (folded in 7f Hungerford Stakes at Newbury): acts
on firm and good to soft ground: effective visored or not: tongue tied: none too consistent.
Saeed bin Suroor

COUNTRYWIDE DREAM (IRE)   2 ch.g. (Mar 28) Definite Article 121 – Gros-   –
venor Miss (IRE) (Tirol 127) [2004 5m 6f 7.5g 7.1f⁵ Jun 21] last in maidens/minor event:
wore cheekpieces last 2 starts. *A. Berry*

COUNTRYWIDE FLYER (IRE)   3 b.g. Revoque (IRE) 122 – Unbidden Melody   **?**
(USA) (Chieftain) [2004 76, a82: p8g⁵ f8.5g* f8.5g² p10g³ a6f a8.5s* a8.5f⁶ a8.5f* a8.5f²   **a91**
a8.5f⁵ a8.5g⁶ Dec 9] strong gelding: fairly useful on all-weather, fair (at 2 yrs) on turf:
successful in handicap at Wolverhampton in January: left T. D. Barron after fourth start:
won claimers at Woodbine in August and October: claimed $40,000 and left R. Biamonte
after ninth outing: stays 8.5f: acts on fibresand/dirt and firm going: blinkered (raced too
freely) on reappearance. *A. R. Katryan, Canada*

COUNTRYWIDE GIRL (IRE)   5 ch.m. Catrail (USA) 123 – Polish Saga 59 (Polish   **51**
Patriot (USA) 128) [2004 –: f6g f8g³ f7g⁵ f5g³ f8g⁶ f7g⁴ f6m³ f7g³ f6g² f7g* f7g⁵ f7g³
f8m⁴ 7g 6g f6g p7.1g* f7g⁶ f7g Dec 16] leggy, quite good-topped mare: modest
performer: won banded races at Wolverhampton in May and November: effective at 7f/
1m: acts on fibresand, lightly raced and, no recent form on turf. *A. Berry*

COUNTRYWIDE LUCK   3 b.g. Inchinor 119 – Thelma (Blakeney 126) [2004 8g⁶   **90**
10.5g² 9.3g* 10g⁶ 12s Oct 23] IR 30,000F, 32,000Y: big, rather leggy gelding: half-
brother to 1¾m winner Furness (by Emarati) and useful German 7f (at 2 yrs) and 11f
winner Orfisio (by Efisio): dam unraced: fairly useful performer: won maiden at Carlisle
in September: good sixth to Flamboyant Lad in handicap at Newmarket next time: should
stay 1½m: well held on soft ground. *N. P. Littmoden*

COUNTRYWIDE STAR (IRE)   6 ch.g. Common Grounds 118 – Silver Slipper 67   –
(Indian Ridge 123) [2004 –: f9.4s Feb 17] sturdy gelding: no form since 2002: tried
visored. *C. N. Kellett*

COUNTRYWIDE SUN   2 b.g. (Mar 21) Benny The Dip (USA) 127 – Sundae Girl   **58**
(USA) 75 (Green Dancer (USA) 132) [2004 5g 6.1s 7g 7m² f7g⁴ 8g 7d Oct 15] smallish,
close-coupled gelding: modest maiden: stays 7f: acts on fibresand and good to firm
going: blinkered third start: wore cheekpieces after: sold 3,000 gns. *N. P. Littmoden*

COUNT WALEWSKI   4 b.g. Polish Precedent (USA) 131 – Classic Beauty (IRE) 65   –
(Fairy King (USA)) [2004 75: 10g p8g May 7] good-bodied gelding: well held in 2004.
S. Dow

COUNTY CLARE   2 ch.f. (Feb 8) Barathea (IRE) 127 – Input (Primo Dominie 121)   **77**
[2004 6m 6f² 7g³ 6.5g 6g⁶ Oct 2] 39,000Y: sturdy filly: second foal: dam, ran once at 2
yrs, out of half-sister to 1m/9f performer Danceabout and French sprinter Pole Position,
both smart: fair maiden: placed at Newbury and Newmarket: should stay 1m: acts on firm
going. *A. M. Balding*

COUNTYKAT (IRE)   4 b.g. Woodborough (USA) 112 – Kitty Kildare (USA) 68   **77**
(Seattle Dancer (USA) 119) [2004 84: f12g⁶ p12g 10.1s 8m² f7g⁴ f7g* 7.9g² 8.3f 8m Jul 19]
lengthy gelding: fair performer: easy winner of minor event at Southwell in June: effective at 7f to 1¼m: acted on fibresand/dirt, raced mainly on good going or firmer on turf:
often wore cheekpieces/visor: carried head awkwardly: dead. *K. R. Burke*

COUP DE CHANCE (IRE)   4 ch.f. Ashkalani (IRE) 128 – Tout A Coup (IRE) 105   **88**
(Ela-Mana-Mou 132) [2004 94: p13g 10m⁵ 18.7m³ 11.7m Aug 15] fairly useful handicapper: creditable efforts second/third starts, upped markedly in trip when 1¾ lengths last
of 3 to High Action at Chester in latter: seems to stay 2¼m, all wins around 1½m: acts on
any ground: usually blinkered: free-going sort: idles in front. *P. A. Blockley*

COUP D'ETAT   2 b.c. (Mar 27) Diktat 126 – Megdale (IRE) 74 (Waajib 121) [2004   **84**
6m⁴ 6g² 7d⁶ 7d⁴ 7s³ Oct 21] good-topped colt: half-brother to several winners, including
3-y-o Frank Sonata and useful 7f (at 2 yrs) to 10.5f (in France) winner Peaceful Paradise
(by Turtle Island): dam, maiden who stayed 1½m, half-sister to very smart miler Alhijaz:
fairly useful maiden: fourth in nursery at Goodwood, best effort: will stay at least 1m:
acts on good to soft ground. *J. L. Dunlop*

COURAGEOUS DUKE (USA)   5 b.g. Spinning World (USA) 130 – Araadh (USA)   **105**
70 (Blushing Groom (FR) 131) [2004 105: 10f³ 10m⁵ 8f 10m² 10m³ 10.3f² 10f² Sep 24]
close-coupled, quite good-topped gelding: useful performer: creditable second in handicaps at Ascot (to Mister Monet) and Doncaster (to Colisay) and in minor event at Ascot
(to Destination Dubai): stays 1¼m: acts on firm ground, below form on good to soft:
consistent. *J. Noseda*

COURAGEOUSLY   2 b.c. (Jan 27) Aljabr (USA) 125 – Eishin Eleuthera (IRE)   **–**
(Sadler's Wells (USA) 132) [2004 5g⁵ May 17] sturdy colt: third foal: half-brother to a
winner in Japan by Mayano Top Gun: dam Japanese 9f winner: green, always behind in
minor event at Windsor. *P. F. I. Cole*

COURANT D'AIR (IRE)   3 b.g. Indian Rocket 115 – Red River Rose (IRE) 51 (Red   **42**
Sunset 120) [2004 52: f8.5g f8g³ f11g⁶ f8g⁵ 7.1g* 7.9m Sep 11] poor performer: won
banded race at Warwick in April: stays 1m: acts on fibresand and good to soft ground:
won over hurdles in October (claimed to join Lucinda Featherstone £5,000) and November. *P. C. Haslam*

COURS DE LA REINE (IRE)   2 b.f. (Mar 25) Fasliyev (USA) 120 – Society Queen   **103**
(IRE) 72 (Law Society (USA) 130) [2004 6m³ 6m 7v* 8m 7s⁴ Nov 2] 30,000Y: tall,
lengthy filly: has a quick action: second foal: dam Irish 1m/1¼m winner: useful performer: won Prix du Calvados Haras du Logis at Deauville in August by short neck from
Royal Copenhagen: 2½ lengths fourth to Stella Blue in Prix Miesque at Maisons-Laffitte:
should stay 1m: easily best efforts on soft/heavy ground: usually races up with pace.
P. W. Chapple-Hyam

COURT CHANCELLOR   3 b.g. Primo Dominie 121 – Welcome Home 55 (Most   **–**
Welcome 131) [2004 –: 8m 8m 6m 7m 7d p12g Nov 27] smallish gelding: little form:
tried visored/blinkered. *P. Mitchell*

COURT EMPEROR   4 b.g. Mtoto 134 – Fairfields Cone (Celtic Cone 116) [2004   **–**
11.8d 10d 14.1s May 14] strong, workmanlike gelding: well held in maidens. *R. J. Price*

COURTINTIME   2 b.f. (Mar 8) Atraf 116 – Royal Girl 67 (Kafu 120) [2004 5m 5g   **–**
Sep 25] 7,200Y: sixth foal: half-sister to fairly useful 2001 2-y-o 5f winner Time Royal
(by Timeless Times): dam 6f/7f winner: well held in maidens. *T. D. Easterby*

COURTLEDGE   9 b.g. Unfuwain (USA) 131 – Tremellick 87 (Mummy's Pet 125)   **–**
[2004 p10g Apr 15] lightly raced and no form on Flat since 4 yrs: tried visored.
M. J. Gingell

COURT MASTERPIECE   4 b.c. Polish Precedent (USA) 131 – Easy Option (IRE)   **116**
115 (Prince Sabo 123) [2004 112: 7g³ 7.1g⁵ 7m⁴ 7g² 7m* 8s⁴ 7m³ 7g⁶ Sep 30] lengthy,

*totesport International Stakes (Handicap), Ascot—Court Masterpiece and Kieren Fallon
lead home top weight Polar Way and Uhoomagoo (No.19) ahead of the favourite Vortex*

angular colt: smart performer: fractured a hind ankle final 3-y-o start: unlucky when short-head second to Material Witness in Bunbury Cup at Newmarket: made amends in totesport International Handicap at Ascot later in July, beating Polar Way by a neck: contested pattern races after, running creditably when 2¾ lengths third to Pastoral Pursuits in Park Stakes at Doncaster: effective at 7f/1m: acts on good to firm going: usually waited with. *E. A. L. Dunlop*

COURT MUSIC (IRE)   5 b. or br.m. Revoque (IRE) 122 – Lute And Lyre (IRE) 96   **41** (The Noble Player (USA) 126) [2004 –: f7g f6g² f6g⁶ f6s Mar 1] rather leggy, angular mare: poor performer: stays 6f: acts on soft ground and fibresand: often wears headgear. *R. E. Barr*

COURT OF APPEAL   7 ch.g. Bering 136 – Hiawatha's Song (USA) (Chief's Crown   **95** (USA)) [2004 80: 13.8g* 12.3d* 12m³ 11.9m² 12m 11.9d² 10.9s⁶ Sep 18] lengthy gelding: useful handicapper: won at Catterick in March and Chester in May: good second at York twice after, beaten head by Mephisto in Queen Mother's Cup (lady riders) fourth start: stays 1¾m: acts on any turf going and fibresand: tongue tied: often races prominently: genuine and consistent. *B. Ellison*

COURT ONE   6 b.g. Shareef Dancer (USA) 135 – Fairfields Cone (Celtic Cone 116)   **50** [2004 44: f12s 11.5m 15g* 14.1m* 14m 14.1f 16.2g 16.2m Sep 6] small, leggy gelding: shows knee action: modest performer: won banded races at Warwick in April and Nottingham in May: stays 2m: acts on firm ground, little promise on all-weather: visored once in 2003: sometimes slowly away. *R. J. Price*

COURT RULER   2 b.g. (Feb 15) Kayf Tara 130 – Fairfields Cone (Celtic Cone 116)   **–** [2004 7g⁵ 8g 10v Oct 20] no form in minor event/maidens: unseated early on second start: slowly away otherwise. *R. J. Price*

COUSTOU (IRE)   4 b.g. In Command (IRE) 114 – Carranza (IRE) (Lead On Time   **65** (USA) 123) [2004 81: 7.1g⁶ 6g 6d 7.1m⁴ 7.2f³ 9.2g³ 9.2f Jul 16] lengthy, good-topped gelding: fair handicapper: effective at 7f to 9f: acts on firm going: occasionally wears cheekpieces/blinkers. *A. R. Dicken*

COVENTINA (IRE)   3 gr.f. Daylami (IRE) 138 – Lady of The Lake 104 (Caerleon   **98** (USA) 132) [2004 90: 10.3g 12.3g 11.6g² 14.1m³ 14m³ 16.1f* Aug 7] rather leggy, quite attractive filly: useful handicapper: best effort when winning at Newmarket in August by 1¼ lengths from Tungsten Strike: suffered leg injury after: will stay beyond 2m: raced only on good ground or firmer (acts on firm). *J. L. Dunlop*

COY (IRE)   3 b.f. Danehill (USA) 126 – Demure (Machiavellian (USA) 123) [2004 88p: **112** 8m⁵ 7g² 8f² 8m* Jul 23] leggy, quite good-topped filly: smart performer: good ½-length second to Celtic Heroine in listed rated stakes at Royal Ascot third start: won listed race on same course next time by neck from same rival, still in rear over 2f out, tending to hang but getting up late on: injured after: stayed 1m: raced only on good ground or firmer: soon off bridle last 2 starts: stud. *Sir Michael Stoute*

CRACKLEANDO   3 ch.g. Forzando 122 – Crackling 57 (Electric 126) [2004 59:   **65** p10g³ p10g 12s³ 14.1s* 14g 14.1m³ 17.1d² 17.1g 15s f14g Nov 22] close-coupled gelding: fair handicapper: won at Nottingham in May: stays 17f: acts on soft going and polytrack, well beaten on fibresand: often races up with pace: none too consistent. *N. P. Littmoden*

CRACOW (IRE)   7 b.g. Polish Precedent (USA) 131 – Height of Secrecy (Shirley   **50 §** Heights 130) [2004 101: 6m 7m 7m 6f⁴ 7.1s a7.5g* Aug 22] rather leggy gelding: modest performer: headstrong, but stays 1¾m: acts on firm and soft ground: wore cheekpieces last 3 starts: untrustworthy. *A. M. Hales*

CRAFTY CALLING (USA)   4 b.c. Crafty Prospector (USA) – Glorious Calling   **59** (USA) (Nijinsky (CAN) 138) [2004 101: 6m 7m 7m 6f⁴ 7.1s a7.5g* Dec 27] tall, quite attractive colt: useful performer at 3 yrs: long way below best in 2004, including when winning claimer at Deauville in December (off 4 months beforehand, having been sold 1,200 gns from P. Cole after previous outing): stays 7.5f: best efforts on turf on good/good to firm going: tried blinkered/tongue tied. *N. Minner, France*

CRAFTY FANCY (IRE)   3 ch.f. Intikhab (USA) 135 – Idle Fancy 79 (Mujtahid   **91** (USA) 118) [2004 90: 5s² 6s³ 6g 8f 7.9g p7g⁶ p8g² Nov 20] smallish, quite good-topped filly: fairly useful performer: placed in listed races at Haydock (rated stakes) and Ascot (third to Millbag) and handicap at Lingfield: stays easy 1m: acts on polytrack, soft and good to firm ground. *D. J. S. ffrench Davis*

CRAFTY POLITICIAN (USA) 7 ch.h. Supremo (USA) 116 – Sauve Qui Peut **50** (CAN) (Cerf Volant (CAN)) [2004 64d: f7g⁴ p6g* p7g² 6m⁵ 5.3g⁶ 5g May 20] modest performer: won banded race at Lingfield in April: stays 7f: acts on polytrack, soft and good to firm ground: often wears blinkers: tried tongue tied. *G. L. Moore*

CRAIC SA CEILI (IRE) 4 b.f. Danehill Dancer (IRE) 117 – Fay's Song (IRE) 84 **74** (Fayruz 116) [2004 82+: 8s 7g 8m 7m⁴ 6g 8.1g⁵ 7g p7.1g* p7.1g⁴ Dec 4] leggy filly: fair handicapper: won at Wolverhampton in November: stays 7f: acts on polytrack, good to firm and soft ground: tried in cheekpieces: headstrong, and sometimes finds little. *M. S. Saunders*

CRAIGMOR 4 br.g. Polar Falcon (USA) 126 – Western Horizon (USA) 58 (Gone West **–** (USA)) [2004 f8.5g f8.5g Jan 19] maiden: tailed off in 2004: tried blinkered. *M. F. Harris*

CRAIL 4 b.g. Vettori (IRE) 119 – Tendency 77 (Ballad Rock 122) [2004 79: 8s³ 8.1d **80** 8m⁴ 8d* 8d 7d p9.5g⁴ p10g⁴ Dec 18] workmanlike gelding: fairly useful handicapper: won apprentice race at Salisbury in August: stays 1¼m: acts on polytrack, soft and good to firm ground. *C. F. Wall*

CRAIOVA (IRE) 5 b.h. Turtle Island (IRE) 123 – Velvet Appeal (IRE) 101 (Petorius **86** 117) [2004 100: 8g 8g 7g 7d 8.1g 7g 7g⁴ 7m Sep 17] strong, lengthy, attractive horse: has a quick action: fairly useful handicapper: effective at 7f/1m: acts on good to firm and good to soft going: tried in cheekpieces: sometimes carries head awkwardly/finds little: sold 6,500 gns. *B. W. Hills*

CRATHES 3 ch.f. Zilzal (USA) 137 – Sweet Dreams 85 (Selkirk (USA) 129) [2004 **53 ?** 6v² 7.1d⁴ f8g⁶ Jun 11] 16,000F: lengthy filly: second foal: dam, 1m winner, half-sister to smart French 1m/1¼m performer Amato: modest maiden: seemingly best effort on debut: should stay 1m. *J. G. Given*

CRATHORNE (IRE) 4 b.g. Alzao (USA) 117 – Shirley Blue (IRE) (Shirley Heights **87 d** 130) [2004 93: 11.9s⁴ 12m³ 12f⁴ 12g 11.9d 12m 9.1d p12.2g 10d Oct 18] deep-girthed gelding: fairly useful handicapper: well below form after second start: stays 1½m: acts on firm and soft going: wears cheekpieces: sometimes slowly away: usually held up: sold 14,000 gns. *J. D. Bethell*

CRAZY LIKE A FOOL (IRE) 5 b.g. Charnwood Forest (IRE) 125 – Shanghai Girl **–** 102 (Distant Relative 128) [2004 8m Jul 5] pulled up (reportedly with breathing problem) both starts in bumpers: tailed off in seller at Musselburgh. *B. Mactaggart*

CREAM OF ESTEEM 2 b.g. (Apr 30) Mark of Esteem (IRE) 137 – Chantilly (FR) **–** (Sanglamore (USA) 126) [2004 7s 6s Nov 6] 12,000F, 9,000Y: smallish, stocky gelding: second living foal: dam unraced half-sister to useful 1m/9f winner Penang Pearl: tongue tied, behind in maidens at Doncaster, slowly away on second occasion. *N. Tinkler*

CREATIVE CHARACTER (USA) 2 b. or br.c. (May 7) Theatrical 128 – Shann- **69** kara (IRE) (Akarad (FR) 130) [2004 7m⁴ 8.1d 7.1m Sep 9] sixth foal: closely related to minor US stakes winner (also second in Grade 2 8.5f event) Tekken (by Nureyev) and half-brother to 2 winners, including useful 1m winner Swan Knight (by Sadler's Wells): dam, 1m winner (including at 2 yrs in France and Grade 3 event in USA), half-sister to Prix Vermeille winner Sharaya: form in maidens only when fourth at Lingfield: slowly away and hung final couple: should stay at least 1m: sent to USA. *P. F. I. Cole*

CREDIT (IRE) 3 b.c. Intikhab (USA) 135 – Tycooness (IRE) 80§ (Last Tycoon 131) **96** [2004 8g³ 8m³ 8m* 8m 8g 10g² 10m* 10g³ 11.9g³ 12g³ 12d Oct 14] 90,000F, 100,000Y: big, good-topped colt: has scope: has a quick, fluent action: second foal: half-brother to 4-y-o Tycoon Hall: dam, untrustworthy 1½m winner, half-sister to Lockinge Stakes winner Broken Hearted: useful performer: won maiden at Newbury in May and handicap at Windsor (beat Portmanteau 1½ lengths) in August: acts on good to firm ground: sold 65,000 gns. *R. Hannon*

CREE 2 b.g. (Mar 12) Indian Ridge 123 – Nightitude 93 (Night Shift (USA)) [2004 **69** 5.2g 5.1g 5m⁵ 5g² 5g⁵ 5s² 6m³ 5.1s* 5m⁴ 6v⁵ 5.1v² p6g Nov 13] 10,000Y: close-coupled, quite good-topped gelding: half-brother to useful Italian 7f/1m winner (including at 2 yrs) Golden Cavern (by Lion Cavern): dam, 2-y-o 5f winner, became one to treat with caution: fair performer: won nursery at Chepstow in September, swerving right: creditable efforts in frame in similar races after: free-going sort, best at 5f/easy 6f: acts on heavy and good to firm ground: blinkered third to fifth starts. *W. R. Muir*

CREEK DANCER 2 b.f. (Apr 10) Josr Algarhoud (IRE) 118 – Dance Land (IRE) **–** (Nordance (USA)) [2004 7g Oct 11] 11,000F: half-sister to several winners, including 3-y-o Grouville and Irish 1½m/1¾m winner Dariole (by Priolo): dam unraced: 100/1, always rear in maiden at Leicester. *R. Guest*

Godolphin's "Crimson Palace"

CREME DE LA CREME (IRE) 2 b.f. (Feb 9) Montjeu (IRE) 137 – Pride of Place **60** (IRE) 71 (Caerleon (USA) 132) [2004 8.2g p7g Oct 28] second foal: dam, ran twice at 2 yrs, half-sister to Oaks and Irish Oaks winner Unite: better effort in maidens when eighth at Nottingham on debut: should be suited by 1¼m+. *D. R. Loder*

CRESKELD (IRE) 5 b.g. Sri Pekan (USA) 117 – Pizzazz 47 (Unfuwain (USA) 131) **72** [2004 87, a96: f8.5s³ 8v 8s 8.3d 8.1g 7.1d 9.2d* 8g⁴ 8.3d 10s⁵ p8.6g p9.5g³ p8.6g f8g³ **a91** Dec 28] sparely-made gelding: fairly useful handicapper on all-weather, fair on turf: won at Hamilton in August: stays 9.5f: acts on all-weather, soft and good to firm going: usually races up with pace: none too consistent. *B. Smart*

CRESSEX KATIE 5 b.m. Komaite (USA) – Kakisa 81 (Forlorn River 124) [2004 76, **–** a61: p7g Feb 7] tailed off only 5-y-o start. *J. R. Best*

CRETAN GIFT 13 ch.g. Cadeaux Genereux 131 – Caro's Niece (USA) 86 (Caro 133) **73** [2004 85: f7g⁵ p6g⁴ p6g³ Dec 27] lengthy gelding: smart performer at best, winner of 15 of 140 career starts: just fair form in 2004: stays 7f: acts on all-weather, firm and soft going: visored/blinkered: tends to start slowly/gets behind. *N. P. Littmoden*

CRETE (IRE) 2 b.c. (Feb 19) Montjeu (IRE) 137 – Paesanella (Seattle Song (USA) **74 p** 130) [2004 8.2v⁴ Nov 4] 125,000Y: sturdy colt: fifth foal: closely related to useful Italian performer up to 1½m Masaniella (by Masad) and half-brother to a winner in Italy by Unfuwain: dam Italian 7f (at 2 yrs) to 9f winner: favourite, 2¼ lengths fourth of 15 to Tawqeet in maiden at Nottingham, green and fading after travelling well: will be suited by 1¼m/1½m: sure to improve. *W. J. Haggas*

CREWES MISS ISLE 3 b.f. Makbul 104 – Riviere Rouge (Forzando 122) [2004 75: **70 d** f6g⁴ 6.1s⁶ f5g* 6s⁵ 5g 6.1g f6g 6m⁵ 5d p6g p7.1g Oct 19] smallish filly: fair performer:

below form after winning minor event at Wolverhampton in April: stays 6f: acts on fibresand and good to firm going. *A. G. Newcombe*

CRIMSON BOW (GER) 2 ch.f. (Feb 4) Night Shift (USA) – Carma (IRE) (Konigs- **49** stuhl (GER)) [2004 6g Aug 5] 20,000Y: first foal: dam, useful German 7f (at 2 yrs) to 1½m winner, sister to Deutsches St Leger winner Caballo: green, ninth in maiden at Haydock: should stay 1m. *J. G. Given*

CRIMSON PALACE (SAF) 5 b.m. Elliodor (FR) 114 – Perfect Guest (SAF) **118** (Northern Guest (USA)) [2004 9f* 8.9m⁴ 10.4s* 8f⁶ 9.5f* Aug 14] tall, rather leggy mare: second known foal: dam won in South Africa: smart performer: won 4 of her 6 starts in South Africa, all at Kenilworth, including Grade 1 Cape Paddock Stakes in December 2002: fourth to Paraca in Majorca Stakes there on only outing in 2003: off nearly a year, won minor event at Nad Al Sheba (by 4¾ lengths from Gateman, sold privately from M. de Kock after) in January, totepool Middleton Stakes at York (by ¾ length from Beneventa) in May and Beverly D Stakes at Arlington (beat Riskaverse by ½ length) in August: fourth to Paolini and Right Approach in Dubai Duty Free at Nad Al Sheba on second start: best form at 9f/1¼m: acted on any going: sweating (ran poorly) fourth outing: reported in October to have suffered a setback: stud. *Saeed bin Suroor*

CRIMSON SILK 4 ch.g. Forzando 122 – Sylhall (Sharpo 132) [2004 103: 6g 6g 7d **100** 7s 7.1g 6m³ 6m 6g³ a6f Nov 8] sturdy gelding: useful performer: third in 2 handicaps at Windsor: left D. Haydn Jones before final outing: effective at 6f/7f: acts on good to firm and good to soft going: wore cheekpieces/blinkers last 6 outings: sometimes early to post. *M. W. Dickinson, USA*

CRIMSON STAR (IRE) 3 b. or br.f. Soviet Star (USA) 128 – Crimson Shower 61 **58** (Dowsing (USA) 124) [2004 8.2s p10g 7m 8.3f 6g³ 7m² p8g² 6m² p7m Dec 8] third living foal: half-sister to 2 winners, including 6-y-o Storm Shower: dam, 1m winner, half-sister to smart 6f to 1m winner Chipaya: modest maiden: effective at 6f to 1m: acts on good to firm ground and polytrack. *C. Tinkler*

CRIMSON SUN (USA) 2 b.c. (Feb 21) Danzig (USA) – Crimplene (IRE) 120 (Lion **104** Cavern (USA) 117) [2004 6s² 6m* 6m* 6s 7g² Sep 30] strong, good-bodied colt: has a quick action: first foal: dam 6f (at 2 yrs) to 1¼m winner (including Irish 1000 Guineas, Coronation and Nassau Stakes): useful performer: won maiden at Doncaster in May and minor event at Newmarket (beat Kings Quay by head, dictating pace) in July: much better effort when after neck second to Diktatorial in Somerville Tattersall Stakes at Newmarket, leading going well over 2f out but headed near finish: stays 7f: acts on good to firm ground: edgy sort. *Saeed bin Suroor*

CRIPSEY BROOK 6 ch.g. Lycius (USA) 124 – Duwon (IRE) 55 (Polish Precedent **91** (USA) 131) [2004 95: 8d⁶ 10.4d⁶ 10m 8.9m 10g² 8m⁸ 10.5g 10g 12m 10.4g⁵ Oct 8] tall gelding: fairly useful handicapper: stays 10.5f: acts on firm and good to soft going: free-going sort: held up: tough and genuine. *Don Enrico Incisa*

CRISPIN HOUSE 4 b.f. Inchinor 119 – Ayr Classic 74 (Local Suitor (USA) 128) **–** [2004 –: 14.1g Jul 24] of little account. *R. J. Price*

CRISTOFORO (IRE) 7 b.g. Perugino (USA) 84 – Red Barons Lady (IRE) (Electric **80** 126) [2004 10.9s* 10d 12f* 12g* 10.1f* 11.6m* Aug 2] big, good-topped gelding: fairly useful handicapper: unraced on Flat in 2003 (won over hurdles): progressed well in 2004, winning at Warwick in April, Folkestone in June, Epsom (2) in July and Windsor (amateur event) in August: effective at 1¼m to 13f: unraced on heavy going, acts on any other turf/all-weather: sometimes slowly away: held up. *B. J. Curley*

CRITICAL STAGE (IRE) 5 b.g. King's Theatre (IRE) 128 – Zandaka (FR) (Doyoun **74** 124) [2004 69, a74: f9.4g³ f11s* f12g³ 12.1m 8.1m⁶ 9.9g⁴ 11.7g⁴ Oct 10] sturdy gelding: fair handicapper: won at Southwell in February: left John Berry after third start: stays 1½m: acts on fibresand, good to firm and good to soft ground: often wears eyeshields on all-weather: usually held up: fair hurdler. *J. D. Frost*

CROCIERA (IRE) 3 b.g. Croco Rouge (IRE) 126 – Ombry Girl (IRE) (Distinctly **60 ?** North (USA) 115) [2004 10v⁴ 12.6s 12g 11.8g Oct 12] lengthy, good-topped gelding: modest maiden: stays 1¼m: acts on good to firm and heavy ground: tried blinkered. *M. H. Tompkins*

CROCODILE DUNDEE (IRE) 3 b.c. Croco Rouge (IRE) 126 – Miss Salsa Dancer **120** 64 (Salse (USA) 128) [2004 90: p7g p8g⁶ 10g³ 11g² 10m² 10d* 12m* Aug 1] sturdy, close-coupled colt: very smart performer: placed 3 times in listed races before improved effort to win similar event at Sandown in July by neck from Silence Is Golden: followed

249

Mr R. W. Huggins' "Crocodile Dundee"

up in Tuborg Scandinavian Open Championship at Copenhagen in August by short head from Maktub, leading near finish: stays 1½m: acts on polytrack, good to firm and good to soft going: held up: game and consistent: sold privately, and joined L. Cumani. *Jamie Poulton*

CROCODILE KISS (IRE) 2 b.f. (Mar 16) Rossini (USA) 118 – Pipe Opener 58 **61** (Prince Sabo 123) [2004 6g⁵ 5.9f⁵ 6g 6v⁶ p6g p6g Dec 3] €40,000Y: fifth foal: half-sister to 3 winners, including useful Irish winner around 7f Sand Partridge (by Desert Style), later successful in USA: dam disappointing maiden: modest maiden: best efforts when fifth: likely to stay 7f. *J. A. Osborne*

CROCOLAT 3 ch.f. Croco Rouge (IRE) 126 – Lamanka Lass (USA) 79 (Woodman **77 p** (USA) 126) [2004 8m 10s 7f⁵ 11.9f² f12g⁴ f12m* f12s* 16g³ 17.1g² Oct 4] 11,000 2-y-o: first foal: dam, 1m winner, out of sister to US Grade 1 9f winner Annoconnor and half-sister to Grand Prix de Paris/Melbourne Cup winner At Talaq: fair form: won claimer at Southwell (claimed from N. Callaghan £10,000) in July and handicap on same course (heavily backed, beat Heathers Girl by 8 lengths) in August: unlucky ¾-length second to Moonshine Beach in handicap at Pontefract final start, short of room before finishing well: stays 17f: acts on fibresand and firm going: open to further improvement. *Mrs Stef Liddiard*

CROIX DE GUERRE (IRE) 4 gr.g. Highest Honor (FR) 124 – Esclava (USA) **56 §** (Nureyev (USA) 131) [2004 59§: 12.6d³ Sep 18] tall gelding: modest performer: stays 12.6f: acts on firm and good to soft going, unraced on softer: effective blinkered or not: quirky: fair hurdler. *P. J. Hobbs*

CROIX ROUGE (USA) 2 b.c. (Mar 8) Chester House (USA) 123 – Rougeur (USA) **75**
(Blushing Groom (FR) 131) [2004 7.1m3 8.3m 7g a8.3g* a8.3g6 Dec 12] smallish,
good-topped colt: seventh foal: half-brother to 3 winners in USA, notably very smart
Grade 1 9f/1¼m winner Flute (by Seattle Slew): dam, 1¼m/1½m winner in France/USA,
half-sister to smart performer up to 2m Eva Luna, dam of 4-y-o Brian Boru: fair perfor-
mer: sold from Mrs A. Perrett 20,000 gns after third start: won maiden at Mijas in
November: should stay 1¼m: looked none too easy ride second/third outings. *R. J. Smith,
Spain*

CROMARTY BAY 3 b.f. Victory Note (USA) 120 – Cromarty 75 (Shareef Dancer **–**
(USA) 135) [2004 10m Jul 15] 700Y: fourth foal: dam, 1½m winner who stayed well,
also successful over hurdles: 66/1, last in maiden at Leicester. *A. P. James*

CRONKYVODDY 3 b.g. Groom Dancer (USA) 128 – Miss Pout (Kris 135) [2004 **53**
7f6 f8g 8.1g6 10.1s4 Aug 30] tall gelding: modest maiden: probably stays 1¼m: acts on
firm and soft ground: tongue tied. *Miss Gay Kelleway*

CROON 2 b.c. (Feb 25) Sinndar (IRE) 134 – Shy Minstrel (USA) (The Minstrel (CAN) **76 p**
135) [2004 p7g6 p7g5 p7.1g* Dec 10] 82,000Y: sixth foal: half-brother to 3 winners
abroad, including useful French 2000 2-y-o 7.5f/1m (Prix d'Aumale) winner Green
Minstrel (by Green Tune): dam won in USA and third in Grade 3 8.5f event at 2 yrs: won
maiden at Wolverhampton by ¾ length from Dudley Docker, making all: likely to be
suited by 1¼m/1½m: should improve. *L. M. Cumani*

CROSS ASH (IRE) 4 ch.g. Ashkalani (IRE) 128 – Priorite (IRE) 85 (Kenmare (FR) **56**
125) [2004 81: 6d 7m f8d 7g 6g 7g6 p8.6d3 f8g p8.6g4 p8m4 p10m3 p9.5g5 Dec 22] strong,
workmanlike gelding: modest performer: stays 1¼m: acts on polytrack and firm ground,
below form on good to soft. *R. Hollinshead*

CROSS MY SHADOW (IRE) 2 b.g. (Apr 22) Cape Cross (IRE) 129 – Shadow- **55**
glow (Shaadi (USA) 126) [2004 8.3m 7s5 7.1g 5.7g 6s 5.1g Oct 10] quite good-topped
gelding: modest maiden: best effort at 5.7f: blinkered final start: tongue tied. *M. F. Harris*

CROSSPEACE (IRE) 2 b.c. (Apr 26) Cape Cross (IRE) 129 – Announcing Peace **94 p**
(Danehill (USA) 126) [2004 6g2 6m* 7s* Oct 23] €23,000Y, 52,000 2-y-o: good-topped
colt: has scope: third foal: half-brother to Italian 5f (at 2 yrs) and 7.5f winner by College
Chapel: dam Irish maiden out of half-sister to high-class 1985 2-y-o November: won
maiden at Newcastle and nursery at Doncaster (beat Top The Charts by ¾ length, making
all) in October: should stay 1m: acts on soft and good to firm ground: should make useful
handicapper as 3-y-o. *M. Johnston*

CROSS THE LINE (IRE) 2 b.c. (Apr 4) Cape Cross (IRE) 129 – Baalbek 76 (Bara- **64 p**
thea (IRE) 127) [2004 p8g4 Oct 25] 34,000Y: first foal: dam, 1m winner, granddaughter
of Irish 1000 Guineas winner Front Row: 11/2, green when fourth to Gryskirk in maiden
at Lingfield: likely to improve. *A. P. Jarvis*

CROSS TIME (USA) 2 b.c. (Mar 18) Cape Cross (IRE) 129 – Reine Maid (USA) **61 p**
(Mr Prospector (USA)) [2004 8v6 Oct 23] $13,000F, €75,000Y: unfurnished colt: closely
related to useful 1994 2-y-o 6f winner Al Nufooth (by Green Desert) and half-brother to
several winners, including useful Italian sprinter Regina Saura (by Wolfhound): dam
French 7f (at 2 yrs)/1m winner: 16/1, sixth to Spear Thistle in maiden at Newbury, green
but getting hang of things late on: should do better. *M. R. Channon*

CROSSWAYS 6 b.g. Mister Baileys 123 – Miami Dancer (USA) (Seattle Dancer **77**
(USA) 119) [2004 p10g4 p13g6 p12g 14.1d4 14.1m2 13.3m2 Jun 9] fair handicapper: won
at Lingfield in February: stays 1¾m: acts on polytrack, firm and good to soft ground.
P. D. Evans

CROWN AGENT (IRE) 4 b.g. Mukaddamah (USA) 125 – Supreme Crown (USA) **70**
(Chief's Crown (USA)) [2004 78: p12g 12g5 11.6d 14.1s p12d Jun 12] leggy, good-
topped gelding: fair maiden: stays 12.6f: acts on polytrack, soft and good to firm going.
A. M. Balding

CROWN CITY (USA) 4 b.f. Coronado's Quest (USA) 130 – Trisha Brown (USA) **–**
(Theatrical 128) [2004 56: f8g p10g f8g 8.1g Apr 23] sturdy filly: maiden: well held in
2004: often tongue tied. *B. P. J. Baugh*

CROWN OF MEDINA 2 ch.c. (Feb 24) Fraam 114 – Medina de Rioseco 70 (Puis- **57**
sance 110) [2004 7g p7.1g6 Oct 19] rather leggy, lengthy colt: modest form in maidens at
Newmarket and Wolverhampton (looked none too keen). *P. W. Harris*

CROW WOOD 5 b.g. Halling (USA) 133 – Play With Me (IRE) 73 (Alzao (USA) 117) **102**
[2004 98: 10.1s 10.3d3 10m3 10m5 11.9g2 13.9s 14g6 14s6 Sep 25] strong, close-coupled

gelding: useful handicapper: best efforts when third to Blue Spinnaker at Redcar on third outing and second to Alkaased at Haydock: stays 1¾m: acts on fibresand, firm and good to soft going, well held on soft: often races handily: sold 50,000 gns. *J. G. Given*

CRUISE DIRECTOR 4 b.g. Zilzal (USA) 137 – Briggsmaid 70 (Elegant Air 119) **92** [2004 88+: p12g³ p12g f12s³ f12g 11.6d* 12g 12.1g 11.9s² 10.5s⁴ 12s⁵ 12s⁵ Nov 6] heavy-topped gelding: fairly useful handicapper: won at Windsor in April: good second to Balkan Knight at York on eighth outing: stays 1½m: acts on all-weather, raced only on good ground or softer on turf: held up. *W. J. Musson*

CRUNCHY (IRE) 6 ch.g. Common Grounds 118 – Credit Crunch (IRE) 51 (Caerleon **–** (USA) 132) [2004 –, a77: 10.3g Mar 25] workmanlike gelding: lightly raced and no form on turf since 3 yrs: tried in cheekpieces: tongue tied. *B. Ellison*

CRUSOE (IRE) 7 b.g. Turtle Island (IRE) 123 – Self Reliance 72 (Never So Bold 135) [2004 –, a76: f8.5s³ f9.4s f8.5s f8s⁴ 10.3g f8g f9.4g⁴ f8.5g² f9.4m 10.5d f8d² f8d **a65** f8g p8m f11g⁴ p9.5g p9.5g Dec 22] small gelding: modest handicapper: probably stays 11f: acts on fibresand, lightly raced and no form on turf after 3 yrs: tried in cheekpieces, usually blinkered. *A. Sadik*

CRUSTY LILY 8 gr.m. Whittingham (IRE) 104 – Miss Crusty 45 (Belfort (FR) 89) **24** [2004 –: p6g³ 6.1m 6f 8d Oct 2] smallish, lengthy mare: bad performer nowadays: tried in cheekpieces. *R. M. H. Cowell*

CRUX 2 b.g. (May 1) Pivotal 124 – Penny Dip 86 (Cadeaux Genereux 131) [2004 5.1g Sep 29] sixth foal: dam, 6f winner, out of smart 2-y-o 5f winner Penny Blessing: 25/1 and green, well held in maiden at Nottingham. *C. W. Thornton*

CRUZSPIEL 4 br.g. Singspiel (IRE) 133 – Allespagne (USA) (Trempolino (USA) 135) **111** [2004 106: 14m³ 14d 14g Sep 18] quite good-topped gelding: smart performer: ran well when 1½ lengths third to Mkuzi in Curragh Cup in June: below form in listed race at Leopardstown and Irish St Leger at the Curragh afterwards: stays 2m: acts on firm and good to soft going: usually blinkered: often races prominently. *J. Oxx, Ireland*

CRYFIELD 7 b.g. Efisio 120 – Ciboure 74 (Norwick (USA) 125) [2004 76: 10.3g 8s **68** 8d⁶ 7g² 8m⁴ 7.5d 7.5g 8.5g* 7.9d⁶ 8.5m⁴ 9.1g³ f8s⁴ 7.9g 10d 7.5m⁶ p8.6g⁶ p8.6d Nov 4] big, good-bodied gelding: fair handicapper: won at Beverley in July: effective at 7f to 9f: acts on any going: sometimes visored: free-going sort. *N. Tinkler*

CRY OF THE WOLF 2 ch.c. (Apr 4) Loup Sauvage (USA) 125 – Hopesay 84 (Warn- **44** ing 136) [2004 6g 6m May 22] poor form in maidens. *N. P. Littmoden*

CRYPTOGAM 4 b.f. Zamindar (USA) 116 – Moss (Alzao (USA) 117) [2004 69d: **45** f12f f16g f8g 9f 8f 12m⁵ 12g 12m Jul 21] smallish filly: poor maiden handicapper: stays 1½m: acts on good to firm ground. *M. E. Sowersby*

CRYSTAL CASTLE (USA) 6 b.g. Gilded Time (USA) – Wayage (USA) (Mr **116** Prospector (USA)) [2004 107: 7d³ 7d³ 6f² 7g⁵ 6.5g 6g⁵ Oct 24] good-topped gelding: smart performer: best effort in 2004 when head second to Fayr Jag in Golden Jubilee Stakes at Royal Ascot (stayed on well after being briefly short of room): first race after leaving J. Hammond in France, respectable 1¾ lengths fifth to I Thee Wed in Grade 2 Nearctic Handicap at Woodbine final outing: effective at 6f/7f: acts on firm and soft going: has had tongue tied: usually waited with: broke out of stall before fifth outing. *D. Vienna, USA*

CRYSTAL CHOIR 4 b.f. Singspiel (IRE) 133 – Crystal Ring (IRE) 83 (Kris 135) **–** [2004 –: 10d 9.9g⁶ 9g Jun 2] rangy filly: little form: sold 34,000 gns. *N. J. Henderson*

CRYSTAL CURLING (IRE) 3 ch.f. Peintre Celebre (USA) 137 – State Crystal **100** (IRE) 114 (High Estate 127) [2004 88p: 11.4d³ 10g³ 12m 10.1s⁵ 10.1g⁵ 8m Sep 25] quite attractive filly: useful performer: best efforts when third in listed races at Chester (4½ lengths behind Hidden Hope) and Newbury (beaten 3¼ lengths by Rave Reviews): should stay 1½m: acts on soft and good to firm ground: tongue tied (well beaten) final outing. *B. W. Hills*

CRYSTAL (IRE) 3 b.f. Danehill (USA) 126 – Solar Crystal (IRE) 110 (Alzao (USA) **88** 117) [2004 85p: 10g² 10g* 12m⁵ 10.1s 10.1g 12s⁵ Nov 6] good-topped filly: fairly useful performer: won maiden at Windsor in April: stiff task, well beaten in Oaks at Epsom next time (subsequently found to have had an infection): well held in listed events last 3 starts, blinkered on final one: stays 1¼m: below form both outings on soft ground: none too consistent. *B. J. Meehan*

CRYSTALLINE 2 b.f. (Apr 28) Green Desert (USA) 127 – Crown of Light 112 (Mtoto **74** 134) [2004 7f³ 7g Aug 13] leggy, close-coupled filly: third foal: half-sister to 4-y-o

Balkan Knight: dam, 7f (at 2 yrs) and 11.5f winner, also third in Oaks: much better effort in maidens when third at Newmarket: dead. *D. R. Loder*

CRYSTAL MYSTIC (IRE)   2 b.g. (Apr 17) Anita's Prince 126 – Out On Her Own 126 (Superlative 118) [2004 7.1m 7.1s^4 p6g 6.1v Nov 4] leggy gelding: modest maiden: fourth at Chepstow, only form: hung right next time: barely stays 7f: blinkered first 3 starts: gelded after final one. *B. Palling*   **55**

CTESIPHON (USA)   3 b.f. Arch (USA) 127 – Beautiful Bedouin (USA) (His Majesty (USA)) [2004 55: 10d 10s f8.5g Jun 4] quite good-topped filly: maiden: well held in 2004: tried blinkered: sold 20,000 gns. *J. G. Given*   **–**

CUBIC CONFESSIONS (IRE)   2 b.f. (Mar 8) Cape Cross (IRE) 129 – Debinnair (FR) (Wolfhound (USA) 126) [2004 p5g^4 p5g^4 5m^4 Jul 22] €6,000Y, resold €34,000Y: leggy, rather unfurnished filly: second foal: sister to fairly useful French 7.5f (at 2 yrs) to 9f winner Vicalex: dam French 2-y-o 6f winner: poor form, including in seller. *J. A. Osborne*   **49**

CUDDLES (FR)   5 b.m. Anabaa (USA) 130 – Palomelle (FR) 112 (Moulin 103) [2004 78, a87: p10g 9.7s^5 12d 8m^4 9d^5 10.2g^3 7.6m 9.9g 8.3d 10.2g^6 10.9d p8g p8.6g Nov 6] leggy mare: fair performer: left C. Brittain after third start: stays 1¼m: acts on any turf going and polytrack: sometimes wears headgear: none too genuine. *K. O. Cunningham-Brown*   **63** **a74**

CUGINA NICOLA   3 b.f. Nicolotte 118 – Cugina 99 (Distant Relative 128) [2004 10g 10.5g 10m Sep 7] quite good-topped filly: first foal: dam 1¼m winner who stayed 1½m: well held in maidens. *G. B. Balding*   **–**

CULCABOCK (IRE)   4 b.g. Unfuwain (USA) 131 – Evidently (IRE) (Slip Anchor 136) [2004 57: 14g Sep 11] modest performer: well held only Flat outing in 2004. *P. Monteith*   **–**

CULMINATE   7 ch.g. Afzal 83 – Straw Blade 66 (Final Straw 127) [2004 –: f7s Feb 17] little form: tried blinkered/in cheekpieces. *J. E. Long*   **–**

CULTURED   3 b.f. Danzero (AUS) – Seek The Pearl 91 (Rainbow Quest (USA) 134) [2004 10s^5 9g^6 May 20] tall filly: seventh foal: half-sister to several winners, including fairly useful 7f/1m winner Diver's Pearl (by Prince Sabo): dam 1¼m winner: modest form in maidens. *Mrs A. J. Bowlby*   **59**

CUMBRIA   3 b.f. Singspiel (IRE) 133 – Whitehaven 116 (Top Ville 129) [2004 11.9d^3 12m^4 May 15] half-sister to 3 winners, including useful French middle-distance stayer/smart hurdler Copeland (by Generous): dam French 1m (at 2 yrs) to 13.5f (Prix de Pomone) winner: fair form in maidens at Haydock and Thirsk: stays 1½m: sold 38,000 gns in December. *M. Johnston*   **74**

CUMBRIAN KNIGHT (IRE)   6 b.g. Presenting 120 – Crashrun (Crash Course 128) [2004 10g Sep 29] fair hurdler: well held in maiden at Nottingham. *J. M. Jefferson*   **–**

CUMBRIAN PRINCESS   7 gr.m. Mtoto 134 – Cumbrian Melody 83 (Petong 126) [2004 36: f12g^4 f8.5g f8.5g p8g* p8g* p8g^3 f8g^6 p10g^3 p10d^6 9d^6 8d p9.5g* p8m^6 p10m p9.5g^3 Dec 22] leggy, sparely-made mare: modest performer: won banded races at Lingfield in March/April and Wolverhampton in November: effective at 1m/1¼m: acts on all-weather, soft and good to firm going: tried blinkered: sometimes wanders: none too reliable. *M. Blanshard*   **55**

CUMMISKEY (IRE)   2 b.c. (Feb 19) Orpen (USA) 116 – Ansariya (USA) 83 (Shahrastani (USA) 135) [2004 5d^5 5.7m^3 5f^4 6.1m^2 6m^2 Sep 12] €75,000F, €180,000Y: lengthy, attractive colt: fifth foal: half-brother to useful French 1m/9f winner Answering (by King's Theatre): dam, Irish 2-y-o 1m winner (later successful in Switzerland), half-sister to very smart French performer up to 1½m Astarabad and to dam of 3-y-o Azamour: fairly useful maiden: second in nurseries at Warwick and Goodwood: will probably stay 7f: acts on firm ground. *J. A. Osborne*   **83**

CUMWHITTON   5 b.m. Jumbo Hirt (USA) 90§ – Dominance (Dominion 123) [2004 –: f11g^5 f11s f11g* f11m^6 May 6] leggy mare: poor performer: won banded race at Southwell in March: stays 11f: acts on fibresand: wore cheekpieces last 2 starts. *R. A. Fahey*   **44**

CUNNING PURSUIT   3 b.g. Pursuit of Love 124 – Mistitled (USA) 54 (Miswaki (USA) 124) [2004 8m f8.5g^6 6.1s^5 8.5m^6 11.5f^2 14g 16g 9.7f* 10m^4 Sep 25] modest performer: won banded race at Folkestone in September: barely stays 11.5f: acts on firm ground: won over hurdles in December. *M. L. W. Bell*   **50**

Stan James Horris Hill Stakes, Newbury—Cupid's Glory puts up the best performance in the race in over fifteen years as he pulls clear of Johnny Jumpup and King Marju

CUPID'S GLORY   2 b.c. (Apr 9) Pursuit of Love 124 – Doctor's Glory (USA)   **116**
91 (Elmaamul (USA) 125) [2004 p7g⁶ p6d* 6.1s* p7g* 6g³ 7s* 8s⁴ Oct 31]

Only three months after finishing sixth of thirteen in a median auction maiden at Lingfield on his debut, Cupid's Glory lined up for the Group 3 Horris Hill Stakes at Newbury with three wins under his belt and looking to have good prospects of making it four. Two of those wins had also come on the polytrack at Lingfield, in a similar event on his second start and a nursery on his fourth, while in between Cupid's Glory had been successful in a minor event at Chester. Cupid's Glory had shown further improvement when defying top weight of 10-0 in the nursery, and matched that form when dropped back to six furlongs in a listed event at the Curragh, finishing third to the subsequent Middle Park Stakes winner Ad Valorem, beaten a length and a half. The Stan James Horris Hill Stakes attracted a field of thirteen, its biggest for over thirty years, and all but one of the runners were previous winners in what was an above-average renewal which, as so often, took place in testing conditions. Cupid's Glory looked a worthy favourite for it, given that he not only had the best form but was also one of the few already proven on soft ground. Seeming well suited by the return to seven furlongs, he improved again to win in very good style. Held up towards the rear, Cupid's Glory responded well when asked for his effort, took the lead over a furlong out and, despite edging right towards the rail, ran on strongly to pull four lengths clear of Johnny Jumpup, who himself had two and a half lengths to spare over third-placed King Marju. The form shown by Cupid's Glory was at least as good as that of any other winner of the race in recent times, though it still leaves him with plenty to find if he is to make an impact in the Two Thousand Guineas, which has been mentioned as a possible target. The Guineas distance shouldn't be beyond him, even though his stamina was stretched when he was tried at a mile on his only outing after Newbury, in the Criterium International at Saint-Cloud, where the ground was again testing. Cupid's Glory made headway round the home turn to dispute the lead but faded in the final furlong to finish fourth to Helios Quercus, beaten a little over two lengths. The Criterium came just nine days after the Horris Hill, and it is possible Cupid's Glory hadn't recovered fully from his exertions in the latter.

	Pursuit of Love	Groom Dancer	Blushing Groom
	(b 1989)	(b 1984)	Featherhill
Cupid's Glory		Dance Quest	Green Dancer
(b.c. Apr 9, 2002)		(b 1981)	Polyponder
	Doctor's Glory (USA)	Elmaamul	Diesis
	(gr 1992)	(ch 1987)	Modena
		Doctor Bid	Spectacular Bid
		(gr 1986)	Fager's Glory

Cupid's Glory, a 48,000-guinea yearling, is a brother to two winners, Courting and Dolzago, and closely related to another in Instructor (by Groom Dancer). Courting was a useful filly at up to a mile and a quarter and Dolzago a fair winner at thirteen furlongs and at up to two and a quarter miles over hurdles in 2004, while the three-year-old Instructor showed fairly useful form over as far as nine and a half furlongs in the latest season. Their dam Doctor's Glory, who won at five furlongs at

Hesmonds Stud's "Cupid's Glory"

two and six furlongs at three, when also showing her form at seven furlongs, is a half-sister to On Call, a filly who developed into a useful stayer and won seven races for Cupid's Glory's trainer in 1998. Cupid's Glory's grandam, the unraced Doctor Bid, is a half-sister to the smart 1986 two-year-old seven-furlong winner Glory Forever, who went on to be third in the Poule d'Essai des Poulains. Cupid's Glory, rather lengthy and good-bodied, looks to have the scope for a bit more improvement and should do well again at three. Yet to race on ground firmer than good, he clearly goes well on soft and also acts on polytrack. *Sir Mark Prescott*

CUP OF LOVE (USA) 2 ch.f. (Feb 25) Behrens (USA) 130 – Cup of Kindness (USA) **50** (Secretariat (USA)) [2004 6g 8m 6s Oct 29] close-coupled filly: half-sister to several winners in USA by Relaunch: dam unraced half-sister to very smart 6f/7f performer Iktamal and smart French 1½m performer First Magnitude: modest form in maidens: needs to settle to stay 1m. *R. Guest*

CURATE (USA) 5 ch.g. Unfuwain (USA) 131 – Carniola 104 (Rainbow Quest (USA) – 134) [2004 49: 10.4m⁶ Jun 11] leggy, quite good-topped gelding: maiden: well held only 5-y-o start: often tongue tied. *A. Dickman*

CURFEW 5 b.m. Marju (IRE) 127 – Twilight Patrol 96 (Robellino (USA) 127) [2004 **94** 102: 5.1g⁴ 5.1g⁵ 5m 5d Jul 31] rather leggy, lengthy mare: just fairly useful performer in 2004: best 5-y-o effort when fourth to Ringmoor Down in listed event at Bath on reappearance: effective at 5f to 7f: acted on firm going: tried tongue tied earlier in career: free-going sort (had been early and quietly to post): held up: stud. *J. R. Fanshawe*

CURRAGH GOLD (IRE) 4 b.f. Flying Spur (AUS) – Go Indigo (IRE) 67 (Cyrano – de Bergerac 120) [2004 52: 10f 10g p16g Sep 18] modest performer: well held in 2004: tried blinkered/in cheekpieces. *Mrs P. N. Dutfield*

255

CURRENCY 7 b.g. Sri Pekan (USA) 117 – On Tiptoes 107 (Shareef Dancer (USA) 85
135) [2004 85: p6g p5g³ p6g² p5g⁴ p7g p7g 6g 5m⁴ 6.1m 6g⁶ 5m³ 5m 6m 6m⁵ 6d² 5.7m*
5f⁴ 6g⁵ 6g 5s p5.1d⁶ f6g p6g³ p6g* p6g* p6m Dec 21] sturdy gelding: fairly useful handicapper: won at Bath in August, Lingfield in November and Wolverhampton in December:
effective at 5f/6f: acts on polytrack, firm and good to soft ground: tried in cheekpieces/
blinkers. *J. M. Bradley*

CURZON LODGE (IRE) 4 ch.g. Grand Lodge (USA) 125 – Curzon Street 70 –
(Night Shift (USA)) [2004 –: p10g 7.1m 8.1m Jul 22] little form in maidens/claimer:
pulled up lame final start: tried tongue tied. *C. Tinkler*

CUSCO (IRE) 3 ch.f. Titus Livius (FR) 115 – John's Ballad (IRE) (Ballad Rock 122) 88 +
[2004 91: 6v² 8.2s⁶ 8f 6m² 7m 7d² 7g 6m Sep 30] sturdy, close-coupled filly: fairly useful
performer: runner-up in minor events at Kempton and Newmarket and handicap (short-
headed by Violet Park) on latter course: effective at 6f to 1m: acts on heavy and good to
firm going. *R. Hannon*

CUSOON 2 b.c. (Apr 5) Dansili 127 – Charming Life 88 (Habitat 134) [2004 5m³ 6f* 78
5.7d⁴ 6m⁴ 7m 7d Oct 10] €8,500Y, 10,000 2-y-o: half-brother to several winners, including smart French 5f (at 2 yrs) to 1m winner Run And Gun (by Lomond) and useful 1¼m
and (in France) 11f winner Caerau (by Nashwan): dam 7f winner: fair performer: won
maiden at Brighton in August by 6 lengths: respectable efforts next 2 starts: should stay
7f: acts on firm and probably good to soft going: slowly away first 3 outings. *G. L. Moore*

CUSP 4 b.f. Pivotal 124 – Bambolona 108 (Bustino 136) [2004 –: 14.4v² Apr 26] tall 54
filly: modest maiden: best effort when second in handicap at Newcastle only 4-y-o start:
stays 1¾m: acts on heavy going. *C. W. Thornton*

CUT AND DRIED 3 ch.g. Daggers Drawn (USA) 114 – Apple Sauce 70 (Prince Sabo 67
123) [2004 60: p5g* p5g* p5g⁶ p5g 5.3m⁵ 5.1f⁴ 5f⁶ 5g⁴ p6g⁵ p6g 6f 5m Sep 11] sturdy
gelding: fair performer: won maiden and handicap at Lingfield in February: free-going
sort, best at 5f/easy 6f: acts on firm ground and polytrack: ran poorly only try in blinkers.
D. M. Simcock

CUTE CAIT 3 b.f. Atraf 116 – Clunk Click 72 (Star Appeal 133) [2004 53: f7d 7.9g⁶ –
Jul 3] close-coupled filly: modest performer: well held in 2004. *Mrs G. S. Rees*

CUTLASS GAUDY 2 br.c. (May 18) Nomination 125 – Cutlass Princess (USA) 41 77
(Cutlass (USA)) [2004 5.1g⁴ 6g 5m² 5g⁵ Oct 5] sturdy colt: brother to useful 1997 2-y-o
5f/6f winner Jimmy Too and half-brother to 5f to 7f winner Princess Efisio (by Efisio):
dam maiden: fair maiden: second to Sharplaw Star in minor event at Beverley, easily best
effort: will prove best at 5f/6f. *R. Hollinshead*

CUT QUARTZ (FR) 7 b.h. Johann Quatz (FR) 120 – Cutlass (IRE) 71 (Sure Blade 117
(USA) 130) [2004 113: 9.8d 14g* 13.5d² 15g* 15.5g⁴ 15s³ 15.5d² 20m² Oct 3] good-
bodied horse: second foal: dam, French 1½m winner, half-sister to smart 1¼m performer
King Adam: smart performer: won Prix Kergorlay at Deauville in 2002 and Prix
Vicomtesse Vigier at Longchamp in 2003: successful in 2004 in apprentice race at
Compiegne in April, minor event at Longchamp in May and listed race at Chantilly (by
short head from Clety) in June: placed last 3 starts behind Gold Medallist in Prix
Kergorlay at Deauville and Westerner in Prix Gladiateur (beaten short neck) and Prix du
Cadran (beaten 3 lengths), both at Longchamp: reportedly suffered fracture in foreleg on
gallops in late-October: stays 2½m, at least when conditions aren't testing: acts on heavy
and good to firm ground: used to be blinkered. *R. Gibson, France*

CUT RIDGE (IRE) 5 b.m. Indian Ridge 123 – Cutting Ground (IRE) 85 (Common 59
Grounds 117) [2004 57: 6g 5m 5d 8m 7.1f³ 6.9f² 7.6f* 6g² 6g⁵ 6.9g 7m Sep 18] lengthy
mare: modest handicapper: won at Lingfield in August: effective at 6f to 7.6f: acts on firm
and good to soft going: tried in cheekpieces, not in 2004: free-going sort. *J. S. Wainwright*

CUT SHORT (USA) 3 b. or br.f. Diesis 133 – Sun And Shade 93 (Ajdal (USA) 130) 86
[2004 7g⁵ 8g⁸ 8.3g³ Aug 9] quite good-topped filly: sixth foal: sister to smart 1997 2-y-o
6f/7f winner Daggers Drawn, and half-sister to 2 winners, including useful 1998 2-y-o 6f
winner Enemy Action (by Forty Niner): dam, 6f (at 2 yrs) and 9f (in USA) winner, half-
sister to Park Hill winner Madame Dubois: fairly useful form: won maiden at Goodwood
in June: creditable third to Tarfah in minor event at Windsor next time: stays 1m: sent to
USA. *J. H. M. Gosden*

CUTTHROAT 4 ch.g. Kris 135 – Could Have Been (Nomination 125) [2004 10m –
May 26] well beaten in maiden at Ripon: joined P. Hobbs 13,000 gns. *T. P. Tate*

CUTTING CREW (USA) 3 ch.c. Diesis 133 – Poppy Carew (IRE) 110 (Danehill 103
(USA) 126) [2004 88: 10d³ 11.9d* 11g⁶ 12g² 12g* Jul 28] rather unfurnished colt: useful

handicapper: won at York in May and Goodwood (valuable event, dictated pace and beat Larkwing by ¾ length) in July: will stay at least 1¾m: unraced on extremes of going: has run well when sweating: genuine. *P. W. Harris*

CUT TO THE CHASE   2 b.g. (Mar 4) Fraam 114 – Chasetown Cailin 59 (Suave Dancer (USA) 136) [2004 6d Aug 27] leggy gelding: 66/1 and tongue tied, well held in maiden at Thirsk. *N. Tinkler*   –

CYBER SANTA   6 b.g. Celtic Swing 138 – Qualitair Ridge (Indian Ridge 123) [2004 12m⁶ 12.1g 12.3s² 12.1s Aug 29] big gelding: modest handicapper: off 21 months before reappearance: stays 13f: acts on polytrack, firm and soft ground. *J. Hetherton*   53

CYCLICAL   2 b.c. (Feb 9) Pivotal 124 – Entwine 92 (Primo Dominie 121) [2004 5d* 6m* 6g³ p5g² Oct 28] good-topped colt: has scope: first foal: dam, 2-y-o 5f winner, half-sister to 5-y-o Feet So Fast and 2-y-o Soar: useful performer: won maiden at Hamilton in August and nursery at Goodwood (under 9-7) in September: respectable efforts in nursery at Newmarket (very much on toes) and minor event at Lingfield (staying-on second to Bond City): stays 6f. *G. A. Butler*   96

CYCLONIC STORM   5 b.m. Catrail (USA) 123 – Wheeler's Wonder (IRE) 43 (Sure Blade (USA) 130) [2004 78: 9.2m³ 9.3g⁴ 8m Jul 6] rather leggy mare: modest handicapper: stays 9.3f: acts on firm and soft going: tried in cheekpieces/blinkers. *R. A. Fahey*   64

CYFRWYS (IRE)   3 b.f. Foxhound (USA) 103 – Divine Elegance (IRE) (College Chapel 122) [2004 80: 7m 6m² f6g² 7.1m⁶ 6d 6m⁶ 6g* 6g f6g⁶ Nov 23] close-coupled filly: fair performer: dead-heated with Sessay in maiden at Catterick in October: effective at 5f to easy 7f: acts on all-weather, good to firm and good to soft ground: tried in tongue tie/visor: carries head high. *B. Palling*   67

CZARINA WALTZ   5 b.m. Emperor Jones (USA) 119 – Ballerina Bay 75 (Myjinski (USA)) [2004 96: 10m² 10m p10g⁶ 8.3d⁷ 10.4g p8g p9.5g p8g² Dec 30] good-topped mare: fairly useful handicapper: left C. Wall after fifth start: best around 1¼m: acts on polytrack and good to firm going, probably on soft: tongue tied last 3 starts: tends to race freely: usually waited with. *Miss Gay Kelleway*   88

CZARS PRINCESS (IRE)   3 b.f. Soviet Star (USA) 128 – Pearl Shell (USA) (Bering 136) [2004 51: p6m Dec 22] tall, leggy filly: maiden: well held only outing in 2004: races freely, and barely stays 7f. *John Berry*   –

CZAR WARS   9 b.g. Warrshan (USA) 117 – Dutch Czarina 45 (Prince Sabo 123) [2004 62, a74: f6g f6g⁶ f6g Apr 2] sturdy gelding: well held in 2004: usually blinkered: tried in cheekpieces and tongue strap: has bled from nose. *J. Balding*   –

CZECH SUMMER (IRE)   3 b.g. Desert Sun 120 – Prague Spring 66 (Salse (USA) 128) [2004 p12g p13g 8.3g Oct 11] tall, leggy gelding: no sign of ability: tried blinkered. *R. M. Flower*   –

D

DABBERS RIDGE (IRE)   2 b.c. (May 5) Indian Ridge 123 – Much Commended 100 (Most Welcome 131) [2004 6s Nov 6] 47,000Y: fourth foal: half-brother to 2 winners in Italy, including 7f winner (including at 2 yrs) Very Cross (by Cape Cross): dam, 2-y-o   66 p

6f winner who stayed 1m, sister to smart performer up to 1½m Prize Giving: 33/1 and very green, seventh of 21 to Bow Wave in maiden at Doncaster, staying on well after being hampered: will stay at least 7f: sure to improve. *B. W. Hills*

DABUS   9 b.g. Kris 135 – Licorne 93 (Sadler's Wells (USA) 132) [2004 –: 12m Aug 3]   –
small, stocky gelding: modest hurdler: well held on Flat since 2002. *M. C. Chapman*

DAFA   8 b.g. Deploy 131 – Linpac North Moor 69 (Moorestyle 137) [2004 f7g* p10g*   **48**
f12g⁶ p10g p13g⁶ f8.5m⁴ May 17] stocky gelding: poor performer: won banded events
at Wolverhampton in January and Lingfield in March: effective at 7f to 1½m: acts on
all-weather: wore blinkers/cheekpieces last 3 starts. *B. J. Curley*

DAFINA (IRE)   4 b.f. Mtoto 134 – Dafayna 121 (Habitat 134) [2004 62: 10.9f⁴ f8m³   **61**
Jul 6] half-sister to 2 winners in Ireland, including 7f/1m winner Darayna (by Shernazar):
dam, won Cork And Orrery Stakes (also successful at 2 yrs), half-sister to 2000 Guineas
winner Doyoun: modest maiden, lightly raced: trained by J. Oxx at 3 yrs: stays 10.9f: acts
on fibresand, firm and good to soft going: sold 95,000 gns. *H. Morrison*

DAFORE   3 b.c. Dr Fong (USA) 128 – Aquaglow 84 (Caerleon (USA) 132) [2004 6s*   **81**
8m 8d 8d Oct 30] 65,000F, 260,000Y: leggy, attractive colt: half-brother to several
winners, including 7f/1m winner Alpenglow (by Ezzoud) and 1m (at 2 yrs) to 1½m (in
USA) winner Attitre (by Mtoto), both useful: dam 7f/1m winner: fairly useful performer:
won maiden at Salisbury in May: not discredited in handicaps last 2 starts: stays 1m: acts
on soft ground: moved poorly to post second start. *R. Hannon*

DAGGERS CANYON   3 ch.g. Daggers Drawn (USA) 114 – Chipewyas (FR) (Bering   **67**
136) [2004 63: 10d² 8.2g 10m* May 25] close-coupled gelding: fair performer: won
handicap at Ripon in May: stays 1¼m: acts on good to firm and good to soft ground.
Julian Poulton

DAGOLA (IRE)   3 b.g. Daggers Drawn (USA) 114 – Diabola (USA) (Devil's Bag   **76**
(USA)) [2004 53: 8.2g* 8.1d 10g 8.3f³ 9g⁴ 8g² 8m⁴ 8.2g p8g⁶ p10g p9.5g* p9.5g
Dec 27] quite good-topped gelding: fair performer: won handicap at Nottingham in
April and (having left C. Cox 8,500 gns after eighth start) seller at Wolverhampton in
November and claimer there in December: stays 9.5f: acts on polytrack and firm going.
C. A. Dwyer

DAHJEE (USA)   3 b.c. Seeking The Gold (USA) – Colorado Dancer 122 (Shareef   **77**
Dancer (USA) 135) [2004 12g⁴ Jun 30] brother to outstanding 1m (including at 2 yrs) and
1¼m winner Dubai Millennium, closely related to 3 winners, including useful French
1¼m winner Denver County (by Mr Prospector) and half-brother to 2 winners: dam, won
13.5f Prix de Pomone, out of outstanding broodmare Fall Aspen: 13/8-favourite and
tongue tied, 4¾ lengths fourth of 9 to Stage Right in maiden at Kempton, slowly away:
left Godolphin, and sent to Japan. *Saeed bin Suroor*

DAHLIYEV (IRE)   2 b.g. (May 7) Fasliyev (USA) 120 – Thaidah (CAN) 105 (Vice   **68**
Regent (CAN)) [2004 6g 7m³ 7d Aug 12] €55,000Y: close-coupled gelding: half-brother
to several winners, including smart 1m winner Kismah (by Machiavellian) and 7-y-o
Mandoob: dam, 5f (at 2 yrs) to 7f winner, half-sister to top-class American filly Glorious
Song (dam of Singspiel) and champion US 1983 2-y-o Devil's Bag: easily best effort
in maidens when third at Lingfield: not sure to stay beyond 7f: gelded after final start.
P. W. Harris

DAHMAN   2 b.c. (Apr 7) Darshaan 133 – Nuriva (USA) 100 (Woodman (USA) 126)   **78**
[2004 7g⁴ 8.1d Aug 12] fifth living foal: half-brother to 3-y-o State Dilemma and 6-y-o
Brave Dane: dam, 2-y-o 6f winner and third in Cork And Orrery, sister to smart 1990
2-y-o Mujtahid: much better effort in maidens when fourth to Oude at Newmarket:
possibly amiss at Sandown: should stay 1m. *Saeed bin Suroor*

DAHTEER (IRE)   2 b.g. (Feb 10) Bachir (IRE) 118 – Reematna 75 (Sabrehill (USA)   **91**
120) [2004 6g⁴ 6f* 6.1m* 7d⁶ 7g 6.1s² 7g³ 6s³ 6g Oct 8] quite good-topped gelding: first
foal: dam, disappointing maiden (might have proved best at 7f/1m), half-sister to Derby
Italiano winner Morshdi: fairly useful performer: won maiden at Brighton in May and
minor event at Chepstow in June: some creditable efforts, including in nursery, after:
probably stays 7f: acts on firm and soft going: visored (below form) fifth outing: gelded
after final one. *M. R. Channon*

DAIMAJIN (IRE)   5 b.g. Dr Devious (IRE) 127 – Arrow Field (USA) (Sunshine   **54 d**
Forever (USA)) [2004 76, a–: f8.5g* f8.5g f8.5s⁵ f12s⁴ f11s 9.9d 10v 8.1v f9.4m 8m
10.1m 8.2d 8g 11.5m 13f⁶ 10f 8m 9.3m p10g 6m Sep 25] modest performer nowadays:
won seller at Wolverhampton in January: left Miss Gay Kelleway after second outing:

mainly well below form subsequently: stays 1¼m: acts on all-weather, soft and good to firm ground: tried in headgear/tongue tied. *Mrs Lucinda Featherstone*

DAINTREE AFFAIR (IRE)   4 b.g. Charnwood Forest (IRE) 125 – Madam Loving 99 (Vaigly Great 127) [2004 66: f5g p5.1g p5g p5.1g Dec 31] little form in 2004: headstrong. *Mrs H. Sweeting*   **–**

DAISY BUCKET   2 b.f. (Feb 8) Lujain (USA) 119 – Masrora (USA) 71 (Woodman (USA) 126) [2004 7g 7m³ 7s* 7g 8d p8.6g⁵ p8.6g⁵ Dec 6] lengthy filly: first foal: dam, maiden (seemed to stay 1½m), out of half-sister to Irish 1000 Guineas winner Trusted Partner: modest performer: won maiden at Brighton in August, wandering/flashing tail: below form after: stays 7f: acts on soft and good to firm going: tried visored. *D. M. Simcock*   **63**

DAISY FOREVER   4 b.f. My Best Valentine 122 – Seymour Ann (Krayyan 117) [2004 p7g Dec 29] half-sister to several winners, including fairly useful 7f (at 2 yrs) and 1¼m winner Captain's Day (by Ballacashtal): dam unraced: 40/1, slowly away and always behind in maiden at Lingfield. *A. P. Jones*   **–**

DAISY POOTER (IRE)   2 b.f. (May 2) Charnwood Forest (IRE) 125 – Idrak 68 (Young Generation 129) [2004 6d p6g³ Dec 27] €8,000F: rather leggy filly: half-sister to several winners, including 7f winner Marguerite Bay (by Darshaan): dam 5f winner: better effort when third in claimer at Wolverhampton: likely to stay 7f. *T. D. Barron*   **57**

DAISYS GIRL   2 b.f. (Jan 21) Inchinor 119 – Andbell (Trojan Fen 118) [2004 6g 5g⁶ 5m⁶ 6d³ Oct 18] 8,500Y: lengthy filly: half-sister to fairly useful but ungenuine 7f to 1¼m winner Willoughby's Boy (by Night Shift) and winner in Norway by Mango Express: dam of little account: modest maiden: should stay 7f: best effort on good to soft going: blinkered penultimate start: tends to get behind. *B. Hanbury*   **52**

DALDINI   2 b.g. (Apr 1) Josr Algarhoud (IRE) 118 – Arianna Aldini (Habitat 134) [2004 6m⁴ 6.1s* 6g² 7s Oct 23] 14,000F, 25,000Y: leggy gelding: half-brother to several winners, including 6-y-o Armagnac and 6f to 1m winner Langtry Lady (by Pas de Seul): dam unraced: fairly useful performer: won maiden at Chepstow in September: good second to Ingleton at York, much better effort in nurseries after: edgy final start (gelded after): should stay 7f: acts on soft ground. *J. A. Osborne*   **85**

DALIDA   3 ch.f. Pursuit of Love 124 – Debutante Days 83 (Dominion 123) [2004 59: f8s 7g⁵ 8s⁵ 7m 7.9f f8g Dec 1] tall, leggy filly: modest maiden: should stay at least 1m: acts on good to soft going. *P. C. Haslam*   **51**

DALISAY (IRE)   3 b.f. Sadler's Wells (USA) 132 – Dabiliya (Vayrann 133) [2004 –p: 10m³ 10m³ p12g² p13g⁶ Oct 1] rangy filly: has scope: fair maiden, lightly raced: will stay 1¾m: acts on good to firm ground and polytrack: carried head high and found little final start: sent to USA. *Sir Michael Stoute*   **76**

DALIYA (IRE)   2 b.f. (May 9) Giant's Causeway (USA) 132 – Dalara (IRE) 114 (Doyoun 124) [2004 7.1m⁶ 6d² Oct 4] leggy filly: seventh foal: half-sister to very smart 1m (at 2 yrs) to 1¾m winner Daliapour and useful 1½m/1¾m winner Dalaram (both by Sadler's Wells) and smart but untrustworthy 1½m and 2m winner Dalampour (by Shernazar): dam, won Prix de Royallieu and stayed 15.5f, closely related to Darshaan: better effort in maidens when second at Windsor: bred to be suited by 1¼m/1½m: blinkered (gave trouble beforehand) on debut, visored next time: hung left both starts. *Sir Michael Stoute*   **70**

DALKEYS LASS   3 gr.f. Wolfhound (USA) 126 – Dalkey Sound (Crash Course 128) [2004 8.3f 9.2f⁴ 9.2d Aug 23] sixth foal: dam staying chaser: little sign of ability. *Mrs L. B. Normile*   **–**

DALLAAH   3 b.f. Green Desert (USA) 127 – Saeedah 75 (Bustino 136) [2004 94: 5m⁶ Jun 12] leggy, close-coupled filly: fluent mover: fairly useful performer at 2 yrs: well held only outing in 2004. *M. A. Jarvis*   **–**

DALLINGTON BROOK   5 b.g. Bluegrass Prince (IRE) 110 – Valetta (Faustus (USA) 118) [2004 6m Apr 25] no sign of ability in bumpers/seller. *Dr J. R. J. Naylor*   **–**

DALLOOL   3 b.c. Unfuwain (USA) 131 – Sardonic 105 (Kris 135) [2004 12d⁵ 11.9d* 11.9d⁴ 11.9d⁴ 11.9g* 12d a9f Dec 16] 55,000Y: good-topped colt: fourth foal: half-brother to useful 7f (in UAE) to 10.5f winner Muwassi (by Grand Lodge) and 7f winner Satyr (by Pursuit of Love): dam, 1¼m winner, daughter of smart performer up to 13f Sardegna: fairly useful performer: won maiden at Haydock (hung right) in April and handicap there in August: ran poorly last 2 starts, leaving M. Jarvis before final one: **90**

should prove at least as effective at 1¼m as 1½m: acts on good to soft going: races up with pace. *D. J. Selvaratnam, UAE*

DALMARNOCK (IRE) 3 ch.g. Grand Lodge (USA) 125 – Lochbelle 70 (Robellino   **56 ?** (USA) 127) [2004 9g 8.5g 8m⁵ Jul 25] big, good-topped gelding: seemingly best effort in maidens on final start. *B. Smart*

DALON (POL) 5 b.g. Winds of Light (USA) 93 – Dikte (POL) (Babant (GER)) [2004   **49** 9.7s f12d⁶ 16.4g p12.2g Nov 26] Polish-bred gelding: poor performer: has won 3 times in Poland, including twice in 2003: stays 1½m: blinkered last 3 outings. *D. B. Feek*

DALPE 3 ch.g. Siphon (BRZ) 130 – Double Stake (USA) (Kokand (USA)) [2004 f11g⁶   **–** Dec 16] 4/1 and tongue tied, well beaten in maiden at Southwell. *H. Morrison*

DALRIATH 5 b.m. Fraam 114 – Alsiba 68 (Northfields (USA)) [2004 ?: f7g f11g⁶   **45** f7g⁶ f8g⁴ f8m² f8m* f8g² 8f⁵ 8m 12d³ f8g⁵ 12m² 12.1m 12.3g f12s⁴ Aug 23] rangy, angular mare: poor performer: won banded event at Southwell in May: effective at 1m to 1½m: acts on fibresand, good to firm and good to soft going: none too consistent. *M. C. Chapman*

DALYAN (IRE) 7 b.g. Turtle Island (IRE) 123 – Salette 110 (Sallust 134) [2004 –:   **–** 8.5m May 24] lightly raced and well held since 2001. *A. J. Lockwood*

DAMASK DANCER (IRE) 5 b.g. Baratbea (IRE) 127 – Polish Rhythm (IRE) 77   **–** (Polish Patriot (USA) 128) [2004 55: p10g p12.2g p10g Dec 20] maiden: no form in 2004: wears blinkers/cheekpieces. *J. A. Supple*

DAMBURGER XPRESS 2 b.c. (Apr 9) Josr Algarhoud (IRE) 118 – Upping The   **69** Tempo (Dunbeath (USA) 127) [2004 7m⁶ p7.1g² p7.1g⁶ Dec 1] 20,000Y: sixth foal: half-brother to 4-y-o Hey Presto and to winner in Turkey by Forzando: dam unraced half-sister to useful sprinter Up And At 'em: best effort in maidens when third at Wolverhampton second start: carried head awkwardly final outing: needs to settle to stay beyond 7f. *D. M. Simcock*

DAME DE NOCHE 4 b.f. Lion Cavern (USA) 117 – Goodnight Kiss 109 (Night   **93** Shift (USA)) [2004 102: 8d⁶ 7.6d 7m³ 7g 6f 6m 5m⁵ 6m³ 6g 5g 5g* 6m⁴ p7g⁴ Oct 28] lengthy, workmanlike filly: fairly useful performer: won minor event at Sandown in September: has won at 1m, best efforts at 5f to 7f: acts on polytrack and firm going: sometimes flashes tail. *J. G. Given*

DAME MARGARET 4 ch.f. Elmaamul (USA) 125 – Pomorie (IRE) 67§ (Be My   **–** Guest (USA) 126) [2004 49: f12g⁵ p12g Feb 23] maiden handicapper: well held in 2004: tends to race freely. *J. A. B. Old*

DAME NOVA (IRE) 3 b.f. Definite Article 121 – Red Note (Rusticaro (FR) 124)   **–** [2004 –: 6s 9.3f⁶ f12d 12.1m 10f Sep 13] tall, quite good-topped filly: little form: slowly away last 2 outings. *P. C. Haslam*

DAMI (USA) 3 b.f. Dynaformer (USA) – Trampoli (USA) 115 (Trempolino (USA)   **83** 135) [2004 70: 8.3m⁵ 11.5f⁵ 8f² 8.1m² 10f* 8.5f* 10g⁵ 10.1g⁵ 10g Oct 2] good-topped filly: fairly useful handicapper: won at Brighton in June and Epsom in July: good efforts last 3 starts: effective at 1m to 11.5f: raced only on good going or firmer: usually wears cheekpieces: reliable. *C. E. Brittain*

DAMSON (IRE) 2 b.f. (Apr 21) Entrepreneur 123 – Tadkiyra (IRE) (Darshaan   **113** 133) [2004 5d* 6m* 5f* 6m* 6g³ Sep 30]
    The Pascal Bary-trained Divine Proportions was the best of her age and sex in Europe but Damson wasn't that far behind, notching two pattern events, including when emulating the French filly by beating the colts in the Independent Waterford Wedgwood Phoenix Stakes. Unlike Divine Proportions, Damson did not remain unbeaten, but she lost little caste in defeat in the Cheveley Park Stakes on her final start. The sturdy and attractive Damson is the type to train on, and, as she will stay at least a mile and has a good turn of foot, she remains a leading candidate for the One Thousand Guineas. Damson's campaign began in mid-April with victory in a five-runner maiden at Cork—she started third favourite—and continued with a smooth two-length defeat of Pictavia in the listed Swordlestown Stud Sprint Stakes over six furlongs at Naas in early-June. Trainer David Wachman straight away stated that Royal Ascot was not on Damson's schedule, but in a rapid about-turn she lined up for the seventeen-runner Queen Mary Stakes at the Royal meeting nine days later, starting joint favourite with once-raced maiden winner Soar in a field containing twelve other winners. The Queen Mary, like the Coventry Stakes,

*Queen Mary Stakes, Royal Ascot—Damson stamps herself as the best
early-season two-year-old filly and gives trainer David Wachman his first Royal Ascot winner;
chasing in vain are Soar, Sharplaw Star and Bunditten (partially hidden near rail)*

was being contested as a Group 2 race for the first time since 1983, an elevation in status which is easier to understand than some which have been instituted over the years. Since 1990, the Queen Mary has been won by the champion two-year-old fillies Gay Gallanta, Blue Duster, Bint Allayl, Queen's Logic and Attraction. Three of that quintet also picked up the Cheveley Park Stakes, as did another winner Marling, while Lyric Fantasy, successful in 1992, landed the Nunthorpe Stakes. Additionally, the Queen Mary is alone among British and Irish pattern races for two-year-olds in having had at least ten runners every year since 1990, with an average of fifteen. The Coventry Stakes is the only one to come close to that,

*Independent Waterford Wedgwood Phoenix Stakes, the Curragh—
Damson enhances her reputation, proving too good for the colts Oratorio (left)
and Russian Blue (spotted cap) and ending Aidan O'Brien's domination of the event*

though in recent years the Flying Childers Stakes, Norfolk Stakes and Rockfel Stakes have all maintained a good average.

The Queen Mary was a plum race, both in quality and competitiveness, so it was appropriate that it fell to Damson. Damson was sweating and taken down steadily and, initially, the return to five furlongs looked like seriously compromising her chances as she was taken off her feet early on after being slightly hampered leaving her stall. Damson had only two behind her at halfway, but when she finally found her stride, weaving through her rivals in eye-catching fashion, she stormed into the lead just inside the final furlong and, despite changing her legs and stumbling slightly, had the race by the scruff of the neck. She passed the post three lengths clear of Soar, eased as her rider celebrated. On the strength of this, Damson was made 20/1 favourite for the One Thousand Guineas. As a point of interest, there was talk after the race that Wachman had a better filly at home in the shape of Intriguing, also successful in a maiden race at Cork. For various reasons, Intriguing, who certainly looked promising and has been rated with a large 'P', was not seen out again, missing the Lowther Stakes among other races. One thing is certain though—Intriguing will have to be pretty smart to surpass her stable-companion, whose Guineas odds contracted to 8/1 after her next performance, in the Phoenix Stakes at the Curragh in early-August. Fillies seemed to have lost the habit of winning the Phoenix Stakes, with Eva Luna in 1994 providing the only success from more than fifty runners from 1990 to 2003. It was very different in the previous thirty years, when nineteen fillies landed the race. Backed as if defeat was out of the question and going off at 11/8-on, Damson did her bit to redress the balance, duly adding her name to the list. For one reason or another (lack of potential reward clearly was not one of them, given the first prize of £111,656), there were no

Mrs John Magnier and Mr M. Tabor's "Damson"

British-trained runners and only two of the five that took Damson on looked to have adequate credentials for a Group 1 race. Both were trained by Aidan O'Brien— Railway Stakes runner-up Russian Blue and Oratorio, successful in the Anglesey Stakes. Damson justified the confidence placed in her but not without having to work harder than previously. Tracking the pace before being pushed on over a furlong out, she kept on to get the better of Oratorio by three quarters of a length, with Russian Blue half a length away third. Predictably, Damson started a hot favourite for the Cheveley Park Stakes at Newmarket at the end of September on her next start. However, she did not take the eye beforehand and, after looking likely to win entering the Dip, proved unable to find extra and finished half a length third to Magical Romance. A possible explanation for a below-par effort was that she had been on the go for a long time.

		Entrepreneur (b 1994)	Sadler's Wells (b 1981)	Northern Dancer Fairy Bridge
Damson (IRE) (b.f. Apr 21, 2002)			Exclusive Order (ch 1979)	Exclusive Native Bonavista
		Tadkiyra (IRE) (b 1989)	Darshaan (br 1981)	Shirley Heights Delsy
			Tremogia (b 1971)	Silver Shark Tonnera III

Damson was bought for €160,000 as a yearling at Goffs; the figure would surely have been considerably higher had she been from her sire Entrepreneur's first crop, which averaged 71,275 guineas at auction and included seventeen lots who sold for 100,000 guineas or more. The Two Thousand Guineas winner looked a fine stallion prospect when retired at the end of his truncated classic campaign in 1997 and was popular enough, getting an average of one hundred foals each year in four seasons at Coolmore. However, his early runners performed with little distinction and his yearlings averaged only 18,000 guineas in 2002 and 12,126 guineas in 2003, by which time he had been packed off to Japan, to some extent another victim of the slings and arrows of outrageous overproduction. Damson is his second Group 1 winner following Vintage Tipple, successful in the 2003 Irish Oaks. Damson comes from a family which served the Aga Khan well, since her unraced grandam Tremogia was a daughter of Prix Saint-Alary winner Tonnera III and produced three pattern winners including Tashtiya (Princess Royal Stakes) and Tassmoun (Prix Messidor). There is no shortage of stamina here. One of Tremogia's daughters produced Tiraaz, successful in the Prix Royal-Oak, and Damson's dam Tadkiyra notched a small race over a mile and a quarter in France. Her two winners before Damson both stayed that distance too. First came Prestige Stakes winner and Musidora Stakes runner-up Geminiani (by another son of Sadler's Wells, King of Kings), then three-year-old Motorway (by Night Shift), successful in a mile-and-a-quarter maiden at Windsor in the summer. The yearling is by King Charlemagne. Further back in the family there is plenty of speed in the shape of Prix de l'Abbaye winners Texana and Texanita, but Damson, who has won on firm and good to soft going, is probably no specialist sprinter herself. *D. Wachman, Ireland*

DANAATT (USA) 2 b.f. (May 18) Gulch (USA) – Agama (USA) 44 (Nureyev (USA) 131) [2004 6g Sep 3] compact filly: half-sister to several winners, including useful 1997 2-y-o 7f/1m winner Setteen (by Robellino) and 3-y-o Waaedah: dam, poor form both starts in Britain, 13.5f winner in France: 33/1, last in maiden at Kempton: sold 3,200 gns, joined K. Burke. *M. P. Tregoning* –

DANAKIL 9 b.g. Warning 136 – Danilova (USA) (Lyphard (USA) 132) [2004 88: p10g p12g 12g 12s 11.9m² 12g⁴ p12g* 12m² 12d² 11.9f⁴ 12d⁶ 12g 12f Sep 24] small gelding: unimpressive mover: fairly useful handicapper: won amateur event at Lingfield in May: stays 1½m: acts on all-weather, firm and soft going: visored (below par) once: usually held up: sometimes hangs. *S. Dow* 81

DANAKIM 7 b.g. Emarati (USA) 74 – Kangra Valley 56 (Indian Ridge 123) [2004 43: f5g⁶ f5g* f6g f5g f5s⁴ f5g f5m 6.1m* 6m⁵ 6g 6g 6.1s 6m 5m 5f⁴ 6m² 5g 6g 6m⁴ 6d 6s³ Oct 30] lengthy, good-quartered gelding: modest performer: won banded event at Southwell in February and seller at Nottingham in May: best at 5f/6f: acts on fibresand and any turf going: tried blinkered: has been early to post/refused to enter stall: races prominently: unreliable. *J. R. Weymes* 54 §

DANCE ANTHEM 2 ch.c. (Feb 22) Royal Academy (USA) 130 – Statua (IRE) 98 **87**
(Statoblest 120) [2004 5d* 6f² 6f 5s Jul 17] 8,500Y: smallish, useful-looking colt: second
foal: dam, 1m winner in USA (third in Rockfel Stakes at 2 yrs), half-sister to useful 7f to
9f performer Bluegrass Prince: fairly useful performer: won maiden at Musselburgh in
May: good second in minor event at Yarmouth, best effort after: should stay 7f: sold
11,000 gns, sent to Saudi Arabia. *M. G. Quinlan*

DANCE AWAY 2 ch.f. (Feb 11) Pivotal 124 – Dance On 93 (Caerleon (USA) 132) **94**
[2004 5g² 5d* 5.2g 6s⁵ Sep 18] small filly: has a quick action: first foal: dam, 5f winner
(ran only at 2 yrs), out of Lowther winner Dance Sequence: fairly useful performer: won
maiden at York in May by 4 lengths: much better effort after when respectable fifth in
Firth of Clyde Stakes at Ayr: should stay 6f. *M. L. W. Bell*

DANCE FLOWER (IRE) 2 b.f. (Feb 11) Cape Cross (IRE) 129 – Ninth Wonder **82**
(USA) (Forty Niner (USA)) [2004 6g² 6m³ 6f⁵ 6.5m⁴ 8f² 7g Oct 2] €12,500F, 58,000Y:
leggy filly: second foal: dam unraced close relative to smart UAE sprinter Conroy out of
Rockfel/Nell Gwyn winner Crystal Gazing: fairly useful maiden: went lame final start:
stays 1m: acts on firm going. *M. R. Channon*

DANCE IN THE SUN 4 b.f. Halling (USA) 133 – Sunny Davis (USA) 71 (Alydar **94**
(USA)) [2004 91: p10g⁶ p12g⁴ p10g² p10g* Mar 19] lengthy filly: fairly useful performer: won handicap at Lingfield in March: effective at 1¼m/1½m: acts on polytrack and
firm ground: consistent: reportedly covered by Vision of Night. *Mrs A. J. Perrett*

DANCEINTHEVALLEY (IRE) 2 b.c. (Mar 16) Imperial Ballet (IRE) 110 – Danc- **–**
ing Willma (IRE) (Dancing Dissident (USA)) 119) [2004 5g 5f Jul 16] well held in
maidens. *G. A. Swinbank*

DANCE LIGHT (IRE) 5 b.m. Lycius (USA) 124 – Embracing 91 (Reference Point **64**
139) [2004 –: p16g 16.1m 19.1f⁵ 16.2d³ 21g 16g 16g⁵ 15.8g Oct 5] angular mare: modest
performer: stays 2m: acts on firm and good to soft going: visored (ran poorly) final outing. *T. T. Clement*

DANCE NIGHT (IRE) 2 b.c. (Mar 27) Danehill Dancer (IRE) 117 – Tiger Wings **104**
(IRE) (Thatching 131) [2004 5g² 5d* 5.1d* 5m⁶ 6.3f 5g⁶ 5s* 6m 5d³ Sep 17] €13,000F,
16,500Y: good-bodied colt: third foal: dam, well beaten in Ireland, out of half-sister to
dam of 5-y-o Mr Dinos: useful performer: won maiden at Beverley in April, minor event
at Chester in May and listed race at York (beat Moscow Music by 1½ lengths) in August:
creditable third to Prince Charming in listed race at Ayr: will prove best at 5f/easy 6f: acts
on soft ground: sold 70,000 gns. *B. A. McMahon*

DANCE ON THE TOP 6 ch.g. Caerleon (USA) 132 – Fern 100 (Shirley Heights **81**
130) [2004 87: p8g* p8g* p7g 8f⁶ p8g⁵ 8f 8.5g 8g Sep 20] close-coupled, good-topped **a103**
gelding: poor mover: useful handicapper on all-weather, fairly useful on turf: won at
Lingfield in January and February, beating Linning Wine by 1¾ lengths in latter: has form
at 1½m, but probably best around 1m: acts on polytrack and firm going: tried visored,
tongue tied nowadays: often front runner. *J. R. Boyle*

DANCE PARTY (IRE) 4 b.f. Charnwood Forest (IRE) 125 – Society Ball 72 (Law **71**
Society (USA) 130) [2004 67: p10g³ p12g³ p10g 10.3g 12d⁴ 10m p10d 11.6f 9.9m p8.6g
Oct 9] good-topped filly: modest maiden handicapper: left A. Balding after eighth start:
stays easy 1½m: acts on polytrack, good to firm and good to soft ground: wore cheekpieces sixth to eighth outings, blinkered (below form) final one. *M. W. Easterby*

DANCER KING (USA) 3 b.g. King of Kings (IRE) 125 – Tigresa (USA) (Tejano **55**
(USA)) [2004 7d⁵ 8g 7m 8s³ 9.9d 13.1s⁶ f8d⁴ Dec 21] good-bodied gelding: modest
maiden: should stay 1¼m: acts on soft ground: tried blinkered. *T. P. Tate*

DANCER'S SERENADE (IRE) 2 b.g. (Mar 7) Almutawakel 126 – Dance Serenade **64**
(IRE) 54 (Marju (IRE) 127) [2004 7.2d³ 7d⁵ 7g 10m Sep 28] €27,000Y: good-topped
gelding: third foal: dam, Irish maiden, half-sister to smart Irish performer up to 1¼m
Pre-Eminent: modest maiden: should stay 1¼m: best efforts on good to soft ground: hung
left third start. *T. P. Tate*

DANCES IN TIME 4 b.f. Danetime (IRE) 121 – Yo-Cando (IRE) 64 (Cyrano de Ber- **43**
gerac 120) [2004 f9.4g f7g⁵ f6g p6g f5s f7s³ f6s Mar 30] third foal: half-sister to fair 2000
2-y-o 5f winner Candothat (by Thatching): dam 2-y-o 6f winner: poor maiden: raced only
on all-weather: blinkered last 2 outings. *C. N. Kellett*

DANCES WITH ANGELS (IRE) 4 b.f. Mukaddamah (USA) 125 – Lady of Leisure **46**
(USA) 76 (Diesis 133) [2004 46: p10g p12g 11.9g³ 12.1m 14.1m 10.9m 10m 8.1s⁶ 10.2s⁴
12s⁵ f12g³ f11d Dec 21] leggy filly: poor maiden: left Mrs A. King after seventh start:
stays 1½m: acts on fibresand, firm and soft going: tried in cheekpieces. *J. W. Unett*

DANCE TO MY TUNE   3 b.f. Halling (USA) 133 – Stolen Melody 74 (Robellino   **76** (USA) 127) [2004 58: f8g⁶ 8s* 8m 9.3f⁴ 10g* 10g² 10f⁴ 10.9s² 11.9g⁴ Oct 8] big, work-manlike filly: fair handicapper: won at Newcastle in May and Nottingham in August: stays 1½m: acts on firm and soft going: visored (ran respectably) final outing in 2003. *M. W. Easterby*

DANCE TO THE BLUES (IRE)   3 br.f. Danehill Dancer (IRE) 117 – Blue Sioux   **60** 69 (Indian Ridge 123) [2004 5.1m 5.1g³ 5m* 5g Aug 22] leggy filly: fourth foal: dam 5f winner: easily best effort when winning maiden at Folkestone in August: raced only at 5f: acts on good to firm going. *B. De Haan*

DANCE WORLD   4 b.g. Spectrum (IRE) 126 – Dansara (Dancing Brave (USA) 140)   **96** [2004 f12g* 12g 14.4v³ 10.2g f12m 10g⁵ 12g* 12.6g f11g² f12g* f12g² Dec 28] useful performer: trained at 3 yrs by M. Zilber in France: won maiden at Southwell in April, and handicaps at Folkestone in August and Southwell in December: good second in handicap at Southwell final start: stays 1¾m: acts on fibresand, raced only on good ground or softer on turf. *Miss J. Feilden*

DANCING BAY   7 b.g. Suave Dancer (USA) 136 – Kabayil 75 (Dancing Brave (USA)   **116** 140) [2004 16.2d* 22.2f² 15.9d² 18m³ 20m⁴ 16s⁴ Oct 16] close-coupled gelding: missed 2003, but developed into a smart performer at 7 yrs: fit from hurdling, won handicap at Haydock in June: in frame after in Queen Alexandra Stakes at Royal Ascot (unlucky second to Corrib Eclipse), Lonsdale Cup at York (best effort when neck second to First Charter), Doncaster Cup (third to dead-heaters Millenary and Kasthari), Prix du Cadran at Longchamp (fourth to Westerner) and Jockey Club Cup at Newmarket (fourth to Millenary): stays 2¾m: acts on any going: has been tongue tied (not since 2001): usually held up (has gone in snatches): sometimes edges left, markedly so for last 2 wins. *N. J. Henderson*

DANCING BEAR   3 b.g. Groom Dancer (USA) 128 – Sickle Moon (Shirley Heights   **52** 130) [2004 –: 10.3g⁴ 10g 10.1m³ 12.1m⁴ p12g p9.5d⁴ f8s⁴ p8m⁶ Dec 8] strong, good-topped gelding: modest maiden: stays 1¼m: blinkered last 4 starts. *Julian Poulton*

DANCING DEANO (IRE)   2 b.g. (Mar 20) Second Empire (IRE) 124 – Ultimate   **60** Beat (USA) (Go And Go) [2004 6g 6g⁶ 7g 6m⁵ Oct 10] good-topped gelding: modest maiden: visored, first home stand side when fifth in nursery at Newcastle: should stay 7f: acts on good to firm ground. *R. M. Whitaker*

DANCING DOLPHIN (IRE)   5 b.m. Dolphin Street (FR) 125 – Dance Model (Un-   **–** fuwain (USA) 131) [2004 10.2d³ f12m⁶ 10v⁶ 10m May 25] rangy, angular mare: maiden: missed 2003: little form in 2004: tried visored. *Julian Poulton*

DANCING FOREST (IRE)   4 br.g. Charnwood Forest (IRE) 125 – Fauna (IRE) 65   **59** (Taufan (USA) 119) [2004 69, a75: p8g p10g⁵ Jan 24] just a modest performer in 2004: stays 1¼m: acts on polytrack, soft and good to firm going: has started slowly/raced freely. *D. K. Ivory*

DANCINGINTHECLOUDS (IRE)   2 b.f. (Apr 9) Rainbow Quest (USA) 134 –   **– p** Ballerina (IRE) 88 (Dancing Brave (USA) 140) [2004 8m Sep 21] sixth foal: sister to 7-y-o Millenary and smart 1½m winner Head In The Clouds and half-sister to 3-y-o Let The Lion Roar: dam, 2-y-o 7f winner, half-sister to Princess Royal winner Dancing Bloom and smart dam of Spectrum (by Rainbow Quest): 10/1, eighth in maiden at New-market, late headway: will be well suited by at least 1½m: sure to do better. *J. L. Dunlop*

DANCING KING (IRE)   8 b.g. Fairy King (USA) – Zariysha (IRE) (Darshaan 133)   **52** [2004 58, a–: f8g⁵ p8g f8.5g⁴ f8.5g f7g⁵ f8g² f7s* f8g³ f8.5s* f8g⁵ f8.5s⁴ p8g f7g f7g⁶   **a58** f8.5g² 7.1d⁶ 8.1v² f9.4m⁵ 8m⁵ 7.1g⁵ 8.1m⁵ 8f⁵ p8m p8.6g 8.2v⁶ f7g⁶ f8s f8g Dec 1] lengthy gelding: modest performer: won banded race and handicap at Wolverhampton in February: stays 8.5f: acts on any turf going and fibresand, well held on polytrack: races prominently. *P. W. Hiatt*

DANCING LYRA   3 b.g. Alzao (USA) 117 – Badaayer (USA) 105 (Silver Hawk   **96** (USA) 123) [2004 85: p8g⁶ p10g⁴ 9.9s* 9g² 10.1m⁴ 9.9m 9.7g⁶ 10g 10v⁵ Oct 20] com-pact gelding: has a quick action: useful performer: won maiden at Lingfield in February and handicap at Salisbury (by 8 lengths) in May: below form last 4 outings: stays 1¼m: acts on polytrack, soft and good to firm going: gelded after final start. *J. W. Hills*

DANCING MOONLIGHT (IRE)   2 b.f. (Jan 23) Danehill Dancer (IRE) 117 – Silver Moon (Environment Friend 128) [2004 5g⁶ f7g 6m p5d 6.1g f7g p6g Dec 29] 15,000Y: unfurnished filly: third foal: half-sister to 5-y-o Sorbiesharry: dam little sign of ability: no form in maidens/minor event: tried in cheekpieces. *Mrs N. Macauley*

DAN

DANCING MYSTERY 10 b.g. Beveled (USA) – Batchworth Dancer 67 (Ballacashtal (CAN)) [2004 97: f5g* p5g³ p5g⁵ 5g 5s 5s 5m 5m* 5.5m⁴ 5g⁵ 5.2f 5g 5.2g 5s² 5.1d 5f 5g³ 5s³ f5s⁴ f5g* Dec 7] close-coupled gelding: useful handicapper on all-weather, fairly useful on turf: won at Southwell in January, Salisbury in June and Southwell (beat Magic Glade by 2½ lengths) in December: best at 5f: acts on all-weather and any turf going: usually blinkered: has spoilt chance by rearing in stall: usually races prominently: tough. *E. A. Wheeler* **88 a107**

DANCING PEARL 6 ch.m. Dancing Spree (USA) – Elegant Rose 72 (Noalto 120) [2004 –: 10d 14s⁵ 19.1f 17.2g³ Jul 3] close-coupled mare: modest maiden, lightly raced on Flat: should stay 2m+: acts on soft ground. *C. J. Price* **51**

DANCING PHANTOM 9 b.g. Darshaan 133 – Dancing Prize (IRE) 99 (Sadler's Wells (USA) 132) [2004 83: f12s³ f12g² Feb 5] quite attractive gelding: modest performer: stays 13f: acts on fibresand, heavy and good to firm going: tried visored: sometimes edgy/on toes: free-going sort, and races prominently. *James Moffatt* **63**

DANCING PRINCE (IRE) 3 b.g. Imperial Ballet (IRE) 110 – Eastern Aura (IRE) 49 (Ahonoora 122) [2004 –: p6g⁵ f8g⁴ p7g p7g f7s Mar 18] quite attractive gelding: modest maiden: likely to prove best at 5f/6f: raced only on all-weather/good to firm ground: tried visored: has raced freely. *A. P. Jarvis* **50**

DANCING RIDGE (IRE) 7 b.g. Ridgewood Ben 113 – May We Dance (IRE) 57 (Dance of Life (USA)) [2004 –: f6s 6v f5g⁵ f5m⁶ f5g May 5] good-topped gelding: maiden: no form since 2002: tried visored/in cheekpieces. *A. Senior* **–**

DANCING ROSE (IRE) 2 b.f. (Apr 21) Danehill Dancer (IRE) 117 – Shinkoh Rose (FR) 67 (Warning 136) [2004 5g² 5.1m³ 5.1d* 6f⁵ 6s Sep 24] €14,000F, 32,000Y: leggy filly: fifth foal: sister to 4-y-o Oh So Rosie, closely related to winner abroad by Danehill and half-sister to 3-y-o Vienna's Boy: dam third at 9f in Ireland: fair performer: won maiden at Bath in August: creditable fifth to Tagula Sunrise in sales race at Doncaster: raced alone final start: stays 6f: acts on firm and good to soft going. *C. G. Cox* **74**

DANCING SHIRL 2 b.f. (Feb 13) Dancing Spree (USA) – Shirl 52 (Shirley Heights 130) [2004 7m⁶ 7m³ 8v³ 8g³ Sep 11] good-topped filly: sixth foal: half-sister to 6f winner Waff's Folly (by Handsome Sailor): dam 1½m winner: modest maiden: likely to stay 1¼m: best effort on good going. *C. W. Fairhurst* **54**

DANCING TILLY 6 b.m. Dancing Spree (USA) – L'Ancressaan 67 (Dalsaan 125) [2004 38: f9.4g⁴ f11g² f11g⁴ p10g⁶ 8m⁴ 9.3m* 10m² 10.1d⁶ p9.5g⁵ f11g⁵ Nov 8] leggy mare: modest performer: won banded race at Carlisle in September: stays 11f: acts on all-weather and firm ground: usually wears cheekpieces: hard ride. *R. A. Fahey* **51**

DANCLARE (USA) 3 ch.f. Stravinsky (USA) 133 – Beyond Temptation (USA) (Sunny's Halo (CAN)) [2004 82p: 7g 7m⁶ 8f⁵ 8m⁴ 8f² Dec 17] good-topped filly: fairly useful performer: ran well when 6¾ lengths fifth to Celtic Heroine in listed rated stakes at Royal Ascot: left J. Gosden before second in allowance race at Hollywood final outing: stays 1m: acts on firm going. *P. Gallagher, USA* **88**

DAN DI CANIO (IRE) 3 b.g. Bahri (USA) 125 – Khudud 61 (Green Desert (USA) 127) [2004 8m⁵ 8.3d 8.1g⁵ 8m⁵ 10f 8g Sep 27] sturdy gelding: modest maiden: best efforts at 1m: tongue tied last 3 starts. *P. W. Harris* **59**

DANDOUCE 3 b.f. Danzero (AUS) – Douce Maison (IRE) 67 (Fools Holme (USA)) [2004 70: 7.1s⁶ 7g³ 8.3m⁴ 7g 6g³ p6m 6g Oct 11] lengthy filly: fair maiden: effective at 6f to 1m: acts on polytrack and good to firm going: tried blinkered/visored, better form when not. *P. W. Chapple-Hyam* **72**

DANDOUN 6 b.h. Halling (USA) 133 – Moneefa 73 (Darshaan 133) [2004 117: 9s 8.2v³ 8s p8g Dec 18] useful-looking horse: smart performer at 5 yrs: best effort in 2004 when third in minor event at Nottingham second start: left J. Dunlop 16,000 gns prior to final outing: stays 9f: acts on soft and good to firm going: has worn crossed noseband: often edgy: takes strong hold. *C. A. Dwyer* **92 ?**

DANDYGREY RUSSETT (IRE) 3 gr.f. Singspiel (IRE) 133 – Christian Church (IRE) (Linamix (FR) 127) [2004 8g 8v⁴ 8s⁴ 10d p8.6g³ p10g* p9.5g² Dec 14] 10,000Y, 46,000 2-y-o: close-coupled, workmanlike filly: first foal: dam, French 2-y-o 1m winner, out of half-sister to smart middle-distance stayer Castle Rising: fair performer: won maiden at Lingfield in November: stays 1¼m: acts on polytrack, raced only on good ground or softer on turf. *G. L. Moore* **79**

DANDY JIM 3 b.c. Dashing Blade 117 – Madam Trilby (Grundy 137) [2004 –: f6s f6g⁵ f7s f6g f8s⁵ 8s⁶ f6m f7g 8.5m May 24] little form: blinkered last 3 starts: dead. *D. W. Chapman* **–**

DANEBANK (IRE)   4 b.g. Danehill (USA) 126 – Snow Bank (IRE) (Law Society   **61**
(USA) 130) [2004 63: 10.2s 10g⁵ 12.6g⁴ 12.1m² 13.1d³ 11.9s 12g² 14.1d³ Oct 15] close-
coupled gelding: modest handicapper: won at Warwick in July: stays 1¾m: acts on good
to firm and good to soft ground: tried visored, in cheekpieces last 5 starts. *J. Mackie*

DANECARE (IRE)   4 b.c. Danetime (IRE) 121 – Nordic Flavour (IRE) 84 (Nordico   **99**
(USA)) [2004 94: 5.8d 6d 6m² 6d⁴ 5m⁵ 6m⁴ 7m Aug 1] small colt: useful performer:
below form in minor event at Haydock fourth start: good fifth to Osterhase in listed
race at Naas next time: slipped up final start: best at 5f/6f: acted on soft and good to firm
ground: dead. *James G. Burns, Ireland*

DANEFONIQUE (IRE)   3 b.f. Danetime (IRE) 121 – Umlaut (Zafonic (USA) 130)   **58**
[2004 55: 10.3g 10d³ 10g² 12.1g² 11.8g⁵ 14.1f⁶ p12d 12m⁴ 9.9d 9.9d² 11.9g⁶ 10s p12.2g   **a44**
p12.2g p10m⁶ p10g⁶ Dec 20] small, strong filly: modest maiden on turf, poor on all-
weather: stays 1½m: acts on polytrack, firm and good to soft going: often slowly away
and usually held up. *D. Carroll*

DANEHILL ANGEL   2 ch.f. (Mar 18) Danehill Dancer (IRE) 117 – Ace Girl 58 (Stan-   **38**
ford 121§) [2004 f5d 6m p7.1g Dec 10] 9,000Y: sixth foal: half-sister to 1998 2-y-o 5f
winner Sound's Ace (by Savahra Sound): dam, 1m winner, half-sister to dam of 3-y-o
Milk It Mick: poor form in maidens. *M. J. Polglase*

DANEHILL DAZZLER (IRE)   2 b.f. (Feb 24) Danehill Dancer (IRE) 117 – Finne-   **65 p**
gans Dilemma (IRE) (Marktingo) [2004 7d⁴ Jun 23] €4,000Y: second foal: dam Irish
bumper winner: not-knocked-about fourth to Maids Causeway in maiden at Kempton:
should improve. *A. P. Jarvis*

DANEHILL FAIRY (IRE)   2 b.f. (Mar 28) Danehill Dancer (IRE) 117 – Turntable   **44**
(IRE) 59 (Dolphin Street (FR) 125) [2004 5v 5s² 5m 5g⁶ 5d³ 6f³ 5m³ 6d² 6m 5s⁴ 6d Aug
30] €5,500Y: sturdy, close-coupled filly: first foal: dam, maiden, out of half-sister to very
smart sprinter Greenland Park: poor maiden: effective at 5f/6f: acts on soft and good to
firm ground: usually blinkered/visored. *Mrs A. Duffield*

DANEHILL LAD (IRE)   4 b.g. Danehill (USA) 126 – River Missy (USA) (River-   **–**
man (USA) 131) [2004 62?, a77: p13g Jan 7] leggy, plain gelding: maiden: pulled up only
4-y-o start: dead. *T. Keddy*

DANEHILL STROLLER (IRE)   4 b.g. Danetime (IRE) 121 – Tuft Hill 92 (Grundy   **84**
137) [2004 98: 6m 6f 6m 6m⁴ 5.2f 6m 7m 6g 6g⁵ p7g Nov 16] angular gelding: just fairly
useful in 2004: effective at 5f/6f (raced too freely at 7f): acts on polytrack, good to firm
and good to soft going: usually wears cheekpieces: usually held up. *R. M. Beckett*

DANEHILL WILLY (IRE)   2 b.c. (Mar 17) Danehill Dancer (IRE) 117 – Lowtown   **84**
(Camden Town 125) [2004 5.2m² 7m 7d 7.1d* 8d* 10d Oct 30] €11,000F, 35,000Y: big,
lengthy colt: has scope: has a round action: half-brother to several winners, including
fairly useful 1999 2-y-o 7f winner Mentiga (by Dancing Dissident) and Irish 13f/1¾m
winner Beebeep (by Distinctly North): dam, Irish 1m/9f winner, also successful over
hurdles: fairly useful performer: won nurseries at Warwick in September and Newmarket
(by head from Atlantic Story) in October, getting up late on both times: raced freely when
seventh in listed race at Newmarket final start: stays 1m: best effort on good to soft going.
N. A. Callaghan

DANELISSIMA (IRE)   3 br.f. Danehill (USA) 126 – Zavaleta (IRE) 97 (Kahyasi   **107**
130) [2004 92: 7s⁵ 10m⁴ 9.5m⁴ 12m* 12f² 11.9g³ 12f⁶ 11.9s⁶ Aug 18] sturdy, close-coupled filly:
fourth foal: sister to useful Irish (at 2 yrs)/French 7f winner Daneleta and half-sister to
2 winners, including fairly useful Irish 6.5f winner Benicio (by Spectrum): dam Irish 6f
(at 2 yrs) to 1m winner who stayed 1¼m: useful performer: won Irish Stallion Farms
Noblesse Stakes at Naas in June by ½ length from Summitville: good 1¼ lengths third to
Pongee in Lancashire Oaks at Haydock following month, running on well after being off
bridle long way out: well held last 2 outings in Irish Oaks at the Curragh (clear lead mid-
race) and Yorkshire Oaks at York (looked far from keen): stays 1½m: acts on firm going:
effective blinkered or not, visored final outing: carries head high: sold 470,000 gns in
December. *J. S. Bolger, Ireland*

DANELOR (IRE)   6 b.g. Danehill (USA) 126 – Formulate 119 (Reform 132) [2004   **90**
96: f8.5s⁴ 8g⁵ 10.1m 11.9m 8m⁵ 7.9d 9.2d* 8.3d 10g⁵ 10.1m 8.9g p9.5g⁵ Dec 11] sturdy,
good-bodied gelding: fairly useful handicapper: won at Hamilton in August: stays 1¼m:
acts on all-weather, firm and good to soft going: free-going sort (has been early to post),
and usually races prominently. *R. A. Fahey*

DANE RHAPSODY (IRE)   3 b. or br.f. Danetime (IRE) 121 – Hil Rhapsody 74   **52 ?**
(Anshan 119) [2004 f6g 5.1g⁵ 6m 5m⁵ 7.1s 5.7f⁵ p6g Oct 18] 4,000Y: rather sparely-made
filly: second foal: closely related to an Italian winner around 7f by Danehill: dam 2-y-o 5f

winner: modest maiden: eased as if something was amiss final start: should stay 6f: acts on firm ground: raced freely fifth outing. *B. Palling*

DANE'S CASTLE (IRE) 2 b.g. (Mar 16) Danetime (IRE) 121 – Faypool (IRE) (Fay **83** ruz 116) [2004 6f³ f6m² 5.3m² p6d³ 5.1g³ 5m* p5.1g⁶ p6g⁵ Dec 30] 8,500Y: fourth foal: **a71** half-brother to fairly useful 2001 2-y-o 7f winner Mr Blue Sky (by Blues Traveller) and 2002 2-y-o 6f seller winner Bond Midnight (by Petardia): dam, maiden in Switzerland, half-brother to smart sprinter Croft Pool: fairly useful on turf, fair on all-weather: made all in maiden at Lingfield in October: seems best at 5f: acts on all-weather and good to firm going: blinkered fifth to seventh starts, hanging right on last of them. *B. J. Meehan*

DANESCOURT (IRE) 2 b.c. (Apr 24) Danetime (IRE) 121 – Faye 79 (Monsanto (FR) **62** 121) [2004 p6d⁵ f6s 6m³ Sep 1] €20,000F, 14,000 2-y-o: brother to 3-y-o Commando Scott and half-brother to several winners, including smart Irish 1m/9f winner Wray (by Sharp Victor): dam, 2-y-o 6f winner, later successful in USA: modest form: third in seller at Lingfield: likely to prove best at 5f/6f. *J. A. Osborne*

DANESMEAD (IRE) 3 b.g. Danehill Dancer (IRE) 117 – Indian Honey (Indian King **91** (USA) 128) [2004 98: 7s⁶ 6m 6m Dec 12] rather leggy, useful-looking gelding: useful performer at 2 yrs: best effort in 2004 when sixth in handicap at York on reappearance: left T. Easterby, gelded and renamed Super King before final outing: likely to prove best at 6f/7f: acts on soft and good to firm going. *S. T. Wong, Hong Kong*

DANE'S ROCK (IRE) 2 b.g. (Mar 24) Indian Danehill (IRE) 124 – Cutting Ground **52** (IRE) 85 (Common Grounds 118) [2004 f5g⁴ 6g 5m⁶ 6g² f6d 7s 8v⁴ f8g f6s⁴ f7g² p7.1g⁵ f7g⁶ Dec 14] modest maiden: left P. Haslam after seventh start: stays 7f: acts on fibresand and good to firm going: sometimes blinkered/visored (has run creditably in both). *Mrs H. Sweeting*

DANETHORPE LADY (IRE) 2 b.f. (Apr 1) Brave Act 119 – Annie's Travels (IRE) **40** (Mac's Imp (USA) 116) [2004 5d⁶ 5m⁴ 6.1g Sep 29] 7,000 2-y-o: third living foal: half-sister to 6-y-o Travel Tardia and 4-y-o Sea The World: dam unraced: poor form in maidens/minor event. *D. Shaw*

DANETIME LADY (IRE) 4 b.f. Danetime (IRE) 121 – Hawattef (IRE) (Mujtahid **36** (USA) 118) [2004 60: p9.5g p9.5g Dec 22] maiden: only poor form at Wolverhampton in 2004: stays 9f: tried in cheekpieces/tongue strap. *Niall Moran, Ireland*

DANETTIE 3 b.f. Danzero (AUS) – Petite Heritiere 43 (Last Tycoon 131) [2004 8.1s **61** 9.2f⁵ 8.3g⁴ 12.3s⁵ 7m⁴ 8m p7.1d Nov 5] third foal: dam, maiden, should have stayed 1½m: modest maiden: stays 1m: acts on good to firm ground. *W. M. Brisbourne*

DANGER BIRD (IRE) 4 ch.f. Eagle Eyed (USA) 111 – Danger Ahead (Mill Reef **–** (USA) 141) [2004 42, a55: f9.4g² f9.4g³ f9.4g f9.4g² f8.5s⁴ f9.4g⁴ f9.4g* f7m⁵ f8g **a61** p8.6g⁶ p12.2g p9.5d p8.6g² p8m p10m⁴ p9.5g⁴ Dec 22] leggy filly: modest performer: won handicap at Wolverhampton in April: stays 1¼m: acts on all-weather, raced only on ground firmer than good on turf: wore cheekpieces (ran creditably) once: free-going sort: sometimes flashes tail. *R. Hollinshead*

DANGEROUS BEANS 4 b.g. Bluegrass Prince (IRE) 110 – A Little Hot (Petong **–** 126) [2004 65: p10m p7m p10g Dec 20] well below form in 2004: tried blinkered. *E. A. Wheeler*

DANGEROUS DAVE 5 b.g. Superpower 113 – Lovely Lilly (Arrasas (USA) 100) **–** [2004 –: 7d Oct 2] of little account. *Jamie Poulton*

DANGER ZONE 2 b.c. (Apr 21) Danzero (AUS) – Red Tulle (USA) 66 (A P Indy **69** (USA) 131) [2004 6g 7.6m 7d⁵ 7m p7g³ Sep 18] rangy colt: third foal: dam, third at 1¼m on debut from 3 starts at 3 yrs, half-sister to US Grade 3 8.5f winner Namaqualand: fair maiden: needs to settle to stay 1m: acts on polytrack and good to soft going. *Mrs A. J. Perrett*

DANGLE (IRE) 3 b.f. Desert Style (IRE) 121 – Dawn Chorus (IRE) (Mukaddamah **102 ?** (USA) 125) [2004 89: 7g² 7g* 7d⁴ 6m 7g² 6d⁵ 7.5v⁴ 6d⁵ 6d Oct 14] €25,000Y: third foal: half-sister to useful Irish 7f (at 2 yrs) to 1¼m winner Solid Approach (by Definite Article) and fairly useful 2002 2-y-o 6f winner La Campanella (by Tagula): dam unraced: useful performer: won maiden at Leopardstown in June: best effort when 1½ lengths fifth to Royal Millennium in Renaissance Stakes at the Curragh sixth start: below form in listed race at Newmarket final outing: effective at 6f to 7.5f: acts on heavy ground: blinkered/visored last 2 starts. *Edward Lynam, Ireland*

DANIELLA 2 b.f. (Mar 17) Dansili 127 – Break Point (Reference Point 139) [2004 7g **– p** Oct 1] deep-girthed filly: third foal: half-sister to fairly useful 1¼m winner Play Time (by

Unfuwain): dam once-raced daughter of smart 1¼m winner Cut Loose, herself sister to St Leger winner Cut Above: 66/1 and in need of run, thirteenth of 23 in maiden won by Rob Roy at Newmarket: should do better. *R. Guest*

DANIELLE'S LAD   8 b.g. Emarati (USA) 74 – Cactus Road (FR) (Iron Duke (FR)   **72** 122) [2004 80, a86: f7g⁴ f8.5g² p7g f7s⁴ f8.5s* f8.5g³ 7d f8.5g³ 7g 8g May 19] strong   **a78** gelding: fair handicapper: won at Wolverhampton in March: effective at 7f to 8.5f: acts on fibresand, heavy and good to firm going: often blinkered: sometimes early to post: has edged right. *B. Palling*

DANIEL THOMAS (IRE)   2 b.c. (Jan 29) Dansili 127 – Last Look (Rainbow Quest   **92** (USA) 134) [2004 7m² 6m² 6s³ 7s² p7g* Oct 28] good-topped colt: has a quick action: fourth foal: half-brother to 3 winners, including 1m to 11.5f winner Littlemissattitude (by Common Grounds) and 4-y-o Ultimata: dam, unraced, out of half-sister to Pursuit of Love: fairly useful performer: third behind Rebuttal and Tremar in maiden at Kempton: won similar event at Lingfield comfortably: should stay 1m: acts on polytrack, soft and good to firm going. *Mrs A. J. Perrett*

DANIFAH (IRE)   3 b.f. Perugino (USA) 84 – Afifah 66 (Nashwan (USA) 135) [2004   **77** 69d: p7g 5.1g 5.7m 6.1g 6.1m⁴ 6m 5.1f 8m⁴ 8.1m⁴ 8m⁶ 7.1s* 6g* 6m³ 7m 8.1s* 6m 8g 7g p7.1d Nov 5] leggy, close-coupled filly: fair handicapper: won at Chepstow and Folkestone in August and Chepstow in September: below form last 4 starts: effective at 6f to 1m: acts on firm and soft going: tried blinkered: usually races up with pace: has looked none too genuine. *P. D. Evans*

DANI RIDGE (IRE)   6 b.m. Indian Ridge 123 – Daniella Drive (USA) (Shelter Half   **91** (USA)) [2004 92: 6d⁴ 5m 6m⁴ 5.1g⁶ 6m Jul 17] good-topped mare: fairly useful handicapper: effective at 6f/7f: acts on polytrack and any turf going. *E. J. Alston*

DANISH MONARCH   3 b.g. Great Dane (IRE) 122 – Moly 64 (Inchinor 119) [2004   **62 d** 79: 8d 7m 6.1m³ 7g 7.1m 6.1d⁶ 6m 7m f6g p7.1g Dec 22] leggy gelding: modest maiden: below form after third start: stays 7.5f: acts on good to firm going. *A. D. W. Pinder*

DANITA DANCER (IRE)   2 b.f. (Apr 24) Barathea (IRE) 127 – Carranita (IRE) 111   **–** (Anita's Prince 126) [2004 8.2m 8g Oct 12] leggy, good-topped filly: third foal: dam 5f/6f winner, including at 2 yrs: well held in maidens. *B. Palling*

D'ANJOU   7 b.g. Marju (IRE) 127 – Rose de Thai (USA) 99 (Lear Fan (USA) 130)   **113** [2004 113: 8m* 8m⁶ a8f 8d* 8g 8f⁶ Jun 27] smart performer: won Group 3 Al Fahidi Fort at Nad Al Sheba in February by 2¼ lengths from One More Round and listed race at Leopardstown in May by ½ length from Meath: below form after: effective at 7f to 1m: acts on firm and good to soft going, ran poorly on dirt debut third start: blinkered once (in 2002). *J. Oxx, Ireland*

DANNY LEAHY (FR)   4 b.g. Danehill (USA) 126 – Paloma Bay (IRE) 92 (Alzao   **63** (USA) 117) [2004 69: f12f⁵ 16.1v 18v Apr 6] strong, good-bodied gelding: modest maiden: stays 1¼m: acts on fibresand and good to firm ground. *M. D. Hammond*

DAN'S HEIR   2 b.g. (Jan 18) Dansili 127 – Million Heiress (Auction Ring (USA) 123)   **56** [2004 5m 7f² 7m 7m² f7g 7m f8g Nov 9] sturdy gelding: modest maiden: stays 7f: acts on firm going: usually wears cheekpieces. *P. C. Haslam*

DANTE'S BATTLE (IRE)   12 b.g. Phardante (FR) 123 – No Battle (Khalkis 127)   **–** [2004 f12m Jul 12] has run only 6 times on Flat: won amateur minor event at Bellewstown in 2000: left N. Meade in Ireland after only start in 2002: well held only 12-y-o start. *Miss K. Marks*

DANTE'S DEVINE (IRE)   3 b.g. Ashkalani (IRE) 128 – Basilea (FR) (Frere Basile   **54** (FR) 129) [2004 63: f9.4g f6s⁶ 8.1s⁵ 8m f8.5g⁴ f7g 6g 7m* 8d² f8g⁴ Dec 1] strong, angular gelding: modest performer: won banded race at Kempton in September: stays 1m: acts on good to firm and good to soft ground: none too reliable. *A. Bailey*

DANTE'S DIAMOND (IRE)   2 b.c. (Mar 25) Orpen (USA) 116 – Flower From   **73** Heaven (Baptism 119) [2004 5.1g² 5g² 6.1s⁵ 5m⁵ 6.1g 7.1d⁴ 7s⁵ 7s Nov 6] €7,000F, €20,000Y: rangy colt: half-brother to several winners, including fairly useful Irish 9f/1¼m winner Angel From Heaven (by Bob Back): dam Irish sprinter: fair maiden: stays 7f: acts on soft going, probably on good to firm: often races up with pace. *F. Jordan*

DANUM   4 b.g. Perpendicular 119 – Maid of Essex 66 (Bustino 136) [2004 59: f11g⁴   **55** f9.4s⁵ f11s p12.2g f11g⁶ p9.5g³ Dec 22] strong, deep-girthed gelding: modest maiden: stays 1¼m: acts on fibresand, soft and good to firm going: usually wears cheekpieces. *R. Hollinshead*

DANZARE 2 b.f. (Feb 12) Dansili 127 – Shot of Redemption (Shirley Heights 130) **61 p**
[2004 7g p8.6g⁴ Oct 7] 11,000Y: fourth foal: half-sister to minor winners in USA by
Brocco and Quest For Fame: dam ran 3 times in USA: modest form in maidens at Kempton (slowly away) and Wolverhampton (hampered early): open to improvement.
M. P. Tregoning

DANZATRICE 2 b.f. (Apr 19) Tamure (IRE) 125 – Miss Petronella (Petoski 135) **59**
[2004 5g 6s⁵ 8s⁵ Oct 30] lengthy, unfurnished filly: sixth foal: sister to 3-y-o Lets Roll:
dam unraced: best effort in maidens at Haydock second start: should be suited by 1¼m/
1½m. *C. W. Thornton*

DANZE ROMANCE 3 b.f. Danzero (AUS) – By Arrangement (IRE) 60 (Bold **62**
Arrangement 127) [2004 8g 9f 8.3m⁵ 9.9g⁴ 11.9s 10v Nov 4] workmanlike filly: fourth
foal: half-sister to 5-y-o Turbo and 1½m winner Its Your Bid (by Dilum): dam 1m to 2m
winner: modest maiden: stays 1¼m: best efforts on good going. *J. L. Dunlop*

DANZIG RIVER (IRE) 3 b.g. Green Desert (USA) 127 – Sahara Breeze 85 **101**
(Ela-Mana-Mou 132) [2004 95: 6d² 6m 6m 6m 5m 6g 6.1g⁴ 6s⁶ 6g 6s² Oct 22] big,
good-bodied gelding: useful handicapper: best effort when head second to Saristar at
Newmarket on reappearance: probably best around 6f: acts on firm and soft going: sold
47,000 gns, then gelded. *B. W. Hills*

DANZIG STAR 4 b.f. Danzig Connection (USA) – Julie's Star (IRE) 45 (Thatching **–**
131) [2004 f8.5g⁶ Feb 2] little sign of ability. *P. R. Chamings*

DANZILI BAY 2 b.c. (Jan 30) Dansili 127 – Lady Bankes (IRE) 69 (Alzao (USA) **80**
117) [2004 5.1f⁴ 5.1m⁴ 5f* 5m Sep 27] 30,000F, 38,000Y: fourth foal: half-brother to
fairly useful 6f (at 2 yrs) to 1m winner Moten Swing (by Kris): dam, 1¼m winner, half-
sister to smart performer up to 1¼m Circle of Gold: fairly useful performer: won maiden
at Redcar in September, best effort: not knocked about final start: should stay 6f.
R. M. Beckett

DAPHNE'S DOLL (IRE) 9 b.m. Polish Patriot (USA) 128 – Helietta 78 (Tyrnavos **–**
129) [2004 38, a–: p8g Mar 29] big mare: well held only 9-y-o start: tried visored/in
cheekpieces. *Dr J. R. J. Naylor*

Lady O Goodwood Cup, Goodwood—
Darasim, Royal Rebel (light cap) and Double Obsession (rail) provide trainer Mark Johnston
with a 1,2,4 to continue his good record in the race; Misternando is third

Mr Markus Graff's "Darasim"

DARAB (POL) 4 ch.g. Alywar (USA) – Damara (POL) (Pyjama Hunt 126) [2004 10f 10m Sep 28] Polish-bred gelding: won 3 races in native country, including 2 in 2003: well held in Britain: tried in cheekpieces. *R. M. H. Cowell* —

DARA GIRL (IRE) 2 b.f. (Mar 15) Key of Luck (USA) 126 – Tavildara (IRE) (Kahyasi 130) [2004 6m 7g 6d Jul 10] €12,000Y: second foal: half-sister to 3-y-o Dark Day Blues: dam unraced: no form in maidens/minor event: tongue tied final start. *Mrs P. N. Dutfield* —

DARA MAC 5 b.g. Presidium 124 – Nishara (Nishapour (FR) 125) [2004 58: 8v 7m² 7f⁶ 8g³ 8d* 8d 8g 8d* 7g 8g⁶ 7.9m 8g⁴ 7.5m 8m 7m Oct 10] rather sparely-made gelding: fair performer: won seller in June and selling handicap in August, both at Thirsk: stays 8.5f: acts on firm and good to soft ground: tried blinkered/in cheekpieces: sometimes starts slowly. *N. Bycroft* **68**

DARASIM (IRE) 6 b.g. Kahyasi 130 – Dararita (IRE) (Halo (USA)) [2004 119: 16.2s⁶ 16g* 20m³ 16m* 18m⁵ 20m⁶ Oct 3] lengthy, quite good-topped gelding: smart performer: successful in Betty Barclay-Rennen at Baden-Baden in May and Lady O Goodwood Cup (beat stable-companion Royal Rebel 2½ lengths, dictating pace, winning for third year running at the meeting) in July: good 4 lengths third to Papineau in Gold Cup at Royal Ascot in between: below best in Doncaster Cup and Prix du Cadran at Longchamp (roused along after missing break) last 2 outings: stays 2½m: acts on firm and good to soft going, probably not on soft: has been blinkered, visored nowadays: best ridden prominently. *M. Johnston* **117**

DARCIE MIA 3 ch.f. Polar Falcon (USA) 126 – Marie La Rose (FR) (Night Shift (USA)) [2004 40: f9.4g Jan 3] rather leggy filly: little form: tried blinkered. *J. R. Weymes* —

DARENEUR (IRE) 4 ch.f. Entrepreneur 123 – Darayna (IRE) (Shernazar 131) [2004 f9.4g 8.1s 9.9g⁵ May 18] 3,500Y: seventh foal: half-sister to 3 winners, notably smart 1m winner Dear Daughter (by Polish Precedent): dam, Irish 7f/1m winner, out of very **57**

smart 6f/7f performer Dafayna, herself half-sister to Doyoun: modest form in maidens. *W. M. Brisbourne*

DARGHAN (IRE)   4 b.g. Air Express (IRE) 125 – Darsannda (IRE) 86 (Kahyasi 130)   77
[2004 82: 8g[4] 8.5f[6] 10g[6] 11f[6] 9g[2] 10.4g 8v[5] 7s p5.1g p8.6g Dec 6] strong gelding: trained by J. Oxx in Ireland in 2003, winning maiden at Listowel: raced in USA for K. McLaughlin first 5 outings in 2004, then fair form in Britain: stays 9f: acts on any going: tongue tied all starts for current stable. *P. D. Evans*

DARING AFFAIR   3 b.f. Bien Bien (USA) 125 – Daring Destiny 113 (Daring March   72
116) [2004 65: f6g[3] f6g[2] f7g* f7g[5] f8.5g* 8.1v[4] f8.5m* May 10] good-topped filly: fair performer: won maiden at Southwell in February and handicaps at Wolverhampton in April and May: stays 8.5f: acts on fibresand and good to soft ground: visored on reappearance. *K. R. Burke*

DARING AIM   3 b.f. Daylami (IRE) 138 – Phantom Gold 119 (Machiavellian (USA)   89
123) [2004 80P: 10d[5] 12m* 14m[5] 11.6m Sep 27] leggy, useful-looking filly: fairly useful performer: won maiden at Newmarket in July: not discredited when fifth of 7 to Astrocharm in Vodafone Fillies' Stakes (Lillie Langtry) at Goodwood penultimate start, though found little: below form final appearance: probably stays 1¾m: acts on good to firm going: reluctant at start last 2 outings: usually flashes tail under pressure (dam showed same trait): temperament under suspicion. *Sir Michael Stoute*

DARING GAMBLE   7 b.m. Barrys Gamble 102 – Rachel Sharp (Daring March 116)   –
[2004 p5m p6g Dec 30] off 3½ years, no form in 2004. *I. W. McInnes*

DARING GAMES   3 b.f. Mind Games 121 – Daira 72 (Daring March 116) [2004   –
11.9m[5] 10m[6] 8g Jul 7] compact filly: first foal: dam 1½m winner: no form in maidens. *B. Ellison*

DARING RANSOM (USA)   2 b.c. (Apr 11) Red Ransom (USA) – Young And Daring   96 p
(USA) (Woodman (USA) 126) [2004 7.9g* Oct 9] tall, unfurnished colt: third living foal: dam, 6f to 9f winner in USA (including minor stakes), half-sister to dam of US Grade 1 winners Victory Ride and River Flyer: 25/1, won maiden at York by 1¼ lengths from Tarraman, moving up smoothly and ridden ahead late on: will stay 1¼m: should progress and win more races. *J. Noseda*

DARIO GEE GEE (IRE)   2 ch.c. (Mar 28) Bold Fact (USA) 116 – Magical Peace   97
(IRE) 80 (Magical Wonder (USA) 125) [2004 5g* 5d[2] 6m[2] 6f 6d[2] 6s* 6d[5] 6m 6m[3] Oct 2] €11,000F, 12,000Y: strong, close-coupled colt: good mover: second foal: dam, Irish 6f winner, out of sister to dam of Vinnie Roe: useful performer: won maiden at Doncaster in March and minor event at Ripon in August: placed in minor events and listed race (third to Obe Gold at Redcar): will probably stay 7f: acts on soft and good to firm going: sold 52,000 gns, sent to Saudi Arabia. *K. A. Ryan*

DARK CHAMPION   4 b.g. Abou Zouz (USA) 109 – Hazy Kay (IRE) 77 (Treasure   67
Kay 114) [2004 67, a57: f6g[2] f7g f6g[4] p6g[6] f6s[5] 6d[3] 6m 5f 6m[4] 6m[5] 5f 6m 5d 6v 6d[4] Oct 15] good-topped gelding: fair maiden: left J. O'Keeffe after fifth start: stays 6f: acts on fibresand, good to firm and good to soft ground: tried in cheekpieces/visor: has raced freely. *R. E. Barr*

DARK CHARM (FR)   5 b.g. Anabaa (USA) 130 – Wardara 107 (Sharpo 132) [2004   96 d
100: 8g[3] 7.9s 8.9m 9g[5] 7.9g Oct 8] tall, quite good-topped gelding: useful handicapper: close third of 24 to Babodana in Lincoln at Doncaster on reappearance: off 5 months, well below form after, looking reluctant on final outing: stays 1m: acts on polytrack, firm and soft going: has been blanketed for stall entry: races freely. *R. A. Fahey*

DARK CHEETAH (USA)   2 b.c. (Apr 18) Storm Cat (USA) – Layounne (USA) (Mt   109
Livermore (USA)) [2004 5m* 5f 6d* Oct 17] tall, leggy colt: second foal: half-brother to winner in USA by Danzig: dam, ran twice in USA, half-sister to smart Irish 6f/7f performer Bernstein and US Grade 3 winners around 1m/9f Caress and Country Cat, all by Storm Cat: won maiden at Cork in May and valuable nursery at Naas (under 9-7, by 2½ lengths from Dipterous) in October: reportedly jarred after seventh in listed race at Royal Ascot: should stay 7f: bordering on smart. *A. P. O'Brien, Ireland*

DARK CUT (IRE)   4 b.g. Ali-Royal (IRE) 127 – Prima Nox (Sabrehill (USA) 120)   –
[2004 60: p10g 12.4v 14.1g 13g 9.2d 10m 7.9m 8.5d Aug 11] fair performer: little form at 4 yrs. *H. Alexander*

DARK DAY BLUES (IRE)   3 ch.g. Night Shift (USA) – Tavildara (IRE) (Kahyasi   69 d
130) [2004 73: 8g 8.5v 8m 7f* 7d 7f[6] 7.1f[5] 8g[5] 7.1g 7g 8.5m 8m 11.9g p9.5g p9.5g Dec 15] workmanlike gelding: fair handicapper: won at Redcar in June: below form after: stays 7f: acts on firm and good to soft going: free-going sort. *M. D. Hammond*

DARK DOLORES 6 b.m. Inchinor 119 – Pingin (Corvaro (USA) 124) [2004 47, a37:   –
p10g⁵ Feb 16] maiden: well held only 6-y-o start. *J. R. Boyle*

DARK EMPRESS (IRE) 3 br.f. Second Empire (IRE) 124 – Good Reference (IRE)   **89**
84 (Reference Point 139) [2004 92: 7.1f⁶ Jun 19] quite attractive filly: fairly useful performer: blinkered, creditable sixth to Lucky Spin in listed race at Warwick only 3-y-o start,
slowly into stride: stays 7f: raced only on good to firm/firm ground: wore cheekpieces
final 2-y-o start (ran creditably): has looked difficult ride. *R. M. Beckett*

DARKO KARIM 2 b.c. (Apr 9) Groom Dancer (USA) 128 – Russian Rose (IRE) 82   **75 §**
(Soviet Lad (USA)) [2004 6m⁴ 7f 6f 7m 8.3d³ 8.3g⁵ 8s Oct 22] 85,000Y: smallish, close-
coupled colt: has a quick action: third foal: half-brother to 4-y-o Hanami: dam 1¼m and
17f winner: fair maiden: stays 1m: acts on good to firm and good to soft ground: visored
fourth start: ungenuine: sold 12,000 gns. *D. R. Loder*

DARK PARADE (ARG) 3 b.c. Parade Marshal (USA) – Charming Dart (ARG)   **51**
(D'Accord (USA)) [2004 7m p10g⁵ 8m f11g⁴ p13m p12m² p13.9g* Dec 22] modest
performer: won banded race at Wolverhampton in December: stays 1¾m: acts on all-
weather: raced freely third start. *G. L. Moore*

DARK RAIDER (IRE) 3 br. or gr.f. Definite Article 121 – Lady Shikari (Kala   **71**
Shikari 125) [2004 77?: 8.2s² 8f⁵ 10m⁵ 9.1g* 10m 9g 8g 9s p12g⁶ p13g p10m⁵ Dec 21]   **a64**
close-coupled filly: fair handicapper: won at Ayr in June: below form after: stays 1¼m:
acts on firm and soft ground. *A. P. Jones*

DARK SHAH (IRE) 4 b.g. Night Shift (USA) – Shanjah (Darshaan 133) [2004 77§:   – §
p8g⁵ p7g 8f 8.1f Jun 19] smallish, sturdy gelding: has been tubed: well held in 2004: tried
in cheekpieces, often tongue tied: has carried head high/found little. *D. M. Simcock*

DARK SOCIETY 6 b.g. Imp Society (USA) – No Candles Tonight 74 (Star Appeal   **54**
133) [2004 8g⁶ 12d6.0d⁴ Oct 9] medium-sized gelding: modest maiden handicapper: stays
1½m: acts on good to soft going: tried visored: has started slowly/hung. *A. W. Carroll*

DARLA (IRE) 3 b.f. Night Shift (USA) – Darbela (IRE) 102 (Doyoun 124) [2004 73:   **75**
7g 6f⁵ 6g² 6m⁶ 6.1d 6m p6m³ Oct 6] close-coupled filly: fair maiden handicapper: stays
6f: acts on polytrack and firm ground: tends to race freely. *J. W. Payne*

DARLING RIVER (FR) 5 b.m. Double Bed (FR) 121 – Oh Lucky Day (Balidar 133)   –
[2004 p8g p7g Oct 28] half-sister to 2 winners in France, including smart miler Si
Symphonie (by Le Glorieux): dam French 1m winner: fair maiden in 2002: well held
since, leaving E. Danel in France prior to reappearance in 2004. *S. Dow*

DARN GOOD 3 ch.g. Bien Bien (USA) 125 – Thimbalina 63 (Salmon Leap (USA)   **78**
131) [2004 73: p10g p10g p12g³ 10.9d 11.8g⁶ 14g 19.1f* 15m* 16.2g² 14.4m 16.4m⁶
16.2g⁶ 15.9g 17.2g* 16g⁴ Sep 30] big gelding: fair handicapper: won at Warwick in
June/July and Bath in September: stays 19f: acts on polytrack and firm ground: usually
visored/blinkered: sometimes carries head awkwardly/finds little. *R. Hannon*

DARSALAM (IRE) 3 ch.c. Desert King (IRE) 129 – Moonsilk (Solinus 130) [2004 –:   **118**
8g² 9g* 10g* 12g* 12g* 14g* 14.6f⁶ 12s³ 14g* Oct 3] big, strong colt: has round action:
trained at 2 yrs by M. Johnston (sold 6,500 gns): much improved for new stable in 2004,
winning 6 races, notably Freudenau Derby in May, Czech Derby at Velka Chuchle in
June, Czech St Leger (by 9 lengths) at latter track in August and Grosser Preis der Dort-
munder Stadtwerke-Deutsches St Leger at Dortmund (by neck from Sword Roche) in
October: smart efforts when 4¼ lengths sixth to Rule of Law in St Leger at Doncaster and
1¼ lengths third to Albanova in Preis von Europa at Cologne: stays 14.6f: acts on firm
and soft ground. *A. M. Savujev, Slovakia*

DARSHARP 2 b.f. (Apr 3) Josr Algarhoud (IRE) 118 – Dizzydaisy 57 (Sharpo 132)   –
[2004 6s⁶ 6s Nov 6] 10,500Y: tall, leggy filly: sixth foal: half-sister to fairly useful 1998
2-y-o 5f winner Aegean Flame (by Anshan) and 1½m winner Aegean Sunrise (by
Deploy): dam maiden who stayed 6f: only a little sign of ability in maidens at Newbury
and Doncaster (edgy). *Miss Gay Kelleway*

DART ALONG (USA) 2 b.c. (Apr 13) Bahri (USA) 125 – Promptly (IRE) 88 (Lead   **75**
On Time (USA) 123) [2004 7f⁵ 7g⁵ 6g⁴ p7g⁴ Oct 28] smallish, stocky colt: fourth foal:
half-brother to 3-y-o Fantastic View and fairly useful 2002 2-y-o 6f/7f winner To The
Rescue (by Cozzene): dam 6f and (US minor stakes) 1m winner: fair maiden: best effort
at Newmarket second start: needs to settle to stay beyond 7f. *R. Hannon*

DARTANIAN 2 b.g. (Apr 6) Jurado (USA) – Blackpool Mamma's 73 (Merdon Melody   **57**
98) [2004 5g 7.1f⁵ 6m⁶ 7m³ p7d 7s* 7s 7m Sep 5] leggy gelding: modest performer: won
seller at Catterick in August: well held in nurseries after: stays 7f: acts on soft going,
probably on polytrack. *P. D. Evans*

DARTING (USA) 3 b.f. Sahm (USA) 112 – Mur Taasha (USA) 108 (Riverman (USA) –
131) [2004 78: p8g Nov 20] attractive filly: fair form at 2 yrs: last of 12 on only outing in
2004: likely to prove best up to 7f. *G. A. Butler*

DASAR 4 ch.f. Catrail (USA) 123 – Rising of The Moon (IRE) 82 (Warning 136) [2004 **57**
58: f7g⁶ f6s⁴ f7g f7m² f7m³ f7g 7.5g f8g² f8g³ f7g³ p7.1g⁵ Dec 22] close-coupled filly:
modest performer: stays 1m: acts on fibresand, raced only on good/good to firm going on
turf: visored/blinkered after reappearance: often races prominently. *M. Brittain*

DASH FOR COVER (IRE) 4 b.g. Sesaro (USA) 81 – Raindancing (IRE) 94 (Tirol **70 d**
127) [2004 75: 9.7s² 10.2g 8.3g 8.1v 8m⁵ 8m⁶ 9g 8d⁵ 8g Sep 2] compact gelding: fair
performer: below form after reappearance: stays 9.7f: acts on soft and good to firm
ground: sold 10,000 gns. *R. Hannon*

DASH FOR GLORY 5 ch.g. Bluegrass Prince (IRE) 110 – Rekindled Flame (IRE) **30**
(Kings Lake (USA) 133) [2004 53: p13g f12g p16g 10.9m 10f³ 12.1g Sep 3] leggy
gelding: poor maiden: left M. Blanshard after third outing: stays 1¼m: acts on polytrack
and good to firm going: tried tongue tied. *J. S. King*

DASHIKI (USA) 3 ch.f. Distant View (USA) 126 – Musicanti (USA) (Nijinsky (CAN) **80**
138) [2004 7g³ Apr 16] lengthy filly: fourth foal: sister to high-class 7f (at 2 yrs, including
Dewhurst Stakes) to 9f winner Distant Music and useful 10.3f winner Fragrant View, and
half-sister to useful 1¼m winner New Orchid (by Quest For Fame): dam French 14.5f
winner: 7/1, bandaged on hind joints and moved fluently to post when 4½ lengths third of
13 to Illustrious Miss in maiden at Newbury: dead. *B. W. Hills*

DASHING DANE 4 b.c. Danehill (USA) 126 – Baldemara (FR) (Sanglamore (USA) –
126) [2004 58: f6g p6g Dec 14] lightly-raced maiden: well held both 4-y-o starts.
D. W. Chapman

DASH OF LIME 2 b.f. (Feb 5) Bold Edge 123 – Green Supreme (Primo Dominie 121) **63 p**
[2004 p6d⁴ Oct 30] half-sister to several winners, including smart sprinter Sampower Star
(by Cyrano de Bergerac) and 5-y-o Fire Up The Band: dam unraced: 7/1, fourth to Pamir
in maiden at Wolverhampton, slowly away: not sure to stay much beyond 6f: should do
better. *S. Kirk*

DASH OF MAGIC 6 b.m. Magic Ring (IRE) 115 – Praglia (IRE) 64 (Darshaan 133) **49**
[2004 52, a46: f12g* f12g⁶ f11g² f12g⁵ f11s* 9.9s 12.1m⁶ 10.5d³ f12d* 14.1g⁵ 12s f12s
Aug 23] leggy, quite good-topped mare: poor performer: won banded races in January
and March and handicap in June, all at Southwell: stays 1½m: acts on fibresand, firm and
good to soft ground: tried blinkered/visored: has been slowly away/looked none too keen.
J. Hetherton

DASH TO THE TOP 2 b.f. (Feb 20) Montjeu (IRE) 137 – Millennium Dash 94 **109 p**
(Nashwan (USA) 135) [2004 8.2g² 8m* 8f³ Sep 25]
      The trainer of Derby winners Kahyasi and High-Rise has fared nothing like
so well in the other Epsom classic. Luca Cumani's first runner in the Oaks, Freeze
The Secret, was beaten three quarters of a length by Dunfermline in 1977, but she
hasn't come so close to winning it since, even though two further representatives
have also finished second: Sudden Love in 1988 and Shamshir in 1991 were troun-
ced by Diminuendo and Jet Ski Lady respectively. Remarkably, Shamshir was the
last Cumani-trained filly to contest the Oaks, but, if all goes well with the promising
Dash To The Top, she will surely be in the line-up at Epsom. Dash To The Top had
three outings in her first season, all within the space of six weeks. Slowly away
when an eye-catching second to Night of Joy in a one-mile maiden fillies' event at
Nottingham on her debut, she went one better in a similar race at Leicester, where
she stayed on to lead over a furlong out, beating Bazelle by half a length, and then
was stepped up markedly in class in the Fillies' Mile at Ascot. Dash To The Top
went off at 16/1 in a nine-runner field for this Group 1 contest, only two of her rivals
at longer odds. Reported to have been a slow learner at home, Dash To The Top's
inexperience showed in the race itself after she was rather rushed up to take a
position on the outer half a mile from home, becoming unbalanced when asked to
extend in the straight, hanging right and causing interference. To her credit, Dash
To The Top did stay on strongly once reorganised and finished third, beaten a length
and three quarters of a length behind Playful Act and Maids Causeway, who on
their previous starts had been first and third respectively in the May Hill Stakes at
Doncaster. Further improvement from Dash To The Top looks likely.

		Sadler's Wells	Northern Dancer
	Montjeu (IRE)	(b 1981)	Fairy Bridge
	(b 1996)	Floripedes	Top Ville
Dash To The Top		(b 1985)	Toute Cy
(b.f. Feb 20, 2002)		Nashwan	Blushing Groom
	Millennium Dash	(ch 1986)	Height of Fashion
	(ch 1997)	Milligram	Mill Reef
		(ch 1984)	One In A Million

Dash To The Top races in the colours of Helena Springfield Ltd, as did all of the mares shown on the bottom line of her pedigree. The black with white spots were carried with particular distinction by two of them, great grandam One In A Million's wins including those in the One Thousand Guineas and Coronation Stakes and grandam Milligram's in the Coronation Stakes, Waterford Crystal Mile and Queen Elizabeth II Stakes. Dash To The Top's dam Millennium Dash wasn't in that league, but she was a fairly useful performer nevertheless and won a mile-and-a-quarter maiden at Bath by ten lengths on the second of her three starts, all as a three-year-old. Millennium Dash, also trained by Cumani, bettered her Bath form when tried at a mile and a half in the Princess Royal Stakes on her final appearance, a never-nearer ninth that day after starting slowly and not having the run of the race. Dash To The Top, the first foal of Millennium Dash and from the first crop of Montjeu, will prove very well suited by a mile and a quarter and further as a three-year-old. Well bred and a very eye-catching sort in appearance, the rangy Dash To The Top looks a good prospect. *L. M. Cumani*

DATAHILL (IRE) 4 b.f. Danehill (USA) 126 – Animatrice (USA) 115 (Alleged (USA) 138) [2004 f12g⁵ Feb 9] half-sister to several winners in France, including useful 1½m (Prix de Royaumont) winner Sadler's Flag (by Sadler's Wells): dam, best at 1½m (third in Oaks), half-sister to very smart 1½m performer Poliglote: best effort in minor events (fairly useful form) when fourth at Saint-Cloud penultimate 3-y-o start: left Mme C. Head-Maarek 50,000 gns, ran poorly only 4-y-o start. *P. W. D'Arcy* **–**

DAUNTED (IRE) 8 b.g. Priolo (USA) 127 – Dauntess (Formidable (USA) 125) [2004 ?, a65: f12g³ f11g* f12g f16g f11g* f12g* f12s* f14g* f12g Dec 28] quite good-topped gelding: fair performer: won amateur handicap, claimers (2) and sellers (2) at Southwell in first half of 2004: effective at 11f to 2m: acts on fibresand, no recent form on turf: usually blinkered prior to 2002: effective with or without cheekpieces: held up. *P. A. Blockley* **? a68**

DAVALA 2 b.c. (Apr 20) Lake Coniston (IRE) 131 – Velvet Heart (USA) 47 (Damister (USA) 123) [2004 6g 6m 7.1d Oct 9] no form in maidens. *A. D. Smith* **–**

DAVE (IRE) 3 b.g. Danzero (AUS) – Paradise News 51 (Sure Blade (USA) 130) [2004 64?: 6m⁶ 6g 7s 5m p9.5d p7.1g Dec 4] lengthy gelding: fair performer: won apprentice handicap at Folkestone in July: ran poorly after: likely to prove best at 5f/6f: acts on good to firm going: withdrawn after breaking out of stall intended second outing. *J. R. Best* **67 d**

DAVENPORT (IRE) 2 b.g. (Apr 7) Bold Fact (USA) 116 – Semence d'Or (FR) (Kaldoun (FR) 122) [2004 p7.1g p7.1g² Dec 10] 2,500F: third foal: half-brother to German 8.5f winner Simonida (by Royal Academy): dam, 2-y-o 7f winner in France on only start, sister to smart winner up to 11f in France/USA See You Soon: better effort in maidens at Wolverhampton when head second to City Zone: hung markedly right on debut. *B. R. Millman* **69**

DAVID JUNIOR (USA) 2 ch.c. (Apr 18) Pleasant Tap (USA) – Paradise River (USA) (Irish River (FR) 131) [2004 7g³ 7f* Sep 24] $175,000 2-y-o: third foal: half-brother to a winner in USA by Swain: dam, maiden in USA, sister to top-class US performer up to 1¼m Paradise Creek and half-sister to very smart US Grade 1 winners Forbidden Apple (1m/1¼m) and Wild Event (9f): favourite, won 5-runner maiden at Ascot by ¾ length from Macabre, dictating pace and idling/hanging left: likely to stay at least 1m: useful prospect. *B. J. Meehan* **89 p**

DAVIDS CHOICE 2 b.g. (Apr 20) Wizard King 122 – Welch's Dream (IRE) 76 (Brief Truce (USA) 126) [2004 7.1d Oct 17] first foal: dam 2-y-o 5f winner who regressed: 100/1, tailed off in maiden at Musselburgh. *A. Berry* **–**

DAVID'S GIRL 3 b.f. Royal Applause 124 – Cheer (Efisio 120) [2004 54d: p8g⁵ 8.2s⁶ 7m⁶ 7g⁵ 7m 8f 7d⁶ 7g⁶ 7m³ 7d² Oct 16] leggy filly: poor maiden: should stay 1m: acts on good to firm and good to soft ground. *D. Morris* **46**

DAVIDS MARK 4 b.g. Polar Prince (IRE) 117 – Star of Flanders (Puissance 110) [2004 64: p6g 6s³ 5.7m⁴ f5g⁴ 6g⁴ 5m* 5d² 5.1m p5.1g p6g³ p5.1g² f5m p6g⁴ p5.1g³ p6m⁶ **65**

Dec 22] fair handicapper: made all at Windsor in August: effective at 5f/6f: acts on all-weather, soft and good to firm going: tried visored/in cheekpieces: sometimes slowly away. *J. R. Jenkins*

DAVID'S SYMPHONY (IRE) 2 ch.g. (Mar 29) Almutawakel 126 – Habemus (FR) – (Bluebird (USA) 125) [2004 6d 7f 8.3m 7.1g Aug 30] no form in minor event/maidens. *R. Hannon*

DAVORIN (JPN) 3 br.c. Warning 136 – Arvola 75 (Sadler's Wells (USA) 132) [2004 79 7d* 8m⁶ p7g 8.5g⁶ 8s Oct 19] 40,000,000 yen Y: leggy, quite attractive colt: seventh foal: brother to 2 winners, notably high-class 6f/7f winner Diktat, and half-brother to winner in Japan by Nashwan: dam, 1m winner, half-sister to high-class miler Cape Cross out of Cheveley Park winner Park Appeal: fair performer: won maiden at Newmarket in July: looked none too keen when below form final start: stays 8.5f: visored (ran poorly) third outing: has been slowly away: sold 25,000 gns. *D. R. Loder*

DAVY CROCKETT 2 b.g. (Feb 9) Polar Prince (IRE) 117 – Sing With The Band 80 63 (Chief Singer 131) [2004 5g 6s 6g⁵ 5.9f⁶ 8g 7m⁶ 6s Oct 22] good-topped gelding: modest performer: trained first 4 starts by Mrs J. Ramsden: won maiden at Newcastle in September: stays 7f: acts on firm going, well beaten on soft. *B. Smart*

DAWN AIR (USA) 3 b.f. Diesis 133 – Midnight Air (USA) 111 (Green Dancer (USA) 53 132) [2004 –: 12d³ 12m 14g 16.2g Jul 19] lengthy filly: form only in maiden at Thirsk on reappearance: tried in cheekpieces. *K. A. Ryan*

DAWN DUEL (IRE) 3 b.f. Daggers Drawn (USA) 114 – Dawn's Folly (IRE) 47 (Blue- – bird (USA) 125) [2004 –: 6s 7.1d May 4] well held in maidens, looking wayward final start. *B. Smart*

DAWN PIPER (USA) 4 b.g. Desert Prince (IRE) 130 – June Moon (IRE) (Sadler's 89 Wells (USA) 132) [2004 87: p8g* p7g p7g² 7d 7.1s² 8.5g 7f⁴ a7f a9f⁵ Dec 16] compact gelding: fairly useful performer: easily landed odds in maiden at Lingfield in January: well below form last 4 starts, leaving D. Loder and off 6 months after seventh outing: may prove best around 1m: acts on polytrack and good to firm going: often visored: front runner. *D. Watson, UAE*

DAWN SURPRISE (USA) 3 b.f. Theatrical 128 – Lignify (ARG) (Confidential Talk 104 (USA)) [2004 78p: 9.9g² 8m* 7m⁵ 8m* 8d* 8g² Oct 1] tall, lengthy, quite attractive filly: has a round action: progressed into a useful performer: won maiden at Salisbury in June and minor events at Kempton and Thirsk (beat Blue Sky Thinking 1¼ lengths) in August: good ½-length second to Royal Prince in minor event at Newmarket final start, racing alone for much of contest: better at 7f/1m than 1¼m: acts on good to firm and good to soft ground: tongue tied last 5 starts: usually races prominently. *Saeed bin Suroor*

DAWTON (POL) 6 br.h. Greinton 119 – Da Wega (POL) (Who Knows 114) [2004 – 11m Jul 16] won 7 times from 19 starts on Flat (up to 1½m) at 3/4 yrs in Poland: well held only start on Flat in Britain: fairly useful hurdler. *T. R. George*

DAYBREAK DANCER (IRE) 2 b.c. (Feb 9) Fasliyev (USA) 120 – Darkling (IRE) 58 60 (Grand Lodge (USA) 125) [2004 7d 7.5s 6d p6g⁴ Dec 15] trained first 3 starts by D. Weld in Ireland: modest maiden: fourth at Wolverhampton, only form: should stay 7f: blinkered penultimate outing. *G. A. Huffer*

DAYBREAKING (IRE) 2 br.c. (Apr 7) Daylami (IRE) 138 – Mawhiba (USA) 63 55 (Dayjur (USA) 137) [2004 p7m 8s⁵ Oct 19] €18,000Y: third foal: dam once-raced close relative to Derby winner Erhaab: modest form in maidens at Lingfield and Bath: will stay at least 1¼m. *R. F. Johnson Houghton*

DAY CARE 3 gr.c. Daylami (IRE) 138 – Ancara 109 (Dancing Brave (USA) 140) [2004 70 p 9.9g² Sep 30] fifth foal: half-brother to 3 winners, including 6-y-o Monolith and 5-y-o Bosphorus: dam French 1¼m and 1½m winner: 5/4 favourite, 4 lengths second to Double Deputy in maiden at Goodwood: should improve. *Mrs A. J. Perrett*

DAYDREAM DANCER 3 gr.f. Daylami (IRE) 138 – Dancing Wolf (IRE) 76 (Wolf- 61 hound (USA) 126) [2004 –: 7.1d⁵ p10g 10m 11.5g 8.1g³ 8.1m 10m* 10m* p12.2d⁴ p9.5g⁵ Nov 20] close-coupled filly: modest handicapper: won at Brighton in August and September: stays 1¼m: acts on good to firm and good to soft ground: blinkered last 6 starts. *C. G. Cox*

DAY FLIGHT 3 b.c. Sadler's Wells (USA) 132 – Bonash 110 (Rainbow Quest (USA) 116 134) [2004 12s* 10.4d* 12g⁴ 11m⁴ Sep 17] good-topped colt: has a short, quick action: fourth live foal: half-brother to useful 1998 2-y-o 7f winner Bionic (by Zafonic): dam French 1m (Prix d'Aumale at 2 yrs) to 1½m (Prix de Malleret) winner: smart form: won maiden at Salisbury and 4-runner listed race at York (by 20 lengths from Mac Regal) in

May: co-favourite, ran well when 1½ lengths fourth to Blue Canari in Prix du Jockey Club at Chantilly in June, leading after home turn: off over 3 months, respectable fourth to Sights On Gold in Arc Trial at Newbury final start: stays 1½m: has worn crossed noseband. *J. H. M. Gosden*

DAYGAR 2 b.c. (Apr 14) Spectrum (IRE) 126 – Milly Ha Ha 106 (Dancing Brave (USA) 140) [2004 7f Jul 21] 5,500Y: seventh foal: half-brother to useful 11f winner Jolly Sharp (by Diesis) and fairly useful 1¼m winner Laughing Girl (by Woodman): dam, 1¼m winner who stayed 1¾m, half-sister to smart stayer Bosham Mill: 25/1, behind in maiden at Leicester, slowly away. *M. G. Quinlan* —

DAY OF RECKONING 3 b.f. Daylami (IRE) 138 – Trying For Gold (USA) 103 (Northern Baby (CAN) 127) [2004 10f³ 10g* Aug 23] half-sister to 3 at least useful winners, including smart 1m (at 2 yrs) to 13f winner Phantom Gold (by Machiavellian), now dam of Oaks runner-up Flight of Fancy: dam, 1½m winner, out of Ribblesdale winner Expansive: confirmed debut promise when winning maiden at Windsor by 2 lengths from Pleasant, getting on top final 1f despite giving flash of tail: will stay 1½m: sent to USA: open to further improvement. *Sir Michael Stoute* **82 p**

DAY ONE 3 b.c. Daylami (IRE) 138 – Myself 110 (Nashwan (USA) 135) [2004 60p: 12f³ 14d⁵ 12d² Oct 17] smallish, compact colt: half-brother to 3 winners, including useful 2-y-o 6f winners Ghayth (in 2000, by Sadler's Wells) and Ego (in 2002, by Green Desert): dam 6f (at 2 yrs) and 7f (Nell Gwyn Stakes) winner: fairly useful maiden: placed at Newmarket (best effort) and Musselburgh: stays 1½m: acts on firm ground: sold 32,000 gns, joined R. Price. *G. Wragg* **80**

DAYTIME GIRL (IRE) 3 gr.f. Daylami (IRE) 138 – Snoozeandyoulose (IRE) 73 (Scenic 128) [2004 7p: 10g³ 12s⁵ 10.3g* 12.3d⁶ 8g⁵ a10f Nov 7] sturdy filly: fairly useful performer: made all in minor event at Chester in June: sold 44,000 gns, left B. Hills after next start: should stay 1½m: acts on good to soft going: blinkered final outing. *E. M. Allain, Canada* **82**

DAY TO REMEMBER 3 gr.c. Daylami (IRE) 138 – Miss Universe (IRE) 99 (Warning 136) [2004 7p: 7g⁵ 8.3m* 8s³ 10d* Oct 4] small, quite attractive colt: fairly useful performer, lightly raced: trained by A. Stewart until after reappearance: won maiden at Windsor in August and handicap there (beat Another Choice by neck, dictating pace) in October: stays 1¼m: act on soft and good to firm going: likely to improve further. *E. F. Vaughan* **93 p**

DAZE 3 b.f. Daylami (IRE) 138 – Proud Titania (IRE) 103 (Fairy King (USA)) [2004 10m³ 12.3s* 11g 14g⁴ Oct 2] big, strong filly: fourth foal: half-sister to 11.7f seller winner Fraternize (by Spectrum): dam Irish 7f winner (including at 2 yrs) who stayed 1m: fair performer: won maiden at Chester in August by 8 lengths: creditable efforts after in handicaps at Newbury (reluctant at stall) and Newmarket (fourth of 11 to Quarrymount): stays 1¾m: acts on soft ground: sold 25,000 gns, sent to USA. *Sir Michael Stoute* **78**

DAZZLING BAY 4 b.g. Mind Games 121 – Adorable Cherub (USA) 58 (Halo (USA)) [2004 107: 6s⁶ 6d 6m³ 6f⁵ 6g² 6m 6s 5m³ 6g 5s Oct 23] big, rather leggy gelding: has a round action: useful performer: good efforts in handicaps at York (third to Circuit Dancer, despite hanging violently right) and Royal Ascot (fifth of 29 to Lafi in Wokingham) and minor event at Haydock (length second to Quito) third to fifth starts: best at 5f/6f: best efforts on good to firm/firm going: effective blinkered or not: has been reluctant to post: usually races prominently. *T. D. Easterby* **106**

DEAL IN FACTS 5 ch.m. So Factual (USA) 120 – Timely Raise (USA) (Raise A Man (USA)) [2004 f7g f6g Jan 20] tall, leggy mare: lighty-raced maiden: no form since 2001: tried blinkered. *C. N. Kellett* —

DEANGATE (IRE) 3 ch.g. Vettori (IRE) 119 – Moonlight (IRE) 69 (Night Shift (USA)) [2004 12m 6.9m Sep 11] pulled up in maiden at Pontefract and tailed off in maiden claimer at Carlisle. *P. T. Midgley* —

DEAR SIR (IRE) 4 ch.g. Among Men (USA) 124 – Deerussa (IRE) (Jareer (USA) 115) [2004 58: 16m Jul 14] maiden: well beaten only start on Flat in 2004. *Mrs P. N. Dutfield* —

DEBBIE 5 b.m. Deploy 131 – Elita (Sharpo 132) [2004 66: f9.4g f11g f9.4g⁴ Feb 2] close-coupled mare: fair on turf in 2003: poor on all-weather: best around 1¼m: acts on fibresand, soft and good to firm going: tends to race freely: fairly useful hurdler. *B. D. Leavy* **43**

DEBONA (IRE) 4 b.f. Nashwan (USA) 135 – Mahalia (IRE) 107 (Danehill (USA) 126) [2004 78: 9v⁵ 9d⁴ 8m 8d 10.2m 8v 10s 8s p9.5g p7.1g Dec 20] IR 18,000Y: third foal: half-sister to French 2000 2-y-o 6f winner Marliana (by Mtoto): dam French sprinter: fair maiden handicapper: left H. Rogers in Ireland, reportedly bled when well beaten both outings in Britain: stays 9f: acts on good to soft going: blinkered once. *J. S. Moore* **72 d**

DEBS BROUGHTON 2 b.f. (Feb 28) Prince Sabo 123 – Coy Debutante (IRE) 58 **57**
(Archway (IRE) 115) [2004 5.1m 6m 6m² 6g 7m⁴ 8g⁵ Sep 16] leggy filly: first foal: dam
maiden who stayed 10.5f: modest maiden: probably stays 1m: acts on good to firm going.
W. J. Musson

DE BULLIONS 2 b.g. (Apr 27) Mujahid (USA) 125 – Stolen Melody 74 (Robellino **–**
(USA) 127) [2004 6g Sep 4] good-topped gelding: well held in maiden at Haydock: sold
1,200 gns. *A. M. Balding*

DECELERATE 4 ch.c. Polar Falcon (USA) 126 – Speed To Lead (IRE) 90 (Darshaan **60 ?**
133) [2004 60: p10g p10g Apr 2] well-made colt: modest performer: finished lame final
start: stays easy 1¼m: acts on all-weather and good to firm ground: sometimes wanders/
carries head high. *A. Charlton*

DECORATION 2 b.c. (May 14) Mark of Esteem (IRE) 137 – Forever Shineing 62 **–**
(Glint of Gold 128) [2004 7g Aug 14] 30,000Y: big, close-coupled colt: sixth foal: half-
brother to 5-y-o Treasure Trail: dam 1½m winner: 12/1, last in maiden at Newbury,
slowly away: sold 4,500 gns. *B. J. Meehan*

DEEDAY BAY (IRE) 2 b.f. (Jan 21) Brave Act 119 – Skerries Bell 71 (Taufan (USA) **78**
119) [2004 6m⁴ 6d⁴ 6d² Aug 28] 22,000Y: good-topped filly: fourth foal: half-sister to
5-y-o Gone'n'Dunnett and winner in Greece by Blues Traveller: dam, Belgian 7f to 9f
winner, half-sister to smart sprinter Indian Rocket: won maiden at Doncaster in June:
creditable efforts when in frame in minor events at Salisbury and Windsor: likely to prove
best at 5f/6f. *C. F. Wall*

DEE DEE GIRL (IRE) 3 b.f. Primo Dominie 121 – Chapel Lawn (Generous (IRE) **–**
139) [2004 60: p8g Feb 18] rather leggy filly: form only when winning claimer at Redcar
in 2003: ran as if amiss only 3-y-o start. *R. Hannon*

DEE EN AY (IRE) 3 ch.g. Shinko Forest (IRE) – Edwina (IRE) 63 (Caerleon (USA) **51 +**
132) [2004 7s 8g 8m⁵ 8.1g⁶ a6d² a6.8d* Dec 19] good-topped gelding: has a quick action:
modest performer: sold from T. Easterby after fourth start: won handicap and minor event
at Taby in December: stays 1m: acts on good to firm going and dirt. *C. Hederud, Sweden*

DEEKAZZ (IRE) 5 b.m. Definite Article 121 – Lyric Junction (IRE) (Classic Secret **37**
(USA) 91) [2004 41: 12m 9.9m 10m⁶ Aug 6] lengthy, angular mare: poor maiden: stays
1¼m: acts on fibresand, best turf efforts on good going or firmer: sometimes blinkered/
visored. *F. Watson*

DEE PEE TEE CEE (IRE) 10 b.g. Tidaro (USA) – Silver Glimpse 108 (Petingo 135) **49**
[2004 8.5d 11.9g³ 10.1d Oct 16] tall gelding: has a round action: unraced in 2003, and
just poor form at 10 yrs: stays 1½m: acts on soft and good to firm going. *M. W. Easterby*

DEEPER IN DEBT 6 ch.g. Piccolo 121 – Harold's Girl (FR) (Northfields (USA)) **80 d**
[2004 79: p8g² p8g⁴ p8g³ p8g³ 8.5s⁵ 8m 8g 9g 9g Jul 14] deep-girthed gelding: fairly
useful performer: well below form last 5 starts: stays easy 1¼m: acts on all-weather, firm
and soft going: tried blinkered/tongue tied: usually races prominently. *J. Akehurst*

DEEP PURPLE 3 b.g. Halling (USA) 133 – Seal Indigo (IRE) 93 (Glenstal (USA) **89 p**
118) [2004 10g* 10d⁴ 11g⁶ Sep 17] 40,000Y: tall, leggy gelding: half-brother to several
winners, including useful 2001 2-y-o 6f winner Prism (by Spectrum) and fairly useful 6f
winner Cielito Lindo (by Pursuit of Love): dam, 10.5f/1½m winner, out of half-sister to
Irish Oaks winner Give Thanks: fairly useful performer: won maiden at Kempton (wandered) in July: similar form in handicaps at Sandown (still green, fourth to Telemachus)
and Newbury (sixth to Solo Flight): will stay at least 1½m: remains open to improvement.
M. P. Tregoning

DEEWAAR (IRE) 4 b.g. Ashkalani (IRE) 128 – Chandni (IRE) (Ahonoora 122) [2004 **49 §**
53§: 10.2s 10f 10.2g Oct 10] workmanlike gelding: poor maiden: stays easy 11f: acts on
polytrack and firm going: tried visored/in cheekpieces: wayward (has tried to run out)
and not to be trusted. *J. C. Fox*

DEFANA 3 b.g. Defacto (USA) – Thalya (Crofthall 110) [2004 48: p8g⁵ 12m³ 10.9g³ **57**
8f 14.1g⁶ 10f* 10m p12.2g Oct 9] leggy gelding: modest handicapper: won seller at **a–**
Redcar in September: stays 1½m: acts on polytrack, firm and good to soft going: wore
cheekpieces (below form) penultimate start. *M. Dods*

DEFERLANT (FR) 7 ch.g. Bering 136 – Sail Storm (USA) 108 (Topsider (USA)) **–**
[2004 12g 13.3m 11.7g Jul 11] ex-French gelding: fairly useful performer in 2001: well
held all 3 Flat starts since: usually visored/in cheekpieces: fair hurdler. *K. Bell*

DEFINING 5 b.g. Definite Article 121 – Gooseberry Pie 63 (Green Desert (USA) 127) **113**
[2004 98: 12m 12m³ 16.1s 13.9s⁴ 14g* 16.2m* 16s⁶ Oct 16] lengthy gelding: smart

stanleybet.com Old Borough Cup Stakes (Handicap), Haydock—Defining records his first win since his three-year-old days; he is chased home by Sergeant Cecil, Lochbuie (rail) and High Action

performer: much improved in 2004, winning handicap at Haydock (by ¾ length from Sergeant Cecil) and listed race at Ascot (beat Swift Tango by 2½ lengths) in September: below form in Jockey Club Cup at Newmarket final outing: effective at 1½m to 2m: acts on polytrack, soft and good to firm going: waited with: genuine and consistent. *J. R. Fanshawe*

DEFINITE GUEST (IRE) 6 gr.g. Definite Article 121 – Nicea (IRE) 90 (Dominion 123) [2004 89: 8.5m³ 8.9m 10d 8m 8m⁵ 8m Aug 7] leggy gelding: fairly useful handicapper: creditable efforts in 2004 only on reappearance and penultimate starts: effective at 1m/1¼m: acts on firm and good to soft going, well held on soft/heavy: blinkered once: tends to wander: held up. *R. A. Fahey* **86 +**

DEFINITELY ROYAL (IRE) 2 b.f. (Mar 28) Desert Prince (IRE) 130 – Specifically (USA) (Sky Classic (CAN)) [2004 p6g p8.6d Oct 30] €12,000Y, 20,000 2-y-o: fifth foal: half-sister to 1¼m winner Thundermill (by Thunder Gulch) and winner in USA by Rhythm: dam, US 2-y-o winner, half-sister to 4-y-o Pride: poor form in minor event at Lingfield (slowly away) and maiden at Wolverhampton. *R. M. H. Cowell* **44**

DEFINITELY SPECIAL (IRE) 6 b.m. Definite Article 121 – Legit (IRE) (Runnett 125) [2004 43, a51: p6g p7g f6s p5g p7g p7g⁶ 7.1d⁴ 8g May 4] poor maiden: stays 1m: acts on polytrack and firm going: wore cheekpieces last 4 starts. *N. E. Berry* **– a38**

DEGREE OF HONOR (FR) 2 ch.f. (Feb 1) Highest Honor (FR) 124 – Sheba Dancer (FR) 117 (Fabulous Dancer (USA) 124) [2004 7.2d p7.1d p5.1g p7.1g Dec 31] €50,000Y, resold €4,000Y, 37,000 2-y-o: close-coupled filly: half-sister to several winners, including useful French performer up to 11f Barings (by Pistolet Bleu): dam, French 1m/9f winner, second in Prix de Diane: poor maiden. *J. G. Given* **39**

DEIGN TO DANCE (IRE) 3 b.f. Danetime (IRE) 121 – Lady Montekin (Montekin 125) [2004 75: p7g⁵ 6.1g 7g 7m⁵ p8d* 8.1g 8.3f³ 8.3m² 9s⁵ 8d⁵ p10g³ Oct 31] strong filly: fair performer: won minor event at Lingfield in June: stays 1¼m: acts on polytrack and firm going, probably on soft: tried in cheekpieces (well below form): sent to Saudi Arabia. *J. G. Portman* **68**

DEJEEJE (IRE) 3 ch.c. Grand Lodge (USA) 125 – Christan (IRE) (Al Hareb (USA) 123) [2004 6m 7f Sep 13] well beaten in maidens at Thirsk and Redcar. *D. W. Chapman* **–**

DELAWARE TRAIL 5 b.g. Catrail (USA) 123 – Dilwara (IRE) (Lashkari 128) [2004 47: f8g 8s Apr 28] big, leggy gelding: maiden: well beaten in 2004: tried in cheekpieces. *J. S. Wainwright* **–**

DELCIENNE 3 b.f. Golden Heights 82 – Delciana (IRE) 61 (Danehill (USA) 126) [2004 53: 8.2g 8.1s 8.5m³ 10f 8f² 8f* 8.5g⁵ 7.9f 8d* 8d p8.6d Nov 3] modest performer: won seller in June and banded race in October, both at Brighton: should stay 1¼m: acts on polytrack, firm and good to soft going: tried tongue tied. *G. G. Margarson* **55**

DELEGATE 11 ch.g. Polish Precedent (USA) 131 – Dangora (USA) 98 (Sovereign Dancer (USA)) [2004 74: 5m 5.7f 5.7f* Jun 23] lengthy gelding: poor mover: fair performer: won minor event at Bath in June: stays 5.7f: acts on any turf going: sometimes slowly away/hangs: usually held up. *N. A. Callaghan* **72**

DELFINIA 3 b.f. Kingsinger (IRE) 94 – Delvecchia (Glint of Gold 128) [2004 10d 12.1m⁴ 12.1m⁶ Jun 21] sixth foal: half-sister to Norwegian 1000 Guineas/Oaks winner Turf Turtle (by Alzao): dam German 2-y-o 7f winner: well held in maidens. *H. S. Howe* —

DELIGHTFUL GIFT 4 b.f. Cadeaux Genereux 131 – Delightful Chime (IRE) 79 (Alzao (USA) 117) [2004 48: 7.5m⁶ f8d 7.5g 8f f7g Dec 12] leggy, close-coupled filly: poor maiden: stays 7.5f: acts on soft ground. *M. Brittain* **42**

DELIGHTFULLY 3 b.f. Definite Article 121 – Kingpin Delight (Emarati (USA) 74) [2004 61: 6d f8.5g² 8f⁴ p12d⁶ 10.9f³ p12d* p12.2g Dec 20] fair performer: won seller at Lingfield in June: left B. Hills prior to tailed off final outing: stays 1½m: acts on all-weather and firm ground: blinkered last 2 starts. *Jean-Rene Auvray* **69**

DELLAGIO (IRE) 3 b.c. Fasliyev (USA) 120 – Lady Ounavarra (IRE) (Simply Great (FR) 122) [2004 81: p5g 6d 6s 7g 5.3m⁴ 5m 7m 5.9m* 7m 5.7f Sep 6] smallish, good-bodied colt: has quick action: modest handicapper nowadays: won at Carlisle in August: stays 6f: acts on firm going: has raced freely. *C. A. Dwyer* **63**

DELLA SALUTE 2 gr.f. (Feb 24) Dansili 127 – Marie Dora (FR) 86 (Kendor (FR) 122) [2004 6g⁶ 7f Jul 29] rather leggy filly: third foal: dam, 1m winner, sister to smart French 1¼m performer Marie de Ken: better effort in maidens when sixth at Newmarket: should stay 1m. *A. M. Balding* **64**

DEL MAR SUNSET 5 b.g. Unfuwain (USA) 131 – City of Angels (Woodman (USA) 126) [2004 78, a93: f9.4g⁴ f8.5s⁵ p8g f8.5g* 9.7s 8g p8.6g* p10g p9.5g³ Dec 31] tall, rather leggy gelding: useful handicapper on all-weather: won at Wolverhampton in March and November (beat Wake by 2 lengths): stays 1¼m: acts on all-weather, had form on turf in 2003 (acts on firm going): blinkered (well held) once, tried in cheekpieces: often front runner: game. *W. J. Haggas* **? a96**

DELPHIE QUEEN (IRE) 3 ch.f. Desert Sun 120 – Serious Delight (Lomond (USA) 128) [2004 77: 6g⁴ 6m³ 7m* 6m² 7d* 7m⁶ 6d⁶ Oct 14] €35,000Y: fourth foal: half-sister to Irish 5f to 7f winner Foxhollow Lady (by Goldmark) and fairly useful 2002 2-y-o 6f/8.5f winner Wathiq (by Titus Livius): dam unraced half-sister to dam of very smart sprinter Pipalong: won maiden at Listowel in 2003 for P. Flynn in Ireland: progressed into a useful performer for new stable, winning handicap at Newmarket in June and minor event at Salisbury (beat Jedburgh by 5 lengths) in July: below form in listed races at Ascot and Newmarket last 2 starts: effective at 6f/7f: acts on good to firm and good to soft ground: tends to hang/carry head high. *S. Kirk* **104 +**

DELSARTE (USA) 4 b.c. Theatrical 128 – Delauncy (Machiavellian (USA) 123) [2004 115: 12m 13.3m² 12g⁵ 13.4s⁶ 12f⁴ Sep 10] tall colt: smart performer: best effort in 2004 when creditable 4 lengths second to The Whistling Teal in listed race at Newbury in May: stays 13.4f: acts on firm and soft going: tongue tied last 4 starts, visored on final one: has early to post: left Godolphin. *Saeed bin Suroor* **112**

Anheuser Busch Railway Stakes, the Curragh—Democratic Deficit overturns odds-on Russian Blue (left), attempting to give Aidan O'Brien a sixth successive win in the race; also in the picture are L'Altro Mondo (rail) and fifth-placed Joyce (dark colours)

DELTA FORCE 5 b.g. High Kicker (USA) – Maedaley 45 (Charmer 123) [2004 55: **55** f16g* f11g² f12f* f11g⁴ f14g⁴ f12s⁵ 11.9m³ 17.2f² 14.1f⁶ Jun 14] fair on all-weather, **a68** modest on turf: won banded race and amateur handicap at Southwell in January: effective at 11f to 17f: acts on fibresand and firm ground: sometimes races freely. *P. A. Blockley*

DELTA LADY 3 b.f. River Falls 113 – Compton Lady (USA) 100 (Sovereign Dancer **35** (USA)) [2004 45: 8s f8m⁶ 9.9m 7m⁵ 7g 8m 8s 7.9m 8f⁶ Sep 16] leggy filly: poor maiden: probably stays 1m: acts on firm and good to soft ground: blinkered (ran respectably) once. *R. Bastiman*

DELTA STAR 4 ch.f. Abou Zouz (USA) 109 – Lamloum (IRE) (Vacarme (USA) 121) – [2004 8.1s p9.5d f7s f7g Dec 12] workmanlike filly: third foal: half-sister to French 9f/ 1¼m winner Anastasia's Shadow (by Theatrical Charmer): dam, French maiden, out of Irish Oaks winner Olwyn: no sign of ability: tried in cheekpieces. *K. A. Ryan*

DELUSION 3 b.f. Hennessy (USA) 122 – Another Fantasy (IRE) 103 (Danehill (USA) **43** 126) [2004 65: 6m⁶ 7m³ 8g 7m 6.9m Aug 2] small filly: fair maiden at 2 yrs: on the downgrade: stays 6f: acts on firm ground. *T. D. Easterby*

DEMATRAF (IRE) 2 gr.f. (May 8) Atraf 116 – Demolition Jo 89 (Petong 126) [2004 **55** f6g* p6g Nov 20] €1,200Y: second foal: dam 6f/7f winner (including at 2 yrs): 40/1, won maiden at Southwell in November: creditable eighth in nursery at Wolverhampton: should stay 7f. *Ms Deborah J. Evans*

DEMOCRATIC DEFICIT (IRE) 2 b.c. (Jan 31) Soviet Star (USA) 128 – Grand- **109** iose Idea (IRE) 89 (Danehill (USA) 126) [2004 6d* 6f* 7m² 7g⁴ 7m⁵ Oct 3] €50,000Y: strong colt: first living foal: dam Irish 1m winner from 2 starts at 2 yrs: useful performer: won maiden at Leopardstown in May and Anheuser Busch Railway Stakes at the Curragh (by ¾ length from Russian Blue) in June: good 2 lengths second to Oratorio in Futurity Stakes at the Curragh: just respectable efforts in National Stakes at the Curragh and Prix Jean-Luc Lagardere at Longchamp: should stay 1m: acts on firm and good to soft ground. *J. S. Bolger, Ireland*

D. H. W. Dobson's "Democratic Deficit"

DEM

DEMOLITION FRANK 2 b.g. (Mar 21) Cayman Kai (IRE) 114 – Something –
Speedy (IRE) 53 (Sayf El Arab (USA) 127) [2004 6.9m 7s Nov 2] no form in maidens.
M. D. Hammond

DEMOLITION MOLLY 3 b.f. Rudimentary (USA) 118 – Persian Fortune 53 **73 d**
(Forzando 122) [2004 75: f5g f5g⁶ p5g 5.1g² f5g* 5.1d 5g p6g p5.1g Nov 13] compact
filly: fair performer: made all in handicap at Southwell in April: ran poorly after: raced
mainly at 5f: acts on all-weather and firm ground: usually tongue tied/in cheekpieces:
very slowly away penultimate outing: races prominently. *R. F. Marvin*

DENEBOLA (USA) 3 br.f. Storm Cat (USA) – Coup de Genie (USA) 114 (Mr Pros- **119**
pector (USA)) [2004 113p: 8g³ 7d² 8g 8g⁴ 7d² 8f Nov 28] close-coupled, quite good-
topped filly: smart performer: won Prix Marcel Boussac at Longchamp at 2 yrs: took time
to find form in 2004 (reportedly suffered with virus in spring) but better than ever at
Longchamp fourth/fifth starts when 1¼ lengths fourth to Grey Lilas in Prix du Moulin
and ¾-length second to Somnus in Prix de la Foret: effective at 7f/1m: acted on soft
ground, ran poorly in Matriarch Stakes at Hollywood on firm final outing: stud. *P. Bary,*
France

DENISE BEST (IRE) 6 ch.m. Goldmark (USA) 113 – Titchwell Lass 57 (Lead On **45**
Time (USA) 123) [2004 63: 12.6g 10.2s⁵ p8g⁵ Sep 18] poor handicapper: left M. Johnston and rejoined former trainer: stays 1½m: acts on fibresand, heavy and good to firm
going: tried in cheekpieces/blinkers: sometimes slowly away. *Miss K. M. George*

DENNICK 2 b.g. (Feb 16) Nicolotte 118 – Branston Dancer (Rudimentary (USA) 118) **55**
[2004 6m⁴ f7g Dec 16] better effort in maidens 6 months apart when fourth at Hamilton:
slowly away both outings: should stay 7f. *P. C. Haslam*

DENOUNCE 3 b.c. Selkirk (USA) 129 – Didicoy (USA) 104 (Danzig (USA)) [2004 **89**
8g² 8m May 2] big, strong colt: has scope: has a quick action: half-brother to several
winners, including 6f (at 2 yrs) to 8.5f (US Grade 2 event) winner Didina (by Nashwan)
and French 1¼m/10.5f winner Espionage (by Zafonic), both smart: dam sprinting half-
sister to Xaar: promising debut when second to United Nations in newcomers event at
Newmarket, leading main group until 1f out: failed to settle early on when only eighth to
Rehearsal in maiden there next time. *H. R. A. Cecil*

DEN PERRY 2 ch.c. (Apr 28) Tipsy Creek (USA) 115 – Beverley Monkey (IRE) 69 –
(Fayruz 116) [2004 5m⁶ 6m 6m 5.1g 7m 6s 6.1s⁵ 5d Aug 31] close-coupled colt: no form,
including in seller: wore cheekpieces penultimate start. *A. Berry*

DEN'S-JOY 8 b.m. Archway (IRE) 115 – Bonvin (Taufan (USA) 119) [2004 75d, a65: –
10s 10g 11.6m 10.1f 8m Jun 18] close-coupled mare: well held at 8 yrs: tried visored/in
cheekpieces: sometimes slowly away. *V. Smith*

DENVER (IRE) 3 b.c. Danehill (USA) 126 – Born Beautiful (USA) (Silver Deputy **95**
(CAN)) [2004 78: p10g f7g² f8g* p7g⁵ p8.6g² Dec 10] improved into a useful handicapper: won at Southwell in March (off 8 months after): good head second to Appalachian
Trail at Wolverhampton final start: stays 8.6f: acts on all-weather and soft ground: usually
blinkered. *B. J. Meehan*

DEO GRATIAS (POL) 4 b.c. Enjoy Plan (USA) – Dea (POL) (Canadian Winter –
(CAN)) [2004 17.2g Jul 11] Polish-bred colt: won twice in native country in 2003: well
held only British start on Flat: best form up to 1¼m. *M. Pitman*

DEPRESSED 2 ch.f. (Apr 20) Most Welcome 131 – Sure Care 62 (Caerleon (USA) **64**
132) [2004 p6g 6g p6g³ p5.1g⁴ p5.1d² p6g⁵ p5.1g p5.1g Dec 13] £3,000Y: quite good-
topped filly: sister to useful 5f to 7f winner Deceitful and 3-y-o Eccentric and half-sister
to 4-y-o Willheconquertoo: dam 13f winner: modest maiden: ran as if amiss final start:
will prove best at 5f/easy 6f: tried in cheekpieces/blinkers: usually front runner. *Andrew*
Reid

DEPUTY OF WOOD (USA) 2 b. or br.f. (Apr 22) Deputy Minister (CAN) – Wood –
of Binn (USA) 105 (Woodman (USA) 126) [2004 5d May 13] $220,000Y: tall filly: fifth
foal: half-sister to Grade 2 winner Distilled (by Hennessy) and Grade 3 winner Three
Wonders (by Storm Cat), both at 9f in USA: dam, French 2-y-o 6.5f (Prix Eclipse) winner,
later second in US 8.5f minor stakes event: favourite, behind in maiden at York, not
knocked about. *P. F. I. Cole*

DERAASAAT 3 ch.f. Nashwan (USA) 135 – Nafhaat (USA) 91 (Roberto (USA) 131) –
[2004 92p: 11.4d 9.9g⁶ 9m Jun 12] lengthy filly: has a powerful, round action: fairly
useful winner at 2 yrs: well held in listed races and handicap in 2004: should have been
suited by 1¼m/1½m: acted on firm going: visits Bahri. *E. A. L. Dunlop*

282

Godolphin's "Descartes"

DERWENT (USA) 5 b.g. Distant View (USA) 126 – Nothing Sweeter (USA) (Darby **72** Creek Road (USA)) [2004 –: 10.3g 12m 9.9d 10m⁴ 9.9g⁶ 10g⁶ 10g 10.1g³ 10m Sep 28] rangy gelding: fair handicapper: stays 1¼m: acts on firm and good to soft going: usually blinkered/visored: sometimes races freely: sold 13,000 gns in October. *J. D. Bethell*

DESCARTES 2 b.c. (Feb 5) Dubai Millennium 140 – Gold's Dance (FR) (Goldneyev **90 P** (USA) 114) [2004 8v* Oct 23] tall colt: has scope: fifth foal: half-brother to 2 winners in France, including smart 1999 2-y-o 9f/1¼m (Criterium de Saint-Cloud) winner Goldamix (by Linamix): dam, French 1¼m/1½m winner, out of smart French middle-distance performer Anitra's Dance: favourite, won 15-runner maiden at Newbury by 1¼ lengths from High Card, slowly away but smooth headway to lead over 1f out: will be suited by 1¼m/1½m: open to considerable improvement, and should make his mark in much stronger company as 3-y-o. *Saeed bin Suroor*

DESERT AIR (JPN) 5 ch.g. Desert King (IRE) 129 – Greek Air (IRE) 107 (Ela- **–** Mana-Mou 132) [2004 11.6g Aug 9] close-coupled gelding: fairly useful performer in 2002: well held only Flat outing since: tried blinkered: fairly useful hurdler. *M. C. Pipe*

DESERT ARC (IRE) 6 b.g. Spectrum (IRE) 126 – Bint Albadou (IRE) 91 (Green **70** Desert (USA) 127) [2004 65: 7.1g 6m* 6m* 6g⁶ 7.2d 6d 6g Sep 25] fair performer: won amateur maiden handicap at Redcar (awarded race) and amateur handicap at Hamilton, both in June: will stay 7f: acts on good to firm ground. *W. M. Brisbourne*

DESERT BATTLE (IRE) 3 ch.g. Desert Sun 120 – Papal (Selkirk (USA) 129) **–** [2004 69: 8.2s 11.6s 8.1d f7g Jun 16] rangy, workmanlike gelding: fair maiden at 2 yrs: well beaten in 2004: blinkered last 2 starts. *M. Blanshard*

DESERT BUZZ (IRE)   2 b.g. (Jan 24) Desert Story (IRE) 115 – Sugar (Hernando   **54**
(FR) 127) [2004 5v 5.1m⁶ 6f 5g⁵ 6g 5d 7d 7.5m 6m⁶ f7g Nov 22] tall gelding: modest
maiden: probably best at 5f/6f: acts on good to firm ground: wore cheekpieces 2 starts
prior to final one. *J. Hetherton*

DESERT CHIEF   2 b.c. (Mar 5) Green Desert (USA) 127 – Oriental Fashion (IRE)   **81 p**
110 (Marju (IRE) 127) [2004 6m² 6d⁶ Oct 14] smallish, good-bodied colt: fluent mover:
second foal: half-brother to 3-y-o Oriental Warrior: dam, 1m winner (including at 2 yrs),
out of close relation to Nayef and half-sister to Nashwan and Unfuwain: fairly useful
form in maidens at Newcastle (second to Crosspeace) and Newmarket (went well long
way in race won by Tomoohat): should stay 7f: likely to do better. *Saeed bin Suroor*

DESERT CITY   5 b.g. Darnay 117 – Oasis (Valiyar 129) [2004 11.9s p10g Nov 13]   **–**
sturdy gelding: maiden: well held both outings since 2002: visored both starts. *P. R. Webber*

DESERT CLASSIC   2 b.f. (Feb 28) Green Desert (USA) 127 – High Standard 83 (Kris   **58**
135) [2004 7m 7g Sep 2] angular, good-topped filly: has a quick action: sixth foal: sister
to fairly useful 7f (at 2 yrs) to 1½m winner Summer Song and half-sister to 1½m winners
Al Moulatham (smart, by Rainbow Quest) and Clever Clogs (useful, by Nashwan): dam,
2-y-o 1m winner who stayed 1½m, out of close relative to Nureyev and half-sister to dam
of Sadler's Wells: better effort in maidens when ninth at Newmarket on debut: should
stay 1m. *E. A. L. Dunlop*

DESERT COMMANDER (IRE)   2 b.c. (Mar 7) Green Desert (USA) 127 – Meadow   **82 p**
Pipit (CAN) 113 (Meadowlake (USA)) [2004 7d⁴ 7g⁶ 6g* Aug 11] fourth foal: closely
related to fairly useful 2002 2-y-o 7f winner Paiyda (by Danehill) and half-brother to
3-y-o Lucky Pipit: dam, 7f to 1¼m winner, out of half-sister to US Grade 1 9f winner
Delta Flag: tongue tied, best effort in maidens when winning at Yarmouth (beat Wavertree
Warrior comfortably by 1¼ lengths): should stay 7f: capable of better. *Saeed bin Suroor*

DESERT CORAL (IRE)   3 ch.f. Desert Story (IRE) 115 – Sleeping Beauty 87 (Mill   **–**
Reef (USA) 141) [2004 f8g Jun 11] €14,500Y: half-sister to several winners, including
useful 7f to 1¼m winner Threadneedle and fairly useful 8.5f to 1½m winner Magic
Junction (both by Danzig Connection): dam 1m winner: 66/1, well beaten in maiden at
Southwell. *P. A. Blockley*

DESERT CRISTAL (IRE)   3 ch.f. Desert King (IRE) 129 – Damiana (IRE) (Thatch-   **94**
ing 131) [2004 82: 8.5s² 8s⁶ 8g³ 7m* 8.3m³ 7s² 8g³ 8.1g 8g* 8s³ Oct 19] sparely-made
filly: fairly useful performer: won maiden at Lingfield in July and minor event at
Goodwood in September: creditable third to Cello in handicap at Bath final start: stays
1m: acts on soft and good to firm ground: tends to hang. *J. R. Boyle*

DESERT DAISY (IRE)   3 gr.f. Desert Prince (IRE) 130 – Pomponette (USA) (Rahy   **53 ?**
(USA) 115) [2004 67: 8g 12.3g 8g 7.1m 5.7g⁶ 5.7s⁶ 6d Nov 5] rather leggy, useful-
looking filly: modest maiden: effective at 6f/7f: tried visored (well beaten). *I. A. Wood*

DESERT DANCE (IRE)   4 b.g. Desert Story (IRE) 115 – Cindy's Star (IRE) 68   **–**
(Dancing Dissident (USA) 119) [2004 73: p8g Apr 3] leggy gelding: maiden: well beaten
only 4-y-o outing: sold 2,200 gns in October, sent to Spain. *G. Wragg*

DESERT DEER   6 ch.h. Cadeaux Genereux 131 – Tuxford Hideaway 102 (Cawston's   **–**
Clown 113) [2004 120: 8m May 15] big, strong horse: very smart performer: won 7 of his
14 races, notably Bet attheraces Mile at Sandown in 2003, when trained by M. Johnston:
fractured near-hind fetlock in Lockinge Stakes at Newbury on reappearance: effective at
1m/1¼m: raced mainly on good going or firmer: front runner: dead. *J. H. M. Gosden*

DESERT DEMON (IRE)   2 b.c. (Mar 26) Unfuwain (USA) 131 – Baldemosa (FR)   **71 p**
(Lead On Time (USA) 123) [2004 6g⁵ 6s³ Sep 14] big, rangy colt: has scope: fifth foal:
half-brother to 6-y-o Caustic Wit: dam, French 1m winner, half-sister to very smart
French sprinter Balbonella, herself dam of Anabaa, Key of Luck and Always Loyal: fair
form in maidens at Newmarket and Salisbury: needs to settle to stay 7f: likely to do better.
B. W. Hills

DESERT DESTINY   4 b.g. Desert Prince (IRE) 130 – High Savannah 77 (Rousillon   **115**
(USA) 133) [2004 109: 7.1g 7m² 7m⁵ 7.1g² 7m⁴ Sep 9] leggy, useful-looking gelding:
smart performer: best effort when ¾-length second to Arakan in Criterion Stakes at Newmarket second start: creditable efforts last 2 outings, unbalanced on descent when fourth
to Mac Love in listed event at Epsom final one: stays 1m: acts on good to firm going: tried
visored, tongue tied last 4 starts: has shown signs of temperament. *Saeed bin Suroor*

DESERT DIPLOMAT (IRE)   3 br.g. Machiavellian (USA) 123 – Desert Beauty
(IRE) 103 (Green Desert (USA) 127) [2004 71p: 8.3s 8.2g Jun 21] big, good-bodied

gelding: form only when fourth in maiden at Leicester second start at 2 yrs: sold 3,500 gns in July. *Sir Michael Stoute*

DESERT DREAMER (IRE) 3 b.g. Green Desert (USA) 127 – Follow That Dream 90 (Darshaan 133) [2004 98: 7.6d⁵ 9g 7m⁶ 7d 7m 7m 6g Sep 20] good-topped gelding: useful performer: below form after second start: likely to prove best up to 1m: acts on good to firm ground: withdrawn after unseating rider/bolting intended sixth outing: sold 18,000 gns in October. *B. W. Hills* **95 d**

DESERT FERN (IRE) 2 b.f. (Apr 8) Desert Style (IRE) 121 – Lady Fern (Old Vic 136) [2004 f6d⁴ f7g Jun 16] 6,500Y: third foal: closely related to 4-y-o Leighton: dam unraced daughter of US Grade 1 2-y-o 6f/7f winner Mrs Warren: poor form in maidens at Southwell. *Ms Deborah J. Evans* **49**

DESERT FURY 7 b.g. Warning 136 – Number One Spot 71 (Reference Point 139) [2004 74d: f8.5g f6g 8f⁶ f8m⁵ 6v p8g⁶ 8s⁴ f8g⁶ f8g⁴ Dec 28] small gelding: just modest nowadays: stays 8.5f: acts on fibresand, soft and good to firm going: tried in cheekpieces, tongue tied 3 starts, also blinkered final one: sometimes slowly away. *R. Bastiman* **50**

DESERT GLORY (IRE) 2 gr.f. (Feb 20) Desert Prince (IRE) 130 – True Love (Robellino (USA) 127) [2004 7g Oct 11] 40,000F, 75,000Y: unfurnished filly: second foal: dam unraced: 66/1, eleventh in maiden at Leicester, not knocked about: should do better. *D. R. Loder* **57 p**

DESERT HAWK 3 b.c. Cape Cross (IRE) 129 – Milling (IRE) 89 (In The Wings 128) [2004 8m 8m 8g⁵ 9g⁴ 10m 9d 9.9s⁶ 8g² 8.1s 8g² 8g Oct 4] €30,000Y: stocky colt: first foal: dam, 9f winner, closely related to smart middle-distance stayer Parthian Springs and half-sister to smart 9f/1¼m winner Pasternak, out of Irish Oaks winner Princess Pati: fair maiden: stays 9f: best efforts on good going. *R. Hannon* **75**

DESERT HEAT 6 b.h. Green Desert (USA) 127 – Lypharitissima (FR) (Lightning (FR) 129) [2004 62: f9.4g f9.4s² f9.4s* f8.5s² f8.5s 10.1v f8.5g⁴ 8g² Apr 29] sturdy, good-bodied horse: fair handicapper: won at Wolverhampton in February: barely stays 1½m: acts on fibresand, good to soft and probably good to firm ground: wears headgear nowadays: none too consistent. *I. Semple* **71**

DESERT IMAGE (IRE) 3 b.c. Desert King (IRE) 129 – Identical (IRE) (Machiavellian (USA) 123) [2004 70: p7g* p10g² f9.4s⁶ 10d 10.9d 10.2g³ 10.2m³ 11.7f² 10.9m⁴ 11.5g 11.7m 10.3g p12m⁶ Dec 22] short-backed colt: fair handicapper: won at Lingfield in January: stays easy 1½m: acts on all-weather and firm ground: tongue tied (ran creditably) final start. *C. Tinkler* **75**

DESERT IMP 2 b.f. (Mar 4) Green Desert (USA) 127 – Devil's Imp (IRE) 84 (Cadeaux Genereux 131) [2004 6d 6g³ 6g³ 6d* Oct 15] leggy, good-topped filly: second foal: dam, 6f and (private sweepstakes at 2 yrs) 7f winner, half-sister to smart 1½m winners Amfortas and Legend Maker from family of High-Rise and In The Wings: fair performer: won maiden at Redcar by 1½ lengths from Fashion House, leading over 1f out: will be suited by 7f/1m. *B. W. Hills* **78**

DESERT ISLAND DISC 7 b.m. Turtle Island (IRE) 123 – Distant Music (Darshaan 133) [2004 84: 10.2g 10g⁴ 12g⁴ 10m 12m³ 12g 9g⁶ 11.9g* 11.9m⁵ 12m* 11.9f* 10d⁶ 12g³ 12g 10g 10s³ 16s p12g Oct 31] sturdy mare: fairly useful performer: won minor event at Brighton and handicaps at Kempton (apprentices) and Brighton in July/August: effective at 1¼m/1½m: acts on any turf going, little form on all-weather: usually races prominently: tough and game. *J. J. Bridger* **84**

DESERT LEADER (IRE) 3 b.g. Green Desert (USA) 127 – Za Aamah (USA) (Mr Prospector (USA)) [2004 8.1m 8.1d f6g² 8.1d 7m 7.2d Sep 16] €125,000Y: good sort: first foal: dam unraced sister to useful 1¼m winner Siyadah out of Yorkshire Oaks winner Roseate Tern: fair maiden: well below form last 2 starts: gelded after: probably stays 1m: acts on fibresand and good to soft going. *B. A. McMahon* **65**

DESERT LIGHT (IRE) 3 b.c. Desert Sun 120 – Nacote (IRE) (Mtoto 134) [2004 46: p6g* f6g³ f6s 5.1g f5g² 5d² p5.1g⁵ f5m² p5.1g³ p5.1g p5.1g Dec 31] sturdy colt: modest performer: won claimer at Lingfield in January: effective at 5f/6f: acts on all-weather and good to soft ground: visored: none too reliable. *D. Shaw* **63**

DESERT LIGHTNING (IRE) 2 ch.c. (Mar 8) Desert Prince (IRE) 130 – Saibhreas (IRE) 83 (Last Tycoon 131) [2004 p7m³ Oct 6] 42,000F, 120,000Y: third foal: dam, Irish 1¼m winner, out of half-sister to top-class sprinter Double Form: 3/1, third to Qadar in maiden at Lingfield: will stay 1m: likely to do better. *J. Noseda* **74 p**

DESERT LORD 4 b.c. Green Desert (USA) 127 – Red Carnival (USA) 109 (Mr Pros- **99**
pector (USA)) [2004 6m⁶ 7f* p6g p6g* p8m³ p7g⁶ Dec 29] lengthy, good-topped colt:
useful performer, lightly raced: missed 2003: won handicaps at Newmarket in August
and (having left Sir Michael Stoute 10,000 gns prior to next outing) Lingfield in December, beating Chateau Nicol by 1¾ lengths in latter: effective at 6f to 1m: acts on polytrack,
firm and good to soft going. *D. Flood*

DESERT LOVER (IRE) 2 b.g. (Mar 6) Desert Prince (IRE) 130 – Crystal Flute **–**
(Lycius (USA) 124) [2004 6m⁶ May 22] 180,000Y: close-coupled gelding: first foal: dam
unraced half-sister to smart performers Pink Cristal (7f/1m winner) and Crystal Hearted
(stayed 1¼m): sixth in maiden at Newmarket, racing freely (gelded after). *J. Noseda*

DESERT MOONBEAM (IRE) 2 b.f. (Feb 24) Desert Prince (IRE) 130 – Pip's **43 ?**
Dream 52 (Glint of Gold 128) [2004 6g⁶ 7.1m 7g Sep 29] 4,000Y: fourth foal: half-sister
to 6-y-o Dream Magic: dam 1¼m/1½m winner: poor form in maidens/minor event.
R. J. Hodges

DESERT MOVE (IRE) 2 b.f. (Apr 30) Desert King (IRE) 129 – Campestral (USA) **72 p**
97 (Alleged (USA) 138) [2004 7d* Aug 27] €50,000Y: close-coupled filly: half-sister
to 3 winners, including smart 10.5f/11f winner Camporese and useful French stayer
Subtle Influence (both by Sadler's Wells): dam 2-y-o 7f winner who stayed 11.5f: 9/2
from 7/1, won maiden at Thirsk, leading over 2f out: should be suited by 1¼m/1½m:
likely to improve. *M. R. Channon*

DESERT OPAL 4 ch.c. Cadeaux Genereux 131 – Nullarbor (Green Desert (USA) 127) **92 d**
[2004 105: 8g 8g 8v⁵ 8g 8.3f⁶ p7.1g Dec 14] useful performer in 2003: well
below form after second start in 2004, leaving J. Gosden 8,000 gns prior to final outing
(ran as though amiss): stays 1m: best form on good/good to soft going: tried visored/
blinkered. *D. W. Chapman*

DESERT PHOENIX (IRE) 2 ch.f. (Feb 1) Desert Story (IRE) 115 – Bird In My Hand **41**
(IRE) 57 (Bluebird (USA) 125) [2004 5g⁶ 6g Jul 22] €15,000Y: sturdy filly: fourth living
foal: half-sister to 2003 2-y-o 5f winner Prince Tara (by Docksider): dam, ran 3 times,
half-sister to very smart stayer Yawa: poor form in maidens at Ripon and Doncaster.
R. A. Fahey

DESERT QUEST (IRE) 4 b.g. Rainbow Quest (USA) 134 – Jumilla (USA) 100 (El **101**
Gran Senor (USA) 136) [2004 102: 12.1d 10.1m² 11.6m⁴ 10.4g 12g* 13.4s⁵ 10d Sep 18]
rather leggy gelding: useful handicapper: won at Ascot in August by neck from Counsel's
Opinion: probably stays 13.4f: acts on soft and good to firm going: visored/blinkered: has
hung under pressure. *A. M. Balding*

DESERT QUILL (IRE) 4 ch.f. In The Wings 128 – Aljood 111 (Kris 135) [2004 53?: **52 ?**
f14.8g² 16m⁵ 11.9g 16.2m 15.8m⁴ Aug 3] sturdy, lengthy filly: modest maiden: stays 2m:
acts on fibresand and good to firm going. *W. M. Brisbourne*

DESERT REIGN 3 ch.g. Desert King (IRE) 129 – Moondance (Siberian Express **80**
(USA) 125) [2004 68: p7g³ 8.5g* 10m⁴ 8.5g² 8v³ Oct 23] workmanlike gelding: fairly
useful performer: off 4 months (gelded), improved when landing gamble in maiden handicap at Epsom in July (wandered): creditable efforts in handicaps after: finds 1m a bare
minimum, and will probably stay 1½m: acts on polytrack, heavy and good to firm going.
A. P. Jarvis

DESERT ROYALTY (IRE) 4 b.f. Alhaarth (IRE) 126 – Buraida 64 (Balidar 133) **96**
[2004 94: 10g² 12g* 11.9m² 12m⁴ 11.9d⁴ 12g 12g 11.9s³ 14.6m Sep 8] close-coupled,
good-bodied filly: useful performer: won handicap at Salisbury in May: good third to
Tarakala in listed race at York on penultimate outing: ran poorly in Park Hill Stakes at
Doncaster final one: stays 1½m: acts on firm and soft going: has been bandaged in front:
free-going sort. *E. A. L. Dunlop*

DESERT SECRETS (IRE) 2 b.f. (Jan 23) Almutawakel 126 – Shaping Up (USA) **64**
89 (Storm Bird (CAN) 134) [2004 p8g p6g p7m⁵ Dec 22] 11,000Y, 17,000£: seventh foal:
half-sister to 3 winners, including fairly useful 1m winner Thaman (by Sri Pekan) and
Irish 9f winner Islamorada (by Persian Bold), both later successful abroad: dam 2-y-o
5.7f winner: modest form in maidens: should stay at least 1m. *J. W. Hills*

DESERT STAR 4 b.g. Green Desert (USA) 127 – Phantom Gold 119 (Machiavellian **108**
(USA) 123) [2004 8f³ 8g Oct 1] big, strong, deep-girthed gelding: has a fluent, round
action: useful performer: impressive winner of maiden at Newmarket at 2 yrs: missed
2003: close third to Calcutta in handicap at Doncaster on return, running on not unduly
punished: well below form in Joel Stakes at Newmarket only outing after: subsequently
gelded: stays 1m: raced only on good ground or firmer. *Sir Michael Stoute*

DESERT TOMMY 3 b.g. Desert King (IRE) 129 – Flambera (FR) (Akarad (FR) 130) [2004 –: p10g p12g Jan 31] soundly beaten in maidens, starting slowly in blinkers/hood final outing. *T. G. Mills* —

DESIGNER CITY (IRE) 3 b.f. Mujadil (USA) 119 – Carnickian (IRE) (Sri Pekan (USA) 117) [2004 60§: 6v 6g 6m 6g 6m 5g⁴ 5d 6g p6g Oct 18] leggy filly: unreliable maiden at 2 yrs: little form in 2004. *A. Berry* — §

DESIGN (FR) 3 ch.g. Machiavellian (USA) 123 – Vitaba (USA) (Northern Baby (CAN) 127) [2004 10v⁴ Oct 20] €220,000Y: fourth foal: half-brother to French 10.5f winner Olympic Candle (by Catrail): dam useful French 2-y-o 5.5f/1m winner who stayed 1¼m: 7/2 favourite from 5/1, green when 5 lengths fourth to Lomapamar in maiden at Nottingham, slowly away, then tiring over 1f out: sold 18,000 gns, joined T. McCourt in Ireland. *Sir Michael Stoute* **55**

DESIREE (IRE) 3 b.f. Desert Story (IRE) 115 – Elba (IRE) (Ela-Mana-Mou 132) [2004 8.2d 10d Oct 4] IR 8,000£, €7,000Y: close-coupled filly: first foal: dam unraced: well held in maidens at Nottingham and Windsor. *John Berry* —

DESIRES DESTINY 6 b.m. Grey Desire 115 – Tanoda 77 (Tyrnavos 129) [2004 47: f8g⁶ f11g f8.5g⁶ f8g³ 9.9s f8m² 9.9m May 24] poor maiden: stays 1¼m: acts on fibresand and soft going. *M. Brittain* **42**

DESPERATION (IRE) 2 b.g. (Mar 17) Desert Style (IRE) 121 – Mauras Pride (IRE) (Cadeaux Genereux 131) [2004 f5g 7s⁵ p8.6g² 9d³ f8g³ f8g³ Dec 11] 1,000Y: good-topped gelding: fifth foal: brother to fairly useful 2000 2-y-o 1¼m winner Deuce of Trumps and half-brother to 5-y-o Wilson Bluebottle: dam unraced from family of William Hill Futurity winner Al Hareb: fair maiden: ran well in nursery at Southwell final start: stays 9f: acts on all-weather and good to soft going. *K. R. Burke* **73**

DESTINATE (IRE) 2 b.c. (Mar 19) Desert Style (IRE) 121 – Double Eight (IRE) 77 (Common Grounds 118) [2004 5g 6m* 7g 7g⁴ 7g⁴ 8.1d² 8m² Sep 11] €46,000Y: good-topped colt: fourth foal: half-brother to 11.6f winner Fiza (by Revoque): dam 1½m winner: useful performer: won maiden at Newmarket in May: good fourth to Shamardal in Vintage Stakes at Goodwood fourth start: respectable second in minor event at Sandown and listed race at Goodwood: likely to stay 1¼m: acts on good to firm going: got loose and withdrawn third intended outing: sold 110,000 gns, sent to Saudi Arabia. *R. Hannon* **101**

DESTINATION DUBAI (USA) 3 br.c. Kingmambo (USA) 125 – Mysterial (USA) (Alleged (USA) 138) [2004 97: 10.5g* 12g³ 12m 11.9d 10.3m 10f* Sep 24] tall, close-coupled colt: useful performer: trained by D. Loder at 2 yrs: won maiden at Haydock in May and minor event at Ascot (beat Courageous Duke ½ length) in September: likely to prove best around 1¼m: acts on firm and good to soft ground: effective visored or not: tongue tied last 3 outings: usually races prominently: looked reluctant latter 2-y-o appearance: said by jockey to be hanging right throughout on penultimate start. *Saeed bin Suroor* **97**

DETONATE 2 b.c. (Apr 1) Mind Games 121 – Bron Hilda (IRE) 50 (Namaqualand (USA)) [2004 5.2g⁶ 5s⁴ 5g 6g⁶ 5.1g³ 5g Aug 14] leggy, close-coupled colt: first foal: dam, maiden, stayed 7f: fair maiden: seems best at 5f: acts on soft going: edgy sort: races freely. *I. A. Wood* **75**

DETROIT DANCER 2 b.c. (Feb 21) Makbul 104 – First Play 59 (Primo Dominie 121) [2004 6m 5g⁵ 6d Aug 4] poor maiden: sold 500 gns, sent to Belgium. *Ronald Thompson* **48**

DEUXIEME (IRE) 3 b.f. Second Empire (IRE) 124 – Kardelle 79 (Kalaglow 132) [2004 7m³ 7g³ 7d⁵ 5.7f² 6g² p6g* p6g⁴ Nov 27] lengthy, quite attractive filly: closely related to 6-y-o King's County and half-sister to a winner in Hong Kong by Salse: dam, maiden who stayed 1¼m, half-sister to smart middle-distance stayer Spout: fair performer: won maiden at Wolverhampton (hung left) in October: free-going sort, and likely to prove best at 5f/6f: acts on polytrack and firm ground: slowly away on debut and fourth outing. *R. Charlton* **74**

DEVANT (NZ) 4 b.f. Zabeel (NZ) – Frenetic (NZ) (Truly Vain (AUS)) [2004 98: 8v 8m⁴ 8m 8m² 8m 10.5s³ 12s⁵ Aug 27] quite good-topped filly: fairly useful handicapper: creditable efforts when in frame: stays 10.5f: acts on soft and good to firm ground: usually held up: has flashed tail: sent to Australia. *M. A. Jarvis* **86**

DEVIL'S BITE 3 ch.g. Dracula (AUS) 121 – Niggle 65 (Night Shift (USA)) [2004 78: p7g f9.4g f8g f5g Dec 14] strong, workmanlike gelding: has a round action: fair maiden —

at 2 yrs: broke blood vessels when pulled up first 2 outings in 2004: left B. Hills, tailed off after. *M. C. Chapman*

DEVIL'S ISLAND 2 b.g. (Mar 2) Green Desert (USA) 127 – Scandalette (Niniski – p (USA) 125) [2004 6.1s⁵ 6m p7m Oct 6] tall gelding: seventh foal: closely related to 7-y-o Gateman and half-brother to 2 winners, including smart 7f/1m winner Surprise Encounter (by Cadeaux Genereux): dam unraced half-sister to high-class sprinter Polish Patriot: slowly away and not knocked about in maidens: gelded after final start: type to do good deal better as 3-y-o. *Sir Mark Prescott*

DEVINE COMMAND 3 b.g. In Command (IRE) 114 – Adriya 94 (Vayrann 133) 63 [2004 p8g p10g p7g² p8g⁵ p9.5g⁴ Dec 17] modest maiden: stays 9.5f: raced only on polytrack. *R. Ingram*

DEVINE LIGHT (IRE) 4 b.f. Spectrum (IRE) 126 – Siskin (IRE) (Royal Academy – (USA) 130) [2004 64?: 10m 9m 11.9f⁶ 6.9f 9.2s 8g 10s Oct 30] leggy filly: no form in 2004: has worn visor/cheekpieces: probably none too genuine. *B. Mactaggart*

DEVIOUS AYERS (IRE) 3 b.g. Dr Devious (IRE) 127 – Yulara (IRE) 99 (Night 58 d Shift (USA)) [2004 62p: f8.5g⁴ 8v 12f 9.2d⁶ p10g p8.6d p8.6g Dec 10] quite good-topped gelding: modest maiden at best: left G. Butler prior to penultimate start: bred to be suited by 1¼m+: acts on all-weather. *J. M. Bradley*

DEVIOUS PADDY (IRE) 4 b.g. Dr Devious (IRE) 127 – Night Arcade (IRE) 77 – (Night Shift (USA)) [2004 75: f8.5s f11g Mar 16] maiden: tongue tied, well held both starts in 2004. *N. Tinkler*

DEVISE (IRE) 5 b.g. Hamas (IRE) 125§ – Soreze (IRE) 102 (Gallic League 119) [2004 95 81: 5.7g* 6g⁶ 6g 5g* 5.7f⁵ 5g⁵ 5m⁴ 5g 5g² 5s³ 5.1d² 5g² 6m Sep 12] smallish, close-coupled gelding: useful performer: won minor event at Bath in April and handicap at Kempton in May: good efforts when placed after: stays 5.7f: acts on soft and good to firm ground: sometimes early to post: game and consistent. *M. S. Saunders*

DEVITO (FR) 3 ch.g. Trempolino (USA) 135 – Snowy (FR) (Wollow 132) [2004 –: 54 11.8m² 12m⁵ 16.2g Jul 19] lengthy gelding: best effort when 11 lengths second in maiden at Leicester. *A. King*

DEVON FLAME 5 b.g. Whittingham (IRE) 104 – Uae Flame (IRE) (Polish Precedent 83 (USA) 131) [2004 72: 6g² 5m* 5.7f² 6g² 6.5g⁴ 6m 6m 5.7m² 6s 5g Sep 20] fairly useful handicapper: won at Windsor in June: creditable efforts when in frame after: best at 5f/6f: acts on good ground: races prominently. *R. J. Hodges*

DEVOTE 6 b.g. Pennekamp (USA) 130 – Radiant Bride (USA) (Blushing Groom (FR) – 131) [2004 10.2g 11.6f⁶ 18d Aug 19] maiden: well held at 6 yrs: tried blinkered. *J. D. Frost*

DEWIN COCH 2 b.g. (Feb 24) Wizard King 122 – Drudwen (Sayf El Arab (USA) 53 127) [2004 7.1g 7.1s 6d⁶ Oct 2] modest form in maidens: best effort at 7f on soft going: tends to race freely. *W. M. Brisbourne*

DEXILEOS (IRE) 5 b.g. Danehill (USA) 126 – Theano (IRE) 114 (Thatching 131) 58 [2004 75: 10.2g 9.7s 8.1v 8.2d 7f 7m 7g 6m³ 6m 7.1s p7.1d³ p7m p7g³ Dec 29] close-coupled gelding: modest maiden: stays 1m: acts on polytrack, soft and good to firm going: tried visored, usually tongue tied. *David Pinder*

DHABYAN (USA) 4 b.g. Silver Hawk (USA) 123 – Fleur de Nuit (USA) (Woodman – (USA) 126) [2004 102: 10.3g Jun 5] good-topped gelding: useful at best: suffered injury after final start in 2003: tailed off only 4-y-o outing: has raced freely. *B. Hanbury*

DHAULAR DHAR (IRE) 2 b.c. (May 6) Indian Ridge 123 – Pescara (IRE) 108 92 p (Common Grounds 118) [2004 7d² 7g* 7s Oct 22] leggy, quite attractive colt: has a round action: second foal: dam French 2-y-o 5.5f winner who stayed 1m: odds on, won maiden at Chester in September easily by 11 lengths, making most and still green: 11/2, only ninth in Horris Hill Stakes at Newbury: will stay 1m: useful prospect. *B. W. Hills*

DHEFAAF (IRE) 2 b.c. (Feb 20) Lujain (USA) 119 – Paparazza (IRE) (Arazi (USA) – 135) [2004 5m May 18] 38,000F, 25,000Y: first foal: dam, little form, half-sister to very smart stayer Solo Mio: behind in maiden at Leicester, slowly away: sold 4,500 gns, sent to Spain. *B. Hanbury*

DHEHDAAH 3 b.g. Alhaarth (IRE) 126 – Carina Clare (Slip Anchor 136) [2004 62: 62 10m 12.1d³ 11.7f⁵ Jul 5] angular gelding: modest maiden: stays 1½m: acts on firm and good to soft going: blinkered final start: sold 14,000 gns, joined Mrs P. Sly. *N. A. Graham*

DIAGON ALLEY (IRE) 4 ro.g. Petong 126 – Mubadara (IRE) 80 (Lahib (USA) 129) –
[2004 –: f9.4s f9.4m⁶ May 17] close-coupled gelding: of no account. *K. W. Hogg, Isle of Man*

DIAL SQUARE 3 b.g. Bluegrass Prince (IRE) 110 – Honey Mill 67 (Milford 119) **?**
[2004 –: f7g p8g* p7g³ p7g² p8g³ p8g* p8g* p10g* 7m 8m 12g p8.6d p8.6g p12.2g **a58**
Nov 15] modest performer: won banded races at Lingfield in February and April (3):
stays 1¼m: acts on polytrack, no form on turf: effective blinkered or not. *P. Howling*

DIAMOND CIRCLE 2 br.f. (Mar 18) Halling (USA) 133 – Canadian Mill (USA) 115 **64 p**
(Mill Reef (USA) 141) [2004 7s⁵ Oct 27] half-sister to 3 winners, notably smart 7f (at 2
yrs) to 1¼m (Musidora Stakes) winner Hawajiss (by Kris): dam, 2-y-o 6f winner, second
in Cheveley Park Stakes: 14/1, 10 lengths fifth to Plea Bargain in maiden at Yarmouth,
slowly away: will stay at least 1m: should do better. *B. W. Hills*

DIAMOND DANCER 3 b.f. Groom Dancer (USA) 128 – Sleepless 92 (Night Shift –
(USA)) [2004 p7g⁶ Dec 29] first living foal: dam winner around 7f: 25/1, always behind
in maiden at Lingfield. *C. A. Dwyer*

DIAMOND DAN (IRE) 2 b.g. (May 11) Foxhound (USA) 103 – Kawther (Tap On –
Wood 130) [2004 6d Oct 14] €11,000Y: smallish gelding: half-brother to several winners,
including 6-y-o Diamond Max: dam little sign of ability: 100/1, never dangerous in
maiden at Newmarket. *John Berry*

DIAMOND DAZZLER 6 br.g. Sula Bula 109 – Dancing Diamond (IRE) 56 (Alzao –
(USA) 117) [2004 f11g Jan 15] well held in seller at Southwell, only outing on Flat.
D. P. Keane

DIAMOND GEORGE (IRE) 3 b.g. Sri Pekan (USA) 117 – Golden Choice (Midyan **52**
(USA) 124) [2004 65: f6g⁵ f7g⁶ 7.1s May 3] close-coupled gelding: modest maiden:
should have stayed 7f: acted on fibresand and good to firm going: dead. *John Berry*

DIAMOND GREEN (FR) 3 b.c. Green Desert (USA) 127 – Diamonaka (FR) 105 **121**
(Akarad (FR) 130) [2004 115p: 8g³ 8g² 8f² 8d² 8g² 8m 8d Oct 30] good-bodied colt: very
smart performer: placed first 5 starts in 2004, running well when second in Poule d'Essai
des Poulains at Longchamp (beaten ½ length by American Post), St James's Palace
Stakes at Royal Ascot (went down by neck to Azamour) and Prix du Moulin de Longchamp (beaten a length by Grey Lilas) second, third and fifth outings: unimpressive in
coat and on toes, well below form in Queen Elizabeth II Stakes at Ascot (took strong
hold): not discredited when eighth to Singletary in Breeders' Cup Mile at Lone Star Park
final start, starting awkwardly and not clearest of runs from home turn: stays 1m: has
form on good to soft going, but very best efforts on good or firmer. *A. Fabre, France*

DIAMOND HERITAGE 2 ch.g. (Apr 1) Compton Place 125 – Eccolina 65 (Formid- **52**
able (USA) 125) [2004 5g 6s 6.1v³ Oct 20] 18,000F, 11,500Y, 16,000 2-y-o: big, strong
gelding: sixth foal: dam, maiden who seemed to stay 1¼m, sister to very smart sprinter
Chilibang: best effort when not-knocked-about fifth in minor event at Nottingham
(gelded after). *J. A. Glover*

DIAMOND HOMBRE (USA) 2 gr.c. (Feb 24) Two Punch (USA) – Flowing (USA) **68**
114 (El Gran Senor (USA) 136) [2004 5f⁴ 6g⁶ p5g Aug 6] $105,000Y: big colt: closely
related to 3 winners, including useful Irish sprinter Lady Shannon (by Mr Prospector)
and half-brother to useful 7f (at 2 yrs) and 1¼m winner Garmoucheh (by Silver Hawk):
dam Irish sprinter: fair form in maidens/minor event: should prove better at 6f than 5f.
J. W. Hills

DIAMOND JOSH 2 ch.g. (Apr 29) Primo Dominie 121 – Exit 82 (Exbourne (USA) **72**
125) [2004 5m³ 6s⁶ Oct 29] sturdy gelding: second foal: dam, 8.5f winner, half-sister to
dam of smart 1998 2-y-o 7f winner Auction House: better effort in maidens when third at
Windsor: refused to enter stall twice after and left P. D. Evans: should stay at least 6f.
John Berry

DIAMOND KATIE (IRE) 2 b.f. (Mar 2) Night Shift (USA) – Fayrooz (USA) 74 **70**
(Gulch (USA)) [2004 6g 6.5g 6g³ Oct 2] 16,000Y: deep-girthed filly: fifth foal: half-sister
to 1¼m winner Beryl (by Bering): dam, 2-y-o 7f winner, out of half-sister to El Gran
Senor and Try My Best: fair form in maidens/sales race: should stay 1m. *R. Guest*

DIAMOND LODGE 3 ch.f. Grand Lodge (USA) 125 – Movieland (USA) 109 (Nure- **98**
yev (USA) 131) [2004 8g⁴ 8.3g* 8.1d² 8.3m* 8g* 9g* 8m⁵ 8m² Sep 4] 47,000Y, 58,000
2-y-o: quite good-topped filly: half-sister to 2 winners, including 1¼m winner Monsieur
Rick (by Sillery): dam, French 2-y-o 1m (Prix des Reservoirs) winner, sister to smart
miler Only Star: useful performer: won maiden at Windsor in May, minor event there in
June and handicaps at Newmarket and Goodwood in July: creditable second to Mystical

Girl in handicap at Kempton final start: should stay 1¼m: acts on good to firm and good to soft going: has worn crossed noseband. *J. Noseda*

DIAMOND MAX (IRE)   6 b.g. Nicolotte 118 – Kawther (Tap On Wood 130) [2004   **85**
96: a7g a8.3g* a8.3g³ 9g 7s⁴ Nov 6] angular gelding: fairly useful performer: won minor
event at Mijas in July: left J. L. Eyre in Spain, creditable fourth in apprentice handicap at
Doncaster final start: barely stays 9f: acts on fibresand/sand, best turf efforts on good
ground or softer (acts on heavy): tried visored. *John Berry*

DIAMOND ORCHID (IRE)   4 gr.f. Victory Note (USA) 120 – Olivia's Pride (IRE)   **63**
(Digamist (USA) 110) [2004 57: f8g³ f12g² f12s⁴ p12g² 10.2s² 11.6m* p10g⁵ 14.1m*
14.1g p16d² 15.9g p12.2g⁴ Oct 9] strong filly: modest handicapper: won at Windsor in
May and Yarmouth in June: stays easy 2m: acts on all-weather, soft and good to firm
going: usually wears cheekpieces/visor: sometimes wanders. *P. D. Evans*

DIAMOND RACKET   4 b.g. Cyrano de Bergerac 120 – Reina 24 (Homeboy 114)   **–**
[2004 –: f5g f5s⁶ f5g f5s Mar 30] good-topped gelding: probably of little account nowadays: usually visored/blinkered. *D. W. Chapman*

DIAMOND RIBBY (IRE)   3 br.f. Desert Sun 120 – Kathleen's Dream (USA) (Last   **–**
Tycoon 131) [2004 –: p8g Mar 9] well held, including in seller at Lingfield at 3 yrs.
P. D. Evans

DIAMOND RING   5 b.m. Magic Ring (IRE) 115 – Reticent Bride (IRE) 71 (Shy   **52**
Groom (USA)) [2004 58: 5.1d⁵ 5m 5.7f³ 5g 5.1g³ 5.1m⁶ 6m² 5.1g⁴ 6.1g 5d Oct 9] quite
good-topped mare: modest performer: best at 5f/6f: acts on soft and good to firm going:
visored once in 2003. *Mrs J. Candlish*

DIAMONDS AND DUST   2 b.c. (Feb 5) Mister Baileys 123 – Dusty Shoes 72 (Sha-   **92**
reef Dancer (USA) 135) [2004 6g⁴ 6g³ 7g⁴ 7m* 7m 6d⁶ Oct 14] 6,000Y: useful-looking
colt: first foal: dam ran twice (should have been suited by 1½m+): fairly useful performer:
won nursery at York in September: very good sixth to Cape Columbine in sales race at
Newmarket: should stay 1m: acts on good to firm and good to soft ground: often races up
with pace. *M. H. Tompkins*

DIAMOND SHANNON (IRE)   3 b.f. Petorius 117 – Balgren (IRE) (Ballad Rock   **65**
122) [2004 47p: 6g 5s 6.1s⁵ f7d⁸ f8g² f7m 6.1d p7.1g p5.1g⁶ p7.1g³ f7g* f8g Dec 28]
leggy filly: fair handicapper: won at Southwell in June and December: stays 1m: best
efforts on fibresand. *D. Carroll*

DIAMONDS WILL DO (IRE)   7 b.m. Bigstone (IRE) 126 – Clear Ability (IRE) 81   **–**
(Be My Guest (USA) 126) [2004 62: 12.1g⁶ Jul 9] poor maiden, lightly raced on Flat:
well held only 7-y-o start. *Miss Venetia Williams*

DIAMOND WAY (USA)   3 ch.c. Boundary (USA) 117 – Discover Silver (USA) (Valid   **67**
Appeal (USA)) [2004 60: p8g* Jan 14] fair performer: visored, won handicap at Lingfield: stayed 1m: acted on polytrack, raced only on good/good to firm ground on turf:
dead. *D. R. Loder*

DIAPHANOUS   6 b.m. Beveled (USA) – Sharp Venita 84 (Sharp Edge 123) [2004 52:   **–**
f5g p5g p5g 5.1f 5g 5m f5g 8.1m 6m 6d⁶ Oct 10] sturdy mare: maiden: little form in 2004:
often blinkered: tried tongue tied. *E. A. Wheeler*

DIATONIC   2 b.g. (Mar 2) Deploy 131 – Vic Melody (FR) (Old Vic 136) [2004 5g p5g   **60**
6m f7g² 8g Sep 11] small gelding: modest maiden: left W. Musson after second in seller
at Southwell: should stay at least 1¼m: easily best effort on fibresand. *D. Carroll*

DICKIE DEADEYE   7 b.g. Distant Relative 128 – Accuracy 83 (Gunner B 126)   **76**
[2004 65: 10.3g⁶ 9.7d⁵ 10v² 10s² 10g³ 12.1g* 12d* 11.9g³ 10m⁴ 11.9g 9.9g³ 11.6d Oct 4]
tall gelding: fair handicapper: made all at Chepstow (apprentice event by 11 lengths)
and Doncaster in July: stays 1½m: acts on polytrack, goes well on good ground or softer.
G. B. Balding

DICK THE TAXI   10 b.g. Karlinsky (USA) – Another Galaxy (IRE) (Anita's Prince   **77**
126) [2004 81: f12g³ 12.3g³ 12.3m 10.3d⁴ a10.5g² a12g² a10.5g⁶ Dec 12] big, good-
topped gelding: fair performer: stays 1½m: acts on all-weather/sand and good to soft
ground: has carried head high: consistent. *R. J. Smith, Spain*

DICTION (IRE)   2 br.f. (Apr 6) Diktat 126 – Waft (USA) 67 (Topsider (USA)) [2004   **–**
6m 6g⁵ f7g* f6d⁴ 7.1f⁵ f7g² p7.1g⁶ f7g³ Dec 14] 3,000Y: quite good-topped filly: fourth   **a71**
foal: dam, third at 1m, half-sister to dam of 4-y-o Papineau and Silver Patriarch: fair
performer: won seller in June and nursery in July, both at Southwell: good efforts when
placed there after: effective at 6f/7f: form only on fibresand. *K. R. Burke*

DIDNT TELL MY WIFE 5 ch.g. Aragon 118 – Bee Dee Dancer (Ballacashtal **76**
(CAN)) [2004 76: 7.1v⁶ p8g⁶ p8d 8.1g⁴ 8g³ 9d* 8d³ 7.9m 8.1d⁶ 8.2v³ 9s p9.5g⁶ p10g⁵
Dec 29] unfurnished gelding: fair handicapper: won at Newbury in August: stays 9f: acts
on all-weather, heavy and good to firm going: blinkered (very slowly away) once in 2002:
usually held up: has edged left/raced freely. *C. F. Wall*

DIDOE 5 br.m. Son Pardo 107 – My Diamond Ring 65 (Sparkling Boy 110) [2004 **56**
57, a46?: 8.1f 8.1m 10m 10.2m* 10m² 8m* 8s 7.1m 8.5m Sep 15] leggy mare: modest
performer: won seller and handicap at Bath in July/August: effective at 1m to 1¼m: acts
on polytrack and firm going. *P. W. Hiatt*

DIEGO CAO (IRE) 3 b.g. Cape Cross (IRE) 129 – Lady Moranbon (USA) (Trempo- **95**
lino (USA) 135) [2004 9.8d² 9.5g* 9.5g⁶ 10g* 10d⁴ 10g² p12g Oct 25] 85,000F: half-
brother to several winners, including 4-y-o Space Cowboy and French 11.5f winner
Anchorage (by Slip Anchor): dam French 9f/1¼m winner: useful performer: won maiden
at Lisieux in April (sold from A. Fabre 6,500 gns in July) and handicap at Sandown in
September: best effort when neck second to Best Be Going in handicap at Windsor penultimate start: well held on all-weather debut final outing: stays 1¼m: won juvenile hurdle
in November. *G. L. Moore*

DIEQUEST (USA) 3 ch.g. Diesis 133 – Nuance (IRE) 70 (Rainbow Quest (USA) 134) **–**
[2004 –: 8.3m 10g 10d p10g Nov 16] little form, and has shown signs of temperament.
Jamie Poulton

DIFFERENT PLANET 3 b.c. Inchinor 119 – Take Heart 84 (Electric 126) [2004 **76**
8m⁴ 8m⁴ 8.3d⁵ Jun 21] 60,000Y: quite good-topped colt: closely related to 4-y-o Indian
Trail and half-brother to 3 winners, including useful 1¼m winner Lonely Heart (by Midyan): dam 7f to 1¼m winner: best effort in maidens when fourth to Credit at Newbury on
debut: sold 4,500 gns in October. *J. W. Hills*

DIGGER (IRE) 5 ch.g. Danzig Connection (USA) – Baliana 75 (Midyan (USA) 124) **–**
[2004 71, a80: f11g* f12g⁴ p12g f12s² f16s⁵ 10.3g 12d Aug 29] big, workmanlike geld- **a80**
ing: fairly useful handicapper on all-weather: won at Southwell in January: left Gay
Kelleway after sixth outing: stays easy 2m: acts on fibresand, good to firm and good to
soft going: tried in headgear: often tongue tied: free-going sort. *Seamus Fahey, Ireland*

DIGITAL 7 ch.g. Safawan 118 – Heavenly Goddess (Soviet Star (USA) 128) [2004 **97**
103: p7g 7s³ 7v⁴ 8g 8v³ 7.6d⁶ 7g 7g 7.1m⁵ 7.2d² 7s² 7g² 7m 7m 7g 7s² 7s² 7m 7g⁵ 7d 7d⁶
7s⁴ Nov 2] workmanlike gelding: useful handicapper: runner-up 5 times in 2004: effective at 7f/1m: acts on polytrack and any turf going: sometimes starts slowly: has raced
freely: carries head awkwardly: waited with: tough. *M. R. Channon*

DIKTATIT 2 b.f. (Jan 31) Diktat 126 – Mystique Smile 78 (Music Boy 124) [2004 **48**
5g 5g⁵ 5.1m Aug 10] 23,000Y: leggy, close-coupled filly: third foal: half-sister to 4-y-o
Earlston: dam 2-y-o 5f winner: poor form in maidens/seller: will stay 6f. *M. R. Channon*

DIKTATORIAL 2 br.c. (Feb 11) Diktat 126 – Reason To Dance 96 (Damister (USA) **105 p**
123) [2004 7m 7.1d* 7g* Sep 30] 45,000Y: tall, angular colt: has a round action: fourth
foal: half-brother to 3 winners, including fairly useful 9f winner Stands To Reason (by
Hernando) and 4-y-o Princess Magdalena: dam 5f (at 2 yrs) and 6.5f (in USA) winner
who stayed 1¼m: progressive type: won maiden at Sandown by 5 lengths, twice veering
left) in August and Somerville Tattersall Stakes at Newmarket (by neck from Crimson
Sun) in September, making running: will stay 1m: has been blanketed/attended by expert
in stall entry at start: smart prospect. *A. M. Balding*

DIL 9 b.g. Primo Dominie 121 – Swellegant 84 (Midyan (USA) 124) [2004 –, a67d: f6g **–**
f7g f6g Nov 8] lengthy, good-topped gelding: well held in 2004: tried tongue tied/visored/
in cheekpieces. *Mrs N. Macauley*

DILIGENT LAD 4 b.g. Secret Appeal – Mohibbah (USA) 86 (Conquistador Cielo **– §**
(USA)) [2004 –§: 12.1g 12.3m May 26] tall, angular gelding: little form: hard ride.
D. W. Barker

DILIZA 5 b.m. Dilum (USA) 115 – Little White Lies 78 (Runnett 125) [2004 59: p8g⁴ **39**
p10g p8g⁶ Feb 3] good-bodied mare: poor performer: stays 1m: acts on polytrack, firm
and good to soft going: sometimes slowly away: none too consistent. *G. B. Balding*

DILYS 5 b.m. Efisio 120 – Ramajana (USA) (Shadeed (USA) 135) [2004 58d: p7g Jan **–**
15] smallish, sturdy mare: well held only outing in 2004: visored once. *W. S. Kittow*

DINE 'N' DASH 3 ch.g. Komaite (USA) – Instinction (Never So Bold 135) [2004 7d **45**
6s⁶ 5.7f p8.6g p7g³ Dec 20] workmanlike gelding: poor maiden: stays 7f: acts on polytrack: tried in cheekpieces. *A. G. Newcombe*

DINGLEY LASS   4 ch.f. Fleetwood (IRE) 107 – Riverine (Risk Me (FR) 127) [2004 **44** –: p10d⁶ 13.1d 16.2m Sep 6] poor maiden, lightly raced. *H. Morrison*

DINNER DATE   2 ch.c. (Apr 1) Groom Dancer (USA) 128 – Misleading Lady (Warn- **– p** ing 136) [2004 7s Oct 22] third foal: half-brother to 3-y-o Lord Mayor: dam twice-raced sister to smart 1½m performer Little Rock and half-sister to smart middle-distance stayer Whitewater Affair: 13/2, behind in maiden at Doncaster, niggled along by halfway: should do better. *Sir Michael Stoute*

DISABUSE   4 ch.g. Fleetwood (IRE) 107 – Agony Aunt 81 (Formidable (USA) 125) **54** [2004 56: f7g² f8f* f11s³ f12s⁴ f12g⁴ 10.1g⁵ 8.2s⁴ 14.1d⁵ f12m f8s 11.9g p8.6d Oct 23] **a63** strong, workmanlike gelding: modest handicapper: won at Southwell in January for S. Williams: left M. Easterby after tenth place: effective at 7f and stays 1¾m: acts on fibre-sand, soft and good to firm ground: wore headgear 5 of last 6 outings: sold 4,500 gns. *D. Shaw*

DISCO DIVA   3 ch.f. Spectrum (IRE) 126 – Compact Disc (IRE) 48 (Royal Academy **59** (USA) 130) [2004 71: p7g 6g 7m 6m 6g 7g² p8.6d² p8g p7.1g⁶ Dec 6] leggy filly: modest performer: stays 8.6f: acts on polytrack and firm going: sometimes races freely: hung left and found little fifth start. *M. Blanshard*

DISCOMANIA   2 b.g. (Apr 18) Pursuit of Love 124 – Discomatic (USA) (Roberto **70** (USA) 131) [2004 7m 7g⁴ 7f⁶ 8d Aug 27] strong gelding: half-brother to 3 winners, not-ably smart 1¾m winner Tuning (by Rainbow Quest): dam, French 9f winner, half-sister to 1987 Phoenix Stakes winner Digamist: fair maiden: should stay 1m: best effort on good going: sold 16,500 gns, then gelded. *R. Charlton*

DISCUSS (USA)   2 b.f. (May 26) Danzig (USA) – Private Line (USA) 105 (Private **77 P** Account (USA)) [2004 6g² Oct 2] tall, lengthy filly: has scope: fourth foal: closely related to smart French 7f to 10.5f (Prix Fille de l'Air) winner Dance Dress (by Nureyev) and half-sister to useful 1¼m winner Conclude (by Distant View) and 4-y-o Colophony: dam 7f (at 2 yrs) to 8.5f (in USA) winner: 5/2, 2½ lengths second to Loyal Love in maiden at Newmarket, slowly away and green in rear but getting hang of things late on: will probably stay 1m: sure to improve significantly and win races. *Sir Michael Stoute*

DISGUISE   2 b.c. (Apr 15) Pursuit of Love 124 – Nullarbor (Green Desert (USA) 127) **78** [2004 6g⁵ 6g² 5.7g⁴ 5.1g² Sep 29] third living foal: half-brother to 4-y-o Desert Opal: dam, French 2-y-o 5.5f winner, half-sister to very smart French/US performer up to 1½m Radevore: fair maiden: tongue tied, short-headed at Nottingham final start: will prove best at 5f/6f. *B. W. Hills*

DISHDASHA (IRE)   2 b.g. (Mar 29) Desert Prince (IRE) 130 – Counterplot (IRE) 91 **52** (Last Tycoon 131) [2004 6m 6m 7g³ f7m 7m 7m p6g⁵ Dec 29] workmanlike gelding: modest maiden: left T. Easterby after third start: stays 7f: acts on polytrack, best turf form on good going. *C. R. Dore*

DISPARITY (USA)   3 b.f. Distant View (USA) 126 – Eternity 77 (Suave Dancer **64** (USA) 136) [2004 10d 10m⁴ p10d² p12g p12g Oct 31] second foal: half-sister to 1½m and 2m winner Etching (by Groom Dancer): dam, 11f/1½m winner, half-sister to May Hill and Fillies' Mile winner Tessla: modest maiden: should stay 1½m: acts on poly-track and good to firm ground: often tongue tied: sent to France. *J. R. Fanshawe*

DISPOL CHARM (IRE)   2 br.f. (Apr 24) Charnwood Forest (IRE) 125 – Phoenix **34** Venture (IRE) 69 (Thatching 131) [2004 5d⁵ 6m p6g f5g Dec 16] €7,000F, 1,500Y: leggy filly: closely related to 6-y-o Cardinal Venture and half-sister to 2 winners abroad: dam, 7f winner, out of sprinting half-sister to 2000 Guineas winner Tirol: poor maiden: left T. D. Barron prior to penultimate start. *D. W. Chapman*

DISPOL EVITA   5 ch.m. Presidium 124 – She's A Breeze 35 (Crofthall 110) [2004 **59 §** 56§, a59§: p12g p10g⁴ p12g² p12g p10g⁴ 11.9f 12g 10f Sep 16] rather leggy, close-coupled mare: modest performer: stays 1½m: acts on all-weather and firm going, probably soft: tried blinkered/in cheekpieces: often slowly away/looks none too keen: inconsistent. *Jamie Poulton*

DISPOL FOXTROT   6 ch.m. Alhijaz 122 – Foxtrot Pie 77 (Shernazar 131) [2004 **73** 9.2g² 8.3d³ May 7] close-coupled mare: bad mover: fair performer: stays 11f: acts on fibresand, best on good ground or softer on turf: has found little/edged right. *Miss V. Scott*

DISPOL IN MIND   2 b.f. (Feb 6) Mind Games 121 – Sans Diablo (IRE) (Mac's Imp **63** (USA) 116) [2004 5m² 5m³ 5.1m* Aug 15] 5,500Y: fifth foal: half-sister to 5f (including at 2 yrs) winner Bonny Ruan (by So Factual): dam unraced: second in seller at Catterick (looked wayward), then left P. Midgley: won maiden at Bath: should stay 6f: tends to be slowly away. *I. A. Wood*

DISPOL ISLE (IRE) 2 gr.f. (Apr 1) Trans Island 119 – Pictina (Petong 126) [2004 **73**
5m⁴ 5g⁴ 5.1g⁴ 5g⁴ 6d³ 7g⁵ 6d⁶ 6s³ Oct 22] 1,000Y: leggy, workmanlike filly: second
living foal: dam unraced out of sister to very smart miler Dominion: fair maiden: third in
nursery/sales race: probably stays 7f: best effort on soft going. *T. D. Barron*

DISPOL KATIE 3 ch.f. Komaite (USA) – Twilight Time (Aragon 118) [2004 88: 5d **85**
6g⁶ 5.1d³ 5f⁵ 5d 5s² 5f 5d Sep 17] tall filly: fairly useful handicapper: should stay 6f: acts
on firm and soft going: often races prominently. *T. D. Barron*

DISPOL PETO 4 gr.g. Petong 126 – Plie 75 (Superlative 118) [2004 67: f7g f7s⁵ f7s² **67**
f7s f7g⁵ 7.1m f7d² f7g f7g⁵ f8g⁵ Dec 28] good-quartered gelding: fair performer: barely
stays 8.5f: acts on fibresand, soft and good to firm going: sometimes blinkered, usually in
cheekpieces: races up with pace: inconsistent. *Ian Emmerson*

DISPOL VELETA 3 b.f. Makbul 104 – Foxtrot Pie 77 (Shernazar 131) [2004 –: f6g³ **75**
f6g f8g* f9.4s⁴ 8.2g* 8g³ 8m 10m f8g* 8s 8.1d f8g 7.9g² Sep 1] good-topped filly: fair
handicapper: won at Southwell (maiden event) in February, Nottingham in March and
Southwell in June: should stay beyond 1m: acts on fibresand, best efforts on turf on good
going. *T. D. Barron*

DISPOL VERITY 4 b.f. Averti (IRE) 117 – Fawley Mist (Suave Dancer (USA) 136) **–**
[2004 f5g 6.1g f8g 6d 8f 8s⁶ Oct 30] small, leggy filly: maiden: well held in 2004.
W. M. Brisbourne

DISSIDENT (GER) 6 b.h. Polish Precedent (USA) 131 – Diasprina (GER) (Aspros **91**
(GER)) [2004 a8g⁴ a8g p10g* 10.9d 11s² 10d² 12g* 14.4v⁴ 12m⁵ 12m⁶ 10.1g⁵ 12g p10g
Dec 30] sturdy horse: half-brother to several winners in Germany, including useful 5f (at
2 yrs) to 7f winner Desidera (by Shaadi): dam German 2-y-o 5f to 1m winner: fairly
useful performer: left H. Blume in Germany after second start: won seller at Lingfield in
April and handicap at Newmarket in May: ran as if amiss last 2 starts: stays 1½m: acts on
polytrack, sand, soft and good to firm going: usually visored: tongue tied (ran well) eighth
start: usually races prominently. *D. Flood*

DISTANT CONNECTION (IRE) 3 b.c. Cadeaux Genereux 131 – Night Owl 73 **97**
(Night Shift (USA)) [2004 79: 10d 7.1s 7.6d 7g⁶ 7.1f* 7m² 8m* 7.1d⁵ 7g³ 7f² 7m p7g*
p7g³ Sep 1] good-topped colt: useful handicapper: won at Sandown in May, Ripon in
June and Lingfield (beat Obrigado comfortably by 2½ lengths) in August: effective at 7f/
1m: acts on polytrack, good to firm and good to soft going: usually races prominently:
raced freely and folded tamely eleventh start: tough and consistent: sold 80,000 gns,
joined M. Al Kurdi in UAE. *A. P. Jarvis*

DISTANT COUNTRY (USA) 5 b.g. Distant View (USA) 126 – Memsahb (USA) **80**
(Restless Native) [2004 82: 7g⁶ 8s⁶ 7d 8m² 6g⁵ 8m² 7m⁵ 8m 7m³ 7m p7.1g² p8.6g³ p7.1g³
p7.1g Dec 20] tall, good-topped gelding: fairly useful handicapper: mostly creditable
efforts in 2004: effective at 7f to 8.6f: acts on polytrack and firm ground: usually wears
cheekpieces: has looked tricky ride/carried head awkwardly: usually held up. *Mrs
J. R. Ramsden*

DISTANT COUSIN 7 b.g. Distant Relative 128 – Tinaca (USA) (Manila (USA)) **70 d**
[2004 72: p12g 12m⁵ 12.3m³ 14.1m 14.6m 12m⁴ 14.1f³ 14.1m 13.9g Oct 9] quite good-
topped gelding: fair handicapper: below form after third start: stays 14.6f: acts on all-
weather, soft and good to firm going: often races freely: visored/blinkered. *M. A. Buckley*

DISTANT KING 11 b.g. Distant Relative 128 – Lindfield Belle (IRE) 78 (Fairy King **–**
(USA)) [2004 –: 6m Jul 31] no longer of much account. *G. P. Kelly*

DISTANT PROSPECT (IRE) 7 b.g. Namaqualand (USA) – Ukraine's Affair (USA) **101**
(The Minstrel (CAN) 135) [2004 100: 18.7d⁴ 16.2d² 16.1s 16.2g 21g³ 18s 12s² Nov 6]
useful handicapper: hasn't won on Flat since 2001 Cesarewitch: mostly creditable efforts
in 2004, 2½ lengths second of 24 to Carte Diamond in November Handicap at Doncaster
final outing: effective at 1½m (given testing conditions) to 21f: acts on any going, though
all wins on good or softer: often sweating: held up: consistent. *A. M. Balding*

DISTANT TIMES 3 b.c. Orpen (USA) 116 – Simply Times (USA) 64 (Dodge (USA)) **81**
[2004 76: 7g⁵ 6.1s* 6d³ 6m 6m 6s⁵ 5m* 5d 5s⁶ 6d Aug 30] big, lengthy colt: fairly useful
performer: won minor events at Warwick in April and Beverley in July: effective at 5f to
easy 7f: acts on soft and good to firm ground: tried blinkered/visored, better form when
not. *T. D. Easterby*

DISTINCTION (IRE) 5 b.g. Danehill (USA) 126 – Ivy Leaf (IRE) 76 (Nureyev **118**
(USA) 131) [2004 112: 12g 13.3m⁵ 13.9g* 12f* 16s⁶ Nov 2] big, strong, good sort: smart
performer, lightly raced: won listed rated stakes at York (by ½ length from Star Member)
in July and listed race at Doncaster (by ¾ length from Compton Bolter, idling) in

orderIT-online.com Troy Stakes, Doncaster—
Distinction earns himself a trip to Australia with this win over Compton Bolter

September: missed Caulfield Cup in October due to a reported low blood count, then respectable sixth of 24 to Makybe Diva in Melbourne Cup at Flemington final outing: will stay beyond 2m: acts on firm going, probably on soft: has wandered/raced freely. *Sir Michael Stoute*

DISTINCTIVE MIND   2 b.g. (Feb 3) Mind Games 121 – Primum Tempus 49 (Primo   **57 p**
Dominie 121) [2004 6g 5m 5.1g Sep 29] big gelding: sixth foal: half-brother to 3 winning sprinters, including 6-y-o Time N Time Again: dam sprint maiden: green, best effort in maidens at Nottingham final start: will prove best at 5f/6f: type to make a better 3-y-o. *T. D. Easterby*

DISTINCTLY GAME   2 b.c. (Jan 28) Mind Games 121 – Distinctly Blu (IRE) 70   **105**
(Distinctly North (USA) 115) [2004 5g² 6g² f6m² 5m* 5g⁴ 6d² 6m² Sep 8] 11,000Y: tall, leggy colt: first foal: dam 5f winner: useful performer: won maiden at York in June: second in nursery at York and sales race at Doncaster (much improved when beaten 2 lengths by Caesar Beware) after: likely to prove best at 5f/6f: acts on fibresand, good to firm and good to soft going: flicked tail/wandered third/fourth starts. *K. A. Ryan*

DISTINCTLYTHEBEST   4 b.g. Distinctly North (USA) 115 – Euphyllia 70 (Super-   **–**
power 113) [2004 –: 9d 9m 7g Sep 7] lengthy gelding: no sign of ability. *F. Watson*

DIUM MAC   3 b.g. Presidium 124 – Efipetite 54 (Efisio 120) [2004 75: 7m 8g⁴ Aug 4]   **–**
leggy gelding: fair maiden at 2 yrs: well held both starts in 2004. *N. Bycroft*

DIVA DANCER   4 ch.f. Dr Devious (IRE) 127 – Catina 102 (Nureyev (USA) 131)   **–**
[2004 –: f8g f11g 10m 16f 17.2g Jul 3] sturdy filly: little form: tried blinkered. *J. Hetherton*

DIVANI (IRE)   2 b.f. (Mar 14) Shinko Forest (IRE) – Supreme Crown (USA) (Chief's   **–**
Crown (USA)) [2004 5g May 17] 20,000Y: good-topped filly: half-sister to several winners, including useful performer up to 13f in Britain/Scandinavia Tough Guy (by Namaqualand): dam unraced: seemed to go amiss in maiden at Windsor: sold 8,000 gns in July. *B. J. Meehan*

DIVERTED   3 b.f. Averti (IRE) 117 – Whittle Rock 91 (Rock City 120) [2004 f8.5s   **–**
p7g 9.7s 7s 8f 8f⁵ 10.1g Aug 11] third foal: sister to a winner in Italy: dam 5f (at 2 yrs) to 7f winner: little form. *M. G. Quinlan*

DIVINA 3 b.f. King's Theatre (IRE) 128 – Heuston Station (IRE) 72 (Fairy King (USA)) [2004 f8g f9.4s p12g 6d p8g⁴ f8d³ f8m² p10g² 8.5m f8g Jul 9] close-coupled filly: poor performer: stayed 1m: acted on all-weather: visored last 6 starts: dead. *S. L. Keightley* — **a41**

DIVINE DIVA 2 b.f. (Mar 29) Diktat 126 – Maid To Dance 62 (Pyramus (USA) 78) [2004 6m 6.1m⁴ Jul 23] 17,500Y: leggy, quite good-topped filly: first foal: dam, ran 3 times, half-sister to very smart performer up to 1½m Filia Ardross, herself dam of Fillies' Mile winner Sunspangled: better effort in maidens when fourth at Chepstow: should stay 1m: sold 800 gns. *R. Hannon* **62**

DIVINE GIFT 3 b.c. Groom Dancer (USA) 128 – Child's Play (USA) (Sharpen Up 127) [2004 89p: 8g* 8d⁴ 8s⁴ 7s Oct 23] good-topped colt: has a quick action: useful performer: clearly best effort, won minor event at Doncaster (beat Gold History 3½ lengths, dictating pace) in March: stays 1m: acts on good to firm and good to soft going. *M. A. Jarvis* **102 ?**

DIVINELY DECADENT (IRE) 2 br.f. (Feb 6) Turtle Island (IRE) 123 – Divine Prospect (IRE) 75 (Namaqualand (USA)) [2004 6g* 7g Oct 2] €27,000Y, 30,000 2-y-o: leggy filly: first foal: dam, 2-y-o 7f winner who stayed 1¼m, half-sister to 6-y-o Vinnie Roe: won maiden at Yarmouth in September by 2 lengths from Peppermint Tea: still green (sweating/on toes), similar form when ninth to Penkenna Princess in listed race at Newmarket, meeting trouble before getting going late: will stay at least 1¼m: should progress. *P. W. Chapple-Hyam* **85 p**

DIVINE PROPORTIONS (USA) 2 b.f. (Mar 13) Kingmambo (USA) 125 – Myth To Reality (FR) (Sadler's Wells (USA) 132) [2004 5d* 5g* 5.5g* 6s* 8m* Oct 3] **119**

    The balance of two-year-old racing at the highest level in Europe has swung so decisively in favour of horses trained in Britain and Ireland that prospects of its changing in the near future seem remote. This is probably an unwelcome development for the French, who have seen an increasing number of important races for juveniles falling to foreign raiders and a decline in the number of leading youngsters trained at home. From 1961 to 1980 French-trained two-year-olds provided the top colt in Europe on eight occasions and the top filly eleven times, with no shortage of others to back up those stars. In the same period, British- or Irish-trained horses won just four top races in France, two of them falling to My Swallow in 1970. By comparison, in the last fifteen years only four colts—Hector Protector, Arazi, Xaar and Bago—and three fillies—Morning Pride, Six Perfections and Divine Proportions—have been top rated, while challengers from abroad have notched twenty-eight Group 1 events. The proportion of French juveniles with a rating of 114 or higher has declined by around half. To some extent this is a

Prix Morny Casinos Barriere, Deauville—Divine Proportions becomes the first since Arazi in 1991 to complete the Robert Papin/Morny double; behind her are Layman, Russian Blue and Captain Hurricane

Prix Marcel Boussac-Criterium des Pouliches Royal Barriere de Deauville, Longchamp—
Divine Proportions extends her unbeaten run to five, landing the odds from Titian Time (No.5),
Fraloga (right) and Intrigued (rail); sixth-placed Queen of Poland is the other filly in the picture

reflection of the increasing internationalisation of the sport (though that should work both ways), the concentration of the best-bred two-year-olds outside France and the fact that the British and Irish patterns have always tended to cater better for precocious youngsters than the French version, which focuses its attention primarily on races over seven furlongs and upwards in the autumn. In an era when pedigrees contain more sprinter-miler elements than ever, that is almost certainly a significant factor. At least Divine Proportions flew the flag in style and did so well in landing all her five starts that she is rated the best juvenile of either sex in her country, as well as being the best two-year-old filly in Europe.

After success in a five-furlong newcomers race at Maisons-Laffitte in May, Divine Proportions really started to show what she was made of in the Prix du Bois at Chantilly at the end of June, putting up a well-above average performance for a filly at the time of year. Opposed by six others, including unbeaten odds-on shot Great Blood and listed winner Salut Thomas, she tracked the pace, quickened ahead in the final furlong and drew clear to beat the favourite impressively by four lengths. Divine Proportions confirmed her standing in the Prix Robert Papin at Maisons-Laffitte a month later, though she was much more workmanlike in defeating Italian-trained filly Shifting Place by a length, needing a few cracks with the whip to lead in the final furlong. The suspicion was that five and a half furlongs was indeed on the sharp side by this stage of the season and, stepped up to six on soft going in the nine-runner Prix Morny Casinos Barriere at Deauville, Divine Proportions put up her best performance. The race was well contested, with six foreign raiders, five of them boasting pattern form, notably Captain Hurricane (July Stakes), Tournedos (Molecomb Stakes) and Russian Blue (third in the Phoenix Stakes), along with Salut Thomas again and five-length Prix de Cabourg victor Layman, who was sent off a warm favourite. Held up and still going well behind the leaders two furlongs out, Divine Proportions accelerated to lead in the final furlong and needed only to be pushed out to beat Layman by a length and a half, with Russian Blue the same distance away third. The first three finished clear and, as Layman went on to be a close third in the Prix Jean-Luc Lagardere, and Russian Blue finished third in the National Stakes, there is little reason to doubt the value of the form.

Despite this, Divine Proportions was only 10/9-on to win the Prix Marcel Boussac-Criterium des Pouliches Royal Barriere de Deauville on Arc day at Long-champ, this with seemingly one of her most serious rivals, Last Rhapsody, a late withdrawal. The predictions of some pundits that she would be hard pressed to stay the trip might have influenced racegoers, as perhaps did the fact that there were some promising fillies among the nine other runners. They included pattern winner Cours de La Reine (Prix du Calvados), pattern-placed Portrayal and Queen of Poland and British maiden winners Intrigued and Titian Time. In the event, Divine Proportions, a smallish, quite attractive filly who was less imposing in appearance than some of her rivals (notably the Chantilly winner Fraloga), won in pretty good

296

style on ground very different to that with which she had coped at Deauville. Close up from the outset, she looked likely to win easily when edging out to challenge in the straight. Soon in front, she did not burst clear and, in fact, tended to idle, eventually beating Titian Time by two lengths with Fraloga, who looks one to follow, a nose further back. Sectional times show that the winner covered the penultimate two hundred metres faster than any other leader on the day, but her final two hundred took almost a second longer, suggesting that she may well have been hanging on by this point. Possibly the going was not entirely in Divine Proportions' favour—she has a fluent and rounded action—but she was still an emphatic winner, the fourth in the last five years for Pascal Bary and the third in a row for the Niarchos Family. Divine Proportions ended the year as 4/1 favourite for the One Thousand Guineas, a short enough price given the sporadic nature of Bary's raids on British races, a record which indicates that the filly's participation at Newmarket is a hope rather than a certainty. If she runs she will command the utmost respect unless underfoot conditions place a particularly heavy premium on stamina.

Divine Proportions (USA) (b.f. Mar 13, 2002)	Kingmambo (USA) (b 1990)	Mr Prospector (b 1970)	Raise A Native
			Gold Digger
		Miesque (b 1984)	Nureyev
			Pasadoble
	Myth To Reality (FR) (b 1986)	Sadler's Wells (b 1981)	Northern Dancer
			Fairy Bridge
		Millieme (b 1977)	Mill Reef
			Hardiemma

Three-year-old Whipper, successful in the Prix Jacques le Marois to add to his Prix Morny victory at two, is still the best of Myth To Reality's progeny, but, with Divine Proportions coming just one year later, there will be interest in the next

Niarchos Family's "Divine Proportions"

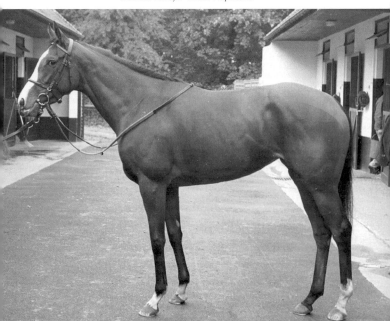

in line, a filly by the sprinter Mt Livermore who did not reach her reserve as a foal at Keeneland and has since been named Anse Victorin. Divine Proportions is closely related to Whipper, since her sire Kingmambo is another son of Miesque and altogether a better racehorse and sire than Miesque's Son; Kingmambo's other winners in the season under review included Russian Rhythm, Rule of Law and leading Japanese three-year-old King Kamehameha. Most of Kingmambo's progeny are effective at a mile and a reason able number—if there is stamina on the distaff side—stay further. Myth To Reality stayed a mile and a half well, as might be expected of a Sadler's Wells filly out of a sister to Shirley Heights, but Whipper, whose essay has more information on the family, is unlikely to stay beyond a mile and Divine Proportions, whose principal asset is speed, will probably follow suit. *P. Bary, France*

DIVINE SPIRIT   3 b.g. Foxhound (USA) 103 – Vocation (IRE) 74 (Royal Academy   **92** (USA) 130) [2004 84: 5.1d 5m 6m 5f³ 5m⁶ 5d* 5m 5.1g³ 5m⁶ 5m 5d³ Aug 12] leggy gelding: fairly useful handicapper: won at Ayr in June: mainly creditable efforts after: effective at 5f (all wins)/6f: acts on firm and good to soft going: effective with or without cheekpieces: consistent. *M. Dods*

DIWAN (IRE)   6 b.g. Be My Guest (USA) 126 – Nectarine (IRE) 95 (Darshaan 133)   **–** [2004 12.6d p8.6g Oct 25] big gelding: lightly-raced maiden. *J. Parkes*

DIXIEANNA   2 ch.f. (Feb 23) Night Shift (USA) – Dixielake (IRE) 84 (Lake Coniston   **79 p** (IRE) 131) [2004 5g² Aug 23] first foal: dam, 1m winner, half-sister to useful 1m winner Lady Fairfax: second in maiden at Windsor, making most: should stay 1m: likely to improve. *B. W. Hills*

DIXIE DANCING   5 ch.m. Greensmith 121 – Daylight Dreams 77 (Indian Ridge 123)   **69** [2004 65: p7g⁵ f8d p8g⁴ p7g² 6g³ Aug 14] sturdy mare: fair performer: effective at 6f to easy 1m: acts on polytrack and good to firm going: free-going sort. *C. A. Cyzer*

DIXIE QUEEN (IRE)   2 b.f. (Feb 14) King of Kings (IRE) 125 – Dixieline City   **56** (USA) (Dixieland Band (USA)) [2004 5v⁵ 6g 7.1g 7g³ 7.9g p8.6g f6s Nov 17] 13,000Y: rather leggy filly: first foal: dam unraced daughter of smart sprinter Central City: modest maiden: stays 7f: blinkered (ran poorly) last 2 starts. *M. Dods*

DIZZY FUTURE   2 b.g. (Apr 5) Fraam 114 – Kara Sea (USA) 70 (River Special   **56** (USA)) [2004 8.3m 6d Oct 14] 8,000Y: good-topped gelding: first foal: dam 1m winner who stayed 1¾m: modest form in maiden at Windsor: last in sales race at Newmarket less than month later: should prove better at 1m to 6f. *W. Jarvis*

DIZZY IN THE HEAD   5 b.g. Mind Games 121 – Giddy 60 (Polar Falcon (USA)   **86 §** 126) [2004 81§: 6s 6v* 5g⁶ 6m³ 5g* 6.1f² 5.5m* 5d 5.1g 5m 6d* 7.1d p6g Dec 27] leggy gelding: fairly useful performer: won claimer at Redcar in May (claimed from J. O'Reilly after next start), handicaps at Beverley and Warwick in June and minor event at Hamilton in August: stays 6f: acts on any turf ground, below form both starts on fibresand: usually wears headgear: often hangs: usually makes running: not one to trust. *Paul Johnson*

DIZZY LIZZY   2 gr.f. (Mar 11) Sendawar (IRE) 129 – Black Velvet (FR) (Black Tie   **–** Affair 128) [2004 7g 5.1g⁴ 8.1s Aug 30] 8,000F: second foal: dam useful French 1m/ 1¼m winner: no form in maidens/minor event. *Nick Williams*

DOCDUCKOUT   4 b.g. Bluegrass Prince (IRE) 110 – Fayre Holly (IRE) 57 (Fayruz   **–** 116) [2004 56: f6g p5.1g Nov 11] pulled up on reappearance and well held second outing in 2004: tried in cheekpieces. *J. W. Unett*

DOCKLANDS BLUE (IRE)   3 ch.f. Cadeaux Genereux 131 – Copious (IRE) (Gener-   **54** ous (IRE) 139) [2004 57: p5g² f6g p5g p6g³ p7g⁶ p7g⁴ p7g³ 7.1s 6g May 14] modest maiden: stays 7f: acts on all-weather, below form both starts on turf: held up: blinkered final start. *N. P. Littmoden*

DOCKLANDS DUDE (IRE)   2 ch.g. (Mar 20) Namid 128 – Cheeky Weeky (Cade-   **43** aux Genereux 131) [2004 5g⁶ 5.1g Apr 8] well-grown, leggy gelding: poor form in seller (for M. Wallace) and claimer. *C. M. Meade*

DOCKLANDS GRACE (USA)   2 gr.f. (May 16) Honour And Glory (USA) 122 –   **62** Afarel (USA) (Runaway Groom (CAN)) [2004 f5m⁵ 5m⁵ 5g³ Aug 13] first foal: half-sister to several winners in USA: dam, US 6f winner, half-sister to Breeders' Cup Sprint runner-up Meafara: modest form in maidens: should stay 6f. *N. P. Littmoden*

DOCK TOWER (IRE)   2 b.g. (Apr 20) Docksider (USA) 124 – Thakhayr (Sadler's   **64** Wells (USA) 132) [2004 p8g p10g⁵ Nov 27] 14,000Y: half-brother to several winners, including fairly useful 6f (at 2 yrs)/7f winner Billy McCaw (by Efisio): dam ran once: green, modest form in maidens at Lingfield, then gelded. *J. W. Hills*

DOCTORATE 3 b.c. Dr Fong (USA) 128 – Aunt Tate (Tate Gallery (USA) 117) [2004 **95** 67: 8g 7s* 7.5m² 8m⁵ p7g³ 8.1g 7d* 7g 7.1d⁴ Oct 17] angular colt: useful performer: won maiden at Folkestone in April and handicap at Newbury in September: creditable fourth to Go Padero in handicap at Musselburgh final start: stays 7.5f: acts on polytrack, soft and good to firm going: tends to edge right: sold 52,000 gns, sent to USA. *E. A. L. Dunlop*

DOCTOR DENNIS (IRE) 7 b.g. Last Tycoon 131 – Noble Lustre (USA) 71 (Lyph- **58 §** ard's Wish (FR) 124) [2004 61d: p6g⁵ p6g* p6g⁶ 7m 6f* 6f 7m⁶ 6g 6d p7.1g p7m p6g³ Dec 20] good-bodied gelding: modest handicapper: won at Lingfield in February and Brighton in June: effective at 6f/7f: acts on all-weather, firm and soft going: usually in headgear: inconsistent. *J. Pearce*

DOCTORED 3 ch.g. Dr Devious (IRE) 127 – Polygueza (FR) 78 (Be My Guest **82** (USA) 126) [2004 59§: p8g p7g p8g⁴ p10g⁶ 7d* f8d* 6s 8f* 10.2g* 10m* 10g* 10g³ 10m 10m⁶ 10g p10g⁴ 10g 14g Oct 2] strong, workmanlike gelding: fairly useful performer: won selling handicap at Folkestone and claimer at Southwell in April, claimer at Bath (left B. Pearce) in May and minor events at Bath, Lingfield and Newmarket in July: stays 1¼m: acts on all-weather, firm and good to soft ground: wears cheekpieces/blinkers: tried tongue tied. *P. D. Evans*

DOCTOR HILARY 2 b.c. (Apr 6) Mujahid (USA) 125 – Agony Aunt 81 (Formid- **92** able (USA) 125) [2004 6.1s⁴ 6m* 6m² 5.1d³ 6m² 6m⁵ Aug 8] 21,000Y, 88,000 2-y-o: strong colt: fourth foal: half-brother to fairly useful 6f winner Cool Tune (by Piccolo), 3-y-o Only If I Laugh and 4-y-o Disabuse: dam 1¼m winner: fairly useful performer: won maiden at Ayr in May: good second in minor event at Kempton and nursery at Ayr: found little final start: stays 6f: acts on good to firm going: visored (slowly away) fourth outing: joined S. Seemar in UAE. *M. L. W. Bell*

DOCTOR JOHN 7 ch.g. Handsome Sailor 125 – Bollin Sophie (Efisio 120) [2004 **55** p12g⁴ f16g² f16.2s* 16.1v⁶ f16.2m² f14m² 14.1m f16g² 16s⁴ 15.8m 15.8g² Oct 5] lengthy gelding: modest handicapper: off 2½ years prior to reappearance: won at Wolverhampton in February: acts on fibresand, heavy and good to firm going: sometimes wears cheek-pieces. *Andrew Turnell*

DOCTOR'S CAVE 2 b.c. (Apr 21) Night Shift (USA) – Periquitum 56 (Dilum (USA) **89** 115) [2004 6m 6m 7m 7.5g 6g* 6s 6g 6d p6g p6g² f8g² Nov 22] 58,000F, 25,000Y: good-topped colt: first foal: dam, ran 3 times, half-sister to smart stayer Primitive Rising: fairly useful performer: won maiden at Goodwood in July: good efforts when runner-up in nursery at Lingfield and minor event at Southwell: effective at 6f to 1m: acts on all-weather, best turf efforts on good going. *C. E. Brittain*

DOCTRINE 3 b.f. Barathea (IRE) 127 – Auspicious 103 (Shirley Heights 130) [2004 **86** 97: 8d⁴ 8f 10.2g⁵ 12f Aug 1] well-made filly: fairly useful performer: respectable efforts in listed/pattern company first 3 starts: stays 1¼m: acts on good to firm ground, probably on good to soft: sold 60,000 gns in December. *J. H. M. Gosden*

DOITFORREEL (IRE) 2 b.f. (May 5) Princely Heir (IRE) 111 – Chehana 78 (Posse **86** (USA) 130) [2004 6f 5.1g 5.1f³ 6d* 6s⁵ 5.1v³ Nov 4] leggy filly: fifth living foal: half-sister to 4-y-o Sahara Prince and 2 winners in Italy, including useful performer up to 11f Veri's Game (by Astronef): dam, 9f winner in Britain, successful up to 11f in USA: fairly useful performer: won maiden at Pontefract in October: very good fifth in listed contest at Newmarket, hanging left: respectable third in nursery at Nottingham final start: barely stays 6f: probably acts on any turf going: refused to enter stall fourth intended outing. *I. A. Wood*

DOITNOW (IRE) 3 b.g. Princely Heir (IRE) 111 – Tonys Gift 73 (Midyan (USA) 124) **94** [2004 6m* 6g² 6m² 6g⁶ 7g⁶ 6.5f Sep 24] €6,000Y: lengthy gelding: half-brother to winner around 1¼m in Italy by King's Theatre: dam, 7f to 15f winner, also won over hurdles: fairly useful performer: won maiden at Ripon in June: runner-up in handicaps at Haydock and Newbury next 2 starts: stays 7f: raced only on good going or firmer. *R. A. Fahey*

DOLCE PICCATA 3 ch.f. Piccolo 121 – Highland Rhapsody (IRE) 78 (Kris 135) **87 d** [2004 88: 6d 6v⁵ 5g⁴ 6g⁵ 6m 6d 5m 5m 5d 5m⁶ p6m Oct 6] workmanlike filly: fairly useful performer: below form after third start: best at 5f: acts on good to firm going, probably on fibresand: tried blinkered, including last 5 outings. *B. J. Meehan*

DOLLAR LAW 8 ch.g. Selkirk (USA) 129 – Western Heights (Shirley Heights 130) **–** [2004 –: 8.2v Oct 20] leggy, short-backed gelding: fair 1m/1¼m handicapper in 2002, well held both Flat starts since. *R. J. Price*

DOLLIVIUS (IRE) 3 b.f. Titus Livius (FR) 115 – Dollar Magic (Fairy King (USA)) **74**
[2004 78: 5m 6d 5f* 5g 5m³ 5m 6m 5d p5.1g⁶ p5.1g p5.1g Dec 4] €4,000Y: sixth foal:
half-sister to 2 winners abroad by Lycius: dam twice-raced half-sister to Ebor winner
Deposki: fair performer: won maiden at Cork in June: left T. McCourt in Ireland 5,000
gns after eighth start: below form last 2 outings: effective at 5f/6f: acts on polytrack and
firm ground. *Ms Deborah J. Evans*

DOLLS HOUSE 2 b.f. (May 20) Dancing Spree (USA) – Kip's Sister (Cawston's **–**
Clown 113) [2004 p6g Nov 16] half-sister to several winners, including 5-y-o Steenberg
and 4-y-o Thingmebob: dam unraced: 12/1 and green, well held in maiden at Lingfield,
not knocked about. *M. H. Tompkins*

DOLLY PEEL 2 b.f. (Feb 20) Josr Algarhoud (IRE) 118 – Transylvania 85 (Wolfhound **–**
(USA) 126) [2004 5d Aug 15] close-coupled filly: third foal: dam 7f/1m winner: well
beaten in maiden at Pontefract, going badly right start. *G. A. Swinbank*

DOLLY WOTNOT (IRE) 3 b.f. Desert King (IRE) 129 – Riding School (IRE) **66**
(Royal Academy (USA) 130) [2004 65: 12.1d⁵ 11.6s 10f⁵ 11.1m³ Jun 9] leggy, sparely-
made filly: fair maiden: stays 1½m: acts on good to firm and good to soft ground.
N. P. Littmoden

DOLPHINELLE (IRE) 8 b.g. Dolphin Street (FR) 125 – Mamie's Joy (Prince Ten- **– §**
derfoot (USA) 126) [2004 –§, a55§: p8g⁴ p8g³ Feb 18] sturdy gelding: modest performer: **a53 §**
stays 1¼m: below form on heavy going, probably acts on any other turf/all-weather: often
blinkered/visored: tends to race lazily: untrustworthy. *Jamie Poulton*

DOLZAGO 4 b.g. Pursuit of Love 124 – Doctor's Glory (USA) 91 (Elmaamul (USA) **–**
125) [2004 50: p13g* p13g² p13g³ 14.4v 13.3g 12g Jul 1] good-bodied gelding: fair **a75**
performer: won maiden at Lingfield in February: stays 13f: acts on polytrack, no recent
form on turf: blinkered last 6 outings. *G. L. Moore*

DOMART (POL) 4 gr.g. Baby Bid (USA) – Dominet (POL) (Dixieland (POL)) [2004 **–**
13.3g Jun 22] Polish-bred gelding: winner of 5 races in native country, including 3 in
2003: well held in handicap at Newbury only 4-y-o start: subsequently gelded. *M. Pitman*

DOMENICO (IRE) 6 b.g. Sadler's Wells (USA) 132 – Russian Ballet (USA) **67**
(Nijinsky (CAN) 138) [2004 82: 16.2m 12m³ 20f p16g⁶ 17.1d 14.8d Aug 27] strong,
close-coupled gelding: just fair performer at 6 yrs: probably stays 2½m: acts on soft and
good to firm ground: blinkered (well beaten) once at 3 yrs: raced too freely fourth start.
J. R. Jenkins

DOMINER (IRE) 2 b.c. (Mar 16) Desert Prince (IRE) 130 – Smart (IRE) (Last Tycoon **–**
131) [2004 5.1m⁶ 5.7f⁶ 5.1f⁶ 6m Sep 12] well held in minor event/maidens: wore
cheekpieces final start. *J. M. Bradley*

DOMIRATI 4 b.g. Emarati (USA) 74 – Julia Domna (Dominion 123) [2004 85: 6m **87**
5.1g⁴ 5g² 5m 5m² 5.2f 5d⁵ p5g³ p6g p6g Dec 13] angular gelding: fairly useful
handicapper: creditable efforts when in frame in 2004: effective at 5f/easy 6f: acts on
polytrack, good to firm and good to soft going: blinkered (pulled hard, well below form)
final outing: has been early to post/had 2 handlers. *R. Charlton*

DONALD (POL) 4 b.g. Enjoy Plan (USA) – Dahira (POL) (Dakota 127) [2004 17.2f³ **63**
13.3m 14.1g⁶ 17.2g Jul 11] ex-Polish gelding: winner of 2 races in Poland at 6f (at 2 yrs)
and 1m: modest form in Britain: stays 17f: acts on firm going: winning hurdler. *M. Pitman*

DON ARGENTO 3 gr.g. Sri Pekan (USA) 117 – Grey Galava 64 (Generous (IRE) **43**
139) [2004 –: 7.1d 10m 7.1g 8.1g 10m³ 10m 10m Aug 16] workmanlike gelding: poor
maiden: stays 1¼m: acts on good to firm going: often slowly away. *Mrs A. J. Bowlby*

DONASTRELA (IRE) 3 b.f. Tagula (IRE) 116 – David's Star (Welsh Saint 126) **74**
[2004 –: p8g⁶ 8.3s 11.5m 10.2f* 10.2g⁴ 10.2m* 12m³ 11.7m³ 14.4m⁵ 12m⁴ 12g Oct 2]
tall, leggy filly: fair handicapper: won at Bath in June and July: stays 1¾m: acts on firm
ground: visored last 8 outings: held up. *A. M. Balding*

DONEGAL SHORE (IRE) 5 b.h. Mujadil (USA) 119 – Distant Shore (IRE) 71 **54**
(Jareer (USA) 115) [2004 –: f6g⁴ f7g² f7g² f8.5s⁴ f8.5g³ f8g 6.1d⁶ f8m 8d⁴ f5g f6g³ p7.1g⁶
f8g² f8g³ Dec 12] rather leggy horse: modest performer: stays 8.5f: acts on fibresand,
heavy and good to firm going: usually tongue tied/visored: none too straightforward.
Mrs J. Candlish

DON FAYRUZ (IRE) 12 b.g. Fayruz 116 – Gobolino (Don 128) [2004 –: p10g Jan **–**
17] good-topped gelding: well held only 12-y-o start. *B. N. Doran*

DON FERNANDO   5 b.g. Zilzal (USA) 137 – Teulada (USA) 61 (Riverman (USA)   **86**
131) [2004 90: 15s 16.2m⁵ 20f 22.2f⁶ 16.1m² Jul 7] tall, good-topped gelding: fairly
useful handicapper: stays 2¾m: acts on firm going: visored once at 3 yrs: usually held up:
sold 1,700 gns in October, then gelded. *M. C. Pipe*

DONNA'S DOUBLE   9 ch.g. Weldnaas (USA) 112 – Shadha 57 (Shirley Heights 130)   **57**
[2004 71, a–: 9.2d⁵ 9.2g⁶ 9.2f³ 7g⁴ 12.1f³ 9.2d⁴ 8s⁶ 9.1d² 9.9m 12g² 12g Oct 4] smallish,
workmanlike gelding: modest performer: stays easy 1½m: acts on firm and soft going,
some promise on fibresand: tried blinkered/visored, usually wears cheekpieces: sometimes carries head awkwardly/finds little: held up: none too consistent. *D. Eddy*

DONNA VITA   3 b.f. Vettori (IRE) 119 – Soolaimon (IRE) 71 (Shareef Dancer (USA)   **85**
135) [2004 78p: 11.5s⁴ 8.1d 10g 10.1g Sep 15] angular filly: fairly useful performer,
lightly raced: left G. Butler after reappearance: ran as though amiss final outing: stays
1¼m: raced only on polytrack and good ground or softer. *P. W. Chapple-Hyam*

DON PASQUALE   2 br.c. (Jan 20) Zafonic (USA) 130 – Bedazzling (IRE) 105 (Dars-   **65 p**
haan 133) [2004 p7g⁵ Oct 28] 90,000Y: first foal: dam, 7f winner (including at 2 yrs),
sister to smart performer up to 1½m Bustan: 25/1 and green, fifth to King's Majesty in
maiden at Lingfield, not knocked about: will stay 1m: sure to improve. *D. R. Loder*

DON PELE (IRE)   2 b.c. (Mar 30) Monashee Mountain (USA) 115 – Big Fandango   **107**
(Bigstone (IRE) 126) [2004 6g 6.1g² 6m* 6m* 6m Sep 8] 18,000Y: good-bodied colt:
third foal: half-brother to 6f (including at 2 yrs) winner Kenley Lass (by Danetime): dam
unraced half-sister to useful performer up to 1m Elegant Warning: useful performer: won
maiden at Windsor in June and listed race at Newbury (much improved when beating
Black Velvet 2 lengths, making most despite edging right) in July: ran as if amiss in sales
race at Doncaster final start: will probably prove best at 5f/6f. *S. Kirk*

DONT CALL ME BABE   2 b.g. (Mar 31) Easycall 115 – Ok Babe 68 (Bold Arrange-   **–**
ment 127) [2004 7s Oct 21] first foal: dam 6f winner, including at 2 yrs: 33/1, slowly
away and well beaten in maiden at Brighton. *R. Rowe*

DONT CALL ME DEREK   3 b.g. Sri Pekan (USA) 117 – Cultural Role 95 (Night   **84 p**
Shift (USA)) [2004 74p: p5g⁵ p5g⁶ p6g 9m 7m 8.1s² f8g* 8d³ 8.2g² 12g* p12.2g* 11.7g*
Oct 10] big, workmanlike gelding: fairly useful handicapper: much improved in second
half of 2004, winning at Southwell in August and Catterick, Wolverhampton (beat Dovedon Hero by 4 lengths) and Bath (readily by length from Mount Benger) within 6 days in
October: effective at 1m to 1½m: acts on all-weather and soft ground: wore blinkers/
eyeshields second start: hung right on bend at Lingfield on reappearance: sold 55,000
gns, joined J. Quinn: probably capable of better still. *S. C. Williams*

DONT LET GO   3 b.f. Danzero (AUS) – Il Doria (IRE) 66 (Mac's Imp (USA) 116)   **–**
[2004 –: 8.3d 7f Jun 25] no sign of ability. *Miss B. Sanders*

DON'T MATTER   4 b.f. Petong 126 – Cool Run 87 (Deep Run 119) [2004 –: 11.6m   **–**
Jun 28] maiden: no form since 2 yrs. *Mrs S. M. Johnson*

DON'T SIOUX ME (IRE)   6 b.g. Sadler's Wells (USA) 132 – Commanche Belle 74   **–**
(Shirley Heights 130) [2004 –: p12g 11.6f⁵ 10g Sep 29] deep-girthed gelding: well held
on Flat since 2002: tried tongue tied: has given trouble in preliminaries: fair hurdler at
best. *C. R. Dore*

DON'T TELL MUM (IRE)   2 b.f. (Feb 14) Dansili 127 – Zinnia (Zilzal (USA) 137)   **90**
[2004 5.1f* 5f⁶ 5.2m² Jul 17] €20,000Y: good-topped filly: first foal: dam, ran once, out
of half-sister to Danzig: won maiden at Bath in May: creditable efforts in Queen Mary
Stakes at Royal Ascot and Super Sprint (beaten ¾ length by Siena Gold) at Newbury:
likely to prove best at 5f/6f. *R. Hannon*

DON'T TELL ROSEY   4 b.g. Barathea (IRE) 127 – Patsy Western 81 (Precocious   **63**
126) [2004 80: p6g Apr 2] compact gelding: fairly useful at 3 yrs: fair form on all-weather
debut only start in 2004: raced only at 5f/6f: acts on firm and soft going: has looked
difficult ride. *M. Blanshard*

DONT TELL SIMON   3 ch.g. Keen 116 – Circumnavigate 41 (Slip Anchor 136)   **–**
[2004 9g 10m 8d Aug 15] close-coupled gelding: no sign of ability. *M. E. Sowersby*

DON'T TELL TRIGGER (IRE)   2 b.f. (Feb 14) Mujadil (USA) 119 – Ordinate   **69**
(Nashwan (USA) 135) [2004 5g 6m⁶ 6.1g* 6m 7m 7m* 6m 8f Sep 6] €4,500F, €3,000Y:
sturdy, lengthy filly: third foal: dam, French 9f winner, granddaughter of Prix Morny
winner Madina: fair performer: won sellers at Chepstow in May and Newmarket in
August: stays 7f: acts on good to firm going: often races up with pace. *J. S. Moore*

totesport Stakes (Handicap), Ascot—
in a thrilling finish, Dorothy's Friend makes it five wins from his last six starts;
close behind are Random Quest (right), Thewhirlingdervish (left) and Promoter (noseband)

DONT WORRY BOUT ME (IRE) 7 b.g. Brief Truce (USA) 126 – Coggle 60 (Kind of Hush 118) [2004 p12g Feb 23] modest performer: missed 2003: well held only 7-y-o start: visored: front runner. *T. G. Mills* —

DONYANA 2 b.f. (Feb 9) Mark of Esteem (IRE) 137 – Albarsha 75 (Mtoto 134) [2004 7g⁵ 7g* 8m⁴ Sep 21] quite good-topped filly: first foal: dam, ran twice (second at 1½m), half-sister to 1000 Guineas winner Ameerat (by Mark of Esteem): won maiden at Salisbury in September: improved again when fourth to Bunny Rabbit in nursery at Newmarket, racing alone: stays 1m: type to make a useful handicapper. *M. A. Jarvis* **89 p**

DOOHULLA (USA) 3 ch.f. Stravinsky (USA) 133 – Viva Zapata (USA) 116 (Affirmed (USA)) [2004 87: 6m⁵ 6m Jul 6] tall filly: useful handicapper: best effort when fifth to Two Step Kid in valuable event at York on reappearance: likely to prove at least as effective at 5f as 6f: acts on polytrack, raced only on good going or firmer on turf: blinkered last 2 starts at 2 yrs: tends to carry head high. *G. A. Butler* **100**

DOOIE DANCER 2 b.c. (Feb 28) Entrepreneur 123 – Vayavaig 78 (Damister (USA) 123) [2004 8s Oct 27] 36,000Y: half-brother to several winners, including useful 6f (at 2 yrs) and 8.5f winner Sweet Prospect (by Shareef Dancer) and fairly useful 6f (including at 2 yrs) winner Wolfhunt (by Wolfhound): dam 2-y-o 6f winner: 20/1, seventh to Very Wise in maiden at Yarmouth, fading and not knocked about late on: sure to do better. *H. R. A. Cecil* **67 p**

DORA CORBINO 4 b.f. Superpower 113 – Smartie Lee 66 (Dominion 123) [2004 50?: f9.4g⁵ f11s³ f12s² f12g f12m⁶ 15g³ 11.9g² 12v⁴ f14g² 12.1m³ 18m⁴ f14m Jul 12] quite good-topped filly: poor maiden: probably stays 2¼m: acts on fibresand and good to firm going. *R. Hollinshead* **47**

DORCHESTER 7 b.g. Primo Dominie 121 – Penthouse Lady (Last Tycoon 131) [2004 83: f7s⁶ 6d⁵ 6.1s May 14] good-topped gelding: fair handicapper: effective at 6f/7f: acts on all-weather, firm and soft going: blinkered once at 3 yrs: tends to edge right. *W. J. Musson* **78**

DORINGO 3 b.c. Prince Sabo 123 – Mistral's Dancer (Shareef Dancer (USA) 135) [2004 –: 7.1d 10g 10m 8g 8s² Oct 15] leggy, sparely-made colt: modest maiden: stays 1m: acts on soft ground. *J. L. Spearing* **54**

302

DORISIMA (FR) 3 ch.f. Mark of Esteem (IRE) 137 – Suhaad 111 (Unfuwain (USA) –
131) [2004 –: 6g 10.1m Oct 10] tall, unfurnished filly: well beaten in maidens: broke
through stall and withdrawn prior to intended reappearance. *M. W. Easterby*

DORIS SOUTER (IRE) 4 b. or br.f. Desert Story (IRE) 115 – Hope And Glory **75**
(USA) 87 (Well Decorated (USA)) [2004 81: p10g² p10g p12g⁵ 12g 10m³ 10m 10m³
10f² Jul 5] close-coupled filly: fair handicapper: stays 1¼m, possibly not 1½m: acts on
polytrack, firm and good to soft going: usually races prominently. *R. Hannon*

DORMY TWO (IRE) 4 b.f. Eagle Eyed (USA) 111 – Tartan Lady (IRE) 88 (Taufan **48**
(USA) 119) [2004 57: 9.9s 16d³ 16m⁶ May 17] good-topped filly: poor maiden: probably
stays easy 2m: usually wears cheekpieces. *J. S. Wainwright*

DORN DANCER (IRE) 2 b.f. (Mar 12) Danehill Dancer (IRE) 117 – Appledorn 99 **77**
(Doulab (USA) 115) [2004 6m 5.1g* 5g⁵ 5g 6.5m 6d⁶ 7g 6s Nov 2] €12,000Y: good-
topped filly: half-sister to several winners, including fairly useful 7f winner Lady Pahia
(by Pivotal) and 2002 2-y-o 1m seller winner Dawn Alibi (by Ali-Royal), later successful
in Italy: dam 6f/7f winner, latter including at 2 yrs: fair performer: won maiden at Chester
in June: creditable effort after on sixth start only: stays 6f: acts on good to soft going:
temperament under suspicion. *D. W. Barker*

DORN HILL 2 b.f. (Apr 20) Lujain (USA) 119 – Benedicite (Lomond (USA) 128) **38 ?**
[2004 5.1m⁵ 5m May 31] quite good-topped filly: sixth foal: half-sister to useful Irish
1m/1¼m winner Brocheta (by Hector Protector) and 6f winner Benedictine (by Primo
Dominie): dam unraced half-sister to very smart performer up to 7f College Chapel: poor
form in minor event/maiden. *Mrs Mary Hambro*

DOROTHY'S FRIEND 4 b.g. Grand Lodge (USA) 125 – Isle of Flame (Shirley **101 p**
Heights 130) [2004 90p: 16.2d 14.8m* 16.2g* 14g 16.2g* 13.9s Aug 18] strong, useful-
looking gelding: useful handicapper: won at Newmarket in June and Ascot in July
(totesport Stakes, beat Random Quest a neck) and August (by length from Double
Obsession): unsuited by shorter trip in Ebor at York final outing: will stay beyond 2m:
acts on firm ground: held up: game: generally progressive, and probably capable of better
still. *R. Charlton*

DORSET (USA) 3 b.f. Deputy Commander (USA) 124 – Draconienne (USA) (Trem- –
polino (USA) 135) [2004 8g 10.2m 12.1m⁶ 11.5g⁵ Aug 9] $160,000Y: fourth foal: half-
sister to winner in USA by Woodman: dam, French 2-y-o 6f and 1m (listed race) winner,
from very good family: little form: sold 5,500 gns from A. Balding before final outing
(blinkered). *R. Gibson, France*

DORUBAKO (IRE) 3 b.c. Danzig (USA) – Spring Pitch (USA) (Storm Cat (USA)) **107**
[2004 6f² 6f² 6f* 6f² 6f² 6f* 5.1g⁴ 6.5g 6g Oct 9] 140,000 2-y-o: first foal: dam, ran
twice in USA, half-sister to high-class miler Selkirk: successful at Chukyo in maiden in
March and minor event in May: useful form when unlucky 2½ lengths fourth to Fire
Up The Band in listed event at Chester seventh start, short of room final 1f: last in Prix
Maurice de Gheest at Deauville next time, other start in Europe: effective at 5f/6f: raced
only on good/firm ground. *H. Mori, Japan*

DOUBLE ASPECT (IRE) 3 b.g. Dr Fong (USA) 128 – Spring 112 (Sadler's Wells **95**
(USA) 132) [2004 10g⁴ 9.9g* 10g⁵ 12d² Aug 15] 65,000Y: tall, good-topped gelding:
seventh foal: half-brother to 3 winners, including smart 1m/1¼m winner Inglenook (by
Cadeaux Genereux) and fairly useful 9f winner Puffin (by Pennekamp): dam, 1½m/1¾m
performer, closely related to Pentire: useful performer: won maiden at Salisbury in June:
good efforts in handicaps after, fourth to Jeepstar at Pontefract final start, racing freely
then carrying head high and edging left: subsequently gelded: stays 1½m: raced only on
good/good to soft going. *Sir Michael Stoute*

DOUBLE BLADE 9 b.g. Kris 135 – Sesame 117 (Derrylin 115) [2004 54: 11m⁶ 16f –
Jul 29] big, angular gelding: well held both starts on Flat in 2004 (won over fences in
between): blinkered (ran poorly) once at 3 yrs: has started slowly/pulled hard/found little.
N. Wilson

DOUBLE DAGGER LADY (USA) 3 b.f. Diesis 133 – Darby Jane (CAN) (Silver **68**
Deputy (CAN)) [2004 10m⁶ 10m⁴ 8.3f⁵ 7d⁶ p7.1d³ f8s² Nov 17] strong filly: second foal:
half-sister to minor winner in North America by Nureyev: dam, won in North America,
sister to Canadian Oaks winner Deputy Jane West: fair maiden: stays 1m: acts on all-
weather and firm ground. *J. Noseda*

DOUBLE DEPUTY (IRE) 3 b.c. Sadler's Wells (USA) 132 – Janaat 74 (Kris 135) **88**
[2004 9.9g* 10.3s* Oct 22] smallish, good-bodied colt: fifth foal: half-brother to very
smart 6f to 1m winner (both including at 2 yrs) Lend A Hand (by Great Commotion): dam

Ascot Stakes (Handicap), Royal Ascot—Double Obsession gains his third course success, and has five lengths to spare over Promoter, in turn clear of the third Penny Pictures (quartered cap)

1½m winner: fairly useful form: successful in maiden at Goodwood (by 4 lengths) in September and handicap at Doncaster (beat Another Choice by neck, well ridden from front) in October: stays 1¼m: acts on soft ground: tongue tied. *Saeed bin Suroor*

DOUBLE HONOUR (FR) 6 gr.g. Highest Honor (FR) 124 – Silver Cobra (USA) **96** (Silver Hawk (USA) 123) [2004 106: 22.2f Jun 19] close-coupled gelding: not a good walker: has a round action: useful performer nowadays: eighth in Queen Alexandra Stakes at Royal Ascot only start on Flat in 2004: stays 2¾m: has form on firm going, possibly ideally suited by good or softer: usually races prominently: useful hurdler/chaser. *P. J. Hobbs*

DOUBLE KUDOS (FR) 2 gr.c. (Apr 24) Highest Honor (FR) 124 – Black Tulip **74** (FR) (Fabulous Dancer (USA) 124) [2004 7m² 7g 9f Sep 13] €30,000Y: half-brother to several winners, notably French 1¼m to 12.5f winner Tulipa (by Alleged) and German 1m/1¼m performer Devil River Peek (by Silver Hawk), both smart: dam French 1¼m/ 1½m winner, including listed events: best effort in maidens when second at Yarmouth: should be suited by 1¼m/1½m. *J. G. Given*

DOUBLE M 7 ch.g. First Trump 118 – Girton Degree 41 (Balliol 125) [2004 57: p7g⁴ **74** p5g* p6g³ p7g p6g² p7g⁴ p6g² p6g* p6g 5d⁶ 5.7m⁵ 5g⁵ 6g³ 5m² 6g* 5g³ 5g⁶ p6g⁶ 5g* 5m² 5.2g 6g 5g 5.7g³ 5g p6g² p5g⁴ p6m* Dec 22] strong, sturdy gelding: fair handicapper: won at Lingfield in January, March and June, Goodwood in July and Lingfield again in December: effective at 5f to easy 7f: acts on all-weather, firm and good to soft ground: has been blinkered, visored nowadays: usually waited with: tough and consistent. *Mrs L. Richards*

DOUBLE OBSESSION 4 b.c. Sadler's Wells (USA) 132 – Obsessive (USA) 102 **111** (Seeking The Gold (USA)) [2004 102: 11.9s 12m 16.2d 20f* 16.2g⁵ 16m⁴ 16.2g² 15s⁴ Aug 22] compact colt: smart performer: won 29-runner Ascot Stakes (Handicap) at Royal Ascot in June by 5 lengths from Promoter: good efforts last 3 starts when 4¼ lengths fourth to Darasim in Goodwood Cup, length second to Dorothy's Friend in handicap at Ascot and 3½ lengths fourth to Gold Medallist in Prix Kergorlay at Deauville: stays 2½m: acts on firm and soft ground: often blinkered/visored: usually races prominently. *M. Johnston*

DOUBLE RANSOM 5 b.g. Bahamian Bounty 116 – Secrets of Honour (Belmez **72** (USA) 131) [2004 64: p8g² p10g³ p8g* p8g⁴ 10.1v² 8.3g* 10d⁶ 9.2d² 8.1g* 9.2d⁶ 10.1d⁵ p9.5g⁶ p8.6g⁶ Dec 27] lengthy, good-topped gelding: fair handicapper: won at Lingfield in February, Hamilton (NH jockeys event) in May and Haydock in August: effective at 1m/1¼m: acts on polytrack and heavy ground: blinkered. *Mrs L. Stubbs*

DOUBLE SPEY 5 b.g. Atraf 116 – Yankee Special 60 (Bold Lad (IRE) 133) [2004 **42** 50: 10.5d⁶ Jun 4] workmanlike gelding: maiden handicapper: just poor form only 5-y-o outing: seems to stay 1¾m: acts on firm and good to soft going: has looked difficult ride. *Miss Kate Milligan*

DOUBLE TURN 4 ch.g. Double Trigger (IRE) 123 – Its My Turn 80 (Palm Track **–** 122) [2004 –: 11.9m⁵ 11.9d 11.1m⁶ Jun 16] lengthy, angular gelding: little form. *W. M. Brisbourne*

DOUBLE VODKA (IRE) 3 b. or br.g. Russian Revival (USA) 125 – Silius (Junius **82** (USA) 124) [2004 65: 8.2s 8m⁶ 8.5m² 8s⁴ 11d 8g* 10g* 8d* 10m 8g³ 10s Oct 11] leggy gelding: fairly useful handicapper: won at Doncaster, Ripon and Pontefract in July/ August, beating Alshawameq by 2½ lengths in last-named: effective at 1m to 11f: acts on soft and good to firm going. *Mrs J. R. Ramsden*

DOUGHTY 2 b.g. (Apr 26) Bold Edge 123 – Marquante (IRE) (Brief Truce (USA) – 126) [2004 5.1g 5.7f 6f 5.7m Jul 22] no promise in maidens: tongue tied final start. *D. J. Wintle*

DOVE COTTAGE (IRE) 2 b.g. (Apr 3) Great Commotion (USA) 123 – Pooka 65 **67** (Dominion 123) [2004 5m⁶ 5f⁵ 5.1f³ 6.1m* 7s² 7f⁵ 8g⁴ Sep 30] 20,000Y: close-coupled gelding: half-brother to 3 winners, including smart German performer up to 1m Chagall (by Fraam): dam placed at 5f at 2 yrs: fair performer: won nursery at Chepstow in August: creditable efforts in similar events after: subsequently gelded: effective at 6f to 1m: acts on firm and soft going: often races prominently. *W. S. Kittow*

DOVEDALE 4 b.f. Groom Dancer (USA) 128 – Peetsie (IRE) (Fairy King (USA)) **68** [2004 8.1s 10.2g⁴ p9.5d⁵ p13.9g Dec 31] lengthy filly: second foal: dam, well beaten in 4 starts on Flat (third in bumper), out of half-sister to 1000 Guineas winner One In A Million: fair maiden, lightly raced: stays easy 1¾m: acts on polytrack. *Mrs Mary Hambro*

DOVEDON HERO 4 ch.g. Millkom 124 – Hot Topic (IRE) (Desse Zenny (USA)) **86** [2004 88: 12g 12g 12m² 12g 14m⁴ 12m⁶ 12g 14.8g² 16.1f 12g³ 14.1m⁴ p12.2g² p13.9g⁴ p12g² p10g p13g* f14g² Dec 7] sturdy, close-coupled gelding: fairly useful handicapper: won at Lingfield in December: good second at Southwell final outing: stays 1¾m: acts on all-weather and firm going: usually blinkered: usually held up. *P. J. McBride*

DOVEDON LASS 3 b.f. Abou Zouz (USA) 109 – Violette Sabo 44 (Prince Sabo 123) – [2004 10.1g May 14] first foal: dam maiden who stayed 7f: 40/1, well beaten in seller at Yarmouth. *P. J. McBride*

DOVER STREET 2 ch.g. (Feb 3) Zafonic (USA) 130 – Seeker 75 (Rainbow Quest **66** (USA) 134) [2004 6m⁵ 6m 6g 8g 10g⁴ 8d Oct 18] 20,000Y: big, lengthy gelding: first foal: dam, 1½m winner, out of half-sister to Kris and Diesis: fair maiden: fourth at Pontefract, best effort: raced freely/not clear run final start: stays 1¼m. *P. W. D'Arcy*

DOWAGER 3 b.f. Groom Dancer (USA) 128 – Rose Noble (USA) 62 (Vaguely Noble **102** 140) [2004 99: 7s⁵ 6f⁴ 6g⁶ m6m³ 7m 6d 6g 6.1g 6g* 6d Oct 14] leggy, useful-looking filly: useful performer: won minor event at Yarmouth in September by ¾ length from Country Reel: probably better at 6f than 7f: acts on firm going: blinkered (pulled hard) once: none too consistent. *R. Hannon*

DOWER HOUSE 9 ch.g. Groom Dancer (USA) 128 – Rose Noble (USA) 62 (Vaguely **85** Noble 140) [2004 90: p10g⁴ p10g⁶ f11s⁵ p10g⁴ p10g p8g⁵ 10g 10.5s 10s Oct 11] lengthy, rather leggy gelding: has a fluent, round action: fairly useful handicapper: well below form only outings on turf in 2004, off 5 months after first of them: effective at 1m/1¼m: acts on polytrack and firm going, probably on soft: sometimes tongue tied: takes good hold: held up. *Andrew Turnell*

DOWNLAND (IRE) 8 b.g. Common Grounds 118 – Boldabsa 96 (Persian Bold 123) **70** [2004 61§: 6v 6v² 7.2m* 6f⁶ 7f⁵ f8g* f7m* f8g³ 7m f7f² 7m⁶ 7.2d⁵ 7m Oct 10] tall, good **a84** sort: fairly useful handicapper on all-weather, fair on turf: won at Ayr in May and Southwell in June and July: effective at 7f/1m: acts on good to firm going, heavy and fibresand: blinkered 3 times at 4 yrs: sometimes early to post/mounted on track. *N. Tinkler*

DOWN TO THE WOODS (USA) 6 ch.g. Woodman (USA) 126 – Riviera Wonder – § (USA) (Batonnier (USA)) [2004 68§: f9.4g 14.1s p10g May 13] tall, angular gelding: temperamental performer. *R. D. E. Woodhouse*

DOYEN (IRE) 4 b.c. Sadler's Wells (USA) 132 – Moon Cactus 118 (Kris 135) **132** [2004 122p: 12m² 12f* 12m* 10m 10s Oct 16]

Sometimes the only way is down, it seems. Doyen was the season's shining star and Horse of the Year-elect after a six-length victory in the Hardwicke Stakes and a dazzling three-length win in the King George VI and Queen Elizabeth Stakes. Whimsically, he was deemed to have fallen from grace so far by the end of the season that he didn't even make the short-list for the Horse of the Year award at the Racehorse Owners' Association's annual dinner in December. Four of the six short-listed in advance for a poll of *Racing Post* readers were Flat horses—Attraction, Haafhd, Ouija Board (the eventual winner of the poll) and Soviet Song—but there was no place for the colt who put up not just the best, but the *two* best performances seen on a racecourse anywhere in Europe during the year. Doyen's most impressive displays at Ascot suggested that he might go on to establish himself as a middle-distance performer right out of the top drawer, possibly even up with the best his owners Godolphin had had over any distance since Dubai Millennium. As anticlimaxes go, Doyen's autumn campaign could hardly have been much worse, his unexplained capitulation when odds on for the Irish Champion Stakes and his comprehensive defeat when favourite again for the Champion Stakes at Newmarket a sad epitaph to his campaign. Doyen is rated in this Annual, not on his last two performances, but on his form in the Hardwicke and King George, victories which lit up the summer and, for which, unless he reaches similar heights on the racecourse as a five-year-old, Doyen looks set to be remembered for longest. His achievements earned him the title of Timeform Horse of the Year.

The 2003 Flat-racing year looked like being a hard act to follow, judged on the quality of the top horses that were around that year. With the two leading three-year-olds Alamshar and Dalakhani retired to stud, along with top older horses Falbrav, High Chaparral and Nayef, the middle-distance scene at the start of the latest season looked a little short of established high-class performers to take on the classic generation. Godolphin's traditionally strong team of older horses was headed by Sulamani, the operation's most successful performer in a decidedly ordinary year in 2003 by its own very high standards (the nine Group/Grade 1 victories worldwide the lowest total since 1997). Doyen ran in Sheikh Mohammed's colours at two and three when trained by Andre Fabre who did not rush him, running him once as a juvenile (fifth in a newcomers race) and five times at three when, after winning his first three starts gradually stepped up in class, he finished second in the Prix Niel and fourth in the Prix de l'Arc de Triomphe, both won by Dalakhani. All Doyen's starts at three were at a mile and a half and, with plenty of stamina in his pedigree and the physical scope to fill out at four, he was earmarked at first by Godolphin as a horse more for the second half of the season. His main objective was said to be the Arc, with Sulamani regarded as the main King George hope. In mid-May the Godolphin stable reported that 'Doyen is not ready to run yet.'

Within two or three weeks, however, Doyen had his first start in the Godolphin royal blue in the Coronation Cup at Epsom. He couldn't have looked any fitter, though he spoiled his appearance by sweating and getting rather on edge. In a race marred by scrimmaging in the closing stages, Doyen rallied after his rider was forced to check when going for a gap over a furlong out; Doyen went down by a length and three quarters to Warrsan but would have finished closer with a clear run. Doyen was sent next to Royal Ascot for the Hardwicke Stakes, run on the final day of the meeting when the going was very firm, the executive having decided not to water the course overnight. In a field reduced to six by the defection of Gamut and Chancellor on account of the going, Doyen turned the Hardwicke into a procession. Looking in really good shape and much calmer in the preliminaries, he burst clear over the last two furlongs after being dropped out as his stablemate Songlark, harried by Systematic, set a good pace. Not hard ridden once the race was in safe keeping, Doyen won by six lengths from the Coronation Cup fourth High Accolade, in the process setting a new time record of 2m 26.53sec for Ascot's mile-and-a-half course. The record held by Stanerra, and set in the same race, had stood since 1983. Regular readers will know, however, that it pays not to get carried away by course records, which are mostly no more than a reflection of the prevailing conditions. Doyen's was no exception. His timefigure of 0.94 fast (equivalent to a timerating of 124) was a high-class one—the fastest at the meeting—but it was 7 lb behind the Timeform rating he earned for the performance. Doyen's victory crowned a magnificent Royal Ascot for Godolphin who won six races, including two Group 1s, the Gold Cup with Papineau and the Queen Anne with Refuse To Bend.

Doyen's Hardwicke performance set the standard for the King George VI and Queen Elizabeth Diamond Stakes over the same course and distance the following month, Doyen looking as if he would be hard to beat, especially as he was progressing with his races and might still have improvement in him. With Derby winner North Light sidelined by injury after being beaten by Grey Swallow (the latter put away for the Irish Champion) in the Irish Derby, the classic generation was represented in the eleven-runner King George only by the Irish Derby third Tycoon. There was nothing third-rate, though, about the older horses that took on 11/10-favourite Doyen. Seven of his rivals had won in Group/Grade 1 company, among them stablemate Sulamani and the Grand Prix de Saint-Cloud winner Gamut, both of whom eventually stood their ground despite worries about the good

Hardwicke Stakes, Royal Ascot—Doyen breaks Stanerra's course record with a top-class performance, coming home six lengths clear of High Accolade, with Persian Majesty (right) third

to firm going. No filly has won the King George since the four-year-old Time Charter in 1983—the latest Oaks winner Ouija Board had successfully completed a classic double in the Irish Oaks the previous weekend—and it was surprising to see French-trained Vallee Enchantee (an unlucky third in the Coronation Cup) start second favourite at 6/1 to Doyen. Next at 13/2 came Warrsan, just thwarted by Refuse To Bend in the Eclipse on his only start since the Coronation Cup; then, on

7/1, came Sulamani (runner-up in the race to Alamshar the previous year), with Gamut and Bandari, winner of the Princess of Wales's Stakes at Newmarket last time from Sulamani, the only others to start at shorter odds than 16/1-shot Tycoon. The King George also attracted the first North American-trained runner in its fifty-four-year history, the Brazilian-bred five-year-old Hard Buck, who had crossed the Atlantic twice before for major races at the Dubai World Cup meeting, finishing ninth (as a four-year-old since he was bred in the southern hemisphere) in the UAE Derby and second in the Dubai Sheema Classic in March. Although a Grade 1 winner in South America and in the States, Hard Buck started at 33/1 for the King George.

Doyen was bandaged on his fore-joints, as on his other starts for Godolphin, but he was a picture again in the paddock, looking noticeably by this stage of the season to be filling out and strengthening. He was full of himself, though not stirred up as at Epsom, and was attended by two handlers. Doyen justified favouritism most impressively, travelling strongly in behind the leaders from the start and being eased to the front a little less than two furlongs out, after moving smoothly through from fifth on the home turn. Soon clear, Doyen stretched out magnificently to win comfortably, Dettori just pushing him along. Doyen had more in hand than the three lengths he was ahead of always-prominent Hard Buck, the American challenger only just holding off the running-on Sulamani by a head for second, with Gamut a further length and three quarters away fourth. Vallee Enchantee came fifth and Tycoon a creditable sixth after becoming pocketed when caught behind the weakening Godolphin pacemaker in the home straight.

The tactics employed on the Godolphin pacemaker Lunar Sovereign were unusual, and also surprising given Doyen's display in a strongly-run Hardwicke. Times taken at various stages of the race confirmed the visual impression that the first part of the King George was very slowly run. Problems with collecting data have held back the advance of meaningful and sophisticated sectional time analysis in Britain—Newmarket (Rowley Mile) is the only track which returns sectional times—but Timeform's race analysts and handicappers take hand-held times at intervals where possible (including for individual horses). Times are taken for the 'in-running' sectionals, with the time deduced for the first sectional from the stalls. The leader covered the first five furlongs of the King George in 67.72sec, farcically slow judged on the standard sectional times used by Timeform. Comparison with the rated stakes handicap over the same distance later on the programme (64.41sec) and with another handicap over the trip on virtually identical going the next day (64.56sec) provide an illustration in themselves of how even simple data collection can reveal plenty about a race. A slow early pace would normally lead to a fast finish but the second sectional taken by Timeform—for the near-four-furlong

King George VI and Queen Elizabeth Diamond Stakes, Ascot—
Doyen records the best performance of the racing year in Europe; American challenger Hard Buck (stripe on sleeves) is second, ahead of the winner's stable-companion Sulamani (rail) and Gamut (right)

stretch approaching the home turn—was remarkably fast. Lunar Sovereign drew a few lengths clear after quickening sharply and covered the section in 43.69sec (compared to 46.56sec for the leader in the rated stakes and 45.17sec for the leader in the handicap). The last section of the King George—about three and a third furlongs in length—took 41.77sec, not particularly good by Ascot standards, and evidenced by the fact that the same section was covered in 41.12 by much inferior animals in the rated stakes (incidentally, Doyen himself recorded 40.85 in the much more truly-run Hardwicke). The way the King George was run was remarkable, the circumstances highly unlikely to be repeated if the runners met again, and the overall time was very poor for the calibre of horses involved. Doyen recorded a timefigure of 0.32 slow, equivalent to a timerating of only 92, compared to a Timeform rating for the performance of 132. The sectionals for the individual horses in the King George, by the way, revealed that, as well as the winner, both Sulamani and Tycoon were probably also deserving of extra credit. One rather unfortunate consequence of Ascot's redevelopment (the King George will be run at Newbury in 2005) is that the track itself is being altered, consigning a mass of useful sectional data collected over recent years to the waste bin! The development of speed-sensing systems, of which more appears in the essay on Iceman, may, it is claimed, mean that those wishing to make a complex study of sectional time, as an aid to understanding some performances, will not have to wait much longer before they get the raw data on a plate.

Doyen's victory in the King George gave the older horses a twenty-seventh success in the race, bringing them level as a group with the classic generation and again emphasising how well, generally, the event has achieved the objective of its architect Sir John Crocker Bulteel of bringing together the different generations in a true championship race. Along with the boosting of the Arc into a race of international importance, the King George challenged the supremacy of the traditional classic races and helped to bring the focus on to weight-for-age competition. From its inception the King George always had the potential to be Britain's most important middle-distance event. As a measure of racing merit, it regularly compares favourably with the other top races in the world's calendar, the latest edition being no exception. Only the Breeders' Cup Classic winner Ghostzapper and the Kentucky Derby and Preakness Stakes winner Smarty Jones earned a higher Timeform rating than Doyen in 2004. Success for Doyen enabled his trainer Saeed bin Suroor to equal the feat of Dick Hern in saddling five winners of the King George. During the ten years that he has held the licence for Sheikh Mohammed's Godolphin operation, Suroor has won one hundred and eleven Group/Grade 1 races around the world and, in the latest season, when Godolphin expanded its stable in Britain from around the usual sixty horses to around two hundred and forty, he was champion trainer for the fifth time in Britain. Godolphin won eleven Group/Grade 1 races worldwide, six of them in Britain. Godolphin's much larger domestic operation played a big part in Frankie Dettori's taking the Jockeys' Association's version of the jockeys' title in Britain (a subject dealt with in the essay on Firebreak). Dettori has ridden four of the five King George winners saddled by Suroor (John Reid rode Swain to the first of his two victories) and he described Doyen as the 'easiest' of his winners, which is not quite the same as saying he is the best. For the record, the Timeform ratings of Godolphin's other King George winners are: Lammtarra 134 (though his King George performance was worth only 125), Swain 134 and 132, and Daylami 138. Dettori's four King George winners put him level with Michael Kinane and Willie Carson on the race's roll of honour, though he still has a long way to go to match Lester Piggott's record seven winners. King George day also provided another landmark for Dettori when he won the opener on Nightfall to record his two thousandth winner in Britain.

Doyen is apparently not noted for being a spectacular worker at home—neither were Daylami and Swain, according to Simon Crisford, Godolphin's racing manager—but he was reported 'in great form' before the Irish Champion Stakes at Leopardstown in September. Well positioned turning for the home, Doyen found little under pressure, dropping out and beating only his pacemaker in the eight-runner field. Dettori reported to the stewards that 'his mount failed to quicken when asked and felt flat from thereon'; the Turf Club vet told the stewards that Doyen was 'post race normal' and a routine dope test subsequently revealed nothing untoward. All that was missing was the classic Irish stewards' statement that 'The stewards accepted the trainer's explanation that he had no explanation,' which would have been apposite in the circumstances. 'The race remains a complete mystery to us, we just don't know what happened,' Simon Crisford said on the eve of Doyen's final appearance five weeks later in the Champion Stakes at Newmarket. 'Before the race he was fine, and he has been fine since.'

Immediately after the triumph in the King George, it seemed hard to envisage a situation in which connections would have to come up with any explanations or excuses for failure for Doyen. But there was more head-scratching after the Champion Stakes in which Doyen again found less at the business end of the race than looked likely for a long way. He was on edge in the paddock (after being relaxed in the preliminaries at Leopardstown) and again performed like a shadow of the horse who had dominated at Ascot in the summer, managing only seventh of the ten finishers. Plans to run Doyen in the Prix de l'Arc Triomphe—for which he had been as short as evens in ante-post betting—had been dropped immediately after defeat at Leopardstown and it had been thought that he would not run again. Notwithstanding that the Champion Stakes might have been something of an afterthought, and that the soft going at Newmarket contrasted sharply with conditions for Doyen's earlier races as a four-year-old, it was impossible to reconcile his performance at either Leopardstown or Newmarket with his Ascot efforts. Some thought they detected an overtrained look about Doyen at Leopardstown but our representatives reported he looked in fine shape; the going at Newmarket was no softer than the surface on which Doyen finished fourth in the 2003 Arc, the best form of his career up to that time; and, although there could have been reservations on pedigree, the drop back to a mile and a quarter looked unlikely to prove an inconvenience given the speed Doyen had shown at crucial stages in a stop-start King George. There is, however, the nagging question of Doyen's temperament. Has he perhaps developed some of his own ideas about the game? Really though, it is not possible to be dogmatic and it remains very much a case of wait and see. After a winter in Dubai, it wouldn't be a big surprise to see Doyen find his best form again as a five-year-old. Let's hope he does so. A top-form Doyen would be a formidable opponent for the classic generation in the big open-aged events at a mile and a quarter and a mile and a half. He is not beholden to the state of the going, which gives his connections a full range of races to aim at, both in Europe and further afield.

		Northern Dancer (b 1961)	Nearctic
	Sadler's Wells (USA) (b 1981)		Natalma
		Fairy Bridge (b 1975)	Bold Reason
Doyen (IRE) (b.c. 2000)			Special
		Kris (ch 1976)	Sharpen Up
	Moon Cactus (b 1987)		Doubly Sure
		Lady Moon (b 1980)	Mill Reef
			Moonlight Night

The tall, rangy Doyen is by the stallion phenomenon Sadler's Wells, whose progeny totted up a further twenty-one pattern wins in Europe in 2004, to bring their sire's career total to two hundred and fifty-two, more than twice the total of his nearest rival, the now-deceased Danehill. Nureyev, Habitat, Riverman and Sadler's Wells' own sire Northern Dancer are the only other stallions whose progeny have won a hundred or more European pattern races. There has been at least one Group 1 winner from each of the seventeen crops by Sadler's Wells to reach the racecourse, Yorkshire Oaks winner Quiff and Fillies' Mile winner Playful Act recording the first such victories for the sixteenth and seventeenth crops respectively in the latest season. The fourteenth sires' championship won by Sadler's Wells in 2004 surpassed the record of thirteen set posthumously by Highflyer in 1798. Sons of Sadler's Wells who have made their mark as stallions remain thin on the ground, but his daughters—most of them naturally enough from very good families—have done well at stud and put him at the top of the table of broodmare sires of pattern winners in Europe in 2004, ahead of Darshaan and Rainbow Quest. 'Breed the best to the *most* and hope for the best' is a modern twist to the old maxim and Sadler's Wells remains among the most active of stallions. His 2003 crop produced one hundred and eleven live foals from one hundred and forty-one mares covered, and he covered one hundred and fifty-nine mares in 2004. The amazing Sadler's Wells story clearly has some way to run, but, although he has always covered large books and had the choicest mares, Sadler's Wells has fully deserved to be recognised for some time as the greatest sire in European bloodstock history.

Sadler's Wells is essentially an influence for stamina and Doyen's dam Moon Cactus, a smart racemare who stayed a mile and a quarter and would have got further, has plenty of stamina in her pedigree too, and comes from a fine family. She is out of Lady Moon, who was carrying Moon Cactus when Sheikh Mohammed bought her for 600,000 guineas at the historic Childwick Bury dispersal at the December Sales in 1986. Another mare purchased from the same draft, the 5,200-guinea Regal Beauty, became the dam of King's Theatre, another of Sadler's Wells's five King George VI and Queen Elizabeth Stakes winners. Lady Moon's purchase price reflected the success her family had had at Childwick Bury. Lady Moon was useful and won three times at around a mile and a half, but, more significantly, her dam the Oaks third Moonlight Night was a daughter of Lovely Light, a half-sister, among others, to Picture Light (dam of Welsh Pageant and Photo Flash), Chandelier (dam of Crocket) and Crystal Palace (dam of Royal Palace, Prince Consort and Selhurst, and grandam of Light Cavalry and Fairy Footsteps). The Lupe Stakes winner Moon Cactus contested an Oaks, but it was at Chantilly, where she finished a promoted second in the Prix de Diane, one of the chief reasons cited for the choice being that right-handed Chantilly was more suitable than Epsom given that Moon Cactus had restricted vision in her left eye.

Kris, the sire of Moon Cactus, was a champion miler but proved quite a strong influence for stamina at stud, among his progeny being the Oaks winners Oh So Sharp (who also won the One Thousand Guineas and St Leger) and Unite (also won the Irish Oaks), as well as the Prix de Diane winner Rafha. Kris was retired

Godolphin's "Doyen"

from stud duties in 2002 and died in 2004. Though he was champion sire in 1985, his influence on pedigrees will continue mostly through his achievements as a sire of broodmares. Oh So Sharp, for example, bred a Prix Saint-Alary winner in Rosefinch, and Rafha became the dam of Haydock Park Sprint Cup winner Invincible Spirit, while Moon Cactus has done even better, breeding not one, but two, Group 1 winners. Doyen is a full brother to the Oaks winner Moonshell, who was the first foal produced by Moon Cactus. In between Moonshell and her seventh foal Doyen, Moon Cactus paid three other visits to Sadler's Wells, producing among others the very smart Hatha Anna, who won the Queen Elizabeth Stakes, an Australian Group 2, for Godolphin as a four-year-old and was a good fourth in the Gold Cup as a five-year-old. Apart from Hatha Anna, the best performer produced by Moon Cactus between Moonshell and Doyen was Ocean of Storms (by Arazi), a smart winner at up to fifteen furlongs in France in his younger days and since successful four times in the United Arab Emirates (only fairly useful form at best in six starts in Britain in latest season). Moon Cactus was barren to Machiavellian in 2001 but there is a two-year-old colt (named Hawksmoor but as yet unraced), a yearling filly and a colt foal, all by In The Wings. *Saeed bin Suroor*

DRAGON FLYER (IRE)   5 b.m. Tagula (IRE) 116 – Noble Rocket (Reprimand 122)   **103**
[2004 105: p5g⁴ 5d² 5.1g 5s 5m 5f 5.1g³ 5m⁴ 5m³ 5m 5.1g⁴ 5m* 5d 5g 5m³ 5d Oct 14] small, sturdy mare: useful performer: won minor event at Leicester in September: good third to Jayanjay in handicap at Epsom penultimate outing: best at 5f: yet to race on heavy going, acts on any other on turf and probably polytrack: hung left eleventh start: often races prominently: game. *M. Quinn*

DRAGON PRINCE   4 b.g. Zamindar (USA) 116 – Nawafell 71 (Kris 135) [2004 10m   **–**
7m 6.9f Jul 16] smallish, stocky gelding: maiden: missed 2003, well held in 2004, refusing to settle. *R. C. Guest*

DRAGON SLAYER (IRE)   2 ch.c. (May 12) Night Shift (USA) – Arandora Star   **67**
(USA) (Sagace (FR) 135) [2004 p6g³ p5g⁶ p6g⁴ p6g² Dec 17] 16,000F, 8,000Y, 46,000 2-y-o: half-brother to 2 winners in France, including 1m winner Arachne (by Shining Steel): dam, French 1¼m winner, half-sister to very smart Hong Kong 1m/1¼m performer Olympic Express: fair maiden: should stay 7f. *P. A. Blockley*

DRALION   2 ch.c. (Mar 10) Dr Fong (USA) 128 – Rosy Outlook (USA) 79 (Trempolino   **60**
(USA) 135) [2004 6m⁵ 5.2m⁵ 6g Aug 9] third foal: half-brother to 3-y-o Orcadian and useful 2001 2-y-o 6f/7f winner Rapscallion (by Robellino): dam 6f winner: modest form on first 2 starts in maidens: should stay 1m. *J. M. P. Eustace*

DRAMATIC QUEST   7 b.g. Zafonic (USA) 130 – Ultra Finesse (USA) 107 (Rahy   **65**
(USA) 115) [2004 77: 10m 11.6m 11.9g 11.9g Oct 8] rangy gelding: fair performer: stays 1½m: acts on polytrack and good to firm going: usually wears cheekpieces nowadays. *Ian Williams*

DRAMATIC REVIEW (IRE)   2 b.g. (Feb 22) Indian Lodge (IRE) 127 – Dramatic   **56**
Shift (IRE) (Night Shift (USA)) [2004 5d⁶ 5d⁵ f6m 8v⁶ 8g Sep 16] close-coupled gelding: modest maiden: best effort at 6f on good to soft going: visored/tongue tied penultimate start: in cheekpieces final one. *P. C. Haslam*

DRAMATICUS   2 b.c. (Feb 17) Indian Ridge 123 – Corinium (IRE) 116 (Turtle Island   **101**
(IRE) 123) [2004 5v³ 6s* 6g 6s Oct 23] strong colt: first foal: dam, 7f/1m (including at 2 yrs) winner, half-sister to Irish 2000 Guineas runner-up Fa-Eq (by Indian Ridge): useful performer: won maiden at Haydock in September: good 6 lengths seventh to Ad Valorem in Middle Park Stakes at Newmarket: tailed off in listed race at Doncaster final start: will probably stay 7f: best effort on good going. *D. R. Loder*

DRAX   2 b.g. (Feb 8) Mark of Esteem (IRE) 137 – Tanasie (Cadeaux Genereux 131)   **72**
[2004 7f³ 7m 7m 7f⁴ Sep 2] 35,000Y: smallish, quite good-topped gelding: has a quick action: second foal: dam, French 1m winner, out of close relative to Most Welcome: fair maiden: fourth in nursery at Redcar, best effort: should stay 1m: slowly away/hung left second start: sold 6,500 gns, sent to Belgium. *D. R. Loder*

DR CERULLO   3 b.g. Dr Fong (USA) 128 – Precocious Miss (USA) 88 (Diesis 133)   **82**
[2004 75: p10g³ p10g³ 10.2g 12.3g² 11.9g⁴ 12.6g⁴ 12g³ 16s Oct 22] fairly useful performer: creditable efforts when in frame in 2004: acts on all-weather and good to firm ground *C. Tinkler*

DR COOL 7 b.g. Ezzoud (IRE) 126 – Vayavaig 78 (Damister (USA) 123) [2004 11.6m – §
12s 14s 14.1f 13.9g Oct 9] quite good-topped gelding: one-time fairly useful winner: no
form in 2004, virtually refusing to race final outing. *J. Akehurst*

DREADNOUGHT 2 b.c. (Apr 21) Slip Anchor 136 – Fleet Amour (USA) (Afleet **67 p**
(CAN)) [2004 p8.6g³ Dec 3] fifth foal: half-brother to 3 winners, including 7f winner
Affaire Royale (by Royal Academy) and 7.5f/1¼m winner Fleet of Light (by Spectrum),
both fairly useful: dam, ran 4 times in USA, closely related to US Grade 1 1m winner
Quiet American: 8/1, 3½ lengths third to Nanton in maiden at Lingfield, green before
staying on: will be well suited by 1¼m/1½m: sure to improve. *J. R. Fanshawe*

DREAM ALIVE 3 b.g. Unfuwain (USA) 131 – Petite Sonnerie 78 (Persian Bold 123) **70**
[2004 10.5g 8.3m³ 9.9s⁴ 11.5g Sep 14] 20,000F, 24,000Y, 26,000 2-y-o: half-brother to
several winners, including useful French performer up to 1½m Petite Speciale (by
Atticus): dam, placed in Britain, later successful in USA (including at 8.5f): fair maiden:
probably stays 1¼m: tongue tied: gelded after final start. *M. Blanshard*

DREAM ALONG 2 b.c. (May 6) Sinndar (IRE) 134 – Dream Quest 102 (Rainbow –
Quest (USA) 134) [2004 8g 8s Oct 19] first foal: dam, 1¼m winner, sister to smart
German 1½m performer Baroon and half-sister to smart sprinters Struggler and Vision of
Night: always rear (after slow start)/unseated leaving stall in maidens. *Mrs A. J. Perrett*

DREAM EASY 3 b.g. Pyramus (USA) 78 – Hush Baby (IRE) 49 (Ballacashtal (CAN)) **65**
[2004 f8g 8m⁵ 7g⁴ 8d⁵ 9.3g³ 10.1m 8s p10g⁵ p10g⁴ p9.5g³ Dec 17] 1,600Y: big workmanlike gelding: fourth foal: half-brother to 1998 French 2-y-o 7f winner El Matar (by
Cosmonaut): dam 1½m winner: fair maiden: stays 1¼m: acts on polytrack, good to firm
and good to soft going: tried blinkered. *P. L. Gilligan*

DREAMER'S LASS 2 b.f. (Mar 20) Pyramus (USA) 78 – Qualitair Dream 80 **51**
(Dreams To Reality (USA) 113) [2004 5.1m² 5.1m 5.7g⁶ 6d 5.7g Sep 13] half-sister to
3 winners, including fairly useful 5f winner (including at 2 yrs) Swynford Dream (by
Statoblest): dam 2-y-o 6f winner who stayed 1m: modest maiden: stays 5.7f: acts on good
to firm going. *J. M. Bradley*

DREAM FALCON 4 br.g. Polar Falcon (USA) 126 – Pip's Dream 52 (Glint of Gold –
128) [2004 –: 10.9s Apr 7] little form on Flat: fairly useful hurdler. *R. J. Hodges*

DREAMING OF YOU (IRE) 3 b.f. Spectrum (USA) 126 – Gay Hellene 111 (Ela- **74**
Mana-Mou 132) [2004 –p: 8.1s* 8m 10m Jun 26] tall filly: won maiden at Warwick in
May: not discredited in handicap at Windsor final start: will be well suited by 1½m+: acts
on soft ground: sent to Australia. *Sir Michael Stoute*

DREAMING WATERS 3 ch.f. Groom Dancer (USA) 128 – Faraway Waters 102 **50**
(Pharly (FR) 130) [2004 62: p10g 8.3m 6.1m⁵ Jun 27] modest performer: should be suited
by at least 1¼m: raced only on good/good to firm ground on turf: refused to enter stall
intended final outing. *R. F. Johnson Houghton*

DREAM MAGIC 6 b.g. Magic Ring (IRE) 115 – Pip's Dream 52 (Glint of Gold 128) **84**
[2004 92: 10g⁴ 10.5d 10g⁵ 10f 10g 9.9g³ 10m² 10d³ 10.1g³ 10g³ 10.5s 10m 10.1s p10g
f11g³ Dec 14] big, good-topped gelding: fairly useful handicapper: stays easy 1½m: acts
on polytrack, firm and soft going: tried visored. *M. J. Ryan*

DREAM OF DUBAI (IRE) 3 b.f. Vettori (IRE) 119 – Immortelle (Arazi (USA) 135) **54 d**
[2004 60: p7g 7m 10m 8.1g p7g p10g 7.1s Sep 20] modest performer at best: probably
stays 1¼m: acts on polytrack and good to firm ground: wore cheekpieces/blinkers last 2
starts. *P. Mitchell*

DREAM OF TOMORROW (IRE) 2 b.f. (Feb 14) Revoque (IRE) 122 – Golden **57 p**
Jorden (IRE) (Cadeaux Genereux 131) [2004 p9.5g³ Nov 15] €9,000Y: second foal: dam
unraced half-sister to useful performer up to 1½m Dashing Chief: 10/1, 1½ lengths third
to Gallantian in maiden at Wolverhampton, staying on: should improve. *John Joseph
Murphy, Ireland*

DREAM SCENE (IRE) 3 b.f. Sadler's Wells (USA) 132 – Highest Accolade 71 **64**
(Shirley Heights 130) [2004 69p: 9f³ p12g⁴ Nov 27] close-coupled filly: fair form when
fourth in maiden at Newbury sole outing at 2 yrs: below that level in similar events at
Redcar and Lingfield in 2004: should stay 1¼m+: sold 21,000 gns. *J. H. M. Gosden*

DREAMS FORGOTTEN (IRE) 4 b.f. Victory Note (USA) 120 – Sevens Are Wild **60 d**
40 (Petorius 117) [2004 63: 10m⁴ 10.1g 8.1g 12g p7g Dec 30] angular filly: modest

maiden: no form after reappearance, leaving G. Margarson before final start: stays 1¼m: acts on fibresand, good to firm and good to soft going. *P. R. Hedger*

DREAMS UNITED 3 br.f. Dancing Spree (USA) – Kaliala (FR) (Pharly (FR) 130) – [2004 39: p8g Feb 3] poor maiden. *A. G. Newcombe*

DREAM TONIC 2 b.c. (Feb 12) Zafonic (USA) 130 – Dream On Deya (IRE) (Dolphin **83** Street (FR) 125) [2004 6m⁶ 8v 8d* Nov 3] lengthy colt: second foal: half-brother to fairly useful 2003 2-y-o 7f winner Wavertree Dream (by Dushyantor): dam tailed off only start: easily best effort in maidens when winning at Musselburgh by 1¾ lengths from Key of Solomon, taking good hold and leading over 1f out: stays 1m: reportedly lame after running on good to firm going. *M. R. Channon*

DREAM VALLEY (IRE) 3 b.f. Sadler's Wells (USA) 132 – Vallee Des Reves (USA) **61** (Kingmambo (USA) 125) [2004 –p: 10g⁶ p12g⁶ 12.1m⁵ p12.2g Nov 19] leggy, lengthy filly: modest maiden: should stay 1½m: wore hood penultimate start. *B. W. Hills*

DREEMON 2 ch.g. (May 3) Tipsy Creek (USA) 115 – Prudence 68 (Grundy 137) [2004 **66** 6m 7g³ 7m p7g 8f 7m Oct 1] half-brother to several winners, including useful 8.5f and 1½m winner Heathyards Rock (by Rock City): dam middle-distance maiden: fair maiden: tended to wander when third at Epsom: needs to settle to stay 1m: acts on good to firm going: sold 3,000 gns. *B. R. Millman*

DRESS PEARL 3 b.f. Atraf 116 – Dress Design (IRE) 84 (Brief Truce (USA) 126) **34** [2004 77d: f5s f6g³ f6m² p6g Dec 22] workmanlike filly: poor maiden: stays 6f: acts on all-weather and heavy going: tried in cheekpieces/blinkers. *J. G. Given*

DR FOX (IRE) 3 b.g. Foxhound (USA) 103 – Eleonora d'Arborea 78 (Prince Sabo – 123) [2004 60: p7g 8.2g 5s 6m 7g 7g p7m Dec 8] short-backed gelding: little form in 2004: tried blinkered/in cheekpieces. *K. A. Morgan*

DRIZZLE 3 ch.g. Hector Protector (USA) 124 – Rainy Sky (Rainbow Quest (USA) – 134) [2004 67: p8g f8g p9.5g p9.5g Nov 26] little form at 3 yrs: tried blinkered. *Ian Williams*

DR JULIAN (IRE) 4 b.g. Sesaro (USA) 81 – Toda 53 (Absalom 128) [2004 53§: f8g **39 §** f14g⁵ f14g f12g 16g⁶ 14d⁴ Jul 13] sturdy, close-coupled gelding: poor maiden: left Miss A. Stokell after fourth start: stays 13.8f: acts on all-weather and firm ground: tried in headgear: ungenuine: fair hurdler. *M. Hourigan, Ireland*

DROOPYS JOEL 2 b.g. (Feb 20) Primo Dominie 121 – Zaima (IRE) 92 (Green Desert – (USA) 127) [2004 p5g 5s 5g Jun 3] strong gelding: well beaten in maidens/claimer. *R. P. Elliott*

DR RAJ 5 ch.g. In The Wings 128 – Tawaaded (IRE) 91 (Nashwan (USA) 135) [2004 – –: f11g f9.4g Feb 9] lightly raced and no form on Flat: tried tongue tied/in cheekpieces. *B. A. McMahon*

DR SHARP (IRE) 4 ch.g. Dr Devious (IRE) 127 – Stoned Imaculate (IRE) 73 (Durgam **88** (USA)) [2004 75: 16d 16.2v* 14.6m² 14g* 16.2g 14g⁶ 15.9s* 14g 16s⁴ 16.5s² Nov 6] good-topped gelding: fairly useful handicapper: won at Beverley in May, Haydock in July and Chester in August: good second to Sendintank at Doncaster final start: races freely, but stays 2m well: acts on heavy and good to firm going: races prominently: game. *T. P. Tate*

DR SYNN 3 br.c. Danzero (AUS) – Our Shirley 84 (Shirley Heights 130) [2004 69p: **75** 7g 6.1s⁶ 6g³ 7g⁶ 6m⁵ 7g 6s² 7g 7s³ 6g⁴ 6d 6d* 7s Oct 27] tall, good-topped colt: fair performer: won maiden at Goodwood in October: effective at 6f/7f: acts on soft and good to firm ground: flashed tail tenth outing, slowly away on eleventh: no easy ride. *J. Akehurst*

DR THONG 3 ch.c. Dr Fong (USA) 128 – Always On My Mind 91 (Distant Relative **91** 128) [2004 74P: 8g⁴ 7g* 7g² 7m⁴ 8m* 7.5g 7.1m⁴ 8s² 8g 7g⁵ Oct 2] tall, lengthy colt: fairly useful performer: won maiden at Doncaster in May and handicap at Leicester (beat Evaluator a head) in July: below form last 2 starts: effective at 7f/1m: acts on soft and good to firm going: free-going sort. *P. F. I. Cole*

DRUID 3 b.g. Magic Ring (IRE) 115 – Country Spirit (Sayf El Arab (USA) 127) [2004 **?** 51: p8g f7f⁶ a8.6g⁶ a8.6g⁴ a8.6g⁵ 9m³ 11g⁵ 7g² a6g⁴ 6g* 7.5g⁴ 6s² 7.5s³ a6.8d a6d⁴ Dec 12] modest performer: sold from P. Haslam after maiden won first 2 starts: won maiden at Copenhagen in September: probably best up to 1m: acts on fibresand: has been blinkered. *A. Jarven, Sweden*

DRUM DANCE (IRE) 2 b.g. (Apr 15) Namid 128 – Socialite (IRE) (Alzao (USA) **80** 117) [2004 5m² 5m² 6s⁴ 6d Oct 15] £35,000Y: sturdy, close-coupled gelding: fourth foal:

half-brother to German 9f/1¼m winner by Dr Devious: dam unraced sister to high-class miler Second Set: fairly useful maiden: second at Leicester and Sandown: should stay 6f: sold 16,000 gns, then gelded. *R. F. Johnson Houghton*

DRURY LANE (IRE)   4 b. or br.g. Royal Applause 124 – Ghost Tree (IRE) 88 (Caerleon (USA) 132) [2004 85: f7g f6s f7g 6s 6m 6m⁴ 7f 6g 6m⁴ 6m 6m 6g 6g Sep 6] modest handicapper nowadays: best at 6f/7f: acts on firm going, below form on all-weather: tried in cheekpieces, usually blinkered: moody. *D. W. Chapman*   **58 §**

DRY ICE (IRE)   2 b.g. (Mar 8) Desert Sun 120 – Snowspin 75 (Carwhite 127) [2004 6m⁵ 7.1m* 7.5g⁵ 7f⁶ 7s Oct 22] 18,000Y: close-coupled gelding: sixth foal: half-brother to 3 winners abroad: dam, 1½m winner who stayed 2m (later successful abroad), half-sister to smart performer up to 1½m Gulland: fairly useful performer: won maiden at Warwick in June: best effort after when creditable sixth in nursery at Doncaster: will stay 1m: acts on firm going: sweating/on toes before final start (gelded after). *H. Candy*   **83**

DRY WIT (IRE)   3 b.f. Desert Prince (IRE) 130 – Nawasib (IRE) 94 (Warning 136) [2004 68: 7m 8.3g⁶ 10.1m 9.9g 8f⁶ Sep 6] smallish filly: just modest form in 2004: stays 1m: acts on firm going. *R. M. Beckett*   **50**

DR ZALO   2 ch.g. (Mar 15) Dr Fong (USA) 128 – Azola (IRE) 63 (Alzao (USA) 117) [2004 6m³ 6d⁵ Oct 4] 18,000Y: sixth foal: half-brother to 5f to 1¼m winner City Reach (by Petong): dam, 1m winner, half-sister to very smart miler Sarab: much better effort in maidens when third at Goodwood (cruised into lead then ran green): reportedly finished lame at Windsor: bred to stay 1m. *P. J. Makin*   **80**

DUAL PURPOSE (IRE)   9 b.g. Rainbows For Life (CAN) – Gracieuse Amie (FR) (Gay Mecene (USA) 128) [2004 11.5g 14m⁶ 7.1d⁴ 8.1s 12g p8.6g f6g⁶ Dec 1] poor maiden: stays 11.5f: tried blinkered/in cheekpieces. *C. Roberts*   **42**

DUBAIAN GIFT   5 b.g. Bahamian Bounty 116 – Hot Lavender (CAN) 67 (Shadeed (USA) 135) [2004 115: 5.2g 5g 5g 5m 5f Jun 15] smallish gelding: smart performer in 2003: well below best in 2004: collapsed and died after finishing last in King's Stand Stakes at Royal Ascot: best at bare 5f: didn't race on soft/heavy ground, acted on all-weather and any other turf going: often forced pace. *A. M. Balding*   **97**

DUBAIAN MIST   3 b.f. Docksider (USA) 124 – Robellino Miss (USA) (Robellino (USA) 127) [2004 55: p7g 6m⁵ 7m² Sep 18] maiden: should stay 1m: acts on good to firm going: joined S. Seemar in UAE. *A. M. Balding*   **60**

DUBAI DREAMER (USA)   2 gr. or ro.c. (Mar 24) Stephen Got Even (USA) 125 – Blacktie Bid (USA) (Black Tie Affair 128) [2004 p7g² Oct 28] $157,000Y, $3,100,000 2-y-o: fourth live foal: half-brother to winners in USA by Tabasco Cat and Victory Gallop: dam, US 2-y-o 5f and 8.5f (minor stakes) winner, half-sister to US Grade 3 6.5f winner Positive Gal: 7/2, 1½ lengths second to King's Majesty in maiden at Lingfield, leading over 1f out until close home: sure to improve. *Saeed bin Suroor*   **82 p**

DUBAI DREAMS   4 b.g. Marju (IRE) 127 – Arndilly 75 (Robellino (USA) 127) [2004 75: f12g⁴ f8f² f9.4g⁵ f11g 12.1g 8g f8s⁶ 10f p7.1g⁶ f7g² f5m f6g f8d* Dec 21] close-coupled gelding: fair performer: left M. Polglase after fourth start: won banded race at Southwell in December: effective at 7f to 1½m: acts on all-weather, firm and good to soft going: often blinkered/visored: tried tongue tied: often races up with pace/finishes weakly. *S. R. Bowring*   **66**

DUBAI ESCAPADE (USA)   2 b.f. (May 10) Awesome Again (CAN) 133 – Sassy Pants (USA) (Saratoga Six (USA)) [2004 5.1g⁵ Jun 2] $75,000Y, $2,000,000 2-y-o: rangy filly: third foal: half-sister to smart US Grade 1 8.5f winner Madcap Escapade (by Hennessy): dam minor sprint stakes winner in USA: 11/4, fifth in maiden at Nottingham, not at all knocked about once tiring: suffered from problem with near-hind curb after: should do better. *Saeed bin Suroor*   **– p**

DUBAI LIGHTNING (USA)   4 br.g. Seeking The Gold (USA) – Heraklia (USA) – (Irish River (FR) 131) [2004 9.1s⁶ p9.5g Dec 1] rangy, useful-looking gelding: fairly useful form at 2 yrs: last in UAE 2000 Guineas at Nad Al Sheba only outing in 2003: left Saeed bin Suroor, little form at 4 yrs, including in seller: wore cheekpieces on reappearance: tried tongue tied. *J. G. M. O'Shea*   **–**

DUBAI SEVEN STARS   6 ch.m. Suave Dancer (USA) 136 – Her Honour 94 (Teenoso (USA) 135) [2004 83§: 18s Oct 16] leggy, workmanlike mare: fair performer: 9 lb out of weights, not discredited when fourteenth to Contact Dancer in Cesarewitch at Newmarket only 6-y-o outing: stays 2¼m: acts on firm and soft going: visored last 7 outings in 2003: held up: ungenuine. *M. C. Pipe*   **77 §**

Maktoum Al Maktoum's "Dubai Success"

DUBAI SUCCESS   4 b.c. Sadler's Wells (USA) 132 – Crystal Spray 75 (Beldale   **117**
Flutter (USA) 130) [2004 114: 12g* 12m⁴ 12m 14m² 13.3g² 14g⁴ 12d Oct 17] lengthy,
quite attractive colt: has a quick action: smart performer: won Dubai Irish Village (John
Porter) Stakes at Newbury in April by short head from Gamut: mostly creditable efforts
after, including 2½ lengths second of 4 to Mubtaker in Geoffrey Freer Stakes at Newbury
fifth outing and 3¾ lengths fourth to Vinnie Roe in Irish St Leger at the Curragh on sixth:
rare below-par effort in Gran Premio del Jockey Club Italiano at Milan final start: stays
1¾m: successful on good to soft going, best efforts on good/good to firm: hung persistently left at Epsom third outing: consistent. *B. W. Hills*

DUBAI SURPRISE (IRE)   2 b.f. (Mar 21) King's Best (USA) 132 – Toujours Irish   **112**
(USA) (Irish River (FR) 131) [2004 7m³ 7m* 7s* 8f 8s² Oct 31] 220,000Y: quite
good-topped filly: third foal: half-sister to fairly useful Irish 1m winner Liffey (by
Desert Prince) and UAE 1m winner Celtic Note (by Singspiel): dam unraced half-
sister to smart French 9f to 1½m winner Athyka (dam of US Grade 1 9f winner Atticus):
smart performer: won maiden at Redcar and Citroen C5 Prestige Stakes at Goodwood
(beat Nanabanana by ½ length) in August: much better effort after when 1½ lengths
second to Helios Quercus in Criterium International at Saint-Cloud: will stay 1¼m: best
efforts on soft going: very edgy penultimate start: joined Godolphin. *D. R. Loder*

DUBAI VENTURE   2 ch.c. (Apr 29) Rainbow Quest (USA) 134 – Bombazine (IRE)   **77 p**
97 (Generous (IRE) 139) [2004 7m⁶ Aug 6] 200,000Y: leggy, unfurnished colt: fluent
mover: fourth foal: brother to French 1½m and 15.5f winner Affirmative Action and
half-brother to 1m winner Camelot (by Machiavellian), both useful: dam, 1¼m winner,
half-sister to Barathea and Gossamer: 8/1, sixth in maiden at Newmarket, going on
strongly having run green: will be suited by 1¼m/1½m: should do better. *Sir Michael
Stoute*

Dr Ali Ridha's "Dubai Surprise"

DUBAWI (IRE)   2 b.c. (Feb 7) Dubai Millennium 140 – Zomaradah 118 (Deploy   **123 p**
131) [2004 6g* 7g* 7g* Sep 19]

After the brilliance he showed on the racecourse, notably when gaining a six-length triumph in the Dubai World Cup and an eight-length victory in the Prince of Wales's Stakes, Dubai Millennium looked a smashing stud prospect. Regrettably, he had just one season at Darley, covering seventy-four out of his book of one hundred and five mares—at £100,000 a time—before succumbing to grass sickness at the end of April 2001, six days after his last covering. For the record, the widely-quoted figure of sixty-five mares ignores nine subsequently covered by other stallions because they were not impregnated by Dubai Millennium. There is no reason why they should be omitted from his total, however. Sheikh Mohammed never made any secret of the esteem in which he held Dubai Millennium, as some of his remarks on the horse's death confirmed: 'He was a very special horse, the best I have ever owned, the best I have ever seen. If you could ever describe a horse as a friend or a counsellor, that was him.' Showing truly exceptional enthusiasm and determination, the Sheikh promptly set out to purchase as many of Dubai Millennium's progeny as possible. The Maktoums and their associates already owned the majority of the fifty-six foals listed in the 2002 *Statistical Record*. The Sheikh obtained two of the remainder at auction, purchased nine privately and, for several others, he bought the in-foal mare. The result was that fifty of the fifty-four surviving foals—two died—ended up with the Maktoums and twenty-eight went into training with Godolphin. Such phenomenal orchestration guarantees nothing unless the stallion can produce the goods but the ploy appears to have worked superbly. Twenty-one of Dubai Millennium's progeny reached the racecourse and

Dunnes Stores National Stakes, the Curragh—Dubawi makes a really good impression and puts himself in the forefront of the betting on the 2005 classics; behind him are Berenson (right), making only his second start, and Russian Blue, placed in a pattern race for the fourth consecutive time

eleven of them won—the only non-Maktoum owned member of the group is Khalid Abdulla's filly Quickfire. Seventeen of Dubai Millennium's runners have a small 'p' added to their rating and one, Descartes, boasts a large 'P'. None ran more than three times, which fits in entirely with Dubai Millennium's profile as a racehorse, since he was not a precocious juvenile and reached his peak at four. The biggest bonus was that a couple showed form in pattern events, and while Champagne Stakes third Oude has some way to go to threaten the best, Dubawi, unbeaten in three races culminating in the National Stakes at the Curragh, unquestionably has the look of a classic colt.

Given the money and energy devoted to obtaining a virtual monopoly, it was inevitable that Godolphin would make every effort to get their Dubai Millennium team off to a perfect start. No sooner said than done, since his first two runners, Dubawi and Belenus, both won—coincidentally it was Quickfire who spoiled the hundred per cent record at Newbury in mid-July. Dubawi lined up for a five-runner maiden event at a Goodwood evening meeting early in June and remarkably, considering his background and the fact that he was Saeed bin Suroor's only runner and Frankie Dettori's only ride on the card, he opened at 5/1 before starting 11/4 second favourite to odds-on Qadar, runner-up to Henrik on the same course on his only start. Dubawi was very green and, after taking time to get the hang of things, he wandered before asserting in the final furlong, beating Fox by a length and a quarter. An encouraging introduction, one on which Dubawi improved significantly when stepped up in class and distance in the Weatherbys Superlative Stakes at the Newmarket July meeting. All his eleven opponents had won, including Rowan Tree from Ireland, Wilko, Henrik and Fox again, and the York winner Pivotal Flame, who started second favourite behind Dubawi. Held up and confidently ridden, Dubawi still seemed greener than most of his rivals when the pace quickened but, knuckling down when driven, made excellent headway to lead near the finish and defeat Henrik by half a length. Dubawi immediately received a 33/1 quote for the Derby, which was down to 20/1 by the time he next appeared in the Dunnes Stores National Stakes at the Curragh over two months later, chosen in preference to the Royal Lodge Stakes.

Recent National Stakes winners, including Desert King, King of Kings, Sinndar, Hawk Wing and Refuse To Bend, have a fine record, making the race second only to the Criterium International as a proving ground in the last few years for top-class horses, for all that it hasn't always had that much strength in depth. Dubawi was not entered at the initial stage and had to be supplemented at a cost of €30,000. None of his six rivals was exceptional, though they included three from Aidan O'Brien's stable, headed by Russian Blue, twice third in Group 1 company. Also in the line-up was Railway Stakes winner Democratic Deficit and Berenson,

318

successful in a maiden at the Curragh on his only start. Dubawi went off at 13/8-on and justified the confidence in style, running on strongly to defeat Berenson pushed out by three lengths, with Russian Blue a length and a half away third. Dubawi still showed signs of inexperience, going on inside the last two furlongs before veering onto the rail two hundred yards out and having to be brought back on to an even keel. His run was still one of the best by a two-year-old during the year and one that augurs very well. Dubawi's Derby odds were cut to 10/1 favourite and by the year's end he was as low as 6/1. So what are his chances of staying the trip? Excellent according to Simon Crisford, Godolphin's racing manager, who claimed: 'He will stay a mile and a half standing on his head.' If Dubawi does that, he is unlikely to win the Derby or any other race unless, like some horses described by connections and/or pundits down the years, he does so 'literally turning handsprings'. Joking apart, Dubai Millennium was raced only once over a mile and a half, when defeated for the only time in his ten-race career in the Derby. As things turned out, he was a naturally free-running sort, a style which gave him little chance of being fully effective beyond a mile and a quarter. That is not to say his offspring will follow suit though. They seem reasonably tractable overall, and the stamina on the distaff side of Dubawi's pedigree is encouraging. Sixteen of the fifty-four survivors by Dubai Millennium are out of Group 1 winners and Dubawi is one of them. He is the first foal of Zomaradah, who showed smart form in Europe and North America,

	Dubai Millennium (b 1996)	Seeking The Gold (b 1985)	Mr Prospector
Dubawi (IRE) (b.c. Feb 7, 2002)			Con Game
		Colorado Dancer (b 1986)	Shareef Dancer
			Fall Aspen
	Zomaradah (b 1995)	Deploy (b 1987)	Shirley Heights
			Slightly Dangerous
		Jawaher (b 1989)	Dancing Brave
			High Tern

Godolphin's "Dubawi"

notching six races at ten and eleven furlongs headed by the Oaks d'Italia, Royal Whip Stakes, E P Taylor Stakes and Premio Lydia Tesio. She also finished third in the Breeders' Cup Filly & Mare Turf. The family contains plenty of horses suited by middle distances. Grandam Jawaher was lightly raced and produced only one foal but she was out of a mare suited by a thorough test of stamina who foaled Derby winner High-Rise and was a half-sister to high-class racemare High Hawk, dam of In the Wings. A fine family, and one whose reputation Dubawi, a well-made, medium-sized, attractive colt who progressed physically between his last two runs, looks sure to boost further at up to a mile and a half. With Shamardal, who gives the impression that he will always be best at up to a mile and a quarter, also now with Godolphin, Dubawi's best chance of British classic success appears to lie in the Derby, and at the time of writing he looks the one to beat at Epsom. By the same token, he is far from devoid of pace and, should anything go wrong with Shamardal, Dubawi would merit considerable respect if lining up for the Two Thousand Guineas. *Saeed bin Suroor*

DUBOIS   3 b.c. Sadler's Wells (USA) 132 – Dazzle 116 (Gone West (USA)) [2004 81: **95 ?** 8g* 10d 8g* 8g Jul 17] good-topped colt: useful performer: trained at 2 yrs by D. Loder: won maiden at Goodwood (made all, despite hanging left) in May and minor event at Ascot (beat Saffron Fox 3 lengths, taken to race alone against far rail and clear when crossing over approaching straight) in July: well below form in handicaps otherwise: stays 1m: best efforts on good going: visored/tongue tied last 4 starts: somewhat way-ward: left Godolphin. *Saeed bin Suroor*

DUBONAI (IRE)   4 ch.g. Peintre Celebre (USA) 137 – Web of Intrigue 66 (Machia- **62** vellian (USA) 123) [2004 62: 12.4s 11.6m 8m³ 8.1m f8m f8s* 6.9g p8.6g⁴ Oct 7] leggy gelding: modest handicapper: won at Southwell in August: acts at 1m to 1½m: acts on all-weather and good to firm going: occasionally tongue tied. *Andrew Turnell*

DUBROVSKY   4 ch.g. Hector Protector (USA) 124 – Reuval 102 (Sharpen Up 127) **90** [2004 90: 8.1d⁴ 8m 8m⁶ 10m Aug 14] lengthy gelding: fairly useful handicapper, lightly raced: creditable fourth at Sandown on reappearance: below form after, markedly so on final start (reportedly had breathing problem): stays 1m: acts on good to firm and good to soft going: tongue tied penultimate outing: usually waited with. *J. R. Fanshawe*

DUCAL DIVA   2 b.f. (May 2) Bahamian Bounty 116 – Lucky Thing (Green Desert **58** (USA) 127) [2004 6g 5f² f5g⁶ 5f 5g p5.1g⁴ p5.1d Oct 23] seventh foal: half-sister to 6-y-o **a49** Little Task: dam unraced: modest maiden on turf, poor on all-weather: probably stays 6f: acts on polytrack and firm going: wore cheekpieces (below form) final start. *J. R. Weymes*

DUCKETT (IRE)   4 b.g. Charnwood Forest (IRE) 125 – Lovat Spring (USA) (Storm **–** Bird (CAN) 134) [2004 f7g p6g Dec 30] little form, leaving J. Burns in Ireland and off 27 months prior to reappearance: blinkered/visored last 2 starts. *Julian Poulton*

DUCK ROW (USA)   9 ch.g. Diesis 133 – Sunny Moment (USA) (Roberto (USA) **114 d** 131) [2004 113: 7.9s² 8.5m 8f⁵ 7g 10d⁶ 8.2v⁴ Nov 4] sturdy, close-coupled gelding: smart performer: good 2 lengths second to Autumn Glory in handicap at York on reappearance: well below form after: effective at 7f to 9f: acts on firm and soft going: usually waited with. *J. A. R. Toller*

DUC'S DREAM   6 b.g. Bay Tern (USA) 86 – Kala's Image 55 (Kala Shikari 125) **62** [2004 71: p12g 13.8g 11.5f* 13.3m 12m 11.5m⁵ 11.6f 10.9d³ 12g³ 12g⁵ p12.2g p12.2g⁶ Nov 15] leggy gelding: modest handicapper: won at Yarmouth in June: effective at 11f to 1¾m: acts on all-weather and any turf going: tried blinkered/visored. *D. Morris*

DUDLEY DOCKER (IRE)   2 b.g. (Apr 3) Victory Note (USA) 120 – Nordic Abu **74** (IRE) 60 (Nordico (USA)) [2004 7f p6g p7.1g² p7g² Dec 20] €10,000F, €17,500Y: seventh foal: half-brother to winners abroad by College Chapel and Danehill Dancer: dam Irish maiden out of smart Irish performer up to 1¼m Noora Abu: fair maiden: second at Wolverhampton and Lingfield: will stay 1m: acts on polytrack. *M. H. Tompkins*

DUE DILIGENCE (IRE)   5 ch.g. Entrepreneur 123 – Kerry Project (IRE) 79 **–** (Project Manager 111) [2004 65d: 7.1g 7m May 31] angular gelding: fair handicapper at best for J. Bolger in Ireland: no form in Britain: stays 1m: acts on firm and good to soft going (well beaten on soft): tried blinkered (pulled hard). *C. W. Fairhurst*

DUELLING BANJOS   5 ch.g. Most Welcome 131 – Khadino (Relkino 131) [2004 **68** 77, a72: f8g 8.3g⁴ 8m 8m 8.3m 10g* 10d p9.5g p10m⁶ Dec 21] fair handicapper: won at Leicester in October: stays 1¼m: acts on all-weather, best efforts on turf on ground softer than good (not discredited on good to firm). *J. Akehurst*

Queen's Vase, Royal Ascot—Duke of Venice is one of six winners at the Royal meeting for Godolphin and Frankie Dettori, who sees he has plenty to spare over Two Miles West and Top Seed

DUE TO ME 4 gr.f. Compton Place 125 – Always Lucky 71 (Absalom 128) [2004 50: p7g⁵ p8g² p8g⁵ p8g* 7v⁴ p10g⁶ 7f³ 7f⁴ 7m 8d 9.7f Sep 4] modest performer: won banded race at Lingfield in April: stays 1m: acts on polytrack, firm and good to soft going: has worn blinkers/eyeshields, in cheekpieces of late: has carried head high. *G. L. Moore* **52**

DUGGAN'S DILEMMA (IRE) 3 b.g. Lake Coniston (IRE) 131 – Miss Ironwood (Junius (USA) 124) [2004 44: f11g f5s⁶ Feb 23] leggy gelding: poor maiden: tried visored. *Ian Emmerson* **–**

DUKE OF MODENA 7 ch.g. Salse (USA) 128 – Palace Street (USA) 103 (Secreto (USA) 128) [2004 100: 8s 8.3d Sep 27] sturdy gelding: useful handicapper in 2003, well held in 2004: has been bandaged. *G. B. Balding* **–**

DUKE OF VENICE (USA) 3 b.g. Theatrical 128 – Rihan (USA) 84 (Dayjur (USA) 137) [2004 109p: 8g* 10m² 16.2m* 12g⁵ 15.9d Aug 17] big, good sort: useful performer: trained at 2 yrs by M. Johnston: won minor event at Doncaster in May and Queen's Vase at Royal Ascot, latter by 6 lengths from Two Miles West: restless in stall, respectable fifth to Maraahel in ABN Amro Stakes (Gordon) at Goodwood penultimate outing: stays 2m: acts on good to firm going, folded tamely in Lonsdale Cup at York on good to soft going final start (gelded after): tongue tied: usually on toes. *Saeed bin Suroor* **109**

DUKES POINT 2 b.c. (Mar 5) Sinndar (IRE) 134 – Dimakya (USA) 83 (Dayjur (USA) 137) [2004 p8g p10g p8m p6g Dec 29] poor maiden. *G. L. Moore* **46 ?**

DUKE'S VIEW (IRE) 3 b.g. Sadler's Wells (USA) 132 – Igreja (ARG) 101 (Southern Halo (USA)) [2004 69: 12.6s 11.6d 10f⁵ 10g⁵ 12.1m 11.9f⁶ 10s 11.5g⁶ 11.9m Sep 23] good-topped gelding: modest maiden: stays 1¼m: acts on firm and good to soft going: sometimes blinkered, looked reluctant to race second outing. *Mrs A. J. Perrett* **58**

DULCE DE LECHE 3 b.g. Cayman Kai (IRE) 114 – Give Us A Treat (Cree Song 99) [2004 60: p5g p7g⁶ f6s⁴ p7g f6g 7d Apr 7] sturdy gelding: just poor maiden in 2004: stays 7f: acts on all-weather: usually wears blinkers. *S. C. Williams* **49**

DULCIMER 3 ch.f. Piccolo 121 – Superspring (Superlative 118) [2004 7g 6s 7g 7m Jun 8] 19,000Y: strong filly: half-sister to 6f (at 2 yrs) to 11f winner Our Destiny (by Mujadil) and 4-y-o Stagnite: dam unraced sister to smart sprinter Superpower: well held in maidens: very free to post on debut. *G. B. Balding* **–**

DUMARAN (IRE) 6 b.g. Be My Chief (USA) 122 – Pine Needle 89 (Kris 135) [2004 104: p10g 8g 10d² 10.4d³ 8.5m⁵ 7.9s 10d⁶ 9g Oct 2] useful handicapper: best efforts of season when placed at Kempton (second to Silence Is Golden in Rosebery Stakes) and York (third to Vintage Premium) in spring: reared and banged head in stall final start: stays 10.4f: acts on polytrack, best turf efforts on good going or softer: visored (below form) twice: sometimes slowly away: has pulled hard. *W. J. Musson* **99**

DUMFRIES 3 ch.g. Selkirk (USA) 129 – Pat Or Else 72 (Alzao (USA) 117) [2004 82p: 11.6g⁵ 12.3d³ 11.9d⁶ 10f⁵ Jun 27] big, good-bodied gelding: fairly useful performer: at least respectable efforts all starts in 2004: will stay 1¾m: best efforts on good/good to soft going: visored final outing: sold 30,000 gns, joined T. Caldwell. *J. H. M. Gosden* **83**

DUMNONI 3 b.f. Titus Livius (FR) 115 – Lamees (USA) (Lomond (USA) 128) [2004 84: p7g 7d⁶ 8.3s³ 9g 7m⁴ 7m* 7.1g³ 7m² 8g² 7g Oct 2] leggy filly: fairly useful handicapper: won at Newmarket in June: ran as if amiss final outing: effective at 7f/1m: acts on all-weather, soft and good to firm going: carried head awkwardly fourth start. *Julian Poulton* **88**

321

totesport Stakes (Handicap), Haydock—enterprisingly-ridden Dunaskin captures this valuable prize; behind him are Coat of Honour (grey), Shahzan House (cheekpieces) and Mutafanen (left)

DUNASKIN (IRE) 4 b.g. Bahhare (USA) 122 – Mirwara (IRE) (Darshaan 133) [2004 **107** 95: 8g 10.3g 11.9s 10m⁵ 11.9d⁶ 12.3d³ 10.1g* 10.5g* 10.4s* 7.9g Oct 8] smallish, workmanlike gelding: useful performer: much improved in 2004, winning minor event at Newcastle in July and handicaps at Haydock (totesport Stakes) and York (beat Zero Tolerance 7 lengths, again dictating pace) in August: reportedly suffered from a poisoned foot in mid-September: well below form final outing: stays 1½m: acts on soft and good to firm ground: used to hang right: front runner: tough and consistent. *D. Eddy*

DUNCANBIL (IRE) 3 b.f. Turtle Island (IRE) 123 – Saintly Guest (What A Guest – 119) [2004 57: f7m f7g 13.8m² 16.2g p10m Dec 8] workmanlike filly: little form in 2004. *J. J. Bridger*

DUNDONALD 5 ch.g. Magic Ring (IRE) 115 – Cal Norma's Lady (IRE) 87 (Lyphard's **35 §** Special (USA) 122) [2004 49§, a59§: f9.4s⁶ f12s f8.5s f8.5s³ f8.5s⁴ f9.4g f8.5g⁶ 12d⁵ **a46 §** 11.5m f8.5m³ 7.1d³ f9.4g³ f11g 8d⁶ p8.6g p10m⁵ p7m⁴ Dec 15] big gelding: poor performer: barely stays 9.4f: acts on fibresand, good to firm and good to soft going: tongue tied: usually wears headgear: often finds little: untrustworthy. *M. Appleby*

DUNDRY 3 b.g. Bin Ajwaad (IRE) 119 – China's Pearl (Shirley Heights 130) [2004 **82** 68p: 9.9g³ 10g³ 10g² 11s² p12g* 11.6m Sep 27] good-topped gelding: fairly useful performer: won maiden at Lingfield in September by 11 lengths: folded tamely in handicap at Windsor after: stays 1½m: raced only on good ground or softer on turf: wore cheekpieces last 3 starts. *G. L. Moore*

DUNEDIN RASCAL 7 b.g. Piccolo 121 – Thorner Lane 86 (Tina's Pet 121) [2004 –, – a80: p7g p6g p7g p6g Feb 4] smallish gelding: well held in 2004: blinkered nowadays: held up. *E. A. Wheeler*

DUNE RAIDER (USA) 3 b.c. Kingmambo (USA) 125 – Glowing Honor (USA) **87** (Seattle Slew (USA)) [2004 10g 10.3m 12.1m* 11.8g⁶ 12s Nov 6] $120,000Y: tall, angular, good-topped colt: half-brother to minor winners in USA by Danzig and Easy Goer: dam, US 9f Grade 2 winner, half-sister to Kentucky Derby winner Sea Hero: fairly useful performer: left Sir Michael Stoute 13,500 gns after second start: won maiden at Chepstow in September: best effort when sixth to Massif Centrale in handicap at Leicester: well beaten in November Handicap at Doncaster final outing: stays 1½m: acts on good to firm going. *K. A. Ryan*

DUNHILL STAR (IRE) 4 b.c. Danehill (USA) 126 – Sueboog (IRE) 109 (Darshaan **101** 133) [2004 114: 12g² Mar 27] well-made, quite attractive colt: smart performer in 2003: length second to Royal Cavalier in minor event at Doncaster on only outing in 2004: should stay 1¾m: successful on polytrack and good to soft going, best form on good to firm: has carried head awkwardly: sold 18,000 gns in October, sent to Bahrain. *B. W. Hills*

DUNLEA DANCER 3 b.g. Groom Dancer (USA) 128 – Be My Lass (IRE) (Be My **71** Guest (USA) 126) [2004 52: 9.9s³ 12.1m⁴ 13.1d² 12.1d* 14g⁶ Jul 2] tall, close-coupled gelding: fair handicapper: won at Hamilton in June by 6 lengths, edging left: should stay 1¾m: acts on firm and soft going: sold 25,000 gns, joined P. Hobbs, won over hurdles in December. *M. Johnston*

322

DUNLEA (IRE) 8 b.g. Common Grounds 118 – No Distractions 78 (Tap On Wood 130) [2004 13m 7d Oct 2] maiden: very lightly raced and no form since 2000, leaving J. Carr in Ireland before final outing. *M. J. Gingell* –

DUNLOWS MINSTREL 2 ch.c. (Mar 3) Opening Verse (USA) 126 – Mary From Dunlow 49 (Nicholas Bill 125) [2004 8.3m Sep 27] last in maiden at Windsor: dead. *Miss D. Mountain* –

DUNMAGLASS (USA) 2 ch.g. (Mar 5) Cat Thief (USA) 126 – Indian Fashion (USA) 71 (General Holme (USA) 128) [2004 7m 7m Jul 17] $50,000Y, resold $90,000Y: workmanlike gelding: half-brother to several winners, including smart 7f (at 2 yrs) and 11.4f winner Solaia (by Miswaki): dam, second at 1m in Britain at 2 yrs, later won in USA and second in Grade 2 1½m event: modest form in maidens at Newbury and Lingfield: will stay at least 1m. *P. F. I. Cole* **62**

DUNMIDOE 4 b.f. Case Law 113 – Rion River (IRE) (Taufan (USA) 119) [2004 –: 8.1g f7g May 5] maiden: well held both starts in 2004: tried in cheekpieces. *C. Drew* –

DUNMORE DERRY (IRE) 2 b.c. (Apr 27) Montjeu (IRE) 137 – Louju (USA) (Silver Hawk (USA) 123) [2004 7m6 6f4 7d 8v5 7g f8g* Dec 11] 50,000Y: fourth foal: half-brother to smart 7f (at 2 yrs) to 9f (Grade 1 in USA) winner Castledale (by Peintre Celebre) and 7f winner Dominion Rose (by Spinning World): dam unraced out of US Grade 1 9f runner-up Secretariat Queen: fair performer: left D. Wachman in Ireland, won maiden at Southwell by short head from Cavan Gael: stays 1m: acts on fibresand and heavy going. *B. J. Meehan* **75**

DUNN DEAL (IRE) 4 b.g. Revoque (IRE) 122 – Buddy And Soda (IRE) 75 (Imperial Frontier (USA) 112) [2004 66§: f5g3 p6g 5d* f5d2 5.1d 5m5 5f 5g6 5g6 5.1g5 f5m p5.1g Nov 29] smallish, sturdy gelding: fair handicapper: won at Warwick in April: best at 5f: acts on fibresand, firm and soft going: tried tongue tied: sometimes wanders. *W. M. Brisbourne* **70**

DUO LEONI 4 ch.f. Vettori (IRE) 119 – La Dolce Vita 76 (Mazilier (USA) 107) [2004 71: p7g6 f7g* Mar 17] fair performer: better effort in 2004 when winning handicap at Wolverhampton: stays 7f: acts on all-weather, firm and good to soft going: free-going sort. *Mrs Stef Liddiard* **67**

DU PRE 3 b.f. Singspiel (IRE) 133 – Child Prodigy (IRE) 87 (Ballad Rock 122) [2004 65: 7d 8g2 8.3f* 10f3 10m Aug 16] smallish, compact filly: fair performer: won handicap at Windsor in July: possibly amiss final start: stays 1¼m: acts on firm ground. *Mrs A. J. Perrett* **78**

DUROOB 2 b.c. (Jan 17) Bahhare (USA) 122 – Amaniy (USA) 96 (Dayjur (USA) 137) [2004 p6d 6.1d3 7.1s3 8d* Oct 15] good-topped colt: fifth foal: half-brother to 6f winner Ikbal (by Indian Ridge) and fairly useful 2003 2-y-o 7f winner Tabadul (by Cadeaux Genereux): dam, 2-y-o 5f/6f winner, half-sister to smart 7f performer Kayrawan: fair performer: won maiden at Redcar, leading final 1f: stays 1m: bit reportedly slipped on debut: sold 22,000 gns. *E. A. L. Dunlop* **77**

DUSK DANCER (FR) 4 b.g. Groom Dancer (USA) 128 – Nightitude 93 (Night Shift (USA)) [2004 67: p7g4 p10g f8.5s Feb 23] rangy, angular gelding: modest maiden: stays 1m: acts on polytrack and good to firm ground: blinkered (pulled hard, ran poorly) final start. *B. J. Meehan* **62**

DUSKY WARBLER 5 br.g. Ezzoud (IRE) 126 – Bronzewing 103 (Beldale Flutter (USA) 130) [2004 110: 14.1g2 16.2s2 16g 20m 15.5d5 Oct 11] big, leggy gelding: smart performer at 4 yrs, just useful in 2004: 18 lengths second of 13 to Risk Seeker in Sagaro Stakes at Ascot on second outing, forcing strong pace and weakening: best effort of season when 3 lengths fifth to Frosted Aclaim in listed race at Maisons-Laffitte final start: stays 2¼m: acts on heavy and good to firm going: usually races prominently: sold 68,000 gns. *M. L. W. Bell* **104**

DUSTINI (IRE) 2 ch.g. (Mar 12) Rossini (USA) 118 – Truly Modest (IRE) (Imp Society (USA)) [2004 5d3 5.3m5 5.1s3 6g p5g Jun 30] modest maiden: likely to prove best at 5f/6f: blinkered/in cheekpieces last 3 starts (best effort on first occasion): gelded after final outing. *W. G. M. Turner* **59**

DUSTY CARPET 6 ch.g. Pivotal 124 – Euridice (IRE) 66 (Woodman (USA) 126) [2004 p12g p12g p12g p16g 10s 9.9g 8.1s Aug 30] sturdy, close-coupled gelding: fairly useful at 3 yrs: off 21 months, fair form at best in 2004: stays easy 1½m: acts on all-weather, firm and soft ground: has carried head awkwardly/edged left under pressure. *M. J. Weeden* **76 d**

DUSTY DANE (IRE) 2 b.g. (Apr 16) Indian Danehill (IRE) 124 – Teer On Eer (IRE) **70**
62 (Persian Heights 129) [2004 5s⁵ 7.5g⁶ 6g⁵ 7g³ f7m 7s⁶ 8.1g⁴ Sep 3] €6,600F, 9,400Y:
workmanlike gelding: third foal: dam, Irish maiden, stayed 7f: fair maiden: stays 1m: best
efforts on good ground: tongue tied first 2 starts: gelded after final one. *W. G. M. Turner*

DUSTY DAZZLER (IRE) 4 ch.f. Titus Livius (FR) 115 – Satinette 109 (Shirley **82**
Heights 130) [2004 93, a102: p6g* p5g⁶ 5.1g 6g⁵ May 14] strong, lengthy filly: fairly **a90**
useful handicapper: won minor event at Lingfield in January: best at 5f/easy 6f: acts on
polytrack: tends to hang right. *W. G. M. Turner*

DUSTY WUGG (IRE) 5 b.m. General Monash (USA) 107 – Welsh Berry (USA) (Sir **43**
Ivor (USA) 135) [2004 59: f6g⁵ f6s³ f6g 7g⁵ 6v Apr 6] leggy mare: poor maiden: stays 7f:
acts on fibresand, firm and soft going: usually slowly away. *A. Dickman*

DUTCH GOLD (USA) 4 ch.c. Lahib (USA) 129 – Crimson Conquest (USA) 85 **112**
(Diesis 133) [2004 112: a9f 12f² 12m 12g 13.9d⁵ 8.5m² 10d⁵ 8g Jul 10] good-topped colt:
smart performer: good second in handicap at Nad Al Sheba in February and Diomed
Stakes at Epsom (beaten 1¼ lengths by Passing Glance) in June: well below form final
start: effective at 1m to 1½m: acts on polytrack and firm going, possibly not on softer
than good: blinkered last 4 outings: tongue tied once at 3 yrs: often races prominently:
occasionally flashes tail: none too consistent: joined M. Al Kurdi in UAE. *C. E. Brittain*

DUTCH KEY CARD (IRE) 3 b.g. Key of Luck (USA) 126 – Fanny Blankers (IRE) **68**
(Persian Heights 129) [2004 79p: 10s 7f⁵ 8g 8d⁵ 8g 7m f5f⁵ p5.1g* p6g p5.1g⁵ Dec 31]
€30,000Y: fifth foal: half-brother to 3 winners, including useful Irish 1½m winner Dutch
Harrier (by Barathea): dam, Irish 2-y-o 7f winner, half-sister to dual Irish St Leger winner
Oscar Schindler: fair performer: trained by K. Prendergast in Ireland until after sixth start:
won maiden at Wolverhampton in November: has form up to 7f, but effective at 5f: acts
on all-weather, best effort on turf on good going: withdrawn after getting loose at start
once, and led to post at Wolverhampton. *G. A. Butler*

DUXFORD 3 ch.g. Young Ern 120 – Marsara (Never So Bold 135) [2004 6m p8m² Oct **66**
6] second foal: dam unraced: better effort in maidens when 4 lengths second to Admiral
Compton at Lingfield, keeping on from mid-field: not bred to stay much beyond 1m.
D. K. Ivory

DVINSKY (USA) 3 b.c. Stravinsky (USA) 133 – Festive Season (USA) (Lypheor 118) **76**
[2004 92p: 5.1g 7m p7.1g⁶ p5.1g⁴ p6g³ p6g⁵ p7.1g Dec 20] compact colt: fairly useful
effort when winning 2-y-o maiden at Goodwood: just fair form in 2004: left G. Butler
after fourth start: should stay 7f: acts on polytrack and good to firm going: tried
tongue tied/blinkered/in cheekpieces: reportedly had breathing problem third outing.
A. W. Carroll

E

EACHY PEACHY (IRE) 5 ch.m. Perugino (USA) 84 – Miss Big John (IRE) (Martin **–**
John) [2004 46: 11.9m⁵ Sep 23] rather leggy mare: maiden: well held only outing in 2004:
often slowly away/carries head high. *J. R. Best*

EAGER ANGEL (IRE) 6 b.m. Up And At 'em 109 – Seanee Squaw (Indian Ridge **60 d**
123) [2004 48: f7g² f8g⁴ f7g f7g* f6g⁵ f7g* f8.5s f7g³ 7s 7v f7g p8.6g f8g f6g Dec 12]
small, good-quartered mare: modest performer: won banded race at Wolverhampton and
handicap at Southwell in February: below form after: stays 7f: acts on fibresand, firm and
soft going: tried in blinkers/tongue tie, usually wears cheekpieces. *R. F. Marvin*

EAGLE FEATHERS 3 b.f. Indian Ridge 123 – Flying Squaw 102 (Be My Chief **–**
(USA) 122) [2004 9g May 16] workmanlike filly: fourth foal: half-sister to 8.5f winner
Flying Carpet (by Barathea): dam 2-y-o 5f/6f winner: 16/1, hampered and always behind
in maiden at Ripon. *T. D. Easterby*

EAGLE RISE (IRE) 4 b.c. Danehill (USA) 126 – Evening Breeze (GER) 99 (Surumu **119**
(GER)) [2004 8s* 8m⁵ 8d³ 8g² 10d⁵ 8s* 8d* 8m Dec 12] smart performer: successful at 3
yrs in minor events at Krefeld and Munich: improved form in 2004, winning listed race at
Cologne in April, Grosse Europa-Meile there (by neck from Putra Pekan) in September
and Premio Ribot at Rome (by short neck from Martillo) in November: best at 1m: acts
on soft ground. *A. Schutz, Germany*

EARL OF LINKS (IRE) 2 ch.c. (Apr 14) Raise A Grand (IRE) 114 – Metroella (IRE) **68**
87 (Entitled 126) [2004 5d³ 5v* 6m⁶ 5.2m 7s⁴ 5.1s⁶ Aug 30] €30,000Y: good-topped

colt: has scope: half-brother to fairly useful Irish 9f and 1½m winner Brogella (by King's Theatre) and Irish 13f winner Czar of Peace (by Brief Truce): dam, Irish 1m winner (including at 2 yrs), also successful over hurdles, half-sister to dam of top-class Irish chaser Beef Or Salmon: fair performer: won maiden at Warwick in May: below form in nurseries/sales race after: should stay 7f: acts on heavy going: sold 7,000 gns, sent to Spain. *R. Hannon*

EARLSFIELD RAIDER   4 ch.g. Double Trigger (IRE) 123 – Harlequin Walk (IRE) **62**
57 (Pennine Walk 120) [2004 62: f12g* p12.2g Nov 8] leggy gelding: modest performer: won maiden at Wolverhampton in February: stays 1½m: acts on fibresand and good to soft ground. *G. L. Moore*

EARLSTON   4 ch.g. Fleetwood (IRE) 107 – Mystique Smile 78 (Music Boy 124) [2004 **47**
73: f7g⁴ f8.5s f7s Feb 20] leggy gelding: just poor form in 2004: tried tongue tied/in cheekpieces/blinkers. *Miss Gay Kelleway*

EARLY MARCH   2 b.c. (Jan 28) Dansili 127 – Emplane (USA) 101 (Irish River **118**
(FR) 131) [2004 7s* 7g* 7m² 8s⁶ Oct 31]
For a long way in the Prix Jean-Luc Lagardere at Longchamp, it looked as though the owner/trainer combination of Khalid Abdulla and Criquette Head-Maarek had every chance of being successful in the race for the second year running. American Post had been a clear-cut winner for connections twelve months earlier, but it was clear from some way out that their representative this time, Early March, was going to be involved in a much tighter finish, successful or not. Early March soon led, but from over a furlong out he began to drift away from the rail and surrendered the lead to Layman soon afterwards. Rallying splendidly, Early March had his head in front again in the closing stages but had no answer to Oratorio's late finish up the rail and went down by a short neck, with Layman just a nose back in third.

Early March had won both his previous starts. He went straight from winning a newcomers race at Clairefontaine in August to taking on five other winners in the Prix La Rochette at Longchamp in September. Two of his rivals had been successful in listed company last time out, the favourite Stop Making Sense at Deauville, and Corsario at La Teste from the subsequent Prix d'Arenberg winner Toupie. Early March ran out a comfortable winner, making the running and just needing to be pushed out once shaken up to beat Stop Making Sense by a length and a half, with the outsider Osidy a close third and Corsario fourth. Early March's narrow defeat in the Prix Jean-Luc Lagardere next time represented further improvement and, with more progress a possibility, he started a short-priced favourite for the Criterium International at Saint-Cloud at the end of October. The step up to a mile should not have posed him any problems and, whilst conditions were much

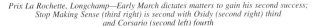

*Prix La Rochette, Longchamp—Early March dictates matters to gain his second success;
Stop Making Sense (third right) is second with Osidy (second right) third
and Corsario (second left) fourth*

softer than for his two outings at Longchamp, he had handled soft ground on his debut. Early March took up his now customary position in front, but he was headed in the straight before dropping away to finish sixth of the eight runners behind Helios Quercus. Early March is a lot better than he showed at Saint-Cloud and his effort there is best forgiven; it's worth noting that his sire Dansili also made a winning debut in the mud but proved best on good or firmer. A big, strong colt, Early March is an imposing type who looked in magnificent shape on Arc day and is just the sort to train on well as a three-year-old. Richard Hughes, who rode him for the first time at Saint-Cloud, described him as the biggest two-year-old he had sat on all year.

Early March (b.c. Jan 28, 2002)	Dansili (b 1996)	Danehill (b 1986)	Danzig
			Razyana
		Hasili (b 1991)	Kahyasi
			Kerali
	Emplane (USA) (b 1995)	Irish River (ch 1976)	Riverman
			Irish Star
		Peplum (b 1988)	Nijinsky
			Chain Store

Early March looks much the best member of Dansili's first crop at this stage. The sire was also represented by the promising Home Affairs in Britain, though interestingly that colt's season also finished with a poor run on soft ground, in the Dewhurst. Dansili was a high-class miler who missed out on a top-level prize but went close on several occasions, including when an unlucky third in the Breeders' Cup Mile on his final start. Incidentally, Dansili's brother Cacique won the Prix Daniel Wildenstein the day before Early March contested the Jean-Luc Lagardere, while his sister Intercontinental won the Matriarch Stakes at Hollywood in November, enhancing their dam Hasili's terrific broodmare record still further. Early March is his dam Emplane's third foal and the second to race after the French eleven-furlong winner Coach Lane (by Barathea). Emplane won a mile maiden at Newmarket from just four starts for Henry Cecil but showed useful form. She should have stayed further too, being a sister to the mile-and-a-quarter performer Boatman, a useful handicapper in Britain before showing smart form in the States, where he finished second in a couple of Grade 1 races. The grandam Peplum won the Cheshire Oaks and was a half-sister to the Irish One Thousand Guineas winner Al Bahathri, who was back in the limelight in the latest season as the dam of Two Thousand Guineas and Champion Stakes winner Haafhd. It is not out of the question that Early March will attempt to give his family a second consecutive Two Thousand Guineas success at Newmarket, though connections may favour taking the route that paid dividends—albeit luckily—with American Post and stay at home for the French version, a race in which Early March's sire finished second. Early March races as though a mile will be the limit of his stamina; like American Post, he is quite an exuberant sort, who went freely to post for the Jean-Luc Lagardere before proving somewhat mulish at the stalls. *Mme C. Head-Maarek, France*

EASIBET DOT NET   4 gr.g. Atraf 116 – Silvery 67 (Petong 126) [2004 72: f12s⁴   **77 §**
12.4v 12m² 10f³ 12m 9.9g⁵ 10.5d³ 12.1f* 12.1s³ 12g⁴ 10.1m³ 12d² f11g⁶ Nov 23] tall gelding: fair handicapper: made all in apprentice event at Hamilton in July: effective at 1¼m/1½m: acts on fibresand, firm and good to soft going: tried visored, usually wears cheekpieces/blinkers: irresolute, and usually carries head high. *I. Semple*

EASILY AVERTED (IRE)   3 b.g. Averti (IRE) 117 – Altishaan (Darshaan 133)   **51 d**
[2004 72: p5g⁵ p5g⁵ p5g p6g 5s 5.3m 7m⁶ 7.6f 5.3s f5g p8m Dec 8] sturdy, close-coupled gelding: fair performer at 2 yrs: well below form in 2004, leaving J. Osborne after reappearance: tried tongue tied/in cheekpieces. *P. Butler*

EASTBOROUGH (IRE)   5 b.g. Woodborough (USA) 112 – Easter Girl (Efisio 120)   **76**
[2004 72+: p12g p10g³ f9.4g* p10g p8g³ f8.5s⁴ 9.7s³ 10.2g⁴ 8.3g⁶ 11.9m⁶ 10m² 11m³ 10.2g² p12g p8.6g² p9.5g³ p10g⁵ p12m² Dec 22] close-coupled, quite good-topped gelding: fair performer: won claimer at Wolverhampton in January: left B. Powell after fifteenth start: effective at 1m to 1½m: acts on all-weather, soft and good to firm going: tried blinkered earlier in career: held up. *Mrs Stef Liddiard*

EAST CAPE   7 b.g. Bering 136 – Reine de Danse (USA) 78 (Nureyev (USA) 131) [2004   **52**
53: f12g⁵ f11g³ f11g f14g* f14s f14g 10.1v 12.4s⁶ 14.1g³ 12.1g⁵ 12.1m² 12.1s⁴ 14.1f

14.1d 10s³ Oct 30] leggy, useful-looking gelding: modest performer: won banded race at Southwell in February: stays 1¾m: acts on fibresand and any turf going: tried visored: sometimes finds little. *Don Enrico Incisa*

EASTERN BLUE (IRE)   5 ch.m. Be My Guest (USA) 126 – Stifen (Burslem 123)   **54**
[2004 62: f6s⁶ p6g⁵ p6g³ Feb 29] sturdy mare: modest handicapper: stays 6f: acts on all-weather, firm and good to soft ground: tried blinkered, often wears cheekpieces: has found little. *Mrs L. Stubbs*

EASTERN BREEZE (IRE)   6 b.g. Sri Pekan (USA) 117 – Elegant Bloom (IRE) 84   **110**
(Be My Guest (USA) 126) [2004 103: p12g⁴ p10g* p10g² p10g 9g⁵ 10.4g 12g* 12m Jul 30] sturdy gelding: smart performer: won handicap at Lingfield in January and minor event at Newmarket (beat Westmoreland Road ¾ length) in July: broke down in listed race at Goodwood final start: stayed 1½m: was at least as effective at shorter: acted on all-weather, soft and good to firm going: dead. *P. W. D'Arcy*

EASTERN DAGGER   4 b.g. Kris 135 – Shehana (USA) 86 (The Minstrel (CAN)   –
135) [2004 78d: 8v f7d 10m 10.1v⁶ 7.5g Jul 2] leggy gelding: well held in 2004, leaving P. Blockley after first outing, J. Turner after second: tried visored. *P. T. Midgley*

EASTERN HOPE (IRE)   5 b.g. Danehill Dancer (IRE) 117 – Hope And Glory (USA)   **69**
87 (Well Decorated (USA)) [2004 76: 10g 7s 8m³ 8.1d 7.5d 8d³ 8g 8s* 8d p9.5g⁵ Dec 20] tall, good-topped gelding: fair performer: won claimer at Newcastle in August: effective at 7f to 9.5f: acts on polytrack, soft and good to firm going: has run well in blinkers: often slowly away. *Mrs L. Stubbs*

EASTERN MAGENTA (IRE)   4 b.g. Turtle Island (IRE) 123 – Blue Heights (IRE)   –
(Persian Heights 129) [2004 –: 10g Mar 31] fairly useful at 2 yrs: lightly raced and well held since. *Mrs L. Stubbs*

EASTERN MANDARIN   2 b.g. (Mar 5) Tipsy Creek (USA) 115 – Hotel Street (USA)   **54**
93 (Alleged (USA) 138) [2004 8v⁵ 8.3d⁵ Sep 27] modest form in claimer at Newcastle (for Mrs L. Stubbs) and maiden at Hamilton (carried head high). *D. Eddy*

EASTERN PEARL   3 ch.f. Wolfhound (USA) 126 – Wild Humour (IRE) 60 (Fayruz   –
116) [2004 75: 5s 5d f5g Jun 11] leggy, lengthy filly: fair performer at 2 yrs: well held in handicaps in 2004. *Mrs L. Stubbs*

EASTERN SCARLET (IRE)   4 b.g. Woodborough (USA) 112 – Cuddles (IRE) 89   **47 §**
(Taufan (USA) 119) [2004 52§: 6d 8.5d⁵ 8d p7.1d⁶ p8.6g⁴ Oct 25] good-bodied gelding: poor performer: left Miss S. Finn in Ireland after second start: stays 9f: acts on polytrack and good to firm ground: sometimes wears cheekpieces, visored final outing: often very slowly away: ungenuine. *V. Smith*

EASTER OGIL (IRE)   9 ch.g. Pips Pride 117 – Piney Pass (Persian Bold 123) [2004   **61**
67, a77: p10g⁵ p12g p10g³ p12g³ p13g² p8g⁴ p10g p10g p10g f8.5s 9.7s 9.7d² 10g⁶ 9.7s⁵   **a70**
12.1d 10d p8.6g⁶ p9.5d⁶ p12g p9.5g p9.5g Dec 6] lengthy, good-topped gelding: fair performer, better on all-weather than turf: effective at 1m, barely at 13f: acts on polytrack and any turf going: tried in visor/cheekpieces: sometimes soon off bridle/gets behind. *Jane Southcombe*

EAST FLARES   4 ch.g. Environment Friend 128 – Ijada Bianca (Absalom 128) [2004   –
66?: f9.4g p10g Feb 14] close-coupled gelding: lightly-raced handicapper: well held in 2004. *J. W. Unett*

EAST RIDING   4 b.f. Gothenberg (IRE) 117 – Bettynouche 69 (Midyan (USA) 124)   **48 d**
[2004 55: 7.1g⁵ f5g⁶ 7.1g⁵ 8.1v³ 10m 10m 12m 12.6m⁵ 9.3g⁵ 9m 6m f7g p9.5g Dec 17] tall, leggy filly: poor maiden: stays 7f: acts on any ground: tried in cheekpieces: has carried head awkwardly. *Miss A. Stokell*

EASTWELL MAGIC   2 b.f. (May 1) Polish Precedent (USA) 131 – Kinchenjunga 67   –
(Darshaan 133) [2004 p7g 8g Sep 3] leggy filly: seventh foal: half-sister to 9.7f to 2¼m winner Eastwell Hall (by Saddlers' Hall): dam, second at 1m on only 2-y-o start, no form afterwards: well held in maidens. *J. G. Given*

EASTWELL VIOLET   4 b.f. Danzig Connection (USA) – Kinchenjunga 67 (Darshaan   –
133) [2004 49: f14m Jul 12] poor maiden: well held only outing in 2004. *R. T. Phillips*

EASY FEELING (IRE)   2 b.f. (Feb 25) Night Shift (USA) – Talena (Zafonic (USA)   **84**
130) [2004 6m³ 5g³ 5d⁴ 6m* 6m⁵ 6.5m Sep 8] €30,000Y: attractive filly: first foal: dam, French maiden who stayed 13f, daughter of Sun Chariot Stakes winner Talented: fairly useful performer: won nursery at Goodwood in July: respectable efforts in sales race at the Curragh and nursery at Doncaster (poorly drawn) after: should stay 7f: acts on good to firm going. *R. Hannon*

EASY MOVER (IRE) 2 ch.f. (Feb 7) Bluebird (USA) 125 – Top Brex (FR) (Top Ville **77** 129) [2004 6g⁵ 6m⁵ 7m* 7.1g² 7m 8d Oct 18] 13,000Y: small filly: third foal: dam French 1½m winner: fair performer: won maiden at Thirsk in September: creditable efforts in minor event at Sandown and nursery at Ascot (not clear run) next 2 starts: should stay at least 1m: acts on good to firm going. *R. Guest*

EAU PURE (FR) 7 b.m. Epervier Bleu 131 – Eau de Nuit (Kings Lake (USA) 133) **41** [2004 –: p13g⁴ Apr 29] poor maiden. *G. L. Moore*

EBINZAYD (IRE) 8 b.g. Tenby 125 – Sharakawa (IRE) (Darshaan 133) [2004 14.1f **70** 16d 14.4s⁵ 17.5d⁵ Sep 17] fair handicapper on Flat nowadays: probably stays 2m: acts on good to firm going, probably on soft: useful hurdler. *L. Lungo*

EBORACUM (IRE) 3 b.f. Alzao (USA) 117 – Fire of London 78 (Shirley Heights **87** 130) [2004 63: 7.5m f7g 8.1g² 10.3d² 12m 10m⁴ 9.2d* 7.9g* 8d* Sep 16] good-topped filly: fairly useful handicapper: much improved last 3 starts, winning at Hamilton in August and at York and Ayr in September: stays 1¼m: acts on good to soft going: blinkered last 4 starts. *T. D. Easterby*

EBORACUM LADY (USA) 4 b.f. Lure (USA) 131 – Konvincha (USA) (Cormorant **48** (USA)) [2004 58?: 10.9m⁶ f8g⁵ 10.1m Jul 26] big, plain filly: just poor maiden in 2004: stays 11f: acts on fibresand and good to firm ground. *J. D. Bethell*

EBORARRY (IRE) 2 b.g. (Mar 7) Desert Sun 120 – Aztec Princess (Indian King **51 ?** (USA) 128) [2004 7.5d⁴ 7.5m 7.5d Aug 11] sturdy gelding: seemingly modest form in minor event/maidens: should stay 1¼m. *T. D. Easterby*

E BRIDE (USA) 2 gr. or ro.f. (Apr 26) Runaway Groom (CAN) – Fast Selection (USA) **58** (Talinum (USA)) [2004 6m⁵ 6.1m⁴ 7s⁴ Nov 1] neat filly: fifth foal: half-sister to winners in USA/Puerto Rico by Fly So Free and Rhythm: dam unraced half-sister to very smart 1¼m performer Montjoy: modest form in maidens: should stay 1m. *J. G. Given*

EBTIKAAR (IRE) 2 b.c. (May 1) Darshaan 133 – Jawlaat (USA) 91 (Dayjur (USA) **73 p** 137) [2004 7m Aug 6] angular, quite attractive colt: fourth foal: half-brother to 3-y-o Thajja and useful 2000 2-y-o 6f winner Khulan (by Bahri): dam, 6f winner (including at 2 yrs), closely related to July Cup winner Elnadim and half-sister to Irish 1000 Guineas winner Mehthaaf, an outstanding family: 14/1 and very green, eighth in maiden at Newmarket, slowly away and never nearer: will stay at least 1m: should do better. *J. L. Dunlop*

ECCENTRIC 3 ch.g. Most Welcome 131 – Sure Care 62 (Caerleon (USA) 132) [2004 **?** –: p8g⁴ p7g* p7g* 6d p6g⁴ p6g² p7g² 7m p7g² p7.1g⁶ p8m* p7g Dec 29] neat gelding: **a95** useful performer: won maiden in February and handicaps in March and December, all at Lingfield: effective at 6f to easy 1m: acts on polytrack, lightly raced and little form on turf: races up with pace. *Andrew Reid*

ECCENTRICITY (USA) 2 ch.f. (Apr 20) Kingmambo (USA) 125 – Shiva (JPN) 127 **61 p** (Hector Protector (USA) 124) [2004 7m⁶ Jul 1] first foal: dam, 8.5f to 10.5f (Tattersalls Gold Cup) winner, sister to very smart middle-distance performer Limnos: 9/2, sixth in maiden at Yarmouth, not knocked about: likely to stay at least 1¼m: should do better. *H. R. A. Cecil*

ECHELON 2 b.f. (Apr 15) Danehill (USA) 126 – Exclusive 115 (Polar Falcon **99 P** (USA) 126) [2004 6g* 8f Sep 25]

Sir Michael Stoute has saddled the winner and the beaten favourite in the last two runnings of the One Thousand Guineas for Cheveley Park Stud in the shape of Russian Rhythm in 2003 and Red Bloom in 2004. In Echelon and Shanghai Lily, connections have leading ante-post fancies for the race again in 2005. If they follow the route taken by Stoute with Russian Rhythm, Red Bloom and Musical Bliss, the winner of the 1989 renewal, they will head to the classic without a prep race. Both Echelon and Shanghai Lily have plenty to prove in terms of form after just two outings each, but they are open to plenty of improvement. Shanghai Lily is available at 20/1 with the major firms at the time of writing, while Echelon is as low as 14/1.

Echelon made a winning debut in a six-furlong maiden at Newmarket on the last Saturday in August, when coincidentally her half-sister Chic beat Nayyir in Goodwood's Celebration Mile. Echelon, the only filly in the line-up, was a 7/1-chance and created a big impression when beating Newsround by two lengths, showing a good turn of foot and being value for further than the winning margin after idling close home. On the strength of this performance, Echelon was sent off 15/8 favourite for Ascot's Fillies' Mile to emulate her aforementioned stablemate

Red Bloom, who won the prize in 2003. Looking in tremendous shape, Echelon had no luck in running and finished seventh, five and a half lengths behind the winner Playful Act. Echelon was short of room early in the straight, when held in by Shohrah, and was forced wide to make her move. Driving her along to improve, her rider was forced to snatch up again when Dash To The Top drifted out to her left, Echelon then able to run on at only one pace when getting in the clear.

Echelon (b.f. Apr 15, 2002)	Danehill (USA) (b 1986)	Danzig (b 1977)	Northern Dancer
			Pas de Nom
		Razyana (b 1981)	His Majesty
			Spring Adieu
	Exclusive (ch 1995)	Polar Falcon (b or br 1987)	Nureyev
			Marie d'Argonne
		Exclusive Order (ch 1979)	Exclusive Native
			Bonavista

Echelon is a lengthy, good sort, a good walker and mover, who has taken a strong hold to post on both her starts. She is the third foal of Exclusive, who also raced for Cheveley Park Stud. Details of Echelon's pedigree can be found in the essay on Chic. Echelon should stay a mile and is clearly better than she was able to show at Ascot. She remains open to plenty of improvement, though her form is some way short of classic standard and she will need to fulfil all her potential to make her mark in the Guineas. *Sir Michael Stoute*

ECHOES IN ETERNITY (IRE)   4 b.f. Spinning World (USA) 130 – Magnificient   **111** Style (USA) 107 (Silver Hawk (USA) 123) [2004 111: 9m⁴ 8m⁴ 9.9m⁵ 14.6m* 12.5m Oct 2] lengthy filly: smart performer: won National Stud Never Say Die Club Park Hill Stakes at Doncaster in September by length from Mazuna: stiffish task, not entirely discredited when last behind Samando in Prix de Royallieu at Longchamp final outing: stays easy 14.6f: acts on good to firm going: usually tongue tied: ran as if amiss second outing: races prominently: left Godolphin. *Saeed bin Suroor*

Godolphin's "Echoes In Eternity"

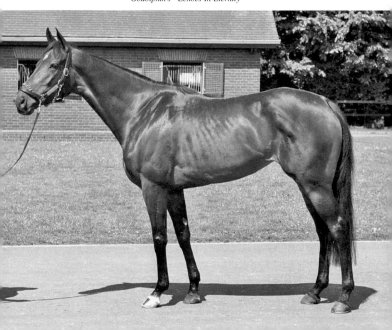

ECHO OF LIGHT 2 b.c. (Mar 7) Dubai Millennium 140 – Spirit of Tara (IRE) 106   **79 p**
(Sadler's Wells (USA) 132) [2004 8d⁴ Oct 15] €1,200,000Y: well-made colt: fourth foal:
half-brother to useful Irish 1m/9f winner Multazem and useful Irish 9f and 1½m winner
Akarem (both by Kingmambo): dam, Irish 1½m winner, sister to Salsabil and half-sister
to Marju: favourite and tongue tied, 8 lengths fourth to Proclamation in maiden at Newmarket, racing wide and staying on not knocked about: will be suited by 1¼m/1½m: sure
to do fair bit better. *Saeed bin Suroor*

ECOLOGICALLY RIGHT 2 b.f. (Feb 3) Entrepreneur 123 – Logic 94 (Slip Anchor   **77**
136) [2004 6d 7.5m⁶ 6.1m⁶ 6s⁶ Oct 23] strong, lengthy filly: third living foal: half-sister
to fairly useful 2002 2-y-o 6f/7f winner Logsdail (by Polish Precedent): dam, maiden ran
only at 2 yrs (bred to stay at least 1¼m), half-sister to useful 1½m winner Port Helene:
fair performer: won maiden at Nottingham in September: raced freely when well held in
listed race at Doncaster final start: should stay 7f: acts on good to firm ground: sold
32,000 gns. *Mrs J. R. Ramsden*

ECOMIUM (IRE) 3 b.c. Sadler's Wells (USA) 132 – Encens (Common Grounds   **118 p**
118) [2004 10d* 10d² Oct 2]

    Ecomium has had his share of problems and, as a result, has been restricted
to just two appearances to date. Yet enough has been seen of him to know that he is
a smart colt at the very least, one fully expected to continue to progress and win
pattern races given a trouble-free season in 2005. The strong, compact Ecomium
took the eye in the paddock on his debut, in an eleven-runner maiden at Newmarket
in April, but not so much as he did in the race itself. He travelled strongly as he
tracked the leader, was the only one still on the bridle when produced to challenge
around the two-furlong marker and quickly drew clear when shaken up a furlong
later. At the line Ecomium was five lengths ahead of the runner-up Buckeye Wonder, and still going away, in the process recording an excellent timefigure (equivalent
to a rating of 110) for a newcomer. The intention was to go for the Derby with Ecomium, taking in the Glasgow Stakes at York. Unfortunately, a minor setback meant
that Ecomium had to miss the Glasgow, and then a corn in his off-fore ruled him out
of the Derby, for which he stood as low as 14/1 in the betting. It was early-October
before Ecomium was seen on the racecourse again. One of fourteen who lined up
for a listed event at the Curragh, he did well to beat all but Mikado, who had
finished fifth in the St Leger on his previous start. Ecomium raced in touch as
Mikado cut out the running and drew almost level a furlong out, but he had been put
to his best to do so and, with the lack of a recent race possibly beginning to tell, was
unable to sustain the effort and went down by a length and a half.

			Northern Dancer	Nearctic
Ecomium (IRE) (b.c. 2001)	Sadler's Wells (USA) (b 1981)		(b 1961)	Natalma
		Fairy Bridge	Bold Reason
		(b 1975)	Special
	Encens (b 1995)	Common Grounds	Kris
		(b 1985)	Sweetly
		Idyllic	Foolish Pleasure
		(b 1982)	Where You Lead

    Both of Ecomium's races took place over a mile and a quarter on good to
soft ground. Later in October, he was taken out of the Group 3 Darley Stakes at
Newmarket because the going was considered too soft for him, while he was also a
late withdrawal from the Canadian International at Woodbine, where he would
have had the opportunity to tackle a mile and a half, a distance he will probably
stay. Ecomium, a €600,000 yearling by Sadler's Wells, is a brother to the four-year-
old filly Epopee, a useful winner at eleven furlongs to an extended fifteen furlongs
in France. They are the first two foals of Encens, a winner over seven furlongs in
France at two. Encens is a half-sister to Scenic (like Ecomium, by Sadler's Wells),
who dead-heated for first in the 1988 Dewhurst Stakes and went on to win over a
mile and a quarter, and to the smart French performer Silent Warrior, who also stayed that far. Ecomium's grandam Idyllic is an unraced daughter of the Musidora
Stakes winner and Oaks runner-up Where You Lead, and granddaughter of the brilliant 1963 Oaks winner Noblesse. Where You Lead is the grandam of Commander
In Chief, Rainbow Quest and Warning. *J. Noseda*

EDDIES JEWEL 4 b.g. Presidium 124 – Superstream (Superpower 113) [2004 51?:   **52**
10m² 8g⁵ 7.5g⁴ 12.1m⁵ 12.1d 9.9d⁶ 9.3m⁴ p7.1g⁴ p8m* f7g Dec 12] strong gelding: mod-

est performer: left H. Alexander after reappearance: won banded race at Lingfield in November: effective at 1m to 1½m: acts on polytrack, good to firm and good to soft going: tried in cheekpieces/visor, blinkered last 3 starts. *J. S. Wainwright*

EDEN STAR (IRE) 2 b.f. (Mar 25) Soviet Star (USA) 128 – Gold Prospector (IRE) 78 (Spectrum (IRE) 126) [2004 5f 6g p6g 5.1f Sep 6] €7,000Y: first foal: dam Irish maiden who stayed 1m: no form in maidens. *D. K. Ivory* — —

EDGED IN GOLD 2 ch.f. (Mar 25) Bold Edge 123 – Piccante (Wolfhound (USA) 126) [2004 5.1s⁶ 5.1d p5.1g³ Nov 27] second foal: dam, unraced, out of sister to very smart middle-distance performer Millkom: easily best effort in maidens when third at Wolverhampton. *P. J. Makin* **64**

EDGE FUND 2 b.g. (Apr 3) Bold Edge 123 – Truly Madly Deeply (Most Welcome 131) [2004 5.1g³ 5s³ 5m³ 6.1m² 6g³ 5.2m 6m³ 5.1m Aug 15] 16,000F, 32,000Y: neat gelding: fourth foal: half-brother to fairly useful 1½m to 15f winner Forever Loved (by Deploy): dam, no form, half-sister to smart 2000 2-y-o sprinter Superstar Leo: fair maiden: stays 6f: acts on soft and good to firm going: wore cheekpieces sixth start: gelded after final outing. *B. R. Millman* **78**

EDGEHILL (IRE) 3 b.g. Ali-Royal (IRE) 127 – Elfin Queen (IRE) 64 (Fairy King (USA)) [2004 60: 7d⁴ 10m² 10f Sep 2] tall, leggy gelding: fair maiden: stays 1¼m: acts on good to firm going: gelded. *C. R. Egerton* **68**

EDGE OF BLUE 2 b.g. (Apr 20) Bold Edge 123 – Blue Goddess (IRE) 94 (Blues Traveller (IRE) 119) [2004 6m⁶ 5m³ 5g 6g⁵ Sep 8] close-coupled colt: first foal: dam, a 2-y-o 6f winner (won all 3 starts), out of close relative to Yorkshire Oaks winner Hellenic, herself dam of Islington and Greek Dance: fair maiden: likely to stay 7f: easily best efforts on good to firm going. *R. Hannon* **69**

EDGE OF ITALY 2 ch.f. (Mar 7) Bold Edge 123 – Brera (IRE) 45 (Tate Gallery (USA) 117) [2004 p6g 5.7g⁶ p6g⁶ p6g⁵ p6g p6g Dec 30] third reported foal: half-sister to 7.5f to 9f winner in Denmark by Nicholas: dam maiden who should have stayed 7f: modest maiden: should stay 7f: acts on polytrack. *K. Bell* **62**

EDIN BURGHER (FR) 3 br.g. Hamas (IRE) 125§ – Jaljuli 107 (Jalmood (USA) 126) [2004 p7.1g p7g⁷ Dec 29] 15,000Y: half-brother to several winners, including 1m winner Jalindi (by Indian Ridge) and 9f winner Royal Jubilee (by King's Theatre), both fairly useful in Ireland: dam, 5f/6f winner at 2 yrs, half-sister to Kooyonga: better effort in maidens when winning at Lingfield by length from Zorn: should stay 1m. *T. T. Clement* **59**

EDITH BANKES 2 ch.f. (Apr 24) Woodborough (USA) 112 – Mayday Kitty 38 (Interrex (CAN)) [2004 8g 8.3g p8.6g⁴ p9.5g Nov 15] fourth foal: dam maiden who stayed 1½m: poor maiden: will stay 1¼m: acts on polytrack. *W. G. M. Turner* **44**

EDMO YEWKAY (IRE) 4 b. or br.g. Sri Pekan (USA) 117 – Mannequin (IRE) 79 (In The Wings 128) [2004 78: 13.8g 14s Apr 10] rangy gelding: has a round action: no form in 2004: often blinkered. *T. D. Easterby* — —

EFFECTIVE 4 ch.g. Bahamian Bounty 116 – Efficacy 62 (Efisio 120) [2004 65, a76: p6g f6g³ p7g f7g⁵ p7g p6g* f6g⁵ 6g² 6m 7m* 6f⁶ Jul 24] lengthy gelding: fair performer: won handicap at Lingfield in April and minor event at Catterick in July: stays 7f: acts on all-weather and good to firm ground: effective visored or not. *A. P. Jarvis* **77**

EFFIE GRAY 5 b.m. Sri Pekan (USA) 117 – Rose Bouquet 78 (General Assembly (USA)) [2004 53?: f12g f8.5s f8.5s⁴ Mar 5] short-backed, workmanlike mare: poor maiden: stays 1½m: acts on firm and soft going: tried visored/blinkered. *J. W. Unett* **41**

EFIDIUM 6 b.g. Presidium 124 – Efipetite 54 (Efisio 120) [2004 76: 7s² 8d 7.1d⁴ 8m² 8m³ 7m* 7m⁵ 7g³ 6.9g⁵ 7.1d⁴ 8m* 8m² 7f 7m Sep 9] small gelding: fairly useful handicapper: won at York in May and Thirsk in July: effective at 6f to 1m: acts on fibresand, firm and soft going: blinkered earlier in career: tough. *N. Bycroft* **81**

EFIMAC 4 b.f. Presidium 124 – Efipetite 54 (Efisio 120) [2004 49: 6g 7m 5d 6m⁴ 5g 6.9f 8.5d 8m³ Sep 4] small, plain filly: poor performer: stays easy 7f: acts on all-weather and good to firm going: tried blinkered/visored: none too consistent. *N. Bycroft* **47**

EFISTORM 3 b.c. Efisio 120 – Abundance 62 (Cadeaux Genereux 131) [2004 6d* 6d⁴ 5d 5m 6s Sep 25] 13,000Y: smallish, quite good-topped colt: second foal: half-brother to 2002 2-y-o 7f winner Xcess Baggage (by Air Express): dam, maiden, stayed 1m: fairly useful performer: won minor event at Milan in March: left M. Marcialis in Italy and rejoined former trainer, well held both starts in Britain: stays 6f: acts on soft ground: sold 12,000 gns. *M. G. Quinlan* **90 d**

totesport Ayr Silver Cup (Handicap), Ayr—one of Brazilian apprentice Nelson de Sousa's four victories on Eisteddfod; it's close for the minor placings between Cd Europe (cheekpieces), Johnston's Diamond (nearest camera) and Balakiref (No.23) in a race dominated by those on the stand side

EFORETTA (GER) 2 ch.f. (Mar 27) Dr Fong (USA) 128 – Erminora (GER) (Highest Honor (FR) 124) [2004 6.1d 6d p7g Oct 28] close-coupled filly: first foal: dam unraced sister to smart German 7f/1m performer Erminius: well beaten in maidens. *D. J. Wintle* —

EFRHINA (IRE) 4 ch.f. Woodman (USA) 126 – Eshq Albahr (USA) (Riverman (USA) 131) [2004 63: 10f 10m 9.9g³ 12s 9.7g² 9.9s p8g 10.2g³ p12.2g⁴ p12.2g³ p9.5d p12.2d⁶ p12.2g⁴ p12.2g³ p12.2g³ f14g⁶ p12.2g⁵ p12.2g p12.2g⁴ p12.2g³ f12g³ Dec 28] useful-looking filly: fair maiden: stays 1½m: acts on all-weather, firm and good to soft ground: tried in cheekpieces. *Mrs Stef Liddiard* **68**

EGERTON (GER) 3 b.c. Groom Dancer (USA) 128 – Enrica 106 (Niniski (USA) 125) [2004 98: 10g⁵ 10g² 12v 10m 10m² 12d² 12s⁴ Sep 26] second foal: half-brother to German 9.3f to 11f winner Esposita (by Sternkonig): dam German 1¼m winner: very smart performer: mostly highly tried and still a maiden: excelled himself when neck second to Warrsan in Grosser Preis von Baden penultimate start, staying on: respectable 1¾ lengths fourth to Albanova in Preis von Europa at Cologne final outing: stays 1½m: acts on soft ground. *P. Rau, Germany* **124**

EGO TRIP 3 b.g. Deploy 131 – Boulevard Rouge (USA) 71 (Red Ransom (USA)) [2004 60: 8s 8m² 10f³ 12m 11.9m⁴ 12g* 12g² 13.8v* 12d⁶ Nov 3] close-coupled colt: fair performer: won handicaps at Newcastle in May and Thirsk in September and minor event at Catterick in October: stays 1¾m: acts on any going: blinkered last 4 starts: sometimes slowly away. *M. W. Easterby* **72**

EGYPTIAN LADY 2 ch.f. (Jan 27) Bold Edge 123 – Calypso Lady (IRE) 88 (Priolo (USA) 127) [2004 7s 5g 7m⁵ Sep 4] 3,500Y: tall filly: third foal: half-sister to winner in Greece by Robellino: dam 2-y-o 6f winner: modest form in maidens: dead. *R. P. Elliott* **57**

EHAB (IRE) 5 b.g. Cadeaux Genereux 131 – Dernier Cri 63 (Slip Anchor 136) [2004 73d: p8g⁶ Feb 29] fair handicapper at best: on downgrade. *G. L. Moore* —

EIDSFOSS (IRE) 2 b.g. (Feb 6) Danehill Dancer (IRE) 117 – Alca Egeria (ITY) (Shareef Dancer (USA) 135) [2004 5.3m⁵ 6g Oct 11] seemingly modest form in maiden at Windsor: ran in seller for N. Callaghan on debut. *T. T. Clement* **53 ?**

EI EI 9 b.g. North Briton 67 – Branitska (Mummy's Pet 125) [2004 –: 12m Jun 5] very lightly raced and no form on Flat after 2000: useful and tremendously tough and game hurdler/chaser, fell fatally in June. *M. C. Chapman* —

332

EIGHT ELLINGTON (IRE) 3 b.g. Ali-Royal (IRE) 127 – Where's Charlotte 53 **55**
(Sure Blade (USA) 130) [2004 59: 6d 6.1m⁴ 5.2m⁶ 6.1m 6.1d p6g⁶ f7g² p9.5g⁴ Dec 22]
quite good-topped gelding: modest maiden: stays easy 9.5f: acts on all-weather, unraced
on extremes of going on turf. *Miss Gay Kelleway*

EIGHT (IRE) 8 ch.g. Thatching 131 – Up To You (Sallust 134) [2004 57, a45: 12.1m **49**
9.9m 14.1m⁴ 12s 8d Nov 5] workmanlike gelding: poor performer nowadays: left
M. Channon after fourth outing: stays 1¾m: acts on polytrack (well held on fibresand),
firm and good to soft going: often visored/blinkered early in career. *J. M. P. Eustace*

EIGHT WOODS (IRE) 6 ch.g. Woods of Windsor (USA) – Cd Super Targeting (IRE) **56**
62 (Polish Patriot (USA) 128) [2004 69: f12g³ f9.4s⁴ Feb 14] just modest form in 2004:
stayed 1½m: acted on fibresand and any turf going: dead. *T. D. Barron*

EIJAAZ (IRE) 3 b.c. Green Desert (USA) 127 – Kismah 111 (Machiavellian (USA) **63 §**
123) [2004 7f 7.1f 8g⁴ 8.2d p12m Oct 6] quite attractive colt: brother to 4-y-o
Tahirah: dam, 1m winner on both starts, out of half-sister to dam of Singspiel: modest
maiden: trained first 3 starts by A. Stewart: stays 1m: most reluctant to race second
outing: one to treat with caution. *G. C. Bravery*

EISTEDDFOD 3 ch.g. Cadeaux Genereux 131 – Ffestiniog (IRE) 96 (Efisio 120) **113 p**
[2004 5s⁵ 6g³ 7d³ 6f* 7d⁸ 6d⁴ 6s* Sep 25] lengthy, good-quartered gelding: second foal:
half-brother to 4-y-o Boston Lodge: dam 6f (at 2 yrs) to 1m winner: most progressive,
winning 5 of 7 starts, namely maiden at Folkestone, minor events at Windsor and Salisbury, and handicaps at Ayr (26-runner totesport Ayr Silver Cup by ¾ length from Cd
Europe) and Haydock (beat Solar Power by ½ length despite idling, pair clear) between
May/September: effective at 5f to 7f: yet to race on heavy ground, acts on any other:
already smart, and capable of better still. *P. F. I. Cole*

EIZAWINA DOCKLANDS 3 b.g. Zilzal (USA) 137 – Sandrella (IRE) (Darshaan **65 d**
133) [2004 8m 8m 8m 8g 8m 10m Jul 3] 7,000Y: second foal: half-brother to 4-y-o San
Hernando: dam unraced half-sister to high-class 1¼m/1½m performer Storming Home:
fair maiden: easily best effort on second start: likely to prove best around 1m: tongue tied
after debut. *N. P. Littmoden*

EJAY 5 b.m. Emperor Jones (USA) 119 – Lough Erne 83 (Never So Bold 135) [2004 –: **48**
f7g f6g⁶ f6s f5g² f5g 5g 5.1d 5v² f6g May 19] poor maiden: best at 5f: acts on fibresand
and heavy going. *Julian Poulton*

EKATERINA 2 b.f. (Apr 11) Merdon Melody 98 – Hsian (Shantung 132) [2004 6m **39**
7d 8s⁶ Oct 30] 500Y: sister to 2 winners, including 1997 2-y-o 7f seller winner Michelee,
and half-sister to 2 winners: dam lightly raced: poor form in maidens/claimer: best effort
at 1m. *W. Storey*

ELA D'ARGENT (IRE) 5 b.m. Ela-Mana-Mou 132 – Petite-D-Argent 91 (Noalto **–**
120) [2004 74: f12g Jan 16] angular, quite good-topped mare: tried tongue tied, including
when well held on only run in 2004. *Miss K. Marks*

ELA FIGURA 4 ch.f. The West (USA) 107 – Chili Bouchier (USA) (Stop The Music **52**
(USA)) [2004 63: 5.3m⁶ 5.7s 6f 5.3f³ 5m⁶ 5f⁵ 5g 5m 5g 5d⁵ 5d³ 5.7s p5m f5g p5m⁵ p5.1g **a47**
Dec 20] good-topped filly: modest maiden: best at 5f: acts on all-weather, firm and good
to soft going: tried visored, often wears cheekpieces. *A. W. Carroll*

ELA JAY 5 b.m. Double Eclipse (IRE) 122 – Papirusa (IRE) (Pennine Walk 120) [2004 **44**
57: f16g⁵ Jan 27] maiden handicapper on Flat: just poor form only outing in 2004: stays
2¼m: acts on polytrack, firm and good to soft going: blinkered (found little) last 2 starts
at 4 yrs: one to treat with caution: fair hurdler. *H. Morrison*

ELA PAPAROUNA 3 b.f. Vettori (IRE) 119 – Pretty Poppy 67 (Song 132) [2004 74: **77**
6s³ 7m 7g⁶ 7d³ 7f² 8f³ 8s³ Sep 14] sturdy filly: fair maiden: stays 1m when conditions
aren't testing: acts on firm and soft ground: has run creditably when sweating. *H. Candy*

ELA RE 5 ch.g. Sabrehill (USA) 120 – Lucia Tarditi (FR) (Crystal Glitters (USA) 127) **50**
[2004 –: f12g⁴ f14g f12d⁴ f12m⁴ p9.5g⁶ f11d³ Dec 21] strong gelding: modest maiden:
stays 1½m: acts on all-weather and soft going. *C. R. Dore*

EL CHAPARRAL (IRE) 4 b.g. Bigstone (IRE) 126 – Low Line 66 (High Line 125) **78**
[2004 7g 6s⁶ 5.1d 7m 8.3m² 7g 10f² 8.3g 10m* 8s 8.3d p10g Sep 7] lengthy gelding: fair
performer: won minor event at Windsor in August: stays 1¼m: acts on firm ground: tried
in cheekpieces (ran poorly): often races freely. *D. K. Ivory*

EL COTO 4 b.c. Forzando 122 – Thatcherella 80 (Thatching 131) [2004 106: 8g 8g* **108**
7.1g⁵ 7.9s⁵ 7m 7.1g 8f 7g⁴ 7m 8m⁴ 7.9s 9g Oct 2] smallish, good-topped colt: useful
handicapper: won Spring Cup at Newbury in April by 1¾ lengths from Serieux: ran well
after when fourth to Material Witness in Bunbury Cup at Newmarket (fared best of those

in stand-side group) and to Ancient World in William Hill Mile at Goodwood: not discredited when ninth in Cambridgeshire at Newmarket (reportedly returned lame) final outing: effective at 7f, and probably stays 10.5f: acts on firm and soft going: effective blinkered or not. *B. A. McMahon*

ELECTION SEEKER (IRE) 2 b.g. (Feb 26) Intikhab (USA) 135 – Scottish Eyes **58** (USA) (Green Dancer (USA) 132) [2004 7m 7d 8s 7s 8g Sep 30] quite good-topped gelding: modest maiden: stays 7f: acts on soft and good to firm going. *G. L. Moore*

ELECTRAS DREAM (IRE) 3 ch.f. Docksider (USA) 124 – Elli Pyrelli (IRE) – (Tenby 125) [2004 7f p10d 10m 7g⁶ Oct 11] compact filly: first foal: dam German 7f/1m winner: mostly well held in maidens. *Mrs C. A. Dunnett*

ELECTRIQUE (IRE) 4 b.g. Elmaamul (USA) 125 – Majmu (USA) 105 (Al Nasr – (FR) 126) [2004 88: 9d 10m p10g p8g p8g Oct 25] leggy, quite good-topped gelding: well held on Flat in 2004: blinkered last 2 starts. *J. A. Osborne*

ELECTROCUTIONIST (USA) 3 b.c. Red Ransom (USA) – Elbaaha 97 (Arazi **125** (USA) 135) [2004 9g* 10m* 11g* 12d² Oct 17]

Stand by for a shock! So far, at least, Electrocutionist has done little to make his name known outside Italy. He has had just four races, and all those have taken place at Milan, just one a contest of any significance on a European scale. It was that final outing, in the Gran Premio del Jockey Club Italiano in October, which put Electrocutionist among the best of his generation over a mile and a half. Only Bago, Cherry Mix, Grey Swallow and North Light showed better form at that trip among the other three-year-olds in Europe, at least the way we read the form-book. Electrocutionist's connections should look forward to 2005 with plenty of optimism, particularly as there may be more to come from this lightly-raced colt.

Electrocutionist had an unbeaten record until the Gran Premio del Jockey Club and he lost it only by a matter of inches. He ranged up to the Deutsches Derby winner Shirocco over a furlong out and the pair fought out a tremendous finish, passing the post together, the short-head verdict going against Electrocutionist. There was more strength in depth to the field than in many an Italian Group 1 contest and the pair pulled clear. The British-trained Imperial Dancer passed the post in third (he was subsequently demoted), five lengths behind, with the Prix Vermeille winner Sweet Stream, former Ganay winner Fair Mix and the Epsom Derby fourth Percussionist the next to finish.

Electrocutionist improved with each of his races, stepping up a furlong in distance for each of them. Starting at nine furlongs, he won a newcomers race in April, then a listed contest in June and a minor event in September after a summer break. He took the last of those races in good style, giving the Derby Italiano fourth Distant Way 4 lb and a six-length beating. Electrocutionist's connections clearly knew they had a good horse on their hands well before he proved it in the autumn. He had been given an entry in the Great Voltigeur Stakes at York, the Ebor meeting holding good memories for his trainer Valfredo Valiani, who won the 2001 Yorkshire Oaks with Super Tassa.

Electrocutionist (USA) (b.c. 2001)	Red Ransom (USA) (b 1987)	Roberto (b 1969)	Hail To Reason
			Bramalea
		Arabia (b 1977)	Damascus
			Christmas Wind
	Elbaaha (ch 1994)	Arazi (ch 1989)	Blushing Groom
			Danseur Fabuleux
		Gesedeh (ch 1983)	Ela-Mana-Mou
			Le Melody

Electrocutionist was improving anyway, but his pedigree strongly suggested that the further he went the better he would be, with a mile and a half likely to suit best of all. He went very close to giving his sire Red Ransom a second consecutive winner of the Gran Premio del Jockey Club after Ekraar's success the year before. Electrocutionist's dam Elbaaha was a useful filly for Michael Jarvis at up to around a mile and three quarters, winning a maiden at Yarmouth over nearly a mile and a half. Electrocutionist is her third foal and only winner so far. Elbaaha is a halfsister to the dam of the Deutsches Derby winner Robertico, who is bred on similar lines to Electrocutionist, being by Robellino, like Red Ransom a son of Roberto. Michael Jarvis also trained Electrocutionist's grandam Gesedeh, a smart filly whose wins included the Pretty Polly Stakes at Newmarket and the Prix de Flore at

Saint-Cloud. She was best at around a mile and a quarter but, as a half-sister to dual Gold Cup winner Ardross, she could have been expected to stay further. Ardross put up one of his best performances to finish second in the Arc, and the same race is likely to be Electrocutionist's main objective in 2005, though he ought already to have made more of a name for himself by then. Electrocutionist acts on good to firm and good to soft ground but has yet to encounter extremes of ground. Italy has struggled to keep hold of its best horses in recent years, Falbrav and Rakti among those to have been transferred or sold abroad, and it is hard to believe that Electrocutionist has not attracted some tempting offers. Italian racing will be hoping he stays put, his four-year-old campaign being awaited with interest. *V. Valiani, Italy*

ELEGANT GRACIE (IRE) 4 ch.f. Desert Prince (IRE) 130 – Elegant Fragrant (IRE) (Be My Guest (USA) 126) [2004 59: p12g² p12g⁶ f11g² f11s⁴ Mar 30] fair maiden: stays 1½m: raced only on all-weather. *R. Guest* **71**

ELEUSIS (USA) 3 b.f. Diesis 133 – Balancing Act (USA) (Spectacular Bid (USA)) [2004 11.5d* 11s² 10.5g* 11g* 12.5s* 12g* 12g* Nov 6] $67,000Y: seventh foal: sister to a winner in USA and half-sister to several winners there: dam, 6.5f winner in USA, half-sister to very smart North American Grade 1 9f winner Peaks And Valleys: smart performer: most progressive, winning newcomers race at Tarbes in April, minor events at Tarbes in May, La Teste in July and Deauville in August, listed race at Chantilly (beat Pink Palace 1½ lengths) in October and Grade 2 Long Island Handicap at Aqueduct (by 2¼ lengths from Literacy) in November: stays 12.5f: capable of better still. *J-C. Rouget, France* **114 p**

ELGIN MARBLES 2 b.g. (Apr 28) Lujain (USA) 119 – Bold Gem 68 (Never So Bold 135) [2004 5.1g* 6d⁶ p7d 6m² 6g² 6d⁵ p6g⁵ Oct 25] €28,000F, 25,000Y: heavy-topped gelding: fifth foal: half-brother to 5-y-o Jessie: dam, 5f winner, half-sister to smart pair Just A Flutter (miler) and Slicious (up to 1½m): fairly useful performer: won maiden at Bath in April: good second in nurseries at Newmarket: should stay 7f: acts on good to firm going, promise on polytrack: races prominently. *R. Hannon* **85**

EL GIZA (USA) 6 ch.g. Cozzene (USA) – Gazayil (USA) 80 (Irish River (FR) 131) [2004 p8g Feb 3] big gelding: poor and lightly-raced maiden on Flat. *J. M. Bradley* **–**

EL HAMRA (IRE) 6 gr.g. Royal Abjar (USA) 121 – Cherlinoa (FR) (Crystal Palace (FR) 132) [2004 –: f7g⁵ 9.7s 16.4g Jul 8] small, strong gelding: lightly raced and no form since 2002: tried blinkered/visored. *M. J. Haynes* **–**

ELIDORE 4 b.f. Danetime (IRE) 121 – Beveled Edge 60 (Beveled (USA)) [2004 80: 6d 7.1m⁵ 6g 8.1d² 8.1s⁴ 8.1d⁵ 10g⁶ 9s 8.2v⁵ p9.5g⁴ Dec 14] rangy filly: only fair nowadays: stays 1¼m: acts on polytrack and any turf going: visored (weakened quickly) third start: often makes running. *B. Palling* **77**

ELISHA (IRE) 2 ch.f. (Apr 4) Raise A Grand (IRE) 114 – Social Butterfly (USA) (Sir Ivor (USA) 135) [2004 5g⁴ 5m⁵ 5g* 5.1d 5m⁶ 7m⁶ 6m² 6m² Sep 23] €4,000F, 5,200Y, resold 9,000Y: sturdy filly: half-sister to several winners abroad, including Hong Kong 1m to 1½m winner Treasure Spring (by Treasure Kay): dam unraced: fair performer: won maiden at Goodwood in May: good second in nurseries at Epsom and Brighton (made running): stays 6f: acts on good to firm going. *D. M. Simcock* **74**

ELITISTA (FR) 3 gr.f. Linamix (FR) 127 – Elacata (GER) 111 (Acatenango (GER) 127) [2004 49: 8.1s May 3] rather unfurnished filly: poor maiden: needs to settle to stay beyond 1m: best effort on polytrack. *E. J. O'Neill* **–**

ELIZABETHAN AGE (FR) 2 b.f. (Mar 29) King's Best (USA) 132 – Dolydille (IRE) 108 (Dolphin Street (FR) 125) [2004 7f² 7g² 7g Oct 2] 85,000Y: tall, rather leggy filly: first foal: dam, Irish 9f to 1½m winner, half-sister to dam of Irish Derby/Eclipse runner-up Sholokhov: short-headed in maidens at Newmarket and Salisbury: forced wide when well held in listed race at Newmarket: will stay 1m. *D. R. Loder* **78**

ELIZABETH'S CHOICE 2 b.f. (Feb 4) Unfuwain (USA) 131 – Nur (USA) 74 (Diesis 133) [2004 7m 6g Jul 14] 25,000Y: sturdy filly: closely related to fairly useful 2001 2-y-o 5f winner Delgado (by Alhaarth), later successful in Spain, and half-sister to several winners, including fairly useful 1999 2-y-o 6f winner Kamareyah (by Hamas): dam, 2-y-o 5f/6f winner, half-sister to Richmond Stakes winner Muqtarib: well held in maidens. *M. A. Jarvis* **–**

ELLAMYTE 4 b.f. Elmaamul (USA) 125 – Deanta In Eirinn (Red Sunset 120) [2004 58: p6g f9.4s p5g f7g⁵ 8.2m p7.1g Dec 14] leggy filly: no form in 2004: left D. Bridgwater after fifth start: sometimes blinkered/visored/tongue tied: has flashed tail. *G. F. Bridgwater* **–**

ELLENARE (IRE)   2 ch.f. (Apr 23) Bahhare (USA) 122 – Lady Ellen-M (IRE) 80   –
(Ballad Rock 122) [2004 5s f6m May 28] €7,000Y: small, plain filly: first foal: dam Irish
7f winner: well held in maidens. *Ms Deborah J. Evans*

ELLE NINO   2 b.f. (Apr 23) Inchinor 119 – Robellino Miss (USA) (Robellino (USA)   **69**
127) [2004 p7g p8g² Nov 13] half-sister to several winners, including 4-y-o Miss Ivanhoe
and useful 1999 2-y-o 7f winner Decision Maid (by Diesis): dam, won up to 9f in USA,
out of close relation to high-class sprinter Silver Fling: fair form in maidens at Lingfield,
1½ lengths second to Sand Fairy: should stay 1¼m. *G. Wragg*

ELLEN MOONEY   5 ch.m. Efisio 120 – Budby 72 (Rock City 120) [2004 79: f8g²   **79 d**
f8g³ f8s⁴ p12g 8.1d 8.3d 7.2f p8.6g p9.5g f8g⁴ f8g Dec 28] workmanlike mare: poor
walker: fair handicapper at best: left B. Smart after second start, R. Elliott after seventh:
barely stays 10.5f: acts on fibresand, soft and good to firm going: often wears cheek-
pieces/blinkers. *Mrs G. S. Rees*

ELLENS ACADEMY (IRE)   9 b.g. Royal Academy (USA) 130 – Lady Ellen 67   **95**
(Horage 124) [2004 85: f6g⁴ f6g⁶ f6g³ f7g⁴ 6g² 6m⁴ 6m⁴ 6d² 6g² 6f³ 6g⁵ 6g⁶ 6d 6g² 6d
Oct 15] big, useful-looking gelding: impresses in appearance: useful performer: in frame
most starts in 2004, best efforts when placed at York in July on ninth and tenth outings
and at Ripon on penultimate: effective at 5f (given test)/6f: acts on fibresand, firm and
good to soft going: occasionally blinkered, not in 2004: sometimes slowly away/wanders:
reportedly resents whip, and usually ridden with hands and heels nowadays. *E. J. Alston*

ELLENS LAD (IRE)   10 b.g. Polish Patriot (USA) 128 – Lady Ellen 67 (Horage 124)   **74 d**
[2004 77: f5s f6g⁵ f6s 5s Mar 27] sturdy, strong-quartered gelding: just fair at best in
2004: stays easy 6f: probably acts on any going: usually blinkered nowadays: often held
up. *W. J. Musson*

ELLENS PRINCESS (IRE)   2 b.f. (Feb 18) Desert Prince (IRE) 130 – Lady Ellen   **69 d**
67 (Horage 124) [2004 7m⁵ 7g⁴ 6g 6g 7d Oct 10] tall filly: half-sister to several winners,
including 9-y-o Ellens Academy and 10-y-o Ellens Lad, both formerly smart: dam,
second at 5f at 2 yrs, half-sister to Indian Ridge: fair maiden: ran badly in nurseries last 2
starts: stays 7f. *R. Hannon*

ELLE ROYAL (IRE)   5 br.m. Ali-Royal (IRE) 127 – Silvretta (IRE) 73 (Tirol 127)   –
[2004 –: p10g p13g f11m⁶ Apr 27] leggy, light-bodied mare: maiden: little form since 2
yrs: tried blinkered. *T. P. McGovern*

ELLERSLIE TOM   2 br.g. (Mar 5) Octagonal (NZ) 126 – Tetravella (IRE) (Groom   **60 ?**
Dancer (USA) 128) [2004 7.9g 8.2v⁵ Oct 20] 8,000Y: second foal: dam, French 1½m and
15f winner, half-sister to useful performer up to 1½m Torcello: seemingly modest form in
maiden at York on debut: well held final start. *O. Brennan*

ELLIEBOW   2 b.f. (Mar 8) Pharly (FR) 130 – Primo Donna Magna (Primo Dominie   –
121) [2004 6f 6g 6d Aug 30] 3,700Y: close-coupled filly: third foal: dam unraced half-
sister to high-class sprinter Kind Music: well held, including in seller. *T. D. Easterby*

ELLINA   3 b.f. Robellino (USA) 127 – Native Flair 87 (Be My Native (USA) 122)   **68**
[2004 –: 8.3s 10s⁴ 10m⁶ 11.9f⁴ 11.5g 11.5g* 12f 11.5g 12g³ p12g⁵ Oct 31] workmanlike
filly: fair handicapper: won at Lingfield in July: should stay 1¾m: acts on polytrack, soft
and good to firm going. *J. Pearce*

ELLIOT'S CHOICE (IRE)   3 b.g. Foxhound (USA) 103 – Indian City 57 (Lahib   **68 d**
(USA) 129) [2004 64: 5s⁴ 5d⁴ 5m 5g 5f⁴ 5d³ 6g⁶ f6g 7f 5d 5d 5s² 6s⁴ 5d 6d⁵ 7m 5m
7.1d⁶ p7.1g f6g Dec 7] close-coupled, useful-looking gelding: fair maiden at best: left
D. Carroll after sixteenth start: effective at 5f/6f: acts on firm and soft going: tried
visored/blinkered: none too genuine: sold £450. *R. M. Stronge*

ELLIOTS WORLD (IRE)   2 b.c. (May 3) King's Best (USA) 132 – Morning Wel-   **106**
come (IRE) (Be My Guest (USA) 126) [2004 7d* 7d* 7f⁶ 8f⁴ 8s Oct 23] €65,000Y: tall
colt: on weak side at 2 yrs: half-brother to several winners, including 6f (at 2 yrs) and 1m
(including Irish 2000 Guineas and Poule d'Essai des Poulains) winner Bachir and 7f (at 2
yrs) to 1¼m winner Albuhera (both smart, by Desert Style): dam Irish maiden who
probably stayed 1½m: useful performer: won maiden at York in July and listed race on
same course (by neck from Oude) in August: highly tried after, creditable effort only
when 3¾ lengths fourth to Perfectperformance in Royal Lodge Stakes at Ascot: effective
at 7f/1m: acts on firm and good to soft ground: edgy sort, tends to race freely: hung left
first 2 starts. *M. Johnston*

ELLIS CAVE   2 gr.g. (Mar 12) Diktat 126 – Cole Slaw (Absalom 128) [2004 6g 6m   **53**
f7g⁴ f6m f6d Jul 23] strong gelding: modest maiden: stays 7f: form only on fibresand:
visored third and final starts. *J. J. Quinn*

ELLOVAMUL   4 b.f. Elmaamul (USA) 125 – Multi-Sofft 30 (Northern State (USA)   **58**
91) [2004 62: 9.2m⁴ 11.5m 12m⁴ 11.5m 10.1m* p10d 11.9s 10m 9.9m 12g 10.1d* p9.5d
p12.2g Nov 15] small, workmanlike filly: modest performer: won handicap in
July and banded race in October, both at Yarmouth: stays easy 1½m: acts on fibresand,
good to firm and good to soft ground: occasionally blinkered (including for last win).
W. M. Brisbourne

ELLWAY HEIGHTS   7 b.g. Shirley Heights 130 – Amina 80 (Brigadier Gerard 144)   **58**
[2004 61: 13m² 12m² 16m² 13g⁵ 13f³ 12s 15.9g⁶ 12.1m 12g Oct 4] angular gelding:
modest handicapper: effective at 1½m to 2m: acts on firm and soft going: reportedly bled
penultimate outing. *W. M. Brisbourne*

ELLWAY PROSPECT   4 ch.f. Pivotal 124 – Littlemisstrouble (USA) (My Gallant   **56**
(USA)) [2004 p16.5g⁴ Nov 6] modest maiden, very lightly raced: will stay beyond 2m:
acts on polytrack. *Miss I. E. Craig*

EL MAGNIFICO   3 b.g. Forzando 122 – Princess Poquito (Hard Fought 125) [2004   **45**
53: p8g⁶ p10g 11.5m 11.8g p12d Aug 9] workmanlike gelding: poor maiden: stays 11.5f:
raced only on all-weather/good to firm ground: tried in headgear. *P. D. Cundell*

ELMS SCHOOLBOY   2 ch.g. (Apr 27) Komaite (USA) – Elms Schoolgirl 79 (Ema-   **47**
rati (USA) 74) [2004 5g 5.1g p6g 6s Oct 29] smallish gelding: poor maiden: should stay
1m: looked none too keen final start. *J. M. P. Eustace*

ELMUSTANSER   3 b.c. Machiavellian (USA) 123 – Elfaslah (IRE) 107 (Green Desert   **104**
(USA) 127) [2004 10d² 10m* 10m² 12g² 12d Oct 14] leggy colt: brother to high-class 7f
(at 2 yrs) to 1¼m (Dubai World Cup) winner Almutawakel and smart 1m (including UAE
1000 Guineas) winner Muwakleh, and half-brother to 3 useful winners: dam, won around
1¼m, half-sister to high-class 1½m performer White Muzzle: useful performer: won
maiden at Newmarket in June: best effort when short-head second to Camrose in minor
event at Kempton penultimate outing: stays 1½m: unraced on extremes of going: tongue
tied: races prominently: joined D. Watson in UAE. *Saeed bin Suroor*

ELOPEMENT (IRE)   2 ch.f. (May 4) Machiavellian (USA) 123 – Melanzane (Arazi   **50 p**
(USA) 135) [2004 p8.6g⁶ Dec 17] 50,000Y, 9,000 2-y-o: first foal: dam, ran once in
France, out of high-class French performer up to 1½m Sierra Roberta: 14/1, sixth in
maiden at Wolverhampton, not knocked about: should do better. *D. J. Daly*

ELOQUENT KNIGHT (USA)   2 b. or br.c. (Feb 12) Aljabr (USA) 125 – Matinee   **– p**
Mimic (USA) (Silent Screen (USA)) [2004 8m 8v Oct 23] $55,000F, €55,000Y: tall,
close-coupled colt: half-brother to several minor winners in USA: dam lightly-raced US
maiden: mid-field in maidens at Newmarket and Newbury (travelled strongly long way):
should do better. *W. R. Muir*

EL PALMAR   3 b.g. Case Law 113 – Aybeegirl 66 (Mazilier (USA) 107) [2004 65:   **70**
5d³ 5s³ 6m 7m* f6g² 7.2d Jun 19] good-topped gelding: fair performer: won claimer at
Thirsk in June (left T. D. Barron): stays 7f: acts on fibresand and good to firm going.
P. A. Blockley

EL PEDRO   5 b.g. Piccolo 121 – Standard Rose 52 (Ile de Bourbon (USA) 133) [2004   **49**
57d, a63d: f12s⁴ f12g³ p10g⁴ f14m f11g² 12.1m⁴ f11g f12d Dec 21] tall gelding: only
poor nowadays: stays easy 1½m: acts on fibresand, firm and good to soft going: often
visored in 2003: blinkered final start: has raced freely/folded. *R. A. Harris*

EL POTRO   2 b.c. (Mar 14) Forzando 122 – Gaelic Air 65 (Ballad Rock 122) [2004 5d   **61**
6s p5.1g p5.1g⁴ Dec 13] easily best effort in maidens when fourth at Wolverhampton: will
stay 6f. *B. A. McMahon*

ELRAFA MUJAHID   2 b.f. (Mar 28) Mujahid (USA) 125 – Fancier Bit (Lion Cavern   **69**
(USA) 117) [2004 p8d³ 8.2g p7g* Sep 18] 2,000Y: third foal: half-sister to 4-y-o
Aragon's Boy: dam unraced out of useful close relation to top-class French/US 1m/9f
winner Thrill Show: fair performer: won maiden at Lingfield, leading close home: stays
1m. *Julian Poulton*

EL REY DEL MAMBO (USA)   2 b.g. (May 4) Kingmambo (USA) 125 – Scarab   **69 p**
Bracelet (USA) (Riverman (USA) 131) [2004 p6g³ Oct 1] $30,000Y, 95,000 2-y-o:
second foal: dam, 8.5f winner in USA, out of US Grade 1 9f winner Chain Bracelet: favourite, third to Emerald Lodge in maiden at Lingfield, tiring late on (gelded after): sure to
improve. *G. A. Butler*

EL REY ROYALE   2 b.g. (Mar 5) Royal Applause 124 – Spanish Serenade 76 (Nash-   **68**
wan (USA) 135) [2004 6g⁸ 6s⁶ 8d Oct 18] 8,000Y: close-coupled gelding: third foal:
half-brother to 2002 2-y-o 7f winner Snugfit Dubarry (by Ali-Royal): dam French 7.5f

337

and 11f winner: 33/1, won maiden at Pontefract in July: well held in minor event/nursery: should stay 1m. *M. D. Hammond*

ELSHADI (IRE) 3 b.c. Cape Cross (IRE) 129 – Rispoto 58 (Mtoto 134) [2004 98: **104** 12m 12m² 10m⁶ 10m² a10f Dec 24] good-topped colt: fluent mover: useful performer: ran well when second in King Edward VII Stakes at Royal Ascot (beaten 4 lengths by Five Dynasties) and minor event at Newmarket (beaten 1¾ lengths by Corriolanus): left M. Tregoning and off 4½ months before final outing: effective at 1¼m/1½m: acts on good to firm going: visored (pulled hard/tailed off in Derby) on reappearance, blinkered otherwise: usually makes running. *D. J. Selvaratnam, UAE*

ELSIE HART (IRE) 2 b.f. (Apr 29) Revoque (IRE) 122 – Family At War (USA) 71 **82** (Explodent (USA)) [2004 5v* 6s³ 5f Jun 15] 18,000Y: leggy, quite good-topped filly: sister to unreliable 2002 2-y-o 5f/6f winner Magic Myth and 1¼m winner Diddymu and half-sister to 3 winners, notably smart 5f winner (including at 2 yrs) Flanders (by Common Grounds): dam 2-y-o 5f winner: won maiden at Newcastle in April: easily best effort when third in minor event at York: in rear in listed race at Royal Ascot: stays 6f. *T. D. Easterby*

ELSIE WAGG (USA) 2 b. or br.f. (Feb 9) Mt Livermore (USA) – Hoedown Honey **67** (CAN) (Country Light (USA)) [2004 5g³ 5g⁴ 5d⁵ 6.1m⁶ 6m Sep 12] 30,000 2-y-o: lengthy filly: half-sister to 2 winners abroad, including useful French 1¼m winner Ares Vallis (by Caerleon): dam, US 1m winner, out of half-sister to dam of Generous: fair maiden: should stay 7f: best efforts on good going. *M. J. Wallace*

ELSINORA 3 b.f. Great Dane (IRE) 122 – Deanta In Eirinn (Red Sunset 120) [2004 **53** 57: p8g 7m 10m 7.9g² 8f⁶ 7m³ 7s⁵ 6m² 7g⁴ 7m² 7d⁵ 8.1d³ 7d* p7.1g Oct 25] workmanlike filly: modest performer: won maiden claimer at Brighton (left H. Morrison) and banded race at Yarmouth, both in October: stays 1m: acts on good to firm and good to soft ground: usually wears headgear: sometimes looks none too keen. *A. G. Juckes*

ELSUNDUS (USA) 6 b.g. Gone West (USA) – Aljawza (USA) 86 (Riverman (USA) **–** 131) [2004 8.3g⁶ Jul 15] fairly useful 1m winner in 2001: tailed off only outing since. *K. A. Morgan*

ELTIHAAB (USA) 3 b. or br.f. Danzig (USA) – Futuh (USA) 95 (Diesis 133) [2004 **53** 8.1g 7m³ 6g⁴ Aug 11] quite good-topped filly: sister to useful 2001 2-y-o 6f winner Far-qad, closely related to 1997 Middle Park Stakes winner Hayil (by Dayjur) and 8-y-o Mizhar and half-sister to 3 winners, including smart 6f (at 2 yrs) and 1¼m (in UAE) winner Tamhid (by Gulch): dam 2-y-o 6f winner: modest form in maidens: should have been suited by 7f+: tongue tied final start: visits Almutawakel. *Saeed bin Suroor*

ELTIZAAM (USA) 2 b. or br.c. (Apr 19) Bahri (USA) 125 – Saffaanh (USA) 87 **74** (Shareef Dancer (USA) 135) [2004 7g⁶ p8d⁵ 7g⁶ 7.1d³ 7m⁵ 7s Oct 16] closely related to useful 7f (at 2 yrs) and 1¼m winner Min Alhawa (by Riverman) and half-brother to 3 winners by Gulch, notably smart 6f (Lowther Stakes at 2 yrs) to 1m (1000 Guineas) winner Harayir: dam, 1½m winner, half-sister to Falmouth Stakes winner Alshakr (by Bahri): fair maiden: should stay 1m: acts on good to firm and good to soft going, some promise on polytrack: sold 13,000 gns, sent to Sweden. *E. A. L. Dunlop*

ELUSIVE DREAM 3 b.g. Rainbow Quest (USA) 134 – Dance A Dream 115 (Sadler's **96** Wells (USA) 132) [2004 58p: f12m* 12g* 11.9m* 13f* 13.9s³ 13.1s* 12m² Sep 26] rangy, useful-looking gelding: has scope: useful performer: progressed well in 2004, winning handicaps at Southwell and Folkestone, minor event at Brighton and handicap at Hamilton within 11 days in July and handicap at Ayr (beat Lets Roll by 5 lengths) in September: again well-backed favourite, good second to Fort in handicap at Ascot final outing (subsequently gelded): effective at 1½m/1¾m: acts on fibresand, firm and soft ground: sometimes hangs right: genuine. *Sir Mark Prescott*

ELUSIVE KITTY (USA) 3 b.f. Elusive Quality (USA) – Al Fahda 93 (Be My Chief **73 d** (USA) 122) [2004 69: p10g⁶ 7m 8.3m³ 9.2d³ 8s⁵ 8m³ 10.1g⁵ 10.2s⁶ p12.2d p9.5g⁶ Nov 20] smallish, lightly-made filly: fair maiden at best: stays 1¼m: acts on polytrack and good to firm going, well held on softer than good: blinkered last 2 starts: tried tongue tied: refused to race second outing: temperamental. *G. A. Butler*

ELVINA 3 b.f. Mark of Esteem (IRE) 137 – Pharaoh's Joy 66 (Robellino (USA) 127) **57** [2004 43p: 5m* 6g p5.1g⁵ p5.1g Dec 31] modest performer, lightly raced: won maiden at Kempton in August: should prove best at 5f/6f: acts on polytrack and good to firm going: swerved left leaving stall second outing. *A. G. Newcombe*

ELVINA HILLS (IRE) 2 ch.f. (Mar 3) Bluebird (USA) 125 – Women In Love (IRE) **61** (Danehill (USA) 126) [2004 5s 5s 6g⁵ 7g⁶ p7g Jul 21] 10,000Y: second foal: dam

Italian 1m/9f winner: modest maiden: best effort at 6f: looked wayward last 2 starts.
W. G. M. Turner

ELVINGTON BOY   7 ch.g. Emarati (USA) 74 – Catherines Well 99 (Junius (USA)   –
124) [2004 72: 5m May 15] quite good-topped gelding: fair form in 2003: reared leaving
stall and unseated rider only 7-y-o outing: effective at 5f/easy 6f: acts on firm going,
possibly not on soft: tried visored/tongue tied: normally fast starter. *M. W. Easterby*

ELZEES   3 b.g. Magic Ring (IRE) 115 – White Flash 39 (Sure Blade (USA) 130) [2004   **68**
p8g 9.9g p10m p10g⁵ Dec 30] brother to 2 winners abroad: dam maiden who stayed 11f:
fair form: should be suited by 1½m. *D. R. C. Elsworth*

EMARADIA   3 ch.f. Emarati (USA) 74 – Rewardia (IRE) 66 (Petardia 113) [2004 55§:   **48 §**
p5g³ f6g* f7g² f7g f5s* f6g² f5s² f5g⁶ f6f⁶ 5.1m f6g³ 5.3d 7m⁴ p7.1g p7.1g³ p7.1d p5.1g   **a62 §**
f6g f6g Dec 12] leggy, good-topped filly: modest performer on all-weather, poor on turf:
won claimer at Wolverhampton (left P. D. Evans) in January and seller there in February:
stays easy 7f, all wins at 5f/6f: acts on all-weather, raced mainly on good going or firmer
on turf: often visored/blinkered: usually front runner: unreliable. *A. W. Carroll*

EMARATI'S IMAGE   6 b.g. Emarati (USA) 74 – Choir's Image 53 (Lochnager 132)   –
[2004 –, a53: p10g p7g⁶ p6g⁴ p5g⁶ f6s⁴ f5g⁶ May 5] big, good-topped gelding: poor   **a43**
nowadays: left R. Stronge after fifth start: best at 5f/6f: acts on all-weather and soft going.
B. Forsey

EMBASSY LORD   3 b.g. Mind Games 121 – Keen Melody (USA) 60 (Sharpen Up   **83**
127) [2004 64: 5.1d⁴ 6m 5m Jun 12] leggy gelding: fairly useful performer: easily best
effort when fourth in handicap at Chester: will prove best at 5f/6f: acts on fibresand,
firm and good to soft going: blinkered: free-going sort, sometimes hangs/finds little.
J. O'Reilly

EMBASSY SWEETS (USA)   3 b.f. Affirmed (USA) – Leaveemlaughing (USA)   **50 ?**
(Dynaformer (USA)) [2004 –: 8.5s⁴ 13.1f p12g Oct 1] seemingly modest form only on
reappearance: should stay at least 1¼m: sent to USA. *P. F. I. Cole*

EMBER DAYS   5 gr.m. Reprimand 122 – Evening Falls 82 (Beveled (USA)) [2004 ?,   **73**
a63: p10g⁵ 10.9d 8s³ 8m 9g² 10.1m³ 10.2f* 9.7g³ 10g⁴ 10f Jul 26] tall mare: fair
handicapper: won at Bath in July: effective at 1m/1¼m: acted on polytrack, firm and soft
going: blinkered second start, subsequently wore cheekpieces: dead. *J. L. Spearing*

EMBOSSED (IRE)   2 b.c. (Mar 23) Mark of Esteem (IRE) 137 – L-Way First (IRE) 59   **104**
(Vision (USA)) [2004 6g⁶ 7.1m* 7g⁶ 7.1d² 7m² 8d² 7s Oct 22] €11,000Y, resold 20,000Y:
close-coupled, good-topped colt: has a quick action: seventh foal: half-brother to 1997
2-y-o 5f winner First Village (by Danehill): dam Irish maiden who stayed 2m: useful
performer: won maiden at Sandown in July: second in Solario Stakes at Sandown (beaten
2½ lengths by Windsor Knot, wandering) and minor events at Doncaster and Newmarket:
probably stays 1m: acts on good to firm and good to soft ground: tends to race lazily: sold
250,000 gns, sent to USA. *R. Hannon*

EMERALD BAY (IRE)   2 b.c. (Jan 27) King's Best (USA) 132 – Belle Etoile (FR)   **61 p**
(Lead On Time (USA) 123) [2004 6g⁴ Aug 7] £24,000Y, resold €90,000Y: fifth foal:
half-brother to fairly useful Irish 1¼m winner Starlight Venture (by Hernando): dam
French 7.5f winner: fourth in maiden at Ayr, fading late on: should improve. *M. Johnston*

EMERALD DANCER   2 b.f. (Jan 31) Groom Dancer (USA) 128 – Green Bonnet   –
(IRE) (Green Desert (USA) 127) [2004 8g Sep 29] 70,000Y: third foal: half-sister to
unreliable 2001 2-y-o 5.7f winner Prince's Passion (by Brief Truce) and 3-y-o Scientist:
dam, French maiden, sister to useful 7f/1m performer Mauri Moon: 25/1 and green, well
held in maiden at Salisbury. *H. Morrison*

EMERALD DESTINY (IRE)   2 b.g. (Apr 30) Key of Luck (USA) 126 – Green Belt   –
(FR) (Tirol 127) [2004 8.1s⁵ 10g 7m Oct 10] tall gelding: well held in maidens. *D. Carroll*

EMERALD FIRE   2 b.c. (Feb 12) Pivotal 124 – Four-Legged Friend 101 (Aragon 118) [2004   **72**
83: p6g⁶ p7g 6d 6g 7s⁵ 6g² f6g Nov 22] small, leggy mare: fair handicapper: effective at
5f (given test)/6f: acts on polytrack, heavy and good to firm going: tried visored.
A. M. Balding

EMERALD LODGE   2 b.c. (Feb 12) Grand Lodge (USA) 125 – Emerald Peace (IRE)   **88**
103 (Green Desert (USA) 127) [2004 5.2m³ 5g⁵ p6g* p6g* Oct 13] 95,000F, 90,000Y:
neat, strong colt: first foal: dam, 5f winner (including at 2 yrs), out of half-sister to
Cheveley Park winner Embassy: fairly useful performer: visored, won maiden and minor
event (beat Middle Earth by 1¼ lengths) at Lingfield, making most: likely to prove best
at 5f/6f: acts on polytrack. *J. Noseda*

EMERALD PENANG (IRE) 2 b.g. (Feb 15) Alzao (USA) 117 – Run To Jane (IRE) **73**
(Doyoun 124) [2004 5d⁵ 6f⁴ 7g* 7m 8d 8.3g Oct 11] €16,000F, 38,000Y: close-coupled
gelding: first foal: dam, well beaten in Ireland, half-sister to dam of smart sprinter Eastern
Purple: fair performer: left B. R. Millman after debut: won maiden at Epsom in July:
below form in nurseries after: stays 7f: acts on firm ground. *P. W. Chapple-Hyam*

EMERAUDE DU CAP 2 b.f. (Mar 21) Tipsy Creek (USA) 115 – High Typha 61 **47**
(Dowsing (USA) 124) [2004 6m 6.1s 5m³ 6s Aug 24] 4,500Y: fourth foal: half-sister to
3-y-o Tyne: dam 7f winner: poor maiden: best effort at 5f. *M. L. W. Bell*

EMILE ZOLA 2 b.c. (Jan 31) Singspiel (IRE) 133 – Ellie Ardensky 100 (Slip Anchor **81 p**
136) [2004 8m* 8.5g⁵ Oct 2] fourth foal: half-brother to 6-y-o Pole Star: dam, 9f/1¼m
winner, closely related to smart performer up to 1½m Lady Shipley out of Lowther Stakes
winner Circus Ring: won maiden at Goodwood in September, short of room and leading
final strides: ran as if amiss in minor event at Epsom: will be suited by 1¼m/1½m:
capable of better. *M. P. Tregoning*

EMILYS DAWN 3 b.f. Komaite (USA) – Spice And Sugar 65 (Chilibang 120) [2004 **47**
54: p7g p8g Jan 28] poor maiden, lightly raced: stays easy 7f: raced only on all-weather:
sometimes slowly away. *D. K. Ivory*

EMINENCE GIFT 2 b.f. (Apr 9) Cadeaux Genereux 131 – Germane 100 (Distant **58**
Relative 128) [2004 6g 6m f7g⁴ f7g² Dec 16] 10,000Y: sixth foal: sister to useful 1m
winner Granted: dam, 2-y-o 7f (Rockfel Stakes) winner, out of half-sister to very smart
performer up to 11f Running Stag: left R. Elliott after second start: easily best effort when
second in maiden at Southwell: will stay 1m. *K. R. Burke*

EMINENT AURA (USA) 3 ch.f. Charismatic (USA) 127 – Perfectly Clear (USA) **–**
(Woodman (USA) 126) [2004 –: f7s Mar 18] strong filly: last in claimer/sellers: tried
visored. *A. Dickman*

E MINOR (IRE) 5 b.m. Blushing Flame (USA) 109 – Watch The Clock 93 (Mtoto **56 d**
134) [2004 77d, a59: f12g⁵ f12g f12s⁶ f16.2g⁶ f12g p13.9g Dec 22] rather leggy, lengthy
mare: handicapper, on the downgrade. *T. Wall*

EMMA'S VENTURE 2 b.f. (Mar 6) Paris House 123 – Emma Amour 67 (Emarati **43**
(USA) 74) [2004 5g⁵ 5s² 5s⁶ 5g⁴ 6m f5s⁴ Aug 23] workmanlike filly: first foal: dam,
maiden, stayed 6f: poor maiden: likely to prove best at 5f/6f: acts on fibresand and soft
going. *M. W. Easterby*

EMMERVALE 5 b.m. Emarati (USA) 74 – Raintree Venture (Good Times (ITY)) **53 d**
[2004 59: 6g⁵ 6f 6f p7g Aug 6] angular mare: modest handicapper: well held after reappearance: stays easy 7f: acts on firm and soft going (yet to race on heavy): visored: often
races prominently. *R. M. H. Cowell*

EMPANGENI 2 b.g. (Apr 8) Mtoto 134 – Shibui (Shirley Heights 130) [2004 7.1d 8s⁵ **61**
p8g Oct 31] 13,000Y: eighth foal: half-brother to 3 winners, including French 1½m
winner Shi Shi (by Alnasr Alwasheek): dam unraced granddaughter of Park Hill winner
Quay Line: modest form in maidens: will be suited by 1½m+: best effort on soft going.
J. L. Dunlop

EMPEROR CAT (IRE) 3 b.g. Desert Story (IRE) 115 – Catfoot Lane 50 (Batshoof **55 §**
122) [2004 60: f6s² f7g³ f6g f6s 8f 7g f7m⁶ 6g⁶ 7.1s f6g² f7g⁵ f6g² f6g p7.1g Dec 14]
close-coupled gelding: modest performer: stays 7f: acts on fibresand and firm going:
sometimes wears headgear: inconsistent. *P. A. Blockley*

EMPEROR'S WELL 5 ch.g. First Trump 118 – Catherines Well 99 (Junius (USA) **70**
124) [2004 64: 9.9m 10s³ 8.5m* 9.9m* f8g² p9.5g p6g Dec 27] well-made gelding: fair
handicapper: won twice at Beverley in September: stays 1¼m: acts on fibresand, soft
and good to firm going: tried visored, blinkered nowadays: sometimes slowly away: races
prominently. *M. W. Easterby*

EMPIRE OF THE SUN 3 b.f. Second Empire (IRE) 124 – Splicing 82 (Sharpo 132) **53**
[2004 p7.1g p7.1g⁴ Nov 19] 10,000Y: fourth foal: half-sister to useful 6f (at 2 yrs) and
1m winner Pairing (by Rudimentary), later won in Spain, and 5-y-o Sholay: dam, 5f/6f
winner, sister to smart sprinter Splice: better effort in maidens at Wolverhampton when 7
lengths fourth to Stage Secret. *P. J. Makin*

EMPIRE'S GHODHA 2 b.c. (Feb 18) Mujadil (USA) 119 – La Caprice (USA) 84 **84**
(Housebuster (USA)) [2004 5g⁵ 5g³ 5m² 5m³ 5.1f* 5m⁵ 5d³ 5g⁴ 6m⁶ 5g 5m 6d⁶ Oct
15] 25,000Y: smallish, good-bodied colt: first foal: dam, 5f winner (including at 2 yrs),
half-sister to useful sprinters Muqtarib and Ra'a: fairly useful performer: won maiden at
Bath in June: in frame in listed race at Sandown (below best) and nursery at York after:

will prove best at 5f/easy 6f: acts on firm going: usually blinkered: usually races prominently: sometimes wanders: sold 20,000 gns, sent to USA. *B. J. Meehan*

EMPIRICAL POWER (IRE) 3 b.c. Second Empire (IRE) 124 – Rumuz (IRE) 67 **96**
(Marju (IRE) 127) [2004 80: 8d⁵ 7m³ 7f* 7.5m* 7m* 7d⁶ Oct 15] 4,000Y: second foal:
dam maiden who stayed 1¼m: useful performer: won handicaps at Roscommon in June
and handicaps at Tipperary in July and Leopardstown in September: respectable sixth in
handicap at Newmarket final start: best around 7f: acts on firm ground, probably on good
to soft. *Edward Lynam, Ireland*

EMPRESS EUGENIE (FR) 3 b.f. Second Empire (IRE) 124 – High Finish 58 (High **72 ?**
Line 125) [2004 8.3s⁴ 10s⁶ 10.1m⁵ May 20] 8,000Y: useful-looking filly: fourth foal:
half-sister to 3 winners, including useful 1¼m winner Rainbow End (by Botanic): dam
lightly-raced half-sister to smart performers Munwar (up to 1½m) and Hateel (up to
1¾m): easily best effort in maidens when fourth at Windsor on debut: should be suited by
1¼m+: acts on soft ground: sold 800 gns. *J. M. P. Eustace*

EMPRESS JOSEPHINE 4 b.f. Emperor Jones (USA) 119 – Valmaranda (USA) (Sir **–**
Ivor (USA) 135) [2004 60: f5g* f5s² f5s⁵ f5d³ 5m 5m p5.1g f5m f6g⁵ Dec 7] fair handi- **a65**
capper: won at Wolverhampton in January: best at 5f: acts on fibresand, no form on turf:
visored: races prominently. *J. R. Jenkins*

EMSAM BALLOU (IRE) 3 ch.f. Bluebird (USA) 125 – Persian Tapestry 70 (Tap On **64 d**
Wood 130) [2004 p7g³ p8g³ 6s³ 7d 6g p7g Oct 28] 30,000F: lengthy filly: sister to 4-y-o
Authority and useful 2000 2-y-o 5f/6f winner Triple Blue and half-sister to 2 winners:
dam, 1¼m winner, half-sister to top-class sprinter Lake Coniston (by Bluebird): modest
maiden: left R. Hannon and off 5 months, well held last 3 starts: stays easy 1m. *V. Smith*

EMTILAAK 3 b.g. Marju (IRE) 127 – Just A Mirage 76 (Green Desert (USA) 127) **80**
[2004 81: p7g² 8g³ 6m* 6m p6g 6f⁴ p6g⁴ a7f a6g Dec 9] big, good-topped gelding: has a
quick action: fairly useful performer: won maiden at Pontefract in May: left B. Hanbury
and off 3½ months after seventh outing: free-going sort, but stays easy 7f: raced only on
polytrack/dirt and good or firmer going on turf. *P. L. Rudkin, UAE*

ENAMOURED 2 b.f. (Apr 27) Groom Dancer (USA) 128 – Ascendancy (Sadler's **60**
Wells (USA) 132) [2004 8s⁵ 8.2m⁵ p8g Nov 13] first foal: dam unraced half-sister to 4-y-o
Polar Bear: modest form in maidens: trained on debut by Mrs A. Perrett: should be suited
by 1¼m/1½m. *M. G. Quinlan*

ENBORNE AGAIN (IRE) 2 ch.c. (May 10) Fayruz 116 – Sharp Ellie (IRE) (Sharp **50**
Victor (USA) 114) [2004 6g 6d 6m Sep 29] €1,000Y, resold €3,500Y: second foal: dam
unraced: modest form at best in maidens: slowly away first 2 outings. *R. A. Fahey*

ENCANTO (IRE) 2 ch.f. (Feb 13) Bahhare (USA) 122 – Born To Glamour (USA) **80**
130) [2004 5g 6.1g⁶ 5.1f² 6.3g² 6d² 6.1g* 6f⁴ 6g⁵ 6.1g³ Sep 29] €10,000Y: small
filly: half-sister to several winners, including useful but untrustworthy 5f (including at 2
yrs) winner Sailing Shoes (by Lahib) and 4-y-o Pawan: dam Irish 2-y-o 6f winner: fairly
useful performer: won maiden at Nottingham in July: creditable efforts in nurseries next
2 starts: should stay 7f: acts on firm ground, probably on good to soft: reared in stall and
withdrawn penultimate intended outing. *J. S. Moore*

ENCHANTED 5 b.m. Magic Ring (IRE) 115 – Snugfit Annie 49 (Midyan (USA) 124) **99**
[2004 96: 6g* 7m* 7f 6f 7m 6g 7m⁴ 5d 6d Oct 14] quite good-topped mare: useful performer: won handicap at Ripon and minor event at Ascot in May: good fourth in listed event
at Doncaster seventh start: best at 6f/7f: acts on firm going, well held on softer than good:
tried tongue tied: has run creditably when sweating: usually held up. *N. A. Callaghan*

ENCHANTED OCEAN (USA) 5 b.m. Royal Academy (USA) 130 – Ocean Jewel **–**
(USA) (Alleged (USA) 138) [2004 10d 12m 12m 12g 13.1d Aug 27] big, leggy mare:
maiden, well held in 2004. *G. B. Balding*

ENCHANTED PRINCESS 4 b.f. Royal Applause 124 – Hawayah (IRE) 68 (Shareef **82**
Dancer (USA) 135) [2004 73: 8.3d 8s⁵ 8m* 8f⁶ 8m Jun 26] well-made filly: fairly useful
performer, lightly raced: won handicap at Ascot in May: stays 1m: best efforts on good to
firm ground: visored (mulish stall)/blinkered last 3 starts: in foal to Dr Fong. *W. J. Haggas*

ENCHANTMENT 3 b.f. Compton Place 125 – Tharwa (IRE) 63 (Last Tycoon 131) **108**
[2004 88: 6s⁵ 6g² 5.1f* 5f* 5m² 5.1g⁴ 5s* 5d⁴ 5m⁴ 5d⁴ Sep 19] lengthy filly: useful performer: much improved in 2004, winning minor event at Bath in May and handicaps at
Redcar in June and York (beat Dispol Katie by 3½ lengths) in August: not discredited
in listed events after: speedy, and best at 5f: acts on firm and soft ground: usually front
runner. *J. M. Bradley*

ENCOMPASS (FR)   3 b.f. Sadler's Wells (USA) 132 – Totality 103 (Dancing Brave   **65**
(USA) 140) [2004 10g 12m³ 11.5g⁶ Jul 21] smallish, good-topped filly: fourth foal:
half-sister to fairly useful 1½m winner Total Care (by Caerleon) and 1¼m winner Total
Devotion (by Desert Prince): dam, 1¾m winner, sister to Derby winner Commander In
Chief and half-sister to Warning and Deploy: fair maiden: stays 1½m: sold 57,000 gns in
December. *H. R. A. Cecil*

ENCORA BAY   3 b.f. Primo Dominie 121 – Brave Revival 93 (Dancing Brave (USA)   **56**
140) [2004 7d⁶ 7.1g³ 7m Sep 7] 8,000F, 20,000Y: sturdy filly: fifth foal: half-sister to
fairly useful 2000 2-y-o 6f winner Bravado (by Zafonic) and 1999 2-y-o 7f winner Vigour
(by Lion Cavern): dam, 1m winner (including at 2 yrs) who stayed 1¼m, half-sister to
very smart sprinter Pivotal: modest form in maidens: should stay 1m. *P. R. Chamings*

ENCORE ROYALE   4 b.f. Royal Applause 124 – Verbena (IRE) (Don't Forget Me   **47 §**
127) [2004 63: f8.5g 9.7s⁵ f9.4m⁶ f7g 8m Jun 12] quite attractive filly: poor maiden
handicapper: stays 1m: acts on firm ground: often slowly away: virtually refused to race
last 2 outings (blinkered first occasion). *J. Jay*

ENCOUNTER   8 br.g. Primo Dominie 121 – Dancing Spirit (IRE) 72 (Ahonoora 122)   **51**
[2004 60, a–: 9.9d 9.2g 8v³ 7.9f⁵ 8g⁶ 8m 8d 9.2f² 9.2f⁵ 8.1g 9.2d 10g⁵ 8f³ 8d⁵ 8.1d² 8d
8s³ Oct 30] lengthy gelding: modest performer: effective at 7f to easy 1¼m: acts on any
turf going, little form on fibresand: sometimes slowly away/pulls hard: usually held up.
J. Hetherton

ENCOURAGEMENT   2 b.f. (Mar 5) Royal Applause 124 – Gentle Persuasion 95   **76**
(Bustino 136) [2004 5.1g 6f³ 5.1d 5g⁴ 6m³ 6g Oct 2] smallish, leggy filly: sister to useful
2001 2-y-o 6f winner Approval and half-sister to several winners, including smart 5f
(including at 2 yrs) to 7f winner Sharp Prod (by Sharpo) and 1¼m winner Punkah (by
Lear Fan): dam, 2-y-o 6f winner, stayed 1m: fair maiden: barely stays 6f: best efforts on
going firmer than good: races prominently: sold 16,000 gns. *R. Hannon*

ENDLESS SUMMER   7 b.g. Sanglamore (USA) 126 – Well Away (IRE) (Sadler's   **94**
Wells (USA) 132) [2004 100d: 6g³ 7m⁵ 7m⁵ 6m 5m⁴ 5.5m⁶ 5g 5.1s² 5g* 6g* 6g p6g⁵ p6g
Dec 4] small, sturdy, attractive gelding: smart for J. Gosden in 2000, and later ran in
USA before having fertility problems at stud: fairly useful nowadays: left K. Ryan after
reappearance, and K. Burke after fifth start: won handicaps at Leicester and Goodwood
within 3 days in September: free-going sort, best at 5f/6f: acts on polytrack, firm and soft
going: tried tongue tied: sometimes carries head awkwardly: broke blood vessel third/
sixth starts in 2003: found to have been foaled on Dec 26 1997, not Jan 2 1998 as
previously stated and age amended accordingly (for more detail see essay on American
Post). *A. W. Carroll*

END OF AN ERROR   5 b.m. Charmer 123 – Needwood Poppy 29 (Rolfe (USA) 77)   **–**
[2004 16m Jul 5] leggy, close-coupled mare: modest at 2 yrs: little form since. *Mrs
Dianne Sayer*

ENFORCER   2 b.c. (Apr 16) Efisio 120 – Tarneem (USA) 87 (Zilzal (USA) 137)   **82**
[2004 6f⁴ 6g⁵ 6g² 7m 7d* 7s Oct 22] 27,000F: tall, leggy colt: fourth foal: brother to fairly
useful 2002 2-y-o 5f winner Lord of The Inn and half-brother to 2 winners, including
3-y-o Innstyle: dam 1m winner: fairly useful performer: won nursery at Goodwood in
October, coming from last to lead on line: never going well final start: will stay 1m: acts
on good to soft ground: quirky. *W. R. Muir*

ENFORD PRINCESS   3 b.f. Pivotal 124 – Expectation (IRE) 59 (Night Shift (USA))   **89**
[2004 86: 6s⁴ 8g 8d³ 7s⁴ 7g 8.1g⁴ 8g⁶ 8d Oct 10] well-made filly: fairly useful performer:
stays 1m: acts on soft ground. *R. Hannon*

ENGLISH FELLOW   2 b.c. (Jan 30) Robellino (USA) 127 – Q Factor 90 (Tragic Role   **71 d**
(USA)) [2004 6.1s³ 5f⁴ 6f⁴ 6m 6g 7m 8d Oct 18] 9,000Y: angular, quite good-topped colt:
third foal: half-brother to 1¼m winner Petite Futee (by Efisio): dam 6f (at 2 yrs) to 1m
winner: fair maiden: well beaten last 4 starts, twice running as if amiss: should stay 1m:
acts on firm and soft going. *B. A. McMahon*

ENGLISH ROCKET (IRE)   3 b.g. Indian Rocket 115 – Golden Charm (IRE) 63   **69**
(Common Grounds 118) [2004 75: 10d 8.2v f8g* p7g Dec 4] fair performer: won maiden
at Southwell in November: well held in handicaps otherwise in 2004: stays 1m: acts on
fibresand and good to soft going. *D. J. S. ffrench Davis*

ENHANCER   6 b.g. Zafonic (USA) 130 – Ypha (USA) (Lyphard (USA) 132) [2004   **79**
10d 11.5g 11.5m³ 10m⁵ 12d⁶ Oct 14] strong, close-coupled gelding: fairly useful form
when successful in 3 bumpers: fair maiden on Flat: may prove best at 1½m/1¾m: acts on
good to firm and good to soft going. *Mrs L. C. Jewell*

ENJOY THE BUZZ 5 b.h. Prince of Birds (USA) 121 – Abaklea (IRE) (Doyoun 124) **57**
[2004 47: f6g⁴ f5g⁴ f6g f6g² f7g³ f6g* f6s² f6s⁴ f6s² 6g 5g* f6g 5.1f² 5g* 6m 6m³ 6f²
6.1g⁵ 6.1g⁵ 6g 5m⁶ Sep 22] small, sturdy horse: has reportedly been to stud: modest
performer: won banded race at Wolverhampton in February and handicaps at Lingfield
in June and Folkestone in July: effective at 5f/6f: acts on fibresand and firm ground.
J. M. Bradley

ENNA (POL) 5 ch.m. Don Corleone 115 – Elba (POL) (Freedom's Choice (USA) 97) **52**
[2004 7s⁴ 10m⁶ f7d 8.1m 8.1g⁴ 7m p10g⁴ 7.6f² 8m 8.1d⁶ 7s 10.9m⁴ p8g³ 10m* Sep 25]
small, close-coupled mare: winner of 3 races in Poland, including 2 in 2003: modest form
in Britain: left A. Juckes after second start: won banded race at Kempton in September:
stays 11f: acts on polytrack, firm and soft going. *Mrs Stef Liddiard*

ENRAPTURE (USA) 3 b.f. Lear Fan (USA) 130 – Cheviot Hills (USA) (Gulch **85**
(USA)) [2004 80p: 7d* 7d* 7d Sep 18] sturdy filly: fairly useful form, lightly raced: won
maiden at Newbury in August: should stay at least 1m: acts on soft and good to firm
going. *Mrs A. J. Perrett*

ENSEMBLE 4 b.g. Polish Precedent (USA) 131 – Full Orchestra 83 (Shirley Heights **55**
130) [2004 –: 15.8g 14.1s* p16.5g f14g Nov 22] strong, useful-looking gelding: form **a–**
only when winning seller at Yarmouth in October: stays 1¾m: acts on soft going, well
held on polytrack: tried blinkered. *D. M. Simcock*

ENTAILMENT 2 b.g. (Mar 12) Kris 135 – Entail (USA) 97 (Riverman (USA) 131) **75 p**
[2004 5d 6d* 7s Oct 23] 30,000Y: rather leggy gelding: first foal: dam 7f/1m winner:
33/1, won maiden at Thirsk in August, leading close home: sweating and better for race,
not knocked about in nursery at Doncaster: should stay at least 7f: sold 20,000 gns: capable of better. *Mrs J. R. Ramsden*

ENTERTAIN 2 b.f. (Apr 15) Royal Applause 124 – Darshay (FR) 87 (Darshaan 133) **54**
[2004 7g 7m Jul 22] 26,000F: half-sister to several winners, including 3-y-o Baileys
Dancer and useful 1m (at 2 yrs)/1¼m winner Deal Fair (by Grand Lodge), later successful
in Germany: dam 9f winner in Belgium: better effort in maidens at Kempton on debut.
M. L. W. Bell

ENTERTAINING 2 b.f. (Feb 25) Halling (USA) 133 – Quaver (USA) 74 (The Mins- **72**
trel (CAN) 135) [2004 6m⁶ 7g⁵ 6.1m² 6g⁵ Oct 11] good-topped filly: half-sister to several
winners, including 6f (at 2 yrs) to 1m winner Dove Tree (by Charnwood Forest) and 2000
2-y-o 1m winner Steel Band (by Kris), both fairly useful: dam 7f winner: fair maiden:
second at Nottingham: barely stays 7f: races prominently. *H. Candy*

ENVIRONMENTALIST 5 b.g. Danehill (USA) 126 – Way O'Gold (USA) (Slew **–**
O' Gold (USA)) [2004 –: 7.1g 6g 7.2m 9m 8f 9.1g Aug 7] of no account. *D. A. Nolan*

ENVIRONMENT AUDIT 5 ch.g. Kris 135 – Bold And Beautiful 105 (Bold Lad **–**
(IRE) 133) [2004 –: f11g f11g 12s 12g 10m 11.5d Aug 26] rather leggy gelding: modest
at best nowadays: effective at 1¼m/1½m: acts on firm and good to soft going: visored last
3 starts. *J. R. Jenkins*

EPALO (GER) 5 b.h. Lando (GER) 128 – Evening Kiss (Kris 135) [2004 117: 10d* **122**
10g* 11g² 10f³ 11d² Sep 11] very smart performer: won listed race at Munich and Singapore Airlines International Cup at Kranji (by 5 lengths from Surveyor) in May: bit below
best next 2 starts, beaten nose by Foreign Affairs in listed race at Cologne and fourth
(promoted to third) behind demoted Powerscourt in Arlington Million: back to best when
1¼ lengths second to Magistretti in Man o'War Stakes at Belmont final start, caught near
finish: missed Cox Plate in October after coming down with a bug: has won at 1¾m but
probably best at 1¼m/11f: acts on dirt, firm and soft going (well beaten on heavy): often
makes running: reliable: winner of 2004 World Series Racing Championship: stays in
training. *A. Schütz, Germany*

EPAMINONDAS (USA) 3 ch.c. Miswaki (USA) 124 – Nora Nova (USA) (Green **68**
Dancer (USA) 132) [2004 82: 6s 7m 7m 10m² 8g 10m⁴ 10g Aug 23] sturdy colt: fair
maiden: stays 1¼m: acts on good to firm going: inconsistent. *R. Hannon*

EPHESUS 4 b.g. Efisio 120 – Composition 82 (Wolfhound (USA) 126) [2004 90: f8.5g³ **88**
f7g f8.5s f12s 8.1s 7g⁶ 8g* 7g⁴ 7.1m² 8g² 8m p8g 8g 8m³ 8g⁶ 10d³ Sep 20] tall gelding:
fairly useful handicapper: won at Goodwood in May: effective at 7f to 1¼m: acts on all-
weather and good to firm ground: usually visored, tried in cheekpieces (ran poorly): sold
20,000 gns. *Miss Gay Kelleway*

EPICES 2 b.g. (Apr 17) Mtoto 134 – French Spice 85 (Cadeaux Genereux 131) [2004 **75 p**
f7g p7.1g⁴ p8.6g² Dec 3] second foal: half-brother to winner in Greece by Hector
Protector: dam, 8.5f to 1½m winner, half-sister to Gold Cup winner Celeric (by Mtoto):

best effort in maidens (not at all knocked about by claimer first 2 starts) when second at Wolverhampton: should stay at least 1½m: open to progress. *Sir Mark Prescott*

EPIPHANY 2 br.f. (Apr 7) Zafonic (USA) 130 – Galette 94 (Caerleon (USA) 132) **81**
[2004 6m² 6g* 6g 7g p7g⁵ Nov 10] useful-looking filly: first foal: dam, 1½m winner from 2 starts, half-sister to Irish 2000 Guineas winner Indian Haven out of Park Hill winner Madame Dubois: fairly useful performer: odds on, won maiden at Ayr in August by short head: respectable effort in nurseries after: should stay 1m: acts on polytrack and good to firm going: tongue tied last 2 starts. *E. A. L. Dunlop*

EPITOMISE 2 b.f. (Feb 20) Mind Games 121 – Yanomami (USA) 71 (Slew O' Gold **60** (USA)) [2004 5g⁶ 5m⁴ 6f 6m⁶ 6.1m p7.1g Nov 12] 16,000Y: half-sister to 2002 2-y-o 5f winner Yarrita (by Tragic Role) and 3-y-o Mirasol Princess: dam 6f winner: modest maiden: form only at 5f: tongue tied last 2 starts. *R. M. Beckett*

EQDAAM (USA) 2 b.c. (Jan 22) Diesis 133 – Awaamir 102 (Green Desert (USA) 127) **80** [2004 7m³ 7g³ 7g* Oct 12] lengthy, attractive colt: fourth foal: dam, 7f (at 2 yrs)/1m winner, granddaughter of US Grade 1 1¼m winner Castilla: marginally best effort in maidens when winning at Leicester, making most: will stay 1m. *J. H. M. Gosden*

EQUILIBRIA (USA) 2 b.c. (May 27) Gulch (USA) – Julie La Rousse (IRE) 114 **50** (Lomond (USA) 128) [2004 p9.5g p8.6g⁶ Dec 17] $28,000Y, 47,000 2-y-o: seventh foal: brother to US Grade 2 11f winner Mariensky, closely related to winner in USA by Mr Prospector and half-brother to useful Irish 9.5f/1¼m winner Julie Jalouse (by Kris S), later US Grade 2 1½m winner: dam, Irish 7f (at 2 yrs) and 1m winner who seemed to stay 1½m, later 9f winner in USA: modest form in maidens at Wolverhampton: raced freely final start. *P. A. Blockley*

EQUUS (IRE) 3 b.g. Desert Style (IRE) 121 – Iolanta (IRE) 77 (Danehill (USA) 126) **–** [2004 69: f12g f14g Jun 16] well-made gelding: fair form in maiden on debut at 2 yrs: has shown nothing since. *L. A. Dace*

ERMINE GREY 3 gr.g. Wolfhound (USA) 126 – Impulsive Decision (IRE) 71 (Nom- **75** ination 125) [2004 70, a82: 10d 8d 8.1d³ f7g⁴ 8g⁴ p9.5g p8.6g³ p7.1g Dec 31] rather leggy **a86** gelding: fairly useful performer on all-weather, fair on turf: stays 9.5f: acts on all-weather, yet to race on extremes of going on turf: usually blinkered/visored. *D. Haydn Jones*

ERRACHIDIA (IRE) 4 b.f. King of Kings (IRE) 125 – Sunset Reigns (IRE) 110 **61** (Taufan (USA) 119) [2004 63: 5d 5m⁶ 6d³ 7s p7.1g p6g⁵ f5g Dec 21] second foal: dam Irish 5f/6f winner: modest performer: won handicap at Cork in 2003: left E. Lynam in Ireland after fourth start: effective at 5f/6f: acts on polytrack, firm and good to soft going: usually blinkered, tried visored: sometimes tongue tied at 3 yrs. *M. J. Wallace*

ERRACHT 6 gr.m. Emarati (USA) 74 – Port Na Blath (On Your Mark 125) [2004 73, **74** a62: f5s f5s⁵ 5.3m* 5m⁶ 5g 5m 5.1g p5g⁵ 5m 5f p6g Dec 20] lengthy mare: fair handi- **a49** capper on turf, poor on all-weather: left K. Burke, won at Brighton in April: below form after: effective at 5f/6f: acts on all-weather and any turf going: often forces pace: sometimes carries head awkwardly. *Mrs H. Sweeting*

ERROL 5 ch.g. Dancing Spree (USA) – Primo Panache (Primo Dominie 121) [2004 **–** 41d: f16s Mar 30] sturdy gelding: bad maiden. *J. F. Coupland*

ERSAAL (USA) 4 ch.g. Gulch (USA) – Madame Secretary (USA) (Secretariat (USA)) **–** [2004 60: p10g f12g³ p10g f12m* p12g³ 12v 12f Jun 25] good-topped gelding: modest **a54** performer: won banded race at Wolverhampton in April: stays easy 1½m: acts on all-weather, no recent form on turf: sometimes blinkered/in cheekpieces: tongue tied last 4 starts. *J. Jay*

ERTE 3 ch.g. Vettori (IRE) 119 – Cragreen (Green Desert (USA) 127) [2004 68: 8d 8g⁶ **57** 10f⁶ 10g³ p12d² 10m 12.1m Jul 27] leggy, useful-looking gelding: modest maiden: stays 1½m: acts on polytrack and firm going: has raced freely: none too consistent: claimed £6,000 final start. *M. R. Channon*

ERUPT 11 b.g. Beveled (USA) – Sparklingsovereign 53 (Sparkler 130) [2004 56§, **43 §** a–§: f9.4g⁵ 11m f8g³ 8m 8.5d 8.3d⁴ 8s³ 9.3m Sep 11] plain, leggy gelding: poor per- **a39 §** former: stays 1¼m: acts on any going: tried blinkered/visored/tongue tied: sometimes slowly away: moody. *R. E. Barr*

ESATTO 5 b.g. Puissance 110 – Stoneydale 83 (Tickled Pink 114) [2004 83: 6m 6g Jul **–** 1] big, quite good-topped gelding: fairly useful handicapper at best: well held in 2004: tried in headgear: usually tongue tied. *M. J. Attwater*

ESCALADE 7 b.g. Green Desert (USA) 127 – Sans Escale (USA) (Diesis 133) [2004 **61** 66, a61: f9.4g 10d⁴ 10m 12m⁵ 10.9d⁴ 12f³ 11m⁴ 12.1g³ 12.1g⁵ 12m⁶ 10m p10m³ p10g

Dec 20] small, compact gelding: modest performer: effective at 9f to 1½m: acts on all-weather and any turf going: often wears cheekpieces/visor: often races freely/wanders/finds little, and usually held up. *W. M. Brisbourne*

ESCAYOLA (IRE) 4 b.g. Revoque (IRE) 122 – First Fling (IRE) 63 (Last Tycoon 131) [2004 99p: 14g 13.9m² 16.1s 16.2g 16m² 16.2m* 18s⁵ Oct 16] good-topped gelding: useful handicapper: won at Ascot in September by head from Mamcazma: good fifth in Cesarewitch at Newmarket final start, ridden with plenty of restraint and nearest at finish: stays 2¼m: acts on firm and soft ground: visored/blinkered: sometimes races freely: tends to hang left: usually waited with. *W. J. Haggas* **99 +**

ESHAADEH (USA) 3 b.f. Storm Cat (USA) – Sarayir (USA) 104 (Mr Prospector (USA)) [2004 7f⁵ 7g Oct 11] third foal: half-sister to fairly useful 1¼m winner Sundus (by Sadler's Wells): dam, 7f (at 2 yrs) and 1¼m winner, closely related to Nayef and half-sister to Nashwan and Unfuwain: tongue tied, well held in maidens at Redcar (3/1-on, flashed tail) and Leicester (mulish to post, reportedly bled): left Godolphin. *Saeed bin Suroor* **–**

ESHER COMMON (IRE) 6 b.g. Common Grounds 118 – Alsahah (IRE) (Unfuwain (USA) 131) [2004 10.3g Mar 25] tall, good-topped gelding: fair performer: missed 2003, tailed off on return: tried visored/tongue tied: races freely/carries head high. *A. E. Price* **–**

ESKDALE (IRE) 2 b.g. (Mar 15) Perugino (USA) 84 – Gilding The Lily (IRE) 58 (High Estate 127) [2004 6g 5m 7s³ 7.1g² 7s⁶ 8g⁴ f8g p9.5g Dec 20] close-coupled gelding: modest maiden: stays 7f: acts on soft ground, well below form on all-weather: sometimes hangs/carries head awkwardly. *R. F. Fisher* **63**

ESKIMO'S NEST 2 b.f. (Mar 1) Polar Falcon (USA) 126 – White House 84 (Pursuit of Love 124) [2004 7g p7.1g² f7g⁴ Nov 23] tall, leggy filly: first foal: dam, 1¼m winner, half-sister to very smart 1½m performer Little Rock: fair form in maidens: second at Wolverhampton: needs to settle to stay beyond 7f. *W. J. Haggas* **66**

ESPADA (IRE) 8 b.g. Mukaddamah (USA) 125 – Folk Song (CAN) (The Minstrel (CAN) 135) [2004 92d: p7g p7g 8.3d 8.3g 7m⁴ 8f⁴ 7g* 8.3m⁵ 8.1m 7g⁴ 7g⁶ 8m 8m 7.1m Sep 9] smallish, strong gelding: modest performer: won handicap at Lingfield in June: effective at 6f (given test) to 1m: acts on polytrack and any turf going: visored once, blinkered last 9 starts: has raced freely/hung left/found little: often makes running. *J. A. Osborne* **56**

ESPERANCE (IRE) 4 ch.g. Bluebird (USA) 125 – Dioscorea (IRE) (Pharly (FR) 130) [2004 68: p10g 10.2s 8.3m⁵ 10.1d⁵ 8m 8m⁵ p10g⁵ 8f² 10f⁴ 8d⁵ p8.6g⁴ p10m p10g⁴ p10g Dec 30] good-topped gelding: modest maiden: stays 11f: acts on polytrack, soft and good to firm going: tried in cheekpieces. *J. Akehurst* **54**

ESPERE D'OR 7 b.g. Golden Heights 82 – Drummer's Dream (IRE) 48 (Drumalis 125) [2004 p6g p7.1g⁶ Dec 14] of no account. *M. Wellings* **–**

ESQUIRE 2 b.c. (Mar 8) Dubai Millennium 140 – Esperada (ARG) (Equalize (USA)) [2004 8g⁶ 7g* Sep 18] tall, attractive colt: second foal: dam won all 3 starts in Argentina (including at 7.5f/1m, champion 2-y-o filly in only season to race): much better effort in maidens when winning at Newbury by 1¾ lengths from Museeb, making all and quickening well: should stay 1m: useful prospect. *Saeed bin Suroor* **92 p**

ESRAR (IRE) 2 b.c. (Apr 3) Mujadil (USA) 119 – Island Desert (IRE) 55 (Green Desert (USA) 127) [2004 7.1d Sep 18] €32,000F, 43,000Y: sixth foal: half-brother to 3 winners, including 5f (at 2 yrs)/6f winner Roundtree (by Night Shift), later successful in USA: dam maiden who stayed 1½m: 10/1, behind in maiden at Warwick: sold 3,700 gns. *M. P. Tregoning* **–**

ESSAY BABY (FR) 4 b.f. Saumarez 132 – Easter Baby (Derrylin 115) [2004 55: p10g⁴ p12g⁴ p12g p13g Mar 23] modest maiden handicapper: stays easy 1½m: acts on polytrack, good to firm and good to soft going: tried blinkered. *P. D. Cundell* **52**

ESSEX STAR (IRE) 3 b.f. Revoque (IRE) 122 – Touch of White 77 (Song 132) [2004 61: 6g f7d³ f8g³ 6g⁵ Aug 22] lengthy filly: poor maiden: effective at 6f to 1m: raced only on fibresand/good/good to firm ground. *Miss J. Feilden* **47**

ESTABLISHMENT 7 b.g. Muhtarram (USA) 125 – Uncharted Waters 68 (Celestial Storm (USA) 132) [2004 90, a–: 16d 12g 16.2m 18g 20f 16.2m 14s⁴ 16m Sep 11] smallish, workmanlike gelding: fair handicapper: stays 2½m: acts on polytrack, firm and soft going: blinkered (below form) once: sometimes sweats/races freely: none too consistent. *C. A. Cyzer* **73**

ESTEBAN 4 b.g. Groom Dancer (USA) 128 – Ellie Ardensky 100 (Slip Anchor 136) **48**
[2004 58: 8v 7m⁴ 8g Jul 5] tall gelding: poor maiden: stays 11f: acts on fibresand and
good to firm going. *J. J. Quinn*

ESTEPONA 3 ch.g. Polar Falcon (USA) 126 – Kingdom Ruby (IRE) 70 (Bluebird **66**
(USA) 125) [2004 8.5s⁴ 7d 8m 10.5g 11.9s Sep 24] strong, workmanlike gelding: first
foal: dam 7f winner: fair maiden: best effort on debut: not bred to need 10.5f. *Miss
J. A. Camacho*

ESTIHLAL 3 b.f. Green Desert (USA) 127 – Ta Rib (USA) 116 (Mr Prospector (USA)) **78**
[2004 –p: 6v 6g⁴ 5.9f* 6g² 6d⁴ 6m* 6m⁴ 6f³ 6g⁵ Aug 14] fair performer: won maiden
at Carlisle in May and handicap at Leicester in July: will prove at least as effective at 5f
as 6f: acts on firm going, below form on softer than good: slowly away last 2 outings.
E. A. L. Dunlop

ESTILO 4 b.g. Deploy 131 – Vilcabamba (USA) (Green Dancer (USA) 132) [2004 –: **–**
12m Jun 7] of little account. *R. M. Flower*

ESTIMATE 4 b.f. Mark of Esteem (IRE) 137 – Mistle Thrush (USA) 90 (Storm Bird **59**
(CAN) 134) [2004 69: f12g f12g f8g 10.1g* 10m 9d 8m² 10.1m² p10d 10d⁴ 9.9s Aug 29] **a–**
tall filly: modest performer: won seller at Yarmouth in May: should stay 1½m: acts on
good to firm ground: usually visored. *John A. Harris*

ESTIMATION 4 b.f. Mark of Esteem (IRE) 137 – Mohican Girl 112 (Dancing Brave **78 d**
(USA) 140) [2004 78: f8g³ f8g⁶ f7g³ f8.5g⁵ p7g 8m p8g p8g f8d Jun 17] tall, lengthy filly:
fair handicapper: below form after reappearance: stays 1m: raced only on all-weather/
good ground or firmer on turf: tried in cheekpieces/visor: sometimes races freely.
R. M. H. Cowell

ESTOILLE 3 b.f. Paris House 123 – Nampara Bay 50 (Emarati (USA) 74) [2004 6m **57**
5m 5d 7m f5f⁶ 5d p5.1g⁴ 6d* f5g² f5g⁵ Dec 1] first foal: dam maiden sprinter: modest
handicapper: won at Yarmouth in November: effective at 5f/6f: acts on all-weather and
good to soft going: tongue tied after second start. *Mrs S. Lamyman*

ESTRELLA LEVANTE 4 ch.g. Abou Zouz (USA) 109 – Star of Modena (IRE) **?**
(Waajib 121) [2004 69, a53: p10g p8g⁵ p8g³ p8g p8g⁶ p7g 8g 10m p10g 7m p8g Sep 18] **a44**
tall, leggy gelding: poor maiden: left G. L. Moore after sixth start: stays 1m: acts on all-
weather and good to firm ground: has worn cheekpieces/blinkers. *R. M. Flower*

ESTUARY (USA) 9 ch.g. Riverman (USA) 131 – Ocean Ballad 104 (Grundy 137) **–**
[2004 p13g 12d f14g Jun 16] big, workmanlike gelding: lightly raced and no form since 6
yrs: tried tongue tied/blinkered. *Ms A. E. Embiricos*

ETAAR 2 b.c. (Mar 12) Zafonic (USA) 130 – Hawayah (IRE) 68 (Shareef Dancer (USA) **83**
135) [2004 7g⁴ 7.5d⁴ 6.1d⁴ Sep 17] 36,000Y: angular colt: has a quick action: half-brother
to several winners, including useful 7f/1m winner Bishr (by Royal Applause) and 4-y-o
Enchanted Princess: dam 2-y-o 7f winner: best effort in maidens at Newmarket on debut
(then left N. Graham): needs to settle to stay beyond 7f.
E. A. L. Dunlop

ETCHING (USA) 4 b.f. Groom Dancer (USA) 128 – Eternity 77 (Suave Dancer (USA) **67**
136) [2004 71: 11.7g* 16d 14.1m 14.1f⁵ 17.2g Sep 27] fair handicapper: dead-heated at
Bath in April: should stay beyond 2m: acts on firm ground, well held on good to soft and
fibresand: sold 5,000 gns. *J. R. Fanshawe*

ETERNAL BEAUTY (USA) 4 b.f. Zafonic (USA) 130 – Strawberry Roan (IRE) **–**
113 (Sadler's Wells (USA) 132) [2004 63: f5s⁶ Jan 8] fair form in minor events in
France at 3 yrs: well held in maidens both British starts: sold 70,000 gns in November.
M. J. Wallace

ETERNAL BLOOM 6 b.m. Reprimand 122 – Forever Roses 70 (Forzando 122) [2004 **55 d**
–: f6g* f7g² f6g f6s f6s f6g³ f7m³ f6m 6.1m May 25] modest performer: best effort when
winning banded stakes at Southwell in January: stays 7f: acts on fibresand: tried visored
(very slowly away). *M. Brittain*

ETERNAL DANCER (USA) 3 b.g. Royal Academy (USA) 130 – Tara Roma (USA) **–**
(Lyphard (USA) 132) [2004 –: f9.4s f8s Mar 14] strong, compact gelding: well held in
maidens/banded race: tried blinkered: sold 1,000 gns, sent to Denmark. *M. Johnston*

ETERNALLY 2 ch.c. (Apr 22) Timeless Times (USA) 99 – Nice Spice (IRE) (Common **40**
Grounds 118) [2004 5g f5d³ f5g⁵ f5g⁵ 6f³ f5g* 5g p5.1g Oct 7] leggy colt: modest on all- **a54**
weather, poor on turf: won seller at Southwell in July: well below form after: likely to
prove best at 5f/easy 6f: acts on fibresand and firm ground: usually wears cheekpieces,
visored final start. *R. M. H. Cowell*

ETERNAL SUNSHINE (IRE) 2 b.f. (Apr 27) Rossini (USA) 118 – Sweet As A **34**
Nut (IRE) 75 (Pips Pride 117) [2004 6g 6f 5m f5g³ f5s Aug 23] €2,000Y: leggy filly:
second foal: dam 2-y-o 5f winner: poor maiden: form only at 5f: visored/blinkered last 2
starts. *R. P. Elliott*

ETESAAL (USA) 4 br.c. Danzig (USA) – Electric Society (IRE) 107 (Law Society **–**
(USA) 130) [2004 114: 9s Oct 16] good-bodied colt: smart performer at best, lightly
raced: left D. Loder and off 15 months, dropped away tamely in Darley Stakes at Newmarket only outing in 2004. *Saeed bin Suroor*

ETLAALA 2 ch.c. (Feb 23) Selkirk (USA) 129 – Portelet 91 (Night Shift (USA)) **119**
[2004 7g* 7f* 7s Oct 16]
Etlaala's performance in the Dewhurst Stakes at Newmarket was reminiscent of the dustcart which proverbially follows the Lord Mayor's Show in London.
Starting a well-backed favourite and looking in fine shape, Etlaala was held up
going freely but went on to run no sort of race, dropping out to finish more than
twenty lengths eighth of nine behind Shamardal, his rider accepting the situation
some way out. As a result, Etlaala's odds for the Two Thousand Guineas were
pushed out to as much as 20/1 from 8/1 joint-favouritism, which may prove to have
been an overreaction given that Etlaala almost certainly failed to act on the testing
ground. His run, like that of Perfectperformance, should probably be forgiven.
Judged on his victory in the SGB Champagne Stakes at Doncaster five weeks
earlier, together with his appearance—he is a big, good-topped colt with plenty of
scope who can be expected to make up into an imposing three-year-old—Etlaala
should on no account be left out of calculations for the Guineas.
Etlaala's announcement as one of the best of his age occurred in a decidedly
short time, less than a month, starting with a ten-runner maiden at Newbury in mid-
August. This was later than his trainer Barry Hills intended but, like a number of
horses in the yard, Etlaala had been affected by coughing. The colt's reputation
preceded him and he started favourite, justifying the confidence in style by making
all, showing plenty of zest in using his long stride to full advantage and soon
quickening clear when given the office two furlongs out to defeat Count Kristo by
two and a half lengths. It is quite a step-up from maiden company, even at a top
course such as Newbury, to the Champagne at Doncaster, a Group 2 which is
consistently one of the best-contested juvenile races in the calendar. Hills rarely
misses a chance, however, to run a good colt in the Champagne Stakes, a race the

SGB Champagne Stakes, Doncaster—
Etlaala puts up an impressive display on only his second start, beating Iceman, Oude and Wilko

stable has won in recent times with Auction House and Distant Music, but the Hills runners usually have more experience than Etlaala—Haafhd finished third after two outings in 2003. In a representative field of ten lacking Shamardal, who had had a minor setback, Etlaala started fourth favourite behind Iceman (carrying a 5-lb penalty), Oude and Elliots World. The other runners included the consistent Wilko. Etlaala won, but only after encountering problems which might have troubled even an experienced colt. Breaking awkwardly, he was held up in last and had no sort of run through when improving on the bridle after halfway, having to be checked several times. By the time Etlaala got clear on the outside, Iceman had quickened into a seemingly decisive lead and showed no sign of stopping. But Etlaala needed only a couple of slaps to catch the leader in the last fifty yards for a half-length success, the pair drawing away from Oude and Wilko. Etlaala came out a worse horse at the weights than the runner-up but there was no denying the style of the win, nor the fact that he would have managed a wider winning margin with a clearer run, and his rating reflects this impression. With such a good turn of foot, Etlaala will surely prove a tough nut to crack over a mile as a three-year-old providing the going is not bottomless—it was firm at Doncaster. One thing Etlaala might need in the Guineas is a strong pace, which would help his rider to settle him.

Etlaala (ch.c. Feb 23, 2002)	Selkirk (USA) (ch 1988)	Sharpen Up (ch 1969)	Atan
			Rocchetta
		Annie Edge (ch 1980)	Nebbiolo
			Friendly Court
	Portelet (b 1992)	Night Shift (b 1980)	Northern Dancer
			Ciboulette
		Noirmant (ch 1987)	Dominion
			Krakow

Mr Hamdan Al Maktoum's "Etlaala"

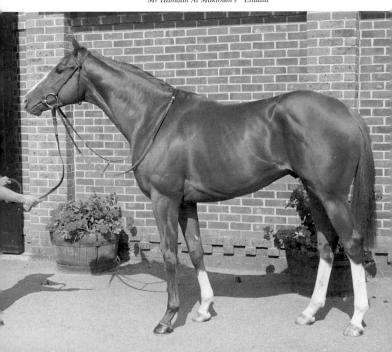

Despite some claims that the sire Selkirk was best with give in the ground, he acted equally well on good to firm and good to soft. Although the fillies Red Bloom and Sulk both won Group 1s over a mile at two, Etlaala is the first colt by Selkirk to win a juvenile pattern event. As that suggests, Selkirk's progeny usually do better at three or even four, another reason to feel confident about Etlaala's prospects. Selkirk was retired to stud in 1993 and the latest season was his best so far, with Altieri, Favourable Terms and Prince Kirk all notching Group 1 prizes. His fee, which started at £8,000, is now £40,000. Etlaala should stay a mile. His dam, Portelet, had speed in excess of stamina, making all to win four five-furlong races, though she showed form over seven, and Etlaala's smart five-year-old brother Selective has won at both seven furlongs and a mile. Portelet's other winner, Over-spect (by Spectrum), was successful over six and seven furlongs at two and over similar distances in Italy at three and four. Portelet was one of five winners out of Noirmant, an unraced half-sister to smart middle-distance stayer Braashee, who won the Yorkshire Cup outright and dead-heated for first in the Prix Royal-Oak. Etlaala cost 160,000 guineas as a yearling at Newmarket. His yearling half-brother by Cadeaux Genereux went for 20,000 guineas less at the same venue in October, two months before his once-raced three-year-old half-sister Bird Key, also by Cadeaux Genereux, sold for 75,000 guineas. Portelet's foal is a filly, also by Selkirk. *B. W. Hills*

ETMAAM 3 b.c. Intikhab (USA) 135 – Sudeley 65 (Dancing Brave (USA) 140) [2004 74P: 7s* 8g⁵ 10.2m² 10.3m² 10.4m* 12m³ 12g 11.9d 11.9g⁶ 10v⁶ Oct 20] sturdy colt: useful performer: won maiden at Newcastle in March, minor event at Bath in May and handicap at York in June: unlucky third in King George V Handicap at Royal Ascot sixth outing: below form last 4 starts, including when tried in blinkers: stays 1½m: acts on soft and good to firm going: usually held up: joined S. Seemar in UAE. *M. Johnston* **99**

ETOILE RUSSE (IRE) 2 b.g. (Mar 27) Soviet Star (USA) 128 – To The Skies (USA) 89 (Sky Classic (CAN)) [2004 6f f8g⁴ f8g³ Dec 11] €19,000F, 11,500Y: third foal: half-brother to useful Italian 1m/1¼m winner Pippo di Lucilla (by Orpen): dam Irish 1¼m winner: in frame in minor event/maiden at Southwell: needs to settle to stay beyond 1m: should improve. *P. C. Haslam* **64 p**

ETON (GER) 8 ch.g. Suave Dancer (USA) 136 – Ermione (Surumu (GER)) [2004 78: 10.3g³ 12v 12d⁵ 10.4m* 12.4v² 11.9g³ 10.1g⁵ 12m² 10g 10.4m⁴ 10m Sep 7] strong, close-coupled gelding: fair performer: won claimer at York in June: effective at 1¼m/1½m: best recent form on good going or firmer: tried blinkered earlier in career: usually races prominently. *D. Nicholls* **76**

ETTRICK WATER 5 ch.g. Selkirk (USA) 129 – Sadly Sober (IRE) 70 (Roi Danzig (USA)) [2004 96: 8.1m⁵ 7g* 7m* 7m 7m* 7m⁶ 7d⁴ p7g Oct 28] strong gelding: useful handicapper: won at Kempton and Newmarket in June and Goodwood (best effort, beat Boston Lodge by 1¾ lengths) in September: best at 7f/1m: acts on firm and soft going, probably on polytrack: tried blinkered, usually visored: effective ridden prominently or waited with. *L. M. Cumani* **108**

EUGENIE 3 ch.f. Primo Dominie 121 – Misty Goddess (IRE) 63 (Godswalk (USA) 130) [2004 –: p6g f7f Jan 22] good-topped filly: well beaten in maidens/seller. *R. Hannon* **–**

EUIPPE 3 b.f. Air Express (IRE) 125 – Myth 89 (Troy 137) [2004 64: 10m 14.1f⁵ 14g* 16.2s⁴ 14.1m Aug 4] tall, rather leggy filly: fair handicapper: won at Haydock in July: stays 2m: acts on soft ground: found little final start. *J. G. Given* **75**

EUKLEIA (USA) 2 ch.f. (Mar 1) Devil His Due (USA) 126 – Good Reputation (USA) (Gran Zar (MEX)) [2004 6g⁶ 6.1g f5g⁵ 5.9g Sep 2] $6,000Y: fifth foal: half-sister to 2 winners, including 4-y-o Wahoo Sam: dam 2-y-o 6f winner in USA: modest maiden: will prove best at 5f/6f. *T. D. Barron* **59**

EUNICE CHOICE 3 b.g. College Chapel 122 – Aquiletta 67 (Bairn (USA) 126) [2004 –: p7g f6g Jun 16] no sign of ability. *M. J. Haynes* **–**

EUROBOUND (USA) 3 b.f. Southern Halo (USA) – Eurostorm (USA) 104 (Storm Bird (CAN) 134) [2004 7.5v⁴ 8f⁴ 12g⁵ 11.7f⁵ Sep 6] 60,000Y: third foal: half-sister to smart 1m/1¼m winner Man O'Mystery (by Diesis) and fairly useful 2000 Irish 2-y-o 6f winner Destorm (by Dehere): dam, Irish 7f (at 2 yrs) to 1¼m winner and later successful in USA, out of Irish St Leger winner Eurobird: fair maiden: left J. Oxx in Ireland after third start: probably stays 1½m: appears to act on any going: tried blinkered: sold 24,000 gns. *D. J. Daly* **70**

EUROLINK ARTEMIS 7 b.m. Common Grounds 118 – Taiga 69 (Northfields (USA)) [2004 63d: f8.5g p10g⁴ p10g f9.4m* 10.2d* f9.4g³ f12d p9.5g p10m f11g Dec 12] useful-looking mare: modest performer on turf, poor on all-weather: left Gay Kelleway and returned to former trainer after reappearance: won banded races at Wolverhampton and Chepstow (apprentices) in April: stays easy 1½m: acts on all-weather, soft and good to firm ground: tried blinkered, wears cheekpieces nowadays. *Julian Poulton* **63 a49**

EUROLINK ZANTE (IRE) 8 b.g. Turtle Island (IRE) 123 – Lady Eurolink 55 (Kala Shikari 125) [2004 63: p8g p8g⁶ p10g 10.9m Sep 6] only poor nowadays: left T. McCarthy after third start: stays 1m: acts on soft and good to firm going, probably on polytrack: tried in cheekpieces/blinkers: usually held up. *A. J. Chamberlain* **45**

EVA JEAN 3 b.f. Singspiel (IRE) 133 – Go For Red (IRE) (Thatching 131) [2004 –p: 8.3g 8.2m⁵ 10s Nov 1] smallish filly: modest maiden: should stay 1¼m. *H. Morrison* **55**

EVALUATOR (IRE) 3 b.g. Ela-Mana-Mou 132 – Summerhill (Habitat 134) [2004 70: 7g⁴ 8.2s³ 8.5v 7m⁶ 7g* 8m² 8d² 8g 8.3g² 8f² Sep 24] useful-looking gelding: progressed into a useful performer: won handicap at Newbury in June: very good neck second to Granston in similar event at Ascot final start, despite edging right (gelded after): stays 1m: acts on polytrack, soft and good to firm ground: has had 2 handlers in paddock/worn crossed noseband. *T. G. Mills* **96**

EVANESCE 2 b.f. (Mar 28) Lujain (USA) 119 – Search Party 78 (Rainbow Quest (USA) 134) [2004 p5g² p5g² 5.2m⁴ 5d² 6g² 6m* 5f² 6g 5.2m 5.2m⁴ 6g 5g 7g Oct 5] €10,000Y: leggy filly: third foal: dam, second at 1m/1¼m from 3 starts, half-sister to US Grade 1 1¼m winner Bequest: fair performer: made all in maiden at Salisbury in June: below form after next start: stays 6f: acts on polytrack and firm ground. *M. R. Channon* **72 d**

EVANGELIST (IRE) 4 b.f. Namaqualand (USA) – Errazuriz (IRE) 94 (Classic Music (USA)) [2004 57d: f7g³ f6g f6s* f6s f6g⁶ p7g Mar 29] quite attractive filly: had a quick action: modest performer: won banded race at Wolverhampton in February: stayed 6f: acted on fibresand, firm and good to soft going: tried in headgear/tongue tie: ungenuine: dead. *Mrs Stef Liddiard* **– § a50 §**

EVA PERON (IRE) 4 b.f. Alzao (USA) 117 – High Flying Adored (IRE) 85 (In The Wings 128) [2004 68§: p7g 8.5d 10.2g⁶ 10m 8f May 27] small, sparely-made filly: poor performer: likely to prove best at 1m/1¼m: acts on fibresand and good to firm going: wore cheekpieces final outing: ungenuine. *W. G. M. Turner* **45 §**

EVASIVE QUALITY (FR) 2 b.f. (Apr 18) Highest Honor (FR) 124 – Exocet (USA) (Deposit Ticket (USA)) [2004 6m Jul 16] €260,000Y: good-topped filly: fourth foal: half-sister to useful 2002 2-y-o 6f (Cherry Hinton Stakes)/7f winner winner Spinola (by Spinning World) and 5-y-o Shot To Fame: dam, sprint winner in USA, out of half-sister to Prix du Cadran winner Molesnes: 7/1, well held in maiden at Newbury, racing freely: likely to do better. *D. R. Loder* **– p**

EVA SONEVA SO FAST (IRE) 2 ch.c. (May 11) In The Wings 128 – Azyaa 101 (Kris 135) [2004 7d 7d⁵ 8m² 8.3m* Sep 27] 21,000Y: sturdy colt: closely related to smart 1½m to 15f winner Samsaam (by Sadler's Wells) and useful 7f (at 2 yrs) and 1¼m winner Al Ihtithar (by Barathea), and half-brother to several winners: dam 7.5f winner: progressive form in maidens: favourite, won at Windsor by ½ length from Phi, getting on top late on: will be suited by 1¼m/1½m: should make a useful 3-y-o handicapper. *J. L. Dunlop* **87 p**

EVEN EASIER 3 gr.f. Petong 126 – Comme Ca (Cyrano de Bergerac 120) [2004 60: p7g p8g p8g⁵ 8g 10m⁶ 7m⁴ 8f⁴ 8g⁵ 10m 8f⁵ 8s Aug 27] modest handicapper: stays 1¼m: acts on polytrack and good to firm ground: usually wears cheekpieces/blinkers: often slowly away. *G. L. Moore* **57 a46**

EVEN HOTTER 3 b.f. Desert Style (IRE) 121 – Level Pegging (IRE) 48 (Common Grounds 118) [2004 –: 5.1m 6m⁵ 6d p8m³ Dec 8] smallish, leggy filly: lightly-raced maiden: should stay 1¼m: easily best effort on polytrack. *D. W. P. Arbuthnot* **63**

EVER CHEERFUL 3 b.g. Atraf 116 – Big Story 50 (Cadeaux Genereux 131) [2004 68: f7g² p6g* p7g p7g⁵ p5g² f5s⁶ p6m 5.7g p5.1g³ p6g* p7.1g⁵ p6g⁶ Dec 30] workmanlike gelding: fluent mover: fair performer: won maiden at Lingfield in January and claimer at Wolverhampton (left W. Turner) in December: effective at 6f/7f: acts on all-weather, raced only on good going or firmer on turf: effective with or without cheekpieces: races freely: sometimes hangs right. *G. C. H. Chung* **71**

EVEREST (IRE) 7 ch.g. Indian Ridge 123 – Reine d'Beaute 97 (Caerleon (USA) 132) [2004 94: 8g 10g 10g 10.3g 7.9g 8m* 8m* 8m 8s⁴ 9g Oct 2] strong, deep-girthed gelding: type to carry condition: fairly useful handicapper: won in large fields at Newmarket (landed gamble) and Newbury (beat Vortex by short head) in July: should stay 1¼m: **93**

acts on any turf going, some promise on all-weather: sometimes races freely: held up.
B. Ellison

EVERY NOTE COUNTS 4 b.g. Bluegrass Prince (IRE) 110 – Miss Mirror 77 (Magic **60**
Mirror 105) [2004 84: 12g 9.9d 10m 8.3m⁶ 10.1s⁶ 8m⁶ p8.6g Nov 13] leggy gelding: just
modest nowadays: stays 1½m: acts on all-weather, firm and soft ground. *J. J. Quinn*

EVIYRN (IRE) 8 b.g. In The Wings 128 – Evrana (USA) (Nureyev (USA) 131) [2004 **–**
16s Apr 20] maiden, lightly raced: tried visored. *J. R. Jenkins*

EVOLUTION EX (USA) 2 b. or br.c. (Apr 23) Bahri (USA) 125 – Zoe's Gold (USA) **74 p**
77 (St Jovite (USA) 135) [2004 p8.6g³ Dec 3] €19,000Y, 31,000 2-y-o: first foal: dam,
9.4f winner, half-sister to top-class miler Half A Year: 6/1, 1½ lengths third to Missata-
cama in maiden at Wolverhampton, making most: should improve. *J. H. M. Gosden*

EVOLVING TACTICS (IRE) 4 b.g. Machiavellian (USA) 123 – Token Gesture **117**
(IRE) 113 (Alzao (USA) 117) [2004 107: 8m* 8.9m 8f Jun 16] leggy, quite good-topped
gelding: smart performer: best effort when winning handicap at Nad Al Sheba in February by 2¾ lengths from Kundooz: only ninth in Dubai Duty Free there penultimate
start, and well held in Hunt Cup at Royal Ascot almost 3 months later: stays 1¼m: acts on
good to firm going: blinkered (ran creditably) final start in 2003, visored final outing in
2004: gelded and sold 42,000 gns, sent to Saudi Arabia. *D. K. Weld, Ireland*

EVOQUE 3 b.f. Revoque (IRE) 122 – Chimere (FR) (Soviet Lad (USA)) [2004 6g Apr **–**
15] 10,000Y: good-topped filly: third foal: half-sister to French 4.5f (at 2 yrs) and 7f
winner Tambour Battant (by Tagula): dam French 2-y-o 1m winner: 100/1, last in maiden
at Newmarket, slowly away. *H. J. Collingridge*

EWAR FINCH (FR) 2 b.f. (Feb 28) Kayf Tara 130 – Ewar Empress (IRE) 57 (Persian **–**
Bold 123) [2004 p8.6g p8.6g p8.6g p9.5g Dec 20] half-sister to 8-y-o Sharp Spice: dam,
temperamental maiden, best at 7f at 2 yrs: well held in maidens at Wolverhampton: blinkered final start. *K. O. Cunningham-Brown*

EXALTED (IRE) 11 b.g. High Estate 127 – Heavenward (USA) (Conquistador **57**
Cielo (USA)) [2004 66: 14.4v⁵ 13.1f⁵ 13g 13g⁶ Jun 24] good-topped gelding: modest
performer: effective at 1½m/1¾m, possibly not 2m: acts on firm and soft ground.
T. A. K. Cuthbert

EXCEED AND EXCEL (AUS) 4 b.c. Danehill (USA) 126 – Patrona (USA) (Lom- **126**
ond (USA) 128) [2004 5.9g* 6g* 6g Jul 8] big, good-topped colt: half-brother to a winner
in Puerto Rico by Honour And Glory: dam, US 6f winner, closely related to Gordon
Stakes winner Stylish Senor: high-class performer: winner of 7 of his 12 starts, including
4 group races in Australia in 2003, notably Group 1 Dubai Racing Club Cup at Caulfield
by 1¾ lengths from Reactive, breaking course record: won Group 2 Royal Sovereign
Stakes at Kensington in February and Group 1 Seppelt Wines Newmarket Handicap at
Flemington (by ½ length from Titanic Jack) in March: changed hands for reported £8m,
then gave impression needed run when well held in July Cup at Newmarket (led long
way) only outing in Britain (had missed Royal Ascot due to a slight virus): stayed 7f
(below form in Group 1 Caulfield Guineas at 1m): acted on good to soft going: front
runner: to stand at Darley Stud, New South Wales, Australia, fee A$55,000 and at
Kildangan Stud, Ireland, fee €10,000, special live foal. *Tim Martin, Australia*

EXCELLENTO (USA) 4 ch.c. Rahy (USA) 115 – Golden Opinion (USA) 127 (Slew **100 ?**
O' Gold (USA)) [2004 108p: 7.9s 8.1f May 31] strong, useful-looking colt: useful
performer: better effort in 2004 when ninth to Putra Kuantan in handicap at Sandown
final outing: will prove best at 7f/1m: acts on good to firm and good to soft ground: has
worn crossed noseband: left Godolphin. *Saeed bin Suroor*

EXCELSIUS (IRE) 4 ch.c. Dr Devious (IRE) 127 – Folgore (USA) 83 (Irish River **100**
(FR) 131) [2004 110: 8g 8.3s³ 8.3m 7.9s 8.1g⁴ 8.1s² 8d⁵ Oct 9] leggy colt: just useful in
2004: tends to race freely, and probably best up to 1m: goes well on soft ground: blinkered
(ran creditably) last 3 starts: none too consistent: sold 35,000 gns. *J. L. Dunlop*

EXCLUSIVE DANIELLE 3 ch.f. Thunder Gulch (USA) 129 – Hasta (USA) (Theat- **78**
rical 128) [2004 73p: 10d⁵ 12g* Sep 7] rather leggy filly: fair performer, lightly raced:
won maiden at Catterick in September: stays 1½m: sold 25,000 gns in December, sent to
USA. *B. W. Hills*

EXCUSEZ MOI (USA) 2 b.c. (Feb 11) Fusaichi Pegasus (USA) 130 – Jiving 69 **77 p**
(Generous (IRE) 139) [2004 p6g² Oct 25] $410,000Y: second foal: dam, maiden,
half-sister to useful performer up to 15f Arrive and to excellent broodmare Hasili: 12/1,
¾-length second to Postgraduate in minor event at Lingfield, leading 1f out until close
home: will stay at least 1m: should improve. *C. E. Brittain*

Prix Ganay, Longchamp—Execute goes one better than in the two previous years; Vespone (rail) is second, ahead of the grey Fair Mix, Vallee Enchantee (second right), Polish Summer (right) and Touch of Land

EXECUTE (FR) 7 ch.h. Suave Dancer (USA) 136 – She's My Lovely (Sharpo 132) **121** [2004 118: 10g² 10.5d* 12m 10d⁶ Nov 7] quite attractive horse: very smart performer: reportedly suffered from knee problems: ¾-length second to Vangelis in Prix d'Harcourt at Longchamp on reappearance: better than ever when winning Prix Ganay there in May (had been runner-up in 2 previous years) by 1½ lengths from Vespone: off 5 months, respectable eleventh of 19 behind Bago in Prix de l'Arc de Triomphe on same course next time: below form in Premio Roma final start: won at 1½m but best around 1¼m: acted on heavy going: held up: to stand at Haras des Fontaines, France, fee €1,000. *J. E. Hammond, France*

EXIT SMILING 2 ch.c. (Mar 4) Dr Fong (USA) 128 – Away To Me (Exit To Nowhere **73** (USA) 122) [2004 5g² 6d³ 5.2m 7m⁵ 8g 7d* 7s f6s⁶ Nov 17] 24,000Y: big colt: fourth foal: half-brother to 3-y-o Here To Me: dam unraced: fair performer: made all in claimer at Redcar in October (left M. Johnston): found little when well below form after: stays 7f: acts on good to soft ground. *D. Nicholls*

EXIT TO HEAVEN 4 ch.f. Exit To Nowhere (USA) 122 – Shona (USA) 60 (Lyphard **51** (USA) 132) [2004 64: f12g f12g⁶ f12g f16g Feb 12] modest maiden: left Gay Kelleway after third start: should stay 1¾m: acts on fibresand, raced only on good going or firmer on turf: tried in cheekpieces: sometimes raced freely: often races prominently. *Mrs Lucinda Featherstone*

EX MILL LADY 3 br.f. Bishop of Cashel 120 – Hickleton Lady (IRE) 64 (Kala **60** Shikari 125) [2004 51: 5s⁴ 5m² 5f² 5m* Jul 7] sturdy filly: modest performer, lightly raced: won maiden at Lingfield in July: should stay at least 6f: unraced on heavy going, probably acts on any other turf (some promise on polytrack). *John Berry*

EXMOOR 2 b.c. (Apr 13) Cape Cross (IRE) 129 – Royal Jade 82 (Last Tycoon 131) **47 p** [2004 p6g Nov 16] fifth foal: half-brother to several winners, including 3-y-o Scottish Exile and 5-y-o Million Percent: dam, 7f winner, half-sister to smart sprinter Averti: 9/1 and green, ninth of 12 to Grand Show in maiden at Lingfield, slowly away and not knocked about: will improve. *R. Charlton*

EXPECTED BONUS (USA) 5 b. or br.g. Kris S (USA) – Nidd (USA) 112 (Known **46** Fact (USA) 135) [2004 –: 9g 9.9g⁴ 10m 8f 8m⁶ 9.7f Sep 4] lengthy gelding: poor nowadays: stays 1¼m: tried blinkered: sometimes carries head awkwardly: usually makes running. *S. C. Williams*

EXPECTEDTOFLI (IRE) 6 b.m. Mujadil (USA) 119 – Zurarah (Siberian Express **–** (USA) 125) [2004 f6m f8g Jun 25] of little account. *T. Wall*

EXPEDITIOUS (USA) 2 b. or br.c. (Mar 25) Forestry (USA) 121 – Nonies Dancer **–** Ali (USA) (Danzatore (CAN) 120) [2004 7g p7g⁶ Oct 28] $175,000Y: strong, close-coupled colt: second foal: dam, US Grade 3 8.5f winner, half-sister to US Grade 2 9f winner Regal Sanction: tongue tied, well held in maidens at Newmarket and Lingfield (blinkered): refused to enter stall intended debut. *Saeed bin Suroor*

EXPERIMENTAL (IRE) 10 b.g. Top of The World 103 – Brun's Toy (FR) (Bruni **77** 132) [2004 12g 12v² 12v⁵ p7.1g* p9.5g Dec 11] formerly useful handicapper: winner of 5 races in Ireland: fair nowadays: won seller at Wolverhampton in November: stays 1½m: acts on polytrack and any turf going. *G. T. Lynch, Ireland*

EXPLICIT (IRE) 3 ch.c. Definite Article 121 – Queen Canute (IRE) (Ahonoora 122) –
[2004 p10d 10g 8.3m f7s p8g Sep 18] little form. *G. C. Bravery*

EXPLODE 7 b.g. Zafonic (USA) 130 – Didicoy (USA) 104 (Danzig (USA)) [2004 57§: **57 §**
8.1v⁴ 8v 8.1g² 9d² 8.2v Nov 4] modest nowadays: stays 1¼m: acts on soft and good to
firm ground: unreliable. *Miss L. C. Siddall*

EXPLOSIVE FOX (IRE) 3 ch.c. Foxhound (USA) 103 – Grise Mine (FR) 121 **72**
(Crystal Palace (FR) 132) [2004 68: 8v 8s 12d³ 11d⁵ 16m 13f² p13g 17.2s p12.2g p12g⁵
p13.9g² p13.9g⁴ Dec 13] half-brother to several winners, including useful Irish 1¼m
winner who stayed 1¾m Pillars of Society (by Caerleon): dam, won Prix Saint-Alary,
half-sister to smart Irish/US 1m to 1¼m performer Kostroma: fair maiden: left T. Stack in
Ireland after sixth start: : stays 1¾m: acts on polytrack, firm and good to soft ground: tried
blinkered/visored. *V. Smith*

EXPONENTIAL (IRE) 2 b.g. (Apr 19) Namid 128 – Exponent (USA) (Exbourne **82 p**
(USA) 125) [2004 5g 5.1g* Aug 16] €14,000Y, 27,000 2-y-o: second foal: dam unraced
from family of Storm Bird: 8/1 from 100/1, much better effort in maidens when winning
at Nottingham by length from Star Duster, always prominent: likely to prove best at 5f/
6f: wears blinkers/eyeshields: should progress. *S. C. Williams*

EXPRESS LILY 5 b.m. Environment Friend 128 – Jaydeeglen 73 (Bay Express 132) –
[2004 12s p12.2g Dec 4] third foal: dam maiden: no sign of ability. *K. R. Burke*

EXTEMPORISE (IRE) 4 ch.c. Indian Ridge 123 – No Rehearsal (FR) (Baillamont **58**
(USA) 124) [2004 47?: f5s f6s³ f7g⁵ 8.1g* 7v* f7g⁶ 7.1m p8.6d² p8.6g* Nov 15] sturdy
colt: modest performer: left P. McBride after third start: won banded races at Warwick in
April, Kempton in May and Wolverhampton in November: stays 8.6f: acts on all-weather
and heavy ground: tried tongue tied. *T. T. Clement*

Ecurie Chalhoub's "Execute"

EXTERIOR (USA)   3 ch.c. Distant View (USA) 126 – Alvernia (USA) (Alydar   **104**
(USA)) [2004 75p: p10d* 9s* 9m⁴ 10v* Oct 20] useful performer, lightly raced: won
maiden at Lingfield and handicap at Goodwood in August and handicap at Nottingham
(beat Haadef by 6 lengths) in October: stays 1¼m: acts on polytrack and heavy going,
probably on good to firm: joined R. Frankel in USA. *Mrs A. J. Perrett*

EXTINGUISHER   5 ch.g. Zamindar (USA) 116 – Xaymara (USA) (Sanglamore   **63**
(USA) 126) [2004 83: 6s 6m 6m 7.5d 9.1d⁵ 7m f6s Aug 23] strong gelding: just modest
nowadays: left D. Nicholls after sixth start: stays 7f: raced mainly on good going or softer:
tried visored: has been difficult at stall. *T. J. Fitzgerald*

EXTRA COVER (IRE)   3 b.g. Danehill Dancer (IRE) 117 – Ballycurrane (IRE)   **76 §**
(Elbio 125) [2004 74p: p8g2 10s² 9.7s² f8g³ f6g* f6m⁶ 6g⁶ p7g 6g p8m⁴ p7.1d⁶ p6g
p7.1g p7.1g³ Dec 4] unfurnished gelding: fair performer: won maiden at Southwell in
July: left R. Charlton after seventh start and N. Callaghan after tenth: has form at 1¼m,
though may prove best around 6f: acts on all-weather and soft ground: usually blinkered:
ungenuine. *Ms Deborah J. Evans*

EXTRA MARK   2 b.g. (Apr 11) Mark of Esteem (IRE) 137 – No Comebacks 70 (Last   **70**
Tycoon 131) [2004 5d² f5g² 5g⁴ 7m 6d f5g⁵ f7g³ Dec 16] 9,000Y: sixth foal: half-brother
to 5-y-o Steely Dan and 7-y-o New Options: dam, 1m to 1½m winner, out of half-sister to
Irish 1000 Guineas winner Katies: fair maiden: will prove best at 5f/6f: acts on fibresand
and good to soft going. *J. R. Best*

EXTREME BEAUTY (USA)   2 ch.f. (Apr 24) Rahy (USA) 115 – Mediation (IRE)   **89**
(Caerleon (USA) 132) [2004 6m⁶ 6f* 6m 6m³ 7f Aug 7] $15,000Y: lengthy filly: fifth
foal: half-sister to winners abroad by Woodman and Gone West: dam, Irish 6f to 1m winner, later successful in USA: fairly useful performer: won maiden at Pontefract in June:
good 5 lengths third to Jewel In The Sand in Cherry Hinton Stakes at Newmarket: should
stay 7f. *C. E. Brittain*

EXTREMELY RARE (IRE)   3 b.f. Mark of Esteem (IRE) 137 – Colourflash (IRE)   **70 ?**
(College Chapel 122) [2004 6g² 6s 6v* 7m 5d 6g 5s⁶ 6d⁶ 6g Oct 11] IR 34,000F,
€32,000Y: rather leggy filly: first foal: dam unraced half-sister to dam of smart sprinter
Eastern Purple: fair performer: won maiden at Redcar in May: left T. Easterby after sixth
start: stays 6f: acts on heavy ground. *M. S. Saunders*

EYES DONT LIE (IRE)   6 b.g. Namaqualand (USA) – Avidal Park 68 (Horage 124)   **– §**
[2004 38§: 12g 12d Oct 17] untrustworthy maiden: tried in headgear/tongue tie.
D. A. Nolan

EYES ONLY (USA)   3 b.f. Distant View (USA) 126 – Yashmak (USA) 118 (Danzig   **89**
(USA)) [2004 8g* Aug 28] third foal: dam, 6f (at 2 yrs) to 1½m (Ribblesdale Stakes)
winner, half-sister to Warning, Commander In Chief and Deploy: 7/4 favourite, impressive when winning maiden at Newmarket by 6 lengths from Thistle, tracking leaders
before asserting over 1f out, only outing: stud. *H. R. A. Cecil*

EZZ ELKHEIL   5 b.g. Bering 136 – Numidie (FR) (Baillamont (USA) 124) [2004   **67 §**
85§: p16g² p12g⁴ p12g³ p13g 12s 12g 10.3g Jun 8] tall, useful-looking gelding: fairly   **a83 §**
useful handicapper on all-weather, fair on turf: stays easy 2m: acts on polytrack, firm and
good to soft going: unreliable (has been reluctant to race). *J. R. Jenkins*

F

FAAYEJ (IRE)   4 b.g. Sadler's Wells (USA) 132 – Russian Ballet (USA) (Nijinsky   **88**
(CAN) 138) [2004 76: 10f* 10m⁴ 10d⁵ 13.1s³ Sep 18] leggy, attractive gelding: fairly
useful handicapper: won at Sandown in May: creditable efforts after, including in cheekpieces: barely stays 13f: acts on firm and soft going: sometimes carries head awkwardly:
sold 50,000 gns. *Sir Michael Stoute*

FABRANESE   4 b.f. Dr Devious (IRE) 127 – Babsy Babe 94 (Polish Patriot (USA) 128)   **–**
[2004 –: p12d 11m⁶ 9g⁵ a12g 8g Oct 16] little form: left P. Howling after reappearance.
Ewa Breitholtz, Sweden

FABRIAN   6 b.g. Danehill (USA) 126 – Dockage (CAN) (Riverman (USA) 131) [2004   **–**
73d: p8g Jan 14] maiden: well held only outing in 2004. *D. W. P. Arbuthnot*

FABULOSO   3 b.f. Dr Fong (USA) 128 – Shafir (IRE) 68 (Shaadi (USA) 126) [2004   **39**
52?: f8g⁵ 7f⁶ 9s 8.5m⁶ 7m⁵ 8.1d p8m Nov 22] leggy, lengthy filly: poor maiden: stays 1m:
acts on polytrack and firm ground. *V. Smith*

FABULOUS EMPEROR (IRE) 2 b.c. (Mar 19) Imperial Ballet (IRE) 110 – Al Cairo (FR) (Vayrann 133) [2004 p6g Dec 4] €7,500F, €12,000 2-y-o: half-brother to 3 winners, including Irish 1½m winner Marinnette (by Be My Guest): dam French 9f (at 2 yrs) to 12.5f winner: 11/2 and green, well held in maiden at Lingfield. *Jamie Poulton* –

FACE THE LIMELIGHT (IRE) 5 b.g. Quest For Fame 127 – Miss Boniface 112 (Tap On Wood 130) [2004 79: 9.9d 10g⁶ 12m Jul 14] leggy, quite good-topped gelding: well held in 2004. *Jedd O'Keeffe* –

FACT AND FICTION (IRE) 2 b.c. (Feb 8) Fasliyev (USA) 120 – Flyleaf (FR) (Persian Bold 123) [2004 6.1g Jun 21] well-made colt: probably amiss in maiden at Nottingham: sold 1,100 gns. *M. Johnston* –

FACTOR TWENTY (IRE) 2 b.f. (Feb 17) Revoque (IRE) 122 – Swirl (Halling (USA) 133) [2004 8s f7g p7g p8.6g⁶ Dec 31] first foal: dam unraced: poor maiden: left M. Halford in Ireland after debut. *W. G. M. Turner* 41

FACTUAL LAD 6 b.g. So Factual (USA) 120 – Surprise Surprise 91 (Robellino (USA) 127) [2004 75: 10g 10.2f 10f* 10m 8f 10.1g 10m³ p12.2g p9.5d² p10.2g p10g p10m Dec 21] close-coupled, workmanlike gelding: fair handicapper on turf, modest on all-weather: won at Brighton in June: stays 1¼m: acts on all-weather, firm and good to soft going: tried blinkered/in cheekpieces. *B. R. Millman* 74 a61

FACTUAL LADY 2 b.f. (Apr 12) Factual (USA) 108 – Shiny Kay 65 (Star Appeal 133) [2004 6f Sep 13] half-sister to several winners, including useful 1995 2-y-o 5f winner Home Shopping and useful winner up to 1m Kayo, both by Superpower: dam 1½m winner: 16/1, very slowly away and always rear in maiden at Redcar. *T. D. Easterby* –

FADAEL (IRE) 2 b.f. (Feb 1) In The Wings 128 – Gift Box (IRE) 63§ (Jareer (USA) 115) [2004 5m 7m⁶ 8.3m³ 7.1g³ 8f p8.6g⁵ p8.6g³ Dec 1] quite good-topped filly: fourth living foal: half-sister to 3-y-o Fadeela: dam, temperamental maiden, half-sister to smart 6f/7f performer Danehill Dancer: fair maiden: stays 8.6f: acts on polytrack and good to firm going. *P. W. D'Arcy* 68

FADEELA (IRE) 3 ch.f. Desert King (IRE) 129 – Gift Box (IRE) 63§ (Jareer (USA) 115) [2004 75: 8d⁵ 7g 7m 6f May 30] good-topped filly: fair handicapper: free-going sort, better at 7f than 1m and should prove effective at 6f: acts on fibresand and good to soft ground, probably on firm: often races prominently. *P. W. D'Arcy* 69

FAILED TO HIT 11 b.g. Warrshan (USA) 117 – Missed Again 84 (High Top 131) [2004 –, a56: f12g³ f16.2g⁴ p13g⁶ Mar 2] lengthy gelding: fair performer at best, winner of 19 (including 14 at Wolverhampton) of 111 career starts: just modest form early in 2004: effective at 1½m to 15f: acted on fibresand, lightly raced and little form in recent seasons on turf: blinkered/visored: often front runner: reportedly retired. *N. P. Littmoden* – a55

FAIR ALONG (GER) 2 b.g. (Mar 23) Alkalde (GER) – Fairy Tango (FR) (Acatenango (GER) 127) [2004 5s 6g 5.1m 8.3m⁴ 8d 8.3g p7.1g p8.6g* Dec 31] rather leggy, quite good-topped gelding: second foal: half-brother to German 7f winner Fair View (by Dashing Blade): dam, German 1¼m winner, half-sister to useful 1½m performer Fair Warning: fair performer: won seller at Wolverhampton: stays 8.6f: acts on polytrack and good to firm going. *W. Jarvis* 65

FAIR COMPTON 3 b.f. Compton Place 125 – Fair Eleanor (Saritamer (USA) 130) [2004 60: 6m⁴ 6f⁶ 5.1g⁵ 6m⁴ 7m⁵ 6f⁵ 6g* 6g Oct 11] quite good-topped filly: fair performer: won handicap at Lingfield in August: stays 6f: raced only on good ground or firmer. *R. Hannon* 65

FAIRGAME MAN 6 ch.g. Clantime 101 – Thalya (Crofthall 110) [2004 68: 5g 5d 5m² 5g 5d⁵ 5g* 5f 5m 5d 5d 5d² f5g p5m⁶ f6g Dec 12] strong gelding: modest handicapper on turf, poor on all-weather: won at Beverley in July: effective at 5f/6f: acts on all-weather, firm and good to soft going: usually wears cheekpieces, visored final start. *J. S. Wainwright* 51 a39

FAIRLAND (IRE) 5 b.g. Blues Traveller (IRE) 119 – Massive Powder (Caerleon (USA) 132) [2004 54: p10g³ 10m⁴ 10.9m p10g⁶ 10.9d 10m 10.1d p12m p10m p10g⁵ Dec 20] modest maiden: trained by J. Crowley in Ireland in 2003: stays 1½m: acts on polytrack, firm and good to soft going: tried blinkered: none too consistent. *S. Dow* 56

FAIRLIE 3 b.f. Halling (USA) 133 – Fairy Flax (IRE) 97 (Dancing Brave (USA) 140) [2004 70: 9.3f⁵ 8.3m 8.5d 7.5g* 10.1d³ 10s Aug 14] lengthy, useful-looking filly: modest performer: won claimer at Beverley (claimed from Mrs J. Ramsden) in July: stays 1¼m: acts on firm and good to soft ground. *Mrs M. Reveley* 64

FAIRLY GLORIOUS 3 b.g. Tina's Pet 121 – Steamy Windows § (Dominion 123) – [2004 f6g f6g f9.4s Feb 20] well held in claimer/maidens. *T. H. Caldwell*

FAIRMILE 2 b.c. (Mar 1) Spectrum (IRE) 126 – Juno Marlowe (IRE) 100 (Danehill **78** (USA) 126) [2004 7g³ 7d³ 7g⁶ 7s⁴ Oct 22] tall colt: has a quick action: first foal: dam, 7f winner (including at 2 yrs), sister to 4-y-o Leporello: fair maiden: slowly away and flashed tail when fourth in nursery at Newbury: likely to be suited by 1¼m/1½m. *P. W. Harris*

FAIR MIX (IRE) 6 gr.h. Linamix (FR) 127 – Fairlee Wild (USA) (Wild Again (USA)) **121** [2004 123: 12m* 12m⁶ 10.5d³ 12g² 12.5v⁶ 10g* 12d⁴ 10d Nov 7] well-made horse: very smart performer: won Burjuman Dubai City of Gold at Nad Al Sheba (by 2 lengths from Prince of War) in March and La Coupe de Maisons-Laffitte (for second time, by short neck from Marshall) in September: best effort in between when respectable 2 lengths third to Execute in Prix Ganay at Longchamp third start: below best last 2 starts in Gran Premio del Jockey Club Italiano at Milan (promoted to fourth behind Shirocco) and Premio Roma: stayed 12.5f: acted on heavy and good to firm going: had worn hood in preliminaries: waited with: to stand at Shade Oak Stud, Shropshire, fee £3,000. *M. Rolland, France*

FAIRMORNING (IRE) 5 b.g. Ridgewood Ben 113 – The Bratpack (IRE) (Mister **47** Majestic 122) [2004 47: f12g² f16.2g⁶ f14g⁵ f12m² Apr 19] smallish, good-topped gelding: poor maiden: stays 2m: acts on fibresand. *J. W. Unett*

FAIR OPTIONS 3 gr.g. Marju (IRE) 127 – Silver Singing (USA) 96 (Topsider (USA)) **66** [2004 6s 6m 6m³ 7f p7g Dec 30] €47,000Y, 60,000 2-y-o: brother to fairly useful Irish 1996 2-y-o 5f winner Nevada (later winner in Hong Kong) and 1m winner Regent Court and half-brother to 2 winners: dam, 5f winner, half-sister to St Leger winner Silver Patriarch and 4-y-o Papineau: fair maiden: clearly best effort when third at Doncaster: left H. Cyzer 2,000 gns after penultimate start: should stay 7f: acts on good to firm ground: blinkered final outing. *D. Flood*

FAIR SHAKE (IRE) 4 b.g. Sheikh Albadou 128 – Shamrock Fair (IRE) 77 (Shavian **76** 125) [2004 71: 6s 7v 6s³ 7.2d⁵ 6d 6g² 6d⁶ 6f² 7.2d 6d 7m Oct 10] close-coupled gelding: fair handicapper: stays 6f: acts on firm and soft ground: often wears cheekpieces/visor: sometimes slowly away. *D. Eddy*

FAIR SPIN 4 ch.g. Pivotal 124 – Frankie Fair (IRE) 73 (Red Sunset 120) [2004 81d: **67** 6g 8.1g³ 8g 8g 7.2s⁵ 8.2v 10s³ Nov 1] smallish, sturdy gelding: fair handicapper: stays 1m: acts on any ground. *M. D. Hammond*

FAIRY MONARCH (IRE) 5 b.g. Ali-Royal (IRE) 127 – Cookawara (IRE) (Fairy **55** King (USA)) [2004 56§: 12.3m² 10.9d 12m² 12g 9.9m 12m⁶ Sep 25] neat gelding: modest performer: stays 1½m: acts on firm and soft ground: tried blinkered, usually wears cheekpieces: tried tongue tied, not in 2004: none too reliable. *P. T. Midgley*

FAIRY QUEST (IRE) 5 b.m. Air Quest 105 – Fairy Glade (IRE) (Fairy King (USA)) **51** [2004 53: 12g 8g³ 8.5d⁴ f8g⁶ p12m p12m Dec 15] first foal: dam unraced: modest performer: left S. Fahey in Ireland after third start: stays 9f: acts on good to firm going: tried blinkered/in cheekpieces. *Mrs L. C. Jewell*

FAIRY WIND (GER) 7 b.h. Dashing Blade 117 – Fairy Bluebird 66 (Be My Guest **40** (USA) 126) [2004 71, a55: p13g f12g f16.2m³ 12m Jun 5] poor performer: stays 1¾m: acts on all-weather and heavy going: tried blinkered/visored, not in 2004. *B. J. Curley*

FAITES VOS JEUX 3 b.f. Foxhound (USA) 103 – Desert Bloom (FR) (Last Tycoon **44** 131) [2004 56: 7.5s 6g 6g⁵ p6g Oct 18] lengthy filly: poor maiden: effective at 5f/6f: acts on fibresand and good to firm ground. *C. N. Kellett*

FAITHFUL FLASH 2 b.f. (Jan 16) Tipsy Creek (USA) 115 – Tudorealm (USA) **44** (Palace Music (USA) 129) [2004 7f⁶ 7.5d 6m⁴ 7m⁶ 6s⁵ Aug 24] quite good-topped filly: seventh foal: half-sister to 3 winners abroad: dam lightly raced: poor maiden: stays 7f: acts on soft and good to firm ground: blinkered (looked wayward but ran creditably) penultimate start. *C. A. Dwyer*

FAITHFULL GIRL (IRE) 2 b.f. (Mar 5) Second Empire (IRE) 124 – Cairde Nua **40 ?** (IRE) 62 (Mukaddamah (USA) 125) [2004 p5g p5g 6f May 28] €5,000Y: first foal: dam ran twice in Ireland: poor form in maidens/seller. *Miss Z. C. Davison*

FAITHFUL WARRIOR (USA) 6 ch.g. Diesis 133 – Dabaweyaa 118 (Shareef Dan- – cer (USA) 135) [2004 102: 8d Oct 15] good-topped gelding: useful 7f/1m handicapper: well held only 6-y-o start: none too reliable: sold only 3,000 gns, joined R. Bouresly in UAE. *B. W. Hills*

FAITH HEALER (IRE) 3 br.f. Key of Luck (USA) 126 – Cindy's Star (IRE) 68 **59**
(Dancing Dissident (USA) 119) [2004 71: 8.2s 8m 11.8g 8f⁴ 10m⁶ f8g* 7g 8f⁶ 8m p7.1g⁶
Oct 19] sturdy filly: modest performer: below form after winning maiden handicap at
Southwell in July: stays 8.5f: acts on fibresand, firm and good to soft ground: usually
wears blinkers/cheekpieces. *V. Smith*

FAITHISFLYING 2 ch.c. (Mar 26) Wolfhound (USA) 126 – Niggle 65 (Night Shift **44**
(USA)) [2004 5g 6g⁶ 5.1m 5m⁶ 6.1v⁶ p7g p8g Nov 20] workmanlike colt: poor maiden:
probably stays 1m. *C. A. Dwyer*

FAIT LE JOJO (FR) 7 b.g. Pistolet Bleu (IRE) 133 – Pretty Davis (USA) (Trempolino **–**
(USA) 135) [2004 14.4m 14.1d Sep 17] useful jumper: soundly beaten on return to Flat.
P. J. Hobbs

FALCON GOER (USA) 2 b.f. (Mar 26) Zamindar (USA) 116 – Elizabeth Eliza **43**
(USA) (Northern Prospect (USA)) [2004 6m 6d 6g Sep 6] $30,000F, €34,000Y: close-
coupled filly: seventh foal: half-sister to winners in North America by Forest Wildcat and
Personal Hope: dam maiden in North America: poor form in maidens. *N. Tinkler*

FALL IN LINE 4 gr.g. Linamix (FR) 127 – Shortfall 103 (Last Tycoon 131) [2004 **96**
66p: f12g* f12g* p13g* f11g* p12g* p10g* Feb 7] big, good-topped gelding: has plenty
of scope: fairly useful form: much improved early in 2004, winning handicaps at Wolverhampton and Southwell (2) and handicap and minor events (2) at Lingfield: completed
6-timer in 13 days when beating Learned Lad by 4 lengths in minor event at Lingfield,
making all: will stay 1¾m: acts on all-weather, shaped well only turf start: looked capable
of better still. *Sir Mark Prescott*

FALLUJAH 2 ch.f. (Apr 13) Dr Fong (USA) 128 – Brilliance 74 (Cadeaux Genereux **–**
131) [2004 7s Oct 27] 20,000F, 40,000Y: third foal: half-sister to useful 7f winner Tora
Bora (by Grand Lodge): dam, 1m winner, half-sister to smart 1m/9f performer Sign of
Hope: 14/1, tailed off in maiden at Yarmouth. *M. Johnston*

FAME 4 ch.g. Northern Amethyst 99 – First Sapphire (Simply Great (FR) 122) [2004 **66 +**
83: 11.7s⁶ Oct 19] tall, lengthy, angular gelding: lightly-raced maiden: just fair form only
outing in 2004: stays 1½m. *P. J. Hobbs*

FAMILIAR AFFAIR 3 b.g. Intikhab (USA) 135 – Familiar (USA) 96 (Diesis 133) **80**
[2004 81: 8.1g 8d 8g* 9.2s³ 8g f8g p8.6g³ Dec 27] leggy, close-coupled gelding: has a
round action: fairly useful performer: won claimer at Ripon (claimed from B. Smart
£20,000) in August: barely stays 9f: acts on polytrack, soft and good to firm going: often
races prominently. *T. D. Barron*

FAMOUS GROUSE 4 b.g. Selkirk (USA) 129 – Shoot Clear 111 (Bay Express 132) **103**
[2004 110: 10g 10.1g⁴ 10.3f⁶ 12g Oct 1] quite attractive gelding: useful performer: best
4-y-o effort when fourth to Sights On Gold in minor event at Epsom: should stay beyond
1¼m: acts on firm and soft ground: sold 23,000 gns, joined P. Bowen and won over
hurdles. *R. Charlton*

FANCY FOXTROT 3 b.c. Danehill Dancer (IRE) 117 – Smooth Princess (IRE) 63 **91**
(Roi Danzig (USA)) [2004 94: p8g* 8m 9g 7m³ 6m p8g 7m 7g p7g⁶ Oct 1] rangy, good
sort: has a rather round action: fairly useful performer: won maiden at Lingfield in April:
good third to Makfool in handicap at Epsom: effective at 7f/easy 1m: acts on firm going
and polytrack: tried in blinkers/cheekpieces: free-going sort: sent to USA. *B. J. Meehan*

FANLING LADY 3 gr.f. Highest Honor (FR) 124 – Pain Perdu (IRE) (Waajib 121) **–**
[2004 75: 8m 10d 10m Aug 7] close-coupled filly: fair maiden at 2 yrs: well held in 2004
(unseated rider to post on reappearance). *D. Nicholls*

FANNY'S FANCY 4 b.f. Groom Dancer (USA) 128 – Fanny's Choice (IRE) 90 (Fairy **94**
King (USA)) [2004 99p: 5.2g 5s 6f 6g³ 6g⁵ 7g⁵ 6d⁵ Oct 14] sturdy, good-quartered filly:
fairly useful performer: best efforts in 2004 when third to Kind in handicap at Newmarket
on fourth outing and fifth to Ruby Rocket in listed race at Newmarket final one: effective
at 5f/6f: acts on polytrack, good to firm and good to soft ground: tried tongue tied: usually
held up. *C. F. Wall*

FANTAISISTE 2 b.f. (Jan 25) Nashwan (USA) 135 – Fantastic Belle (IRE) 79 (Night **81**
Shift (USA)) [2004 7m 7f³ p6g² p6m* p8g Nov 16] first foal: dam, 6f winner, half-sister
to smart performer up to 1½m Germano: made all in nursery at
Lingfield in October by ½ length from Bahamian Magic: left Sir Mark Prescott 110,000
gns before racing freely final start: bred to stay 1m: acts on polytrack, promise on firm
going. *P. F. I. Cole*

Godolphin's "Fantastic Love"

FANTASIA'S FOREST (IRE) 2 b.f. (Mar 17) Shinko Forest (IRE) – Persian Fantasia (Alzao (USA) 117) [2004 7f 7g 7s Oct 21] second foal: dam, well beaten, half-sister to useful stayer Height of Fantasy: slowly away and well held in maidens. *J. L. Dunlop* —

FANTASTIC LOVE (USA) 4 b.g. Peintre Celebre (USA) 137 – Moon Flower (IRE) 95 (Sadler's Wells (USA) 132) [2004 110p: 9.9g 13.9s 14.6f³ 12g² 12.5v* 12v² Nov 13] quite good-topped gelding: smart performer: trained at 3 yrs by M. Johnston (gelded after): not seen out in 2004 until July: good efforts when placed in Mallard (Handicap) at Doncaster (third to Lost Soldier Three) and listed race at Newmarket (head second to Private Charter, making most before wandering) prior to winning Group 2 Queen Elizabeth Stakes (Handicap) at Flemington in November by a short neck from Manawa King: good 2¼ lengths second to Count Ricardo in Sandown Classic at Sandown (Australia) final outing: best around 1½m: acts on any going: blinkered last 2 outings: tongue tied at 4 yrs. *Saeed bin Suroor* **115**

FANTASTIC LUCK (IRE) 2 b.g. (Apr 20) Josr Algarhoud (IRE) 118 – Fantastic Fantasy (IRE) 85 (Lahib (USA) 129) [2004 8m 8g 8s Oct 27] tall, close-coupled gelding: first foal: dam, 1¼m to 1¾m winner, half-sister to 3 useful performers out of sister to dam of Derby winner Oath: best effort in maidens when never-nearer tenth at Yarmouth final start (gelded after): will be suited by 1¼m/1½m: likely to do better as 3-y-o. *J. L. Dunlop* **53 p**

FANTASTIC NIGHT (DEN) 2 ch.f. (Mar 3) Night Shift (USA) – Gaelic's Fantasy (IRE) (Statoblest 120) [2004 7g 6s Oct 29] third foal: half-sister to 3-y-o Torquemada and 4-y-o Pooka's Daughter: dam, Italian 1m winner, half-sister to smart miler Bachir: well held in maidens at Leicester and Newmarket. *R. Guest* —

FANTASTICO (IRE) 4 b.f. Bahhare (USA) 122 – Minatina (IRE) 78 (Ela-Mana-Mou 132) [2004 71: 14m⁴ 13g 16.1d³ 17.1d 16.1g⁶ Sep 6] good-topped filly: modest handicapper: stays 2m: acts on all-weather, firm and soft ground: wore cheekpieces last 3 starts. *Mrs K. Walton* **63**

358

FANTASTIC STAR   2 b.f. (Mar 3) Lahib (USA) 129 – Fervent Fan (IRE) 65 (Soviet   –
Lad (USA)) [2004 5d 6m f7d Jul 23] third foal: dam 2-y-o 6f winner: no form in maidens/
seller. *J. G. Given*

FANTASTIC VIEW (USA)   3 ch.c. Distant View (USA) 126 – Promptly (IRE) 88   **109**
(Lead On Time (USA) 123) [2004 113: 8g⁵ 8f⁴ Sep 10] small, sturdy colt: useful performer: off 5 months (reportedly scoped badly after reappearance in Craven Stakes), much
better effort in 2004 when 1¾ lengths fourth to Secret Charm in minor event at Doncaster:
stays 1m: acts on firm going: joined D. Watson in UAE. *R. Hannon*

FANTASY BELIEVER   6 b.g. Sure Blade (USA) 130 – Delicious 51 (Dominion 123)   **107**
[2004 102: 7v 7d 6g 7m 6m 6d⁴ 6m* 6.5g 6g* 6m² 6d 5.6m 6s² 6g⁶ 6g³ Oct 9] sturdy
gelding: useful handicapper: won at Newbury (by 2½ lengths from Caustic Wit) and
Newcastle (by neck from Fair Shake) in July: runner-up after in Stewards' Cup at Goodwood (beaten 1¼ lengths by Pivotal Point) and Ayr Gold Cup (beaten 2 lengths by Funfair
Wane): best at 6f/7f: acts on any going: sometimes hangs/carries head awkwardly:
usually held up nowadays. *J. J. Quinn*

FANTASY CRUSADER   5 ch.g. Beveled (USA) – Cranfield Charger (Northern State   **66**
(USA) 91) [2004 58: 7m 10m³ 10m³ 10.1f 10f³ 10f³ p10g² 10g 8g 10f³ 10m* 8m³ 9m* p8.6g
p8g* p12g p10g Nov 13] fair performer: won handicaps at Lingfield (for second successive year) in August and Goodwood (amateur event) in September and minor event at
Lingfield in October: stays 1¼m: acts on firm ground and polytrack: usually wears
cheekpieces: tried tongue tied: none too consistent. *Mrs A. C. Gilbert*

FANTASY DEFENDER (IRE)   2 b.g. (Apr 20) Fayruz 116 – Mrs Lucky (Royal   **56**
Match 117) [2004 5s 5v 6m 7g 6d 6m⁵ 7f f6g⁴ p7m p8.6g p7.1g f8d² Dec 21] good-topped
gelding: modest maiden: barely stays 8.6f: acts on all-weather, good to firm and good to
soft going: in cheekpieces last 3 starts. *J. J. Quinn*

FANTASY RIDE   2 b.c. (Jan 31) Bahhare (USA) 122 – Grand Splendour 79 (Shirley   **98**
Heights 130) [2004 7m 8s* 8f⁵ 10d² Oct 30] 2,000F: rather leggy, quite attractive colt:
has a markedly round action: third foal: half-brother to 5-y-o Smith N Allan Oils: dam
1¼m winner at 4 yrs: useful performer: won maiden at Yarmouth in August by 11 lengths:
better effort in listed races when 5 lengths second to Ayam Zaman at Newmarket,
slowly away and staying on well: likely to stay 1½m: acts on soft ground. *J. Pearce*

FANTORINI (USA)   2 b.c. (Feb 18) Theatrical 128 – Beyrouth (USA) (Alleged (USA)   **77 p**
138) [2004 7g 8.1g⁴ Sep 15] third foal: half-brother to 5-y-o Golden Dixie and fairly
useful 2002 2-y-o 7f winner (later winner in USA) Air Adair (by Storm Cat): dam, useful
French 1m winner and Grade 2 9f winner in USA, half-sister to smart 1¼m performer
Flame Valley: better effort in maidens when fourth at Sandown, fading final 1f having
led: should progress. *J. H. M. Gosden*

FARAWAY ECHO   3 gr.f. Second Empire (IRE) 124 – Salalah 62 (Lion Cavern (USA)   **55**
117) [2004 60: 8.2g f7g⁶ 8.2s³ 8.1m 8m⁵ 12.1s⁵ f8f2s⁵ Aug 23] rather leggy filly: modest
handicapper: left M. Bell, won apprentice race at Hamilton in August: stays 1½m: acts on
soft and good to firm ground: ran creditably both tries in visor. *James Moffatt*

FARAWAY LOOK (USA)   7 br.g. Distant View (USA) 126 – Summer Trip (USA) 117   –
(L'Emigrant (USA) 129) [2004 a74: f9.4g⁴ f8g⁵ f12f f12f Jan 22] good-bodied gelding: **a58**
modest handicapper: left J. O' Shea after reappearance: effective at 9.4f to 1½m: acts
on fibresand, best turf efforts on good/good to firm going: tried in cheekpieces/visor:
sometimes carries head high. *D. Shaw*

FAREWELL GIFT   3 b.c. Cadeaux Genereux 131 – Daring Ditty (Daring March 116)   **85**
[2004 98: 6g⁴ 6s³ 7g² 6g³ 6m² 6d³ 7m³ 6f³ 6s* 7d Sep 18] big, good-topped colt: fairly
useful performer: won maiden at Kempton in August: effective at 6f/7f: acts on soft and
good to firm going: visored last 2 starts. *R. Hannon*

FAR FOR LULU   3 ch.f. Farfelu 103 – Shady Habitat (Sharpo 132) [2004 41: f7f p7g   –
Feb 3] no form at 3 yrs. *W. R. Muir*

FARNBOROUGH (USA)   3 b.g. Lear Fan (USA) 130 – Gretel 100 (Hansel (USA))   **53**
[2004 p8g⁵ p7g 7g 7m 9.9g 7.9f 8d⁴ 10.2s⁵ p7.1g f11g² f12g³ Dec 1] modest maiden:
trained only 2-y-o start by A. Fabre in France: left D. Elsworth and gelded after fourth
outing: stays easy 1½m: acts on all-weather and soft ground. *R. J. Price*

FARNE ISLE   5 ch.m. Midnight Legend 118 – Biloela 67 (Nicholas Bill 125) [2004   **68**
11.9d⁴ 12.3m³ 8g 11.9f Jul 24] leggy mare: third foal: dam 1¼m winner: bumper
winner: fair maiden on Flat: stays 1½m: acts on good to firm and good to soft ground.
G. A. Harker

359

FAR NOTE (USA) 6 ch.g. Distant View (USA) 126 – Descant (USA) (Nureyev **71** (USA) 131) [2004 70: f6g⁶ f5s² f5g f6g f5g⁴ f6s⁶ f5g* 6s f5d* 6d⁴ 5f⁴ 5g 5g⁴ 6m 7.1d p6g **a83** f5g Dec 14] sturdy, well-made gelding: fairly useful handicapper on all-weather, fair on turf: won at Southwell in March and April: effective at 5f/6f: acts on fibresand, good to firm and good to soft going: tried in cheekpieces, usually blinkered: tried tongue tied. *S. R. Bowring*

FARRIERS CHARM 3 b.f. In Command (IRE) 114 – Carn Maire 83 (Northern Pros- **71** pect (USA)) [2004 58: f7g* 7m 8.3m 9s* 8.3d⁵ 9.9g p8.6g Nov 6] fair handicapper: won at Wolverhampton in April and Kempton in August: stays 9f: acts on fibresand, soft and good to firm going. *D. J. Coakley*

FARTHING (IRE) 2 b.f. (Apr 27) Mujadil (USA) 119 – Neat Shilling (IRE) (Bob Back **73** (USA) 124) [2004 5.2m² 5m⁴ 5.1f² 5g³ p5.1g p6g Dec 3] 21,000Y: first foal: sister to 3-y-o Mr Jack Daniells and 4-y-o Tidy: dam unraced sister to useful Irish middle-distance stayer Fill The Bill: fair maiden: should stay at least 6f: acts on firm going. *G. C. Bravery*

FASCINATION STREET (IRE) 3 b.f. Mujadil (USA) 119 – Loon (FR) (Kaldoun **69** (FR) 122) [2004 6d⁶ 8.3v⁵ 7d 7m² 6m³ 8.1m² 7m* 8.2g⁶ Sep 29] 170,000Y: half-sister to several winners, including very smart 9f to 1¼m winner in Ireland/USA Golden Apples (by Pivotal) and winner 1¼m (at 2 yrs) to 14.6f winner Alexander Three D (by Penne-kamp): dam French 1m (at 2 yrs) to 1½m winner: fair performer: left A. Fabre in France after third start: won maiden at Catterick in September: stays 1m: acts on good to firm and good to soft ground. *M. A. Jarvis*

FASHION HOUSE (USA) 2 b.f. (Apr 19) Quiet American (USA) – Polish Style **73** (USA) (Danzig (USA)) [2004 6g⁵ 6d² Oct 15] strong, lengthy filly: sixth living foal: half-sister to 3 winners, including 1999 Irish 2-y-o 7f winner Polish Panache (by Gone West) and winner up to 9f in USA/UAE Danuta (by Sunday Silence), both useful: dam, French 6f winner (including at 2yrs), out of champion US filly Family Style: fair form in maidens at Yarmouth and Redcar (walked to post when second to Desert Imp, making running): should stay 7f. *Saeed bin Suroor*

FAST GATE (USA) 5 gr.h. Gate Dancer (USA) – Myshiphascomin (USA) (Premier- **91 +** ship (USA)) [2004 6g² a7g* a6.5s* p7g 6d² 6d² 5d* a6.8g* a6.8g* 6m a7g* a6.8g* a7.5g* Nov 29] $15,000Y: fifth foal: half-brother to 3 winners in USA: dam won in USA: won 6 races in Italy in 2003 and prolific winner again in 2004, successful in minor events at Rome and Cagnes-sur-Mer early in year, Florence in May, Corridonia (3) in the summer, and Rome, Corridonia and Varese in autumn: fairly useful form when eighth of 15 to What-A-Dancer in handicap at Lingfield fourth start: effective at 5f to 7.5f: acts on soft going, goes well on sand: has been blinkered/tongue tied. *L. Pantuosco, Italy*

FAST HEART 3 b.c. Fasliyev (USA) 120 – Heart of India (IRE) (Try My Best (USA) **96** 130) [2004 98: 5g 5s 6m⁴ 6m Jun 12] good-bodied colt: useful performer: fourth to Moss Vale in listed race at Haydock: barely stays 6f: acts on good to firm going: usually tongue tied: usually waited with. *B. J. Meehan*

FAST LANE (IRE) 5 ch.g. Hamas (IRE) 125§ – Rainstone 57 (Rainbow Quest (USA) **–** 134) [2004 7s 8.5d f8s Nov 17] lengthy gelding: well held in 4 starts in Hong Kong in 2002/3: no form in Britain, including in blinkers/cheekpieces. *J. S. Wainwright*

FASYLITATOR (IRE) 2 b.c. (Apr 8) Fasliyev (USA) 120 – Obsessed 80 (Storm **75** Bird (CAN) 134) [2004 7m⁶ 6m³ 6d⁶ 7m p6m⁴ 7s⁶ f8g* p7.1g⁴ f8g⁴ Dec 11] €85,000F, 36,000Y: close-coupled colt: third foal: half-brother to winner in Greece by Pursuit of Love: dam 2-y-o 6f winner: fair performer: won nursery at Southwell in November: stays 1m: acts on all-weather and good to firm going: often races up with pace. *J. A. Osborne*

FATAYAAT (IRE) 3 b.f. Machiavellian (USA) 123 – Maraatib (IRE) 93 (Green Desert **–** (USA) 127) [2004 65p: 8f May 27] small filly: some promise only 2-y-o start, none on only outing in 2004: sold 14,000 gns in December. *B. W. Hills*

FATEHALKHAIR (IRE) 12 ch.g. Kris 135 – Midway Lady (USA) 126 (Alleged **–** (USA) 138) [2004 –: 12v Apr 6] leggy, angular gelding: one-time fair handicapper on Flat/fairly useful jumper: well held only 12-y-o start. *B. Ellison*

FATHER SEAMUS 6 b.g. Bin Ajwaad (IRE) 119 – Merry Rous 66 (Rousillon (USA) **–** 133) [2004 p10g Jul 17] maiden: no form in 2 races on Flat since 2001: tried in cheek-pieces. *P. Butler*

FATTAAN (IRE) 4 b.g. Danehill (USA) 126 – Bintalshaati 95 (Kris 135) [2004 64: **–** 16.2m Jul 23] compact gelding: maiden: well held only 4-y-o start. *J. G. M. O'Shea*

FAVOUR   4 b.f. Gothenberg (IRE) 117 – Prejudice 83 (Young Generation 129) [2004   **79**
82+: 6m² 7m 6m⁶ 7d 7g 6f³ 5m 6g Oct 11] leggy, quite good-topped filly: fair handicapper: best effort in 2004 on reappearance: effective at 6f/7f: acts on firm and good to
soft going: free-going sort: wears crossed noseband. *Mrs J. R. Ramsden*

FAVOURABLE   3 b.f. Mark of Esteem (IRE) 137 – Top Society (High Top 131) [2004   **–**
8.3g 10.2g 10.2g Oct 10] big, workmanlike filly: sixth living foal: half-sister to 3 winners,
including useful 7f (at 2 yrs) and 1¼m winner Forthwith (by Midyan): dam unraced: well
beaten in maidens, leaving B. Meehan after debut. *A. W. Carroll*

FAVOURABLE TERMS   4 b.f. Selkirk (USA) 129 – Fatefully (USA) 110   **120**
(Private Account (USA)) [2004 110: 8f* 8m⁶ 9.9m* Jul 31]

    One of the races introduced in 2004 to encourage more owners and breeders
to keep their fillies and mares in training in Europe after the age of three was staged
at Royal Ascot, and it proved a welcome addition to the programme. The Group 2
Windsor Forest Stakes run over the straight mile attracted a field of ten of which
only 100/1-shot Starbeck was making up the numbers, the remainder having all
shown themselves to be at least useful. Among them were two overseas challengers, Actrice from France and Marbye from Italy, while one of Godolphin's two
entries was the ex-South African Crimson Palace, who had won a Grade 1 event in
her native country. Also doubly represented was Sir Michael Stoute, with Chic and
Favourable Terms, the latter making her seasonal reappearance and the mount of
stable-jockey Kieren Fallon. Crimson Palace was all the rage and went off favourite
at 6/5, but Favourable Terms, despite having been off the course for over eight
months, wasn't without her supporters and came next in the betting at 13/2.

    Unraced at two, Favourable Terms had made just five appearances in her
first season, showing smart form and winning a maiden at Goodwood, a listed event
at Sandown and the Group 2 Matron Stakes at Leopardstown. As the least experienced in the Windsor Forest line-up, Favourable Terms had the potential to win it,
though several of her opponents, notably Crimson Palace, proved to be nowhere
near their best, and Chic, who by season's end had shown herself superior to her
stable companion, lost all chance when almost coming down just over two furlongs
out. Yet Favourable Terms still deserves plenty of credit for winning in good style,
coming through to lead a furlong out and pulling two lengths clear of Monturani,
who in turn finished three and a half lengths clear of third-placed Soldera. It is
possible that Favourable Terms was still feeling the effects of this race when well
held behind Soviet Song in the Falmouth Stakes at the beginning of July, but
she was back to her best for another Group 1 contest at the end of the month, the
Vodafone Nassau Stakes at Goodwood. This event, though, was hardly worthy of
its status, only six fillies turning up, of which three faced a stiff task. Favourable
Terms, who looked in fine shape, was held up as Echoes In Eternity, a stable-
companion of second favourite Zosima, forced the pace, preventing the favourite
Chorist from adopting her usual front-running tactics. On her only other attempt at
a mile and a quarter in the previous season, Favourable Terms had finished second
to Chorist, seeming barely to stay the trip in quite testing conditions. With the
emphasis more on speed this time, Favourable Terms's stamina held out, though

Windsor Forest Stakes, Royal Ascot—
Favourable Terms takes the first running of this event in good style from Monturani; Soldera is third

Vodafone Nassau Stakes, Goodwood—
Favourable Terms (centre) gives Sir Michael Stoute his third successive win in the race;
Silence Is Golden (right) runs her best race in second with Chorist (left) a close third

only just. She looked likely to win readily when coming through to lead under two furlongs out, but edged right under pressure and at the line had only a short head to spare over the fast-finishing Silence Is Golden, with Chorist, squeezed slightly by the winner late on, a neck behind in third. Favourable Terms provided a third successive Nassau Stakes win for her trainer, following those of Islington and Russian Rhythm. Unfortunately, Favourable Terms's second season turned out to be even shorter than her first, a recurrence of a minor back injury one of the reasons she wasn't seen again after Goodwood. However, she stays in training.

Favourable Terms (b.f. 2000)	Selkirk (USA) (ch 1988)	Sharpen Up (ch 1969)	Atan
			Rocchetta
		Annie Edge (ch 1980)	Nebbiolo
			Friendly Court
	Fatefully (USA) (b 1993)	Private Account (b 1976)	Damascus
			Numbered Account
		Fateful (b 1988)	Topsider
			Fate's Reward

Favourable Terms is yet another pattern winner for her sire Selkirk, whose dam Annie Edge had to be put down in October at the age of twenty-four. Annie Edge was every bit as good a racemare as Favourable Terms, though in contrast to the well-bred Favourable Terms hers was a rags-to-riches story. Bought for just IR 6,800 guineas as a yearling, Annie Edge, trained by Derek Haydn Jones, won the Kiveton Park Stakes at Doncaster and was sold at the end of her three-year-old season for 330,000 guineas. She continued racing in the States, where she won two graded events. Favourable Terms's dam Fatefully was a smart winner over seven furlongs and a mile at three, and showed that she probably stayed a mile and a quarter when finishing fourth in the Sun Chariot Stakes at four. Fatefully's first foal Opportunist (by Machiavellian) is a useful performer, successful over six and a half furlongs in the States and subsequently at up to a mile and a quarter in the UAE. Her third foal Have Faith, a three-year-old sister to Opportunist, is a fairly useful performer who stays a mile. Favourable Terms's grandam Fateful was a fairly useful winner over six and seven furlongs, while her great grandam Fate's Reward won at up to nine furlongs. Favourable Terms, a sturdy filly, acts on firm and good to soft ground. *Sir Michael Stoute*

FAVOURING (IRE) 2 ch.c. (Apr 1) Fayruz 116 – Peace Dividend (IRE) (Alzao (USA) **69** 117) [2004 5g⁴ 5v 5.9f 6s² 5d⁴ 6d 6g⁶ Oct 4] 6,500Y: sturdy colt: fourth foal: half-brother to 2 winners, including Irish 6.5f to 1m (latter at 2 yrs) winner Badger Kennedy (by Perugino): dam ran once (at 2 yrs) in Ireland: fair maiden: second in nursery at Catterick, best effort: stays 6f: acts on soft going: visored (found little) final start. *R. A. Fahey*

FAVOURITA 2 b.f. (Mar 4) Diktat 126 – Forthwith 104 (Midyan (USA) 124) [2004 **103** 7f* 7s⁴ 8m⁵ 7g² 7s³ Oct 16] leggy filly: fifth foal: half-sister to 3 winners, including smart 1½m winner (stayed 2m) Time Zone (by Shirley Heights) and 3-y-o Forthright: dam 7f (at 2 yrs) and 1¼m winner: useful performer: won maiden at Brighton in August: best efforts when placed in listed race and Rockfel Stakes (rallied when ¾-length third to Maids Causeway) at Newmarket: should stay 1m: edgy sort: somewhat reluctant to post second and third outings. *C. E. Brittain*

FAVOURITE NATION (IRE) 3 ch.c. Cadeaux Genereux 131 – Fernanda 95 (Be **95** My Chief (USA) 122) [2004 95+: 6m 7f⁶ 8f 8g²* 8m³ 7m⁵ 6d 7v⁴ Oct 31] €320,000Y: strong colt: third foal: half-brother to smart 6f (at 2 yrs) to 1¼m (in UAE) winner Mubeen (by Barathea): dam, 6f (at 2 yrs) and 1m winner, half-sister to smart performer up to 1m Chipaya: useful performer: won maiden at Tipperary at 2 yrs and minor event at Limerick in July: respectable sixth to Kheleyf in Jersey Stakes at Royal Ascot second outing: stays 1m: acts on good to firm ground: tried blinkered. *D. K. Weld, Ireland*

FAYR FIRENZE (IRE) 3 b.g. Fayruz 116 – Shillay (Lomond (USA) 128) [2004 56: **47** p7g f7g⁴ p6g⁶ f6g² 7.1g⁵ p6g² 7g² 7m⁴ p6g Dec 22] poor maiden: stays 7f: acts on all-weather and good to firm going: usually wears blinkers/visor. *M. F. Harris*

FAYR JAG (IRE) 5 b.g. Fayruz 116 – Lominda (IRE) 80 (Lomond (USA) 128) **116** [2004 115: 6s 6f* 6g 5s 6d 6v Oct 3]

A thriving youth system should be the lifeblood of any sport, but, in sprinting at least, racing could cater better than it does for its budding talent. Oddly, sprinting is alone in failing to provide a single pattern race in Europe restricted to three-year-olds, though three-year-old sprinters are admittedly closer to full maturity than their counterparts over longer distances. Milers, middle-distance horses and stayers all have ample opportunity to contest pattern races in their own age group at three, and even seven-furlong horses have a chance to do so after the Guineas trials—in the Jersey Stakes—but not sprinters. Inevitably, the lack of a nurturing ground beyond their two-year-old season sees some horses fall by the wayside. Others among the faster youngsters each year with no classic pretensions are sold abroad, to the detriment of sprinting in the long run judged by the relatively low level of performances which have sometimes been good enough to win the top races at five and six furlongs in recent seasons.

The general standard of sprinting nowadays means the gap between the form of the top handicaps and pattern races is nearly always smaller than over other distances. In 2004, two of Britain's three Group 1 races at six furlongs were won by horses who had graduated from handicaps the previous season, Fayr Jag taking the Golden Jubilee at Royal Ascot and Frizzante the July Cup at Newmarket. Prize money for the Golden Jubilee was brought into line with the other top races at the fixture when the race was elevated to Group 1 status but, in three runnings since, only the Australian-trained Choisir has bettered the sort of performance usually needed to win the race in its days as the Group 2 Cork And Orrery. Fayr Jag followed in the footsteps of Harmonic Way, winner of the final Cork And Orrery in 2001, in adding the £145,000 first prize to success at the fixture the previous season in the Wokingham Handicap. Despite his bid having slipped with outright victory in sight, Fayr Jag dead-heated with Ratio in a strong renewal of the Wokingham under 9-6, and he had to show little or no improvement on that smart form to win the

Golden Jubilee Stakes, Royal Ascot—Fayr Jag gains a second Royal Ascot success,
following a dead heat in the 2003 Wokingham; running him very close are
Crystal Castle (No.6) and Hong Kong raider Cape of Good Hope (No.4),
who is placed at Royal Ascot for the second time in a week; Country Reel (far side) is fourth

Golden Jubilee twelve months on. In a field of fourteen, he started at 12/1 after finishing towards the rear behind Monsieur Bond in the Duke of York Stakes in May. Significant absentees at Royal Ascot included his stable-companion Somnus and Patavellian, both Group 1 winners in 2003, as well as the former Australian sprinter Exceed And Excel, ante-post favourite after being acquired by Sheikh Mohammed, only to be ruled out by a blood abnormality indicating a slight virus. Patavellian's stable-companion the Prix du Gros-Chene winner Avonbridge started favourite at 100/30. Airwave, runner-up to Choisir in 2003, came next at 9/2, with Monsieur Bond at 6/1 and the Hong Kong-trained Cape of Good Hope at 13/2. Fayr Jag had shaped reasonably well on his first run for seven months at York, and he looked in fine shape at Ascot. With nothing to blaze the trail as Choisir had done, the Golden Jubilee field was still well bunched towards the stand rail as Fayr Jag burst through between horses two furlongs out. Taking a definite advantage inside the last furlong, Fayr Jag began to edge right on the very firm ground, but responded gamely to pressure from Willie Supple to hold on by a head from the French-trained Crystal Castle, who came from last two furlongs out, with Cape of Good Hope another head further back in third. The race was another sprinting triumph for Yorkshire trainer Tim Easterby, who won the Sprint Cup at Haydock in 2003 with Somnus and in 2000 with Pipalong, another bargain buy beaten two short heads in the July Cup the same season.

		Song (b 1966)	Sing Sing, Intent
	Fayruz (b 1983)	Friendly Jester (ch 1973)	Be Friendly, Lady Jester
Fayr Jag (IRE) (b.g. 1999)		Lomond (b 1980)	Precipitic, Miss Prince
	Lominda (IRE) (b 1988)	Olinda (ch 1977)	Sassafras, Jodee Zee

The Golden Jubilee turned out to be Fayr Jag's only placing in six starts. Despite his win, he started at 25/1 in the July Cup next time, being hampered early on before finishing thirteenth of twenty. Down the field in the Nunthorpe at York in August, he started second favourite to the home-trained Lucky Strike in the Goldene Peitsche at Baden-Baden early the following month, but could manage only ninth, never a threat. In October, Fayr Jag's connections took up an invitation to the extremely valuable Sprinters Stakes at Nakayama in Japan in anticipation of more favourable ground than for the Abbaye at Longchamp, but a pre-race typhoon turned the going heavy and Fayr Jag finished last, weakening quickly soon after the turn and being eased.

Despite his 2004 form figures, Fayr Jag, whose name is trucker's slang for a heavy load, has been largely reliable when he has had conditions in his favour, though he did rear and unseat his rider leaving the stalls once as a three-year-old. A close-coupled gelding, he has form on good to soft going but seems in his element on ground firmer than good. He has put up his best efforts at six furlongs. Like his stable-companion Somnus, another gelding, he should be around for a lot longer yet and, though he may not be easy to place under a Group 1 penalty in 2005, as an 8,000-guinea yearling, connections are unlikely to lose much sleep over that now. They won't have so far to travel should Fayr Jag tackle the Golden Jubilee in 2005, when the Royal meeting will be run at York. *T. D. Easterby*

FAYRWAY RHYTHM (IRE) 7 b.g. Fayruz 116 – The Way She Moves (North Stoke 130) [2004 44: f16g Jan 4] strong gelding: well held only 7-y-o start: tried visored/tongue tied/in cheekpieces. *Ian Emmerson*   **–**

FAYRZ PLEASE (IRE) 3 ch.g. Fayruz 116 – Castlelue (IRE) (Tremblant 112) [2004 56: f6g4 f5g4 f6g 7g 5m 6g Oct 5] lengthy gelding: modest maiden: effective at 5f/6f. *M. C. Chapman*   **58**

FEAAT 3 b.f. Unfuwain (USA) 131 – Trois Heures Apres (Soviet Star (USA) 128) [2004 9.9g3 10m* 12m6 12g6 14m4 Jul 31] 190,000Y: big, lengthy filly: fourth foal: half-sister to 2 winners abroad, including useful French 1m to 1¼m winner Rising Talent (by Bering): dam unraced half-sister to Oaks and Yorkshire Oaks third Mezzogiorno (by Unfuwain): fairly useful performer: won maiden at Redcar in June: best efforts when sixth to Punctilious in Ribblesdale Stakes at Royal Ascot third start and fourth to Astrocharm in Vodafone Fillies' Stakes (Lillie Langtry) at Goodwood final one: stays easy 1¾m: raced only on good/good to firm going: sold 30,000 gns in December, sent to Denmark. *J. H. M. Gosden*   **94**

FEARBY CROSS (IRE) 8 b.g. Unblest 117 – Two Magpies 43 (Doulab (USA) 115) [2004 76: p7g6 p7g 7s4 7g5 7d 7m 6m5 6d4 6g6 7s* 7g5 7s Oct 27] strong gelding: poor mover: fair handicapper: won at Salisbury in September: effective at 6f/7f: acts on poly-track, firm and soft ground: blinkered 3 times, including at Salisbury: usually held up: sometimes looks none too keen. *W. J. Musson*   **75**

FEARLESS SPIRIT (USA) 2 ch.f. (Feb 5) Spinning World (USA) 130 – Hot Princess 101 (Hot Spark 126) [2004 8.2m5 Sep 28] tall, unfurnished filly: half-sister to several winners, notably top-class 1m/1¼m winner Rodrigo de Triano (by El Gran Senor), also 6f/7f winner at 2 yrs: dam, Irish 5f to 7f winner, later successful in USA: 15/2 from 12/1, fifth to Sharaiji Blossom in maiden at Nottingham, staying on not knocked about: sure to improve. *J. H. M. Gosden*   **71 p**

FEAST OF ROMANCE 7 b.g. Pursuit of Love 124 – June Fayre (Sagaro 133) [2004 –, a59: p8g3 f7g3 f7g* f7g3 f7g2 p8g6 f7g2 f7g* f8.5s5 p7g 7m3 6s 7f6 6f4 f7m 7g2 p7g p6g f6g2 f7g4 Dec 16] sturdy gelding: modest performer: won sellers at Wolverhampton in January and Southwell in February: left P. Howling after ninth start, C. Allen after fifteenth: barely stays 1m: acts on all-weather and good to firm going: often wears blinkers/cheekpieces. *G. A. Huffer*   **54 a64**

FEED THE METER (IRE) 4 b.f. Desert King (IRE) 129 – Watch The Clock 93 (Mtoto 134) [2004 –: 6m 9.9g2 11.6m* 12g 10g Jul 16] big, good-bodied filly: modest performer, lightly raced: won handicap at Windsor in June: stays 11.6f: acts on soft and good to firm going. *T. T. Clement*   **61**

FEELING BLUE 5 b.m. Missed Flight 123 – Blues Indigo 103 (Music Boy 124) [2004 51: f5g f5g Feb 24] leggy, angular mare: modest 5f performer: well beaten in 2004. *B. N. Pollock*   **–**

FEEL THE NEED 2 ch.c. (Apr 4) Chocolat de Meguro (USA) 98 – Mary Miller 71 (Sharpo 132) [2004 5m Jul 31] tailed off in maiden at Thirsk. *M. A. Barnes*   **–**

FEET SO FAST 5 ch.g. Pivotal 124 – Splice 114 (Sharpo 132) [2004 117: 7g5 a6f3 6.5m*dis 6.5m* a6f 7g3 May 16] lengthy gelding: smart performer on turf, useful on dirt: returned to former trainer before reappearance: first past post in handicaps at Nad Al Sheba in February (beat Cat Belling 1¾ lengths but disqualified for weighing in light) and March (beat Boston Lodge by 2¼ lengths): in rear in Dubai Golden Shaheen at Nad   **118 a100 +**

Al Sheba next time, then respectable 2 lengths third to Win Radius in Keio Hai Spring Cup at Tokyo final outing: effective at 6f/7f: acts on good to firm and good to soft going: visored final 3-y-o start: has been tongue tied. *S. Seemar, UAE*

FEI MAH 2 b.f. (Feb 12) Vettori (IRE) 119 – Bluewain Lady 76 (Unfuwain (USA) – 131) [2004 p6g p7m Dec 22] first foal: dam 1½m winner who stayed 1¾m: tailed off in maidens at Lingfield. *J. R. Jenkins*

FELICITY (IRE) 4 b.f. Selkirk (USA) 129 – Las Flores (IRE) 102 (Sadler's Wells **108** (USA) 132) [2004 106: 9m 10.2m³ 11.9m⁴ 10.2g* 10s Aug 22] big, close-coupled filly: useful performer: won Oakgrove Stud Golden Daffodil Stakes at Chepstow in July by neck from Kinnaird (pair clear), rallying gamely: well held in Prix Jean Romanet at Deauville only subsequent outing: takes strong hold (raced too freely on reappearance), and better at 1¼m than 1½m: has form on good to firm ground, best efforts on good or softer: sometimes has 2 handlers: races prominently. *J. H. M. Gosden*

FELIDAE (USA) 4 ch.c. Storm Cat (USA) – Colcon (USA) (Pleasant Colony (USA)) – [2004 43: f12g f8.5g Feb 6] close-coupled colt: maiden: well held in 2004: tried blinkered/tongue tied. *M. Brittain*

FELLBECK FRED 2 gr.c. (Mar 23) Paris House 123 – Wyse Folly (Colmore Row **33** 111) [2004 5d 6g 5m f5g⁴ f7g Dec 14] close-coupled colt: poor maiden: form only at 5f: tried blinkered. *C. W. Thornton*

FELLOW SHIP 4 b.g. Elmaamul (USA) 125 – Genoa 96 (Zafonic (USA) 130) [2004 – § 83§: p8g p10m p10g Dec 30] close-coupled gelding: well held in claimers/seller in 2004: tried tongue tied/in cheekpieces/blinkers: temperamental. *P. Butler*

FEMINIST (IRE) 2 b.f. (Apr 17) Alhaarth (IRE) 126 – Miss Willow Bend (USA) **74 d** (Willow Hour (USA)) [2004 5s⁵ 5g³ 5.1f 5.7m p5.1g p7m Dec 22] 32,000Y: sister to 3-y-o Almond Willow and half-sister to several winners, including fairly useful 5f/6f winner (including at 2 yrs) Willow Dale (by Danehill): dam winning sprinter in USA: fair maiden: third at Kempton, only form: left M. Channon after fourth start: should stay 6f. *J. M. Bradley*

FENDER 3 b.c. Rainbow Quest (USA) 134 – Rockfest (USA) 104 (Stage Door Johnny **52** (USA)) [2004 10g 14d Oct 10] blinkered, modest form in maidens: wandered second start: sold 4,500 gns. *H. R. A. Cecil*

FEN GAME (IRE) 2 b.c. (Feb 15) Montjeu (IRE) 137 – Hatton Gardens 96 (Auction **72** Ring (USA) 123) [2004 8.2d⁶ 7g Oct 1] 50,000Y: quite good-topped colt: closely related to smart Irish 7f (at 2 yrs) and 12.5f winner Lime Gardens (by Sadler's Wells) and half-brother to several winners, including 4-y-o Squirtle Turtle: dam, Irish 6f to 1m winner, half-sister to high-class 7f/1¼m performer Kooyonga: better effort in maidens when sixth at Nottingham: likely to be suited by 1¼m/1½m. *J. H. M. Gosden*

FEN GYPSY 6 b.g. Nashwan (USA) 135 – Didicoy (USA) 104 (Danzig (USA)) [2004 **79** 73: p8g⁵ p10g⁴ p8g p8g p10g 8.3d² 7s* 8.1v² 8.1d⁴ 7.1m⁵ 7g* 7.6g² 7g⁴ 8.3m* 8m⁴ 7s⁴ **a65** 8.1s³ 7.9m 8g Oct 16] good-topped gelding: fair performer: won seller at Southwell in April, apprentice handicap at Kempton in July and handicap at Windsor in August: effective at 7f to easy 1¼m: acts on polytrack, firm and soft ground: tongue tied once: tried blinkered: often races up with pace: tough and reliable. *P. D. Evans*

FENRIR 2 ch.g. (Mar 12) Loup Solitaire (USA) 117 – Whoops (Shernazar 131) [2004 **81** 7.5m 7.2s* 7g⁵ 8d³ 8g 10g Oct 11] first foal: dam no form: fairly useful performer: won maiden at Ayr in August: creditable third of 4 in minor event there, only other form: will stay 1¼m: possibly needs going softer than good: gelded after final start. *J. R. Weymes*

FEN SHUI (UAE) 2 b.f. (Mar 17) Timber Country (USA) 124 – Crystal Gazing (USA) **96 p** 114 (El Gran Senor (USA) 136) [2004 7g* 7s Oct 16] strong, well-made filly: eighth foal: half-sister to 3 winners, including smart UAE 5f/6f winner Conroy (by Gone West) and useful Irish 1¼m winner Dark Veil (by Gulch): dam won Nell Gwyn and third in 1000 Guineas: favourite, won maiden at Kempton in September easily by 6 lengths from Abide: ran no sort of race in Rockfel Stakes at Newmarket: will stay 1m: capable of better. *Saeed bin Suroor*

FENWICKS PRIDE (IRE) 6 b.g. Imperial Frontier (USA) 112 – Stunt Girl (IRE) **59** (Thatching 131) [2004 –: 6.1s³ 6m 5d 6d 6.9g 5d Oct 17] strong, lengthy gelding: modest handicapper: well below form last 3 starts: effective at 5f/6f: acts on soft and good to firm going (well held on fibresand): often visored. *R. A. Fahey*

FERNERY 4 b.f. Danehill (USA) 126 – Fern 100 (Shirley Heights 130) [2004 78: 10.5s⁴ **78** 10g Apr 26] strong, angular filly: fair performer: should stay 1½m: raced only on good ground or softer: sold 70,000 gns in December. *L. M. Cumani*

FERN HOUSE (IRE) 2 b.c. (May 3) Xaar 132 – Certain Impression (USA) (Forli (ARG)) [2004 5g Sep 2] 25/1, behind in maiden at Carlisle, slowly away. *James Moffatt* —

FERRARA FLAME (IRE) 2 b.f. (Mar 29) Titus Livius (FR) 115 – Isolette (Wassl 125) [2004 5.7m f6s 6m 8.3g² p8.6d p9.5g⁴ p8.6g p8.6g Dec 31] €4,000F, €10,000Y: third foal: half-sister to fairly useful Irish 10.5f and 1½m winner Gwapa (by Imperial Frontier): dam third in Irish bumper: modest maiden: left J. Osborne after second in seller at Windsor: stays 9.5f: acts on polytrack, best turf effort on good going. *R. Brotherton* **59 a54**

FERRYBRIDGE (IRE) 2 br.f. (Mar 14) Mister Baileys 123 – Final Shot 91 (Dalsaan 125) [2004 p7.1g p5.1g Nov 27] half-sister to several winners, including smart sprinters Double Action (by Reprimand) and Sir Nicholas (by Cadeaux Genereux), latter also successful up to 1¼m in Hong Kong: dam won Ayr Gold Cup: last in maidens at Wolverhampton. *D. R. Loder* —

FESTIVE AFFAIR 6 b.g. Mujadil (USA) 119 – Christmas Kiss 82 (Taufan (USA) 119) [2004 –, a56: f5g³ f6s f6g⁴ Apr 2] modest performer: has reportedly had 3 wind operations: stays 6f: acts on fibresand and heavy going: tried tongue tied. *B. Smart* **a51**

FESTIVE CHIMES (IRE) 3 b.f. Efisio 120 – Delightful Chime (IRE) 79 (Alzao (USA) 117) [2004 6d 7m³ f6g 6.1d 6.9m⁶ 7m Sep 18] fifth foal: dam, Irish 2-y-o 1m winner, sister to Cheveley Park/Moyglare Stud winner Capricciosa: modest maiden: stays 7f: acts on good to firm ground: tried in cheekpieces. *J. J. Quinn* **55**

FEU DUTY (IRE) 3 b.f. Fayruz 116 – Fire Reply (IRE) (Royal Academy (USA) 130) [2004 64: 5g⁶ 5f* 5d 5m 5f 5f 6f Sep 2] workmanlike filly: fair handicapper: well below form after winning at Carlisle in May: best at 5f: acts on firm going: tried in blinkers. *T. J. Etherington* **69 d**

FFIFFIFFER (IRE) 6 b.h. Definite Article 121 – Merry Twinkle (Martinmas 128) [2004 p13g⁴ f12g* f14g 15.4s Apr 20] tall, good-topped horse: ran in Spain in 2002 (winning twice) and 2003 for current handler: fair form when winning handicap at Wolverhampton in March: stays 1½m: acts on all-weather, firm going, good to soft and sand: tried visored. *C. Tinkler* **63**

FFIZZAMO GO 3 b.g. Forzando 122 – Lady Lacey 66 (Kampala 120) [2004 12m⁶ 14.1m⁴ 11.7d⁶ Aug 27] little form: blinkered all starts. *R. M. Beckett* —

FIAMMA ROYALE (IRE) 6 b.m. Fumo di Londra (IRE) 108 – Ariadne 79 (Bustino 136) [2004 69: f6g⁴ p6g p6g 5.7s 5.1f⁶ 5.1m Jul 22] leggy, quite good-topped mare: just a modest handicapper at best nowadays: effective at 5f/6f: acts on any turf going/all-weather: tried in cheekpieces: sometimes carries head high/finds little: usually races up with pace. *M. S. Saunders* **46 a52**

FICTIONAL 3 b.c. Fraam 114 – Manon Lescaut 56 (Then Again 126) [2004 80p: 5m* 6m⁶ Jun 28] sturdy colt: fairly useful performer: won handicap at Leicester in June by neck from Tony The Tap: effective at 5f/6f: acts on good to firm ground, possibly not on good to soft going: races prominently. *B. A. McMahon* **92**

FIDDLE ME BLUE 3 ch.f. Bluebird (USA) 125 – Fiddle-Dee-Dee (IRE) (Mujtahid (USA) 118) [2004 77p: 5s⁵ 5g 6m 5m 5.1m⁵ 5g³ 5.2g⁶ 6d 5d² p5.1g⁴ Nov 13] strong filly: fairly useful performer: won handicap at Bath in August: effective at 5f/6f: acts on polytrack, soft and good to firm ground: effective visored or not. *H. Morrison* **86**

FIDDLERS CREEK (IRE) 5 b.g. Danehill (USA) 126 – Mythical Creek (USA) (Pleasant Tap (USA)) [2004 70, a82: f11g⁶ p12g 10.1v 14g 9.1s* 12d⁴ p9.5g* Dec 27] quite good-topped gelding: fair on all-weather, modest on turf: won seller at Ayr in October and handicap at Wolverhampton in December: effective at 9f to 1½m: acts on all-weather, soft and good to firm going: often wears cheekpieces/visor: tried tongue tied. *R. Allan* **61 a78**

FIDDLERS FORD (IRE) 3 b.g. Sadler's Wells (USA) 132 – Old Domesday Book 93 (High Top 131) [2004 –: p10g³ p10g² p10g² p10g⁶ p12g⁴ 12.4v p10d⁴ 11.6d 18m⁴ p13g p12.2g⁵ Dec 14] strong, good-bodied gelding: fairly useful performer: first past post in maiden at Lingfield (demoted for hanging left close home) in January: won similar event at Warwick in June: subsequently left J. Noseda 32,000 gns: stays 2¼m: acts on polytrack and good to firm going: visored on debut. *T. Keddy* **80**

FIDDLES MUSIC 3 b.f. Fraam 114 – Fiddles Delight 45 (Colmore Row 111) [2004 –: p8g 10.1m* 10.2f⁴ 8f⁵ 12g⁶ 11.9f⁵ p10g 8s* 9.7f⁶ 10m Sep 23] sparely-made filly: modest performer: left M. Channon after fourth start: won seller at Yarmouth in April and handicap at Brighton in August: stays 1¼m: acts on firm and soft going: races prominently. *Miss S. West* **57 ?**

FID

FIDRA (IRE) 2 gr.f. (Apr 22) Vettori (IRE) 119 – Doon Point (Kenmare (FR) 125) **47 p**
[2004 7d p8m⁴ Dec 21] 55,000Y: half-sister to several winners in France, including fairly
useful 1996 2-y-o 1m winner Dounreay (by Lomond): dam French 1¼m winner: better
effort in maidens (trained on debut by D. Wachman in Ireland) when fourth at Lingfield,
pulling hard: should improve. *H. Morrison*

FIEFDOM (IRE) 2 br.c. (Jan 21) Singspiel (IRE) 133 – Chiquita Linda (IRE) **94**
(Mujadil (USA) 119) [2004 5.1g⁵ 6s⁴ 6m* 6g² 7m⁴ 8.5g³ 8d Oct 18] strong, compact colt:
has a quick action: first foal: dam, Italian 5.5f (including listed race at 2 yrs)/6f winner,
half-sister to very smart 6f/7f performer Mount Abu: fairly useful performer: won maiden
at Doncaster in June despite hanging left: good second in nursery at Ascot, comfortably
best effort after: should stay 1m: acts on soft and good to firm ground: usually races up
with pace. *M. Johnston*

FIELD SPARK 4 b.g. Sillery (USA) 122 – On The Top (High Top 131) [2004 68: **64**
14.1g⁶ 11.8m* 12.3m⁵ 12m² 12f³ 11.9g 12d² 12.1s 11.5g 12g⁴ p12.2g² p12.2d³ p12g³
p12.2g⁵ p16.5g³ p12.2g² Dec 15] good-bodied gelding: modest handicapper: won at
Leicester in May: effective at 1½m to 2m: acts on polytrack, firm and good to soft
ground: tried visored, usually wears cheekpieces: free-going sort: usually held up: tough.
J. A. Glover

FIENNES (USA) 6 b. or br.g. Dayjur (USA) 137 – Artic Strech (USA) (Arctic Tern **–**
(USA) 126) [2004 –, a47: f5g f5g p6g Feb 16] small, sparely-made gelding: poor performer: effective at 5f to easy 7f: acts on good to firm going and fibresand: usually wears
visor/cheekpieces: tried tongue tied. *Mrs N. Macauley*

FIERY ANGEL (IRE) 3 ch.f. Machiavellian (USA) 123 – Flaming June (USA) 69 **–**
(Storm Bird (CAN) 134) [2004 6d p7.1g p6g Dec 14] €130,000Y, 23,000 3-y-o: fourth
foal: dam, lightly-raced maiden, half-sister to useful performer up to 1¼m Majmu, herself
dam of high-class miler Muhtathir: well held in maidens. *A. G. Newcombe*

FIFE AND DRUM (USA) 7 b. or br.g. Rahy (USA) 115 – Fife (IRE) 95 (Lomond **52**
(USA) 128) [2004 69: p8g p10g 10m⁶ 10m 10.1f 8.1m Jul 2] smallish gelding: just
modest form at best in 2004: best at 1m/1¼m: acts on polytrack (well held on fibresand),
best turf efforts on good going or firmer: tried blinkered, usually wears cheekpieces:
usually races prominently. *Miss J. Feilden*

FIFTH COLUMN (USA) 3 b.g. Allied Forces (USA) 123 – Miff (USA) (Beau **57 ?**
Genius (CAN)) [2004 –p: 8m 8.5g 8.2g 8g⁵ 10s Oct 11] compact, attractive gelding:
modest form in maidens, leaving J. Fanshawe: pulled up final
outing: stays 1m: acts on good to firm ground. *D. W. Thompson*

FIGARO'S QUEST (IRE) 2 b.c. (Mar 15) Singspiel (IRE) 133 – Seren Quest 90 **62**
(Rainbow Quest (USA) 134) [2004 8.1d⁶ 8g p8.6g Oct 16] close-coupled colt: sixth foal:
half-brother to 3 useful or better winners at 1¼m+, including 7-y-o Saddlers' Quest: dam
1¼m winner: form in maidens only when sixth at Sandown: should be suited by 1¼m/
1½m. *P. F. I. Cole*

FIGGY'S BREW 2 ch.f. (Jan 17) Ashkalani (IRE) 128 – Marabela (IRE) 79 (Shernazar **56**
131) [2004 7g Oct 11] second living foal: half-sister to 3-y-o Betty Stogs: dam 1m winner
from 4 starts: 125/1, thirteenth of 19 in maiden at Leicester. *C. G. Cox*

FIGHTING TOM CAT (USA) 2 ch.c. (May 4) Storm Cat (USA) – Elizabeth Bay **78**
(USA) 116 (Mr Prospector (USA)) [2004 6g 6g⁶ 6d* Aug 29] lengthy, angular colt: fourth
foal: half-brother to 3 winners, including 3-y-o Bayeux and useful 7f (at 2 yrs) and 1m
winner Jahaam (by Danzig): dam, French 1m/9f performer who also won in USA, out of
US Grade 1 9f/1¼m winner Life At The Top: best effort in maidens when winning at
Yarmouth by short head from Love Thirty, making most: should stay 7f: tongue tied:
looked none too straightforward first 2 starts. *Saeed bin Suroor*

FIGHT THE FEELING 6 ch.g. Beveled (USA) – Alvecote Lady 50 (Touching Wood **63 d**
(USA) 127) [2004 66: f12g⁴ f12f² f12f² f12g² f12s p12g f12g⁵ 11.8m 14.1m⁶ 14.1g 14.6m⁵
12.6d p12.2g Nov 29] angular gelding: modest handicapper: well below form after third
start: best efforts around 1½m: acts on fibresand, heavy and good to firm ground: often
visored/blinkered. *J. W. Unett*

FIGHT YOUR CORNER 5 b.h. Muhtarram (USA) 125 – Dame Ashfield 90 (Grundy **108**
137) [2004 114: 12.1d 14.1g³ Sep 2] tall, angular, useful-looking horse: fluent mover: just
useful performer nowadays: fractured hind cannon bone final 3-y-o outing: better effort
at 5 yrs when 1¾ lengths third to Barolo in minor event at Salisbury: stays 1¾m: acts on
firm and good to soft going: tongue tied in 2004: has worn crossed noseband: tends to
carry head awkwardly. *Saeed bin Suroor*

FIGURA 6 b.m. Rudimentary (USA) 118 – Dream Baby (Master Willie 129) [2004 79d: **65 d**
p10g p10g³ p12g⁵ p10g⁶ p10g⁶ p10g⁶ p10g⁵ 10m 10.1f 8f 8.5g p10g⁵ p10d Jul 31] big,
leggy mare: fair handicapper, well below form after sixth outing: effective at 1¼m/1½m:
acts on polytrack and firm going: tried visored/tongue tied: usually held up. *R. Ingram*

FILEY BUOY 2 b.g. (May 8) Factual (USA) 108 – Tugra (FR) (Baby Turk 120) [2004 **39**
6s 7m 7d 7d Oct 15] workmanlike gelding: poor maiden: form only when visored final
start. *R. M. Whitaker*

FILLIEMOU (IRE) 3 gr.f. Goldmark (USA) 113 – St Louis Lady 71 (Absalom 128) **60**
[2004 65: 7m 9.9g 7m 8.1g⁵ 8.3f² 8f⁴ 8.3m⁴ 7.1m p8.6g 8s Oct 29] quite good-topped
filly: modest maiden handicapper: stays 1m: acts on firm and soft ground: tried visored.
A. W. Carroll

FINAL DIVIDEND (IRE) 8 b.g. Second Set (IRE) 127 – Prime Interest (IRE) (Kings **57**
Lake (USA) 133) [2004 61: 12.3m 11.5m⁵ 10m⁶ 12.1m⁵ 12s⁶ Aug 13] close-
coupled gelding: modest performer: won ladies claimer at Brighton in August: effective
at 1½m to easy 2m: acts on firm and soft going, probably better on polytrack than fibresand: tried in cheekpieces, not in 2004. *J. M. P. Eustace*

FINAL LAP 8 b.g. Batshoof 122 – Lap of Honour 100 (Final Straw 127) [2004 –: f12s **34**
f8.5s³ f12m Apr 19] poor performer: stays 1½m: acts on fibresand and good to soft
ground: tried in blinkers, not in 2004. *S. T. Lewis*

FINAL OVERTURE (IRE) 2 b.f. (Mar 7) Rossini (USA) 118 – Two Magpies 43 **–**
(Doulab (USA) 115) [2004 6m Jun 20] €3,600F, €7,000Y: leggy filly: half-sister to
several winners, including 8-y-o Fearby Cross and 1¼m winner Dangerman (by Pips
Pride): dam Irish 7f and 1¼m winner: 20/1 and backward, behind in maiden at Pontefract,
slowly away. *J. S. Wainwright*

FINAL PROMISE 2 b.c. (Apr 17) Lujain (USA) 119 – Unerring (Unfuwain (USA) **67**
131) [2004 7s 7g 6s⁴ Oct 22] 6,000Y: tall, close-coupled colt: second foal: dam unraced: best effort when fourth to Bailey Gate in maiden at Newbury: should stay 7f.
G. B. Balding

FINANCIAL FUTURE 4 b.g. Barathea (IRE) 127 – In Perpetuity 90 (Great Nephew **72**
126) [2004 103+: 12g 12m 12m 11m 12.3m 12m 12m Sep 18] strong, close-coupled
gelding: just fair form in 2004: stays 1½m: acts on good to firm and good to soft going:
blinkered last 2 outings: usually races prominently. *M. Johnston*

FINANCIAL TIMES (USA) 2 b.c. (Mar 18) Awesome Again (CAN) 133 – Investa- **82 p**
bull (USA) (Holy Bull (USA) 134) [2004 6m² Jun 10] $190,000Y: strong, attractive colt:
second foal: dam unraced half-sister to US Grade 2 8.5f winner Follow The Money: 3/1,
staying-on second to Perfect Choice in maiden at Newbury: underwent knee surgery
after: should stay 1m: likely to improve. *Saeed bin Suroor*

FINDERS KEEPERS 3 b.g. Selkirk (USA) 129 – La Nuit Rose (FR) 109 (Rainbow **82**
Quest (USA) 134) [2004 87: p7g² p7g³ 7.1g* 6s 7m 7f p6g* p7g 5d Sep 27] tall, rangy
gelding: fairly useful performer: won maiden at Musselburgh in April and handicap
at Lingfield (beat The Jobber ¾ length) in August: effective at 6f/easy 7f: acts on polytrack, good to firm and good to soft ground: sometimes early to post: free-going sort: sold
13,000 gns. *E. A. L. Dunlop*

FINE FRENZY (IRE) 4 b.f. Great Commotion (USA) 123 – Fine Project (IRE) 92 **38**
(Project Manager 111) [2004 53: 8.5d f7g⁴ 7m May 18] rather leggy, useful-looking filly:
just poor form in 2004: tried visored/in cheekpieces. *Miss S. J. Wilton*

FINE LADY 2 ch.f. (Jan 30) Selkirk (USA) 129 – Rua d'Oro (USA) 103 (El Gran **70**
Senor (USA) 136) [2004 8.1s⁶ 7.1m² 8.3d³ 7v² Oct 16] 24,000Y: plain, unfurnished filly:
half-sister to 3 winners, including useful performer up to 1½m Gypsy Passion (by Woodman), later successful in Saudi Arabia: dam Irish 6f (at 2 yrs) and 1m winner: fair maiden:
second at Chepstow and Catterick: should stay 1m: acts on heavy and good to firm going:
races up with pace. *M. Johnston*

FINE PALETTE 4 ch.c. Peintre Celebre (USA) 137 – Filly Mignonne (IRE) (Nashwan **100**
(USA) 135) [2004 79p: 10s* 10m* 12m⁵ 10d⁵ 10m³ 10.5g Aug 7] big, strong, lengthy
colt: useful performer: won maiden at Lingfield and handicap at Leicester (hung right) in
May: best form when 2¾ lengths third to Mister Monet in handicap at Ascot fifth start:
barely stays 1½m: acts on soft and good to firm ground: free-going sort, usually held up:
sold 16,000 gns. *H. R. A. Cecil*

FINE SILVER (IRE) 3 gr.c. Intikhab (USA) 135 – Petula 103 (Petong 126) [2004 **108**
83: 7s⁴ 8m 8f* 8m⁴ 8g² 9.9m² 9g³ 8.2v² Nov 4] angular, quite good-topped colt: useful
performer: won minor event at Ayr in May: good efforts after, including when 1½ lengths

third of 32 to Spanish Don in Cambridgeshire at Newmarket and 3½ lengths second to St Andrews in minor event at Nottingham last 2 starts: stays 1¼m: acts on any going: consistent. *P. F. I. Cole*

FINE THANKS 3 b.f. Danzig Connection (USA) – Dim Ots 92 (Alhijaz 122) [2004 – p9.5g p8.6g Nov 27] £1,200Y: second foal: sister to 4-y-o How's Things: dam 5f (at 2 yrs) and 6f winner: well beaten in maiden/seller. *D. Haydn Jones*

FINGER OF FATE 4 br.g. Machiavellian (USA) 123 – La Nuit Rose (FR) 109 (Rain- **49** bow Quest (USA) 134) [2004 –: f12g f8.5g f16g p10g f6s p6g f5m² f5d⁶ f6g⁴ f6g⁶ 5m 5g f5m³ 7g 7m³ 6f 7.1g Sep 26] sparely-made gelding: poor performer: effective at 5f to easy 7f: acted on fibresand and good to firm going: often wore blinkers/cheekpieces: dead. *M. J. Polglase*

FINISHED ARTICLE (IRE) 7 b.g. Indian Ridge 123 – Summer Fashion 84 (Moore- **96** style 137) [2004 104: 8g 8g⁵ 8.1f³ 8f 8.1d 8m 8.1d 8d⁴ 8d Oct 30] workmanlike gelding: useful handicapper: unlucky in running several times in 2004, weaving through from rear when creditable fourth to Kamanda Laugh at Newmarket penultimate outing: subse- quently left D. Elsworth 12,000 gns: best at 1m/1¼m: acts on firm and good to soft going: held up. *W. J. Musson*

FINLAND (UAE) 2 b.c. (Jan 30) Timber Country (USA) 124 – Najm Al Bahar (FR) **65 p** 64 (Caerleon (USA) 132) [2004 p9.5g Nov 13] second foal: dam, French 10.5f/11.5f winner, sister to Park Hill Stakes winner Noble Rose: 12/1, seventh to Liberty Run in maiden at Wolverhampton, fading: joined Mrs A. Duffield 15,000 gns: will stay at least 1½m: should do better. *M. Johnston*

FINNEGANS RAINBOW 2 ch.c. (May 9) Spectrum (IRE) 126 – Fairy Story (IRE) **– p** 80 (Persian Bold 123) [2004 8g Oct 12] big, good-topped colt: half-brother to useful 7f/ 1m winner Welenska (by Danzig Connection) and 4-y-o Zietory: dam, 7f winner (includ- ing at 2 yrs), out of half-sister to dam of Shaamit: 16/1, burly and green, behind in maiden at Leicester: likely to do better. *P. F. I. Cole*

FINNFOREST (IRE) 4 ch.g. Eagle Eyed (USA) 111 – Stockrose (Horage 124) [2004 59: p16g Sep 1] well-made gelding: maiden: well held only 4-y-o start: tried blinkered. *Mrs A. J. Bowlby*

FINNINGLEY CONNOR 4 b.g. Cosmonaut – Arroganza 62 (Crofthall 110) [2004 –: f7g 8.5d 7s Apr 20] of little account nowadays. *Ronald Thompson*

FIORE DI BOSCO (IRE) 3 b.f. Charnwood Forest (IRE) 125 – Carabine (USA) **73** (Dehere (USA) 121) [2004 79: 6d⁵ 6m 7m⁴ 6m⁴ 5.9g⁶ Jul 3] tall, rangy filly: fair handi- capper: should stay 7f: acts on fibresand and good to firm ground. *T. D. Barron*

FIRE AT WILL 2 b.c. (Apr 16) Lugana Beach 116 – Kahyasi Moll (IRE) 35 (Brief **41** Truce (USA) 126) [2004 5.1m 5.1f 5d 8g Sep 13] poor maiden: visored penultimate start. *A. W. Carroll*

FIREBELLY 3 b.f. Nicolotte 118 – Desert Delight (IRE) (Green Desert (USA) 127) [2004 86: p8g⁵ 7m 6m Sep 10] smallish, sturdy filly: fairly useful performer at 2 yrs: little form in 2004: tried visored. *M. J. Wallace*

FIREBIRD 3 b.f. Soviet Star (USA) 128 – Al Corniche (IRE) 62 (Bluebird (USA) **66** 125) [2004 6g³ Jul 24] 28,000Y: fifth foal: half-sister to 2 winners, including useful 1999 2-y-o 6f to 1m winner Whyome (by Owington): dam 2-y-o 5f winner who stayed 1¾m: 16/1, 1¼ lengths third to Kostar in maiden at Salisbury: will stay 7f: looked sure to improve. *H. Candy*

FIREBIRD RISING (USA) 3 b.f. Stravinsky (USA) 133 – Capable (USA) (Capote **62 d** (USA)) [2004 66: 6m⁵ 5m 6.9f³ 6.9g⁶ 6d 6.9m⁴ 7s 7.5s 6.9m³ 7m p8m⁴ p8.6g Dec 22] tall, lengthy filly: modest maiden: below form after third start, leaving T. D. Barron after tenth one: stays easy 1m: acts on polytrack and firm going: ungenuine. *R. Brotherton*

FIREBREAK 5 b.h. Charnwood Forest (IRE) 125 – Breakaway 98 (Song 132) **125** [2004 118: a8f* 8m⁴ 7m² 7s* 8m* Dec 12]
Although arguably one of the lesser lights in a glittering season for Godol- phin, Firebreak developed into a high-class performer, his campaign culminating in success in the Cathay Pacific Hong Kong Mile at Sha Tin in December, his first win at Group 1 level. Always handy under Frankie Dettori, who was returning from a month's suspension for careless riding in the Melbourne Cup, Firebreak took up the running inside the final furlong to triumph by three quarters of a length and a short head, without having to be at his best, from the locally-trained pair Perfect Partner and The Duke. It was the perfect end to a fine year for Firebreak's rider, one which

saw him widely recognised as champion jockey in Britain for a third time. The season begins on January 1st and runs to December 31st and the champion jockey —as with the champion owner and champion trainer—should be decided over the calendar year, though the Jockeys' Association arbitrarily recognises a championship that covers only races between the end of March and the beginning of November. Dettori won that title with one hundred and ninety-two winners. During the winter, when jockeys' championships of any kind were not regarded as a target by Dettori himself, he was not even quoted in bookmakers' ante-post lists for the Jockeys' Association title.

Dettori had not been champion since 1995—the year before he became the face of British racing when riding all seven winners on the Saturday of the Ascot Festival—and had not finished in the top five since the light aircraft accident in which he could easily have lost his life in 2000, insisting he would never travel by such means again. Throughout the latest hectic summer, Dettori was at a disadvantage with his main rival Kieren Fallon in travelling to two meetings a day by road, though he made occasional use of a helicopter. What helped Dettori to his highest tally (he rode one hundred and ninety-five winners in all) since his last championship year, was a renewed determination. He gave up his role as team captain on the television series *A Question of Sport* to concentrate on riding after describing his 2003 campaign in his autobiography as 'disastrous', admitting that he came in for serious criticism from David Loder for the way he was riding. Dettori, who rode only twelve horses for Loder in 2004, set out to prove his critics wrong and gave himself a target of one hundred and fifty winners. He was assisted by a vastly increased Godolphin string which included most of the owners' two-year-olds (a change of policy discussed in the essay on Librettist). Dettori rode seventy-seven winners for Godolphin in Britain in 2004, compared to seventeen in 2003 and fifteen in 2002. He also rode for one hundred and twenty-four different trainers in Britain during the year.

Dettori did not ride at Doncaster's Lincoln meeting because of the Dubai World Cup at Nad Al Sheba but he still got off to a flying start, chalking up twenty-five winners in April, the highlight a 947/1 five-timer at Folkestone, after which he was shortened to 7/1 for the championship. Dettori broke a finger when unseated from Chinkara at Goodwood in May and, returning eleven days later, had lost his place at the top of the table to Fallon who led by two. Fallon was seventeen clear of Dettori in the Jockeys' Association championship by the end of June and Seb Sanders looked likeliest to push Fallon closest. Though Dettori made up some ground in July, by the end of evening racing in August Fallon had a seemingly secure fifteen-winner lead. A superb September for Dettori saw him ride forty-two winners, helped by Godolphin's two-year-old string really beginning to fire. Dettori's twenty-two individual two-year-old winners in this period included

Godolphin Mile, Nad Al Sheba—Firebreak records a much more decisive win in the race than in 2003; Tropical Star, Excessivepleasure (third left) and the grey Estimraar follow him home

Victor Chandler Challenge Stakes, Newmarket—
Firebreak gives weight away all round and wins readily from Keltos (grey), Polar Bear and Polar Way

fifteen trained by Saeed bin Suroor. With less than a month to go, the title race seemed as good as over when Dettori rode a treble at Leicester and Fallon was unseated and stood down by the doctor at the same meeting. Despite Dettori's ban, picked up when riding Mamool into seventh at Melbourne in early-November, he was crowned Jockeys' Association champion four days later.

Fallon, who went on to reach two hundred for the year, had conceded the championship on the weekend that Firebreak and Dettori won the Victor Chandler Challenge Stakes at Newmarket in October by a length from Keltos, with Polar Bear back in third. Settling nicely, Firebreak bowled along from the start and pulled out extra after momentarily idling when Keltos came at him inside the final furlong.

Firebreak's season had also started on a high note when he collected the Godolphin Mile on dirt at the Dubai World Cup meeting for a second successive year. Taking up the running two furlongs out, he pulled four and a half lengths clear of Tropical Star. Shipped to Newmarket after wintering in Dubai with the rest of the Godolphin string, Firebreak reappeared in the Lockinge Stakes at Newbury, along with his shorter-priced stablemate Refuse to Bend. Tracking the leaders under Kerrin McEvoy, Firebreak looked a possible winner three furlongs out, but his effort petered out inside the final furlong and he finished fourth, a length and three quarters behind the winner Russian Rhythm. Firebreak was not seen out again until the Park Stakes at Doncaster in September, when he was sent off a well-supported 5/2 favourite. Racing prominently as usual, he tracked Naahy in the centre of the track, holding every chance, but was unable to contain the three-year-old Pastoral Pursuits, who was receiving 5 lb more than weight-for-age, going down by a length and a quarter.

Cathay Pacific Hong Kong Mile, Sha Tin—Firebreak (third left) keeps on well to win from the locals
Perfect Partner (second left), The Duke (outside, star on cap) and Scintillation (left)

Firebreak (b.h. 1999)	Charnwood Forest (IRE) (b or br 1992)	Warning (b 1985)	Known Fact
			Slightly Dangerous
		Dance of Leaves (b 1987)	Sadler's Wells
			Fall Aspen
	Breakaway (b 1985)	Song (b 1966)	Sing Sing
			Intent
		Catherine Howard (ch 1977)	Tower Walk
			Righteous Girl

Firebreak is a smallish, leggy, quite attractive horse who was tongue tied on all his starts in 2004. He remains in training in 2005, when a bid for a third successive Godolphin Mile is likely to be on his agenda before contesting some of the better mile races in Europe. He is the seventh foal out of the useful sprinter Breakaway and is a half-brother to several winners, notably the useful miler Sharplaw Venture (by Polar Falcon). Firebreak is effective at six furlongs to a mile. He is unraced on heavy but acts on any other turf going and on dirt. He is game and consistent. *Saeed bin Suroor*

FIRE CAT 5 ch.g. Beveled (USA) – Noble Soul 67 (Sayf El Arab (USA) 127) [2004 58: f7g f6g 5.1d 6s 5g 5f⁶ Jun 25] little form in 2004: occasionally wears cheekpieces. *A. P. Jones* —

FIRE DOME (IRE) 12 ch.g. Salt Dome (USA) – Penny Habit (Habitat 134) [2004 72: p7g Feb 28] rangy gelding: on the downgrade, and well held only 12-y-o start: tried blinkered/visored/tongue tied. *Andrew Reid* —

FIRE DRAGON (IRE) 3 b.g. Sadler's Wells (USA) 132 – Cattermole (USA) (Roberto (USA) 131) [2004 –: 11s⁴ 12d* 12.3d⁵ 14d⁴ Aug 12] half-brother to several winners, including smart French 1½m/13f winner Spendent (by Generous) and useful 1½m winner Scattergun (by Rainbow Quest): dam, French 8.5f winner, half-sister to very smart 7f performer Condrillac from very good US family: fairly useful performer: won handicap at Killarney in May on final start for D. Wachman in Ireland: creditable efforts in Britain after (wandered final outing): probably stays 1¾m: acts on good to soft going: wore blinkers/cheekpieces in 2004: fair hurdler. *Jonjo O'Neill* — **80**

FIRE FINCH 3 ch.f. Halling (USA) 133 – Fly For Fame (Shaadi (USA) 126) [2004 8g⁶ 10g⁶ 8f 12m⁶ Jul 14] third foal: half-sister to 1¼m winner Fittonia (by Ashkalani) and French 6f (at 2 yrs) to 9.8f winner Charlepierre (by Bering): dam useful French 1¼m (at 2 yrs)/1½m winner: signs of ability (sixth of 7 in listed race at Newbury second start): has looked reluctant. *M. R. Channon* —

FIRENZE 3 ch.f. Efisio 120 – Juliet Bravo 61 (Glow (USA)) [2004 5.2m f6g* Jul 23] strong, lengthy filly: first foal: sister to 5-y-o Frizzante, closely related to fairly useful 5f/6f winner Glowing (by Chilibang) and half-sister to 7.6f (at 2 yrs) to 1¼m winner Colonel Mustard (by Keen): dam 2-y-o 5f winner: much better effort in maidens (fair form) when winning at Southwell by ¾ length from Stargem, leading inside final 1f after slow start: should improve further. *J. R. Fanshawe* — **69 p**

FIRESONG 2 b.c. (Mar 21) Dansili 127 – Leaping Flame (USA) (Trempolino (USA) 135) [2004 7g⁶ Oct 12] big, leggy colt: has a round action: second foal: half-brother to 3-y-o Zaffeu: dam, French 7f winner, half-sister to smart performers up to/around 1m Apple of Kent and War Zone: 40/1, burly and very green, sixth to Eqdaam in maiden at Leicester, slowly away and going on strongly at finish despite wandering: will stay 1m: sure to do better. *S. Kirk* — **71 p**

FIRE UP THE BAND 5 b.h. Prince Sabo 123 – Green Supreme (Primo Dominie 121) [2004 116: p5g 6g 6g³ 6s⁴ 6f 5.1g* 5m 5s 5.8g 6s Sep 18] lengthy, good-topped horse: useful performer: won listed race at Chester (beat Talbot Avenue by short head) in July: effective at 5f/6f: acts on polytrack, firm and good to soft going, below form on soft: tried visored: often makes running: none too consistent. *D. Nicholls* — **102**

FIREWIRE 6 b.g. Blushing Flame (USA) 109 – Bay Risk (Risk Me (FR) 127) [2004 71: 8.3m* 9g Jul 7] smallish, workmanlike gelding: fair handicapper: won at Windsor in June: effective at 1m/1¼m: acts on good to firm going, and below good and polytrack: has been slowly away/reluctant to race: usually waited with. *Miss B. Sanders* — **70**

FIREWORK 6 b.g. Primo Dominie 121 – Prancing 98 (Prince Sabo 123) [2004 72: p6g p6g p6g 6s⁶ 6m 6f* 6m 6g⁴ 6.1m⁴ p6g Dec 4] quite attractive gelding: fair performer: won claimer at Folkestone in June: raced mainly at 6f: acts on fibresand, firm and soft ground: tried blinkered/visored: usually wears cheekpieces: races up with pace. *J. Akehurst* — **64**

FIROZI 5 b.m. Forzando 122 – Lambast 70 (Relkino 131) [2004 54: 7.9m⁵ Aug 2] **51**
smallish, workmanlike mare: modest handicapper: stays 1¼m: acts on firm going, probably on soft: tried blinkered/in cheekpieces. *R. A. Fahey*

FIRST CANDLELIGHT 3 b.f. First Trump 118 – No Candles Tonight 74 (Star **78 ?**
Appeal 133) [2004 82p: 8s 7m 7m 7.1m Aug 11] tall, quite good-topped filly: fair performer: should stay at least 1m: acts on good to firm and good to soft ground. *J. G. Given*

FIRST CENTURION 3 b.c. Peintre Celebre (USA) 137 – Valley of Hope (USA) **85**
(Riverman (USA) 131) [2004 68p: 8v* 10m 11.9d 10m⁴ 13.1s⁵ p12g Oct 25] sturdy colt:
fairly useful performer: won maiden at Kempton in May by 5 lengths: failed to repeat
form in handicaps: should stay 13f: acts on heavy going, below form on polytrack: sold
30,000 gns. *J. W. Hills*

FIRST CHARTER 5 b.h. Polish Precedent (USA) 131 – By Charter 104 (Shirley **119**
Heights 130) [2004 119: 13.4d 12m* 12m² 15.9d* 14g³ Sep 18] lengthy, quite attractive
horse: smart performer: won listed race at Newmarket (by ½ length from Westmoreland
Road) in June and Weatherbys Insurance Lonsdale Cup at York (by neck from Dancing
Bay, leading over 1f out and edging left) in August: good placed efforts when neck second
to Alkaased in listed race at Goodwood and 3 lengths third to Vinnie Roe in Irish St Leger
at the Curragh: stays 2m: acts on good to firm and good to soft going: reportedly sold, and
to join T. McEvoy in Australia. *Sir Michael Stoute*

FIRST CLASS GIRL 5 b.m. Charmer 123 – Boulevard Girl 80 (Nicholas Bill 125) **–**
[2004 f12g⁴ 10m May 31] tall, quite good-topped mare: no form. *C. B. B. Booth*

FIRST CLASS LADY 4 ch.f. Lion Cavern (USA) 117 – Tino-Ella 73 (Bustino 136) **–**
[2004 51: p8g⁵ p12g Feb 23] maiden: no form in 2004. *P. Mitchell*

FIRST COUNSEL 3 b.g. Wolfhound (USA) 126 – Supreme Kingdom 85 (Take A Reef **75**
127) [2004 8.1m⁵ 8.1d³ Jun 4] tall, lengthy gelding: half-brother to 3 winners, including
fairly useful 7f to 9f winner Equerry (by Midyan): dam 2-y-o 7f winner who became
temperamental: fair form in maidens at Haydock, coltish and edgy when third to Invasian:
subsequently gelded: not sure to stay beyond 1m. *M. A. Jarvis*

FIRST DAWN 3 ch.f. Dr Fong (USA) 128 – Delight of Dawn 74 (Never So Bold 135) **57**
[2004 68: 7m 7g 8g 8.1g Sep 3] leggy filly: just modest maiden at 3 yrs. *M. R. Channon*

FIRST DYNASTY (USA) 4 br. or b.c. Danzig (USA) – Willow Runner (USA) (Aly- **74**
dar (USA)) [2004 77: f9.4g* 8.1s 8.5m⁶ 10g³ 11.7s Oct 19] $325,000Y: closely related/ **a80**
half-brother to several winners in USA, notably very smart US Grade 2 9f winner who
stayed 1¼m Trail City (by Red Ransom): dam minor winner in USA: fairly useful on
all-weather, fair on turf: left A. O'Brien in Ireland prior to winning maiden at Wolverhampton in April: stays 9.4f: acts on fibresand, firm and soft ground: wore cheekpieces
(failed to stay) final outing. *Miss S. J. Wilton*

FIRST EAGLE 5 b.g. Hector Protector (USA) 124 – Merlin's Fancy 62 (Caerleon **44**
(USA) 132) [2004 –, a54: f9.4g 10f³ Sep 16] rather unfurnished gelding: poor maiden:
left Mrs N. Macauley after reappearance: barely stays 1½m: acts on all-weather and firm
ground: usually wears headgear. *A. L. Forbes*

*Weatherbys Insurance Lonsdale Cup, York—First Charter responds well to win his first pattern race,
beating Dancing Bay (right) narrowly; Millenary (left) is third with Swing Wing fourth*

FIRST ECLIPSE (IRE) 3 b.f. Fayruz 116 – Naked Poser (IRE) 83 (Night Shift – (USA)) [2004 66d: 5m 5g Jul 31] good-topped filly: modest performer: well held in 2004: blinkered (slowly away) once. *J. Balding*

FIRST FOUGHT (IRE) 2 b.g. (Apr 26) Germany (USA) 124 – Royal Flame (IRE) – p 72 (Royal Academy (USA) 130) [2004 8s Oct 27] first foal: dam 1¼m winner: 33/1, well held in maiden at Yarmouth, green then fading: likely to do better. *M. Johnston*

FIRST MAITE 11 b.g. Komaite (USA) – Marina Plata (Julio Mariner 127) [2004 66, **57** a79: f8g⁶ f8.5g⁶ f8s⁶ f12g⁴ 10m³ 8.1f² f8g³ 10m⁵ p7.1g⁵ Nov 29] tall, lengthy gelding: **a69** has a round action: fair on all-weather, modest on turf: stays 1¼m: acts on fibresand, soft and firm going: occasionally blinkered/visored: tried tongue tied. *S. R. Bowring*

FIRST OF MAY 3 b.f. Halling (USA) 133 – Finger of Light 89 (Green Desert (USA) **52** 127) [2004 60p: p7g³ p8g⁴ p8g⁶ p8m p10m⁶ Dec 15] unfurnished filly: modest maiden: left M. Jarvis after third start: probably stays 1¼m. *Miss Z. C. Davison*

FIRST ORDER 3 b.g. Primo Dominie 121 – Unconditional Love (IRE) 104 (Polish **105 d** Patriot (USA) 128) [2004 99: 5g² 5m 5.1g⁶ 5g² Sep 15] quite good-topped gelding: useful performer: best effort when neck second to Connect in handicap at Newmarket on reappearance: disappointing after, carrying head high and finding little when second to Ok Pal in claimer at Sandown (claimed to join Andrew Reid £20,000) final start: should stay 6f: acts on firm ground: tends to swish tail. *Sir Mark Prescott*

FIRST RHAPSODY (IRE) 2 b.f. (Apr 14) Rossini (USA) 118 – Tinos Island (IRE) **58** (Alzao (USA) 117) [2004 5m 6f p6g⁴ p7.1g p8.6g⁵ Dec 1] €5,500Y: good-bodied filly: third foal: half-sister to 3-y-o Mister Trickster: dam ran 3 times: modest maiden: barely stays 8.6f: acts on polytrack. *T. J. Etherington*

FIRST ROW (IRE) 2 b.c. (Feb 1) Daylami (IRE) 138 – Ballet Society (FR) (Sadler's **73 p** Wells (USA) 132) [2004 7.1m⁵ Jul 21] 220,000Y: seventh foal: half-brother to 3 winners, including fairly useful 1¼m/1½m winner Secret Ballot (by Taufan) and 4-y-o Swift Tango: dam, ran once, closely related to 2000 Guineas runner-up Enrique out of smart sprinter Gwydion: 20/1, fifth in maiden at Sandown, not knocked about (bolted to post/blanketed for stall entry): should improve. *B. J. Meehan*

FIRST RULE 2 ch.c. (Mar 21) Primo Dominie 121 – Tarsa 81 (Ballad Rock 122) [2004 **67** 5v 5m⁴ 5m⁴ 5m 6m Sep 21] 29,000F, 37,000Y: compact colt: brother to Italian 1994 2-y-o 6f winner Nota Azzurra and half-brother to several winners, including 3-y-o Burley Flame: dam, 6f winner, later successful in Italy: fair maiden: should stay 6f: acts on good to firm ground: sent to Oman. *C. F. Wall*

FISBY 3 ch.g. Efisio 120 – Trilby 72 (In The Wings 128) [2004 –: p8g⁵ 8.3f⁵ 6d 8g 8m **77** p8.6d* p7.1g² p9.5g* Dec 6] sturdy gelding: fair performer: won minor event at Wolverhampton in November and handicap on same course in December: should stay 1¼m: acts on polytrack. *S. Kirk*

FISHER'S DREAM 3 b.g. Groom Dancer (USA) 128 – Cremets 94 (Mummy's Pet – 125) [2004 55: f6g f6g Dec 1] leggy, angular gelding: maiden: well held in 2004: usually visored. *J. R. Norton*

FISHLAKE FLYER (IRE) 3 b.f. Desert Style (IRE) 121 – Millitrix 82 (Doyoun **59 §** 124) [2004 76§: 5s⁴ 5m³ 5f⁴ Jul 21] lengthy, useful-looking filly: modest maiden: raced only at 5f: acts on firm and good to soft going: below form in visor: temperamental. *J. G. Given*

FISIO THERAPY 4 b.g. Efisio 120 – Corn Lily 78 (Aragon 118) [2004 90: 8g 10.5d⁴ **85** 10.3d May 6] smallish, good-topped gelding: fairly useful handicapper: stayed 10.5f: acted on soft and good to firm ground: dead. *M. Johnston*

FISSION 3 ch.f. Efisio 120 – Area Girl 76 (Jareer (USA) 115) [2004 68, a77: f6g⁶ f7g³ **76** p7g* p7g 6m² 6s p6g⁴ Nov 12] lengthy filly: fair performer: won claimer at Lingfield in February: stays easy 7f: acts on all-weather and good to firm ground: often blinkered: often gives trouble at start and was banned from Flat races started with stalls for 6 months after fourth outing (final one for J. Osborne). *Mrs Stef Liddiard*

FITTING GUEST (IRE) 3 ch.g. Grand Lodge (USA) 125 – Sarah-Clare 67 (Reach **76** 122) [2004 64: 10s⁶ 9.9g² 10m² 10m* 8m Jun 17] good-topped gelding: unimpressive mover: fair performer: won minor event at Leicester in June: stays 1¼m: acts on good to firm going: usually races prominently: sold 20,000 gns in October, then gelded. *G. G. Margarson*

FIT TO FLY (IRE) 3 b.g. Lahib (USA) 129 – Maid of Mourne (Fairy King (USA)) **79 d** [2004 72: f6s² p7g⁵ f6s* 8.1m⁵ f7g⁶ 10s 8g⁵ 10.5g f8g 8g p12.2g p7.1d f8g⁴ f8s⁶ p8.6g

Nov 27] fair performer: won maiden at Southwell in March: claimed from S. Kirk £14,000 seventh start: below form after: stays 1m: acts on all-weather and good to firm going: tried in cheekpieces/visor. *Mrs J. Candlish*

FITZ THE BILL (IRE)   4 b.f. Mon Tresor 113 – In The Sky (IRE) 70 (Imp Society (USA)) [2004 –: p8g p12g p10g3 10.1g3 10m 10.1m 16m Jul 26] sparely-made filly: poor maiden: stays 1¼m: tried blinkered/tongue tied. *N. B. King*   **45**

FITZWARREN   3 b.g. Presidium 124 – Coney Hills 35 (Beverley Boy 99) [2004 72: 6m 5d3 5d 5g 6g3 6m6 6f 5f6 6.1m 7d Oct 15] small gelding: fair handicapper at best: effective at 5f/6f: acts on firm and good to soft going: often visored, tried tongue tied: sometimes slowly away: often races up with pace. *N. Bycroft*   **70 d**

FIVE DYNASTIES (USA)   3 b.c. Danehill (USA) 126 – Star Begonia 110 (Sadler's Wells (USA) 132) [2004 98p: 11.5s3 12g 12m* 12f Jun 27] quite good-topped, attractive colt: second foal: brother to Irish 1¼m winner/Irish Derby third Roosevelt: dam, 1½m winner (second in Ribblesdale Stakes), sister to very smart French winner up to 1½m Poliglote: smart performer: won maiden at Tralee at 2 yrs: creditable eighth in Prix du Jockey Club at Chantilly second start: justified favouritism in 5-runner King Edward VII Stakes at Royal Ascot in June by 4 lengths from Elshadi, tending to hang but driven clear from over 1f out: well held in Irish Derby at the Curragh final start: stays 1½m: acts on firm and good to soft going: seemed unsuited by track at Lingfield on reappearance: sent to Hong Kong. *A. P. O'Brien, Ireland*   **111**

FIVE GOLD (IRE)   3 b.g. Desert Prince (IRE) 130 – Ceide Dancer (IRE) 79 (Alzao (USA) 117) [2004 75: 7.1g 7m 7m 7.1d 10s Oct 30] workmanlike gelding: little form in 2004, leaving B. R. Millman after fourth start. *A. C. Whillans*   **–**

FIVEOCLOCK EXPRESS (IRE)   4 gr.g. Woodborough (USA) 112 – Brooks Masquerade (Absalom 128) [2004 92, a100: p7g4 7d2 7s 7m 8f5 p8g2 7m 6g 8d 7g p8.6g p12g p9.5g p7.1g3 p7.1g f8g Dec 28] deep-girthed gelding: useful performer at best on all-weather, fairly useful on turf: effective at 7f/1m: acts on all-weather, firm and good to soft going: often wears visor/cheekpieces: becoming temperamental. *Miss Gay Kelleway*   **86 d / a95 d**

FIVE YEARS ON (IRE)   3 b.g. Desert Sun 120 – Snowspin 75 (Carwhite 127) [2004 68p: 8g4 8g4 8g5 Oct 9] good-topped gelding: fair maiden: stays 1m: acts on polytrack, best turf effort on good going. *W. J. Haggas*   **73**

FIZZY LADY   3 b.f. Efisio 120 – The Frog Lady (IRE) 52 (Al Hareb (USA) 123) [2004 70: p8g4 f6g4 7g7* 7m 8.1g 7m 8d 7.1g 8.1m2 10.2s4 10m 10g* 11d f8g p12.2g Nov 29] small, sturdy filly: modest performer: won seller at Southwell (sold from B. Hills 8,000 gns) in February and apprentice selling handicap at Nottingham in September: stays 1¼m: acts on all-weather, good to firm and good to soft ground: often tongue tied, including for first win: unreliable. *N. E. Berry*   **58 §**

FIZZY LIZZY   4 b.f. Cool Jazz 116 – Formidable Liz 66 (Formidable (USA) 125) [2004 52d: 6m f6g 6d 5.9f* f6g p6g Dec 30] dipped-backed filly: poor performer: won claimer at Carlisle (claimed from J. O'Keeffe £2,500) in July: effective at 5f/6f: acts on firm going: tried in cheekpeices: none too consistent. *G. A. Ham*   **42**

FIZZY POP   5 b.m. Robellino (USA) 127 – Maria Isabella (FR) (Young Generation 129) [2004 7m6 9.2d Aug 23] 24,000F, 35,000Y: half-sister to several winners, including 1½m winner Rain In Spain and 7.5f (at 2 yrs) to 10.5f winner in Italy Streisand (both useful, by Unfuwain): dam French maiden: looked temperamental in bumpers: always behind in maidens: withdrawn after refusing to enter stalls in September. *W. S. Cunningham*   **–**

King Edward VII Stakes, Royal Ascot—
Five Dynasties justifies favouritism from Elshadi, Barati, Haadef (right) and Gold History (rail)
in a disappointing turn-out following the withdrawal of African Dream and Rule of Law

FLAG LIEUTENANT   2 b.c. (Feb 26) Machiavellian (USA) 123 – Fairy Godmother **79 p**
113 (Fairy King (USA)) [2004 7g² Oct 12] strong, compact colt: first foal: dam, 1¼m
winner, half-sister to very smart middle-distance stayer Blueprint from family of Nashwan, Nayef and Unfuwain: 12/1, green and shade coltish, ½-length second to Eqdaam in
maiden at Leicester, held up and running on strongly: should stay at least 1¼m: sure to
improve, and should win a race or 2. *Sir Michael Stoute*

FLAG POINT (IRE)   2 b.c. (Apr 4) Indian Danehill (IRE) 124 – Bianca Cappello **68**
(IRE) (Glenstal (USA) 118) [2004 7g³ 7.6m 7g 8g 8d Nov 5] 18,000Y: leggy, close-
coupled colt: closely related to fairly useful 7f winner Gemini Future (by Flying
Spur) and half-brother to useful 2000 2-y-o 6f/6.5f winner Potaro (by Catrail), later
successful up to 1¼m in USA: dam, no form, half-sister to smart Irish 7f to 1¼m performer Idris: fair maiden: probably stays 1m: best efforts on good going. *J. L. Dunlop*

FLAMAND (USA)   2 ch.f. (Mar 23) Miswaki (USA) 124 – Sister Sorrow (USA) (Holy **72**
Bull (USA) 134) [2004 6f5 p7.1g⁴ p7.1g² Nov 27] $7,000F, $16,00Y resold €45,000Y:
angular, quite good-bodied filly: fluent mover: third foal: half-sister to a winner in
Canada by Honour And Glory: dam unraced: fair maiden: made running when 1½ lengths
second to Triple Two at Wolverhampton: should stay at least 1m. *L. M. Cumani*

FLAMBE   6 b.g. Whittingham (IRE) 104 – Uae Flame (IRE) (Polish Precedent (USA) **–**
131) [2004 –, a56: f8g⁴ Jan 5] good-topped gelding: modest handicapper: stayed 9.4f: **a60**
acted on fibresand and firm going: tried blinkered/tongue tied: dead. *P. C. Haslam*

FLAMBOYANT LAD   3 ch.c. Nashwan (USA) 135 – Cheeky Charm (USA) 56 (Nur- **95**
eyev (USA) 131) [2004 86p: 10.3g³ 10m³ 10g³ 10m² 10f* 10g* 12d* Oct 14] big, lengthy
colt: has a quick action: useful performer: won maiden at Pontefract in September and 2
handicaps at Newmarket in October, beating Big Moment by head for final success: stays
1½m: acts on firm and soft ground. *B. W. Hills*

FLAMENCO BRIDE   4 b.f. Hernando (FR) 127 – Premier Night 102 (Old Vic 136) **76**
[2004 79: 12d 16.2m 14.4m³ 14.1g Sep 29] good-topped filly: fair handicapper: stays
1¾m: acts on good to firm ground: front tongue tied: sold 8,500 gns. *D. R. C. Elsworth*

FLAME OF ZARA   5 ch.m. Blushing Flame (USA) 109 – Sierra Madrona (USA) **57**
(Woodman (USA) 126) [2004 60?: 16.1v 14.1g⁴ 15s Oct 11] lengthy mare: modest maid-
en: left M. Reveley after second outing: stays 1¾m: best efforts on good ground or
softer: carries head awkwardly. *James Moffatt*

FLAME PRINCESS   4 ch.f. Bluegrass Prince (IRE) 110 – Rekindled Flame (IRE) **46**
(Kings Lake (USA) 133) [2004 –: p6g³ p6g p8g p7g Mar 14] poor maiden: stays 6f: acts
on polytrack. *J. R. Boyle*

FLAME QUEEN   3 b.f. The West (USA) 107 – Red Cloud (IRE) 61 (Taufan (USA) **57**
119) [2004 73: 7m 8.1g 8.3f 7f⁴ 8d 10m⁴ 10.1g 8m 8g Oct 12] leggy filly: modest maiden:
left Miss K. Boutflower after fourth start: free-going sort, and barely stays 1m: acts on
firm ground: races up with pace. *Mrs C. A. Dunnett*

FLAMING EYES (GER)   3 b.f. Imperial Ballet (IRE) 110 – Fantastic Flame (IRE) **72**
79 (Generous (IRE) 139) [2004 78: 10m 10m 7m 8v p12.2g* p13g Dec 29] 155,000Y:
third foal: half-sister to useful 2002 2-y-o 8.5f winner Bahamian Dancer (by Bering),
later successful up to 1½m in Hong Kong, and fairly useful 1½m winner Flaming Salsa
(by Salse): dam, 1¼m winner, sister to smart 1¼m/1½m performer Germano: fair performer: left D. Weld in Ireland after fourth start: won maiden at Wolverhampton in
December on British debut, dictating: stays easy 1½m: acts on polytrack and firm going:
tried blinkered. *W. R. Swinburn*

FLAMINGO PALACE   3 ch.g. Croco Rouge (IRE) 126 – Chantilly (FR) (Sanglamore **–**
(USA) 126) [2004 12m May 22] big, workmanlike gelding: tailed off in maiden at
Newmarket. *P. J. McBride*

FLAMING SPIRT   5 b.m. Blushing Flame (USA) 109 – Fair Test 95 (Fair Season **57 §**
120) [2004 –§: p10d⁴ 11.6g⁴ 10d² 10s Aug 24] lengthy mare: modest handicapper: stays
11.6f: acts on all-weather and good to soft going: sometimes slowly away: unreliable.
J. S. Moore

FLAMING WEAPON   2 b.g. (Mar 22) Unfuwain (USA) 131 – Flame Valley (USA) **–**
112 (Gulch (USA)) [2004 p8g p8.6g Dec 17] 35,000Y: good-bodied colt: fourth foal:
half-brother to fairly useful 2001 2-y-o 1m winner Aglow (by Spinning World): dam,
1¼m winner, out of sister to Prix de la Salamandre winner Common Grounds and half-
sister to dam of Derby winner Kris Kin: well held in maidens: withdrawn after refusing to
enter stall intended debut. *J. W. Hills*

FLAMJICA (USA)   3 ch.f. Real Quiet (USA) 131 – Fiamma (IRE) 97 (Irish River   **72** (FR) 131) [2004 81?: 8m⁴ 8m² Jun 19] leggy filly: fair maiden, lightly raced: should stay at least 1¼m. *J. A. R. Toller*

FLAPDOODLE   6 b.m. Superpower 113 – My Concordia 58 (Belfort (FR) 89) [2004   **53** 63: 5g⁵ 5.1f 5.1m 5m 5g³ 6d 5d⁵ p5.1g Oct 25] modest performer: best at 5f: acts on fibresand, firm and good to soft going: sometimes blinkered/visored: races prominently: sometimes hangs. *A. W. Carroll*

FLARAN   4 b.g. Emarati (USA) 74 – Fragrance (Mtoto 134) [2004 67: 5m 6g 5g³ 6g³   **72** p5.1g² Nov 11] smallish, rather dipped-backed gelding: fair handicapper: trained by A. Stewart on reappearance: best at 5f/6f: acts on polytrack and good to firm ground. *E. F. Vaughan*

FLASHING BLADE   4 b.f. Inchinor 119 – Finlaggan 83 (Be My Chief (USA) 122)   **71** [2004 90?: 6g 6s 5.1g 6g 6f 8.2g* 8.2s 7d⁶ 7m⁵ 6d 8m² Sep 4] good-topped filly: fair performer: won maiden at Nottingham in June: stays 1m: acts on firm and good to soft going: races freely: visored in cheekpieces: usually tongue tied: sold 36,000 gns. *B. A. McMahon*

FLASH RAM   3 b.g. Mind Games 121 – Just A Gem (Superlative 118) [2004 64: 5.1g⁶   **68** 7m⁴ 6m² 7d² 6m⁶ 6.9f* 6g⁶ 7.1g³ 7.9m Sep 5] lengthy gelding: fair performer: won maiden at Carlisle in July: finished lame final start: effective at 6f/7f: acts on firm and good to soft going: effective blinkered/visored or not: consistent. *T. D. Easterby*

FLAUNTING IT (IRE)   2 ch.f. (Jan 25) Alhaarth (IRE) 126 – Ide Say (IRE) (Grand   **58 d** Lodge (USA) 125) [2004 7m⁵ 7d 6s⁴ 7g⁶ f8g p6g⁴ p7.1g Nov 26] 18,000F, 40,000Y: lengthy filly: second foal: dam unraced half-sister to smart 1m/1¼m performer Spindrift: modest maiden: should stay 1m: best effort on good to firm going: tried blinkered: sometimes slowly away, markedly so final outing. *J. A. Osborne*

FLAUNT N FLIRT   2 b.f. (Apr 20) Erhaab (USA) 127 – Lets Fall In Love (USA) (Nor-   **68** thern Baby (CAN) 127) [2004 6g p7g p7.1d² p7.1g Nov 20] half-sister to several winners, including 1996 2-y-o 5f winner Heart Throb (by Statoblest), later 7f winner in Germany, and 2003 2-y-o 1m winner Good To Go (by Deploy): dam winning sprinter in USA: fair maiden: second at Wolverhampton: will stay 1m: twice slowly away. *M. P. Tregoning*

FLAXBY   2 b.g. (Apr 30) Mister Baileys 123 – Harryana 79 (Efisio 120) [2004 6s 6g   **73** 6m⁴ 6s Oct 22] 9,000Y: strong gelding: first foal: dam 2-y-o 5f winner: fair maiden: good eighth in sales race at Doncaster final start: likely to stay 7f. *J. D. Bethell*

FLEET ANCHOR   3 b.c. Fleetwood (IRE) 107 – Upping The Tempo (Dunbeath   **61** (USA) 127) [2004 67: 6.1m 6d 6m 7.1s² 6.1d⁵ 8g³ 8.1s⁵ 8d Oct 29] good-topped colt: modest maiden handicapper: stays 1m: acts on soft going. *J. M. Bradley*

FLEETFOOT MAC   3 b.g. Fleetwood (IRE) 107 – Desert Flower (Green Desert   **68** (USA) 127) [2004 61: 12.1d* 11.6s* 14d 12.3g f12g³ 11.6g⁴ 12.1m 16.2g Aug 30] compact gelding: fair performer: won claimer at Chepstow in April and handicap at Windsor in May: stays 1½m: acts on fibresand, soft and good to firm going: visored (ran poorly) final start: usually races prominently. *P. D. Evans*

FLEETING MOON   4 ch.f. Fleetwood (IRE) 107 – Aunt Judy (Great Nephew 126)   **70** [2004 –p: p12g² p13g² f11s* p16g³ 13.1m² p12g⁴ Jul 7] fair performer: won maiden at Southwell in February: stays 2m: raced only on all-weather and good to firm ground. *A. M. Balding*

FLEETWOOD BAY   4 b.g. Fleetwood (IRE) 107 – Caviar And Candy 47 (Soviet Star   **74** (USA) 128) [2004 76: 7d 6s 8.1s⁶ 7.6g³ 7g⁶ 7.1g 8m² 8m⁶ 8d 6.1g p7g Dec 4] workman-like gelding: has a round action: fair handicapper: stays 1m: acts on polytrack, soft and good to firm going: tried tongue tied: usually races prominently. *B. R. Millman*

FLETCHER   10 b.g. Salse (USA) 128 – Ballet Classique (USA) 84 (Sadler's Wells   **52 d** (USA) 132) [2004 49, a–: p13g 11.9m⁵ p16g* 14.1m 12f 17.2f 14.1f⁴ Jul 29] useful-looking gelding: modest performer: won banded race at Lingfield in April: below form after: effective at 1½m to 2m: acts on polytrack, firm and soft ground: tried visored/in cheekpieces: sometimes looks none too keen. *H. Morrison*

FLIGHT COMMANDER (IRE)   4 b.g. In The Wings 128 – Lucrezia (IRE) 89   **60** (Machiavellian (USA) 123) [2004 65: 9.2d⁵ 10.1g 11.9s 15s 12d Nov 3] modest maiden: reportedly split a pastern after final appearance in 2003: well held last 3 outings, including in visor: should stay 1¾m. *I. Semple*

FLIGHT OF ESTEEM   4 b.g. Mark of Esteem (IRE) 137 – Miss Up N Go (Gorytus   **100** (USA) 132) [2004 99: p12g² p12g² Jan 24] lengthy, quite good-topped gelding: useful handicapper: good second at Lingfield both starts in 2004, beaten 1½ lengths by Cold

Turkey in latter: stays 1½m: acts on polytrack, raced only on good going or firmer on turf: carries head awkwardly: races prominently: consistent. *P. W. Harris*

FLIGHTY FELLOW (IRE) 4 ch.g. Flying Spur (AUS) – Al Theraab (USA) 81 **103** (Roberto (USA) 131) [2004 101: 8g 8v⁶ 8.5g* 8f 8.1g⁶ 7.9d² 8m⁴ 10.5g 8f⁴ 8m³ 7.9g Oct 8] tall, quite good-topped gelding: useful handicapper: won at Beverley in May by 1¾ lengths from Ace of Hearts: some good efforts after, including when third to Welcome Stranger at Ascot penultimate outing: effective at 1m to easy 1¼m: acts on firm and soft ground: effective blinkered or not: no easy ride (tends to wander). *T. D. Easterby*

FLING 3 b.f. Pursuit of Love 124 – Full Orchestra 83 (Shirley Heights 130) [2004 10s* **89** 10m⁵ 10m² 12d² 10.5s⁴ 14.1s⁵ 16d³ 16.5s⁴ Nov 6] leggy filly: sister to 2000 2-y-o 8.5f winner Seductive, later 1m to 10.5f winner in Switzerland, and half-sister to several winners, including useful 6f (at 2 yrs) and 9f winner Rudimental (by Rudimentary): dam 1¼m winner: fairly useful performer: won maiden at Southwell in April: mostly creditable efforts after: stays 2m: acts on soft and good to firm ground: often slowly away: looks difficult ride. *J. R. Fanshawe*

FLINT RIVER 6 b.g. Red Ransom (USA) – She's All Class (USA) (Rahy (USA) 115) **82** [2004 83, a93: f6g² f6g f8.5s p7g f7g* 7.1g² 7.6d⁴ 7g 7g 8f² 8s² 8.5g⁵ p7.1g p8.6g Nov 8] **a92** close-coupled gelding: fairly useful handicapper, better on all-weather than turf: won at Wolverhampton in March: effective at 6f to easy 8.5f: acts on all-weather, firm and soft going: tried blinkered earlier in career. *H. Morrison*

FLIPANDO (IRE) 3 b.g. Sri Pekan (USA) 117 – Magic Touch (Fairy King (USA)) **98** [2004 79: 6s⁴ 6m² 7m² 6g* 6g⁵ 7g³ 8g* Sep 11] tall gelding: useful handicapper: steadily progressive, and won at Haydock in July and Musselburgh (beat Mrs Moh by ½ length) in September: effective at 6f to 1m: acts on firm going: sometimes races freely: genuine. *T. D. Barron*

FLIP FLOP AND FLY (IRE) 3 b.g. Woodborough (USA) 112 – Angelus Chimes **88** 80 (Northfields (USA)) [2004 94: 8g 6s 7m* 7m 8d⁶ 7.1m² 7.1m⁵ 8m Sep 4] strong, sturdy gelding: fairly useful handicapper: won at Lingfield in May: stays 7f: acts on good to firm going: blinkered (well beaten) once: sometimes hangs left, markedly so final start: sold 26,000 gns, sent to Switzerland. *S. Kirk*

FLITE OF ARABY 7 b.g. Green Desert (USA) 127 – Allegedly Blue (USA) 106 **40** (Alleged (USA) 138) [2004 p9.5g Dec 20] leggy, close-coupled gelding: maiden: off 3 years (had been hurdling), poor form only outing in 2004: stays 1½m: acts on all-weather, firm and soft going: tried visored: has played up in stall/taken good hold. *R. J. Price*

FLOOSIE (IRE) 2 b.f. (Apr 29) Night Shift (USA) – German Lady (Mon Tresor 113) **–** [2004 5m 6m p7.1g p8.6g Dec 17] 15,000Y: first foal: dam, German 7.5f/1m winner, out of half-sister to 2000 Guineas winner King of Kings: tongue tied, well held in maidens. *N. P. Littmoden*

FLORENZAR (IRE) 6 b.m. Inzar (USA) 112 – Nurse Tyra (USA) (Dr Blum (USA)) **–** [2004 58: f9.4g p10g Feb 4] modest maiden: well held in 2004. *P. D. Evans*

FLORIAN 6 b.g. Young Ern 120 – Murmuring 69 (Kind of Hush 118) [2004 74: p8d **52** 8.3m 7g 8f⁵ 7s⁶ 5.7f 6g Sep 16] rangy gelding: modest performer: stays easy 1m: acts on all-weather and good to firm going: tried in cheekpieces: often makes running: sometimes looks none too keen. *T. G. Mills*

FLORIDA HEART 3 ch.f. First Trump 118 – Miami Dancer (USA) (Seattle Dancer **72** (USA) 119) [2004 75: 8m⁴ 9d⁶ Jun 23] rather leggy, quite good-topped filly: fair handicapper: stays 1m: acts on good to firm going. *A. M. Balding*

FLOSSYTOO 2 b.f. (Mar 29) Royal Applause 124 – Nite-Owl Dancer 75 (Robellino **66 d** (USA) 127) [2004 5g 5d* 5m 5m 5g p5.1g Dec 20] leggy filly: fifth foal: half-sister to 6f winner Nite-Owl Mate (by Komaite) and 6-y-o Nite-Owl Fizz: dam 5f winner: fair performer: won maiden at Haydock in April: little other form, leaving J. O'Reilly after fifth start: should stay 6f: sometimes hangs left. *J. Balding*

FLOTTA 5 ch.g. Elmaamul (USA) 125 – Heavenly Goddess (Soviet Star (USA) 128) **93** [2004 93: p13g⁴ 12g⁵ 12m 14m⁴ 13.9m⁴ 12m³ 14d 12g* 12g⁶ 11g⁵ 12m 12d 12s⁶ p13g² Nov 10] big, plain gelding: fairly useful handicapper: won at Pontefract in August: effective at 1½m to 14.6f: acts on polytrack and firm ground, possibly not on softer than good: usually held up: consistent. *M. R. Channon*

FLOWERDRUM (USA) 4 b.f. Mister Baileys 123 – Norelands (USA) (Irish River **92** (FR) 131) [2004 90p: 7v 8m* 8.1m⁴ 8d* 8m 8m⁵ 10.1s 8m⁵ Sep 25] tall filly: fairly useful performer: won handicaps at Yarmouth in April and Salisbury in June: creditable fifth to Brindisi in listed race at Bath sixth start: stays 1m: acts on all-weather, good to firm and good to soft going: waited with: game: sent to Australia. *W. J. Haggas*

FLOWER SEEKER 2 b.f. (Apr 25) Lujain (USA) 119 – Kingpin Delight (Emarati –
(USA) 74) [2004 7.1g 7.1s 8g Sep 29] 15,000Y: fourth foal: half-sister to 3 winners,
including useful Irish 2002 2-y-o 6f winner Dixie Evans (by Efisio) and 3-y-o Delightfully: dam unraced: well held in maidens. *C. Tinkler*

FLUR NA H ALBA 5 b.g. Atraf 116 – Tyrian Belle 77 (Enchantment 115) [2004 91§: 89 §
7.2f* 7.2d 7.2g³ 6g⁴ 7.2s p7.1g³ p8.6g Nov 20] smallish, strong gelding: fairly useful
performer: won handicap at Ayr in May: effective at 6f to 1m: acts on polytrack, firm
and soft ground: tried blinkered, usually wears cheekpieces: usually races prominently:
unreliable. *I. Semple*

FLUSHING MEADOWS (USA) 3 b.c. Grand Slam (USA) 120 – Sheepish Grin 85 ?
(USA) (Our Native (USA)) [2004 6g⁵ Sep 14] half-brother to several winners in North
America, including minor stakes winner Pure Wool (by Relaunch): dam minor stakes
winner in USA: fairly useful performer: won maiden at Hollywood and allowance race at
Saratoga at 2 yrs for E. Harty in US: tongue tied, seemingly creditable fifth to Dowager in
minor event at Yarmouth only 3-y-o start: best efforts at 6f: acts on dirt. *Saeed bin Suroor*

FLYING ADORED 3 b.f. Polar Falcon (USA) 126 – Shining High 90 (Shirley Heights 87
130) [2004 74: 7s³ 8m 8g² 8s* 8.1g⁵ 10d³ 10.3s Oct 22] quite good-topped filly: fairly
useful handicapper: won twice at Goodwood in August, beating Dr Thong by 2 lengths
on second occasion: stays 1¼m: acts on soft and good to firm going. *J. L. Dunlop*

FLYING BANTAM (IRE) 3 b.g. Fayruz 116 – Natural Pearl (Petong 126) [2004 76: 88
6d² 6m² 6m² 6m⁴ 6g 6g² 5.1g⁴ 6d 6f⁴ 6g* 6g³ p6d⁴ 6s² Nov 1] small, well-made gelding:
progressed into a fairly useful performer: won maiden at Ripon in September and handicap at Wolverhampton in October: good neck second to Sir Desmond in handicap at
Redcar final start, finishing strongly: stays 6f: acts on polytrack, firm and soft ground:
tried in cheekpieces: sometimes looks difficult ride. *R. A. Fahey*

FLYING DANCER 2 b.f. (Mar 17) Danzero (AUS) – Alzianah 102 (Alzao (USA) 65
117) [2004 6m³ p6g⁴ 6f 6s p6g² Dec 29] 58,000Y: strong, close-coupled filly: sister to
fairly useful 2003 2-y-o 6f winner Desperate Dan and half-sister to several winners,
including fairly useful 5f (including at 2 yrs) winner Leozian (by Lion Cavern): dam 5f/
6f winner (including at 2 yrs): fair maiden: left A. King before second at Lingfield: will
probably stay 7f: acts on polytrack and good to firm going. *R. A. Harris*

FLYING EDGE (IRE) 4 b.g. Flying Spur (AUS) – Day Is Dawning (IRE) (Green 63
Forest (USA) 134) [2004 68: f6g f7g² f7s 6g⁵ 7m 6m⁶ 5.9f⁵ 7m 6.9g 7m 6g⁴ 6d⁴ 6d p7.1g⁴
f6g⁶ p6g⁴ Dec 17] close-coupled gelding: modest handicapper: effective at 6f/7f: acts on
all-weather, firm and soft going: tried blinkered at 3 yrs. *E. J. Alston*

FLYING EXPRESS 4 ch.c. Air Express (IRE) 125 – Royal Loft 105 (Homing 130) 91
[2004 98: 7d⁶ 8.1d 7m² 7g 7.1m³ 7.6m p7g 7m 10.5m⁶ Dec 12] lengthy, good-topped
colt: fairly useful performer: left B. Hills 13,500 gns before final outing: stays 7f: acts on
firm and good to soft going: sometimes carries head awkwardly: usually races prominently. *G. Bietolini, Italy*

FLYING FAISAL (USA) 6 b.h. Alydeed (CAN) 120 – Peaceful Silence (USA) 45
(Proper Reality (USA)) [2004 60, a54: f6g p6g f6g f6s⁶ p6g f6s⁴ p7g f6s f5g³ f5g f6m⁴
5.1d⁶ 6m* 5.3g 6g 7m 6.1m 6.1g Jun 21] sturdy horse: poor performer: won seller at
Brighton in April: effective at 5f to easy 7f: acts on fibresand, good to firm and good to
soft going: tried blinkered/tongue tied/in cheekpieces: sold £2,800. *J. M. Bradley*

FLYING HEART 2 ch.f. (Apr 9) Bahamian Bounty 116 – Flying Wind 51 (Forzando 49
122) [2004 6g 6g 6s p6g⁴ Dec 29] sixth foal: half-sister to 6f winner Master Luke (by
Contract Law) and 7f winner My Emily (by King's Signet): dam maiden who stayed 1m:
poor maiden: should stay 7f. *M. R. Channon*

FLYING HIGHEST 2 b.f. (Mar 1) Spectrum (IRE) 126 – Mainly Sunset (Red Sunset – p
120) [2004 6.1s Sep 20] 36,000Y: half-sister to several winners, including 5f winner
Antonia's Double (by Primo Dominie) and Irish 5f/6f winner Musical Sunset (by Music
Boy), both fairly useful: dam lightly-raced half-sister to very smart sprinter Bolshoi:
favourite, very green when last in maiden at Chepstow: sold 20,000 gns: should do better.
H. Candy

FLYING PASS 2 b.g. (Apr 11) Alzao (USA) 117 – Complimentary Pass 80 (Danehill 73
(USA) 126) [2004 5v 6g³ 6m 7g² p7g² 7m⁵ 6d⁶ 8f⁴ 10m² 8.3d Oct 4] 15,000F, 17,000Y:
close-coupled gelding: has a quick action: second foal: dam, ran twice, closely related to
useful sprinter Daawe: fair maiden: stays 1¼m: acts on polytrack, firm and probably good
to soft going: visored (ran respectably) seventh start. *D. J. S. ffrench Davis*

FLYING PATRIARCH   3 gr.g. Silver Patriarch (IRE) 125 – Flying Wind 51 (For-   –
zando 122) [2004 –: 10g 14g Jun 11] no form: tried blinkered. *G. L. Moore*

FLYING RED (IRE)   3 b.f. Entrepreneur 123 – Mary Ellen Best (IRE) 64 (Danehill   –
(USA) 126) [2004 11.1g Apr 26] €1,200Y: neat filly: fifth foal: dam, Irish maiden, half-
sister to Moyglare Stud Stakes winner Gayle Gal: tailed off in maiden at Hamilton.
P. A. Blockley

FLYING RIDGE (IRE)   2 ch.f. (Apr 9) Indian Ridge 123 – Jarrayan 64 (Machia-   **75**
vellian (USA) 123) [2004 6m 6g⁵ 6.1g⁵ 5g* Sep 2] 22,000Y: third foal: half-sister to
4-y-o Lark In The Park and 3-y-o Invasian: dam, maiden best at 6f at 2 yrs, out of half-
sister to dam of 7-y-o Mubtaker: fair performer: won maiden at Carlisle despite flashing
tail repeatedly: likely to prove best at 5f/6f. *A. M. Balding*

FLYING SPIRIT (IRE)   5 b.g. Flying Spur (AUS) – All Laughter (Vision (USA))   **85**
[2004 67: 11.9m* 11.9f* 12g* 11.7m 12g² Aug 30] quite good-topped gelding: fairly
useful performer: improved in 2004, winning handicap in May and amateur minor event
in June, both at Brighton, and handicap at Epsom in July: good second to Tender Falcon
in amateur handicap at Epsom final start: stays 1½m: acts on firm and good to soft going
(well held on polytrack): tried in headgear, not in 2004: races prominently. *G. L. Moore*

FLYING SPUD   3 ch.g. Fraam 114 – Lorcanjo 36 (Hallgate 127) [2004 –: f6g⁵ f7g⁴   **54**
8.1s⁵ 8.2s* 11g f8.5g 8.1m 8.5g² 8.5d 7.9g 8d⁵ p9.5d⁵ Oct 23] modest on turf, poor on   **a47**
all-weather: won selling handicap at Nottingham in May: stays 9.5f: acts on all-weather
and soft ground: none too consistent. *J. L. Spearing*

FLYING TACKLE   6 ch.g. First Trump 118 – Frighten The Life (Kings Lake (USA)   **58**
133) [2004 59: p6g 6s 5g 6f³ 5g² 5.1f* 5g 5f 5m 6g 5m² 5m p6g⁶ Dec 30] strong, lengthy
gelding: modest handicapper: won apprentice event at Bath in July: left M. Dods 2,000
gns before final start: effective at 5f/6f: acts on any turf going: usually wears headgear.
I. W. McInnes

FLYING TARA   2 b.f. (Feb 1) Kayf Tara 130 – Arcady 69 (Slip Anchor 136) [2004   –
6m May 24] third foal: dam, 13f to 2m winner, half-sister to 7-y-o Atavus: 100/1, tailed
off in maiden at Leicester. *John A. Harris*

FLYING TREATY (USA)   7 br.h. You And I (USA) 118 – Cherie's Hope (USA) (Fly-   **63 d**
ing Paster (USA)) [2004 83, a100: f6g f7g f8.5g f12s⁶ 7g 7.1g p8g⁵ 8g⁶ 10f f12s p9.5g   **a75 d**
Dec 4] useful-looking horse: has reportedly been hobdayed/had soft palate operation: just
fair performer at best in 2004: left Miss A. Stokell after sixth start: best efforts around 7f/
1m: acts on good to firm ground, better form on fibresand than polytrack: tried in headgear: usually races prominently: inconsistent. *J. L. Spearing*

FLYING WITH EAGLES   3 ch.g. Most Welcome 131 – Super Sol (Rolfe (USA) 77)   –
[2004 6m 6m 7f f7d⁶ 16.2g Jul 19] little form. *J. Jay*

FLY KICKER   7 ch.g. High Kicker (USA) – Double Birthday (Cavo Doro 124) [2004   –
40: 17.2g 15g⁶ Jul 20] poor maiden handicapper: usually wears checkpieces. *W. Storey*

FLY ME TO DUNOON (IRE)   2 b.f. (Mar 4) Rossini (USA) 118 – Toledana (IRE)   **39 ?**
(Sure Blade (USA) 130) [2004 7.1f 6d⁶ p8g Sep 22] €5,000F, €18,000Y: half-sister to 3
winners, including useful Irish 5f (including at 2 yrs)/6f winner Newpark Lady (by Foxhound): dam ran once in Ireland: seemingly poor form in maidens: visored last 2 starts.
K. R. Burke

FLY MORE   7 ch.g. Lycius (USA) 124 – Double River (USA) (Irish River (FR) 131)   –
[2004 87: 6d 5d p5.1g Nov 13] very big, lengthy gelding: well held in 2004. *J. M. Bradley*

FLYOFF (IRE)   7 b.g. Mtoto 134 – Flyleaf (FR) (Persian Bold 123) [2004 53: p12g   –
11.8m Jul 15] well held in 2004: usually blinkered/visored: makes running. *K. A. Morgan*

FLY SO HIGH   3 b.f. Danzero (AUS) – Fly The Flag (NZ) (Sir Tristram 115) [2004   **53**
p7g p7g 6g 10m 12.5s⁵ 11d⁶ 12.3s Oct 25] 11,000 2-y-o: good-topped filly: second foal:
dam, won in New Zealand, sister to Melbourne Cup winner Brew out of Japan Cup
winner Horlicks: modest maiden: left D. Shaw 26,000 gns after fourth outing: stays 12.5f:
tried visored/blinkered. *R. Pritchard-Gordon, France*

FLY TO DUBAI (IRE)   2 b.c. (Apr 13) Fly To The Stars 124 – Morna's Fan (FR)   **52**
(Lear Fan (USA) 130) [2004 6g 6d⁶ p7g Jul 21] €13,000Y: first foal: dam unraced out of
half-sister to Kentucky Derby runner-up Casual Lies: form in maidens only when sixth at
Ayr: should stay at least 1m. *E. J. O'Neill*

FOCUS GROUP (USA)   3 b.g. Kris S (USA) – Interim 117 (Sadler's Wells (USA)   **78 p**
132) [2004 9f* Sep 2] strong gelding: fourth foal: brother to French 10.5f winner Indem-

nity and half-brother to useful 1¼m/1½m winner Staging Post (by Pleasant Colony), later smart up to 1¾m in USA, and 9f winner Introducing (by Deputy Minister): dam, 1m to 1½m (US Grade 2) winner, half-sister to very smart 6f to 1m performer Interval: 9/2, won maiden at Redcar by length from Namat, staying on from rear to lead final 1f: will stay at least 1¼m: withdrawn after refusing to enter stalls (blanketed and attended by stalls expert) later in September (gelded after): should progress if temperament allows. *H. R. A. Cecil*

FOKINE (USA) 3 b.c. Royal Academy (USA) 130 – Polar Bird 111 (Thatching 131) **114** [2004 115: p7g² 7g² 7m* 7f² 6m* Dec 18] smallish, rather leggy, lengthy colt: smart performer: won listed race at Newmarket in May by neck from Peak To Creek: favourite, good 1¾ lengths second to Kheleyf in Jersey Stakes at Royal Ascot next time, leading over 1f until final 100 yds: left B. Hills, very leniently treated when winning handicap at Sha Tin in December: effective at 6f/7f: raced only on good ground or firmer on turf. *C. H. Yip, Hong Kong*

FOLD WALK 2 ch.f. (Apr 27) Paris House 123 – Georgia (Missed Flight 123) [2004 **45** 5s 5s⁴ 5g 6m 5g⁵ f6s³ 7d 7.5m Sep 15] lengthy, sparely-made filly: first foal: dam ran once in bumper: poor maiden: stays 6f: best effort on fibresand. *M. W. Easterby*

FOLEY MILLENNIUM (IRE) 6 ch.g. Tagula (IRE) 116 – Inshirah (USA) 90 (Caro **81** 133) [2004 54: 5s 5v* 5.7f* 5f* 5g* 5.1g 6m² 5.1g* 6f⁴ 5.1g² 5d 5.2g⁵ 5m⁵ 5d Oct 18] tall, lengthy gelding: fairly useful performer: won banded event at Kempton in May, seller at Bath and handicap at Warwick in June and handicap at Haydock and minor event at Nottingham in July: effective at 5f/easy 6f: acts on any going: usually front runner. *M. Quinn*

FOLEY PRINCE 3 b.g. Makbul 104 – Princess Foley (IRE) 64 (Forest Wind (USA) **77** 111) [2004 71: p7g p7g³ f7g 8.3s* 8.3m² 8.1m² 8.2g³ 8m⁶ Jul 3] lengthy gelding: fair handicapper: left D. Flood, won at Windsor in May: stays 1m: acts on polytrack, soft and good to firm ground: sometimes edgy/races freely: usually races up with pace. *Mrs Stef Liddiard*

FOLGA 2 b.f. (Mar 21) Atraf 116 – Desert Dawn 108 (Belfort (FR) 89) [2004 5f³ 5d **70** 5g* 5m⁵ Sep 27] half-sister to several winners abroad, including useful French 1m (including at 2 yrs) to 11f winner Desert Mixa (by Linamix): dam 5f performer: fair performer: trained by R. Elliott first 2 starts: won maiden at Musselburgh in September: creditable fifth in nursery at Windsor: likely to prove best at 5f: acts on good to firm going. *J. G. Given*

FOLIO (IRE) 4 b.g. Perugino (USA) 84 – Bayleaf 104 (Efisio 120) [2004 87: 7f⁶ p8m **91** Dec 21] rather leggy, useful-looking gelding: fairly useful handicapper: stays 7f: best form on good going or firmer. *W. J. Musson*

FOLLOWING FLOW (USA) 2 b. or br.g. (Mar 4) King of Kings (IRE) 125 – Sign **83** Here (USA) (Private Terms (USA)) [2004 7m p7g³ 7m* 7s² 8m 7s Oct 16] 42,000Y: good-topped gelding: first foal: dam, 6.5f winner in USA, out of Lowther winner Miss Demure: fairly useful performer: won maiden at Catterick in August: creditable second at Chester, best effort in nurseries after: should stay 1m: acts on polytrack, soft and good to firm ground: gelded after final start. *W. Jarvis*

FOLLOW MY LEAD 2 b.f. (Mar 2) Night Shift (USA) – Launch Time (USA) **51** (Relaunch (USA)) [2004 5m 5.2m 6g Sep 3] 38,000F, 50,000Y: leggy filly: sixth foal: half-sister to 3 winners in USA: dam, placed in USA, half-sister to high-class Irish/US performer up to 1¼m Executive Pride: modest form in maidens: will probably stay 1m. *B. W. Hills*

FOLLOW THE GAME 2 b.c. (Apr 16) Mind Games 121 – Play The Game 70 **–** (Mummy's Game 120) [2004 p7g Oct 28] 20/1, very slowly away when last in maiden at Lingfield. *P. W. Harris*

FONG SHUI 2 ch.c. (Mar 13) Dr Fong (USA) 128 – Manila Selection (USA) (Manila **75** (USA)) [2004 6g⁴ p7g 7g* 7.1d⁴ 6d Oct 14] 8,000Y: workmanlike colt: second foal: half-brother to 3-y-o Insubordinate: dam unraced out of half-sister to very smart performer up to 1¼m in Britain/USA Montjoy: fair performer: won maiden at Folkestone in August: will stay 1m: acts on polytrack, probably on good to soft going: visored (edgy, below form) final start: sold 22,000 gns. *P. J. Makin*

FONG'S THONG (USA) 3 b.c. Dr Fong (USA) 128 – Bacinella (USA) (El Gran **113** Senor (USA) 136) [2004 7m* 8m* 7m⁵ 8m Sep 25] $290,000Y: strong colt: has a fluent action: third foal: half-brother to a winner in Belgium by Selkirk: dam unraced close relative to smart 1½m winner Xtra: smart performer: blinkered, won maiden at Arlington at 2 yrs on final outing for F. Brothers in US: won minor event at Newbury and listed race at Goodwood (beat Mandobi 2 lengths) in July: not discredited when fifth to Pastoral Pursuits in Park Stakes at Doncaster in September, appearing to go wrong inside final 1f: tongue tied, well held in Queen Elizabeth II Stakes at Ascot final start: effective at 7f/1m: raced only on dirt and good to firm ground: has worn crossed noseband: races up with pace. *B. J. Meehan*

FONGTASTIC 2 ch.c. (Apr 24) Dr Fong (USA) 128 – Kelso Magic (USA) 98 (Distant View (USA) 126) [2004 6g³ 7m* Jul 30] 30,000Y: smart-looking colt: first foal: dam 2-y-o 5f winner: better effort in maidens when making all at Newmarket: will stay 1m: sold privately, and sent to USA: should improve. *B. J. Meehan* — **87 p**

FONTHILL ROAD (IRE) 4 ch.g. Royal Abjar (USA) 121 – Hannah Huxtable (IRE) (Master Willie 129) [2004 78: 6m⁶ 6g* 7.1d³ 6g² 6s² 6d* 6g* 6d⁶ 6g Sep 29] strong gelding: fairly useful performer: steadily progressive, and won minor event at Hamilton in June and handicaps at York (beat Watching by short head) and Newmarket (beat Nisr by head) in August: effective at 6f/7f: acts on fibresand, soft and good to firm ground: usually waited with. *R. A. Fahey* — **88**

FOODBROKER FOUNDER 4 ch.g. Groom Dancer (USA) 128 – Nemea (USA) 97 (The Minstrel (CAN) 135) [2004 112: 9.9g 10m⁶ 10d⁶ 9.9g 11.6d⁶ 10.1g 10f Sep 24] good-bodied gelding: useful performer: well below form last 4 starts: stays 1¼m: acts on firm and good to soft ground: often races prominently. *D. R. C. Elsworth* — **101 d**

FOOLISH GROOM 3 ch.g. Groom Dancer (USA) 128 – Scared (Royal Academy (USA) 130) [2004 8.1s³ 8.1m⁴ 8.1d⁵ 9g⁶ 8.1d³ 8g⁵ 7.6m 8.1s² 8g³ p8.6g p8.6g⁵ p9.5g Nov 20] 6,500Y: quite good-topped gelding: half-brother to 5-y-o Lady Protector and useful 7f/1m performer Lord Protector (by Nicolotte): dam unraced: fair maiden: stays 8.6f: acts on polytrack, good to firm and soft going: sometimes wears cheekpieces/tongue tie. *R. Hollinshead* — **73**

FOOLISH THOUGHT (IRE) 4 b.g. Green Desert (USA) 127 – Trusted Partner (USA) 114 (Affirmed (USA)) [2004 69: p7g⁶ p7g⁵ f9.4g⁴ f6s* f7s⁵ p7g p7g 6.1s Jul 3] modest performer: won claimer at Wolverhampton (claimed from R. Fahey £2,000) in February: well below form after: stays 7f: acts on all-weather and good to firm ground: often wears tongue tie/visor/cheekpieces. *I. A. Wood* — **59 d**

FOOLS ENTIRE 3 ch.g. Fraam 114 – Poly Blue (IRE) 82 (Thatching 131) [2004 73: p7g² p7g p7g³ 8g⁶ 8.2g 7g 6m p7g p6g f6f³ 7s⁴ 8d⁵ 7m 6s 6d f6g⁶ p7.1g f7g⁶ f8d Dec 21] tall, leggy gelding: modest performer: gradually regressed after third start: stays 7f: acts on all-weather, firm and soft ground: tried in visor/cheekpieces: sometimes looks reluctant. *Mrs A. C. Gilbert* — **70 d**

FOOTBALL CRAZY (IRE) 5 b.g. Mujadil (USA) 119 – Schonbein (IRE) 60 (Persian Heights 129) [2004 95: 12s 14.1d May 15] lengthy, quite good-topped gelding: just fair form at best in 2004: stays 1½m: acts on soft and good to firm going: tried blinkered: won 6 times over hurdles between May and October. *P. Bowen* — **72 ?**

FOOT FAULT (IRE) 3 b.f. Danehill (USA) 126 – Mockery (Nashwan (USA) 135) [2004 59: p7g p10g⁴ p10g⁴ p10g⁴ Mar 29] modest maiden: stays easy 1¼m: acts on polytrack, raced only on good to firm ground on turf: found little third start. *N. A. Callaghan* — **54**

FOOTSTEPSINTHESAND 2 b.c. (Feb 15) Giant's Causeway (USA) 132 – Glatisant 104 (Rainbow Quest (USA) 134) [2004 6d* 7s* Oct 25] — **114 p**

It is important to look for value in the classics as it is when betting on any other event. Those following Aidan O'Brien's shortest-priced runners in the Two Thousand Guineas have certainly come unstuck in recent years. Since 1998, when King of Kings gave him the first of his two successes in the race, O'Brien has saddled five beaten favourites in six renewals at Newmarket, while his other winner in that period, Rock of Gibraltar, went off at 9/1. Among the favourites, Giant's Causeway and Hawk Wing lost no caste in finishing second, but Orpen, Hold That Tiger and One Cool Cat trailed home well beaten. The reputation of the stable has seen bookmakers overreact to the performances of O'Brien's classic prospects as two-year-olds at times, but the market has been slower to spot the potential of one of Ballydoyle's latest crop, Giant's Causeway's son Footstepsinthesand, still available at the time of writing at 20/1 for Newmarket.

Footstepsinthesand's two victories as a juvenile were gained in Ireland in October, away from the glare of the most prestigious events, but there was no denying the promise of them. The betting caused as much of a stir as the race in the first, a six-furlong maiden at Naas. Partnered by Colm O'Donoghue in a field of

*Killavullan Stakes, Leopardstown—Footstepsinthesand makes a good impression;
Gaff is the only one to make a race of it*

twenty, Footstepsinthesand opened at 10/1 on course in a market headed by another
Ballydoyle-trained newcomer Olympic, the mount of Jamie Spencer. By the off,
Footstepsinthesand had shortened rapidly to 3/1 favourite, and he gave his supporters few anxious moments. In front soon after halfway, though running green, he
drew clear to beat Olympic easily by four and a half lengths. There were no fancy
prices about Footstepsinthesand when he stepped up in class for the Group 3
Killavullan Stakes over seven furlongs at Leopardstown only eight days later, and
he went off at 5/4-on in a field of six. His main market rival was listed winner Gaff,
representing Dermot Weld, successful in the race twelve months earlier with Grey
Swallow. O'Brien hinted at concern about the favourite on the soft ground beforehand, saying 'he's a lovely, big, rangy colt, but he's a good-moving horse.' Footstepsinthesand dispelled his trainer's fears in no uncertain manner. He had to be
niggled along at times by Spencer, still seeming green, but shot to the front when
shaken up from the turn and was already clear when given a couple of cracks in the
final furlong, beating Gaff by two lengths with the third seven lengths further back.
Spencer was excited afterwards claiming that 'the world is his oyster and when he
gets fast ground he will be in business.'

		Storm Cat	Storm Bird
	Giant's Causeway (USA)	(b or br 1983)	Terlingua
	(ch 1997)	Mariah's Storm	Rahy
Footstepsinthesand		(b 1991)	Immense
(b.c. Feb 15, 2002)		Rainbow Quest	Blushing Groom
	Glatisant	(b 1981)	I Will Follow
	(b 1991)	Dancing Rocks	Green Dancer
		(b 1979)	Croda Rosa

Giant's Causeway drew the comment 'the world should be his oyster as a
sire' in *Racehorses of 2000*, and he made a flying start in 2004, also being represented by Shamardal and Maids Causeway among others. Giant's Causeway never
raced beyond a mile and a quarter, but, interestingly, he got winners at up to that
distance in his first crop of two-year-olds. Footstepsinthesand, just inside the top
twenty highest-priced yearlings when sold for 170,000 guineas at Tattersalls, will

be well suited by a step up to a mile and should stay at least a mile and a quarter. His dam, the Rainbow Quest mare Glatisant, did her winning in a six-furlong maiden and the Group 3 Prestige Stakes over seven furlongs as a two-year-old, but she was out of Dancing Rocks, winner of the Nassau Stakes and fourth in the Yorkshire Oaks. Glatisant's first foal, Frappe (by Inchinor), won over six furlongs as a two-year-old, and her third, Theme Song (by Singspiel), gained two successes over two miles in Ireland as a four-year-old and showed similar form in winning over a mile and a half in 2004. Glatisant was talked of as a classic prospect at two, only to be troubled by injury, showing signs of temperament on her belated return at three, but Footstepsinthesand looks to have plenty to recommend him as a three-year-old, when he should make a very smart colt at least. *A. P. O'Brien, Ireland*

FORA SMILE 3 ch.c. Forzando 122 – Don't Smile 76 (Sizzling Melody 117) [2004 — f6g f7g p7g f8.5s p6g 7d5 p10g Apr 15] little form: tried visored. *M. D. I. Usher*

FORBEARING (IRE) 7 b.g. Bering 136 – For Example (USA) 66 (Northern Baby (CAN) 127) [2004 83: 11.8m3 10.2m2 12.1m6 p12.2g6 Dec 27] good-topped gelding: **60** carries plenty of condition: just a modest performer in 2004: claimed from M. Pipe after second start and left J. O'Shea after penultimate one: stays 1½m: acts on fibresand, firm and good to soft going: tried visored/in cheekpieces: free-going sort: none too genuine. *F. Jordan*

FORCE NINE (USA) 2 br.c. (Mar 8) Stormin Fever (USA) 116 – Screener (USA) **66 p** (Major Impact (USA)) [2004 8g5 Sep 16] $38,000Y, 80,000 2-y-o: quite good-topped colt: second foal: brother to winner in USA: dam 1m winner in USA: 16/1, fifth in maiden at Yarmouth, slowly away and not knocked about: joined S. Seemar in UAE: should improve. *J. Noseda*

FORCE OF NATURE (USA) 4 b.f. Sadler's Wells (USA) 132 – Yashmak (USA) **83** 118 (Danzig (USA)) [2004 83: 9.9g 11.9m2 12.3m4 Jun 16] strong filly: fairly useful maiden: beaten ¾ length by Tarandot at York second start: well below form otherwise in 2004: stayed 1½m: raced only on good ground or firmer: stud. *H. R. A. Cecil*

FOREHAND (IRE) 2 b.f. (Mar 23) Lend A Hand 124 – Set Trail (IRE) 76 (Second **44** Set (IRE) 127) [2004 7s p8.6g Nov 26] 15,000Y: third foal: half-sister to 4-y-o Toro Bravo: dam 2-y-o 7f winner: poor form in maidens. *E. F. Vaughan*

FOREIGN AFFAIRS 6 ch.h. Hernando (FR) 127 – Entente Cordiale (USA) (Affir- **112** med (USA)) [2004 107: 12s* 15.5s3 12g4 12d5 11g* 12m* 12g2 12s2 Nov 6] rather leggy, good-topped horse: smart performer: won listed races at Longchamp (by ½ length from Jazz d'Allier) in March and at Cologne (by nose from Epalo) and Leopardstown (held on by neck from Vinnie Roe) in August: short-headed by Collier Hill in Stockholm Cup

*Ballyroan Stakes, Leopardstown—Foreign Affairs lives up to his name
by winning his third listed race of 2004 in as many different countries;
Vinnie Roe (blinkers) finishes to such effect that the margin is only a neck at the line*

International at Taby seventh start: not at best when 5 lengths second to Big Moment in listed race at Doncaster final outing: effective at 1¼m to 1¾m: acts on fibresand, soft and good to firm ground: blinkered (bit below form) once: often makes running/races prominently. *Sir Mark Prescott*

FOREST AIR (IRE) 4 br.f. Charnwood Forest (IRE) 125 – Auriga 73 (Belmez 51 (USA) 131) [2004 49: 9.2g 8g* 8v 9.2m 8m⁵ 10g² 10g⁶ 9.1g Aug 7] workmanlike filly: modest performer: won seller at Ayr in April: effective at 1m/1¼m: raced mainly on good ground or firmer: wore cheekpieces last 3 starts. *Miss L. A. Perratt*

FOREST DANE 4 b.g. Danetime (IRE) 121 – Forest Maid (Thatching 131) [2004 – 66: f6s p5.1g Nov 29] smallish, good-topped gelding: maiden: reportedly suffered pelvic injury after final 3-y-o start: well held in 2004. *P. W. Hiatt*

FOREST DELIGHT (IRE) 2 ch.f. (Apr 12) Shinko Forest (IRE) – Laurel Delight 58 104 (Presidium 124) [2004 5g 5m 5.1s p5.1g Nov 12] 11,000Y: fifth foal: half-sister to 3 winners, notably smart US performer up to 11f Mr O'Brien (by Mukaddamah): dam, 5f winner (including at 2 yrs), half-sister to very smart sprinter Paris House: modest maiden: best effort on debut: should stay 6f. *C. Tinkler*

FOREST HEATH (IRE) 7 gr.g. Common Grounds 118 – Caroline Lady (JPN) (Caro – § 133) [2004 –§: p10g p12g Mar 9] quite good-topped gelding: little form in 3 races on Flat since 2002: usually wears headgear: temperamental. *H. J. Collingridge*

FORESTIER (FR) 4 ch.c. Nikos 124 – Forest Hills (FR) (Sicyos (USA) 126) [2004 117 105: 15.5d* 15.5g² 15.5g* 15d* Jul 17] brother to useful French 7f (at 2 yrs) to 9.5f winner Nik Hills and half-brother to several winners in France, including 2000 2-y-o 7.5f/ 1m winner Forestnikov (by Baryshnikov): dam French maiden: smart performer: won 3 times at 3 yrs, including listed race at Maisons-Laffitte: improved further in 2004, winning minor event at Saint-Cloud in March, Prix Vicomtesse Vigier at Longchamp (beat Westerner a neck in receipt of 4 lb) in May and 4-runner Prix Maurice de Nieuil at Maisons-Laffitte (made all, beat Royal Fantasy 2 lengths) in July: stays 15.5f: raced only on good ground or softer. *E. Danel, France*

FOREST MAGIC (IRE) 4 b.c. Charnwood Forest (IRE) 125 – Adultress (IRE) 99 (Ela-Mana-Mou 132) [2004 12g⁴ 12g 13.4d⁵ 13.3m May 15] good-topped colt: useful performer: missed 2003: stiff tasks in 2004 and similar form first 3 outings, well-beaten fifth to Systematic in Ormonde Stakes at Chester on last occasion: probably stays 13.4f: acts on soft going: wears crossed noseband: hung left in front for both wins at 2 yrs. *P. W. D'Arcy*

FOREST QUEEN 7 b.m. Risk Me (FR) 127 – Grey Cree 64 (Creetown 123) [2004 –: – f8.5s f8.5m 5g f8m Jul 6] of no account nowadays. *K. W. Hogg, Isle of Man*

FOREST RAIL (IRE) 4 b.f. Catrail (USA) 123 – Forest Heights 81 (Slip Anchor – § 136) [2004 43§: 5m 6g Sep 14] quite good-topped filly: well held in 2004: tried blink-ered: has refused to enter stall several times, and has served a ban from Flat racing. *John A. Harris*

FOREST TUNE (IRE) 6 b.g. Charnwood Forest (IRE) 125 – Swift Chorus (Music 56 d Boy 124) [2004 69, a74: 10.3g 9.7d 11.9m 11.8m⁶ 10f p10d 10.3d⁶ 10g⁴ 10m⁵ 9.7m³ Aug 5] well-made, attractive gelding: modest handicapper: stays 1¼m: acts on all-weather, soft and good to firm ground: tried blinkered/tongue tied. *B. Hanbury*

FOREST VIKING (IRE) 2 b.g. (Mar 6) Orpen (USA) 116 – Berhala (IRE) (Doyoun 48 124) [2004 6m⁵ 6m 6f 6m 6s Oct 22] tall, rather leggy gelding: poor maiden: should stay 7f: acts on good to firm going. *J. S. Wainwright*

FOREVER FREE (GER) 4 ch.g. Platini (GER) 126 – Forever Nice (GER) (Grein- 101 ton 119) [2004 108?: 8s 8.5g⁵ 8.5d⁵ 7g* 8v* 8d 8d* 8g 8d* 6s 7d⁶ p7g p9.5g⁵ Dec 31] useful performer: winner of 5 races, including 3 minor events at Munich and a listed race at Baden-Baden (by ½ length from Activo in September) in 2004: left D. Richardson in Germany after eleventh outing: barely stays easy 9.5f: acts on polytrack and heavy going. *P. Mitchell*

FOREVER MY LORD 6 b.g. Be My Chief (USA) 122 – In Love Again (IRE) 86 – (Prince Rupert (FR) 121) [2004 64, a57: p10g p12g p13g 13.1f⁶ May 22] good-bodied gelding: well held in 2004: tried blinkered/tongue tied earlier in career: often slowly away. *J. R. Best*

FOREVER PHOENIX 4 b.f. Shareef Dancer (USA) 135 – With Care 78 (Warning 106 136) [2004 76: f7g⁵ p6g⁶ f6g⁵ p6g* p6g² p5g* 5s³ 5s* 6.1d² 5m 6m 5m² 5m³ 6g 5.1g³ 5d⁶ 5g* 5.6m⁶ 5d⁶ 6m³ 5d⁵ Oct 14] strong, lengthy filly: useful performer: won handicaps at Southwell and Lingfield in February, Lingfield in March and May and Haydock (beat Devise by 1¼ lengths) in September: effective at 5f/6f: acts on all-weather, soft and good to firm ground: waited with: left at start in Temple Stakes at Epsom (tape start, facing wrong way when starter let them go) tenth outing: tough and consistent. *R. M. H. Cowell*

FORFEITER (USA) 2 ch.g. (Mar 19) Petionville (USA) – Picabo (USA) (Wild Again (USA)) [2004 5g2 5g6 7f2 7.1f2 7s3 7s f7g* f8g5 Dec 28] $15,000F, 13,000Y: work-manlike gelding: sixth foal: brother to winners abroad by River Special and Private Terms: dam unraced: fairly useful performer: won maiden at Southwell in December by 7 lengths: probably stays easy 1m: acts on fibresand, firm and soft going: blinkered/ visored 5 of last 6 starts. *T. D. Barron* **78 a85**

FORGED (IRE) 3 b.c. Peintre Celebre (USA) 137 – Imitation (Darshaan 133) [2004 10.2g 12.1g3 10.3m2 12m* Jul 23] €80,000Y: good-bodied, attractive colt: type to carry condition: second foal: half-brother to 4-y-o Stealing Beauty: dam unraced sister to smart miler Darnay: fairly useful form: placed in maidens prior to winning handicap at Thirsk by 9 lengths from Classic Event: stays 1½m: acts on good to firm going: sold only 9,000 gns in October. *L. M. Cumani* **94**

FORGE LANE (IRE) 3 b.g. Desert Style (IRE) 121 – March Fourteenth (USA) 61 (Tricky Creek (USA)) [2004 p7g p8g 7s 8m p12d 10m4 10m2 10f 10m p10g 10.9d Sep 18] modest maiden: left C. Weedon after second outing: well beaten last 4 starts: stays 1¼m: acts on good to firm going: wore cheekpieces/blinkers last 5 outings. *G. L. Moore* **59**

FORGERY (IRE) 2 ch.c. (Apr 9) Dr Devious (IRE) 127 – Memory Green (USA) (Green Forest (USA) 134) [2004 8s3 p8.6g* Nov 26] 130,000Y: fifth foal: brother to useful 1m (at 2 yrs) to 1¼m winner Dr Greenfield and half-brother to fairly useful 13f/ 1¾m winner Forum Chris (by Trempolino): dam, won around 1¼m in USA, out of sister to Glint of Gold and Diamond Shoal: favourite, won maiden at Wolverhampton by head from Heat of The Night: will stay at least 1¼m: capable of better. *G. A. Butler* **85 p**

FOR LIFE (IRE) 2 b.c. (Feb 19) Bachir (IRE) 118 – Zest (USA) (Zilzal (USA) 137) [2004 6g3 6m Sep 8] 15,000Y: strong, sturdy colt: third foal: half-brother to Italian 7f (including at 2 yrs) to 1m winner by Ali-Royal: dam lightly-raced maiden (reluctant to race once): fairly useful form in maiden at York (green, finished well) and sales race at Doncaster (poorly drawn and short of room): will stay at least 7f: should progress and win a race or 2. *A. P. Jarvis* **88 p**

FORMALISE 4 b.g. Forzando 122 – Esilam 62 (Frimley Park 109) [2004 77: 5g 6m 6.1m5 6g 6d5 6m 5.7m 5g4 5.7g 5m f6g p6g Dec 17] good-topped gelding: just modest handicapper in 2004: left until after tenth outing by G. Balding: effective at 5f/6f: acts on firm and good to soft ground: sometimes wears cheekpieces: often races prominently: none too reliable. *J. A. Geake* **64 d**

FORMERIC 8 ch.g. Formidable (USA) 125 – Irish Limerick 89 (Try My Best (USA) 130) [2004 –: f8g f7g 6v3 7v 6d 6d Aug 17] big, workmanlike gelding: poor performer: best recent form at 6f: acts on heavy and good to firm going: usually visored/blinkered: inconsistent. *Miss L. C. Siddall* **45**

FORMIDABLE WILL (FR) 2 b.g. (Mar 26) Efisio 120 – Shewillifshewants (IRE) (Alzao (USA) 117) [2004 6d p7.1g Oct 19] well held in maidens: subsequently gelded. *C. G. Cox* **–**

FOR NOWT 2 b.c. (Mar 4) Forzando 122 – Angel Chimes 77 (Most Welcome 131) [2004 5g6 6g 7g 6m 7s Aug 13] lengthy colt: poor maiden. *T. D. Easterby* **30**

FORPETESAKE 2 ch.g. (Feb 22) Primo Dominie 121 – Showcase 68 (Shareef Dancer (USA) 135) [2004 5g 6f6 7.5d6 7.5m 7g6 8.3d 10g p8.6g Nov 20] good-topped gelding: modest maiden: left Mrs J. Ramsden after third start: best efforts at 7.5f: tried visored. *Ms Deborah J. Evans* **52**

FORREST GUMP 4 ch.g. Zilzal (USA) 137 – Mish Mish (Groom Dancer (USA) 128) [2004 –: 8g 6g2 6d f8g4 Dec 16] good-bodied gelding: modest maiden: clearly best effort when second at Ripon: stays 6f: tried blinkered/visored. *C. J. Teague* **56**

FORT 3 ch.g. Dr Fong (USA) 128 – Chief's Quest (USA) (Chief's Crown (USA)) [2004 89: 8.2s3 10.1m 12g3 12m2 12g 10.3m5 12m* 12g6 Oct 1] leggy, close-coupled, rather plain gelding: useful handicapper: best effort when winning at Ascot in September by 2½ lengths from Elusive Dream: free-going sort, not sure to stay beyond 1½m: acts on good to firm going, probably on soft: has worn crossed noseband/had 2 handlers: races prominently: sold 85,000 gns, sent to Saudi Arabia. *M. Johnston* **104**

FORT CHURCHILL (IRE) 3 b.g. Barathea (IRE) 127 – Brisighella (IRE) (Al Hareb **83** (USA) 123) [2004 –: 11.5g⁵ 11.5f³ 10g⁴ 12s² 12.6g 12s* 10.5s 14g² 13.1s Oct 12] big, good-topped gelding: fairly useful performer: made all in claimer at Salisbury (claimed from M. Tompkins £31,000) in September by 13 lengths: should stay 2m: acts on firm and soft ground: blinkered last 6 starts: usually races prominently. *B. Ellison*

FORT DIGNITY (USA) 3 b.c. Seeking The Gold (USA) – Kitza (IRE) 113 (Danehill **109** (USA) 126) [2004 93p: 7g⁴ 10.4d⁴ May 13] good-topped colt: useful performer: winner of only start at 2 yrs: best effort when 2¼ lengths fourth to Salford City in Greenham Stakes at Newbury on reappearance, rallying after racing freely: favourite, 30 lengths last of 4 to Day Flight in listed race at York next time: bred to stay at least 1m: unraced on extremes of going. *Sir Michael Stoute*

FORTHRIGHT 3 b.g. Cadeaux Genereux 131 – Forthwith 104 (Midyan (USA) 124) **93** [2004 85: p10g* a8f a8.5f⁴ 10d⁵ 8m⁶ 8g 10m 8d p7g⁶ 8f 8g⁶ Oct 4] tall, good sort: fairly useful performer: won handicap at Lingfield in January: good sixth to Mandobi in Britannia Handicap at Royal Ascot fifth start: found little in claimer at Pontefract final one: stays 1¼m: acts on polytrack, dirt and firm ground: wore cheekpieces/blinkers last 6 starts: sold 18,000 gns, joined Gay Kelleway. *C. E. Brittain*

FORTISZAMO 2 b.g. (Feb 15) Forzando 122 – Flamingo Times 60 (Good Times **64 p** (ITY)) [2004 p7.1g⁵ Dec 31] sixth foal: half-brother to 6f/7f (at 2 yrs) winner Miss Jingles (by Muhtarram) and French 1½m winner Kaigani (by Pharly): dam 1½m winner: 20/1, fifth in maiden at Wolverhampton, not knocked about: sure to do better. *A. W. Carroll*

FORT McHENRY (IRE) 4 b.g. Danehill Dancer (IRE) 117 – Griqualand (Con- **75** naught 130) [2004 76: 6s 6m 6f* p7d a7.5g a6.5g² Dec 28] big, strong, lengthy gelding: fair performer: made all in claimer at Yarmouth in August: sold from N. Callaghan 8,000 gns after next start: effective at 5f to 7f: acts on all-weather at Deauville, firm and good to soft going: sometimes wears cheekpieces: usually races prominently. *Ecurie Farnese, France*

FORTNUM 2 b.c. (Apr 7) Forzando 122 – Digamist Girl (IRE) (Digamist (USA) 110) **58** [2004 5v⁵ 5s³ 6m 7f⁵ 6d³ 7m Oct 1] modest maiden: stays 7f: acts on firm and soft going: looked less than keen penultimate start. *R. Hannon*

FORTUNA MEA 4 b.f. Mon Tresor 113 – Veni Vici (IRE) (Namaqualand (USA)) **–** [2004 41, a–: 10.2d⁶ f14.8m May 10] angular filly: well held in 2004. *W. M. Brisbourne*

FORTUNATE DAVE (USA) 5 b.g. Lear Fan (USA) 130 – Lady Ameriflora (USA) **–** (Lord Avie (USA)) [2004 62: p13g Feb 11] leggy, quite good-topped gelding: well held only 5-y-o start. *Ian Williams*

FORTUNATE ISLE (USA) 2 ch.c. (May 2) Swain (IRE) 134 – Isla Del Rey (USA) **79 p** 103 (Nureyev (USA) 131) [2004 7g² Oct 1] quite good-topped colt: fifth foal: half-brother to 4-y-o Island Light and smart 1m/9f (in USA) winner L'Oiseau d'Argent (by Silver Hawk): dam, 6f (in UAE)/7f (including at 2 yrs in Ireland) winner, 66/1, 2½ lengths second to Rob Roy in maiden at Newmarket, challenging 2f out and staying on: will stay at least 1m: should improve. *B. W. Hills*

FORTUNE POINT (IRE) 6 ch.g. Cadeaux Genereux 131 – Mountains of Mist (IRE) **64 §** 80 (Shirley Heights 130) [2004 71§: p10g⁴ f8.5g f8g² p10g* p12g³ p10g² 11.6d 10d p8d⁴ **a69 §** 8m f8d⁶ 10f² 10.2g Sep 3] strong, angular gelding: fair handicapper: won at Lingfield in February: effective at 1m to easy 1½m: acts on all-weather and any turf going: tried visored/tongue tied: usually races prominently: unreliable. *A. W. Carroll*

FORTUNES FAVOURITE 4 ch.f. Barathea (IRE) 127 – Golden Fortune 102 (For- **50 §** zando 122) [2004 54: f16g f14g³ f12s⁴ f14g 10d* 12.4s 11m p9.5g p10m p10m Dec 15] **a39 §** modest performer: won seller at Ripon in April: left G. M. Moore after seventh start: effective at 1¼m/1½m: acts on fibresand and soft ground: unreliable. *J. E. Long*

FORTUNE'S PRINCESS 3 b.f. Desert Prince (IRE) 130 – Golden Fortune 102 **80** (Forzando 122) [2004 10m² 10m² 10m² 10g* 10m² 10m Sep 4] angular filly: fairly useful performer: won maiden at Pontefract in July: should be as effective at 1m as 1¼m: raced only on good/good to firm ground: sent to Saudi Arabia. *M. J. Wallace*

FORTY FORTE 8 b.g. Pursuit of Love 124 – Cominna (Dominion 123) [2004 71d: **58 §** f9.4g f8.5g f8.5s f11s³ 10.9s f8.5g* f8.5g* f8.5m p12.2g Dec 27] modest performer: won seller at Wolverhampton in May: best at 1m/1¼m: acts on fibresand, heavy and good to firm ground: sometimes wears cheekpieces/tongue strap: free-going sort, and needs to dominate: unreliable. *Miss S. J. Wilton*

FORWARD MOVE (IRE) 2 ch.c. (May 8) Dr Fong (USA) 128 – Kissing Gate (USA) **97 p**
62 (Easy Goer (USA)) [2004 8g² 8m* Sep 21] big, lengthy colt: has plenty of scope:
fourth foal: half-brother to 3-y-o Turnstile and a winner up to 1½m in Sweden by Green
Desert: dam, 2-y-o 8.5f winner, half-sister to very smart sprinter Keen Hunter and smart
performers up to 1¼m Altibr and Marnor: confirmed promise when winning 18-runner
maiden at Newmarket by 5 lengths from My Putra, forging clear from 1f out: likely to be
suited by 1¼m/1½m: type to make better 3-y-o, and should win more races. *R. Hannon*

FORZEEN 2 ch.g. (Mar 5) Forzando 122 – Mazurkanova 63 (Song 132) [2004 f5g³ **92**
5.1f⁴ 5f² p5g³ 5m* 5g⁴ 5m 6m 5m* 5m 6g² p6g² p6g* 8f⁵ Nov 27] 19,000Y: leggy
gelding: brother to fairly useful 2002 2-y-o 5f winner Fortune Bay and half-brother to 2
winners, including 5f/6f winner (including at 2 yrs) Matthew David (by Indian Forest):
dam 2-y-o 6f winner who stayed 7.5f: fairly useful performer: won nurseries at Lingfield
in July and Windsor in September, claimer at Wolverhampton in October and nursery at
Lingfield (final outing for J. Osborne) in November: respectable fifth in Grade 3 Generous Stakes at Hollywood: effective at 5f, seemingly at 1m: acts on all-weather and firm
going: tough and game. *J. M. Cassidy, USA*

FORZENUFF 3 b.g. Mujadil (USA) 119 – Sada 74 (Mujtahid (USA) 118) [2004 68: **59 d**
p5g⁵ p6g⁶ p8g 5g 5m 7m 6g p7m⁴ p6g⁵ Dec 20] small gelding: modest performer:
below form after reappearance: stays easy 7f: acts on polytrack, raced only on good going
or firmer on turf: tried tongue tied/visored. *J. R. Boyle*

FORZNAR RIDGE 4 b.g. Forzando 122 – Narbonne 60 (Rousillon (USA) 133) [2004 **–**
p12.2g f11g Dec 16] well held in maidens. *C. Roberts*

FOSSGATE 3 ch.g. Halling (USA) 133 – Peryllys 67 (Warning 136) [2004 73: 8g² **72**
8.5v 8.5m³ 10g⁶ 9.3f⁴ 8d⁴ 8g⁴ 7d Oct 15] angular gelding: fair maiden: stays 9.3f: acts on
firm and soft ground: wore cheekpieces/visor last 4 outings: has looked none too genuine.
J. D. Bethell

FOUR AMIGOS (USA) 3 b.g. Southern Halo (USA) – Larentia 58 (Salse (USA) 128) **88**
[2004 78: 6d⁵ 5s* 6d 5d⁶ 6g³ 5.1g 6s 5s 5s⁴ 5g 5d Sep 27] compact gelding: fairly useful
performer: below form after winning handicap at Thirsk in April: best at 5f/6f: acts on
soft ground, possibly not on firmer than good: sold 17,000 gns, then gelded. *J. G. Given*

FOUR JAYS (IRE) 4 b.g. Alzao (USA) 117 – Paparazzi (IRE) 68 (Shernazar 131) **–**
[2004 89d: p7g p7g Jan 10] good-bodied gelding: on downgrade in 2003 and no form in
2004: often wears cheekpieces. *N. P. Littmoden*

FOUR KINGS 3 b.c. Forzando 122 – High Cut 84 (Dashing Blade 117) [2004 p5g⁵ 6s **64 d**
6m³ 8.3m³ 8m 9f⁶ 7d 12s Aug 13] modest maiden: left J. Eustace after
fifth start: stays 1m: acts on good to firm ground: usually tongue tied. *R. Allan*

FOUR PENCE (IRE) 3 b.c. Rainbow Quest (USA) 134 – American Queen (FR) **71**
(Fairy King (USA)) [2004 71p: 12.6m⁴ 12m² p12g⁶ Sep 1] smallish, good-bodied colt:
fair maiden: stays 1½m: acts on good to firm going: sold 6,500 gns. *B. W. Hills*

FOUR PLEASURE 2 ch.f. (Mar 27) King's Best (USA) 132 – Please (Kris 135) [2004 **–**
6g 7g Oct 1] close-coupled filly: second foal: dam, ran twice (signs of ability), out of
sister to smart middle-distance stayer Spring and close relation of Pentire: well held in
maidens at Yarmouth and Newmarket. *C. A. Dwyer*

FOURSQUARE (IRE) 3 b.g. Fayruz 116 – Waroonga (IRE) (Brief Truce (USA) 126) **93**
[2004 86p: 5d⁸ 5.1d⁵ 5m 5m⁴ 6g 5g³ 5m Dec 18] robust gelding: fairly useful handicapper: won at Haydock in April: left J. Mackie before final start: best at 5f: unraced on
heavy going, acts on any other: front runner. *T. W. Leung, Hong Kong*

FOURSWAINBY (IRE) 3 b.g. Foxhound (USA) 103 – Arena 86 (Sallust 134) [2004 **38 ?**
–: 8g⁶ 8s³ May 12] seemingly some ability on second start. *B. Ellison*

FOURTH DIMENSION (IRE) 5 b.g. Entrepreneur 123 – Isle of Spice (USA) 74 **86**
(Diesis 133) [2004 94: 11.9d 12m⁴ 14g 13.9m 10.4g f12g Dec 16] sturdy gelding: fairly
useful handicapper: stays 1¾m: best form on ground firmer than good: usually held up.
D. Nicholls

FOX 2 b.c. (May 15) Diktat 126 – Badawi (USA) 103 (Diesis 133) [2004 6g² 7m* 7g⁴ **101**
7g³ 7.1d⁶ Aug 21] tall, quite good-topped colt: has scope: closely related to useful 1m
winner Badagara (by Warning) and half-brother to several winners, including 3-y-o Badminton: dam 1m/9f winner: useful performer: odds on, won maiden at Newmarket in
June: good efforts in Superlative Stakes on same course (fourth to Dubawi) and Vintage
Stakes at Goodwood (tended to hang when 3¾ lengths third to Shamardal): will stay 1m:
acts on good to firm ground: edgy sort. *C. E. Brittain*

FOX

FOX COVERT (IRE) 3 b.g. Foxhound (USA) 103 – Serious Contender (IRE) (Tenby **61**
125) [2004 72: 6g 6d 7s 5.9f² 6m³ 6g⁵ 6m 6g⁴ 5m 6d 5g³ 6g* 5m Sep 22] workmanlike
gelding: modest handicapper: won at Thirsk in September: effective at 5f/6f: acts on
firm and good to soft going: tried in cheekpieces, usually visored: races up with pace.
D. W. Barker

FOXHAVEN 2 ch.c. (Feb 21) Unfuwain (USA) 131 – Dancing Mirage (IRE) 83 **92**
(Machiavellian (USA) 123) [2004 7d³ 8g² 8g² 7g* 7s⁶ Oct 22] 40,000Y: strong colt: first
foal: dam, 2-y-o 7f winner, out of half-sister to very smart French miler Shaanxi: fairly
useful performer: won 3-runner minor event at Leicester in October by 1½ lengths from
Red Peony, dictating pace: not discredited when sixth to Cupid's Glory in Horris Hill
Stakes at Newbury: stays 1m: best efforts on good going. *P. R. Chamings*

FOX HOLLOW (IRE) 3 b.c. Foxhound (USA) 103 – Soignee (Night Shift (USA)) **–**
[2004 –: p8g p6g f7g³ f8.5g² 7d⁶ f9.4g² f11g³ 11.6m f12d p10g 10.1g Sep 15] workman- **a51**
like colt: modest maiden: stays 11f: acts on fibresand, no form on turf. *M. J. Haynes*

FOXIES FUTURE (IRE) 3 b.f. General Monash (USA) 107 – Indescent Blue 63 **49**
(Bluebird (USA) 125) [2004 65: f6g³ 6d f6g f6g⁴ Dec 17] leggy, close-coupled filly: poor
performer: stays 6f: acts on fibresand: tried in cheekpieces: tends to start slowly.
J. R. Weymes

FOXILLA (IRE) 3 ch.f. Foxhound (USA) 103 – Lilissa (IRE) (Doyoun 124) [2004 **68**
56: p10g p10g 10m³ 10m* 11.6m⁴ 10m³ 10f² Aug 1] good-bodied filly: fair handicapper:
won at Windsor in June: will stay 1½m: acts on firm going, below form on polytrack.
D. R. C. Elsworth

FOXY GWYNNE 2 b.f. (Feb 11) Entrepreneur 123 – Nahlin (Slip Anchor 136) [2004 **69**
p6g 7.1m³ 7s² Oct 16] leggy, quite good-topped filly: fourth foal: half-sister to German
winner around 7f Mumbles (by Efisio): dam, French maiden, half-sister to useful stayer
Warfield and German 1000 Guineas winner Princess Nana: fair form in maidens: made
most when second at Catterick: should stay 1m. *A. M. Balding*

FOXY TRIX 5 b.m. Mind Games 121 – Hill Vixen 69 (Goldhill 125) [2004 f12s Feb **–**
16] half-sister to several winning jumpers: dam 1½m winner: well held in maiden at
Wolverhampton. *J. W. Unett*

FRAAMBUOYANT (IRE) 2 b.f. (Feb 4) Fraam 114 – River Maiden (USA) (River- **31**
man (USA) 131) [2004 f7g 7m p7.1g 7s⁶ Nov 2] 2,500Y: fifth foal: half-sister to Irish 9f
winner Zaidaan (by Ezzoud): dam French 2-y-o 6f winner: poor maiden: visored final
start. *C. W. Fairhurst*

FRAAMTASTIC 7 b.m. Fraam 114 – Fading (Pharly (FR) 130) [2004 –, a37: f7g² **49**
f11g⁴ f8g* f8g⁶ f7g f8.5g* f8g* 7.1d² Apr 23] angular mare: poor mover: modest **a54**
performer: won banded races at Southwell in February, Wolverhampton in March and
Southwell in April: stays 8.5f: acts on all-weather, good to firm and good to soft going:
usually wears headgear. *B. A. Pearce*

FRABROFEN 3 b.f. Mind Games 121 – Oh My Oh My (Ballacashtal (CAN)) [2004 **59 ?**
5d² p6g 5s Nov 2] quite good-topped filly: half-sister to 3 winning sprinters, including 5f
winner (including at 2 yrs) Cartmel Park (by Skyliner) who became temperamental: dam
sprint maiden: form only when 3½ lengths second to Mr Wolf in maiden at Newcastle:
off nearly 6 months after. *James Moffatt*

FRAGRANT STAR 3 gr.f. Soviet Star (USA) 128 – Norfolk Lavender (CAN) 80 **–**
(Ascot Knight (CAN) 130) [2004 78: 7g 10m 8m 8g 7f Aug 5] tall, useful-looking filly:
fair performer at 2 yrs: well held in 2004. *C. E. Brittain*

FRALOGA (IRE) 2 b.f. (Mar 20) Grand Lodge (USA) 125 – Fragrant Hill 104 (Shirley **107 p**
Heights 130) [2004 7.5d⁴ 8m* 8m³ Oct 3] angular, good-topped filly: has scope: half-
sister to several winners in France, including very smart 10.5f to 1½m winner Fragrant
Mix and useful performers up to around 1½m Farfala, Fracassant and Fascinating Mix
(all by Linamix): dam 7f (at 2 yrs) and 11f winner: won minor event at Chantilly in
September in good style by 4 lengths: good 2 lengths third to Divine Proportions in Prix
Marcel Boussac at Longchamp (blanketed for stall entry): will be well suited by 1¼m/
1½m: sure to improve, and win more races. *A. Fabre, France*

FRAMBO (IRE) 3 b.f. Fraam 114 – Wings Awarded 67 (Shareef Dancer (USA) 135) **46**
[2004 53: f11g f11g p10g⁵ 10d 12v⁶ p12g⁴ p12d⁴ 12.1m⁴ 16g³ 12.1d³ 16.2s⁶ Aug 30]
leggy filly: poor maiden: stays 2m: acts on all-weather and good to firm going: usually
wears blinkers/cheekpieces/tongue strap. *J. G. Portman*

FRAMBROISE   2 ch.f. (Mar 16) Diesis 133 – Applaud (USA) 105 (Rahy (USA) 115)   **– p**
[2004 6g Sep 15] sturdy filly: fifth foal: half-sister to winner in USA by Gone West:
dam 2-y-o 5f/6f (Cherry Hinton Stakes) winner: 16/1 and visored, well held in maiden at
Yarmouth, hampered early but travelling well long way: sent to France: should do better.
D. R. Loder

FRANCIS CADELL   2 b.c. (Mar 11) Cadeaux Genereux 131 – Ruby Affair (IRE) 68   **84 p**
(Night Shift (USA)) [2004 p7.1g⁴ p6g* Nov 27] 55,000Y: third foal: half-brother to 3-y-o
Khabfair: dam, second at 7f, half-sister to 2000 Guineas winner Island Sands: much
better effort in maidens at Wolverhampton when winning by 4 lengths from Bentley
Brook, taking good hold: should stay 7f: likely to improve. *D. R. Loder*

FRANCIS FLUTE   6 b.g. Polar Falcon (USA) 126 – Darshay (FR) 87 (Darshaan 133)   **58**
[2004 59: 8.3g 7.2m² 8g⁴ 8d 7.2g 9.2f 7.2s Oct 12] modest performer: effective at 7f to
easy 9f: acts on good to firm and good to soft going: headstrong, and often makes running.
B. Mactaggart

FRANELA   2 b.f. (Apr 27) Dansili 127 – Pernilla (IRE) 104 (Tate Gallery (USA) 117)   **–**
[2004 7g 7s a7.5g Dec 18] deep-girthed filly: closely related to 1998 2-y-o 5f winner
Paula's Joy (by Danehill) and half-sister to 7f winner (including at 2 yrs) Hunting Tiger
(by Pursuit of Love) and French 1¼m winner Sort (by Halling): dam Irish 6f/7f performer: well held in maidens, leaving D. Loder before final start. *L. A. Urbano Gajales,
France*

FRANGIPANI (IRE)   3 b.f. Sri Pekan (USA) 117 – Sharkashka (IRE) 84 (Shardari   **–**
134) [2004 76: 8f³ 11.6f 11.6f 8.1g Aug 5] tall filly: fair maiden: little form in 2004:
tried tongue tied: withdrawn after bursting through stall on intended reappearance: sent
to Saudi Arabia. *P. F. I. Cole*

FRANKIES WINGS (IRE)   3 b.g. In The Wings 128 – River Fantasy (USA) (Irish   **–**
River (FR) 131) [2004 –p: 10d 11.1g⁶ 14.1f 12g 10m Jul 14] useful-looking gelding: little
form: tried blinkered: sold 2,500 gns, sent to Italy. *T. G. Mills*

FRANKLINS GARDENS   4 b.c. Halling (USA) 133 – Woodbeck 90 (Terimon 124)   **114**
[2004 111: 10d⁴ 10.5g⁴ 12.5v 12f⁶ 12m⁶ 16s² 15.5s⁶ Oct 24] rather leggy, close-coupled
colt: smart performer: best efforts in 2004 when fourth to Chancellor in Gordon Richards
Stakes at Sandown on reappearance and 1¼ lengths second to Millenary in Jockey Club
Cup at Newmarket sixth outing: stays 2m: acts on soft and good to firm ground: usually
held up. *M. H. Tompkins*

FRANKSALOT (IRE)   4 ch.g. Desert Story (IRE) 115 – Rosie's Guest (IRE) (Be My   **83**
Guest (USA) 126) [2004 76: 7m 7f* 7g⁴ 8g⁵ 7f⁴ p7d² 8.5g⁵ 8.5g³ 8g p8g⁶ p8g p7g p6g³
p6m³ Dec 21] close-coupled gelding: fairly useful handicapper: won at Brighton in June
and Lingfield in August: effective at 6f to easy 1m: acts on polytrack, firm and good to
soft going: tends to edge left. *Miss B. Sanders*

FRANKSKIPS   5 b.g. Bishop of Cashel 122 – Kevins Lady (Alzao (USA) 117) [2004   **63**
74: p7g f8.5g⁵ p7g p8g p8g³ p7g³ p8g Mar 31] tall, close-coupled gelding: modest handicapper: stays 1m: acts on all-weather, firm and soft going: tried tongue tied earlier in
career. *Miss B. Sanders*

FRANK SONATA   3 b.c. Opening Verse (USA) 126 – Megdale (IRE) 74 (Waajib 121)   **110**
[2004 93: 8g⁶ 10.4s* 11m³ 11.9d* 11.9s* 14.6f 12s 12v² Oct 23] good-bodied colt: smart
performer: won handicaps at York in May and Haydock in June and listed race at Haydock (by neck from Pukka) in July: last of 9 in St Leger at Doncaster (moved poorly to
post) sixth start: 15 lengths second to Orcadian in St Simon Stakes at Newbury final one:
should stay 1¾m: best form on ground softer than good. *M. G. Quinlan*

FRANK'S QUEST (IRE)   4 b.g. Mujadil (USA) 119 – Questuary (IRE) 63 (Rainbow   **65**
Quest (USA) 134) [2004 62: f7g f11g² f8.5s³ p10g³ p8g⁶ 8.5d f8.5g⁴ 8s f9.4m² f8.5m*
f8g* f8d 7g p7g³ f8s p9.5g⁶ Dec 6] sturdy gelding: fair performer: left J. Harris after
second outing: won seller at Wolverhampton in May and apprentice handicap at Southwell in June: stays 1¼m: acts on all-weather and good to soft ground. *A. B. Haynes*

FRANSISCAN   2 ch.g. (Feb 17) Fraam 114 – Ordained 66 (Mtoto 134) [2004 6d 6m   **40**
7g⁶ 8v 7.5m⁵ Sep 15] poor maiden: stays 7.5f: acts on good to firm going: visored/in
cheekpieces last 3 starts. *P. C. Haslam*

FRANTIC   2 ch.f. (Mar 22) Fraam 114 – Carn Maire 83 (Northern Prospect (USA))   **56**
[2004 5.1g 6m⁴ 5.1s⁴ Jul 3] rangy filly: has scope: half-sister to several winners, including
fairly useful 1999 2-y-o 5f winner Passion Flower (by Forzando) and 3-y-o Farriers
Charm: dam 2-y-o 5f winner: modest form in maidens: will probably stay 7f: sent to
France. *T. D. Easterby*

FRASCATI 4 b.f. Emarati (USA) 74 – Fizzy Fiona (Efisio 120) [2004 81: f5s f5g f5g **85** f5g[4] 5g* 5v 5d[2] 5m[3] 5m 5m* 5.1d* 5g[2] 5.1d 5.1s 5.1g[4] 5d[3] 5m 5d Oct 17] robust filly: fairly useful handicapper: won at Musselburgh in April and at Doncaster and Chester in June: seemed to run very well when third to Kind in listed event at Hamilton in September: best at 5f: acts on all-weather, firm and good to soft going: sometimes flashes tail. *A. Berry*

FRATERNITY 7 b.g. Grand Lodge (USA) 125 – Catawba 98 (Mill Reef (USA) 141) – [2004 45: f9.4g[6] f11g f12s Feb 2] well held in 2004: tried blinkered/visored: races prominently. *J. A. Pickering*

FREAK OCCURENCE (IRE) 3 b.g. Stravinsky (USA) 133 – Date Mate (USA) **87** (Thorn Dance (USA) 107) [2004 85: 8g 9v[3] 7.9d[4] 8.1m[6] 8.1d[3] 10.1m 8.3g[6] 8.3d p7g 7d 8d 6s f6g* p7g p6g[5] Dec 3] good-topped gelding: has a round action: fairly useful performer: won handicap at Southwell in November: effective at 6f to 9f: acts on all-weather, heavy and good to firm ground: effective visored or not. *Miss E. C. Lavelle*

FREDDIE FRECCLES 3 ch.g. Komaite (USA) – Leprechaun Lady 57 (Royal Blend **62** 117) [2004 65: p8g[6] 8.5m f8s p12.2g[3] p13.9g Dec 10] lengthy gelding: modest performer: stays 1½m: acts on all-weather. *J. G. Given*

FREDERICK JAMES 10 b.g. Efisio 120 – Rare Roberta (USA) 118 (Roberto (USA) – 131) [2004 7s 6.1m 7m 8.1d Aug 19] of little account nowadays. *H. E. Haynes*

FRED'S FIRST 3 b.g. Nomination 125 – Perecapa (IRE) 44 (Archway (IRE) 115) – [2004 –: f8.5m[5] 12.1m f12m Jul 12] little sign of ability. *B. Palling*

FREEDOM NOW (IRE) 6 b.g. Sadler's Wells (USA) 132 – Free At Last 115 (Shirley **75** Heights 130) [2004 86: 16d 13.9s 16m[6] 14.1f 16m Jul 31] compact gelding: fair handicapper: stays 1¾m: acts on firm and good to soft going: fair hurdler. *M. D. Hammond*

FREE LIFT 2 ch.f. (Apr 8) Cadeaux Genereux 131 – Step Aloft 87 (Shirley Heights **76** 130) [2004 6m* 6g Sep 2] angular filly: fourth foal: half-sister to fairly useful 7f winner Chief Yeoman (by Machiavellian) and German 7f winner by Barathea: dam, 1¼m winner at 4 yrs, half-sister to smart performers up to 1¼m Starlet and Unknown Quantity: won maiden at Newbury in July by ¾ length from Quickfire: possibly amiss in listed event at Salisbury, hanging left: should stay 1m. *R. Charlton*

FREELOADER (IRE) 4 b.g. Revoque (IRE) 122 – Indian Sand (Indian King (USA) **89** 128) [2004 84: 10g 10.5d[4] 10m[3] 9g 9g* 8g[4] 8.3d[5] 10g[4] 8.9g[3] p8.6g* p8.6g Dec 10] strong, lengthy gelding: fairly useful performer: won handicap at Kempton in July and minor event at Wolverhampton (best effort, beat Templet by 2½ lengths) in November: effective at 1m to 1¼m: acts on all-weather, firm and good to soft going: held up: reliable. *J. W. Hills*

FREE OPTION (IRE) 9 ch.g. Indian Ridge 123 – Saneena 80 (Kris 135) [2004 76, – a83: p8g[5] f8.5g p8g[3] p10g[3] p7g* p8g[5] May 26] fair performer: won claimer at Lingfield **a79** in April: effective at 7f to easy 1¼m: acts on polytrack, firm and good to soft going: tried blinkered. *W. J. Musson*

FREE STYLE (GER) 4 ch.f. Most Welcome 131 – Furiella 70 (Formidable (USA) **59** 125) [2004 f9.4g[6] f11g[3] f14g p12g* f12s[4] p12g[5] p13g[5] 11.9m[2] 11.7s 11.8m[4] 12m[5] 14.1m 12.6g p12.2g[2] f11g[5] p12m* p12.2g Dec 20] sixth foal: half-sister to several winners in Germany: dam 6f winner: modest performer: won maiden at 3 yrs when trained by U. Stoltefuss in Germany: won banded races at Lingfield in February and December: left K. Burke (after seventh start) in between: stays 1½m: acts on all-weather, good to firm and good to soft ground. *Mrs H. Sweeting*

FREE TRIP 3 ch.c. Cadeaux Genereux 131 – Well Away (IRE) (Sadler's Wells (USA) **100** 132) [2004 81: 7g* 7g[6] 7.6d 7m[2] 7m[5] 8m[5] 7m[5] 7.1m[2] 8.1g* 7m Sep 25] compact, attractive colt: useful handicapper: won at Doncaster (idled/drifted left) in March and Sandown (beat Take A Bow 1½ lengths) in September: stays 1m: acts on good to firm and good to soft going: waited with: consistent: sold 100,000 gns. *J. H. M. Gosden*

FREE WHEELIN (IRE) 4 b.g. Polar Falcon (USA) 126 – Farhana 109 (Fayruz 116) **58** [2004 93: 6g 6d[3] 6.1s f6d 5d 6g Aug 23] lengthy, useful-looking gelding: only modest in 2004: stays 6f: acts on soft and good to firm ground: sometimes slowly away: inconsistent. *W. Jarvis*

FREE WILL 7 ch.g. Indian Ridge 123 – Free Guest 125 (Be My Guest (USA) 126) – [2004 12m Jun 30] well-made gelding: well held only 7-y-o start. *R. C. Guest*

FREMEN (USA) 4 ch.g. Rahy (USA) 115 – Northern Trick (USA) 131 (Northern **98** Dancer) [2004 102p: 8g 7g 8d Oct 15] big, lengthy, quite good-topped gelding: useful handicapper: off 6 months, best 4-y-o effort when seventh to Wizard of Noz in handicap at Newmarket second start: stays 1m: raced mainly on good going or firmer: free-going sort: sold 14,500 gns, then gelded. *Sir Michael Stoute*

FRENCH GIGOLO   4 ch.g. Pursuit of Love 124 – French Mist 71 (Mystiko (USA) 124) [2004 –: p8g⁴ p10g⁶ Aug 21] sturdy gelding: modest maiden: barely stays 1¼m: acts on firm ground and polytrack. *C. N. Allen*   **55**

FRENCH GOLD   2 b.f. (Mar 7) Bien Bien (USA) 125 – Shalad'or 97 (Golden Heights 82) [2004 8g 8s Oct 19] £5,500Y: second foal: dam 7f (at 2 yrs)/1m winner: poor form in maidens at Bath. *P. F. I. Cole*   **40**

FRENCH HORN   7 b.g. Fraam 114 – Runcina (Runnett 125) [2004 70: p8g* f8.5g⁴ f9.4g³ p8g⁵ p10g³ p8g Feb 29] workmanlike gelding: modest performer: won seller at Lingfield (sold from M. Ryan 3,000 gns) in January: pulled up final outing: stayed 1¼m: best turf efforts on ground softer than good, and acted on all-weather: tried blinkered, often wore cheekpieces: dead. *M. Wigham*   **54**

FRENCH KISSES   2 b.f. (Mar 2) Paris House 123 – Clashfern (Smackover 107) [2004 6f 6g 8.5s Aug 29] 9,200Y: close-coupled filly: fifth foal: half-sister to 2 winners, including fairly useful 2001 2-y-o 5f winner Shuffling Kid (by Rock City), later Grade 3 6.5f winner in USA: dam unraced: poor form in maidens. *Ronald Thompson*   **36**

FRENCHMANS LODGE   4 b.g. Piccolo 121 – St Helena (Monsanto (FR) 121) [2004 60d: f7g 7s 5.3g 5v 6m² 6m⁵ 5.7f⁶ f5g⁶ Jun 28] modest maiden: effective at 5f/6f: acts on good to firm ground: often blinkered. *J. M. Bradley*   **50**

FRENCH RISK (IRE)   4 b.g. Entrepreneur 123 – Troyes 81 (Troy 137) [2004 53: f12g 10.1f Jun 2] strong, lengthy gelding: well held in 2004: tried blinkered. *W. M. Brisbourne*   **–**

FRENCH SCHOOL   2 b.f. (Jan 17) Desert Prince (IRE) 130 – Bint Shihama (USA) 78 (Cadeaux Genereux 131) [2004 7m p7g⁴ Sep 7] third foal: half-sister to 4-y-o Cheese 'N Biscuits and a winner in Greece by Sabrehill: dam, 7f winner, out of sister to 1000 Guineas winner Sayyedati and half-sister to high-class 1¼m/1½m winner Golden Snake: easily better effort in maidens when fourth at Lingfield, making most. *D. R. Loder*   **66**

FRESH CONNECTION   3 b.f. Danzig Connection (USA) – Naturally Fresh 91 (Thatching 131) [2004 p8g p6g p8g 10.1m⁵ p8g⁴ Apr 27] 800Y: close-coupled filly: half-sister to 3 winners abroad, including German winner up to 10.5f Never To Louse (by Petoski): dam 2-y-o 5f winner: poor maiden: tried in cheekpieces. *G. G. Margarson*   **–**

FRIAR TUCK   9 ch.g. Inchinor 119 – Jay Gee Ell 78 (Vaigly Great 127) [2004 68d: 6v 6g 7.1g 6g* 6m⁴ 7.2f⁶ 6g⁴ 6m 6g 6g 6g⁴ 6g 6g Aug 7] leggy, lengthy gelding: has reportedly had several wind operations: modest handicapper: won at Hamilton in May: best at 5f/6f: acts on any going: unreliable. *Miss L. A. Perratt*   **60 §**

FRIDA   2 b.f. (Apr 14) Lujain (USA) 119 – Ishona (Selkirk (USA) 129) [2004 6m Jul 28] 4,800Y: second foal: dam unraced: well held in maiden at Leicester, slowly away. *P. D. Cundell*   **–**

FRIDAY'S TAKINGS   5 ch.g. Beveled (USA) – Pretty Pollyanna (General Assembly (USA)) [2004 60, a80: f8g f8f 8.1d p8.6d Nov 4] well held in 2004: usually blinkered/visored. *B. Smart*   **–**

FRIENDS HOPE   3 ch.f. Docksider (USA) 124 – Stygian (USA) 73 (Irish River (FR) 131) [2004 64: 12g 10s* 10m⁵ 6.9f² p9.5g Nov 20] 800F, €6,000Y: third foal: half-sister to 6-y-o Ambersong: dam, 5f/6f winner (ran only at 2 yrs), out of sister to top-class miler Northjet: modest performer: trained at 2 yrs by J. Burns in Ireland, winning claimer at Down Royal: won handicap at Southwell (very slowly away) in April: effective at 7f to 1¼m: acts on firm and soft going, probably on polytrack. *P. A. Blockley*   **62**

FRIMLEY'S MATTERRY   4 b.g. Bluegrass Prince (IRE) 110 – Lonely Street 93 (Frimley Park 109) [2004 54: f7g6 f8g 7.1g⁶ 6v⁶ 6m⁶ 6g⁵ 8d 6m³ 6m* 6d⁶ 6g⁶ 6g Sep 6] modest handicapper: won at Redcar in August: effective at 6f/7f: acts on all-weather and good to firm going, below form on softer than good: tried visored, not in 2004: races prominently. *R. E. Barr*   **57**

FRISBY RIDGE (IRE)   2 b.f. (Jan 16) Monashee Mountain (USA) 115 – Suave Lady (FR) (Suave Dancer (USA) 136) [2004 5d 5s⁵ 6m 6m⁵ 5d⁵ 5f⁴ 7.5d 6m³ Aug 7] €14,000R, 3,000Y: leggy filly: first foal: dam unraced: poor maiden: edged right when third in seller at Redcar, best effort: stays 6f: sometimes blinkered: sold 2,000 gns, sent to Sweden. *T. D. Easterby*   **47**

FRITH (IRE)   2 b.c. (Mar 20) Benny The Dip (USA) 127 – Melodist (USA) 118 (The   **99**
Minstrel (CAN) 135) [2004 7m² 7m³ 8f⁵ 8s Oct 23] good-topped colt: half-brother to 3
winners, including fairly useful 1¾m winner Melodica (by Machiavellian) and useful
Irish 1½m winner Song of The Sword (by Kris): dam won Oaks d'Italia and dead-heated
for first in Irish Oaks: placed in maidens at Newmarket: edgy, best effort when 5 lengths
fifth to Perfectperformance in Royal Lodge Stakes at Ascot: tailed off in Racing Post
Trophy at Doncaster: will be suited by 1¼m/1½m: acts on firm ground. *B. W. Hills*

FRIXOS (IRE)   4 ch.g. Barathea (IRE) 127 – Local Lass 106 (Local Suitor (USA) 128)   **– §**
[2004 56§, a80§: p10g⁶ 16.2m⁶ 12.1m 8.1m Sep 9] big gelding: ungenuine performer.
M. Scudamore

FRIZZANTE   5 b.m. Efisio 120 – Juliet Bravo 61 (Glow (USA)) [2004 106p: 6g²   **121**
5g* 5f³ 6g* 6.5g 6g Sep 4]
     Nearly forty years on from the first use of starting stalls in Britain, racing is
still wrestling with the vagaries of the draw, though it is becoming increasingly
clear that fixed draw biases are a rarity, particularly on straight courses. Familiarity
with, and consideration of, the draw has become an everyday part of betting. Controversy over unevenly-watered surfaces and watering in general has also contributed to making examination and discussion of the draw pivotal to interpreting the
outcome of some races. But there seems even more to it nowadays. The comprehensive availability of television pictures has gradually brought into question some of
the conclusions traditionally drawn from results in the form-book. Conclusions
now tend to be drawn from meeting to meeting, day by day, or even race by race,
though anticipating apparent bias from one contest to the next often backfires.
Races can be decided by fractions of a second and by split-second decisions by
riders. Any influence the draw might have in shaping a race early on, by encouraging the runners to one rail or another in a sprint, or perhaps to bunch up the middle,
is usually outweighed by runners making a quick start or a sudden quickening of
the pace in mid-race.
     Newmarket's July meeting has often been a hot-bed in recent seasons for
discussion of draw bias, only for advantages seemingly established in earlier races
at the fixture to end up being turned on their head. On the final day of the July
meeting in 2004, in the handicap which opened the card, runners drawn in single
figures filled the first five places, and the first two home in the Bunbury Cup two
races later were also drawn low. In the meeting's feature event later in the afternoon, the Darley July Cup, punters took the apparent hint. In a field of twenty,
Sheikh Mohammed's Australian import Exceed And Excel, drawn in stall three,
was made favourite at 4/1 on his first run in Britain. Aidan O'Brien's Antonius
Pius, dropping back to sprinting after his third in the St James's Palace Stakes,
was second favourite at 5/1, drawn five. Shortest-priced of those drawn high was
Patavellian, winner of the previous year's Prix de l'Abbaye. He was at 7/1, with
Jersey Stakes winner Kheleyf at 8/1. Somnus was at 12/1 along with Nayyir, with
Frizzante, Monsieur Bond and Moss Vale at 14/1. Twenty millimetres of overnight
rain had eased the ground to good, less testing than the official good to soft. As the

*Darley July Cup, Newmarket—in the biggest field ever for the race,
with runners from six different countries, Frizzante (left) comes from near last to first
to beat 50/1-shot Ashdown Express, Balmont (No.17) and Cape of Good Hope (hidden by runner-up)*

runners broke, Exceed And Excel was the first to show from his low draw, but he was soon being taken on for the lead by the free-running Patavellian from stall twelve. Individual runners who do not necessarily go on to be concerned in the finish can have a significant influence on the running of a tightly-matched sprint. Patavellian's move encouraged others drawn high to race closer up than they might have done had Exceed And Excel dictated. Perhaps crucially as well, Patavellian stayed longer to the fore than the favourite and, as Balmont came to seize the initiative on Patavellian's outside from stall sixteen, others drawn high began their challenges too. Inside the final half furlong, the race was between Frizzante, drawn eighteen, and Ashdown Express, drawn eleven. The 100/1-shot Ashdown Express momentarily looked the winner, but Frizzante, who had been held up, found extra under pressure, challenging on his outside, and she was a neck to the good at the line, with Balmont third and Cape of Good Hope fourth. Some of those drawn low never looked like finding their stride fully, some becoming pocketed on the inside, and seventh-placed Antonius Pius was the only one in the first ten drawn in single figures.

Although there was a maximum field—Dorubako, one of two Japanese-trained declarations, and American-trained Lydgate were eliminated by using international handicap classifications—the July Cup was nothing like the defining sprint race of the season it sometimes is. Frizzante, whose success ended a losing run for fillies in the race going back to Habibti in 1983, came two lengths clear with Ashdown Express, but, in receipt of 3 lb, her form was as modest as had been needed to win the race in many years, having more in common with the performances of such as Agnes World and Continent, among recent winners, rather than with the likes of Mozart and Oasis Dream. Little over a length covered the next eight home, with Somnus, in fifth, clearly not in the form he showed later in the season. Frizzante showed the best of her form otherwise in the first part of the season. After a close second to Arakan in the listed Abernant Stakes over six furlongs on the Rowley Mile in April, she returned to Newmarket to gain her first pattern success in the Group 3 Victor Chandler Palace House Stakes over five furlongs on Two Thousand Guineas day. Ridden by Johnny Murtagh, her regular jockey in 2004 after the Abernant, she overcame a sluggish start to beat Avonbridge by a short head, bursting through against the rail as the pair came four lengths clear. On the strength of that effort, Frizzante started favourite for the King's Stand Stakes at Royal Ascot, where she again ran well, once more doing her best work at the finish and gaining ground all the way to the line, after having to be switched to the rail late on, failing by a neck to take second behind the length-and-a-half winner The Tatling. Frizzante failed to give her running in two races after the July Cup, never getting in a blow when tenth to Somnus in the Prix Maurice de Gheest at Deauville in August and, though still looking in the pink of condition, beating only two home in a field of nineteen for the Sprint Cup at Haydock in September.

	Efisio (b 1982)	Formidable (b 1975)	Forli
			Native Partner
		Eldoret (b 1976)	High Top
Frizzante (b.m. 1999)			Bamburi
	Juliet Bravo (b 1990)	Glow (br 1983)	Northern Dancer
			Glisk
		Countess Olivia (b 1978)	Prince Tenderfoot
			Coralivia

Frizzante was knocked down to London Thoroughbred Services for 500,000 guineas at the Newmarket December Sales, which represented a handsome return on the original investment for her owner-breeders who paid 2,100 guineas for her dam as a yearling. Juliet Bravo won only a five-furlong maiden at Ayr as a two-year-old from twenty-four starts, but she did well at stud even before producing Frizzante. Her first foal Glowing (by Chilibang) showed fairly useful form for Frizzante's trainer at up to seven furlongs, though doing all her winning at shorter, while her second Colonel Mustard (by Keen) won at seven furlongs to a mile and a quarter. Juliet Bravo died after foaling her final produce, the two-year-old Zidane (by Danzero), who was unraced in 2004; her three-year-old filly Firenze, a sister to Frizzante, won a maiden on the all-weather over six furlongs in July. Frizzante's grandam Countess Olivia, successful at up to a mile and a quarter, has bred several

Mrs Jan Hopper & Mrs Elizabeth Grundy's "Frizzante"

winners apart from Juliet Bravo, easily the best of them Donna Viola, winner of the Matron Stakes at the Curragh and the Prix de l'Opera at Longchamp as well as the Grade 1 Yellow Ribbon Stakes and the Gamely Handicap in the States. Frizzante's sire Efisio is in the veteran stage now, but his fee has been raised from £10,000 to £12,000 for 2005 after he was also represented in 2004 by Attraction. Efisio raced mainly at seven furlongs and a mile, but he has produced good sprinters before Frizzante, including the Prix de l'Abbaye winner Hever Golf Rose. The good-topped Frizzante was probably as effective at five furlongs as six and raced only on good ground or firmer. She tended to be sluggishly away and rather slow to warm up, but was game, as well as reliable, on the whole, winning seven of only fifteen starts after a belated debut as a three-year-old. She progressed well at four, her only defeats from six starts coming when recording good efforts—unfavourably drawn as the races panned out—in the Stewards' Cup and in the Ayr Gold Cup. *J. R. Fanshawe*

FROGS' GIFT (IRE) 2 gr.f. (Apr 30) Danehill Dancer (IRE) 117 – Warthill Whispers **43**
59 (Grey Desire 115) [2004 6g 5.9g⁶ 6m Jul 23] leggy filly: fourth foal: dam, sprint maiden, one to treat with caution: poor form in maidens. *G. M. Moore*

FROMSONG (IRE) 6 b.g. Fayruz 116 – Lindas Delight 54 (Batshoof 122) [2004 93: **101**
5.1g² 5.2g⁴ 5g⁴ 6m⁴ 5m⁴ 6m 5d 5g⁶ 5m⁶ 5d Oct 14] tall, angular gelding: useful performer: best 6-y-o efforts when fourth to Frizzante in Palace House Stakes at Newmarket third start and to Boogie Street in listed race at Kempton fifth one: reportedly had breathing problem eighth outing: best at 5f: acts on soft and good to firm going: tongue tied (ran badly) once at 4 yrs: has worn crossed noseband. *B. R. Millman*

FROM THE NORTH (IRE)   3 ch.f. Foxhound (USA) 103 – Best Swinger (IRE)   **47**
(Ela-Mana-Mou 132) [2004 –: 6d 5m⁵ 5d 5.9m⁴ 6.9m 6g Sep 14] lengthy filly: poor
maiden: should stay 7f: acts on good to firm ground: wore visor/cheekpieces last 5 starts.
A. Dickman

FRONTIER   7 b.g. Indian Ridge 123 – Adatiya (IRE) (Shardari 134) [2004 83: 10m²   **80**
10.3g* 10.2m² 11.6m³ Jun 26] well-made gelding: fairly useful handicapper: won at
Chester in June: effective at 1¼m to 11.6f: acts on soft and good to firm ground: often
tongue tied: fair hurdler. *B. J. Llewellyn*

FRONTLINEFINANCIER   4 b.g. Bluegrass Prince (IRE) 110 – Bunny Gee (Last   **46**
Tycoon 131) [2004 f12g p13.9g⁴ Dec 22] poor maiden, lightly raced: seems to stay 1¾m:
acts on polytrack. *N. I. M. Rossiter*

FRONT STAGE (IRE)   2 b. or br.c. (Feb 23) Grand Lodge (USA) 125 – Dreams 88   **92 p**
(Rainbow Quest (USA) 134) [2004 7g 8g³ Sep 3] 65,000Y: good-topped colt: fifth foal:
half-brother to useful winner around 1¼m First Fantasy (by Be My Chief): dam,
untrustworthy 1¼m winner, half-sister to Melbourne Cup winner Jeune and smart winner
up to 1½m Beneficial: easily better effort in maidens (green on debut) when third to
Humourous at Kempton, no extra only late on: likely to be suited by 1¼m/1½m: should
progress and win a race or 2. *Sir Michael Stoute*

FRUHLINGSSTURM   4 b.c. Unfuwain (USA) 131 – Fruhlingserwachen (USA)   **114**
(Irish River (FR) 131) [2004 116: 12m⁵ 10.1d* 10m 10d³ 10g⁴ 9s⁴ 10d⁵ p10g Nov 20]
close-coupled colt: half-brother to 2 winning sprinters, including fairly useful 2000 2-y-o
5f/6f winner Preferred (by Distant Relative): dam French 1m winner out of half-sister to
Running Stag: smart performer: won minor event at Hanover, Dutch Derby at Duindigt
and Ernst & Young Euro-Cup at Frankfurt when trained by P. Rau in Germany in 2003:
won minor event at Epsom in July by short head from Imtiyaz: also ran well when 5¼
lengths third to Ancient World in Winter Hill Stakes at Windsor fourth outing and 2½
lengths fifth to Soldier Hollow in Premio Roma: probably best around 1¼m: acts on any
turf ground, ran as if amiss on polytrack. *M. A. Jarvis*

FRUIT OF GLORY   5 b.m. Glory of Dancer 121 – Fresh Fruit Daily 92 (Reprimand   **99**
122) [2004 97: 6.5f 8m⁵ 6.5m⁴ 6g⁴ 5s³ 6g 7g⁴ 6m² 5.1d* 6g⁴ 6g² 6d² 5s⁵ 6.1g⁴ 6m 5d³
p7g p5g² p6g Nov 26] sturdy, lengthy mare: useful performer: trained by M. Channon
first 3 starts (all at Nad Al Sheba): won handicap at Nottingham in July by ½ length from
Paradise Isle: in frame in listed races at Pontefract twelfth start and Chester fourteenth
one: effective at 5f to easy 7f: acts on polytrack, firm and soft going: usually races
prominently: tough and consistent. *J. R. Jenkins*

FUBOS   3 b.g. Atraf 116 – Homebeforemidnight (Fools Holme (USA)) [2004 71: p7g⁵   **58 ?**
p8g⁶ 7g May 14] workmanlike gelding: modest maiden: stays 1m: acts on polytrack and
good to soft ground: visored in 2004. *Julian Poulton*

FUEL CELL (IRE)   3 b.c. Desert Style (IRE) 121 – Tappen Zee (Sandhurst Prince   **76**
128) [2004 8g 8m 9m³ 8m³ 8.3f 9.7m* 10m³ 10d⁵ 10m 10g³ Oct 12] IR 23,000F,
€100,000Y: compact colt: sixth foal: brother to fairly useful Irish 7f winner Zacholiv and
half-brother to 2 winners, including useful 7f/1m winner Mawingo (by Taufan): dam,
Irish 7f winner, half-sister to smart 7f/1m winner Cape Town (by Desert Style): fair
performer: won maiden at Folkestone in July: stays 1¼m: acts on good to firm going:
blinkered last 4 starts: sometimes carries head awkwardly/hangs left. *R. Hannon*

FU FIGHTER   3 b.g. Unfuwain (USA) 131 – Runelia (Runnett 125) [2004 69p: 10g   **76 d**
14d⁵ 14g⁴ 18m³ 18d 16s 11.5g² Sep 14] rather leggy gelding: fair maiden: claimed to join
C. Popham £9,000 final start: stays 1¾m: acts on good to soft going. *J. A. Osborne*

FULLANDBY (IRE)   2 b.c. (Mar 8) Monashee Mountain (USA) 115 – Ivory Turner   **65 p**
(Efisio 120) [2004 p7.1g² Oct 25] €4,000F, €6,000Y: third foal: dam Italian 5f (at 2 yrs)
to 1m winner: 9/1, second in maiden at Wolverhampton, slowly away and staying on:
should improve. *T. J. Etherington*

FULL EGALITE   8 gr.g. Ezzoud (IRE) 126 – Milva 56 (Jellaby 124) [2004 –: p12g⁴   **40**
p12g⁶ Apr 19] smallish, sturdy gelding: poor performer: stays 13f: acts on all-weather,
soft and good to firm ground: often blinkered/visored. *B. R. Johnson*

FULL OF ZEST   2 ch.f. (Apr 21) Pivotal 124 – Tangerine 70 (Primo Dominie 121)   **77 p**
[2004 7s² Oct 22] 12,000F, 40,000Y: strong, lengthy filly: first foal: dam 2-y-o 5.7f
winner: 8/1 and backward, 2½ lengths second to Ballinteni in maiden at Doncaster,
disputing lead most of way: sure to improve. *Mrs A. J. Perrett*

FULL PITCH   8 ch.g. Cadeaux Genereux 131 – Tricky Note 97 (Song 132) [2004 f6g   **74 d**
f6s 6d⁵ 5v* 5.1d f6m 5g 6.1g p6g p6g p6g f5g Dec 21] fair performer: successful on only

start in 1999: missed next 4 seasons: 50/1-winner of minor event at Warwick in May: below form after: form only at 5f on soft/heavy ground: tried in cheekpieces: inconsistent. *W. Jenks*

FULL SPATE 9 ch.g. Unfuwain (USA) 131 – Double River (USA) (Irish River (FR) 131) [2004 79: 5.7g⁶ 6d 6.1v⁵ 6.1s⁴ 6m⁶ 6g⁴ 6g⁶ 6m³ 6.1m² 6m 6m 7.1m 6m² 6g* 6g⁶ 6d 6.1g 6d p6g 6g⁴ Oct 11] tall, good-topped gelding: fair handicapper: won at Haydock in August: best at 6f: acts on any turf going, probably on polytrack: well held in blinkers/cheekpieces earlier in career: sometimes slowly away: usually held up. *J. M. Bradley*   **77**

FULLY FLEDGED 4 b.f. Fraam 114 – Alarming Motown (Warning 136) [2004 46: 11.7g Apr 27] leggy, plain filly: well held only 4-y-o start. *G. B. Balding*   **–**

FULVIO (USA) 4 b.g. Sword Dance – One Tuff Gal (USA) (Lac Ouimet (USA)) [2004 76: p8d 7g 8m p8g³ p7d 6d 7s p7.1g⁴ f7g³ f6g⁵ p7.1g⁵ Dec 14] big gelding: modest performer: left Jamie Poulton after seventh outing: effective at 6f to easy 1m: acts on all-weather, firm and good to soft going: often visored: inconsistent. *P. D. Evans*   **56**

FU MANCHU 2 b.c. (Feb 13) Desert Style (IRE) 121 – Robsart (IRE) 91 (Robellino (USA) 127) [2004 7g 7d* Aug 13] 75,000Y: smallish, well-made colt: second foal: half-brother to fairly useful 2002 2-y-o 5f winner (stayed 1m) Tourmalet (by Night Shift): dam, 7f and 1¼m winner, out of smart French 1¼m winner Sharp Girl: much better effort in maidens when winning at Newmarket by ½ length from Mister Genepi, leading close home: will stay 1m: should progress. *D. R. Loder*   **82 p**

FUNFAIR 5 b.g. Singspiel (IRE) 133 – Red Carnival (USA) 109 (Mr Prospector (USA) 123) [2004 114: 8f² 8g³ 8d⁶ Oct 30] strong, lengthy gelding: smart performer: left Sir Michael Stoute and off almost 14 months before reappearance: ran well when neck second to Calcutta in handicap at Doncaster and 2 lengths third to Polar Ben in Joel Stakes at Newmarket: hampered in listed race at Newmarket final outing: stays 1m: winner on soft ground, best form on good or firmer (acts on firm): refused to enter stall once at 2 yrs (has been blanketed since): has run well when sweating. *Mrs A. J. Perrett*   **113**

FUNFAIR WANE 5 b.g. Unfuwain (USA) 131 – Ivory Bride 86 (Domynsky 110) [2004 102?: 7m 5d 5m⁴ 5m 6m 5g⁶ 5.6m 6s* 6d⁶ Sep 27] strong, lengthy gelding: has a long stride: useful performer: clearly best effort in 2004 when winning totesport Ayr Gold Cup (also won race in 2002) in September by 2 lengths from Fantasy Believer, soon clear, edging right and flashing tail then reasserting final 100 yds: best at 5f/6f: acts on good to firm and soft ground: often edgy: has had 2 handlers/been early to post: has run well when sweating: races prominently: unreliable. *D. Nicholls*   **107 §**

FUN TO RIDE 3 ch.f. Desert Prince (IRE) 130 – Zafaaf 105 (Kris 135) [2004 80: 6g* 6.1d² 6m 6m 5.6m Sep 8] leggy, useful-looking filly: useful performer: won maiden at Newmarket in April: good length second to Lake Garda in handicap at Chester next time: stays 6f: acts on good to soft going: sold 37,000 gns. *B. W. Hills*   **96**

FURL AWAY 2 b.g. (Mar 17) Squared Away 55 – Miss Pel (Pelder (IRE) 125) [2004 7g Jul 25] 100/1, raced freely when tenth in maiden at Newmarket. *J. W. Payne*   **58 ?**

FURNITURE FACTORS (IRE) 4 b.g. Magic Ring (IRE) 115 – Make Hay (Nomination 125) [2004 –: 10s f9.4m May 28] no form since 2 yrs: tried tongue tied/in cheekpieces. *Ronald Thompson*   **–**

totesport Ayr Gold Cup, Ayr—2002 winner Funfair Wane makes all,
and provides David Nicholls with his fourth win in the race in five years;
Fantasy Believer is second, ahead of 2001 winner Continent, Mutawaqed and 2003 winner Quito (rail)

FURTHER OUTLOOK (USA)   10 gr.g. Zilzal (USA) 137 – Future Bright (USA) **94**
(Lyphard's Wish (FR) 124) [2004 76: 5s* p6g³ 6g 5.1d 5g 5g⁴ 5m² 5g³ 6m 5g 5.2f 6g⁶ **a80**
5.2g⁵ 5s* 5.1d⁵ 5g 5g³ 5s⁵ 5s² 5d⁴ 5s Oct 23] big, strong gelding: carries condition: fairly
useful performer: won handicap in March and minor event in August, both at Kempton:
best at 5f/6f: acts on all-weather, good to firm and heavy ground: tried tongue tied, not in
2004: wore cheekpieces last 3 starts: races up with pace. *D. K. Ivory*

FUSILLADE (IRE)   4 ch.g. Grand Lodge (USA) 125 – Lili Cup (FR) (Fabulous
Dancer (USA) 124) [2004 –: 7d 12m Jul 21] sturdy, lengthy gelding: little sign of ability.
A. J. Lockwood

FUSS   3 b.f. Unfuwain (USA) 131 – First Sapphire (Simply Great (FR) 122) [2004 10v⁶
Oct 23] fifth foal: half-sister to useful 1¼m winner Rolling Stone (by Northern Amethyst)
and fairly useful 11.6f winner First Impression (by Saddlers' Hall): dam of no account:
9/1, well held in maiden at Newbury. *W. Jarvis*

FUTOO (IRE)   3 b.g. Foxhound (USA) 103 – Nicola Wynn 83 (Nicholas Bill 125) **74**
[2004 71: 8.5v⁶ 8m⁵ 8.1d* 7.2g³ 7.5g 9.9g* 10g³ 9.9d⁴ 10d² 10.1g 10.1m Oct 10] tall,
useful-looking gelding: fair handicapper: won at Haydock in June and Beverley in July:
stays 1¼m: acts on good to firm and good to soft going: tried visored at 2 yrs: races up
with pace. *G. M. Moore*

FUTURE DEAL   3 b.f. First Trump 118 – Katyushka (IRE) 73 (Soviet Star (USA) **66**
128) [2004 7d⁴ 6m³ p6g⁷ Oct 18] 6,000Y: strong, workmanlike filly: second foal: dam,
7f winner, out of smart 5f performer Welsh Note: fair performer: won maiden at Wolverhampton by length from Imtalkinggibberish: should stay 7f. *C. A. Horgan*

FUTURE TO FUTURE (IRE)   4 gr.g. Linamix (FR) 127 – Finir En Beaute (FR) **–**
(Groom Dancer (USA) 128) [2004 12s p16g Sep 1] maiden: trained by X. T. Demeaulte
in France in 2003: well held both starts in Britain: tried blinkered. *L. A. Dace*

FUTURISTIC   4 b.g. Magic Ring (IRE) 115 – Corn Futures 78 (Nomination 125) [2004 **?**
67: f8.5g² f8.5s 8d Apr 24] quite good-topped gelding: modest performer: stays 8.5f: acts **a64**
on fibresand and good to soft going: tried visored. *J. Pearce*

FYODOR (IRE)   3 b.g. Fasliyev (USA) 120 – Royale Figurine (IRE) 107 (Dominion **77**
Royale 112) [2004 86p: 5m 6g⁶ 5m 5f 6g 5m⁴ 5d 7s Oct 27] tall, good-topped gelding:
just fair performer in 2004: barely stays 6f: acts on good to firm going: none too
consistent. *W. J. Haggas*

G

GABANA (IRE)   3 br.f. Polish Precedent (USA) 131 – Out West (USA) 103 (Gone **72**
West (USA)) [2004 71: 7g 8g⁶ 8.3m 8f³ 8g² 8.1g³ 8m³ Jul 22] lengthy, rather unfurnished
filly: fair maiden: should stay 1¼m: acts on firm and good to soft going: carries head
high: difficult ride. *C. F. Wall*

GABANNA (USA)   2 b.c. (Feb 1) Kingmambo (USA) 125 – Star Begonia 110 (Sadler's **72**
Wells (USA) 132) [2004 8.3m⁶ 10v³ Oct 20] $1,200,000Y: third foal: half-brother to very
smart Irish 1¼m winner (Irish Derby third) Roosevelt (by Danehill) and 3-y-o Five
Dynasties: dam, 1½m winner (second in Ribblesdale Stakes), sister to very smart French
winner up to 1½m Poliglote: better effort in maidens when third to Louise Rayner at
Nottingham: will stay at least 1½m. *Saeed bin Suroor*

GABLESEA   10 b.g. Beveled (USA) – Me Spede (Valiyar 129) [2004 10.5s Jul 17] tall **–**
gelding: no longer of any account. *B. P. J. Baugh*

GABOR   5 b.g. Danzig Connection (USA) – Kiomi 65 (Niniski (USA) 125) [2004 69: **–**
11.9m 12m 11.9m⁵ Aug 16] tall gelding: well below form in 2004: tried blinkered: fair
hurdler. *G. L. Moore*

GAELIC PRINCESS   4 b.f. Cois Na Tine (IRE) 101 – Berenice (ITY) (Marouble 116) **83**
[2004 91: f6g p7g 6g⁶ 6m 6m 6f 7m 6d⁵ p7g⁴ p8g³ p6g Dec 27] good-bodied filly: fairly
useful handicapper: stays easy 1m: acts on all-weather and firm going. *A. G. Newcombe*

GAELIC PROBE (IRE)   10 b.g. Roi Danzig (USA) – Scottish Gaelic (USA) (High- **–**
land Park 124) [2004 –: f14.8g⁶ Jan 3] fair winner in Ireland in 1997: little show both
Flat outings since: tried blinkered/in cheekpieces. *R. M. H. Cowell*

GAELIC ROULETTE (IRE)   4 b.f. Turtle Island (IRE) 123 – Money Spinner (USA) **72**
61 (Teenoso (USA) 135) [2004 78: 11.8m³ 14m 12g Aug 11] rather leggy filly: fair

handicapper: ran as if amiss final outing: stays 1¾m: raced only on good going or firmer on turf: often slowly away. *P. W. Harris*

GAFF (USA) 2 b.c. (Mar 28) Maria's Mon (USA) 121 – Ionlyhaveeyesforu (CAN) **109**
(Tunerup (USA)) [2004 a4.5f 7d* 7s² Oct 25] $7,000F, $100,000Y: fourth foal: half-brother to winners in USA by Belong To Me and Cryptoclearance: dam, won in USA, sister to US Grade 3 6f winner Ifyoucouldseemenow: seventh of 10 in maiden at Keeneland for S. Asmussen: won listed race at Fairyhouse in September by ½ length from Zelkova, shuffled back at halfway before asserting close home: improved again when 2 lengths second (clear of remainder) to Footstepsinthesand in Killavullan Stakes at Leopardstown: will stay 1m: useful. *D. K. Weld, Ireland*

GAIETY GIRL (USA) 3 b.f. Swain (IRE) 134 – Knoosh (USA) 113 (Storm Bird **56**
(CAN) 134) [2004 69: 9.9g 10f⁶ 13.1d⁵ 8.1g 6.9f 6g 10.1m Oct 10] rather leggy filly: modest maiden: should stay 1½m: acts on firm going: blinkered (found little) fifth start: slowly away first 2 outings. *T. D. Easterby*

GALANDORA 4 b.f. Bijou d'Inde 127 – Jelabna (Jalmood (USA) 126) [2004 56: **58**
12s⁵ 12d⁶ 16s* 16.2v 16m* 13.9m² 14m 16.4g³ 17.2g³ 16m 16.2m p16g⁵ p16g Oct 13] **a52**
close-coupled filly: modest handicapper: won at Southwell in April and Musselburgh (apprentice event) in May: stays 17f: acts on polytrack, firm and soft going: tried tongue tied: usually held up. *Dr J. R. J. Naylor*

GALA SUNDAY (USA) 4 b.g. Lear Fan (USA) 130 – Sunday Bazaar (USA) (Nure- **–**
yev (USA) 131) [2004 105: 8s 10g 10.4d 9.9d 10g 9d⁶ 9.3f 8m⁶ 7.9m 7.5m 8m Oct 2] smallish, well-made gelding: little form in 2004: blinkered eighth start. *M. W. Easterby*

GALAXY FALLON 6 b.m. Dancing Spree (USA) – No Comebacks 70 (Last Tycoon **32**
131) [2004 f11g⁶ f7g 10m⁶ May 25] tall, quite good-topped mare: poor maiden: stays 1¼m: acts on good to firm going. *M. Dods*

GALEOTA (IRE) 2 b.c. (Apr 5) Mujadil (USA) 119 – Refined (IRE) 95 (Stato- **111**
blest 120) [2004 5g⁴ 6g* 6s⁵ 6m⁵ 6f* 6g* Sep 18]
Who next? It is difficult to become champion jockey without the backing of a major stable. Frankie Dettori rode for Godolphin when reclaiming the Jockeys' Association crown from Kieren Fallon in 2004, Fallon had the backing of Sir Michael Stoute and prior to that Henry Cecil when champion before him (he also rode most winners in the latest calendar year), though Kevin Darley, the only other former title holder still riding, managed it in 2000, when Fallon and Dettori were

Dubai Duty Free Mill Reef Stakes, Newbury—
Galeota provides jockey Ryan Moore with a second pattern-race success on the day;
Mystical Land and Rebuttal are placed

Mr J. A. Lazzari's "Galeota"

both sidelined. While Dettori and Fallon remain in top jobs, they will continue to set standards which will be hard to beat, but there is no shortage of talent among the younger jockeys waiting in the wings. Ryan Moore is one who has caught the eye in particular. R. L. Moore, as he appears in the race card, is from a family of professional jockeys, including his father Gary, now a trainer, and brother Jamie, both successful riders over jumps. Ryan partnered his first winner as a sixteen-year-old in 2000, on his only ride over hurdles so far, and rode his first winner on the Flat as an amateur at the same age before becoming champion apprentice in 2003. Moore's first full year out of his claim evoked memories of Dettori's early career. Moore partnered 125 winners during the course of the turf season—and 132 during the calendar year—and he was, along with Seb Sanders and Darryll Holland, one of only three riders, apart from Dettori and Fallon, to record a century during the turf season in 2004. By all accounts, a sober and unassuming character and an avid form student, Moore already shows the confidence to go beyond merely riding to instructions or to a set formula, which, given his age, is all the more encouraging for his future.

Around a third of Moore's winners in 2004 were provided by his retaining stable, that of Richard Hannon. Although enjoying fewer highlights than in some years, Hannon reached a century of winners for the seventh consecutive season in 2004. As usual two-year-olds played a significant part, including Galeota, on whom Moore was seen to particularly good effect in the Group 2 Dubai Duty Free Mill Reef Stakes at Newbury in September. Galeota looked up against it on form at Newbury, starting at 7/1 in a field of nine which included Salsa Brava and Andronikos, runner-up in the Lowther Stakes and the Gimcrack at York respectively. After winning a maiden at Windsor in July, following defeat at odds on first time out, Galeota came only fifth in the Gimcrack and the Sirenia Stakes at Kempton on his two starts in pattern company before Newbury, being tried in cheekpieces on the second occasion. He had shown some improvement when making all to beat Rajwa by two lengths in a minor event at Doncaster on St Leger day on his most recent start. Many riders shy away from front-running, especially when partnering two-year-olds on the more testing tracks, but Moore seized the opportunity to steal a march in the Mill Reef with both hands. In a race run in a downpour, Galeota was asked to dictate a steady pace early on, taking a good hold, before quickening sharply to go a couple of lengths clear under two furlongs out. Galeota and Moore always looked in control thereafter and Galeota held second favourite Mystical Land by a length. Rebuttal suffered most as a result of the various tactics employed, finishing strongly but all too late a short head further back, the trio two and a half lengths clear of the disappointing favourite Salsa Brava, with Andronikos only seventh. The win completed a twenty-first birthday double for Moore, successful earlier on The Tatling on the card's only other pattern race, the Group 3 Dubai International Airport World Trophy.

			Storm Bird		Northern Dancer
	Mujadil (USA)		(b 1978)		South Ocean
	(b 1988)		Vallee Secrete		Secretariat
Galeota (IRE)			(b 1977)		Midou
(b.c. Apr 5, 2002)			Statoblest		Ahonoora
	Refined (IRE)		(b 1986)		Statira
	(b 1995)		Annsfield Lady		Red Sunset
			(b 1985)		Petit Eclair

Galeota was purchased at Tattersalls October Sales by Peter Doyle, a long-term buyer of yearlings for Hannon's operation. A good-topped colt, Galeota must have taken the eye, making 150,000 guineas, the top price for any of Mujadil's progeny sold in Britain and Ireland in 2003 which averaged around 20,000 guineas. Mujadil is also the sire of Galeota's sister Vermilliann, the first foal of the dam, Refined. Vermilliann showed fairly useful form for Hannon as a two-year-old in 2003, winning twice over five furlongs. Refined is a half-sister to the smart Pipe Major, a winner at six furlongs (at two years) to a mile, out of the Irish nine-furlong and mile-and-a-quarter winner Annsfield Lady. Refined also won over five furlongs as a juvenile, showing similar form. Both Refined and Vermilliann failed to win as three-year-olds and Mujadil, whose stock has a reputation for precocity, was also best at two, when he won the Cornwallis Stakes over five furlongs. Galeota clearly got better as his first season went on but, all the same, with a Group 2 penalty, he probably won't be easy to place as a three-year-old. Effective on firm ground and probably on soft, he is likely to prove best at five/six furlongs. *R. Hannon*

GALEY RIVER (USA) 5 ch.g. Irish River (FR) 131 – Carefree Kate (USA) (Lyphard (USA) 132) [2004 –: p8g p7g p8g⁵ p10g p10g⁵ p10g* p10g⁶ f9.4g² f9.4g³ p10g⁵ 9g 10m⁴ 11m⁵ 10g 10f⁶ p10d⁴ 10d⁵ p13m³ p13.9g² p12m Dec 8] strong, close-coupled gelding: modest performer: won banded race at Lingfield in April: stays easy 1¾m: acts on all-weather and firm going: tried in cheekpieces/blinkers: fair hurdler. *J. J. Sheehan* **54**

GALLANT BOY (IRE) 5 ch.g. Grand Lodge (USA) 125 – Damerela (IRE) (Alzao (USA) 117) [2004 90, a95: p12g p12g p12g⁴ p12g p12g 10.3g⁵ 12.6f 10f⁶ 14.4g⁴ 10.3g 14.8g⁵ 10f⁴ 12.3m⁴ 11.7m⁴ 12g⁴ 15.9g 11.6d p12m 11.7g 12d p13.9g⁶ p12.2g Nov 26] rather leggy, quite good-topped gelding: good walker: easy mover: fair performer: below form after fifteenth start: stays 14.4f: acts on all-weather, firm and good to soft going: tried blinkered, usually visored/tongue tied: held up. *P. D. Evans* **76 d**

GALLANTIAN (IRE) 2 gr.g. (Jan 18) Turtle Island (IRE) 123 – Galletina (IRE) 74 (Persian Heights 129) [2004 p7g 7s 7s p9.5g* Nov 15] second foal: half-brother to 4-y-o Gondolin: dam, Irish 1¾m/2m winner, also won over hurdles: fair form in maidens: won at Wolverhampton: will be suited by 1¼m/1½m: capable of better. *G. A. Butler* **69 p**

GALLAS (IRE) 3 b.c. Charnwood Forest (IRE) 125 – Nellie's Away (IRE) 72 (Magical Strike (USA) 114) [2004 69d: 8.5v 7.9m 8.5g 7.5g² 8m 7.9f 8.5d Aug 11] sturdy colt: modest maiden: stays 1m: acts on good to firm going: usually visored. *J. S. Wainwright* **52**

GALLEGO 2 br.c. (Apr 20) Danzero (AUS) – Shafir (IRE) 68 (Shaadi (USA) 126) [2004 6g p7g 5s Aug 12] strong, close-coupled colt: no form in maidens/claimer: blinkered/visored last 2 starts. *S. L. Keightley* **–**

GALLEON BEACH   7 b.g. Shirley Heights 130 – Music In My Life (IRE) 59 (Law   –
Society (USA) 130) [2004 –: 16.2d⁴ 16.2g 21g Jul 28] sturdy, deep-girthed gelding: little
form since 2002: tried blinkered/visored: tongue tied: reportedly bled both starts at 6 yrs.
B. D. Leavy

GALLERY BREEZE   5 b.m. Zamindar (USA) 116 – Wantage Park 104 (Pas de Seul   **78**
133) [2004 74: 7m* 7m p7d 8s 7s p8m⁵ p7.1g² p8.6g* f6g p8.6g² Dec 27] leggy mare:
fair performer: won handicap at Doncaster in June and, having left J. Spearing after
seventh start, minor event at Wolverhampton (idled/flashed tail) in November: stays
8.6f: acts on polytrack, firm and soft going: tried in cheekpieces, sometimes blinkered.
P. A. Blockley

GALLERY GOD (FR)   8 ch.g. In The Wings 128 – El Fabulous (FR) 111 (Fabulous   **71**
Dancer (USA) 124) [2004 106: 10d 12m 22.2f 12m 12s 10.1m Sep 9] rangy gelding: has
a quick action: form in 2004 only when ninth in handicap at Epsom final start: best at
1½m/1¾m: acts on any going: fairly useful novice hurdler. *S. Dow*

GALLEY LAW   4 ch.g. Most Welcome 131 – Miss Blitz 83 (Formidable (USA) 125)   **54**
[2004 –: f12s³ f12g² f11g⁴ f8g² f12s² f12g⁴ Apr 16] sturdy gelding: modest performer:
won banded race at Southwell in February: stays 1½m: raced only on fibresand and good/
good to firm going. *R. Craggs*

GALLOWAY MAC   4 ch.g. Environment Friend 128 – Docklands 91 (On Your Mark   **68**
125) [2004 f8g³ f7g³ f6g f8g* f7g² 9.7s⁴ 9.7d⁶ f8g p8g⁵ Oct 13] fair performer: won
maiden at Southwell in February: likely to prove best at 7f/1m: acts on all-weather and
soft going: sold 7,800 gns, then gelded. *W. A. O'Gorman*

GALVANISE (USA)   3 b.c. Run Softly (USA) 114 – Shining Bright 98 (Rainbow Quest   **91**
(USA) 134) [2004 78p: 8g⁶ 10m* 10m 10g³ 10.3m Sep 8] close-coupled, good-topped
colt: has a quick action: fairly useful performer: won maiden at Ripon in June: good third
to Stretton in handicap there: tongue tied, hampered/reportedly lost a shoe final outing:
should stay 1½m: raced only on good/good to firm going: sold 11,500 gns. *B. W. Hills*

GAMBLE OF THE DAY (USA)   2 ch.c. (May 15) Cozzene (USA) – Sue Warner   **71 p**
(USA) (Forli (ARG)) [2004 7s⁶ Oct 22] $260,000Y: rangy colt: half-brother to several
winners abroad, including useful French 1m winner Lady Ilsley (by Trempolino) and
the dam of Breeders' Cup Juvenile winner Action This Day: dam unraced half-sister to
very smart performer up to 7f Beaudelaire: 9/1 and green, 5¼ lengths sixth to Tasdeed
in maiden at Doncaster, not knocked about: will stay at least 1m: sure to do better. *Sir
Michael Stoute*

GAMBLING SPIRIT   2 ch.f. (Mar 26) Mister Baileys 123 – Royal Roulette 77 (Risk   **– p**
Me (FR) 127) [2004 8.2m Sep 28] 8,000Y: big filly: second foal: dam 1m to 2m winner:
16/1 and backward, behind in maiden at Nottingham, not knocked about: should improve.
H. Candy

GAME DAME   3 ch.f. Nashwan (USA) 135 – Gentle Dame 75 (Kris 135) [2004 78:   **77**
10m⁴ 8.1m* 10g⁵ Aug 2] lengthy, rather sparely-made filly: fair performer: won maiden
at Chepstow in June: stays 1¼m: raced only on good going or firmer: raced freely final
start: sold 14,000 gns, sent to Saudi Arabia. *B. W. Hills*

GAME FLORA   3 b.f. Mind Games 121 – Breakfast Creek 63 (Hallgate 127) [2004   **56**
55d: 6s⁸ 6.1s⁴ 6m 6m⁵ 5m 5.9m⁶ f6s 7.5s² p9.5d Oct 23] leggy filly: modest performer: **a–**
won maiden at Pontefract in April: good second in claimer at Beverley in August: stays
7.5f (pulled too hard over 9.5f): acts on firm and soft going. *M. E. Sowersby*

GAME GURU   5 b.g. First Trump 118 – Scarlett Holly 81 (Red Sunset 120) [2004 –,   **64**
a71: f8g f8g* f8s³ f7g* f7s⁴ f8.5s⁶ f11g²⁶ 10.9d 11s⁵ f11g⁵ May 15] leggy, quite good-   **a73**
topped gelding: fair on all-weather, modest on turf: won apprentice claimer in January
(left T. D. Barron after next start), handicap in February and seller in March, all at Southwell: stays easy 11f: acts on all-weather and soft going: effective with/without blinkers or
cheekpieces. *P. A. Blockley*

GAME LAD   2 b.g. (Apr 2) Mind Games 121 – Catch Me 75 (Rudimentary (USA)   **86**
118) [2004 f5m³ 6d⁴ 6d 7m³ 6g 7s² 7s* 7s⁴ Nov 6] big, lengthy gelding: has scope: second
foal: half-brother to 3-y-o Pay Attention: dam, 2-y-o 7f winner, half-sister to smart performer up to 9f Missile: fairly useful performer: won maiden at Redcar in November,
idling: good fourth in nursery at Doncaster final start, hanging left (gelded after): stays
7f: acts on soft and good to firm going. *T. D. Easterby*

GAMESET'N'MATCH   3 b.g. Hector Protector (USA) 124 – Tanasie (Cadeaux   **51**
Genereux 131) [2004 71: 8.5g⁶ p6g 7f⁴ 6g³ Aug 30] lengthy gelding: modest maiden:
barely stays 7f: acts on firm going: usually blinkered/in cheekpieces. *W. G. M. Turner*

Grand Prix de Saint-Cloud—Gamut gives Britain its first win in the race for eleven years; Policy Maker is next, followed by Visorama (second left) and Short Pause (No.2)

GAMUT (IRE) 5 b.h. Spectrum (IRE) 126 – Greektown (Ela-Mana-Mou 132) **124**
[2004 121: 12g² 12m* 12d* 12m⁴ 12d⁵ Sep 5]

'Cats and monkeys—monkeys and cats—all human life is there!' The creator of novelty statuettes, combining 'sculpture and satire' and each featuring a cat and a monkey, in Henry James's short story *The Madonna of the Future* claimed not to know 'whether the cats and monkeys imitate us, or whether it's we who imitate them.' The *News of the World* adopted 'All human life is there' as its slogan in the 'fifties and many of its stories down the years must have left its readers in no doubt about man's propensity to imitate cats and monkeys. The *News of the World*'s quest to uncover scandal and expose wrongdoing has taken it into the seamier side of horseracing on occasions and it turned its attention to the sport again in March when publishing allegations about a 'tipping scandal' involving six-times champion jockey Kieren Fallon and fellow rider John Egan. The story, which also contained other allegations about the pair, was drawn from accounts—in time-honoured *News of the World* fashion—by 'undercover' reporters, on this occasion masquerading as Middle Eastern punters. The story was given front-page treatment following Fallon's riding earlier in the week of Ballinger Ridge in a weakly-contested maiden at a regional fixture on the all-weather at Lingfield. Ballinger Ridge turned for home ten lengths in front and would have won had Fallon driven him out fully in the straight. Caught on the line and beaten a short head by the favourite, Fallon was found by the stewards to have 'failed to ride out for first place' and was referred to the Jockey Club, the race also involving reports of irregular betting patterns.

Fallon was handed a twenty-one-day ban for the riding offence and also faced—along with Egan—a Jockey Club investigation into allegations of accepting money or benefit in kind for tips, and a wider one of bringing racing into disrepute as a result of the revelations in the *News of the World*. Fallon went to great lengths to defend himself—with his wife alongside him—in an invited interview broadcast on ITV news programmes a few days after the *News of the World* story; one of the points he made was that 'it would be impossible to fix a race.' If Fallon thought the worst of his troubles were over, he was in for a surprise. In August, he was the best known among sixteen arrested—a number which had risen to twenty-five by early-December—by City of London police as part of a large-scale criminal inquiry into alleged fixing of races (eighty was the number mentioned), combined with the laying of horses on betting exchanges. The police became involved after Jockey Club security—which has very limited powers over individuals not bound by the *Rules of Racing*—purported to have uncovered evidence of criminal activity that 'could undermine the integrity of racing.'

There is a feeling, among some in racing, that the sport has been here before. Three jump jockeys were arrested in similarly dramatic fashion in January 1998 but all protested their innocence at the time and charges were eventually dropped. Whatever the outcome of the latest investigation, however, it would be amazing if the Jockey Club and police had not learned lessons from those earlier acutely embarrassing cases, in which Jamie Osborne, Dean Gallagher and Leighton Aspell all shamefully had their licences suspended by the Jockey Club, a decision quickly reversed after widespread anger over such treatment. Innocent until proven guilty is a fundamental principle of the British justice system, and it is as well to point out that none of the twenty-five arrested had actually been charged with any offence at the time of going to press. Judgement needs to be reserved until cases are brought before a court of law when, unfortunately, racing will be in line for a further bout of unwelcome headlines. In the long term, of course, racing's integrity and public image would be strengthened by any miscreants being punished. Kieren Fallon's solicitors seem very confident that he himself has nothing to fear. After the Jockey Club—'having taken advice from our legal team'—dropped plans in December for a formal inquiry into whether Fallon and Egan brought racing into disrepute, Fallon's solicitors set out to obtain a retraction from the *News of the World*. 'All there is left now is to resolve the police matter and then begin legal proceedings,' the spokesman added.

The first weekend in July was a good one for Kieren Fallon. He and John Egan heard that they would not face Jockey Club charges of accepting money or benefit in kind for tips following the *News of the World* allegations, though, at the time, the disrepute investigation was continuing. Fallon also celebrated a Group 1 victory on the five-year-old Gamut in the Grand Prix de Saint-Cloud. The reliable Gamut, a late developer who was still improving at the age of five, has been ridden in twelve of his fourteen races so far by Fallon, including when runner-up as a four-year-old in the Irish St Leger on his only start in Group 1 company before Saint-Cloud. Gamut went close to winning the first pattern race of his career on his reappearance, going down by a short head to Dubai Success in the John Porter at Newbury. Gamut didn't have much longer to wait, going one better in the UltimateBet.com Jockey Club Stakes at Newmarket on One Thousand Guineas day, winning by a length and a quarter from Systematic, with Warrsan third and Dubai Success, unable to reproduce his Newbury effort, fourth. Gamut missed his next intended start—in the Hardwicke at Royal Ascot—because of the very firm

Mrs G. Smith's "Gamut"

going, and there were concerns about the good to soft going for the Grand Prix de Saint-Cloud. Gamut had done nearly all his racing on good going or firmer and had turned in a disappointing effort in a listed event on good to soft at Doncaster the previous November (when he was Pat Eddery's last ride). Gamut dispelled the theory that he might be unsuited by ground softer than good with a clear-cut success at Saint-Cloud, leading soon after the home turn and winning in good style by three lengths from Policy Maker. He showed even better form when a very good fourth to Doyen in the King George VI and Queen Elizabeth Stakes at Ascot three weeks later. His participation was in doubt until the day of the race because of his trainer's fears about the firmish going, but 12/1-shot Gamut, well ridden by Fallon, ran every bit as well as could have been expected, in the right place to track the winner through in the home straight, but lacking the finishing speed at the end of a muddling race. Gamut's campaign ended on a low note when he was a below-form fifth behind Warrsan in the Grosser Preis von Baden in September, the first time he has finished out of the frame in his career. A plan to tackle the Canadian International was dropped.

		Spectrum (IRE) (b 1992)	Rainbow Quest (b 1981)	Blushing Groom
Gamut (IRE) (b.h. 1999)				I Will Follow
			River Dancer (b 1983)	Irish River
				Dancing Shadow
		Greektown (ch 1985)	Ela-Mana-Mou (b 1976)	Pitcairn
				Rose Bertin
			Edinburgh (b 1974)	Charlottown
				Queen's Castle

The strong, well-made Gamut, who has a quick but unimpressive action and is usually tongue tied, formerly carried the colours of Lord Weinstock and is a product of the Ballymacoll Stud, his dam the mile-and-a-quarter and mile-and-a-half winner Greektown being a half-sister to the Prix du Cadran winner Sought Out, the dam of Derby winner North Light, in whose essay more details on the family can be found. Gamut is the best of five winners bred by Greektown, including two winners by Rainbow Quest, the sire of Gamut's sire Spectrum, easily the better of them the Geoffrey Freer Stakes winner Multicoloured (the lightly raced but fairly useful filly Rainbow City is the other). Gamut is also a half-brother to the useful winner at up to ten furlongs Athens Belle and to the fair winning three-year-old filly at a mile and a half Wedding Cake, both of whom are by Groom Dancer. Gamut stays a mile and three quarters and acts on firm and good to soft going. He stays in training. *Sir Michael Stoute*

GANYMEDE 3 gr.c. Daylami (IRE) 138 – Germane 100 (Distant Relative 128) [2004 **83 §** 7p: 10d² 12s³ 10m² 11g² 10g² 10g 12f⁴ 12g³ 12g⁶ Sep 22] close-coupled colt: fairly useful maiden: mostly creditable efforts at 3 yrs: stays 1½m: acts on good and good to soft going: tried visored: sold 22,000 gns. *M. L. W. Bell*

GARANCE 2 b.f. (Jan 27) Zafonic (USA) 130 – Arletty 63 (Rainbow Quest (USA) **59 ?** 134) [2004 7m 7f 8.1s 8g Sep 29] leggy, good-topped filly: fourth foal: dam, maiden who stayed 1½m, half-sister to high-class miler Shavian and Gold Cup winner Paean: modest maiden: form on first 2 starts only: should stay 1m. *R. Hannon*

GARDASEE (GER) 2 gr.g. (May 23) Dashing Blade 117 – Gladstone Street (IRE) **47** (Waajib 121) [2004 f6d 6s f7m⁶ Jul 6] big, strong gelding: poor form in maidens: twice slowly away. *T. P. Tate*

GARDEN SOCIETY (IRE) 7 ch.g. Caerleon (USA) 132 – Eurobird 118 (Ela-Mana- **82** Mou 132) [2004 6m 8m 7.9m 8.2g 10g⁵ 10.3s p12.2g* p13.9g* p13.9g⁴ Dec 31] small gelding: fairly useful handicapper: missed 2003: left W. O'Gorman, then won twice at Wolverhampton in December, beating Indalo Grey by 7 lengths on second occasion: stays 1¾m: acts on polytrack, firm and soft going: tried visored. *P. L. Gilligan*

GARGOYLE GIRL 7 b.m. Be My Chief (USA) 122 – May Hills Legacy (IRE) 68 **64** (Be My Guest (USA) 126) [2004 68: f12g 14g⁵ 16d* 12.4s 14m⁶ 16.1v 16g⁴ 13.9g⁶ 16d⁶ Nov 3] big, good-topped mare: modest handicapper: won at Musselburgh in May: stays 2m: acts on firm and good to soft going: tried visored/in cheekpieces: sometimes slowly away: usually waited with. *J. S. Goldie*

GARHOUD 2 b.c. (Apr 25) Grand Lodge (USA) 125 – Puce 112 (Darshaan 133) [2004 **59** 8d p10g p8.6g Dec 17] 95,000Y: fourth foal: half-brother to 3 winners, including 3-y-o Pukka and 4-y-o Pongee: dam 1¼m/1½m winner who stayed 14.6f: best effort in maidens when seventh at Lingfield second start: will stay at least 1½m. *E. A. L. Dunlop*

GARNETT (IRE) 3 b.g. Desert Story (IRE) 115 – In Behind (IRE) 52 (Entitled 126) **72**
[2004 11.6f⁴ 12m³ 14m³ 14.4m p12g³ 16m⁵ p13g Dec 29] €8,500Y, 12,500 2-y-o: fourth
foal: half-brother to 2 winners, including fairly useful Irish 2001 2-y-o 7f winner
Shauna's Vision (by Dolphin Street): dam 1½m to 2m winner: fair maiden: won juvenile
hurdle and then left A. King prior to final Flat start: stays 1½m: acts on good to firm
going. *D. E. Cantillon*

GARNOCK BELLE (IRE) 3 b.f. Marju (IRE) 127 – Trojan Relation (Trojan Fen **–**
118) [2004 –: f6g f8g 8.5s⁵ f8.5g Mar 22] little form: hung markedly second start.
A. Berry

GARNOCK VENTURE (IRE) 3 b.c. Mujadil (USA) 119 – Stay Sharpe (USA) **55**
(Sharpen Up 127) [2004 57: f6g⁴ f7f f7g f7s* f6g 5g³ 5d 6m f6g* 6s 7.1m f6g⁵ 6.9m⁵ 7.5s **a71**
Aug 29] fair on all-weather, modest on turf: won seller in March and claimer in June, both
at Southwell: below form after: effective at 5f to easy 7f: acts on fibresand and firm going:
blinkered. *A. Berry*

GARRIGON 3 b.g. Hector Protector (USA) 124 – Queen of The Keys 56 (Royal **63**
Academy (USA) 130) [2004 68, a64: p7g⁵ p7g p8g⁴ p7g p7g⁴ p7g⁶ p10g² p9.5g⁵ p10m
Dec 22] workmanlike gelding: modest maiden: stays easy 1¼m: acts on polytrack, good
to firm and good to soft going: tried in cheekpieces/blinkers: slowly away, sometimes
markedly so: none too genuine. *N. P. Littmoden*

GARRYURRA 3 gr.f. Daylami (IRE) 138 – Tropical 122 (Green Desert (USA) 127) **64**
[2004 75p: 9.9g⁵ 12.1g May 31] smallish, lengthy filly: modest form in maidens: ran as if
amiss in handicap final start: should stay 1¼m: raced only on good/good to firm going:
sent to Australia. *Sir Michael Stoute*

GARSTON STAR 3 ch.g. Fleetwood (IRE) 107 – Conquista 87 (Aragon 118) [2004 **69**
54: 10m³ 11g* 11.9f² 12d² 14m 11.9m⁵ 11g* f12f⁶ 16g⁶ Sep 30] good-topped gelding: **a–**
fair handicapper: won selling event in May and apprentice race in August, both at Goodwood: stays 1½m: acts on firm and good to soft going: front runner. *J. S. Moore*

GARW VALLEY 5 b.m. Mtoto 134 – Morgannwg (IRE) 86 (Simply Great (FR) 122) **–**
[2004 –: p13.9g Nov 29] rather leggy mare: maiden: little form since 2002: tried blinkered. *M. Wigham*

GASPARINI (IRE) 3 ch.c. Docksider (USA) 124 – Tarjou (Marju (IRE) 127) [2004 **59**
60: 6s 7g 6m 9g⁴ 6.9g³ 7.5g 7m³ 6m Jul 30] quite attractive colt: has a quick action:
modest maiden: barely stays 9f: acts on good to soft going: sometimes races freely: sold
2,000 gns, sent to Sweden. *T. D. Easterby*

GATEMAN 7 b.g. Owington 123 – Scandalette (Niniski (USA) 125) [2004 116: 9f² **118**
8m⁶ 8.9m 8g² 9g* 8.1d² 8m 8.5m³ 8.3m* 8g² 10m² 10d² 9.8m² 10d³ Nov 7] big, well-
made gelding: smart performer: won Weatherbys Earl of Sefton Stakes at Newmarket (by
length from Kalaman) in April and listed race at Windsor (rallied to beat Shot To Fame a
head) in June: good second in Group 2 events at Sandown (beaten a neck by Hurricane
Alan in Mile), Ayr (length behind Kalaman in Scottish Derby) and Longchamp (went

Weatherbys Earl of Sefton Stakes, Newmarket—
Gateman (nearer camera) finds more under pressure than odds-on Kalaman; Hurricane Alan takes third

down by a neck to Touch of Land in Prix Dollar) on sixth, eleventh and penultimate starts: effective at 1m/1¼m: acts on firm and soft going: usually heavily bandaged behind: front runner: tough, game and consistent, a credit to his connections. *M. Johnston*

GATWICK (IRE) 3 b.c. Ali-Royal (IRE) 127 – Airport (Warpath 113) [2004 71p: 8g* 8g³ 9g* 8.1m* 12m 10m⁶ 9.9m 10v⁵ 9.9d* 10d⁵ 9g 9s Oct 16] rather leggy colt: has a quick action: smart performer: won maiden at Doncaster in March and valuable handicaps at Goodwood and Haydock (totesport Silver Bowl) in May and Beverley (beat Invasian by a length despite meeting trouble) in August: good fifth to Spuradich in John Smith's Handicap at Newbury and seventh to Spanish Don in Cambridgeshire at Newmarket (second home in far-side group) next 2 starts: stays 1¼m (stiff task at 1½m in Derby at Epsom): acts on good to firm and good to soft going: often stirred up in preliminaries: races lazily: sold 270,000 gns, joined S. Woods in Hong Kong. *M. R. Channon* **115**

GAUDALPIN (IRE) 2 b.f. (Mar 28) Danetime (IRE) 121 – Lila Pedigo (IRE) 62 (Classic Secret (USA) 91) [2004 p5g³ 5g⁴ 5g 6.1s⁴ 6m 6.1d 5g² p6g² p5.1d p5.1g⁴ p6g⁴ Nov 20] 3,000Y: workmanlike filly: second foal: dam 6f (at 2 yrs) and 1¼m winner: modest maiden: trained first 2 starts by M. Wallace: will prove best at 5f/easy 6f: acts on polytrack and soft going: often races up with pace. *M. J. Attwater* **62**

GAVIOLI (IRE) 2 b.c. (Mar 12) Namid 128 – Pamina (IRE) (Perugino (USA) 84) [2004 6m⁵ 6.1g 6.1m⁴ 6.1g² 6d 6m 6.1m³ 6.1d⁵ Aug 12] big, workmanlike colt: modest maiden: needs to settle to stay 7f: acts on good to firm ground: usually tongue tied: none too consistent. *J. M. Bradley* **63**

GAVROCHE (IRE) 3 b.c. Docksider (USA) 124 – Regal Revolution 105 (Hamas (IRE) 125§) [2004 67: f9.4g* f8.5g² f9.4s³ f12g⁵ 10m² 9v² 11.9d⁵ 10.3m* 9.9g* 10f⁴ 10.3g* 9.9m 9.7g 9.9d Aug 28] close-coupled colt: useful handicapper: won at Wolverhampton in January (left M. Wallace after fourth start), Doncaster in May, Goodwood in June and Chester (beat Hatch A Plan a length) in July: stays 10.3f: acts on fibresand and any turf going: visored (raced freely) once: sometimes slowly away: held up: reliable. *C. A. Dwyer* **95**

GAYLE STORM (IRE) 3 b.f. Mujadil (USA) 119 – Mercy Bien (IRE) 63 (Be My Guest (USA) 126) [2004 59: p7g p8g p8g f8g⁵ Feb 17] leggy, close-coupled filly: poor maiden: stays 1m: raced only on all-weather/good to firm going: often slowly away: races freely. *C. Tinkler* **48**

GAY ROMANCE 3 ch.f. Singspiel (IRE) 133 – Gaijin 97 (Caerleon (USA) 132) [2004 7d 8.3f 9f⁶ 10d⁵ 8.2g³ 8s p7.1g* Dec 11] tall filly: half-sister to several winners, notably high-class US 1m/9f performer Hawksley Hill (by Rahy), previously 7f to 11f winner in Britain: dam, 2-y-o 6f winner, best at 7f: fair performer: won maiden at Wolverhampton in December: stays 9f: acts on polytrack and firm going. *B. W. Hills* **71**

GDANSK (IRE) 7 b.g. Pips Pride 117 – Merry Twinkle (Martinmas 128) [2004 83: 6v 6d 6g May 3] leggy, sparely gelding: no form in 2004: usually slowly away: unseated leaving stalls second outing, and twice refused to enter them at 7 yrs: banned from Flat races started from stalls until Feb 16 2005. *A. Berry* **– §**

GEE BEE EM 2 b.f. (Jan 11) Piccolo 121 – Cibenze 74 (Owington 123) [2004 6g² 5.7f* 6g⁴ 5.1m⁴ 6m p6m Oct 6] first foal: dam, maiden, effective at 7f/1m: fair performer: won maiden at Bath in June: well below form in nurseries last 2 starts (left M. Channon in between): likely to prove best at 5f/6f: acts on firm going. *G. P. Enright* **71 d**

GEESPOT 5 b.m. Pursuit of Love 124 – My Discovery (IRE) (Imperial Frontier (USA) 112) [2004 46: f6g p7g⁴ p7g p8g p8g p8g³ p7g p7g Mar 29] small mare: poor performer: stays easy 1m: acts on all-weather, soft and good to firm going: tried visored/ in cheekpieces: none too consistent. *D. J. S. ffrench Davis* **46**

GEISHA LADY (IRE) 2 b.f. (Apr 5) Raise A Grand (IRE) 114 – Mitsubishi Style (Try My Best (USA) 130) [2004 5g⁶ 5.7g³ 6.1m² 6.1m⁴ 7.1g² 8d Oct 18] €11,500F, £3,200Y: smallish filly: half-sister to several winners, including fairly useful 2001 2-y-o 5f winner Northern Tara (by Fayruz) and 4-y-o Harry The Hoover: dam third at 1m in Ireland: fair maiden: stays 7f: acts on good to firm going. *R. M. Beckett* **71**

GELLER 3 b.g. Mind Games 121 – Time To Tango 73 (Timeless Times (USA) 99) [2004 80: 10.2g⁵ 9.9m⁴ 8m 8.5g 7f⁵ Jul 31] tall, leggy gelding: modest maiden: stays 1m: acts on good to firm and good to soft going. *R. Hannon* **64**

GEM BIEN (USA) 6 b.g. Bien Bien (USA) 125 – Eastern Gem (USA) (Jade Hunter (USA)) [2004 91: 8d 8m 8.5d³ f7f p8.6g f8g Dec 16] rather leggy gelding: only poor form in 2004: left A. Turnell after second outing: stays 1¼m: acts on soft and good to firm going: tongue tied once at 3 yrs. *D. W. Chapman* **53**

totesport Silver Bowl (Handicap), Haydock—
Gatwick does well to come from behind to beat stable-companion Makfool (hidden)

GEMI BED (FR)   9 b.g. Double Bed (FR) 121 – Gemia (FR) (King of Macedon 126) **55**
[2004 54: p13g⁶ p16g* p16g⁵ 12s⁴ Mar 30] modest handicapper: won at Lingfield in February: effective at 1½m to 2m: acts on polytrack and soft going: blinkered. *G. L. Moore*

GEMINI GIRL (IRE)   3 b.f. Petardia 113 – Miss Sabre (Sabrehill (USA) 120) [2004 **48 d**
55: 5.1g 5m 5f 5d 7.2g 8m 7.9f 5g Aug 2] small filly: disappointing maiden handicapper: tried visored. *M. D. Hammond*

GEMINI LADY   4 b.f. Emperor Fountain 112 – Raunchy Rita (Brigadier Gerard 144) **52 §**
[2004 54: 8v 8.2m² 8m 8.1g 7.9m 7m⁴ 8m p7.1d Oct 23] strong, close-coupled filly: modest maiden: effective at 7f to 1¼m: acts on firm and good to soft going: blinkered last 3 outings: unreliable. *Mrs G. S. Rees*

GEMMA   4 b.f. Petong 126 – Gem 58 (Most Welcome 131) [2004 –: p10g p13g Feb 3] **–**
rather leggy filly: maiden: no form in 2004: tried in cheekpieces. *P. J. Makin*

GEMS BOND   4 b.g. Magic Ring (IRE) 115 – Jucinda 58 (Midyan (USA) 124) [2004 **79**
92: a8f a8f 8g 8f 7m 8.1s 7.1g⁵ 10g p8g Oct 25] leggy, quite good-topped gelding: fair **a?**
handicapper: ran in UAE first 4 starts in 2004 for P. Rudkin: form back in Britain only when fifth at Sandown: effective at 7f/1m: acts on firm going, no form on dirt/polytrack. *J. S. Moore*

GENERAL   7 b.g. Cadeaux Genereux 131 – Bareilly (USA) (Lyphard (USA) 132) [2004 **79**
f8.5s* f12g² p12g 10g⁵ 12s² 12.1g 12m 11.9g 12d⁵ f8d³ 9v² 11.9s 10g 9s⁶ f12g³ f12s⁶ **a75**
p12.2g Nov 26] strong, heavy-bodied gelding: fair performer: won seller at Wolverhampton (left Mrs N. Smith) in March: left N. Littmoden after tenth start: stays 1½m: acts on fibresand and any turf going: tried blinkered: sometimes slowly away: none too consistent. *C. R. Dore*

GENERAL FEELING (IRE)   3 b.g. General Monash (USA) 107 – Kamadara (IRE) **82**
(Kahyasi 130) [2004 67p: 5s³ 5.1m³ 6.1m 6m⁴ 7m* 8f* 8s⁴ 7d Sep 18] good-bodied gelding: fairly useful handicapper: won at Galway in July and Brighton (wandered) in August: reportedly made a noise when below form final start: stays 1m: acts on firm and soft going. *S. Kirk*

GENERAL FLUMPA   3 b.g. Vettori (IRE) 119 – Macca Luna (IRE) 78 (Kahyasi **67**
130) [2004 58: 7.1d⁶ f9.4g³ 11.6s³ f12g⁵ 10.9m² 10d⁶ 10.1g³ 10d⁴ Aug 26] fair maiden: stays 1½m: acts on fibresand, soft and good to firm going. *C. F. Wall*

GENERAL HAIGH 2 b.g. (Mar 21) Mujahid (USA) 125 – Stygian (USA) 73 (Irish **68**
River (FR) 131) [2004 p5d6 5g4 6g4 p6m Oct 6] 20,000Y: fourth foal: half-brother to
6-y-o Ambersong and 3-y-o Friends Hope: dam, 5f/6f winner (ran only at 2 yrs), out of
sister to top-class miler Northjet: fair maiden: best effort when fourth at Lingfield third
start: will probably stay 7f: refused to enter stall fourth intended outing. *J. R. Best*

GENERAL JUMBO 2 b.c. (Apr 17) Dansili 127 – Aunt Jemima (Busted 134) [2004 **88 p**
8v2 p8g* Nov 13] 11,500F, 17,000Y: half-brother to 3 winners, notably useful 6f (at 2
yrs) to 1½m winner Azhar (by Night Shift): dam unraced half-sister to 7-y-o Compton
Bolter: won maiden at Lingfield impressively by 5 lengths from Indebted: sold privately
after, and was due to run in Hollywood Futurity Dec 18, but withdrawn on morning of
race: should stay 1¼m: likely to make a useful 3-y-o. *B. J. Meehan*

GENERAL MAX (IRE) 2 b.c. (Apr 8) General Monash (USA) 107 – Sawaki 71 **60**
(Song 132) [2004 6f3 7m 6s 7m Sep 5] useful-looking colt: modest maiden: best effort at
6f on firm going. *A. Crook*

GENERAL NUISANCE (IRE) 2 ch.g. (Feb 28) General Monash (USA) 107 – **55**
Baywood (Emarati (USA) 74) [2004 5g2 5.1g6 5v4 5m5 7f4 6f3 6m2 6m 6g3 6s Aug
24] sturdy gelding: modest maiden: trained by P. Murphy second start only: effective at
5f/6f: acts on any going: blinkered/in cheekpieces last 7 starts. *J. S. Moore*

GENERAL SMITH 5 b.g. Greenmith 121 – Second Call 67 (Kind of Hush 118) –
[2004 68: 8v 7.1d 8m 6m 5m Jul 27] little form in 2004: tried in cheekpieces: reared and
got trapped in stall final appearance. *G. A. Harker*

GENEROUS GESTURE (IRE) 3 b.f. Fasliyev (USA) 120 – Royal Bounty (IRE) 80 **71 d**
(Generous (IRE) 139) [2004 69: f6g* p7g5 6.1g6 f6d* 7m 7f6 f7g5 6m6 7g 6.1d 6g 6d Nov **a86**
5] lengthy, quite good-topped filly: fairly useful on all-weather, fair at best on turf: won
maiden in March and handicap (by 2 lengths from Marinate, hung left) in April, both at
Southwell: barely stays 7f: acts on all-weather and firm going, probably on good to soft:
effective visored or not: often slowly away/races freely: sold 13,000 gns. *M. L. W. Bell*

GENEROUS MEASURE 2 b.c. (Apr 6) Largesse 112 – Stormy Heights 62 (Golden –
Heights 82) [2004 7s p8.6g Nov 26] well held in maidens. *J. M. P. Eustace*

GENEROUS OPTION 2 ch.f. (Feb 11) Cadeaux Genereux 131 – Easy Option (IRE) **85**
115 (Prince Sabo 123) [2004 6m5 6.1m* 6m3 6d4 6d4 6d Oct 15] strong, lengthy filly:
fourth foal: half-sister to 3 winners, including 4-y-o Court Masterpiece and useful French
winner around 5f (including at 2 yrs) Maybe Forever (by Zafonic): dam, 5f winner (including at 2 yrs), twice fourth in Prix de l'Abbaye: fairly useful performer: won maiden
at Nottingham in July: good efforts in frame in nurseries: will probably stay 7f: acts on
good to firm and good to soft going. *M. Johnston*

GENEROUS SHARE 4 ch.f. Cadeaux Genereux 131 – Marl 94 (Lycius (USA) 124) –
[2004 –: f7g6 Jan 5] maiden: no form since 2yrs. *M. S. Saunders*

GENEROUS SPIRIT (IRE) 3 ch.c. Cadeaux Genereux 131 – Miss Rossi (Artaius **55**
(USA) 129) [2004 7d 6s 5s 6m6 6m Jul 22] modest maiden: stays 7f: acts on good to firm
and good to soft going: slowly away final outing. *J. A. Osborne*

GENGHIS (IRE) 2 ch.g. Persian Bold 123 – Cindy's Baby 36 (Bairn (USA) 126) **87**
[2004 89+: 12m2 14g5 11m2 11.9d 11.9g3 14.1d3 12f2 Sep 24] rather leggy gelding: fairly
useful maiden handicapper: good efforts in 2004 when placed: stays 1¾m: acts on firm
and good to soft going: sometimes races freely/wanders: usually makes running: sold
30,000 gns, joined P. Bowen. *H. Morrison*

GENNIE BOND 2 b.f. (Apr 21) Pivotal 124 – Miriam 59 (Forzando 122) [2004 6m4 **73**
6g3 6f2 6f 6.5m 6.5g Sep 18] 37,000Y: good-topped filly: half-sister to several winning
sprinters, including 3-y-o Ivory Lace and 6-y-o Viewforth: dam 5f winner, including at 2
yrs: fair maiden: ran poorly last 3 starts: should prove best at 5f/6f: acts on firm ground.
R. Hannon

GENTLEMAN GEORGE 3 b.c. Kingsinger (IRE) 94 – Miss Bigwig 84 (Distinctly –
North (USA) 115) [2004 50: p8g p5g Jan 14] sturdy colt: maiden: last in sellers at 3 yrs.
D. K. Ivory

GENTLEMAN'S DEAL (IRE) 3 b.c. Danehill (USA) 126 – Sleepytime (IRE) 121 **88 p**
(Royal Academy (USA) 130) [2004 8g4 7.1d* p9.5g* Oct 18] 460,000Y: big, strong,
good-topped colt: has an unimpressive, quick action: third foal: dam, won 1000 Guineas
(7f winner at 2 yrs), sister to high-class miler Ali-Royal and half-sister to very smart
1¼m/1½m performer Taipan: won maiden at Chepstow in August and handicap at Wol-

verhampton in October: plenty of improvement when beating Miss Polaris comfortably by 3 lengths in latter, leading 2f out: will stay 1¼m: useful prospect. *E. A. L. Dunlop*

GENTLE RAINDROP (IRE) 3 b.f. College Chapel 122 – Dream Chaser 92 (Record Token 128) [2004 8m 7m⁵ 7m 8.1g 8.3m 6d 10.2g p8.6g Oct 16] half-sister to several winners, including 5f winner Cradle Days (by Dance of Life) and smart 7f (at 2 yrs) and 1m winner King's Ironbridge (by King's Theatre): dam suited by 6f: seemingly modest maiden: stays 1m: blinkered 2 of last 3 starts. *S. Kirk* — **58 ?**

GENTLE RESPONSE 4 b.f. Puissance 110 – Sweet Whisper 63 (Petong 126) [2004 59: p6g p5g p6g⁶ p6g³ p7g* p7g p6g⁵ p7g⁶ 6d p8m p7m Dec 15] good-bodied filly: modest performer: left C. Dwyer after second start: won banded race at Lingfield in March: stays 7f: acts on polytrack and firm going: blinkered/visored after second outing. *B. R. Johnson* — **53**

GENTLE WARNING 4 b.f. Parthian Springs 114 – Manx Princess 47 (Roscoe Blake 120) [2004 8.1m 9.9s 10m Sep 7] sparely-made filly: fourth foal: dam maiden, including over hurdles: tailed-off last in maidens, in blinkers final outing. *M. Appleby* — **–**

GENUINELY (IRE) 3 b.f. Entrepreneur 123 – Fearless 53 (Groom Dancer (USA) 128) [2004 –: p7g 8.3s p12d⁶ 11.5m³ 16g 16.2s³ Aug 30] workmanlike maiden: stays 1½m: acts on polytrack and good to firm going: visored last 3 starts. *W. J. Musson* — **43**

GEOGRAPHY (IRE) 4 ch.g. Definite Article 121 – Classic Ring (IRE) 50 (Auction Ring (USA) 123) [2004 52: p10g f9.4s p10g⁶ p12g 11.9m 10d Oct 2] poor maiden: stays easy 1½m: acts on all-weather, soft and good to firm going: wears cheekpieces. *P. Butler* — **45**

GEOJIMALI 2 ch.c. (Mar 16) Compton Place 125 – Harrken Heights (IRE) (Belmez (USA) 131) [2004 6g⁶ 7.2m⁶ 6g⁵ Aug 7] heavy-topped colt: well held in maidens at Ayr. *J. S. Goldie* — **–**

GEORDIE DANCER (IRE) 2 b.g. (Feb 25) Dansili 127 – Awtaar (USA) 67 (Lyphard (USA) 132) [2004 5g 8g⁵ 7m Sep 29] good-bodied gelding: burly, modest form in maidens: probably stays 1m: gelded after final start. *A. Berry* — **51**

GEORGE STUBBS (USA) 6 b. or br.g. Affirmed (USA) – Mia Duchessa (USA) (Nijinsky (CAN) 138) [2004 80: p16g f12g⁶ f12s² f14g³ f12s⁶ f12g⁴ 18g 15s³ 16d* 13g³ 13.9s⁵ 16m⁵ 13.1d⁵ 16.1m Jul 17] leggy, quite good-topped gelding: fair handicapper: won at Ripon in April: stays 2m: acts on all-weather, soft and good to firm going: tried in blinkers/cheekpieces at 5 yrs: often races up with pace. *M. J. Polglase* — **72**

GEORGE THE BEST (IRE) 3 b.g. Imperial Ballet (IRE) 110 – En Retard (IRE) 97 (Petardia 113) [2004 86: 6d 6g⁶ 6d⁴ 6d 6g⁶ 7.5g 6s 6d 5d⁵ 5s⁶ Nov 2] workmanlike gelding: fair performer: effective at 5f/6f: acts on good to soft going: sometimes slowly away. *M. D. Hammond* — **69**

GEORGIE BELLE (USA) 2 ch.f. (Jan 28) Southern Halo (USA) – Saabikah (USA) (Dayjur (USA) 137) [2004 5d³ 5d³ p7g Oct 28] 11,000Y: compact filly: first foal: dam unraced out of half-sister to high-class 1m/1¼m performer Lahib: modest form when third in maidens, then off 6 months: should stay 7f. *C. Tinkler* — **56**

GEORGINA 2 ch.f. (Mar 13) Polish Precedent (USA) 131 – Rose Bourbon (USA) (Woodman (USA) 126) [2004 7m 7m 7f Aug 5] 42,000Y: fifth foal: half-sister to useful 2002 2-y-o 7f winner Bourbonnais (by Singspiel): dam, useful French maiden who should have stayed 1m, half-sister to Poule d'Essai des Pouliches winner Baiser Vole: modest form in maidens: needs to settle to stay beyond 7f. *M. A. Jarvis* — **59**

GERMANICUS 2 b.g. (Feb 3) Desert King (IRE) 129 – Simacota (GER) (Acatenango (GER) 127) [2004 p8.6d p7.1g p8.6g⁴ Nov 26] 70,000Y: first foal: dam, German 10.5f winner, sister to very smart German/US 1¼m/1½m performer Sabiango and half-sister to high-class German 1¼m/1½m performer Silvano: best effort in maidens at Wolverhampton when never-dangerous fourth to Bridegroom, not knocked about: will be well suited by 1¼m/1½m: should do better. *R. Charlton* — **57 p**

GERONIMO 7 b.g. Efisio 120 – Apache Squaw 54 (Be My Guest (USA) 126) [2004 –, a71: f6s² f6g f7s³ f8.5s* f8.5s f7g⁴ f8g f6g p6g Dec 27] sparely-made gelding: fair handicapper: won at Wolverhampton in February: below form after: effective at 6f to 8.5f: acts on fibresand (raced only on all-weather since 2002): tried blinkered, often wears cheekpieces: sometimes slowly away: often gets behind. *Miss Gay Kelleway* — **– a69**

GET STUCK IN (IRE) 8 b.g. Up And At 'em 109 – Shoka (FR) 86 (Kaldoun (FR) 122) [2004 –§: 6s 5g 5v Apr 20] leggy gelding: fairly useful sprint handicapper at 6 yrs: no form since: tried in blinkers/cheekpieces: not one to trust. *Miss L. A. Perratt* — **– §**

411

GET TO THE POINT 3 ch.g. Daggers Drawn (USA) 114 – Penny Mint 79 **77 d**
(Mummy's Game 120) [2004 65: f7g 6s² 6m² 6m⁵ 6f 6.1g 7f 5f⁵ 7m f6g f7g* f8d Dec 21]
sturdy, lengthy gelding: fair performer: below best after third outing (left P. D'Arcy after
eighth one), including when winning claimer at Southwell in December: stays easy 7f:
acts on fibresand, soft and good to firm going: tried visored/blinkered. *Miss J. Feilden*

GHAILL FORCE 2 b.g. (Mar 20) Piccolo 121 – Coir 'a' Ghaill 38 (Jalmood (USA) **67 p**
126) [2004 8m² Sep 25] eighth foal: brother to winner in Italy: dam staying maiden: 66/1,
neck second to Bold Counsel in maiden at Kempton: should improve. *J. G. Portman*

GHANTOOT 3 ch.c. Inchinor 119 – Shall We Run 59 (Hotfoot 126) [2004 8g 6.1s **78**
7.5g 8m 9g³ 10g* 10g³ 10.3s Oct 22] 54,000Y: good-bodied colt: eighth foal: brother to
6-y-o Bannister (useful at 2 yrs, won Gimcrack) and half-brother to 2 winners, including
useful 1999 2-y-o 5f/6f winner Roo (by Rudimentary): dam lightly-raced half-sister to
very smart but temperamental sprinter Dead Certain): fair handicapper: won at Brighton
in July: should stay 1½m: best efforts on good going: visored last 4 starts: no easy ride:
sold 32,000 gns. *L. M. Cumani*

GHASIBA (IRE) 2 gr.f. (Mar 3) Daylami (IRE) 138 – Night Owl 73 (Night Shift **76**
(USA)) [2004 6m⁶ 7g² 6s 6.5m 8f Sep 25] 54,000Y: close-coupled filly: has a fluent,
round action: third foal: half-sister to 3-y-o Distant Connection: dam, headstrong maiden
who stayed 6f, half-sister to useful 1½m/1¾m winner Lord Jim and smart French performer up to 10.5f Audacieuse: fair maiden: highly tried third (seemed to run well) and
final starts: should stay 1m: acts on soft going. *C. E. Brittain*

GHOSTZAPPER (USA) 4 b.c. Awesome Again (CAN) 133 – Baby Zip (USA) **137**
(Relaunch (USA)) [2004 126: a7f* a9s* a9f* a10f* Oct 30] fifth foal: half-brother to 3
winners in USA, including smart performer up to 1m City Zip (by Carson City), Grade 1
7f winner at 2 yrs: dam US 6f winner, including minor stakes at 2 yrs: outstanding
performer: won 4 of his 6 starts in 2002/3, including 6.5f Vosburgh Stakes at Belmont
at 3 yrs: reportedly bruised a foot in April 2004, but won all 4 races after, Grade 2 Tom
Fool Handicap at Belmont in July, Grade 3 Philip H. Iselin Breeders' Cup Handicap at
Monmouth (by 10¾ lengths) in August, Woodward Stakes at Belmont (odds on, beat
Saint Liam by a neck, pair well clear, after a good battle) in September and Breeders' Cup
Classic Powered by Dodge at Lone Star Park in October: gave impressive display of front
running when beating Roses In May and Pleasantly Perfect by 3 lengths and 4 lengths in
last-named event, quickening on home turn and drawing clear final 1f, still full of running
passing post: stays 1¼m: acts well in sloppy/muddy conditions: wears visor/blinkers:
tended to come from well off pace in 2003, but raced more prominently since stepped up
in trip: stays in training. *R. J. Frankel, USA*

GHURRA (USA) 2 b.f. (Mar 31) War Chant (USA) 126 – Futuh (USA) 95 (Diesis **85**
133) [2004 6f* 6g 6d⁴ Oct 15] lengthy filly: closely related to 3 winners, including 1997
Middle Park winner Hayil (by Dayjur), and half-sister to 3 winners, including smart 6f
(at 2 yrs) and 1¼m winner Tamhid (by Gulch): dam 2-y-o 6f winner: won maiden at
Yarmouth in August: similar form in listed race at Salisbury and nursery at Newmarket
(fourth to Ingleton): should stay 7f. *E. A. L. Dunlop*

GIANT'S ROCK (IRE) 2 ch.g. (Apr 29) Giant's Causeway (USA) 132 – En Garde **71**
(USA) 82 (Irish River (FR) 131) [2004 7f³ p7.1g⁶ p10g Nov 27] 58,000Y: third foal:
half-brother to 4-y-o Rifleman: dam, 2-y-o 5.7f winner who stayed 1¼m, half-sister to
top-class miler Observatory: best effort in maidens when third at Ascot (gave trouble at
start): refused to enter stall next intended outing: should stay 1m: blinkered (found little)
final appearance. *G. A. Butler*

GIBRALTAR BAY (IRE) 2 b.f. (May 15) Cape Cross (IRE) 129 – Secrets of Honour **58**
(Belmez (USA) 131) [2004 7m 8.3m⁴ 8.2g Aug 18] €18,000Y, 15,000 2-y-o: half-sister
to 5-y-o Double Ransom and 6-y-o Another Secret: dam unraced half-sister to high-class
sprinter Mr Brooks: best effort in maidens when fourth at Windsor: likely to stay 1¼m:
joined T. Mills. *G. G. Margarson*

GIDAM GIDAM (IRE) 2 b.g. (May 11) King's Best (USA) 132 – Flamands (IRE) **66**
92 (Sadler's Wells (USA) 132) [2004 7g⁶ 8g⁶ 10.2g³ Sep 27] €38,000Y, 35,000 2-y-o: tall
gelding: fifth foal: half-brother to useful 1½m/1¾m winner Dune (by Desert King):
dam, 1½m/1¾m winner, sister to smart 1¼m performer Casey Tibbs: best effort in
maidens when third at Bath, slowly away (gelded after): will be suited by at least 1½m.
C. E. Brittain

GIFTED FLAME 5 b.g. Revoque (IRE) 122 – Little Lady Leah (USA) (Shareef **80**
Dancer (USA) 135) [2004 79§: 9.9d 8.3d 7.9f⁴ 8g 8g 8.5m³ 7.9m* 9.1g⁴ 7.5d³ 7.9g⁶ 8g
7.5m* 8m Oct 2] rangy gelding: fairly useful handicapper: won at Carlisle (ladies event)

in August and Beverley in September: stays 9f: acts on firm and good to soft going: tried visored/in cheekpieces: sometimes slowly away/races freely: waited with. *T. D. Barron*

GIFTED GAMBLE   2 b.c. (Jan 28) Mind Games 121 – Its Another Gift 64 (Primo Dominie 121) [2004 5s 5g³ 5m³ 5.1g³ 5g² 5f² 5m* 6m⁵ 5g 6d² 6m 6d³ 6s⁴ 6s⁵ Nov 16] 8,000Y: leggy colt: first foal: dam, maiden best at 5f, out of useful sprinter Margaret's Gift: fairly useful performer: won maiden at Lingfield in July: good efforts when in frame in nursery, sales race (third to Cape Columbine at Newmarket) and listed event (fourth to Andronikos at Doncaster) after: likely to prove best at 5f/6f: acts on firm and soft going: blinkered third to eighth starts, wore cheekpieces on eleventh: often races up with pace. *K. A. Ryan*   **93**

GIFTED LASS   2 b.f. (Mar 11) Bold Edge 123 – Meeson Times 71 (Enchantment 115) [2004 6d p7.1g p5.1g p5.1g² f5g⁴ Dec 16] 5,000Y: good-bodied filly: fourth foal: half-sister to fairly useful 2000 2-y-o 5f winner Mise En Scene (by Lugana Beach): dam 5f and (including at 2 yrs) 6f winner: fair maiden: best effort when second at Wolverhampton: will prove best at 5f. *J. Balding*   **65**

GIFTED MUSICIAN   2 b.c. (Mar 7) Sadler's Wells (USA) 132 – Photogenic 93 (Midyan (USA) 124) [2004 8f* Oct 23] quite good-topped colt: third foal: dam, Irish 6f/7f winner (ran only at 2 yrs), out of half-sister to Bella Colora (dam of Stagecraft) and Colorspin (dam of Kayf Tara and Opera House): 10/1, 8¼ lengths fourth to Descartes in maiden at Newbury, green in rear before staying on well: will be suited by 1¼m/1½m: sure to improve. *J. L. Dunlop*   **75 p**

GIFT HORSE   4 ch.g. Cadeaux Genereux 131 – Careful Dancer (Gorytus (USA) 132) [2004 87: 7g 7g² 7d³ 8m 8.1s⁴ 9g Oct 2] lengthy, angular gelding: fairly useful handicapper: ran well when length second to Ettrick Water and ¾-length third to Chateau Nicol, both at Kempton in June: stays 1m: acts on good to firm going, probably on soft: held up: sold 25,000 gns. *J. R. Fanshawe*   **92**

GIFT OF LIFE (FR)   4 b.f. Android (USA) 116 – Teardrops Fall (FR) (Law Society (USA) 130) [2004 p9.5g Dec 22] half-sister to 2 winners in France by The Wonder, including 9f winner Star of Wonder: dam French maiden: well held in 2 outings for R. Hobson in France at 2 yrs, and in claimer at Wolverhampton. *C. J. Gray*   **–**

GIFT VOUCHER (IRE)   3 ch.g. Cadeaux Genereux 131 – Highland Gift (IRE) 95 (Generous (IRE) 139) [2004 10g 12g³ 10g 12m² 11.5m* Aug 16] useful-looking gelding: fourth foal: half-brother to 2000 Guineas/King George VI and Queen Elizabeth Stakes winner Golan (by Spectrum), fairly useful 1¼m winner Mount Street (by Pennekamp) and 4-y-o Highland Games: dam, 1¼m winner, half-sister to smart middle-distance stayer Bonny Scot: fairly useful performer: landed odds in maiden at Yarmouth in August, making all to beat Samaria 1½ lengths: good second to Stolen Hours in handicap at Newmarket penultimate start: should stay 1¾m: tongue tied last 2 outings: seemed to try to bite rivals third appearance: sold 70,000 gns, then gelded. *Sir Michael Stoute*   **86**

GIG HARBOR   5 b.g. Efisio 120 – Petonica (IRE) 77 (Petoski 135) [2004 84, a96: p12g* p12g p12g* p10g⁵ p13g⁶ 11.6m 9g⁴ 8m 9.9g p12g⁴ p10g p12.2g² Dec 17] good-bodied gelding: poor mover: useful handicapper on all-weather, fairly useful on turf: won in January and February (beat Barry Island ¾ length) at Lingfield (has gained all 4 wins there): left Miss E. Lavelle after ninth start: creditable efforts after when in frame: stays easy 13f: acts on polytrack, good to firm and good to soft going: usually races prominently. *P. R. Chamings*   **86 a101**

GIKO   10 b.g. Arazi (USA) 135 – Gayane 125 (Nureyev (USA) 131) [2004 50: p13g p12g³ p12g p12g⁶ p12g 12g⁶ 12m² 12.6m³ 17.2g 14.1d 12f 8s² 12m Sep 25] leggy gelding: poor performer: stays 13f: acts on all-weather, firm and soft going: tried blinkered/tongue tied: none too consistent. *Jane Southcombe*   **46**

GILDAS FORTUNA   2 b.f. (Feb 8) Fort Wood (USA) 117 – Gleaming Sky (SAF) (Badger Land (USA)) [2004 6d⁴ Oct 15] 5,500Y: good-bodied filly: second foal: dam won 8 races in South Africa, including Group 2 1½m event: 50/1, 2¼ lengths fourth to Desert Imp in maiden at Redcar: open to improvement. *P. C. Haslam*   **71 p**

GILDED COVE   4 b.c. Polar Prince (IRE) 117 – Cloudy Reef 57 (Cragador 110) [2004 78: f6g f6g f6g³ f6s³ f6s⁵ f6g* f5g* f6m⁴ f6d⁴ p5.1g* p5.1g Dec 10] strong colt: reportedly has only one eye: fair performer: won claimers in March and April and handicap in November, all at Wolverhampton: fell final outing: effective at 5f/6f: acts on all-weather and good to firm going: sometimes slowly away. *R. Hollinshead*   **76**

GILLY'S GENERAL (IRE) 4 ch.g. General Monash (USA) 107 – Good Aim (IRE) **49**
(Priolo (USA) 127) [2004 49: f7g⁴ p7g f7m* f7g⁶ 7.1m f7d 7f p7.1g³ p7.1g Dec 22]
sturdy gelding: poor performer: won banded race at Wolverhampton in April: stays 7f:
acts on all-weather, raced only on good going or firmer on turf: tried blinkered/in cheekpieces: often front runner. *J. W. Unett*

GIMASHA 2 b.f. (Mar 23) Cadeaux Genereux 131 – First Waltz (FR) 117 (Green **75**
Dancer (USA) 132) [2004 6.1m⁴ 6g² 5.1s Oct 19] rangy filly: half-sister to several
winners, including useful 1m winners Atlantic Rhapsody (by Machiavellian) and Gaitero
(in France, by Groom Dancer): dam won Prix Morny: fair form at Nottingham and Windsor first 2 starts in maidens: reportedly distressed final one: likely to prove best at 5f/6f.
M. R. Channon

GINGER COOKIE 2 ch.f. (Mar 17) Bold Edge 123 – Pretty Pollyanna (General **–**
Assembly (USA)) [2004 6m Sep 5] 5,000Y: tall, lengthy filly: closely related to 5-y-o
Friday's Takings and half-sister to 3 winners, including useful 1m (including at 2 yrs)
winner Peculiarity (by Perpendicular): dam unraced: 33/1, well held in maiden at York.
B. Smart

GINGER ICE 4 ch.g. Bahamian Bounty 116 – Sharp Top 62 (Sharpo 132) [2004 –: **45**
p10g³ p10g⁵ p16g p8m⁵ p10m Dec 8] tall, leggy gelding: poor maiden: stays 1¼m: acts
on polytrack, raced only on good/good to firm going on turf: tried in cheekpieces/visor:
often slowly away. *G. G. Margarson*

GINGIEFLY 2 b.c. (Feb 9) Sinndar (IRE) 134 – Native Ring (FR) (Bering 136) [2004 **67**
7m 8.3m³ Sep 27] 15,000Y: leggy colt: first foal: dam, French 10.5f winner, out of close
relative to very smart performer up to 1½m Antheus: much better effort in maidens when
third at Windsor: will be suited by 1¼m/1½m. *J. L. Dunlop*

GINGKO 7 b.g. Pursuit of Love 124 – Arboretum (IRE) 83 (Green Desert (USA) 127) **69**
[2004 69, a78: p10g* p10g⁵ p10g p12g³ 10.1d³ f11g⁴ p10g⁵ Dec 18] fair performer: won **a76**
minor event at Lingfield in January: effective at 1¼m/1½m: acts on all-weather, good to
firm and good to soft going: consistent. *P. R. Webber*

GINNER MORRIS 9 b.g. Emarati (USA) 74 – Just Run (IRE) 45 (Runnett 125) **– §**
[2004 –§: f8g⁶ Jan 12] lengthy gelding: no longer of much account: usually blinkered.
J. Hetherton

GIN 'N' FONIC (IRE) 4 ch.g. Zafonic (USA) 130 – Crepe Ginger (IRE) 67 (Sadler's **–**
Wells (USA) 132) [2004 69: 7.1m Jul 23] big, workmanlike gelding: well held over
unsuitable trip only outing in 2004: tried in cheekpieces. *J. D. Frost*

GIOCOSO (USA) 4 b.c. Bahri (USA) 125 – Wing My Chimes (USA) (Flying Paster **89 ?**
(USA)) [2004 91: 7g⁶ 9g 10g 8m* 8.1s⁴ 8.3g⁵ 7.1s⁴ 8g 8s⁶ Oct 19] quite good-topped
colt: fairly useful performer: won handicap at Leicester in August by 1½ lengths from
Concer Eto: stays 9f: acts on firm and soft going: probably best when able to dominate.
B. Palling

GIRLSWEEKEND 2 b.f. (Mar 12) Benny The Dip (USA) 127 – Snoozy (Cadeaux **57**
Genereux 131) [2004 p6g p7g p6g³ Dec 4] 10,000Y: second foal: half-sister to Swedish
11f winner by Inchinor: dam unraced: modest form in maidens at Lingfield: should stay
at least 1m. *Mrs L. J. Mongan*

GIRL WARRIOR (USA) 3 ch.f. Elusive Quality (USA) – Qhazeenah 101 (Marju **?**
(IRE) 127) [2004 76p: 7g⁶ 8f⁴ 10m a8f* a8.5f⁴ a8.5f* Dec 10] tall filly: fair performer:
below form first 3 starts in 2004: left P. Cole, won maiden at Del Mar in September and
allowance race at Hollywood in December: stays 8.5f: acts on dirt. *N. D. Drysdale, USA*

GIRONDE 3 b.c. Sadler's Wells (USA) 132 – Sarah Georgina 79 (Persian Bold 123) **91**
[2004 67p: 10d⁴ 10g³ 12m 11.6g³ 12s* Aug 13] rangy, good-topped colt: fairly useful
performer: visored, landed odds easily in maiden at Catterick in August: best effort when
1¼ lengths third to Settlement Craic in handicap at Windsor penultimate start: should stay
at least 1¾m: acts on soft going: slowly away first 2 outings. *Sir Michael Stoute*

GITCHE MANITO (IRE) 2 b.c. (Mar 28) Namid 128 – Chasing Rainbows (Rainbow **79**
Quest (USA) 134) [2004 7d³ 7d 7m⁵ 7m² Sep 23] 26,000 2-y-o: strong, well-made colt:
third foal: half-brother to useful German 7f/1m winner Cashua (by Bishop of Cashel):
dam unraced half-sister to smart performers Precede (at 1¼m/1½m) and Warm Feeling
(1½m to 2½m): fair maiden: raced up with strong pace when second at Brighton: will
probably stay 1m: acts on good to firm and good to soft going. *A. King*

GIUNCHIGLIO 5 ch.g. Millkom 124 – Daffodil Fields (Try My Best (USA) 130) **74**
[2004 79: p10g³ 10g* 9g 10.3d³ 10.3g⁶ 9g 10m⁴ 12.3s* 10.3g⁶ 10.9s p12.2g⁴ 10d Oct 18]

tall gelding: fair handicapper: won at Kempton in May and Chester (amateur event, went in snatches/wandered) in August: stays 1½m: acts on polytrack, firm and soft going: tried visored at 4 yrs. *W. M. Brisbourne*

GIUST IN TEMP (IRE)   5 b.h. Polish Precedent (USA) 131 – Blue Stricks (Bluebird **43** (USA) 125) [2004 58d: f9.4g⁴ f9.4g² f9.4g f9.4s⁶ 10m 10.2m⁴ 9.7m 8.5d Aug 11] quite attractive horse: poor maiden: stays easy 1¼m: acts on fibresand and firm going. *P. W. Hiatt*

GIVE HIM CREDIT (USA)   4 b.g. Quiet American (USA) – Meniatarra (USA) 68   **–** (Zilzal (USA) 137) [2004 72: f6g⁵ 8m 7m 6m 7g⁶ Jul 24] small, sturdy gelding: well held in 2004, including in seller: tried in headgear. *Mrs A. Duffield*

GIVEMETHEMOONLIGHT   5 ch.m. Woodborough (USA) 112 – Rockin' Rosie   **66** 59 (Song 132) [2004 57: f9.4g² p10g⁵ f9.4g² f8.5g* f9.4g³ p10g⁵ f8.5g³ f9.4g⁶ f7s* f9.4s² f7s³ f8.5s⁶ f8.5s³ p7.1g f8g³ f8g Dec 28] sturdy mare: fair performer: won claimer in January and handicap in February, both at Wolverhampton: effective at 7f to 9.4f: acts on all-weather: tried blinkered/in cheekpieces, usually visored. *Mrs Stef Liddiard*

GIVEN A CHANCE   3 b.g. Defacto (USA) – Milly Molly Mango (Mango Express   **48** 106) [2004 37: f8g⁴ f8g⁵ f7g 12v⁵ 8.1v³ 10s⁴ 8.5m² 8.5m⁶ 10m 8.1g⁶ 8.5g³ Jul 13] close-coupled gelding: poor maiden: left J. Given after third start: effective at 1m/1¼m: acts on heavy and good to firm going. *Mrs S. Lamyman*

GIVEN A CHOICE (IRE)   2 b.c. (Mar 29) Trans Island 119 – Miss Audimar (USA)   **79** (Mr Leader (USA)) [2004 7m⁴ 8.2d 8g⁵ Sep 30] 65,000Y: big, strong colt: good mover: half-brother to numerous winners, notably 5-y-o Bandari: dam winner up to 11f in USA and graded stakes-placed: fair form in maidens at Newmarket (2) and Nottingham: stays 1m: pulled hard second start. *J. G. Given*

GIVERAND   5 b.m. Royal Applause 124 – Petersford Girl (IRE) 84 (Taufan (USA)   **–** 119) [2004 48: 7s 5.1g 5g Jul 12] no form in 2004. *Miss Jacqueline S. Doyle*

GJOVIC   3 br.g. Singspiel (IRE) 133 – Photo Call 73 (Chief Singer 131) [2004 73p: **76** p10g² 8.1s⁵ 7.9d 10.5m⁴ 9.9g³ 12m³ 11.6d 11g⁶ Sep 22] sturdy maiden: fair maiden: stays 1½m: acts on polytrack, soft and good to firm going: tried blinkered: gelded after final start. *B. J. Meehan*

GLAD BIG (GER)   2 b.c. (Feb 27) Big Shuffle (USA) 122 – Glady Sum (GER)   **74 p** (Surumu (GER)) [2004 6m³ 6s Sep 24] €52,000Y: rangy colt: brother to several winners abroad, including useful German performer up to 1m Glady Beauty, and half-brother to useful German 8.5f winner Glad Hunter (by Laroche): dam German 1m (at 2 yrs) to 11f winner: better effort in maidens when third at Lingfield, slowly away: restless stall, tended to hang at Haydock: should stay 7f: likely to do better. *J. A. Osborne*

GLADS IMAGE   2 ch.f. (Feb 3) Handsome Ridge 121 – Secret So And So (So Factual   **–** (USA) 120) [2004 8.2m 7.1d⁶ Oct 9] first foal: dam unraced: well held in maidens. *D. J. Daly*

GLADYS AYLWARD   4 b.f. Polar Falcon (USA) 126 – Versami (USA) (Riverman   **–** (USA) 131) [2004 63d: f11g⁵ f12g Feb 5] lengthy filly: little form since fourth start at 3 yrs: tried blinkered/in cheekpieces. *A. Crook*

GLANWORTH (IRE)   3 ch.g. Woodman (USA) 126 – Leo Girl (USA) 100 (Seattle   **–** Slew (USA)) [2004 11.5g 12m⁶ 8m f8g Jun 16] lengthy gelding: little sign of ability in maidens/handicap (blinkered): gelded after final start. *N. A. Callaghan*

GLARAMARA   3 b.g. Nicolotte 118 – Digamist Girl (IRE) (Digamist (USA) 110)   **100** [2004 93: p7g 7d² 8g 7.6d³ 6m 7f 7g⁴ 6g⁴ 7.6g⁴ 7.6s 6s p6g Dec 18] big, good-topped gelding: useful performer: some creditable efforts in 2004, including when length third to Oasis Star in handicap at Chester in May and fourth to Paradise Isle in Shergar Cup Sprint (Handicap) at Ascot (eighth outing): effective at 6f to 7.5f: acts on good to firm and good to soft going: blinkered (raced freely) on reappearance: hung right fifth start: usually waited with. *A. Bailey*

GLASS NOTE (IRE)   6 b.m. Spectrum (IRE) 126 – Alice En Ballade (Tap On Wood   **–** 130) [2004 –: p12.2g Dec 27] fair handicapper in 2002 for T. Stack in Ireland: well held since. *S. T. Lewis*

GLASSON LODGE   2 b.f. (Apr 16) Primo Dominie 121 – Petrikov (IRE) (In The   **52** Wings 128) [2004 f5g⁴ 5s⁵ 5f⁶ 6.1g³ 6m⁴ 5.1m² 5.1f² 6m⁶ 6.1m 6g⁴ f7g⁶ Nov 22] 3,000Y: quite good-topped filly: fourth foal: half-sister to winner in Holland by Bishop of Cashel: dam unraced out of sister to 1000 Guineas/Oaks winner Midway Lady: poor maiden:

effective at 5f/6f: acts on fibresand, firm and soft ground: visored fifth and tenth starts: sometimes looks none too genuine. *P. D. Evans*

GLEBE GARDEN 3 b.f. Soviet Star (USA) 128 – Trounce (Barathea (IRE) 127) [2004 **83** 86: 8s⁵ 8.2s⁵ 7m⁶ 8g 8.1m 7f* 7d² 7g p7g Oct 1] leggy filly: fairly useful handicapper: won at Yarmouth in August: again dictated pace when good neck second to Princess Galadriel there next time: stays 1m: acts on firm and soft going: carried head high on reappearance: sold 14,500 gns. *M. L. W. Bell*

GLENCAIRN STAR 3 b.c. Selkirk (USA) 129 – Bianca Nera 107 (Salse (USA) 128) **68** [2004 64: 7s 8d 8m p6g* f5m* f6g⁴ f7g* Dec 11] sturdy, good sort: fair performer: won banded race at Wolverhampton (made all) in November then handicaps at Southwell in November and December: stays 7f: acts on all-weather, probably on good to soft going. *J. S. Goldie*

GLENCALVIE (IRE) 3 ch.g. Grand Lodge (USA) 125 – Top of The Form (IRE) 79 **78** (Masterclass (USA) 116) [2004 8m 8g⁵ 8g 7m⁴ 7m* 6m* p7g Oct 1] 75,000F, 225,000Y: strong, well-made gelding: second foal: dam, 5f (at 2 yrs)/6f winner, half-sister to useful 5f performers Double Quick and Speedy James: fair handicapper: much improved when winning at Yarmouth in August and Lingfield in September: ran poorly final start: stays 7f: visored last 3 outings: sold 38,000 gns, then gelded. *J. Noseda*

GLENCOE SOLAS (IRE) 4 ch.f. Night Shift (USA) – Boranwood (IRE) (Exhibi- **80** tioner 111) [2004 77: 6.1s⁶ 6s⁴ 5.7f² 6f² 6m* 6m⁵ 6.1m³ 6d² 5.7g⁶ 6g Jul 24] sturdy filly: fairly useful handicapper: won at Doncaster in June: good short-head second to Jayanjay at Epsom eighth start: stays 6f: acts on firm and good to soft going: tried blinkered. *S. Kirk*

GLENDALE 3 ch.g. Opening Verse (USA) 126 – Kayartis 57 (Kaytu 112) [2004 73: **57** p8g* 10d 10g 8.5v 8.5m f8g⁵ 10g 10m p7g p9.5g⁵ p8.6g p10m⁵ Dec 21] big, strong, workmanlike gelding: modest performer: won maiden at Lingfield in February, hanging badly right: left C. Dwyer after seventh start: stays easy 1¼m: acts on polytrack and good to firm going: tried in cheekpieces/visor: none too reliable. *D. K. Ivory*

GLEN IDA 2 ch.c. (Mar 17) Selkirk (USA) 129 – Yanka (USA) (Blushing John (USA) **83** 120) [2004 7.1d³ 8.1g² 8m* Sep 29] 62,000Y: tall, rangy colt: fourth foal: half-brother to 3-y-o Song of Vala and a winner in USA by Geri: dam, US 1½m winner, out of close relation to July Cup winner Ajdal: fairly useful form in maidens: won at Newcastle by ¾ length from Tamatave, leading over 1f out: should stay 1¼m: carried head awkwardly/wandered first 2 starts. *M. L. W. Bell*

GLEN INNES (IRE) 3 b.f. Selkirk (USA) 129 – Shinko Hermes (IRE) (Sadler's **97** Wells (USA) 132) [2004 8v* 8s² 10.4s² 8.5m 10m 10.3s⁴ Nov 6] leggy filly: third foal: half-sister to 2 winners abroad by Sunday Silence, including French 13f winner Shinty: dam, ran once in Japan, half-sister to Generous: useful performer: won maiden at New- castle in April by 11 lengths: raced in listed/pattern company after, best effort when 6 lengths second to Punctilious in Musidora Stakes at York third start: found little when fourth to Mango Mischief in listed race at Doncaster final start: stays 10.4f: acts on heavy going: sometimes races freely/edges left. *D. R. Loder*

GLEN VALE WALK (IRE) 7 ch.g. Balla Cove 119 – Winter Harvest (Grundy 137) **49** [2004 55: 10.5m⁶ 11.8m³ 10.9m⁵ Jun 14] leggy gelding: poor handicapper: stays 1½m: acts on fibresand, firm and soft going: blinkered: sometimes slowly away/races freely/ finds little: held up. *Mrs G. S. Rees*

GLENVIEWS POLLY (IRE) 4 b.f. Poliglote 121 – Fun Board (FR) (Saumarez 132) **–** [2004 –: f7g⁶ f7g f7g Jan 19] leggy filly: no longer of much account. *Ian Emmerson*

GLENVIEWS SURLAMI (IRE) 3 gr.f. Daylami (IRE) 138 – Surmise (USA) 75 **–** (Alleged (USA) 138) [2004 9.5g f8g f11g p9.5g Dec 22] half-sister to winners abroad by Be My Guest and Royal Academy: dam 7f winner: well held in maidens/claimer, leaving Miss I. Oakes in Ireland after debut. *A. Berry*

GLESNI 5 gr.m. Key of Luck (USA) 126 – Llwy Bren (Lidhame 109) [2004 –: p10g **–** Jan 24] well held in 2 maidens at Lingfield. *S. C. Williams*

GLIDE 3 ch.g. In The Wings 128 – Ash Glade (Nashwan (USA) 135) [2004 72p: 10.9d³ **74** 11.9d 14g³ Jun 11] compact gelding: fair maiden handicapper: creditable third at War- wick (hung left) and Goodwood (visored): tailed off in between: stays 1¾m: acts on good to firm and good to soft going: sold 60,000 gns, joined J. Old. *R. Charlton*

GLIDING BY 3 ch.f. Halling (USA) 133 – Waft (USA) 67 (Topsider (USA)) [2004 –: **–** 10g 10f 11.9f Aug 4] little form. *P. R. Chamings*

GLIMMER OF LIGHT (IRE) 4 b.g. Marju (IRE) 127 – Church Light 88 (Caerleon   **73**
(USA) 132) [2004 79: 10.3g⁶ 10m 10m 10m 10.2g Sep 3] leggy gelding: fair handicapper: weakened tamely last 2 starts, in blinkers final one: stays 1¼m: raced only on good
ground or firmer: sold 9,000 gns. *P. W. Harris*

GLINTING DESERT (IRE) 2 b.f. (Mar 28) Desert Prince (IRE) 130 – Dazzling Park   **73**
(IRE) 116 (Warning 136) [2004 6d 7g⁴ 6m⁶ 5s³ 6d⁵ 6d 7p7m* Dec 22] second foal: dam,
1m (including at 2 yrs)/9f winner and second in Irish Champion Stakes, half-sister to
Japanese Group 1 6f winner Shinko Forest out of Phoenix Champion Stakes winner Park
Express: fair performer: left J. Burns in Ireland, won maiden at Lingfield by ½ length
from Gulchina: stays easy 7f: acts on polytrack, soft and good to firm going. *D. J. Daly*

GLOBAL ACHIEVER 3 b.g. Key of Luck (USA) 126 – Inflation 68 (Primo Dominie   **77**
121) [2004 f8.5g³ f7s² f7g² f6s* 6d 5g 7g f6m 6f 6g p7.1g p5.1d* p5.1g³ p6g² p5.1g³ p6g⁵
Dec 13] 13,000Y: first foal: dam sprint maiden: fair performer: won maiden in February
and handicap in November, both at Wolverhampton: effective at 5f to 7f: acts on all-
weather, little form on turf: tried blinkered/tongue tied. *G. C. H. Chung*

GLOBAL BANKER (IRE) 2 b.c. (Feb 2) Desert Prince (IRE) 130 – Luisa Demon   **–**
(IRE) (Barathea (IRE) 127) [2004 6f p5d⁵ Jul 31] well held in maidens: tongue tied final
start. *G. C. H. Chung*

GLOBE BEAUTY (IRE) 6 b.m. Shalford (IRE) 124§ – Pen Bal Duchess (Chap-   **–**
arly (FR)) [2004 p10g⁶ f7g Feb 9] first foal: dam unraced: last in maiden/seller.
A. D. W. Pinder

GLOBE TREKKER (USA) 2 gr.f. (Apr 6) Aljabr (USA) 125 – Amazonia (USA)   **74**
(Deputy Minister (CAN)) [2004 6g 7.9g⁴ 8m⁴ 8s Oct 11] $18,000Y, 15,000 2-y-o:
lengthy filly: third foal: dam unraced half-sister to smart performers up to around 1¼m
Dr Massini and Weigh Anchor: fair maiden: best effort at York on second start: needs to
settle to stay beyond 1m. *James Moffatt*

GLORIA NIMBUS 2 b.f. (Feb 19) Cloudings (IRE) 112 – Glorious Aragon 88   **44**
(Aragon 118) [2004 5d 6m 5.1g⁶ 5.7g 5g Oct 5] compact filly: fifth foal: half-sister to
winner in Spain by Petong: dam 5f winner: poor maiden: needs to settle to stay beyond
5f. *M. Mullineaux*

GLORIOUS STEP (USA) 2 b.f. (Apr 6) Diesis 133 – Bessie's Chips (USA) (Rakeen   **91 p**
(USA) 99) [2004 7m³ 8.3m* 7v 8f* Sep 23] $35,000Y: leggy filly: first foal: dam, 5f
winner in USA, half-sister to US 2-y-o Grade 3 6f winner Annie Cake: won maiden at
Windsor in August and nursery at Pontefract (beat Dance Flower by neck) in Septem-
ber: stays 1m: acts on firm ground, stiff task on heavy: should make a useful 3-y-o.
J. H. M. Gosden

GLORY GIRL 4 ch.f. Factual (USA) 108 – Glory Gold 59 (Hittite Glory 125) [2004   **41**
50: f6m⁶ 6.1s⁶ May 7] poor maiden: will probably stay 7f: acts on soft going. *M. Brittain*

GLORY QUEST (USA) 7 b.g. Quest For Fame 127 – Sonseri 95 (Prince Tenderfoot   **81**
(USA) 126) [2004 83: f12g² f12g f16s³ f14g⁵ f12s² f16.2s² f12s* 12g 14.1d³ 12m⁴ 14d*
20f 14.1g³ 14.6m* 18s p13.9g p13g f14g Dec 7] good-topped gelding: fairly useful
handicapper: won at Southwell in March, and Haydock and Doncaster (beat Dr Sharp a
short head) in June: effective at 1½m to easy 2m: acts on all-weather, firm and soft going:
sometimes wears headgear. *Miss Gay Kelleway*

GLOVED HAND 2 b.f. (Mar 26) Royal Applause 124 – Fudge (Polar Falcon (USA)   **86**
126) [2004 5.1g* 5f 5g 5m⁶ Sep 21] quite good-topped filly: third foal: half-sister to 3-y-o
Jackie Kiely: dam unraced half-sister to dam of 3-y-o Salford City and Irish Derby second
Definite Article: fairly useful performer: won maiden at Nottingham in June by head
from Castelletto: well held after: should stay 6f. *J. G. Given*

GO BANANAS 3 b.g. Primo Dominie 121 – Amsicora (Cadeaux Genereux 131) [2004   **83**
89: 7.1m⁶ 7m⁴ p7g 7m Sep 17] workmanlike gelding: fairly useful handicapper: stayed
7f: acted on firm and good to soft going: dead. *B. J. Meehan*

GO BETWEEN 3 b.f. Daggers Drawn (USA) 114 – Pizzicato 64 (Statoblest 120)   **91**
[2004 77: 7m² 7m 6m⁶ 7f⁶ 7.1f* 7d 7g Sep 2] good-topped filly: fairly useful handicapper: won at Musselburgh in July by 1¾ lengths from Bint Royal: well below form
after: will prove best at 6f/7f: acts on firm and good to soft going: sometimes slowly
away/races freely: sold 62,000 gns. *E. A. L. Dunlop*

GOBLIN 3 b.g. Atraf 116 – Forest Fantasy 61 (Rambo Dancer (CAN) 107) [2004 73:   **76**
6s⁴ f8g* 10.2g⁵ 9.9g* 12f³ 10m⁵ 10.9f* 10.9m³ p10g Nov 13] sturdy, lengthy gelding:
fair performer: won minor event at Southwell (idled) in April and handicaps at Beverley

in May and Warwick in June: stays 1½m: acts on all-weather and firm going: edged left/
carried head awkwardly penultimate start: held up. *D. E. Cantillon*

GO CLASSIC 4 b.f. Classic Cliche (IRE) 128 – Edraianthus 78 (Windjammer (USA))   –
[2004 67: p16g 14.4s 11.8m May 18] good-bodied filly: maiden: little form since third
start at 3yrs. *A. M. Hales*

GODSEND 2 b.f. (Mar 13) Royal Applause 124 – Gracious Gift 96 (Cadeaux Generoux   **76**
131) [2004 5g² 5m⁶ 6.1m² 6.1m³ 7g Oct 2] sparely-made filly: second foal: half-sister to
3-y-o Instinct: dam, 2-y-o 6f/7f winner, half-sister to smart performer up to 7f Sharp Prod:
fair performer: won maiden at Warwick in July: good placed efforts in nurseries next 2
starts: stays 6f: acts on good to firm going: sold 26,000 gns, sent to USA. *R. Hannon*

GO FOR GOLD (IRE) 3 b.c. Machiavellian (USA) 123 – Kithanga (IRE) 117 (Dar-   **118**
shaan 133) [2004 81p: 10.4d³ 12g² 11.9d³ 14.6f Sep 11] 525,000Y: tall, rather leggy,
attractive colt: fourth foal: half-brother to high-class 7f (at 2 yrs) to 14.6f (St Leger)
winner Milan (by Sadler's Wells): dam, won St Simon Stakes and third in Irish St Leger,
out of half-sister to dam of Kahyasi: smart performer: won maiden at Gowran only 2-y-o
start: much improved after reappearance: 1½ lengths second to Maraahel in ABN Amro
Stakes (Gordon) at Goodwood, 4 lengths third to Rule of Law in Great Voltigeur Stakes
at York and 7¼ lengths seventh to Rule of Law in St Leger Stakes at Doncaster: stays
14.6f: acts on good to soft going, probably on firm: has had 2 handlers/worn crossed
noseband: joined M. Al Kurdi in UAE. *A. P. O'Brien, Ireland*

GO FREE 3 b.g. Easycall 115 – Miss Traxdata (Absalom 128) [2004 –: f7d² f8m⁵ 8f   **53**
f6g⁵ 7.1d 7g f8g⁶ Nov 23] modest maiden: stays easy 1m: acts on all-weather, no form on
turf. *A. M. Hales*

GO GARUDA 3 b.g. Air Express (IRE) 125 – Free As A Bird 62 (Robellino (USA)   **70**
127) [2004 8.1g³ 8.3f p7g* Dec 29] 10,000Y: good-topped gelding: third foal: half-
brother to fairly useful 2001 2-y-o 6f winner Greenhills (by Greensmith): dam, maiden
who stayed 7f, half-sister to useful 7f/1m performers Cragganmore and Hoh Chi Min: fair
performer: off 5 months and gelded, won maiden at Lingfield, carrying head awkwardly,
but leading late on: stays 1m. *D. W. P. Arbuthnot*

GOGETTER GIRL 2 b.f. Wolfhound (USA) 126 – Square Mile Miss (IRE)   **66**
51 (Last Tycoon 131) [2004 5g⁶ 5s² 5d⁴ 5s 5m⁴ 5m⁶ p6g 5f 6.1d 6m 8s p8.6d⁶ p8.6g⁵   **a61**
p7m³ p7.1g² p7.1g³ p7.1g⁶ p7g Dec 29] 800Y: close-coupled filly: second foal: dam 7f/
1m winner: fair maiden on turf, modest on all-weather: stays 7f: acts on polytrack,
soft and good to firm going: wore cheekpieces/blinkers after seventh start. *J. Gallagher*

GO GO GIRL 4 ch.f. Pivotal 124 – Addicted To Love 73 (Touching Wood (USA)   **74**
127) [2004 67: 5.7s* 6d Oct 4] fair handicapper: won at Bath in May: stays 6f: acts on
firm and soft going. *L. G. Cottrell*

GO GREEN 3 ch.f. Environment Friend 128 – Sandra Mac (Marju (IRE) 127) [2004   **61**
f8g 8.1s 10.2g 10.3d 8f⁵ 8.2g 8.1g² 10.2m* 10m⁴ 10g³ 10s² 10.2s⁶ 10.2m 12s³ 10d² 12g   **a–**
11.8g⁶ 11.5d⁴ f11g⁶ p12m Dec 15] good-topped filly: first foal: dam unraced: modest
performer on turf: won seller at Chepstow in August: stays 11.5f: acts on soft and good to
firm going, no form on all-weather: tongue tied after sixth start: sometimes slowly away:
none too consistent. *P. D. Evans*

GOJO (IRE) 3 b.f. Danetime (IRE) 121 – Pretonic 73 (Precocious 126) [2004 71:   **70**
6.1g⁴ 6.1s² 5.7s 6m 6.1d 6d p6m Oct 6] leggy filly: fair maiden handicapper: below form
after second start: should stay 7f: acts on soft and good to firm going: fell on bend when
tried in cheekpieces final outing. *B. Palling*

GOLANO 4 gr.g. Linamix (FR) 127 – Dimakya (USA) 83 (Dayjur (USA) 137) [2004   **82**
86: p10d² 11.6m 10d 11.9g⁶ 10.5s Sep 24] rather leggy, quite good-topped gelding: fairly
useful handicapper: best effort of 2004 when runner-up at Lingfield: reportedly struck
into second start, then left C. Wall: effective at 1¼m/1½m: acts on polytrack, heavy and
good to firm going: usually waited with. *P. R. Webber*

GOLBAND 2 b.f. (Jan 26) Cadeaux Generoux 131 – Hatheethah (IRE) (Machiavellian   –
(USA) 123) [2004 6m⁵ Jun 9] first foal: dam, maiden, half-sister to useful 7f/1m performer Arzoo: 3/1, well held in maiden at Hamilton. *L. M. Cumani*

GOLDBRICKER 4 b.g. Muhtarram 109 – Sally Slade 80 (Dowsing (USA)   **65**
124) [2004 67: f8g⁶ f8.5g⁵ f9.4s* Feb 17] tall, leggy gelding: fair performer: won maiden
at Wolverhampton in February, reportedly finishing lame: stays 1¼m: acts on fibresand,
raced only on good going or firmer on turf. *W. M. Brisbourne*

GOLD CARD 3 b.g. First Trump 118 – Fleuve d'Or (IRE) (Last Tycoon 131) [2004 71: **66** f8s² 11.1d² 12.3g⁵ 12.4g⁵ 12.1d² 10g* Jul 12] fair performer: won claimer at Ayr (claimed £10,000) in July: stays 1½m: acts on good to firm and good to soft going: visored last 2 starts: sold 4,000 gns in October. *J. R. Weymes*

GOLDEN ANTHEM (USA) 2 ch.f. (Mar 19) Lion Cavern (USA) 117 – Bacinella **93** (USA) (El Gran Senor (USA) 136) [2004 5v* 6m 6m³ 7.1m⁶ 6s⁶ 7g 6s Oct 29] 4,500Y: leggy filly: fourth foal: half-sister to 3-y-o Fong's Thong and winner in Belgium by Selkirk: dam unraced close relative to smart 1½m winner Xtra: fairly useful performer: won maiden at Kempton in May: creditable efforts in listed races and Firth of Clyde Stakes at Ayr third to fifth starts: ran poorly last 2: barely stays 7f: acts on heavy and good to firm going. *J. Pearce*

GOLDEN APPLAUSE (FR) 2 b.f. (Mar 18) Royal Applause 124 – Golden Circle **51** (USA) 72 (Theatrical 128) [2004 6.1m Jul 23] €5,000F, €22,000Y, resold 26,000Y: third foal: half-sister to 10.5f winner Glitter Ice (by Intikhab) and 15f winner Adria (by Grand Lodge), both in France: dam Irish 10.5f winner: seventh in maiden at Chepstow: refused to enter stall in August. *Mrs A. L. M. King*

GOLDEN ASHA 2 ch.f. (Feb 16) Danehill Dancer (IRE) 117 – Snugfit Annie 49 **66 +** (Midyan (USA) 124) [2004 5m³ 5m Oct 1] half-sister to 5-y-o Enchanted: dam third in 6f seller at 2 yrs: much better effort in maidens when strong-finishing third at Beverley: favourite, only seventh at Lingfield: should stay at least 6f. *N. A. Callaghan*

GOLDEN BANKES (IRE) 3 ch.f. Foxhound (USA) 103 – Semence d'Or (FR) (Kal- **–** doun (FR) 122) [2004 7m 6g f6s f8g Dec 7] 8,000F, €18,000Y: second foal: half-sister to German 8.5f winner Simonida (by Royal Academy): dam, 2-y-o 7f winner in France on only start, sister to smart winner up to 11f in France/USA See You Soon: little form: hinted at temperament in cheekpieces last 2 starts. *W. G. M. Turner*

GOLDEN BOOT 5 ch.g. Unfuwain (USA) 131 – Sports Delight (Star Appeal 133) **67** [2004 78: 12.1g⁶ 14.1s 13g 11.9f* May 28] big, strong gelding: fair performer: won ladies claimer at Brighton in May: effective at 1½m to easy 2m: acts on any going: wears head-gear: often slowly away: free-going sort, usually held up. *A. Bailey*

GOLDEN BOUNTY 5 b.h. Bahamian Bounty 116 – Cumbrian Melody 83 (Petong **62** 126) [2004 96: 6g 6.1m⁶ 6g 6d 5g f5f p5.1g³ Dec 31] good-bodied horse: just modest form in 2004, leaving R. Hannon after fifth start: barely stays 6f: acts on polytrack, firm and good to soft going: tried tongue tied: none too consistent. *N. Wilson*

GOLDEN CHALICE (IRE) 5 ch.g. Selkirk (USA) 129 – Special Oasis (Green **96** Desert (USA) 127) [2004 99: f8.5g⁵ p6g⁶ 8g 7d 7s* 7m 7g 7d Oct 15] rather leggy, close-coupled gelding: useful handicapper: won at Lingfield in May by ¾ length from Oakley Rambo: below form after: effective at 7f/1m: acts on soft and good to firm going: visored (wandered/found little) second start: sold 16,000 gns, joined Miss E. Lavelle. *A. M. Balding*

GOLDEN CHANCE (IRE) 7 b.g. Unfuwain (USA) 131 – Golden Digger (USA) 66 **57** (Mr Prospector (USA)) [2004 55: 12.3m 11.5m* Jul 1] sturdy gelding: modest handicapper: won amateur event at Yarmouth in July: stays 2m: acts on firm and good to soft going. *M. W. Easterby*

GOLDEN DIXIE (USA) 5 ch.g. Dixieland Band (USA) – Beyrouth (USA) (Alleged **88** (USA) 138) [2004 97: 6m 6d² 6m⁵ 6d⁵ 6m 6d 6g 7g p6g* p5.1g* p7.1g f5f Dec 28] **a80** good-bodied gelding: fairly useful performer: left A. Balding, then won 2 claimers at Wolverhampton in November: effective at 5f to 7f: acts on polytrack, good to firm and good to soft going: sometimes edges right. *C. A. Dwyer*

GOLDEN DRIFT 3 ch.f. Inchinor 119 – Carpet of Leaves (USA) (Green Forest (USA) **64** 134) [2004 –: 8.3g 8m⁵ 11.6d 10m² 10.1g⁵ 10f 12.1m³ 14.1m⁶ Oct 2] big, lengthy filly: modest maiden: stays 1½m: acts on good to firm going: sold 6,500 gns. *G. Wragg*

GOLDEN DUAL 4 b.g. Danehill (USA) 126 – Golden Digger (USA) 66 (Mr Pros- **60** pector (USA)) [2004 72: p10g p10g p12g⁶ f14g p12g p12g p13g² 12s 14.1g p12d Aug 9] lengthy, good-topped gelding: modest maiden: left S. Dow before final outing: stays easy 13f: acts on polytrack and firm going: tried blinkered/visored. *C. L. Tizzard*

GOLDEN DYNASTY 2 ch.c. (Feb 28) Erhaab (USA) 127 – Ajeebah (IRE) (Mujtahid **69** (USA) 118) [2004 7g 7g 8.1s⁶ 8g p7.1g⁴ p7.1g Dec 6] sturdy colt: second living foal: half-brother to useful 2001 2-y-o 5f/6f winner Shukran (by Hamas): dam, ran 3 times, half-sister to useful performer up to 10.5f Cape Grace: fair maiden: fourth in nursery at Wolverhampton: barely stays 1m: acts on polytrack. *R. Hannon*

TSG Firth of Clyde Stakes, Ayr—Golden Legacy shows improved form in a race upgraded to Group 3; Castelletto and Nufoos are close behind

GOLDEN EMPIRE (USA) 3 br.g. Red Ransom (USA) – Golden Gorse (USA) (His **61** Majesty (USA)) [2004 78p: f9.4g² 12g² 11.9d⁴ 11.1g* 11.6d 11.5g Jul 21] close-coupled gelding: just fair performer in 2004: won maiden at Hamilton in April: stays 1½m: acts on good to firm going: tried visored: somewhat irresolute. *E. A. L. Dunlop*

GOLDEN FEATHER 2 ch.c. (Feb 1) Dr Fong (USA) 128 – Idolize 92 (Polish Pre- **76** cedent (USA) 131) [2004 7s³ p8g Nov 13] first foal: dam, 1m (at 2 yrs) and 1¼m winner, sister to very smart performer up to 1½m Riyadian out of Irish Oaks winner Knight's Baroness: 3½ lengths third to Tasdeed in maiden at Doncaster, travelling well long way: odds on, only ninth at Lingfield: should stay at least 1m. *J. H. M. Gosden*

GOLDEN FIELDS (IRE) 4 b.f. Definite Article 121 – Quickstep Queen (FR) (Pam- **43** pabird 124) [2004 57d: 16s 10.9m 12.1m 10s³ p12.2g⁴ p12.2g f11g⁶ Dec 11] lengthy filly: poor performer: stays 11f: acts on firm and soft going: usually blinkered/visored. *Mrs J. Candlish*

GOLDEN FURY 2 ch.c. (Feb 18) Cadeaux Genereux 131 – Galaxie Dust (USA) 86 **85** (Blushing Groom (FR) 131) [2004 6m⁴ 7m³ 8g⁴ 8.1g² 8m³ Sep 29] angular, good-bodied colt: half-brother to several winners, including very smart 6f (at 2 yrs) to 1½m winner Zimzalabim (by Damister), 7f (at 2 yrs) to 1½m winner Dust Dancer (by Suave Dancer) and 7f (at 2 yrs) and 1¼m winner Bulaxie (by Bustino), last 2 both smart: dam 2-y-o 6f winner: fairly useful maiden: best efforts second to fourth starts (runner-up at Sandown): stays 1m. *J. L. Dunlop*

GOLDEN GATE (IRE) 2 b.g. (Apr 21) Giant's Causeway (USA) 132 – Bay Queen **–** 85 (Damister (USA) 123) [2004 8s 8.2v Nov 4] tall, close-coupled gelding: half-brother to 8-y-o Prairie Wolf and 11f winner Dance Master (by Nureyev): dam 9f to 11f winner: well held in maidens, then gelded. *M. L. W. Bell*

GOLDEN GRACE 3 b.c. Green Desert (USA) 127 – Chief Bee 89 (Chief's Crown **94** (USA)) [2004 87p: 10g 10.4s⁴ 10m⁴ 12m 8.1g 10g Oct 11] well-made colt: fairly useful handicapper: good fourth in handicaps at York (beaten 2¾ lengths by Frank Sonata) and Ascot in May: no form after, twice running as if amiss: stays 10.4f: acts on soft and good to firm going: sold 40,000 gns. *E. A. L. Dunlop*

GOLDEN ISLAND (IRE) 3 ch.f. Selkirk (USA) 129 – Daftiyna (IRE) 74 (Darshaan **99** 133) [2004 59p: 9g³ 10g² 10.3d* 10g⁵ 8f* 8m 7g³ 8m² Sep 25] tall filly: useful performer:

420

GOL

won maiden at Chester in June and handicap at Newmarket (beat Summer Shades a neck) in August: excellent head second to Tarfah in listed handicap at Ascot final start: stays 1¼m: acts on firm and good to soft going. *J. W. Hills*

GOLDEN KEY   3 b.g. Rainbow Quest (USA) 134 – Keyboogie (USA) 97 (Lyphard (USA) 132) [2004 10g 10.2g Jun 3] tall, lengthy, quite good-topped gelding: soundly beaten in maidens at Newbury and Chepstow (reportedly lost action): should be suited by 1½m: sold 4,500 gns and gelded. *Sir Michael Stoute*   –

GOLDEN LEGACY (IRE)   2 b.f. (Apr 4) Rossini (USA) 118 – Dissidentia (IRE) (Dancing Dissident (USA) 119) [2004 6f² 6m 6m* 6.1m* 6.1g³ 6s* 6g⁴ Sep 30] leggy, workmanlike filly: third living foal: half-sister to winner in Italy by Paris House: dam 5f winner in Belgium/France: useful performer: won maiden at Catterick in July, nursery at Chester (under 9-7) in August and TSG Firth of Clyde Stakes at Ayr (beat Castelletto by ¾ length) in September: good close fourth to Magical Romance in Cheveley Park Stakes at Newmarket, finishing well despite edging right: will probably stay 7f: acts on soft and good to firm going. *R. A. Fahey*   **107**

GOLDEN LEGEND (IRE)   7 b.g. Last Tycoon 131 – Adjalisa (IRE) 65 (Darshaan 133) [2004 f7m p12g May 13] useful-looking gelding: no longer of much account. *R. J. Price*   –

GOLDEN NUN   4 b.f. Bishop of Cashel 122 – Amber Mill 96 (Doulab (USA) 115) [2004 105: 6g 7s² 7s³ 6.1d* 6d³ 6f* 6d 7m⁵ 6.5g 6d⁵ 7m⁴ 6f 7s Oct 16] angular filly: useful performer: won listed race at Nottingham (by short lead from Forever Phoenix) in May and Kerry Group Ballyogan Stakes at Cork (by 1½ lengths from Simianna) in June: mostly creditable efforts in pattern races after, 4¼ lengths fourth to Pastoral Pursuit in Park Stakes at Doncaster eleventh start: effective at 6f/7f: acts on firm and soft going: wears cheekpieces/blinkers: upset in stall seventh outing: sometimes slowly away: best held up: rather quirky. *T. D. Easterby*   **108**

GOLDEN OLDIE (IRE)   6 b.g. Old Vic 136 – Misty Gold (Arizona Duke) [2004 p8g Mar 9] well held in 2 bumpers, and in seller at Lingfield (blinkered). *D. Flood*   –

GOLDEN QUEEN   3 b.f. Unfuwain (USA) 131 – Queen Linear (USA) (Polish Navy (USA)) [2004 p10g 10.1g³ 10.2g Sep 27] 55,000Y, 7,000 3-y-o: leggy, angular filly: sixth foal: half-sister to 1m winner Ellway Queen (by Bahri) and winner in USA by Miner's Mark: dam winning sprinter in USA: form only when third in seller at Yarmouth. *M. D. I. Usher*   **47**

GOLDEN QUEST   3 ch.g. Rainbow Quest (USA) 134 – Souk (IRE) 98 (Ahonoora 122) [2004 –p: f12s* p12g²* 12.3g 14d* 12m⁵ Jun 17] strong gelding: fairly useful performer: won maiden at Wolverhampton (slowly away) and handicap at Lingfield in March and handicap at Sandown (wandered) in June: good fifth to Admiral in King George V Handicap at Royal Ascot final start: gelded after: stays 1¾m: acts on all-weather, good to firm and good to soft going. *M. Johnston*   **88**

GOLDEN SAHARA (IRE)   3 b.c. Green Desert (USA) 127 – Golden Digger (USA) 66 (Mr Prospector (USA)) [2004 101p. 8g 7d³ 7m* 7m³ 7g Oct 1] strong, lengthy colt: useful performer: won minor event at Goodwood in July by ½ length from Material Witness: good third to Ettrick Water in handicap there next time: below form final start: stays 7f: acts on firm going, probably on good to soft: visored first 2 outings in 2004: wears tongue tie: has had 2 handlers/been on toes in paddock. *Saeed bin Suroor*   **104**

GOLDEN SHELL   5 ch.m. Hatim (USA) 121 – Sonnenelle 71 (Sonnen Gold 121) [2004 7.2s Oct 30] of little account. *A. C. Whillans*   –

GOLDEN SPECTRUM (IRE)   5 ch.g. Spectrum (IRE) 126 – Plessaya (USA) (Nureyev (USA) 131) [2004 –: 6g³ 7.2f⁵ 5.9f 8g 7m³ 6m 7s 6.9g 8.5m³ 8m 9d Oct 15] leggy, quite good-topped gelding: modest handicapper: stays 8.5f: acts on all-weather and firm going: tried in headgear/tongue tied: none too consistent. *D. Nicholls*   **61**

GOLDEN SQUARE (IRE)   5 ch.g. Spectrum (IRE) 126 – Cherish Me 88 (Polar Falcon (USA) 126) [2004 6s 6g⁶ f7g p8.6g⁶ p8m⁶ p8.6g⁴ Dec 31] workmanlike gelding: second foal: dam 6f winner: fair maiden: stays 8.6f: acts on polytrack: blinkered fourth and final starts, found little/hung left in between: not one to trust. *B. J. Meehan*   **65 §**

GOLDEN SQUAW   2 ch.f. (Jan 26) Grand Lodge (USA) 125 – Wig Wam (IRE) (Indian Ridge 123) [2004 7.5g⁶ 6g 7d 7.5m Sep 15] 3,500Y: sparely-made filly: first foal: dam unraced out of close relative of Saddlers' Hall and half-sister to Sun Princess: poor maiden: bred to stay at least 1¼m: blinkered final start. *T. D. Easterby*   **45**

421

Slatch Farm Stud Flying Fillies' Stakes, Pontefract—
a second listed-race success of the year for Goldeva, who gets the better of Fruit of Glory

GOLDEVA 5 gr.m. Makbul 104 – Gold Belt (IRE) 61 (Bellypha 130) [2004 99: 6g* 6s⁵ 6d 6d⁵ 6.1m⁴ 6d* 6.1g⁵ 6d 6s⁶ Nov 6] leggy mare: has a quick action: useful performer: won listed races at Doncaster (by neck from Orientor) in March and Pontefract (beat Fruit of Glory 2½ lengths) in August: best at 6f: acts on any going: tried tongue tied: slowly away last 2 outings: best held up off strong pace. *R. Hollinshead* **103**

GOLD GUEST 5 ch.g. Vettori (IRE) 119 – Cassilis (IRE) (Persian Bold 123) [2004 79: p10g* p10g 7.1m 11g⁴ 10.4m⁵ 11.7g⁶ 12v² p12.2g⁶ p9.5g⁶ p10m³ Dec 21] leggy gelding: fair performer: won handicap at Lingfield in January: left P. D. Evans after eighth outing: stays 11.7f: acts on all-weather, heavy and good to firm going: tried visored: sometimes slowly away/races freely. *J. Hetherton* **68 a72**

GOLD GUN (USA) 2 b.c. (Mar 5) Seeking The Gold (USA) – Possessive Dancer 118 (Shareef Dancer (USA) 135) [2004 8g 8d Oct 15] big, useful-looking colt: closely related to UAE 6f/7f winner Morshid (by Gulch) and half-brother to 2 winners, notably smart but temperamental 7f (at 2 yrs) to 1½m winner Maylane (by Mtoto): dam won Italian and Irish Oaks: burly, well held in maidens at Newmarket: likely to do better. *M. A. Jarvis* **– p**

GOLDHILL PRINCE 2 b.g. (Apr 10) Prince Sabo 123 – Lady Mabel 34 (Inchinor 119) [2004 5g 5.1g⁴ 5.1g f5m² 6g* 6f* 5g* 6f* 7f³ f6d⁶ 7m⁵ 6m³ 6m p6g⁴ Dec 27] 500Y: useful-looking gelding: third foal: dam, maiden, stayed 1m: fair on turf, modest on all-weather: won sellers at Ripon and Ayr in May and claimers at Hamilton and Brighton in June: mostly respectable efforts after: seems best at 5f/6f: acts on all-weather and firm ground: wore cheekpieces after debut: often races up with pace. *W. G. M. Turner* **69 a58**

GOLD HISTORY (USA) 3 b.c. Seeking The Gold (USA) – Battle Hymn (USA) (Danzig (USA)) [2004 96: 8g2 9g* 10d³ 12m⁵ 8m 9.9m 10.4s⁶ 9.9d⁵ 9m* 10f Sep 24] big colt: useful performer: won listed race at Newmarket (made all to beat Psychiatrist ¾ length) in April and handicap at Goodwood (by head from King's County) in September: stays 1¼m (raced freely when below form over 1½m): acts on good to firm and good to soft going: usually races prominently: sold 75,000 gns, joined M. Al Kurdi in UAE. *M. Johnston* **100**

GOLD MAJESTY 2 b.f. (Apr 27) Josr Algarhoud (IRE) 118 – Calcutta Queen 51 (Night Shift) [2004 5d 6g 5.7m 7s 5.7g p7.1g Nov 26] €58,000Y: strong, compact filly: fifth foal: half-sister to 3-y-o Majestic Desert: dam third at 1m: modest maiden: best effort at 5.7f on good going: flashed tail final start. *M. R. Channon* **50**

GOLD MASK (USA) 3 b. or br.c. Seeking The Gold (USA) – Leo's Gypsy Dancer (USA) 113 (Leo Castelli (USA)) [2004 70?: 7d⁶ 8g² 8g* 8m Jun 17] compact colt: fluent **83**

mover: fairly useful performer: visored, made most to land odds in maiden at Goodwood in June by 1½ lengths from Admiral Compton: blinkered, weakened after making most in far-side group in Britannia Stakes (Handicap) at Royal Ascot final start: stays easy 1m: yet to race on extremes of going: races freely: sent to USA. *J. H. M. Gosden*

GOLD MEDALLIST　4 ch.g. Zilzal (USA) 137 – Spot Prize (USA) 108 (Seattle Dancer (USA) 119) [2004 107: 13.3m⁶ 16.4d 16.2g⁴ 15s* 15.5d⁵ 16s⁵ Oct 16] big, strong gelding: smart performer: career-best effort when making most to win Prix Kergorlay at Deauville in August by 1½ lengths from Brian Boru: respectable fifth in Prix Gladiateur at Longchamp (to Westerner) and Jockey Club Cup at Newmarket (beaten 7¼ lengths by Millenary) last 2 outings: will stay beyond 2m: acts on firm and soft going: races prominently: joined P. Hobbs, won over hurdles in December. *D. R. C. Elsworth*　**116**

GOLD QUAY (IRE)　2 b.f. (Mar 16) Docksider (USA) 124 – Viaticum (IRE) 110 (Scenic 128) [2004 6m² 5f⁴ 5.1g⁶ Jul 9] 10,000 2-y-o: workmanlike filly: fifth foal: dam Irish 6f (at 2 yrs) and 1¼m winner: fair form in frame in seller at York (for P. Haslam) and minor event at Windsor: poor effort final start: will stay 7f: sent to USA. *N. P. Littmoden*　**75**

GOLD QUEEN　2 b.f. (Feb 12) Grand Lodge (USA) 125 – Silver Colours (USA) 94 (Silver Hawk (USA) 123) [2004 6d³ 7.5d* Aug 28] 120,000Y: compact filly: first foal: dam, 2-y-o 1m winner, half-sister to smart Japanese Group 2 7f winner God of Chance: refused to enter stall intended debut: won maiden at Beverley (beat Musical Day by short head): should stay 1¼m. *M. R. Channon*　**81**

GOLD RELIC (USA)　3 b.f. Kingmambo (USA) 125 – Gold Bust (Nashwan (USA) 135) [2004 8.3f 10.2g Sep 13] first foal: dam, useful French 1¼m winner, closely related to smart French miler Gold Splash and granddaughter of Arc winner Gold River: soundly beaten in maidens at Windsor and Bath (raced freely). *A. M. Balding*　**–**

GOLD RING　4 ch.g. Groom Dancer (USA) 128 – Indubitable 87 (Sharpo 132) [2004 95: 12g 12.1g² 11.9s³ 14g⁶ 13.9m⁵ 11.9d³ 11m³ 12f⁶ 13.9s² 13d⁴ 12d Oct 14] leggy, workmanlike gelding: useful handicapper: won at Newbury in July by 2½ lengths from Genghis: best effort when short-head second to Mephisto in Ebor at York in August, receiving slight bump from winner close home: effective at 11f to 1¾m: acts on soft and good to firm going: usually races prominently. *G. B. Balding*　**103**

GOLFAGENT　6 b.g. Kris 135 – Alusha 88 (Soviet Star (USA) 128) [2004 –: f16s⁴ 15g⁶ Apr 23] small gelding: poor maiden: stays 17f: acts on fibresand and firm going: tongue tied. *Miss K. Marks*　**39**

GOLNESSA　3 b.f. Pyramus (USA) 78 – My Pretty Niece (Great Nephew 126) [2004 f8s 7.1d 8.2s⁶ May 7] fourth living foal: dam of little account: tailed off in maidens. *Mrs N. Macauley*　**–**

GO MO (IRE)　2 br.g. (May 3) Night Shift (USA) – Quiche 83 (Formidable (USA) 125) [2004 6m 6g⁶ p6g⁶ 7m 8.3d 6v² 6s² Nov 2] €26,000Y: quite good-topped gelding: half-brother to several winners, including smart 6f performer Lionhearted (by Catrail) and useful 5f to 7f winner (in Ireland/France) Symboli Kildare (by Kaldoun): dam 6f winner: fair maiden: second in nurseries at Newbury and Catterick: should stay 7f: acts on heavy going: gelded after final start. *S. Kirk*　**76**

GONDOLIN (IRE)　4 b.g. Marju (IRE) 127 – Galletina (IRE) 74 (Persian Heights 129) [2004 92: 13.3d 15.9s Aug 21] workmanlike gelding: fairly useful up to 10.6f at 3 yrs: well held in 2 handicaps over further in 2004: tried tongue tied/visored. *G. A. Butler*　**–**

Prix Kergorlay, Deauville—complete outsider Gold Medallist wins in the Persian Punch colours; Brian Boru is short of room, but takes second ahead of 2002 winner Cut Quartz (noseband), with Double Obsession and Clety next

GONE FISHING (IRE)   2 ch.f. (Feb 21) Cadeaux Genereux 131 – Dabbing (USA)   **76**
(Cure The Blues (USA)) [2004 6m 7d² 7.5d³ p7g³ Sep 7] €110,000Y: sister to smart Hong
Kong 5f to 1m winner New Trumps: dam, winning sprinter in USA, half-sister to smart
French stayer Molesnes and to dam of very smart French 6f/7f performer Cherokee Rose:
fair maiden: odds on, bit below best final start: stays 7.5f: acts on good to soft going: races
up with pace. *M. A. Jarvis*

GONE LOCO   3 b.f. Piccolo 121 – Missed Again 84 (High Top 131) [2004 –: 8.1m   **–**
Jun 21] compact filly: little sign of ability. *H. S. Howe*

GONE'N'DUNNETT (IRE)   5 b.g. Petardia 113 – Skerries Bell 71 (Taufan (USA)   **67**
119) [2004 76: p5g f6s f5g f5s 6s 6g f6m⁶ 6f⁶ 6f* 5m 6m³ 5.3g* 6g 5.3f⁵ 5.3d² 5.2g 5f
6.1m p5g p6m³ Dec 22] strong gelding: fair handicapper: won at Yarmouth in June and
Brighton in July: best at 5f/6f: acts on all-weather, firm and good to soft going: tried
blinkered, usually visored/in cheekpieces: often races prominently. *Mrs C. A. Dunnett*

GONE TOO FAR   6 b.g. Reprimand 122 – Blue Nile (IRE) 70 (Bluebird (USA) 125)   **58**
[2004 52: 15g* Jul 20] sparely-made gelding: modest handicapper: won at Ayr in July:
stays easy 2m: acts on firm and good to soft going: often blinkered/visored: fair hurdler/
chaser. *P. Monteith*

GONFILIA (GER)   4 b.f. Big Shuffle (USA) 122 – Gonfalon (Slip Anchor 136) [2004   **109**
107: 8m 9m* 7s² 8g* 8.5m* 8f 7m⁴ 7m² 7m* Oct 2] leggy filly: useful performer: won
valuable minor event at Nad Al Sheba in March, listed event at Goodwood in May,
Princess Elizabeth Stakes at Epsom (beat Kunda by 2½ lengths) in June and listed event
at Redcar (beat Twilight Blues by 1¾ lengths) in October: effective at 7f to 9f: acts on
dirt, soft and good to firm going: tongue tied: usually races up with pace: tough and
reliable. *Saeed bin Suroor*

Godolphin's "Gonfilia"

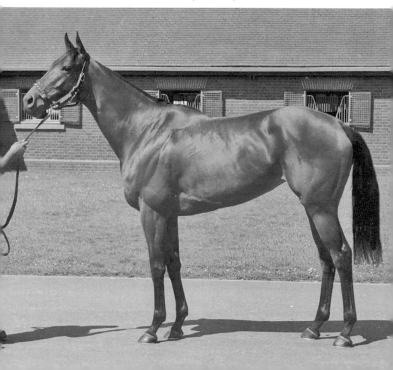

GOOD ARTICLE (IRE) 3 b.g. Definite Article 121 – Good News (IRE) 61 (Ajraas — (USA) 88) [2004 –: 10s 9.7s 10d 8g Jun 17] sturdy gelding: blind in near-side eye: little form: tried tongue tied. *A. P. Jones*

GOODBYE BEN 2 b.c. (Mar 31) Benny The Dip (USA) 127 – Alifandango (IRE) 78 **55 p** (Alzao (USA) 117) [2004 7d p9.5g⁶ Nov 15] 4,000Y: big, good-topped colt: third foal: half-brother to 4-y-o Miss Poppets: dam 1m winner: better effort in maidens when sixth at Wolverhampton, weakening: type to make a better 3-y-o. *J. H. M. Gosden*

GOODBYE MR BOND 4 b.g. Elmaamul (USA) 125 – Fifth Emerald 54 (Formidable **85** (USA) 125) [2004 64: f9.4g⁵ f8g⁶ f8.5s³ 8v⁴ 8d³ 8v⁴ 8g* 8.3m* 8g* 7.9g* 8m³ 9.3f² 8d⁶ 8.1g* 8.9g 8d⁶ Oct 15] strong, lengthy gelding: fairly useful handicapper: won at Newcastle, Hamilton, Redcar and Carlisle within 22 days in June and at Haydock (best effort, beat African Sahara 1½ lengths) in September: stays 9.3f: acts on fibresand and any turf going: visored (raced freely) second start: waited with: tough. *E. J. Alston*

GOODBYE MRS CHIPS 5 ch.m. Zilzal (USA) 137 – Happydrome (Ahonoora 122) — [2004 7.2g⁶ Apr 29] rather leggy, quite good-topped mare: maiden: well held only start since 2002: tongue tied. *Mrs L. B. Normile*

GOODENOUGH MOVER 8 ch.g. Beveled (USA) – Rekindled Flame (IRE) (Kings **97** Lake (USA) 133) [2004 81: p6g² 7g* 7m² 7.1g² 7.1m* 7m* 7.1g⁵ 7.1m² 7d 7.1g 6g* p7g* p7g³ p6g⁵ p7g⁴ Dec 29] rangy gelding: useful handicapper: better than ever in 2004, winning at Salisbury in May, Chepstow in June, Newbury in July, Salisbury in September and Lingfield (by head from Khabfair) in October, ridden by claimer Hayley Turner on 4 of those occasions: best at 6f/7f: acts on polytrack, soft and firm going: usually races prominently: tough. *J. S. King*

GOODENOUGH STAR 4 b.f. Stronz (IRE) 62 – Goodenough Girl (Mac's Imp — (USA) 116) [2004 –: f11g Jan 6] maiden: well held only start in 2004. *A. P. Jones*

GOOD FORM (IRE) 4 b.g. Danetime (IRE) 121 – Faapette (Runnett 125) [2004 — 47: f9.4g⁵ f7g⁶ p6g Feb 3] maiden: no form at 4 yrs: tried blinkered/tongue tied. *Miss K. M. George*

GOOD INVESTMENT 2 b.g. (Mar 5) Silver Patriarch (IRE) 125 – Bundled Up **65** (USA) (Sharpen Up 127) [2004 6g³ 7d⁵ 7.2s p8.6g Oct 7] 12,500Y: unfurnished gelding: half-brother to several winners, including 3-y-o Tytheknot and fairly useful but temperamental 5f to 7f winner Rififi (by Aragon): dam French 2-y-o 9.7f winner: fair maiden: best effort on debut: should stay 1m. *P. C. Haslam*

GOOD LOSER (IRE) 4 b.g. Mujadil (USA) 119 – Cockney Star (IRE) (Camden — Town 125) [2004 64: 8.5d 10.1g May 14] close-coupled gelding: well held in sellers in 2004. *C. R. Dore*

GOODRICKE 2 b.c. (Apr 12) Bahamian Bounty 116 – Star 83 (Most Welcome 131) **92** [2004 5d² 5d* 6.1s¹* 6f Jun 15] 110,000Y: smallish, attractive colt: good walker: has a quick action: fourth foal: brother to 3-y-o Pastoral Pursuits: dam, 5f winner, ran only at 2 yrs: fairly useful performer: won maiden at Leicester in April and minor event at Nottingham in May: respectable ninth in Coventry Stakes at Royal Ascot: stays 6f: acts on soft going. *D. R. Loder*

GOOD TIME BOBBY 7 b.g. Primitive Rising (USA) 113 – Goodreda 58 (Good **51 d** Times (ITY)) [2004 8m³ f14.8g 6.9f⁴ 5m 6m 5d 7m 7.9m f6g Nov 8] sturdy gelding: maiden: showed little after third start: stays 1m: acts on firm going. *J. O'Reilly*

GOOD TIMING 6 bl.g. Timeless Times (USA) 99 – Fort Vally 58 (Belfort (FR) 89) **45** [2004 –: f9.4g² f11g f9.4g 7.5m 10.9d Jun 18] lengthy, sparely-made gelding: poor maiden: stays 9.4f: acts on fibresand and any turf going. *J. Hetherton*

GOOD VIBRATIONS 3 b.f. Bijou d'Inde 127 – Showcase 68 (Shareef Dancer **52 +** (USA) 135) [2004 54: p7g³ f7g⁵ p7g⁶ p6g a6g* 6g* a6.8g² 5.8g* 5.8g² 5.8m³ a6.8g 5.8g⁴ Sep 28] modest performer: sold from P. Cole 1,600 gns after fourth start: won maiden at Taby and minor events at Gothenberg and Taby in May/June: best around 6f: acts on polytrack and dirt (well below form on fibresand), raced only on good/good to firm ground on turf: wore cheekpieces final start in Britain. *M. Kahn, Sweden*

GOOD WEE GIRL (IRE) 2 b.f. (Mar 14) Tagula (IRE) 116 – Auriga 73 (Belmez **71** (USA) 131) [2004 5.7f 6.1s 6m² 6m* 6.1m⁵ 7s* 8d 7m 8g p7.1g f6g p7g³ Nov 16] **a51** 8,000Y: leggy filly: half-sister to 3 winners, including 3-y-o Morse and 4-y-o Forest Air: dam, maiden who should have stayed beyond 7f, half-sister to smart performer up to 1½m Beldale Star: fair on turf, modest on all-weather: won maiden at Leicester in July and claimer at Chester (then left S. Kirk) in August: claimed by S. Woodman final start (wore cheekpieces): stays 7f: acts on polytrack, soft and good to firm going: sometimes slowly away/looks less than keen. *P. S. McEntee*

GOODWOOD FINESSE (IRE) 3 b.f. Revoque (IRE) 122 – Key To Paris (ARG) **77** (Profit Key (USA)) [2004 70p: 9g* 10m⁵ 14s⁶ 11g³ 12s⁶ Oct 29] lengthy filly: fair performer: won maiden at Goodwood in June: stays 1½m: acts on soft going: sold 9,000 gns. *J. L. Dunlop*

GOODWOOD PRINCE 4 b.g. Emperor Jones (USA) 119 – Scarlet Lake 60 (Reprimand 122) [2004 81, a70: p5g⁵ p6g 6d 5g 5g 6f 7f p6g p6d Nov 5] smallish, sturdy gelding: handicapper: mostly well held after reappearance: stays 7f: acts on polytrack, soft and good to firm going: tried in headgear. *S. Dow* **63 d**

GOODWOOD SPIRIT 2 b.c. (Mar 6) Fraam 114 – Rechanit (IRE) (Local Suitor **82** (USA) 128) [2004 6g² 5.7m² 6g³ 7m* 7m⁵ Sep 26] 28,000Y: seventh foal: half-brother to several fairly useful winners, including 4-y-o Hip Hop Harry: dam, Italian 5f to 7f winner, half-sister to very smart middle-distance stayer Sapience: fairly useful performer: odds on, won maiden at Epsom in September: not run of race when creditable fifth in nursery at Ascot: will probably stay 1m. *J. L. Dunlop*

GOOSE CHASE 2 b.g. (Feb 8) Inchinor 119 – Bronzewing 103 (Beldale Flutter (USA) **62** 130) [2004 7g 7s⁶ 7s Oct 27] quite good-topped gelding: half-brother to several winners, including 3-y-o Snow Goose, 5-y-o Dusky Warbler and smart 7f (at 2 yrs) and 1¼m winner Merry Merlin (by Polar Falcon): dam 6f and 1m winner: modest form in maidens: will stay at least 1m: best effort on good going. *M. L. W. Bell*

GOOSE ISLAND (IRE) 3 b.f. Kahyasi 130 – Sabrata (IRE) (Zino 127) [2004 –: **51** 11.9d⁵ 12d² f11g Nov 8] €4,500Y: fifth foal: half-sister to fairly useful 2001 2-y-o 7f/7.5f winner Receivedwiththanx (by Celtic Swing), later 1m/1¼m winner in Spain, and 7f seller winner Head Scratcher (by Alhijaz): dam French 2-y-o 4.5f winner: modest maiden: below form in banded race at Southwell final start: stays 1½m: form only on good to soft going. *Patrick Martin, Ireland*

GO PADERO (IRE) 3 ch.c. Night Shift (USA) – Watch The Clock 93 (Mtoto 134) **96** [2004 82p: 7.1d* 8d⁴ 7s* Nov 2] big, heavy-topped colt: useful handicapper, lightly raced: won at Musselburgh (by short head from Azreme) in October and Catterick (by ¾ length from King Harson) in November: stays 1m: acts on soft going. *M. Johnston*

GORDY'S JOY 4 b.f. Cloudings (IRE) 112 – Beatle Song 70 (Song 132) [2004 –: **–** f14.8g³ 17.2f 16.2m Jul 23] maiden: little form. *G. A. Ham*

GORGEOUS BOY (IRE) 2 ch.c. (Jan 31) Forzando 122 – Instil (Rudimentary (USA) **51 p** 118) [2004 f7g⁵ Dec 16] 2,500F, 2,500Y: first foal: dam unraced: 33/1, fifth in maiden at Southwell, prominent 5f: should improve. *P. L. Gilligan*

GORTUMBLO 2 b.g. (Feb 4) Sri Pekan (USA) 117 – Evergreen (IRE) 74 (Lammtarra **78 d** (USA) 134) [2004 5g* 6m³ 6g 6m 7g 6m Sep 23] 8,000Y: close-coupled gelding: has a quick, fluent action: first foal: dam 1m winner: fair performer: won maiden at Goodwood in May: creditable third in listed race at Epsom: ran poorly after (blinkered final start): should stay 7f. *D. J. S. ffrench Davis*

GOSLAR 3 ch.f. In The Wings 128 – Anna of Brunswick 78 (Rainbow Quest (USA) **92** 134) [2004 9.9g³ 12.1m* 12g⁴ 11.9s⁴ 14.1s⁴ Oct 27] rather leggy, useful-looking filly: fourth foal: half-sister to 1m/9f winner in Germany by Salse: dam, 9.7f winner who stayed 1¾m, half-sister to dams of very smart performers up to 1½m Annaba and Annus Mirabilis: fairly useful performer: won maiden at Chepstow in June: creditable fourth in listed races at Newmarket, York and Yarmouth (beaten 4 lengths by Modesta) after: stays 1¾m: acts on soft and good to firm going: slowly away on debut. *H. Candy*

GO SOLO 3 b.c. Primo Dominie 121 – Taza (Persian Bold 123) [2004 83: 7g 7m³ **82** 8.1m³ 10.5g⁵ 8.5f³ 8.5g 10d 8g Oct 4] workmanlike colt: has a quick action: fairly useful performer: below form after third start, including in claimers: stays 1m: acts on good to firm and good to soft going: sold 23,000 gns. *B. W. Hills*

GOSSIP QUEEN (IRE) 2 ch.f. (Feb 11) Daggers Drawn (USA) 114 – Kifenia (IRE) **60 p** (Hatim (USA) 121) [2004 p7.1g p7m⁵ Dec 22] half-sister to fairly useful Irish 1½m winner Kimu (by Ela-Mana-Mou) and Italian 1m/1¼m winner by In The Wings: dam unraced half-sister to smart 1995 2-y-o 6f winner Kahir Almaydan: better effort in maidens when fifth at Lingfield, slowly away: races freely, but should stay 1m: capable of better. *J. R. Fanshawe*

GO SUPERSONIC 3 b.f. Zafonic (USA) 130 – Shirley Superstar 94 (Shirley Heights **66** 130) [2004 8.1d⁴ 10.2g⁴ Sep 13] half-sister to very smart 1m (at 2 yrs) to 1½m (Oaks) winner Lady Carla (by Caerleon) and 9f winner Azores (by Polish Precedent): dam, 7f winner (at 2 yrs), out of smart performer up to 1¾m Odeon: favourite, fourth in maidens at Sandown (better effort) and Bath (wandered). *Sir Michael Stoute*

GO TECH 4 b.g. Gothenberg (IRE) 117 – Bollin Sophie (Efisio 120) [2004 91: 8g 7v 7d⁶ 7m 8.1d⁶ 10m² 10.1v⁴ 10s⁶ 7.9d 10.3g⁴ 10g² 10f* 10m* 10.4g* 12s Nov 6] rather leggy gelding: shows plenty of knee action: fairly useful handicapper: right back to best in autumn, winning at Pontefract, Redcar and York (beat Beat The Heat by 1½ lengths, idling): stays 10.4f: acts on any going: sometimes races freely: held up. *T. D. Easterby* **94**

GOT ONE TOO (FR) 7 ch.g. Green Tune (USA) 125 – Gloria Mundi (FR) (Saint Cyrien (FR) 128) [2004 80: 16.2m² 20f Jun 15] big, plain gelding: fair handicapper: stays 2m: acts on soft and good to firm going: blinkered on debut: tried tongue tied in 2000: front runner: smart chaser. *N. J. Henderson* **76 +**

GOT TO BE CASH 5 ch.m. Lake Coniston (IRE) 131 – Rasayel (USA) 79§ (Bering 136) [2004 53: f9.4g⁴ 9.9s² 9.7s* 10m 10m⁵ 9.9g³ 9.7f 10.5s 10.2s** 10g⁴ 9v 10.9d Sep 18] strong, lengthy mare: modest handicapper: won at Folkestone in May and Chepstow (apprentice event) in August: stays 12.4f: acts on firm and soft going: usually waited with. *W. M. Brisbourne* **59**

GOTYA 4 b.f. Gothenberg (IRE) 117 – Water Well 96 (Sadler's Wells (USA) 132) [2004 –: f12s Feb 16] angular filly: tailed off in 2 maidens. *J. R. Weymes* **–**

GOVERNMENT (IRE) 3 b.g. Great Dane (IRE) 122 – Hidden Agenda (FR) 55 (Machiavellian (USA) 123) [2004 8m 10m⁴ 7g⁵ 6g Oct 5] well-made gelding: seemingly best effort in maidens when fifth at Catterick, first start after leaving J. Gosden: blinkered second outing. *M. C. Chapman* **49 ?**

GO YELLOW 3 b.g. Overbury (IRE) 116 – Great Lyth Lass (IRE) 67 (Waajib 121) [2004 76: 7g 6.1d 6m⁵ 6.1m² 7g⁴ 7m⁶ 7m* 6m⁴ 7.1m 7g² p7.1g 7d⁶ p8.6g⁶ f7g p6g p7g Dec 31] close-coupled gelding: fair performer: won maiden at Yarmouth in July: barely stays 8.6f: acts on polytrack, good to firm and good to soft going. *P. D. Evans* **74 a67**

GRACE DARLING 3 b.f. Botanic (USA) – Light On The Waves 71 (Greensmith 121) [2004 –: 12.1d⁵ Apr 23] tailed off in seller/claimer. *Miss E. C. Lavelle* **–**

GRACEFUL AIR (IRE) 3 b.f. Danzero (AUS) – Samsung Spirit 79 (Statoblest 120) [2004 65: f6g⁴ 6v⁵ 7.1d² 8m² 7.5m⁴ 8f 7.2g⁵ 8m⁴ 9.2g⁴ 7.1f⁵ 7.1g 7.9g 8g³ 8g² 9d f8g⁴ p8.6g Nov 15] workmanlike filly: modest maiden: probably stays 9f: acts on fibresand, firm and good to soft going: tried in cheekpieces/visor: tail flasher: consistent. *J. R. Weymes* **56**

GRACEFUL FLIGHT 2 gr.f. (Apr 4) Cloudings (IRE) 112 – Fantasy Flight (Forzando 122) [2004 6d 6f Sep 13] first reported foal: dam no form: well held in maidens. *P. T. Midgley* **–**

GRACIA 5 gr.m. Linamix (FR) 127 – Francia 59 (Legend of France (USA) 124) [2004 78: 8.3d 8m 8.5s⁴ Apr 21] lengthy, angular mare: just modest form in 2004: effective at 1m to 1¼m: acts on polytrack, good to firm and good to soft going. *S. C. Williams* **61**

GRACIE'S GIFT (IRE) 2 b.g. (Feb 24) Imperial Ballet (IRE) 110 – Settle Petal (IRE) (Roi Danzig (USA)) [2004 5m⁴ 5m⁴ f6s³ p7.1g Dec 1] modest maiden: best effort when third in claimer at Southwell: stays 6f, possibly not 7f. *P. C. Haslam* **62**

GRACILIS (IRE) 7 b.g. Caerleon (USA) 132 – Grace Note (FR) 99 (Top Ville 129) [2004 f16s 18.7d 14.6s Oct 22] heavy-topped gelding: fairly useful handicapper at best: unraced in 2003: well held at 7 yrs. *G. A. Swinbank* **–**

GRACIOUS AIR (USA) 6 b.m. Bahri (USA) 125 – Simply Bell (USA) (Simply Majestic (USA)) [2004 46: p10g f8g* f8g⁵ f8g³ f9.4s³ f8s Mar 14] tall, leggy, good-topped mare: modest performer: won apprentice banded stakes at Southwell in February: effective at 1m to easy 1½m: acts on fibresand, probably on any turf going: wore headgear last 7 starts. *J. R. Weymes* **56**

GRADY 5 ch.g. Bluegrass Prince (IRE) 110 – Lady Sabina 61 (Bairn (USA) 126) [2004 –: 8.1d⁶ 12.3m⁶ 12.3g 10.9d⁶ 11.5m 12.1g 12m Aug 3] sturdy gelding: disappointing maiden: tried blinkered/in cheekpieces. *W. M. Brisbourne* **–**

GRAFT 5 b.g. Entrepreneur 123 – Mariakova (USA) 84 (The Minstrel (CAN) 135) [2004 75: 10.1v 9.9d⁶ 10d² 12f 12.3m 9g* 7m p12g⁵ p9.5g p10g⁶ p10m* Dec 21] quite good-topped gelding: fair handicapper: won at Kempton (amateur event on first start after leaving M. Easterby) in June and Lingfield in December: best around 9f/1¼m: **72**

acts on polytrack, firm and soft going: wore blinkers/cheekpieces 8 of last 9 outings.
Mrs P. Townsley

GRAHAM ISLAND 3 b.g. Acatenango (GER) 127 – Gryada 93 (Shirley Heights **90**
130) [2004 74p: 11g* p12g 12.3d[6] 11g[6] 13.1d 11.6m[5] p12g[4] p12g Nov 20] strong, lengthy
gelding: has a round action: fairly useful performer: won maiden at Newbury in April by
2 lengths from Strike: several respectable efforts after, including in listed company and
handicaps: stays 1½m: acts on polytrack and good to firm ground: free-going sort: has
shown signs of temperament. *G. Wragg*

GRALMANO (IRE) 9 b.g. Scenic 128 – Llangollen (IRE) 87 (Caerleon (USA) 132) **82**
[2004 94, a89: p12g 18.7d 13.9m[6] 20f Jun 15] strong gelding: unimpressive mover: fairly
useful handicapper: form in 2004 only when sixth to Star Member at York: stays easy
2¼m: acts on all-weather, firm and good to soft going: tried visored/blinkered earlier in
career: heavily bandaged fore joints last 2 starts: edgy sort: races prominently. *K. A. Ryan*

GRAMADA (IRE) 2 b.f. (Apr 12) Cape Cross (IRE) 129 – Decatur (Deploy 131) **–**
[2004 6m Aug 2] 12,000Y: first foal: dam unraced close relative to useful stayer Georgia
Venture: 25/1 and green, well held in maiden at Windsor. *M. J. Wallace*

GRAMPIAN 5 b.h. Selkirk (USA) 129 – Gryada 93 (Shirley Heights 130) [2004 12.3d[2] **111**
12.1d[6] 10.3g[2] 11.9g[3] 13.9s 14.1g[2] 12m[5] Sep 26] rather leggy, good-topped horse: smart
performer: unraced in 2003 (reportedly kicked a wall early in year): best efforts at 5yrs
when runner-up in minor events at Ripon, Doncaster (5 lengths behind Muqbil) and
Salisbury (went down by neck to Barolo) and third in Old Newton Cup at Haydock
(beaten 4¼ lengths by Alkaased): stays easy 1¾m: acts on firm and good to soft going:
slowly away second outing: held up. *J. G. Given*

GRANARY GIRL 2 b.f. (Feb 8) Kingsinger (IRE) 94 – Highland Blue 55 (Never So **43**
Bold 135) [2004 5.1g 6.1g p7.1g[6] f7g Dec 16] £1,000Y: second foal: dam, ran 3 times,
half-sister to smart sprinter Lord Kintyre: poor maiden. *B. Palling*

GRANATO (GER) 3 b.c. Cadeaux Genereux 131 – Genevra (IRE) 107 (Danehill **89**
(USA) 126) [2004 89p: 6d 6d 8m[4] 7.1m[4] a6f a6g Dec 9] strong colt: fluent mover: fairly
useful handicapper: creditable fourth at Newmarket and Sandown (raced freely) in
summer (trained by A. Stewart): off 4 months, tailed off on dirt last 2 starts: effective at
7f/1m: acts on firm and good to soft. *D. J. Selvaratnam, UAE*

GRAN CLICQUOT 9 gr.m. Gran Alba (USA) 107 – Tina's Beauty 41 (Tina's Pet **56**
121) [2004 54: p8g p10g p8g[2] 10m 9g* 8.1f 9g[2] 8m 9.7f 8m Sep 25] modest handicapper:
won amateur event at Goodwood in June: stays 11f: acts on polytrack, raced only on good
going or firmer on turf: tried in cheekpieces at 7 yrs. *G. P. Enright*

GRANDALEA 3 b.f. Grand Lodge (USA) 125 – Red Azalea 95 (Shirley Heights 130) **85**
[2004 81: 8.3m[5] 8.3g[3] p7g* 8.5g[6] Aug 30] tall, heavy-topped filly: fairly useful performer: won minor event at Lingfield in July be runs from Eccentric, best effort: stays 1m:
acts on polytrack and firm going. *Sir Michael Stoute*

GRAN DANA (IRE) 4 b.g. Grand Lodge (USA) 125 – Olean (Sadler's Wells (USA) **85 d**
132) [2004 11.8d[2] 12g* 12.1g 13.9s 12.1m 11.9g 10.1g 15s Oct 11] big, strong gelding:
fairly useful performer: won maiden at Musselburgh in April: well below form in handicaps after third start: should stay 1¾m: acts on good to soft going: sold 5,000 gns, joined
G. Prodromou. *M. Johnston*

GRAND APOLLO 3 ch.f. Grand Lodge (USA) 125 – Narva (Nashwan (USA) 135) **70**
[2004 67p: 8f[2] 8m[5] p8g[6] p8.6g[5] p10g Oct 31] quite attractive filly: fair maiden: should
stay 1¼m: acts on polytrack, raced only on ground firmer than good on turf: slowly away
second outing. *J. H. M. Gosden*

GRAND BUT ONE (IRE) 3 ch.c. Grand Lodge (USA) 125 – Unscathed (Warning **89**
136) [2004 8g[6] 8m[2] 8m[2] 8m[3] 8g* 8m[6] 8g* p8.6g Nov 8] €75,000Y: close-coupled colt:
first foal: dam unraced out of close relative to Poule d'Essai des Pouliches winner Houseproud: fairly useful performer: won maiden at Ripon (dictated pace) in July and claimer
at Pontefract (beat Patterdale 1¼ lengths) in October: stays easy 1¼m: acts on good to
firm going: reportedly broke blood vessel final start: sent to USA. *B. W. Hills*

GRAND CENTRAL (IRE) 2 b.c. (Apr 7) Sadler's Wells (USA) 132 – Rebecca **97 p**
Sharp 122 (Machiavellian (USA) 123) [2004 7s* Oct 25] fourth foal: half-brother to
useful 6f (at 2 yrs) and 1m winner Miss Pinkerton (by Danehill): dam 7f/1m (Coronation
Stakes) winner: 5/2-on, won 7-runner maiden at Leopardstown easily by 4 lengths from
Conscript, leading over 1f out and soon well on top: will stay at least 1m: sure to improve.
A. P. O'Brien, Ireland

GRANDE ROCHE (IRE)   2 b.c. (May 17) Grand Lodge (USA) 125 – Arabian Lass   **– p**
(SAF) (Al Mufti (USA) 112) [2004 6s Nov 6] €75,000Y: well-made colt: second living
foal: dam champion 2-y-o filly/Group 1 1m winner in South Africa: 18/1 and green,
behind in maiden at Doncaster, slowly away and not knocked about: type to do better.
B. W. Hills

GRANDE TERRE (IRE)   3 b.f. Grand Lodge (USA) 125 – Savage (IRE) 98 (Polish   **–**
Patriot (USA) 71: 8.1s 10.5g 8m 9s 12g 16.1m Sep 29] leggy filly: maiden:
little form at 3 yrs. *J. G. Given*

GRAND FROMAGE (IRE)   6 ch.g. Grand Lodge (USA) 125 – My First Paige (IRE)   **58 +**
53 (Runnett 125) [2004 16.2m 18g 15.9g³ Jul 10] quite good-topped gelding: fairly useful
handicapper at 4 yrs (visored 3 times, including when successful): missed 2003: just
modest form in 2004: stays 2m: acts on firm and good to soft going. *A. King*

GRAND GIRL   2 b.f. (Mar 2) Mark of Esteem (IRE) 137 – Ayunli 81 (Chief Singer   **46**
131) [2004 7g 7s 7.1s p7.1g⁵ Oct 16] 8,000Y: lengthy filly: fifth foal: half-sister to fairly
useful 2001 2-y-o 5f winner Ayzal (by Zilzal) and US 8.5f/9f winner Helms Deep (by
Royal Applause): dam 8.5f to 15.5f winner: poor maiden: will stay 1m. *B. W. Duke*

GRAND IDEAS   5 br.g. Grand Lodge (USA) 125 – Afrafa (IRE) (Lashkari 128) [2004   **63**
p7g² f7g p10m⁶ Dec 21] fair maiden: unraced at 4 yrs: stays 1½m: acts on polytrack,
raced only on good to soft/soft going on turf. *Julian Poulton*

GRAND LASS (IRE)   5 b.m. Grand Lodge (USA) 125 – Siskin (IRE) (Royal Academy   **55 §**
(USA) 130) [2004 73d: f9.4g³ f12g⁴ f9.4g* f8.5s² f8.5s⁵ f9.4g⁴ 12d³ 10.9s 11s f12g⁴ Apr
26] compact mare: modest performer: won claimer at Wolverhampton (left T. D. Barron)
in February: should stay 1¾m: acts on fibresand, good to firm and good to soft going:
usually wears headgear: has refused to enter stall on several occasions, and banned from
Flat racing from stalls until mid-Jan 2005. *A. Sadik*

GRANDMA LILY (IRE)   6 b.m. Bigstone (IRE) 126 – Mrs Fisher (IRE) 94 (Salmon   **65**
Leap (USA) 131) [2004 87: f5s³ f5g f6g f6g 7g 5g 6.1s³ 8g 6.1m³ 7s⁴ p7.1d⁴ f6g* p6g⁶   **a77**
Dec 11] big, lengthy mare: fair handicapper: left M. Chapman after ninth outing: won at
Southwell in November: probably best at 5f/6f: acts on all-weather, soft and good to firm
going: visored last 2 starts: sometimes carries head awkwardly: often races up with pace:
none too consistent. *D. Carroll*

GRAND MARQUE (IRE)   2 ch.c. (Feb 23) Grand Lodge (USA) 125 – Royal Fizz   **99**
(IRE) (Royal Academy (USA) 130) [2004 7m⁵ 7m* 7m* 8g² 7f⁵ 8f Sep 25] 80,000F:
well-made colt: fourth foal: half-brother to winner in Belgium by Brief Truce: dam,
French 2-y-o 6.5f winner, out of sister to high-class middle-distance stayers Diamond
Shoal and Glint of Gold: useful performer: won maiden and minor event (beat Blues And
Royals a neck) at Newbury in July: 3 lengths second of 3 to Perfectperformance in listed
race at Salisbury: respectable efforts in Champagne Stakes at Doncaster and Royal Lodge
Stakes at Ascot last 2 starts: stays 1m: acts on firm going. *R. Hannon*

GRANDMA RYTA   2 br.f. (Apr 23) Cyrano de Bergerac 120 – Tamara 83 (Marju (IRE)   **28**
127) [2004 5m 5g Oct 5] close-coupled filly: second foal: dam 2-y-o 5f winner: burly,
poor form in maidens. *John Berry*

GRANDMA'S GIRL   2 b.f. (Mar 30) Desert Style (IRE) 121 – Sakura Queen (IRE)   **64**
52 (Woodman (USA) 126) [2004 6g 7f⁴ 7.1m⁵ 8m 8.3d Oct 4] half-sister to several
winners, including 3-y-o Son of Thunder and 1½m winner Reine Cerise (by Shareef
Dancer): dam, maiden who stayed 1¼m, half-sister to dam of Rock of Gibraltar: modest
maiden: stays 1m: acts on firm ground: hung left third start. *R. Guest*

GRAND MUSIC (IRE)   4 b.g. Grand Lodge (USA) 125 – Abury (IRE) 104 (Law   **–**
Society (USA) 130) [2004 12f p13g p12.2g Dec 4] lengthy gelding: well held in maidens:
blinkered last 2 starts. *J. J. Sheehan*

GRAND OPTION   2 ch.c. (Feb 3) Compton Place 125 – Follow The Stars 86 (Sparkler   **73**
130) [2004 p5g 5s³ 5d² 5.1g³ 5g² 5g⁵ 5.2m 6m 7.1g⁴ 7.1d⁶ 7m 6d* Oct 18] 8,000Y:
compact colt: half-brother to numerous winners, including useful 5f (at 2 yrs) to 1¼m
winner Brigante di Cielo (by Robellino) and fairly useful 5f (at 2 yrs)/6f winner Montserrat (by Aragon): dam 8.5f and 1¼m winner: fair performer: won maiden at Pontefract:
probably best at 5f/6f: acts on soft and good to firm going: blinkered (below form)
seventh, tenth and eleventh starts. *B. W. Duke*

GRANDOS (IRE)   2 b.c. (May 13) Cadeaux Genereux 131 – No Reservations (IRE)   **60**
87 (Commanche Run 133) [2004 6g 7s⁵ 6d Aug 27] 37,000Y: tall colt: fifth foal: half-
brother to smart 6f/7f winner Hot Tin Roof (by Thatching): dam, 6f (at 2 yrs)/7f winner,

half-sister to smart sprinters Hanu and Sanu: modest form in maidens: reportedly lost action final start: stays 7f. *T. D. Easterby*

GRAND PASSION (IRE)   4 b.g. Grand Lodge (USA) 125 – Lovers' Parlour 83   **113**
(Beldale Flutter (USA) 130) [2004 110: p10g² p10g* p10g 10.3d 8g⁴ 10m² 8f* 8m³ 8g⁶
p10g* Nov 20] good-bodied gelding: smart performer: won minor event at Lingfield in
February and listed races at the Curragh (by length from Solskjaer) in June and Lingfield
(asserted final 1f to beat Compton Bolter 1¼ lengths) in November: effective at 1m/1¼m:
acts on polytrack, firm and good to soft going: waited with. *G. Wragg*

GRAND PLACE   2 b.g. (Mar 26) Compton Place 125 – Comme Ca (Cyrano de Berge-   **77**
rac 120) [2004 6m 5g⁴ 5.2m 5g* 6g 6f⁴ 6.1d⁴ 5m⁵ Oct 2] 15,000Y: leggy, lengthy gelding:
second foal: half-brother to 3-y-o Even Easier: dam unraced: fair performer: landed odds
in maiden at Folkestone in August: good close fourth in sales race at Doncaster 2 starts
later: will prove best at 5f/6f: acts on firm going. *R. Hannon*

GRAND PRAIRIE (SWE)   8 b.g. Prairie – Platonica (ITY) (Primo Dominie 121)   **54 ?**
[2004 ?: p13g⁵ Jan 31] Swedish-bred gelding: winner of 12 races in Sweden/Spain:
modest form only start on Flat in 2004: stays 1½m: acts on sand, polytrack and good to
firm going. *G. L. Moore*

GRAND RAPIDE   3 ch.f. Grand Lodge (USA) 125 – Vax Rapide 80 (Sharpo 132)   **62**
[2004 6g⁶ 7d 8.3f 7.1s⁴ 8d* 9.9m p9.5g 8d Nov 5] leggy filly: first foal: dam, 2-y-o 5f
winner, out of useful sprinter Vax Lady: modest performer: won handicap at Bath in
August, easily best effort: stays 1m: acts on good to soft going. *J. L. Spearing*

GRAND REWARD (USA)   3 b. or br.c. Storm Cat (USA) – Serena's Song (USA)   **107**
126 (Rahy (USA) 115) [2004 112: 7m² 8m⁵ 7f 6m⁶ 6m 6m³ 5m⁶ 6d³ 5m 6d² a7f Dec 26]
smallish, angular, good-topped colt: useful performer: landed odds in minor event at Naas
in July: some creditable efforts after, including when ¾-length third to Royal Millennium
in Renaissance Stakes at the Curragh eighth start and 3½ lengths second to Striking
Ambition in listed race there penultimate one (final outing for A. O'Brien in Ireland):
best up to 7f (not discredited when fifth in Irish 2000 Guineas over 1m second appearance): acts on good to firm and good to soft going (short to post, ran as though amiss on
firm ground in Jersey Stakes at Royal Ascot third start), stiff task on dirt: refused to race
fifth outing (fitted with blanket after): has worn crossed noseband and tongue tie:
blinkered last 4 starts. *D. W. Lukas, USA*

GRAND SHOW   2 b.c. (Apr 25) Efisio 120 – Christine Daae 74 (Sadler's Wells   **77 p**
(USA) 132) [2004 6f⁴ 6s⁵ p6g⁵ Nov 16] strong colt: brother to fairly useful 5f winner
Annette Vallon and half-brother to several winners, including smart sprinter To The Roof
(by Thatching) and useful 5f (at 2 yrs) and 1m winner Risque Lady (by Kenmare): dam
1¼m winner: progressive form in maidens (trained by P. Harris first 2 starts), winning
12-runner event at Lingfield by 2 lengths from Latin Express: should stay 7f: will improve. *W. R. Swinburn*

GRAND VIEW   8 ch.g. Grand Lodge (USA) 125 – Hemline 77 (Sharpo 132) [2004   **45**
49: p6g⁶ f7g 6v⁴ 6.1g² p6g* 6g 6.1m 7g 6.1d 6m Jul 31] poor performer: won banded
event at Lingfield in April: stays 6f: acts on all-weather and any turf going: tried blinkered, wore cheekpieces at 8 yrs: hung markedly left final outing. *J. R. Weymes*

GRAND WELCOME (IRE)   2 b.g. (Mar 12) Indian Lodge (IRE) 127 – Chocolate   **62**
Box 70 (Most Welcome 131) [2004 5.1g 6.1s 7g 7s² 7m² 8s p8.6g p8m⁵ Dec 8] 6,000Y:
smallish gelding: third foal: dam, 13f winner, sister to very smart stayer Arctic Owl:
modest maiden: second at Brighton and Newcastle, making running: should stay 1m: acts
on soft and good to firm going: blinkered last 5 starts. *C. Tinkler*

GRAND WIZARD   4 b.g. Grand Lodge (USA) 125 – Shouk 94 (Shirley Heights 130)   **54**
[2004 68+: p12g⁴ 14.1s 11.5f 12.3s 10d⁶ Sep 20] close-coupled, quite good-topped   **a72**
gelding: fair on all-weather, modest on turf: stays 1½m: acts on polytrack and good to soft
going: tried tongue tied: has hinted at temperament: sold 7,500 gns. *W. Jarvis*

GRANITA   2 b. or br.f. (Mar 22) Machiavellian (USA) 123 – Actualite (Polish Precedent   **–**
(USA) 131) [2004 6g Aug 11] €135,000Y: half-sister to several winners, including 4-y-o
Ali Bruce and 7-y-o Shamrock City: dam French 10.5f winner: behind in maiden at
Salisbury, travelling comfortably 3f. *M. Blanshard*

GRANSTON (IRE)   3 b. or gr.g. Revoque (IRE) 122 – Gracious Gretclo 54 (Common   **87**
Grounds 118) [2004 74: 7g³ 8g* 8m⁶ 8m⁶ 7m 7f² 7g⁵ 7m³ 8f* Sep 24] tall, leggy, quite
good-topped gelding: fairly useful handicapper: won at Ripon in April and Ascot (beat
Evaluator by a neck) in September: stays 1m: acts on firm going: sometimes races freely.
J. D. Bethell

GRANT (IRE)   4 b.g. Bahamian Bounty 116 – Verify 94 (Polish Precedent (USA) 131)   **73**
[2004 69: f7s⁵ p5g⁶ 7d 5d⁵ 5.8d² 5f⁴ 5s Sep 16] fair handicapper: won claimer at Ballinrobe in 2003: respectable efforts at Wolverhampton and Lingfield first 2 starts at 4 yrs:
stays 7f: acts on firm and soft going, probably on all-weather: often blinkered/in cheekpieces: reportedly lame final outing. *P. Morris, Ireland*

GRANUAILE O'MALLEY (IRE)   4 b.f. Mark of Esteem 137 – Dame Laura   **–**
(IRE) 100 (Royal Academy (USA) 130) [2004 53: f7g Jan 8] maiden: tailed off in banded
race only start in 2004. *P. W. D'Arcy*

GRASP   2 b.c. (Apr 15) Kayf Tara 130 – Circe 73 (Main Reef 126) [2004 8s⁴ 10.1d p10g   **59**
Nov 27] modest form in maidens: should be suited by 1½m+: tongue tied. *R. M. Beckett*

GRASSLANDIK   8 b.g. Ardkinglass 114 – Sophisticated Baby 39 (Bairn (USA) 126)   **–**
[2004 62, a49: f5g Apr 5] lengthy gelding: handicapper: well held only outing in 2004:
wears headgear. *Miss A. Stokell*

GRASS WIDOW (IRE)   2 b.f. (Apr 16) Mujadil (USA) 119 – Noble Clare (IRE)   **–**
(The Noble Player (USA) 126) [2004 7s p6g Nov 19] 8,000Y: sixth foal: half-sister to 3
winners, including useful 2002 2-y-o 7f winner Bigalothegigalo (by Desert Story): dam
unraced: well held in maiden/seller: dead. *J. J. Quinn*

GRAVARDLAX   3 ch.g. Salse (USA) 128 – Rubbiyati 56 (Cadeaux Genereux 131)   **78**
[2004 89: 8d 10.2g⁴ 11m 8f p10g² p12g³ f11g³ Dec 14] leggy, quite good-topped gelding:
good mover: just fair maiden at 3 yrs: stays easy 1½m: acts on all-weather and good to
firm going: tried blinkered/in cheekpieces. *B. J. Meehan*

GRAZE ON   2 b.g. (Mar 19) Factual (USA) 108 – Queens Check 69 (Komaite (USA))   **82**
[2004 5m² 5d* 5s² 5g⁵ 6g 6s Oct 22] 500Y, resold 1,200Y: lengthy gelding: third foal:
dam 5f winner, including at 2 yrs: fairly useful performer: won maiden at Pontefract in
August: creditable efforts in nurseries next 2 starts (runner-up at Beverley): should stay
6f: acts on soft going. *J. J. Quinn*

GREAT AS GOLD   5 b.g. Goldmark (USA) 113 – Great Land (USA) (Friend's   **69**
Choice (USA)) [2004 69: 21.6v* 16.2v² May 8] good-topped gelding: fair handicapper:
won at Pontefract in April: stays 21.6f: acts on fibresand, heavy and good to firm
going: wears cheekpieces: tried blinkered/tongue tied earlier in career: usually held up.
B. Ellison

GREAT BELIEF (IRE)   2 b.c. (Apr 30) Namid 128 – Fairy Lore (IRE) 89 (Fairy King   **75**
(USA)) [2004 5g³ 5f⁶ 6g⁴ p5.1g⁶ Nov 27] €21,000F, 12,000Y: fifth foal: half-brother to 2
winners in Italy, including useful 7f (including at 2 yrs) to 15f winner Cauchemar de Chat
(by Tenby): dam Irish 1m winner: fair maiden: best efforts when in frame at Windsor:
stays 6f: hung/found little final start. *T. D. McCarthy*

GREAT BLASKET (IRE)   3 b.f. Petardia 113 – Alexander Goddess (IRE) (Alzao   **–**
(USA) 117) [2004 56: 8.3f 8s 8d 10f f8d Dec 21] little form at 3 yrs: visored final start.
E. J. O'Neill

GREATCOAT   2 ch.g. (May 27) Erhaab (USA) 127 – Vaula 49 (Henbit (USA) 130)   **– p**
[2004 7s Oct 22] big, useful-looking gelding: has plenty of scope: half-brother to several
winners, including 5f/6f winner Flak Jacket (by Magic Ring) and 7f winner Time Again
(by Then Again), both fairly useful: dam won at 13f at 4 yrs: 50/1, coltish and very green,
well held in maiden at Doncaster: should do better. *J. G. Given*

GREATEST BY PHAR   3 b.g. Pharly (FR) 130 – Greatest Friend (IRE) (Mandalus   **–**
110) [2004 p8g p10g Feb 11] showed little in maidens at Lingfield. *J. Akehurst*

GREAT EXHIBITION (USA)   3 b.c. Gone West (USA) – Touch of Greatness (USA)   **75**
(Hero's Honor (USA)) [2004 88: a9f 8v 7f³ 7m² 6d² Oct 10] close-coupled colt: fair
maiden: effective at 6f/7f: acts on firm and good to soft going: tongue tied in 2004: left
Godolphin. *Saeed bin Suroor*

GREAT FOX (IRE)   3 b.c. Foxhound (USA) 103 – Good Enough (IRE) (Simply   **81**
Great (FR) 122) [2004 80: 6g 6s⁶ 5d³ p5.1g² p5.1g Nov 26] big, strong colt: fairly useful
performer: good ¾-length second to Cherokee Nation at Wolverhampton penultimate
start: effective at 5f/6f: acts on polytrack, soft and good to firm going: tongue tied on
reappearance: hung left first 2 outings. *P. L. Gilligan*

GREAT GENERAL (IRE)   2 ch.g. (Jan 27) General Monash (USA) 107 – Racing   **44**
Brenda 72 (Faustus (USA) 118) [2004 6d 7.1d p6g p6g Dec 13] poor maiden: visored/
tongue tied (ran poorly) final start. *S. L. Keightley*

GREAT GIDDING 3 b.g. Classic Cliche (IRE) 128 – Arcady 69 (Slip Anchor 136) **52**
[2004 14.1s 11.8m³ 9.7m 14g 11.6f⁵ 16g Jul 30] leggy gelding: modest maiden: below
form after third start, in blinkers final one: should stay beyond 1½m. *H. Morrison*

GREAT OPINIONS (USA) 2 b.f. (Apr 11) Rahy (USA) 115 – Gracie Lady (IRE) **76**
(Generous (IRE) 139) [2004 5.1g 7m² 7m 7g Aug 13] $75,000Y, resold $180,000Y:
leggy, quite good-topped filly: third foal: dam, French maiden who stayed 1¼m, half-
sister to Poule d'Essai des Poulains winner No Pass No Sale: fair maiden: second at
Yarmouth, only form: should stay 1m: blinkered final start: sold 10,000 gns, sent to USA.
J. H. M. Gosden

GREAT SCOTT 3 b.g. Fasliyev (USA) 120 – Arabis 88 (Arazi (USA) 135) [2004 90: **86**
7d 7.1d 10m⁵ 10.3g³ 10g⁴ 10.3s 7.1g 8.3d 8g⁵ 10s Oct 11] leggy, lengthy gelding: fairly
useful performer: below form after sixth start, in claimers last 2 (wore cheekpieces final
one): stays 10.3f: acts on firm and soft going: blinkered (raced too freely) seventh outing:
sold 6,000 gns. *M. Johnston*

GREAT VIEW (IRE) 5 b.g. Great Commotion (USA) 123 – Tara View (IRE) (Wassl **72**
125) [2004 64, a50: p10g p13g* 10.9s² 11.9m* 11.7s² 11.8m⁴ 12f 12.6m² 11.9m³ 12m **a55**
12.6g² 11.5g⁴ 12g Oct 2] lengthy gelding: fair handicapper on turf, modest on all-
weather: won amateur event at Lingfield in March and ladies race at Brighton in April:
stays easy 13f: acts on all-weather, firm and soft going: usually blinkered/visored: held
up: reliable. *Mrs A. L. M. King*

GREEK STAR 3 b.g. Soviet Star (USA) 128 – Graecia Magna (USA) 109 (Private **–**
Account (USA)) [2004 –: 11.8m⁴ 10m 12f 11.9m⁶ Sep 23] big, strong gelding: little form.
K. A. Morgan

GREENBOROUGH (IRE) 6 b.g. Dr Devious (IRE) 127 – Port Isaac (USA) 64 **–**
(Seattle Song (USA) 130) [2004 –: f12s f9.4s Feb 17] tall gelding: no longer of much
account: tried in cheekpieces. *Mrs P. Ford*

GREEN CONVERSION (IRE) 3 ch.g. Desert King (IRE) 129 – Blue Bangor (IRE) **–**
(Thatching 131) [2004 15.8m Aug 3] 33/1, pulled up in seller at Catterick. *G. Fierro*

GREEN FALCON 3 b.c. Green Desert (USA) 127 – El Jazirah (Kris 135) [2004 p7g **60 d**
p7g³ p8g³ 7g 10.3m 8.1m 8m 9.9s Aug 29] 10,000Y: strong, good-bodied colt: fourth
foal: half-brother to useful 1¼m to 13f (in France) winner Mount Elbrus (by Barathea)
and 7f winner Christaleni (by Zilzal): dam unraced sister to Prix de Diane winner Rafha:
modest maiden: below form after third start: stays 1m: acts on polytrack and good to firm
going: tried visored/tongue tied. *J. W. Hills*

GREEN GINGER 8 ch.g. Ardkinglass 114 – Bella Maggio (Rakaposhi King 119) **–**
[2004 52: 8.1d f11g p9.5g Dec 22] well held in 2004: tried visored. *C. N. Kellett*

GREEN MANALISHI 3 b.g. Green Desert (USA) 127 – Silca-Cisa 93 (Hallgate **95**
127) [2004 83: p5g⁴ p5g² 5.1d² 5g* 5m 5m³ 5m* 6m⁵ 5.1g⁵ 5m 5m 5g 5g Sep 30] sturdy
gelding: useful handicapper: won at Windsor (hung left) in May and Newmarket (beat
Tony The Tap by a neck) in June: speedy, and best at bare 5f: acts on polytrack, firm and
good to soft going: gelded after final start. *D. W. P. Arbuthnot*

GREEN MASTER (POL) 4 bl.g. Who Knows 114 – Green Fee (GER) (Windwurf **?**
(GER)) [2004 6.5g* 8g 12g 13g p12.2d p10m f11g Dec 11] Polish-bred gelding: winner
twice in native country, including on 4-y-o reappearance: well held in 2 banded races and
a claimer in Britain: usually blinkered. *A. Sadik*

GREEN 'N' GOLD 4 b.f. Cloudings (IRE) 112 – Fishki 36 (Niniski (USA) 125) [2004 **60**
55: 18v* 21.6v 16.1m⁴ 14.1m 18m 16m 17.1d Aug 15] smallish, sturdy filly: modest
handicapper: won at Pontefract in April: stays 2¼m: acts on fibresand and any turf going:
tried in cheekpieces. *M. D. Hammond*

GREEN OCEAN 4 gr.f. Environment Friend 128 – Northern Swinger (Northern State **–**
(USA) 91) [2004 48: 9.9s 11.6f p9.5g Dec 17] smallish filly: maiden: no form in 2004:
tried blinkered. *J. W. Unett*

GREEN PIRATE 2 b.g. (Apr 16) Bahamian Bounty 116 – Verdura 63 (Green Desert **–**
(USA) 127) [2004 7m Sep 21] 26,000Y: leggy gelding: first foal: dam, maiden who
stayed 9f, half-sister to useful 11f winner North Wind: 50/1, well held in maiden at
Newmarket, racing freely: gelded after. *D. R. Loder*

GREEN RIDGE 3 b.f. Muhtarram (USA) 125 – Top of The Morning 56 (Keen 116) **53**
[2004 70: 6v² 5.2m⁴ 5m 5g 8.1s p7g Oct 13] leggy filly: modest maiden: no form after
leaving P. D'Arcy fourth outing: probably stays 7f: acts on fibresand and good to firm
going. *Miss A. M. Newton-Smith*

GREENSLADES 5 ch.h. Perugino (USA) 84 – Woodfield Rose 41 (Scottish Reel 123) **101**
[2004 94: 7d⁴ 6g⁴ 7m² 6f 7g³ 7m 8g⁶ 7g⁶ 7m 7g⁵ p7g³ p7g p7g Nov 20] big, strong horse: good
walker: useful handicapper: several good efforts in 2004, including ¾-length second to
Mine in Victoria Cup at Ascot and 1¼ lengths third to Material Witness in Bunbury Cup
at Newmarket third/fifth starts: effective at 6f/7f: acts on polytrack, soft and good to firm
going: usually races prominently. *P. J. Makin*

GREEN SWALLOW (FR) 3 b.f. Green Tune (USA) 125 – Green Sails (IRE) (Slip **105**
Anchor 136) [2004 107: 8d⁶ 9.3d³ 10g May 23] leggy, close-coupled filly: half-sister to 2
winners, including French/Belgian 1m winner Silverchore (by Priolo): dam ran 3 times in
France: useful performer: won Prix du Calvados at Deauville and fourth in Prix Marcel
Boussac at Longchamp at 2 yrs: best effort in 2004 when 2½ lengths third to Latice in Prix
Vanteaux at Longchamp: left P. Demercastel in France before contesting void running of
Prix de la Nonette at Deauville Aug 22: should have stayed 1¼m: acted on soft ground,
also successful on good to firm: visits Danehill Dancer. *D. Loder*

GREENWICH MEANTIME 4 b.g. Royal Academy (USA) 130 – Shirley Valentine **85**
104 (Shirley Heights 130) [2004 86: 16g 16d³ 13.9s 14g 14.1f³ 11.9g 16.2g 16m⁵ **a76**
16.2d⁶ 16d 16.1g⁴ 12m³ p12.2d* p13.9g³ p16.5g* p13.9g³ Dec 31] sturdy gelding: fairly
useful handicapper: won at Wolverhampton in November (flashed tail) and December:
effective at 1½m to 16.5f: acts on polytrack, firm and good to soft going: waited with.
Mrs J. R. Ramsden

GREENWOOD 6 ch.g. Emarati (USA) 74 – Charnwood Queen 61 (Cadeaux Genereux **86**
131) [2004 93, a86: f6g p7g³ 7g p8g p8g⁶ 7g⁶ 7f² p8g p7.1g⁵ p7g⁴ p7.1g⁵ Dec 11] strong, **a82**
lengthy gelding: fairly useful handicapper: best effort in 2004 when second at Brighton in
May: stays 7f: acts on all-weather, firm and good to soft going: blinkered earlier in career.
P. G. Murphy

GREGORIAN (IRE) 7 b.g. Foxhound (USA) 103 – East River (FR) (Arctic Tern **55**
(USA) 126) [2004 55: 11.6m May 24] well held only start on Flat in 2004.
J. G. M. O'Shea

GRELE (USA) 3 gr.f. Loup Sauvage (USA) 125 – Fiveblushingroses (USA) (Runaway **47**
Groom (CAN)) [2004 –: 7d 7.6g⁵ 7.9f⁶ 9.3g⁴ 7.9m 10g Sep 29] close-coupled filly: poor
maiden: stays 9f: probably acts on firm going. *R. Hollinshead*

GRETNA 3 ch.f. Groom Dancer (USA) 128 – Llia 94 (Shirley Heights 130) [2004 64p: **77 d**
9.7s* 9g 10m 9d 10g Aug 14] leggy filly: fair performer: won maiden at Folkestone in
March: tailed off in handicaps last 3 starts, looking temperamental in blinkers final one:
stays 9.7f: acts on soft going. *J. L. Dunlop*

GREY ADMIRAL (USA) 3 gr.g. Cozzene (USA) – Remarkable Style (USA) 99 **67**
(Danzig (USA)) [2004 69: 9.9g 12.1g Jul 9] workmanlike gelding: fair maiden: seems to
stay 1¼m: acts on good to firm ground: free-going sort. *A. M. Balding*

GREY BOY (GER) 3 gr.g. Medaaly 114 – Grey Perri 103 (Siberian Express (USA) **61 ?**
125) [2004 53: 7s 7.5g⁵ May 18] seemingly modest form in maidens: should stay 1m:
raced freely final one. *G. C. Bravery*

GREY CLOUDS 4 gr.f. Cloudings (IRE) 112 – Khalsheva 55 (Shirley Heights 130) **84**
[2004 76: 9.9d⁴ 10s² 10g 10m* 9.9d² 10m³ 10.3g² 10.4f² 9.2d⁵ 10.1g 10f Sep 23] tall,
rather leggy filly: fairly useful performer: won handicap at Pontefract in May: good
efforts next 4 starts: stays 10.4f: acts on firm and soft going. *T. D. Easterby*

GREY COSSACK 7 gr.g. Kasakov – Royal Rebeka (Grey Desire 115) [2004 88: 7d **84 d**
6s* 5v 6m 6d⁵ 6m 6m 6d 6d⁵ 6g 7m Oct 10] leggy, good-topped gelding: fairly useful
handicapper: won at Redcar in April: below form after, leaving P. Midgley prior to final
start: probably best at 6f: acts on heavy and good to firm going: tried visored at 3 yrs:
often slowly away. *N. Wilson*

GREYFIELD (IRE) 8 b.g. Persian Bold 123 – Noble Dust (USA) (Dust Commander **59**
(USA)) [2004 12f⁵ 10.2m 12m⁶ 14.1g 12.1m Aug 5] leggy gelding: fairly useful handicapper at best: unraced on Flat in 2002/3: just modest form at 8 yrs: probably best at 1½m:
acts on firm and soft going: sometimes slowly away. *K. Bishop*

GREY FORTUNE 5 gr.m. Grey Desire 115 – Mere Melody 88 (Dunphy 124) [2004 8d **42**
7v⁴ 6g f7g⁵ p9.5g f8g Dec 12] leggy mare: third foal: sister to 9-y-o Melodian: dam, 2-y-o
5f/6f winner who became unreliable: poor maiden: stays 7f: acts on fibresand. *M. Brittain*

GREY GURKHA 3 gr.c. Kasakov – Royal Rebeka (Grey Desire 115) [2004 5s⁶ 6g **–**
5d⁶ Jul 3] little form in maidens. *P. T. Midgley*

GREY LILAS (IRE)   3 gr.f. Danehill (USA) 126 – Kenmist 105 (Kenmare (FR) **120**
125) [2004 8g* 8g* 8g² 10.5g³ 10v* 8g* 10m² Oct 3]

    When Grey Lilas made a winning reappearance in the Prix du Louvre, a
minor event over a mile at Longchamp in early-April, she was still practically
unknown. Her two outings as a two-year-old, in which she had finished last of six
on her debut at Deauville and then second at the lesser track of Fontainebleau, gave
no indication of the heights she was to reach as a three-year-old when she developed into one of the best fillies in Europe. Of more significance at the time was that
Grey Lilas' win was the first on French soil for the new association of American
Hall of Fame jockey Gary Stevens with the top French stable of Andre Fabre. Fabre
and Stevens had linked up successfully as long ago as 1988, when Nasr El Arab
won the Oak Tree Invitational at Santa Anita, and two years after that In The Wings
had provided the combination with a Breeders' Cup victory in the Turf. The more
permanent partnership between the two got off to the best possible start when
Stevens rode Polish Summer to victory in the Dubai Sheema Classic at Nad Al
Sheba a week before Grey Lilas set the ball rolling on home turf.

    A move to France was the latest change of direction in the American
jockey's colourful career. Stevens was no stranger to riding in Europe, and had
made successful flying visits to Royal Ascot in both 1997, winning the Hardwicke
Stakes on Predappio, and 2003 when winning the Jersey Stakes with Membership.
He had also enjoyed a more sustained spell in Britain in 1999 when joining Sir
Michael Stoute, though what had started out as a long-term commitment lasted
barely three months. Stevens had hoped that riding on turf would be easier on his
arthritic knee than American dirt tracks, but the condition worsened to the extent
that, back in the States at the end of the same year, he announced his retirement.
However, by the end of 2000, Stevens was back in the saddle and gaining further
big-race successes, including that year's Breeders' Cup Mile on War Chant and the
2001 Kentucky Derby on Point Given. Another career-break followed when
Stevens took the role of jockey George Woolf in the film *Seabiscuit*, and there was
further speculation that he was set to pursue an acting career before the surprise
news of his link-up with the Fabre stable early in 2004.

    It is fair to say that by the end of the season, Grey Lilas enjoyed a happier
campaign than her rider but, to start with, Stevens and Grey Lilas teamed up to good
effect. Three weeks after the Prix du Louvre, Grey Lilas took a step up in class and
provided Stevens with his first pattern win in France when winning the Prix de la
Grotte at Longchamp. A defeat of rivals who for the most part had already won at
listed or pattern level, notably the Prix Marcel Boussac winner Denebola who was
only third, showed Grey Lilas to be very much on the upgrade and, as a result, she
started a short-priced favourite (coupled with Nyramba) for the Poule d'Essai des
Pouliches back at Longchamp in May. Although beaten there, Grey Lilas ran well
in finishing a length and a half second to Torrestrella, another filly who had made
rapid improvement in the spring. Grey Lilas ran an even better race in defeat on her
next start when a close third to Latice in the Prix de Diane at Chantilly. Ridden

*NetJets Prix du Moulin de Longchamp—Grey Lilas gets first run on her rivals,
who include Diamond Green (nearest camera), Antonius Pius and Denebola (rail);
it is trainer Andre Fabre's only Group 1 win of the year in France*

prominently as usual, Grey Lilas took over in front two furlongs out but was headed inside the last before being beaten a length and a quarter by the unbeaten favourite, Grey Lilas giving the impression that her stamina had been stretched somewhat by the extended ten furlongs.

Grey Lilas returned from a summer break to contest the Prix de la Nonette at Deauville at the end of August, a Group 3 race which would not normally be one to dwell on in the campaign of a filly who contested several races of better quality. However, the Nonette and the events surrounding it were of some note. Heavy ground meant that the field was already depleted, with only six of the nine declared fillies going to post, Latice the most notable absentee. After one of the stalls opened a fraction late, a false start was signalled but it went unheeded by half the field. In a situation similar to the void Grand National of 1993, the three riders who had missed the recall flag proceeded to complete the 'race' to general confusion in the stands, whilst Stevens and the two other riders pulled up and returned to the start. Whilst the stewards declared the race void and took disciplinary action against the jockeys who had completed the course, they also chose to re-run the event two days later, instead of letting the three riders who had heeded the false start try again there and then—much to the annoyance of those connected with the horses who had obeyed the signal, Stevens among them. In the event, only one of those who had completed in the void race lined up again forty-eight hours later, making a field of four for the re-run, which took place without betting as the first race on the card. Grey Lilas made short work of the depleted field, winning by five lengths. Stevens showed that he had learned to play the French jockeys at their own game, setting what was, even by French standards, a funereal pace in the still heavy ground and quickening best from the home turn; the time was some ten seconds slower than a claimer over the same trip later on the card. Events took another dramatic turn the same day when Stevens announced that he would be returning forthwith to the States. It looked as though Grey Lilas would go down as his last winner in France, as well as his first, though he ultimately stayed on another week to see out the remainder of the Deauville meeting, his final win coming instead on the Fabre-trained two-year-old Stop Making Sense in a listed race.

So what had gone wrong? An unseasonably wet and miserable Deauville August meeting had seemingly not yielded the hoped-for results for the stable, and perhaps the fiasco over the Prix de la Nonette had been the last straw. Both Fabre and Stevens stressed that there had been no falling-out between them (Stevens rode Polish Summer for Fabre again at Belmont in October) and the rider singled out the Lagardere family and Sheikh Mohammed to thank for their backing, whilst implying that other owners had given him much less support. The offer of television work back in the States had seemingly also been a reason for Stevens' decision to quit, while he had also admitted to homesickness and difficulties with the language in an interview at the beginning of August, in which he had otherwise seemed upbeat about his future in France. 'I am enjoying the start of what I would like to call the twilight of my career. I would like the opportunity to stay next year.' Stevens rode a total of fifty-one winners in France during the year, his impressive ratio of winners to rides (around 21%), interestingly, virtually identical to the one he had in Britain when associated with the Stoute stable. The Deauville meeting had not been a complete disaster either. The Group 1 success of Somnus in the Prix Maurice de Gheest for Tim Easterby was the most important of seven listed- or pattern-race victories for Stevens during the meeting. There had, though, been other events which must have tested Stevens' commitment to remaining in Europe. The seemingly trivial matter of wearing breeches bearing the American and French flags brought him into conflict with the French officials and a more serious brush with the stewards came at Rome later in May. Stevens refused to take the ride in a Group 3 sprint there after his mount had bolted to post, leaving both himself and the horse, in his opinion, in no fit state to take part in the race. The stewards gave Stevens a twenty-day suspension as a result, though various appeals meant the ban had still not taken effect by the end of the year.

Gary Stevens' French season might have been over by the end of August, but the highlight of Grey Lilas' campaign was still to come. When Stevens heard the result of the NetJets Prix du Moulin de Longchamp at the beginning of September, he must have been wishing he had delayed his return to the States by another week. Grey Lilas was supplemented for the race, her first against colts and older rivals. Of the four older horses in the field, the Luca Cumani-trained Italian import Le Vie dei Colori was the most prominent in the betting, but it was the three-year-old contingent which made the Moulin a competitive-looking race. The recent Jacques le Marois winner Whipper started favourite, and American Post, Diamond Green and Antonius Pius, who had all been involved in a dramatic Poule d'Essai des Poulains in the spring, all held strong claims as well. The Mark Johnston-trained Lucky Story was the other three-year-old colt in the line-up, with Denebola the only three-year-old filly besides Grey Lilas.

A change of rider did not mean a change of tactics for Grey Lilas, and having her prominent proved crucial in a race where it paid to be handily placed. Taking over from Lucky Story, whom she had tracked, turning into the home straight, Grey Lilas got first run on all the other principals. The challenges of first American Post and then Martillo petered out as Grey Lilas kept on well to win by a length. The next eight home were covered by around two lengths, with just a nose between Diamond Green and Antonius Pius, who kept on for the places ahead of Denebola. Whipper and the German horse Paolini (who fared best of the older brigade) finished strongly for fifth and sixth. Stevens' place on Grey Lilas was taken by Eric Legrix, another jockey with an interesting story. Legrix had returned to France only the year before, originally just to have surgery on a knee after a ten-year stint in Hong Kong, but ended up making a permanent return. The Moulin was his first Group 1 success in France since Caerlina's Prix de Diane thirteen years earlier. Andre Fabre picks up Group 1 events on a much more regular basis, though surprisingly, the Moulin, which he had won the year before with Nebraska Tornado, was his only domestic success at that level in 2004, something which did not, however, prevent his winning an eighteenth consecutive French trainers' title. Many more titles and the French equivalent of the Monopolies Commission, the Conseil de la Concurrence, might be asked to look into Fabre's dominance! Legrix had the ride again when Grey Lilas made her final appearance of the season back at a mile and a quarter in the Prix de l'Opera on Arc day. Grey Lilas ran another good race under conditions firmer than she had met before, but simply found Alexander Goldrun too strong in the closing stages and went down by a length.

			Danzig		Northern Dancer
	Danehill (USA)		(b 1977)		Natalma
	(b 1986)		Razyana		His Majesty
Grey Lilas (IRE)			(b 1981)		Spring Adieu
(gr.f. 2001)			Kenmare		Kalamoun
	Kenmist		(gr 1975)		Belle of Ireland
	(gr 1994)		Mistral's Collette		Simply Great
			(b 1987)		Kitty's Sister

Having an American jockey for most of her races brought an even more international flavour to Grey Lilas' already cosmopolitan background. Bred in Ireland but raised at an Italian stud and sent to the sales at Deauville as a yearling, she was bought back for €170,000 before being sold privately to her German owners. Her dam Kenmist was trained in Britain by Luca Cumani and was a useful filly. She won a maiden at Milan on her debut over a mile and a quarter but proved best at a mile, winning a listed rated stakes at Ascot and finishing third in the Group 3 Premio Bagutta back at Milan. Grey Lilas is her second foal after close relative Stendhal (by Polish Precedent), who has won at up to around nine furlongs in France. Kenmist was one of the top lots at the latest December Sales at Newmarket where she was sold in foal to Rock of Gibraltar for 775,000 guineas. Kenmist is a half-sister to several winners in Italy, the best of them the useful stayer Jar. Grandam Mistral's Collette began her career in Ireland, winning a six-furlong maiden at Phoenix Park and finishing third in the Killavullan Stakes, before she too was sent to the December Sales. Sold for the more modest sum of 57,000 guineas at the end of her two-year-old season, she continued her career in Italy, where she won three more races, including a nine-furlong listed event at Milan and took fourth place in the Italian St Leger. Mistral's Collette is out of a sister to the Lowther winner Kittyhawk, whose son Nomadic Way won the Cesarewitch before proving top class over hurdles, finishing second in two Champion Hurdles before winning the Stayers'.

Gestut Ammerland's "Grey Lilas"

The rather leggy, good-topped Grey Lilas did not run a bad race all year and looks worth keeping in training for another season. Effective at both a mile and a mile and a quarter, there are now plenty of opportunities in Europe for good older fillies over both those distances, though Grey Lilas has already proved that she does not need to be kept to races restricted to her own sex to win a good prize. She is effective on good to firm ground and clearly handled heavy conditions well enough at Deauville. *A. Fabre, France*

GREY ORCHID   3 gr.f. Opening Verse (USA) 126 – Marjorie's Orchid 49 (Petong   –   126) [2004 –: 8d 6m⁶ 5d 7.1m 9.9d Aug 28] good-bodied filly: little form. *T. J. Etherington*

GREY PEARL   5 gr.m. Ali-Royal (IRE) 127 – River's Rising (FR) 88 (Mendez (FR)   **91**   128) [2004 80: f7g⁵ p7g* p7g* p7g³ p7g⁶ p7g⁴ 8m⁶ a6f 6m⁴ 6m* 7m 6.1g 5m Sep 21] sturdy mare: fairly useful performer: won 2 handicaps at Lingfield in January and minor event at Newmarket (by ½ length from Cusco) in June: stiff tasks after: effective at 6f/7f: acts on all-weather and firm going: tried tongue tied/visored/in cheekpieces: usually races up with pace. *Miss Gay Kelleway*

GREY SAMURAI   4 gr.g. Gothenberg (IRE) 117 – Royal Rebeka (Grey Desire 115)   –   [2004 11.9m⁶ 11.9d 10g 10.9m 14.1g Jul 24] no form: tried in cheekpieces. *P. T. Midgley*

GREY SWALLOW (IRE)   3 gr.c. Daylami (IRE) 138 – Style of Life (USA) (The   **127**   Minstrel (CAN) 135) [2004 116p: 8s* 8g⁴ 8m³ 12f* 10m⁴ 12m Oct 3]

For the fifth year in a row, the Budweiser Irish Derby was won by a home-trained runner. The portents did not look good beforehand in a line-up including the first four in the Epsom Derby, all of whom were trained in Britain. With one-time Derby favourite Yeats ruled out for the season by the time the Irish Derby came along, Ballydoyle, which had won three of the last seven renewals, had to rely on a quintet of outsiders. The other runner in a field of ten was the Dermot Weld-trained Grey Swallow who had finished in the frame in the Two Thousand Guineas at both Newmarket and the Curragh but was regarded by most as having missed his chance of classic success. His form was no better than smart and, with more speed than stamina on the dam's side of his pedigree, Grey Swallow looked far from certain to be fully effective stepped up to a mile and a half. Not only did Grey Swallow dispel any stamina doubts in the Irish Derby, he also stepped up considerably on his earlier classic efforts to upset the odds laid on the Epsom Derby winner North Light, becoming at 10/1 the longest-priced winner of the race since 20/1-shot Zagreb in 1996, also trained by Weld.

'You would think at this stage that a mile would be his trip . . . he's a naturally fast horse,' Grey Swallow's trainer had said when discussing the horse's prospects at the beginning of the season. After winning both his outings as a two-year-old—a maiden by ten lengths and the Group 3 Killavullan Stakes by eight—Grey Swallow took the same route to the Two Thousand Guineas as the stable's Guineas winner Refuse to Bend the previous year. Like Refuse To Bend, Grey Swallow maintained an unbeaten record in the Leopardstown 2000 Guineas Trial in April, though his scrambling victory over Meath hardly enhanced his Newmarket claims. Refuse to Bend had been only workmanlike but, at the time, he was not a certain runner at Newmarket, connections seeming to be leaning more towards going straight to Epsom. No such reservations were entertained with Grey Swallow who looked well forward, in grand shape, at Leopardstown. In stark contrast to some observers, our representative reported that Grey Swallow didn't blow to any great degree after the race. Grey Swallow's winter odds for the Two Thousand Guineas had been no longer than 6/1, but there was a lack of market confidence in him after Leopardstown and, though again taking the eye beforehand, he was sent off at 10/1 on the day, his trainer widely quoted beforehand as saying that the race might come a little too soon ('A few of the horses have had head colds and I was very careful with Grey Swallow before his trial'). Slowly away and held up, Grey Swallow made ground into the firing line a furlong out but could produce

Leopardstown 2000 Guineas Trial Stakes—Grey Swallow only just maintains his unbeaten record; Meath (right) battles on to hold second, with Amarula Ridge (left) and Medicinal next

Budweiser Irish Derby, the Curragh—Grey Swallow steps up in trip and beats a field that includes the first four at Epsom; odds-on North Light (pale colours) is second, with 150/1-shot Tycoon (right) third, Rule of Law (rail) fourth and Let The Lion Roar (visor) fifth

no extra and finished fourth behind Haafhd, Snow Ridge and Azamour. Haafhd and Snow Ridge bypassed the Irish Two Thousand Guineas in which Azamour and Grey Swallow met for a second time. There wasn't much between them again but they finished in the same order, third-placed Grey Swallow half a length behind Azamour, the pair beaten by the Newmarket seventh Bachelor Duke. Grey Swallow was keeping on more strongly at the finish than he had at Newmarket, after taking a while to respond when the pace quickened over three furlongs out.

The Prix Jean Prat over nine furlongs on Prix du Jockey Club day was said to be the next possible target for Grey Swallow but, although he appeared in the five-day declarations for both the Prix Jean Prat and the Prix du Jockey Club, he did not appear between the Irish Guineas and the Irish Derby five weeks later. No British-trained runner has won the Irish Derby since the filly Balanchine in 1994, but hopes were high with Britain represented by the principals at Epsom, North Light, Rule of Law, Let The Lion Roar and Percussionist. The Derby finishing order was repeated, Rule of Law and Let The Lion Roar filling fourth and fifth this time (Percussionist finished tailed off). North Light was up there all the way, as at Epsom, but the more patiently-ridden Grey Swallow improved from fifth on the home turn and stayed on strongly under pressure to head North Light inside the final furlong, keeping on to beat him by half a length. The 150/1-shot Tycoon came out best of the Ballydoyle quintet, finishing a length and a half behind North Light in third, following in the footsteps of other rank outsiders who had been placed in the race for his stable in the two previous years, 150/1-shot Roosevelt (third to Alamshar) and 200/1-shot Sholokhov (runner-up to High Chaparral).

North Light more or less replicated his Epsom running with Rule of Law, with Let The Lion Roar beaten further, and there seemed no reason to think that North Light had run below his Derby form (though his jockey thought the going was too firm for him and it was reported that North Light returned home very sore). Grey Swallow undoubtedly recorded a high-class performance at the Curragh and he started at considerably shorter odds than Azamour when the pair met for the third time in the Irish Champion Stakes at Leopardstown in September. Having his first outing for ten weeks, Grey Swallow again finished behind Azamour, whose only outing between the Irish Guineas and the Irish Champion had come at Royal Ascot in the St James's Palace Stakes, which he had won, turning the tables on the

Newmarket and Curragh Guineas winners. The defeat of odds-on Doyen in the Irish Champion focused closer attention on Grey Swallow's respectable fourth to Azamour, as the Prix de l'Arc de Triomphe—for which Doyen had been a short-priced ante-post favourite—was Grey Swallow's next target. Grey Swallow ran as though his first run for nearly eleven weeks at Leopardstown would put an edge on him, but, unfortunately, his preparation between the Irish Champion and the Arc was hampered by a slight training setback and, joining the Arc line-up at the supplementary stage, he ran as if something was amiss, already beaten when bumped early in the straight and coming home eighteenth of nineteen.

		Daylami (IRE) (gr 1994)	Doyoun (b 1985)	Mill Reef
Grey Swallow (IRE) (gr.c. 2001)				Dumka
			Daltawa (gr 1989)	Miswaki
				Damana
		Style of Life (USA) (b 1985)	The Minstrel (ch 1974)	Northern Dancer
				Fleur
			Bubinka (b 1976)	Nashua
				Stolen Date

The close-coupled, good-topped Grey Swallow is a good walker and a fluent mover with a quick action in his faster paces. He raced in the colours of American-based Mrs Rochelle Quinn, who missed his Irish Derby victory because of illness. The trainer's mother Gita and one-time flamboyant gambler Terry Ramsden were minority partners, though Grey Swallow will race in new ownership as a four-year-old after reportedly being purchased by Geneva-based Jean Pierre Regli. Gita Weld, Grey Swallow's breeder, has retained a ten per cent interest. Mrs Weld's small Piper's Hill Stud consigned Grey Swallow to the Houghton Yearling Sales in 2002 and he went through the ring, with a sale recorded for 150,000 guineas to McKeever St Lawrence, who purchased the colt for Paul and Susan Roy. Tattersalls' conditions of sale lay down, among other things, that 'the purchasers

Mrs Rochelle Quinn's "Grey Swallow"

may only return the lot if . . . it has not been removed from the premises and a notice in writing from the purchaser has been received within 24 hours from the fall of the hammer that he requires an examination . . . a certificate in writing from a veterinary surgeon must be received before 5pm on the fourth day after the day on which the lot was sold alleging the lot to be a whistler and/or roarer.' Grey Swallow's return meant that the Roys missed out but they did enjoy success in the latest season with the two-year-old Wilko, although a majority share in that horse had been sold by the time of the Breeders' Cup. Grey Swallow provided Daylami with his first classic winner from his first crop and Piper's Hill Stud with its most important winner since Roll of Honour, who won the Grand Prix de Paris and came second in the Prix du Jockey Club in 1970. Grey Swallow's dam, the Irish six- and seven-furlong winner Style of Life, was owned by Mrs Weld and trained by Dermot Weld. Style of Life has done well at stud, breeding seven winners so far, including the useful performers Stylish Ways (by Thatching) and Rustic (by Grand Lodge), both best at up to seven furlongs, and Central Lobby (by Kenmare) and Style For Life (by Law Society), both of whom showed useful form at up to a mile and a half. Style of Life is a sister to the smart Seasonal Pickup—also trained by Weld—who was best at sprint distances. Their dam Bubinka, a sister to the smart Stoshka and a half-sister to Taufan, was trained in France and was a Group 3 winner at a mile in Italy; Style of Life's grandam Stolen Date was a half-sister to Best In Show, dam of pattern winners Malinowski, Monroe and Gielgud (none of whom won beyond a mile), and also to Sex Appeal, who, in turn, bred the brothers El Gran Senor and Try My Best, among others. El Gran Senor won the Irish Derby as well as the Two Thousand Guineas, so Grey Swallow's fourth dam Stolen Hour now features in the extended pedigree of two Irish Derby winners. Grey Swallow stays a mile and a half and acts on firm and soft going. *D. K. Weld, Ireland*

GREZIE   2 gr.f. (Apr 26) Mark of Esteem (IRE) 137 – Lozzie (Siberian Express (USA)   **59** 125) [2004 5g⁴ p5g⁴ 5d³ 7g f8g p7m p8m* f7g* f8g⁶ Dec 28] 2,500Y: workmanlike filly: third foal: dam unraced half-sister to high-class middle-distance colt Raami: modest performer: trained on debut by A. Smith: won claimer at Lingfield (left J. Best) and seller at Southwell in December: stays 1m: acts on all-weather and good to soft going. *G. G. Margarson*

GRIGOROVITCH (IRE)   2 b.c. (Mar 8) Fasliyev (USA) 120 – Hasty Words (IRE)   **83 p** 103 (Polish Patriot (USA) 128) [2004 6g p5.1g* Nov 27] neat colt: first foal: dam 5f (at 2 yrs) and 1m winner: much better effort in maidens 4 months apart (slowly away/raced freely on debut) when winning at Wolverhampton by 3½ lengths from Gifted Lass: will stay 6f: likely to do better still. *B. W. Hills*

GRIST MIST (IRE)   3 gr.f. Imperial Ballet (IRE) 110 – Ard Dauphine (IRE) (Forest   **–** Wind (USA) 111) [2004 58: 10d 10.2g 11.6s 11g² 9g Jun 4] maiden: well held in 2004: reportedly had breathing problem second start, tongue tied after. *Mrs P. N. Dutfield*

GRIZEBECK (IRE)   2 b.g. (Apr 10) Trans Island 119 – Premier Amour 111 (Salmon   **–** Leap (USA) 131) [2004 8.1g Sep 3] €20,000F: big, strong gelding: half-brother to several winners abroad, including German 8.5f to 10.5f winner Primeur (by Lando): dam French 9f (including at 2 yrs) to 11f winner: 66/1 and very backward, last in maiden at Haydock. *R. F. Fisher*

GRIZEDALE (IRE)   5 ch.g. Lake Coniston (IRE) 131 – Zabeta (Diesis 133) [2004   **98 d** 104: 7g⁵ 7m 7s 7m 7m 7g 6s⁶ Oct 22] strong gelding: useful handicapper: creditable effort in 2004 only on reappearance, when fifth to Material Witness in Bunbury Cup at Newmarket in July: best at 7f: acts on any going: tongue tied: free going sort: usually waited with: none too reliable. *J. Akehurst*

GROOMS AFFECTION   4 b.c. Groom Dancer (USA) 128 – Love And Affection   **91** (USA) (Exclusive Era (USA)) [2004 80p: 10m* 11.6m⁶ 12m 13.3d 14.8d Aug 27] good-bodied colt: reportedly cracked a bone in a leg in 2003: fairly useful handicapper, lightly raced: won at Sandown in June by 1¼ lengths from Say What You See: stays 11.6f: acts on soft and good to firm going: tongue tied (tailed off) final outing: sold 11,000 gns. *P. W. Harris*

GROOMSMAN   2 b.g. (Mar 29) Groom Dancer (USA) 128 – Trois Heures Apres   **76** (Soviet Star (USA) 128) [2004 8g⁴ 8v Oct 23] 40,000Y: quite good-topped gelding: fifth foal: half-brother to 3 winners, including 3-y-o Feaat and useful French winner up to 1¼m Rising Talent (by Bering): dam unraced half-sister to Oaks third Mezzogiorno, herself dam of 5-y-o Monturani: much better effort in maidens when fourth at Leicester (fractious preliminaries): should stay at least 1¼m. *H. Morrison*

GROOM TESSE 3 gr.c. Groom Dancer (USA) 128 – Vicomtesse Mag (FR) 106 (Highest Honor (FR) 124) [2004 99: 10d* 10.5d² 12m* 12m Jun 20] second foal: half-brother to Italian winner up to 9f Vid (by Wolfhound): dam French 1m winner who stayed 1¼m: smart performer: won 4 times at 2 yrs, notably Premio Guido Berardelli at Rome: successful there in minor event on reappearance in April and Derby Italiano (easily best effort, by 2½ lengths from Dayano) in May: disappointing in Gran Premio di Milano final start (reportedly thought to have injured his testicles when whipping round on way to start): stays 1½m: acts on soft and good to firm ground: has been blinkered. *F. & L. Camici, Italy* **117**

GROSVENOR SQUARE (IRE) 2 b.c. (Mar 20) Dubai Millennium 140 – Embassy 114 (Cadeaux Genereux 131) [2004 6g⁶ 7m* Sep 21] close-coupled, useful-looking colt: third foal: dam, 6f (including Cheveley Park Stakes) winner at 2 yrs, out of Cheveley Park winner/Poule d'Essai des Pouliches runner-up Pass The Peace: much better effort in maidens when winning at Newmarket by 4 lengths from Councellor, making all and quickening well: should stay 1m: will progress. *Saeed bin Suroor* **97 p**

GROUNDCOVER 2 b.c. (Mar 30) Zafonic (USA) 130 – Moss (Alzao (USA) 117) [2004 8m 8g Oct 12] heavy-topped colt: sixth foal: half-brother to useful 1m winner Mossy Moor (by Sanglamore) and 8-y-o Javelin: dam, French 1¼m winner, half-sister to St Leger winner Toulon: slowly away, modest form in maidens at Goodwood and Leicester: likely to be suited by 1¼m/1½m: sold 12,000 gns. *Mrs A. J. Perrett* **62**

GROUND PATROL 3 b.g. Ashkalani (IRE) 128 – Good Grounds (USA) (Alleged (USA) 138) [2004 –p: p8g³ p8g⁴ p10g³ 10d⁶ 11g f8g 8m⁴ p10g⁶ p10g⁴ p12.2g Nov 11] good-topped gelding: fair maiden: left A. Balding after sixth start: stays 1¼m (pulled hard over 1½m): acts on polytrack, good to firm and good to soft going: tried visored: tongue tied last 4 outings: sometimes slowly away. *G. L. Moore* **69**

GROUND RULES (USA) 2 b.c. (Mar 31) Boundary (USA) 117 – Gombeen (USA) (Private Account (USA)) [2004 7.1d² 7m Jul 30] sturdy colt: third foal: dam, placed in USA, half-sister to Danehill: much better effort in maidens when strong-finishing second at Sandown: will stay 1m. *B. W. Hills* **81 +**

GROUP CAPTAIN 2 b.c. (Apr 16) Dr Fong (USA) 128 – Alusha 88 (Soviet Star (USA) 128) [2004 6d⁵ 7.1m⁴ 7.1g² 7m² 7g 7g² 8.1g³ 7s Oct 22] 12,000Y: rather leggy colt: fifth foal: half-brother to useful 1¼m/1½m winner Scheming (by Machiavellian), 1m winner Proxima (by Cadeaux Genereux) and 3-y-o Verkhotina: dam, 2-y-o 6f winner (stayed 1¼m), half-sister to smart performer up to 1½m Prize Giving: fairly useful maiden: below form after fourth start: should stay 1m: acts on good to firm ground: sold 66,000 gns. *S. Kirk* **82**

GROUVILLE 3 b.g. Groom Dancer (USA) 128 – Dance Land (IRE) (Nordance (USA)) [2004 p8g* p8g 10d Apr 1] 13,500Y: leggy gelding: half-brother to 3 winners, including Irish 1½m/1¾m winner Dariole (by Priolo) and 2001 2-y-o 5f winner My Dancer (by Alhaarth): dam unraced half-sister to grandam of Attraction: won maiden at Lingfield in January: well held in minor event and handicap (blinkered, set strong pace) after: should stay 1¼m: sold 14,000 gns. *B. J. Meehan* **64**

GROWLER 3 ch.g. Foxhound (USA) 103 – Femme Femme (USA) (Lyphard (USA) 132) [2004 67: 8d 7f³ 8.5g 7f² 6s* 6m 7m Sep 29] sturdy gelding: fair performer: won maiden at Goodwood in August, easily best effort: stays 6f: acts on firm and soft going: visored last 4 outings: sold 12,500 gns. *J. L. Dunlop* **79**

GRUB STREET 8 b.g. Barathea (IRE) 127 – Broadmara (IRE) 91 (Thatching 131) [2004 f7g³ f8g⁴ f8g* f11s Mar 14] big, lengthy gelding: poor performer: won apprentice handicap at Southwell in March: stays 1m: acts on fibresand and good to soft going. *J. Parkes* **42**

GRUFF 5 ch.g. Presidium 124 – Kagram Queen 64 (Prince Ragusa 96) [2004 –: f5g f6g f5g 6v 6.1m f7g 6.1d Jul 10] sturdy gelding: no longer of much account. *P. T. Midgley* **–**

GRUMPYINTMORNING 5 b.g. Magic Ring (IRE) 115 – Grecian Belle 53 (Ilium 121) [2004 60+: 7d 7s 8.1f 10.9m Jul 2] tall gelding: maiden: little form at 5 yrs: blinkered final outing. *Mrs P. Townsley* **–**

GRYSKIRK 2 b.g. (Feb 25) Selkirk (USA) 129 – Gryada 93 (Shirley Heights 130) [2004 5d⁴ 5g⁶ 6g³ 7.1m 7g 7m p7d³ f7g 7m⁵ 8g p8g* Oct 25] 9,000Y: big, workmanlike gelding: has a round action: fourth foal: brother to 5-y-o Grampian and half-brother to useful 1¼m/1½m winner Guaranda (by Acatenango) and 3-y-o Graham Island: dam, **69**

2-y-o 7f/1m winner, closely related to useful stayer Gondolier: fair performer: won maiden at Lingfield by ¾ length from Kandidate: will stay 1¼m: acts on polytrack and good to firm ground: sometimes slowly away/looks none too keen: sold 21,000 gns. *P. W. D'Arcy*

GUADALOUP 2 ch.f. (Mar 20) Loup Sauvage (USA) 125 – Rash (Pursuit of Love 124) [2004 6m Sep 5] 11,000Y: big, lengthy filly: fourth foal: half-sister to fairly useful 1m winner Loveleaves (by Polar Falcon) and 2002 2-y-o 5f winner Foolhardy (by Primo Dominie): dam unraced: 33/1 and green, well held in maiden at York, slowly away and not knocked about. *M. Brittain* —

GUADIARO (USA) 2 b.c. (Mar 25) El Prado (IRE) 119 – Splendid (IRE) (Mujtahid (USA) 118) [2004 5g 6v Nov 6] $60,000F, €160,000Y: good-topped colt: third foal: half-brother to a winner in USA by Polish Numbers: dam, ran 3 times, from excellent family of Russian Rhythm: burly, never dangerous in maidens at Haydock and Doncaster: should do better. *B. W. Hills* – p

GUARD 4 b.g. Night Shift (USA) – Gaijin 97 (Caerleon (USA) 132) [2004 –: 7f p10d Aug 9] of little account: tried tongue tied. *N. P. Littmoden* —

GUARDIAN SPIRIT 5 b.m. Hector Protector (USA) 124 – Amongst The Stars (USA) 107 (Proctor (USA)) [2004 –: 8.2d p7g Aug 6] rather leggy mare: of little account. *D. Shaw* —

GUILDED FLYER 5 b.g. Emarati (USA) 74 – Mo Ceri 63 (Kampala 120) [2004 89: 10g 10.3d* 10.1m 9g³ 10g Jul 14] big, lengthy gelding: fairly useful handicapper: won at Chester in May by 2½ lengths from Petrula: good 1½ lengths third to Spanish Don at Kempton: effective at 9f to easy 1½m: acts on all-weather, good to firm and good to soft going: usually races prominently: sold 46,000 gns, sent to Saudi Arabia. *W. S. Kittow* 94

GUILDENSTERN (IRE) 2 b.c. (Apr 8) Danetime (IRE) 121 – Lyphard Abu (IRE) 78 (Lyphard's Special (USA) 122) [2004 6.1m 6d⁴ 6s⁵ Oct 29] €32,000F, 13,000Y: well-made colt: fourth foal: dam, Irish 1½m/13f winner, half-sister to smart Irish performer up to 1¼m Noora Abu: best effort in maidens when fourth at Windsor: needs to settle to stay beyond 6f. *H. Morrison* 68

GUINEA A MINUTE (IRE) 2 ch.f. (Feb 22) Raise A Grand (IRE) 114 – Repique (USA) 88 (Sharpen Up 127) [2004 6m 6d³ 6f⁶ 7m⁶ f7g⁵ 8s³ 8s³ 8d Nov 5] 20,000Y: angular filly: half-sister to useful Irish 5f winner Give A Whistle (by Mujadil) and 4-y-o Roman Mistress: dam 6f/7f winner, half-sister to high-class 7f to 9f performer Indian Lodge: fair maiden: left M. Bell before poor effort final start: stays 1m: acts on soft going, probably on fibresand. *P. D. Evans* 66

GULCHINA (USA) 2 b. or br.f. (Mar 22) Gulch (USA) – Harda Arda (USA) 66 (Nureyev (USA) 131) [2004 7d⁴ p7m² Dec 22] $75,000F: sturdy filly: third foal: half-sister to a minor winner in USA by Smart Strike: dam, Irish 9f winner, half-sister to smart Irish/ US middle-distance performer Phantom Breeze: fair form in maidens at Newmarket and Lingfield (½-length second to Glinting Desert): will stay at least 1m: should improve. *D. R. C. Elsworth* 72 p

GULF (IRE) 5 ch.g. Persian Bold 123 – Broken Romance (IRE) (Ela-Mana-Mou 132) [2004 110: 16d 13.3m³ 16.4d⁵ 14.1g² Sep 2] big, strong gelding: useful performer: creditable effort in 2004 only when never-nearer 4½ lengths third to The Whistling Teal in listed event at Newbury in May: stays 2m: acts on firm going: tongue tied final outing: usually waited with. *D. R. C. Elsworth* 109

GUNNERBERGKAMP 2 b.g. (Apr 21) Defacto (USA) – Judys Girl (IRE) (Simply Great (FR) 122) [2004 7m 6m 7s Aug 13] seems of little account. *M. D. Hammond* —

GUNNHILDR (IRE) 4 ch.f. In Command (IRE) 114 – Queen Canute (IRE) (Ahonoora 122) [2004 60: 6g May 14] strong filly: maiden: tailed off only start at 4 yrs: tried visored. *P. J. Makin* —

GUN SALUTE 4 b.g. Mark of Esteem (IRE) 137 – Affair of State (IRE) 99 (Tate Gallery (USA) 117) [2004 61: p6g p6g* p6g p6g⁴ p7g⁶ 6s 7m⁶ 6f 6g Jun 12] modest performer at best: won claimer at Lingfield in February: best around 6f: acts on polytrack: tried blinkered, usually wears cheekpieces: sold 3,200 gns. *G. L. Moore* 61 d

GUNS BLAZING 5 b.g. Puissance 110 – Queen of Aragon 76 (Aragon 118) [2004 68: 5.3m 5v 5.1d* 5g³ 5.3f⁶ 5f 5m* 5.3g 5m 5g Jul 28] leggy gelding: fair handicapper: won at Nottingham in May and Lingfield in June: best at 5f: acts on firm and soft going: usually wears headgear: usually forces pace. *D. K. Ivory* 76

GURRUN 2 b.c. (Mar 12) Dansili 127 – Mashmoon (USA) 80 (Habitat 134) [2004 7m **56**
7g 7d 7g 6m⁶ f8g f8g Dec 11] good-topped colt: has a markedly round action: modest
maiden: should stay 1m: acts on good to firm and good to soft going. *N. A. Callaghan*

GUSTAVO 3 b.g. Efisio 120 – Washita (Valiyar 129) [2004 7d 7g 7s 8.1g f8s² 10.9d² **64**
Sep 18] quite attractive gelding: has a round action: seventh foal: half-brother to 1994
2-y-o 7f winner Last Roundup (by Good Times) and 1¾m/15f winner Los Alamos (by
Keen): dam, maiden, should have stayed further than 11f: modest maiden: best efforts in
blinkers last 2 starts: stays 11f: acts on fibresand and good to soft going. *B. W. Hills*

GUYANA (IRE) 2 br.c. (Mar 24) Lend A Hand 124 – Romora (FR) (Sillery (USA) **58**
122) [2004 7m 7.1m p6d³ 7m 6v Oct 23] 34,000Y: quite good-topped colt: second foal: **a70**
half-brother to useful 2003 2-y-o 5f/6f winner Clifden (by Gold Away): dam unraced: fair
maiden on all-weather, modest on turf: probably stays 7f. *S. Kirk*

GWAZI 4 b.g. Pennekamp (USA) 130 – Made of Pearl (USA) 107 (Nureyev (USA) 131) **–**
[2004 –: f11g f9.4s³ 8.5d f7m⁶ May 17] little form: tried visored/in cheekpieces: tongue
tied. *Miss D. A. McHale*

GWEN JOHN (USA) 3 ch.f. Peintre Celebre (USA) 137 – River Jig (USA) 98 (Irish **70**
River (FR) 131) [2004 68p: 8g⁵ 9g³ 10m 9.3f 10.2s Oct 19] tall filly: fair maiden: well
below form last 3 starts, in blinkers penultimate one: should stay at least 1¼m: acts on
good to firm going. *H. Morrison*

GWYNETH 2 b.f. (Feb 4) Zafonic (USA) 130 – Llyn Gwynant 115 (Persian Bold 123) **62**
[2004 7d⁵ 7m Jul 29] half-sister to several winners, including useful 2m/17f winner
Lady of The Lake (by Caerleon) and fairly useful 1994 2-y-o 7f winner Llia (by Shirley
Heights): dam best at 1m/9f: modest form in maidens at Kempton (slowly away) and
Goodwood. *J. L. Dunlop*

GYPSY FAIR 2 b.f. (Feb 22) Compton Place 125 – Marjorie's Memory (IRE) 76 (Fairy **62**
King (USA)) [2004 5s 5d p6g p5.1g³ Dec 13] 21,000Y: sturdy filly: sixth foal: half-sister
to 3 winners by Petong, including 6-y-o Pay The Silver: dam 5f winner, including at 2
yrs: modest maiden: easily best effort when third at Wolverhampton: likely to prove best
at 5f/6f. *T. D. Barron*

GYPSY JOHNNY 2 gr.c. (Apr 26) Bachir (IRE) 118 – Gentle Gypsy 94 (Junius (USA) **79**
124) [2004 7.5d* 8s Sep 18] 10,000E, 16,000Y, 34,000 2-y-o: lengthy colt: half-brother
to several winners, including useful 5f (including at 2 yrs) to 1m (in Scandinavia) winner
Coconut Johnny (by King of Spain) and 7f winner Automatic (by Clantime): dam 2-y-o
5f winner: won 4-runner minor event at Beverley in July by 4 lengths: visored, last in
nursery at Ayr, free to post and in lead early: joined M. Al Kurdi in UAE. *M. L. W. Bell*

GYPSY ROYAL (IRE) 2 b.f. (Feb 9) Desert Prince (IRE) 130 – Menominee (Soviet **42**
Star (USA) 128) [2004 6f 7.1m 5.7g Sep 27] €50,000Y: leggy filly: fifth foal: half-sister
to smart 1m winner Touch And Fly (by Catrail) and 11f to 1¾m winner Count de Money
(by Last Tycoon): dam unraced half-sister to Prix Royal-Oak winner Mersey and Prix
Saint-Alary winner Muncie: poor form in maidens. *R. Ingram*

H

HAADEF 3 b.c. Sadler's Wells (USA) 132 – Taqreem (IRE) 73 (Nashwan (USA) 135) **101**
[2004 10g³ 10d* 12m⁴ 11.9g 11.8g 10v² Oct 20] stocky, round-barrelled colt: fifth foal:
half-brother to useful 7f winner Ma-Arif (by Alzao) who stayed 1¼m: dam, middle-
distance maiden, half-sister to Ibn Bey and Roseate Tern: useful performer: won maiden
at Sandown in June: better efforts in frame after in King Edward VII Stakes at Royal
Ascot (7 lengths behind Five Dynasties) and handicap at Nottingham (beaten 6 lengths
by Exterior): effective at 1¼m/1½m: acts on heavy and good to firm ground: blinkered
last 2 starts: reportedly injured near-fore fourth outing (Old Newton Cup): sold 85,000
gns, joined J. Howard Johnson. *J. H. M. Gosden*

HAAFHD 3 ch.c. Alhaarth (IRE) 126 – Al Bahathri (USA) 123 (Blushing Groom **129**
(FR) 131) [2004 115+: 8g* 8g* 8f⁴ 8g 10s* Oct 16]
 Shooting stars rarely burst back to life once they have faded, leaving only
the memory of a spectacular one-off performance. Having begun to pale by com-
parison with some of those left in his wake in the Two Thousand Guineas in May,
Haafhd proved an exception. Azamour, Grey Swallow, Whipper and Bachelor

Duke went on to win five Group 1 races between them, in hindsight making the Guineas look a better race than the Derby and one of the strongest renewals in depth in a long time, but Haafhd's efforts in the spring seemed to catch up with him. Freshened up by a break, however, he confirmed himself a good classic winner, and just about the best three-year-old of 2004 in Britain and Ireland, with victory in the Champion Stakes at Newmarket in October, retiring with his reputation revitalised after a second performance which everyone could stand back and admire.

Haafhd was available at 33/1 for the Guineas at the beginning of the year. After winning his first two starts as a two-year-old, he finished only third in pattern company in the Champagne Stakes at Doncaster and the Dewhurst at Newmarket. All the same, a well-bred colt with a stable renowned for its horses coming to hand early, he looked the type to make his mark in a trial at least and duly showed himself an improved performer with a decisive success in the bet365 Craven Stakes at Newmarket in April. It has become far from unusual for the Guineas to be won by horses making their reappearance at three, but some trainers still see a trial in the spring as good preparation. Barry Hills bemoaned the removal of the Thirsk Classic Trial after the course lost television coverage for its April fixture; Hills had been regularly represented since winning it with his previous Guineas winner Tap On Wood in 1979. Historically, the Craven itself has lost some significance since Tirol became its fourth winner to go on to Guineas success in six years in 1990, but Haafhd put himself strongly in the picture to be another to complete the double. With the Guineas a little over two weeks away, he looked well and very fit beforehand, visibly sharper than some of his opponents, and he started joint second favourite behind Dewhurst runner-up Three Valleys in a field of five. Sent off to make the running for the first time, he settled well over the longer trip and turned Dewhurst form round in no uncertain terms, quickly opening up a clear lead two furlongs out and drawing further away near the finish, merely pushed out firmly to beat the favourite by five lengths. On the face of it, Haafhd could hardly have won in better style, but to some extent he had the run of things, something which was far from sure to be repeated in the Guineas, and he was top-priced 7/1 for the first classic afterwards.

Thirteen rivals took on Haafhd in the Two Thousand Guineas, sponsored for the first time by UltimateBet.com. In a field containing ten pattern winners, Ballydoyle's One Cool Cat dominated the market, as he had all winter, going off at 15/8 for his first outing since the last of his run of four successes from five starts as a juvenile in the National Stakes at the Curragh in September. Haafhd went off at 11/2 along with Salford City, another to have shortened considerably in the betting after his impressive success in the Greenham Stakes at Newbury. Godolphin's Snow Ridge, winner of the Royal Lodge Stakes for Marcus Tregoning at two, had also been shortened after coasting home in a private trial at Nad Al Sheba in Dubai for new connections. He was at 8/1, with French-trained Whipper at 9/1 after his impressive victory in the listed Prix Djebel at Maisons-Laffitte. Dermot Weld's Grey Swallow, who had scrambled home on his reappearance at Leopardstown—in the same race won by his stable's Refuse To Bend prior to success at Newmarket twelve months earlier—was at 10/1. Dewhurst winner Milk It Mick started at 12/1 after two defeats in the spring.

bet365 Craven Stakes, Newmarket—Haafhd makes all as his rivals barely challenge; Three Valleys is second, ahead of Peak To Creek and Imperial Stride

UltimateBet.com 2000 Guineas Stakes, Newmarket—in a good renewal, Haafhd (striped cap) is clear after quickening decisively over two furlongs out; Snow Ridge (second left) briefly looks a threat to him, while Azamour (second right) and Grey Swallow (noseband) come from behind to finish third and fourth; Whipper (left), Salford City (right) and Bachelor Duke (light colours) are next

At a meeting condensed to two days from its traditional three, the ground was good for the start of Guineas weekend after rain through the week had prevented the need for watering. Newmarket deliberately denied the Guineas field the full width of the Rowley Mile, narrowing the course, and placed the stalls in the centre in the hope of avoiding a repeat of the trouble which had marred its classics twelve months earlier. As things turned out, in the smallest Guineas field since 1996, luck in running proved no issue, though the race was given a tactical element by the presence of pacemakers for One Cool Cat and Snow Ridge. Pacemakers in a field sometimes encourage jockeys to act as if any amount of ground can be conceded early on, and the Guineas field was stretched out over an unusually long distance, the field in two distinct lines by halfway. Riding tactics were tempered slightly on Haafhd (who, looking in still better shape than in the Craven, had attracted a bet of £50,000 to £8,000), but he raced close up in the leading group, which also included Whipper, Bachelor Duke and Three Valleys. Again travelling with tremendous zest, Haafhd began his effort in earnest over two furlongs out and quickly took the initiative. Clear in the Dip, he responded well to pressure and, though Snow Ridge came out of the pack, nothing got to Haafhd, who held on well up the hill, winning by a length and three quarters from Snow Ridge, with 25/1-shot Azamour, making his reappearance, finishing well to be a length further back, the same distance ahead of Grey Swallow, who pipped the fading Whipper for fourth. One Cool Cat trailed throughout, reportedly found afterwards to have an irregular heartbeat.

Haafhd's success in the Guineas was the most decisive since King's Best won by three and a half lengths in 2000, and, even at the time, he looked a good Guineas winner, more or less on a par with King's Best as well as Zafonic and Pennekamp, the best winners in the 'nineties. Haafhd's timefigure of 1.14 fast was also a good one, the best of the season in any age group, and provided confirmation of his form rating. It confirmed as well that the race had been truly run, though there were grounds for arguing that some of Haafhd's opponents had been set a little too much to do, Azamour the most striking example. Patient tactics are usually no disadvantage in a well-run race, but it's another matter to be dropped out so far as to be virtually in another contest. As races on the Rowley Mile tend to do, the way the Guineas was run attracted criticism, chiefly, on this occasion, because the runners fanned out centre to far side. However, the lack of bunching was a refreshing change from some other recent renewals, and the race was better for it. The 2004 Guineas not only proved solid form, but also a good pointer to stamina, which was to prove significant with Haafhd in the autumn. The tactics, of course, were of the riders' own making. For his part, Richard Hills, whose twin brother Michael also won a classic, the Irish One Thousand Guineas, for father Barry on Nicer in 1993, has tended to attract scant praise in the saddle over the years, but his riding at Newmarket in particular, where races are regularly won and lost in the Dip, has often been exemplary. Haafhd was Hills's third victory in a Newmarket classic, following success in the One Thousand Guineas on Harayir and Lahan, both also owned by Hamdan Al Maktoum, to whom Hills is first jockey. Reflecting on his first British classic win with one of his sons and a job well done through the winter and spring, Barry Hills called it 'the sweetest day since Rheingold won the Arc in 1973.'

Hills had gone on record before Newmarket as saying Haafhd was as good as any miler he had trained, but further evidence of that and of the reliability of the Guineas form had to wait. Although made a short-priced favourite, Haafhd missed the Irish Guineas to wait for the St James's Palace Stakes at Royal Ascot. With talk of the Derby quashed soon after Newmarket, Haafhd became only the third Guineas winner to line up in the St James's Palace in the last ten years. In a field of eleven, he was backed from 2/1 to 6/4 favourite to emulate Rock of Gibraltar in 2002 but, despite looking in good shape, had to work to edge past the front-running outsider Castleton in the straight and was overtaken inside the last furlong, albeit going down by little over a length in fourth to Azamour. Haafhd had moved well on the good ground at Newmarket, both in the Craven and the Guineas, showing a fluent action, the sort often associated with a horse at home on firm going, but the firm surface at Ascot seemed not to suit him, and he carried his head a little more awkwardly than usual in the closing stages. Conditions were more like they had been at Newmarket for his next outing in the Sussex Stakes at Goodwood, but Haafhd was even further below form. Soviet Song and Nayyir would have found Haafhd hard to beat at his best, but he clearly wasn't himself and already looked beaten when hampered a furlong out, finishing ninth and reportedly losing his action. Haafhd was absent for ten weeks after Goodwood, reportedly giving the odd cough, along with others in the yard. In the autumn, connections in hindsight concluded he had 'lightened up a bit before the Sussex, not looking so full and well as he does now.'

After some deliberation amid reports of mixed home work—a similar scenario occurred before his St James's Palace defeat—Haafhd was declared for the Queen Elizabeth II Stakes at Ascot in September, only to be withdrawn on the day because of the unseasonably firmish ground. Conditions were far more autumnal for the Emirates Airline Champion Stakes at Newmarket in October. The feature event on Champions Day is worth considerably less than its equivalent at Leopardstown in September, but it still carries a deal of prestige as the last all-aged Group 1 run in Britain. King George winner Doyen started favourite at 3/1, despite disappointing in the Irish Champion Stakes behind Azamour, who drifted out to 6/1 at Newmarket amid concerns over the soft ground. Lucky Story started second favourite at 9/2 after his fine second to Rakti in the Queen Elizabeth, while his stable-companion, the improving Mister Monet, was also preferred to Azamour at 5/1, with Refuse To Bend next at 7/1. Stepped up in trip and tackling testing conditions, Haafhd was the forgotten horse after his defeats at Royal Ascot and Goodwood, going off at 12/1. As Naheef made the pace towards the centre, Haafhd soon started to make his odds look generous and was still travelling well as most began to tread water. Even as the mare Chorist went for home, it seemed only a matter of whether or not Haafhd would stay, and, though drifting left to the rail once he finally came under pressure, he ran on strongly from the Dip to win by two and a half lengths. Azamour closed only late on for third, beaten a further length, though he finished six lengths clear of Norse Dancer in fourth. In the end, few of his main rivals gave their running, but Haafhd's performance was hard to fault and only a little behind the best in the race in recent years. After Storming Home in 2002, he became a second winner for his trainer in three runnings, and a second for Richard Hills and Hamdan Al Maktoum in four, also following Nayef.

Emirates Airline Champion Stakes, Newmarket—
Haafhd returns to his best and has two and a half lengths to spare over Chorist; Azamour is third

Haafhd's Guineas success went some way to compensating for defeat in the same colours in the Newmarket classics for his sire and dam. Dewhurst winner Alhaarth was only fourth behind Mark of Esteem at Newmarket when favourite, while Al Bahathri was beaten a short head by Oh So Sharp before going on to success in the Irish Guineas and the Coronation Stakes. Oh So Sharp became the grandam of Shantou, successful in the St Leger, but Al Bahathri is the first winner of a major European classic to become the dam of a British classic winner since Snow Bride, promoted from second in the Oaks, produced the 1995 Derby winner Lammtarra. Alhaarth came only fifth in the Derby, and did his winning at three and four over a mile and nearly a mile and a quarter, but he has produced winners over a range of distances at stud, including good ones over a mile and a half in 2004 in Bandari and Phoenix Reach. Alhaarth got King's Stand winner Dominica in his first crop after being retired to his owner's Derrinstown Stud in Ireland at the equivalent of €6,000 in 1998. His fee in 2005 will be €30,000.

Haafhd (ch.c. 2001)	Alhaarth (IRE) (b 1993)	Unfuwain (b 1985)	Northern Dancer / Height of Fashion
		Irish Valley (ch 1982)	Irish River / Green Valley
	Al Bahathri (USA) (ch 1982)	Blushing Groom (ch 1974)	Red God / Runaway Bride
		Chain Store (b 1972)	Nodouble / General Store

Not surprisingly, Haafhd is comfortably the best produce of his dam, who was bought by Sheikh Hamdan as a yearling at Keeneland for 650,000 dollars. That said, most of Al Bahathri's previous foals have been winners, several of them well

Mr Hamdan Al Maktoum's "Haafhd"

above average. Al Bahathri's first foal Hasbah (by Kris) was a smart performer at seven furlongs and a mile, finishing second in the Coronation Stakes. Munir (by Indian Ridge), successful in the Greenham and the Challenge Stakes as well as finishing sixth in the Guineas, was also smart, while in between the pair, Goalwah (by Sadler's Wells), Mithali (by Unfuwain) and Za-Im (by Green Desert) were all useful. Al Bahathri has been covered again by Alhaarth and has also produced a colt by King's Best. As a racehorse, the unimposing Al Bahathri was renowned for her gameness, her free-going nature and her exaggerated, long stride, making her well suited to being allowed to bowl along up front. A game sort, like his dam, Haafhd could front run too, as he did in the Craven, and he was also a fine sight in full flow, though he was inclined to look about him in the lead and tuck his head back, sometimes carrying it a little high. Haafhd did not stand his racing quite so well as Rodrigo de Triano, another chestnut with a fine turn of foot, who was the last before Haafhd to complete the Two Thousand Guineas/Champion Stakes double; Rodrigo de Triano won the Irish Guineas and the Juddmonte International in between. The strong, lengthy, medium-sized Haafhd was untried beyond a mile and a quarter; he won on good to firm ground, but showed his best form on good and soft. He has been retired to his owner's Nunnery Stud in Norfolk, where his grandsire Unfuwain stood until his death in 2002. Haafhd's fee is £20,000. *B. W. Hills*

HAATMEY 2 b.c. (Feb 9) Josr Algarhoud (IRE) 118 – Raneen Alwatar 80 (Sadler's **90** Wells (USA) 132) [2004 7m³ 7.2s⁴ 9f² 10.2g* 10g⁴ Oct 11] good-topped colt: eighth foal: half-brother to fairly useful 1998 2-y-o 1m winner Raneen Nashwan (by Nashwan): dam, 1½m winner, out of sister to Coronation Stakes winner Flame of Tara, herself dam of Salsabil and Marju: fairly useful performer: won maiden at Bath in September: creditable fourth to Sunday Symphony in minor event at Leicester final start, hanging right: will stay 1½m: best efforts on good going. *M. R. Channon*

HABANERO 3 b.c. Cadeaux Genereux 131 – Queen of Dance (IRE) (Sadler's Wells **81** (USA) 132) [2004 73: 10d 10d 8.3s⁵ 8.3m³ 8.1m* 10g³ 8.1m³ 8.5f* 8g⁶ 8.5g 8f p10g⁶ Oct 31] good-topped, quite attractive colt: fairly useful handicapper: won at Sandown in June and Epsom (beat Pickle by ½ length, dictating pace) in July: stays 1¼m: acts on firm going, showed promise on polytrack: front runner: game. *R. Hannon*

HABIBTI SARA 4 ch.f. Bijou d'Inde 127 – Cut Velvet (USA) (Northern Dancer) **–** [2004 –: f12s Feb 2] leggy filly: little sign of ability. *A. W. Carroll*

HABITUAL DANCER 3 b.g. Groom Dancer (USA) 128 – Pomorie (IRE) 67§ (Be **68** My Guest (USA) 126) [2004 53: 7g⁶ 10d* 12s² 12.1d³ 14g 17.1d⁵ 16g 15s* Oct 11] good-bodied gelding: fair handicapper: won at Southwell in April and Ayr (edged left) in October: probably stays 17f: acts on soft going, probably on good to firm. *Jedd O'Keeffe*

HABITUAL (IRE) 3 b.g. Kahyasi 130 – Kick The Habit 94 (Habitat 134) [2004 –p: **60** p7g p8g 16.2g⁴ 11.5f⁵ p16g* 16.1m p12.2g Oct 16] rangy gelding: modest performer: best effort when winning banded race at Lingfield in September: stays easy 2m: acts on polytrack: raced freely final outing: sold 14,000 gns. *Sir Mark Prescott*

HABSHAN (USA) 4 ch.g. Swain (IRE) 134 – Cambara 97 (Dancing Brave (USA) **80** 140) [2004 79: 8m 8m⁴ 8m³ 8.2s⁵ 8m* 8.2g 8g³ Sep 2] good-topped gelding: fairly useful handicapper: won at Newmarket in July then left N. Graham: good third at Salisbury final outing: should prove as effective at 7f as 1m (bred to stay much further): acts on soft and good to firm going. *C. F. Wall*

HACHITA (USA) 2 ch.f. (Jan 18) Gone West (USA) – Choice Spirit (USA) 105 (Dan- **88** zig (USA)) [2004 7m* 7.1m³ 7.6g² Sep 11] first foal: dam, French 1m winner, half-sister to Zafonic and Zamindar (both by Gone West): won maiden at Kempton in July: better efforts in minor events at Sandown and Chester (made most and rallied when second to Johnny Jumpup): will stay 1m. *H. R. A. Cecil*

HADRIAN (IRE) 2 b.c. (Mar 6) King's Best (USA) 132 – Wanton 106 (Kris 135) **86** [2004 6d⁶ 7f² 7g⁶ 7s Oct 16] 90,000Y: small, good-topped colt: half-brother to numerous winners, including Irish 1000 Guineas winner Classic Park (by Robellino) and 3-y-o Birthday Suit: dam, sprinter (best at 2 yrs), half-sister to smart sprinter Easy Option: fairly useful performer: made all in maiden at Thirsk in September: never going well in nursery final start: stays 7f: acts on firm going. *M. Johnston*

HAENERTSBURG (IRE) 2 b.f. (Apr 2) Victory Note (USA) 120 – Olivia's Pride **50** (IRE) (Digamist (USA) 110) [2004 6m 6d 7m p5.1g⁵ Dec 13] €6,000Y: sturdy filly: sister to 4-y-o Diamond Orchid and half-sister to 1998 2-y-o 5f winner Ladycake (by Peru-gino): dam unraced: modest maiden: needs to settle to stay 7f. *A. Berry*

HAGLEY PARK 5 b.m. Petong 126 – Gi La High 68 (Rich Charlie 117) [2004 57: f5g² f5g² f5g⁶ f5g⁵ p5g⁴ f5g³ f5g f5g³ f5g* f5g 5.1f 6f 5.1m⁵ p7g p5.1g⁵ p5m Dec 15] smallish mare: modest performer: won banded race at Wolverhampton in May: left M. Quinn after twelfth outing: best at 5f: acts on all-weather, firm and good to soft going: tried visored: often forces pace: unreliable. *Miss K. M. George* **55 §**

HAIBAN 2 b.c. (Mar 20) Barathea (IRE) 127 – Aquarela (Shirley Heights 130) [2004 8.3d⁴ 7s² 8.3d³ Sep 19] quite good-topped colt: third foal: dam ran once: placed in maidens at Chester (carried head high) and Hamilton: should be suited by 1¼m/1½m. *G. A. Butler* **69**

HAIL THE CHIEF 7 b.h. Be My Chief (USA) 122 – Jade Pet 90 (Petong 126) [2004 –: f8.5g* f8.5g⁴ p10g 8g³ 7.6d 9m⁶ 10m 8.5g 7m 8.3m Sep 27] rather sparely-made horse: good mover: useful on all-weather nowadays, only fair on turf: won minor event at Wolverhampton (by 4 lengths from Lakota Brave) in January: left D. Nicholls after fifth start: best at 1m/1¼m: acts on dirt, fibresand, soft and good to firm going: has been bandaged in front. *J. Akehurst* **69 a102**

HAITHEM (IRE) 7 b.g. Mtoto 134 – Wukk (IRE) (Glow (USA)) [2004 –§: f8g⁶ f8g f8.5g f12g f9.4g³ f9.4g f8g⁶ f9.4s p8g⁵ p8g⁶ p8g* p10g p8g p8.6g f7g p10m Dec 8] close-coupled gelding: modest performer: won banded race at Lingfield in March: stays 9.4f: acts on all-weather and good to firm ground: tried blinkered: often tongue tied/in eyeshields: temperamental. *D. Shaw* **51 §**

HAJEER (IRE) 6 b.g. Darshaan 133 – Simouna (Ela-Mana-Mou 132) [2004 55: f16g⁵ f14.8g² Jan 16] lengthy, angular gelding: poor performer: stays 2m: acts on all-weather: tried in blinkers/cheekpieces. *P. W. Hiatt* **44**

HALABALOO (IRE) 3 b.f. Intikhab (USA) 135 – Outcry 73 (Caerleon (USA) 132) [2004 66p: 7g⁵ 8s 7g³ 8d⁶ 8.1d⁶ Aug 21] angular filly: fair maiden: should stay 1m: best efforts on good ground: had to be led to start in blinkers on final outing (raced freely during race): looked less than keen under pressure third start: sent to Sweden. *G. Wragg* **73**

HALCYON EXPRESS (IRE) 2 b.c. (Apr 13) Mujadil (USA) 119 – Hakkaniyah 84 (Machiavellian (USA) 123) [2004 6d 7.1d⁴ Nov 3] 17,000Y: fourth foal: half-brother to a winner abroad by Grand Lodge: dam, 2-y-o 6f winner, closely related to useful French performer up to 1¼m Elanaaka: better effort in maidens (tongue tied) when fourth at Musselburgh: will probably stay 1m. *P. F. I. Cole* **68**

HALCYON MAGIC 6 b.g. Magic Ring (IRE) 115 – Consistent Queen 55 (Queen's Hussar 124) [2004 63, a–: 6s² 6.1s 8f 8m² 7m 7g⁶ 8g 7g* 7.1s⁵ Sep 20] sturdy gelding: modest handicapper: left Miss J. Feilden: won apprentice race at Yarmouth in September: effective at 6f (given bit of a test) to 1m: acts on firm and soft going: blinkered: unreliable. *M. Wigham* **58 § a– §**

HALF A HANDFUL 3 b.g. Victory Note (USA) 120 – Enaam 65§ (Shirley Heights 130) [2004 p6g 6d 6s 6m⁶ 6m³ 6m³ 7.2g² 6m³ 8m Jul 28] 7,000Y: sixth living foal: half-brother to 3 winners, notably useful 1997 2-y-o 6f winner Linden Heights (by Distinctly North): dam, ungenuine maiden, should have stayed beyond 1¼m: fair maiden handi-capper: creditable efforts when placed: acts on good to firm going: visored last 2 starts: has looked tricky ride/carried head high: often slowly away: gelded after final outing. *M. J. Wallace* **70**

HALF INCH 4 b.f. Inchinor 119 – Anhaar (Ela-Mana-Mou 132) [2004 68: p10g 9.7d⁴ 9.9s 12d Jul 8] lengthy filly: fair handicapper: stays 1¼m: acts on good to firm and good to soft going: tried in visor, usually wears cheekpieces: sometimes looks reluctant: none too consistent. *B. I. Case* **65**

HALICARDIA 3 br.f. Halling (USA) 133 – Pericardia 60 (Petong 126) [2004 94p: 8d³ 9.9g* 10m² Jun 10] rather leggy, quite attractive filly: good walker: has a quick, fluent action: useful performer: won listed Lupe Stakes at Goodwood in May by neck from Spotlight: placed in similar events at Kempton and Newbury (¾-length second to Inch-eni): stays 1¼m: acts on good to firm ground: tended to hang second 2-y-o start and at Goodwood: usually held up: sold 64,000 gns in November. *P. W. Harris* **104**

HALLAHOISE HYDRO (IRE) 3 ch.g. Lake Coniston (IRE) 131 – Flo Bear (IRE) (Prince Rupert (FR) 121) [2004 –: 6d⁵ 5d 7m 7m 6d 6g Sep 14] strong, close-coupled gelding: modest handicapper: won at Down Royal in April: below form after, leaving D. Gillespie in Ireland after fourth start: stays 6f: acts on good to soft ground. *B. S. Roth-well* **61 d**

HALLAND 6 ch.g. Halling (USA) 133 – Northshiel 85 (Northfields (USA)) [2004 –: **83**
12f 16g 18s Oct 16] quite attractive gelding: useful at 3 yrs: unraced in 2002 (reportedly
had another operation on hind joint): well beaten both starts at 5 yrs: fairly useful form
in 2004: probably stays 2¼m: acts on any going: well beaten only try in cheekpieces.
N. P. Littmoden

HALLA SAN 2 b.g. (Mar 14) Halling (USA) 133 – St Radegund 85 (Green Desert **74**
(USA) 127) [2004 5m 5d 6d⁵ 7g⁴ 8d³ Oct 14] 37,000Y: angular, gelding: has a quick
action: second foal: half-brother to 3-y-o Chubbes; dam, 7f winner from 2 starts, out of
1000 Guineas and Sussex Stakes winner On The House: fair maiden: third in nursery at
Newmarket: better at 1m than shorter. *Mrs J. R. Ramsden*

HALLE BOP 2 b.f. (Apr 4) Dubai Millennium 140 – Napoleon's Sister (IRE) 101 **85 p**
(Alzao (USA) 117) [2004 6d2 6g* Sep 3] compact filly: third foal: half-sister to fairly
useful 2002 2-y-o 1m winner Louis Napoleon (by Indian Ridge): dam, 1¼m winner, half-
sister to Derby winner Oath and high-class performer up to 10.5f Pelder: favourite,
confirmed promise when winning maiden at Kempton comfortably by 1¼ lengths from
Holly Springs, making all: should stay at least 1m: useful prospect. *Saeed bin Suroor*

HALLHOO (IRE) 2 gr.c. (Mar 3) Indian Ridge 123 – Nuit Chaud (USA) (Woodman **91**
(USA) 126) [2004 6m³ 7g* 8.1g² 8s² 8d Oct 15] 210,000Y: angular colt: fourth foal: half-
brother to 3-y-o Arrgatt and winner in USA by Fastness: dam, ran twice in USA, half-
sister to dam of Danehill Dancer: fairly useful performer: made all in maiden at Newbury
in August: good second in nurseries at Haydock and Ayr: ran no sort of race final outing:
will stay 1¼m: acts on soft going: hung right first 2 starts. *M. R. Channon*

HALLINGS OVERTURE (USA) 5 b.g. Halling (USA) 133 – Sonata (Polish Pre- **84**
cedent (USA) 131) [2004 p10g⁶ p10g 7g² 8g Sep 2] robust gelding: fairly useful maiden,
lightly raced: unraced in 2003: best effort when second to Poule de Luxe at Kempton in
April: effective at 7f to 1¼m: acts on polytrack, raced only on good/good to firm ground
on turf. *C. A. Horgan*

HALLOWED DREAM (IRE) 2 b.f. (Feb 3) Alhaarth (IRE) 126 – Salul (Soviet **85**
Star (USA) 128) [2004 8f 7d 8m 8m² 8d⁶ Oct 15] 15,000F: big, strong filly: fifth foal:
half-sister to several winners, including useful 6f to 1m winner Senator's Alibi (by Caerleon) and 7f winner Forge Valley Lady (by Hamas): dam unraced: fairly useful maiden:
second at Newmarket: showed up well long way final start: stays 1m: acts on good to firm
going. *C. E. Brittain*

HALLUCINATE 2 b.c. (Apr 13) Spectrum (IRE) 126 – Swift Spring (FR) 56 (Bluebird **79**
(USA) 125) [2004 5m 6f⁴ 7f² 7m³ 7s⁴ 7.9g³ Sep 1] 14,000Y: leggy colt: half-brother to 3
winners, including 5-y-o Swing Wing and fairly useful but ungenuine 11.5f winner
Spring Anchor (by Slip Anchor): dam, 7f winner who seemed to stay 2m, half-sister to
smart French performer up to 15.5f Philanthrop: fair maiden: will stay at least 1¼m: best
effort on good going. *R. Hannon*

HALMAHERA (IRE) 9 b.g. Petardia 113 – Champagne Girl 67 (Robellino **107**
(USA) 127) [2004 107: 6g 6s² 5v⁴ 6d⁶ 6m⁶ 6f 5d⁵ 5m 6m⁶ 6s 5.6m* 5g 6d 6s p6g
f5g⁴ Dec 7]
    The Yorkshire town of Thirsk, the model for Darrowby in the James Herriot
books written by Alf Wright who lived and worked there, lost one of its best loved
characters in 2004. The amateur weather forecaster Bill Foggitt died in September
at the age of ninety-one. Foggitt's predictions were based on weather records kept
by his family since 1830 and on his knowledge of country lore. Swallows appearing
early in April and rooks nesting higher in the treetops, for example, were signs of a
good summer, waxwings coming to Britain from Scandinavia were an indicator of
a cold winter, the closing of pine cones heralded rain, while an increase in mole
activity was a forerunner of warmer weather. The re-emergence of the area around
Thirsk as a training centre has made some of its racehorses household names as
well, none more so than Halmahera who became the first horse to win the Portland
Handicap three years in a row. Halmahera's third triumph, carrying joint-second
top weight of 9-10 and setting a course record (one of five on the day), even put
Frankie Dettori in the shade. Dettori, who incidentally rode Halmahera to the
second of his Portland wins, landed a four-timer at Doncaster but the headlines next
day were all about Halmahera, who put up his best effort of the year, coming with a
very strong run to snatch a typically competitive Portland in the last few strides by
a head from Texas Gold. Halmahera got up in a blanket finish, with runners across

451

totesport Portland (Handicap), Doncaster—Halmahera (left) achieves a remarkable third successive win in this typically strongly-contested event; Texas Gold (right of centre; spots on sleeves) is second, ahead of Ptarmigan Ridge (No. 22), Whistler (cheekpieces) and Whitbarrow (right; blinkered)

the full width of the track, after still having plenty to do a furlong out, though his rider Neil Callan incurred the displeasure of the stewards, picking up a one-day ban for improper use of the whip.

Apart from a share of the spoils in a handicap at Ascot in 2003, the three Portlands (sponsored by totesport in 2004) have been the only races won by Halmahera in the past five seasons. After a prompt start to his racing career as a two-year-old—finishing fourth at Kempton's Easter meeting—Halmahera established himself as a tough and genuine juvenile, winning four races (including the

Mr J. Duddy and Mrs G. Quinn's "Halmahera"

Cornwallis Stakes) from eight starts. But he didn't win again until he was four, when he picked up the Chipchase Stakes, then a listed event, at Newcastle and started to establish himself as a regular in the traditional big sprint handicaps. Runner-up in both the Wokingham and the Stewards' Cup that year, he finished runner-up for a second time in the Stewards' Cup as a six-year-old before changing hands for 40,000 guineas at the Newmarket Autumn Sales, bought out of Ian Balding's yard. Since moving to Kevin Ryan—who saddled the gelding to fill the runner-up spot for a third time in the Stewards' Cup—Halmahera has raced in the colours of John Duddy and Gillian Quinn, wife of ex-footballer Niall, who described Halmahera's third Portland win as being 'as good as any day I've had in sport.' The present owners stepped in when another prospective client backed out because of Halmahera's age. Halmahera, who finished sixth in the latest Stewards' Cup, had the ninety-third and final outing of his career when a creditable fourth behind Dancing Mystery in a useful handicap at Southwell in December. He has now been retired.

Halmahera (IRE) (b.g. 1995)	Petardia (b 1990)	Petong (gr 1980)	Mansingh
			Iridium
		What A Pet (b 1981)	Mummy's Pet
			Moben
	Champagne Girl (b 1991)	Robellino (b 1978)	Roberto
			Isobelline
		Babycham Sparkle (b 1980)	So Blessed
			Effervescence II

Halmahera is a good-topped gelding with a round action, by the now-deceased Petardia, a sprinter-miler who became mainly a sire of sprinters, though the best horse he produced, The Deputy, won the Santa Anita Derby over nine furlongs. Halmahera's dam, the two-year-old five-furlong winner Champagne Girl, has bred three other winning sprinters including Speedy Gee, a full brother to Halmahera who was fairly useful at two, but didn't go on. Halmahera was effective at five furlongs on an easy seven and acted on any turf going and fibresand. Tried visored and blinkered, though at least as effective when not, the tough Halmahera was sometimes slowly away and carried his head awkwardly. He was best held up in races run at a strong gallop. *K. A. Ryan*

HAMAASY 3 b.g. Machiavellian (USA) 123 – Sakha 109 (Wolfhound (USA) 126) **58** [2004 71: 6m⁵ 5d 5g 5d Aug 9] quite attractive gelding: modest maiden: effective at 5f to 7f: acts on good to firm going: tongue tied second/final 2-y-o outings: free-going sort. *D. Nicholls*

HAMAIRI (IRE) 3 ch.c. Spectrum (IRE) 126 – Handaza (IRE) 93 (Be My Guest **112** (USA) 126) [2004 8s⁴ 7s² 7.5m* 7m² 8m² 7.5v* Oct 3] strong, good-topped colt: third foal: half-brother to smart Irish 6f/1m winner Hanabad (by Cadeaux Genereux), 7f winner at 2 yrs: dam Irish 1m winner: smart performer: won maiden at Tipperary in May and Coolmore Home of Champions Concorde Stakes there (by 2½ lengths from Fearn Royal) in October: second at Leopardstown in between in Ballycorus Stakes (beaten ½ length by Naahy) and Desmond Stakes (beaten 2 lengths by easy winner Ace): stays 1m: acts on good to firm ground. *J. Oxx, Ireland*

HAMBLEDEN 7 b.g. Vettori (IRE) 119 – Dalu (IRE) 72 (Dancing Brave (USA) 140) **105** [2004 109: 10.3d⁶ 12g 12f⁴ 11.9g⁴ 14g 12g⁶ 13.4s³ Aug 21] strong, angular gelding: useful handicapper: in frame at Ascot (Duke of Edinburgh Stakes, fourth to Wunderwood), Haydock (Old Newton Cup, fourth to Alkaased) and Chester (third to Swift Tango): stays 1¾m: acts on fibresand, firm and soft going: usually races prominently: tough. *M. A. Jarvis*

HAMBURG SPRINGER (IRE) 2 b.g. (Mar 1) Charnwood Forest (IRE) 125 – Kyra **33** Crown (IRE) (Astronef 116) [2004 6m 5m⁵ 5m 5g 7.9g Oct 9] close-coupled gelding: poor maiden. *M. J. Polglase*

HAMMER OF THE GODS (IRE) 4 ch.g. Tagula (IRE) 116 – Bhama (FR) (Habitat **69** 134) [2004 7m³ 6s³ 7g p5m* p5.1g⁴ p5g² Dec 18] strong gelding: poor mover: fair performer: unraced in 2003: won banded race at Lingfield in November: will stay 6f: acts on polytrack: tongue tied: visored (looked wayward) second start, blinkered last 3. *Julian Poulton*

HANA DEE 3 b.f. Cadeaux Genereux 131 – Jumairah Sun (IRE) 98 (Scenic 128) [2004 **58** 72p: p7g 8m 7m⁶ 8m 7f 7.2g⁴ 8g⁵ 8g³ 8m 8d 10m⁴ p8g⁵ p8.6d p12.2g⁶ f8g³ p8g p8.6g Dec

27] big, workmanlike filly: modest maiden: stays 1m: acts on polytrack and good to firm ground: usually held up: none too genuine. *M. R. Channon*

HANAMI 4 b.f. Hernando (FR) 127 – Russian Rose (IRE) 82 (Soviet Lad (USA)) [2004 108: 8m³ 10m⁶ 10s Aug 22] smallish, quite attractive filly: useful performer: respectable third to Soviet Song in Ridgewood Pearl Stakes at the Curragh on reappearance: poor efforts after in Pretty Polly Stakes at same course (had won race year before) and Prix Jean Romanet at Deauville: likely to prove best around 1¼m: acts on soft and good to firm going. *J. A. R. Toller* **99**

HANAZAKARI 3 b.c. Danzero (AUS) – Russian Rose (IRE) 82 (Soviet Lad (USA)) [2004 11.5m p12g⁵ Sep 1] well held in maidens at Yarmouth and Lingfield. *J. A. R. Toller* **–**

HAND CHIME 7 ch.g. Clantime 101 – Warning Bell 88 (Bustino 136) [2004 89, a99: f6g f7g p7g⁵ 7s 7s 7m² 6d 7s 7g⁶ 7s Oct 27] angular gelding: fairly useful handicapper on all-weather, fair on turf: best form at 7f: yet to race on heavy going, acts on any other turf/all-weather: sometimes slowly away: free-going sort: has reportedly bled. *W. J. Haggas* **75 a92**

HANDSOME CROSS (IRE) 3 b.c. Cape Cross (IRE) 129 – Snap Crackle Pop (IRE) 87 (Statoblest 120) [2004 89: 7.1s⁵ 7m⁵ 6g⁶ 7m 5m³ 5g 5s Oct 16] strong colt: fairly useful handicapper: third to Jimmy Ryan at Goodwood in July: likely to prove best at 5f/6f: acts on good to firm ground: races prominently. *H. Morrison* **85**

HANDSOME LADY 2 ch.f. (Feb 27) Handsome Ridge 121 – Il Doria (IRE) 66 (Mac's Imp (USA) 116) [2004 5g⁴ 5m⁶ 5m 5.1d⁵ 5g⁶ 5g⁴ 5d 5d³ Oct 17] smallish, sturdy filly: good mover: fourth dam, sprint maiden, half-sister to smart 5f performer Palacegate Episode: fair performer: won maiden at Ayr in April: fourth in nursery at Musselburgh, only creditable effort after: needs to settle to stay beyond 5f: best efforts on good going: visored fifth start. *I. Semple* **74**

HANNAH'S DREAM (IRE) 2 b.f. (Apr 29) King's Best (USA) 132 – Meritxell (IRE) (Thatching 131) [2004 6g⁶ 7.5m² 7m³ Oct 10] 14,000Y: sturdy filly: second foal: dam, French 1½m maiden, half-sister to very smart 1m/1¼m performer Almushtarak: fair form, racing prominently, when placed in maidens at Beverley and Newcastle (looked bit wayward): will stay at least 1m: sold 20,000 gns, sent to Sweden. *M. Johnston* **69**

HANNAH'S TRIBE (IRE) 2 b.f. (Apr 17) Daggers Drawn (USA) 114 – Cala-Holme (IRE) (Fools Holme (USA)) [2004 5.9f 7d 7.1d p8.6g Nov 26] €2,200F, 4,000Y: third foal: dam no form in 3 starts: poor form in maidens: should stay 1m. *B. Smart* **46**

HANSEATIC LEAGUE (USA) 2 b.g. (Feb 26) Red Ransom (USA) – Rhine Valley (USA) 101 (Danzig (USA)) [2004 5m² 5d² 5d⁶ 6d* Oct 4] good-topped gelding: third foal: dam, Irish 5f/6f winner, half-sister to useful Irish performer up to 2m Lowlander: fairly useful performer: made all in maiden at Windsor (gelded after): will probably stay 7f. *M. Johnston* **82**

HANSOMELLE (IRE) 2 b.f. (Mar 12) Titus Livius (FR) 115 – Handsome Anna (IRE) 67 (Bigstone (IRE) 126) [2004 5f⁴ 6f* 5.9g² 6d⁴ 7g²* 7s³ Oct 23] workmanlike filly: first foal: dam, Irish maiden who probably stayed 8.5f, out of very smart disqualified Coronation Stakes winner Buz Kashi: fairly useful performer: won minor event at Hamilton in July and nursery at Catterick in October: good third in nursery at Doncaster: will probably stay 1m: acts on firm and soft going. *B. Mactaggart* **80**

HANZANO (IRE) 6 b.g. Alzao (USA) – Movie Legend (USA) (Affirmed (USA)) [2004 111: a8g a8.7f⁵ 8g⁵ 7s⁴ 8d* 6d³ 8d⁶ 6.8g 8s⁵ a8g³ 7s⁴ a6.8g² p7g Oct 28] well-made gelding: useful performer: won minor event at Ovrevoll in June: good third after in listed races won by Steve's Champ at Ovrevoll and Vortex at Taby: well held in handicap at Lingfield final start: best at 6f to 1m: acts on dirt and soft going: has had tongue tied/been blinkered. *A. Hyldmo, Norway* **106**

HAPPY AS LARRY (USA) 2 b. or br.c. (Mar 10) Yes It's True (USA) 116 – Don't Be Blue (USA) (Henbane (USA) 91) [2004 p7g* Oct 13] $155,000Y, $525,000 2-y-o: third foal: dam, ran twice in USA, sister to US Grade 3 1m winner Leave It To Beezer: 5/1 and tongue tied, won maiden at Lingfield easily by 2½ lengths from Karen's Caper, slowly away but quickening to lead over 1f out: will probably prove best up to 1m: useful prospect at least. *Saeed bin Suroor* **93 p**

HAPPY BANKER (IRE) 2 gr.c. (Feb 4) With Approval (CAN) – Tropical Paradise (USA) (Manila (USA)) [2004 7d Jul 10] well held in maiden at Salisbury: dead. *M. R. Channon* **–**

HAPPY CAMPER (IRE) 4 b.g. Pennekamp (USA) 130 – Happy Dancer 95 (Seattle Dancer (USA) 119) [2004 p6g p6g p7g⁶ p7g⁵ 7v³ 7m p10g 8.1d⁵ f8s p7g² Dec **46**

20] neat gelding: poor performer nowadays: winner in Britain at 2 yrs: raced in Spain at 3 yrs: left C. Von Der Recke in Germany after reappearance: stays 7f: acts on sand (probably on polytrack), good to firm and good to soft going: has worn blinkers. *J. J. Best*

HAPPY CRUSADER (IRE)   3 b.g. Cape Cross (IRE) 129 – Les Hurlants (IRE)   **102** (Barathea (IRE) 127) [2004 103: 8g² 11g⁴ 10m 5m 7m Dec 12] well-made gelding: useful performer: creditable efforts when in frame in minor event at Doncaster (1¾ lengths second to Duke of Venice) and listed race at Goodwood (3¼ lengths fourth to Manyana, though seemed not to stay): left P. Cole after next outing: may prove best around 1m: acts on good to firm going: races prominently. *D. Oughton, Hong Kong*

HAPPY EVENT   2 b.g. (Feb 5) Makbul 104 – La Belle Vie 73 (Indian King (USA)   **85** 128) [2004 6m* 6g 5.2m 5.7d* 7g⁴ Sep 20] 15,000Y: tall gelding: seventh foal: brother to 3-y-o La Vie Est Belle and 5-y-o Maktavish and half-brother to fairly useful 5f winner Paradise Lane (by Alnasr Alwasheek): dam 6f/7f winner: fairly useful performer: won maiden at Windsor in June and minor event at Bath (beat Bold Minstrel a length) in August: will prove best at 5f/6f: acts on good to firm and good to soft ground: sometimes slowly away: gelded after final start. *B. R. Millman*

HARAMBEE (IRE)   4 b.f. Robellino (USA) 127 – Hymenee (USA) (Chief's Crown   – (USA)) [2004 11.9s 9.9d 10m 11.9g Jul 1] leggy filly: first foal: dam, 1¼m winner in France, daughter of high-class French 2-y-o Hippodamia: fairly useful performer: won maiden at Questembert and minor event at Craon in 2003 for E. Lellouche in France: well beaten both completed starts in 2004: stays 11.5f. *B. S. Rothwell*

HARBOUR HOUSE   5 b.g. Distant Relative 128 – Double Flutter 92 (Beldale Flutter   **51** (USA) 130) [2004 63d, a50: p6g p8g² p7g p8g⁶ p6g³ 5.3g* 5v³ 6f 5.3g² 5m⁶ 6f⁶ 7s⁵ 5.7s Oct 19] leggy gelding: modest performer: won banded race at Brighton in May: effective at 5f to 1m: acts on polytrack and any turf going: tried blinkered/visored. *J. J. Bridger*

HARBOUR LEGEND   2 b.f. (Mar 24) Dansili 127 – English Harbour 81 (Sabrehill   – (USA) 120) [2004 6f 7m⁶ 7.2s Aug 20] 4,000F, €8,000Y: smallish, sturdy filly: first foal: dam, 1¼m winner, half-sister to high-class 1¼m/1½m performer Environment Friend: well held in maidens/minor event: blinkered final start. *J. G. Given*

HARBOUR PRINCESS   3 b.f. Bal Harbour 113 – Gipsy Princess 65 (Prince Daniel   **30** (USA)) [2004 f6g p5g⁶ f5s⁶ f8g⁶ p7g³ 8g⁴ p10g May 13] second foal: dam 2-y-o 7f winner: poor maiden: stays 7f: acts on all-weather: visored final start. *M. F. Harris*

HARCOURT (USA)   4 b.c. Cozzene (USA) – Ballinamallard (USA) 112 (Tom Rolfe)   **77** [2004 99: 10.1s 12m p12.2g p10m Dec 22] rangy colt: lightly raced: useful handicapper at 3 yrs, just fair in 2004: should stay 1½m: acts on polytrack, good to firm and good to soft going. *P. F. I. Cole*

HARD BUCK (BRZ)   5 b. or br.h. Spend A Buck (USA) – Social Secret 69   **127** (Secreto (USA) 128) [2004 a8.5s⁴ 11f* 12m² 8.5d² 11f⁵ 12m² Jul 24]

Inconvenience, lower prize money and the absence of suitable races on an artificial surface dictate that not many horses trained in North America try their luck in Europe, whatever inducements are offered. It would be naive to imagine that there will be any change in this state of affairs in the foreseeable future. The best hope, a genuine European championship on dirt, remains a distant prospect. The same can be said about: supersonic travel which would make a round trip of at least six thousand miles less of an obstacle; a funding increase large enough to make transatlantic raids a genuine attraction; and an upheaval in the international bloodstock business under which success in a Group 1 event in Europe would add significantly to a North American-raced stallion's appeal in Kentucky. At present, transatlantic challenges from America are prompted by a spirit of adventure, undoubtedly admirable but, in truth, not a sound basis in a sport dominated increasingly by commercial considerations. The results achieved so far have not been encouraging to would-be challengers. Two dirt specialists, Kentucky Derby winner Reigh Count and Triple Crown winner Omaha, respectively won the 1929 Coronation Cup and finished second in the 1936 Gold Cup during lengthy campaigns, Omaha having been transferred to Cecil Boyd-Rochfort, but, in the last forty years, only one runner from a total of getting on for twenty has hit the target, while only a handful have gained places in stakes races. The winner was Fourstars Allstar, trained by Leo O'Brien, in the 1991 Irish Two Thousand Guineas, the placed horses were Zadracarta in the 1989 Prix de l'Abbaye, Diamonds Galore in the 1992 Nunthorpe Stakes, America America in four listed races in 2003, and Hard Buck.

Very few turf specialists aged four and up have tried their luck, and Hard Buck's challenge for the King George VI and Queen Elizabeth Stakes was the first in a championship middle-distance event since El Senor ran ninth in the 1991 Arc. All credit, then, to Hard Buck's connections for having a go, and even more credit to the five-year-old, who put up his best performance to chase home Doyen with six Group/Grade 1 winners behind him. After holding a prominent position behind the pacemaker, Hard Buck led briefly two furlongs out before being swamped by Doyen and going down by three lengths, a head in front of third-placed Sulamani.

Hard Buck wasn't merely the first North American-trained runner in the King George—he also had novelty value as an ex-Brazilian whose career in his native country had put him near the top of the tree, with five victories from nine starts, all at La Gavea in Rio de Janeiro. The pick of the five was the Grade 1 Grande Premio Linneo de Paula Machado over a mile and a quarter in October 2002. That race was worth less than £10,000 to the winner, compared to the £165,000 Hard Buck picked up for his second at Ascot. Hard Buck also finished second in a Grade 1 over a mile behind another local horse who went on to make a mark in the States in the season under review, Pico Central. After being sold and having an abortive run in the UAE Derby in spring 2003, Hard Buck was raced in the States and won four of his first five starts there, three in the autumn and the Gulfstream Park Breeders' Cup Handicap in February. Receiving 5 lb in that race he defeated Grade 1 winner Balto Star by a head, a performance which suggested Hard Buck was a little behind the best on turf in his new country. A second trip to Nad Al Sheba at the end of March proved much more fruitful than the first as Hard Buck led in the final furlong of the Dubai Sheema Classic before having no answer to Polish Summer's turn of foot, losing out by half a length. The next four home were Scott's View, Razkalla, Warrsan and Fair Mix, so this was a creditable run, but Hard Buck

Team Victory's "Hard Buck"

proceeded to lose his next two starts, including when only fifth, after not getting the run of the race in the United Nations Stakes, at Monmouth Park three weeks before Ascot. Unfortunately Hard Buck was not seen out again after the King George. Plans to run him in the Grosser Preis von Baden and the Prix de l'Arc de Triomphe came to nothing, reportedly because the trip to England and back had taken a lot out of him. In the run-up to the Canadian International the announcement came that he had been retired because of an unspecified injury.

Even with his impressive record, Hard Buck may find life difficult at stud. After reports that he would be standing in Ireland, Hard Buck will be based at Cloverleaf Farms II in Florida at 2,500 dollars, less than half the fee of ex-British Running Stag in the same state and five hundred dollars behind fellow Cloverleaf resident Impeachment, whose best efforts came when third in two North American classics. Hard Buck's fee is also lower than that of such new European sires as Masterful, Needwood Blade, Deportivo and Fair Mix, none of whom had form to match his. To some extent this is symptomatic of the way turf specialists are largely regarded as second-class citizens in the States, stud fees rarely bearing comparison with those of horses who excelled on dirt. At the highest level, fourteen dirt specialists stand at a fee of 60,000 dollars or higher in 2005, whereas only five turf horses fit this category. Four of them—in fee order Kingmambo, Giant's Causeway, El Prado and Rahy—made their name in Europe, though both Giant's Causeway and Rahy performed to some effect on dirt as well. Breeders' Cup Mile winner War Chant, a son of the fashionable Danzig, is the only home-grown turf horse in the list. He is at the bottom end of the scale on 60,000 dollars, but that is vastly better than another Breeders' Cup Mile winner, Silic, whose fee is a paltry 3,500 dollars. Two other Brazilian exports with similar profiles to Hard Buck have struggled, with Siphon available at 10,000 dollars and the now-deceased Sandpit standing at 7,500 dollars in his final season.

Hard Buck (BRZ) (b. or br.h. 1999)	Spend A Buck (USA) (b 1982)	Buckaroo (b 1975)	Buckpasser
			Stepping High
		Belle de Jour (b 1973)	Speak John
			Battle Dress
	Social Secret (b 1986)	Secreto (b 1981)	Northern Dancer
			Betty's Secret
		Expediency (b or br 1976)	Vaguely Noble
			Gazala

Hard Buck's pedigree should be familiar to breeders in the States, though it is insufficiently fashionable to guarantee him patronage. His sire Spend A Buck, winner of the Kentucky Derby, failed to live up to his reputation in Kentucky and was exiled to Brazil in 2001 after shuttling there for several years. He died in 2002. Spend A Buck is also sire of Pico Central, a very different kettle of fish whose principal asset is his speed, used to good effect to land three Grade 1 races at up to a mile. Social Secret, Hard Buck's dam, showed little ability in five starts in Britain, appearing not to stay a mile and a half, and was sold for 7,000 guineas at the end of her three-year-old season. Hard Buck's grandam Expediency produced the tough mile- to mile-and-a-quarter horse Bin Shaddad, successful in three pattern races in Germany, and the stayer Oh So Risky, who won the Prix Gladiateur and, over jumps, the Triumph Hurdle. Expediency, though only lightly raced, was well bred, a sister to Mississipian (Grand Criterium) and Gonzales (Irish St Leger) and half-sister to Eclipse Award winner Youth, whose outstanding classic campaign in 1976 included victories in the Prix Lupin, Prix du Jockey Club, Canadian International and Washington DC International. Hard Buck's great grandam Gazala was out of the top drawer, with a tally of five races highlighted by the Poule d'Essai des Pouliches and Prix de Diane. The lengthy Hard Buck, who stayed a mile and a half, acted on firm and good to soft going. *K. G. McPeek, USA*

HARD TO CATCH (IRE)   6 b.g. Namaqualand (USA) – Brook's Dilemma 80   **82** (Known Fact (USA) 135) [2004 80: p6g p6g p7g² p7g⁴ p6g* p6g p6g⁴ p7g⁵ 5.7g⁵ 6.1s   **a77** 5g 5.3f* 5m* 6.1f³ 5.3f³ 6d 6m⁶ 6m³ p7g 6m p7g Sep 7] close-coupled gelding: fairly useful handicapper on turf, fair on all-weather: won at Lingfield (apprentices) in February, Brighton in May and Folkestone in June: effective at 5f to 7f: acts on all-weather, firm and good to soft going: visored once, usually blinkered. *D. K. Ivory*

HARD TOP (IRE)   2 b.c. (Apr 17) Darshaan 133 – Well Head (IRE) (Sadler's Wells   **74 P**
(USA) 132) [2004 8d⁵ Oct 15] leggy, angular colt: brother to fairly useful 1½m winner
Spring Symphony and half-brother to 3 at least useful winners, including 9-y-o Ionian
Spring: dam unraced half-sister to Spectrum and to dam of Petrushka, an excellent fam-
ily: 20/1, fifth to Proclamation in maiden at Newmarket, held up running green and never
nearer: will be well suited by 1¼m/1½m: sure to do good deal better. *Sir Michael Stoute*

HARELDA   4 ch.f. Hector Protector (USA) 124 – Hen Harrier 94 (Polar Falcon (USA)   **71 +**
126) [2004 82: f12g* f12s⁶ 12g Apr 14] fair performer: won maiden at Southwell in February by 14 lengths: well beaten in handicaps after: should stay 1¾m: sold 5,000 gns in
July, resold 7,500 gns in December. *H. Morrison*

HARFORD BRIDGE   3 ch.g. Bandmaster (USA) 97 – Double Or Bust 42 (Presidium   **–**
124) [2004 f8.5s Mar 13] 66/1, well beaten in maiden at Wolverhampton, very slowly
away. *R. J. Baker*

HARIBINI   4 b. or br.f. Groom Dancer (USA) 128 – Mory Kante (USA) (Icecapade   **–**
(USA)) [2004 56: p10g 10g May 22] maiden: no form in 2004, starting slowly: tried
blinkered. *J. J. Bridger*

HARIK   10 ch.g. Persian Bold 123 – Yaqut (USA) 77 (Northern Dancer) [2004 47, a85:   **48**
p16g⁶ 17.2f² 16.4g p13g Dec 29] rather leggy gelding: just poor form in 2004: stays
17.2f: acts on all-weather and firm ground: sometimes visored/blinkered/tongue tied.
G. L. Moore

HARIPUR   5 b.h. Rainbow Quest (USA) 134 – Jamrat Jumairah (IRE) 91 (Polar Fal-   **–**
con (USA) 126) [2004 75+, a108: p10g Jan 31] lengthy, quite good-topped horse: useful
on all-weather, fairly useful on turf in 2003, winning 5 times at Lingfield: well held only
5-y-o outing: tried tongue tied: raced prominently: dead. *Andrew Reid*

HARLESTONE LINN   2 ch.g. (May 3) Erhaab 122 – Harlestone Lake 78   **– p**
(Riboboy (USA) 124) [2004 7g 8s Oct 19] compact gelding: half-brother to 3 winners,
including smart stayer Harlestone Grey (by Shaamit) and fairly useful 1½m to 2½m
winner Harlestone Brook (by Jalmood): dam out-and-out stayer: signs of ability in mid-
field in maidens at Newmarket and Bath: should do better at 1½m+. *J. L. Dunlop*

HARLOT   4 b.f. Bal Harbour 113 – Queen of The Quorn 53 (Governor General 116)   **–**
[2004 64: p10g p12g Feb 14] maiden: well held both starts in 2004: tried in cheekpieces.
John Berry

HAROLDINI (IRE)   2 b.g. (Mar 5) Orpen (USA) 116 – Ciubanga (IRE) (Arazi (USA)   **77 d**
135) [2004 5.1g 6g⁴ 5m² 6m⁶ f6d² 7m 6.1d p6g Oct 19] €8,500Y: lengthy gelding: first
foal: dam, Italian maiden, half-sister to useful Italian sprinter/miler Imprevedibile: fair
maiden: below form last 3 starts, leaving Mrs P. N. Dutfield after first of them: should stay
7f: acts on fibresand and good to firm going: wore cheekpieces final outing. *J. Balding*

HARRINGTON BATES   3 ch.g. Wolfhound (USA) 126 – Fiddling 82 (Music Boy   **65**
124) [2004 5m⁴ 6m⁶ 7d 5m⁵ Jul 14] 26,000Y, 25,000 2-y-o: strong, compact gelding:
half-brother to 2002 2-y-o 5f winner Good Health (by Magic Ring): dam, 5f winner, sister
to useful sprinter Clantime: fair maiden, lightly raced: likely to prove best at 5f: acts on
good to firm going. *R. M. Whitaker*

HARRISON POINT (USA)   4 b.c. Nureyev (USA) 131 – Maid's Broom (USA)   **94**
(Deputy Minister (CAN)) [2004 84: p7g* p8g* 8m² 7g² 8m p7d* 7m 7g⁶ Oct 9] rangy
colt: fairly useful handicapper: won at Lingfield in February, March and August (beat
Bob's Buzz by 1¼ lengths): raced at 7f/1m, should prove effective at 6f: acts on polytrack, raced only on good going or firmer on turf: tried visored at 3 yrs: consistent: sold
38,000 gns, sent to UAE. *P. W. Chapple-Hyam*

HARRISON'S FLYER (IRE)   3 b.g. Imperial Ballet (IRE) 110 – Smart Pet 77   **86**
(Petong 126) [2004 69?: 6m 5d² 7.5g 5f² 6m 6m² 5g 5m 5g 5.3s⁴ p5.1g* 5d* Nov 3]
good-topped gelding: fairly useful performer: improved in the autumn, winning handicaps at Brighton (hung left), Wolverhampton and Musselburgh (beat Fiddle Me Blue
1¼ lengths): effective at 5f/6f: acts on polytrack, firm and soft ground: tried blinkered/
visored: effective with or without cheekpieces: has shown temperament (reluctant and
unseated rider leaving stall seventh outing). *R. A. Fahey*

HARRY CAME HOME   3 b.g. Wizard King 122 – Kirby's Princess (Indian King   **–**
(USA) 128) [2004 p12g 11.1g 12s 8f 7m p12d 8d 8.1g 10m Sep 27] compact gelding: no
form: tried blinkered. *J. C. Fox*

HARRYCAT (IRE)   3 b.g. Bahhare (USA) 122 – Quiver Tree 68 (Lion Cavern (USA)   **75**
117) [2004 8g 8g⁵ 8g⁶ 12d² 10s³ Nov 1] leggy gelding: second foal: dam French 8.5f
winner: fair maiden: stays 1½m: acts on soft going. *V. Smith*

HARRY LAD 3 ch.g. Then Again 126 – Silly Sally (Music Boy 124) [2004 f9.4s⁵ –
f12s⁵ 12s⁶ Apr 16] close-coupled gelding: little form. *P. D. Evans*

HARRY POTTER (GER) 5 b.g. Platini (GER) 126 – Heavenly Storm (USA) (Storm **87**
Bird (CAN) 134) [2004 f9.4g p7g p8g³ 8v 8s* 7d 8.1d 9.1d³ 8g* 8.2g* 8m⁵ 8.3g
8.9m³ 8s 8.9g p8.6g* p8.6g⁵ Nov 20] ex-German gelding: fairly useful performer:
won handicaps at Thirsk in April and Ayr in July, and minor events at Nottingham later in July
and Wolverhampton in November: stays 9f: acts on polytrack, soft and good to firm
going: blinkered/visored nowadays: usually waited with: has hung left. *K. R. Burke*

HARRY'S GAME 7 gr.g. Emperor Jones (USA) 119 – Lady Shikari (Kala Shikari –
125) [2004 –: p10g Dec 20] fairly useful winner in Ireland at 2 yrs: lightly raced and no
form since 2002: tried blinkered/tongue tied. *A. P. Jones*

HARRYS HOUSE 2 gr.g. (Feb 25) Paris House 123 – Rum Lass 54 (Distant Relative **76**
128) [2004 5m⁴ 5d 7s⁴ 6.9m³ 5g* 6s Nov 2] close-coupled gelding: first foal: dam, sprint
maiden, half-sister to smart winner up to 1m Smart Predator and 5-y-o Smart Hostess:
fair performer: won maiden at Catterick in October, best effort: carried head awkwardly
final start: likely to prove best at 5f/6f: acts on soft and good to firm ground. *J. J. Quinn*

HARRY'S SIMMIE (IRE) 2 ch.f. (May 5) Spectrum (IRE) 126 – Minstrels Folly –
(USA) (The Minstrel (CAN) 135) [2004 7m 6g p8.6g Oct 7] €5,000F, €6,000Y:
half-sister to several winners in Ireland, including 1m/9f winner Marching Orders (by
Nashwan) and winner up to 2m Musical Mayhem (by Shernazar), both useful: dam Irish
1m winner: well beaten in maidens. *R. Hollinshead*

HARRY THE HOOVER (IRE) 4 b.g. Fayruz 116 – Mitsubishi Style (Try My Best **59 ?**
(USA) 130) [2004 –: p8g p8.6g p8.6g⁵ Dec 10] fairly useful winner at 2 yrs, probably just
modest in 2004: stays 8.6f: acts on polytrack. *M. J. Gingell*

HARRY TU 4 b.g. Millkom 124 – Risky Tu 62 (Risk Me (FR) 127) [2004 –: f8f p10g – §
f11g⁵ Dec 16] no form: left Gay Kelleway prior to final outing: tried in tongue tie:
ungenuine. *E. R. Oertel*

HARRY UP 3 ch.c. Piccolo 121 – Faraway Lass 94 (Distant Relative 128) [2004 96: **93**
6d² 5s³ 5.1d 6.1d³ 5f⁴ 6m 5m Jul 30] strong colt: fairly useful performer: ran poorly last 2
starts: best form at 5f: acts on firm and soft ground. *J. G. Given*

HARTSHEAD 5 b.g. Machiavellian (USA) 123 – Zalitzine (USA) 98 (Zilzal (USA) **89**
137) [2004 70?: 6d² 6m 5.9f⁶ 6g* 5.9g* 6g⁴ 6m* 7f* 7.1g² 7g³ Oct 9] leggy gelding:
unraced at 2/3 yrs: fairly useful performer: in good form in 2004, winning maiden at
Redcar, minor event at Carlisle and handicap at Thirsk in June/July and minor event at
Redcar in September: effective at 6f/7f: acts on firm and good to soft ground: usually
waited with: consistent. *G. A. Swinbank*

HARVEST WARRIOR 2 br.g. (Feb 28) Mujahid (USA) 125 – Lammastide 93 (Mar- **101**
tinmas 128) [2004 5v² 5.1g² 6g* 6d⁵ 6m 6s² Oct 23] 21,000F, 23,000Y: leggy, quite
good-topped gelding: half-brother to several winners, including ungenuine 2001 2-y-o
6f winner La Perla (by Royal Applause) and fairly useful 7f winner Amber Fort (by
Indian Ridge): dam 2-y-o 5f winner: useful performer: won maiden at Haydock in July
by 5 lengths: good efforts after only when second in nursery at Haydock and listed race
at Doncaster (beaten 2 lengths by Andronikos): should stay 7f: acts on soft ground.
T. D. Easterby

HASAIYDA (IRE) 3 b.f. Hector Protector (USA) 124 – Hasainiya (IRE) 109 (Top **84**
Ville 129) [2004 9m* 10g⁴ 10m* 12g 10g Sep 15] lengthy filly: fifth foal: half-sister to 3
winners, including useful 11f and 13f winner Hasanpour (by Dr Devious) and fairly useful 1m winner Hasik (by Ashkalani): dam Irish 1¼m winner: fairly useful performer: won
maiden at Lingfield in May and handicap at Sandown (beat Nordwind by a length) in
August: should stay 1½m: acts on good to firm going: reportedly struck into penultimate
start. *Sir Michael Stoute*

HASAYIS 3 b.f. Danehill (USA) 126 – Intizaa (USA) 77 (Mr Prospector (USA)) [2004 **71 +**
59: 8.1s⁷ 7g 7f⁴ 8m Aug 15] sturdy, angular filly: fair performer, lightly raced: won
maiden at Warwick in April: best effort in handicap penultimate start: effective at 7f/1m:
acts on firm and good to soft ground: sold 18,000 gns in December. *J. L. Dunlop*

HASHID (IRE) 4 b.g. Darshaan 133 – Alkaffeyeh (IRE) (Sadler's Wells (USA) 132) **68**
[2004 84: 11.8d⁶ 10.2g³ 14.8m 12d 12.1m⁶ 13.1d⁵ Aug 27] big gelding: fair maiden
handicapper: will stay 1¾m: acts on good to firm and good to soft going: tried blinkered/
visored: fair hurdler. *P. C. Ritchens*

HASHIMA (USA) 2 b.f. (May 12) Kingmambo (USA) 125 – Fairy Heights (IRE) 110 **70**
(Fairy King (USA)) [2004 7g³ p7g⁴ Oct 28] $90,000Y: sixth foal: closely related to
French 1m winner (including at 2 yrs) Fairy West (by Gone West): dam 2-y-o 7f/1m
(Fillies' Mile) winner: fair form in maidens at Folkestone and Lingfield: should stay 1m.
C. E. Brittain

HASHIMIYA (USA) 2 b.f. (Feb 24) Gone West (USA) – Touch of Greatness (USA) **64 p**
(Hero's Honor (USA)) [2004 7g⁶ Oct 11] $3,800,000Y: tall, rangy filly: sister to US
Grade 3 7f/1m winner Elusive Quality and useful 6f (including at 2 yrs) winner Ghazal,
and closely related to several winners, notably smart Irish 1999 2-y-o 5f/6f winner Rossini (by Miswaki): dam unraced half-sister to high-class middle-distance performer Gold
And Ivory: 15/8, 6 lengths sixth to Corcoran in maiden at Leicester, slowly away and one
paced late on: sure to improve. *Saeed bin Suroor*

HASTY PRINCE 6 ch.g. Halling (USA) 133 – Sister Sophie (USA) (Effervescing **?**
(USA)) [2004 90: 12g Sep 20] tall gelding: useful at best: slipped up only start on Flat in
2004: stays 1½m: acts on firm and soft going: smart hurdler. *Jonjo O'Neill*

HATCH 3 ch.c. Cadeaux Genereux 131 – Footlight Fantasy (USA) 68 (Nureyev (USA) **91**
131) [2004 86p: f7g² p7g² p7g* 6d³ 7.1g* 7.1g³ 9g 7.1m⁴ p8g 6g 8.5g⁴ Nov 26] big,
lengthy colt: fairly useful performer: left R. Charlton after reappearance: won maiden at
Lingfield in March and minor event at Musselburgh in April: left R. Cowell before final
outing: best around 7f: acts on polytrack and firm going: tongue tied penultimate start:
sometimes plays up in preliminaries/pulls hard/looks none too keen. *P. J. Oliver, USA*

HATCH A PLAN (IRE) 3 b.g. Vettori (IRE) 119 – Fast Chick 93 (Henbit (USA) **83**
130) [2004 69p: p6g 8d 10f 10m* 10.3g² 10g² 11.8m⁴ 12d 10g 11.6d⁵ Oct 4] leggy
gelding: fair performer: won minor event at Windsor in June: stays 1½m: best efforts on
good/good to firm ground: wore cheekpieces final outing: clipped heels and unseated
rider second start: sold 22,000 gns. *R. M. Beckett*

HATHLEN (IRE) 3 b.c. Singspiel (IRE) 133 – Kameez (IRE) 72 (Arazi (USA) 135) **79**
[2004 77: 12.4v 12.3g⁶ 12s⁶ 12m⁵ 14d⁶ 14g* 14m⁵ 16d⁶ 16g 16g⁶ Sep 26] leggy colt:
fairly useful handicapper: won at Goodwood in June: stays 2m: well held on soft/heavy
going, acts on any other turf: sold 17,000 gns. *M. R. Channon*

HATHRAH (IRE) 3 gr.f. Linamix (FR) 127 – Zivania (IRE) 101 (Shernazar 131) **113**
[2004 101p: 8d* 8m³ May 2] rangy filly: took the eye in appearance both starts in 2004:
smart performer: on toes, improved to win listed race at Kempton in April by 9 lengths
from Coqueteria: good length third to Attraction in 1000 Guineas at Newmarket final
start, always close up: sustained leg injury after: should stay 1¼m: acts on good to firm
and good to soft going: stays in training. *J. L. Dunlop*

HAT TRICK MAN 3 gr.c. Daylami (IRE) 138 – Silver Kristal 81 (Kris 135) [2004 **69**
61: 10f⁶ 10m 11.5d³ Nov 5] fair maiden, lightly raced: probably stays 11.5f: acts on firm
and good to soft ground. *J. Akehurst*

HAULAGE MAN 6 ch.g. Komaite (USA) – Texita 65 (Young Generation 129) [2004 **64**
73: 6m 6d² 8d 6f² 6g 6f 6d Oct 12] tall gelding: modest performer: effective at 6f to 1m:
acts on firm and good to soft going: sometimes wears cheekpieces, including last 4 starts:
often slowly away. *D. Eddy*

HAUNTING MEMORIES (IRE) 2 b.c. (Feb 1) Barathea (IRE) 127 – King of All **99**
(IRE) (King of Clubs 124) [2004 6m⁴ 6s* 7g² 8d³ Oct 18] 30,000Y: good-topped colt:
has a round action: first foal: dam, 6f/7f winner in Italy, out of sister to high-class miler
Noalcoholic: useful performer: won maiden at York in August by ½ length from Rajwa:
respectable efforts in minor event at Leicester (hung right) and listed contest at Pontefract
(7½ lengths third to Comic Strip) after: probably stays 1m: acts on soft going: races up
with pace. *M. A. Jarvis*

HAUNT THE ZOO 9 b.m. Komaite (USA) – Merryhill Maid (IRE) 71 (M Double M **–**
(USA)) [2004 –, a67: 8g⁵ f8d f8d³ f8g f8m f8g f8d⁵ Dec 21] tall mare: modest handi- **a61**
capper on all-weather: stays 9.4f: acts on fibresand, lightly raced and little recent form on
turf: reared leaving stalls on reappearance: usually held up. *John A. Harris*

HAVANA ROSE (IRE) 4 b.f. Goldmark (USA) 113 – Roses Red (IRE) 64 (Exhibi- **–**
tioner 111) [2004 26: f8g f5s Mar 1] IR 1,100Y: half-sister to 3 winners abroad: dam ran
twice in Ireland: bad maiden: tried in cheekpieces. *P. Morris, Ireland*

HAVANTADOUBT (IRE) 4 ch.f. Desert King (IRE) 129 – Batiba (USA) (Time For **44**
A Change (USA)) [2004 76: 9.7s 10g 9.7g 9.7f⁵ 10.9d 12m Sep 25] workmanlike filly:
only poor form in 2004: barely stays 1½m: acts on firm and good to soft ground: tried
visored/in cheekpieces/tongue tied. *M. R. Bosley*

HAVE FAITH (IRE) 3 b.f. Machiavellian (USA) 123 – Fatefully (USA) 110 (Private **87** Account (USA)) [2004 87: 8m³ 8m⁶ 8g⁶ 10v Oct 20] tall, leggy filly: fairly useful performer: good third to Distant Connection in handicap at Ripon on reappearance: well below form last 2 starts: stays 1m: acts on good to firm going. *B. W. Hills*

HAVE SOME FUN 4 ch.g. Bering 136 – Hilaris (Arazi (USA) 135) [2004 43: p8g³ **63 d** p10g² 8m 8g p7d p7d Aug 9] modest maiden: stays 1¼m: acts on polytrack: blinkered (slowly away, ran poorly) final start: sold £550. *P. R. Chamings*

HAVETOAVIT (USA) 3 b.g. Theatrical 128 – Summer Crush (USA) (Summer Squall **74** (USA)) [2004 64: 12d⁵ 12.3g³ 12.1m² 12.3m⁴ 11d 12m⁴ 10m* 10f² 10.3g 10.1m Oct 10] useful-looking gelding: fair handicapper: won maiden event at Redcar in August, dictating pace: stays 1½m: acts on fibresand, firm and good to soft going: tends to race freely up with pace: sold 15,000 gns. *J. D. Bethell*

HAVOC 5 b.g. Hurricane Sky (AUS) – Padelia (Thatching 131) [2004 –: f8s Mar 18] tall **–** gelding: maiden: no form since 2002: blinkered/tongue tied both 4-y-o starts. *Ronald Thompson*

HAWAAJES 3 b.g. Royal Applause 124 – Aegean Blue (Warning 136) [2004 8m 7.5g³ **79** 6g* 6m⁴ 6s Jul 17] 45,000F, 90,000Y: lengthy gelding: second foal: dam unraced: fair performer: won maiden at Haydock in June: stays 6f: acts on good to firm going, tailed off on soft: joined S. Seemar in UAE. *B. Hanbury*

HAWADETH 9 ch.g. Machiavellian (USA) 123 – Ghzaalh (USA) 87 (Northern Dan- **84** cer) [2004 16d⁵ 20f Oct 11] sturdy, angular gelding: fairly useful hurdler: of similar merit on Flat, first outing since 2001 when creditable fifth in handicap at Kempton, better effort in 2004: stays 2m: acts on soft to soft ground: tried blinkered, wore cheekpieces last 2 starts. *V. R. A. Dartnall*

HAWK 6 b.g. A P Jet (USA) – Miss Enjoleur (USA) (L'Enjoleur (CAN)) [2004 87d: **–** p6g p6g f6g f5s 5.7f p7.1g Dec 6] big, good-bodied gelding: fairly useful sprinter at best: well below form in 2004: visored (ran poorly) once: tried tongue tied/in cheekpieces. *A. G. Juckes*

HAWK ARROW (IRE) 2 ch.c. (Jan 13) In The Wings 128 – Barbizou (FR) (Selkirk **68 p** (USA) 129) [2004 8g Oct 12] 27,000Y: stocky colt: first foal: dam unraced half-sister to smart French 5f performer Run And Gun: 33/1 and better for race, seventh in maiden at Leicester, slowly away and not knocked about: should do better. *H. Morrison*

HAWKES BAY 2 b.c. (Apr 2) Vettori (IRE) 119 – Nordico Princess 71 (Nordico **74 p** (USA)) [2004 6m 8g³ Oct 12] 4,400F: big, close-coupled colt: fifth foal: half-brother to 3 winners, including ungenuine 1999 2-y-o 5f/6f winner City Princess (by Rock City): dam 5f/6f winner: better effort in maidens when strong-finishing third to River Alhaarth at Leicester: likely to stay 1¼m: should progress. *M. H. Tompkins*

HAWKIT (USA) 3 b.g. Silver Hawk (USA) 123 – Hey Ghaz (USA) (Ghazi (USA)) **82** [2004 72: f8.5s⁵ f8.5s² f8.5s* p8g 9.2g⁴ 10m² 8m 10g 7.6s⁵ p7.1g p9.5g Dec 4] rather **a74** leggy gelding: fairly useful performer on turf, fair on all-weather: won maiden at Wolverhampton in March and claimer at Hamilton (left J. Osborne) in May: left P. D. Evans prior to final outing: stays 1¼m: acts on all-weather and good to firm going: tongue tied last 3 starts. *J. Hetherton*

HAWKS TOR (IRE) 2 b.c. (Feb 26) Danehill (USA) 126 – Born Beautiful (USA) **–** (Silver Deputy (CAN)) [2004 7.2d⁶ Jun 19] 480,000Y: second foal: brother to 3-y-o Denver: dam unraced half-sister to dam of Cheveley Park winner Pas de Reponse and Poule d'Essai des Poulains winner Green Tune, an excellent family: favourite, sixth of 7 in maiden at Ayr (unsettled by rival at start): sent to UAE. *M. Johnston*

HAWRIDGE KING 2 b.g. (Feb 18) Erhaab (USA) 127 – Sadaka (USA) 77 (King- **63** mambo (USA) 125) [2004 6m³ 7.1m⁵ 8.3m⁶ p7g⁵ 8s⁵ Sep 14] 8,000Y: quite a good-topped gelding: first foal: dam, 1m winner, out of Cheveley Park Stakes third Basma: modest maiden: stays 1m: acts on polytrack, soft and good to firm ground: signs of temperament. *W. S. Kittow*

HAWRIDGE PRINCE 4 b.g. Polar Falcon (USA) 126 – Zahwa 72 (Cadeaux Gener- **105** eux 131) [2004 84p: 10g* 9.9g* 10g² 12g⁴ 11.6d² 10d Sep 18] big, lengthy gelding: smart performer: lightly raced: improved in 2004, winning handicaps at Newbury (by 1¾ lengths from Shredded) in May and Salisbury (by 6 lengths from Blue Marine) in June: good efforts next 3 starts, particularly when 1½ lengths second to Naheef in listed race at Windsor on penultimate: stays 1½m: acts on good to soft going. *L. G. Cottrell*

461

HAWRIDGE SENSATION 2 ch.g. (Apr 17) Polish Precedent (USA) 131 – Looks **– p**
Sensational (USA) (Majestic Light (USA)) [2004 8.3m Sep 27] 18,000F, 32,000Y:
half-brother to several winners, including fairly useful 1992 2-y-o 5f winner Yakin and
useful French 7f/1m performer Special Discount (both by Nureyev): dam twice-raced
half-sister to US Grade 1 1¼m winner Awe Inspiring: 33/1 and green, never dangerous in
maiden at Windsor: likely to do better as 3-y-o. *L. G. Cottrell*

HAWRIDGE STAR (IRE) 2 b.g. (Feb 22) Alzao (USA) 117 – Serenity 98 (Selkirk **75**
(USA) 129) [2004 7g⁶ 7s² 8g Oct 10] €16,000F, 46,000Y: close-coupled gelding: second
foal: half-brother to 4-y-o Camille Pissarro: dam 2-y-o 6f winner: best effort in maidens
when second at Salisbury: should stay at least 1m: gelded after final start. *W. S. Kittow*

HAYDN (USA) 3 b.g. Stravinsky (USA) 133 – Circular (USA) (What A Pleasure **78 d**
(USA)) [2004 96?: f6g⁵ f6d 6s 6g⁵ 6m 10g⁶ 10f 8d Aug 29] €200,000Y: lengthy gelding:
half-brother to several winners in USA, including Grade 2 7f winner Star of The Crop
(by Relaunch): dam, minor US stakes winner, out of US Grade 1 9f winner Convenience:
trained at 2 yrs by A. O'Brien in Ireland, winning minor event at Tipperary on debut:
below form in 2004 after reappearance, leaving P. Chapple-Hyam after fifth start and
C. Allen after sixth one: stays 6f: acts on fibresand and soft going. *G. A. Huffer*

HAYRAAN (IRE) 2 b.c. (Mar 25) Bluebird (USA) 125 – Alma Latina (IRE) 73 **59**
(Persian Bold 123) [2004 7m 7s Oct 27] €9,000F, 11,000 2-y-o: third foal: dam, Irish
maiden, half-sister to top-class middle-distance performer Celestial Storm and dam of
Sakhee: seventh in maidens, better effort behind Plea Bargain at Yarmouth on final start.
G. C. Bravery

HAYSTACKS (IRE) 8 b.g. Contract Law (USA) 108 – Florissa (FR) (Persepolis (FR) **41**
127) [2004 –: 13.1g³ 16m May 17] close-coupled gelding: poor performer: stays 2m: acts
on any turf going: usually visored/in cheekpieces: difficult ride. *James Moffatt*

HAZARISTA (IRE) 3 b.f. Barathea (IRE) 127 – Hazaradjat (IRE) 82 (Darshaan 133) **113**
[2004 66p: 7d⁴ 8m* 10.2m* 12f³ 11.9s³ 10g Sep 19] tall, leggy filly: half-sister to several
winners, including 1m winner Handaza (by Be My Guest) and 13f winner Hazarama
(by Kahyasi), both fairly useful in Ireland: dam Irish 7f (at 2 yrs) and 1¼m winner: smart
performer: won maiden at Gowran and Irish Stallion Farms EBF Blue Wind Stakes at
Cork (by 2 lengths from Cache Creek) in May: creditable third in Irish Oaks (beaten 1¾
lengths by Ouija Board) at the Curragh and Yorkshire Oaks (12½ lengths behind Quiff) at
York: reportedly struck into in Blandford Stakes at the Curragh final outing: stays 1½m:
unraced on heavy going, acts on any other. *J. Oxx, Ireland*

HAZE BABYBEAR 4 b.f. Mujadil (USA) 119 – River's Rising (FR) 88 (Mendez (FR) **–**
128) [2004 64: f6d f6g f5m⁶ Jul 12] leggy filly: well held in 2004: blinkered final start.
R. A. Fahey

HAZEWIND 3 gr.g. Daylami (IRE) 138 – Fragrant Oasis (USA) 113 (Rahy (USA) **78**
115) [2004 –: p6g p7g⁴ p7g² p7g* 9g 7.1s 7m 7m 9.9g² 10.2m⁵ 8.1g* 7g* 8g⁶ 7g⁴ 7m*
8s⁶ p8.6g⁴ p7.1g⁴ p9.5g³ p7.1d³ Nov 4] smallish, stocky gelding: fair performer: won
minor event at Lingfield in February and handicaps at Warwick and Newmarket in July
and York in September: effective at 7f to 1¼m: acts on polytrack, soft and good to firm
going: usually visored/tongue tied: tough and consistent. *P. D. Evans*

HAZYVIEW 3 b.c. Cape Cross (IRE) 129 – Euridice (IRE) 66 (Woodman (USA) 126) **112**
[2004 69p: 10d² 10g* 10d³ 10g* 11.5s² 10m* 12m 10d³ 10f⁶ Aug 14] strong, attractive
colt: smart performer: vastly improved in 2004, winning handicaps at Newmarket and
Sandown in April and 2 listed races at Newmarket in May, beating Duke of Venice 1¾
lengths for final success: creditable 3½ lengths third to Valixir in Prix Eugene Adam at
Maisons-Laffitte on penultimate outing: below form in Secretariat Stakes at Arlington
final appearance: may prove best at 1¼m (not discredited when eighth in Derby at Epsom
at 1½m): acts on good to firm and good to soft going, probably on soft: retained 350,000
gns in October. *N. A. Callaghan*

HEAD BOY 3 ch.g. Forzando 122 – Don't Jump (IRE) 71 (Entitled 126) [2004 58: p7g⁴ **62**
p8g p8g 6d⁵ 8d⁶ 7s⁵ 7g⁴ 7m² 7.6f 7s 8.1g 7.1d⁶ p7.1d³ p8.6g p7.1g p7g Dec 30] sturdy
gelding: modest performer: stays 7f: acts on polytrack, good to firm and good to soft
going: none too consistent. *S. Dow*

HEADLAND (USA) 6 b. or br.g. Distant View (USA) 126 – Fijar Echo (USA) (In **63**
Fijar (USA) 121) [2004 63§, a88d: f7g⁴ f8.5g² f6f f7g f7g³ f6s f7g³ f7d f7g⁶ 6.1s² f6m²
7m* 7s⁵ f6f⁵ f6s* 7g 6.1m⁵ 7.2s f6g f7g Dec 11] well-made gelding: modest handicapper:
won at Thirsk in July and Southwell in August: effective at 6f to easy 1m: acts on all-
weather, soft and good to firm going: tried visored, blinkered nowadays: tried tongue

tied: sometimes very slowly away: refused to race once at 5 yrs: none too consistent. *D. W. Chapman*

HEAD OF STATE 3 b.g. Primo Dominie 121 – Lets Be Fair 94 (Efisio 120) [2004 53: p5g f5g f6s* p6g f6s³ 6d f5g 6g⁵ Jun 18] strong gelding: modest performer: won handicap at Southwell in February: stays 6f: acts on fibresand, no form on turf: visored last 6 outings: sold 4,000 gns. *R. M. Beckett* — **a64**

HEAD TO KERRY (IRE) 4 b.g. Eagle Eyed (USA) 111 – The Poachers Lady (IRE) (Salmon Leap (USA) 131) [2004 77: 14.1d 16m 14m 13.3g³ 15m⁵ 12m³ 12.1m⁴ 12m² 14.4m⁴ 12s⁵ 9.9s⁴ 10.3g p12.2g⁶ Oct 19] lengthy gelding: modest handicapper: effective at 1¼m (granted bit of a test) and stays 2m: acts on fibresand, firm and soft going: tried tongue tied/in cheekpieces: sometimes races freely. *D. J. S. ffrench Davis* — **64**

HEALEY (IRE) 6 ch.g. Dr Devious (IRE) 127 – Bean Siamsa (Solinus 130) [2004 49: 10m 8g 10s Aug 24] lengthy, quite good-topped gelding: poor performer: left P. Wood prior to final start: stays 1½m: acts on any going: tried blinkered/tongue tied/in cheekpieces: none too consistent. *I. W. McInnes* — **–**

HEARTBEAT 3 b.f. Pursuit of Love 124 – Lyrical Bid (USA) 77 (Lyphard (USA) 132) [2004 –: p6g⁴ p7g f8.5s 10d⁴ 8.5d⁴ 10m⁵ 11.8g 11.5f 8f³ Jun 23] good-bodied filly: modest maiden: stays 1¼m: acts on all-weather, good to firm and good to soft ground: visored (temperamental display) third start, blinkered last 2 (found little first occasion), also tongue tied final one (slowly away). *P. J. McBride* — **51**

HEARTBREAKER (IRE) 4 b.g. In Command (IRE) 114 – No Hard Feelings (IRE) 86 (Alzao (USA) 117) [2004 –: f14g Jul 9] strong gelding: no form. *M. W. Easterby* — **–**

HEARTHSTEAD DREAM 3 ch.g. Dr Fong (USA) 128 – Robin Lane 98 (Tenby 125) [2004 72: 8m 11.9f³ 8g² 11.1m* 8.3m⁵ 12.4v* 11.1g² 12.3g* 12.3s³ 16g³ 12.1m⁴ 13.9g³ 14.1d Oct 15] long-backed gelding: fair performer: left M. Johnston after second start: won claimers at Hamilton and Newcastle (claimed from J. O'Shea) in June and handicap at Ripon in August: creditable efforts in frame after: barely stays 2m: acts on any going: effective blinkered or not: quirky (carries head high), but is consistent: sold 18,000 gns. *J. D. Bethell* — **77**

HEARTHSTEAD WINGS 2 b.c. (Mar 15) In The Wings 128 – Inishdalla (IRE) 103 (Green Desert (USA) 127) [2004 6g* 7f⁴ 7g⁶ 8m* 8d³ Oct 17] rangy colt: half-brother to winners in USA by Irish River and St Jovite: dam, Irish 6f (at 2 yrs)/7f winner, later successful in USA: useful performer: won maiden at Ripon in May and listed event at Goodwood (made most, beat Destinate by 1¼ lengths) in September: good third to Konigstiger in Gran Criterium at Milan: will probably stay 1¼m: acts on firm and good to soft ground: edgy sort, tends to sweat. *M. Johnston* — **104**

HEART OF ETERNITY (IRE) 2 b.f. (Apr 13) Namid 128 – Kurfuffle (Bluebird (USA) 125) [2004 5g 5s⁴ 6m Aug 16] €31,000Y: second foal: half-sister to fairly useful Irish 2003 2-y-o 5f winner Kurlicue (by Imperial Ballet): dam unraced half-sister to useful performer up to 1¼m Shemozzle: poor form in maidens. *J. R. Boyle* — **44**

HEART'S DESIRE (IRE) 3 b.f. Royal Applause 124 – Touch And Love (IRE) (Green Desert (USA) 127) [2004 79p: 8g⁶ 7.6g² 9f⁵ 8m Oct 2] fair maiden: best effort at 7f on soft ground (at 2 yrs): sold 10,000 gns. *B. W. Hills* — **66**

HEARTSONFIRE 2 bl.f. (Mar 24) Bold Fact (USA) 116 – Jazirah (Main Reef 126) [2004 5d³ 5d³ 6g 6m⁴ 5.1g 7m 6.1g⁴ p6g* p7g p6g* p6g Dec 3] €4,600F, €7,000Y: good-topped filly: half-sister to 3 winners, including Irish 1¼m to 13f winner Biddy Blackhurst (by Imp Society) and 7f/1m winner Finsbury Flyer (by Al Hareb): dam unraced: fair performer: left D. Gillespie in Ireland after third start: won maiden in October and nursery in November, both at Wolverhampton: best form at 6f: acts on polytrack, good to firm and good to soft going: sometimes wanders. *P. W. D'Arcy* — **68**

HEART SPRINGS 4 b.f. Parthian Springs 114 – Metannee 63 (The Brianstan 128) [2004 –: 11.9m 10m 15m p16g⁴ p16d⁵ 18d² 16.2m 16d Oct 10] leggy filly: modest maiden: stays 2¼m: acts on polytrack and good to soft going: sometimes slowly away. *Dr J. R. J. Naylor* — **50**

HEART STOPPING (USA) 2 b.f. (Jan 20) Chester House (USA) 123 – Clog Dance 103 (Pursuit of Love 124) [2004 7d Oct 30] tall, lengthy filly: has scope: first foal: dam, maiden who stayed 1¼m, half-sister to smart Ebor winner Tuning: 16/1, seventh to Read Federica in maiden at Newmarket, tiring late on: sure to improve. *B. W. Hills* — **69 p**

HEAT ALERT (USA) 2 b. or br.f. (Feb 12) Valid Expectations (USA) – Melt My Heart (USA) (Peterhof (USA) 116) [2004 p7g p7m⁶ Dec 22] half-sister to 3 winners in — **54**

USA: dam, minor winner in USA, half-sister to 1979 Queen Mary winner Abeer: better effort in maidens at Lingfield when sixth (tongue tied, slowly away). *A. M. Balding*

HEATHERS FURIO (IRE) 2 b.f. (May 9) Spectrum (IRE) 126 – Almi Ad (USA) 78 (Silver Hawk (USA) 123) [2004 p7.1g Dec 31] second foal: dam, ran twice at 2 yrs, second at 1m: 100/1, last of 12 in maiden at Wolverhampton. *R. P. Elliott* — **–**

HEATHERS GIRL 5 ch.m. Superlative 118 – Kristis Girl 76 (Ballacashtal (CAN)) [2004 f7g f9.4s* f8.5s⁶ f9.4g² 10.9g⁴ f11g² f12d² f12g⁴ p12.2g p12.2g⁴ f16s⁵ p13.9g Nov 27] modest performer: won seller at Wolverhampton in February: stays 1½m: acts on all-weather, very lightly raced on turf: tried blinkered. *D. Haydn Jones* **45 a56**

HEATHWOOD (IRE) 2 b.c. (Feb 9) Green Desert (USA) 127 – Woodsia 97 (Woodman (USA) 126) [2004 p7m Oct 6] third foal: brother to 4-y-o Wood Fern and half-brother to fairly useful 2001 2-y-o 1m winner Lahooq (by Indian Ridge), later successful in USA: dam, Irish 1¼m winner, half-sister to useful 5f performer Millstream: 25/1, ninth in maiden at Lingfield, slowly away and not knocked away: should do better. *J. H. M. Gosden* **– p**

HEATHYARDSBLESSING (IRE) 7 b.g. Unblest 117 – Noble Nadia (Thatching 131) [2004 53: p6g f6g⁶ f6s⁵ f6s f5s³ f6g⁵ f5g⁵ f6g p5m⁶ Dec 15] quite good-topped gelding: just poor nowadays: stays 6f: acts on fibresand, firm and good to soft ground: tried in cheekpieces: has carried head awkwardly/looked none too keen. *R. Hollinshead* **47**

HEATHYARDS JOY 3 ch.f. Komaite (USA) – Heathyards Lady (USA) 76 (Mining (USA)) [2004 –: f7f f7g f7s⁴ f8s⁴ 7.1g² 7g⁵ 6v⁵ f6m⁶ 7.5m 7.5g³ 8m² p7m³ p8m² Dec 15] poor maiden: stays 1m: acts on all-weather and good to firm going. *R. Hollinshead* **47**

HEATHYARDS PRIDE 4 b.g. Polar Prince (IRE) 117 – Heathyards Lady (USA) 76 (Mining (USA)) [2004 43p: f9.4g* 10.9s 7.9f⁴ 11.7g⁵ 10.9m* 12g* p12.2g* p12.2g* Nov 11] fair performer: won maiden at Wolverhampton in January, claiming handicap at Warwick in September, handicaps at Pontefract and Wolverhampton in October, and minor event at Wolverhampton in November: should stay 1¾m: acts on all-weather and firm ground: tends to idle. *R. Hollinshead* **73 +**

HEAT OF THE NIGHT 2 b.f. (May 12) Lear Fan (USA) 130 – Hot Thong (BRZ) (Jarraar (USA) 78) [2004 7g⁴ 7m 7.1m² 7m⁵ p8.6g² Nov 26] quite attractive filly: fourth foal: dam, Brazilian Grade 3 7f winner and third in 1000 Guineas, out of close relative to smart 1½m winner Ninotchka: fair maiden: second at Warwick and Wolverhampton: stays 8.6f: acts on polytrack and good to firm going. *P. W. Chapple-Hyam* **79**

HEAVENS WALK 3 ch.c. Compton Place 125 – Ghost Dancing (Lion Cavern (USA) 117) [2004 5m⁵ 6s 6s⁴ p6g³ f5g⁶ p5.1g Nov 29] strong colt: first foal: dam, ran once, half-sister to useful sprinter Royal Beacon: modest maiden: stays 6f: acts on polytrack: tongue tied final start. *P. J. Makin* **61**

HEBENUS 5 b.g. Hamas (IRE) 125§ – Stinging Nettle 90 (Sharpen Up 127) [2004 50: 7.2g² 6m 7.9m 6s⁴ Oct 30] lengthy gelding: poor performer: stays 1m: acts on firm and good to soft going: tried blinkered. *T. A. K. Cuthbert* **47**

HEDINGHAM KNIGHT (IRE) 2 b.g. (Mar 13) Fasliyev (USA) 120 – Exclusive Davis (USA) (Our Native (USA)) [2004 5f⁶ 6m Jun 18] strong gelding: modest form in maidens: gelded after final start. *N. A. Callaghan* **52**

HEFIN 7 ch.g. Red Rainbow 105 – Summer Impressions (USA) 70 (Lyphard (USA) 132) [2004 74: p13.9g p13.9g⁵ p13.9g Dec 31] rather sparely-made gelding: has reportedly had leg trouble: fair handicapper: left B. Powell prior to final start: stays 2m: acts on polytrack, firm and good to soft going: usually waited with. *Mrs Stef Liddiard* **69**

HEIDENHEIM (IRE) 2 b.f. (May 17) Cape Cross (IRE) 129 – Solar Attraction (IRE) 60 (Salt Dome (USA)) [2004 p6g p7.1g⁶ Nov 27] €37,000Y: half-sister to several winners, including 5-y-o Neckar Valley and 3-y-o Zweibrucken: dam third at 5f in Ireland at 2 yrs: better effort in maidens when sixth at Triple Two at Wolverhampton. *S. Kirk* **56**

HEIDI'S DASH (IRE) 2 b.f. (Mar 16) Green Desert (USA) 127 – Child Prodigy (IRE) 87 (Ballad Rock 122) [2004 5g 5f⁴ p5g⁴ Nov 20] 140,000Y: sturdy filly: good walker: third foal: half-sister to fairly useful 2002 2-y-o 8.5f winner Menuhin (by Royal Academy) and 3-y-o Du Pre: dam, 6f (at 2 yrs) and 1m (in USA) winner, half-sister to very smart 1¼m/1½m performer Kutub: modest form in maidens: will stay at least 6f. *R. Charlton* **62**

HEIGHT OF SPIRITS 2 b.c. (Apr 28) Unfuwain (USA) 131 – Kimono (IRE) (Machiavellian (USA) 123) [2004 p8m Dec 21] 3,000Y: third foal: half-brother to useful French 11f/1½m winner Briviesca (by Peintre Celebre): dam, ran twice, out of smart 1½m **64 p**

winner Kilinski: 25/1, seventh to Alessano in maiden at Lingfield, slowly away and not knocked about: will be suited by 1¼m/1½m: should improve. *T. D. McCarthy*

HEIR TO BE 5 b.g. Elmaamul (USA) 125 – Princess Genista 108 (Ile de Bourbon (USA) 133) [2004 84: 15s⁵ 16g 16d⁶ Apr 24] angular gelding: fair handicapper nowadays: stays 2m: best on good going or softer: found less than seemed likely final start. *J. L. Dunlop* **72**

HEISSE 4 b.c. Darshaan 133 – Hedera (USA) 90 (Woodman (USA) 126) [2004 101: 12g⁵ 16d 12s 14.6f 12g Oct 1] sturdy colt: fairly useful performer, lightly raced: good fifth in minor event at Doncaster on reappearance: well below form after: stays 12.4f: acts on good to firm going: visored third start: sold 10,000 gns. *D. R. Loder* **94**

HE JAA (IRE) 3 gr.f. Daylami (IRE) 138 – Calpella 81 (Ajdal (USA) 130) [2004 8g 10m May 2] 32,000Y: tall, quite good-topped filly: half-sister to useful 1m (at 2 yrs) and 1¼m winner Naskhi (by Nashwan) and a winner abroad by Darshaan: dam 1m winner: 7 lengths seventh to Mudawin in maiden at Newbury on debut: suffered serious injury in listed event at Newmarket next time: dead. *C. E. Brittain* **68**

HEKTIKOS 4 ch.g. Hector Protector (USA) 124 – Green Danube (USA) 92 (Irish River (FR) 131) [2004 –: p12g p8g p8g⁵ Apr 19] sturdy, quite attractive gelding: no form since 2 yrs. *S. Dow* **–**

HELDERBERG (USA) 4 b.f. Diesis 133 – Banissa (USA) (Lear Fan (USA) 130) [2004 79: 8m 9f⁵ 8.5g⁶ Jun 17] lengthy, good-topped filly: fair handicapper: stays 11f: acts on firm ground, probably on heavy: none too reliable: sold 10,000 gns in December. *B. S. Rothwell* **69**

HELEN HOUSE 2 b.f. (May 5) Tipsy Creek (USA) 115 – Tiempo 50 (King of Spain 121) [2004 6s 6d³ p6g Nov 16] big, strong filly: half-sister to fairly useful 1997 2-y-o 1m winner Ten Bob (by Bob Back) and winner in Denmark by Idris: dam, sprint maiden, half-sister to smart sprinter Grey Desire: best effort in maiden third to Westland at Yarmouth, racing prominently: not sure to stay much beyond 6f. *M. H. Tompkins* **64**

HELEN SHARP 2 ch.f. (Apr 10) Pivotal 124 – Sunny Davis (USA) 71 (Alydar (USA)) [2004 7d Oct 30] 115,000Y: well-made filly: half-sister to several winners, including useful 6f (at 2 yrs) to 1m (in Sweden) winner Warming Trends (by Warning) and 4-y-o Dance In The Sun: dam 2-y-o 7f winner: 7/1, ran as if in need of race when behind in maiden at Newmarket (reluctant stall): should do better. *M. A. Jarvis* **– p**

HELIOS QUERCUS (FR) 2 b.c. (May 12) Diableneyev (USA) 112 – Criss Cross (FR) (Crystal Palace (FR) 132) [2004 4.5s* 5s* 5g⁴ 6s* 5s⁴ 7s* 8d* 8s* Oct 31] **118**
The story of Helios Quercus is the sort which inspires the dreams of small owners in their unequal struggle with the big battalions. Unfashionably bred and from a stable in the French Provinces better known for its jumpers, Helios Quercus started out in March, winning the first two-year-old race of the season at Maisons-Laffitte, and seven outings and seven months later he took the Group 1 Criterium International at Saint-Cloud, an event won in its first three years by Act One, Dalakhani and Bago. Neither Helios Quercus' owner nor his trainer had ever had a runner in a Group 1 event on the Flat and his jockey Alexandre Roussel had never ridden in one.
Dalakhani and Bago, who both went on to win the following year's Arc for the Aga Khan and the Niarchos Family respectively, won the Prix des Chenes over a mile at Longchamp on their way to the Criterium International. The Prix des Chenes was the race which first brought Helios Quercus and his connections to the attention of a wider French racing public. He lined up at Longchamp as the winner of four of his six starts, having followed up his victory at Maisons-Laffitte—over four and a half furlongs—with others in minor events at Fontainebleau in April and Maisons-Laffitte in June, before landing a valuable contest at Deauville in August from the subsequent Prestige Stakes runner-up Nanabanana. Starting at 98/10 in a field of seven for the Prix des Chenes, Helios Quercus held off Musketier by a short neck after getting first run when sent ahead over a furlong out. Both Musketier and the Prix des Chenes third Vatori won pattern races before Helios Quercus lined up at Saint-Cloud where, in a field of eight, he started fifth in the betting behind hot favourite Early March, runner-up in the Prix Jean-Luc Lagardere on Arc day. The Prestige Stakes winner Dubai Surprise was also in the International—she started at 26/1—and she chased home Helios Quercus who made his run up the rail as the

Criterium International, Saint-Cloud—Helios Quercus gains his sixth and most important success of the year; British challenger Dubai Surprise (centre) is second and Walk In The Park (No.6) third; Cupid's Glory (rail), another trained in Britain, weakens to finish fourth ahead of Stop Making Sense and Early March (left)

leader Early March edged out over a furlong out. Helios Quercus beat Dubai Surprise by a length and a half with Walk In The Park a close third, Cupid's Glory fourth and a below-form Early March fading back into sixth. The form of the latest Criterium International cannot be rated so highly as that of its immediate predecessor and Helios Quercus doesn't look anything like so exciting a prospect as Act One, Dalakhani and Bago, all of whom ended their first season unbeaten. However he fares from now on, though, Helios Quercus has proved himself a smart and genuine colt. Were he to go on and win the Prix du Jockey Club, his main target in the next season, Helios Quercus would be imprinted indelibly on the list of big-race winners who have provided food for the optimists down the years.

Helios Quercus (FR) (b.c. May 12, 2002)	Diableneyev (USA) (b or br 1995)	Nureyev (b 1977)	Northern Dancer
			Special
		La Pitie (b or br 1989)	Devil's Bag
			Empiracle
	Criss Cross (FR) (gr 1982)	Crystal Palace (gr 1974)	Caro
			Hermieres
		Zelide (b 1976)	Lyphard
			Zelinda

Helios Quercus was bred by the Haras du Bois aux Proux, which also bred the highest-rated four-year-old hurdler of 2003/4 in Europe, the filly Maia Eria. Many of the stud's colts include Quercus (a generic name for oak) in their name, while many of the stud's fillies have Eria (a genus of orchid) in theirs. Helios Quercus is a half-brother to several winners in France, including the useful mile-and-a-half and thirteen-furlong winner Ares Quercus (by Hero's Honor). The dam Criss Cross won at eleven furlongs in France and the grandam Zelide, who contested the Poule d'Essai des Pouliches, was placed in listed company over a mile and a quarter. The great grandam of Helios Quercus, Zelinda, won the Prix d'Astarte over a mile. Helios Quercus is by the smart sprinter Diableneyev, who spent most of his racing career in listed and minor pattern company. He probably owed his chance at stud—he stood his first season at only €915 and reportedly had a first crop of fourteen—just as much to the fact that he was by Nureyev out of a good family, the dam being a granddaughter of Queen Empress (champion two-year-old filly in America in 1964) out of a half-sister to the excellent broodmare Royal Dilemma (dam of Prix de l'Abbaye winner Silver Fling among others). The fact that the Prix du Jockey Club will be run over an extended mile and a quarter in 2005, instead of the traditional mile and a half, is probably in Helios Quercus' favour. Judged on pedigree, he is likely to stay a mile and a quarter but isn't certain to be so effective at a mile and a half. He acts on soft going and wears ear plugs. *C. Diard, France*

HELIXALOT (IRE)   3 ch.g. College Chapel 122 – Last Ambition (IRE) 29 (Cadeaux Genereux 131) [2004 p13g Oct 1] 66/1, tailed off in maiden at Lingfield. *G. P. Enright*   –

HELLBENT   5 b.g. Selkirk (USA) 129 – Loure (USA) 66 (Lyphard (USA) 132) [2004 –: f7g f6g p7g p6g p8g⁵ p10g⁶ p12g³ 10.2d⁴ f9.4g⁶ p12g⁵ p8.6g f6g⁶ Dec 28] poor maiden: left J. Osborne after eleventh start: effective at 6f and probably stays easy 1½m: **44**

466

acts on all-weather and good to firm ground: tried blinkered: sometimes slowly away. *A. W. Carroll*

HELLO IT'S ME 3 ch.g. Deploy 131 – Evening Charm (IRE) (Bering 136) [2004 **97**
78p: 10g² 10.4s 8.1g² 8.2g⁵ 10f⁴ 9.9d³ 12f⁵ 10g p12g* p12.2g* Dec 17] good-bodied
gelding: useful handicapper: in cheekpieces, won at Lingfield in November and Wolverhampton (beat Gig Harbor by head) in December: stays 1½m: acts on polytrack, firm and
good to soft going (well below form on soft). *H. J. Collingridge*

HELLO ROBERTO 3 b.f. Up And At 'em 109 – Hello Hobson's (IRE) 67 (Fayruz **77 d**
116) [2004 66, a80: p7g p6g² f6g p6g² p5g⁵ 5d³ 5d 5.1g* 5f 5m p6g f5f⁴ 5.1g 5g 5s Nov
1] quite good-topped filly: fair performer: won handicap at Chester in July: below form
last 2 starts, leaving M. Polglase prior to final one: effective at 5f/6f: acts on all-weather,
good to firm and good to soft ground: sometimes slowly away. *N. Tinkler*

HELLO SID 3 ch.g. Hello Mister 106 – Moving Up (IRE) 61 (Don't Forget Me 127) **–**
[2004 p5g Feb 14] 50/1 and blinkered, slowly away and tailed off throughout in maiden
at Lingfield. *T. E. Powell*

HELLO TIGER 3 b.g. Terimon 124 – Blue Peru (IRE) 48 (Perugino (USA) 84) [2004 **–**
f8s 8m f8m 7m⁵ Jul 22] no sign of ability: tried in cheekpieces. *J. A. Supple*

HELM (IRE) 3 b.g. Alhaarth (IRE) 126 – Pipers Pool (IRE) 94 (Mtoto 134) [2004 10d **68**
p13g⁴ 14d⁶ p13g⁶ p16g Nov 30] IR 66,000€, €260,000Y: good-bodied gelding: fifth foal:
half-brother to 3 winners, including fairly useful Irish 6f winner Pipewell (by Lake Coniston) and useful French 1m winner Miss Chryss (by Indian Ridge), later successful in
USA: dam, maiden who stayed 1¼m, closely related to smart middle-distance stayer
Pipsted: fair maiden: left L. Cumani after debut: should stay 2m: acts on polytrack.
R. Rowe

HENESEYS LEG 4 b.f. Sure Blade (USA) 130 – Away's Halo (USA) (Sunny's Halo **85**
(CAN)) [2004 70: 8.1s* 10m* 9.3g* p10g⁵ 10s³ 12m Sep 4] quite good-topped filly:
fairly useful handicapper: won at Warwick and Lingfield in May and Carlisle (beat Route
Sixty Six by 4 lengths) in June: best up to 1¼m: acts on polytrack, firm and soft ground:
consistent. *John Berry*

HENNDEY (IRE) 3 b.g. Indian Ridge 123 – Del Deya (IRE) 117 (Caerleon (USA) **83**
132) [2004 –: 7s² 7s² a5.5f a8f Dec 18] good-bodied gelding: fairly useful maiden at best: **a–**
left M. Jarvis and off 7½ months after second outing: stays 7f: acts on soft going, tailed
off both times on dirt: carried head awkwardly only 2-y-o appearance. *D. J. Selvaratnam,
UAE*

HENRIK 2 b.c. (Mar 21) Primo Dominie 121 – Clincher Club 77 (Polish Patriot **114 p**
(USA) 128) [2004 6g* 7g² 8s³ Oct 23]
    Both Henrik and the footballer after whom he is named, Henrik Larsson,
were the subject of transfers in 2004, with the progressive two-year-old colt moving
from Mick Channon to Saeed bin Suroor and the prolific goalscorer from Celtic to
Barcelona. Whereas Larsson is coming towards the end of what has been an
illustrious career, Henrik is just starting out, and, from the little we have seen of him
so far, he looks to have a bright future. Henrik made his debut in May in a six-
furlong maiden at Goodwood, for which another newcomer, Qadar, started a hot
favourite. The pair fought out the finish and Henrik came out on top, though there
was only a short head in it and the outcome would have been different had Qadar
not met trouble. Henrik, on the other hand, enjoyed a clear run, showing good speed
to dispute the lead until edging ahead over a furlong out and responding well to
pressure.
    Stepped up in both distance and class on his next start, in the seven-furlong
Superlative Stakes at Newmarket in July, Henrik left his Goodwood form well
behind in finishing second, splitting Dubawi and Wilko in a very close finish to this
Group 3 event. After making up his ground smoothly, Henrik looked to be going
better than Dubawi when taking the lead approaching the final furlong but was
outstayed up the hill and beaten half a length. Although he changed hands privately
after this race, Henrik was still with Channon when he made his final appearance of
the season, in the Racing Post Trophy over a mile at Doncaster in October. He had
been due to contest the Dewhurst Stakes the previous week, but was a late withdrawal because the ground at Newmarket was considered too soft for him. As it
turned out, Henrik encountered a similar surface at Doncaster, where he acquitted
himself very well in finishing third behind Motivator and Albert Hall, eight lengths

and more clear of the five other runners. Henrik would have done even better under less testing conditions—his stamina gave out after he had briefly looked a serious threat to the winner at the two-furlong marker—and he has been rated accordingly. Motivator beat him by three and a half lengths, Albert Hall by a length. With the emphasis on speed at the trip, Henrik could well win a good race over a mile, but a return to shorter may provide him with a better opportunity to do so. The Greenham Stakes run over seven furlongs at Newbury would have been a highly suitable race for him in the early part of the next season, but the Godolphin team will not be back from winter in Dubai in time.

Henrik (b.c. Mar 21, 2002)	Primo Dominie (b 1982)	Dominion (b 1972)	Derring-Do Picture Palace
		Swan Ann (ch 1971)	My Swanee Anna Barry
	Clincher Club (b 1993)	Polish Patriot (b 1988)	Danzig Maria Waleska
		Merry Rous (br 1988)	Rousillon Merry Weather

Henrik, a 100,000-guinea yearling, is the fourth foal of Clincher Club, a fair performer as a two-year-old when successful in a five-furlong maiden, but only modest at three when she won a claimer over seven and a half furlongs. Two of Clincher Club's earlier foals are fairly useful winners. Spritzeria (by Bigstone) was successful over six furlongs at two and a mile at three, while Bishop's Lake (by Lake Coniston) won twice over six furlongs as a two-year-old but didn't train on. Henrik's grandam Merry Rous, also a two-year-old six-furlong winner, is a half-sister to the smart sprinter Tina's Pet. Henrik, a leggy sort, is nothing special on looks and didn't particularly take the eye in the paddock at Doncaster, where he sweated. He acts on soft going and has yet to race on ground firmer than good. *M. R. Channon*

HENRY AFRIKA (IRE)   6 b.g. Mujadil (USA) 119 – Floralia 81 (Auction Ring (USA) 123) [2004 80: f8.5g f7s 9.5g* 8m 9.5m⁶ Jun 6] fairly useful handicapper nowadays: ran at Wolverhampton first 2 starts in 2004 (as if amiss second occasion): best effort for some time when winning ladies race at Gowran in May: stays 9.5f: acts on fibresand and good to firm ground: tried blinkered/in cheekpieces: none too consistent. *G. M. Lyons, Ireland*   **88**

HENRY HALL (IRE)   8 b.h. Common Grounds 118 – Sovereign Grace (IRE) 101 (Standaan (FR) 118) [2004 103: 5.1g³ 5d 5s³ 5m 5m³ 5d 5g 5g 5g 5s 5m 5d Oct 17] leggy horse: has a round action: useful handicapper: several creditable efforts in 2004, particularly when placed at York third and fifth starts: well below form last 3 outings: best at 5f: acts on firm and soft going: visored (well beaten) once: usually waited with. *N. Tinkler*   **99**

HENRY ISLAND (IRE)   11 ch.g. Sharp Victor (USA) 114 – Monterana 99 (Sallust 134) [2004 77: 15.4s⁵ 17.2f 16.2g⁴ 14m 16.4m 16.2g² 15.9g 17.2g⁴ 16d f16s Nov 17] workmanlike gelding: good mover: just modest handicapper in 2004: stays 19f: acts on fibresand, soft and good to firm going: tends to sweat: waited with: sometimes finds little. *Mrs A. J. Bowlby*   **62**

HENRY TUN   6 b.g. Chaddleworth (IRE) 103 – B Grade 59 (Lucky Wednesday 124) [2004 44§, a68§: f5g³ p5g⁵ f5g f5g² f5s* f5g³ f5g f5g² 5.1d 5g 5m⁶ 5.7f f5g f5m³ p5.1g f5g⁴ Dec 21] tall gelding: modest on all-weather, poor on turf: won seller at Southwell in February: left J. Balding after sixth start and rejoined him from N. Berry prior to fourteenth: effective at 5f/easy 6f: acts on fibresand and firm going: usually wears headgear: tried tongue tied earlier in career: usually races prominently: sometimes looks none too keen: unreliable. *J. Balding*   **43 §**   **a59 §**

HERENCIA (IRE)   2 b.c. (Apr 10) Victory Note (USA) 120 – Originality (Godswalk (USA) 130) [2004 6g 6m 5d 7d⁴ 7m² 8s⁶ f8g Nov 9] modest maiden: stayed 1m: acted on soft and good to firm ground: wore cheekpieces last 3 starts: dead. *P. A. Blockley*   **53**

HERES HARRY   4 b.c. Most Welcome 131 – Nahla (Wassl 125) [2004 6g 5m Jun 11] no sign of ability in bumpers/claimers. *Miss Jacqueline S. Doyle*   **–**

HERES THE PLAN (IRE)   2 b.f. (Feb 4) Revoque (IRE) 122 – Fanciful (IRE) (Mujtahid (USA) 118) [2004 6m* 6m 7m⁶ 7d p8.6g⁴ Oct 9] 4,500Y: lengthy filly: fourth foal: half-sister to 3 winners, including 3-y-o Queenstown and 2000 2-y-o 7.5f winner The   **79**

Fancy Man (by Definite Article): dam ran once at 2 yrs in Ireland: fair performer: won maiden at Newmarket in May: creditable efforts next 2 starts: stays 7f, probably not quite 8.6f: acts on good to firm going: sometimes races freely. *M. G. Quinlan*

HERETIC   6 b.g. Bishop of Cashel 122 – Barford Lady 93 (Stanford 121§) [2004 110: **108** 8s* 8s⁴ 7g 7s Aug 19] good-bodied gelding: has a short, round action: useful performer: lightly raced: nearly as good as ever when winning minor event at Thirsk in April by ½ length from Mine: ran as if amiss all 3 starts after, visored on final one: best around 1m: has form on good to firm going, very best efforts on good or softer (yet to race on heavy): usually waited with. *J. R. Fanshawe*

HERE TO ME   3 ch.f. Muhtarram (USA) 125 – Away To Me (Exit To Nowhere (USA) **78** 122) [2004 73: 7m⁵ 7m³ 7g⁴ 8f⁴ 7g² 6.1m¹¹ 7g³ p6g⁵ 7s⁶ 8.1d² p7.1g Oct 9] rather leggy, workmanlike filly: fair performer: won maiden at Warwick in July: effective at 6f to 1m: acts on polytrack, firm and soft going: often races prominently: consistent. *R. Hannon*

HERIOT   3 b.g. Hamas (IRE) 125§ – Sure Victory (IRE) 75 (Stalker 121) [2004 8v 8g **55 ?** 7.1f 6g Jul 24] modest form only on final outing: blinkered/visored after debut. *H. Candy*

HERMITAGE COURT (USA)   3 ch.g. Out of Place (USA) – Russian Act (USA) **90** (Siberian Express (USA) 125) [2004 8g* 10g⁴ 8.5g⁶ 8f Sep 24] $48,000YS, $100,000 2-y-o: first foal: dam, US maiden, out of Prix de Minerve winner Gamberta: fairly useful performer: won maiden at Newmarket in July: good fourth to Nightspot in handicap at Newbury next time: below form in similar event at Ascot final start: stays 1¼m: raced freely penultimate outing. *B. J. Meehan*

HERNANDITA   6 b.m. Hernando (FR) 127 – Dara Dee 87 (Dara Monarch 128) [2004 **64** 17.1f⁴ 20f 15m⁶ Jul 2] close-coupled mare: modest handicapper nowadays: stays 17f: acts on firm and soft going: tried visored: fair hurdler. *Miss E. C. Lavelle*

HERNANDO'S BOY   3 b.g. Hernando (FR) 127 – Leave At Dawn (Slip Anchor 136) **62** [2004 64p: 10v⁵ 9.9s 10v 11d 12.3g² Aug 2] workmanlike gelding: fair maiden handicapper: will be suited by 1¾m+: raced mainly on good going or softer: fair juvenile hurdler. *Mrs M. Reveley*

HERNE BAY (IRE)   4 b.g. Hernando (FR) 127 – Charita (IRE) 103 (Lycius (USA) **68** 124) [2004 64: f16g* 14.1m 15.9g⁵ Jul 10] angular gelding: fair performer: won handicap at Southwell in May: stays 2m well: acts on fibresand and good to firm ground: tried in cheekpieces (below form). *A. Bailey*

HERODOTUS   6 b.g. Zafonic (USA) 130 – Thalestria (FR) 91 (Mill Reef (USA) 141) **– §** [2004 92§, a97§: 12m 11.6m 12d 14.1g p9.5g p13g Nov 10] big gelding: useful at best: no form in 2004: occasionally tongue tied/blinkered: unreliable. *K. O. Cunningham-Brown*

HERON'S WING   3 ch.g. Hernando (FR) 127 – Celtic Wing (Midyan (USA) 124) **57** [2004 p10g Jan 24] 12,000Y: third living foal: dam unraced half-sister to Celtic Swing: 50/1 and green, not knocked about when eighth to Baawrah in maiden at Lingfield (subsequently gelded). *Lady Herries*

HER OWN KIND (JPN)   2 b.f. (Feb 12) Dubai Millennium 140 – The Caretaker 113 **89 p** (Caerleon (USA) 132) [2004 7m² 7m³ 8s* Oct 22] angular, unfurnished filly: half-sister to high-class 1m (at 2 yrs) to 14.6f (St Leger) winner Mutafaweq (by Silver Hawk) and smart 7f to 1¼m winner in Ireland/USA Dimitrova (by Swain): dam Irish 7f (including at 2 yrs)/1m winner: confirmed promise when landing odds in maiden at Doncaster comfortably by 3 lengths from Twyla Tharp, pulling clear final 2f: will stay at least 1¼m: useful prospect. *Saeed bin Suroor*

HE'S A DIAMOND   2 ch.g. (Feb 16) Vettori (IRE) 119 – Azira 45 (Arazi (USA) 135) **74** [2004 6m⁵ 7g²* 7m³ 7f 7m 8g Sep 16] 5,000Y, 25,000 2-y-o: leggy gelding: first foal: dam sprint maiden: fair performer: won maiden at Brighton in July: creditable effort in nurseries after on next start only: should stay 1m: acts on good to firm going. *T. G. Mills*

HE'S A ROCKET (IRE)   3 b.g. Indian Rocket 115 – Dellua (IRE) 69 (Suave Dancer **64 d** (USA) 136) [2004 51: p6g⁶ 6d⁵ 5s⁵ 5g* 5d³ 6m⁶ 5d 5d 5f⁶ 5m 5s² 5d 5m 5m 5.7g f5g⁵ f5g Dec 1] close-coupled gelding: modest performer: won claimer at Folkestone (then left Mrs C. Dunnett) and handicap at Musselburgh in April: best efforts at 5f: acts on soft going, probably on firm: wears headgear: none too reliable. *K. R. Burke*

HE'S A STAR   2 ch.g. (Jan 28) Mark of Esteem (IRE) 137 – Sahara Belle (USA) (Sang- **60** lamore (USA) 126) [2004 6.1g 5.3f⁴ 6m 7f⁶ 7m⁶ 8g Sep 30] modest maiden: should stay 1¼m: acts on firm going: gelded after final start. *R. Hannon*

HEVERSHAM (IRE) 3 b.c. Octagonal (NZ) 126 – Saint Ann (USA) 66 (Geiger **83 d**
Counter (USA)) [2004 f7g⁴ p8g* p8g² 9s 8m 8m 7f⁴ 8m² 10m⁵ 8g 7d 7.9g 7.9m 8g² 8.5m²
8m 8s p7.1g f8g p9.5g⁵ p9.5g⁶ p7.1g Dec 20] quite good-topped colt: second foal: dam,
ran 4 times at 2 yrs (looked temperamental), out of half-sister to very smart sprinter Primo
Dominie: fairly useful on all-weather, fair on turf: won maiden at Lingfield in February:
left W. Haggas after eighth outing: stays 9.5f: acts on polytrack and firm going: usually
races up with pace: none too reliable. *J. Hetherton*

HE WHO DARES (IRE) 6 b.g. Distinctly North (USA) 115 – Sea Clover (IRE) 77 **75**
(Ela-Mana-Mou 132) [2004 69: p10g² p7g p10g³ p8g⁴ 8v³ 7s* 10.2f² May 21] rather
leggy, quite good-topped gelding: fair handicapper: dead-heated in ladies event at Lingfield in May: was effective at 7f to 1¼m: acted on polytrack and any turf going: sometimes started slowly/raced freely: dead. *A. W. Carroll*

HEYBROOK BOY (USA) 2 ch.g. (Feb 15) Woodman (USA) 126 – Liberada (USA) **77**
(Spend A Buck (USA)) [2004 6s 6g⁴ 7.1f² Jul 29] $22,000Y, resold 14,000Y: close-
coupled gelding: fourth foal: closely related to winners in USA by Silver Ghost and
Conquistador Cielo, and half-brother to winner in USA by Private Terms: dam US 7f to
9f (minor stakes) winner: fair form in maidens: second at Musselburgh: will stay at least
1m: acts on firm going: gelded after final start. *M. Johnston*

HEY PRESTO 4 b.g. Piccolo 121 – Upping The Tempo (Dunbeath (USA) 127) [2004 **78**
88: 6m 6m 5g 6g⁵ 6m⁶ 7m* 7f 7s 7m 7g Sep 30] strong, good-topped gelding: usually
takes the eye: fair handicapper: won 25-runner ladies event at Ascot in July: stays 7f: acts
on firm going: blinkered (below form) final 3-y-o start: sold 16,000 gns. *C. G. Cox*

HEYWARD PLACE 4 b.f. Mind Games 121 – Ginny Binny 113 (Ahonoora 122) **–**
[2004 f7g 8m 9.7s May 6] 4,800Y: half-sister to several winners, including useful 6f
(including at 2 yrs)/7f winner Carrie Pooter (by Tragic Role): dam Italian sprinter: no
form in maidens: tongue tied last 2 starts. *T. Keddy*

HEZAAM (USA) 3 b.c. Red Ransom (USA) – Ashraakat (USA) 105 (Danzig (USA)) **87**
[2004 84p: 7g 8m⁵ 9.9g 10d* 12.3s* 12s² 14s⁴ 11.7s Oct 19] quite attractive colt: fairly
useful handicapper: won at Sandown in July and Ripon in August: good head second
to Jack of Trumps at Goodwood next time: stays 1½m: raced mainly on good or softer
ground: has been bandaged in front: sold 38,000 gns, joined C. Fairhurst. *J. L. Dunlop*

H HARRISON (IRE) 4 b.g. Eagle Eyed (USA) 111 – Penrose (IRE) 75 (Wolfhound **86 §**
(USA) 126) [2004 95: 7g 7.1g⁶ 7.1s⁴ 7f.6d⁵ 7m⁴ 7g* 6m 7m 7g³ 6m⁵ 7.6m 7.6s p7g⁶ 8g⁵
7.1g 7g³ p7.1d⁶ 7s p6g p6g p7m Dec 21] smallish gelding: fairly useful handicapper: won
at Chester in June: probably stays 1m: acts on polytrack, firm and good to soft going: tried
in cheekpieces/blinkers: often hangs left/carries head high: unreliable. *I. W. McInnes*

HIAMOVI (IRE) 2 b.g. (Feb 24) Monashee Mountain (USA) 115 – Dunfern (Wolver **56**
Hollow 126) [2004 5.1g f7g⁵ f6s² 6m p6g f6s f8g f5f² Dec 28] modest maiden: second in
claimer/seller at Southwell: needs to settle to stay 7f: acts on fibresand: wore cheekpieces
sixth start, blinkered final one (slowly away). *R. M. H. Cowell*

HIATS 2 b.c. (Apr 25) Lujain (USA) 119 – Naulakha (Bustino 136) [2004 5g 5s⁶ 5g Jun **–**
2] well-grown, leggy colt: no form in minor event/maidens. *J. O'Reilly*

HIAWATHA (IRE) 5 b.g. Danehill (USA) 126 – Hi Bettina 96 (Henbit (USA) 130) **80**
[2004 84: f11g⁴ f9.4g* p10g³ p10g p8g 10f* 10m 10.3d⁵ 9.2d 10d p9.5g p9.5g
Dec 27] fairly useful performer: won claimer at Wolverhampton in January (claimed
from T. D. Barron) and handicap at Ayr in May: effective at 1m/1¼m: acts on all-weather,
firm and soft ground: tried blinkered: reportedly had breathing problem ninth outing.
P. A. Blockley

HIBERNATE (IRE) 10 ch.g. Lahib (USA) 129 – Ministra (USA) (Deputy Minister **45**
(CAN)) [2004 12.1m 12f⁶ 12m⁴ 12m 12m 13f⁵ Jul 28] big, lengthy gelding: poor performer nowadays: stays 1½m: acts on polytrack, firm and good to soft going: occasionally
visored: front runner: moody. *C. J. Teague*

HICCUPS 4 b.g. Polar Prince (IRE) 117 – Simmie's Special 75 (Precocious 126) [2004 **87**
84: 5s² 6g 6m³ 6m* 6g 6m⁶ 6g³ 6s³ 5g Aug 26] tall, quite good-topped gelding: fairly
useful performer: won minor event at Doncaster in May: left Mrs J. Ramsden, creditable
third to Smokin Beau at Ripon on penultimate start: effective at 5f/6f: unraced on heavy
going, acts on any other: usually wears cheekpieces, not last 2 outings: sometimes slowly
away/carries head awkwardly: upset in stall final appearance: usually waited with.
D. Nicholls

Letheby & Christopher Cheshire Oaks, Chester—Hidden Hope shows plenty of improvement stepped up from maiden company; subsequent Oaks d'Italia winner Menhoubah is second

HICKERTHRIFTCASTLE   5 ch.g. Carlingford Castle 126 – Sun Sprite (Morston (FR) 125) [2004 11.6m Jun 7] little show in bumper/novice hurdles, and claimer at Windsor. *V. Smith*   –

HI DARL   3 ch.f. Wolfhound (USA) 126 – Sugar Token 66 (Record Token 128) [2004 52: 8.1g 7f 7.1s 5m 7m 6d 6s⁵ Oct 30] strong, lengthy filly: poor performer: stays 6f: acts on soft ground: tends to carry head awkwardly. *W. M. Brisbourne*   **40**

HIDDEN CHANCE   2 ch.f. (Feb 28) Hernando (FR) 127 – Catch (USA) (Blushing Groom (FR) 131) [2004 7g 7m* 8d 7m 10m⁴ 8d Oct 18] 15,000Y: close-coupled filly: seventh foal: half-sister to 3 winners in USA: dam 6.5f winner in USA: fair performer: won maiden at Folkestone in July: creditable efforts in nurseries after on fourth and fifth starts only: stays 1¼m: acts on good to firm going, possibly not on good to soft. *R. Hannon*   **67**

HIDDEN DRAGON (USA)   5 b.g. Danzig (USA) – Summer Home (USA) (Easy Goer (USA)) [2004 108: p7g² p7g² 7m 7m 6s⁶ 5m⁴ 6s 6g Sep 25] big, lengthy gelding: useful performer: good second in handicap and minor event at Lingfield first 2 outings: below form on turf subsequently: probably best around 6f: acts on polytrack, firm and soft ground: tried blinkered, wore cheekpieces final outing: has been bandaged: tends to hang. *P. A. Blockley*   **107 d**

HIDDEN HOPE   3 ch.f. Daylami (IRE) 138 – Nuryana 107 (Nureyev (USA) 131) [2004 62p: 8.3s² 11.4d* 12m⁵ 11.9g⁴ 12.5d² 12f³ Sep 24] quite good-topped filly: useful performer: won listed Cheshire Oaks at Chester in May by 2½ lengths from Menhoubah: creditable efforts after, ½-length second to Lune d'Or in Prix de Pomone at Deauville and 1½ lengths third to Mazuna in Princess Royal Stakes at Ascot last 2 starts: should stay 1¾m: acts on firm and good to soft ground. *G. Wragg*   **108**

HIDDEN JEWEL   2 ch.g. (May 17) Forzando 122 – Manhattan Diamond 54 (Primo Dominie 121) [2004 5m f6d⁶ f7g⁶ 7m 6s² 6.1v³ p5.1g* Nov 12] 9,500Y: well-made gelding: fourth foal: half-brother to 4-y-o Kaymich Perfecto: dam, maiden, effective at 6f to 8.5f: fairly useful performer: won maiden at Wolverhampton: best effort when head second to Pivotal Flame in sales race at Doncaster: likely to prove best at 5f/6f: acts on polytrack and soft ground. *B. A. McMahon*   **82**

HIDDENSEE (USA)   2 b.c. (Feb 11) Cozzene (USA) – Zarani Sidi Anna (USA) 113 (Danzig (USA)) [2004 8g Oct 12] strong, lengthy colt: seventh foal: half-brother to French 1½m winner Swallowtailed Kite (by Silver Hawk) and winner in USA by Gone West: dam, 6f winner (including at 2 yrs) and later successful in USA, out of half-sister to champion US older horse Bates Motel: 40/1, burly and green, tailed off in maiden at Leicester. *M. Johnston*   –

HIDDEN STAR   2 br.c. (Feb 12) Lujain (USA) 119 – Inimitable 66 (Polish Precedent (USA) 131) [2004 6f³ 6g⁶ Jul 16] 4,000F, 21,000Y: good-bodied colt: fourth foal: half-brother to fairly useful 1m winner Inverness (by Inchinor), 1m (at 2 yrs)/1¼m winner   **62 p**

Royal Approval (by Royal Applause) and 3-y-o Trew Class: dam, 1¼m winner, out of half-sister to Melbourne Cup winner Jeune: modest form in minor event at Windsor (very slowly away) and maiden at Pontefract (favourite, tired late on): likely to do better. *F. Jordan*

HIGGYS PRINCE 2 b.g. (Mar 16) Prince Sabo 123 – Themeda 69 (Sure Blade (USA) – 130) [2004 5g 5g Jun 2] well beaten in maidens: failed 2 stall tests after, and banned from Flat racing from stalls until March 1 2005. *D. Flood*

HIGH ACCOLADE 4 b.c. Mark of Esteem (IRE) 137 – Generous Lady 98 (Generous (IRE) 139) [2004 122: 12m⁴ 12f² 12m³ 12m 12g² 18m⁴ 12m* Sep 26] small, sturdy colt: very smart performer: won Barnardo's Cumberland Lodge Stakes at Ascot by neck from Self Defense, rallying after being bumped by runner-up 1f out: other good efforts in 2004 when fourth to Warrsan in Coronation Cup at Epsom, 6 lengths second to Doyen in Hardwicke Stakes at Royal Ascot, 3 lengths third to Bandari in Princess of Wales's Stakes at Newmarket and ¾-length second to Albanova in Rheinland-Pokal at Cologne: stays 1¾m, below form in Doncaster Cup at 2¼m on penultimate start: raced only on good ground or firmer (acts on firm): sometimes blinkered/visored, tongue tied: carries head awkwardly: has gone in snatches: consistent. *M. P. Tregoning* **122**

HIGH ACTION (USA) 4 ch.g. Theatrical 128 – Secret Imperatrice (USA) (Secretariat (USA)) [2004 102: 12g 10.3g 16.2g 14.8g* 18.7m* 14g 14.6f⁵ Sep 10] strong, close-coupled gelding: useful handicapper: won at Newmarket in July and Chester in August, beating Thewhirlingdervish by ¾ length in 3-runner race for latter, dictating pace: stays 18.7f: raced only on good ground or firmer: tongue tied last 5 outings: usually races prominently. *Ian Williams* **95**

HIGHBURY LASS 2 ch.f. (Mar 18) Entrepreneur 123 – Princess Victoria 61 (Deploy 131) [2004 5m 7f⁶ 7s Aug 13] 8,500Y: small, good-topped filly: first foal: dam 2-y-o 5f seller winner: well beaten in maiden/sellers. *P. C. Haslam*

HIGHCAL 7 gr.g. King's Signet (USA) 110 – Guarded Expression 51 (Siberian Express (USA) 125) [2004 –: f14g Nov 22] good-bodied gelding: modest in 2002: well held both starts since: tried blinkered. *Ronald Thompson*

Barnardo's Cumberland Lodge Stakes, Ascot—High Accolade (left) gains a repeat success; Self Defense excels in second and Bandari (right) is a creditable third giving weight away all round

HIGH CANE (USA) 4 ch.f. Diesis 133 – Aerleon Jane 89 (Caerleon (USA) 132) [2004 **60 d**
70: p10g 7s³ 8s 6s 7v f8d Jun 10] leggy, lengthy filly: modest maiden: trained by
J. Noseda at 3 yrs: form in 2004 only when third at Newcastle: effective at 7f/1m: acts on
soft ground, ran as if amiss on firm on debut: blinkered (looked none too keen) final 3-y-o
start. *M. D. Hammond*

HIGH CARD 2 b.g. (Apr 18) So Factual (USA) 120 – High Cut 84 (Dashing Blade **88**
117) [2004 p7m p8.6g⁶ 8v² Oct 23] quite good-topped gelding: fourth foal: brother to 7f
winner in Spain: dam lightly-raced maiden who should have stayed beyond 7f: easily best
effort in maidens when 1¼ lengths second to Descartes at Newbury: should stay 1¼m.
J. M. P. Eustace

HIGH CHART 2 b.f. (Apr 9) Robellino (USA) 127 – Bright Spells 93 (Salse (USA) **67**
128) [2004 5g* 6s⁴ 5m⁴ 5f 5.2m³ 6f 6g⁶ 7m 6.5g 5m 8.3g p6g p6g⁴ Dec 18] 7,500F,
10,000Y: close-coupled filly: fifth foal: half-sister to Irish 1997 2-y-o 7f winner Cultural
Role (by Night Shift) and Irish 1½m/13f winner Stutter (by Polish Precedent): dam, 6f
winner at 2 yrs, stayed 1¾m: fair performer: won maiden at Windsor in April: below form
in second half of 2004, leaving G. Margarson prior to penultimate start: will stay 7f: acts
on firm ground: sometimes tongue tied. *T. G. Mills*

HIGH CHARTER 3 b.g. Polish Precedent (USA) 131 – By Charter 104 (Shirley **55**
Heights 130) [2004 10v p9.5g f12g² Dec 11] 78,000Y: brother to 5-y-o First Charter,
closely related to 1995 2-y-o 7f winner Green Charter (by Green Desert) and half-brother
to several winners: dam, 2-y-o 7f winner who seemed to stay 1½m, daughter of Time
Charter: modest form in maidens: stays 1½m: acts on all-weather. *J. R. Fanshawe*

HIGH CLASS PET 4 b.f. Petong 126 – What A Pet (Mummy's Pet 125) [2004 8g **–**
9d⁶ Aug 4] 7,000Y: leggy filly: sister to 3 winners, notably smart performer up to 1m
Petardia, 5f to 7f (Champagne Stakes) winner at 2 yrs, and half-sister to winner in France:
dam French 1m winner: no sign of ability in maidens. *F. P. Murtagh*

HIGH DAWN (IRE) 2 b.g. (Mar 20) Namid 128 – Highbrook (USA) 88 (Alphabatim **–**
(USA) 126) [2004 5d⁶ Apr 5] 15,500Y: fourth foal: half-brother to 4-y-o Pink Sapphire
and 7-y-o Niagara: dam,1¼m to 13f winner, useful over hurdles: well held in maiden at
Windsor, slowly away. *R. M. Beckett*

HIGH DIVA 5 b.m. Piccolo 121 – Gifted (Shareef Dancer (USA) 135) [2004 58: p10g⁶ **42**
f12f⁴ f16s⁶ f9.4s⁵ p8g p8g⁵ Mar 2] tall mare: fluent mover: poor maiden: left B. Johnson
after reappearance: stays 1¼m: acts on all-weather, raced only on good/good to firm
going on turf: tried in tongue tie/cheekpieces: usually held up: has raced freely. *J. R. Best*

HIGH DRAMA 7 b.g. In The Wings 128 – Maestrale (Top Ville 129) [2004 42: 17.2f* **45**
16.4g² 17.1d⁴ Aug 15] leggy gelding: poor handicapper: won ladies event at Bath in June:
stays 2¼m: acts on firm and good to soft going: blinkered once: usually held up, ridden
more prominently in 2004. *P. Bowen*

HIGH DYKE 2 b.g. (Apr 3) Mujahid (USA) 125 – Gold Linnet 69 (Nashwan (USA) **69**
135) [2004 6g 5m⁵ 7f⁶ 7.1g⁵ 7.1d p7.1g⁴ f8g³ Dec 28] 8,000F, 6,000Y, 7,000 2-y-o: quite
good-topped gelding: sixth foal: half-brother to 3 winners, including Irish 1½m winner
Little Linnet (by Be My Guest): dam, second once from 2 starts at 1¼m, out of very smart
middle-distance stayer Banket: fair maiden: good third in nursery at Southwell: stays easy
1m: acts on all-weather and firm going. *D. Haydn Jones*

HIGHER LOVE (IRE) 2 b.f. (Feb 1) Sadler's Wells (USA) 132 – Dollar Bird (IRE) **73 p**
103 (Kris 135) [2004 8m⁶ 8.1s² Sep 25] €340,000Y: good-topped filly: first foal: dam,
2-y-o 1m winner who stayed 1¾m, half-sister to smart French middle-distance stayer
Legend Maker (by Sadler's Wells) out of sister to High Hawk, herself dam of In The
Wings (also by Sadler's Wells): fair form in maidens at Leicester and Haydock (second to
Tcherina): will be suited by 1¼m/1½m: should progress. *M. L. W. Bell*

HIGH ESTEEM 8 b.g. Common Grounds 118 – Whittle Woods Girl 80 (Emarati **–**
(USA) 74) [2004 55, a65: f6g⁴ f6g f6m 5s Aug 13] big gelding: modest maiden: **a50**
effective at 5f to 7f: acts on fibresand and any turf going: wore headgear in 2004: tongue
tied penultimate outing: often races prominently: has hung left/looked difficult ride.
M. A. Buckley

HIGHEST (IRE) 5 b.h. Selkirk (USA) 129 – Pearl Kite (USA) 106§ (Silver Hawk **110**
(USA) 123) [2004 121: 13.9d 20m Jun 17] big, strong horse: very smart performer at
best: better effort in 2004 when seventh to Papineau in Gold Cup at Royal Ascot (put
down after reportedly rupturing a ligament): was effective at 1½m/1¾m: unraced on soft/
heavy going, very best form on good or firmer: tried visored/tongue tied. *Saeed bin
Suroor*

HIGHEST REGARD 2 b.c. (Mar 19) Mark of Esteem (IRE) 137 – Free As A Bird **72** 62 (Robellino (USA) 127) [2004 p7.1g 6d p7m⁵ p7.1g² p7.1g² Dec 15] 3,000Y: third foal: half-brother to 3-y-o Go Garuda and fairly useful 2001 2-y-o 6f winner Greenhills (by Greensmith): dam, maiden who stayed 7f, half-sister to useful 7f/1m performers Cragganmore and Hoh Chi Min: fair maiden: second at Wolverhampton, unlucky in nursery final start: stays 7f: acts on polytrack. *P. L. Gilligan*

HIGHEST RETURN (USA) 2 b. or br.g. (Feb 3) Theatrical 128 – Hasene (FR) 108 **63** (Akarad (FR) 130) [2004 7.2m⁴ 7m Jul 30] €70,000Y: leggy gelding: first foal: dam, French/US 1m/1¼m winner, half-sister to 7-y-o Execute: better effort in maidens when fourth at Ayr: should be suited by 1¼m/1½m: gelded after final start. *M. Johnston*

HIGH FINANCE (IRE) 4 b. or br.f. Entrepreneur 123 – Phylella (Persian Bold 123) **68 ?** [2004 85: 7.1g⁵ 7m⁶ p7g Aug 26] rather leggy, useful-looking filly: just fair at best in 2004: effective at 7f/easy 1m: acts on all-weather, raced only on good going or firmer on turf: patiently ridden: sold 26,000 gns in December. *J. W. Hills*

HIGHFLUTING 3 b.f. Piccolo 121 – Vilcabamba (USA) (Green Dancer (USA) 132) **–** [2004 p10g 9.9g 10.2m 11.9m May 23] smallish filly: third foal: half-sister to 1½m winner Harry B (by Midyan): dam French 9f winner: well held in maidens. *R. M. Flower*

HIGH FREQUENCY (IRE) 3 ch.g. Grand Lodge (USA) 125 – Freak Out (FR) **60** (Bering 136) [2004 8g 8g⁶ 8.1g May 31] €110,000Y: tall gelding: second foal: brother to French 13f winner Lodgina: dam French 1¼m/11f winner: modest form in mid-division in newcomers event/maidens: should be suited by 1¼m+. *W. R. Muir*

HIGH HOPE (FR) 6 ch.g. Lomitas 129 – Highness Lady (GER) (Cagliostro (GER)) **76** [2004 89: p12g 14s⁵ Aug 29] leggy gelding: fair handicapper: effective at 1¼m to 15f: acts on polytrack, raced mainly on good going or softer on turf: tried blinkered/in cheekpieces. *G. L. Moore*

HIGHLAND CASCADE 2 ch.f. (Feb 24) Tipsy Creek (USA) 115 – Highland Hannah **75** (IRE) (Persian Heights 129) [2004 6g* 6f³ 6f² 6.5m 6g³ 6d Oct 14] good-topped filly: first foal: dam unraced out of half-sister to 7-y-o Compton Bolter: fair performer: won maiden at Yarmouth in May: placed in minor events/nursery: stays 6.5f: acts on firm ground. *J. M. P. Eustace*

HIGHLAND DIVA (IRE) 2 ch.f. (Feb 19) Selkirk (USA) 129 – Drama Class (IRE) **67 P** 102 (Caerleon (USA) 132) [2004 7g⁴ Sep 2] strong, lengthy filly: first foal: dam, 1¼m winner who stayed 1½m, out of sister to high-class performer up to 1¼m Prince of Dance and granddaughter of Sun Princess: 20/1 and green, 4 lengths fourth to Almansoora in maiden at Salisbury, forced wide before finishing well: likely to be suited by 1¼m/1½m: sure to do good deal better and win races. *Sir Michael Stoute*

HIGHLAND GAMES (IRE) 4 b.g. Singspiel (IRE) 133 – Highland Gift (IRE) 95 **96** (Generous (IRE) 139) [2004 89: 14g² 13.9s 12m² 12m⁴ 12f⁵ 12f³ 16.2g³ 14.6f 16.2m Sep 25] strong, well-made gelding: useful handicapper: good third to Dorothy's Friend at Ascot seventh outing: ran as though amiss last 2 starts: stays 2m: acts on firm going, possibly not soft. *J. G. Given*

HIGHLAND LASS 3 b.f. Nicolotte 118 – Portvasco 90 (Sharpo 132) [2004 6m 7m **–** 7d⁶ 6g 6g p6g f6g Nov 23] sturdy filly: closely related to 6f/7f winner Oare Sparrow (by Night Shift) and half-sister to 3 winners, including fairly useful 5f (at 2 yrs)/6f winner who stayed 1m Midwich Cuckoo (by Midyan): dam 6f winner: little form. *Mrs H. Sweeting*

HIGHLAND REEL 7 ch.g. Selkirk (USA) 129 – Taj Victory 68 (Final Straw 127) **94 §** [2004 94§: 8g* 8.1f 8f 8d⁴ 8m 8g³ 8m⁴ 9s⁴ Aug 29] leggy gelding: fairly useful handicapper: won at Goodwood in May: good close third to Pango at same course sixth start: effective at 1m/1¼m: acts on any going: sometimes hangs right: usually waited with: looked reluctant final outing: unreliable. *D. R. C. Elsworth*

HIGHLAND WARRIOR 5 b.h. Makbul 104 – Highland Rowena 59 (Royben 125) **80** [2004 66: 6s³ 7.1g³ 5v² 5d³ 6d⁴ 6m* 5m⁶ 6g 5m 6g⁴ 6d⁶ 6g⁶ 6m³ 6g 6s² 5d⁶ 6d⁴ 5s² 5d⁶ Nov 3] big, leggy horse: fairly useful handicapper: won at Ayr in May (has gained both other successes there): best at 5f/6f nowadays: acts on heavy and good to firm going: usually slowly away: moves races freely: waited with. *J. S. Goldie*

HIGHLIGHT GIRL 3 ch.f. Forzando 122 – Norska 67 (Northfields (USA)) [2004 **–** 10s 8.1m Jun 21] half-sister to several winners, including 5-y-o Mrs Cube and 1¾m winner Eponine (by Sharpo): dam maiden who stayed 1¼m: no sign of ability in maidens at Windsor and Chepstow. *A. W. Carroll*

HIGH MINDED   2 b.g. (May 17) Mind Games 121 – Pips Way (IRE) 83 (Pips Pride 54
117) [2004 5m 5g⁶ Jun 17] useful-looking gelding: first foal: dam 6f (at 2 yrs) to 9f
winner: modest form at Ripon on first start in maidens. *K. R. Burke*

HIGH PETERGATE (IRE)   2 b.f. (Mar 21) Mujadil (USA) 119 – Anamara (IRE) 68 55
(Fairy King (USA)) [2004 5m⁵ 5f⁴ 6d 6g Oct 4] €13,000F, €40,000Y: small, workmanlike filly: third foal: half-sister to winner up to 1¼m in Italy by Sri Pekan: dam, Irish
maiden (stayed 7f), out of half-sister to Cadeaux Genereux: modest maiden: best effort
when fourth at Redcar: should stay 6f. *M. W. Easterby*

HIGH POINT (IRE)   6 b.g. Ela-Mana-Mou 132 – Top Lady (IRE) 83 (Shirley Heights 86
130) [2004 87: p12g p12g p12g p16g² 16d³ 13.9s³ 16m³ 16.1m⁶ 16.2m 14.8d⁵ 16g* 18s³
Oct 16] leggy gelding: fairly useful handicapper: won at Yarmouth (by ½ length from
Astyanax) in September: very good close third of 34 to Contact Dancer in Cesarewitch at
Newmarket final start: effective at 1½m to 2¼m: acts on polytrack, soft and good to firm
going: usually held up: tough and reliable. *G. P. Enright*

HIGH POLICY (IRE)   8 ch.g. Machiavellian (USA) 123 – Road To The Top 84 (Shir- 67
ley Heights 130) [2004 60, a73: f16g⁴ f14g³ Jun 16] well-made gelding: fair handicapper:
effective at 1¾m/2m: acts on fibresand, heavy and good to firm going: tried visored,
usually wears cheekpieces: no easy ride (often slowly away/flashes tail): held up.
R. Hollinshead

HIGH REACH   4 b.g. Royal Applause 124 – Lady of Limerick (IRE) (Thatching 131) 100
[2004 98+: 6g³ 6g⁶ 6f³ 6m 6m³ 5.2g 5g p7g Oct 28] strong, compact gelding: useful performer: good efforts when third in Wokingham at Royal Ascot (to Lafi) and Stewards'
Cup at Goodwood (beaten 1½ lengths by Pivotal Point, making virtually all in far-side
group) third/fifth starts, and when ninth of 11 in Group 3 event at Newbury on sixth:
effective at 5f to 7f: acts on polytrack and firm going. *T. G. Mills*

HIGH RESERVE   3 b.f. Dr Fong (USA) 128 – Hyabella 111 (Shirley Heights 130) 80 p
[2004 71p: 8g³ 8s* Sep 14] fairly useful form: won minor event at Salisbury readily by
length from Giko, stumbling leaving stall and quickening well when finally getting in
clear over 1f out: likely to stay 1¼m: acts on soft and good to firm ground: capable of
better still. *J. R. Fanshawe*

HIGH RHYTHM   2 b.f. (Jan 9) Piccolo 121 – Slave To The Rythm (IRE) 63 (Hamas 55
(IRE) 125§) [2004 6g⁶ p6g⁶ p6g Dec 15] first foal: dam, ran twice, daughter of use-
ful sprinter Silver Singing, herself half-sister to St Leger winner Silver Patriarch and
Gold Cup winner Papineau: modest form in maidens: likely to prove best at 5f/6f.
S. C. Williams

HIGH RIDGE   5 ch.g. Indian Ridge 123 – Change For A Buck (USA) 83 (Time For A 81
Change (USA)) [2004 68: 6.1v 5.7m* 7.1g⁵ 5.7f* 6m² 5.5m³ 5.7g⁴ 6g* 6m² 6m² 6m⁴ 6g
6d 6g Oct 11] fairly useful performer: won handicaps at Bath in May and June and minor
event at Pontefract in July: has form up to 1¼m, but best efforts around 6f: acts on firm
and soft going: usually wears cheekpieces: waited with: tough. *J. M. Bradley*

HIGH SCHOOL   3 b.f. Sadler's Wells (USA) 132 – High Hawk 124 (Shirley Heights 76
130) [2004 9.7s² 12s⁶ 9.9g⁴ 10m² 11.9m⁶ Jul 19] sister to several winners, notably high-
class 1½m performer In The Wings, closely related to 2 winners, including fairly useful
1m winner Eaglesham (by Barathea), and half-sister to 2 winners: dam, Ribblesdale and
Park Hill Stakes winner, half-sister to dam of High-Rise: fair maiden: stays 1½m: acts on
soft and good to firm ground: sent to Australia. *D. R. Loder*

HIGH TREASON (USA)   2 ch.c. (Feb 14) Diesis 133 – Fabula Dancer (USA) (North- 59 ?
ern Dancer) [2004 7m 8m 7g 7.9g Oct 9] 50,000Y: tall colt: half-brother to several
winners in Germany, including smart performer up to 1½m Flamingo Road (by Acatenango) and useful stayer Flamingo Paradise (by Rainbow Quest): dam won in Germany:
seemingly modest form in maidens: will stay at least 1¼m. *J. G. Given*

HIGH VIEW (USA)   3 ch.c. Distant View (USA) 126 – Disco Doll (USA) (Diesis –
133) [2004 8v 10g 10m 8.1d 12g 8s 12.6d Sep 18] lengthy colt: no form: refused to enter
stall intended sixth outing. *F. Jordan*

HIGH VOLTAGE   3 ch.g. Wolfhound (USA) 126 – Real Emotion (USA) (El Prado 103
(IRE) 119) [2004 93: 6d⁸ 6m³ 6m⁶ 5m 6m 6g 6.1g* 5.6m 6s Sep 25] good-topped gelding: useful handicapper: won at Ripon in April and Chester (beat Compton's Eleven by
short head) in August: best at 5f/easy 6f: acts on firm and good to soft ground, possibly
not on soft: has been tongue tied: tends to carry head high: races up with pace. *K. R. Burke*

HILARIOUS (IRE)   4 b.f. Petorius 117 – Heronwater (IRE) 73 (Ela-Mana-Mou 132) 48 d
[2004 60: 8.1v⁵ f7m⁴ 8m⁵ f8g⁶ 10f⁴ p10d 10.2s⁶ 7s 12f 10d Oct 2] good-topped filly: just

poor maiden in 2004: left B. R. Millman after third start, below form after fifth: barely stays 1¼m: acts on fibresand, firm and good to soft going: sometimes races freely: tried blinkered/in cheekpieces. *Dr J. R. J. Naylor*

HILBRE ISLAND 4 b.c. Halling (USA) 133 – Faribole (IRE) 106 (Esprit du Nord (USA) 126) [2004 115: 14.1g³ 12g 16.2s 16.4f⁵ 16m Jul 29] sturdy colt: fluent mover: just useful performer in 2004, best effort when fifth to Papineau in Henry II Stakes at Sandown: looked irresolute in Goodwood Cup final outing: seems to stay 2m: acts on firm and good to soft going: blinkered (raced too freely in testing conditions and pulled up) third start. *B. J. Meehan* **109**

HILITES (IRE) 3 ch.f. Desert King (IRE) 129 – Slayjay (IRE) 94 (Mujtahid (USA) 118) [2004 85: 6v³ 6g 6g³ 5m 7m 7m⁶ 7.1m³ 9g 8.5f⁴ 6d 7g 6d p6d⁶ p7g p8g Nov 30] leggy, close-coupled filly: fairly useful handicapper: effective at 6f/7f: acts on polytrack and any turf going: wore cheekpieces last 5 starts. *J. S. Moore* **80**

HILLABILLA (IRE) 2 b.f. (Apr 18) Imperial Ballet (IRE) 110 – London Rose (USA) (Machiavellian (USA) 123) [2004 6.1d 7g Sep 2] €13,000Y: first foal: dam unraced granddaughter of Oaks winner Unite: well held in maidens. *M. Blanshard* **–**

HILL FAIRY 2 ch.f. (Jan 27) Monsun (GER) 124 – Homing Instinct (Arctic Tern (USA) 126) [2004 6g⁶ 8.2g⁴ 8.1s⁵ Sep 25] €46,000Y: leggy, close-coupled filly: third foal: dam, 11f/1½m winner in France, half-sister to very smart French 1¼m performer Gunboat Diplomacy: modest form in maidens/minor event: should stay at least 1½m. *T. P. Tate* **62**

HILLSIDE HEATHER (IRE) 2 ch.f. (Mar 9) Tagula (IRE) 116 – Danzig Craft (IRE) (Roi Danzig (USA)) [2004 5g⁴ 5m³ 5g² 5d 5m² 6m⁴ 5.1g⁵ 5s 5f⁶ 5g* Sep 26] €5,000Y: lengthy filly: third foal: half-sister to Swedish 6f winner by Lake Coniston: dam unraced out of half-sister to smart 5f to 7f performer Blue Siren: fair performer: won maiden at Musselburgh, coming from off strong pace: effective at 5f/6f: acts on good to firm going: wore cheekpieces last 3 starts. *A. Berry* **65**

HILLS OF ARAN 2 b.c. (Apr 2) Sadler's Wells (USA) 132 – Danefair 109 (Danehill (USA) 126) [2004 7d³ 8.5g* 8s⁴ Oct 23] strong, well-made colt: half-brother to 3-y-o Well Known and half-brother to 4-y-o Trade Fair: dam, French 1¼m/1½m (Prix Minerve) winner, sister to 5-y-o Vortex: won maiden at Galway in September by 4½ lengths from Sky High Flyer: 11½ lengths fourth to Motivator in Racing Post Trophy at Doncaster: should be suited by 1¼m/1½m: likely to progress. *A. P. O'Brien, Ireland* **103 p**

HILLS OF GOLD 5 b.g. Danehill (USA) 126 – Valley of Gold (FR) 117 (Shirley Heights 130) [2004 74: 7s⁴ 8d* 7s 7.9d³ 8d² 9.9g² 7g* 8.3d⁴ 8.1g⁶ 7.2s⁶ 8.9g 7v Oct 16] big, lengthy gelding: has a quick, fluent action: fairly useful handicapper: won at Ripon in April and Chester (apprentice event, for second successive year) in August: effective at 7f to 1¼m on firm and soft ground: tried tongue tied, not in 2004. *M. W. Easterby* **83**

HILLS SPITFIRE (IRE) 3 b. or br.g. Kahyasi 130 – Questina (FR) (Rainbow Quest (USA) 134) [2004 95p: 10m³ Jul 6] lengthy, quite good-topped gelding: useful form at 2 yrs: odds on but better for race, below that form when third to Apsara in maiden at Pontefract only 3-y-o start: gelded after: will stay at least 1½m: raced only on good/good to firm ground: slowly away all 3 outings. *P. W. Harris* **80**

HILLTIME (IRE) 4 b.g. Danetime (IRE) 121 – Ceannanas (IRE) 77 (Magical Wonder (USA) 125) [2004 –: 6d 6m 5d 8d 8.2g³ 7m f8g⁵ p8.6g⁵ Nov 15] modest maiden: stays 1m: acts on polytrack and good to firm ground: tried visored. *J. J. Quinn* **58**

HILLTOP RHAPSODY 3 b.f. Bin Ajwaad (IRE) 119 – Saferjel (Elmaamul (USA) 125) [2004 8g 10.3m 8.3f* 10.5g 8.3m⁴ Sep 27] big, useful-looking filly: first foal: dam, ran 3 times, out of 1½m winner: fair performer: won maiden at Windsor in July: good fourth to Omaha City in handicap there final start: stays 1m: acts on firm going. *D. J. Daly* **76**

HILLY BE 3 b.f. Silver Patriarch (IRE) 125 – Lolita (FR) (Hellios (USA)) [2004 –: 8.1s Apr 7] tailed off in maidens. *J. R. Jenkins* **–**

HINCHLEY WOOD (IRE) 5 b.g. Fayruz 116 – Audriano (IRE) (Cyrano de Bergerac 120) [2004 p7g⁶ f9.4s p7g p10g p7g⁵ p6g⁵ p7g⁴ p6g² p6g⁶ Apr 19] poor performer: stays 7f: acts on polytrack, well held only outing on turf: blinkered last 3 outings. *R. E. Best* **49**

HINODE (IRE) 3 ch.c. Vettori (IRE) 119 – Juvenilia (IRE) 55 (Masterclass (USA) 116) [2004 8g 8m f8g³ 11.9s⁵ 11.5g⁴ 14.1g 11.8g Oct 12] lengthy colt: third foal: half-brother to 4-y-o Riquewihr: dam third at 7f both starts: modest maiden: stays 11.5f: acts on fibresand, best effort on turf on good going: sold 8,000 gns. *J. A. R. Toller* **61**

HIP HOP HARRY   4 b.c. First Trump 118 – Rechanit (IRE) (Local Suitor (USA) 128)   **95**
[2004 84: f11g p12g² p10g* p12g² 12g 10m 12g⁵ Aug 4] sturdy colt: useful handicapper:
won at Lingfield in February: good ¾-length second to Millville on same course following day: well held returned to turf after: stays 1½m: successful on good to firm going, best
form on polytrack: visored 3 of last 5 starts: sold 11,000 gns in October. *E. A. L. Dunlop*

HIRAYNA   5 b.m. Doyoun 124 – Himaya (IRE) (Mouktar 129) [2004 11g³ 7.1m 7.6g⁴   **52**
8m⁴ 10s 9.9m 8m Sep 25] big mare: sixth foal: sister to fairly useful Irish 1¼m winner
Hisar and half-sister to useful 1½m to 2m winner Hirapour (by Kahyasi): dam second at
1½m from 2 starts in Ireland: bumper winner: modest maiden on Flat: should stay 1¼m:
acts on good to firm going: edged left fourth outing. *W. M. Brisbourne*

HIS MAJESTY   2 ch.c. (Mar 24) Case Law 113 – Eternal Triangle (USA) 76 (Bara-   **58**
chois (CAN)) [2004 p5g 5m³ 6g² 6s⁶ 7m f6s p8.6g p6g Dec 27] strong colt: modest   **a40**
maiden on turf, poor on all-weather: stays 6f: best effort on good going: blinkered final
outing. *N. P. Littmoden*

HISTORIC PLACE (USA)   4 b.g. Dynaformer (USA) – Captive Island 116 (North-   **83**
fields (USA)) [2004 11.9d² 9.9g⁴ 12g 17.5d³ 18s 16.5s⁶ Nov 6] workmanlike gelding:
fairly useful bumper winner: fairly useful maiden on Flat: stays 17.5f: acts on good to soft
going. *G. B. Balding*

HITS ONLY CASH   2 b.c. (Feb 24) Inchinor 119 – Persian Blue 64 (Persian Bold   **66**
123) [2004 5m⁶ 5g 6d⁵ 6s 5.2s⁴ 5.1v⁵ p7.1g² p7.1g Nov 26] 20,000F, 12,000Y, 18,000
2-y-o: close-coupled colt: third foal: half-brother to 3-y-o Maluti: dam, maiden, stayed
1½m: fair maiden: second in nursery at Wolverhampton: will need to settle to stay beyond
7f: acts on polytrack and heavy ground. *P. A. Blockley*

HIT'S ONLY MONEY (IRE)   4 br.g. Hamas (IRE) 125§ – Toordillon (IRE) 69 (Con-   **75**
tract Law (USA) 108) [2004 106: 7.1d 8g 7m 7s 6m 6g f5s p6g Nov 26] workmanlike
gelding: usually looks well: just fair form in 2004: best efforts at 6f on good/good to firm
ground. *P. A. Blockley*

HOBART JUNCTION (IRE)   9 ch.g. Classic Secret (USA) 91 – Art Duo 86 (Artaius   **–**
(USA) 129) [2004 12.1m Aug 5] unraced on Flat in 2003: tailed off only outing in 2004:
sometimes blinkered. *J. A. T. de Giles*

HOH BLEU DEE   3 b.g. Desert Style (IRE) 121 – Ermine (IRE) 86 (Cadeaux Gener-   **80**
eux 131) [2004 89: 7g 8.1d⁶ 10d 8g² 8g* 8f 7d⁴ 12s p6m⁶ Dec 21] smallish, well-made
gelding: fairly useful performer: won claimer at Salisbury in July: left S. Kirk prior to
final start: stays 1m: acts on good to firm and good to soft going: effective with or without
blinkers. *T. Keddy*

HOH HEDSOR   2 ch.f. (May 9) Singspiel (IRE) 133 – Ghassanah 73 (Pas de Seul
133) [2004 7g 8v Oct 23] half-sister to several winners, including 5f/6f winner (including
at 2 yrs) Alzianah (by Alzao) and 6f/7f (latter at 2 yrs) winner Return of Amin (by Salse),
both useful: dam 7f winner: only a trifle sign of ability in maidens. *S. Kirk*

HOH HOH HOH   2 ch.c. (Mar 14) Piccolo 121 – Nesting 47 (Thatching 131) [2004   **95**
5.7f* May 21] 21,000Y: first foal: dam ran 3 times: favourite, won maiden at Bath by 7
lengths from Come Good: fractured a knee after. *A. M. Balding*

HOH MY DARLING   2 br.f. (Apr 28) Dansili 127 – Now And Forever (IRE) (Kris   **63**
135) [2004 7d 8.3m⁴ 8d Oct 15] useful-looking filly: fourth living foal: half-sister to
useful 1999 2-y-o 7f winner (stayed 1½m) Everlasting Love (by Pursuit of Love): dam
unraced half-sister to smart stayer Witness Box out of close relative to Dahlia: modest
form in maidens: fourth at Windsor: should stay 1¼m. *M. L. W. Bell*

HOH NELSON   3 b.g. Halling (USA) 133 – Birsay (Bustino 136) [2004 70?: 8g³ 11.6g   **66**
11.8g 18d⁶ 16s⁴ Aug 28] strong, angular gelding: fair maiden: stays 2m: acts on soft
ground, probably on good to firm: joined C. Mann. *H. Morrison*

HOH'S BACK   5 b.g. Royal Applause 124 – Paris Joelle (IRE) (Fairy King (USA))   **70 d**
[2004 76, a80: f8g f8.5g f8g 8s² f8.5g 7.1d⁶ f8g 8g f8d⁵ f8g.1f 7.5g 7.6g 8f 9v 8m 7.9m⁵
Sep 11] well-made gelding: fair performer at best: below form after fourth outing: stays
9.4f: acts on all-weather, soft and good to firm ground: wears cheekpieces: unreliable.
Paul Johnson

HOLBECK GHYLL (IRE)   2 ch.c. (Apr 30) Titus Livius (FR) 115 – Crimada (IRE)   **73**
(Mukaddamah (USA) 125) [2004 6.1g³ 5m 5g³ Jun 23] €6,000F, 13,000Y: rather leggy,
good-topped colt: second foal: half-brother to a winner in Greece by Goldmark: dam
unraced sister to Monte Lemos (sprinter) and half-sister to Gone For A Burton (stayed

1½m), both useful: fair form in Norfolk Stakes (eighth) at Royal Ascot and maidens: suffered niggling problems after: should prove best at 5f/6f. *A. M. Balding*

HOLDERNESS GIRL   11 b.m. Lapierre 119 – Isobel's Choice 58 (Green God 128)   –
[2004 8m⁶ f8g Jun 16] smallish mare: poor maiden in 1998: well held both outings on Flat since. *M. E. Sowersby*

HOLD THE LINE   3 b.g. Titus Livius (FR) 115 – Multi-Sofft 30 (Northern State   73
(USA) 91) [2004 72: p10g⁶ f8s* f8g⁶ Apr 15] big gelding: fair performer: won maiden at Southwell in March: should stay 1½m: acts on all-weather, some promise on good to firm going second 2-y-o start: wore cheekpieces last 3 starts. *W. G. M. Turner*

HOLD UP   3 ch.f. Daggers Drawn (USA) 114 – Select Sale (Auction Ring (USA) 123)   –
[2004 –p: 10m 11.6f 10m 8.3f 7f 8g 8d p9.5g⁶ f12g Dec 1] leggy, attractive filly: little form: blinkered last 2 starts. *Miss J. Feilden*

HOLIDAY CAMP (USA)   2 b.c. (Feb 7) Chester House (USA) 123 – Arewehaving-   74 p
funyet (USA) (Sham (USA)) [2004 6s³ Oct 22] tall, good-topped colt: has scope: half-brother to several winners, including French 11f winner Morina (by Lyphard), herself dam of very smart middle-distance stayer Mons: dam US Grade 1 2-y-o 8.5f winner: favourite, 6 lengths third to Bailey Gate in maiden at Newbury, slowly away and no extra only late on: will stay 1m: sure to progress. *B. W. Hills*

HOLIDAY COCKTAIL   2 b.g. (Apr 28) Mister Baileys 123 – Bermuda Lily 78 (Dun-   – p
beath (USA) 127) [2004 5m Sep 15] 30,000F: closely related to fairly useful 1997 2-y-o 6f winner Bermuda Boy (by Robellino), later successful over 7f in Hong Kong where known as Toymark, and half-brother to several at least fairly useful winners, including useful 1m/1¼m winner Sir Talbot (by Ardross): dam 2-y-o 5f winner: 20/1, well held in maiden at Beverley, very slowly away: should do better. *S. C. Williams*

HOLLINGWOOD SOUL   2 ch.f. (Mar 6) Timeless Times (USA) 99 – Crystal Chan-   31
delier (Pivotal 124) [2004 5g 6m 5d 7.5d 7m Jul 21] 1,200Y: sparely-made filly: first foal: dam, ran 3 times, out of half-sister to smart performer up to 7f Atraf: poor maiden. *Ronald Thompson*

HOLLOW JO   4 b.g. Most Welcome 131 – Sir Hollow (USA) (Sir Ivor (USA) 135)   70
[2004 77: 7s 6d 5g⁴ 6m May 31] strong, lengthy gelding: fair handicapper: creditable effort in 2004 only when fourth at Kempton: effective at 5f to 7f: acts on firm and good to soft going: tends to wander. *J. R. Jenkins*

HOLLY ROSE   5 b.m. Charnwood Forest (IRE) 125 – Divina Luna 96 (Dowsing   66 §
(USA) 124) [2004 67§: 6s 10m² 10.2f⁴ 10m 10.9m⁴ 10g⁴ 9.7g² 9.9m p10d 10s Aug 24] sturdy mare: modest handicapper: stays 11f: acts on polytrack and good to firm going: tried blinkered/visored, usually wears cheekpieces nowadays: temperamental. *D. E. Cantillon*

HOLLY SPRINGS   2 b.f. (Feb 4) Efisio 120 – Anotheranniversary 95 (Emarati (USA)   81
74) [2004 6g² 6.5g 6g² Oct 11] 40,000F, 120,000Y: sturdy filly: third foal: half-sister to 3-y-o Royal Challenge: dam 2-y-o 5f winner: fairly useful form in sales race and maidens (second at Kempton and Windsor): not sure to stay much beyond 6.5f. *J. H. M. Gosden*

HOLLY WALK   3 ch.f. Dr Fong (USA) 128 – Holly Blue 107 (Bluebird (USA) 125)   53
[2004 46: 8s 12.1s² 14.1s⁵ 12.1g⁵ 10f⁴ f12d³ f12g² 12m f12f³ f12g⁴ Dec 1] sturdy filly: modest maiden handicapper: stays 1½m: acts on fibresand, soft and good to firm going: usually wears headgear: wandered seventh outing. *M. Dods*

HOLLYWOOD CRITIC (USA)   3 b.g. Theatrical 128 – Lyphard's Starlite (USA)   62
(Lyphard (USA) 132) [2004 8g 10.5g 8.3f⁵ 11.1s³ Aug 17] leggy gelding: half-brother to several winners in USA, including Escrito (by Cox's Ridge), also useful 6f to 1¼m winner in Ireland: dam unraced half-sister to top-class sprinter/miler Moorestyle: modest maiden: stays 11f: acts on soft ground: raced freely last 2 starts, reared leaving stall final one. *P. Monteith*

HOLLYWOOD HENRY (IRE)   4 b.g. Bahhare (USA) 122 – Takeshi (IRE) 67   63
(Cadeaux Genereux 131) [2004 –: 8.1m* 8.5d⁶ 8m p8g⁴ p9.5d⁴ p9.5g Nov 27] well-made gelding: modest performer nowadays: won handicap at Warwick in June: stays 1m: acts on polytrack, soft and good to firm going: tried blinkered, wore cheekpieces in 2004. *J. Akehurst*

HOLY ORDERS (IRE)   7 b.g. Unblest 117 – Shadowglow (Shaadi (USA) 126) [2004   109 §
114: 14m⁴ 22.2f⁴ 12m⁶ 14g* 20m⁵ 15.5s 16d⁴ Nov 3] smallish gelding: useful performer nowadays: won listed race at Fairyhouse (beat Mzuki by 3½ lengths) in August: credit-able fifth to Westerner in Prix du Cadran at Longchamp (unimpressive to post) next time:

below form in Prix Royal-Oak on same course and listed race at Musselburgh after: stays 2m (well below best in Queen Alexandra Stakes at Royal Ascot second start): acts on heavy and good to firm going: blinkered: held up: travels strongly, and sometimes finds little: sometimes slowly away: ridden by claimer D. Condon (unable to claim 6 of 7 outings in 2004): unreliable. *W. P. Mullins, Ireland*

HOME AFFAIRS 2 b.c. (Mar 2) Dansili 127 – Orford Ness 107 (Selkirk (USA) 129) [2004 7g⁵ 7g* 7s Oct 16] close-coupled, quite attractive colt: good walker: third foal: half-brother to very smart French winner around 1¼m Weightless (by In The Wings) and fairly useful French 10.5f winner Castle Rising (by Indian Ridge): dam, won Prix de Sandringham, also 1m winner at 2 yrs: landed odds in maiden at Yarmouth in September in good style by 3 lengths from Notability: 12/1, last of 9 in Dewhurst Stakes at Newmarket, failing to settle: should stay 1m: well regarded, and probably a useful prospect at least. *Sir Michael Stoute* **94 p**

HOMEBRED STAR 3 ch.g. Safawan 118 – Celtic Chimes (Celtic Cone 116) [2004 8.3d 7g 7.1m Aug 5] well held in maidens, starting slowly. *P. Bowen* **–**

HOME BY SOCKS (IRE) 5 ch.m. Desert King (IRE) 129 – Propitious (IRE) 101 (Doyoun 124) [2004 7s 10.3m Jun 26] leggy, close-coupled mare: maiden: no form since 2 yrs. *M. C. Chapman* **–**

HOME COMING 6 br.g. Primo Dominie 121 – Carolside 108 (Music Maestro 119) [2004 –: f6g⁶ f7g Jan 14] little form: tried visored. *P. S. Felgate* **–**

HOME FRONT (IRE) 3 b.g. Intikhab (USA) 135 – Felicita (IRE) 97 (Catrail (USA) 123) [2004 5d Aug 28] 66/1 and very green, showed little in maiden at Beverley. *Ms Deborah J. Evans* **–**

HOMERIC TROJAN 4 ch.c. Hector Protector (USA) 124 – Housefull 81 (Habitat 134) [2004 –: f8f⁶ f11s 16.1v f12g⁶ f16.2m⁶ Apr 19] tall, quite good-topped colt: little form. *M. Brittain* **–**

HOMEWARD (IRE) 3 ch.f. Kris 135 – Home Truth 98 (Known Fact (USA) 135) [2004 –p: 7.1m⁵ 8g Aug 28] sturdy filly: half-sister to several winners, including very smart 6f/7f winner Susu (by Machiavellian) and useful 6f winner Cadeaux Cher (by Cadeaux Genereux): dam 7f/1m winner: poor maiden: should stay 1m: raced only on good/good to firm ground. *A. M. Balding* **49**

HOMME DANGEREUX 2 b.c. (Mar 17) Royal Applause 124 – Happy Lady (FR) 72 (Cadeaux Genereux 131) [2004 f6g³ 5m f5m⁵ 7.1d p6g⁴ Dec 17] modest maiden: stays 6f: acts on all-weather, no form on turf: blinkered (ran creditably) final start. *C. R. Egerton* **55**

HONEST INJUN 3 b.c. Efisio 120 – Sioux 76 (Kris 135) [2004 77p: f7g* 8.3s⁴ 9v⁴ 8m 7.9d⁵ 8g⁴ 8d⁵ 7d² 8d² 8g⁵ p7.1g Dec 11] sturdy colt: fairly useful performer: won maiden at Wolverhampton in January: creditable efforts last 6 turf starts (claimed from B. Hills £20,000 after fourth of them): should stay 1¼m: acts on fibresand and heavy ground. *J. G. M. O'Shea* **80**

HONEYMOONING 3 b.f. Groom Dancer (USA) 128 – Ever Genial 117 (Brigadier Gerard 144) [2004 10s 12m⁴ 12.1g³ 10s Aug 5] useful-looking filly: half-sister to several winners, including 5f and 7f winner Present Laughter (by Cadeaux Genereux) and 1¾m and 2¼m winner Receptionist (by Reference Point): dam 7f/1m winner, including May Hill and Hungerford Stakes: clearly best effort in maidens when fourth to Larkwine at Newmarket second start: should stay 1¾m: acts on good to firm ground. *H. R. A. Cecil* **70**

HONEY RYDER 2 b.f. (Feb 5) Compton Place 125 – Urania 66 (Most Welcome 131) [2004 6m² 5.2m² 6.5g 6g⁴ Sep 30] 42,000Y: leggy filly: fluent mover: third foal: half-sister to smart German 6f to 1m winner Lucky Strike (by Petong) and fairly useful 1999 2-y-o 5f winner Caxton Lad (by Cyrano de Bergerac): dam placed at 1m/1¼m: fair maiden: needs to settle to stay beyond 6f: best efforts on good to firm going. *D. R. Loder* **77**

HONEY'S GIFT 5 b.m. Terimon 124 – Honeycroft (Crofter (USA) 124) [2004 –: p10g Mar 2] rather leggy mare: maiden: lightly raced and little form since 2002: tried in cheekpieces. *G. G. Margarson* **–**

HONEYSTREET (IRE) 4 b.f. Woodborough (USA) 112 – Ring of Kerry (IRE) 67 (Kenmare (FR) 125) [2004 62: 12.3g 9g Jun 30] sparely-made filly: well held both starts in 2004: wore cheekpieces last 6 outings in 2003. *J. D. Frost* **–**

HONORINE (IRE) 4 b.f. Mark of Esteem (IRE) 137 – Blue Water (USA) 104 (Bering 136) [2004 89: 8f⁶ 9g 8g⁵ 10g* 10d 10.3s Nov 6] tall, leggy filly: fairly useful handi- **86**

capper: won at Nottingham in September: stays 1¼m: acts on good to firm and good to soft ground: usually held up: sold 50,000 gns. *J. W. Payne*

HONOR ROUGE (IRE) 5 ch.m. Highest Honor (FR) 124 – Ayers Rock (IRE) 95 (In The Wings 128) [2004 86: 12g⁶ 11.9f Aug 3] good-topped mare: well below form both starts on Flat in 2004. *D. G. Bridgwater* —

HONOUR HIGH 2 gr.g. (Feb 18) Cloudings (IRE) 112 – Meant To Be 84 (Morston (FR) 125) [2004 8m 8g 7.1d⁵ Oct 9] seemingly modest form on first start in maidens: should stay at least 1¼m. *Lady Herries* **56 ?**

HOOPS AND BLADES 3 gr.c. Peintre Celebre (USA) 137 – Mare Aux Fees (Kenmare (FR) 125) [2004 8g 8m 8g 10.5g 18d Aug 19] shallow-girthed colt: well held in maidens/handicap: tried tongue tied: sold 4,000 gns, sent to Sweden. *N. P. Littmoden* —

HOPE AN GLORY (IRE) 2 ch.c. (Feb 23) Nashwan (USA) 135 – Susi Wong (IRE) (Selkirk (USA) 129) [2004 p8g⁴ p8.6g⁴ Dec 3] 11,000Y: second foal: half-brother to 3-y-o La Petite Chinoise: dam German 1m winner: fair form in maidens at Lingfield and Wolverhampton (not knocked about): will stay at least 1¼m. *W. R. Swinburn* **72**

HOPELESSLY DEVOTED 2 b.f. (Apr 14) Compton Place 125 – Alpi Dora (Valiyar 129) [2004 6g 5g⁶ 5s* f6s 5.9g⁵ 5f⁴ Sep 13] good-topped filly: half-sister to several winners, including fairly useful 2003 2-y-o 6f winner Vilamoura (by Forzando) and 17f winner Windmill Lane (by Saddlers' Hall): dam Italian 7.5f (at 2 yrs) and 8.5f winner: modest performer: won claimer at Haydock in August: respectable fourth in nursery at Redcar: should stay 6f: acts on soft going, probably on firm. *P. C. Haslam* **57**

HOPE SOUND (IRE) 4 b.g. Turtle Island (IRE) 123 – Lucky Pick 69 (Auction Ring (USA) 123) [2004 68?: 16.1v 15.8m⁴ p16g Nov 30] modest maiden: probably stays 2m: acts on good to firm and good to soft going: visored final 3-y-o start, wore cheekpieces in 2004. *B. Ellison* **61**

HORIZONTAL (USA) 4 ch.g. Distant View (USA) 126 – Proud Lou (USA) (Proud Clarion) [2004 59: p6g⁶ p5g⁶ 5s 8.1v 7f⁵ p10g f6g Dec 7] sturdy gelding: modest maiden: left H. Collingridge after reappearance, V. Smith after fifth start and R. Ingram prior to final one: free-going sort, and probably best at short of 1m: acts on firm and soft ground. *N. A. Twiston-Davies* **57**

HORMUZ (IRE) 8 b.g. Hamas (IRE) 125§ – Balqis (USA) 93 (Advocator) [2004 66, a56: 8v 7.1f 7.6g 9.3m Sep 11] big, heavy-topped gelding: no form in 2004: tried in cheekpieces. *Paul Johnson* —

HORNER (USA) 3 b.c. Rahy (USA) 115 – Dynashore (CAN) (Dynaformer (USA)) [2004 79: 8g 11.6g⁴ 12.1g² 12.1g² 12.6m* 12d 12m³ 12g² Sep 8] good-bodied colt: fairly useful performer: won maiden at Warwick in June: good second to Nordwind in handicap at Epsom final start: stays 12.6f: acts on good to firm going: blinkered (raced freely) penultimate outing: usually waited with: sold to Saudi Arabia. *P. F. I. Cole* **88**

HORNINGSHEATH 2 ch.f. (Mar 22) Royal Applause 124 – Pacifica 90 (Robellino (USA) 127) [2004 6d 7s Oct 27] 32,000Y: good-topped filly: third foal: dam, 2-y-o 5f winner, out of half-sister to smart miler Nicolotte: better effort in maidens when tenth at Yarmouth final start, racing freely. *C. F. Wall* **52**

HORNPIPE 2 b.c. (Mar 10) Danehill (USA) 126 – Dance Sequence (USA) 105 (Mr Prospector (USA)) [2004 5m⁶ 6.1g* Jun 21] close-coupled colt: fourth foal: half-brother to fairly useful 2000 2-y-o 5f winner Dance On (by Caerleon) and useful 1¼m/1½m winner Sequential (by Rainbow Quest): dam, 2-y-o 6f (Lowther Stakes) winner who stayed 1m, sister to smart American performers around 1m Souvenir Copy and Gold Tribute: much better effort in maidens when winning at Nottingham easily by 5 lengths, making most: should stay 1m: sure to progress. *Sir Michael Stoute* **86 p**

HORS LA LOI (FR) 8 ch.g. Exit To Nowhere (USA) 122 – Kernia (IRE) (Raise A Cup (USA)) [2004 10m May 18] ex-French gelding: won maiden and minor event at Lyon Villeurbanne at 2 yrs: left N. Clement's stable after second start in 1999: fairly useful jumper nowadays: well held on belated return to Flat, slowly away. *Ian Williams* —

HOT LIPS PAGE (FR) 3 b.f. Hamas (IRE) 125§ – Salt Peanuts (IRE) (Salt Dome (USA)) [2004 72?: 7m⁵ 8.1m* 8.3f⁴ 8f 8.3d p8g p8g² p9.5g p8.6g Dec 27] leggy, close-coupled filly: fair performer: won handicap at Chepstow in June: claimed from R. Hannon after seventh start: stays 1m: acts on polytrack and firm going: well held in cheekpieces final outing: none too reliable. *N. P. Littmoden* **78**

HOUDINI BAY (IRE) 2 b.f. (Feb 17) Indian Lodge (IRE) 127 – Do The Right Thing 71 (Busted 134) [2004 5d f5m 6f² f8g p8.6g⁶ Dec 11] 6,500Y: fourth foal: half-sister to **42**

5-y-o Nemo Fugat and 3-y-o Lady Bahia: dam 1½m winner: poor maiden: probably stays 8.6f. *R. P. Elliott*

HOUSE MARTIN 2 b.f. (Mar 29) Spectrum (IRE) 126 – Guignol (IRE) 80 (Anita's **73**
Prince 126) [2004 7m⁴ 7g Sep 2] good-topped filly: first foal: dam, Irish 5f winner, half-
sister to smart French/Italian miler Sole Che Sorgi and useful Italian sprinter Sotabras-
ciet: better effort in maidens when staying-on fourth to Fongtastic at Newmarket: likely
to stay 1m. *A. M. Balding*

HOUSE OF BLUES 3 b.g. Grand Lodge (USA) 125 – Sartigila 67 (Efisio 120) [2004 **55**
59: 10.2g f12m 10m⁵ 15.8m³ Aug 3] close-coupled, useful-looking gelding: modest
maiden: stays 2m: acts on polytrack and good to firm ground. *J. A. Osborne*

HOUT BAY 7 ch.g. Komaite (USA) – Maiden Pool 85 (Sharpen Up 127) [2004 62: **83**
f5s* p6g³ f6g⁶ 5d² 5.1s⁴ 5d* 5d* 5d³ 5d* 5d⁶ 5s p5.1g Nov 13] big, lengthy gelding: fairly
useful handicapper: won at Southwell (dead-heat) in January, Newmarket and Beverley
on consecutive days in August and Ayr (beat Mr Wolf by 1¼ lengths) in September: best
at 5f/easy 6f: acts on all-weather, firm and good to soft going: blinkered final 6-y-o start:
usually waited with: consistent. *R. A. Fahey*

HOV 4 gr.g. Petong 126 – Harifa (Local Suitor (USA) 128) [2004 88: f9.4g f11s 8v 7s² **79**
6s⁶ 8.1s 8m May 18] leggy, quite good-topped gelding: fair performer: stays 8.5f: acts
on all-weather, best efforts on turf on going softer than good: tried in cheekpieces: often
races freely: inconsistent. *J. J. Quinn*

HOWARDS DREAM (IRE) 6 b.g. King's Theatre (IRE) 128 – Keiko 76 (Generous **–**
(IRE) 139) [2004 53: 14g 10g⁴ 7.2m 11.1g⁶ 13m 12m 13g 12.1f⁵ 10.9s⁴ 13.1s Oct 30]
little form in 2004. *D. A. Nolan*

HOWARDS PRINCESS 2 gr.f. (Feb 28) Lujain (USA) 119 – Grey Princess (IRE) **65**
92 (Common Grounds 118) [2004 6g⁵ 5d² 5d² 5g⁴ 5g Sep 25] neat filly: first foal: dam
2-y-o 5f/6f winner: fair maiden: should stay 6f: best efforts on good to soft going.
J. S. Goldie

HOWARDS ROCKET 3 ch.g. Opening Verse (USA) 126 – Houston Heiress (USA) **–**
(Houston (USA)) [2004 9.2d 8.1g 8.3f⁶ 9.1g 7.2s Aug 20] little form in maidens/
handicaps, leaving I. Semple after debut. *J. S. Goldie*

HOWS THAT 2 ch.f. (Mar 23) Vettori (IRE) 119 – Royalty (IRE) (Fairy King (USA)) **61**
[2004 6g 7m 6s 7g 6d² 6m* f6g p8g⁴ f8g* p8.6g Dec 31] angular filly: first foal: dam
unraced sister to useful Irish 7f/1m performers Crown Regent and Mysterious Ways:
modest performer: left P. McBride after fifth start: won selling nursery at Newcastle in
October and claimer at Southwell in November: stays 1m: acts on fibresand (poor efforts
on polytrack), good to firm and good to soft going. *K. R. Burke*

HOW'S THINGS 4 b.g. Danzig Connection (USA) – Dim Ots 92 (Alhijaz 122) [2004 **?**
78: f8.5s⁶ 8.1g 9d 8.1s p7.1d² p8.6g Nov 13] good-topped gelding: fair performer: stays **a74**
9.4f: acts on all-weather, little form on turf in 2004: tried visored/in cheekpieces: sometimes races freely. *D. Haydn Jones*

HSI WANG MU (IRE) 3 ch.f. Dr Fong (USA) 128 – Oh Hebe (IRE) 74 (Night Shift **48**
(USA)) [2004 50: f9.4s² f8.5s⁵ 10d 10s⁵ 8f 10.2f p8.6g Nov 6] sparely-made filly: modest **a61**
maiden: stays 1¼m: acts on fibresand, soft and good to firm going. *R. Brotherton*

HUBOOB (FR) 2 b. or br.g. (Jan 16) Almutawakel 126 – Atnab (USA) 64 (Riverman **– p**
(USA) 131) [2004 8g Sep 22] third foal: dam, 1½m winner, half-sister to useful middle-
distance stayer Thari: 16/1 and very green, always behind in maiden at Goodwood,
slowly away: gelded after: likely to do better. *M. P. Tregoning*

HUGGIN MAC (IRE) 3 b.f. Spectrum (IRE) 126 – Little Love (Warrshan (USA) 117) **45 ?**
[2004 7s⁶ 7.5m Jun 2] IR 8,500F: unfurnished filly: second foal: dam unraced: poor form
in maidens at York and Beverley. *N. Bycroft*

HUGO THE BOSS (IRE) 2 ch.g. (Apr 15) Trans Island 119 – Heartland 72 (North- **–**
fields (USA)) [2004 p7g p7g p8g p6g Nov 16] well held in maidens at Lingfield:
blinkered final start. *J. R. Boyle*

HUGS DESTINY (IRE) 3 b.g. Victory Note (USA) 120 – Embracing 91 (Reference **75**
Point 139) [2004 7.9m⁵ p10d² Jun 26] IR 7,500F, 28,000Y: strong, sturdy gelding: fifth
foal: half-brother to smart Hugs Dancer (by Cadeaux Genereux), winner at 12.4f to 21f in
Britain and Group 2 1m winner in Australia, and 5-y-o Dance Light: dam 1½m/1¾m
winner: fair form in maidens at York and Lingfield: will stay at least 1½m. *J. G. Given*

betfred.com Mile, Sandown—a well-contested renewal goes to Hurricane Alan (third left) from Gateman (second left), Soviet Song (rail) and Norse Dancer (right)

HULA BALLEW 4 ch.f. Weldnaas (USA) 112 – Ballon 63 (Persian Bold 123) [2004 **70** 70: 8v 8d⁵ 8.3g 8g 7.2g⁵ 8m⁵ 7m 8m* 8g⁵ 10.1m⁵ 7.9g² 8g³ 8m Sep 29] smallish filly: fair handicapper: won at Pontefract in July: best around 1m: acts on good to firm and good to soft ground: wore cheekpieces last 8 starts. *M. Dods*

HUMBLE OPINION 2 br.c. (Apr 5) Singspiel (IRE) 133 – For More (FR) (Sangla- **78 p** more (USA) 126) [2004 p7g² p8m* Dec 21] first foal: dam French 9f to 12.5f and hurdles winner: confirmed debut promise when winning maiden at Lingfield by 3½ lengths from Mickehaha, making all: likely to stay at least 1¼m: open to improvement. *B. J. Meehan*

HUMDINGER (IRE) 4 b.f. Charnwood Forest (IRE) 125 – High Finish 58 (High **–** Line 125) [2004 71d, a66d: f12g f8g p12g 10g p10m f11g Dec 12] fair winner at 3 yrs, no form in 2004: tried visored. *D. Shaw*

HUMID CLIMATE 4 ch.g. Desert King (IRE) 129 – Pontoon 89 (Zafonic (USA) 130) **–** [2004 80: 7s 8f 10g 10d Oct 18] strong, good-bodied gelding: type to carry condition: no form on Flat since winning 1¼m maiden at 3 yrs: very early to post and reluctant to race second outing. *R. A. Fahey*

HUMILITY 3 b.f. Polar Falcon (USA) 126 – Rich In Love (IRE) 95 (Alzao (USA) 117) **–** [2004 –p: 5.1m May 17] well held in maidens at Ascot and Bath. *C. A. Cyzer*

HUM (IRE) 3 ch.f. Cadeaux Genereux 131 – Ensorceleuse (FR) (Fabulous Dancer **–** (USA) 124) [2004 63: 8m 8.5g p8m Dec 8] leggy filly: little form since 2-y-o debut: tried in cheekpieces. *Miss D. A. McHale*

HUMOUROUS (IRE) 2 b.c. (Feb 2) Darshaan 133 – Amusing Time (IRE) 104 **97** (Sadler's Wells (USA) 132) [2004 7m⁵ 8g* 8d Oct 18] well-made colt: second foal: half-brother to 4-y-o Not Amused: dam, French 1¼m winner, sister to smart performer up to 1¼m Musalsal out of Prix Robert Papin winner Ozone Friendly: favourite, won maiden at Kempton in September by short head from Forward Move, making most: ran no sort of race in listed event at Pontefract final outing: will be suited by 1¼m/1½m: tongue tied all starts. *Saeed bin Suroor*

HUNIPOT 2 ch.f. (Apr 5) Aragon 118 – Acinom (Rambo Dancer (CAN) 107) [2004 **–** 5s 5v 5d 5m 5m⁶ 6m Aug 7] 1,100Y: leggy filly: first foal: dam unraced: seems of little account. *M. E. Sowersby*

HUNTER'S VALLEY 3 b.f. Nicolotte 118 – Down The Valley 73 (Kampala 120) **71** [2004 79: 8m 7m² 8m⁴ 8m 8.3m⁴ 7.9g⁴ p8m³ 8g Oct 10] good-bodied filly: fair maiden: stays 7f: raced only on good/good to firm going on turf: folded tamely fourth/fifth starts: sold 10,000 gns. *R. Hannon*

HUNTING LODGE (IRE) 3 ch.g. Grand Lodge (USA) 125 – Vijaya (USA) (Lear **–** Fan (USA) 130) [2004 99: 8g Jul 8] strong gelding: useful performer at 2 yrs: well held in handicap at Newmarket only 3-y-o start: gelded after: should be suited by 1¼m/1½m: visored last 2 starts in 2003. *D. R. Loder*

482

HUNTING PINK 3 b.f. Foxhound (USA) 103 – Dancing Bluebell (IRE) 79 (Bluebird **49** (USA) 125) [2004 52: f7f² f8g³ f8g⁴ f7g³ Feb 19] close-coupled, good-bodied filly: poor maiden: stays 1m: acts on all-weather, raced only on going firmer than good on turf: blinkered (raced freely) final start: tried tongue tied. *H. Morrison*

HURRICANE ALAN (IRE) 4 b. or br.c. Mukaddamah (USA) 125 – Bint Al Balad **118** (IRE) 113: 9g³ 8h⁵ 8f 8g³ 8g 8d³ 8s³ 10m] good-topped colt: smart performer: won betfred.com Mile at Sandown in April by a neck from Gateman: several good efforts after, notably when 2 lengths third to Norse Dancer in Sovereign Stakes at Salisbury seventh start and ½-length second to Cacique in Prix Daniel Wildenstein at Longchamp: stays 1m: acts on firm ground, probably on soft: has been attended by 2 handlers: sometimes races freely. *R. Hannon*

HURRICANE COAST 5 b.g. Hurricane Sky (AUS) – Tread Carefully 51 (Sharpo **87** 132) [2004 68§: f6g* f6g* p6g* p6g³ p5g* f5g³ f6g² p7g f6g p5g⁴ f6s* f6s 7s* 6d⁶ 8v⁶ 7.1g⁴ p6g⁶ p6g p8g p7g Dec 29] tall gelding: fairly useful performer: won seller and claimer (left P. Blockley) at Southwell, apprentice claimer and handicap at Lingfield, and handicaps at Wolverhampton (dead-heated) and Southwell in first half of 2004: best at 5f to 7f: acts on all-weather, firm and soft going: usually blinkered nowadays: edgy sort: carries head awkwardly/tends to hang: tough. *D. Flood*

HURRICANE FLOYD (IRE) 6 ch.g. Pennekamp (USA) 130 – Mood Swings **73 §** (IRE) 77 (Shirley Heights 130) [2004 98§: 7d 8v 7f 7m 8m⁴ 6g² 7.2s p7.1g p7g Dec 4] smallish, sturdy gelding: has a quick action: just fair form in 2004: trained by D. Loder first 5 starts, claimed from D. Nicholls £15,000 after sixth: stays 1m: acts on firm ground, probably not on softer than good: usually tongue tied in 2002/3: tried visored/blinkered: edgy sort (has worn ear plugs): usually slowly away, sometimes markedly so: waited with: unreliable. *D. Flood*

HURSLEY 2 b.f. (Feb 20) Compton Place 125 – Kilcoy (USA) (Secreto (USA) 128) **53** [2004 7.6m 7g Aug 13] 10,000F: half-sister to several winners, including smart 1999 2-y-o 6f/7f winner Sheer Hamas (by Hamas) and fairly useful 1¾m/2m winner Decoy (by Double Eclipse): dam unraced: modest form at Folkestone final start in maidens. *S. Kirk*

HUSKY (POL) 6 b.g. Special Power – Hallo Bambina (POL) (Neman (POL)) [2004 **51** 53: f12g⁵ p10g* p10g³ p10g 10f⁵ 10m⁴ Aug 6] Polish-bred gelding: modest performer: won banded event at Lingfield in April: stays 1¼m: acts on polytrack and good to firm going: tried visored/tongue tied: wears cheekpieces nowadays. *R. M. H. Cowell*

HUXLEY (IRE) 5 b.g. Danehill Dancer (IRE) 117 – Biddy Mulligan (Ballad Rock 122) **82** [2004 87+: 8v 8g 8s 10g 8g⁴ 8.2g 8g* 8.9g Oct 9] leggy gelding: fairly useful handicapper, trained in 2003 by P. Roche in Ireland: best effort in 2004 when winning at Thirsk in September: stays 1¼m: acts on firm and soft going: tried blinkered: tongue tied on third and last 3 starts. *M. G. Quinlan*

HYMN OF VICTORY (IRE) 2 b.c. (Mar 29) Bluebird (USA) 125 – Vaga Follia **59** (IRE) (Alzao (USA) 117) [2004 5f 5g⁵ 6d² 6m⁶ 5g² 5g 6d⁴ p6g⁵ Dec 1] quite attractive colt: modest maiden: should stay 7f: acts on good to soft ground. *T. J. Etherington*

HYMNS AND ARIAS 3 b.f. Mtoto 134 – Ewenny 71 (Warrshan (USA) 117) [2004 **–** 47: f8.5s f11g⁴ 10d 10s f8m 7m Jun 4] smallish filly: poor winner at 2 yrs: little form in 2004: tried in cheekpieces. *Ronald Thompson*

HYPNOTIC 2 ch.c. (Mar 16) Lomitas 129 – Hypnotize 103 (Machiavellian (USA) **99** 123) [2004 p6g⁴ p7g* p7d* p7g³ 8.3d* 8d Sep 18] first foal: dam, 2-y-o 7f winner, closely related to smart performer up to 1m Dazzle: useful performer: won maiden at Lingfield in July, nursery (made most) in August and listed race at Craon (by ½ length from River Bride) in September: last of 7 in Prix des Chenes at Longchamp: will probably stay 1¼m: acts on polytrack and good to soft going. *Sir Mark Prescott*

I

IAMBACK 4 b.f. Perugino (USA) 84 – Smouldering (IRE) (Caerleon (USA) 132) **56** [2004 –§: f9.4g² f7g⁶ f8.5g* f9.4s⁶ f8.5s f8g⁴ f8.5g³ 8.1d f9.4g* f9.4g* p10g f9.4m 7g p8.6g f8g⁶ p8.6g f7g⁴ p8.6g³ Dec 22] leggy filly: modest performer: won maiden in February and 2 banded races in May, all at Wolverhampton: stays 9.4f: acts on all-weather, good to firm and good to soft ground: tried blinkered, usually wears cheekpieces: races prominently: none too genuine. *Miss Gay Kelleway*

IAM FOREVERBLOWING   2 ch.f. (Mar 20) Dr Fong (USA) 128 – Farhana 109 **41** (Fayruz 116) [2004 5s⁵ 5s⁴ 5.7f⁵ f6m 5f 6g 5.1g Aug 19] 14,000F, 23,000Y: third foal: half-sister to 4-y-o Free Wheelin: dam 5.5f/6f (latter including at 2 yrs) winner: poor maiden: form only at 5f on soft going. *S. C. Burrough*

IANINA (IRE)   4 b.f. Eagle Eyed (USA) 111 – Ice Dream (GER) (Mondrian (GER) **102** 125) [2004 8g⁶ 8s 8g 8g² 8g² 8f³ 8m² 8f⁵ 8m² 8d 8s* Nov 7] quite good-topped filly: first foal: dam German 6.5f (at 2 yrs) and 1m winner: useful performer: won listed race at Cologne in November by head from Golden Rose: 25/1, well held in similar event at Goodwood third start: stays 1m: acts on firm and soft ground. *R. Rohne, Germany*

IBERUS (GER)   6 b.g. Monsun (GER) 124 – Iberica (GER) (Green Dancer (USA) **75** 132) [2004 ?: 8g 10.3g 7m 7g⁵ 8.5g⁴ 10.5g² 12f 10g 8.2v⁴ Oct 20] leggy, angular gelding: fair handicapper: effective at 1m to 1½m: acts on any going: tried blinkered/in cheek-pieces: found little seventh/eighth outings. *S. Gollings*

ICANNSHIFT (IRE)   4 b.g. Night Shift (USA) – Cannikin (IRE) 82 (Lahib (USA) **63** 129) [2004 98d: p7g p10g p10g⁶ 9.7d 9.7s² 10d⁴ 10.2s³ 10g 10f³ 9g⁶ 10m³ p10g 10.1d³ 10m 10.1f⁴ 10.9m² 9m⁶ 8g⁵ p10m Dec 21] small, good-bodied gelding: modest handi-capper: made all at Leicester in April: left S. Dow prior to final outing: stays 1¼m: acts on firm and soft going: tried visored: usually races up with pace. *T. M. Jones*

ICARUS DREAM (IRE)   3 ch.g. Intikhab (USA) 135 – Nymphs Echo (IRE) (Muj- **75** tahid (USA) 118) [2004 8m⁴ 9g⁶ 9f² 12f 9s² 10f 11g 16s Aug 28] leggy gelding: fair maiden: left D. Weld in Ireland after fifth start, well held on Flat after: stayed 9f: acted on firm and soft going: blinkered third/fourth outings, wore cheekpieces seventh one (raced freely): won twice over hurdles in autumn: dead. *P. R. Hedger*

ICE AND FIRE   5 b.g. Cadeaux Genereux 131 – Tanz (IRE) 79 (Sadler's Wells (USA) **–** 132) [2004 63?: f11s Feb 26] quite good-topped gelding: well held only 5-y-o outing: tried in cheekpieces, blinkered last 2 outings. *B. D. Leavy*

ICECAP   4 b.f. Polar Falcon (USA) 126 – Warning Light (High Top 131) [2004 60: f8m **58** 7f* 8m 7.1g 7m Sep 9] lengthy filly: modest performer: left Miss E. Lavelle after reap-pearance: won handicap at Brighton in August: effective at 7f to easy 1¼m: acts on all-weather and firm ground. *W. G. M. Turner*

ICED DIAMOND (IRE)   5 b.g. Petardia 113 – Prime Site (IRE) (Burslem 123) [2004 **59** 60: f7g* f7s 8m 7m 7.6g 7g 7m⁴ 7.6m⁴ 7g 6.9g² 7.1m⁶ p7g⁵ f7g⁶ p7g⁶ Dec 30] good- **a65** topped gelding: fair handicapper on all-weather, modest on turf: won at Wolverhampton in February: best recent efforts at 6f/7f: acts on all-weather and firm going: tried in head-gear/tongue tied: sometimes slowly away: often races freely: wayward. *W. M. Brisbourne*

ICE DRAGON   3 b.f. Polar Falcon (USA) 126 – Qilin (IRE) 94 (Second Set (IRE) 127) **–** [2004 73: 7f 7s p7g Dec 4] fair maiden at 2 yrs: well held in 2004. *M. H. Tompkins*

ICEMAN   2 b.c. (Mar 27) Polar Falcon (USA) 126 – Virtuous 92 (Exit To Nowhere **117** (USA) 122) [2004 5.1s² 6m* 6f* 7f² 6g³ 7s⁴ Oct 16]
        The Iceman cometh. Well, that was certainly true for much of Iceman's first season, as he quickly developed into a smart performer, but defeats in the Middle Park Stakes and Dewhurst Stakes at Newmarket on his last two starts saw earlier enthusiasm about his classic prospects melt away. Now it is a question of where does he go from here? Iceman started favourite for the Middle Park, but was found wanting for speed on his return to six furlongs and finished just over three lengths third to Ad Valorem, pushed along more or less from the off, dropping back to last place two out before running on strongly on meeting the rising ground. The extra furlong of the Dewhurst showed Iceman in a better light and he matched the pick of his earlier form when finishing fourth to Shamardal, again beaten a little over three lengths.
        Iceman was close to missing the Middle Park, his trainer John Gosden having threatened to withdraw him because he considered the ground, which had been watered earlier in the week, to have become very poached following rain, particularly on the far side of the course where the stalls had been placed for the first day of the three-day fixture. After the stewards decided to have the stalls moved to the centre of the course for the remainder of the meeting, as Gosden publicly requested, Iceman was allowed to take his chance. After the Dewhurst, Gosden was

Coventry Stakes, Royal Ascot—Iceman is about to overhaul Council Member (right) in the opening race of the Royal meeting; Capable Guest (left) is about to do likewise to Tony James (No.13) for third

to make his feelings known about another very different matter. On a day which saw the first live broadcast using a prototype speed-sensing system, which purports to pinpoint a horse's position during a race as well as its speed and the exact distance it travels, Gosden refused to allow Iceman to carry the transmitter used to send signals to fixed-point receivers. Aidan O'Brien hadn't allowed his runner in the previous race, the Champion Stakes, to carry the transmitter either but had a change of heart with his Dewhurst representative, Oratorio, who went on to finish second. A week later the connections of Self Defense and Sharp As A Tack refused to let their horses run with a speed-sensing chip at Newbury. There was no rule saying that horses had to carry the chip, and, unless one is introduced, it seems unlikely that Gosden will change his mind as he feels the device used is too cumbersome. While Channel 4 sees the displaying of speed-sensing information as a novel development, the on-screen graphics have so far disappeared from view—presumably for some technical reason—in the last two furlongs or so, the most significant section of any race, in Britain at least, for anyone studying times. Back in 1998 we enthused about electronic sectional timing becoming available on the Rowley Mile at Newmarket, but that equipment did not operate when the new speed-sensing system was in use for televised races, denying accurate and vital information for sectional analysis. The Rowley Mile, incidentally, remains the only turf course in Britain with equipment necessary for comprehensive sectional timing. Hopefully, 2005 will see overdue progress made.

Incidentally, Gosden was also one of the trainers most critical of the BHB's recently instituted (albeit very selectively) forty-eight-hour declaration system, making his feelings known when taking Percussionist out of the Chester Vase because he considered the ground would be too firm for the colt. Had there been an overnight declaration stage for the race then Gosden would have run Percussionist, as by that time the ground had eased to good to soft following heavy rain. In November, the BHB announced that it would reduce the number of races with the forty-eight-hour declaration stage. From January 1st, Group 2 and Group 3 races and heritage handicaps will revert to a twenty-four-hour final declaration, though courses staging a heritage handicap may stick with the forty-eight-hour declaration if they wish. The forty-eight-hour system will remain for all Sunday racing and Group 1s, and was in place for all-weather racing from November 2004 to March 2005.

Iceman was a promising second to Johnny Jumpup in a maiden at Bath on his debut and went one better in a similar event at Newbury on his next start before being sent to Royal Ascot for the Coventry Stakes, a race re-elevated to Group 2 status. It attracted thirteen runners, of which all bar Capable Guest were winners, including the Godolphin representative Council Member, successful in a maiden at Newcastle on his only start. There was nothing to choose between Iceman and Council Member in the betting, the pair going off joint favourites at 5/1, and there was little between them at the finish. Iceman was unable to go the early pace and was one of the first off the bit, but he eventually weaved his way through, causing minor interference when switched right over a furlong out. By this time Council Member had got to the front, but Iceman, running on strongly, collared him near the finish and won going away by half a length. Iceman looked sure to benefit from a step up to seven furlongs and, following a three-month break, he duly improved again when given the opportunity to tackle that trip in the Champagne Stakes at Doncaster. A penalty for his Coventry Stakes win meant that Iceman had to concede 5 lb to all nine of his rivals, and, despite the longer trip, he was again soon in rear and off the bridle. Iceman did come through to lead just inside the final furlong and kept on strongly, though edging left, only to be picked off close home and beaten half a length by Etlaala, who had met trouble in running. This performance marked the end of Iceman's improvement for the season, but there may be better to come from him at three, when another step up in trip should suit.

		Nureyev	Northern Dancer
	Polar Falcon (USA)	(b 1977)	Special
	(b or br 1987)	Marie d'Argonne	Jefferson
Iceman		(ch 1981)	Mohair
(b.c. Mar 27, 2002)		Exit To Nowhere	Irish River
	Virtuous	(b 1988)	Coup de Folie
	(b 1995)	Exclusive Virtue	Shadeed
		(b 1988)	Exclusive Order

Iceman may stay a mile and a quarter. While his sire Polar Falcon showed plenty of speed, he also possessed enough stamina to win the Lockinge Stakes over a mile and has been responsible for plenty of winners who stay better than he himself did. Iceman's dam Virtuous won a one-mile maiden at Nottingham at two, having finished fourth in the May Hill Stakes on her previous start; easily her better performance at three was when third in a listed event at Lingfield

Cheveley Park Stud's "Iceman"

run over a distance just short of a mile and a half. The grandam Exclusive Virtue, a seven-furlong winner at two who stayed a mile and a half, is a half-sister to the Two Thousand Guineas winner Entrepreneur, to the Coronation Stakes winner Exclusive (also by Polar Falcon, and now the dam of Chic and the very promising two-year-old Echelon) and to the smart middle-distance performers Dance A Dream and Sadler's Image. The great grandam Exclusive Order was a French six-furlong to seven-furlong winner who stayed a mile. Iceman is the third foal of Virtuous. Her first was Peace (by Sadler's Wells), a fairly useful filly who won a ten-furlong maiden at three; her second, Liberty (by Singspiel), won a six-furlong maiden at Windsor on the second of two starts at two. Iceman, named after the top American jockey George 'Iceman' Woolf, who was played by Gary Stevens in the 2003 film *Seabiscuit*, has yet to encounter heavy going but has shown already that he is effective on any other turf surface. Iceman was one of the best-looking individuals among the 2004 juveniles, being a strong, good-bodied individual. He was also one of the best movers, showing a quick, fluent action. *J. H. M. Gosden*

ICENASLICE (IRE) 3 b.f. Fayruz 116 – Come Dancing 48 (Suave Dancer (USA) 136) [2004 60: 5d 5m* f5g4 5d* 5m 5m4 5s 5d* Sep 27] leggy filly: fair performer: won handicaps at Thirsk (apprentice event) and Newcastle in June: best at 5f: acts on good to firm and good to soft on fibresand: edgy (below form) penultimate outing: usually races up with pace. *J. J. Quinn* — **78**

ICENI WARRIOR 2 b.g. (Mar 22) Lake Coniston (IRE) 131 – Swing Job 58 (Ezzoud (IRE) 126) [2004 p5g5 Mar 26] first foal: dam, maiden, stayed 1½m: green, fifth in maiden at Lingfield. *T. G. Mills* — **47**

ICE PALACE 3 ch.f. Polar Falcon (USA) 126 – White Palace 80 (Shirley Heights 130) [2004 99+: 8.5g3 8f2 10.1s* 10.1s4 9g Oct 2] tall, leggy filly: fluent mover: useful performer, lightly raced: won listed event at Newcastle (beat Blue Oasis a neck) in June: good fourth to Posteritas in listed handicap at Yarmouth penultimate outing, ending up isolated against far rail: below form in Cambridgeshire at Newmarket final start: stayed 1¼m: unraced on heavy going, acted on any other turf: stud. *J. R. Fanshawe* — **100**

ICE PLANET 3 b.c. Polar Falcon (USA) 126 – Preference (Efisio 120) [2004 7s 5s3 7d5 6d 6g5 Jul 22] 22,000F, 9,000 2-y-o: useful-looking colt: first foal: dam unraced sister to smart 6f/7f performer Casteddu: fair maiden: good fifth to Commando Scott in handicap at Doncaster final start, keeping on from poor position: stays 6f: raced only on good ground and softer: lightly raced, and capable of better still. *D. Nicholls* — **67 p**

ICE RUBY 2 b.f. (Feb 20) Polar Prince (IRE) 117 – Simply Style (Bairn (USA) 126) [2004 5g 5g f5m May 10] 500Y, resold 1,500Y: close-coupled filly: sister to 4-y-o Stylish Prince and half-sister to 3 winners, including 1997 2-y-o 5f winner Lady Moll (by King's Signet), later successful in USA: dam unraced: well beaten in maidens/claimer: unruly and withdrawn in September. *D. Shaw* — **–**

ICEY RUN 4 b.g. Runnett 125 – Polar Storm (IRE) 76 (Law Society (USA) 130) [2004 –: 14m p16g6 p12m Dec 8] little form. *D. G. Bridgwater* — **–**

ICING 2 br.f. (Feb 21) Polar Falcon (USA) 126 – Dance Steppe (Rambo Dancer (CAN) 107) [2004 6.1d6 p6d4 p7g* 7g Oct 2] 54,000F: useful-looking filly: third foal: half-sister to useful performer up to 1m in Italy/USA La Martina (by Atraf): dam no form: fair performer: won maiden at Lingfield in September: poorly drawn in nursery final start: should stay 1m: acts on polytrack. *W. J. Haggas* — **74**

IDEALISTIC (IRE) 3 b.f. Unfuwain (USA) 131 – L'Ideale (USA) (Alysheba (USA)) [2004 10g 10.5m2 12.1m2 12.1m2 11.5g2 11.7m* Aug 15] lengthy, angular filly: fourth living foal: half-sister to smart 1¼m/11f winner Shagraan (by Darshaan) and useful 8.5f to 1¼m winner Aegean Dream (by Royal Academy): dam, ran twice in France, half-sister to high-class French performer up to 1½m Loup Sauvage: fairly useful performer: runner-up 3 times prior to landing odds at Bath comfortably by 2½ lengths from Turn 'N Burn, dictating pace: stays 1½m: raced only on good/good to firm going. *L. M. Cumani* — **85**

IDLE JOURNEY (IRE) 3 b.g. Mujadil (USA) 119 – Camassina (IRE) 62 (Taufan (USA) 119) [2004 –: 6v 7m 7m* 8.5g2 8v 8m4 10.1d Oct 16] modest performer: won handicap at Down Royal in June: left R. Donohoe in Ireland prior to penultimate start: stays 8.5f: acts on good to firm ground, well beaten on heavy: tried tongue tied. *M. Scudamore* — **53**

IDLE POWER (IRE) 6 b. or br.g. Common Grounds 118 – Idle Fancy 79 (Mujtahid (USA) 118) [2004 97d: 6s 7.6d 6g* 7f* 6m 7g2 6.5g3 6m 6m 7s2 p7g* 7g* p7.1g p6g — **92**

Oct 31] close-coupled gelding: fairly useful handicapper: won at Goodwood and Brighton (within 48 hrs) in May, and at Lingfield and Goodwood (beat Concer Eto by neck) in September: effective at 6f/7f: acts on polytrack, soft and good to firm going: tried blinkered, usually wears cheekpieces. *J. R. Boyle*

IF BY CHANCE 6 ch.g. Risk Me (FR) 127 – Out of Harmony 79 (Song 132) [2004 **84** 72: f6s 6s² 6s⁴ 6s⁴ 6d* 5g 5m p6g 5s⁴ p6g* p6g Dec 3] strong, close-coupled gelding: poor mover: fairly useful handicapper: better than ever in 2004, winning at Thirsk in May and Wolverhampton in November: best at 5f/6f: acts on all-weather, heavy and good to firm going: usually visored/blinkered: usually front runner. *R. Craggs*

IFFRAAJ 3 b.c. Zafonic (USA) 130 – Pastorale 91 (Nureyev (USA) 131) [2004 88p: **93** 7g⁴ Apr 15] good-bodied colt: fairly useful performer: twice raced at 2 yrs: good fourth to Oasis Star in handicap at Newmarket only outing in 2004: injured after, but stays in training: raced only at 7f. *M. A. Jarvis*

IFFY 3 b.g. Orpen (USA) 116 – Hopesay 84 (Warning 136) [2004 58: p7g⁴ 8m 8.5g⁴ **68** 10m* 10m³ p8.6d p9.5g² p10m Dec 21] workmanlike gelding: fair handicapper: won at Ascot in July: stays 1¼m: acts on polytrack and good to firm going. *P. D. Cundell*

IFIT (IRE) 2 b.f. (Apr 13) Inchinor 119 – Robin (Slip Anchor 136) [2004 7f 6f 7g 8m **52** 7d³ p9.5g Dec 20] €50,000Y: leggy filly: first foal: dam unraced half-sister to very smart performer up to 1¾m Top Class: modest maiden: should stay 1¼m: acts on firm and good to soft ground. *M. R. Channon*

IF PARADISE 3 b.c. Compton Place 125 – Sunley Stars (Sallust 134) [2004 102: 5s* **107** 6g 5m6 5f 5m 5m 5m² 5d² 6s Oct 22] sturdy, useful-looking colt: useful performer: won listed rated stakes at Haydock (beat Crafty Fancy by 2½ lengths) in April: creditable efforts after when runner-up in minor event at Beverley and handicap at Newmarket (beaten ½ length by Corridor Creeper): best at 5f: acts on soft and good to firm going: sometimes bandaged in front: often races prominently. *R. Hannon*

IFTERADH 3 b.c. Bahhare (USA) 122 – Matila (IRE) 98 (Persian Bold 123) [2004 **95** p7g* 7g² Apr 15] useful-looking colt: good walker: half-brother to several winners, including smart 7f (at 2 yrs) to 8.5f winner Easaar (by Machiavellian): dam 6f winner: successful debut in maiden at Lingfield in March: useful form when neck second to Oasis Star in handicap at Newmarket only other start: raced only at 7f: dead. *B. Hanbury*

IFTIKHAR (USA) 5 b.g. Storm Cat (USA) – Muhbubh (USA) 108 (Blushing Groom **60** (FR) 131) [2004 61: 10.5m 8.1g 10.5s 10f⁴ 10.4m 10g 9d 10s p12.2g² p12.2g² p12.2g⁵ p9.5g² p9.5g² Dec 22] big, strong gelding: modest maiden: stays 1½m: acts on polytrack and firm ground: blinkered (raced freely) seventh outing: sometimes slowly away. *W. M. Brisbourne*

IGNITION 2 ch.f. (Apr 28) Rock City 120 – Fire Sprite 83 (Mummy's Game 120) **62** [2004 6m⁵ 7s⁴ 7.1g³ 6.9m⁴ 7m 7g Oct 5] 6,200Y: leggy, workmanlike filly: sister to 5-y-o TBM Can and half-sister to 3 winners, including useful 6f winner Always Alight (by Never So Bold): dam 2-y-o 5f winner: modest maiden: stays 7f: acts on soft ground. *W. M. Brisbourne*

I GOT RHYTHM 6 gr.m. Lycius (USA) 124 – Eurythmic 58 (Pharly (FR) 130) [2004 **–** 45: 16s 14.4v Apr 26] leggy mare: has a round action: lightly raced on Flat in recent years: no form in 2004. *Mrs M. Reveley*

I HAD A DREAM 3 b.f. Bering 136 – Dirigeante (FR) (Lead On Time (USA) 123) **96** [2004 8g³ 10s³ 10s* 8s 10d² 10.3s Nov 6] €250,000Y: rangy filly: sixth foal: half-sister to several winners abroad, notably smart French 1m/1¼m performer Al Namix (by Lina-mix): dam French 7f winner: useful performer: won minor event at Longchamp in June: left Mme C. Head-Maarek in France, good ½-length second to Sundrop in listed race at Newmarket (mulish stall) on British debut: well below form in similar event at Doncaster final start: stays 1¼m: acts on soft ground. *M. A. Jarvis*

I HAD A SISTER (BEL) 3 ch.g. Bid For Blue 107 – Texas Cowgirl (IRE) 60 (Salt **58** Dome (USA)) [2004 p9.5g p9.5g⁴ p12.2g Dec 4] best effort in maidens at Wolverhampton second start: should stay 1¼m. *P. S. McEntee*

IKAN (IRE) 4 br.f. Sri Pekan (USA) 117 – Iktidar 80 (Green Desert (USA) 127) [2004 **92** 98: p5g 5d³ 5.1g 5s May 12] workmanlike filly: unimpressive mover: fairly useful performer: easily best effort of 2004 when creditable third to Proud Boast in minor event at Beverley second start: below form after: best at 5f: acted on firm and soft going: usually waited with: visits Exceed And Excel. *N. P. Littmoden*

IKHTYAR (IRE) 4 b.c. Unfuwain (USA) 131 – Sabria (USA) (Miswaki (USA) 124) **123**
[2004 124: 8s³ 8m⁶ 10d² 10f³ 10d⁶ 10m³ Jul 19] good-topped, attractive colt: very smart
performer: best efforts in 2004 when neck second to Bandari (pair clear) in Brigadier
Gerard Stakes at Sandown and 2½ lengths third to Rakti in Prince of Wales's Stakes at
Royal Ascot, both in June: visored, below-form third to Kalaman in Scottish Derby at
Ayr final start, wandering: stays 1¼m: acts on firm and good to soft going: sometimes
edges left: became increasingly warm and swished tail in preliminaries at Royal Ascot.
J. H. M. Gosden

IKTIBAS 3 b.c. Sadler's Wells (USA) 132 – Bint Shadayid (USA) 109 (Nashwan **88**
(USA) 135) [2004 8g* 10s⁵ Oct 29] leggy colt: third foal: half-brother to 1¼m winner
Khams-Alhawas (by Marju) who stayed 1½m: dam, 2-y-o 6f/7f winner and third in 1000
Guineas (stayed 1¼m), out of 1000 Guineas winner Shadayid from good family: fairly
useful form: won maiden at Thirsk in September by 9 lengths (slowly away): similar form
when fifth to Spanish Don in listed race at Newmarket, soon beaten as pace picked up
and flashing tail before eased: bred to stay 1½m: tongue tied both starts: left Godolphin.
Saeed bin Suroor

IKTITAF (IRE) 3 b.c. Alhaarth (IRE) 126 – Istibshar (USA) 78 (Mr Prospector (USA)) **88**
[2004 8m 10.2g³ 10.3d* 10m 10g 10.3s³ Oct 22] strong, lengthy colt: fifth living foal:
closely related to fairly useful 7f (in UAE) and 1½m winner Mostabshir (by Unfuwain)
and half-brother to 2 winners, including fairly useful 7f winner Furaat (by Danehill):
dam, 6f winner, sister to US Grade 3 8.5f winner Namaqualand: fairly useful performer:
won maiden at Chester in May: good third to Double Deputy in handicap at Doncaster
final start: will stay 1½m: acts on soft and good to firm ground: sold 85,000 gns.
J. H. M. Gosden

IL CAVALIERE 9 b.g. Mtoto 134 – Kalmia (Miller's Mate 116) [2004 68: 16.2v⁵ 17.1f **–**
Jun 7] good-topped gelding: well held both starts on Flat in 2004. *Mrs M. Reveley*

IL COLOSSEO (IRE) 2 b.g. (Feb 14) Spectrum (IRE) 126 – Valley Lights (IRE) **93**
(Dance of Life (USA)) [2004 7g³ 7.2s⁴ p7.1d* p7.1g* Dec 14] €14,500F: seventh foal:
half-brother to 3 winners, including useful 6f (including at 2 yrs) winner Masha-Il (by
Danehill) and 6-y-o Mumbling: dam, lightly-raced Irish maiden, half-sister to high-class
miler Then Again: fairly useful performer: made all in maiden in November and minor
event (beat Chief Exec by 1¼ lengths) in December, both at Wolverhampton: needs to
settle to stay 1m: acts on polytrack. *Mrs L. Stubbs*

ILE FACILE (IRE) 3 b.c. Turtle Island (IRE) 123 – Easy Pop (IRE) (Shernazar 131) **74**
[2004 f6g² f7g⁴ p7g² f7s⁴ p6g* p8g 10f² 10g 10.5g⁴ 12m* 11.5g⁴ 10g⁵ Jul 30] €18,000Y,
62,000 2-y-o: sturdy colt: third foal: brother to fairly useful Irish 7f winner All Pop and
half-brother to useful 2002 2-y-o 1m/8.5f winner Grand (by Grand Lodge): dam unraced
half-sister to very smart Irish St Leger third Lord Duke: fair performer: won maiden
at Lingfield in February and handicap at Catterick in July: stays easy 1½m: acts on
all-weather and firm going: tongue tied 5 of last 6 starts: sold 20,000 gns in October.
N. P. Littmoden

ILE MICHEL 7 b.g. Machiavellian (USA) 123 – Circe's Isle (Be My Guest (USA) **67**
126) [2004 98: f8.5s 7g 10.2g⁴ 10.4m³ 8.3m 8g p7.1g⁵ p7.1g⁶ p7.1d Nov 4] good-topped
gelding: fair performer: stays easy 1¼m: acts on polytrack and firm ground (possibly not
on softer than good): sometimes carries head high/hangs left. *J. G. M. O'Shea*

I'LL DO IT TODAY 3 b.g. Mtoto 134 – Knayton Lass 94 (Presidium 124) [2004 10v⁶ **–**
10s Nov 1] well held in maidens at Nottingham and Redcar. *J. M. Jefferson*

ILLEANA (GER) 3 ch.f. Lomitas 129 – Illyria (IRE) 66 (Nashwan (USA) 135) [2004 **62**
–p: 9.7s⁴ 10.2g 11.6s 12.4g* 11.5g p12g³ 16g 16g p12.2g⁶ Nov 8] modest performer: won
apprentice minor event at Newcastle in June: should stay 1¾m: acts on polytrack and soft
going: raced freely third start: none too reliable. *W. R. Muir*

I'LL FLY 4 ch.g. Polar Falcon (USA) 126 – I'll Try 71 (Try My Best (USA) 130) [2004 **–**
10d Apr 24] lengthy, rather sparely-made gelding: poor form over hurdles: well held in
maiden at Leicester on Flat debut. *J. R. Fanshawe*

ILLICIUM (IRE) 5 b.m. Fourstars Allstar (USA) 122 – Sweet Mignonette 80 (Tina's **–**
Pet 121) [2004 12g⁶ 8.5s 12.1g 13.9m May 28] third foal: dam, 1m to 1¼m winner, also
successful over hurdles: well held in maidens/handicap: dead. *Mrs M. Reveley*

ILLUSIONIST 6 b.g. Mujtahid (USA) 118 – Merlin's Fancy 62 (Caerleon (USA) 132) **– §**
[2004 49§: f7g f9.4s⁵ f12g⁵ Feb 24] little form in 2004: usually blinkered/visored: looks
none too keen. *Mrs N. Macauley*

ILLUSIVE (IRE)   7 b.g. Night Shift (USA) – Mirage 60 (Red Sunset 120) [2004 72:   **69**
p6g f6g p6g³ p7g⁵ p6g p6g p7g² p7g² p6g⁶ 5.7m² p6g 5g 6m⁴ 6m p6g⁵ Jul 21] sturdy
gelding: fair performer: stays easy 7f: acts on all-weather, firm and good to soft going:
usually blinkered: sometimes looks none too keen. *M. Wigham*

ILLUSTRIOUS DUKE   6 b.g. Dancing Spree (USA) – Killick 69 (Slip Anchor 136)   **–**
[2004 –, a61: p6g f7g f9.4s f8.5g f7g⁶ f8g f7g² f6g Apr 24] workmanlike gelding: poor   **a44**
performer: effective at 7f to 8.5f: acts on fibresand, little form on turf: has worn cheek-
pieces/blinkers: often forces pace: none too reliable. *M. Mullineaux*

ILLUSTRIOUS MISS (USA)   3 b.f. Kingmambo (USA) 125 – Our Wildirish Rose   **115**
(USA) (Irish Tower (USA)) [2004 64, a60: 12g f14m³ 12m⁵ 12m 12.1m⁶ 16s⁶ Aug 9] workmanlike
(USA) (Irish Tower (USA)) [2004 7g* 7s* 8m³ 8m⁵ Jul 6] $600,000Y: tall, good sort:
sixth foal: half-sister to 3 winners in USA, including Grade 3 8.5f/9f winner Nani Rose
(by Peteski): dam unraced half-sister to US Grade 1 9f/1¼m winner Political Ambition:
smart performer: won maiden at Newbury in April and totesport Chartwell Fillies' Stakes
at Lingfield (beat Gonfilia 2½ lengths, quickening well) in May: creditable 3 lengths third
to Attraction in Irish 1000 Guineas at the Curragh, soon flat out in rear but battling on
well: pulled hard when well-held fifth to Soviet Song in Falmouth Stakes at Newmarket
final start: stayed 1m: acted on soft and good to firm going: had worn crossed noseband:
stud. *D. R. Loder*

ILOVETURTLE (IRE)   4 b.g. Turtle Island (IRE) 123 – Gan Ainm (IRE) 92 (Mujadil   **54**
(USA) 119) [2004 64, a60: 12g f14m³ 12m⁵ 12m 12.1m⁶ 16s⁶ Aug 9] workmanlike   **a43**
gelding: modest handicapper on turf, poor on all-weather: stays 1½m: acts on fibresand,
good to firm and good to soft going: blinkered (slowly away/looked difficult ride) third
3-y-o start: none too reliable. *M. C. Chapman*

Sheikh Mohammed's "Illustrious Miss"

IL PRANZO 2 b.c. (Mar 27) Piccolo 121 – St Helena (Monsanto (FR) 121) [2004 p5g **76**
5g⁶ 5.2m³ 5.1m⁵ 5.7g 5.1g⁴ p5.1d* 5.2s³ p6g p5.1g p6g* Dec 27] 4,000Y: half-brother to
several winners, including 5f (including at 2 yrs)/6f winner Swino (by Forzando) and 5f
(at 2 yrs) to 7f winner Oriel Girl (by Beveled): dam Italian 5f/6.5f winner: fair performer:
won maiden in October and claimer (claimed by D. Flood) in December, both at Wolverhampton: likely to prove best at 5f/easy 6f: acts on polytrack, soft and good to firm going.
S. Kirk

ILTRAVITORE (IRE) 3 ch.g. Daggers Drawn (USA) 114 – May Hinton 82 (Main **52**
Reef 126) [2004 7g 6s⁵ 5g 6m 5.7g Oct 10] modest maiden: should prove best at 5f/
6f: twice slowly away. *D. R. C. Elsworth*

ILWADOD 3 b.g. Cadeaux Genereux 131 – Wedouah (IRE) 80 (Sadler's Wells (USA) **67**
132) [2004 –: 10s* 8s² 11.8g² 14.1f² 12.3m² 14g Jul 2] lengthy, good-bodied gelding: fair
handicapper: won at Nottingham in May: creditable efforts after: should stay 2m: acts on
firm and soft ground: visored last 2 starts: soon off bridle fourth/fifth outings: sold 26,000
gns. *M. R. Channon*

I'M A DARK HORSE 3 b.g. Alzao (USA) 117 – Romoosh 69 (Formidable (USA) **–**
125) [2004 12m 9.3f⁵ 13.8m Jul 7] well held in maidens. *K. A. Ryan*

I'M AIMEE 2 ch.f. (Apr 8) Timeless Times (USA) 99 – Marfen (Lochnager 132) [2004 **76 d**
p5g² 5s⁶ 5s³ 5.1d 5m⁴ 5m 5.1g² 5s² 5g² 6.1m² 6s³ 5.1g 5.1s⁴ 5.1f⁴ 5.7g⁵ p6g p6g
p6g Dec 27] 3,400Y: leggy filly: seventh foal: sister to 2 winners, including fairly useful
but unreliable 5f/6f winner (latter including at 2 yrs) Ramsey Hope: dam unraced: fair
maiden: below form last 7 starts: likely to prove best at 5f/6f: acts on polytrack, soft and
good to firm going: often races prominently. *P. D. Evans*

I'M DANCING 3 b.f. Polish Precedent (USA) 131 – Dancing Heights (IRE) 80 (High **65**
Estate 127) [2004 61: f8g 10v² May 10] good maiden: stays 1¼m: acts
on heavy and good to firm going: sold 6,500 gns. *T. D. Easterby*

IMPELLER (IRE) 5 ch.g. Polish Precedent (USA) 131 – Almaaseh (IRE) 63 (Danc- **105**
ing Brave (USA) 140) [2004 98: 8g 8g 8.1f² 8.5m⁶ 8f 8m⁵ 9.9g² 8m² 10.1g* 10f³ 9g 8d²
p10g⁵ p10g⁴ Nov 30] tall gelding: useful performer: better than ever in 2004: won minor
event at Epsom (by neck from Mango Mischief) in September: good efforts last 3 starts,
including when fifth to Grand Passion in listed race at Lingfield: effective at 1m/1¼m:
acts on polytrack, firm and good to soft going: blinkered (well below form) once: carries
head high: travels strongly, and usually waited with: consistent. *W. R. Muir*

IMPERATIVE (USA) 4 ch.g. Woodman (USA) 126 – Wandesta 121 (Nashwan **–**
(USA) 135) [2004 89?: p12g⁴ f12s⁶ f12s³ f12s³ p12.2g Nov 11] fairly useful maiden at
best: showed little in 2004: left I. Williams after second start and Gay Kelleway prior to
final one: tried blinkered/tongue tied. *M. J. Gingell*

IMPERATRICE 2 b.f. (Feb 20) Emperor Jones (USA) 119 – Fine Honor (FR) (High- **41**
est Honor (FR) 124) [2004 f5g 6m⁶ 5.3m⁶ 6m Oct 1] first foal: dam French 1¼m winner:
poor maiden: wore cheekpieces final start. *R. M. H. Cowell*

IMPERIAL DANCER 6 b.h. Primo Dominie 121 – Gorgeous Dancer (IRE) (Nordico **118**
(USA)) [2004 123: 12g³ 10g⁶ 12m 10d 10m³ 10.4d 8.9g³ 10m⁶ 11m² 12m 12d⁵ 10d² 12m
Dec 12] smallish, angular horse: had a quick action: smart performer: mostly creditable
efforts in 2004, notably in John Porter Stakes at Newbury (3 lengths third to Dubai
Success) on reappearance, Grosser Dallmayr-Preis at Munich (2½ lengths third to Intendant) fifth start, Dubai Duty Free Arc Trial at Newbury (length second behind Sights On
Gold) and Premio Roma at Rome (1½ lengths second to Soldier Hollow): effective at
1¼m/1½m: acted on any going: sometimes carried head awkwardly: usually held up: to
stand at Lavington Stud, West Sussex, fee £3,000 special live foal. *M. R. Channon*

IMPERIAL DRAGON (USA) 4 b.g. Meadowlake (USA) – South Cove (Forli **54**
(ARG)) [2004 p8g 7s⁴ 7g Apr 12] good-topped gelding: modest form in maidens: should
be as effective at 6f as 7f: slowly away on debut, raced freely final start: unruly in stall
and withdrawn intended debut at 3 yrs. *W. A. O'Gorman*

IMPERIAL DYNASTY (USA) 2 b.c. (Apr 3) Devil's Bag (USA) – Leasears (USA) **69**
(Lear Fan (USA) 130) [2004 6g 6g⁵ 7.2s 7f f7g² Dec 14] $20,000F, $25,000Y: fifth foal:
half-brother to 2 winners in USA by Lake George: dam French 6f winner: fair maiden:
best effort when second in nursery at Southwell: stays 7f: acts on fibresand. *T. D. Barron*

IMPERIAL ECHO (USA) 3 b.g. Labeeb 124 – Regal Baby (USA) (Northern Baby **92**
(CAN) 127) [2004 88: 7.1g 6m 6m⁴ 6m 6g² 5g² 5m 6m³ 5s⁴ 6d* 6s³ 6s⁴ 5d⁵ Nov 3]
leggy, quite good-topped gelding: fairly useful handicapper: won at Ripon (beat unlucky
Trojan Flight by neck) in August: creditable efforts after: best at 5f/6f: acts on firm and

soft ground: tried in blinkers/visor, better form without: sometimes slowly away: edged left seventh start. *T. D. Barron*

IMPERIALISTIC (IRE) 3 b.f. Imperial Ballet (IRE) 110 – Shefoog 90 (Kefaah (USA) 124) [2004 89: 7g⁴ 8.1s* 7.5s* 8.5m 8.1d⁵ 8d⁵ 8.1s³ 8d 10.3s⁶ Nov 6] leggy, close-coupled filly: useful performer: won handicaps at Haydock and Beverley in April: stays 1m, not 1¼m: acts on fibresand and heavy going, possibly not on firmer than good: often wears cheekpieces: carries head awkwardly/sometimes hangs: seemed unsuited by course at Epsom fourth outing. *K. R. Burke* **97 +**

IMPERIAL MISS (IRE) 2 b.f. (Mar 12) Imperial Ballet (IRE) 110 – Miss Flite (IRE) (Law Society (USA) 130) [2004 6m 6m⁶ 7g 7m⁶ 7m 7m f8g p8g Nov 20] smallish filly: seventh foal: half-sister to 3 winners, including 4-y-o Coppington Flyer: dam unraced: modest maiden: well below form last 4 starts: should stay 1m: acts on good to firm ground. *B. W. Duke* **58 d**

IMPERIAL PRINCESS (IRE) 3 b.f. Imperial Ballet (IRE) 110 – Rose Tint (IRE) (Salse (USA) 128) [2004 –: p6g Jan 28] little form: tried visored. *D. K. Ivory* **–**

IMPERIAL ROYALE (IRE) 3 ch.g. Ali-Royal (IRE) 127 – God Speed Her (Pas de Seul 133) [2004 61: 11.9d⁵ 11.8g 10s⁶ 12m 10g 12s 10.4m 8g p9.5g p13.9g p13.9g⁵ p13.9g Dec 22] leggy gelding: modest maiden: stays 11.9f: probably acts on soft going: tried in cheekpieces. *P. L. Clinton* **56**

IMPERIAL SOUND 2 b.c. (Mar 26) Efisio 120 – Final Trick (Primo Dominie 121) [2004 5g* 5g² 5.2m 6g* 6m 5g⁶ Sep 13] 21,000F, 36,000Y: rather leggy colt: first foal: dam twice-raced daughter of useful sprinter Tricky Note: fairly useful performer: won minor events at Beverley in June and Ripon (by 5 lengths) in August: effective at 5f/6f: dead. *T. D. Barron* **92**

IMPERIAL STRIDE 3 b.c. Indian Ridge 123 – Place de L'Opera 98 (Sadler's Wells (USA) 132) [2004 113p: 8g⁴ 9s 8d Oct 30] tall, good-bodied, attractive colt: has scope: lightly raced: smart performer at 2 yrs: just useful form in Group 3 races/listed event in 2004, off 6 months after reappearance (fourth of 5 in Craven Stakes at Newmarket): likely to stay 1¼m: acts on good to firm ground: tends to race freely. *Sir Michael Stoute* **100**

IMPERIAL WIZARD 3 ch.g. Magic Ring (IRE) 115 – Paula's Joy 75 (Danehill (USA) 126) [2004 p6g 5m 6s 5.7f 7m Sep 25] little form. *M. D. I. Usher* **–**

IMPERIOLI 2 b.c. (Apr 18) Fraam 114 – Jussoli (Don 128) [2004 7m 8.3d⁶ 8d Oct 15] quite good-topped colt: no form in maidens: slowly away first 2 outings. *P. A. Blockley*

IMPERIUM 3 b.g. Imperial Ballet (IRE) 110 – Partenza (USA) (Red Ransom (USA)) [2004 79§: p7g⁴ p6g p2g5 5.7g 5.1g 5.7s⁵ 5.3m* 5.3m* 5.1g³ 5m 5g p6g 6f⁶ 5m 5.3f² 5s³ 5m Sep 11] leggy gelding: fair handicapper: won twice at Brighton in May: effective at 5f to easy 7f: acts on polytrack, firm and soft going: tried blinkered/tongue tied: ungenuine. *Mrs Stef Liddiard* **76 §**

IMPERSONATOR 4 b.g. Zafonic (USA) 130 – Conspiracy 98 (Rudimentary (USA) 118) [2004 90: 8.1d 7.6s⁴ 8.1g³ 8.3d³ 10g 10d³ Oct 15] good-bodied gelding: has a long, round stride: fairly useful handicapper: good efforts third/fourth starts: stays 1m: raced mainly on good going or softer (acts on heavy): blinkered (well below form) second start: sold 18,000 gns. *J. L. Dunlop* **84**

IMPISH JUDE 6 b.m. Imp Society (USA) – Miss Nanna 56§ (Vayrann 133) [2004 14.1s⁴ Apr 30] leggy mare: poor maiden: stays 13f: probably acts on any turf going. *J. Mackie* **49**

IMPRESSIVE FLIGHT (IRE) 5 b.m. Flying Spur (AUS) – Certain Impression (USA) (Forli (ARG)) [2004 95: 6g 6s 5g 6m⁶ 6f⁵ 6g 6m Sep 30] lengthy mare: fairly useful handicapper: creditable efforts in 2004 only on fourth and sixth outings: found little in blinkers final one: stays 6f: acts on firm and soft going: often starts slowly: sent to USA. *T. D. Barron* **89**

IMPROVISE 2 b.f. (Feb 23) Lend A Hand 124 – Mellow Jazz 86 (Lycius (USA) 124) [2004 6m⁶ p7g² 6m² Sep 21] strong filly: first foal: dam 6f (at 2 yrs) and 1m winner: fair form in maidens: second at Lingfield and Newmarket (finished well): should stay 1m. *C. E. Brittain* **76**

IMPULSIVE BID (IRE) 3 b.f. Orpen (USA) 116 – Tamburello (IRE) (Roi Danzig (USA)) [2004 67?: 6d⁴ 6.1g 7s² 7m 6.9g⁵ 9.9g 8g 10.5g Sep 4] useful-looking filly: modest maiden handicapper: stays 7f: best efforts on ground softer than good. *Jedd O'Keeffe* **62**

IMSHY (IRE) 3 ch.f. Daggers Drawn (USA) 114 – Paganina (FR) (Galetto (FR) 118) [2004 92: 6s 5.5d⁶ 5.5d² 6v⁴ 6g⁴ 6d Oct 14] fairly useful performer: several creditable **89**

efforts in 2004, including second in handicap at Deauville third start: well held in listed race at Newmarket final outing: has won at 7f, seems best at shorter: acts on heavy going. *R. Pritchard-Gordon, France*

I'M SO LUCKY 2 b.g. (Mar 18) Zilzal (USA) 137 – City of Angels (Woodman (USA) 126) [2004 6d 7.1g* 8g² 8s⁴ Oct 22] 10,000Y: tall gelding: seventh foal: brother to 1¼m winner Charmer Venture and half-brother to 3 winners, including 5-y-o Del Mar Sunset: dam unraced: won minor event at Warwick in July: in frame in nurseries at Musselburgh and Doncaster (close fourth to Alpine Gold, finishing well), then gelded: likely to be suited by 1¼m/1½m: has scope to make a useful 3-y-o. *M. Johnston*   **90 p**

IM SPARTACUS 2 b.g. (Apr 16) Namaqualand (USA) – Captivating (IRE) 63 (Wolfhound (USA) 126) [2004 p5g 5.1g² 5.3m* 6.1s⁶ 6m⁵ 6g 7g⁶ 7m⁵ 7m⁴ 7.1d* 8.1g⁵ 7m⁴ 8.3g² 8s⁵ p8g* f8g* Dec 11] leggy gelding: second foal: half-brother to 5-y-o Antony Ebeneezer: dam, maiden, best at 2 yrs, later had form up to 17f: fairly useful on all-weather, fair on turf: won maiden at Brighton in April and nurseries at Sandown in August and (having left I. Wood 25,000 gns) Lingfield in November and Southwell in December: should stay 1¼m: acts on all-weather, soft and good to firm ground: blinkered last 2 starts, wore cheekpieces previous 3: tough and consistent. *D. Flood*   **77** **a86**

IMTALKINGGIBBERISH 3 b.g. Pursuit of Love 124 – Royal Orchid (IRE) 74 (Shalford (IRE) 124§) [2004 7d 7s⁵ 7f 6f² 6s 6m⁵ 6d⁴ p6g² p7.1g⁵ f6s² p6g² f6g³ Dec 28] 9,500Y: big, close-coupled, workmanlike gelding: third foal: half-brother to 4-y-o Maddie's A Jem: dam, maiden who stayed 7f, out of half-sister to smart sprinter Mistertopogigo: fairly useful maiden: seemed flattered when eighth in Jersey Stakes at Royal Ascot on third start: runner-up 4 times: effective at 6f/7f: acts on all-weather and firm going: sometimes carries head awkwardly: none too resolute. *J. R. Jenkins*   **73**

IMTIHAN (IRE) 5 ch.g. Unfuwain (USA) 131 – Azyaa 101 (Kris 135) [2004 –: 10.9s 18g Jun 3] good-topped gelding: fairly useful at 3 yrs: well held since: tried in blinkers/cheekpieces/tongue strap. *S. C. Burrough*

IMTIYAZ (USA) 5 ro.h. Woodman (USA) 126 – Shadayid (USA) 122 (Shadeed (USA) 135) [2004 116: 8g² 10.1d² 10m⁴ Aug 6] leggy horse: smart performer: creditable efforts when runner-up in listed race at Goodwood (beaten ¾ length by Kalaman) and minor event at Epsom (beaten short head by Fruhlingssturm): unable to dominate when below form in minor event at Newmarket: stays 10.4f: acts on dirt, firm and good to soft going: effective visored or not: usually tongue tied: often makes running: joined K. McLaughlin in USA. *Saeed bin Suroor*   **112**

IMTOUCHINGWOOD 3 b.f. Fleetwood (IRE) 107 – Shanuke (IRE) 56 (Contract Law (USA) 108) [2004 10m May 24] second foal: dam 1½m seller winner: always behind in maiden at Windsor, slowly away. *P. R. Hedger*   **–**

INAGH 2 b.f. (Jan 25) Tipsy Creek (USA) 115 – Compton Amber 78 (Puissance 110) [2004 5m⁶ 6.1s³ p8.6g Oct 7] 6,000Y: second foal: dam, temperamental maiden (placed at 2 yrs at 5f to 7f), half-sister to 4-y-o Golden Nun: form in maidens only when third at Chepstow. *M. Wallace*   **64**

INCA WOOD (UAE) 2 b.f. (Apr 8) Timber Country (USA) 124 – Lady Icarus (Rainbow Quest (USA) 134) [2004 8s² 8.5g² 8g 8s⁴ Oct 11] third foal: dam unraced close relative to smart milers Sharman and Hazaam out of high-class miler Sonic Lady: fair maiden: second at Yarmouth and Epsom: likely to be suited by 1¼m/1½m: acts on soft going. *M. Johnston*   **76**

INCH BY INCH 5 b.m. Inchinor 119 – Maid Welcome 81 (Mummy's Pet 125) [2004 65: 6m p5g⁴ 5g 5.1m* 5g* 6.1m* p6d* p5.1g* p5.1g³ Nov 26] smallish mare: fair performer: won handicaps at Chepstow and Goodwood (apprentices) and minor events at Nottingham and Wolverhampton (2) between September and November: effective at 5f/6f: acts on all-weather and firm ground: blinkered. *P. J. Makin*   **71**

INCHCAPE ROCK 2 ch.c. (Mar 17) Inchinor 119 – Washm (USA) (Diesis 133) [2004 5g p7g 6.1d 8.1s² 10.2g Sep 27] 18,000Y: lengthy colt: fourth foal: half-brother to 2003 2-y-o 7f winner Sioux River (by Indian Ridge): dam, ran twice at 2 yrs, out of half-sister to Irish 1000 Guineas winner Enscone: fair maiden: form only when second at Chepstow: stays 1m: acts on soft ground: free-going sort. *L. G. Cottrell*   **72**

INCHCONNEL 3 b.g. Inchinor 119 – Sharanella (Shareef Dancer (USA) 135) [2004 67: 10.3g 12d 10s May 7] strong, lengthy, rather dipped-backed gelding: no form since second 2-y-o start: tried blinkered. *V. Smith*   **–**

INCHCOONAN 6 b.m. Emperor Jones (USA) 119 – Miss Ivory Coast (Sir Ivor (USA) 135) [2004 –, a69: f8g⁴ f7g⁴ f6s² f7s² Mar 8] strong mare: modest performer   **–** **a53**

nowadays: stays 1m: acts on all-weather and firm going, probably not on soft: sometimes wears visor/cheekpieces: sometimes races freely: tends to idle in front. *K. R. Burke*

INCHDURA 6 ch.g. Inchinor 119 – Sunshine Coast 86 (Posse (USA) 130) [2004 78: 7s 7g 7d[6] 8g 10.1m p9.5d[5] f8g Nov 9] quite attractive gelding: fair handicapper: effective at 7f/1m: best form on going firmer than good: tried tongue tied: usually waited with. *N. Tinkler* **69 ?**

INCHENI (IRE) 3 b.f. Nashwan (USA) 135 – Inchmurrin 114 (Lomond (USA) 128) [2004 71p: 7g[2] 8m 8g[3] 10m* 10.2g[4] 9.9g[6] Aug 11] good-bodied filly: useful performer: 3 lengths second to Silca's Gift in Nell Gwyn Stakes at Newmarket on reappearance: won listed event at Newbury (beat Halicardia by ¾ length) in June: below form after, tending to hang and looking none too keen on final one: stays 1¼m: acts on polytrack, raced only on good ground or firmer on turf. *G. Wragg* **100**

INCHING 4 b.f. Inchinor 119 – Tshusick 81 (Dancing Brave (USA) 140) [2004 69d: f5s[4] p6g[4] p6g f5g 6g 5m 5m[2] 5m[6] 5.3f 5g[2] 5f 5m Jun 26] modest maiden handicapper: effective at 5f/6f: acts on all-weather, raced only on good ground or firmer on turf: tried in cheekpieces/visor/tongue strap: unreliable. *R. M. H. Cowell* **55 §**

INCHINNAN 7 b.m. Inchinor 119 – Westering 54 (Auction Ring (USA) 123) [2004 68: p10g[5] 9.2g 12.4s[5] May 12] small mare: modest handicapper, lightly raced nowadays: left C. Weedon 4,000 gns after reappearance: stays 10.5f: has form on firm going, seems at very best on soft/heavy and acts on polytrack. *James Moffatt* **61**

INCH LODGE 2 ch.c. (Feb 6) Grand Lodge (USA) 125 – Legaya 94 (Shirley Heights 130) [2004 p7.1g* Nov 13] second live foal: half-brother to 5-y-o Legal Approach: dam Irish 1½m winner out of Oaks winner Jet Ski Lady: odds on, won maiden at Wolverhampton comfortably by 1¼ lengths from Eskimo's Nest, travelling well tracking pace and leading over 1f out: will stay at least 1¼m: sure to progress. *Sir Michael Stoute* **74 p**

INCHLOSS (IRE) 3 b.g. Imperial Ballet (IRE) 110 – Earth Charter 60 (Slip Anchor 136) [2004 7g 8.1s[4] 6.1s* 7.9d[2] 8m 7m 8g[6] 8.2d* 8.2g[2] 8.1g[2] 9.9d[4] 10.3m 10g Oct 2] €25,000Y, 7,000 2-y-o: smallish, sturdy gelding: fifth foal: half-brother to winners abroad by Fayruz and Blues Traveller: dam maiden who should have stayed further than 6f: fairly useful performer: won maiden in April and minor event in July, both at Nottingham: creditable efforts often in frame after: stays 1¼m: acts on soft going, possibly unsuited by firmer than good. *B. A. McMahon* **89**

INCHNADAMPH 4 b.g. Inchinor 119 – Pelf (USA) 79 (Al Nasr (FR) 126) [2004 –: 9.9v[6] 10.5d[2] 10.9d[2] 13g* 13g* 11.9f[5] 13.9g 13.8s[2] Nov 2] sturdy gelding: fair handicapper: won at Hamilton in June (ladies) and July: stays 1¾m: acts on firm and soft going: usually tongue tied. *T. J. Fitzgerald* **70**

INCHPAST 3 ch.c. Inchinor 119 – Victor Ludorum (Rainbow Quest (USA) 134) [2004 67: 8.3s 11.6d 12m[4] 11.5m* 12f[2] 12.1d* 13.8g* 14.1f* Sep 13] workmanlike colt: fair performer: won handicap at Yarmouth in July, minor event at Beverley in August, and handicaps at Catterick and Redcar (beat Most Definitely by ½ length) in September: stays 1¾m: acts on polytrack and firm ground: blinkered last 6 starts. *M. H. Tompkins* **80**

INCISE 3 ch.f. Dr Fong (USA) 128 – Pretty Sharp 64 (Interrex (CAN)) [2004 89: 5.1g[6] 5.1d 5m 5m[4] 5m[4] 5m 5m[5] Aug 16] good-topped filly: fairly useful performer: mostly creditable efforts in 2004: likely to prove best at 5f/easy 6f: acts on good to firm and good to soft going: tried tongue tied: ill at ease on track at Epsom third start: edgy sort. *B. J. Meehan* **86**

INCISOR 3 b.g. Dracula (AUS) 121 – Last Night's Fun (IRE) (Law Society (USA) 130) [2004 55: 10g[5] 10m* p10g* f8.5g* 10m Jun 14] compact gelding: fair performer: won handicaps at Brighton in April, Lingfield in May and Wolverhampton in June: stayed easy 1¼m: acted on all-weather: raced only on good/good to firm going on turf: dead. *S. Kirk* **77**

INCLINE (IRE) 5 b.g. Danehill (USA) 126 – Shalwar Kameez (IRE) (Sadler's Wells (USA) 132) [2004 92: p7g[6] 7v[5] 7d 8d[5] 7v[2] 8v Oct 31] fairly useful performer: sold from T. Mills 8,000 gns after reappearance: stays 1m: acts on polytrack and heavy ground. *R. McGlinchey, Ireland* **84 a87**

INCROYABLE 3 gr.f. Linamix (FR) 127 – Crodelle (IRE) (Formidable (USA) 125) [2004 –p: 10.1g[2] 10d* 12g Oct 2] tall filly: has scope: fair performer, lightly raced: won minor event at Nottingham (by neck from Mambina) in September: ran poorly in apprentice handicap at Epsom final start: should stay 1½m: acts on good to soft going. *Sir Mark Prescott* **69**

INCURSION 3 b.g. Inchinor 119 – Morgannwg (IRE) 86 (Simply Great (FR) 122) **86**
[2004 79: 10s* 10m 10g³ 11.6g 12d Aug 20] sturdy gelding: fairly useful performer: won
maiden at Windsor in May: stays 11.6f: acts on soft and good to firm going. *A. King*

INDALO GREY (IRE) 8 gr.g. Toca Madera 111 – Pollyfaster (Polyfoto 124) [2004 **69**
14d⁶ 14m⁴ 16f⁵ p13.9g⁵ p13.9g f14g p16.5g⁴ p13.9g⁴ p13.9g² p12.2g Dec 20] fair maiden **a61**
on turf, modest on all-weather: ran just once on Flat prior to 2004: trained by G. Kyne in
Ireland prior to fourth outing: probably stays 2m: acts on polytrack and firm going: tried
in cheekpieces: tongue tied last 3 starts. *Mrs Stef Liddiard*

INDEBTED 2 b.f. (Apr 6) Royal Applause 124 – Briggsmaid 70 (Elegant Air 119) **68 p**
[2004 p8g² Nov 13] 24,000Y: sixth foal: half-sister to several winners, including fairly
useful 1¼m/1½m winner Kez (by Polar Falcon) and 4-y-o Cruise Director: dam 1½m to
2m winner: 12/1, 5 lengths second to General Jumbo in maiden at Lingfield, slowly away
and forced wide: should stay 1¼m: sure to improve. *J. Noseda*

IN DEEP 3 b.f. Deploy 131 – Bobbie Dee 93 (Blakeney 126) [2004 80: 10.3g 10.1m **68**
11.6d⁶ 10m 10g² Aug 16] leggy filly: fair maiden: stays 1¼m: best efforts on good/good
to soft going. *Mrs P. N. Dutfield*

INDEPENDENT SPIRIT 2 ch.g. (Mar 23) Wolfhound (USA) 126 – Kigema (IRE) **–**
58 (Case Law 113) [2004 5.1s 6g p5.1g p7.1g Oct 16] small gelding: well held in
maidens/sellers. *R. P. Elliott*

INDESATCHEL (IRE) 2 b.c. (Apr 2) Danehill Dancer (IRE) 117 – Floria (IRE) **108**
(Petorius 117) [2004 5s⁴ 7g*⁵ 6.3f³ 6m² 6m³ 6g² 8d⁴ Oct 10] €21,000F, €72,000Y: tall,
close-coupled colt: third foal: brother to a winner in Turkey: dam well held in bumpers/
over hurdles in Ireland: useful performer: won maiden at the Curragh in June: placed
on same course in Anglesey Stakes (1¼ lengths third to Oratorio), sales race (found little
when second to Beaver Patrol), Round Tower Stakes (third to Cherokee) and listed
event (length second to Ad Valorem): stays 7f, possibly not 1m: acts on firm going.
D. Wachman, Ireland

INDIANA BLUES 3 ch.f. Indian Ridge 123 – Blue Siren 113 (Bluebird (USA) 125) **70**
[2004 90p: 7g⁴ 6g 5.2m 8g³ 7g⁵ 6.1d³ 6.1g⁴ 5.7f³ 7m² 6m* p7.1d³ Nov 5] good-topped
filly: just fair form in 2004: won maiden at Windsor in September: barely stays easy 7f:
acts on polytrack, good to firm and good to soft ground: tried blinkered: has carried head
high. *A. M. Balding*

INDIAN BAZAAR (IRE) 8 ch.g. Indian Ridge 123 – Bazaar Promise 58 (Native **58 §**
Bazaar 122) [2004 55: 5g 5m 6g² 5g 5f 5m² 6f 5.1g⁶ 5.1m 6m 6d 5.7m 5.7f 5.1m 5g Sep
22] big, good-topped gelding: modest handicapper: effective at 5f/6f: acts on firm and
soft going, well held on heavy: tried blinkered/in cheekpieces: has edged left: usually
races prominently: unreliable. *N. E. Berry*

INDIAN BLAZE 10 ch.g. Indian Ridge 123 – Odile (Green Dancer (USA) 132) [2004 **60**
73d: p13g⁶ p10g² p8g* p10g² p8g p8g³ p8g⁶ p8g 9g⁶ p10d 8m p8.6g p10m² p8m⁵ p10m³
p8g⁵ p10m Dec 21] workmanlike gelding: modest handicapper: won at Lingfield in February: stays easy 1¼m: acts on any turf going/all-weather: tried blinkered. *Andrew Reid*

INDIAN CALL 3 ch.g. Classic Cliche (IRE) 128 – Crees Sqaw (Cree Song 99) [2004 **–**
64: 10.3g 10d 7.1d p8.6g f5f Dec 28] big, lengthy gelding: maiden: well held in 2004.
B. A. McMahon

INDIAN CHASE 7 b.g. Terimon 124 – Icy Gunner (Gunner B 126) [2004 p16g² 14.1s⁶ **50**
10d 18m 12d 16.2m⁴ p16d 18d* p16g² p16g Oct 13] leggy gelding: modest performer:
won maiden handicap at Chepstow in August: stays 2¼m: acts on polytrack and good to
soft going: visored first 4 outings: sometimes races freely. *Dr J. R. J. Naylor*

INDIAN DOVE (IRE) 2 b.f. (May 10) Indian Danehill (IRE) 124 – African Dance **45**
(USA) (El Gran Senor (USA) 136) [2004 p8g⁶ 8s p7.1g Nov 13] €32,000Y: half-sister to
3 winners, including fairly useful 1996 2-y-o 6f winner Telemania (by Mujtahid): dam
Irish maiden: poor form in maidens. *G. A. Butler*

INDIAN EDGE 3 ch.g. Indian Rocket 115 – Beveled Edge 60 (Beveled (USA)) [2004 **62 d**
68: p7g 6.1s⁵ 6.1s² 7m 6m 6.1d 8.1g p6g p8.6g⁶ Nov 15] good-topped gelding: modest
maiden: below form after third outing: best at 6f: acts on polytrack and soft ground: looks
hard ride. *B. Palling*

INDIAN HAVEN 4 ch.c. Indian Ridge 123 – Madame Dubois 121 (Legend of France **110 ?**
(USA) 124) [2004 119: 8.1d⁵ 8m 7d⁶ May 27] tall, good-bodied colt: smart performer:
won Irish 2000 Guineas at the Curragh in 2003: just respectable efforts in betfred.com
Mile at Sandown (fifth to Hurricane Alan) and Lockinge Stakes at Newbury (edged left)

first 2 starts in 2004: below form in Prix du Palais-Royal at Longchamp final outing: reportedly underwent surgery to remove a bone fragment in near-fore after: stayed 1m: acted on good to firm and good to soft going: usually waited with: to stand at Irish National Stud, Co. Kildare, fee €6,000. *P. W. D'Arcy*

INDIAN LILY 3 ch.f. Compton Place 125 – Princess Lily 65 (Blakeney 126) [2004 **51 ?** 6d⁵ 7s 5s⁶ 6.1m 6m 6g 7g 10m Sep 25] lightly-made filly: half-sister to several winners by Risk Me, including fairly useful 5f (at 2 yrs) to 8.5f winner Risk Free and 1m to 2m winner Royal Roulette: dam maiden who stayed 1½m: modest maiden: should stay 7f: acts on soft and good to firm ground: tried tongue tied. *C. F. Wall*

INDIAN MAIDEN (IRE) 4 br.f. Indian Ridge 123 – Jinsiyah (USA) 98 (Housebuster **72** (USA)) [2004 75: p6g 6m⁴ 5.7g 6g 6g* Oct 11] tall, leggy filly: fair performer: best effort in 2004 when winning handicap at Leicester (slowly away): best at 5f/6f: acts on fibresand (probably on polytrack), good to firm and good to soft going. *M. S. Saunders*

INDIAN MUSIC 7 b.g. Indian Ridge 123 – Dagny Juel (USA) 75 (Danzig (USA)) **47 §** [2004 39§, a45§: f8.5s⁶ f6s* 6v⁵ f6g⁴ f6m⁴ f7m³ f6g³ f6g² f7d⁴ f6g⁶ f6g² f6m 6m f6g⁶ 6v⁵ **a54 §** 6d 6s f6g f6d⁵ Dec 21] stocky gelding: modest on all-weather, poor on turf: won banded race at Southwell in March: effective at 6f to 9.4f: acts on fibresand and probably any turf going: tried blinkered/in cheekpieces: carries head high: unreliable. *A. Berry*

INDIANNIE STAR 2 b.f. (Jan 17) Fraam 114 – Ajig Dancer 86 (Niniski (USA) 125) **89** [2004 5.2g² 5m* 5f⁵ 5f 5g⁵ 5.1g* 6m³ 7f⁵ Aug 7] leggy, quite attractive filly: second foal: dam, 5f (at 2 yrs) to 7f winner, out of sister to smart sprinter Puissance: fairly useful performer: won maiden at Lingfield in May and minor event at Chepstow in July: creditable efforts in listed event at Newbury and Sweet Solera Stakes at Newmarket (fifth to Maids Causeway) last 2 starts: stays 7f: acts on firm and good going: sent to USA. *M. R. Channon*

INDIAN OAK (IRE) 3 b.f. Indian Rocket 115 – Marathon Maid 82 (Kalaglow 132) **–** [2004 –: p5g p5g p7g p7g Mar 4] no form. *M. P. Muggeridge*

INDI ANO STAR (IRE) 3 b.g. Indian Rocket 115 – Audriano (IRE) (Cyrano de Ber- **45 ?** gerac 120) [2004 7s⁶ 8.1s⁶ 8v⁶ 8m 7m⁵ 9.1g⁵ 10s Nov 1] IR 7,000F, 10,500 2-y-o: leggy gelding: poor maiden: stays 1m: acts on soft ground: visored penultimate start. *D. Carroll*

INDIAN PEARL (IRE) 2 b.f. (Apr 24) Indian Lodge (IRE) 127 – Thatchabella **–** (IRE) (Thatching 131) [2004 5.1f May 27] 16,000Y: third foal: half-sister to a winner in Hong Kong by Alzao: dam unraced out of close relation to smart Irish 1991 2-y-o El Prado and half-sister to high-class 1¼m performer Entitled: 66/1, last in maiden at Bath. *R. J. Hodges*

INDIAN PIPE DREAM (IRE) 2 br.c. (Apr 29) Indian Danehill (IRE) 124 – Build **63 p** A Dream (USA) (Runaway Groom (CAN)) [2004 8g 8g⁶ Sep 29] €50,000F, 70,000Y: strong, lengthy colt: closely related to fairly useful Italian winner up to 1½m Luis Butarat (by Flying Spur) and half-brother to several other winners abroad: dam Italian maiden half-sister to dam of smart sprinter Pharaoh's Delight: modest form when never dangerous in maidens at Kempton and Salisbury: likely to do better. *J. H. M. Gosden*

INDIAN SHORES 5 b.m. Forzando 122 – Cottonwood 80 (Teenoso (USA) 135) **–** [2004 66d: f6g f6g f5g⁶ f7g f5g p6g 7m 6g 6d p12.2g Nov 8] neat mare: one-time fair 6f winner: no form in 2004: tried in cheekpieces. *M. Mullineaux*

INDIAN SKY (IRE) 2 b.f. (Feb 10) Indian Lodge (IRE) 127 – Bolero (Rainbow Quest **54 ?** (USA) 134) [2004 p7m Dec 22] 11,000Y: first foal: dam unraced out of Irish Oaks winner Bolas: 33/1, tenth in maiden at Lingfield, not knocked about. *B. R. Millman*

INDIAN'S LANDING (IRE) 3 b.g. Barathea (IRE) 127 – We've Just Begun (USA) **58** (Huguenot (USA) 121) [2004 5m 8m 10m 10d 10v³ 10s⁵ f12g⁵ p12.2g Dec 15] modest maiden: left Michael Cunningham in Ireland after fourth start: stays 1¼m: acts on heavy going, probably on polytrack. *K. A. Morgan*

INDIAN SMOKE 2 b.g. (May 21) Makbul 104 – Indian Flower 87 (Mansingh (USA) **–** 120) [2004 5m May 31] tall gelding: behind in maiden at Leicester. *J. A. Pickering*

INDIAN SOLITAIRE (IRE) 5 b.g. Bigstone (IRE) 126 – Terrama Sioux (Relkino **77** 131) [2004 81: 12g³ 11.9s 10m⁶ 9.9g 12d Oct 15] good-bodied gelding: fair handicapper: left R. Fahey 9,000 gns prior to final start (wore cheekpieces): stays 1¾m: has form on good to firm ground, but very best efforts on good going or softer: tried blinkered, usually visored in 2004. *B. P. J. Baugh*

INDIAN SPARK 10 ch.g. Indian Ridge 123 – Annes Gift (Ballymoss 136) [2004 110: **98 d** 5.1g⁴ 6g 6d⁴ 5m⁴ 6d⁶ 6f 5d 6g 6g⁶ 6d 6d 5m 6s Nov 1] close-coupled gelding: poor mover (reportedly fractured off-fore joint earlier in career): one-time smart performer:

very much on the downgrade: best at 5f/6f: acts on any going: often gets behind. *J. S. Goldie*

INDIAN STEPPES (FR) 5 b.m. Indian Ridge 123 – Ukraine Venture 96 (Slip Anchor 136) [2004 84: 6.1d⁶ 7m⁶ 6m⁴ 6m³ 6g 6m⁶ 6g³ f6g² f6g³ p6g² p6m⁵ Dec 21] angular mare: fairly useful on all-weather, fair on turf: best at 6f/7f: acts on dirt, all-weather, soft and good to firm going: tried in cheekpieces: has run well sweating. *Julian Poulton* **75 a86**

INDIAN TRAIL 4 ch.g. Indian Ridge 123 – Take Heart 84 (Electric 126) [2004 89: 7m 6m* Jul 17] strong gelding: fairly useful performer: won handicap at Newbury by ¾ length from Doitnow: effective at 6f/7f: acts on firm and soft going. *D. R. C. Elsworth* **93**

INDIAN WARRIOR 8 b.g. Be My Chief (USA) 122 – Wanton 106 (Kris 135) [2004 52: f7g* p7g f7g p6g⁴ f6s f6g⁵ p7g⁵ 7v 8.2m 6d³ Oct 16] small gelding: poor performer: won banded race at Wolverhampton in January: effective at 6f/7f: acts on any turf going/ all-weather: tried visored/tongue tied, usually blinkered: often starts slowly. *J. Jay* **46**

INDIAN WELCOME 5 ch.g. Most Welcome 131 – Qualitair Ridge (Indian Ridge 123) [2004 86: p8g Mar 26] big gelding: fairly useful at 4 ys: well held only start in 2004: usually wears blinkers/cheekpieces: races prominently. *H. Morrison* **–**

INDIAN WELL (IRE) 2 b.g. (Apr 8) Indian Ledge (IRE) 127 – Pride of Pendle 80 (Grey Desire 115) [2004 7.1g Aug 30] 6,000Y: third foal: dam 6f (at 2 yrs) to 9f winner: 20/1, well held in maiden at Warwick, slowly away and not knocked about: likely to do better. *S. Kirk* **– p**

INDIBAR (IRE) 3 b.g. Indian Ridge 123 – Barbara Frietchie (IRE) (Try My Best (USA) 130) [2004 10m Jun 1] tailed off in maiden at Redcar. *Andrew Turnell* **–**

INDIBRAUN (IRE) 2 b.g. (Apr 9) Indian Rocket 115 – The Aspecto Girl (IRE) 53 (Alzao (USA) 117) [2004 5s⁵ 6m* 6m⁴ 7.1f⁴ f7m 7s³ 7.1g⁴ 6.1d p6g⁶ Oct 7] 10,500Y: sturdy gelding: half-brother to 2000 2-y-o 6f/7f winner Cedar Tsar and 1m seller winner Another Aspect (both by Inzar): dam maiden half-sister to useful 7f to 1¼m performer Canaska Star: fair performer: won maiden at Doncaster in May: creditable efforts after on third and sixth starts only: stays 7f: acts on soft and good to firm going: wore cheekpieces penultimate outing: sold 8,000 gns, sent to Sweden. *P. C. Haslam* **74**

INDIENA 2 ch.f. (Jan 14) Indian Ridge 123 – Aliena (IRE) (Grand Lodge (USA) 125) [2004 6g⁴ 6m⁵ 6g² 6.1g⁴ 6.5m² 6.1m³ p6g⁵ Nov 8] 75,000Y: small, sturdy filly: first foal: dam French/US 2-y-o 7f/1m winner: fair maiden: second in minor event/nursery: stays 6.5f: acts on good to firm going: sometimes races freely/finds little. *B. J. Meehan* **78**

INDIVIDUAL TALENTS (USA) 4 ch.f. Distant View (USA) 126 – Indigenous (USA) 56 (Lyphard (USA) 132) [2004 77p: 12s 14.1d 12m May 21] smallish filly: fair handicapper at 3 yrs: well held in 2004, seemingly amiss last 2 starts. *S. C. Williams* **–**

INDONESIA 2 ch.g. (Apr 22) Lomitas 129 – Idraak (Kris 135) [2004 8.5s 9f 7.9g⁵ Oct 9] strong, useful-looking gelding: seventh foal: half-brother to 3 winners, including smart 1½m performer Iscan (by Caerleon), 7f winner at 2 yrs, and 4-y-o Legacy: dam, French middle-distance maiden, half-sister to Oaks winner Snow Bride, herself dam of Lamm-tarra: easily best effort in maidens when fifth at York (gelded after): will be well suited by 1¼m/1½m: should do better. *M. Johnston* **65 p**

INDRANI 3 b.f. Bijou d'Inde 127 – Tea And Scandals (USA) (Key To The Kingdom (USA)) [2004 52: f6g f7g⁶ f6g⁴ f6s f5g f6g⁴ p6g 6v² f6m 6m⁵ 6g 6g 6g 6s² f7g Sep 14] unfurnished filly: poor maiden: stays 6f: acts on fibresand, heavy and good to firm going: tried in cheekpieces: sometimes slowly away: ungenuine. *John A. Harris* **44 §**

INDRAPURA STAR (USA) 4 b.g. Foxhound (USA) 103 – Royal Recall (USA) (Native Royalty (USA)) [2004 –: f8g⁶ p10g Mar 9] no sign of ability. *Miss J. Feilden* **–**

IN DREAM'S (IRE) 2 b.g. (Feb 24) Dr Fong (USA) 128 – No Sugar Baby (FR) (Crystal Glitters (USA) 127) [2004 5g 6f 8m 6d⁵ p7g Oct 13] 35,000Y rather unfurnished gelding: half brother to several winners, including useful stayer Sweetness Herself (by Unfuwain): dam French maiden: modest maiden: best effort at 6f on good to soft ground: sometimes looks wayward. *B. Gubby* **63**

INESCAPABLE (USA) 3 b.c. Cape Town (USA) 125 – Danyross (IRE) 99 (Danehill (USA) 126) [2004 6g 6m 7g⁴ 7.1g 7g* 8d 7g Oct 12] modest performer: won seller at Leicester in September: stays 7f: best efforts on good going. *W. R. Muir* **55**

IN EVERY STREET (USA) 3 br.f. Favorite Trick (USA) 121 – Hit The Bid (USA) (Lear Fan (USA) 130) [2004 p8g 10g⁶ Jul 24] second foal: dam, maiden in USA, sister to Kentucky Derby runner-up Casual Lies: well held in maidens at Lingfield and Notting-ham: joined J-P. Gallorini in France. *M. A. Magnusson* **–**

IN EXCELSIS (USA) 2 b.c. (Feb 14) Fusaichi Pegasus (USA) 130 – Lakeway (USA) **92**
119 (Seattle Slew (USA)) [2004 5v* 7f⁵ 7g⁵ Sep 19] $950,000Y: rather leggy, quite good-
topped colt: on the weak side at 2 yrs: has a fluent, rather round action: sixth foal: closely
related/half-brother to winners in USA by Seeking The Gold and Storm Cat: dam US
Grade 1 1m/9f winner: landed odds in maiden at Tipperary in April: fifth in listed race at
Royal Ascot (to Whazzat) and National Stakes at the Curragh (best effort, behind
Dubawi): should stay 1m: sent to USA. *A. P. O'Brien, Ireland*

INFIDELITY (IRE) 3 b.f. Bluebird (USA) 125 – Madaniyya (USA) 96 (Shahrastani **61**
(USA) 135) [2004 73: p10g⁶ p10g 10.3g 12.3d 9.9g⁶ 10m 9.2m⁶ 9.1g³ 11.9g⁵ 10m 10.3g⁴
p9.5g p8.6d⁴ p12.2g p12.2g Dec 15] leggy, lengthy filly: modest handicapper: stays
1¼m: acts on polytrack, firm and good to soft going: tried in cheekpieces/visor. *A. Bailey*

INGLETON 2 b.c. (Feb 14) Komaite (USA) – Dash Cascade (Absalom 128) [2004 5.1g **101**
6m⁴ 6d* 6g* 6d* Oct 15] 10,000Y: strong colt: seventh foal: half-brother to 3 winners,
including 1999 2-y-o 6f winner Red Typhoon (by Belfort) and 1998 2-y-o 1m seller
winner (later won in Sweden) Swiss Toni (by Petong): dam unraced: useful performer:
won maiden at Ayr in September and nurseries at York and Newmarket (beat Our Fugitive
by neck) in October: likely to stay 7f: acts on good to soft ground: often races prominently: sold 55,000 gns. *B. A. McMahon*

INGLEWOOD 4 ch.g. Fleetwood (IRE) 107 – Preening 62 (Persian Bold 123) [2004 **–**
40: f14.8g Jan 3] poor maiden on Flat. *C. W. Thornton*

INGRANDIRE (JPN) 5 b.h. White Muzzle 129 – Marilyn Momoko (JPN) (Real Sha- **122**
dai (USA) 126) [2004 115: a12s² 16f* 20m a11.5g² Aug 12] big, good-topped Japanese-
bred horse: very smart performer: won 4 Group 2/3 events in 2003, and Group 1 Tenno
Sho (Spring) at Kyoto in May by 7 lengths from subsequent Japan Cup winner Zenno
Rob Roy: 1½ lengths second to Time Paradox (who rec 4 lb) in Group 2 event at Asahi-
kawa final start: weakened quickly after leading long way when well held in Gold Cup at
Royal Ascot (wore hood in paddock) penultimate outing: stays 2m: acts on firm ground
and dirt. *Y. Shimizu, Japan*

INISTRAHULL ISLAND (IRE) 4 b.g. Flying Spur (AUS) – Dolcezza (FR) (Lich- **68 d**
ine (USA) 117) [2004 69: p6g³ p7g⁶ p8g 6m⁶ 8d Jun 24] fair maiden: below form after
reappearance: effective at 6f to 1m: acts on polytrack, firm and good to soft ground: tried
visored/blinkered. *M. H. Tompkins*

INKA DANCER (IRE) 2 ch.f. (Mar 31) Intikhab (USA) 135 – Grannys Reluctance **71**
(IRE) 63 (Anita's Prince 126) [2004 5.7g³ 5.7g⁴ 6g³ Oct 11] second foal: dam, maiden
who stayed 1m, half-sister to smart Italian/French performer up to 1m Sole Che Sorgi:
fair form in maidens: should stay 1m. *B. Palling*

INK IN GOLD (IRE) 3 b.g. Intikhab (USA) 135 – Your Village (IRE) 64 (Be My **66**
Guest (USA) 126) [2004 8.1g 7v⁵ 12.3d 8.1s 7.1d p9.5d⁴ p8.6g³ p9.5g³ f12g* p12.2g⁵
f12g² Dec 1] €18,000Y: fourth foal, dam, Irish middle-distance maiden, half-sister to
Middle Park winner Mister Majestic and Grand Prix de Paris winner Homme de Loi:
fair performer: won maiden at Southwell in November: stays 9.5f: acts on all-weather.
P. A. Blockley

IN LUCK 6 b.m. In The Wings 128 – Lucca (Sure Blade (USA) 130) [2004 68, a–: f12g **–**
Jan 12] lengthy mare: maiden: well held only outing in 2004: none too genuine. *B. Smart*

INMOM (IRE) 3 b.f. Barathea (IRE) 127 – Zakuska 96 (Zafonic (USA) 130) [2004 **58**
63?: 8.2s³ 12m f8d⁴ 10g⁶ 9.9g⁶ f8m 9.9d 10s⁶ p13.9g Nov 29] good-topped filly: modest
maiden: stays 1¼m: acts on fibresand, soft and good to firm going: tried tongue tied.
S. R. Bowring

INNCLASSIC (IRE) 3 b.f. Stravinsky (USA) 133 – Kyka (USA) (Blushing John **63**
(USA) 120) [2004 72p: 6g 6m f6g³ 6.1m* f5m² 5.1m 5.1m 6g p5.1g p5.1d Nov 3] close-
coupled filly: modest performer: won claimer at Warwick in June: left B. Meehan after
fifth start: effective at 5f/6f: acts on all-weather and good to firm going: blinkered last 8
starts: usually races prominently. *Jane Southcombe*

INN FOR THE DANCER 2 b.g. (Apr 23) Groom Dancer (USA) 128 – Lady Joyce **57**
(FR) (Galetto (FR) 118) [2004 p8.6d p7.1g p8.6g p7m Dec 22] modest maiden: best
efforts at 7f: slowly away other outings. *J. A. Glover*

INNOCENT REBEL (USA) 3 ch.g. Swain (IRE) 134 – Cadeaux d'Amie (USA) 115 **66**
(Lyphard (USA) 132) [2004 8g p10g⁴ 9.7g³ 14.1g Sep 29] rather leggy gelding: half-
brother to several winners, notably French 1m (won 1000 Guineas) to 1½m (second in
Breeders' Cup Turf) performer Hatoof and French/US 1m/9f performer Irish Prize (both
very smart, by Irish River): dam, French 1m (at 2 yrs) and 1¼m winner, half-sister to Mrs

Penny: fair maiden: seems to stay 1¾m: raced only on polytrack/good ground: sold 14,000 gns, then gelded. *E. A. L. Dunlop*

INNOCENT SPLENDOUR   2 b.f. (Jan 26) Mtoto 134 – Maureena (IRE) (Grand Lodge (USA) 125) [2004 7m² 7g* 8g Sep 30] 18,000Y: first foal: dam unraced half-sister to 4-y-o Chappel Cresent: won maiden at Folkestone in August: improved again when never-dangerous seventh in nursery at Goodwood: should stay at least 1¼m: should progress. *E. A. L. Dunlop*   **78 p**

INNPURSUIT   2 b.c. (Feb 16) Inchinor 119 – Quest For The Best (Rainbow Quest (USA) 134) [2004 p8.6d p10g⁶ Nov 12] 16,000Y: fifth foal: half-brother to 6f/7f winner Best Quest (by Salse): dam well beaten: modest form in maidens at Wolverhampton (slowly away) and Lingfield: likely to stay 1½m: should improve. *J. M. P. Eustace*   **60 p**

INNSTYLE   3 b.f. Daggers Drawn (USA) 114 – Tarneem (USA) 87 (Zilzal (USA) 137) [2004 74: 6g⁶ 5f 6m 5.7f³ 5.7g 6m 5.7g* p6g p7.1d Nov 5] leggy, close-coupled filly: fair performer: won claimer at Bath in October: effective at 5f to easy 7f: acts on firm going: tried blinkered: has shown signs of temperament (refused to enter stall once at 2 yrs). *J. L. Spearing*   **69**

IN RHUBARB   2 ch.g. (Mar 30) Piccolo 121 – Versami (USA) (Riverman (USA) 131) [2004 5.2m⁶ 5g 5g Oct 5] quite good-topped gelding: poor form in maidens: tongue tied on debut: slowly away first 2 outings. *I. W. McInnes*   **41**

INSIGNIA (IRE)   2 b.c. (Jan 30) Royal Applause 124 – Amathea (FR) (Exit To Nowhere (USA) 122) [2004 5m⁵ 6m⁵ p6g Aug 26] modest form in maidens: best effort on debut: should stay at least 6f: sold 8,000 gns in November. *J. H. M. Gosden*   **58**

INSIGNIFICANCE   4 b.g. Bishop of Cashel 122 – Summer Pageant 81 (Chief's Crown (USA)) [2004 54: f8.5s p8g 5d 10g² 11.9m⁵ 7f May 27] modest maiden handicapper: stays 1¼m: acts on good to firm going, below form on all-weather in Britain, including first 2 starts in 2004: tried blinkered/tongue tied. *John A. Quinn, Ireland*   **52**

INSINUATION (IRE)   2 b.f. (Apr 10) Danehill (USA) 126 – Hidden Meaning (USA) (Gulch (USA)) [2004 7g⁶ Sep 4] 260,000Y: tall filly: has scope: fourth foal: dam unraced half-sister to very smart Irish 7f to 1¼m performer Fair Judgment: 17/2, sixth of 7 to Joint Aspiration in minor event at Kempton, slowly away, very green and not given hard race: type to do considerably better as 3-y-o. *Sir Michael Stoute*   **66 P**

INSPECTOR BLUE   6 ch.g. Royal Academy (USA) 130 – Blue Siren 113 (Bluebird (USA) 125) [2004 –: 11.5f Aug 5] leggy, quite good-topped gelding: no form: tried in cheekpieces. *T. Keddy*   **–**

IN SPIRIT (IRE)   6 b.g. Distinctly North (USA) 115 – June Goddess (Junius (USA) 124) [2004 64: f12g Jan 12] handicapper: well held only outing in 2004: sometimes blinkered/visored. *B. J. Curley*   **–**

INSTANT HIT   5 b.g. Indian Ridge 123 – Pick of The Pops 109 (High Top 131) [2004 74: 7d 8d² 10s 10s p9.5g Dec 13] fair handicapper: runner-up at the Curragh second start: poor efforts otherwise in 2004, including at Wolverhampton final outing: stays 1m: acts on good to firm and good to soft going: often tongue tied: wore cheekpieces on reappearance: has raced freely. *M. Woods, Ireland*   **73**

INSTANT RECALL (IRE)   3 ch.c. Indian Ridge 123 – Happy Memories (IRE) (Thatching 131) [2004 p7g³ p7g* p7g 6.1d⁴ 6g⁵ 6g⁴ 6m⁵ p6g* 6g² 6g⁴ 6d p7g Sep 7] 140,000Y: lengthy, quite attractive colt: second foal: dam unraced half-sister to smart Irish 1¼m/1½m performer Topanoora: fairly useful performer: won maiden in March and handicap in June, both at Lingfield: effective at 6f/7f: acts on polytrack, good to firm and good to soft going: blinkered last 6 starts: sold 35,000 gns, sent to UAE. *B. J. Meehan*   **84 a88**

INSTINCT   3 b.g. Zafonic (USA) 130 – Gracious Gift 96 (Cadeaux Genereux 131) [2004 65p: p7g⁵ p7g 6s³ 6d 6g 7.1g 7f³ 8f³ 6.1d² 6g* 6d Oct 4] fair performer: won maiden at Yarmouth in September, looking none too keen: effective at 6f, barely at 1m: acts on firm and soft going: sometimes slowly away: sold 6,500 gns. *R. Hannon*   **67**

INSTRUCTOR   3 ch.g. Groom Dancer (USA) 128 – Doctor's Glory (USA) 91 (Elmaamul 125) [2004 76: p7g² p8g* 9g 8.1d 7g p9.5g⁶ p8.6g⁶ p9.5g⁵ Dec 27] unfurnished gelding: easy mover: fairly useful performer: won maiden at Lingfield in April: left R. Hannon 14,000 after sixth start: stays 9.5f: acts on polytrack and good to firm ground: usually races up with pace. *R. A. Fahey*   **82**

INSUBORDINATE   3 ch.g. Subordination (USA) 120 – Manila Selection (USA) (Manila (USA)) [2004 63: 8.2g 7s* 7.2s Oct 12] good-bodied gelding: modest performer: won handicap at Newcastle in May: should stay 1m: acts on fibresand, firm and soft going: effective with or without cheekpieces. *J. S. Goldie*   **61**

INTAVAC BOY 3 ch.g. Emperor Fountain 112 – Altaia (FR) 90 (Sicyos (USA) 126) **75**
[2004 6d⁶ 5.1g⁶ 5d⁴ 6g 8m² 8d² Oct 18] workmanlike gelding: half-brother to 3 winners,
including fairly useful 8.5f/1½m winner Alessandro Severo (by Brief Truce): dam 6f/7f
winner: fair maiden: runner-up in handicap at Newcastle and minor event at Pontefract
last 2 starts: much better at 1m than 6f: acts on good to firm and good to soft going.
C. W. Thornton

INTELLIBET ONE 4 b.f. Compton Place 125 – Safe House 81§ (Lyphard (USA) 132) **60**
[2004 68, a–: 6m 5f 5g³ 6f⁴ 5g 6m 5g 5m Aug 2] leggy filly: modest handicapper nowa- **a–**
days: effective at 5f/6f: acts on polytrack, firm and soft going: tried visored: sometimes
looks none too keen. *P. D. Evans*

INTENDANT (GER) 3 b.c. Lando (GER) 128 – Incenza (GER) (Local Suitor (USA) **120**
128) [2004 10g* 11g³ 11d⁴ 12v 10m* Aug 1] third foal: brother to German 1m winners
Interent and Internet: dam German 1m winner: very smart performer: won maiden at
Frankfurt in April and showed plenty of improvement when winning Grosser Dallmayr-
Preis at Munich in August, leading inside final 1f to beat idling Powerscourt 1½ lengths:
reportedly operated on subsequently for a chip: may prove best around 1¼m (soundly
beaten at 1½m on heavy ground in Deutsches Derby). *Frau A. Bertram, Germany*

INTENDED 2 b.f. (Mar 2) Singspiel (IRE) 133 – Introducing 78 (Mtoto 134) [2004 7g **63**
p10g⁴ Nov 27] fourth foal: dam, 1¼m winner in France, sister to very smart performer up
to 13f (also third in Derby) Presenting: modest form in maidens at Salisbury and Lingfield: will be suited by at least 1½m. *A. M. Balding*

INTENSITY 8 b.g. Bigstone (IRE) 126 – Brillante (FR) 118 (Green Dancer (USA) **62**
132) [2004 68: p12g³ f11s 10.3g 14.1g² 11.9m Apr 25] leggy, useful-looking gelding:
handicapper, just modest form in 2004: stays 1¾m: acts on polytrack, firm and good to
soft going: usually held up: found little penultimate start: sold 8,000 gns. *P. A. Blockley*

INTERCEPTOR 4 ch.c. Hector Protector (USA) 124 – Moorish Idol 90 (Aragon 118) **95**
[2004 95: 10g 8.5f³ 9f* 9f 11f³ Sep 3] useful-looking colt: useful performer: carried head
awkwardly when below form in handicap at Newmarket on reappearance, then left
J. Hills: won allowance race at Hollywood in July: creditable third in optional claimer at
Del Mar final outing: stays 9.7f: raced only on good or firmer going. *P. Gallagher, USA*

INTERIM PAYMENT (USA) 2 b.f. (Apr 25) Red Ransom – Interim 117 **73 p**
(Sadler's Wells (USA) 132) [2004 8m⁵ Sep 7] close-coupled filly: fifth foal: closely
related to 2 winners by Kris S, including 3-y-o Focus Group, and half-sister to 2 winners,
including useful 1¼m/1½m winner Staging Post (by Pleasant Colony), later smart up to
1¾m in USA: dam 1m to 1½m (US Grade 2) winner: 20/1 and better for race, fifth to
Dash To The Top in maiden at Leicester, not knocked about: likely to be suited by 1¼m/
1½m: should do better. *R. Charlton*

INTERNATIONALGUEST (IRE) 5 b.g. Petardia 113 – Banco Solo (Distant Rela- **88 d**
tive 128) [2004 91: p12g p12g² p12g p8g p12g p10g² 8g 11.6d 10.1v⁵ 10f⁵ 9.9g⁵ 11.6g
10.1d p10g 10d Oct 18] tall, close-coupled gelding: fairly useful performer: below form
after sixth outing: stays easy 1½m: acts on polytrack and good to firm going, goes well on
soft/heavy: usually in headgear: sold 13,000 gns. *G. G. Margarson*

INTERSTICE 7 b.g. Never So Bold 135 – Mainmast 63 (Bustino 136) [2004 58+, **?**
a72: f11g³ f12f⁶ f9.4s⁵ Feb 16] modest handicapper: effective at 1¼m/1½m: acts on soft **a55**
ground, better form on fibresand than polytrack: wore cheekpieces last 2 starts: free-
going sort. *A. G. Newcombe*

INTER VISION (USA) 4 b.g. Cryptoclearance (USA) – Fateful (USA) 90 (Topsider **88**
(USA)) [2004 99: 5g 6v 6m⁵ 6g 6d 6m⁴ 6g² 7m 5f 6g p6g⁶ p6g⁶ Dec 13] tall gelding: just
fairly useful handicapper in 2004: only placing when short-head second to Bygone Days
at Ripon (carried head awkwardly and hung in behind winner): best at 5f/6f: acts on
polytrack and firm going: usually held up: tried in cheekpieces. *A. Dickman*

INTERWOVEN (IRE) 2 b.c. (May 1) Woodman (USA) 126 – Woven Silk (USA) 104 **–**
(Danzig (USA)) [2004 6g 7g Oct 12] lengthy colt: has a quick action: signs of only a little
ability in maidens at Redcar and Leicester, slowly away: sold 1,500 gns. *M. Johnston*

IN THE FAN (USA) 2 b.g. (Mar 15) Lear Fan (USA) 130 – Dippers (USA) 86 (Polish **92**
Numbers (USA)) [2004 7m² 7g* 7m³ 8.2g² Aug 16] strong, sturdy gelding: first foal:
dam, Irish 2-y-o 5f winner, out of half-sister to high-class sprinter Committed: fairly
useful performer: made all in maiden at Epsom in July: creditable efforts in minor events
at Newmarket (on toes and free to post) and Nottingham (2 lengths second to Northern
Splendour) after: stays 1m. *J. L. Dunlop*

IN THE KNOW 2 b.c. (Apr 8) Desert Prince (IRE) 130 – Evocatrice 91 (Persepolis **76**
(FR) 127) [2004 6s p8m² Dec 21] tall, lengthy colt: half-brother to several winners
abroad, including useful French 1¼m/1½m winner Edouna (by Doyoun): dam, French
2-y-o 7f winner who stayed 1¼m, out of top-class filly up to 1½m Northern Trick: better
effort in maidens when length second to Alessano at Lingfield, making running: very
slowly away on debut. *J. H. M. Gosden*

IN THE LEAD (USA) 2 b. or br.f. (Mar 19) Bahri (USA) 125 – Air de Noblesse (USA) **55 p**
(Vaguely Noble 140) [2004 7g Sep 18] $8,000Y: tall, leggy filly: half-sister to several
winners, including fairly useful French 1¼m winner L'Arrosee (by Woodman): dam,
French maiden, half-sister to smart performers up to 1m Rami and Crack Regiment and
very smart sprinter La Grande Epoque: 50/1, seventh in maiden at Newbury, never a
threat: likely to do better. *W. S. Kittow*

IN THE PINK (IRE) 4 gr.f. Indian Ridge 123 – Norfolk Lavender (CAN) 80 (Ascot **80**
Knight (CAN) 130) [2004 74: 7.1v 8m 7g* 7m² 7m 7g² 8f 7d⁴ 7m⁵ 7m³ Sep 29] close-
coupled, quite good-topped filly: fairly useful performer: won handicap at Goodwood in
June: effective at 7f/1m: acts on firm going: sometimes races freely. *M. R. Channon*

IN THE SHADOWS 2 b.f. (Mar 2) Lujain (USA) 119 – Addicted To Love 73 –
(Touching Wood (USA) 127) [2004 5.7d 7g p7m Oct 6] 13,000Y: workmanlike filly:
sixth foal: half-sister to 3 winners, including Go Go Girl and 7f/1m winner Unchain
My Heart (by Pursuit of Love): dam 1¼m and 1¾m winner: well held in minor event/
maidens. *W. S. Kittow*

IN THE STARS (IRE) 6 ch.g. Definite Article 121 – Astronomer Lady (IRE) (Monte- –
kin 125) [2004 64?: p10g Jan 28] maiden handicapper, lightly raced: well held only 6-y-o
outing (visored). *P. R. Webber*

INTIMATE FRIEND (USA) 3 b.f. Expelled (USA) 116 – Intimate (USA) (Topsider –
(USA)) [2004 85: p7.1g Dec 11] lengthy, rather sparely-made filly: maiden, disappointing since debut at 2 yrs: tailed off only outing in 2004. *Miss Gay Kelleway*

INTITNICE (IRE) 3 b.g. Danehill Dancer (IRE) 117 – Gathering Place (USA) –
(Hawaii) [2004 52: f8.5g p6g 8g 7.1s Aug 12] smallish gelding: modest maiden at 2 yrs:
well beaten in 2004: often wears blinkers/cheekpieces. *Miss K. M. George*

INTO THE BREEZE (IRE) 4 b.g. Alzao (USA) 117 – Catalane (USA) (Septieme –
Ciel (USA) 123) [2004 103: 7m May 22] good-bodied gelding: useful handicapper at
best: last in Victoria Cup at Ascot only 4-y-o outing (reportedly finished lame). *J. W. Hills*

INTO THE DARK 3 ch.c. Rainbow Quest (USA) 134 – Land of Dreams 115 **119 p**
(Cadeaux Genereux 131) [2004 10.3m* 10g* 11.9g* 10.9s* Sep 18]
    The St Leger winner and Derby second Rule of Law and the Two Thousand
Guineas runner-up Snow Ridge were Godolphin's leading three-year-olds in 2004,
but Into The Dark might have gone on to show himself their equal given further
opportunities, such was the progress he made in a period of less than three months.
Into The Dark was unbeaten in four appearances and is already verging on very
smart, though he hasn't even contested a pattern race yet, let alone won one. He will
surely be making his presence felt in such events in 2005.
    The Derby had been run by the time Into The Dark came out of the shadows.
A slow learner by all accounts, he was fitted with a visor to help him concentrate, as
well as a tongue strap, when making his debut at the end of June in a maiden at

Weatherbys Bank Stakes (Doonside Cup), Ayr—Into The Dark extends his unbeaten run to four
with success over Derby fourth Percussionist; Bonecrusher finishes well clear of the others in third

Godolphin's "Into The Dark"

Doncaster. Into The Dark showed no signs of inexperience when winning by five lengths there, making most, and he was also fitted with both aids in his remaining races. The first of these was a competitive-looking handicap for three-year-olds at Newmarket, where he gave another impressive front-running display to win by a length and a half from Art Trader. On his third start, Into The Dark provided more of the same when stepped up from a mile and a quarter to a mile and a half at York in another handicap. Sent off the even-money favourite, despite having to concede weight to nine useful rivals, Into The Dark dictated the pace and soon had the opposition in trouble when asked to quicken in the straight, striding out most impressively to win by two and a half lengths from Secretary General. At this stage, Into The Dark still had a St Leger entry, and was as low as 12/1 for the race, but with Rule of Law to represent them it was never likely that Into The Dark's connections would ask him to take such a big step up in class so early in his career. The Weatherbys Bank Stakes (Doonside Cup), a listed event run over nearly eleven furlongs at Ayr, provided a much more suitable alternative. Three of the six runners were no-hopers, and neither the smart handicapper Bonecrusher nor the Derby fourth Percussionist, himself a one-time leading fancy for the St Leger, were arguably coming into the race in top form. One of the outsiders set a steady pace, tracked by Into The Dark, and it wasn't until the latter was sent on turning out of the back straight that the race began in earnest. Percussionist was in trouble the moment Into The Dark, in receipt of 7 lb, increased the tempo, and neither he nor Bonecrusher looked particularly enthusiastic under pressure. Into The Dark, on the other hand, went about his work with a will and was never seriously challenged in winning by five lengths from Percussionist. Into The Dark might well have been flattered to some extent, given the way the race unfolded, but, even allowing for that, he showed that he was still very much on the upgrade.

Into The Dark (ch.c. 2001)	Rainbow Quest (USA) (b 1981)	Blushing Groom (ch 1974)	Red God
			Runaway Bride
		I Will Follow (b 1975)	Herbager
			Where You Lead
	Land of Dreams (b 1995)	Cadeaux Genereux (ch 1985)	Young Generation
			Smarten Up
		Sahara Star (b 1989)	Green Desert
			Vaigly Star

Into The Dark may stay beyond a mile and a half and clearly gets his stamina from his sire Rainbow Quest, the bottom line of his pedigree being all speed. He is the first foal of Land of Dreams, who won over six furlongs on her debut but was best at five, showing smart form and winning the Flying Childers Stakes and King George Stakes at the latter trip. Into The Dark's grandam Sahara Star won the Molecomb Stakes for Sir Michael Stoute, while his great grandam Vaigly Star and her half-brother Vaigly Great were even more successful for the same trainer. Vaigly Star was a smart sprinter, Vaigly Great a high-class one. The second foal of Land of Dreams is a colt by Selkirk named Only Make Believe. He showed fairly useful form in a couple of runs over seven furlongs in Ireland for Jim Bolger, winning a maiden at Gowran first time up. Into The Dark, a lengthy, rather leggy, quite attractive individual, acts on soft and good to firm going. *Saeed bin Suroor*

INTO THE SHADOWS 4 ch.f. Safawan 118 – Shadows of Silver 89 (Carwhite 127) [2004 8v³ 12.1g³ 9.2d⁴ 10.1m* 12s* Oct 29] quite good-topped filly: third foal: dam, 1½m/1¾m winner, also bumper winner: second in 3 bumpers: progressive form: won maiden at Newcastle and handicap at Newmarket (by ½ length from Reem One) in October: should stay 1¾m: acts on soft and good to firm going: held up: capable of better still. *K. G. Reveley*   **77 p**

INTOXICATING 2 b.c. (Apr 27) Mujahid (USA) 125 – Salalah 62 (Lion Cavern (USA) 117) [2004 6g* 6d³ Jul 10] 20,000Y second foal: half-brother to 3-y-o Faraway Echo: dam, 7f winner, half-sister to useful 1995 sprinting 2-y-o Flying Squaw: very green, won maiden at Leicester in June: similar form when third to Johnny Jumpup in minor event at Salisbury: likely to stay 7f. *R. F. Johnson Houghton*   **82**

INTREPID JACK 2 b.c. (Feb 27) Compton Place 125 – Maria Theresa (Primo Dominie 121) [2004 8v p6g* Nov 8] 20,000Y: lengthy colt: first foal: dam unraced half-sister to smart 7f/1m performer Nicobar: better effort in maidens when winning at Wolverhampton by ¾ length from Seamless, edging left: open to improvement. *H. Morrison*   **70 p**

INTRICAT 4 ch.g. Bluegrass Prince (IRE) 110 – Noble Soul 67 (Sayf El Arab (USA) 127) [2004 42: p7.1g Nov 15] poor maiden: well held in banded race only 4-y-o start: tried visored. *A. P. Jones*   **–**

INTRICATE WEB (IRE) 8 b.g. Warning 136 – In Anticipation (IRE) 93 (Sadler's Wells (USA) 132) [2004 82: f9.4g* f9.4g* f11s² f12s⁴ 10.5s⁶ 10.5d 10.9g* 8.1m³ 8.1d³ 8.9m 10g* 8.1g 10.3g 10.5g 8f⁵ 10.5s⁶ 10.4g Oct 8] sturdy, angular gelding: fairly useful handicapper: won at Wolverhampton (twice) in January, Ripon in May and Redcar in June: stays 11f: well beaten on heavy ground, acts on any other turf/fibresand: tried in headgear, not recently: races lazily, and comes from behind. *E. J. Alston*   **86 a90**

INTRIGUED 2 gr.f. (Feb 2) Darshaan 133 – Last Second (IRE) 121 (Alzao (USA) 117) [2004 7.5d³ 8.5g* 8m⁴ Oct 3]   **105 p**

It is just possible there could be a most unusual sighting at Epsom racecourse in June, that of a horse trained by Sir Mark Prescott taking part in a British classic. Several Group 1 wins have come along since Pivotal provided Prescott with his first at that level, in the 1996 Nunthorpe Stakes, but the classics have continued to take place without a single runner from Heath House. Of course, the stable isn't one to pitch its horses in at the highest level unless they can be considered serious prospects, and rightly so. It would be surprising, though, if the master of Heath House isn't harbouring hopes that his promising filly Intrigued will develop into one good enough to be worth her place in the Oaks. Whether or not Intrigued makes into an Oaks filly, she is a good-looking individual with an excellent pedigree and will definitely step up on the useful form she showed in a light first season. It will be a surprise if she fails to win a good race or two in 2005.

Intrigued had clearly pleased in her work prior to her debut, in a twelve-runner maiden fillies' event at Beverley at the end of August, for she came in for

Mr Faisal Salman's "Intrigued"

		Shirley Heights (b 1975)	Mill Reef Hardiemma
	Darshaan (br 1981)	Delsy (br 1972)	Kelty
Intrigued (gr.f. Feb 2, 2002)		Alzao (b 1980)	Lyphard Lady Rebecca
	Last Second (IRE) (gr 1993)	Alruccaba (gr 1983)	Crystal Palace Allara

good support and went off at slight odds on. That Intrigued failed to justify the support was mainly because of her inexperience, but she did shape very well in a close third behind Gold Queen, running on strongly when finally getting the hang of things. She started at even shorter odds when reappearing eleven days later in a five-runner maiden at Epsom, Intrigued making no mistake this time. Even though she still looked green, taking time to warm to her task then edging left down the camber after she was nudged into the lead under three furlongs out, Intrigued still drew clear under hands and heels and had the remainder well strung out at the finish, five lengths the winning margin over Inca Wood. A far stiffer task faced Intrigued on her next start, in the Prix Marcel Boussac at Longchamp on Arc day. In finishing two and a half lengths fourth of ten to Divine Proportions, the leading two-year-old filly in Europe in 2004, Intrigued showed further marked improvement. Patiently ridden, Intrigued took a while to find her stride once in line for home, but she was staying on strongly at the death. All three of Intrigued's races at two were at or around a mile, but judged both on pedigree and style of racing she will prove very well suited by a mile and a quarter or more in her second season and should get the Oaks trip.

Two of Intrigued's relatives have finished a close second in the Oaks very recently. Quarter Moon (by Sadler's Wells) was beaten half a length by Kazzia in

2002, and her full sister and stable-companion Yesterday looked unlucky when failing by a neck to peg back Casual Look the following year. Jude, the dam of Quarter Moon and Yesterday, is a half-sister to Intrigued's dam Last Second, as is Alouette, the dam of two Prescott-trained Group 1 winners in Alborada and Albanova. Alborada won the Champion Stakes twice, while Albanova was successful in three Group 1s in Germany in the latest season. Last Second also did Prescott proud on the racecourse. Said by her trainer to be a fragile individual, the lightly-raced Last Second won both her starts at two, and the Nassau Stakes and Sun Chariot Stakes at three, when she was also a very close second in the Coronation Stakes. Retired to stud after disappointing on both her outings as a four-year-old, Last Second produced three foals prior to Intrigued, all of them fillies. Two managed only one outing between them, but Intrigued's full sister Approach was a useful performer who won at seven furlongs as a two-year-old and a mile and a quarter in listed company at three, also running well over a mile and a half when fourth in the Prix de Malleret. Intrigued's grandam Alruccaba raced only at two, winning a six-furlong maiden, while the great grandam Allara won over seven furlongs in the French Provinces and is a half-sister to the dam of Aliysa, who was first past the post in the 1989 Oaks but much later disqualified on technical grounds. Alruccaba's numerous other winners include the Prescott-trained filly Alleluia, successful in the 2001 Doncaster Cup. This is an excellent family, and the strong, rangy Intrigued already looks a worthy addition to it. *Sir Mark Prescott*

INTRIGUING GLIMPSE 3 b. or br.f. Piccolo 121 – Running Glimpse (IRE) 84 **85** (Runnett 125) [2004 72: 6s³ 5g² 5.3m² 5m² 6f Jul 29] strong filly: fairly useful handicapper: head second to Baron Rhodes at Sandown fourth start, best effort: effective at 5f/ 6f: acts on polytrack, soft and good to firm ground: waited with. *Miss B. Sanders*

INTRIGUING (IRE) 2 b.f. (Mar 11) Fasliyev (USA) 120 – Sea Mistress (Habitat 134) **87 P** [2004 6m* May 14] 240,000Y: half-sister to several winners, notably smart Irish 6f to 1m

Mr M. Tabor & Mrs John Magnier's "Intriguing"

winner Nautical Pet (by Petorius): dam unraced: odds on, won maiden at Cork very easily by 2½ lengths from Gouache, making all: well regarded, and capable of good deal better. *D. Wachman, Ireland*

INTRODUCTION   3 b.g. Opening Verse (USA) 126 – Cartuccia (IRE) (Doyoun 124)   –
[2004 47: p8g 11.6m 16.2g 12.1d⁵ 11.7d Aug 27] quite good-topped gelding: of little account nowadays: left W. Musson after second start: visored final outing. *R. J. Price*

IN TUNE   4 b.g. Distinctly North (USA) 115 – Lingering 96 (Kind of Hush 118) [2004   –
58: 10.2g 10.2s f6g 7.1m 8.1g p10g Jul 17] maiden: no form in 2004: tried blinkered/tongue tied: sometimes slowly away. *S. C. Burrough*

INVADER   8 b.g. Danehill (USA) 126 – Donya 74 (Mill Reef (USA) 141) [2004 90§,   **70 §**
a95§: f7g p10g f8.5g⁶ f8.5s 8.1d 7.6g p8g* 10g 7m⁶ 8g⁶ 8.5g 8.3m Sep 27] big gelding: **a81 §**
fairly useful on all-weather, fair on turf: won minor event at Lingfield in June: well below form after: best at 1m/easy 1¼m: acts on all-weather, firm and good to soft going: tried visored, usually blinkered/tongue tied: lazy sort, sometimes finds little: unreliable: sold 4,000 gns. *C. E. Brittain*

INVASIAN (IRE)   3 ch.c. Desert Prince (IRE) 130 – Jarrayan 64 (Machiavellian   **103**
(USA) 123) [2004 –p: 4.1d* 8m² 8g 7m 9.7g* 9.9d² 9.5s Oct 13] close-coupled, quite attractive colt: useful performer: made all in maiden at Haydock in June and minor event at Folkestone (beat Secretary General 2½ lengths) in August: good length second to Gatwick in valuable handicap at Beverley penultimate start: well beaten in Prix Andre Baboin at Bordeaux final start: stays 1¼m: acts on good to firm and good to soft going: game front-runner. *H. R. A. Cecil*

INVER GOLD   7 ch.h. Arazi (USA) 135 – Mary Martin (Be My Guest (USA) 126)   –
[2004 60, a79: f12s f12d Dec 21] lengthy horse: poor mover: fair winner in 2003: well held both 7-y-o starts: often takes while to warm up. *A. G. Newcombe*

INVERTIEL (USA)   2 br.c. (Apr 3) Royal Academy (USA) 130 – Intriguing (USA)   **74**
(Deputy Minister (CAN)) [2004 6g⁴ 6f² 7.2s 6d 7m 7.1d⁶ a8g* Nov 14] $17,000Y, 20,000 2-y-o: fifth foal: half-brother to winners in USA by Woodman and Unbridled's Song: dam, US maiden, half-sister to US Grade 1 1m winner Quiet American: fair performer: below form after second start, though won 3-runner minor event at Taby on first outing after leaving I. Semple: stays 1m: acts on firm ground and dirt: visored penultimate appearance. *Pia Brandt, Sweden*

INVESTMENT AFFAIR (IRE)   4 b.g. Sesaro (USA) 81 – Superb Investment (IRE)   –
(Hatim (USA) 121) [2004 68: 10.3g Sep 11] close-coupled, good-topped gelding: fair handicapper in 2003: well held only Flat outing in 2004: has wandered: fair hurdler. *D. McCain*

INVITATION   6 b.g. Bin Ajwaad (IRE) 119 – On Request (IRE) 53 (Be My Guest   **80**
(USA) 126) [2004 83: 12g 11.6d⁶ 14.1s⁴ 10s² 10g 14g² 20f Jun 15] angular gelding: fairly useful handicapper: stays 1¾m: acts on heavy and good to firm going: tried in cheekpieces: usually held up. *A. Charlton*

INVITING (USA)   3 b.f. Exploit (USA) 117 – Raging Apalachee (USA) (Apalachee   **55**
(USA) 137) [2004 8g Jul 16] $250,000F, $430,000Y: good-topped filly: half-sister to several winners, notably Breeders' Cup Sprint winner Artax (by Marquetry): dam unraced: 20/1, modest form when fourteenth of 20 in maiden at Newmarket, racing freely: sent to Australia. *R. Charlton*

INVOGUE (FR)   4 b.f. Bin Ajwaad (IRE) 119 – Wenda (IRE) 93 (Priolo (USA) 127)   –
[2004 –: 8s 12g f12m⁶ f8d Jul 23] 3,500Y: first foal: dam 2-y-o 6f winner who stayed 11.5f: lightly raced and no form (left J. Coogan in Ireland after second start). *R. A. Fahey*

IO CALLISTO   3 br.f. Hector Protector (USA) 124 – Queen Shirley (IRE) (Fairy King   –
(USA)) [2004 43: 5d Jul 3] no form since debut in 2003. *R. A. Fahey*

IONIAN SPRING (IRE)   9 b.g. Ela-Mana-Mou 132 – Well Head (IRE) (Sadler's   **98**
Wells (USA) 132) [2004 93: 10g* 10g 10.5d* 10.4g 10.5g 10.4s⁵ 8.9m Sep 5] sturdy gelding: has reportedly suffered from broken blood vessels: useful handicapper: won at Newbury in April and Haydock (career-best effort, beat Ofaraby short head) in June: below form after next start: effective at 1¼m/easy 1½m: acts on firebsand, firm and good to soft going: sometimes early to post/races freely: tends to edge left: held up. *C. G. Cox*

IPHIGENIA (IRE)   3 b. or br.f. Orpen (USA) 116 – Silver Explosive (Rock Hopper   **78**
124) [2004 60: 8f 8f⁵ 7f 7f² 8.1g⁴ 8.5g⁵ 7.1m³ 7m* 7s² 7g⁶ 7g⁶ Sep 8] fair handicapper: won at Folkestone in August: best effort at 7f: acts on firm and soft going. *P. W. Hiatt*

IPLEDGEALLEGIANCE (USA)   8 b.g. Alleged (USA) 138 – Yafill (USA) 80   **40**
(Nureyev (USA) 131) [2004 70d: f12g² f11g⁵ f12g³ f11g⁶ f12g⁵ f12s p12g f12s f11s⁵
p10g⁵ 13.1g 10m⁵ 13m⁵ 14.1g² 12m 16m³ f14m² 15g 13f Jul 28] leggy gelding: poor
performer nowadays: stays 2m: acts on fibresand, firm and soft ground: blinkered last
7 outings: sometimes slowly away: usually held up: moody efforts last 2 starts: none too
reliable. *D. W. Chapman*

IPSA LOQUITUR   4 b.f. Unfuwain (USA) 131 – Plaything 69 (High Top 131) [2004   **64**
63: 10d 10d⁴ 11.8m May 18] good-topped filly: modest maiden: reportedly had irregular
heartbeat when pulled up on final start: should be suited by at least 1½m: acts on
polytrack and good to soft going. *S. C. Williams*

IQTE SAAB (USA)   3 b.c. Bahri (USA) 125 – Shuhrah (USA) 101 (Danzig (USA))   **106**
[2004 96p: 7d* 7m⁶ 6m 7m⁵ 7m³ Oct 2] rather leggy, quite attractive colt: keen walker:
useful performer: won minor event at Newmarket (beat Glaramara by 3 lengths) in April:
creditable efforts in listed races at Epsom (fifth to Mac Love) and Redcar (2¾ lengths
third to Gonfilia) last 2 starts: stays 7f: acts on good to firm and good to soft going: races
freely: joined D. Watson in UAE. *J. L. Dunlop*

IRANOO (IRE)   7 b.g. Persian Bold 123 – Rose of Summer (IRE) (Taufan (USA) 119)   **–**
[2004 12d May 4] close-coupled gelding: maiden: well held only Flat start since 2000:
tried blinkered: tongue tied. *R. Allan*

IRELAND'S EYE (IRE)   9 b.g. Shareef Dancer (USA) 135 – So Romantic (IRE) 97   **–**
(Teenoso (USA) 135) [2004 –: f14g³ f16.2g⁴ Jan 14] small gelding: maiden: no form in 3
runs since 2001: tried visored: fair hurdler. *J. R. Norton*

IRIE RASTA (IRE)   5 ch.g. Desert King (IRE) 129 – Seeds of Doubt (IRE) (Night   **–**
Shift (USA)) [2004 75: 10v p12.2g Nov 29] big, strong gelding: fair handicapper at 4 yrs:
well held both starts in 2004: sometimes finds little. *S. Kirk*

IRISH BALLAD   2 b.c. (Apr 20) Singspiel (IRE) 133 – Auenlust (GER) (Surumu   **62**
(GER)) [2004 8s 8.2d p8.6g⁴ Oct 16] 35,000Y: neat colt: half-brother to 4-y-o Aries and
several other winners in Germany: dam, German 1m winner, half-sister to dam of smart
5f/6f winner Auenklang: form in maidens only when fourth at Wolverhampton: will stay
1¼m. *P. W. Harris*

IRISH BLADE (IRE)   3 b.c. Kris 135 – Perle d'Irlande (FR) (Top Ville 129) [2004   **83**
–p: 10s⁴ 12s³ 10f 11.9g 10g 16s³ 15.9g² 14.1g* 16d⁵ 16s⁶ Oct 22] close-coupled colt:
fairly useful handicapper: won at Salisbury in September: seems best at 1¾m: acts on
firm and soft going: sold 50,000 gns. *H. Candy*

IRISH CHAPEL (IRE)   8 b.g. College Chapel 122 – Heart of Flame (Top Ville 129)   **–**
[2004 8m f11d Jun 17] of little account. *H. E. Haynes*

IRISH CRACK (IRE)   4 ch.f. Fumo di Londra (IRE) 108 – Polish Crack (IRE) (Polish   **–**
Patriot (USA) 128) [2004 –: 10s p8.6g Nov 27] IR 500Y: fourth foal: dam unraced: no
form, including at Wolverhampton. *Miss G. Lee, Ireland*

IRISH PLAYWRIGHT (IRE)   4 b.g. King's Theatre (IRE) 128 – Marino Waltz   **58**
(Thatching 131) [2004 7.1m p13g p9.5d³ p8.6g² p10m p9.5g Dec 6] modest maiden:
stays 9.5f: acts on polytrack: blinkered/visored last 4 starts. *D. G. Bridgwater*

IRON TEMPTRESS (IRE)   3 ch.f. Piccolo 121 – River Divine (USA) 59 (Irish River   **–**
(FR) 131) [2004 73: 7m f8g 13.8g⁶ 12.1m 13.8m Sep 18] tall, workmanlike filly: fair
performer at 2 yrs: little form in 2004: tried blinkered: had looked none too keen: dead.
G. M. Moore

IRON WARRIOR (IRE)   4 b.g. Lear Fan (USA) 130 – Robalana (USA) (Wild Again   **–**
(USA)) [2004 62: 12g Oct 4] workmanlike gelding: maiden: well beaten only 4-y-o
outing: tried in blinkers/cheekpieces. *G. M. Moore*

IRONY (IRE)   5 gr.g. Mujadil (USA) 119 – Cidaris (IRE) (Persian Bold 123) [2004 98:   **89**
7s 8.1d 8.5g⁴ 8.5m 8d Jun 23] good-topped gelding: fairly useful handicapper: suffered
hairline crack of cannon bone after last outing: stays easy 1m: acts on firm and good to
soft going: tried tongue tied: front runner. *A. M. Balding*

IROQUOIS PRINCESS   2 ch.f. (Feb 28) Polish Precedent (USA) 131 – Chelsea   **–**
(USA) (Miswaki (USA) 124) [2004 6d p7.1g 6.1v f6g Nov 8] 3,200Y: workmanlike filly:
fourth foal: closely related to 6f (at 2 yrs) and 1m winner Cedar Rangers (by Anabaa):
dam, French 9f winner, half-sister to US Grade 1 1¼m winner Super Staff and very smart
performer up to 12.5f in France/USA Public Purse: well beaten in maidens. *D. Shaw*

IRREVERSIBLE   2 b.f. (Feb 26) Diktat 126 – Amsicora (Cadeaux Genereux 131)   **68**
[2004 p7g⁶ p7.1g Nov 13] 32,000Y: second foal: half-sister to 3-y-o Go Bananas: dam, unraced, out of sister to very smart 7f/1m winner Efisio: better effort in maidens when sixth at Lingfield. *J. H. M. Gosden*

IRUSAN (IRE)   4 br.g. Catrail (USA) 123 – Ostrusa (AUT) (Rustan (HUN)) [2004 7g⁶   **68**
6m 6g f6g⁴ f7m⁶ f6m⁵ 7.2s p8.6g² p7.1g* f7g p7.1g⁵ p8.6g³ Dec 17] good-topped gelding: fair handicapper: won at Wolverhampton in October: stays 8.6f: acts on all-weather and good to firm going: blinkered last 5 outings. *Jedd O'Keeffe*

ISA'AF (IRE)   5 b.g. Darshaan 133 – Shauna's Honey (IRE) 88 (Danehill (USA) 126)   **73**
[2004 61d: f12g* f14g² 11s* 14.1s* 12m 13g² 12.1m⁴ 11.8g⁴ 14.1d* 12g⁶ 12s 12.6g 15.9g⁴ 16g² 13.9g 18d⁴ Oct 18] neat gelding: fair performer: won banded event at Wolverhampton in March and handicaps at Southwell (apprentices) and Nottingham in April and Nottingham in July: barely stays 2¼m: acts on fibresand, soft and good to firm going: tough. *P. W. Hiatt*

ISAZ   4 b.c. Elmaamul (USA) 125 – Pretty Poppy 67 (Song 132) [2004 ?: 7d⁵ 6s⁵ 6m⁵   **67**
6m 6f Jul 5] strong, good sort: lightly-raced maiden: just fair form in 2004: effective at 6f/7f: acts on good to firm ground, probably on soft: sold 4,700 gns in October, sent to Belgium. *H. Candy*

I SEE NO SHIPS   4 b.f. Danzig Connection (USA) – Killick 69 (Slip Anchor 136)   **–**
[2004 –: 6m 11.7g Jul 11] close-coupled filly: no sign of ability. *M. Mullineaux*

ISIDORE BONHEUR (IRE)   3 b.c. Mtoto 134 – Way O'Gold (USA) (Slew O' Gold   **99**
(USA)) [2004 99: 9g⁴ 10g⁴ 12.3d⁴ 14.8m⁴ 8f 10g Oct 2] big, strong, close-coupled colt: fluent mover: useful performer: creditable fourth in 2 listed races at Newmarket and Chester Vase (beaten 7¼ lengths by Red Lancer) first 3 starts in 2004: well below form fourth and final outings: races freely, but seems to stay 1½m: acts on good to firm and good to soft ground: tried blinkered: difficult ride: none too reliable: sold 47,000 gns. *B. W. Hills*

ISITLOVEYOURAFTER (IRE)   2 b.f. (Feb 23) Orpen (USA) 116 – Pericolo (IRE)   **–**
92 (Kris 135) [2004 6d 5g⁵ 7.1f⁶ 5f f6g Nov 8] €2,500F, €6,000Y: half-sister to several winners, including 5f (at 2yrs) to 6.5f (in UAE) winner Nantucket (by Turtle Island): dam third at 2 yrs on only start: well held in maidens/nursery: blinkered final outing. *R. P. Elliott*

ISKANDER   3 b.g. Danzero (AUS) – Amber Mill 96 (Doulab (USA) 115) [2004 91:   **86 d**
6d⁶ 7s 7m 6m 6g 6s⁶ 8.1g⁴ 8g 9.2s⁵ 8g 8g⁴ p9.5g Oct 18] leggy gelding: fairly useful handicapper: below form after reappearance: stays 1m: acts on good to firm and good to soft going, ran poorly on all-weather debut final start: often blinkered: sometimes slowly away: usually waited with. *K. A. Ryan*

ISLAND HOUSE (IRE)   8 ch.h. Grand Lodge (USA) 125 – Fortitude (IRE) (Last   **107**
Tycoon 131) [2004 115: 10g³ 10d 9.9g⁵ 12m³ 12g³ Jul 16] tall, quite good-topped horse: smart performer at best: just useful form in 2004: third in listed race at Kempton (behind Scott's View) on reappearance and in similar contest (behind First Charter) and minor event (to Eastern Breeze) at Newmarket last 2 outings: effective at 1¼m/1½m: acts on any going: has idled/edged left/carried head awkwardly: usually waited with. *G. Wragg*

ISLAND LIGHT (USA)   4 ch.g. Woodman (USA) 126 – Isla Del Rey (USA) 103   **–**
(Nureyev (USA) 131) [2004 94§: 12g 10.3g 10g 10.5d Jun 3] compact gelding: fairly useful in 2003: well held in 2004: wore cheekpieces final outing: sometimes slowly away: headstrong. *Mrs M. Reveley*

ISLAND RAPTURE   4 b.f. Royal Applause 124 – Gersey (Generous (IRE) 139)   **77**
[2004 87: 8.1d 8m 9g⁴ 10m p8g³ 8m² 8m⁶ 8.5g p8g² p8.6g³ p8g⁵ p9.5g⁶ p8g* Nov 30] quite attractive filly: fair handicapper: won at Lingfield in November: stays 1¼m: acts on polytrack, firm and soft going: sometimes slowly away: usually waited with: consistent. *J. A. R. Toller*

ISLANDS FAREWELL   4 b.g. Emarati (USA) 74 – Chief Island 62 (Be My Chief   **58**
(USA) 122) [2004 –: 9g 8v 8.3f² 8f⁵ f8s 8s³ 10f² 11.9m² Sep 23] lengthy gelding: modest maiden: left Mrs M. Reveley after second start: stays 1½m: acts on firm and soft going, well held on fibresand. *D. Nicholls*

ISLAND SOUND   7 b.g. Turtle Island (IRE) 123 – Ballet 61 (Sharrood (USA) 124)   **104**
[2004 104: 10m⁶ 10.1g³ 9d³ Sep 18] lengthy, angular gelding: has a round action: useful performer: best effort in 2004 when third to Sights On Gold in minor event at Epsom second start: races mainly at 1¼m nowadays: acts on heavy and good to firm going: tried visored/in cheekpieces: usually front runner. *D. R. C. Elsworth*

ISLAND SPELL 3 b.f. Singspiel (IRE) 133 – Shifty Mouse 44 (Night Shift (USA)) **55**
[2004 75: 7d³ 7m⁵ 6d³ 5d 5m 6m Jul 23] close-coupled filly: fair maiden at 2 yrs, only
modest in 2004: should stay 1m: acts on firm going: wore cheekpieces final start: sold
1,200 gns. *C. Grant*

ISLAND STAR (IRE) 4 b.g. Turtle Island (IRE) 123 – Orthorising (Aragon 118) **44**
[2004 67d: p8g p6g p7g p10g⁴ 11.9g⁶ May 4] sturdy gelding: poor maiden: stays 1m: acts
on polytrack and firm ground: tried visored: often races prominently. *G. P. Enright*

ISLAND SWING (IRE) 2 ch.f. (Mar 19) Trans Island 119 – Farmers Swing (IRE) **82**
(River Falls 113) [2004 5g 6g* 6m* 6m⁴ 6g 6.1g 6g³ 6m⁴ 6.1v* 6v p6g Dec 30] €7,000F,
7,500Y: leggy, lengthy filly: good mover: first foal: dam, Norwegian 8.5f winner, half-
sister to useful performer up to 1m Scarteen Fox: fairly useful performer: won sellers at
Haydock and York in June and minor event at Nottingham in October: well held in
nurseries last 2 starts: should stay 7f: acts on heavy and good to firm going. *J. L. Spearing*

ISLAND WARRIOR (IRE) 9 b.g. Warcraft (USA) – Only Flower § (Warpath 113) **–**
[2004 p12.2g Dec 27] well held both outings on Flat: tried tongue tied. *B. P. J. Baugh*

ISLE DREAM 2 ch.f. (Mar 17) Forzando 122 – La Volta 86 (Komaite (USA)) [2004 **–**
5f 6f p5.1d Oct 23] 900Y: strong filly: second foal: dam 5f to 7f winner, including at 2
yrs: no form in maidens. *J. Balding*

ISLEOFHOPEANTEARS (IRE) 5 b.g. College Chapel 122 – Fontaine Lodge **–**
(IRE) 55 (Lafontaine (USA) 117) [2004 8.5m⁵ 10g 10.2g Oct 10] no form in 3 maidens,
trained by N. Glynn in Ireland first 2: very slowly away final outing. *A. E. Jones*

ISLE OF LIGHT (IRE) 2 b.f. (Apr 23) Trans Island 119 – Singled Out (IRE) (Fairy **–**
King (USA)) [2004 6m f5s Aug 23] second foal: dam unraced: well beaten in maiden/
seller, racing freely. *W. R. Muir*

ISMAHAAN 5 ch.m. Unfuwain (USA) 131 – River Divine (USA) 59 (Irish River (FR) **67**
131) [2004 10m⁶ 12.3d⁵ Aug 30] 150,000Y: big, lengthy mare: second foal: dam ran once
at 2 yrs: little form in bumpers, refusing to race once: seemingly better effort on Flat in
maiden at Windsor on debut: should stay at least 1½m. *G. Wragg*

ISSY BLUE 2 b.f. (Feb 14) Primo Dominie 121 – Mountain Bluebird (USA) 79 (Clever Trick **53**
(USA)) [2004 7m 6g 7d Aug 12] 18,000Y: quite good-topped filly: half-sister to several
winners, including 5f (at 2 yrs) to 7.5f winner Waxwing (by Efisio) and useful stayer
Anchor Clever (by Slip Anchor): dam 1m winner: modest form on first 2 starts in
maidens: should stay 1m. *J. A. Osborne*

ITALIAN COUNSEL (IRE) 7 b.g. Leading Counsel (USA) 122 – Mullaghroe (Tar- **43**
boosh (USA)) [2004 p10g p12g⁴ May 13] fairly useful hurdler: first form on Flat in
banded race at Lingfield final outing: stays 1½m. *L. A. Dace*

ITALIAN MIST (FR) 5 b.g. Forzando 122 – Digamist Girl (IRE) (Digamist (USA) **47**
110) [2004 46§: f6g* f6g³ p6g⁵ f6s* f7g² p7g f5g* 5s³ f6g* 6s f5d⁴ f6m 5.7s p5.1g⁴ **a69**
p5g⁵ Dec 18] fair on all-weather, poor on turf: won banded race at Wolverhampton, 2
handicaps at Southwell and handicap at Wolverhampton in first half of 2004: effective at
5f to easy 7f: acts on all-weather and good to firm going, probably on soft: tried blinkered/
in cheekpieces: sometimes carries head awkwardly. *Julian Poulton*

ITALIAN TOUCH (IRE) 2 b.g. (Apr 25) Rossini (USA) 118 – Attached (IRE) (For- **57**
est Wind (USA) 111) [2004 6.1m 6.1d 5.1g 7v p7.1g p6g p6g Dec 18] quite good-topped **a44**
gelding: modest maiden on turf, poor on all-weather: should stay 6f: acts on polytrack,
best turf effort on good going: visored (below form) penultimate start. *J. A. Glover*

I T CONSULTANT 6 b.g. Rock City 120 – Game Germaine (Mummy's Game 120) **– §**
[2004 56, a–: 5v Apr 20] strong gelding: tailed off only start in 2004: tried blinkered/
tongue tied. *Miss L. A. Perratt*

ITHACA (USA) 3 ch.f. Distant View (USA) 126 – Reams of Verse (USA) 121 (Nure- **100**
yev (USA) 131) [2004 97: 7d³ 11.4d⁶ 10g⁵ 8.1d³ 8m⁴ 7m³ 7m⁵ Oct 2] smallish, close-
coupled filly: useful performer: best efforts when third in listed races at Sandown (2¼
lengths behind Antediluvian) and Doncaster (beaten 1½ lengths by Attune) on fourth/
sixth starts: stayed 1m: acted on firm and good to soft going: stud. *H. R. A. Cecil*

IT MUST BE SPEECH 3 b.g. Advise (FR) – Maiden Speech (Pitskelly 122) [2004 **–**
–: f11g⁵ f12s² f12g⁵ 8.5m 12g Oct 5] good-bodied gelding: fair maiden on all-weather: **a65**
stays 1½m: acts on fibresand, little form on turf. *S. L. Keightley*

IT'S A BLESSING 3 b.f. Inchinor 119 – Benedicite (Lomond (USA) 128) [2004 –: –
p10g Jan 10] well beaten in maidens at Doncaster and Lingfield. *N. P. Littmoden*

ITSA MONKEY (IRE) 2 b.g. (Apr 5) Merdon Melody 98 – Gracious Imp (USA) **44**
(Imp Society (USA)) [2004 p5g 6f⁶ f5g² 7m 7m f7g 8.5s 6.9m 7.5m f8g Nov 23] poor
maiden: trained by N. Littmoden first 2 starts: stays 8.5f: acts on fibresand and soft going:
wore cheekpieces fifth outing, blinkered last 4. *M. J. Polglase*

ITS A MYSTERY (IRE) 5 b.m. Idris (IRE) 118 – Blue Infanta (Chief Singer 131) –
[2004 –: 11.5f Aug 5] tall, workmanlike mare: no form: tried tongue tied. *R. J. Smith*

IT'S BLUE CHIP 3 b.g. Polar Falcon (USA) 126 – Bellateena 57 (Nomination 125) **68**
[2004 –: f9.4g³ p10g 11.6s* 14.6g⁴ 11.6s⁶ f12g⁴ f12g* 11.6g 12f 12.1d 13.9g p12.2d Nov
4] workmanlike gelding: fair handicapper: won at Windsor in April and Southwell in
June: below form after, very slowly away final outing: stays 1½m: acts on fibresand and
soft going: joined Miss H. Knight. *P. W. D'Arcy*

IT'S DEFINITE (IRE) 5 b.g. Definite Article 121 – Taoveret (IRE) (Flash of Steel –
120) [2004 88: 18s Oct 16] big, lengthy gelding: fairly useful handicapper at best: well
held in Cesarewitch at Newmarket only Flat outing in 2004: tried visored/in cheekpieces:
usually held up. *P. Bowen*

ITS ECCO BOY 6 ch.g. Clantime 101 – Laena 72 (Roman Warrior 132) [2004 73, **62 d**
a62: p6g⁴ f7g⁴ f6s* f7s f6s p7g 5m 6m 7m 6m f6m p8m⁶ p8g p7.1g⁶ Oct 25] tall gelding:
modest performer: won handicap at Southwell in February: below form after: effective
at 6f/7f: acts on all-weather, firm and good to soft going: tried visored/in cheekpieces.
P. Howling

ITS MY SON 3 b.g. Sea Raven (IRE) 75 – Fay Eden (IRE) 60 (Fayruz 116) [2004 10m –
Aug 2] tailed-off last in maiden at Windsor. *L. G. Cottrell*

ITSONLYAGAME 4 b.g. Ali-Royal (IRE) 127 – Mena 58 (Blakeney 126) [2004 68: **56**
p10g* p10g p13g p10g⁵ p12g p10g² 11.7s May 4] modest performer: won maiden at
Lingfield in January: stays 11.6f: acts on polytrack, firm and good to soft going: visored
(well held) 2 of last 3 starts: gelded after final outing. *R. Ingram*

IT'S PEGGY SPEECH 2 b.f. (Apr 2) Bishop of Cashel 122 – Marsara (Never So –
Bold 135) [2004 6s Nov 6] third foal: dam unraced: 66/1, well held in maiden at Doncaster. *S. L. Keightley*

IT'S THE LIMIT (USA) 5 b.g. Boundary (USA) 117 – Beside (USA) (Sportin' Life **97**
(USA)) [2004 98: 12m⁴ 14g 16.2m⁴ 18s Oct 16] rangy, good sort: useful performer,
lightly raced: creditable fourth in handicaps at Ascot in July and September, beaten 3½
lengths by Escayola in latter: stays 2m: acts on good to firm going: reared leaving stall
second outing. *Mrs A. J. Perrett*

IVANA ILLYICH (IRE) 2 ch.f. (Apr 29) Tipsy Creek (USA) 115 – Tolstoya (North- **72**
fields (USA)) [2004 5s⁵ 5g 6m⁴ 6m 6g³ 7.1d³ 7m 7m f8g p8.6g Nov 29] €25,000Y: **a–**
close-coupled filly: half-sister to several winners, including useful 6f winner (including
at 2 yrs) Wildwood Flower (by Distant Relative) and fairly useful 7f winner Zaretski (by
Pursuit of Love): dam Irish 2-y-o 5f winner: fair maiden: shapes as if will stay 1m: acts
on good to firm and good to soft going, well below form on all-weather. *S. Kirk*

IVORY COAST (IRE) 3 b.f. Cape Cross (IRE) 129 – Ivory League 47 (Last Tycoon **61**
131) [2004 56: p10g⁴ p10g* 9.3f² 10m 10m 10.2g 10.1m⁵ 10.1g 10s* 10d Sep 20] tall,
leggy filly: modest performer: won handicap at Lingfield in January and seller at Brighton in August: stays 1¼m: acts on all-weather, firm and soft going: blinkered last 2 starts:
sometimes races freely: sold 5,000 gns. *W. R. Muir*

IVORY LACE 3 b.f. Atraf 116 – Miriam 59 (Forzando 122) [2004 70: p5g⁵ p5g² f5g **79**
p5g* p6g³ 5.1g* 5.1g* 5.3m⁴ 5.1g* 5d⁵ 5g 6g p6m⁴ Oct 6] rather leggy filly: fair perfor- **a72**
mer: won seller at Lingfield in February (left D. Ivory after next start) and handicaps at
Bath (2) and Chepstow in June: effective at 5f/easy 6f: acts on polytrack and firm
going, probably on good to soft: blinkered (well held) once at 2 yrs. *S. Woodman*

IVORY VENTURE 4 b.f. Reprimand 122 – Julietta Mia (USA) 72 (Woodman (USA) **46**
126) [2004 57: p6g p5g p7g p8g p5g* p7g Feb 23] poor performer: form in 2004 only
when winning banded stakes at Lingfield in February: best efforts at 5f: acts on all-
weather, firm and good to soft going: blinkered last 3 starts. *D. K. Ivory*

IVORY WOLF 2 ch.g. (Mar 6) Wolfhound (USA) 126 – Ashkernazy (IRE) 60 (Salt –
Dome (USA)) [2004 5.3f 5f 7g Jul 8] well held in maidens: slowly away first 2 outings:
wore cheekpieces final one. *J. L. Spearing*

IVY HOUSE LAD (IRE)   4 b.g. Presidium 124 – Nice Spice (IRE) (Common   –
Grounds 118) [2004 p10g⁵ Mar 29] well beaten in bumper, and in claimer at Lingfield.
I. W. McInnes

IVY LEAGUE STAR (IRE)   3 b.f. Sadler's Wells (USA) 132 – Ivy (USA) (Sir Ivor   74
(USA) 135) [2004 59p: 12m⁵ f12g 11.9s* p12.2g⁵ 14.1d⁵ p13g⁵ Nov 10] leggy filly: fair
handicapper: won at Haydock in September: stays 1¾m: acts on polytrack, soft and good
to firm going: threatened to run out fourth outing: sold 135,000 gns. *B. W. Hills*

IVY MOON   4 b.f. Emperor Jones (USA) 119 – Bajan Rose 89 (Dashing Blade 117)   48
[2004 64: f8.5g³ f7g⁶ p8g 6g³ 7m⁵ 7.1m³ 8.1m⁴ 7m 8.1m⁵ 8f Sep 6] leggy filly: poor
performer: effective at 6f to 1m: acts on firm ground and fibresand: often slowly away/
pulls hard: ran out third 3-y-o outing. *B. J. Llewellyn*

I WISH   6 ch.m. Beveled (USA) – Ballystate 71 (Ballacashtal (CAN)) [2004 73: p7g   65
p7g⁵ p7g 5.7s⁴ 6g* 5m⁵ 7g⁵ 6m³ 6f 7f² 6g² 6g⁶ p7g⁴ p7g Nov 27] tall, leggy mare: fair
performer: won claimer at Windsor in May: effective at 5f to 1m: acts on polytrack, firm
and good to soft going: tried in cheekpieces: often races freely. *M. Madgwick*

I WISH I KNEW   3 br.g. Petong 126 – Hoh Dancer 66 (Indian Ridge 123) [2004 57:   –
f7s⁶ 7.1s 6m 7m 6f Jun 14] modest maiden at 2 yrs: little form in 2004: visored last 2
starts: dead. *D. J. Coakley*

I WON'T DANCE (IRE)   3 b.c. Marju (IRE) 127 – Carnelly (IRE) 101 (Priolo (USA)   74
127) [2004 84p: 6g 7f 8d 7m⁴ p7g Sep 1] leggy colt: fair performer: acts on good to firm
ground: slowly away third outing: sold 10,000 gns. *R. Hannon*

IZMAIL (IRE)   5 b.g. Bluebird (USA) 125 – My-Lorraine (IRE) 77 (Mac's Imp (USA)   74 §
116) [2004 79§: 5s 5d 5m 5f 5.3g 5f* 5m 5.1s 5.7f 5.1m 5.1g⁵ 5g p5.1d p5.1g p5.1g Nov
19] useful-looking gelding: fair handicapper: won at Carlisle in July: left D. Nicholls
after next start: best at 5f/easy 6f: acts on firm and good to soft going: tried visored/
blinkered: sometimes slowly away/races freely: unreliable. *P. D. Evans*

IZZA   3 br.f. Wizard King 122 – Nicholas Mistress 56 (Beveled (USA)) [2004 –: f6g Feb   –
15] unfurnished filly: probably of no account. *W. Storey*

IZZET MUZZY (FR)   6 ch.g. Piccolo 121 – Texanne (BEL) 66§ (Efisio 120) [2004   –
f5s Jan 15] good-bodied gelding: missed 2003 and well held only 6-y-o outing: tried
visored. *D. Shaw*

J

JAAMID   2 b.g. (Feb 14) Desert Prince (IRE) 130 – Strictly Cool (USA) (Bering 136)   79
[2004 7m⁴ 6d 8s² Oct 19] 60,000Y: big, good-topped gelding: half-brother to useful
winner in France/Ireland around 1¼m Heezapistol (by Pistolet Bleu) and fairly useful
French 7f winner Highest Cool (by Highest Honor): dam French 2-y-o 9f winner: fair
form in maidens: second at Bath, making most and tending to hang: will stay 1¼m: acts
on soft and good to firm ground: sold 35,000 gns, then gelded. *M. Johnston*

JABAAR (USA)   6 gr.g. Silver Hawk (USA) 123 – Sierra Madre (FR) 119 (Baillamont   96
(USA) 124) [2004 96: 8g 10.3g³ 10.4d⁵ 10m⁶ 10.3d² 10.4g⁵ 11.9d 10g 10d² 10.4g 12s 12s
Nov 6] strong, lengthy gelding: useful handicapper: left D. Nicholls after sixth start: best
at 1¼m/1½m: acts on firm and good to soft going: effective visored/blinkered or not.
M. W. Easterby

JABRAAN (USA)   2 b.c. (Mar 1) Aljabr (USA) 125 – Miss Zafonic (FR) 98 (Zafonic   69 p
(USA) 130) [2004 7g Oct 12] angular colt: good mover: third foal: dam, 6f (at 2 yrs) and
7f winner, half-sister to smart sprinter Central City: odds on, eighth to Eqdaam in maiden
at Leicester, fading closing stages: should do better. *Saeed bin Suroor*

JACARANDA (IRE)   4 ch.g. Bahhare (USA) 122 – Near Miracle (Be My Guest   77
(USA) 126) [2004 86: 7d 7s⁵ 7.1m 9g 10.1d² 9.9g⁴ 10m* 10m³ 11.7m⁶ 10g 12f⁵ 11.6d
Oct 4] unfurnished gelding: fair handicapper: won amateur event at Newmarket in July:
stays 1¼m: acts on fibresand, firm and soft going. *Mrs A. L. M. King*

JACKADANDY (USA)   2 b.g. (May 11) Lear Fan (USA) 130 – Chandra (CAN)   63
(Morning Bob (USA)) [2004 7d⁴ 8.3d³ 8m Sep 4] $11,000Y, 30,000 2-y-o: leggy gelding:
has a round action: third foal: dam, ran twice in North America, out of half-sister to US

Grade 1 9f winner Technology: modest form first 2 starts in maidens: will stay 1¼m.
J. Howard Johnson

JACK DAWSON (IRE)   7 b.g. Persian Bold 123 – Dream of Jenny 73 (Caerleon   **83**
(USA) 132) [2004 81: 14m* 16.1f Aug 7] neat gelding: fairly useful handicapper: won at
Musselburgh in May: effective at 1½m to easy 2m: seems best on good going or firmer:
held up: tough and consistent: useful handicap hurdler. *John Berry*

JACK DURRANCE (IRE)   4 b.g. Polish Precedent (USA) 131 – Atlantic Desire   **43**
(IRE) 100 (Ela-Mana-Mou 132) [2004 79: 10.2g 10.2g 11.6m⁴ 12.6m 17.2g 14.1g Jul 24]
small, strong gelding: only poor form in 2004: should stay 1½m: tried visored. *G. A. Ham*

JACKIE KIELY   3 ch.g. Vettori (IRE) 119 – Fudge (Polar Falcon (USA) 126) [2004   **70**
–: p7g p10g⁶ p10g² p10g 11.6s⁵ 12.6s⁵ 11.5m⁴ 10f² f12d* 10.2f 10m* 10g* 12m 11.5m   **a60**
10f³ 10m 8.5g⁴ 10m 9m³ 8.5g⁵ p9.5g p12g p9.5g p12.2g Nov 29] leggy gelding: fair
performer: left T. Mills after eighth outing: won handicaps at Southwell in June and at
Brighton and Newmarket in July: stays 1½m: acts on all-weather and firm ground: tongue
tied nowadays: held up. *P. S. McEntee*

JACK OF TRUMPS (IRE)   4 b.c. King's Theatre (IRE) 128 – Queen Caroline (USA)   **80**
67 (Chief's Crown (USA)) [2004 70+: p10g* p10g 9.7d 12m⁴ 12d* 11.9f* 12s* 12g
Sep 13] strong colt: fairly useful performer: won maiden at Lingfield in January and
handicaps at Salisbury (edged left), York and Goodwood in July/August: found little final
start: should stay 1¾m: acts on polytrack, firm and soft ground: free-going sort. *G. Wragg*

JACK'S CHECK   3 b.g. Factual (USA) 108 – Ski Baby (Petoski 135) [2004 8.1s 8g   **–**
Oct 4] tall gelding: well held in maidens at Haydock and Pontefract. *N. Tinkler*

JACKS DELIGHT   4 b.g. Bettergeton 97 – Impromptu Melody (IRE) (Mac's Imp   **–**
(USA) 116) [2004 –: f7g 6m f6g Jun 4] of little account. *B. D. Leavy*

JACK SULLIVAN (USA)   3 ch.g. Belong To Me (USA) – Provisions (USA) (Devil's   **96**
Bag (USA)) [2004 96: a8f² a9f⁴ 7f.1g⁴ 7m 8m⁵ p7g* p8g⁴ Dec 18] strong, good-topped   **a115**
gelding: smart performer on all-weather, useful on turf: gelded and off 4 months, best
effort when winning handicap at Lingfield in November by a length from Moayed: also
in frame in UAE 2000 Guineas (2½ lengths second to Little Jim) and UAE Derby (5¼
lengths fourth behind Lundy's Liability) at Nad Al Sheba first 2 starts: best effort on turf
when fifth to Fong's Thong in listed race at Goodwood (blinkered, raced freely): stays 9f:
acts on polytrack and dirt, raced only on good/good to soft ground on turf: tongue tied
fourth/fifth starts: often races prominently. *G. A. Butler*

JACK THE GIANT (IRE)   2 b.c. (May 4) Giant's Causeway (USA) 132 – State   **60 p**
Crystal (IRE) 114 (High Estate 127) [2004 6f 7d Aug 27] tall, quite good-topped colt:
fluent mover: sixth living foal: half-brother to 3-y-o Crystal Curling and 1¼m winner
True Crystal and 1½m winner Time Crystal (both fairly useful, by Sadler's Wells): dam,
7f (at 2 yrs) and 1½m (Lancashire Oaks) winner, half-sister to Fillies' Mile winner
Crystal Music and smart middle-distance stayer Tchaikovsky: modest form in maidens
at Windsor and Newmarket: should be suited by 1¼m/1½m: type to make a better 3-y-o.
B. W. Hills

JACOBIN (USA)   3 b.c. Tamayaz (CAN) 121 – Simply Follow Me (USA) (Green Dan-   **–**
cer (USA) 132) [2004 10m 12f Aug 7] tailed off in maidens at Sandown and Newmarket.
P. J. McBride

JACOB (IRE)   3 b.g. Victory Note (USA) 120 – Persian Mistress (IRE) (Persian Bold   **46 ?**
123) [2004 62: f6g⁵ f8s⁴ f7g Mar 22] compact gelding: just poor form at 3 yrs (reportedly
broke blood vessel final start): stays 6f. *P. A. Blockley*

JADAN (IRE)   3 b.g. Imperial Ballet (IRE) 110 – Sports Post Lady (IRE) 72 (M   **86**
Double M (USA)) [2004 73: 5s 5.1d 5g³ 5d⁶ 5d⁶ 5d* 5m⁵ 5d 6.1g 5d* 5s⁶ Oct 16] sturdy
gelding: fairly useful performer: won handicap at Haydock in July and minor event at
Hamilton in September: best at 5f: acts on good to firm and good to soft ground, probably
on soft. *E. J. Alston*

JADEERON   5 b.g. Green Desert (USA) 127 – Rain And Shine (FR) 78 (Rainbow   **69**
Quest (USA) 134) [2004 64: p13g² f12g² f12s² p13g³ 16g⁴ 14g⁴ 16d 12m p12.2g⁶ p12m⁶
p13.9g³ p13g⁵ p13.9g* p13.9g⁵ p13.9g⁶ Dec 31] useful-looking gelding: fair handicapper: won at Wolverhampton in December: stays 2m: acts on all-weather and firm going,
probably on good to soft: tried blinkered/tongue tied: often wears cheekpieces: reportedly
finished lame eighth outing. *Miss D. A. McHale*

JADE STAR (USA) 4 b.f. Jade Hunter (USA) – Danzig's Girl (USA) (Danzig (USA)) **59**
[2004 55, a45: f12f⁴ f9.4g* p10g f9.4g² f9.4g⁶ 9.9s⁴ 11.5m⁴ 9.7g 10.1m³ f8m 10m f8g
Dec 1] modest handicapper: won at Wolverhampton in February: left Gay Kelleway after
ninth start, trained by P. Burgoyne tenth one only: stays 1¼m: acts on fibresand, soft and
good to firm going: sometimes wears cheekpieces: often makes running. *A. B. Haynes*

JAGGED (IRE) 4 b.g. Sesaro (USA) 81 – Latin Mass (Music Boy 124) [2004 67: p6g **72**
6.1v 5.7m f6g² 6m³ f5g* f6s² 5.7f² 5.7g⁴ p5.1d* p6g p5.1g Nov 26] workmanlike gelding: fair handicapper: left K. Burke after reappearance, Mrs H. Sweeting after
third start: won at Southwell in August and Wolverhampton in November: has form at
7f, but best at 5f/6f nowadays: acts on all-weather, firm and good to soft ground: tried
blinkered, usually visored nowadays: races up with pace. *J. R. Jenkins*

JAGGER 4 gr.g. Linamix (FR) 127 – Sweetness Herself 106 (Unfuwain (USA) 131) **107**
[2004 109p: 16.1s 14g³ 13.9s 12m⁴ 14g Sep 18] smallish, quite attractive gelding: useful
performer: unlucky length third to Mephisto in handicap at Goodwood second start: stiff
task, ran as well as could be expected when 5¾ lengths last of 4 to Mamool in September
Stakes at Kempton penultimate outing: always behind in Irish St Leger at the Curragh
fortnight later (gelded after): should stay 2m: acts on polytrack, firm and good to soft
going, possibly unsuited by soft: edgy type, often has 2 handlers: held up. *G. A. Butler*

JAHANGIR 5 b.g. Zamindar (USA) 116 – Imperial Jade 105 (Lochnager 132) [2004 **48**
60d: p8g² p7g³ p6g p6g p8g Mar 9] close-coupled gelding: poor maiden: stays 7f: acts on
all-weather and good to firm ground: tried visored/blinkered: sometimes troublesome at
stall: free-going sort: none too trustworthy. *B. R. Johnson*

JAHIA (NZ) 5 br.m. Jahafil 114 – Lana (NZ) (Tristrams Heritage (NZ)) [2004 8v 10f **–**
9d 8g p10g Nov 13] very long-backed New Zealand-bred mare: ran 4 times in native
country, winning at 5f/6f at 3 yrs: little sign of ability in Britain, leaving R. C. Guest after
reappearance. *M. Madgwick*

JAILBIRD 3 b.f. Nicolotte 118 – Grace Browning 84 (Forzando 122) [2004 57: 5.7f **–**
6.1m Jun 14] smallish, sturdy filly: lightly-raced maiden: last in handicaps in 2004:
visored final start. *R. M. Beckett*

JAIR OHMSFORD (IRE) 5 b.g. Hamas (IRE) 125§ – Harry's Irish Rose (USA) **82**
(Sir Harry Lewis (USA) 127) [2004 68+: f9.4g* f9.4g⁴ f12s* f12g* 12v⁴ 10d³ f12g³
Dec 16] lengthy gelding: fairly useful performer: won handicap at Wolverhampton in
January and minor event and handicap at Southwell in February: ran well after lay-off
final start: stays 1½m: acts on fibresand, raced only on good going or softer on turf: ridden
by M. Fenton for all wins. *W. J. Musson*

JAKARMI 3 b.g. Merdon Melody 98 – Lady Ploy 42 (Deploy 131) [2004 58: **76**
f8.5g* f7g⁶ f8.5s* f8.5s³ 8.2g² f8g² 10.2g² 8.3s³ f12g² 10g* 10s* 10d 10g 11g⁵ 11.6m
Sep 27] heavy-topped gelding: fair performer: won seller and claimer at Wolverhampton
in January/February, maiden at Leicester in June and minor event at Nottingham in July:
barely stays easy 1½m: acts on fibresand and soft going. *B. Palling*

JAKEAL (IRE) 5 b.g. Eagle Eyed (USA) 111 – Karoi (IRE) (Kafu 120) [2004 67: p7g **60**
8s⁴ 8d 7.5g 7.5g² 8.2v Nov 4] strong gelding: probably stays 1m: acts on
firm and soft ground: wore cheekpieces (ran creditably) penultimate start: has been
awkward leaving stall: has worn severe bridle. *R. M. Whitaker*

JAKE BLACK (IRE) 4 b.g. Definite Article 121 – Tirhala (IRE) (Chief Singer 131) **70**
[2004 57: f12g f8.5s* f9.4g* f8g⁵ 10.1v³ 10s* 10.2s⁵ 10m 12.4g⁴ 10g⁴ 10.4m* 10.3g 10d
10.1m Oct 10] workmanlike gelding: fair performer: won 2 banded races (first one amateur event) at Wolverhampton in March and apprentice handicaps at Pontefract in April
and York in September: stays 1¼m: acts on fibresand, heavy and good to firm going:
twice visored, including when successful: fair hurdler. *J. J. Quinn*

JALAMID (IRE) 2 b.c. (Mar 30) Danehill (USA) 126 – Vignelaure (IRE) 74 (Royal **75 +**
Academy (USA) 130) [2004 7.1m* 7g Jul 8] 300,000Y: big, lengthy colt: third foal: half-
brother to useful Irish 1m winner La Pieta (by Spectrum): dam, third at 1m (at 2 yrs) from
2 starts in Ireland, half-sister to smart Irish miler Fatherland out of Coronation Stakes
winner Lisadell, a very good family: won maiden at Sandown in June, doing just enough
in front: well held in Superlative Stakes at Newmarket: should stay 1m: tongue tied both
starts. *J. H. M. Gosden*

JALISSA 2 b.f. (May 13) Mister Baileys 123 – Julia Domna (Dominion 123) [2004 **66 p**
p7g⁴ Sep 7] fourth foal: half-sister to 7-y-o Vintage Premium and 4-y-o Domirati: dam,

no form, half-sister to very smart 7f/1m performer Norwich: 14/1 and green, fourth in maiden at Lingfield, slowly away and not knocked about: should improve. *R. Charlton*

JALONS STAR (IRE) 6 b.g. Eagle Eyed (USA) 111 – Regina St Cyr (IRE) (Doulab (USA) 115) [2004 10m 10.1f 11.6m Aug 2] tall gelding: fair handicapper in 2001: well held on return in 2004. *M. R. Channon*   –

JALOUHAR 4 b.g. Victory Note (USA) 120 – Orient Way (IRE) 61 (Danehill (USA) 126) [2004 67: f6g⁵ f6g⁴ f7g⁶ p6g⁵ p7g f6s⁵ f5g 6m² 6.1m 8.2g⁶ 6d 6m² 7.1m 6g 7g⁶ 6g 6g 6g f6g p7.1g Dec 22] compact gelding: modest performer at best in 2004: effective at 6f/7f: acts on all-weather and good to firm going: has worn visor/cheekpieces: usually races prominently. *B. P. J. Baugh*   **57 d**

JALOUSIE DREAM 3 b.f. Easycall 115 – Forest Maid (Thatching 131) [2004 10d 9g⁵ 10m³ 12m 13.8g Sep 7] quite lightly-made filly: third foal: dam unraced out of half-sister to high-class 7f to 9f performer Indian Lodge: little form. *G. M. Moore*

JAMAARON 2 ch.c. (Mar 28) Bachir (IRE) 118 – Kentmere (FR) (Galetto (FR) 118) [2004 7g³ 7m 8s⁴ 8g Sep 30] 30,000Y: lengthy colt: sixth foal: half-brother to 3 winners, including fairly useful 2001 2-y-o 6f winner Danemere (by Danehill) and 1½m/13f winner Love Bitten (by Darshaan): dam, French 1m (at 2 yrs) and 11f winner, half-sister to Prix de Diane winner Lypharita: fair performer: won maiden at Goodwood in August: bit reportedly slipped final start: likely to stay 1¼m: acts on soft going. *R. Hannon*   **77**

JAMAICAN FLIGHT (USA) 11 b.h. Sunshine Forever (USA) – Kalamona (USA) (Hawaii) [2004 61, a55: f16g³ f16g⁴ f12s⁴ 18v⁴ 21.6v⁴ f16g⁵ 18f⁵ 15.8g Oct 5] leggy horse: moderate handicapper, on the downgrade: stays 21f: acts on fibresand/any turf going: tried in visor, better without: has been too free to post/given trouble start: front runner. *Mrs S. Lamyman*   **52 d**

JAMAICAN (UAE) 2 ch.g. (Feb 18) Timber Country (USA) 124 – Notting Hill (Lammtarra (USA) 134) [2004 p7m Dec 22] £2,500 2-y-o: first foal: dam unraced half-sister to smart Irish performer up to 1½m Exaltation: 40/1, eleventh of 13 in maiden at Lingfield. *I. A. Wood*   **53 ?**

JAMES CAIRD (IRE) 4 ch.g. Catrail (USA) 123 – Polish Saga 59 (Polish Patriot (USA) 128) [2004 94: 10m⁶ 10m² 8.9m² 9g² 8m 10.5g 10.3m³ 10f² Sep 23] tall, leggy gelding: useful handicapper: ran well in 2004 when placed: stays 1¼m: acts on fibresand and firm going: blinkered (below form) once at 3 yrs: held up. *M. H. Tompkins*   **95**

JAMESTOWN 7 b.g. Merdon Melody 98 – Thabeh 57 (Shareef Dancer (USA) 135) [2004 66, a54: f8g⁵ f11g f8f f8s f8.5g f11g 7m f9.4m⁴ 8.1m 9.2g⁴ f8f 8.1d Oct 9] workmanlike, close-coupled gelding: just poor form in 2004: best at 7f to 9f: acts on all-weather, firm and soft going: none too reliable. *M. J. Polglase*   **45 a47**

JAN BRUEGHEL (USA) 5 ch.g. Phone Trick (USA) – Sunk (USA) (Polish Navy (USA)) [2004 –, a76: f7g³ f7g⁴ f7g Jan 30] big, strong gelding: just poor form in 2004, finding little (reportedly again broke blood vessel final start): stays easy 7f: acts on fibresand and good to firm going, probably on heavy. *T. D. Barron*   **a46**

JANE JUBILEE 2 b.f. (Feb 19) Mister Baileys 123 – Elsie Bamford 57 (Tragic Role (USA)) [2004 5v³ 6f⁵ 6m² 7m² 7m* 7.1f* 7d⁵ 7s 7g 6d Oct 14] 5,500Y: smallish, lengthy filly: first foal: dam, won around 1¾m, out of half-sister to very smart 1m/1¼m performer Radetzky: fairly useful performer: won nurseries at Catterick (by 5 lengths) and Musselburgh (under 9-11) in July: more highly tried after, running poorly last 3 starts: will stay at least 1m: acts on firm going. *M. Johnston*   **91**

JANES VALENTINE 4 b.f. My Best Valentine 122 – Jane Herring (Nishapour (FR) 125) [2004 63d: p10g⁴ p7g p7g⁴ p7g p7g 7v p6g⁶ May 13] maiden: only poor form in 2004: stays 7f: acts on polytrack and firm going: tried in cheekpieces/visor. *J. J. Bridger*   **40**

JANGO MALFOY (IRE) 3 ch.g. Russian Revival (USA) 125 – Sialia (IRE) (Blue-bird (USA) 125) [2004 61: p7g p8g f8g 12m 16g Jul 30] maiden: no form in 2004: tried blinkered/tongue tied. *B. W. Duke*   –

JAOLINS 3 b.f. Groom Dancer (USA) 128 – On The Top (High Top 131) [2004 45: p6g* p7g² p7g f6s p7g⁵ 7.1s 5.7s 6m 7m 7g f8g⁶ f8d⁵ 9.7f 8.1d⁴ f8g p8.6g p10m Dec 8] leggy filly: modest performer: won seller at Lingfield in February: left R. Hannon after next outing: stays 1m: acts on polytrack, best turf effort on good ground: free-going sort: looks wayward. *P. G. Murphy*   **52**

JARRAAF 4 ch.g. Desert Story (IRE) 115 – Bee Off (IRE) 59 (Wolfhound (USA) 126) [2004 64, a68: f8g⁵ f9.4g⁵ Mar 27] good-bodied gelding: modest maiden: stayed 9.4f: acted on fibresand, good to firm and good to soft ground: dead. *J. W. Unett*   **55**

JARVO 3 b.g. Pursuit of Love 124 – Pinkie Rose (FR) (Kenmare (FR) 125) [2004 66: **67**
10s² f8.5g⁵ 7.1f⁴ 8m 8.5g 8m² 7d³ 8m p8.6g⁴ p7.1g⁴ p9.5g² Dec 22] sturdy gelding: fair
maiden: stays 1¼m: acts on polytrack, firm and soft going: tried tongue tied. *N. P. Litt-moden*

JASMICK (IRE) 6 ch.m. Definite Article 121 – Glass Minnow (IRE) 59 (Alzao (USA) **77**
117) [2004 94: 12m⁵ 14.4m 16.4m 12d⁶ 13.1d 14s² Aug 29] smallish mare: fair handicapper: probably best at 1½m/1¾m: acts on firm and soft going: reportedly covered by
Averti. *H. Morrison*

JASMINE HILL 2 ch.f. (Apr 30) Timeless Times (USA) 99 – Coney Hills 35 (Bever- **43**
ley Boy 99) [2004 5d 5m⁶ 5d 5f Sep 2] 1,600Y: third foal: half-sister to 3-y-o Fitzwarren:
dam, maiden, stayed 7f: poor maiden. *N. Bycroft*

JASMINE PEARL (IRE) 3 b.f. King of Kings (IRE) 125 – Tumbleweed Pearl 96 **45**
(Aragon 118) [2004 68: f7g³ p6g⁶ p7g 6s p6g⁴ 6m 6f² 6m⁵ 6m⁶ 7f⁶ 6g 6m p7g Dec 20]
workmanlike filly: poor maiden: left B. Meehan after reappearance: effective at 6f/easy
7f: acts on all-weather and firm going (well beaten on soft). *T. M. Jones*

JATH 3 b.f. Bishop of Cashel 122 – Night Trader (USA) (Melyno 130) [2004 84p: 8m **85**
10m⁶ 8.1d 7.1m⁶ 7s* 8f 7g 7s Nov 2] big, leggy, close-coupled filly: fairly useful performer: won 4-runner minor event at Yarmouth in August: not sure to stay further than 1m:
acts on firm and soft going. *Julian Poulton*

JAVA DANCER 3 b.g. Danehill Dancer (IRE) 117 – Evasive Step 70 (Batshoof 122) **48**
[2004 8.1g 8m⁶ f8g⁶ Aug 19] poor form in maidens. *T. D. Easterby*

JAVA DAWN (IRE) 4 b.f. Fleetwood (IRE) 107 – Krakatoa (Shirley Heights 130) **44**
[2004 –: 11.7s p12g p12d³ 16.4g⁶ 12.1m Aug 5] poor maiden: stays 1½m: acts on polytrack and good to firm going: tried visored: sometimes slowly away: none too genuine.
T. E. Powell

JAVA GOLD 3 ch.f. The West (USA) 107 – Another Jade 79 (Beveled (USA)) [2004 **–**
5.7m 5.7g p5.1g Nov 6] fourth foal: dam 5f (at 2 yrs)/6f winner: well beaten in claimers.
W. G. M. Turner

JAVELIN 8 ch.g. Generous (IRE) 139 – Moss (Alzao (USA) 117) [2004 58: 12.6m⁶ **46**
14.1d⁵ 13.1d Aug 27] strong gelding: poor handicapper in 2004: stays 12.6f: acts on firm
and good to soft going (modest form on fibresand in 2000): wore cheekpieces/blinkers
last 2 starts: fair hurdler. *Ian Williams*

JAWWALA (USA) 5 b.m. Green Dancer (USA) 132 – Fetch N Carry (USA) (Alleged **– §**
(USA) 138) [2004 69§: 17.1d 16.2g Aug 30] leggy, close-coupled, sparely-made
mare: ungenuine handicapper: refused to race on reappearance: tried in cheekpieces.
J. R. Jenkins

JAYANJAY 5 b.g. Piccolo 121 – Morica 88 (Moorestyle 137) [2004 88: p6g f6g⁴ 5.3f³ **94**
6m⁴ 6g³ 6d* 5m⁵ 5.3f² 6g² 5s⁵ 5g 5m* p6g⁴ p5g⁵ p6g² p6g² Dec 13] close-coupled
gelding: fairly useful handicapper: won at Epsom in July and October, beating Corridor
Creeper a neck in latter: good second at Wolverhampton final start: effective at 5f/6f:
acts on polytrack, firm and soft going: tried blinkered/visored, not in 2004: tough.
Miss B. Sanders

JAYCEE STAR (IRE) 3 ch.f. Idris (IRE) 118 – Shantung (IRE) 65 (Anshan 119) **–**
[2004 p6g p6g p7g p7g Dec 29] first foal: dam, probably stayed 1¼m, disappointing
maiden: beat only 1 home in 4 maidens at Lingfield. *Miss A. M. Newton-Smith*

JAYER GILLES 4 br.g. Busy Flight 122 – Jadidh 64 (Touching Wood (USA) 127) **85**
[2004 12.1m² 12m² 12f⁵ 16s Oct 22] leggy gelding: fluent mover: fairly useful maiden:
should stay beyond 1½m: started slowly on debut. *H. Candy*

JAY GEE'S CHOICE 4 b.g. Barathea (IRE) 127 – Llia 94 (Shirley Heights 130) **97**
[2004 104: 8g⁶ 8g 8v 7m³ 8.5m 8m⁴ 7d 7g⁴ 7.1s⁶ 8f* 8g³ 7g⁴ p7.1g* Oct 18] sturdy, well-
made gelding: sort to carry condition: has a quick action: useful performer: won minor
event at Pontefract in September and handicap at Wolverhampton in October: stays 1m:
acts on polytrack, firm and good to soft ground, well held on soft/heavy: usually races
prominently: sold 32,000 gns, joined B. Powell. *M. R. Channon*

JAY (IRE) 2 ch.f. (Mar 31) Bluebird (USA) 125 – Welsh Dawn (Zafonic (USA) 130) **55 §**
[2004 6m 6m 7f² 7m 6m² 7m 6g* 7f 7m Sep 7] strong filly: second foal: half-sister to
Italian 1¼m winner by Orpen: dam, ran 3 times in Italy, half-sister to smart French
middle-distance performer Ordinance: modest performer: won seller at Yarmouth in

August: should stay 1m: acts on firm going: often blinkered/in cheekpieces: often slowly away (very much so for win): unreliable: sent to Oman. *N. A. Callaghan*

JAZIL 9 b.g. Nashwan (USA) 135 – Gracious Beauty (USA) 67 (Nijinsky (CAN) 138) – [2004 f11g⁶ 12m 11.8m 16.2m 14.1d Oct 16] big, strong, rangy gelding: useful performer at 3 yrs: tongue tied, no form in 2004: tail swisher: sometimes visored. *K. A. Morgan*

JAZRAWY 2 b.c. (Feb 2) Dansili 127 – Dalila di Mare (IRE) (Bob Back (USA) 124) **75** [2004 6m⁴ 7.6m⁴ p8.6g* p8g² Nov 16] 65,000F, 85,000Y: second foal: half-brother to Italian winner up to 1m by Sri Pekan: dam Italian 1m to 11f winner: fair performer: won maiden at Wolverhampton in October: good second in nursery at Lingfield: will stay 1¼m. *L. M. Cumani*

JAZZ MESSENGER (FR) 4 bl.g. Acatenango (GER) 127 – In The Saltmine (FR) **100** (Damister (USA) 123) [2004 104: 8.1d⁶ 7.9s 7g 7.9s 10.1g⁶ Sep 8] tall, leggy gelding: useful handicapper: creditable efforts in 2004 only on first and third starts: effective at 1m/1¼m: acts on heavy and good to firm ground: has been early to post: has worn crossed noseband: races freely, and usually held up: sent to France. *G. A. Butler*

JAZZ PRINCESS (IRE) 2 b. or br.f. (Mar 4) Bahhare (USA) 122 – Jazz Up (Cade- **108 p** aux Genereux 131) [2004 6.5v* 8.5g* 7d* Oct 2] €9,200Y: first foal: dam, unraced, out of useful close relative to Cheveley Park winner Blue Duster and Middle Park winner Zieten: won minor events at Sligo in August and Galway in September and C. L. Weld Park Stakes at the Curragh (useful form when making all and beating Saoire by 3 lengths) in October: stays 8.5f: should progress. *Mrs J. Harrington, Ireland*

JAZZ SCENE (IRE) 3 b.c. Danehill Dancer (IRE) 117 – Dixie Jazz 51 (Mtoto 134) **101** [2004 91p: 7g 8m 7d² 7.1d² 8m⁴ 8m⁵ 7d² 8d p8.6g⁶ Nov 8] rangy colt: useful performer: runner-up 4 times in 2004, to Young Mr Grace in handicap and to Sabbeeh in minor event (raced lazily, beaten short head), both at Ayr, on last 2 occasions: effective at 7f/1m: acts on firm and soft ground, respectable effort on polytrack: visored ninth/tenth starts. *M. R. Channon*

JAZZY MILLENNIUM 7 ch.g. Lion Cavern (USA) 117 – Woodcrest 82 (Niniski **68** (USA) 125) [2004 65: 6d 6f³ 7f⁶ 5.3g³ 7m³ 5.1m 6m⁴ 6f* 7s² 7m² 6.1m p7g⁵ Oct 28] quite attractive gelding: fair handicapper: won at Lingfield in August: effective at 5f to easy 7f: well beaten on heavy going, acts on any other turf/all-weather: usually blinkered/visored: reportedly bled seventh outing at 6 yrs: effective ridden up with pace or waited with. *B. R. Millman*

JEDBURGH 3 b.c. Selkirk (USA) 129 – Conspiracy 98 (Rudimentary (USA) 118) **105** [2004 93p: 8g 8m³ 7g³ 7d² 7m 7.6g² 7m⁵ 7g Oct 1] strong, compact colt: useful performer: best effort when length second to Peter Paul Rubens in minor event at Chester sixth start: should be at least as effective at 7f as 1m: acts on good to firm and good to soft going. *J. L. Dunlop*

JEDEYDD 7 b.g. Shareef Dancer (USA) 135 – Bilad (USA) (Riverman (USA) 131) **67** [2004 73d: 7.1m 7m 7.5d⁴ 7.5g 7m⁶ 8m⁴ 6.9f 7m 7m 6g* 6g Sep 6] lengthy gelding: fair performer: won claimer at Haydock in August: effective at 6f to 1m: acts on firm and good to soft ground: tried in cheekpieces, blinkered last 3 starts: tongue tied nowadays: sold 1,300 gns. *M. Dods*

JEEPSTAR 4 b.g. Muhtarram (USA) 125 – Jungle Rose 90 (Shirley Heights 130) [2004 **86** 85: 12s 12.3d 12m⁶ 10g² 10f² 12d* 13.9m 12g* 14.6s² 12s⁴ Nov 6] leggy, lightly-made gelding: fairly useful handicapper: won at Pontefract in August and Musselburgh (for second successive year) in September: stays 14.6f: acts on firm and good to soft ground: has given trouble in preliminaries/been early to post: front runner: game. *T. D. Easterby*

JEFFSLOTTERY 2 b.g. (Mar 15) Rock City 120 – Thieves Welcome 61 (Most Wel- **55** come 131) [2004 7d 8.3d⁶ 7s 8s² f8g Nov 9] quite good-topped gelding: modest maiden: best effort when second at Ayr: likely to stay 1¼m: blinkered last 2 starts (ran as if amiss final one). *J. R. Weymes*

JELANI (IRE) 5 b.h. Darshaan 133 – No Rehearsal (FR) (Baillamont (USA) 124) **108** [2004 12g 12m⁶ 13.9d³ May 13] big, good-topped horse: smart performer at 3 yrs: suffered tendon injury and missed 2003: just useful in 2004, best effort when 7 lengths third to Millenary in Yorkshire Cup at York final outing: stays 1¾m: yet to race on heavy going, acts on any other. *Andrew Turnell*

JELLY BABY 3 b.f. Marju (IRE) 127 – Daisy May (In The Wings 128) [2004 10s – p12g* p12d* 12.3g a8.5g* Dec 8] workmanlike filly: first living foal: dam unraced: fair **a66 +**

form: won seller and handicap at Lingfield in June: sold out of W. Haggas' stable 11,000 gns and off 5 months, won claimer at Hollywood in December: stays 1½m: acts on polytrack/dirt, tailed off both outings on turf: blinkered last 4 starts. *T. Yakteen, USA*

JEM'S LAW 5 b.m. Contract Law (USA) 108 – Alnasr Jewel (USA) (Al Nasr (FR) 126) [2004 8.3d 10m May 31] leggy mare: fourth foal: dam unraced: visored, well held in sellers. *J. R. Jenkins* —

JENAVIVE 4 b.f. Danzig Connection (USA) – Promise Fulfilled (USA) 90 (Bet Twice (USA)) [2004 55: p13g Mar 23] big, good-bodied filly: maiden handicapper: stays 1¾m: acts on firm ground: races freely. *N. J. Hawke* —

JENNA STANNIS 2 ch.f. (Mar 28) Wolfhound (USA) 126 – Darling Splodge (Elegant Air 119) [2004 7g 7g 8.2m Sep 28] workmanlike filly: seventh foal: half-sister to 6-y-o Starry Mary and 2m/17f winner Our Monogram (by Deploy): dam unraced: best effort in maidens when eighth at Salisbury on second start: should be suited by 1¼m/1½m. *R. M. Beckett* **65**

JENNVERSE 2 b.f. (Feb 4) Opening Verse (USA) 126 – Jennelle 97 (Nomination 125) [2004 5.1s⁶ p5g⁶ p5g⁵ Nov 20] first foal: dam 5f winner, including at 2 yrs: modest form in maidens: should stay 6f. *D. K. Ivory* **57**

JEROME 3 b.g. Nicolotte 118 – Mim 39 (Midyan (USA) 124) [2004 71: 8.5v May 8] smallish, sturdy gelding: fair maiden at 2 yrs: below form only run in 2004: not sure to stay beyond 1m: acts on firm ground: blinkered (ran creditably) last 2 starts at 2 yrs. *T. D. Easterby* **59**

JERRY'S GIRL (IRE) 2 ch.f. (Jan 31) Danehill Dancer (IRE) 117 – Lurgoe Lady (IRE) (Spectrum (IRE) 126) [2004 5f³ 6m⁶ 6g⁴ 5f* 6m Aug 8] close-coupled filly: first foal: dam unraced half-sister to useful performer up to 1½m Abury: fair performer: won maiden at Musselburgh in July: should stay 6f: acts on firm going: hung left third start. *Miss L. A. Perratt* **66**

JESSE SAMUEL 3 ch.g. First Trump 118 – Miss Kellybell 48 (Kirchner 110) [2004 51: 7.1s 7.1g⁴ 7s May 6] lengthy gelding: poor maiden: barely stays 7f: best efforts on good going. *J. R. Jenkins* **41**

JESSIAUME 2 gr.f. (Mar 17) Mister Baileys 123 – Jucinda 58 (Midyan (USA) 124) [2004 6s⁴ Oct 29] quite good-topped filly: third foal: half-sister to 4-y-o Gems Bond: dam, 15.4f winner, sister to Goodwood Cup winner Tioman Island: 14/1, fourth to Tucker in maiden at Newmarket, green but staying on: should stay at least 1m: likely to improve. *H. Candy* **67 p**

JESSICA'S STYLE (IRE) 2 b.f. (Feb 26) Desert Style (IRE) 121 – Mugello 96 (Emarati (USA) 74) [2004 6f f5g 6g Aug 28] €28,000Y: third foal: half-sister to 3-y-o Miss Judgement and 9f/1¼m winner in Spain by Revoque: dam 2-y-o 5f winner who didn't train on: poor form in maidens. *J. G. Given* **40**

JESSIE 5 ch.m. Pivotal 124 – Bold Gem 68 (Never So Bold 135) [2004 54: f7g⁵ f7g⁶ f8g⁵ f8s² f7g² f7s² f7s⁴ 7v f7d⁵ 7m⁴ 8g³ 7.9m Sep 11] workmanlike mare: poor handicapper: best at 7f/1m: acts on fibresand, firm and soft ground: tried tongue tied, visored last 4 starts: sometimes slowly away. *Don Enrico Incisa* **45**

JESSINCA 8 b.m. Minshaanshu Amad (USA) 91§ – Noble Soul 67 (Sayf El Arab (USA) 127) [2004 53: f9.4g f7g f8s⁶ f7d 9.7f³ 10g² 9.7g 10.2m⁵ 10s Aug 24] smallish, sturdy mare: poor handicapper: barely stays 1¼m: acts on fibresand, firm and soft going: tried visored: usually waited with. *A. P. Jones* **45**

JE SUIS BELLE 2 ch.f. (Mar 15) Efisio 120 – Blossom (Warning 136) [2004 6f 5d³ 6s² 6d* 7g Oct 2] quite attractive filly: first foal: dam unraced out of half-sister to very smart middle-distance colt Apache: fair performer: won nursery at Ayr in September: poorly drawn final start: should stay 7f: acts on soft ground: sold 9,000 gns, joined Gay Kelleway. *B. W. Hills* **70**

JEUNE LOUP 2 b.g. (Apr 26) Loup Sauvage (USA) 125 – Secret Waters 100 (Pharly (FR) 130) [2004 6g 7g⁴ 6s Aug 18] 22,000Y: rather leggy gelding: eighth foal: halfbrother to 3 winners, including 3-y-o Carini: dam, 12.5f to 1¾m winner, half-sister to dam of Tenby: best effort in maidens when fourth at Newcastle: will stay at least 1m. *P. C. Haslam* **70**

JEWEL IN THE SAND (IRE) 2 b.f. (Mar 27) Bluebird (USA) 125 – Dancing Drop 103 (Green Desert (USA) 127) [2004 5f⁵ 6m* 6m* 7m 6g Sep 30] €65,000Y: strong, sturdy filly: has a quick action: fourth foal: half-sister to useful German 6f (including at 2 yrs)/6.5f winner Davignon (by Highest Honor) and fairly useful Irish 2002 2-y-o 5f **107**

Chippenham Lodge Stud Cherry Hinton Stakes, Newmarket—
Jewel In The Sand (right) shows a good turn of foot to win from Salsa Brava, Extreme Beauty (No.2),
Shivaree (hidden by runner-up) and Arabian Dancer (striped sleeves)

winner Triton Dance (by Hector Protector): dam 2-y-o 6f winner who stayed 1m: useful performer: won maiden at Sandown in May, listed event at Royal Ascot (beat Spirit of Chester by 1½ lengths) in June and Chippenham Lodge Stud Cherry Hinton Stakes at Newmarket (by head from Salsa Brava, quickening well then idling) in July: well below form in Moyglare Stud Stakes at the Curragh (reportedly in season) and Cheveley Park Stakes at Newmarket: likely to prove best at 5f/6f. *R. Hannon*

JEWEL OF INDIA 5 ch.g. Bijou d'Inde 127 – Low Hill (Rousillon (USA) 133) [2004 93: p8g p10g 8.3g⁶ Aug 9] leggy, sparely-made gelding: fairly useful performer: below best in 2004: stays easy 1¼m: acts on all-weather and soft going, probably on good to firm: usually blinkered prior to 2004, though effective without. *Mrs A. L. M. King* **81 ?**

JEZADIL (IRE) 6 b.m. Mujadil (USA) 119 – Tender Time (Tender King 123) [2004 51§: p12g p13g 10.2d³ 13.1g 12.1g⁶ Jun 22] sparely-made mare: no longer of much account. *Mrs L. Stubbs* **– §**

JIDIYA (IRE) 5 b.g. Lahib (USA) 129 – Yaqatha (IRE) (Sadler's Wells (USA) 132) [2004 73: 12m 8m 10g² 12g 10.5g³ 10f³ 11.9g p10g p10g* Dec 29] big, workmanlike gelding: fair performer: trained by J. Kiely in Ireland in 2003: won apprentice handicap at Lingfield in December: effective at 1¼m to 2m: acts on polytrack and good to firm going. *S. Gollings* **73**

JILLY WHY (IRE) 3 b.f. Mujadil (USA) 119 – Ruwy 77 (Soviet Star (USA) 128) [2004 64: f6s 6g⁴ 6m* 5.1g* 6f 6s 5d² p6g⁴ 5d p6d⁵ p5.1d⁶ f6g⁵ p5.1g² p5.1g p7.1g p6g Dec 27] workmanlike filly: fairly useful on turf, fair on all-weather: won maiden at Thirsk and handicap at Chester, both in September: effective at 5f/6f: acts on all-weather, firm and good to soft going: usually races up with pace. *Ms Deborah J. Evans* **80 a75**

JIM LAD 4 b.g. Young Ern 120 – Anne's Bank (IRE) 77 (Burslem 123) [2004 –: 10.2d⁵ Apr 23] little from: blinkered/visored: none too keen. *Dr J. R. J. Naylor* **–**

JIMMY BYRNE (IRE) 4 ch.g. Red Sunset 120 – Persian Sally (IRE) (Persian Bold 123) [2004 78: 7d 10v⁴ 10.1v* 10m 10m⁵ 12.3m⁶ 10.5g* 10.5d* 10.5s³ 10g⁶ 10d Sep 17] workmanlike gelding: fairly useful performer: won minor event at Newcastle (dead-heat) in April and claimer and handicap at Haydock in July: stays 10.5f: acts on heavy and good to firm ground: tried in cheekpieces: carries head high. *B. Ellison* **83**

JIMMY HAY 3 b.g. Bluegrass Prince (IRE) 110 – Priory Bay 54 (Petong 126) [2004 7.1m p10g 10m 12.6d Oct 9] small gelding: probably of no account. *J. C. Fox* **–**

JIMMY RYAN (IRE) 3 b.c. Orpen (USA) 116 – Kaysama (FR) (Kenmare (FR) 125) [2004 85p: 6g 6.1g 5m* 5g² 5m* Jul 30] lengthy, quite good-topped colt: useful handicapper: won at Newmarket (hung badly right) in June and Goodwood (sweating, beat Treasure Cay comfortably by 1½ lengths) in July: best at 5f: raced only on good/good to firm going: has been early to post: tried to duck out on debut: free-going sort. *T. D. McCarthy* **104**

JINKSONTHEHOUSE 3 b.f. Whittingham (IRE) 104 – Aldwick Colonnade 62 (Kind of Hush 118) [2004 59: 5.7s⁴ 6g 5.1f* 6.1g 5.7f⁴ 5g 5m* 5.1m⁴ 5m² 5.1m⁴ 5.1g p5.1g Dec 31] close-coupled filly: modest performer: won claimer at Bath in May and seller at Musselburgh in June: effective at 5f/easy 6f: acts on firm going. *M. D. I. Usher* **59**

JOANS JEWEL 3 ch.f. Wolfhound (USA) 126 – Chatter's Princess (Cadeaux Genereux 131) [2004 p6g⁵ p5g⁵ p7g⁶ 6g 6m 6g 7m 7d Oct 16] third foal: half-sister to **45**

4-y-o Surdoue: dam unraced: poor maiden: acts on polytrack: tried in cheekpieces. *G. G. Margarson*

JOE CHARLIE   3 ch.g. Daggers Drawn (USA) 114 – La Ballerine 62 (Lafontaine (USA) 117) [2004 53: f6s Feb 10] close-coupled gelding: modest form only on debut in 2003: well beaten since: blinkered only 3-y-o outing. *K. A. Ryan*   –

JOE JO STAR   2 b.c. (Feb 20) Piccolo 121 – Zagreb Flyer (Old Vic 136) [2004 5.1g⁶ 5v⁶ 5g 6.1d Sep 17] compact colt: modest maiden: should stay 6f: best efforts on good going. *P. A. Blockley*   50

JOELY GREEN   7 b.g. Binary Star (USA) – Comedy Lady 46 (Comedy Star (USA) 121) [2004 60§, a75§: f16.2g⁵ p13g p12g⁶ p13g⁶ p16g⁶ 11.9m 16m² 17.1f 17.2f 19.1f 16.4g 11.9f⁴ p16g Sep 18] tall, workmanlike gelding: modest handicapper: effective at 1½m, probably at 19f: acts on all-weather and firm going, possibly not on good to soft: usually wears headgear: sometimes slowly away/wanders/runs in snatches: unreliable. *N. P. Littmoden*   54 § a59 §

JOE NINETY (IRE)   2 ch.g. (Mar 30) Daggers Drawn (USA) 114 – Sea Idol (IRE) 65 (Astronef 116) [2004 p5g⁵ p5g⁶ 5s 6.1g 7f³ 6m 7g 6s⁴ 6m Sep 1] poor maiden: stays 7f: acts on polytrack, firm and soft going: below form in blinkers/cheekpieces sixth and final starts. *J. S. Moore*   47

JOEY PERHAPS   3 b.g. Danzig Connection (USA) – Realms of Gold (USA) (Gulch (USA)) [2004 72: 8.2s 5.9f 10.2f 8.5g⁶ 9.9g³ 9f² 7.9m³ p10d⁶ Aug 9] tall, leggy gelding: modest maiden: barely stays 1¼m: acts on polytrack, raced mainly on good ground or firmer on turf: sometimes slowly away. *J. R. Best*   60

Sand Associates' "Jewel In The Sand"

JOEY THE SCHNOZE   6 ch.g. Zilzal (USA) 137 – Linda's Design (Persian Bold   –
123) [2004 p13g 12m Jul 6] well held in maidens, leaving G. Margarson after reappearance: tried tongue tied. *Miss D. A. McHale*

JOHANNIAN   6 b.g. Hernando (FR) 127 – Photo Call 73 (Chief Singer 131) [2004 –:   **81**
8.1s 8m 8m³ 8.3m⁶ 10m 8.2s² 9g 8.3m⁴ 8.1s⁶ 8s³ 8.1s² 8m* 8g² 8v p8g Nov 10] quite
good-topped gelding: unimpressive mover: smart performer in prime: fairly useful
handicapper nowadays: won apprentice event at Goodwood in September in good style:
effective at 1m/1¼m: acts on firm and soft ground: tried tongue tied: sometimes bandaged off-hind. *J. M. Bradley*

JOHN FORBES   2 b.c. (Mar 1) High Estate 127 – Mavourneen (USA) (Dynaformer   **82 §**
(USA)) [2004 7f 6d* 7g 7m 8s 6g 8s 6s 7s⁵ Nov 6] 8,500Y, 20,000 2-y-o: strong, useful-
looking colt: first foal: dam, unraced, out of Musidora winner Marillette, herself out of
half-sister to Storm Bird: fairly useful performer: won maiden at Newcastle in June: stays
7f: probably acts on soft ground: blinkered sixth/seventh outings: unreliable. *B. Ellison*

JOHNNY ALLJAYS (IRE)   3 b.g. Victory Note (USA) 120 – It's Academic 73   **36**
(Royal Academy (USA) 130) [2004 –: 8s 8.5m 7m 6f 8f 8f⁴ 7f⁴ 8m Aug 16] big gelding:
poor maiden: stays 1m: acts on firm ground: has worn blinkers/cheekpieces last 6 starts.
J. S. Moore

JOHNNY CHI (IRE)   2 ch.c. (Mar 25) Indian Lodge (IRE) 127 – Bring Me Home   –
(IRE) (Charnwood Forest (IRE) 125) [2004 7d Oct 30] €6,000F, 25,000Y: unfurnished
colt: first foal: dam unraced: 33/1, last in maiden at Newmarket. *P. W. D'Arcy*

JOHNNY JUMPUP (IRE)   2 ch.c. (Feb 18) Pivotal 124 – Clarice Orsini (Common   **105**
Grounds 118) [2004 5.1s* 6d* 7.1d 7.6g²* 7s² Oct 22] 15,000F, 11,000Y: close-coupled
colt: second foal: half-brother to 4-y-o Ally Makbul: dam third at 1m in France: useful
performer: won maiden at Bath (from Iceman) in May and minor events at Salisbury in
July and Chester (4 ran, beat Hachita 2½ lengths) in September: good 4 lengths second
to Cupid's Glory in Horris Hill Stakes at Newbury: should stay 1m: acts on soft going:
game. *R. M. Beckett*

JOHNNY PARKES   3 b.g. Wolfhound (USA) 126 – Lucky Parkes 108 (Full Extent   **88**
(USA) 113) [2004 77: 5.1g* 5.1d 5m³ 5f Jun 1] big, strong gelding: fairly useful handicapper: won at Nottingham in March: also ran well third start: will prove best at 5f/easy
6f: acts on good to firm going (below form on good to soft): upset in stall (below form)
final outing. *Mrs J. R. Ramsden*

JOHNNY ROOK (IRE)   3 ch.g. Woodman (USA) 126 – Tani (USA) (Theatrical 128)   –
[2004 p10g May 29] reportedly had sore shins in spring: 14/1, seventh in maiden at
Lingfield, bit slowly away, only outing: sold 4,000 gns in October. *E. A. L. Dunlop*

JOHN O'GROATS (IRE)   6 b.g. Distinctly North (USA) 115 – Bannons Dream   **66 d**
(IRE) (Thatching 131) [2004 88: 5s 5d 5m 6m 7.2f 5f 5.9f 5g 5g 5f5g 5m 5d 6s* Oct 30]
tall, close-coupled, good-topped gelding: only fair at best in 2004: on downgrade (left
M. Dods after ninth start, D. Chapman after twelfth one) but still won banded race at Ayr
in October: effective at 5f/6f: acts on firm and soft going: tried in headgear: held up.
B. Mactaggart

JOHN ROBIE (USA)   2 ch.c. (Apr 27) Rahy (USA) 115 – Diamond Flower (USA)   **76**
(Fly So Free (USA) 122) [2004 5m⁶ 6m³ 6p4 Oct 25] $14,000Y, 17,000 2-y-o: rangy
leggy colt: first foal: dam, 5.5f winner in USA, half-sister to US Grade 1 winner at 7f to
9f Exotic Wood (by Rahy): fair form in maidens/minor event at Lingfield and York: will
probably stay 7f. *G. A. Butler*

JOHN'S CHAMP (IRE)   4 b.g. Mujadil (USA) 119 – Big Buyer (USA) 67 (Quest   –
For Fame 127) [2004 53: 10.1v Jun 24] modest maiden: tailed off only run in 2004: tried
visored. *R. E. Barr*

JOHNSTON'S DIAMOND (IRE)   6 b.g. Tagula (IRE) 116 – Toshair Flyer 88   **95**
(Ballad Rock 122) [2004 91: f6g f6g f6s* f6s 5d4 5.1d⁶ 6m² 6m 6f 6f 6d 5g 5.1g 6d³ 5s⁶   **a85**
6d³ 7g 6s³ p6g³ p6g Dec 13] big, workmanlike gelding: useful on turf, fairly useful on
all-weather: won handicap at Wolverhampton in February: best at 5f/6f (raced too freely
at 7f): acts on all-weather, firm and soft ground: blinkered (below form) once: tongue tied
last 2 starts: races prominently. *E. J. Alston*

JOINT ASPIRATION   2 ch.f. (May 2) Pivotal 124 – Welcome Home 55 (Most Wel-   **103**
come 131) [2004 7d* 7g² 8f⁶ Sep 25] 36,000Y: angular filly: fourth foal: dam, 1½m
winner, half-sister to smart sprinter Two Clubs: won maiden at Salisbury in August and
minor event at Kempton (by 1½ lengths from Tahrir) in September: further improvement

when 3¾ lengths sixth to Playful Act in Fillies' Mile at Ascot, taking good hold early: stays 1m: useful. *M. R. Channon*

JOINT DESTINY (IRE) 3 b.f. Desert Prince (IRE) 130 – Brogan's Well (IRE) (Caerleon (USA) 132) [2004 70d: f9.4g⁵ p7g p8g² p10g* 11.5f 9.2m⁴ 10.1m 8.5f⁶ Jul 29] angular, quite good-topped filly: modest performer: won banded race at Lingfield in May: stays easy 1¼m: acts on polytrack and firm ground. *E. J. O'Neill*   **52**

JOLIE (IRE) 2 b.f. Orpen (USA) 116 – Arabian Dream (IRE) (Royal Academy (USA) 130) [2004 6.1m Sep 28] good-topped filly: fourth foal: half-sister to fairly useful Irish 7f (including at 2 yrs) to 9.5f winner Like A Dream (by Alzao): dam unraced granddaughter of Arc winner Allez France: 80/1, behind in maiden at Nottingham, starting slowly. *R. Dickin*   **–**

JOLIZERO 3 br.g. Danzero (AUS) – Jolis Absent 57 (Primo Dominie 121) [2004 –: 8.2g⁴ 10d 12f³ 12.1d² 14.1d⁵ 10.9s p12g⁶ 10v* Oct 23] big, good-bodied gelding: fair performer: easily best effort when winning maiden at Newbury (by 17 lengths): stays 1½m: acts on any going: sold 30,000 gns. *P. W. Chapple-Hyam*   **75 ?**

JOMACOMI 3 b.c. Hector Protector (USA) 124 – Stylish Rose (IRE) 65 (Don't Forget Me 127) [2004 f12s* 11.6g³ 11.9d⁶ 11.9d 12.3g⁶ Jul 5] big, workmanlike colt: second foal: half-brother to 2001 2-y-o 1m winner Celtic Style (by Celtic Swing): dam won at 1m: fair performer: won maiden at Wolverhampton in February: stays 1½m: acts on fibresand: has wandered off bridle/looked hard ride: sold 8,000 gns in October. *M. Johnston*   **78**

JOMUS 3 b.g. Soviet Star (USA) 128 – Oatey 68 (Master Willie 129) [2004 67: p7g⁵ f8g² p8g* f8g² 7m 8.1m 8.3f 7.6m⁴ 8.5f 8.1g³ 10d⁵ 10g p8.6d⁶ p10m² Dec 21] close-coupled, quite good-topped gelding: fair performer: won handicap at Lingfield in March: stays 1¼m: acts on all-weather, raced mainly on good going or firmer on turf: often slowly away: races freely: inconsistent. *L. Montague Hall*   **71**

JONANAUD 5 b.g. Ballet Royal (USA) – Margaret Modes (Thatching 131) [2004 p13g⁶ 10.2g Oct 10] fairly useful hurdler: fair form in maidens at Lingfield and Bath, only outings on Flat: will be suited by 1¾m+. *H. J. Manners*   **65**

JONNY EBENEEZER 5 b.g. Hurricane Sky (AUS) – Leap of Faith (IRE) 65 (Northiam (USA)) [2004 86, a74: f7g 6s 6s 7s² 7.1v 7m² 7m* 7f f7d³ f6m* 6.1d 5g² 7g² 5m* 6m* f6m⁴ 6m* 6g* 6s 5.6m 6s 5s* 7g³ 6g* 6d⁶ p6g⁵ Dec 4] tall gelding: useful on turf, fairly useful on all-weather: had an excellent season, winning seller at Brighton and (having left R. Cowell after ninth start) handicaps at Southwell, Sandown, Newmarket (2), Windsor, Haydock and York (quickened impressively to beat Talbot Avenue ½ length): effective at 5f to 7f: acts on all-weather, soft and good to firm going: below form in cheekpieces, usually blinkered nowadays: tough and genuine. *D. Flood*   **108** **a86 +**

JONNYEM 3 b.g. Emarati (USA) 74 – Deerlet 64 (Darshaan 133) [2004 9.3g 8g⁴ 7m 12g Oct 5] seemingly modest maiden. *G. A. Swinbank*   **54 ?**

JONNY FOX'S (IRE) 2 ch.g. (Mar 6) Foxhound (USA) 103 – Lala Salama (IRE) 62 (College Chapel 122) [2004 p5g⁶ 5d 5m⁶ 5g 5.3m Sep 23] poor maiden: left J. Boyle after debut: should stay 6f: blinkered third and final starts. *J. Gallagher*   **47**

Coral Sprint Trophy (Handicap), York—Jonny Ebeneezer (left),
revitalised by second-season trainer David Flood, gains his eighth win of the year;
top weight Talbot Avenue is next, then come Fantasy Believer (right) and Connect (dark blinkers)

JON

JONQUIL (IRE) 2 ch.c. (May 3) Machiavellian (USA) 123 – Jumilla (USA) 100 (El **95 p** Gran Senor (USA) 136) [2004 7m⁴ 7m* 7f Sep 10] 130,000Y: sturdy colt: fifth foal: half-brother to 4-y-o Desert Quest and French 1¼m winner Jolan's Wish (by Woodman): dam, 2-y-o 6f winner who stayed 1¼m, half-sister to dam of 5-y-o Passing Glance: won maiden at Goodwood in July by 1½ lengths from Looks Could Kill: travelled strongly long way when respectable eighth in Champagne Stakes at Doncaster: will probably stay 1m: should make a useful 3-y-o. *J. H. M. Gosden*

JOOLS 6 b.g. Cadeaux Genereux 131 – Madame Crecy (USA) (Al Nasr (FR) 126) **85** [2004 85: p8g p8g 8.3d* 8.1d⁵ 7.6s³ 10m 10f 8.3m⁴ 8.3f⁴ 9g⁶ 7g⁵ 8m 8.3m 8f⁶ 8.3g 8.5g Aug 30] rather leggy gelding: fairly useful performer: won minor event at Windsor in April: barely stays 1¼m: acts on all-weather, firm and soft going: visored once: none too consistent. *D. K. Ivory*

JORDANS ELECT 4 ch.g. Fleetwood (IRE) 107 – Cal Norma's Lady (IRE) 87 **84** (Lyphard's Special (USA) 122) [2004 78?: 9.2g⁵ 8.3d* 8m 9.2g* 8.3m⁴ 8m 8.3d⁴ 9.2f³ Jul 31] tall, rather leggy, useful-looking gelding: fairly useful handicapper: won at Hamilton in May and June (best effort, beat Takes Tutu 2 lengths): effective at 1m to 1¼m: acts on firm and good to soft ground. *I. Semple*

JORDANS SPARK 3 ch.g. Opening Verse (USA) 126 – Ribot's Pearl (Indian Ridge **62** 123) [2004 11.1g⁵ 10m 10.5g 11.1s⁶ 9.2d* 10.1g⁶ 8m p8.6d⁶ Nov 5] workmanlike gelding: second foal: dam 7f/1m winner in Italy: modest performer: won claimer at Hamilton in September: stays 1¼m: acts on good to soft going: effective in cheekpieces, blinkered (folded tamely) final start. *I. Semple*

JOROBADEN (FR) 4 gr.g. Poliglote 121 – Mercalle (FR) 108 (Kaldoun (FR) 122) **95** [2004 p10g² 10d* 12g⁶ 14.4v* 13.9s 16.2d⁶ 16.1s 14g Sep 4] close-coupled, quite good-topped gelding: useful performer: missed 2003: won maiden at Leicester in April and handicap at Kempton (best effort, beat Linens Flame 3½ lengths) in May: should stay 2m: yet to race on ground firmer than good: sold 17,000 gns, joined Mrs H. Dalton. *C. F. Wall*

JOSEAR 2 b.c. (Feb 6) Josr Algarhoud (IRE) 118 – Real Popcorn (IRE) 52 (Jareer **50** (USA) 115) [2004 5s⁴ 5g 5m Jun 14] good-topped colt: modest form in maidens: should stay 1½m (dam 1½m winner): best effort on soft going. *S. C. Williams*

JOSEPH HENRY 2 b.g. (Mar 3) Mujadil (USA) 119 – Iris May 87 (Brief Truce (USA) **100** 126) [2004 5g* 5.1s* 6g⁴ 5s⁴ 6s³ 6s⁵ Oct 29] well-made gelding: second foal: dam, 5f winner (including at 2 yrs), half-sister to smart 5f winner Cathedral: useful performer: won maiden at Musselburgh and minor event at Nottingham (by 7 lengths) in April, injured after latter: creditable efforts in frame in listed events at York and Doncaster and Cornwallis Stakes (fourth to Castelletto) at Newmarket: likely to prove best at 5f/6f: acts on soft going: races up with pace: gelded after final start. *M. Johnston*

JOSEPHUS (IRE) 3 ch.c. King of Kings (IRE) 125 – Khulasah (USA) (Affirmed **–** (USA)) [2004 103p: 8d Oct 30] strong, good-bodied colt: useful winner at 2 yrs (also second in Horris Hill Stakes at Newbury): off 12 months, last of 11 in listed race at Newmarket only run in 2004: should stay 1m. *R. Charlton*

JOSH 2 b.c. (Apr 3) Josr Algarhoud (IRE) 118 – Charlie Girl 70 (Puissance 110) [2004 **104** 6s* 6m³ 6m 6g* 6g⁶ 6.5s³ Oct 20] 36,000Y: good-topped colt: second foal: half-brother to 2003 2-y-o 7f seller winner Gone To Ground (by Foxhound): dam, 2-y-o 5f winner, out of half-sister to high-class French 1¼m performer Creator: useful performer: won maiden at Haydock in July and minor event at Yarmouth (beat Army of Angels by neck in 4-runner contest, edging right) in September: creditable efforts in Middle Park Stakes at Newmarket and listed event at Deauville (third to Campo Bueno) after: should stay 7f: acts on soft and good to firm going. *M. A. Jarvis*

JOSHAR 2 b.f. (Apr 10) Paris House 123 – Penny Hasset 73 (Lochnager 132) [2004 5s **48** 5s³ 5d f6g³ 6m³ 6m⁴ 6m Jun 11] strong, lengthy filly: half-sister to fairly useful 1999 2-y-o 5f/6f winner Happy Times (by Timeless Times): dam 5f/6f winner: poor maiden: stays 6f: acts on fibresand, soft and good to firm ground. *M. W. Easterby*

JOSHUAS BOY (IRE) 4 ch.g. Bahhare (USA) 122 – Broadway Rosie 101 (Absalom **43** 128) [2004 –: 6g³ 7.2m 6m Aug 7] big, strong gelding: poor maiden: tried blinkered/in cheekpieces. *K. A. Ryan*

JOSHUA'S GOLD (IRE) 3 b.g. Sesaro (USA) 81 – Lady of The Night (IRE) 54 **63** (Night Shift (USA)) [2004 54: p7g² 7.1d³ 8m⁶ 8.2g 7m 7f 7.9f* 7m⁴ 7.1g² 6.9g³ 7m 8g⁵ 8.5m 8m Sep 29] sturdy, close-coupled gelding: modest handicapper: won at Carlisle in July: barely stays 8.5f: acts on polytrack, firm and good to soft going: visored 6 of last 7 starts: usually waited with. *D. Carroll*

JOSTLE 2 b.g. (Mar 23) Josr Algarhoud (IRE) 118 – Russell Creek 80 (Sandy Creek – **p**
123) [2004 7m Sep 21] 2,000F, 26,000Y: close-coupled gelding: half-brother to several
winners, including 3-y-o Among Dreams: dam 1m winner: 25/1, tongue tied and very
green, well held in maiden at Newmarket, very slowly away (gelded after): likely to do
better. *D. R. Loder*

JOY AND PAIN 3 b.g. Pursuit of Love 124 – Ice Chocolate (USA) 77 (Icecapade **77**
(USA)) [2004 p7g p10g p8g⁶ p7g p7g* 6s⁶ 7g² 7m³ 8m 6g 7s p7g* Nov 27] 6,000F,
13,500Y, 7,000 2-y-o: brother to a winner up to 1¼m in Italy and half-brother to several
winners, including 1¼m/1½m winner Ice Rebel (by Robellino): dam 1m winner at 4 yrs:
fair performer: won handicap in March and minor event in November, both at Lingfield: better at 7f than 1m: acts on polytrack and good to firm ground: has raced freely.
G. L. Moore

JOYCE'S CHOICE 5 b.g. Mind Games 121 – Madrina 70 (Waajib 121) [2004 56: 5g² **55**
6g 5d 5g⁵ 5m⁴ 5d 5g 5d 5f² 5m⁶ 5d* f5g* f5g* f5g Dec 21] leggy gelding: modest
performer: won banded races at Warwick in October and Southwell in December: best
at 5f: acts on fibresand, firm and soft going: tried in cheekpieces/blinkers: refused to race
last 4 starts: refused to race third outing, unseated rider and bolted to post fifth one.
J. S. Wainwright

JOYEAUX 2 b.f. (Mar 18) Mark of Esteem (IRE) 137 – Divine Secret (Hernando (FR) **62**
127) [2004 p7g 6s⁶ p6g⁴ p6g² p6g⁶ p7m Dec 21] leggy filly: first foal: dam unraced out of
sister to smart French sprinter Monde Bleu and half-sister to high-class sprinter Sayf El
Arab: modest maiden: second in nursery at Wolverhampton: stays 6f. *S. L. Keightley*

J R STEVENSON (USA) 8 ch.g. Lyphard (USA) 132 – While It Lasts (USA) 78 **88 d**
(Foolish Pleasure (USA)) [2004 93: p8g² p10g 8s⁴ 10g⁶ 8.3d⁵ 8m 8g⁶ 8d* p8.6g
p9.5g² p10m² p10g² Dec 30] strong, close-coupled gelding: has a quick action: fairly
useful performer: below best after reappearance, though won claimer at Yarmouth (left
M. Wigham) in November: effective at 1m/1¼m: acts on polytrack, soft and good to firm
going: tried visored earlier in career: sometimes finds little: probably best held up. *Miss
Gay Kelleway*

JUANTORENA 2 ch.c. (May 23) Miswaki (USA) 124 – Millyant 114 (Primo Dominie **92**
121) [2004 6m² 5g² 5f⁴ 6g³ 5g⁴ 5g² 5m* Sep 15] 66,000 2-y-o: sturdy colt: fifth foal:
half-brother to 4-y-o Millybaa: dam, 5f performer, half-sister to very smart sprinter
Prince Sabo: fairly useful performer: good fourth in listed race at Royal Ascot third start:
favourite, won maiden at Beverley by short head: will prove best at 5f/easy 6f: acts on
firm going: joined M. Al Kurdi in UAE. *M. L. W. Bell*

JUBILEE COIN 2 ch.f. (Mar 16) Fumo di Londra (IRE) 108 – Money Supply (Brig- –
adier Gerard 144) [2004 6g 6g Sep 30] leggy filly: half-sister to several winners,
including 7f (at 2 yrs) to 1½m winner Credit Squeeze (by Superlative): dam unraced: last
in maidens at Newbury and Goodwood. *G. B. Balding*

JUBILEE STREET (IRE) 5 b.g. Dr Devious (IRE) 127 – My Firebird (Rudimentary **67**
(USA) 118) [2004 57: f7g 6g⁴ 7.2m³ 7m* 7m 8.5g 7m⁶ 7m* 7.5d² 7g* 7.5m 7m 7v Oct
16] big gelding: fair handicapper: won at Doncaster (apprentices) in May and Catterick in
August and September: stays 7.5f: acts on firm and good to soft ground: visored last 2
outings in 2003. *Mrs A. Duffield*

JUBILEE TREAT (USA) 4 b.f. Seeking The Gold (USA) – Dance Treat (USA) 115 –
(Nureyev (USA) 131) [2004 86: 8m 10m 10.1s⁶ Jun 26] rather leggy, useful-looking filly:
fairly useful performer at 3 yrs: well held in 2004. *G. Wragg*

JUDDA 3 b.g. Makbul 104 – Pepeke 78 (Mummy's Pet 125) [2004 6m 7f f7d 10v f6s –
Nov 17] no form in maidens: tried in cheekpieces/tongue tie. *R. F. Marvin*

JUDD STREET 2 b.g. (Feb 21) Compton Place 125 – Pudding Lane (IRE) 64 (College **69 p**
Chapel 122) [2004 p6g⁴ p6g* Dec 4] 2,500Y: first foal: dam maiden who stayed 7f (ran
only at 2 yrs): won maiden at Lingfield by neck from Belly Dancer: likely to stay 7f:
should improve further. *R. F. Johnson Houghton*

JUDGE DAMUSS (IRE) 2 ch.c. (May 22) Tagula (IRE) 116 – Acicula (IRE) 96 –
(Night Shift (USA)) [2004 6s 8d Oct 15] sturdy colt: last in maidens at Ripon and Redcar.
A. Crook

JULES LEE 2 ch.g. (May 13) Bluegrass Prince (IRE) 110 – Jade's Girl (Emarati (USA) –
74) [2004 7g 8.3g Oct 11] well beaten in claimer/seller: wore cheekpieces final start.
W. G. M. Turner

JUMBO'S FLYER 7 ch.g. Jumbo Hirt (USA) 90§ – Fragrant Princess (Germont) – [2004 5.9f Jul 29] close-coupled, sturdy gelding: fair handicapper at 3 yrs: lightly raced and well held on Flat since: tried visored. *F. P. Murtagh*

JUMEIRAH SCARER 3 b.g. Tagula (IRE) 116 – Mountain Harvest (FR) 64§ **69** (Shirley Heights 130) [2004 64p: p8g² p8g² Jan 17] placed in 3 maidens on polytrack at Lingfield: should stay 1¼m. *M. R. Channon*

JUN FAN (USA) 2 br.c. (Mar 10) Artax (USA) 126 – Ringside Lady (NZ) (Clay Hero **61** (AUS)) [2004 5m⁵ 6f⁶ Jun 8] $20,000Y, 13,000 2-y-o: good-bodied colt: fifth foal: half-brother to 2 winners in Australia, including 6f minor stakes winner She's Purring (by Flying Spur): dam 5f minor stakes winner in Australia: modest form in maidens at Redcar, not unduly punished: bred to be best at 5f/6f. *B. Ellison*

JUNGLE JIM 3 b.g. Atraf 116 – Enchanting Melody 71 (Chief Singer 131) [2004 **52** p7.1g⁶ p7.1g⁴ Dec 11] last in bumper: modest form in maidens at Wolverhampton. *Miss Gay Kelleway*

JUNGLE LION 6 ch.g. Lion Cavern (USA) 117 – Star Ridge (USA) (Storm Bird **55** (CAN) 134) [2004 –: f8.5g⁶ f11g² f14g f12s* f12s f14g* f12g⁶ 14.1g f16g⁶ f11d² Dec 21] lengthy, quite good-topped gelding: modest nowadays: won banded race at Southwell in February and handicap there in April: left J. Harris before final start: stays 1¾m: acts on fibresand and soft going: tried in headgear: tongue tied: has worn near-side pricker/hung left: free-going sort: none too consistent. *J. R. Norton*

JUNIPER BANKS 3 ch.g. Night Shift (USA) – Beryl 77 (Bering 136) [2004 66: 5g⁶ **63** 6g⁶ 5d 6d p5.1g³ p5.1d p5.1g⁶ f5g p9.5g p8.6g p6g Dec 20] good-topped gelding: modest maiden: stays 6f: acts on polytrack and good to firm going: tongue tied at 2 yrs after debut: got worked up in cheekpieces final 2-y-o start: probably temperamental. *Miss A. Stokell*

JUST A FLUKE (IRE) 3 b.g. Darshaan 133 – Star Profile (IRE) 100 (Sadler's Wells **78 §** (USA) 132) [2004 78P: 10d⁴ 10s 9.3f² 10.1v³ 10.1g 9.3f⁵ 9.2d² 8g* 8.3d⁴ Sep 27] strong, lengthy gelding: fair performer: won maiden at Musselburgh in September: stays 1¼m: acts on any going: tried tongue tied: has hung markedly: ungenuine: sold 8,500 gns, then gelded. *M. Johnston*

JUST A GLIMMER 4 b.f. Bishop of Cashel 122 – Rockin' Rosie 59 (Song 132) **93** [2004 85: f7g³ f7g f7s* f7g² 7.1d 7.1s* 7g 7g p7.1g p7.1g Dec 31] lengthy filly: fairly useful performer: won handicap at Wolverhampton in March and minor event at Warwick in May: best form around 7f: acts on all-weather and soft ground, probably on good to firm. *L. G. Cottrell*

JUSTALORD 6 b.g. King's Signet (USA) 110 – Just Lady 72 (Emarati (USA) 74) **85** [2004 72, a88: f5s f5g² p5g* p5g² p5g³ 5s 5f⁶ 5m* 5.1g 5g* f5g f5g³ Dec 14] lengthy **a96** gelding: useful handicapper on all-weather, fairly useful on turf: won at Lingfield in February, Catterick in July and Musselburgh in August: best at 5f: acts on all-weather, firm and good to soft ground: wears cheekpieces/blinkers: sometimes early to post: refused to enter stall intended eleventh outing: usually races up with pace/carries head high: consistent. *J. Balding*

JUSTAQUESTION 2 b.f. (Feb 3) Pursuit of Love 124 – Queenbird 90 (Warning 136) **92** [2004 5g 5d* 6s* 6m 7.1g³ 7m² 7g* 7s⁵ 6.5g 7s⁶ 8d⁴ Oct 30] £6,800Y: leggy, workman-like filly: sister to 6-y-o Temper Tantrum and half-sister to 5-y-o Pants: dam, 2-y-o 5f to 7f winner, became untrustworthy: fairly useful performer: won maiden at Warwick in April and minor events at York in May and Ascot (beat Beaver Patrol a head) in August: more highly tried after, respectable fourth to Squaw Dance in listed event at Newmarket: barely stays 1m: acts on soft and good to firm going: sometimes sweating. *I. A. Wood*

JUST A TRY (USA) 2 ch.c. (Feb 27) Lure (USA) 131 – Boubasis (USA) (Diesis 133) **71** [2004 7m 7d⁶ 8.1g p7m² Dec 21] 41,000 2-y-o: strong colt: first foal: dam, ran twice in North America, out of half-sister to very smart French performer up to 10.5f Bint Alnasr: fair maiden: best effort when second in nursery at Lingfield: should stay 1m. *R. Hannon*

JUST BEWARE 2 b.f. (Mar 4) Makbul 104 – Bewails (IRE) 53 (Caerleon (USA) 132) **47** [2004 6m 7d p7g p7g p8g Nov 30] seventh foal: dam ran twice: poor maiden: stays 1m: acts on polytrack. *Miss Z. C. Davison*

JUST BONNIE 2 b.c. (Apr 1) Lujain (USA) 119 – Fairy Flight (IRE) 86 (Fairy King – (USA)) [2004 6.1m⁶ 5f 6m 6.1d Sep 17] leggy colt: no form in minor event/maidens: signs of temperament. *J. M. Bradley*

JUST CLIFF   2 b.c. (Feb 15) Handsome Ridge 121 – Justfortherecord (Forzando 122)   **58**
[2004 p6g 7.1d⁴ p7.1g⁴ p7g p6g p6g Dec 18] modest maiden: below form last 3 starts:
needs to settle to stay 1m: blinkered final start. *W. R. Muir*

JUST DANCE ME (FR)   3 gr.f. Linamix (FR) 127 – Reine de La Ciel (USA) (Con-   **60**
quistador Cielo (USA)) [2004 –p: 9.2g² 8.3g⁶ Oct 11] tall filly: modest maiden, lightly
raced: off 4 months and left W. Haggas before poor effort final start: sent to France.
R. Charlton

JUST DASHING   5 b.g. Arrasas (USA) 100 – Smitten 72 (Run The Gantlet (USA))   **–**
[2004 9.9g 6m 10d p10g p10m Dec 15] compact gelding: no form. *J. E. Long*

JUST DO IT (UAE)   2 b.c. (Jan 29) Timber Country (USA) 124 – Poised (USA) (Rahy   **71**
(USA) 115) [2004 p8d⁶ 8d² 8.1s⁵ 7m 8.3d Oct 4] first foal: dam, ran twice in France,
sister to Noverre and closely related to Arazi: fair maiden: second at Salisbury, easily best
effort: will stay 1¼m: sometimes soon off bridle/carries head awkwardly. *M. R. Channon*

JUST ELIZABETH   2 b.f. (May 19) Aragon 118 – Collison Lane 80 (Reesh 117)   **–**
[2004 6s 7v 6s Nov 6] workmanlike filly: sixth foal: dam 5f (at 2 yrs)/6f winner: well held
in maidens. *M. E. Sowersby*

JUSTENJOY YOURSELF   2 b.f. (Apr 30) Tipsy Creek (USA) 115 – Habibi 50   **43**
(Alhijaz 122) [2004 5s⁶ 5m f5g⁶ 5m⁴ 6s 6s³ 7.5m Sep 15] 5,000Y: third foal: dam 2-y-o
6f seller winner: poor maiden: stays 6f: acts on soft and good to firm ground. *C. A. Dwyer*

JUSTE POUR L'AMOUR   4 ch.g. Pharly (FR) 130 – Fontaine Lady 41 (Millfontaine   **81**
114) [2004 87: 8m 7f⁴ 10m 7m 8g 6m⁴ 6m 6m 8m* 8s⁵ 8.5g² 7m⁶ 8g⁴ p8g⁵ p7g p7g⁵
Dec 4] sturdy, workmanlike gelding: fairly useful performer: won apprentice handicap at
Brighton in August: best at 7f/1m: acts on polytrack and firm going: blinkered (below
form) fourth start. *P. L. Gilligan*

JUST FLY   4 b.g. Efisio 120 – Chrysalis 66 (Soviet Star (USA) 128) [2004 88: p6g²   **83**
f7g² p7g² 8s 7g³ 7g 7.1g 7m 7s 7m 8g 8.3m² p6g⁵ p6g² p8.6g p6g⁵ p8m p7g Dec 29]   **a94**
sturdy gelding: fairly useful handicapper, better on all-weather than turf: stays 1m: acts
on all-weather and good to firm going. *S. Kirk*

JUSTICE JONES   3 b.g. Emperor Jones (USA) 119 – Rally For Justice (Dominion   **–**
123) [2004 f8.5s 7.1d 10.2g 10s 10f 7m 6.1d Jul 10] no form, including in sellers: tried
blinkered. *J. L. Spearing*

JUST JAMES   5 b.g. Spectrum (IRE) 126 – Fairy Flight (IRE) 86 (Fairy King (USA))   **101**
[2004 120: 6s 8f 7g Aug 14] strong, compact gelding: very smart at 4 yrs: just useful form
in 2004: effective at 6f/7f: acts on firm and soft going: held up: quirky. *J. Noseda*

JUST ONE LOOK   3 b.f. Barathea (IRE) 127 – Western Sal 75 (Salse (USA) 128)   **60**
[2004 77: p7g 6.1g 6g 7g f8g 8.1g⁶ 8.1d 7.1g⁵ 8s p8.6g³ p8.6d³ p9.5g Nov 20] smallish,
quite good-topped filly: modest performer: stays 8.6f: acts on polytrack and firm ground:
sold 5,000 gns. *M. Blanshard*

JUST ONE SMILE (IRE)   4 b.f. Desert Prince (IRE) 130 – Smile Awhile (USA)   **64 d**
(Woodman (USA) 126) [2004 71: 6v 7v³ 6m⁶ 7.2f 6g 6m 6m Jul 15] lengthy, useful-
looking filly: just modest handicapper in 2004: below form after second outing: stays 1m,
as effective at 6f/7f: acts on polytrack and any turf going: blinkered last 2 starts: has raced
freely/looked difficult ride. *T. D. Easterby*

JUST RED   6 ch.g. Meqdaam (USA) – Orchard Bay 47 (Formidable (USA) 125) [2004   **–**
–: f12g Jan 9] well held in 3 maidens. *R. Hollinshead*

JUST TIM (IRE)   3 ch.c. Inchinor 119 – Simply Sooty 78 (Absalom 128) [2004 76:   **77**
p10g⁴ 8g⁸ 8.1d⁴ 8m 8.1g* 8m⁵ 8.3m 8g Jul 27] useful-looking colt: fair performer: won
maiden at Bath in April and minor event at Chepstow in May: effective at 1m/easy 1¼m:
acts on polytrack, unraced on extremes of going on turf: tongue tied final start: often races
prominently: sold 8,500 gns. *R. Hannon*

JUST WAZ (USA)   2 ch.g. (Mar 13) Woodman (USA) 126 – Just Tops (USA) (Topsider   **67**
(USA)) [2004 7.5d 7s* 8g⁵ 8s Oct 22] $40,000F, 45,000Y: quite good-topped gelding:
fifth foal: closely related to winner by Crafty Prospector and half-brother to winner by
Formal Gold, both in USA: dam, 6.5f to 8.5f winner in USA, out of very smart French/
US performer up to 9f Justicara: fair performer: won maiden at Newcastle in August: well
held in nurseries after: should stay 1m: acts on soft going. *R. M. Whitaker*

JUST WIZ   8 b.g. Efisio 120 – Jade Pet 90 (Petong 126) [2004 48, a79: p12g⁶ f12g³   **–**
p10g f8.5s² f9.4g³ 8.3d f12g² f8.5g⁵ p8.6g p12.2g⁴ Dec 27] small gelding: fair performer: **a70 d**
below form after reappearance: barely stays easy 1½m: acts on fibresand, tried rarely on
turf nowadays: wears blinkers/visor: held up. *N. P. Littmoden*

JUWWI   10 ch.g. Mujtahid (USA) 118 – Nouvelle Star (AUS) (Luskin Star (AUS)) **74 d**
[2004 82: p6g p5g⁴ p6g p5g f6s⁴ f5g⁴ 6s f5g⁶ 5.7f² f6g⁶ 6d⁶ f5g 5.1g 5d Jul 15] robust
gelding: handicapper: on the downgrade: best at 5f/6f: acts on all-weather/any turf going:
sometimes wears cheekpieces: usually claimer ridden/slowly away/gets behind: reportedly broke blood vessel final 9-y-o outing: unreliable. *J. M. Bradley*

K

KABEER   6 ch.g. Unfuwain (USA) 131 – Ta Rib (USA) 116 (Mr Prospector (USA)) **73**
[2004 7f⁴ 7.1f³ 7.1m 8m p7d⁵ 8.3m⁶ 10g p7g⁶ p7g⁵ Nov 27] big, lengthy gelding: fair
maiden: should stay beyond 1m: acts on polytrack and firm going: tongue tied last 2
starts. *P. S. McEntee*

KABIS AMIGOS   2 ch.c. (Mar 14) Nashwan (USA) 135 – River Saint (USA) 73§ (Irish **60**
River (FR) 131) [2004 8g 8v Oct 23] 22,000Y: tall, leggy colt: second foal: dam, unreliable maiden who should have stayed 1m, half-sister to champion US filly Serena's Song
(best up to 9f), herself dam of Coronation Stakes winner Sophisticat: tongue tied, modest
form in maidens at Leicester (slowly away) and Newbury. *H. R. A. Cecil*

KABIS DANCER   3 ch.c. Night Shift (USA) – Perfect Welcome (Taufan (USA) **63**
119) [2004 77: 10m³ 11d Oct 10] sturdy colt: maiden: fair form on debut: just modest at
best in 3 races since: should stay beyond 1m: sold 800 gns. *H. R. A. Cecil*

KABREET   3 b.c. Night Shift (USA) – Red Rabbit 86 (Suave Dancer (USA) 136) [2004 **84**
79: p7g³ p6g* 6g 6m 6g 5d Aug 12] sturdy colt: fairly useful performer: won handicap at
Lingfield in January: well below form on turf after: best at 6f/7f: acts on polytrack, best
effort on turf on good to soft going: visored final start. *E. A. L. Dunlop*

KAFIL (USA)   10 b. or br.g. Housebuster (USA) – Alchaasibiyeh (USA) 85 (Seattle **–**
Slew (USA)) [2004 –: p6g p7g p6g May 13] leggy gelding: no longer of any account.
J. J. Bridger

KAGGAMAGIC   2 ch.g. (Apr 19) Abou Zouz (USA) 109 – Meadmore Magic 68 **62 d**
(Mansingh (USA) 120) [2004 6f⁵ 6s⁴ 7.1g 5.9g 6m f6g p9.5g Nov 15] small gelding:
modest maiden: below form after third start: stays 7f: acts on firm going, probably on
soft. *J. R. Norton*

KAGOSHIMA (IRE)   9 b.g. Shirley Heights 130 – Kashteh (IRE) 79 (Green Desert **45**
(USA) 127) [2004 38: f16g² f14g² f14g³ f16g³ f16.2s⁶ Feb 20] deep-bodied gelding: poor
performer: stays 2m: acts on fibresand and firm ground: visored. *J. R. Norton*

KAHIRA (IRE)   2 ch.f. (Apr 22) King's Best (USA) 132 – Sine Labe (USA) (Vaguely **80 p**
Noble 140) [2004 8g 7g² Oct 11] big, leggy filly: half-sister to high-class sprinter (also 7f
winner at 2 yrs) Tamarisk (by Green Desert) and fairly useful 1m/1¼m winner Grand
Selection (by Cricket Ball), later successful in USA: dam, ran twice in France, half-
sister to Prix Saint-Alary winner Treble out of half-sister to Triptych: much better effort
in maidens when neck second to Corcoran at Leicester, green before finishing strongly:
should stay 1m: likely to progress. *M. L. W. Bell*

KAHLUA BEAR   2 b.g. (Apr 10) Mister Baileys 123 – Crystal Magic 92 (Mazilier **53 p**
(USA) 107) [2004 p6g⁴ Dec 29] 11,000Y: fifth foal: half-brother to 6f winner O B Comfort (by College Chapel) and 1m winner I'm Magic (by First Trump): dam, 2-y-o 5f
winner, out of sister to high-class sprinter Petong: 11/2, fourth to Aggravation in maiden
at Lingfield, not knocked about once held: should improve. *W. J. Haggas*

KAHYASI PRINCESS (IRE)   4 b.f. Kahyasi 130 – Dungeon Princess (IRE) 62 **–**
(Danehill (USA) 126) [2004 92: 14g⁵ Apr 30] sturdy filly: fairly useful performer at 3
yrs: well held only run in 2004: races prominently. *M. Johnston*

KAID (IRE)   9 b.g. Alzao (USA) 117 – Very Charming (USA) (Vaguely Noble 140) **–**
[2004 f12g Feb 9] good-topped gelding: poor maiden: tried blinkered/visored. *R. Lee*

KAIETEUR (USA)   5 b.h. Marlin (USA) 124 – Strong Embrace (USA) (Regal Emb- **108**
race (CAN)) [2004 121: 10d⁶ 10f 10m⁵ 10.3f⁴ Sep 10] big, strong, well-made horse: very
smart performer in 2003 (reportedly finished lame final start): only useful in 2004, fourth
of 6 to Big Bad Bob in minor event at Doncaster final outing: best around 1¼m: has form
on firm going, best efforts on good or softer: tends to sweat: blinkered penultimate start
(reportedly found to have had a quarter crack problem after). *B. J. Meehan*

KAJUL   3 b.f. Emperor Jones (USA) 119 – Andbell (Trojan Fen 118) [2004 7d p8m
Oct 6] good-topped filly: half-sister to fairly useful but ungenuine 7f to 1¼m winner

Willoughby's Boy (by Night Shift) and winner in Norway by Mango Express: dam of little account: well beaten in maidens. *C. A. Horgan*

KALAMAN (IRE) 4 b.c. Desert Prince (IRE) 130 – Kalamba (IRE) (Green Dancer (USA) 132) [2004 126: 9g² 8g* 10d³ 10m* 10.4d⁶ 8m Dec 12] well-made, attractive colt: impresses in appearance: very smart performer: won listed race at Goodwood (edged right, beat Imtiyaz ¾ length) in May and Daily Record Scottish Derby at Ayr (idled and hung left after quickening to lead 1f out, beat Gateman by length) in July: creditable 4¼ lengths third to Refuse To Bend in Eclipse Stakes at Sandown in between, staying on strongly after being forced to check over 3f out: below form last 2 starts in International Stakes at York (final outing for Sir Michael Stoute, found little) and Hong Kong Mile at Sha Tin (renamed Oriental Magic): stays 1¼m: acts on firm and good to soft going: occasionally found less than expected. *D. A. Hayes, Hong Kong* **120**

KALAMANSI (IRE) 3 b.f. Sadler's Wells (USA) 132 – Musk Lime (USA) 97 (Private Account (USA)) [2004 9g⁶ 10m 7f 9.2m 11.5f Aug 5] 60,000Y: compact filly: second foal: dam, Irish 2-y-o 7f winner, out of half-sister to Breeders Cup Distaff winner Inside Information: little form. *N. A. Callaghan* **–**

KALANISHA (IRE) 4 ch.g. Ashkalani (IRE) 128 – Camisha (IRE) 82 (Shernazar 131) [2004 –: 10d 12v⁶ f12d f14g³ p10g⁵ Sep 18] strong, lengthy gelding: poor maiden: left N. Graham after fourth start: should stay 1½m: blinkered last 2 starts. *John Berry* **40**

KALANI STAR (IRE) 4 b.g. Ashkalani (IRE) 128 – Bellissi (IRE) 77 (Bluebird (USA) 125) [2004 83: 8g⁶ 7d 7.5m³ 8f 7m⁴ a7g⁵ p7.1d f7g² p8.6g⁵ Dec 27] just fair form in 2004, leaving Timothy Doyle in Ireland after sixth start: probably stays 1m: acts on all-weather, firm and good to soft going: wore tongue tie in 2003, when also tried blinkered. *I. Semple* **75 +**

KALI 3 gr.f. Linamix (FR) 127 – Alkarida (FR) (Akarad (FR) 130) [2004 71p: 9.7s³ 8.3g³ 7g² 7.1f* 7d⁶ p7g⁴ 7s⁶ p8.6g² p8g⁴ p8g² p8.6g⁵ Dec 10] leggy filly: fairly useful performer: won maiden at Warwick (hung left) in June: stays 8.6f: acts on polytrack, firm and good to soft going. *R. Charlton* **83**

KALIKA (IRE) 2 b.f. (Mar 31) Bachir (IRE) 118 – Ruwy 77 (Soviet Star (USA) 128) [2004 f6m⁶ 6f f7g 7m Oct 2] 1,800F, 8,500Y: leggy, angular filly: fifth foal: half-sister to fairly useful 7f/1m winner Freya's Dream (by Danehill Dancer) and 3-y-o Jilly Why: dam 1m winner: poor maiden: sometimes unruly in preliminaries (twice withdrawn as a consequence). *Ms Deborah J. Evans* **36**

KALIMENTA (USA) 3 ch.f. Rahy (USA) 115 – Toujours Elle (USA) (Lyphard (USA) 132) [2004 8s⁴ 8g² 9.5s⁶ 10m⁶ 10.2m 9s 10.2g Sep 3] eighth foal: half-sister to 3 winners, including fairly useful 7f (at 2 yrs) and 2m (in Ireland) winner Al Towd (by Kingmambo): dam, French maiden, closely related to Elnadim and Mehthaaf and granddaughter of Fall Aspen: modest maiden: trained by H-A. Pantall in France first 3 starts: seems to stay 1¼m: tried blinkered: looks tricky ride: sent to USA. *S. Kirk* **54**

KALISHKA (IRE) 3 b.c. Fasliyev (USA) 120 – Andromaque (USA) 111 (Woodman (USA) 126) [2004 66?: 8.5s⁶ 8m⁵ 8g 10g 8.5m 10g Oct 11] leggy, angular colt: just modest maiden in 2004: should stay 1¼m: tried blinkered: sold 4,800 gns. *Andrew Turnell* **54 ?**

Daily Record Scottish Derby, Ayr—
Kalaman gains his first pattern-race success despite idling in front; Gateman is a good second

KALLISTA'S PRIDE 4 b.f. Puissance 110 – Clan Scotia 47 (Clantime 101) [2004 –: **64**
7m 5m² 5g 6d* 6f 5.1g⁶ 5d 5g⁵ 5g 6.1m p6g p5.1g⁴ p6g⁵ p6g³ p6g² Dec 30] modest handicapper: left M. Bosley after second start: won amateur event at Salisbury in July: stays 6f:
acts on polytrack, good to firm and good to soft ground: sometimes visored. *J. R. Best*

KALMINI (USA) 2 b. or br.f. (Apr 25) Rahy (USA) 115 – Kilma (USA) 97 (Silver **73**
Hawk (USA) 123) [2004 7m 7m² 7g* 8s⁵ 7.1g⁴ 8g Sep 30] lengthy filly: fourth foal: dam,
won around 1½m, out of US Grade 2 9f winner Nikishka: fair performer: won maiden at
Folkestone in August: stays 1m: acts on soft and good to firm going: visored (ran poorly)
final start. *M. R. Channon*

KALOU (GER) 6 b.g. Law Society (USA) 130 – Kompetenz (IRE) (Be My Guest **54**
(USA) 126) [2004 56: p10g³ 10g 10m³ 11.6g 10.9d Sep 18] modest handicapper: stays
11f: acts on all-weather, heavy and good to firm and good to firm ground: tried blinkered (not in Britain):
possibly not straightforward. *B. J. Curley*

KALUANA COURT 8 b.m. Batshoof 122 – Fairfields Cone (Celtic Cone 116) [2004 **57**
80: 17.2g 13.9g 18s 12s p13.9g p16.5g Dec 30] good-topped mare: only modest handicapper in 2004: stays 17f: best efforts on good/good to firm going: usually held up.
R. J. Price

KALUSH 3 b.g. Makbul 104 – The Lady Vanishes (Robin Des Pins (USA) 119) [2004
66: 8g 10s 10.3m⁶ 8m Jul 25] tall, leggy gelding: maiden: no form in 2004. *Ronald
Thompson*

KAMAKIRI (IRE) 2 b.c. (Feb 18) Trans Island 119 – Alpine Flair (IRE) (Tirol 127) **100 p**
[2004 7d 7m* 7.1m* Aug 11] €50,000F, 35,000Y: tall, close-coupled colt: second living
foal: dam unraced half-sister to useful Italian filly up to 9f Fair Weather: won maiden at
Ascot (by 2 lengths from Capable Guest) in July and minor event at Sandown (4 ran,
comfortably by 2½ lengths from Active Asset) in August: should stay 1m: useful already,
and should progress. *R. Hannon*

KAMALA 5 b.m. Priolo (USA) 127 – Fleeting Vision (IRE) 79 (Vision (USA)) [2004 **–**
–: f12g⁶ Jan 13] maiden: lightly raced and no form since 2002: tried visored: temperament
under suspicion. *R. Brotherton*

KAMANDA LAUGH 3 ch.g. Most Welcome 131 – Kamada (USA) (Blushing Groom **93 p**
(FR) 131) [2004 66: p6g* 7.1s² 7m* 8g* 8d* 8d⁵ Oct 30] strong gelding: fairly useful
form: progressed in 2004, winning maiden at Lingfield in March and handicaps at
Doncaster in May, Leicester in June and Newmarket in October: creditable fifth to Zero
Tolerance in handicap at Newmarket final outing: stays 1m: acts on polytrack, soft and
good to firm going: races prominently: likely to improve further at 4 yrs. *B. W. Hills*

KAMA'S WHEEL 5 ch.m. Magic Ring (IRE) 115 – Tea And Scandals (USA) (Key **–**
To The Kingdom (USA)) [2004 46, a–: 8g 8m 7.9m⁶ 8.1d Aug 19] workmanlike mare:
poor maiden: well held in 2004: has worn cheekpieces: edgy sort: often slowly away.
John A. Harris

KAMENKA 3 ch.f. Wolfhound (USA) 126 – Aliuska (IRE) 70 (Fijar Tango (FR) 127) **72 d**
[2004 66+: 6d⁴ 5g⁴ 5d⁴ 6d 6s 6g³ 6d³ p6g⁶ Oct 18] close-coupled filly: fair maiden: well
below form after third start: effective at 5f/6f: acts on good to firm and good to soft going:
visored last 2 starts. *R. A. Fahey*

KAMES PARK 2 b.g. (Apr 28) Desert Sun 120 – Persian Sally (IRE) (Persian **86**
Bold 123) [2004 8.1g⁴ 8.3d² 7.2s* Oct 12] €16,000F, 3,500Y, 7,500 2-y-o: good-bodied
gelding: fourth foal: half-brother to 3 winners, including 3-y-o Come What July and 4-y-o
Jimmy Byrne: dam unraced: best effort in maidens when winning at Ayr by length from
Alrafidain: should stay 1m: slowly away first 2 starts: tends to carry head high. *I. Semple*

KANAD 2 b.g. (Apr 14) Bold Edge 123 – Multi-Sofft 30 (Northern State (USA) 91) **80**
[2004 6g³ 5.1m² 6m 6m² 6m⁵ 7s* Oct 16] 13,000Y: compact gelding: half-brother to
several winners, including 4-y-o Ellovamul and 3-y-o Hold The Line: dam maiden who
probably stayed 1¾m: fairly useful performer: blinkered, improved slightly to win
maiden at Catterick: stays 7f: acts on soft and good to firm going: tongue tied. *B. Hanbury*

KANDIDATE 2 b.c. (Apr 15) Kabool 119 – Valleyrose (IRE) (Royal Academy (USA) **98**
130) [2004 7m 7m³ 7g 8f⁶ p8g² p8g* Nov 16] 30,000F, 26,000Y: good-topped colt: has a
quick action: third foal: half-brother to 6-y-o Star Valley: dam French 1m/9f winner: useful performer: won nursery at Lingfield under 9-7: best effort when sixth in Royal Lodge
Stakes at Ascot: stays 1m: acts on polytrack and firm going. *C. E. Brittain*

KANGARILLA ROAD 5 b.g. Magic Ring (IRE) 115 – Kangra Valley 56 (Indian **74**
Ridge 123) [2004 78: 5g 5m 5f² 5m 5g 5m Jun 30] leggy, good-topped gelding: fair handi-
capper: best at bare 5f: acts on firm ground: sometimes races freely: usually waited with.
Mrs J. R. Ramsden

KANGRINA 2 b.f. (Jan 13) Acatenango (GER) 127 – Kirona 107 (Robellino (USA) **77**
127) [2004 p8g⁵ p8.6g⁴ p8.6d* p8g⁶ Nov 16] €34,000Y: first foal: dam German 7f/1m
winner, including at 2 yrs: fair performer: won maiden at Wolverhampton in October:
good sixth in nursery at Lingfield: likely to be suited by 1¼m/1½m. *Sir Mark Prescott*

KANZ WOOD (USA) 8 ch.g. Woodman (USA) 126 – Kanz (USA) 115 (The **–**
Minstrel (CAN) 135) [2004 59, a74: p7g p8g⁵ p8g 8.1d⁵ 7v⁵ f8.5g³ f8.5m⁴ f7g³ f8g⁶ **a50**
f7d Jun 17] strong gelding: has had breathing operation: modest performer: stays 8.5f:
acts on all-weather, good to firm and good to soft going: tongue tied once in 2002: visored
last 3 starts: sometimes carries head high: none too reliable. *A. W. Carroll*

KAPAJE 2 b.f. (Apr 17) Lake Coniston (IRE) 131 – Reina 24 (Homeboy 114) [2004 **60**
6m 6.1m⁵ 7g³ 8m Sep 25] 3,000Y: half-sister to several winners, including 1999 2-y-o 5f
winner Richard Ansdell (by Absalom) and 4-y-o Diamond Racket: dam maiden who
stayed 7f: modest maiden: left M. Channon after debut: stays 7f: acts on good to firm
going. *P. D. Evans*

KAPAROLO (USA) 5 ch.g. El Prado (IRE) 119 – Parliament House (USA) (General **–**
Assembly (USA)) [2004 78: 16.2v 16d Oct 10] strong gelding: handicapper, well below
form in 2004. *Mrs A. J. Perrett*

KARA DOOT 3 b.f. Bijou d'Inde 127 – Meghdoot 75 (Celestial Storm (USA) 132) **– p**
[2004 p10g Dec 4] first reported foal: dam 1½m winner: 33/1, tenth in maiden at Lingfield, racing freely and not knocked about: open to improvement. *H. J. Collingridge*

KARAKUM 5 b.g. Mtoto 134 – Magongo 103 (Be My Chief (USA) 122) [2004 –: **–**
12.6m⁴ 11.7g 11.9m Sep 23] close-coupled gelding: poor maiden: tried blinkered.
A. J. Chamberlain

KARAMEA (SWI) 3 gr.f. Rainbow Quest (USA) 134 – Karapucha (IRE) (Kaldoun **75**
(FR) 122) [2004 76p: 10g³ 12d* 11.8m⁵ 12d 11.9g Sep 3] leggy, close-coupled filly: fair
performer: won maiden at Thirsk in May: ran as if amiss last 3 starts: stays 1½m: unraced
on extremes of going. *J. L. Dunlop*

KARAOKE (IRE) 4 b.g. Mujadil (USA) 119 – Kayoko (IRE) 74 (Shalford (IRE) **82**
124§) [2004 84: p10g p10g p10g* 10.2g 10g 8.1d⁵ 10g⁴ 10.2f² 10m² 10m 10s 9g
10g³ 10f* 10f 11.9f⁵ p8.6g⁴ p9.5g³ p10m* Dec 22] good-bodied gelding: fairly useful
handicapper: won at Lingfield in March, Windsor in July and Lingfield in December:
effective at 1m, barely stays 1½m: acts on all-weather and firm going. *S. Kirk*

KARAOKE KING 6 ch.h. King's Signet (USA) 110 – Brampton Grace 80 (Tachypous **52**
128) [2004 71: f7g⁶ p7g p6g p7g 7s May 8] workmanlike horse: modest performer in
2004: best at 6f/easy 7f: acted on all-weather, good to firm and good to soft going: often
raced prominently: dead. *J. E. Long*

KARASHINKO (IRE) 3 b.g. Shinko Forest (IRE) – Kayoko (IRE) 74 (Shalford **–**
(IRE) 124§) [2004 8m 5m Jun 5] tailed off in maidens at Newmarket and Doncaster.
R. Guest

KARATHAENA (IRE) 4 b.f. Barathea (IRE) 127 – Dabtara (IRE) 88 (Kahyasi 130) **53**
[2004 78?: p7g p8g 8.3d 9.9s 8s 11.9s 12g Oct 4] good-bodied filly: disappointing
maiden: left J. Hills after fifth start: should prove best around 1¼m: acts on soft ground:
tried visored: has worn crossed noseband/raced freely: possibly none too genuine.
M. E. Sowersby

KAREEB (FR) 7 b.g. Green Desert (USA) 127 – Braari (USA) 97 (Gulch (USA)) **80**
[2004 90: p8g⁶ 7d 6s 7m⁴ 7m 7g⁶ 7f 7s⁶ 7m⁴ 7m p7g³ Dec 4] smallish, robust gelding:
fairly useful handicapper: better at 7f than 1m: acts on polytrack, firm and soft going:
tried blinkered at 3 yrs: held up: inconsistent. *W. J. Musson*

KARELIAN 3 gr.g. Linamix (FR) 127 – Kalikala (Darshaan 133) [2004 10.5d 11s **72**
11s⁴ 11g* 10s³ 16d⁶ Nov 3] half-brother to several winners, including French 1¼m/10.5f
winner Kalajana (by Green Dancer) and 7f (at 2 yrs) to 1½m winner Kalabo (by Trempolino), both smart: dam, French 1½m winner, half-sister to dam of Kahyasi: fair performer:
left A. Fabre 105,000 gns and gelded after winning handicap at Lyon-Parilly in June:
creditable third in similar event at Ayr 4 months later: likely to stay 1½m (seemed not to
stay 2m): raced only on good ground or softer: effective blinkered or not. *K. A. Ryan*

KAREN'S CAPER (USA) 2 b.f. (May 13) War Chant (USA) 126 – Miss Caerleona **80 p**
(FR) (Caerleon (USA) 132) [2004 p7g² p8g* Oct 31] fourth foal: half-sister to winner in
USA by Storm Cat: dam useful performer around 1¼m in France, later US Grade 3 9f
winner at 4 yrs: landed odds in maiden at Lingfield impressively by 5 lengths from Obezyana, leading 2f out: will probably stay 1¼m: sure to progress. *J. H. M. Gosden*

KARITA 2 ch.f. (Jan 22) Inchinor 119 – Ebba 88 (Elmaamul (USA) 125) [2004 5s Apr – 17] £9,000Y: leggy filly: first foal: dam 2-y-o 5f/6f winner: well held in claimer at Thirsk, slowly away: sold 2,000 gns in July, sent to Spain. *M. L. W. Bell*

KARLU (GER) 2 ch.c. (Feb 1) Big Shuffle (USA) 120 – Krim (GER) (Lagunas) [2004 **72 p** 7m 7.1s* Sep 20] 25,000F, 32,000Y: fourth foal: brother to 2 winners in Germany, including 7f to 8.5f winner Kayo: dam unraced sister to dam of 1000 Guineas/Oaks winner Kazzia: confirmed promise when winning maiden at Chepstow by ½ length from Spectait, travelling comfortably and leading late on: should stay 1m: likely to progress. *J. L. Dunlop*

KARMA CHAMELIAN (USA) 3 b.f. Diesis 133 – Wild Rumour (IRE) 89 (Sadler's **38** Wells (USA) 132) [2004 –: 8m 7.1f⁵ 6.1m Jun 27] good-topped filly: poor form in maidens/claimer: slowly away/took good hold final outing. *J. W. Hills*

KARMINSKEY PARK 5 b.m. Sabrehill (USA) 120 – Housefull 81 (Habitat 134) **71** [2004 71: 5v⁵ 5v² 5v⁶ 5m⁵ 5f³ 5g² 5g* 5g 5.1d 5g 5g 5d 6g⁵ 6g p6d⁶ Nov 5] heavy-bodied mare: fair handicapper: won at Hamilton in June: effective at 5f/easy 6f: acts on all-weather and any turf going: sometimes flashes tail. *T. J. Etherington*

KARYON (IRE) 4 b.f. Presidium 124 – Stealthy 73 (Kind of Hush 118) [2004 40: **43** 12.3m⁵ f14m 14.1f Jul 29] good-topped filly: poor maiden: may prove best short of 1¼m: winning hurdler. *Miss Kate Milligan*

KASHIMO (GER) 5 br.h. Lomitas 129 – Kardia (Mister Rock's (GER)) [2004 p12g⁵ **62** p12g³ 11.5m⁴ Apr 12] ex-German horse: half-brother to several winners in Germany, including smart 1m to 1¼m performer Kalatos (by Big Shuffle): dam, German 7f (at 2 yrs) to 11f winner, half-sister to German Group 1 1½m winner Kamiros: won at Frankfurt (twice) and Cologne in 2003: left A. Bolte in Germany, modest form in handicaps in Britain: stays 1½m: some promise on polytrack, below form on going softer than good: ran in snatches final outing. *G. L. Moore*

KASHMAR FLIGHT 2 b.f. (Mar 17) Fraam 114 – Evasive Step 70 (Batshoof 122) **53** [2004 5s 6m 7f⁶ 7m⁵ 8f Sep 23] leggy filly: second foal: dam, maiden who stayed 1m and possibly none too genuine, out of half-sister to high-class stayer and Champion Hurdle winner Royal Gait: modest maiden: stays 7f: acts on soft and good to firm going: signs of temperament. *T. D. Easterby*

KASHTANKA (IRE) 2 ch.c. (Apr 8) Ashkalani (IRE) 128 – Spark (IRE) 79 (Flash **47** of Steel 120) [2004 6d 7d⁶ 7m⁶ Sep 4] strong colt: poor form in maidens: should stay at least 1m. *J. J. Quinn*

KASKA (IRE) 3 b.f. King of Kings (IRE) 125 – Antiguan Jane 71 (Shirley Heights **68** 130) [2004 8g 10g⁶ May 14] 77,000Y: rangy unfurnished filly: has a quick, unimpressive action: second foal: half-sister to a winner in USA by Crafty Prospector: dam, easily best effort at 1¼m, sister to useful performer up to 1¾m (also US Grade 3 11f winner) Party Season: fair form in newcomers event at Newmarket and maiden at Newbury, sixth to Remaadd in latter: sold 9,500 gns in December. *B. W. Hills*

KASTHARI (IRE) 5 gr.g. Vettori (IRE) 119 – Karliyka (IRE) (Last Tycoon 131) [2004 **117** 113: 18m⁴ 16s Oct 16] tall, lengthy gelding: smart performer, lightly raced: left Sir Michael Stoute, and won twice over hurdles in 2003/4: better than ever when dead-heating with Millenary in GNER Doncaster Cup in September, rallying gamely as pair pulled clear: ran poorly in Jockey Club Cup at Newmarket subsequent start: stays 2¼m: acts on soft ground, best efforts on good to firm: has edged left. *J. Howard Johnson*

KATALI 7 ch.m. Clantime 101 – Portvally (Import 127) [2004 –: p6g Feb 3] lightly- – raced maiden: no sign of ability. *A. Bailey*

KATANA 2 b.f. (Feb 5) Spectrum (IRE) 126 – Karlaska (Lashkari 128) [2004 8.2g 8s **62** p8g⁵ 7.9g² Oct 9] 10,000Y: workmanlike filly: fourth foal: half-sister to 2 winners in Italy, including 1¼m winner by Halling: dam useful French 1½m winner: modest maiden: should stay 1¼m: tends to carry head high. *I. A. Wood*

KATAVI (USA) 3 b.f. Stravinsky (USA) 133 – Halholah (USA) 65 (Secreto (USA) **56** 128) [2004 p7g⁵ p7.1g³ p8.6g⁶ Nov 13] $160,000F, $230,000Y: half-sister to several winners, including smart 6f (at 2 yrs) to 10.5f winner Murajja and fairly useful 1m and 15f winner Yanabi (both by Silver Hawk): dam maiden who stayed 1¼m: reportedly suffered an injury in 2003, and had another setback in spring 2004: modest form in maidens at Lingfield and Wolverhampton (2) in autumn. *J. Noseda*

KATAYEB (IRE) 3 b.f. Machiavellian (USA) 123 – Fair of The Furze 112 (Ela- – Mana-Mou 132) [2004 10g Sep 10] 560,000Y: half-sister to several winners, notably high-class 1½m performer White Muzzle (by Dancing Brave), smart 7f (at 2 yrs)/1¾m

(Deutsches St Leger) winner Fair Question (by Rainbow Quest) and useful dam of Dubai World Cup winner Almutawakel: dam 1m/1¼m winner who stayed 1½m: 10/1, well held in maiden at Sandown, slowly away: visits Green Desert. *M. P. Tregoning*

KATHOLOGY (IRE) 7 b.g. College Chapel 122 – Wicken Wonder (IRE) 71 (Distant Relative 128) [2004 96, a–: 5m 5m⁶ 5g 5d 5m³ 5.2f⁵ 5d p6g p5g⁵ Dec 18] smallish, sturdy gelding: fairly useful handicapper on turf, fair on all-weather: effective at 5f/6f: acts on soft and firm going, and on all-weather: usually races prominently: none too consistent. *D. R. C. Elsworth*   **84 a75 +**

KATHRYN JANEWAY (IRE) 2 b.f. (Mar 15) In The Wings 128 – Freak Out (FR) (Bering 136) [2004 7g 8s⁶ Oct 22] €32,000Y: good-topped filly: third foal: half-sister to French 13f winner Lodgina (by Grand Lodge): dam French 1¼m/11f winner: modest form, not knocked about, in maidens at Leicester and Doncaster: should be suited by 1¼m/1½m: likely to progress. *W. R. Muir*   **57 p**

KATHYS JOB 2 b.f. (Apr 18) Silver Wizard (USA) 117 – Kathy Fair (IRE) 46 (Nicholas Bill 125) [2004 5g Mar 25] fifth foal: half-sister to ungenuine 5f (at 2 yrs) and 7f winner Quite Remarkable (by Danzig Connection): dam maiden who stayed 1¼m: ninth in minor event at Doncaster. *A. D. Smith*   **50**

KATIE BOO (IRE) 2 br.f. (Mar 5) Namid 128 – Misty Peak (IRE) 83 (Sri Pekan (USA) 117) [2004 5m³ 5m² 5f* 6g³ 5.1g⁵ 5f² 5m² 6.1g⁹* Aug 19] €11,000Y: lengthy filly: first foal: dam, Irish maiden (probably stayed 7f), half-sister to useful Irish 1½m winner Golly Gosh: fairly useful performer: won minor events at Carlisle in June and Chester (made all) in August: second in nurseries in between: effective at 5f/easy 6f: acts on firm going. *A. Berry*   **87**

KATIE KAI 3 b.f. Cayman Kai (IRE) 114 – Yemaail (IRE) (Shaadi (USA) 126) [2004 8s⁵ Oct 11] third reported foal: dam unraced: 200/1, tailed off in minor event at Ayr, slowly away. *Miss S. E. Forster*   **–**

KATIE KILLANE 2 ch.f. (Apr 9) Komaite (USA) – Efficacy 62 (Efisio 120) [2004 5.1s 6m 5.1g p5.1g Oct 7] fourth foal: half-sister to 4-y-o Effective: dam 6f winner at 4 yrs: only a little sign of ability in maidens/minor event: wore cheekpieces final start. *M. Wellings*   **–**

KATIE MERNAGH (IRE) 4 b.f. Danetime (IRE) 121 – White Jasmin 53 (Jalmood (USA) 126) [2004 –: 14.1s⁵ Oct 27] half-sister to 3 winners, including 1996 2-y-o 7f winner The Deejay and 1½m/2m winner Ludere (both by Desse Zenny): dam 2m winner: well held in maidens at 3 yrs for P. Nolan in Ireland, and in seller at Yarmouth (blinkered, slowly away). *P. S. McEntee*   **–**

KATIE'S BATH TIME 3 b.f. Lugana Beach 116 – Eucharis 41 (Tickled Pink 114) [2004 39: f6s 5g Mar 31] good-topped filly: little form. *Ian Emmerson*   **–**

KATIE'S BISCUIT 2 b.f. (Apr 28) Cayman Kai (IRE) 114 – Peppers (IRE) 71 (Bluebird (USA) 125) [2004 6m⁶ 7m 7s⁶ Nov 1] workmanlike filly: first foal: dam maiden who stayed 1½m: modest form in maidens: likely to stay 1m. *Ian Emmerson*   **53**

GNER Doncaster Cup—a rousing finish ends in a dead heat between the grey Kasthari and Millenary; Dancing Bay, High Accolade (hidden) and Darasim are next

KATIE'S ROLE   3 b.f. Tragic Role (USA) – Mirkan Honey 83 (Ballymore 123) [2004   **45**
60: f7g³ f7f⁴ f7g⁴ f8.5g³ 10.3g 10d Apr 5] plain, leggy filly: poor maiden: stays easy 8.5f:
acts on fibresand and good to soft ground, possibly not on good to firm. *Ian Emmerson*

KATIYPOUR (IRE)   7 ch.g. Be My Guest (USA) 126 – Katiyfa (Auction Ring (USA)   **85**
123) [2004 81: p10g p10g³ p8g* p8g² 8.5s 8m* 8.3m⁴ 10.1g 10.1f³ 8f⁴ 9d⁵ 10.1g 10.1m
p10g³ Sep 22] quite attractive gelding: fairly useful handicapper: won at Lingfield in
March and Brighton in May: effective at 1m to easy 1½m: acts on all-weather, firm and
good to soft going: sometimes visored in 2002: sometimes slowly away: has raced freely:
carries head high. *Miss B. Sanders*

KATY JEM   2 b.f. (Mar 26) Night Shift (USA) – Top Jem 85 (Damister (USA) 123)   **–**
[2004 7d Oct 30] big, strong filly: second foal: half-sister to 4-y-o Polar Jem: dam, 9f/
1¼m winner, half-sister to smart performer up to 1½m Polar Red: 33/1, behind in maiden
at Newmarket, slowly away and hanging left. *D. M. Simcock*

KATY O'HARA   5 b.m. Komaite (USA) – Amy Leigh (IRE) 78 (Imperial Frontier   **51**
(USA) 112) [2004 59d: f6s f6g² f6s⁶ 7m f7g⁵ Dec 12] good-bodied mare: modest handicapper: stays 6f: acts on all-weather and good to firm going: tried visored: sometimes
slowly away. *Miss S. E. Hall*

KATZ PYJAMAS (IRE)   3 b.f. Fasliyev (USA) 120 – Allepolina (USA) (Trempo-   **– §**
lino (USA) 135) [2004 51§: 6.1d 8f Sep 6] leggy, workmanlike filly: inconsistent maiden
at 2 yrs: soundly beaten in 2004: blinkered (good effort) once in 2003. *G. F. H. Charles-
Jones*

KAURI FOREST (USA)   3 ch.g. Woodman (USA) 126 – Kentucky Fall (FR) 76   **82**
(Lead On Time (USA) 123) [2004 7g³ 8g² 7g² p8m³ p7g⁴ Oct 25] €30,000Y: lengthy
gelding: third foal: dam, 6f winner, half-sister to 8-y-o Tillerman: fairly useful maiden:
well below form at Lingfield last 2 outings: has form at 1m, worth a try at 6f: carries head
high/finds little: sold 15,000 gns. *J. R. Fanshawe*

KAVI (IRE)   4 ch.g. Perugino (USA) 84 – Premier Leap (IRE) 56 (Salmon Leap (USA)   **62**
131) [2004 61: p10g p10g p12g Feb 24] small, strong gelding: modest performer: stays
easy 1¼m: acts on all-weather, good to firm and good to soft going: blinkered (ran creditably) penultimate start. *Simon Earle*

KAYF ARAMIS   2 b.c. (Apr 27) Kayf Tara 130 – Ara (Birthright) [2004 7.1m Jun 12]   **–**
50/1, tailed off in maiden at Sandown, very slowly away. *I. A. Wood*

KAYMICH PERFECTO   4 b.g. Sheikh Albadou 128 – Manhattan Diamond 54   **61**
(Primo Dominie 121) [2004 a10g a8g* a8g³ a9g² a8g² a8g 8.2g 10.1m p7.1g⁶ p8.6g⁵
f7g f8g² Dec 16] ex-Spanish gelding: won handicap at Mijas in March: modest form
in Britain: stays 9f: acts on all-weather and sand: blinkered/in cheekpieces last 4 starts.
R. M. Whitaker

totejackpot On Saturday Stakes (Handicap), Ascot—
with the construction of the new track under way in the background,
Kehaar wins from Kool (spots on cap), Mine (chevrons), Traytonic (No.9) and Naahy (rail)

KAY TWO (IRE) 2 ch.c. (Feb 20) Monashee Mountain (USA) 115 – Tricky 66 (Song **103**
132) [2004 5v² 5m² 6f⁴ 5m* 6.3f⁵ 5s* 5v* 5s³ 6s Oct 29] €9,000F: neat colt: half-brother
to 3 winners, including 1m winner Colonel North (by Distinctly North) and 5f (including
at 2 yrs) winner Magic Orb (by Primo Dominie), both fairly useful: dam, third at 5f at 2
yrs, sister to smart sprinter Jester: useful performer: won maiden in July, minor event in
August and listed race (beat Tournedos by 2 lengths) in October, all at Tipperary: good 2
lengths third to Castelletto in Cornwallis Stakes at Newmarket: will prove best at 5f/easy
6f: probably acts on any turf going: usually races up with pace. *Ms F. M. Crowley, Ireland*

KEDROSS (IRE) 3 ch.f. King of Kings (IRE) 125 – Nom de Plume (USA) 116 (Nod- **–**
ouble (USA)) [2004 63: f7g f6g f8g 11.8m⁵ f7m 7m Jun 8] close-coupled filly: little form
at 3 yrs, leaving R. Elliott after reappearance: tried blinkered. *J. Jay*

KEELUNG (USA) 3 b.g. Lear Fan (USA) 130 – Miss Universal (IRE) 107 (Lycius **94**
(USA) 124) [2004 66p: p8g⁴ p8g² 10.3g² 10.1v* 9.9s³ 10d² 12m 11.9g 10d 10g Oct 22]
lengthy, good-topped gelding: fairly useful performer: landed odds (by 16 lengths) in
maiden at Newcastle in April: below form last 4 starts: likely to stay 1½m: acts on heavy
ground: has been early to post: tends to hang/race freely, and proved virtually unrideable
seventh start: usually races prominently. *M. A. Jarvis*

KEEPASHARPLOOKOUT (IRE) 2 b.g. (Mar 23) Rossini (USA) 118 – Zoyce **51**
(Zilzal (USA) 137) [2004 5s⁴ 5g⁴ 6s 5d⁴ Jun 9] leggy gelding: modest maiden: should
stay at least 6f: acts on soft going: gelded after final start. *Mrs L. Stubbs*

KEEP BACCKINHIT (IRE) 2 b.f. (Mar 30) Raise A Grand (IRE) 114 – Taispeain **80**
(IRE) 86 (Petorius 117) [2004 6m³ 5.7g 6f³ 7m* 7.1d⁵ 6.5m 6m⁴ 7d⁶ Oct 10] 10,000
2-y-o: third foal: half-sister to fairly useful Irish 2003 2-y-o 5f winner Chained Emotion
(by Danetime): dam Irish 2-y-o 6f winner who stayed 7f: fairly useful performer: won
nursery at Goodwood in July: creditable efforts in similar events last 2 starts: stays 7f:
acts on good to firm and good to soft going. *G. L. Moore*

KEEPERS KNIGHT (IRE) 3 b.c. Sri Pekan (USA) 117 – Keepers Dawn (IRE) 103 **65**
(Alzao (USA) 117) [2004 62: p10g* p10g³ p10g⁵ f12g 10.9d 8.3f 9.7m³ 9.7g⁵ 11d⁴ 10.3s⁵ **a70**
10v f13.9g f11g⁴ Dec 11] rangy colt: fair handicapper: won at Lingfield in January: stays
11f: acts on all-weather, good to firm and good to soft going: tried blinkered/tongue tied:
no easy ride. *P. F. I. Cole*

KEEPER'S LODGE (IRE) 3 ch.f. Grand Lodge (USA) 125 – Gembira (USA) (Aly- **77**
sheba (USA)) [2004 73: 7d⁴ 8m 8m 8.1g* 6s 8g³ 10.3s⁵ 9.9s² 10.5g Sep 4] stocky filly:
fair handicapper: won at Haydock in July: stays 1¼m: acts on soft ground, probably not
on good to firm. *B. A. McMahon*

KEEP ME WARM 2 ch.g. (Mar 19) Atraf 116 – Little Greenbird 39 (Ardkinglass **73**
114) [2004 5.1s⁴ p6d² f7g³ p7.1g⁴ p7.1g⁶ Dec 31] 3,000F: first foal: dam maiden: fair
maiden: stays 7f: acts on all-weather. *W. G. M. Turner*

KEEP ON MOVIN' (IRE) 3 b.f. Danehill Dancer (IRE) 117 – Tormented (USA) **79**
(Alleged (USA) 138) [2004 73: 10d⁵ 12.1d 11.8m² 12g 12g⁴ 14.4m Sep 4] tall, rather
leggy filly: fair handicapper: ran as if amiss final outing: effective at 1¼m/1½m: acts on
polytrack, good to firm and good to soft going. *T. G. Mills*

KEEP THE PEACE (IRE) 6 br.g. Petardia 113 – Eiras Mood 57 (Jalmood (USA) **–**
126) [2004 –: 12.1m Jul 23] of little account nowadays. *K. G. Wingrove*

KEHAAR 3 ch.c. Cadeaux Genereux 131 – Lighthouse 92 (Warning 136) [2004 7m* **108 p**
8g* 7m 7m* Sep 25] 170,000Y: big, good-topped colt: first foal: dam, won at 1m from 3
starts, half-sister to Middle Park winner First Trump: useful form: won maiden at
Newbury in June and handicaps at Newmarket (beat Mister Monet short head) in July and
Ascot (beat Kool by 1¾ lengths in totejackpot On Saturday Stakes) in September: well
below form in minor event at Goodwood on other start: likely to prove best up to 1m: has
worn crossed noseband: sold 525,000 gns, joined Godolphin: lightly raced, and capable
of better still. *M. A. Magnusson*

KELBROOK 5 b.g. Unfuwain (USA) 131 – Pidona (Baillamont (USA) 124) [2004 **65 ?**
45: 8d⁵ 11.9m 10g⁴ Jun 17] lengthy, sparely-made gelding: fair maiden: seemingly easily
best effort at 1m on good to soft ground. *A. Bailey*

KELLY NICOLE (IRE) 2 b.f. (Mar 17) Rainbow Quest (USA) 134 – Banquise (IRE) **–**
(Last Tycoon 131) [2004 p9.5g Dec 20] €32,000Y: fourth foal: half-sister to fairly useful
Irish winner around 9f Cold Cold Woman (by Machiavellian): dam, French 2m winner,
half-sister to very smart French 1½m performer Modhish and smart French performer up
to 10.5f Truly Special: 33/1, well held in maiden at Wolverhampton. *K. A. Ryan*

KELSEAS KOLBY (IRE)   4 b.g. Perugino (USA) 84 – Notre Dame (IRE) (Classic   **66**
Music (USA)) [2004 66: 7d 7d 7m* 8m⁴ 8f³ 8d⁴ 7.9m⁴ 7m² 8m² p8g⁵ 8m³ 9.9g Sep
29] leggy gelding: fair performer: won seller at Leicester (left J. Glover) in May: left
P. Blockley after eighth start: stays 1m: acts on polytrack, soft and firm ground: tried
blinkered/in cheekpieces, usually visored: tends to hang/sometimes looks none too keen.
P. Butler

KELTIC FLUTE   5 b.g. Piccolo 121 – Nanny Doon (Dominion 123) [2004 f8.5g f7g⁴   **32**
f8.5g f7s⁶ p7g f6g⁶ f7g Apr 16] poor maiden: effective at 7f/1m: acts on all-weather and
good to firm ground: has been blinkered, visored nowadays. *Mrs Lucinda Featherstone*

KELTIC RAINBOW (IRE)   3 b.f. Spectrum (IRE) 126 – Secrets of Honour (Belmez   **–**
(USA) 131) [2004 58: f9.4s⁴ 10s⁶ f8.5g 11.6f 12.1d⁴ 8s⁵ 12.1g 10g p10g Dec 20] leggy
filly: little form in 2004: tried visored/in cheekpieces: hung markedly left on reappearance. *D. Haydn Jones*

KELTOS (FR)   6 gr.h. Kendor (FR) 122 – Loxandra 76 (Last Tycoon 131) [2004 7d*   **118**
8m² 8d² 8v² 7d³ 8m⁵ 7s² 8s³ 8s* Nov 23] close-coupled, useful-looking horse: put up
top-class performance when winning Lockinge Stakes at Newbury in 2002: missed rest
of that year and reportedly had fertility problems at stud in 2003: just smart form on
return: won minor event at Maisons-Laffitte in April and listed race at Saint-Cloud (beat
Salon Turtle ¾ length) in November: placed most starts in between, including when
second in Prix Quincey at Deauville (beaten short neck by Autumn Glory) on fourth
outing and Challenge Stakes at Newmarket (went down by a length to Firebreak) on
seventh: effective at 7f/1m: unraced on firm going, acts on any other turf: usually held up.
C. Laffon-Parias, France

KELUCIA (IRE)   3 ch.f. Grand Lodge (USA) 125 – Karachi (SPA) (Zino 127) [2004   **92**
101: 8g⁵ 8m 8m⁵ 8m⁶ 8.1d⁶ 10m⁶ 8m⁶ 8g 7.9g Oct 8] lengthy filly: fairly useful
performer: mostly highly tried in 2004, probably best effort when sixth to Attraction in
Coronation Stakes at Royal Ascot on fourth outing: should stay 1¼m: acts on firm going:
edgy sort, sometimes early to post/slowly away/flashes tail. *J. S. Goldie*

KEMPSEY   2 ch.c. (Apr 4) Wolfhound (USA) 126 – Mockingbird 64 (Sharpo 132)   **66**
[2004 5m 5m⁶ p5g⁴ 5m⁴ 5s⁴ 6m⁶ 5m 6d p8g⁶ p6g² p5.1g² p6g³ Dec 29] 3,000F, 5,500Y:
good-bodied colt: fifth foal: half-brother to 5-y-o Ridicule: dam 2-y-o 6f winner: fair
maiden: likely to prove best at 5f/6f: acts on polytrack, soft and good to firm ground:
wore cheekpieces fifth to seventh appearances, ran creditably in visor last 3. *J. J. Bridger*

KENMORE   2 b.c. (Mar 12) Compton Place 125 – Watheeqah (USA) 60 (Topsider   **95 p**
(USA)) [2004 6m⁴ 6d² Oct 14] 16,000F, 38,000Y: strong, good sort: has a quick action:
fifth foal: half-brother to 3-y-o Nounou: dam 5f winner: much better effort in maidens at
Newmarket when 1¼ lengths second to Tomoohat, travelling strongly close up long way:
not sure to stay much beyond 6f: open to progress, and sure to win a race or 2. *B. W. Hills*

KENNINGTON   4 ch.g. Compton Place 125 – Mim 39 (Midyan (USA) 124) [2004   **66**
f7g* f7g f6s⁴ f7g 6d³ f6g⁴ f6g 7m 6f² f6g 6f 5d⁴ 5m f5g² 5.2d⁴ 6g⁵ f5m² f6g² p5.1g²
f6g p5.1g² Dec 10] small, sturdy gelding: fair performer: missed 2003: won maiden at
Southwell in January: effective at 5f to easy 7f: acts on all-weather, firm and good to soft
ground: usually visored/blinkered: races prominently: has looked tricky ride: consistent.
Mrs C. A. Dunnett

KENNY THE TRUTH (IRE)   5 b.g. Robellino (USA) 127 – Just Blink (IRE) (Fairy   **55**
King (USA)) [2004 –, a53: f8g³ f8g² f8g³ f8g³ f8.5s⁴ f9.4s⁵ f8s* f8g⁴ 8.1d³ f8g³ 8.2m
f12d f8g⁶ f8m⁵ 10.5s p9.5g Dec 22] robust gelding: modest performer: won banded race
at Southwell in March: left Mrs J. Candlish before final start: should be suited by 9f+:
acts on fibresand and good to soft going: usually tongue tied. *A. Dickman*

KEN'S DREAM   5 b.g. Bin Ajwaad (IRE) 119 – Shoag (USA) (Affirmed (USA))   **87 +**
[2004 10g 10m³ 10m⁴ 10m* 11m⁴ 10f⁶ Jul 31] workmanlike gelding: fairly useful
handicapper: missed 2003: won at Newmarket in June: probably best around 1¼m: acts
on firm and soft ground: tends to race freely (has worn crossed noseband): consistent.
Ms A. E. Embiricos

KENSINGTON (IRE)   3 b.g. Cape Cross (IRE) 129 – March Star (IRE) 109 (Mac's   **67**
Imp (USA) 116) [2004 75: 7s⁶ 6.1s³ 6m² 6.1m⁶ 6g* p6m⁶ p6d⁵ f6g Nov 23] leggy
gelding: fair performer: trained by D. Weld in Ireland at 2 yrs: won maiden at Ripon in
September: stays 6f: acts on polytrack, soft and good to firm ground: tried blinkered/in
cheekpieces. *R. Guest*

KENTMERE (IRE)   3 b.g. Efisio 120 – Addaya (IRE) (Persian Bold 123) [2004 72:   **77**
8m⁶ p10d* Jun 26] good-topped gelding: fair performer: blinkered, won maiden at Ling-

field in June: stays 1¼m: acts on polytrack, firm and good to soft going: tongue tied (folded tamely) on reappearance: sold 34,000 gns, joined P. Webber. *W. J. Haggas*

KENTUCKY BANKES 2 b.c. (Apr 25) Bluegrass Prince (IRE) 110 – Countess Bankes 50 (Son Pardo 107) [2004 f5g 6.1g⁶ 6m Jul 13] seems of little account. *W. G. M. Turner* —

KENTUCKY BLUE (IRE) 4 b.g. Revoque (IRE) 122 – Delta Town (USA) (Sanglamore (USA) 126) [2004 93: 10.5d³ 11.9s 10g Aug 31] lengthy, good-topped gelding: fairly useful handicapper: form in 2004 only when third at Haydock on reappearance: stays 1½m: acts on soft and good to firm going, ran poorly on firm: often races prominently. *T. D. Easterby* **89**

KENTUCKY BULLET (USA) 8 b.g. Housebuster (USA) – Exactly So (Caro 133) [2004 38§, a56§: f11g³ f12f f12s⁶ f12g³ f12g⁶ f12d f12m⁵ f12m⁵ f12d³ Dec 21] leggy, angular gelding: modest performer on all-weather, poor on turf: barely stays 14.8f: acts on fibresand, good to firm and good to soft ground: tried blinkered/in cheekpieces/tongue tied: sometimes hangs/flashes tail: unreliable. *A. G. Newcombe* **?** **a55 §**

KENTUCKY EXPRESS 3 b.c. Air Express (IRE) 125 – Hotel California (IRE) 58 (Last Tycoon 131) [2004 7m 6g² 6m³ Jun 16] 27,000Y: sturdy colt: seventh foal: half-brother to fairly useful 5.7f (at 2 yrs) and 7f winner Goldie (by Celtic Swing) and 9f to 13.5f winner in Italy by First Trump: dam 2-y-o 7.5f winner: clearly best effort in maidens when 1¼ lengths second to Hawaajes at Haydock: should stay 7f. *T. D. Easterby* **72**

KENTUCKY KING (USA) 4 b.g. Tale of The Cat (USA) 113 – Anna's Honor (USA) (Alleged (USA) 138) [2004 86: f6g⁶ f8.5s⁶ p10g p8g* p8g 8.3d³ 10g 8.1s 8m 10.1g³ p7d⁵ 8.3g² 11.7m 8.2g⁴ 10g Aug 23] strong, lengthy gelding: fairly useful performer: dead-heated with African Sahara in minor event at Lingfield in March: stays 1¼m: acts on all-weather and good to soft ground: refused to race on 2 of last 3 outings: one to treat with caution. *P. W. Hiatt* **87 §**

KENWYN 2 b.g. (Apr 27) Efisio 120 – Vilany 87 (Never So Bold 135) [2004 5g 6g Jul 12] good-topped gelding: little sign of ability in maidens. *M. Blanshard* —

KEON (IRE) 2 b.c. (May 20) Rossini (USA) 118 – Lonely Brook (USA) (El Gran Senor (USA) 136) [2004 7s p7.1g⁴ Dec 1] €21,000Y: rather leggy colt: third foal: half-brother to Irish 7f winner Stovash (by Thatching) and winner in Italy by Brief Truce: dam French 7f winner: fair form in maidens at Doncaster and Wolverhampton (not at all knocked about): should do better. *R. Hollinshead* **66 p**

KERASHAN (IRE) 2 b.c. (May 1) Sinndar (IRE) 134 – Kerataka (IRE) 103 (Doyoun 124) [2004 7m⁸ 8g² 8s Oct 27] smallish, attractive colt: first foal: dam, Irish 1m winner, out of smart 7f performer Kerita: fair form at Kempton in minor event and maiden (neck second to Australian) first 2 starts: not knocked about final one: should be suited by 1¼m/1½m. *Sir Michael Stoute* **79**

KERESFORTH 2 b.g. (Feb 19) Mind Games 121 – Bullion 85 (Sabrehill (USA) 120) [2004 f5d 5d 5g² 5m* 5m 5m² 6m Jul 26] rather leggy gelding: modest performer: trained by T. Easterby first 3 starts: won seller at Folkestone in June: likely to prove best at 5f: acts on good to firm going: usually blinkered. *I. A. Wood* **61**

KERGOLAY (IRE) 2 b.c. (Mar 2) King's Theatre (IRE) 128 – Trim Star (Terimon 124) [2004 p8.6g⁶ p8g Oct 25] only a little sign of ability in maidens at Wolverhampton and Lingfield: sold 12,000 gns. *W. R. Muir* —

KERNEL DOWERY (IRE) 4 b.g. Sri Pekan (USA) 117 – Lady Dowery (USA) (Manila (USA)) [2004 72: 10.2g 10d 10m² 10.1f* 10f* 10.1m 10f 10s⁴ 10m⁵ 9.9g p12.2g⁴ p12g p12.2g Nov 19] just modest performer in 2004: won handicap at Yarmouth and minor event at Brighton in June: trained by P. Harris until after twelfth start: stays easy 1½m: acts on polytrack, firm and good to soft going: sometimes wears cheekpieces: sometimes hangs left/finds little: usually races prominently: none too consistent. *W. R. Swinburn* **64**

KERNY (IRE) 2 b.c. (Mar 24) Rossini (USA) 118 – Queen of Sweden (IRE) (Solid Illusion (USA) 117) [2004 f5g 5m⁶ 5.1g 5g Sep 7] smallish, well-made colt: signs of only a little ability in maidens/nursery. *J. J. Quinn* —

KERRISTINA 3 b.f. So Factual (USA) 120 – Arch Angel (IRE) 55 (Archway (IRE) 115) [2004 8.1s 8f 8m p12d 10m 10.2m Aug 5] second foal: dam 2-y-o 6f/7f seller winner: little form: tried visored. *D. J. S. ffrench Davis* **?**

KERRY'S BLADE (IRE) 2 ch.g. (Apr 27) Daggers Drawn (USA) 114 – Treasure (IRE) 72 (Treasure Kay 114) [2004 6g 6g⁵ 6d⁶ 8g² 8g⁶ p8.6g p7.1g f8g Dec 11] €9,000Y, **68** **a54**

6,500 2-y-o: tall, leggy gelding: fifth foal: dam, third at 1¼m in Ireland, sister to Italian 1000 Guineas winner Treasure Hope: fair maiden on turf, modest on all-weather: second in nursery at Musselburgh: stays 8.6f: acts on polytrack, best turf effort on good going: wandered/found little fifth start, looked ungenuine in blinkers final one. *P. C. Haslam*

KESHYA 3 b.f. Mtoto 134 – Liberatrice (FR) (Assert 134) [2004 66: 8g³ 10.2g⁴ f8.5m² **69** 8.1g⁴ Jul 9] leggy filly: fair maiden handicapper: stays 1¼m: acts on fibresand and good to soft going: carried head high/edged left final 2-y-o start. *D. J. Coakley*

KEW GREEN (USA) 6 b. or br.g. Brocco (USA) 124 – Jump With Joy (USA) (Link- **90 +** age (USA)) [2004 p9.5g* Dec 4] rangy gelding: fairly useful handicapper: off 26 months, won at Wolverhampton in December: stays 10.5f: acts on polytrack, firm and soft ground: tried tongue tied: wandered penultimate 4-y-o outing: sometimes races freely. *P. R. Webber*

KEW THE MUSIC 4 b.g. Botanic (USA) – Harmonia (Glint of Gold 128) [2004 74: **74** 6s 6d 7g 7m 8.1g 6v 6.1g 6g* 5f 6g p6g p5.1g* p7.1g* p7g³ Nov 27] lengthy gelding: fair performer: won handicap at Yarmouth in September and 2 minor events at Wolverhampton in November: stays 7f: acts on polytrack and good to firm ground (well beaten on heavy): effective visored or not: often gets behind early. *M. R. Channon*

KEYAKI (IRE) 3 b.f. Shinko Forest (IRE) – Woodie Dancer (USA) (Green Dancer **83** (USA) 132) [2004 7g⁶ 7s⁶ 7f* 7m* 8g⁴ 7s⁴ 7d 7s Oct 23] IR 5,800F, €14,000Y: leggy, rather unfurnished filly: third foal: dam, French maiden, out of smart performer up to 1¼m in Ireland/USA Happy Bride: fairly useful performer: won maiden at Yarmouth and handicap at Lingfield in June: should stay 1m: acts on firm ground, probably on soft. *C. F. Wall*

KEYALZAO (IRE) 2 b.f. (Apr 3) Alzao (USA) 117 – Key Partner (Law Society **32** (USA) 130) [2004 6s 6m 7g 7m Oct 2] €7,500Y, 12,500 2-y-o: small filly: half-sister to several winners, including useful Irish 7f winner Blast of Storm (by Perugino): dam Irish 6f (at 2 yrs) to 12.5f winner, also won over hurdles: poor maiden. *A. Crook*

KEY FACTOR 3 b.f. Defacto (USA) – Onemoretime (Timeless Times (USA) 99) **49 ?** [2004 6m⁴ 7.5d 7f f6s f7g Nov 8] sturdy filly: second foal: dam little form: no form after debut: unsteerable third outing. *M. W. Easterby*

KEY IN 3 ch.f. Unfuwain (USA) 131 – Fleet Key (Afleet (CAN)) [2004 8g 10.2g⁶ **a60** p13g³ 13.8v⁶ Oct 16] 30,000Y: lengthy filly: second foal: dam Italian 7f (including at 2 yrs) to 9f winner: modest maiden: form only on polytrack: sold 6,000 gns. *B. W. Hills*

KEYNES (JPN) 2 ch.c. (Apr 8) Gold Fever (USA) 119 – Eternal Reve (USA) 116 **74** (Diesis 133) [2004 f7g³ p7g 7.6m² a8.3g⁴ a8.3g Dec 12] half-brother to several winners, including 3-y-o Romaric and useful 6f (at 2 yrs) and 1m winner (in UAE) Infinite Spirit (by Maria's Mon): dam, French 6f (at 2 yrs) to 1m winner, half-sister to US Grade 1 9f winner Eternity Star: fair maiden: best effort when visored third start (sold from J. Gosden 16,000 gns after): stays 7.6f: tended to hang second outing. *E. J. Creighton, Spain*

KEY OF GOLD (IRE) 3 b.g. Key of Luck (USA) 126 – Damaslin (Camden Town **63** 125) [2004 78: f7g 6g 6g⁴ 7g 6g Aug 28] close-coupled gelding: just fair performer in 2004: stays 1m: acts on fibresand. *D. Carroll*

KEY OF SOLOMON (IRE) 2 ch.c. (Jan 25) Machiavellian (USA) 123 – Minerva **79 p** (IRE) (Caerleon (USA) 132) [2004 8g⁶ 8s³ 8d² Nov 3] first foal: dam, unraced, closely related to US Grade 2 11f winner Sword Dancer, out of half-sister to smart Irish miler Fatherland: fair form in maidens: staying-on second at Musselburgh (tongue tied previously): will be well suited by 1¼m/1½m: should do better. *H. Morrison*

Jersey Stakes, Royal Ascot—Kheleyf makes his first appearance in the Godolphin colours a winning one; Fokine, Cartography (far side) and Bahiano make up the frame

KEY PARTNERS (IRE)　3 b.g. Key of Luck (USA) 126 – Teacher Preacher (IRE) 37　**83**
(Taufan (USA) 119) [2004 74p: 7.1d* 10m 7s² 7m 8.1g p9.5g Dec 11] quite good-topped
gelding: fairly useful performer: won maiden at Warwick in April: stays 7f: very best
form on ground softer than good (shaped quite well after lay-off on polytrack final start).
P. A. Blockley

KEY SECRET　2 ch.f. (Mar 3) Whittingham (IRE) 104 – Foxkey 61 (Foxhound (USA)　**95**
103) [2004 f5m* 5m* 5g* 5m⁴ 5g⁴ 5g* 5.5m⁶ 5d 5s³ Oct 15] smallish, workmanlike filly:
first foal: dam 2-y-o 5f seller winner: useful performer: won claimers at Wolverhampton
and Leicester (for M. Usher) in May and nurseries at York in July and Windsor (by 5
lengths) in August: below best when 8 lengths third to Centifolia in listed race at
Maisons-Laffitte: will probably stay 6f: acts on fibresand and good to firm going:
sometimes wanders. *M. L. W. Bell*

KHABFAIR　3 b.c. Intikhab (USA) 135 – Ruby Affair (IRE) 68 (Night Shift (USA))　**110**
[2004 94: 6m⁴ 6m* 6g³ 6g⁶ 6g 6.5f* p7g² Oct 28] good-bodied colt: smart handicapper: won at Ascot in July and September (beat Compton's Eleven by a head): good
head second to Goodenough Mover at Lingfield final start: stays 7f: raced only on polytrack and good ground or firmer (acts on firm): sometimes carries head awkwardly.
Mrs A. J. Perrett

KHAFAYIF (USA)　3 b.f. Swain (IRE) 134 – Copper Play (USA) (Fast Play (USA))　**62 ?**
[2004 7g 7.5m³ 7d 7g⁵ Aug 14] $75,000Y, €240,000Y: workmanlike filly: fourth foal:
half-sister to winners in USA by Carson City and Broad Brush: dam, minor stakes-placed
winner in USA, half-sister to smart sprinter Tipsy Creek: seemingly best effort in maidens
when third at Beverley: sold 6,000 gns in December. *B. Hanbury*

KHALIDIA (USA)　3 b.g. Boundary (USA) 117 – Maniches Slew (USA) (Slew O'　**82**
Gold (USA)) [2004 59p: 6m* 6m² p6g Dec 13] strong, good-bodied gelding: has scope:
won maiden at Doncaster in June: good second to Mahmoom in handicap at Newmarket
later in month: not discredited after lay-off final start: likely to prove best at 5f/6f: acts on
good to firm going. *M. A. Magnusson*

KHANJAR (USA)　4 ch.g. Kris S (USA) – Alyssum (USA) (Storm Cat (USA)) [2004　**84**
76: 9g² 8g⁴ 10m f7f* 8g² 7.2s 8.9g² p8g² p9.5g⁴ p8.6g² f8g⁵ Dec 28] sturdy, attractive
gelding: fairly useful performer: left D. Loder prior to winning minor event at Southwell in August: stays 9f: acts on all-weather, dirt and firm going, well below form on
soft: visored first 3 starts: sometimes slowly away/found little for previous stable, but is
consistent. *K. R. Burke*

KHARISH (IRE)　2 b.c. (Mar 20) Desert Prince (IRE) 130 – Moy Water (IRE) 87　**88**
(Tirol 127) [2004 7g⁴ 7g³ 8.1d² 8g* 8m⁴ Sep 9] €300,000Y: lengthy, quite good-topped
colt: fifth foal: half-brother to 3 winners, including 1999 German 2-y-o 5f/6f winner
Mona Em (by Catrail) and Irish 7f winner (stayed 1¼m) Maumee (by Indian Ridge), both
useful: dam Irish 1m (at 2 yrs) and 9f winner: fairly useful performer: won maiden at
Kempton in September: good fourth to Singhalese in nursery at Doncaster final start:
stays 1m: acts on good to firm going. *J. Noseda*

KHELEYF (USA)　3 br.c. Green Desert (USA) 127 – Society Lady (USA) 75 (Mr Pros-　**116**
pector (USA)) [2004 114: 7f* 6g 7g³ 8d⁶ 7g⁵ Sep 30] big, good-topped colt: impressed in
appearance: smart performer: trained by D. Loder at 2 yrs: won Jersey Stakes at Royal
Ascot by 1¾ lengths from Fokine, quickening impressively: respectable 1½ lengths third
to Byron in Betfair Cup (Lennox) at Goodwood, best effort after (met plenty of trouble in
July Cup at Newmarket on second outing): best at 6f/7f: acted on firm going: had worn
crossed noseband/had 2 handlers: waited with: to stand at Kildangan Stud, Co Kildare,
Ireland, fee €7,000. *Saeed bin Suroor*

KHUZDAR (IRE)　5 ch.g. Definite Article 121 – Mariyda (IRE) (Vayrann 133) [2004　**?**
72d: f16g p16g³ f12g² f12s p13g⁵ 12f* 12g* 14g² 10m² 12m³ Aug 30] modest performer:　**a48 §**
left A. Bailey, won handicaps at Les Landes in Jersey in April/May: stays easy 2m: acts
on all-weather, firm and good to soft going: found little in cheekpieces fourth/fifth
starts: has started slowly/carried head awkwardly: ungenuine. *Mrs A. Malzard, Jersey*

KIAMA　2 b.f. (Feb 24) Dansili 127 – Catriona 75 (Bustino 136) [2004 8.2m 8v⁶ Oct　**69 p**
23] 10,000F: second foal: dam, 7f winner, out of sister to top Irish 1982 2-y-o Danzatore:
better effort in maidens when sixth to Descartes at Newbury, helping set pace: not sure to
stay much beyond 1m: likely to progress. *H. Morrison*

KIBRYAA (USA)　3 ch.c. Silver Hawk (USA) 123 – Fleur de Nuit (USA) (Woodman　**86**
(USA) 126) [2004 79: 8m⁶ 8s² 7.5g² 8.1m⁴ 8.1g⁵ 8g a8f a7.5f Dec 30] good-topped colt:
fairly useful performer: creditable efforts second to fifth starts, though persistently short

of room last 2 occasions: left M. Jarvis after sixth outing: stays 1m: acts on soft and good to firm going, well held on dirt: tried in cheekpieces: sometimes carries head awkwardly. *D. J. Selvaratnam, UAE*

KID'Z'PLAY (IRE)   8 b.g. Rudimentary (USA) 118 – Saka Saka (Camden Town 125) [2004 73: 12g 12.1g³ 10.1s⁴ 11.1g² 10g* 10.1s⁵ 10g³ 12.1s⁴ 13d⁵ 10.9s⁶ 16d Nov 3] workmanlike gelding: fair handicapper: won at Ayr in June: stays 13f: acts on any going: wore cheekpieces (below form) penultimate outing: sometimes early to post: usually makes running. *J. S. Goldie*   **73**

KIEV (IRE)   4 b.g. Bahhare (USA) 122 – Badrah (USA) 69 (Private Account (USA)) [2004 f12g Nov 22] modest form in bumpers: tailed off on Flat debut. *D. G. Bridgwater*   **–**

KIKIS GIRLS (IRE)   3 b.f. Spectrum (IRE) 126 – Jane Heller (USA) (Halo (USA)) [2004 10g 8.2d Sep 17] IR 3,200F, 2,500Y: smallish, plain filly: fifth foal: half-sister to 3 winners, including French 1m and (at 2 yrs) 1¼m winner Saint Andrew (by St Jovite): dam unraced out of very smart French performer up to 1½m Treizieme: tailed off in maidens at Nottingham, leaving Miss M. Rowland after debut. *M. Wigham*   **–**

KILCULLEN LASS (IRE)   3 ch.f. Fayruz 116 – Foretell (Tirol 127) [2004 –: p8g 8g 9g May 12] strong, workmanlike filly: little form: left P. D. Evans after second start. *W. A. Murphy, Ireland*   **–**

KILDARE CHILLER (IRE)   10 b.g. Shahrastani (USA) 135 – Ballycuirke (Taufan (USA) 119) [2004 12d⁶ Apr 5] one-time fair handicapper in Ireland: well held only outing on Flat since 2001. *P. R. Hedger*   **–**

KILINDINI   3 gr.g. Silver Patriarch (IRE) 125 – Newlands Corner 65 (Forzando 122) [2004 9.7s⁶ 9.7m 10f⁵ 10d⁴ 13.1f Sep 6] first foal: dam 6f winner: fair maiden: should stay 1½m: acts on firm and good to soft going: reared and unseated rider at start second outing. *Miss E. C. Lavelle*   **70**

KILKENNY KITTEN (IRE)   2 b.f. (Feb 15) Blue Ocean (USA) 87 – El Tina (Unfuwain (USA) 131) [2004 5s⁶ f5g 5m May 28] €7,000Y: second foal: half-sister to winner in Italy by Tagula: dam 2-y-o 7f winner in Italy: tongue tied, poor form in maidens: should have stayed 6f: dead. *N. Tinkler*   **44**

KILLALA (IRE)   4 b.g. Among Men (USA) 124 – Hat And Gloves (Wolver Hollow 126) [2004 72: 7.1m³ 7.1m⁵ 7.1m⁵ 7g² 8f² 7m⁴ 10.3g p8.6g p7.1g Dec 22] fair performer: on downgrade in 2004, leaving I. Semple after fifth start: stays easy 1m: acts on firm and good to soft going. *R. N. Bevis*   **70 d**

KILLENA BOY (IRE)   2 b.g. (Mar 17) Imperial Ballet (IRE) 110 – Habaza (IRE) 68 (Shernazar 131) [2004 p6d 6m 7.5m⁴ 6d Oct 14] €6,500F, 9,500Y: good-bodied gelding: second foal: dam ran 3 times in Ireland: modest maiden: fourth at Beverley, only form: stays 7.5f. *W. Jarvis*   **63**

KILLERBY NICKO   3 ch.g. Pivotal 124 – Bit of A Tart (Distant Relative 128) [2004 62: f6g⁶ 5g 5.9f⁶ 6m f8g⁵ 6s 7.1m³ 7.5g 6d⁵ Jul 17] heavy-topped gelding: poor maiden: stays 1m: acts on fibresand, firm and good to soft going: blinkered last 4 starts: upset in stall and unseated rider after start sixth outing. *T. D. Easterby*   **48**

KILLING JOKE   4 b.c. Double Trigger (IRE) 123 – Fleeting Vision (IRE) 79 (Vision (USA)) [2004 80: 18v 16d Apr 24] lengthy colt: fairly useful handicapper at 3 yrs: well held in 2004: sold 4,000 gns. *J. G. Given*   **–**

KILLING ME SOFTLY   3 b.g. Kingsinger (IRE) 94 – Slims Lady 59 (Theatrical Charmer 114) [2004 55: f8.5g² f11g 10.9d⁴ 11.8g p8.6d p9.5g Nov 27] modest performer: stays 10.9f: acts on fibresand and good to soft ground: inconsistent. *J. Gallagher*   **56**

KILLINGTON (IRE)   2 ch.g. (Feb 5) Kris 135 – Miss Pickpocket (IRE) 64 (Petorius 117) [2004 5m² p6g 6m Oct 1] fourth foal: half-brother to 2000 2-y-o 5f winner Western Hero (by Lake Coniston), later winner in Denmark, and 5-y-o Zamyatina: dam 2-y-o 5f winner who stayed 7f: form in maidens only when second at Sandown: tongue tied next time: needs to settle to stay beyond 5f. *G. A. Butler*   **65**

KILLMOREY   3 ch.g. Nashwan (USA) 135 – Zarma (FR) (Machiavellian (USA) 123) [2004 8m 8m 8m² 10g⁶ 12.4s* Aug 30] big, workmanlike gelding: has an unimpressive, round action: second foal: dam, useful French 1¼m performer (later also winner in USA), out of very smart French 1½m performer Zartota: fair performer: won 4-runner handicap at Newcastle in August, despite still looking green: will stay 1¾m: acts on soft and good to firm ground: lightly raced, and capable of further improvement. *S. C. Williams*   **73 p**

KILLOCH PLACE (IRE) 3 b.g. Compton Place 125 – Hibernica (IRE) 69 (Law **37**
Society (USA) 130) [2004 –: 10d 10.9d 8s 7f 6m³ 7.1m⁴ 8.5g 7g Sep 14] tall gelding: poor
maiden: best efforts at 6f on going firmer than good: blinkered/visored after reappearance. *J. A. Glover*

KILMEENA LAD 8 b.g. Minshaanshu Amad (USA) 91§ – Kilmeena Glen (Beveled **73**
(USA)) [2004 76: p7g² p6g⁵ Jan 14] good-quartered gelding: fair handicapper, lightly
raced nowadays: effective at 6f to easy 1m: acts on polytrack and any turf going: tried
blinkered earlier in career: tends to edge left: has run well sweating: has reared leaving
stall. *J. C. Fox*

KILMEENA ROSE 4 ch.f. Compton Place 125 – Kilmeena Glen (Beveled (USA)) **–**
[2004 –: p8g Dec 4] unfurnished filly: no form. *J. C. Fox*

KILMEENA STAR 6 b.g. So Factual (USA) 120 – Kilmeena Glen (Beveled (USA)) **58**
[2004 43: p6g f7g p7g p7g⁴ p6g* p6g² 5v p6g p6g Dec 20] modest performer:
won handicap at Lingfield in March: stays 7f: acts on polytrack and firm going: tried in
cheekpieces, blinkered last 7 starts: none too consistent. *J. C. Fox*

KILMINCHY LADY (IRE) 3 b.f. Cape Cross (IRE) 129 – Lace Flower (Old Vic **–**
136) [2004 –: 10f⁵ 8f 8m Aug 4] little form. *W. R. Muir*

KILMOVEE 2 gr.f. (Mar 5) Inchinor 119 – Christmas Rose (Absalom 128) [2004 6g⁵ **59**
6f 5g⁵ 5m⁵ 5.9g 5f 6s Sep 24] 7,000Y, 25,000 2-y-o: second foal: half-sister to 3-y-o
Snow Wolf: dam ran twice: modest maiden: best form at 5f: acts on good to firm going.
N. Tinkler

KIMBERLEY HALL 2 ch.f. (Mar 4) Bachir (IRE) 118 – Sedna (FR) (Bering 136) **–**
[2004 5m 5d 6g 6.1m Sep 28] €5,000Y: first foal: dam French 10.5f winner: well held in
minor event/maidens. *J. A. Glover*

KIMOE WARRIOR 6 ch.g. Royal Abjar (USA) 121 – Thewaari (USA) 68 (Eskimo **–**
(USA)) [2004 –: f12m⁵ f8g Jun 25] tall, close-coupled gelding: maiden: no form in 3 runs
since 2001. *M. Mullineaux*

KINBRACE 3 b.f. Kirkwall 118 – Cache (Bustino 136) [2004 –p: 7.1f⁶ 8.3f⁵ 8g⁵ p8g **61**
Oct 25] unfurnished filly: modest maiden: bred to be suited by 1¼m/1½m, but needs to
learn to settle: probably quirky: sold 5,000 gns. *M. P. Tregoning*

KIND EMPEROR 7 br.g. Emperor Jones (USA) 119 – Kind Lady 56 (Kind of Hush **69**
118) [2004 69: 7m 10.1g⁴ 10.1d 11.5g² 10m⁶ 10.1d⁶ p12g Nov 13] leggy, sparely-made
gelding: fair performer: effective at 7f, seemingly at 11.5f: acts on firm and soft going (no
recent form on all-weather): visored twice, refusing to race first occasion: tends to hang
right: front runner. *P. L. Gilligan*

KIND (IRE) 3 b.f. Danehill (USA) 126 – Rainbow Lake 113 (Rainbow Quest (USA) **100 p**
134) [2004 77p: 7g³ 7g* 6g* 6d* 6g* 5d* Sep 19] strong, good-topped filly: useful performer: progressed markedly, winning maiden in May and 2 minor events in June, all at
Kempton, and handicap at Newmarket in July and listed race at Hamilton (beat Autumn
Pearl by ½ length) in September: free-going sort, and best at 5f/6f: yet to race on extremes
of going: races prominently: capable of better still. *R. Charlton*

KINDLELIGHT DEBUT 4 b.f. Groom Dancer (USA) 128 – Dancing Debut 83 **81 d**
(Polar Falcon (USA) 126) [2004 84: 7.6g 7m 7g³ 8f 8g 7m 7m p8g³ 7m p8g⁶ p7.1d p8g
p7m⁴ Dec 21] smallish filly: fairly useful handicapper: easily best effort in 2004 on third
start: stays easy 1m: acts on polytrack and firm ground, unraced on softer than good: tried
in cheekpieces. *D. K. Ivory*

KINDLELIGHT DREAM (IRE) 2 b.f. (Apr 9) Tagula (IRE) 116 – Dioscorea (IRE) **58 §**
(Pharly (FR) 130) [2004 5s p7g⁶ p7g p8g Nov 20] €6,000Y: third foal: dam unraced half-
sister to useful French 1m winner Dirca: form in maidens only when sixth at Lingfield:
refused to race last 2 outings, in blinkers final one. *D. K. Ivory*

KINDLING 2 br.f. (May 11) Dr Fong (USA) 128 – Isle of Flame (Shirley Heights 130) **77 p**
[2004 6f⁵ 7m⁴ 9d* Oct 17] small filly: half-sister to several winners, including smart
French 9f/1¼m winner Thattinger (by Salse), 4-y-o Dorothy's Friend and 3-y-o River of
Babylon: dam unraced: won maiden at Musselburgh comfortably by 3½ lengths from
Caribbean Dancer, making most: likely to stay at least 1½m: acts on good to firm and
good to soft going: should progress. *M. Johnston*

KINDNESS 4 ch.f. Indian Ridge 123 – Kissing Gate (USA) 62 (Easy Goer (USA)) **56 §**
[2004 60: p8g⁶ 8.1v 8f 8m² 9.7f² 10m 8.5f² 8m 9.7f 8g 8.3g⁶ p8.6d⁴ Oct 23] modest
maiden: should stay 1¼m: acts on polytrack, firm and soft going: often races up with
pace: unreliable. *A. D. W. Pinder*

KINFAYRE BOY 2 b.g. (Apr 18) Grey Eagle – Amber Gambler (ITY) (Nijin (USA)) – [2004 7g Jun 19] tailed off in seller at Redcar. *K. W. Hogg, Isle of Man*

KING AFTER 2 b.g. (Mar 25) Bahamian Bounty 116 – Child Star (FR) 58 (Bellypha 65 130) [2004 p5g* 5d⁶ 5.1d⁶ 6m 5m 6m 5m p7g p7g⁵ p6g⁶ p8g² p8.6g² p7.1g* p7m³ p7g⁴ Dec 29] 9,000F, 6,000Y: leggy gelding: fifth foal: half-brother to 3 winners, including 2000 2-y-o 5f winner Animal Cracker and 5-y-o Vandenberghe: dam 14.6f/2m winner on Flat and winning hurdler: fair performer: won maiden at Lingfield in March and nursery at Wolverhampton in December: stays 8.6f: acts on polytrack, probably on soft going: consistent. *J. R. Best*

KING AT LAST 2 b.g. Zamindar (USA) 116 – Louis' Queen (IRE) 102 (Tragic Role 52 ? (USA)) [2004 p8m p7g Oct 25] good-topped gelding: modest form at best in 3 maidens: flashed tail final outing. *K. Bell*

KING CARNIVAL (USA) 3 ch.c. King of Kings (IRE) 125 – Miss Waki Club (USA) 90 ? (Miswaki (USA) 124) [2004 92: 7g 8.1f 7.1m 7g Aug 14] close-coupled colt: fairly useful handicapper: seemed to run creditably in 2004 only on second start: stays 1m: raced only on good going or firmer: sold only 5,000 gns in November. *R. Hannon*

KINGDOM OF DREAMS (IRE) 2 b.c. (Feb 12) Sadler's Wells (USA) 132 – Regal 59 p Portrait (IRE) 57 (Royal Academy (USA) 130) [2004 7s Oct 22] 300,000Y: close-coupled, attractive colt: sixth foal: brother to useful 7f (at 2 yrs) and 8.5f (in USA) winner Atarama who stayed 1½m and half-brother to useful Italian sprinter King's Ivory (by Lake Coniston): dam lightly-raced half-sister to King's Theatre (by Sadler's Wells) and High Estate: 6/1, seventh to Ballinteni in maiden at Doncaster, green: likely to be suited by 1¼m/1½m: should improve. *Sir Michael Stoute*

KING EGBERT (FR) 3 b.g. Fasliyev (USA) 120 – Exocet (USA) (Deposit Ticket 64 (USA)) [2004 66d: 5m⁴ 5m 5m³ 5g p5.1g⁶ 6d⁵ Nov 5] lengthy, good-bodied gelding: fair maiden handicapper: should stay 6f: acts on firm going: tried blinkered. *A. W. Carroll*

KING EIDER 5 b. or br.g. Mtoto 134 – Hen Harrier 94 (Polar Falcon (USA) 126) [2004 85 97: 16g 12g 18s Oct 16] good-topped gelding: fairly useful handicapper: stays 2m: unraced on heavy going, acts on any other: usually races prominently: fairly useful hurdler. *B. Ellison*

KING FLYER (IRE) 8 b.g. Ezzoud (IRE) 126 – Al Guswa 98 (Shernazar 131) [2004 85 85, a–: p16g 16g² 16g³ 14g 18g² 20f 16.1m 14.8g 16g⁵ p12g³ p12g⁶ p16.5g⁴ p13.9g⁶ Dec a65 10] leggy, workmanlike gelding: fairly useful on turf, fair on all-weather: finds 1½m a minimum, and stays 2¼m: acts on polytrack, firm and good to soft going: occasionally blinkered: has been tongue tied, not in 2004: held up. *Miss J. Feilden*

KING FOREVER 2 b.c. (Feb 3) King's Best (USA) 132 – Elude (Slip Anchor 136) 72 p [2004 7m⁶ Jul 6] 65,000Y: strong, close-coupled colt: second foal: half-brother to 3-y-o Baffle: dam unraced close relation to smart 1¼m performer Perpendicular out of half-sister to Kris and Diesis: 8/1, burly and green, sixth to Belenus in maiden at Newmarket, taking good hold and not knocked about: should improve if all is well. *J. Noseda*

KING GABRIEL (IRE) 2 b.g. (Apr 10) Desert King (IRE) 129 – Broken Spirit (IRE) 69 (Slip Anchor 136) [2004 7g 8s⁶ Oct 19] 10,000F: fifth foal: half-brother to fairly useful Irish 9.5f to 2m winner Ballintry Guest (by Be My Guest) and Irish 6f/7f winner Detatch (by Thatching): dam unraced: better effort in maidens when never-dangerous sixth at Bath: likely to stay at least 1½m. *D. J. S. ffrench Davis*

KING HALLING 5 b.h. Halling (USA) 133 – Flower Fairy (FR) (Fairy King (USA)) 58 [2004 12f 15.9g⁶ 12.1m 10.5g⁴ p12.2g⁵ Oct 9] big horse: modest handicapper: at least as effective at 1¼m as 1½m: acts on polytrack, firm and good to soft going: tried in cheek-pieces/blinkers. *R. Ford*

KINGHAM 4 ch.g. Desert Prince (IRE) 130 – Marie de Flandre (FR) 109 (Crystal – Palace (FR) 132) [2004 –: p8g p6g Jan 17] leggy, lengthy gelding: fairly useful winner in 2002: lightly raced and well held since. *Mrs Mary Hambro*

KING HARSON 5 b.g. Greensmith 121 – Safari Park 43 (Absalom 128) [2004 90: 7d 93 § 7m² 7m 7m 7m⁶ 7g 7s* 7s⁵ 7.2s 7g 7s² Nov 2] close-coupled, good-bodied gelding: fairly useful handicapper: won at Chester in August: effective at 6f to 7.5f: acts on any ground: has been blinkered, visored nowadays: often makes running: unreliable. *J. D. Bethell*

KING HENRIK (USA) 2 b.g. (Feb 15) King of Kings (IRE) 125 – Ma Biche (USA) 63 d 125 (Key To The Kingdom (USA)) [2004 7f⁴ 7m⁶ 7.2m 7m Sep 18] close-coupled gelding: modest maiden: form only on debut: probably temperamental. *A. Crook*

KING JOCK (USA) 3 b.c. Ghazi (USA) – Glen Kate 118 (Glenstal (USA) 118) [2004 **98**
84: 8m* 8m 6.3f 7m⁵ 7m⁵ 5f* Sep 4] leggy, quite good-topped colt: sixth foal: half-
brother to several winners, including useful Irish 7f winner Perfect Touch (by Miswaki)
and French 1997 2-y-o 9f winner Trempkate (by Trempolino): dam 6f to 7f winner, including in USA: useful performer: won maiden at Leopardstown in May and handicap at
Down Royal (by a neck from Budelli) in September: mid-division in Britannia Stakes at
Royal Ascot second start: successful at 1m, best effort at 5f: acts on firm and good to soft
going. *D. K. Weld, Ireland*

KINGKOHLER (IRE) 5 b.g. King's Theatre (IRE) 128 – Legit (IRE) (Runnett 125) **78**
[2004 82p: p12g⁶ Mar 31] lightly-raced gelding: fairly useful winner in 2003: fair form
only outing in 2004: stays 1½m: acts on fibresand (probably on polytrack), raced only on
good or softer ground on turf. *K. A. Morgan*

KING MARJU (IRE) 2 b.c. (Apr 17) Marju (IRE) 127 – Katoushka (IRE) (Hamas **103**
(IRE) 125§) [2004 7m⁶ 6.1m² 6m* 7d² 7s³ Oct 22] 30,000Y, 34,000 2-y-o: lengthy colt:
second foal: dam unraced half-sister to smart performers Tajasur (sprinter) and Cayman
Kai (up to 1m): useful performer: odds on, made all in maiden at Newmarket in September: placed in nursery at Goodwood and Horris Hill Stakes at Newbury (excellent 6½
lengths third to Cupid's Glory, no extra late on) after: effective at 6f/7f: acts on soft and
good to firm going: free-going sort. *P. W. Chapple-Hyam*

KING NICHOLAS (USA) 5 b.g. Nicholas (USA) 111 – Lifetime Honour (USA) **69**
(Kingmambo (USA) 125) [2004 67d: f8g f6s* 7g 6v⁴ 6.1s* 6.1d 6g⁶ f6g 7.5d⁶ p8.6g*
p8.6g⁴ f8s⁵ p8.6g² f8g* Dec 28] good-topped gelding: fair performer: won seller at
Southwell in March and handicaps at Nottingham (apprentices) in May, Wolverhampton
in October and Southwell in December: effective at 6f to 8.6f: acts on all-weather and
heavy going: usually wears headgear/tongue tie. *J. Parkes*

KING OF BLUES (IRE) 2 ch.c. (Feb 10) Bluebird (USA) 125 – Highly Respected **80**
(IRE) 57 (High Estate 127) [2004 6m 7f p7g⁴ 7f* 7.1d 8m³ Sep 21] €46,000F, €80,000Y:
third foal: half-brother to 2 winners, including 4-y-o Sir Night: dam, maiden who should
have stayed at least 1m, closely related to smart Irish 1¼m performer Make No Mistake:
fairly useful performer: won nursery at Newbury in August: creditable third at Newmarket, much better effort in similar events after: stays 1m: acts on firm ground: tongue
tied last 4 starts. *M. A. Magnusson*

KING OF CASHEL (IRE) 3 b.c. King of Kings (IRE) 125 – Jaya (USA) (Ela-Mana- **87**
Mou 132) [2004 92: 7.1m³ 7.1d Jul 3] good-bodied colt: fairly useful performer: stayed
1m: acted on good to firm and good to soft going: dead. *R. Hannon*

KING OF DIAMONDS 3 b.c. Mtoto 134 – Capricious Lass (Corvaro (USA) 124) **84**
[2004 p6g² p7g⁶ p6g² 7.6g 8.1m 8g* 7g 8.5g⁴ 8g p12g² p10g² p10g⁶ p10m p8g⁵ Dec 30]
leggy colt: second known foal: dam ran once in Ireland: fairly useful handicapper: won
at Newmarket in August: stays easy 1½m: raced only on polytrack and good/good to firm
ground: sometimes pulls hard. *J. R. Best*

KING OF DREAMS (IRE) 3 b.c. Sadler's Wells (USA) 132 – Koniya (IRE) (Doy- **103**
oun 124) [2004 79p: 10.3g* 10g 10g* 10.5g⁵ 11.9d Aug 17] leggy, quite attractive colt:
useful performer: won maiden at Doncaster in March and handicap at Newmarket (beat
Anna Pallida 1¾ lengths) in July: broke leg at York final start: stayed 10.5f: raced mostly
on good ground or firmer: dead. *M. Johnston*

KING OF FIRE 2 b.g. (Feb 16) Magic Ring (IRE) 115 – Alaskan Princess (IRE) 70 **38**
(Prince Rupert (FR) 121) [2004 6g May 22] ninth in maiden at Kempton: dead. *Miss
B. Sanders*

KING OF KNIGHT (IRE) 3 gr.g. Orpen (USA) 116 – Peace Melody (IRE) 69 **70**
(Classic Music (USA)) [2004 65: 8m⁴ 8d⁵ 7g 12m 10.1g 8d⁴ p12g² p12g⁴ p9.5g² f11g⁴
Dec 16] quite good-topped gelding: fair maiden: barely stays 1½m: acts on polytrack
(found little on fibresand final start), good to firm and good to soft ground. *G. Prodromou*

KING OF LOVE 2 b.c. (Apr 17) King's Best (USA) 132 – Fadaki Hawaki (USA) 60 **76 p**
(Vice Regent (CAN)) [2004 5.9g* Jun 23] 46,000Y: seventh foal: half-brother to unreliable 7.5f winner Sutton Common (by Common Grounds) and French 1¼m winner
Premiership (by Zinaad): dam, maiden who stayed 1m, closely related to smart 1990
2-y-o sprinter Mujadil and half-sister to high-class 1½m performer Fruits of Love: 4/1,
won maiden at Carlisle comfortably by 1¼ lengths (struck into, wound took long time to
heal, but fully recovered): should stay 1m: likely to improve. *M. Johnston*

KING OF MEZE (IRE) 3 b.g. Croco Rouge (IRE) 126 – Cossack Princess (IRE) 72 **–**
(Lomond (USA) 128) [2004 p8g p6g⁶ f6g f12d 8.1d Oct 9] little form: tongue tied final
start. *G. Prodromou*

KING OF MUSIC (USA) 3 ch.g. Jade Hunter (USA) – Hail Roberta (USA) (Roberto **70** (USA) 131) [2004 73: 7f 7g 8d[6] p8g[2] f8s* f8g[4] Dec 16] rather leggy, angular gelding: fair handicapper: won at Southwell in November: stays 1m: acts on all-weather and good to firm ground. *G. Prodromou*

KING PRIAM (IRE) 9 b.g. Priolo (USA) 127 – Barinia (Corvaro (USA) 124) [2004 **43 §** 66d: f12g f12g[4] f12g* f8g[4] f11g[5] f16g f12g[6] f12g[6] f14g[4] f12g[5] f14g[4] 12g f12g f14m[6] f12g[6] f14g f14g[6] f11d Dec 21] sturdy gelding: poor mover: poor performer: won claimer at Southwell in January: effective at 1½m to 2m: acts on all-weather/any turf going: wears headgear: tried tongue tied: often gets behind: has bled: unreliable. *M. J. Polglase*

KING REVO (IRE) 4 b.g. Revoque (IRE) 122 – Tycoon Aly (IRE) 70 (Last Tycoon **87** 131) [2004 89: 12.1g* 11.9s May 11] tall, useful-looking gelding: fairly useful handicapper: won at Hamilton in April: tailed off subsequent outing: stays 1½m: acts on polytrack, firm and soft ground: sometimes hangs: useful hurdler. *P. C. Haslam*

KING'S ACCOUNT (USA) 2 ch.g. (May 13) King of Kings (IRE) 125 – Fighting **87** Countess (USA) (Ringside (USA)) [2004 7d[2] 7.2s[2] 8.1g[2] 7.5m* 8s* Oct 12] 9,000Y, 15,000 2-y-o: well-made, good sort: sixth foal: half-brother to 3 winners in USA: dam, 7.5f minor stakes winner in USA, half-sister to Breeders' Cup Juvenile Fillies winner Countess Diana: fairly useful performer: won maiden at Beverley in September and nursery at Ayr in October, from Stancomb Wills both times: stays 1m: acts on soft and good to firm going: races prominently: gelded after final start. *M. Johnston*

KING'S BALLET (USA) 6 b.g. Imperial Ballet (IRE) 110 – Multimara (USA) **55 d** (Arctic Tern (USA) 126) [2004 75d: p6g f5g f5s[2] f5g f5g[4] 5d 5s 5v 6g May 17] strong, lengthy gelding: modest handicapper: on downgrade: best at 5f/6f: acts on fibresand and good to firm going, though all wins on softer than good: tried blinkered/visored/tongue tied, usually wears cheekpieces nowadays. *P. R. Chamings*

KING'S CAPRICE 3 ch.g. Pursuit of Love 124 – Palace Street (USA) 103 (Secreto **97** (USA) 128) [2004 91p: 6s 6m[3] 6m[4] 6m* 7.1d 6f[4] 6g[4] 7s* 7s[5] 6s 7d[2] 6s Oct 22] rather leggy gelding: has a round action: useful performer: won maiden at Windsor in June and handicap at Kempton in August: effective at 6f/7f: acts on firm and soft going. *G. B. Balding*

KINGS COLLEGE BOY 4 b.g. College Chapel 122 – The Kings Daughter 79 **79** (Indian King (USA) 128) [2004 68: 6d 6m 5m[3] 5m[2] 5g[3] 5d 6m[3] 5g 5g[3] 5d 5.1s* 5d 5.1g[2] 5d[4] 5d 5g[4] 5s Nov 1] well-made gelding: fair handicapper: won at Chester in August: best at 5f/6f: acts on soft and good to firm going: usually blinkered/visored: usually comes from off pace. *R. A. Fahey*

KING'S COUNTY (IRE) 6 b.g. Fairy King (USA) – Kardelle 79 (Kalaglow 132) **101** [2004 109: 8g[3] 7.9s 7f[3] 8f 8m 9m[2] 9g Oct 2] strong, good-topped gelding: useful performer: creditable efforts when placed in 2004: stays 9f: acts on firm and soft going: tried blinkered/visored: has worn dropped noseband: often races freely: sold 40,000 gns, sent to USA. *L. M. Cumani*

KINGSCROSS 6 ch.g. King's Signet (USA) 110 – Calamanco 71 (Clantime 101) [2004 **89** 83: 6s[4] 6d[2] 6g* 6m 6d[5] 6s 6s[2] 6g[2] 6g[6] 6g[4] 7g[4] 7d Oct 30] strong, good-bodied gelding: fairly useful handicapper: won at Doncaster in May: stays 7f: acts on soft and good to firm going: usually held up. *M. Blanshard*

KINGSDON (IRE) 7 b.g. Brief Truce (USA) 126 – Richly Deserved (IRE) (Kings **70** Lake (USA) 133) [2004 57d: f12s p10g* p10g p10g[4] 10.1v[4] 10g* p10g* p10g* 10.1s* 9.9d[3] f11g p12.2g Dec 20] sturdy, useful-looking gelding: fair performer: won banded races at Lingfield in February and May and Ayr in April, and handicaps at Lingfield and Newcastle in June: stays 1¼m: acts on polytrack and any turf going: has been blinkered, visored/tongue tied nowadays. *T. J. Fitzgerald*

KINGS EMPIRE 3 b.g. Second Empire (IRE) 124 – Dancing Feather 72 (Suave **85** Dancer (USA) 136) [2004 86p: 10d 10.3g[4] 10.5s 10.3s p8g f8g[2] p9.5g* f8g f8g Dec 28] sturdy gelding: fairly useful handicapper: won at Wolverhampton in December: broke leg final start: was best at 1m/1¼m: acted on all-weather, well held on soft going: was sometimes tongue tied: dead. *D. Carroll*

KING'S ENVOY (USA) 5 b.g. Royal Academy (USA) 130 – Island of Silver (USA) **69** 107 (Forty Niner (USA)) [2004 –: 9g[4] 9g[3] 12m[5] 10.1g 9v 10.9s Sep 16] tall gelding: fair maiden: stays 9f: raced mainly on good/good to firm going: visored once in 2002. *Mrs J. C. McGregor*

KING'S GAIT 2 b.g. (Apr 5) Mujahid (USA) 125 – Miller's Gait 74§ (Mill Reef (USA) **83**
141) [2004 5g⁶ 5s* 6.1s⁴ May 14] leggy, quite good-topped gelding: half-brother to
several winners, including useful 6f (at 2 yrs)/7f winner Welton Arsenal (by Statoblest)
and smart stayer Bold Gait (by Persian Bold): dam, ungenuine middle-distance maiden,
half-sister to high-class stayer/hurdler Royal Gait: fair form: won maiden at Pontefract in
April: good fourth in minor event at Nottingham: should stay 7f. *T. D. Easterby*

KINGSGATE BAY (IRE) 2 b.g. (Mar 12) Desert Sun 120 – Selkirk Flyer (Selkirk **99 p**
(USA) 129) [2004 6m p5g⁵ 5m⁵ 5.9g* p6g* p7m* p6g* Dec 30] €9,500F, 21,000Y: third
foal: half-brother to Italian 6f/7f winner (including at 2 yrs) by Sesaro: dam unraced:
useful performer: won nursery at Carlisle (hung left/swished tail) in September, minor
event at Lingfield in November and 2 nurseries at Lingfield in December, beating Beau
Marche readily by 3 lengths on final occasion: stays easy 7f: acts on polytrack: sold
privately to USA: open to further progress. *J. R. Best*

KINGSHOLM 2 ch.c. (Feb 19) Selkirk (USA) 129 – Putuna 98 (Generous (IRE) 139) **70**
[2004 7.1m⁶ 8.1d³ 8m Sep 4] sturdy colt: has a quick action: second foal: dam, 8.5f and
1¼m winner, half-sister to useful sprinter Lochonica and to dam of 5-y-o Funfair Wane:
fair form at Sandown on first 2 starts in maidens: shapes as if will stay at least 1¼m.
A. M. Balding

KING'S KAMA 2 b.c. (May 2) Giant's Causeway (USA) 132 – Maid For The Hills **78**
101 (Indian Ridge 123) [2004 6g⁴ 7.1m⁴ p7g³ Oct 13] 350,000Y: leggy colt: fifth foal:
half-brother to 3 winners, including useful 7f (at 2 yrs) and 1¼m winner Maid To Perfection (by Sadler's Wells) and 4-y-o Artistic Lad: dam 2-y-o 6f winner: fair form in
maidens: third to Happy As Larry at Lingfield: will stay at least 1m. *Sir Michael Stoute*

KINGSMAITE 3 b.g. Komaite (USA) – Antonias Melody 86 (Rambo Dancer (CAN) **76**
107) [2004 66, a79: 7g 7.5s⁴ 7m 6.1g⁵ 6g* f7f³ 6f 8.5m⁵ 7m p6d² p7.1g* p6g f5g⁴ **a85**
Dec 14] workmanlike gelding: fairly useful handicapper on all-weather, fair on turf: won
at Redcar in June and Wolverhampton in November: effective at 6f to 1m: acts on all-
weather and good to firm ground: blinkered nowadays. *S. R. Bowring*

KING'S MAJESTY (IRE) 2 b.c. (Mar 5) King's Best (USA) 132 – Tiavanita (USA) **89 P**
(J O Tobin (USA) 130) [2004 7m p7g² p7g* Oct 28] €240,000Y: well-made colt:
half-brother to several winners, notably 2000 Guineas winner Island Sands (by Turtle
Island), 6f winner at 2 yrs: dam French maiden half-sister to very smart middle-distance
performer Corrupt: progressive form in maidens: favourite (having been unlucky on
same course time before), won at Lingfield comfortably by 1½ lengths from Dubai
Dreamer, going bit in snatches before leading final 1f: will stay at least 1m: at least a
useful prospect and sure to win more races. *Sir Michael Stoute*

KING'S MINSTREL (IRE) 3 b.g. Cape Cross (IRE) 129 – Muwasim (USA) (Mea- **56**
dowlake (USA)) [2004 8m 8m 9.9g 8.3g p10m⁴ p10m⁵ Dec 15] modest maiden: left
M. Channon after second start: stays 1¼m: acts on polytrack. *R. Rowe*

KING'S MOUNTAIN (USA) 4 b.g. King of Kings (IRE) 125 – Statistic (USA) (Mr **–**
Prospector (USA)) [2004 –: 10.9d 14.1g Jun 19] close-coupled gelding: fairly useful
winner in Ireland at 2 yrs: no form in Britain: tried blinkered. *Mrs A. L. M. King*

KING SPINNER (IRE) 7 b.g. Mujadil (USA) 119 – Money Spinner (USA) 61 (Teen- **– §**
oso (USA) 135) [2004 14.1d Jul 10] lengthy gelding: fair but unreliable handicapper in
2001: last only start since: visored 3 times in 2001. *Mrs A. J. Bowlby*

KINGS POINT (IRE) 3 b.c. Fasliyev (USA) 120 – Rahika Rose 91 (Unfuwain (USA) **106**
131) [2004 103: p8g⁵ 7g 8g⁵ 6m³ 7m 7m⁴ 7g 8m³ 7m 7g 7g Sep 30] strong, compact colt:
useful performer: best efforts when 3 lengths equal-fourth to Arakan in Criterion Stakes
at Newmarket in June and 2 lengths third to Fong's Thong in listed race at Goodwood
(edgy) in July: stays easy 1m: raced mainly on good or firmer ground on turf: blinkered
(respectable effort) final outing: sold 70,000 gns (privately). *R. Hannon*

KINGS QUAY 2 b.c. (Feb 4) Montjeu (IRE) 137 – Glen Rosie (IRE) 102 (Mujtahid **101**
(USA) 118) [2004 5g⁸ 6f 6m² 7d⁴* 7g⁶ Sep 30] 32,000Y: unfurnished colt: has a quick
action: first foal: dam, 2-y-o 5f winner who stayed 1m, half-sister to smart French/US
performer around 1m Hello Soso: useful performer: won maiden at Sandown in June and
listed event at Newbury (by ½ length from Wilko, leading over 1f out then wandering) in
August: ran lacklustre race final start, tending to hang left: will stay at least 1m: acts on
good to firm and good to soft going. *R. Hannon*

KINGS ROCK 3 ch.g. Kris 135 – Both Sides Now (USA) (Topsider (USA)) [2004 **69**
66: f8g² f9.4s⁶ p10g 8.2g 7s⁶ 8g³ 8.1g 8f* 8f² 7.5s* 7m 7s 8g Oct 4] rather leggy, useful-
looking gelding: has a quick action: fair performer: won seller at Leicester in July and

claimer at Beverley (left K. Ryan) in August: stays 1m: acts on fibresand, firm and soft going: blinkered last 6 outings. *Mrs Lucinda Featherstone*

KINGS SQUARE 4 b.g. Bal Harbour 113 – Prime Property (IRE) 60 (Tirol 127) [2004 –: 11.9g Sep 1] strong, workmanlike gelding: no sign of ability. *M. W. Easterby*

KING'S THOUGHT 5 b.h. King's Theatre (IRE) 128 – Lora's Guest 99 (Be My Guest (USA) 126) [2004 105: 12g6 10d 10.1s4 10g6 10.3d4 10.3g4 8m3 Jun 20] angular, good-topped horse: useful performer: ran creditably last 3 starts: best at 1m/1¼m: acts on polytrack, firm and soft ground: has been bandaged on fore joints: front runner. *S. Gollings* **103**

KINGSTON HARBOUR (IRE) 3 b.g. Danehill (USA) 126 – Kallavesi (USA) 64 (Woodman (USA) 126) [2004 8m4 7g p9.5g* p13g5 Dec 29] third foal: half-brother to fairly useful Irish 1m winner Marie Pavie (by Entrepreneur), later successful in Saudi Arabia: dam, Irish maiden (best effort at 1m), sister to smart Irish middle-distance performer Campo Catino: left C. O'Brien in Ireland, off 4 months and gelded, won maiden at Wolverhampton in December: seems to stay easy 13f. *V. Smith* **67**

KINGSTON TOWN (USA) 4 ch.g. King of Kings (IRE) 125 – Lady Ferial (FR) 67 (Carwhite 127) [2004 77: p10g f9.4g f8s4 f11s 10.1f6 10.1m f8f2 8s5 p10g f12g2Dec 16] leggy, close-coupled gelding: fair performer: left N. Littmoden after ninth start: stays easy 1½m: acts on all-weather and good to firm ground: usually wears cheekpieces/blinkers. *M. C. Pipe*

KINGS TOPIC (USA) 4 ch.g. Kingmambo (USA) 125 – Topicount (USA) (Private 57 Account (USA)) [2004 –: p10g2 p10g* p10g* 10m May 12] deep-bodied gelding: modest performer: won 2 banded events at Lingfield in April: stays 1¼m: acts on polytrack. *P. Burgoyne*

KING SUMMERLAND 7 b.g. Minshaanshu Amad (USA) 91§ – Alaskan Princess 44 (IRE) 70 (Prince Rupert (FR) 121) [2004 8.3s5 9.1s4 Oct 12] winner of 8 races in Germany/Holland for J. Pubben, including handicap at Hamburg in 2003: poor form over hurdles/on Flat in Britain: effective at 6f, also won up to 1½m earlier in career: acts on soft ground. *B. Mactaggart*

KING'S WELCOME 6 b.g. Most Welcome 131 – Reine de Thebes (FR) 67 (Darshaan 133) [2004 12v6 10.1s f12g Nov 9] rather leggy, quite good-topped gelding: useful in 2002: well held in claimers/minor event on return: tried blinkered. *C. W. Fairhurst*

KINGSWORD (USA) 3 bl.c. Dynaformer (USA) – Western Curtsey (USA) (Gone 105 West (USA)) [2004 89p: 10.3g5 10m2 9.9m Jul 28] tall, lightly-made colt: useful form: best effort when 1¾ lengths second to Mutasallil in minor event at Pontefract: well held in ladbrokes.com Handicap at Goodwood subsequent outing: should stay 1½m: raced only on good/good to firm going: sold 13,000 gns, sent to Denmark. *Sir Michael Stoute*

KING TOP 3 b.g. Inchinor 119 – Panorama (Shirley Heights 130) [2004 11g4 Jun 18] 25/1 and very green, tailed-off last of 4 in maiden at Redcar. *T. D. Easterby*

KING ZAFEEN (IRE) 2 b.c. (Feb 15) Lend A Hand 124 – Groom Dancing (Groom 71 Dancer (USA) 128) [2004 7m 8m4 8g 8s Nov 1] €32,000F, 50,000Y: neat colt: has a quick action: first foal: dam French 7.5f (at 2 yrs) and 9f winner: fair maiden: easily best effort when fourth at Thirsk: left M. Channon before final start: should stay 1¼m: tongue tied second/third outings. *M. W. Easterby*

KINISKA 3 b.f. Merdon Melody 98 – Young Whip (Bold Owl 101) [2004 62: 8g p8m – p7.1g p7.1g Dec 14] close-coupled filly: modest form in 2 maidens at 2 yrs: well held in 2004. *B. Palling*

KINKOZAN 3 ch.c. Peintre Celebre (USA) 137 – Classic Design (Busted 134) [2004 49 –: 8.1g6 p10g Jul 24] quite good-topped colt: poor maiden: stays 1m: reportedly had breathing problem on debut. *N. P. Littmoden*

KINNAIRD (IRE) 3 ch.f. Dr Devious (IRE) 127 – Ribot's Guest (IRE) (Be My Guest 111 (USA) 126) [2004 105p: 8m4 8m5 10.2g2 10d2 10g2 Sep 19] sturdy filly: smart performer: fourth in Irish 1000 Guineas at the Curragh (4 lengths behind Attraction) and runner-up in Golden Daffodil Stakes at Chepstow (beaten a neck by Felicity), Prix de Psyche at Deauville (went down by a length to Quilanga) and Blandford Stakes at the Curragh (tongue tied, beaten ½ length by Monturani): stays 1¼m: unraced on heavy going, probably acts on any other turf: genuine: stays in training. *P. C. Haslam*

KINRANDE (IRE) 2 b.c. (Jan 23) Sri Pekan (USA) 117 – Pipers Pool (IRE) 94 (Mtoto 71 134) [2004 8.3m3 p8g3 p10g* Nov 27] €17,000F, €44,000Y: sixth foal: half-brother to 3 winners, including fairly useful Irish 6f winner Pipewell (by Lake Coniston) and useful

French 1m winner Miss Chryss (by Indian Ridge), later successful in USA: dam, maiden who stayed 1¼m, closely related to smart middle-distance stayer Pipsted: favourite, won maiden at Lingfield by 2½ lengths from Sandy's Legend: stays 1¼m. *P. J. Makin*

KINSMAN (IRE) 7 b.g. Distant Relative 128 – Besito 79 (Wassl 125) [2004 56, a67: p7g² p7g* p8g⁵ p7g⁴ 7f⁶ 7g 7f 7.6f p7g⁵ p7g² Dec 30] leggy, useful-looking gelding: modest performer: won handicap at Lingfield in February: effective at 7f to easy 1¼m: acts on all-weather, firm and soft going: wears headgear: tried tongue tied: often starts slowly: sometimes carries head high/hangs: held up. *T. D. McCarthy* **50 a63**

KINTORE 3 ch.g. Inchinor 119 – Souadah (USA) (General Holme (USA) 128) [2004 –: 9.2d⁶ 9.1g⁴ 9m Jul 5] quite good-topped gelding: little form: gelded after final start. *J. S. Goldie* **–**

KIPSIGIS (IRE) 3 b.g. Octagonal (NZ) 126 – Kisumu (Damister (USA) 123) [2004 10g 10g⁴ p13g⁴ p12g Nov 27] 16,000Y: sixth foal: half-brother to very smart Italian/US performer up to 1½m Timboroa (by Salse): dam unraced half-sister to very smart 7f/1m performer Efisio and US Grade 1 1¼m winner Mountain Bear: modest maiden: stays 13f: acts on polytrack: tended to hang third start. *Lady Herries* **62**

KIRAT 6 b.g. Darshaan 133 – Kafsa (IRE) (Vayrann 133) [2004 p12g p12g⁴ Feb 18] tall, leggy gelding: little form in 3 races on Flat (reportedly finished lame final start): stays 1½m: raced only on polytrack/good to firm ground. *G. L. Moore* **–**

KIRKBY'S TREASURE 6 gr.g. Mind Games 121 – Gem of Gold 52 (Jellaby 124) [2004 67§: 7.1g* 7.1m² 7.1m* 5.9f³ 7.9g 7.1m* 6.9g² 7g 7.1f² 6g² 7.6s⁶ 6d 7.1g³ 7.1d⁵ 7s³ 7s² Nov 6] tall, leggy gelding: has a round action: fairly useful handicapper: won at Musselburgh in April, May and June: effective at 6f to 1m: acts on fibresand, firm and soft ground: often wore cheekpieces/blinkers in 2003: sometimes wanders: normally held up: tough and consistent. *A. Berry* **84**

KIRKHAM ABBEY 4 b.g. Selkirk (USA) 129 – Totham 84 (Shernazar 131) [2004 74: 10m 10g³ 10f² 10m⁶ 9.2f⁵ 10f* 10.1m 10m* Sep 28] fair handicapper: won at Brighton in August and Nottingham in September: effective at 9f to 1½m: acts on fibresand and firm going: tried in cheekpieces/blinkers, effective visored or not: sold 32,000 gns. *M. A. Jarvis* **76**

KIRKHAMMERTON (IRE) 2 ch.g. (Mar 28) Grand Lodge (USA) 125 – Nawara 75 (Welsh Pageant 132) [2004 6g 6d 6m 6.1d Sep 17] sturdy gelding: well held in maidens. *J. A. Osborne* **–**

KIROV KING (IRE) 4 b.c. Desert King (IRE) 129 – Nymphs Echo (IRE) (Mujtahid (USA) 118) [2004 85: 11.6d 14.4v 12m 10f 11.9m⁶ 9.9s Aug 29] IR 50,000Y: half-brother to 2 winners in Ireland, including useful 1m/1¼m winner Sonorous (by Ashkalani): dam unraced: fairly useful performer at 3 yrs for D. Weld in Ireland: well held in 2004: stays 1½m: acts on soft and good to firm going: tried blinkered: won over hurdles in September. *B. G. Powell* **–**

KISS AGAIN 3 b.f. Halling (USA) 133 – Kissogram 120 (Caerleon (USA) 132) [2004 p7.1g p9.5g⁵ Nov 26] first foal: dam, 1m/1¼m (Sun Chariot Stakes) winner, grand-daughter of top-class miler Milligram: better effort in maidens when fifth to Lytham at Wolverhampton. *L. M. Cumani* **48**

KISSES FOR ME (IRE) 3 b.f. Sadler's Wells (USA) 132 – Fanny Cerrito (USA) (Gulch (USA)) [2004 80p: 10m⁵ 8m 12m 9f³ 12f³ 11.9s 9.5d³ 8d 10s Oct 25] well-made filly: has a short, round action: second foal: dam unraced daughter of US Grade 1 9f/1¼m winner Sabin: useful performer: won maiden at Navan only start in 2003: creditable efforts in 2004 in listed races when fifth to Ouija Board at Newmarket in May and when third at the Curragh (to Tropical Lady), Cork (behind My Renee) and Gowran (beaten 2 lengths by Cache Creek): acted as pacemaker when tailed off in Oaks at Epsom third start: stays 1½m: acts on firm and good to soft ground: tongue tied last 3 starts: sent to USA. *A. P. O'Brien, Ireland* **99**

KISSING A FOOL 2 b.g. (Apr 24) Tipsy Creek (USA) 115 – Amathus Glory 76 (Mummy's Pet 125) [2004 5s⁵ 5s* 5d f6g⁵ May 15] good-topped gelding: modest per-former: made all in claimer at Newcastle in April: should stay 6f. *W. G. M. Turner* **50**

KISSING LIGHTS (IRE) 2 b.f. (Mar 10) Machiavellian (USA) 123 – Nasaieb (IRE) 89 (Fairy King (USA)) [2004 6m⁵ 5m* 6m⁶ 6m³ 6s 5f³ Sep 11] 110,000Y: good-bodied filly: first foal: dam, lightly-raced 2-y-o 5f winner, half-sister to smart 7f/1m performer Raise A Grand: useful performer: won maiden at Warwick in June: good third to Soar (beaten 2 lengths) in Princess Margaret Stakes at Ascot and to Chateau Istana (not clear **99**

run when beaten 2¾ lengths) in Flying Childers Stakes at Doncaster: effective at 5f/6f: acts on firm going. *M. L. W. Bell*

KISS THE RAIN   4 b.f. Forzando 122 – Devils Dirge 68 (Song 132) [2004 60: f6g⁶   **44** f6g 7g 6g f5g Dec 1] small filly: poor performer: left R. Brotherton after reappearance: best at 5f/6f: acts on fibresand, firm and soft ground: usually visored. *P. A. Blockley*

KISWAHILI   2 ch.f. (Feb 16) Selkirk (USA) 129 – Kiliniski 119 (Niniski (USA) 125)   **89 p** [2004 7g² 8.3d* Sep 27] half-sister to 3 winners, including useful 1¼m and 11.7f winner Robe Chinoise (by Robellino) who stayed 1¾m: dam, 1½m winner (also in frame in Oaks and Yorkshire Oaks), out of half-sister to Nureyev and dam of Sadler's Wells: better effort in maidens when winning at Hamilton comfortably by 9 lengths from Aire de Mougins, going clear 3f out: will be suited by 1¼m/1½m: useful prospect. *Sir Mark Prescott*

KITCHEN SINK (IRE)   2 ch.g. (Feb 13) Bold Fact (USA) 116 – Voodoo Rocket 56   **59 p** (Lycius (USA) 124) [2004 6g 5.1s p5.1g⁵ Nov 12] €12,000Y: third living foal: half-brother to 2 winners abroad, including Italian 7f (at 2 yrs)/1m winner by Mujadil: dam, maiden, probably stayed 9f: modest form in maidens: fourth to Hidden Jewel at Wolverhampton, considerably handled: should stay 6f: likely to do better. *P. J. Makin*

KITLEY   3 b.c. Muhtarram (USA) 125 – Salsita (Salse (USA) 128) [2004 68: 10s 8.3s   **61** 7m⁶ 8m p10d Jun 26] close-coupled colt: maiden, only modest at best in 2004: free-going sort, but stays 1m: acts on polytrack and good to firm going (poor efforts on soft): sometimes awkward leaving stall. *B. G. Powell*

KITTYLEE   5 b.m. Bal Harbour 113 – Courtesy Call (Northfields (USA)) [2004 –:   **–** f12g f14g⁶ Jan 8] no sign of ability. *M. A. Buckley*

KITTY O'SHEA   2 b.f. (Apr 23) Sadler's Wells (USA) 132 – Eva Luna (USA) 114   **87 P** (Alleged (USA) 138) [2004 8s* Oct 13] fourth foal: sister to 4-y-o Brian Boru and half-sister to smart French 10.5f to 12.5f (Prix de Royallieu) winner Moon Search (by Rainbow Quest): dam 11.5f to 14.6f (Park Hill Stakes) winner: 7/2, won 18-runner maiden at Navan by head from Maria Luisa, looking like winning well when leading over 1f out but idling/flashing tail and ridden out: will be well suited by 1¼m/1½m: useful prospect at least. *A. P. O'Brien, Ireland*

KNEAD THE DOUGH   3 b.g. Wolfhound (USA) 126 – Ridgewood Ruby (IRE) 77   **58** (Indian Ridge 123) [2004 p6g² 5.7f⁶ 7.1d 6g² 6g p6g⁵ f5g² f5m⁶ f6g³ f5g³ Dec 21] smallish, strong gelding: modest maiden: barely stays 6f: acts on all-weather, firm and good to soft going: effective with or without cheekpieces: has run well when sweating: usually races prominently. *D. E. Cantillon*

KNICKYKNACKIENOO   3 b.g. Bin Ajwaad (IRE) 119 – Ring Fence 74 (Polar   **67** Falcon (USA) 126) [2004 ?: f7s⁴ 7.1s² 7s² 9g 7m³ 8g* 8.3f 8g² 8m⁵ p8g³ 8m p7.1g⁴ p7g Dec 30] big, plain gelding: fair handicapper: won apprentice race at Salisbury in June: stays 1m: acts on all-weather, firm and soft going: sometimes pulls hard. *A. G. Newcombe*

KNIGHT OF HEARTS (IRE)   3 gr.g. Idris (IRE) 118 – Heart To Heart (IRE)   **52** (Double Schwartz 128) [2004 f12g⁵ f9.4g⁵ 8m f8m 11.1s⁴ 16.2s p9.5d² p9.5g Nov 20] leggy gelding: modest maiden: left R. Peacock after third start: stays 11f: acts on polytrack and soft going. *P. A. Blockley*

KNIGHT OF SILVER   7 gr.g. Presidium 124 – Misty Rocket 75 (Roan Rocket 128)   **–** [2004 17.2g Jul 11] maiden: has shown little in 2 Flat runs since 1999. *J. D. Frost*

KNIGHT ONTHE TILES (IRE)   3 ch.g. Primo Dominie 121 – Blissful Night (Cadeaux Genereux 131) [2004 77, a67: p7g⁷ f7g 6m 7.5g 7m 6f Aug 7] fair performer at 3 yrs: no form in 2004: often blinkered. *J. R. Best*

KNIGHTSBRIDGE HILL (IRE)   2 b.c. (Mar 22) Raise A Grand (IRE) 114 –   **74** Desert Gem 87 (Green Desert (USA) 127) [2004 7m⁵ 8d⁶ 7.1m⁴ 8g Sep 30] €20,000F, €22,000Y, 11,000 2-y-o: eighth foal: half-brother to 3 winners, including 5f (at 2 yrs) and 6f (seller) winner Risky Whisky and 7.5f winner in Italy (both by Risk Me): dam maiden who stayed 1m: fair maiden: last in nursery final start: best effort at 7f. *A. King*

KNIGHT TO REMEMBER (IRE)   3 ch.g. Fayruz 116 – Cheerful Knight (IRE)   **49 d** (Mac's Imp (USA) 116) [2004 –: f7f³ f7g⁴ f8.5g 5s 7.5m⁵ 7m f6g⁵ 7.9g 8m Jul 23] angular gelding: poor maiden: left K. Ryan after third start, K. Burke after fifth: stays 7f: acts on fibresand, good to firm going: tried in cheekpieces. *R. E. Barr*

KNOCKANURE LAD (IRE)   4 ch.c. Titus Livius (FR) 115 – Bannons Dream (IRE)   **53** (Thatching 131) [2004 67: 7d 8.5m 14m 9s⁵ f8s Nov 17] modest maiden: well held in handicap at Southwell final start: stays 9f: acts on any going: tried blinkered/in cheekpieces. *Frederick John Bowles, Ireland*

KNOCK BRIDGE (IRE) 2 b.f. (Mar 15) Rossini (USA) 118 – Touraneena (Robellino **70** (USA) 127) [2004 6m⁴ 5m² 5m 5.1s³ 5.1g 7s* 7s Nov 6] 5,500Y: leggy filly: third foal: half-sister to Irish 9f winner Twilight Breeze (by Night Shift): dam ran once at 2 yrs: fair performer: left M. Wallace after second start: won nursery at Catterick in October: well held in similar event final start: stays 7f: acts on soft going, probably on good to firm: sometimes slowly away. *P. D. Evans*

KNOCKDOO (IRE) 11 ch.g. Be My Native (USA) 122 – Ashken (Artaius (USA) – 129) [2004 48: f12g f16.2g³ Feb 6] poor performer: well held in 2004: tried visored. *J. S. Goldie*

KNOCKTOPHER ABBEY 7 ch.g. Pursuit of Love 124 – Kukri (Kris 135) [2004 – p13g 9s 12g p13.9g Nov 12] angular, plain gelding: fair performer at 5 yrs: lightly raced and little form since, leaving B. R. Millman after reappearance: often blinkered. *A. G. Newcombe*

KNOT IN DOUBT (IRE) 3 b.g. Woodborough (USA) 112 – In The Mind (IRE) – (Taufan (USA) 119) [2004 –: 7.5g 7m Jun 4] close-coupled gelding: no solid form. *J. A. Glover*

KNOT IN WOOD (IRE) 2 b.c. (Feb 7) Shinko Forest (IRE) – Notley Park 71 (Wolf- **72** hound (USA) 126) [2004 6g 6f⁶ 6g³ Oct 8] 10,000Y: sturdy colt: third foal: half-brother to 4-y-o Mulan Princess: dam, maiden who stayed 7.5f, half-sister to smart sprinter Notley: best effort in maidens when third at York: will probably stay 7f. *R. A. Fahey*

KNOWN MANEUVER (USA) 6 b.g. Known Fact (USA) 135 – Northern Mane- – uver (USA) (Al Nasr (FR) 126) [2004 –: f12g⁴ f12g⁴ f14s Mar 14] smallish gelding: fair winner in 2002: little form since: tried blinkered. *M. C. Chapman*

KODIAC 3 b.c. Danehill (USA) 126 – Rafha 123 (Kris 135) [2004 82p: 7m* 8f 7d Oct **86** 30] smallish, sturdy colt: fairly useful form, lightly raced: off 14 months, won maiden at Lingfield in September: better effort after when seventh in handicap at Ascot next time, edging right: should prove at least as effective at 7f as 1m: took good hold to post on debut. *J. L. Dunlop*

KOFI 2 br.g. (May 16) Emperor Fountain 112 – La Vie En Primrose 104 (Henbit **36** (USA) 130) [2004 p7.1g Dec 10] 2,500F: half-brother to 1¾m winner Influence Pedler (by Keen): dam 1¼m winner: 40/1, ninth of 12 in maiden at Wolverhampton. *Miss K. M. George*

KOLYMA (IRE) 2 ch.f. (Apr 3) Grand Lodge (USA) 125 – Koniya (IRE) (Doyoun **61** 124) [2004 6g 7g⁵ 8m Sep 7] leggy filly: second foal: half-sister to 3-y-o King of Dreams: dam, French 15f winner, half-sister to dam of High Chaparral: modest form in maidens: should be suited by 1¼m/1½m. *J. L. Dunlop*

KOMAC 2 b.c. (Mar 9) Komaite (USA) – Star of Flanders (Puissance 110) [2004 5s⁶ 5f² **71** 5g⁴ 5.1s⁶ 15g* 5m 6m Oct 2] 5,500Y: sturdy colt: third foal: half-brother to 4-y-o Davids Mark: dam unraced: fair performer: won maiden at Southwell in August: virtually pulled up final start: will prove best at 5f: acts on fibresand and firm going: races up with pace: sometimes carries head high: sold 9,500 gns. *B. A. McMahon*

KOMATI RIVER 5 b.g. Wesaam (USA) 95 – Christening (IRE) (Lahib (USA) 129) – [2004 62: f12f 11.7s 12g May 22] lightly-raced maiden: well held in 2004. *J. Akehurst*

KOMENA 6 b.m. Komaite (USA) – Mena 58 (Blakeney 126) [2004 56: p6g⁵ p6g f6s **45** 6f 6.1g 6.1s⁵ 7m 6g 7m Sep 4] tall, lengthy mare: poor performer: effective at 6f to 1m: acts on fibresand, firm and soft going: tried blinkered: carries head awkwardly: none too genuine. *J. W. Payne*

KOMOTO 3 b.g. Mtoto 134 – Imperial Scholar (IRE) 94 (Royal Academy (USA) 130) **69 d** [2004 p8g* 8m 11.7m 11.9s⁴ 17.2g Sep 27] third foal: half-brother to useful 8.5f and 1¼m (in Sweden) winner Gryngolette (by Linamix): dam, maiden, bred well. fair form when winning maiden at Lingfield in July: well held in handicaps after: should be suited by 1¼m+: visored/blinkered last 2 starts: sold 2,000 gns. *G. A. Butler*

KOMREYEV STAR 2 b.c. (Mar 11) Komaite (USA) – L'Ancressaan 67 (Dalsaan **– p** 125) [2004 6g 6m 6.1v Nov 4] sturdy colt: eighth foal: brother to fairly useful 1m/1¼m winner Komreyev Dancer and half-brother to 6-y-o Dancing Tilly and 7f winner Mr Cospector (by Cosmonaut): dam 2-y-o 6f winner: signs of ability in maidens, not knocked about: type to do better. *R. A. Fahey*

KONG (IRE) 2 b.c. (Feb 19) Sadler's Wells (USA) 132 – Hill of Snow 80 (Reference **81 p** Point 139) [2004 8.1s⁴ 8g³ Oct 12] strong, good-bodied colt: has plenty of scope: power-ful galloper: fifth foal: half-brother to 3 winners, including Irish 7f (Moyglare Stud

Stakes)/1m winner (stayed 1¼m) Preseli (by Caerleon) and 1000 Guineas second Snow-fire (by Machiavellian), 7f winner at 2 yrs, both smart: dam Irish 1¼m winner: better effort in maidens (very green on debut) when third to Luis Melendez at Leicester, hanging left but running on well: will be suited by 1¼m/1½m: type to make a useful 3-y-o, and should win races. *J. L. Dunlop*

KONIGSTIGER (GER)   2 b.c. (Mar 3) Tiger Hill (IRE) 127 – Kittiwake 98 (Barathea (IRE) 127) [2004 7.5d* 8d* Oct 17] second foal: half-brother to useful German 1m/9f performer Kitcat (by Monsun): dam, 1¼m winner, closely related to smart middle-distance stayer Spring and half-sister to Pentire: won maiden at Baden-Baden in September and 10-runner Gran Criterium at Milan (led close home to beat stable-companion Idealist a head) in October: will stay 1¼m: smart prospect. *P. Schiergen, Germany*   **106 p**

KONKER   9 ch.g. Selkirk (USA) 129 – Helens Dreamgirl 95 (Caerleon (USA) 132) [2004 72: 10.1v³ Apr 26] fair handicapper, lightly raced: well below form only Flat run in 2004: usually waited with: sold 6,000 gns. *Mrs M. Reveley*   –

KOODOO   3 gr.g. Fasliyev (USA) 120 – Karsiyaka (IRE) (Kahyasi 130) [2004 –: 8d 7m⁶ 10f 9m 7.9f 9.2d⁵ 10s Oct 30] angular gelding: seemingly modest maiden: left A. Crook after sixth start: barely stays 1¼m: acts on firm and good to soft ground: tried in cheekpieces. *K. A. Ryan*   **53 ?**

KOOL ACCLAIM   3 b.f. Royal Applause 124 – Carrie Kool 69 (Prince Sabo 123) [2004 6m² 6g* 5g Sep 15] fifth foal: half-sister to 3 winners, including 7-y-o Loch Inch and 2000 2-y-o 5f winner Screamin' Georgina (by Muhtarram): dam 2-y-o 5f winner who stayed 7f: fair form: won maiden at Yarmouth in August by ¾ length from Antigua Bay, hanging left: not discredited in handicap at Sandown subsequent outing, not getting clearest of runs after slow start: stays 6f. *S. C. Williams*   **75**

KOOL (IRE)   5 b.g. Danehill Dancer (IRE) 117 – New Rochelle (IRE) 65 (Lafontaine (USA) 117) [2004 7.1d³ 7d 7s⁵ 7m⁵ 7g³ 7m⁵ 7.1m⁴ 7f 7g² 7s³ 7m⁶ 7m² Sep 25] well-made gelding: useful performer: missed 2003: creditable efforts nearly all starts in 2004: effective at 6f to easy 1m: acts on firm going, probably on soft: has worn crossed noseband: consistent: sold 37,000 gns, joined M. Al Kurdi in UAE. *P. F. I. Cole*   **98**

KOOL OVATION   2 b.g. (Apr 19) Royal Applause 124 – Carrie Kool 69 (Prince Sabo 123) [2004 6f 5g³ 6m³ Sep 29] 3,000Y: workmanlike gelding: on weak side at 2 yrs: sixth foal: brother to 3-y-o Kool Acclaim and half-brother to 3 winners, including 7-y-o Loch Inch: dam 2-y-o 5f winner who stayed 7f: fair form in maidens: third at Haydock and Newcastle: not sure to stay much beyond 6f. *A. Dickman*   **73**

KOSTAR   3 ch.g. Komaite (USA) – Black And Amber 45 (Weldnaas (USA) 112) [2004 6m⁴ 6g* 6d 6g⁴ p5.1d² p6g* p6g² Dec 13] second foal: dam lightly-raced maiden: fairly useful performer: won maiden at Salisbury in July and minor event at Wolverhampton in December: ran well final outing: effective at 5f/6f: acts on polytrack. *C. G. Cox*   **89**

KRASIVI'S BOY (USA)   2 b. or br.c. (Apr 1) Swain (IRE) 134 – Krasivi (USA) (Nijinsky (CAN) 138) [2004 p8d 8s² p8g⁴ 8.3g Oct 11] $15,000Y, 15,000 2-y-o: fifth foal: half-brother to 2 minor winners in USA: dam, minor winner in USA, out of smart French performer up to 1¼m/US Grade 1 winner La Koumia: fair maiden: second at Goodwood, beaten only ½m in nursery final start: will stay at least 1¼m. *G. L. Moore*   **71**

KRATAIOS (FR)   4 b.c. Sabrehill (USA) 120 – Loxandra 76 (Last Tycoon 131) [2004 110: 7g* 8d⁴ 8m May 15] big, heavy-topped colt: fifth foal: brother to useful French 7f/1m performer Iridanos and half-brother to 6-y-o Keltos and smart French 1¼m to 12.5f winner Loxias (by Saumarez): dam 1m winner: useful performer: reportedly suffered hairline fracture after good 2½ lengths third to Clodovil in Poule d'Essai des Poulains at Longchamp final start in 2003: won minor event at Longchamp in April before creditable 2¼ lengths fourth to Martillo in Prix du Muguet at Saint-Cloud: bandaged in front, below form when twelfth of 15 behind Russian Rhythm in Lockinge Stakes at Newbury: stays 1m: acts on good to soft ground. *C. Laffon-Parias, France*   **109**

KRISTALCHEN   2 b.f. (Mar 10) Singspiel (IRE) 133 – Crystal Flite (IRE) 76 (Darshaan 133) [2004 7m 8.2g 8m 10v⁴ Oct 20] first foal: dam 1½m winner: modest form in maidens: will be suited by 1½m+: acts on heavy and good to firm ground. *J. G. Given*   **62**

KRISTAL'S DREAM (IRE)   3 b.f. Night Shift (USA) – Kristal's Paradise (IRE) 100 (Bluebird (USA) 125) [2004 77p: 10m³ 10.2m⁵ 10.3g 11.6m² 12m⁵ 12g Aug 11] sturdy, compact filly: has a round action: fairly useful performer: best effort when head second to Feed The Meter in handicap at Windsor: should stay 1½m: raced only on good/good to firm ground: ran as if amiss in tongue tie final start: usually races up with pace. *J. L. Dunlop*   **81**

KRISTENSEN 5 ch.g. Kris S (USA) – Papaha (FR) 103 (Green Desert (USA) 127) **88**
[2004 93: 16d⁵ 18.7d 16.2m⁶ 14m² 16.1s⁵ 16.2g 21g 11.9d³ 17.5d 16g² 18s 16d³ p16.5g⁴
f14g* Dec 7] smallish, sturdy gelding: fairly useful handicapper: won at Southwell
in December: effective at 1¾m to 21f: acts on all-weather, firm and soft going: effective
with or without cheekpieces: usually tracks leaders: consistent. *D. Eddy*

KRISTIANSAND 4 b.g. Halling (USA) 133 – Zonda 100 (Fabulous Dancer (USA) **68**
124) [2004 71: 9.2g 9.2f⁶ 9.2f⁴ 9.2d Aug 17] fair handicapper: stays 1¼m: raced mainly
on good going or firmer: slowly away second/third outings: has made running. *P. Monteith*

KRISTIKHAB (IRE) 2 ch.g. (Feb 21) Intikhab (USA) 135 – Alajyal (IRE) (Kris **69 d**
135) [2004 5s 5d⁵ 6f⁴ 5g² f6g 6.3g 5f 6f⁵ 5s 5.9g 6d 5.1v Nov 4] leggy, quite good-topped
gelding: fair maiden: ran badly after second in claimer at Hamilton: should stay 6f: acts
on firm going: tried in cheekpieces: often slowly away: unreliable. *A. Berry*

KRISTINEAU 6 ch.m. Cadeaux Genereux 131 – Kantikoy (Alzao (USA) 117) [2004 **48**
13.9m⁵ 17.1f 13m⁶ 17.2g 10m Jul 6] lengthy, good-topped mare: poor maiden handicapper: missed 2002/2003: stays 13f: acts on soft and good to firm going: tried in
cheekpieces: tongue tied in 2004. *Mrs Dianne Sayer*

KRISTINOR (FR) 2 ch.g. (Mar 28) Inchinor 119 – Kristina 92 (Kris 135) [2004 7m⁶ **72**
8g 12g Sep 29] big, lengthy gelding: second foal: dam, 2-y-o 1m winner who stayed 1¾m,
out of half-sister to smart French sprinter Derniere Danse and very smart sprinter/miler
Pursuit of Love: much better effort in maidens when sixth at Newmarket: needs to settle
to stay 1m: edgy sort, refused to enter stall second intended outing: gelded after final one.
J. R. Fanshawe

KRISTOFFERSEN 4 ch.g. Kris 135 – Towaahi (IRE) (Caerleon (USA) 132) [2004 **–**
82: p12g p12g Mar 8] fairly useful performer at 3 yrs: well held in 2004, in blinkers final
start: tends to carry head high. *R. M. Stronge*

KRUGERRAND (USA) 5 ch.g. Gulch (USA) – Nasers Pride (USA) (Al Nasr (FR) **94**
126) [2004 92§: p10g 8g 8.3d 8s 8.9m* 8.3f³ 10g⁶ 9.9g 10.3g⁵ 8.3g* 9m⁵ 9g 8d Oct 30]
big, lengthy gelding: fairly useful performer: won handicap at York (for second successive year) in June and minor event at Windsor in August: stays 9f: acts on firm and good
to soft going: tongue tied at 2 yrs: headstrong: sometimes slowly away, markedly so
final outing: held up: none too genuine. *W. J. Musson*

KRULLIND (IRE) 2 b.g. (Apr 29) Rossini (USA) 118 – Jemima Yorke (Be My Guest **59 p**
(USA) 126) [2004 6d 7d⁶ 6d⁶ Nov 5] 21,000Y: close-coupled gelding: half-brother to
several winners abroad, including German 10.5f winner Jugendliebe (by Persian Bold):
dam Irish maiden who stayed 1¼m: modest form in maidens: late headway not knocked
about final start: should do better. *P. W. Chapple-Hyam*

KRUMPET 2 b.f. (Mar 13) Mujahid (USA) 125 – Dame Jude 76 (Dilum (USA) 115) **56**
[2004 7m 7g Aug 13] second foal: half-sister to 3-y-o Bertocelli: dam 2-y-o 5f winner:
green, modest form in maidens at Folkestone. *G. G. Margarson*

KRYNICA (USA) 2 br.f. (May 10) Danzig (USA) – Bionic 105 (Zafonic (USA) 130) **80**
[2004 6m* 6d⁴ 7g Sep 14] neat filly: second foal: dam, 2-y-o 7f winner on only start, out
of smart French performer up to 1½m Bonash: won maiden at Pontefract in June: best
effort when fourth to Abraxas Antelope in minor event at Doncaster, carrying head awk-
wardly/edging right: ran as if amiss final start: should have stayed 7f: stud. *Sir Michael
Stoute*

KRYSSA 3 ch.f. Kris 135 – Alessandra 101 (Generous (IRE) 139) [2004 p6g⁴ p5g* p7g³ **80**
5.1g³ 6g⁵ 7g* 7g³ 8.1g* 8.5f³ 8.3m* 8.1g p10g⁶ Sep 22] smallish, leggy filly: third foal:
dam, 1½m winner, closely related to Park Hill winner Casey and to dam of 4-y-o Avonbridge and 6-y-o Patavellian: fairly useful performer: won maiden at Lingfield in March
and handicaps at Kempton in June, Chepstow in July and Windsor in August: should stay
easy 1¼m: raced only on polytrack and good ground or firmer on turf. *G. L. Moore*

KSCHESSINKA (USA) 3 br.f. Nureyev (USA) 131 – Gran Dama (USA) (Rahy **87**
(USA) 115) [2004 –p: 6m* 6m³ 6d⁶ Jul 19] sturdy filly: fairly useful form, lightly raced:
won maiden at Newbury in June: good third to Mahmoom in handicap at Newmarket next
time: raced only at 6f: acts on good to firm ground: raced freely final outing: sent to USA.
W. J. Haggas

KUDBEME 2 b.f. (Jan 26) Forzando 122 – Umbrian Gold (IRE) 83 (Perugino (USA) **40**
84) [2004 5m 7m⁶ Oct 10] 2,000Y: good-topped filly: first foal: dam 7f winner: poor form
in maidens at York and Newcastle (late headway). *N. Bycroft*

KUMAKAWA 6 ch.g. Dancing Spree (USA) – Maria Cappuccini 70 (Siberian Express – §
(USA) 125) [2004 –§, a52§: p7g f8s⁵ p8g f8g³ p10g p10g f8g² p8g⁶ f8g 8.3d 8g 8d⁵ p9.5d **a55 §**
f8g f7g² p7m p8g Dec 20] tall gelding: modest performer: left E. Wheeler after eleventh
start: stays 9.4f: acts on fibresand, soft and good to firm going: usually wears headgear:
difficult ride: unreliable. *D. K. Ivory*

KUMALA OCEAN (IRE) 2 ch.f. (Apr 14) Blue Ocean (USA) 87 – Kumala (IRE) **54**
(Simply Great (FR) 122) [2004 f7d² 7.1f⁵ 7g 6.9m² 7m f6g⁵ p9.5g Nov 15] €1,100Y,
resold 2,000Y: fourth foal: dam ran once in Ireland: modest maiden: likely to stay 1m:
acts on fibresand and firm going: blinkered sixth start. *P. A. Blockley*

KUMARI (IRE) 3 b.f. Desert Story (IRE) 115 – Glow Tina (IRE) (Glow (USA)) [2004 –
48: f6g Jan 19] close-coupled filly: poor maiden at 2 yrs: well held only outing in 2004.
W. M. Brisbourne

KUNDA (IRE) 3 b.f. Intikhab (USA) 135 – Ustka 60 (Lomond (USA) 128) [2004 96: **95**
7g⁶ 8.5m² 7.1f³ 8.1d 8m 8m Aug 15] rather leggy filly: useful performer: good placed
efforts in Princess Elizabeth Stakes at Epsom (2½ lengths second to Gonfilia) and listed
race at Warwick (4¼ lengths third behind Lucky Spin) in June: stays 8.5f: acts on firm
going: sent to USA. *R. Hannon*

KURINGAI 3 b.g. Royal Applause 124 – Talighta (USA) 62 (Barathea (IRE) 127) **70**
[2004 72: p6g p6g⁴ 5.1g³ 6d 6g 6f 6m 5.1g Jul 30] small, good-bodied gelding: fair
performer: effective at 5f/6f: acts on polytrack, firm and good to soft ground: sometimes
wanders: often races prominently. *B. W. Duke*

KUSSHARRO 3 ch.g. Case Law 113 – Risking 48 (Risk Me (FR) 127) [2004 7g⁵ 6g **?**
Sep 25] well-made gelding: 4 lengths fifth in maiden at Mulheim before well beaten in
similar event at Ripon. *Bruce Hellier, Germany*

KUSTER 8 b.g. Indian Ridge 123 – Ustka 60 (Lomond (USA) 128) [2004 97: 11.9s **95**
11.9m⁶ 10m* 13.9g⁶ Jul 10] good-bodied gelding: unimpressive mover: useful performer: won 4-runner claimer at Windsor in June: stays 1½m: acts on firm and soft going:
usually blinkered: usually held up. *L. M. Cumani*

KUSTOM KIT FOR HER 4 b.f. Overbury (IRE) 116 – Antonias Melody 86 (Rambo –
Dancer (CAN) 107) [2004 –, a54: f7g⁶ f6g f6s f12g f12g² f9.4s³ f8g² f11s² p10g⁴ f8s f8d **a51**
f8f Aug 20] modest maiden: seems to stay easy 1½m: acts on fibresand and firm ground:
tried blinkered/tongue tied. *S. R. Bowring*

KWAHERI 6 b.m. Efisio 120 – Fleeting Affair 98 (Hotfoot 126) [2004 14.1d Aug 12] –
smallish, sturdy mare: lightly-raced maiden. *Mrs P. N. Dutfield*

KWAI BABY (USA) 3 gr.f. Charnwood Forest (IRE) 125 – Roses In The Snow (IRE) –
101 (Be My Guest (USA) 126) [2004 –: 9.9m 9.9g 8.3g 17.2s Oct 19] of little account.
J. J. Bridger

KWAME 2 b.f. (Mar 15) Kingsinger (IRE) 94 – Admire 77 (Last Tycoon 131) [2004 **77**
5m² 5g* 5.1g² 5g 5d² 6g⁵ 6m³ 6g p6g⁵ Oct 13] workmanlike filly: third foal: dam, 2-y-o
1m winner, became temperamental: fair performer: won maiden at Lingfield in June:
some creditable efforts, including in nurseries, after: likely to prove best at 5f/6f: acts on
good to firm and good to soft going: visored last 3 starts: sold 20,000 gns, sent to USA.
Miss E. C. Lavelle

KYALAMI (IRE) 5 b.g. Kylian (USA) – Nikkicola (USA) (Damascus 86) [2004 –: **41**
f16g³ f14g⁴ Jan 8] no form. *M. J. Polglase*

KYBER 3 ch.g. First Trump 118 – Mahbob Dancer (FR) (Groom Dancer (USA) 128) **61**
[2004 13.8m⁵ 8m⁴ 9d³ 12s³ 16.1m 10s⁶ 12d⁴ 13.8s⁵ f12g⁴ Dec 11] €14,000Y: fourth
foal: half-brother to fairly useful 2000 2-y-o 6f winner Hamadeenah (by Alhijaz): dam
unraced: modest maiden: stays 1½m: acts on soft and good to firm ground: usually races
prominently. *R. F. Fisher*

KYLE OF LOCHALSH 4 gr.g. Vettori (IRE) 119 – Shaieef (IRE) 66 (Shareef Dancer **62 d**
(USA) 135) [2004 64: p8g³ p10g 10g 10m 9m⁵ 10.1m⁵ 9.7m 10s⁶ Oct 30] leggy gelding:
modest handicapper, showed little after reappearance: left G. Margarson after seventh
start: stays easy 1¼m: raced on polytrack and good/good to firm ground: tried in
cheekpieces/blinkered: none too consistent. *J. S. Goldie*

KYLKENNY 9 b.g. Kylian (USA) – Fashion Flow (Balidar 133) [2004 92: f12g³ **79**
11.6d 10g 10m⁶ 11.9m⁵ 10m³ 12d⁴ 10m⁴ 9.9g⁴ 11.9g 12f 10g p12g p9.5g f11g* f12g⁵
Dec 28] angular, workmanlike gelding: only fair nowadays: won claimer at Southwell in
December: effective at 1¼m/easy 1½m: acts on fibresand, firm and good to soft going:
usually tongue tied: sometimes wanders. *H. Morrison*

KYTHIA (IRE) 3 b.f. Kahyasi 130 – Another Rainbow (IRE) 72§ (Rainbows For Life **77**
(CAN)) [2004 73: 10.2m⁴ 10m³ 11.9g² 11.9m 12.6g⁶ 12.1m 9.9g Sep 29] small filly: fair
performer: stays 1½m: raced only on good/good to firm going. *H. Morrison*

L

LAABBIJ (USA) 3 ch.c. Shuailaan (USA) 122 – United Kingdom (USA) 93 (Danzig **74**
(USA)) [2004 71p: 8g⁶ 10s 10m⁵ 10m³ 12.1s² Aug 12] sturdy, useful-looking colt: fair
maiden: stays 1½m: acts on soft and good to firm going: blinkered last 2 starts: joined
D. Selvaratnam in UAE. *M. P. Tregoning*

LAAWARIS (USA) 3 b.g. Souvenir Copy (USA) 113 – Seattle Kat (USA) (Seattle **–**
Song (USA) 130) [2004 78p: 10d 9v 11g p9.5g Dec 27] tall, rather leggy, close-coupled
gelding: no form in handicaps in 2004: often slowly away. *J. A. Osborne*

LA BELLA GRANDE (IRE) 2 ch.f. (Feb 6) Giant's Causeway (USA) 132 – La **64**
Belle Otero (USA) 60 (Nureyev (USA) 131) [2004 7d p8g⁴ Nov 13] big, lengthy filly:
third foal: half-sister to fairly useful 2001 2-y-o 7f winner Brown Eyes (by Danehill):
dam, ran once, half-sister to US Grade 3 9f winner Summer Matinee: better effort in
maidens (very green and slowly away on debut) when fourth at Lingfield: should stay
1¼m. *R. Charlton*

LA BELLA ROSA (IRE) 2 b.f. (May 11) Revoque (IRE) 122 – Tempesta Rossa **–**
(IRE) (Persian Heights 129) [2004 5v 6g 6m Jun 13] 3,500Y: lengthy filly: seventh foal:
dam lightly-raced maiden: no form in maidens/seller (visored). *J. S. Wainwright*

LABELLED WITH LOVE 4 ch.g. Zilzal (USA) 137 – Dream Baby (Master Willie **57**
129) [2004 –: 10m² 10f⁵ 8m⁶ p8g p7g⁵ 8d² p8.6g² f7g* f7g* Dec 12] tall gelding: modest
performer: left W. Turner after second start: won 2 banded races at Southwell in December: barely stays 1¼m: acts on all-weather, good to firm and good to soft ground: tongue
tied last 5 outings: sometimes slowly away/carries head awkwardly: free-going sort.
J. R. Boyle

LABRETT 7 b.g. Tragic Role (USA) – Play The Game 70 (Mummy's Game 120) [2004 **90**
92, a89: p8g³ p10g p8g⁵ p8g² f7g³ f8.5g p8g Dec 30] good-topped gelding: fairly useful
handicapper: creditable efforts in 2004 when placed: best at 7f to 9f: acts on all-weather,
firm and soft going: blinkered earlier in career: often tongue tied/in cheekpieces: usually
waited with. *Miss Gay Kelleway*

LA CALERA (GER) 3 ch.f. Big Shuffle (USA) 122 – La Luce (Niniski (USA) 125) **50**
[2004 7.5m³ a7.5g* 7v 8d 7f⁵ 6.9m³ 8s³ 6m 7g 10m⁵ 8.1d 7d⁴ f7g⁴ f7g⁵ p7m Dec 8]
€9,500Y: second foal: dam unraced: fair in Germany at 2 yrs: won maiden at Neuss in
February, then left M. Hofer after fourth start: modest form in Britain, leaving M. Harris
after sixth outing: stays 1m: acts on dirt, fibresand, soft and good to firm going: usually
wears headgear. *G. C. H. Chung*

LA CONCHA (IRE) 3 b.g. Kahyasi 130 – Trojan Crown (IRE) 105 (Trojan Fen 118) **–**
[2004 p8g p12g p10g 10s 14.1s 11.5f Jun 10] little form in maidens/handicaps: visored
final start. *Mrs L. C. Jewell*

LACONIA (IRE) 3 b.f. Orpen (USA) 116 – Mislead (IRE) 77 (Distinctly North (USA) **74**
115) [2004 64: p5g⁴ 5g⁵ 5.1g² 5s⁶ 5.1g² 5.1m⁶ 5.1g² 5m 5f p5.1d Nov 3] big filly: fair
maiden: below form after fifth start: best at 5f: acts on polytrack and good to firm going.
J. S. Moore

LACONICOS (IRE) 2 ch.c. (Jan 31) Foxhound (USA) 103 – Thermopylae 81 (Tenby **73**
125) [2004 5d² 5.1m³ 7f² 7m p6g p7.1g Nov 26] €28,000F: leggy, rather unfurnished
colt: first foal: dam, maiden who should have stayed 1½m, half-sister to very smart 1½m
performer Posidonas: fair maiden: visored, ran poorly fourth start, then left D. Loder:
stays 7f: acts on firm and good to soft going: led to post/slowly away penultimate outing.
J. A. Osborne

LA CORUNA 3 b.f. Deploy 131 – Valencia 79 (Kenmare (FR) 125) [2004 92p: 6v⁴ May **–**
3] neat, attractive filly: won both starts at 2 yrs: well below form only outing in 2004:
stud. *R. Charlton*

LA CUCARACHA 3 b.f. Piccolo 121 – Peggy Spencer 77 (Formidable (USA) 125) **100**
[2004 95+: 5.1g² 6g⁶ 6m³ May 24] good-topped filly: useful performer: good ¾-length
second to Ringmoor Down in listed event at Bath in April: repeatedly short of room when
sixth to So Will I in listed event at Newbury next time: just respectable third to Celtic Mill
in similar race at Windsor final start: stays 6f: raced only on good/good to firm going.
B. W. Hills

LA CYGNE BLANCHE (IRE) 2 gr.f. (Feb 4) Saddlers' Hall (IRE) 126 – Ivory's **46**
Promise 74 (Pursuit of Love 124) [2004 6.1m p7g p6g⁶ p6g Dec 29] lengthy filly: second
foal: dam, 5f winner, ran only at 2 yrs: poor maiden: should stay at least 7f. *Mrs
N. Macauley*

LA DANSEUSE 3 b.f. Groom Dancer (USA) 128 – Alik (FR) 113 (Targowice (USA) **50**
130) [2004 49: p10g⁵ Jan 10] sturdy filly: modest maiden: stays 1¼m: raced only on all-
weather/good to firm going. *G. C. Bravery*

LADEENA (IRE) 2 b. or br.f. (Feb 20) Dubai Millennium 140 – Aqaarid (USA) 116 **80 p**
(Nashwan (USA) 135) [2004 7d² Oct 30] rangy filly: fifth foal: half-sister to fairly useful
2000 2-y-o 1m winner Elmonjed (by Gulch), later winner at 7f in UAE: dam, won Fillies'
Mile and second in 1000 Guineas, from good family: 12/1, 2½ lengths second to Songthrush in maiden at Newmarket, travelling well and first home in main pack: will stay 1m:
should progress and win a race or 2. *J. L. Dunlop*

LADIES KNIGHT 4 b.g. Among Men (USA) 124 – Lady Silk 67 (Prince Sabo 123) **–**
[2004 –, a64: f5g⁶ p5g³ p6g² f5g⁵ p6g p6g⁶ f5g³ p6g f5g⁵ f6g p6g⁴ p5.1g Dec 31] leggy, **a65**
angular gelding: fair performer: effective at 5f/6f: acts on all-weather and good to firm
going: tried visored: sometimes slowly away. *D. Shaw*

LADRUCA 2 b. or br.f. (Apr 26) Dracula (AUS) 121 – Promissory (Caerleon (USA) **57 d**
132) [2004 6m 6g 7m⁵ 7g* 7f p7.1g p7.1g Dec 15] leggy, close-coupled filly: sister to
Italian 5.5f and (at 2 yrs) 7f winner Dracula Gold and half-sister to fairly useful 1m winner Kathinka (by Bin Ajwaad): dam, maiden, out of sister to smart sprinter Jester: modest
performer: won claimer at Salisbury in August by 5 lengths, then left R. Hannon: ran
poorly in nurseries after: likely to stay 1m: acts on good to firm going. *G. G. Margarson*

LADY ALRUNA (IRE) 5 ch.m. Alhaarth (IRE) 126 – In Tranquility (IRE) (Shalford **–**
(IRE) 124§) [2004 61d: f7g Jan 3] maiden: on the downgrade: tried in headgear.
P. T. Midgley

LADY ANN SUMMERS (USA) 2 ch.f. (Feb 13) Two Punch (USA) – Why Walk **80 d**
(USA) (Zilzal (USA) 137) [2004 5f 5g³ 6g⁴ 5g p7g Aug 26] $60,000F, $165,000 2-y-o:
rather leggy filly: second foal: sister to winner in USA: dam ran 3 times in USA: fairly
useful maiden: blinkered/in cheekpieces, ran badly in nurseries last 2 starts: stays 6f: acts
on firm going: sometimes slowly away: sent to USA. *B. J. Meehan*

LADY ARNICA 5 b.m. Ezzoud (IRE) 126 – Brand (Shareef Dancer (USA) 135) [2004 **–**
–: f14g p16g Feb 26] lengthy, angular mare: lightly raced and little form: tried visored.
A. W. Carroll

LADY AT LEISURE (IRE) 4 ch.f. Dolphin Street (FR) 125 – In A Hurry (FR) (In **45**
Fijar (USA) 121) [2004 –: p10g⁶ p8g p10g p10g⁴ p10g* 10v May 10] leggy, quite good-topped
filly: poor performer: won banded race at Lingfield in April, first start after leaving Julian
Poulton: stays 1¼m: acts on polytrack and good to firm going. *M. J. Ryan*

LADY BAHIA (IRE) 3 b.f. Orpen (USA) 116 – Do The Right Thing 71 (Busted 134) **71**
[2004 69: f9.4s p10g⁶ f6s* f5g f5s* Mar 13] big, good-topped filly: has a short, unimpressive action: fair performer: won handicap at Southwell (wandered/flashed tail) in
February and claimer at Wolverhampton in March: effective at 5f to 1m: acts on fibresand
and firm going. *R. P. Elliott*

LADY BLADE (IRE) 3 b.f. Daggers Drawn (USA) 114 – Singhana (IRE) (Mouktar **64**
129) [2004 64: 8f p10d⁴ 12g 10f⁵ 9s p8g p8.6g Oct 19] tall, angular filly: modest maiden:
stays 1¼m: acts on polytrack and firm going: tried blinkered: sold 6,800 gns. *B. Hanbury*

LADY CHEF 2 ch.f. (Apr 24) Double Trigger (IRE) 123 – Dundeelin 46 (Dunbeath **75**
(USA) 127) [2004 5g 6.1g⁵ 7g* 7m³ 8f 8.3d Oct 4] £2,400Y: workmanlike filly: second
foal: dam 2-y-o 5f seller winner: fair performer: won maiden at Lingfield in June: good
third at Goodwood, only form in nurseries after: stays 7f: acts on good to firm ground:
often races prominently. *B. R. Millman*

LADY DAN (IRE) 2 b.f. (Feb 9) Danzero (AUS) – Dubai Lady 78 (Kris 135) [2004 **72**
5v⁴ 5m³ 5m² 7.5g 5g⁶ 6m 5g³ 5g Sep 25] small, strong filly: closely related to smart 1m
(including at 2 yrs)/1¼m winner Ela-Aristokrati (stayed 1½m) and useful 1¾m winner
L'Evangile (stayed 2m), both by Danehill: dam middle-distance maiden: fair maiden:
form only at 5f: acted on heavy and good to firm ground: dead. *M. W. Easterby*

LADY DORIS WATTS 2 b.f. (Mar 26) Emarati (USA) 74 – Wrong Bride (Reprimand **60**
122) [2004 6g 7.1d² 6d 6s⁶ f6g⁵ p6g p6g f5f⁶ Dec 28] leggy filly: fourth foal: half- **a44**
sister to 4-y-o Lucky Leo: dam, ran once, half-sister to 5-y-o Funfair Wane: modest

maiden on turf, poor on all-weather: stays 7f: acts on all-weather and good to soft going. *M. R. Channon*

LADY DOUBLE U   4 b.f. Sheikh Albadou 128 – Bollin Victoria 51 (Jalmood (USA)   –
126) [2004 7g f7g f7g 6s 5m 6m Jun 1] strong, sturdy filly: poor maiden: stays 6f: form only on good to firm going. *T. D. Easterby*

LADY DULCET   4 b.f. Thowra (FR) – Freedom Weekend (USA) (Shahrastani (USA)   –
135) [2004 –: 8.1d Apr 23] of little account. *D. Burchell*

LADY EDGE (IRE)   2 ch.f. (Apr 7) Bold Edge 123 – Lady Sheriff 90 (Taufan (USA)   –
119) [2004 5g Oct 5] quite good-topped filly: fourth foal: dam 5f winner, including at 2 yrs: 50/1, backward and green, tailed off in maiden at Catterick. *M. W. Easterby*

LADY ELLENDUNE   3 b.f. Piccolo 121 – Eileen's Lady 50 (Mtoto 134) [2004 43:   –
f6g Jan 14] smallish filly: maiden: tailed off only start at 3 yrs: tried blinkered/in cheek-pieces. *D. J. S. ffrench Davis*

LADY ERICA   2 b.f. (Apr 22) Komaite (USA) – Zamarra 59 (Clantime 101) [2004   56
f5g² 5s⁵ f5m⁴ p5g³ 5.1s 5g Oct 5] 6,000Y: small filly: fourth foal: half-sister to 2002 2-y-o 5f winner Double Assembly (by Presidium): dam, lightly-raced maiden at 2 yrs, best at 5f: modest maiden: will probably prove best at 5f: acts on fibresand and soft ground: visored (ran badly) final start. *K. R. Burke*

LADY FILLY   2 ch.f. (Apr 7) Atraf 116 – Just Lady 72 (Emarati (USA) 74) [2004 5s*   92
5s* 5s* 5f 5d⁵ 6s⁵ Oct 23] big filly: has a quick, fluent action: fourth living foal: half-sister to 6-y-o Justalord: dam 2-y-o 5f winner: won maiden at Kempton in March and minor events at Thirsk in April and Salisbury in May: ran poorly in listed races last 2 starts (lame on first occasion): will prove best at 5f: acts on soft ground, probably on firm: usually races up with pace. *W. G. M. Turner*

LADY FRANPALM (IRE)   4 b.f. Danehill Dancer (IRE) 117 – Be Nimble (Wattle-   49 ?
field 117) [2004 53: 7g 7s 7m f6f 6d Oct 10] leggy filly: maiden: poor form in 2004. *M. J. Haynes*

LADY GEORGINA   3 gr.f. Linamix (FR) 127 – Georgia Venture 98 (Shirley Heights   88
130) [2004 75: 8d³ 8.2d⁶ 7m* 7m² 7g* 7m⁵ Jul 1] small, angular filly: fairly useful per-former: won minor events at Lingfield in May and Goodwood in June: best effort when 1½ lengths second to Delphie Queen in handicap at Newmarket in between: stays 7f: acts on good to firm and good to soft going: tried tongue tied at 2 yrs: waited with. *J. R. Fanshawe*

LADY HECCLES   5 b.m. Sayaarr (USA) – Rae Un Soleil (Rushmere 92) [2004 p8g   –
Mar 2] first foal: dam no sign of ability: tailed off in bumper, and in maiden at Lingfield. *M. R. Hoad*

LADY HEN   2 b.f. (Apr 16) Efisio 120 – Royale Rose (FR) 75 (Bering 136) [2004 6g   66
6m⁶ 6.1m p7m² Dec 22] 20,000Y: well-made filly: fourth foal: half-sister to 4-y-o Vin du Pays and fairly useful French 9f winner Antioquia (by Singspiel): dam, 1m winner, sister to useful French miler Rouen: fair maiden: left M. Wallace, best effort when second at Lingfield: should stay 1m. *Miss J. Feilden*

LADY HOPEFUL (IRE)   2 b.f. (Apr 30) Lend A Hand 124 – Treble Term 66 (Lion   63
Cavern (USA) 117) [2004 5d⁵ 5m⁴ f7g² 7.1m² 5.1g 6f⁵ 5g⁵ 7g 6d⁴ 5.1v p5.1g⁶ Nov 12] 6,500 2-y-o: good-topped filly: fourth foal: dam, maiden who stayed 6f, out of half-sister to Poule d'Essai des Poulains winner Victory Note: modest maiden: stays easy 7f: acts on fibresand, good to firm and good to soft ground: visored sixth start, blinkered last 3. *R. P. Elliott*

LADY INDIANA (IRE)   2 b.f. (Mar 11) King's Theatre (IRE) 128 – Najeyba 80   –
(Indian Ridge 123) [2004 6g 6m 7g 8.5s Aug 29] €6,000Y: compact filly: first foal: dam 6f winner: no form, slowly away, in maidens/sellers. *J. S. Wainwright*

LADY JEANNIE   7 b.m. Emarati (USA) 74 – Cottonwood 80 (Teenoso (USA) 135)   –
[2004 8.2m 9.7f 9.7g p16g Jul 24] sturdy mare: modest at best: unraced in 2003: little form at 7 yrs. *M. J. Haynes*

LADY JUSTICE   4 b.f. Compton Place 125 – Zinzi (Song 132) [2004 66: 6.1s 5.1g⁴   52
6m p5g 5m⁶ Aug 5] lengthy filly: modest maiden: raced only at 5f/6f: acts on good to firm and good to soft going: tried blinkered. *W. Jarvis*

LADY KARR   3 b.f. Mark of Esteem (IRE) 137 – Percy's Lass 120§ (Blakeney 126)   70 p
[2004 9f 10.1m³ 12s* Nov 2] 16,000Y: sister to fairly useful Irish 9f to 11f winner Love Token and half-sister to useful 1m/1¼m winner Blue Lion (by Lomond): dam 6f (at 2 yrs)

to 11f winner who became temperamental: fair form in maidens: won at Catterick in November by 6 lengths, making running and idling/edging left: stays 1½m: acts on soft and good to firm going: should progress at 4 yrs. *M. Johnston*

LADY KORRIANDA 3 ch.f. Dr Fong (USA) 128 – Prima Verde 81 (Leading Counsel (USA) 122) [2004 61: 6d p7g Oct 31] maiden: showed little in 2004. *Lady Herries* –

LADY LAKOTA (IRE) 2 b.f. (Feb 24) Indian Lodge (IRE) 127 – Milady Lillie (IRE) 65 (Distinctly North (USA) 115) [2004 6g Sep 15] 12,000Y: well-made filly: first foal: dam, 7f winner, out of Irish 1000 Guineas runner-up Millingdale Lillie: 50/1, well held in maiden at Yarmouth. *A. P. Jarvis* –

LADY LAKSHMI 4 ch.f. Bahhare (USA) 122 – Polish Honour (USA) 61 (Danzig Connection (USA)) [2004 52: f12m³ p13g² p10g³ Sep 18] sturdy filly: poor maiden: left R. Guest after second start: should stay 1¾m: acts on all-weather and good to firm going: tongue tied final outing. *M. Madgwick* **48**

LADY LE QUESNE (IRE) 2 ch.f. (Mar 12) Alhaarth (IRE) 126 – Lady Moranbon (USA) (Trempolino (USA) 135) [2004 6m⁶ 5.2m² 6d* 5.1m* 6.5g 7g 8f⁵ Nov 26] 16,000Y: smallish filly: half-sister to several winners, including 3-y-o Diego Cao: dam French 9f/1¼m winner: fair performer: won maiden at Epsom and minor event at Bath in July: sold from A. Balding 35,000 gns, respectable fifth in Grade 3 Miesque Stakes at Hollywood: probably stays 1m: acts on firm and good to soft going: races prominently. *D. E. Hofmans, USA* **78**

LADY LEXIE 3 b.f. Cape Cross (IRE) 129 – Lady of The Land 75 (Wollow 132) [2004 8m⁶ May 22] 15,000Y: angular filly: half-sister to several winners, including 7-y-o Pays d'Amour and fairly useful 5f to 7.6f winner Jawhari (by Lahib): dam 1m winner: 33/1, sixth in maiden at Newmarket, running very green: sold 1,500 gns. *R. Guest* –

LADY LIESEL 4 b.f. Bin Ajwaad (IRE) 119 – Griddle Cake (IRE) 62 (Be My Guest (USA) 126) [2004 54: p8g p6g p8g³ p8g p7g p8g⁴ p8g 9.7f p10g 8d Oct 2] leggy, plain filly: poor maiden: stays 1m: acts on polytrack and firm going. *J. J. Bridger* **43**

LADY LONDRA 2 b.f. (Mar 15) Fumo di Londra (IRE) 108 – Lady Phyl 67 (Northiam (USA)) [2004 6f 6g Aug 9] fifth foal: dam 2-y-o 6f winner, later successful in Holland: better effort in maidens at Windsor when ninth on final start: should stay 7f. *D. K. Ivory* **63**

LADY LUCINDA 3 b.f. Muhtarram (USA) 125 – Lady Phyl 67 (Northiam (USA)) [2004 –: 9.9s 10m Sep 7] big, leggy filly: little form in maidens. *John A. Harris* –

LADY LUISA (IRE) 2 b.f. (Feb 18) Lujain (USA) 119 – Lady of Dreams (IRE) 84 (Prince Rupert (FR) 121) [2004 7m 7m⁵ 7.1g 8.1g 7m p7m p8.6g² p8m⁴ p8.6g f8d Dec 21] €4,700Y: half-sister to 3 winners, including 4-y-o Trance: dam, 1¼m winner, out of half-sister to very smart miler Pennine Walk: modest maiden: second in seller at Wolverhampton: left J. S. Moore after next start: stays 8.6f: acts on polytrack and good to firm going: wore cheekpieces last 4 outings. *Miss A. Stokell* **53**

LADY MCNAIR 4 b.f. Sheikh Albadou 128 – Bonita Bee 50 (King of Spain 121) [2004 86: 11.6d⁴ 10g 10m² 10f⁴ May 31] workmanlike filly: fairly useful handicapper: stays 1¼m: acts on good to soft going. *P. D. Cundell* **82**

LADY MISHA 2 b.f. (Jan 26) Mister Baileys 123 – Hakone (IRE) 78 (Alzao (USA) 117) [2004 5d⁵ 6.1s⁵ 6f 7.5g³ 7d* 8s² 8s⁵ 8s Oct 22] 6,000Y: close-coupled filly: fifth foal: closely related to Irish 1¼m winner Casa Que Canta (by Robellino) and half-sister to 2 winners, including 4-y-o Mysterinch: dam, Irish maiden (stayed 1m), sister to smart 9f to 1½m performer Cicerao: fair performer: won nursery at Newcastle in August: good second there, best effort in similar events after: should stay 1¼m: acts on soft going. *Jedd O'Keeffe* **73**

LADY MO 3 b.f. Young Ern 120 – Just Run (IRE) 45 (Runnett 125) [2004 58§: p6g⁵ p8g³ f8g⁵ f8s* f7g* p7g f7g* f8.5g² 7g³ 7g 8g⁶ 7g* 7.6m² 7f² 7f³ 7d⁵ 7m Sep 9] leggy, good-topped filly: fair performer: won sellers at Southwell (2, left A. Reid after first) in February and Wolverhampton in April and, having left K. Ryan after ninth start, claimer at Epsom in July: barely stays 8.5f: acts on all-weather, firm and good to soft going: tried tongue tied. *G. G. Margarson* **71** **a79**

LADY MYTTON 4 ch.f. Lake Coniston (IRE) 131 – The In-Laws (IRE) 90 (Be My Guest (USA) 126) [2004 75: 8s⁵ 7.2s Sep 18] lengthy filly: showed little in 2004. *A. Bailey* –

LADY NATILDA 4 ch.f. First Trump 118 – Ramajana (USA) (Shadeed (USA) 135) [2004 59: f6s⁴ f6g³ f6s f7g⁶ Feb 6] modest handicapper: stays 6f: acts on fibresand and firm going: tried in headgear. *D. Haydn Jones* **52**

LADY NETBETSPORTS (IRE)   5 b.m. In The Wings 128 – Auntie Maureen (IRE)   **67**
73 (Roi Danzig (USA)) [2004 75, a–: 9.9g 13g³ 14.6m 16.2d² 14d 16.2s Jul 17] leggy   **a–**
mare: fair maiden handicapper: stays 2m: acts on any going: tried visored at 4 yrs: races
up with pace. *B. S. Rothwell*

LADY OF THE LINKS (IRE)   3 b.f. Desert Style (IRE) 121 – Itkan (IRE) (Marju   **–**
(IRE) 127) [2004 53: 5d⁴ 6s 8s⁵ 6m 7.2s f6g Nov 8] good-bodied filly: maiden: little form
in 2004: tried visored/tongue tied. *N. Tinkler*

LADY ORIANDE   3 b.f. Makbul 104 – Lady Roxanne 65 (Cyrano de Bergerac 120)   **54**
[2004 59: p6g⁶ 6d p7g p6g³ Nov 30] modest maiden: may prove best at 5f/6f: acts on
fibresand and good to firm going: sometimes slowly away. *A. M. Balding*

LADY PEACHES   3 ch.f. Bien Bien (USA) 125 – Upper Club (IRE) 59 (Taufan (USA)   **67**
119) [2004 –: 10m 10s³ 10m 11.5g⁴ 11.9m⁵ p9.5g⁶ Dec 17] plain filly: fair maiden:
stays 11.5f: acts on soft and good to firm going: sometimes slowly away/races freely.
D. Mullarkey

LADY PEKAN   5 b.m. Sri Pekan (USA) 117 – Cloudberry 88 (Night Shift (USA))   **69 d**
[2004 69: f6s⁶ p5g³ f5g⁵ f5s⁶ p5g f5g 5g2 5s² 5.3m 5s 5m³ 5.3f⁵ 5m³ 5m 5f 5g p5.1g
f5m⁶ p5.1g p5.1g⁶ Dec 31] smallish, strong mare: fair handicapper: best at 5f: acts on all-
weather, firm and soft going: wears headgear: sometimes carries head high: front runner.
P. S. McEntee

LADY PILOT   2 b.f. (Apr 5) Dansili 127 – Mighty Flyer (IRE) (Mujtahid (USA) 118)   **67**
[2004 7.1m 6g 6g⁶ 7m Oct 1] 21,000F, 40,000Y: workmanlike filly: third foal: half-sister
to French 10.5f winner Reddy Blue (by Unfuwain): dam French 9f winner: fair maiden:
stays 7f: best efforts on good to firm going. *C. E. Brittain*

LADY PISTE (IRE)   3 ch.f. Ali-Royal (IRE) 127 – Alpine Lady (IRE) (Tirol 127) [2004   **58**
67: p7g p6g⁴ p5g² p6g⁵ p7g³ p7g* p7g 7m* 8m⁴ Jun 25] leggy filly: modest performer:
won claimers at Lingfield in March and May (left P. D. Evans): barely stays 1m: acts on
polytrack, good to firm and good to soft going: tried blinkered, usually visored/tongue
tied. *G. G. Margarson*

LADY PREDOMINANT   3 b.f. Primo Dominie 121 – Enlisted (IRE) 83 (Sadler's   **46 d**
Wells (USA) 132) [2004 66d: p10g⁴ p8g⁴ p8g p7g⁶ p7g f8s* 8.2g f8.5m⁵ 8f 8d 6m p9.5d
p12.2g p7.1g Dec 14] sturdy filly: poor performer: won banded race at Southwell in
March: no form after, leaving A. Reid after eighth start: stays 1m: acts on all-weather and
firm going: tried visored/tongue tied. *G. F. Bridgwater*

LADY PROTECTOR   5 b.m. Sri Pekan (USA) 117 – Scared (Royal Academy (USA)   **63**
130) [2004 59, a44: f5g⁴ f5g* f5g f5g³ f5s f5d 5d 5m* 5m* 5m³ 5g³ 5.1m³ 5.1g 5m
Sep 29] leggy mare: modest performer: won banded race at Southwell in January and
handicaps at Newcastle and Lingfield in May: effective at 5f/6f: acts on fibresand, good
to firm and good to soft going: tried visored/blinkered at 4 yrs. *J. Balding*

LADY REDERA (IRE)   3 b.f. Inzar (USA) 112 – Era 70 (Dalsaan 125) [2004 55:   **–**
8.2d 8m 10.2m Jul 22] close-coupled filly: maiden: no form in handicaps in 2004: tried
blinkered. *H. S. Howe*

LADYSTGEORGE   5 b.m. Mind Games 121 – Indiahra 76 (Indian Ridge 123) [2004   **–**
–: f6g Jan 3] little form. *M. Mullineaux*

LADY STRATAGEM   5 gr.m. Mark of Esteem (IRE) 137 – Grey Angel (Kenmare   **48**
(FR) 125) [2004 14.1g 10m 12.1m³ 13.8m 11.9g 9.3m Sep 11] sturdy mare: poor maiden:
stays 1½m: acts on good to firm and good to soft going: none too consistent. *E. W. Tuer*

LADY STRIPES   3 gr.f. Alzao (USA) 117 – Shamaya (IRE) (Doyoun 124) [2004 63:   **52**
p7g p10g⁶ f6g p10g 8.5m⁴ 11.9m³ 9d Aug 28] strong filly: modest maiden: left
M. Wallace after fourth start: stays 1¼m: acts on polytrack and good to firm going.
A. J. Martin, Ireland

LADY SUESANNE (IRE)   2 b.f. (Apr 27) Cape Cross (IRE) 129 – Lady At War   **42**
(Warning 136) [2004 6g f7g 7m 6g Sep 15] €11,000Y: strong filly: third foal: closely
related to 2003 2-y-o 6f winner Seeking Answers (by Shinko Forest) and half-sister to 6f/
7f (latter including at 2 yrs) winner Sir Northerndancer (by Danehill Dancer), both fairly
useful: dam unraced: poor maiden: should stay at least 7f. *C. A. Dwyer*

LADY SUNSET (IRE)   3 b.f. Entrepreneur 123 – Sunset Reigns (IRE) 110 (Taufan   **–**
(USA) 119) [2004 66: 5g 5s 8m 5.9f May 24] good-bodied filly: maiden: little form at 3
yrs: tried blinkered/in cheekpieces. *K. A. Ryan*

LADY'S VIEW (USA)   3 b.f. Distant View (USA) 126 – Karasavina (IRE) (Sadler's   85
Wells (USA) 132) [2004 85p: 7f³ 7m 10.1g 8d⁶ Oct 10] $21,000Y, resold 35,000Y: leggy
filly: third foal: half-sister to winner in USA by Red Ransom: dam unraced sister to Royal
Lodge winner Desert Secret out of half-sister to Seattle Slew and Lomond: fairly useful
performer: won maiden at Leopardstown at 2 yrs: best effort in 2004 when close seventh
in handicap at same course second start, then left J. Oxx in Ireland: stays easy 1m: acts on
good to firm and good to soft going. *D. J. Daly*

LADY TAVERNER   3 b.f. Marju (IRE) 127 – Prompting 76 (Primo Dominie 121)   53 ?
[2004 8.3g 10g 8m⁵ 7m 8m Sep 23] 15,000Y: leggy filly: seventh foal: half-sister to 3
winners, including useful German 6f to 1m performer Sharp Domino (by Sharpo): dam,
2-y-o 5f winner (later winning sprinter in Switzerland), half-sister to useful sprinter Sharp
Prod: seemingly modest maiden: stays 1m: slowly away most outings. *H. J. Cyzer*

LADY TILLY   7 b.m. Puissance 110 – Lady of Itatiba (BEL) (King of Macedon 126)   –
[2004 –: 7.2s Oct 30] workmanlike mare: no longer of any account. *D. A. Nolan*

LADY VEE (IRE)   2 b.f. (May 16) Rossini (USA) 118 – Dama de Noche (Rusticaro   49
(FR) 124) [2004 6d 6g⁵ 8m 6m Oct 10] €1,600Y, resold €4,000Y: leggy filly: half-sister
to 3 winners in Italy: dam Italian 7f (at 2 yrs) and 9f winner: poor maiden: best effort at 6f
on good going: slowly away final outing. *P. D. Niven*

LADYWELL BLAISE (IRE)   7 b.m. Turtle Island (IRE) 123 – Duly Elected (Persian   49 §
Bold 123) [2004 54§: p8g p8g³ p8g⁶ Feb 3] sturdy mare: poor performer: stays easy 1¼m:
acts on all-weather, firm and good to soft going: blinkered once: unreliable. *J. J. Bridger*

LADY WEST   4 b.f. The West (USA) 107 – Just Run (IRE) 45 (Runnett 125) [2004 –:   –
8.3m Jun 28] lengthy filly: no longer of any account. *Dr J. R. J. Naylor*

LADY XANTHIA   3 ch.f. Bien Bien (USA) 125 – Carmosa (USA) 65 (Blushing John   –
(USA) 120) [2004 50: f7g p10g⁴ p13g Apr 29] maiden: little form at 3 yrs: tried blinkered.
I. A. Wood

LAFFAH (USA)   9 b.g. Silver Hawk (USA) 123 – Sakiyah (USA) (Secretariat (USA))   –
[2004 –: 18g Jun 3] heavy-topped gelding: handicapper: showed little both starts since
2001: tried visored/blinkered, often tongue tied. *G. L. Moore*

LAFI (IRE)   5 ch.g. Indian Ridge 123 – Petal Girl 96 (Caerleon (USA) 132) [2004   107
106p: 6m 6m³ 6f* Jun 19] good-topped gelding: useful handicapper: won Wokingham at
Royal Ascot by 1½ lengths from Coconut Penang, quickening to lead final 1f: best at 6f/
7f: acts on firm going: reported in early-July to have suffered an injury. *D. Nicholls*

Wokingham Stakes (Handicap), Royal Ascot—
Lafi lands a massive gamble from two on the stand side, Coconut Penang (nearer rail) and High Reach;
Royal Storm (far side) takes fourth ahead of Dazzling Bay (blaze) and the grey Pic Up Sticks

LA FONTEYNE 3 b.f. Imperial Ballet (IRE) 110 – Baliana 75 (Midyan (USA) 124) **43**
[2004 –: 6v⁵ 8.1d f6g² 7g f6g⁵ 6g 7v³ 7d 7.2s⁴ Oct 30] smallish filly: poor maiden: stays
7f: acts on fibresand and heavy going. *C. B. B. Booth*

LAGGAN BAY (IRE) 4 b.g. Alzao (USA) 117 – Green Lucia 116 (Green Dancer **77**
(USA) 132) [2004 82: 14.1s 12m⁶ 11.9d 14.8d 18s 16s² p16.5g⁵ p12g p16.5g⁵ Dec 3]
small gelding: fluent mover: fair handicapper: left J. Fox after fourth start: stays 16.5f:
acts on polytrack, firm and soft going: sometimes blinkered/visored: usually held up.
J. S. Moore

LAGGAN MINSTREL (IRE) 6 b.g. Mark of Esteem (IRE) 137 – Next Episode **–**
(USA) (Nijinsky (CAN) 138) [2004 –: f8s 7m May 18] tall, close-coupled gelding:
mostly well held since 2002, including in sellers, leaving P. Blockley after reappearance:
tried in cheekpieces/tongue tie. *B. J. Llewellyn*

LAGO DI COMO 7 b.g. Piccolo 121 – Farmer's Pet 90 (Sharrood (USA) 124) [2004 **62**
f11m* p12g May 25] sturdy gelding: modest performer: unraced in 2002/03: won banded
event at Southwell in May: stays 11f: acts on fibresand and firm going: tried blinkered/
visored: tongue tied at 7 yrs: front runner. *Mrs P. Townsley*

LAGO D'ORTA (IRE) 4 ch.g. Bahhare (USA) 122 – Maelalong (IRE) 77 (Maelstrom **107**
Lake 118) [2004 115+: 8g⁶ 9g4 10.3d 9.9g 8f⁶ 8m⁶ 8d 7g 8d Oct 15] close-coupled, quite
good-topped gelding: just useful performer in 2004, best efforts when sixth in handicaps
at Royal Ascot (close up behind Mine in Hunt Cup) and Newbury (to Everest) fifth/sixth
starts: stays 9.3f: acts on any going: edgy sort: often slowly away: sold 61,000 gns, then
gelded. *C. G. Cox*

LAGOSTA (SAF) 4 ch.g. Fort Wood (USA) 117 – Rose Wine 91 (Chilibang 120) **–**
[2004 –: 12m May 15] quite good-topped gelding: little form on Flat. *G. M. Moore*

LA HERMANA 3 ch.f. Hernando (FR) 127 – La Candela (GER) (Alzao (USA) 117 **103**
[2004 8g⁵ 8d⁵ 11g4 10s4 9.9g 8g² 10s² Oct 17] second foal: dam, German 5f (at 2 yrs)
and 7f winner, out of half-sister to high-class German 1½m performer Lomitas: useful
performer: won maiden at Mulheim in 2003: ran well when 1¾ lengths fourth to Amarette
in Preis der Diana at Hamburg third start: well below form in listed race at Salisbury 2
outings later, before good second in similar events at Bremen and Munich: stays 11f:
raced only on good going or softer. *A. Wohler, Germany*

LAHOB 4 ch.g. First Trump 118 – Mystical Song 68 (Mystiko (USA) 124) [2004 61: **51**
12m 14.8g⁵ 12f 14.1m 12.6d p9.5g³ p9.5g f8g Dec 1] small, strong gelding: modest
maiden: left P. Howling after sixth start: stays 1½m: acts on polytrack and good to firm
going: tried in cheekpieces/blinkers: usually front runner: gelded after final outing.
N. B. King

LAIRD DARA MAC 4 b.c. Presidium 124 – Nishara (Nishapour (FR) 125) [2004 –: **–**
f12s Feb 29] sturdy colt: little sign of ability: tried blinkered. *N. Bycroft*

LAKAAM 3 b.f. Danzero (AUS) – Langtry Lady 91 (Pas de Seul 133) [2004 p10g p12g **57**
11.8d³ Apr 1] 1,000F: leggy filly: half-sister to 3 winners, including 8-y-o Nowell House
and 1996 2-y-o 6f winner Sharp Return (by Sharpo), later useful sprinter in Scandinavia:
dam 6f to 9f winner: modest form in maidens, pulling hard last 2 starts. *G. P. Enright*

LAKE CAREZZA (USA) 2 b.c. (Apr 18) Stravinsky (USA) 133 – May Wedding **68 p**
(USA) (French Deputy (USA) 118) [2004 6g⁵ 6d Nov 5] $50,000Y, resold 110,000Y:
smallish, strong colt: first foal: dam, 1m winner in USA, out of close relative to very
smart French 1½m performer Husband: better effort in maidens when strong-finishing
fifth at York: not knocked about again final start: should do better. *J. Noseda*

LAKE CHARLOTTE (USA) 3 b.f. Danzig (USA) – Quinpool (USA) (Alydar **68**
(USA)) [2004 7g³ 7m² 6g³ 5d* 6f⁶ Sep 16] rather leggy, lengthy filly: fourth foal: half-
sister to winner in USA by Capote: dam US 8.5f/9f winner and third in 9f Kentucky Oaks:
fair performer: made all in maiden at Beverley in August: effective at 5f to easy 7f: acts
on firm and good to soft ground: tongue tied final start: free-going sort: sent to Australia.
D. R. Loder

LAKE CHINI (IRE) 2 b.c. (Mar 10) Raise A Grand (IRE) 114 – Where's The Money **79 p**
87 (Lochnager 132) [2004 p7m 7g 6s² Oct 29] €33,000F, 70,000Y: strong, good sort: has
a round action: half-brother to 3 winners, including 4-y-o Vanished and fairly useful 5f
(at 2 yrs) and 7f winner Promised (by Petardia): dam 2-y-o 5f winner: best effort in maidens when staying-on second to Tucker at Newmarket: should stay 7f: likely to progress.
M. A. Jarvis

LAKE DIVA 3 ch.f. Docksider (USA) 124 – Cutpurse Moll 76 (Green Desert (USA) **70**
127) [2004 –: 8g³ 9.2d⁴ 8d p8.6d* p9.5g* p9.5g p9.5g⁶ Dec 14] fair performer: won
minor event (flashed tail) and handicap at Wolverhampton in November: folded tamely
in handicap there final start: stays 9.5f: acts on polytrack, raced only on good/good to soft
going on turf. *J. G. Given*

LAKE EYRE (IRE) 5 b.m. Bluebird (USA) 125 – Pooh Wee 71 (Music Boy 124) **49**
[2004 52: f6g⁵ f6g f6f f6m⁵ f6g⁵ f6g³ f6d² Dec 21] poor maiden: stays 7f: acts on fibresand, good to firm and good to soft going: tried visored. *J. Balding*

LAKE GARDA 3 b.c. Komaite (USA) – Malcesine (IRE) 46 (Auction Ring (USA) **94**
123) [2004 83: 5s⁵ 5d³ 6.1d* 6.1d* 5.6m Sep 8] good-topped colt: fairly useful performer:
won handicap at Chester (by length from Fun To Ride) and minor event at Nottingham
(beat Morse by short head) in May: ran as if amiss in handicap at Doncaster final start:
effective at 5f/6f: acts on soft and good to firm going: usually races prominently: sold
28,000 gns. *B. A. McMahon*

LAKE IMPERIAL (IRE) 3 b.g. Imperial Ballet (IRE) 110 – Lakes of Killarney **–**
(IRE) (Ahonoora 122) [2004 p12.2g Dec 4] 25/1, slowly away and well held in maiden at
Wolverhampton. *Mrs H. Dalton*

LAKELANDS LADY (IRE) 4 ch.f. Woodborough (USA) 112 – Beautyofthepeace **45**
(IRE) (Exactly Sharp (USA) 121) [2004 76d: f6g f5g f5g 6m 5d 5d 6d⁴ p7.1d⁴ p6g Nov
15] close-coupled filly: poor performer: stays 1m: acts on fibresand, soft and good to firm
going: tried blinkered/in cheekpieces. *J. Balding*

LAKE OF DREAMS 5 b.g. Polish Precedent (USA) 131 – Rainbow Lake 113 (Rain- **–**
bow Quest (USA) 134) [2004 10d 10m f14g⁵ Jul 9] little sign of ability. *Dr J. R. J. Naylor*

LAKE 'O' GOLD 5 ch.m. Karinga Bay 116 – Ginka 57 (Petoski 135) [2004 52: 15.8g **–**
Oct 5] workmanlike mare: modest maiden handicapper: well held only start at 5 yrs.
D. W. Thompson

LAKESDALE (IRE) 2 b.f. (Feb 13) Desert Style (IRE) 121 – Option (IRE) 52 (Red **59 d**
Ransom (USA)) [2004 5g 6.1g² 7f² 6.1s 7m⁴ 7m 7m² 7s³ p6g⁶ 6m* 7g 8g 6m f8g p7.1g⁴
p7g p6g Dec 18] 8,000Y: strong filly: first foal: dam, lightly-raced maiden who probably
stayed 1½m, out of half-sister to Oaks second All At Sea: modest performer: trained first
2 starts by M. Channon, third by C. Gray and until after seventh by Mrs C. Dunnett: won
seller at Lingfield in September: below form after: stays 7f: acts on polytrack and firm
ground: sometimes sweating. *Miss D. Mountain*

LAKESIDE GUY (IRE) 3 b.g. Revoque (IRE) 122 – Glen of Imaal (IRE) (Common **59**
Grounds 118) [2004 –: p7g p6g p5g⁴ f5g 5f³ 5g⁵ 5f⁶ 5m² 6g p6g³ p5.1g⁴ p5.1g⁵ p6g⁴
Dec 1] modest maiden: stays 6f: acts on polytrack and firm going: tried tongue tied.
P. S. McEntee

LAKE VERDI (IRE) 5 ch.g. Lake Coniston (IRE) 131 – Shore Lark (USA) (Storm **56**
Bird (CAN) 134) [2004 70d: 6g p6g⁴ 5g³ 5.1m 6m 6f² 6d⁶ 6m f6d Dec 21] quite good-
topped gelding: modest performer: left B. Hanbury after sixth start: effective at 5f to 7f:
acts on polytrack, firm and good to soft going: tongue tied: tried blinkered: sometimes
slowly away. *Miss Gay Kelleway*

LAKE WAKATIPU 2 b.f. (Feb 20) Lake Coniston (IRE) 131 – Lady Broker 54 **54**
(Petorius 117) [2004 6m 6d⁴ 7g³ 8.1s⁶ 7.2s⁶ Oct 12] lengthy filly: sixth foal: half-sister to
fairly useful 6f (including at 2 yrs) and 7.5f winner Lady Boxer (by Komaite): dam 7f
winner: modest maiden: stays 7f: acts on soft going: signs of temperament final start.
M. Mullineaux

LAKOTA BRAVE 10 ch.g. Anshan 119 – Pushkinia (FR) 95 (Pharly (FR) 130) [2004 **70**
72, a98: f8.5g² p10g⁴ f8.5g p10g f8.5s 7s⁶ 8s⁴ 8g 8d² p8.6g⁶ p9.5g p8g³ p10m Dec 22] **a93 d**
leggy, lengthy gelding: fairly useful on all-weather, fair on turf: stays easy 1¼m: acts on
all-weather, firm and soft ground: tried tongue tied: free-going sort. *Mrs Stef Liddiard*

LA LANDONNE 3 b.f. Fraam 114 – Le Pin 59 (Persian Bold 123) [2004 77: 6.1s⁴ **72**
8.1m³ 6m⁶ p7g⁶ 7m 8d p8.6g² Oct 19] fair performer: stays 8.6f: acts on polytrack and
good to firm going: tried visored: has hinted at temperament. *P. M. Phelan*

LAMA ALBARQ (USA) 2 ch.c. (Mar 17) Nureyev (USA) 131 – Nuts In May (USA) **–**
63 (A P Indy (USA) 131) [2004 6f 6m⁶ p7m Oct 6] €420,000Y: first foal: dam, second
at 6f from 4 starts, half-sister to 6-y-o Pleasantly Perfect out of Prix Morny winner
Regal State, herself half-sister to dam of Distant View: signs of only a little ability in
maidens: trained first 2 starts by Saeed bin Suroor: sold 8,000 gns, sent to Kazakhstan.
E. A. L. Dunlop

LA MAGO 4 b.f. Wizard King 122 – Dancing Dancer 45 (Niniski (USA) 125) [2004 – 9.3g Sep 2] third foal: dam, lightly raced on Flat, winning selling hurdler: well held in bumpers, and in maiden at Carlisle. *F. P. Murtagh*

LAMBRIGGAN LAD 2 b.g. (May 4) Mazurek 80 – Alfs Classic (FR) (Sanglamore – (USA) 126) [2004 8g p7g 10v p10g Nov 27] well held in maidens. *Miss Victoria Roberts*

LAMH EILE (IRE) 2 b.f. (Mar 2) Lend A Hand 124 – Mothers Footprints (IRE) **88** (Maelstrom Lake 118) [2004 6d* 7m* 7g³ 6.5m Sep 8] leggy, quite good-topped filly: fourth foal: half-sister to winner in Italy by Goldmark: dam unraced: fairly useful performer: won maiden at Ayr in June and minor event at Catterick in July: good third in minor event at Ascot: possibly amiss final start: stays 7f: races prominently. *T. D. Barron*

LA MOTTA (IRE) 4 b.c. Sesaro (USA) 81 – Cheviot Indian (IRE) 71 (Indian Ridge **70** 123) [2004 74: 6m 6f 5d 5s² 5d 5s² f5g⁵ Nov 9] first foal: dam Irish maiden who stayed 7f: fair maiden: tongue tied, below form at Southwell final start: best at 5f: acts on soft and good to firm going: tried blinkered/in cheekpieces. *S. J. Mahon, Ireland*

LAMPOS (USA) 4 b. or br.g. Southern Halo (USA) – Gone Private (USA) (Private **60** Account (USA)) [2004 61, a51: f12g³ f14g* f16g² f16g⁵ f14g 16s 14.4v p12.2g p16.5g Nov 6] good-topped gelding: modest performer: won banded event at Southwell in January: stays 2m: acts on all-weather, good to firm and good to soft going: tried in headgear: none too consistent. *Miss J. A. Camacho*

LA MUETTE (IRE) 4 b.f. Charnwood Forest (IRE) 125 – Elton Grove (IRE) (Astro- – nef 116) [2004 87?: f16s 12.4v 8d 10.9d Apr 12] well-made filly: no form in 2004. *M. Appleby*

LA MUSIQUE 2 b.c. (Mar 16) Merdon Melody 98 – Daleside Ladybird 66 (Tolomeo – 127) [2004 8m p8g Oct 31] workmanlike colt: slowly away when last in maidens. *P. J. McBride*

LANAS TURN 2 b.f. (Apr 16) Mister Baileys 123 – Lana Turrel (USA) (Trempolino **46** (USA) 135) [2004 5m f7g⁵ 7.5g 6.1s 7m⁴ 7d⁶ 7.5m Sep 15] 1,200Y, resold 800Y: strong filly: fifth foal: half-sister to 7f winner Salsa (by Salse) and 1m winner in Germany by Grand Lodge: dam winner over jumps in France: poor maiden: stays 7f: acts on good to firm going: blinkered (ran respectably) last 2 starts. *T. D. Easterby*

LAND ARMY (IRE) 3 b.f. Desert Style (IRE) 121 – Family At War (USA) 71 (Explo- – dent (USA)) [2004 8.3g May 17] 40,000Y: half-sister to several winners, including smart 5f winner (including at 2 yrs) Flanders (by Common Grounds) and fairly useful 2002 2-y-o 5f/6f winner Magic Myth (by Revoque): dam 2-y-o 5f winner: 100/1, showed nothing in maiden at Windsor. *Miss J. Feilden*

LANDESCENT (IRE) 4 b.g. Grand Lodge (USA) 125 – Traumerei (GER) 70 (Sur- **57** umu (GER)) [2004 75d: p13g f14.8g⁴ p13g⁵ p10g* p10g* f9.4g⁵ 10.2f⁶ May 21] small-ish, sturdy gelding: modest performer: left M. Quinn after third start: won banded race at Lingfield in February and March: effective at 1¼m/easy 1½m: acts on all-weather and soft going: tried blinkered/visored: often runs in snatches. *Miss K. M. George*

LANDING STRIP (IRE) 4 b.g. Dolphin Street (FR) 125 – Funny Cut (IRE) (Sure – Blade (USA) 130) [2004 88: 6g 6s 5.7f⁵ 5.3g 6m 5.3d p6g Oct 7] tall gelding: fairly useful sprinter at 3 yrs: mostly well held in 2004: tried in cheekpieces: sold 7,000 gns. *J. M. P. Eustace*

LANDINIUM (ITY) 5 b.m. Lando (GER) 128 – Hollywood Girl (Cagliostro (GER)) **108** [2004 103: 10g⁴ 10.4s⁴ 12m* 12m³ 10m² 11m* 10g² 10g⁵ Oct 24] leggy mare: useful performer: won minor event at Milan in June (final outing for C. Wall) and listed race at Merano (by neck from Norina) in August: respectable staying-on 6 lengths fifth to Lune d'Or in Premio Lydia Tesio at Rome final start: effective at 1¼m/1½m: acts on firm and soft going: has worn crossed noseband/tongue tie: edgy sort: has wandered/looked less than keen. *V. Valiani, Italy*

LAND 'N STARS 4 b.g. Mtoto 134 – Uncharted Waters 68 (Celestial Storm (USA) **90** 132) [2004 75: 14.4v 16.2m⁴ 20f⁵ 16.1m⁴ 16m* 16g³ 18s⁶ 16s⁵ Oct 29] leggy, close-coupled gelding: fairly useful handicapper: won at Ascot in May and Goodwood (beat Escayola a head) in September: good efforts at Yarmouth and Newmarket (sixth to Contact Dancer in Cesarewitch) next 2 starts: stays 2½m: acts on firm and soft going: usually held up. *Jamie Poulton*

LAND OF FANTASY 5 ch.g. Hernando (FR) 127 – Height of Folly 81 (Shirley **65** Heights 130) [2004 70d: p16g* f16g² p16g³ Feb 26] close-coupled, quite good-topped gelding: fair handicapper: won at Lingfield in January: stays easy 2m: acts on all-weather: tried visored/blinkered. *Lady Herries*

LANDOFHEARTSDESIRE (IRE) 5 b.m. Up And At 'em 109 – Ahonita 90 (Aho-noora 122) [2004 55d: f7g⁶ f7g 8.2m May 25] smallish, good-topped mare: no form in 2004: wears headgear. *J. S. Wainwright*   –

LAND OF NOD (IRE) 3 b.f. Barathea (IRE) 127 – Rafif (USA) 68 (Riverman (USA) 131) [2004 67p: 8.1s⁴ 10m 12m 7s⁵ 8.1g⁶ 8g Sep 22] modest maiden: stays 1m: acts on polytrack and soft going: blinkered/visored last 4 starts, running as if amiss final one: sometimes races freely: sold £4,200. *G. A. Butler*   52

LANDUCCI 3 b.g. Averti (IRE) 117 – Divina Luna 96 (Dowsing (USA) 124) [2004 70p: f8.5g² 8.3s 8.3m⁶ 7s* 7g³ 6m⁴ 7m p7.1d² p6g⁶ Nov 27] big, close-coupled gelding: fair performer: won minor event at Brighton in August: best at 6f/7f: acts on polytrack, soft and good to firm going: tongue tied last 6 starts: sometimes edges left: gelded after final start. *J. W. Hills*   70

LANE MARSHAL 2 gr.g. (Feb 26) Danzig Connection (USA) – Evening Falls 82 (Beveled (USA)) [2004 5v⁶ 5s⁵ 6g 5m 7.5d 5m⁶ 7s⁵ f6s 6d⁵ f8d⁵ Dec 21] close-coupled gelding: poor maiden: left M. Sowersby prior to final outing: stays 1m: acts on fibresand and soft going: blinkered fifth to ninth starts: ungenuine. *J. O'Reilly*   42 §

LANGE BLEU (FR) 5 ch.g. Beyssac (FR) – Dear Blue (FR) (Cyborg (FR)) [2004 12.1g 9g Sep 13] ran 3 times in France for J. Barbe, best effort when runner-up in 12.5f maiden at Argentan only 3-y-o outing: tailed off in maiden/claimer in Britain. *Mrs S. C. Bradburne*   –

LANGFORD 4 ch.g. Compton Place 125 – Sharpening 72 (Sharpo 132) [2004 87: 8m² 8m* 8f 8m 8.3g⁸* 8.1g⁴ 9m 10d 8m⁵ 9g Oct 2] well-made gelding: fairly useful performer: won handicap at Ripon in May and minor event at Hamilton in July: good length fourth to Young Mr Grace in handicap at Haydock: effective at 1m, barely at 11f: acts on firm going: sometimes finds little. *M. H. Tompkins*   93

LANGSTON BOY 2 b.g. (Jan 31) Namid 128 – Blinding Mission (IRE) 70 (Marju (IRE) 127) [2004 5d⁴ 5d² 5v³ 7g p7g² 7g⁴ 8d Oct 14] 50,000Y: big, lengthy gelding: first foal: dam, maiden who should have stayed 1¼m, out of half-sister to smart 7f/1m per-former Hadeer: fair maiden on all-weather, modest on turf: will stay 1m: acts on polytrack and heavy going: sometimes finds little/looks less than keen. *M. L. W. Bell*   62 a74

LANOS (POL) 6 ch.g. Special Power – Lubeka (POL) (Milione (FR) 62) [2004 70: f12g⁵ p12g⁵ 14.4s⁵ Mar 27] angular gelding: just modest handicapper in 2004: left R. Ford after second start: stays easy 15.4f: acts on all-weather, firm and soft going: tried blinkered: tongue tied: slowly away second outing. *Miss S. West*   64

LAPADAR (IRE) 5 b. or br.m. Woodborough (USA) 112 – Indescent Blue 63 (Blue-bird (USA) 125) [2004 –: f16g⁶ f12g⁴ Jan 20] rather leggy mare: no longer of much account. *J. R. Weymes*   –

LAPDANCING 3 ch.f. Pursuit of Love 124 – Petrikov (IRE) (In The Wings 128) [2004 –: 9g 9.2g May 2] no form in maidens/claimer. *Miss L. A. Perratt*   –

LA PEREGRINA 3 b. or br.f. Zafonic (USA) 130 – Flawless 107 (Warning 136) [2004 p7g² p8g⁵ Feb 14] second foal: dam 2-y-o 7f winner who stayed 1m: modest form in maidens at Lingfield: carried head awkwardly on debut: sold 7,000 gns in July, in foal to Medicean, and sent to France. *Sir Mark Prescott*   55

LA PERSIANA 3 gr.f. Daylami (IRE) 138 – La Papagena (Habitat 134) [2004 73p: 8m⁵ 8m² 10.3m⁶ 10f* 10.4f* 10.1s² 10.1g³ Sep 15] angular filly: useful performer: won minor event at Doncaster and handicaps at Windsor and York in June/July: good length second to Posteritas in handicap, better effort in listed races at Yarmouth after: stays 10.4f: acts on firm and soft going: sometimes races freely/idles in front: races prominently: tough. *W. Jarvis*   103

LA PETITE CHINOISE 3 ch.f. Dr Fong (USA) 128 – Susi Wong (IRE) (Selkirk (USA) 129) [2004 68: p7g⁶ p7g 9.1f⁴ 11.1m² 11.5g² 12m⁵ 11.5m⁶ 11m* 12g* 14g³ 9s² a12g* Nov 7] useful performer: won handicap at Lingfield in August (final start for R. Guest), then successful twice at Copenhagen, notably in Dansk Oaks in September, and won listed race at Jagersro (from Gryngolette) in November: stays 1¾m (third in Dansk St Leger): acts on polytrack/dirt, firm and soft ground: blinkered second start: consistent. *L. Kelp, Denmark*   99

LA PROFESSORESSA (IRE) 3 b.f. Cadeaux Genereux 131 – Fellwah (IRE) 66 (Sadler's Wells (USA) 132) [2004 67: 8f⁶ 7.1m 10m 10m⁵ 9s³ 10.2g Sep 3] tall filly: 60 modest maiden handicapper: weakened quickly final start: barely stays 1¼m: acts on firm and soft going: sometimes races freely. *Mrs P. N. Dutfield*

LA PROVIDENCE 2 b.f. (Mar 29) Takhlid (USA) 91 – Petite Danseuse 79 (Aragon 118) [2004 f5s 7.1g p7.1g f6g p8g Nov 20] first foal: dam 5f (at 2 yrs) to 7f winner: of little account. *D. W. Chapman* —

LA PUCE 3 b.f. Danzero (AUS) – Verbena (IRE) (Don't Forget Me 127) [2004 60: f8g⁴ p10g f8.5s* f8.5s* f8.5g⁴ 8f⁶ 7f 7f 7m p7.1g² 8s* p8.6g² p9.5g Dec 4] tall, leggy filly: fair handicapper: won at Wolverhampton in February and March and, having left Gay Kelleway after tenth start, Newmarket (apprentices) in October: stays 8.6f: acts on all-weather, soft and good to firm going: tried in cheekpieces/tongue strap: sometimes slowly away. *M. J. Attwater* **72**

LARA BAY 4 b.f. Polish Precedent (USA) 131 – Way O'Gold (USA) (Slew O' Gold (USA)) [2004 64: 10m p12g 10m Jun 26] close-coupled filly: maiden: showed little in handicaps at 4 yrs, in tongue strap final start. *A. M. Balding* —

LARAD (IRE) 3 br.g. Desert Sun 120 – Glenstal Priory 53 (Glenstal (USA) 118) [2004 53d: p8g³ p10g⁵ p8g p8g p8g⁵ p8g⁵ p10g* p8g³ f9.4g³ 8.1s⁴ 7s⁶ 9.9m* 10.5d 10f⁶ 10.2f 10d⁶ 10m⁵ 10g 10.1d⁴ p9.5d* p8.6g* p10m* p9.5g* Dec 15] good-bodied gelding: modest performer: won banded races at Lingfield and Beverley in spring and Wolverhampton (2) and Lingfield in autumn, and minor event at Wolverhampton in December: stays 1¼m: acts on all-weather, soft and good to firm going: tried in cheekpieces, blinkered in 2004. *J. S. Moore* **52 a63 +**

LARA FALANA 6 b.m. Tagula (IRE) 116 – Victoria Mill 59 (Free State 125) [2004 78, a67: p7g p10g² p10g⁵ 10m⁴ 10f² p10d⁶ 9.7f⁴ p10g* 9g p9.5g p9.5g⁴ p10g Dec 18] smallish, good-topped mare: fair handicapper: won at Lingfield in July: stays 1¼m: acts on polytrack, firm and good to soft going: tried tongue tied/blinkered: effective ridden prominently or held up. *Miss B. Sanders* **72 a68**

LARA'S GIRL 2 b.f. (Apr 20) Tipsy Creek (USA) 115 – Joe's Dancer (Shareef Dancer (USA) 135) [2004 6f 7f⁴ 6m 7m 7g³ 7d³ 8g p8.6g Nov 20] 1,000Y: stocky filly: first foal: dam unraced: modest maiden: stays 7f: acts on good to soft going: none too consistent. *I. A. Wood* **50**

LARGO (IRE) 4 ch.f. Selkirk (USA) 129 – Lady of The Lake 104 (Caerleon (USA) 132) [2004 94: 12g 12g⁵ May 13] close-coupled filly: has a short action: fairly useful handicapper: stays 14.5f: acts on good to firm and good to soft going. *J. L. Dunlop* **90**

LARGS 4 ch.f. Sheikh Albadou 128 – Madam Zando 51 (Forzando 122) [2004 57: f7g f6g³ f7g³ f6g² 6s⁶ f6g³ f7m² p6g f6g f7g⁶ Dec 12] good-bodied filly: modest maiden: stays easy 7f: acts on fibresand and good to firm going, probably on soft: tried in cheekpieces. *J. Balding* **58**

LARKING ABOUT (USA) 4 ch.f. Silver Hawk (USA) 123 – Milly Ha Ha 106 (Dancing Brave (USA) 140) [2004 66: 9.9v 10.2f 12f 14m⁶ 14.1m 16s² 14.1f Sep 2] maiden handicapper: just modest form in 2004: ran as if amiss final start: stays 2m: acts on polytrack, soft and good to firm going: blinkered last 3 outings. *W. J. Musson* **57**

LARK IN THE PARK (IRE) 4 ch.f. Grand Lodge (USA) 125 – Jarrayan 64 (Machiavellian (USA) 123) [2004 57: p8g 8.1d 8m 8m⁵ 8m 9.3m Sep 11] lengthy filly: handicapper, only poor form in 2004: stays 1m: acts on firm going: tried tongue tied: none too consistent. *W. M. Brisbourne* **37**

LARKWING (IRE) 3 b.c. Ela-Mana-Mou 132 – The Dawn Trader (USA) 70 (Naskra (USA) 70) [2004 70p: 10d² 10.3d³ 12m⁶ 12g² 11.9g⁵ 12g 12g Oct 1] leggy, close-coupled colt: fairly useful performer: landed odds in maiden at Newmarket in May: best effort when ¾-length second to Cutting Crew in cantorodds.com Handicap at Goodwood next time: should stay 1¾m: acts on good to firm and good to soft going: has shown signs of temperament. *G. Wragg* **94**

LARKY'S LOB 5 b.g. Lugana Beach 116 – Eucharis 41 (Tickled Pink 114) [2004 –, a65: f6g² f7g* f7g⁴ f7g⁵ f7g³ f6s² f7g⁴ f7s⁶ f6s³ f6m* f6m² f6g² f5g* f6d⁶ 5g² 5d³ p6g⁵ 5d p5.1d Nov 4] leggy, plain gelding: fair on all-weather, modest on turf: won apprentice banded races at Southwell in January and (having left P. Johnson after ninth start) in April, and handicap at Wolverhampton in June: effective at 5f to 7f: acts on all-weather and good to soft going: tried in headgear: front runner. *J. O'Reilly* **52 a73**

LA ROSE 4 b.f. Among Men (USA) 124 – Marie La Rose (FR) (Night Shift (USA)) [2004 42: f12s⁶ Jan 8] small filly: maiden: well held only start in 2004: tried visored. *J. W. Unett* —

LASANGA   5 ch.g. Zamindar (USA) 116 – Shall We Run 59 (Hotfoot 126) [2004 85:   **70**
8.3g 10m 8.3g² p7.1d⁶ Nov 4] fair maiden, lightly raced: best at 1m: acts on good to firm
going: slowly away/raced freely final outing. *Lady Herries*

LASKA (IRE)   3 br.f. Fasliyev (USA) 120 – Dacian (Diesis 133) [2004 6m⁴   **60**
6m⁴ 7.1f Jun 19] leggy filly: second foal: dam no form in 4 starts: modest form in
maidens: tailed off in listed race at Warwick final start. *M. J. Wallace*

LAS RAMBLAS (IRE)   7 b.g. Thatching 131 – Raise A Warning 57 (Warning 136)   –
[2004 58: 5m 5d 6d 6s Oct 30] compact gelding: no longer of much account. *D. A. Nolan*

LASSER LIGHT (IRE)   4 b.g. Inchinor 119 – Light Ray (Rainbow Quest (USA)   –
134) [2004 –: 9.9g 8.3g 11s⁵ 11.9m p8.6d p9.5g Nov 15] tall gelding: mostly well beaten,
including in banded races: tried blinkered. *D. G. Bridgwater*

LASSO   2 ch.f. (Feb 19) Indian Ridge 123 – Rosse 100 (Kris 135) [2004 p6g⁵ p6g Dec   **54 p**
15] first foal: dam, 7f winner (stayed 1m), half-sister to very smart 7f/1m performer
Rebecca Sharp: modest form in maidens at Lingfield and Wolverhampton (not knocked
about): will stay 1m: should improve. *R. Charlton*

LAST APPOINTMENT (USA)   4 b.c. Elusive Quality (USA) – Motion In Limine   **84**
(USA) (Temperence Hill (USA)) [2004 82+: 7g⁵ 7g p7d³ p7g Aug 26] tall colt: fairly
useful performer, lightly raced: best effort in handicaps in 2004 when third at Lingfield in
August, making running/carrying head awkwardly: stays 7f: acts on polytrack and firm
going: sold 7,000 gns. *J. M. P. Eustace*

LAST CHAPTER (IRE)   2 b.g. (Feb 15) Desert Story (IRE) 115 – Dutosky 80 (Dou-   –
lab (USA) 115) [2004 7d p10g Nov 27] stocky gelding: well held in maidens. *John Berry*

LASTING DELIGHT   3 b.f. Robellino (USA) 127 – Last Result (Northern Park   –
(USA) 107) [2004 69: p10g Jan 28] strong, workmanlike filly: soundly beaten only 3-y-o
start. *Sir Mark Prescott*

LASTING IMAGE   2 br.f. (Mar 14) Zilzal (USA) 137 – Minsden's Image 78 (Dancer's   – p
Image (USA)) [2004 6g Sep 15] close-coupled filly: half-sister to several winners,
including fairly useful 6f/7f winner Swift Dispersal (by Shareef Dancer): dam 2m winner:
50/1 and burly, well held in maiden at Yarmouth: likely to do better. *S. C. Williams*

LASTOFTHEWHALLEYS   6 b.m. Noble Patriarch 115 – Pride of Whalley (IRE)   –
61 (Fayruz 116) [2004 f7s Mar 8] strong mare: no longer of any account. *K. W. Hogg, Isle
of Man*

LAST PIONEER (IRE)   2 b.g. (Mar 5) New Frontier (IRE) 110 – Toordillon (IRE)   **65**
69 (Contract Law (USA) 108) [2004 6g 7d 8.3d⁴ 8s⁴ Oct 12] €5,800F: strong gelding:
fourth foal: half-brother to 4-y-o Hit's Only Money: dam Irish 1½m winner: fair maiden:
will stay 1¼m: acts on soft going. *T. P. Tate*

LAST REBEL (IRE)   5 b.g. Danehill (USA) 126 – La Curamalal (IRE) 76 (Rainbow   –
Quest (USA) 134) [2004 p7g⁶ 11.6m Jun 7] fairly useful in Germany for P. Schiergen,
winning maiden at Hoppegarten and minor event at Leipzig at 2 yrs: well beaten in
claimers in 2004: has been blinkered. *R. T. Phillips*

LAST RHAPSODY (IRE)   2 b.f. (Feb 21) Kris 135 – Lobmille (Mill Reef (USA)   **108 p**
141) [2004 8g* Sep 5] €250,000Y: sister to useful 7f winner (including at 2 yrs, also Nell
Gwyn Stakes) Lil's Jessy and half-sister to several winners, including smart French miler
Lone Bid (by Priolo): dam unraced daughter of sister to Highclere: impressive winner of
newcomers race at Longchamp by 6 lengths from Scartara, close up and quickening clear
over 1f out: withdrawn from Prix Marcel Boussac on day of race due to a foot abscess:
joined Godolphin after: not sure to stay much beyond 1m: smart prospect, and should
make her mark in stronger company as 3-y-o. *E. Libaud, France*

LA SYLPHIDE   7 ch.m. Rudimentary (USA) 118 – Primitive Gift 38 (Primitive   **94**
Rising (USA) 133) [2004 84: 10.5d² 11.9s⁵ 10.5d⁶ 10m 10g² 10.5s* 10d³ 12s⁴ Nov 6]
strong, workmanlike mare: fairly useful performer: better than ever at 7 yrs, winning
handicap at Haydock in September by ¾ length from Tartouche: length third to Sundrop
at Newmarket, easily better effort in listed races after: barely stays 1½m: acts on fibresand
and soft going: front runner. *G. M. Moore*

LATALOMNE (USA)   10 ch.g. Zilzal (USA) 137 – Sanctuary (Welsh Pageant 132)   **80**
[2004 ?: 12.3m* 13g⁴ 11.7m 13.9m Sep 5] strong, powerful, round action:
fairly useful handicapper: won ladies event at Ripon in June by 2 lengths from Sualda:
should stay 1¾m: acts on firm and good to soft going: tried visored: high-class chaser at
best, fairly useful nowadays. *N. Wilson*

LATE ARRIVAL   7 b.g. Emperor Jones (USA) 119 – Try Vickers (USA) 72 (Fuzz-   **45**
buster (USA)) [2004 –: 8d 8.3d 7.9f 7.9f f8m² f8m⁶ 9.9m 12s⁴ 10f Sep 16] tall gelding:
poor handicapper: stays 1½m: acts on fibresand, firm and soft going; sometimes blink-
ered/visored. *M. D. Hammond*

LATEEN SAILS   4 ch.g. Elmaamul (USA) 125 – Felucca 94 (Green Desert (USA)   **–**
127) [2004 116: 10d 8f 10.5g⁵ Aug 7] strong, lengthy gelding: has a markedly round
action: smart performer in 2003: tongue tied, well held in pattern races at 4 yrs (gelded
after final outing): stays 10.4f: acts on firm and good to soft going: often makes running.
Saeed bin Suroor

LATE OPPOSITION   3 b.c. Unfuwain (USA) 131 – Hawa (USA) (Woodman (USA)   **76**
126) [2004 63: 10d⁴ 11.6s² 11.6g² 11.6s² 9.9g 10g 10d³ 11.1s* 14.4s² 17.5d² 14g p13g
a10f* Dec 18] good-bodied colt: fair performer: won maiden at Hamilton in August and,
having left E. Dunlop, minor event at Nad Al Sheba in December: effective at 1¼m to
17.5f: acts on dirt and soft going: visored nowadays: tail flasher, and none too reliable.
A. Al Raihe, UAE

LATERAL THINKER (IRE)   2 b.f. (Apr 20) Desert Sun 120 – Miss Margate (IRE)   **71**
60 (Don’t Forget Me 127) [2004 p5g² 5g² 5g³ f5m⁴ 6m* 5.2m 6m⁵ p7d² p7g⁶ 7g 6m⁶
8.3g⁴ p7.1g* p8.6g Dec 1] second foal: half-sister to 4-y-o Best Before: dam, Irish maiden
who stayed 2m, half-sister to smart performer up to 2m Shambo: fair performer: won
nursery at Lingfield in July and seller at Wolverhampton (then left J. Osborne) in October: ran as if amiss final start: should stay 1m: acts on polytrack and good to firm going.
P. D. Evans

LATICE (IRE)   3 ch.f. Inchinor 119 – Laramie (USA) 63 (Gulch (USA)) [2004   **121**
110p: 9.3d* 10.5g* 12d 12m 10m Dec 12]

    Latice kept her unbeaten record and put up a very smart performance,
confidently ridden, to win the Prix de Diane Hermes in June, but she did not go on
from that success. She had won both her starts at two, a newcomers race at Fontainebleau in September and the Group 3 Prix de Conde at Longchamp the
following month, the latter by half a length and two lengths from Voix du Nord and
Prospect Park, form which was to look very good by the time of the Diane. Latice
had also made a satisfactory reappearance in the Prix Vanteaux at Longchamp in
early-May, landing the odds smoothly by a length from Asti, and she started a short-
priced favourite at 18/10 in the Diane at Chantilly. In a seventeen-runner field,
which equalled the largest since 1974, and was the same number as in 1978 and
1983, Latice’s main rivals appeared to be Alexander Goldrun, stepping up to a mile
and a quarter after chasing home Attraction in the Irish One Thousand Guineas,
Torrestrella and Grey Lilas, who had fought out the finish of the Poule d’Essai des
Pouliches, and the Prix Saint-Alary winner Ask For The Moon. Latice was held
up by Christophe Soumillon, a long way off the pace, and was moved wide in the
straight two furlongs out before producing a good turn of foot to catch Millionaia
and win by three quarters of a length, with Grey Lilas another half length away in
third and Alexander Goldrun fourth. Latice gave her trainer Jean-Marie Beguigne
his first classic win, though he was also responsible for the Prix Vermeille winners
Indian Rose and Young Mother, as well as the dual Prix Ganay winner Saint
Andrews.

Prix de Diane Hermes, Chantilly—Latice maintains her unbeaten record;
Millionaia (left), Grey Lilas and Alexander Goldrun (blaze) follow her home

Mr George Strawbridge's "Latice"

Latice wasn't seen out again until the Prix Vermeille, having missed the Prix de la Nonette in August because of the soft ground. The Vermeille at Longchamp was opened to four-year old fillies for the first time. Despite the change, the field looked little stronger than in recent years and Latice again started favourite (the shortest-priced four-year-old was Whortleberry at 13/1). Latice looked set to put herself in contention for the Arc when, ridden more prominently than in the Diane, she was eased into the lead off the home turn, still on the bridle, looking set to win comfortably. However, she weakened markedly inside the last hundred yards, managing only eighth, beaten under two lengths by the winner Sweet Stream, who led home a one, two, three for the four-year-olds. Her trainer reported that 'It's flagrantly obvious she didn't stay. She won't run in the Arc, but will go to the Prix de l'Opera.' However, in the weeks after the Vermeille, connections had a change of heart and Latice took her chance in the Arc. Starting at 40/1 and partnered for the first time by Michael Kinane, she moved short to post but ran better than in the Vermeille without quite reproducing her Diane form, finishing just over four lengths seventh to Bago. Suited by a return to exaggerated waiting tactics, Latice only briefly looked dangerous after weaving her way through the field before keeping on at one pace. The Prix de l'Opera, the third race on Longchamp's Arc card, was won by Alexander Goldrun from Grey Lilas, fourth and third respectively in the Prix de Diane.

Latice gave her sire Inchinor, who died in 2003, his second Group 1 winner after Summoner, a 33/1 winner of the Queen Elizabeth II Stakes in 2001. No better than smart himself, Inchinor was well represented in 2004 by smart performers Satchem and sprinters Cape of Good Hope and Orientor and, as well as Latice, he

564

was also responsible for a couple of other notable three-year-old fillies in Felicity and Secret Melody, both Group 3 winners in Germany. Latice is the first foal of Laramie, a modest maiden who ran twice over seven furlongs in Ireland. Her grandam Light The Lights was a very smart three-year-old in France who was third in the Vermeille and ninth in the Arc. Unlike her granddaughter, though, stamina was the forte of Light The Lights and she was a winner at up to thirteen and a half furlongs, notably in the Prix de Pomone.

		Ahonoora	Lorenzaccio
	Inchinor	(ch 1975)	Helen Nichols
	(ch 1990)	Inchmurrin	Lomond
Latice (IRE)		(b 1985)	On Show
(ch.f. 2001)		Gulch	Mr Prospector
	Laramie (USA)	(b 1984)	Jameela
	(b 1994)	Light The Lights	Shirley Heights
		(b 1985)	Lighted Glory

The leggy, quite good-topped Latice, who has worn a crossed noseband, was entered in the December Sales at Newmarket, but was purchased privately by George Strawbridge before finishing tenth in the Hong Kong Cup at Sha Tin in December, never better than mid-division. She now continues her career in North America and, although she stays a mile and a half, is likely to be campaigned at shorter distances in 2005. She has yet to race on extremes of going. *J-M. Beguigne, France*

LATIF (USA) 3 b.c. Red Ransom (USA) – Awaamir 102 (Green Desert (USA) 127) **71** [2004 82p: 8g 7m⁴ May 22] strong, good-topped colt: fair maiden, lightly raced: should stay at least 1m: tongue tied final start: sold 3,000 gns. *J. H. M. Gosden*

LATIN EXPRESS (IRE) 2 b.c. (Apr 29) Marju (IRE) 127 – Sea Port (Averof 123) **74** [2004 5.7g 6d p6g² p5g² p5.1g⁴ p7g Dec 29] 70,000Y: workmanlike colt: brother to very smart Hong Kong performer up to 1½m Indigenous, 1m winner in Ireland at 2 yrs, and half-brother to several winners: dam once-raced half-sister to high-class stayer Sea Anchor: fair maiden: second at Lingfield: barely stays 7f. *W. R. Muir*

LATIN QUEEN (IRE) 4 b. or br.f. Desert Prince (IRE) 130 – Atlantic Dream (USA) **51** (Muscovite (USA) 105) [2004 61: 12m⁵ 10.9m 10f⁵ 12.1m⁵ 10d Aug 13] IR 20,000Y: half-sister to 2 winners, including smart 6f (including at 2 yrs) winner Storiths (by Double Schwartz), later winner up to 1m in USA: dam Irish 2-y-o 6f winner: modest maiden: left E. Lynam in Ireland prior to reappearance: barely stays 1½m: acts on good to firm and good to soft going: tongue tied once at 2 yrs. *J. D. Frost*

LATIN REVIEW (IRE) 3 ch.f. Titus Livius (FR) 115 – Law Review (IRE) 63 (Case **83 ?** Law 113) [2004 87: 6m p6g Dec 4] strong, deep-girthed filly: fairly useful performer: stiff tasks in handicaps (6 months apart) in 2004: stays 6f: acts on good to firm going, seemingly on polytrack. *A. P. Jarvis*

LAUGH 'N CRY 3 b.f. In The Wings 128 – The Kings Daughter 79 (Indian King **60** (USA) 128) [2004 10g 9g⁵ Jun 18] 15,000Y: half-sister to several winners, including 5-y-o Wicked Uncle and winner up to 11.5f in Italy by Slip Anchor: dam 5f/6f winner: still green, better effort in maidens when fifth at Goodwood. *C. A. Cyzer*

LAURA LEA 4 b.g. Bishop of Cashel 122 – Kirriemuir 51 (Lochnager 132) [2004 **–** f9.4s 7g May 3] showed little in maidens (pulled up lame on debut). *Ronald Thompson*

LAUREL DAWN 6 gr.g. Paris House 123 – Madrina 70 (Waajib 121) [2004 64, a71: **66** f5s f6g 5d 5f 5g* 5m⁵ 5g² 5.7g⁵ 5g 5m⁶ 6m 5d 6g 5.1s 5d 6g³ 6g³ p6m p5.1g Dec 31] leggy, plain gelding: fair handicapper: won apprentice event at Beverley in June: effective at 5f/6f: acts on all-weather, firm and good to soft going. *I. W. McInnes*

LAUREN LOUISE 2 b.f. (Jan 27) Tagula (IRE) 116 – Movie Star (IRE) (Barathea **–** (IRE) 127) [2004 6s f7g 7.9g Sep 1] 7,000Y: leggy, good-topped filly: second foal: dam, well beaten only start, out of half-sister to dam of Lit de Justice, Colonel Collins and Commander Collins: tongue tied, well held in maidens. *N. Tinkler*

LAURENS GIRL (IRE) 3 b.f. Imperial Ballet (IRE) 110 – Tresor Vert (USA) (Storm **61** Cat (USA)) [2004 p8g 9.7m⁶ 10m⁴ Jul 3] IR 2,800F: close-coupled filly: third foal: half-sister to German 9f winner by Kahyasi: dam Italian 5f (at 2 yrs) to 7.5f winner: modest form in maidens/claimer: stays 9.7f: slowly away on debut: raced freely second start. *M. G. Quinlan*

LAURO 4 b.f. Mukaddamah (USA) 125 – Lapu-Lapu 62 (Prince Sabo 123) [2004 82: **84**
f8.5g³ 8.3d² 9.9d⁴ 8d⁴ 8.1g 9.2s* 10s p8.6g⁵ p9.5g⁴ p9.5g Dec 1] strong filly: fairly useful
performer: won claimer at Hamilton in September: best effort when 1¼ lengths second
to Celtic Heroine in handicap there in May: stays easy 9.5f: acts on all-weather, soft and
firm going. *Miss J. A. Camacho*

LAUROLLIE 2 b.f. (Feb 8) Makbul 104 – Madonna Da Rossi 53 (Mtoto 134) [2004 **47**
7m 7g 8.1g 6d p8.6g⁵ p9.5g⁶ Dec 20] 5,000Y, 2,000 2-y-o: half-sister to 6f (seller at 2 yrs)
and 1m winner Impish Lad (by Imp Society): dam placed at 7f: poor maiden: easily best
effort when sixth at Wolverhampton: stays 9.5f. *Dr J. R. J. Naylor*

LA VIE EST BELLE 3 b.f. Makbul 104 – La Belle Vie 73 (Indian King (USA) 128) **71**
[2004 80: p5g⁶ 6.1d 6.1g⁴ 6d 8.3m 6g⁶ 5s* 5m 6.1d⁴ p6m⁵ 5.7g² Oct 10] leggy filly: fair
handicapper: won at Goodwood in August: stays 6.5f: acts on firm and soft going: usually
races prominently: sold 6,500 gns. *B. R. Millman*

LA VIGNA (IRE) 3 ch.g. Woodborough (USA) 112 – Bona Fide (Sharpo 132) [2004 **–**
–: p7g f5g p6g Mar 29] compact gelding: little form. *Mrs Lucinda Featherstone*

LA VIOLA 2 b.f. (Apr 21) Fraam 114 – Arasong 76 (Aragon 118) [2004 6d⁶ 7.1d⁵ **60**
p7.1g³ Nov 13] quite good-topped filly: fourth foal: half-sister to 7f winner (including
at 2 yrs) Annie's Song (by Farfelu): dam 5f winner, including at 2 yrs: modest form in
maidens: stays 7f. *K. R. Burke*

LAVISH TIMES 3 ch.c. Timeless Times (USA) 99 – Lavernock Lady (Don't Forget **56 d**
Me 127) [2004 59§: p5g f5g⁵ f5s³ 5g f5g⁶ 5.1g³ 5g⁶ 5d 5f⁶ 5m⁵ f5m 5.9m p6g Dec 22]
leggy colt: modest performer: well below form last 7 starts: probably best at 5f: acts on
fibresand and firm going: tried in cheekpieces, usually blinkered: ungenuine. *A. Berry*

LAWAAHEB (IRE) 3 b.g. Alhaarth (IRE) 126 – Ajayib (USA) 84 (Riverman (USA) **–**
131) [2004 71: 12g 10g p10g 10.1g p12g Nov 13] rangy gelding: maiden: mostly well
beaten in 2004, leaving J. Dunlop after second start: tried in cheekpieces. *B. R. Johnson*

LAW BREAKER (IRE) 6 ch.g. Case Law 113 – Revelette (Runnett 125) [2004 97: **97**
p6g⁵ p5g⁵ 6g² 6g 6d 6g 5g 6g p6g Oct 31] leggy gelding: useful performer: some
creditable efforts at 6 yrs, short-head second to Steel Blue in handicap at Doncaster in
March: best at 5f/6f: acts on all-weather: soft and good to firm going: tried visored/in
cheekpieces. *J. A. Gilbert*

LAWGIVER (IRE) 3 b.c. Definite Article 121 – Marylou Whitney (USA) (Fappiano **–**
(USA)) [2004 –: 10s 10m May 25] good-topped colt: of little account. *T. J. Fitzgerald*

LAW MAKER 4 b.g. Case Law 113 – Bo' Babbity 75 (Strong Gale 116) [2004 –: f6g **52**
f5g f6g p6g p6g⁶ p6g p6g⁴ p5g² 5m³ 5.1g 5m⁴ 5m³ 5g⁶ 5f² 5m 5m Jul 25] good-topped
gelding: modest maiden: best at 5f: acts on polytrack and firm going: usually blinkered/
visored. *M. A. Buckley*

LAWOOD (IRE) 4 gr.g. Charnwood Forest (IRE) 125 – La Susiane (Persepolis (FR) **82**
127) [2004 85: p8g⁴ f7s 10g* 12s² 10.5m⁴ 10.3g 11.9m Jun 12] good-topped gelding: has
a quick action: fairly useful performer: trained by F. Ennis in Ireland at 3 yrs: won minor
event at Nottingham in March: stays 1½m: acts on polytrack, soft and good to firm going:
tried in blinkers/cheekpieces: sold 29,000 gns, joined C. Mann. *K. A. Ryan*

LAWRENCE OF ARABIA (IRE) 4 b.g. Desert King (IRE) 129 – Cumbres (FR) **61**
(Kahyasi 130) [2004 9g 11.9f⁶ 14.1m⁶ 16s 14.1f 11.8g Oct 12] tall, close-coupled
gelding: shows knee action: modest maiden: missed 2003: dropped away tamely last 3
outings: should stay 2m: acts on firm going: sold 10,500 gns. *Sir Mark Prescott*

LAY DOWN SALLY (IRE) 6 ch.m. General Monash (USA) 107 – Sally Fay (IRE) **43 §**
66 (Fayruz 116) [2004 56§: f6g⁶ p6g Feb 16] sturdy mare: poor performer: stays 7f: acts
on all-weather, firm and good to soft going: tried in cheekpieces: sometimes blinkered:
usually slowly away: sometimes looks less than keen: unreliable. *J. White*

LAYED BACK ROCKY 2 ch.c. (Mar 27) Lake Coniston (IRE) 131 – Madam Taylor **57**
81 (Free State 125) [2004 6m⁶ 7s 7g² 8.1s⁶ 6.1v⁶ p6g Nov 8] workmanlike colt: modest
maiden: stays 7f: acts on heavy going: slowly away final outing. *M. Mullineaux*

LAYMAN (USA) 2 ch.c. (Apr 7) Sunday Silence (USA) – Laiyl (IRE) 85 (Nure- **117**
yev (USA) 131) [2004 7d* 6g* 6s² 7m³ Oct 3]
It is now twelve years since Andre Fabre last won France's most important
two-year-old race of the summer, the Prix Morny at Deauville. Zafonic was his last
winner in 1992, and in the latest season he looked to have one of his best chances of
winning it again with the even-money favourite Layman. Only two runnings of the

Morny have gone by since Zafonic's win without the trainer being represented, and on three occasions since then he has been double-handed. That made Layman the thirteenth member of the stable to line up in the race since Zafonic but, like Zafonic's brother Zamindar in 1996, and one of Zafonic's first-crop sons Xaar a year later, Layman had to settle for second place. There was no disgrace in that, though, as the winner Divine Proportions remained unbeaten in her five starts and was the best French-trained two-year-old of either sex. Layman attempted to make all in the Morny but, on softer ground than he had met previously, he began to wander approaching the final furlong. Edging first towards the rail, he then shifted back towards the centre of the track and, when joined by the filly with around a hundred yards to run, had to give best and was beaten a length and a half.

Like the stable's other runners-up in the race, Layman had earned favouritism for the Morny by winning the Prix de Cabourg over the same course and distance three weeks earlier. He did so impressively, making all and drawing clear for what was officially a five-length success, though it looked more like four. The placed horses, Inhabitant and Salut Thomas, had both already won listed races. Layman came to the Prix Cabourg as the winner of his only start, a newcomers race in July, also at Deauville, the same race, incidentally, which the Fabre stable had won the previous year with Diamond Green, another colt who went on to much better things. Layman's debut had been over seven furlongs and he looked likely to be suited by the return to that trip for his final start in the Prix Jean-Luc Lagardere at Longchamp. He ran another fine race in defeat, beaten just a short neck and a nose by Oratorio and Early March after actually having his head in front in the closing stages before Early March rallied, only for Oratorio to collar them both.

Layman is by Sunday Silence, whose domination of Japan's breeding industry makes even Sadler's Wells' position in Britain and Ireland look unastonishing by comparison. Sunday Silence died in 2002, but in 2004 (when he secured a tenth consecutive sires' championship in Japan) he was as omnipotent as ever. His three-year-olds had a virtual monopoly of Japan's classics, finishing first and second in the One Thousand Guineas, winning both the Two Thousand Guineas and Oaks as well, and filling second to seventh places in the Derby! He was also responsible for the Japan Cup winner Zenno Rob Roy, the top older miler Durandal, the best older filly Admire Groove and the best two-year-old filly Shonan Peintre. Layman is a rare representative of Sunday Silence in Europe, though he is one of several that Sheikh Mohammed has raced here successfully in either his own colours or those of Godolphin, either as a result of sending a mare to the sire (as in Layman's case) or from a purchase at auction. Another in the latest season was the

Prix de Cabourg, Deauville—Layman is a clear-cut winner from Inhabitant and Salut Thomas (rail)

LAY

One Thousand Guineas runner-up Sundrop. Layman is his dam's second foal and the result of her second visit to Sunday Silence after the fairly useful French mile-and-a-quarter winner Silent. Their dam Laiyl ran just twice, making an impressive debut in a mile-and-a-quarter maiden at Ayr on heavy ground. She then started favourite for a listed race over a mile and a half but finished last after racing freely. Laiyl is closely related to the Prix Cleopatre winner Allurement out of the Irish Oaks winner Alydaress. This is an excellent family that has produced Group 1 performers on a regular basis. Two of Alydaress's half-sisters won the Cheveley Park Stakes before making a name for themselves at stud as well, Park Appeal as the dam of Cape Cross and grandam of Diktat, and Desirable as the dam of Shadayid. Another half-sister to Alydaress, the unraced Balistroika, is the dam of Russian Rhythm and the latest season's Royal Lodge winner Perfectperformance.

		Sunday Silence (USA) (b or br 1986)	Halo (b or br 1969)	Hail To Reason
Layman (USA) (ch.c. Apr 7, 2002)				Cosmah
			Wishing Well (b 1975)	Understanding
				Mountain Flower
		Laiyl (IRE) (gr 1996)	Nureyev (b 1977)	Northern Dancer
				Special
			Alydaress (gr 1986)	Alydar
				Balidaress

Layman has now joined Perfectperformance in the Godolphin team for 2005. He fills the eye, being a strong, good-bodied colt and a striking chestnut. Layman is bred to stay at least a mile and a quarter but is a strong-running sort who did not look in need of much further than seven furlongs, at least as a two-year-old. Sunday Silence has got good winners over all kinds of trips in Japan, sprinters

Sheikh Mohammed's "Layman"

included. Layman's three-year-old campaign will no doubt depend upon how he fares in Godolphin's trials in the spring, but he looks the type to train on well. *A. Fabre, France*

LAZZAZ 6 b.g. Muhtarram (USA) 125 – Astern (USA) 67 (Polish Navy (USA)) [2004 62, a68: f11g⁴ f12g³ f12g⁵ f12g³ p13g³ f14g³ f12s p12g² 11.8m 12.3m⁵ 12f⁶ 12m⁴ 10m³ 11.7g⁴ 12.1m² 9.9m⁶ 13.8m⁵ 10s⁵ 16.2m* 12.6d* 12g p16g⁶ p12.2d p16.5g p12.2g Nov 29] fair performer on all-weather, modest on turf: won apprentice handicap and minor event at Warwick in September: stays easy 2m: acts on all-weather, firm and soft going: tried blinkered/in cheekpieces: usually races prominently. *P. W. Hiatt* **59 a66**

LEAGUE OF NATIONS (IRE) 2 b.c. (Jan 22) Indian Danehill (IRE) 124 – Athens Belle (IRE) 101 (Groom Dancer (USA) 128) [2004 6m f6m⁵ 7.1f² Jun 20] €42,000Y: good-bodied colt: seventh foal: half-brother to fairly useful 7f/1m winner Shalimar (by Indian Ridge): dam, 7f (at 2 yrs) and 1¼m winner, closely related to smart performer up to 13f Multicoloured and half-sister to 5-y-o Gamut: fair form in maidens: will stay 1m: ran poorly on fibresand. *P. F. I. Cole* **73**

LEAH'S PRIDE 3 b.f. Atraf 116 – First Play 59 (Primo Dominie 121) [2004 f7s Nov 17] 500 2-y-o: sixth foal: half-sister to winners abroad by Wolfhound and Emarati: dam 6f winner: 50/1, well held in seller at Southwell. *Miss D. A. McHale* **–**

LEAPING BRAVE (IRE) 3 b.g. Indian Rocket 115 – Island Heather (IRE) 77 (Salmon Leap (USA) 131) [2004 77: 7.1s⁴ 8.1g² 7.1m⁴ 8m 7.1m 8.1m Aug 5] rather leggy gelding: fair handicapper: stays 1m: acts on polytrack, soft and good to firm going. *B. R. Millman* **73**

LEARNED LAD (FR) 6 ch.g. Royal Academy (USA) 130 – Blushing Storm (USA) 102 (Blushing Groom (FR) 131) [2004 61, a74: p10g² p10g⁵ p10g p8g 10f 9g 9g 9g 8g 8g Sep 22] big gelding: fair handicapper: no form after third start: barely stays 1½m: acts on polytrack, firm and good to soft going: tried blinkered: sold 3,000 gns. *Jamie Poulton* **73 d**

LEARN THE LINGO 8 b.g. Teenoso (USA) 135 – Charlotte Gray (Rolfe (USA) 77) [2004 f9.4g Mar 27] little sign of ability in bumpers/over hurdles: 66/1 and wearing cheekpieces/tongue tie, tailed off in maiden at Wolverhampton. *Mrs H. Dalton* **–**

LEBENSTANZ 4 b. or br.f. Singspiel (IRE) 133 – Reamur 68 (Top Ville 129) [2004 p8g⁶ 9.9g⁶ 10m⁶ 12.2g⁶ 16.1d 14.1m 13.5d² 9.5v Dec 26] leggy filly: seventh foal: closely related to smart 1¼m to 2¼m winner Boreas (by In The Wings) and half-sister to French 1996 2-y-o 6f to 9f winner Redeem (by Doyoun): dam maiden who stayed 1½m: fair maiden: left L. Cumani after sixth start: should stay at least 1¾m. *D. de Watrigant, France* **66**

LE CHIFFRE (IRE) 2 br.c. (May 6) Celtic Swing 138 – Implicit View 63 (Persian Bold 123) [2004 7m³ Oct 10] €40,000Y: seventh foal: half-brother to winners in Italy by Brief Truce and Bigstone: dam, Irish maiden, sister to useful 1m performer Arpero: 7/1, 9¾ lengths third to Real Quality in maiden at Newcastle, staying on from rear: should improve. *D. R. Loder* **71 p**

LE CORVEE (IRE) 2 b.c. (Mar 5) Rossini (USA) 118 – Elupa (IRE) 98 (Mtoto 134) [2004 7g* 8.2g³ 7m⁴ p8.6g² Oct 9] €16,000Y, 27,000 2-y-o: compact colt: fifth foal: half-brother to Irish 1½m winner Ishkasullus (by Persian Bold): dam, Irish 1½m and 2m winner, half-sister to grandam of Soviet Song: fairly useful performer: won maiden at Doncaster in July: creditable efforts in minor events, head second to Watchmyeyes at Wolverhampton: will probably stay 1¼m. *A. King* **90**

LEFONIC 2 ch.c. (Jan 30) Zafonic (USA) 130 – La Adrada (Arazi (USA) 135) [2004 p10g p9.5g Dec 20] tenth in maidens at Lingfield (slowly away) and Wolverhampton. *G. C. H. Chung* **53 ?**

LEGACY (JPN) 4 b.g. Carnegie (IRE) 129 – Idraak (Kris 135) [2004 105: 9f a8f 8f 8.2v Nov 4] sturdy ex-Irish gelding: useful at best: won maiden at Listowel in 2002 and handicap at Gowran in 2003: well beaten in 2004 (first 2 starts at Nad Al Sheba), leaving J. Oxx after third outing. *T. T. Clement*

LEGAL APPROACH 5 b.h. Zafonic (USA) 130 – Legaya 94 (Shirley Heights 130) [2004 12.3d⁴ 12.1d May 14] lengthy, good sort: smart at 3 yrs: missed following season: well below form in 2004: sold 1,500 gns, joined R. Bouresly in UAE. *M. Johnston* **–**

LEGAL BELLE 2 ch.f. (Mar 17) Superpower 113 – Legal Sound 85 (Legal Eagle 126) [2004 6d⁴ Nov 5] half-sister to 3 winners, including 8-y-o Zucchero: dam 6f winner: 50/1, fourth to Westland in maiden at Yarmouth, keeping on: should improve. *J. L. Spearing* **58 p**

Gallagher Equine Ltd's "Leitrim House"

LEGALIS (USA) 6 ch.g. Gone West (USA) – Loyalize (USA) 105 (Nureyev (USA) – 131) [2004 –, a62: f6g³ f6f² p6g f6g³ f7g* f7s³ f7s⁶ f6s⁴ f7g² Mar 22] modest performer: **a61** won seller at Southwell in February: stays easy 7f: acts on dirt, fibresand and good to soft going: wears cheekpieces/blinkers: sold 5,500 gns. *K. A. Ryan*

LEGALITY 4 b.f. Polar Falcon (USA) 126 – Lady Barrister (Law Society (USA) 130) **45** [2004 63?: p10g 10.1m⁶ 10g f11g p8.6g Nov 15] lengthy filly: poor performer: probably best at 1m: acts on all-weather and good to firm going: tried tongue tied/visored/in cheek-pieces. *Julian Poulton*

LEGALLY FAST (USA) 2 b.c. (Apr 29) Deputy Minister (CAN) – Earthly Angel – (USA) (Crafty Prospector (USA)) [2004 8d 8g Oct 10] useful-looking colt: first foal: dam unraced sister to US Grade 2 11f winner Mr Bluebird: well held in maidens at Newmarket and Bath. *P. F. I. Cole*

LEGAL SET (IRE) 8 gr.g. Second Set (IRE) 127 – Tiffany's Case (IRE) 65 (Thatch- **68** ing 131) [2004 74: p6g⁴ p7g p6g⁵ p6g p7g² 6g 7.2m 7.2f 6g 5m 6m⁴ 6g² 6g* 6m⁴ 6g **a63** 6m² 6g⁴ 6f 6g 6m² 7m 6d⁴ 6s⁵ 6g 6f 7g² 8g⁴ 7.5m 10f 8m⁵ 7v² p6g⁵ p7g p7g p7.1g p6g³ Dec 30] rather leggy, close-coupled gelding: fair on turf, modest on all-weather: left W. Musson after fifth start: won handicap at Hamilton in June: effective at 6f to easy 1m: acts on polytrack and any turf going: tried visored, usually tongue tied: tough. *Miss A. Stokell*

LEGEND OF DANCE 2 b.f. (Jan 23) Dansili 127 – Hard Task 82 (Formidable (USA) **52 ?** 125) [2004 7g 8m p8g Sep 22] 14,000Y: sixth foal: half-sister to 3 winners, including useful 1m/9f winner Gryffindor (by Marju) and 4-y-o Complication: dam, 1½m winner, half-sister to smart middle-distance stayer Midnight Legend: modest form at best in maidens. *B. J. Meehan*

LEGION OF HONOUR (IRE) 5 b.h. Danehill (USA) 126 – Total Chic (USA) (Far – North (CAN) 120) [2004 –: 8f f12m 10.9m Sep 6] leggy horse: no longer of any account. *Miss S. J. Wilton*

LEG SPINNER (IRE) 3 b.g. Intikhab (USA) 135 – Road Harbour (USA) (Rodrigo **88 +** de Triano (USA) 130) [2004 8m³ 9.3f³ 11.7f* 14m 11.8m* 14.4m* Sep 4] 25,000Y: tall gelding: first foal: dam unraced daughter of US Grade 2 11f winner Revasser: fairly useful performer: won maiden at Bath in June, minor event at Leicester (idled) in August and handicap at Kempton (beat Red Damson a head) in September: stays 14.4f: sometimes edges left: sold 60,000 gns. *M. R. Channon*

LEICESTER SQUARE (IRE) 3 ch.c. Gone West (USA) – Stage Manner 104 (In **107** The Wings 128) [2004 106: 8m² 10m Jun 17] leggy colt: useful performer: better effort in listed races at 3 yrs when neck second to Tahreeb at Kempton: stays 1m: raced only on good going or firmer: tongue tied in 2004: carries head awkwardly: left Godolphin. *Saeed bin Suroor*

LEIGHTON BUZZARD 2 b.g. (Mar 20) Cyrano de Bergerac 120 – Winsome Woos- **56 p** ter 71 (Primo Dominie 121) [2004 6.1d 5.1g p6g p5.1g⁴ Nov 27] compact gelding: second living foal: dam 5f (at 2 yrs) to 7f winner: modest form in maidens, not knocked about when fourth at Wolverhampton: should stay 7f: probably capable of better. *P. W. Chapple-Hyam*

LEIGHTON (IRE) 4 b.g. Desert Story (IRE) 115 – Lady Fern (Old Vic 136) [2004 **80** 92: 10.5s 10g⁵ 10f⁴ 10.1v 9.2g² 10f 11.8m³ 12.6g 12g p10g p13g Dec 29] tall gelding: fairly useful performer: left J. Bethell after fifth start: stays 1½m: acts on firm going, shaped quite well both starts on polytrack: tried tongue tied/in cheekpieces: none too genuine. *R. M. Stronge*

LEITRIM HOUSE 3 ch.c. Cadeaux Genereux 131 – Lonely Heart 101 (Midyan **114** (USA) 124) [2004 92: p8g* 7m* 8m⁴ 7f Jun 16] quite attractive colt: smart performer: won listed race at Lingfield (beat Milk It Mick 1¼ lengths) in April and Rock of Gibraltar EBF Tetrarch Stakes at the Curragh (made all, beat Grand Reward comfortably by 3½ lengths) in May: creditable 3 lengths fourth to Bachelor Duke in Irish 2000 Guineas at the Curragh next time, then well below form in Jersey Stakes at Royal Ascot: stays 1m: acts on polytrack, raced only on good going or firmer on turf: has worn crossed noseband. *B. J. Meehan*

LEITRIM ROCK (IRE) 4 b.g. Baratheea (IRE) 127 – Kilshanny 70 (Groom Dancer **32 §** (USA) 128) [2004 59§: 10.9d 8f 10f⁴ 8.1g⁶ 8m Aug 4] quite good-topped gelding: poor performer: stays 1¼m: acts on all-weather, soft and good to firm going: tried blinkered/in cheekpieces: virtually refused to race on reappearance, slowly away all other outings at 4 yrs: ungenuine. *A. G. Newcombe*

LEKKA DING (IRE) 2 b. or br.f. (Mar 4) Raise A Grand (IRE) 114 – Non Dimenticar **60 p** Me (IRE) 63 (Don't Forget Me 127) [2004 p7g 7s Oct 22] 16,000Y: tall, unfurnished filly: fifth foal: half-sister to several winners, including useful 1999 2-y-o 5f/6f winner Master Fay (by Fayruz), later successful at 7f in Hong Kong, and 6-y-o Zarin: dam 5f winner who stayed 7f: better effort in maidens when eighth at Doncaster final start, again not knocked about: should do better. *C. F. Wall*

LEMARATE (USA) 7 b.g. Gulch (USA) – Sayyedati 122 (Shadeed (USA) 135) [2004 **40** –: f7g³ f6g³ f8g f7g f8g⁵ Feb 15] quite attractive gelding: poor maiden: effective at 6f to 8.5f: acts on fibresand, soft and good to firm going: often blinkered. *D. W. Chapman*

LE MERIDIEN (IRE) 6 ch.m. Magical Wonder (USA) 125 – Dutch Queen (Aho- **58** noora) [2004 66: 5m⁵ 5g 5d 5.5g 5g⁶ 5d⁵ 6m* 5m 6f³ 6d Aug 15] robust mare: modest handicapper: won at Thirsk in July: effective at 5f to 7f: acts on firm and soft going: tried tongue tied, often wears visor/cheekpieces. *J. S. Wainwright*

LENNEL 6 b.g. Presidium 124 – Ladykirk 78 (Slip Anchor 136) [2004 74: 10.9d⁵ 12s **76** 9.2g⁴ 10d 10f 12.3g⁴ 10.3g 10.5d⁶ 10.5s⁴ 10g* 10.1m³ 11.9f² 10.5g³ 12.3s³ 12g 10d⁵ 13.1s⁶ 12g² f12g⁵ Dec 16] leggy, close-coupled gelding: fair handicapper: won at Ayr in July: stays 1½m: acts on any going: tried in cheekpieces/visor, usually blinkered: often slowly away: held up. *A. Bailey*

LENWADE 3 gr.f. Environment Friend 128 – Branitska (Mummy's Pet 125) [2004 **54** 53: 10d 10g p10g³ p10g 8.5g 8m 8f⁴ 10.1g⁵ 10m² 9.7f² 10.1g* 10m³ 10d² 10.1d² Oct **a44** 16] leggy filly: modest performer: won seller at Yarmouth in September: stays 1¼m: acts on good to firm and good to soft going: tried blinkered: usually waited with. *G. G. Margarson*

LEOBALLERO 4 ch.g. Lion Cavern (USA) 117 – Ball Gown 98 (Jalmood (USA) **96** 126) [2004 78: 8m⁵ 7m³ 7m⁵ 8.3g⁴ 10m 7g² 8d Oct 15] tall gelding: useful handicapper: best effort when length second to Wizard of Noz at Newmarket in October, wandering: effective at 7f/1m: acts on polytrack and good to firm going: usually tongue tied (reportedly had breathing problem final outing): sometimes carries head high: held up. *D. J. Daly*

LEONALTO (IRE) 2 ch.g. (Mar 22) Raise A Grand (IRE) 114 – Chrismas Carol (IRE) **55** 72 (Common Grounds 118) [2004 5d 5d⁵ 5.3m³ 5.1g⁶ 5f⁵ 5.1m Aug 10] neat gelding: modest maiden: should stay 6f: blinkered last 4 starts (best effort on first occasion): signs of temperament. *B. J. Meehan*

LEONORA TRUCE (IRE) 5 b.m. Brief Truce (USA) 126 – Eleonora d'Arborea 78 **–** (Prince Sabo 123) [2004 –, a53: f8.5g f6g f7s Feb 17] rather leggy mare: no form at 5 yrs: tried visored/blinkered. *R. P. Elliott*

LEOPARD CREEK 3 ch.f. Weldnaas (USA) 112 – Indigo 86 (Primo Dominie 121) **59 d** [2004 60p: 6g 6.1s 5f² 6m 5d² 5g 5g 7g 5.9m f5g⁵ Aug 19] lengthy filly: modest maiden: will prove best at 5f/6f: acts on firm and good to soft going: tried in cheekpieces/visor: often slowly away: probably ungenuine: sold 17,000 gns. *Mrs J. R. Ramsden*

LEOPARD SPOT (IRE) 6 b.g. Sadler's Wells (USA) 132 – Savoureuse Lady 111 **–** (Caerleon (USA) 132) [2004 14g 17.1d 13d Aug 23] close-coupled gelding: maiden: useful at best for A. O'Brien in Ireland at 2/3 yrs: lightly raced and little form since: tried blinkered/tongue tied/in cheekpieces. *I. Semple*

LEOPHIN DANCER (USA) 6 b.g. Green Dancer (USA) 132 – Happy Gal (FR) **47** (Habitat 134) [2004 47: f12g⁶ f12g f12g p12g* p12g² p12g² p13g³ 11.9g⁴ May 4] tall, leggy gelding: poor performer: won banded event at Lingfield in April: stays 2m: acts on all-weather, firm and good to soft going: often tongue tied at 4 yrs: free-going sort: sometimes finds little. *P. W. Hiatt*

LEO'S LUCKY STAR (USA) 2 b.c. (Feb 28) Forestry (USA) 121 – Leo's Lucky **98** Lady (USA) (Seattle Slew (USA)) [2004 6f* 6m* 7.1d 7f Sep 10] $200,000Y: rangy colt: has scope: half-brother to several winners, including useful 7f (at 2 yrs) and 1¼m winner Leo's Luckyman (by Woodman): dam, winner in USA up to 6f (including at 2 yrs), out of 1000 Guineas second Konafa from family of Awaasif, Hector Protector and Bosra Sham: useful performer: long odds on, made all in maiden at Ayr in May and minor event at Pontefract in June in good style: last in Solario Stakes at Sandown and Champagne Stakes at Doncaster: should stay at least 7f: acts on firm going. *M. Johnston*

LEPORELLO (IRE) 4 b.c. Danehill (USA) 126 – Why So Silent (Mill Reef (USA) **116** 141) [2004 118p: 10.3d³ 8.5m Jun 5] sturdy colt: has a moderate, quick action: smart performer: won 6 races in 2003: creditable 3 lengths third to Bandari in listed event at Chester on reappearance: below form in Diomed Stakes at Epsom final start (injured): stays 10.5f: acts on good to firm and good to soft going: travels strongly and has a fine turn of foot: genuine: stays in training. *P. W. Harris*

LERIDA 2 ch.g. (Apr 18) Groom Dancer (USA) 128 – Catalonia (IRE) 76 (Catrail **–** (USA) 123) [2004 5g⁶ Apr 26] 3,000Y: close-coupled gelding: first foal: dam, 7f winner, half-sister to smart performer up to 1½m The Glow Worm: last in maiden at Hamilton, slowly away. *T. D. Barron*

LES ARCS (USA) 4 br.g. Arch (USA) 127 – La Sarto (USA) (Cormorant (USA)) **85** [2004 98: 8v 10.3g 9.9g² 8.3d* 8.5g³ 10.3g⁶ 11.9d 8f⁶ 8.3d 7.1d³ p10g p8.6g* Dec 6] tall, quite good-topped gelding: fairly useful performer: won minor event at Hamilton in June and handicap at Wolverhampton in December: effective at 7f to 1¼m: acts on polytrack, good to firm and good to soft ground: tried in cheekpieces, tongue tied last 3 starts: free-going sort: waited with: none too consistent. *R. C. Guest*

L'ESCAPADE (IRE) 2 ch.c. (May 23) Grand Lodge (USA) 125 – Brief Escapade **78** (IRE) 95 (Brief Truce (USA) 126) [2004 7m³ 7.6g⁵ 7m⁴ 8g³ Sep 20] rather leggy colt: has a quick action: third foal: dam, 1m winner, half-sister to high-class 7f to 9f performer Indian Lodge and very smart French middle-distance performer Sarhoob: fair maiden: stays 1m: acts on good to firm going. *A. M. Balding*

LESLINGTAYLOR (IRE) 2 b.g. (Apr 2) Orpen (USA) 116 – Rite of Spring 86 **72** (Niniski (USA) 125) [2004 5d⁵ 6g³ 6m* 7s⁵ 7s Nov 6] €8,000F, €6,000Y: good-topped gelding: second foal: brother to Irish 6f winner Artistic Belle: dam 1½m winner: fair performer: won maiden at Catterick in September: creditable fifth there, better effort in nurseries after: stays 7f: acts on soft and good to firm going. *J. J. Quinn*

L'ETANG BLEU (FR) 6 gr.g. Graveron (FR) – Strawberry Jam (FR) (Fill My Hopes **–** (FR)) [2004 p13g Mar 2] ran once at 2 yrs in France for J. Bertran de Balanda: wearing cheekpieces/tongue strap, well held only start on Flat since. *P. Butler*

LE TISS (IRE) 3 b.g. Croco Rouge (IRE) 126 – Manarah 76 (Marju (IRE) 127) [2004 **95** 81: 9s⁴ 11m 12g² 14.1m* 12m⁴ 12g 13.9s Aug 19] tall, quite good-topped gelding: fairly useful handicapper: won at Salisbury in June: finished strongly when close fourth to Admiral in King George V Handicap at Royal Ascot later in month: found little next time, tailed off final start: gelded after: stays 1¾m: acts on good to firm going, probably on soft. *M. R. Channon*

LET IT BE 3 ch.f. Entrepreneur 123 – Noble Dane (IRE) 79 (Danehill (USA) 126) **57** [2004 –: 10d² 10s⁵ 12.1m 10f⁵ 12m* 12m* 12m⁵ 14.1g² 12g 16.1m⁵ Sep 29] compact filly: modest handicapper: won at Pontefract (seller) in June and Catterick (apprentice race) in July: stays 2m: acts on firm and soft going: held up. *K. G. Reveley*

LET ME TRY AGAIN (IRE) 4 b.g. Sadler's Wells (USA) 132 – Dathiyna (IRE) **102** (Kris 135) [2004 110: 12g 16.2s⁴ Apr 28] good-bodied gelding: smart performer at 3 yrs: much better effort in 2004 when eighth to Dubai Success in John Porter Stakes at Newbury: reported in late-May to have suffered a setback: stays 13.3f: acts on polytrack and good to firm going: visored twice at 3 yrs: has worn crossed noseband: tends to sweat/get on edge. *T. G. Mills*

LETS GET IT ON (IRE) 3 b.f. Perugino (USA) 84 – Lets Clic Together (IRE) 90 **82** (Don't Forget Me 127) [2004 80: 7g 5s 6d⁵ 6d² 6m 6m 6g⁵ 6g³ 5g 5s⁶ Nov 1] compact filly: fairly useful performer: below form last 3 starts: best at 5f/6f: acts on good to firm and good to soft going: sometimes slowly away. *J. J. Quinn*

LET SLIP 2 b.f. (Mar 13) Second Empire (IRE) 124 – Loose Talk 68 (Thatching 131) **– p** [2004 7d Oct 30] good-topped filly: fourth foal: half-sister to winner in Greece by Common Grounds: dam, sprint maiden, closely related to dam of Irish 1000 Guineas winner Classic Park: 33/1 and burly, behind in maiden at Newmarket: should do better. *W. Jarvis*

LET'S PARTY (IRE) 4 b.f. Victory Note (USA) 120 – Mashoura (Shareef Dancer **–** (USA) 135) [2004 60d: 8.5s 8s 7.6g Jul 9] rather leggy filly: maiden: no longer of much account: tried blinkered: usually tongue tied. *P. L. Clinton*

LET'S PRETEND 3 b.f. Rainbow Quest (USA) 134 – Imaginary (IRE) 94 (Dancing **69** Brave (USA) 140) [2004 11.7f⁴ Sep 6] fifth foal: sister to smart 1½m to 2¼m winner Rainbow High and half-sister to useful French 9f (at 2 yrs) to 11f winner Imaginative (by Last Tycoon): dam, 1¼m winner, half-sister to Lowther Stakes winner Kingscote, herself dam of very smart performer up to 9f Rainbow Corner: 8/1, 8½ lengths fourth to Simonda in maiden at Bath, recovering from slow start to race close up, only outing: stud. *B. W. Hills*

LETS ROLL 3 b.g. Tamure (IRE) 125 – Miss Petronella (Petoski 135) [2004 69: 8g² **90** 10d⁶ 8m² 9m² 8s³ 11d* 12.3d* 13.9s⁵ 13.1s² 11.8g⁴ Oct 11] rather leggy gelding: fairly useful handicapper: won at Redcar and Ripon (beat Party Ploy 2 lengths) in July: creditable efforts last 2 starts, strong-finishing fourth to Massif Centrale at Leicester final one: stays 13f: acts on soft and good to firm going: held up: tough. *C. W. Thornton*

LET THE LION ROAR 3 b.c. Sadler's Wells (USA) 132 – Ballerina (IRE) 88 **122** (Dancing Brave (USA) 140) [2004 97p: 10g* 10.4s³ 12m³ 12f⁵ 11.9d² 14.6f Sep 11]

Courage can't usually be found in the cups of blinkers or a visor—normally it has to come from the horse, especially in a race as tough as the Derby. The preliminaries at Epsom might not be so protracted nowadays, but one of the enduring demands of the Derby is that, given the strong pace at which it is usually run and the contours of the course, it tests the runners' mettle throughout. Blinkers or a visor are not necessarily evidence of temperament or unwillingness, but they often do little more than paper over the cracks in those that are inclined to shirk the issue once racing. No horse has won the Derby in blinkers or a visor since Aboyeur was awarded the race on the disqualification of Craganour in the 'suffragette Derby' of 1913, and the last to pass the post first was St Amant in 1904. Six horses have worn headgear in the last ten renewals, including Let The Lion Roar, a 14/1-shot at Epsom when visored for the first time. Let The Lion Roar proved more free-going in the early stages at Epsom than previously, able to travel comfortably closer to the front from the rear in the field of fourteen. However, he lost his place badly after coming off the bit running down Tattenham Hill, turning for home last but two. For much of the straight, Let The Lion Roar remained out of touch with the leaders, despite his rider's efforts, but he finally ran on when switched wide, storming home to snatch third, a head behind another strong finisher Rule of Law, the pair beaten a length and a half by North Light, who had been perfectly placed throughout.

Let The Lion Roar briefly met some trouble approaching the straight at Epsom and failure to handle the downhill section of the track was also offered as an explanation for his performance. However, he looked a difficult ride throughout the season, and showed increasing waywardness as it wore on. It had seemed reasonable to assume he was still green when scrambling home from Top Seed in a minor event at Newbury on his reappearance in April, but Let The Lion Roar was on and off the bridle from an early stage when third to North Light when favourite for the Dante Stakes at York the following month. After Epsom, Let The Lion Roar was sent to the Curragh for the Irish Derby, in which the more conventional course failed to bring about any improvement. Far from reversing the Epsom form, Let The Lion Roar managed only fifth to Grey Swallow, over four lengths behind runner-up North Light, and two and a half lengths behind Rule of Law in fourth. After a break, he ran creditably when second of seven to Rule of Law in the Great Voltigeur Stakes at York in August, going down by two and a half lengths, but appearing not to be putting it all in under pressure. On his final outing, Let The

	Sadler's Wells (USA) (b 1981)	Northern Dancer (b 1961)	Nearctic Natalma
Let The Lion Roar (b.c. 2001)		Fairy Bridge (b 1975)	Bold Reason Special
	Ballerina (IRE) (b 1991)	Dancing Brave (b 1983)	Lyphard Navajo Princess
		Dancing Shadow (b 1977)	Dancer's Image Sunny Valley

Mr L. Neil Jones's "Let The Lion Roar"

Lion Roar started third favourite at 9/2 in a field of nine to emulate his half-brother Millenary by winning the St Leger at Doncaster in September, but he found a new way to make life difficult for his rider, his response to pressure even more disappointing. Difficult to settle early on this time, Let The Lion Roar was beaten in strides after making headway briefly in the straight, trailing in last but one.

Let The Lion Roar, who has a two-year-old half-sister by Rainbow Quest called Dancingintheclouds, is the third well-above-average performer out of his dam, the two-year-old seven-furlong winner Ballerina, a half-sister to Princess Royal Stakes winner Dancing Bloom and smart French performer at up to a mile River Dancer, herself the dam of Spectrum. As well as Millenary, Ballerina has also produced Head In The Clouds, like Millenary by Rainbow Quest. Head In The Clouds was also trained by John Dunlop and won the Princess Royal Stakes over a mile and a half and was second in the Prix de Pomone over thirteen and a half furlongs. Millenary was still going strongly for the stable as a seven-year-old entire in Cup races in 2004, when he did all his winning in blinkers. He has won pattern races from a mile and a half to two and a quarter miles. Let The Lion Roar's sire Sadler's Wells is, if anything, more of an influence for stamina than Rainbow Quest and Let The Lion Roar would certainly have stayed the Leger trip at four, though he is unlikely to be asked to do so as he has been sent to the States to be trained by Christophe Clement. A tall, quite good-topped colt, with a round action, Let The Lion Roar has yet to show his best form on firm ground, but he acts on good to firm and good to soft and shaped well on soft in the Dante. Let The Lion Roar, who was visored on his last four outings, has more than enough ability to win good races in America in 2005, though his resolution is clearly open to question. *J. L. Dunlop*

LEVANTINE (IRE) 7 b.g. Sadler's Wells (USA) 132 – Spain Lane (USA) 115 (Seeking The Gold (USA)) [2004 53: f7g³ f6s⁵ f8g⁶ p8g* 8m² 8d⁴ p8.6g f7g p8.6g Dec 22] modest performer: left A. Newcombe after third start: won banded race at Lingfield in September: stays 8.5f: acts on dirt, all-weather, soft and good to firm going: tried in headgear. *Miss J. Feilden* **55**

LEVELLED 10 b.g. Beveled (USA) – Baino Charm (USA) (Diesis 133) [2004 –: f5g f5s f6s p6g p5g⁴ f5g⁵ f5s⁵ f5g f5g² f5m³ f6g³ f5m* f6g 5d⁶ f6m⁵ 5g 5d⁶ 6m⁴ f5g 5d Oct 9] angular gelding: modest performer: won banded event at Wolverhampton in May: effective at 5f/6f: acts on dirt/all-weather/any turf going: tried blinkered. *D. W. Chapman* **47 a52**

LE VIE DEI COLORI 4 b.c. Efisio 120 – Mystic Tempo (USA) 76 (El Gran Senor (USA) 136) [2004 119: 8.5g* 8d* 10g⁴ 8g³ 8g 7d³ Oct 9] workmanlike colt: very smart performer, winner of 12 of his 15 starts when trained in Italy, including Premio Parioli at Rome and Premio Vittorio di Capua at Milan at 3 yrs, and minor event and listed race at Rome in April: left R. Brogi after third start: good third in Sussex Stakes at Goodwood (beaten 2½ lengths by Soviet Song) and Prix de la Foret at Longchamp (beaten 1¾ lengths by Somnus) after: pulled too hard in Prix du Moulin at Longchamp in between: best around 7f/1m: acts on firm and good to soft going: genuine. *L. M. Cumani* **121**

LEVITATOR 3 b.c. Sadler's Wells (USA) 132 – Cantilever 107 (Sanglamore (USA) 126) [2004 –p: 10g 12.6m² 14.4g² 14m 14d* 14.1d⁴ Aug 29] quite attractive colt: fair performer: won handicap at Sandown in August: stays 14.4f: acts on good to firm and good to soft going: sold 60,000 gns. *Sir Michael Stoute* **79**

LEWIS ISLAND (IRE) 5 b.g. Turtle Island (IRE) 123 – Phyllode (Pharly (FR) 130) [2004 10d 10.4g p12g⁴ p13g² f12g Dec 16] angular, lengthy gelding: fair handicapper: unraced on Flat in 2003: will stay 1¾m: acts on polytrack, soft and good to firm ground: free-going sort: none too reliable: fairly useful hurdler. *B. Ellison* **79**

LEXICON 4 ch.f. Weldnaas (USA) 112 – Swift Move (Move Off 112) [2004 9.1d Sep 16] first reported foal: dam tailed off both starts on Flat: 150/1, tailed off in claimer at Ayr. *Miss Lucinda V. Russell* **–**

LEYAALY 5 ch.m. Night Shift (USA) – Lower The Tone (IRE) 74 (Phone Trick (USA)) [2004 –: f12g⁶ p12g 10.2d f9.4g* f7d² f8g⁴ 9g Jun 30] poor performer: won amateur banded race at Wolverhampton in May: stays 9.4f: form only on fibresand: tried tongue tied/in cheekpieces. *B. A. Pearce* **45**

LIABILITY (IRE) 2 b.f. (May 4) Bluebird (USA) 125 – Madaniyya (USA) 96 (Shahrastani (USA) 135) [2004 7d 7.9g⁶ 7m⁶ Sep 29] €5,500Y: big, leggy filly: sixth foal: sister to 3-y-o Infidelity and half-sister to 1997 2-y-o 7f winner Madjamilla (by Doyoun) and **39**

Irish 1½m/13f winner Madalyar (by Darshaan), both fairly useful: dam Irish 9f/1¼m winner: poor form in maidens. *N. Tinkler*

LIAKOURA (GER)   2 b.g. (Feb 3) Royal Academy (USA) 130 – Lady Member (FR)   **95 p**
(Saint Estephe (FR) 123) [2004 7d* 7m 8g* Sep 2] 58,000Y: rather leggy, quite attractive
gelding: sixth foal: half-brother to 3 winners, including fairly useful 7f to 8.5f winner
(successful at 1m at 2 yrs) Master Soden (by Pembroke): dam French 2-y-o 1m winner,
later won in USA: won maiden in July and minor event in September (in cheekpieces,
beat Sun Kissed by length, edging left/flashing tail but strong run to lead final 1f), both at
Salisbury: should stay 1¼m: stirred up when below form second outing: gelded after final
one: useful, and probably capable of better. *Mrs A. J. Perrett*

LIAMELISS   2 ch.f. (Mar 1) Dr Fong (USA) 128 – Ivory Palm (USA) 93 (Sir Ivor   **45 ?**
(USA) 135) [2004 6m⁶ 7g 7m 6m Sep 4] 1,000Y: half-sister to fairly useful 1998 2-y-o 5f
winner Tamara (by Marju) and 9-y-o Tommy Carson: dam 7f (at 2 yrs) and 12.5f winner:
poor maiden: tended to hang third start. *M. A. Allen*

LIBERA   3 b.f. Turtle Island (IRE) 123 – Princess Louise 86 (Efisio 120) [2004 7d Jun   **–**
23] 13,000Y: first foal: dam, 2-y-o 6f winner on only start, out of useful winner up to 1m
Louis' Queen: length second to Rumba Loca in 5f maiden at Milan on debut: below that
form in Premio Dormello there later at 2 yrs, and in maiden at Salisbury only start in
2004: sold 1,500 gns. *M. G. Quinlan*

LIBERTY FLAG (USA)   3 b.f. Kingmambo (USA) 125 – Banner Dancer (USA)   **79**
(Danzig (USA)) [2004 8.3f² 8.1m* Aug 11] sixth foal: closely related to winners in USA
by Forty Niner and Gulch and half-sister to winner there by A P Indy: dam, maiden in
USA, half-sister to Breeders' Cup Distaff winner Sacahuista: fair form: landed odds in
maiden at Sandown by ¾ length from Alenushka: would probably have stayed 1¼m:
stud. *J. H. M. Gosden*

LIBERTY ROYAL   5 b.g. Ali-Royal (IRE) 127 – Hope Chest 70 (Kris 135) [2004 85:   **71**
p8g⁶ 8.3d 8.5s⁶ 9g³ 9g 8f³ 8m⁴ 8g* 8.1d p8g Oct 13] fair handicapper: won at Salisbury
in September: effective at 1m/1¼m: acts on all-weather and firm going: wore cheekpieces last 7 starts: sold 6,500 gns. *P. J. Makin*

LIBERTY RUN (IRE)   2 ch.c. (Mar 19) Grand Lodge (USA) 125 – Bathe In Light   **74 p**
(USA) 72 (Sunshine Forever (USA)) [2004 8d p7g³ p9.5g* Nov 13] 32,000F, 160,000Y:
neat colt: fourth foal: dam, 1½m/1¾m winner, out of sister to King Edward VII Stakes
winner Open Day: won maiden at Wolverhampton by neck from Chocolate Caramel: will
stay at least 1½m: should progress. *N. A. Callaghan*

LIBERTY SEEKER (FR)   5 ch.g. Machiavellian (USA) 123 – Samara (IRE) 108   **64**
(Polish Patriot (USA) 128) [2004 71?: 10v 12m 15g² Jul 20] angular gelding: modest
maiden handicapper: barely stays 15f: acts on soft and good to firm giong: tried in cheekpieces: fairly useful hurdler/chaser. *P. D. Niven*

LIBRE   4 b.g. Bahamian Bounty 116 – Premier Blues (FR) 35 (Law Society (USA) 130)   **84**
[2004 80: 10.3g 10.1v⁵ 10s⁴ 10.5m 7m f8g 7.5g* 9.2d 6.9f 7d p7.1g* p9.5g* p9.5g²
p8.6g* Dec 27] leggy gelding: fairly useful handicapper: won at Beverley in June and
Wolverhampton in November (first start after rejoining present trainer from R. C. Guest)
and December (twice): stays 9.5f: acts on polytrack and any turf going: often blinkered/in
cheekpieces/tongue tied: has shown signs of temperament, but looks reformed character.
F. Jordan

LIBRETTIST (USA)   2 b.c. (Apr 17) Danzig (USA) – Mysterial (USA) (Alleged   **114 p**
(USA) 138) [2004 7g* 7m* 7s⁵ Oct 16]
Godolphin had a radical change in policy, training and running two-year-
olds 'in house' with Saeed bin Suroor at Newmarket rather than relying on other
yards, and focusing much more on winning races rather than using a juvenile campaign principally as a precursor to one in the classics. The policy reaped dividends,
with Frankie Dettori the most obvious beneficiary. His successful challenge for
the Jockeys' Association title was boosted significantly by riding forty juvenile
winners for his retaining stable, including three on the all-weather. No fewer than
ninety-one two-year-olds ran for Suroor, around forty more than for Aidan O'Brien,
including a dozen on the all-weather, for an overall tally of fifty-eight victories in
Britain (plus one in Ireland) achieved by forty-eight horses. In the five previous
seasons Suroor had only eight individual two-year-old runners in Britain, seven of
those in 2003. The quality of the latest, active team was pretty high too, with two
pattern winners, Dubawi and Perfectperformance, several pattern-placed perform-

McKeever St Lawrence Conditions Stakes, Doncaster—
Librettist, a half-brother to Dubai Destination, sees off the useful Embossed

ers and a hefty number of promising once-raced maiden winners, notably Afrashad, Ballinteni, Belenus, Centaurus, Descartes, Potent Heir and Saywaan. Then there was Librettist, second only to Dubawi in the team in terms of the form shown on the racecourse and a colt who looks sure to train on and make a mark at up to a mile as a three-year-old, always assuming he gets the chance, given the embarrassment of riches in the stable.

With Dettori riding Royal Lodge Stakes winner Perfectperformance, 10/1-chance Librettist clearly was not Godolphin's first string in the Dewhurst Stakes at Newmarket in October—the Somerville Tattersall Stakes had been mentioned as a more likely target earlier in the month—but he outperformed his stable companion. Prominent from the outset, Librettist was still disputing the lead under a furlong out but faded to finish four lengths fifth to his future stablemate Shamardal. In all probability, inexperience played a part in this performance, since Librettist had not contested a pattern race, nor come under serious pressure, in winning his previous starts. The races involved were an eleven-runner maiden at Newmarket in July, when he ran green but scored comfortably by two and a half lengths from Baradore, and a five-runner minor event at Doncaster in September, when he made all to justify short-priced favouritism by a length and a half from Embossed, needing only firmish hand riding.

Librettist is one of the best-looking of the Godolphin team, a big, strong colt with a fluent, round action, and he is also one of the best-bred in a stable where purple pedigrees are two a penny—a comment on numbers, not value. Like Middle Park winner Ad Valorem, Librettist is a son of Danzig, who was retired from stud duties in the latest season, but, unlike Ad Valorem, Librettist comes from a top-notch family on the distaff side. Danzig's career is dealt with in more detail in the essay on Ad Valorem, but speed was his hallmark as a stallion, the average distance of races won by his three-year-olds and upwards being just under a mile. His Group 1 winners in Europe include no fewer than six winners of the July Cup. Librettist is the fourth foal out of the twice-raced Mysterial, dam of two previous winners for Godolphin, both by Kingmambo, who is more of an influence for stamina than Danzig. Dubai Destination won the Champagne Stakes over seven furlongs at two, making Rock of Gibraltar look pretty ordinary that day, and, after being restricted by injuries to just one outing at three, came back to win the Queen Anne Stakes over a mile at four, though he ran nowhere near his Royal Ascot form in two races afterwards. Mysterial's three-year-old Destination Dubai showed useful form in scoring twice at around a mile and quarter, winning a maiden at Haydock and a minor event at Ascot from six starts. The dam is by Alleged, an influence for stamina, out of the maiden Mysteries who was raced only four times,

577

Godolphin's "Librettist"

Librettist (USA) (b.c. Apr 17, 2002)	Danzig (USA) (b 1977)	Northern Dancer (b 1961)	Nearctic Natalma
		Pas de Nom (b or br 1968)	Admiral's Voyage Petitioner
	Mysterial (USA) (b or br 1994)	Alleged (b 1974)	Hoist The Flag Princess Pout
		Mysteries (b 1986)	Seattle Slew Phydilla

putting up her best performance when third in the Musidora Stakes, showing smart form. Mysteries was a keen, active type who gave the impression she might have proved ideally suited by distances short of a mile and a quarter, and she has made her mark as a broodmare through the achievements of July Cup and Prix de l'Abbaye winner Agnes World, by Danzig incidentally, and the very smart Japanese sprinter-miler Hishi Akebono. Librettist's great grandam Phydilla was a high-class miler, though one of her half-brothers Observation Post was runner-up in the Irish Derby and the Coronation Cup. Phydilla was also a half-sister to Royal Suzuka, another leading performer in Japan. *Saeed bin Suroor*

LIEUDAY 5 b.g. Atraf 116 – Figment 75 (Posse (USA) 130) [2004 58: f7m⁵ 8.2d 7m³ 7.1f Jun 21] rather leggy gelding: modest maiden: stays 7.6f: acts on soft and good to firm going: tried visored, usually wears cheekpieces. *W. M. Brisbourne*   **53**

LIFE IS BEAUTIFUL (IRE) 5 b.m. Septieme Ciel (USA) 123 – Palombella (FR) (Groom Dancer (USA) 128) [2004 50§: 9.9s⁶ 12.1m* 9.9g⁵ 12.1g* 12.1g⁶ 14.1m² 11.9g⁴ 9.9m² Sep 21] smallish, sturdy mare: modest performer: won banded event in May and claimer in June, both at Beverley: stays 1¾m: acts on soft and good to firm going: goes well (last 4 wins) for R. Winston. *W. H. Tinning*   **55**

578

LIFTED WAY 5 b.g. In The Wings 128 – Stack Rock 111 (Ballad Rock 122) [2004 **85**
87: p8g 8.1d* p8g* 8.1f 7d⁶ 8m⁵ 7.1d⁴ 8.1d 7.1g Sep 10] fairly useful handicapper: won
at Sandown in April and Lingfield in May: effective at 7f (given bit of a test) to 1¼m: acts
on polytrack, good to firm and good to soft going: usually races prominently: gelded after
final start. *P. R. Chamings*

LIGHT BRIGADE 5 b.g. Kris 135 – Mafatin (IRE) 74 (Sadler's Wells (USA) 132) **–**
[2004 63: f14g⁶ f12g p12g p12g⁵ 8.1m Jul 2] maiden: little form in 2004: tried visored.
J. M. P. Eustace

LIGHTED WAY 2 b.f. (Apr 15) Kris 135 – Natchez Trace 52 (Commanche Run 133) **66**
[2004 6m 6.1d⁶ 5.1d⁶ 5.7g² 5.1s² Sep 20] 15,000Y: half-sister to 3 winners, including
7-y-o Connect and 1½m winner Be True (by Robellino): dam third at 7f (bred to stay
much further): fair maiden: likely to prove best at 5f/6f: acts on soft going: races prominently. *A. M. Balding*

LIGHTENING FIRE (IRE) 2 b.g. (Apr 28) Woodborough (USA) 112 – Glowlamp **54 ?**
(IRE) 93 (Glow (USA)) [2004 6g 7.1f 8m 7.9g Oct 9] smallish, sturdy gelding: modest
maiden: best effort on debut: should stay 1m. *T. J. Etherington*

LIGHTHORNE LAD 2 ch.c. (Apr 13) Hornbeam 107 – Give Me A Day (Lucky Wed- **–**
nesday 124) [2004 5f 5m 6m Aug 16] well held in maidens. *J. R. Jenkins*

LIGHTNING PROSPECT 2 ch.f. (Mar 31) Zaha (CAN) 106 – Lightning Blaze 58 **–**
(Cosmonaut) [2004 5d Aug 31] 12,000Y: good-bodied filly: first foal: dam 2-y-o 5f
winner: 10/1 and backward, well held in maiden at Ripon, slowly away. *P. C. Haslam*

LIGHTNING STAR (USA) 9 b.g. El Gran Senor (USA) 136 – Cuz's Star (USA) **–**
(Galaxy Libra 104) [2004 11.6f Jul 19] fair at best: little form since 5 yrs (unraced on Flat
in 2002/3): blinkered: modest hurdler. *G. L. Moore*

LIGHT OF DUBAI (USA) 2 b.f. (Feb 22) Gone West (USA) – A P Assay (USA) **77 p**
115 (A P Indy (USA) 131) [2004 7g⁴ Sep 3] $1,600,000Y: strong, well-made filly: second
foal: dam, US Grade 2 7f winner, half-sister to very smart US performer up to 1¼m Came
Home (by Gone West): 7/2, fourth of 7 to Joint Aspiration in minor event at Kempton,
going well in lead long way before weakening: sure to do fair bit better. *Saeed bin Suroor*

LIGHT OF MORN 3 gr.f. Daylami (IRE) 138 – My Emma 118 (Marju (IRE) 127) **99**
[2004 12s² 11.9m³ 11.5g* 12f⁴ 14.6m⁶ 12g⁴ Oct 1] tall, leggy filly: third foal: half-sister
to 4-y-o Moments of Joy: dam, 1½m (Yorkshire Oaks/Prix Vermeille) winner, half-sister
to St Leger and Gold Cup winner Classic Cliche: useful performer: won maiden at Lingfield in July: good efforts in listed event at Newbury (fourth to Sahool), Park Hill Stakes
at Doncaster (sixth to Echoes In Eternity) and listed event at Newmarket (3 lengths fourth
to Private Charter): stays 14.6f: acts on firm and soft going: held up. *R. Guest*

LIGHT THE DAWN (IRE) 4 ch.f. Indian Ridge 123 – Flaming June (USA) 69 **48**
(Storm Bird (CAN) 134) [2004 –: 8.1s 6g 8.2g 7g⁵ f7g p8.6g Nov 15] lengthy, workmanlike filly: poor maiden: stays 7f. *W. M. Brisbourne*

LIGHT WIND 3 ch.f. Unfuwain (USA) 131 – River Spey 96 (Mill Reef (USA) 141) **89**
[2004 12s⁵ 12.1m* 11.6f* 12f⁵ 10.5s⁶ 12d³ 14.1s⁶ Oct 27] rangy filly: half-sister to
numerous winners, including smart 7f (at 2 yrs) to 1¾m winner Jahafil and useful 1¼m/
1½m winner Mondschein (both by Rainbow Quest): dam 2-y-o 7f winner who stayed
1½m: fairly useful performer: won maiden at Chepstow in June and minor event at Windsor in July: ran creditably after, 6½ lengths sixth to Modesta in listed race at Yarmouth
final start: barely stays 1¾m: acts on firm and soft going: slowly away first 2 outings.
Mrs A. J. Perrett

LIGNE D'EAU 3 ch.c. Cadeaux Genereux 131 – Miss Waterline 77 (Rock City 120) **63**
[2004 69: 6s 6.1m⁵ 6g³ 6g6 7.1m⁶ 6.1d 8.1s⁶ 6d* p5.1g⁶ p6g* p6m² p7g⁴ Dec 30] sturdy,
close-coupled colt: modest performer: won maiden at Redcar (made most/wandered) in
October and minor event at Wolverhampton in December: should prove best at 6f/7f: acts
on polytrack, good to firm and good to soft going: tried visored, blinkered last 5 starts.
P. D. Evans

LILIAN 4 b.f. First Trump 118 – Lillibella 64 (Reprimand 122) [2004 53: f9.4g⁶ f8g⁵ **42**
f9.4s⁶ p10g 11.8m 14.1g 8m⁶ p10g Dec 20] leggy, quite good-topped filly: poor maiden:
stays 1¼m: acts on polytrack and firm going: usually wears headgear: tried in tongue tie.
Miss Z. C. Davison

LILLAS FOREST 2 b.g. (Mar 5) Forestry (USA) 121 – Lines of Beauty (USA) (Line **63 ?**
In The Sand (USA)) [2004 7g 7.9g p8.6g p8m Dec 8] small gelding: first foal: dam US

Grade 3 9f winner: seemingly modest form in maiden at York on second start: well held otherwise, including in claimers. *P. C. Haslam*

LILLEBROR (GER)   6 b.g. Top Waltz (FR) 119 – Lady Soliciti (GER) (Solicitor (FR) 121) [2004 –: 14s 16.2g 14m³ 16.4m Aug 11] small gelding: modest handicapper: stays 1¾m: acts on heavy and good to firm going: tried visored/in cheekpieces: won novice hurdle in October. *B. J. Curley*   **60**

LILLIANNA (IRE)   3 ch.f. Barathea (IRE) 127 – Machikane Akaiito (IRE) (Persian Bold 123) [2004 8.2s⁴ 8.3g 8.5g³ 10m 10d 11.5g Sep 14] €9,000Y: smallish filly: second foal: dam, placed in Japan, out of useful half-sister to high-class 1m/1¼m performer Kooyonga: modest maiden: stays 8.5f: sold 2,000 gns. *H. R. A. Cecil*   **64**

LILLI MARLANE   4 b.f. Sri Pekan (USA) 117 – Fiveofive (IRE) 61 (Fairy King (USA)) [2004 82: 8s² 8.3d⁶ 10m 10m 9.7f* 10s 10.1g 10m⁵ p8g p8g⁴ p8g p8g⁴ p8g* p8.6g p9.5g⁴ p8.6g⁶ Dec 27] fair handicapper: won at Folkestone in June and Lingfield in November: effective at 1m/1¼m: acts on polytrack, firm and good to soft going: blinkered (slowly away) third outing, respectable effort in cheekpieces final one: usually held up: none too consistent. *N. A. Callaghan*   **79**

LILL'S STAR LAD   6 ch.g. Kasakov – Lady Khadija (Nicholas Bill 125) [2004 –: f7g 10m May 25] of no account. *P. R. Wood*   **–**

LILLY GEE (IRE)   3 b.f. Ashkalani (IRE) 128 – Welsh Mist 102 (Damister (USA) 123) [2004 p5.1g p6g* p5.1g Dec 31] 12,000Y: fourth foal: half-sister to 3 winners, including 7f and 8.5f winner Brighter Future (by Night Shift) and 4-y-o Soyuz, both useful: dam 5f (including at 2 yrs)/6f winner: best effort at Wolverhampton when winning maiden by head: should stay at least 7f: slowly away on debut. *R. P. Elliott*   **56**

LILTING PROSE (IRE)   2 ch.f. (Mar 28) Indian Ridge 123 – Kirkwood (Selkirk (USA) 129) [2004 6f⁵ 6g Oct 2] 45,000Y: neat filly: first foal: dam, useful French 6f winner, out of sister to US Grade 1 1¼m winner Spanish Fern: green, modest form in maidens at Windsor and Newmarket. *R. Hannon*   **55**

LILY LENAT   2 b.f. (Mar 20) Josr Algarhoud (IRE) 118 – Rushing River (USA) (Irish River (FR) 131) [2004 5g 5g⁴ 5g³ 6g 7m p6m⁵ p7.1g Nov 12] 13,000Y: fifth foal: dam unraced: fair maiden: ran as if amiss final outing: should stay 7f: acts on polytrack, best turf effort on good going: wore cheekpieces last 3 starts. *J. R. Boyle*   **71**

LILY OF THE GUILD (IRE)   5 ch.m. Lycius (USA) 124 – Secreto Bold (Never So Bold 135) [2004 62: p7g p7g p7g² p7g⁴ 5.7f⁴ 7g⁵ 6d 7.1m 6m p7.1g² p8.6g³ p8m² Dec 8] close-coupled mare: modest performer: stays 8.6f: acts on polytrack, firm and good to soft going: wore cheekpieces last 3 starts: sometimes slowly away/races freely. *W. S. Kittow*   **56 a61**

LIMERICK BOY (GER)   6 b.g. Alwuhush (USA) 121 – Limoges (GER) (Konigsstuhl (GER)) [2004 13.4d⁶ May 7] smart performer at best, winner of Dr Busch Memorial at Krefeld and Preis der Deutschen Einheit at Hoppegarten in 2001: left A. Schutz after final 4-y-o start, then developed into smart hurdler: well held in Ormonde Stakes at Chester, only outing on Flat since 2002: stays 11f: acts on heavy ground: tried blinkered. *Miss Venetia Williams*   **–**

LIMIT DOWN (IRE)   3 b.g. Desert Story (IRE) 115 – Princess Raisa (Indian King (USA) 128) [2004 55: f9.4s⁶ f6g³ p6g³ p5g⁶ Feb 4] modest maiden: stays 7f: raced only on all-weather and good to soft going: tried visored. *M. J. Wallace*   **51**

LIMITED MAGICIAN   3 b.f. Wizard King 122 – Pretty Scarce (Handsome Sailor 125) [2004 –: f6g f6g Apr 15] workmanlike filly: last in maidens/claimer. *C. Smith*   **–**

LIMIT (IRE)   2 b.f. (May 11) Barathea (IRE) 127 – Orlena (USA) (Gone West (USA)) [2004 8.1s³ 8s p8g² p7.1d⁶ p7.1g* Nov 13] €38,000Y: first foal: dam, French 2-y-o 7f winner, out of US Grade 3 8.5f/9f winner Cox Orange: fair performer: won maiden at Wolverhampton, hanging left: will probably stay 1¼m. *M. R. Channon*   **69**

LIMONIA (GER)   2 b.f. (May 2) Perugino (USA) 84 – Limoges (GER) (Konigsstuhl (GER)) [2004 5v⁵ 5g⁵ 5.1g 5g⁶ 5.1s Sep 20] 8,000Y: rather leggy filly: half-sister to several winners in Germany, notably 6-y-o Limerick Boy: dam German 10.5f winner: modest maiden: needs to settle to stay beyond 5f: best efforts on good going: signs of waywardness. *D. K. Ivory*   **62**

LINBY LAD (IRE)   4 ch.g. Dolphin Street (FR) 125 – Classic Look (IRE) 58 (Classic Music (USA)) [2004 –: p10g p10g Mar 24] useful-looking gelding: lightly raced and little form since 2 yrs: tried blinkered. *J. A. Glover*   **–**

LINCOLN DANCER (IRE) 7 b.g. Turtle Island (IRE) 123 – Double Grange (IRE) **91**
(Double Schwartz 128) [2004 94d: f7g f7g 7g⁴ 6s³ 6v⁴ 6g* 6g May 3] compact, sturdy
gelding: poor mover: fairly useful performer: won minor event at Windsor in April by
neck from Morse: best at 6f/7f: has form on good to firm going, goes well on softer than
good: tried visored. *D. Nicholls*

LINCOLNEUROCRUISER 2 b.c. (Feb 7) Spectrum (IRE) 126 – Rush Hour (IRE) **85**
(Night Shift (USA)) [2004 5g⁵ 5s² 6.1s³ 6f* 6m Jul 15] 4,500Y: good-topped colt:
first foal: dam unraced out of sister to smart 1¼m performer Perpendicular: fairly useful
performer: won maiden at Redcar in June: good second in minor event at Hamilton, much
better effort after: should stay 1m: acts on firm and soft ground: usually races prominently. *J. O'Reilly*

LINDA GREEN 3 b.f. Victory Note (USA) 120 – Edge of Darkness 62 (Vaigly Great **62**
127) [2004 61: 5g* 5g⁴ Apr 30] rather leggy filly: modest performer: won minor event at
Catterick in March: likely to prove best at 5f/easy 6f: acts on fibresand and good to firm
going. *P. A. Blockley*

LINDA'S COLIN (IRE) 2 b.c. (Mar 20) Xaar 132 – Capable Kate (IRE) (Alzao **77**
(USA) 117) [2004 7m p8.6g² p8.6d² p8.6g* Dec 6] 10,000Y: lengthy colt: sixth living
foal: half-brother to 3 winners, including 3-y-o Obe Bold: dam unraced: won maiden at
Wolverhampton by ¾ length from Ten Cents: likely to stay 1¼m. *W. D'Arcy*

LINDEN'S LADY 4 b.f. Compton Place 125 – Jubilee Place (IRE) 76 (Prince Sabo **55**
123) [2004 82: 6g 6m⁶ 6f 8f⁵ 7g⁶ 6g⁵ 5g 7m⁵ 6.9g⁴ 7g³ 7m p6d Oct 23] leggy filly: modest
performer: stays easy 1m: acts on firm going: tried visored/blinkered. *J. R. Weymes*

LINE AHEAD (IRE) 2 b.f. (Mar 22) Sadler's Wells (USA) 132 – Alignment (IRE) **– p**
98 (Alzao (USA) 117) [2004 8.2g Aug 18] third foal: dam, headstrong maiden (fourth in
Musidora Stakes), half-sister to smart performer up to 14.6f Bonny Scot and to dam of
Golan out of half-sister to Prix du Cadran winner Sought Out (herself dam of 3-y-o North
Light): 12/1, well held in maiden at Nottingham, not knocked about: will be well suited
by 1¼m/1½m: likely to do fair bit better. *Sir Michael Stoute*

LINE DRAWING 3 b.c. Unfuwain (USA) 131 – Fine Detail (IRE) 93 (Shirley Heights **81**
130) [2004 10.3d² 10m⁴ 10.9f³ 10g³ 12.3d² Aug 30] big, good-topped colt: fourth foal:
half-brother to fairly useful 7f winner Fine Arts (by Cadeaux Genereux) and 4-y-o
Artistic Style: dam, 1½m winner on only start, half-sister to French performer up to 12.5f
De Quest and US Grade 1 9f/1¼m winner Wandesta, both very smart: fairly useful
maiden: in frame all starts: stays 1½m: acts on good to firm and good to soft going: looks
temperamental: sold 32,000 gns. *B. W. Hills*

LINENS FLAME 5 ch.g. Blushing Flame (USA) 109 – Atlantic Air (Air Trooper 115) **78**
[2004 –: 14.4s* 15.4s* 14.4v² 16m 14g 12g 16s⁴ 16s Oct 29] fair handicapper: won at
Kempton in March and Folkestone in April: stays 2m: acts on heavy ground: usually
races prominently. *B. G. Powell*

LIN IN GOLD (IRE) 3 b.g. Second Empire (IRE) 124 – Wasmette (IRE) (Wassl 125) **–**
[2004 80: 8m⁵ Apr 25] lengthy gelding: won maiden at Brighton on debut at 2 yrs: looked
headstrong when below that form both starts since: sent to Macau. *P. A. Blockley*

LINNET (GER) 2 b.f. (Apr 14) Dr Fong (USA) 128 – Lauderdale (GER) (Nebos **71 p**
(GER) 129) [2004 7d⁶ Oct 30] 23,000F, €100,000Y: rangy filly: fourth foal: half-sister to
German winners Ladino (up to 11f) and Lareda (up to 1½m), both by Acatenango: dam,
German 9.5f winner, half-sister to dam of Deutsches Derby winners Lando and Laroche:
14/1, 6 lengths sixth to Songthrush in maiden at Newmarket, slowly away, green and not
knocked about: likely to be suited by 1¼m/1½m: should improve. *Mrs A. J. Perrett*

LINNGARI (IRE) 2 ch.c. (Apr 1) Indian Ridge 123 – Lidakiya (IRE) 105 (Kahyasi **93 p**
130) [2004 7m³ p7g* 7.1g* Sep 15] first foal: dam, lightly-raced 1¼m/1½m winner,
half-sister to smart Irish 1m/1¼m winner Livadiya: won minor events at Lingfield in
August and Sandown (4 ran, beat Easy Mover comfortably by 3½ lengths) in September:
will stay at least 1m: useful prospect. *Sir Michael Stoute*

LINNING WINE (IRE) 8 b.g. Scenic 128 – Zallaka (IRE) (Shardari 134) [2004 91, **87**
a103: p10g p8g² 8g⁴ 10.3d 8m⁶ 8m⁴ 8.3g⁵ 8.1d⁵ 9s⁵ p7.1g p7g* p7g p7.1g* p9.5g² Dec **a103**
31] lengthy gelding: useful on all-weather, fairly useful on turf: won claimers at Lingfield
(left B. Powell) in October and Wolverhampton in December: good second in handicaps
at Lingfield (behind Dance On The Top) on second outing and at Wolverhampton (to
Compton Bolter) final start: effective at 7f to 1½m: acts on polytrack, good to firm and
good to soft going: held up, and sometimes finds little. *P. A. Blockley*

LINZIS LAD 2 ch.g. (Feb 24) Magic Ring (IRE) 115 – Come On Katie (Cadeaux Genereux 131) [2004 7m 7.1d p8.6g³ f7g⁶ Dec 16] quite good-topped gelding: modest maiden: third in seller at Wolverhampton: stays 8.6f: acts on polytrack and good to soft going: wore cheekpieces/blinkers last 2 starts. *K. A. Ryan* **50**

LION HUNTER (USA) 5 b.g. Quest For Fame 127 – Prodigious (FR) (Pharly (FR) 130) [2004 p10g p10g⁶ 10g 10g³ 12m May 15] tall, rather leggy gelding: fairly useful performer: missed 2003: best effort when very close third to Tawny Way in minor event at Windsor: stays 1¼m: acts on polytrack, firm and soft going. *Miss E. C. Lavelle* **92**

LION'S DOMANE 7 b.g. Lion Cavern (USA) 117 – Vilany 87 (Never So Bold 135) [2004 69d, a–§: f6g f7g⁵ f6s⁶ f7s 7g f7m 7.1d 8d 8m 7.2g 7.2g Aug 7] strong, workmanlike gelding: unreliable performer: little form in 2004: tried visored/in cheekpieces: front runner. *A. Berry* **– §**

LIQUIDATE 3 b.g. Hector Protector (USA) 124 – Cut And Run (Slip Anchor 136) [2004 58: 12g* 12.3g 14d Jun 1] good-bodied gelding: fair handicapper: form in 2004 only when winning at Catterick in March: should stay 1¾m: tried tongue tied at 2 yrs. *H. Morrison* **73**

LIQUID FORM (IRE) 4 b.g. Bahhare (USA) 122 – Brogan's Well (IRE) (Caerleon (USA) 132) [2004 93: 7.1s 10.5d 10g 10m⁶ 10m 10.1g⁵ 10g Sep 29] small, sturdy gelding: fair handicapper: best at 1¼m/11f: acts on firm going: sold 19,000 gns, sent to Switzerland. *B. Hanbury* **75**

LIQUID LOVER (IRE) 2 b.c. (Apr 10) Night Shift (USA) – New Tycoon (IRE) (Last Tycoon 131) [2004 6m 7g 7m 7m Sep 7] sturdy colt: modest maiden: form only on debut: should stay 7f: tends to be awkward away. *R. Hannon* **53 ?**

LIRAGE 2 b.f. (Feb 9) Wizard King 122 – Diamond Rouge 53 (Puissance 110) [2004 6s Sep 24] workmanlike filly: first foal: dam sprint maiden: 100/1 and burly, well held in maiden at Haydock. *M. Mullineaux* **–**

LISA MONA LISA (IRE) 2 b.f. (Feb 1) Desert Style (IRE) 121 – Amneris (IRE) 73 (Alzao (USA) 117) [2004 5g* 5s⁴ 7f* 7g f6d⁴ 7m* 7s 8g⁶ Sep 11] strong, lengthy filly: first foal: dam, maiden (likely to have stayed 1¾m), out of half-sister to high-class middle-distance performer Emmson: fair performer: won sellers at Doncaster in March and Yarmouth in June and nursery at Folkestone in August: well below form last 2 starts: stays 7f: acts on firm and soft going, probably on fibresand: sold 1,000 gns. *V. Smith* **72**

LISEBERG (IRE) 2 b.c. (May 12) Gothenberg (IRE) 117 – Read And Approved (IRE) (Husyan (USA) 115) [2004 7d Aug 27] sturdy colt: well held in seller at Thirsk, slowly away. *I. A. Wood* **–**

LISSAHANELODGE 5 br.g. Grand Lodge (USA) 125 – Lissahane Lass (Daring March 116) [2004 p12g* p13g² 11.9m 11.6m⁶ 13.3m⁶ 14.1m⁶ Jun 30] modest on allweather, poor on turf: missed 2003: won banded race at Lingfield in March: stays 13.3f: acts on polytrack and good to firm going: wore cheekpieces (stumbled badly) final start: sometimes slowly away. *P. R. Hedger* **45 a52**

LISTEN TO ME 2 gr.g. (Feb 3) Petong 126 – Time Clash 67 (Timeless Times (USA) 99) [2004 5d⁵ 5.1s 7g⁵ 6m p8.6g f8g f7g Dec 12] sturdy, close-coupled gelding: poor maiden: barely stays 7f: acts on fibresand: visored last 2 starts. *D. Haydn Jones* **46**

LISTEN TO REASON (IRE) 3 b.g. Mukaddamah (USA) 125 – Tenalist (IRE) 69 (Tenby 125) [2004 57: 7m⁸ 8m 7m 7.1g f8g⁵ p9.5g² p9.5m⁶ Dec 6] strong, lengthy gelding: fair performer: won maiden at Catterick in July: stays 9.5f: acts on polytrack, raced only on good/good to firm going on turf. *J. G. Given* **66**

LITERATIM 4 b.c. Polish Precedent (USA) 131 – Annie Albright (USA) (Verbatim (USA)) [2004 7g⁴ 7g* 8.1d² 10.3m 7.9g³ Oct 8] strong, close-coupled colt: half-brother to useful 5f (at 2 yrs) and 6f winner Shamanic (by Fairy King) and French 11.5f winner Belmonte (by Belmez): dam, Irish sprint maiden, half-sister to smart performer up to 1m Crystal Gazing: useful performer: won maiden at Doncaster in July: good efforts after when placed in handicaps at Sandown (¾-length second to Norton) and York (1¼ lengths third to Nashaab, wandering): should stay 1¼m: acts on good to soft going: lightly raced, and should improve further. *L. M. Cumani* **95 p**

LITERATURE (USA) 2 b.f. (Mar 29) Notebook (USA) – Deputy's Mistress (USA) (Deputy Minister (CAN)) [2004 7.1m* Sep 6] $310,000 2-y-o: tall, quite good-topped filly: sister to 2 winners in USA, including 8.5f minor stakes winner Backatem, and halfsister to 3 winners there: dam unraced out of half-sister to outstanding broodmare Fall **78 p**

Aspen: 7/2, won maiden at Warwick comfortably by 1¾ lengths from Lysandra, leading final 1f: should stay 1m: likely to improve. *Saeed bin Suroor*

LITHOS 2 ch.c. (Mar 16) Inchinor 119 – Leisure (FR) (Fast Topaze (USA) 128) [2004 **80** 8.3m² 8s⁶ 8.1g⁵ 8g* Sep 13] €27,000Y: leggy, workmanlike colt: third foal: half-brother to smart French 1¼m to 1½m winner Levitski (by Vettori); dam, French 1¼m winner, half-sister to very smart French stayer Alesso: fairly useful performer: won maiden at Musselburgh by 2 lengths from Maneki Neko: will stay at least 1¼m: acts on good to firm going: coltish/edgy second and third starts: sold 30,000 gns. *J. A. Osborne*

LITTLE BISCUIT (IRE) 2 br.f. (Mar 20) Indian Lodge (IRE) 127 – Arjan (IRE) 88 **62** (Paris House 123) [2004 f5g* 5s* 5m² 5m⁵ 6m⁴ 5f² 5.1g⁶ 5s⁴ 5.1g 5.1v f5f* Dec 28] small, sturdy filly: first foal: modest performer: won seller at Wolverhampton in March, claimer at Thirsk in April and seller at Southwell in December: will prove best at 5f/easy 6f: acts on fibresand, firm and soft going. *K. R. Burke*

LITTLE BOB 3 ch.g. Zilzal (USA) 137 – Hunters of Brora (IRE) 102 (Sharpo 132) **78** [2004 –: 8g⁴ 8d⁴ 9.1f² 10.3m³ 9d 9d* 8.1g 10d 10s Oct 11] good-topped gelding: fair performer: won maiden at Newcastle in August: stays 1¼m: acts on firm and good to soft going: often slowly away. *J. D. Bethell*

LITTLE DALHAM 2 b.c. (Feb 24) Diktat 126 – Almost Amber (USA) 88 (Mt **80** Livermore (USA)) [2004 7m⁴ 6d² 6f* 7.1d⁶ 6v⁴ Oct 23] 13,000Y: sturdy, close-coupled colt: second foal: dam, 2-y-o 5f winner, became temperamental: fairly useful performer: won maiden at York in July: below form in nurseries after: needs to settle to stay 7f: acts on firm and good to soft going: sold 39,000 gns. *P. W. Chapple-Hyam*

LITTLE EDWARD 6 gr.g. King's Signet (USA) 110 – Cedar Lady (Telsmoss 91) **97 d** [2004 106: 8g⁵ 5.2g 5g⁵ 5m 6m 6m⁵ 5d 5m 5.2f 6g⁵ 5m⁶ 6m⁴ 5g⁶ 7m Sep 17] angular gelding: useful performer: fifth to Moss Vale in listed race at Salisbury sixth start: mostly well below form after: best at 5f/6f: acts on polytrack, firm and good to soft going: none too consistent. *B. G. Powell*

LITTLE ENGLANDER 4 b.g. Piccolo 121 – Anna Karietta 82 (Precocious 126) **64** [2004 65: 10s⁵ 11.8m 10g 8.2g⁵ 8.2s* 8m 8m 8.2g⁴ 7g⁴ 8.2v⁵ p8.6g Dec 17] rather leggy, close-coupled gelding: modest handicapper: won at Nottingham in July: ran as if amiss final start (visored), first after leaving H. Candy: stays 1¼m: acts on heavy and good to firm going. *M. Hill*

LITTLE EYE (IRE) 3 b.g. Groom Dancer (USA) 128 – Beaming 93 (Mtoto 134) **71** [2004 69: p10g⁴ p10g p7g³ 7m p8d⁶ 8.3f⁴ 8.5g 9.7m² 10m* Aug 4] sturdy, close-coupled gelding: fair handicapper: won at Kempton in August: effective at 7f to 1¼m: acts on all-weather, raced only on good going or firmer on turf: visored last 4 starts. *J. R. Best*

LITTLE FLUTE 3 b.c. Piccolo 121 – Nordic Victory (USA) (Nordico (USA)) [2004 **51** 52: p5g⁴ f5g f6s p6g p7g f6g* 6f⁶ 6m⁶ 5d⁴ 6d⁵ Oct 16] smallish, compact colt: modest performer: won banded event at Wolverhampton in April: stays 6f: acts on all-weather, good to firm and good to soft going: very slowly away fifth outing. *T. Keddy*

LITTLE FOX (IRE) 9 br.m. Persian Bold 123 – Dance Land (IRE) (Nordance (USA)) **–** [2004 11.6f⁶ 11.9f p16d Aug 9] fair at best: missed 2003: no form at 9 yrs. *J. J. Bridger*

LITTLE GANNET 3 ro.f. Bien Bien (USA) 125 – Lady Kalliste (Another Realm 118) **–** [2004 p10d 11.5g Jul 21] fourth foal: half-sister to 1¼m/11.5f winner Lady Jo (by Phountzi): dam no form: well held in maidens at Lingfield. *S. Dow*

LITTLE GOOD BAY 4 b.c. Danehill (USA) 126 – Brave Kris (IRE) 104 (Kris 135) **103** [2004 110: p7g p7g⁶ Nov 20] smallish colt: useful handicapper: better effort at Lingfield in autumn when sixth to Jack Sullivan: probably best around 7f: acts on polytrack, raced only on good going or firmer on turf: visored/blinkered last 7 starts: has had 2 handlers: sometimes slowly away/races freely. *J. H. M. Gosden*

LITTLE INDY 2 ch.c. (May 20) Forzando 122 – Indian Nectar 68 (Indian Ridge 123) **53 ?** [2004 5g 7g 7.1m 7.1s⁶ p6g f7g Dec 14] small colt: modest maiden: seemingly best effort at 7f on good to firm going. *R. Brotherton*

LITTLE JIMBOB 3 b.g. Desert Story (IRE) 115 – Artistic Licence (High Top 131) **85** [2004 71: 9.3f* 8g² 8.5d⁴ 8.2g³ 7g⁵ 8g² 10d⁴ p10g Oct 31] close-coupled gelding: fairly useful performer: won maiden at Carlisle in June: mostly creditable efforts in handicaps after, second at Leicester and Pontefract: stays 1¼m: acts on firm and good to soft going: races prominently. *R. A. Fahey*

LITTLE LONDON   3 b.g. Bahhare (USA) 122 – North Kildare (USA) (Northjet 136)   –
[2004 77: 8s Aug 29] useful-looking gelding: fair maiden: pulled up only start in 2004:
stayed 1m: acted on firm going: dead. *J. L. Dunlop*

LITTLE MISS GRACIE   2 gr.f. (Apr 22) Efisio 120 – Circled (USA) 83 (Cozzene   93
(USA)) [2004 7d³ 7d³ 8.3m² 8v⁴ 8f* 8d⁴ Oct 18] 9,000Y: tall, leggy filly: fourth foal:
sister to 1¼m winner in South Africa and half-sister to 2 winners, including 3-y-o Scott:
dam 2-y-o 7f winner who stayed 1½m: fairly useful performer: trained first 3 starts by
P. Burgoyne: won maiden at Pontefract in September by 5 lengths: good fourth in listed
races at Deauville and Pontefract (beaten 8¼ lengths by Comic Strip): will probably stay
1¼m: acts on any turf going. *A. B. Haynes*

LITTLE MISS LILI   3 b.f. Danzig Connection (USA) – Little Miss Rocker 65 (Rock   –
Hopper 124) [2004 8m 10g Sep 29] first foal: dam, 1½m winner, half-sister to useful
performer up to 2m Rada's Daughter: last in maidens. *G. G. Margarson*

LITTLE MISS TRICKY   5 br.m. Magic Ring (IRE) 115 – Mistook (USA) (Phone   –
Trick (USA)) [2004 –: p10g Feb 16] little sign of ability. *P. Mitchell*

LITTLE RICHARD (IRE)   5 b.g. Alhaarth (IRE) 126 – Intricacy 65 (Formidable   48
(USA) 125) [2004 60d: f12g f14g p13g⁴ f12g³ p16g* p12g⁴ p12g p12g² p13g³ p16g⁵
f14.8g⁴ 14.1d p12m Dec 15] small, workmanlike gelding: poor performer: won banded
race at Lingfield in February: effective at 1½m to 2m: acts on all-weather and good to
firm going: usually wears headgear. *M. Wellings*

LITTLE RIDGE (IRE)   3 b.g. Charnwood Forest (IRE) 125 – Princess Natalie 78   86
(Rudimentary (USA) 118) [2004 84p: 6g 6g p7g 5s* p5.1d³ p5g⁵ p5.1g⁵ f5f² Dec 28]   a81
close-coupled gelding: fairly useful performer: won minor event at Redcar (beat Highland Warrior by 1¾ lengths) in November: best at 5f: acts on all-weather, soft and good to
firm going: sometimes wanders: front runner. *H. Morrison*

LITTLE SKY   7 gr.m. Terimon 124 – Brown Coast (Oats 126) [2004 53?: p12g 12f   –
14.1m Jun 30] no form since debut (at 6 yrs). *D. Mullarkey*

LITTLESTAR (FR)   3 b.g. Robellino (USA) 127 – Green Charter 77 (Green Desert   59
(USA) 127) [2004 57: 10d 11.6s 11.6s 11.5m 10g² Sep 5] sturdy gelding: modest
maiden: form in 2004 only when neck second in handicap at Brighton in July, final start
for J. Dunlop: stays 1¼m: tried blinkered. *A. Dickman*

LITTLE TASK   6 b.g. Environment Friend 128 – Lucky Thing (Green Desert (USA)   45
127) [2004 –: 8.5m³ 10m* 12.3m⁴ 12f* 12m 12.1g⁴ 11.1g⁶ 12.1m p9.5g Oct 25] smallish,
close-coupled gelding: poor performer: won apprentice banded race at Nottingham in
May and handicap at Musselburgh in June: stays 1½m: acts on fibresand and firm going:
tried blinkered. *J. S. Wainwright*

LITTLE TOBIAS (IRE)   5 ch.g. Millkom 124 – Barbara Frietchie (IRE) (Try My   59 §
Best (USA) 130) [2004 61§: 16s⁶ 14.1s 14.1f* 16.1g³ 15.8m³ 17.1g 15s⁴ Oct 11]
smallish, good-topped gelding: modest handicapper: won apprentice event at Carlisle in
July: stays 2m: acts on firm and soft going: ungenuine. *Andrew Turnell*

LITTLETON LIBERTY   3 b.f. Royal Applause 124 – Lammastide 93 (Martinmas   –
128) [2004 –: p7g f5g Apr 22] little form: tried blinkered/in cheekpieces. *Andrew Reid*

LITTLETON TELCHAR (USA)   4 ch.c. Atticus (USA) 121 – Miss Waikiki (USA)   83
(Miswaki (USA) 124) [2004 9f⁵ 10m* 10f 10m 12s Aug 27] $14,000F, 350,000 francs Y,
2,500 3-y-o: quite good-topped colt: half-brother to 3 winners in USA: dam, won in USA
at 2 yrs, half-sister to smart 1¼m performer Husyan and to dam of 7-y-o Mubtaker: fairly
useful performer: trained on debut by H. O'Driscoll in Ireland: 50/1, won maiden at
Windsor in June by ¾ length from Summer Serenade: well below form in handicaps after:
stays 1¼m: acts on good to firm going. *M. J. Ryan*

LITTLETON VALAR (IRE)   4 ch.g. Definite Article 121 – Fresh Look (IRE) 64   43 §
(Alzao (USA) 117) [2004 49§: f9.4g 10d⁴ f11g⁴ 10m May 25] poor maiden: stayed 1¼m:
acted on good to firm and good to soft going: tried blinkered/in cheekpieces: inconsistent:
won over hurdles in May: dead. *J. R. Weymes*

LITTLETON ZEPHIR (USA)   5 b.m. Sandpit (BRZ) 129 – Miss Gorgeous (IRE)   64
76 (Damister (USA) 123) [2004 57: f7g f9.4g² f8.5g f9.4s p8g* f7m⁵ f8g 9.7g 9.9m p8m⁵
p8g* Dec 20] sturdy mare: modest performer: won banded events at Lingfield in April
(amateurs) and December: effective at 1m/1¼m: acts on all-weather: tried in headgear.
Mrs P. Townsley

LITTLE VENICE (IRE)   4 b.f. Fumo di Londra (IRE) 108 – Petrine (IRE) (Petorius   91
117) [2004 85: 6g 7g⁵ 7m³ 8m* 8m 8m 8.3g 8g* Sep 15] lightly-made filly: fairly useful

handicapper: won at Newmarket (by 7 lengths) in June and Yarmouth (by ¾ length from Johannian) in September: stays 1m: acts on firm and good to soft going: usually races prominently. *C. F. Wall*

LITTLE WALTHAM   2 ch.f. (May 28) Tomba 119 – Post Impressionist (IRE) 63   – (Ahonoora 122) [2004 6m p8d 6d Aug 29] sixth foal: dam 1½m and 2m winner: well held in maidens. *K. A. Morgan*

LITTLE WARNING   2 b.f. (Apr 7) Piccolo 121 – Iltimas (USA) 95 (Dayjur (USA)   **62** 137) [2004 5.1m 5.1f 5.1g⁵ 6s Oct 22] 8,000Y: fifth foal: closely related to 1999 2-y-o 5f winner Cautionary (by Warning) and half-sister to 4-y-o Zoom Zoom: dam, 5f and (including at 2 yrs) 6f winner, half-sister to Queen Mary winner Nadwah: modest maiden: should stay 6f: acts on firm ground. *R. M. Beckett*

LITTLE WIZZY   2 b.f. (Mar 27) Wizard King 122 – Little Unknown (Known Fact   **69 §** (USA) 135) [2004 5g³ 5.1g 5s* 5s³ 5g⁶ 5.1g 6v 6g⁵ p6g⁵ p6g p5.1g Dec 20] leggy filly: **a53 §** seventh living foal: dam unraced: fair on turf, modest on all-weather: won maiden at Warwick in May: likely to prove best at 5f/easy 6f: acts on polytrack and soft going: carries head awkwardly: no battler. *P. D. Evans*

LITZINSKY   6 b.g. Muhtarram (USA) 125 – Boulevard Girl 80 (Nicholas Bill 125)   – [2004 –: p16g 16g Mar 31] rather leggy, lengthy gelding: fair handicapper at best: lightly raced and little form since 2002. *C. B. B. Booth*

LIVE IN HOPE   2 b.f. (Apr 12) High Estate 127 – Movieland (USA) 109 (Nureyev   – (USA) 131) [2004 6m 6f 6g Jul 16] lengthy, slightly hollow-backed filly: half-sister to 3 winners, including 3-y-o Diamond Lodge: dam French 2-y-o 1m (Prix des Reservoirs) winner: no sign of ability in maidens. *Jedd O'Keeffe*

LIVELY FELIX   7 b.g. Presidium 124 – Full of Life 85 (Wolverlife 115) [2004 49d: – f6g⁴ f7g f7s⁶ f7g p7g p7g Apr 6] poor maiden: little form in 2004: tried visored/blinkered. *D. G. Bridgwater*

LIVE WIRE LUCY (USA)   3 b. or br.f. King of The Heap (USA) 116 – Approach   **?** The Bench (USA) (Majestic Light (USA)) [2004 8.5f 8.5f³ 6m 7d 10f 10g 10g 8g Sep 27] leggy filly: half-sister to 2 winners abroad by Muhtarram, including German winner up to 1m Friedrich August: dam maiden in USA: raced only at Calder at 2 yrs, winning maiden on turf: third in allowance race at Gulfstream in January: left J. Nazareth, now in USA and off 5 months after: well held in listed race/handicaps in Britain: stays 8.5f: acts on firm going: sent to Spain. *C. Tinkler*

LIVIA (IRE)   3 b.f. Titus Livius (FR) 115 – Passing Beauty 83 (Green Desert (USA)   **52 §** 127) [2004 p7g p10g⁶ p8g p7g⁴ 6s 7.1s⁶ 7s 7g 8f 10g 8.1d² p8.6g⁴ p8.6d Nov 3] €21,000Y: second foal: dam 1m winner in France: modest maiden: stays 1m: acts on polytrack and soft going: wore headgear last 7 starts: unreliable. *J. G. Portman*

LIVVIES LADY (IRE)   2 b.f. (Feb 9) Opening Verse (USA) 126 – Indian Wardance   – (ITY) (Indian Ridge 123) [2004 p7g p7g Oct 28] third foal: half-sister to fairly useful 2002 2-y-o 7f winner Vespasian (by Dashing Green Jones): dam Italian maiden: well held in maidens at Lingfield, slowly away. *D. K. Ivory*

LIWA'S LAKE (USA)   2 ch.f. (Feb 20) Greenwood Lake (USA) 119 – Champagne   **63 ?** Sweep (USA) (End Sweep (USA)) [2004 5f³ 5m 5d Aug 9] $80,000U, $300,000 2-y-o: tall, quite good-topped filly: first foal: dam, maiden in North America, sister to Canadian Grade 1 1m winner Dark Ending: form in maidens only when third at Sandown: tongue tied next time: sweating final start: left Godolphin, and sent to USA. *Saeed bin Suroor*

LIZARAZU (GER)   5 b.h. Second Set (IRE) 127 – Lilly (GER) (Motley (USA) 123)   **46** [2004 8.2d 8m 8m 8.3d 7s p7.1g f7g f8d Dec 21] third foal: half-brother to German 9.5f winner Loraine (by Goofalik): dam, German 9f/1¼m winner, half-sister to Deutsches Derby winner Lebos: useful performer at best: winner of 2 races from 27 outings in Germany, both in 2002: left J. Mayer after final start at 4 yrs: poor form on balance in Britain, in cheekpieces last 2 outings: stays 1¼m: acts on soft going. *F. Jordan*

LIZHAR (IRE)   3 b.f. Danetime (IRE) 121 – Amelesa (IRE) 65 (Perugino (USA) 84)   – [2004 55, a72: f6g⁴ f5g⁶ p5g⁴ f6g p5g⁴ f5s² f5s f6s⁴ p6g⁶ 5.1g 6m Jul 3] compact filly: **a63** modest performer: left M. Polglase before final outing: stays 6f: acts on fibresand and good to soft going: tried in cheekpieces/blinkers. *J. J. Quinn*

LLAMADAS   2 b.g. (Mar 23) Josr Algarhoud (IRE) 118 – Primulette 82 (Mummy's   **66 §** Pet 125) [2004 5d³ 5m 6d³ f7m⁴ 7g 5g³ 5g⁶ 5g⁶ 7m p5.1g² p6g p5.1g p6g p8m Dec 8]   **a59 §** 16,000Y: close-coupled gelding: half-brother to numerous winners, including 6f and 1m winner Proletariat (by Petong): dam 5f (at 2 yrs) and 1m winner: fair maiden on turf, modest on all-weather: left M. Dods after tenth start: stays 6f: acts on polytrack and good to soft going: usually wears headgear: ungenuine. *Mrs Stef Liddiard*

LOADED GUN   4 ch.g. Highest Honor (FR) 124 – Woodwardia (USA) 93 (El Gran Senor (USA) 136) [2004 –: f8f 10s^2 11.9g^4 10.9s 10s^3 9s^4 p9.5g p12.2g^4 p9.5g Nov 27] modest maiden: left Miss J. Feilden after reappearance: best efforts at 1$\frac{1}{4}$m: acts on polytrack and soft going. *W. M. Brisbourne*   **64**

LOADERFUN (IRE)   2 br.g. (Feb 21) Danehill Dancer (IRE) 117 – Sideloader Special 66 (Song 132) [2004 5m^4 6g^2 6s* 6g^2 Sep 25] 15,000F, 23,000 2-y-o: sturdy gelding: half-brother to several winners, including 1995 2-y-o 5f winner Jessica's Song (by Colmore Row) and unreliable 1$\frac{1}{2}$m seller winner Trumble (by Tragic Role): dam 6f winner: fairly useful performer: won maiden at Salisbury in September by 5 lengths from Anchor Date, making all: heavily eased when beaten 16 lengths by Country Rambler in 2-runner minor event at Ripon final start (gelded after): will probably stay 7f: acts on soft going. *H. Candy*   **93**

LOBENGULA (IRE)   2 b.g. (Feb 1) Spectrum (IRE) 126 – Playwaki (USA) (Miswaki (USA) 124) [2004 6g 7s^5 Nov 1] €15,000Y: second foal: dam unraced out of close relative to Secreto and Istabraq: modest form in maidens at York (slowly away) and Redcar: should stay at least 1m. *H. Alexander*   **62**

LOCAL POET   3 b.c. Robellino (USA) 127 – Laugharne (Known Fact) 135) [2004 92+: 6g* 7d^5 5.1d 6m^5 6m 6m 5g Aug 7] sturdy colt: fairly useful performer: landed odds in maiden at Doncaster in March, edging right: creditable fifth to Moss Vale in listed race at Haydock fourth start: tongue tied, well held in handicaps after: probably stays 7f: acts on good to firm and good to soft going. *B. A. McMahon*   **88**

LOCATOR (IRE)   3 b.g. Mujadil (USA) 119 – Lifeboat (IRE) (Petorius 117) [2004 60p: 8d 8m p10g Nov 13] tall gelding: has a quick action: maiden: form only on sole start at 2 yrs. *J. M. P. Eustace*   **–**

LOCHBUIE (IRE)   3 b.c. Definite Article 121 – Uncertain Affair (IRE) 79 (Darshaan 133) [2004 73p: 10.3g^4 12.3g* 12.3d* 12d^3 14m* 13.9s^4 14g^4 14g^3 Sep 30] big, good-bodied colt: useful performer: won handicaps at Ripon in April, Chester in May and Goodwood (by $\frac{3}{4}$ length from Yoshka) in July: creditable efforts after, fourth in handicaps at York (to Lost Soldier Three in Melrose Rated Stakes) and Haydock (behind Defining), then 5 lengths third to Tungsten Strike in listed race at Newmarket: stays 1$\frac{3}{4}$m: acts on soft and good to firm going: held up: reliable. *G. Wragg*   **103**

LOCH INCH   7 ch.g. Inchinor 119 – Carrie Kool 69 (Prince Sabo 123) [2004 62: 5g 5.3f 5m 5f^4 5.3g 5g^4 5.1m^2 6m^3 5m^3 5.7m Aug 15] smallish gelding: modest handicapper: broke leg final start: best at 5f/6f: acted on fibresand, firm and good to soft going: usually wore headgear: dead. *J. M. Bradley*   **60**

LOCH LAIRD   9 b.g. Beveled (USA) – Daisy Loch (Lochnager 132) [2004 62: p6g p6g p7g* p7g 6s^5 7f 7g 7m^5 8d^4 7s^3 7.1g p7g Sep 18] lengthy gelding: modest handicapper: won at Lingfield in March: stays 7f: acts on polytrack, firm and soft going: tried in headgear. *M. Madgwick*   **57**

LOCH QUEST (IRE)   2 ch.g. (Apr 18) Giant's Causeway (USA) 132 – Taibhseach (USA) 94 (Secreto (USA) 128) [2004 8m^5 8g 8g Oct 10] $150,000Y: sixth foal: half-brother to winner in USA by Woodman: dam, Irish 2-y-o 7f winner who probably stayed 1$\frac{1}{4}$m, half-sister to US Grade 1 1$\frac{1}{4}$m winner Mi Selecto: easily best effort in maidens when fifth at Goodwood, slowly away: gelded after final start: should stay 1$\frac{1}{4}$m. *Mrs A. J. Perrett*   **78**

LOCHRIDGE   5 ch.m. Indian Ridge 123 – Lochsong 129 (Song 132) [2004 110: 5m^2 5f 6f 6d^3 6g^2 6d^4 6g Sep 4] workmanlike mare: useful performer: creditable efforts in 2004 in listed race at Kempton (length second to Boogie Street), Summer Stakes at York (4 lengths third to Tante Rose) and minor event at Doncaster (neck second to Mac Love): stiff task in Sprint Cup at Haydock final start: probably best around 6f: acts on firm and good to soft going: usually races prominently. *A. M. Balding*   **106**

LOCKSTOCK (IRE)   6 b.g. Inchinor 119 – Risalah (Marju (IRE) 127) [2004 74: f8s p10g 8s* 8g 7.1m 7.1g 8.3m^5 8g^4 Oct 10] quite good-topped gelding: fair handicapper: won at Bath in May: stays 9.4f: acts on fibresand, heavy and good to firm going: usually wears blinkers/cheekpieces. *M. S. Saunders*   **77**

LOCOMBE HILL (IRE)   8 b.g. Barathea (IRE) 127 – Roberts Pride 62 (Roberto (USA) 131) [2004 74: p7g f8g^2 8v 7.1m 6m^5 7.5g 6g^4 6d^4 6.9f 7.2s* 7.5d^5 7m^3 7.2d* 6d^2 7.2s^2 8v f8s^6 Nov 17] very big, rather dipped-backed gelding: fair handicapper on turf, modest on all-weather: left D. Nicholls after ninth start: won at Ayr in August and Sept-   **79**   **a62**

ember: best at 6f to 1m: acts on fibresand and any turf going: tried visored: withdrawn having been unruly in stall intended third outing: takes good hold, and usually races prominently. *N. Wilson*

LODGER (FR) 4 ch.c. Grand Lodge (USA) 125 – Light River (USA) (Irish River **94**
(FR) 131) [2004 101: 11.9d 12m⁶ 12f⁴ 14g 16.2m Sep 25] big, good-topped colt: just fairly useful performer in 2004: stays 1¾m: acts on firm going: held up. *J. Noseda*

LODGICIAN (IRE) 2 b.c. (Apr 3) Grand Lodge (USA) 125 – Dundel (IRE) 82 (Mach- **63**
iavellian (USA) 123) [2004 6d⁴ 7d³ 7.5m 8g⁴ 7m 6g Oct 4] 80,000Y: useful-looking colt: fourth foal: half-brother to French 1m winner Wing And Wing (by Singspiel): dam, 7f winner, out of sister to high-class middle-distance stayer High Hawk, herself dam of In The Wings: has a quick action: modest maiden: should stay 1¼m: best efforts on good/good to soft going. *J. J. Quinn*

LOGGER RHYTHM (USA) 4 b.g. Woodman (USA) 126 – Formidable Dancer **–**
(USA) (Danzig (USA)) [2004 8g 10d 12d⁴ 11.8m 8.1s p12.2g Dec 15] compact gelding: little form. *R. Dickin*

LOGISTICAL 4 b.c. Grand Lodge (USA) 125 – Magic Milly 60 (Simply Great (FR) **53**
122) [2004 81: 7.1v 7m 7.1m⁵ 7m 7g 7.1g 7.1m p7g p8m p8.6g Dec 22] close-coupled colt: modest performer: stays 7f: acts on good to firm going, probably on soft: tried tongue tied: sometimes slowly away. *A. D. W. Pinder*

LOITOKITOK 2 b.g. (Mar 12) Piccolo 121 – Bonita Bee 50 (King of Spain 121) **59 ?**
[2004 p8d 8g 8g Sep 20] sturdy, close-coupled gelding: seemingly best effort in maidens when eighth at Kempton final start: slowly away all outings. *P. D. Cundell*

LOJO 2 ch.f. (Apr 24) Pivotal 124 – Myhat 71 (Factual (USA) 108) [2004 6m 6g³ 6f² **61**
7f* Jun 22] 5,000Y: leggy filly: first foal: dam a 2-y-o 6f winner who probably stayed 7f: modest performer: left R. Elliott, won 4-runner claimer at Brighton: stays 7f: acts on firm going. *C. A. Dwyer*

LOLA LOLA (IRE) 3 b.f. Piccolo 121 – French Gift 99 (Cadeaux Genereux 131) **–**
[2004 –: 8g f8g 7.1s Aug 12] lengthy filly: no form in maidens/handicaps. *J. L. Dunlop*

LOLA SAPOLA (IRE) 2 b.f. (Feb 9) Benny The Dip (USA) 127 – Cutpurse Moll 76 **77**
(Green Desert (USA) 127) [2004 6g 7g 7d 7m* 8d⁴ 8d Nov 5] angular, workmanlike filly: half-sister to several winners, including 5-y-o Colonel Cotton and useful 6f winner Cyclone Connie (by Dr Devious): dam, 7f winner, out of useful 1m/1¼m winner Pretty Pol: fair performer: won maiden at Brighton in September, coming from well off strong pace: creditable efforts in nurseries after: likely to stay 1¼m: acts on good to firm and good to soft ground: held up. *N. A. Callaghan*

LOLA'S DESTINY 3 b.f. Mark of Esteem (IRE) 137 – Kristiana (Kris 135) [2004 **38**
43: f9.4g⁵ f8g⁶ f8s Feb 10] quite good-topped filly: poor maiden: should have stayed at least 1m: dead. *P. A. Blockley*

LOMAPAMAR 3 b.f. Nashwan (USA) 135 – Morina (USA) (Lyphard (USA) 132) **71**
[2004 76: 11s³ 11g p13g 10v* Oct 20] leggy filly: fair performer: won maiden at Notting-ham in October: should stay 1½m: acts on heavy and good to firm going: ran as if amiss second/third starts: sold 23,000 gns. *Mrs A. J. Perrett*

LOMMEL (UAE) 3 b.c. Lomitas 129 – Idrica 88 (Rainbow Quest (USA) 134) [2004 **–**
84: 8g 7.1g Apr 30] smallish colt: won minor event at Yarmouth on debut: well below that form all 3 starts since: sold 4,700 gns. *D. R. Loder*

LONDONER (USA) 6 ch.g. Sky Classic (CAN) – Love And Affection (USA) (Exclu- **66**
sive Era (USA)) [2004 72?: p10g p8g p10g p12g p8g³ 7m² 7f² 7f* 8.1m 8.1f⁵ 7f³ 7.6m⁵ **a72**
8f² 8f 8s p8g* 8m⁶ p8.6g² p10g Dec 29] tall gelding: fair performer: won handicap at Brighton in June and apprentice minor event at Lingfield in September: effective at 7f, barely at 1½m: acts on polytrack, firm and good to soft going: tried tongue tied: usually races prominently: often finishes weakly. *S. Dow*

LONE PIPER 9 b.g. Warning 136 – Shamisen 86 (Diesis 133) [2004 47: f5g f5g **–**
f5g f5g⁶ f5s⁴ f5s³ f5g⁶ f5g⁶ 5.1d 6m⁶ 6.1m May 25] small gelding: poor mover: poor **a46**
performer: stays 7f: acts on fibresand and firm going: tried tongue tied/in headgear. *J. M. Bradley*

LONER 6 b.g. Magic Ring (IRE) 115 – Jolis Absent 57 (Primo Dominie 121) [2004 60, **62**
a–: 8d 8f² 7m Aug 3] strong gelding: modest handicapper: stays 1m: acts on firm and soft **a–**
going, probably on all-weather: tried blinkered, usually wears cheekpieces. *R. A. Fahey*

LONGRIDGE (GER) 6 ch.g. Surumu (GER) – La Paz (GER) (Roi Dagobert 128) **108**
[2004 108: a11.5g* a10g 9.3g* 10d² 12s 11d⁴ p10g³ Nov 20] useful performer: has won 8
races, including minor events at Neuss in January and Cologne in August: good efforts in
Group 3 event at Baden-Baden (¾-length second to Soldier Hollow) and listed race at
Lingfield (1¼ lengths third to Grand Passion, finishing strongly): stays 1½m: acts on
polytrack, sand and good to soft going. *M. Hofer, Germany*

LONG ROAD (USA) 3 b.g. Diesis 133 – Tuviah (USA) (Eastern Echo (USA)) [2004 **92**
8m² 8m² 8s² 10m* Jul 6] strong, good-topped gelding: third foal: brother to 1¼m/11f
winner Literacy: dam, placed in USA, half-sister to 9-y-o Duck Row (by Diesis): fairly
useful performer: second in maidens before winning similar event at Newmarket in July
by 3½ lengths from Mikao: gelded after: stays 1¼m: acts on soft and good to firm going:
flashed tail penultimate start. *J. Noseda*

LONG WEEKEND (IRE) 6 b.g. Flying Spur (AUS) – Friday Night (USA) (Trempo- **44**
lino (USA) 135) [2004 54, a–: f6g p6g⁶ f7g⁶ p6g² p6g* p5g* p6g⁴ p6g⁶ 6s 5.7m⁶ 6g 6f **a59**
6g 6m p6d⁴ p7.1g³ p7m p7.1g⁴ p6g* p6g² Dec 27] sturdy, angular gelding: modest on
all-weather, poor on turf: won banded races in March (2) and December, all at Lingfield:
stays easy 7f: acts on all-weather and good to firm going: often wears headgear. *D. Shaw*

LOOK AGAIN 3 ch.g. Zilzal (USA) 137 – Last Look (Rainbow Quest (USA) 134) **92**
[2004 10g* 10.3m⁴ Sep 8] rather leggy gelding: third foal: half-brother to 1m to 11.5f
winner Littlemissattitude (by Common Grounds) and 4-y-o Ultimata: dam unraced out of
half-sister to very smart sprinter/miler Pursuit of Love: fairly useful form: green, won
maiden at Nottingham in August by 4 lengths from Dundry: ran well when 3¼ lengths
fourth to Tartouche in minor event at Doncaster, taking strong hold: not sure to stay much
beyond 1¼m. *Mrs A. J. Perrett*

LOOK AT THE STARS (IRE) 2 b.g. (Apr 21) Bachir (IRE) 118 – Pizzazz 47 (Un- **81**
fuwain (USA) 131) [2004 6g 6g* 6m Aug 21] €30,000Y: half-brother to 3 winners,
including 5-y-o Creskeld and 4-y-o Somerset West: dam lightly-raced half-sister to Nell
Gwyn winner Thrilling Day: won maiden at Haydock in August by length from Molly
Marie: always behind in sales race at the Curragh final start, then gelded: will stay 7f.
C. G. Cox

LOOK HERE'S CAROL (IRE) 4 ch.f. Safawan 118 – Where's Carol 67 (Anfield **99**
117) [2004 94: 6g³ 6.1d³ 6d⁶ 7.1m³ 7g* 7f 7s⁵ 7g² 7m 7m Sep 26] leggy filly: useful
performer: won handicap at York in July by head from Digital: mostly creditable efforts
otherwise at 4 yrs, including when 1½ lengths third to Golden Nun in listed race at
Nottingham second start: effective at 6f/7f: acts on firm and soft going: sometimes slowly
away: consistent. *B. A. McMahon*

LOOKING DOWN 4 ch.f. Compton Place 125 – High Stepping (IRE) (Taufan (USA) **–**
119) [2004 87: 7s 7m May 31] lengthy filly: well held in 2004, including in seller: won
over hurdles in July. *P. C. Haslam*

LOOKING GREAT (USA) 2 b.g. (Mar 14) Gulch (USA) – Shoofha (IRE) 70 (Blue- **47**
bird (USA) 125) [2004 5g 6g 8.3m 8s Aug 28] poor maiden. *R. F. Johnson Houghton*

LOOKOUTHEREICOME 3 b.f. Rudimentary (USA) 118 – Sylvatica 99 (Thatch- **–**
ing 131) [2004 p8g p8g 11.6f 10m 8.1m Sep 6] half-sister to 3 winners, including fairly
useful Irish 1m winner Taajreh (by Mtoto): dam Irish 2-y-o 6f winner who stayed 1¼m:
little form in maidens. *T. T. Clement*

LOOKS COULD KILL (USA) 2 b. or br.g. (Feb 14) Red Ransom (USA) – Mingling **91**
Glances (USA) 106 (Woodman (USA) 126) [2004 7m² 8.3d* 8.1g⁴ 8s³ 7s² Oct 22]
40,000 2-y-o: good-topped gelding: first foal: dam Irish 1m winner who was later successful in USA (probably stayed 1¼m): fairly useful performer: won maiden at Hamilton
in August: in frame in nurseries after, good second at Newbury (gelded after): stays 1m:
acts on soft and good to firm going: found little penultimate start. *G. A. Butler*

LOOKS THE BUSINESS (IRE) 3 b.g. Marju (IRE) 127 – Business Centre (IRE) **71**
58 (Digamist (USA) 110) [2004 67: p10g² f9.4s⁴ p10g⁵ 10d 7.5d 10.2m May 17] workmanlike gelding: fair maiden: stays 1¼m: acts on polytrack and firm going: tongue tied
until final start. *W. G. M. Turner*

LORD ARTHUR 3 b.g. Mind Games 121 – Flower O'Cannie (IRE) 87 (Mujadil **49**
(USA) 119) [2004 –: f6g f6g⁴ f6m 6v 7.9g Sep 2] tall, leggy gelding: poor maiden: should
stay 7f: acts on fibresand: blinkered (raced too freely) final start. *M. W. Easterby*

LORD BASKERVILLE 3 b.g. Wolfhound (USA) 126 – My Dear Watson (Chilibang **59**
120) [2004 59: p7g p6g 5g⁶ 6v 5g³ 5.9f 5d 5d 5m 6m² 6g² 6d⁴ 7.9f 7.5s⁴ 6g⁴ 8m 8m 8m

Oct 10] leggy gelding: modest maiden: left M. Quinlan after second start: stays 6f: acts on good to firm going, probably on soft. *W. Storey*

LORD CHALFONT (IRE) 2 ch.g. (Feb 25) Daggers Drawn (USA) 114 – Byproxy (IRE) (Mujtahid (USA) 118) [2004 5g f5d f6d f7g 7m 8.3m 8.5s 8g Sep 16] strong gelding: no form in maidens/selling nursery: trained by D. Flood first 2 starts: usually blinkered/in cheekpieces. *M. J. Polglase*   **–**

LORD CHAMBERLAIN 11 b.g. Be My Chief (USA) 122 – Metaphysique (FR) (Law Society (USA) 130) [2004 65: f8.5g² f7g* f8f⁴ f8.5g⁴ p7g f7s² f8.5s² f8g 8f³ 8f⁴ 7.1m⁴ 7g 7.1f³ 8d 8.1m² 8.1g 8.1m* 7.6f⁴ 8.1d 7.1g² 9m⁵ 7g Sep 15] big gelding: fair handicapper: won apprentice event at Wolverhampton in January and ladies race at Chepstow in August: stays 8.5f: acts on fibresand and any turf going: blinkered: sometimes slowly away. *J. M. Bradley*   **68**

LORD CONYERS (IRE) 5 b.m. Inzar (USA) 112 – Primelta 55 (Primo Dominie 121) [2004 12d 10.1v 8s⁴ 8m⁴ May 28] leggy mare: poor maiden: stays 1¼m: acts on fibresand, firm and soft going: tried in headgear. *B. Ellison*   **42**

LORD DUNDEE (IRE) 6 ch.g. Polish Precedent (USA) 131 – Easy To Copy (USA) 108 (Affirmed (USA)) [2004 13.1d 11.9g 11.9f⁴ Jul 16] tall, well-made gelding: fairly useful winner in 2002: subsequently underwent minor surgery on knee, and showed little on return in 2004: visored on debut, tongue tied last 2 starts. *R. C. Guest*   **–**

LORD ELROND 2 b.c. (Mar 9) Magic Ring (IRE) 115 – Cactus Road (FR) (Iron Duke (FR) 122) [2004 5m May 24] last in minor event at Windsor. *P. W. Chapple-Hyam*   **–**

LORD EUROLINK (IRE) 10 b.g. Danehill (USA) 126 – Lady Eurolink 55 (Kala Shikari 125) [2004 83: 10g 10d Oct 18] strong, lengthy gelding: handicapper: well held at 10 yrs: usually visored in 2000: tried tongue tied. *M. H. Tompkins*   **–**

LORD GIZZMO 7 ch.g. Democratic (USA) 101 – Figrant (USA) (L'Emigrant (USA) 129) [2004 50: f12g f12g⁶ f12s Feb 14] handicapper: showed little in 2004. *P. W. Hiatt*   **–**

LORD GREYSTOKE (IRE) 3 b.g. Petardia 113 – Jungle Story (IRE) 74 (Alzao (USA) 117) [2004 62: p10g 8.3s 8.1g 12.6d 10g Sep 29] good-bodied gelding: maiden: showed little in 2004, in blinkers final start. *C. P. Morlock*   **–**

LORD JOHN 2 b.c. (May 1) Piccolo 121 – Mahbob Dancer (FR) (Groom Dancer (USA) 128) [2004 5g 5d⁴ 5m 6m⁴ f6d 7d 6s⁴ 5.9g 5g² 5f³ Sep 13] 900Y: sparely-made colt: fifth foal: half-brother to fairly useful 2000 2-y-o 6f winner Hamadeenah (by Alhijaz): dam unraced: modest maiden: effective at 5f/6f: acts on firm and soft going: blinkered (ran creditably) last 2 starts. *M. W. Easterby*   **62**

LORD KINTYRE 9 b.g. Makbul 104 – Highland Rowena 59 (Royben 125) [2004 92: 5.1d Aug 27] good-topped gelding: smart sprinter at best: well below form only 9-y-o outing: wore cheekpieces last 6 starts in 2003. *B. R. Millman*   **–**

LORD LAHAR 5 b.g. Fraam 114 – Brigadiers Bird (IRE) (Mujadil (USA) 119) [2004 –: 10m⁶ 11.8m 16m 12.1m 8.5d⁵ 10.2s 13.1f⁴ 15.8m p12.2g² 14.1d⁶ p12.2g* p12.2d Nov 3] modest handicapper: won at Wolverhampton in October, then left M. Channon: ran as if amiss final start: stays 13f: acts on polytrack, firm and good to soft going. *M. A. Buckley*   **56**

LORD LAMB 12 gr.g. Dunbeath (USA) 127 – Caroline Lamb 74 (Hotfoot 126) [2004 71: 16f³ 12.4v⁴ 16d 12m⁵ 16.2m³ Jul 23] tall, good-topped gelding: modest performer: stays 2m: acts on heavy and good to firm going: carries head high and no easy ride. *Mrs M. Reveley*   **55**

LORD LINKS (IRE) 3 ch.g. Daggers Drawn (USA) 114 – Lady From Limerick (IRE) 61 (Rainbows For Life (CAN)) [2004 84: 7g⁴ 8m 8g 7m 8g 7g⁴ 7d 8.5g³ 8d* p8.6g Nov 20] strong, workmanlike gelding: fairly useful handicapper: won at Goodwood in October by neck from Master Theo: stays 8.5f: acts on good to firm and good to soft going. *R. Hannon*   **86**

LORD MAYFAIR (USA) 2 b. or br.g. (Apr 16) Silic (FR) 125 – Spring Wedding (USA) (Prized (USA)) [2004 6d² 7g⁵ 6s⁶ Sep 24] $7,500J, resold $17,000Y: quite good-topped gelding: first foal: dam unraced out of half-sister to very smart 9f to 11f performer Running Stag: easily best effort in maidens when second at Hamilton: found little last 2 starts: should stay 7f. *T. D. Barron*   **80**

LORD MAYOR 3 b.g. Machiavellian (USA) 123 – Misleading Lady (Warning 136) [2004 92p: 10.4s³ 10.1m* 10m⁵ 11.9s⁵ 10v⁶ Aug 21] quite good-topped gelding: useful performer: won valuable handicap at Epsom in June in good style by 1¾ lengths from Royal Warrant, edging left: good 3¼ lengths fifth to Moscow Ballet in listed race at Royal   **104**

Vodafone Live! Stakes (Handicap), Epsom—a perfect start to Derby Day for Stoute and Fallon as Lord Mayor wins easing down from Royal Warrant (left) and Mystical Girl (far side)

Ascot next time: raced too freely in similar event at Haydock and Prix Guillaume d'Ornano at Deauville after: subsequently gelded: should stay 1½m: acts on polytrack and good to firm going, probably on heavy: held up. *Sir Michael Stoute*

LORD MELBOURNE (IRE)   5 b.g. Lycius (USA) 124 – Adana (IRE) (Classic **57 §**
Music (USA)) [2004 50§: f6g2 p7g* p6g4 f7g3 p7g p7g5 f6s* f8.5s6 f7d Jun 17] sturdy
gelding: modest performer: won banded race at Lingfield in January and (having been
claimed from J. Osborne after sixth start) claimer at Wolverhampton in March: effective
at 6f/7f: acts on all-weather and firm going: tried blinkered/in cheekpieces: unreliable.
A. G. Juckes

LORD NELLSSON   8 b.g. Arctic Lord 114 – Miss Petronella (Petoski 135) [2004 **64**
11.7f4 11.8m 11.5g 18d5 13.1f 17.2g Sep 27] modest maiden: stays 2¼m: acts on good to
soft going. *J. S. King*

LORD NORMACOTE   2 b.g. (Apr 30) Loup Sauvage (USA) 125 – Blessed Event **61**
117 (Kings Lake (USA) 133) [2004 6g 7g 7m4 8d 7m 8g a8g* Dec 12] 6,000F, 14,000Y:
unfurnished gelding: half-brother to several winners, including smart 8.5f to 12.5f winner
Sacrament (by Shirley Heights) and to dam of 5-y-o Chorist: dam, 1¼m winner, second
in Yorkshire Oaks: modest performer: left C. Dwyer before winning minor event at Gran
Canaria: stays 1m: blinkered final start in Britain. *J. Guerra, Spain*

LORD OF ADVENTURE (IRE)   2 b.c. (Mar 28) Inzar (USA) 112 – Highly Fashion- **51**
able (IRE) 68 (Polish Precedent (USA) 131) [2004 6m p8m5 Dec 21] better effort in
maidens when fifth at Lingfield. *Jamie Poulton*

LORD OF DREAMS (IRE)   2 ch.c. (Feb 1) Barathea (IRE) 127 – The Multiyorker **72**
(IRE) 72 (Digamist (USA) 110) [2004 6.1m 8s5 6f p8g3 8.3d4 8d2 Oct 18] 27,000Y: strong
colt: fifth foal: half-brother to fairly useful 2000 2-y-o 6f winner Siptitz Heights (by
Zieten), later successful in USA, and winner up to 1¾m in France/Belgium Courrier
du Tsar (by Ashkalani): dam, 7f winner (including at 2 yrs), out of sister to 2000 Guineas
winner Tap On Wood: fair maiden: good second in nursery at Pontefract, wandering:
stays 1m: acts on polytrack and soft going. *D. W. P. Arbuthnot*

LORD OF METHLEY   5 gr.g. Zilzal (USA) 137 – Paradise Waters 73 (Celestial **50**
Storm (USA) 132) [2004 57: 8.5d 8s 12.3m 8.3d* Aug 17] leggy, good-topped gelding:

590

modest performer: won seller at Hamilton: effective at 1m/1¼m: acts on soft and good to firm going, probably on fibresand: usually wears headgear: sold £7,500. *R. M. Whitaker*

LORD OF THE EAST 5 b.g. Emarati (USA) 74 – Fairy Free (Rousillon (USA) 133) **80** [2004 73, a–: 7d 7s³ 6d² 6m 7f* 6m³ 6g² 6d³ 7g² 6g* 6f 6m 7m Sep 9] lengthy gelding: **a–** fairly useful performer: won handicap at Thirsk in June and minor event at Doncaster (by ¾ length from Armagnac) in July: stays 7f: acts on firm and soft going: tried tongue tied/blinkered/in cheekpieces: usually races prominently: goes well (4 wins) at Epsom. *D. Nicholls*

LORD OF THE FENS 4 b.g. Danzig Connection (USA) – Zizi (IRE) 87 (Imp Society **–** (USA)) [2004 6m 8.1g 6m⁶ Jun 17] no form in maidens. *C. N. Kellett*

LORD OF THE SEA (IRE) 3 b.g. Perugino (USA) 84 – Sea Mistress (Habitat 134) **74 d** [2004 73: p8g³ p10g³ p8g⁴ p10g 11g 9.9g 8g⁴ 7m 8s⁶ 8m p8m p7g p6m p6g Dec 30] tall, leggy gelding: fair maiden: below form after third start: stays easy 1¼m: acts on polytrack, best turf efforts on good going: blinkered last 3 starts. *Jamie Poulton*

LORD WISHINGWELL (IRE) 3 b.g. Lake Coniston (IRE) 131 – Spirito Libro **38 +** (USA) 89 (Lear Fan (USA) 130) [2004 –: 10d 6v³ 6m³ 6s 7m⁴ 5m⁶ 6g 7.9m 7d 6d Oct 15] strong, workmanlike gelding: poor maiden: stays 7f: acts on good to firm going: usually visored/in cheekpieces. *J. S. Wainwright*

LORD ZINC 3 b.g. Forzando 122 – Zolica 60 (Beveled (USA)) [2004 5.1m May 17] **–** 66/1, tailed off in maiden at Bath. *D. W. P. Arbuthnot*

LORIEN HILL (IRE) 3 b.f. Danehill (USA) 126 – Lothlorien (USA) 80 (Woodman **78** (USA) 126) [2004 69: 8.3s⁶ 8.2d⁵ 7.5m* 7m 7m² 7g 7.1m³ 7g 8g⁵ p10g Nov 10] strong filly: fair performer: won maiden at Beverley in June: effective at 7f/1m: acts on polytrack, good to firm and good to soft going: consistent. *B. W. Hills*

LORNA DUNE 2 b.f. (Feb 21) Desert Story (IRE) 115 – Autumn Affair 100 (Lugana **67** Beach 116) [2004 6s³ 6f⁵ 5g 5f⁶ f7g 7m³ 8g* 10m 8.3g⁵ p8.6g p8.6g⁴ p8.6g p8.6g² Dec **a53** 11] 11,000Y: quite good-topped filly: fourth foal: half-sister to 1¼m winner Portacasa (by Robellino): dam 2-y-o 6f winner who stayed 1m: fair on turf, modest on all-weather: left Mrs J. Ramsden prior to winning selling nursery at Yarmouth in September: stays 8.6f: acts on all-weather, best turf effort on good going: wore headgear 5 of last 6 outings. *J. G. M. O'Shea*

LOS ORGANOS (IRE) 2 br.f. (Mar 6) Turtle Island (IRE) 123 – Spicebird (IRE) 67 **81** (Ela-Mana-Mou 132) [2004 8v³ 8d Oct 30] leggy filly: first foal: dam, Irish 1½m winner, half-sister to Horris Hill Stakes winner Sapieha and French stayer Dajraan, both smart: fairly useful form in maiden at Newbury (third to Descartes) and listed race at Newmarket (last of 8 to Squaw Dance): will be suited by 1¼m/1½m. *P. W. Chapple-Hyam*

LOST SOLDIER THREE (IRE) 3 b.g. Barathea (IRE) 127 – Donya 74 (Mill Reef **107** (USA) 141) [2004 8m⁶ 10.2g* 10f⁵ 10g⁴ 13.3d² 13.9s* 14.6f* 14g⁴ Sep 30] close-coupled gelding: half-brother to several winners, including 10.5f/1½m winner Altaweelah (by Fairy King) and 1995 2-y-o 6f winner Jedaal (by Soviet Star), both useful: dam, ran twice (at 1¼m and 1½m), out of Prix de Diane winner Dunette: useful performer: won maiden at Chepstow in June and handicaps at York (Kone PLC Melrose Rated Stakes by 3½ lengths from Peak of Perfection) in August and Doncaster (beat Sergeant Cecil by 1¼

totepool Mallard Stakes (Handicap), Doncaster—the progressive Lost Soldier Three defies a 10-lb rise in his mark to beat the strong-finishing Sergeant Cecil (No.8), Fantastic Love (rail) and Trust Rule

lengths in totepool Mallard Stakes) in September: favourite and sweating, below form in listed race won by Tungsten Strike at Newmarket final start: will stay 2m: acts on firm and soft going: waited with. *L. M. Cumani*

LOST SPIRIT   8 b.g. Strolling Along (USA) – Shoag (USA) (Affirmed (USA)) [2004 –
54, a36: p10g 11.8m May 31] strong gelding: well held in 2004: tried blinkered.
P. W. Hiatt

LOTTIE   3 b.f. Robellino (USA) 127 – Montserrat 81 (Aragon 118) [2004 7g 7m⁵ 7g⁴ –
6g 7g Sep 20] 1,200 3-y-o: fourth foal: half-sister to 2002 2-y-o 6f winner Sarayat (by
Polar Falcon) and 6f (at 2 yrs) to 1m winner Terfel (by Lion Cavern), both useful: dam 5f
(at 2 yrs) and 6f winner: little form. *Miss V. Haigh*

LOTTIE DUNDASS   2 ch.f. (Mar 23) Polar Falcon (USA) 126 – Sand Grouse (USA)   72
(Arctic Tern (USA) 126) [2004 6m⁵ 7g² 7.1m 8f⁴ 8g⁴ p7g⁴ Nov 16] 42,000Y: rather
leggy, lengthy filly: sister to smart French/Spanish performer up to 1m Sand Falcon and
half-sister to several winners: dam French 1¼m winner: fair maiden: stays 1m: acts on
all-weather and firm going. *W. R. Swinburn*

LOUGHLORIEN (IRE)   5 b.g. Lake Coniston (IRE) 131 – Fey Lady (IRE) (Fairy   61
King (USA)) [2004 66: 5m 6f 5g 5g 6.1s 6m³ 5m³ 5m⁴ 6m 5m* 6g² 5s³ f5m Nov 22]
close-coupled, good-topped gelding: modest performer: won banded event at Carlisle in
September, first start after leaving R. Fahey: effective at 5f/6f: acts on firm and soft going:
sometimes wears headgear (all wins without). *R. E. Barr*

LOUISE PARIS (IRE)   2 b.f. (Apr 28) Soviet Star (USA) 128 – Avantage Service   –
(IRE) (Exactly Sharp (USA) 121) [2004 p8d p8g Nov 13] €4,000Y: half-sister to several
winners in Greece/Turkey: dam unraced close relative to dam of 5-y-o Epalo: 100/1, well
held in maidens at Lingfield: trained by M. Attwater on debut. *P. Butler*

LOUISE RAYNER   2 b.f. (Jan 22) Vettori (IRE) 119 – Showery 76 (Rainbow Quest   71
(USA) 134) [2004 7f⁵ 7.5g⁴ 7f p7d 10v* Oct 20] fifth foal: half-sister to useful 1m winner
(including at 2 yrs) Bestam (by Selkirk) and winner in Hong Kong by Cadeaux Genereux:
dam, 6f winner, half-sister to 6-y-o Adiemus: fair performer: won maiden at Nottingham
by length from Sand Repeal: will stay at least 1½m: acts on heavy ground: sold 12,000
gns. *M. L. W. Bell*

LOUIS GEORGIO   5 b.g. Royal Applause 124 – Swellegant 84 (Midyan (USA) 124)   –
[2004 5.3m f6g 6.1m May 25] smallish gelding: fair at 3 yrs: ran in Spain for J. Brown at
4 yrs, winning handicap at Mijas: well held in 2004. *M. R. Hoad*

LOUISIADE (IRE)   3 b.g. Tagula (IRE) 116 – Titchwell Lass 57 (Lead On Time (USA)   65
123) [2004 74: 5s 6d³ 6.1g 6g 8m³ 8m³ 8s 8g f7g⁵ f7g⁵ f8g⁵ Dec 28] strong, lengthy gelding: fair performer: stays 1m: acts on firm going, probably on fibresand. *T. D. Easterby*

LOUIS PRIMA   3 gr.g. Paris House 123 – Chanson d'Amour (IRE) (High Estate 127)   –
[2004 –: 5f 5.9m 5g 6s Sep 19] smallish gelding: little form: tried in headgear. *Miss
L. A. Perratt*

LOUISVILLE PRINCE   3 ch.g. Bluegrass Prince (IRE) 110 – Noble Soul 67 (Sayf   –
El Arab (USA) 127) [2004 p10g p7.1g p7g⁵ Dec 29] poor form in maidens/seller: should
stay 1m. *A. P. Jones*

LOUPHOLE   2 ch.g. (Apr 4) Loup Sauvage (USA) 125 – Goodwood Lass (IRE) 71   91
(Alzao (USA) 117) [2004 5m³ 6m⁴ 5.3m* 5.1g 6m 5m³ 5m* 6d p6g* Nov 8] 2,500Y:
close-coupled gelding: fourth foal: half-brother to 2001 2-y-o 7.5f winner Silent Gift (by
Brief Truce): dam 7f (at 2 yrs) and 1½m winner: fairly useful performer: won maiden at
Brighton in July and nurseries at Epsom in October and Wolverhampton (by short head
from Forzeen) in November: likely to prove best at 5f/6f: acts on polytrack and good to
firm going. *P. J. Makin*

LOVE AFFAIR (IRE)   2 b.f. (Apr 4) Tagula (IRE) 116 – Changing Partners 58 (Rain-   73
bow Quest (USA) 134) [2004 7m² 7d 6f 7g² Oct 2] 26,000Y: lengthy, useful-looking
filly: fourth living foal: half-sister to 2 winners, including German 6f (at 2 yrs) to 9f winner Glockenbach (by Doyoun): dam 1½m winner: fair maiden: second at Goodwood and
Newmarket (nursery, edged right): should stay 1m: acts on good to firm going. *R. Hannon*

LOVE ALWAYS   2 b.f. (Feb 18) Piccolo 121 – Lady Isabell 62 (Rambo Dancer (CAN)   75
107) [2004 7g⁴ 7g² Sep 20] tall, attractive filly: second foal: half-sister to 4-y-o Vengeance: dam maiden who should have been suited by at least 1m: fair form in maidens at
Salisbury and Kempton (second to Quickfire): should stay 1m. *Mrs A. J. Perrett*

LOVE AND HONOUR 2 b.f. (Feb 20) Silver Patriarch (IRE) 125 – Fox Star (IRE) –
61 (Foxhound (USA) 103) [2004 8s Oct 27] first foal: dam, maiden, stayed 7f: 100/1,
tailed off in maiden at Yarmouth. *Julian Poulton*

LOVE AND LAUGHTER (IRE) 2 b.f. (Mar 1) Theatrical 128 – Hoh Dear (IRE) **74**
106 (Sri Pekan (USA) 117) [2004 6s⁶ 7m* 7f Sep 11] €60,000Y: smallish filly: first
foal: dam 2-y-o 5f to 1m (Canadian Grade 3 event) winner: won maiden at Chester in
August, soon off bridle but leading final 1f: possibly amiss final start: will stay at least
1m. *T. D. Easterby*

LOVE ANGEL (USA) 2 b. or br.c. (Jan 31) Woodman (USA) 126 – Omnia (USA) **76**
85 (Green Dancer (USA) 132) [2004 6m⁴ 6g³ Jul 20] good-topped colt: sixth foal: closely
related/half-brother to winners in USA by Miswaki and Pleasant Colony: dam, 7f winner,
half-sister to smart performer up to 1m Firm Pledge: fair form in minor event at Newmarket and maiden at Ayr (third to Madame Topflight): should stay 1m. *M. Johnston*

LOVE ATTACK (IRE) 2 b.f. (Mar 18) Sri Pekan (USA) 117 – Bradwell (IRE) 76 **39**
(Taufan (USA) 119) [2004 p7.1g⁶ p7.1g⁶ 6s Nov 6] €5,000F, €5,200Y: seventh foal: half-
sister to 3 winners, including fairly useful Irish 2002 2-y-o 5f winner Ryan's Academy
(by Ali-Royal): dam 5f winner who probably stayed 7f: poor form in seller/maidens.
D. Carroll

LOVE BEAUTY (USA) 2 b.c. (Apr 10) Seeking The Gold (USA) – Heavenly **77**
Rhythm (USA) (Septieme Ciel (USA) 123) [2004 6m⁴ 7m 8.1s² 8d⁵ Nov 3] big, leggy
colt: on the weak side at 2 yrs: has a quick action: fifth foal: half-brother to 2000 2-y-o 7f
winner Rebel Storm (by Storm Bird): dam unraced half-sister to very smart Irish miler
Prince of Birds: fair maiden: second at Haydock, easily best effort: stays 1m: acts on soft
ground. *M. Johnston*

LOVE FROM RUSSIA 2 b.g. (Feb 7) Xaar 132 – Heart 87 (Cadeaux Genereux 131) **39**
[2004 6d 8m 6m 6g Oct 8] small, sturdy gelding: poor maiden: should stay 1m. *A. Berry*

LOVE IN SEATTLE (IRE) 4 b.c. Seattle Slew (USA)) – Tamise (USA) 113 (Time **81 d**
For A Change (USA)) [2004 84: 10.1v 8g* 8m 8m 8.3m 10.4g Oct 8] big, rangy colt:
fairly useful performer, lightly raced: made all in minor event at Musselburgh in April:
dropped away tamely all starts after: effective at 1m/1¼m: acts on good to firm going:
races prominently: none too reliable. *M. Johnston*

LOVE IN THE MIST (USA) 3 b.f. Silver Hawk (USA) 123 – Fast Nellie (USA) –
(Ack Ack (USA)) [2004 69: p7g Jan 3] workmanlike filly: maiden: well below form only
start in 2004. *E. A. L. Dunlop*

LOVEISDANGEROUS 3 b.f. Pursuit of Love 124 – Brookhead Lady 73 (Petong **48**
126) [2004 54: f5g⁵ 5d 6m May 26] rather unfurnished filly: poor performer: will prove
best at 5f/6f: acts on firm going, probably on fibresand: tried in cheekpieces. *Don Enrico
Incisa*

LOVELORN 2 b.g. (Feb 22) Mind Games 121 – Love Letters 81 (Pursuit of Love 124) **58**
[2004 f6d³ 5.9f 5.1g Aug 16] modest form in maidens: will need to settle to stay beyond
6f: best effort on fibresand. *M. W. Easterby*

LOVE ME TENDER 2 b.f. (Jan 9) Green Desert (USA) 127 – Easy To Love (USA) **66**
86 (Diesis 133) [2004 7m 7d⁵ 6s Oct 29] smallish, strong, lengthy filly: first foal: dam,
11.5f winner, sister to Oaks winner Love Divine out of useful close relative to Champion
Stakes winner Legal Case: easily best effort in maidens when fifth to Thakafaat at Newmarket: found little there final start: bred to stay 1m. *H. R. A. Cecil*

LOVE OF LIFE 3 b.f. Spectrum (IRE) 126 – Night Over Day 57 (Most Welcome **52 §**
131) [2004 9.7s 7d 8m⁶ 7m 6.9m² 8d p7.1d Nov 5] 4,200F: second foal: half-sister to
fairly useful Italian 1m to 1¼m winner Mrs Seek (by Unfuwain): dam, Irish maiden out
of half-sister to smart 1¼m performer Sasuru, stayed 9f: modest maiden: left M. Quinlan
after second start: visored, refused to race final outing: stays 7f: acts on good to firm
going: one to treat with caution. *Julian Poulton*

LOVE PALACE (IRE) 2 b.c. (Mar 23) King's Best (USA) 132 – Vijaya (USA) (Lear **95**
Fan (USA) 130) [2004 7.5d² 8.3d² 7g⁴ 8.3d* 8d⁵ Oct 15] €110,000Y: big, good-topped
colt: has a quick action: fourth foal: half-brother to 3-y-o Hunting Lodge: dam 1m/9f
winner in France (later successful in USA): useful performer: won maiden at Hamilton in
September by 9 lengths from Kames Park, making all: paid for racing up with good pace
in minor event at Newmarket final start: stays 1m. *M. Johnston*

LOVERS WALK (USA) 3 b.f. Diesis 133 – Starlight Way (USA) (Green Dancer **50**
(USA) 132) [2004 p7.1g⁶ f8g⁵ Nov 23] $65,000Y: fifth foal: sister to fairly useful 1m

winner Silent Crystal, later successful in USA, and half-sister to 2 winners in North America, including Canadian Grade 1 2000 2-y-o 8.5f winner Salty You (by Salt Lake): dam, 1m/8.5f winner in USA, half-sister to top-class performer up to 1m Moorestyle: better effort in maidens when sixth at Wolverhampton: should stay 1m: sold 42,000 gns. *W. J. Haggas*

LOVE'S DESIGN (IRE)   7 b. or br.g. Pursuit of Love 124 – Cephista 61 (Shirley Heights 130) [2004 ?, a60: f12s f8.5g6 f9.4g f7g f9.4g5 f8.5s5 7m4 May 18] poor performer: best at 7f to 8.5f: acts on all weather, firm and soft going: sometimes wears headgear: held up: often finds little. *Miss S. J. Wilton*   **47**

LOVES TRAVELLING (IRE)   4 b.g. Blues Traveller (IRE) 119 – Fast Love (IRE) (Second Set (IRE) 127) [2004 85: 12g2 11.9g* 11.9d2 14g 12m Sep 26] leggy gelding: useful handicapper: won at Carlisle in June: good neck second to Carte Diamond at York third start, hanging left: ran as if amiss final start: stays 1¾m: acts on polytrack, firm and good to soft going: held up: sold 37,000 gns. *L. M. Cumani*   **95**

LOVE THIRTY   2 b.f. (Mar 3) Mister Baileys 123 – Polished Up 51 (Polish Precedent (USA) 131) [2004 6f6 6d2 6.5g5 6g* Sep 30] 120,000Y: leggy filly: first foal: dam, maiden who stayed 1¼m, half-sister to Cadeaux Genereux: fairly useful performer: odds on, won maiden at Goodwood by short head from Cape Columbine: best effort when fifth to Salamanca in sales race at Newbury: will probably stay 7f. *M. R. Channon*   **86**

LOVE TRIANGLE (IRE)   3 ch.g. Titus Livius (FR) 115 – Kirsova (Absalom 128) [2004 82: 7.1f3 6d 7.1d 8d 8g4 10m5 p10g p13.9g Dec 31] smallish, good-topped gelding: fair performer: left D. Elsworth after penultimate start: stays 1¼m: acts on firm and good to soft going: tongue tied (ran creditably) final start. *Mrs Stef Liddiard*   **81**

LOVE YOU ALWAYS (USA)   4 ch.g. Woodman (USA) 126 – Encorenous (USA) (Diesis 133) [2004 10v 10.3f6 10d Sep 20] lengthy gelding: useful at 2 yrs: missed following season: showed more temperament than ability in 2004, leaving D. Loder after reappearance. *Miss J. Feilden*   **–**

LOVEYOULONGTIME   3 gr.f. Compton Place 125 – Sky Red 75 (Night Shift (USA)) [2004 6m 5.2m 5m4 Jul 7] 40,000Y: good-topped filly: second foal: dam, 5f winner, sister to useful sprinter Night Haven: poor form in maidens. *A. M. Balding*   **38**

LOW CLOUD   4 b.g. Danehill (USA) 126 – Raincloud (Rainbow Quest (USA) 134) [2004 83: 10.3d6 10g 7m3 7.9f5 8.5g* 7.1m4 8d3 10.3g4 9m 8.3d 10d p9.5g Dec 4] useful-looking gelding: fair performer: won minor event at Beverley in June: sometimes ran as if amiss after, leaving D. Nicholls after tenth start: stays 1¼m: acts on firm and good to soft going, probably on polytrack: effective visored or not. *J. J. Quinn*   **79**

LOWESTOFT PLAYBOY   2 ch.g. (Mar 16) Pivotal 124 – Red Typhoon 75 (Belfort (FR) 89) [2004 5f 6m6 5g5 5m 6m p6g4 p5.1d5 8d p5.1g2 p6g6 Dec 3] 4,500Y: leggy gelding: first foal: dam 2-y-o 6f winner: fair maiden: likely to prove best at 5f/6f: acts on polytrack and good to firm ground: often races prominently. *Mrs C. A. Dunnett*   **68**

LOYAL LOVE (USA)   2 br.f. (May 11) Danzig (USA) – Always Loyal (USA) 113 (Zilzal (USA) 137) [2004 6g6 6g* Oct 2] good-topped filly: fourth foal: dam, won Poule d'Essai des Pouliches (and stayed 10.5f), sister to minor winner in USA: half-sister to top-class French sprinter Anabaa (by Danzig) and to high-class 1m/1¼m winner in USA/Dubai Key of Luck: much better effort in maidens when winning at Newmarket by 2½ lengths from Discuss, making all in far-side group: will stay 7f, probably 1m: useful prospect. *Saeed bin Suroor*   **85 p**

LOYAL TYCOON (IRE)   6 br.g. Royal Abjar (USA) 121 – Rosy Lydgate 53 (Last Tycoon 131) [2004 97: 6g 6v 6g2 6m5 6m 7m 6g* 6.5g 6f5 6f5 6m 6m2 Aug 16] robust, close-coupled gelding: useful performer: won handicap at Epsom in July by 5 lengths from Lord of The East: claimed £26,000 final outing: effective at 6f/7f: acts on all-weather, firm and soft going: tried visored at 4 yrs: usually held up: tough. *D. Nicholls*   **97**

LOYALTY LODGE (IRE)   2 ch.g. (Apr 7) Grand Lodge (USA) 125 – Gaily Grecian (IRE) (Ela-Mana-Mou 132) [2004 6s 6m6 7d 7f Sep 2] good-topped gelding: has a quick action: modest maiden: form only when sixth at Ripon: should stay at least 1m. *J. D. Bethell*   **50**

LUALUA   3 ch.g. Presidium 124 – Tawny 81 (Grey Ghost 98) [2004 77: 6g4 5m2 6.1g3 5m 5d4 5d3 5m 5d 5m6 Oct 2] sturdy gelding: fairly useful performer: best efforts when placed in handicaps at Thirsk and Nottingham second/third starts: effective at 5f/6f: acts on good to firm going: visored (looked temperamental) penultimate outing: usually slowly away. *T. D. Barron*   **83**

LUAS LINE (IRE) 2 b.f. (Feb 26) Danehill (USA) 126 – Streetcar (IRE) 69 (In The **102** Wings 128) [2004 6d 6f* 7m² 7s Aug 29] €150,000Y: neat filly: third foal, dam, lightly raced at 2 yrs in Ireland, half-sister to smart but untrustworthy 6f to 1m winner Intimate Guest: useful performer: odds on, won maiden at Cork in August: best effort when ½-length second to Silk And Scarlet in Debutante Stakes at the Curragh: only seventh in Prestige Stakes at Goodwood final start: stays 7f: acts on firm ground. *D. Wachman, Ireland*

LUBECK 2 b.g. (Jan 18) Lujain (USA) 119 – Milling (IRE) 89 (In The Wings 128) **79** [2004 6g⁵ 6g* 6d Aug 17] 15,000F, €110,000Y: strong gelding: second foal: dam, 9f winner, closely related to smart middle-distance stayer Parthian Springs and half-sister to smart 9f/1¼m winner Pasternak, out of Irish Oaks winner Princess Pati: made all in maiden at Newmarket in July (beat Disguise by a neck): slowly away when only ninth in nursery at York (gelded after): should stay 7f. *D. R. Loder*

LUBINAS (IRE) 5 b.g. Grand Lodge (USA) 125 – Liebesgirl (Konigsstuhl (GER)) **–** [2004 ?: 14.1s f14.8m⁵ May 10] big gelding: maiden: little form on Flat in Britain: fair hurdler. *F. Jordan*

LUCAYAN BELLE 3 b.f. Cadeaux Genereux 131 – Floppie (FR) (Law Society **–** (USA) 130) [2004 10d Apr 24] 25,000Y: sixth foal: closely related to fairly useful Irish 7f winner Still Going On (by Prince Sabo) and half-sister to several winners, including 5-y-o Ringmoor Down: dam French 1m winner: 5/1 and visored, well held in seller at Ripon. *M. L. W. Bell*

LUCAYAN DANCER 4 b.g. Zieten (USA) 118 – Tittle Tattle (IRE) 80 (Soviet Lad **67** (USA)) [2004 85d: 7d⁶ 8v⁵ 9.9d⁵ 8g 10s* 10.9s⁴ 10f* 10.1m² 10.3s³ 10s⁴ Nov 1] leggy gelding: has a markedly round action: fair performer: won amateur handicap at Brighton in August and apprentice minor event at Pontefract in September: stays 1¼m: acts on any going: tried in cheekpieces/blinkers at 3 yrs. *D. Nicholls*

LUCAYAN LEGEND (IRE) 3 b.c. Docksider (USA) 124 – Capo di Monte 118 **98** (Final Straw 127) [2004 8v⁶ 8g³ 8m* 8m² 9.9m Jul 29] 16,500F, 42,000Y: strong colt: has a quick, unimpressive action: half-brother to several winners, including useful 5f to 7f winner Daawe (by Danzig) and fairly useful 1¼m winner Lace Wing (by Caerleon): dam 6f (at 2 yrs) to 11f (US Grade 3 event) winner: useful performer: won maiden at Ripon in May: good length second of 27 to Mandobi in Britannia Stakes (Handicap) at Royal Ascot, finishing strongly: moved poorly to post when well held in ladbrokes.com Handicap at Goodwood final start: jarred up after: likely to stay 1¼m: acts on good to firm going. *R. Hannon*

LUCAYAN MONARCH 6 ch.g. Cadeaux Genereux 131 – Flight Soundly (IRE) 78 **63** (Caerleon (USA) 132) [2004 73: f7g² f7g* f7g* f7g² f7g⁵ f8.5g p7g p8g² p7g³ p8g² p8g³ p7g⁶ p7g⁵ p7g² Apr 19] lengthy gelding: modest performer: won seller and claimer at Southwell in January: reportedly finished lame fifth start, then left P. Blockley: probably best at 7f/1m: acts on all-weather, firm and soft going: tried blinkered (ran poorly), usually wears cheekpieces. *P. S. McEntee*

LUCEBALL (IRE) 4 b.f. Bluebird (USA) 125 – Mysterious Plans (IRE) (Last **51** Tycoon 131) [2004 54: p6g p6g 5f 5.8g 5g* 5g Jul 1] modest handicapper: won at Down **a?** Royal in June: below form otherwise at 4 yrs, including at Lingfield first 2 starts: effective at 5f/6f: acts on good to firm going: sometimes blinkered/tongue tied. *P. Morris, Ireland*

LUCEFER (IRE) 6 b.g. Lycius (USA) 124 – Maharani (USA) (Red Ransom (USA)) **59** [2004 55: p8g 7m 9.7s³ 10m⁴ 8.2m⁴ 9g 8m³ 8s* 8.1s 7g⁵ 8g 8d p8.6d⁵ p10m⁵ Nov 22] leggy gelding: modest performer: won handicap at Brighton in August: stays 1¼m: acts on polytrack, firm and soft going: tried blinkered at 3 yrs: sometimes tongue tied: sometimes carries head high. *G. C. H. Chung*

LUCE (IRE) 3 b.f. Sadler's Wells (USA) 132 – Onaga (USA) (Mr Prospector (USA)) **59** [2004 12.5d p10g⁴ Dec 30] third foal: half-sister to 2 winners abroad, including useful French 2001 2-y-o 5.5f winner Sashimi (by Mt Livermore): dam, US maiden, sister to dam of One Cool Cat: much better effort in maidens (left J. Oxx in Ireland after debut) when 3½ lengths fourth to Silver Palace at Lingfield. *H. Morrison*

LUCHI 3 ch.f. Mark of Esteem (IRE) 137 – Penmayne 95 (Inchinor 119) [2004 p6g⁶ **45 ?** p6g Feb 4] 16,000Y: first foal: dam 2-y-o 6f winner: modest maiden at Lingfield when slow-starting sixth: refused to enter stall intended debut. *A. Charlton*

LUCID DREAMS (IRE) 5 b.g. Sri Pekan (USA) 117 – Scenaria (IRE) (Scenic 128) **67** [2004 63: p7g⁵ f7g p7g⁴ p8g* p8g² p8g³ p8g* p8g⁵ Mar 31] rather leggy, good-topped gelding: fair handicapper: won at Lingfield in February and March: stays easy 1m: acts on all-weather and firm going: tried blinkered in 2003, wore cheekpieces last 3 outings: consistent. *M. Wigham*

LUCIFEROUS (USA) 2 ch.f. (Feb 17) Devil's Bag (USA) – Vital Laser (USA) **64** (Seeking The Gold (USA)) [2004 6g⁵ 6g⁶ Aug 21] $25,000F, 10,000Y: third foal: half-sister to winner in Japan by Louis Quatorze: dam unraced: modest form in maidens at Salisbury (made most) and Lingfield (slowly away): will probably stay 7f. *Jane Southcombe*

LUCIUS VERRUS (USA) 4 b.g. Danzig (USA) – Magic of Life (USA) 118 (Seattle **57** Slew (USA)) [2004 55: f5s³ p7g f5g⁵ 5v f6g⁵ f5g² f6g f6g⁵ f6m⁶ 6g f6s³ p6g² p7m⁶ f6g² p6g⁴ Dec 20] modest performer: won maiden claimer at Wolverhampton in April: should stay 7f: acts on all-weather and good to firm going: visored/blinkered after fourth start. *D. Shaw*

LUCKILY (IRE) 5 br.m. Key of Luck (USA) 126 – Sarapaka (IRE) 71 (Kahyasi 130) **–** [2004 61: 7g 12v p9.5g Dec 13] IR 7,400Y: first foal: dam Irish 11f winner: lightly-raced maiden: well held in 2004, at Wolverhampton final start. *M. Woods, Ireland*

LUCKY AGAIN (IRE) 3 br.g. Be My Guest (USA) 126 – Persian Fantasia (Alzao **–** (USA) 117) [2004 8g 9.7s⁴ 9.7m 11.9f⁵ Jun 22] small, sturdy gelding: little form in maidens/handicap. *J. L. Dunlop*

LUCKY ARCHER 11 b.g. North Briton 67 – Preobrajenska 93 (Double Form 130) **41** [2004 72d: 10g 8.1f 8.1m 10.2m 10f⁶ f11g Nov 8] smallish, well-made gelding: poor performer: stays 1¼m: acts on firm and good to soft going: blinkered once at 3 yrs: none too consistent. *Ian Williams*

LUCKY ARTHUR (IRE) 3 ch.f. Grand Lodge (USA) 125 – Soltura (IRE) (Sadler's **62** Wells (USA) 132) [2004 10s 10.2m⁵ 10m 11.1m³ 11.7f² 12.1g³ 12m 12g 12d p9.5g³ p9.5g Dec 15] €10,000Y, 8,000 2-y-o: sixth foal: half-sister to fairly useful Irish 7f winner Alcadia (by Thatching) and Irish 1¼m winner Urban Hymn (by College Chapel): dam unraced close relative of US Grade 2 11f winner Sword Dance: modest maiden: should stay 1¾m: acts on polytrack, firm and good: below form in visor/cheekpieces (folded tamely): sometimes slowly away. *J. G. M. O'Shea*

LUCKY EMERALD (IRE) 2 b.f. (Apr 17) Lend A Hand 124 – Anita's Love (IRE) **68** 53 (Anita's Prince 126) [2004 5.1s² 5g 5.1m* 6.1m 5.1g⁵ p6g Oct 25] seventh foal: half-sister to 5f winners Monte Verde (by Whittingham) and Thornaby Girl (at 2 yrs, by Fayruz): dam sprint maiden: fair performer: won maiden at Chepstow in August: creditable fifth in nursery at Bath, only form after: likely to prove best at 5f/easy 6f: acts on good to firm going: tongue tied last 2 starts. *B. Palling*

LUCKY JUDGE 7 b.g. Saddlers' Hall (IRE) 126 – Lady Lydia 66 (Ela-Mana-Mou **75** 132) [2004 12.4v⁴ 12.1g 16d* f14g⁵ 16.1v* 16d* 15.9s⁶ 16d⁵ Aug 27] close-coupled gelding: fair handicapper: missed 2003: won at Thirsk in May, Newcastle in June and Redcar in July: stays 2m: acts on any turf going: visored once: held up. *G. A. Swinbank*

LUCKY LARGO (IRE) 4 b. or br.g. Key of Luck (USA) 126 – Lingering Melody **62 §** (IRE) 59 (Nordico (USA)) [2004 74: 10.1v 8.5d⁵ 9.2g 8.3g 8m⁴ 8g 9.1d² 12m⁶ 10.9g 10g 8f 9.2d 10s 7.9m 10.9s Sep 16] leggy gelding: modest maiden: left S. Gollings after second start: stays easy 1½m: acts on good to firm and good to soft going: usually blinkered: ungenuine. *Miss L. A. Perratt*

LUCKY LEO 4 b.g. Muhtarram (USA) 125 – Wrong Bride (Reprimand 122) [2004 **76** 75?, a–: 10d 12m* 11m* 12g Jul 8] lengthy gelding: fair handicapper: won at Doncaster **a–** in May and Newbury (apprentice event) in July: stays 1½m: acts on soft and good to firm going: held up. *Ian Williams*

LUCKY LUCKY (IRE) 2 ch.f. (Apr 25) Lil's Boy (USA) 109 – Join The Party (Be **–** My Guest (USA) 126) [2004 p6g Dec 15] seventh foal: dam Irish 2-y-o 5f winner: 33/1, slowly away and well held in maiden at Wolverhampton. *R. P. Elliott*

LUCKY PIPIT 3 b.f. Key of Luck (USA) 126 – Meadow Pipit (CAN) 113 (Meadow- **102** lake (USA)) [2004 102: 7g⁵ 7.1f² 7m* 7m 7m⁴ 7m Oct 2] leggy filly: useful performer: won minor event at Yarmouth (beat Three Secrets by 8 lengths) in July: good 3 lengths second to Lucky Spin in listed race at Warwick second start: below form last 4 outings: stays 7f: acts on firm and good to soft going: edgy sort: front runner: sent to USA. *B. W. Hills*

LUCKY PISCEAN 3 b.g. River Falls 113 – Celestine 62 (Skyliner 117) [2004 7s⁵ **48 ?** 8.5s 7g 9.9d 16.1m Sep 29] tall, leggy gelding: poor maiden: seems to stay 8.5f: acts on soft going. *C. W. Fairhurst*

LUCKY RED PEPPER   2 b.c. (Mar 15) Barathea (IRE) 127 – Mutige (Warning 136)   **80**
[2004 7f* Jul 21] 30,000Y: first foal: dam, German 7f and 1¼m winner, out of sister to
Prix de Diane winner Lacovia: 12/1, won maiden at Leicester by ¾ length from Hallucinate, leading 1f out: split a pattern after: will stay 1m. *P. W. Chapple-Hyam*

LUCKY ROMANCE   5 b.m. Key of Luck (USA) 126 – In Love Again (IRE) 86   **37**
(Prince Rupert (FR) 121) [2004 –: f9.4g⁵ f8.5g Jan 14] tall mare: poor maiden: stays 9.4f:
acts on all-weather: tried blinkered: headstrong and a tricky ride. *B. J. Meehan*

LUCKY SPIN   3 b.f. Pivotal 124 – Perioscope (Legend of France (USA) 124) [2004   **107**
7g² 7s* 7g* 7.1f* 7m 7g³ Sep 17] 16,500Y: quite attractive filly: half-sister to several
winners, including 1995 Irish 2-y-o 7f winner Chuffed (by Batshoof), later winner up to
9f in Hong Kong, and 2001 2-y-o 6f winner Fangio's Quest (by Piccolo): dam placed at
6f in Scandinavia: useful performer: won maiden at Lingfield in May and minor event at
Leicester (made all) and listed race at Warwick (by 3 lengths from Lucky Pipit) in June:
ran as if amiss in Oak Tree Stakes at Goodwood, then respectable length third to Royal
Storm in listed event at Newbury: likely to prove best at 6f/7f: acts on firm and soft going.
R. Hannon

LUCKY STORY (USA)   3 br.c. Kris S (USA) – Spring Flight (USA) (Miswaki   **128**
(USA) 124) [2004 119p: 8d² 8g 8m² 10s 16]
    While One Thousand Guineas success for Attraction made Mark Johnston's
day at Newmarket on the first Sunday in May, giving her trainer a classic to add to
Mister Baileys' win in the 1994 Two Thousand Guineas, Haafhd's victory in the
colts' equivalent twenty-four hours earlier must have left Johnston with decidedly
mixed feelings. The Johnston-trained Lucky Story had beaten the winner into third,
conceding him 4 lb, in the Champagne Stakes at Doncaster on his final outing as a
two-year-old. Sidelined with injury as Haafhd showed improved form at Newmarket, success eluded Lucky Story on his belated return. But, despite failing to
win a race at all in 2004, Lucky Story's second to Rakti in the Queen Elizabeth II
Stakes at Ascot in September was one of the performances of the year at a mile, and
suggested he might well have proved a thorn in Haafhd's side had he been able to
take his chance in similar form in the Guineas.
    Successful on the last four of his five starts as a juvenile, Lucky Story had
been denied the opportunity to cap his two-year-old season in the Dewhurst when
withdrawn in the week of the race, and he was ruled out of the Guineas in
early-April. Diagnosed with a 'bony reaction on his right tibia', then a corn in a
foot, he looked in excellent shape when finally reappearing in the well-contested
Group 3 Sovereign Stakes at Salisbury in mid-August, albeit giving the strong
impression the race would bring him to a peak. In losing out only on the nod to the
four-year-old Norse Dancer, Lucky Story put up a fine effort in the circumstances,
seeming to lose concentration once in front over a furlong out and, as he had as a
juvenile, wandering under pressure before rallying. Promoted to Group 1 company
for the first time in the Prix du Moulin at Longchamp early the following month,
Lucky Story ran only respectably in finishing over two lengths seventh of eleven to
Grey Lilas, but he returned to show his true colours at Ascot next time. In a market
dominated for once by older horses, Lucky Story started at 16/1 in a field of eleven,
but he ran the race of his life. Looking in good shape, though, not for the first time,
sweating more as the preliminaries wore on, he was soon well placed in a much
more truly-run race than at Longchamp. Though unable to match Rakti's burst from
the front early in the straight, Lucky Story rallied strongly in the closing stages,
going down by only half a length, despite edging right. Lucky Story finished two
and a half lengths clear of third-placed Refuse To Bend, with Nayyir over a length
further behind in fourth and Ace, the next three-year-old, well back in fifth. Lucky
Story had one more outing after Ascot, starting second favourite when tackling a
mile and a quarter for the first time in the Champion Stakes at Newmarket in
October. Still looking well, he ran no sort of race on the very soft ground, coming
back tailed off behind Haafhd.
    In common with his stable-companion the Dewhurst winner Shamardal,
Lucky Story ran in the colours of Maktoum Al Maktoum's Gainsborough Stud at
Newmarket. Both horses had previously been seen in the orange silks of Abdulla
Buhaleeba, whose family was the subject of newspaper stories speculating on
reports of gambling activities in a London casino in 2004. Both Lucky Story and

Gainsborough Stud's "Lucky Story"

Lucky Story (USA) (br.c. 2001)	Kris S (USA) (b 1977)	Roberto (b 1969)	Hail To Reason Bramalea
		Sharp Queen (b 1965)	Princequillo Bridgework
	Spring Flight (USA) (b 1987)	Miswaki (ch 1978)	Mr Prospector Hopespringseternal
		Coco La Investment (b 1975)	Coco La Terreur Great Investment

Shamardal were to be trained by Godolphin in 2005. Unfortunately, Lucky Story suffered an injury over the winter and has been retired to Tweenhills Stud, Gloucestershire, at a fee of £4,000 with live foal terms. His pedigree was discussed in full in the 2003 annual. In summary, he is a brother to Dr Fong, also runner-up in the Queen Elizabeth II Stakes as a three-year-old after winning the St James's Palace Stakes and two races at a mile and a quarter, notably the Prix Eugene Adam. Lucky Story took after Dr Fong in that he tended to sweat, though that was less pronounced in 2004 (he wore ear plugs in the preliminaries at Newmarket). A well-made, attractive colt, Lucky Story stayed a mile thoroughly and would have been well worth another try at a mile and a quarter. Usually soon to the fore, he acted on good to firm and good to soft ground, and never tackled firm. *M. Johnston*

LUCKY SUSPECT (IRE)   2 b.f. (Apr 10) Lucky Guest 109 – Suspiria (IRE) 87   –
(Glenstal (USA) 118) [2004 p7.1g Nov 11] €2,200Y: half-sister to 1999 2-y-o 7f winner Gin Oclock (by Bin Ajwaad) and winner in Turkey by Anshan: dam, 5f winner in Italy at 2 yrs, half-sister to smart miler Ventiquattrofogli: 33/1, very slowly away when well held in maiden at Wolverhampton (reportedly finished lame). *E. A. L. Dunlop*

LUCKY VALENTINE   4 b.f. My Best Valentine 122 – Vera's First (IRE) 69 (Exodal   54
(USA)) [2004 51: 5.3f² 5.3f⁴ 5.1f³ p5g³ 6f⁶ Aug 5] modest handicapper: effective at 5f/6f: acts on polytrack and firm going: usually blinkered/in cheekpieces. *G. L. Moore*

LUCRETIUS 5 b.g. Mind Games 121 – Eastern Ember 85 (Indian King (USA) 128) **47**
[2004 53?: p8g p6g p7g p8g⁴ 6.1g⁴ Apr 23] poor maiden: stays easy 1m: raced only on
polytrack and good/good to firm going: tried in cheekpieces. *D. K. Ivory*

LUCY PARKES 2 ch.f. (Feb 16) Piccolo 121 – Janette Parkes 39 (Pursuit of Love **49**
124) [2004 5s 5g⁴ 5d 5m 5g Sep 25] good-topped filly: first foal: dam, ran once, half-
sister to useful sprinters Lucky Parkes and Summerhill Parkes: poor maiden: likely to
prove best at 5f/easy 6f: acts on good to soft going. *E. J. Alston*

LUGANA POINT 2 b.c. (Apr 5) Lugana Beach 116 – Raisa Point 60 (Raised Socially **–**
(USA)) [2004 5m p6d p5.1g Nov 27] little form in maidens. *J. Balding*

LUIS MELENDEZ (USA) 2 ch.c. (Mar 8) Horse Chestnut (SAF) 119 – Egoli (USA) **86**
93 (Seeking The Gold (USA)) [2004 8g⁴ 8.1g³ 8g* Oct 12] $35,000F: good-topped colt:
second foal: dam, 7f (at 2 yrs) and 9f (in USA) winner, half-sister to Poule d'Essai des
Pouliches winner Rose Gypsy: favourite, won maiden at Leicester by ¾ length from
Barbary Coast, making most: likely to stay 1¼m. *P. F. I. Cole*

LUJAIN ROSE 2 b.f. (Mar 9) Lujain (USA) 119 – Rose Chime (IRE) 58 (Tirol 127) **58 p**
[2004 8.2m Sep 28] 6,000F, €15,000Y: unfurnished filly: fourth foal: half-sister to 4-y-o
Plum and 5-y-o Tiger Tops: dam 2-y-o 6f/7f winner: 50/1, ninth in maiden at Nottingham,
not knocked about: should improve. *H. Morrison*

LUKE AFTER ME (IRE) 4 b.g. Victory Note (USA) 120 – Summit Talk (Head For **60 §**
Heights 125) [2004 66: f8g 7g² 7.1g³ 7.1g 7d² 7.2m 7.2f⁴ 7m³ 7f 7.1f 7m Aug 8] angular, **a?**
good-topped gelding: modest maiden: stays 7f: acts on firm and good to soft going:
ungenuine. *G. A. Swinbank*

LUKE SHARP 3 gr.g. Muhtarram (USA) 125 – Heaven-Liegh-Grey 90 (Grey Desire **–**
115) [2004 –: 6g 7.1m f6g Jul 23] leggy gelding: little form: tried blinkered. *K. A. Ryan*

LUMBACK (IRE) 5 b.g. Desert Style (IRE) 121 – Bellingham Jester (Jester 119) **–**
[2004 6.9f Jul 16] no sign of ability in 2 bumpers, and in maiden at Carlisle (tongue tied).
N. Wilson

LUNA BLU (IRE) 2 b.f. (Jan 30) Mujahid (USA) 125 – Blu Tamantara (USA) **–**
(Miswaki (USA) 124) [2004 7g Aug 22] 800Y: third foal: half-sister to winner in Italy by
Unfuwain: dam Italian 7f winner: 100/1, well held in maiden at Folkestone, slowly away.
M. Wigham

LUNAR EXIT (IRE) 3 gr.g. Exit To Nowhere (USA) 122 – Moon Magic 62 (Polish **89**
Precedent (USA) 131) [2004 95p: 10.4m⁶ 10m 12g⁶ 12g Oct 1] good-bodied gelding:
fairly useful performer: sixth in handicap at York and minor event at Kempton: ran as if
amiss other starts in 2004, in blinkers final one: should stay 1¾m: raced only on good/
good to firm going: tends to hang left. *Lady Herries*

LUNAR LEADER (IRE) 4 b.f. Mujadil (USA) 119 – Moon River (FR) (Groom **–**
Dancer (USA) 128) [2004 78: 10g 11s 12s 8.3g 12m 8.1m 10.1d Jul 8] quite good-topped
filly: well held in 2004: tried tongue tied/in headgear. *M. J. Gingell*

LUNAR LORD 8 b.g. Elmaamul (USA) 125 – Cache (Bustino 136) [2004 –: 10.3g **56**
10.2g 14.1m 10.2m 12g⁴ 14.1d² 14.1g² 12.1m 12.6d⁶ 12m Sep 25] close-coupled gelding:
modest performer: stays 2m: acts on fibresand and any turf going: tried in cheekpieces.
D. Burchell

LUNAR SKY (USA) 2 b.f. (Apr 27) Lemon Drop Kid (USA) 131 – Celestial Bliss **69**
(USA) 50 (Relaunch (USA)) [2004 7m 7g⁶ 9f⁴ 10m Sep 28] leggy filly: sixth foal:
half-sister to winner in USA by Irish River: dam, ran twice in Ireland at 3 yrs, half-sister
to Arlington Million winner Paradise Creek: fair maiden: should stay 1¼m: acts on firm
going. *C. E. Brittain*

LUNAR SOVEREIGN (USA) 5 b. or br.h. Cobra King (USA) 122 – January Moon **115**
(CAN) (Apalachee (USA) 137) [2004 121: 12m³ 12m 10f 12m Jul 24] lengthy, attractive
horse: very smart performer in 2003, successful at Belmont in allowance race and Man
o'War Stakes (career-best effort, beat Slew Valley 2¾ lengths) for K. McLaughlin:
rejoined former trainer, respectable 3½ lengths third to Fair Mix in Dubai City of Gold at
Nad Al Sheba on reappearance: below form in Dubai Sheema Classic there next time and
when acting as pacemaker last 2 starts: barely stays 1½m: acts on firm and soft going:
blinkered once in 2002: tongue tied at 5 yrs: won from Saeed bin Suroor

LUNDY'S LANE (IRE) 4 b.g. Darshaan 133 – Lunda (IRE) 60 (Soviet Star (USA) **99**
128) [2004 108: f8.5g⁴ 8g 8g 10.4g 8f 9g Oct 2] lengthy, good-topped gelding: useful
performer: best effort in 2004 when seventh to Calcutta in handicap at Doncaster
penultimate start: effective at 1m to 1½m: acts on all-weather and dirt, raced only on good

going or firmer on turf: has won in tongue tie: tried blinkered: sold 52,000 gns, joined S. Seemar in UAE. *C. E. Brittain*

LUNE D'OR (FR) 3 b.f. Green Tune (USA) 125 – Luth d'Or (FR) (Noir Et Or 125) **116** [2004 10.5s³ 10g* 12d* 12.5d* 12d 10g* 12f Nov 28] leggy, useful-looking filly: half-sister to several winners in France, including 1¾m winner Cavalier d'Or (by Diesis): dam, French 11f to 12.5f winner, half-sister to high-class miler/Arc third Luth Enchantee: smart performer: won minor event at Chantilly in June, Prix de Malleret at Saint-Cloud (beat Buoyant a neck) in July, Prix de Pomone at Deauville (by ½ length from Hidden Hope) in August and Premio Lydia Tesio at Rome (led over 1f out to beat Walkamia 2 lengths) in October: not discredited when 4¾ lengths seventh to Zenno Rob Roy in Japan Cup at Tokyo final start: stays 12.5f: acts on firm and good to soft ground, showed promise on soft: held up: reportedly suffered from throat infection after fifth outing (Prix Vermeille). *R. Gibson, France*

LUPINE HOWL 3 b.c. Wolfhound (USA) 126 – Classic Fan (USA) (Lear Fan (USA) **41** 130) [2004 66: 6g 7m 5.9f 7f 10g⁶ 7m Jul 28] good-topped colt: just poor maiden in 2004: tried in cheekpieces. *B. A. McMahon*

LUTEUR DES PICTONS (FR) 5 ch.g. Ragmar (FR) 117 – Ezera (FR) (Chamberlin **–** (FR)) [2004 p12g Jan 31] sixth of 13 in non-thoroughbred event at Angers with part in France in 2003 (when trained by T. Lerner): well held in maiden at Lingfield. *B. G. Powell*

LUXI RIVER (USA) 4 b.g. Diesis 133 – Mariella (USA) 106 (Roberto (USA) 131) **48** [2004 60: f12g⁵ f12g⁵ f11g⁴ f12g⁴ 16g Jul 2] big gelding: poor maiden: left P. Blockley after fourth outing: stays 1½m: acts on fibresand, raced only on good going or firmer on turf: dropped away tamely second/third starts. *Michael McElhone, Ireland*

LUXOR 7 ch.g. Grand Lodge (USA) 125 – Escrime (USA) 92 (Sharpen Up 127) [2004 **–** –: 10.5m 9.1d 10.3g 10g 10g 10.5g 10.3g Sep 11] rangy gelding: handicapper: little form since 2002, leaving W. M. Brisbourne after third start at 7 yrs: tried in headgear/tongue tie. *Mrs G. S. Rees*

LYCA BALLERINA 3 b.f. Marju (IRE) 127 – Lovely Lyca 76 (Night Shift (USA)) **72 d** [2004 76: 7g⁵ 8.1s³ 7m⁴ 7.5d* 8s 7m³ 8.5m 7m⁶ 7.5s 7d 7v Sep 22] quite attractive filly: fair performer: won maiden at Beverley in June: left B. Hills after sixth start: below form after: effective at 7f/1m: acts on soft and good to firm going: wore cheekpieces last 2 starts: sold 19,000 gns. *Andrew Slattery, Ireland*

LYDGATE (USA) 4 b.c. Pulpit (USA) 117 – Mariuka (USA) (Danzig (USA)) [2004 **108** 6.5f² 8f⁴ 6.5f¹ 6.5f² 5g* 5f 6m⁴ 5d Oct 14] $500,000Y: stocky colt: second foal: half-brother to winner in USA by Woodman: dam, won in USA (including 1m minor stakes), closely related to high-class miler Mukaddamah: useful performer: unraced at 2 yrs (reportedly injured a shin): successful in maiden at Santa Anita in 2003 and Grade 3 Aegon Turf Sprint Stakes at Churchill Downs in April: respectable efforts in Britain last 3 starts, leaving E. Harty in USA after first of them: 3½ lengths fourth to Var in listed race at Goodwood: stays 6.5f: better on turf than dirt (acts on firm going): tried tongue tied. *Saeed bin Suroor*

LYDIA'S LOOK (IRE) 7 b.m. Distant View (USA) 126 – Mrs Croesus (USA) (Key **55** To The Mint (USA)) [2004 49: p6g p5g⁵ p6g⁵ p6g⁴ 5m⁵ 5d* 5g⁶ 5g 5.1g Aug 18] **a47** close-coupled mare: modest performer: won handicap at Beverley in June: effective at 5f/6f: acts on all-weather, firm and soft going: reportedly in foal to Bahamian Bounty. *T. J. Etherington*

LYES GREEN 3 ch.g. Bien Bien (USA) 125 – Dissolve 48 (Sharrood (USA) 124) **–** [2004 12.1s⁴ p13g p12g Nov 10] soundly beaten in maidens. *R. M. Beckett*

LYFORD LASS 3 b.f. Bahamian Bounty 116 – Ladykirk 78 (Slip Anchor 136) [2004 **64 d** 8v² 8v* 8.3d 10s 10s p8.6g p8.6g f6g Dec 7] leggy filly: third foal: half-sister to 6-y-o Lennel: dam 2-y-o 1m winner who stayed 1½m: modest performer: won maiden at Newcastle in April: below form after, in sellers (visored/in cheekpieces) last 2 starts: stays 1m: acts on heavy going. *I. Semple*

LYGETON LAD 6 b.g. Shaamit (IRE) 127 – Smartie Lee 66 (Dominion 123) [2004 **70** 85, a112: p10g⁵ p12g⁵ p10g⁶ p7g⁵ p7g* 8.5s 7s 8m 7m 7m⁴ 7g⁶ p7g⁵ p7g⁴ p8g* p7g Dec **a110** 29] tall gelding: smart on all-weather, fair on turf: won minor events at Lingfield in April and December: good 2¾ lengths fourth to Jack Sullivan in handicap there thirteenth start: effective at 7f to easy 1¼m: better on polytrack than fibresand, and acts on good to firm and good to soft going: usually tongue tied: has been bandaged: sometimes races freely: tough and genuine. *Miss Gay Kelleway*

LYNS RESOLUTION 4 b.g. Awesome 73 – Our Resolution (Caerleon (USA) 132) **63 ?**
[2004 8.1m 8.2m⁴ Sep 28] well held in 2 bumpers: seemingly better effort on Flat when
fourth in maiden at Nottingham, wandering: refused to enter stalls intended final outing.
D. Burchell

LYONELS GLORY 3 b.c. Green Desert (USA) 127 – La Virginia (GER) (Surumu **109**
(GER)) [2004 10v² 10d³ 12g³ 12g⁶ 10d* 10d³ Sep 18] big, good-bodied colt: seventh
foal: half-brother to 3 winners, notably high-class Deutsches Derby winner Lavirco and
smart German performer up to 1¾m Laveron (both by Konigsstuhl), later also high-class
hurdler in France: dam German 1¼m winner: unraced at 2 yrs: useful performer: won
Furstenberg-Rennen at Baden-Baden in August by ½ length from Saldentigerin: not
discredited time before when sixth to Maraahel in ABN Amro Stakes (Gordon) at Goodwood: good 3 lengths third to Delfos in Prix du Prince d'Orange at Longchamp final start,
making most: stays 1½m, may be ideally suited by 1¼m: raced only on good ground or
softer. *U. Suter, Germany*

LYRICAL GIRL (USA) 3 b.f. Orpen (USA) 116 – Lyric Theatre (USA) (Seeking **58**
The Gold (USA)) [2004 64: p10g* p10g⁵ 10.2m 7m⁶ 8.1m 12.1g Sep 3] sturdy filly: modest performer: won claimer at Lingfield (left M. Channon) in January: below form after:
stays 1¼m: acts on all-weather, raced only on good going or firmer on turf. *H. J. Manners*

LYRICAL LADY 3 b.f. Merdon Melody 98 – Gracious Imp (USA) (Imp Society **–**
(USA)) [2004 58: 5.1m 6.1g 6.1m 8.1m 8d Oct 2] well-made filly: maiden: no form in
2004: tried blinkered/in cheekpieces. *Mrs A. J. Bowlby*

LYRICAL WAY 5 b.g. Vettori (IRE) 119 – Fortunate (Reference Point 139) [2004 67: **65**
p10g⁴ p10g p10g⁵ 10g 10g⁶ 11.9f⁴ p10m Dec 21] leggy gelding: fair performer: very best
form at 1¼m: acts on polytrack, firm and good to soft going: usually blinkered/visored.
P. R. Chamings

LYRIC DANCES (FR) 2 ch.f. (Apr 6) Sendawar (IRE) 129 – Romanche (FR) (Galetto **–**
(FR) 118) [2004 6.1d Aug 19] €60,000Y: fourth foal: brother to 3 winners abroad,
including US Grade 2 1m winner Reine de Romance (by Vettori): dam useful French 1m/
1¼m winner: 33/1, well held in maiden at Chepstow. *J. Jay*

LYSANDER'S QUEST (IRE) 6 br.g. Doyoun (USA) – Haramayda (FR) **51**
(Doyoun 124) [2004 56: 10m 14m p12g⁵ 12f* 12m p12m⁵ p12m⁴ Dec 15] tall gelding:
modest performer: won banded event at Folkestone in September: effective at 1½m/
1¾m: acts on polytrack, firm and good to soft going: tried visored/in cheekpieces: held
up. *R. Ingram*

LYSANDRA (IRE) 2 b.f. (Mar 17) Danehill (USA) 126 – Oriane 109 (Nashwan **77 p**
(USA) 135) [2004 7.1m² 7d⁴ Oct 30] deep-girthed filly: fourth foal: half-sister to 3-y-o
Barati and fairly useful 2001 2-y-o 7f winner Cassirer (by Zafonic): dam, Irish 1m
winner, half-sister to smart miler Killer Instinct out of smart half-sister to Irish Oaks
winner Colorspin, herself dam of Opera House and Kayf Tara: fair form in maidens at
Warwick (green when second to Literature) and Newmarket (fourth to Songthrush): will
stay 1m: should progress. *Sir Michael Stoute*

LYTHAM (IRE) 3 b.g. Spectrum (IRE) 126 – Nousaiyra (IRE) (Be My Guest (USA) **75**
126) [2004 8m 10d⁴ 9g 9g 10m 8s³ p8.6d² p12g p9.5g* Nov 26] €30,000Y: second foal:
dam, second at 1¼m in France, half-sister to very smart 1½m performer Narwala: fair
performer: left C. O'Brien in Ireland after sixth start: won maiden at Wolverhampton in
November, carrying head awkwardly/hanging left: stays 9.5f: acts on polytrack and soft
going. *M. J. Wallace*

M

MA'AM (USA) 2 ch.f. (Feb 27) Royal Anthem (USA) 135 – Hide The Bride (USA) **63 p**
(Runaway Groom (CAN)) [2004 p8g p8g⁵ Nov 13] 8,000Y: second foal: dam Canadian
Grade 3 6f winner: still green, better effort in maidens when never-nearer fifth to General
Jumbo at Lingfield, very slowly away: will stay at least 1¼m: should do better. *I. A. Wood*

MABELLA (IRE) 2 b.f. (Mar 23) Brave Act 119 – Wee Merkin (IRE) (Thatching **60**
131) [2004 6m 5m⁵ 6g 5.7m⁴ 6.1g 7m Sep 22] 15,000Y: first foal: dam unraced half-sister
to smart 7f/1m performer Tempting Fate: modest maiden: seems to stay 7f: acts on good
to firm going. *B. R. Millman*

MABEL RILEY (IRE)   4 b.f. Revoque (IRE) 122 – Mystic Dispute (IRE) (Magical   **39**
Strike (USA) 114) [2004 63d: f8.5g⁵ f8.5g 7s Apr 20] poor performer: stays 8.5f: acts
on fibresand, good to firm and good to soft going: tried in headgear: difficult ride.
M. A. Buckley

MAC   4 ch.g. Fleetwood (IRE) 107 – Midnight Break 78 (Night Shift (USA)) [2004 93:   **–**
16.2m 12d Oct 14] good-bodied gelding: handicapper: well held in 2004, in blinkers on
reappearance: sold 25,000 gns. *M. P. Tregoning*

MACABRE   2 b.c. (Mar 13) Machiavellian (USA) 123 – Lady In Waiting 113 (Kylian   **87 p**
(USA)) [2004 7f² Sep 24] 280,000Y: first foal: dam, 5f (at 2 yrs) to 10.4f winner, closely
related to 5-y-o Savannah Bay: 9/4, ¾-length second of 5 to David Junior in maiden at
Ascot, carried left: should stay at least 1¼m: sure to improve. *Saeed bin Suroor*

MACARONI GOLD (IRE)   4 b.g. Rock Hopper 124 – Strike It Rich (FR) 88 (Rhein-   **65**
gold 137) [2004 75: p16g f14g⁴ p16g⁴ f16.2s⁵ 16g 14.1s³ f16g³ 16g⁶ 14.1d⁶ p16.5g²   **a70**
f14g* Dec 11] unfurnished gelding: fair handicapper: won at Southwell in December:
stays 16.5f: acts on all-weather and soft going: effective blinkered or not: sometimes
slowly away/races freely. *W. Jarvis*

MACAULAY (IRE)   2 ch.c. (Feb 16) Zafonic (USA) 130 – Wigging 96 (Warning 136)   **81 p**
[2004 p7g³ Oct 28] 30,000Y: third foal: half-brother to 3-y-o Warbreck: dam, 7f winner,
half-sister to very smart 5f to 7f performer Bluebook: 33/1, 1½ lengths third to King's
Majesty in maiden at Lingfield, slowly away and staying on: will stay 1m: should
improve. *R. Charlton*

MACCHIATO   3 br.f. Inchinor 119 – Tereyna 58 (Terimon 124) [2004 59: 12.1d 11.5g⁵   **51**
10.2g p10g 11.5f f14g 12f Sep 4] leggy filly: modest maiden: should stay at least 1½m:
acts on firm going: blinkered last 2 outings. *R. F. Johnson Houghton*

MAC COIS NA TINE   2 b.g. (Feb 6) Cois Na Tine (IRE) 101 – Berenice (ITY) (Mar-   **68**
ouble 116) [2004 5s 6m² 7.5g³ 7g Jul 8] 17,000Y: leggy, quite good-topped gelding: sixth
foal: brother to 4-y-o Gaelic Princess and half-brother to 6f winner (including at 2 yrs)
Berenice (by College Chapel) and 6f (at 2 yrs) to 11f winner The Bomber Liston (by
Perugino), both useful in Ireland, latter also winner in Italy: dam unraced: fair maiden:
stays 7f: acts on good to firm going: gelded after final start. *K. A. Ryan*

MACHINIST (IRE)   4 br.g. Machiavellian (USA) 123 – Athene (IRE) 83 (Rousillon   **93**
(USA) 133) [2004 88: 6m 7m 8m 6m* 6f² 6s⁴ 6s⁵ 6d Sep 17] leggy, useful-looking
gelding: fairly useful handicapper: won at Ayr in July by 3 lengths from Foley Millennium: good second to Mutawaqed at York, best effort after: should prove as effective at 5f
as 6f: acts on polytrack, firm and soft going. *D. Nicholls*

MACLEAN   3 b.g. Machiavellian (USA) 123 – Celtic Cross 100 (Selkirk (USA) 129)   **85**
[2004 80p: 8m² 9g²* 8m³ 10d⁶ 8g⁵ 8.3m⁶ 10.3s* 10.1g Aug 30] tall, good-topped gelding:
fairly useful performer: won maiden at Musselburgh in April and handicap at Chester
(made most to beat Tarfah 2½ lengths) in August: should stay 1½m: acts on soft and good
to firm going: visored/wore cheekpieces last 4 starts: sometimes looks temperamental:
sold 30,000 gns. *Sir Michael Stoute*

MAC LOVE   3 b.g. Cape Cross (IRE) 129 – My Lass 91 (Elmaamul (USA) 125) [2004   **117**
104: 6d⁵ 6s⁴ 6g² 6m² 6m⁶ 6m⁶ 6g* 6g 7m* 6f 7g* Sep 30] strong, compact gelding:
improved into a smart performer: won minor event at Doncaster in July, and listed race at
Epsom (beat Peter Paul Rubens by a neck) and Citigroup Charlton Hunt Supreme Stakes
at Goodwood (by 2 lengths from Vanderlin) in September: below form in Sprint Cup at
Haydock and Diadem Stakes at Ascot eighth/tenth starts: effective at 6f/7f: acts on firm
going: held up: tough. *J. Akehurst*

MACPURSIE   3 br.f. Botanic (USA) – Jeethgaya (USA) 61 (Critique (USA) 126)   **54**
[2004 f7g⁵ f8g⁴ 10f³ 12g⁶ 12g Jul 22] half-sister to 2 winners, including 6f (at 2 yrs) to
1m winner Calko (by Timeless Times): dam, maiden, best around 1¼m: modest maiden:
left T. D. Barron after second start: clearly best effort at 1¼m: acts on firm going: tried
tongue tied. *T. G. McCourt, Ireland*

MAC REGAL (IRE)   3 b.c. King's Theatre (IRE) 128 – Shine Silently (IRE) (Bering   **80**
136) [2004 10g³ 10d⁶ 8g⁵ 12m 10m² 9.5d⁵ Nov 16] 14,000F, €28,000Y: smallish, leggy
colt: first foal: dam unraced out of sister to very smart stayer Assessor: fairly useful
performer: won maiden at Milan at 2 yrs: third in minor event at Newbury (carried head
awkwardly) and 20 lengths second of 4 to Day Flight in listed race at York first 2 starts
in 2004: well held in Derby Italiano at Rome next outing, final one for M. Quinlan:
creditable efforts in minor events for new stable: stays 10.4f: acts on good to firm and
good to soft ground. *A. Renzoni, Italy*

MAC'S ELAN 4 b.g. Darshaan 133 – Elabella (Ela-Mana-Mou 132) [2004 –: 7g 7.1d⁵ **66** p10g 10d⁶ 8.3g² 12s² p12g⁴ f8s p12.2g Dec 4] fair maiden: stays 1½m: acts on polytrack, raced only on good going or softer on turf. *A. B. Coogan*

MAC'S TALISMAN (IRE) 4 ch.c. Hector Protector (USA) 124 – Inherent Magic **79** (IRE) 95 (Magical Wonder (USA) 125) [2004 75: 6g p6g 6m f7g² 8m³ 8g 6.1g p7g* p8.6g* p8.6g² Nov 13] sturdy colt: fair performer: won minor event at Lingfield (landed gamble) in October and handicap at Wolverhampton in November: stays 8.6f: acts on all-weather, raced only on good going or firmer on turf: tried blinkered, wore cheekpieces/tongue strap last 3 starts: waited with. *V. Smith*

MAC THE KNIFE (IRE) 3 b.g. Daggers Drawn (USA) 114 – Icefern 88 (Moorestyle – 137) [2004 80: 6d 6s 7m 7m 8f 7g Sep 20] compact, well-made gelding: no form in 2004, including in sellers, leaving R. Hannon after fifth start. *A. W. Carroll*

MAD 3 br.f. Pursuit of Love 124 – Emily-Mou (IRE) 80 (Cadeaux Genereux 131) [2004 **63** p12g 8s p8m p7g⁶ p7m p8m* p10m² p10m³ Dec 21] £1,000Y: tall filly: third living foal: half-sister to 1¾m seller winner Dangerous Deploy (by Deploy): dam 1¼m winner: modest performer: won banded race at Lingfield in December: stays 1¼m. *Andrew Reid*

MADAAR (USA) 5 b.g. Spinning World (USA) 130 – Mur Taasha (USA) 108 (River- – man (USA) 131) [2004 54: f8g 10m Jul 6] maiden: no form in 2004: often visored at 4 yrs. *R. Bastiman*

MADAEH (USA) 3 b. or br.f. Swain (IRE) 134 – Tamgeed (USA) 66 (Woodman **87** (USA) 126) [2004 97: 9.9g⁴ 8f Jun 16] strong filly: fairly useful performer: better effort in 2004 when respectable fourth to Halicardia in listed event at Goodwood, though weakening quickly: best form at 7f: raced only on good going or firmer: sold 8,000 gns in December. *J. L. Dunlop*

MADALYAR (IRE) 5 b.g. Darshaan 133 – Madaniyya (USA) 96 (Shahrastani (USA) – 135) [2004 –: f8.5s Feb 20] leggy, angular gelding: fairly useful at 1½m/13f in Ireland at 3 yrs: no form since: tried blinkered. *Jonjo O'Neill*

MADAM CAVERSFIELD 2 b.f. (Mar 8) Pursuit of Love 124 – Madam Alison 90 **71** (Puissance 110) [2004 5.1f⁵ 6m 7.1m³ 7g⁴ 7m⁴ 7f⁶ 8.1s² 8s Oct 19] first foal: dam 6f (at 2 yrs) and 1m winner: fair maiden: stays 1m: acts on soft and good to firm ground: sometimes wanders. *R. Hannon*

MADAME FATALE (IRE) 2 br.f. (Feb 15) Daggers Drawn (USA) 114 – Taajreh – (IRE) 89 (Mtoto 134) [2004 7.9g p8.6d Oct 30] close-coupled filly: fourth foal: half-sister to Italian 2001 2-y-o 5f/5.5f winner Royal Rhapsody (by Ali-Royal): dam Irish 1m winner: well beaten in maidens at York and Wolverhampton. *Jedd O'Keeffe*

MADAME GUILLOTINE 2 b.f. (Apr 17) Sure Blade (USA) 130 – Delicious 51 – (Dominion 123) [2004 6d p6d Oct 30] fifth foal: sister to 6-y-o Fantasy Believer: dam, maiden, stayed 1¾m: burly, well beaten in maidens at Redcar and Wolverhampton. *J. Balding*

MADAME MARIE (IRE) 4 b.f. Desert King (IRE) 129 – Les Trois Lamas (IRE) **58** (Machiavellian (USA) 123) [2004 55: 9.7d 7s 8.2d² 8.1m 9g⁶ 9.7g p10d p12g p16g **a50** 11.9m⁴ p9.5g⁴ p13m Nov 22] modest maiden: should stay 1½m: acts on polytrack, soft and good to firm going: visored last 2 starts: sometimes slowly away. *S. Dow*

MADAME ROUX 6 b.m. Rudimentary (USA) 118 – Foreign Mistress (Darshaan 133) – [2004 –: f6g⁶ p6g⁵ May 13] angular mare: maiden: no longer of much account. *C. Drew*

MADAME TOPFLIGHT 2 b.f. (Feb 19) Komaite (USA) – Jamarj 113 (Tyrnavos **101** 129) [2004 5.1g 5g² 6g* 6.1m⁵ 5v² 6s 6g 6s* Nov 29] leggy, quite good-topped filly: half-sister to winner in Turkey by Pursuit of Love: dam 5f (at 2 yrs) to 9f winner: useful performer: won maiden at Ayr in July and, after being sold from Mrs G. Rees 14,500 gns, minor event at Fontainebleau (by 4 lengths) in November: ½-length equal-second to Beautifix in listed race at Deauville fifth start: effective at 5f/6f: acts on heavy ground: often races up with pace. *R. Pritchard-Gordon, France*

MADAMOISELLE JONES 4 b.f. Emperor Jones (USA) 119 – Tiriana (Common **73** Grounds 118) [2004 76: 10.3g 8.2d⁴ 7m⁵ 8m* 8g⁶ 8.5d⁴ 8.3m⁶ 8.3d 8.5g Sep 8] close-coupled filly: fair handicapper: won at Leicester in May: stays 8.5f: acts on polytrack, soft and good to firm going. *H. S. Howe*

MAD CAREW (USA) 5 ch.g. Rahy (USA) 115 – Poppy Carew (IRE) 110 (Danehill **79** (USA) 126) [2004 82: p12g⁵ p10g* p10g p12g⁴ 10.1s 8g⁵ 10m⁵ 8g⁴ 9m 12g⁵ 10s⁴ p10g⁴ **a86** p10m⁴ Dec 22] sturdy gelding: fairly useful handicapper on all-weather, fair on turf:

won at Lingfield in February: effective at 1m to easy 1½m: acts on polytrack, firm and soft going: tried in cheekpieces, usually blinkered: held up: tough. *G. L. Moore*

MADDIE'S A JEM 4 b.f. Emperor Jones (USA) 119 – Royal Orchid (IRE) 74 (Shalford (IRE) 124§) [2004 72: 6s* 5s* 6.1s³ 6f⁵ 6m⁶ 6f⁴ 6g² 5.1g* 5.2d⁶ 6f² f6g p6g⁵ p6m Dec 21] deep-girthed filly: fairly useful performer: won handicap and minor event at Folkestone in March/April and minor event at Nottingham in August: effective at 5f/6f: acts on all-weather, firm and soft going: visored (ran poorly) final start: sometimes slowly away (all but refused to race fifth 3-y-o outing). *J. R. Jenkins* **82 a76**

MADGE 2 b.f. (Jan 25) Marju (IRE) 127 – Aymara 85 (Darshaan 133) [2004 7m⁶ p9.5g⁵ p8.6g² p8.6g³ Dec 17] rather unfurnished filly: first foal: dam, 1½m winner, out of smart performer up to 1m Chipaya: modest maiden: second at Wolverhampton: stays 8.6f: races up with pace. *J. H. M. Gosden* **63**

MADHAHIR (IRE) 4 b.g. Barathea (IRE) 127 – Gharam (USA) 108 (Green Dancer (USA) 132) [2004 72: f16g p16g 12s* 11.5m³ 14.1s 16.2v 11.8m 12.4g⁶ 9g 9s 11.3s Oct 20] good-topped gelding: fair handicapper: won apprentice event at Folkestone in March: below form after next outing: left C. Dwyer after eighth start: stays easy 2m: acts on fibresand, soft and good to firm going: tried in headgear: inconsistent. *Mervyn Torrens, Ireland* **68 d**

MADHAVI 2 gr.f. (Jan 30) Diktat 126 – Grey Galava 64 (Generous (IRE) 139) [2004 6g 6m³ 6g⁵ 6g 6.5g 6d Oct 14] 24,000Y: well-grown, good-topped filly: fourth foal: half-sister to 4-y-o Millagros and German 2000 2-y-o 7.5f winner Greese (by Mukaddamah): dam 1¾m winner: fair maiden: should stay 7f: acts on good to firm going: blinkered (signs of temperament) last 2 starts. *R. Hannon* **71**

MADIBA 5 b.g. Emperor Jones (USA) 119 – Priluki 65 (Lycius (USA) 124) [2004 70: f11g* f12g⁶ p13g f14g² f16.2s² f16.2s² 16g 16d² f16g² 16.2m 14.1m 16.1m 16m 16s⁵ 16.1g² 15.8g⁶ 16d² p12g⁶ p12.2g² f16s* p16.5g⁶ f14g³ f12g⁶ p13g Dec 29] leggy, useful-looking gelding: fairly useful on all-weather, modest on turf: won maiden in January and handicap (by 13 lengths) in November, both at Southwell: stays 16.5f: acts on all-weather, firm and soft going: tried visored/blinkered. *P. Howling* **64 a83**

MADID (IRE) 3 br.c. Cape Cross (IRE) 129 – Waffle On 89 (Chief Singer 131) [2004 8m* 7.1g* 8f Jun 15] 150,000Y: strong, well-made colt: fifth foal: closely related to useful 7f winner Desert Alchemy (by Green Desert) and half-brother to 2 winners, including useful French 9.5f winner La Frou Frou (by Night Shift), later successful in USA: dam 2-y-o 6f winner: smart form: won maiden at Newbury in May and listed race at Sandown (beat Pastoral Pursuits by ½ length, leading close home) in June: ninth of 11 behind Azamour in St James's Palace Stakes at Royal Ascot final start: stayed 1m: raced only on good ground or firmer: moved poorly to post and drifted markedly left on debut: dead. *J. H. M. Gosden* **119**

MAD MARTY WILDCARD 2 ch.c. (Apr 8) Komaite (USA) – Done And Dusted (IRE) 75 (Up And At 'em 109) [2004 6g 6s Oct 22] close-coupled colt: well held in maidens at Windsor and Newbury. *R. Brotherton* **–**

MAD MAURICE 3 ch.g. Grand Lodge (USA) 125 – Amarella (FR) (Balleroy (USA) 115) [2004 57p: 7g 7s 10.5m 11.5f 12f Sep 4] sturdy gelding: some promise only 2-y-o start: no form in 2004: tried in cheekpieces/blinkers. *B. J. Curley* **–**

MADRA RUA (IRE) 3 b.g. Foxhound (USA) 103 – Fun Fashion (IRE) 64 (Polish Patriot (USA) 128) [2004 71: 6d 5f 5d Oct 11] fair maiden at 2 yrs for J. Coogan in Ireland: well held in 2004: seems to stay 7f: acts on firm and good to soft going: tried blinkered/in cheekpieces. *Miss L. A. Perratt* **–**

MADRASEE 6 b.m. Beveled (USA) – Pendona 72 (Blue Cashmere 129) [2004 84, a74: p5g² p6g p5g p6g⁴ p6g⁵ 5s⁵ 5s⁵ 6m 6g 5g 6g⁶ 6s 5g⁶ 5.3s² p5.1g³ p6g³ p5g² Dec 18] leggy mare: fair handicapper: effective at 5f/6f: acts on polytrack, firm and soft going: usually races prominently: tough. *L. Montague Hall* **73**

MAEVEEN (IRE) 4 b.f. Flying Spur (AUS) – Cool Gales 85 (Lord Gayle (USA) 124) [2004 –: 11.9m 12f p10g⁴ Sep 18] half-sister to several winners, including 7-y-o What-A-Dancer: dam, maiden, probably stayed 1½m: poor maiden: trained by D. Wachman in Ireland until after second start: stays 1¼m: acts on polytrack. *V. Smith* **32**

MAFAHEEM 2 b.c. (Feb 27) Mujahid (USA) 125 – Legend of Aragon 67 (Aragon 118) [2004 6g* Oct 8] 33,000F: strong, well-made colt: fourth foal: half-brother to UAE 1¼m winner Spanish Bells (by Robellino): dam 2-y-o 5f winner who stayed 1m: 10/1, won maiden at York by length from Pivotal's Princess, green before getting on top final 1f: should stay 1m: probably a useful prospect. *M. Johnston* **91 p**

MAFRUZ   5 ch.g. Hamas (IRE) 125§ – Braari (USA) 97 (Gulch (USA)) [2004 76d: 10.1s 8m Jul 5] good-topped gelding: fair performer at best: well held in 2004: tried blinkered/in cheekpieces. *R. A. Fahey*

MAGANDA (IRE)   3 b.f. Sadler's Wells (USA) 132 – Minnie Habit (Habitat 134)   **77** [2004 84p: 10d* 11m⁶ 8m 8.9g Oct 9] useful-looking filly: fair performer: won maiden at Ripon in April: well below form last 2 starts: should stay 1½m: unraced on extremes of going: sent to France. *M. A. Jarvis*

MAGARI   3 b.f. Royal Applause 124 – Thatcher's Era (IRE) 57 (Never So Bold 135)   **53** [2004 59p: 7m⁴ 8.3g f8s 6.9m⁵ 8g³ 8d⁴ Oct 16] lengthy filly: modest maiden: stays 1m: acts on good to firm and good to soft ground. *J. G. Given*

MAGDELAINE   2 b.f. (Mar 24) Sinndar (IRE) 134 – Crystal Drop 101 (Cadeaux Gener-eux 131) [2004 8.2g p8.6g p7.1g Oct 19] 20,000Y: fourth foal: dam, French 1m winner who stayed 11f, out of close relation to Irish 1000 Guineas winner Ensconse: well beaten in maidens. *P. M. Phelan*   **–**

MAGENTA RISING (IRE)   4 ch.f. College Chapel 122 – Fashion Queen (Chilibang 120) [2004 79d: f12f 8d Aug 9] modest performer: well beaten in 2004, leaving D. Burchell after reappearance: tried tongue tied/visored. *D. W. Thompson*   **–**

MAGGIE JORDAN (USA)   2 b.f. (Mar 13) Fusaichi Pegasus (USA) 130 – Pharapache (USA) (Lyphard (USA) 132) [2004 6s* Oct 29] $120,000Y: lengthy filly: has scope: sixth foal: half-sister to 3 winners in USA by Bertrando, including smart performer up to 1m Cliquot: dam, French 1¼m winner, closely related to very smart French middle-distance performer Antheus: 7/2, won 10-runner maiden at Newmarket by 2 lengths from Puya, travelling strongly, leading 1f out then green: likely to stay at least 1m: useful prospect. *B. J. Meehan*   **86 p**

MAGGIE MAQUETTE   4 ch.f. Atraf 116 – Bronze Maquette (IRE) 66 (Ahonoora 122) [2004 –: p6g⁵ p5g⁶ f5g Apr 5] modest maiden: stays 6f: acts on polytrack: has shown signs of temperament. *W. S. Kittow*   **50**

MAGGIE'S PET   7 b.m. Minshaanshu Amad (USA) 91§ – Run Fast For Gold (Deep Run 119) [2004 ?, a56: f8.5g² f9.4g⁵ f8g² f9.4s² p8g⁴ f8s⁵ f8.5g* f7m⁶ May 28] modest performer: won amateur handicap at Wolverhampton in April: effective at 1m to 11f: acts on all-weather: usually tongue tied. *K. Bell*   **? a54**

MAGGIE TULLIVER (IRE)   2 b.f. (Apr 18) Spectrum (IRE) 126 – Eliza Acton 70 (Shirley Heights 130) [2004 6f 7g 7g p8.6d* Nov 5] neat filly: second foal: dam, 2-y-o 1m winner, sister to useful stayer Top Cees and closely related to dam of 4-y-o Leporello: fair performer: won maiden at Wolverhampton by 5 lengths from Sandy's Legend, leading over 2f out: should stay at least 1¼m: best effort on polytrack. *P. W. Harris*   **69**

MAGHANIM   4 b.c. Nashwan (USA) 135 – Azdihaar (USA) 81 (Mr Prospector (USA)) [2004 –: 7g⁵ 8.2g³ 7m² 7g 7m 9m Sep 11] lengthy, quite attractive colt: useful performer: best effort when 5 lengths second of 28 to Unscrupulous in valuable handicap at Royal Ascot, making most: below form after, though second home on stand side when tenth in Bunbury Cup at Newmarket next time: races freely and probably best short of 1m: raced only on good/good to firm going: usually races up with pace: has shown signs of temperament: joined S. Seemar in UAE. *J. L. Dunlop*   **108 ?**

MAGICAL MIMI   3 b.f. Magic Ring (IRE) 115 – Naval Dispatch (Slip Anchor 136) [2004 75: 8g 8m 8.2m 8m⁴ 9.3f⁵ 10g 8g⁵ 8g Sep 14] useful-looking filly: fair handicapper: stays 1m: raced only on good ground or firmer: inconsistent. *Jedd O'Keeffe*   **70**

MAGICAL QUEST   4 b.c. Rainbow Quest (USA) 134 – Apogee 113 (Shirley Heights 130) [2004 11.5g 14m* 16m Sep 11] fourth living foal: brother to useful French 1½m/ 12.5f winner Space Quest and half-brother to useful French 11f winner Light Ballet and smart French 1¼m to 12.5f (Prix de Royallieu) winner Dance Routine (both by Sadler's Wells): dam French 1¼m/1½m (Prix de Royaumont) winner: fairly useful performer, very lightly raced: won maiden at Lingfield in August by 6 lengths from Red Damson, making all: well held in handicap at Goodwood only subsequent outing: should stay 2m: sold 30,000 gns. *Mrs A. J. Perrett*   **82**

MAGICAL ROMANCE (IRE)   2 b.f. (Feb 5) Barathea (IRE) 127 – Shouk 94   **110** (Shirley Heights 130) [2004 5m⁴ 6g* 6m⁶ 6g* 6g* Sep 30]

Pacemakers apart, the usual fate of outsiders in Group 1 events is to make up the numbers, but there are instances where outsiders have achieved a great deal more. In the last fifteen years alone, six have hit the bull's-eye in a British Group 1 race at odds of 40/1 or longer, namely Maroof, Generous, Jet Ski Lady, Compton

Sky Bet Cheveley Park Stakes, Newmarket—a big upset as Magical Romance shows further marked improvement; Suez (white sleeves) also beats odds-on Damson (right), with Golden Legacy (stars), Slip Dance (rail) and Soar next home

Place, Moonax and, the latest addition to the list, Magical Romance. There have been seven just at the Breeders' Cup—Arcangues, Spain, Caressing, One Dreamer, Volponi, Miss Alleged and Adoration—which confirms that tilting at windmills can sometimes be rewarded. Together with Slip Dance, Magical Romance at 40/1 was the longest-priced of the seven runners for the Sky Bet Cheveley Park Stakes at Newmarket in late-September, and her victory, though gamely achieved, did nothing to upset the pecking order among the British- and Irish-trained juvenile fillies. The market was headed by unbeaten Queen Mary Stakes and Phoenix Stakes winner Damson at odds on, followed by Soar (Princess Margaret Stakes and Lowther Stakes), Suez (listed event at Salisbury), Jewel In The Sand (Cherry Hinton Stakes) and Golden Legacy (Firth of Clyde Stakes). In other words, most fillies who should have been there were there. Magical Romance, who had two handlers beforehand, chased front-running Suez from the off, looked likely to be outpaced when Damson challenged over a furlong out, but battled on under pressure to edge past Suez by a neck with Damson, who failed to find anything in the last fifty yards, the same distance back in third. Soar and Jewel In The Sand ran way below form, occupying the last two places, and the favourite did not reproduce her best either, but all credit to Magical Romance for seizing the opportunity.

Magical Romance was twice the odds of the two longest-priced Cheveley Park winners in living memory, Embla in 1985 and Night Off in 1964, and provided the first victory in any Group 1 for her rider Robert Winston, who had replaced the injured Jimmy Fortune. Trainer Brian Meehan was also notching his first British Group 1, though Bad As I Wanna Be, Kaieteur and Tomba had all produced the goods in top races abroad. In the aftermath, Magical Romance received quotes between 16/1 and 25/1 for the One Thousand Guineas. She will need to progress a fair bit further to win a classic, since she is one of the more lowly rated Cheveley Park winners of recent times. She may, though, have some improvement in her, given the way she left her earlier form behind when winning the race. The best of that earlier form, around a stone inferior, had come ten days earlier in a thirteen-runner nursery at Leicester, in which Magical Romance made all and quickened clear to score by three lengths under second top weight of 9-6 in a good time for the grade. Before that, she had finished fourth behind Roodeye in a fillies' median auction maiden race at Windsor at the end of June, then convincingly landed a similar event at Kempton in July before running as if something was amiss when tailed-off last of six in the Princess Margaret Stakes at Ascot.

Magical Romance provided her sire Barathea with a second Group 1 winner over six furlongs, following the Stanleybet Sprint Cup success of Tante Rose.

Mr F. C. T. Wilson's "Magical Romance"

		Sadler's Wells	Northern Dancer
	Barathea (IRE)	(b 1981)	Fairy Bridge
	(b 1990)	Brocade	Habitat
Magical Romance (IRE)		(b 1981)	Canton Silk
(b.f. Feb 5, 2002)		Shirley Heights	Mill Reef
	Shouk	(b 1975)	Hardiemma
	(br 1994)	Souk	Ahonoora
		(b 1988)	Soumana

Judged on the distaff side of her pedigree, however, Magical Romance is unlikely to shine over sprint distances as a three-year-old, when a mile should be well within her capabilities. The dam Shouk, a daughter of Shirley Heights, won a maiden race over ten and a half furlongs on soft and is closely related to Puce, a listed winner over a mile and a half and third in the Park Hill Stakes and Ebor Handicap at around a mile and three quarters. To an earlier mating with Barathea, Puce produced the smart four-year-old Pongee, successful in the Lancashire Oaks and runner-up in the Yorkshire Oaks. Shouk's two other runners have both won. Grand Wizard (by Grand Lodge) was on the mark at a mile and a quarter and three-year-old Saree (also by Barathea) scored over seven furlongs and finished a close second in the Grade 3 Natalma Stakes over a mile as a juvenile. She also landed an allowance race over a mile at Delaware Park in July. The grandam Souk was successful twice at seven furlongs and stayed a mile. Souk was out of an unraced half-sister to Poule d'Essai des Pouliches winner Dumka, dam of Doyoun. Magical Romance cost 125,000 guineas as a yearling at Newmarket; her closely-related sister by Barathea's sire Sadler's Wells fetched 420,000 guineas at the same venue in October. Magical Romance, a leggy, quite good-topped filly, has raced only on good going or good to firm. *B. J. Meehan*

607

MAGICAL WIT (IRE)   4 ch.f. Bahhare (USA) 122 – Saleemah (USA) 96 (Storm **40**
Bird (CAN) 134) [2004 7g 5s p7g⁶ Dec 20] third foal: half-sister to fairly useful 5f (in
UAE) to 1m winner Medraar (by Machiavellian): dam won around 1m: poor maiden: left
P. Cluskey in Ireland before final start: stays 7f. *V. Smith*

MAGIC AMIGO   3 ch.g. Zilzal (USA) 137 – Emaline (FR) 105 (Empery (USA) 128) **81**
[2004 75: f7g² 9.7s* 10m 10.3g² 10.3m³ f12m 9.9g⁴ 10g³ 10m⁶ 9.7g² 10.1d⁶ p10g Sep
22] tall, leggy gelding: fairly useful performer: won maiden at Folkestone in May: stays
1¼m: acts on fibresand, soft and good to firm ground. *J. R. Jenkins*

MAGIC AMOUR   6 ch.g. Sanglamore (USA) 126 – Rakli 84 (Warning 136) [2004 **64**
71: 7m² 8m⁶ 8m 7m⁴ 7m 7m 6.1g* 7m 6g p8.6g Nov 13] strong, lengthy gelding: modest
handicapper: won at Warwick in August: effective at 6f to 1m: acts on firm going, well
held on softer than good: tried blinkered/visored: usually races up with pace. *Ian Williams*

MAGIC BOX   6 b.g. Magic Ring (IRE) 115 – Princess Poquito (Hard Fought 125) [2004 **–**
f8m Jul 12] strong, good-bodied gelding: one-time fair performer: well held only Flat run
since 2001: tried visored. *Miss Kate Milligan*

MAGIC CHARM   6 b.m. Magic Ring (IRE) 115 – Loch Clair (IRE) 53 (Lomond **43 d**
(USA) 128) [2004 47: f12g p13g f13g 12f 12m⁶ 12.3m 12m 14.1g⁶ f11g Dec 14]
angular mare: poor handicapper: left A. Newcombe after third start: barely stays 13f: acts
on all-weather and firm ground, below form on softer than good: tried visored/blinkered:
looks no easy ride. *Jedd O'Keeffe*

MAGIC COMBINATION (IRE)   11 b.g. Scenic 128 – Etage (Ile de Bourbon (USA) **89**
133) [2004 16.1v² 14.1f⁵ 18m² 16d² 14d* 14g* 13.9m Sep 5] leggy gelding: fairly useful
handicapper: unraced on Flat in 2003: won at Haydock in July and August: stays 2¼m:
acts on any turf going: blinkered once at 4 yrs. *L. Lungo*

MAGIC EAGLE   7 b.g. Magic Ring (IRE) 115 – Shadow Bird 70 (Martinmas 128) **37**
[2004 f6g⁵ f6g f6s f5g 7g f7g May 19] quite good-topped gelding: poor performer: best at
6f: acts on all-weather, soft and good to firm going: tried visored: usually races prominently. *P. T. Midgley*

MAGIC FLO   2 ch.f. (Mar 19) Magic Ring (IRE) 115 – Moore Stylish 65 (Moorestyle **56**
137) [2004 6g p7m⁶ 7d Oct 30] workmanlike filly: half-sister to 8-y-o Mr Stylish and a
winner in Sweden by Be My Chief: dam, middle-distance maiden, winning hurdler:
modest form in maidens: likely to stay 1m. *G. C. Bravery*

MAGIC GENIE (IRE)   2 b.f. (Mar 14) Lujain (USA) 119 – Haut Volee (Top Ville **47**
129) [2004 6m⁵ 6g 5g Jul 19] €12,000F: workmanlike filly: sixth foal: half-sister to 3
winners, including 5-y-o Cat's Whiskers and 7-y-o Stormville: dam German 2-y-o 6f and
1m winner: poor form in seller/claimers. *M. W. Easterby*

MAGIC GLADE   5 b.g. Magic Ring (IRE) 115 – Ash Glade (Nashwan (USA) 135) **95**
[2004 81: f6g f5g* p5g² 5g* 5m³ 5m 5m 5m³ f5s⁵ p5.1g⁶ f5g² f5g* Dec 14] compact
gelding: useful handicapper: left C. Dore after eighth outing: won at Southwell in February, Musselburgh in April and Southwell (beat Tag Team by length) in December:
effective at 5f/6f: acts on all-weather, raced only on good going or firmer on turf: reportedly bled sixth/seventh starts: usually races prominently. *R. Brotherton*

MAGIC MAMMA'S TOO   4 b.g. Magic Ring (IRE) 115 – Valona Valley (IRE) (Rep- **70 d**
rimand 122) [2004 70: f8g² f7g⁵ f8g³ f8g⁴ 7.1g 8d⁵ 7.9m Aug 2] rather leggy gelding:
inconsistent maiden: easily best effort in 2004 on reappearance: left T. D. Barron after
sixth start: stays 1m: acts on fibresand and firm going: tried in cheekpieces/visor:
sometimes plays little. *J. R. Weymes*

MAGIC MERLIN   3 b.g. Magic Ring (IRE) 115 – St James's Antigua (IRE) 79 (Law **84**
Society (USA) 130) [2004 8f³ 8.1g* 8g⁴ Jun 24] 5,500F, 9,000Y: seventh foal: brother to
a 7f winner in Italy and half-brother to 3 winners, including 1¼m winner Ibin St James
(by Salse) and 6-y-o Sashay: dam 1m winner: fairly useful form: won maiden at Chepstow in May: good fourth in handicap at Leicester subsequent start: gelded after: bred to
stay 1¼m. *P. W. Harris*

MAGIC MUSIC (IRE)   5 b.m. Magic Ring (IRE) 115 – Chiming Melody 71 (Cure **66 ?**
The Blues (USA)) [2004 82: 6g 6m 6m Jul 23] good-topped mare: just fair form at best in
2004, leaving Mrs H. Dalton after reappearance: raced mainly at 6f: acts on any going:
usually races prominently. *W. M. Brisbourne*

MAGICO   3 ch.g. Magic Ring (IRE) 115 – Silken Dalliance 91 (Rambo Dancer (CAN) **53 §**
107) [2004 54: p8g p6g f7d 8f³ 8f² 8f 7d p7.1g Nov 15] quite good-topped gelding: mod- **a36 §**
est maiden on turf, poor on all-weather: left A. Balding after second start, *P. Burgoyne*

after fifth: stays 1m: acts on firm ground: tried visored/blinkered: often races freely: unreliable. *A. B. Haynes*

MAGIC RED 4 ch.g. Magic Ring (IRE) 115 – Jacquelina (USA) 66 (Private Account **62** (USA)) [2004 –: f14g* f14m* p16d⁴ f14g² f14g² f16g³ Dec 14] big, rather leggy gelding: has a round action: modest handicapper: won twice within 4 days at Southwell in July: stays 2m: acts on all-weather and good to firm ground: tried in headgear: raced prominently in 2004, running in snatches final outing. *M. J. Ryan*

MAGIC SPIN 4 b.f. Magic Ring (IRE) 115 – Moon Spin 83 (Night Shift (USA)) **59** [2004 6d⁶ 7.1g⁵ p8m⁶ Oct 6] fifth foal: half-sister to 3 winners, including useful 1m (at 2 yrs) and 1¼m winner Golden Sparrow (by Elmaamul) and fairly useful 1¾m to 2¼m winner Rosa Canina (by Bustino): dam 1m to 1½m winner: modest form in maidens: reluctant at stall and wandered penultimate outing. *R. F. Johnson Houghton*

MAGIC STING 3 ch.g. Magic Ring (IRE) 115 – Ground Game 95 (Gildoran 123) **81** [2004 67: 10d⁵ f8.5g⁵ 11.6g⁶ 10v* 11.1g* 10g 10.3g³ 9.9d³ 10d² 10.2g* 9.2s² 10d⁵ Oct 4] smallish, workmanlike gelding: fairly useful performer: won handicap at Redcar in May, minor event at Hamilton in June and handicap at Chepstow in September: stays 11f: acts on heavy and good to firm ground: races freely. *M. L. W. Bell*

MAGIC STONE 4 br.g. Magic Ring (IRE) 115 – Ridgewood Ruby (IRE) 77 (Indian **42** Ridge 123) [2004 –: p7g p8g⁴ Mar 2] poor maiden, lightly raced: acts on polytrack. *A. Charlton*

MAGIC TREE (UAE) 2 ch.f. (Jan 25) Timber Country (USA) 124 – Moyesii (USA) **52 p** (Diesis 133) [2004 7g Jul 7] first foal: dam, French 9f winner, half-sister to smart miler Bowman (later 11f winner in UAE) out of Haydock Sprint Cup winner Cherokee Rose: 20/1, thirteenth in maiden at Kempton, fading: should do better. *M. R. Channon*

MAGIC VERSE 3 ch.f. Opening Verse 126 – Festival Sister (Belmez (USA) **61** 131) [2004 8m 10m f8g⁴ f8g⁴ f8g⁴ 10f⁵ 8s⁴ 8d* 8s 8d Nov 5] good-topped filly: second foal: half-sister to 4-y-o Never Without Me: dam, Italian 1¼m winner, half-sister to Lancashire Oaks winner Squeak, later very smart US Grade 1 9f/1¼m winner: modest performer: won banded race at Brighton in October: should stay 1¼m: acts on fibresand and good to soft going. *R. Guest*

MAGIC WARRIOR 4 b.g. Magic Ring (IRE) 115 – Clarista (USA) 67 (Riva Ridge **?** (USA)) [2004 58, a64: p8g³ p10g⁴ p10g⁶ p10g 8.1m 8m Sep 25] modest performer: stays **a62** easy 1¼m: acts on polytrack, best turf effort on good going. *J. C. Fox*

MAGISTRETTI (USA) 4 b.c. Diesis 133 – Ms Strike Zone (USA) (Deputy Minister **124** (CAN)) [2004 124: 12m⁶ 12m⁴ 10m⁴ 10f² 11d* 12d² 12d⁴ Oct 30] big, strong colt: very smart performer: just respectable efforts at best first 4 starts in 2004, including when sixth to Warrsan in Coronation Cup at Epsom and third (promoted to second) when demoted Powerscourt in Arlington Million (left N. Callaghan after): returned to best when winning Man o' War Stakes at Belmont in September by 1¼ lengths from Epalo, quickening in fine style to lead close home: in frame after 1m Turf Classic at Belmont (creditable 2½ lengths second to Kitten's Joy) and Breeders' Cup Turf at Lone Star Park (bit below best when 5 lengths fourth to Better Talk Now, squeezed for room as winner went by early in straight): barely stays 1½m: acts on firm and good to soft going: blinkered last 4 starts: sometimes sweats: gave trouble entering stall at Epsom: reportedly lost a shoe third outing. *P. L. Biancone, USA*

MAGNETIC POLE 3 b.c. Machiavellian (USA) 123 – Clear Attraction (USA) (Lear **84** Fan (USA) 130) [2004 88P: 10.2g² 9g³ 12.3d 12g² 10f² 11.9s* Oct 15] well-made colt: fairly useful performer: won maiden at Brighton in October by 21 lengths: stays 1½m: acts on soft and good to firm ground: blinkered fifth start: found little third to fifth outings: sold 48,000 gns. *Sir Michael Stoute*

MAGPIE BRIDGE 2 b.f. (May 17) Bandmaster (USA) 97 – Peapod (Krayyan 117) **–** [2004 p7.1g p7.1g p7m 8g.6g Dec 31] first reported foal: dam unraced: soundly beaten in maidens/seller, leaving B. R. Millman after second start. *N. I. M. Rossiter*

MAHARAAT (USA) 3 b.c. Bahri (USA) 125 – Siyadah (USA) 106 (Mr Prospector **84** (USA)) [2004 8g⁵ 10s⁵ 9.7m² Jun 7] third foal: half-brother to 4-y-o Musanid: dam, 1¼m winner, out of Yorkshire Oaks winner Roseate Tern, herself half-sister to high-class middle-distance performer Ibn Bey: fairly useful maiden: short-headed by Whitsbury Cross at Folkestone, best effort: tongue tied all 3 starts, also visored final one: sold 25,000 gns in July, resold 22,000 gns in October. *Sir Michael Stoute*

MAHLSTICK (IRE) 6 b.g. Tagula (IRE) 116 – Guv's Joy (IRE) 72 (Thatching 131) **43** [2004 p8g⁶ p7g³ p7g⁴ p6g⁴ 6.1m 8d Oct 2] good-topped gelding: poor maiden: best at 6f/

7f: acts on polytrack, best turf efforts on good going or firmer: tried visored/tongue tied. *D. W. P. Arbuthnot*

MAHMJRA 2 b.c. (Feb 24) Josr Algarhoud (IRE) 118 – Jamrat Samya (IRE) 79 (Sadler's Wells (USA) 132) [2004 7.9g 8s p8g Oct 31] big, strong colt: fourth foal: dam, ran once, out of sister to dam of Salsabil and Marju: seemingly modest form in maidens. *M. R. Channon* **56 ?**

MAHMOOM 3 ch.c. Dr Fong (USA) 128 – Rohita (IRE) 94 (Waajib 121) [2004 94: 7g 8m 6.1d⁶ 6m 6m* 6m² 7m⁶ 6g² Aug 14] strong, attractive colt: useful handicapper: won at Newmarket in June: ran well when second at same course after, beaten a neck by Alderney Race on second occasion: best at 6f: acts on good to firm going: visored fourth/fifth starts: joined D. Selvaratnam in UAE. *M. R. Channon* **100**

MAIDANNI (USA) 2 b. or br.c. (Mar 30) Private Terms (USA) – Carley's Birthday (USA) (Marfa (USA)) [2004 8m⁴ 7.9g* 8s Oct 22] $20,000Y, $425,000 2-y-o: rangy colt: on weak side at 2 yrs: fifth foal: half-brother to winner in USA by All Gone: dam 5f (at 2 yrs)/6f winner in USA: odds on, won maiden at York in October by ½ length from Aylmer Road, flashing tail: weakened quickly late on in nursery final start: likely to prove best at 7f/1m: probably capable of better. *Saeed bin Suroor* **79 p**

MAID FOR LIFE (IRE) 4 b.f. Entrepreneur 123 – Arandora Star (USA) (Sagace (FR) 135) [2004 66: 10f⁶ 9.9s⁶ 8g Sep 27] fair maiden at 3 yrs: well held in 2004, looking very reluctant. *M. J. Wallace* **– §**

MAIDS CAUSEWAY (IRE) 2 ch.f. (Mar 11) Giant's Causeway (USA) 132 – Vallee Des Reves (USA) (Kingmambo (USA) 125) [2004 6m² 7d⁵ 7.1m² 7f* 8m³ 8f² 7s* Oct 16] tall filly: has scope: third foal: dam unraced half-sister to very smart French performers Vetheuil (miler) and Verveine (up to 1½m), latter dam of 4-y-o Vallee Enchantee: smart performer: won maiden at Kempton in June, Sweet Solera Stakes at Newmarket (beat Slip Dance 1¼ lengths) in August and Owen Brown Rockfel Stakes at Newmarket (by short head from Penkenna Princess, making most and rallying) in October: good placed efforts behind Playful in May Hill Stakes at Doncaster and Fillies' Mile at Ascot fifth and sixth starts: likely to stay 1¼m: acts on firm and soft going: tends to sweat/get on edge: game and consistent. *B. W. Hills* **111**

MAIDSTONE MIDAS (IRE) 3 b.c. Nashwan (USA) 135 – Be Mine (Wolfhound (USA) 126) [2004 10g 11.5s⁴ p10g⁵ 10.9f⁶ Jun 19] modest maiden: best effort at 1¼m: seemingly tended to hang left final outing: joined M. Pipe. *W. S. Kittow* **60**

MAID THE CUT 3 ch.f. Silver Wizard (USA) 117 – Third Dam (Slip Anchor 136) [2004 –: f8g⁴ f7g 7.1s 8d⁵ 10m⁶ 12.6d⁵ p10m Dec 8] poor maiden: stays 1¼m: acts on fibresand, good to firm and good to soft ground. *A. D. Smith* **44**

MAID TO TREASURE (IRE) 3 b.f. Rainbow Quest (USA) 134 – Maid For The Hills 101 (Indian Ridge 123) [2004 77p: 10d⁴ 10d⁶ 10v³ 12s p10g Nov 16] attractive filly: disappointing maiden: should be suited by 1½m+. *J. L. Dunlop* **71 d**

*Owen Brown Rockfel Stakes, Newmarket—game and consistent Maids Causeway (right)
rallies splendidly to beat Penkenna Princess, Favourita (breastgirth) and Bibury Flyer*

Mr Martin S. Schwartz's "Maids Causeway"

MAJESTICAL (IRE)   2 b.g. (Apr 7) Fayruz 116 – Haraabah (USA) 99 (Topsider **59**
(USA)) [2004 p5g³ 5.3m⁴ 5m 5m 6f⁴ 5.1m² 5.7g⁴ 5m 5.1g⁶ p5.1g⁵ p5.1g⁶ Dec 20] tall
gelding: modest maiden: left W. Muir after ninth start: stays 5.7f: acts on polytrack and
good to firm going: carries head high. *J. M. Bradley*

MAJESTIC DESERT   3 b.f. Fraam 114 – Calcutta Queen 51 (Night Shift (USA)) **113**
[2004 108: 7g* 8m 8m 8m² 7d² 8g² 8d⁴ 8g⁴ 8m² Oct 10] smallish, leggy filly: has a round
action: smart performer: won Dubai Duty Free Stakes (Fred Darling) at Newbury in April
by length from Nyramba: several good efforts after, including when second in Coronation
Stakes at Royal Ascot (2½ lengths behind Attraction), Brownstown Stakes at Leopards-

Dubai Duty Free Stakes (Fred Darling), Newbury—
Majestic Desert justifies favouritism and books her place in the Guineas field;
Nyramba finishes strongly in second, with Nataliya (second right) and Spotlight (rail) next

town (beaten a neck by Tropical Lady), Prix d'Astarte at Deauville (went down by ½ length to Marbye) and Premio Vittorio di Capua at Milan (1¼ lengths behind Ancient World) and when 4 lengths fourth to Whipper in Prix Jacques le Marois at Deauville on seventh outing: stays 1m: acts on good to firm and good to soft going: held up: game and consistent. *M. R. Channon*

MAJESTIC MISSILE (IRE)   3 b.c. Royal Applause 124 – Tshusick 81 (Dancing   **112** Brave (USA) 140) [2004 116p: 5f⁵ 5m 5.2g⁶ Sep 18] tall, quite good-topped colt: smart performer: best effort in 2004 when respectable 2½ lengths fifth to The Tatling in King's Stand Stakes at Royal Ascot: races freely, and best at 5f: raced only on good ground or firmer: has been bandaged hind joints/taken steadily to post: carried head high and edged right penultimate start. *W. J. Haggas*

MAJESTIC MOVEMENT (USA)   2 ch.c. (Apr 5) Diesis 133 – Zarara (USA) (Man-   **68** ila (USA)) [2004 8.1d⁵ 7s 10g³ 8s⁵ f8g⁵ Nov 9] sturdy colt: first foal: dam unraced half-sister to Oaks winner Ramruma (by Diesis): fair maiden: stays 1¼m: acts on soft ground: sold 7,000 gns. *J. H. M. Gosden*

MAJESTIC STAR   3 b.f. Fraam 114 – Fun While It Lasts (Idiot's Delight 115) [2004   – 10v p10g Dec 30] leggy filly: third foal: dam modest novice hurdler: well held in maidens at Newbury and Lingfield. *M. J. Ryan*

MAJESTIC VISION   3 ch.g. Desert King (IRE) 129 – Triste Oeil (USA) 103 (Raise   **74** A Cup (USA)) [2004 73: 10s 14.1d⁶ 13.8m² 16g⁵ 14.1g³ 14.1d p13.9g Nov 11] close-coupled, quite good-topped gelding: fair maiden handicapper: trained until after sixth start by P. Harris: stays 2m: acts on good to firm and good to soft ground: usually races up with pace. *W. R. Swinburn*

MAJHOOL   5 b.g. Mark of Esteem (IRE) 137 – Be Peace (USA) (Septieme Ciel   **60** (USA) 123) [2004 77: p5g p7g⁴ p7g⁵ 7m* 7f 7g Sep 7] tall gelding: only modest: left G. L. Moore, won seller at Brighton in March: left T. Mills after fifth start: stays easy 7f: acts on polytrack and firm ground: has been early to post. *I. W. McInnes*

MAJIK   5 ch.g. Pivotal 124 – Revoke (USA) 70 (Riverman (USA) 131) [2004 77: f6g   **75** f7g³ f7g⁴ 6s 6s⁴ 6s 7s⁴ 6g⁵ 5.7s³ f6g⁴ p6g³ Nov 20] close-coupled gelding: fair handicapper, better on all-weather than turf: effective at 6f/7f: acts on fibresand, soft and good to firm ground: tried in visor/cheekpieces. *D. J. S. ffrench Davis*

MAJLIS (IRE)   7 b.g. Caerleon (USA) 132 – Ploy 87 (Posse (USA) 130) [2004 74:   **73 §** p12g p12g p13g⁵ 14g 11.9m May 12] fair handicapper: should stay 1¾m: acts on all-weather and good to firm going: one to treat with caution. *R. M. H. Cowell*

MAJOR BLADE (GER)   6 b.g. Dashing Blade 117 – Misniniski (Niniski (USA)   – 125) [2004 64?: 10g 10g 10f Jul 19] one-time fairly useful performer in Germany: well held in handicaps in 2004. *B. G. Powell*

MAJORCA   3 b.c. Green Desert (USA) 127 – Majmu (USA) 105 (Al Nasr (FR) 126)   **94** [2004 73p: 6g³ 6m² 6g⁴ 7f* 8s* 8g Jul 8] tall, rather leggy, quite good-topped colt: poor walker: has a round, unimpressive action: fairly useful form: won maiden at Thirsk and handicap at Newcastle in June: stays 1m: unraced on heavy going, acts on any other: sold 16,000 gns in October. *J. H. M. Gosden*

MAJOR EFFORT (USA)   3 b.c. Rahy (USA) 115 – Tethkar 75 (Machiavellian (USA)   **80** 123) [2004 79p: 8m⁴ 8.1d Jun 1] good-topped colt: fairly useful maiden, lightly raced: will stay 1¼m: acts on good to firm and good to soft going: sold 10,000 gns in August. *Sir Michael Stoute*

MAJOR FAUX PAS (IRE)   2 b.g. (Mar 12) Barathea (IRE) 127 – Edwina (IRE) 63   **85 p** (Caerleon (USA) 132) [2004 p7.1g* f8g* Nov 22] €35,000Y: half-brother to fairly useful 7f (in Ireland)/1m winner Your The Lady (by Indian Ridge) and useful 7f/1m (including in UAE) winner Seihali (by Alzao): dam, maiden, half-sister to useful sprinter Roger The Butler: won maiden at Wolverhampton in November and minor event at Southwell (by ¾ length from Doctor's Cave) in December: should stay 1¼m: open to improvement. *J. A. Osborne*

MAJOR PROJECT (IRE)   3 b.g. General Monash (USA) 107 – Mini Project (IRE)   – 94 (Project Manager 111) [2004 –: f8g 8.5m May 24] no form. *P. C. Haslam*

MAJORS CAST (IRE)   3 b.c. Victory Note (USA) 120 – Ziffany 68 (Taufan (USA)   **102 p** 119) [2004 7.1m³ 7g* 7s³ p7g* 6.5f³ Sep 24] IR 38,000F, 190,000Y: good-topped colt: third foal: half-brother to smart 5f/6f winner Jessica's Dream (by Desert Style): dam, 7f seller winner, ran only at 2 yrs: useful performer: won maiden at Goodwood in August and handicap at Lingfield (by neck from Eccentric) in September, idling both times: shaped well when third to Khabfair in handicap at Ascot final start, held up and forced wide, finishing strongly when checked well inside final 1f: effective at 6f/7f: progressive, and likely to do better still. *J. Noseda*

MAKARIM (IRE) 8 ch.g. Generous (IRE) 139 – Emmaline (USA) (Affirmed (USA)) **64 §** [2004 76§: p13g p16g f16.2s³ f16.2s⁵ p13g 15m⁴ 17.2g 14.1m⁵ p13.9g Dec 10] tall gelding: modest handicapper: stays easy 2m: acts on all-weather and firm ground: tried blinkered/visored, wears cheekpieces nowadays: ungenuine. *M. R. Bosley*

MAKE IT HAPPEN NOW 2 b. or br.f. (Mar 14) Octagonal (NZ) 126 – Whittle **43 ?** Woods Girl 80 (Emarati (USA) 74) [2004 5.1s 5.1m⁴ 5f 6g f5g 8f Sep 6] 13,000Y: sixth foal: half-sister to 8-y-o High Esteem and 4-y-o Zagala: dam, 6f winner, sister to useful 6f/7f performer Emerging Market and half-sister to smart sprinter Atraf: poor maiden. *S. C. Burrough*

MAKE IT SNAPPY 2 b.f. (Mar 22) Mujadil (USA) 119 – Snap Crackle Pop (IRE) **65** 87 (Statoblest 120) [2004 7d 7g p7g³ Oct 28] 24,000Y: unfurnished filly: fourth foal: half-sister to 3-y-o Handsome Cross and 2001 2-y-o 6f winner Snip Snap (by Revoque): dam 2-y-o 5f winner: easily best effort in maidens when third to Royal Jelly at Lingfield: shapes as if will stay 1m. *P. W. Harris*

MAKE MY HAY 5 b.g. Bluegrass Prince (IRE) 110 – Shashi (IRE) 79 (Shaadi (USA) **56** 126) [2004 51: f11g³ p13g⁶ 12v* 11.6m² 12f⁵ 12.6g⁵ 12m⁵ 12g⁶ 12m² 11.9s⁴ f12g⁵ Dec 1] leggy, sparely-made gelding: modest performer: left J. White after second start: won banded race at Kempton in May: stays 1½m: acts on all-weather, heavy and good to firm going: tried blinkered: held up. *J. Gallagher*

MAKEPEACE (IRE) 2 b.c. (Apr 9) Xaar 132 – Marillette (USA) 108 (Diesis 133) **60** [2004 6m 7.2d⁴ 7s 7m Sep 7] modest maiden: should stay 1m: best effort on good to soft going. *M. R. Channon*

MAKES PERFECT (IRE) 2 b.f. (Feb 13) Orpen (USA) 116 – Practice (USA) 97 **48** (Diesis 133) [2004 5.7m 6f⁶ Aug 3] half-sister to several minor winners in USA: dam 2-y-o 5f/6f winner (later successful in USA): poor form in maidens: dead. *S. Kirk*

MAKE US FLUSH 2 b.f. (Feb 14) Mind Games 121 – Pearls (Mon Tresor 113) [2004 **75** 5d⁴ 6m 6g⁴ 6m 6g* 5s* 6.1m 5g² 6s* 6d 6d 6s⁶ p6g Oct 7] leggy filly: fourth foal: sister to fairly useful 2001 2-y-o 6f winner Perle d'Azur and closely related to 2000 2-y-o 6f winner Wilson Blyth (by Puissance, later successful in Spain): dam unraced: fair performer: won claimer at Haydock in July and nurseries there in July and August: effective at 5f/6f: acts on good going, probably on good to firm. *A. Berry*

MAKFOOL (FR) 3 b.c. Spectrum (IRE) 126 – Abeyr 106 (Unfuwain (USA) 131) **101** [2004 98: p7g 8g³ 7d⁴ 7.6d 8.1m² 7m* 8m 7g 7m Jul 29] rather leggy, useful-looking colt: has a round action: useful handicapper: won at Epsom in June by ¾ length from Mandobi: below form after: stays 1m: yet to race on extremes of going on turf, well below form only start on polytrack: joined D. Selvaratnam in UAE. *M. R. Channon*

MAKHLAB (USA) 4 b.c. Dixieland Band (USA) – Avasand (USA) (Avatar (USA)) **109 ?** [2004 108+: 8g⁵ 7d⁵ 7.1g⁴ 7.1g² 7g² 7g Aug 14] rangy, good sort: poor mover: useful performer: best efforts in 2004 when second in listed race at Haydock (beaten ½ length by Suggestive) and minor event at Chester (blinkered, beaten 1¾ lengths by Vanderlin): effective at 7f/1m: has won on good to firm going, possibly best on good or softer (though yet to race on heavy): joined A. Al Raihe in UAE. *B. W. Hills*

MAKSAD (IRE) 4 b.c. Machiavellian (USA) 123 – Balaabel (USA) 83 (Sadler's **90** Wells (USA) 132) [2004 7.6d² 7m 6g³ a7.5g² a7f⁶ a6.5f³ Dec 23] fifth foal: half-brother to useful 2000 2-y-o 7f (Rockfel Stakes) winner Sayedah (by Darshaan) and to fairly useful 7f winner Marasem (by Cadeaux Genereux): dam, 1m winner, half-sister to US Grade 2 7f winner Kayrawan: fairly useful performer: ran for Saeed bin Suroor in UAE only on debut at 3 yrs: won minor events at Deauville and Lyon Parilly later in 2003: well held in Victoria Cup (Handicap) at Ascot second start in 2004 (well backed): creditable efforts next 2 outings in minor events at Chantilly (amateurs) and Deauville (apprentices), then left J. Hammond in France: stays 1m: acts on good to firm and good to soft going, and on dirt/all-weather at Deauville: tongue tied last 2 appearances. *E. Charpy, UAE*

MAKTAVISH 5 b.g. Makbul 104 – La Belle Vie 73 (Indian King (USA) 128) [2004 **92** 83, a89: f5g* 5g* 5g² 5s* 5.1d³ 5m 5m 5.1d 5g⁴ 5g⁶ 5g 5g 5d f5g Dec 14] close-coupled gelding: fairly useful performer: won handicaps at Southwell in February and Doncaster in March and minor event at Thirsk in April: left I. Semple prior to final start: best at 5f: acts on fibresand and probably any turf going (all 6 turf wins on good or softer): wears cheekpieces: has run well when sweating: races up with pace: tends to hang right. *J. Mackie*

MAKTU 2 ch.g. (Mar 9) Bien Bien (USA) 125 – Shalateeno 80 (Teenoso (USA) 135) **68**
[2004 8.3m^5 8.1s^3 8m^4 Sep 25] £4,000Y: second foal: dam 1¼m/1½m winner who stayed 2m: fair form in maidens: should stay at least 1½m: best effort on soft going. *P. F. I. Cole*

MAKTUB (ITY) 5 b.h. Love The Groom (USA) 123 – Carmen The Best (IRE) (Waajib **118**
121) [2004 118: 16.2s 13.9d^6 12m^2 10d 12m^2 12f^2 12d Oct 2] close-coupled, good-topped ex-Italian horse: smart performer: well held all 3 starts in Britain in 2004 (acted as pacemaker in Eclipse Stakes at Sandown fourth time), but good second in Gran Premio di Milano (beaten 2½ lengths by Senex), Scandinavian Open Championship at Copenhagen (short-headed by Crocodile Dundee) and Bosphorus Cup at Veliefendi (beaten ½ length by Senex): tailed-off last in Turf Classic at Belmont final outing: effective at 11f to 15f: has won on soft ground, best recent form on good or firmer: has worn tongue tie. *M. A. Jarvis*

MAKULU (IRE) 4 b.g. Alzao (USA) 117 – Karinski (USA) (Palace Music (USA) 129) **73**
[2004 83: 11.6d 16g 10.4m^2 10.3d Jun 26] rather leggy, useful-looking gelding: fair performer: stays 11.6f: acts on polytrack and soft going: tried blinkered, wore cheekpieces last 2 starts: joined C. Mann and won over hurdles. *B. J. Meehan*

MAKYBE DIVA 6 b.m. Desert King (IRE) 129 – Tugela (USA) (Riverman (USA) **125**
131) [2004 7g^5 8g^3 10g^6 10g^3 12g^3 16g^4 7g^4 8v^2 10g 12d^2 16s^4 Nov 2] first foal: dam twice-raced daughter of smart performer up to 1¼m Rambushka: high-class mare: won twice in Group 1 company at Randwick (including a Sydney Cup at Randwick in April (by short neck from Manawa King, left D. Hall after) and Melbourne Cup (Handicap) at Flemington (beat Vinnie Roe by 1¼ lengths) in November, in latter race justifying favouritism to become first horse since Think Big in 1975, and first female in race's history, to win in successive years, quickening to lead 1f out and having bit in hand: beaten narrowly by Elvstroem in Caulfield Cup (Handicap) on penultimate start: stays 2m: raced mainly on good or softer going: has flashed tail: has good turn of foot. *D. L. Freedman, Australia*

MALAAH (IRE) 8 gr.g. Pips Pride 117 – Lingdale Lass 60 (Petong 126) [2004 –: p8g **41**
p6g p7g^4 f6g p7g Mar 29] good-topped gelding: poor performer: stays 1m: acts on polytrack and firm going: blinkered/visored. *Julian Poulton*

MALAHIDE EXPRESS (IRE) 4 gr.g. Compton Place 125 – Gracious Gretclo 54 **66**
(Common Grounds 118) [2004 69: f5s^4 f6g^5 f5s f5g^2 7.1g 5v^5 5d^5 5m^4 5m* 5m 5g 5m^3 p5.1g Oct 18] angular gelding: fair performer: left M. Polglase after fourth start: won at Hamilton in June: best at 5f: acts on all-weather, good to firm and good to soft ground: tried in cheekpieces and often blinkered before joining present stable: often pulls hard/hangs: often makes running. *E. J. Alston*

MALAIKA 2 b.f. (Apr 11) Polar Prince (IRE) 117 – Gold Belt (IRE) 61 (Bellypha 130) **65**
[2004 5d^5 5.1g^4 5.1s^3 Oct 19] smallish, good-topped filly: sister to 4-y-o Prince of Gold and half-sister to several winners, including 5-y-o Goldeva and 7-y-o Royal Cavalier: dam 1m winner: in frame in maidens at Nottingham and Bath: likely to prove best at 5f/easy 6f. *R. Hollinshead*

MALAK AL MOULOUK (USA) 4 ch.g. King of Kings (IRE) 125 – Honor To Her **72**
(USA) (Sir Ivor (USA) 135) [2004 67: 10m^4 10f^2 11.6g 8g Sep 2] fair maiden, lightly raced: stays 1¼m: acts on all-weather and firm going: hung left second outing. *J. M. P. Eustace*

MALAPROPISM 4 ch.g. Compton Place 125 – Mrs Malaprop 83 (Night Shift (USA)) **97**
[2004 93: 5g^6 5m 6m 5d 5g^6 5m 5.2f^4 5g 5.2g^6 5.1d^6 5f* 5.2g 5m^6 5s* 5d* 5s p6g Oct 31] well-made gelding: useful handicapper: won at Doncaster in September, and Catterick and Musselburgh (within 24 hrs) in October, best effort when beating Corridor Creeper 1¾ lengths in last-named: best at 5f: unraced on heavy going, acts on any other: sometimes rears in stall: usually races prominently: tends to hang/carry head awkwardly: tough. *M. R. Channon*

MALARKEY 7 b.g. Mukaddamah (USA) 125 – Malwiya (USA) (Shahrastani (USA) **80**
135) [2004 p12g^5 16g^8 15s^2 16g* 16m^5 18g^3 20f Jun 15] tall, rather angular gelding: has a high knee action: fairly useful handicapper: missed 2003: left A. Crook after reappearance: won at Nottingham in March and Newbury in April: stays 17f: acts on all-weather, soft and good to firm ground: blinkered once at 4 yrs, has worn cheekpieces/blinkers (not for present stable): usually held up. *Mrs Stef Liddiard*

MALCHEEK (IRE) 2 br.c. (Apr 24) Lend A Hand 124 – Russland (GER) (Surumu **71 p**
(GER)) [2004 6m⁴ Jun 12] €27,000Y: rangy colt: has scope: half-brother to several
winners, including French 9f (at 2 yrs) to 1½m winner Nastroenie (by Be My Guest):
dam, German 2-y-o 6f winner, half-sister to German Group 3 11f winner Romano: 25/1,
fourth in maiden at York: will stay 1m: should do better if all is well. *T. D. Easterby*

MALIBU (IRE) 3 b.g. Second Empire (IRE) 124 – Tootle (Main Reef 126) [2004 84?: **79**
9g⁴ 10.1m⁶ 10g⁵ 10d 8m* 8.5f⁵ 9d 7g 8f p9.5g³ p8.6g³ p9.5g Dec 15] €2,500Y: tall, good-
topped gelding: half-brother to 3 winners, including fairly useful 1993 2-y-o 7f winner
Suaad (by Fools Holme): dam French 5.5f winner: fair performer: trained at 2 yrs by
J. Crowley in Ireland: won handicap at Brighton in July: stays 9.5f: acts on polytrack and
good to firm ground: tried in headgear. *S. Dow*

MALINSA BLUE (IRE) 2 b.f. (Mar 29) Desert Style (IRE) 121 – Talina's Law (IRE) **80**
83 (Law Society (USA) 130) [2004 6.1s⁶ 6m² 6g² 6m⁶ 7m² 7f* 7g Oct 2] €20,000Y:
workmanlike filly: half-sister to 3 winners, including useful Irish 1¾m winner Queen
Astrid (by Revoque): dam, Irish 2m winner and winning hurdler, out of half-sister to 2000
Guineas winner Zino: fairly useful performer: won nursery at Doncaster in September:
poorly drawn and soon off bridle final start: should stay 1m: acts on firm going.
J. A. Glover

MALLARD (IRE) 6 b.g. Tagula (IRE) 116 – Frill (Henbit (USA) 130) [2004 69, a82: **70**
8g³ 7.5g p8g² 8.1g⁶ 7.6g 7d p7g p7g⁴ p7.1g³ Oct 2] good-bodied gelding: fairly useful **a81**
performer on all-weather, fair on turf: effective at 7f to 8.5f: acts on all-weather, best turf
efforts on good ground: sold 14,500 gns, sent to Saudi Arabia. *J. G. Given*

MALLIA 11 b.g. Statoblest 120 – Pronetta (USA) (Mr Prospector (USA)) [2004 55§: **53 §**
6v⁴ f6g* f7d⁶ f6g³ f6m² f6m⁴ 6g 6d Aug 17] lengthy, dipped-backed gelding: modest
performer: won seller at Wolverhampton in June: best at 6f: acts on fibresand/any turf
going: tried in headgear (not in 2004): slowly away/finds little: held up. *T. D. Barron*

MALMAND (USA) 5 ch.g. Distant View (USA) 126 – Bidski (USA) (Explosive Bid **?**
(USA)) [2004 ?, a52§: f9.4g f9.4g* p10g f9.4g⁴ f9.4s Mar 8] compact, quite attractive **a45 §**
gelding: poor performer: won banded race at Wolverhampton in January: stays 9.4f: acts
on fibresand, soft and good to firm going: tried blinkered/in cheekpieces, visored nowadays: reportedly bled once at 4 yrs: unreliable. *R. Brotherton*

MALUTI 3 ch.g. Piccolo 121 – Persian Blue 64 (Persian Bold 123) [2004 52: 5.1g **58**
6m⁶ 6f³ 5.3f* 5d⁴ 5.1m² 5m p5.1d⁵ p5.1g Nov 13] small, close-coupled gelding: modest
handicapper: won at Brighton in June: effective at 5f/6f: acts on polytrack, firm and good
to soft going. *R. Guest*

MALVERN LIGHT 3 b.f. Zieten (USA) 118 – Michelle Hicks 92 (Ballad Rock 122) **102**
[2004 87p: 7g⁴ 7s 6d 7m³ Jul 6] good-topped filly: useful performer, lightly raced:
5¼ lengths fourth to Silca's Gift in Nell Gwyn Stakes at Newmarket on reappearance:
best effort when 2¼ lengths third to Peeress in handicap at Newmarket: stays 7f: acts
on good to firm and good to soft ground: has worn crossed noseband: free-going sort.
W. J. Haggas

MAMBAZO 2 b.c. (Mar 24) Dansili 127 – Kalindi 102 (Efisio 120) [2004 6g 6.1d 7g **71**
8.3m p6g² Oct 19] 60,000Y: stocky colt: first foal: dam 5f (at 2 yrs) and 7f winner: fair
maiden: clearly best effort when second to Captain Johnno at Wolverhampton: likely to
prove best at 6f/7f: acts on polytrack. *S. C. Williams*

MAMBINA (USA) 3 ch.f. Kingmambo (USA) 125 – Sonata (Polish Precedent (USA) **74**
131) [2004 74: p8g 10.9d⁴ 10s⁴ 11.6s⁵ 10f 10g⁴ 10.5g 9.9d² 11.1s² 10.2g³ 10d² 10f⁴
10.1g* 10.1m* 10d⁶ 10.3s⁶ 10v³ p10g⁶ p9.5g Nov 20] compact filly: fair performer: won
maiden at Epsom and handicap at Newcastle in October: stays 11f: acts on heavy and
good to firm going, well held on polytrack: has raced freely/wandered/carried head
awkwardly. *M. R. Channon*

MAMBO PRINCESS (USA) 2 b.f. (Feb 15) Kingmambo (USA) 125 – Tuzla (FR) **60 p**
121 (Panoramic 120) [2004 p7m⁶ Dec 22] first foal: dam US Grade 1 9f winner and
second in Breeders' Cup Mile: 5/1 and green, sixth to Glinting Desert in maiden at Lingfield, slowly away: should do better. *J. H. M. Gosden*

MAMBO'S MELODY 2 b.f. (Mar 15) Kingmambo (USA) 125 – Key Academy 103 **– p**
(Royal Academy (USA) 130) [2004 7g Oct 11] 100,000Y: angular filly: first foal: dam,
1½m winner (later successful in USA), half-sister to Lancashire Oaks/US Grade 1 9f/
1¼m winner Squeak: 40/1 and backward, well held in maiden at Leicester: likely to do
better. *P. W. Chapple-Hyam*

Pentax UK September Stakes, Kempton—Mamool shows himself to be almost as good as ever in beating Alkaased and Bandari, with Jagger last of the four runners

MAMCAZMA 6 gr.g. Terimon 124 – Merryhill Maid (IRE) 71 (M Double M (USA)) **95** [2004 102: 12m 16.1s 13.9g⁴ 14g 16.1f 14.8d 14.1d 16.2m² 16s p16.5g* p12g Nov 20] strong, lengthy gelding: fairly useful handicapper: won at Wolverhampton in November: effective at 1½m to 2m: acts on fibresand, soft and firm going: blinkered (below form) once: waited with: sometimes carries head awkwardly. *D. Morris*

MAMOOL (IRE) 5 b.h. In The Wings 128 – Genovefa (USA) 107 (Woodman (USA) **118** 126) [2004 122: 10s³ 12m* 12m 16s Nov 2] good-topped horse: smart performer: found to have fractured off-hind fetlock final 4-y-o start: back to near best to win 4-runner Pentax UK September Stakes at Kempton by ½ length from Alkaased: not discredited after in Prix de l'Arc de Triomphe at Longchamp (took strong hold when fifteenth of 19) and Melbourne Cup at Flemington (7¼ lengths seventh behind Makybe Diva): effective at 1½m to 2m (failed to stay 2½m in Gold Cup): acts on soft and good to firm going: has been tongue tied: has worn crossed noseband: sometimes bandaged: game. *Saeed bin Suroor*

MAMORE GAP (IRE) 6 b.g. General Monash (USA) 107 – Ravensdale Rose (IRE) **67** (Henbit (USA) 130) [2004 81: p8g p10g 10g 8g⁵ 9.9g 10g⁵ 8.1s⁵ 8.3m Sep 27] smallish gelding: fair performer: effective at stiff 7f, barely stays 1¼m: acts on firm and soft ground: sold 3,000 gns, then gelded. *R. Hannon*

MANAAR (IRE) 4 b.g. Titus Livius (FR) 115 – Zurarah (Siberian Express (USA) 125) **90** [2004 97: 7d 7m⁵ 7m 7g² 7.2g 7g² 7g Oct 9] good-quartered gelding: fairly useful performer: stays 7f: acts on polytrack and good to firm ground: blinkered (looked reluctant) final outing: has worn crossed noseband: usually held up nowadays: temperament under suspicion. *J. Noseda*

MANA D'ARGENT (IRE) 7 b.g. Ela-Mana-Mou 132 – Petite-D-Argent 91 (Noalto **95** 120) [2004 97: 16d 18.7d⁵ 13.9s 20f 16.2g 16.2m* 21g⁵ 16.2m 18s 17s⁵ p13.9g Nov 27] small gelding: good walker: unimpressive mover: useful handicapper on his day: has gained all 6 successes at Ascot, including in July (beat stable-companion Riyadh by short head): creditable fifth in Chester Cup second start: effective at 1½m to 21f: acts on fibresand and any turf going: blinkered/visored earlier in career: usually held up: sometimes wanders: none too consistent. *M. Johnston*

MANASHIN 4 b.f. Whittingham (IRE) 104 – Montagne 49 (Midyan (USA) 124) [2004 **–** –: f8g f12s⁴ Mar 8] workmanlike filly: well beaten in maidens, leaving B. Smart after reappearance. *R. P. Elliott*

MAN AT ARMS (IRE) 3 b.c. Daggers Drawn (USA) 114 – Punta Gorda (IRE) (Roi **81** Danzig (USA)) [2004 69: 10.2m⁴ 11.9f* 12g⁴ 12.3g 11.6g 14m⁴ 14m⁶ 14.4m 12g 14g Oct 2] well-made colt: fairly useful handicapper: won at Brighton in June: stays 1¾m: raced only on good ground or firmer: well below form when tried visored/in cheekpieces: held up. *R. Hannon*

MAN CRAZY (IRE) 3 b.f. Foxhound (USA) 103 – Schonbein (IRE) 60 (Persian **56** Heights 129) [2004 76: p6g p7g⁶ 6.1g 7g 6g 6d⁴ 6m 5.7m 5g⁴ 7g 6s 6d⁴ f6g² f6g⁶ Dec 7] sturdy filly: modest maiden: left R. Beckett after ninth start: stays 7f: acts on polytrack, firm and good to soft going: tried blinkered: often races prominently. *C. A. Dwyer*

MANDAHAR (IRE) 5 b.g. Bluebird (USA) 125 – Madiriya 119 (Diesis 133) [2004 **–** p8g p7g 6s 7g p10g f11d Jun 17] workmanlike gelding: little form: visored final start. *A. W. Carroll*

616

MANDARIN SPIRIT (IRE) 4 b.g. Primo Dominie 121 – Lithe Spirit (IRE) 74 **78**
(Dancing Dissident (USA) 119) [2004 82+: 6g 7f[5] 7m[5] 6g 7g[5] 7m* p6g[4] 7s[3] p6g p7.1g*
p7.1g[6] Dec 20] fair performer: won handicap at Epsom in September and claimer at
Wolverhampton in December: effective at 6f/7f: acts on all-weather and firm going:
usually blinkered. *G. C. H. Chung*

MANDATUM 3 b.g. Mtoto 134 – Reamur 68 (Top Ville 129) [2004 12.3m[2] 10g[2] 12f* **84 p**
14.6s[4] Oct 22] rather leggy, lengthy gelding: eighth foal: half-brother to 2 winners, notably smart 1¼m to 2¼m winner Boreas (by In The Wings): dam maiden who stayed
1½m: fairly useful form: won maiden at Newmarket in August by ½ length from Turnstile, making most despite wandering: creditable fourth to Winged d'Argent in handicap
at Doncaster subsequent outing, still seeming inexperienced: should be suited by 1¾m+:
remains type to develop into a useful handicapper. *L. M. Cumani*

MANDINKA 4 b.g. Distinctly North (USA) 115 – Primo Panache (Primo Dominie **65**
121) [2004 –: 8g 9.9d[4] 10.9m 10f f11g[2] f11d* Dec 21] big, good-topped gelding: fair
performer: won banded race at Southwell in December by 8 lengths: stays 11f: acts on
fibresand, good to firm and good to soft going: sometimes slowly away. *J. F. Coupland*

MANDOBI (IRE) 3 ch.c. Mark of Esteem (IRE) 137 – Miss Queen (USA) (Miswaki **111**
(USA) 124) [2004 95: 6.1d[4] 7m[2] 8m* 8m[2] a7.5f[3] Dec 16] sturdy, close-coupled colt:
smart performer: won Britannia Stakes (Handicap) at Royal Ascot by length from Lucayan Legend: good 2 lengths second to Fong's Thong in listed race at Goodwood next time
(trained by A. Stewart): off 4½ months, respectable third in handicap at Nad Al Sheba on
dirt debut final outing: stays 1m: yet to race on extremes of going on turf: usually held up,
and has good turn of foot. *D. J. Selvaratnam, UAE*

MANDOOB 7 b.g. Zafonic (USA) 130 – Thaidah (CAN) 105 (Vice Regent (CAN)) **75 §**
[2004 72: f12g[4] f12g* f12s* f12s 14.4s f12g[2] 11.9m p12g[4] p12d[4] p16d[6] Aug 9] big,
close-coupled gelding: fair performer: won claimer and handicap at Wolverhampton on
consecutive days in February: below form after: barely stays 14.8f: acts on all-weather/
any turf ground: usually wears headgear: sometimes tongue tied: has given trouble at
stall/hung: sometimes slowly away: not one to trust. *B. R. Johnson*

MANDURO (GER) 2 br.c. (Mar 9) Monsun (GER) 124 – Mandellicht (IRE) (Be My **115 p**
Guest (USA) 126) [2004 7g* 8d* Oct 17] €130,000Y: fourth foal: half-brother to 2
winners in Germany, including useful 10.5f/11f winner who stayed 13.5f Mandela (by
Acatenango): dam German 7.5f winner: won maiden at Munich (by 6 lengths) in September and Oppenheim Pramerica - Preis des Winterfavoriten at Cologne (beat Kahn
comfortably by 5 lengths, leading over 2f out) in October: will be suited by 1¼m/1½m:
sure to progress and win more good races in 2005. *P. Schiergen, Germany*

MANDY'S COLLECTION 5 ch.m. Forzando 122 – Instinction (Never So Bold 135) **–**
[2004 –: f5g p6g f6g[5] f5m May 17] maiden: well held since 2002: jinked and unseated
rider at start second outing. *A. G. Newcombe*

MANEKI NEKO (IRE) 2 b.g. (Feb 22) Rudimentary (USA) 118 – Ardbess (Balla **76**
Cove 119) [2004 6g[4] 6m[2] 8g[2] 7d f8g[3] p8.6g[3] Nov 26] €15,000Y: first foal: dam unraced:
fair maiden: stays 1m: acts on good to firm going: blinkered (below form) final start:
tends to wander. *M. H. Tompkins*

Britannia Stakes (Handicap), Royal Ascot—
Mandobi provides trainer Alec Stewart with his last big-race victory;
next to finish are Lucayan Legend (left), Thyolo (rail), Fine Silver (spots on sleeves) and Free Trip

MANGO MISCHIEF (IRE)   3 ch.f. Desert King (IRE) 129 – Eurolink Mischief 84   **99**
(Be My Chief (USA) 122) [2004 84p: 9.9m* 10m² 9.9g⁴ 10.1g² 10f 10.3s* 10.5s Nov 27]
tall, leggy filly: has scope: useful performer: won minor event at Salisbury in June
and listed race at Doncaster (beat Star of Normandie by 3½ lengths) in November: below
form in listed race at Saint-Cloud final outing: will stay 1½m: acts on soft and good to
firm ground: waited with. *J. L. Dunlop*

MANGROVE CAY (IRE)   2 b.g. (Apr 16) Danetime (IRE) 121 – Art Duo 86 (Artaius   **65**
(USA) 129) [2004 7g 7.1g⁴ p6g⁵ p6g⁵ f8g Nov 9] €20,000Y, resold 17,000Y: half-brother
to several winners, including useful 6f (at 2yrs) to 10.4f winner Amyas (by Waajib):
dam, maiden, best at 7f at 2yrs: fair maiden: left D. Loder after fourth start: stays 7f:
acts on polytrack: visored (ran creditably) penultimate start: tends to wander/find little.
J. Hetherton

MANGUS (IRE)   10 b.g. Mac's Imp (USA) 116 – Holly Bird (Runnett 125) [2004 –§,   **– §**
a44§: f5g³ p5g f5s⁶ f5g p5g 5.3g⁵ May 4] workmanlike gelding: poor performer: raced   **a41 §**
mainly at 5f: acts on all-weather, firm and soft going: tried tongue tied/in cheekpieces/
blinkers: sometimes starts slowly: not an easy ride, and not one to trust. *K. O. Cunningham-Brown*

MANHATTAN JACK   3 ch.g. Forzando 122 – Manhattan Diamond 54 (Primo   **70**
Dominie 121) [2004 9g 10m⁵ 11.1m² 11d Jul 4] €11,000Y: quite good-topped gelding:
third foal: half-brother to 4-y-o Kaymich Perfecto: dam, maiden, effective at 6f to 8.5f:
fair performer: stays 11f: best effort on good to firm going. *G. A. Swinbank*

MANIATIS   7 b.g. Slip Anchor 136 – Tamassos 67 (Dance In Time (CAN)) [2004   **78**
f12g⁶ 12d* f12g* 11.9s f11d² f12g* 10m³ Jun 28] tall, good sort: useful performer in
2002: missed 2003: fair form in 2004, winning claimers at Southwell (amateurs) and
Wolverhampton (left Mrs J. Candlish) in April and Southwell in June: raced mainly at
1¼m/1½m: acts on fibresand, soft and good to firm going: visored last 6 starts: has been
taken steadily to post/blanketed for stall entry: tends to hang. *Andrew Reid*

MANIC   2 br.f. (Apr 26) Polar Falcon (USA) 126 – Gentle Irony 65 (Mazilier (USA) 107)   **59**
[2004 5m p6g* 6.1v³ 8d p7.1g⁵ p7.1g³ p7m Dec 21] £2,800Y: half-sister to 3 winners,   **a67**
including 6f to 8.5f winner (including 7f at 2 yrs) Violent (by Deploy) and 3-y-o
Certifiable: dam 7f (including at 2 yrs) to 11f winner: fair on all-weather, modest on turf:
won maiden at Wolverhampton in October: probably stays 1m: acts on polytrack and
heavy going. *Andrew Reid*

MANIKATO (USA)   10 b.g. Clever Trick (USA) – Pasampsi (USA) (Crow (FR) 134)   **–**
[2004 45d, a–: f7g f9.4g f8.5s 10.9m 10.2m Aug 5] close-coupled gelding: no form in
2004: tried tongue tied/in cheekpieces/visor. *K. G. Wingrove*

MANNORA   4 b.f. Prince Sabo 123 – Miss Bussell 65 (Sabrehill (USA) 120) [2004 70?:   **57 d**
6g⁴ 6f 6g 6.1g 6m p5g Jul 21] workmanlike filly: modest performer: below form after
reappearance: free-going sort, best at 5f/6f: acts on good to firm going. *P. Howling*

MANNY   4 b.g. Emarati (USA) 74 – Needwood Nymph 45 (Bold Owl 101) [2004 f12m   **–**
14.4v f9.4g⁵ May 11] leggy gelding: of little account. *Miss A. Stokell*

MANNYMAN (IRE)   3 b. or br.f. Dr Devious (IRE) 127 – Lithe Spirit (IRE) 74 (Danc-   **–**
ing Dissident (USA) 119) [2004 –: 7.1g 7g p7g Oct 13] workmanlike filly: little form.
W. Jarvis

MAN OF LETTERS (UAE)   3 b.c. Belong To Me (USA) – Personal Business (USA)   **80**
(Private Account (USA)) [2004 66p: 8g⁴ 8.1s³ 7.5s² 7.1g² 7.1d* 10m² 10d⁵ 8.5d³ 10g Jul
16] strong, compact colt: fairly useful performer: won maiden at Musselburgh in May:
left M. Johnston before final outing: stays 1¼m: acts on soft and good to firm going.
G. G. Margarson

MANORSHIELD MINX   2 b.f. (May 14) Pursuit of Love 124 – Polly's Teahouse 68   **50 ?**
(Shack (USA) 118) [2004 6f 8.1m 7s 8m Sep 25] close-coupled filly: half-sister to several
winners by Weldnaas, including fairly useful 5f (including at 2 yrs) winner Polly Golightly and temperamental 7f winner Tea For Texas: dam sprint maiden: modest maiden:
seemingly best effort at 6f. *S. Kirk*

MANORSON (IRE)   5 ch.g. Desert King (IRE) 129 – Familiar (USA) 96 (Diesis 133)   **98**
[2004 12m 12m 12g² 12d⁴ Oct 14] sturdy gelding: useful performer, lightly raced: missed
2003: best effort of 2004 when creditable second in handicap at Newmarket: stays 1½m:
acts on soft going and polytrack: tongue tied last 3 starts: has been bandaged: often makes
running: sold 55,000 gns, joined O. Sherwood and won over hurdles. *M. A. Magnusson*

MANRIQUE (USA) 2 ch.c. (Jan 22) Rahy (USA) 115 – Dance Trick (USA) 101 –
(Diesis 133) [2004 6s Nov 6] smallish, sturdy colt: third foal: dam, 2-y-o 6f winner (both
her starts), half-sister to smart performer up to 7f Woodborough: 8/1 and green, well held
in maiden at Doncaster: joined D. Watson in UAE. *M. Johnston*

MANSFIELD PARK 3 br.f. Green Desert (USA) 127 – Park Appeal 122 (Ahonoora   **107**
122) [2004 71: 12s² 10d⁵ 8m³ 8g* Oct 12] tall, good-topped filly: useful performer, lightly
raced: left D. Loder and off 13 months after 2 yrs: good efforts when third in minor event
at Doncaster and listed handicap at Ascot (beaten 1¼ lengths by Tarfah): landed odds
easily in minor event at Leicester final outing: stays 1m: raced only on good going or
firmer: has worn crossed noseband. *Saeed bin Suroor*

MANSIYA 2 ch.f. (May 8) Vettori (IRE) 119 – Bay Shade (USA) 90 (Sharpen Up 127)   **65**
[2004 7m² 8.2m⁶ Sep 28] smallish filly: half-sister to several winners, including 1998
2-y-o 7f winner Forest Shadow (by Sadler's Wells) and 7f (at 2 yrs) and 11.4f winner
Abury (by Law Society), both useful: dam 2-y-o 7f winner, later won Italian 1m listed
event: modest form in maidens at Folkestone and Nottingham: likely to stay 1¼m.
C. E. Brittain

MANTEL MINI 5 b.m. Reprimand 122 – Foretell (Tirol 127) [2004 p8g 10.1d⁶ p8g   –
6m Jul 31] 800Y: first foal: dam unraced: little sign of ability, starting slowly: tried in
headgear. *B. A. Pearce*

MAN THE GATE 5 b.g. Elmaamul (USA) 125 – Girl At The Gate 53 (Formidable   **62**
(USA) 125) [2004 71: 12s² 10d⁵ 14.1s 11.8m³ 12f⁶ 11m² 12d* 12g⁵ 11.6g 11g 12g p12.2g
Nov 29] leggy gelding: modest handicapper: won apprentice event at Epsom in July,
hanging markedly left: stays 1½m: acts on polytrack, soft and good to firm ground:
usually held up: tricky ride. *P. D. Cundell*

MANTILLA 7 b.m. Son Pardo 107 – Well Tried (IRE) 43 (Thatching 131) [2004 –:   **40**
p13g Apr 6] maiden on Flat: tried visored: fair hurdler. *Ian Williams*

MANTLES PRIDE 9 b.g. Petong 126 – State Romance 67 (Free State 125) [2004 62d: – §
8.1d Apr 23] ungenuine performer: well held only outing in 2004: usually visored/
blinkered: sometimes slowly away. *Dr P. Pritchard*

MANTLES PRINCE 10 ch.g. Emarati (USA) 74 – Miami Mouse (Miami Springs   –
121) [2004 f16.2s⁶ Mar 5] tall, good-topped gelding: fairly useful in 2000: well below
form both Flat outings since: effective blinkered or not. *A. G. Juckes*

MANTON LASS 5 b.m. Rakaposhi King 119 – My Muszka 68 (Viking (USA)) [2004   –
p9.5g Dec 22] sixth foal: dam 1¼m/hurdles winner: tailed off in bumpers and in claimer
at Wolverhampton. *M. Mullineaux*

MANYANA (IRE) 3 b.c. Alzao (USA) 117 – Sometime (IRE) (Royal Academy (USA)   **108**
130) [2004 97p: 10g⁵ 11g* 12g 12g Jul 27] smallish, sturdy, close-coupled colt: useful
performer, lightly raced: won listed race at Goodwood (by head from Crocodile Dundee)
in May: respectable 7½ lengths eleventh to Blue Canari in Prix du Jockey Club at
Chantilly next time, but last of 8 in ABN Amro Stakes (Gordon) at Goodwood: should
stay 1½m: reportedly swallowed tongue on reappearance, tongue tied after (reportedly
had breathing problem final outing): joined Godolphin. *M. P. Tregoning*

MANY THANKS 4 b.f. Octagonal (NZ) 126 – Answered Prayer (Green Desert (USA)   –
127) [2004 73: f12s⁵ f12g⁶ Feb 19] lengthy, quite good-topped filly: maiden: no form in
2004: tried in cheekpieces. *B. S. Rothwell*

MAPLE BRANCH (USA) 2 b.f. (Jan 17) Stravinsky (USA) 133 – Galanty Show 76   **63**
(Danehill (USA) 126) [2004 7g² p7m p6g Dec 29] second foal: half-sister to 3-y-o
Chatshow: dam 6f winner: form in maidens only when second at Le Touquet (then left
P. Bary, France): not sure to stay beyond 7f. *G. G. Margarson*

MAPLE SYRPLE (CAN) 3 b.f. American Chance (USA) 117 – Sweet And   **93**
Lowdown (USA) (Stalwart (USA)) [2004 110: 7.1f a6f⁴ a6f⁶ a8f⁵ Oct 7] $40,000Y,
$350,000 2-y-o: first foal: dam US 6f (including at 2yrs)/7f winner: smart form at 2 yrs,
when trained by M. Casse in Canada, winning maiden and valuable restricted event at
Woodbine, and 3 lengths second to Ashado in Grade 2 Schuylerville Stakes at Saratoga:
just fairly useful form in 2004, including in listed race at Warwick and non-graded event
at Belmont on first 2 starts: should stay 7f: acts on sloppy going: left Godolphin. *Saeed
bin Suroor*

MARAAHEL (IRE) 3 b.c. Alzao (USA) 117 – Nasanice (IRE) 97 (Nashwan (USA)   **121**
135) [2004 87p: 11m² 12m² 12g* 14.6f⁴ Sep 11] quite good-topped colt: has a fluent,
round action: very smart performer: progressed well in 2004, second in handicaps at

ABN Amro Stakes (Gordon), Goodwood—the progressive Maraahel stakes his St Leger claims with victory over the lightly-raced pair Go For Gold and the grey Remaadd; Mikado (partly hidden) and Duke of Venice are next

Newbury (to Pukka) and Royal Ascot (top weight, beaten a neck by Admiral in King George V Stakes) prior to winning ABN Amro Stakes (Gordon) at Goodwood in July by 1½ lengths from Go For Gold: good 2¾ lengths fourth behind Rule of Law in St Leger at Doncaster final start: stays 14.6f: raced mainly on good ground or firmer (acts on firm): likeable sort. *Sir Michael Stoute*

MARAAKEB (FR) 3 gr.c. Linamix (FR) 127 – Raheefa (USA) 75 (Riverman (USA) 131) [2004 84P: 10.3m⁶ 10g* Sep 10] big, strong colt: fairly useful form in maidens, winning at Sandown in September impressively by 3 lengths from Barathea Blue, making all and merely nudged clear: may prove best around 1¼m: raced only on good/good to firm going: ran as if amiss on reappearance: remains capable of better. *J. H. M. Gosden*   **84 p**

MARABAR 6 b.m. Sri Pekan (USA) 117 – Erbaya (IRE) (El Gran Senor (USA) 136) [2004 87: f7g f7g⁶ f7g⁵ p6g f5g 6v* 7s 5v 5v³ f7m* f6g² f7d² f7d⁶ 8f⁶ 6m 5d⁴ 6g p7.1d f6g f7g³ f5g⁵ Dec 21] big, strong mare: just fair performer in 2004: won seller at Pontefract in April and banded race at Wolverhampton in May: effective at 5f to 7f: acts on fibresand, heavy and good to firm going: often wears cheekpieces/blinkers: unreliable. *D. W. Chapman*   **65 §**

MARAJUANA 2 b.f. (Mar 8) Robellino (USA) 127 – Mara River 86 (Efisio 120) [2004 5m* Jun 14] good-topped filly: fourth foal: half-sister to 3-y-o Border Music: dam 6f to 1m winner: won maiden at Windsor, making most: suffered setback after: bred to stay 1m: should progress. *A. M. Balding*   **82 p**

MARAKASH (IRE) 3 b.g. Ashkalani (IRE) 128 – Marilaya (IRE) 96 (Shernazar 131) [2004 –: p8g² p8g p8g⁶ Mar 9] modest maiden: should stay 1¼m: acts on all-weather and soft going: tried in cheekpieces/tongue tie. *M. R. Bosley*   **54**

MARAUD 10 ch.g. Midyan (USA) 124 – Peak Squaw (USA) 75 (Icecapade (USA)) [2004 f16g⁵ f16.2g³ Jan 14] lightly raced and little form on Flat since 1996. *R. Hollinshead*   **–**

MARAVEDI (IRE) 4 ch.f. Hector Protector (USA) 124 – Manuetti (IRE) 86 (Sadler's Wells (USA) 132) [2004 –: f9.4g p8g f14g 13.1s p9.5g⁵ Dec 14] modest maiden: left S. Keightley after third start: stays 9.5f: acts on polytrack: tried visored. *W. M. Brisbourne*   **54**

MARBLE ARCH 8 b.g. Rock Hopper 124 – Mayfair Minx (St Columbus 98) [2004 91: 16d Nov 3] tall, lengthy gelding: very smart hurdler (second in 2002 Champion Hurdle): fairly useful form on Flat in 2003: well held in handicap only Flat run in 2004: tried in cheekpieces: carries head awkwardly: usually held up. *H. Morrison*   **–**

MARBURYANNA 4 ch.f. Classic Cliche (IRE) 128 – Lake Mistassiu 86 (Tina's Pet 121) [2004 8.1s p7.1g p8.6g p6g Dec 4] small filly: half-sister to 7f (at 2 yrs) to 11f winner Santiburi Girl (by Casteddu): dam 5f winner, including at 2 yrs: no sign of ability. *M. Mullineaux*   **–**

MARBUSH (IRE) 3 ro.c. Linamix (FR) 127 – Fig Tree Drive (USA) 94 (Miswaki (USA) 124) [2004 8g³ 9g² 8m* 8g⁵ 10m³ a8f⁴ a9g* Dec 10] 160,000Y: strong colt: third foal: half-brother to 4-y-o Sublimity: dam, 2-y-o 6f winner (her only start), out of sister to US Grade 1 winners De La Rose (9f) and Upper Nile (1¼m): useful performer: won   **98**

maiden at Musselburgh (tended to hang) in May and, having left M. Jarvis after fifth start, handicap at Jebel Ali in December: effective at 1m/1¼m: raced only on dirt and good/ good to firm going: tongue tied fifth outing. *D. J. Selvaratnam, UAE*

MARBYE (IRE) 4 b.f. Marju (IRE) 127 – Hambye 97 (Distant Relative 128) [2004 **114** 111: 9g* 8s⁴ 8m* 8f⁵ 8g* 8m⁶ 10g Oct 24] second foal: half-sister to Italian 2001 2-y-o 5f/7f winner Halzal (by Zilzal): dam Italian sprinter: smart performer: winner of 7 races at Milan at 2/3 yrs, including 2 listed races and Premio Sergio Cumani in 2003: successful in 2004 in minor event at Rome in March, Premio Emilio Turati at Milan (beat Honey Bunny 3½ lengths) in June and Prix d'Astarte at Deauville (best effort, beat Majestic Desert ½ length) in August: below form otherwise, including in Windsor Forest Stakes at Royal Ascot fourth start: effective at 1m/9f: acted on good to firm and good to soft ground: has had tongue tied: usually held up: stud in Japan. *B. Grizzetti, Italy*

MARCELA ZABALA 2 b.f. (Mar 11) Zaha (CAN) 106 – Bay Bianca (IRE) (Law **56** Society (USA) 130) [2004 f5g 5m* p6g 6s* 6.1d 6s Oct 22] 8,000Y: leggy filly: sixth foal: half-sister to 3 winners, including 4-y-o Pertemps Bianca and 3-y-o The Job: dam German 6f winner: modest performer: won sellers at Leicester in July and Yarmouth (nursery) in August: ran as if amiss final start: likely to stay 7f: acts on soft and good to firm ground (well beaten on all-weather): sold 1,800 gns. *J. G. Given*

MARCHETTA 2 b.f. (Mar 23) Mujadil (USA) 119 – My Lewicia (IRE) 100 (Taufan **69** (USA) 119) [2004 7g⁶ 7g⁵ 7.1d³ Sep 18] quite good-topped filly: fourth foal: dam, 1m winner, half-sister to smart sprinter To The Roof: fair form in maidens/minor event: likely to stay 1m. *P. W. Harris*

MARCHING SONG 2 b.c. (Feb 23) Royal Applause 124 – Marl 94 (Lycius (USA) **90** 124) [2004 5.2g⁵ 5m³ 5m² 7g⁴ 6g² 6m* 6g² 6g⁵ Sep 29] good-topped colt: fifth foal: half-brother to smart 7f/1m winner Green Line (by Green Desert) and 6-y-o Snow Bunting: dam, 2-y-o 5f winner, best at 6f: fairly useful performer: won maiden at Folkestone in August: good second in nursery at Newmarket, better effort after: barely stays 7f: acts on good to firm going: often races prominently: sometimes edges left. *R. Hannon*

MARCUS EILE (IRE) 3 b.g. Daggers Drawn (USA) 114 – Sherannda (USA) (Trem- **73** polino (USA) 135) [2004 86: p10g⁴ f8.5g⁴ f8.5s 7s p7.1g⁴ f7g⁵ Dec 14] sturdy gelding: fair performer: stays 1m: acts on polytrack and firm going: tried in headgear: none too reliable. *K. R. Burke*

MARDONICDECLARE 3 b.g. Perpendicular 119 – Daisy Girl 69 (Main Reef 126) **–** [2004 8m Jul 25] 40/1, tailed off in maiden at Pontefract. *P. S. Felgate*

MARENGO 10 b.g. Never So Bold 135 – Born To Dance 76 (Dancing Brave (USA) **–** 140) [2004 47, a54d: f12g f11g⁶ f11g f9.4s 10s⁶ 8g⁴ f8m 10g f8f 6g f11g Dec 14] small gelding: no longer of much account. *M. J. Polglase*

MAREN (USA) 3 b.g. Gulch (USA) – Fatina 98 (Nashwan (USA) 135) [2004 88p: **85** 7.1g 8g 8.5g Oct 2] angular gelding: fairly useful handicapper, lightly raced: not seen out until September: ran badly last 2 starts: should stay at least 1m: raced only on good/good to firm going: tongue tied: sold 1,500 gns, then gelded. *E. F. Vaughan*

MARGALITA (IRE) 4 b.f. Sesaro (USA) 81 – Mamma Luigi (IRE) (Classic Music **76 d** (USA)) [2004 86: p6g⁶ 6s 8m 5g⁶ 6m 7g 5m 5g p7g p6d p9.5g p8g⁶ Dec 20] just fair form at best in 2004: stays 8.5f: acts on heavy going, sand and polytrack: tried blinkered/ tongue tied. *P. Mitchell*

Prix d'Astarte, Deauville—a race that lacked the really big names despite its new status as a Group 1; Marbye (left) makes up for her disappointing run at Royal Ascot by beating Majestic Desert (third left), Nebraska Tornado (second right), Monturani (fourth right), Martha Stewart (blinkers), Cattiva Generosa (diamonds on sleeves) and Denebola (right)

MAR

MARGARET'S DREAM (IRE) 3 b.f. Muhtarram (USA) 125 – Acidanthera 81 **55**
(Alzao (USA) 117) [2004 61: 10m 9g 7m 8f 5s⁴ 6d³ f7g Dec 11] €2,200Y: second foal:
dam 7.5f winner: modest maiden handicapper: better effort in Britain when third at
Yarmouth: stays 7f: acts on firm and soft going. *Ms Caroline Hutchinson, Ireland*

MARGARETS WISH 4 gr.f. Cloudings (IRE) 112 – Gentle Gain 58 (Final Straw **46**
127) [2004 45: f8g p10g⁴ p10g f8.5s 10.2d* 10v 10.5d 10.2m 8.1g 10.2m⁶ 10.2s Aug 12]
poor performer: won banded race at Chepstow in April: stays 1¼m: acts on firm and good
to soft going, probably on polytrack: blinkered last 2 starts: inconsistent. *T. Wall*

MARGERY DAW (IRE) 4 b.f. Sri Pekan (USA) 117 – Suyayeb (USA) (The Minstrel **56**
(CAN) 135) [2004 70: p8g⁵ 10.3d p10g 11.9m 11.8m⁶ 11.9f³ 12f 10f 8f⁵ 10s 9.7f p10g
10d p10m* p10m⁴ p10g² f11d p8.6g⁴ Dec 22] close-coupled filly: modest performer: left
M. Tregoning after reappearance: won banded race at Lingfield in December: stays 1¼m:
acts on polytrack and firm going: tried blinkered. *P. S. McEntee*

MARGOLD (IRE) 4 ch.f. Goldmark (USA) 113 – Arcevia (IRE) 85 (Archway (IRE) **54**
115) [2004 56: f8g f14g 12.3m³ 12m 12m Jul 21] leggy filly: modest maiden: stays easy
1¾m: unraced on extremes of going on turf. *R. Hollinshead*

MARHABA MILLION (IRE) 2 gr.c. (Apr 21) Linamix (FR) 127 – Modelliste **– p**
(Machiavellian (USA) 123) [2004 8g Sep 29] fifth foal: half-brother to 3 winners, including fairly useful 2000 2-y-o 1m winner Samara Middle East (by Marju) and 2002 2-y-o
6f winner Moujoudh (by Mujadil): dam, 1m winner in UAE, closely related to smart
7f winner Beraysim: 20/1, behind in maiden at Salisbury, fading: should improve.
M. R. Channon

MARHOON (USA) 2 ch.c. (Feb 15) Lion Cavern (USA) 117 – United Kingdom **80**
(USA) 93 (Danzig (USA)) [2004 6d⁴ 7s² p8g* Oct 31] sixth foal: closely related to fairly
useful 1m winner Hakeyma (by Gone West) and UAE 7f/1m winner Mannjam (by
Gulch): dam, 1m (in France) and 1¼m winner, closely related to smart 1¼m winner La
Confederation out of Oaks winner Unite: best effort in maidens when winning at Lingfield by 3 lengths from Rollerbird, leading final 1f and hanging right: stays 1m: acts on
polytrack: tongue tied last 2 starts: joined D. Selvaratnam in UAE. *E. F. Vaughan*

MARIA BONITA (IRE) 3 b.f. Octagonal (NZ) 126 – Nightitude 93 (Night Shift **65**
(USA)) [2004 72: 10s⁴ 10.2m 10.2f⁴ 10m p10g⁴ 11.5g³ 11d³ p12.2d³ p12g f12g⁶ p12.2g⁴ **a59**
p9.5g Dec 15] modest maiden: left R. Beckett after sixth start: stays easy 1½m: acts on
polytrack, firm and good to soft ground: tried blinkered. *Mrs Stef Liddiard*

MARIA DELFINA (IRE) 2 ch.f. (Mar 2) Giant's Causeway (USA) 132 – Photo- **60 +**
graphie (USA) (Trempolino (USA) 135) [2004 p8g³ p8g⁶ Nov 13] third foal: dam, French
maiden, sister to Prix Marcel Boussac winner Juvenia and closely related to very smart
French 1m/9f performer In Extremis: modest form in maidens at Lingfield, shaping well
on first occasion: should be suited by 1¼m/1½m. *J. H. M. Gosden*

MARIA MARIA (IRE) 3 ch.f. Among Men (USA) 124 – Yiayia's Girl (Smackover **–**
107) [2004 –: f9.4g f8s 8.2s⁴ 11.5f f8g Jul 9] little form: tried in cheekpieces. *Mrs
N. Macauley*

MARIANIS 2 b.f. (Apr 4) Lujain (USA) 119 – Without Warning (IRE) (Warning 136) **55**
[2004 6g⁴ 6m 7g⁵ Jul 8] 13,000Y: rangy, rather unfurnished filly: fifth foal: half-sister to
2 winners, including useful 7f (at 2 yrs)/1m winner Judge Davidson (by Royal Applause):
dam ran once: modest form in maidens: likely to stay 1m. *J. G. Portman*

MARIAN'S GIFT 2 ch.f. (May 3) Bold Edge 123 – Thimbalina 63 (Salmon Leap **–**
(USA) 131) [2004 5m May 28] half-sister to several winners, including 3-y-o Darn Good:
dam 1¼m/1½m winner: 33/1, well held in maiden at York. *M. W. Easterby*

MARIANS MAID (IRE) 2 b.f. (Mar 26) Monashee Mountain (USA) 115 – Speedy **47**
Action (Horage 124) [2004 6m 6m⁶ 7m Jul 26] €900Y: ninth foal: half-sister to 1998
2-y-o 6f/7f winner Vale of Leven (by Fayruz) and 1m winner Bustle'em (by Burslem):
dam 1¼m winner: modest form in maidens: should stay 7f. *J. S. Moore*

MARIAS MAGIC 3 b.f. Mtoto 134 – Majoune (FR) 105 (Take Risks (FR) 116) [2004 **76**
7m⁶ 10.2g²* 10.1d Nov 5] first foal: dam, French 1m (at 2 yrs) to 11f (Prix Corrida)
winner, half-sister to smart French filly up to 1½m Mousse Glacee (by Mtoto): won
maiden at Bath in October by 1½ lengths from Safirah, running green: left J. Oxx in
Ireland, well held in handicap at Yarmouth next time: should stay 1½m. *M. Johnston*

MARIDAY 3 br.g. Trifolio 99 – Classic Hand (Some Hand 119) [2004 9.9m⁶ p13g **63**
11.9s⁶ p12g⁵ p16.5g Dec 4] modest maiden: easily best effort on fourth start: stays 1½m:
acts on polytrack. *Lady Herries*

MARINAITE 3 b.f. Komaite (USA) – Marina's Song (Savahra Sound 111) [2004 f8f² **82**
f7s* 7d⁵ 6.1g² f6d² 5.1d 8.2m³ 7f 8g³ 7v 6s f6g⁶ f6g⁶ p8.6g Dec 6] second foal: dam,

622

ran twice, half-sister to useful sprinter First Maite (by Komaite): fairly useful performer: won maiden at Southwell in February: barely stays 1m: acts on fibresand and good to firm ground, well below form on soft/heavy: tried blinkered. *S. R. Bowring*

MARINE CITY (JPN) 3 b.f. Carnegie (IRE) 129 – Marienbad (FR) (Darshaan 133) **77** [2004 –p: 12s* 12.3d⁶ 11m⁶ 12.4s³ 16g⁴ 16m³ 16s⁵ Oct 22] tall, quite good-topped filly: fair performer: won maiden at Folkestone in April: stays 2m: acts on soft and good to firm going, though has looked ill at ease on latter: wore cheekpieces last 3 starts: wandered markedly penultimate outing. *M. A. Jarvis*

MARINNETTE (IRE) 3 ch.f. Be My Guest (USA) 126 – Al Cairo (FR) (Vayrann **92** 133) [2004 80: 9v⁵ 10m 10g⁴ 12f⁵ 12v* 12d⁶ 10.3s Nov 6] eighth foal: half-sister to 2 winners abroad, including French winner up to 16.5f Alexandrin (by Exit To Nowhere): dam French 9f (at 2 yrs) to 12.5f winner: fairly useful performer: won maiden at Tralee in August: best efforts starts either side when fifth in Irish Oaks (beaten 12¾ lengths by Ouija Board) and sixth in listed event, both at the Curragh: tailed off in listed race at Doncaster final outing: should stay beyond 1½m: acts on any going. *M. P. Sunderland, Ireland*

MARINO MOU (IRE) 4 b.c. Darshaan 133 – Lia's Dance (Lead On Time (USA) **47** 123) [2004 f9.4g f9.4g f12g⁶ 15.4s³ 16d 16.1m May 20] poor maiden: stays 15.4f: acts on soft ground: tried blinkered. *Miss D. Mountain*

MARITA 3 ch.f. Dancing Spree (USA) – Maria Cappuccini 70 (Siberian Express (USA) **34** 125) [2004 53: f8.5g⁵ f8g Jan 27] leggy, close-coupled filly: poor maiden: should stay 1¼m: form only on fibresand: tried visored: covered by Zaha, sold 800 gns in July and sent to Italy. *J. G. Given*

MARITIMA 2 b.f. (Apr 7) Darshaan 133 – Armeria (USA) 79 (Northern Dancer) [2004 **– p** 7g Oct 11] good-topped filly: half-sister to several winners, most at least useful, notably Racing Post Trophy/Chester Vase winner and St Leger second Armiger (by Rainbow Quest): dam, 1¼m winner, half-sister to Park Hill winner I Want To Be: 8/1, hampered and unseated over 1f out in maiden at Leicester, signs of ability and staying on at time: will be suited by 1¼m+: sure to do better. *Sir Michael Stoute*

MARITIME BLUES 4 b.g. Fleetwood (IRE) 107 – Dixie d'Oats 66 (Alhijaz 122) **68 §** [2004 78: 10g 9.9d 10d 12m* 12m 12f⁶ 12d³ 11.9f 10f 10s* 10g 10.1g⁵ 10.9s p12.2g 10s² f11g Nov 23] small, strong gelding: fair handicapper: won at Doncaster in May and Ayr in August: effective at 1¼m/1½m: acts on fibresand, soft and good to firm going: unreliable. *J. G. Given*

MARKER 4 ch.g. Pivotal 124 – Palace Street (USA) 103 (Secreto (USA) 128) [2004 **85** 96: 7s⁶ 6g 6g 7s⁴ 6m 7d⁴ 7m 7.1g 6s⁴ 6s* 6s Nov 1] sturdy, close-coupled gelding: fairly useful handicapper: won at Goodwood in August: effective at 6f/7f: acts on firm and soft ground: effective visored or not. *G. B. Balding*

MARKET AVENUE 5 b.m. Factual (USA) 108 – The Lady Vanishes (Robin Des **68** Pins (USA) 119) [2004 78: 10m⁶ 10m 9.2g⁵ 8g 9.1g⁵ 10.1g* 10.3g 10m 10.1m⁶ p9.5g⁶ p8.6g⁴ p9.5g Dec 31] lengthy, angular mare: has a quick action: fair handicapper: won at Newcastle in September: best at 9f to 11f: acts on firm and good to soft going: tried in cheekpieces: has pulled hard/hung left: waited with. *R. A. Fahey*

MARKET LEADER 3 b.f. Marju (IRE) 127 – I Will Lead (USA) (Seattle Slew **72** (USA)) [2004 72: 12m³ 14s³ 12.1m³ 14d³ Oct 10] tall, good-topped filly: has a round, unimpressive action: fair maiden: will stay 2m: acts on soft and good to firm going: blinkered (raced too freely) third outing: sold 26,000 gns. *Mrs A. J. Perrett*

MARKET TREND 2 b.f. (Jan 11) Selkirk (USA) 129 – Equity Princess 106 (Warning **82** 136) [2004 6g² 7.2d⁶ 7g 8d Oct 14] big, useful-looking filly: third foal: dam, 1m (at 2 yrs) and 9f winner, out of useful stayer Hawait Al Barr: fairly useful performer: won maiden at Ayr in September, idling: creditable effort at Catterick next time, much better effort in nurseries after (despite seeming ill at ease on track): should stay at least 1m. *M. Johnston*

MARKO JADEO (IRE) 6 b.g. Eagle Eyed (USA) 111 – Fleeting Quest (Rainbow **88** Quest (USA) 134) [2004 92: 6m³ 5m 6.3f 6g³ 6m³ a7g* 8g p7g p6g p8m p7.1g⁶ Dec 31] workmanlike ex-Irish gelding: fairly useful performer: claimed from P. J. Flynn in Ireland €22,100 after winning claimer at Laytown in September: below form in Britain: effective at 6f/7f: acts on sand, firm and good to soft ground. *K. A. Morgan*

MARKSGOLD (IRE) 3 b.g. Goldmark (USA) 113 – Lady of Shalott 61 (Kings Lake **54** (USA) 133) [2004 50: 7.1d³ f7g⁶ 5.7s⁶ 7g p12g⁵ 7g Jun 24] modest maiden: should stay 1m: acts on good to soft ground, probably on all-weather. *P. F. I. Cole*

MARK YOUR CARD 2 ch.f. (Apr 20) Mark of Esteem (IRE) 137 – Charolles 82 – (Ajdal (USA) 130) [2004 6s 7d 7.9g 6g Sep 14] 10,000Y: quite good-topped filly: half-sister to several winners, including fairly useful 6f (at 2 yrs)/7f winner Chantilly Myth (by Sri Pekan): dam maiden who stayed 1m: signs of only a little ability in maidens. *T. D. Easterby*

MARK YOUR WAY 4 b.g. Spectrum (IRE) 126 – Titania's Way 91 (Fairy King (USA)) [2004 59?: 9.9g 10.2s 10.9m Sep 6] maiden: no form since debut. *P. R. Chamings*

MARLENES GIRL (IRE) 2 b.f. (Mar 16) Foxhound (USA) 103 – Premier Place **47** (USA) (Out of Place (USA)) [2004 5g 5g⁶ 5d Aug 15] €13,000Y, 18,000 2-y-o: leggy filly: first foal: dam French maiden who stayed 1m: poor form in maidens: should stay at least 6f. *A. Berry*

MARMADUKE (IRE) 8 ch.g. Perugino (USA) 84 – Sympathy 77 (Precocious 126) **68** [2004 63: f16.2g² p16g⁵ p12g⁴ Mar 4] tall handicapper: fair handicapper: was effective at 1½m, seemingly at 2¼m: acted on all-weather and probably any turf going: tried visored: tended to race freely: usually raced prominently: dead. *M. Pitman*

MARNE (IRE) 2 b.g. (Mar 14) Mtoto 134 – Perfect Poppy 73 (Shareef Dancer (USA) – 135) [2004 f5g⁴ Mar 27] last in seller at Wolverhampton. *J. M. P. Eustace*

MARNIE 7 ch.m. First Trump 118 – Miss Aboyne 64 (Lochnager 132) [2004 62, a52: **58** p8g p8g* p8g³ p8g 8f² 8f² 8f⁵ 8g⁵ 8.5f⁵ 8m 8m⁶ p8m p8g² Dec 20] sturdy, lengthy mare: modest handicapper: won at Lingfield in March: effective at 7f/1m: acts on polytrack, firm and good to soft going: tends to race freely/hang. *J. Akehurst*

MAROMITO (IRE) 7 b.g. Up And At 'em 109 – Amtico (Bairn (USA) 126) [2004 65: **69** f5g f6s f7g³ p5g* f5m* 5g f5g 5m³ 5m 5g* 5.1m⁴ 5g Sep 22] well-made gelding: fair performer: won banded races at Lingfield and Southwell in April and apprentice handicap at Salisbury in September: best at 5f: acts on all-weather, firm and good to soft going: tried blinkered at 6 yrs: sometimes sweats/on edge/early to post: has hung left: front runner. *R. Bastiman*

MARON 7 b.g. Puissance 110 – Will Be Bold 79 (Bold Lad (IRE) 133) [2004 –: p6g⁵ **46** f5s² p6g⁴ Apr 15] rather leggy gelding: poor performer: stays easy 6f: acts on all-weather and any turf going: tried tongue tied/blinkered/in cheekpieces. *F. Jordan*

MARREL 6 b.g. Shareef Dancer (USA) 135 – Upper Caen (High Top 131) [2004 44: **48** 16m⁵ 12.1m⁶ Aug 5] strong, workmanlike gelding: poor handicapper: stays 2m: acts on fibresand, best turf efforts on ground firmer than good: often blinkered/visored: fair hurdler. *D. Burchell*

MARSAD (IRE) 10 ch.g. Fayruz 116 – Broad Haven (IRE) (Be My Guest (USA) **95** 126) [2004 98: 6g 6d³ 6m 6m² 6m 6m 6g 6g² 6g 6g 6s⁴ Oct 22] lengthy, good-topped gelding: useful handicapper: ran creditably in 2004 when placed, all 3 of those runs at York: effective at 6f/easy 7f: acts on any going: has run creditably when sweating: reared as stall opened penultimate outing. *J. Akehurst*

MARSHAL BOND 6 b.g. Celtic Swing 138 – Arminda (Blakeney 126) [2004 57d: – f9.4s Feb 2] workmanlike gelding: no longer of any account. *B. Smart*

MARSHALL (FR) 4 b.c. Anabaa (USA) 130 – Monitrice (FR) (Groom Dancer **117** (USA) 128) [2004 115: 8d* 8d 8d 9.5g² 10g 10s* 10d 10g² 9.5s² 10g* Nov 13] fifth foal: closely related to French 1½m winner Mysterieux (by Petit Loup) and half-brother to 3 winners in France, including at around 1½m Monitoring (by Linamix): dam lightly-raced half-sister to smart French 7f/1m performer Malaspina: smart performer: successful in Prix de Guiche at Longchamp at 3 yrs: won minor event at Saint-Cloud in February and listed races at Compiegne in June and Marseille Borely (by 3½ lengths from Rislew) in November: best effort when beaten short neck by Fair Mix in La Coupe de Maisons-Laffitte eighth start: stays 1¼m: acts on soft and good to firm ground. *C. Laffon-Parias, France*

MARSHALLSPARK (IRE) 5 b.g. Fayruz 116 – Lindas Delight 54 (Batshoof 122) **80** [2004 78: 5d 6m 6f 6g⁵ 6m* 6m 6g* 5f⁶ 6g² 6g p5.1g p6g p7.1g Dec 20] sturdy, lengthy **a68** gelding: fairly useful handicapper on turf, fair on all-weather: won at Leicester in July and Ayr in August: also ran well when second to Endless Summer at Goodwood: effective at 6f/7f: acts on firm and good to soft going: tried blinkered at 3 yrs. *R. A. Fahey*

MARSHMAN (IRE) 5 ch.g. College Chapel 122 – Gold Fly (IRE) (Be My Guest **98** (USA) 126) [2004 99: 8g 7d³ 7s 7f 7m 7f 7g 7s³ 7.1s³ 7.2s⁵ 7g* 7d⁵ p7g⁶ Oct 28] good-topped gelding: useful handicapper: won at York in October by 5 lengths from Cd Flyer: effective at 6f/7f: acts on polytrack, firm and soft going: tried blinkered: usually waited with. *M. H. Tompkins*

MAS

MARSH ORCHID   3 b.g. Lahib (USA) 129 – Majalis 79 (Mujadil (USA) 119) [2004   **75**
7d⁵ 8.2g² 9m² 10.1d Aug 29] 8,500Y: smallish, workmanlike gelding: first foal: dam 5f
winner who stayed 1m : fair maiden: stays 9f: sold 11,000 gns in October. *W. Jarvis*

MARTALINE   5 gr.h. Linamix (FR) 127 – Coraline (Sadler's Wells (USA) 132) [2004   **115**
118: 12m 12m⁵ 12.5d* 12.5v² 10g 12s⁶ Oct 17] strong, good-topped horse: carried plenty
of condition: had a markedly round action: smart performer: more patiently ridden than
usual first 2 starts, taking strong hold when respectable fifth to Gamut in Jockey Club
Stakes at Newmarket on second occasion: didn't have to be at best to win listed race at
Deauville in August (made all) but ran creditably when 4 lengths second to Cherry Mix
in Grand Prix de Deauville later in month: well below form last 2 starts: had form at 15f,
best around 1½m: probably acted on any going: usually raced prominently: to stand at
Haras de la Reboursiere et Montaigu, France, fee €3,500, live foal. *A. Fabre, France*

MARTHA REILLY (IRE)   8 ch.m. Rainbows For Life (CAN) – Debach Delight 97   **–**
(Great Nephew 126) [2004 f16g⁶ p16g Feb 16] smallish, sparely-made mare: lightly
raced and no form on Flat since 2000: tried blinkered. *Mrs Barbara Waring*

MARTILLO (GER)   4 b.c. Anabaa (USA) 130 – Maltage (USA) (Affirmed (USA))   **119**
[2004 119: 8.9m⁵ 8d* 8f 8g* 8g 8d² 8m⁶ Dec 12] big, strong colt: smart performer:
creditable fifth to Paolini and Right Approach in Dubai Duty Free at Nad Al Sheba on
reappearance: won Prix du Muguet at Saint-Cloud (by head from Sarre) in May and
Berlin Brandenburg-Trophy at Hoppegarten (for second year running, by head from
Assiun) in July: only ninth in Queen Anne Stakes at Royal Ascot in between: ran well
when short-neck second to Eagle Rise in Premio Ribot at Rome before respectable sixth
to Firebreak in Hong Kong Mile at Sha Tin: effective at 1m/9f: acts on good to firm and
good to soft going. *R. Suerland, Germany*

MARTIN HOUSE (IRE)   5 b.g. Mujadil (USA) 119 – Dolcezza (FR) (Lichine (USA)   **–**
117) [2004 –: 7m 10.5s Jul 17] tall, leggy gelding: useful performer at 3 yrs: mostly well
held on Flat since: tried visored/tongue tied. *A. W. Walton*

MARTON MERE   8 ch.g. Cadeaux Genereux 131 – Hyatti 74 (Habitat 134) [2004 –:   **–**
12m 12m Aug 3] angular gelding: no longer of much account. *A. J. Lockwood*

MARY CARLETON   3 ch.f. Halling (USA) 133 – Anne Bonny 105 (Ajdal (USA)   **–**
130) [2004 7f 7f⁶ 7d 10m p12.2d Oct 23] strong, lengthy filly: sixth foal: half-sister to
6-y-o Random Quest and 8-y-o Who Cares Wins: dam 1m/1¼m winner out of Yorkshire
Oaks winner Sally Brown: no form. *R. M. H. Cowell*

MARY GRAY   2 gr.f. (Mar 25) Mujahid (USA) 125 – Ancestry (Persepolis (FR) 127)   **61**
[2004 6m⁵ 7m 7m 8s Nov 1] 14,000F, 9,000Y: tall, quite good-topped filly: half-sister to
several winners, including useful 5f/6f winner Night Flight (by Night Shift) and fairly
useful 6f (at 2 yrs) to 1¼m winner Devilry (by Faustus): dam unraced: modest maiden:
below form last 2 starts, in nursery final one: should stay 1m. *M. Johnston*

MARY READ   2 ch.f. (Mar 30) Bahamian Bounty 116 – Hill Welcome 52 (Most Wel-   **100**
come 131) [2004 5v³ 5g* 5m³ 5f* 5g₂ 5d² 6d Oct 14] 10,000Y: leggy, angular filly:
first foal: dam, maiden who stayed 7f, half-sister to Middle Park winner Stalker: useful
performer: won maiden at Musselburgh in April and minor event at Windsor in June: best
efforts when second in Molecomb Stakes at Goodwood (beaten neck by Tournedos) and
listed race at Ayr (length behind Prince Charming): probably best at 5f: acts on firm and
good to soft ground: races up with pace: tends to hang left. *B. Smart*

MARYSIENKA   3 b.f. Primo Dominie 121 – Polish Romance (USA) 83 (Danzig   **72**
(USA)) [2004 78: 6g 6g⁵ 5d 5m³ 5g⁴ 5g p6g Oct 16] compact filly: fair maiden: best at 5f:
acts on soft and good to firm ground: wore cheekpieces (ran creditably) penultimate outing. *J. Balding*

MASAFI (IRE)   3 b.g. Desert King (IRE) 129 – Mrs Fisher (IRE) 94 (Salmon Leap   **97**
(USA) 131) [2004 –p: p8g² f8m* 9.3f* 10m* 9.7m* f8g* 9f* 9.3f* 8f⁵ 10f Sep 23]
    'Training is the only business I know that when things are going wrong you
must do less.' Sir Mark Prescott's decision to close down his stable in the middle of
May for seven weeks, while the horses recovered fully from a viral infection, paid
dividends. 'Everybody tries to make you do the wrong thing, the Press keep ringing
to ask when you're having runners, your friends enquire whether you've retired—
but it's no good getting to work on the horses if they're not right.' By the time the
yard resumed operations at the beginning of July, it had had only four runners on
the turf in Britain in 2004. The Prescott stable had a splendid July, sending out
nineteen winners (one of them Albanova in the Deutschlandpreis at Dusseldorf)

St James Security Classified Stakes, Carlisle—
Masafi completes a remarkable sequence of wins during an eighteen-day spell in July;
third- and fourth-placed Millagros (visor) and Fossgate are also in the picture

from fifty-three runners, and continued in fine form through into the autumn, ending the year with seventy-six winners at home and abroad. If July was a splendid month for the Prescott stable generally, it was most notable for one of its inmates in particular, the three-year-old Masafi. He won seven races in a row in the space of eighteen days, bettering the achievement of seven wins (from nine starts) in nineteen days recorded by Chaplins Club in 1988. Back then, weights for handicaps were published three weeks beforehand and trainers and owners could plan further in advance than they have been able to do since the introduction of the five-day entry system. The Prescott stable still managed to exploit to the full the BHB mark allotted to Masafi. He started the season on a mark of 52 after finishing out of the first six in three runs over six furlongs as a two-year-old and was raised just 1 lb after being beaten a short head in a modest Lingfield handicap, stepped up to a mile on his reappearance in March.

When Masafi was seen again, it was in a similarly modest handicap at Southwell, run on a Monday, leaving the maximum eleven-day gap before any amended BHB handicap mark could come into operation. Masafi won in good style at Southwell and when he followed up under a fixed 6-lb penalty on the Friday at Carlisle his trainer still had up to the Friday of the next week to run him off the same mark (with the penalty). A further three wins followed in the second week at Brighton, Folkestone and Southwell (Monday, Thursday and Friday), Masafi starting odds on (as for all his last six successes) and winning readily. A five-timer in twelve days became a six-timer in seventeen when Masafi won at Musselburgh off a new mark of 75, taking into account the form of his first two wins. The record came the next day at Carlisle, not in a handicap but in a classified stakes for horses rated 0-75. Masafi's winning run came to an end when he managed only fifth in a more valuable event at Brighton the following week, running off a mark (including a penalty) which was still 13 lb below the mark of 92 which the BHB handicapper had allotted for future races and which by then took into account the improved form of his sixth and seventh wins. Masafi was seen out only once after Brighton, when below form seven weeks later at Pontefract.

Masafi (IRE) (b.g. 2001)	Desert King (IRE) (b 1994)	Danehill (b 1986)	Danzig
			Razyana
		Sabaah (ch 1988)	Nureyev
			Dish Dash
	Mrs Fisher (IRE) (b 1989)	Salmon Leap (ch 1980)	Northern Dancer
			Fish-Bar
		Amboselli (b 1980)	Raga Navarro
			Late Spring

Masafi's owner Graham Waters also owned another prolific Prescott-trained winner, the admirable Spindrifter who won thirteen races as a two-year-old in 1980, including ten in a row. Spindrifter, who was put down as a three-year-old after fracturing a leg on the gallops, was a half-brother to Masafi's grandam Amboselli who was third at five furlongs as a two-year-old. Amboselli and Masafi's dam, the fairly useful seven-furlong winner Mrs Fisher, who won six races and was placed a further five times from her twelve starts, were also trained by Prescott. Mrs Fisher is the dam of two other fairly useful winners at their best, the miler Pedro (by Brief Truce) and the six-year-old Grandma Lily, successful at five to seven furlongs. Masafi's trainer, incidentally, was reportedly the prime target of a convoluted and silly new rule announced—and sensibly later dropped—to prevent three-year-old maidens being stepped up considerably in trip in handicaps and classified stakes after acquiring their mark from runs down the field over shorter. According to the BHB, the proposed rule would have affected only nine horses who made winning debuts as three-year-olds in the two previous seasons. It would not have affected Masafi who began his run of success at a mile and is yet to race beyond a mile and a quarter (though he may well stay further). The Prescott stable had a good year with its two-year-olds but it has earned a reputation for exploiting lenient BHB marks with well-bred horses who don't begin to come into their own until three over middle distances, after being qualified for handicaps while still green, and sometimes backward, at two. It would be much better, and more straightforward, for the BHB handicappers to follow the instruction set out in the *Racing Calendar* not to allot a mark if, in their opinion, there is insufficient information upon which to make an assessment. It will be interesting to see how much more improvement his trainer can extract from the good-bodied Masafi as a four-year-old. Even after seven wins, he didn't look handicapped out of things on his best form and was among the stable's entries for the Cambridgeshire. Masafi, who was gelded after his last run, usually races prominently and has run only on the all-weather and on going firmer than good on turf. *Sir Mark Prescott*

MASA (USA) 2 gr. or ro.f. (Feb 20) Dixie Union (USA) 121 – My Yellow Diamond (USA) (Housebuster (USA)) [2004 6m* 6m 6m⁶ Jul 6] good-topped filly: not a good walker: has a fluent, round action: third foal: half-sister to winner in USA by Gilded Time: dam, 6f winner in USA, half-sister to Oaks d'Italia winner Miss Gris: won maiden at Lingfield in May easily by 5 lengths from Tesary, making all: below that form in listed race at Royal Ascot and Cherry Hinton Stakes at Newmarket: suffered foot problems after: bred to stay 7f. *Saeed bin Suroor* **92**

MASJOOR 4 ch.g. Unfuwain (USA) 131 – Mihnah (IRE) 87 (Lahib (USA) 129) [2004 58: p12g f12g² 14.1s Apr 30] lengthy gelding: modest maiden: stays 1½m: acts on all-weather and good to firm ground: sold 8,000 gns in July. *N. A. Graham* **64**

MASKED (IRE) 3 b.g. Soviet Star (USA) 128 – Moon Masquerade (IRE) 69 (Darshaan 133) [2004 10g 10s 8.1g⁴ 11.1m* 12.3g⁵ 12m² 14.4m² 14.4m 14g Oct 2] 42,000Y: good-bodied, quite attractive gelding: second foal: dam, maiden who stayed 1¾m, sister to useful middle-distance stayer Shaandar: fairly useful performer: won maiden at Hamilton in June: stays 1¾m: acts on soft and good to firm going: gelded after final start. *J. W. Hills* **84**

MAS O MENOS (IRE) 2 b.g. (Mar 19) King's Theatre (IRE) 128 – Promising Lady 91 (Thunder Gulch (USA) 129) [2004 5v² f6m 6g 6m² 5g 6m Oct 10] quite good-topped gelding: modest maiden: form only when second: should stay at least 1m: acts on heavy and good to firm ground. *Ms Deborah J. Evans* **60**

MASQUERADER (USA) 2 ch.c. (Mar 21) Unbridled (USA) 128 – Guise (USA) (Believe It (USA)) [2004 7d Jul 9] $200,000Y: tall, quite good-topped colt: fifth foal: **– p**

half-brother to 3 minor winners in USA: dam, 1m winner in USA, sister to US Grade 3 2-y-o 1m winner Swear: 11/4, well held in maiden at York, becoming unbalanced and not knocked about: suffered minor ligament problem after: should do better. *Saeed bin Suroor*

MASSEY 8 br.g. Machiavellian (USA) 123 – Massaraat (USA) (Nureyev (USA) 131) **54 d**
[2004 –, a103: f6g* f6g f6g* 6g 6m 7m 7.2s 5m p7g f5s p6g p7.1g⁵ Dec 6] big gelding: **a100 c**
useful on all-weather, modest on turf: won handicap at Wolverhampton in January and
minor event at Southwell in February: well held after: best at 6f/7f: acts on fibresand and
good to firm going: tried visored: front runner. *T. D. Barron*

MASSIF CENTRALE 3 ch.c. Selkirk (USA) 129 – Madame Dubois 121 (Legend of **104**
France (USA) 124) [2004 12s 10g² 12m 12m* 12g 14g⁵ 11.8g* 12v⁶ Oct 23] 82,000Y:
big, lengthy colt: closely related to 1½m winner Richelieu (by Kris) and half-brother
to numerous winners, notably 4-y-o Indian Haven: dam won Park Hill Stakes: useful
performer: won maiden at Newbury in July and well-contested handicap at Leicester
(beat Zeitgeist 1¼ lengths) in October: creditable eleventh in Derby at Epsom (sweating)
on third start: stays 1½m: acts on good to firm going, tailed off on heavy (in St Simon
Stakes at Newbury). *D. R. C. Elsworth*

MASTER COBBLER (IRE) 2 b.c. (Apr 20) Alhaarth (IRE) 126 – Lady Joshua **83**
(IRE) 88 (Royal Academy (USA) 130) [2004 5.2m⁴ 6g² 10.2g² 9d⁴ Oct 17] €50,000Y:
quite good-topped colt: fifth foal: brother to winner in Australia and half-brother to 3-y-o
Privy Seal and fairly useful 1½m/1¾m winner Lord Joshua (by King's Theatre): dam,
maiden who stayed 1½m, closely related to very smart performer up to 1¾m Sapience:
fairly useful maiden: best effort at Bath penultimate start: odds on, hung right/looked
ungenuine final one: will stay 1½m: edgy sort. *G. A. Butler*

MASTER JOSEPH 2 b.c. (Apr 12) Komaite (USA) – Petit Peu (IRE) (Kings Lake **63**
(USA) 133) [2004 5.7f⁴ 6m 7g 7d 8d² 7f⁵ Sep 2] 800F, 18,000Y: lengthy colt: half-brother
to 3 winners, including 1¼m winner Silvery (by Petong): dam, ran once over hurdles in
Ireland, half-sister to smart performer up to 1m Petardia: modest maiden: stays 1m: acts
on firm and good to soft going. *M. R. Channon*

MASTER MAHOGANY 3 b.g. Bandmaster (USA) 97 – Impropriety (Law Society **67**
(USA) 130) [2004 p6g 8.1s⁴ 10.2g 10.2m 9g⁶ 12m⁵ 10g⁴ 10.2g⁶ 8g 8m³ 8.1g 8g* 8g⁶ Sep
27] brother to an 11f/1½m winner in Italy and half-brother to 3 winners, including 1½m
winner Wildmoor (by Common Grounds): dam unraced: fair handicapper: won at Bath in
September: stays 1¼m: acts on good to firm ground. *R. J. Hodges*

MASTERMAN READY 3 b.g. Unfuwain (USA) 131 – Maria Isabella (FR) (Young **74**
Generation 129) [2004 54p: 10g 9.9g 12d⁶ 14.1g 14.1m* 14.1d³ 14.1f⁶ 16g* Sep 30] neat
gelding: fair handicapper: won at Yarmouth (maiden event) in August and Goodwood in
September: stays 2m: acts on good to firm and good to soft going. *P. W. Harris*

MASTER MARVEL (IRE) 3 ch.c. Selkirk (USA) 129 – Insijaam (USA) 112 (Secre- **93**
tariat (USA)) [2004 8g² 9g* 8m* 10.1m 8m 8.1g⁶ 10g Oct 2] good-topped colt: fifth foal:
half-brother to useful performer up to 9f in UAE Janadel (by Machiavellian), 6.5f winner
in USA at 2 yrs: dam, French 9f (at 2 yrs) and 1¼m winner, half-sister to very smart 1m
to 1½m performer Hatoof: fairly useful performer: won maiden at Musselburgh in April
and handicap at Newmarket in May: should stay 1¼m: sold 10,000 gns. *M. Johnston*

MASTER NIMBUS 4 b.g. Cloudings (IRE) 112 – Miss Charlie 59 (Pharly (FR) 130) **–**
[2004 –: 7.9m Sep 11] strong, angular gelding: maiden: well held in banded event only
outing in 2004: stays 6f: acts on good to firm ground: inconsistent. *J. J. Quinn*

MASTER OF THE RACE 2 ch.c. (Apr 29) Selkirk (USA) 129 – Dust Dancer 116 **94 p**
(Suave Dancer (USA) 136) [2004 7d² Oct 30] 200,000Y: strong, close-coupled colt:
fourth foal: half-brother to 3 winners, including 3-y-o Spotlight and useful 7f winner
Tyranny (by Machiavellian): dam, 7f to 1½m winner (including 1¼m Prix de la Nonette),
half-sister to very smart performer up to 1½m Zimzalabim: 7/1, 1¼ lengths second of 19
to Centaurus in maiden at Newmarket, tacked across from wide draw and running on
well: will be suited by 1m/1¼m: useful prospect, sure to win races. *Sir Michael Stoute*

MASTER RAT 3 b.g. Thowra (FR) – Race Against Time (Latest Model 115) [2004 **–**
7.1g 5g 5.7g Oct 10] tailed off in maiden/claimers. *R. J. Hodges*

MASTER RATTLE 5 b.g. Sabrehill (USA) 120 – Miss Primula 81 (Dominion 123) **55 §**
[2004 64§: p7g p6g f7g p6g⁵ p7g² p7g p7g f7m 5.5g* 6.1m² May 25] modest performer:
won in Jersey in May: stays easy 7f: acts on polytrack, soft and good to firm ground: tried
blinkered: often races prominently: unreliable. *Jane Southcombe*

MASTER ROBBIE   5 b.g. Piccolo 121 – Victoria's Secret (IRE) 70 (Law Society   **95**
(USA) 130) [2004 104: 7s 7d 6g 7m 7f* 7g⁶ 7m 7g 7m 7m 7f 7g 7m 7g 7g⁴ 7g p7g* Nov
16] tall, close-coupled gelding: useful handicapper: won at Newmarket (by ½ length
from Obrigado) in May and Lingfield (by 1¼ lengths from Soyuz) in November: best
around 7f: acts on polytrack and firm going, probably not on softer than good: tried
visored: effective held up or making running: often soon off bridle. *M. R. Channon*

MASTER ROLE (IRE)   4 ch.c. Master Willie 129 – Calaloo Sioux (USA) 100 (Our   **72**
Native (USA)) [2004 88: f9.4g² f12s⁶ Mar 5] tall, lengthy colt: brother to useful Irish 1m
winner Master Tribe and half-brother to several winners, including fairly useful 1¼m/
1½m winner Double Colour (by Doyoun): dam 7.6f winner: lightly-raced maiden: left
C. Collins in Ireland, fair form when second at Wolverhampton on reappearance: ran as if
amiss subsequent start: stays 9.4f: acts on fibresand, yet to race on extremes of going on
turf. *M. A. Jarvis*

MASTER THEO (USA)   3 b.g. Southern Halo (USA) – Lilian Bayliss (IRE) 100   **85**
(Sadler's Wells (USA)) [2004 72: 8m 8m³ 7.5d³ 8s³ 8g³ 7f 8d³ p8m⁴ 8d² p8.6g*
p9.5g* Dec 15] small, sturdy gelding: fairly useful performer: in cheekpieces, won minor
events at Wolverhampton in November and December: stays 9.5f: acts on polytrack, good
to firm and good to soft ground. *H. J. Collingridge*

MASTER T (USA)   5 b.g. Trempolino (USA) 135 – Our Little C (USA) (Marquetry   **–**
(USA) 121) [2004 –, a66: p10g p13g Feb 11] sparely-made gelding: poor on Flat nowa-   **a41**
days: will prove best short of 13f: acts on polytrack and firm going (below form on softer
than good): has been tongue tied. *G. L. Moore*

MASTER WELLS (IRE)   3 b.g. Sadler's Wells (USA) 132 – Eljazzi 92 (Artaius   **85**
(USA) 129) [2004 10s* 11.9d 11.9d 12.3d² 12.3g 14m 15.9s² 16d* 17.5d⁴ 13.1s 16.5s
Nov 6] €55,000Y: smallish, close-coupled gelding: brother to smart performer up to 2m
Chiang Mai and useful Irish 1½m winner Chamela Bay and closely related/ half-brother
to several winners, notably very smart 8.5f to 11.5f winner (including Prix de Diane)
Rafha (by Kris), now good broodmare: dam 2-y-o 7f winner who stayed 1¼m: fairly
useful performer: won maiden at Pontefract in April and handicap at Thirsk in August:
stays 17.5f: acts on soft ground: held up. *J. D. Bethell*

MASTMAN (IRE)   2 ch.c. (Apr 8) Intikhab (USA) 135 – Spanker 71§ (Suave Dancer   **94**
(USA) 136) [2004 7m² 7m⁵ 7f⁴ 7.6g* 8g³ Sep 17] 24,000F, 35,000Y: tall colt: second
foal: half-brother to Irish 1¼m winner Skerries (by Dr Fong): dam, irresolute maiden
(stayed 1½m), out of smart performer up to 1¼m Yawl: fairly useful performer: won
minor event at Chester in August by short head from Skidrow, making most: very good
third to Merchant in similar contest at Newbury: stays 1m: best effort on good going:
tongue tied last 3 starts: sold 48,000 gns. *B. J. Meehan*

MATCH BALL (USA)   2 br.f. (May 6) Grand Slam (USA) 120 – Glitters (USA)   **– p**
(Glitterman (USA)) [2004 5d Jul 17] $160,000Y: first foal: dam 5f (at 2yrs) to 6.5f winner
in USA: 4/1, ran as if amiss in maiden at Ripon: suffered ligament problem after: should
do better. *Saeed bin Suroor*

MATERIAL WITNESS (IRE)   7 b.g. Barathea (IRE) 127 – Dial Dream (Gay   **108**
Mecene (USA) 128) [2004 95: 6g 7s 7g² 6m 7g* 7.1m* 7g* 7m² 6m 7s⁴ 7s* 7m⁶ 7g 7m
Sep 25] angular gelding: useful performer: won handicap at Goodwood, minor event at

*Ladbrokes Bunbury Cup (Handicap), Newmarket—Material Witness (white nose) completes a hat-trick
by beating Court Masterpiece; behind them are Greenslades (partially hidden by winner), El Coto (left),
Grizedale (blaze), Royal Storm (stars) and Amandus (spots)*

Warwick and Ladbrokes Bunbury Cup (Handicap) at Newmarket (beat Court Master-piece short head) in June/July and handicap at Goodwood (beat Digital ¾ length) in August: effective at 6f/7f: acts on polytrack, firm and soft going: tried blinkered/visored ealier in career: carries head high: front runner. *W. R. Muir*

MATHMAGICIAN 5 ch.g. Hector Protector (USA) 124 – Inherent Magic (IRE) 95 **39** (Magical Wonder (USA) 125) [2004 –, a45: f8g⁴ f8g⁵ f7s⁴ f8g f11s⁴ f11g⁶ f16s⁶ 11s f8m³ f8m⁵ May 6] strong gelding: poor maiden: stays 11f: acts on fibresand, probably on soft going: wears blinkers/cheekpieces: inconsistent. *R. F. Marvin*

MATOURAKA (FR) 3 b. or br.f. Great Palm (USA) 119 – Madragoa (FR) (Kaldoun **72** (FR) 122) [2004 9g a12g* 12d a11.5g* 9s Oct 22] lengthy filly: second foal: sister to French 1¼m winner Melodya: dam unraced: fair performer: claimed from A. Fracas in France after winning claimers on all-weather at Deauville in July and August: claimed: favourite, reportedly finished lame in apprentice handicap at Newbury on British debut: stays 1½m. *P. W. Chapple-Hyam*

MATRIARCHAL 4 ch.f. Presidium 124 – Mayor 86 (Laxton 105) [2004 41: 7m 6m⁵ **–** f7g 5m 6g Aug 6] neat filly: little form in 2004: tried tongue tied. *Don Enrico Incisa*

MATRIMONY 3 b.c. Groom Dancer (USA) 128 – Zonda 100 (Fabulous Dancer **?** (USA) 124) [2004 10.1m a7g* a11g a17g³ Dec 12] closely related to useful French 1m winner Zambesi (by Rahy) and half-brother to several winners, including smart 6f (at 2 yrs) to 1m (in UAE) winner Zoning (by Warning): dam 5f to 8.5f (in USA) winner: pulled up on debut (only outing for E. Dunlop): won minor event at Gran Canaria in October: stays 17f. *S. Hernandez, Spain*

MATSUNOSUKE 2 b.c. (Feb 25) Magic Ring (IRE) 115 – Lon Isa 80 (Grey Desire **61** 115) [2004 6f 6d Oct 14] fifth foal: dam, maiden who stayed 1½m, half-sister to useful middle-distance winner Naked Welcome: fell before halfway on debut: tenth to Tomo-ohat in maiden at Newmarket: should stay 1m. *A. B. Coogan*

MATTY TUN 5 b.g. Lugana Beach 116 – B Grade 59 (Lucky Wednesday 124) [2004 **98** 96: 5d 5g⁵ 5s⁵ 5m 6f 5d 5d⁵ 5g 5f 5d 5s* f5s Nov 17] strong gelding: useful handicapper: won at Doncaster in October by ¾ length from Whitbarrow: best at 5f: acts on fibresand and any turf going: tongue tied once at 3 yrs: sometimes slowly away: tends to carry head awkwardly/idle. *J. Balding*

MAUNBY RAVER 3 ch.g. Pivotal 124 – Colleen Liath (Another Realm 118) [2004 **58 ?** 65: p7g 6m⁴ 6m p6g p6g Dec 17] workmanlike gelding: has a round action: modest performer: should stay 7f: acts on all-weather, unraced on extremes of going on turf: tried visored. *P. C. Haslam*

MAUNBY REVELLER 2 b.g. (Mar 6) Benny The Dip (USA) 127 – Aunt Tate (Tate **–** Gallery (USA) 117) [2004 f7g Dec 12] half-brother to useful 7f winner Doctorate (by Dr Fong) and 2002 2-y-o 7f winner Lodge Keeper (by Grand Lodge), later useful up to 1½m in UAE: dam, ran twice, out of smart French 1¼m winner Aunty: well held in maiden at Southwell. *P. C. Haslam*

MAUNBY ROCKER 4 ch.g. Sheikh Albadou 128 – Bullion 85 (Sabrehill (USA) **–** 120) [2004 60: p10g f8s f7s⁶ f12s⁵ Feb 29] small gelding: no longer of much account. *P. C. Haslam*

MAUREEN ANN 4 b.f. Elmaamul (USA) 125 – Running Glimpse (IRE) 84 (Runnett **51 ?** 125) [2004 59: 7.5g 7.5g 8.1g 7g 7m Sep 18] quite good-topped filly: modest performer: best at 7f/1m: acts on good to firm and good to soft going, well held on all-weather: has worn hood: sometimes slowly away: has looked hard ride: inconsistent. *T. J. Fitzgerald*

MAUREEN'S LOUGH (IRE) 2 b.f. (Apr 13) Bachir (IRE) 118 – Tadjnama (USA) **55** (Exceller (USA) 129) [2004 5s³ 5g⁶ 7f* 7g⁵ 7.5d⁴ 7m⁴ 7m* 7m 7d⁵ 5.9g 7m 7.5m² 8g⁶ Sep 26] leggy, plain filly: sixth foal: half-sister to 1996 2-y-o 5f winner Fruitana (by Distinctly North), later successful abroad, and 6-y-o Warlingham: dam lightly-raced Irish maiden: modest performer: won seller at Redcar in June and claimer at Thirsk (then left T. D. Barron) in July: second in selling nursery at Beverley, only form after: stays 7.5f: acts on firm and good to soft going. *J. Hetherton*

MAURO (IRE) 2 b.f. (Mar 3) Danehill Dancer (IRE) 117 – Stop The Traffic (IRE) 66 **56** (College Chapel 122) [2004 5d⁴ 5.1s² 5g⁴ 6d⁶ 5.1g Aug 16] €12,000Y: smallish filly: first foal: dam maiden best at 6f/7f: modest maiden: should stay 6f: acts on soft going. *P. M. Phelan*

MAWHOOB (USA) 6 gr.g. Dayjur (USA) 137 – Asl (USA) 114 (Caro 133) [2004 –§, **– §** a51§: f12g Jan 8] good-bodied gelding: no longer of much account. *Mrs N. Macauley*

MAXAMILLION (IRE)   2 b.c. (Feb 20) Mujadil (USA) 119 – Manazil (IRE) 98   **82**
(Generous (IRE) 139) [2004 7.1s⁵ 8s⁴ 7s* 7s⁶ Nov 6] €20,000F, 10,000Y, 31,000 2-y-o:
fourth foal: half-brother to 6f winner Mystical Charm (by Indian Ridge): dam, 1m/1¼m
winner, half-sister to useful performers Jalaab (miler) and Takamaka Bay (up to 1½m):
fairly useful performer: won maiden at Brighton in October by 3½ lengths from Marhoon: respectable sixth in nursery at Doncaster: should stay 1m. *S. Kirk*

MAXILLA (IRE)   4 b. or br.f. Lahib (USA) 129 – Lacinia 107 (Groom Dancer (USA)   **78**
128) [2004 77: 10s⁴ 10s 9.9d⁵ 9.7g⁶ 11.9g² 13.9m⁴ Sep 5] rangy filly: fair performer:
stays 1¾m: acts on polytrack, soft and good to firm ground: carried head awkwardly
penultimate start: sold 24,000 gns. *L. M. Cumani*

MAXIMINUS   4 b.g. The West (USA) 107 – Candarela 41 (Damister (USA) 123) [2004   **70**
–: 9.7s⁴ p12d 11.6f⁶ 11.6f p16g Sep 18] fair maiden: stays 11.6f: unraced on heavy going,
seems to act on any other on turf, below form all 3 starts on polytrack: has carried head
high. *M. Madgwick*

MAXI'S PRINCESS (IRE)   3 b.f. Revoque (IRE) 122 – Harmer (IRE) 72 (Alzao   **51**
(USA) 117) [2004 60: 5.1g⁶ 5.3m 5f Jun 27] modest maiden: stays 6f: acts on fibresand,
best turf effort on good going: tried tongue tied, poor effort in cheekpieces final start.
P. J. Makin

MAYADEEN (IRE)   2 b.c. (Jan 28) King's Best (USA) 132 – Inaaq 109 (Lammtarra   **75 p**
(USA) 134) [2004 7g³ 8g* Oct 10] good-topped colt: first foal: dam, 1¼m winner who
stayed 1½m, half-sister to Dubai World Cup winner Almutawakel and 1000 Guineas
runner-up Muwakleh: fair form in maidens at Newbury and Bath (favourite, edged
right when beating Tranquilizer by ¾ length): likely to stay 1¼m: should improve.
M. P. Tregoning

MA YAHAB   3 ch.c. Dr Fong (USA) 128 – Bay Shade (USA) 90 (Sharpen Up 127)   **82**
[2004 72p: 9.9g³ 10.1g³ 12.3m 10.5g⁴ 9f⁴ p10g² Sep 22] good-topped colt: fairly useful
maiden: best effort final outing: stays 1¼m: acts on polytrack and firm going: ran as
though amiss third outing: sold 45,000 gns, joined Venetia Williams. *L. M. Cumani*

MAYBE SOMEDAY   3 ch.g. Dr Fong (USA) 128 – Shicklah (USA) 106 (The Minstrel   **–**
(CAN) 135) [2004 60, a74: p10g³ f9.4g⁴ p7g⁴ p7g⁶ p10g³ p8g² p10g f7s² 8.1d f7d 7m 7m Jul   **a70**
28] fair performer: left I. Wood after seventh start: effective at 7f to easy 1¼m: acts on
all-weather, best turf effort on good to soft going: wore cheekpieces/blinkers last 7
outings. *J. Balding*

MAYFAIR MAUNDY   4 ch.f. The West (USA) 107 – Mayfair Ballerina 53 (King's   **–**
Signet (USA) 110) [2004 7g⁴ 5v May 10] of little account. *W. G. M. Turner*

MAY MORNING (IRE)   2 b.f. (May 3) Danehill (USA) 126 – Golden Digger (USA)   **78**
66 (Mr Prospector (USA)) [2004 5.1d⁴ 5.1d⁶ f2 Sep 13] fifth foal: closely related to 3-y-o
Golden Sahara and half-sister to 2 winners, notably 5-y-o Naheef: dam, maiden who
failed to progress from only 2-y-o start, sister to dam of Irish Oaks/Nassau Stakes winner
Lailani and half-sister to very smart pair Always Fair and Faithful Son: better effort in
maidens when second to Amalie at Redcar: should stay 7f. *B. W. Hills*

MAYNOOTH PRINCE (IRE)   2 b.g. (Feb 1) Spectrum (IRE) 126 – Muffle 70   **–**
(Sadler's Wells (USA) 132) [2004 7m 8d Oct 15] sturdy gelding: well beaten in maidens
at Newcastle and Redcar. *H. Alexander*

MAYS DREAM   2 b.f. (Apr 17) Josr Algarhoud (IRE) 118 – Amber Mill 96 (Doulab
(USA) 115) [2004 7.2d Sep 17] 27,000Y: workmanlike filly: half-sister to several
winners, including 4-y-o Golden Nun and 3-y-o Iskander: dam 5f/6f winner, including at
2 yrs: 25/1, well held in maiden at Ayr (moved poorly to post). *D. Nicholls*

MAYSTOCK   4 ch.f. Magic Ring (IRE) 115 – Stockline (Capricorn Line 111) [2004   **77**
80: p13g* p12g p10g³ 11.7g 12g 10.1m³ 12g 10g 11.7s p13g* p13.9g⁶ p12.2g Dec 14]   **a83**
sturdy filly: fairly useful handicapper on all-weather, fair on turf: won at Lingfield in
January and November: will stay 1¾m: acts on polytrack, good to soft and good to firm
ground: often visored: tried tongue tied. *G. A. Butler*

MAYZIN (IRE)   4 b.g. Fayruz 116 – Peep of Day (USA) (Lypheor 118) [2004 60: p7g³   **54**
p7g² p6g⁴ p7g* p7g² p7g³ p6g³ p6g* p6g⁴ 5.7m 7m 5g 6m 6m 7.6f 5d³ 6m⁵ Sep 4]   **a75**
lengthy, angular gelding: fair on all-weather, modest on turf: won maiden in February and
handicap in March, both at Lingfield: effective at 5f to 7f: acts on polytrack, soft and good
to firm ground: usually wears cheekpieces: races prominently. *R. M. Flower*

MAZEPA (IRE) 4 b.c. Indian Ridge 123 – Please Believe Me 93 (Try My Best (USA) **102**
130) [2004 97: 6g⁶ 6m³ 6d 6m⁵ 7g 6s Oct 22] rangy, good-topped colt: has a quick action:
useful handicapper: good third to Royal Storm at Newmarket on second start: below
form after: effective at 5f/6f: acts on polytrack, good to firm and good to soft going: sold
16,000 gns, sent to USA. *N. A. Callaghan*

MAZINDAR (USA) 2 b. or br.g. (Apr 7) Zamindar (USA) 116 – Fantastic Bloom **54**
(VEN) (Imperial Ballet (IRE) 110) [2004 p7.1g p8.6g Dec 17] modest form in maidens at
Wolverhampton: slowly away on debut: hung left final start. *D. J. Coakley*

MAZRAM 5 b.m. Muhtarram (USA) 125 – Royal Mazi 58 (Kings Lake (USA) 133) **–**
[2004 –: 8.5d 6.9m 7d Oct 2] no sign of ability: blinkered last 2 starts. *I. W. McInnes*

MAZUNA (IRE) 3 b.f. Cape Cross (IRE) 129 – Keswa 94 (Kings Lake (USA) 133) **110**
[2004 56: 11.5g* 10m² 12m³ 10g² 14.6m² 12f* 10g⁶ Oct 24] neat filly: smart performer:
won handicap at Lingfield in June and Princess Royal John Doyle Stakes at Ascot (by
short head from My Renee) in September: creditable length second to Echoes In Eternity
in Park Hill Stakes at Doncaster fifth start: needs further than 1¼m and stays 14.6f: acts
on polytrack, firm and good to soft going. *C. E. Brittain*

MBOSI (USA) 3 b.g. Kingmambo (USA) 125 – April Starlight (USA) 94 (Storm Bird **88**
(CAN) 134) [2004 81+: 8f³ 8.5d³ 8d 10.1g² 10.3g 10g³ 8.3d 8.5g a8f⁶ a6.5f⁴ a7.5f⁶ Dec **a69**
30] quite good-topped gelding: has short, quick action: fairly useful performer on turf,
fair on dirt: left M. Johnston after eighth outing: stays 1¼m: acts on firm and good to soft
going: blinkered seventh/eighth starts. *E. Charpy, UAE*

MCCRACKEN (IRE) 8 b.g. Scenic 128 – Sakanda (IRE) (Vayrann 133) [2004 21.6v⁶ **–**
Apr 19] lightly raced and little form on Flat since 2001: tried blinkered/tongue tied.
R. Ford

Mr Saeed Manana's "Mazuna"

MCELDOWNEY 2 b.g. (Apr 24) Zafonic (USA) 130 – Ayodhya (IRE) (Astronef **78**
116) [2004 6m³ 7.5g² 7.1m² 6f² 6g³ 7g 7m 7.1g² 6d⁵ 7s* Nov 2] 20,000Y: rangy gelding:
half-brother to several winners, including useful 1999 2-y-o 6f winner Acrobatic (by
Warning), later 1m winner in Hong Kong, and fairly useful 1½m winner Amalianburg
(by Hector Protector): dam French 2-y-o 6f/7f winner: fair performer: made all in maiden
at Catterick: will probably stay 1m: acts on firm and soft going: blinkered (below form)
seventh start: none too consistent. *M. Johnston*

MCQUEEN (IRE) 4 ch.g. Barathea (IRE) 127 – Bibliotheque (USA) 79 (Woodman **81**
(USA) 126) [2004 85: p12g 9.7s⁶ 10d 11.6m f8d⁶ f12m 10g² 8s* 10.2s* 10.3g 10.5s⁵
9s* 10s* 10v² Nov 4] lengthy gelding: fairly useful handicapper: won at Goodwood
(amateurs) and Chepstow within 4 days in August, at Newbury (apprentices) in October
and Redcar in November: effective at 1m/1¼m: acts on all-weather and heavy going:
tough. *Mrs H. Dalton*

MEADAAF (IRE) 3 b.c. Swain (IRE) 134 – Virgin Hawk (USA) (Silver Hawk (USA) **85**
123) [2004 72: 10m* 12.3g² 10f³ 11d⁶ 13.3d³ a8f a10f Dec 18] rangy colt: fairly useful **a–**
performer on turf: won minor event at Brighton in April: left E. Vaughan before
penultimate outing: stays 13f: acts on firm and good to soft going, no form on dirt: has
raced freely. *D. J. Selvaratnam, UAE*

MEADOW END BOY 3 b.g. Great Dane (IRE) 122 – Bettynouche 69 (Midyan **–**
(USA) 124) [2004 f11g p10g Dec 30] well held in maidens at Southwell and Lingfield.
Bob Jones

MEADOW HAWK (USA) 4 b.g. Spinning World (USA) 130 – Sophonisbe (Wollow **–**
132) [2004 73: 14.1s May 14] tall, leggy gelding: lightly-raced maiden: fair form for
A. O'Brien in Ireland in 2002/3: showed nothing only outing in 2004. *Ian Williams*

MEASURED LEAP 3 br.f. Inchinor 119 – Lochspring (IRE) (Precocious 126) [2004 **40**
10m 10g 9.6d 7f⁵ 5s³ f6g Nov 8] 1,800 2-y-o: fourth living foal: half-sister to fairly useful
6f winner Locharati (by Emarati): dam unraced half-sister to Nunthorpe winners Lochsong and Lochangel: poor maiden: well beaten in banded race at Wolverhampton final
start. *Patrick Martin, Ireland*

MEATH (IRE) 3 b.c. Sadler's Wells (USA) 132 – Twyla 101 (Habitat 134) [2004 96p: **108**
8s² 8d² 10m* 12m Jun 5] smallish, stocky, short-coupled colt: brother to useful Irish
1m winner Dalcassian and half-brother to smart 7f (at 2 yrs) to 12.3f winner Twist And
Turn (by Groom Dancer) and 13f winner High Pyrenees (by Shirley Heights): dam, 2-y-o
6f winner, sister to smart sprinter Defecting Dancer: useful performer: runner-up in
listed races at Leopardstown (beaten a head by Grey Swallow on first occasion) prior to
winning Airlie Stud Gallinule Stakes at the Curragh in May by 1½ lengths from Cairdeas:
tailed-off last in Derby at Epsom subsequent start: stays 1¼m: acts on firm and soft going:
has worn crossed noseband: sent to Hong Kong. *A. P. O'Brien, Ireland*

MECCA'S MATE 3 gr.f. Paris House 123 – Clancassie (Clantime 101) [2004 –: 5d⁵ **62**
7g⁶ 6g⁵ 5d* 6s³ Sep 19] leggy, lengthy filly: modest perfomer: won apprentice handicap
at Thirsk in August, tending to edge right: best at 5f/6f: acts on soft ground: has been
slowly away. *D. W. Barker*

MEDALLA (FR) 4 gr.c. Medaaly 114 – Sharp Cracker (IRE) 80 (Hamas (IRE) 125§) **72 ?**
[2004 8d³ 9.9s⁵ 8g 10.1m Oct 10] 4,500Y: workmanlike colt: first foal: dam 6f (at 2 yrs)/
1m winner: 100/1, third in maiden at Pontefract on debut, easily best effort. *M. Brittain*

MEDALLIST 5 b.g. Danehill (USA) 126 – Obsessive (USA) 102 (Seeking The Gold **62**
(USA)) [2004 77: 8.1d⁶ 10.1s⁶ May 12] lengthy gelding: only modest nowadays: stays
10.5f: acts on firm and good to soft going: tried blinkered: sold 2,500 gns. *B. Ellison*

MEDIA HORA (CHI) 4 ch.g. Somersham (USA) – Membrana (CHI) (The Great **102**
Shark (USA)) [2004 6.5g a5g 5.8g 6v a1.5g* 3f* 3f* a5g* 5s a6g* p6g Dec 18] Chilean-
bred gelding: useful performer: winner of 4 races in Chile at 3 yrs: successful in 2004 in
minor events at Copenhagen (2) and Jagersro (3) between July and November, reportedly
breaking track record when beating Pipoldchap 2½ lengths on last occasion: eleventh in
handicap at Lingfield final start: effective at very short distances and stays 6f: acts on dirt
and firm going: usually blinkered. *F. Castro, Sweden*

MEDIA PUZZLE (USA) 7 ch.g. Theatrical 128 – Market Slide (USA) 94 (Gulch **113**
(USA)) [2004 10m⁵ 14g 16s 12v³ Nov 13] big, strong, lengthy gelding: fluent mover:
smart performer: reportedly fractured pelvis at 3 yrs and has suffered with leg problems
(missed 2003 and reportedly fired on both tendons): respectable efforts in 2004, seventh

to Vinnie Roe in Irish St Leger at the Curragh, twelfth to Makybe Diva in Melbourne Cup at Flemington (had won race in 2002) and 3¼ lengths third to Count Ricardo in Group 2 Sandown Classic at Sandown (Australia): effective at 1½m to 2m: acts on any going: often blinkered. *D. K. Weld, Ireland*

MEDICA BOBA   3 b.f. Dr Fong (USA) 128 – Silly View (IRE) 75 (Scenic 128) [2004   **57** 8m 8.3f 8.3f 8.3g 10.2m 16g³ p16g Oct 13] half-sister to fairly useful 6f/7f performer Kulachi (by Royal Applause) and 2 winners abroad: dam, Irish 9f winner, half-sister to dam of Racing Post Trophy winner Seattle Rhyme: modest maiden: sold 4,000 gns. *H. Morrison*

MEDITATION   2 ch.f. (Apr 2) Inchinor 119 – Trojan Desert 97 (Troy 137) [2004 7m   **71** p7g p7m p7g* 7s Nov 6] half-sister to untrustworthy 1¼m winner Alberkinnie (by Ron's Victory) and to winners abroad by Kalaglow and Local Suitor: dam 7f winner, later successful in USA: fair performer: won maiden at Lingfield in October by short head from King's Majesty, dictating pace: should stay 1m: acts on polytrack, no form on turf. *I. A. Wood*

MEDUSA   4 b.f. Emperor Jones (USA) 119 – Diebiedale 58 (Dominion 123) [2004 73:   **–** 6.1s 7m 7f Jun 22] lengthy filly: maiden handicapper: well held in 2004. *D. Morris*

MEELUP (IRE)   4 ch.g. Night Shift (USA) – Centella (IRE) (Thatching 131) [2004 64:   **66 d** p7g p7g² p8g* p10g p8g 8.3g 8.5g² 8.3d² 8.1d 7.1m 8.1g 7.1g 8g p8.6g p9.5g Dec 6] sturdy, deep-girthed gelding: unimpressive mover: fair performer: left A. Newcombe after second start: won handicap at Lingfield in March: well below form last 7 outings: stays 1m: acts on polytrack, soft and firm going: wears cheekpieces: sometimes makes running: inconsistent. *Jane Southcombe*

MEGABOND   3 b.g. Danehill Dancer (IRE) 117 – Apple Peeler (IRE) 56 (Rainbows   **63 ?** For Life (CAN)) [2004 64: f6s⁵ f7g f6g⁴ 6m 6g 6.9m* 8m p7.1g⁵ p7g p7.1g f8g⁴ Nov   **a59** 23] lengthy, attractive gelding: modest performer: left B. Smart after winning claimer at Carlisle in September: effective at 6f to 1m: acts on all-weather and good to firm ground: wore cheekpieces/visor last 6 starts. *C. A. Dwyer*

MEGAN'S MAGIC   4 b.f. Blue Ocean (USA) 87 – Hot Sunday Sport 42 (Star Appeal   **74** 133) [2004 70: 8v⁶ 9.9s* 8d² 8.3d 10m 10m³ 10d⁶ 10g⁴ 9.9s⁴ 10.1g 8g⁵ Sep 14] leggy filly: fair performer: won at Beverley in April: stays 1¼m: acts on firm and soft ground: blinkered last 2 starts: often slowly away and usually held up: sold 3,000 gns, joined M. Sowersby. *W. Storey*

MEGELL (IRE)   2 b.f. (Apr 28) Entrepreneur 123 – Shalwell (IRE) (Shalford (IRE)   **64** 124§) [2004 5v⁶ 6g² 5g 7m⁵ 6m* 6.1d Sep 17] €7,500Y: lengthy filly: second foal: dam unraced half-sister to Poule d'Essai des Poulains/Irish 2000 Guineas winner Bachir: modest performer: won claimer at Yarmouth in August: barely stays 7f: acts on good to firm going: sometimes races freely. *M. G. Quinlan*

MEHMAAS   8 b.g. Distant Relative 128 – Guest List 85 (Be My Guest (USA) 126)   **55 §** [2004 72d, a–§: 8.3g 8v 8m 7m 8g⁴ 8d f8m 7g* 7d 7m 8.3d⁵ 8s Aug 30] smallish, sturdy gelding: modest performer: won apprentice claimer at Newcastle in July: stays 1m: acts on any turf going and fibresand: usually wears headgear: often front runner: unreliable. *R. E. Barr*

MEISSEN   3 ch.f. Amfortas (IRE) 115 – Musetta (IRE) 107 (Cadeaux Genereux 131)   **77** [2004 68p: 10m² 12g² p13g* Oct 1] big, strong, lengthy filly: has scope: fairly useful performer, lightly raced: trained by A. Stewart first 2 starts: won maiden at Lingfield in October: stays easy 13f: raced only on polytrack and good/good to firm ground. *E. F. Vaughan*

MEKURIA (JPN)   3 b.f. Carnegie (IRE) 129 – Noble Air (IRE) (Lycius (USA) 124)   **74** [2004 84p: 11.9d 11.9g 10s⁴ Jul 3] well-made filly: lightly raced: stays 1¼m: acts on soft ground: sold 16,000 gns, sent to Germany. *M. Johnston*

MELAINA   3 b.f. Whittingham (IRE) 104 – Oh I Say 74 (Primo Dominie 121) [2004   **65** 54: f6g² f6g f6g6 f6g* f6g* 6.1g⁵ 6m Jul 3] fair handicapper: won at Wolverhampton in April and Folkestone in May: stays 6f: acts on fibresand, firm and soft ground: wears cheekpieces: usually makes running: sold 1,000 gns in October. *M. S. Saunders*

MELALCHRIST   2 b.g. (Jan 28) Almaty (IRE) 113§ – Lawless Bridget 62 (Alnasr   **92** Alwasheek 117) [2004 5v⁴ 5m² 5g² 5g* 6f³ 6d 6s Oct 22] 4,500Y: compact gelding: second foal: dam, maiden, best effort at 6f at 2 yrs: fairly useful performer: won maiden at Beverley in May and minor event there in July: probably best at 5f: acts on heavy and good to firm going: sometimes races freely. *J. J. Quinn*

MELANDRE 2 b.f. (Jan 30) Lujain (USA) 119 – Talighta (USA) 62 (Barathea (IRE) **74**
127) [2004 5d⁶ 5d 5m⁴ 5m⁵ 5g* 5g² 5m Oct 2] 3,700F, 6,200Y: close-coupled filly:
second foal: half-sister to 3-y-o Kuringai: dam Irish sprint maiden: fair performer: won
nursery at Catterick in September: good second at Ripon, much better effort in similar
events after: likely to prove best at 5f: best form on good going: usually races prominently. *M. Brittain*

MELFORD RED (IRE) 4 b.g. Sri Pekan (USA) 117 – Sunflower (IRE) (Fairy King –
(USA)) [2004 –: f8g f8s Nov 17] lengthy gelding: no sign of ability: tried in cheekpieces.
R. F. Marvin

MELINDA'S GIRL 3 b.f. Intikhab (USA) 135 – Polish Honour (USA) 61 (Danzig –
Connection (USA)) [2004 44: 8.1s 10m⁶ 8s Oct 15] good-topped filly: well held in 2004:
tried visored. *A. P. Jarvis*

MELODIAN 9 b.h. Grey Desire 115 – Mere Melody 88 (Dunphy 124) [2004 71: f11g⁵ **72**
10.1v⁴ 9.9d⁵ 10v* 9.9v² 10.1s³ 10.1d² 10.5g* 9v⁶ 12.1s 10.1g 11.9g 10s Nov 1] leggy
horse: fair handicapper: won at Pontefract in April and Haydock in August: stays 10.5f:
has won on firm going, best efforts on good or softer: wears blinkers, visored once:
usually races up with pace. *M. Brittain*

MELODY KING 3 b.g. Merdon Melody 98 – Retaliator 80 (Rudimentary (USA) **70 d**
118) [2004 70: 6d 5.7f³ 5.1g² 5.1g⁵ 5.7f⁴ 5g³ 5.1g⁶ 5.1m⁵ 5.1g 5.7m 6.1g⁶ 5m 7g⁴ 5.7g 6d
Nov 5] rather leggy gelding: fair performer: regressed in 2004: best at 5f/6f: acts on firm
going: tried visored, usually blinkered: tends to hang left: races up with pace. *P. D. Evans*

MELODY QUE (IRE) 2 b.f. (Mar 24) Sadler's Wells (USA) 132 – Bex (USA) 116 **58 p**
(Explodent (USA)) [2004 7.5d⁶ Aug 28] €400,000Y: strong, close-coupled filly: sister to
3 winners in France, including smart 1¼m/1½m winner Hijaz, closely related to French
1¼m winner Janadriyah (by Fairy King) and half-sister to 2 winners, including smart
French 1¼m/1½m winner Crimson Quest (by Rainbow Quest): dam 1m to 10.5f winner:
12/1, sixth in maiden at Beverley, not knocked about: will be suited by 1¼m/1½m: should
improve. *J. Howard Johnson*

MELOGRANO (IRE) 4 ch.g. Hector Protector (USA) 124 – Just A Treat (IRE) 47 **55**
(Glenstal (USA) 118) [2004 50: f11m² f12d 10.9d 10m p12.2d* p12m³ Dec 8] modest
performer: won banded race at Wolverhampton in October: stays 1½m: acts on all-
weather and heavy ground: inconsistent. *Mark Campion*

MELROSE AVENUE (USA) 2 b.c. (Apr 30) Kris S (USA) – Sham Street (USA) **95**
(Sham (USA)) [2004 7.1m⁵ 7.1d* 7m⁵ 8d⁴ Sep 16] 80,000F, 80,000Y: big, close-coupled colt:
looked weak at 2 yrs: not the best of walkers: closely related to winner in USA by
Dynaformer and half-brother to several winners, including 5f (useful at 2 yrs in Ireland)
to 1¼m winner Shahik (by Spectacular Bid): dam 8.5f/9f winner: useful performer:
won maiden at Sandown in July by 6 lengths from Ground Rules, making all: last in
Futurity Stakes at the Curragh and minor event at Ayr (hung right early) after: should stay
at least 1m. *M. Johnston*

MEL'S MOMENT (USA) 2 b.c. (Apr 17) Storm Creek (USA) – One Moment In **78**
Time (USA) (Magesterial (USA) 116) [2004 7s 8g⁶ p7g p7.1g⁴ p8.6d⁶ Oct 30] $40,000Y:
good-topped colt: half-brother to several winners, including fairly useful 2002 2-y-o 1m
winner Senor Sol (by El Prado): dam 6f to 1m winner in USA: fair maiden:
stays 1m: best effort on good going. *Mrs A. J. Perrett*

MELVINO 2 b.g. (Apr 6) Josr Algarhoud (IRE) 118 – Safe Secret 50 (Seclude (USA)) **71**
[2004 6d⁴ 5m 6m³ 6f⁴ 6d 6f Sep 10] 7,500F, 16,000Y: rather leggy gelding: fourth foal:
half-brother to 5-y-o The Mog and winning sprinter in Italy by General Monash: dam,
maiden who seemed to stay 1½m, winning hurdler: fair maiden: below form last 3 starts
(visored first 2 of them): likely to stay 7f: acts on good to firm going. *T. D. Barron*

MEMBERSHIP (USA) 4 ch.c. Belong To Me (USA) – Shamisen 86 (Diesis 133) **107**
[2004 119: a6f 7.5f⁵ 8.9m⁵ 8m² 7s 8f Nov 27] strong, lengthy colt: has a quick action:
smart performer at 3 yrs, only useful in 2004: raced at Nad Al Sheba first 4 starts, second
to Walmooh in handicap on last of them: better effort after 7-month break when eighth of
15 in stakes event at Tokyo final outing: best at 6f/7f: acts on polytrack and firm going,
possibly not on softer than good: blinkered once at 2 yrs: free-going sort, best held up.
C. E. Brittain

MEMORY MAN 3 b.g. Primo Dominie 121 – Surrealist (ITY) (Night Shift (USA)) **65**
[2004 6g 7.1m⁴ p8g³ 7m 6.9m Sep 11] 33,000Y: fourth foal: half-brother to 2 winners,
including 5-y-o Mitsuki: dam unraced: fair maiden: stays 1m: acts on polytrack and good
to firm ground: sold 1,500 gns. *W. R. Muir*

Oaks d'Italia, Milan—after some good efforts in defeat,
Menhoubah gains a deserved success in a race carrying more prize money than the Epsom version;
Step Danzer is second, while the other British-trained runner, fifth-placed Tamarillo, is also in the picture

MENAI STRAIGHTS 3 ch.g. Alhaarth (IRE) 126 – Kind of Light 83 (Primo Dominie **67** 121) [2004 69: f9.4g⁶ 7.5d 8m⁶ 8m³ 7f⁵ 6.9g* 7.2g³ 6.9f 7m⁶ 7m⁶ 7d p7g² p7g⁴ p9.5g p8.6g Dec 17] lengthy, good-topped gelding: fair handicapper: won at Carlisle in July: effective at 7f/1m: acts on polytrack, firm and good to soft going: tried in cheekpieces, tailed off in blinkers final start. *R. F. Fisher*

MENEEF (USA) 3 b.c. Kingmambo (USA) 125 – Black Penny (USA) (Private **80** Account (USA)) [2004 82p: 7m³ 8.2d² 8g³ Oct 4] strong, close-coupled colt: fairly useful maiden: reportedly suffered injury problems and off 9 months before reappearance: will stay 1¼m: joined K. McLaughlin in USA. *M. P. Tregoning*

MENELAUS 3 b.c. Machiavellian (USA) 123 – Mezzogiorno 108 (Unfuwain (USA) **–** 131) [2004 11.5m⁶ Aug 16] 8/1, well held in maiden at Yarmouth: sold 23,000 gns in October. *D. R. Loder*

MENHOUBAH (USA) 3 b.f. Dixieland Band (USA) – Private Seductress (USA) **107** (Private Account (USA)) [2004 102: a8f² a9f³ a9f 11.4d² 11m* 10.5g 9.9m⁶ 11.9s 10m Oct 3] good-bodied filly: has a quick action: useful performer: second in UAE 1000 Guineas at Nad Al Sheba and listed race at Chester (beaten 2½ lengths by Hidden Hope) first/fourth starts: best effort when winning Oaks d'Italia at Milan in May by 1¼ lengths from Step Danzer: well held after in Prix de Diane at Chantilly, Nassau Stakes at Goodwood, Yorkshire Oaks at York and Prix de l'Opera at Longchamp: stays 11.4f: acts on dirt, firm and good to soft going: often wears cheekpieces: sweating/wandered fourth 2-y-o start: often races up with pace. *C. E. Brittain*

MENNA 2 b.f. (Mar 13) Mark of Esteem (IRE) 137 – Pounelta 91 (Tachypous 128) **55 ?** [2004 5.1g⁵ 6g Jul 1] 20,000F, €36,000Y: rather unfurnished filly: half-sister to several winners, notably very smart 7f (including at 2 yrs) winner Lots of Magic (by Magic Ring): dam, 2-y-o 7f winner who probably stayed 1½m, half-sister to very smart but temperamental sprinter Dead Certain: seemingly modest form in maiden at Chester and minor event at Haydock: needs to settle to stay beyond 6f. *R. Hollinshead*

MENOKEE (USA) 3 b.c. Cherokee Run (USA) 122 – Meniatarra (USA) 68 (Zilzal **111 p** (USA) 137) [2004 102p: 10s² Oct 29] good-topped colt: smart performer, lightly raced: best effort when ¾-length second to Spanish Don in listed race at Newmarket only outing in 2004, running green: will stay 1½m: acts on soft going, yet to race on firmer than good: probably has further improvement in him. *Sir Michael Stoute*

Mr Saeed Manana's "Menhoubah"

MEPHISTO (IRE) 5 b.g. Machiavellian (USA) 123 – Cunning 118 (Bustino 136) **111 p**
[2004 87: 12g 12m⁵ 11.9m* 12g* 14g* 13.9s* Aug 18] good-bodied gelding: progressed into a smart handicapper in 2004: won at York (Queen Mother's Cup) in June, Newmarket and Goodwood (Tatler Summer Season Stakes by ½ length from Sergeant Cecil) in July and York (totesport Ebor, beat Gold Ring by short head despite edging left)

Tatler Summer Season Stakes (Handicap), Goodwood—progressive Mephisto overcomes trouble in running to beat Sergeant Cecil, Jagger (No.3), Santando and Self Defense

*totesport Ebor (Handicap), York—a controversial finish involving Mephisto (hooped sleeves)
and Gold Ring, the former edging left and giving the runner-up a slight bump;
the result stood after a stewards' inquiry and an appeal by the latter's connections;
Mikado (hidden) is third with Defining (stars) fourth*

in August: stays 1¾m: acts on soft and good to firm ground: has taken strong hold: sold
220,000 gns in October, joined J. Howard Johnson: probably capable of better still.
L. M. Cumani

MERCARI 2 ch.f. (Mar 5) Bahamian Bounty 116 – Aonach Mor (Anabaa (USA) 130) **60**
[2004 6m 6.1d 6f 5.1g⁶ 6m⁴ f6g p6g Nov 19] first foal: dam unraced out of half-sister to
very smart middle-distance stayer Sapience: modest maiden: effective at 5f/6f: acts on
good to firm ground: wore cheekpieces final start. *G. M. Moore*

MERCHANT (IRE) 2 ch.c. (Mar 6) Tagula (IRE) 116 – Easy Pop (IRE) (Shernazar **103**
131) [2004 7g⁵ 6g³ 5.9f² 6d* 7s* 8d* 8g* 8d⁴ 8s Oct 31] €28,000Y, 17,000 2-y-o: well-
made colt: fourth foal: half-brother to 3 winners, including 3-y-o Ile Facile and useful
2002 2-y-o 1m winner Grand (by Grand Lodge): dam unraced half-sister to very smart
Irish St Leger third Lord Duke: useful performer: won maiden at Hamilton and nurseries
at York and Newmarket in August and minor event at Newbury (wandered when landing
odds by 2½ lengths from Noble Duty) in September: creditable fourth to Konigstiger in
Gran Criterium at Milan, better effort after: stays 1m: acts on soft going. *M. L. W. Bell*

MERCURIOUS (IRE) 4 ch.f. Grand Lodge (USA) 125 – Rousinette (Rousillon **58**
(USA) 133) [2004 48: p13g⁴ f16.2m* 15g⁵ f16.2m⁴ f14g² f16g* 16s² f14g⁵ 15.8g* Oct 5]
strong filly: modest performer: won banded race at Wolverhampton in April, apprentice
handicap at Southwell in July and handicap at Catterick in October: effective at 1½m
to 2m: acts on all-weather, raced only on good ground or softer on turf (acts on soft).
J. Mackie

MERDIFF 5 b.g. Machiavellian (USA) 123 – Balwa (USA) 101 (Danzig (USA)) **65**
[2004 70: 7d 9f f8d f7m² 7.6g* f7m² 7.6m p7d⁴ 7g² 7.2d 8.2g p6d* p6g² p6g p6g³ **a75**
p7.1g² p6g Dec 27] big gelding: fair performer: won apprentice handicap at Chester in
July and minor event at Wolverhampton in November: effective at 6f to 1m: acts on all-
weather and firm ground: tongue tied when winning at 4 yrs: usually races prominently.
W. M. Brisbourne

638

MERGER (USA) 2 gr.c. (Mar 16) Mr Greeley (USA) 122 – Toledo Queen (IRE) 81 **112 p**
(El Gran Senor (USA) 136) [2004 8d* 8d² Oct 10] $210,000Y: sixth foal: half-brother to
winners in USA by Strike The Gold and Black Tie Affair: dam 7f winner (including at 2
yrs), later successful in USA: won maiden at Thurles in September by 5 lengths: plenty of
improvement when ½-length second of 5 to Albert Hall (pair clear) in Beresford Stakes
at the Curragh, slowly into stride and still green: should stay 1¼m: should progress and
win more races. *D. K. Weld, Ireland*

MERLIN'S CITY 4 b.f. Merdon Melody 98 – Sharp Ego (USA) (Sharpen Up 127) –
[2004 6d 10s p8.6g f6g p6g Dec 14] half-sister to several winners, including fairly
useful 6f winner Ego Night (by Night Shift): dam Irish 5f winner: of little account.
Miss L. C. Siddall

MERLIN'S DANCER 4 b.g. Magic Ring (IRE) 115 – La Piaf (FR) (Fabulous **94**
Dancer (USA) 124) [2004 84: 6g 6.1s⁵ 6m* 5m 5g 5m 5g⁴ 6m* 5.6m Sep 8] good-bodied
gelding: unimpressive mover: fairly useful performer: won minor event at Ripon in May
and handicap at Goodwood (best effort, beat High Ridge 1¼ lengths) in July: effective at
5f/6f: acts on firm and good to soft ground: blinkered (below form) once: often makes
running. *D. Nicholls*

MERLINS PROFIT 4 b.g. Wizard King 122 – Quick Profit 78 (Formidable (USA) **50**
125) [2004 54: 7.2g⁵ 11m⁴ 9.9m² 10.9d 8.3d 9.2d⁴ 9.3m³ 10d⁶ 9.1s Oct 12] rather unfurnished gelding: modest maiden: stays 1¼m: acts on good to firm going: tried blinkered.
M. Dods

MERMAID'S CRY 2 b.f. (Feb 11) Danzero (AUS) – Little Tramp (Trempolino (USA) **46 d**
135) [2004 6m² 5g f6d 5m f7g Nov 22] sturdy filly: third foal: half-sister to 5f winner Red
China (by Inchinor): dam unraced: poor maiden: form only on debut (for J. Glover): ran
as if amiss after: stays 6f. *R. Brotherton*

MERRYMADCAP (IRE) 2 b.g. (Apr 22) Lujain (USA) 119 – Carina Clare (Slip **58**
Anchor 136) [2004 6m 7g⁵ 7g⁶ 7m⁶ 8.1s 7s⁶ 7m 6m Oct 1] leggy gelding: modest maiden:
should stay 1m: acts on soft and good to firm ground: blinkered (below form) final start.
M. Blanshard

MERRYMAKER 4 b.g. Machiavellian (USA) 123 – Wild Pavane (Dancing Brave **88**
(USA) 140) [2004 70: 11.9m⁴ 12m⁶ 11.5f⁴ 12f 13.1d* 11.9g² 12m* 11.9f 11.9g 12.1s³
12g⁵ 13.1s⁵ p12.2g* 11.7s⁵ p13.9g* p12g p12.2g³ p12.2g⁴ Dec 17] angular gelding: fairly
useful handicapper: won at Ayr (apprentice maiden) in June and Newbury (apprentice
event) in July and at Wolverhampton in October and November: stays 1¾m: acts on polytrack, firm and soft going: effective visored/blinkered or not. *W. M. Brisbourne*

MERSEY SOUND (IRE) 6 b.g. Ela-Mana-Mou 132 – Coral Sound (IRE) 67 (Glow –
(USA)) [2004 77: 16g 14.1s May 2] rather leggy, quite attractive gelding: fair handicapper at 5 yrs: well held in 2004: tried visored earlier in career: usually held up. *S. Kirk*

Haynes, Hanson and Clark Conditions Stakes, Newbury—
Merchant gains his fourth win in a row at the expense of newcomer Noble Duty (left), with Mastman,
another debutant Pittsburgh (noseband) and Takhleed (right) completing the field

MERWAHA (IRE) 3 b.f. Green Desert (USA) 127 – Samheh (USA) 62 (Private **72**
Account (USA)) [2004 8g⁴ 8m³ 8.1m⁴ Aug 11] fifth foal: sister to 5-y-o Ajeel and half-
sister to 1999 2-y-o 7f winner Marah (by Machiavellian), both fairly useful: dam, maiden
who stayed 1¼m, out of US Grade 1 7f (at 2 yrs) and 9f winner Lucky Lucky Lucky: fair
form in maidens: blinkered final start (raced freely). *M. P. Tregoning*

MESAYAN (IRE) 3 ch.c. Grand Lodge (USA) 125 – Missish (Mummy's Pet 125) **59**
[2004 8m 8.1g⁴ Jul 1] 100,000Y: good-bodied colt: half-brother to several winners,
including 10-y-o Andreyev and 5f winner (including at 2 yrs) Moscow Road (both by
Presidium): dam unraced: backward, signs of ability in maidens at Newmarket (very
green) and Haydock (coltish, again slowly away): tongue tied: joined D. Selvaratnam in
UAE. *A. C. Stewart*

MESHAHEER (USA) 5 b.h. Nureyev (USA) 131 – Race The Wild Wind (USA) 121 **111**
(Sunny's Halo (CAN)) [2004 113: 7.1g 7g² 7s* Oct 23] close-coupled horse: has a round
action: smart performer: ran well when ½-length second to Royal Storm in listed event at
Newbury (had to wait for an opening): won minor event at Doncaster (by 2 lengths from
Millennium Force) following month: stays 7f: acts on soft and good to firm going: usually
tongue tied: has worn crossed noseband/raced freely: joined M. Tregoning. *Saeed bin
Suroor*

MESMERISED 4 b.f. Merdon Melody 98 – Gracious Imp (USA) (Imp Society (USA)) **– §**
[2004 57d: f5g f6g f6g f6g f5g⁶ f7g 5m 10m May 31] leggy, workmanlike filly: modest
and unreliable at 3 yrs: no form in 2004: tried in cheekpieces. *Miss A. Stokell*

MESSE DE MINUIT (IRE) 3 ch.c. Grand Lodge (USA) 125 – Scrimshaw (Selkirk **77**
(USA) 129) [2004 76p: 12.3g 9.9g³ 11.7m⁶ Aug 10] quite attractive colt: fair performer:
should stay 1½m: acts on polytrack, probably on soft and good to firm going: sold 15,000
gns. *R. Charlton*

METEORITE SUN (USA) 6 b.g. Miesque's Son (USA) 117 – Myth To Reality **77 d**
(FR) (Sadler's Wells (USA) 132) [2004 10.1v 10v³ 12.5s 10.5g 10d a12g 10g⁵ 12g 10.5d
10s⁶ 12s 10s 9.5d Dec 15] leggy gelding: fairly useful form for J. Hammond in France in
2001: off nearly 2½ years prior to reappearance, better effort for Mrs J. Ramsden in handicaps when third at Pontefract second start: regressed back in France afterwards (rejoined
J. Hammond third/fourth outings only): stays 1½m: raced only on good ground or softer
on turf: blinkered final start. *G. Lellouche, France*

METHODICAL 2 b.f. (Apr 5) Lujain (USA) 119 – Simple Logic 73 (Aragon 118) **62**
[2004 6g⁴ 6g 6g⁵ 6v Oct 23] close-coupled filly: third foal: dam 2-y-o 6f winner: modest
maiden: fifth at Newbury, best effort: likely to stay 7f. *I. A. Wood*

METICULOUS 6 gr.g. Eagle Eyed (USA) 111 – Careful (IRE) 59 (Distinctly North **–**
(USA) 115) [2004 –: f7g f8g f12f f12g f7g f8g f5s 7s 6g f7g⁶ May 19] of no account.
M. C. Chapman

METOLICA 4 b.f. (Apr 15) Diktat 126 – South Sea Bubble (IRE) 75 (Bustino 136) **32**
[2004 f5d 6g 7.5d f7g Dec 14] 2,700Y: workmanlike filly: fourth foal: dam 1¼m winner:
poor maiden. *C. Smith*

MEXICAN PETE 4 b.g. Atraf 116 – Eskimo Nel (IRE) 75 (Shy Groom (USA)) [2004 **87**
81: 12s 12.3d³ 14.1d 12m² 12g 12d⁴ 12g⁴ 11.8f³ 12g² 11.8m⁶ 12m Sep 4] close-coupled
gelding: fairly useful performer: stays 1½m: acts on firm and good to soft going, below
form only outing on polytrack: usually waited with: consistent. *P. W. Hiatt*

MEXICAN (USA) 5 b.g. Pine Bluff (USA) – Cuando Quiere (USA) (Affirmed (USA)) **43**
[2004 55: 9.9d 7.2g f8g³ f12m⁵ f8m² 8s Oct 30] quite attractive gelding: poor maiden:
stays 1¼m: acts on fibresand and firm going: tried tongue tied/in cheekpieces/visor.
M. D. Hammond

MEZEREON 4 b.f. Alzao (USA) 117 – Blown-Over 41 (Ron's Victory (USA) 129) **55**
[2004 60: p10g f9.4g Apr 17] quite good-topped filly: modest performer: stays easy
1½m: acts on all-weather, raced only on good ground or firmer on turf. *D. Carroll*

MEZUZAH 4 b.g. Barathea (IRE) 127 – Mezzogiorno 108 (Unfuwain (USA) 131) **64 §**
[2004 96: 8v 8.1d⁵ 8d 10.4g 7v 10s Nov 1] lengthy gelding: useful handicapper at 3 yrs:
well below best in 2004, leaving G. Wragg after third outing: stays 1¼m: acts on heavy
and good to firm going: carries head high: sometimes slowly away: one to treat with
caution. *M. W. Easterby*

M FOR MAGIC 5 ch.g. First Trump 118 – Celestine 62 (Skyliner 117) [2004 48§: **49 §**
6m⁵ 6v² 7f⁴ 6g⁵ 6d Oct 15] useful-looking gelding: poor maiden: best efforts at 6f:
acts on heavy and good to firm ground: tried blinkered/in cheekpieces: unreliable.
C. W. Fairhurst

MICHABO (IRE) 3 b.g. Robellino (USA) 127 – Mole Creek 91 (Unfuwain (USA) **83**
131) [2004 –: 9m⁴ 10m³ 9.9g² 10g⁶ 10m² 10d* 12s³ 11g Sep 22] strong, good sort: fairly
useful performer: won maiden at Sandown in August: free-going sort, but stays 1½m:
acts on soft and good to firm going: usually makes running. *D. R. C. Elsworth*

MICHAELS DREAM (IRE) 5 b.g. Spectrum (IRE) 126 – Stormswept (USA) 74 **51 §**
(Storm Bird (CAN) 134) [2004 50, a71: f14g⁶ 10m³ 12m³ 12m 12f⁴ 12.3m 12.1s Aug 29] **a?**
smallish gelding: modest performer: effective at 1¼m to 1¾m: acts on fibresand, firm
and good to soft going: usually wears headgear (effective without): often races freely:
unreliable. *J. Hetherton*

MICHAELS PRIDE (IRE) 2 b.f. (May 1) Distant View (USA) 126 – Ruacana Falls **56**
(USA) 86 (Storm Bird (CAN) 134) [2004 8.2v p8.6g⁵ Dec 6] second foal: dam, 2-y-o 1m
winner, closely related to Chester Vase winner Panama City: better effort in maidens
when fifth at Wolverhampton. *M. Johnston*

MICHELLE MA BELLE (IRE) 4 b.f. Shareef Dancer (USA) 135 – April Magic **83**
(Magic Ring (IRE) 115) [2004 88: p7g p7g² 7d² 7g 8m 7m 6m* 6g 6s 6g Sep 22] sturdy
filly: fairly useful handicapper: won at Windsor in August: best at 6f/7f: acts on polytrack, firm and soft going: blinkered last 5 outings: sometimes races freely: has carried
head awkwardly: usually waited with. *S. Kirk*

MICKEHAHA 2 b.c. (May 9) Lake Coniston (IRE) 131 – Minnehaha (Be My Chief **69**
(USA) 122) [2004 7g p8m³ p8m² Dec 21] second foal: half-brother to 3-y-o Morag: dam
unraced half-sister to very smart performer up to 13f Water Jump: placed at Lingfield in
claimer and maiden (best effort when second to Humble Opinion): will probably stay
1¼m. *I. A. Wood*

MICKEY BOGGITT 2 b.g. (Feb 12) Mind Games 121 – Valldemosa 81 (Music Boy **–**
124) [2004 5m 7f Jun 8] close-coupled gelding: no form in maiden/seller. *A. Berry*

MICKEY PEARCE (IRE) 2 b.c. (Jan 30) Rossini (USA) 118 – Lucky Coin 73 **43**
(Hadeer 118) [2004 6f 6.1m 7d 7s Aug 20] close-coupled colt: poor maiden: best effort at
7f on soft going. *J. G. M. O'Shea*

MICKLEDO 2 b.c. (Apr 19) Perryston View 114 – Ever So Lonely 63 (Headin' Up) **54**
[2004 6s 5d Aug 15] leggy colt: better effort in maidens when ninth at Pontefract on final
start: bred to prove best at 5f/6f. *A. Bailey*

MICKLEDOR (FR) 4 ch.f. Lake Coniston (IRE) 131 – Shamasiya (FR) (Vayrann **60**
133) [2004 49: 6m 6m 5d³ 7.1f 6.1s* 6g* 6m 6m 6v³ 6g⁶ 7m⁵ 6d⁶ Sep 27] sparely-made
filly: modest handicapper: won seller at Nottingham and apprentice race at Hamilton,
both in July: stays 7f: acts on any going: wears headgear. *M. Dods*

MICKLEGATE 3 b.f. Dracula (AUS) 121 – Primulette 82 (Mummy's Pet 125) [2004 **59**
59: 6.9f⁴ 6.9g⁴ 7.5g 6.9m Sep 11] quite good-topped filly: modest maiden: will stay 1m:
acts on good to firm and good to soft ground: sold 1,300 gns. *J. D. Bethell*

MIDAS WAY 4 ch.g. Halling (USA) 133 – Arietta's Way (IRE) 71 (Darshaan 133) **100**
[2004 106: 13.4s² 14.6f 16.2m³ 18s Oct 16] rather leggy gelding: useful handicapper:
creditable efforts when placed at Chester and Ascot: ran poorly in Cesarewitch final start:
should stay beyond 2m: acts on good and soft going. *P. R. Chamings*

MIDCAP (IRE) 2 b.f. (Mar 9) Entrepreneur 123 – Tis Juliet (USA) (Alydar (USA)) **70**
[2004 6m 7m⁶ 7g 7.1m³ 7m⁶ Oct 1] tall, lengthy filly: half-sister to 3 winners abroad:
dam, US Grade 1 9f winner, out of champion US sprinter My Juliet: fair maiden: should
stay 1m: acts on good to firm going: flashed tail third appearance. *B. W. Hills*

MIDDLE EARTH (USA) 2 ch.c. (Feb 9) Dixieland Band (USA) – Lite Twilight **77**
(USA) (Twilight Agenda (USA) 126) [2004 5f² 6s p6g² Oct 13] $100,000Y: first foal:
dam minor sprint stakes winner in USA: fair form when second in maiden at Windsor and
minor event (tongue tied) at Lingfield: will stay 7f. *A. M. Balding*

MIDDLE EASTERN 2 b.c. (Mar 29) Mujahid (USA) 125 – Swissmatic 54 (Petong **63**
126) [2004 6d⁵ 6g⁴ 5g 6d Sep 17] 7,000F, €9,000Y, 11,000 2-y-o: big, leggy colt: third
foal: half-brother to 2002 2-y-o 5f seller winner Schematic (by Brief Truce): dam ran
4 times: modest maiden: fourth at Haydock, best effort: not sure to stay much beyond 6f.
P. A. Blockley

MIDDLEHAM PARK (IRE) 4 b.g. Revoque (IRE) 122 – Snap Crackle Pop (IRE) **59**
87 (Statoblest 120) [2004 68d: f8g² 7m 8g 12m p8.6d⁴ Nov 4] lengthy gelding: modest
maiden: best around 1m: acts on polytrack, raced only on good/good to firm ground on
turf. *P. C. Haslam*

MIDDLEHAM ROSE 3 b.f. Dr Fong (USA) 128 – Shallop 55 (Salse (USA) 128) **34**
[2004 –: f9.4g⁶ f8g⁶ f12g² 10f f12f⁵ Aug 20] tall filly: poor maiden: stays 1½m: acts on
fibresand: has been slowly away/carried head awkwardly. *P. C. Haslam*

MIDDLEMARCH (IRE) 4 ch.c. Grand Lodge (USA) 125 – Blanche Dubois (Nash- **106 ?**
wan (USA) 135) [2004 114: 8g 10g⁴ 10.4d 8.9m⁵ 8f Jun 27] tall, angular colt: smart
performer at 3 yrs in Ireland: A. O'Brien in Ireland: useful for present stable, running creditably
only when fifth to Krugerrand in handicap at York: stays 1¼m: acts on firm and good to
soft ground: often wears headgear. *J. S. Goldie*

MIDDLEMISS (IRE) 4 b.f. Midhish 109 – Teresa Deevey 50 (Runnett 125) [2004 –: **33**
10.2d p8g 7g² May 4] poor maiden: tried in cheekpieces. *J. W. Mullins*

MIDDLETHORPE 7 b.g. Noble Patriarch 115 – Prime Property (IRE) 60 (Tirol 127) **70**
[2004 74: 12g* 13.8g⁵ 14s⁶ 11.9g 11.9g Oct 8] rather sparely-made gelding: poor mover:
fair handicapper: won apprentice race at Doncaster (for second time in 3 years) in March:
effective at 1½m/1¾m: acts on heavy and good to firm going, below form on firm/fibre-
sand: blinkered: tends to wander: fairly useful hurdler. *M. W. Easterby*

MIDDLETON GREY 6 gr.g. Ashkalani (IRE) 128 – Petula 103 (Petong 126) [2004 **78**
74, a97: f9.4g f6s³ f7s² 7d 7.1g³ 7m⁵ 7.1d² 6g* 7d p6g* p6g³ p6g Dec 18] leggy gelding: **a99**
useful handicapper on all-weather, fair on turf: won twice at Newmarket in August and Wolverhampton in November: good third to Moayed at latter track penultimate start: effective
at 6f to 8.5f: acts on all-weather, unraced on extremes of going on turf: usually wears
headgear. *A. G. Newcombe*

MIDGES PRIDE 4 b.g. Puissance 110 – It's All Academic (IRE) 91 (Mazaad 106) **–**
[2004 51: f8g Feb 19] maiden: well held only outing in 2004: tried visored. *Mrs
A. Duffield*

MIDMAAR (IRE) 3 b.c. Cape Cross (IRE) 129 – Khazinat El Dar (USA) 78 (Slew **–**
O' Gold (USA)) [2004 86: f12m f8g p10d f8s Aug 23] well held in Britain. *M. Wigham*

MIDNIGHT ARROW 6 b.m. Robellino (USA) 127 – Princess Oberon (IRE) 91 **–**
(Fairy King (USA)) [2004 7.6g 6.9f f8g Dec 1] leggy, useful-looking mare: fairly useful
winner in 2000: lightly raced and no form since: blinkered once. *A. Berry*

MIDNIGHT BALLARD (USA) 3 b. or br.g. Mister Baileys 123 – Shadow Music **84 d**
(USA) (Shadeed (USA) 135) [2004 87: 6g⁶ 6d⁴ 7m² 7m 7f* 7m 6m p7g p6g Oct 16]
good-topped gelding: fairly useful performer: below form after third start, though won
maiden at Folkestone in June: likely to prove best at 6f/7f: acts on firm going: blinkered
(ran poorly) last 3 starts: sold 2,000 gns. *R. F. Johnson Houghton*

MIDNIGHT IN MOSCOW (IRE) 2 b.g. (Mar 18) Soviet Star (USA) 128 – Solar **–**
Display (Diesis 133) [2004 6m⁶ 6s Aug 18] good-bodied gelding: well held in
minor event/maidens: edgy, free-going sort. *P. C. Haslam*

MIDNIGHT LACE 2 ch.f. (Mar 20) Tomba 119 – Royal Passion 78 (Ahonoora 122) **65**
[2004 5m 6.1d 6.1m³ 6v p6g³ p7m⁴ p7g Dec 29] lengthy filly: seventh living foal: half-
sister to 3 winners, including 6f to 1¼m winner Attache (by Wolfhound), 7f winner at 2
yrs, and 5f (including at 2 yrs)/6f winner Tadeo (by Primo Dominie), both smart: dam
1¼m winner: fair maiden: likely to stay 1m: acts on polytrack and good to firm ground.
R. Hannon

MIDNIGHT MAMBO (USA) 4 b.f. Kingmambo (USA) 125 – Witching Hour (FR) **50**
(Fairy King (USA)) [2004 53+: f7g⁵ p10g⁵ f9.4g 8m 10.2s 9.7f² Sep 4] modest maiden:
stays 1¼m: acts on polytrack and good to firm ground: tried blinkered. *R. Guest*

MIDNIGHT PARKES 5 b. or br.g. Polar Falcon (USA) 126 – Summerhill Spruce 70 **78**
(Windjammer (USA)) [2004 80: 6d 6f⁴ 5g³ 5.5m⁵ 6g 6m³ 5g* 5g 6f 5f³ 5m 5f Oct
12] strong, lengthy gelding: type to carry condition: fair handicapper: won at Pontefract
in July: effective at 5f/6f: acts on firm and good to soft going: sometimes wears blinkers/
cheekpieces: usually races up with pace: none too consistent: sold 9,000 gns. *E. J. Alston*

MIDNIGHT PRINCE 3 b.g. Dracula (AUS) 121 – Phylian 77 (Glint of Gold 128) **49**
[2004 59: 7m⁶ 7.9f⁵ 9.9d Aug 11] good-topped gelding: has scope: fluent mover: poor
maiden: stays 1m: raced mainly on ground firmer than good. *M. W. Easterby*

MIDNIGHT PROMISE 3 b.g. Aragon 118 – Uninvited 73 (Be My Guest (USA) 126) **–**
[2004 f7g p7g Feb 18] well beaten in maidens at Southwell and Lingfield. *J. A. Glover*

MIDNIGHT TYCOON 2 b.g. (Feb 27) Marju (IRE) 127 – Midnight Allure 85 (Ara- **81**
gon 118) [2004 5d* 5m³ 6g⁴ 5s Jul 17] 7,000Y: rather leggy, useful-looking gelding: first
foal: dam, 1m winner, sister to smart sprinter Midnight Escape: fairly useful performer:
won maiden at Hamilton in May: in frame in minor events: ran as if amiss final start
(gelded after): probably stays 6f: acts on good to firm and good to soft going. *B. Smart*

MIDSHIPMAN 6 b.h. Executive Man 119 – Midler (Comedy Star (USA) 121) [2004 **71**
–: f8.5g p12g f12g 11.6d 16d 10s³ 10d 11.5f f8d² f8g² f12m² f8g⁴ 10.2s 8g⁶ p12.2g⁵
p9.5g* p12.2g⁵ p9.5g* p9.5g Dec 6] good-topped horse: fair handicapper: won at Wolverhampton in November and December: effective at 1m to 1½m: acts on all-weather and
soft ground: tried blinkered, usually visored/tongue tied. *A. W. Carroll*

MIDSHIPMAN EASY (USA) 3 ch.g. Irish River (FR) 131 – Winger 70 (In The **74 d**
Wings 128) [2004 –p: 10s³ 10s² 10d 12.3d 12d⁶ 10m 11.9s Oct 15] useful-looking
gelding: fair maiden: well below form after second start: should stay 1½m: acts on soft
ground: has been slowly away/looked wayward: sold 2,500 gns, sent to Holland.
P. W. Harris

MIGHTY EMPIRE (IRE) 2 b.c. (Feb 28) Second Empire (IRE) 124 – Barnabas **82**
(ITY) (Slip Anchor 136) [2004 6m 5g 7f⁴ 7m* 8m² 8m Sep 21] €15,000F, €7,000Y: quite
good-topped colt: third foal: dam unraced half-sister to Japanese St Leger winner That's
The Plenty: fairly useful performer: won nursery at Newmarket in August: good second
to Singhalese at Doncaster, better effort in similar races after: stays 1m: acts on good to
firm going: tends to race freely: sent to USA. *M. H. Tompkins*

MIGHTY MAX 6 b.g. Well Beloved 86 – Jokers High (USA) (Vaguely Noble 140) **–**
[2004 f16.2g Jan 9] poor maiden: stays 1¼m: tried tongue tied. *G. A. Ham*

MIGHTY MOVER (IRE) 2 ch.c. (Feb 22) Bahhare (USA) 122 – Ericeira (IRE) **50**
(Anita's Prince 126) [2004 p8.6g⁶ Dec 6] €3,000Y: first foal: dam unraced: 20/1, sixth in
maiden at Wolverhampton: held up and not knocked about. *B. Palling*

MIGHTY PIP (IRE) 8 b.g. Pips Pride 117 – Hard To Stop 77 (Hard Fought 125) [2004 **47**
57: 10.9d 10d⁵ p12.2g p9.5g Nov 15] poor performer: stays 11f: acts on polytrack, heavy
and good to firm going: tried blinkered/tongue tied: has been slowly away: usually held
up. *M. R. Bosley*

MIGRATION 8 b.g. Rainbow Quest (USA) 134 – Armeria (USA) 79 (Northern Dan- **–**
cer) [2004 49: 14.1s f16g 12.6g 10g Jul 16] tall gelding: no longer of much account on
Flat: fairly useful hurdler. *Mrs S. Lamyman*

MIJDAAF (FR) 3 b.c. Mtoto 134 – Zobaida (IRE) 77 (Green Desert (USA) 127) [2004 **82**
10m⁶ 10m² Jul 6] quite good-topped colt: second foal: dam, 7f winner who stayed 8.5f,
out of half-sister to Zilzal: fairly useful form in maidens: 3 lengths second to Apsara at
Pontefract: started slowly on debut. *A. C. Stewart*

MIKADO 3 b.c. Sadler's Wells (USA) 132 – Free At Last 115 (Shirley Heights 130) **121**
[2004 106p: 14m⁴ 12g⁴ 13.9s³ 14.6f⁵ 10d* Oct 2] smallish, quite attractive colt: very
smart performer: won listed race at the Curragh in October by 1½ lengths from Ecomium,

Stanleybet Diamond Stakes, the Curragh—Mikado holds off Ecomium in this listed event

making virtually all: had improved with each run earlier in the year, fourth to Mkuzi in Curragh Cup and to Maraahel in ABN Amro Stakes (Gordon) at Goodwood, third to Mephisto in Ebor Handicap at York (hung left/carried head high, beaten 2½ lengths) and fifth to Rule of Law in St Leger at Doncaster (beaten 2¾ lengths): reportedly sold privately after: needs good test at 1¼m and stays 14.6f: acts on firm and soft going: has worn crossed noseband and been attended by 2 handlers. *A. P. O'Brien, Ireland*

MIKAO (IRE) 3 b.g. Tagula (IRE) 116 – Oumaladia (IRE) 84 (Waajib 121) [2004 8m⁵ **85** 7.9m³ 10m² 10.5g⁴ p12g² 10d* Oct 4] 12,000F, €35,000Y: rather leggy, useful-looking gelding: second foal: dam Irish 1½m winner: fairly useful performer: didn't need to be at best when winning maiden at Windsor in October: stays 1½m: acts on polytrack, good to firm and good to soft ground. *M. H. Tompkins*

MIKASA (IRE) 4 b.g. Victory Note (USA) 120 – Resiusa (ITY) (Niniski (USA) 125) **41** [2004 –: f7g p12g 12d 12d³ 11m f8.5m 10.9d⁵ 17.2g 12m 15g 15.8m⁶ Aug 3] tall, quite good-topped gelding: poor maiden: stays 1½m: tried in blinkers/cheekpieces. *R. F. Fisher*

MIKES MATE 3 b.g. Komaite (USA) – Pitcairn Princess (Capricorn Line 111) [2004 **–** –: 7d 9g 11.9d f8g Dec 16] rather unfurnished gelding: no sign of ability. *C. J. Teague*

MILITARY TWO STEP (IRE) 3 b.g. General Monash (USA) 107 – Con Dancer **–** (Shareef Dancer (USA) 135) [2004 63: 8.2g 8.2s 7s 7m 7d 7d Oct 16] sturdy gelding: little form in 2004: sometimes wears cheekpieces: sold 500 gns, sent to Denmark. *K. R. Burke*

MILK AND SULTANA 4 b.f. Millkom 124 – Premier Princess 45 (Hard Fought **67** 125) [2004 62, a67: 8.1d 10.2m⁶ 12.6f 12.6g 11.7g² 12.1m 11.6f² 12.3s⁴ 10.5g* 10.3g* 10d⁴ 9.9g p12.2g³ 11.7g p13.9g p12g Nov 16] fair handicapper: left W. M. Brisbourne after reappearance: won at Haydock (amateur event) and Chester in September: stays easy 1½m: acts on all-weather and firm going, probably good to soft. *G. A. Ham*

MILK IT MICK 3 b.c. Millkom 124 – Lunar Music 67 (Komaite (USA)) [2004 120: **112** p8g² 7g⁵ 8g 6g³ 7.6g³ 8f² Sep 10] big, good-topped colt: impresses in appearance: smart performer: won Dewhurst Stakes at Newmarket at 2 yrs: best efforts in 2004 when second in listed race at Lingfield (beaten 1¼ lengths by Leitrim House) and minor event at Doncaster (went down by ½ length to Secret Charm): stays easy 1m: acts on polytrack, firm and good to soft going: edgy sort, and sometimes has 2 handlers in paddock (wore net muzzle and sweating when only eighth in 2000 Guineas at Newmarket third outing): free-going sort, best held up: reportedly finished distressed fifth outing. *J. A. Osborne*

MILLAFONIC 4 b.c. Zafonic (USA) 130 – Milligram 130 (Mill Reef (USA) 141) **101** [2004 97: 10m⁶ 10m 10d 10v 8s⁴ 10.6d* Dec 11] useful-looking colt: useful performer: good sixth to Blue Spinnaker at Redcar on reappearance: below best next 3 starts, then sold from L. Cumani 25,000 gns: won minor event at Marseilles Vivaux in December: stays 10.6f: acts on good to firm and good to soft going: visored third start. *T Clout, France*

MILLAGROS (IRE) 4 b.f. Pennekamp (USA) 130 – Grey Galava 64 (Generous **82** (IRE) 139) [2004 86+: 8.3d 10m⁴ 8m⁴ 9.1d⁶ 9.2g³ 9.3f³ 8s* 8m³ 8g³ 10s⁴ p8.6g p9.5g Nov 13] lengthy, good-bodied filly: fairly useful performer: won minor event at Ayr in August: effective at 1m/1¼m: acts on firm and soft going: visored/in cheekpieces last 7 starts: has hung left: sometimes finds little. *I. Semple*

MILLBAG (IRE) 3 b. or br.cc. Cape Cross (IRE) 129 – Play With Fire (FR) (Priolo **105** (USA) 127) [2004 98: 6s* 6m 5f⁵ Jun 27] good-bodied colt: has a quick action: useful performer: won listed event at Ascot in April by 3 lengths from Moonlight Man: below form in similar events after: stays 7f: acts on firm and soft going: usually races up with pace: joined D. Selvaratnam in UAE. *M. R. Channon*

MILL BY THE STREAM 2 b.g. (Mar 6) Lujain (USA) 119 – Lonesome 60 (Night **58** Shift (USA)) [2004 6g 5m 6f 8f⁶ 6g 6d p8g² p7.1g Dec 6] close-coupled gelding: modest maiden: easily best effort when second in seller at Lingfield, making running: stays 1m: acts on polytrack: visored last 3 starts. *A. P. Jarvis*

MILL EMERALD 7 b.m. Old Vic 136 – Milinetta (Milford 119) [2004 f14g Jan 20] **–** no longer of any account on Flat. *Mrs G. Harvey*

MILLEMIX (FR) 3 gr.c. Linamix (FR) 127 – Milesime (USA) (Riverman (USA) 131) **119** [2004 102p: 10.5g² 10.5g* 10.5g² May 16] half-brother to several winners in France, including smart 1m (at 2 yrs) to 1½m winner Mayaro (by Saumarez): dam, French 9f and 1¼m winner, half-sister to very smart 1m/9f performer In Extremis and 1998 Prix Marcel Boussac winner Juvenia: smart performer: successful twice at 2 yrs, including in listed race at Fontainebleau: beaten a head by Prospect Park in similar event at Longchamp on reappearance: won Prix Greffulhe there in April by 2 lengths from demoted Esperanto: best effort when beaten a nose by Voix du Nord in Prix Lupin on same course: would have stayed 1½m: acted on soft ground: put down after reportedly fracturing off-hind later in May. *Mme C. Head-Maarek, France*

MILLENARY   7 b.h. Rainbow Quest (USA) 134 – Ballerina (IRE) 88 (Dancing   **121**
Brave (USA) 140) [2004 121: 16.2s³ 13.9d* 15.9d³ 18m* 16s* Oct 16]
    The 2004 season was disappointing overall for the John Dunlop stable, and it would have been even worse but for the oldest horse in the yard Millenary. The 2000 St Leger winner was just about as good as ever at the age of seven and he took his total of pattern-race victories to nine with outright wins in the Yorkshire and Jockey Club Cups and a dead heat in the Doncaster Cup. In each of those races Millenary was ridden by Richard Quinn, renewing the partnership following the retirement of Pat Eddery. Quinn had been successful on the only occasions he had ridden Millenary prior to 2004, in the Gordon Stakes and the St Leger. Both jockeys have won five races each on Millenary, Eddery's wins including those in the Jockey Club Stakes in 2001 and the Princess of Wales's Stakes in 2002 and 2003. Millenary gave Quinn and Eddery the opportunity to display their skills on a horse who is by no means a straightforward ride. Millenary travels strongly but doesn't always find as much as expected, and is best produced as late as possible.
    Following an encouraging reappearance in gruelling conditions in the Sagaro Stakes at Ascot, Millenary lined up for the Emirates Airline Yorkshire Cup re-equipped with blinkers, which he had worn twice the previous season, including when successful. Of his nine opponents, seven had won pattern races, the 2003 Gold Cup winner Mr Dinos amongst them. Whereas the steady gallop didn't suit Mr Dinos, it played into Quinn's hands on Millenary, who produced easily the best finishing speed to win by three lengths from Alcazar, Quinn taking a pull to ensure that his mount, who had been travelling best from a long way out, didn't hit the front too soon. Millenary also wore blinkers on his three subsequent starts, the first of which was the Lonsdale Cup, also at York. With Quinn out through injury, Michael Kinane came in for the mount on Millenary, who looked the likely winner when the race began in earnest, only to find little off the bridle and finish third behind First Charter and Dancing Bay, beaten a neck and three lengths. With Quinn back on board, Millenary turned the tables on Dancing Bay in both the Doncaster and Jockey Club Cups, the latter finishing third and fourth respectively. In the GNER Doncaster Cup Millenary was the only runner able to make significant headway from the rear in a race which came down to a test of finishing speed. Millenary did well to peg back Kasthari after the latter got first run when sent to the front over two furlongs out, and Quinn resisted the temptation to go for the whip as the pair pulled clear. Kasthari rallied gamely, but Millenary, ridden vigorously with hands and heels, found enough to force a dead heat. Millenary and Kasthari met again in the Persian Punch Jockey Club Cup, a race renamed in honour of the horse who won it for a third time when beating Millenary a short head in the 2003 renewal. Kasthari, a close third that day, finished last of eleven in the latest running whereas Millenary, showing no signs of his exertions at Doncaster, gave a very smooth performance in winning by a length and a quarter from Franklins Gardens, asked for his effort running into the Dip and soon settling matters. This success, which ended a losing run of forty-eight for the Dunlop stable, took Millenary's win prize

Emirates Airline Yorkshire Cup, York—Millenary has quickened clear of Alcazar and Jelani

*Persian Punch Jockey Club Cup, Newmarket—Millenary wins his ninth pattern race with a typical display;
the others in the photo (from left to right) are Gold Medallist (fifth),
Franklins Gardens (second) and Dancing Bay (fourth)*

money earnings to close to £600,000. With a stud career having been put off for
another year, he will surely be adding to that in 2005.

Millenary (b.h. 1997)	Rainbow Quest (USA) (b 1981)	Blushing Groom (ch 1974)	Red God, Runaway Bride
		I Will Follow (b 1975)	Herbager, Where You Lead
	Ballerina (IRE) (b 1991)	Dancing Brave (b 1983)	Lyphard, Navajo Princess
		Dancing Shadow (b 1977)	Dancer's Image, Sunny Valley

Millenary's half-brother and stable-companion Let The Lion Roar (by
Sadler's Wells) also showed very smart form in the latest season and finished third
in the Derby, though he failed miserably when attempting to emulate Millenary
in the St Leger. Let The Lion Roar, like Millenary, is not a straightforward ride, and
wore a visor on his last four starts. Their dam Ballerina, who gained her sole success
in two seasons' racing in a seven-furlong maiden on her only start at two, is also
responsible for the smart Head In The Clouds, a full sister to Millenary who won
the Princess Royal Stakes. Millenary, a good walker and a fluent mover in his faster
paces, hasn't encountered heavy ground, but he has shown himself fully effective
on any other turf surface. A leggy, attractive horse, he stays two and a quarter miles,
at least when conditions aren't testing. He may be found wanting for stamina should
connections ever give him the opportunity to tackle two and a half miles in the Gold
Cup. *J. L. Dunlop*

MILL END CHATEAU 2 ch.g. (May 18) Paris House 123 – Mill End Quest 65 – (King's Signet (USA) 110) [2004 5m 6m Jun 11] leggy, lengthy gelding: reportedly lost action when well held in maiden/seller. *M. W. Easterby*

MILL END TEASER 3 b.f. Mind Games 121 – Mill End Quest 65 (King's Signet – (USA) 110) [2004 40: f5g Feb 2] lengthy, good-topped filly: poor maiden: raced only at 5f on fibresand/good going or firmer: tried blinkered: has looked none too keen. *M. W. Easterby*

MILLENIO (GER) 4 ch.g. Big Shuffle (USA) 122 – Molto In Forma (GER) (Surumu 75 (GER)) [2004 a7.5g³ a5.5g³ a5.5g³ 7s⁶ p8d² f8d Jun 17] won maiden at Dresden and handicap at Neuss in 2003: left C. Von Der Recke in Germany, fair form when second in minor event at Lingfield on debut in Britain: virtually refused to race subsequent outing: stays 1m: joined Gay Kelleway, and gelded. *D. Flood*

MILLENNIUM FORCE 6 b.g. Bin Ajwaad (IRE) 119 – Jumairah Sun (IRE) 98 111 (Scenic 128) [2004 115: 7.1g 7.9s 7.1g⁴ 7g² 7g³ 7f³ 7g 8.1g 7d⁴ 7m 7.5v⁵ 7s² 6s² Nov 6] tall, lengthy gelding: smart performer: nearly as good as ever in 2004, running well when second in Prix de La Porte Maillot at Longchamp (beaten short head by Charming

646

Groom) and listed event at Doncaster (beaten 1¼ lengths by Quito) on fourth/final starts, and 2 lengths third to Trade Fair in Minstrel Stakes at the Curragh on sixth: effective at 6f to 1m: visored (ran well) once at 3 yrs: usually held up: sometimes wanders. *M. R. Channon*

MILLENNIUM HALL 5 b.g. Saddlers' Hall (IRE) 126 – Millazure (USA) 71 (Day-jur (USA) 137) [2004 66: 9.2g 8.3g⁶ 12.4s³ 13g³ 12.1m* 13m* 11.9g 11.9g⁶ 13g⁶ 9.2d 13d⁶ 14g 16g⁶ Sep 13] leggy gelding: has a quick action: fair handicapper: won twice at Hamilton in June: stays 13f: acts on any ground: tried in cheekpieces at 4 yrs: usually waited with. *P. Monteith* **69**

MILLER HILL 2 b.g. (Apr 9) Prince Sabo 123 – Atlantic Heiress (Thowra (FR)) [2004 5v f6g² 5g 7d⁶ 8s Aug 26] 2,800F, 2,200Y: leggy gelding: half-brother to winning sprinter in Italy by Great Dane: dam unraced: modest maiden: second in seller at Southwell: left M. Easterby after next start: stays 7f. *J. Naouri, Netherlands* **64**

MILLFIELDS DREAMS 5 b.g. Dreams End 93 – Millfields Lady 75 (Sayf El Arab (USA) 127) [2004 55?: 6.1m* 6g 7.1g 6m 6f 5.7m⁶ 6.1g 8.1m 5m 7.1d⁵ Oct 9] fair performer: won handicap at Chepstow in June: below form after: stays 6f: acts on good to firm going: wore cheekpieces final outing. *R. Brotherton* **65**

MILLIETOM (IRE) 3 b.g. General Monash (USA) 107 – June Lady (Junius (USA) 124) [2004 –: f5g Feb 8] no form: tried in cheekpieces/blinkers. *K. A. Ryan* **–**

MILLINSKY (USA) 3 ch.f. Stravinsky (USA) 133 – Millyant 114 (Primo Dominie 121) [2004 5m⁶ 5.2m³ 5m² 5g³ 6m² Sep 27] rather leggy, lengthy filly: fourth foal: half-sister to 4-y-o Millybaa: dam, 5f performer, half-sister to very smart sprinter Prince Sabo: fair maiden: stays 6f. *R. Guest* **68**

MILLIONAIA (IRE) 3 b.f. Peintre Celebre (USA) 137 – Moonlight Dance (USA) 111 (Alysheba (USA)) [2004 10.5g² 10.5s² 10s* 10.5g² Jun 13] fifth foal: half-sister to smart French 1999 2-y-o 1m winner Memory Maker (by Lure) and to French 1¼m winner Memoire (by Sadler's Wells): dam, won Prix Saint-Alary, out of high-class French filly Madelia: smart form: won minor event at Chantilly in May: considerable improvement when ¾-length second to Latice in Prix de Diane there final start, improving to have every chance 1f out: stays good around 1¼m. *E. Lellouche, France* **119**

MILLION PERCENT 5 b.g. Ashkalani (IRE) 128 – Royal Jade 82 (Last Tycoon 131) [2004 91: 6g 6m⁶ 6m² 6m² 6m⁶ 6d⁶ 6d p6g⁴ p6m² Dec 21] small, strong gelding: fairly useful performer: second in minor events at Doncaster and Newmarket and handicap at Lingfield: best at 6f/easy 7f: acts on polytrack, firm and soft going: tried in cheekpieces/visor: has been slowly away. *K. R. Burke* **86**

MILLKOM ELEGANCE 5 b.m. Millkom 124 – Premier Princess 45 (Hard Fought 125) [2004 48: 12m 8d³ 8f p12.2g³ f11d Dec 21] small, quite good-topped mare: poor performer: left K. Ryan after third start: stays easy 1½m: acts on polytrack, firm and good to soft going: blinkered/visored last 6 starts. *G. A. Ham* **45**

MILLQUISTA D'OR 2 b.f. (May 15) Millkom 124 – Gild The Lily 83 (Ile de Bour-bon (USA) 133) [2004 8m p8.6g p9.5g p8.6g⁶ Nov 26] 4,000 2-y-o: half-sister to 1½m winner Ronquista d'Or (by Ron's Victory) and winner in Greece by Environment Friend: dam 9f and (in Ireland) 1½m winner who seemed to stay 2m: poor maiden: best effort at 8.6f. *G. A. Ham* **44**

MILLSTREET 5 ch.g. Polish Precedent (USA) 131 – Mill Path (Mill Reef (USA) 141) [2004 111: 12m 10.4d⁵ 10m Sep 11] leggy gelding: smart performer: ran creditably in 2004 only when 7¼ lengths fifth to stable-companion Sulamani in International Stakes at York: stays 1½m: acts on firm and good to soft going: tongue tied nowadays: often makes running/acts as pacemaker. *Saeed bin Suroor* **112**

MILLVILLE 4 ch.g. Millkom 124 – Miss Top Ville (FR) (Top Ville 129) [2004 p10g* p7g p12g* p13g* 12g 12f⁵ 11.9d⁴ 14g⁵ 12g 12s² 12s Nov 6] tall, leggy gelding: fairly useful performer: won maiden and 2 handicaps at Lingfield in January/March: good second to Tempsford in handicap at Doncaster: stays 1¾m: acts on polytrack, firm and soft going: held up. *M. A. Jarvis* **92**

MILLYBAA (USA) 4 b.f. Anabaa (USA) 130 – Millyant 114 (Primo Dominie 121) [2004 105: 6d² 6.1d⁴ 5g 6d 6g⁴ 6d 6s 6s Nov 6] lengthy, quite good-topped filly: useful performer: short-head second to Abunawwas in listed race at Naas on reappearance: below form after, mostly in similar events: stays 6f: acts on soft ground: has been blanketed for stall entry: blinkered (well held) penultimate start. *R. Guest* **100 d**

*Royal Hunt Cup (Handicap), Royal Ascot—heads and short heads separate the first five;
from the far side they are Amandus (fourth), Camp Commander (fifth), Zonergem (third),
Mine (first) and Able Baker Charlie (second)*

MILLY GOLIGHTLY 3 b.f. Mind Games 121 – Milliscent 49 (Primo Dominie 121) –
[2004 8d 10.1m⁶ 7f Jun 15] 10,000Y: leggy filly: first foal: dam, maiden who stayed 1m,
half-sister to useful sprinter Amber Mill: well held in maidens. *M. Dods*

MILLY'S LASS 6 b.m. Mind Games 121 – Millie's Lady (IRE) (Common Grounds – §
118) [2004 39§: f5g Jan 5] sparely-made mare: poor performer: effective at 5f/6f: acts on
all-weather and any turf going: tried in cheekpieces/blinkers: unreliable. *J. M. Bradley*

MILLY WATERS 3 b.f. Danzero (AUS) – Chilly Waters (Polar Falcon (USA) 126) 87 ?
[2004 88: 8g⁵ p8g⁵ p8.6g Nov 8] tall, leggy filly: fairly useful performer: off nearly 12
months before reappearance (suffered lung infection): form in 2004 only when fifth
to Miss George in listed race at Lingfield: probably stays 1m: acts on all-weather and
good to firm ground: has run well when sweating: game: joined M. de Kock in UAE.
W. M. Brisbourne

MIMAS GIRL 5 b.m. Samim (USA) 84 – Cocked Hat Girl 47 (Ballacashtal (CAN)) 37
[2004 43: f6g⁵ f6g f8.5g⁵ f6g³ f8g f8g p7g f7g³ f7g⁶ Apr 16] poor maiden: effective at 6f
to 1m: acts on fibresand and firm ground: tried in blinkers/cheekpieces: usually tongue
tied. *S. R. Bowring*

MIMIC 4 b.f. Royal Applause 124 – Stripanoora (Ahonoora 122) [2004 83: 6d 5.7f 6m 74
6m 6d* 5.1g⁵ 6f 6g p6g³ p7g p6g Nov 27] angular filly: fair handicapper: won apprentice
event at Salisbury in August: best at 6f: acts on polytrack, good to firm and good to soft
ground: usually races up with pace. *R. Guest*

MIMI MOUSE 2 br.f. (Mar 17) Diktat 126 – Shifty Mouse 44 (Night Shift (USA)) 89
[2004 5s⁶ 6m⁴ 5m³ 5m* 5f* 6m 5d Sep 17] 14,000Y: smallish, close-coupled filly: third
foal: half-sister to winner in Hungary by Eagle Eyed: dam, ran twice at 2 yrs, out of sister
to Nassau and Musidora Stakes winner Triple First: fairly useful performer: won maiden
at Pontefract in June and nursery at York in July, hanging right: had excuses in sales race/
listed event after: will prove best at 5f/easy 6f: acts on firm ground: sometimes on toes/
early to post: races up with pace. *T. D. Easterby*

MINA ALSALAAM 2 b.f. (Feb 2) Lujain (USA) 119 – Rain And Shine (FR) 78 (Rain- –
bow Quest (USA) 134) [2004 6.1d 6f Aug 1] fourth foal: half-sister to 5-y-o Jadeeron:
dam, Irish 1½m winner who stayed 2m, out of sister to dam of Dubai Millennium: well
beaten in maidens: sold 800 gns. *M. R. Channon*

MIND ALERT 3 b.g. Mind Games 121 – Bombay Sapphire (Be My Chief (USA) 122) 70
[2004 73: 6m 6m² 6g 7f 6s 5m 7d⁵ p7g* p8.6g⁵ p7.1g⁴ p7g Dec 30] good-topped gelding:
fair handicapper: left T. Easterby after sixth start: won apprentice event at Lingfield in

648

October: effective at 6f/7f: acts on polytrack, good to firm and good to soft ground: tried in blinkers/cheekpieces, better form without. *Miss J. A. Camacho*

MINDFUL   2 b.c. (Mar 15) Mind Games 121 – Blushing Victoria 74 (Weldnaas (USA) 112) [2004 5g f5g⁶ f6d 5d Aug 31] good-topped colt: poor maiden: signs of temperament. *M. J. Polglase*   **36**

MIND PLAY   3 b.f. Mind Games 121 – Diplomatist 69 (Dominion 123) [2004 –: f8s⁶ f11g Feb 17] small filly: little form: tried blinkered. *M. E. Sowersby*   **–**

MINDSET (IRE)   3 b.f. Vettori (IRE) 119 – Eden (IRE) 88 (Polish Precedent (USA) 131) [2004 78: 7d 8s 8s 8s Nov 27] leggy, angular filly: well held in 2004, leaving L. Cumani after reappearance. *C. Laffon-Parias, France*   **–**

MIND THE TIME   3 b.g. Mind Games 121 – Rare Indigo 80 (Timeless Times (USA) 99) [2004 –: f6g f6s⁶ f5g⁶ 5f Jul 21] bad performer. *J. Hetherton*   **28**

MINE BEHIND   4 b.g. Sheikh Albadou 128 – Arapi (IRE) 89 (Arazi (USA) 135) [2004 84: 6s⁴ 6g⁶ 6m² 6m² 5m 6m 6m 5.7g⁴ 6f 6g 6m 5.2g⁵ 5g⁴ 6g 5d⁴ p6g⁵ Dec 4] lengthy gelding: useful handicapper: won at Windsor (apprentices) in April, Bath in July and Yarmouth in September: effective at 5f/6f: acts on polytrack, firm and soft going: tried in cheekpieces. *J. R. Best*   **95**

MINE (IRE)   6 b.h. Primo Dominie 121 – Ellebanna 69 (Tina's Pet 121) [2004 111: 8s² 7.9s³ 7m* 8f* 8.1d⁵ 8f² 7s 8f⁵ 7m³ Sep 25] tall, useful-looking horse: smart handicapper: won totesport Victoria Cup at Ascot (beat Greenslades by ¾ length) in May and Royal Hunt Cup at Royal Ascot (by head from Able Baker Charlie) in June: good efforts in handicaps last 2 starts, fifth to Calcutta at Doncaster and third to Kehaar at Ascot: effective at 7f/1m: acts on firm and soft going, possibly not on heavy: usually visored: waited with, and travels strongly: tough and reliable, and a credit to connections. *J. D. Bethell*   **116**

MINEKO   2 b.f. (Apr 15) Nashwan (USA) 135 – Musetta (IRE) 107 (Cadeaux Genereux 131) [2004 7d Oct 30] fifth foal: half-sister to 3-y-o Meissen and 2001 2-y-o 6f winner Mameyuki (by Zafonic), both fairly useful: dam 7f (at 2 yrs) and 1¼m winner who was fourth in Oaks: 33/1, eighth to Read Federica in maiden at Newmarket, not knocked about: should be suited by 1¼m/1½m: likely to do better. *E. F. Vaughan*   **69 p**

MINERAL STAR (IRE)   2 b.c. (Apr 3) Monashee Mountain (USA) 115 – Summit Talk (Head For Heights 125) [2004 7m 7.9g³ Oct 9] €5,500F, €13,000Y: eighth foal: half-brother to 3 winners, including 1m/1¼m winner Talk Back (by Bob Back): dam Irish 7.5f winner: much better effort in maidens when third to Mister Genepi at York: not sure to stay much beyond 1m. *M. H. Tompkins*   **75**

MING THE MERCILESS   4 b.g. Hector Protector (USA) 124 – Sundae Girl (USA) 75 (Green Dancer (USA) 132) [2004 –: f8g⁵ f11g⁶ Jan 15] big, strong gelding: maiden: little form since 2 yrs: tried blinkered. *J. G. Given*   **–**

MINGUN (USA)   4 b. or br.c. A P Indy (USA) 131 – Miesque (USA) 133 (Nureyev (USA) 131) [2004 117: 10d³ 10s 8.5f⁴ Nov 27] tall, angular, quite good-topped colt: smart performer, lightly raced: off over a year, respectable efforts when 3 lengths third to Mikado in listed race at the Curragh on October and 2 lengths fourth to Leroidesanimaux in Citation Handicap at Hollywood (started slowly and pulled hard) in November: dropped away tamely in Champion Stakes at Newmarket in between: stays 10.4f: probably acts on any going. *A. P. O'Brien, Ireland*   **114**

MING VASE   2 b.c. (Apr 12) Vettori (IRE) 119 – Minstrel's Dance (CAN) (Pleasant Colony (USA)) [2004 5v⁶ f7g² f7m⁵ 6s⁶ 8s 6g⁵ 6d³ Oct 18] 4,200F, 8,000Y: strong colt: third foal: half-brother to winner in Scandinavia by Green Dancer: dam unraced: modest maiden: stays 7f: acts on fibresand and good to soft going: carried head awkwardly final start. *D. Carroll*   **62**

MINIBULE (FR)   4 ch.f. Funambule (USA) 118 – Mipour (FR) (Shakapour 125) [2004 10.8g 16g 12g 11.5g 12g* f12d Dec 21] 20,000 francs Y: half-sister to French winner around 1½m Aucarque (by Easter Sun): dam French 11f/1½m winner: fair performer: successful 3 times in France, including in claimer at Saint-Cloud in May, then left Mme C. Barande Barbe: well held in claimer at Southwell final outing: stays 13f: acts on good to soft going: was usually blinkered in France. *N. Wilson*   **73**

MINIMUM BID   3 b.f. First Trump 118 – La Noisette (Rock Hopper 124) [2004 61: 5m 5g 5g² 6m p5g² 6m 7m Sep 9] modest maiden handicapper: should stay 6f: raced only on polytrack/good ground or firmer. *Miss B. Sanders*   **58**

MINIRINA   4 b.f. Mistertopogigo (IRE) 118 – Fabulous Rina (FR) (Fabulous Dancer (USA) 124) [2004 64d: f5s f5g⁴ f5g⁴ f5m 5g p5.1g Dec 20] leggy filly: poor maiden: **33**

raced only at 5f: acts on fibresand, good to firm and good to soft going: tried blinkered: unreliable. *C. Smith*

MINIVET 9 b.g. Midyan (USA) 124 – Bronzewing 103 (Beldale Flutter (USA) 130) **63** [2004 63: f16g 12f⁵ 13d⁴ 14g* 12d Nov 3] workmanlike gelding: modest handicapper: left T. Easterby after second outing: won at Musselburgh in September: effective at 1¼m to 2m: acts on soft and good to firm going: tried blinkered: often slowly away/held up: none too reliable. *R. Allan*

MINK MITTEN 2 b.f. (Apr 23) Polish Precedent (USA) 131 – Trefoil (FR) (Blakeney — 126) [2004 7m 7m Oct 10] 9,000Y: close-coupled, useful-looking filly: half-sister to several winners, including 4-y-o Anak Pekan and useful 1½m winner Firecrest (by Darshaan): dam, French 10.5f to 1½m winner, half-sister to dam of Melbourne Cup winner Jeune: tongue tied, only a little sign of ability in maidens at Newmarket and Newcastle (possibly amiss). *D. J. Daly*

MINNESINGER 2 b.f. (Apr 15) Fraam 114 – Rose Alto 98 (Adonijah 126) [2004 8s — Oct 22] 2,200Y, resold €6,500Y: half-sister to useful 10.5f and 1½m winner Musician (by Shirley Heights): dam 1¼m to 11.5f winner: 80/1 and very green, well held in maiden at Doncaster. *R. M. Beckett*

MINNESOTA (USA) 2 ch.c. (Apr 20) Silver Hawk (USA) 123 – Coco (USA) 105 **78 +** (Storm Bird (CAN) 134) [2004 5.7f² 7m* 8g³ 7.1g³ Sep 15] first foal: dam 1m winner, later successful in USA: fair performer: won maiden at Lingfield in July: not-knocked-about third in listed race at Salisbury (last to Perfectperformance, probably bit flattered) and minor event at Sandown: should stay 1¼m: acts on firm going: usually races prominently: sent to Barbados. *H. Candy*

MINORITY REPORT 4 b.g. Rainbow Quest (USA) 134 – Queen Sceptre (IRE) 97 **81** (Fairy King (USA)) [2004 8.1g³ 8.2g 8.1m² 11.7m Aug 15] stocky gelding, type to carry condition: best effort in maidens when head second to Serre Chevalier at Sandown: neither placed to challenge nor knocked about in ladies handicap at Bath subsequent outing (reportedly lost a shoe and badly bruised a foot): should be suited by 1¼m+: sold 30,000 gns in October. *L. M. Cumani*

MINSTREL HALL 5 b.m. Saddlers' Hall (IRE) 126 – Mindomica 63 (Dominion **55** 123) [2004 12d⁴ 10g⁵ 10g Jul 20] tall mare: modest performer: stays 1½m: acts on heavy and good to firm going. *P. Monteith*

MINSTREL'S DOUBLE 3 ch.g. Jumbo Hirt (USA) 90§ – Hand On Heart (IRE) 62 — (Taufan (USA) 119) [2004 6.9f⁵ 12.3d Aug 30] sturdy gelding: well held in 2 maidens. *F. P. Murtagh*

MINTLAW 2 b.f. (Feb 11) Mujahid (USA) 125 – Rynavey 67 (Rousillon (USA) 133) **80 p** [2004 6g² 8s⁶ 7.1d* Nov 3] half-sister to several winners, including useful performer up to 9f in Scandinavia Dipple (by Komaite), 6f winner in Britain at 2 yrs: dam, middle-distance maiden, half-sister to smart middle-distance stayer Applecross, herself dam of Invermark and Craigsteel: best effort in maidens when winning at Musselburgh by 3½ lengths from Consider This, leading 1f out and wandering: likely to prove best up to 1m: should progress. *I. Semple*

MI ODDS 8 b.g. Sure Blade (USA) 130 – Vado Via 56 (Ardross 134) [2004 55, a99: **?** f8.5g* f8.5s⁵ p10g 10.3g 10.5m 10.5d 11.5g f5s p12.2g p9.5g Dec 31] tall gelding: useful **a102** on all-weather, modest on turf: won minor event at Wolverhampton in January by 4 lengths from Countrywide Flyer: good fifth to Vortex in handicap on same course: mostly well held after: effective at 8.5f to 1½m: acts on fibresand and good to firm going: tried in cheekpieces at 7 yrs. *Mrs N. Macauley*

MIRACLE BABY 2 b.f. (Jun 5) Atraf 116 – Musica 82 (Primo Dominie 121) [2004 **51 p** 6.1v Nov 4] strong filly: fifth foal: half-sister to fairly useful 2-y-o 5f winners Coco de Mer (in 1999, by Prince Sabo) and Piccatune (in 2002, by Piccolo): dam 5f winner, including at 2 yrs: 40/1, backward and green, seventh in maiden at Nottingham: should do better. *G. B. Balding*

MIRAGE PRINCE (IRE) 2 ch.g. (Apr 20) Desert Prince (IRE) 130 – Belle Bijou **65** 61 (Midyan (USA) 124) [2004 5d⁶ 6m 7.1m⁶ 7.5m⁵ 7.6g⁴ 7.1g Aug 30] 100,000Y: rather leggy gelding: third living foal: dam, 1¼m winner who stayed 13f, half-sister to high-class 1m/1¼m performer Bijou d'Inde: fair maiden: will stay at least 1m: acts on good to firm ground. *W. M. Brisbourne*

MIRASOL PRINCESS 3 ch.f. Ali-Royal (IRE) 127 – Yanomami (USA) 71 (Slew **80** O' Gold (USA)) [2004 83: 6g 5g 5.1f⁴ 5m⁶ 5g⁶ p6g⁶ 5.1m⁴ 5m 5m* 5s 5g³ 5m p5g⁶ p6g⁶ p5g³ p6m Dec 21] smallish filly: fairly useful handicapper: won at Windsor in August: effective at 5f/6f: acts on polytrack and good to firm going. *D. K. Ivory*

John Smith's Northumberland Plate (Handicap), Newcastle—the first three are always to the fore; Mirjan (nearest camera) lands this very valuable prize from Swing Wing and Anak Pekan (rail)

MIRJAN (IRE) 8 b.g. Tenby 125 – Mirana (IRE) (Ela-Mana-Mou 132) [2004 16g³ **98** 16.1s* 18s Oct 16] small, sturdy gelding: useful performer: trained by L. Cumani as 3-y-o, only previous year of racing on Flat: won John Smith's Northumberland Plate at Newcastle in June by head from Swing Wing: good seventh in Cesarewitch at Newmarket final outing: barely stays 2¼m: acts on soft and good to firm going: blinkered last 2 starts (usually wears headgear over hurdles). *L. Lungo*

MISARO (GER) 3 b.g. Acambaro (GER) 118 – Misniniski (Niniski (USA) 125) [2004 **80** 80: 5v 7.5m⁵ 7d⁶ 6d² 6d⁴ 5d p7.1g p6g* Dec 17] leggy gelding: fairly useful performer: visored, won seller at Wolverhampton in December: best around 6f: acts on polytrack and good to soft going: races up with pace. *P. A. Blockley*

MISBEHAVIOUR 5 b.g. Tragic Role (USA) – Exotic Forest 66 (Dominion 123) [2004 **–** –: p7g p8g p10g Mar 2] leggy gelding: maiden: well held all 4 outings since 2002: tried in cheekpieces/visor. *P. Butler*

MIS CHICAF (IRE) 3 b.f. Prince Sabo 123 – Champagne Season (USA) 54 (Vaguely **101** Noble 140) [2004 70: 6d² 6m* 6m* 6m Jun 12] strong, workmanlike filly: useful handicapper: won at Doncaster and York (clearly best effort, beat Bridgewater Boys impressively by 7 lengths) in May: stays 6f: acts on good to firm and good to soft going: races prominently. *J. S. Wainwright*

MISCHIEF 8 ch.g. Generous (IRE) 139 – Knight's Baroness 116 (Rainbow Quest **– §** (USA) 134) [2004 44§: 12.3m 14.1m Aug 4] compact gelding: unreliable handicapper: well held in 2004: sometimes blinkered/visored: has looked reluctant: unreliable. *K. Bell*

MISHAP 2 b.f. (Apr 20) Mark of Esteem (IRE) 137 – Classic Colleen (IRE) 79 (Sadler's **–** Wells (USA) 132) [2004 8d Oct 16] 16,000F, 5,000Y: fifth foal: half-sister to 3 winners, including 6-y-o Classic Millennium and unreliable 1¼m winner Sculptor (by Salse): dam, maiden who stayed 1¾m, half-sister to very smart miler Alhijaz: 16/1, last in maiden at Yarmouth. *W. Jarvis*

MISHKA 6 b.g. Mistertopogigo (IRE) 118 – Walsham Witch 61 (Music Maestro 119) **67** [2004 –: p6m³ Dec 22] strong, close-coupled gelding: fair handicapper: good third to Pawan at Lingfield only 6-y-o outing: best around 6f: acts on all-weather, heavy and good to firm ground: blinkered/visored: usually races prominently. *Julian Poulton*

MISKINA 3 b.f. Mark of Esteem (IRE) 137 – Najmat Alshemaal (IRE) 98 (Dancing **59** Brave (USA) 140) [2004 57: 8g f8.5g³ 9.2d f7m* 8s⁵ 8m p7.1d⁴ p8.6g⁶ p7.1g Nov 19] rather leggy filly: modest handicapper: won at Wolverhampton in May: stays easy 8.6f: acts on all-weather, good to firm and good to soft going: tried tongue tied. *W. M. Brisbourne*

MISS ADELAIDE (IRE) 3 b.f. Alzao (USA) 117 – Sweet Adelaide (USA) 98 (The **77**
Minstrel (CAN) 135) [2004 85: p8g⁴ 8v⁴ 10m² 8.1m p7.1g² p7.1g³ p5.1g* p5.1g* Dec
31] fair performer: won maiden and handicap at Wolverhampton in December, edging
left both times: has form at easy 1¼m, may prove best at 5f/6f: acts on polytrack and good
to firm going: has found little. *B. W. Hills*

MISS ATACAMA (IRE) 2 b.f. (Mar 14) Desert Style (IRE) 121 – Delta Town (USA) **73**
(Sanglamore (USA) 126) [2004 p7g⁴ p8g⁵ p8.6g* Dec 3] €10,000Y: fifth foal: half-sister
to 4-y-o Kentucky Blue: dam French maiden daughter of smart French performer up to
1¼m Daeltown: best effort in maidens when winning at Wolverhampton by 1½ lengths
from Epices: will stay 1¼m. *D. J. Daly*

MISS BEAR (IRE) 2 b.f. (Apr 29) Orpen (USA) 116 – The Poachers Lady (IRE) –
(Salmon Leap (USA) 131) [2004 7m 7.9g Oct 9] €20,000Y: good-bodied filly: half-sister
to several winners, including 7-y-o Sir Ninja and fairly useful 1m winner Chalom (by
Mujadil): dam Irish 1¼m/1½m winner: signs of only a little ability in maidens at Thirsk
and York. *B. Smart*

MISS CASSIA 2 b.f. (Feb 14) Compton Place 125 – Miller's Melody 86 (Chief Singer **75**
131) [2004 5g³ 5g² 5.7g 5.3m³ 5s* 6.5g 5m⁶ Sep 27] 42,000Y: good-topped filly: half-
sister to several winners, including 6-y-o Top Dirham and useful German 1¼m/1½m
performer Metaxas (by Midyan): dam disappointing maiden: fair performer: won nursery
at Goodwood in August: good sixth in similar event at Windsor: should stay 6f: acts on
soft and good to firm ground: sold 55,000 gns, sent to USA. *R. Hannon*

MISS CELERITY 4 b.f. Compton Place 125 – Film Buff 60 (Midyan (USA) 124) –
[2004 –: p8g p6g p8g⁴ p8g 8.3d p7g f8f Aug 20] of little account. *M. J. Haynes*

MISS CEYLON 4 b.f. Brief Truce (USA) 126 – Five Islands 62 (Bairn (USA) 126) –
[2004 –: f6g 5g 5d 5m 5d 5m 5s Nov 2] angular, close-coupled filly: fair performer at
2 yrs: little form since: tried in headgear: has been reluctant to race/very slowly away.
S. P. Griffiths

MISS CHAMPERS (IRE) 4 b. or br.f. Grand Lodge (USA) 125 – Katherine Gorge –
(USA) (Hansel (USA)) [2004 47, a75: f8.5g f8s* f8s* f9.4g⁴ p7g Mar 4] leggy filly: fair **a77**
on all-weather, poor on turf: won apprentice claimer in January (left P. D. Evans) and
handicap in February, both at Southwell: best short of 9.4f: acts on fibresand, best turf
form on good to soft ground. *P. A. Blockley*

MISS CHANCELOT 3 b.f. Forzando 122 – Suedoro 51 (Hard Fought 125) [2004 –
6m 7m 6g p6g Oct 18] second foal: dam 5f/6f winner: tailed off in maidens. *S. P. Griffiths*

MISS CHILDREY (IRE) 3 ch.f. Dr Fong (USA) 128 – Blazing Glory (IRE) (Glow **97 d**
(USA)) [2004 95: 7s⁵ 7d³ 8m 6f 9.5d 8f 7m Sep 26] leggy filly: useful performer: close
third to Alexander Goldrun in 1000 Guineas Trial at Leopardstown in May: well below
form after, leaving F. Ennis in Ireland prior to final start: stays 1m: acts on good to firm
and good to soft going: tried tongue tied: sold 62,000 gns in November. *D. J. S. ffrench
Davis*

MISS COTSWOLD LADY 2 b.f. (Mar 30) Averti (IRE) 117 – Celtic Bay (USA) 63 **69 d**
(Green Dancer (USA) 132) [2004 5g⁵ 5m⁴ 6m² 5g 6.1m 7m p5.1g p6g Dec 1] 5,200Y:
leggy, quite good-topped filly: first foal: dam maiden who should have stayed 1½m: fair
maiden: trained by A. Jarvis fifth to seventh starts only: ran badly last 3: stays 6f: acts on
good to firm going: visored penultimate outing. *A. W. Carroll*

MISS CUISINA 2 b.f. (Apr 20) Vettori (IRE) 119 – Rewardia (IRE) 66 (Petardia 113) **36**
[2004 7g f7g 7s Aug 20] 6,200Y: third foal: half-sister to 3-y-o Emaradia: dam, maiden,
probably stayed 1¼m: poor form in maidens/claimer. *P. D. Evans*

MISS DANBYS 9 b.m. Charmer 123 – Dohty Baby (Hittite Glory 125) [2004 f11g⁶ –
May 19] fourth foal: dam, 6f seller winner, also successful in selling hurdles: poor maiden
hurdler: well beaten in seller at Southwell on Flat debut. *J. M. Jefferson*

MISS DANGEROUS 9 b.m. Komaite (USA) – Khadine 79 (Astec 128) [2004 f5g Mar –
29] rather dipped-backed mare: fair performer at best: behind in handicap at Wolverhampton on only run since 2000: effective blinkered or not. *M. Quinn*

MISS DE BOIS 7 ch.m. Elmaamul (USA) 125 – Petite Melusine (IRE) 50 (Fairy King –
(USA)) [2004 12m 10g 8.1m Sep 9] third foal: dam maiden (second at 5f at 2 yrs): well
beaten in claimers/seller. *W. M. Brisbourne*

MISS DEFYING 2 b.f. (Apr 2) Shambo 113 – Dugy (Risk Me (FR) 127) [2004 8.2d –
p10g Nov 27] first foal: dam unraced out of half-sister to dam of Queen Mary/Molecomb
winner Risky: well beaten in maidens at Nottingham (burly) and Lingfield. *R. Curtis*

MISS DINAMITE 2 b.f. (May 28) Polar Prince (IRE) 117 – Over The Moon 64 – (Beveled (USA)) [2004 8m Sep 25] first foal: dam 7f to 11f winner: 66/1, well held in maiden at Kempton. *M. J. Attwater*

MISSED A BEAT 2 b.f. (Mar 20) Mister Baileys 123 – Lonely Heart 101 (Midyan 74 (USA) 124) [2004 6g 6m⁴ 7f 6m* 6s⁵ 6v Oct 23] 9,000Y: close-coupled filly: fourth foal: half-sister to 3 winners, including 3-y-o Leitrim House and 5-y-o Ace of Hearts: dam 1¼m winner: fair performer: won maiden at Lingfield in September: creditable fifth at Haydock, much better effort in nurseries after: should stay 7f: acts on soft and good to firm going. *M. Blanshard*

MISSED TURN 2 b.f. (Feb 9) Mind Games 121 – Miss Beverley (Beveled (USA)) 54 [2004 f5d⁵ 5d⁴ f6g⁴ 5f⁶ 6m 7g p8g² p8.6g p7g Dec 29] 14,000Y: good-topped filly: third foal: sister to 2002 2-y-o 6f winner Night Games: dam unraced: modest maiden: trained first 3 starts by K. Ryan: second in seller at Lingfield, making running: stays 1m: acts on all-weather and good to soft ground. *J. M. P. Eustace*

MISSELLA (IRE) 2 gr.f. (May 14) Danehill (USA) 126 – Delage (Bellypha 130) 63 [2004 7g 8s⁴ p8.6g⁵ p8.6g² Dec 17] €70,000Y: tall, leggy filly: fifth foal: sister to 3-y-o Alqwah and half-sister to 2 winners, including fairly useful 1¼m/11.6f winner Mystic Mile (by Sadler's Wells): dam unraced half-sister to very smart performer up to 7f College Chapel: modest maiden: should stay 1¼m. *M. Johnston*

MISS ELOISE 3 b.f. Efisio 120 – Zaima (IRE) 92 (Green Desert (USA) 127) [2004 67 61: 8.1v⁶ 8.1d² 8m⁶ 8s 9.9g* 10d 9.9g 9.9d 10.5g Sep 4] smallish, stocky filly: fair handicapper: won at Beverley in July: stays 1¼m: acts on good to firm and good to soft going: blinkered penultimate start. *T. D. Easterby*

MISS FAYE 4 b. or br.f. Puissance 110 – Bingo Bongo 60 (Petong 126) [2004 –: 7.1d – 7g³ 6.1m May 25] of little account. *J. M. Bradley*

MISS FLEURIE 4 b.f. Alzao (USA) 117 – Miss Sancerre 95 (Last Tycoon 131) [2004 50 f6s 7s f8g f12m² 12m⁶ 12g 12m 10s² f11d Dec 21] good-topped filly: modest maiden: a43 missed 2003: stays 1½m: acts on fibresand and good to soft ground. *R. Craggs*

MISS GEORGE 6 b.m. Pivotal 124 – Brightside (IRE) 99 (Last Tycoon 131) [2004 88 93: p7g* 6g p7g 6g³ 7s 6m 6m⁶ 5m 6f³ 6g 5s³ p7g 6m p7g³ p7.1g² p8g* p8.6g p7g Nov a99 20] big mare: useful on all-weather, fairly useful on turf: won minor event at Lingfield in March and listed race (by length from Tahitiah) on same course in October: ran well when seventh to Jack Sullivan in handicap there final start: effective at 6f to easy 1m: acts on all-weather and firm going, little form on softer than good: ran poorly in cheekpieces earlier in career: sometimes slowly away/hangs left: tough and game. *D. K. Ivory*

MISS GLORY BE 6 b.m. Glory of Dancer 121 – Miss Blondie (USA) (Stop The Music 50 (USA)) [2004 53, a68: p10g f8.5g³ f8s⁵ f8m² p10d³ p10d³ f8s 9.7f⁶ 10.1d³ p9.5g* p9.5g³ a61 p8.6g* p7g Dec 30] modest performer: left Gay Kelleway after third start: won minor event in November and handicap in December, both at Wolverhampton: stays easy 1¼m: acts on all-weather, firm and good to soft going: usually wears cheekpieces, tailed off when visored: sometimes carries head awkwardly. *E. R. Oertel*

MISS GOOD TIME 2 gr.f. (Feb 28) Timeless Times (USA) 99 – Fort Vally 58 (Belfort 50 (FR) 89) [2004 5.2m 5d⁶ 6.1s 6g⁶ 6d⁶ 6m⁵ 7.5m⁶ Sep 15] 2,200Y: leggy filly: sixth foal: sister to 7f winner Time Vally: dam 1m/9f winner: modest maiden: stays 6f: acts on soft going: blinkered last 2 starts. *J. G. Given*

MISS GRACE 4 ch.f. Atticus (USA) 121 – Jetbeeah (IRE) 95 (Lomond (USA) 128) 60 [2004 64: 8.3g p10g⁴ 8m 9g³ Jun 2] leggy filly: fair on all-weather, modest on turf: stays a74 1¼m: acts on polytrack, unraced on extremes of going. *J. J. Sheehan*

MISS HERMIONE 2 ch.f. (May 25) Bahamian Bounty 116 – Try Vickers (USA) 72 57 (Fuzzbuster (USA)) [2004 p6g 8d 6d⁵ Nov 5] half-sister to several winners, including 5f/ 6f (including at 2 yrs) winner Nordico Princess (by Nordico) and 3-y-o Boris The Spider: dam, maiden, stayed 1¼m: form in maidens only when fifth at Yarmouth: will probably stay 7f. *Mrs C. A. Dunnett*

MISS HOOFBEATS 3 b.f. Unfuwain (USA) 131 – Oiselina (FR) (Linamix (FR) – 127) [2004 –: 10g f12d p12d 10m Jul 23] unfurnished filly: no form. *Miss J. Feilden*

MISSIE 4 ch.f. Compton Place 125 – About Face (Midyan (USA) 124) [2004 48?: 7m – 5g Jun 3] good-topped filly: maiden: well held in 2004. *G. A. Swinbank*

MISSIE BAILEYS 2 ch.f. (Apr 6) Mister Baileys 123 – Jilly Woo 60 (Environment 66 Friend 128) [2004 6d⁶ p7g⁵ 7g 8.3g* Oct 11] close-coupled filly: third foal: half-sister to 4-y-o Private Benjamin: dam maiden who stayed 1¼m: fair performer: won seller at Windsor comfortably: stays 1m: acts on good to soft going, probably on polytrack. *D. R. C. Elsworth*

MISS INKHA 3 b.f. Intikhab (USA) 135 – Santi Sana 80 (Formidable (USA) 125) **66** [2004 7g 8m 8g6 8g6 10s2 10.5g 11.9s3 11.7g5 Oct 10] 40,000Y: strong filly: sixth foal: half-sister to 1998 2-y-o 7f winner Minnesota (by Danehill) and 1m winner Sandenista (by Diesis): dam, 7f winner, sister to very smart 7f/1m winner Efisio: fair maiden: stays 1½m: acts on soft ground. *R. Guest*

MISSIN MARGOT 2 b.f. (Feb 6) Fraam 114 – Abstone Queen 66 (Presidium 124) **49** [2004 6m5 p6g 5g6 Oct 5] 10,000Y: third foal: sister to 3-y-o Amber Legend: dam 6f (including at 2 yrs)/7f winner: poor form in maidens: tends to flash tail. *Ms Deborah J. Evans*

MISSION AFFIRMED (USA) 3 ch.g. Stravinsky (USA) 133 – Affirmed Legacy **66** (USA) (Affirmed (USA)) [2004 –: f6g f7g* f8g5 f8g* 8.5v f8g4 8.1d 9f5 f8g2 7g3 8.2g **a70** Sep 29] good-bodied gelding: fair handicapper: won at Southwell in March and April: stays 1m: acts on fibresand, best turf efforts on good ground. *T. P. Tate*

MISSION MAN 3 b.c. Revoque (IRE) 122 – Opopmil (USA) 68 (Pips Pride 117) **81** [2004 81: 7g4 7d2 6.1s* 7m4 6m 8g4 8.1m5 8d 7g Aug 28] big, strong colt: fairly useful performer: won maiden at Nottingham in May: mostly creditable efforts otherwise: stays 1m: acts on soft and good to firm ground. *R. Hannon*

MISSION TO MARS 5 b.g. Muhtarram (USA) 125 – Ideal Candidate 80 (Celestial **102** Storm (USA) 132) [2004 83: p12g* p12g* f12s3 Mar 5] quite good-topped gelding: useful performer: has won 6 of last 8 starts, including handicaps at Lingfield in January and February, latter by 1¼ lengths fron Nawamees: good third to Mr Mischief in similar event at Wolverhampton: stays 1½m: acts on all-weather and firm going. *P. R. Hedger*

MISS ISSY (IRE) 4 b.f. Victory Note 120 – Shane's Girl (IRE) (Marktingo) **62** [2004 69: p7g3 Jan 10] lengthy filly: fair performer at best: was effective at 7f to 8.5f: acted on all-weather and good to firm going: visored last 4 starts: tended to pull hard: dead. *J. Gallagher*

MISS IVANHOE (IRE) 4 b.f. Selkirk (USA) 129 – Robellino Miss (USA) (Robellino **97** (USA) 127) [2004 107+: 7d 7s6 7.9g Oct 8] big, good-topped filly: useful performer: below best in 2004, markedly so last 2 outings: best at 7f/1m: acts on good to firm and good to soft going. *G. Wragg*

MISS JELLYBEAN (IRE) 2 b.f. (Apr 16) Namid 128 – Elfin Queen (IRE) 64 (Fairy **–** King (USA)) [2004 5m 5g 5s Oct 16] €3,800Y, 12,000 2-y-o: fourth foal: half-sister to winner in Greece by Dolphin Street: dam sprint maiden: only a little sign of ability in maidens/minor event. *N. Tinkler*

MISS JUDGED 2 b.f. Case Law 113 – Marie's Crusader (IRE) (Last Tycoon 131) **46** [2004 46: p7g 8.5g f6g6 f6g f5g Feb 12] poor maiden: tried tongue tied/blinkered. *A. P. Jones*

MISS JUDGEMENT (IRE) 3 b.f. Revoque (IRE) 122 – Mugello 96 (Emarati (USA) **72** 74) [2004 59: p6g5 6m3 6.1m2 6.1g* 6m3 p6g 7f 6f* 6m 5.7f 6.1d 5.7g Oct 10] neat filly: **a?** fair performer: won handicap at Nottingham in June and minor event at Lingfield (hung right) in August: stays 6f: acts on firm going: well below form on all-weather. *W. R. Muir*

MISS KOEN (IRE) 5 b.m. Barathea (IRE) 127 – Fanny Blankers (IRE) (Persian **59** Heights 129) [2004 –: f8.5s6 p13g3 p12g* p10g 12s3 12d 14.1g 13.1m p13.9g Nov 29] modest performer: won claimer at Lingfield in March: stays 1½m: acts on polytrack and soft ground: blinkered once: tongue tied after reappearance. *D. L. Williams*

MISS LADYBIRD (USA) 3 b. or br.f. Labeeb 124 – Bird Dance (USA) (Storm Bird **–** (CAN) 134) [2004 64: 8.1s Aug 12] quite good-topped filly: modest performer: well held only run at 3 yrs: barely stays 8.5f: acts on fibresand, good to firm and good to soft going. *J. G. Given*

MISS LANGKAWI 3 gr.f. Daylami (IRE) 138 – Miss Amanpuri 92 (Alzao (USA) **75** 117) [2004 76p: 9g 11.6g 12s3 10.3s Nov 6] rather leggy filly: fair performer: will stay 1¾m: acts on soft going, probably on firm: sold 10,000 gns. *G. Wragg*

MISS L'AUGEVAL 2 b.f. (Mar 17) Zilzal (USA) 137 – Miss Sancerre 95 (Last Tycoon **89** 131) [2004 6m4 7m* 7s 7g 8.2v2 Oct 20] lengthy filly: fourth foal: sister to 5-y-o Mr Mistral: dam, 2-y-o 7f winner, out of sister to very smart sprinter Cyrano de Bergerac: fairly useful performer: won maiden at Goodwood in July: very good neck second of 5 to Public Forum in minor event at Nottingham: stays 1m: acts on heavy and good to firm going: sold 40,000 gns. *G. Wragg*

MISS LEHMAN   6 ch.m. Beveled (USA) – Lehmans Lot (Oats 126) [2004 –: 8.5m⁶   –
May 24] well-made mare: no form: seems headstrong. *Mrs M. Reveley*

MISS LIBRATE   6 b.m. Librate 91 – Hayley's Lass (Royal Boxer 112) [2004 8g   –
f8.5g Apr 17] third foal: dam poor novice hurdler: well beaten in bumpers/maidens.
J. M. Bradley

MISS LYVENNET   3 ch.f. Then Again 126 – Precious Girl 76 (Precious Metal 106)   –
[2004 55: 7g Mar 31] workmanlike filly: modest maiden at 2 yrs: well held in seller only
run in 2004: likely to prove best at 5f/6f. *M. Todhunter*

MISS MADAME (IRE)   3 b.f. Cape Cross (IRE) 129 – Cosmic Countess (IRE) 74   **74**
(Lahib (USA) 129) [2004 62?: f7g3 5.3m3 5.1g6 7.6m* 8f2 7g* 8m6 8g Sep 20] fair
performer: won minor event at Lingfield in July and handicap at Yarmouth in August:
effective at 7f/1m: acts on fibresand and firm ground. *R. Guest*

MISS MALONE (IRE)   2 b.f. (Feb 9) Daggers Drawn (USA) 114 – Queen Molly 53   **70**
(Emarati (USA) 74) [2004 6m 6.3g 6g2 6m4 7m 6.5m 5.1s5 6m Oct 1] €15,000F,
€32,000Y: tall filly: first foal: dam, second at 6f from 3 starts, half-sister to dam of Sussex
Stakes winner Reel Buddy: fair maiden: likely to prove best at 5f/6f: acts on good to firm
ground, probably on soft: often races prominently. *R. Hannon*

MISS MAMBO (USA)   3 b.f. Kingmambo (USA) 125 – Troika (USA) (Strawberry   **110**
Road (AUS) 128) [2004 8g* 8g* 8g3 8g2 8g2 8g5 8d* Oct 17] $220,000Y: lengthy,
angular filly: first foal: dam, US 8.5f to 1¼m winner, daughter of Arlington Million
winner Estrapade: smart performer: won minor events at Longchamp and Chantilly in
April and listed race at Naas (by length from Bywayofthestars) in October: good efforts
in between when 3½ lengths third to Torrestrella in Poule d'Essai des Pouliches at Longchamp, second to Baqah in Prix de Sandringham at Chantilly (final start for E. Libaud in
France) and second to Troubadour in listed race at the Curragh: stays 1m: raced only on
good ground or softer: possibly amiss in Sun Chariot Stakes at Newmarket penultimate
start: blinkered final outing. *D. K. Weld, Ireland*

MISS MEGGY   2 b.f. (Apr 15) Pivotal 124 – Selkirk Rose (IRE) 74 (Pips Pride 117)   **97**
[2004 5m* 5m* 5f 6m5 5s5 6.5m6 6s4 Sep 18] 10,000F, €25,000Y, 20,000 2-y-o: leggy
filly: first living foal: dam 5f (at 2 yrs)/6f winner: useful performer: won minor event at
Thirsk in May and listed race at Beverley (beat Taguta Sunrise a neck) in June: visored,
very good fourth to Golden Legacy in Firth of Clyde Stakes at Ayr: barely stays testing
6f: acts on firm and soft going. *T. D. Easterby*

MISS MERENDA   3 b.f. Sir Harry Lewis (USA) 127 – Cool Merenda (IRE) (Glacial   **51**
Storm (USA) 127) [2004 8m 11.5g 9.7m p9.5d4 p13m Nov 22] first foal: dam unraced:
modest maiden: seems to stay at least 9.5f: acts on polytrack. *D. E. Cantillon*

MISS MILLIETANT   3 b.f. Up And At 'em 109 – Annie Hall (Saddlers' Hall (IRE)   –
126) [2004 –: p10g p7g6 f7g Mar 23] compact filly: little form: tried visored. *L. Montague
Hall*

MISS MONICA (IRE)   3 ch.f. Grand Lodge (USA) 125 – Bea's Ruby (IRE) 86 (Fairy   **68**
King (USA)) [2004 8.1s6 9g4 10f3 8.1g 10g Oct 12] 32,000Y: rather sparely-made filly:
second foal: half-sister to Irish 1m winner Kilmannin (by College Chapel): dam 7f/1m
winner: fair maiden: not sure to stay beyond 1¼m: acts on firm going: sold 2,800 gns.
H. R. A. Cecil

MISS MONZA   3 b.f. Hazaaf (USA) 62 – Monstrosa 70 (Monsanto (FR) 121) [2004   **64 ?**
6g 7d 6d3 5.7f 6m Sep 27] half-sister to several winners, including fairly useful 5f to
7f winner Champagne Grandy (by Vaigly Great): dam 2-y-o 5f winner who stayed 1m:
seemingly modest form in maidens only on third start. *B. R. Millman*

MISS MYTTON (USA)   3 ch.f. Mt Livermore (USA) – Sisterella (USA) (Diesis 133)   –
[2004 72: 7g f7s Nov 17] close-coupled, workmanlike filly: fair maiden: no form in 2004:
tried blinkered: sometimes slowly away (from tape start on reappearance). *A. Bailey*

MISS NOTERIETY   4 b.f. Victory Note (USA) 120 – Mystic Maid (IRE) 62 (Muj-   –
tahid (USA) 118) [2004 –: f7d 6m f5m Jul 12] unfurnished filly: of little account.
C. J. Teague

MISS OCEAN MONARCH   4 ch.f. Blue Ocean (USA) 87 – Faraway Grey 99   **45 §**
(Absalom 128) [2004 47: f7g f8m f9.4g f8.5m 8.5m2 8f 9.9g 12m 12.1m Jul 27] angular
filly: poor performer: stays 1¼m: acts on firm and soft going: wore blinkers last 2 starts,
refusing to settle on penultimate: tends to edge left: unreliable. *D. W. Chapman*

MISS PARTICULAR (IRE)   2 b.f. (Apr 20) Sadler's Wells (USA) 132 – Viz (USA)   **57 p**
(Kris S (USA)) [2004 7g Oct 1] rangy filly: fifth living foal: sister to smart 2000 2-y-o 7f

winner Relish The Thought, also third in Oaks, closely related to 5-y-o Valiant Effort and half-sister to 3-y-o Secret Charm: dam, US 2-y-o 1m winner and third in Grade 1 1m event, out of half-sister to Breeders' Cup Juvenile winner Brocco: 12/1 and wrong in coat, eleventh to Rob Roy in maiden at Newmarket, slowly away: should be suited by 1¼m/1½m: will do better. *B. W. Hills*

MISS PATRICIA 2 b.f. (Mar 17) Mister Baileys 123 – Zoena 67 (Emarati (USA) 74) **78** [2004 5.7g 6f 6d⁴ 7g³ Sep 14] first foal: dam 5f/6f winner: fair maiden: third in nursery at Yarmouth: stays 7f: acts on good to soft going. *J. G. Portman*

MISS PEACHES 6 b.m. Emperor Jones (USA) 119 – Dear Person (Rainbow Quest **53** (USA) 134) [2004 –: p8g² p8g p8g* p8g³ p8g⁵ p8g⁴ 7m⁶ 8f⁵ 10g Jun 30] quite good-topped mare: modest performer: won banded race at Lingfield in February: stays 1m: acts on polytrack, and probably any turf going. *G. G. Margarson*

MISS PEBBLES (IRE) 4 ch.f. Lake Coniston (IRE) 131 – Sea of Stone (USA) 71 **82** (Sanglamore (USA) 126) [2004 78: 9.7s* 9.7s⁴ 10s 8g 8m⁵ 10m* 10m² 10s⁵ 10d 12g Sep 22] sturdy filly: fairly useful performer: won minor event at Folkestone in March and handicap at Windsor in June: left B. Johnson after seventh outing: stays 1¼m: acts on polytrack, soft and good to firm ground: visored fifth to ninth starts: has run well in cheekpieces: held up. *S. C. Williams*

MISSPERON (IRE) 2 b.f. (Feb 21) Orpen (USA) 116 – Secret Hideaway (USA) **77** (Key To The Mint (USA)) [2004 6m⁵ 6f³ 6m* 5g³ 6.1m⁴ 6f 6d² Sep 17] 18,000Y: lengthy filly: half-sister to several winners, including useful 6f (at 2 yrs) and 1m winner Lagoon (by Common Grounds) and fairly useful 5f (at 2 yrs) to 1m (in UAE) winner Muchtarak (by Try My Best): dam unraced: fair performer: won maiden at Pontefract in June: creditable efforts in frame in nurseries after: stays 6f: acts on good to firm and good to soft ground: in cheekpieces final start. *K. A. Ryan*

MISS POLARIS 3 b.f. Polar Falcon (USA) 126 – Sarabah (IRE) 83 (Ela-Mana-Mou **81** 132) [2004 8.2d⁶ 8g* p9.5g² Oct 18] 30,000Y: lengthy filly: sister to 3 useful winners, including 5f to 7f (including at 2 yrs) winner Cryhavoc and unreliable 7f (at 2 yrs) to 9f winner Ice and closely related/half-sister to 3 winners, including useful 7f (at 2 yrs) and 1¼m winner Saratov (by Rudimentary): dam, 1¼m winner, half-sister to smart 7f/1m performer Gothenberg: fairly useful form: won maiden at Pontefract in October: good second in handicap at Wolverhampton subsequent start: stays 9.5f. *P. W. Harris*

MISS POPPETS 4 ch.f. Polar Falcon (USA) 126 – Alifandango (IRE) 78 (Alzao **61 ?** (USA) 117) [2004 62, a73: p6g p7g Apr 2] lengthy, sparely-made filly: just modest form in 2004: probably better at 6f than further: acts on fibresand, firm and good to soft ground: sold £4,000. *D. R. C. Elsworth*

MISS PORCIA 3 ch.f. Inchinor 119 – Krista 73 (Kris 135) [2004 –: 7m* 7.2g² 8g f8s **62** p8m* p8g³ Dec 20] tall, lengthy, unfurnished filly: modest performer: won maiden at Thirsk in June and banded race at Lingfield in December: stays 1m: acts on polytrack and good to firm going: tongue tied final outing at 2 yrs. *P. W. Chapple-Hyam*

MISS PRIM 3 ch.f. Case Law 113 – Calamanco 71 (Clantime 101) [2004 6g p6g f5g **–** f6s Nov 17] deep-girthed filly: fifth foal: half-sister to 5-y-o Artie and 6-y-o Kingscross: dam 5f winner: well held in maidens. *G. P. Kelly*

MISS PROCURER (IRE) 3 b.f. Entrepreneur 123 – Kariyh (USA) 96 (Shadeed **59 §** (USA) 135) [2004 72?: 7g⁵ 8m 7m⁴ 8.1g⁵ 10s³ Aug 24] sturdy filly: modest maiden: should stay 1m: acts on good to firm going: tried tongue tied: inconsistent, and looked far from willing final outing: sent to Saudi Arabia. *P. F. I. Cole*

MISS ROSIE 2 b.f. (Apr 4) Xaar 132 – Disallowed (IRE) 76 (Distinctly North (USA) **67** 115) [2004 6m⁴ 7.5m⁴ 7d Aug 9] 24,000Y: tall, leggy filly: good mover: third foal: dam 9f and hurdles winner: fair form in maidens: should stay 1m. *T. D. Easterby*

MISS SHANGRI LA 3 b.f. Rainbow Quest (USA) 134 – Miss Rinjani 83 (Shirley **43** Heights 130) [2004 7g 10m 10f⁶ 10m p8.6g Nov 13] leggy, quite good-topped filly: fifth foal: half-sister to 3 winners, notably smart 1¼m/13f winner St Expedit (by Sadler's Wells) and 6-y-o Asian Heights: dam 2-y-o 7f winner who stayed 1½m: poor maiden: sold 28,000 gns. *G. Wragg*

MISS SHARAPOVA (IRE) 2 b.f. (Apr 26) Almutawakel 126 – Dolcezza (FR) **69** (Lichine (USA) 117) [2004 7m⁴ Jul 29] €15,000Y resold 11,000Y, 75,000 2-y-o: tall, useful-looking filly: half-sister to several winners, including 5-y-o Martin House: dam unraced close relation to smart French performer up to 10.5f Caprarola: fourth in maiden at Goodwood, racing freely: joined M. Al Kurdi in UAE. *G. A. Butler*

MISS ST ALBANS 3 b.f. Robellino (USA) 127 – Alieria (IRE) (Lomond (USA) 128) [2004 10g 9.7s 7f 9.7m 7d Oct 16] 5,500Y: leggy filly: sixth foal: half-sister to 3 winners abroad, including Hong Kong 6f winner Villager (by Glitterman): dam French 2-y-o 1m winner later successful in USA: no form, leaving T. Clement after fourth start. *M. Wigham*

MISS SUDBROOK (IRE) 2 ch.f. (Apr 20) Daggers Drawn (USA) 114 – Missed Opportunity (IRE) (Exhibitioner 111) [2004 5.7m 7.1s⁴ p6g Oct 2] €1,800F, €7,500Y: half-sister to 7f winner Mother Corrigan (by Paris House) and fairly useful 1¼m winner Peradventure (by Persian Bold): dam Irish 2-y-o 1m winner: form in maidens only when fourth at Chepstow. *D. Haydn Jones* **59**

MISS THE BOAT 2 b.f. (Mar 6) Mtoto 134 – Missed Again 84 (High Top 131) [2004 7g² Sep 2] sturdy filly: eighth foal: half-sister to 3 winners, including 6-y-o Canterloupe and 11-y-o Failed To Hit: dam, 1¼m winner, half-sister to smart performers Desert Shot (up to 1½m) and Mojave (up to 7f): 50/1 and edgy, always-prominent 2 lengths second to Donyana in maiden at Salisbury: likely to be suited by 1¼m/1½m: should improve. *J. L. Dunlop* **78 p**

MISS TILLY 3 b.f. Nicolotte 118 – Little White Lies 78 (Runnett 125) [2004 –: 6s 7m Jun 8] leggy filly: no sign of ability. *G. B. Balding* **–**

MISS TOLERANCE (USA) 2 ch.f. (Feb 5) Mt Livermore (USA) – Acquiesce (Generous (IRE) 139) [2004 7g 6g³ p6g p6g³ p6g p7g³ Dec 29] fourth foal: half-sister to useful 2002 2-y-o 7f winner (stayed 1¼m) Oblige (by Robellino) and fairly useful 2001 2-y-o 7f winner I Do (by Selkirk): dam unraced half-sister to 7-y-o Endless Summer out of sister to Scenic: fair maiden: left Sir Michael Stoute after third outing: should be suited by 1m: acts on polytrack. *P. W. D'Arcy* **74 a67**

MISS TRENDSETTER (IRE) 2 b.f. (Feb 6) Desert Style (IRE) 121 – Chummy's Friend (IRE) 47 (Be My Guest (USA) 126) [2004 6g 7m 7s f7g Dec 14] €9,000Y: good-bodied filly: sixth foal: half-sister to 5f/6f winner Prince Nico (by Nicolotte): dam poor maiden: bad maiden: tried in cheekpieces. *K. A. Ryan* **26**

MISS TRIAL 2 b.f. (May 3) Zafonic (USA) 130 – Perfect Alibi (Law Society (USA) 130) [2004 6s⁶ 6.1m³ 7m³ 6d³ p7g Nov 10] 20,000Y: well-made filly: half-sister to several winners, including 6f (including at 2 yrs) winner Likely Story (by Night Shift) and 1m winner Beggars Belief (by Common Grounds), both fairly useful: dam, unraced, from an excellent family: fair maiden: barely stays 7f: acts on soft and good to firm ground. *M. A. Jarvis* **73**

MISS TRINITY 4 b.f. Catrail (USA) 123 – Rosy Sunset (IRE) (Red Sunset 120) [2004 59: p7g f5g p6g 7m 7d 7g⁶ 8.5g⁶ 7g 8v a6g⁶ Dec 19] maiden: little form in 2004, leaving C. Allen after fourth start: tried blinkered/in cheekpieces. *Yvonne Bos, Netherlands* **–**

MISS TRUANT 2 b.f. (Mar 19) Zaha (CAN) 106 – Miss Runaway 73 (Runnett 125) [2004 5.2m⁶ 5g⁶ Apr 26] 13,000Y: half-sister to fairly useful 5f/6f winner The Fugative (by Nicholas): dam 6f winner: modest form, slowly away, in maidens at Yarmouth and Windsor (reportedly sore after). *M. L. W. Bell* **56**

MISSUS LINKS (USA) 3 b.f. Lure (USA) 131 – Cozisaidso (USA) (Cozzene (USA)) [2004 69p: 6.1g⁵ 6g² 7.1f⁵ 6m 6d⁶ 6d⁴ 6g p7g⁶ p8g³ p7g⁶ p6g Dec 11] good-topped filly: fair handicapper: stays easy 1m: acts on polytrack, firm and good to soft going: visored (seemed reluctant to race) final outing: usually races prominently. *R. Hannon* **77**

MISS WIZZ 4 b.f. Wizard King 122 – Fyas 52 (Sayf El Arab (USA) 127) [2004 38: f8g f7g⁴ f6g* 6s⁶ f5m⁴ 5g⁴ 5d⁵ 16d* 7m 6m 16s 6s Oct 30] lengthy filly: modest performer: won banded race at Southwell in February and claimer at Newcastle in June: should stay 7f: acts on fibresand, good to firm and good to soft ground: wore cheekpieces after reappearance. *W. Storey* **50**

MISS WONG ONE (IRE) 4 b.f. Eagle Eyed (USA) 111 – Fakhira (IRE) 83 (Jareer (USA) 115) [2004 61: f6g 5d² 5d Apr 24] modest maiden: stays 7f: acts on fibresand and good to soft ground: ran as if amiss at Southwell on reappearance: blinkered last 2 outings, very slowly away penultimate one. *Frederick John Bowles, Ireland* **63**

MISS WOODPIGEON 8 b.m. Landyap (USA) 112 – Pigeon Loft (IRE) 47 (Bellypha 130) [2004 –: 11.6f³ 10.2m Aug 5] fair bumper winner: poor maiden on Flat: stays 11.6f: acts on firm going: *J. D. Frost* **41**

MISSY CINOFAZ 2 ch.f. (Apr 16) Zafonic (USA) 130 – Dancing Wolf (IRE) 76 (Wolfhound (USA) 126) [2004 7g p7m⁴ p7m³ Dec 22] 5,500F: lengthy, angular filly: third foal: half-sister to 3-y-o Daydream Dancer: dam, maiden effective at 7f/1m, half-sister to useful dam of 5-y-o Monturani: left I. Wood, best effort in maidens when third to Glinting Desert at Lingfield: bred to stay 1m. *A. M. Balding* **70**

Petros Rose of Lancaster Stakes, Haydock—the fast-improving Mister Monet makes a successful step up to pattern company; Muqbil is clear of the rest

MISTBLACK 4 b.f. Wizard King 122 – Dear Heart (Blakeney 126) [2004 f5m Jul 12] –
half-sister to several winners abroad, including French 8.5f winner Parisian Lover (by
Gallic League): dam unraced: 66/1 and green, well held in seller at Southwell. *A. Senior*

MISTER ARJAY (USA) 4 b.c. Mister Baileys 123 – Crystal Stepper (USA) (Fred –
Astaire (USA)) [2004 86: 8d 9.9d⁶ p12.2g 10s Nov 1] smallish, good-bodied colt: fairly
useful performer at 3 yrs: well held in 2004: tried blinkered: has hung right: possibly none
too genuine. *B. Ellison*

MISTER AZIZ (IRE) 2 b.c. (Apr 10) Mister Baileys 123 – Aziz Presenting (IRE) 86 **59**
(Charnwood Forest (IRE) 125) [2004 6g f7m 5m⁵ 6.1m p7.1g Nov 12] modest maiden:
easily best effort when fifth at Sandown: likely to prove best at 5f/6f: slowly away penultimate outing. *J. M. P. Eustace*

MISTER BELL 2 gr.c. (Apr 4) Lujain (USA) 119 – Zaragossa 80 (Paris House 123) **48**
[2004 5d³ 5.1f⁶ 6.1m 5.7g 5.1g Oct 10] poor maiden: probably stays 5.7f. *J. G. M. O'Shea*

MISTER BENJI 5 b.g. Catrail (USA) 123 – Katy-Q (IRE) 58 (Taufan (USA) 119) **60**
[2004 69: f8.5g f7g⁵ p8.6d f8g³ f8g³ f8g f8g³ Dec 28] quite good-topped gelding: modest
performer: stays easy 1m: acts on fibresand, good to firm and good to soft going: tried in
headgear. *B. P. J. Baugh*

MISTER BUZZ 2 b.c. (Mar 16) Mind Games 121 – Compact Disc (IRE) 48 (Royal **54**
Academy (USA) 130) [2004 6f 6s 6g 6m⁴ 6g⁴ 5.9g 8s Nov 1] workmanlike colt: modest
maiden: not sure to stay beyond 6f: acts on good to firm ground. *M. D. Hammond*

MISTER CHALK 3 gr.c. Silver Patriarch (IRE) 125 – B B Glen 52 (Hadeer 118) [2004 **41**
10d f12g p9.5g⁵ Dec 13] poor maiden: should be suited by 1½m+: looked reluctant on
debut. *T. Keddy*

MISTER CLINTON (IRE) 7 ch.g. Lion Cavern (USA) 117 – Thewaari (USA) 68 **66**
(Eskimo (USA)) [2004 62: p7g p8g p10g p8g p7g⁶ 7f³ 7f⁴ 10g 8g* 7m² 7.6m 8f* 7s⁶ 7m
8.3m 8.2g Sep 29] tall, lengthy gelding: fair performer: has good record at Brighton,
winning handicap in July and minor event in August: stays easy 1¼m: acts on polytrack,
firm and good to soft going: tried in headgear: held up: none too consistent. *D. K. Ivory*

MISTER COMPLETELY (IRE) 3 b.g. Princely Heir (IRE) 111 – Blue Goose **56**
(Belmez (USA) 131) [2004 52: p6g² p7g⁶ p7g⁵ 6s 6m p10g 7g p12g 8f* f8m⁶ 16g p10g*
10s 10m⁵ 10g³ 14.1s³ f12g⁵ p10m Nov 22] modest handicapper: won at Bath (selling
event) in June and Lingfield in August: stays 1¼m: acts on polytrack and firm going:
inconsistent. *J. R. Best*

MISTER ELEGANT 2 b.c. (Mar 25) Fraam 114 – Risky Valentine 68 (Risk Me (FR) **64**
127) [2004 6m 8g⁴ 8d⁶ Oct 16] 2,800Y: first foal: dam 5f (at 2 yrs)/6f winner: best effort
in maidens when fourth at Salisbury: likely to prove best up to 1m. *J. L. Spearing*

MISTER GENEPI 2 b.c. (Mar 23) Mister Baileys 123 – Ring Queen (USA) (Fairy **104**
King (USA)) [2004 7d⁵ 7g² 7d² 7g³ 7f 7g³ 7.9g* Oct 9] 40,000Y: leggy, short-backed
colt: good mover: second foal: dam unraced close relation to very smart 1m/9f winner
in France/USA Special Ring: useful performer: excellent third, beaten narrowly by
Diktatorial, in Somerville Tattersall Stakes at Newmarket penultimate outing: odds on, won
maiden at York readily by 5 lengths from William Tell: stays 1m: best effort on good
going: tended to go freely early starts. *W. R. Muir*

MISTER GRAHAM 9 b.g. Rock Hopper 124 – Celestial Air 96 (Rheingold 137) **48**
[2004 12d p16g⁴ p10g⁶ Apr 29] fourth in seller at Lingfield, only form: tried in cheekpieces: slowly away all 3 outings. *K. F. Clutterbuck*

MISTER LINKS (IRE) 4 b.c. Flying Spur (AUS) – Lady Anna Livia (Ahonoora 122) **110**
[2004 105: 6g³ 7m* May 24] tall, good sort: smart performer: left R. Hannon and off 12
months prior to reappearance: won 4-runner minor event at Leicester in May by 6 lengths
from St Andrews, making all: will prove best up to 7f (pulled too hard in 2000 Guineas at
3 yrs): acts on soft and good to firm going: genuine. *Saeed bin Suroor*

MISTER MAL (IRE) 8 b.g. Scenic 128 – Fashion Parade (Mount Hagen (FR) 127) **68**
[2004 63, a69: f7s 7g⁶ 6v* 6m 6m 5d³ f6f* 5d² 5d p5.1g f6g Dec 7] big, strong, lengthy
gelding: fair handicapper: won at Newcastle in April and Southwell in August: best at
stiff 5f to 7f: acts on fibresand and any turf going: effective with or without headgear:
often unruly at stall, and has been withdrawn after giving trouble to post: sometimes
slowly away: free-going sort, usually races prominently. *B. Ellison*

MISTER MARMADUKE 3 b.g. Marju (IRE) 127 – Lalique (IRE) (Lahib (USA) **83**
129) [2004 83: 5m 7.1f⁴ 6.1g³ 5g⁵ 8g 7.1g p6g p6g³ p6g Dec 27] 5,000Y: first foal: dam
unraced half-sister to smart French 7f to 1¼m performer Goofalik: fairly useful performer: left J. Harley in Ireland after reappearance: likely to prove best at 5f/6f: acts on
polytrack and firm going. *I. Semple*

MISTER MERLIN (IRE) 3 ch.g. Titus Livius (FR) 115 – Official Secret (Polish Pat- **–**
riot (USA) 128) [2004 –: 12g 12m Sep 25] sturdy gelding: little sign of ability. *D. Carroll*

MISTER MINTY (IRE) 2 b.c. (May 13) Fasliyev (USA) 120 – Sorb Apple (IRE) **–**
79 (Kris 135) [2004 6g Aug 5] 33/1 and very green, tailed off in maiden at Haydock.
D. Carroll

MISTER MONET (IRE) 3 b.c. Peintre Celebre (USA) 137 – Breyani 101 (Comman- **123**
che Run 133) [2004 92p: 8g² 9.2g* 10m* 10.5g* 10v* 10s Oct 16] strong colt: very smart
performer: reportedly had a problem with right fetlock in spring and not seen out until
July: most progressive on return, winning minor event at Hamilton and handicap at Ascot
later in month, and Rose of Lancaster Stakes at Haydock (beat Muqbil 1½ lengths, despite
hanging left/idling markedly) and Prix Guillaume d'Ornano at Deauville (beat Delfos in
very good style by 4 lengths, making all) in August: broke near-hind at halfway in
Champion Stakes at Newmarket in October: stayed 1¼m: acted on heavy and good to
firm going: raced prominently: dead. *M. Johnston*

MISTER MUJA (IRE) 3 gr.g. Mujadil (USA) 119 – Remiss (IRE) (Indian Ridge 123) **65**
[2004 7d 7.1g⁶ p7g* p7.1g⁶ Nov 19] €65,000Y: good-bodied gelding: first foal: dam, ran
3 times in Ireland, closely related to Rockfel winner/1000 Guineas third Negligent: fair
performer: won maiden at Lingfield in October: ran respectably in handicap next time:
will stay 1m: tongue tied: reportedly broke blood vessel second start. *W. R. Swinburn*

MISTERNANDO 4 b.c. Hernando (FR) 127 – Mistinguett (IRE) 77 (Doyoun 124) **113**
[2004 109: 16.2s 18.7d² 16.4f⁶ 20m 16.4d³ 16m³ Jul 29] compact colt: smart performer:
ran at least respectably at 4 yrs in Chester Cup (5 lengths second to Anak Pekan), Henry
II Stakes at Sandown, Gold Cup at Royal Ascot, listed race at Sandown and Goodwood
Cup (best effort, travelled better than usual when 3¼ lengths third to Darasim): reported
in early-September to have suffered a leg injury: stays 2½m: acts on firm and good to soft
going: visored last 2 starts: has run well when sweating: tends to hang/race lazily: usually
comes from behind: tough and consistent. *M. R. Channon*

MISTER PUTT (USA) 6 b. or br.g. Mister Baileys 123 – Theresita (GER) (Surumu **65**
(GER)) [2004 69: 15.4s² 16d Oct 10] big, strong gelding: fair maiden handicapper: barely
stays 2¼m: acts on firm and soft ground: blinkered last 4 starts. *Mrs N. Smith*

*Prix Guillaume d'Ornano, Deauville—Mister Monet is well in command after setting a steady pace;
Delfos and Islero Noir are second and third*

MISTER REGENT 3 b.g. Mind Games 121 – River of Fortune (IRE) 68 (Lahib (USA) **59**
129) [2004 6s³ 6d 7m 7m 7.1g 7.1m f7g⁶ f8d Dec 21] tall, angular gelding: modest
maiden: stays 7f: acts on fibresand, soft and good to firm ground: sometimes blinkered:
has looked wayward under pressure. *K. A. Ryan*

MISTER RIGHT (IRE) 3 ch.g. Barathea (IRE) 127 – Broken Spirit (IRE) (Slip **61**
Anchor 136) [2004 –: 8.3g³ 10.1d Nov 5] lengthy, plain gelding: modest maiden: lightly
raced: should stay 1¼m: pulled hard final start. *K. Bell*

MISTER RUSHBY 4 b.g. Hamas (IRE) 125§ – Final Rush 66 (Final Straw 127) [2004 **– §**
–§: f6g f12g f8m Apr 27] close-coupled gelding: no longer of any account. *Miss V. Haigh*

MISTER SAIF (USA) 3 ch.g. Miswaki (USA) 124 – Shawgatny (USA) 83 (Danzig **91**
Connection (USA)) [2004 85: 7g 8m 7s⁵ 8.1d 7m⁴ 7.1m² 6.5g 7m Jul 29] rather leggy
gelding: fairly useful performer: best effort when ¾-length second to Oasis Star in minor
event at Sandown: stays 1m: acts on polytrack, soft and good to firm going: sometimes
wanders: usually races prominently: gelded and joined D. Watson in UAE. *R. Hannon*

MISTERS SISTER 2 b.f. (Apr 6) Robellino (USA) 127 – Baileys On Line 60 (Shareef **42**
Dancer (USA) 135) [2004 7.9g 10v 10.1d p8.6g Nov 26] good-topped filly: first foal:
dam, maiden who stayed 1¾m, closely related to Irish Oaks winner Bolas: poor form in
maidens: blinkered last 2 starts (looked none too keen on first occasion). *J. G. Given*

MISTER SWEETS 5 ch.g. Nashwan (USA) 135 – Keyboogie (USA) 97 (Lyphard **78**
(USA) 132) [2004 87: 6d⁶ 6m 7m* 7g⁵ 6d f7f⁶ 6g 8m 7m 7s f8g Nov 9] lengthy
gelding: fair handicapper: won apprentice race at Newmarket in June: below form after
next start: effective at 6f to easy 9f: acts on all-weather, firm and good to soft going: tried
tongue tied: has been slowly away (awkward and nearly unseated penultimate outing).
D. Carroll

MISTER TRICKSTER (IRE) 3 b.c. Woodborough (USA) 112 – Tinos Island (IRE) **64**
(Alzao (USA) 117) [2004 60: 10d⁶ 10.9d 11.6s 7.1g* 7g 8m 8.1d 8m³ Sep 23] sturdy,
close-coupled colt: modest handicapper: won at Chepstow in June: effective at 7f/1m:
acts on firm and good to soft going: sometimes slowly away. *R. Dickin*

MISTER TROUBRIDGE 2 ch.c. (May 18) Mister Baileys 123 – So True 116 (So **–**
Blessed 130) [2004 7s 7g 7s Oct 21] strong colt: only a little sign of ability in maidens/
minor event. *G. B. Balding*

MIST OPPORTUNITY (IRE) 2 b.g. (Apr 11) Danetime (IRE) 121 – Lady of The **–**
Mist (IRE) 46 (Digamist (USA) 110) [2004 5m 7f 7g 7d Aug 27] tall gelding: little sign
of ability in maidens/seller: hung badly right second start. *P. C. Haslam*

MISTRAL SKY 5 b.g. Hurricane Sky (AUS) – Dusk In Daytona 64 (Beveled (USA)) **85**
[2004 78: p7g² p7g f6s 7d² 7g 7m⁴ 7m³ 7.1m³ 7.6g⁵ 7m⁴ 7g 6m* 6m² 6f² 6d* p6g²
p6d p7.1g p6g p7g⁶ p6g² p7.1g* Dec 20] angular gelding: fairly useful performer: won
minor event at Leicester (third course success) in July, and handicaps at Newmarket in
August and Wolverhampton in December: best at 6f/7f: acts on polytrack (well beaten on
fibresand), firm and good to soft going: wears headgear (usually visor): tends to wander:
tough. *Mrs Stef Liddiard*

MISTRESS HOLLIE (IRE) 3 b.f. Titus Livius (FR) 115 – Soden (IRE) 73 (Mujadil **–**
(USA) 119) [2004 –: p8g Feb 21] smallish, strong filly: well held in maidens/claimers:
wore cheekpieces last 3 starts. *Mrs P. N. Dutfield*

MISTRESS TWISTER 3 b.f. Pivotal 124 – Foreign Mistress (Darshaan 133) [2004 **82**
75: 7f³ 6g³ 7m 6.9f³ 7.9g 8m* Oct 2] leggy, unfurnished filly: fairly useful handicapper:
won 26-runner event at Redcar in October by ½ length from Mount Vettore: stays 1m:
raced only on good ground or firmer. *T. D. Barron*

MISTY BAY 2 b.f. (Mar 13) Namaqualand (USA) – Paris Mist (Paris House 123) [2004 **–**
5g Jul 5] 1,400Y: close-coupled filly: second foal: dam unraced: 100/1, well held in
maiden at Ripon. *J. Balding*

MISTY MAN (USA) 6 ch.g. El Gran Senor (USA) 136 – Miasma (USA) 92 (Lear **45**
Fan (USA) 130) [2004 33: f12g³ f9.4g⁵ f12g* f11m⁴ 10v⁵ f11g⁵ p9.5g f8g Dec 1]
lengthy, angular gelding: poor performer: won selling handicap at Wolverhampton in
January: stays 1½m: acts on all-weather: tried visored/tongue tied, blinkered nowadays.
Miss J. Feilden

MISTY MILLER 2 b.c. (Feb 15) Mind Games 121 – Antonia's Folly 64 (Music Boy **59**
124) [2004 5s⁵ 5g 6m⁶ Jun 12] good-topped colt: modest form at best in maidens: dead.
T. D. Easterby

MISTY PRINCESS   2 gr.f. (Feb 18) Paris House 123 – Miss Whittingham (IRE) 68   **57**
(Fayruz 116) [2004 5g 5g⁵ 5s⁶ 5g f6g 6.1d p5g Aug 6] tall, leggy filly: fourth foal: sister
to fairly useful 1999 2-y-o 5f winner Singsong: dam 5f/6f winner: modest maiden: best
efforts at 5f: acts on polytrack and soft going: edgy sort: sometimes carries head high.
M. J. Polglase

MITCHAM (IRE)   8 br.g. Hamas (IRE) 125§ – Arab Scimetar (IRE) (Sure Blade   **–**
(USA) 130) [2004 98: 6g Apr 12] strong gelding: usually impresses in appearance: useful
performer: off 9 months prior to well held only outing in 2004: effective at 5f/6f: acts on
firm going, probably on soft: blinkered once as 4-y-o: sometimes finds little. *T. G. Mills*

MITCHELLAND   2 b.f. (May 7) Namaqualand (USA) – Precious Girl 76 (Precious   **72**
Metal 106) [2004 5g⁴ 5v* 5.1d 5m⁶ 6g⁶ 5s³ 7d⁵ 6d⁵ 6s⁵ 6s p5.1g⁵ p7.1g² p7.1g* p7.1g
Nov 20] leggy, close-coupled filly: fifth foal: half-sister to 6-y-o Cark and 4-y-o Rosie's
Result: dam 5f/6f winner: fair performer: won minor event at Newcastle in April and
nursery at Wolverhampton in November: stays 7f: acts on polytrack and heavy going:
visored (below form) ninth/tenth starts. *James Moffatt*

MITH HILL   3 b.c. Daylami (IRE) 138 – Delirious Moment (IRE) 90 (Kris 135) [2004   **82**
10.5g 9.9d* p12m* p12g* 12s Nov 6] 90,000Y: second foal: dam, 1m winner who stayed
1¼m, out of half-sister to very smart Irish performer up to 1¼m Executive Perk: fairly
useful performer: won maiden at Beverley in August and 2 handicaps at Lingfield in
October: raced freely when well held in November Handicap at Doncaster final outing:
stays 1½m: raced only on polytrack and good ground or softer. *E. A. L. Dunlop*

MITRAILLETTE (USA)   2 ch.f. (Feb 20) Miswaki (USA) 124 – Crockadore (USA)   **87**
102 (Nijinsky (CAN) 138) [2004 6m⁶ 6.1g⁵ 7g⁴ 7m* Sep 7] unfurnished filly: closely
related to several winners, including fairly useful Irish 2001 2-y-o 7f/1m winner Crooked
Wood (by Woodman), and half-sister to Irish 1¾m winner Circus Maximus (by Pleasant
Colony): dam, Irish 1m/US Grade 2 1½m winner, closely related to smart sprinter Flowing: fairly useful performer: improved to win nursery at Lingfield in quite good style by
½ length from Watchmyeyes: should stay 1m. *Sir Michael Stoute*

MITRASH   4 b.g. Darshaan 133 – L'Ideale (USA) (Alysheba (USA)) [2004 55: 12.3d   **–**
Aug 30] little sign of ability in 2 maidens 15 months apart. *D. McCain*

MITSUKI   5 b.m. Puissance 110 – Surrealist (ITY) (Night Shift (USA)) [2004 83: 6g   **63**
6m⁵ 6m 5d Aug 27] big mare: only modest in 2004: effective at 5f/6f: acts on firm going,
possibly not on good to soft: visored (well held) once: tends to get behind, and best with
strong pace: sometimes carries head awkwardly. *J. D. Bethell*

MITZI CASPAR   3 ch.f. Kirkwall 118 – Petrovna (IRE) 78 (Petardia 113) [2004 f8s   **?**
8g 8.3s 8m f6m³ f7g² f7d* f8g 6g f8s 7g Sep 14] first foal: dam 2-y-o 5f winner: modest   **a51**
performer: won maiden at Southwell in June: best efforts at 7f on fibresand. *P. L. Gilligan*

MIX IT UP   3 b.f. Linamix (FR) 127 – Hawayah (IRE) 68 (Shareef Dancer (USA) 135)   **–**
[2004 –p: 8g Apr 8] well beaten in 2 maidens. *R. M. Beckett*

MIZHAR (USA)   8 b. or br.g. Dayjur (USA) 137 – Futuh (USA) 95 (Diesis 133) [2004   **57**
70: f7g f6g⁵ f7g² f7g⁵ f6s 6v f7g* f7m³ f8.5g² 6.1m May 25] sturdy gelding: just modest
performer in 2004: won seller at Wolverhampton in April: stays 8.5f: easy 8.5f:
acted on all-weather, firm and good to soft going: often wore headgear: held up: bled final
start: dead. *J. J. Quinn*

MIZZ TEE (IRE)   2 b.f. (Mar 27) Orpen (USA) 116 – D D's Jakette (USA) (Deputy   **80**
Minister (CAN)) [2004 5d² 5m* 5m⁵ Jun 2] 15,000F, 15,000Y: strong, lengthy filly:
fluent mover: fourth foal: half-sister to fairly useful Irish 7f winner Zaraglen (by Lear
Fan): dam winner in USA: injured in stall intended debut: won maiden at Ripon in May:
creditable fifth to Miss Meggy in listed race at Beverley, slowly away: will stay at least
6f. *T. D. Easterby*

MKUZI   5 ch.h. Halling (USA) 133 – African Peace (USA) (Roberto (USA) 131) [2004   **112**
113: 10m⁶ 12f⁶ 12m 10d⁵ 12f* 14m* 12m³ 14g² 16s Oct 16] strong, close-coupled horse:
has a round action: smart performer: won listed race at Limerick in May by 3 lengths from
demoted Tarakala and Sharp Minds Betfair Curragh Cup in June by ½ length from Dubai
Success: placed after in listed races at Leopardstown (length third to Foreign Affairs) and
Fairyhouse (3½ lengths second to Holy Orders): well below form in Jockey Club Cup at
Newmarket final outing: stays 1¾m: acts on firm and good to soft going: blinkered final
4-y-o start. *J. Oxx, Ireland*

MOANING MYRTLE   3 br.f. Desert King (IRE) 129 – Grinning (IRE) (Bellypha   **53**
130) [2004 p12g⁴ p13g Oct 1] leggy filly: half-sister to several winners, including useful

1m/1¼m winner Jokesmith (by Mujadil) and fairly useful Irish 7f/8.5f winner Smiling Brave (by Indian Ridge): dam unraced: better effort in maidens at Lingfield on debut: folded quickly subsequent start. *J. R. Fanshawe*

MOAYED 5 b.g. Selkirk (USA) 129 – Song of Years (IRE) 89 (Shareef Dancer (USA) **93 +** 135) [2004 90: p8g* p10g² p10g⁶ p7g³ 7v³ 6g* 5m 7.1m⁴ 7d p6g* f5s² p7g² p6g* f5g p6g **a111** p7g* Dec 29] smart on all-weather, fairly useful on turf: won seller at Lingfield in February and handicaps at Newmarket in May, Lingfield in October, Wolverhampton (beat Quito by ¾ length) in November and Lingfield (beat Chateau Nicol cosily by 1¼ lengths) in December: has form at 1¼m but best at 6f/7f: acts on all-weather, heavy and good to firm going: blinkered/tongue tied: sometimes slowly away: held up. *N. P. Littmoden*

MOBANE FLYER 4 b.g. Groom Dancer (USA) 128 – Enchant 92 (Lion Cavern **73** (USA) 117) [2004 74: 7g 7g 8.5d⁶ 9v³ 10.4m³ 8g* 8m³ 8.2v² 10.3s² 10v⁶ Nov 4] fair performer: left D. Weld in Ireland after 3 yrs: won minor event at Musselburgh in September: stays 10.3f: acts on any going. *R. A. Fahey*

MOBARHEN (USA) 2 b. or br.c. (Feb 26) Red Ransom (USA) – Fit For A Queen **89** (USA) 81 (Fit To Fight (USA)) [2004 7g⁵ 8d⁵ 8m² 8g³ 8d Oct 14] £325,000Y: quite attractive colt: has a quick action: closely related to smart US performer up to 1½m (third in Belmont Stakes) Royal Assault (by Kris S) and half-brother to several winners in USA: dam, 6f winner in Britain, later US Grade 2 8.5f winner: fairly useful maiden: placed at Thirsk and Yarmouth (nursery, did very well from poor draw): ran badly final start: stays 1m: acts on good to firm ground: sold 44,000 gns, sent to USA. *Sir Michael Stoute*

MOBO-BACO 7 ch.g. Bandmaster (USA) 97 – Darakah 78 (Doulab (USA) 115) [2004 **64** 74: 10.2g⁴ 8s⁴ 8m 8f 7.1m 8.1f 8.1m* 8.1g⁵ 7m 7.6f⁶ 8s 7.1g⁴ 8.1m³ 8g² p8.6d² p8.6g³ p9.5g⁴ p8.6g⁵ Dec 17] good-bodied gelding: modest performer: won selling handicap at Warwick in July: effective at 7f to 1¼m: acts on all-weather, firm and soft going: has wandered/raced freely: often races prominently. *R. J. Hodges*

MOCCA (IRE) 3 b.f. Sri Pekan (USA) 117 – Ewan (IRE) (Indian Ridge 123) [2004 77: **97** 10g⁴ 11m⁵ 10m* 12f⁶ 10.3m² 10f⁶ 10s³ 10.3s⁵ Nov 6] tall, leggy filly: useful performer: won handicap at Sandown in June: good efforts after when placed in minor event at Doncaster (½-length second to Tartouche) and listed race at Munich (third to Spatzolita): stays 1¼m: acts on good to firm ground. *D. J. Coakley*

MOCHACCINO (IRE) 2 b.f. (Feb 18) Tagula (IRE) 116 – Cafe Solo 51 (Nomination **–** 125) [2004 f5g 5d 6.1m p5.1d Oct 23] 3,500Y: fourth foal: dam 6f/7f winner: well held in maidens: visored final start: sold 700 gns, sent to Denmark. *D. Shaw*

MODAFFAA 4 b.g. Darshaan 133 – Irish Valley (USA) (Irish River (FR) 131) [2004 **75 p** p12g* Nov 10] half-brother to Alhaarth: won bumper at Ludlow in October: 4/1, won maiden at Lingfield readily by 1¾ lengths from Samaria: should improve. *P. R. Webber*

MODEL FIGURE (USA) 3 b.f. Distant View (USA) 126 – Sylph (USA) 110 (Alleged (USA) 138) [2004 70: 7m Jul 31] fair performer: off over 10 months, well held in handicap at Lingfield only 3-y-o start: will stay at least 1m: wandered when winning final 2-y-o outing: sold 37,000 gns in December, sent to USA. *B. W. Hills*

MODEM (IRE) 7 b.g. Midhish 109 – Holy Water (Monseigneur (USA) 127) [2004 –, **–** a49: f12g p10g Mar 2] sturdy gelding: poor performer: was probably best at 7f/1m: acted on all-weather, soft and firm going: tried blinkered, usually visored: dead. *D. Shaw*

MODESTA (IRE) 3 b.f. Sadler's Wells (USA) 132 – Modena (USA) (Roberto (USA) **105** 131) [2004 10g⁴ 11.5g* 11.9d² 12m 13.9s⁶ 14.6m⁵ 14.1s* Oct 27] rangy filly: has a rather round, unimpressive action: closely related to 2 winners, including very smart 7f (at 2 yrs, when also successful in Fillies' Mile) to 1½m (Oaks) winner Reams of Verse (by Nureyev), and half-sister to several winners, including high-class 7f (at 2 yrs) to 1¼m (Eclipse) winner Elmaamul (by Diesis): dam unraced half-sister to smart 7f/1m performer Zaizafon, herself dam of Zafonic: useful performer: won maiden at Yarmouth in May and listed race there (beat Corrine by 1½ lengths) in October: good fifth to Echoes In Eternity in Park Hill Stakes at Doncaster penultimate start: stayed 14.6f: acted on soft and good to firm going: stud. *H. R. A. Cecil*

MODESTY BLAISE (SWE) 4 br.f. Mango Express 106 – Singoalla (IRE) 69 (Alwuhush (USA) 121) [2004 56: f7g* f8g f7s⁵ p12.2g p8g p10g Dec 18] rather leggy, workmanlike filly: fair performer: easily best effort when winning maiden at Wolverhampton in January: left Gay Kelleway after third start: stays 7f: acts on fibresand. *C. A. Horgan* **71 d**

MODRAJ 2 b.f. (Apr 27) Machiavellian (USA) 123 – Saleela (USA) 85 (Nureyev **81** (USA) 131) [2004 6m 6d³ Aug 13] leggy, useful-looking filly: second living foal: closely related to winner in USA by Miswaki: dam, 12.5f winner, half-sister to 2000 Guineas winner King's Best and Arc winner Urban Sea, herself dam of Galileo: better effort in maidens at Newbury when third to Salamanca: will stay at least 1m. *J. L. Dunlop*

MODULOR (FR)   12 gr.g. Less Ice 113 – Chaumontaise (FR) (Armos) [2004 12.1m   –
12v Oct 16] ex-French gelding: well beaten in seller/claimer in Britain. *L. R. James*

MOKABRA (IRE)   3 b.c. Cape Cross (IRE) 129 – Pacific Grove 89 (Persian Bold   **100**
123) [2004 106: 7g⁶ 7m³ 8g 8m Jun 17] smallish colt: useful performer: 5½ lengths third
of 5 to Leitrim House in Tetrarch Stakes at the Curragh, only respectable effort in 2004:
stays 7f, probably not 1m: acts on good to firm going, ran respectably on soft: visored
final outing: joined D. Selvaratnam in UAE. *M. R. Channon*

MOKARABA   2 ch.f. (Feb 18) Unfuwain (USA) 131 – Muhaba (USA) 96 (Mr Pros-   **86**
pector (USA)) [2004 7f⁴ 8.2g⁴ 8.1m² 8s² Oct 22] quite good-topped filly: third foal: dam,
2-y-o 1m winner, sister to US Grade 2 9f winner Sahm out of Salsabil: fairly useful
maiden: second at Chepstow and Doncaster (nursery): will be suited by 1¼m/1½m: best
effort on soft going. *J. L. Dunlop*

MOLCON (IRE)   3 b.g. Danetime (IRE) 121 – Wicken Wonder (IRE) 71 (Distant Rela-   **89**
tive 128) [2004 75: 6d⁵ 6s* 6s⁵ 6m³ 7m⁴ 7m⁴ 7d 7m* 7f 7s 8g 7s Oct 23] leggy gelding:
fairly useful handicapper: won at Ascot in April and Lingfield (by a head from Apex) in
July: stays 7f: acts on firm and soft ground: sold 18,000 gns. *N. A. Callaghan*

MOLEHILL   3 b.f. Salse (USA) 128 – Mountain Lodge 120 (Blakeney 126) [2004   **60**
11.9d 12m⁵ 12m⁴ 17.1d 16s Aug 28] small, leggy filly: half-sister to several winners, notably smart 1½m/13f winner Compton Ace (by Pharly) and useful 7f (at 2 yrs) and 1¼m
winner Mayville Thunder (by Zilzal): dam won Irish St Leger and Cesarewitch: modest
maiden: probably stays 17f: acts on good to firm and good to soft ground: sold 7,500 gns.
J. G. Given

MOLEM   2 b.g. (Apr 4) Green Desert (USA) 127 – Injaad (Machiavellian (USA) 123)   **70**
[2004 7m⁶ 8.2v⁴ Oct 20] neat gelding: first foal: dam unraced half-sister to 3-y-o Bull
Run: fair form in minor events at Kempton and Nottingham: not sure to stay beyond 1m:
sold 20,000 gns, then gelded. *Sir Michael Stoute*

MOLINIA   3 b.f. Nicolotte 118 – Themeda 69 (Sure Blade (USA) 130) [2004 54: 8.3s   **67**
8.2m 7m⁴ 8.2g 7g⁴ 7m 7m³ 7g p7.1g* p8.6g* f8g² f8g Dec 28] workmanlike filly: fair
performer: won banded race in October and (having left R. Beckett) minor event in
November, both at Wolverhampton: stays 8.6f: acts on polytrack and good to firm going:
tongue tied last 6 starts (reportedly had breathing problem on second occasion): sometimes slowly away. *Mrs Stef Liddiard*

MOLLY DANCER   2 b.f. (Jan 22) Emarati (USA) 74 – Perfect Partner (Be My Chief   **56**
(USA) 122) [2004 6g 6m 6m³ 5.1s⁵ 5m⁶ Sep 15] strong, lengthy filly: first foal: dam
unraced half-sister to 5-y-o Funfair Wane: modest maiden: likely to prove best at 5f/6f:
acts on good to firm going: signs of temperament. *M. R. Channon*

MOLLY MARIE (IRE)   2 b.f. (Apr 5) Fasliyev (USA) 120 – Snoozeandyoulose (IRE)   **75**
73 (Scenic 128) [2004 5g² 6m⁴ 5d⁶ 6g² 7s 6.5m 6f 6s² Sep 24] 9,000F, 34,000Y: tall filly:
fifth foal: half-sister to 3-y-o Daytime Girl: dam Irish 7f winner: fair maiden: should stay
7f: acts on firm ground. *T. D. Easterby*

MOLLY MOON (IRE)   3 br.f. Primo Dominie 121 – Snowing 88 (Tate Gallery (USA)   **72**
117) [2004 84: 5m 5.1g 6f Jul 19] smallish, compact filly: just fair form in 2004: best at
5f: acts on good to firm going, yet to race on ground softer than good. *M. Blanshard*

MOLLY'S SECRET   6 b.m. Minshaanshu Amad (USA) 91§ – Secret Miss 55 (Beve-   **59**
led (USA)) [2004 58: f12g* f12g f12s p10g 10g³ 12m 12.1m³ 10s⁶ 10.9m³ p12.2g* f12d²
p12.2g² Dec 27] workmanlike mare: fair performer: won handicap in January and seller
in November, both at Wolverhampton, leaving C. Cox after latter: stays 1½m: acts on all-
weather and good to firm ground: tried blinkered, usually wears cheekpieces: free-going
sort: sometimes carries head awkwardly. *Miss S. J. Wilton*

MOLLZAM (IRE)   2 b.c. (Apr 1) Danehill (USA) 126 – Matilda Bay (IRE) (Indian   –
Ridge 123) [2004 7g 7d Jul 10] sturdy colt: only a little sign of ability in maidens.
M. P. Tregoning

MOLOTOV   4 b.g. Efisio 120 – Mindomica 63 (Dominion 123) [2004 –, a69d: 5m*   **64**
f5g 6.1g 5m⁴ 5.3d* 6m³ 5m³ 6g⁴ 5d* p5.1g f5m Nov 22] modest performer: won banded
race at Beverley in May, handicap at Brighton in August and minor event at Musselburgh
in October: speedy, and best at 5f: acts on all-weather, good to firm and good to soft

going: ran poorly only start in blinkers: has refused to go to post: races up with pace. *I. W. McInnes*

MOMBASSA (IRE) 4 b.g. Mujadil (USA) 119 – Twilight Tango (Groom Dancer **102** (USA) 128) [2004 103: 7m⁴ 6m⁶ 5m 7m 7m 7g⁵ 8d⁴ 8d* 8d 7v² Oct 31] small, sturdy gelding: useful performer: won apprentice handicap at the Curragh in October easily by 4 lengths from Instant Hit: met trouble in handicap at Newmarket, then below best when 6 lengths second to Fearn Royal in listed race at Leopardstown last 2 starts: stays 1m: acts on firm and good to soft going: tongue tied on debut. *Edward Lynam, Ireland*

MOMENTS I TREASURE (USA) 3 ch.f. Mt Livermore (USA) – Munnaya – (USA) 101 (Nijinsky (CAN) 138) [2004 68: p8g⁶ 12.1d Apr 14] smallish, sparely-made filly: maiden: raced only 4 times, easily best effort on debut at 2 yrs: sent to Australia. *E. A. L. Dunlop*

MOMENTS OF JOY 4 b.f. Darshaan 133 – My Emma 118 (Marju (IRE) 127) [2004 – 113: 12m May 2] big, good-bodied filly: smart performer, lightly raced: last in Jockey Club Stakes at Newmarket only outing in 2004: will stay 2m: raced only on good ground or firmer. *R. Guest*

MOMMKIN 3 b.f. Royal Academy (USA) 130 – Walimu (IRE) 82 (Top Ville 129) **78** [2004 78: 11g⁵ 10.3g⁵ 9.9d⁵ 9.7m⁴ 11.7m Aug 10] big, lengthy, good-topped filly: has plenty of scope: fair maiden: below form after reappearance: stays 11f: visored final start. *M. R. Channon*

MOMTIC (IRE) 3 ch.c. Shinko Forest (IRE) – Uffizi (IRE) (Royal Academy (USA) **93** 130) [2004 77: 9g³ 8.1d³ 9g 10d⁴ 8m⁴ 9g* 8g² 9.7g⁵ Aug 13] well-made colt: fairly useful handicapper: won at Kempton in July: stays 1¼m: acts on firm and good to soft ground: sometimes races freely: consistent. *W. Jarvis*

MONAD (IRE) 2 b.f. (Mar 2) General Monash (USA) 107 – Moon River (FR) (Groom **47** Dancer (USA) 128) [2004 7d 7.1g 7s p8g Sep 22] €9,500Y: strong filly: third foal: half-sister to 2 winners, including 4-y-o Lunar Leader: dam third at 2m in France: modest maiden. *Mrs P. N. Dutfield*

MONA LISA 2 ch.f. (Mar 6) Giant's Causeway (USA) 132 – Colorsnap (Shirley **108** Heights 130) [2004 7m⁴ 7m² 8f⁴ a8.5f Oct 30] 1,250,000Y: close-coupled, good sort: has a quick action: half-sister to several winners, including useful performer up to 1½m Croeso Cariad (by Most Welcome) and fairly useful Irish 1997 2-y-o 6f/7f winner Photogenic (by Midyan): dam unraced half-sister to Irish Oaks winner Colorspin, herself dam of Opera House and Kayf Tara: useful maiden: odds on first 2 starts: easily best effort when 1¾ lengths fourth to Playful Act in Fillies' Mile at Ascot (hampered 2f out): always behind in Breeders' Cup Juvenile Fillies at Lone Star Park: will be suited by 1¼m/1½m. *A. P. O'Brien, Ireland*

MONASHEE MISS 2 ch.f. (Jan 4) Monashee Mountain (USA) 115 – Most Uppitty **43** 69 (Absalom 128) [2004 5.1s⁴ f6g 7g³ f7m f7d Jul 23] 950Y: sixth foal: half-sister to winner in Germany by Revoque: dam 5f (at 2 yrs)/6f winner: poor maiden: dead. *J. A. Pickering*

MONASHEE PRINCE (IRE) 2 ch.g. (Feb 18) Monashee Mountain (USA) 115 – **76** Lodema (IRE) (Lycius (USA) 124) [2004 5.2m² 5g* 5.1d⁵ 5m³ 5m⁴ 5g 6g 6d p7g⁶ p8g p8g⁴ Nov 30] tall, leggy gelding: first foal: dam unraced granddaughter of Irish Oaks winner Knight's Baroness: fair performer: won maiden at Hamilton in April: stays 1m: acts on polytrack, good to firm and good to soft going: often races up with pace. *R. A. Best*

MONASHEE ROSE (IRE) 2 br.f. (Feb 14) Monashee Mountain (USA) 115 – Thorn **78** Tree (Zafonic (USA) 130) [2004 5m 5m* 5g* 5.7g² 5g 5m 5v⁶ Oct 3] €1,500Y: first foal: dam unraced granddaughter of Queen Mary and Flying Childers winner Abeer: fair performer: won maiden at Carlisle and nursery at Musselburgh in August: good second in nursery at Bath: will prove best at 5f/easy 6f: acts on good to firm going, probably on heavy. *J. S. Moore*

MONASH GIRL (IRE) 3 b.f. General Monash (USA) 107 – Maricica (Ahonoora – 122) [2004 –: 8f⁶ 8.3f 8s Oct 15] little form. *B. R. Johnson*

MONASH LAD (IRE) 2 ch.g. (Mar 24) General Monash (USA) 107 – Story Time **74** (IRE) (Mansooj 128) [2004 5m 6m⁵ 6m³ 6g³ 6m⁴ 6s³ p7g Nov 10] €11,500Y: rather leggy gelding: fifth foal: half-brother to 2001 Italian 2-y-o 6f to 7.5f winner by Perugino: dam unraced: fair maiden: stays 6f: acts on soft and good to firm ground. *M. H. Tompkins*

MONDURU 7 b.g. Lion Cavern (USA) 117 – Bint Albadou (IRE) 91 (Green Desert **55** (USA) 127) [2004 42: p10g f8.5g* p10g² p10g² p10g³ f9.4g² p10g* a10.5g a9g⁶ a16.5g² a12g³ a10.5g* a10.5g Sep 26] good-topped gelding: modest performer: won banded event at Wolverhampton in February, claimer at Lingfield (final start for G. L. Moore) in April and handicap at Mijas in August: probably best up to 10.5f: acts on all-weather/sand and any turf going: blinkered latter starts in Britain: sometimes carries head high. *P. Haley, Spain*

MONICA GELLER   6 b.m. Komaite (USA) – Rion River (IRE) (Taufan (USA) 119) [2004 63+, a–: p8.6g6 Dec 22] leggy mare: just poor form only outing in 2004: should stay 1¼m: acts on all-weather, soft and good to firm going: tried visored: sometimes slowly away: refused to enter stall intended final 5-y-o outing. *M. Dods*   **38**

MONICA'S REVENGE (IRE)   2 b.f. (Feb 2) Josr Algarhoud (IRE) 118 – Unimpeachable (IRE) 65 (Namaqualand (USA)) [2004 6.1m 7.1s p8.6g Oct 7] leggy filly: first foal: dam 2-y-o 1m seller winner: poor form in maidens. *R. M. Beckett*   **41 ?**

MONKEY MADGE   2 br.f. (Feb 22) Cape Cross (IRE) 129 – Runelia (Runnett 125) [2004 6g² 6d Oct 18] 8,500Y: leggy filly: half-sister to several winners, including useful 1¼m/1½m winner (including in UAE) Kumatour (by Batshoof): dam lightly-raced maiden: much better effort in maidens when second at Thirsk: should stay 7f. *B. Smart*   **63**

MONKEY OR ME (IRE)   3 b.g. Sri Pekan (USA) 117 – Ecco Mi (IRE) (Priolo (USA) 127) [2004 –: f7g f8g f7g⁴ f8g² 7.1g³ f7g³ 8.5m⁴ 9.9d 7.9m Sep 11] poor maiden: stays 8.5f: acts on fibresand and good to firm going. *P. T. Midgley*   **36**

MONOLITH   6 b.g. Bigstone (IRE) 126 – Ancara 109 (Dancing Brave (USA) 140) [2004 13.1d³ 18s Oct 16] fairly useful performer: best effort on Flat when third in handicap at Ayr: should be suited by 2m+: acts on heavy ground: useful hurdler. *L. Lungo*   **87**

MON PLAISIR   2 br.f. (May 13) Singspiel (IRE) 133 – Mademoiselle Chloe 106 (Night Shift (USA)) [2004 p7g 7s Oct 27] half-sister to 3 winners, including smart 6f (at 2 yrs) to 1m winner French Fellow (by Suave Dancer), later 1m winner in Hong Kong: dam 2-y-o 5f winner: well beaten in maidens at Lingfield and Yarmouth, green and slowly away. *C. F. Wall*

MONSAL DALE (IRE)   5 ch.g. Desert King (IRE) 129 – Zanella (IRE) 87 (Nordico (USA)) [2004 64: f12g f16s 14.1g p16g6 Apr 21] strong gelding: modest performer at best, no Flat form in 2004: sometimes wears cheekpieces: sometimes races freely. *N. E. Berry*   **–**

MON SECRET (IRE)   6 b.g. General Monash (USA) 107 – Ron's Secret 92 (Efisio 120) [2004 69: f8g⁴ f7g 7.1d 7.1m6 7.5d 8f6 6.9g* 8.5m p8.6g p9.5d6 Nov 4] sparely-made gelding: fair handicapper: won at Carlisle in September: effective at 7f (all wins since 2 yrs)/1m: acts on all-weather and good to firm ground. *B. Smart*   **61 a65**

MONSIEUR BOND (IRE)   4 ch.c. Danehill Dancer (IRE) 117 – Musical Essence 65 (Song 132) [2004 115: 6g⁵ 7s* 6s* 6f 6g6 6.5g 6g⁵ 7d⁴ Oct 9] close-coupled, useful-looking colt: very smart performer: won Castlemartin/La Louviere Studs Gladness   **120**

Duke of York Hearthstead Homes Stakes, York—
Monsieur Bond (right) follows up a win in Ireland to land his second pattern race of the year;
Steenberg (left), Arakan (white cap), Welsh Emperor (blinkers) and Goldeva (grey) are next

Stakes at the Curragh (by 7 lengths from Steenberg) in April and Duke of York Hearth-stead Homes Stakes at York (by 1½ lengths from same horse, hanging left) in May: creditable efforts in blinkers last 2 starts when 2½ lengths fifth to Tante Rose in Sprint Cup at Haydock and 2 lengths fourth to Somnus in Prix de la Foret at Longchamp: effective at 6f/7f: acted on soft and good to firm going, seemingly not on firm: raced prominently: to stand at Whitsbury Manor Stud, Hampshire, fee £3,500. *B. Smart*

MONSIEUR MIRASOL 2 b.g. (Mar 18) Mind Games 121 – Nom Francais 39§ (First   **78** Trump 118) [2004 5g³ 5g³ 5f⁵ 6s* 6m 6s² 5s⁴ 7m 6m⁵ 6m 6v Oct 23] 21,000Y: leggy gelding: first foal: dam, maiden who seemed to stay 2m (probably ungenuine), closely related to smart sprinter Perryston View: fair performer: won maiden at Newcastle in June: creditable efforts after only when in frame in nurseries: stays 6f: acts on soft going: blinkered (very stiff task) penultimate outing. *K. A. Ryan*

MONSOON RAIN (USA) 2 b.c. (Jan 18) Old Trieste (USA) 122 – Smokey Mirage **103 p** (USA) (Holy Bull (USA) 134) [2004 7m² 8m* Sep 8] $95,000F, $550,000Y: leggy, close-coupled colt: has a quick, fluent action: second foal: dam, 5f (minor stakes at 2 yrs) to 6.5f winner in USA, sister to smart UAE 7f to 9f winner Estimraar: second to Windsor Knot in maiden at Newmarket: won similar event at Doncaster by ¾ length from Shannon Springs, getting on top final 1f: will stay 1¼m: potentially smart, and should win more races. *Saeed bin Suroor*

MONTANA 4 b.g. Puissance 110 – Mistral's Dancer (Shareef Dancer (USA) 135) [2004   **57 §** 80d: 5g 6m⁴ 6g Sep 16] tall gelding: ungenuine maiden: stays 6f: acts on good to firm ground: gelded after final start. *J. L. Spearing*

MONTARA (IRE) 5 b.g. Perugino (USA) 84 – Tatra (Niniski (USA) 125) [2004 –: 9f⁶ **55**
10g³ 10.5g² 12d p9.5g* p9.5d⁵ Nov 4] modest performer: won banded race at Wolverhampton in October: stays 10.5f: acts on polytrack and soft ground: tried blinkered/
tongue tied at 3 yrs, wore cheekpieces last 5 starts. *Lindsay Woods, Ireland*

MONTECITO 2 b.f. (Feb 24) Montjeu (IRE) 137 – Dancing Fire (USA) (Dayjur **78**
(USA) 137) [2004 6d 7g 6g³ 6d Oct 14] 34,000Y: lengthy filly: second foal: dam unraced
daughter of Poule d'Essai des Pouliches winner Danseuse du Soir: fair maiden: easily
best effort when staying-on third in minor event at Salisbury: should stay at least 7f.
R. Hannon

MONTECRISTO 11 br.g. Warning 136 – Sutosky 78 (Great Nephew 126) [2004 83: **77**
12g 11.9g 11.6d 11.7s⁴ 13.8s⁴ p12g³ p13g⁴ f14g⁶ p13g Dec 29] leggy, close-coupled
gelding: fair nowadays: effective at 1½m to 2m: acts on all-weather/dirt, heavy and good
to firm going: held up: has won twice for lady rider: consistent. *R. Guest*

MONTE MAJOR (IRE) 3 b.g. Docksider (USA) 124 – Danalia (IRE) 78 (Danehill **67**
(USA) 126) [2004 53: p7g³ p7g⁴ f8s² p7g* 6d² 6d May 1] fair performer: won maiden at **a77**
Lingfield in March: ran as though amiss final start: stays 7f: raced only on all-weather/
good to soft ground: has raced freely: sold 14,000 gns in July. *M. A. Jarvis*

MONTE MAYOR LAD (IRE) 4 b.g. Sesaro (USA) 81 – Alcalali (USA) 96 (Sep- **59**
tieme Ciel (USA) 123) [2004 71: 6.1s 6m f8d Jun 10] good-bodied gelding: just modest
maiden in 2004: stays 7f: acts on all-weather, good to firm and good to soft going: tried
blinkered/in cheekpieces. *D. Haydn Jones*

MONTGOMERY 3 b.g. In Command (IRE) 114 – Lightening Reef (Bon Sang (FR) **47**
126) [2004 11.7m⁶ 9s⁶ 9.9m⁵ 10m p8.6g p10m Dec 8] poor maiden: seems to stay 9f:
tried in cheekpieces. *A. G. Newcombe*

MONTGOMERY'S ARCH (USA) 2 b. or br.c. (Jan 30) Arch (USA) 127 – **118**
Inny River (USA) (Seattle Slew (USA)) [2004 7g* 6m* 7m⁴ 7s³ Oct 16]
    'One owner complained that his horse's ears were too thin. He'd ask me
how it could be expected to run when it had no muscle on its ears.' Apart from a
fund of anecdotes, Peter Chapple-Hyam had little to show for his stint in Hong
Kong, where he found it difficult in new surroundings, training only a trickle of
winners from a poor string of horses in each of his four seasons. Chapple-Hyam
again found himself on unfamiliar ground on his return to Britain in 2004, basing
himself in Newmarket at St Gatien stables, but he wasted little time showing that
he had not lost his touch. Eight of his first seventeen runners, up until the end of
April, were successful, and he ended the season with thirty on the board (plus one at
Deauville), reviving memories of his best days with five pattern successes, African
Dream, the first of them, winning the Betfred Classic Trial at Sandown in April
shortly after the death of Chapple-Hyam's former leading patron at home, Robert
Sangster. Chapple-Hyam married into the Sangster family and enjoyed great suc-

*Richmond Stakes, Goodwood—one of 30 winners in Britain
for Peter Chapple-Hyam in his first season back following a spell in Hong Kong;
Montgomery's Arch (rail) foils Mystical Land with Silver Wraith staying on well for third*

cess when taking over from Barry Hills at Sangster's Manton training establishment. He had still to turn thirty when saddling Dr Devious to win the Derby in 1992, little over a year after taking out a licence, and won the Two Thousand Guineas at Newmarket and the Curragh, as well as the International Stakes at York and the Champion Stakes at Newmarket, with Sangster's Rodrigo de Triano in the same season. Chapple-Hyam left for Hong Kong under a cloud after being replaced at Manton by John Gosden in 2000, but he reportedly sought Sangster's advice before taking the decision to return to Britain, and he trained Harrison Point, who won three times in the Sangster colours in 2004.

A string of other big-race successes for Chapple-Hyam in his first spell as a trainer also included the Middle Park, the Dewhurst and the Racing Post Trophy, and three of his pattern winners in 2004 came in juvenile events. He won the Prix du Calvados at Deauville in August with Cours de La Reine, after taking the July Stakes at Newmarket with Captain Hurricane and the Group 2 Richmond Stakes at Glorious Goodwood with Montgomery's Arch. Chapple-Hyam was well aware of the strength of his two-year-olds when Montgomery's Arch made his debut in a seven-furlong maiden at Folkestone the day after Captain Hurricane's Newmarket success, Montgomery's Arch starting favourite in a field of ten and winning comfortably by two and a half lengths. 'I told everyone there are two certainties—we die and this horse wins at Folkestone,' said Chapple-Hyam afterwards. Moved up sharply in class, Montgomery's Arch was only fourth favourite at 13/2 for the Rich-

Franconson Partners' "Montgomery's Arch"

mond, over six furlongs three weeks later, in a market dominated by Blue Dakota and Mystical Land, first and second in the Norfolk Stakes at Royal Ascot. With only eight runners, the early pace proved steady, but Montgomery's Arch was soon to the fore and, though headed by Mystical Land around a furlong out, he kept on gamely under strong pressure from Jimmy Fortune to peg back Mystical Land by a neck, the pair two lengths clear. After a two-month break, Montgomery's Arch was returned to seven furlongs and moved up again to Group 1 company for his final two starts of the year. He ran creditably when under three lengths fourth of six to Oratorio in the Prix Jean-Luc Lagardere at Longchamp in October and turned in his best effort when third to Shamardal in the Dewhurst at Newmarket later in the month. Sweating and very much on his toes beforehand at Newmarket, Montgomery's Arch got much closer to Oratorio than he had at Longchamp, rallying late on to be beaten a neck by him for second behind the two-and-a-half-length winner.

Montgomery's Arch (USA) (b. or br.c. Jan 30, 2002)	Arch (USA) (b 1995)	Kris S (b 1977)	Roberto Sharp Queen
		Aurora (b 1988)	Danzig Althea
	Inny River (USA) (b 1995)	Seattle Slew (b or br 1974)	Bold Reasoning My Charmer
		Golden Petal (ch 1981)	Mr Prospector Hattons Rose

Montgomery's Arch has already proved quite a bargain. Led out unsold at 42,000 guineas at Newmarket as a yearling, he ended up with Chapple-Hyam after being knocked down for 20,000 guineas at the Newmarket Breeze-Up Sales in April. He is the third foal of his dam Inny River, a lightly-raced close relative to the very smart North American performer at up to a mile and a quarter Golden Larch, as well as half-sister to another winner Golden Gorse, the dam of Prince of Wales's Stakes winner Lear Spear. Inny River's first foal, by Hennessy, was a winner over a mile as a two-year-old in North America, and a yearling out of her by Cozzene sold for 250,000 dollars at Keeneland in September. Montgomery's Arch's sire, Arch, a son of Kris Kin's sire Kris S, showed high-class form at a mile and a quarter, winning the Grade 1 Super Derby on dirt, and was also represented in Europe in 2004 by the three-year-old Art Trader, who showed smart form at a mile and a quarter. Montgomery's Arch will be suited by a step up to a mile and will probably stay a mile and a quarter. A tall, quite good-topped colt, he acts on soft ground and has yet to race on firm. *P. W. Chapple-Hyam*

MONTJEU BABY (IRE)   2 b.f. (Mar 23) Montjeu (IRE) 137 – Catch The Lights 86   **60** (Deploy 131) [2004 6.1d 7g 7.1m 8g⁶ p7.1g Nov 12] fourth foal: dam, 7f/1m winner, half-sister to smart performer up to 1m King's Ironbridge: modest maiden: form only at 1m. *R. Hannon*

MONTMARTRE (IRE)   4 b.f. Grand Lodge (USA) 125 – French Quarter (Ile de   **–** Bourbon (USA) 133) [2004 98: 13.9g 8m Jul 31] tall, angular filly: useful performer at 3 yrs: well held in handicaps in 2004: races up with pace: bolted to post and withdrawn on intended reappearance. *J. Howard Johnson*

MONTOSARI   5 ch.g. Persian Bold 123 – Sartigila 67 (Efisio 120) [2004 44: p13g*   **63** p10g⁶ p12g³ p12g* p10g² 11.6m p16g³ 12m p16g p12g⁴ p16g* Nov 30] modest performer: won banded races in February and April and amateur handicap in November, all at Lingfield: stays 2m: acts on all-weather and good to firm ground: sometimes races freely. *P. Mitchell*

MONT SAINT MICHEL (IRE)   2 b.c. (Mar 2) Montjeu (IRE) 137 – Band of Angels   **70 p** (IRE) (Alzao (USA) 117) [2004 7g 8g⁶ Oct 12] 140,000F, 62,000Y: strong, close-coupled colt: third foal: half-brother to fairly useful Irish 2003 2-y-o 7f winner Dance On The Moon (by Fasliyev): dam unraced half-sister to Derby winner Dr Devious: burly, better effort in maidens when sixth to Luis Melendez at Leicester, not knocked about: should be suited by 1¼m/1½m: type to do better as 3-y-o. *G. Wragg*

MONTURANI (IRE)   5 b.m. Indian Ridge 123 – Mezzogiorno 108 (Unfuwain   **112** (USA) 131) [2004 108: 8d³ 10.5g⁶ 8f² 8m⁴ 8g⁴ 10s⁵ 10g* 10g Oct 24] big, good-topped mare: smart performer: suffered stress fracture of off-hind tibia after final 3-y-o start: won Irish National Stud Blandford Stakes at the Curragh in September by ½ length from

Irish National Stud Blandford Stakes, the Curragh—
Monturani and Kinnaird make it a British-trained 1,2

Kinnaird: creditable efforts otherwise when 2 lengths second to Favourable Terms in Windsor Forest Stakes at Royal Ascot and when fourth to Soviet Song in Falmouth Stakes at Newmarket and to Marbye in Prix d'Astarte at Deauville: effective at 1m to 10.5f: acts on firm ground, has run respectably on soft: has worn crossed noseband/had 2 handlers: usually tracks leaders. *G. Wragg*

MOON BIRD   2 b.f. (Feb 18) Primo Dominie 121 – Time For Tea (IRE) 73 (Imperial **62** Frontier (USA) 112) [2004 6f p6g⁴ p6g³ Dec 15] fourth foal: half-sister to fairly useful 7f/ 1m winner Frazzled (by Greensmith), later successful in Spain, and 3-y-o Trifti: dam maiden who stayed 1¼m: modest form when in frame in maidens: needs to settle to stay 7f. *C. A. Cyzer*

MOON DAZZLE (USA)   3 b.f. Kingmambo (USA) 125 – June Moon (IRE) (Sadler's **104** Wells (USA) 132) [2004 8m* 8m⁴ 8.1d⁵ 8m⁵ 8m² 8m⁶ Sep 25] smallish, leggy, close-coupled filly: half-sister to several winners, including milers Pacino, Zachariah (in Japan) and Dupont (won Italian/German 2000 Guineas), all smart and by Zafonic: dam unraced daughter of 1000 Guineas runner-up and smart sprinter Kerrera: useful performer: won maiden at Newmarket in May: best effort when 6 lengths fourth to Attraction in Coronation Stakes at Royal Ascot: not sure to stay beyond 1m: acts on good to firm going: edged left final start: joined M. de Kock in UAE. *W. J. Haggas*

MOON EMPEROR   7 b.g. Emperor Jones (USA) 119 – Sir Hollow (USA) (Sir Ivor **91 d** (USA) 135) [2004 102: p12g p12g⁶ 16d 13.9s⁴ 14g⁶ 14m⁶ 16m 16g 16d Oct 10] tall, close-coupled gelding: useful handicapper at best: on downgrade: stays 2m: acts on polytrack, firm and soft going: visored third/fourth outings: held up. *J. R. Jenkins*

MOONFLEET (IRE)   2 b.f. (Mar 26) Entrepreneur 123 – Lunasa (IRE) 82 (Don't **58** Forget Me 127) [2004 7.5g 6d³ 7.9g 8s p7m Nov 22] 2,400 2-y-o: third living foal: closely related to winner in Greece by In The Wings: dam, Irish 1¾m winner, out of half-sister to Moon Madness and Sheriff's Star: modest maiden: should stay at least 1¼m: acts on good to soft going. *M. F. Harris*

MOON FOREST (IRE)   2 br.c. (May 2) Woodborough (USA) 112 – Ma Bella Luna **82** 76 (Jalmood (USA) 126) [2004 7.1g² 6d⁴ 7.1d* 7s* Oct 22] €12,000Y: good-topped colt: sixth foal: brother to fairly useful 2001 2-y-o 5f winner Woodsmoke and half-brother to winner abroad by Goldmark: dam 1m winner: fairly useful performer: made all in maiden at Warwick and nursery at Newbury (beat Looks Could Kill by head, edging left) in October: stays 7f: acts on soft going. *P. W. Chapple-Hyam*

MOONGLADE (USA) 4 ch.f. Carson City (USA) – Moonshine Girl (USA) 97 **36 ?**
(Shadeed (USA) 135) [2004 –: f6g p6g 6.1g 6.1m⁵ 7g 5.3f⁶ 6m Jul 19] poor maiden:
sometimes wears headgear/tongue tie. *Miss J. Feilden*

MOON LEGEND (USA) 3 ch.f. Gulch (USA) – Highland Legend (USA) 93 (Storm **70**
Bird (CAN) 134) [2004 68p: 7f 7m³ 7f 7m* 6m p7.1g⁶ Oct 9] tall, close-coupled filly:
fair performer: won maiden at Thirsk in July: should stay 1m: acts on polytrack and good
to firm going: sometimes slowly away. *W. Jarvis*

MOONLIGHT APPEAL (IRE) 2 ch.f. (Apr 12) Bahamian Bounty 116 – Divine **–**
Appeal (El Gran Senor (USA) 136) [2004 6g Oct 8] 3,500Y: lengthy filly: first foal:
dam, fairly useful 1½m winner in France, showed little later in Britain: 66/1, tailed off in
maiden at York. *J. S. Wainwright*

MOONLIGHT MAN 3 ch.c. Night Shift (USA) – Fleeting Rainbow 65 (Rainbow **103**
Quest (USA) 134) [2004 104: 7g² 6s² 7m 6m 7m² 7m⁴ 7m² 8f⁶ 7m Oct 2] leggy, quite
attractive colt: useful performer: runner-up 4 times at 3 yrs, in listed Free Handicap at
Newmarket (to Brunel), listed race at Ascot (behind Millbag), minor event at Newbury
(3½ lengths behind Fong's Thong) and handicap at Leicester (beaten a length by My
Paris): should stay 1m: acts on firm and soft going. *R. Hannon*

MOONLIGHT SONG (IRE) 7 b.m. Mujadil (USA) 119 – Model Show (IRE) 82 **45 d**
(Dominion 123) [2004 –: 7.2g³ 7v f8.5m f7d 7m 7.5g f7m Jul 12] small mare: poor performer: well held after reappearance: effective at 7f/1m: acts on fibresand, heavy and
good to firm going: tried in cheekpieces/blinkers. *John A. Harris*

MOONLIGHT TANGO (USA) 3 br.f. Benny The Dip (USA) 127 – Summer Dance **77**
86 (Sadler's Wells (USA) 132) [2004 76: 10.2g⁵ 9.9g⁵ 12.1g⁴ May 31] leggy, unfurnished
filly: fair maiden: probably stays 1½m: raced only on good/good to firm going: carried
head high final outing: sold 21,000 gns in July, sent to Australia. *J. H. M. Gosden*

MOONMAIDEN 2 ch.f. (Feb 13) Selkirk (USA) 129 – Top Table 65 (Shirley Heights **71**
130) [2004 7g 8.1s⁵ 8.2d⁵ 7m Oct 2] leggy, angular filly: closely related to 1½m winner
Manama Rose and 6f (at 2 yrs) and 1m winner Krispy Knight (both useful, by Kris) and
half-sister to 2 winners: dam, second at 1½m, half-sister to smart miler Centre Stalls: fair
maiden: easily best effort when fifth at Nottingham: should be suited by 1¼m/1½m: acts
on good to soft ground. *M. R. Channon*

MOON MISCHIEF (IRE) 2 b.f. (Feb 28) Desert Sun 120 – Moonlight Path (IRE) **64**
(Fairy King (USA)) [2004 6m f5g³ 5.1d 6m p6g Dec 27] 15,000Y: smallish filly: third
foal: dam unraced: modest maiden: ran poorly last 2 starts: should stay 6f: best effort on
fibresand. *N. P. Littmoden*

MOON ROYALE 6 ch.m. Royal Abjar (USA) 121 – Ragged Moon 72 (Raga Navarro **–**
(ITY) 119) [2004 48, a31: f6g f7g f11g 8.5d Aug 11] close-coupled mare: no form in
2004: has worn cheekpieces. *Mrs N. Macauley*

MOONSHAFT (USA) 3 br.c. Capote (USA) – Moonshine Girl (USA) 97 (Shadeed **70**
(USA) 135) [2004 10d 10d 10s⁴ 12.1m 9.2d⁴ p8.6g⁵ p7g Oct 25] tall, lengthy colt: has a
fluent, quick action: third foal: brother to US 2001 2-y-o 5.5f winner Glimmering Bay:
dam 2-y-o 5f winner who stayed 7f: fair maiden: stays 1¼m: acts on polytrack and good
to soft going: visored (raced too freely) final outing. *E. A. L. Dunlop*

MOONSHINE BEACH 6 b.g. Lugana Beach 116 – Monongelia 98 (Welsh Pageant **81**
132) [2004 71: 15s⁴ 21.6v 14.1d⁶ 16m³ 18g⁶ 17.2f⁵ 19.1f⁴ 15m 16.2g* 17.2g* 16.2m
16m³ 16.2d* 16.2g* 16m 17.2g³ 17.1g* 18d* Oct 18] leggy, lengthy gelding: fairly useful handicapper: had a good season, winning at Warwick and Bath within 4 days in
July, Beverley (carried head high and edged left) and Warwick in August and twice at
Pontefract in October: stays 2¼m: acts on polytrack, firm and good to soft going: wore
cheekpieces third to sixth outings. *P. W. Hiatt*

MOONSHINE BILL 5 ch.g. Master Willie 129 – Monongelia 98 (Welsh Pageant **59**
132) [2004 63: 10.9s³ 10v Apr 19] lengthy, workmanlike gelding: modest handicapper:
should stay 1½m: acts on soft and good to firm ground: found little final start. *P. W. Hiatt*

MOON SHOT 8 gr.g. Pistolet Bleu (IRE) 133 – La Luna (USA) (Lyphard (USA) 132) **77**
[2004 66+: f12s* f12s² p12g⁴ 10s May 10] good-bodied gelding: fair performer, lightly
raced nowadays: won minor event at Wolverhampton in February: stays 1½m: acts on
all-weather, firm and good to soft going: blinkered once at 4 yrs: has been tongue tied:
sometimes races freely/finds little. *A. G. Juckes*

MOO

MOONSIDE 2 gr.f. (Apr 11) Docksider (USA) 124 – Moon Magic 62 (Polish Precedent (USA) 131) [2004 5.7g 7g 7d Oct 30] 7,000Y: lengthy filly: seventh foal: half-sister to 3 winners, including 3-y-o Lunar Exit and 4-y-o Once: dam, ran once, half-sister to Sheriff's Star and Moon Madness: well held in maidens: visored final start. *G. B. Balding* –

MOON SPINNER 7 b.m. Elmaamul (USA) 125 – Lunabelle (Idiot's Delight 115) [2004 11.7f 8.2m p7.1g 14.1s Oct 27] second foal: dam winning hurdler/chaser up to 2¼m: modest winning hurdler: no form on Flat. *Andrew Reid* –

MOONSTRUCK 2 ch.c. (Apr 4) Fraam 114 – Easter Moon (FR) (Easter Sun 122) [2004 p8g Sep 22] 20/1, seventh of 11 in maiden at Lingfield. *J. M. P. Eustace* 42

MOORS MYTH 3 b.g. Anabaa (USA) 130 – West Devon (USA) (Gone West (USA)) [2004 67p: 7d³ 7d⁶ 7.1m⁵ 8.3m⁶ 7f* p7g Oct 1] big, good-topped gelding: has scope: fair performer: won maiden at Redcar in September: stays 7f: takes strong hold: has looked awkward ride: sold 12,500 gns, then gelded. *B. W. Hills* 73

MOOSE MALLOY 7 ch.g. Formidable (USA) 125 – Jolimo 92 (Fortissimo 111) [2004 p8g⁵ Apr 21] big, workmanlike gelding: no form on Flat: tried in cheekpieces. *M. J. Ryan* –

MORAG 3 b.f. Aragon 118 – Minnehaha (Be My Chief (USA) 122) [2004 70: 8d⁴ 10.2m 8.3m 7f 8.1d⁶ 8m⁶ 7m² 7s 7m 9m 7g p7.1g p9.5g p7m⁶ Dec 8] fair performer: well below form last 5 starts: stays 1m: acts on good to firm and good to soft going: tried in cheekpieces/blinkers/tongue tie. *I. A. Wood* 66

MORAHIB 6 ch.h. Nashwan (USA) 135 – Irish Valley (USA) (Irish River (FR) 131) [2004 99: 10.1m² 10g Aug 23] strong, well-made horse: lightly-raced handicapper, useful at 5 yrs for M. Tregoning: well below best in claimers in 2004: best efforts around 1m: acts on good to firm ground. *W. J. Musson* 72

MORGAN LEWIS (IRE) 3 b.g. Orpen (USA) 116 – Party Piece (Thatch (USA) 136) [2004 65: 5m 6g* 6d³ 5s² 5d³ Sep 27] fairly useful performer, lightly raced: won handicap at Haydock in August: effective at 5f/6f: acts on soft and good to firm going: usually waited with: edged right final start. *G. B. Balding* 78

MORITAT (IRE) 4 b.g. Night Shift (USA) – Aunty Eileen (Ahonoora 122) [2004 60?: f6d 5.1m⁶ 5f³ 6f⁵ 6g⁶ 6.1g³ 5.1m 6g Oct 5] good-topped gelding: modest maiden: stays 6f: acts on firm going: sometimes tongue tied. *P. D. Evans* 60

MORNING AFTER 4 b.f. Emperor Jones (USA) 119 – Onefortheditch (USA) 79 (With Approval (CAN)) [2004 82: 8m p8g⁶ 7m⁶ p8g⁴ Sep 22] fair performer: stays 1m: raced only on polytrack and good/good to firm ground on turf. *J. R. Fanshawe* 70

MORNING HAWK (USA) 3 b.f. Silver Hawk (USA) 123 – Dawn Aurora (USA) (Night Shift (USA)) [2004 51: p8g f11g⁴ f9.4g⁵ p10g⁶ 16.2g 16g⁴ 14.1m 16.2s⁴ 10d Oct 2] workmanlike filly: poor maiden: stays 2m: acts on fibresand and good to firm ground: blinkered last 4 outings. *J. S. Moore* 44

MORNING MAJOR (USA) 2 b.g. (Mar 18) Parade Ground (USA) 124 – North of Seattle (USA) (Northern Baby (CAN) 127) [2004 6s 7g 7d Aug 27] good-topped gelding: poor form in maidens: sold 1,000 gns. *T. D. Barron* 43

MORNING SUN 4 b.f. Starborough 126 – Malham Tarn (Riverman (USA) 131) [2004 –: f9.4g Jan 5] workmanlike filly: little form. *K. O. Cunningham-Brown* –

MORNING WORLD 2 b.c. (Jan 29) Bahamian Bounty 116 – Snap Cracker 82 (Inchinor 119) [2004 5g 5d 5m⁶ May 21] sturdy, close-coupled colt: well held in maidens. *J. R. Weymes* –

MORNIN RESERVES 5 b.g. Atraf 116 – Pusey Street Girl 87 (Gildoran 123) [2004 108: 5g 5f 5d Jul 3] tall, angular gelding: useful performer: below best in 2004, trained by R. Allan on reappearance only: speedy, and best at 5f: acts on any ground: usually leads. *I. Semple* 96 ?

MOROZOV (USA) 5 b.h. Sadler's Wells (USA) 132 – High Hawk 124 (Shirley Heights 130) [2004 115: 16.2s 13.9d May 13] smart performer for A. Fabre at 4 yrs: pulled up in Sagaro Stakes at Ascot and Yorkshire Cup at York in 2004: stayed 15.5f: acted on soft and good to firm going: blinkered (ran poorly) final outing in 2003: swerved and unseated rider penultimate 4-y-o appearance: to stand at Blackhall Stud, Co Wexford, Ireland. *C. N. Allen* –

MORRIS DANCING (USA)   5 b.g. Rahy (USA) 115 – Summer Dance 86 (Sadler's   –
Wells (USA) 132) [2004 –: f11g f9.4g f12g f8g p10g⁵ p12g f8m f9.4g f11g³ f12g⁵ 12.6m
Jul 2] little form since 2002: tried in cheekpieces/visor/tongue tie. *B. P. J. Baugh*

MORSE (IRE)   3 b.g. Shinko Forest (IRE) – Auriga 73 (Belmez (USA) 131) [2004 79:   **91**
7g 6d² 6g² 6g³ 6s* 6.1d² 6m p6g 6.5g⁶ 6m 6.1g 8.1g 7.1d* 6s p7.1g² 7s⁵ Oct 23]
close-coupled gelding: fairly useful performer: won handicap at Lingfield in May and
claimer at Warwick in September: effective at 6f/easy 7f: acts on polytrack, soft and good
to firm ground: races prominently: gelded after final start. *J. A. Osborne*

MORSON BOY (USA)   4 b.g. Lear Fan (USA) 130 – Esprit d'Escalier (USA) (Diesis   **95**
133) [2004 110p: 12.1d 16.2d 13.9g 14g 16.2g Aug 7] tall, leggy gelding: smart handicapper in 2003: off 10 months and gelded, well below best in 2004, though saddle
reportedly slipped last 2 starts: should stay at least 2m: acts on good to firm ground:
ungainly galloper, and sometimes wanders: joined P. Nicholls. *M. Johnston*

MORVERN (IRE)   4 ch.g. Titus Livius (FR) 115 – Scotia Rose (Tap On Wood 130)   **53**
[2004 65: p12g⁴ f14g 14.1m⁵ 13.1d⁶ Jun 18] strong gelding: modest maiden: stays easy
1½m: acts on polytrack and good to firm ground: tried in cheekpieces/visor: has raced
freely. *J. G. Given*

MOSCOW BALLET (IRE)   3 b.c. Sadler's Wells (USA) 132 – Fire The Groom   **111**
(USA) 115 (Blushing Groom (FR) 131) [2004 109: 10.4s⁶ 9g⁶ 10m* 12f 10f³ Aug 14]
close-coupled, attractive colt: has a quick action: smart performer: back to form to win
listed race at Royal Ascot in June by 1¼ lengths from Crocodile Dundee, well ridden
from front: respectable efforts after when seventh to Grey Swallow in Irish Derby at the
Curragh and 4½ lengths third to Kitten's Joy in Secretariat Stakes at Arlington: stays
1¼m: acts on firm going: sweating/edgy on reappearance: wears crossed noseband:
joined D. Hayes in Hong Kong. *A. P. O'Brien, Ireland*

MOSCOW BLUE   3 ch.g. Soviet Star (USA) 128 – Aquamarine 89 (Shardari 134)   **57**
[2004 –p: 8.5s⁶ 8.1m May 21] big, close-coupled gelding: modest form in maidens: bred
to stay at least 1¼m: sold 6,500 gns, gelded and joined Venetia Williams. *J. H. M. Gosden*

MOSCOW MARY   3 b.f. Imperial Ballet (IRE) 110 – Baileys Firecat 67 (Catrail   –
(USA) 123) [2004 63: f5g f6g 6.1m 7f 6m 8.1d Oct 17] small, leggy, close-coupled filly:
modest winner at 2 yrs, little form in 2004. *A. G. Newcombe*

MOSCOW MUSIC   2 ch.c. (Mar 3) Piccolo 121 – Anna Karietta 82 (Precocious 126)   **100**
[2004 5.2g² 5s* 5f² 6m³ 6m³ 7g⁵ Sep 30] 14,000F, 23,000Y: rather leggy, quite
good-topped colt: brother to 4-y-o Little Englander and half-brother to several winners,
including useful German 6f/7f performer Just Heaven's Gate (by Slip Anchor): dam 6f/7f
winner: useful performer: landed odds in maiden at Lingfield in May: creditable placed
efforts after in listed races at Sandown and York and sales event (third to Caesar Beware)
at Doncaster: good fifth in Somerville Tattersall Stakes at Newmarket: barely stays 7f:
acts on firm and soft going: joined C. Yip in Hong Kong. *M. G. Quinlan*

MOSCOW TIMES   3 b.g. Soviet Star (USA) 128 – Bargouzine 67 (Hotfoot 126) [2004   **79**
74: 6g⁶ 7g⁵ 8g 8g* 8m³ 8g p7g⁵ Oct 1] well-made gelding: has scope: fair handicapper:
won at Salisbury in July: stays 1m: raced only on polytrack/good ground or firmer:
sometimes slowly away/carries head high: usually held up: none too straightforward: sold
6,000 gns. *D. R. C. Elsworth*

MOSHKIL (IRE)   2 b.c. (Apr 27) In The Wings 128 – Brentsville (USA) (Arctic Tern   **65**
(USA) 126) [2004 7.1m 8d 8g⁶ Sep 13] 40,000Y: half-brother to several winners,
including useful 5f/6f winner Sylva Paradise (by Dancing Dissident): dam, Irish 2-y-o 6f
winner, half-sister to smart performer up to 1¼m Young Senor: best effort in maidens
when sixth at Bath: will probably stay 1¼m: sold 8,200 gns. *M. P. Tregoning*

MOSSMANN GORGE   2 b.g. (Apr 24) Lujain (USA) 119 – North Pine (Import 127)   **64**
[2004 5f 6g⁶ 6m⁵ 7.1d² p6g⁴ f7g⁴ Dec 16] 9,000Y, 15,000 2-y-o: quite good-topped
gelding: half-brother to several winners, including fairly useful 5f winner (including
at 2 yrs) Heaven-Liegh-Grey (by Grey Desire): dam poor half-sister to top-class sprinter
Lochnager: modest maiden: left G. A. Swinbank after fourth start: stays 7f: acts on
all-weather, good to firm and good to soft going: seems no easy ride. *D. Flood*

MOSS VALE (IRE)   3 b.c. Shinko Forest (IRE) – Wolf Cleugh (IRE) 65 (Last Tycoon   **118**
131) [2004 99: 6d⁴ 5.1d* 6m* 6m* 6g 5s 6d² 6d² Oct 15] strong colt: has a quick action:
smart performer: won handicap at Chester and listed race at Haydock in May and listed
event at Salisbury (beat Mac Love by ¾ length) in June: below form in July Cup at

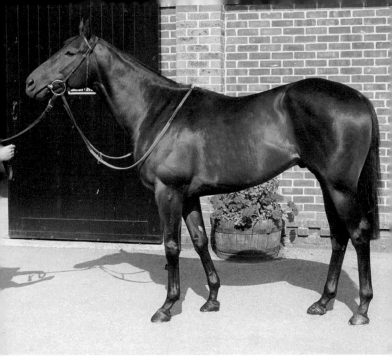

Mr John C. Grant & Cheveley Park Stud's "Moss Vale"

Newmarket and Nunthorpe Stakes at York next 2 starts: good efforts when runner-up to Royal Millennium in Renaissance Stakes at the Curragh (beaten ½ length) and Bentinck Stakes at Newmarket (short-headed) last 2 starts: effective at 5f/6f: acts on soft and good to firm ground: races prominently. *B. W. Hills*

MOSTANAD 2 b.g. (Feb 12) Alhaarth (IRE) 126 – Jeed (IRE) 86 (Mujtahid (USA) 118) [2004 6g Jul 10] 12/1, hampered twice when behind in maiden at York: sold 6,500 gns. *E. A. L. Dunlop* –

MOSTARSIL (USA) 6 ch.g. Kingmambo (USA) 125 – Naazeq 80 (Nashwan (USA) 135) [2004 78: 16d 14.1s⁶ 16.2m³ 14g⁴ 14m* 11.9g⁶ 14.4g 11.9f⁶ Aug 3] workmanlike gelding: fair handicapper: won at Sandown in June: probably needs further than 1½m nowadays and stays 2m: acts on polytrack, firm and soft going: tried blinkered/visored, wears cheekpieces: usually held up. *G. L. Moore* **75**

MOSTASHAAR (FR) 2 b.c. (Feb 13) Intikhab (USA) 135 – Nasanice (IRE) 97 (Nashwan (USA) 135) [2004 7m 7g⁵ Oct 12] fluent mover: third foal: half-brother to useful 2002 2-y-o 7f winner Huja (by Alzao) and 3-y-o Maraahel: dam Irish 9f winner: better effort in maidens at Leicester when fifth to Eqdaam: will stay at least 1m: should progress. *Sir Michael Stoute* **76 p**

MOST DEFINITELY (IRE) 4 b.g. Definite Article 121 – Unbidden Melody (USA) (Chieftain) [2004 64: 14.1f² 16.1v 16d⁶ 16m² 14g³ 14.1f² 14.1m² 14.1d* 16d² Nov 3] leggy gelding: fairly useful handicapper: won at Redcar in October, wandering: stays 17f: acts on firm and good to soft going: tried blinkered: sometimes finishes weakly. *T. D. Easterby* **81**

MOST-SAUCY 8 br.m. Most Welcome 131 – So Saucy 59 (Teenoso (USA) 135) [2004 83, a78: 11s⁶ 11.7g⁶ 11.9m⁵ 11.8m 11.8m³ 12m⁴ 12.6f⁵ 13.3g 12g⁴ p16g³ 12m³ 11.9f **64 a61**

674

p16g* 17.2g p16g Oct 13] lengthy mare: fair handicapper: won at Lingfield in September: effective at 1½m to 2m: acts on all-weather, firm and soft going: usually held up. *I. A. Wood*

MOTARASSED   2 b.c. (Apr 1) Green Desert (USA) 127 – Sayedati Eljamilah (USA) **87**
64 (Mr Prospector (USA)) [2004 6m³ 6g* 7m⁵ Sep 8] lengthy colt: first foal: dam twice-raced half-sister to Derby winner Erhaab: won maiden at Salisbury in July by 1½ lengths from Marching Song, leading close home: jumped shadow and lost action final start (sustained injury): will stay at least 7f. *J. L. Dunlop*

MOTH BALL   2 b.c. (Apr 3) Royal Applause 124 – Chrysalis 66 (Soviet Star (USA) **110**
128) [2004 6m² 6g³ 6g* 6.1g 5g³ 6m* 6m⁴ 6g* Oct 9] 110,000Y: lengthy colt: third foal: half-brother to 3-y-o Western Roots and 4-y-o Just Fly: dam, maiden who stayed 1m, out of half-sister to Arc winner Saumarez: smart performer: won maiden at Goodwood in August, nursery at Brighton in September and listed event at York (comfortably, by 1¼ lengths from Nufoos) in October: sold privately for 205,000 gns later in October, and joined J. Cassidy in USA: likely to stay 7f: acts on good to firm going: often edgy at stall, and was withdrawn from Grade 3 Generous Stakes at Hollywood in November after causing trouble at start. *J. A. Osborne*

MOTHECOMBE DREAM (IRE)   2 b.c. (Jan 28) Foxhound (USA) 103 – Another **67**
Shadow (IRE) (Topanoora 118) [2004 7m 8g 8s p8g⁶ p6g³ p6g* p6g² Dec 27] €19,000F, 30,000Y: sturdy colt: first foal: dam unraced: fair performer: won seller at Lingfield (sold from B. Meehan) in December: good second in claimer at Wolverhampton final start: should stay 7f: acts on polytrack and soft going: blinkered last 4 starts: tends to carry head awkwardly/hang. *C. A. Dwyer*

MOTIVATOR   2 b.c. (Feb 22) Montjeu (IRE) 137 – Out West (USA) 103 (Gone **122 p**
West (USA)) [2004 8d* 8s* Oct 23]
'Racing over a mile at two is harmful for classic hopes' was one of the objections raised when the race now known as the Racing Post Trophy, the final Group 1 of the year in Britain, was first run in 1961. The field for the inaugural running—as the Timeform Gold Cup—turned out to include the subsequent winners of both the Derby and St Leger, Larkspur and Hethersett, and the race has been won since by such as Noblesse, Vaguely Noble, Pretendre, High Top, Reference Point, King's Theatre, Celtic Swing and, in the three runnings immediately before the latest one, by subsequent classic winners High Chaparral, Brian Boru and American Post. Some of the others who didn't win have included, since the 'eighties, Shergar, Assert, Mendez, Sheriff's Star, Assessor, Benny The Dip, Mutamam, Holding Court, Ekraar and Grandera, all Group 1 winners. The race was not designed, by the way, with the aim of providing a good guide to the following year's top races. Its purpose, in the words of Timeform's founder Phil Bull, was 'to provide a worthwhile opportunity for high-class two-year-olds bred to stay to compete for a valuable prize over a distance commensurate with their stamina.'

Racing Post Trophy, Doncaster—in testing conditions,
Motivator justifies favouritism, winning from Albert Hall and Henrik (almost obscured)

High Chaparral, Brian Boru, American Post and the latest winner Motivator were all arguably bred to stay a mile and a half as three-year-olds (though American Post failed to do so when sixth to North Light in the Derby). While American Post won the Racing Post Trophy on his fourth start and Brian Boru and High Chaparral won it on their third, Motivator had only one outing under his belt when he lined up at Doncaster. The impression created by his six-length success in a maiden over a mile at Newmarket in August marked him down as a colt with a big future. The race effectively developed into a three-furlong sprint but Motivator was in a different league to his rivals, quickly settling matters when set alight two furlongs out and eased near the finish. The runner-up Sunday Symphony won his next two races. Motivator missed the Royal Lodge Stakes at Ascot in September because connections felt that the firm underfoot conditions placed too much emphasis on speed. Soft ground at Doncaster and a good gallop made the Racing Post Trophy a thorough test of stamina and the runners finished well strung out. Despite understandably still showing signs of greenness, and wandering a little after moving to the front over two furlongs out, Motivator established himself as one of the season's top juveniles with a two-and-a-half-length success, eased near the line, over the O'Brien-trained Beresford Stakes winner Albert Hall. The pair had dominated the betting—Motivator starting at 6/4 and Albert Hall at 5/2—and, of the six other runners, only third-placed 12/1-shot Henrik (who had missed the Dewhurst the previous week) managed to finish within ten lengths of Motivator. The second O'Brien-trained challenger Hills of Aran came fourth while the last two places were filled by the Royal Lodge fourth and fifth, Elliots World and Frith. Motivator's Timeform rating was the highest recorded in the Racing Post Trophy since Celtic Swing's year, and was confirmed by the timefigure for the performance of 0.81 fast (equivalent to a timerating of 120), bettered only by Dewhurst winner Shamardal among the season's juveniles, though it must be noted that the field at Doncaster raced on fresh ground on the far side of the straight course for the first four furlongs. One final point before leaving the Racing Post Trophy. The race has been run on the straight mile at Doncaster since 2001, but it would be more in keeping with the original concept if it were to return to the round course. Not only would the race be a better spectacle for those on the course, but it would also provide a better education—as it was designed to do—for a prospective stayer who will have to race round turns as a three-year-old.

Motivator (b.c. Feb 22, 2002)	Montjeu (IRE) (b 1996)	Sadler's Wells (b 1981)	Northern Dancer
			Fairy Bridge
		Floripedes (b 1985)	Top Ville
			Toute Cy
	Out West (USA) (br 1994)	Gone West (b 1984)	Mr Prospector
			Secrettame
		Chellingoua (b 1983)	Sharpen Up
			Uncommitted

Motivator cost 75,000 guineas as a yearling and is a tall, good sort. He was still a shade on the weak side as a two-year-old and has the scope for further physical development at three. He is from the promising first crop of Arc and King George winner Montjeu, who was third behind Pivotal and Giant's Causeway in the sires' two-year-old earnings list. His other progeny include Ayam Zaman, Dash To The Top, Kings Quay and Where With All. Montjeu's stamina-laden pedigree and racing record made it likely that, if he was to sire a Group 1 two-year-old winner in Britain, it would be in the Racing Post Trophy. His sire Sadler's Wells, not generally credited as a sire of two-year-olds, has had five winners of the race, King's Theatre, Commander Collins, Aristotle, High Chaparral and Brian Boru. If Motivator takes after his sire and most of the offspring of his grandsire, he will do better still as a three-year-old. Although he will stay at least a mile and a quarter, and probably get a mile and a half, Motivator is not short of speed and should not be ruled out of the Two Thousand Guineas, if that becomes his target, for which he is on offer at 16/1 at the time of writing. Motivator is the third foal produced by the useful Out West, who won over seven and a half furlongs as a two-year-old and was successful in a listed event over a mile at Goodwood at three when trained by Henry Cecil. Out West's first two foals were by the miler Polish Precedent: the first was the filly Warsaw Girl, a minor winner over six furlongs in the States, and the second was the

The Royal Ascot Racing Club's "Motivator"

fair maiden three-year-old Gabana who has done most of her racing at around a mile. Out West's sire Gone West has sired winners over a range of distances but has made his name mostly as an influence for speed, while Out West's dam the lightly-raced maiden Chellingoua, who was placed at a mile in France, is a half-sister to the successful sire Wavering Monarch, winner of the Grade 1 Haskell Invitational over nine furlongs. Motivator's fourth dam Lady Be Good, who is the great grandam of Polish Precedent, was a foundation mare for the Phipps family. She bred ten winners herself and appears in the extended pedigrees of numerous notable performers including two other tip-top milers Posse (grandam) and Zilzal (great grandam). While soft ground would place the emphasis on stamina at Newmarket and would be in Motivator's favour, it is worth bearing in mind that he has yet to encounter going firmer than good to soft and his effectiveness under the firmish conditions that often prevail on Guineas day would have to be taken on trust, as he is reportedly unlikely to have a preparatory race. Motivator is understandably at shorter odds for the Derby—14/1 available—and makes slightly more appeal for that classic. Were connections to consider a tilt at the Prix du Jockey Club, which will be run over an extended mile and a quarter in 2005, there would be even stronger grounds for being optimistic about Motivator's prospects of joining the roll of honour of classic winners. *M. L. W. Bell*

MOTIVE (FR) 3 ch.c. Machiavellian (USA) 123 – Mistle Song 112 (Nashwan (USA) **94**
135) [2004 8v⁵ 10m* 10.4m² 10m 10g 11.8g Oct 11] 250,000Y: lengthy, good-topped

colt: first foal: dam 1½m and 14.6f (Park Hill Stakes) winner: fairly useful performer: won maiden at Windsor in May: beaten a head by Etmaam in handicap at York next time: should stay 1½m: acts on good to firm going: found little final outing: sold 120,000 gns, joined J. Howard Johnson. *Sir Michael Stoute*

MOTORWAY (IRE)   3 b.c. Night Shift (USA) – Tadkiyra (IRE) (Darshaan 133)   **84** [2004 10.2g⁶ 10f* 10m⁵ Aug 8] 270,000Y: fifth foal: half-brother to useful 2002 2-y-o 7f winner Geminiani (by King of Kings): dam, French 1¼m winner, half-sister to Princess Royal Stakes winner Tashtiya: fairly useful form: won maiden at Windsor in July by ¾ length from News Sky: respectable fifth in handicap there subsequent start: should stay 1½m: sold 70,000 gns in October. *R. Charlton*

MOTU (IRE)   3 b.g. Desert Style (IRE) 121 – Pink Cashmere (IRE) (Polar Falcon   **68** (USA) 126) [2004 79: 6d 6s 8m 7m 8.2d 7.5d 8.1d³ 8d⁶ 7g p8.6g⁴ Dec 17] good-topped gelding: fair performer: left J. Dunlop after eighth start: stays 1m: acts on good to firm and good to soft going, probably on polytrack: tried blinkered. *P. R. Chamings*

MOUFTARI (USA)   3 b.c. Miswaki (USA) 124 – Nature's Magic (USA) (Nijinsky   **79** (CAN) 138) [2004 68p: 8g⁵ 10.3d⁴ 10.5m⁵ 10.2f² p12g³ 10g⁵ Sep 29] well-made colt: fair maiden: stays 1¼m: acts on polytrack, firm and good to soft going: blinkered final start: sold 12,000 gns. *B. W. Hills*

MOUNTAIN BREEZE   2 b.f. (Mar 30) Monashee Mountain (USA) 115 – Breezy   **–** Louise 60 (Dilum (USA) 115) [2004 7.5d p8.6g 6d Oct 18] 1,500F, 3,500Y: big filly: first foal: dam 5f winner, including at 2 yrs: no form in maidens. *D. Shaw*

MOUNTAIN MEADOW   3 ch.g. Deploy 131 – Woodwardia (USA) 93 (El Gran   **79** Senor (USA) 136) [2004 83p: 10g² 12.1g* Jun 17] sturdy gelding: fairly useful form: won maiden at Beverley in June: stayed 1½m: raced only on good going: dead. *Mrs A. J. Perrett*

MOUNT ARAFAT   2 b. or br.g. (Mar 25) Erhaab (USA) 127 – Cache (Bustino 136)   **–** [2004 8.1s 8g 10.2g Sep 27] well held in maidens: tongue tied final start. *M. Salaman*

MOUNT BENGER   4 ch.g. Selkirk (USA) 129 – Vice Vixen (CAN) (Vice Regent   **70** (CAN)) [2004 66: 10g⁶ 10.2m 10.1d⁴ 10.5s* 12s 10g³ 10.9s 11.7g² Oct 10] tall, leggy gelding: fair handicapper: won at Haydock in July: stays easy 1½m: acts on all-weather and soft ground: visored final start, wore cheekpieces previous 5 outings: usually held up: sold 20,000 gns. *R. M. Beckett*

MOUNT BUTLER (IRE)   2 b.g. (Apr 17) Celtic Swing 138 – Baylands Sunshine   **44** (IRE) (Classic Secret (USA) 91) [2004 6m 7.9g 10v⁶ Oct 20] leggy, workmanlike gelding: poor form in maidens. *J. G. Given*

MOUNTCHARGE (IRE)   3 b.g. Intikhab (USA) 135 – Zorilla (Belmez (USA) 131)   **63** [2004 81: 8m 7m 8m⁵ 10g 8.1d Sep 18] stocky gelding: modest performer: left C. Allen after third start: should stay 1¼m: acts on polytrack and good to firm going: very slowly away second outing at 2 yrs (gave trouble at start). *G. A. Huffer*

MOUNT COTTAGE   3 b.f. Cape Cross (IRE) 129 – Brecon Beacons (IRE) 71   **44** (Shirley Heights 130) [2004 8m⁶ 8.1s⁴ 9.9s⁶ 10.1d f12g f14g Dec 11] 12,500Y: sixth foal: half-sister to winners abroad by Wolfhound and Royal Academy: dam maiden best at 2 yrs (should have stayed at least 1¼m): poor maiden: tried visored. *J. G. Given*

MOUNT EPHRAM (IRE)   2 b.g. (Apr 4) Entrepreneur 123 – Happy Dancer (USA)   **66 §** 95 (Seattle Dancer (USA) 119) [2004 5v⁴ 6s⁵ 6m⁶ 7g⁴ 7.1m* 7m⁴ 7m² 8g 7.1d 8s p8.6g* p8.6g³ f8g⁵ p8.6g p8.6g Dec 11] €20,000Y: rather leggy gelding: third foal: half-brother to 4-y-o Happy Camper: dam 2-y-o 1m winner in France/Italy: fair performer: won maiden at Musselburgh in June and claimer at Wolverhampton in November: stays 8.6f: acts on all-weather, soft and good to firm going: tried blinkered, has won in cheekpieces: sometimes reluctant stall/hangs: not to be trusted. *R. F. Fisher*

MOUNT HILLABY (IRE)   4 b.f. Mujadil (USA) 119 – Tetradonna (IRE) 102 (Teen-   **74** oso (USA) 135) [2004 67: f7g* f8f 8.1g 8.2g² 9v 7.9m* 7.5m 7m⁵ p8.6g* f8g p9.5g³ p8.6g* Dec 27] good-topped filly: fair handicapper: won at Wolverhampton (apprentices) in January, York in September and Wolverhampton in November and December: stays 8.6f: acts on all-weather, good to firm and good to soft ground. *M. W. Easterby*

MOUNT KELLET (IRE)   2 ch.g. (Feb 20) Bluebird (USA) 125 – Antinnaz (IRE)   **42** 111 (Thatching 131) [2004 6d p5.1g p7.1g Oct 18] poor form in maiden/sellers: sold 500 gns, sent to Sweden. *J. G. Given*

MOUNT LOGAN   9 b.h. Shareef Dancer (USA) 135 – Double Entendre 81 (Dominion   **–** 123) [2004 –: p10g Jan 7] well held in 3 maidens. *R. Curtis*

MOUNT PEKAN (IRE) 4 b.g. Sri Pekan (USA) 117 – The Highlands (FR) (High **50 §**
Line 125) [2004 64§: 9.9d 8.3d³ 9.2g 8g⁶ 8.1g 7.2g⁵ 7g 7d 8.3d Aug 17] leggy gelding:
unreliable maiden: stays 1m: acts on good to soft ground: sometimes races freely/looks
less than keen. *J. S. Goldie*

MOUNT ROYALE (IRE) 6 ch.g. Wolfhound (USA) 126 – Mahabba (USA) 74 (Elo- **61**
cutionist (USA)) [2004 60, a69: f8g f8g f6f⁶ f7g³ f7g* f7s* f7s 7g 6d⁶ f7g² f7g² 7.1g² **a70**
7d³ p6d f8g f7g² f7g² Dec 14] close-coupled gelding: has knee action: fair handicapper
on all-weather, modest on turf: won at Southwell and Wolverhampton in February:
effective at 6f/7f: acts on fibresand (ran poorly on polytrack), firm and soft going: tried
blinkered, usually visored/tongue tied. *N. Tinkler*

MOUNT SUPERIOR (USA) 8 b.g. Conquistador Cielo (USA) – Zum Solitair (USA) **45**
(Vice Regent (CAN)) [2004 43: f6g* f6g⁵ f6g⁶ p8g f6s Mar 30] poor performer nowadays:
won amateur banded race at Southwell in January: stays 7f: acts on fibresand: tried
tongue tied, often blinkered. *P. W. D'Arcy*

MOUNT VETTORE 3 br.g. Vettori (IRE) 119 – Honeyspike (IRE) 79 (Chief's Crown **84**
(USA)) [2004 64p: f6g* 7g² 8.1s 8m 8m 10f 8.5d 7g⁶ 8m⁶ 7m³ 8m² Oct 2] strong gelding:
fluent mover: fairly useful performer: won maiden at Wolverhampton in January: stays
1m: acts on fibresand and good to firm ground: none too trustworthy: sold 24,000 gns,
joined K. Reveley, and won over hurdles in December. *Mrs J. R. Ramsden*

MOUSEMAN 3 b.g. Young Ern 120 – Scottish Royal (IRE) (Night Shift (USA)) **–**
[2004 59: 5.3m⁵ 6.1m 5m Jul 14] good-bodied gelding: modest performer at 2 yrs: well
held in 2004: sometimes blinkered. *C. N. Kellett*

MOVIE KING (IRE) 5 ch.g. Catrail (USA) 123 – Marilyn (IRE) 72 (Kings Lake **70**
(USA) 133) [2004 80, a93: 12.3d 10g 10g² 10.3g 10g 10m⁶ 10g³ 8g Sep 14] workmanlike **a?**
gelding: fair handicapper: best at 1m/1¼m: acts on polytrack and firm going: tried
visored/in cheekpieces: races up with pace. *S. Gollings*

MOYNE PLEASURE (IRE) 6 b.g. Exit To Nowhere (USA) 122 – Ilanga (IRE) 92 **47**
(Common Grounds 118) [2004 58: f16.2g f12s f8g f12s⁶ f11s 16.1v f11m² 11.9g f9.4g²
f12m³ f9.4m* 8.5m⁴ 10.1g⁶ f12d f8g 12f 10.1s Jun 25] small, sparely-made gelding: poor
performer nowadays: won banded race at Wolverhampton in May: effective at 9.4f to 2m:
well held on heavy going, acts on any other turf and fibresand: usually wears cheekpieces:
sometimes looks none too keen, refused to race final outing. *Paul Johnson*

MOZAFIN 2 b.c. (Mar 12) Zafonic (USA) 130 – Bedara 83 (Barathea (IRE) 127) [2004 **85**
5g⁶ 6m² 6s⁴ 7m³ 7.1d² 7s 7g² 8.1s* 7.5g Dec 12] 58,000Y: sturdy colt: first foal: dam
10.5f winner out of useful French stayer Cutting Reef: fairly useful performer: favourite,
made all in maiden at Haydock on debut: sold from M. Channon before below form
in listed race at Pisa: stays 1m: acts on soft and good to firm going: visored/blinkered last
3 starts. *Annelies Mathis, Austria*

MPENZI 2 b.f. (Jan 12) Groom Dancer (USA) 128 – Muschana 100 (Deploy 131) [2004 **62 p**
7g 8v Oct 23] well-made filly: first foal: dam, 1¼m winner, half-sister to Melbourne Cup
winner Jeune and King Edward VII Stakes winner Beneficial: better effort in maidens
when strong-finishing seventh to Rob Roy at Newmarket on debut (got loose before start
and slowly away): should be suited by 1¼m/1½m: likely to do better. *J. L. Dunlop*

MR AITCH (IRE) 2 b.c. (Apr 6) Soviet Star (USA) 128 – Welsh Mist 102 (Damister **72**
(USA) 123) [2004 8.3m² p8g⁴ p9.5g⁴ Nov 13] €77,000Y: fifth foal: closely related
to 3-y-o Lilly Gee and half-brother to 3 winners, including useful 7f and 8.5f winner
Brighter Future (by Night Shift) and 4-y-o Soyuz: dam 5f (including at 2 yrs)/6f winner:
fair form in maidens: seems barely to stay 9.5f. *J. A. Osborne*

MR BELVEDERE 3 b.g. Royal Applause 124 – Alarming Motown (Warning 136) **54 §**
[2004 70: 8.2g 7m 8g 7m³ 8f² 8m p10g⁴ 10m 9s Oct 22] sturdy gelding: modest maiden:
left R. Hannon after fifth start: stays easy 1¼m: acts on polytrack, firm and good to soft
ground: tried in headgear: has hung left: unreliable. *A. J. Lidderdale*

MR BOUNTIFUL (IRE) 6 b.g. Mukaddamah (USA) 125 – Nawadder 73 (Kris 135) **59**
[2004 67: 7g 7d 7.2m⁴ 7f 7m 6m⁶ 5.9f⁴ 7m p6d⁴ p6g p6g⁵ p7g⁵ Dec 30] angular gelding:
modest performer: effective at stiff 5f to 7f: acts on all-weather, firm and soft going: tried
blinkered, usually in cheekpieces: tongue tied last 7 starts. *M. Dods*

MR DINGLAWI (IRE) 3 b.g. Danehill Dancer (IRE) 117 – Princess Leona (IRE) **65 ?**
(Naiyli (IRE)) [2004 p7g p8g p12g⁵ 11.9s Oct 15] IR 8,000F, 52,000Y, 3,500 2-y-o:
second foal: brother to useful 2002 2-y-o 5f/6f winner Miss Takeortwo: dam unraced:
possibly flattered when fifth in maiden at Lingfield: no form otherwise: may prove best
short of 1½m: tried blinkered (raced freely)/tongue tied. *D. B. Feek*

MR DINOS (IRE) 5 b.h. Desert King (IRE) 129 – Spear Dance (Gay Fandango (USA) **118**
132) [2004 124: 13.9d⁴ 16.4f² 20m⁶ Jun 17] good-topped horse: very smart performer:
won Henry II Stakes at Sandown and Gold Cup at Royal Ascot (reportedly sore after) in
2003: encouraging 1½ lengths second to Papineau in Henry II Stakes at Sandown in May:
favourite, disappointing sixth behind same horse in Gold Cup at Royal Ascot (reportedly
very sore after) final outing: stays 2½m: acts on any going: has worn crossed noseband:
races prominently: game. *P. F. I. Cole*

MR DIP 4 b.g. Reprimand 122 – Scottish Lady (Dunbeath (USA) 127) [2004 66?: p8g **53**
f8s⁶ 8.1s 10.2m 10.9m⁵ 12.1g² 10.5s⁶ 12.1m Aug 5] leggy gelding: modest maiden: stays
1½m: acts on soft and good to firm ground: sometimes slowly away: found little final
outing. *A. W. Carroll*

MR ED (IRE) 6 ch.g. In The Wings 128 – Center Moriches (IRE) 74 (Magical Wonder **88**
(USA) 125) [2004 86: 14m² 14d² 14.4m* 14.1d² 18s² Oct 16] angular gelding: fairly
useful handicapper: won at Kempton in August, idling: good second to Contact Dancer in
Cesarewitch at Newmarket final outing: stays 2¼m: acts on soft and good to firm going:
tried blinkered, has worn cheekpieces last 4 starts: sometimes slowly away/wanders: held
up: smart hurdler. *P. Bowen*

MR FLEMING 5 b. or br.g. Bin Ajwaad (IRE) 119 – Fabulous Night (FR) (Fabulous **35**
Dancer (USA) 124) [2004 49: p10g³ p10g 10g Jul 16] poor maiden: stays 11.5f: raced
mainly on polytrack/good to firm ground: blinkered last 4 starts: sold 1,200 gns, sent to
Denmark. *Dr J. D. Scargill*

MR FORTYWINKS (IRE) 10 ch.g. Fools Holme (USA) – Dream On 54 (Absalom **48**
128) [2004 67: 16d 16d⁵ 13.9m 16m⁶ 16f³ Jul 29] sparely-made gelding: poor handicapper nowadays: stays 17f: acts on fibresand and any turf going: tried tongue tied: tends
to sweat: usually races up with pace. *B. Ellison*

MR HULLABALOU (IRE) 3 b.g. Princely Heir (IRE) 111 – Lomalou (IRE) (Light- **68**
ning Dealer 103) [2004 p6g 6d 6s⁴ 7f² 7g⁵ 6g 7.6g 6m 7g 6m* f6g p7g p6m Dec 22] IR
7,000F, €4,000Y: first foal: dam unraced: fair performer: won maiden at Lingfield in
July: should stay 7f: acts on soft and good to firm ground. *R. Ingram*

MR INDEPENDENT (IRE) 3 b.g. Cadeaux Genereux 131 – Iris May 87 (Brief **53**
Truce (USA) 126) [2004 66: 8.2s 10m 9g 9.5d Dec 24] close-coupled gelding: modest
maiden: sold from E. Dunlop after third start (visored). *E. Castelli, Italy*

MR JACK DANIELLS (IRE) 3 b.g. Mujadil (USA) 119 – Neat Shilling (IRE) **83**
(Bob Back (USA) 124) [2004 70: 7.1s³ 8m⁶ 8m³ 8g 8m⁴ 8.1m* 10m⁴ 10g 8.1g³ 7d Sep
18] big gelding: fairly useful performer: won minor event at Sandown in July: stays 1¼m:
acts on soft and good to firm ground: blinkered (ran poorly) final start: sold 38,000 gns.
W. R. Muir

MR KALANDI (IRE) 2 gr.c. (Mar 10) Grand Lodge (USA) 125 – Singhana (IRE) **65**
(Mouktar 129) [2004 6m³ 6m 7m 6.1m⁶ 7.1d p7.1g² Nov 26] 22,000Y: quite good-topped
colt: sixth foal: dam, Irish 1¾m winner, half-sister to dam of Sinndar (by Grand Lodge):
fair maiden: should stay at least 1m: acts on polytrack and good to firm going: tongue tied
final start. *P. W. D'Arcy*

MR KAYOS 2 b.g. (Mar 23) Kayf Tara 130 – Highland Heights (IRE) (Lomond (USA) **–**
128) [2004 p9.5g p7.1g Dec 31] fourth foal: dam bad maiden hurdler: 100/1, well beaten
in maidens at Wolverhampton. *Mrs J. Candlish*

MR LAMBROS 3 ch.g. Pivotal 124 – Magical Veil 73 (Majestic Light (USA)) [2004 **90**
78p: p7g* p7g² 6.5f 7g 6s Oct 22] fairly useful performer: won maiden at Lingfield
in January: has pulled hard, and should be as effective at 6f as 7f: acts on polytrack, poor
effort on soft going: gelded after final start. *A. M. Balding*

MR LEAR (USA) 5 b.g. Lear Fan (USA) 130 – Majestic Mae (USA) (Crow (FR) 134) **–**
[2004 82: 12.3d 12m 10v Nov 4] sturdy gelding: fairly useful handicapper at 4 yrs for
T. D. Barron: little form in 2004. *R. A. Fahey*

MR LEHMAN 7 ch.g. Presidium 124 – Lehmans Lot (Oats 126) [2004 f8f f11g Jan **–**
29] modest form in bumpers: soundly beaten in maiden and seller at Southwell. *Mrs M.
Reveley*

MR LEWIN 3 ch.g. Primo Dominie 121 – Fighting Run (Runnett 125) [2004 67p: **53**
7.2g 8.1s p9.5g⁵ 8s p7.1g Oct 25] big gelding: modest maiden: barely stays 9.5f: acts on
polytrack and good to firm going. *R. A. Fahey*

MR LOVERMAN (IRE) 4 ch.g. Spectrum (IRE) 126 – Soviet Artic (FR) 84§ (Bering **§§**
136) [2004 –§: p8g f8.5m f7d Jun 10] temperamental maiden. *Miss V. Haigh*

MR MALARKEY (IRE) 4 b.g. Pivotal 124 – Girl Next Door 58 (Local Suitor (USA) **89**
128) [2004 88: 6d⁴ 6g 6g⁴ 6m⁶ 6m³ 6g³ 5m 6g⁶ 6m* 5s 6m⁶ 5.2g Sep 14] plain gelding:
fairly useful handicapper: won at Yarmouth in August: effective at 5f/6f: acts on firm and
good to soft going: has worn cheekpieces/visor, usually blinkered: tends to hang left:
usually races prominently: quirky. *Mrs C. A. Dunnett*

MR MARUCCI (USA) 2 b.c. (Mar 17) Miner's Mark (USA) 120 – Appealing Style **59**
(USA) (Valid Appeal (USA)) [2004 7d⁵ 7m p8.6g⁵ Oct 7] tall, leggy colt: on weak side at
2 yrs: modest form in maidens: raced freely second start: stays 8.6f. *B. Ellison*

MR MAXIM 2 ch.g. (Mar 13) Lake Coniston (IRE) 131 – White Hare 56 (Indian Ridge **56**
123) [2004 6m 5.9g⁵ 7d 7.1g 7.5m⁴ 10g Oct 4] workmanlike gelding: modest maiden:
barely stays 1¼m: acts on good to firm going. *R. M. Whitaker*

MR MAYFAIR (IRE) 2 ch.g. (Jan 23) Entrepreneur 123 – French Gift 99 (Cadeaux **53**
Genereux 131) [2004 7.1d p8g Oct 31] modest form in maidens at Warwick and
Lingfield: not sure to stay much beyond 1m. *J. A. Osborne*

MR MIDASMAN (IRE) 3 b.c. Entrepreneur 123 – Sifaara (IRE) (Caerleon (USA) **67**
132) [2004 75: 10.3g⁶ 7.5d 8.2s 8.5v 7m 8g⁴ f8g⁶ 10.5g³ 10.3g³ p9.5d³ p12.2g* p12.2g⁶
Nov 29] sturdy colt: fair handicapper: won at Wolverhampton in November: finds 1m a
minimum and stays 1½m: acts on polytrack and good to soft ground. *R. Hollinshead*

MR MIDAZ 5 ch.g. Danzig Connection (USA) – Marmy 43 (Midyan (USA) 124) **48**
[2004 10.5s⁵ 14.1f⁵ 11.9g⁵ Sep 2] good-bodied gelding: poor maiden: stays 1¾m: acts on
firm and soft ground: tried blinkered: usually races prominently. *D. W. Whillans*

MR MISCHIEF 4 b.g. Millkom 124 – Snow Huntress 80 (Shirley Heights 130) [2004 **–**
72, a93: p12g³ p12g f12s* 12s Aug 13] leggy gelding: useful on all-weather, modest on **a97**
turf: won handicap at Wolverhampton (beat Glory Quest by 2½ lengths) in March: stays
14.8f: acts on all-weather (unbeaten in 5 starts on fibresand), unraced on extremes of
going on turf. *P. C. Haslam*

MR MISCHIEVOUS 3 b.g. Magic Ring (IRE) 115 – Inya Lake 101 (Whittingham **47 ?**
(IRE) 104) [2004 –: p6g p7.1g f6g p6g⁵ Dec 22] poor form: tried visored. *M. D. I. Usher*

MR MISTRAL 5 b.g. Zilzal (USA) 137 – Miss Sancerre 95 (Last Tycoon 131) [2004 **92**
7f² 8s* 7m Jul 24] fairly useful performer, very lightly raced: won 4-runner maiden at
Newcastle in June: stays 1m: best effort on soft ground. *G. Wragg*

MR MOON 3 b.g. Pursuit of Love 124 – Sound of Sleat (Primo Dominie 121) [2004 –: **–**
f7g⁶ 8m⁶ 7.9f 10f 13.1d 8m⁶ 6.9m 9.9d⁵ 10f 10g f11g Dec 11] good-bodied gelding: little
form: left M. Hammond after seventh outing: tried visored/blinkered. *J. Parkes*

MR PERRY (IRE) 8 br.g. Perugino (USA) 84 – Elegant Tune (USA) 51 (Alysheba **34 ?**
(USA)) [2004 f12s f8.5s⁵ f8g Mar 23] lightly raced and poor on Flat nowadays: has been
blinkered/visored. *Mrs P. Ford*

MR PERTEMPS 6 b.g. Primo Dominie 121 – Amber Mill 96 (Doulab (USA) 115) **53 +**
[2004 63: f6s³ f6g* f6g² f5g⁵ 6.1g p6g 5d⁶ Oct 17] tall, lengthy gelding: fair handicapper **a68**
on all-weather, modest on turf: won at Wolverhampton in January: left R. Fahey after
fourth start: probably best at 6f: acts on fibresand (probably on polytrack) and soft going:
often wears cheekpieces: tongue tied once earlier in career: carries head high: sold 3,000
gns, sent to Holland. *J. J. Quinn*

MR REIN (IRE) 2 b.c. (Apr 14) Indian Danehill (IRE) 124 – Lady's Vision (IRE) 93 **55 p**
(Vision (USA)) [2004 p9.5g³ Dec 20] €24,000, 26,000Y: fifth foal: half-brother to 3
winners, including 3-y-o Peruvian Style: dam Irish 7f (at 2 yrs) to 11f winner, also won
over hurdles: 22/1 and green, 4¼ lengths third to Truckle in maiden at Wolverhampton:
should improve. *J. A. Osborne*

MRS BOZ 4 b.f. Superpower 113 – Bar None (Rabdan 129) [2004 –: p6g⁴ 7f 7f Aug 3] **–**
of little account. *A. W. Carroll*

MRS BROWN 3 b.f. Royal Applause 124 – Shifting Mist 76 (Night Shift (USA)) [2004 **60**
f7g³ f8g⁵ f7g⁶ 12m p10d⁵ p10d p8.6g⁴ 8s⁵ 8s Oct 29] sixth foal: half-sister to 5-y-o Cal
Mac and winner in Poland by Bin Ajwaad: dam 1¼m to 1¾m winner: modest maiden:
probably stays 1¼m: acts on all-weather: sometimes slowly away. *Sir Mark Prescott*

MRS CEE (IRE) 3 b.f. Orpen (USA) 116 – Cutleaf 81 (Kris 135) [2004 71d: f7g Jan **–**
13] lengthy filly: fair at best at 2 yrs: started very slowly/looked reluctant in blinkers only
run in 2004. *M. G. Quinlan*

MRS CHIPPY (IRE) 2 ch.f. (Jan 27) Docksider (USA) 124 – Pile (USA) 62 (Shadeed – (USA) 135) [2004 7d Oct 30] €5,500Y: lengthy filly: first foal: dam ran 4 times in Ireland: 66/1 and very green, well held in maiden at Newmarket. *M. H. Tompkins*

MRS CUBE 5 ch.m. Missed Flight 123 – Norska 67 (Northfields (USA)) [2004 42: **54** f9.4s* f8.5s* f8s³ f9.4g³ p10g⁴ 10m 10.1f Jun 2] well-grown mare: modest performer: won 2 banded races at Wolverhampton in March: stays 9.4f: acts on fibresand and good to firm going: blinkered last 2 starts at 4 yrs. *P. Howling*

MRS KEPPLE 2 b.f. (Jan 23) King's Best (USA) 132 – Sabayik (IRE) 93 (Unfuwain – (USA) 131) [2004 5d⁴ 5m 7.5g Jun 22] €40,000Y: seventh foal: half-sister to 3 winners, including useful 1m/1¼m winner Khibrah (by Lahib): dam 1m winner who stayed 1½m: no form in maidens. *M. Johnston*

MR SMITHERS JONES 4 br.g. Emperor Jones (USA) 119 – Phylian 77 (Glint of **62** Gold 128) [2004 –: f11g² f14g* f12f³ f14g³ Mar 16] close-coupled, quite good-topped gelding: modest performer: won maiden at Southwell in January: stays easy 1¾m: raced only on all-weather/soft ground: sold 7,000 gns. *S. C. Williams*

MRS MOH (IRE) 3 b.f. Orpen (USA) 116 – My Gray (FR) (Danehill (USA) 126) **95** [2004 85: 6d 7s 7m⁵ 7d* 7f³ 8.1g* 8g² 8.3s² 7.9g 7s⁴ Oct 23] sturdy, quite attractive filly: useful handicapper: won at Chester in July and Haydock in August: stays 1m: acts on fibresand, firm and soft going: game. *T. D. Easterby*

MRS PANKHURST 3 b.f. Selkirk (USA) 129 – Melodist (USA) 118 (The Minstrel **73** (CAN) 135) [2004 67: 10.3g⁵ 10s 9.9g⁵ 8m⁶ 8.1g 8d⁴ 10d⁵ p10g Oct 31] leggy, useful-looking filly: fair handicapper: stays 1¼m: best efforts on good/good to soft ground: inconsistent. *B. W. Hills*

MRS PHILIP 5 b.m. Puissance 110 – Lightning Legacy (USA) 78 (Super Concorde **56** (USA) 128) [2004 11.7f 10.2g 10d 10.2g Oct 10] 1,000F, 3,800Y: half-sister to several winners, including useful performer up to 1½m Black Monday (by Busted): dam, maiden, stayed 1m: modest winning hurdler: modest maiden on Flat. *P. J. Hobbs*

MR SPLIFFY 5 b.g. Fayruz 116 – Johns Conquerer (IRE) 74 (Conquering **54 d** Hero (USA) 116) [2004 71§, a53§: f5g f5g⁵ p5g* p6g p5g f5s⁵ 6s 5m 5m 5g 5m 5m 5m 6m 5m² f5g f6g Dec 12] close-coupled gelding: modest performer: won claimer at Lingfield in January: left K. Burke after sixth start: best at 5f: acts on all-weather, firm and good to soft going: sometimes visored, found little in cheekpieces: has bolted/been early to post: usually races prominently: no easy ride. *M. C. Chapman*

MRS SHILLING 3 b.f. Dr Fong (USA) 128 – Papaha (FR) 103 (Green Desert (USA) **75** 127) [2004 60p: 7d³ 7m⁴ 7.5m² 8g⁴ p8.6g³ Oct 16] useful-looking filly: fair maiden: stays 1m: acts on polytrack, unraced on extremes of going on turf: sold 14,500 gns, sent to USA. *J. R. Fanshawe*

MRS SPENCE 3 b.f. Mind Games 121 – Maid O'Cannie 72 (Efisio 120) [2004 63: 5s – 5d⁶ 7v 6.1m 5d Oct 11] tall, leggy filly: maiden: little form in 2004: blinkered (dropped away tamely) final start. *M. W. Easterby*

MRS ST GEORGE (IRE) 3 b.f. Orpen (USA) 116 – Tamarzana (IRE) (Lear Fan **87** (USA) 130) [2004 74: 6d⁴ 6d² 6m 6d* 6m* 5m² 6g 5d 6d⁵ Oct 10] €3,200Y: fifth foal: half-sister to winners abroad by Turtle Island and Ezzood: dam French 7f winner: fairly useful handicapper: won at Ballinrobe in June and Naas in July: below form at Ascot seventh start: effective at 5f/6f: acts on heavy and good to firm going. *James G. Burns, Ireland*

MR STROWGER 3 b.c. Dancing Spree (USA) – Matoaka 72 (Be My Chief (USA) **52** 122) [2004 –: 8.1s⁶ 11g³ 8d 10.2s p13m⁵ p10m⁴ p10m* Dec 15] modest performer: left A. Charlton after sixth start: won banded race at Lingfield in December: stays easy 13f: acts on polytrack, raced only on good ground or softer on turf. *J. C. Fox*

MR STYLISH 8 b.g. Mazilier (USA) 107 – Moore Stylish 65 (Moorestyle 137) [2004 **38 §** 64§: f7g⁶ f7g⁶ Feb 9] lengthy gelding: poor performer nowadays: effective at 6f/7f: acts on fibresand and any turf going: tried blinkered/in cheekpieces, usually visored/tongue tied: sometimes pulls hard: carries head awkwardly: unreliable. *J. S. Moore*

MRS WILLY NILLY 2 ch.f. (May 16) Timeless Times (USA) 99 – Laena 72 (Roman – Warrior 92) [2004 5g 5s 6.1d Jul 10] 1,000Y: seventh foal: half-sister to 3 winning sprinters by Clantime, notably useful Cape Merino: dam third at 7f at 2 yrs: last in maidens: looked wayward in cheekpieces final start: sold £1,000. *J. M. Bradley*

MR TAMBOURINE MAN (IRE) 3 b.g. Rainbow Quest (USA) 134 – Girl From **89** Ipanema 106 (Salse (USA) 128) [2004 82: 10g⁶ 9.9s 10d 10m* 10.1g³ 10m* 12g⁴ 12g²

11g 11.6m Sep 27] rangy gelding: fluent mover: fairly useful handicapper: won at Windsor in June and Pontefract in July: should stay 1¾m: acts on good to firm going: has run well when sweating: sometimes races freely: gelded after final start. *P. F. I. Cole*

MR UPPITY 5 b.g. Shareef Dancer (USA) 135 – Queenfisher 101 (Scottish Reel 123) **48**
[2004 52: f5g f5g f6s² f7m⁴ f6m⁵ f6g³ 6.1m⁶ 6f⁵ f6g⁴ 6m² 7m 6m⁵ f6g⁴ f6g² Dec 12] poor maiden: effective at 5f to 7f: acts on fibresand and good to firm going: usually wears headgear. *Julian Poulton*

MR VELOCITY (IRE) 4 b.g. Tagula (IRE) 116 – Miss Rusty (IRE) (Mukaddamah **92**
(USA) 125) [2004 79: 8.1d³ 8.2d² 7g* 7g 8m⁶ 8.5g³ 8.5g* 8g* 8v² 7s⁶ Nov 6] compact, quite attractive gelding: fairly useful performer: won minor event at Redcar in June (trained until after next start by A. Stewart) and handicap at Epsom and minor event at Musselburgh in September: stays 8.5f: acts on heavy and good to firm going. *E. F. Vaughan*

MR WHIZZ 7 ch.g. Manhal – Panienka (POL) 70 (Dom Racine (FR) 121) [2004 46: **48**
p10g f8g* f8.5g⁴ f8s⁴ f8g³ 10.2d² 10v² 10.2f 16.4g⁵ 11.9f* 17.1d 12.1g⁴ 10d Oct 2] lengthy gelding: poor performer: won banded race at Southwell in January and selling handicap at Brighton in August: stays 1½m: acts on fibresand, any turf going: tried tongue tied: usually wears headgear. *A. P. Jones*

MR WOLF 3 b.g. Wolfhound (USA) 126 – Madam Millie 99 (Milford 119) [2004 65: **82**
5g² 5s² 5d* 6d* 5m⁶ 6m⁶ 6g 5.1g 6d 5d⁵ 5d² 5d⁶ Sep 27] tall, leggy gelding: fairly useful performer: won maiden at Newcastle in April and minor event at Thirsk in May: best at 5f/6f: acts on firm and soft going: races up with pace. *D. W. Barker*

MS POLLY GARTER 2 b.f. (Feb 9) Petong 126 – Utopia (Primo Dominie 121) **51 d**
[2004 5.1s⁴ 5g 5.1f⁶ 5m 5.1s 5.1g Oct 10] 2,100Y: first foal: dam unraced: modest maiden: form only on debut. *J. M. Bradley*

MS THREE 2 b.f. (May 2) Josr Algarhoud (IRE) 118 – Swing Along 86 (Alhijaz 122) **52**
[2004 6g f5s⁶ 5m⁵ 5g⁶ 6m p5.1d f6g p6g f5f Dec 28] 4,000Y: first foal: dam 7f and 9.4f **a45**
winner: modest maiden on turf, poor on all-weather: probably stays 6f: acts on fibresand and good to firm going: wore cheekpieces final start. *R. Ford*

MT DESERT 2 b.c. (Jan 15) Rainbow Quest (USA) 134 – Chief Bee 89 (Chief's **69 p**
Crown (USA)) [2004 8g⁶ 8g⁶ Oct 12] 90,000Y: strong, lengthy colt: has scope: fifth foal: brother to 6-y-o Beekeeper and 4-y-o Argonaut and half-brother to 2 winners, including 3-y-o Golden Grace: dam, 9f to 14.6f winner, sister to Racing Post Trophy winner Be My Chief: better effort in maidens when sixth to River Alhaarth at Leicester final start: will be suited by 1¼m+: sort to make a better 3-y-o. *J. H. M. Gosden*

MTILLY 3 br.f. Mtoto 134 – Corn Lily 78 (Aragon 118) [2004 8g 10v p10g⁵ Dec 4] **55 p**
lengthy filly: seventh foal: half-sister to 4-y-o Fisio Therapy: dam, effective at 1½m/ 1¾m, also successful over hurdles: best effort in maidens when fifth at Lingfield: bred to stay 1½m+: weakened tamely having pulled too hard second start: should improve. *M. Johnston*

MUBTAKER (USA) 7 ch.h. Silver Hawk (USA) 123 – Gazayil (USA) 80 (Irish **122**
River (FR) 131) [2004 132: 13.3g* 12d 12g⁴ Oct 24]
  The 2001 season remains the only one in which Mubtaker has completed a full campaign, numerous training troubles having severely curtailed his appearances otherwise. It says much for the skill and patience of those connected with Mubtaker that he has achieved as much as he has, his record now standing at nine wins from twenty starts, in the process earning around £600,000 in total prize money. Restricted to three outings, covering a period of just over two months in the latest season, Mubtaker couldn't reproduce the improved form shown in 2003, when he won all three of his starts before putting up a top-class performance to finish runner-up to Dalakhani in the Prix de l'Arc de Triomphe.
  For the second year running, injury prevented Mubtaker from appearing at the Dubai World Cup meeting in March, tendonitis the problem this time around, and it was August before he finally made it to the racecourse. The race chosen for his return was the Stan James Geoffrey Freer Stakes, a Group 2 event in which he had been successful in each of the two previous years. Mubtaker at long odds on to account for three smart rivals, Compton Bolter, Dubai Success and The Great Gatsby, and Mubtaker did just that without needing to produce anything like his best form. Making a rare appearance in a crossed noseband, Mubtaker raced freely in the early stages of a steadily-run contest, but moved easily past the pace-

setter Dubai Success two furlongs out and needed only to be kept up to his work until eased near the finish to win by two and a half lengths from that horse. The September Stakes at Kempton, which Mubtaker had won in 2003, looked like being his next race but, after figuring among the five-day entries, he ran instead in the following day's Grosser Preis von Baden at Baden-Baden, for which he started odds on. Mubtaker, without the crossed noseband, pulled hard and weakened after leading until a furlong and a half out, holding his head awkwardly and racing with his tongue lolling out as he dropped back to seventh, the first time he had finished out of the first three in his career. He was to do so again on his only subsequent outing. After missing the Arc because his trainer felt the horse wasn't in good enough shape to do himself justice, Mubtaker was sent over for the Canadian International at Woodbine where he ran below his best in finishing fourth to Sulamani, beaten a little over four lengths. Mubtaker is to stay in training, but, as an eight-year-old, time isn't on his side.

Mubtaker (USA) (ch.h. 1997)	Silver Hawk (USA) (b 1979)	Roberto (b 1969)	Hail To Reason / Bramalea
		Gris Vitesse (gr 1966)	Amerigo / Matchiche II
	Gazayil (USA) (ch 1985)	Irish River (ch 1976)	Riverman / Irish Star
		Close Comfort (b 1979)	Far North / Caterina

Mubtaker's pedigree has been well documented in previous annuals. Suffice to say here that he is the fifth foal of Gazayil, a two-year-old seven-furlong winner later successful in Australia, and a half-brother to several winners, notably the useful Irish 1998 two-year-old seven-furlong winner and Irish One Thousand Guineas fourth Crystal Downs (by Alleged). Mubtaker is an unimpressive mover—connections reportedly blamed the rough ground for his below-par effort at Baden-Baden—but that hasn't stopped him from showing his form on going ranging from firm through to heavy. A lengthy horse, he is effective at a mile and a quarter to thirteen furlongs and is thoroughly genuine. *M. P. Tregoning*

MUDAWIN (IRE) 3 b.g. Intikhab (USA) 135 – Fida (IRE) (Persian Heights 129) **100** [2004 73P: 8g 8g* 8m 10m* 12m Jun 17] big, lengthy, good-topped gelding: has plenty of scope: has a round action: useful performer: won maiden at Newbury in April and handicap at Ascot (beat Ganymede by 3½ lengths) in May: well beaten otherwise in 2004, including in King George V Handicap at Royal Ascot final outing: stays 1¼m: unraced on extremes of going. *M. P. Tregoning*

MUDDY (IRE) 2 ch.g. (Apr 27) Monashee Mountain (USA) 115 – Schonbein (IRE) **58** 60 (Persian Heights 129) [2004 6d⁵ 6.1m 7g 6.1v p6g Nov 8] good-topped gelding: modest maiden: will probably prove best up to 7f: acts on good to soft going: wore cheekpieces final start. *G. A. Huffer*

MUESTRA (IRE) 2 ch.f. (Apr 7) Raise A Grand (IRE) 114 – Iva's Flyer (IRE) 71 **31** (Imperial Frontier (USA) 112) [2004 5g 5.1s 5v 5.1f 6m⁵ f7d³ 7g 7d Oct 15] €5,000Y: **a51** leggy filly: seventh foal: half-sister to fairly useful Irish 5f/6f (including at 2 yrs) winner Reptar (by Elbio): dam 2-y-o 5f winner: modest maiden on all-weather, poor on turf: stays 7f: acts on fibresand and good to firm going: sold 700 gns. *Mrs P. N. Dutfield*

MUFREH (USA) 6 b.g. Dayjur (USA) 137 – Mathkurh (USA) 97 (Riverman (USA) **63** 131) [2004 –, a88: f7g* f7g⁵ f6s² 7d⁴ 7s p6g Dec 13] strong, lengthy gelding: fairly useful **a93**

handicapper on all-weather, modest on turf: won at Southwell in January: effective at 6f/ 7f: acts on fibresand, raced mainly on going softer than good on turf. *A. G. Newcombe*

MUGEBA 3 b.f. Primo Dominie 121 – Ella Lamees 61 (Statoblest 120) [2004 60: f7g⁵ **64** p8g⁵ 7m* 6m² 7f² 6g 7s⁶ p7.1g³ p7.1g p8.6g⁵ Dec 15] modest performer: won seller at Yarmouth (left W. Musson) in June: effective at 6f/7f: acts on polytrack and firm going: tried blinkered, sometimes tongue tied. *Miss Gay Kelleway*

MUHAREB (USA) 5 ch.g. Thunder Gulch (USA) 129 – Queen of Spirit (USA) **99** (Deputy Minister (CAN)) [2004 106: 12m⁵ 12g 10.1g 10f⁵ 12g 12d Oct 14] rather leggy, lengthy gelding: useful performer: form in 2004 only when fifth at Ascot in handicap (to Always Waining) and minor event (behind Destination Dubai): stays 1½m: acts on all-weather, firm and good to soft going: tongue tied (ran creditably) once at 4 yrs: has run well when sweating: usually races prominently: sold 11,000 gns. *C. E. Brittain*

MUHAYMIN (USA) 3 ch.c. A P Indy (USA) 131 – Shadayid (USA) 122 (Shadeed **80** (USA) 135) [2004 89p: 10g 8m 9.9g⁴ 8g Jun 24] rather leggy, good-topped colt: fair handicapper: best form at 1m: acts on good to firm going: usually races up with pace: joined K. McLaughlin in USA. *J. L. Dunlop*

MUJAGEM (IRE) 8 br.m. Mujadil (USA) 119 – Lili Bengam (Welsh Saint 126) **–** [2004 f7g Jan 4] tall mare: little form since 2000: often blinkered. *M. W. Easterby*

MUJALINA (IRE) 6 b.g. Mujadil (USA) 119 – Talina's Law (IRE) 83 (Law Society **–** (USA) 130) [2004 18s Oct 16] leggy gelding: fairly useful performer: first run on Flat since 2001 when well held in Cesarewitch at Newmarket: blinkered (ran poorly) once at 2 yrs. *M. C. Pipe*

MUJAWER (USA) 3 b.g. Gulch (USA) – Good Cents (USA) (Deputy Minister **65 ?** (CAN)) [2004 7g⁵ 9f 7.1g Aug 30] $350,000Y: fourth foal: closely related/half-brother to 3 minor winners in USA: dam unraced out of half-sister to Irish 2000 Guineas winner Prince of Birds: clearly best effort in maidens when fifth at Newmarket on debut: should stay 1m: blinkered (showed little) final start: sold 5,500 gns. *M. P. Tregoning*

MUJAZAF 2 b.c. (Apr 25) Grand Lodge (USA) 125 – Decision Maid (USA) 105 **67 p** (Diesis 133) [2004 8f³ Sep 23] 150,000Y: quite good-topped colt: first foal: dam, 2-y-o 7f winner, closely related to 4-y-o Miss Ivanhoe: 11/4, third in maiden at Pontefract (moved poorly to post): should improve. *M. R. Channon*

MUJIMAC (IRE) 2 b.g. (Apr 29) Mujadil (USA) 119 – Cross Dall (IRE) 58§ (Blues **55 ?** Traveller (IRE) 119) [2004 p7m Dec 22] 33/1, ninth of 13 to Resplendent Prince in maiden at Lingfield. *J. R. Boyle*

MUJKARI (IRE) 8 ch.g. Mujtahid (USA) 118 – Hot Curry (USA) (Sharpen Up 127) **44** [2004 58: p9.5d p8.6g p7m⁶ p10g⁶ Dec 20] lengthy gelding: poor performer nowadays: effective at 7f to 1¼m: acts on all-weather, firm and good to soft going: tried visored, blinkered nowadays: sometimes races moodily. *J. M. Bradley*

MUKAFEH (USA) 3 b.c. Danzig (USA) – Bint Salsabil (USA) 110 (Nashwan (USA) **105** 135) [2004 96p: 7g 8m² 7f⁵ Jun 16] angular, well-made colt: fluent mover: has had hocks pin-fired: useful performer, lightly raced: ran well when ½-length second to Almuraad in minor event at Newmarket and 5 lengths fifth to Kheleyf in Jersey Stakes at Royal Ascot (sweated), making running both times: stays 1m: acts on firm going. *J. L. Dunlop*

MUKTASB (USA) 3 b.g. Bahri (USA) 125 – Maghaarb 104 (Machiavellian (USA) **56** 123) [2004 72: f5g f6s³ f6g p6g p5.1g³ Dec 20] good-topped gelding: maiden: just modest form at 3 yrs: should stay 7f: acts on all-weather: tried in blinkers/cheekpieces. *D. Shaw*

MULAN PRINCESS (IRE) 4 b.f. Mukaddamah (USA) 125 – Notley Park 71 (Wolf- **–** hound (USA) 126) [2004 66d: p6g Jan 31] leggy filly: fair at best at 3yrs: well held only outing in 2004. *S. C. Burrough*

MULBERRY LAD (IRE) 2 b.g. (Jan 28) Entrepreneur 123 – Taisho (IRE) 96 (Nam- **66** aqualand (USA)) [2004 5m⁵ 5.1f² 5.3m⁴ 6f² 6m p6m⁶ p6g⁶ Oct 19] 10,000Y: first foal: dam Irish 6f/7f winner, including at 2 yrs: fair maiden: should stay 7f: acts on polytrack and firm going: tongue tied fifth start, blinkered last 4. *W. R. Muir*

MULBERRY WINE 2 b.f. (Feb 12) Benny The Dip (USA) 127 – Top Berry 87 (High **65** Top 131) [2004 7d⁶ 7g⁴ 7m⁵ 6d 7m 8g Sep 30] half-sister to several winners, including fairly useful 7f (at 2 yrs) and 1m winner Derryquin (by Lion Cavern) and 3-y-o Blaeberry: dam 1m winner: fair maiden: should stay at least 1m: acts on good to firm going. *M. Blanshard*

MULSANNE 6 b.g. Clantime 101 – Prim Lass 65 (Reprimand 122) [2004 –: 10.9m Sep 6] no form. *P. A. Pritchard* —

MULTAHAB 5 b. or br.g. Zafonic (USA) 130 – Alumisiyah (USA) 93 (Danzig (USA)) [2004 55: p5g² p5g⁴ p5g² p5g⁴ 5.1d 5m 6m 6m 5d 5.3d⁶ p5.1g p6g p5.1g p5.1g² Dec 20] smallish gelding: modest maiden: trained by P. McEntee eighth to twelfth starts then rejoined former stable: effective at 5f/6f: acts on all-weather: tried blinkered/in cheekpieces: usually tongue tied. *Miss Gay Kelleway* — 49 a64

MULTICOLOUR 4 ch.f. Rainbow Quest (USA) 134 – Raymouna (IRE) (High Top 131) [2004 58: 10.2s May 4] angular filly: modest maiden: soundly beaten only run in 2004: found little last 2 starts at 3 yrs. *R. Hannon* —

MULTIPLE CHOICE (IRE) 3 ch.g. Woodborough (USA) 112 – Cosmona (Dominion 123) [2004 85: p5g 6d 5d 5g f8g² f8d⁴ 6.9m⁶ f8g⁴ 6.1g p6m p7g Oct 13] well-made gelding: just fair at best in 2004: stays 1m: acts on fibresand and firm going: sometimes wears tongue tie/blinkers: sold 5,000 gns. *N. P. Littmoden* — 53 ? a63

MUMBLING (IRE) 6 ch.g. Dr Devious (IRE) 127 – Valley Lights (IRE) (Dance of Life (USA)) [2004 82: 12g Sep 22] strong, lengthy gelding: fairly useful performer at best: well below form only run in 2004: tried blinkered. *B. G. Powell* —

MUNAAHEJ (IRE) 3 b.c. Soviet Star (USA) 128 – Azyaa 101 (Kris 135) [2004 69: 7g p7.1g f6g p6g Dec 22] smallish colt: maiden: well held in 2004. *K. A. Morgan* —

MUNAAWASHAT (IRE) 3 b.f. Marju (IRE) 127 – Simaat (USA) 72 (Mr Prospector (USA)) [2004 68: 10f³ 8.3m* 8.3d² 10g 8.3m* 8.3d* 8m 8d⁶ p8g Nov 20] close-coupled filly: fairly useful performer: won minor event at Hamilton in June and (having left M. Johnston after third start) 2 handicaps at Windsor in August: best form at around 1m: acts on good to firm and good to soft going: got worked up before disappointing once at 2 yrs: usually races prominently. *K. R. Burke* — 86

MUNAAWESH (USA) 3 b.g. Bahri (USA) 125 – Istikbal (USA) (Kingmambo (USA) 125) [2004 71: p8g 6d³ f8g 7s 8.1v 8m f8d 10g f12g 11d⁴ 9m² 9.9g 9f⁴ 10m² 14.1m² 10f 13.8g⁴ 12g⁵ 15.8g f11g p12.2g f14g⁵ Nov 24] sturdy gelding: modest maiden: stays 1¾m: acts on firm and good to soft ground: often blinkered, wore cheekpieces final start: gelded after: has found little. *D. W. Chapman* — 60 a51

MUNADDAM (USA) 2 ch.c. (Apr 9) Aljabr (USA) 125 – Etizaaz (USA) 117 (Diesis 133) [2004 6f² 6g² 5.7g* Sep 27] sturdy colt: second foal: dam, 7f (at 2 yrs)/1m winner who was second in Prix Vermeille, out of half-sister to Swain: landed odds at Bath easily by 5 lengths, leading well over 1f out: should stay at least 7f: useful already, and should progress. *Saeed bin Suroor* — 95 p

MUNFARID (IRE) 4 ch.g. Alhaarth (IRE) 126 – Meursault (IRE) (Salt Dome (USA)) [2004 ?: f12g² p13g p13g⁴ f12s 14.4s 15s f14g Aug 19] fair maiden: trained by K. Prendergast in Ireland in 2003: probably stayed 13f: acted on good to firm and good to soft going, probably on polytrack: tongue tied: dead. *P. G. Murphy* — 63

MUNGO JERRY (GER) 3 b.g. Tannenkonig (IRE) 111 – Mostly Sure (IRE) (Sure Blade (USA) 130) [2004 –: 10.5g³ 10.5m⁶ 11.8g³ Jun 24] tall gelding: fair performer: stays 11.8f: raced only on good ground or firmer: gelded after final start. *J. G. Given* — 73

MUNSEF 2 b.c. (Mar 18) Zafonic (USA) 130 – Mazaya (IRE) 105 (Sadler's Wells (USA) 132) [2004 6d 7s³ Oct 27] close-coupled colt: second foal: dam 1½m winner out of half-sister to Prix Vermeille winner Sharaya: green, better effort in maidens when third to Plea Bargain at Yarmouth, slowly away and late headway: will stay at least 1m: likely to do fair bit better. *J. L. Dunlop* — 74 p

MUQARRAR (IRE) 5 ch.h. Alhaarth (IRE) 126 – Narjis (USA) 87 (Blushing Groom (FR) 131) [2004 63?: f7g⁶ f8f⁶ f8f⁶ f8g 8d 8s* Oct 30] workmanlike horse: performer: visored and tongue tied, won banded race at Ayr in October: should stay 1¼m: acts on fibresand, soft and good to firm going: tried in blinkers. *T. J. Fitzgerald* — 57

MUQBIL (USA) 4 ch.c. Swain (USA) 134 – Istiqlal (USA) (Diesis 133) [2004 118: 10d 10.3g* 10m* 10.5g² 9.9m⁴ 12m⁵ Sep 26] lengthy, quite attractive colt: good walker/mover: very smart performer: won minor event at Doncaster (by 5 lengths from Grampian) in June and listed race at Newbury (by ¾ length from Vespone) in July: creditable 1½ lengths second to Mister Monet in Rose of Lancaster Stakes at Haydock: below form in Select Stakes at Goodwood and Cumberland Lodge Stakes at Ascot last 2 starts: stays 1¼m: raced mainly on good ground or firmer: has twice hung markedly right at Newmarket: waited with: joined K. McLaughlin in USA. *J. L. Dunlop* — 120

MUQTADI (IRE) 6 b.g. Marju (IRE) 127 – Kadwah (USA) 80 (Mr Prospector **59**
(USA)) [2004 59§: f8.5g p6g³ p7g p6g⁶ p7g p8g⁴ p8g* p10g⁵ p8g f7g p10g⁴ 8.3d⁵ 6s⁴
7v 8f⁶ 8.1f 8.1m 8.1g Jul 9] leggy gelding: modest performer: won seller at Lingfield
in February: effective at 6f to easy 1¼m: acts on polytrack, firm and soft going: usually
slowly away, and held up: none too reliable. *M. Quinn*

MURAABET 2 b.c. (Mar 5) Dubai Millennium 140 – Mahasin (USA) 90 (Danzig **88 p**
(USA)) [2004 8d³ 7s⁶ Oct 27] big, lengthy colt: has scope: half-brother to several winners, including smart 1¼m/1½m winner Elhayq (by Nashwan) and useful Irish 1m
winner Shibl (by Arazi): dam, 7f/1m winner, half-sister to William Hill Futurity winner
Al Hareb: much better effort in maidens when third to Proclamation at Newmarket,
leading briefly 3f out: odds on, found little at Yarmouth just 12 days later: will stay at
least 1¼m: probably a useful prospect. *J. L. Dunlop*

MURAQEB 4 ch.g. Grand Lodge (USA) 125 – Oh So Well (IRE) (Sadler's Wells **51**
(USA) 132) [2004 61: p10g p10g p12g f14s⁵ 16g 16s 8.1d 10.3s⁶ Oct 22] sturdy gelding:
modest maiden: stays 10.3f: acts on soft and good to firm ground: tried visored/blinkered:
has looked none too keen. *Mrs Barbara Waring*

MURASHAH (USA) 4 ch.c. Storm Cat (USA) – Shadayid (USA) 122 (Shadeed **– §**
(USA) 135) [2004 82p: 8m Jun 26] good-topped, compact colt: won maiden at Not-
tingham only run in 2003 (gave flash of tail): very slowly away and refused to race at
Doncaster only outing at 4 yrs: wore crossed noseband/tongue tied both starts: joined
K. McLaughlin in USA. *Saeed bin Suroor*

MURBAAT (IRE) 3 b.c. Deploy 131 – Ozette 99 (Dancing Brave (USA) 140) [2004 **78**
8m³ 10m² Jun 17] strong, angular, good-bodied colt: fourth foal: half-brother to fairly
useful 1999 2-y-o 7f/1m winner who stayed 1¼m Osood (by Caerleon): dam, Irish 11f
to 1¾m winner, half-sister to smart French performer up to 1½m Tafka Yahmed: fair form
when placed in maidens at Ripon, still green when 4 lengths second to Galvanise: should
stay 1¼m: joined D. Selvaratnam in UAE. *A. C. Stewart*

MURDINGA 5 br.g. Emperor Jones (USA) 119 – Tintinara (Selkirk (USA) 129) [2004 **–**
60: p10g Mar 4] tall gelding: lightly-raced maiden: blinkered (well held) only run in
2004. *A. M. Hales*

MURZIM 5 b.g. Salse (USA) 128 – Guilty Secret (IRE) 109 (Kris 135) [2004 83d: **–**
p13g Feb 28] angular gelding: fairly useful handicapper at best: on the downgrade: tried
in headgear. *J. Gallagher*

MUSAHIM (USA) 2 b.c. (Mar 10) Dixieland Band (USA) – Tabheej (IRE) 100 (Muj- **74**
tahid (USA) 118) [2004 6g 6g³ Sep 6] strong, compact colt: first foal: dam, 5f/6f winner
at 2 yrs, sister to useful 1995 2-y-o 5f winner Mubhij: fair form in maidens at Newmarket
and Newcastle: likely to prove best at 5f/6f. *B. W. Hills*

cantorodds.com Steventon Stakes, Newbury—
Muqbil and Vespone (visor) are clear of the others, led by Musanid

MUSANID (USA) 4 ch.c. Swain (IRE) 134 – Siyadah (USA) 106 (Mr Prospector **111** (USA)) [2004 100: 10g³ 12f⁶ 10m³ 12g³ Aug 14] strong, close-coupled, quite attractive colt: has a fluent, round action: smart performer, lightly raced: best effort when 1½ lengths third to Bandari in minor event at Newmarket on reappearance: has raced freely, and probably doesn't stay 1½m: acts on firm and good to soft going: edgy sort: inconsistent: joined K. McLaughlin in USA. *Sir Michael Stoute*

MUSARDIERE 2 b.f. (Apr 23) Montjeu (IRE) 137 – Majestic Image 86 (Niniski **62 p** (USA) 125) [2004 6f 6.1m⁵ 7m Oct 2] 34,000Y: leggy, close-coupled filly: half-sister to several winners, including 1¾m/2m winner Mbele (by Mtoto) and German 1½m to 2m winner Montalban (by Mondrian), both smart: dam 1¾m/2m winner: modest form in maidens, not knocked about: should be well suited by 1¼m+: likely to do better. *Mrs J. R. Ramsden*

MUSEEB (USA) 2 b.c. (May 8) Danzig (USA) – Elle Seule (USA) 122 (Exclusive **87 p** Native (USA)) [2004 6g⁴ 7g² Sep 18] big, lengthy colt: brother to 2 winners, notably high-class 6f winner (including July Cup) Elnadim, closely related to several winners, notably very smart 6f (at 2 yrs) to 1m (including Irish 1000 Guineas) winner Mehthaaf (by Nureyev), and half-brother to 2 winners by Storm Cat, including useful 6f/7f winner (including at 2 yrs) Khulood: dam, French 1m (Prix d'Astarte) to 10.5f winner, half-sister to dam of Dubai Millennium out of outstanding broodmare Fall Aspen: better effort in maidens when second to Esquire at Newbury: will probably stay 1m: sure to progress. *J. L. Dunlop*

MUSHAJER 2 gr.g. (Apr 14) Linamix (FR) 127 – Luxurious (USA) (Lyphard (USA) **85** 132) [2004 6m³ 7g⁴ Jun 24] 35,000F, 78,000G: rather leggy, angular gelding: good walker: half-brother to several winners abroad, notably smart French/US performer up to 1¾m Persianlux (by Persian Bold): dam, French maiden, daughter of Prix Marcel Boussac winner Tropicaro: better effort in maidens when third to Iceman at Newbury: odds on, found little at Salisbury (gelded after): should stay at least 1m. *M. P. Tregoning*

MUSICAL DAY 2 ch.f. (Mar 3) Singspiel (IRE) 133 – Dayville (USA) 86 (Dayjur **80** (USA) 137) [2004 7m 7m 7g 7.5d² 6.5g 7g⁴ p8.6g³ p8g⁸ Oct 25] 20,000Y: lengthy filly: fourth foal: half-sister to Irish 5f winner Alexander Ballet (by Mind Games) and 1¼m/ 1½m winner My Daisychain (by Hector Protector), both fairly useful: dam, 6f winner (including at 2 yrs), half-sister to smart filly up to 1¼m Spanish Fern out of sister to Irish 1000 Guineas winner Al Bahathri: fairly useful performer: blinkered, workmanlike winner of maiden at Lingfield: best efforts when in frame, including in nursery at Newmarket sixth start: stays 8.6f: acts on polytrack and good to soft going. *B. J. Meehan*

MUSICAL FAIR 4 b.f. Piccolo 121 – Guarded Expression 51 (Siberian Express (USA) **82** 125) [2004 81: 6g 6g 6g 5m² 5m* 5m⁵ 5m⁶ 5g 5d 5g³ 5f 5.2g³ p6g⁵ p5.1d Nov 4] sturdy, close-coupled filly: fairly useful handicapper: won at Thirsk in May: barely stays easy 6f: acts on polytrack and firm ground: visored (hung markedly left) eighth start: usually waited with. *J. A. Glover*

MUSICAL GIFT 4 ch.g. Cadeaux Genereux 131 – Kazoo 108 (Shareef Dancer (USA) **75** 135) [2004 67: f9.4g* p7g⁴ f8.5s⁴ p8g⁵ 8.3d p7.1d p8g⁵ p7.1g p10m Dec 22] fair performer: won maiden at Wolverhampton in January: left C. Allen after fifth start: stays easy 1¼m: acts on all-weather, well held only start on turf: tried in cheekpieces: usually races prominently. *G. A. Huffer*

MUSICAL LYRICS (USA) 3 b.f. Quiet American (USA) – Foreign Courier (USA) **–** (Sir Ivor (USA) 135) [2004 67: 9.2d May 7] small, sturdy filly: maiden: form only when third at 2 yrs: should stay at least 7f: sent to Australia. *M. Johnston*

MUSICAL TOP (USA) 4 ch.f. Mt Livermore (USA) – Brief Escapade (IRE) 95 **59** (Brief Truce (USA) 126) [2004 46: 6d 6m 6.9m³ 7s 5.7f 8g⁴ p8.6g⁵ Oct 9] first foal: dam, 1m winner, half-sister to high-class 7f to 9f performer Indian Lodge and very smart French performer up to 1½m Sarhoob: modest maiden: left J. Oxx in Ireland after second start: stays 8.6f: acts on polytrack, good to firm and good to soft going. *H. Morrison*

MUSICANNA 3 b.f. Cape Cross (IRE) 129 – Upend 120 (Main Reef 126) [2004 8m² **81 p** 8.1s* Sep 24] 60,000Y: good-topped filly: half-sister to several winners, including 10-y-o Al Azhar and useful 1¼m/10.5f winner Shortfall (by Last Tycoon): dam, 1¼m/1½m (St Simon Stakes) winner, half-sister to dam of high-class stayer/Champion Hurdle winner Royal Gait: reportedly had knee problem at 2 yrs: favourite, but backward after 3½-month break, won maiden at Haydock in September by 1¾ lengths from Foolish Groom, still having lot to do at halfway and asserting readily final 1f: had earlier shown better form when second to Castleton in maiden at Newmarket: will be suited by 1¼m+: changed hands 26,000 gns in October: remains capable of better. *J. R. Fanshawe*

MUSIC MAID (IRE)   6 b.m. Inzar (USA) 112 – Richardstown Lass (IRE) (Muscatite   **70**
122) [2004 70: 8m 7m* 7g 7g 7g 7.1g 8g Sep 20] angular mare: fair handicapper: won at
Newbury in June: effective at 7f to 8.5f: acts on firm and good to soft going: often slowly
away: sometimes races freely/swishes tail/wanders. *H. S. Howe*

MUSIC MIX (IRE)   3 b.c. Linamix (FR) 127 – Baldemara (FR) (Sanglamore (USA)   **60**
126) [2004 64: 8.3s 10g p10d* 12g⁴ 10g⁴ 10d 12g Sep 5] leggy colt: fair handicapper: **a69**
won apprentice event at Lingfield in August: stays 1¼m: raced only on all-weather/good
ground or softer: visored (below form) final outing: usually waited with: sold 16,000 gns.
E. A. L. Dunlop

MUSICO (IRE)   2 ch.c. (Feb 13) Bold Fact (USA) 116 – Scherzo Impromptu (Music   **73**
Boy 124) [2004 6.1g⁴ 6m⁶ 6f⁴ 7f² 6.1d³ 6f 8.3d Oct 4] €14,500F, 28,000Y: neat colt: half-
brother to Italian sprint winner Golden Stevens (by Catrail): dam twice-raced half-sister
to smart sprinter Governor General: fair maiden: stayed 7f: acted on firm and good to soft
going: dead. *B. R. Millman*

MUSIC TEACHER   2 ch.f. (Jan 17) Piccolo 121 – Duena (Grand Lodge (USA) 125)   **66 p**
[2004 6g p5g* Nov 10] 40,000Y: quite good-topped filly: first foal: dam unraced half-
sister to 4-y-o Presto Vento out of close relative to smart French sprinter Pole Position:
showed up well long way on debut: won maiden at Lingfield by ½ length from Small
Stakes: will stay 6f: should do better. *H. Morrison*

MUSIOTAL   3 ch.c. Pivotal 124 – Bemuse 89 (Forzando 122) [2004 –: 7.1g 5g⁵ 5d⁵   **58**
6m 6s² 7.2g* 6g 8s⁴ 5d 7.2s Oct 12] lengthy, useful-looking colt: modest handicapper:
won at Ayr in July: effective at 6f (given a test) and seems to stay 1m: acts on soft ground.
J. S. Goldie

MUSKATSTURM (GER)   5 b.g. Lecroix (GER) 112 – Myrthe (GER) (Konigsstuhl   **–**
(GER)) [2004 –: 15s 12s 14.8g 14.1d Aug 29] tall, leggy ex-German gelding: little form
in Britain: usually blinkered before 2004. *B. J. Curley*

MUSKETIER (GER)   2 gr.c. (Mar 15) Acatenango 127 – Myth And Reality   **114**
(Linamix (FR) 127) [2004 8d⁴ 8v* 8d² 9s* 10s⁵ Nov 6] €52,000Y: second foal: dam,
French 2-y-o 7.5f winner, half-sister to US Grade 2 9f winner Miatuschka: smart performer: won minor event at Deauville in August and Prix de Conde at Longchamp (4 ran,
beat Doctor Dino by 6 lengths) in October: beaten short neck by Helios Quercus in Prix
des Chenes at Longchamp in between: only fifth to Paita in Criterium de Saint-Cloud:
should stay 1¼m: acts on heavy going. *P. Bary, France*

MUSLIN   3 ch.f. Bien Bien (USA) 125 – Moidart 90 (Electric 126) [2004 10g 9.7s³   **58**
p12d 14g 11.5m² 14.1f⁵ 12g⁶ p16g Oct 13] sixth foal: half-sister to 3 winners, including
9f (at 2 yrs) to 2m winner Eileen Shona (by Suave Dancer) and 1¾m winner Mosca (by
Most Welcome): dam 11f and 2m winner: modest maiden: stays 1¾m: acts on polytrack
and firm ground: has looked awkward under pressure: sold 9,500 gns. *J. R. Fanshawe*

MUSTAJED   3 b.g. Alhaarth (IRE) 126 – Jasarah (IRE) 70 (Green Desert (USA) 127)   **85 ?**
[2004 87: 7g⁶ 8m May 29] sturdy gelding: fairly useful form: won maiden at Newbury
only run at 2 yrs: suffered fractured near-hind pastern after: respectable efforts in minor/
listed events in 2004 (visored second start): should stay 1m. *M. P. Tregoning*

MUSTAKHLAS (USA)   3 ch.g. Diesis 133 – Katiba (USA) 99 (Gulch (USA)) [2004   **–**
8g Apr 14] rangy gelding: 10/1, never-nearer eleventh in newcomers event at Newmarket: sold 2,700 gns in July, joined B. Baugh and gelded. *J. L. Dunlop*

MUSTANG ALI (IRE)   3 ch.g. Ali-Royal (IRE) 127 – Classic Queen (IRE) (Classic   **72**
Secret (USA) 91) [2004 67: 10g⁶ 11.6g 12g³ 14g⁵ 10m⁵ 11.7f³ 11.5g⁵ 11.5m⁶ 10.2m⁶
11.7g 11.9s p12.2g* p13.9g p12.2g p13g Dec 29] workmanlike gelding: fair handicapper:
won at Wolverhampton in November: stays 1½m: acts on polytrack and firm going:
sometimes soon off bridle. *S. Kirk*

Prix de Conde, Longchamp—Musketier has his three rivals well strung out;
Doctor Dino is second, with the John Hills-trained Wingman third

MUST BE MAGIC 7 b.g. Magic Ring (IRE) 115 – Sequin Lady (Star Appeal 133) **?**
[2004 74, a69: p10g⁴ p10g⁵ p10g 8m 9g 9g 12s 10.9d p9.5g³ Dec 15] smallish, good- **a66**
topped gelding: fair handicapper: below form after second start: effective at 1m/easy
1¼m: acts on polytrack, soft and good to firm going: usually visored. *H. J. Collingridge*

MUST BE SO 3 b.f. So Factual (USA) 120 – Ovideo 58 (Domynsky 110) [2004 52: **44 ?**
p7g⁵ p8g p7g p6g p6g⁶ 6v 5.3f⁴ 5.3f 7m 6f⁵ 5m Sep 11] close-coupled filly: poor performer: best at 6f/7f: acts on polytrack and good to firm going: tried tongue tied. *J. J. Bridger*

MUSTGODOWNTOTHESEA (IRE) 2 ch.f. (Apr 19) Raise A Grand (IRE) 114 **–**
– Rainery (IRE) 56 (Fairy King (USA)) [2004 6v 7v 7s p6g Nov 19] €1,500Y: fourth foal:
dam Irish maiden who stayed 2m: only a little sign of ability in maidens/Wolverhampton
seller. *Frederick John Bowles, Ireland*

MUTABARI (USA) 10 ch.g. Seeking The Gold (USA) – Cagey Exuberance (USA) **–**
(Exuberant (USA)) [2004 55d: f8.5g p8g f9.4g 7m 7f 7m 7f 8s Aug 27] rangy gelding: no
longer of any account. *J. L. Spearing*

MUTAFANEN 3 gr.c. Linamix (FR) 127 – Doomna (IRE) 97 (Machiavellian (USA) **108**
123) [2004 85: 10.3g⁴ 10.1s³ 9g³ 10m³ 10.4g 9.9m⁴ 10.5g⁴ 9.9d 14g⁶ Sep 30] medium-
sized, quite good-topped colt: smart performer: won handicap at Doncaster in March:
good efforts when third to Moscow Ballet in listed race at Royal Ascot fourth outing
and when fourth in ladbrokes.com Handicap at Goodwood (to Art Trader) and totesport
Handicap at Haydock (beaten 2¾ lengths by Dunaskin): well below form last 2 starts:
stays 1¼m: acts on good to firm and good to soft ground: tried visored, including at
Haydock: joined E. Charpy in UAE. *E. A. L. Dunlop*

MUTAHAYYA (IRE) 3 b.c. Peintre Celebre (USA) 137 – Winsa (USA) 80 (Riverman **104**
(USA) 131) [2004 109: 8d² 11g⁵ 10m 9s Oct 16] good-topped colt: useful performer:
ran creditably in 2004 only when length second to Privy Seal in listed race at Kempton:
free-going sort, best around 1m: acts on firm and good to soft going: joined P. Rudkin in
UAE. *J. L. Dunlop*

MUTAJAMMEL (FR) 2 b.c. (May 1) Kingmambo (USA) 125 – Irtifa 71 (Lahib **87 P**
(USA) 129) [2004 7d⁴ 8.1g* Sep 15] 525,000Y: big, good-topped colt: has plenty of
scope: fourth foal: half-brother to 3 winners, including fairly useful French 12.5f winner
Sayuri (by Sadler's Wells): dam, 2-y-o 6f winner who stayed 1m, out of useful half-sister
to champion US older mare Glorious Song, herself dam of Singspiel: still green,
confirmed promise when justifying favouritism in maiden at Sandown by ¾ length from
Golden Fury, leading over 1f out and responding well to pressure despite wandering:
likely to be suited by 1¼m/1½m: type to do very much better at 3 yrs, and will win more
races. *Sir Michael Stoute*

MUTAMAASEK (USA) 2 b. or br.c. (Mar 19) Swain (IRE) 134 – Tamgeed (USA) **78**
66 (Woodman (USA) 126) [2004 7g⁵ 8d 8.2d⁴ 10g⁵ Oct 4] smallish, strong colt: second
foal: brother to 3-y-o Madaeh: dam, maiden (best effort at 1¼m), out of close relative of
Mehthaaf and Elnadim: fair maiden: best effort when fourth at Nottingham: led briefly 2f
out final start: stays 1m: acts on good to soft going: sold 19,000 gns. *J. L. Dunlop*

MUTAMARED (USA) 4 ch.c. Nureyev (USA) 131 – Alydariel (USA) (Alydar **97**
(USA)) [2004 84?: 7m³ 7m³ 7d Oct 30] lengthy colt: fairly useful performer: won maiden
at Thirsk in May: much better effort after (similar form) when very close third to Chateau
Nicol in handicap at Newbury 4 months later: has form at 1m, but may prove best at 6f/
easy 7f: acts on good to firm ground: tongue tied last two 3-y-o starts. *M. P. Tregoning*

MUTANABI (USA) 2 b.c. (May 12) Wild Rush (USA) 123 – Freudenau (USA) **76 p**
(Meadowlake (USA)) [2004 p6d² p7m³ Oct 6] $6,200F, $45,000Y, $1,600,000 2-y-o:
third foal: half-brother to minor winner in USA by Lit de Justice: dam unraced out of
half-sister to US Grade 2 1m winner Kyle's Our Man: fair form in maidens at Lingfield,
no extra after leading travelling strongly both times: likely to prove best up to 7f: will do
better. *Saeed bin Suroor*

MUTARAFAA (USA) 5 b.g. Red Ransom (USA) – Mashaarif (USA) (Mr Prospector **63 d**
(USA)) [2004 64: f8.5s⁴ f8g³ f8.5g² f8.5g⁴ p10g p8g p8g f8s² p7g f8g 8.2v f8s f8g f7g
p8g Dec 20] strong gelding: modest performer, below form after fourth start: effective at
7f to 8.5f: acts on all-weather and good to firm going: usually wears headgear: inconsistent. *D. Shaw*

MUTARED (IRE) 6 b.g. Marju (IRE) 127 – Shahaada (USA) 57 (Private Account **–**
(USA)) [2004 83d: f9.4g 9g f8g 10m 7.9m 8m Aug 16] lengthy gelding: fairly useful
handicapper at best: no form in 2004: tried in headgear: often owner ridden. *N. P. Littmoden*

MUTASALLIL (USA) 4 ch.c. Gone West (USA) – Min Alhawa (USA) 108 (River- **109**
man (USA) 131) [2004 10m* 10m* 10m² 10.5g 12f* Sep 11] good-topped colt: third
foal: closely related to 5-y-o Tasneef: dam, 7f (at 2 yrs) and 1¼m winner, half-sister to
1000 Guineas winner Harayir: smart performer, lightly raced: won maiden at Ripon in
May, minor event at Pontefract in June and handicap at Doncaster (beat Pagan Dance by
short head) in September: stays 1½m: raced only on dirt and good ground or firmer:
tongue tied: often makes running: joined D. Watson in UAE. *Saeed bin Suroor*

MUTASSEM (FR) 3 b.c. Fasliyev (USA) 120 – Fee Eria (FR) (Always Fair (USA) **66**
121) [2004 73p: p8g 7d 7g 8d 7g 6m 6g² 8p.6g p7g 6d p6g³ p6g⁵ Dec 27] workmanlike **a58**
colt: fair maiden on turf, modest on all-weather: left E. Dunlop after third outing: effective at 6f/7f: acts on polytrack, good to firm and good to soft going: wore cheekpieces last
2 starts. *T. Keddy*

MUTAWAFFER 3 b.c. Marju (IRE) 127 – Absaar (USA) 76 (Alleged (USA) 138) **104 ?**
[2004 102: 10.4s 7s⁴ Oct 23] strong, well-made colt: useful performer, lightly raced:
seemed to run well when 2½ lengths fourth to Meshaheer in minor event at Doncaster
(dictated pace): should stay 1m: acts on soft going. *B. W. Hills*

MUTAWAQED (IRE) 6 ch.g. Zafonic (USA) 130 – Waqood (USA) 75 (Riverman **99**
(USA) 131) [2004 95: 6d 6m⁴ 6m² 6d 6f* 6m 5s² 5.6m 6g⁴ 6g Oct 9] heavy-bodied
gelding: useful handicapper: won at York in July by length from Machinist: mostly ran
well otherwise in 2004, fourth to Funfair Wane in Ayr Gold Cup penultimate start: reportedly broke blood vessel final outing: has won at 1m, but best at 5f/6f: acts on all-weather,
firm and soft going: tried visored/blinkered, not in 2004: tongue tied: usually bandaged:
best held up (tends to idle): consistent. *M. A. Magnusson*

MUTAWASSEL (USA) 3 b.c. Kingmambo (USA) 125 – Danzig Darling (CAN) **97**
(Danzig) [2004 97p: 10d⁴ 10.3d³ 9.9m Jul 29] tall, good-topped, quite attractive
colt: has a round action: useful performer: ran creditably in frame behind African Dream
in Classic Trial at Sandown (took strong hold) and Dee Stakes at Chester (2¼ lengths last
of 3): stays 1¼m: unraced on extremes of going: blinkered (ran poorly) final start: has
hung right/flashed tail: sold 26,000 gns, sent to Bahrain. *B. W. Hills*

MUTAYAM 4 b.g. Compton Place 125 – Final Shot 91 (Dalsaan 125) [2004 42: 6g⁶ 5g **57**
5g⁶ 5f 5g⁸ 5d 6d Sep 27] modest performer: won maiden at Newcastle in September: best
at 5f: acts on firm ground: tongue tied: usually races prominently: none too consistent.
D. A. Nolan

MUYASSIR (IRE) 9 b.g. Brief Truce (USA) 126 – Twine (Thatching 131) [2004 76, **–**
a66: p10g p8g* 8g 8m 8g 8g p8g p8.6g p8g Dec 20] deep-bodied gelding: modest **a60**
performer: won handicap at Lingfield in January: effective at 1m/1¼m: acts on firm
going and polytrack: tried in blinkers/cheekpieces/tongue strap, not in 2004: none too
reliable. *Miss B. Sanders*

MUY BIEN 3 ch.c. Daggers Drawn (USA) 114 – Primula Bairn 77 (Bairn (USA) 126) **79**
[2004 67, a78: f6g² f6g² f6g f5s³ 6d* 6.1s² 6s³ 7s f6g f5f³ Dec 28] tall, useful-looking
colt: fair handicapper: won at Windsor in April: effective at 6f/7f: acts on all-weather and
soft ground: tried visored/blinkered: sometimes looks none too keen: often races up
with pace. *J. R. Jenkins*

MUZIO SCEVOLA (IRE) 3 ch.g. Titus Livius (FR) 115 – Dancing Sunset (IRE) **62**
111 (Red Sunset 120) [2004 p12g² 11.8d⁵ 11g⁵ 14.6g⁶ 16m³ 17.1g Oct 4] strong, angular **a70**
gelding: fourth foal: half-brother to 2000 2-y-o 6f/7f winner Lady of Kildare (by Mujadil)
and 7f winner Islandagore (by Indian Ridge), both useful in Ireland: dam, Irish 1¼m/
1½m winner, from family of Ajdal and Arazi: fair performer on all-weather, modest on
turf: stays 2m: acts on polytrack. *M. R. Channon*

MY ACE 6 b.m. Definite Article 121 – Miss Springtime 65 (Bluebird (USA) 125) [2004 **–**
9g⁶ Apr 8] 8,000Y: second foal: dam, 7f/1m winner, became one to treat with caution:
poor winning hurdler: well beaten in maiden at Musselburgh. *James Moffatt*

MYANNABANANA (IRE) 3 ch.g. Woodborough (USA) 112 – Raging Storm (Hor- **45**
age 124) [2004 44, a66: p10g⁵ f9.4g³ f11g⁴ f8.5s⁴ f8g 10d⁵ 8s 10g 9g 10d 10f 13.8m 10g **a63 d**
10s f8g p9.5g Dec 22] quite good-topped gelding: modest at best on all-weather, poor on
turf: seems to stay 1¼m: acts on fibresand, good to firm and good to soft going: wears
headgear. *J. R. Weymes*

MY BAYARD 5 ch.g. Efisio 120 – Bay Bay 101 (Bay Express 132) [2004 63, a76: **67**
f8.5s⁶ f7s² f8.5s⁵ 12g f7g* 7m 6g⁴ 5.9g³ 5f 6d³ Aug 17] plain gelding: fairly useful on **a84**
all-weather, fair on turf: won minor event at Wolverhampton in April: had form at 11f,
probably best at 6f to 1m: acted on fibresand and good to soft going, probably on firm:

tried blinkered/tongue tied: joined J. Balding, and due to have first outing for new trainer when 'kidnapped' from Wolverhampton racecourse stables Nov 20 (ownership dispute): soon returned to Balding's stable, but put down in December due to colitis. *J. O'Reilly*

MY BOO   2 b.f. (Feb 7) Sri Pekan (USA) 117 – Malwiya (USA) (Shahrastani (USA) 135) [2004 p8.6g Dec 17] 5,200Y: half-sister to several winners, including 7-y-o Malarkey: dam unraced: 33/1, well held in maiden at Wolverhampton. *T. Keddy*   –

MY COUNTRY CLUB   7 b.h. Alzao (USA) 117 – Merry Rous 66 (Rousillon (USA) 133) [2004 7s⁶ 7m⁶ f8.5m 6.1d 10.2m⁶ Aug 5] winner of 8 races in Poland: little form in Britain: effective at 6f/7f: tried blinkered. *A. G. Juckes*   –

MY DREAM (IRE)   2 b.f. (Mar 15) King's Theatre (IRE) 128 – Dream Chaser 92 (Record Token 128) [2004 5.1f⁴ Jun 12] sister to smart but ungenuine 7f (including at 2 yrs)/1m winner King's Ironbridge and half-sister to 3 winners, including fairly useful 5f winner Cradle Days (by Dance of Life): dam best at 6f: 12/1 and green, last in minor event at Bath. *R. Hannon*   –

MY DUBAI (IRE)   2 ch.f. (Mar 11) Dubai Millennium 140 – Pastorale 91 (Nureyev (USA) 131) [2004 7d³ Oct 30] rather leggy, lengthy filly: half-sister to several winners, including 1998 2-y-o 7f winner Kareymah (by Zafonic) and 1m winner Jathaabeh (by Nashwan), both useful: dam, 7f winner from 3 starts, half-sister to Cape Cross and closely related to dam of Diktat, an excellent family: 6/1 and tongue tied, ¾-length third of 19 to Read Federica in maiden at Newmarket, travelling well and first home in stand-side group: will stay 1m: sure to progress. *Saeed bin Suroor*   **76 p**

MY GACHO (IRE)   2 b.c. (Feb 17) Shinko Forest (IRE) – Floralia 81 (Auction Ring (USA) 123) [2004 6g 7.1g³ 6f³ 6d p6g³ p5g³ Nov 20] 8,500Y: good-topped colt: half-brother to several winners, including 6-y-o Henry Afrika: dam, 7f and 9f winner, half-sister to smart Performer Sugarfoot: fair maiden: effective at 6f/7f: acts on polytrack and firm going: wandered fourth start: races prominently. *Mrs P. N. Dutfield*   **78**

MY GALLIANO (IRE)   8 b.g. Muharib (USA) 97 – Hogan Stand (Buckskin (FR) 133) [2004 78: 10s 9.9g³ 10.1d⁶ 10.1f⁵ Jul 29] compact gelding: fair handicapper: effective at 1¼m/1½m: acts on polytrack and good to firm going: tends to pull hard. *B. G. Powell*   **70**

MY GIRL PEARL (IRE)   4 b.f. Sri Pekan (USA) 117 – Desert Bloom (FR) (Last Tycoon 131) [2004 55: p7g f7g² f7m⁴ 7m² 6.1m 6.1s⁶ 7m⁴ 6m* 6f 6g³ 6.1g⁶ 7.1m* 7g⁴ 7.1s Sep 20] angular filly: modest handicapper: won at Brighton (NH jockeys event) in July and Chepstow in September: stays 7f: acts on fibresand and firm going: blinkered (well below form) twice. *M. S. Saunders*   **58**

MY HOPE (IRE)   3 b.f. Danehill (USA) 126 – Lady Elgar (IRE) (Sadler's Wells (USA) 132) [2004 69p: 8v 8m 8.2g 8.1g 10.2m³ 8g Aug 4] leggy filly: fair maiden: barely stays 1¼m: acts on good to firm going: sold 22,000 gns in November. *R. Charlton*   **67**

MY LAST BEAN (IRE)   7 gr.g. Soviet Lad (USA) – Meanz Beanz (High Top 131) [2004 68: 10.9d⁶ 12g Oct 4] just modest form in 2004: stays 13f: acts on fibresand, soft and good to firm ground: usually blinkered, not in 2004: races prominently: fair hurdler. *B. Smart*   **50**

MY LEGAL EAGLE (IRE)   10 b.g. Law Society (USA) 130 – Majestic Nurse 80 (On Your Mark 125) [2004 –: f14.8g* f14.8m⁴ f16.2m² 13.9m* 14.1m* 13.3m* 14g² Jul 1] smallish gelding: fair performer: won banded race at Wolverhampton and handicaps at York (apprentices), Nottingham and Newbury in May/June: stays 17f: acts on fibresand, heavy and good to firm going: occasionally blinkered earlier in career: usually held up. *R. J. Price*   **65**

MY LILLI (IRE)   4 b.f. Marju (IRE) 127 – Tamburello (IRE) (Roi Danzig (USA)) [2004 57?: p10g³ p10g⁴ p12g p12g⁶ p8g⁴ p8g* p10g³ 8f p10g p8.6g p10m Dec 21] tall, close-coupled filly: modest handicapper on all-weather: won at Lingfield in April: ran as if amiss last 3 starts: effective at 1m to 1½m: acts on polytrack, well held on turf: tried visored. *P. Mitchell*   **46 a59**

MY LINE   7 b.g. Perpendicular 119 – My Desire 88 (Grey Desire 115) [2004 70: 18v Apr 6] lengthy gelding: fair handicapper: blinkered (tailed off) only Flat run in 2004: has a low head carriage: won over hurdles later in April. *Mrs M. Reveley*   –

MY LITTLE SOPHIA   4 b.f. Wizard King 122 – David James' Girl 65 (Faustus (USA) 118) [2004 f7s⁵ 8.1s 11.9m f7d Jun 17] 500Y: workmanlike filly: second foal: dam 5f (at 2 yrs) to 1m winner: no sign of ability: wore cheekpieces final start. *M. Mullineaux*   –

MY MAITE (IRE)   5 b.g. Komaite (USA) – Mena 58 (Blakeney 126) [2004 66d, **52**
a77d: p10g² p10g⁴ p10g p10g 8.2m* 10f⁶ 8.3m 9g⁴ 8m⁵ 9.7m 10m³ 9.7f³ 10m³ p9.5g⁴ **a62**
p9.5g⁶ p9.5g² p12.2g⁵ p10m Dec 21] modest performer: won banded race at Nottingham
in May: stays easy 1½m: acts on polytrack, good to firm and good to soft ground: wears
headgear/tongue tie: has found little. *R. Ingram*

MY MICHELLE   3 b.f. Ali-Royal (IRE) 127 – April Magic (Magic Ring (IRE) 115) **57**
[2004 74: 6d 8f 8.2g⁴ 10g⁵ 8.1m⁴ 10g⁶ Nov 6] leggy, quite good-topped filly:
modest maiden: stays easy 1m: acts on good to firm and good to soft ground. *B. Palling*

MYND   4 b.g. Atraf 116 – Prim Lass 65 (Reprimand 122) [2004 68: f5s* f5g* f5s² p6g **72**
5d² 5g* 5d 5v 5f⁶ 5d⁴ 5g 5d⁵ 5d 6g 5s p5.1g p5g Dec 18] workmanlike gelding: fair
performer: won maiden and handicap at Wolverhampton in January and handicap
(apprentices) at Ripon in April: probably best at 5f: acts on all-weather and soft going:
tried in cheekpieces: usually races prominently: sometimes slowly away. *R. M. Whitaker*

MY ONLY SUNSHINE   5 b.g. First Trump 118 – Fivesfive (IRE) 61 (Fairy King **–**
(USA)) [2004 p6g Dec 13] dipped-backed gelding: fairly useful handicapper in 2002:
off 29 months, well beaten only 5-y-o start: sometimes carries head high/wanders.
M. J. Wallace

MY PARIS   3 b.g. Paris House 123 – My Desire 88 (Grey Desire 115) [2004 –: f7g³ **101**
f7g² 7d² 9g² 8m⁵ 10.3m² 10m² 9d* 7m* 7g* Aug 28] leggy gelding: useful performer:
won maiden at Ripon in July and handicaps at Leicester (dictated pace) and Newmarket
(clearly best effort, beat Alfonso by short head, despite being slowly in stride and then
hanging left when in front) in August: effective at 7f to 1¼m: acts on fibresand, good to
firm and good to soft going: usually races prominently. *K. A. Ryan*

MY PENSION (IRE)   3 b.g. Orpen (USA) 116 – Woodenitbenice (USA) (Nasty And **80**
Bold (USA)) [2004 8v 7s⁴ 7.2f³ 8.1d 8d 10.1g⁶ p8.6g³ p8g* p8.6d² p8.6g* p7g p9.5g²
p9.5g⁵ Dec 27] €18,000Y: lengthy, rather sparely-made gelding: half-brother to several
winners, including 1m to 1¼m winner Special Promise (by Anjiz): dam unraced: fairly
useful performer: won minor event at Lingfield in October and handicap at Wolverhampton in November: probably stays 1¼m: acts on polytrack and any turf ground. *P. Howling*

MY PORTFOLIO (IRE)   2 b.g. (Mar 7) Montjeu (IRE) 137 – Elaine's Honor (USA) **68**
(Chief's Crown (USA)) [2004 8d⁴ 8g 8g Oct 12] 50,000Y: quite good-topped gelding:
half-brother to several winners, including useful 1999 2-y-o 5f winner Areydha (by Cadeaux Genereux) and 4-y-o Brazilian Terrace: dam French winner around 8.5f: best effort
in maidens when fourth at Salisbury: likely to be suited by 1¼m/1½m. *R. Charlton*

MY PRINCESS (IRE)   2 b.f. (May 3) Danehill Dancer (IRE) 117 – Shanoora (IRE) **83**
53 (Don't Forget Me 127) [2004 6m³ 6m⁵ 6m³ 7f* 6d 8d⁵ 8m⁵ 7g² 7s Oct 16] 24,000Y:
close-coupled filly: fourth foal: half-sister to Irish 7f winner She's So Beautiful (by Bluebird): dam 2-y-o 5f winner who stayed 1m: fairly useful performer: won maiden at
Brighton in August: unlucky third (promoted a place) in nursery at Catterick: lacklustre
effort final start: probably stays 1m: acts on firm and good to soft ground. *N. A. Callaghan*

MY PUTRA (USA)   2 b. or br.c. (Jan 31) Silver Hawk (USA) 123 – Petite Triomphe **82 p**
(USA) (Wild Again (USA)) [2004 6s³ 8m² Sep 21] $170,000Y: tall, quite good-topped
colt: has a round action: first foal: dam, 6.5f winner in USA, half-sister to useful French
performer up to 10.5f Petite Speciale: fairly useful form in maidens at York and Newmarket (5 lengths second to Forward Move, travelling strongly long way): should
progress. *P. F. I. Cole*

MY RASCAL (IRE)   2 b.g. (Mar 23) Imperial Ballet (IRE) 110 – Derena (FR) (Crystal **57**
Palace (FR) 132) [2004 7m 7d 7.1m p7g Oct 13] big, strong gelding: modest maiden:
should stay 1m: best efforts on good to firm going. *M. J. Wallace*

MY RENEE (USA)   4 b. or br.f. Kris S (USA) – Mayenne (USA) (Nureyev (USA) **109**
131) [2004 107: 14m³ 12f* 12f² Sep 24] useful performer, lightly raced: won listed race
at Cork in August by neck from Tarakala: good short-head second to Mazuna in Princess Royal Stakes at Ascot final outing: stays 1½m: acts on firm going: sent to USA.
M. J. Grassick, Ireland

MY RISK (FR)   5 b.h. Take Risks (FR) 116 – Miss Pat (FR) (Vacarme (USA) 121) **119**
[2004 120: 8d⁴ 8d⁵ 8g* 8d³ 8m Oct 2] smart performer: won Prix Edmond Blanc at Saint-
Cloud (by head from Art Moderne) in March and Prix du Chemin de Fer du Nord at
Chantilly (by head from Charming Groom) in June: good 2½ lengths third to Whipper
in Prix Jacques le Marois at Deauville: stayed 1m: acted on heavy going (below form
in Prix Daniel Wildenstein at Longchamp final start, only outing on firmer than good):

held up: genuine and reliable: to stand at Haras de Victot, France, fee €2,200, live foal. *J-M. Beguigne, France*

MYRTUS 5 ch.g. Double Eclipse (IRE) 122 – My Desire 88 (Grey Desire 115) [2004 – –: f12g³ f16g f16g⁵ Jul 23] lengthy gelding: little form. *J. R. Weymes*

MY SHARP GREY 5 gr.m. Tragic Role (USA) – Sharp Anne 74§ (Belfort (FR) 89) [2004 62: p10g Feb 7] modest maiden: well held only Flat run in 2004: tried blinkered: modest winning hurdler. *J. Gallagher*

MYSTERINCH 4 b.g. Inchinor 119 – Hakone (IRE) 78 (Alzao (USA) 117) [2004 96: **96** 8s³ 10g 8.5m 7.1m² 8.1g 7.9d 7f 8d⁴ Aug 22] good-topped gelding: useful performer: reportedly sustained minor injury only 3-y-o start: some creditable efforts in 2004, including short-head second to Material Witness in minor event at Warwick: effective at 7f, barely at 1¼m: acts on polytrack, soft and good to firm ground. *Jedd O'Keeffe*

MYSTERIUM 10 gr.g. Mystiko (USA) 124 – Way To Go 69 (Troy 137) [2004 51: **49** f14.8g³ p16g⁴ f16.2s* f16.2m⁵ p16g⁶ Apr 27] tall, leggy gelding: poor performer: won banded race at Wolverhampton in March: stays 17f: acts on all-weather and good going: visored: sometimes slowly away: held up: often looks none too keen. *N. P. Littmoden*

MYSTERLOVER (IRE) 4 b.g. Night Shift (USA) – Jacaranda City (IRE) 88 (In **54** The Wings 128) [2004 52?: p10g p12g p13g p16g Mar 8] modest maiden, lightly raced: stays 13f: raced only on all-weather: tongue tied last 2 starts. *N. P. Littmoden*

MYSTERY LOT (IRE) 2 b.f. (Mar 18) Revoque (IRE) 122 – Mystery Bid (Auction **74** Ring (USA) 123) [2004 p7g⁶ 7d² 7.1s² 8.3g³ Oct 11] 9,500Y: well-made filly: half-sister to several winners, including fairly useful 1998 2-y-o 7f winner Spy (by Mac's Imp) and 1½m winner Secret Service (by Classic Secret): dam Irish maiden who stayed 1½m: fair maiden: will stay 1¼m: acts on soft going. *A. King*

MYSTERY MAID (IRE) 2 b.f. (Feb 24) King's Theatre (IRE) 128 – Duly Elected – (Persian Bold 123) [2004 5.1g 6g⁶ 6m 6g 7g Sep 20] €2,500Y: close-coupled filly: half-sister to several winners, including fairly useful 1998 2-y-o 6f winner Kangaroo Island (later successful in USA, by Turtle Island) and 7-y-o Ladywell Blaise: dam fourth at 1m/ 9f in Ireland: little sign of ability in maidens. *H. S. Howe*

MYSTERY MOUNTAIN 4 b.g. Mistertopogigo (IRE) 118 – Don't Jump (IRE) 71 **41** (Entitled 126) [2004 62: f6g f7g⁵ f6s⁴ Mar 1] poor maiden: should be suited by 7f+: raced only on fibresand and good/firm ground. *Mrs J. R. Ramsden*

MYSTERY PIPS 4 b.f. Bin Ajwaad (IRE) 119 – Le Shuttle 49 (Presidium 124) [2004 **50** 57: 5d 5m 5m 5d 5f⁴ 5g 5g 5m⁴ 5m³ 5d 5d p5.1g Oct 25] poor performer: effective at 5f/ easy 6f: acts on firm and good to soft ground: wears blinkers/visor. *N. Tinkler*

MYSTERY SOLVED (USA) 4 b.f. Royal Academy (USA) 130 – Golden Rhyme 87 – (Dom Racine (FR) 121) [2004 57: 12d f8g May 15] closely related/half-sister to several winners, notably very smart 1991 2-y-o 6f/1m (Racing Post Trophy) winner Seattle Rhyme (by Seattle Dancer): dam 7f winner: modest maiden in Ireland for D. Wachman in 2003: no form in Britain: stays 1m: acts on soft ground. *P. A. Blockley*

MYSTICAL GIRL (USA) 3 ch.f. Rahy (USA) 115 – Miss Twinkletoes (IRE) (Zafo- **102** nic (USA) 130) [2004 73: 8g³ 8.5v³ 8m* 11g² 8.1d* 10.1m³ 8f 10m⁶ 8m 10.1s⁵ 8m* p9.5g⁶ Dec 31] lengthy, good-topped filly: useful performer: won handicap at Thirsk in May, minor event at Sandown in June and handicap at Kempton (beat Diamond Lodge by 2 lengths) in September: barely stays easy 9.5f: acts on polytrack, heavy and good to firm ground: races up with pace. *M. Johnston*

MYSTICAL LAND (IRE) 2 b.c. (Feb 24) Xaar 132 – Samsung Spirit 79 (Statoblest **108** 120) [2004 5s² 5g* 5m² 6m³ 6m² 6s⁵ 6g² Sep 18] 20,000Y: sturdy, useful-looking colt: fourth foal: half-brother to fairly useful 2002 2-y-o 6f winner (stayed 1m) Spiritual Air (by Royal Applause): dam, 6f winner (including at 2 yrs), half-sister to dam of smart 6f/ 7f performer Indian Rocket: useful performer: won minor event at Doncaster in May: good second after in Norfolk Stakes (beaten neck by Blue Dakota) at Royal Ascot, Richmond Stakes (same margin behind Montgomery's Arch) at Goodwood and Mill Reef Stakes (visored, beaten length by Galeota) at Newbury: stays 6f: acts on good to firm ground, possibly not on soft: sometimes swishes tail in preliminaries. *J. H. M. Gosden*

MYSTIC LAD 3 gr.g. Magic Ring (IRE) 115 – Jilly Woo 60 (Environment Friend **67** 128) [2004 p8g² 8g p7g⁴ Dec 29] second foal: half-brother to 4-y-o Private Benjamin: dam maiden who stayed 1¼m: easily best effort in maidens when second at Lingfield: off over 8 months after next start. *Jamie Poulton*

MYSTIC MAN (FR)   6 b.g. Cadeaux Genereux 131 – Shawanni 105 (Shareef Dancer **94** (USA) 135) [2004 99: f7g f8.5s 8g 8d 8m* 8m³ 7m 7s⁴ 6g³ 6m 6d 7.9g Oct 8] strong, angular gelding: fairly useful performer: won minor event at Doncaster in May by 2½ lengths from Langford: effective at 6f to 1m: acts on fibresand, soft and good to firm going: sometimes tongue tied/wears crossed noseband: usually held up: tends to race freely. *K. A. Ryan*

MYSTIC MOON   3 br.f. First Trump 118 – Misty Moon (Polar Falcon (USA) 126) **56 d** [2004 –: p7g p7g 9.7s⁶ 8.2g 10s⁴ 10s p10g 10.1m⁴ 10.1g 10g 8s 10.2g Sep 13] modest maiden at best: stays 1¼m: acts on soft going. *J. R. Jenkins*

MYSTIC PROMISE (IRE)   3 gr.g. Among Men (USA) 124 – Ivory's Promise 74 **36** (Pursuit of Love 124) [2004 –: f6g f6s f8g f8g⁵ p10g f8g³ f7g⁴ f7m⁵ f9.4g⁶ f8g Jun 11] leggy, lengthy gelding: poor performer: stays 1m: acts on fibresand: tried in headgear/tongue tie. *Mrs N. Macauley*

MY SUNSHINE (IRE)   3 b.f. Alzao (USA) 117 – Sunlit Ride (Ahonoora 122) [2004 **60 d** 62: 10d 7.9m 8m p8g 8g 8g Sep 27] smallish, lengthy filly: modest maiden: regressed after second outing: bred to be suited by 1¼m/1½m: tried blinkered. *B. W. Hills*

MYTHICAL CHARM   5 b.m. Charnwood Forest (IRE) 125 – Triple Tricks (IRE) **65** 70 (Royal Academy (USA) 130) [2004 63, a58: f9.4g⁶ p10g p8g p10g p10g⁶ p10g³ p8g³ **a53** 8m 9g 8.3m 6f³ 7g⁵ 8g 6g 8s² 8m² 8m 9s Oct 22] good-topped mare: fair on turf, modest on all-weather: effective at 6f to 1½m: acts on all-weather, firm and soft ground: often tongue tied: sometimes slowly away. *J. J. Bridger*

MYTHICAL KING (IRE)   7 b.g. Fairy King (USA) – Whatcombe (USA) 88 **56** (Alleged (USA) 138) [2004 59: 12.4s 10d⁶ p12.2g Oct 19] deep-girthed gelding: modest handicapper: best at 1¼m/1½m: acts on firm and good to soft going. *R. Lee*

Sheikh Mohammed's "Mystical Land"

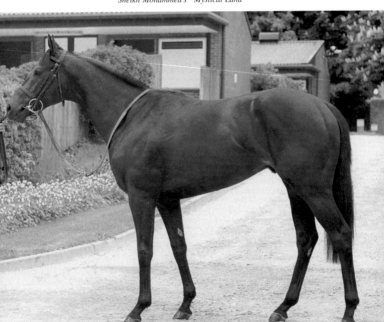

MYTORI 2 ch.f. (Apr 26) Vettori (IRE) 119 – Markievicz (IRE) 73 (Doyoun 124) [2004 – 7m 8.2g⁶ 6.1s⁶ Sep 20] 600 2-y-o: half-sister to 5-y-o Oases and 9-y-o Paarl Rock: dam Irish 6.5f winner: well held in maidens/minor event. *D. Shaw*

MY TRUE LOVE (IRE) 5 b.g. Beneficial 117 – Elfi (IRE) (Le Moss 135) [2004 **50** 18m⁵ 12g 14m⁴ 16.2m Sep 6] big, heavy-topped gelding: runner-up in bumper: modest maiden on Flat. *R. J. Baker*

MYTTON'S BELL (IRE) 2 b.f. (Mar 17) Bold Edge 123 – Ionian Secret 56 (Mystiko **67** (USA) 124) [2004 6m² f6m³ 6s 6.1m³ 6g 7.1g⁵ 6d 7.1d³ 7s* 5.1v f8g² p7.1g p7.1g f7g Dec 14] 7,000Y: quite good-topped filly: second foal: dam, lightly-raced maiden, half-sister to smart sprinter Northern Goddess: fair performer: won maiden at Catterick in November: stays 1m: acts on fibresand, soft and good to firm going: usually races up with pace. *A. Bailey*

MYTTON'S DREAM 2 br.f. (Mar 21) Diktat 126 – Courtisane (Persepolis (FR) **56** 127) [2004 5d⁶ 5.1d⁶ 5g* 5.1d 6m⁴ 7d 7m f7g³ p6g⁵ f7g⁶ Dec 14] 7,000F, 15,000Y: leggy **a47** filly: half-sister to several winners, including 2001 2-y-o 5f winner Dangerous Liaison (by Great Commotion) and 6f winner (including at 2 yrs) Charming Lotte (by Nicolotte): dam French 2-y-o 7f winner: modest on turf, poor on all-weather: won seller at Beverley in May: barely stays 7f: acts on fibresand, good to firm and good to soft going. *A. Bailey*

MY WILD ROVER 4 b.g. Puissance 110 – June Fayre (Sagaro 133) [2004 –: p6g f5g – 5s 6.1m May 25] of no account. *K. A. Morgan*

N

NAADDEY 3 b.c. Seeking The Gold (USA) – Bahr 119 (Generous (IRE) 139) [2004 98: **93** 9g 8m⁶ 8.2g⁴ a7f⁶ Dec 4] neat, attractive colt: fairly useful performer: left M. Channon after third start: should stay 1¼m: best efforts on good to firm going (ran respectably on dirt): tried visored (looked reluctant on both occasions). *D. J. Selvaratnam, UAE*

NAAHY 4 ch.c. Bahamian Bounty 116 – Daffodil Fields (Try My Best (USA) 130) **110** [2004 111: 7g³* 7m* 7m 7f⁴ 7g⁴ 6.5g⁶ 8s 7m 7m⁵ 7g Dec 26] quite attractive colt: smart performer: reportedly chipped a bone in knee after final start in 2003: won minor event at Goodwood (by 1¾ lengths from Suggestive) in May and Ballycorus Stakes at Leopardstown (beat Hamairi by ½ length) in June: creditable efforts when fourth in Minstrel Stakes at the Curragh (to Trade Fair) and Betfair Cup (Lennox) at Goodwood (behind Byron) and fifth to Kehaar in valuable handicap at Ascot: left M. Channon 82,000 gns after: best at 7f: acts on firm and good to soft going: tends to sweat: has handled left-hand turn poorly at Catterick and Epsom: game front runner. *M. Al Kurdi, UAE*

NABTAT SAIF 3 b.f. Compton Place 125 – Bahawir Pour (USA) (Green Dancer **63** (USA) 132) [2004 70: a8f a7.5f⁴ a9f 10m 7m 10f Jul 26] lengthy filly: fair maiden: trained by D. Watson first 3 starts, seventh in UAE 1000 Guineas and UAE Oaks at Nad Al Sheba in February/March: rejoined former trainer, below form in handicaps last 3 outings: stays 1m: raced only on good or firmer ground on turf: tried visored/tongue tied. *R. Hannon*

NADESZHDA 4 ch.f. Nashwan (USA) 135 – Ninotchka (USA) 110 (Nijinsky (CAN) **91** 138) [2004 83: p12g³¹ 11s 10f* 10f² 12f² Nov 25] fairly useful performer: well backed, won handicap at Lingfield (beat Regal Gallery comfortably by ¾ length) in July: tailed off in listed race at Krefeld 11 days later (left Sir Mark Prescott after): off 3 months, improved in US, winning allowance race at Santa Anita in October: good 1½ lengths second to Uraib in non-graded handicap at Hollywood following month: should stay 1¾m: acts on all-weather and firm ground, well beaten both starts on softer than good: free-going sort: attempted to run out final 3-y-o outing. *N. D. Drysdale, USA*

NADIR 3 b.c. Pivotal 124 – Amid The Stars 61 (Midyan (USA) 124) [2004 81p: 8g 8g⁶ **65** 10d p9.5g³ p9.5g p8.6g⁵ Dec 17] tall, close-coupled colt: fairly useful form sole 2-y-o start: just fair form in 2004: should stay 1¼m: acts on polytrack. *P. Howling*

NAFFERTON GIRL (IRE) 3 b.f. Orpen (USA) 116 – Petomi 75 (Presidium 124) **41** [2004 51: 6d⁴ f9.4g p10g 10.2f Jun 23] lengthy filly: poor maiden: should stay 7f: slowly away second outing: sold 6,000 gns. *J. A. Osborne*

NAFFERTON HEIGHTS (IRE) 3 b.c. Peintre Celebre (USA) 137 – Gold Mist 85 **47** (Darshaan 133) [2004 –: 7s 9.9s⁵ 12.1g 14.1m 16.2g 12.1m⁶ 8g Aug 4] smallish, leggy colt: poor maiden: stays 1½m: best effort on good going: blinkered (found little) penultimate start. *M. W. Easterby*

NAHEEF (IRE)   5 b.g. Marju (IRE) 127 – Golden Digger (USA) 66 (Mr Prospector **109**
(USA)) [2004 116: a10f³ 10.5m⁵ 12m 11.6d* 9.9g⁵ 10s Oct 16] well-made, quite attractive gelding: just useful form in 2004: won listed event at Windsor (beat Hawridge Prince
by 1½ lengths) in August: only fifth to Alkaadhem in similar race at Goodwood penultimate start: stays 11.6f: acts on good to firm and good to soft going: visored/tongue tied:
usually races prominently (acted as pacemaker in Champion Stakes final outing): gelded
after. *Saeed bin Suroor*

NAIVETY   2 ch.f. (May 23) Machiavellian (USA) 123 – Innocence 73 (Unfuwain **78**
(USA) 131) [2004 7d² 7.5m Sep 15] 70,000Y: rather unfurnished filly: fifth foal: half-
sister to 3 winners, including fairly useful 6f winner Najeyba (by Indian Ridge): dam,
maiden who stayed 1½m, half-sister to smart middle-distance performers Beneficial and
Jeune, latter also winner of Melbourne Cup: much better effort in maidens when second
to Playful Act at Newmarket: favourite, raced freely in slowly-run race at Beverley:
should stay at least 1m. *C. E. Brittain*

NAJAABA (USA)   4 b.f. Bahhare (USA) 122 – Ashbilya (USA) (Nureyev (USA) **90**
131) [2004 69: f8g* f8g* f9.4g* f8g* p10g⁵ f8.5g* 8d⁵ 9m⁶ 8.3d⁵ 8g p8g p8g⁵ p8.6g⁴
f8g² Dec 28] smallish, sturdy filly: carries plenty of condition: fairly useful performer:
won handicaps at Southwell (3) and Wolverhampton (2) between January and March:
also ended year in good form: stays 9.4f: acts on all-weather, good to firm and good to
soft ground: effective held up/ridden close to pace: tough and reliable. *Miss J. Feilden*

NAJEEBON (FR)   5 ch.g. Cadeaux Genereux 131 – Jumairah Sun (IRE) 98 (Scenic **87**
128) [2004 98: 6g 6m 6m 6m³ 6m⁶ 6m³ 6.5g 6m 6g 6m² 6g³ 6g Sep 29] lengthy, well-
made gelding: fairly useful handicapper: effective at 6f/7f: acts on firm going, probably
on soft: tried visored/tongue tied: sometimes slowly away/soon off bridle: none too
reliable: sold 32,000 gns. *M. R. Channon*

NAKWA (IRE)   6 b.g. Namaqualand (USA) – Cajo (IRE) (Tirol 127) [2004 61: f12g* **72**
f12g² f12g² f14g⁵ 12.4v³ 14s² 13g² 14m* 14d² 14g⁶ 16.1m 13f 10.9s 18s Oct 16] tall
gelding: fair performer: won banded race at Wolverhampton in January and handicap
at Haydock in May: stays 1¾m: acts on fibresand, soft and good to firm going: has
reportedly broken blood vessels: often makes running. *E. J. Alston*

NAMAT (IRE)   3 b.f. Daylami (IRE) 138 – Masharik (USA) 93 (Caerleon (USA) 132) **74 p**
[2004 9f² 10.2g* Sep 27] lengthy filly: third foal: half-sister to fairly useful 1m winner
Glamorous Girl (by Darshaan): dam, 1¼m winner, half-sister to high-class middle-
distance stayer Ibn Bey and Yorkshire Oaks winner Roseate Tern: fair form: confirmed
debut promise when winning maiden at Bath by head from Principessa, taking while to
find full stride and getting up on line: should stay 1½m: slowly away on debut: sold
31,000 gns in December: remains open to improvement. *M. P. Tregoning*

NAMED AT DINNER   3 ch.g. Halling (USA) 133 – Salanka (IRE) 68 (Persian **–**
Heights 129) [2004 75: 9.9s 8m 6m 7.9g 7g 6.9m 7g 10g Sep 29] close-coupled gelding:
little form in 2004: blinkered/visored last 2 starts. *Mrs A. Duffield*

NAMKING   2 b.g. (May 3) Namid 128 – Kingdom Queen (IRE) 65 (Night Shift (USA)) **54**
[2004 5d 5m f6m⁶ p7.1g⁴ Dec 15] modest maiden: should stay 1m. *C. W. Thornton*

NAMROC (IRE)   3 b.c. Indian Ridge 123 – Hesperia (Slip Anchor 136) [2004 8m* **97 p**
8d⁴ 8f² 10g⁴ 10v Oct 23] 85,000Y: strong colt: fourth foal: half-brother to 2002 7f 2-y-o
winner Lucky Date (by Halling): dam, useful 11f/1½m winner in Italy, out of half-sister
to champion US filly Go For Wand: useful performer: won maiden at Newmarket in June:
good second to Jay Gee's Choice in minor event at Pontefract: stays 1¼m: acts on firm
and good to soft ground, well held on heavy final outing: sort to do better at 4 yrs.
E. F. Vaughan

NAMROUD (USA)   5 b.g. Irish River (FR) 131 – Top Line (FR) (Top Ville 129) [2004 **86 d**
103: 6g 7v⁶ 8.1m 7m 7.1m 8.1g 7.6s⁴ 7.2s 7.1d⁶ 7s p7.1g p6g Nov 13] tall gelding: only
fairly useful at best in 2004: effective at 7f/1m: acts on good to firm and good to soft
going, probably on heavy and polytrack: well held both starts in blinkers: none too consistent. *R. A. Fahey*

NANABANANA (IRE)   2 b.f. (Feb 8) Anabaa (USA) 130 – Tanabata (FR) (Shining **100**
Steel 123) [2004 6d⁴ 7v² 7d* 7s² 7s² 6s² 6s Nov 16] €95,000Y: rather leggy filly: third
foal: dam, French maiden (second at 7f and 9f), sister to smart French/US performer up
to 1¼m Gold And Steel: useful performer: won minor event at Clairefontaine in July:
second after in minor event at Deauville (beaten 1½ lengths by Helios Quercus), Prestige
Stakes at Goodwood (beaten ½ length by Dubai Surprise) and listed race at Newmarket

(edgy, beaten head by Bahia Breeze): last of 8 in listed race at Saint-Cloud final outing: stays 7f: raced only on going softer than good. *Mme C. Head-Maarek, France*

NAN JAN 2 b.f. (Apr 27) Komaite (USA) – Dam Certain (IRE) 61 (Damister (USA) 123) [2004 6m 6g 6.1m² p6g⁴ p7.1g⁴ p7m³ Dec 22] compact filly: fifth living foal: half-sister to 2 winners, including 5-y-o Red Storm: dam 7f to 9f winner: fair maiden: stays 7f: acts on polytrack and good to firm ground: tongue tied last 4 starts. *R. Ingram* **76**

NANNA (IRE) 3 b.f. Danetime (IRE) 121 – Pre Catelan 53 (Polar Falcon (USA) 126) [2004 43: f7g⁵ f6g² f6s f6s³ f5g f5g² 5.1m* 5.7f⁶ f5g² 5d* 5m* 5g⁶ 5d 5m³ p5.1d p5.1g⁶ f5m⁵ Nov 22] fair on turf, modest on all-weather: won maiden at Bath in May and handicaps at Redcar and Catterick in July: best efforts at 5f: acts on all-weather, good to firm and good to soft going: races up with pace. *R. Hollinshead* **74 a58**

NANTON (USA) 2 gr. or ro.c. (Mar 18) Spinning World (USA) 130 – Grab The Green (USA) (Cozzene (USA)) [2004 8g p8g⁶ p9.5g³ p8.6g³ p8.6g* p8g* Dec 18] $75,000Y: leggy, quite good-topped colt: fifth foal: closely related to a winner in Japan by Theatrical and half-brother to 2 winners in USA: dam US Grade 3 8.5f winner: fairly useful performer: won maiden at Wolverhampton and minor event at Lingfield (strong late burst to beat Reaching Out by length) in December: barely stays 9.5f: acts on polytrack. *P. F. I. Cole* **82 p**

NANTUCKET SOUND (USA) 3 b.g. Quiet American (USA) – Anna 97 (Ela-Mana-Mou 132) [2004 68: 8d 8.3s⁴ 10.2f* 10g 11.6g f8g² f11g* f12g* Dec 28] workmanlike gelding: fair performer: won handicap at Bath in May then claimer (claimed from M. Pipe £5,000) and handicap, both at Southwell in December: stays 1½m: acts on fibresand, firm and soft going: visored last 3 starts. *P. Howling* **79**

NAPAPIJRI (FR) 2 gr.f. (Apr 15) Highest Honor (FR) 124 – Les Marettes (FR) (Baillamont (USA) 124) [2004 7d⁵ 8.1s 8g⁴ Oct 10] €28,000 2-y-o: good-topped filly: has a quick action: fifth foal: half-sister to 2 winners in France, including 9f to 11.5f winner Legende d'Automne (by Valanour): dam French 1m to 11f winner: modest form in maidens: fourth at Bath: should be suited by 1¼m/1½m: ran no sort of race on soft going. *D. P. Keane* **58**

NARCISO (GER) 4 b.g. Acatenango (GER) 127 – Notturna (Diu Star) [2004 8.1d 7.5d f6g 6.9f 14.1f⁶ 10.4m 15.8m⁶ Sep 18] tall, leggy gelding: modest maiden: should stay 2m: acts on firm ground. *M. W. Easterby* **52**

NARRATIVE (IRE) 6 b.h. Sadler's Wells (USA) 132 – Barger (USA) (Riverman (USA) 131) [2004 109: 13.4d 8.2g⁴ 8m⁶ 10.4g Jul 10] strong, lengthy, good-bodied horse: trained by Saeed bin Suroor at 4/5 yrs, when sometimes used as pacemaker: just useful nowadays: creditable efforts in 2004 only in minor event at Nottingham (fourth to Shot To Fame) and handicap at Pontefract (sixth to Ace of Hearts): effective at 1m and stays 1¾m: yet to race on heavy going, acts on any other turf/dirt: tried tongue tied: races freely (pulled too hard in Ormonde Stakes at Chester on reappearance). *D. R. Loder* **105**

NASHAAB (USA) 7 b.g. Zafonic (USA) 130 – Tajannub (USA) 104 (Dixieland Band (USA)) [2004 100, a81: p10g p8g 6g 6g 7.6d² 8g³ 7.6m* 7s⁵ 7m 8m 9g 7.9g* 8d p8.6g³ p9.5g² Nov 27] small, quite attractive gelding: useful handicapper on turf, fairly useful on all-weather: first past post at Chester in August, York (beat Adaikali ¾ length) in October and Wolverhampton (demoted to second) in November: effective at 7f to 9.5f: acts on all-weather, firm and soft going: sometimes visored/blinkered, including last 5 starts: sometimes bandaged in front: often slowly away: held up: joined M. Al Kurdi in UAE. *P. D. Evans* **101 a89**

NASSAU STREET 4 gr.g. Bahamian Bounty 116 – Milva 56 (Jellaby 124) [2004 44: f9.4s³ f12g 10.2s 7m³ f8g Dec 1] poor maiden: stays 9.4f: acts on fibresand and good to firm going: tried visored. *D. J. S. ffrench Davis* **44**

NASSEEM DUBAI (USA) 2 ch.c. (Mar 10) Silver Hawk (USA) 123 – Fleur de Nuit (USA) (Woodman (USA) 126) [2004 5.9f 7s⁶ 7d² 8m⁵ 7.2d³ p6m 6d a6g² Dec 9] 35,000Y: strong, sturdy colt: fourth foal: brother to 4-y-o Dhabyan and 3-y-o Kibryaa: dam, US 6f (at 2 yrs) to 9f (Grade 3 event) winner, out of Poule d'Essai des Pouliches winner Pearl Bracelet: fair maiden: left Mrs A. Duffield before final outing: likely to prove best short of 1m: acts on polytrack/dirt and good to soft going: sometimes races freely. *R. Bouresly, Kuwait* **74**

NASSIRIA 3 b.f. Singspiel (IRE) 133 – Naskhi 102 (Nashwan (USA) 135) [2004 8m⁶ 10.4s⁶ 10m 12g 10.1m 10f³ p12g³ p10g² p9.5g² f11g* Nov 23] workmanlike filly: second foal: half-sister to 1m winner in Italy by Machiavellian: dam 1m (at 2 yrs) and 1¼m win- **83**

ner: fair handicapper: won at Southwell in November: stays 11f: acts on all-weather and firm going: tried in cheekpieces: effective ridden prominently or held up. *C. E. Brittain*

NATALIE JANE (IRE) 2 ch.f. (Mar 7) Giant's Causeway (USA) 132 – Kirk 79 **89** (Selkirk (USA) 129) [2004 8.2m 8g³ 10v* 10d³ a9f⁶ Nov 27] rather leggy filly: second foal: half-sister to winner in Greece by Fasliyev: dam, 1m winner, closely related to smart performer up to 1¼m Carmelite House: fairly useful performer: made all in maiden at Nottingham in October: good 7 lengths third to Ayam Zaman in listed race at Newmarket next time: well-held sixth in Grade 2 Demoiselle Stakes at Aqueduct final outing: will stay at least 1½m: acts on heavy going. *G. A. Butler*

NATALIYA 3 b.f. Green Desert (USA) 127 – Ninotchka (USA) 110 (Nijinsky (CAN) **104** 138) [2004 97: 7g³ 8m 8.1d 8m⁴ 6d 7m Sep 9] good-bodied filly: useful performer: sustained injury after final 2-y-o start: creditable efforts in 2004 in Dubai Duty Free Stakes (Fred Darling) at Newbury (2 lengths third to Majestic Desert), 1000 Guineas at Newmarket (4¼ lengths seventh to Attraction on second outing) and listed race at Ascot (2½ lengths fourth to Coy) in April and also in listed race at Doncaster (visored): stayed 1m: acted on good to firm going, well held both starts on good to soft. *J. L. Dunlop*

NATHAN BRITTLES (USA) 4 ch.g. Cat's Career (USA) – Doc's Answer (USA) **84** (Dr Schwartzman (USA)) [2004 77: 7g* Mar 31] rangy gelding: fairly useful performer: upped in trip, improved form to win handicap at Catterick (beat Sarraaf by ½ length) only 4-y-o outing: fractured a pedal bone after, but is said to have made a complete recovery: stays 7f: acts on firm ground: races prominently. *T. D. Barron*

NATHAN DETROIT 4 b.g. Entrepreneur 123 – Mainly Sunset (Red Sunset 120) **49** [2004 –: 6m 5.7m p8g⁴ Dec 20] poor maiden nowadays: stays 7f: acts on polytrack: tried blinkered/in cheekpieces: slowly away second outing, gelded prior to final one. *P. J. Makin*

NATIONAL CURRENCY (SAF) 5 b.h. National Assembly (CAN) – Enchanted **124** Dollar (USA) (Spend A Buck (USA)) [2004 123: a6f* Feb 5] very smart perfomer: one of South Africa's top sprinters: successful in 2003 in Grade 1 Computaform Sprint at Turffontein, minor event there, Grade 1 Mercury Sprint at Clairwood (by 5¼ lengths from Honour The Guest) and minor event at Durbanville: very good length second to Silent Witness in Hong Kong Sprint at Sha Tin final 4-y-o start: best effort when winning listed race at Nad Al Sheba in February by 6½ lengths from Persuasivo Fitz, showing plenty of speed to lead before gradually pulling clear: reportedly developed abscess in a foot later in month and was put down due to suspected laminitis in March: stayed 6f: acted on good to firm going and dirt: usually raced prominently. *M. Azzie, South Africa*

NATIONAL TRUST 2 b.c. (May 6) Sadler's Wells (USA) 132 – National Treasure **– p** 72 (Shirley Heights 130) [2004 7d Oct 30] good-bodied colt: fourth foal: dam, ran 3 times at 3 yrs, sister to smart performer up to 1¼m Free At Last and half-sister to very smart miler Barathea and Irish 1000 Guineas winner Gossamer (both by Sadler's Wells): 12/1, behind in maiden at Newmarket, very green and not knocked about: sure to do better. *Sir Michael Stoute*

NATIVE AMERICAN 2 b.c. (Jan 27) Indian Lodge (IRE) 127 – Summer Siren (FR) **–** (Saint Cyrien (FR) 128) [2004 p8g p8m Dec 21] 20/1, well held in maidens at Lingfield: slowly away on debut. *M. A. Jarvis*

NATIVE TITLE 6 b.g. Pivotal 124 – Bermuda Lily 78 (Dunbeath (USA) 127) [2004 **95** 88: 5.1d⁴ 6m 6m* 6f 6d 6g³ 6m 6d 5s Oct 23] big, close-coupled gelding: has had breathing operation: useful handicapper: best effort when winning at Epsom (beat Mutawaqed by 1½ lengths) in June: most effective at 5f/6f: acts on firm and soft going: blinkered once at 4 yrs: usually travels strongly. *D. Nicholls*

NATIVE TURK (USA) 3 b.c. Miswaki (USA) 124 – Churn Dat Butter (USA) (Un- **74** bridled (USA) 128) [2004 66p: 8m 7g f8g² 8.5m⁵ Sep 9] compact colt: fair maiden: stays 1m: acts on fibresand: blinkered (tailed off) second start: sent to USA. *J. A. R. Toller*

NATMSKY (IRE) 5 b.g. Shadeed (USA) 135 – Cockney Lass 117 (Camden Town 125) **–** [2004 –: 12m 12m 8m Sep 4] quite good-topped gelding: no longer of any account: tried in headgear. *G. A. Harker*

NAUGHTY GIRL (IRE) 4 b.f. Dr Devious (IRE) 127 – Mary Magdalene 78 (Night **54 §** Shift (USA)) [2004 79§: p7g f6g f8s 5.7s 6g 5m 5.7f 8m⁵ 8.3g⁴ 7.2g⁴ 8m 8.1m² 8m 8f* 8f 7g p7.1g⁵ p7m² Dec 15] smallish, sturdy filly: modest handicapper: won selling event at Bath in September: stays 1m: acts on polytrack, good to firm and good to soft going: usually wears headgear/tongue strap: unreliable. *P. D. Evans*

NAUTICAL 6 gr.g. Lion Cavern (USA) 117 – Russian Royal (USA) 108 (Nureyev **73** (USA) 131) [2004 –: 10.9d 10.2s p10g⁴ 10g⁶ 8g⁴ 8m³ 8m 8.3m² 6g 7.1g* p8.6g* p8g p7.1g² Oct 16] fair handicapper: won at Chepstow in September and Wolverhampton in October: effective at 7f to 1¼m: acts on dirt, polytrack and good to firm going: tried visored/blinkered: often tongue tied prior to 2004: often slowly away/races freely. *A. W. Carroll*

NAUTICAL STAR 9 b.g. Slip Anchor 136 – Comic Talent 105 (Pharly (FR) 130) **37** [2004 13.1g⁵ Apr 29] good-topped gelding: poor performer: stays 2m: acts on firm and soft going: tried visored: usually makes running. *A. C. Whillans*

NAVAL ATTACHE 2 b.g. (May 20) Slip Anchor 136 – Cayla (Tumble Wind) [2004 **–** 7.9g 8s Oct 27] well held in maidens at York and Yarmouth. *N. P. Littmoden*

NAVAL FORCE 2 b.g. (Mar 1) Forzando 122 – Barsham 94 (Be My Guest (USA) **70** 126) [2004 6f p7g⁴ 5.9f³ 6g 7s Oct 22] 11,500F, 22,000Y: brother to fairly useful 1998 2-y-o 5f winner Bemuse and half-brother to several winners, including useful 1996 2-y-o 6f and 1m winner Falkenham (by Polar Falcon), later winner around 9f in USA: dam 1¼m winner: fair maiden: well held in nurseries last 2 starts: acts on polytrack and firm going: tongue tied after debut: gelded after final start. *H. Morrison*

NAVIGATION (IRE) 2 ch.c. (Apr 20) Bahamian Bounty 116 – Bridge Pool 74 (First **59** Trump 118) [2004 6m 6m⁶ p5.1d p6g Nov 20] lengthy colt: modest maiden: should prove better at 6f than 5f: acts on polytrack and good to firm going. *T. J. Etherington*

NAWAAEM (USA) 2 b.f. (Mar 21) Swain (IRE) 134 – Alattrah (USA) (Shadeed **71 p** (USA) 135) [2004 7d⁵ Oct 30] compact filly: second foal: dam unraced sister to 1000 Guineas winner Shadayid: 8/1, 2 lengths fifth to Read Federica in maiden at Newmarket, second home stand side: should stay 1¼m: should progress. *B. W. Hills*

NAWAMEES (IRE) 6 b.g. Darshaan 133 – Truly Generous (IRE) 104 (Generous (IRE) **95** 139) [2004 83: p16g⁴ p12g² 11.6m² 14g 12m Sep 26] useful handicapper: runner-up at Lingfield and Windsor (best effort, beaten 1½ lengths by Vengeance): effective at 11.6f to easy 2m: acts on polytrack and good to firm going: wore cheekpieces last 3 starts: found little last 2 outings: useful hurdler. *G. L. Moore*

NAWOW 4 b.g. Blushing Flame (USA) 109 – Fair Test 95 (Fair Season 120) [2004 87: **81** p12g 16g³ 16g⁵ 13.9s⁶ 11g 12g² 14.1g 11.6d⁴ Oct 4] tall, good-topped gelding: fairly useful performer: barely stays 2m: acts on polytrack and good to firm ground. *P. D. Cundell*

NAYYIR 6 ch.g. Indian Ridge 123 – Pearl Kite (USA) 106§ (Silver Hawk (USA) **126** 123) [2004 126: 8.9m³ 6g 8g² 8s² 8m⁴ 7d⁶ Oct 9]

The two best geldings in training in Europe, Somnus and Nayyir, enjoyed contrasting fortunes in 2004. While Somnus won two Group 1s, the Prix Maurice de Gheest and the Prix de la Foret, Nayyir had a luckless season, recording at least four good-class efforts without tasting victory. Somnus won the Maurice de Gheest by a neck and the Foret by three quarters of a length. Nayyir went down by a neck in both the Dubai Duty Free (worth £434,783 to the winner) and the Sussex Stakes (£174,000). It was a very fine line between success and failure at Nad Al Sheba in March, when only a length or so covered the first six home in the Dubai Duty Free. Nayyir got his nose in front briefly inside the final furlong only for the dead-heaters Paolini and Right Approach to sweep by close home, Nayyir beaten into third. The Sussex was Nayyir's main target in the summer and, after shaping quite well until hampered and eased in the July Cup in his only outing in the interim, he started at 12/1 in a good renewal at Goodwood. Nayyir turned in a cracking performance, just failing to catch Soviet Song after being checked and switched to make his challenge. Nayyir was gaining all the way to the line and looked a little unfortunate. He wasn't much below his Sussex form when a hot favourite for the Celebration Mile on his return to Goodwood in August, when, again, he had to settle for second, beaten a length and a quarter by the very strong-finishing Chic, having quickened clear two furlongs out and looked all over the winner entering the final furlong. Third-placed Hurricane Alan was five lengths adrift. Nayyir's lot in the Queen Elizabeth II Stakes at Ascot in September was to finish a never-nearer fourth behind Rakti after losing ground by fly-jumping leaving his stall and then being forced to come wide, with a lot to do, off the home bend. A frustrating campaign ended when Nayyir managed only sixth of seven, having no apparent excuses, behind Somnus in the Foret.

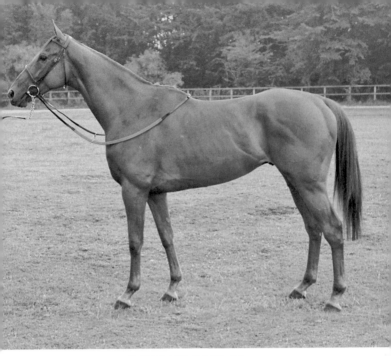

Mr Abdulla Al Khalifa's "Nayyir"

Nayyir (ch.g. 1998)	Indian Ridge (ch 1985)	Ahonoora (ch 1975)	Lorenzaccio Helen Nichols
		Hillbrow (ch 1975)	Swing Easy Golden City
	Pearl Kite (USA) (b 1991)	Silver Hawk (b 1979)	Roberto Gris Vitesse
		Spur Wing (ch 1984)	Storm Bird Equal Change

The strong, lengthy, angular Nayyir, who has a round action, did not see a racecourse until he was four, but he soon made up for lost time, winning the Diomed Stakes, the Lennox Stakes and the Challenge Stakes at that age. He won the Lennox at Goodwood for the second time as a five-year-old when he made a belated comeback after being struck down by a severe form of colitis at the end of his four-year-old campaign while in Hong Kong. Nayyir takes much more after his sire Indian Ridge than his dam Pearl Kite. Indian Ridge won the Jersey Stakes at three and the Duke of York and the King's Stand at four, and the majority of his offspring prove best at up to a mile. Nayyir's dam the Ribblesdale third Pearl Kite showed useful form at up to a mile and three quarters and her two best offspring apart from Nayyir, the ill-fated Highest (by Selkirk) and the smart filly Shamaiel (by Lycius), both stayed that trip, Highest finishing second in the St Leger. Details of the extended family can be found in earlier *Racehorses* essays on Highest and Nayyir. Nayyir has shown his form at six and a half furlongs to an easy nine furlongs and he is also fairly versatile as regards going requirements, acting on polytrack, soft and good to firm going (withdrawn twice as a five-year-old because of very firm). Nayyir, who has worn a crossed noseband and been attended by two handlers, can sometimes race too freely early on, pulling hard, and is best covered up, a racing style that means his fortunes can be influenced more than most by luck in running. *G. A. Butler*

NAZAAHA (USA) 2 gr.f. (Feb 5) Elnadim (USA) 128 – Taatof (IRE) (Lahib (USA) 129) [2004 6f⁴ Aug 1] first foal: dam unraced out of Princess Royal Stakes winner Labibeh: 11/1, fourth to Swan Nebula in maiden at Newbury, slowly away and not knocked about: should improve. *J. L. Dunlop* **71 p**

NAZZWAH 3 ch.f. Rahy (USA) 115 – Baaderah (IRE) 102 (Cadeaux Genereux 131) [2004 7m⁶ 9g⁶ 8g Jul 4] lengthy filly: fourth foal: closely related to fairly useful 1m winner Badr Rainbow (by Rainbow Quest): dam 6f (including at 2 yrs) winner who stayed 1m: best effort in maidens on debut: sold 4,500 gns, sent to Italy. *M. R. Channon* **57**

NDOLA 5 b.g. Emperor Jones (USA) 119 – Lykoa (Shirley Heights 130) [2004 f9.4g* f11g p10g p10g³ Apr 6] rather leggy, quite good-topped gelding: modest performer: off 14 months, won banded race at Wolverhampton in January: stays easy 1¼m: acts on all-weather and heavy ground. *B. J. Curley* **52**

NEAP TIDE 3 br.g. Zafonic (USA) 130 – Love The Rain (Rainbow Quest (USA) 134) [2004 75: 10.2g 7m Jun 9] good-bodied, attractive gelding: fair maiden at 2 yrs: weakened tamely both starts in 2004: sold 11,000 gns. *J. H. M. Gosden* **–**

NEARLY A FOOL 6 b.g. Komaite (USA) – Greenway Lady (Prince Daniel (USA)) [2004 74, a60: p7g* p6g* p7g p7g² f7g* p7g 7d* 8.2g³ 8.2g⁴ p7d 7g⁵ 7.5m 8g⁵ p7g* p7g² f8g f8g p7m Dec 21] close-coupled gelding: fair performer: won 2 handicaps at Lingfield in January, minor event at Southwell in March, handicap at Southwell in April and minor event at Lingfield in October: left G. Margarson after fifteenth start: effective at 7f/1m: acts on all-weather and any turf going: tried blinkered, visored nowadays: tough. *P. Howling* **76**

NEATH 3 b.f. Rainbow Quest (USA) 134 – Welsh Autumn 107 (Tenby 125) [2004 10g⁵ 10g³ 10.2s Oct 19] lengthy filly: second foal: sister to useful 1m (at 2 yrs)/9f winner Rainwashed Gold: dam, French 1m winner (including at 2 yrs), half-sister to Tillerman: best effort in maidens when third to Maraakeb at Sandown: raced only at 1¼m: slowly away on debut: stud. *Mrs A. J. Perrett* **72**

NEBRASKA CITY 3 b.g. Piccolo 121 – Scarlet Veil 75 (Tyrnavos 129) [2004 65: p6g 5.7f⁶ 8.3f 6m⁴ 7m⁶ 6m 6d Aug 12] compact gelding: modest maiden: trained by P. Mitchell third to sixth starts, then returned to former trainer: seems to stay 7f: acts on good to firm ground: tried in cheekpieces/visor/tongue tie. *B. Gubby* **54**

NEBRASKA TORNADO (USA) 4 br.f. Storm Cat (USA) – Media Nox 98 (Lycius (USA) 124) [2004 123: 9.3g⁵ 8f⁴ 8g³ 8g³ a9f Oct 30] tall, leggy filly: smart performer: won 4 of 5 starts in 2003, notably Prix de Diane at Chantilly and Prix du Moulin de Longchamp: creditable efforts in 2004 only when 2 lengths fourth to Refuse To Bend in Queen Anne Stakes at Royal Ascot and 1¾ lengths third of 5 to Attraction in Sun Chariot Stakes at Newmarket on second/fourth starts: favourite when third to Marbye in Prix d'Astarte at Deauville in between: effective at 1m to 10.5f: acted on firm going, winner on soft (well held only start on dirt in Breeders' Cup Distaff at Lone Star Park): proved stubborn at stalls on several occasions and sometimes ridden in paddock: raced prominently: stud. *A. Fabre, France* **119**

NECKAR VALLEY (IRE) 5 b.g. Desert King (IRE) 129 – Solar Attraction (IRE) 60 (Salt Dome (USA)) [2004 85: 10d Sep 17] lengthy, quite good-topped gelding: fairly useful handicapper at 4 yrs, well held only start in 2004. *R. A. Fahey* **–**

NECKLACE 3 b.f. Darshaan 133 – Spinning The Yarn 70 (Barathea (IRE) 127) [2004 105p: 8m 8m⁶ 12m⁴ 9.5f³ 9g⁴ Sep 12] rather leggy, close-coupled filly: smart performer: won Moyglare Stud Stakes at the Curragh at 2 yrs: ran well last 2 starts in 2004, ¾-length third to Crimson Palace in Beverly D Stakes at Arlington and 2¼ lengths fourth to Lucifer's Stone in Garden City Breeders' Cup Handicap at Belmont: had earlier finished sixth in Irish 1000 Guineas at the Curragh and fourth to Ouija Board in Oaks at Epsom (beaten 12 lengths): best efforts around 9f: acts on firm going. *A. P. O'Brien, Ireland* **115**

NEEDLES AND PINS (IRE) 3 b.f. Fasliyev (USA) 120 – Fairy Contessa (IRE) 63 (Fairy King (USA)) [2004 104: 6g⁴ 6.1d 6d⁵ 5m 5s Aug 18] smallish filly: fairly useful performer: best effort in 2004 when seventh of 10 to Airwave in listed race at Ayr penultimate start: will prove best at 5f/easy 6f: acts on good to firm and good to soft going. *M. L. W. Bell* **90**

NEEDWOOD BUCOLIC (IRE)   6 br.g. Charnwood Forest (IRE) 125 – Greek Icon   –
87 (Thatching 131) [2004 5g 7.1m 5m f6g 6g 7.2g 7.2g Aug 7] won 5f event in Greece at
4 yrs: well held in Britain in 2004: tried blinkered. *R. Allan*

NEEDWOOD MYSTIC   9 b.m. Rolfe (USA) 77 – Enchanting Kate (Enchantment   **68**
115) [2004 75, a–: 11.9f² Jun 10] smallish, workmanlike mare: fair performer: effective   **a–**
at 1½m to 16.5f: acts on polytrack, firm and soft going: tried tongue tied. *Mrs A. J. Perrett*

NEEDWOOD SPIRIT   9 b.g. Rolfe (USA) 77 – Needwood Nymph 45 (Bold Owl   –
101) [2004 40: 11.9g 15.8m Sep 18] smallish gelding: poor handicapper: well held in
2004: visored once. *Mrs A. M. Naughton*

NEE LEMON LEFT   2 b.f. (Apr 21) Puissance 110 – Via Dolorosa (Chaddleworth   **60 d**
(IRE) 103) [2004 5g² 5g⁶ 5m³ 5m 5g⁶ 5d⁴ 5g Aug 26] second foal: dam last on only start:
modest maiden: form on first and third outings only: likely to prove best at 5f/6f: wore
cheekpieces fifth start, blinkers final one: probably ungenuine. *A. Berry*

NEFERURA   2 b.f. (Mar 24) Mister Baileys 123 – Boadicea's Chariot (Commanche   **49**
Run 133) [2004 6g 7m 8s Oct 27] useful-looking filly: sixth foal: half-sister to useful
1999 2-y-o 7f winner Agrippina (by Timeless Times): dam Irish 1½m winner/winning
hurdler: poor form in maidens: best effort at 7f. *W. J. Haggas*

NEGAS (IRE)   2 b.g. (Apr 29) Titus Livius (FR) 115 – Alzeam (IRE) 61 (Alzao (USA)   –
117) [2004 5m 5f 7g 6s Aug 14] sturdy gelding: well held in maidens. *J. Howard Johnson*

NEGWA (IRE)   3 b.f. Bering 136 – Ballet 61 (Sharrood (USA) 124) [2004 76: 10.3g⁵   –
10m 8d Aug 13] tall, leggy, close-coupled filly: has a quick action: no form in 2004:
refused to enter stall once at 2 yrs: sold 5,200 gns. *M. R. Channon*

NEIL'S LEGACY (IRE)   2 br.f. (May 3) Second Empire (IRE) 124 – Eliade (IRE)   **62**
82 (Flash of Steel 120) [2004 f7g⁶ p8.6g⁴ Dec 17] fifth foal: half-sister to 6-y-o Blushing
Prince and Italian 11f winner by Victory Note: dam, French 9f winner, half-sister to smart
sprinter Don't Worry Me: modest form in maidens at Southwell and Wolverhampton
(fourth to Pocketwood). *Miss L. A. Perratt*

NELLA FANTASIA (IRE)   2 ch.f. (Mar 5) Giant's Causeway (USA) 132 – Paper   **65**
Moon (IRE) 92 (Lake Coniston (IRE) 131) [2004 5.1g⁶ 6g⁶ Jun 24] 78,000F, €55,000Y:
neat filly: first foal: dam, Irish 1m winner, half-sister to Prix Marcel Boussac winner
Mary Linoa: better effort in maidens at Leicester final start: will stay 1m: sent to South
Africa. *G. C. Bravery*

NELLIE GWYN   2 b.f. (May 10) King's Best (USA) 132 – On Tiptoes 107 (Shareef   –
Dancer (USA) 135) [2004 6s Nov 6] half-sister to several winners, including useful 6f
(including at 2 yrs)/7f winner Caballero and fairly useful 7f winner Cadeaux des Mages
(both by Cadeaux Genereux): dam 5f (including Queen Mary Stakes) winner: 12/1, edgy
and green, well held in maiden at Doncaster, slowly away. *J. G. Given*

NELSON'S LUCK   3 b.g. Young Ern 120 – A Little Hot (Petong 126) [2004 7m Sep   –
7] last of 15 in maiden at Lingfield, soon well outpaced. *E. A. Wheeler*

NEMO FUGAT (IRE)   5 b.g. Danehill Dancer (IRE) 117 – Do The Right Thing 71   **68**
(Busted 134) [2004 79: 6s 6m 8g⁵ 8.3m⁶ 9.1d 6m² 6m⁵ 6.9m² 7s 7s 7.9m³ 8g Sep 13] big,
strong, lengthy gelding: fair performer nowadays: effective at 6f to 1m: acts on firm and
good to soft ground: tried blinkered, visored last 7 starts. *D. Nicholls*

NEON BLUE   3 b. or br.g. Atraf 116 – Desert Lynx (IRE) 79 (Green Desert (USA)   **75**
127) [2004 71: 6d⁵ 6m* 7.5m 6m³ 6g³ 6s³ 7f* 7g⁶ 7f 8d 7d Oct 15] smallish, compact
gelding: fair performer: won maiden at Doncaster in May and handicap at York in July:
effective at 6f/easy 7f: acts on firm and soft going. *R. M. Whitaker*

NE OUBLIE   2 b.c. (Apr 14) Makbul 104 – Parkside Prospect 65 (Piccolo 121) [2004   **67**
5d⁶ 5m⁴ 5d³ 5g Aug 26] sturdy colt: first foal: dam 2-y-o 5f/6f winner: fair maiden: likely
to prove best at 5f: acts on good to firm and good to soft going. *J. Mackie*

NEPAL (IRE)   2 ch.f. (Feb 12) Monashee Mountain (USA) 115 – Zetonic 79 (Zafonic   **65**
(USA) 130) [2004 6f⁶ 7m² 7m⁴ Oct 10] €10,500Y: tall filly: first foal: dam 11f/1½m
winner in France/Ireland: easily best effort in maidens when second at Newcastle: needs
to settle to stay 1m. *T. D. Barron*

NEPHETRITI WAY (IRE)   3 b.f. Docksider (USA) 124 – Velvet Appeal (IRE) 101   **77**
(Petorius 117) [2004 92: 8s 7g⁵ 7.1m⁵ 8m⁵ Jul 13] rather leggy, quite good-topped filly:
just fair form in 2004: should stay 1m: acts on good to firm going. *P. R. Chamings*

NEPTUNE   8 b.g. Dolphin Street (FR) 125 – Seal Indigo (IRE) 93 (Glenstal (USA) 118)   **44**
[2004 p16g⁵ p12g p12g p12g² p12g⁴ 12v⁵ p12g³ p12d⁵ 11.7g³ p12m⁶ p13.9g Dec 22]   **a51**

leggy gelding: modest on all-weather, poor on turf: stays 2m: acts on all-weather, firm and good to soft going: has given trouble at stall/looked difficult ride. *J. C. Fox*

NEQAAWI 3 br.f. Alhaarth (IRE) 126 – Jinsiyah (USA) 98 (Housebuster (USA)) [2004 60: 7.5m⁵ 6.9f* 6.9g a8.3g⁴ a6g a8.3g a10.5g⁴ a6g⁶ a10.5g* a9g⁵ Dec 12] fair handicapper: won at Carlisle in June and, after being sold from B. Hanbury 8,500 gns after next start, Mijas in November: stays 10.5f: acts on sand, raced only on good ground or firmer on turf: has had tongue tied: has raced freely/carried head awkwardly. *J. Bidgood, Spain* — **72**

NERO'S RETURN (IRE) 3 b.g. Mujadil (USA) 119 – Snappy Dresser (Nishapour (FR) 125) [2004 104p: 8d⁶ 7g 6m⁶ 6m 10d 6m⁵ 6g Aug 7] rather leggy gelding: useful performer: respectable efforts in 2004 only in Greenham Stakes at Newbury (eighth to Salford City) second start and handicap at Sandown fifth one: gelded after final outing: barely stays 1¼m: acts on firm and good to soft ground: blinkered penultimate appearance: none too reliable. *M. Johnston* — **96**

NESNAAS (USA) 3 ch.g. Gulch (USA) – Sedrah (USA) 82 (Dixieland Band (USA)) [2004 68: 7m 7g Jun 22] big, workmanlike gelding: fair maiden at 2 yrs: well held in 2004: sold 10,000 gns, joined M. Rimell. *B. Hanbury* — **–**

NESSEN DORMA (IRE) 3 b.g. Entrepreneur 123 – Goldilocks (IRE) (Caerleon (USA) 132) [2004 76: p10g⁴ p10g⁵ 12.3g⁵ 11.8d² 14.6g* 11.9d³ 14d³ 16.2m 16.2g 13.1s Sep 18] lengthy gelding: fairly useful handicapper: won at Doncaster in May: should stay 2m: acts on all-weather and good to soft going: visored (ran respectably) eighth start. *J. G. Given* — **85**

NEUTRAL NIGHT (IRE) 4 b.f. Night Shift (USA) – Neutrality (IRE) (Common Grounds 118) [2004 54, a46: f6g³ p8g f6s f7g⁵ f7s³ f7s² f8.5g⁴ f6s³ f7g³ f7g* f6g² f7m² f7d f7g p7m Dec 15] modest performer: won banded race at Wolverhampton in May: effective at 6f/7f: acts on all-weather, raced only on good ground or firmer on turf: wears blinkers/visor: tried tongue tied. *R. Brotherton* — **50**

NEUTRINO 2 b.c. (Apr 28) Mtoto 134 – Fair Seas 72 (General Assembly (USA)) [2004 7g 7s⁴ p7.1d⁴ Nov 3] 18,000Y: rather leggy colt: sixth foal: half-brother to 11f winner Blue Anchor (by Robellino): dam, maiden on Flat (best at 1¼m), winning hurdler: fair form in maidens, not knocked about each time: will be well suited by 1¼m/1½m: should do better. *L. M. Cumani* — **75 p**

NEVADA DESERT (IRE) 4 b.g. Desert King (IRE) 129 – Kayanga (Green Desert (USA) 127) [2004 78: 10g⁴ 8m⁵ 10d² 11.9f 8.3d* 8d 10d 8.3d 7s⁶ p7.1g⁵ f8g³ f8g⁴ p10g² Dec 18] useful-looking gelding: fair handicapper: won at Hamilton in August: effective at 1m to 11f: acts on all-weather, good to firm and good to soft ground: effective with or without cheekpieces: usually races up with pace: has carried head high. *R. M. Whitaker* — **79**

NEVER AWAY 2 b.f. (May 17) Royal Applause 124 – Waypoint 95 (Cadeaux Genereux 131) [2004 6g 6g 7g 6g 7g 5g 14] useful-looking filly: fourth foal: half-sister to useful 2002 2-y-o 5f/5.5f (Prix Robert Papin) winner Never A Doubt (by Night Shift) and 3-y-o Primo Way: dam, 6f/7f winner, half-sister to smart sprinter Acclamation: modest maiden: probably stays 7f: signs of temperament. *N. A. Callaghan* — **51**

NEVER CRIED WOLF 3 b.g. Wolfhound (USA) 126 – Bold Difference 66 (Bold Owl 101) [2004 p8g⁶ p8g p7g p8g⁶ p8g Mar 14] poor maiden: tried in cheekpieces: sometimes slowly away. *D. R. C. Elsworth* — **48 ?**

NEVER FORGET BOWIE 8 b.g. Superpower 113 – Heldigvis 63 (Hot Grove 128) [2004 9.2d 6d 7.2s⁵ f7g p9.5g* Dec 22] big gelding: modest performer: missed 2003: form in 2004 only when winning banded race at Wolverhampton in December: stays 9.5f: acts on polytrack. *R. Allan* — **52**

NEVERLETME GO (IRE) 2 b.f. (Mar 13) Green Desert (USA) 127 – Cassandra Go (IRE) 119 (Indian Ridge 123) [2004 5.1g⁴ 6g⁵ Sep 3] strong filly: first foal: dam, 5f (including Temple Stakes/King's Stand) to 7f winner, half-sister to Irish 2000 Guineas second Verglas: fair form in maidens at Nottingham and Kempton (went well long way): likely to prove best at 5f/easy 6f. *G. Wragg* — **75**

NEVER PROMISE (FR) 6 b.m. Cadeaux Genereux 131 – Yazeanhaa (USA) 68 (Zilzal (USA) 137) [2004 40: 9.3m⁶ 8s Oct 30] smallish mare: poor performer: stays 1¼m: acts on firm going: visored/blinkered. *C. Roberts* — **35**

NEVER WILL 3 b.c. Cadeaux Genereux 131 – Answered Prayer (Green Desert (USA) 127) [2004 –p: 7.1g² 8m² 9.2d* 9g 8m Jun 17] strong, lengthy colt: fairly useful performer: won maiden at Hamilton in May: well held in handicaps at Goodwood and — **85**

Royal Ascot after: stays 9f: acts on good to firm and good to soft ground: sold 5,000 gns. *M. Johnston*

NEVER WITHOUT ME   4 ch.g. Mark of Esteem (IRE) 137 – Festival Sister (Belmez (USA) 131) [2004 56: f6s⁶ f6s⁴ f5s⁵ f5g² f5g* 5g f6d³ 6.1v⁴ f6d* f6g* 6m² 6m⁴ 5g² 5.2d² 5g⁶ 6g Sep 25] tall gelding: fair performer: left P. McBride after fourth start: won handicap at Southwell in April and minor event and handicap at same course in June: effective at 5f/6f: acts on fibresand, good to firm and good to soft going: effective visored or not: sometimes slowly away. *J. F. Coupland*   **76**

NEVINSTOWN (IRE)   4 b.g. Lahib (USA) 129 – Moon Tango (IRE) 81 (Last Tycoon 131) [2004 –: p8g Feb 16] lightly-raced maiden: poor form at Lingfield only outing in 2004: tried visored/blinkered/tongue tied. *Niall Moran, Ireland*   **38**

NEWCLOSE   4 b.g. Barathea (IRE) 127 – Wedgewood (USA) (Woodman (USA) 126) [2004 46: f8.5g³ f7g³ f11g³ f12s⁴ 8.1g Apr 23] well-made gelding: poor maiden: stays easy 11f: acts on fibresand and good to firm going: tongue tied. *N. Tinkler*   **43**

NEWCORP LAD   4 b.g. Komaite (USA) – Gleam of Gold (Crested Lark 78) [2004 78: 8s 10.1v⁴ 8m 10.3g 9.2d 9.2g⁴ 8g⁴ 8.2g² 8.1g⁴ 7.9g 8g³ 8m* 8m⁴ 8m Oct 10] strong gelding: fair handicapper: made all at Newcastle in September: best around 1m: acts on any going: visored tenth start, wore cheekpieces last 3: often races up with pace. *Mrs G. S. Rees*   **76**

NEWCORR (IRE)   5 b.g. Magical Wonder (USA) 125 – Avionne 59 (Derrylin 115) [2004 –: p8g p12g p8g⁶ p8g³ 8g² p7g⁴ 7f 10.2s Aug 12] fair performer at best in Ireland for M. Hourigan: poor form in Britain: stays 9f: acts on heavy ground and polytrack: tried blinkered/in cheekpieces. *J. J. Bridger*   **35**

NEW DAY DAWNING   3 ch.f. First Trump 118 – Tintinara (Selkirk (USA) 129) [2004 61?: 6.1s 5m 5d 6m f8g f6g Dec 7] close-coupled filly: little form at 3 yrs: tried blinkered. *C. Smith*   **–**

NEW MEXICAN   3 ch.g. Dr Fong (USA) 128 – Apache Star 96 (Arazi (USA) 135) [2004 99: 8g⁴ 9g⁵ 7m⁶ Nov 28] tall, close-coupled gelding: useful performer: found less than seemed likely but creditable efforts in minor event at Doncaster (wore cheekpieces) and listed race at Newmarket (2¾ lengths fifth to Gold History) first 2 starts, then left Mrs J. Ramsden: off over 7 months, renamed Golden Sun, below form final outing: barely stays 9f: acts on good to firm and good to soft going: carries head high, and temperament under suspicion. *C. H. Yip, Hong Kong*   **96**

NEW MORNING (IRE)   3 b.f. Sadler's Wells (USA) 132 – Hellenic 125 (Darshaan 133) [2004 73p: 11.5g² 11.8m* 12m⁴ 11.9g⁵ 9.9g* 10g⁶ Sep 19] good-bodied filly: useful performer: won maiden at Leicester in May and listed event at Salisbury (by 1¾ lengths from Tahtheeb) in August: creditable fourth to Punctilious in Ribblesdale Stakes at Royal Ascot and fifth to Pongee in Lancashire Oaks at Haydock in between: below form when sixth to Monturani in Blandford Stakes at the Curragh (at 1¼m/1½m): acts on good to firm going: races up with pace (took strong hold first and third outings). *M. A. Jarvis*   **109**

NEWNHAM (IRE)   3 ch.g. Theatrical 128 – Brief Escapade (IRE) 95 (Brief Truce (USA) 126) [2004 8.3g² 10g² 12.1m² 12d³ Oct 17] second foal: dam, 1m winner, half-sister to high-class 7f to 9f performer Indian Lodge and very smart French middle-distance performer Sarhoob: fair maiden: runner-up at Windsor and Chepstow: found little final start: stays 1½m: acts on good to firm going. *L. M. Cumani*   **70**

NEW OPTIONS   7 b.g. Formidable (USA) 125 – No Comebacks 70 (Last Tycoon 131) [2004 –, a74: f6s⁵ f6g⁴ f6g f6s⁵ p6g p6g³ 6v p7g³ 6s 10d f7g f6g⁵ Jun 25] strong gelding: fair performer: below form after reappearance: stays easy 7f: acts on all-weather, dirt and good to firm going: often wears blinkers/cheekpieces: tends to carry head high/finish weakly: sold 3,000 gns. *W. J. Musson*   **– a67 d**

NEW ORDER   3 b.f. Singspiel (IRE) 133 – Eternal (Kris 135) [2004 7s³ 8.1g* 7s* 8f⁶ 10.3s Oct 22] rather leggy filly: seventh foal: half-sister to 5f winner Furnish and 1¼m to 1½m winner Wadi (both by Green Desert) and 2000 2-y-o 7f winner Never End (by Alzao): dam once-raced half-sister to Derby winner Quest For Fame: fairly useful performer: won maiden at Haydock in July and handicap at Goodwood (by 1¾ lengths from Sabrina Brown, carrying head awkwardly) in August: reportedly finished lame final start: stayed 1m: acted on firm and soft going: stud. *B. W. Hills*   **84**

NEW PROSPECTIVE   6 b.g. Cadeaux Genereux 131 – Amazing Bay 100 (Mazilier (USA) 107) [2004 47: f7g Jan 8] poor performer: well beaten only 6-y-o outing: tried tongue tied/in cheekpieces: free-going sort. *D. Nicholls*   **–**

NEW REALM (USA) 2 b.c. (Mar 7) Red Ransom (USA) – Mystery Rays (USA) 122 **– p**
(Nijinsky (CAN) 138) [2004 7d Oct 30] $32,000Y: tall colt: has scope: half-brother to
several winners, notably smart 7f (at 2 yrs)/1m winner King of Happiness (by Spinning
World) and 4-y-o Anani: dam French 1m (at 2 yrs) to 1½m (Prix Minerve) winner: 33/1
and backward, always rear in maiden at Newmarket: likely to do better. *E. F. Vaughan*

NEW SEEKER 4 b.g. Green Desert (USA) 127 – Ahbab (IRE) 81 (Ajdal (USA) 130) **106**
[2004 111p: 8s² 7m⁴ 8g 7m⁶ 6m Aug 21] tall, good sort: impresses in appearance: useful
performer: at least respectable efforts first 3 starts in 2004, including when 4 lengths
second to Putra Pekan in listed race at Ascot and fourth of 28 to Unscrupulous in handicap
at Royal Ascot (well-backed favourite, first home on stand side): gelded after final
outing: better form at 7f than 1m, and should prove effective at 6f: acts on good to firm
and good to soft ground: blinkered (below form) fourth start: has been taken last/steadily
to post: races prominently. *C. G. Cox*

NEW SOUTH WALES 4 b.c. In The Wings 128 – Temora (IRE) 90 (Ela-Mana-Mou **112**
132) [2004 107: 16.4f³ 20m Jun 17] good-topped, attractive colt: smart performer: good
3 lengths third to Papineau in Henry II Stakes at Sandown: soundly beaten behind same
horse in Gold Cup at Royal Ascot only other 4-y-o start: stays 2m: acts on firm and good
to soft going: usually tongue tied. *Saeed bin Suroor*

NEWSROUND 2 ch.c. (Feb 24) Cadeaux Genereux 131 – Ring The Relatives 75 **95**
(Bering 136) [2004 6g² 6g* 6g Oct 9] 220,000Y: well-made colt: first foal: dam, second
at 1¼m (ran twice), out of smart half-sister to very smart 1¼m performer One So Wonderful: second to Echelon in maiden at Newmarket: odds on, made all in similar event at
Newbury in September, beating Oranmore Castle 2½ lengths: easy to back, only seventh
in listed race at York, hanging left: will stay 7f, probably 1m. *M. A. Jarvis*

NEWS SKY (USA) 3 b.c. Gone West (USA) – Dubian 120 (High Line 125) [2004 8g **82**
8.1g² 10f² 10g³ 10.1g³ 10.2g Oct 10] close-coupled, rather leggy colt: brother to smart 7f
(at 2 yrs)/1m winner Race Leader, closely related to winner in UAE by Gulch and half-
brother to several winners, notably 1000 Guineas winner Sayyedati (by Shadeed) and
high-class 1m (at 2 yrs) to 1½m winner Golden Snake (by Danzig): dam 7f (at 2 yrs) to
1½m winner: fairly useful maiden: best effort at Windsor third start: stays 1¼m: acts on
firm going: tried in cheekpieces: sold 22,000 gns, sent to Bahrain. *B. W. Hills*

NEWTONIAN (USA) 5 ch.g. Distant View (USA) 126 – Polly Adler (USA) (House- **–**
buster (USA)) [2004 77: f12g³ p12g 12v⁴ f11g² Dec 14] well-made gelding: fair perfor- **a74**
mer: stays 1½m: acts on fibresand, well held on turf and polytrack: tends to wander.
J. Parkes

NEWTON (IRE) 3 b.c. Danehill (USA) 126 – Elite Guest (IRE) (Be My Guest (USA) **101 §**
126) [2004 101: 7s* 7m⁴ 8g⁶ 8m⁶ 8f 6d 7.5v Oct 3] good-bodied, attractive colt: useful
performer: won listed race at the Curragh (by ½ length from Dabiroun) in April: sixth in
Poule d'Essai des Poulains at Longchamp (acted as pacemaker and flattered when beaten
only 3¼ lengths by American Post) and Irish 2000 Guineas at the Curragh (7½ lengths
behind Bachelor Duke): well held last 3 starts, reluctant to race and tailed off in St James's
Palace Stakes at Royal Ascot on first of them: stays 1m: acts on soft and good to firm
ground: sometimes blinkered/visored: temperamental: sent to Australia. *A. P. O'Brien,
Ireland*

NEWTOWN CHIEF 3 b.g. So Factual (USA) 120 – Polish Descent (IRE) (Danehill **–**
(USA) 126) [2004 –: 7m 12m p10g 8m Aug 4] trained by M. Halford in Ireland at 2 yrs:
little sign of ability: tried in cheekpieces/blinkered. *N. P. Littmoden*

NEW WISH (IRE) 4 b.g. Ali-Royal (IRE) 127 – False Spring (IRE) (Petorius 117) **61**
[2004 93d: 8.2g⁵ 7m 7m 8m Oct 10] rather leggy, quite good-topped gelding: only modest
form in 2004: should stay 1¼m: acts on good to firm going: sometimes slowly away/races
freely. *M. W. Easterby*

NEW YORK CITY (IRE) 3 b.c. Alzao (USA) 117 – Eurolinka (IRE) (Tirol 127) **–**
[2004 10g Aug 18] well beaten in maiden at Nottingham, slowly away: sold 3,200 gns.
L. M. Cumani

NEW YORK (IRE) 3 b.f. Danzero (AUS) – Council Rock 74 (General Assembly **56**
(USA)) [2004 72: 7g 7m 7g³ 8m⁵ 6d Oct 15] leggy, attractive filly: modest maiden:
stays 1m: acts on good to firm ground: tongue tied 3 starts prior to blinkered final one.
W. J. Haggas

NEXT FLIGHT (IRE) 5 b.g. Woodborough (USA) 112 – Sans Ceriph (IRE) 75 **56**
(Thatching 131) [2004 50: f11g⁶ f14g² f11g³ f14s² 12g³ 14.4v* 12.4s⁵ 14.1m³ f14g²
16.1v³ 16m⁴ f14m⁶ 13.8m Aug 3] good-bodied gelding: modest handicapper: won at
Newcastle in April: stays 14.5f: acts on all-weather, heavy and good to firm going: tried
visored: usually races prominently. *R. E. Barr*

NEXT TIME AROUND (IRE)   2 b. or br.c. (Mar 31) Namid 128 – In Due Course   **92**
(USA) (A P Indy (USA) 131) [2004 5g* 5d³ 5f⁵ 5f 5d⁴ 6g Oct 9] good-topped colt:
unimpressive mover: second foal: dam unraced half-sister to smart French performer up
to 1½m Dark Nile out of half-sister to very smart 1¼m performer Kefaah: fairly useful
performer: won minor event at Doncaster in March: good fourth to Prince Charming in
listed race at Ayr: should stay 6f: acts on firm and good to soft ground: sometimes looks
ungenuine. *Mrs L. Stubbs*

NEXT TIME (IRE)   2 b.f. (Apr 23) Danetime (IRE) 121 – Muckross Park 41 (Nomina-   **54 d**
tion 125) [2004 5g⁴ 5g⁵ 5d 6m 5m⁴ 5f⁴ 5.1g 5g p5.1g f5f Dec 28] 20,000Y: small,
useful-looking filly: sixth foal: sister to 4-y-o No Time and half-sister to winners abroad
by Petardia and Mac's Imp: dam sprint maiden: modest maiden: well below form last 6
outings: should prove best at 5f: acts on good to firm ground: often races prominently.
M. J. Polglase

NIAGARA (IRE)   7 b.g. Rainbows For Life (CAN) – Highbrook (USA) 88 (Alphaba-   **64**
tim (USA) 126) [2004 69, a64: 12v 10.1m⁶ 10g Jul 16] stocky gelding: modest handicapper: stays 1½m: acts on polytrack and any turf going: usually races prominently.
M. H. Tompkins

NIBBLES (IRE)   2 b.g. (Mar 26) Soviet Star (USA) 128 – Tumbleweed Pearl 96 (Ara-   **–**
gon 118) [2004 f6s Aug 23] well held in claimer at Southwell, rearing start. *R. P. Elliott*

NICE TUNE   2 b.f. (Apr 18) Diktat 126 – Military Tune (IRE) (Nashwan (USA) 135)   **89**
[2004 7g³ 8m⁴ 7g 7v⁵ Oct 23] 23,000Y: big, good-topped filly: sixth foal: half-sister to
4-y-o Play That Tune and useful French 11f winner Filly Bergere (by Sadler's Wells):
dam unraced half-sister to Prix Saint-Alary winner Muncie and Prix Royal-Oak winner
Mersey: fairly useful maiden: best effort when fourth in listed race at Goodwood: stays
1m: acts on good to firm going. *C. E. Brittain*

NICHOLAS NICKELBY   4 gr.g. Fayruz 116 – Alasib 93 (Siberian Express (USA)   **67**
125) [2004 67: 7.1v 7m⁶ 8m² 11.9m 8d f7g⁴ 6.1d³ 6g⁴ 5d⁴ 6.9m² 6g⁵ 8g f6g* f6g⁴ f7g Dec
14] strong, lengthy gelding: fair performer: won handicap at Southwell in November:
effective at 6f to 1m: acts on fibresand, good to firm and good to soft going: often wears
cheekpieces. *M. J. Polglase*

NICIARA (IRE)   7 b.g. Soviet Lad (USA) – Verusa (IRE) (Petorius 117) [2004 f16g   **–**
f16g f6b 8] lengthy gelding: little form on Flat since 2000. *M. C. Chapman*

NICKEL SUNGIRL (IRE)   4 b.f. Petorius 117 – Sharp Hint 60 (Sharpo 132) [2004   **–**
51, a–: f8g Jan 4] leggy filly: maiden: well held only 4-y-o start. *R. Hollinshead*

NICK THE SILVER   3 gr.c. Nicolotte 118 – Brillante (FR) 118 (Green Dancer (USA)   **– §**
132) [2004 69: 10d 11.6g⁶ 13.3m 12d 14.1g 12f Jul 31] big colt: fair maiden at 2 yrs: well
held in handicaps in 2004: ran out fourth outing: temperamental. *G. B. Balding*

NIETZSCHE (IRE)   3 b.c. Sadler's Wells (USA) 132 – Wannabe 84 (Shirley Heights   **78**
130) [2004 10d 10g² 10m⁵ 10v² Oct 23] 300,000Y: lengthy colt: fifth foal: closely related
to useful 2001 2-y-o 1m winner Assaaf (by Night Shift) and half-brother to 2 winners,
including Cheveley Park winner/1000 Guineas second Wannabe Grand (by Danehill):
dam, 1m and (in France) 1¼m winner, half-sister to Cheveley Park runner-up Tanami:
fair maiden: runner-up at Windsor (best effort) and Newbury: raced only at 1¼m.
J. Noseda

NIFTY ROY   4 b.g. Royal Applause 124 – Nifty Fifty (IRE) 97 (Runnett 125) [2004   **–**
10m 7.9f f6m 6g Jul 10] modest maiden at 2 yrs: missed 2003 and well beaten in
handicaps in 2004. *K. W. Hogg, Isle of Man*

NIGHT AIR (IRE)   3 b.g. Night Shift (USA) – Pippas Song 75 (Reference Point 139)   **86**
[2004 7d* 7m⁵ 7f² 7d² Sep 18] 44,000F, 110,000Y: sturdy gelding: sixth foal: brother to
useful 5f to 7f winner Nightbird and half-brother to fairly useful 2001 2-y-o 1m winner
Shanty (by Selkirk): dam, 1½m winner, half-sister to smart 11.4f winner Rockerlong:
fairly useful performer, lightly raced: won maiden at Thirsk in May: good efforts when
runner-up in minor event at Redcar and handicap at Newbury (beaten 1½ lengths by
Doctorate, hanging left) last 2 starts: raced only at 7f: acts on firm and good to soft going:
changed hands 15,000 gns. *D. R. Loder*

NIGHT CAP (IRE)   5 ch.g. Night Shift (USA) – Classic Design (Busted 134) [2004   **47 §**
57, a68?: p6g⁶ p5g p6g p6g² p6g 6g³ 6m 6f⁴ 6d p6g f6g p6g⁵ Dec 30] modest performer: **a51 §**
best at 6f/7f: acts on all-weather and firm going: tried in cheekpieces/blinkers: usually
races prominently: unreliable. *T. D. McCarthy*

NIGHT CLUB QUEEN (IRE) 2 ch.f. (May 14) Night Shift (USA) – Play The Queen –
(IRE) (King of Clubs 124) [2004 6m 6d 6g Sep 3] sturdy filly: half-sister to several
winners, including 4-y-o Terraquin and fairly useful 6f (at 2 yrs) to 1m winner Salty Jack
(by Salt Dome): dam Irish 7f winner: little sign of ability in maidens. *J. W. Hills*

NIGHT DANCE 12 ch.g. Weldnaas (USA) 112 – Shift Over (USA) 62 (Night Shift –
(USA)) [2004 8g Jul 16] good-topped gelding: one-time useful performer: modest in
Britain in 1999: failed to win in Germany (including over jumps) prior to well beaten only
12-y-o start: tried tongue tied. *M. Wigham*

NIGHT DRIVER (IRE) 5 b.g. Night Shift (USA) – Highshaan (Pistolet Bleu (IRE) –
133) [2004 –: 8s 8g 8.1d 10g 9.7m p12d Aug 9] big, strong gelding: little form in 2004:
tried in cheekpieces/blinkers. *G. L. Moore*

NIGHT EXPLOSION (IRE) 6 ch.g. Night Shift (USA) – Voodoo Rocket 56 (Lycius ?
(USA) 124) [2004 a6g³ a7g a6g a6g* a7g⁶ a6g a6g a7g f7g Dec 16] winner of several
races when trained in Greece, including in March: well held after, including in seller at
Southwell on British debut: stays 7f: acts on sand: tried blinkered. *D. J. S. ffrench Davis*

NIGHTFALL (USA) 2 b.c. (Mar 11) Rahy (USA) 115 – Quality Gift (Last Tycoon 80
131) [2004 6m* 6m⁶ p7g Aug 26] sturdy colt: second foal: half-brother to useful French
2003 2-y-o 1m winner Bright Abundance (by Quiet American): dam, French 11f winner,
half-sister to National Stakes winner Manntari: won maiden at Ascot in July: well held in
minor event/nursery: should stay 7f: tongue tied. *Saeed bin Suroor*

NIGHT FROLIC 3 b.f. Night Shift (USA) – Miss d'Ouilly (FR) (Bikala 134) [2004 68
–: 8v* 9.3f³ 10m 8.1g⁶ 8.3m⁶ 8d 8.1s⁴ 8m² 8s⁵ Oct 29] leggy filly: fair performer: won
maiden at Kempton in May: stays 9.3f: acts on any going: tried tongue tied: raced freely
final start. *J. W. Hills*

NIGHT GUEST (IRE) 2 b.c. (Apr 27) Danehill Dancer (IRE) 117 – Meadow Grass 63 ?
(IRE) (Thatching 131) [2004 7.1d 8g 8g Sep 29] €24,000F, 48,000Y: well-made colt:
sixth foal: brother to 2002 2-y-o 5f winner Countrywide Dancer and half-brother to
Italian 9f/1¼m winner by Catrail: dam ran 3 times: seemingly modest form only on debut
in maidens: ran as if amiss final start: sold 1,000 gns. *R. Hannon*

NIGHT HOUR (IRE) 2 b.c. (Mar 15) Entrepreneur 123 – Witching Hour (IRE) 88 89 p
(Alzao (USA) 117) [2004 8g⁴ 8g⁶ 8d Oct 15] strong, rangy colt: fourth foal: brother to
German 1¼m winner Moonlight Prince and half-brother to fairly useful 9f winner
Unafraid (by Unfuwain): dam, 2-y-o 6f winner who stayed 1m, half-sister to very smart
1m/1¼m performer Great Dane: confirmed considerable promise when winning maiden
at Salisbury in September by 1½ lengths from Top Gear: only seventh in minor event at
Newmarket, free to post and early in race: needs to settle to stay beyond 1m: should make
a useful 3-y-o. *M. P. Tregoning*

NIGHT KISS (FR) 4 ch.f. Night Shift (USA) – Roxy (Rock City 120) [2004 71: 8v 51
7g 8m May 22] just modest in 2004: stays 1m: acts on good to firm and good to soft
going, and polytrack. *R. Hannon*

NIGHT MAIL 4 b.g. Shaamit (IRE) 127 – Penlanfeigan (Abutammam 85) [2004 42: 40
f11g⁶ 9.3m Sep 11] leggy gelding: poor maiden: stays 13.8f: acts on fibresand and firm
ground: tried blinkered: sometimes slowly away: none too reliable. *M. W. Easterby*

NIGHT MARKET 6 ch.g. Inchinor 119 – Night Transaction 59 (Tina's Pet 121) 58 §
[2004 66d: f8g 8.1f* 10m 7.9m 10s 7.9m⁶ Sep 11] strong gelding: modest performer: won
amateur handicap at Warwick in June: stays 1¼m: acts on fibresand and firm going, not
on softer than good: tried blinkered/in cheekpieces: sometimes races freely/finds little.
N. Wilson

NIGHT OF JOY (IRE) 2 b.f. (Feb 5) King's Best (USA) 132 – Gilah (IRE) (Saddlers' 87
Hall (IRE) 126) [2004 6m⁴ 7m⁴ 8.2g* 8s* 8.1g 8s Oct 22] 70,000Y: lengthy filly: first
foal: dam unraced half-sister to smart 1¼m winner Cocotte, herself dam of Pilsudski:
fairly useful performer: won maiden at Nottingham and nursery at Newcastle in August:
below form in nurseries after, racing freely on first occasion: stays 1m: acts on soft going.
M. A. Jarvis

NIGHT OUT (FR) 2 b.f. (Mar 3) Night Shift (USA) – My Lucky Day (FR) (Darshaan 55
133) [2004 5d 6m⁶ 5.1m Aug 15] €35,000Y: first foal: dam French 11.5f/12.5f winner:
modest form in maidens: bred to stay 1m. *G. C. Bravery*

NIGHT PEARL (IRE) 3 b.f. Night Shift (USA) – Miss Pickpocket (IRE) 64 (Petorius 47
117) [2004 72: p7.1g p6g f7g⁴ p6g Dec 17] leggy filly: just poor maiden in 2004: barely
stays 7f: acts on all-weather, firm and good to soft going: tongue tied: blinkered (ran
poorly) final 2-y-o start: edgy sort. *E. J. Alston*

NIGHT PROSPECTOR   4 b.c. Night Shift (USA) – Pride of My Heart 74 (Lion   **110 ?**
Cavern (USA) 117) [2004 97: 5s 5m* 5d 5s 5m Sep 9] close-coupled, good-topped colt:
smart performer: 33/1, seemingly improved form when winning Vodafone Temple Stakes
at Epsom in June by 1¼ lengths from Autumn Pearl, soon well placed from tape start and
leading 1f out: well held after, blinkered final outing: best at 5f: acts on firm and good to
soft going: races prominently: tends to wander. *J. W. Payne*

NIGHTS CROSS (IRE)   3 b.g. Cape Cross (IRE) 129 – Cathy Garcia (IRE) (Be My   **107**
Guest (USA) 126) [2004 103: 5s⁴ 6g³ 5f 6f 6m 5m 6.1m³ 6m³ 6g³ 5s 6v 5g* 6d Oct 10]
compact gelding: useful performer: won listed race at Newmarket in September by ½
length from Steve's Champ: several creditable efforts earlier, including when 1¾ lengths
third to One Cool Cat in Phoenix Sprint Stakes at the Curragh eighth outing: effective at
5f/6f: best on good ground or firmer: blinkered/visored last 6 starts: sold 52,000 gns, then
gelded. *M. R. Channon*

Vodafone Temple Stakes, Epsom—the transfer from Sandown results in significant absentees
and a substandard renewal, and there's also industrial action by stalls handlers which means
the race is started by tape; Night Prospector takes the measure of Autumn Pearl (rail)
while Bishops Court (left) is an unlucky third ahead of Boston Lodge (blinkers)
(Note: for more detail on the race, see the essay on Patavellian)

NIGHT SIGHT (USA) 7 b.g. Eagle Eyed (USA) 111 – El Hamo (USA) (Search For **78**
Gold (USA)) [2004 76: 12m 12m² 12g³ 14.6m⁴ 12d⁴ 10g* 11.9g⁵ 12m* 12f⁴ 10m⁵ 11.9g²
f12s³ Nov 17] smallish, stocky gelding: fluent mover: fair handicapper: won at Pontefract
(amateurs) in August and Thirsk in September: best at 1¼m/1½m: acts on all-weather,
probably on turf going: blinkered once: sometimes races freely: held up: tough. *Mrs
S. Lamyman*

NIGHTSPOT 3 ch.g. Night Shift (USA) – Rash Gift 78 (Cadeaux Genereux 131) **89**
[2004 80: 10.4s⁶ 10m³ 10g² 10g* 12s⁶ 12g Sep 8] tall, quite attractive gelding: fairly
useful handicapper: won at Newbury in August by neck from Mazuna: well below form
both starts after: stays 1¼m: acts on polytrack, soft and good to firm ground. *R. Charlton*

NIGHT STORM 3 b.f. Night Shift (USA) – Monte Calvo 85 (Shirley Heights 130) **69**
[2004 70: p10g⁵ p8g³ p8g³ p7g³ p8g⁶ 7s p7.1d* p8.6g p8g⁵ p7g p7m Dec 21] smallish,
workmanlike filly: fair performer: won minor event at Wolverhampton in November:
effective at 7f/1m: acts on polytrack and good to firm ground: tongue tied at 2 yrs. *S. Dow*

NIGHT WARRIOR (IRE) 4 b.g. Alhaarth (IRE) 126 – Miniver (IRE) (Mujtahid **?**
(USA) 118) [2004 82, a77: p10g f12g⁴ p12g⁴ f12g² p12g f11g p13g f16g Dec 14] fair **a71**
performer: well below form last 4 starts: stays 1½m: acts on all-weather, raced only on
good ground or firmer on turf: tried in cheekpieces/visor: usually waited with. *D. Flood*

NIGHT WOLF (IRE) 4 gr.g. Indian Ridge 123 – Nicer (IRE) 113 (Pennine Walk **73 d**
120) [2004 78: p8g⁶ 8v 8m 7.1m³ 8g 7m 7g 6m 6f⁵ 7g 8m Sep 4] fair handicapper: little
form after fourth start: stays 1m: acts on polytrack and good to firm going: inconsistent.
M. R. Channon

NIGHT WORKER 3 b.c. Dracula (AUS) 121 – Crystal Magic 92 (Mazilier (USA) **50**
107) [2004 66: 6d⁶ 6s 8.3s 7m 6f 7m⁶ 5f⁵ 6f 7.1s 8d 7.1s Sep 20] strong, compact colt:
unimpressive mover: modest maiden: stays 7f: acts on firm and soft going. *R. Hannon*

NIKIFOROS 3 b.c. Inchinor 119 – Putout 69 (Dowsing (USA) 124) [2004 7m 8m⁶ **61**
8.1g p7g⁴ 7.1m⁴ 6.1d 6m Sep 1] modest maiden: stays 1m: acts on polytrack, good to firm
and good to soft going: wore cheekpieces third start, tongue tied on sixth: sent to Cyprus.
J. W. Hills

NIMBUS TWOTHOUSAND 4 b.f. Cloudings (IRE) 112 – Blueberry Parkes 71 **43 §**
(Pursuit of Love 124) [2004 48§: f8g⁵ Apr 2] poor maiden: stays 11f: acts on fibresand,
firm and good to soft ground: blinkered last 5 starts: wayward and not one to trust.
P. R. Wood

NIMELLO (USA) 8 b.g. Kingmambo (USA) 125 – Zakota (IRE) (Polish Precedent **84 §**
(USA) 131) [2004 ?, a96§: p10g f8.5s f8.5g* 8s 8.5d* 8.2g 8v p6g f8g⁶ Dec 28] smallish, **a95 §**
well-made gelding: useful handicapper on all-weather, fairly useful on turf nowadays:
won at Wolverhampton (apprentices), beat Samuel Charles by length) in April and Epsom
in July: best at 1m/9f: has won on firm ground, goes particularly well on softer than good
and fibresand: tried blinkered: tends to carry head high/find little/wander: unreliable.
A. G. Newcombe

NINA FONTENAIL (FR) 3 gr.f. Kaldounevees (FR) 118 – Ninon Fontenail (FR) **51**
(Turgeon (USA) 123) [2004 –: 11.1g 10.2s 8.1g 12.1m⁵ 11.7m⁴ p10g² 8.1d⁵ p13m⁴
p12m⁴ p12m Dec 15] leggy, close-coupled filly: modest maiden: trained by N. Hawke
first 4 starts: probably stays 13f: acts on polytrack and good to firm going. *B. R. Millman*

NINAH 3 b.f. First Trump 118 – Alwal (Pharly (FR) 130) [2004 69, a59: 7.1s 6.1g 8.1m **–**
5.7f 8g 7.5s p8.6d Nov 5] tall, leggy filly: maiden: little form in 2004: often races freely.
J. M. Bradley

NINAH'S INTUITION 2 b.c. (May 2) Piccolo 121 – Gina of Hithermoor (Reprimand **56**
122) [2004 5g⁴ 5v⁴ 5g Jun 30] modest form in maidens: should stay 6f: best effort on
heavy going. *J. M. Bradley*

NINE RED 3 b.f. Royal Applause 124 – Sarcita 111 (Primo Dominie 121) [2004 57: **54**
7m 7.1f 8m f7g² 7s 7.1g Aug 30] leggy, good-topped filly: modest maiden: left B. Hills **a63**
after fourth outing: stays 7f: acts on fibresand and firm going: reluctant to post last 2
appearances: difficult ride. *J. M. Bradley*

NINJA STORM (IRE) 2 b.c. (Mar 2) Namid 128 – Swan Lake (IRE) 65 (Waajib 121) **74**
[2004 5g⁴ 5f⁵ p5g⁶ 5d Aug 20] €15,000Y, 40,000G 2-y-o: second foal: dam sprint maiden:
fair maiden: very much caught the eye after slow start penultimate outing: likely to prove
best at 5f/6f: best effort on firm going. *G. L. Moore*

NIOBE'S WAY 3 b.f. Singspiel (IRE) 133 – Arietta's Way (IRE) 71 (Darshaan 133) **74**
[2004 10g 8m⁴ 10d³ 14d² 17.2s⁶ Oct 19] 20,000Y: third foal: half-sister to 1m winner

Leisurely Way (by Kris) and 4-y-o Midas Way: dam, ran 4 times, half-sister to smart performers Court of Honour (up to 2m) and Single Empire (up to 1¾m): fair maiden: should stay 2m: acts on good to soft going. *P. R. Chamings*

NIP NIP (IRE)   2 b.f. (Mar 10) Royal Applause 124 – Rustie Bliss (Kris 135) [2004 7d   –
5.7d Aug 27] 2,000Y: leggy filly: third foal: dam unraced from family of Irish 1000
Guineas/Yorkshire Oaks winner Sarah Siddons: well held in maiden/minor event.
A. D. Smith

NIPPY NIPPER   3 b.f. Fraam 114 – Elite Hope (USA) 84 (Moment of Hope (USA))   –
[2004 7g p8.6g 8d p6g Nov 12] first foal: dam 6f and (including at 2yrs) 7f winner: well
held in seller/claimers (trained by M. Quinn on debut): tried tongue tied. *Miss J. Feilden*

NISR   7 b.g. Grand Lodge (USA) 125 – Tharwa (IRE) 63 (Last Tycoon 131) [2004 6g²   83
Aug 28] lengthy gelding: fairly useful performer: reportedly had shoulder problem final
5-y-o start: very good ½-length second to Fonthill Road in handicap
at Newmarket only 7-y-o start: effective at 6f/7f: acts on polytrack, firm and good to soft
going. *J. W. Payne*

NISTAKI (USA)   3 ch.c. Miswaki (USA) 124 – Brandywine Belle (USA) (Trempolino   79 p
(USA) 135) [2004 7s⁴ 7.9m⁶ 8.5g⁴ 6m² Aug 8] 30,000 2-y-o: strong, compact colt:
second foal: dam, placed at 6f in USA, out of half-sister to smart 1m to 1¼m performer
Baronet: fair form: left Miss V. Haigh after debut: good second to Obe Bold in handicap
at Redcar final start, travelling strongly long way and finishing well: will prove best at 6f/
7f: acts on soft and good to firm going: open to further improvement. *T. D. Easterby*

NITEOWL DREAM   4 ch.f. Colonel Collins (USA) 122 – Nite-Owl Dancer 75 (Rob-   38
ellino (USA) 127) [2004 –: 7.5m⁴ f7d 8m f5g Jun 28] tall, leggy filly: poor maiden: stays
7.5f: acts on fibresand, soft and good to firm going: tried blinkered. *J. O'Reilly*

NITEOWL EXPRESS (IRE)   3 b.f. Royal Applause 124 – Nordan Raider 81 (Dom-   38
ynsky 110) [2004 –: f6g f6g⁶ f8g⁵ f6m⁴ 6.1d 7g Jul 24] poor maiden: tried blinkered.
J. O'Reilly

NITE-OWL FIZZ   6 b.g. Efisio 120 – Nite-Owl Dancer 75 (Robellino (USA) 127)   –
[2004 –, a69: f8.5g⁴ f8.5g² f8.5g f8.5s⁴ Feb 14] modest performer: stays 8.5f: acts on   a51
fibresand: often races prominently. *J. O'Reilly*

NITEOWL LAD (IRE)   2 ch.g. (Apr 17) Tagula (IRE) 116 – Mareha (IRE) 95 (Cade-   64
aux Genereux 131) [2004 5v 6s 5f² 5m⁵ Jul 25] €20,000F, 6,000Y: lengthy gelding: fifth
foal: half-brother to winner in Greece by Night Shift: dam 7f/1m winner: modest maiden:
likely to prove best at 5f: acts on firm going. *J. O'Reilly*

NIVERNAIS   5 b.g. Forzando 122 – Funny Wave 65 (Lugana Beach 116) [2004 92:   81
6s 6g 5g 5m 6m⁶ 7m 5.2f⁶ 6d³ 6g* 6m⁵ Sep 4] smallish, lengthy gelding: fairly useful
handicapper: won at Windsor in August: effective at 5f to easy 7f: acts on firm and good
to soft going: tried visored/tongue tied. *H. Candy*

NOBBLER   2 br.c. (Mar 3) Classic Cliche (IRE) 128 – Nicely (IRE) 94 (Bustino 136)   65
[2004 8.1m 7.9g 10.1d⁶ Nov 5] fluent mover: first foal: dam, 1m (at 2 yrs) and 2m winner,
out of half-sister to very smart 9f to 1½m winner Terimon: best effort in maidens when
sixth at Yarmouth: will be suited by 1½m+. *J. W. Hills*

NOBELIX (IRE)   2 gr.g. (Mar 14) Linamix (FR) 127 – Nataliana 103 (Surumu (GER))   69 p
[2004 p8m⁴ Dec 21] €50,000Y: fifth foal: half-brother to 2 winners abroad, including
German 1¼m winner Nobleblue (by Bluebird): dam 9.5f/1¼m winner: 6/1,
fourth to Alessano in maiden at Lingfield, not given hard time: should improve.
J. R. Fanshawe

NOBLE CALLING (FR)   7 b.g. Caller I D (USA) – Specificity (USA) 103 (Alleged   61
(USA) 138) [2004 61: p10g 17.2f³ 10m 17.2f³ 15m² Jul 2] angular gelding: modest
handicapper: seemingly stays 17.2f: acts on firm and good to soft ground: sometimes
blinkered/visored (not of late): gelded after final start. *R. J. Hodges*

NOBLE CYRANO   9 ch.g. Generous (IRE) 139 – Miss Bergerac (Bold Lad (IRE)   – §
133) [2004 43§, a48§: f11g⁶ f11g Jan 15] tall, angular gelding: poor performer: well held
both starts in 2004: unreliable. *Jedd O'Keeffe*

NOBLE DESERT (FR)   3 b.f. Green Desert (USA) 127 – Sporades (USA) 117 (Vagu-   –
ely Noble 140) [2004 –: 7s 6g⁵ f6s 7.9m 8d 8.1d Oct 9] smallish, workmanlike filly: little
form. *R. Guest*

NOBLE DUTY (USA)   2 b.c. (Feb 9) Dubai Millennium 140 – Nijinsky's Lover (USA)   91 p
(Nijinsky (CAN) 138) [2004 8g² 7.9g³ Oct 9] tall, good sort: half-brother to several

winners, including smart French/US 6f and 1m winner Naninja (by Alysheba) and 1999 US 2-y-o Grade 2 6f winner Dance Master (by Gone West): dam, minor US 1m stakes winner, half-sister to dam of Dolphin Street and Saffron Walden: fairly useful form in minor event at Newbury (second to Merchant) and maiden at York (odds on, led long way when third to Daring Ransom): not sure to stay much beyond 1m: type to make a useful 3-y-o, and should win races. *Saeed bin Suroor*

NOBLE LOCKS (IRE)   6 ch.g. Night Shift (USA) – Imperial Graf (USA) (Blushing John (USA) 120) [2004 –, a80: f6s f6g f7s f6g f6g⁴ f6m p7.1g Dec 20] smallish gelding: fair handicapper: form in 2004 only on fifth start: effective at 6f to 8.5f: acts on fibresand, no recent form on turf: tried blinkered/visored/tongue tied. *J. W. Unett* — **a67**

NOBLE MIND   3 b.g. Mind Games 121 – Lady Annabel 54 (Alhijaz 122) [2004 8.3d² 7.1m 10f f8g³ p8.6d Nov 4] leggy gelding: first foal: dam little worthwhile form: fair form when second in maiden at Windsor on debut: well below that level after: may prove best around 1m: slowly away final outing. *P. G. Murphy* — **78 ?**

NOBLE MOUNT   3 b.g. Muhtarram (USA) 125 – Our Poppet (IRE) 58 (Warning 136) [2004 p6g⁵ f6g 5s 5g³ f6g p7g p6g p6g* Dec 20] modest performer: left R. Guest after fifth start: won banded race at Lingfield in December: bred to be suited by 7f+: acts on all-weather: wore cheekpieces last 2 outings. *A. B. Haynes* — **59**

NOBLE PENNY   5 b.m. Pennekamp (USA) 130 – Noble Form (Double Form 130) [2004 64d: 8v 8.2d⁶ 7m² 7m 8g⁴ 8g⁶ 7d⁵ Aug 4] well-made mare: modest maiden: effective at 7f/1m: acts on firm and good to soft ground: wore cheekpieces (not discredited) penultimate start. *Mrs K. Walton* — **54**

NOBLE PHILOSOPHER   4 ch.g. Faustus (USA) 118 – Princess Lucy 42 (Local Suitor (USA) 128) [2004 –: f11m May 6] big, angular gelding: little form. *K. Bell* — **–**

NOBLE PURSUIT   7 b.g. Pursuit of Love 124 – Noble Peregrine (Lomond (USA) 128) [2004 82d: f8s² f8g² f7g f9.4s f8.5s³ p12g⁵ f8s⁵ f8g 7f 8d² 7.5g⁴ 10m 7g³ 7.9m 8d 8s Aug 30] workmanlike gelding: modest performer: on downgrade: left P. Blockley after eighth start: effective at 7f/1m: acts on all-weather, soft and good to firm going: tried in cheekpieces: sometimes slowly away/races freely: unreliable. *R. E. Barr* — **60 d**

NOBRATINETTA (FR)   5 b.m. Celtic Swing 138 – Bustinetta 89 (Bustino 136) [2004 75: 14s 16d⁴ 14.1d May 15] fair performer, lightly raced: will stay beyond 2m: acts on good to soft ground: wore cheekpieces (found little) final start. *Mrs M. Reveley* — **78**

NOCATEE (IRE)   3 b.g. Vettori (IRE) 119 – Rosy Sunset (IRE) (Red Sunset 120) [2004 45: f9.4g³ f11g³ f11g⁴ 14.1s³ 14.1m* p12.2g³ p13.9g⁶ p13.9g⁵ Dec 22] tall gelding: modest performer: won nursery handicap at Redcar in June: stays 1¾m: acts on all-weather, soft and good to firm going: tried in visor/cheekpieces: tends to wander. *P. C. Haslam* — **58**

NO CHANCE TO DANCE (IRE)   4 b.g. Revoque (IRE) 122 – Song of The Glens (Horage 124) [2004 –: 10d 8f 8m⁴ 9.2d³ 8g⁶ 9.7m⁶ 9.2d 10.1d Oct 16] good-topped, lengthy gelding: modest maiden: stays 9.7f: acts on good to firm and good to soft going: tongue tied last 7 starts. *H. J. Collingridge* — **54**

NO COMMISSION (IRE)   2 b.g. (Feb 7) General Monash (USA) 107 – Price of Passion 83 (Dolphin Street (FR) 125) [2004 5s 5g⁵ 6m⁴ 6d f6g⁵ 6g⁴ 5g 6g² 6f* 7m 7s⁵ 5.9g 6d p7.1g⁶ Dec 6] 18,000Y: sturdy gelding: first foal: dam, 5f winner (including at 2 yrs), out of useful 5f winner Food of Love: fair performer: won nursery at Hamilton in July: respectable effort final start, best effort in similar events after: should stay 7f: acts on firm going. *R. F. Fisher* — **71**

NO DILEMMA (USA)   3 ch.g. Rahy (USA) 115 – Cascassi (USA) 91 (Nijinsky (CAN) 138) [2004 61: 10d Apr 5] leggy gelding: modest maiden in 2004: tailed off only 3-y-o outing. *E. A. L. Dunlop* — **57**

NODINA   2 br.c. (May 10) Primo Dominie 121 – Princess Tara 85 (Prince Sabo 123) [2004 6.1m 5m⁵ 6g Oct 11] 28,000Y: good-topped colt: half-brother to several winners, including useful 1998 2-y-o 5f/6f winner El Tango (by Risk Me) and 3-y-o Compton's Eleven: dam 6f (at 2 yrs) and 1m winner: best effort in maidens when fifth at Lingfield: should stay 6f. *S. C. Williams* — **65**

NOD 'N' A WINK   6 b.g. Factual (USA) 108 – Singing Reply (USA) 67 (The Minstrel (CAN) 135) [2004 p8g Jan 7] tailed off in bumper, and in seller at Lingfield. *C. A. Dwyer* — **–**

NOD'S NEPHEW   7 b.g. Efisio 120 – Nordan Raider 81 (Domynsky 110) [2004 63, a55: f8g² f8s 8.5d² 10.9g² Apr 23] lengthy gelding: modest performer: effective at 1m, — **58 a55**

barely at 11f: acts on all-weather and any turf going: often tongue tied: sometimes races freely. *D. E. Cantillon*

NOD'S STAR 3 ch.f. Starborough 126 – Barsham 94 (Be My Guest (USA) 126) [2004 **47** 8v⁵ 7g 8m f12d 9.9g 14.1g³ 15.8g Oct 5] 10,500Y: close-coupled filly: half-sister to several winners, including useful 1996 2-y-o 6f to 1m winner Falkenham (by Polar Falcon), later 9f winner in USA, and fairly useful 1¼m winner Jameel Asmar (by Rock City): dam 1¼m winner: poor maiden: barely stays 1¾m: best effort on good going. *Miss J. A. Camacho*

NOFA'S MAGIC (IRE) 4 b.f. Rainbow Quest (USA) 134 – Garah 107 (Ajdal (USA) **71** 130) [2004 92: 12.4v³ 10g Apr 26] smallish filly: lightly-raced maiden: fairly useful form on debut (at 3 yrs): best effort after when eighth in minor event at Windsor final start: should stay 1½m. *J. L. Dunlop*

NO GROUSE 4 b.g. Pursuit of Love 124 – Lady Joyce (FR) (Galetto (FR) 118) [2004 **76** 83: f7g f8.5s⁵ f7s 7g 7.1g³ 7m 6f 7.9g 7m 7m 7.6m⁵ 7m 7m⁵ 7.5m⁴ 7m² 7v⁵ p7.1g* Dec 4] strong gelding: fair performer: left R. Fahey 8,500 gns and rejoined former trainer, won minor event at Wolverhampton in December: stays 7.5f: acts on all-weather and good to firm ground: often wore cheekpieces in 2004, not when successful: sometimes wanders: none too consistent. *E. J. Alston*

NOODLES 2 b.c. (Feb 5) Mind Games 121 – Salacious (Sallust 134) [2004 6d 5.9g² **64** 6g 5m 6s Aug 14] 36,000Y: rather leggy colt: brother to 2000 2-y-o 5f winner Quizzical Lady (later 1m winner in Spain) and half-brother to several winners: dam Irish 7f (at 2 yrs) and 9f winner: modest maiden: will probably stay 7f: visored (only form) second/ third starts, blinkered final one. *T. D. Easterby*

NOORAIN 2 ch.f. (Apr 5) Kabool 119 – Abeyr 106 (Unfuwain (USA) 131) [2004 **77** 5m³ 5.7g⁴ 7m² 7m Aug 6] strong, useful-looking filly: fifth foal: half-sister to 3 winners, including useful 7f winner Raheema (by Lion Cavern) and 3-y-o Makfool: dam 7f/1m winner: fair maiden: second at Thirsk, best effort: possibly amiss final start: will stay 1m: sold 7,000 gns. *M. R. Channon*

NOORA (IRE) 3 ch.f. Bahhare (USA) 122 – Esteraad (IRE) 90 (Cadeaux Genereux **83** 131) [2004 59p: 7d² 7g 7g² 7d⁴ 8.1d³ p8m* p8g⁴ p9.5g* p10m Dec 22] good-topped filly: has scope: fairly useful performer: won maiden at Lingfield in October and handicap at Wolverhampton in December: stays 9.5f: acts on polytrack, raced only on good ground or softer on turf: consistent. *W. Jarvis*

NOPEKAN (IRE) 4 b.g. Sri Pekan (USA) 117 – Giadamar (IRE) (Be My Guest (USA) **97 d** 126) [2004 100: 12d⁵ 10.2m⁶ 12f 10.5g 12.3m 10g Aug 16] leggy gelding: useful performer: left T. Mullins in Ireland, well below form last 4 starts: stays 1¼m: acts on firm and good to soft going, probably on soft: tried blinkered/in cheekpieces. *Miss K. Marks*

NOPLEAZINU 4 ch.f. Sure Blade (USA) 130 – Vado Via 56 (Ardross 134) [2004 6g⁵ **–** 8.2m p9.5d⁶ p9.5g Dec 13] second foal: sister to 8-y-o Mi Odds: dam, 1½m winner, also fairly useful staying hurdler: well held in maidens. *Mrs N. Macauley*

NORCROFT 2 b.g. (Feb 21) Fasliyev (USA) 120 – Norcroft Joy 82§ (Rock Hopper **75** 124) [2004 5d² 5.1g* 5s⁶ 6.1s 6g 6f 7.1d⁴ 6m 8m p7.1g³ 10d f6g² f5g⁴ p6g³ Dec 30] leggy, good-topped gelding: first foal: dam 1½m/1¾m winner: fair performer: won maiden at Nottingham in April and (having left N. Callaghan after tenth start and P. McEntee after twelfth) nursery at Wolverhampton in December: stays 7f: acts on polytrack, firm and good to soft ground: blinkered seventh to ninth starts, wore cheekpieces on last 3. *Mrs C. A. Dunnett*

NORDHOCK (USA) 2 gr.f. (Mar 1) Luhuk (USA) 114 – Starlight Dreams (USA) **57** (Black Tie Affair 128) [2004 6m⁶ 6m* 7m⁶ 7m³ Aug 6] workmanlike filly: first foal: dam, US 1m winner, out of close relative to dam of Sakhee: modest performer: won seller at Yarmouth in July: creditable third in nursery at Newmarket: will stay 1m: sent to Oman. *N. A. Callaghan*

NORDWIND (IRE) 3 b.c. Acatenango (GER) 127 – Narola (GER) (Nebos (GER) **98** 129) [2004 8.1m³ 8.1d⁴ p8g* 10g* 10m² 12g* 11g** 11.8g Oct 11] 110,000Y: good-topped, attractive colt: half-brother to several winners, including useful German performer up to 1½m National Academy (by Royal Academy) and 4-y-o Numitas: dam German 11f winner: useful performer: won maiden at Lingfield and handicap at Nottingham in July and handicaps at Epsom and Goodwood (beat Quadrant by 1½ lengths) in September: folded tamely in handicap at Leicester final start: stays 1½m: acts on polytrack and good to firm going: sometimes wanders/idles (can look ungainly in finish). *P. W. Harris*

NO REFUGE (IRE) 4 ch.g. Hernando (FR) 127 – Shamarra (FR) (Zayyani 119) [2004 **110** 112p: 14d³ 15s* 18s Oct 16] rather leggy gelding: smart performer: off 11 months prior to reappearance: won listed race at Cologne in September by 2 lengths from Le Royal: raced freely when well held in Cesarewitch at Newmarket final start: stays 15f: acts on all-weather/dirt and soft ground: blinkered last 2 starts: slowly away/ran in snatches fifth 3-y-o outing: has idled: sold 180,000 gns, joined J. Howard Johnson: useful form over hurdles. *Sir Mark Prescott*

NORMA SPEAKMAN (IRE) 4 ch.f. Among Men (USA) 124 – Bride Bank (IRE) **–** (Statoblest 120) [2004 12m 9.9g⁶ 12m 12m Aug 3] workmanlike filly: maiden: missed 2003: no form in 2004. *E. W. Tuer*

NORSE DANCER (IRE) 4 b.c. Halling (USA) 133 – River Patrol 96 (Rousillon **125 §** (USA) 133) [2004 118: 8.1d⁴ 8m³ 8f 10d⁴ 8g⁴ 8d* 10.4d² 10m² 8m 10s⁴ Oct 16]
Norse Dancer's career brings to mind a couple of lines by that noted Australian poet of the outback 'Banjo' Paterson:

> *'The rule holds good in everything in life's uncertain fight;*
> *You'll find the winner can't go wrong, the loser can't go right'.*

For a horse with his ability (rated 101p at two and 118 at three), earnings (around £500,000) and nine first-four placings in Group 1 company, beaten less than a length on four of those occasions, Norse Dancer is distinctly short of victories, with just three from twenty-one starts. There is a natural tendency with a runner possessing such a record to put the failures down to the horse being faint-hearted, something of a shirker. Norse Dancer has certainly been on the receiving end of plenty of critical barbs, many of them—to be blunt—justified. The summary of his eccentricities contained in the *Black Book* noteform comment each week during the latest season was lengthier than the full comment for a good many horses, running as follows: 'sometimes slowly away/races lazily, and often waited with . . . has wandered/carried head awkwardly: has found little/not gone through with effort.' It is a shade ironic that Norse Dancer's connections happen to be precisely the same as those of Persian Punch, a horse who showed relentless enthusiasm and a willingness to battle. Equally, while life would be easier for punters if every horse resembled Persian Punch, one of the sport's strengths is its variety, and characters

totesport Sovereign Stakes, Salisbury—a competitive event for its first running as a Group 3;
Norse Dancer (second left) has just a short head to spare over Lucky Story, making an excellent comeback
after eleven months off; Hurricane Alan (behind winner), Passing Glance (stripe on cap),
Shot To Fame (behind runner-up) and Autumn Glory (rail) are next

such as Nasrullah, Zucchero, Red God, Knockroe, Buzzards Bay, Hamas and Royal Rebel in years gone by, and Norse Dancer, Antonius Pius and Salselon now, add a touch of entertainment, even though their quirkiness can be infuriating.

Praise where it is due with Norse Dancer, though. Three successive runs at the height of the summer saw him at his very best, better in fact in two of those than when he made the frame in the Two Thousand Guineas, Derby and Sussex Stakes as a three-year-old. Because of injury Richard Quinn missed the ride on Norse Dancer in the totesport Sovereign Stakes at Salisbury in August. He had partnered the colt on his five previous starts, one atrocious run in the Queen Anne Stakes at Royal Ascot and four respectable ones. These had included a three-quarters-of-a-length third to Russian Rhythm in the Lockinge Stakes at Newbury despite being on and off the bridle and failing to put everything into his finishing effort, and never-dangerous fourth places in the Eclipse at Sandown and the Sussex at Goodwood. John Egan deputised at Salisbury in a race upgraded to Group 3 which also attracted Lucky Story on his reappearance, the favourite Ancient World, Hurricane Alan and Passing Glance. The change of jockey seemed to work wonders, proof perhaps that not all horses are suited to all jockeys, even when the riders concerned are out of the top drawer. Responding well to driving with a quarter of a mile to go, Norse Dancer came away with Lucky Story and got the better of a fine final-furlong tussle, showing no inclination to down tools, eventually scoring by a short head. Egan rode Norse Dancer in his remaining races and, brought out quickly for the Juddmonte International at York, Norse Dancer excelled himself. There was a change of tactics, too, as he kept closer to the pace than usual in third. Taking it up over a furlong out and galloping on unswervingly, Norse Dancer was caught by the final flourish of Sulamani, who beat him by three quarters of a length. Those behind included Bago, Cacique and Kalaman. If anything, the horses Norse Dancer accounted for on his next outing, in the Baileys Irish Champion Stakes at Leopardstown the following month, were even better. He still could not manage to get his head in front though. Close up from the outset, Norse Dancer responded well under pressure to go on inside the final furlong, saw off Powerscourt but then had no answer to the finishing burst of Azamour, who got up to beat him by a half a length. Powerscourt, Grey Swallow, Rakti and Doyen, all Group 1 winners during the year, were behind and, even if they did not all run to form, Norse Dancer had still put up a cracking display. Unfortunately Norse Dancer fell sharply from grace on his final two starts. Perhaps the novelty of a new man on his back was wearing off. Either way, Norse Dancer became agitated in the preliminaries of the Queen Elizabeth II Stakes at Ascot and took no interest in proceedings, trailing in last but one. He finished closer to the principals in the Champion Stakes at Newmarket, in fourth behind Haafhd, but the way he went about his task was less than impressive, as he again showed a distinct lack of enthusiasm only to run on strongly once Egan had more or less given up on him with two furlongs left.

Norse Dancer (IRE) (b.c. 2000)	Halling (USA) (ch 1991)	Diesis (ch 1980)	Sharpen Up Doubly Sure
		Dance Machine (b 1982)	Green Dancer Never A Lady
	River Patrol (b 1988)	Rousillon (b 1981)	Riverman Belle Dorine
		Boathouse (b 1978)	Habitat Ripeck

There is little to add to the analysis of Norse Dancer's pedigree contained in *Racehorses of 2003*. His sire Halling had only two other pattern winners during the year, Chancellor and Mkuzi, which suggests he needs to get moving if he is to leave his mark, and the dam River Patrol did not have any other runners. Her three foals following Norse Dancer—she is based in Germany—are River Blue (by Ashkalani, third in Germany as a two-year-old on his only start), Rosewater (by Winged Love) and a yearling filly also by Winged Love. Norse Dancer is effective at a mile to a mile and a half, though not his best form at a mile and a quarter; he has not been tried over further since the Derby. He acts on good to firm and good to soft going and has been below form on very firm and very soft, though because of his attitude no definite conclusions should yet be drawn about his effectiveness under such conditions. He has been tried in a visor and blinkers but is better without, and has also run creditably when sweating. In appearance Norse Dancer looks the part for a potential Group 1 winner, being a big, rangy, good sort with a quick action. He also has more than enough ability to win a race at the top level but whether he does so is likely to depend as much on the way he applies himself, as upon the strength of his opponents. *D. R. C. Elsworth*

NORTHANGER ABBEY (IRE) 2 ch.c. (Mar 15) In The Wings 128 – Glenstal **65** Priory 53 (Glenstal (USA) 118) [2004 7d 7.1m 10.2g⁵ 10g Oct 4] 90,000Y: sturdy colt: half-brother to several winners, including fairly useful 1999 2-y-o 5f winner Duke of Aston (by Shalford) and 3-y-o Larad: dam 2m/2¼m winner: form in maidens only when fifth at Bath: should stay 1½m: sold 24,000 gns. *J. H. M. Gosden*

NORTHERN DESERT (IRE) 5 b.g. Desert Style (IRE) 121 – Rosie's Guest (IRE) **87** (Be My Guest (USA) 126) [2004 –: 8.1s 7.9g 7s p7g³ p8.6g Nov 20] lengthy, quite good-topped gelding: useful at 3 yrs, missed 2003: fairly useful nowadays: stays 1m: acts on polytrack, firm and good to soft going, probably on soft. *P. W. Hiatt*

NORTHERN GAMES 5 b.g. Mind Games 121 – Northern Sal 59 (Aragon 118) [2004 **86** 68: 8m 7f 6m* 6.9m⁴ 6.1g² 7g⁴ 7.2d² 6d* 7v* 6s 6dg Dec 3] leggy, useful-looking gelding: fairly useful handicapper: won at Catterick in July, and at Ayr and Catterick in October: effective at 6f/7f: acts on all-weather and any turf going: often wears blinkers/cheekpieces: very slowly away sixth outing. *K. A. Ryan*

NORTHERN NYMPH 5 b.g. Makbul 104 – Needwood Sprite 58 (Joshua 129) **71** [2004 80: f16s² f16.2s³ 18g 14s 14.1s⁵ 16.2v⁶ 14m² 14d³ 14g⁴ 14d 15.9g⁵ 17.2g⁵ 13.9g² **a86** Oct 9] good-topped gelding: fairly useful handicapper on all-weather, fair on turf: stays 2m: acts on fibresand, soft and good to firm going: tried tongue tied. *R. Hollinshead*

NORTHERN REVOQUE (IRE) 2 b.f. (Apr 24) Revoque (IRE) 122 – Delia (IRE) **41** (Darshaan 133) [2004 5g⁵ 6g 6m f5g⁵ 6d 7m 7s⁴ 7s 7d 8s Oct 30] €2,000Y: workman-like filly: second foal: half-sister to Irish 2002 2-y-o 5f winner Katies Crown (by Royal Abjar): dam third at 6f in Germany at 2 yrs: poor maiden: stays 7f: acts on soft ground: sometimes blinkered/in cheekpieces. *A. Berry*

NORTHERN SECRET 2 b.f. (Feb 23) Sinndar (IRE) 134 – Northern Goddess 111 **70** (Night Shift (USA)) [2004 7m 7g³ 7d 7m Oct 1] 20,000Y: leggy, close-coupled filly: eighth foal: half-sister to smart 1¼m/1½m winner in France/USA Northern Quest (by Rainbow Quest) and French 5.5f (at 2 yrs) to 10.5f winner Nortolixa (by Linamix): dam sprinter: fair maiden: needs to settle to stay beyond 7f: best effort on good going. *A. M. Balding*

NORTHERN SPIRIT 3 b.g. Kadeed (IRE) – Elegant Spirit 31 (Elegant Air 119) **56** [2004 58: 10g 14.1s⁶ 12.3g 14.1m³ 16.2g 12.1m* Jul 27] tall gelding: modest handicapper: won selling event at Beverley (claimed 6,200 gns) in July: stays 1¾m: acts on good to firm going: wore cheekpieces/blinkers last 3 starts. *K. A. Ryan*

NORTHERN SPLENDOUR (USA) 2 ch.c. (Apr 17) Giant's Causeway (USA) **99** 132 – Ribbonwood (USA) 100 (Diesis 133) [2004 6m³ 7d* 8.2g* Aug 16] smallish, strong colt: sixth foal: half-brother to smart 7f (in Ireland at 2 yrs) to 1½m (in UAE) winner Broche (by Summer Squall), 7f winner in Ireland at 2 yrs, and 7f (at 2 yrs) and 11f (in UAE) winner Crown of Trees (by Chief's Crown): dam, 2-y-o 6f winner, half-sister to Preakness/Belmont Stakes winner Risen Star: won maiden at Redcar in July and minor event at Nottingham (comfortably, by 2 lengths from In The Fan) in August: will probably stay 1¼m: races prominently: useful. *Saeed bin Suroor*

NORTHERN SUMMIT (IRE) 3 b.g. Danehill Dancer (IRE) 117 – Book Choice **–** (North Summit) [2004 –: 12g f12d⁶ f12g⁶ May 11] workmanlike gelding: little form. *J. R. Norton*

NORTHERN SVENGALI (IRE) 8 b.g. Distinctly North (USA) 115 – Trilby's **48** Dream (IRE) (Mansooj 118) [2004 46: 5f 5m 5m 5g⁵ 5g⁵ 6g⁶ Jul 10] small, sturdy gelding: poor performer: effective at 5f to easy 7f: acts on any turf going/all-weather: tried blinkered/in cheekpieces: usually tongue tied. *D. A. Nolan*

NORTH LANDING (IRE) 4 b.g. Storm Bird (CAN) 134 – Tirol Hope (IRE) 100 **–** (Tirol 127) [2004 63d: f7m 10.1d Aug 4] leggy, quite good-topped gelding: maiden: well held on Flat in 2004: tried in cheekpieces. *R. C. Guest*

NORTH LIGHT (IRE) 3 b.c. Danehill (USA) 126 – Sought Out (IRE) 119 (Rain- **126** bow Quest (USA) 134) [2004 95P: 10.4s* 12m* 12f2 12m⁵ Oct 3]
'It can be said that the Derby course and distance provide an admirable test of the thoroughbred. A true-run mile and a half—there is seldom any loitering in the Derby—demands speed as well as stamina, and eliminates the fast short-runner

and the plodder devoid of acceleration.' Little has changed with the Derby test since the precise period-English description given to it by Roger Mortimer in *The History of the Derby Stakes* when reviewing the inaugural running over the present-day lay-out, first used in 1872. Inevitably, the same can't be said of the world in general. The racing landscape, for example, has altered dramatically from the one the Derby towered over in its prime. The top open-aged events in Europe, principally the Arc and the King George, are now the benchmark at a mile and a half, and, further afield, more recent innovations such as the Breeders' Cup, first run in 1984, have broadened horizons still further. As racing and breeding in America, with its bias more towards speed, has had an increasing worldwide influence, top races at a mile and a quarter, such as the Juddmonte International and the Irish Champion Stakes, have also risen in prominence, while the low-key record of recent Derby winners as sires, in comparison with other top winners with form at shorter distances, has even brought into question whether the Derby should remain in its traditional form and still be run over Epsom's mile and a half.

In 2004 the increasing sense of isolation of the Derby, felt in some quarters, was heightened by the announcement in September by the authorities in France that the French Derby, the Prix du Jockey Club, was being reduced in distance to an extended mile and a quarter from 2005, and was having a substantial boost in prize money, offering a new and viable alternative for horses for whom the Derby distance might be considered too severe a test. Peter Savill, former chairman of the BHB, who switched Celtic Swing from Epsom to Chantilly in 1995, voiced support for the Derby to follow suit. Pressed for an immediate response, Epsom talked of 'the sacred trust we must maintain'. In the light of events, it is perhaps timely to reflect on the Derby winners of the last twenty-five years, the second quarter of a century of increased prominence for the top all-aged events. At a watershed for the first quarter, at the time of the 200th Derby, *Racehorses of 1979* challenged the fading claims of the Derby to be labelled as 'the world's greatest race'; the essay on Troy noted that he was only the seventh winner in twenty-five years that, by the end of the season, could reasonably be referred to as the best three-year-old in Europe over a mile and a half—the others, for the record, Crepello, Sea Bird II, Royal Palace, Nijinsky, Mill Reef and Grundy. At least the situation is no worse now, indeed it might be better. In the twenty-five years since, using the same criteria, it can reasonably be said of eight Derby winners, nine counting one jointly top, that they were the best of their age over a mile and a half in Europe. The list doesn't include the unlucky Dancing Brave, of course, or Nashwan, pipped as the best of the year in 1989 by Old Vic. Interestingly, of those on the list—Shergar, Slip Anchor, Reference Point, Generous, Lammtarra, High-Rise, Sinndar, Galileo and High Chaparral (jointly with Sulamani)—eight could reasonably be said to be the best three-year-old in Europe *at any distance* among those racing that year.

The standing of Derby winners among their contemporaries in general has also remained high of late. In the ten years prior to 2004, Lammtarra, High-Rise, Sinndar and Galileo, as noted above, were the best three-year-olds of their year and,

totesport Dante Stakes, York—North Light puts himself firmly in the Derby picture with a comfortable success from Rule of Law (right), Let The Lion Roar (left) and Top Seed

among the Derby winners that fell short of that, the lowest in the pecking order was Oath, joint sixth best in 1999. Interestingly, the standing of horses with form at a mile and a half generally in the same period has also remained high. During the ten years from 1994 to 2003, *Racehorses* allotted a rating of 130 or more to twenty-five European-trained three-year-olds, fourteen of which showed their form at the Derby distance, from only seventeen to tackle a mile and a half. Six of the seven rated 134 or higher as three-year-olds in that ten-year period—Lammtarra, Helissio, Peintre Celebre, Montjeu, Sinndar and Galileo—showed their best form at a mile and a half, all bar Helissio among those successful in the Derby at home or in France along the way. Irrespective of the types of horses breeders may be trying to produce, it seems there is no shortage among the top horses of those able to excel at a mile and a half.

A more disturbing worry for the Derby, in the light of the shortening of the distance of the Prix du Jockey Club, is that it might develop an image as more of a race for stayers than for horses with a combination of speed and stamina. If so, it will almost certainly lead to a fall in the number of horses the Derby attracts from the Two Thousand Guineas. The record of Guineas runners in the Derby of late— Nashwan was the last to do the double in 1989—encourages the idea that racing is becoming more specialised. Interestingly, in the last twenty-five years, only two Derby winners also took part in the Two Thousand Guineas—the other, Generous, finished fourth at Newmarket in 1991. In contrast, in the 'seventies alone, five Derby winners ran in the Guineas, Nijinsky—in 1970 the third in four years to do the double—followed by Mill Reef, Roberto, Grundy and The Minstrel, who were all placed at Newmarket.

What is the explanation? The pooling of good horses in a select number of stables is one possibility, though the variety of trainers winning the Derby of late seems no less than it was in the 'seventies when Vincent O'Brien alone won three. A bigger shift has come in the way Derby winners are campaigned prior to Epsom. In the 'seventies, all bar three Derby winners made their debut as two-year-olds by July, and all bar Morston, unraced at two, ran in a pattern race as juveniles, seven of them winning at least one. Since then, the further growth in importance of the all-aged championship events and the prospect of a longer season at three, and of staying in training at four, has seemingly driven a wedge between Derby winners and two-year-old racing, as it has done with the other British classics. Of the last ten Derby winners, only two made their debut as two-year-olds before August and only Benny The Dip, Sinndar and High Chaparral ran in a pattern race, each winning one over a mile, incidentally.

The modern approach to the Derby has been reflected in Sir Michael Stoute's successes in the race. Of his four Derby winners, none ran more than twice as a juvenile, and only Shergar, runner-up in what is now the Racing Post Trophy, tackled a pattern race. Like Stoute's 2003 winner Kris Kin, North Light contested two maiden races as a juvenile. After going down by a short head over seven furlongs at Sandown on his debut in late-August, North Light won comfortably over a mile at Goodwood in September. He held entries in the Royal Lodge Stakes and the Racing Post Trophy but, already surpassing his brother Researched and half-brother Cover Up in winning as a juvenile, he was put away for the winter. North Light reportedly suffered with cracked heels in the spring, and his early progress at three had to be followed in gallop reports, appearing regularly from mid-April. There was no media fanfare for his reappearance in the totesport Dante Stakes at York in mid-May, though he had already been backed from 40/1 to 20/1 with Ladbrokes for Epsom. A strong, well-made colt, North Light stood out in the paddock at York, looking in very good shape, and he started fourth favourite at 6/1 in a field of ten. Withdrawn on the previous Saturday from the Lingfield Derby Trial, reportedly to avoid a hard race over virtually the full Derby distance on soft ground, North Light revelled in similar underfoot conditions over the Dante trip. Pressing the leader before halfway, he was sent on turning for home and was already clear when Fallon gave him a couple of slaps inside the last furlong, holding Rule of Law comfortably by half a length, with favourite Let The Lion Roar two and a half lengths further away in third. Briefly 12/1 for Epsom afterwards, North Light was generally 8/1 by the following day to become the first since Benny The Dip in 1997 to complete the Dante/Derby double.

Vodafone Derby Stakes, Epsom—as they come into the straight North Light is poised to take over from Meath (right); Hazyview (rail), American Post and Pukka are following, while Let The Lion roar (visor) and Rule of Law (white cap) on his outside have a lot to do

The Dante was much the most competitive of the middle-distance trials in Britain. Chester's Dee Stakes and the Vase were won by geldings (ineligible for the Derby) in small fields, and the listed Glasgow Stakes over the Dante course and distance maintained its record of having attracted a field bigger than six only once since Commander In Chief used it as a stepping stone to Derby success in 1993, York threatening to ditch the race in 2005. A shortage of runners is nothing new in Derby trials—Troy beat seven in two races in 1979—but one benefit of reducing the number of them might be to entice more horses bred to stay beyond a mile back to the Guineas.

The public's lack of familiarity nowadays with many Derby winners beforehand does little for the publicity surrounding the race. America, and half the world it seemed, became engrossed with Smarty Jones in the spring. He was the sixth horse in eight years to win the first two legs of the American Triple Crown, the third leg of which, the Belmont Stakes, was shown live in Britain on satellite station Racing UK. Publicity surrounding the Vodafone Derby at around the same time was humdrum by comparison. Much of it centred on the on-off participation of long-time ante-post favourite Yeats, winner of two trials in small fields in Ireland, and the on-off industrial action by stalls handlers, which threatened to bring about the first tape start to a Derby since 1966 (now that would have made the news!). Epsom's promotional exercise 'Breakfast with the Stars', featuring a gentle workout on the course for a few intended runners in front of the media and invited members of the public, scheduled for the week before the race, had to be cancelled because of an outbreak of the potentially fatal equine disease 'strangles' in a non-racing stable nearby.

Derby week saw the publication of a newspaper article by outspoken trainer Bill O'Gorman, claiming the Derby had 'lost its buzz' and suggesting, among other things, a 'young stayers series' for two-year-olds over a mile and a quarter to promote breeding for stamina, and a return to a Wednesday Derby, which, critics of Saturday argue, enjoyed greater exclusivity. Epsom has labelled the idea of a return to the traditional mid-week Derby a 'red-herring, not worth talking about', and it is probably right, since its management has been able to revitalise attendances, dwindling before the switch to a Saturday Derby in 1995, and can anticipate a crowd regularly reaching 100,000, most on the Downs, many of them allowed in free, and admittedly drawn as much through modern marketing which underlines the carnival aspect of Derby Day as much as it promotes the Derby as Europe's richest horserace. Epsom has also taken steps to keep the Derby to the first Saturday in June, avoiding a clash with other major sporting events until at least 2006, though the off-time in 2004 was moved from four o'clock to four twenty, to coincide with half time in an England versus Iceland football friendly, broadcast live on satellite television. Epsom is also committed to improving the viability of the Derby meeting's first day, Oaks day, but switching the Group 2 Temple Stakes from its traditional home at Sandown to Epsom's Friday card proved short-lived, with the race moving back to Sandown in 2005.

Derby Day received a boost when *The Sun*, Britain's biggest selling daily newspaper, declared 'It's Derby Day' on its front page, though the biggest news story of the weekend was the sixtieth anniversary of the D-Day landings, commemorations attended by the Queen, usually at Epsom for the Derby. The front page of the *Racing Post* carried a picture of Frankie Dettori in Godolphin silks, taken over his shoulder from behind, imposed on another picture of the teeming Downs. In the absence of Guineas winner Haafhd, and of Azamour and Grey Swallow, two others who made the frame at Newmarket, Dettori's mount Snow Ridge represented the Guineas form after his good second, and he started joint favourite at 7/2 to give his rider a first Derby winner. In a field of fourteen, North Light was also at 7/2, with American Post, the first French-trained runner in five years, at 13/2 after his somewhat fortuitous win in the Poule d'Essai des Poulains. Percussionist, wide margin winner of the four-runner Lingfield Derby Trial in North Light's absence, was at 7/1, with Guineas sixth Salford City at 8/1 and the well-backed Pukka at 10/1. Gatwick and Hazyview, both supplemented for £75,000, were among the others.

North Light looked in fine shape and was full of beans to post, Fallon sensibly pulling him up six furlongs from the stalls and walking him the rest of the way. North Light certainly lived up to the traditions of the race, showing the best blend of speed and stamina on the day. Drawn six, North Light was soon second as Yeats' stand-in Meath set a good pace. North Light's extravagant action had raised doubts beforehand as to whether he would handle the course, but, even on ground slightly firmer than the official good, North Light was full of running on the descent to Tattenham Corner. Pushed to the front three furlongs out, North Light briefly had

Vodafone Derby Stakes, Epsom—
inside the final furlong, North Light looks in no danger of being pegged back;
Rule of Law (white cap) and Let The Lion Roar (visor) are making good late headway on the outside
to overtake Percussionist (spots on cap), Salford City (striped cap) and American Post (rail)

Vodafone Derby Stakes, Epsom—at the finish,
North Light gives Sir Michael Stoute and Kieren Fallon their second successive win in the race;
Rule of Law is partially hidden by the winner and Let The Lion Roar is on the left

American Post in his slipstream going well, but soon shook him off. As Fallon finally picked up his whip in earnest a furlong and a half out, North Light continued to run on strongly, despite changing his legs once, and, though Percussionist and Salford City flattered either side of him, he was never threatened. The strong-finishing Rule of Law was a length and a half back at the line, with Let The Lion Roar, also finishing well a further head away, completing the same one, two, three as the Dante. Percussionist finished a head behind Let The Lion Roar in fourth. Following the previous Derby successes of Shergar, Shahrastani and Kris Kin, Sir Michael Stoute equalled Henry Cecil's tally of four, the pair two behind Vincent O'Brien, the most successful post-war Derby trainer. Stoute became the second trainer, after Aidan O'Brien, to win the Derby in successive years since Dick Hern in 1980.

Fallon returned to the winner's enclosure with three fingers raised in salute. The man sometimes referred to in the saddle as 'the assassin' has executed his job well from seven mounts in the Derby, his successes on Oath in 1999 and Kris Kin in 2003 coming on the only others to start at shorter than 25/1. Fallon, who also won the Oaks on Ouija Board, was the first since Willie Carson on Troy and Henbit to win the Derby two years in a row, but he chose to mimic Lester Piggott afterwards when asked when he thought he had the race won, replying 'about three weeks ago,' a quote borrowed, as Fallon confessed, from Piggott's success on Sir Ivor in the Washington International in 1968. With the Queen absent, Piggott was the most famously enduring face at Epsom on Derby Day, signing copies of his book *Lester's Derbys*, which provides some timely reminders of the publicity Piggott brought to the race over a long period, from his first win as an eighteen-year-old on Never Say Die fifty years ago to his last Derby ride in 1994. 'I'll need a gun to stop Wollow' was the headline reproduced in the book from the back page of the *Evening Standard* before the seventh of the nine wins by 'the housewives' choice' on Empery in 1976. Fallon's own third success came in the wake of charges of 'bringing racing into disrepute', a story covered in the essay on Gamut, publicity which can't have helped betting turnover on the Derby which had been widely considered to have been boosted by the 'Fallon factor' in the gamble on Kris Kin in

2003. That year, the Derby regained second place behind the Grand National in the list of the year's top betting races. Viewing figures for the Derby in 2004 on the BBC did not match the surge in numbers that had watched the 2004 Grand National, rising only slightly to 3.1m from three million in 2003, though still nearly double the numbers that watched Best Mate's historic third win in the Cheltenham Gold Cup in March and higher than the 2.4m that viewed the 2001 Derby, the last on Channel 4. The BBC, which extended its contract for the Derby until 2009 in May, once again dedicated its flagship sports programme to the race, drawing praise for its greater focus on the Derby itself, as opposed to the trappings of the day, coverage again including a preview show on Friday night and highlights late on Saturday.

As he stood unsaddled in the winner's circle at Epsom, North Light was surrounded by three generations of the female side of the Weinstock family, providing a poignant moment. Lord Arnold Weinstock, for many years chairman of GEC, died aged seventy-seven in 2002, when North Light was a yearling, six years after the death of his son Simon, another key figure in the Ballymacoll Stud operation, which had been acquired, along with one hundred and thirty horses, including broodmares, for £250,000 by Lord Weinstock and his father-in-law Sir Michael Sobell in 1960. Ballymacoll Stud has bred twenty-five Group 1 winners, most of which have carried the same pale blue colours worn by North Light, including Troy, the 1983 Oaks and St Leger winner Sun Princess and 2001 Two Thousand Guineas winner Golan, the last-named also trained by Sir Michael Stoute. North Light's Derby was a particular triumph for Ballymacoll given that it also bred Snow Ridge, sold to Godolphin at the end of his two-year-old career, and also Ballerina, the dam of third-placed Let The Lion Roar. Ballymacoll Stud headed the breeders' table in Britain the year Troy won the Derby, ahead of Lord Howard de Walden, with the Queen fourth. Times change, but, interestingly in view of the debate on the over-emphasis of breeding for speed, the leading sires in Britain and Ireland that year were Petingo (Troy's sire), Habitat, Sharpen Up, Sallust and Thatch, all milers.

Troy was magnificent on Derby Day, winning by seven lengths, but North Light was only an average Derby winner on form, though he scored with authority and his timefigure of 0.99 fast (equivalent to a timerating of 125) provided confirmation of the level of his ability on the day. As a lightly-raced colt from a late-maturing family, there seemed the promise of better to come. North Light reportedly took the race in his stride, and he started at 11/8-on in a field of ten for the Irish Derby the following month, attempting to follow in the footsteps of Sinndar, Galileo and High Chaparral, the last three to tackle the double. The form of the Derby proves reliable more often than not, and North Light beat those reopposing from Epsom, but he couldn't become the fifteenth Derby winner to complete the double since the Irish Derby became a race of major international significance in the 'sixties. On ground firmer than the official good to firm, North Light was pushed along sooner than at Epsom and, though he led under two furlongs out, he went down by half a length, rallying at the finish, to Grey Swallow. North Light finished a length and a half ahead of Tycoon, with Rule of Law fourth, Let The Lion Roar fifth and Percussionist tailed-off last.

While Derby winners contesting the Guineas beforehand have become a rarity, there has been no knock-on benefit for the St Leger, the third leg of the triple crown, Reference Point in 1987 the last Derby winner to go on to Doncaster. North Light was made a 10/1-shot in early St Leger betting, which reflected the slim prospect of his running, rather than his chance of winning. His odds were down to as low as 5/1, though, before connections announced at the end of July that Doncaster was not on the agenda. Ballymacoll Stud manager Peter Reynolds was quoted as saying 'Sun Princess won the Leger but Lord Weinstock always said it cost her the Arc.' Winning the Arc would be the crowning glory in racing for the Weinstock family, whose colours have also been carried to victory in the King George, and have been associated with a run of good efforts at Longchamp. Weinstock horses have been placed six times in the Arc, with Homeric (1972), Troy (1979), Ela-Mana-Mou (1980), closest of them when beaten only half a length when third behind Detroit, Sun Princess (1983) and Pilsudski (1996 and 1997). Golan, fourth after being runner-up in the Derby, won the Prix Niel on the way, but North Light went straight to Longchamp from the Curragh. Reportedly 'lame on his right hind after Ireland, after which the muscles on his quarters were very sore', North Light

Ballymacoll Stud's "North Light"

had missed the King George and needed further physiotherapy when the injury flared up again later in the summer. After appearing between races on a day at Newmarket in September when the ground was too firm for him to do more than breeze along, North Light completed his preparation at home and looked in magnificent shape on Arc day, starting second favourite at just over 5/1 behind the surprise favourite, Prix du Jockey Club runner-up Prospect Park. Bustled along to secure the early lead, North Light was soon taken on, not surprisingly in a field of nineteen, the Japanese-trained Tap Dance City harrying him for the lead from a long way out. With Fallon keen to keep his place against the rail, North Light began to race in earnest well before the straight and, though he stuck to his task well in the circumstances (Fallon arguably guilty of overdoing things) as Tap Dance City dropped away tamely from the turn, he was swallowed up under two furlongs out, edging left a little as he held on for fifth, three and a half lengths behind the winner Bago, two lengths behind third-placed Ouija Board. North Light's form was a little below that which he showed in the Derby and Irish Derby.

North Light ended the season the fourth best three-year-old in Europe at a mile and a half, behind Bago, Arc runner-up Cherry Mix and Grey Swallow. As a matter of interest, North Light was also a little inferior among his age group to Haafhd, Azamour and Lucky Story. He was the second Derby winner running, following Kris Kin, to end the season without another win, but, unlike Kris Kin, he remains in training at four, joining Henbit, Teenoso, Slip Anchor, Quest For Fame, High-Rise and High Chaparral among the others to do so in the last twenty-five years. Among those, only Teenoso and High Chaparral added significantly to their reputations, Teenoso winning the King George and High Chaparral the Irish Champion Stakes, over a mile and a quarter, and dead-heating to earn a second

723

Breeders' Cup Turf. Forcing the pace, North Light probably has fair prospects of winning a Group 1 at a mile and a quarter himself, particularly on testing going, though, equally, he will stay beyond a mile and a half, in the unlikely event of his being required to do so. His dam Sought Out was a front runner, ideally suited by soft ground, and a renowned tail swisher, a trait North Light shows slight signs of himself, though, like his dam, he has proved thoroughly genuine. Still lightly raced, North Light is the first Derby winner his trainer has had as a four-year-old, and, not surprisingly, given his patient approach, Stoute has a reputation for excelling with older horses.

Among Derby winners in the 'seventies, Nijinsky and Mill Reef went on to have exceptional careers at stud, and Shirley Heights a good one, all of them siring at least one Derby winner as well. Nijinsky was responsible for Golden Fleece, Shahrastani and Lammtarra. Derby winners since have had nothing like a comparable record, several in the 'nineties being sold to Japan, including Generous after making a promising start, siring nearly forty horses rated 100+ in *Racehorses* in his first four crops. Generous is back in Europe now, along with Erhaab and High-Rise, the latest to return from Japan. Sinndar made a slow start with his first crop and following on, to try to pick up the baton, are Galileo, whose yearlings sold well in 2004, then High Chaparral, who, like Galileo, has the considerable backing of Coolmore. North Light's Derby success was a fitting tribute to his sire Danehill, fatally injured in a paddock at Coolmore in May 2003 when already at the top of the tree as a sire in Australia and second only to Sadler's Wells in Europe. Danehill's only other British classic success has been Guineas winner Rock of Gibraltar, though Danehill will have three-year-old runners until 2007. Danehill's first important winner in the northern hemisphere was Desert King, successful in the Irish Guineas and Irish Derby in 1997, and he has also had two winners of the Poule d'Essai des Poulains in Clodovil and Landseer. Danehill is unusual among sires of Derby winners in that he showed his best form at sprint distances—Ahonoora, responsible for Dr Devious in 1992, had previously been the first sprinter to sire an Epsom Derby winner since 1958—but Danehill did finish a close third also to Nashwan in the Guineas before winning the Haydock Sprint Cup. Danehill's sire Danzig was a strong influence for speed himself, though he is also grandsire of the 1994 Derby winner Erhaab, through his son Chief's Crown, and the great grandsire of Sinndar, through Chief's Crown's son Grand Lodge. Through his son Danewin, Danehill was the grandsire of Queensland Derby winner Toulouse Lautrec in 2004 in Australia, where Danehill was one of the Coolmore stallions at the forefront of the shuttle boom.

North Light (IRE) (b.c. 2001)	Danehill (USA) (b 1986)	Danzig (b 1977)	Northern Dancer
			Pas de Nom
		Razyana (b 1981)	His Majesty
			Spring Adieu
	Sought Out (IRE) (b 1988)	Rainbow Quest (b 1981)	Blushing Groom
			I Will Follow
		Edinburgh (b 1974)	Charlottown
			Queen's Castle

Ballymacoll Stud has been renowned over the years as one of the few not to make wholesale concessions to the fashionable trend of breeding for speed, with many of its best horses bred for and suited by middle distances. On the dam's side, North Light traces back to Coventry Belle, one of two foundation mares of the stud. Coventry Belle is the grandam of Country House, dam of Ballymacoll's first top-class horse of the Sobell/Weinstock era Reform, one of the most popular performers of his day and the best three-year-old miler of 1967, when his wins also included the Champion Stakes. Country House is the grandam of Edinburgh, a smart two-year-old in France, winning the Prix des Reservoirs over a mile. Edinburgh is the dam of several significant broodmares at Ballymacoll, including Greektown, dam of the five-year-old Gamut, and Scots Lass, the grandam of Ballymacoll's most recent King George winner Golan. Edinburgh is also North Light's grandam. Neither Edinburgh nor her dam Queen's Castle raced at much beyond a mile and a quarter, but, sent to Rainbow Quest—sire of the dam of Kris Kin as well as sire of 1994 Derby winner Quest For Fame—Edinburgh produced the out-and-out stayer Sought Out, winner of the Prix du Cadran over two and a half miles, as well as the Prix Kergorlay, as a four-year-old for John Hammond in France after being third in the Ribblesdale Stakes and winning the Prix de Lutece for Sir Michael Stoute as a three-year-old. Sought Out's first foal Treasure Chest (by Last Tycoon), an unreliable dual-purpose performer, was finally successful on the Flat over two miles as a six-year-old, and her second Hidden Bounty (by Generous) is a fairly useful staying hurdler/chaser. Sought Out's third foal, Cover Up (by Machiavellian), also took after his dam, winning the Ascot Stakes and two editions of the Queen Alexandra Stakes, Britain's longest Flat race, showing smart form. Sought Out's fifth foal, Researched (by Danehill), developed into a smart four-year-old at up to a mile and three quarters, though doing his winning at a mile and a quarter/a mile and a half. Researched was thought good enough at the time to take his chance in the Chester Vase at three, a sign of things to come perhaps, as Sought Out's next foal, also by Danehill, was North Light. Her 2002 foal Paper Hunt (by Indian Danehill) died as a yearling, and her 2003 filly foal by Kalanisi is in training with Stoute. Many of the Ballymacoll stock are fine-looking animals, and North Light is no exception. His great grandsire Northern Dancer now appears on the sires' side in the extended pedigrees of fifteen Derby winners, including Nijinsky, who was from his first crop. North Light was no Nijinsky on Derby Day, nor a Troy, but he was a splendid sight all the same as he tackled the historic course and distance. *Sir Michael Stoute*

NORTH POINT (IRE)   6 b.g. Definite Article 121 – Friendly Song 48 (Song 132)   **48**
[2004 65: 11.9m 17.2f 11.9f⁴ Jun 29] smallish, useful-looking gelding: poor handicapper: stays easy 2m: acts on firm and good to soft going: tried in headgear. *R. Curtis*

NORTH SEA (IRE)   3 b.f. Selkirk (USA) 129 – Sea Spray (IRE) 101 (Royal Academy   **60**
(USA) 130) [2004 –p: 9.7s 8m Jun 19] tall, quite good-topped filly: modest maiden, lightly raced: should stay 1¼m. *M. R. Channon*

NORTH SHORE (IRE)   2 b.c. (Apr 26) Soviet Star (USA) 128 – Escape Path (Wolver   **75**
Hollow 126) [2004 7m⁶ 8m⁵ 6d Oct 4] 37,000Y: tall, quite-good topped colt: half-brother to 3 winners, including smart 5f (at 2 yrs) to 7f winner Sergeyev (by Mulhollande) and useful 1999 2-y-o 7f winner Michele Marieschi (by Alzao): dam maiden half-sister to William Hill Futurity winner Sandy Creek: best effort in maidens when fifth at Doncaster: veered left start final outing: stays 1m. *R. Hannon*

NORTHSIDE LODGE (IRE)   6 b.g. Grand Lodge (USA) 125 – Alongside 58 (Slip   **84**
Anchor 136) [2004 91: p10g² p10g² p10g p10g³ 10.1s 10.3d 10m³ 10m⁵ 12g² 12g 12.3d   **a95**
11.9f 12m⁵ 10d p10g⁵ p10g² p9.5g² p10m⁶ Dec 22] good-topped gelding: useful handicapper on all-weather, fairly useful on turf: placed 7 times in 2004: effective at 1¼m (all 8 wins)/1½m: acts on polytrack and firm going, below form on softer than good: won in blinkers in 2001. *W. R. Swinburn*

NORTON (IRE)   7 ch.g. Barathea (IRE) 127 – Primrose Valley 99 (Mill Reef (USA)   **103**
141) [2004 113: 8g 8g⁵ 10.1s 8v⁴ 8f 8d 7.1d³ 8.1d* 8m 8d Oct 30] strong, useful-looking gelding: smart handicapper at best, useful nowadays: won at Sandown (beat Literatim by ¾ length, dictating pace) in August: effective at 7f to 10.4f: acts on polytrack, firm and soft going: visored (found little) sixth start: effective held up or making running: game. *T. G. Mills*

NORTON ROSE   2 ch.f. (Mar 18) Dr Fong (USA) 128 – Bonica 56 (Rousillon (USA)   **49**
133) [2004 6s f7g p7.1g p7.1g⁶ Dec 10] 7,500Y: half-sister to several winners, including fairly useful 6f to 1¼m winner Bacchus (by Prince Sabo): dam, maiden, half-sister to smart performer up to 1m Chipaya: poor maiden: should stay 1m. *T. J. Fitzgerald*

NORWEGIAN   3 b.c. Halling (USA) 133 – Chicarica (USA) 112 (The Minstrel (CAN)   **75**
135) [2004 f8.5g⁵ f8s* p10g⁴ p8g³ 8m May 15] good-topped colt: sixth living foal: half-brother to 3 winners, including 2001 2-y-o 5f winner Morouj (by Gone West) and 6f (at 2 yrs) and 1m (in France) winner Court Lane (by Machiavellian), both fairly useful: dam won Cherry Hinton Stakes: fair performer: won maiden at Southwell in January: stays 1m: acts on fibresand: visored last 2 starts: sold 9,000 gns. *D. R. Loder*

NOSSENKO (USA)   3 b.f. Stravinsky (USA) 133 – Humble Fifteen (USA) (Feather   **?**
Ridge (USA)) [2004 –p: p6g² 8.5f a8.5f⁵ a6f³ a7f* a6.5f⁴ a6f5 a6f⁵ a8f a6f⁶ Dec 3] modest form when second in maiden at Lingfield in January: left J. Noseda 14,000 gns before next outing: won maiden at Del Mar in July: claimed out of J. Cassidy's stable $16,000 after next start: stays 7f: acts on dirt/polytrack, well held only outing on turf: blinkered last 8 appearances. *R. Becerra, USA*

NOSTRADAMUS (USA) 5 b. or br.g. Gone West (USA) – Madam North (CAN) (Halo (USA)) [2004 16.2g Aug 7] close-coupled, good-topped gelding: useful form at 3 yrs when trained by A. O'Brien: tailed off at Ascot only 5-y-o outing: stays 1¼m. *K. Burke, Ireland* –

NOTA BENE 2 b.c. (Apr 23) Zafonic (USA) 130 – Dodo (IRE) 90 (Alzao (USA) 117) [2004 6g² 6g* 6s* Oct 29] 14,000Y: strong colt: third foal: half-brother to 4-y-o Tarjman and 3-y-o Porthcawl: dam, 6f winner, out of very smart but temperamental sprinter Dead Certain: won maiden at Windsor and minor event at Newmarket (contest for 2- and 3-y-os, by neck from Word Perfect despite idling/carrying head high), both in October: will stay 7f: useful prospect. *D. R. C. Elsworth* **94 p**

NOTABILITY (IRE) 2 b.c. (May 20) King's Best (USA) 132 – Noble Rose (IRE) 113 (Caerleon (USA) 132) [2004 8d 7g² 8g* Oct 10] quite good-topped colt: fifth living foal: half-brother to fairly useful 2002 2-y-o 6f winner Illustria (by Seeking The Gold) and UAE 1¼m winner Riordan (by Theatrical): dam, 7f (at 2 yrs) to 14.6f (Park Hill Stakes) winner, half-sister to smart 1¼m/1½m performer Simeon: best effort in maidens when winning at Bath by 1½ lengths from Rain Stops Play, quickening to lead 1f out: should stay 1¼m. *M. A. Jarvis* **85**

NOTABLE GUEST (USA) 3 b.c. Kingmambo (USA) 125 – Yenda 116 (Dancing Brave (USA) 140) [2004 91p: 10s⁵ 10g³ 9.2f* Jul 31] strong, useful-looking colt: has a quick action: 10/1-on, comfortably won maiden at Hamilton: best effort when 2¾ lengths third to Into The Dark in handicap at Newmarket previous start: will stay 1½m: acts on firm ground, below form on soft: remains capable of better. *Sir Michael Stoute* **95 p**

NOT AMUSED (UAE) 4 ch.g. Indian Ridge 123 – Amusing Time (IRE) 104 (Sadler's Wells (USA) 132) [2004 85: 11.7s Oct 19] big, lengthy gelding: fairly useful at 3 yrs, tailed off only 4-y-o outing: sometimes races freely/carries head awkwardly. *Ian Williams* –

NOT DECENT (IRE) 2 b.g. (Apr 22) Desert Style (IRE) 121 – My Trelawny (IRE) 78 (Dowsing (USA) 124) [2004 f7g f7g Dec 14] tongue tied, well held in sellers at Southwell. *N. Tinkler* –

NOTHING DAUNTED 7 ch.g. Selkirk (USA) 129 – Khubza 86 (Green Desert (USA) 127) [2004 56: 6d Jun 25] quite attractive gelding: one-time useful handicapper: well held only 7-y-o outing. *T. A. K. Cuthbert* –

NOTHING MATTERS 3 b.f. Foxhound (USA) 103 – Dawn Alarm 47 (Warning 136) [2004 43: p8g⁶ p8g f7f Jan 22] rather leggy filly: maiden: little form at 3 yrs. *P. R. Chamings* –

NO TIME (IRE) 4 b.c. Danetime (IRE) 121 – Muckross Park 41 (Nomination 125) [2004 105, a96: p6g⁶ f6g⁶ p7g⁶ p5g² p5g* p5g⁵ 5g 5g 6m 5m p6g f5g p6g Dec 18] smallish, good-topped colt: useful on all-weather, just fairly useful at best on turf in 2004: won handicap and minor event at Lingfield in February/March, latter by short head from Speed Cop: effective at 5f/6f: acts on firm and good to soft going, and dirt/polytrack, probably not on fibresand: has flashed tail: usually races prominently. *M. J. Polglase* **82 a106**

NOTJUSTAPRETTYFACE (USA) 2 b. or br.f. (Mar 23) Red Ransom (USA) – Maudie May (USA) (Gilded Time (USA)) [2004 5g⁵ 5.2g⁴ 6s⁴ 5d Sep 17] 45,000 2-y-o: sturdy filly: has a quick action: second foal: dam, 8.5f winner in USA, half-sister to smart 1994 2-y-o Sri Pekan (by Red Ransom): useful performer: won maiden at Kempton in July: good fourth in listed race at Newbury and Lowther Stakes (beaten 4 lengths by Soar) at York: possibly amiss final start: will prove best at 5f/6f: acts on soft going. *H. Morrison* **98**

NOTNOWCATO 2 ch.c. (Mar 25) Inchinor 119 – Rambling Rose 111 (Cadeaux Genereux 131) [2004 7.1m² 7g³ Sep 29] lengthy, well-made colt: second foal: dam 1m (at 2 yrs) and 1½m winner: fair form in maiden at Warwick and minor event (third to Sudden Dismissal) at Salisbury: will stay at least 1m. *Sir Michael Stoute* **83**

NOT SO DUSTY 4 b.g. Primo Dominie 121 – Ann's Pearl (IRE) 81 (Cyrano de Bergerac 120) [2004 93: p5g⁶ p5.1g Dec 4] sturdy, quite attractive gelding: fairly useful performer: should prove best at 5f: acts on all-weather and good to firm going: blinkered final start at 3 yrs. *P. J. Makin* **82**

NOUL (USA) 5 ch.g. Miswaki (USA) 124 – Water Course (USA) (Irish River (FR) 131) [2004 74, a82: f9.4g f9.4g² f12g⁵ 10.3g⁵ 12.4v⁵ 9.2g Apr 26] sturdy gelding: only modest form in 2004: barely stays 9.4f: acts on fibresand, soft and good to firm going: wears blinkers/cheekpieces: waited with. *K. A. Ryan* **64**

NOUNOU 3 b.c. Starborough 126 – Watheeqah (USA) 60 (Topsider (USA)) [2004 7s f7g⁵ 10.2m 7.1g 9.7g⁵ 12g⁵ 12g⁵ 11.9s⁵ Oct 15] 15,000F, 30,000Y: quite good-topped colt: fourth foal: dam 5f winner: fair performer: won apprentice handicaps at Folkestone in August and Epsom in October: stays 1½m: best efforts on good ground. *D. J. Daly* **75**

NOUVEAU RICHE (IRE)   3 ch.f. Entrepreneur 123 – Dime Bag 87 (High Line 125)   **84**
[2004 8g² 8m³ 8.3f* 8d² 8.1g³ 10.5s⁵ Sep 25] 47,000Y: sturdy filly: half-sister to several
winners, including maiden 6f (at 2 yrs) to 1m winner Guys And Dolls (by Efisio) and 7-y-o
Pawn Broker: dam 1½m to 2m winner: fairly useful performer: won maiden at Windsor
in July: good efforts in handicaps after: stays 1¼m: yet to race on heavy ground, acts on
any other: edgy final start. *H. Morrison*

NOVA TOR (IRE)   2 b.f. (Apr 24) Trans Island 119 – Nordic Living (IRE) 53 (Nordico   **86**
(USA)) [2004 f5g⁴ 5d* 5m 5.1d⁴ 5.1g* 6m⁵ 5f⁴ 6.1m 5g* 5d³ 5g 6.3g⁶ 6g f5g Dec 7]
€5,000Y: strong, close-coupled filly: half-sister to several winners, including 7-y-o Alfie
Lee and 5.5f (in USA) to 7f (at 2 yrs) winner Sylvan Girl (by Case Law): dam ran 4 times
in Ireland: fairly useful performer: won maiden at Southwell in April, claimer at Thirsk
(then left P. Haslam) in May and nurseries at Chester in July and Newmarket in August:
best at 5f: acts on fibresand, firm and good to soft going: tried in cheekpieces: usually
races up with pace. *N. P. Littmoden*

NOVELINA (IRE)   2 b.f. (May 4) Fusaichi Pegasus (USA) 130 – Novelette (Darshaan   **57 p**
133) [2004 p8.6d³ Nov 5] second foal: dam, French 1m winner, sister to useful dam of
very smart 1m/1¼m performer Best of the Bests: 9/1, third to Maggie Tulliver in maiden
at Wolverhampton: should improve. *W. J. Haggas*

NOWADAY (GER)   2 b.g. (Mar 2) Dashing Blade 117 – Notre Dame (GER) (Acate-   **61**
nango (GER) 127) [2004 6d 7.5g⁶ 7.5d⁶ 7d Aug 27] €20,000Y: quite good-topped
gelding: first foal: dam, German 11f/1½m winner, half-sister to smart German middle-
distance performer Noroit: modest maiden: best effort penultimate start: will probably be
suited by 1¼m/1½m. *T. P. Tate*

NOW AND AGAIN   5 b.g. Shaamit (IRE) 127 – Sweet Allegiance 59 (Alleging (USA)   **55**
120) [2004 f8g³ f7g⁴ f9.4g³ p7.1g³ p8.6g³ p10m f8g p10g³ Dec 20] showed little in
bumpers/over hurdles: modest maiden: left M. Easterby prior to fourth start: stays 8.6f:
acts on fibresand. *I. W. McInnes*

NOWELL HOUSE   8 ch.g. Polar Falcon (USA) 126 – Langtry Lady 91 (Pas de Seul   **83**
133) [2004 88, a73: f12g⁶ 11.9s⁶ May 11] smallish, lengthy gelding: fairly useful   **a?**
handicapper on turf, fair on all-weather: stays 13f: best form on good ground or softer:
visored (well below form) once: has pulled hard/carried head awkwardly/wandered.
M. W. Easterby

NOW LOOK AWAY (IRE)   3 b.g. Dushyantor (USA) 123 – Where's Carol 67   **–**
(Anfield 117) [2004 10.5g f8g Dec 7] well beaten in maidens at Haydock (slowly away)
and Southwell. *B. A. McMahon*

NUFOOS   2 b.f. (Feb 4) Zafonic (USA) 130 – Desert Lynx (IRE) 79 (Green Desert   **101**
(USA) 127) [2004 5d³ 6m* 6m 6m 5s* 6s² 6g² Oct 9] 100,000F: good-topped filly: third
foal: half-sister to 4-y-o Valiant Romeo and 3-y-o Neon Blue: dam, 6f winner, half-sister
to smart sprinter Watching: useful performer: won maiden at Leicester in May and
nursery at Beverley in August: good efforts in Firth of Clyde Stakes (third, promoted a
place, to Golden Legacy) at Ayr and listed race (1¼ lengths second to Moth Ball) at York
last 2 starts: likely to stay 7f: acts on soft and good to firm ground: game. *M. Johnston*

NUIT SOMBRE (IRE)   4 b.g. Night Shift (USA) – Belair Princess (USA) (Mr   **72**
Prospector (USA)) [2004 99: 8.1d 8.1s⁵ 8.1d⁴ 8m⁶ Jun 13] good-topped gelding: just fair
handicapper in 2004: effective at 1m to 10.4f: acts on firm and good to soft ground: ran
poorly both starts in blinkers: often finishes weakly: joined N. Henderson, won novice
hurdle in November. *M. Johnston*

NUKHBAH (USA)   3 b.f. Bahri (USA) 125 – El Nafis (USA) 73 (Kingmambo (USA)   **73 d**
125) [2004 75: 8.3s³ 8.1s⁴ 9.1f⁵ 10m 8.1g p9.5g f12g Dec 28] leggy filly: fair maiden at
best: left Lady Herries 8,000 gns prior to fifth start: may prove best around 1m: acts on
soft going. *A. G. Newcombe*

NUMERO DUE   2 b.c. (Mar 13) Sinndar (IRE) 134 – Kindle (Selkirk (USA) 129)   **72**
[2004 10g⁶ 8.2v³ Oct 20] 10,000Y: compact colt: first foal: dam, French maiden who
stayed 9.5f, half-sister to smart stayer Arden: better effort when third of 5 in minor event
at Nottingham: will be suited by 1½m+. *G. M. Moore*

NUMITAS (GER)   4 b.c. Lomitas 129 – Narola (GER) (Nebos (GER) 129) [2004 102:   **95**
18.7d 20f Jun 15] leggy, workmanlike colt: useful performer: creditable eighth to Anak
Pekan in Chester Cup on reappearance: poor effort in Ascot Stakes only other 4-y-o start:
stays 18.7f. acts on firm and good to soft going: sometimes races freely: sold 20,000 gns
in November: fairly useful hurdler. *P. J. Hobbs*

Golan EBF Mooresbridge Stakes, the Curragh—
Nysaean records his second successive win in the race at the chief expense of Latino Magic and Akshar

NUMPTY (IRE) 3 b.g. Intikhab (USA) 135 – Atsuko (IRE) (Mtoto 134) [2004 –: **39** f6g⁵ f6s⁵ p10g 10g 8s f7g⁶ May 19] strong gelding: poor maiden: stays 6f: tongue tied. *N. Tinkler*

NUNKI (USA) 3 ch.g. Kingmambo (USA) 125 – Aqua Galinte (USA) (Kris S (USA)) **91** [2004 10d³ 10.5m* 10.4m 10.1g 10g⁴ 10v³ Oct 20] smallish, good-topped gelding: first foal: dam unraced out of smart French miler Hydro Calido, herself half-sister to Machiavellian and Exit To Nowhere: fairly useful performer: won maiden at Haydock in May: good fourth to Honorine in handicap at Nottingham penultimate start: raced only around 1¼m: acts on good to firm ground, probably on heavy: visored last 2 starts: sold 26,000 gns. *H. R. A. Cecil*

NUTLEY QUEEN (IRE) 5 b.m. Eagle Eyed (USA) 111 – Secret Hideaway (USA) **54** (Key To The Mint (USA)) [2004 59d: 10d 8v 12g 7f 10g⁶ p10g² Dec 20] 9,000Y: half-sister to several winners, including useful 6f (at 2 yrs) and 1m winner Lagoon (by Common Grounds): dam unraced: modest maiden: left J. Gorman in Ireland before final start: stays 1¼m: acts on polytrack, good to firm and good to soft going: tried in blinkers/ cheekpieces. *C. N. Kellett*

NUTS FOR YOU (IRE) 3 b.f. Sri Pekan (USA) 117 – Moon Festival 74 (Be My **72** Guest (USA) 126) [2004 67: 10.2m* p12.2g Oct 2] lengthy filly: fair performer: won handicap at Chepstow in September: upped in trip, well below form in similar event at Wolverhampton, taking good hold: stays 1¼m: sold 22,000 gns. *R. Charlton*

NUTTY TIMES 2 ch.f. (Apr 24) Timeless Times (USA) 99 – Nuthatch (IRE) 36 **51** (Thatching 131) [2004 f5g² f5g³ 5.1g³ 5g f6g 5.1f Jul 5] 800Y: sister to 5f (at 2 yrs) and 1m winner Algunas Veces: dam, maiden, should have stayed 1m: modest maiden: likely to prove best at 5f/6f. *W. G. M. Turner*

NUZOOA (USA) 3 b. or br.f. A P Indy (USA) 131 – Min Alhawa (USA) 108 (River- **99** man (USA) 131) [2004 83p: 10m* 12g⁵ 10.1g 10.1g 12d* Oct 10] leggy, quite attractive filly: easy mover: useful performer: won maiden at Newbury in June and handicap at Goodwood (beat Sand And Stars 3½ lengths, edging left) in October: stays 1½m: acts on good to firm and good to soft going: blinkered (ran poorly) penultimate start: acts on good to firm and good to soft going: joined K. McLaughlin in USA. *M. P. Tregoning*

NUZZLE 4 b.f. Salse (USA) 128 – Lena (USA) (Woodman (USA) 126) [2004 70§: f8g **52 §** f9.4g p10g 11.7g⁵ p10g 10.5m² 10.2f⁶ 10m 8f³ 8f 8m³ 10.3g 10.2m 10m p8.6g⁵ Oct 25] good-topped filly: modest performer: stays 1¼m: acts on all-weather and firm going: sometimes visored: usually races prominently/freely: unreliable. *M. Quinn*

NYRAMBA 3 b.f. Night Shift (USA) – Maramba 97 (Rainbow Quest (USA) 134) [2004 **107** 107: 7g² 8g⁵ 8g⁵ 7m² 6d⁵ 7m⁵ a6.5g³ a7f Dec 27] quite good-topped filly: useful performer: good efforts first 4 starts, including in Dubai Duty Free Stakes (Fred Darling) at Newbury (length second to Majestic Desert), Poule d'Essai des Pouliches at Longchamp (4 lengths fifth to Torrestrella on second start) and Oak Tree Stakes at Goodwood (went down by ½ length to Phantom Wind): below form after, leaving J. Gosden following sixth outing: stays 1m: acts on firm going. *N. D. Drysdale, USA*

NYSAEAN (IRE) 5 b.h. Sadler's Wells (USA) 132 – Irish Arms (FR) (Irish River **118** (FR) 131) [2004 118: 10d⁵ 10g⁴ 10g⁵ 10d² 10g* 10.5m³ 10d⁴ 10d⁵ 12d³ 11m⁶ Sep 17] good-topped horse: carries plenty of condition: smart performer: good neck second to Chancellor in Gordon Richards Stakes at Sandown fourth start: won Golan EBF Mooresbridge Stakes at the Curragh (for second year running, beat Latino Magic comfortably by 2½ lengths) in May: best effort after when respectable third of 4 to Policy Maker in Prix Foy at Longchamp penultimate start: barely stays 1½m: has form on going firmer than good, but probably best on good or softer nowadays: usually races prominently. *R. Hannon*

O

OAKLEY ABSOLUTE 2 ch.c. (Mar 28) Bluegrass Prince (IRE) 110 – Susie Oakley **64** VII (Damsire Unregistered) [2004 7.1s 8g 8v p7m⁴ Dec 22] strong non-thoroughbred colt: fourth known foal: dam unraced: modest maiden: should stay 1m: acts on polytrack. *R. Hannon*

OAKLEY RAMBO 5 br.g. Muhtarram (USA) 125 – Westminster Waltz (Dance In **85 ?** Time (CAN)) [2004 85, a76: 7d⁵ 8.1d 8s⁶ 7s² 7g 8.1g⁶ 7g 8.1s 7s p7.1g Oct 9] leggy **a–** gelding: fairly useful performer: well below form after fourth start: effective at 7f/1m: acts on polytrack and any turf going: sold 3,000 gns. *R. Hannon*

OASES 5 ch.g. Zilzal (USA) 137 – Markievicz (IRE) 73 (Doyoun 124) [2004 68: f7g 6s² **64 §** 6g 6.1v⁶ 6s 7m 6m 7g³ 7.1m⁵ 7m⁶ 7s 7.5d⁴ 7g p7.1d⁵ p7m³ p8m³ p7.1g³ Dec 22] rather **a55 §** leggy, quite good-topped gelding: modest performer: barely stays 1m: acts on polytrack, heavy and good to firm going: sometimes wears headgear: usually slowly away: unreliable. *D. Shaw*

OASIS STAR (IRE) 3 b.f. Desert King (IRE) 129 – Sound Tap (IRE) (Warning 136) **95** [2004 76p: 7g* 7.6d⁴ 8.1m⁵ 7.1m* 7m² 8.2g 7g⁵ 6.5f⁵ 7d Oct 15] good-topped filly: useful performer: won handicaps at Newmarket in April and Chester in May and minor event at Sandown (edged left) in June: mostly creditable efforts after, though probably flattered when 2 lengths fifth to Royal Storm in listed event at Newbury seventh start: barely stays 1m: acts on firm and good to soft going: waited with. *P. W. Harris*

OASIS WAY (GR) 2 b.f. (Feb 13) Wadood (USA) 97 – Northern Moon 76 (Ile de **67** Bourbon (USA) 133) [2004 7g⁵ 8.1m⁵ 6.5g 8.3d⁶ 7s Oct 22] £12,000Y: smallish filly: sister to useful Greek 5f (at 2 yrs) to 9f winner Denebola Way: dam 11.5f winner: fair maiden: stays 1m: acts on good to firm going, probably on soft. *P. R. Chamings*

OATCAKE 2 ch.f. (Apr 7) Selkirk (USA) 129 – Humble Pie 92 (Known Fact (USA) **68 p** 135) [2004 6s³ Nov 6] 2,800Y: leggy filly: sister to 4-y-o Arran and to untrustworthy 7f/ 1m winner Rimatara, closely related to smart sprinter Leap For Joy (by Sharpo) and half-sister to 3 winners, including useful 7f winner (including at 2 yrs) Pie High (by Salse): dam, 2-y-o 6f winner, half-sister to very smart 6f/7f performer College Chapel: 10/1 and bandaged behind, 2 lengths third to Bow Wave in maiden at Doncaster, staying on having run green: should stay 1m: sure to improve. *G. A. Butler*

OBAY 3 ch.g. Kingmambo (USA) 125 – Parade Queen (USA) (A P Indy (USA) 131) **91** [2004 80p: 10d⁴ 12s* 11g⁴ 12m² 11.6f³ 12.1d² 14.1d Sep 17] rangy gelding: has a round action: fairly useful performer: won maiden at Thirsk in April by 11 lengths: mostly creditable efforts after, 3 lengths second to Portrait of A Lady in handicap at Newbury fourth outing: stays 1½m: acts on soft and good to firm going: tried blinkered: sold 28,000 gns, joined B. Powell. *E. A. L. Dunlop*

*betfair.com Two-Year-Old Trophy, Redcar—Obe Gold (visor) denies odds-on Caesar Beware;
they are followed by Dario Gee Gee (noseband), Moth Ball (left, partially hidden by winner)
and Beaver Patrol (star on cap)*

OBE BOLD (IRE)   3 b.f. Orpen (USA) 116 – Capable Kate (IRE) (Alzao (USA) 117)   **73**
[2004 71: f5g⁴ f6d³ 5m 6m² 6g 5d f6g* 5g⁵ 5d 6g⁴ 5m³ 5g 6m* 6.1g 6d 6f⁴ 6s p6d f6g   **a65**
p5.1g Dec 31] small, lengthy filly: fair performer: won claimer at Southwell in June and
handicap at Redcar in August: effective at 5f/6f: acts on fibresand, firm and good to soft
going: tried tongue tied: sometimes slowly away/hangs right. *A. Berry*

OBE GOLD   2 b.c. (Mar 26) Namaqualand (USA) – Gagajulu 75 (Al Hareb (USA) 123)   **104**
[2004 5v³ 5g* 6m⁴ 6m² 7m⁴ 6m 6d³ 6f³ 6g* 6m* 6d² 6s⁵ Oct 29] useful-looking colt: fifth
foal: half-brother to 3-y-o Under My Spell: dam 2-y-o 5f winner: useful performer: won
maiden at Salisbury in May, nursery at Newmarket in September and listed betfair.com
Two-Year-Old Trophy at Redcar (by length from Caesar Beware) in October: also first
past post in Premio Primi Passi at Milan in June (demoted a place for causing interference): good second to Cape Columbine in sales race at Newmarket: stays 6f: acts on good
to firm and good to soft going: visored sixth (unseated rider) and last 4 starts: often races
up with pace: tough. *M. R. Channon*

OBE ONE   4 b.g. Puissance 110 – Plum Bold 83 (Be My Guest (USA) 126) [2004 87:   **74**
5g 6g 6m 6m⁶ 5m⁴ 5.1g 5m² 5g³ 6g 5d⁶ 5g 5g⁴ 6m 5g⁴ 6f⁴ 5m⁵ 6d 5f⁵ p6g Oct 9] leggy
gelding: fair handicapper: effective at 5f/6f: acts on firm going, probably on good to soft:
blinkered final start: usually held up. *A. Berry*

OBEZYANA (USA)   2 ch.c. (Feb 22) Rahy (USA) 115 – Polish Treaty (USA) (Danzig   **71**
(USA)) [2004 8d p8g² Oct 31] $25,000Y, 46,000 2-y-o: sixth foal: dam, won 1m minor
stakes in USA, out of half-sister to 1000 Guineas winner Quick As Lightning: still green,
much better effort in maidens when 5 lengths second to Karen's Caper at Lingfield:
should stay 1¼m. *G. A. Huffer*

OBLIQUE (IRE)   2 b.f. (Apr 25) Giant's Causeway (USA) 132 – On Call 103 (Alleged   **59 p**
(USA) 138) [2004 p7g p7g 6.1v⁴ Nov 4] angular filly: third foal: half-sister to 4-y-o One
Off and 3-y-o Optimal: dam 1½m to 2m winner: modest form in maidens: slowly away
and never dangerous final start: sure to do better at 1¼m+. *Sir Mark Prescott*

OBOE   3 ch.f. Piccolo 121 – Bombay (Be My Chief (USA) 122) [2004 –: p6g p6g p8g⁶   **–**
Apr 19] little form. *T. Keddy*

OBRIGADO (USA)   4 b.g. Bahri (USA) 125 – Glorious Diamond (USA) (His Majesty   **87**
(USA)) [2004 89+: 8m 7f² 7m 7.2g* 8m p7g² p7g Sep 7] big, leggy gelding: fairly useful
performer: won minor event at Ayr in July by neck from Winning Venture, flashing tail:
stays 1m: acts on polytrack, firm and good to soft going: visored fifth start: tends to sweat:
races freely. *W. J. Haggas*

OBSERVATION   3 ch.f. Polish Precedent (USA) 131 – Search Party 78 (Rainbow   **–**
Quest (USA) 134) [2004 9.7s 8.3s 10.2g 12.6d Oct 9] second foal: dam, second at 1m/
1¼m from 3 starts, half-sister to US Grade 1 1¼m winner Bequest: no form in maidens/
claimer, leaving M. Jarvis after second start. *Mrs J. Candlish*

OBSERVER (IRE) 2 b.c. (Feb 23) Distant View (USA) 126 – Virgin Stanza (USA) **76**
(Opening Verse (USA) 126) [2004 5d* 6.1m³ 6g Jul 10] 23,000F, 95,000Y: close-coupled
colt: second foal: dam, 8.5f winner in USA, granddaughter of top-class 1m/1¼m performer Rose Bowl: fair performer: won maiden at Folkestone in April: creditable efforts
after (visored next time): bred to stay 1m: sold 6,000 gns. *D. R. Loder*

OBSTREPEROUS WAY 2 ch.g. (Mar 26) Dr Fong (USA) 128 – Fleet Key (Afleet **35**
(CAN)) [2004 f7g Dec 16] 33/1, tenth in maiden at Southwell, slowly away and green.
P. R. Chamings

OCEAN AVENUE (IRE) 5 b.g. Dolphin Street (FR) 125 – Trinity Hall 67 (Hallgate **92**
127) [2004 86: 12g* 12f 14.4m⁶ 12g* 12g Sep 20] strong gelding: fairly useful handicapper: won at Kempton in May and September, career-best effort when beating Blaze of
Colour by 2 lengths in latter: effective at 1½m to 14.4f: acts on firm going: front runner:
consistent. *C. A. Horgan*

OCEANCOOKIE (IRE) 2 b.f. (Feb 10) Dashing Blade 117 – Sankaty Light (USA) **58 p**
55 (Summer Squall (USA)) [2004 6m⁵ p7g⁵ 6s⁶ Oct 22] 3,600Y: big, unfurnished filly:
second foal: dam maiden who should have stayed beyond 1m: modest form in maidens/
sales race: not knocked about final start: should stay 1m: type to do better as 3-y-o.
A. M. Balding

OCEAN GIFT 2 b.g. (Feb 23) Cadeaux Genereux 131 – Sea Drift (FR) 72 (Warning **85 ?**
136) [2004 6g⁶ 7g⁴ 6g 8d Oct 15] 56,000F: quite good-topped gelding: first foal: dam, 7f
winner, out of useful sprinter Night At Sea: seemingly best effort when never-dangerous
eighth in Mill Reef Stakes at Newbury on third start: fair form in maidens otherwise:
should stay 7f. *D. R. C. Elsworth*

OCEANICO DOT COM (IRE) 2 br.f. (Feb 12) Hernando (FR) 127 – Karen Blixen **75**
(Kris 135) [2004 5.1g 6.1s 5d² 5d* 5g³ 5g* 5g⁶ 6g p6g Nov 8] €10,000Y: small, sturdy
filly: first foal: dam unraced: fair performer: won maiden at Ripon in August and nursery
at Musselburgh in September: last in nursery final start: seems best at 5f: acts on good to
soft going: often races prominently. *A. Berry*

OCEAN OF STORMS (IRE) 9 b. or br.h. Arazi (USA) 135 – Moon Cactus 118 (Kris **85 §**
135) [2004 8f² a10f* 8.5m 12f 10.1g⁴ 11m⁵ 9m² 9.9g a8f a9f⁴ Dec 30] smart in 1999: has
won 4 times at Nad Al Sheba since, including in handicap in April: raced in Britain next 6
starts, second in apprentice handicap at Goodwood: effective at 1m, and stayed 15f earlier
in career: acts on dirt, winner on soft and good to firm ground: often slowly
away (refused to race final outing in 2003): one to treat with caution. *C. Wroe, UAE*

OCEAN ROCK 3 b.c. Perugino (USA) 84 – Polistatic 53 (Free State 125) [2004 –: **63 d**
p12g 10g 10d 12m 12.6d Sep 18] strong, workmanlike colt: maiden: well beaten after
reappearance. *C. A. Horgan*

OCEAN TIDE 7 b.g. Deploy 131 – Dancing Tide (Pharly (FR) 130) [2004 –: f16s³ **79**
18g³ 16g⁴ 16.2v⁴ 18g 18m³ 15.8m⁵ 16.2g² 16.2s⁵ Jul 17] angular gelding: fair handicapper: stays 2¼m: acts on any going: usually visored/blinkered. *R. Ford*

OCHIL HILLS DANCER (IRE) 2 b.f. (Apr 24) Bluebird (USA) 125 – Classic **58**
Dilemma (Sandhurst Prince 128) [2004 5m 6g⁵ 5g 5d⁴ 6f⁵ 5g⁶ 5g 6d Sep 19] €4,000F,
5,000Y, 17,000 2-y-o: half-sister to winners abroad by Soviet Lad and Good Thyne: dam
Irish 2-y-o 6f winner: modest maiden: should stay 7f: acts on good to firm going: tongue
tied last 3 starts. *A. Crook*

OCOTILLO 4 b.g. Mark of Esteem (IRE) 137 – Boojum 101 (Mujtahid (USA) 118) **–**
[2004 57: 10s Oct 12] better effort in maidens 20 months apart when fifth at Lingfield at
3 yrs. *Mrs L. B. Normile*

OCTENNIAL 5 gr.g. Octagonal (NZ) 126 – Laune (AUS) 68 (Kenmare (FR) 125) **– §**
[2004 60§: 6.1s 6.1d Jul 10] leggy gelding: well held in sellers in 2004: tried in visor/
cheekpieces: ungenuine. *C. Smith*

OCTOBER MIST (IRE) 10 gr.g. Roselier (FR) – Bonny Joe (Derring Rose 97) [2004 **76**
68: 12.4v* Apr 3] strong gelding: useful hurdler/fairly useful chaser at best: fair form on
Flat: won maiden at Newcastle in April: will stay at least 1¾m: raced only on going softer
than good. *Mrs M. Reveley*

ODABELLA (IRE) 4 b.f. Selkirk (USA) 129 – Circe's Isle (Be My Guest (USA) **76**
126) [2004 81: 8m³ 8.3d 10m 13.1d⁴ Jun 18] tall, useful-looking filly: fair maiden: stays
1¼m: acts on polytrack and good to firm going: tongue tied final start. *John Berry*

ODDSMAKER (IRE) 3 b.g. Barathea (IRE) 127 – Archipova (IRE) (Ela-Mana-Mou **93**
132) [2004 74: 8.1s³ 10s² 12.3d⁵ 7.9d* 8m 8m* 8.1g⁵ 8g³ 7f 9.9m 10.3m 8s⁶ Sep 18]

angular gelding: fairly useful performer: won handicap at York in May and minor event at Doncaster (beat Devant by 1½ lengths) in June: third to Diamond Lodge in handicap at Newmarket, best effort after: effective at 1m/1¼m: acts on soft and good to firm going: tried in cheekpieces/blinkers at 2 yrs: usually takes strong hold: sometimes hangs. *P. D. Evans*

ODIHAM 3 b.g. Deploy 131 – Hug Me 96 (Shareef Dancer (USA) 135) [2004 77p: 10d* 12m 12g⁴ 11.9g 11.8g⁵ 12s⁴ Oct 23] tall, leggy gelding: fairly useful handicapper: won at Sandown in June by 2 lengths from Keelung: mostly creditable efforts after, though flicked tail at Leicester penultimate start: should stay at least 1¾m: acts on soft going: has been bandaged hind joints. *H. Morrison*   **93**

OEUF A LA NEIGE 4 b.g. Danehill (USA) 126 – Reine de Neige 96 (Kris 135) [2004 76: 6d⁵ 7m 6m⁶ 6m* 6.9m⁵ 6g 5.7g* 6d* 5g⁵ 6g 6s p7.1g⁴ p6g⁴ p6g p8.6g Dec 6] leggy gelding: fairly useful handicapper: won at Thirsk (apprentices) in July, Bath in September and Windsor in October: effective at 5f to 1m: acts on polytrack, good to firm and good to soft going: sometimes slowly away: none too consistent. *G. C. H. Chung*   **80**

OFARABY 4 b.g. Sheikh Albadou 128 – Maristax 74 (Reprimand 122) [2004 87: p10g³ 10.1v* 12s⁶ 10.3d⁴ 10.5d² 10g⁵ 10.5g 10g³ 10.1s* Oct 27] leggy gelding: useful performer: won handicap at Newcastle in March and minor event at Yarmouth (beat Wiggy Smith by ¾ length) in October: effective at 1¼m: acts on all-weather, raced only on good going or softer on turf: sometimes wanders: consistent. *M. A. Jarvis*   **95**

OFF BEAT (USA) 3 ch.g. Mister Baileys 123 – Off Off (USA) (Theatrical 128) [2004 79: p7g⁶ p7g³ 6d 5.7f 7m 7g 8g 10.2m 8m⁶ p10g 12d p9.5g f8g⁶ f8g Dec 28] close-coupled gelding: fair performer at best: left F. J. Houghton after tenth start: probably stays 1¼m: acts on polytrack and firm going: sometimes blinkered. *T. D. Barron*   **79 d**

OFF COLOUR 2 b.c. (Apr 15) Rainbow Quest (USA) 134 – Air of Distinction (IRE) 99 (Distinctly North (USA) 115) [2004 7.1d⁴ 7.1m 8g⁶ Sep 3] good-topped colt: fifth foal: brother to useful yearling colt 2001 2-y-o 1m winner Him of Distinction and closely related to useful 6f (at 2 yrs) and 1m winner Man of Distinction (by Spectrum): dam Irish 6f winner, including Anglesey Stakes at 2 yrs: modest form in maidens: stays 1m. *Mrs A. J. Perrett*   **62**

OFF HIRE 8 b.g. Clantime 101 – Lady Pennington 51 (Blue Cashmere 129) [2004 57, a49: f5g² f5s³ f5g⁴ f5g 6f 5g⁵ 5g f5m f5g⁶ f6d* Dec 21] leggy, angular gelding: modest performer: won handicap race at Southwell: best at 5f/6f: acts on fibresand and any turf going: visored. *C. Smith*   **54**

OFFICER'S PINK 4 ch.f. Grand Lodge (USA) 125 – Arethusa 101 (Primo Dominie 121) [2004 79: 6m 6m 6f Jul 26] strong, lengthy filly: good walker: handicapper: well held in 2004: usually tongue tied. *P. F. I. Cole*   **–**

OGILVY (USA) 3 ch.c. Distant View (USA) 126 – Shoogle (USA) 86 (A P Indy (USA) 131) [2004 8g 10m 9f² Aug 1] strong, sturdy colt: first foal: dam, 2-y-o 7f winner who stayed 1¼m, sister to high-class US performer up to 1½m Aptitude: easily best effort in maidens when 1¼ lengths second to Tahtheeb at Newbury: will stay 1¼m: sold 18,000 gns, sent to Bahrain. *J. H. M. Gosden*   **81**

OH BOY (IRE) 4 b.c. Tagula (IRE) 116 – Pretty Sally (IRE) 51 (Polish Patriot (USA) 128) [2004 64: 8.3d 7g 8.1d⁵ 8m* 8m* 8m 7m 7s 8g 8s Sep 14] good-bodied colt: fair handicapper: won twice at Newbury in June, hanging left both times: well below form after: stays 1m: acts on good to firm going: has flashed tail/found little: sold 3,000 gns. *R. Hannon*   **78**

OH DARA (USA) 2 b.f. (Jan 25) Aljabr (USA) 125 – Sabaah Elfull 75 (Kris 135) [2004 5m⁵ 5.1g⁵ 5.2g 5g⁵ Aug 26] 9,000Y, 26,000 2-y-o: strong filly: fourth foal: half-sister to UAE 6f/7f winner Outlaw (by Danehill): dam, 5f winner who stayed 7.5f, closely related to smart French sprinter Pole Position: fairly useful performer: won maiden at Catterick in June: creditable efforts after, including in nursery final start: will prove best at 5f: races up with pace. *P. A. Blockley*   **85**

OH GOLLY GOSH 3 ch.g. Exit To Nowhere (USA) 122 – Guerre de Troie (Risk Me (FR) 127) [2004 67: 8.1s² 8v² 8m 8m⁴ 7.2f² 10.1m 8.2g⁵ 9m³ f7s* 7m p7.1g Oct 9] workmanlike gelding: fair performer: won maiden at Southwell in August: best efforts when in frame in first half of 2004: stays 1m: acts on all-weather/any turf going: wore cheekpieces/visor after second start. *N. P. Littmoden*   **74**

OH SO HARDY 3 b. or br.f. Fleetwood (IRE) 107 – Miss Hardy (Formidable (USA) 125) [2004 10g 11.9m⁴ 12.1m³ p13m Nov 22] third foal: dam unraced: little form in maidens/banded race. *M. A. Allen*   **–**

OH SO ROSIE (IRE)   4 b.f. Danehill Dancer (IRE) 117 – Shinkoh Rose (FR) 67   **66**
(Warning 136) [2004 69: 7d⁴ 8.3d³ 8.1d³ 7s 8m³ 8f² 8f⁵ 9g 8m 8m* 7.9m 8.1m 8m⁴ 8d²
8m⁵ p8g² 7s p8.6d p8g⁵ p7g Dec 30] small, angular filly: fair handicapper: won at Yarmouth in July: effective at 7f/1m: acts on polytrack, firm and good to soft going: tried
visored, usually wears cheekpieces. *J. S. Moore*

OK PAL   4 b.g. Primo Dominie 121 – Sheila's Secret (IRE) 97 (Bluebird (USA) 125)   **91**
[2004 95: p5g f6s³ 5d 6g 5s⁶ 5g 5.1g⁶ 5g* 5g² 6g³ 5d* Oct 18] lengthy gelding: fairly
useful performer: won claimer at Sandown in September and handicap at Pontefract (beat
Corps de Ballet ½ length) in October: effective at 5f/6f: acts on all-weather and good to
soft going: blinkered sixth (hung left)/seventh starts: races prominently. *T. G. Mills*

OKTIS MORILIOUS (IRE)   3 b.g. Octagonal (NZ) 126 – Nottash (IRE) 74 (Royal   **59**
Academy (USA) 130) [2004 –: f7f f9.4g p8g⁴ p10g* p10g² 12.1d³ p10g⁴ 11g² 11.9f⁶   **a48**
10.2f² 10.2f⁵ 10.9g* 10m 11.7m⁴ 10g 11.7d* 10.1g 16.1m⁴ 17.1g⁶ f14g p13.9g Dec 22]
sparely-made gelding: modest performer: left J. Osborne after second start: won banded
race at Lingfield in March and sellers at Warwick in July and Bath in August: left
A. Carroll after seventeenth start: barely stays 17f: acts on polytrack, firm and good to
soft going. *C. R. Dore*

OLD BAILEY (USA)   4 gr.g. Lit de Justice (USA) 125 – Olden Lek (USA) (Cozzene   **54**
(USA)) [2004 54: 6v⁶ 6s 7.1d⁵ 7.2m f7g* 5.9f f7g f7m 6g⁵ 6m⁵ 6m f8f³ 6v* p7.1g f6g*   **a71**
f7g⁴ Dec 14] good-topped gelding: fair handicapper on all-weather, modest on turf: won
at Wolverhampton in June, Newcastle (apprentices) in August and Southwell in December: stays 7f: acts on fibresand and any turf going: wears headgear: none too consistent.
T. D. Barron

OLDENWAY   5 b.g. Most Welcome 131 – Sickle Moon (Shirley Heights 130) [2004   **81**
90, a?: p10g p10g 10.3g² 10g² 12m⁴ 10m² 9.9d* 10g⁴ 11.9g 9.2g* Jul 15] lengthy   **a64**
gelding: fairly useful on turf, modest on all-weather: won handicap at Beverley in June
and claimer at Hamilton (claimed £30,000) in July: stays 1½m: acts on polytrack, firm
and good to soft going: tends to race freely: sold 8,000 gns. *R. A. Fahey*

OLD HARRY   4 b.g. Case Law 113 – Supreme Thought 68 (Emarati (USA) 74) [2004   **–**
62: 7m 5.1m 6f 6m Sep 25] close-coupled gelding: maiden: mostly well held in 2004:
tried visored/tongue tied. *P. C. Ritchens*

OLDSTEAD FLYER (IRE)   2 b. or br.c. (Apr 29) Foxhound (USA) 103 – Princess   **–**
Tycoon (IRE) 77 (Last Tycoon 131) [2004 5m f6g⁶ 7m f7m Jul 6] leggy colt: no form in
maidens. *D. Carroll*

OLIGARCH (IRE)   2 b.c. (Feb 23) Monashee Mountain (USA) 115 – Courtier   **83**
(Saddlers' Hall (IRE) 126) [2004 6d² 6m 8g³ 8s* 7s Nov 6] €12,500F, 60,000Y: sturdy
colt: second foal: half-brother to 3-y-o Barbajuan: dam unraced: fairly useful performer:
won maiden at Brighton in October: only seventh in nursery final start: barely stays 1m:
acts on soft ground: made running last 2 starts. *N. A. Callaghan*

OLIMP (POL)   8 ch.g. Saphir (GER) – Olgierda (POL) (Sentyment (POL)) [2004   **–**
f16.2g Feb 6] Polish-bred gelding: successful 8 times at 1m/1¼m in Poland: well held in
selling handicap on British Flat debut: temperamental hurdler. *Miss A. M. Newton-Smith*

OLIVANDER   3 b.g. Danzero (AUS) – Mystic Goddess (USA) 94 (Storm Bird (CAN)   **74**
134) [2004 83: 7s 7f³ 9m 8m² Sep 23] small, close-coupled gelding: fair maiden: left
G. Butler after third outing: should stay 1¼m: acts on firm going: blinkered last 3 starts,
tongue tied final one: sold 15,500 gns. *R. M. Beckett*

OLIVIA ROSE (IRE)   5 b.m. Mujadil (USA) 119 – Santana Lady (IRE) 72 (Blakeney   **90**
126) [2004 70: 9.9s 10s* 10s³ 10m* 10m² 9.9d³ 10m* 10m⁴ 10d* 10.1g³ 10f 10.1g 10g
Sep 29] lengthy mare: fairly useful handicapper: won at Nottingham in April, Redcar in
May and Ripon in June and July (best effort, beat Nevada Desert 1½ lengths): probably
best at 1¼m: acts on fibresand and any turf going: tried visored: usually held up. *J. Pearce*

OLIVIA TWIST   2 ch.f. (Jan 21) Fraam 114 – Tricata (Electric 126) [2004 7g Jul 8]   **–**
ninth foal: half-sister to useful 7f (at 2 yrs) to 11.5f winner Kingston Venture (by Interrex)
and 1999 2-y-o 5f winner Kingston Bill (by Then Again): dam unraced: last in maiden at
Folkestone. *W. G. M. Turner*

OLLIJAY   3 b.g. Wolfhound (USA) 126 – Anthem Flight (USA) (Fly So Free (USA)   **–**
122) [2004 7g⁶ 7.1d⁶ 7.1g 7g p9.5d Nov 5] little form. *Mrs H. Dalton*

O'L LUCY BROON   3 b.f. Royal Applause 124 – Jay Gee Ell 78 (Vaigly Great 127)   **50**
[2004 62: 5g 6g 5m 5d p6d⁵ p8.6g⁶ f7g Dec 1] modest maiden: stays 6f: acts on polytrack,
good to firm and good to soft going: tried visored. *J. S. Goldie*

OLYMPIAS (IRE) 3 b.f. Kahyasi 130 – Premier Amour 111 (Salmon Leap (USA) **56**
131) [2004 9.7s⁵ 12s 9g 14g⁶ 12g⁴ 18d 13.1f³ 17.2g Sep 27] IR 15,000F, 25,000Y: lengthy
filly: half-sister to several winners abroad, including German 8.5f to 10.5f winner
Primeur (by Lando): dam French 9f (including at 2 yrs) to 11f winner: modest maiden:
should stay 2m: acts on firm and soft going: blinkered last 2 starts: sometimes slowly
away. *H. Morrison*

OMAHA CITY (IRE) 10 b.g. Night Shift (USA) – Be Discreet (Junius (USA) 124) **81**
[2004 92: p8g 8g p8g² 8g* 8m 8g 8m 7.1g 7m 8.3m* p8m² p8g* p8g³ Nov 10] strong
gelding: fairly useful handicapper: won at Goodwood in June, Windsor in September and
Lingfield in October: stays 1m: acts on polytrack, firm and soft going: tried visored: edgy
sort: usually held up. *B. Gubby*

OMAN GULF (USA) 3 b.g. Diesis 133 – Dabaweyaa 118 (Shareef Dancer (USA) **68 +**
135) [2004 84: 10.4s 8f⁴ 8d 7s Nov 6] rather unfurnished gelding: suffered stress fracture
of cannon bone after winning only 2-y-o start: below that form in 2004, leaving B. Hills
after third start: stays 1m: acts on firm going. *J. G. Given*

OMAN SEA (USA) 3 b.f. Rahy (USA) 115 – Ras Shaikh (USA) 105 (Sheikh Albadou **–**
128) [2004 81: 7.6g⁵ Aug 19] well-made filly: suffered fracture of pastern after winning
minor event at York on second start at 2 yrs: tailed off in similar race at Chester 15 months
later. *B. W. Hills*

OMASHERIFF (IRE) 2 ch.c. (Feb 18) Shinko Forest (IRE) – Lady of Leisure (USA) **100**
76 (Diesis 133) [2004 5g* 6s* 6.5g² 6m⁴ Sep 8] 4,000Y: strong colt: second foal: dam,
1¼m winner, out of sister to Mujadil and half-sister to Fruits of Love: useful performer:
won maiden at Baden-Baden in May and listed race at Hamburg (by ½ length from Rue
d'Alsace) in July: second in listed race at Cologne and fourth (to Caesar Beware, best
effort) in sales race at Doncaster: stays 6.5f: wears blinkers. *B. Hellier, Germany*

ON ACTION (USA) 2 b.c. (Feb 22) Miswaki (USA) 124 – Dancing Action (USA) **57**
96 (Danzatore (CAN) 120) [2004 6m³ 6f⁵ a6g Dec 9] quite good-topped colt: modest
maiden: left Mrs A. Duffield after second outing: should stay 1m. *R. Bouresly, Kuwait*

ONCE AROUND (IRE) 3 b. or br.g. Grand Lodge (USA) 125 – Lady Lucre (IRE) **–**
73 (Last Tycoon 131) [2004 –: p10g p8g 12s p12g May 29] little form in maidens/seller.
T. G. Mills

ONCE (FR) 4 gr.g. Hector Protector (USA) 124 – Moon Magic 62 (Polish Precedent **76**
(USA) 131) [2004 83: 14m³ 20f 16.2m 11g 13.1f 10m p13.9g p12.2g* p12.2g p12.2g **a64**
Dec 20] leggy, quite good-topped gelding: fair performer: made all in minor event at
Wolverhampton in November: stays 1¾m: acts on polytrack, raced only on good going or
firmer on turf: tried blinkered: none too reliable. *J. A. Osborne*

ON CLOUD NINE 3 ro.f. Cloudings (IRE) 112 – Princess Moodyshoe 72 (Jalmood **70**
(USA) 126) [2004 9.7s² 12.1g⁶ 10d 9.7g 12m⁴ 12.1d³ 12.1g* 12g⁵ p12.2d Nov 4] sixth
foal: half-sister to useful 1999 2-y-o 5f to 1m winner Misbehave (by Reprimand) and
fairly useful but ungenuine 2m/2¼m winner Trained Bythe Best (by Alderbrook): dam,
winner around 1½m, also successful over hurdles: fair performer: won claimer at Chepstow (left M. Bell) in September: stays 1½m: acts on soft and good to firm going:
free-going sort: sometimes wanders: held up. *J. G. M. O'Shea*

ONE ALONE 3 b.f. Atraf 116 – Songsheet 74 (Dominion 123) [2004 –: f9.4s 7m 7m **50**
8.3m p10g⁴ p12d² Aug 9] modest maiden: left J. Given after reappearance: stays 1½m:
form only on polytrack: visored/blinkered last 2 starts. *Jean-Rene Auvray*

ONE COOL CAT (USA) 3 b.c. Storm Cat (USA) – Tacha (USA) (Mr Prospector **123**
(USA)) [2004 118p: 8g 8m⁵ 6m* 5s³ 6g⁶ Sep 4]
'Please don't hurt the cat.' Roy Horn, one half of tiger-taming double act
Siegfried and Roy, had thoughts only for his white tiger Montecore as he was
stretchered away in a critical condition after being badly mauled by the tiger during
a Las Vegas show in 2003. Horn defended the tiger, claiming it had been trying to
help him after he had fallen. Horn's belief that the tigers, given the freedom of the
double-act's 10,000,000-dollar estate (including the house), looked upon him as
one of their own stemmed from the close relationships developed with the tigers in
his care from an early age. 'Mine is the first voice they hear, the first touch they
feel, to them I am a tiger on two legs.' Aidan O'Brien seems to cultivate a similarly
close affinity with the horses in his care. Patently meticulous and devoted, O'Brien
can watch his horses in their boxes from his house on CCTV and is inclined to keep
his

leading hope in the box nearest his house. Like Horn with his tigers, O'Brien tends to be protective of his horses' behaviour to the last. As a result, the trainer needed a thick skin of his own at times in 2004 as he and One Cool Cat seemed set against the world, O'Brien getting the mauling as Ballydoyle's leading classic hope turned tail in the Guineas before showing his claws only briefly as a sprinter.

The die was cast with One Cool Cat's two-year-old season the previous year. 'He's a unique colt' and 'I've never come across a horse with such a blast of speed as this fellow,' were just two of the glowing references O'Brien gave him as a juvenile. One Cool Cat won the last four of his five starts as a two-year-old, the last three in pattern company, including two Group 1 races, the Phoenix Stakes over six furlongs and the National Stakes over seven, both at the Curragh. He showed a good turn of foot each time, but the form looked no better than smart and his winter odds of 7/4 for the Two Thousand Guineas seemed nonsensical. On the day, without a preparatory race, One Cool Cat dominated the betting at Newmarket, starting at 15/8 in a field of fourteen. Rumours had persisted about his well-being, but he looked in excellent shape in the paddock, though it looked as if his heels had been treated with what appeared to be gentian violet, an antiseptic used for minor cuts. Held up as usual, One Cool Cat performed lamentably, behind throughout, and returning tailed-off last but one. On examination immediately afterwards, One Cool Cat was reportedly found to have an irregular heartbeat. Withdrawn from the Irish Two Thousand Guineas with a 'low-grade infection', One Cool Cat missed Royal Ascot as well and was not seen out again until the Group 3 International Stakes over a mile at the Curragh in July. Starting odds on, he managed only fifth of the seven runners, finding little once asked to improve and beaten over six lengths behind Red Feather, again reportedly returning with an irregular heartbeat.

There was talk of retirement for One Cool Cat after this second defeat of the season over a mile, but he leapt back into the headlines on the track when returned to six furlongs in the Group 3 Patrick P O'Leary Memorial Phoenix Sprint Stakes at the Curragh in August. Although again favourite, One Cool Cat faced no easy task under an 8-lb penalty for his juvenile successes and showed improved form, putting up a very smart effort. Ridden confidently by Spencer, One Cool Cat was switched back inside, rather than taken wide, a furlong out and soon stormed through, idling in front as he had as a two-year-old, as he held The Kiddykid by a length with Nights Cross third and Osterhase fourth. Passing the post, Spencer turned sideways in the saddle to wave his whip, as if with indignation, at the crowd, the tensions inside the camp underlined by Coolmore supremo John Magnier's comments afterwards. 'I'd had enough after the Curragh in July. I said to Aidan, look I don't want to run him. He's 1000/1!' O'Brien had reportedly replied 'I know what you're

Patrick P. O'Leary Memorial Phoenix Sprint Stakes, the Curragh—dropped back in trip, One Cool Cat impresses as he overcomes the British-trained pair The Kiddykid and Nights Cross (visor), with Osterhase (rail) fading into fourth; Ulfah is fifth

saying, but I am looking at him everyday and I think he should.' O'Brien also added, after the race, 'I can't tell you the relief. My heart has gone beyond putting a monitor on it.'

Returned to Group 1 company in Britain, in a year lacking a top-class sprinter, One Cool Cat started favourite in the Nunthorpe Stakes at York, going off at 3/1 in a field of twelve. Back at five furlongs for the first time since his racecourse debut, he was switched left from a high draw at the start and was still last of the main bunch a furlong and a half out before weaving his way through, still closing at the finish as he went down by a neck and a length to Bahamian Pirate and The Tatling. In the circumstances, One Cool Cat recorded a creditable effort at the least, but O'Brien, who had spent a lengthy period beforehand pacing the course assessing the soft ground, with a mobile phone pressed to his ear, seemed to feel obliged to defend One Cool Cat as the media confronted him afterwards. 'We knew he was a fast-ground horse. I worry about the trainer making an awful dog's mess. That's the reality of it. How could I have got it so wrong with him?' To the outside observer, it was hard to see where O'Brien had gone so badly wrong at York, or earlier in the season for that matter. On his only run after York, One Cool Cat ended his campaign as he had begun it, going off at cramped odds in the Stanleybet Sprint Cup, in which he started at 6/4 in a field of nineteen. Little over two weeks on from York, he could finish only sixth, beaten over three lengths after having every chance. Beforehand, a cartoon of One Cool Cat, whose racing character had been a debating point all season, appeared in the *Racing Post*, showing him reclined in a psychiatrist's chair. By the end of September there came an announcement that One Cool Cat was retired, after reportedly suffering a condylar fracture of a near-hind during final preparations for the Prix de l'Abbaye.

One Cool Cat (USA) (b.c. 2001)	Storm Cat (USA) (b or br 1983)	Storm Bird (b 1978)	Northern Dancer
			South Ocean
		Terlingua (ch 1976)	Secretariat
			Crimson Saint
	Tacha (USA) (b or br 1992)	Mr Prospector (b 1970)	Raise A Native
			Gold Digger
		Savannah Dancer (b or br 1982)	Northern Dancer
			Valoris

One Cool Cat has a largely American pedigree—his dam Tacha, a minor winner over an extended mile, is a daughter of Savannah Dancer, successful in the Del Mar Oaks—but he will stand at Coolmore in Ireland at a fee of €17,500. Several other colts by his sire Storm Cat who were trained at Ballydoyle already stand at Coolmore's Ashford Stud in America, including Giant's Causeway, champion first season sire in Britain and Ireland in 2004. Although Storm Cat made less impact at Ballydoyle with his two-year-olds than in recent seasons, he was represented in the States by the Breeders' Cup Juvenile Fillies winner Sweet Catomine, as well as Consolidator, successful in the Grade 1 Lane's End Breeders' Futurity at Keeneland in October. Storm Cat, whose sire Storm Bird died in December, was also responsible in 2004 for the most expensive yearling ever sold at the Keeneland September Sale, a colt from the family of A P Indy knocked down for eight million dollars. Coolmore, who dropped out of the bidding for the record-breaking colt at seven million, paid 3,100,000 dollars for One Cool Cat at the Keeneland July Sale, making him their most expensive yearling purchase in North America in 2002. One Cool Cat should more than recoup the original outlay at stud. One correspondent questioned whether a horse with a history of heart problems should have the opportunity to be a stallion at all, but history is littered with successful sires whose supposed defects have been long forgotten—Danehill, for example, was said to be 'back at the knee' and his early stock to have 'crab knees'. A big, angular, good-topped colt, One Cool Cat should have stayed a mile on pedigree, but he clearly had plenty of speed. Effective on firm ground and probably on soft, he was inclined to wander and carry his head awkwardly under pressure, as well as having a tendency to idle once in front. He usually took the eye in the preliminaries, and looked in particularly fine shape at York; O'Brien considered that One Cool Cat's tendency to sweat on occasions was exaggerated by his colour, nearer black than his registered bay. What glistens isn't always pure gold it seems! *A. P. O'Brien, Ireland*

ONE FOR ME 6 br.m. Tragic Role (USA) – Chantallee's Pride (Mansooj 118) [2004 –
–: 21g Jul 28] handicapper: little form on Flat since 4 yrs (fair hurdler in 2003): tried
tongue tied. *Jean-Rene Auvray*

ONEFORTHEBOYS (IRE) 5 b.g. Distinctly North (USA) 115 – Joyful Prospect **47**
(Hello Gorgeous (USA) 128) [2004 –: f8g p8g f8g⁶ p5g² p6g⁴ p6g p6g p6g³ p7g p5g⁶
p6g³ 6f 6.1d Jul 10] poor maiden: should stay 7f: acts on polytrack: tried tongue tied:
reared leaving stall last 2 outings. *D. Flood*

ONE GOOD THING (USA) 2 b.c. (Feb 14) Touch Gold (USA) 127 – Once To Often **73**
(USA) (Raise A Native) [2004 6g 8g⁵ 8s Oct 27] $550,000Y: quite attractive colt: half-
brother to numerous winners, including US 1m minor stakes winner Boom Town Girl (by
Unbridled): dam, Canadian 4.5f (at 2 yrs) and 6.5f winner, closely related to Breeders'
Cup Sprint third Exclusive Enough: best effort in maidens when fifth at Leicester, making
most: soon off bridle final start: not sure to stay beyond 1m. *Saeed bin Suroor*

ONE GREAT IDEA (IRE) 2 b.g. (Mar 17) Night Shift (USA) – Scenaria (IRE) **76**
(Scenic 128) [2004 5g² 6g⁵ 5m² Sep 15] 30,000F, 35,000Y: tall gelding: third foal:
half-brother to 5-y-o Lucid Dreams and 1m winner in Hong Kong by Grand Lodge: dam
unraced: fair form in maidens: second at Haydock and Beverley: likely to prove best at
5f/6f: tended to hang penultimate start. *T. D. Barron*

ONEIRO WAY (IRE) 2 b.g. (Mar 15) King's Best (USA) 132 – Koumiss (Unfuwain **57 ?**
(USA) 131) [2004 7.1d 8g Sep 29] seemingly modest form on first start in maidens:
slowly away final one. *P. R. Chamings*

ONE LAST TIME 4 b.g. Primo Dominie 121 – Leap of Faith (IRE) 65 (Northiam **69**
(USA)) [2004 80?: 7d 8d 8.3g 6m² 5f 5m Jul 25] good-topped gelding: has a quick action:
fair handicapper: stays 1m: acts on good to firm and good to soft going: none too consistent. *R. Bastiman*

ONE 'N' ONLY (IRE) 3 b.f. Desert Story (IRE) 115 – Alpina (USA) 69 (El Prado **52**
(IRE) 119) [2004 54: 7.1g⁴ 5g⁵ 9.2g⁴ 8m³ May 21] quite good-topped filly: modest
maiden: stays 1m: raced only on good going or firmer. *Miss L. A. Perratt*

ONE OF DISTINCTION 3 b.f. Nashwan (USA) 135 – Air of Distinction (IRE) 99 **– p**
(Distinctly North (USA) 115) [2004 10m Aug 2] fourth foal: closely related to fairly
useful 2-y-o 1m winner Him of Distinction (by Rainbow Quest) and half-sister to useful
6f (at 2 yrs) and 1m winner Man of Distinction (by Spectrum): dam Irish 6f winner, including Anglesey Stakes at 2 yrs: 16/1 and green, tailed off in maiden at Windsor: should
do better. *E. A. L. Dunlop*

ONE OF EACH (IRE) 2 ch.f. (Apr 19) Indian Lodge (IRE) 127 – Indian City 57 **60**
(Lahib (USA) 129) [2004 5f⁵ 5d⁵ f5g Aug 20] 4,000Y: leggy filly: second foal: dam 2-y-o
6f winner: modest maiden: should stay 6f: well held on fibresand. *D. Carroll*

ONE OFF 4 b.g. Barathea (IRE) 127 – On Call 103 (Alleged (USA) 138) [2004 94p: **87**
14g 18f⁴ Sep 16] well-made gelding: progressive handicapper at 3 yrs, winning 6 times
within 2 months: respectable seventh to Holy Orders in listed race at Fairyhouse on
reappearance: ran as if amiss in minor event at Pontefract following month: should stay
beyond 2m: acts on fibresand and good to firm going: sent to USA. *Sir Mark Prescott*

ONE OF THEM 5 ch.g. Pharly (FR) 130 – Hicklam Millie 49 (Absalom 128) [2004 **–**
10s p12g May 25] successful over 9f/1¼m in Germany at 3 yrs: left B. Hellier, no form in
blinkers in Britain. *J. S. Moore*

ONE PUTRA (IRE) 2 b.c. (Mar 3) Indian Ridge 123 – Triomphale (USA) (Nureyev **99**
(USA) 131) [2004 6g⁵ 6g* 6.1s³ 6g⁶ Sep 18] 200,000Y: strong colt: second living foal:
half-brother to 3-y-o Rondelet, dam, French 2-y-o 6f winner, closely related to smart
French/US performer up to 1¼m Tresoriere: useful performer: won maiden at Windsor in
August by 1½ lengths from Rebuttal: respectable efforts in minor event at Chester (weakened late on) and Mill Reef Stakes at Newbury (sixth to Galeota) after: will probably stay
7f. *M. A. Jarvis*

ONESHOTTWOLIONS (IRE) 2 b.c. (Feb 2) Giant's Causeway (USA) 132 – Fern- **56**
anda 95 (Be My Chief (USA) 122) [2004 7g a7f⁴ Dec 30] better effort in maidens when
fourth at Nad Al Sheba: trained by E. Dunlop on debut: will stay 1m. *M. Al Kurdi, UAE*

ONE SO MARVELLOUS 3 ch.f. Nashwan (USA) 135 – Someone Special 105 **86 p**
(Habitat 134) [2004 8g 10g 10m* 10g² Sep 29] well-made filly: sister to very smart 7f (at
2 yrs) to 1¼m winner One So Wonderful, closely related to fairly useful 1m winner You
Are The One (by Unfuwain), and half-sister to several winners, including smart 7f (at 2
yrs) to 10.4f winner Alnasr Alwasheek (by Sadler's Wells): dam, 7f winner who stayed

1m, half-sister to top-class miler Milligram: won maiden at Leicester in September by neck from Flamboyant Lad: creditable length second to Honorine in handicap at Nottingham final start: stays 1¼m: should make a useful 4-y-o. *L. M. Cumani*

ONE TO WIN (IRE) 2 b.f. (Feb 17) Cape Cross (IRE) 129 – Safe Exit (FR) (Exit To   **73 p**
Nowhere (USA) 122) [2004 p7g² Sep 7] €18,000F, €45,000Y: first foal: dam, French 11.5f winner, half-sister to dam of Prix Vermeille winner Volvoreta: 15/2, ½-length second to Icing in maiden at Lingfield, held up and staying on: will stay at least 1m: sure to improve. *J. Noseda*

ONE UPMANSHIP 3 ch.g. Bahamian Bounty 116 – Magnolia 52 (Petong 126)   **68**
[2004 69: 6g 6f 7m 7.1m⁶ 6.1m³ 7m² 7.6m⁶ 8.1g* p10g² 9s³ p10g p8.6d p8g⁵ p10g p10m⁵ Dec 22] fair performer: won maiden claimer at Haydock in August: stays easy 1¼m: acts on polytrack, soft and good to firm going: tried in cheekpieces/blinkers. *J. G. Portman*

ON EVERY STREET 3 b.g. Singspiel (IRE) 133 – Nekhbet 74 (Artaius (USA) 129)   **81**
[2004 –p: 10m⁴ 11g³ 10.9f* 10g⁴ 8.9m⁶ 9.2s 10.3s 10s Nov 1] close-coupled gelding: fairly useful performer: tongue tied, won maiden at Warwick (left H. Cecil) in June: mostly well held after, often running as if amiss: should stay at least 1½m: acts on firm going: visored/blinkered first 6 starts at 3 yrs. *R. Bastiman*

ONE WAY TICKET 4 ch.c. Pursuit of Love 124 – Prima Cominna 86 (Unfuwain   **77 §**
(USA) 131) [2004 74§: 8.3g 7.1v 7m 6m³ 6m² 6m 5.7f³ 6.1m* f6g 5.7g 6m 5.1m⁴ 5.3d⁵ 5g 5g² Sep 22] lengthy, workmanlike colt: fair handicapper: won at Chepstow in June: also first past post in void race (stalls opened at different times) at Brighton in August: has won at 7f, probably best at 5f/6f: acts on firm and soft going: wears cheekpieces: usually races up with pace: carries head high: unreliable. *J. M. Bradley*

ON GUARD 6 b.g. Sabrehill (USA) 120 – With Care 78 (Warning 136) [2004 69, a48:   **52**
p10g³ p12g⁶ 10.9s 10.2s f9.4g⁴ 11.6m May 24] neat gelding: modest performer: barely stayed 1½m: acted on all-weather, firm and good to soft going: tried in cheekpieces, often visored: held up: dead. *P. G. Murphy*

ONIZ TIPTOES (IRE) 3 ch.g. Russian Revival (USA) 125 – Edionda (IRE) (Magical   **43**
Strike (USA) 114) [2004 –: 6m 12m⁶ 10g⁴ 12.1m² 12g Aug 13] close-coupled gelding: poor maiden: stays 1½m: raced only on good going or firmer on turf: wore headgear last 4 starts. *J. S. Wainwright*

ONLINE INVESTOR 5 b.g. Puissance 110 – Anytime Baby 56 (Bairn (USA) 126)   **79 d**
[2004 87: 6v 7d 6g⁵ 5m² 7.2f 5m⁵ 5f⁵ 5m 5d 5f 5g 6m 5d² 5.3d⁴ 5m⁴ 5f 6d⁶ p6g⁵ Dec 4] leggy, quite good-topped gelding: fair performer: below form after fourth start: best at 5f/6f: acts on firm and good to soft ground: tried blinkered/visored: often slowly away: free-going sort: ungenuine. *D. Nicholls*

ONLY FOR GOLD 9 b.g. Presidium 124 – Calvanne Miss 48 (Martinmas 128) [2004   **30**
53, a–: f5s⁵ f7g Mar 23] rangy gelding: poor performer nowadays: tried visored/in cheekpieces. *Dr P. Pritchard*

ONLY FOR SUE 5 ch.g. Pivotal 124 – Barbary Court (Grundy 137) [2004 59: f12g   **64**
f12g 14.1g³ 11.7s* 14.1m Jun 2] rather leggy, angular gelding: modest handicapper: lightly raced: won at Bath in May: stays 1¾m: acts on fibresand and soft going: wore cheekpieces/blinkers last 3 starts. *W. S. Kittow*

ONLY IF I LAUGH 3 ch.g. Piccolo 121 – Agony Aunt 81 (Formidable (USA) 125)   **72 §**
[2004 77: p5g³ f5g⁴ 5s 5.1f² f6g³ 5d 5g⁵ 5m³ 5g p5.1d⁴ p5.1g⁴ p6g⁵ Nov 27] big, strong gelding: fair performer: left B. Meehan after fourth start: best at 5f/easy 6f: acts on all-weather, firm and good to soft going: sometimes blinkered/hooded, visored final outing: unreliable. *P. A. Blockley*

ONLY ONE LEGEND (IRE) 6 b.g. Eagle Eyed (USA) 111 – Afifah 66 (Nashwan   **50 §**
(USA) 135) [2004 77§, a82§: p6g f5g f6g f6g p6g 6s³ 6g 6.1m³ f7d* f7g⁵ f7m 6m 7m   **a67 §**
Aug 3] lengthy gelding: fair on all-weather, modest on turf: won claimer at Southwell in June: stays 7f: acts on all-weather, firm and good to soft going: wears blinkers/cheekpieces: no easy ride: unreliable. *K. A. Ryan*

ONLYTIME WILL TELL 6 ch.g. Efisio 120 – Prejudice 83 (Young Generation 129)   **101**
[2004 108, a–: p8g 6d⁵ 7g⁴ 6m² 8m 6m* 6g⁴ 6s⁶ 6s* 6s p7.1g Nov 12] lengthy gelding: **a74**
useful on turf, fair on all-weather: won claimer at Windsor in August and handicap at Newbury (beat Danzig River by ¾ length) in October: best at 6f/7f: acts on fibresand/any turf going: sometimes wanders: usually held up. *D. Nicholls*

ONLY WORDS (USA) 7 ch.g. Shuailaan (USA) 122 – Conversation Piece (USA)   **–**
(Seeking The Gold (USA)) [2004 16.2d⁶ Jul 3] sturdy gelding: maiden: well held only start on Flat since 2002: tried tongue tied. *A. J. Lockwood*

ON THE BRIGHT SIDE   2 b.f. (Mar 14) Cyrano de Bergerac 120 – Jade Pet 90   **60 p**
(Petong 126) [2004 5g³ Jul 3] 13,000Y: sixth foal: half-sister to 7-y-o Hail The Chief and
8-y-o Just Wiz: dam, 5f winner, including at 2 yrs, half-sister to dam of smart sprinter
Sampower Star (by Cyrano de Bergerac): 20/1, third in maiden at Carlisle, very slowly
away and not knocked about: should do better. *D. Nicholls*

ON THE FAIRWAY (IRE)   5 b.m. Danehill Dancer (IRE) 117 – Asta Madera (IRE)   **–**
67 (Toca Madera 111) [2004 –: p8m p6g p7m Dec 15] tall mare: no longer of much
account. *J. J. Bridger*

ON THE LEVEL   5 ch.m. Beveled (USA) – Join The Clan 95 (Clantime 101) [2004   **–**
47: f5g p5g 6f Jun 10] maiden: no form at 5 yrs: tried in cheekpieces/blinkers. *Mrs
N. Macauley*

ON THE TRAIL   7 ch.g. Catrail (USA) 123 – From The Rooftops (IRE) (Thatching   **66**
131) [2004 f5s f6s f5g f6s f6s* f6g³ f6g* f6g² f6d* f6g³ f7d⁴ 5g³ f6m³ 5g* 5d* 5d⁴
6g⁵ 6f² 6g 6g* 6d² p7.1g⁴ p6d³ p5.1g⁴ Nov 13] strong gelding: fair performer: won
banded event at Wolverhampton in March, 2 sellers at Southwell in April and handicaps
at Pontefract (2) in August and Catterick (apprentices) in October: best at 5f/6f: acts on
all-weather, firm and good to soft going: tried tongue tied at 4/5 yrs, well held in blinkers:
usually races up with pace: tough. *D. W. Chapman*

ON THE WATERFRONT   3 ch.c. Docksider (USA) 124 – Film Buff 60 (Midyan   **69**
(USA) 124) [2004 p8g⁵ p10g⁵ p7g⁴ 8m² 8m 8.1d⁴ 8.3m² 8g⁵ Aug 14] 11,000Y: sturdy
colt: first foal: half-brother to winner in USA by Robellino: dam, maiden who stayed
1¾m, out of sister to dam of Oaks winner Lady Carla: fair maiden: stays 1m: acts on
polytrack, good to firm and good to soft going: sometimes races freely. *J. W. Hills*

ON THE WATERLINE (IRE)   2 b.f. (Apr 18) Compton Place 125 – Miss Waterline   **79**
77 (Rock City 120) [2004 5.1g² 5.1d³ 5m 6g⁴ 5.1g² 6g 6.5m 6d* p6g⁶ 6d Oct 15] leggy
filly: third foal: half-sister to 3-y-o Ligne d'Eau: dam, 2-y-o 6f winner, half-sister to smart
sprinters Double Action and Sir Nicholas: fair performer: made all in maiden at Windsor
in October: below form after: stays 6f: acts on good to soft going: visored last 3 starts.
P. D. Evans

ON THE WING   3 b.f. Pivotal 124 – Come Fly With Me (Bluebird (USA) 125) [2004   **–**
78: 8g p10g Nov 10] tall, leggy filly: fair at 2 yrs: well held in 2004. *A. P. Jarvis*

ONTOS (GER)   8 b. or br.g. Super Abound (USA) – Onestep (GER) (Konigsstuhl   **–**
(GER)) [2004 18v Apr 6] successful 4 times up to 11f in Germany at 3/4 yrs for Frau
E. Schnakenberg: tailed off in handicap at Pontefract on British Flat debut: fairly useful
hurdler. *Miss V. Scott*

ONWARD TO GLORY (USA)   4 b.c. Zabeel (NZ) – Landaria (FR) (Sadler's Wells   **72**
(USA) 132) [2004 12d 14m 11.5m⁴ 11.9s⁶ 11.7g 13.8s* p13.9g⁴ Nov 11] $310,000Y: first
foal: dam, fairly useful French maiden (stayed 1½m), half-sister to very smart French
stayer Alesso out of high-class French 1½m performer Leandra: fairly useful form in 3
starts for A. Fabre in France at 2/3 yrs: fair form in Britain: won handicap at Catterick in
November: stays 1¾m: acts on polytrack, heavy and good to firm going. *J. L. Dunlop*

ONYA   4 ch.f. Unfuwain (USA) 131 – Reel Foyle (USA) 77 (Irish River (FR) 131) [2004   **–**
–: p7g Jan 3] lengthy, angular filly: little form: tongue tied only start in 2004. *J. W. Hills*

ONYERGO (IRE)   2 b.c. (Mar 15) Polish Precedent (USA) 131 – Trick (IRE) 76 (Shir-   **76**
ley Heights 130) [2004 7s³ 7.2s³ 8d³ Nov 3] 7,500Y: sturdy colt: fifth foal: half-brother
to 3 winners, including useful 2001 2-y-o 6f winner White Rabbit (by Zilzal) and fairly
useful 6f (at 2 yrs) to 1½m winner Cap Ferrat (by Robellino): dam 1¼m winner: fair form
in maidens at Newcastle, Ayr and Musselburgh: probably stays 1m. *J. R. Weymes*

ONYX   3 b.g. Bijou d'Inde 127 – Prime Surprise 35 (Primo Dominie 121) [2004 6g⁶   **–**
6.1s p6g p6g p6g Dec 20] small gelding: little form in maidens/banded event. *W. de Best-
Turner*

OOPS (IRE)   5 b.g. In The Wings 128 – Atsuko (IRE) (Mtoto 134) [2004 ?: 14.1g   **52**
16.2d⁴ 16.2s⁶ 16m² 16s³ 16g² 16.2m⁴ 15.8m⁴ 15.8g Oct 5] good-topped gelding: modest
handicapper: won at Beverley in July: stays 2m: acts on soft and good to firm going: tried
blinkered: races freely/carries head awkwardly. *J. F. Coupland*

OOS AND AHS   4 b.f. Silver Wizard (USA) 117 – Hot Feet (Marching On 101) [2004   **–**
–: f12g Jan 8] sparely-made filly: well held in maiden/claimer 3 months apart. *C. W. Fairhurst*

OPEN BOOK   3 br.f. Mark of Esteem (IRE) 137 – Sweetness Herself 106 (Unfuwain   **54**
(USA) 131) [2004 12s 10.2m 10m 11g 12f³ p16g 12m³ Sep 25] second foal: half-sister to

4-y-o Jagger: dam 1½m to 16.5f winner: modest maiden: probably stays easy 2m: acts on polytrack and firm going: sold 9,000 gns. *H. Morrison*

OPEN HANDED (IRE) 4 b.g. Cadeaux Genereux 131 – Peralta (IRE) (Green Desert 59 (USA) 127) [2004 64d: f7g6 f8.5s 7g 8.5d* 8d 7m5 7.5g5 8d 8s 9.1s Oct 12] modest performer: won seller at Beverley in April: stays 8.5f: acts on soft going: tried in cheekpieces: usually tongue tied: wayward. *B. Ellison*

OPENING CEREMONY (USA) 5 m.m. Quest For Fame 127 – Gleam of Light 79 (IRE) 81 (Danehill (USA) 126) [2004 80: 10m6 10g2 10.1s4 9d2 10.3g* 10.5d5 10.3g* 10m5 10.1d2 10d4 p10g Sep 22] angular mare: fair handicapper: won at Chester and Doncaster in July: stays 10.6f: acts on firm and good to soft going: tried in cheekpieces: sometimes races freely/carries head high. *R. A. Fahey*

OPEN MIND 3 b.f. Mind Games 121 – Primum Tempus 49 (Primo Dominie 121) 49 [2004 64d: 5g4 5.9f3 5m 6.1m6 6d 6g Sep 14] leggy, plain filly: poor maiden: effective at 5f/easy 6f: acts on firm going. *E. J. Alston*

OPEN VERDICT (IRE) 2 b.g. (Apr 21) Mujadil (USA) 119 – Law Review (IRE) 63 51 (Case Law 113) [2004 5m 5.1g4 5.7g p5.1g p8.6g Dec 11] heavy-topped gelding: modest maiden: form only when fourth at Chester: withdrawn on vet's advice next intended start: should stay 6f: sometimes tongue tied. *A. P. Jarvis*

OPERA BABE (IRE) 3 b.f. Kahyasi 130 – Fairybird (FR) 70 (Pampabird 124) [2004 – 65: 14.6g 12g Aug 11] good-bodied filly: maiden: well held in handicaps in 2004 (reportedly gurgled on reappearance): tried tongue tied. *H. S. Howe*

OPERA COMIQUE (FR) 3 b.f. Singspiel (IRE) 133 – Grace Note (FR) 99 (Top – Ville 129) [2004 100p: 10m6 14.6m 14.1s Oct 27] lengthy, good-bodied filly: useful at 2 yrs: showed little in 2004 in listed races at Newmarket and Yarmouth and Park Hill Stakes at Doncaster in between: left Godolphin, and sent to USA. *Saeed bin Suroor*

OPERASHAAN (IRE) 4 b.g. Darshaan 133 – Comic Opera (IRE) (Royal Academy – (USA) 130) [2004 –: p10g Jan 7] tall gelding: lightly raced and little form. *G. L. Moore*

OPERA STAR (IRE) 3 b.f. Sadler's Wells (USA) 132 – Adjalisa (IRE) 65 (Darshaan 56 133) [2004 –p: p8g5 10.2g 11.7f3 18m6 f12s p12g p12.2g Nov 19] modest maiden: stays easy 1½m: acts on polytrack and firm going: reportedly had breathing problem fifth start: none too consistent. *B. W. Hills*

OPHISTROLIE (IRE) 2 b.c. (May 13) Foxhound (USA) 103 – Thoughtful Kate 64 – (Rock Hopper 124) [2004 8v Oct 23] 15,000 2-y-o: fourth foal: half-brother to 3-y-o Biscar Two: dam, maiden who stayed 1½m, half-sister to Captain Rio: 33/1, well held in maiden at Newbury. *S. Kirk*

OPIUM CREEK (IRE) 3 b.f. Darshaan 133 – Zaizafonic Davis (IRE) (Law Society 61 (USA) 130) [2004 63: 10d 10d 12d4 p12.2g f14g3 p12g Nov 27] €55,000Y: third foal: dam French maiden out of sister to dam of Zafonic: modest maiden: left C. O'Brien in Ireland after third start: barely stays 1¾m: acts on all-weather, firm and good to soft going. *P. W. Chapple-Hyam*

OPTIMAITE 7 b.g. Komaite (USA) – Leprechaun Lady 57 (Royal Blend 117) [2004 70 § 76§: p12g6 May 25] tall, workmanlike gelding: easy mover: fair handicapper: barely stays 1¾m: acts on polytrack, firm and good to soft going: visored (reluctant to race) once, tried in cheekpieces: tongue tied: often slowly away: ungenuine. *B. R. Millman*

OPTIMAL (IRE) 3 gr.f. Green Desert (USA) 127 – On Call 103 (Alleged (USA) 138) 69 [2004 57p: 10.2g 11.5g6 10f* 10f Sep 2] lengthy, useful-looking filly: has a short, round action: fair handicapper: won at Brighton in August: reportedly suffered nasal discharge when tailed off final outing: should stay 1½m: acts on firm going: blinkered last 2 starts. *Sir Mark Prescott*

OPTIMUM (IRE) 2 b.g. (Apr 30) King's Best (USA) 132 – Colour Dance (Rainbow 57 Quest (USA) 134) [2004 7m 8f5 p7m Oct 6] close-coupled gelding: modest form in maidens: best effort at 1m. *D. R. Loder*

OPTIMUM NIGHT 5 b.g. Superlative 118 – Black Bess (Hasty Word 84) [2004 –: 28 9g 10g3 f9.4g f7g4 8.5m5 10.9d Jun 18] bad maiden: stays 1¼m: acts on good to firm going and fibresand: wore cheekpieces last 3 starts. *P. D. Niven*

OPTIMUS (USA) 2 ch.c. (May 6) Elnadim (USA) 128 – Ajfan (USA) 112 (Woodman 80 (USA) 126) [2004 p6g5 p7m2 p7g4 Oct 28] €52,000Y: seventh foal: half-brother to 3 winners, including smart 5f/6f winner in Britain/UAE Mutamayyaz (by Nureyev) and useful 1¼m winner El Laoob (by Red Ransom): dam, 7f (at 2 yrs)/1m winner who was third in 1000 Guineas, half-sister to St Leger second Minds Music: fairly useful form in maidens at Lingfield: will probably stay 1m. *G. A. Butler*

ORANGE TOUCH (GER) 4 b.c. Lando (GER) 128 – Orange Bowl (General Assembly (USA)) [2004 99: 10g⁶ 12g² 14s* 14g Sep 18] well-made colt: smart performer, lightly raced: won 4-runner minor event at Newmarket (by 6 lengths from Remaadd) and 5-runner listed race at Goodwood (beat Swift Tango by 11 lengths) in August: below form in Irish St Leger at the Curragh final start: stays 1¾m: acts on soft and good to firm going. *Mrs A. J. Perrett* **115**

ORANGINO 6 b.g. Primo Dominie 121 – Sweet Jaffa 73§ (Never So Bold 135) [2004 50: 6d 6m² 8g 6g² 6m 6d 8m Oct 2] modest maiden: stays 1m: acts on soft and good to firm going: tried blinkered in 2001: unreliable. *J. S. Haldane* **50 §**

ORANMORE CASTLE (IRE) 2 b.c. (Jan 29) Giant's Causeway (USA) 132 – Twice The Ease 46 (Green Desert (USA) 127) [2004 6g² 6s⁶ Oct 29] €150,000Y: good-topped colt: first foal: dam, ran twice in Ireland, half-sister to smart Irish performer up to 1¼m Two-Twenty-Two: much better effort in maidens when 2½ lengths second to Newsround at Newbury: favourite, found little at Newmarket: bred to stay at least 1m, but needs to settle. *B. W. Hills* **87**

ORATION 3 b.g. Singspiel (IRE) 133 – Blush Rambler (IRE) (Blushing Groom (FR) 131) [2004 10g Jul 14] 12/1, tailed off in maiden at Kempton. *Sir Michael Stoute* **–**

ORATORIO (IRE) 2 b.c. (Apr 29) Danehill (USA) 126 – Mahrah (USA) 89 (Vaguely Noble 140) [2004 6m² 6f 6.3f* 6m² 7m* 7m* 7s² Oct 16] **119**

Aidan O'Brien's team did not enjoy its accustomed success internationally, but that is not to say the trainer experienced a bad year, especially as he notched his sixth successive Irish championship and his seventh in all. Against that, by the start of October, Ballydoyle runners had picked up only one Group 1 race, with Powerscourt in the Tattersalls Gold Cup (the colt had also been disqualified from first in the Arlington Million). One Cool Cat had not lived up to expectations and early Derby favourite Yeats had been sidelined by injury since before Epsom. Given that the principal aim of the whole Ballydoyle operation is to create stallions to be retired to Coolmore, the lack of success in 2004 must have been a worry. Moreover,

Galileo EBF Futurity Stakes, the Curragh—a fifth win in the race in eight years for Aidan O'Brien as Oratorio sees off his rivals; Democratic Deficit is second in front of Elusive Double (right) and the winner's stablemate Carnegie Hall (rail)

Prix Jean-Luc Lagardere (Grand Criterium), Longchamp—
just a short neck and a nose separate Oratorio (far side), Early March and Layman (No.2)

by the start of October, the two-year-olds were doing worse than in 2003, which had itself been a below-par year by O'Brien's exceptional standards. The closest the latest crop of juveniles had come to success at the top level was Oratorio's second behind Damson in the Phoenix Stakes. Things took a turn for the better when Ad Valorem showed himself one of the best of his age by winning the Middle Park Stakes, and two days later Oratorio crowned a season of splendid endeavour with a nail-biting success in the Prix Jean-Luc Lagardere at Longchamp. Oratorio might not be the top juvenile in training, and he will have to improve a bit to come up trumps in a classic, but he defers to none of his peers in courage or consistency.

Oratorio was at his best at the end of the campaign, finishing a fine second to Shamardal in the Dewhurst Stakes at Newmarket two weeks after his victory at Longchamp. The season started fairly early for him and, by the end of August, he looked pretty well exposed and no certainty to make up into a leading challenger for the best autumn prizes. Admittedly, at the height of the summer, Oratorio landed the Dubai Duty Free Anglesey Stakes and the Galileo EBF Futurity Stakes, both at the Curragh. In the former he started at 9/1 and beat his better-fancied stable-companion Cougar Cat by a length after leading a quarter of a mile out, and in the latter he had little difficulty defeating four rivals headed by Railway Stakes winner Democratic Deficit, making most of the running and striding out well to score by two lengths. On his first two starts, Oratorio landed the odds convincingly in a seven-runner maiden at the Curragh towards the end of May, before running an inexplicably lacklustre race when seventh in the Coventry Stakes at Royal Ascot.

Oratorio's record was not enough to make him favourite for the Prix Jean-Luc Lagardere, which still carries the old race title Grand Criterium, albeit in brackets. As usual, the event did not attract a large field and this time there were no Group 1 winners in the field either, though all six who lined up had at least one pattern victory to their name. Early March, successful in the Prix La Rochette, shaded favouritism from Layman, a five-length winner of the Prix de Cabourg before chasing home Divine Proportions in the Prix Morny. Next came Oratorio, then Montgomery's Arch (Richmond Stakes), Democratic Deficit (fourth in the National Stakes on his last start) and Tony James (Gimcrack Stakes). Different tactics were applied on Oratorio. Held up while Early March set a sound gallop, Oratorio obtained a perfect run up the rails and finished strongly to catch the leader and Layman, all three involved in a tremendous tussle, on the line. The margins were a short neck and a nose. This performance indicated that Oratorio would be suited by an even stiffer test of stamina, a conclusion which his final appearance confirmed. Encountering soft going for the first time, and showing a tactical versatility that is another point in his favour, Oratorio raced prominently up the centre in the Dewhurst, a part of the course where the runners kicked up more divots than on the rails where Shamardal set a strong pace. Driven hard to go after the leader two furlongs out, Oratorio went a length up on his group in the centre but could not reach Shamardal, edging left in the final hundred yards and, going down by two and a half lengths, a neck ahead of Montgomery's Arch. A creditable run, which looked even better afterwards as it transpired that Oratorio had pulled a muscle in his hind quarters.

			Danzig	Northern Dancer
	Danehill (USA)		(b 1977)	Pas de Nom
	(b 1986)		Razyana	His Majesty
Oratorio (IRE)			(b 1981)	Spring Adieu
(b.c. Apr 29, 2002)			Vaguely Noble	Vienna
	Mahrah (USA)		(b 1965)	Noble Lassie
	(b 1987)		Montage	Alydar
			(b 1981)	Katonka

Oratorio looks the part, being a strong, good-bodied colt with a quick action. He has yet to race on heavy going but acts on any other. His pedigree supports the belief that he will be suited by further than seven furlongs and will probably stay a mile and a quarter. The progeny of his now-deceased sire Danehill had another cracking season, with around thirty pattern or graded winners globally over a wide range of distances. Oratorio's dam Mahrah, by an influence for stamina in Vaguely

Mrs John Magnier & Mr M. Tabor's "Oratorio"

Noble, won a maiden race over a mile at Ripon and has produced five other winners. Fahim (by another son of Danzig, Green Desert) set a track record over a mile and a quarter in winning the Fort McHenry Handicap at Laurel and finished second in the Grade 1 Sword Dancer Handicap over two furlongs further. Mowaadah (by Alzao) won three races at a mile including a listed rated stakes at Ascot in 2001, three-time winner Hadeb (by Unfuwain) stayed a mile and three quarters and three-year-old filly Glimmering (by Sadler's Wells) got off the mark in a maiden race over a mile and a half at Limerick in late-October. Glimmering fetched 175,000 guineas at the December Sales a month later. Apart from Mowaadah, the only other one of the quintet who did not stay middle distances was Miss Mirage (by Alhaarth), successful over six furlongs as a three-year-old. Oratorio's grandam Montage, who produced Blandford Stakes winner Andros Bay, was a daughter of Katonka, a smart winner of eleven races who produced two Grade 2 scorers. *A. P. O'Brien, Ireland*

ORCADIAN 3 b.g. Kirkwall 118 – Rosy Outlook (USA) 79 (Trempolino (USA) 135) **111 ?** [2004 105: 8m³ 7m 7m⁶ 9s⁵ 12v* Oct 23] well-made gelding: fluent mover: smart performer, lightly raced: 33/1, seemingly improved form when winning Stan James St Simon Stakes in testing conditions at Newbury in October by 15 lengths from Frank Sonata: 5½ lengths fifth to Autumn Glory in Darley Stakes at Newmarket penultimate start: stays 1½m: acts on heavy and good to firm going: front runner. *J. M. P. Eustace*

ORCHESTRATION (IRE) 3 ch.g. Stravinsky (USA) 133 – Mora (IRE) 100 (Second **51** Set (IRE) 127) [2004 73: p6g⁴ f6s⁴ 7g 5f 6g p8.6g⁶ p8.6d f6g⁵ p6g² Dec 22] compact gelding: modest maiden: probably stays 8.6f: acts on polytrack and firm going: tried blinkered/in cheekpieces. *A. W. Carroll*

ORIENTAL MOON (IRE) 5 ch.m. Spectrum (IRE) 126 – La Grande Cascade (USA) **– §** (Beaudelaire (USA) 125) [2004 –§: p12g Apr 15] leggy mare: maiden: little form since 2002: tried in headgear. *M. J. Gingell*

ORIENTAL WARRIOR 3 b.c. Alhaarth (IRE) 126 – Oriental Fashion (IRE) 110 **106 p** (Marju (IRE) 127) [2004 101p: 8f⁵ Sep 10] good-bodied, angular colt: useful form, lightly raced: 3½ lengths fifth to Secret Charm in minor event at Doncaster only 3-y-o start, stumbling slightly: stays 1m: raced only on good going or firmer: should make a smart 4-y-o, all being well. *M. P. Tregoning*

ORIENTOR 6 b.h. Inchinor 119 – Orient 106 (Bay Express 132) [2004 112: 6g² 7s⁴ **118** 6s⁵ 6s 6m⁵ 5f³ 5d* 5s⁵ 6g 5m⁶ Oct 3] close-coupled horse: smart performer: won Champagne Laurent-Perrier Sprint Stakes at Sandown in July by 2½ lengths from Ringmoor Down: 1½ lengths fifth to Bahamian Pirate in Nunthorpe Stakes at York next time, beginning to stay on very strongly when running out of room in final 1f: ran respectably when seventh to Tante Rose in Sprint Cup at Haydock and sixth to Var in Prix de l'Abbaye at Longchamp last 2 starts: effective at 5f (given test)/6f: has form on firm going, but all wins on good or softer: usually held up. *J. S. Goldie*

ORIGINAL SIN (IRE) 4 b.g. Bluebird (USA) 125 – Majakerta (IRE) (Shernazar 131) **–** [2004 64?: p10g p7g p8g Feb 3] lengthy gelding: maiden: no form in 2004, including in seller. *S. Dow*

ORINOCOVSKY (IRE) 5 ch.g. Grand Lodge (USA) 125 – Brillantina (FR) (Crystal **62** Glitters (USA) 127) [2004 73: f11g* f12g f12g³ p16g f12s² p12g³ f14g² 10.9s f12g* f12g³ 11.9f Aug 3] rangy gelding: modest performer: won sellers at Southwell (left C. Egerton) in January and Wolverhampton (apprentices) in April: stays 1¾m: acts on all-weather, firm and good to soft going: blinkered once: free-going sort: usually races prominently: successful over fences in September. *N. P. Littmoden*

Champagne Laurent-Perrier Sprint Stakes, Sandown—there's no danger to Orientor in the final furlong; Ringmoor Down is the winner's closest pursuer in a race upgraded to Group 3

ORION EXPRESS 3 b.c. Bahhare (USA) 122 – Kaprisky (IRE) (Red Sunset 120) **65 d**
[2004 56: 6g⁶ 7.5d⁶ 8.5v 9.9g 7f⁴ 8g⁶ 8.1d⁴ 9.9g⁶ 10.1d⁶ 7.9g p9.5g p9.5g f8g⁵ Dec 16]
lengthy colt: fair maiden at best: stays 1¼m: acts on any going: tried blinkered.
M. W. Easterby

ORION'S BELT 4 ch.g. Compton Place 125 – Follow The Stars 86 (Sparkler 130) **59**
[2004 –: p7g p6g³ p7g 10g³ 8.5g 8v² 10d 9.5d 8s Oct 26] modest maiden: left G. Balding
after third start: stays 1¼m: acts on polytrack, heavy and good to firm going. *P. A. Fahy,
Ireland*

ORLAR (IRE) 2 b.f. (Apr 16) Green Desert (USA) 127 – Soviet Maid (IRE) (Soviet **73**
Star (USA) 128) [2004 7.1m⁵ 8.1s p7g³ p8g⁴ Nov 16] 100,000Y: sturdy filly: sixth foal:
closely related to a winner in Turkey by Hamas and half-sister to 2 winners, including
2000 2-y-o 7f winner Ridgeway Dawn (by Mujtahid): dam unraced half-sister to very
smart 1½m/1¾m performer Air Marshall: fair maiden: fourth in nursery at Lingfield:
stays 1m: well held on soft going. *J. A. Osborne*

ORO STREET (IRE) 8 b.g. Dolphin Street (FR) 125 – Love Unlimited (Dominion **44**
123) [2004 f12g⁵ f12g³ Feb 24] big, lengthy gelding: fair at 3/4 yrs: unraced on Flat
between 2001 and 2003: poor from at 8 yrs: stays 1½m: acts on fibresand, soft and good
to firm going. *G. F. Bridgwater*

ORO VERDE 3 ch.c. Compton Place 125 – Kastaway 91 (Distant Relative 128) [2004 **91**
91, a86: 6s 6s⁶ 5m³ 5m 7d Oct 15] small, strong colt: fairly useful performer: good 2¾
lengths third to Benbaun in minor event at Sandown in June: below form in handicaps
after: best at 5f/6f: acts on polytrack and good to firm going: sold 6,000 gns. *R. Hannon*

ORPEN ANNIE (IRE) 2 b.f. (Apr 21) Orpen (USA) 116 – Nisibis (In The Wings **62**
128) [2004 5g 6m³ 7g⁶ f6d 7m⁴ 7m 8g² Sep 16] smallish, workmanlike filly: second foal:
dam, well beaten in 3 starts, half-sister to smart performer up to 9f Nijo: modest maiden:
stays 1m: acts on good to firm going. *Miss J. Feilden*

ORPENBERRY (IRE) 3 b.f. Orpen (USA) 116 – Forest Berries (IRE) (Thatching **–**
131) [2004 75: 6m 6.1g 8g 7g 7g Sep 20] good-topped filly: well held in 2004 (left
J. Balding after second start), in seller final outing. *E. J. Alston*

ORPENDONNA (IRE) 2 b.f. (Jan 19) Orpen (USA) 116 – Tetradonna (IRE) 102 **75**
(Teenoso (USA) 135) [2004 6d 8.2m³ 7.9g⁶ p6g⁶ p7.1g² Dec 6] strong,
lengthy filly: fifth living foal: half-sister to 3 winners, including useful 8.5f (at 2 yrs) to
2m winner Alberich (by Night Shift) and 4-y-o Mount Hillaby: dam, second in Nell
Gwyn Stakes but disappointing after, stayed 1½m: fair maiden: second in nursery at
Wolverhampton: stays 1m: acts on polytrack and good to firm going. *K. A. Ryan*

ORPEN WIDE (IRE) 2 b.g. (Mar 26) Orpen (USA) 116 – Melba (IRE) 62 (Nam- **74**
aqualand (USA)) [2004 6g 6g³ 7g³ 8g 6d 6.1v² 6s⁵ f5g* Dec 16] 5,500 2-y-o: strong
gelding: first foal: dam ran 3 times: fair performer: well backed, improved to win nursery
at Southwell on first start since gelded, drifting right: should prove best at 5f/6f: acts
on fibresand and heavy going: tongue tied fourth outing: often races up with pace.
M. C. Chapman

ORPHAN (IRE) 2 b.g. (Feb 28) Orpen (USA) 116 – Ballinlee (IRE) (Skyliner 117) **68 p**
[2004 6d 6s⁵ 5g⁴ 5g⁴ Oct 5] 5,200F, 1,000Y: tall gelding: fourth foal: half-brother to
useful 7f winner Alfie Boy and 1¼m winner Charlie Simmons (both by Forest Wind):
dam unraced sister to smart sprinter Blyton Lad: modest form in maidens, fading after
good speed each time: likely to prove best at 5f: type to do better in handicaps as 3-y-o.
K. R. Burke

OSCAR PEPPER (USA) 7 b.g. Brunswick (USA) 119 – Princess Baja (USA) (Con- **76**
quistador Cielo (USA)) [2004 73, a96: 8.1g⁵ 8m 9f⁶ 9.2g³ 10m⁴ 10g⁵ 8d² 9.2f⁴ 9.9m* **a96**
10g⁴ 8m³ 7.9m Sep 5] close-coupled gelding: useful handicapper on all-weather, fair on
turf: won ladies race at Beverley in July: stays 1¼m: acts on fibresand, firm and good to
soft going: tried in blinkers/cheekpieces, visored last 9 starts. *T. D. Barron*

OSLA 3 ch.f. Komaite (USA) – Orlaith 68 (Final Straw 127) [2004 6.1m f7d 7g 10m **–**
10.9g⁶ 8f Jul 21] 500 2-y-o: half-sister to 3 winners, including 1¼m winner Telopea (by
Teenoso): dam third over 6f only start: little form, including in sellers, leaving H. Candy
after debut: blinkered final start. *R. Brotherton*

O'SO NEET 6 b.g. Teenoso (USA) 135 – Unveiled 76 (Sayf El Arab (USA) 127) [2004 **–**
p7g 10v May 10] neat gelding: of little account. *P. Burgoyne*

Ladbrokes Rockingham Handicap, the Curragh—Osterhase defies top weight of 10-1 and puts up the best handicap performance in Ireland in 2004; Jacks Estate is second

OSTERHASE (IRE) 5 b.g. Flying Spur (AUS) – Ostrusa (AUT) (Rustan (HUN)) **120** [2004 111: 5v 6m⁶ 5m* 5f* 5m* 6m⁴ 5m³ 5m⁴ 5m Dec 12] big, good-topped gelding: very smart performer: won listed races at Naas (by short head from Benbaun) and the Curragh (broke long-standing track record, beat Moon Unit 4 lengths) in June and handicap at the Curragh (under 10-1, beat Jacks Estate 1½ lengths for best performance in a handicap in Ireland during year) in July: good 1¾ lengths fourth to Var in Prix de l'Abbaye at Longchamp penultimate start, best effort after: best at 5f on good going or firmer: blinkered: front runner. *J. E. Mulhern, Ireland*

OTAGO (IRE) 3 b.g. Desert Sun 120 – Martino 44 (Marju (IRE) 127) [2004 6m³ 7f **74** 5f⁴ 6g⁵ 7g 8f⁴ 8d² 7.9g* 8m 8m* 8d p8.6d⁵ p9.5g⁴ p9.5g⁵ p10m⁴ p13g* Dec 29] IR 6,000F, 14,000Y, 30,000 2-y-o: strong gelding: third foal: dam, Irish maiden, stayed 13f: fair performer: won handicap at Carlisle and minor event at Brighton in September, and handicap at Lingfield in December: stays 13f: acts on polytrack, firm and good to soft going: visored last 2 starts. *J. R. Best*

OTYLIA 4 ch.f. Wolfhound (USA) 126 – Soba 127 (Most Secret 119) [2004 57: f6g⁵ **49** f6s⁴ f6s 6m 6d 5.7s f5g f6g⁶ Dec 7] smallish, strong, lengthy filly: poor maiden: left A. Berry after second start: stays 6f: acts on fibresand and firm going: sometimes in cheekpieces/visor. *R. M. H. Cowell*

OUDE (USA) 2 b. or br.c. (Mar 16) Dubai Millennium 140 – Chosen Lady (USA) **105 p** (Secretariat (USA)) [2004 7g* 7d² 7f³ Sep 10] leggy, quite attractive colt: half-brother to several winners in USA, notably smart Grade 1 8.5f winner Well Chosen (by Deputy Minister): dam, lightly-raced US maiden, sister to US Grade 2 1¼m winner Academy Award: won maiden at Newmarket in July in good style by neck from Shannon Springs: useful form in listed race at York and Champagne Stakes (3 lengths third to Etlaala, racing freely and leading briefly 2f out) at Doncaster: should stay 1m: likely to progress. *Saeed bin Suroor*

OUIJA BOARD 3 b.f. Cape Cross (IRE) 129 – Selection Board 75 (Welsh Pageant **125** 132) [2004 98: 10m* 12m* 12f* 12m³ 11d* Oct 30]

Not all the famous ancestors of the 19th Earl of Derby were imbued with the same love of horse racing. The 15th Earl, for example, was said to have dismissed the sport as an 'appalling extravagance', though, as Lord Stanley in 1851, he was one of five ancestors of the present Lord Derby to win the Oaks, an achievement emulated by the current incumbent with the home-bred Ouija Board. The 15th Earl, incidentally, served (as Lord Stanley) in all three fairly short-lived governments formed by his father, the 14th Earl, in the 1850s and 1860s. The 14th Earl was regarded as a weak prime minister ('It was said that he bore the imprint of the last person who sat on him') and Disraeli was a leading figure in all three of his governments, holding the post of Chancellor of the Exchequer. The famous 'black, white cap' colours—which also have one white button—were first registered in the eighteenth century by the 12th Earl of Derby, who gave his name to Flat racing's most famous event, first run in 1780 (over a mile), after he and Sir Charles Bunbury—

who won the first Derby with Diomed—were said to have tossed a coin to decide whose name the race should carry. A year earlier, the 12th Earl had founded the Oaks—named after the country house he leased in Surrey—for three-year-old fillies over a mile and a half and won its first running with Bridget (he was successful in the race again in 1794). The 16th Earl won the 1896 and 1906 runnings and the 17th Earl also won the race twice, firstly in 1928 and then in 1945 with Sun Stream, the last horse before Ouija Board to carry the family's colours to victory in a classic.

The 17th Earl of Derby was named 'Man of the Century' in the John Randall/Tony Morris work *A Century of Champions*, published in conjunction with Timeform to provide a millennial perspective on the sport. At number five was the trainer George Lambton, who had a forty-year partnership with the 16th and 17th Earls; and at number seven was Walter Alston, stud manager for about thirty years to the 16th and 17th Earls, who was responsible for many of the decisions which made the Stanley Stud operation such an influence on twentieth-century racing. The 17th Earl inherited the title and the Stanley family's bloodstock when his father the 16th Earl died in 1908. The 17th Earl, secretary of state for war in the Lloyd George government, was influential in securing the resumption of racing after its cessation for a time in 1917. Lord Derby's home-bred sprinter Phalaris, the best older horse in training in 1917 and 1918, went on to exert a massive influence at stud, *A Century of Champions* naming him 'Sire of the Century'. The brothers Pharos and Fairway, both products of Lord Derby's stud, were by Phalaris and, like him, became champion sires, Nearco (through Nasrullah, Nearctic and Royal Charter) spreading the influence of Pharos, and Fair Trial and his sons spreading the influence of Fairway. Nearctic became the sire of the prepotent Northern Dancer. Nearly all the horses raced by the 17th Earl of Derby were home-bred—from a band of broodmares usually numbering only around thirty at any one time—and he won a record-equalling number of classics, both as an owner (twenty) and breeder (nineteen), between 1910 and 1945. Leading breeder ten times and leading owner on seven occasions, Lord Derby also bred and owned the outstanding 1933 Derby and St Leger winner Hyperion, who went on to become champion sire on six occasions between 1940 and 1954 (Sun Stream was the last of his four Oaks winners).

The 17th Earl of Derby also bred Alycidon, who won the Ascot Gold Cup in 1949, the year after the 17th Earl's death, and was later champion sire in Britain. The 18th Earl, uncle of the current Lord Derby, was the winning owner (as Lord Stanley) in the 1935 Oaks with the leased Quashed and he bred and owned the top-class miler of the 'eighties Teleprompter, a full brother to Ouija Board's dam Selection Board. But more of Ouija Board's family later.

The dukes and lords of British racing enjoyed something of a classic revival in 2004. As well as Ouija Board's victories in both the Oaks and the Irish Oaks —she was Lord Derby's only horse in training incidentally—the Duke of Roxburghe's Attraction completed the Anglo-Irish Guineas double, the colours of the late Duke of Devonshire were carried to success by Bachelor Duke in the Irish Two Thousand Guineas, and the Derby went to North Light in the silks which Lord

Vodafone Oaks, Epsom—the famous 'black, white cap' of Lord Derby is carried to victory in a classic for the first time since 1945; Kieren Fallon looks round and sees no danger on Ouija Board, with All Too Beautiful, Punctilious, Necklace and Crystal strung out behind

Darley Irish Oaks, the Curragh—Ouija Board completes the Oaks double, landing the odds from Punctilious, Hazarista and All Too Beautiful

Weinstock helped to make famous. The latest season does not herald a return to the old aristocratic order, but it provided an interesting interlude, a year when the usually dominant battalions of Godolphin and Ballydoyle mustered a single success in the British and Irish classics between them—with Rule of Law in the St Leger. Ouija Board showed only useful form as a two-year-old—winning once from three starts—and she was available at 40/1 in the ante-post market for the Vodafone Oaks at the end of April. A much improved performance in one of the lesser Oaks trials, the Pretty Polly Stakes over a mile and a quarter at Newmarket on One Thousand Guineas day, caused a drastic revision of those odds after Ouija Board showed a fine turn of foot and demolished her field by six lengths, the rest led home by Sahool. A tilt at the Prix de Diane was reportedly considered because of doubts about Ouija Board's stamina, but the feeling expressed by connections that 'there is only one Oaks' always made it more likely she would line up at Epsom.

There had not been a smaller field for the Oaks since the peerless Pretty Polly beat just three opponents at 100/8-on (the shortest odds ever returned in a British classic) exactly a century before. The seven runners for the latest renewal, the same number as in 1916, when Fifinella won, and as in 1992, User Friendly's year, included three from Ballydoyle and two representing Godolphin. The superbly-bred All Too Beautiful, a sister to Galileo, had won both her starts—the second a listed event at Navan—and started 11/4 favourite to provide Aidan O'Brien with his third Oaks winner. Saeed bin Suroor, also seeking a third win in the race, provided the second and third favourites ahead of 7/2-shot Ouija Board, the One Thousand Guineas runner-up Sundrop starting at 3/1 and the Musidora Stakes winner Punctilious at 100/30. Sundrop and Punctilious had finished second and third in the Fillies' Mile at two when O'Brien's second string in the Oaks, the 10/1-shot Necklace, had won the Moyglare Stud Stakes. Sundrop and Necklace (unplaced in the Guineas at both Newmarket and the Curragh), along with the Ballydoyle pacemaker Kisses For Me, were the only Oaks runners who had previously contested a classic. After being taken down last and quietly to post, Ouija Board put up a breathtaking performance, taking a while to warm to her task but coming back on the bridle early in the straight and settling the issue in a matter of strides after being sent into the lead two furlongs out. The margin of victory over All Too Beautiful was seven lengths, one bettered only six times in the Oaks since official distances were first published for the race in 1842 (Sun Princess won by twelve in 1983; Formosa, Noblesse and Jet Ski Lady by ten in 1868, 1963 and 1991 respectively; Lady Carla by nine in 1996; and Saucy Sue by eight in 1925). Blue Wind also won by seven in 1981. Ouija Board's performance was the best recorded in the Oaks since User Friendly beat All At Sea by three and a half lengths, with the third a further twenty lengths away; third-placed Punctilious finished ten and a half lengths behind Ouija Board in the latest edition, fourth-placed Necklace was beaten twelve by the winner with a further gap of eighteen back to fifth-placed Crystal, Sundrop beating only the pacemaker.

User Friendly went on to win the Irish Oaks, the Yorkshire Oaks and the St Leger after her triumph at Epsom, before coming an excellent second in the Arc and ending her three-year-old campaign with sixth in the Japan Cup. Ouija Board was not entered for the St Leger—there had never seemed much prospect of her having the stamina—but, otherwise, the remainder of her campaign followed along similar lines to User Friendly's. Both fillies are relatively rare in being Oaks winners who enhanced their reputation after Epsom. Of the eleven Oaks winners between User Friendly and Ouija Board, for example, only Intrepidity, Balanchine, Ramruma and Kazzia won a race afterwards (Moonshell and Imagine both had training setbacks and did not run again as three-year-olds after Epsom). Balanchine (also winner of the One Thousand Guineas) beat the colts in the Irish Derby on her only subsequent three-year-old start; Ramruma emulated User Friendly by completing the Oaks Group 1 treble, following up at the Curragh and York, and then finishing second in the St Leger; Intrepidity came fourth in the Irish Oaks, won the Vermeille, finished fourth in the Arc and unplaced in the Breeders' Cup Turf; Kazzia (who had won the One Thousand Guineas) managed only fourth in the Yorkshire Oaks, missed the St Leger with foot trouble and had her last two outings in North America, winning the Flower Bowl Invitational but failing to do herself justice in the Breeders' Cup Filly & Mare Turf, coming only sixth after an interrupted preparation. The campaigns of User Friendly, Intrepidity and Kazzia emphasised the internationalism of modern racing. There is more to aim at, particularly in the last quarter of the season, and, while a classic victory still carries great prestige, the programme for a top three-year-old which keeps its form and steers clear of illness and injury extends right through to late-autumn. Ouija Board wasn't seen on a British racecourse after Epsom, though she was declared at the forty-eight-hour stage for the Yorkshire Oaks before being a late withdrawal because of soft going. That denied her the chance of the Group 1 Oaks treble achieved by User Friendly and Ramruma, and before them by Fair Salinia and Diminuendo (who dead-heated at the Curragh). But Ouija Board did become the tenth to complete the Oaks/Irish Oaks double, following, as well as those mentioned, Masaka, Altesse Royale, Juliette Marny, Blue Wind and Unite. The latest Irish Oaks, sponsored by Darley, was essentially a rematch between the principals at Epsom, the supplemented Ouija Board odds on to defeat six rivals including All Too Beautiful and Punctilious, the latter successful in the Ribblesdale at Royal Ascot in the interim. Punctilious turned the tables on a below-form All Too Beautiful, who was beaten for third by the Aga Khan-owned 20/1-shot Hazarista. Despite being slowly away, Ouija Board ran out quite a comfortable winner, though tending to drift to the right, across the runner-up, after hitting the front over a furlong out, and having only a length to spare at the line. Ouija Board was her trainer's second Irish Oaks winner in four years, following Lailani in 2001. Dunlop saddled the Poule d'Essai des Pouliches winner Ta Rib in 1996, the year he also enjoyed Group 1 success with Iktamal in the Haydock Park Sprint Cup.

After missing the Yorkshire Oaks and the Vermeille ('I'm not convinced we should go to France twice'), Ouija Board was targeted at Longchamp's Arc week-end programme, taking her place, after some deliberation, in a nineteen-runner field for the Arc itself, rather than tackling the shorter Prix de l'Opera, a Group 1 restricted to fillies and mares, originally announced as the more likely option. The unconsidered four-year-old Urban Sea in 1993 (the year Intrepidity was fourth) was the last of her sex to land the Arc—and the only one to do so since fillies won five in a row between 1979 and 1983—but the so-called 'weaker sex' have a sound record in the Arc historically. That said, no British-trained filly has won the race. The five-year-old Park Top was an unlucky second to Levmoss in 1969, Awaasif finished third to Akiyda in 1982, Sun Princess was runner-up to All Along in 1983 (when the first four were all fillies), User Friendly went down by a neck to Subotica in 1992, and Leggera (who was also fourth the following year) by the same distance to Sagamix in 1998. The Nassau Stakes and Yorkshire Oaks winner Islington was the best of her sex trained in Britain in 2002 when she came a creditable fifth in the Arc, followed by third in the Breeders' Cup Filly & Mare Turf (a race she returned to win as a four-year-old when she bypassed the Arc). Awaasif and Leggera were both trained by John Dunlop, who also saddled the New Zealand Derby winner Balmerino when he was second in the 1977 Arc. Ouija Board, whose trainer is the elder of John Dunlop's two surviving sons, added to the Dunlop family's collection of placed horses in the Arc. With her regular rider as a three-year-old Kieren Fallon claimed for Derby winner North Light, Ouija Board was ridden by Johnny Murtagh at Longchamp (as she would have been if she had taken her chance in the Yorkshire Oaks in which Fallon was also claimed by the Stoute stable). Ouija Board finished strongly for third, beaten half a length and a length, still making ground at the line, by the French-trained three-year-old colts Bago and Cherry Mix (North Light was back in fifth). Ouija Board's high-class effort was on a par with the form she showed in the Oaks at Epsom but she might well have finished even closer had she not lost ground after becoming involved in some scrimmaging rounding the home turn, and then had to be switched wide to make her challenge in the straight. Ouija Board was held up, and for most of the way was not far behind the eventual winner who enjoyed an uninterrupted run.

Breeders' Cup wins used to be a rarity for British-trained horses, the victories of the filly Pebbles in the 1985 Turf and of Sheikh Albadou in the Sprint on dirt in 1991 being the only ones in the first ten years. In the eleven years since, the winners have come more regularly—Barathea (Mile, 1994), Pilsudski (1996, Turf), Daylami (1999, Turf), Kalanisi (2000, Turf), Fantastic Light (2001, Turf), Islington (2003, Filly & Mare Turf) and, in the twenty-first Breeders' Cup, Ouija Board in the Filly & Mare Turf and, more surprisingly, the seemingly exposed Wilko in the Juvenile on dirt. The Breeders' Cup organisers revel in labelling the meeting the 'World Thoroughbred Championships' but there are rival attractions nowadays, including the Champion Stakes at Newmarket and events in Canada, Australia, Japan (which is opening more of its richly-endowed races to international competition nowadays) and Hong Kong. For the first time since 1997, Saeed bin Suroor did not have a Breeders' Cup runner, Sulamani aimed instead at the Canadian International the previous weekend, while Doyen and Refuse To Bend tackled the Champion Stakes. The difficulties of travelling horses long distances to warmer climates have largely been overcome with experience and the Breeders' Cup suffers more from the dramatic changes that have taken place in the international landscape. Back in 1984, only two other races in America—the Arlington Million and the Hollywood Futurity—offered a million-dollar purse. The first Breeders' Cup had five one million-dollar races, the two-million dollar Breeders' Cup Turf and the three-million dollar Breeders' Cup Classic. Two decades on, there are at least a dozen million-dollar races in North America, apart from the eight now staged at the Breeders' Cup. At least sixty races worldwide now offer purses of a million dollars or more. Prize money for some of the Breeders' Cup races has risen in recent years but entry fees have gone up too, with some owners now questioning

VO5 Breeders' Cup Filly & Mare Turf, Lone Star Park—a third win in the race in four years for Europe and another notable success for Ouija Board who beats her elders; Film Maker (right) is second ahead of Wonder Again (almost completely hidden by winner) and Moscow Burning (rail)

the worth of stumping up five- and six-figure entry fees to run horses who were either not nominated as foals, or whose sires were not nominated.

Connections of Ouija Board, who had to be supplemented, deliberated over whether to tackle the Filly & Mare Turf (added as an eighth race in 1999) or the Breeders' Cup Turf, one of the factors being the difference between the final supplementary entry fees, 180,000 dollars for the Turf and 90,000 dollars for the mares race. Ouija Board, reunited with Fallon, was the only three-year-old in the twelve-runner line-up for the Filly & Mare Turf, but she was the form choice and, handy throughout in a steadily-run affair, landed the odds at Lone Star Park by a length and a half from Film Maker, adapting well to the sharp track and proving herself on good to soft going (the first time she had raced on anything softer than good). 'She has been round Epsom and will adapt,' her trainer said beforehand, expressing more concern about the likely effects of the heavy rain that fell in the days before the meeting.

One further point before leaving the Breeders' Cup. Concerns were expressed from the outset about North American racing's policy on drugs—or 'medication'—and, twenty-one years on, the Breeders' Cup organisers are still no nearer to coming into line. Pretty well all American horses race on the diuretic drug lasix (salix)—claimed to be beneficial for those who suffer bleeding in their lungs when racing—and use of the pain-masking drug bute is also almost universal. Both are banned in every other major country. Unlike the previous year at Santa Anita, bute didn't have to be declared at Lone Star Park. It was, nonetheless, disappointing to see the trainers of most of the twelve European challengers (a smaller number than usual) again adopting a 'when in Rome' approach to lasix. Andre Fabre has stood out conspicuously against 'medication' and his runners Nebraska Tornado and Diamond Green both raced 'clean', as did another French-trained challenger Aubonne. The two other French challengers, Six Perfections and Whipper, and the five Ballydoyle representatives raced on lasix, as did Ouija Board and Wilko. Whether lasix aided either Ouija Board or Wilko, or any of the six home-trained winners, is impossible to know for certain, but the permissive approach of the Breeders' Cup organisers will always detract from the meeting's considerable value to international racing. The domestic television audience, incidentally, for a five-hour programme on NBC was reportedly the lowest ever recorded for a Breeders' Cup.

The tall, leggy Ouija Board is from the first crop of the high-class miler Cape Cross, whose first three-year-olds did him proud, nine of his forty-one runners earning a rating of 100 or more. The average distance of races won by the Cape Cross three-year-olds in Britain was around eight and a half furlongs, in line with most expectations given the pedigree and racing record of Cape Cross. Ouija Board wasn't alone, however, in staying further than her sire who also had two runners in the Derby, the smart Hazyview, not discredited in eighth, and Elshadi, and was also represented in the latest season by Privy Seal, third in the Derby Italiano. Another of Cape Cross's fillies, the useful Mazuna out of a mare who won at a mile and a half, won the Princess Royal Stakes and was second in the Park Hill. Breeders who have used Cape Cross, in the last two seasons in particular, will be hoping that Ouija Board and others continue to keep his name in lights. Cape Cross covered 97 mares in his second season (compared with 120 in his first), but that number rose sharply in 2002 (138) and 2003 (136) before another big jump in 2004, when he covered no fewer than 188 mares. Little surprise then that, after the latest covering season, Darley announced that Cape Cross would not be shuttled to Australasia for the 2004 southern hemisphere breeding season. 'He's done nine consecutive seasons [in two hemispheres] and the timing just seemed right to give him a break,' said the managing director of Kildangan. Perhaps some breeders deserve a break too: none should have to enter into a contract to use a stallion without receiving a guarantee of the maximum number of mares the stallion will cover that season. General over-production contributed to a fall in demand at the 2004 yearling sales in Britain and Ireland and, with even bigger crops from the most fashionable stallions in the pipeline, the situation for vendors looks set to worsen before it can get better.

Ouija Board's family was introduced into the Stanley House studs in 1950 when the 18th Earl and French breeder Elisabeth Couturie swapped two seven-year-old mares, a half-sister to Alycidon crossing the Channel one way in exchange for the winning mare Gradisca, whose dam was a half-sister to the good sire Rialto, among others. Mme Couturie got very much the better of the deal at first. She exercised an option to purchase if a filly was produced to Gradisca's service by Tornado while still in France. The English-foaled filly, named Tahiti II, was returned to France and went on to finish second in the Poule d'Essai des Pouliches and win the Prix de Diane in Mme Couturie's colours; the foal produced by the daughter of Alycidon, a colt called Antares, did not run as a two-year-old but finished second for Mr R. B. Strassburger in the Prix du Jockey Club a week after Tahiti won the Prix de Diane. Gradisca's stud career in England was a disappointment. She produced only two winners, both gelded sons of Hyperion, and had only two daughters, both by Alycidon. The twice-raced Almah was weeded out after being well beaten in maidens but later became the grandam of the outstanding Australian performer Kingston Town. Almah's unraced year-older sister Samanda remained at the stud after being blinded as a result of charging through a paddock fence with her dam as a foal. Caroline Silver's book *Classic Lives*, which followed the progress of seven foals bred by the Stanley House stud operation as hopefuls for the 1968 Derby, explains the arrangements that had to be made for Samanda. Because she could not have defended herself, Samanda was kept on her own, with a loosebox opening on to a paddock. She found her way round using her hearing and sense of smell, and had no trouble walking freely in and out of her stable. Samanda's foals were equipped with a bell on their head collar and, because the mare suffered from claustrophobia, her foals mostly slept out from being a few days old. Because of their early isolation, they apparently rarely suffered from any of the illnesses common to foals, though they often caught the ailments after weaning, when running with others.

The foal by Samanda who was a subject for *Classic Lives*, a colt called Rainhill, never ran, badly injuring himself on a flight to Ireland as a foal and then having to be put down as a yearling after developing severe laminitis. Samanda produced twelve foals in all, nine of whom won, two of her daughters being Sam's Song and Ouija. Sam's Song was a useful stayer who became great grandam of July Cup winner Owington, sold as a yearling by Stanley House for 56,000 guineas. Already among the descendants of Samanda at the time were those notable performers out of Ouija's daughter Rosia Bay, the four-time Group 1 winner and Breeders' Cup Classic runner-up Ibn Bey and Roseate Tern, winner of the Yorkshire Oaks and placed in the Oaks and St Leger. Useful on her day, Rosia Bay had been obtained by Lord Carnarvon for only 6,200 guineas at the Doncaster Sales after carrying Lord Derby's colours successfully at two and three. Rosia Bay was the first foal out of Ouija, a useful winner at a mile and probably just the best of Samanda's offspring on the racecourse. Ouija's third foal was Teleprompter who carried Lord Derby's colours with great distinction. Ineligible as a gelding for Group 1 events in Europe, the front-running Teleprompter gained his biggest triumph in the Arlington Million in 1985 after winning the Queen Elizabeth II Stakes (then a Group 2) at Ascot the previous year. The ban on geldings was relaxed in Britain in 1986 but the move came just too late for Teleprompter who was by then a six-year-old; nonetheless, he put up creditable efforts that year to finish third to Dancing Brave and Triptych in the Eclipse, and second to Sure Blade in the Queen Elizabeth II Stakes. Teleprompter raced for six seasons in all, earning nearly £800,000 in prize money, a record at the time for a British-trained gelding.

After Rosia Bay (whose more distant descendants include the smart three-year-old Red Bloom) and Teleprompter, Ouija went on to produce four other winners who also raced for the 18th Earl of Derby, a minor winner over six furlongs called Indian Sign (later successful at a mile and a quarter), the useful milers Riot Squad and Message Pad, and the Brigadier Gerard Stakes winner Chatoyant. Ouija was sent back to Teleprompter's sire Welsh Pageant immediately after producing Indian Sign and the resultant offspring was Ouija Board's dam Selection Board, who came a close second in an Ayr maiden on her only start at two but made only one other racecourse appearance, when down the field thirteen months later in a back-end maiden over a mile at Haydock. The now-deceased Selection Board had a career at stud that was nothing to write home about until Ouija Board—her penultimate foal—added another memorable chapter in the story of the Samanda family. Selection Board had six winners before Ouija Board, the pick of them the

66,000-guinea yearling Star Selection (by Rainbow Quest), a useful performer at up to a mile and a half on the Flat whose varied record included a sixth in the Two Thousand Guineas in 1994, when he also contested the Derby for Paul Cole's stable, and a lengthy career over jumps in which he won both over hurdles and fences. Also useful was the Inchinor filly Cruinn A Bhord who won two quite valuable handicaps at Newmarket over seven furlongs as a four-year-old in Lord Derby's colours; Cruinn A Bhord is now one of Lord Derby's eight-strong band of broodmares and, coincidentally, is due to foal to Cape Cross in 2005. Selection Board produced offspring who won over a variety of distances. Star Selection's brother the fairly useful Spectrometer stayed a mile and three quarters and has also won over hurdles and fences. The lesser lights Officer Cadet (by Shernazar) and Coalition (by Polish Precedent) won at up to eleven furlongs and a mile and three quarters respectively, while Draft Board, the first of three winners by Rainbow Quest out of Selection Board, ran only at three and gained her only victory dropped back to six furlongs after starting her campaign at ten and a half furlongs. Selection Board's final offspring, a gelding by Inchinor named Illuminati who is in training with Willie Jenks and has yet to race, fetched only 5,500 guineas as a yearling, the week before Ouija Board gained the first win of her career in a minor event at Yarmouth as a two-year-old.

		Green Desert	Danzig
	Cape Cross (IRE)	(b 1983)	Foreign Counter
	(b 1994)	Park Appeal	Ahonoora
Ouija Board		(br 1982)	Balidaress
(b.f. 2001)		Welsh Pageant	Tudor Melody
	Selection Board	(b 1966)	Picture Light
	(b 1982)	Ouija	Silly Season
		(b 1971)	Samanda

The precedents are not particularly encouraging for Ouija Board's four-year-old campaign. User Friendly went on to win the Grand Prix de Saint-Cloud

Lord Derby's "Ouija Board"

as a four-year-old but neither Intrepidity, Balanchine, Moonshell, Lady Carla nor Ramruma, the other recent Oaks winners kept in training at four, managed to win a race. Much more encouragement can, however, be taken from the success of Islington, who turned out to be at least as good at four when she won the Yorkshire Oaks as well as the Breeders' Cup Filly & Mare Turf, after an interrupted training programme in the spring. The fact that Ouija Board is effective at a mile and a quarter to a mile and a half, and is now proven on going ranging from firm to good to soft, gives her connections a fairly wide range of targets to aim at. Incidentally, as Ouija Board's name suggests, Lord and Lady Derby are somewhat superstitious and, on race days in the latest season, were kitted out in clothes and adornments identical to those they wore when Ouija Board won the Pretty Polly Stakes. It was a chilly day on the Rowley Mile so, if the practice is continued, it is to be hoped none of Ouija Board's races in the next summer coincides with a heatwave! *E. A. L. Dunlop*

OULTON BROAD   8 b.g. Midyan (USA) 124 – Lady Quachita (USA) (Sovereign Dancer (USA)) [2004 f12g f16g⁵ p16g⁶ f16.2m⁶ May 17] poor performer: stays 1½m: acts on all-weather and heavy going: visored once at 3 yrs, wore cheekpieces in 2004. *F. Jordan*   **39**

OUNINPOHJA (IRE)   3 b.g. Imperial Ballet (IRE) 110 – Daziyra (IRE) (Doyoun 124) [2004 10.3m⁴ 8g³ 6.9f² 10m⁵ 10s* Oct 12] good-topped gelding: fourth foal: half-brother to fairly useful Irish 2001 2-y-o 5f winner Dangerous Years (by Ali-Royal): dam ran once in France: fair performer: landed odds in maiden at Ayr in October: stays 1¼m: acts on soft and good to firm going. *G. A. Swinbank*   **78 +**

OUR CHELSEA BLUE (USA)   6 ch.m. Distant View (USA) 126 – Eastern Connection (USA) (Danzig Connection (USA)) [2004 54, a66: f6s f5g³ f5s⁶ p6g f5g p6g Apr 19] modest performer: left A. Carroll after third start: stays easy 7f: acts on all-weather and good to firm going: sometimes tongue tied: often slowly away. *I. A. Wood*   **–**
   a54

OUR CHOICE (IRE)   2 b.c. (Mar 15) Indian Danehill (IRE) 124 – Spring Daffodil 97 (Pharly (FR) 130) [2004 5d 5g⁴ 6m p7d⁶ 8d 8d⁶ Oct 15] €28,000F, 28,000Y: tall, good-topped colt: half-brother to several winners, including useful 1m to 1¼m winner Pantar (by Shirley Heights): dam Irish 7f/1m winner, later successful in USA: modest maiden: stays 1m: acts on polytrack, best turf effort on good to soft going. *N. P. Littmoden*   **62**

OUR DESTINY   6 b.g. Mujadil (USA) 119 – Superspring (Superlative 118) [2004 58: f8.5g³ f9.4g² f12g⁴ f9.4s f8g* f8.5g* f8g⁶ 8.3d³ f8.5g* 10.2g² 10.2s⁴ 11.9m³ 10m* 10.1f 10f⁴ 10g* 12.6g 10f⁵ 8f⁶ 10f⁶ 10.2g 8.1m⁴ 10.9d p12.2d⁵ p9.5g³ p9.5g⁴ p12.2g³ p9.5g² p12.2g⁴ p9.5g Dec 15] strong, lengthy gelding: fair performer: won claimers at Southwell (amateurs, left D. Burchell) and Wolverhampton (apprentices), seller at Wolverhampton and handicaps at Brighton and Lingfield (apprentices) in first half of 2004: stays easy 1½m: acts on all-weather, firm and soft going: effective visored or not: tough. *A. W. Carroll*   **65**

OUR EMMY LOU   3 ch.f. Mark of Esteem (IRE) 137 – Regent's Folly (IRE) 101 (Touching Wood (USA) 127) [2004 56: 12m² 11.9m⁴ 12.1d⁵ f12s⁶ 11.5g* 10f⁵ p12g Oct 1] leggy, good-topped filly: fair performer: won claimer at Yarmouth in September: stays 1½m: acts on good to firm going: blinkered (raced too freely) fourth start: sold 13,000 gns. *Sir Mark Prescott*   **70**

OUR FRED   7 ch.g. Prince Sabo 123 – Sheila's Secret (IRE) 97 (Bluebird (USA) 125) [2004 62§, a75§: p5g⁶ p5g 5g Jun 24] lengthy gelding: fair handicapper on all-weather, modest on turf: barely stays 6f: acts on all-weather, firm and good to firm going: tried visored: often blinkered: usually races up with pace: unreliable: sold 2,000 gns. *T. G. Mills*   **?**
   a69 §

OUR FUGITIVE (IRE)   2 gr.c. (Apr 12) Titus Livius (FR) 115 – Mystical Jumbo (Mystiko (USA) 124) [2004 5.1s⁴ 5m 5f³ 5.1m² 5.1s* 6d² Oct 15] third foal: leggy colt: half-brother to useful 2002 2-y-o 6f/7f winner Leitrim Lakes (by Mujadil): dam unraced: useful performer: won nursery at Chepstow in August: excellent neck second to Ingleton in similar event at Newmarket final start: effective at 5f/6f: acts on soft ground, probably on firm: swerved markedly right fourth outing: races up with pace. *A. W. Carroll*   **97**

OUR GAMBLE (IRE)   3 b.f. Entrepreneur 123 – Manilia (FR) (Kris 135) [2004 84: 6v⁶ 7g 6g 6d 7f⁵ 5g Sep 15] leggy filly: fluent mover: modest performer: probably stays 7f: acts on good to firm going: sold 2,500 gns. *R. Hannon*   **59**

OUR GLENARD   5 b.g. Royal Applause 124 – Loucoum (FR) 93 (Iron Duke (FR) 122) [2004 58§: f11g² p10g² f12g f11g⁵ p13g⁶ p10g⁴ 9.9v p10g 9.9m⁴ May 24] smallish,   **51 §**

sturdy gelding: modest performer: stays 13f: acts on all-weather and good to firm going: tried tongue tied: slowly away last 3 outings: untrustworthy. *S. L. Keightley*

OUR IMPERIAL BAY (USA) 5 b.g. Smart Strike (CAN) 121 – Heat Lightning (USA) (Summer Squall (USA)) [2004 –: p16g 14.4s f11s* f12g p16g³ 8.1f f12g³ f14g⁶ f14m³ 16.2m 12.1g 12.1m⁵ f12g p12.2g p13.9g f12g f11g⁴ Dec 12] tall gelding: modest performer: won seller at Southwell in March: left R. Stronge after fifth start: stays easy 2m: acts on all-weather, soft and good to firm going: wears headgear: ungenuine. *Mrs J. Candlish*   **49 §** **a56 §**

OUR JAFFA (IRE) 3 br.f. Bin Ajwaad (IRE) 119 – Griddle Cake (IRE) 62 (Be My Guest (USA) 126) [2004 10g⁴ 8f* 8.2m* 8m² p7g⁵ 8.1g 8g⁶ Oct 1] 700Y, 2,600 2-y-o: tall filly: sixth foal: sister to winner up to 1½m in Sweden: dam, maiden who stayed 1½m, half-sister to smart middle-distance performers Bonny Scot and Mary Stuart, and to dam of Golan: fairly useful performer: won maiden at Bath in May and handicap at Nottingham in June: ran at least respectably in handicaps/minor event after: stays 1m: acts on firm going and polytrack. *D. J. Daly*   **87**

OUR KES (IRE) 2 gr.f. (Apr 18) Revoque (IRE) 122 – Gracious Gretclo 54 (Common Grounds 118) [2004 5m 8g 8m 8.3m⁴ 7.9g p8g p7.1g* p7g* Dec 29] 13,000Y: strong, lengthy filly: fourth living foal: sister to 3-y-o Granston and half-sister to 4-y-o Malahide Express: dam maiden who stayed 6f: fair on all-weather, modest on turf: trained by A. Berry on debut: won maiden at Wolverhampton and nursery at Lingfield in December: barely stays 1m: acts on polytrack and good to firm going. *P. Howling*   **61** **a76**

OUR KID 3 ch.g. Pursuit of Love 124 – Flower Princess (Slip Anchor 136) [2004 63: 9.9s 12.3g f12m⁶ 7m 7s 7s Oct 26] workmanlike gelding: maiden: little form in 2004, leaving T. Easterby after third start: tried blinkered: often slowly away. *T. G. McCourt, Ireland*

OUR LITTLE ROSIE 3 b.f. Piccolo 121 – Villella (Sadler's Wells (USA) 132) [2004 p8g p8g p10g⁵ f12g* 10.9d f12g 10.5g p12g p12.2g Nov 8] half-sister to French 10.5f/11.5f winner Periwinkle (by Bering) and 1½m winner Brunston Castle (by Hector Protector): dam unraced out of smart performer up to 1½m Ghaiya: modest performer: won maiden at Wolverhampton in March: mostly well held after: stays 1½m: acts on all-weather. *M. Blanshard*   **62 d**

OUR LITTLE SECRET (IRE) 2 ch.f. (May 8) Rossini (USA) 118 – Sports Post Lady (IRE) 72 (M Double M (USA)) [2004 5g⁵ p5.1g³ p5.1d³ p5.1g Nov 12] €1,500F, 2,200Y: half-sister to 3-y-o Jadan and 2 winners abroad: dam best at 5f: modest maiden: likely to prove best at 5f. *A. Berry*   **59**

OUR LOUIS 2 b.f. (Feb 9) Abou Zouz (USA) 109 – Ninfa of Cisterna (Polish Patriot (USA) 128) [2004 5s⁶ 5s 5g⁵ 5m⁴ 5f* 5g⁵ 5g 5m 5s 5g 5f Sep 13] €3,000Y: compact filly: third foal: dam, Italian 5f/6f (including at 2 yrs) winner, out of half-sister to Poule d'Essai des Poulains winner Victory Note: modest performer: won seller at Musselburgh in June: below form after: will prove best at 5f: acts on firm going: wore cheekpieces fourth start: races up with pace. *J. S. Wainwright*   **52**

OUR NIGEL (IRE) 2 gr.g. (Feb 13) Namid 128 – Mystical 77 (Mystiko (USA) 124) [2004 5g 5.1f 5d 5.7g Sep 27] well held in maidens/seller. *Mrs P. N. Dutfield*   **–**

OUR OLD BOY (IRE) 4 br.g. Petorius 117 – Minzal Legend (IRE) 84 (Primo Dominie 121) [2004 f5g f5g f7s Feb 17] small gelding: little form. *J. A. Gilbert*   **–**

OUR PLACE (IRE) 5 b.g. Distinctly North (USA) 115 – Simplyhectic (IRE) (Simply Great (FR) 122) [2004 f16.2s Mar 5] lengthy, good-topped gelding: lightly raced and little form. *B. N. Doran*   **–**

OUR SION 4 b.g. Dreams End 93 – Millfields Lady 75 (Sayf El Arab (USA) 127) [2004 6s 6m 6.1m May 25] of no account. *R. Brotherton*   **–**

OUR TEDDY (IRE) 4 ch.g. Grand Lodge (USA) 125 – Lady Windley (Baillamont (USA) 124) [2004 103: p8g⁴ 8g 8g 8.1f⁵ 8.9m⁴ 10m⁴ 8.1d 8m p10g⁵ Nov 27] lengthy gelding: useful handicapper: best effort in 2004 when fourth to Dance On The Top at Lingfield on reappearance: stays easy 1¼m: acts on polytrack and firm going: visored (folded) second start, blinkered most outings after: unreliable. *A. M. Balding*   **99 §**

OUR WILDEST DREAMS 2 b.f. (Apr 9) Benny The Dip (USA) 127 – Imperial Scholar (IRE) 94 (Royal Academy (USA) 130) [2004 8m Sep 29] 1,000Y: fourth foal: half-sister to 3-y-o Komoto and fairly useful 8.5f winner Gryngolette (by Linamix), later successful in Scandinavia: dam, maiden, best effort at 7f: 100/1, well held in maiden at Newcastle. *C. W. Fairhurst*   **–**

OUT AFTER DARK 3 b.g. Cadeaux Genereux 131 – Midnight Shift (IRE) 73 (Night **90** Shift (USA)) [2004 75p: 6s⁵ 6g* 5s* 6g³ 5g² 6.5f⁶ Sep 24] strong, useful-looking gelding: has a quick action: fairly useful performer: won minor event at Pontefract and handicap at Sandown (beat Morgan Lewis by 1¼ lengths) in August, making most both times: creditable efforts last 3 starts, sixth to Khabfair in handicap at Ascot final one: effective at 5f to 6.5f: acts on firm and soft going. *C. G. Cox*

OUTEAST (IRE) 4 b.f. Mujadil (USA) 119 – Stifen (Burslem 123) [2004 –: 5s⁴ Aug **44** 13] angular filly: fair at 2 yrs: form since only in claimer on sole outing in 2004: best at 5f: acts on soft and good to firm going: tried in cheekpieces. *G. A. Harker*

OUTER HEBRIDES 3 b.g. Efisio 120 – Reuval 102 (Sharpen Up 127) [2004 86: 7g **91** 8m 7m⁴ p7g² 7s² Oct 27] sturdy gelding: has round action: fairly useful handicapper: tongue tied, improved form when runner-up at Lingfield and Yarmouth (beaten ½ length by Ask The Clerk) last 2 starts: should stay 1m: acts on all-weather, soft and good to firm going: effective visored or not. *D. R. Loder*

OUT FOR A STROLL 5 b.g. Zamindar (USA) 116 – The Jotter 99 (Night Shift **73** (USA)) [2004 87: 8s 7s 7g 8.2g 7g Oct 11] sturdy, deep-girthed gelding: fair handicapper: best at 7f/1m: acts on firm going. *S. C. Williams*

OUT OF INDIA 2 b.f. (Feb 21) Marju (IRE) 127 – Tide of Fortune (Soviet Star (USA) **61 p** 128) [2004 p8.6g Dec 3] 18,000Y: sixth foal: half-sister to 6-y-o Starbeck and winner in Greece by Barathea: dam unraced granddaughter of top-class 1m/1¼m performer Rose Bowl: 25/1, seventh to Nanton in maiden at Wolverhampton, fading having raced freely: should do better. *B. Smart*

OUT OF MY WAY 3 ch.f. Fraam 114 – Ming Blue 52 (Primo Dominie 121) [2004 –: **–** p7g p7g p8g p10g⁴ 11.5g Jun 30] probably of little account. *T. M. Jones*

OUT OF TUNE 4 ch.g. Elmaamul (USA) 125 – Strawberry Song 87 (Final Straw 127) **–** [2004 –: p7g 5m May 17] of little account. *Mrs L. B. Normile*

OUTRAGEOUS FLIRT (IRE) 2 b.f. (Apr 4) Indian Lodge (IRE) 127 – Sofia **64** Aurora (USA) (Chief Honcho (USA)) [2004 5m 5g 5g 6d³ 7.5m³ 7s² Nov 2] €14,000Y: sturdy filly: second foal: half-sister to 3-y-o Queen of Bulgaria: dam Italian 2-y-o 9f winner: modest maiden: easily best effort when second at Catterick, racing freely: stays 7f: acts on soft going. *A. Dickman*

OUTSIDE HALF (IRE) 2 ch.g. (Mar 10) Raise A Grand (IRE) 114 – Lindas Delight **58** 54 (Batshoof 122) [2004 p8m Dec 21] 40/1, ninth in maiden at Lingfield. *W. J. Musson*

OUTSIDE INVESTOR (IRE) 4 b. or br.g. Cadeaux Genereux 131 – Desert Ease **–** (IRE) 94 (Green Desert (USA) 127) [2004 80: p8g 10f 12g Aug 22] fairly useful maiden for D. Weld in Ireland at 2/3 yrs: no form in 2004, leaving T. McGovern after second start: usually blinkered in Ireland. *N. J. Gifford*

OUTWARD (USA) 4 b.g. Gone West (USA) – Seebe (USA) 112 (Danzig (USA)) **–** [2004 62: 8d 8m 12.3m 10m 16f Jul 29] leggy gelding: maiden: little form in 2004. *R. Bastiman*

OVAMBO (IRE) 6 b.g. Namaqualand (USA) – Razana (IRE) 71 (Kahyasi 130) [2004 **105** 11.6d⁴ 12m⁶ 12g⁴ Oct 1] sturdy gelding: smart at 4 yrs: missed 2003 (reportedly with serious foot problems): just useful form in 2004, best effort when 4¼ lengths fourth to Vinando in handicap at Newmarket final start: effective at 1½m/1¾m: acts on firm and good to soft going: usually held up: sold 51,000 gns, sent to Saudi Arabia. *P. J. Makin*

OVERDRAWN (IRE) 3 b.g. Daggers Drawn (USA) 114 – In Denial (IRE) (Mael- **88 d** strom Lake 118) [2004 96: 8.1d 8m 8.1m 7m 7m 7m 8f 8d p7.1d⁵ Nov 5] leggy, quite good-topped gelding: fairly useful handicapper: below form after third start: stays 1m: acts on fibresand, good to firm and good to soft going: tried blinkered: sometimes slowly away. *J. A. Osborne*

OVERJOY WAY 2 b.f. (May 7) Cadeaux Genereux 131 – May Light 62 (Midyan **58** (USA) 124) [2004 7.1m 8.3m p7g⁵ Oct 13] 32,000Y: tall filly: seventh foal: half-sister to 3-y-o Bygone Days and fairly useful 1998 2-y-o 1m winner Trio (by Cyrano de Ber- gerac): dam maiden who stayed 7f: modest form in maidens: needs to settle to stay 1m. *P. R. Chamings*

OVER RATING 4 ch.f. Desert King (IRE) 129 – Well Beyond (IRE) 101 (Don't **53** Forget Me 127) [2004 74, a67: f9.4g f12g p10g⁶ Jan 24] maiden: modest form at 4 yrs, looking reluctant in cheekpieces final start: stays 1¼m: acts on fibresand, raced only on good ground or firmer on turf. *K. A. Ryan*

OVERRIDE (IRE)   4 b.c. Peintre Celebre (USA) 137 – Catalonda (African Sky 124)   **78**
[2004 85d: p7g* 7m⁵ Jul 3] rather leggy colt: fair performer: won claimer at Lingfield in
February, hanging right: stays 7f: acts on polytrack, raced only on good going or firmer
on turf: sold 18,500 gns. *J. M. P. Eustace*

OVERSTRAND (IRE)   5 b.g. In The Wings 128 – Vaison La Romaine 100 (Arctic   **75**
Tern (USA) 126) [2004 86: 16g⁵ Apr 8] lengthy gelding: fair handicapper: stays 2m: acts
on polytrack, firm and good to soft going. *Mrs M. Reveley*

OVER THE LIMIT (IRE)   2 b.f. (Apr 28) Diktat 126 – Premiere Cuvee 109 (Formid-   **61**
able (USA) 125) [2004 6s p6g p7g Nov 27] strong filly: half-sister to several winners,
including Italian miler She Bat (by Batshoof) and 7f/1m winner Cask (by Be My Chief),
both useful: dam sprinter: modest form in maidens/minor event: should stay 1m.
Mrs A. J. Perrett

OVER THE RAINBOW (IRE)   3 b.c. Rainbow Quest (USA) 134 – Dimakya (USA)   **87**
83 (Dayjur (USA) 137) [2004 86: p10g* 10.1m 12m 10d 10.1g⁶ 10d 11.7s Oct 19] quite
good-topped colt: has a quick action: fairly useful performer: won maiden at Lingfield in
March: only a couple of creditable efforts in handicaps after: stays 1¼m: acts on polytrack and good to firm going: tried blinkered/in cheekpieces/tongue strap: free-going sort:
sold 10,000 gns, sent to Spain. *B. W. Hills*

OVER THE YEARS (USA)   3 b.g. Silver Hawk (USA) 123 – Sporting Green (USA)   **38**
(Green Dancer (USA) 132) [2004 –: 12s⁵ 14.1s⁴ 16.2g 14.1g Aug 28] big, good-topped
gelding: poor form: tried blinkered. *T. P. Tate*

OVER TIPSY   2 b.g. (Apr 12) Tipsy Creek (USA) 115 – Over Keen 58 (Keen 116)   **45**
[2004 6.1d 6m 7g 8s Oct 19] poor maiden: form only at 6f. *R. Hannon*

OVERTOP WAY (GR)   2 b.g. (Mar 10) Denebola Way (GR) – Dada (GR) (Ice Reef)   **58**
[2004 7.1g p8.6g Oct 7] modest form at Wolverhampton on final start in maidens (gelded
after). *P. A. Chamings*

OVER TO YOU BERT   5 b.g. Overbury (IRE) 116 – Silvers Era 72 (Balidar 133)   **49**
[2004 48: f8g p6g⁶ f8.5s⁵ p8g* 8.3d⁴ 8.1d 8.2m 7.1m 8.1m³ 8.1g³ 8g* 7.1m 10f⁴ 10d   **a54**
8.1m⁶ Sep 9] modest on all-weather, poor on turf: won seller at Lingfield in March and
handicap at Bath in July: probably best at 1m: acts on all-weather, good to firm and good
to soft going: tried in cheekpieces/visor at 4 yrs. *R. J. Hodges*

OVIGO (GER)   5 b.g. Monsagem (USA) 117 – Ouvea (GER) (Konigsstuhl (GER))   **77**
[2004 74: f8.5s* f7g⁴ f8.5g⁶ f9.4g³ f8.5s Feb 14] fair handicapper: won apprentice event
at Wolverhampton in January: stayed 9.4f: acted on fibresand and good to soft going:
tried blinkered: dead. *P. A. Blockley*

OWED   2 b.c. (Feb 2) Lujain (USA) 119 – Nightingale (Night Shift (USA)) [2004 6d 6g   **54**
6g⁴ Sep 14] good-topped colt: best effort in maidens when fourth at Thirsk: tongue tied
first 2 starts: tends to hang left. *Mrs G. S. Rees*

OWN LINE   5 b.g. Classic Cliche (IRE) 128 – Cold Line 74 (Exdirectory 129) [2004   **–**
53: 15.8g Oct 5] good-topped gelding: handicapper: well held only start in 2004: tried in
cheekpieces. *J. Hetherton*

OXFORD STREET PETE (IRE)   2 b.g. (Apr 15) Rossini (USA) 118 – Thabeh 57   **58**
(Shareef Dancer (USA) 135) [2004 7m³ 7s 7g Sep 11] leggy gelding: form in maidens
only when third at Chester. *A. Bailey*

P

PAARL ROCK   9 ch.g. Common Grounds 118 – Markievicz (IRE) 73 (Doyoun 124)   **–**
[2004 f16.2s f12g f16.2m Apr 19] quite good-topped gelding: modest handicapper in
2001: no form on belated return: often blinkered/visored. *S. T. Lewis*

PABLO   5 b.h. Efisio 120 – Winnebago 63 (Kris 135) [2004 117: 8g 7.1d* 8.1d 7.9s   **97 d**
8.1d 8d 10s 8v Oct 31] good-bodied horse: smart performer at best: just useful form when
winning minor event at Warwick in April: below even that level subsequently, leaving
B. Hills 58,000 gns first start (and all 5 wins) on good ground or
softer: wore cheekpieces second to fourth starts. *P. O. Brady, Ireland*

PACIFIC OCEAN (ARG)   5 b.h. Fitzcarraldo (ARG) – Play Hard (ARG) (General   **58**
(FR)) [2004 56: f9.4g² f9.4g³ f12s³ 8g⁶ 9.7s 8.1m⁴ 10.9m³ 10f⁶ 10m 9.9g f8s³ Aug 23]   **a68**
fair maiden on all-weather, modest on turf: stays 11f: acts on fibresand and good to firm

going: tried blinkered/in cheekpieces: usually tongue tied, races freely: sold £7,800. *Mrs Stef Liddiard*

PACIFIC PIRATE (IRE)   2 b.c. (Feb 4) Mujadil (USA) 119 – Jay And-A (IRE) 98   **62**
(Elbio 125) [2004 6g 6m⁶ 7m Oct 10] 12,000Y, 20,000 2-y-o: useful-looking colt: second
foal: dam Irish 5f/6f winner: modest form first 2 starts in maidens: not sure to stay 7f.
M. G. Quinlan

PACIFIC RUN (USA)   3 b.c. Gone West (USA) – Miss Union Avenue (USA) (Steinlen   **–**
127) [2004 10d 11.9s Oct 15] well held in maidens. *B. J. Meehan*

PACIFIC STAR (IRE)   2 b.g. (Apr 14) Tagula (IRE) 116 – Acidanthera 81 (Alzao   **64**
(USA) 117) [2004 6g 7.1m⁶ 7f⁵ 7g⁶ Jul 4] €30,000Y: third foal: dam 7.5f winner: modest
maiden: likely to stay 1m: sent to Spain. *E. A. L. Dunlop*

PACKIN EM IN   6 b.h. Young Ern 120 – Wendy's Way 53 (Merdon Melody 98) [2004   **49 §**
–: f7g³ p6g² f6g p7g⁸ p6g 7v 6m Aug 16] poor performer: won banded race at Lingfield
in March: stays 7f: acts on all-weather: tried blinkered: unreliable. *J. R. Boyle*

PADDY BOY (IRE)   3 br.g. Overbury (IRE) 116 – Arts Project (IRE) 66 (Project   **–**
Manager 111) [2004 f8.5g³ p10g 9.9g 11.6f f12m p10m f11d Dec 21] smallish gelding: **a42**
poor maiden: probably stays 1¼m: visored last 2 starts. *J. R. Boyle*

PADDY MUL   7 ch.h. Democratic (USA) 101 – My Pretty Niece (Great Nephew 126)   **55**
[2004 43: f12g² f14g* f16g⁴ f14g³ f14s⁴ 16.1v⁵ 12.4v³ 12m³ 16m* f14m⁴ 13f⁴ 16m Jul   **a45**
31] sparely-made horse: modest performer on turf, poor on all-weather: won banded race
at Southwell in January and handicap at Musselburgh in July: ran as if amiss final outing:
stays 2m: acts on fibresand and any turf going: tried visored: tongue tied. *W. Storey*

PADDY OLIVER (IRE)   2 b.g. (Mar 17) Petorius 117 – Creggan Vale Lass (Simply   **–**
Great (FR) 122) [2004 7.1d p9.5g p8.6g Dec 6] well held in maidens/seller. *B. Palling*

PADDY'S TERN   2 b.c. (May 2) Fraam 114 – Great Tern 59 (Simply Great (FR) 122)   **–**
[2004 6f Jul 26] 100/1, tailed off in maiden at Windsor. *N. M. Babbage*

PADDYWACK (IRE)   7 b.g. Bigstone (IRE) 126 – Millie's Return (IRE) 71 (Ballad   **81**
Rock 122) [2004 86: 6s 5v⁴ 6m 6m³ 6m⁵ 5m³ 6g 5g* 5d* 6g 5g³ 6g⁶ 5d³ 5.1g³ 5f 5d⁴ 5g⁵
5s⁵ f6g p5.1g⁴ p6g⁴ p6g⁶ Dec 13] small gelding: fairly useful handicapper: won at Thirsk
in June and Beverley in July: effective at 5f/6f: acts on all-weather and any turf going:
blinkered: sometimes slowly away. *D. W. Chapman*

PADRAO (IRE)   2 b.c. (Mar 21) Cape Cross (IRE) 129 – Dazilyn Lady (USA) 105 (Zil-   **60 p**
zal (USA) 137) [2004 6g Aug 28] 50,000F, 130,000Y: close-coupled colt: first foal: dam
2-y-o 6f winner (stayed 1m): 20/1 and better for race, eleventh in maiden at Newmarket,
prominent to halfway: should do better. *D. R. Loder*

PAGAN CEREMONY (USA)   3 ch.g. Rahy (USA) 115 – Delightful Linda (USA)   **–**
(Slew O' Gold (USA)) [2004 –: 12.3d 12s p13g Oct 1] lengthy gelding: probably of little
account. *Mrs A. J. Perrett*

PAGAN DANCE (IRE)   5 b.g. Revoque (IRE) 122 – Ballade d'Ainhoa (FR) (Al Nasr   **101**
(FR) 126) [2004 101: p12g³ 12s⁴ 12g² 12f² 16.1s⁶ 16.2g 13.9s 12f² 12m⁴ Sep 26] strong
gelding: useful handicapper: mostly ran well in 2004, including when 3½ lengths second
to Wunderwood in Duke of Edinburgh Stakes at Royal Ascot on fourth start and short-
head second to Mutasallil at Doncaster on penultimate: stays 2m: acts on polytrack, firm
and soft going: wears cheekpieces: tends to carry head awkwardly/hang: usually held up.
Mrs A. J. Perrett

PAGAN MAGIC (USA)   3 b.g. Diesis 133 – Great Lady Slew (USA) (Seattle Slew   **80**
(USA)) [2004 68p: 10s³ 9g 12g* 10d 12d⁵ 12g⁴ 12g p12g³ p16.5g Nov 8] quite good-
topped gelding: fairly useful handicapper: won at Kempton in June: some creditable
efforts after: stays 1½m: acts on polytrack, raced mainly on good ground or softer (acts
on soft) on turf. *J. A. R. Toller*

PAGAN PRINCE   7 br.g. Primo Dominie 121 – Mory Kante (USA) (Icecapade (USA))   **84**
[2004 81: 8.1d 8.3d* 8g⁴ 8g⁶ 8.9g⁴ 8s⁵ a8.3g Nov 14] leggy gelding: fairly useful handicapper: won at Windsor in August: sold from J. Toller 16,500 gns before final start: raced
mainly at 1m/9f: acts on fibresand, firm and soft going: usually waited with: consistent.
P. Haley, Spain

PAGAN QUEST   2 b.c. (Apr 20) Lujain (USA) 119 – Rohita (IRE) 94 (Waajib 121)   **59**
[2004 6g 6d Oct 14] sturdy, close-coupled colt: better effort in maidens when seventh at
Newbury on debut. *J. A. R. Toller*

PAGAN SKY (IRE) 5 ch.g. Inchinor 119 – Rosy Sunset (IRE) (Red Sunset 120) [2004 **91**
97+: 10g 10m 10m⁶ 10d⁴ 12g⁵ 10v³ 12s Nov 6] close-coupled gelding: fairly useful
handicapper: effective at 1¼m/1½m: acts on any going: usually held up. *J. A. R. Toller*

PAGAN STORM (USA) 4 ch.g. Tabasco Cat (USA) 126 – Melodeon (USA) (Alydar **63 §**
(USA)) [2004 78§: p7g p7g 7.1g 6g 6d⁵ 6m 7.2f 6m 7m³ 7g 8m 7.1m 8m p7.1d⁶ p7.1g² **a50 §**
p8m⁴ Nov 22] lengthy, sparely-made gelding: fluent mover: modest performer: effective
at 6f/7f: acts on polytrack, firm and good to soft going: tried tongue tied/blinkered/in
cheekpieces: sometimes slowly away/hangs left: unreliable. *Mrs L. Stubbs*

PAGAN SWORD 2 ch.c. (Apr 3) Selkirk (USA) 129 – Vanessa Bell (IRE) (Lahib **62**
(USA) 129) [2004 7d p8g Nov 13] 22,000F, €85,000Y: well-made colt: fourth foal: half-
brother to 4-y-o Angelica Garnett: dam, 6f winner in Italy at 2 yrs, out of half-sister to
disqualified Oaks winner Aliysa, herself grandam of Alamshar: better effort in maidens
when eighth at Lingfield final start. *Mrs A. J. Perrett*

PAGEANT 7 br.m. Inchinor 119 – Positive Attitude 82 (Red Sunset 120) [2004 56§, **– §**
a–§: f8.5g f7g⁶ f8g⁵ p8g⁴ p8g f8.5g f7s⁵ f8g Feb 24] rather leggy, useful-looking mare: **a31 §**
modest when last ran on turf, poor on all-weather: effective at 7f/1m: acts on fibresand
and probably any turf going: blinkered last 3 starts: often front runner: has looked none
too keen: unreliable. *J. M. Bradley*

PAINTBOX 3 b.f. Peintre Celebre (USA) 137 – Photogenic 93 (Midyan (USA) 124) **69**
[2004 8m⁶ 8.3g³ 8.5m² 10.2g⁶ p10g Oct 13] second foal: dam, Irish 6f/7f winner (ran only
at 2 yrs), out of half-sister to Bella Colora (dam of Stagecraft), Colorspin (dam of Kayf
Tara and Opera House) and Cezanne: fair maiden: should stay 1¼m: acts on good to firm
going: raced freely on debut: hung right penultimate start. *Mrs A. J. Perrett*

PAINTBRUSH (IRE) 4 b.f. Groom Dancer (USA) 128 – Bristle 96 (Thatch (USA) **40**
136) [2004 48: p10g⁵ p10g⁴ Mar 2] poor maiden: probably stays 1¼m: sometimes slowly
away. *Mrs L. Stubbs*

PAINTED MOON (USA) 3 ch.f. Gone West (USA) – Crimson Conquest (USA) 85 **–**
(Diesis 133) [2004 –: 7g Jul 17] well held in maidens at Folkestone (trained by D. Loder)
and Newmarket 11 months apart. *C. E. Brittain*

PAINT THE LILY (IRE) 3 b.f. Barathea (IRE) 127 – Chocolate Box 70 (Most Wel- **–**
come 131) [2004 10g 10d 10.3d⁴ 12g 15.8m Sep 18] €50,000Y: second foal: dam, 13f
winner, sister to very smart performer up to 2m Arctic Owl: little form: left J. Hills after
fourth start. *F. Watson*

PAIRING (IRE) 6 ch.g. Rudimentary (USA) 118 – Splicing 82 (Sharpo 132) [2004 p7g **?**
a8g a8.3g⁴ a8.3g* a8g⁴ a8.3g⁶ a8.3g² a6g a8.3g Dec 12] smallish, lengthy gelding: useful
performer in 2002: has won 4 times since at Mijas, including in handicap in August: only
beaten in handicap at Lingfield on reappearance, only outing for G. L. Moore: effective at
1m/1¼m: acts on fibresand/sand and good to firm going: has been blinkered. *P. Haley,
Spain*

PAITA 2 b.f. (Feb 16) Intikhab (USA) 135 – Prada (GER) (Lagunas) [2004 9v* 10s* **108 p**
Nov 6] 10,000Y, 32,000 2-y-o: fifth foal: half-sister to 2 winners in Germany, notably
useful 11f (Preis der Diana) winner Puntilla (by Acatenango): dam German 9.5f to 11f
winner: won newcomers race at Milan (by 6 lengths) in October and Criterium de Saint-
Cloud (by ¾ length from Yehudi, coming from rear to lead final 1f) in November: will
stay 1½m: smart prospect, and should win more races. *M. Hofer, Germany*

PALABELLE (IRE) 3 b.f. Desert Prince (IRE) 130 – Moviegoer 104 (Pharly (FR) **54**
130) [2004 8.3g 8f 8.1m 8.1g⁵ 10m Jul 14] €80,000Y: rather leggy filly: half-sister to
several winners, including 7f to 9.4f winner Salim (by Salse) and 1993 2-y-o 5.7f winner
Kissininthebackrow (by Trempolino), both fairly useful: dam, 7f winner, half-sister to
dam of Oaks winner Lady Carla: modest maiden: stays 1m. *P. W. Harris*

PALACE THEATRE (IRE) 3 b.g. Imperial Ballet (IRE) 110 – Luminary (Kalaglow **80**
132) [2004 74p: 6s 6d³ May 8] useful-looking gelding: fairly useful performer, lightly
raced: raced only at 6f: acts on good to firm and good to soft ground. *T. D. Barron*

PALACE WALK (FR) 2 b.c. (Mar 31) Sinndar (IRE) 134 – Page Bleue (Sadler's **65 ?**
Wells (USA) 132) [2004 8g 7.9g⁶ 8v Oct 23] quite good-topped colt: half-brother to
several winners, including 7.5f (at 2 yrs) and 1¼m winner Page Nouvelle (by Spectrum)
and useful German/French 1m (at 2 yrs) to 1¼m winner Page's King (by Konigsstuhl):
dam French 2-y-o 7f winner: seemingly best effort in maidens when sixth at York: should
be suited by 1¼m/1½m. *A. M. Balding*

PALANZO (IRE) 6 b.g. Green Desert (USA) 127 – Karpacka (IRE) 99 (Rousillon (USA) 133) [2004 –§: 5d⁵ 6d 6f Jun 7] lengthy gelding: just fair handicapper nowadays: stays 7f: acts on any ground: blinkered (ran poorly) once: sometimes slowly away: ungenuine. *D. Nicholls* **72 §**

PALATINATE (FR) 2 br.g. (Mar 15) Desert Prince (IRE) 130 – Dead Certain 123§ (Absalom 128) [2004 6g⁴ 7d³ 7s* 7g⁴ Sep 29] strong, sturdy gelding: good walker: half-brother to several winners, including 1998 2-y-o 5f/6f winner Deadly Nightshade (by Night Shift) and Irish 7f and 1¼m winner Hamad (by Sadler's Wells), both useful, and 7-y-o True Night: dam, won Cheveley Park Stakes, became temperamental: fairly useful performer: won maiden at Salisbury in September: good fourth to Sudden Dismissal in minor event on same course final start, never nearer (gelded after): should stay 1m: acts on soft going. *H. Candy* **83**

PALAWAN 8 br.g. Polar Falcon (USA) 126 – Krameria 72 (Kris 135) [2004 92: f5g p5g p5g⁶ 5s 5.1d 5m 5m 5.1d 5f 5g p5g⁶ Dec 18] lengthy gelding: fairly useful performer: well below form in 2004 after third start: has won at 7f, seems best at 5f: acts on all-weather and firm ground: tried in headgear: often makes running. *A. M. Balding* **85 d**

PALVIC MOON 3 ch.f. Cotation – Palvic Grey (Kampala 120) [2004 59§: 6s⁵ 6v³ f6g⁶ 6d 5d 7g Oct 12] leggy, workmanlike filly: poor maiden: stays 6f: acts on heavy and good to firm going: blinkered/in cheekpieces last 2 starts: ungenuine. *C. Smith* **48 §**
a– §

PAMIR (IRE) 2 b.g. (Apr 20) Namid 128 – Mijouter (IRE) (Coquelin (USA) 121) [2004 6m 6d³ p6d* p7.1g⁴ Nov 12] €30,000F, 50,000Y: good-topped gelding: sixth foal: half-brother to several winners, including 6f winner Hopeful Star (by Pips Pride): dam unraced half-sister to dam of very smart miler Pennine Walk: fair performer: won maiden at Wolverhampton in October: ran well but looked wayward in nursery there final start: not sure to stay much beyond 7f: acts on polytrack, better turf effort on good to soft going. *L. M. Cumani* **75**

PANCAKEHILL 5 ch.m. Sabrehill (USA) 120 – Sawlah (Known Fact (USA) 135) [2004 66: p7g p8g f8f p8g p8g⁶ p6g p10g f8s Mar 18] quite good-topped mare: just modest form at best in 2004: effective at 7f to 1¼m: acts on good to firm going and all-weather: has worn blinkers/cheekpieces/tongue tie: temperament under suspicion. *D. K. Ivory* **57 d**

PANCAKE ROLE 4 b.g. Tragic Role (USA) – My Foxy Lady 37 (Jalmood (USA) 126) [2004 –: 12.6m⁶ 10m 11.5m 10d Aug 13] tall, rather leggy gelding: poor maiden. *A. W. Carroll* **–**

PANFIELD BELLE (IRE) 3 b.f. Danetime (IRE) 121 – Make Hay (Nomination 125) [2004 5m⁶ Jul 7] €1,200Y: seventh foal: half-sister to 5f winner Mount Park (by Colonel Collins) and winner in Japan by Kefaah: dam unraced: 33/1, last in maiden at Lingfield. *H. J. Collingridge* **–**

PANGLOSS (IRE) 3 ch.g. Croco Rouge (IRE) 126 – Kafayef (USA) 46 (Secreto (USA) 128) [2004 72: 11.6s³ 9.9g 12d⁵ 12f 12d⁴ 16s⁵ 12s⁶ 11d⁶ Oct 10] sturdy gelding: fair maiden: best form up to 1½m: acts on soft and good to firm going: wore cheekpieces/blinkers last 5 starts: has carried head awkwardly/looked none too keen. *G. L. Moore* **69**

PANGO 5 ch.g. Bluegrass Prince (IRE) 110 – Riverine (Risk Me (FR) 127) [2004 79: 8g² 8.3m² 7g* 7.1g* 8g* 7.6s² 7m⁴ 8m 7.9g Oct 8] fairly useful handicapper: improved in 2004 and won at Epsom, Chepstow and Goodwood (by ½ length from Ringsider) in July: probably best at 7f/1m nowadays: acts on all-weather, firm and soft going: consistent. *H. Morrison* **92**

PANJANDRUM 6 b.g. Polar Falcon (USA) 126 – Rengaine (FR) (Music Boy 124) [2004 53, a74: p5g p5g³ p6g⁵ f6g* f6s p5g⁶ f5g p6g 5.3m⁴ 5v 5g p5.1g* p5.1g p6g Dec 27] lengthy, sparely-made gelding: fair performer: won claimers at Southwell in February and Wolverhampton in November for N. Berry: effective at 5f/6f: acts on all-weather and firm going: tried visored earlier in career. *R. A. Harris* **61**
a70

PANSHIR (FR) 3 ch.g. Unfuwain (USA) 131 – Jalcamin (IRE) (Jalmood (USA) 126) [2004 –: 8g⁵ 8g 7g³ 8m 7m* 8m⁶ 7g² 7m⁶ Jul 28] tall, leggy gelding: fairly useful handicapper: won at Newbury in June: races freely, and better at 7f than 1m: acts on good to firm going: hung left final start: usually waited with. *C. F. Wall* **88**

PANTS 5 b.m. Pivotal 124 – Queenbird 90 (Warning 136) [2004 54, a65: p7g p7g p7g Jan 28] sparely-made mare: modest performer: best at 6f/7f: acts on all-weather, good to firm and good to soft going: visored once: sometimes slowly away. *Andrew Reid* **–**
a56

*Dubai Duty Free, Nad Al Sheba—strong finishers Paolini (light colours, two hoops on sleeve)
and Right Approach (on Paolini's right) sweep through on the outside to share the spoils;
Nayyir (centre), Crimson Palace (partially hidden by Nayyir), Martillo (right) and
Checkit (behind Martillo) all finish within a length or so of the dead-heaters*

PANZER (GER) 3 b.g. Vettori (IRE) 119 – Prompt (Old Vic 136) [2004 10d⁶ Apr 1] **61**
8,000Y: strong, angular gelding: fourth foal: half-brother to 2001 2-y-o 6f winner Frodo
(by Magic Ring) and winner in Greece by Efisio: dam once-raced half-sister to smart
1¼m winner Baron Ferdinand out of half-sister to Shirley Heights: 50/1 and green, 12
lengths sixth to Jorobaden in maiden at Leicester, late headway under considerate
handling: suffered setback after. *R. Charlton*

PAOLINI (GER) 7 ch.h. Lando (GER) 128 – Prairie Darling (Stanford 121§) [2004 **118**
121: 8.9m* 10m 10g 8g⁶ 10.2g Oct 23] strong, good-bodied horse: carries plenty of
condition: very smart performer at best: winner of Premio Presidente della Repubblica at
Rome and Gran Premio di Milano in 2001: numerous good efforts in top company around
the world in meantime but only success afterwards when dead-heating with Right
Approach in Dubai Duty Free at Nad Al Sheba in March: below form next 2 starts, then
off over 4 months with reported leg injury: not at all discredited last 2 outings when
staying-on sixth to Grey Lilas in Prix du Moulin de Longchamp and close tenth to Savabeel in Cox Plate at Moonee Valley: ideally suited by further than 1m and stayed 1½m:
acted on firm and good to soft going: effective blinkered or not: held up: tough (raced in
11 different countries): retired as Germany's leading all-time money-earner: to stand at
Gestut Hof Ittlingen, Germany, fee €4,750, Oct 1st. *A. Wohler, Germany*

PAPALITY 2 b.f. (Feb 10) Giant's Causeway (USA) 132 – Papabile (USA) 104 (Chief's **66**
Crown (USA)) [2004 6g⁵ 7g Sep 20] good-topped filly: has scope: first foal: dam, 1m
winner, sister to Grand Lodge: fair form in maidens at Newmarket and Kempton: should
stay 1m. *W. Jarvis*

PAPARAAZI (IRE) 2 b.c. (Feb 19) Victory Note (USA) 120 – Raazi 46 (My Genera- **71**
tion 111) [2004 7.5m⁵ 7m p7.1g³ f8g⁴ p7.1g* p6g³ Dec 3] €3,200Y: lengthy colt: first
foal: dam maiden who stayed 7f: fair performer: won nursery at Wolverhampton in
November: stays 1m: acts on all-weather, some promise on turf: sometimes looked none
too keen early starts. *R. A. Fahey*

PAPEETE (GER) 3 b.f. Alzao (USA) 117 – Prairie Vela (Persian Bold 123) [2004 74: **61**
8g⁴ 8f⁴ 11.5g 10m 11.9s* 16g p12.2d² p12.2g⁶ p13.9g Dec 13] leggy, close-coupled filly:
modest handicapper: left W. Haggas after second start: won at Brighton in August: stays
1½m: acts on polytrack, soft and good to firm going: tried blinkered. *Miss B. Sanders*

PAPER TALK (USA) 2 br.c. (Mar 4) Unbridled's Song (USA) 125 – Journalist (IRE) **87**
102 (Night Shift (USA)) [2004 6m³ 7g² Sep 1] angular, useful-looking colt: first foal:
dam, 2-y-o 6f winner, half-sister to useful sprinter Sheer Viking: placed in maidens at
Newmarket and York (second to Subpoena, making most): not sure to stay much beyond
7f. *B. W. Hills*

bonusprint.com Henry II Stakes, Sandown—
Papineau drifts across Mr Dinos as New South Wales keeps on for third ahead of Risk Seeker

PAPINEAU 4 ch.c. Singspiel (IRE) 133 – Early Rising (USA) (Grey Dawn II 132) **124**
[2004 107: 12g* 16.4f* 20m* Jun 17]

      For the fourth time in nine years the Gold Cup at Royal Ascot went the way of Godolphin, one of their three representatives, Papineau, winning it with a performance at least as good as those put up by Classic Cliche in 1996 and Kayf Tara in 1998 and 2000. Not that Papineau can be rated quite so highly overall as that pair, who both bettered their Gold Cup form in some of the other races they contested. Not yet, anyway. If injury had not prevented Papineau from racing after Royal Ascot there is a possibility that he, too, could have gone on to achieve a higher rating than the one we are able to give him at present. Fortunately, he should have plenty of opportunities to prove the point when he returns to action in 2005.

      Papineau, unraced at two, ran four times as a three-year-old for Sheikh Mohammed before joining Godolphin, all four of those runs taking place in France, where he was trained by Andre Fabre. He won a minor event at Saint-Cloud on his second start and a listed race at Longchamp on his third, but wasn't seen out again after finishing fifth behind Dalakhani in the Prix du Jockey Club, having sustained a knee injury during that race. It was almost twelve months before Papineau was seen on a racecourse again. The race chosen for his return was a minor event at Goodwood, though it was well contested with all of his thirteen opponents either useful or smart. Papineau made them look ordinary. One of only a few able to get into contention from off the pace, he still had around four lengths to make up when eventually switched wide to get a run over a furlong out, but quickened so well that his winning margin was two and a half lengths over the runner-up, stable-companion Songlark, with Persian Majesty third. Having raced only at a mile and a half so far, Papineau was stepped up to two miles on his next outing, in the bonusprint.com Henry II Stakes at Sandown, for which he was supplemented, and he showed his effectiveness at the trip in winning by a length and a half from Mr Dinos, who had won the same race, as well as the Gold Cup, the previous year. Papineau had the speed to take full advantage when a race in which the pace steadied markedly in the

Gold Cup, Royal Ascot—in an international field, Papineau shows further improvement,
stepped up again in trip; Westerner and Darasim are his nearest pursuers

back straight began in earnest only off the home turn, whereas Mr Dinos took most of the straight to get fully opened out; Papineau drifted to the right across Mr Dinos inside the final furlong, which led to a two-day suspension for his rider Frankie Dettori, but the result wasn't affected.

Mr Dinos would have finished a bit closer to Papineau but for the interference, and many were of the opinion that the placings would be reversed in the Gold Cup. Not only would Papineau be re-opposing on worse terms, but there was also an extra half mile to be covered, which seemed likely to suit Mr Dinos more than it would Papineau. The betting reflected that, with Mr Dinos going off favourite at 5/4 and Papineau second favourite at 5/1. Not that it was a two-horse race by any means. The thirteen-runner field also included France's top stayer Westerner, the 2003 St Leger winner Brian Boru and the dual Gold Cup winner Royal Rebel, who had missed all of the 2003 season through injury, this trio the next three in the betting in what looked an up-to-standard renewal. The pace, set by the Japanese challenger Ingrandire, wasn't a strong one and the runners were quite well bunched on the home turn. Papineau, who impressed in appearance, took the preliminaries calmly and settled far better than his half-brother My Patriarch had done when well held in the same race ten years earlier. At the turn Papineau was just behind the leaders, still travelling strongly. It wasn't until Westerner was sent for home early in the straight that Papineau was asked for his effort, and he quickened well to peg him back entering the final furlong, running on willingly after a brief battle to win by a length and a half, with Darasim a further two and a half lengths back in third. The plan now was for Papineau to follow in the footsteps of Classic Cliche, who had contested the King George VI and Queen Elizabeth Stakes after winning the Gold Cup, finishing an excellent second to Pentire. Doubts about Papineau's participation due to a bruised foot began to increase in the lead-up to that race, however, and it came as no surprise when he was taken out at the five-day stage.

Godolphin's "Papineau"

Papineau will probably prove fully effective back at a mile and a half, and, while he will need to progress again to win one of the top races at that distance, there is every chance he could do so, given that he has made just seven appearances to date.

Papineau (ch.c. 2000)	Singspiel (IRE) (b 1992)	In The Wings (b 1986)	Sadler's Wells High Hawk
		Glorious Song (b 1976)	Halo Ballade
	Early Rising (USA) (gr 1980)	Grey Dawn II (gr 1962)	Herbager Polamia
		Gliding By (b 1975)	Tom Rolfe Key Bridge

Papineau, bought as a foal for 85,000 guineas, is a half-brother to numerous winners apart from the aforementioned My Patriarch (by Be My Guest), a smart stayer who also won the Henry II Stakes. The pick of them is the 1997 St Leger winner and Derby runner-up Silver Patriarch (by Saddlers' Hall), who also went on to show high-class form at four and five, doing the majority of his racing at a mile and a half. It's a remarkable success story for their dam Early Rising, who won only one small race, at around a mile, as a three-year-old in the United States. Early Rising had produced four foals (three of whom won) before she was purchased by the late Peter Winfield for 160,000 dollars at the Keeneland November Sale in 1988. She had been owned previously by Paul Mellon, and is from one of his most successful families, her grandam being Key Bridge, the dam of Fort Marcy, Key To The Mint, Key To The Kingdom and Key To Content. Fort Marcy was champion turf horse in the States in 1967 and 1970, while Key To The Mint was their champion three-year-old in 1972, Key To The Kingdom the sire of Ma Biche and Key To Content the very smart winner of over 350,000 dollars. Another of Key Bridge's offspring, Silver Patriarch's grandam Gliding By, was reportedly a twin who had just one race, which she won. Papineau, a strong, rangy colt who impresses in appearance, acts on firm and good to soft going. He was tongue tied for all of his races in the latest season. *Saeed bin Suroor*

PAPPUS (GER) 7 b.g. Acatenango (GER) 127 – Pariana (USA) (Bering 136) [2004 108: a9.5g² a9.8g* a9.5g* 10m⁶ 10g² 10d² p10g Nov 20] useful performer: has won 7 races, including minor event at Dortmund in January and listed race at Neuss (by 1½ lengths from Grantley) in February: not discredited when eighth to Grand Passion in similar event at Lingfield final start, never dangerous: stays 1¼m: acts on polytrack/sand, good to firm and good to soft going: tried blinkered. *M. Hofer, Germany* **106**

PAPPY (IRE) 3 b.f. Petardia 113 – Impressive Lady 98 (Mr Fluorocarbon 126) [2004 63d: f8g⁴ 8.3f 7.1s³ 6.1g 7m 8.1d Oct 9] big, leggy filly: poor maiden: left J. Given after reappearance: probably stays 7f: acts on good to firm ground, probably on soft: blinkered (missed break) final 2-y-o outing: races freely. *A. W. Carroll* **46**

PARACHUTE 5 ch.g. Hector Protector (USA) 124 – Shortfall 103 (Last Tycoon 131) [2004 91: 11.7s Oct 19] big, strong, lengthy gelding: fairly useful performer at 4 yrs for Sir Mark Prescott: well beaten only run in 2004. *J. A. B. Old* **–**

PARADISE BREEZE 3 b.f. Perugino (USA) 84 – Paradise Forum 78 (Prince Sabo 123) [2004 –p: 6m 7g 6m⁵ Jul 31] little form. *C. A. Horgan* **–**

PARADISE FLIGHT (IRE) 3 ch.f. In The Wings 128 – Aloft (IRE) (Ela-Mana-Mou 132) [2004 –: 11.9m⁵ 10m⁶ 14g 12d⁵ 16v 17.8g* f16s Nov 17] IR 32,000F, €38,000Y: first foal: dam, unraced half-sister to smart 1m/1¼m performer Siege, out of half-sister to Yorkshire Oaks winner Hellenic, herself dam of Islington: fair performer: best effort when winning handicap at Downpatrick in August on final outing for Ms J. Morgan in Ireland: ran in snatches when soundly beaten in similar event at Southwell on British debut: stays 2¼m: wore cheekpieces third/fourth starts. *K. A. Ryan* **65**

PARADISE GARDEN (USA) 7 b.g. Septieme Ciel (USA) 123 – Water Course (USA) (Irish River (FR) 131) [2004 –: 11s f11m⁵ f8m⁴ 10m³ 10.5d Jun 4] tall gelding: poor performer: stays 1½m: tried in headgear. *P. L. Clinton* **40**

PARADISE ISLE 3 b.f. Bahamian Bounty 116 – Merry Rous 66 (Rousillon (USA) 133) [2004 96: 5m 5m⁴ 5.1d² 6g* 6.1g 6m* 6d³ Oct 14] rather sparely-made filly: useful performer: won handicaps at Ascot in August and Newmarket (beat Solar Power by ½ length) in September: first home in far-side group when 4 lengths third to Ruby Rocket in **109**

listed race at Newmarket final outing: effective at 5f/6f: acts on firm and good to soft going: tends to carry head high: ridden up with pace nowadays. *C. F. Wall*

PARADISE MILL (USA) 2 b.f. (Mar 9) Horse Chestnut (SAF) 119 – Eaton Place (IRE) 74 (Zafonic (USA) 130) [2004 7s² Oct 27] first foal: dam, 1¼m winner from 2 starts, half-sister to Grand Prix de Paris winner Grape Tree Road, smart middle-distance stayer Red Route and smart stayer Windsor Castle: 17/2, ½-length second to Zalongo in maiden at Yarmouth, leading most of final 1f: should stay at least 1m: will progress. *J. H. M. Gosden* **81 p**

PARADISE VALLEY 4 b.g. Groom Dancer (USA) 128 – Rose de Reve (IRE) (Persian Heights 129) [2004 66§: f12s* f12s⁶ p12g p10g⁵ f16.2g p10g² 10.9s 11.7s⁵ 11.9m⁴ 14.1m³ 11.6m* Jun 7] good-bodied gelding: modest performer: won claimers at Wolverhampton in January and Windsor in June: stays easy 1¾m: acts on all-weather and firm ground: usually tongue tied, tried visored: has been slowly away/carried head awkwardly: reportedly gurgled when tailed off fifth outing: none too reliable. *Mrs Stef Liddiard* **54 a58**

PARAGON OF VIRTUE 7 ch.g. Cadeaux Genereux 131 – Madame Dubois 121 (Legend of France (USA) 124) [2004 88: p10g³ p10g⁴ p10g p8g³ p10g⁶ p8g⁵ May 7] lengthy gelding: fairly useful handicapper: effective at 1m to 1½m: acted on polytrack, soft and good to firm going: dead. *P. Mitchell* **85**

PARALLEL LINES (IRE) 3 ch.g. Polish Precedent (USA) 131 – Phone Booth (USA) (Phone Trick (USA)) [2004 61: p8g f6s p6g p6g⁴ p5g 7.1s p6g³ 5.1f⁶ 6m 5m Jun 4] poor maiden: stays 6f: acts on polytrack, firm and good to soft ground: tried blinkered/visored: temperamental. *P. D. Evans* **44 §**

PARASOL (IRE) 5 br.g. Halling (USA) 133 – Bunting 102 (Shaadi (USA) 126) [2004 119: 10.3d² 9.9g 8.5m 9d⁴ Sep 18] big, rangy gelding: usually takes the eye: easy mover: smart performer: off 10 months, creditable 1¾ lengths second to Bandari in listed event at Chester on reappearance: well held after: stays 1¼m, not 1½m: acts on polytrack, soft and good to firm going: has been bandaged hind joints: visored: races prominently: carries head high, and sometimes finds little: joined D. Watson in UAE. *D. R. Loder* **112**

PARC AUX BOULES 3 b.g. Royal Applause 124 – Aristocratique 71 (Cadeaux Genereux 131) [2004 –p: f6g⁴ Dec 28] big, good-bodied gelding: better effort in maidens 14 months apart when 1¼ lengths fourth of 13 to Quincannon at Southwell in December, still green and running on well under 7-lb claimer. *R. Charlton* **57 +**

PARCHMENT (IRE) 2 ch.g. (Jan 20) Singspiel (IRE) 133 – Hannalou (FR) 70 (Shareef Dancer (USA) 135) [2004 5v⁴ Aug 27] 18,000F, 100,000Y: third foal: dam, maiden best at 7f, out of sister to dam of Dolphin Street and Saffron Walden: 9/1, last in minor event at Newcastle: gelded after. *J. Howard Johnson* **–**

PARDISHAR (IRE) 6 b.g. Kahyasi 130 – Parapa (IRE) (Akarad (FR) 130) [2004 10g Apr 26] useful at 3 yrs: lightly raced on Flat since. *G. L. Moore* **–**

PARDON MOI 3 ch.f. First Trump 118 – Mystical Song 68 (Mystiko (USA) 124) [2004 52: f7g³ p6g⁴ f6g⁴ p6g 5s 6m⁴ 6v* 6g 6m⁴ 6f 6m 6f⁶ 6g 6g 6m 7d Oct 16] stocky filly: poor performer: won banded race at Kempton in May: stays 7f: acts on fibresand, heavy and good to firm going: has hung left/looked none too keen: tried cheekpieces: sometimes slowly away: none too consistent. *Mrs C. A. Dunnett* **48**

PAR INDIANA (IRE) 3 b.f. Indian Rocket 115 – Paryiana (IRE) (Shernazar 131) [2004 61p: 9g³ 11.1d³ 11.1m⁶ 9.2d⁶ Sep 27] modest maiden: stays 11f: acts on fibresand, yet to race on extremes of going on turf: has raced freely. *I. Semple* **61**

PARIS BELL 2 b. or br.g. (Mar 24) Paris House 123 – Warning Bell 88 (Bustino 136) [2004 5s³ 5v⁵ 5f 7m 6s⁴ 5f 6d* 6v* 6s* Nov 2] rather leggy gelding: half-brother to several winners, including 7-y-o Hand Chime and fairly useful 1m/1¼m winner Virtual Reality (by Diamond Shoal): dam 1¼m winner: fairly useful performer: won nurseries at Ayr and Newbury in October and Catterick (by short head from Go Mo, slowly away) in November: gelded after: stays 6f: goes well on ground softer than good: tends to race freely. *T. D. Easterby* **84**

PARIS DREAMER 3 b.f. Paris House 123 – Stoprovoreltate 65 (Scorpio (FR) 127) [2004 –: f6g f9.4g f11g Feb 12] tall, leggy filly: little form. *M. W. Easterby* **–**

PARIS HEIGHTS 2 gr.g. (Feb 15) Paris House 123 – Petra Nova 51 (First Trump 118) [2004 7f 7d⁶ 7g⁴ 7m 6g 8d Oct 15] quite good-topped gelding: modest maiden: ran badly last 3 starts (visored one): stays 7f: acts on good to soft ground. *R. M. Whitaker* **60**

PARISIAN PLAYBOY 4 gr.g. Paris House 123 – Exordium (Exorbitant 81) [2004 59: f7g 7m 8.1v 8.2m 8d* 8g² 7d* 8.1g 8g 7.2s Oct 12] tall gelding: modest handicapper: **55**

won at Redcar (apprentices) in July and Newcastle in August: stays 1m: acts on soft ground: usually waited with. *Jedd O'Keeffe*

PARISI PRINCESS 3 ch.f. Shaddad (USA) 75 – Crambella (IRE) 30 (Red Sunset – 120) [2004 9.9s 13.8m 10g f12g Nov 9] third foal: dam, maiden, stayed 1½m: well held, including in seller. *G. P. Kelly*

PARIS LATINO (FR) 5 b.g. Nikos 124 – Tarbelissima (FR) (Tarbes (FR)) [2004 p5g – p8g Mar 20] well held in maidens at Lingfield: tried tongue tied. *C. L. Tizzard*

PARIS TAPIS 2 gr.f. (Feb 26) Paris House 123 – Time of Night (USA) 70 (Night Shift **61** (USA)) [2004 6f f7d⁴ 6m² 5s² f5s* p5.1g 5.2s⁶ p6g Nov 13] 1,300Y: lengthy filly: first foal: dam 7f/1m winner: modest performer: below form after winning seller at Southwell (left K. Ryan) in August: effective at 5f/6f: acts on fibresand, soft and good to firm going. *P. S. McEntee*

PAR JEU 2 b.f. (Feb 11) Montjeu (IRE) 137 – Musical Twist (USA) 97 (Woodman **56** (USA) 126) [2004 7g Jul 7] 13,000F, 4,000Y: third foal: half-sister to a winner in Greece by Atticus: dam, maiden (stayed 1m), out of Cherry Hinton/Fred Darling winner Music-ale: 11/2, tenth in maiden at Kempton. *D. J. Daly*

PARK APPROACH (IRE) 2 gr.f. (Feb 23) Indian Ridge 123 – Abyat (USA) (Sha- **77** deed (USA) 135) [2004 6d⁴ 5g³ 5g² Sep 10] €140,000Y: lengthy filly: third foal: sister to fairly useful Irish 1¼m winner Indian Belle and half-sister to 3-y-o Poetical: dam unraced half-sister to Middle Park Stakes winner Hayil: fair form in maidens: second at Sandown, racing freely/carrying head high: likely to prove best at 5f/6f. *J. Noseda*

PARK AVE PRINCESS (IRE) 3 b.f. Titus Livius (FR) 115 – Satinette 109 (Shirley **62 d** Heights 130) [2004 63: p7g² p8g² p7g⁵ p7g⁵ p7g² f5f 7.9g 6f p7.1g p7.1g p7.1g f7g Dec 14] workmanlike filly: modest handicapper: below form after leaving N. Littmoden fifth start: stays 1m: acts on polytrack, firm and good to soft going: tried in cheekpieces final start. *M. J. Polglase*

PARKER 7 b.g. Magic Ring (IRE) 115 – Miss Loving 89 (Northfields (USA)) [2004 **70 d** 75: p7g⁴ f7s³ f7g⁶ p7g f7g⁶ 8s f6m⁵ 7.1g 7m 7.1m Sep 9] neat gelding: fluent mover: fair performer: below form after second start: effective at 6f to easy 1m: acts on all-weather, firm and good to soft going: tried in tongue tie/cheekpieces, usually blinkered: often races prominently: sometimes looks none too keen: none too consistent. *B. Palling*

PARK LAW (IRE) 2 b.f. (Mar 14) Fasliyev (USA) 120 – Blanche Dubois (Nashwan **94** (USA) 135) [2004 7d² 7g* 7.1m⁵ 8m⁶ Sep 11] third living foal: half-sister to 4-y-o Middlemarch and useful 2001 2-y-o 7f winner (stayed 1¼m) Lady High Havens (by Bluebird): dam unraced half-sister to Irish 2000 Guineas winner Indian Haven: fairly use-ful performer: made all in maiden at Kempton in July: much better effort in listed races after when good fifth at Sandown: wandered final start: should stay 1m. *J. H. M. Gosden*

PARK ROMANCE (IRE) 2 b.f. (Feb 1) Dr Fong (USA) 128 – Park Charger 105 **95** (Tirol 127) [2004 6g² 6m* 6m⁵ 7f³ Aug 7] 200,000F: well-made filly: half-sister to seve-ral winners, including 2002 2-y-o 6f winner Pakhoes (by College Chapel) and 6f (at 2 yrs)/7f winner Rum Charger (by Spectrum), both useful in Ireland: dam Irish 1m/1¼m winner: useful performer: won maiden at Newmarket in June: good 1¾ lengths third to Maids Causeway in Sweet Solera Stakes at Newmarket, racing lazily early: should stay 1m: acts on firm going. *B. J. Meehan*

PARKSIDE PURSUIT 6 b.g. Pursuit of Love 124 – Ivory Bride 86 (Domynsky 110) **78** [2004 79: 5.1d 5g* 5f* 5m 6m⁴ 6.1f* 5.7f³ 5.3f* 5g 6m 5g 5g 5.3s p6g p5.1d⁵ p6g⁴ Nov 30] lengthy, dipped-backed gelding: fair performer: won handicaps at Goodwood (apprentices) and Ayr in May, and minor event at Warwick and handicap at Brighton in June: best at 5f/6f: acts on firm and good to soft going: often held up. *J. M. Bradley*

PARK STAR 4 b.f. Gothenberg (IRE) 117 – Miriam 59 (Forzando 122) [2004 68, a63: **57** f5g⁶ f6g³ p6g² p6g 5g 6d 6.1s⁴ 7v⁴ 7m p6d f6g⁴ p6g³ f6g⁴ Dec 12] leggy, good-topped **a62** filly: modest handicapper: stays easy 7f: acts on all-weather, best turf runs on going softer than good: tried visored. *D. Shaw*

PARKVIEW LOVE (USA) 3 b. or br.c. Mister Baileys 123 – Jerre Jo Glanville **100 d** (USA) (Skywalker (USA)) [2004 103: p8g 7g³ 7s 8.1m 7m 8m 7m 9.9g⁴ 8g⁵ 10f³ 10g 7s p9.5g p8.6g p12.2g⁶ p9.5g Dec 27] leggy, good-topped colt: useful performer: 5¼ lengths third to Brunel in listed European Free Handicap at Newmarket second start: mostly well below form otherwise in 2004, leaving M. Johnston after twelfth outing: stays 1¼m: acts on firm and good to soft going, seemingly not on soft: blinkered/in cheekpieces last 5 starts: usually races prominently: ungenuine. *D. Shaw*

PARLIAMENT ACT (IRE)   3 b.g. Mujadil (USA) 119 – Law Student (Precocious   –
126) [2004 6m 5.1g 6.1m Jun 27] workmanlike gelding: little form in maidens/claimer:
tongue tied. *B. A. McMahon*

PARLIAMENT SQUARE (IRE)   3 b.c. Sadler's Wells (USA) 132 – Groom Order   93 ?
(Groom Dancer (USA) 128) [2004 10d³ 10g⁵ p13g² Oct 1] 600,000Y: big, rangy colt:
fifth foal: closely related to 3 winners, including smart Irish 6f (at 2 yrs) to 1m winner
Beckett (by Fairy King) and useful Irish 7f and 1m (latter at 2 yrs) winner Barring Order
(by Barathea): dam unraced daughter of half-sister to 2000 Guineas winner Entrepreneur
(by Sadler's Wells): fairly useful form when third to Ecomium in maiden at Newmarket
in April: well below par after, racing freely final start: sold 31,000 gns. *D. R. Loder*

PARNASSIAN   4 ch.g. Sabrehill (USA) 120 – Delphic Way 63 (Warning 136) [2004   85
71: 8v 8.3g 8.1s³ 7s³ 8.2d* 8m³ 9g 8m⁵ 8.1g* 8d* 9m⁵ 8m⁴ 8.1d³ 8.5g 8s³ 8g* 8v Oct 23]
angular gelding: fairly useful handicapper: won at Nottingham (apprentice maiden event)
in May, Haydock and Doncaster in July and Bath (best effort) in October: should stay 9f:
well beaten on heavy going, acts on any other: waited with. *G. B. Balding*

PARSLEY'S RETURN   2 b.g. (Feb 9) Danzero (AUS) – The Frog Queen 64 (Bin   –
Ajwaad (IRE) 119) [2004 6f 6f⁵ 7m Jun 19] good-topped gelding: last in minor events/
maiden. *N. A. Callaghan*

PARTNERS IN JAZZ (USA)   3 ro.c. Jambalaya Jazz (USA) 111 – Just About   93
Enough (USA) (Danzig (USA)) [2004 88p: 6m⁵ 6g 6s 5s⁵ 6g* 6s⁴ 6g Oct 9] tall colt:
fairly useful handicapper: won at York in September: effective at 5f/6f: acts on good to
firm and good to soft ground, probably on soft: sometimes makes running. *T. D. Barron*

PART TIME LOVE   2 b.c. (Jan 31) Royal Applause 124 – Keen Melody (USA) 60   62
(Sharpen Up 127) [2004 6g⁶ 6f* Jun 2] 36,000F: compact colt: half-brother to 3 winners,
including 5f/6f winner Mutasawwar (by Clantime) and 3-y-o Embassy Lord: dam, maid-
en, stayed 1m: sixth in maiden at Goodwood: favourite, won seller at Yarmouth despite
slow start/wandering (sold 20,000 gns and joined P. Chapple-Hyam): will probably stay
7f. *M. R. Channon*

PARTY BOSS   2 gr.c. (Mar 11) Silver Patriarch (IRE) 125 – Third Party 63 (Terimon   74
124) [2004 7m p7.1g³ f7g* Nov 23] close-coupled colt: third foal: half-brother to 7f
winner Party Turn (by Pivotal): dam, 6f winner, half-sister to smart sprinter Passion For
Life: won maiden at Southwell by head from Buster Hyvonen: will stay 1m. *C. E. Brittain*

PARTY PLOY   6 b.g. Deploy 131 – Party Treat (IRE) 69 (Millfontaine 114) [2004 72:   75
14.1s 14.1d 14.1m² 13g* 12f* 11.9g 10.9g* 12.3d² 11.8f* 11.9f 10.1d⁴ 12m⁴ p12.2g⁵
Oct 7] small gelding: poor mover: fair handicapper: won at Hamilton and Thirsk in June
and Ayr and Leicester in July: effective at 11f to 1¾m: acts on all-weather, firm and soft
going: tried in visor/cheekpieces: usually races prominently. *K. R. Burke*

PARTY PRINCESS (IRE)   3 b.f. Orpen (USA) 116 – Summer Queen 80 (Robellino   71
(USA) 127) [2004 65: 6d 7s 6m* 6m⁴ 5m 6m 6g 6d 6.1d p6g* Oct 25] strong filly: fair
handicapper: won at Ripon in May and Lingfield (apprentices) in October: stays 6f: acts
on polytrack and good to firm ground. *J. A. Glover*

PASCALI   4 b.f. Compton Place 125 – Pass The Rose (IRE) (Thatching 131) [2004 61p: 55
5.7m May 17] lengthy, quite good-topped filly: modest performer, lightly raced: respectable effort only outing in 2004: better at 6f than 1m. *H. Morrison*

PAS DE SURPRISE   6 b.g. Dancing Spree (USA) – Supreme Rose 95 (Frimley Park   61 d
109) [2004 71: f8.5g³ f8.5g p8g⁵ p8g⁵ p8g⁴ f8.5g 7m 9g⁵ 9g⁴ 7.6g⁴ 9g⁵ 8g⁴ 8g 8.1m 8.5m
9.1d p8.6g⁶ p9.5d Nov 4] modest performer: on downgrade: stays 9f: acts on all-weather,
firm and good to soft going: tried in headgear. *P. D. Evans*

PASO DOBLE   6 b.g. Dancing Spree (USA) – Delta Tempo (IRE) (Bluebird (USA)   73
125) [2004 69: f11g⁵ f9.4g f8.5g² f8.5s⁶ f9.4s² p12g 9g⁵ 7m⁴ f8g² 9g 10m 11.6m p12g
f8g⁵ p9.5g p6g² f8g* Dec 28] fair performer: won handicap at Southwell in December:
effective at 6f to 11f: acts on all-weather and firm going: effective in cheekpieces: often
races prominently: none too reliable. *B. R. Millman*

PASSANDO   4 b.f. Kris 135 – Iota 83 (Niniski (USA) 125) [2004 64: p10g Jan 17] big,   –
strong filly: lightly-raced maiden: well held only run in 2004. *A. M. Balding*

PASS GO   3 b.g. Kris 135 – Celt Song (IRE) (Unfuwain (USA) 131) [2004 73p: 7.1g 5s   –
5.1g 6f p10g Jul 24] fair form, only run at 2 yrs: well held in 2004: tried tongue tied/in
blinkers: joined J. Lambe in Ireland. *G. A. Butler*

Vodafone Diomed Stakes, Epsom—front-running Passing Glance dominates proceedings;
Dutch Gold (blinkers) and Gateman take the minor placings, ahead of Checkit (second left),
Vanderlin (noseband) and Beauchamp Pilot

PASSING GLANCE   5 b.h. Polar Falcon (USA) 126 – Spurned (USA) 91 (Robellino   **119** (USA) 127) [2004 118: 8.5m* 8g 8d⁴ 8s⁵ Aug 28] tall, rather leggy horse: impressed in appearance: smart performer: won Vodafone Diomed Stakes at Epsom in June by 1¼ lengths from Dutch Gold, very well ridden from front: creditable 2 lengths fourth to Norse Dancer in Sovereign Stakes at Salisbury penultimate start: well held otherwise in 2004: probably best around 1m: acted on firm and soft going, well held only start on polytrack: had worn crossed noseband/carried head awkwardly: front runner: genuine: to stand at National Stud, Newmarket, fee £3,000. *A. M. Balding*

PASSIONATELY ROYAL   2 b.c. (Feb 27) Royal Applause 124 – Passionelle 56   **50 p** (Nashwan (USA) 135) [2004 5g 6.1v p6g⁶ Nov 27] 24,000Y: strong, close-coupled colt: third foal: dam twice-raced close relative to useful middle-distance stayer Treble Heights: best effort in maidens when sixth to Francis Cadell at Wolverhampton, not clear run: should stay 7f. *R. A. Fahey*

PASSION FRUIT   3 b.f. Pursuit of Love 124 – Reine de Thebes (FR) 67 (Darshaan   **57** 133) [2004 58: 7.9g 7m 8g 8s⁶ 7.2s* Oct 30] close-coupled, good-topped filly: modest performer: blinkered, won claimer at Ayr in October: should stay 1m: acts on soft and good to firm going. *C. W. Fairhurst*

PASS THE PORT   3 ch.g. Docksider (USA) 124 – One of The Family 73 (Alzao   **81** (USA) 117) [2004 8v⁵ f8g* 8g⁶ 8s p9.5g⁵ Dec 1] 22,000Y: leggy gelding: first foal: dam, maiden who should have stayed at least 1¼m, sister to smart performer up to 1¼m Relatively Special and half-sister to very smart 1¼m performers One So Wonderful and Alnasr Alwasheek: fairly useful performer: won maiden at Southwell in June: left J. Fanshawe after fourth start: stays 9.5f: acts on all-weather. *D. Haydn Jones*

PASTORAL PURSUITS   3 b.c. Bahamian Bounty 116 – Star 83 (Most Welcome   **123** 131) [2004 110p: 7.1g² 6m* 7m* 7d⁵ Oct 9]

    Pastoral Pursuits, operated on after chipping a bone in his off-fore knee when winning the Sirenia Stakes at Kempton on his final outing at two, made a complete recovery and returned to show even better form at three. His connections had hoped he might be back in time to contest the Two Thousand Guineas, and that he wasn't is no cause for regret. Pastoral Pursuit is a very smart performer at up to seven furlongs, but, judged on his pedigree and style of racing, it is unlikely that he will be so effective over a mile. Not that he needs to be. There will be more than enough opportunities for Pastoral Pursuits to add to his two pattern-race successes kept to six and seven furlongs in 2005, perhaps even at Group 1 level.

    Off nine months after the Sirenia, in which he completed a hat-trick, Pastoral Pursuits was stepped up from six to seven furlongs on his reappearance, in a listed race at Sandown. Notably weak in the market, Pastoral Pursuits produced a fine effort to finish a half-length second to Madid, collared late on having quickened from off the pace to lead a furlong out. A return to six furlongs in another listed race, this time at Newbury, provided Pastoral Pursuits with a good opportunity to go one better, and he was sent off favourite despite his antics beforehand. According to his trainer Hughie Morrison, Pastoral Pursuits doesn't like being saddled, and

GNER Park Stakes, Doncaster—
Pastoral Pursuits comes from behind to account for Firebreak and Court Masterpiece (No.2)

on this occasion he reportedly proved very troublesome and damaged his saddling box. Neither this, nor a kick from Twilight Blues at the start, had any ill-effect on Pastoral Pursuits who was soon travelling strongly on the heels of the leaders after dwelling and, after edging ahead over a furlong out, held on by a head from Cartography. Pastoral Pursuits faced stiffer tasks in his two subsequent starts, both of which were in pattern company over seven furlongs. First up came the Group 2 GNER Park Stakes at Doncaster, in which his seven opponents included the high-class Firebreak, who started favourite despite carrying a 4-lb penalty. Pastoral Pursuits, niggled along in the early stages following another slowish start, had too much finishing speed for all of them, coming from off the pace to lead inside the final furlong and win by a length and a quarter from Firebreak. Once again he played up in the preliminaries, but not to the same extent as at Newbury. Pastoral Pursuits, described as 'very boisterous' by Morrison, managed to get to France in one piece for the Group 1 Prix de la Foret at Longchamp and ran only a little below his best in finishing fifth of seven to Somnus, beaten three lengths. Good to soft ground placed the emphasis more on stamina than at Doncaster, and Pastoral Pursuits couldn't sustain his effort after briefly going second over a furlong out. Pastoral Pursuits had been due to sign off for the season in the Challenge Stakes at Newmarket, but he was withdrawn because the soft ground was considered unsuitable for him.

Pastoral Pursuits (b.c. 2001)	Bahamian Bounty (ch 1994)	Cadeaux Genereux (ch 1985)	Young Generation
			Smarten Up
		Clarentia (ch 1984)	Ballad Rock
			Laharden
	Star (b 1995)	Most Welcome (ch 1984)	Be My Guest
			Topsy
		Marista (b 1977)	Mansingh
			Evendo

The well-made Pastoral Pursuits acts on good to firm and good to soft going and is by the smart six-furlong performer Bahamian Bounty, winner of the Prix Morny and Middle Park, out of a mare who won a five-furlong maiden at Nottingham on the first of her three starts, all of them at two years. The dam, Star, is a half-sister to Superstrike, who made a winning debut on the all-weather before being transferred to America, where he won Grade 3 races, and to the useful five-furlong performer Four-Legged Friend. Pastoral Pursuits is Star's third foal, and he was her first winner. She didn't have to wait long for her second, Pastoral Pursuits' full brother Goodricke showing himself a fairly useful two-year-old when winning at Leicester and Nottingham in the spring. *H. Morrison*

PATANDON GIRL (IRE) 4 b.f. Night Shift (USA) – Petite Jameel (IRE) (Ahonoora – 122) [2004 66: p6g p6g Jan 21] small, close-coupled filly: modest handicapper: well held in 2004: stays 7f: acts on firm ground: visored twice. *A. Bailey*

PATAU   2 ch.c. (Mar 11) Inchinor 119 – Haste (Halling (USA) 133) [2004 7m Jul 30]   –
good-topped colt: 33/1, well held in maiden at Newmarket. *M. J. Wallace*

PATAVELLIAN (IRE)   6 b.g. Machiavellian (USA) 123 – Alessia 91 (Caerleon   **123**
(USA) 132) [2004 124: 5g³ 6g 6g³ 5m 6s³ Oct 29]
'. . . who can deny that he was one of the toughest to race here for many
years? He ran fourteen times in all, the same number as in 1969, on courses as far
apart as Lanark and Longchamp, and how well he stood up to his racing.' The
sporting spirit of yesteryear reflected in the tribute paid to Raffingora in *Racehorses
of 1970* sometimes seems less prevalent nowadays—the legendary grey won the
Temple Stakes at Sandown and the King George Stakes at Goodwood in 1970, in
between setting an electronically-timed world record for five furlongs under ten
stone in a handicap at Epsom on firm ground in June. 'There is no way we will
risk jarring up either with the thrills and spills of the mighty bacon slicer,' wrote
owner-breeder Philip Deer about leading sprinters Patavellian and Avonbridge
in a letter to the *Racing Post* in February. The letter was in response to the decision
taken by Epsom's owners, Racecourse Holdings Trust, to move the Group 2 Temple
Stakes to Epsom's Friday card from its traditional home at Sandown, another of its
courses, in order to bolster Oaks day. The switch also brought criticism from trainer
Henry Candy, successful in the race in 2003 with Airwave, Candy reportedly
calling the decision 'absolutely ridiculous'. When it was announced that the race
would return to Sandown in 2005, trainer John Gosden said the move to Epsom had
shown a 'total disregard for race-planning and horse requirements.'
Airwave was one of several notable absentees from the Temple Stakes,
along with Avonbridge, The Trader and The Tatling, first, third and fourth in the
Prix du Gros-Chene at Chantilly two days after Epsom, as well as Patavellian, winner of the Prix de l'Abbaye in 2004. Not surprisingly, with a first prize of £63,800,
all twelve five-day entries for Epsom stood their ground, though the field looked
substandard, only the ten-year-old Repertory a previous pattern winner. In a farcical
race, begun by a tape start because of industrial action by stalls handlers, Dragon
Flyer and Forever Phoenix took virtually no part, and the prize went to 33/1-shot
Night Prospector, no better than eighth in three subsequent starts. Sponsors Vodafone offered a £200,000 bonus to any horse breaking Spark Chief's time of 53.7
seconds achieved when lowering Raffingora's world record in a handicap at Epsom
in 1983, but, with the course executive undertaking watering to achieve officially
good ground for the start of the two-day Derby fixture, their money was fairly safe!

		Machiavellian (USA)	Mr Prospector	Raise A Native	
		(b 1987)	(b 1970)	Gold Digger	
Patavellian (IRE)			Coup de Folie	Halo	
(b.g. 1998)			(b 1982)	Raise The Standard	
		Alessia	Caerleon	Nijinsky	
		(b 1992)	(b 1980)	Foreseer	
			Kiss	Habitat	
			(b 1978)	Miss Petard	

As things turned out, Patavellian failed to add to the previous season's
successes in 2004, but he proved himself more or less as good as ever, showing very
smart form in defeat on two of his first three starts. Returned to Longchamp for his
reappearance in the Prix de Saint-Georges in May, Patavellian went down by two
lengths and a length and a half to The Trader and The Tatling, conceding them 9 lb
and 5 lb respectively. After missing Royal Ascot due to the baked ground, then
finishing only tenth in the July Cup at Newmarket, with the stable troubled by a
virus, Patavellian wasn't seen again until the Haydock Sprint Cup in September.
Starting at 14/1, he was ridden with a bit more restraint than usual at Haydock and
turned in an excellent effort in the hottest sprint of the season, having every chance
as he finished third, three quarters of a length behind his stable-companion Tante
Rose, who won by a short head from Somnus. Patavellian was only seventh when
returned to Longchamp for the Prix de l'Abbaye in October. On much firmer
ground than the year before, he was reported by his jockey to have 'taken a false
step' after about fifty yards, and he was considerably handled once held, finishing
two places behind Avonbridge and beaten under four lengths by the winner Var.
Patavellian's final race of the year was also in France, in the Prix de Seine-et-Oise

at Maisons-Laffitte, where he turned in a rather laboured effort, albeit finishing third, beaten a length and a half by Miss Emma and stable-companion Striking Ambition.

Patavellian's sire Machiavellian, responsible for ten Group/Grade 1 winners, one of them Chic in 2004, and Patavellian's dam Alessia both died during the year. Alessia had also produced Avonbridge, sired by Averti (who succumbed to a heart attack late in the year), runner-up in the same blue and white diamond colours of his owner in the Prix de l'Abbaye in 1998. A tall, useful-looking gelding, Patavellian, who is usually blinkered nowadays, and has worn a crossed noseband, has shown his best form at five and six furlongs, though he won the Bunbury Cup over seven in 2003, and he acts on firm and soft going (unraced on heavy). A genuine sort, still quite lightly raced, he will be unpenalised in pattern company in 2005, when it's more likely the Temple Stakes will be on his agenda. *R. Charlton*

PATRICIAN DEALER 2 br.g. (Apr 2) Millkom 124 – Double Fault (IRE) 54 (Zieten (USA) 118) [2004 7.1s p8.6g Oct 16] well held in maidens at Chepstow and Wolverhampton. *M. S. Saunders* —

PATRIXPRIAL 3 gr.c. Linamix (FR) 127 – Magnificent Star (USA) 122 (Silver Hawk (USA) 123) [2004 –p: 10.3d⁵ 12m⁵ 14.1d* 16g 13.1s⁴ 16s⁶ Oct 29] well-made colt: fairly useful performer: won handicap at Yarmouth in August: stays 1¾m, probably not 2m: acts on good to soft going. *M. H. Tompkins* **83**

PATRIXTOO (FR) 3 gr.c. Linamix (FR) 127 – Maradadi (USA) (Shadeed (USA) 135) [2004 60p: 10d 10d⁵ 7m 10.1g² 10.5g⁴ 12.1m 12d⁵ Oct 15] leggy gelding: modest maiden: stays 10.5f: acts on good to soft ground: sometimes makes running/takes strong hold. *M. H. Tompkins* **64**

PATRONAGE 2 b.c. (Feb 19) Royal Applause 124 – Passionate Pursuit 85 (Pursuit of Love 124) [2004 7d⁵ 7g⁵ 8m⁵ Sep 21] 160,000Y: good-topped colt: first foal: dam, 1¼m winner who stayed 1f, half-sister to very smart US performer up to 9f Jumron: best effort in maidens when third to Forward Move at Newmarket, soon off bridle: shapes as if will stay 1¼m. *M. L. W. Bell* **82**

PATRONOFCONFUCIUS (IRE) 2 b.g. (Apr 21) Imperial Ballet (IRE) 110 – Shefoog 90 (Kefaah (USA) 124) [2004 7g 7s Sep 14] tall gelding: well held in minor event at Ascot and maiden at Salisbury. *J. R. Boyle* —

PAT'S MIRACLE (IRE) 4 ch.f. College Chapel 122 – Exemplaire (FR) (Polish Precedent (USA) 131) [2004 –: p12g Jan 15] no form: tried blinkered. *John Berry* —

PAT'S NEMESIS (IRE) 3 b.f. Sri Pekan (USA) 117 – Exemplaire (FR) (Polish Precedent (USA) 131) [2004 –: 6d 7s f7d Jun 10] little form. *B. R. Johnson* —

PATTERDALE 3 b.g. Octagonal (NZ) 126 – Baize 95 (Efisio 120) [2004 81: 7d² 6m* 7g 8g² 10g⁶ 8v⁶ Oct 23] leggy gelding: fair performer: won maiden at Brighton in August: effective at 6f, barely stays 1¼m: acts on good to firm and good to soft going: sold 15,000 gns, sent to Belgium. *W. J. Haggas* **79**

PATTERNMAKER (USA) 2 b. or br.g. (Mar 10) Elnadim (USA) 128 – Attasliyah (IRE) (Marju (IRE) 127) [2004 6d⁶ Oct 4] $67,000F, 30,000Y: first foal: dam unraced half-sister to useful performer up to 7f Al Ihsas: 40/1, sixth in maiden at Windsor, green and not knocked about: should improve. *W. Jarvis* **60 p**

PATTERN MAN 3 b.c. Wizard King 122 – Quick Profit 78 (Formidable (USA) 125) [2004 –: 14.1s 16.2g f14g Aug 19] good-bodied colt: little form. *J. R. Norton* —

PATTERSON (IRE) 3 br.f. Turtle Island (IRE) 123 – Richmond Lillie (Fairbairn) [2004 10m p12g 12.1m⁶ Sep 9] half-sister to several winners, including 4-y-o Richmond Lodge: dam Irish maiden half-sister to Cheveley Park and Irish 1000 Guineas runner-up Millingdale Lillie: well held in maidens. *M. Madgwick* —

PATXARAN (IRE) 2 b.f. (Mar 17) Revoque (IRE) 122 – Stargard (Polish Precedent (USA) 131) [2004 6f 6g⁵ 7m⁴ 8s⁶ 8f³ 10m⁶ 8s Nov 1] €10,000Y: strong, lengthy filly: third foal: sister to 3-y-o Restart: dam, French maiden, half-sister to smart stayer Give Notice: fair maiden: ran as if amiss final start: will stay at least 1½m: acts on firm and soft going: sometimes hangs. *P. C. Haslam* **66**

PAULA 4 b.f. Compton Place 125 – Be My Bird 65 (Be My Chief (USA) 122) [2004 8v 12d⁶ 9.9g⁶ 9f Jun 1] 3,500Y: lengthy filly: fourth foal: half-sister to 2001 2-y-o 7f seller winner Birdlip Hill (by Prince Sabo) and 1m winner Timeless Chick (by Timeless —

Times): dam third at 7f/8.5f at 2 yrs: well held in maidens/handicap: tried in cheekpieces/visor. *M. Dods*

PAULA JO   2 b.f. (May 11) Factual (USA) 108 – Superstream (Superpower 113) [2004   **47**
5g⁶ 5g 6g 5d 5f Sep 13] fifth foal: half-sister to 3-y-o Baron Rhodes, 4-y-o Eddies Jewel and 6-y-o Tommy Smith: dam unraced: poor maiden: will prove best at 5f/6f: wore cheekpieces final start. *J. S. Wainwright*

PAULA LANE   4 b.f. Factual (USA) 108 – Colfax Classic 48 (Jareer (USA) 115) [2004   **–**
73: f12g f16s⁵ 10.9s 15.4s⁶ Apr 20] fair performer at 3 yrs: well held in 2004. *R. Curtis*

PAULINE'S PRINCE   2 b.c. (Mar 12) Polar Prince (IRE) 117 – Etma Rose (IRE)   **68**
(Fairy King (USA)) [2004 5f⁶ 7g⁴ 7m⁴ 6g 7s f8g⁵ p7.1g⁶ p7.1g⁵ p7m⁴ Dec 21] leggy colt: third foal: dam of little account: fair performer: won maiden at Southwell in June: mostly creditable efforts in nurseries after: stays easy 1m: acts on all-weather, probably on soft going: wore cheekpieces final start. *R. Hollinshead*

PAVILION   2 b.f. (Feb 20) Robellino (USA) 127 – Chiltern Court (USA) (Topsider (USA)) [2004 7g Sep 20] 3,500Y: close-coupled filly: fourth foal: half-sister to 1m winner Circlet (by Lion Cavern): dam unraced out of sister to Thatch and Special, latter dam of Nureyev and grandam of Sadler's Wells: 33/1, well held in maiden at Kempton. *B. J. Meehan*

PAWAN (IRE)   4 ch.g. Cadeaux Genereux 131 – Born To Glamour (Ajdal (USA) 130)   **72**
[2004 61: 6s⁵ f6g² 6s² f6g 5v³ 6s⁵ 7m³ 6m 7.1m² 7.1g 7.1m* 8.1f⁶ 7.9g⁶ 7.1m³ 7m 9d⁵ 7.9d 10.1g⁵ 10.3g 8m 7.2s p7.1g p8.6g p8.6d f7g f6g* p10m p8g p6m* p7g Dec 30] lengthy, angular gelding: fair performer: left N. Tinkler after second start: won minor events at Warwick in June and Redcar in July and banded race at Southwell and handicap at Lingfield in December: effective at 6f to 9f: acts on all-weather, heavy and good to firm ground: usually races prominently: tough. *Miss A. Stokell*

PAWN BROKER   7 ch.g. Selkirk (USA) 129 – Dime Bag 87 (High Line 125) [2004   **110**
107+: p10g 8f* 10d⁴ 9.9m⁶ 9g 9s Oct 16] rather leggy gelding: smart performer: won minor event at Newmarket in July by length from Mine, easily best effort in 2004: effective at 1m to 1½m: acts on polytrack and any turf going: tried blinkered earlier in career: sometimes races freely, and often finds little. *D. R. C. Elsworth*

PAWN IN LIFE (IRE)   6 b.g. Midhish 109 – Lady-Mumtaz (Martin John) [2004 –,   **–**
a72: f7g f7g f7g f7s² f7s f6s f8g⁶ f7g f7g³ f8g Dec 28] lengthy gelding: fair handicapper: **a69**
stays 1m: acts on all-weather, no form on turf: sometimes wears headgear: sometimes slowly away. *T. D. Barron*

PAX   7 ch.g. Brief Truce (USA) 126 – Child's Play (USA) (Sharpen Up 127) [2004 90:   **90**
5g⁶ 5s⁶ 5d 6m* 6m 6m 6f 5m 6m 6g 5d 5s Oct 16] tall gelding: fairly useful handicapper: won at York in May by length from Romany Nights: effective at stiff 5f/6f: acts on firm and good to soft going: often blinkered in 2001: often slowly away: usually held up. *D. Nicholls*

PAY ATTENTION   3 b.f. Revoque (IRE) 122 – Catch Me 75 (Rudimentary (USA)   **68**
118) [2004 57: 8s⁴ 10s 10s² 9.3f 9.9g² 10.1d* 12.1d⁴ 9.9s⁵ Aug 29] quite good-topped filly: fair performer: won apprentice minor event at Newcastle in August: best around 1¼m: unraced on heavy going, acts on any other turf. *T. D. Easterby*

PAYOLA (USA)   3 b.f. Red Ransom (USA) – Bevel (USA) (Mr Prospector (USA))   **74**
[2004 66p: 10g* 11.9s⁶ 12g⁵ 10s⁶ Oct 15] rather leggy, close-coupled filly: fair performer: won maiden at Ripon in August: probably stays 1½m: acts on soft going, probably on good to firm. *C. E. Brittain*

PAYS D'AMOUR (IRE)   7 b.g. Pursuit of Love 124 – Lady of The Land 75 (Wollow   **71 d**
132) [2004 76: f5g 7s 6g* 6m f7d³ f6d 6d⁵ 7m 6m 6g² 5d 6s 6d 6d Oct 12] strong gelding: unimpressive mover: fair performer: won claimer at Doncaster in May: left D. Nicholls and below form after: best at 6f/easy 7f: acts on firm and soft going: tried tongue tied: usually held up. *Miss L. A. Perratt*

PAY THE SILVER   6 gr.g. Petong 126 – Marjorie's Memory (IRE) 76 (Fairy King   **72**
(USA)) [2004 82, a60: 10.9d 8.1s⁴ 8m p12g² 9g 11.9f³ 12g³ p16g 11.9f Aug 3] close-   **a63**
coupled, good-bodied gelding: fair handicapper: stays 1½m: acts on polytrack (probably on fibresand), firm and soft going: tried visored, wears cheekpieces nowadays: often races freely: held up: has good record at Epsom. *I. A. Wood*

PAY TIME   5 ch.m. Timeless Times (USA) 99 – Payvashooz 78 (Ballacashtal (CAN))   **37**
[2004 56d: 6v⁶ 5m 5g 7m⁵ 6g⁶ 6d 5s Nov 2] dipped-backed mare: poor maiden: stays 6f: acts on fibresand and good to firm ground: tried tongue tied. *R. E. Barr*

PEACEFUL FRONTIER   2 b.f. (Jan 6) Monashee Mountain (USA) 115 – Edge of   –
Darkness 62 (Vaigly Great 127) [2004 5g 5m 6m Aug 7] half-sister to 3 winners, including 3-y-o Linda Green and 8-y-o Salford Flyer: dam 1¼m to 2m winner: little sign of
ability in maidens/seller. *C. Smith*

PEACE LILY   2 b.f. (Apr 25) Dansili 127 – Shall We Run 59 (Hotfoot 126) [2004   67
6g⁵ 7d Oct 30] strong, close-coupled filly: half-sister to several winners, including 6-y-o
Bannister, 3-y-o Ghantoot and useful 1999 2-y-o 5f/6f winner Roo (by Rudimentary):
dam lightly-raced half-sister to very smart but temperamental sprinter Dead Certain:
better effort in maidens when fifth at Windsor. *R. F. Johnson Houghton*

PEACE TREATY (IRE)   3 b.f. Turtle Island (IRE) 123 – Beautyofthepeace (IRE)   –
(Exactly Sharp (USA) 121) [2004 –: f8g f8g f9.4g f8g 8.5m 5m⁶ 7g Jun 24] small filly:
little form: tried blinkered/tongue tied. *S. R. Bowring*

PEAK OF PERFECTION (IRE)   3 b.g. Deploy 131 – Nsx 74 (Roi Danzig (USA))   97
[2004 –: 10g⁵ f8.5g³ 12g⁵ p12d* 12.3d* 14m* 13.9s² 16.2m 14.6s⁶ Oct 22] good-bodied
gelding: useful performer: won maiden at Lingfield and handicaps at Chester and Sandown in June/July: good second to Lost Soldier Three in Melrose Rated Stakes at York
next time: should stay 2m: acts on polytrack (probably on fibresand), soft and good to
firm ground: free-going sort, races up with pace. *M. A. Jarvis*

PEAK PARK (USA)   4 b. or br.g. Dynaformer (USA) – Play Po (USA) (Play On   53
(USA)) [2004 56: 16m 18m 14.1m² 16.4g 16s³ p16g² p16g² p16.5g³ f16g⁶ f16g* Dec 14]   **a63**
strong, close-coupled gelding: modest handicapper: best effort when winning by 6
lengths at Southwell in December: stays 2m: acts on all-weather, best turf form on ground
firmer than good: sometimes visored: tends to race freely. *J. A. R. Toller*

PEAK TO CREEK   3 b.c. Royal Applause 124 – Rivers Rhapsody 104 (Dominion   118
123) [2004 112: 8g³ 7m² 7.1g³ Jun 3] smallish, quite attractive colt: smart performer:
placed in Craven Stakes at Newmarket (6¼ lengths third to Haafhd) and listed races on
same course (beaten a neck by Fokine) and Sandown (3 lengths third to Madid): best
short of 1m: acts on firm going, probably on good to soft: usually held up: sometimes
races freely: consistent. *J. Noseda*

PEARL FARM   3 b.f. Foxhound (USA) 103 – Trinity Hall 67 (Hallgate 127) [2004 6s   57
p7g³ Oct 25] fourth foal: half-sister to 5-y-o Ocean Avenue: dam, 6f winner, half-sister to
smart 5f/6f performer Emma Peel: third in maiden at Lingfield, looking green then
staying on well final 1f: will stay 1m. *C. A. Horgan*

PEARL GREY   3 gr. or ch.f. Gone West (USA) – Zelanda (IRE) 108 (Night Shift   98
(USA)) [2004 98: 6.1g³ 7m² 6d Oct 14] smallish, sturdy filly: useful performer: trained at
2 yrs by D. Loder: good efforts in 2004 when placed in listed races at Chester (third to
Simianna) and Ascot (3 lengths second behind Badminton): well held in similar event at
Newmarket: left Godolphin after: not sure to stay beyond 7f: unraced on extremes of
going: tongue tied in 2004. *Saeed bin Suroor*

PEARL ISLAND (USA)   3 b.g. Kingmambo (USA) 125 – Mother of Pearl (IRE) 113   **51 ?**
(Sadler's Wells (USA) 132) [2004 –: 7.1d 8.1s f6s⁵ p5.1g p7.1g⁶ Dec 22] sturdy geld-
ing: seemingly modest maiden: should stay 7f: acts on fibresand: usually slowly away.
D. J. Wintle

PEARL OF LOVE (IRE)   3 b.c. Peintre Celebre (USA) 137 – Aunt Pearl (USA)   101
(Seattle Slew (USA)) [2004 112: 9g 8f Jun 15] strong, good-bodied colt: has a quick
action: smart performer at 2 yrs, winner of Gran Criterium at Milan: beat only home in
both Prix Jean Prat at Chantilly and St James's Palace Stakes at Royal Ascot in June 2004:
reported later in month to be suffering from recurrence of hoof injury to off-fore: stays
1m: acts on firm going: usually races up with pace: game. *M. Johnston*

PEARL OF YORK (DEN)   3 b.f. Richard of York 123 – Laser Show (IRE) (Wassl   67
125) [2004 54: 10g 10m 10f² f12d⁵ 9m* 9.3f³ 10.1d⁵ 12g⁶ 10s* 9g* Oct 4] leggy filly:
fair performer: won handicap at Musselburgh in July and, having left R. Guest after
seventh start, minor events at Ovrevoll in September and Copenhagen in October: stays
1¼m: acts on all-weather, soft and good to firm going. *S. Jensen, Denmark*

PEARL PRIDE (USA)   3 ch.f. Theatrical 128 – Spotlight Dance (USA) (Miswaki   –
(USA) 124) [2004 71: 10v 10m 7.5g 12.1d Aug 11] tall, rather leggy filly: fair maiden at
2 yrs: little form in 2004: sent to USA. *M. Johnston*

PEARL'S A SINGER (IRE)   2 ch.f. (Feb 9) Spectrum (IRE) 126 – Cultured Pearl   66
(IRE) 72 (Lammtarra (USA) 134) [2004 7.6m 8.2g⁵ 7.5m⁵ 8g Sep 30] first foal: dam,
maiden who should have stayed 1¼m, daughter of Prix Marcel Boussac and Poule

d'Essai des Pouliches winner Culture Vulture: fair maiden: form only when fifth: should stay 1¼m. *M. L. W. Bell*

PEARNICKITY 3 b.f. Bob's Return (IRE) 123 – The Robe 54 (Robellino (USA) 127) [2004 10m 12.1m 10m 11.7d Aug 27] first foal: dam, staying maiden on Flat, winner over hurdles: well held in maidens/seller. *A. W. Carroll* —

PEARSON GLEN (IRE) 5 ch.g. Dolphin Street (FR) 125 – Glendora (Glenstal (USA) 118) [2004 65: 8m Oct 2] good-topped gelding: fair handicapper: well held only run at 5 yrs. *G. A. Swinbank* —

PEARTREE HOUSE (IRE) 10 b.g. Simply Majestic (USA) – Fashion Front (Habitat 134) [2004 66, a–: f8g f8f f8.5g f7g 8s⁶ f7g⁶ 8.2m⁶ 8f f7g 8m 8f Sep 16] rangy gelding: poor nowadays: effective at 7f to easy 9f: acts on firm and soft ground: visored once in 1998: has pulled hard. *D. W. Chapman* **42 a–**

PEBBLE MILL (IRE) 2 b.c. (Mar 3) Cape Cross (IRE) 129 – Mill Path (Mill Reef (USA) 141) [2004 6m 8g Oct 12] angular, useful-looking colt: only a little sign of ability in maidens: sold 3,500 gns. *M. Johnston* —

PEDLAR OF DREAMS (IRE) 2 b.f. (Apr 28) Fayruz 116 – Beautyofthepeace (IRE) (Exactly Sharp (USA) 121) [2004 5d³ 5g⁵ 6.1m Sep 28] seventh foal: half-sister to 3 winners, including 4-y-o Lakelands Lady and fairly useful but unreliable 1m (at 2 yrs) to 15f winner Windshift (by Forest Wind): dam unraced: modest form on first 2 starts in maidens: should stay 6f. *T. D. Barron* **63**

PEDLER'S PROFILES 4 br.g. Topanoora 118 – La Vie En Primrose 104 (Henbit (USA) 130) [2004 p10g p8g p7g Mar 9] rather dipped-backed gelding: little form: tried in blinkers. *Miss K. M. George* —

PEDRILLO 3 b.g. Singspiel (IRE) 133 – Patria (USA) 76 (Mr Prospector (USA)) [2004 91p: 8m³ 8.3s* 9g Oct 2] tall gelding: useful performer, lightly raced: won minor event at Hamilton in September impressively by 5 lengths from Mrs Moh: gambled-on 7/2 favourite, ran poorly in Cambridgeshire at Newmarket final outing, racing freely: may prove best up to 1m: acts on soft and good to firm going: carried head awkwardly at 2 yrs. *Sir Mark Prescott* **107**

PEDRO JACK (IRE) 7 b.g. Mujadil (USA) 119 – Festival of Light (High Top 131) [2004 83, a92: 6s f6g* 6g 6g 6m 6f³ f6m Jul 26] tall gelding: modest performer: won claimer at Wolverhampton (left B. Meehan) in April: best at 6f: acts on all-weather, best on good ground or firmer on turf: tried blinkered/visored/tongue tied (not in 2004): sometimes slowly away (virtually refused to race once as 5-y-o): none too consistent. *M. A. Buckley* **58 a63**

PEE JAY'S DREAM 2 ch.g. (Apr 22) Vettori (IRE) 119 – Langtry Lady 91 (Pas de Seul 133) [2004 f5g⁶ 6g 6g 6g Oct 4] sturdy gelding: poor maiden: should stay at least 1m. *M. W. Easterby* **48**

PEEP SHOW 2 b.f. (Feb 15) In The Wings 128 – Arderelle (FR) 80 (Pharly (FR) 130) [2004 p8g Nov 13] sister to smart 1m (at 2 yrs)/1¼m winner Aldwych and half-sister to several winners, including smart 7f (at 2 yrs) to 1½m winner Spout (by Salse): dam 1¼m winner: 25/1, never dangerous in maiden at Lingfield: will be suited by 1¼m/1½m: should do better. *R. Charlton* **– p**

PEEPTOE (IRE) 2 ch.f. (Mar 25) Machiavellian (USA) 123 – Alfaguara (USA) (Red Ransom (USA)) [2004 5d³ 6.1d² 6d⁵ 6m⁴ 5.1g Sep 29] €125,000F, €150,000Y: smallish filly: first foal: dam, French 1m winner, half-sister to dam of 3-y-o Bachelor Duke: fair maiden: should stay 7f: acts on good to firm and good to soft going. *J. L. Dunlop* **73**

PEERESS 3 ch.f. Pivotal 124 – Noble One 107 (Primo Dominie 121) [2004 86p: 8f* 8f* 7m* 7m³ p8g⁴ Oct 31] strong, rangy filly: has a quick action: useful performer: won maiden at Bath in May and handicaps at Thirsk in June and Newmarket (idled when beating Oasis Star 1¼ lengths) in July: better than result suggests when third to Peter Paul Rubens in handicap at Goodwood and length fourth to Miss George in listed race at Lingfield (slowly away and finished strongly once switched) after: effective at 7f/1m: acts on polytrack, raced only on good ground or firmer on turf: remains a smart performer in the making, sure to win more races. *Sir Michael Stoute* **105 p**

PELLA 3 ch.f. Hector Protector (USA) 124 – Norpella 95 (Northfields (USA)) [2004 9.7s 11.1g 10s⁶ 8.2m² 8.1m⁵ 8.1g³ 9g² 10g³ 8.3m 8d* 8g 8.5m* 8d⁴ p10g⁵ p9.5g Nov 13] quite good-topped filly: half-sister to several winners, including smart 6f (at 2 yrs) to 1m winner Sugarfoot (by Thatching) and useful 5f (at 2 yrs) to 1m winner Ultimo Imperatore (by Cadeaux Genereux): dam 1¼m/1½m winner who stayed 15f: fair performer: won **71**

minor event at Yarmouth in August and handicap at Beverley in September: stays 1¼m: acts on polytrack, good to firm and good to soft going. *M. Blanshard*

PENALTY CLAUSE (IRE) 4 b.g. Namaqualand (USA) – Lady Be Lucky (IRE) 57 **39** (Taufan (USA) 119) [2004 –: f14g⁵ Jan 12] leggy gelding: fair maiden in Ireland at 2 yrs, poor nowadays: stays 1½m: acts on soft ground: tried blinkered/tongue tied/in cheekpieces: has been slowly away. *K. A. Morgan*

PENALTY KICK (IRE) 2 b.c. (Apr 30) Montjeu (IRE) 137 – Dafrah (USA) 78 **75** (Danzig (USA)) [2004 7g 7.1d⁶ 8g 10m* 8.3d⁵ Oct 4] 50,000F, 82,000Y: tall colt: has scope: half-brother to 1999 2-y-o 1m winner Peacock Jewel and 1¼m winner Bold Demand (both useful, by Rainbow Quest): dam 1m winner: fair performer: won nursery at Nottingham in September: respectable fifth in similar event at Windsor final start: will stay 1½m: acts on good to firm going: blinkered (raced too freely) third outing. *N. A. Callaghan*

PENANG SAPPHIRE 2 b.g. (Apr 11) Spectrum (IRE) 126 – Penang Pearl (FR) 106 **60** (Bering 136) [2004 p6d⁶ 6.1d 6m 5.1v* p6g⁶ Dec 1] useful-looking gelding: first foal: dam 1m/9f winner: modest performer: 40/1-winner of nursery at Nottingham in November: possibly amiss final start: should stay 6f: acts on heavy going. *G. A. Butler*

PENDING (IRE) 3 b.g. Pennekamp (USA) 130 – Dolcezza (FR) (Lichine (USA) 117) **68** [2004 78p: 8.2g³ 8.2d 8m⁶ 8d 10s³ 11.5g Sep 14] tall, lengthy gelding: fair maiden: stays 1m: acts on good to firm going, probably on soft: wore cheekpieces 3 of last 4 starts: sold 13,000 gns. *J. R. Fanshawe*

PENEL (IRE) 3 b.g. Orpen (USA) 116 – Jayess Elle 55 (Sabrehill (USA) 120) [2004 **63** 57: p7g⁶ 8.2g 7.1d² 6m⁵ p8.6g f6s⁴ p7.1g³ f6g* Dec 7] smallish gelding: modest performer: won seller at Southwell in December (bought by P. Blockley 6,200 gns): probably best at 6f/7f: acts on all-weather and good to soft going: effective blinkered or not: consistent. *B. R. Millman*

PENINSULAR (FR) 2 ch.c. (Feb 5) Giant's Causeway (USA) 132 – Blue Note (FR) **60** 122 (Habitat 134) [2004 5.2g Apr 16] sturdy colt: half-brother to several winners, notably 5f (at 2 yrs) to 7f winner Blue Duster and 5f (at 2 yrs) to 1m winner Zieten (both smart, by Danzig): dam French 5f to 7f winner: seventh of 8 in maiden at Newbury: dead. *J. H. M. Gosden*

PENKENNA PRINCESS (IRE) 2 b.f. (May 2) Pivotal 124 – Tiriana (Common **105** Grounds 118) [2004 6g 6g* 6m³ 7g* 7s² Oct 16] 16,000Y, 60,000 2-y-o: tall, leggy filly: third foal: half-sister to 4-y-o Madamoiselle Jones and 3-y-o Salut Saint Cloud: dam, third at 1m in France, half-sister to useful 1996 2-y-o 5f winner Head Over Heels: useful performer: won maiden at Kempton in September and listed race at Newmarket (by ½ length from Favourita) in October: good short-head second to Maids Causeway in Rockfel Stakes at Newmarket, leading briefly final 1f: should stay 1m: acts on soft and good to firm going. *R. M. Beckett*

PENNAUTIER (IRE) 2 gr.f. (Feb 26) Paris House 123 – Traci's Castle (IRE) (Ajraas **41 p** (USA) 88) [2004 p6g Nov 27] €1,300Y: third foal: half-sister to winners abroad by Pharly and Colonel Collins: dam ran twice: 33/1, eighth in maiden at Wolverhampton, held up after slow start and not knocked about: should do better. *P. A. Blockley*

PENNESTAMP (IRE) 2 b.c. (Jan 15) Pennekamp (USA) 130 – Sopran Marida (IRE) **61** (Darshaan 133) [2004 5g 6m⁶ 6d⁵ 5m⁴ 6m⁴ 5g³ 6.1d 6m⁵ 8.3g Oct 11] neat colt: modest maiden: likely to prove best at 5f/6f: acts on good to firm going: tends to hang right. *Mrs P. N. Dutfield*

PENNY CROSS 4 b.f. Efisio 120 – Addaya (IRE) (Persian Bold 123) [2004 99: 7s 8d **82** 8g 7m 9.3g³ Jun 23] smallish, good-topped filly: just fairly useful form in handicaps in 2004: stays 9f: acts on firm going: races prominently: sometimes carries head awkwardly. *J. G. Given*

PENNY ISLAND (IRE) 2 b.c. (Feb 2) Trans Island 119 – Sparklingsovereign 53 **72** (Sparkler 130) [2004 7f 7m⁶ 8s³ 8m⁵ 7d Oct 10] €20,000F, €30,000Y: leggy colt: half-brother to 3 winners, including smart Irish 9f to 11f winner Golden Rule (by Emarati): dam second in 7f seller: fair maiden: stays 1m: acts on firm and soft ground: free-going sort. *A. King*

PENNY PICTURES (IRE) 5 b.g. Theatrical 128 – Copper Creek 78 (Habitat 134) **91** [2004 20f³ 16.2g⁵ 18s Oct 16] close-coupled, quite good-topped gelding: useful performer at 3 yrs: not seen on Flat in 2003, and just fairly useful form in 2004, including third to Double Obsession in Ascot Stakes at Royal Ascot: reared leaving stall when well held in Cesarewitch at Newmarket final outing: stays 2½m: acts on firm going. *M. C. Pipe*

totescoop6 Stakes (Handicap), Sandown—
under a well-judged ride from Frankie Dettori, Pentecost (left) collars St Andrews

PENNY PIE (IRE) 4 b.f. Spectrum (IRE) 126 – Island Lover (IRE) (Turtle Island (IRE) 123) [2004 67: p10g Jan 7] deep-girthed filly: fair maiden at 3 yrs: visored, raced freely when well held only outing in 2004. *P. W. Harris* –

PENNY'S CROWN 5 b.m. Reprimand 122 – Two And Sixpence (USA) 74 (Chief's Crown (USA)) [2004 f12d p12.2g Dec 27] 300Y: fifth foal: half-sister to 2 winners, including 7f winner Sarah's Song (by Warning): dam 17f winner: poor hurdler: well held in claimer at Southwell and seller at Wolverhampton (visored). *G. A. Ham* –

PENNY STALL 3 b.f. Silver Patriarch (IRE) 125 – Madiyla 73 (Darshaan 133) [2004 67p: 10m 14g⁴ 16.2s² 17.1d⁶ 14.1g⁴ p16.5g Dec 3] big, good-topped filly: easy mover: fair maiden: left J. Dunlop after fifth start: stays 17f: acts on polytrack, soft and good to firm going: found little fourth outing. *Miss E. C. Lavelle* **69**

PENNY VALENTINE 4 ch.f. My Best Valentine 122 – Precision Finish 63 (Safawan 118) [2004 39: p8g p10g⁶ p12g Feb 23] modest maiden at 2 yrs: no longer of much account. *J. R. Best* –

PENNY WEDDING (IRE) 2 b.f. (Feb 6) Pennekamp (USA) 130 – Eilean Shona 102 (Suave Dancer (USA) 136) [2004 8m 7.9g⁶ Oct 9] small, workmanlike filly: first foal: dam 9f (at 2 yrs) to 2m winner: late headway when well held in maidens at Newmarket and York: will be suited by 1¼m/1½m: should do better. *J. R. Fanshawe* **– p**

PENRITH (FR) 3 b.c. Singspiel (IRE) 133 – Queen Mat (IRE) (Fairy King (USA)) [2004 85p: 8m* 9.9m³ 9g 8m³ 8m⁵ 10.5g 8.3d² 8g³ 7.9g⁴ 8d Oct 15] smallish, close-coupled colt: fairly useful handicapper: won at Pontefract in May: creditable efforts when in frame after: should stay 1¼m: acts on good to firm and good to soft ground: sold 30,000 gns. *M. Johnston* **93**

PENSION FUND 10 b.g. Emperor Fountain 112 – Navarino Bay 102 (Averof 123) [2004 66d: 9.9v⁵ 10.5d⁵ 8.1f⁶ 10m⁴ Jul 6] tall gelding: modest handicapper: races at 1m/1¼m nowadays: acts on fibresand, probably on any turf going: blinkered twice (including when racing freely/finding little), below form once in cheekpieces: sometimes slowly away: no easy ride. *M. W. Easterby* **57**

PENTECOST 5 ch.g. Tagula (IRE) 116 – Boughtbyphone 62 (Warning 136) [2004 108: 8g 7.9s⁶ 8f 8.1d* 8g⁴ 8m 8g* 8d 8f 9d* 8g Oct 1] sturdy, close-coupled gelding: smart performer: won totescoop6 Stakes (Handicap) at Sandown (by head from St Andrews) in July, valuable handicap at Ascot (second year running, by 1¼ lengths from Vortex) in August and minor event at Newbury (beat Checkit ¾ length) in September: stays 9f: yet to race on heavy going, acts on any other: tried visored, not in 2004: has been bandaged/worn dropped noseband: sometimes races freely. *A. M. Balding* **114**

PENWELL HILL (USA) 5 b.g. Distant View (USA) 126 – Avie's Jill (USA) (Lord Avie (USA)) [2004 78: f8g* f9.4g f8s² f8.5s² 8s 10m⁶ 10m 8g 8f³ 7.9m* 9d f8g* p9.5g Dec 11] quite good-topped gelding: fairly useful on all-weather, modest on turf: won handicap at Southwell in January, banded event at Carlisle in September and handicap at Southwell (best effort) in November: best form at 7f to 8.5f: acts on fibresand and firm going: game front runner. *T. D. Barron* **59 a87**

PENZANCE 3 ch.g. Pennekamp (USA) 130 – Kalinka (IRE) 88 (Soviet Star (USA) 128) [2004 77: 9v⁶ 10.3g⁴ 10g* 12g 10m 11g Sep 17] good-bodied gelding: fairly useful handicapper: won at Nottingham in June: stays 1¼m: acts on firm and good to soft going: joined A. King. *J. R. Fanshawe* **83**

PEOPLETON BROOK   2 b.c. (Apr 12) Compton Place 125 – Merch Rhyd-Y-Grug   **64 d**
(Sabrehill (USA) 120) [2004 5.1f⁵ p5g⁶ 5.2m 6.1d 7m 6d Oct 18] 9,500Y: leggy colt:
third foal: half-brother to 3-y-o Three Welshmen: dam no form: modest maiden: form
only on debut: needs to settle to stay beyond 5f: blinkered final start. *D. W. P. Arbuthnot*

PEPE (IRE)   3 b.f. Bahhare (USA) 122 – Orange And Blue 50 (Prince Sabo 123) [2004   **58**
50: f9.4g⁶ f11g⁶ f12g³ 10.9d f12d* f12m⁴ f12d f12f 13.8m* Sep 18] tall filly: modest
performer: won handicap at Southwell in April and seller at Catterick in September: stays
easy 1¾m: acts on fibresand, unraced on extremes of going on turf: effective with or without cheekpieces: sent to Ukraine. *R. Hollinshead*

PEPPERMINT TEA (IRE)   2 b.f. (May 15) Intikhab (USA) 135 – Karayb (IRE) 93   **79**
(Last Tycoon 131) [2004 6m 6g 6g² Sep 15] €38,000Y: compact filly: fifth foal: half-
sister to 3 winners, including useful French 1¼m winner Ghyraan (by Cadeaux Genereux) and 2002 2-y-o 1m winner Red Chief (by Lahib): dam 6f (at 2 yrs)/7f winner: easily
best effort in maidens when second to Divinely Decadent at Yarmouth, racing alone and
making most: bred to stay 7f. *M. L. W. Bell*

PEPPER ROAD   5 ch.g. Elmaamul (USA) 125 – Floral Spark 69 (Forzando 122)   **62**
[2004 61: 8d 7d 7.9f* 6.9f² 7.9m² 7.1m² 8m p8g⁶ p7.1d Nov 5] modest handicapper: won
at Carlisle in June: effective at 7f/1m: acts on polytrack, firm and good to soft going: tried
in cheekpieces (below form): often taken early to post: found little final start. *R. Bastiman*

PEPPERSTORM (GER)   3 b.c. Big Shuffle (USA) 122 – Pasca (GER) (Lagunas)   **116**
[2004 103: 7.5g³ 8g⁴ 8d² 8g* 8s* Aug 31] brother to 3 winners in Germany, notably smart
milers Peppercorn and Peppershot: dam German 2-y-o 6.5f winner: smart performer:
successful at 2 yrs in maiden at Krefeld and national listed races at Cologne and Dusseldorf: progressive form in 2004, winning Globetrotter-Meile at Cologne (by neck from
Eagle Rise) and Darley Oettingen-Rennen at Baden-Baden (in good style, by 2 lengths
from Checkit) in August: stays 1m: acts on soft ground: joined Godolphin. *U. Ostmann,
Germany*

PEQUENITA   4 b.f. Rudimentary (USA) 118 – Sierra Madrona (USA) (Woodman   **65**
(USA) 126) [2004 70: 10s⁶ 9s⁵ Oct 22] leggy filly: fair performer: stays 1½m: acts on
fibresand and soft ground: blinkered last 4 starts: often makes running: winning hurdler:
sold £6,000. *G. L. Moore*

PERCHERON (IRE)   2 ch.g. (Apr 3) Perugino (USA) 84 – Silvery Halo (USA) 68   **80**
(Silver Ghost (USA)) [2004 6d 7d 5g³ p5.1g* Nov 19] €4,500F, 16,000Y: good-topped
gelding: third foal: closely related to Italian 2002 2-y-o 7.5f winner by Eagle Eyed: dam,
Irish maiden, stayed 1m: fairly useful performer: easily best effort when making all in
nursery at Wolverhampton: will prove best at 5f/easy 6f: acts on polytrack: carried head
high third start. *P. A. Blockley*

PERCUSSIONIST (IRE)   3 b.c. Sadler's Wells (USA) 132 – Magnificient Style   **121**
(USA) 107 (Silver Hawk (USA) 123) [2004 79p: 12d* 11.5s* 12m⁴ 12f 10.9s² 15m³ 12d⁶
15.5s⁵ Oct 24] tall, close-coupled colt: has a powerful, round action: very smart performer: won maiden at Newmarket in April and Gallagher Group Ltd Derby Trial at
Lingfield in May, beating Hazyview 10 lengths in latter despite cocking jaw and hanging
markedly right: unimpressive to post, good 1¾ lengths fourth to North Light in Derby at
Epsom next time, staying on strongly: rather disappointing after, best effort in autumn
when 5 lengths second behind Into The Dark in listed race at Ayr: should stay at least
1¾m: acts on soft ground, ran well on good to firm at Epsom but well below form both
starts after on ground firmer than good: blinkered (respectable effort) final outing: edgy
sort (wears crossed noseband/gets on toes/tends to sweat): not an easy ride (has hung
right/often soon off bridle): has worn ear plugs/American halter: sold 340,000 gns in
November, joined J. Howard Johnson. *J. H. M. Gosden*

*Gallagher Group Ltd Derby Trial Stakes, Lingfield—Percussionist hangs badly right
but still pulls well clear of Hazyview and Five Dynasties in a four-runner field*

Hackney Empire Royal Lodge Stakes, Ascot—
Perfectperformance (left) stays on too strongly for Scandinavia, Wilko and Elliots World (rail)

PERCY DOUGLAS 4 b.c. Elmaamul (USA) 125 – Qualitair Dream 80 (Dreams To **40** §
Reality (USA) 113) [2004 77d: f5g f5s 6d 5v 5f 8d 10m⁶ 8m 5g 5d 5m⁵ 5g 6m 6d⁶ 5.1g
6g Aug 28] good-topped colt: poor nowadays: effective at 5f to 1m: acts on fibresand
and firm ground: sometimes visored/wears cheekpieces: tongue tied last 7 starts: tends to
edge right: not one to trust. *Miss A. Stokell*

PERCY-VERANCE (IRE) 6 ch.g. Dolphin Street (FR) 125 – Sinology (Rainbow **39**
Quest (USA) 134) [2004 11m⁵ 17.2g⁴ Jul 3] poor performer: stays 17.2f. *J. J. Quinn*

PEREGIAN (IRE) 6 b.g. Eagle Eyed (USA) 111 – Mo Pheata (Petorius 117) [2004 **54**
58: f8.5g⁵ p7g³ 7.1g 7m Jul 13] stocky gelding: modest performer: left J. Akehurst after
second start: effective at 7f to easy 1¼m: acts on polytrack, firm and good to soft going
(below form on soft): tried blinkered/in cheekpieces (raced freely): sometimes hangs.
Andrew Reid

PEREGRINE HAWK (IRE) 3 ch.g. Perugino (USA) 84 – Follow The Wind (Artaius **37**
(USA) 129) [2004 –: 6s 10s 5s p8m⁶ p10m Dec 8] poor maiden: seems to stay 1¼m: acts
on polytrack: tried in blinkers/cheekpieces. *P. Morris, Ireland*

PERELANDRA (USA) 4 ch.f. Cadeaux Genereux 131 – Larentia 58 (Salse (USA) **76**
128) [2004 76: 11.5d* 12m 13.1s⁴ 12g⁴ Sep 26] rather leggy, useful-looking filly: fair
performer, lightly raced: won seller at Lingfield in August: barely stays 13.1f: acts on
polytrack, soft and good to firm going: took good hold penultimate outing, hung left final
start: sold 8,500 gns. *M. J. Wallace*

PERERIN 3 b.g. Whittingham (IRE) 104 – Antithesis (IRE) 75 (Fairy King (USA)) **48**
[2004 –: 6s 7g* 7m 7f 7m 8f³ 8f 8d⁶ 8.1d 7d 8d³ p7.1g³ p8m² p7m³ p8m⁵ Dec 15] sturdy,
close-coupled gelding: poor performer: won banded race at Brighton in May: left I. Wood
after eleventh start: stays 1m: acts on polytrack, firm and good to soft ground: usually
blinkered/visored. *N. B. King*

PERESTROIKA (IRE) 6 ch.g. Ashkalani (IRE) 128 – Licentious 45 (Reprimand **56**
122) [2004 f16s 12g 12m⁴ 14m 14d⁴ 13.8m Aug 3] leggy gelding: missed 2003 and just
modest in 2004: stays 14.4f: acts on firm going: tried in cheekpieces at 4 yrs. *B. Ellison*

PEREZ (IRE) 2 b.c. (Mar 31) Mujadil (USA) 119 – Kahla (Green Desert (USA) 127) **69**
[2004 6m 6g 7m⁶ 5.7g Sep 13] €36,000F: good-bodied colt: second foal: dam unraced
half-sister to Grand Prix de Paris winner Dancehall: best effort in maidens when sixth at
Leicester: hung left second start: stays 7f. *R. Hannon*

PERFECT BALANCE (IRE) 3 b. or br.g. Shinko Forest (IRE) – Tumble (Mtoto **64**
134) [2004 53: 8.2g 8s* 10g⁶ 9.2d⁵ 10v⁴ f12g 9g 14g f11g⁴ Dec 14] close-coupled
gelding: modest handicapper: won at Redcar in April: stays 1¼m: raced only on good
going or softer (acts on heavy). *N. Tinkler*

PERFECT CHOICE (IRE) 2 gr.c. (May 1) Daylami (IRE) 138 – Fairy Contessa **88**
(IRE) 63 (Fairy King (USA)) [2004 6m 6m* 7f 7m⁶ Jul 30] 155,000Y: leggy, quite good-
topped colt: has a quick action: second foal: half-brother to 3-y-o Needles And Pins: dam,
maiden (stayed 7f), half-sister to Gimcrack winner River Falls: fairly useful performer:
won maiden at Newbury in June: creditable sixth to Brecon Beacon in minor event at
Newmarket, only other form: likely to stay 1m. *B. J. Meehan*

PERFECT HINDSIGHT (IRE) 3 b.g. Spectrum (IRE) 126 – Vinicky (USA) (King- **–**
mambo (USA) 125) [2004 68: 6d 7m 6.1m 6m p9.5g Dec 22] quite good-topped gelding:
fair maiden at 2 yrs: little form in 2004: left C. Cox prior to final outing: blinkered
penultimate start. *C. J. Gray*

PERFECT LOVE   4 b.f. Pursuit of Love 124 – Free Spirit (IRE) (Caerleon (USA)   **59**
132) [2004 84: 6.9f 7g 7f 7m 5m Sep 29] fairly useful at 3 yrs: modest form at best in
2004 (hung badly right third start): should stay 1m: acts on polytrack: tried blinkered.
E. J. Alston

PERFECTPERFORMANCE (USA)   2 ch.c. (Feb 24) Rahy (USA) 115 – Balis-   **112**
troika (USA) (Nijinsky (CAN) 138) [2004 7g* 7m² 8g* 8f* 7s Oct 16] $1,100,000Y:
strong, good-bodied colt: type to carry condition: has fluent, quick action: closely related
to a winner in USA by Mt Livermore and half-brother to several winners, notably 4-y-o
Russian Rhythm: dam unraced half-sister to Cheveley Park winners Park Appeal and
Desirable, and to Irish Oaks winner Alydaress, an excellent family: smart performer: won
maiden at Salisbury in June, listed event there in August and Hackney Empire Royal
Lodge Stakes at Ascot (edgy/sweating, beat Scandinavia by 1½ lengths, leading over 1f
out) in September: soon off bridle when behind in Dewhurst Stakes at Newmarket: should
stay at least 1¼m: acts on firm going: blanketed for stall entry: tends to edge right. *Saeed
bin Suroor*

PERFECT PORTRAIT   4 ch.g. Selkirk (USA) 129 – Flawless Image (USA) 109 (The   **77**
Minstrel (CAN) 135) [2004 84p: 7d³ 7s 7g 7f⁴ Jun 1] compact gelding: fair performer,
lightly raced: should stay 1m: has been visored: sold 10,500 gns in July. *D. R. Loder*

PERFECT PUNCH   5 b.g. Reprimand 122 – Aliuska (IRE) 70 (Fijar Tango (FR) 127)   **74**
[2004 73, a77: 10d² 10m 11.8g 11.5g 14.1g² 13.9g Oct 9] fair handicapper: stays 1¾m: **a?**
acts on polytrack, unraced on extremes of going on turf: sold 24,000 gns, joined K. Reveley. *C. F. Wall*

PERFECT SETTING   4 b.g. Polish Precedent (USA) 131 – Diamond Park (IRE) 91   **63 ?**
(Alzao (USA) 117) [2004 74d: 5.1g⁶ 5m 5.1g Jul 11] useful-looking gelding: lightly-
raced maiden: only modest nowadays: raced only at 5f: acts on good to firm ground:
looked none too keen in blinkers final start in 2003. *P. J. Makin*

Godolphin's "Perfectperformance"

PERFECT SOLUTION (IRE) 2 ch.f. (Feb 12) Entrepreneur 123 – Pearl Barley **61**
(IRE) 79 (Polish Precedent (USA) 131) [2004 6m p6g Oct 25] €32,000F, €30,000Y,
25,000 2-y-o: sturdy filly: first foal: dam, Irish 6.5f winner, half-sister to 4-y-o Nayyir
and 5-y-o Highest: better effort when eighth in minor event at Lingfield final start: should
stay 1m. *J. A. R. Toller*

PERFECT STORM 5 b.g. Vettori (IRE) 119 – Gorgeous Dancer (IRE) (Nordico **100**
(USA)) [2004 101: 12g 12g 12g⁵ 12.1d⁴ 11.6m 12d 10v 8d Oct 30] lengthy gelding: useful performer: ran creditably in 2004 only when fourth to Collier Hill in listed handicap at
Hamilton in May: stays 1½m: acts on firm and soft going: blinkered (well beaten) once:
gelded, joined M. Pipe. *M. Blanshard*

PERFECT STORY (IRE) 2 b.f. (Apr 9) Desert Story (IRE) 115 – Shore Lark (USA) **66 p**
(Storm Bird (CAN) 134) [2004 p7m⁴ Dec 22] 25,000Y: fourth foal: half-sister to 5-y-o
Lake Verdi and a winner in Greece by Sri Pekan: dam unraced half-sister to smart sprinter
Tipsy Creek: 33/1, encouraging fourth to Glinting Desert in maiden at Lingfield, waited
with and keeping on but not knocked about: should improve. *J. A. R. Toller*

PERFECT TONE (USA) 2 ch.f. (Mar 26) Silver Hawk (USA) 123 – Copper Cachet **73 p**
(USA) (Sheikh Albadou 128) [2004 7.9g⁵ Oct 9] $150,000F, 170,000Y: smallish, lengthy
filly: third foal: half-sister to winner in USA by Wild Rush: dam unraced half-sister to
very smart 1¼m to 1¾m performer Red Bishop (by Silver Hawk): 25/1 and green, fifth to
Daring Ransom in maiden at York: should do better. *M. A. Magnusson*

PERFIDIOUS (USA) 6 b.g. Lear Fan (USA) 130 – Perfolia (USA) 104 (Nodouble **79**
(USA)) [2004 81: p10g³ p12g² p12g⁵ p10g³ 10.1g Jul 15] sturdy gelding: fair performer:
best at 9f to 1½m: acts on all-weather and firm going: often leads, and tends to race
moodily when unable to do so. *J. R. Boyle*

PERFORMING ART 2 b.c. (Mar 21) Sadler's Wells (USA) 132 – Charming Life **– p**
(NZ) (Sir Tristram 115) [2004 8m Sep 8] 50,000Y: big, strong, rangy colt: has plenty of
scope: brother to very smart 1¼m/1½m winner Wellbeing and half-brother to several
winners, including very smart 1¼m/1½m winner Kingfisher Mill (by Riverman): dam,
Australian 7f winner, sister to Zabeel and half-sister to Baryshnikov, both Australian
Group 1 winners: 12/1 and burly, well held in maiden at Doncaster, very green before and
during race: type to do better. *P. W. Chapple-Hyam*

PERIANTH (IRE) 2 ch.c. (Mar 21) Bluebird (USA) 125 – Meandering Rose (USA) **60**
(Irish River (FR) 131) [2004 5s⁴ 5m 6m p7d 5.7g³ 6m 6g f6g⁴ p6g Dec 13] lengthy colt: **a53**
modest maiden: effective at 5f/6f: acts on fibresand, best turf effort on good going:
blinkered last 2 starts. *B. J. Meehan*

PERIDA (IRE) 4 b.f. Perugino (USA) 84 – Razida (IRE) 106 (Last Tycoon 131) [2004 **45**
59: 12d⁵ 12f 17.2g 11.5m p8m f11g Dec 11] third foal: sister to a winner in Switzerland:
dam Irish 2-y-o 7f winner who stayed 1m: poor maiden: left C. Swan in Ireland after
reappearance and B. Powell after fourth start: stays 1½m: acts on firm and good to soft
ground: tried visored. *D. Carroll*

PERLE D'OR (IRE) 3 b.f. Entrepreneur 123 – Rose Society (Caerleon (USA) 132) **88**
[2004 72: 7m* 8f* 8g* 8m⁵ Sep 4] leggy, quite attractive filly: fairly useful performer:
won maiden at Redcar in May and handicaps at Yarmouth in June and Doncaster in July:
below form final outing: stays 1m: raced only on good ground or firmer. *W. J. Haggas*

PERRYWINKLE 2 b.f. (Mar 14) Perryston View 114 – Crab 'n Lobster (IRE) 40 **–**
(Waajib 121) [2004 6d Aug 4] tall, lengthy filly: second reported foal: dam maiden who
probably stayed 2m: tailed off in maiden at Newcastle. *James Moffatt*

PERRYWINKLE BOY 3 b.g. Piccolo 121 – Flower Arrangement (Lomond (USA) **–**
128) [2004 8g⁴ᵈ 8d 7v 10s 7.2s Oct 30] lengthy gelding: well held in maidens/claimer:
tongue tied last 2 starts. *M. D. Hammond*

PERSARIO 5 b.m. Bishop of Cashel 122 – Barford Lady 93 (Stanford 121§) [2004 **96**
91p: 6g* 6g May 1] lengthy mare: useful handicapper: won at Kempton in April readily
by ½ length from Zilch: unsuited by run of race at Newmarket subsequent outing: probably better at 6f than 7f: acted on good to firm and good to soft going: sometimes slowly
away: usually waited with: stud. *J. R. Fanshawe*

PERSEPHONE HEIGHTS 4 br.f. Golden Heights 82 – Jalland (Jalmood (USA) **–**
126) [2004 76?, a51: p10m Nov 22] fair handicapper at best: off 12 months, tailed off
only outing in 2004. *M. Madgwick*

PERSIAN CARPET 2 b.f. (Feb 9) Desert Style (IRE) 121 – Kuwah (IRE) 77 (Be My **61**
Guest (USA) 126) [2004 7g 7.1m⁴ 6g² 6g² 6m⁶ 6.5g 6d Oct 14] 3,000Y: workmanlike

filly: sixth foal: half-sister to 3 winners, including 5-y-o Sunnyside Royale: dam, Irish 1½m winner, closely related to smart 1¼m/1½m winner Suhaad: modest maiden: below form last 3 starts: effective at 6f/7f: acts on good to firm going: usually races prominently. *I. A. Wood*

PERSIAN DAGGER (IRE)   3 b.g. Daylami (IRE) 138 – Persian Fantasy 94 (Persian   **68** Bold 123) [2004 –: 10d 10s 10s⁶ 11.9f⁵ 15m³ Jul 2] smallish gelding: fair maiden: gelded after final start: stays 15f: acts on soft and good to firm ground. *J. L. Dunlop*

PERSIAN GENIE (IRE)   3 br.f. Grand Lodge (USA) 125 – Persia (IRE) (Persian   **61** Bold 123) [2004 –: 10d 10g 10g 10f 12s 12s² 12g⁶ Oct 4] leggy filly: modest maiden: stays 1½m: acts on soft going. *G. B. Balding*

PERSIAN KHANOOM (IRE)   2 b.f. (Mar 4) Royal Applause 124 – Kshessinskaya   **59** 99 (Hadeer 118) [2004 p8g⁶ p7.1g⁶ Nov 13] 10,000F, 15,000Y: fifth living foal: half-sister to French/Italian winner up to 1½m Noble Doble (by Shareef Dancer): dam 11.5f winner: modest form in maidens at Lingfield and Wolverhampton, not knocked about. *J. A. Osborne*

PERSIAN KING (IRE)   7 ch.g. Persian Bold 123 – Queen's Share (Main Reef 126)   **67** [2004 85?: 11.6d 12s 12g 14g 13.3g⁶ 12g³ 11.5m⁴ Aug 6] sturdy gelding: just fair in 2004: stays 14m: acts on good to firm and good to soft ground: tried tongue tied (has reportedly had a wind operation): fair hurdler/chaser. *J. A. B. Old*

PERSIAN LIGHTNING (IRE)   5 b.g. Sri Pekan (USA) 117 – Persian Fantasy 94   **114** (Persian Bold 123) [2004 109: 10g⁴ 12g⁴ 10.1m* 10m⁴ 12m⁶ Jul 30] strong, angular gelding: usually impresses in appearance: smart performer: best effort when winning valuable handicap at Epsom in June by head from Desert Quest: best around 1¼m: raced mainly on good ground or firmer: has been early to post/raced too freely: effective ridden prominently or held up. *J. L. Dunlop*

PERSIAN MAJESTY (IRE)   4 b.c. Grand Lodge (USA) 125 – Spa (Sadler's Wells   **119** (USA) 132) [2004 114p: 10d⁶ 12g³ 12f³ 12m⁵ 12m⁴ 12m Sep 26] strong, attractive colt: smart performer: won listed event at Royal Ascot only 3-y-o outing, hanging markedly right: operated on for hairline fracture of knee after: good efforts in 2004 when 3¼ lengths third to Papineau in minor event at Goodwood and 6½ lengths third to Doyen in Hardwicke Stakes at Royal Ascot: just respectable fifth to Bandari in Princess of Wales's Stakes at Newmarket, then below form in listed race at Goodwood and Cumberland Lodge Stakes at Ascot (blinkered): stays 1½m: acts on firm ground, probably on good to soft: usually comes from behind. *P. W. Harris*

PERSIAN PUNCH (IRE)   11 ch.g. Persian Heights 129 – Rum Cay (USA) 75   **–** (Our Native (USA)) [2004 120: 16.2s Apr 28]

Desert Deer (fractured fetlock), Highest (ruptured ligament) and Mister Monet (broken near-hind) all suffered fatal injuries in high profile races on the Flat in Britain in 2004, while the Two Thousand Guineas runner-up Snow Ridge was put down in September after developing severe laminitis. Their deaths made a significant impression at the time, and readers will no doubt recall others that were personally poignant for them. Undoubtedly, though, the saddest loss for the sport as a whole was that of the redoubtable front-running veteran Persian Punch, who collapsed and died in the Sagaro Stakes at Ascot in April on his reappearance. Persian Punch never won at Ascot, though he was successful in the Sagaro Stakes in 1998 when it was run at Newmarket. He ran in the Gold Cup seven times and was twice runner-up (to Royal Rebel after a rousing set-to in 2001 and to Mr Dinos in 2003). The latest season would have been Persian Punch's ninth on the track in a career which saw him win twenty of his sixty-three starts and build up a marvellous record in staying races, his victories including three each in the Henry II Stakes at Sandown and the Jockey Club Cup at Newmarket, and two each in the Goodwood Cup and the Lonsdale Stakes at York. He also won the Doncaster Cup and the Prix Kergorlay at Deauville in accumulating a record-equalling thirteen European pattern races, in the process beating Teleprompter's long-standing record for the most prize money earned on the Flat by a British-trained gelding. Persian Punch's last victory came on Champions' Day at Newmarket in 2003, in the Jockey Club Cup, in which he took his total earnings past the £1m mark. The race was renamed the Persian Punch Jockey Club Cup in the latest season and was won by Millenary, whom Persian Punch had beaten in typical style twelve months earlier, rallying splendidly to get back up on the line. The five previous essays in *Racehorses* on renowned battler Persian Punch contain numerous heart-stirring examples of his snatching victory from the jaws of defeat. Racing is unlikely to forget him in a hurry. His trainer, incidentally, paid 22,000 guineas at the Tattersalls October Yearling Sales for a half-brother to Persian Punch by Mozart, now named Classic Punch. The dam Rum Cay had her eighth winner when French-trained two-year-old Grand Bahama (by Singspiel) won over nine furlongs at Longchamp in October. *D. R. C. Elsworth*

PERSIAN ROCK (IRE) 2 b.g. (Mar 15) Namid 128 – Cairo Lady (IRE) (Persian **86** Bold 123) [2004 5g² 6f* 6.1d* 6m 7m Sep 26] £10,000F, 37,000Y: rather leggy, quite good-topped gelding: fourth foal: dam ran twice in Ireland: fairly useful performer: won maiden at Windsor in July and nursery at Chepstow (made most) in August: creditable efforts after: stays 7f: acts on firm and good to soft ground: sold 42,000 gns, then gelded. *J. A. Osborne*

PERSONIFY 2 ch.c. (Feb 10) Zafonic (USA) 130 – Dignify (IRE) 105 (Rainbow **81** Quest (USA) 134) [2004 6m* 7.6g⁴ 6d Oct 15] rather leggy colt: first foal: dam, French 2-y-o 7f/1m (Prix d'Aumale) winner who stayed 11f, out of Prix de Diane runner-up Her Ladyship, herself half-sister to Prix de la Salamandre winner Lord of Men: won maiden at Yarmouth in June: seemed to run creditably when last in minor event at Chester next time: visored/tongue tied, well below form final start: bred to stay 1m. *Saeed bin Suroor*

PERTEMPS BIANCA 4 b.f. Dancing Spree (USA) – Bay Bianca (IRE) (Law Society **–** (USA) 130) [2004 47?: p8g⁶ f12g f7g Feb 19] leggy filly: fair winner at 2 yrs: no longer of any account. *A. D. Smith*

PERTEMPS MAGUS 4 b.f. Silver Wizard (USA) 117 – Brilliant Future 58 (Welsh **72** Saint 126) [2004 71d: 7m³ 7s* 7.2s⁶ 7d³ 7.2d⁶ p7g⁶ p7g⁴ 6g² p6g* Dec 27] sparely-made filly: fair handicapper: won at Catterick in August and Wolverhampton (amateurs) in December: stays 7f: acts on polytrack, soft and good to firm going: visored/in cheek-pieces last 5 starts: has pulled hard/carried head high. *R. A. Fahey*

PERTEMPS RED 3 ch.c. Dancing Spree (USA) – Lady Lullaby (IRE) (Ballad Rock **–** 122) [2004 –: p12g 7.1d Apr 12] tailed off in seller and maidens. *A. D. Smith*

PERTEMPS SIA 4 b.c. Distinctly North (USA) 115 – Shamrock Dancer (IRE) 36 **43** (Dance of Life (USA)) [2004 40: 17.2f 17.2g⁵ 14.1g³ Jul 24] leggy, sparely-made colt: poor maiden: stayed 17f: best efforts on good going: tried tongue tied: often slowly away: wayward: dead. *A. D. Smith*

PERTEMPS WIZARD 4 br.g. Silver Wizard (USA) 117 – Peristyle 59 (Tolomeo **–** 127) [2004 –: f8g Feb 19] lengthy gelding: lightly-raced maiden, no form since 2 yrs. *A. D. Smith*

PERTINO 8 b.g. Terimon 124 – Persian Fountain (IRE) 67 (Persian Heights 129) **–** [2004 11.8m May 31] workmanlike gelding: fair hurdler/chaser: lightly raced and little form on Flat in cheekpieces. *J. M. Jefferson*

PERUVIA (IRE) 4 b.f. Perugino (USA) 84 – Dane's Lane (IRE) (Danehill (USA) **58** 126) [2004 86: 10s f11d⁵ 9.2d a8g* a13g⁹ Nov 7] strong, workmanlike filly: just modest form in 2004: sold from R. Beckett 2,500 gns after third start: won minor events at Gran Canaria in October/November: stays 13f: acts on good to firm and good to soft going, and on sand: visored/tongue tied last 2 starts in Britain. *D. Ramirez, Spain*

PERUVIAN BREEZE (IRE) 3 b.g. Foxhound (USA) 103 – Quietly Impressive **63** (IRE) 66 (Taufan (USA) 119) [2004 62: 9g⁵ 11.1g⁶ p12g⁵ 11.9f f12g 11.6f² Jul 19] tall, good-topped gelding: modest performer: won seller at Lingfield in May: left N. Littmo-den after fifth start: stays easy 1½m: acts on polytrack and firm going. *J. Gallagher*

PERUVIAN CHIEF (IRE) 7 b.g. Foxhound (USA) 103 – John's Ballad (IRE) **100** (Ballad Rock 122) [2004 107, a113: a6f a5f⁶ 6.5m a6f p5g 5.2g² 5g 5g 5m 6m 5g 5.6m 6m³ 6g Sep 25] good-topped gelding: useful handicapper: best efforts in 2004 when placed at Newbury (short-head second to Bishops Court) and Goodwood (1¾ lengths third to Texas Gold): effective at 5f to sharp 7.6f: acts on all-weather, firm and good to soft going: tried blinkered, usually visored: unseated rider leaving stall tenth outing, awkward exiting next time: sometimes wanders: comes from off pace: sold 27,000 gns. *N. P. Littmoden*

PERUVIAN PRINCESS 5 gr.m. Missed Flight 123 – Misty View 73 (Absalom 128) **–** [2004 p8.6g Nov 13] second foal: dam 7f (at 2 yrs) and 1¼m winner: tailed off in bumpers, and in maiden at Wolverhampton. *C. N. Kellett*

PERUVIAN PRINCE (USA)   2 b.c. (Apr 22) Silver Hawk (USA) 123 – Inca Dove   **86 p**
(USA) (Mr Prospector (USA)) [2004 7m² Sep 4] $45,000Y: strong, well-made colt: third
foal: brother to a winner in Japan and half-brother to fairly useful French winner around
1¼m Goleador (by Arch): dam lightly-raced sister to US Grade 3 8.5f winner Namaqualand: 12/1, 3½ lengths second to Storm Silk in minor event at Kempton, not unduly
knocked about: will stay at least 1m: sure to improve. *J. A. R. Toller*

PERUVIAN STYLE (IRE)   3 b.g. Desert Style (IRE) 121 – Lady's Vision (IRE) 93   **77**
(Vision (USA)) [2004 77: p5g* p5g* 6d 6g⁵ 6g 5d 5.1m⁶ 6f⁵ 6f² 5m 7g* 6g p7g⁴ p6g⁴ p6g   **a85**
p6g² Dec 30] strong gelding: fairly useful handicapper on all-weather, fair on turf: won at
Lingfield in March (twice) and at Epsom in September: effective at 5f to 7f: acts on poly-
track and firm going, below form both starts on ground softer than good: tried blinkered.
N. P. Littmoden

PESQUERA   2 b.f. (Apr 12) Green Desert (USA) 127 – Rose Des Andes (IRE) (Royal   **71**
Academy (USA) 130) [2004 6g 6d³ Oct 4] 60,000Y: lengthy filly: second foal: dam,
French 1m winner, out of sister to Prix Vermeille winner Indian Rose: much better effort
in maidens when third to Hanseatic League at Windsor (mulish stall, no extra late on):
should stay at least 7f. *J. Noseda*

PETANA   4 br.f. Petong 126 – Duxyana (IRE) (Cyrano de Bergerac 120) [2004 49§:   **54 §**
6g⁵ 5m 5g⁴ 5d 5f* p5g 5m 5m f5g Dec 21] compact filly: modest handicapper: won at
Musselburgh in June: stays 6f: acts on firm and good to soft ground: usually blinkered/in
cheekpieces: unreliable. *R. P. Elliott*

PETARDIAS MAGIC (IRE)   3 ch.c. Petardia 113 – Alexander Confranc (IRE) 73   **92**
(Magical Wonder (USA) 125) [2004 83: p8g⁴ 6d* 6d³ 6d 6s² 6g⁴ 6d 5s p7g f8g Dec 28]
strong, compact colt: fairly useful performer: won handicap at Kempton in April: left
E. O'Neill, below form last 4 starts: best form at 6f: acts on polytrack, soft and good to
firm ground: free-going sort. *C. A. Dwyer*

PETER PAUL RUBENS (USA)   3 ch.c. Belong To Me (USA) – Skybox (USA)   **113**
(Spend A Buck (USA)) [2004 8v 7s⁴ 7m* 7m⁵ 7.1m* 7m* 7.6g* 7m² Sep 9] $65,000Y:
big, strong colt: seventh foal: half-brother to several winners in USA: dam sprint winner
at 2 yrs in USA: smart performer: won maiden at Ascot in May, handicaps at Sandown
and Goodwood (by 1½ lengths from Compton's Eleven) in July and minor event at
Chester (beat Jedburgh a length) in August: good neck second to Mac Love in listed race
at Epsom final outing: free-going sort, and should prove as effective at 6f as 7.6f: acts on
good to firm ground: races up with pace and with plenty of enthusiasm. *P. F. I. Cole*

PETER ROUGHLEY (IRE)   2 b.g. (Jan 16) Indian Lodge (IRE) 127 – Dahabiah 57   **62**
(Soviet Star (USA) 128) [2004 8.3d 7s⁴ 7s² p6g⁶ p7.1g Dec 1] €6,000F, €8,500Y, €5,200
2-y-o: first foal: dam, ran 3 times (best effort at 7.5f), out of Ribblesdale winner Queen
Midas: best effort in maidens when second at Catterick: not sure to stay 1m. *A. Berry*

PETERS CHOICE   3 ch.g. Wolfhound 126 – Dance of The Swans (IRE) 69   **69**
(Try My Best (USA) 130) [2004 86p: 5g 5s 5g⁵ 5f 5d 5f² 5f Jul 29] sturdy gelding: fairly
useful on all-weather at 2 yrs, only fair on turf in 2004: will prove best at 5f: acts on fibresand and firm ground: wore cheekpieces third start, blinkered last 2 outings: sometimes
looks difficult ride. *I. Semple*

PETERS DELITE   2 b.c. (Mar 10) Makbul 104 – Steadfast Elite (IRE) 58 (Glenstal   **65**
(USA) 118) [2004 6g 5m³ 5v³ 6.1m Sep 6] 31,000Y: quite good-topped colt: brother to
2000 2-y-o 6f winner Ebullience and 5f (at 2 yrs) and 7f winner Dudleys Delight: dam 5f
(at 2 yrs) to 11f winner, also won over hurdles: fair maiden: best efforts when third:
should stay 6f. *R. A. Fahey*

*Albert Stakes (Handicap), Goodwood—one of four wins during the year for Peter Paul Rubens
as he and Compton's Eleven are first and second virtually throughout; Peeress is closing in third*

PETER'S IMP (IRE) 9 b.g. Imp Society (USA) – Catherine Clare 58 (Sallust 134) **53**
[2004 –: 12m* 16f⁵ 12m³ 16m⁴ 15.8m 12v³ Oct 16] good-bodied gelding: modest performer: won claimer at Catterick in July: stays 2m: acts on any going: tried blinkered/
visored earlier in career: usually held up. *A. Berry*

PETERS PLOY 4 ch.g. Deploy 131 – Alpi Dora (Valiyar 129) [2004 f6g 10m p12g **–**
p12g Sep 1] well held in maidens. *T. Keddy*

PETITE COLLEEN (IRE) 3 b.f. Desert Sun 120 – Nishiki (USA) (Brogan (USA) **65**
110) [2004 69: 10.9d 10m⁴ 10g 11.6g⁶ 11.6f 8.1d⁵ 10.2g p8.6d⁴ f12g² p12.2g⁴ f12g Dec
28] leggy filly: fair maiden: stays easy 1½m: acts on all-weather and good to firm ground:
tried in cheekpieces/visor. *D. Haydn Jones*

PETITE ELLE 2 b.f. (Mar 11) Wolfhound (USA) 126 – Start Again (IRE) (Cyrano de **?**
Bergerac 120) [2004 f5g³ 6f⁴ f7g⁴ 6m³ a6g* a8g³ a8g³ a6.8d* a6g* Dec 14] 1,200Y:
fourth living foal: half-sister to a winner in Denmark by Perugino: dam unraced: modest
performer: trained first 4 starts by P. McBride: won at Taby in maiden in August and
minor events in November/December: seems best around 6f: acts on sand: visored second
start. *M. Kahn, Sweden*

PETITE GIRL 2 gr.f. (Feb 15) Daylami (IRE) 138 – Pagoda (FR) (Sadler's Wells **–**
(USA) 132) [2004 6.1m Sep 28] small filly: first foal: dam, fairly useful French maiden
who stayed 1½m, sister to Dewhurst dead-heater Scenic out of half-sister to outstanding
broodmare Slightly Dangerous and the dam of Rainbow Quest: 50/1, well held in maiden
at Nottingham. *J. L. Spearing*

PETITE MAC 4 b.f. Timeless Times (USA) 99 – Petite Elite 47 (Anfield 117) [2004 **–**
59: 5d 5d Aug 27] small filly: modest performer at 3 yrs: well held both starts in 2004:
below form only run in cheekpieces. *N. Bycroft*

PETITE NOIRE 2 b.f. (Jan 27) Lujain (USA) 119 – Coffee Cream 87 (Common **32**
Grounds 118) [2004 5.1g f7g⁶ p6g⁵ Aug 6] 6,800Y: second foal: half-sister to 3-y-o Carte
Noire: dam 7f (at 2 yrs)/1m winner: poor form in claimer/sellers: tongue tied last 2 starts.
J. G. Portman

PETITE ROSE (IRE) 3 b.f. Turtle Island (IRE) 123 – Double Grange (IRE) (Double **88**
Schwartz 128) [2004 6d* 6g² 6.1d May 15] 35,000F, €75,000Y: leggy filly: sixth foal:
sister to 7-y-o Lincoln Dancer and 6f and 8.5f winner Velvet Island: dam of little account
in Ireland: fairly useful form: won maiden at Folkestone in April: ½-length second to
Bonne de Fleur at Ripon, easily better effort in listed events after: should prove best at 5f/
6f: sold 27,000 gns in October. *J. H. M. Gosden*

PETITE SPECTRE 2 ch.f. (Jan 24) Spectrum (IRE) 126 – Petite Epaulette 80 (Night **74**
Shift (USA)) [2004 6d p7g p6g* p8g Nov 30] half-sister to several winners, including
useful 2002 2-y-o 5f to 7f winner Rag Top (by Barathea) and 3-y-o Red Top: dam, 5f
winner, ran only at 2 yrs: fair performer: best effort when winning maiden at Wolverhampton in November: should stay 1m. *R. Hannon*

PETONGSKI 6 b.g. Petong 126 – Madam Petoski 61 (Petoski 135) [2004 58§: 5g 5v **– §**
6v May 10] good-bodied gelding: little form in 2004: tried in headgear: has reportedly
had breathing problem: sometimes hangs right/flashes tail. *B. Ellison*

PETRION 3 b.f. Petong 126 – Rion River (IRE) (Taufan (USA) 119) [2004 6m 7f f7d³ **41**
8f⁶ 7d Oct 16] 2,500 2-y-o: seventh foal: half-sister to 3 winners, including 6-y-o Monica
Geller: dam Irish 1¼m winner: poor maiden: should stay 1m. *R. Guest*

PETROLERO (ARG) 5 gr.g. Perfect Parade (USA) – Louise (ARG) (Farnesio **–**
(ARG)) [2004 54?: 10.5g Aug 5] tall gelding: maiden: well held only outing in 2004: has
been tongue tied. *James Moffatt*

PETROLINA (IRE) 3 b.f. Petardia 113 – Arbitration (IRE) (Bigstone (IRE) 126) **53**
[2004 6.1s p12d f8m⁴ f8m 7d Aug 27] 21,000Y: good-topped filly: first foal: dam unraced
half-sister to useful performer up to 1½m Kill The Crab: modest maiden: stays 1m: acts
on fibresand. *H. Morrison*

PETROSA (IRE) 4 ch.f. Grand Lodge (USA) 125 – Top Brex (FR) (Top Ville 129) **78**
[2004 71: 9g⁴ 9.9g⁵ 11g 8.3m³ 10d⁵ Oct 4] leggy, good-topped filly: fair maiden: stays
1¼m: acts on good to firm ground: has been edgy/walked to post: held up: not a straightforward ride: sold 6,500 gns. *D. R. C. Elsworth*

PETRULA 5 ch.g. Tagula (IRE) 116 – Bouffant (High Top 131) [2004 84: 10.3d² 10g⁶ **86**
12m 10d 10.4g Oct 8] good-bodied gelding: fairly useful handicapper: below form after
reappearance: best form around 1¼m: acts on firm and soft going: visored once in 2003,
usually blinkered in 2004: races up with pace: sometimes finishes weakly. *K. A. Ryan*

PETTICOAT HILL (UAE) 2 b.f. (Mar 2) Timber Country (USA) 124 – Crinolette   –
(IRE) (Sadler's Wells (USA) 132) [2004 p7g Oct 13] fourth foal: half-sister to useful
2003 2-y-o 6f winner Cedarberg (by Cape Cross): dam, ran once, half-sister to very smart
Irish 6f/7f performer Desert Style: 20/1 and green, well held in maiden at Lingfield.
J. H. M. Gosden

PEVENSEY (IRE) 2 b.g. (Mar 14) Danehill (USA) 126 – Champaka (IRE) (Caerleon   **91**
(USA) 132) [2004 6d⁶ 6g 8g* 10g³ Oct 11] €220,000Y: quite attractive gelding: second
foal: brother to useful French 7.5f (at 2 yrs) to 10.5f (Prix Cleopatre) winner Steel Princess: dam unraced half-sister to smart performer up to 1¼m Casey Tibbs: fairly useful
performer: much improved to win maiden at Newmarket in September: creditable
½-length third to Sunday Symphony in minor event at Leicester, leading briefly 1f out:
stays 1¼m: blinkered after second start: sold 42,000 gns. *J. H. M. Gosden*

PHANTOM FLAME (USA) 4 b.g. Mt Livermore (USA) – Phantom Creek 92 (Mr   **45**
Prospector (USA)) [2004 80d: f7g⁵ f9.4g² f7g f8g Feb 19] leggy, quite good-topped
gelding: poor maiden nowadays: likely to prove best up to 1m: acts on all-weather and
good to firm going: tried visored: usually races prominently. *M. Johnston*

PHANTOM SONG (IRE) 2 gr.c. (Mar 16) Shinko Forest (IRE) – Natural Pearl   –
(Petong 126) [2004 6g 5d Aug 15] well held in maidens at Haydock and Pontefract.
D. Carroll

PHANTOM STOCK 4 b.g. Alzao (USA) 117 – Strike Alight (USA) (Gulch (USA))   **70**
[2004 72p: f16g² f16.2g* p13g⁴ f16g² f16g* f16.2s 18g⁴ Mar 26] good-bodied gelding:
fair handicapper: won amateur event at Wolverhampton in January and apprentice event
at Lingfield in March: best around 2m: raced only on all-weather and good/good to firm
ground. *W. Jarvis*

PHANTOM WIND (USA) 3 b.f. Storm Cat (USA) – Ryafan (USA) 121 (Lear Fan   **111**
(USA) 130) [2004 96p: 7g⁶ 6m⁵ 7m* 8m³ 9g⁴ Oct 16] strong, close-coupled filly: had a
quick action: smart performer: sweating, won Oak Tree Stakes at Goodwood in July by ½
length from Nyramba: good efforts after, 5½ lengths third to Soviet Song in Matron
Stakes at Leopardstown then 2 lengths fourth behind Ticker Tape in Queen Elizabeth II
Challenge Cup at Keeneland: stayed 9f: raced only on good ground or firmer: tongue tied
(mulish) to post/almost refused to race) on debut at 2 yrs: had worn crossed noseband:
stud. *J. H. M. Gosden*

PHARAOH HATSHEPSUT (IRE) 6 b.m. Definite Article 121 – Maid of Mourne   –
(Fairy King (USA)) [2004 f7g 16g 9.2g 7v 9.1d 9m⁶ 7.2g 6.9f 6g⁶ 5s Aug 13] good-
topped mare: little form in 2004: tried blinkered/visored. *James Moffatt*

PHARLY REEF 12 b.g. Pharly (FR) 130 – Hay Reef 72 (Mill Reef (USA) 141) [2004   –
–: 10.2d⁴ Apr 23] lightly raced and little form on Flat since 1999: tried visored.
D. Burchell

PHAROAH'S GOLD (IRE) 6 b.g. Namaqualand (USA) – Queen Nefertiti (IRE)   **58**
61 (Fairy King (USA)) [2004 –, a72: f8g² f8.5g f7g⁵ 7d f8g³ f8.5g 9.2g* 8.1v 8.3d p10d   **a66**
9.1d⁴ 7m 7s 9.2d 8g 7.9g 7.1s p8.6g Oct 7] smallish, strong gelding: fair handicapper on
all-weather, modest on turf: won at Hamilton in April: stays 9f: acts on all-weather, soft
and good to firm going: usually wears visor/cheekpieces: none too consistent. *D. Shaw*

*Oak Tree Stakes, Goodwood—in the race's first running as a Group 3, two three-year-olds,
Phantom Wind and Nyramba (left), fight out the finish ahead of four-year-olds Chic (No.3),
Gonfilia (rail) and Golden Nun (blinkers)*

PHECKLESS 5 ch.g. Be My Guest (USA) 126 – Phlirty (Charly (FR) 130) [2004 65, **62** a78: f7g p7g³ p6g⁴ p5g p8g p6g 6s³ 6g 7g p7g p7.1g Nov 19] fair performer: left **a65** F. J. Houghton after second start: tends to race freely, and best at 6f/7f: acts on polytrack (well below form on fibresand), soft and good to firm going: sometimes slowly away. *J. M. Bradley*

PHILHARMONIC 3 b.g. Victory Note (USA) 120 – Lambast 70 (Relkino 131) [2004 **102** 99p: 5d⁴ 6m 6s 6d⁵ 6g Oct 9] strong, lengthy gelding: useful performer, lightly raced: good fourth to Caribbean Coral in Gosforth Park Cup (Handicap) at Newcastle on reappearance: below form after, including in Ayr Gold Cup: effective at 5f/6f: acts on firm and good to soft ground: waited with. *R. A. Fahey*

PHILLY DEE 3 b.f. Bishop of Cashel 122 – Marbella Beach (IRE) (Bigstone (IRE) – 126) [2004 48: p5g³ p6g p5g f6s p5g 5.1m f6g 6m Aug 16] smallish filly: poor mover: poor maiden: left J. Jay after reappearance: stays easy 6f: acts on fibresand, raced only on good/good to firm ground on turf: sometimes blinkered: sometimes slowly away. *N. E. Berry*

PHILOSOPHIC 10 b.g. Be My Chief (USA) 122 – Metaphysique (FR) (Law Society (USA) 130) [2004 p16g p13g p13g Feb 11] fair staying handicapper in 1999: lightly raced and well beaten since: tried in visor/cheekpieces. *Mrs L. C. Jewell*

PHI PHI (IRE) 2 b.f. (Feb 25) Fasliyev (USA) 120 – Council Rock 74 (General **58** Assembly (USA)) [2004 5m Jun 14] quite attractive filly: half-sister to several winners, including smart 2000 2-y-o 5f winner Superstar Leo (by College Chapel) and useful 6f to 8.5f winner (7f winner at 2 yrs) Royal Artist (by Royal Academy): dam, maiden best at 1¼m, out of Nassau Stakes winner Dancing Rocks: 4/1, seventh in maiden at Windsor, starting slowly. *W. J. Haggas*

PHI (USA) 2 b. or br.c. (Feb 17) Rahy (USA) 115 – Salchow (USA) (Nijinsky (CAN) **86** 138) [2004 7g 8.3m² 8g⁵ 10s* 10s⁵ Nov 27] big, rangy colt: has scope: half-brother to smart French 1998 2-y-o 6.5f and 1m (Grand Criterium) winner Way of Light (by Woodman, stayed 1½m) and French 1¼m winner Simadartha (by Gone West): dam unraced half-sister to Machiavellian and Exit To Nowhere: fairly useful performer: left Sir Michael Stoute before winning maiden at Durtal in November: stays 1¼m: acts on soft and good to firm ground. *D. Sepulchre, France*

PHLAUNT 2 b.f. (Apr 24) Faustus (USA) 118 – Phlirty (Charly (FR) 130) [2004 6g⁴ 5m **61** 6g³ 7s³ p7g Sep 18] £1,000Y: small filly: sixth foal: sister to 5f (at 2 yrs) to 1½m winner Pheisty and half-sister to 3 winners, including 3-y-o Phluke: dam tailed off both starts: modest maiden: well below form last 2 starts: should stay 7f. *R. F. Johnson Houghton*

PHLUKE 3 b.g. Most Welcome 131 – Phlirty (Charly (FR) 130) [2004 76: p7g⁵ f7s³ p7g **75** 6s⁵ 7.5d* 8d² 7.1s 9g⁴ 8m 8m⁶ 7m 8.2g Sep 29] good-bodied gelding: fair handicapper: won at Beverley in April: probably best at 7f/1m: acts on all-weather, good to firm and good to soft ground: races prominently. *R. F. Johnson Houghton*

PHOEBE WOODSTOCK (IRE) 2 ch.f. (Apr 22) Grand Lodge (USA) 125 – Why **76 p** So Silent (Mill Reef (USA) 141) [2004 7g³ Sep 20] leggy, quite good-topped filly: half-sister to several winners, notably 4-y-o Leporello and smart 7f (at 2 yrs) to 1½m winner Poppy Carew (by Danehill): dam unraced close relative to useful stayer Top Cees: 20/1, third to Fen Shui in maiden at Kempton, green but finishing well: should be suited by 1¼m/1½m: will improve. *P. W. Harris*

PHOENIX EYE 3 b.c. Tragic Role (USA) – Eye Sight 67 (Roscoe Blake 120) [2004 – –: 10.3d 10.5m 7.5d p7.1g Oct 25] close-coupled colt: well held in maidens/banded event. *M. Mullineaux*

PHOENIX NIGHTS (IRE) 4 b.g. General Monash (USA) 107 – Beauty Appeal – (USA) (Shadeed (USA) 135) [2004 54: f9.4g f9.4g⁵ f8.5g f12s 10.3g⁶ 12g⁴ 9g⁴ 8d⁶ 9g 8.3s⁶ Sep 19] smallish, workmanlike gelding: little form in 2004: tried blinkered. *A. Berry*

PHOENIX REACH (IRE) 4 b.c. Alhaarth (IRE) 126 – Carroll's Canyon (IRE) **120** (Hatim (USA) 121) [2004 122p: 10f⁶ 12d⁶ 12m 12f⁶ 12m* Dec 12]
Phoenix Reach rose phoenix-like from the ashes of a hitherto unproductive season to win the Cathay Pacific Hong Kong Vase at Sha Tin in December. Connections are now eyeing the Queen Elizabeth II Cup worth HK$14m on the same course in April, and for which Phoenix Reach would receive a further million-dollar bonus should he complete the double. No easy task, of course, especially as the trip is a mile and a quarter, over which Phoenix Reach has not won before.

Cathay Pacific Hong Kong Vase, Sha Tin—a valuable prize for Phoenix Reach who holds Sights On Gold, with Vallee Enchantee and Sweet Stream next

It says much for Phoenix Reach, and those involved with him at Park House, that he has overcome various setbacks to achieve as much as he has. His prospects of racing again looked no better than fifty-fifty when he split a pastern shortly after his only appearance as a two-year-old, an injury which required the insertion of three screws and a pin in his near-fore fetlock. Yet he returned in 2003 to win three races, including the Gordon Stakes at Goodwood and the Canadian International at Woodbine, as well as finishing third in the St Leger. A recurrence of that pastern injury meant Phoenix Reach required further surgery early in 2004, and his reappearance was delayed. Respectable efforts when sixth in the Prince of Wales's Stakes and the Grand Prix de Saint-Cloud suggested that Phoenix Reach would be spot-on for his first major target, the King George VI and Queen Elizabeth Stakes, only for him to run some way below form. Subsequently found to have suffered significant internal bleeding during the race, Phoenix Reach was back on the easy list and didn't return to action until four months later, in the Japan Cup at Tokyo. There he acquitted himself well enough, in finishing sixth behind Zenno Rob Roy, to make a trip to Hong Kong worthwhile, and he was one of nine European entries in the twelve-runner Vase, for which the previous year's winner Vallee Enchantee started favourite. Phoenix Reach was one of the outsiders, but he returned to his best to win by half a length from Sights On Gold, with Vallee Enchantee a length and a half further back in third. Held up in touch in a race run at a steady pace, Phoenix Reach improved to track the leaders towards the end of the back straight and ran on well after taking the lead over a furlong out to gain his second success at Group 1 level.

Phoenix Reach (IRE) (b.c. 2000)	Alhaarth (IRE) (b 1993)	Unfuwain (b 1985)	Northern Dancer / Height of Fashion
		Irish Valley (ch 1982)	Irish River / Green Valley
	Carroll's Canyon (IRE) (ch 1989)	Hatim (ch 1981)	Exclusive Native / Sunday Purchase
		Tuna (ch 1969)	Silver Shark / Vimelette

Phoenix Reach is the seventh foal of the unraced Carroll's Canyon and easily her best, though she has produced three other winners including the fairly useful but ungenuine Capriolo (by Priolo), successful at up to a mile and a half. Carroll's Canyon herself is a half-sister to the 1989 Arc winner Carroll House. Phoenix Reach, who acts on firm and good to soft ground, has done most of his racing over a mile and a half and showed in the St Leger that he is effective over as far as a mile and three quarters. He wore blinkers or a visor in the Canadian International, the King George, the Japan Cup and the Hong Kong Vase. *A. M. Balding*

PHONE TAPPING   3 b.g. Robellino (USA) 127 – Miss Party Line (USA) (Phone Trick (USA)) [2004 8m 8.5g[6] 8g[6] 10.5g 10s p12.2g[4] Nov 19] lengthy gelding: modest maiden: stays 1½m: acts on polytrack and soft going. *M. H. Tompkins*   **58**

PHOTOFIT   4 b.g. Polish Precedent (USA) 131 – Photogenic 93 (Midyan (USA) 124) [2004 76: 7d[6] 8s Apr 28] quite attractive gelding: fair maiden, lightly raced: stays 1m: acts on good to firm and good to soft going. *J. L. Dunlop*   **65**

PHRED   4 ch.g. Safawan 118 – Phlirty (Pharly (FR) 130) [2004 77: 8.3d[6] 8.1g[4] 7s[6] 8m[5] 7.1g[4] 8.3m[2] 8m 9g 9d[5] 8.1g 9m p8.6g p8.6g p8m Dec 8] leggy gelding: fair performer: left F. J. Houghton after twelfth start: well held last 5 outings, including in tongue tie: stays 1m: acts on heavy and good to firm going: tried blinkered: usually races prominently. *I. A. Wood*   **65 d**

PHRENOLOGIST   4 gr.g. Mind Games 121 – Leading Princess (IRE) 55 (Double Schwartz 128) [2004 74: p7g 7m p6g p6g p7.1g p7.1g p6g[2] p6g Dec 30] modest performer: left J. Fanshawe after reappearance: stays 6f: acts on polytrack, lightly raced on turf: wore blinkers/cheekpieces last 5 starts. *Andrew Reid*   **55**

PHYSICAL (IRE)   2 b.c. (Apr 2) Efisio 120 – St Clair (Distant Relative 128) [2004 6s 6d p6g* Nov 16] €26,000F, 60,000Y: good-bodied colt: second foal: dam unraced half-sister to useful sprinters Baize and Bayleaf (both by Efisio): easily best effort in maidens when winning at Lingfield by short head from Reaching Out: needs to settle to stay beyond 6f. *Mrs A. J. Perrett*   **71**

PIANOFORTE (USA)   2 b.g. (Feb 24) Grand Slam (USA) 120 – Far Too Loud (CAN) (No Louder (CAN)) [2004 6g[6] 7m[2] 8s[4] Aug 24] $190,000Y: strong, close-coupled gelding: fourth foal: dam Canadian 1m stakes winner: best effort in maidens when second at Leicester: odds on, finished tired when fourth at Yarmouth (then gelded): should stay 1m: acts on good to firm going. *D. R. Loder*   **84**

PIANO STAR   4 b.g. Darshaan 133 – De Stael (USA) 93 (Nijinsky (CAN) 138) [2004 105: 10g 10.3d May 6] tall, rather leggy gelding: fluent mover: useful performer at 3 yrs: below form in listed events at Kempton and Chester (visored, looked reluctant) in 2004: stays 1½m: acts on firm ground: needs treating with caution: sold 55,000 gns in July. *Sir Michael Stoute*   **93 §**

PICCLED   6 b.g. Piccolo 121 – Creme de Menthe (IRE) (Green Desert (USA) 127) [2004 91, a103: f6s 5g[3] 5g 5v 5.1g 5m* 5d 5m[5] 5m 5g 5f 5d[3] Sep 17] good-topped gelding: useful handicapper at best on all-weather, fairly useful on turf: won at York in June by 1¾ lengths from Obe One: best at 5f: acts on fibresand, firm and good to soft going: sometimes races prominently: reluctant to race ninth outing, refused to race next time. *E. J. Alston*   **92 § a?**

PICCLEYES   3 b.g. Piccolo 121 – Dark Eyed Lady (IRE) 82 (Exhibitioner 111) [2004 65: 7m 7m 6.1m 6g* 6f 7g 5g[3] 5m[6] 6m 6m[3] 6.1m[2] f5m f6g f6g Dec 7] fair performer on turf, modest on all weather: won maiden at Lingfield in June: left R. Hannon after eleventh start: best at 5f/6f: acts on fibresand, good to firm and good to soft going: usually blinkered. *M. J. Polglase*   **69 a56**

PICCOLOMINI   2 b.c. (Mar 23) Diktat 126 – La Dama Bonita (USA) 87 (El Gran Senor (USA) 136) [2004 7.1d[3] f8g[5] Nov 22] 18,000Y: closely related to smart 5f to 1m winner in UAE Conflict (by Warning), earlier successful up to 10.5f in Britain, and half-brother to winners abroad by Machiavellian and Lion Cavern: dam, 5f (at 2 yrs) and 7f winner, closely related to high-class French 6f to 1m performer Polar Falcon: better effort when third in maiden at Musselburgh: should stay 1m. *M. Johnston*   **70**

PICCOLO PRINCE   3 ch.g. Piccolo 121 – Aegean Flame 86 (Anshan 119) [2004 56: f6g f5g* f5g[2] f6g* f6s[2] 6d* 5d[2] 6.1d 6m[2] 6m 6g 5g[5] 6d 6s[5] Sep 19] strong, stocky gelding: fair performer: won handicaps in January/March and minor event in April, all at Southwell: effective at 5f/6f: acts on fibresand, good to firm and good to soft going. *E. J. Alston*   **70**

PICK A BERRY   3 b.f. Piccolo 121 – Bonne de Berry (Habitat 134) [2004 –: p7g 6v 6.1m[6] 7.6m 6g Aug 11] neat filly: modest maiden: raced very freely fourth start. *G. Wragg*   **50**

PICKAPEPPA   2 ch.f. (Jan 20) Piccolo 121 – Cajole (IRE) 72 (Barathea (IRE) 127)   **69**
[2004 6m 7g⁵ Sep 20] close-coupled filly: first foal: dam maiden who stayed 7f: much
better effort in maidens when fifth to Quickfire at Kempton, no extra late on: not sure to
stay beyond 7f: gave trouble/withdrawn intended debut. *R. F. Johnson Houghton*

PICKLE   3 b.f. Piccolo 121 – Crackle 85 (Anshan 119) [2004 p6g³ p6g p6v⁴ 7s* 6g 7g³   **84**
7m³ 8.3f⁶ 7g* 7f* 8m* 8.5f² 8.1g 8.5g⁴ Oct 2] workmanlike filly: first foal: dam, 5.7f
(at 2 yrs) to 1¼m winner, stayed 1½m: fairly useful handicapper: won at Folkestone in
May and Epsom, Leicester and Newmarket in July: stays 8.5f: acts on firm and soft going:
usually waited with: sold 34,000 gns, sent to USA. *S. C. Williams*

PICK OF THE CROP   3 ch.g. Fraam 114 – Fresh Fruit Daily 92 (Reprimand 122)   **74**
[2004 72: f6g* f7g² p7g 9g 7d 7g Oct 11] tall gelding: fair performer: won maiden at
Southwell in January: effective at 6f/7f: acts on fibresand, raced mainly on good/good to
firm ground on turf: sometimes slowly away. *J. R. Jenkins*

PICO ALTO   3 b.f. Lugana Beach 116 – Noble Canonire 58 (Gunner B 126) [2004   **–**
8.1m 7.1d p8m p8.6g Oct 25] second foal: dam 11f seller winner at 4 yrs: of little account.
B. Palling

PICOT DE SAY   2 b.g. (Mar 28) Largesse 112 – Facsimile 67 (Superlative 118) [2004   **63**
6m 6m 8g 8.3g³ 8s² 8d⁵ Nov 5] unfurnished gelding: second foal: dam maiden who stayed
1m: modest maiden: will stay at least 1¼m: acts on soft ground. *John Berry*

PIC UP STICKS   5 gr.g. Piccolo 121 – Between The Sticks 83 (Pharly (FR) 130)   **104**
[2004 108d: 6.5f³ 6.5m* 6.5m⁶ 5.2g³ 6f⁶ 5m 6m 5.6m 6g* 6g 5d 6s⁵ Oct 22] tall gelding:
useful handicapper: won at Nad Al Sheba in February and Ripon (beat Ellens Academy
by length) in September: mostly ran creditably when raced in 2004: effective at 5f to 6.5f:
acts on firm and good to soft ground: effective held up or ridden prominently: sold 42,000
gns. *M. R. Channon*

PIDDIES PRIDE (IRE)   2 b.f. (Apr 7) Indian Lodge (IRE) 127 – Fairybird (FR) 70   **73**
(Pampabird 124) [2004 5d⁵ 6m⁶ 6g⁶ 6g⁴ 6m* 5m* 6m³ 6f² 7f 6d⁴ 6.1m 6m⁵ p6g 6s 5.2s²   **a66**
5.1v p7.1g² p7g p6g² p7.1g p6g Dec 3] 4,000Y: smallish, lengthy filly: fifth foal: half-
sister to winners abroad by Persian Bold and Sri Pekan: dam, 5f winner, ran only at 2 yrs:
fair performer: won sellers at Brighton (for I. Wood) and Folkestone in July: creditable
efforts when in frame in nurseries after: effective at 5f to easy 7f: acts on polytrack, firm
and soft going: visored third/fourth starts: none too consistent. *P. S. McEntee*

PIE CORNER   2 ch.g. (Mar 18) Fumo di Londra (IRE) 108 – Ballystate 71 (Ballacashtal (CAN)) [2004 5.1s 5g 7f 5.7m Jul 22] no form in maidens: gelded after final start.
M. Madgwick

PIETER BRUEGHEL (USA)   5 b.g. Citidancer (USA) – Smart Tally (USA) (Smar-   **94**
ten (USA)) [2004 99: 7m 6m⁴ 6d 6m 6g* 6f³ 6g³ 6s² 6d 6g Sep 25] big, good-topped gelding: fairly useful handicapper: won at York in July by ½ length from Ellens Academy:
creditable efforts after when placed, including second to Smokin Beau in Great St Wilfrid
at Ripon: probably best around 6f: acts on firm and soft ground (well held on heavy): has
been tongue tied: races up with pace. *D. Nicholls*

PIKE BISHOP (IRE)   2 b.c. (Mar 23) Namid 128 – Pink Cashmere (IRE) (Polar   **103 p**
Falcon (USA) 126) [2004 5m* 5m* Jun 16] 62,000Y: fifth foal: half-brother to 3 winners,
including useful German 2001 2-y-o 6f winner Medina (by Pennekamp) and 3-y-o Motu:
dam unraced half-sister to very smart sprinter Owington: won minor events at Windsor in
May and Ripon (by 3 lengths from Beckermet) in June in good style: suffered respiratory
disease in second half of season: will prove best at 5f/6f: probably capable of making his
mark in stronger company. *R. Charlton*

PILCA (FR)   4 ch.g. Pistolet Bleu (IRE) 133 – Caricoe (Baillamont (USA) 124) [2004   **–**
10g Sep 29] well beaten in maiden at Argentan for T. Trapenard in France sole Flat outing
in 2003, and in similar event at Nottingham in 2004: fair hurdler. *I. W. McInnes*

PILGRIM PRINCESS (IRE)   6 b.m. Flying Spur (AUS) – Hasaid Lady (IRE) 69   **51**
(Shaadi (USA) 126) [2004 55: f6g³ f6g⁵ f7g⁴ f6g⁶ f7s f7g 6v f6g⁴ 5.9f⁵ Jul 29] rather
angular, good-quartered mare: modest performer: effective at 6f/easy 7f: acts on fibresand, firm and heavy going: tried blinkered/in cheekpieces: often races prominently:
sometimes finds little/drifts right: reportedly bled seventh 5-y-o start. *E. J. Alston*

PILGRIMS PROGRESS (IRE)   4 b.g. Entrepreneur 123 – Rose Bonbon (FR) (High   **79**
Top 131) [2004 87: 14g⁴ 13d 16g⁵ 15s 13.8s Nov 2] lengthy gelding: fairly useful
performer when trained by T. Stack in Ireland in 2003, winning handicap at Killarney:
just fair form at best in 2004: stays 1¾m: acts on heavy going. *D. W. Thompson*

PILLARS OF WISDOM   2 ch.c. (Apr 26) Desert Prince (IRE) 130 – Eurolink Mis- **76 p**
chief 84 (Be My Chief (USA) 122) [2004 7m 7m³ Sep 21] tall, good-topped colt: half-
brother to several winners, including 5-y-o Bonecrusher and 3-y-o Mango Mischief: dam
1½m winner: better effort in maidens when third to Grosvenor Square at Newmarket: will
stay at least 1m: refused to enter stall on intended debut: should progress. *J. L. Dunlop*

PINAFORE   2 ch.f. (Jan 11) Fleetwood (IRE) 107 – Shi Shi (Alnasr Alwasheek 117) **62**
[2004 6g³ p7g² 6d² p5.1d⁴ Oct 23] first foal: dam French 1½m winner: modest maiden:
stays 7f: acts on polytrack and good to soft going. *H. Morrison*

PINCHBECK   5 b.g. Petong 126 – Veuve Hoornaert (IRE) 88 (Standaan (FR) 118) **92**
[2004 82: 6d 6g⁴ 6g* 6m 6d* 6g⁴ 6g⁶ 6g Sep 1] strong, good sort: fairly useful handicapper: won at Yarmouth in May and Haydock (best effort, beat Golden Dixie 1¼
lengths) in July: best at 6f: acts on good to firm and good to soft ground: effective
blinkered or not, usually wears cheekpieces nowadays. *M. A. Jarvis*

PINCHING (IRE)   3 ch.f. Inchinor 119 – Input (Primo Dominie 121) [2004 7g⁴ 8.2s³ **77**
8.3g² 9d³ 8g 8g² p8.6g⁵ p9.5g⁵ Nov 20] 55,000Y: leggy filly: first foal: dam, ran once at 2
yrs, out of half-sister to 1m/9f performer Danceabout and French sprinter Pole Position,
both smart: fair maiden: stays 9f: acts on good to soft going, below form on polytrack:
visored last 6 outings: tended to wander first 2 starts, found little fifth one: sold 5,000 gns.
H. R. A. Cecil

PINE BAY   3 b.f. Sure Blade (USA) 130 – Opuntia (Rousillon (USA) 133) [2004 7m⁶ **68**
8g p10d 7d 6m* Sep 27] 14,500Y: seventh foal: sister to useful 6f winner (including
at 2 yrs) Boomerang Blade and half-sister to several winners, including 9-y-o Point of
Dispute: dam unraced: fair performer: trained by P. Mitchell on third start only: won
maiden at Windsor in September, best effort. *B. Gubby*

PINK BAY   2 b.f. (Apr 4) Forzando 122 – Singer On The Roof 62 (Chief Singer 131) **63**
[2004 6m⁴ p6g² Oct 2] 5,000Y: sixth foal: half-sister to German 9.5f and 12.5f winner
(ungenuine in Britain) Sole Singer (by Slip Anchor) and 6.5f winner abroad by Bluebird:
dam, 1m winner, half-sister to Prix Saint-Alary winner Air de Rien: modest form in maidens at Folkestone and Wolverhampton (second to Manic): will stay 7f. *W. S. Kittow*

PINK SAPPHIRE (IRE)   3 ch.f. Bluebird (USA) 125 – Highbrook (USA) 88 (Alpha- **77**
batim (USA) 126) [2004 63+: 6d 8m² 7.1f⁴ 10g⁶ 7g⁴ 6g Oct 11] good-bodied filly:
fair handicapper: probably best around 1m: acts on firm ground: blinkered final outing.
D. R. C. Elsworth

PINK SUPREME   3 ch.f. Night Shift (USA) – Bright Spells 93 (Salse (USA) 128) **51**
[2004 70: 7g 6m 6m 7m 6m 7.5g⁶ 6m 6g⁴ 6g 6m Sep 4] good-bodied filly: modest maid-
en: stays 6f: acts on soft and good to firm ground: tongue tied second to fifth starts.
I. A. Wood

PINS 'N NEEDLES (IRE)   3 gr.f. Mark of Esteem (IRE) 137 – Khalisiyn 96 (Shaka- **53**
pour 125) [2004 p7g p10g⁶ 10.2g p12.2d p9.5g p8m Dec 8] 10,000Y: closely related to
useful Irish performer up to 1½m Khalafiya and fairly useful Irish 1½m winner Khali-
khoum (both by Darshaan) and half-sister to 3 winners: dam 7f/1m winner: modest
maiden: stays 1¼m: acts on polytrack: raced very freely second start. *C. A. Cyzer*

PINTLE   4 b.f. Pivotal 124 – Boozy 111 (Absalom 128) [2004 69: 5.7f⁴ 7m* 7m* 8g⁶ **82**
7.1g⁴ 7m* Sep 29] smallish filly: fairly useful performer: won handicaps at Yarmouth and
Leicester in July and minor event at Newcastle in September: best at 6f/7f: raced only on
good ground or firmer: usually races prominently. *J. L. Spearing*

PIPER   4 ch.g. Atraf 116 – Lady-H (Never So Bold 135) [2004 –: 7d Aug 4] no form: **–**
tried in cheekpieces. *D. W. Barker*

PIPER GENERAL (IRE)   2 br.g. (Apr 27) General Monash (USA) 107 – Pipewell **–**
(IRE) 84 (Lake Coniston (IRE) 131) [2004 7.1d Oct 9] 40/1, well held in maiden at
Warwick, slowly away. *J. S. Moore*

PIPER LILY   2 b.f. (Feb 3) Piccolo 121 – Polly Golightly 84 (Weldnaas (USA) 112) **72 d**
[2004 5.1d⁵ 5d* 5f⁶ 5.1g 6g 5.2s p5.1g Nov 19] small filly: first foal: dam 5f winner,
including at 2 yrs: fair performer: won maiden at Haydock in June: below form in minor
event/nurseries after: likely to prove best at 5f/easy 6f: best effort on good to soft going:
blinkered final start. *M. Blanshard*

PIPER'S ASH (USA)   2 b.f. (Apr 13) Royal Academy (USA) 130 – Merida (Warning **84 p**
136) [2004 6f⁶ 5m* Aug 11] sixth foal: half-sister to useful 6f winner Como (by Cozzene): dam, 1m winner in France/USA, half-sister to smart performer up to 1m in Britain/
USA Tychonic: much better effort in maidens when winning 6-runner event at Sandown

by 7 lengths from Killington, quickening well: likely to prove best at 5f/6f: suffered respiratory disease in second half of season, but remains a useful prospect. *R. Charlton*

PIPS PEARL (IRE) 2 b.f. (Apr 9) Lil's Boy (USA) 109 – Penka (IRE) 85 (Don't **43**
Forget Me 127) [2004 6g 6f 6d 8.3m 6m⁵ 7d Oct 15] €9,000Y: lengthy filly: fifth foal: half-sister to 3 winners in Ireland by Desert Style, including useful 7f (at 2 yrs)/1m winner Galanta: dam Irish 2-y-o 6f winner: poor maiden: visored/tongue tied last 2 starts (only form on first occasion). *Mrs P. N. Dutfield*

PIPSSALIO (SPA) 7 b.g. Pips Pride 117 – Tesalia (SPA) (Finissimo (SPA)) [2004 45: **49**
f16g⁶ f12s² 14.1s⁶ 12v² f12d 16d Oct 10] workmanlike gelding: poor performer: seems to stay 2m: acts on fibresand, best on soft/heavy going on turf: sometimes blinkered, usually tongue tied nowadays. *Jamie Poulton*

PIPS SONG (IRE) 9 ch.g. Pips Pride 117 – Friendly Song 48 (Song 132) [2004 69d: **58 ?**
f6g f6g f6g* f6s f7g p6g³ p6g f6g⁵ f6g f6g⁶ Jun 4] lengthy gelding: poor mover: just modest nowadays: won seller at Wolverhampton in January: effective at stiff 5f to 7f: acts on all-weather, probably on good ground or softer: tried blinkered/visored. *P. W. Hiatt*

PIQUET 6 br.m. Mind Games 121 – Petonellajill 73 (Petong 126) [2004 46: p10g³ **41**
p8g* p7g⁶ p8g⁶ p10g p8g 10m 11.9f⁶ p10g³ 10f p10d* 10f p10d 9.7f 10m p10m **a60**
p8g⁴ p8m² p10m² p8g⁶ Dec 20] modest on all-weather, poor on turf: won banded race in February and handicap in December, both at Lingfield: effective at 7f to easy 1¼m: acts on polytrack and firm going. *J. J. Bridger*

PIRAN (IRE) 2 b.g. (Apr 13) Orpen (USA) 116 – Dancing At Lunasa (IRE) 70 (Danc- **66**
ing Dissident (USA) 119) [2004 7.1m 7g 8.3m⁵ 8s Oct 15] €15,000F, €17,000Y: lengthy gelding: sixth foal: half-brother to 6f (seller winner at 2 yrs)/7f winner Tough Nut (by Sri Pekan): dam Irish 5f winner: fair maiden: form only when fifth at Windsor: stays 1m: acts on good to firm going. *B. J. Meehan*

PIRI PIRI (IRE) 4 b. or br.f. Priolo (USA) 127 – Hot Curry (USA) (Sharpen Up 127) **75**
[2004 75: 10m⁶ 11.5f² 12.1m³ 10m 12m³ 10f² 10m 11.5g 10m p9.5g⁵ p9.5g* Dec 1] rather leggy, workmanlike filly: fair performer: won minor event at Wolverhampton in December: stays 1½m: acts on polytrack, firm and good to soft going: usually held up: has looked none too keen, but is consistent. *P. McBride*

PIRLIE HILL 4 b.f. Sea Raven (IRE) 75 – Panayr (Faraway Times (USA) 123) [2004 **60**
43: 6g³ 6g⁴ f6g 6f² 5f⁵ 6g 5g* 5m⁶ 5f 5g⁴ 5g⁴ 5f 5g⁶ 5f⁵ 6g 6d 5m Sep 11] good-bodied filly: modest handicapper: won at Hamilton in June: barely stays 6f: raced mainly on good ground or firmer on turf: sometimes slowly away: tends to hang right. *Miss L. A. Perratt*

PIROETTA 2 b.f. (Jan 29) Averti (IRE) 117 – Bint Albadou (IRE) 91 (Green Desert **–**
(USA) 127) [2004 7.1m Sep 6] 33,000Y: fifth foal: sister to 4-y-o Badou and half-sister to 3 winners, including 6-y-o Desert Arc: dam Irish 2-y-o 6f winner: 16/1 and backward, slowly away when always rear in maiden at Warwick. *J. A. Osborne*

PIROUETTES (IRE) 4 b.f. Royal Applause 124 – Dance Serenade (IRE) 54 (Marju **48**
(IRE) 127) [2004 61: p7g 8g 6m p10d p7g⁴ 8d f8g p10m² p10m⁵ Dec 15] big, lengthy filly: poor maiden: left Gay Kelleway after reappearance: stays easy 1¼m: acts on all-weather, good to firm ground and good to soft going: tried tongue tied/in headgear. *E. R. Oertel*

PISTE BLEU (FR) 4 b.f. Pistolet Bleu (IRE) 133 – Thamissia (FR) (Riverman (USA) **60**
131) [2004 65: f12s 12v 12m 12.3m* 11.8m⁶ 12.1g⁴ 11.7g 10m Sep 25] smallish, close-coupled filly: just modest handicapper in 2004: won selling event at Ripon in May: stays 1½m: acts on firm ground: tried tongue tied. *R. Ford*

PITCAIRN ISLAND 2 ch.f. (Apr 14) Indian Ridge 123 – Girl From Ipanema 106 **52**
(Salse (USA) 128) [2004 7s 6s p7.1g Nov 27] tall, leggy filly: has scope: fifth foal: half-sister to 3 winners, including useful 1m/1¼m winner Wondrous Joy (by Machia-vellian) and 3-y-o Mr Tambourine Man: dam 7f (at 2 yrs) and 1m winner: modest form in maidens last 2 starts: should stay 1m. *M. Johnston*

PITCH UP (IRE) 2 b.g. (Feb 9) Cape Cross (IRE) 129 – Uhud (IRE) (Mujtahid **86**
(USA) 118) [2004 5g 5m⁴ 6f* 5m* p5g* 5g⁵ 5f 6d 5s Oct 16] 40,000Y: strong, angular **a100**
gelding: third foal: half-brother to 11f winner in Italy by Distinctly North: dam unraced: useful on all-weather, fairly useful on turf: won maiden at Sandown in July and minor event at Lingfield (by 1½ lengths from Sundance) in August: stiffish tasks and mostly well held after: likely to prove best at 5f/easy 6f: acts on polytrack and firm going: blink-ered (seemed to run creditably) seventh appearance: usually races up with pace: gelded after final start. *T. G. Mills*

PITTON MILL   4 b.g. Millkom 124 – Sea Song (Prince Sabo 123) [2004 p12d 11.6f –
Jun 27] well beaten in maidens at Lingfield and Windsor. *W. G. M. Turner*

PITTSBURGH   2 ch.c. (Mar 17) Nashwan (USA) 135 – Oatey 68 (Master Willie 129) **87**
[2004 8g⁴ 8g Oct 10] 24,000Y: strong colt: second living foal: half-brother to 3-y-o
Jomus: dam, 5f winner, half-sister to 1½m to 2m performer Hateel and winner up to 11.5f
Munwar, both smart: clearly better effort when fourth of 5 to Merchant in minor event at
Newbury, getting hang of things late on: only seventh in maiden at Bath: likely to be
suited by 1¼m/1½m. *A. M. Balding*

PIVOTAL FLAME   2 b.c. (May 3) Pivotal 124 – Reddening 82 (Blushing Flame **102**
(USA) 109) [2004 6s* 7g⁵ 7.1d⁴ 7g* 6m⁶ 6s* Oct 22] 24,000F, 50,000Y: angular, good-
topped colt: has scope: first foal: dam 2m winner: useful performer: won maiden at York
in May, minor event at Leicester (hung left) in September and sales race at Doncaster
(nowhere near best when beating Hidden Jewel by head) in October: creditable 5¼
lengths fourth to Windsor Knot in Solario Stakes at Sandown: barely stays 7f: acts on soft
and good to firm ground. *B. A. McMahon*

PIVOTAL POINT   4 b.g. Pivotal 124 – True Precision 84 (Presidium 124) [2004 **121**
100: 6d 6m 5g* 5m² 6m* 5g* 5.2g⁵ 6f* 5m Dec 12]

    In the modern age, the traditional 'building-block' of form study, the
handicap, isn't quite so weighty as it used to be. From September 1st, the BHB
revised the structure of bread-and-butter handicaps, narrowing the maximum
weight range in most to 15 lb, 10 lb for the lowest grade of races. Under the new
structure, in which prize money for races is distributed in proportion to the class of
race, in theory rewarding handicappers working their way up the ladder more than
those snaking their way down, the main bone of contention became the number of
horses missing out on a run, either because they were rated too highly for one band
of race or being balloted out of oversubscribed events for which they were eligible.
As a result, the BHB took a step back and relaxed the parameters, allowing more
flexibility. All the same, the numbers of horses running from similar official marks
left many handicaps looking more like conditions races, with only a few pounds
separating runners.

    Some of the problems with oversubscription under the new system could
have been anticipated by looking at the example of the so-called heritage handicaps, the weight range in which was kept at 30 lb. In reality, the difference between
the imposts carried by those at the top and bottom of the weights for the most presti-

*Vodafone Stewards' Cup (Handicap), Goodwood—Pivotal Point lands a gamble;
Fantasy Believer (far side, star on cap) and High Reach (No. 17) are next to finish,
while Two Step Kid (No. 19) takes fourth, ahead of Simianna (cheekpieces) and Halmahera (No.6)*

*GNER Diadem Stakes, Ascot—Pivotal Point caps a fine season with an impressive display;
Airwave, The Tatling (centre) and Celtic Mill (cheekpieces) fight out the minor placings
in a race run on the round course due to track alterations*

gious or heritage handicaps has been shrinking. When King's Signet equalled a
weight-carrying record in victory under 9-10 in the Stewards' Cup at Goodwood in
1993, 30 lb separated him from the bottom weight. In the 2004 running, the range
between top and bottom was 18 lb. It is perhaps an illustration of the growth in the
horse population in general that to achieve the same weight range in the Stewards'
Cup in 2004 as in 1993, around fifty horses among those declared at the five-day
stage would have needed to take part.

The one-hundred-and-four five-day declarations for the Stewards' Cup—
Goodwood also stages a consolation event earlier in the week for those balloted
out—is also an indication of the popularity of the race. With two withdrawals on
the day, twenty-eight lined up in 2004, the bottom weight carrying 8-6. The draw
takes place two days in advance nowadays, connections choosing from available
stalls after picking lots. Since King's Signet famously made the most of a fresher
strip of ground towards the far rail, traditionally opened up halfway through the
Glorious Goodwood fixture, the majority of runners have tended to converge on
that part of the track and eight of the eleven winners since King's Signet have been
drawn sixteen or higher. With three of the first four home in the consolation
Stewards' Sprint Stakes, run twenty-four hours earlier, drawn in single figures, the
market in 2004 was less reflective than it has been of stalls positions. Co-favourites
at 7/1, Pivotal Point, Pic Up Sticks and High Reach, were drawn one, eleven and
twenty-eight respectively. Available at 14/1 in the morning, Pivotal Point was the
best-backed among them. Like other recent winners of the race, he was one of the
runners to have shown improved form since the publication of the weights in June.
Even with a 3-lb penalty for his win in a five-furlong handicap at Ascot, Pivotal
Point's Goodwood mark was still 5 lb lower than when he had finished a neck
second of twenty-four to Baltic King in the valuable Hong Kong Jockey Club
Sprint back at Ascot on his latest start. For once in the Stewards' Cup, the field split
into two equal groups. For most of the way, if anything, the far-side bunch looked
to hold a slight edge, but Pivotal Point, who recovered quickly from a slow start and
travelled strongly, responded well to pressure over a furlong out and stormed
through on the stand side to win by a length and a quarter. Fantasy Believer, drawn
twenty-four, finished strongly from well back to be first home of those on the far
side, a neck in front of High Reach with Two Step Kid fourth.

Pivotal Point wasted little time after Goodwood in making his mark in
pattern company. His next start came back at five furlongs in the Group 3 Prix du
Petit Couvert at Longchamp in September. In a field of nine, with Dettori replacing
Seb Sanders, he started second favourite and made the most of the 5 lb received
from market leader The Tatling, travelling strongly and leading over a furlong out,
driven out to beat the favourite by a length. Pivotal Point renewed rivalry with The
Tatling in the Group 2 Diadem Stakes at Ascot later in the month. Along with
French-trained Ratio, Pivotal Point was second favourite at 11/2 behind Airwave,
narrowly preferred to The Tatling on terms 1 lb worse than at Longchamp, despite
having been only fifth behind him in the Dubai International Airport World Trophy
at Newbury in the meantime. The Breeders' Cup Sprint is run round a bend, but it is
unusual to see sprinters taking a turn in European pattern races, something forced

793

on the Diadem by the start of Ascot's refurbishment. In a field restricted to twelve, the draw didn't prove crucial but, not surprisingly, a handy position into the short straight helped. Pivotal Point showed himself better than ever, soon travelling strongly in second as Celtic Mill made the running, then settling the issue in a matter of strides once leading over a furlong out, beating Airwave by three lengths with The Tatling third. A tilt at the Prix de l'Abbaye at Longchamp was considered after Ascot, but Pivotal Point was kept instead for the very valuable Hong Kong Sprint at Sha Tin in December, in which he never got into things, trailing home thirteenth of fourteen.

	Pivotal (ch 1993)	Polar Falcon (b or br 1987)	Nureyev Marie d'Argonne
		Fearless Revival (ch 1987)	Cozzene Stufida
Pivotal Point (b.g. 2000)			
	True Precision (b 1990)	Presidium (b 1982)	General Assembly Doubly Sure
		Madam Muffin (b 1983)	Sparkler Northern Lady

Despite the strides made, Pivotal Point was only the second best sprinter of the year, behind Somnus, of those sired by the highly successful Pivotal, though he was rated higher than his sire's other pattern winner at sprint distances in 2004, the filly Ringmoor Down. Pivotal Point's dam True Precision, fairly useful at up to seven furlongs, finished down the field behind King's Signet in the Stewards' Cup as a three-year-old after winning over five and six furlongs earlier in the year. True Precision bred three winners before Pivotal Point—five-furlong winners Uncle Exact (by Distant Relative) and Hot Pants (by Rudimentary), as well as the fairly useful six-furlong/seven-furlong winner Foreign Editor (by Magic Ring). Her latest

Mr R. A. Bernard's "Pivotal Point"

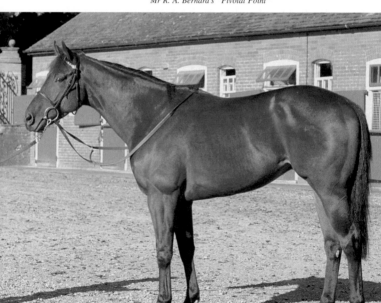

foal to race, Foreign Editor's sister True Magic, also showed fairly useful form in 2004, winning twice over five furlongs as a three-year-old.

Pivotal Point, who made only 9,000 guineas at Doncaster Sales as a yearling, was originally trained in Scotland by Linda Perratt but proved difficult at the stalls, being withdrawn at the start on his intended debut as a two-year-old. Gelded after joining Peter Makin, Pivotal Point was attended at the start as a three-year-old by 'horse whisperer' Gary Witherford, and he won a maiden over six furlongs at Windsor on only his second outing. A strong, close-coupled gelding with a quick, fluent action, he is still quite lightly raced and there may be further improvement in him as a five-year-old. Effective at five and six furlongs, Pivotal Point acts on firm ground. He was below form on his reappearance as a four-year-old on his only start on good to soft and was reportedly considered unsuited by 'loose' going by connections on a wet day at Newbury. *P. J. Makin*

PIVOTAL'S PRINCESS (IRE) 2 ch.f. (Feb 12) Pivotal 124 – Art Princess (IRE) (Fairy King (USA)) [2004 5d³ 5g³ 6g² Oct 8] 11,000Y: small, sturdy filly: third foal: half-sister to winner in Norway by Coneybury: dam, maiden in Norway, out of sister to 2000 Guineas winner Tap On Wood: best effort in maidens when length second to Mafaheem at York, making most: will probably stay 7f. *B. A. McMahon* **83**

PIZAZZ 3 ch.c. Pivotal 124 – Clare Celeste 73 (Coquelin (USA) 121) [2004 74p: 6g⁵ 8v² 8m⁵ 7.1f² 7m² 8m 7m³ 7m* 7m 7g Sep 17] angular, workmanlike colt: useful handicapper: won at Kempton in July by 5 lengths from Dumnoni, making all: below form after, though stiff task final start: stays 1m: acts on any going: blinkered last 3 appearances: looked difficult ride second outing: sold 17,000 gns. *B. J. Meehan* **98**

PLACE COWBOY (IRE) 3 b.c. Compton Place 125 – Paris Joelle (IRE) (Fairy King (USA)) [2004 69: 6g⁸ 6f⁵ 7m² 7.1d⁴ 7g⁶ 9f 8.5f² Nov 28] useful-looking colt: fairly useful performer in Britain: won maiden at Catterick in March: good efforts in frame in handicaps at Newmarket and Sandown in June/July: left J. Osborne, appeared to run very well when 2¾ lengths seventh to Blackdoun in Grade 2 Del Mar Derby in September: beaten a nose in allowance race at Hollywood final outing: stays 9f: acts on firm and good to soft going, promising second on fibresand on debut: has carried head awkwardly. *J. M. Cassidy, USA* **84 +**

PLAIN CHANT 7 b.g. Doyoun 124 – Sing Softly 112 (Luthier 126) [2004 19.1f Jun 19] lightly-raced maiden: well held only run on Flat since 2001. *C. Roberts* **–**

PLANET (IRE) 2 b.g. (Feb 21) Soviet Star (USA) 128 – Laurentia (USA) 97 (St Jovite (USA) 135) [2004 7g p7m p8.6g² Oct 16] 24,000F, 115,000Y: well-made gelding: first foal: dam Irish 1¼m/1½m winner: easily best effort in maidens when second to Jazrawy at Wolverhampton (gelded after): should stay 1¼m. *Sir Michael Stoute* **68**

PLANET TOMATO (IRE) 2 b.c. (Feb 14) Soviet Star (USA) 128 – Via Splendida (IRE) 80 (Project Manager 111) [2004 5.2g³ 5v² May 3] 84,000F, 58,000Y: big, strong colt: second foal: half-brother to fairly useful Irish 2002 2-y-o 7f winner Alexander Diamond (by Linamix): dam Irish maiden (stayed 1m): fairly useful form in maidens at Newbury and Kempton: dead. *P. F. I. Cole* **83**

PLANTERS PUNCH (IRE) 3 br.c. Cape Cross (IRE) 129 – Jamaican Punch (IRE) (Shareef Dancer (USA) 135) [2004 –p: 7g 10.2g 10m 10g* 11.6d 10m 10g 10d³ 10m² 10g² 10d² Oct 18] strong, useful-looking colt: fair handicapper: won at Leicester in June: stays 1¼m: yet to race on extremes of going: tried visored, better form without: sometimes slowly away: sold 30,000 gns. *R. Hannon* **77**

PLATEAU 5 b.g. Zamindar 116 – Painted Desert 89 (Green Desert (USA) 127) [2004 91: 6g⁶ 6g 5m² 5m 6m 5g³ 5d Sep 17] good-bodied gelding: fairly useful handicapper: best efforts of 2004 at Epsom, when short-head second to Caribbean Coral and close third to Atlantic Viking: effective at 5f/6f: acts on good to firm and good to soft ground: sometimes early to post. *D. Nicholls* **90**

PLATINUM BOY (IRE) 4 b.g. Goldmark (USA) 113 – Brown Foam (Horage 124) [2004 –, a61d: p12g f12g f12s p10g p10g³ p8g p10g p10g⁶ 10m p10m⁶ p10m p10g⁵ Dec 20] compact gelding: poor performer: stays 1¼m: acts on all-weather and good to firm going: tried blinkered/visored, wears cheekpieces nowadays. *M. Wellings* **a43**

PLATINUM CHARMER (IRE) 4 b.g. Kahyasi 130 – Mystic Charm (Nashwan (USA) 135) [2004 76d: f12g² f12g* p12g f16.2g² 12d⁴ f11g⁴ 11m² 11.9f⁴ 12.4g 12f³ 11.5m² 11.9f⁵ 12m* 12s 15s⁶ 13.8v⁵ f11g f12g⁶ Dec 1] compact gelding: modest performer: won seller at Southwell in January and (having left K. Ryan after fourth start) **63**

claimers at Musselburgh in May and Catterick in August: stays 1½m, probably not 13.8f: acts on all-weather, firm and soft going: usually wears cheekpieces, visored final outing: has wandered: usually waited with. *K. R. Burke*

PLATINUM CHIEF   3 b.g. Puissance 110 – Miss Beverley (Beveled (USA)) [2004   **38** 53: f8.5g⁶ f8g⁶ f7g⁵ f8s f9.4g⁵ f7m³ f8m⁴ f9.4g⁴ 8.5m May 24] close-coupled gelding: poor maiden: stays 9.4f: raced only on fibresand/good ground or firmer on turf: tried blinkered/in cheekpieces. *A. Berry*

PLATINUM PIRATE   3 b.g. Merdon Melody 98 – Woodland Steps 86 (Bold Owl   **67** 101) [2004 49: p10g² p10g p10g² 10s* 10s³ 9.9s⁶ 10v⁵ 11.1m⁴ p10g p10g* 10d* 10s³ 10v p9.5g p9.5g Dec 6] sturdy, close-coupled gelding: fair performer: won handicap at Redcar in April and claimers at Lingfield (idled) and Leicester (wandered) in September: stays 1¼m: acts on polytrack (below form on fibresand) and heavy going: blinkered/visored: carries head high. *K. R. Burke*

PLATTOCRAT   4 b.g. Dancing Spree (USA) – No Comebacks 70 (Last Tycoon 131)   **–** [2004 f8s⁵ f6g 8d f6f 7g Sep 7] workmanlike gelding: no form. *R. P. Elliott*

PLAUSABELLE   3 b.f. Royal Applause 124 – Sipsi Fach 100 (Prince Sabo 123) [2004   **58** 51: 8s 8s² 12.4s 12m 9.9d³ 10f² p7m p9.5g² Dec 15] modest maiden: left T. Easterby after sixth start: stays 1¼m: acts on polytrack, firm and soft ground: tried blinkered. *A. W. Carroll*

PLAY BOUZOUKI   3 b.f. Halling (USA) 133 – Balalaika 108 (Sadler's Wells (USA)   **70** 132) [2004 8.2g³ 8g⁴ 10.2g p8.6g⁶ Oct 16] third foal: half-sister to 4-y-o Alkaadhem and useful 1m/1¼m winner Lookalike (by Rainbow Quest): dam, 9f winner who stayed 1½m, sister to high-class 1¼m performer Stagecraft: fair maiden: should stay 1¼m: acts on polytrack: slowly away on debut. *L. M. Cumani*

PLAYFUL ACT (IRE)   2 b.f. (Apr 12) Sadler's Wells (USA) 132 – Magnificient   **113 p** Style (USA) 107 (Silver Hawk (USA) 123) [2004 7g² 7d* 8m* 8f* Sep 25]

Few owner-breeders in any era make a sufficient mark to be called 'a pioneer', 'a visionary' and 'a man who revolutionised international racing and breeding', but it is an eloquent testimony to Robert Sangster's influence that all these descriptions were applied, and applied accurately, to him by leading racing personalities after his death aged sixty-seven in April. The bare facts are impressive enough. Sangster was leading owner in Britain five times between 1977 and 1984 and had his colours carried to victory in around one hundred and thirty Group 1 races internationally, including in twenty-three British, Irish and French classics. Nine of his horses were Timeform champions and the highest rated—not all of them champions, admittedly—were Alleged (138), El Gran Senor (136), The Minstrel (135), Assert (134), Storm Bird (134), Golden Fleece (133), Caerleon and Sadler's Wells (132), Detroit and Thatching (131), Rodrigo de Triano (130) and Try My

betfair.com May Hill Stakes, Doncaster—Playful Act (right) proves well suited by the step up in trip, beating Queen of Poland (centre), Maids Causeway and Cassydora

Meon Valley Stud Fillies' Mile, Ascot—Playful Act gets the better of Maids Causeway once again; Dash To The Top (right) pips Mona Lisa (No.7) for third

Best (130). As the owner of Swettenham Stud, Sangster was leading breeder in Britain—and Europe—in 1992 thanks to Rodrigo de Triano and Derby winner Dr Devious, whom he had sold at a time when his formerly prodigious level of owner-ship was being scaled down. Sangster also bred one of the best milers of the 'eighties, Kings Lake; two more classic winners that he sold after their two-year-old campaigns, Balanchine and Cape Verdi; and, even more significantly, Sadler's Wells, the most influential sire of modern times in Europe.

It was the radical approach leading to this phenomenal success that truly set Sangster apart since, as he reasonably reflected in 1977, 'I came up with an idea that is so simple I'm surprised no one thought of it before—turn breeding into a strictly commercial venture.' This policy involved linking up with Vincent O'Brien and John Magnier in the early-'seventies and developing Coolmore through the purchase of American-bred yearlings to race on turf in Europe and then standing or selling them to generate a return on the capital. Northern Dancer was the key—nine of the twelve horses named above were from his line—and the effect the policy had on the yearling market was astonishing. At the Keeneland July Sale in 1974, the average price was 53,489 dollars and the aggregate was 17,000,000 dollars. Ten years later, the average was 544,681 dollars, the aggregate was 176,000,000 dollars and thirty-three yearlings fetched at least a million, including two to Sangster and his associates for 8,250,000 and 5,400,000, plus one at Saratoga for 4,600,000. Not all of these expensive purchases excelled—Seattle Dancer, the world-record priced yearling at 13,100,000 dollars in 1985, recouped only a fraction of the expense—and once the Maktoums arrived on the scene in the early-'eighties Sangster's dom-inance came under strong pressure. But the pluses outweighed the minuses for nearly a decade, thanks to such as The Minstrel (200,000-dollar yearling, Derby, Irish Derby, King George VI & Queen Elizabeth Stakes, syndicated for 9,000,000 dollars), Alleged (175,000-dollar two-year-old, two Prix de l'Arc de Triomphes, syndicated for 16,000,000 dollars), Storm Bird (million-dollar yearling, cham-pion juvenile, syndicated for around 30,000,000 dollars), Assert (approximately £16,000, Prix du Jockey Club, syndicated for 25,000,000 dollars) and Golden Fleece (775,000-dollar yearling, Derby, syndicated for 28,000,000 dollars). Sangster was also instrumental in pioneering the practice of shuttling stallions to the southern hemisphere to increase income, and it is a fact that without his foresight and contribution Coolmore would be nothing like so powerful as it is nowadays. Good news for some, of course, is not necessarily good news for all and the consequences of the revolution initiated by Sangster and his partners have included inflated auction prices, inflated stallion fees and inflated stallion books in both the short- and long-term. The value of these developments for the sport as a whole is questionable, but that does nothing to diminish the impact Sangster had overall. If for no other reason, he deserves praise and gratitude for being instru-mental in bringing a string of horses across the Atlantic without whose contribution the sport in Britain and Ireland and, more widely, in Europe would have been inestimably less interesting.

797

Sangster ended his business links with Coolmore around a decade ago but retained several shares in Sadler's Wells. The sire came up with yet another Group 1 winner in the familiar blue and green colours in September, Playful Act, owned by the Sangster Family. Playful Act is game, thoroughly likeable and favourite for the Oaks after landing three of her four starts. Her first two appearances, in seven-furlong maiden events at Newmarket in August, take little describing. Both times she looked green, running on from off the pace to be second to Cassydora, then making all to land the odds convincingly from Naivety. Everything about Playful Act suggested she would be suited by a mile and deserved a crack at a pattern race. Her chance came in the betfair.com May Hill Stakes at Doncaster in September, when she started only fifth favourite at 8/1. Two of her seven rivals, market leader Queen of Poland and Maids Causeway, had won stakes races and the latter carried a 3-lb penalty for her success in the Sweet Solera Stakes. Red Peony, third in the Prestige Stakes, and Cassydora also started at shorter odds, but none of them could cope with Playful Act. She tracked the strong pace, took over inside the final furlong and stayed on strongly to account for Queen of Poland by three quarters of a length, with Maids Causeway a close third.

The May Hill Stakes is a natural precursor to the Meon Valley Stud Fillies' Mile at Ascot later in the month but, oddly, only four fillies had completed the double, Height of Fashion, Tessla, Reams of Verse and Teggiano. Playful Act and Maids Causeway, now at levels, were the most exposed of a pretty inexperienced field of nine at Ascot. Prestige Stakes winner Dubai Surprise was the only other with pattern experience, the remainder consisting of four maiden and/or minor winners, notably the favourite Echelon, successful at Newmarket, and two who had yet to win a race, including Irish challenger Mona Lisa. The race proved rather rough, with Echelon one of the sufferers, but Playful Act was always in the right place to avoid any shenanigans as she set off in front, and she galloped on resolutely

Sangster Family's "Playful Act"

to beat Maids Causeway by a length, at no stage looking like being caught. Dash To The Top was third and Mona Lisa fourth after a troubled run—she should have finished closer but would never have beaten the winner. Maids Causeway went on to land the Rockfel Stakes, stamping the form of the Fillies' Mile. After the May Hill Stakes, trainer John Gosden said that Playful Act would not be trained for the One Thousand Guineas but would be prepared especially for the Oaks (for which she's generally 8/1 favourite at the time of writing), a reasonable decision given the way the filly races, and her pedigree. Now apparently the plan is to go for the Guineas, connections seemingly feeling that there is nothing to lose in training her for that race. Given the emphasis on speed in the Guineas, the Oaks will surely offer Playful Act the best chance of hitting the classic mark.

Playful Act (IRE) (b.f. Apr 12, 2002)	Sadler's Wells (USA) (b 1981)	Northern Dancer (b 1961)	Nearctic
			Natalma
		Fairy Bridge (b 1975)	Bold Reason
			Special
	Magnificient Style (USA) (b 1993)	Silver Hawk (b 1979)	Roberto
			Gris Vitesse
		Mia Karina (b or br 1983)	Icecapade
			Basin

Like the vast majority of Sadler's Wells' progeny, Playful Act will be suited by a mile and a quarter and more. She is well bred on the dam's side too, with no shortage of stamina. Her three-year-old brother Percussionist finished fourth in the Derby, while her four-year-old half-sister Echoes In Eternity, by the miler Spinning World, has won important pattern races over a mile (Sun Chariot Stakes) and a mile and three quarters (Park Hill Stakes). Their dam Magnificient Style, a 410,000-dollar purchase for Swettenham as a four-year-old, was not easy to train and ran below form on her only outing over a mile and a half, a trip she should have stayed, judged on the way she made all to win the Musidora Stakes. Magnificient Style has a one hundred per cent record with her foals, since the first one, by Storm Cat, is a minor stakes winner in the States. Since Playful Act the mare has foaled a filly by Danehill and a colt by Peintre Celebre before being returned to Sadler's Wells, to whom she is reportedly in foal again. The family contains numerous Group or Grade 1 winners including Magnificient Style's half-brother Siberian Summer and, more remotely, such as Sleepytime and Ali-Royal. A rather leggy filly, Playful Act has worn a crossed noseband. She acts on firm and good to soft going but was none too impressive in her slower paces at Ascot; there is a possibility that her powerful, round action may not prove ideal for the gradients of Epsom. Be that as it may, Playful Act also has a bit of improvement to make to reach normal Oaks-winning standard, though she has less to make than the other leading winter Oaks fancies. Playful Act does look likely to improve, and it will be interesting to see how she turns out, and whether the Sangster colours can be first past the post in an Epsom classic yet again. *J. H. M. Gosden*

PLAYFUL DANE (IRE) 7 b.g. Dolphin Street (FR) 125 – Omicida (IRE) (Danehill (USA) 126) [2004 64: 6m* 6m⁵ 6g 5m* 6f³ 5m* 5m² 5g* Oct 8] good-topped gelding: **88** not raced on Flat until 2002: developed into a fairly useful handicapper in 2004, winning at Redcar in May, Thirsk in July, Newcastle in September and York in October, last-named by neck from Prince of Gold: successful at 6f, but best at bare 5f: acts on fibresand and firm ground, probably on good to soft: has been slowly away: races up with pace. *W. S. Cunningham*

PLAYFUL SPIRIT 5 b.m. Mind Games 121 – Kalimat 74 (Be My Guest (USA) 126) **56** [2004 56: f6g f6g⁶ f6f³ f6s³ f5g f6g f5g³ 6m 5m 6m f6g 5d 6d Oct 16] leggy mare: modest performer: effective at 5f to 1m: acts on fibresand and good to firm going: visored: no easy ride. *J. Balding*

PLAY MASTER (IRE) 3 b.g. Second Empire (IRE) 124 – Madam Waajib (IRE) **77** (Waajib 121) [2004 f7g² f8.5g* f8.5s² 10.3g 8.3s* 7.9d f8g³ 7m 8.1g⁵ Sep 3] 15,000Y: tall, rather leggy, useful-looking gelding: first foal: dam showed signs of a little ability at 2 yrs: fair performer: won maiden at Wolverhampton in January and handicap at Windsor in April: should stay 1¼m: acts on fibresand and soft going: has raced freely/idled. *D. Haydn Jones*

PLA

PLAY THAT TUNE 4 ch.f. Zilzal (USA) 137 – Military Tune (IRE) (Nashwan (USA) **95**
135) [2004 97: 7.9s 9g⁵ 8.3g⁴ 7.9d³ 7d³ 7s Aug 19] strong, angular filly: useful performer:
ran well in 2004 only when third in handicaps at York (to St Petersburg) and Doncaster
(to Scotland The Brave): left M. Johnston after latter and returned to former trainer: free-
going sort, best at 7f/1m: acts on good to firm and good to soft ground. *H. R. A. Cecil*

PLAY THE BALL (USA) 2 ch.g. (Mar 15) Boundary (USA) 117 – Copper Play **72 p**
(USA) (Fast Play (USA)) [2004 p7.1g* Dec 31] $65,000F, €70,000Y: fifth foal: half-
brother to winners in USA by Carson City and Broad Brush: dam, won at around 6f in
USA (including at 2 yrs), half-sister to smart sprinter Tipsy Creek: 9/2, won maiden at
Wolverhampton by 1½ lengths from Cavan Gael, slowly away and leading final 1f: will
stay 1m: sure to improve. *G. A. Butler*

PLAY THE MELODY (IRE) 3 b. or br.g. Revoque (IRE) 122 – Dumayla 78 (Sher- **72**
nazar 131) [2004 9.7s³ 9.7g* Aug 22] eighth foal: half-brother to 3 winners, including
fairly useful 1½m winner Conwy Castle (by Sri Pekan): dam, third at 1m/1¼m (only
starts), half-sister to Doyoun: won maiden at Folkestone by neck from Efrhina: will be
suited by 1½m. *C. Tinkler*

PLAYTIME BLUE 4 b.g. Komaite (USA) – Miss Calculate 67 (Mummy's Game 120) **77 d**
[2004 69: f6s² p6g³ p5g⁶ f5s* f6s² f5s* 5s⁴ 5d³ 5v 5g⁶ 5m 5m⁵ 5g³ 5f³ 5g 5g 5.7m p6g
p5.1d p5.1g p5.1g p5g⁶ p6m⁵ Dec 22] lengthy, good-quartered gelding: fair handicapper:
won twice at Wolverhampton in February: below form subsequently (left K. Burke after
eighth start): effective at 5f/6f: acts on all-weather, firm and good ground: sometimes
edges left: often makes running. *Mrs H. Sweeting*

PLAY UP POMPEY 2 b.g. (Mar 3) Dansili 127 – Search For Love (FR) (Groom **53**
Dancer (USA) 128) [2004 7g 6m p7g 7g 8s 6s Sep 14] angular gelding: modest maiden:
seemingly best effort at 7f on polytrack. *J. J. Bridger*

PLEA BARGAIN 2 b.c. (Feb 24) Machiavellian (USA) 123 – Time Saved 89 (Green **100 p**
Desert (USA) 127) [2004 8g³ 7s* Oct 27] 425,000Y: first foal: dam, 1¼m winner, half-
sister to smart performers Time Allowed (at 1½m) and Zinaad (stayer) out of Time Charter: favourite, won maiden at Yarmouth easily by 5 lengths from Polish Eagle, always
close up: should stay at least 1¼m: already useful, and should go on to better things.
J. H. M. Gosden

PLEASANT 3 b.f. Topanoora 118 – Devon Peasant 74 (Deploy 131) [2004 10m⁴ 10g² **72**
10.2g 10d Oct 4] 1,000Y: first foal: dam, maiden on Flat (stayed 1¼m), winning hurdler:
fair maiden: best effort when second at Windsor: stays 1¼m. *L. G. Cottrell*

PLEASANTLY PERFECT (USA) 6 b.h. Pleasant Colony (USA) – Regal State **130**
(USA) 122 (Affirmed (USA)) [2004 126: a9f* a10f* a8.5f² a10f* a10f³ Oct 30]
A change of approach by Godolphin, which normally has a host of runners
at the Dubai World Cup meeting, resulted in smaller fields than usual for some of
the races. Godolphin fielded only nine contenders on the heavily-endowed, six-race
card and its only victory came courtesy of Firebreak's second successive win in the
Godolphin Mile, which like the UAE Derby had a single-figure field. The meeting
at Nad Al Sheba in March, the finale to the new and very successful nine-week
Dubai International Racing Carnival featuring a major meeting each week, attracted forty-six runners trained outside the United Arab Emirates. Coincidentally, this
was the same number as the previous year when plans for a dozen Japanese runners
were scrapped at the eleventh hour because of the proximity of Dubai to the war
zone in Iraq. Japan was among thirteen countries represented, including the host
nation, at the latest World Cup, two fewer than in 2003. The day's winners came
from five different countries (there was one dead heat) and the only country to win
two events outright was the United States, which again provided the biggest foreign
contingent on the day with thirteen runners (all bar two of them in the four dirt
races). The Americans took the two events in which they were most strongly
represented, with five and four runners respectively. Our New Recruit led home a
one, two, four in the Dubai Golden Shaheen, American-trained sprinters also filling
sixth and eighth in the twelve-runner field. The finish of the ninth running of the
Dubai World Cup, the world's most valuable race with first prize of £1,956,522,
was fought out by top-class American dirt performers Pleasantly Perfect and Medaglia d'Oro.
　　The Dubai World Cup field of twelve was drawn from six nations, though,
for the first time, none of the major European racing countries was represented.

Probably the main achievement of the Dubai World Cup has been its success in attracting top quality challengers from North America. Though traditionally insular, North American racing warmed to the Dubai World Cup meeting from the start, its challengers generally proving suited to the artificial sand-based surface at Nad Al Sheba and acquitting themselves well. Pleasantly Perfect and Medaglia d'Oro had finished first and second in the Breeders' Cup Classic the previous October and dominated the World Cup field, along with the in-form South African challenger Victory Moon, winner of the UAE Derby the previous year and successful in the second and third rounds of the Maktoum Challenge at Nad Al Sheba during the carnival. Pleasantly Perfect had been successful in the Grade 2 San Antonio Handicap at Santa Anita in January but had then been forced to miss the Santa Anita Handicap in March with a high temperature. He started at 5/2 with British bookmakers, shaded in the betting by 2/1 favourite Medaglia d'Oro, who had won the Donn Handicap at Gulfstream Park in authoritative style in February. Victory Moon was at 4/1, with the best of the three Japanese-trained runners, top dirt performer Admire Don, at 11/1, and the only Godolphin challenger Grand Hombre next at 12/1 (half the field started at odds between 22/1 and 66/1). Pleasantly Perfect confirmed Breeders' Cup placings with Medaglia d'Oro, getting the better of him by three quarters of a length after a good duel over the final furlong. Pleasantly Perfect became the second horse, following inaugural World Cup winner Cigar, to win the world's two most important all-aged races on dirt, Cigar having also won the previous autumn's Breeders' Cup Classic. Nothing got near Pleasantly Perfect and Medaglia d'Oro in the World Cup, third-placed Victory Moon finishing five lengths away in third and Grand Hombre a further seven and three quarter lengths back in fourth, with the remainder strung out, the three Japanese challengers coming eighth, ninth and last. Pleasantly Perfect was the fourth North American-trained winner of the Dubai World Cup (following also Silver Charm and Captain Steve) and provided a first winner for his trainer Richard Mandella, who has also saddled three runners-up, Soul of The Matter (second to Cigar), Siphon and Malek (who also finished fourth in a World Cup), as well as a third in Sandpit.

The 2003 Breeders' Cup Classic at Santa Anita—one of four wins on a red-letter day for his trainer who also won the Turf (dead heat) and the two Juveniles—was the first Grade 1 success of Pleasantly Perfect's career. A 725,000-dollar yearling, he didn't reach the racecourse at two and made an inauspicious debut (on turf) on his only outing at three when pulled up. He won four times at four, including the Grade 2 Goodwood Breeders' Cup Handicap at local course Santa Anita in the autumn, but a series of minor injuries, which plagued him for much of his career, including as a four-year-old, restricted his appearances again at five. He had missed the Classic as a four-year-old, banned from racing by a 'thirty-day' rule in Illinois after bleeding at Santa Anita, and had only three outings before the 2003 Classic, though they included a repeat win in the Goodwood Handicap. His victory in the Classic still caused a surprise and was thought at the time to have been

Dubai World Cup, Nad Al Sheba—Pleasantly Perfect (left) and Medaglia d'Oro fight out the closest finish to the race for five years; Victory Moon is third

assisted by Medaglia d'Oro and another leading fancy Congaree cutting each other's throats by battling for the lead from early on. After the Dubai World Cup, Pleasantly Perfect was given a break and began his build-up to another tilt at the Breeders' Cup Classic at the Del Mar meeting in August. Beaten three quarters of a length when conceding 10 lb to Choctaw Nation in the San Diego Handicap, over a trip possibly short of his best, Pleasantly Perfect then gained his fourth major win in ten months in the Grade 1 Pacific Classic, scoring a shade comfortably from Whitney Handicap runner-up Perfect Drift and Hollywood Gold Cup winner Total Impact, with previously unbeaten Choctaw Nation in fourth. Pleasantly Perfect managed only third in a very good renewal of the Breeders' Cup Classic at Lone Star Park, repeating Pacific Classic form with fourth-placed Perfect Drift but unable to make any impression in the straight on the front-running pair Ghost-zapper and Whitney Handicap winner Roses In May, who had both come into the race unbeaten during the season. Pleasantly Perfect reportedly injured his off-fore at Lone Star Park and he has now been retired to Lane's End Farm, Kentucky, where he will stand at a fee of 40,000 dollars in 2005.

Pleasantly Perfect (USA) (b.h. 1998)	Pleasant Colony (USA) (b 1978)	His Majesty (b 1968)	Ribot Flower Bowl
		Sun Colony (b 1968)	Sunrise Flight Colonia
	Regal State (USA) (ch 1983)	Affirmed (ch 1975)	Exclusive Native Won't Tell You
		La Trinite (ch 1976)	Lyphard Promessa

Pleasantly Perfect is by a former Lane's End inmate, the Kentucky Derby and Preakness winner Pleasant Colony, who was retired from stud duties in 1999 and is now dead. He sired plenty of major winners in North America and easily the best of his European representatives, which have been relatively few and far between, was the Irish Derby and King George winner St Jovite. Pleasantly Perfect is the seventh foal out of the Prix Morny winner Regal State, who is herself a half-sister to another Prix Morny winner in Seven Springs, the dam of high-class miler and successful sire Distant View. The best of Regal State's previous winners was her fifth foal, the Prix Eclipse winner Hurricane State (by Miswaki), a lightly-raced sprinter/miler trained by Peter Chapple-Hyam; Regal State was also represented on the racecourse in the latest season by the three-year-old Swagger Stick (by Cozzene) who won twice at up to almost a mile and a half for John Dunlop. The game and consistent Pleasantly Perfect, who won nine of his eighteen races, stayed a mile and a quarter. Usually held up, he wore blinkers or a visor in recent seasons and had worn a tongue tie. He was reported more than once to have bled in his races and was habitually raced on bute and lasix in North America, 'medication' forbidden in the Dubai World Cup. *R. E. Mandella, USA*

PLEASURE SEEKER   3 b.f. First Trump 118 – Purse 78 (Pursuit of Love 124) [2004 –: 6s 8f 8f 7d 10.2s⁶ Sep 20] leggy filly: little form: usually slowly away. *M. D. I. Usher*   **–**

PLEASURE TIME   11 ch.g. Clantime 101 – First Experience 58 (Le Johnstan 123) [2004 56: f5g⁵ f5g p6g f5s* f5g⁶ 6f p5.1g Oct 25] leggy, good-topped gelding: poor performer: won banded race at Southwell in March: best at 5f: acts on fibresand, best turf form on good going or firmer: has worn blinkers, visored nowadays: often a front runner. *C. Smith*   **48**

PLENTY CRIED WOLF   2 b.g. (Mar 2) Wolfhound (USA) 126 – Plentitude (FR) (Ela-Mana-Mou 132) [2004 6g 6d 7m⁴ 6.9m 7m³ p8.6g⁶ 7s³ Nov 2] workmanlike gelding: modest maiden: barely stays 8.6f: acts on polytrack, soft and good to firm going. *R. A. Fahey*   **64**

PLOVERS LANE (IRE)   3 b.g. Dushyantor (USA) 123 – Sweet Alma 67 (Alzao (USA) 117) [2004 –: 10g 12.1g May 31] good-bodied gelding: fluent mover: well held in maidens: in cheekpieces final start. *M. P. Tregoning*   **–**

PLUM   4 br.f. Pivotal 124 – Rose Chime (IRE) 58 (Tirol 127) [2004 69: 7s* 7v Oct 16] rather leggy filly: fair performer, lightly raced: won handicap at Brighton in August: may prove best up to 7f: acts on firm and soft ground: sold 3,000 gns. *E. F. Vaughan*   **75**

PLUMMET (USA)   3 b.f. Silver Hawk (USA) 123 – Fairy Heights (IRE) 110 (Fairy King (USA)) [2004 10m⁴ 10g² 10m³ p10g Dec 4] fifth foal: half-sister to French 1m   **83**

winner (including at 2 yrs) Fairy West (by Gone West): dam 2-y-o 7f/1m (Fillies' Mile) winner: fairly useful maiden: best effort when head second at Kempton. *J. H. M. Gosden*

PLUMPIE MAC (IRE) 3 b.f. Key of Luck (USA) 126 – Petrine (IRE) (Petorius 117) – [2004 –: 7d⁶ 7.5g 7.9f Jul 29] close-coupled filly: little form. *N. Bycroft*

PLUNGINGTON TAVERN (IRE) 2 b.c. (Mar 9) Josr Algarhoud (IRE) 118 – Hever Golf Lady 62 (Dominion 123) [2004 7.2d Sep 17] lengthy colt: 66/1 and burly, well held in maiden at Ayr, racing freely. *P. A. Blockley*

PLUTOCRAT 8 b.g. Polar Falcon (USA) 126 – Choire Mhor 100 (Dominion 123) 75 [2004 16g² 12m May 17] leggy, shallow-girthed gelding: fair handicapper: stays 2m: best efforts on good going or firmer: ran poorly in visor final start. *L. Lungo*

POACHER'S PARADISE 3 ch.g. Inchinor 119 – Transylvania 85 (Wolfhound – (USA) 126) [2004 52: f6g f6g 10d⁶ 8s Apr 12] lengthy gelding: maiden: little form at 3 yrs. *M. W. Easterby*

POCKETWOOD 2 b.g. (Apr 25) Fleetwood (IRE) 107 – Pocket Venus (IRE) (King's 72 Theatre (IRE) 128) [2004 7.1m p10g p8.6g* Dec 17] first foal: dam ran 3 times at 2 yrs: best effort in maidens when winning at Wolverhampton by ½ length from Sinnomore, leading close home: should stay at least 1¼m. *Jean-Rene Auvray*

POETICAL (IRE) 3 ch.f. Croco Rouge (IRE) 126 – Abyat (USA) (Shadeed (USA) 103 135) [2004 94: 8m³ 8m* 7m 7.5v³ 8d Oct 17] €20,000Y: second foal: half-sister to Irish 1¼m winner Indian Belle (by Indian Ridge): dam unraced half-sister to Middle Park winner Hayil: useful performer: won maiden at the Curragh in August: best effort when 3 lengths third to Hamairi in Concorde Stakes at Tipperary penultimate start: well held in listed race at Doncaster third outing: stays 1m: acts on any ground. *M. J. Grassick, Ireland*

POETRY 'N PASSION 3 b.f. Polish Precedent (USA) 131 – Ghassanah 73 (Pas de 50 Seul 133) [2004 8.1d 6d p7g 11.5d⁵ p9.5g p10m Dec 15] 12,000Y: good-topped filly: half-sister to several winners, including 5f/6f winner (including at 2 yrs) Alzianah (by Alzao) and 6f/7f (latter at 2 yrs) winner Return of Amin (by Salse), both useful: dam 7f winner: modest maiden: barely stays 11.5f. *C. A. Cyzer*

POINT CALIMERE (IRE) 3 b.g. Fasliyev (USA) 120 – Mountain Ash 107 (Dom- 68 inion 123) [2004 80: p5g 6s⁴ 5d⁵ 7g f6g* 5d 6m 7g 5d 7s² Oct 25] angular gelding: fair performer: won maiden at Southwell in June, swishing tail and edging right (left C. Egerton after): stays 7f: acts on fibresand, firm and soft going: wore cheekpieces (good effort) final outing, blinkers 5 previous starts. *L. McAteer, Ireland*

POINTED (IRE) 3 br.f. Selkirk (USA) 129 – Tragic Point (IRE) 89 (Tragic Role – (USA)) [2004 7g 9.9g 10m³ f14g Aug 19] 16,000Y: leggy, close-coupled filly: fifth foal: half-sister to fairly useful 7f winner Desdemona (by Lahib): dam Irish 2-y-o 1m winner: little form: left T. Easterby after third start. *Mrs J. Candlish*

POINT MAN (IRE) 4 b.g. Pivotal 124 – Pursuit of Truth (USA) 69 (Irish River (FR) 44 ? 131) [2004 –: f6m 8g³ f7g⁴ p7.1g⁶ Dec 14] sturdy, quite attractive gelding: poor maiden: stays 1m: blinkered on reappearance. *J. W. Payne*

POINT OF DISPUTE 9 b.g. Cyrano de Bergerac 120 – Opuntia (Rousillon (USA) 88 § 133) [2004 88§: 7m⁵ 7m² 7.1d p7g⁴ p7g p7.1g³ p7.1g⁴ p7.1g² Dec 6] tall gelding: fairly useful performer: best at 6f/7f: acts on all-weather, firm and good to soft going: visored: sometimes sweats: often slowly away/held up: irresolute. *P. J. Makin*

POISE (IRE) 3 b.f. Rainbow Quest (USA) 134 – Crepe Ginger (IRE) 67 (Sadler's 93 p Wells (USA) 132) [2004 93P: 10m* Aug 2] rather leggy, lengthy filly: fairly useful form in just 2 races: as low as 12/1 for Oaks when reportedly suffered an infection in May: landed odds in maiden at Windsor in August easily by 5 lengths from Michabo: will stay 1½m: raced only on good to firm going: should still make a useful performer, all being well. *Sir Michael Stoute*

POKER 3 ch.g. Hector Protector (USA) 124 – Clunie 84 (Inchinor 119) [2004 –: f8g* 55 8s 7.1g p9.5g Oct 2] modest performer: landed gamble in maiden handicap at South-well in February: well beaten after, leaving W. Haggas before third start: should stay 1¼m: acts on fibresand and good to firm ground: sold 1,500 gns, sent to Denmark. *Mrs J. Candlish*

POKER PLAYER (IRE) 2 ch.g. (Mar 16) Raise A Grand (IRE) 114 – Look Non- 80 p chalant (IRE) 61 (Fayruz 116) [2004 6d⁵ Oct 14] €11,500F: useful-looking gelding: has a quick action: fourth foal: half-brother to fairly useful Irish 9f and 1½m winner Nonchalant (by Magical Wonder) and 2001 2-y-o 5f winner Case Study (by Case Law): dam, Irish maiden, probably stayed 1m: 20/1, fifth to Tomoohat in maiden at Newmarket, slowly away and green but finishing well: will be suited by 7f/1m: should improve. *B. J. Meehan*

POLANSKI MILL 5 b.g. Polish Precedent (USA) 131 – Mill On The Floss 117 (Mill — Reef (USA) 141) [2004 –: 14.4s 13.3m 17.2g 16m p16d Aug 9] lightly-raced maiden: little form in 2004: wore cheekpieces/tongue tie final start. *C. A. Horgan*

POLAR BEAR 4 ch.g. Polar Falcon (USA) 126 – Aim For The Top (USA) 111 (Irish 117 River (FR) 131) [2004 101p: 7s³ 8f 7s* 7s* 8m 7s³ Oct 16] tall, rather unfurnished gelding: smart performer: missed cut when ante-post favourite for Victoria Cup at Ascot on intended second start: won handicap at Newcastle (by 5 lengths from Digital) in June and listed event at York (beat Welsh Emperor by short head) in August: good 1¼ lengths third to Firebreak in Challenge Stakes at Newmarket final outing, finishing best of all: effective at 7f/1m: winner on good to firm going, very best efforts on soft: held up. *W. J. Haggas*

POLAR BEN 5 b.g. Polar Falcon (USA) 126 – Woodbeck 90 (Terimon 124) [2004 118 118: 7d² 7.1g² 7m 8g²* 7s Oct 16] rather leggy, useful-looking gelding: smart performer: second in listed races at Leicester (behind Tout Seul) and Haydock (short-headed by Rockets'n Rollers) on first 2 outings: off 3 months before winning Shadwell Stud Joel Stakes at Newmarket in October by ¾ length from Salsalson: raced too freely and carried head awkwardly when well below form in Challenge Stakes at same course final start: effective at 7f/1m: has won on good to firm going, best on good or softer: held up. *J. R. Fanshawe*

POLAR DANCER 3 b.f. Polar Falcon (USA) 126 – Petonica (IRE) 77 (Petoski 135) 63 [2004 71: 11.6s 10m³ 12f 12g 9.9m³ 9.9g³ 11d Oct 10] modest maiden: stays 1¼m: acts on polytrack and good to firm ground: sold 15,000 gns, sent to Germany. *Mrs A. J. Perrett*

POLAR DAWN 2 b.f. (Apr 23) Polar Falcon (USA) 126 – Leave At Dawn (Slip 72 Anchor 136) [2004 6m² 6.1m⁶ 7d⁴ 7.1g* 6d Oct 14] leggy filly: sixth foal: half-sister to 2 winners in Scandinavia, including Nassau Night (by Bahamian Bounty), also 1m winner in Britain: dam unraced out of half-sister to smart miler Trojan Fen: fair performer: won maiden at Warwick in August: not run of race in sales event at Newmarket final start: stays 7f: acts on good to firm and good to soft going. *B. R. Millman*

POLAR FORCE 4 ch.g. Polar Falcon (USA) 126 – Irish Light (USA) 91 (Irish River 68 (FR) 131) [2004 82d: p6g⁴ p6g p6g p6g³ 5g 6m³ 6f Jun 10] neat gelding: useful performer at 2 yrs, just fair nowadays: left M. Channon after sixth start: stays 6f: acts on polytrack: best turf efforts on softer than good: sometimes slowly away. *Miss K. B. Boutflower*

POLAR GALAXY 3 br.f. Polar Falcon (USA) 126 – June Brilly (IRE) (Fayruz 116) 51 ? [2004 58: 7m 8f⁵ 7.9f 6g⁴ f6g Aug 19] leggy filly: modest maiden: free-going sort, barely stays 7f: acts on good to firm ground: tried in cheekpieces. *C. W. Fairhurst*

POLAR HAZE 7 ch.g. Polar Falcon (USA) 126 – Sky Music 85 (Absalom 128) [2004 48 § 44, a60: p6g⁴ f6g² f6h⁵ f6g⁵ f6s f6g⁴ f6g⁵ f6d⁵ 7m 6.1m⁴ 6f 6d² f6g p6g f6g³ p6g a65 § Dec 17] lengthy, good-quartered gelding: fair on all-weather, poor on turf: won seller at Southwell in February: probably best around 6f: acts on all-weather, firm and soft going: blinkered/visored: unreliable. *J. Pearce*

POLAR IMPACT 5 br.h. Polar Falcon (USA) 126 – Boozy 111 (Absalom 128) [2004 81 84: a7g⁵ 7g 6g⁵ 6m* 5m⁴ 6g⁵ 6s a6g² a5g* a6g² Nov 28] strong, short-backed horse: fairly useful performer: won minor events at Dos Hermanas in January (final outing for J. Brown), Windsor in June and, after leaving G. L. Moore after seventh start, Mijas in October: has won at 7f, best recent form at 5f/6f: acts on soft and good to firm going, and on sand, ran as if amiss on firm: has been early to post. *P. Haley, Spain*

POLAR JEM 4 b.f. Polar Falcon (USA) 126 – Top Jem 85 (Damister (USA) 123) 102 [2004 75: 10s³ 10s⁴ 10m* 10m* 9g* 10m* 10.4g6 10g³ 12f² 10.1g* 12f⁶ Sep 24] leggy filly: useful performer: much improved in 2004, winning minor event and handicaps at Kempton, Sandown and Newmarket in May/June, and listed event at Yarmouth (beat Shamara by ½ length) in September: effective at 9f to 1½m: acts on firm and soft ground: front runner: genuine and consistent. *G. G. Margarson*

POLAR KINGDOM 6 b.g. Pivotal 124 – Scarlet Lake 60 (Reprimand 122) [2004 80: 81 + f6g³ f6g* f7g* f6g 6g 6g³ 6d Jun 26] rangy gelding: usually looks well: useful handi- a97 capper on all-weather, fairly useful on turf: won twice at Southwell in February, best effort when beating Prima Stella 2½ lengths in latter: effective at 6f to 7.6f: acts on fibresand and soft going: tried visored/blinkered/tongue tied. *T. D. Barron*

POLAR MAGIC 3 ch.c. Polar Falcon (USA) 126 – Enchant 92 (Lion Cavern (USA) 91 p 117) [2004 7d⁴ 7g² p7g* Oct 1] 37,000Y: second foal: half-brother to 4-y-o Mobane

804

Flyer: dam, 7f winner who stayed 1¼m, closely related to smart performer up to 1m Dazzle: won maiden at Thirsk in June and handicap at Lingfield (beat Outer Hebrides by 2 lengths, quickening impressively) in October: bred to stay 1m: useful performer in making. *J. R. Fanshawe*

POLAR PASSION 2 b.f. (Apr 29) Polar Prince (IRE) 117 – Priorite (IRE) 85 (Kenmare (FR) 125) [2004 7g⁵ 6s Sep 24] workmanlike filly: third foal: half-sister to 4-y-o Cross Ash: dam Irish 2-y-o 7f winner: poor form in maidens at Chester (reared start) and Haydock. *R. Hollinshead* **40**

POLAR SUN 3 b.g. Polar Falcon (USA) 126 – Barford Lady 93 (Stanford 121§) [2004 7f⁶ 7g³ 6s⁶ Aug 18] lengthy, quite attractive gelding: sixth foal: half-brother to 5-y-o Persario, 6-y-o Heretic and smart 7f winner Warningford (by Warning): dam 7f/1m winner: best effort in maidens when third to Surreptitious at Newmarket. *J. R. Fanshawe* **67**

POLAR TRYST 5 ch.m. Polar Falcon (USA) 126 – Lovers Tryst 91 (Castle Keep 121) [2004 72: 13.1f* 12f p13g⁴ Nov 10] leggy, lengthy mare: fair handicapper: off 14 months prior to winning at Bath in September by 6 lengths: stays 13f: acts firm and good to soft ground, probably on polytrack: races up with pace. *Lady Herries* **75**

POLAR WAY 5 ch.g. Polar Falcon (USA) 126 – Fetish 85 (Dancing Brave (USA) 140) [2004 114: 6f 7m³ 7m² 7g 7.1g* 7g³ 7s⁴ Oct 16] angular, workmanlike gelding: unimpressive mover in slower paces: very smart performer: excellent neck second under 9-7 to Court Masterpiece in totesport International Stakes at Ascot in July: landed odds in 5-runner minor event at Warwick in August comfortably by ½ length from Desert Destiny: respectable efforts in Supreme Stakes at Goodwood (2 lengths third to Mac Love) and Challenge Stakes at Newmarket (4 lengths fourth to Firebreak) last 2 starts: barely stays testing 7f: unraced on heavy going, acts on any other turf. *Mrs A. J. Perrett* **120**

POLE STAR 6 b. or br.g. Polar Falcon (USA) 126 – Ellie Ardensky 100 (Slip Anchor 136) [2004 114: 16s Oct 16] tall, angular gelding: smart performer: reportedly found to be lame final start at 5 yrs: well beaten in Jockey Club Cup at Newmarket only outing on Flat in 2004: stays 2½m: acts on any going: usually held up: normally reliable: won over hurdles in December. *J. R. Fanshawe* **–**

POLESWORTH 2 b.f. (Mar 16) Wizard King 122 – Nicholas Mistress 56 (Beveled (USA)) [2004 f7d⁵ 7s 7.1m Sep 6] second foal: dam 6f winner: poor form, including in seller. *C. N. Kellett* **36**

POLICY MAKER (IRE) 4 b.c. Sadler's Wells (USA) 132 – Palmeraie (USA) (Lear Fan (USA) 130) [2004 117: 10g⁵ 12g* 12d² 12d* 12m 12f⁴ Nov 28] tall, rather leggy colt: smart performer: won Grand Prix de Chantilly (by short neck from Fair Mix) in June and 4-runner Prix Foy Gray d'Albion Barriere at Longchamp (set very slow pace, beat Short Pause 2 lengths) in September: also ran well when 3 lengths second to Gamut in Grand Prix de Saint-Cloud in between and when just over 3 lengths fourth to Zenno Rob Roy in Japan Cup at Tokyo final start: well beaten (for second year running) in Prix de l'Arc de Triomphe at Longchamp penultimate outing: stays 12.5f well: acts on soft and firm going: has worn ear plugs. *E. Lellouche, France* **119**

POLISH BARON (IRE) 7 b.g. Barathea (IRE) 127 – Polish Mission (Polish Precedent (USA) 131) [2004 f12g⁶ Jan 8] useful-looking gelding: fair performer in 2002: missed 2003 Flat season: acted on fibresand, soft and good to firm going: barely stayed 2m: joined J. R. Cornwall, and won over fences in April/May: dead. *J. White* **–**

POLISH EAGLE 2 b.c. (Jan 14) Polish Precedent (USA) 131 – Tinashaan (IRE) 100 (Darshaan 133) [2004 8d 7s² Oct 27] 60,000Y: leggy colt: fourth foal: half-brother to fairly useful 7f to 1½m winner Pantone (by Spectrum): dam, 1½m winner, half-sister to useful stayer Life of Riley: much better effort in maidens when 5 lengths second to Plea Bargain at Yarmouth: likely to be suited by 1¼m/1½m: should progress. *E. A. L. Dunlop* **83 p**

POLISH EMPEROR (USA) 4 ch.g. Polish Precedent (USA) 131 – Empress Jackie (USA) (Mount Hagen (FR) 127) [2004 81: p6g⁴ f5g² p5g² 5s⁵ 5.7g 5.3m⁵ 5m* 6m 5m 5g 5d⁶ 5.2g 5m* p5.1d p5g⁴ p5.1g* p5.1g* 6p Dec 18] lengthy gelding: useful performer: won handicap at Thirsk in May, minor event at Redcar in October and handicaps at Wolverhampton in November and December (best effort, beat Treasure Cay ½ length): has won at 6f, best at 5f: acts on all-weather, firm and soft ground: sometimes blinkered: races prominently. *W. R. Swinburn* **99**

POLISH INDEX 2 b.c. (Apr 13) Polish Precedent (USA) 131 – Glossary (Reference Point 139) [2004 8m Sep 21] angular colt: 100/1 and in need of race, well held in maiden at Newmarket. *J. R. Jenkins* **–**

*Dubai Sheema Classic, Nad Al Sheba—Polish Summer (left) is very confidently ridden
to beat Hard Buck (stripe on sleeve) and Scott's View (star on cap),
giving Andre Fabre and Gary Stevens a fine start to their new partnership*

POLISH LEGION 11 b.g. Polish Precedent (USA) 131 – Crystal Bright 75 (Bold Lad –
(IRE) 133) [2004 47: 6g p6g f7g Dec 16] big gelding: poor nowadays: left H. O'Driscoll
in Ireland after reappearance: best at 5f/6f: acts on any turf going: has looked hard ride.
M. J. Ryan

POLISH RHAPSODY (IRE) 3 b.f. Charnwood Forest (IRE) 125 – Polish Rhythm –
(IRE) 77 (Polish Patriot (USA) 128) [2004 –: p8g p7g 10v⁶ p10g p10g Dec 20] quite
good-topped filly: of no account. *J. A. Supple*

POLISH ROSE 3 ch.f. Polish Precedent (USA) 131 – Messila Rose (Darshaan 133) 55
[2004 7m 8m⁵ 10v Oct 23] angular filly: first foal: dam unraced: modest form in maidens
first 2 starts, tailed off (heavy ground) subsequent outing: bred to be suited by 1m+.
E. F. Vaughan

POLISH SPIRIT 9 b.g. Emarati (USA) 74 – Gentle Star 77 (Comedy Star (USA) 121) 68
[2004 –: 9g 8.2g 9.9g⁶ 9.9s* 11.7g f11g⁵ p12.2g Dec 11] lengthy, workmanlike gelding:
fair handicapper: won at Goodwood in August: stays 11f: acts on fibresand and probably
any turf going (most wins on good or softer): usually races prominently. *B. R. Millman*

POLISH SUMMER 7 b.h. Polish Precedent (USA) 131 – Hunt The Sun (Rainbow 120
Quest (USA) 134) [2004 118: 10d* 12m* 10.5d⁵ 12d 12d⁴ 12d⁵ 12m⁶ Dec 12] strong,
good sort: very smart performer: won Prix Exbury at Saint-Cloud (by short head from
Bright Sky) and Dubai Sheema Classic at Nad Al Sheba (by ½ length from Hard Buck,
leading inside final 1f after challenging on bridle) in March: below best afterwards, fifth
to Kitten's Joy in Turf Classic at Belmont and sixth to Phoenix Reach in Hong Kong Vase
at Sha Tin last 2 outings: best at 1¼m to 12.5f: acted on soft and good to firm going:
visored (ran creditably) final outing in 2002: to stand at Haras de Mortree, France, fee
€2,200. *A. Fabre, France*

POLKA PRINCESS 4 b.f. Makbul 104 – Liberatrice (FR) (Assert 134) [2004 –: 48
f9.4g f11g p13g p16g³ p12g p12g p12g p12g f14.8g⁵ May 5] small, angular filly: poor
nowadays: stays 2m: acts on all-weather, raced only on good going or firmer on turf:
sometimes wears cheekpieces/blinkers. *M. Wellings*

POLLITO (IRE) 2 b.g. (Mar 15) Rossini (USA) 118 – Bezee (Belmez (USA) 131) 70
[2004 6f⁵ 6m⁶ 7g⁴ p8g³ Sep 22] €26,000F, 25,000Y: fifth foal: half-brother to fairly
useful 1¼m winner Lafayette (by General Monash) and a winner in Italy by Efisio: dam
unraced: fair maiden: should stay 1¼m: acts on polytrack, best turf effort on good going.
B. J. Meehan

POLLY ALEXANDER (IRE) 2 ch.f. (Apr 2) Foxhound (USA) 103 – Fiveofive 85
(IRE) 61 (Fairy King (USA)) [2004 5s⁵ 5s* 5d* 5.2g³ 5.5g² 6g* 6m 6g 6d Oct 14]
9,000Y: close-coupled filly: seventh foal: half-sister to 3 winners, including fairly useful
2001 2-y-o 7f winner My Only Sunshine (by First Trump) and 4-y-o Lilli Marlane: dam
5f (at 2 yrs) and 1m winner: fairly useful performer: won maiden at Warwick and minor
event at Ripon in April and minor event at Salisbury (beat Captain Hurricane by head) in
June: stiffish tasks and well below form last 3 starts: stays 6f: acts on soft ground: sold
40,000 gns, sent to USA. *M. J. Wallace*

POLLY PERKINS (IRE)   2 b.f. (Feb 28) Pivotal 124 – Prospering 50 (Prince Sabo   **100**
123) [2004 5m* 5f* 5f 6m 5d* Jul 2] 25,000Y, 17,000 2-y-o: close-coupled, workmanlike
filly: second foal: dam 7f winner: useful performer: won maiden at Musselburgh and
listed races at Sandown in May and July (came from off strong pace when beating Southern Africa by 8 lengths): should stay 6f: acts on firm and good to soft going: sold 115,000
gns in October. *N. P. Littmoden*

POLONIUS   3 b.g. Great Dane (IRE) 122 – Bridge Pool 74 (First Trump 118) [2004   **–**
94p: 7d⁶ Jul 10] fairly useful performer at 2 yrs: last in minor event at Salisbury only run
in 2004: likely to prove best up to 7f. *H. Candy*

POLYGONAL (FR)   4 b.g. Octagonal (NZ) 126 – Sectarine (FR) (Maelstrom Lake   **102**
118) [2004 10d* 10g³ 8.9m⁶ 10.4g 10m⁵ 10m* 10.3f Sep 11] quite good-topped gelding:
useful performer: successful in minor event at Longchamp in March (left E. Lellouche in
France after next start) and handicap at Newmarket (best effort, by 6 lengths from Elmustanser) in August: reportedly finished lame subsequent outing: stays 1½m: acts on good
to firm and good to soft ground: tried blinkered, better form without. *Mrs J. R. Ramsden*

POMFRET LAD   6 b.g. Cyrano de Bergerac 120 – Lucky Flinders 77 (Free State 125)   **94 d**
[2004 108: 5g 5.1d 6d 5.6m 6s 7g 6g 5d Oct 18] tall, good-topped gelding: just fairly
useful for new trainer: stays 7f: acts on good to firm and good to soft ground:
blinkered (well held) twice: inconsistent. *D. Nicholls*

POMPEY BLUE   3 b.f. Abou Zouz (USA) 109 – Habla Me (IRE) (Fairy King (USA))   **59**
[2004 71: f6g⁵ p6g⁵ p5g 6g 5g 5f 5d p6g Dec 20] modest performer: will prove best at 5f/
6f: acts on all-weather and good to firm ground: looked none too keen sixth start.
P. J. McBride

POMPEY CHIMES   4 b.g. Forzando 122 – Silver Purse 67 (Interrex (CAN)) [2004   **49 ?**
45p: 6s⁴ 7d 5.7m May 17] poor maiden, lightly raced. *G. B. Balding*

PONDERON   4 ch.g. Hector Protector (USA) 124 – Blush Rambler (IRE) (Blushing   **94**
Groom (FR) 131) [2004 102: 16d 18.7d⁶ 16.2d Jun 5] lengthy gelding: useful handicapper at 3 yrs: best effort in 2004 when sixth to Anak Pekan in Chester Cup: ran as if amiss
subsequent outing: likely to prove best at 1¾m/2m: acts on polytrack and good to soft
going, probably on firm. *R. F. Johnson Houghton*

PONENTE   2 b.f. (Apr 8) Robellino (USA) 127 – Polmara (IRE) (Polish Precedent   **62**
(USA) 131) [2004 6d⁶ 7.1m 7v³ Oct 16] close-coupled filly: first foal: dam ran once:
modest form in maidens: best effort at 6f. *B. W. Hills*

PONGEE   4 b.f. Barathea (IRE) 127 – Puce 112 (Darshaan 133) [2004 96: 12g³ 11.9m*   **110**
11.9g* 14m² 11.9s² Aug 18] quite attractive filly: smart performer: won listed race at
Haydock in May by 2½ lengths from Desert Royalty and Lancashire Oaks there in July by
length from Sahool: creditable second after in Vodafone Fillies' Stakes (Lillie Langtry) at
Goodwood (went down by ¾ length to Astrocharm) and Yorkshire Oaks at York (beaten
11 lengths by Quiff): stays 1¾m: acts on firm and good to soft going: game and reliable.
L. M. Cumani

---

*bet365 Lancashire Oaks, Haydock—Pongee makes a successful step up to pattern level, beating Sahool;
the other filly in the photo is New Morning, who weakens to finish fifth*

PON MY SOUL (IRE) 2 b.g. (Mar 22) Imperial Ballet (IRE) 110 – Erin Anam Cara **64**
(IRE) 56 (Exit To Nowhere (USA) 122) [2004 7.5d* 7m⁶ 8g 8.3g⁶ Oct 11] workmanlike
gelding: modest performer: won seller at Beverley in July: creditable efforts in similar
events when sixth after: stays 1m. *M. G. Quinlan*

PONT ALLAIRE (IRE) 3 b.f. Rahy (USA) 115 – Leonila (IRE) 113 (Caerleon (USA) **78**
132) [2004 72p: 8.2s* 10g 8m⁵ Jun 26] leggy filly: fair performer, lightly raced: won
maiden at Nottingham in April: well held after: should stay at least 1¼m: acts on firm and
soft ground: sold 22,000 gns in December. *H. Candy*

PONT NEUF (IRE) 4 b.f. Revoque (IRE) 122 – Petite Maxine 70 (Sharpo 132) [2004 **73**
68: p10g p12g f12s⁴ 11.6f² 12m⁵ 11.6g* 11.6f* 11.6m 11.6g² 12s³ 11.9g 13.9g p12.2g
p12.2d Nov 3] tall, angular filly: fair performer: won seller (left J. Hills) and handicap at
Windsor in July: stays 1½m: acts on fibresand, firm and soft ground: usually tongue tied.
P. D. Evans

POOKA'S DAUGHTER (IRE) 4 b.f. Eagle Eyed (USA) 111 – Gaelic's Fantasy **–**
(IRE) (Statoblest 120) [2004 63d: f8g⁵ 7g f8f p6g 8.5g f7s² p7g f7g Mar 23] poor **a36**
performer: stays 8.5f: acts on fibresand and good to soft going: tried in blinkers/cheek-
pieces: none too consistent. *J. M. Bradley*

POPE'S HILL (IRE) 3 b.c. Sadler's Wells (USA) 132 – Ghost Tree (IRE) 88 (Caer- **77**
leon (USA) 132) [2004 11.9m⁴ 12.1m⁴ 12g⁶ 11.5g³ 16.4m⁴ 16m⁶ Sep 11] €80,000Y:
tall colt: half-brother to several winners, including 4-y-o Drury Lane: dam, 7f winner,
sister to very smart Japanese miler Zenno El Cid: fair maiden: once raced for A. Renzoni
in Italy at 2 yrs: blinkered final start: stayed 2m: acted on good to firm and good to soft
going: dead. *L. M. Cumani*

POPPYFIELDS 2 b.f. (May 16) Danzero (AUS) – Shalverton (IRE) (Shalford (IRE) **–**
124§) [2004 7.1g Aug 30] third foal: dam ran 3 times: last in maiden at Warwick, slowly
away. *M. Blanshard*

POPPYLINE 4 b.f. Averti (IRE) 117 – Shalverton (IRE) (Shalford (IRE) 124§) [2004 **58**
69: p7g 8g 7.9f 8f³ 8m⁶ 8g³ 7m 8f 6g⁶ 6m⁵ Sep 4] close-coupled filly: modest
maiden: stays 1m: acts on polytrack and firm ground: blinkered last 4 starts. *W. R. Muir*

POPPYS FOOTPRINT (IRE) 3 ch.f. Titus Livius (FR) 115 – Mica Male (ITY) **85**
(Law Society (USA) 130) [2004 85: 7g 7g 6d 7.9d⁵ 7m³ 7.5m⁴ 7m 8.1g 8m* 8d Sep 16]
leggy, workmanlike filly: fairly useful handicapper: won at Thirsk in September: stays
1m: yet to race on extremes of going: got upset stall when pulled up amiss eighth outing:
sometimes slowly away/carries head high. *K. A. Ryan*

POP UP AGAIN 4 ch.f. Bahamian Bounty 116 – Bellair (Beveled (USA)) [2004 83+: **69**
7.2f 8m 7s 6m 7.2s p8g p7g⁴ Dec 30] unfurnished filly: just fair nowadays: below form
after reappearance: stays 7f: acts on firm and soft ground: has looked none too keen.
G. A. Swinbank

PORLEZZA (FR) 5 ch.m. Sicyos (USA) 126 – Pupsi (FR) (Matahawk 127) [2004 **117**
117: 5g* 5g² 6g 6.5g Aug 8] strong mare: smart performer: won listed race at Chantilly
in April by neck from Swedish Shave: good ½-length second to Avonbridge in Prix du
Gros-Chene at Chantilly next time (attempting hat-trick in race), then far from discredited
(met trouble) when mid-division in July Cup at Newmarket: well held (reportedly sustained leg fracture) when going for second win in Prix Maurice de Gheest at Deauville
final outing: stayed 6.5f: acted on soft and good to firm going: sometimes reared in stall
and usually put in late: usually raced prominently: stud. *Y. de Nicolay, France*

PORT D'ARGENT (IRE) 2 b.f. (Apr 22) Docksider (USA) 124 – Petite-D-Argent **– p**
91 (Noalto 120) [2004 7.1d Nov 3] half-sister to several winners, including 3-y-o Winged
d'Argent and 7-y-o Mana d'Argent: dam 6f (at 2 yrs), 7f winner: 10/1, tenth in maiden
at Musselburgh, prominent until past halfway: should do better. *M. Johnston*

PORTHCAWL 3 b.f. Singspiel (IRE) 133 – Dodo (IRE) 90 (Alzao (USA) 117) [2004 **89**
–p: 8.1d* 8.1g* 8m Sep 25] fairly useful form, lightly raced: won maiden at Sandown in
August and handicap there (idled) in September: stays 1m: unraced on extremes of going:
found little final start. *Mrs A. J. Perrett*

PORTICHOL PRINCESS 4 b.f. Bluegrass Prince (IRE) 110 – Barbrallen 38 (Rambo **–**
Dancer (CAN) 107) [2004 –: p10g⁶ Mar 9] no form in 4 all-weather maidens: tried tongue
tied. *R. M. Stronge*

PORTMANTEAU 3 b.f. Barathea (IRE) 127 – Dayanata (Shirley Heights 130) [2004 **96**
70p: 8.3s 9.9g* 9g 10f* 10m² Aug 8] good-bodied, close-coupled filly: useful performer,
lightly raced: won maiden at Beverley in May and handicap at Newbury in August: good

second to Credit in handicap at Windsor: will stay 1½m: acts on firm ground. *Sir Michael Stoute*

PORTMEIRION 3 b.f. Polish Precedent (USA) 131 – India Atlanta (Ahonoora 122) **– p**
[2004 8.2d Sep 17] leggy filly: half-sister to several winners, notably smart performer up to 9f Ventiquattrofogli (by Persian Bold): dam unraced half-sister to smart German miler Sinyar: 12/1, signs of ability when tenth in steadily-run maiden at Nottingham, not knocked about: should do better. *E. F. Vaughan*

PORT MORENO (IRE) 4 b.g. Turtle Island (IRE) 123 – Infra Blue (IRE) (Bluebird **–**
(USA) 125) [2004 57, a50: f16g⁵ f12s 17.2g Jul 11] rather sparely-made gelding: modest performer at best: well held in 2004: visored/blinkered: has looked none too keen. *J. G. M. O'Shea*

PORT NATAL (IRE) 6 b.g. Selkirk (USA) 129 – Play Around (IRE) 105 (Niniski **53 d**
(USA) 125) [2004 53: f7g f6g² f8.5s f6s 8d* 8v⁶ 5.8m 6d 8s Oct 26] modest performer nowadays: ran on all-weather in Britain first 4 starts in 2004: won handicap at Thurles in March: no form after: effective at 6f to 1¼m: acts on fibresand, firm and good to soft going: sometimes wears blinkers/cheekpieces (not for wins). *P. Morris, Ireland*

PORT 'N STARBOARD 3 ch.g. Polar Falcon (USA) 126 – Sally Slade 80 (Dowsing **66**
(USA) 124) [2004 11g⁴ 10g⁵ 10g⁴ 11s⁴ p12.2g p10g Oct 13] £4,000Y: fourth foal: half-brother to 3 winners, including 6-y-o Summer Shades and 4-y-o Goldbricker: dam 5f winner, including at 2 yrs: fair maiden: stays 1¼m: tried visored, hung markedly right second/fifth starts. *C. A. Cyzer*

PORTRAIT OF A LADY (IRE) 3 ch.f. Peintre Celebre (USA) 137 – Starlight **95**
Smile (USA) (Green Dancer (USA) 132) [2004 69: 12s³ 12m* 12.1g³ 12m* 11.8m* 12g³ 14m⁶ Jul 31] neat filly: useful performer: won maiden at Thirsk in May and handicaps at Newbury in June and Leicester in July: good 5 lengths third to Beneventa in listed race at Newmarket penultimate start: tailed off in Lillie Langtry Stakes at Goodwood final outing: stays 1½m: acts on soft and good to firm going: sold 72,000 gns in November. *H. R. A. Cecil*

PORTRAYAL (USA) 2 b.f. (Mar 11) Saint Ballado (CAN) – True Glory (IRE) 84 (In **105**
The Wings 128) [2004 6d³ 6d* 5.5g³ 7v⁴ 8g² 8m⁵ Oct 3] big, lengthy filly: has plenty of scope: fourth foal: dam, 11f winner, closely related to high-class smart Wareed and half-sister to smart middle-distance performers Jaydoom and Truly A Dream: useful performer: won minor event at Chantilly in July: good efforts after when keeping-on 1¾ lengths third to Divine Proportions in Prix Robert Papin at Maisons-Laffitte, 1½ lengths second to Birthstone in Prix d'Aumale at Chantilly and 2¾ lengths fifth behind Divine Proportions in Prix Marcel Boussac at Longchamp: should stay 1½m: below form on heavy going: joined Godolphin. *A. Fabre, France*

PORT SODRICK 3 b. or br.g. Young Ern 120 – Keepsake (IRE) 58 (Distinctly North **61**
(USA) 115) [2004 p8g⁶ 8.2g⁶ p10d⁴ 10.1g⁵ 10m 12.6d 17.2s² f16s³ p16g Nov 30] sturdy gelding: first foal: dam 1½m winner: modest maiden: left M. Usher after seventh start: seems to stay 17f: acts on all-weather and soft going: sometimes slowly away. *C. L. Tizzard*

PORT ST CHARLES (IRE) 7 b. or br.g. Night Shift (USA) – Safe Haven (Blakeney **69 d**
126) [2004 83: f6g⁵ f6g f6g f6s f8.5g⁴ 5.7g⁴ 6s 6g 5.3f⁴ 5g³ 5m 5m 5g 6m⁴ 5m 5.3f⁶ 5d **a83 d**
f6g² 6.1g p6g² f6g* p7m Dec 21] tall gelding: fairly useful handicapper, below best after reappearance: trained by C. Dore ninth to eighteenth start before rejoining former trainer: dead heated at Southwell in December: effective at 5f to easy 7f: acts on all-weather and any turf going: tried blinkered: free-going sort: sometimes starts slowly/looks wayward: none too consistent. *P. R. Chamings*

POSH NOSH (IRE) 3 b.f. Alzao (USA) 117 – Frenzy (Zafonic (USA) 130) [2004 **–**
10m 10g 8d 10m f8g Nov 8] IR 7,500F: first foal: dam unraced half-sister to Fillies' Mile winner/Oaks runner-up Shamshir: no form, including at Southwell final outing. *Patrick Martin, Ireland*

POSH SHEELAGH 3 b.f. Danzero (AUS) – Button Hole Flower (IRE) (Fairy King **–**
(USA)) [2004 –: f7g Jan 12] well beaten in seller at Southwell (slowly away) and maiden at Wolverhampton. *J. G. Given*

POSTERITAS (USA) 3 b.f. Lear Fan (USA) 130 – Imroz (USA) 99 (Nureyev (USA) **91**
131) [2004 8g³ 8m² 10m* 10g⁵ 10.1s* 10.3m⁶ 12g Sep 20] smallish, attractive filly: second foal: half-sister to 2002 2-y-o 7f winner Apex Star (by Diesis): dam, 6f (at 2 yrs)/7f winner, out of Prix du Moulin/Musidora Stakes winner and Oaks runner-up All At Sea: fairly useful performer: won maiden at Pontefract in June and listed rated stakes at

Yarmouth (by length from La Persiana) in August: well below form final outing: stayed 10.3f: acted on soft and good to firm going: stud. *H. R. A. Cecil*

POSTGRADUATE (IRE) 2 b.c. (Apr 11) Almutawakel 126 – Institutrice (IRE) 87 **83 p** (College Chapel 122) [2004 p7m⁵ p6g* Oct 25] €76,000F, €50,000Y: second foal: half-brother to 3-y-o Bella Tutrice: dam, Irish maiden who seemed to stay 1¼m, half-sister to useful Irish performer up to 1½m Cheviot Amble: confirmed promise when winning minor event at Lingfield by ¾ length from Excusez Moi, leading close home: should stay 7f, probably 1m: will progress. *H. Morrison*

POTENT HEIR (USA) 2 b.c. (Feb 20) Forest Wildcat (USA) 120 – Penniless Heiress **90 p** (USA) (Pentelicus (USA)) [2004 6g* Sep 6] $475,000Y: fifth foal: brother to 3 winners, including US 2001 Grade 3 2-y-o 6f winner Forest Heiress and US Grade 1 6f winner Wildcat Heir: dam, minor winner in USA, half-sister to US Grade 2 winners Meritocrat (6f) and On To Royalty (8.5f): favourite, won maiden at Newcastle by length from Crosspeace, green but quickening well: should stay 7f: useful prospect. *Saeed bin Suroor*

POTSDAM 6 ch.g. Rainbow Quest (USA) 134 – Danilova (FR) 89 (Lyphard (USA) **55** 132) [2004 53: f8.5g f7g² 8v 7f⁴ 8m* 7f Jun 8] modest performer: won handicap at Tralee in June: pulled up lame 2 days later: bred to stay further than 9f, but races freely: acts on fibresand (ran creditably at Wolverhampton first 2 starts) and any turf going: tongue tied. *Niall Moran, Ireland*

POUILLY FUME 3 b.f. Polish Precedent (USA) 131 – Feather Bride (IRE) (Groom **–** Dancer (USA) 128) [2004 10s May 10] 8,000F, 11,000Y: fifth foal: half-sister to several winners, including smart 7f (including at 2 yrs)/US Grade 3 1m winner Millennium Dragon (by Mark of Esteem) and fairly useful 1¼m winner Bless The Bride (by Darshaan): dam French 10.5f winner: 50/1, slowly away and always behind in maiden at Windsor. *D. J. S. ffrench Davis*

POULE DE LUXE (IRE) 3 b.f. Cadeaux Genereux 131 – Likely Story (IRE) 94 **75** (Night Shift (USA)) [2004 60: 7g* 7s Sep 14] close-coupled filly: fair performer, lightly raced: won maiden at Kempton in April: should stay at least 1m: sold 52,000 gns. *J. L. Dunlop*

POWER AND DEMAND 7 b.g. Formidable (USA) 125 – Mazurkanova 63 (Song **–** 132) [2004 f8.5m⁴ f7g Apr 22] maiden handicapper: well held both starts on Flat since 2001: used to be blinkered: tried tongue tied. *K. G. Wingrove*

POWER BIRD (IRE) 4 b.f. Bluebird (USA) 125 – Polynesian Goddess (IRE) **55** (Salmon Leap (USA) 131) [2004 88d: p7g² p7g p8g 7m f7d 6f⁵ 8.1m Jul 2] modest maiden: left D. Flood after reappearance: stayed 1m: acted on polytrack and good to soft going: tried blinkered/visored: joined R. Flint: dead. *B. R. Johnson*

POWERFUL PARRISH (USA) 3 b.f. Quiet American (USA) – Parish Business **72** (USA) (Phone Trick (USA)) [2004 92: 8m 8.1m² 10.2f⁴ 10m 10f 11.7f Sep 6] tall, leggy filly: fair maiden: should stay 1¼m: raced only on good ground or firmer: tried tongue tied. *P. F. I. Cole*

POWER NAP 3 b.f. Acatenango (GER) 127 – Dreams Are Free (IRE) 71 (Caerleon **–** (USA) 132) [2004 –: 10.3d⁶ 7g 12m 10m 7g Sep 20] little sign of ability: tried visored/blinkered/tongue tied. *N. Tinkler*

POWERSCOURT 4 b.c. Sadler's Wells (USA) 132 – Rainbow Lake 113 (Rain- **124** bow Quest (USA) 134) [2004 122: 10.5m* 10f² 10d⁵ 10m² 10f⁴ 10m³ 12d³ 12f 10m⁴ Dec 12]

'Don't worry son, the shirt will carry you round the pitch.' A first full season in silks for Jamie Spencer as stable jockey to Aidan O'Brien proved less straightforward than legendary football manager Bill Shankly made things sound for nervous young players stepping out in the red of Liverpool in the 'sixties and 'seventies. In a torrid season for Spencer at Ballydoyle, adding a first jockeys' championship in Ireland to the apprentice title he won there in 1999, before coming to Britain, went virtually unnoticed in the face of the criticism which came his way after some high profile reverses and a string of riding bans. He resigned in the winter and looks set to continue his career in Britain. Nowadays, the leading stables campaign worldwide and Spencer, whose stable drew a blank in the classics in Britain, Ireland and France, suffered a particularly trying time in America on Powerscourt, losing the Arlington Million at Chicago in August in the stewards' room and being heavily criticised for his tactics when third on him in the Breeders' Cup Turf at Lone Star Park in November.

Successful in the Great Voltigeur Stakes at York and third in the Irish St Leger at the Curragh on his last two starts as a three-year-old, Powerscourt began his season at four with a win at home in the Group 1 Tattersalls Gold Cup at the Curragh in May, following in the footsteps of his stable's Black Sam Bellamy twelve months earlier. Under an enterprising ride, Powerscourt coped well with the mile and a quarter at the Curragh, making all to win by six lengths from Livadiya, albeit left with little to beat, odds-on Nysaean a below-par third in an already weak-looking field of six. Powerscourt ran next in the Prince of Wales's Stakes at Royal Ascot. Somewhat surprisingly ridden with restraint, he ran very well all the same, particularly so in a race in which the early pace was fairly steady, staying on strongly to go down by two lengths to Rakti. Powerscourt ran only respectably in two more runs before the Arlington Million, beaten over four lengths when fifth behind Refuse To Bend in the Coral-Eclipse at Sandown in July and a length and a half when second at odds on to the home-trained three-year-old Intendant when front-running tactics were used again in the Grosser Dallmayr-Preis at Munich in August. Powerscourt idled at Munich and was tried in headgear for the first time at Arlington later in the month. Worth over £300,000 to the winner, and celebrating its twenty-second running, the Arlington Million drew a handful of very smart older horses in a field of thirteen, Powerscourt starting second favourite at 46/10 behind the German-trained Epalo, winner of the Singapore Airlines International at Kranji in May. Wearing a visor, Powerscourt missed the break, but was still travelling strongly as he improved wide on the turn. Early in the straight, he swept to the front but hung left with Spencer riding vigorously with his whip in his right hand. Although Powerscourt seemed barely to touch Epalo on his inside, the favourite also hung left, cannoning into the home-trained Kicken Kris against the rail. As Spencer belatedly pulled his whip through once he was clear, Powerscourt held Kicken Kris by a length and a half. Powerscourt looked the winner on merit, and would almost certainly have kept the race had it been run in Britain, but the local stewards demoted him. After an objection by Kicken Kris's rider, Kent Desormeaux, who had remonstrated wildly with Spencer as the runners pulled up, Powerscourt was put back to fourth, a place behind Epalo. When asked how he was feeling as he waited for the stewards' decision, Spencer had reportedly told the Press, 'If he loses it, I'll cry.'

Tattersalls Gold Cup, the Curragh—Powerscourt makes a sparkling return;
Livadiya (right) is second ahead of Nysaean, Napper Tandy (left) and Naheef (partially hidden)

Arlington Million Stakes—Powerscourt wins on merit but is demoted to fourth for causing interference inside the final furlong; runner-up Kicken Kris, whose rider lambasts Spencer, is the main beneficiary of the stewards' decision

At twenty-four, Spencer is far younger and less experienced than the man he replaced at Ballydoyle, Michael Kinane, especially in the big arenas, and he thanked his employers publicly for their sympathetic viewing of events at Arlington. Powerscourt had only one more run before being returned to America for the Breeders' Cup, reportedly pulling a muscle when finishing a good third to Azamour and Norse Dancer in the Irish Champion Stakes at Leopardstown in September. Powerscourt was blinkered when going down only by half a length and a neck, despite hanging left after going clear briefly off the turn. After missing the Arc, Powerscourt started second favourite at Lone Star Park behind the home-trained Kitten's Joy, winner of the Joe Hirsch Turf Classic at Belmont the time before. With the pace steady, Powerscourt was rushed up to take the lead towards the end of the back straight, Spencer clearly sensing the chance to steal the race. Clear briefly into the straight, Powerscourt had nothing to give when tackled, again edging left as he went down by a length and three quarters and a length to the rank outsider Better Talk Now and the odds-on Kitten's Joy. The manner of Spencer's fifth defeat on the card, which had earlier included a narrow one on the frustrating Antonius Pius in the Mile, brought many of the season's problems home to roost, including with some members of the American press. In his review of the Breeders' Cup meeting, Steven Crist in the *Daily Racing Form* wrote 'Spencer looked like an Aqueduct winter apprentice on a bad day' and 'Spencer's on-going clueless riding in America.' After the Breeders' Cup, Spencer spent time in New York, reportedly at the suggestion of his employers, riding track work under the gaze of trainer Todd Pletcher and the legendary Angel Cordero Jnr, spending up to five hours a day with Cordero, watching races and talking about riding and tactics. Spencer had two opportunities to put what he had learned to use on Powerscourt. Drawn wide, the partnership could never mount a challenge in the Japan Cup at Tokyo in November, finishing tenth. Powerscourt ran much better in the Hong Kong Cup at Sha Tin in December, though he was unable to make the most of an inside draw and had to be switched wide on the turn before finishing strongly, despite meeting trouble back inside, beaten only two lengths behind Alexander Goldrun in fourth.

Powerscourt (b.c. 2000)	Sadler's Wells (USA) (b 1981)	Northern Dancer (b 1961)	Nearctic
			Natalma
		Fairy Bridge (b 1975)	Bold Reason
			Special
	Rainbow Lake (b 1990)	Rainbow Quest (b 1981)	Blushing Groom
			I Will Follow
		Rockfest (ch 1979)	Stage Door Johnny
			Rock Garden

Powerscourt's stable-companion 2003 St Leger winner Brian Boru, whom he pipped in the Voltigeur, has been retired to stud as a National Hunt stallion, but Powerscourt stays in training. Powerscourt's pedigree was covered in last year's annual, but an important update is that his three-year-old half-sister Kind (by Danehill) progressed markedly into a useful performer, winning her last five starts and looking capable of better still. Contrary to expectations, she proved best kept to sprinting. Effective at a mile and a quarter to a mile and three quarters, Powerscourt has won on soft going, but his very best efforts have come on firmer than good. Visored or blinkered for his last five starts, he has worn a crossed noseband and sweated slightly/swished his tail in the paddock. A medium-sized, good-topped colt, who did well from three to four, Powerscourt took the eye more than once with his exceptional condition in 2004. Undoubtedly very smart, his consistency is hard to fault, though at times he looked less straightforward at four than at three, slow

Mrs John Magnier's "Powerscourt"

starts becoming one trait, and he certainly proved somewhat frustrating, particularly for his rider, who will be hoping he enjoys a less troubled season—though he won't be riding Powerscourt in 2005. *A. P. O'Brien, Ireland*

POWER TO BURN   3 b.g. Superpower 113 – Into The Fire 74 (Dominion 123) [2004 **50** 56: f6g³ f6s⁵ 6d 6.1d p6g Dec 17] modest maiden: stays 6f: acts on fibresand and good to firm ground: tried tongue tied/visored/in cheekpieces. *K. Bell*

PRAGMATICA   3 b.f. Inchinor 119 – Isabella Gonzaga 75 (Rock Hopper 124) [2004 **51** f8g⁴ f8g⁵ p8.6g³ Dec 27] first foal: dam 1¼m/1½m winner: modest form in maidens at Southwell (2) and Wolverhampton. *R. M. H. Cowell*

PRAGUE   6 b.g. Cyrano de Bergerac 120 – Basenite (Mansingh (USA) 120) [2004 p10g **–** Jan 17] lightly-raced maiden: has been slowly away. *J. R. Boyle*

PRAIRIE FALCON (IRE)   10 b.g. Alzao (USA) 117 – Sea Harrier (Grundy 137) **91** [2004 94: 12g³ 12m 16.2d 14.8m Jun 19] attractive gelding: good mover: fairly useful handicapper, winner of 9 races: below form in 2004 after reappearance: broke hind leg in June: stayed 2¼m: acted on firm and soft going: was effective racing prominently or held up: dead. *B. W. Hills*

PRAIRIE LAW (GER)   4 b.g. Law Society (USA) 130 – Prairie Charm (IRE) (Thatching 131) [2004 a11.5g² a9.5g a11.5g 10g⁶ 9.7m⁴ 10d³ 16.2m 12g Sep 14] won maiden at **48** Neuss in January: left M. Hofer in Germany after third start: poor form in Britain: stays 12.5f: acts on sand, good to firm and good to soft going: blinkered in Germany. *Ian Williams*

PRAIRIE OYSTER   3 b.f. Emperor Jones (USA) 119 – Soba Up 74 (Persian Heights **–** 129) [2004 9g May 20] strong, close-coupled filly: fourth foal: half-sister to useful 1½m/1¾m winner Saint Alebe (by Bishop of Cashel): dam, 1¼m/1½m winner, out of high-class sprinter Soba: 16/1 and backward, well held in maiden at Goodwood. *D. R. C. Elsworth*

PRAIRIE SUN (GER)   3 b.f. Law Society (USA) 130 – Prairie Flame (IRE) 85 (Marju **60** (IRE) 127) [2004 55: f12g⁴ 12.1d⁴ 14.6g⁵ 12.1g⁴ 12.4g f12d 9.9g 12m⁶ 12m 13.8m⁶ 13.8g³ Sep 7] quite good-topped filly: modest handicapper: won at Beverley in May: stays 13.8f: acts on good to firm and good to soft ground, well held on fibresand: tried visored/in cheekpieces: won over hurdles in December. *Mrs A. Duffield*

PRAIRIE WOLF   8 ch.g. Wolfhound (USA) 126 – Bay Queen 85 (Damister (USA) **82** 123) [2004 93: 10.1s 10.3g 10m 10m 10g⁵ 9.9g* 9.9g 9.9g 10.1m 10s Oct 15] big, strong gelding: useful performer at best, winner of 7 races, including minor event at Beverley in July: stayed 11f: acted on fibresand, firm and good to soft going (below form on soft/heavy): often sweated up: usually raced prominently: reportedly retired to British Racing School, Newmarket. *M. L. W. Bell*

PRAKARA (IRE)   2 ch.f. (Feb 16) Indian Ridge 123 – Prima Volta 80 (Primo Dominie **– p** 121) [2004 p6g p6g Nov 27] heavy-bodied filly: fourth foal: half-sister to useful 5f (at 2 yrs) to 1m winner Bouncing Bowdler (by Mujadil): dam 6f (at 2 yrs) and 9f winner: green and not knocked about in maidens: likely to do better. *L. M. Cumani*

PRALIN STAR (IRE)   2 ch.g. (Apr 24) Daggers Drawn (USA) 114 – Polaregina (FR) **45** (Rex Magna (FR) 129) [2004 7m 7s⁴ 8m p7.1g Nov 26] poor maiden: form only at 7f on soft going: in cheekpieces final start. *Mrs H. Sweeting*

PRAYERFUL   5 b.m. Syrtos 106 – Pure Formality 84 (Forzando 122) [2004 –: 10.9g⁵ **40** Apr 23] workmanlike mare: poor maiden: stays 11f: acts on good to soft going, well beaten only run on fibresand: winning hurdler. *B. N. Doran*

PRECIOUS FREEDOM   4 b.g. Ashkalani (IRE) 128 – Prayers'n Promises (USA) **?** (Foolish Pleasure (USA)) [2004 60, a–: f6g f6g f5g 6.5g² 7g⁴ 8.3g³ 7.8g⁴ 6.5f* 5.8g 6.5m⁵ 6.5g 7m Sep 18] sturdy gelding: modest performer: sold from J. Balding after third start: won handicap at Odense in July: best around 6f: acts on firm and soft ground: wore headgear last 10 starts in Britain. *Pia Lillelund, Denmark*

PRECIOUS MYSTERY (IRE)   4 ch.f. Titus Livius (FR) 115 – Ascoli (Skyliner **71** 117) [2004 65: 11.6m⁴ 11.9s² p12m 11.9s* 13.8s⁶ p12g² Nov 16] fair handicapper: won at Brighton in October: should stay at least 1¾m: acts on polytrack, soft and good to firm going. *A. King*

PRECIOUS SAMMI   2 b.g. (Apr 8) Mark of Esteem (IRE) 137 – Night Over Day 57 **65** (Most Welcome 131) [2004 7g p7m⁵ 8d p7g p7m² p6g Dec 10] 1,700Y: third foal: half-brother to fairly useful Italian 1m/1¼m winner Mrs Seek (by Unfuwain): dam, Irish maiden, stayed 9f: fair maiden: best effort when second at Lingfield, making running: stays 7f: wore cheekpieces last 2 starts. *Julian Poulton*

PRE EMINANCE (IRE)　3 b.c. Peintre Celebre (USA) 137 – Sorb Apple (IRE) 79　**64**
(Kris 135) [2004 7p8: 8m⁶ May 29] useful-looking colt: fair form in maidens at New-
market (better effort) and Kempton 7 months apart: bred to be suited by 1¼m/1½m.
C. R. Egerton

PREGNANT PAUSE (IRE)　3 b.g. General Monash (USA) 107 – Dissidentia (IRE)　**56**
(Dancing Dissident (USA) 119) [2004 70: p5g⁴ p7g 8f⁴ 8m⁵ 8f⁴ p9.5g p8.6g Dec 27]
smallish, good-topped gelding: has a quick action: modest maiden: likely to prove best at
6f/7f: acts on polytrack and firm ground. *S. Kirk*

PRELUDE　3 b.f. Danzero (AUS) – Dancing Debut 83 (Polar Falcon (USA) 126) [2004　**65**
7d⁵ 8g 8.1m 10.3g⁶ 12m⁶ 10.9g⁶ 10d* 12.1m⁵ 12g Oct 5] 2,600 2-y-o: good-topped filly:
fourth foal: half-sister to 4-y-o Kindlelight Debut: dam, maiden who stayed 1¼m well,
out of half-sister to 2000 Guineas winner Entrepreneur: fair handicapper: won at Ripon
in August: effective at 1¼m/1½m: yet to race on extremes of going: carries head awkwardly, and has found little. *W. M. Brisbourne*

PREMIER DREAM (USA)　3 ch.c. Woodman (USA) 126 – Marina Duff (Caerleon　**71**
(USA) 132) [2004 8.1s⁶ 8g⁶ 8.5s³ 8.1v* 8m 8g⁴ 8.1s 10.2m Sep 9] sturdy colt: brother to
winner in Italy and half-brother to 3 winners, including useful Italian/US performer up to
1½m Sopran Mariduff (by Persian Bold): dam Italian 6f and 1m (including Group 3 event
at 2 yrs) winner: fair handicapper: won at Warwick in May: left M. Johnston after sixth
start, ran as if amiss subsequently: stays 8.5f: acts on heavy going. *J. G. M. O'Shea*

PREMIER FANTASY　2 b.c. (Feb 19) Pivotal 124 – Hemaca (Distinctly North (USA)　**93 p**
115) [2004 6d⁶ 5g* Sep 23] 60,000Y: quite good-topped colt: first foal: dam unraced out of
half-sister to smart performer up to 1m Kahir Almaydan: confirmed promise when
winning maiden at Haydock comfortably by 1¼ lengths from Juantorena, leading 1f out
and drifting left: should stay at least 6f: useful prospect, and should win more races as
3-y-o. *T. D. Barron*

PREMIER ROUGE　3 b.g. Croco Rouge (IRE) 126 – Petit Point (IRE) 78 (Petorius　**75**
117) [2004 7.5d⁴ 8.1g⁴ 9.9d³ 8d² 8.1s³ 8g Oct 10] 90,000Y: strong, short-backed gelding:
third foal: half-brother to 5-y-o Seel of Approval: dam, 6f winner, half-sister to dam of
very smart 1½m performer Kutub: fair maiden: trained by A. Stewart first 2 starts: bred
to stay further than 1m. *E. F. Vaughan*

PREMIER TIMES　2 ch.g. (Apr 14) Timeless Times (USA) 99 – Lady Magician (Lord　**55 d**
Bud 121) [2004 5g⁵ 6d* 7.1f⁶ 6m 7s f7g p8.6g Dec 11] modest performer: won seller at
Ripon in July: well held after: stays 6f: acts on good to soft going. *M. D. Hammond*

PRENUP (IRE)　3 ch.f. Diesis 133 – Mutual Consent (IRE) 107 (Reference Point 139)　**81**
[2004 60p: 11.6s⁴ 10f* 12.1d* 12m² 11d² 12g 12m⁶ Sep 4] lengthy, quite good-topped
filly: fairly useful handicapper: won at Brighton in May and Beverley in June: stays 1½m:
acts on polytrack, firm and soft going: races freely (found little penultimate start), often
up with pace. *L. M. Cumani*

PRESENT 'N CORRECT　11 ch.g. Cadeaux Genereux 131 – Emerald Eagle 78　**–**
(Sandy Creek 123) [2004 42, a–: f7g f7g f6s Feb 2] workmanlike gelding: well held in
2004: sometimes blinkered/in cheekpieces. *J. M. Bradley*

PRESENT ORIENTED (USA)　3 ch.g. Southern Halo (USA) – Shy Beauty (CAN)　**75**
(Great Gladiator (USA)) [2004 86: 10g⁵ 10.2g Jun 3] strong, close-coupled gelding: has
a fluent, round action: lightly-raced maiden, disappointing in 2004: needs to settle to stay
beyond 1m: sold 3,000 gns in October, and gelded. *H. R. A. Cecil*

PRESKANI　2 b.g. (Mar 15) Sri Pekan (USA) 117 – Lamarita 92§ (Emarati (USA) 74)　**39**
[2004 7m f5g 6.1d p6g Oct 2] poor form in maidens: in cheekpieces final start.
Mrs N. Macauley

PRESS EXPRESS (IRE)　2 ch.c. (Mar 11) Entrepreneur 123 – Nawaji (USA) 45　**76**
(Trempolino (USA) 135) [2004 7d 7d⁶ 7.1m** 8g 6d 7s Oct 23] strong colt: fourth foal:
dam, maiden who stayed 13f, sister to smart 9f to 1½m performer Triarius: fair performer:
won maiden at Chepstow in September: creditable effort in nurseries after on next start
only: stays 1m: acts on good to firm and good to soft ground: edgy, free-going sort.
M. R. Channon

PRESTON HALL　3 b.g. Accordion – Little Preston (IRE) 53 (Pennine Walk 120)　**51**
[2004 p10g p10g 7g⁶ 9.7m⁵ 12g Aug 13] modest maiden: stays easy 1¼m. *Mrs
L. C. Jewell*

PRESTO SHINKO (IRE)　3 b. or br.g. Shinko Forest (IRE) – Swift Chorus (Music　**90**
Boy 124) [2004 75: p6g⁶ 6.1d⁶ 6s³ 6.1g² 6g* 6f³ 6g⁴ 6g Sep 29] tall gelding: fairly useful

performer: won maiden at Lingfield in March and handicap at Goodwood in June: should prove as effective at 5f as 6f: acts on polytrack, firm and soft going. *R. Hannon*

PRESTO VENTO 4 b.f. Air Express (IRE) 125 – Placement (Kris 135) [2004 99: 6m – 7s May 8] close-coupled filly: fluent mover: useful performer at 2/3 yrs: well held in 2004. *R. Hannon*

PRESUMPTIVE (IRE) 4 b.g. Danehill (USA) 126 – Demure (Machiavellian (USA) **89** 123) [2004 84: 7s⁵ 8d³ 8m 7.1d* 7.2s 7g Oct 9] leggy, useful-looking gelding: fairly useful performer, lightly raced: won handicap at Sandown in August: effective at 7f/1m: acts on good to soft going: blinkered (seemed to take little interest) penultimate start: sold 21,000 gns, and gelded. *R. Charlton*

PRETTY FLAMINGO (IRE) 4 ch.f. Lycius (USA) 124 – Scribbling (USA) 88 **53** (Secretariat (USA)) [2004 –: 8v⁴ 10g⁵ 16v 12.5d p13.9g³ Nov 29] fourth reported living foal: dam 1¼m winner: modest maiden: ran creditably in minor event at Wolverhampton final start: stays 1¾m: acts on polytrack and heavy going. *T. Cooper, Ireland*

PRETTY KOOL 4 b.f. Inchinor 119 – Carrie Kool 69 (Prince Sabo 123) [2004 –: **56** 8.2g 6m⁵ p7g³ 6g* 7.1g 6g Sep 16] good-topped filly: modest handicapper: won at Folkestone in August: stays 7f: acts on polytrack, yet to race on extremes of going on turf. *S. C. Williams*

PRETTY STAR (GER) 4 b.c. Lando (GER) 128 – Pretty Ballerina (Sadler's Wells **96** (USA) 132) [2004 12g 12d² 11.9d Aug 17] half-brother to several winners abroad, including useful German/French 1¼m/1½m performer Pretty Fighter (by Kornado): dam, Irish maiden who stayed 1½m, out of half-sister to very smart middle-distance filly Dubian: useful performer: won maiden at Dresden, handicap at Hoppegarten and listed race at Dresden in 2003: left E. Groschel in Germany after reappearance: easily better effort in Britain within 3 days when second in handicap at Pontefract: stays 1½m: acts on good to soft going: usually blinkered in Germany: joined A. King. *M. Johnston*

PRETTY WOMAN (IRE) 2 ch.f. (May 13) Night Shift (USA) – Kind of Cute 52 **45** (Prince Sabo 123) [2004 5m 5m p5g p5.1g Nov 27] sixth foal: half-sister to useful French 1¼m/11f winner Abou Safian (by Bluebird) and 6-y-o Travelling Band: dam, third at 6f at 2 yrs (only season to race), sister to Mill Reef Stakes winner Princely Hush: poor maiden. *S. C. Williams*

PRIDE (FR) 4 b.f. Peintre Celebre (USA) 137 – Specificity (USA) 103 (Alleged (USA) **117** 138) [2004 96?: 10g⁴ 10d* 10.5g³ 12d⁵ 10s² 12d³ 12m 12s* Oct 17] leggy, sparely-made filly: smart performer: trained by G. Butler at 3 yrs: much improved to win Prix Allez France at Chantilly (by 1½ lengths from Russian Hill) in May and won Prix du Conseil de Paris at Longchamp (quickened clear in good style to beat Simplex 5 lengths) in October: best efforts in between on fifth/sixth starts when 2 lengths second to Whortleberry in Prix Jean Romanet at Deauville and unlucky length third (hampered, then finished well) to Sweet Stream in Prix Vermeille at Longchamp: effective at 1¼m/1½m: acts on soft going, probably on good to firm, below form on polytrack: held up: consistent. *A. de Royer Dupre, France*

PRIDE OF KINLOCH 4 ch.f. Dr Devious (IRE) 127 – Stormswept (USA) 74 (Storm **65 §** Bird (CAN) 134) [2004 80, a–: f6g f7g⁶ 7s 8d⁴ 8.1v 7m³ 7m 6m 6g 6d³ 6m² 6m⁶ 6f 8.2v **a46 §** f7g Dec 1] strong filly: unreliable maiden: effective at 6f to 1m: acts on good to firm and good to soft going, has shown little on fibresand: sometimes slowly away: has looked reluctant: one to treat with caution. *J. Hetherton*

PRIDE OF LONDON (IRE) 2 b.f. (Jan 28) Danetime (IRE) 121 – Kavana (IRE) **52** (Marju (IRE) 127) [2004 6.1s 7m 7d Aug 12] €5,000Y: compact filly: second foal: dam unraced half-sister to 5-y-o Camp Commander: form in maidens only when eighth at Yarmouth second start: needs to settle to stay beyond 7f. *I. A. Wood*

PRIDE OF POONA (IRE) 2 b.f. (May 2) Indian Ridge 123 – Scandalous (Warning **43** 136) [2004 p6g p7g p7g f7g Nov 22] €21,000Y, 28,000 2-y-o: second foal: dam unraced sister to Cheveley Park Stakes winner Prophecy out of Lancashire Oaks winner Andaleeb: poor maiden: visored final start. *R. M. H. Cowell*

PRIDEWOOD DOVE 5 b.m. Alderbrook 120 – Flighty Dove (Cruise Missile) – [2004 10.2s 18m Jun 27] second foal: dam ran once in bumpers: temperamental hurdler: has shown nothing in maidens on Flat (pulled up final start). *R. J. Price*

PRIDEYEV (USA) 4 ch.g. Nureyev (USA) 131 – Pride of Baino (USA) (Secretariat – (USA)) [2004 56: f16.2s Mar 5] good-topped gelding: lightly-raced maiden: well held only outing in 2004. *B. J. Llewellyn*

PRIMARILY   2 b.c. (Feb 12) Mind Games 121 – Prim N Proper (Tragic Role (USA)) **64**
[2004 5m 6s⁵ 6d² 7s³ p6g⁶ Nov 8] quite good-topped colt: modest maiden: stays 7f: acts
on soft ground. *A. Berry*

PRIMA STELLA   5 br. or gr.m. Primo Dominie 121 – Raffelina (USA) (Carson City   **?**
(USA)) [2004 74: f6g⁴ f6g* p7g f7g² f6s⁶ p7g⁶ p6g 6m 6f Jul 5] leggy mare: fairly useful   **a85**
handicapper on all-weather: won at Southwell in January: free-going sort, but stays easy
7f: acts on all-weather, lightly raced and little form on turf since 2002: sometimes slowly
away. *J. A. R. Toller*

PRIMATECH (IRE)   3 b.f. Priolo (USA) 127 – Ida Lupino (IRE) (Statoblest 120)   **44**
[2004 5m 7g 7m 7f 9g 7.1s 7.9m⁴ 8.1d 7d³ p7m p6g7m⁴ Dec 20] €1,400Y: second foal:
half-sister to 5f winner in Italy (including at 2 yrs) by Marju: dam soundly beaten: poor
maiden: left Michael Cunningham in Ireland after sixth start: stays 1m: wore cheek-
pieces/visor last 5 starts. *K. A. Morgan*

PRIME CONTENDER   2 b.c. (Apr 21) Efisio 120 – Gecko Rouge (Rousillon (USA)   **72 p**
133) [2004 6s 6s⁵ Nov 6] 7,500F, €30,000Y: tall, good-topped colt: has scope: third foal:
dam, seemed of little account, out of half-sister to high-class stayer Sea Anchor: better
effort in maidens when fifth to Bow Wave at Doncaster, slowly away: likely to stay at
least 1m: should do better. *B. W. Hills*

PRIMED UP (IRE)   2 b.g. (Feb 25) Rainbow Quest (USA) 134 – Cape Mist (USA)   **–**
(Lure (USA) 131) [2004 7m Jul 30] €110,000F, 18,000Y: tall gelding: first foal: dam
unraced out of half-sister to very smart 1¼m/1½m performer Infamy: 50/1 and backward,
last in maiden at Goodwood. *G. L. Moore*

PRIME OFFER   8 b.g. Primo Dominie 121 – Single Bid 68 (Auction Ring (USA)   **73**
123) [2004 f7g p8g² p8g⁴ 8f* 7f² 8m* 8d⁵ 8f⁴ 7s² 8m Oct 2] useful-looking gelding: fair   **a66**
handicapper: trained in Spain in 2003: won at Yarmouth and Newmarket (apprentices) in
June: stays 1m: acts on all-weather, soft and firm going: tried blinkered in 2002: usually
races prominently. *J. Jay*

PRIME POWERED (IRE)   3 b.g. Barathea (IRE) 127 – Caribbean Quest 90 (Rain-   **93 §**
bow Quest (USA) 134) [2004 90: 10g⁵ 10.1m⁵ 12g 9.9g² 10.1g 11g⁴ 10v p12g Nov 20]
close-coupled gelding: has a round action: fairly useful handicapper: barely stays 1½m:
acts on good to firm and good to soft going: tried in cheekpieces/blinkers: has hung left all
4 runs at Epsom: looked reluctant to race last 3 outings, and needs treating with caution.
G. L. Moore

PRIME RECREATION   7 b.g. Primo Dominie 121 – Night Transaction 59 (Tina's   **78 §**
Pet 121) [2004 78: f5s⁶ f5g f5g⁶ f5s 5s 5d 5.1d³ 5g 5g 5g⁴ 5.1g 5d 5.2d* 5.2g 5s³ Nov 1]
strong, rangy gelding: fair performer: won handicap at Yarmouth in August: best at 5f:
acts on fibresand, heavy and good to firm going: tried in cheekpieces: sometimes slowly
away/finds little: hung markedly right penultimate outing: probably best when able to
lead: unreliable. *P. S. Felgate*

PRIMESHADE PROMISE   3 ch.f. Opening Verse (USA) 126 – Bonnie Lassie 74   **54**
(Efisio 120) [2004 8.3f 10f 7.1m³ 8.1s 8g Oct 12] second foal: half-sister to 2001 2-y-o 5f
winner Michaels Girl (by Bluebird), later successful in Spain: dam 2-y-o 1m winner:
modest maiden: best effort at 7f on good to firm going. *D. Burchell*

PRIMO WAY   3 b.c. Primo Dominie 121 – Waypoint 95 (Cadeaux Genereux 131)   **92**
[2004 77: 6s* 6g³ 6.1g⁶ 7m³ 7m 7d³ 7g p7.1g Oct 18] tall, rather unfurnished colt: fairly
useful maiden: won maiden at Southwell in April: stays 7f: acts on firm and good to soft going:
wore cheekpieces final start: sometimes slowly away. *B. W. Hills*

PRIMUS INTER PARES (IRE)   3 b.g. Sadler's Wells (USA) 132 – Life At The   **105**
Top 107 (Habitat 134) [2004 98p: 8.1g* 8g Jul 8] smallish, close-coupled gelding: useful
performer, lightly raced: won handicap at Haydock (beat Hello It's Me 1½ lengths) in
July: left J. Fanshawe, last in similar event at Newmarket 6 days later (poorly drawn):
gelded after: will stay at least 1¼m: raced only on polytrack and good/good to firm going:
reportedly jarred up final 2-y-o start. *D. Nicholls*

PRINCE AARON (IRE)   4 b.g. Marju (IRE) 127 – Spirito Libro (USA) 89 (Lear Fan   **102**
(USA) 130) [2004 60: p6g* p6g* p6g⁶ p6g² p6g* 6m³ 6m* 6m⁵ 6.5g* 6g* 6s Sep 18]
angular gelding: useful performer: much improved and had excellent season, winning
handicaps at Lingfield in January (2) and March, Kempton in May and Ascot in July and
listed race at Newmarket (confidently ridden to beat Atavus by ½ length) in August: stays
6.5f: acts on polytrack and good to firm going, tailed off in Ayr Gold Cup (weak in
market) on soft final start: held up. *C. N. Allen*

PRINCEABLE LADY (IRE) 2 b.f. (Apr 26) Desert Prince (IRE) 130 – Saucy Maid **53** (IRE) 69 (Sure Blade (USA) 130) [2004 6m 6.1d 6m 5g Aug 6] 41,000Y: rather unfurnished filly: sixth foal: half-sister to 3 winners, including fairly useful 2001 2-y-o 6f winner Sophorific (by Danehill) and 11f winner La Mondotte (by Alzao): dam, maiden who stayed 1¼m, half-sister to dam of Pilsudski: modest maiden: no form after debut. *T. D. Easterby*

PRINCE ALBERT 6 ch.g. Rock City 120 – Russell Creek 80 (Sandy Creek 123) [2004 **45 ?** –: 8.3d 9.7s 10v³ May 10] leggy, lengthy gelding: poor maiden: stays 1¼m: acts on soft and good to firm ground: tried tongue tied. *J. R. Jenkins*

PRINCE CHARMING 2 b.c. (Mar 24) Royal Applause 124 – Miss Primula 81 (Dom- **105** inion 123) [2004 5d* 5s* 5f 5v⁶ 5d* 6g 5s⁵ 6s⁴ Oct 29] 110,000Y: smallish, well-made colt: half-brother to several winners, including useful Irish 5f/6f winner Tinker Amelia (by Damister) and fairly useful German winner up to 7.5f Magic Grey (by Petong): dam 5f/6f winner: useful performer: won maiden at Kempton and minor event at Ascot in April and listed race at Ayr (beat Mary Read by length) in September: more highly tried and bit below form last 3 starts, fourth in Criterium de Maisons-Laffitte: likely to prove best at 5f/easy 6f: acts on heavy going, ran as if amiss on firm. *J. H. M. Gosden*

PRINCE CYRANO 5 b.g. Cyrano de Bergerac 120 – Odilese 82 (Mummy's Pet 125) **79 §** [2004 93§: 6g 6g 6g 7s⁶ 7f 6m³ 6m⁵ 5d² 5d 5g 5g Oct 8] quite good-topped gelding: fair handicapper: best at 5f/6f: acts on firm and soft going: tried blinkered: often slowly away/ pulls hard/finds little: needs treating with caution. *W. J. Musson*

PRINCE DAYJUR (USA) 5 b. or br.g. Dayjur (USA) 137 – Distinct Beauty (USA) **82 §** (Phone Trick (USA)) [2004 –§: 6m 6g* 5m 6m Jul 19] close-coupled, quite attractive gelding: fairly useful handicapper: won at Kempton in June: below form otherwise in 2004: should stay 7f: raced mainly on good/good to firm going: visored last 3 starts: virtually refused to race on reappearance: unreliable. *M. J. Wallace*

PRINCE DU SOLEIL (FR) 8 b.g. Cardoun (FR) 122 – Revelry (FR) (Blakeney 126) **41 §** [2004 45§: p8g⁶ p8g⁶ p10g 7f Jun 2] quite attractive gelding: poor performer: probably best around 1m: acts on polytrack, heavy and good to firm going: tried in visor/cheekpieces/tongue tied: ungenuine. *J. R. Jenkins*

PRINCE HECTOR 5 ch.g. Hector Protector (USA) 124 – Ceanothus (IRE) 61 (Blue- **88** bird (USA) 125) [2004 90: 6s 6g² 7m⁶ 8m² 7m⁴ Jul 22] strong, close-coupled gelding: fairly useful winner of 3 races: effective at 7f/1m: acted on firm and good to soft going: was inconsistent: dead. *W. J. Haggas*

PRINCE HOLING 4 ch.g. Halling (USA) 133 – Ella Mon Amour 65 (Ela-Mana-Mou **66** 132) [2004 94: 10v⁵ 13.1d 11.9g 12d 13.8m Aug 3] rangy gelding: fairly useful performer at 2/3 yrs: below form in 2004, leaving Venetia Williams after reappearance: stayed 1½m: acted on firm going: tried tongue tied: sometimes slowly away/raced freely: dead. *M. Todhunter*

PRINCE IVOR 4 b.g. Polar Falcon (USA) 126 – Mistook (USA) (Phone Trick (USA)) **– §** [2004 42§: p10g p10g p10g 10d p13g p10m Dec 15] workmanlike gelding: ungenuine maiden: left J. Fox after second outing: tried visored/blinkered/tongue tied. *M. J. Gingell*

PRINCE KIRK (FR) 4 b.c. Selkirk (USA) 129 – Princess Manila (CAN) (Manila **122** (USA)) [2004 115: 10m* 10s³ 9.3g* May 23] sixth living foal: half-brother to 3 winners in France/Italy: dam, ran once in North America, half-sister to Derby Italiano winner Hailsham: very smart performer: successful in minor event and listed race at Milan in 2003, when also good second in Premio Parioli at Rome and Prix Jean Prat at Chantilly: won listed race at Pisa in March and Prix d'Ispahan at Longchamp in May: blinkered, career-best effort when beating Six Perfections ½ length in latter despite losing footing and brushing rail inside final 1f: 4¼ lengths third to Altieri in listed race at Milan in between: stays 1¼m: has won on good to soft going, but best efforts on good or firmer. *E. Borromeo, Italy*

PRINCELET (IRE) 2 b.c. (Mar 4) Desert Prince (IRE) 130 – Soeur Ti (FR) 109 (Kal- **72 p** doun (FR) 122) [2004 8s⁴ Oct 27] €80,000Y: third foal: half-brother to French 9f winner Sin El Fil (by Night Shift): dam French 7f (at 2 yrs) to 9f winner: 14/1, 6¼ lengths fourth to Very Wise in maiden at Yarmouth, staying on not knocked about: sure to improve. *M. A. Jarvis*

PRINCELY VALE (IRE) 2 b.g. (Apr 29) Princely Heir (IRE) 111 – Lomalou (IRE) **72** (Lightning Dealer 103) [2004 5g 6.1g⁴ 6f* 7g* 6f* 6m³ 7.1f⁴ 6s⁵ 5.1s² Aug 30] €3,500F, 3,000Y: leggy gelding: second foal: brother to 3-y-o Mr Hullabalou: dam unraced half-sister to useful Italian performer up to 1m Fay Breeze: fair performer: won sellers at

Thirsk and Redcar and claimer at Brighton in June: mostly creditable efforts after: effective at 5f to easy 7f: acts on firm and soft ground: usually in cheekpieces: hung right penultimate outing: gelded after final outing. *W. G. M. Turner*

PRINCELYWALLYWOGAN   2 b.c. (Mar 25) Princely Heir (IRE) 111 – Dublivia   **55** (Midyan (USA) 124) [2004 7g⁶ Aug 22] third foal: half-brother to Irish 7f winner Tashadelek (by Victory Note): dam little form: 25/1, sixth in maiden at Folkestone, slowly away and behind long way. *I. A. Wood*

PRINCE MINATA (IRE)   9 b.g. Machiavellian (USA) 123 – Aminata 98 (Glenstal   **40** (USA) 118) [2004 ?, a54: f12g p10g f8g³ f8g 12d⁴ f8.5g p8g⁶ Apr 29] sturdy gelding: poor performer: barely stays 1¼m: acts on all-weather, firm and soft going: tried tongue tied: has reportedly broken blood vessels: none too consistent. *P. W. Hiatt*

PRINCE NAMID   2 b.c. (Mar 28) Namid 128 – Fen Princess (IRE) 72 (Trojan Fen   **75** 118) [2004 5g⁴ 5s³ 5v* May 10] sturdy colt: closely related to useful 7f to 8.5f (in USA) winner Ben's Ridge (by Indian Ridge) and half-brother to 3 winners, including useful 9f to 15f winner Fiori (by Anshan): dam 15f winner: made all in 3-runner minor event at Redcar: should stay at least 6f. *Mrs A. Duffield*

PRINCE NASSEEM (GER)   7 b.h. Neshad (USA) 108 – Penola (GER) (Acatenango   **–** (GER) 127) [2004 –: f16.2s Mar 5] no form in Britain. *A. G. Juckes*

PRINCE NUREYEV (IRE)   4 b.g. Alzao (USA) 117 – Annaletta 89 (Belmez   **96** (USA) 131) [2004 102: 10.4d 10.4d 12f 10d² Jul 2] angular, quite good-topped gelding: has a short, choppy action: useful performer: best effort in handicaps in 2004 when 2½ lengths second to Silvaline at Sandown (edged right): effective at 1¼m, barely at 1¾m: acts on firm and soft ground: sometimes races freely, and is held up. *B. R. Millman*

PRINCE OF ARAGON   8 b.g. Aragon 118 – Queens Welcome 60 (Northfields   **–** (USA)) [2004 f8g Jun 28] tall, leggy gelding: modest at 3 yrs: very lightly raced and well held on Flat since: often visored/blinkered: tends to carry head high: won over hurdles in August. *Miss Suzy Smith*

PRINCE OF BLUES (IRE)   6 b.g. Prince of Birds (USA) 121 – Reshift 94 (Night   **65** Shift (USA)) [2004 84d, a89d: f6s p5g² f5g f6s f5s p5g⁴ 5d 5s⁴ 6g⁵ 5s 5m 6d³ 5.1g³ 6g⁵   **a70** 5.1d 10.3g 6m³ 6m 6s³ 5.1s³ 5g 5.1g 5g Sep 20] good-topped, useful-looking gelding: poor mover: fair performer: probably best at 5f/6f: acts on all-weather, firm and soft going: usually wears blinkers/cheekpieces: sometimes slowly away: usually races prominently: none too reliable. *M. Mullineaux*

PRINCE OF GOLD   4 b.c. Polar Prince (IRE) 117 – Gold Belt (IRE) 61 (Bellypha   **74** 130) [2004 79: 10g f8g⁵ 8d 8.2d 7m⁶ 8.1d 7.5d* 8.1f 8.1g 10.3g 8.5m 8m 7.5d 7.5m⁵ 6g³ 5g² 7v p6g* p6d² p6g⁶ p7m Dec 21] good-topped colt: fair performer: won handicap at Beverley in June and minor event at Wolverhampton in October: effective at 5f to 8.5f: acts on all-weather, firm and good to soft going: tried blinkered, usually wears cheekpieces nowadays: usually waited with. *R. Hollinshead*

Prix d'Ispahan, Longchamp—
Italian-trained Prince Kirk loses his footing but still has half a length to spare over Six Perfections

PRINCE OF PERLES 3 b.g. Mind Games 121 – Pearls (Mon Tresor 113) [2004 42§: f8g p7g f6g³ p7g f6d³ Dec 21] poor maiden: stays 6f: blinkered/visored: pulled hard on reappearance: sometimes slowly away: ungenuine. *D. Shaw* **46 §**

PRINCE OF THEBES (IRE) 3 b.g. Desert Prince (IRE) 130 – Persian Walk (FR) (Persian Bold 123) [2004 87: 8m* 9.7g³ Aug 13] good-topped gelding: useful performer, lightly raced: suffered pelvic injury after final 2-y-o start: won handicap at Ascot in July: free-going sort, may prove best up to 1m: raced only on good/good to firm ground. *A. M. Balding* **96**

PRINCE OF THE MAY 2 ch.g. (May 16) Bluegrass Prince (IRE) 110 – Maytime 55 (Pivotal 124) [2004 f8g Dec 11] first foal: dam, maiden, stayed 1m: 16/1, well held in maiden at Southwell. *H. Morrison* **–**

PRINCE OF THE WOOD (IRE) 4 ch.g. Woodborough (USA) 112 – Ard Dauphine (IRE) (Forest Wind (USA) 111) [2004 56, a42: p16g² f16.2m* 13.9m⁴ 18g 17.1f⁵ 16d 15g⁴ p13.9g⁶ f16g⁴ Dec 14] workmanlike gelding: modest performer: won banded race at Wolverhampton in May: stays 17f: acts on all-weather, firm and good to soft ground: tried blinkered/in cheekpieces. *A. Bailey* **56**

PRINCE PROSPECT 8 b.g. Lycius (USA) 124 – Princess Dechtra (IRE) 65 (Bellypha 130) [2004 –§, a54§: f9.4g f9.4g* f9.4g² f12s² f12g f9.4g 9.1s p12.2g Nov 15] sturdy gelding: modest performer: won banded race at Wolverhampton in February: effective at 9.4f to easy 1½m: acts on all-weather, firm and good to soft going: visored once at 2 yrs: wayward and unreliable. *Mrs L. Stubbs* **– §** **a56 §**

PRINCE PYRAMUS 6 b.g. Pyramus (USA) 78 – Rekindled Flame (IRE) (Kings Lake (USA) 133) [2004 –: 5v 5m May 24] well-made gelding: fair performer at best: well held since 2002: tried tongue tied/blinkered/in cheekpieces. *C. Grant* **41**

PRINCE RENESIS 3 b.g. Mind Games 121 – Stoneydale 83 (Tickled Pink 114) [2004 5.7s 7f 6m 10s⁶ 10g p8.6g⁵ p13m p10g Dec 20] poor maiden: left J. S. Moore after debut: stays 8.6f: acts on polytrack and good to firm going: blinkered (tailed off) once. *I. W. McInnes* **41**

PRINCE SAMOS (IRE) 2 b.c. (Apr 22) Mujadil (USA) 119 – Sabaniya (FR) (Lashkari 128) [2004 6m⁴ 6g 6s⁵ p6g³ 6d³ Oct 15] €65,000Y: neat colt: fifth foal: brother to fairly useful 2000 2-y-o 5f winner Chaguaramas: dam, Irish bumper winner, half-sister to high-class French 1¼m/1½m winner Sadjiyd and to grandam of Sinndar: fairly useful maiden: third at Lingfield and Newmarket (nursery): should stay 7f: acts on polytrack, soft and good to firm going. *R. Hannon* **82**

PRINCE SHAAMAAL 6 b.g. Shaamit (IRE) 127 – Princess Alaska (Northern State (USA) 91) [2004 p13g Dec 4] tall, leggy gelding: fair winning form only run at 2 yrs: lightly raced and mainly well held on Flat since: has looked none too keen: one to treat with caution. *K. Bell* **– §**

PRINCE SLAYER 8 b.g. Batshoof 122 – Top Sovereign (High Top 131) [2004 p10g Feb 7] well-made gelding: well held only outing on Flat since 2001: tried blinkered: tends to carry head high: has drifted right. *T. P. McGovern* **–**

PRINCESS ALINA (IRE) 3 b.f. Sadler's Wells (USA) 132 – Eilanden (IRE) (Akarad (FR) 130) [2004 66: p10g p10g a6f 8.5f⁴ a9f⁴ 8.5f⁵ 9g⁵ 8f⁵ 8.5f⁶ Nov 5] strong filly: modest maiden: left A. Balding after second outing: seems to stay 1¼m: acts on polytrack and firm going: blinkered in US. *R. R. Root, USA* **60**

PRINCESS BANKES 3 b.f. Vettori (IRE) 119 – Lady Bankes (IRE) 69 (Alzao (USA) 117) [2004 p8g f8.5g⁶ 6g f7m 7f 9.7f⁴ 11.9m³ 10.2g 10.1d f11g⁵ p10m⁶ f11d Dec 21] third foal: half-sister to fairly useful 6f (at 2 yrs) to 1m winner Moten Swing (by Kris): dam, 1¼m winner, half-sister to dam of 3-y-o Rule of Law: poor maiden: trained by D. Sepulchre in France at 2 yrs (fair form): probably stays 1½m: acts on all-weather, firm and good to soft ground. *Miss Gay Kelleway* **44**

PRINCESS ERICA 4 b.f. Perpendicular 119 – Birichino (Dilum (USA) 115) [2004 63: 6.1s 6g f6g 6m⁴ 6.1m 6m Jun 1] big, good-topped filly: poor maiden: stays 6f: acts on fibresand, heavy and good to firm ground: tried visored, wore cheekpieces last 5 starts. *J. Balding* **49**

PRINCESS GALADRIEL 3 b.f. Magic Ring (IRE) 115 – Prim Lass 65 (Reprimand 122) [2004 49: 6s² 6g* 6m³ 8f² 9.7f 11.5g⁶ 7m³ 7g⁶ 7d* 8.5m³ 8.2v 8s² p8.6d p9.5g Nov 13] rather leggy filly: fair handicapper: won at Yarmouth in May and August: stays 8.5f: acts on soft and good to firm ground, well held on all-weather: usually held up: temperament under suspicion. *J. R. Best* **74**

PRINCESS ISMENE 3 b.f. Sri Pekan (USA) 117 – Be Practical 83 (Tragic Role **58 d** (USA)) [2004 61: p8g* p8g⁵ f7g² f7g² p7g⁴ p10g³ 10.1m³ f8g⁴ 10g 8.2s⁵ 11g⁴ 11.5f⁶ 7m 9.9s 8.1m p9.5d Nov 5] small filly: modest performer: won seller at Lingfield in January: left J. Jay after third run, P. Blockley after thirteenth, deteriorating in both form and temperament (refused to race 3 of last 4 outings): barely stays 1¼m: acts on all-weather and good to firm going: blinkered/visored. *M. Appleby*

PRINCESS KAI (IRE) 3 b.f. Cayman Kai (IRE) 114 – City Princess 62§ (Rock City **57** 120) [2004 58: p5g* p5g p6g p5g³ 5.1g⁴ 5g² 5.3m² 5m⁶ 6m Jun 7] modest performer: won maiden at Lingfield in January: should stay easy 6f: acts on polytrack, firm and good to soft ground: blinkered: usually races prominently: sometimes wanders. *R. Ingram*

PRINCESS KARLA (IRE) 2 b.f. (Mar 20) Fayruz 116 – Mystique Air (IRE) 66 **49** (Mujadil (USA) 119) [2004 p7m p7.1g Dec 31] €5,200F, 10,000Y: third foal: dam 7f and 9f winner: poor form in maidens at Lingfield and Wolverhampton. *J. W. Unett*

PRINCESS KIOTTO 3 b.f. Desert King (IRE) 129 – Ferghana Ma 62 (Mtoto 134) **74** [2004 –: 8g⁵ f12d² 14g³ 16.2g* 16.1m* 18d² Oct 18] rather leggy filly: fair handicapper: won at Beverley (maiden event) in July and Newcastle in September: stays 2¼m: acts on fibresand, good to firm and good to soft going. *T. D. Easterby*

PRINCESS LINKS 2 b.f. (Mar 12) Bahamian Bounty 116 – Miss Prism 60 (Niniski **–** (USA) 125) [2004 8v Oct 23] 5,000F, 35,000Y: fifth foal: half-sister to 1m winner Island Light (by Inchinor) and Swedish 6f to 1m winner Royal Gold (by Emarati), both useful: dam maiden who stayed 2m: 25/1, tailed off in maiden at Newbury: sold 9,500 gns, sent to Kazakhstan. *R. Hannon*

PRINCESS MAGDALENA 4 ch.f. Pennekamp (USA) 130 – Reason To Dance 96 **–** (Damister (USA) 123) [2004 60: 8s 11.6m 9.7f 11.6g Jul 12] leggy, close-coupled filly: modest 1¼m winner at 3 yrs: well held since. *L. G. Cottrell*

PRINCE TUM TUM (USA) 4 b.c. Capote (USA) – La Grande Epoque (USA) 120 **104** (Lyphard (USA) 132) [2004 115: 7.9s 7m⁶ 7m⁴ 7.1g³ Aug 30] lengthy, quite attractive colt: smart performer at best: useful in 2004, best effort when 2½ lengths third to Polar Way in minor event at Warwick: stays 1m: acts on firm ground: sold 17,500 gns. *J. L. Dunlop*

PRINCE VALENTINE 3 b.g. My Best Valentine 122 – Affaire de Coeur 55 (Imperial **56 d** Fling (USA) 116) [2004 67: p10g p7g 8.1s³ 8.1v⁵ 10f⁴ 10f 10m⁴ p10g 10s 8m Sep 25] modest maiden at best in 2004: stays 1¼m: acts on polytrack and firm going: tried blinkered/in cheekpieces. *D. B. Feek*

PRINCE VECTOR 2 b.c. (Mar 19) Vettori (IRE) 119 – The In-Laws (IRE) 90 (Be My **67 p** Guest (USA) 126) [2004 7g Oct 12] 31,000Y: tall foal: half-brother to 4-y-o Lady Mytton: dam, 2-y-o 7f winner, stayed 1¼m: 100/1, eleventh in maiden at Leicester, never dangerous and not knocked about: likely to do better. *A. King*

PRINCE VETTORI 2 b.g. (Feb 8) Vettori (IRE) 119 – Bombalarina (IRE) (Barathea **67** (IRE) 127) [2004 7g 8.1g p8g⁶ p8.6g⁴ Dec 1] 20,000Y: angular gelding: first foal: dam unraced half-sister to useful 1997 2-y-o 6f and 1m winner Silent Tribute out of half-sister to Middle Park winner Balla Cove: fair maiden: good fourth in nursery at Wolverhampton, still green: likely to stay 1¼m. *D. J. Coakley*

PRINCIPAL WITNESS (IRE) 3 b.g. Definite Article 121 – Double Eight (IRE) **82** 77 (Common Grounds 118) [2004 8g 8m⁴ 8m² 8m p10d⁵ 8g Jul 8] €125,000Y: strong, useful-looking gelding: third foal: half-brother to 11f winner Fiza (by Revoque): dam 1½m winner: fairly useful maiden: well below form last 3 starts: gelded after: races freely, and may prove best up to 1m: acts on good to firm ground. *W. R. Muir*

PRINCIPESSA 3 b.f. Machiavellian (USA) 123 – Party Doll 108 (Be My Guest (USA) **74** 126) [2004 68p: 8.3s⁵ 10.2g 10.2m 10m 10g² 9.9g² 10m 11.7m² 12.3s⁴ 10.2g³ 10.2g² 12g **a65** p12g p12.2g⁵ f11g³ Dec 16] leggy, close-coupled filly: fair maiden: stays 11.7f: acts on soft and good to firm going: usually races prominently. *B. Palling*

PRINS WILLEM (IRE) 5 b.g. Alzao (USA) 117 – American Garden (USA) (Alleged **95** (USA) 138) [2004 97: 12g² 12g³ 16.2d⁴ 13.9g⁵ 11.9d 12g 12d³ Oct 15] sturdy gelding: useful handicapper: below form last 3 starts: best at 1½m/1¾m: acts on good to firm and good to soft going: tried visored/tongue tied: usually waited with. *J. R. Fanshawe*

PRINTSMITH (IRE) 7 br.m. Petardia 113 – Black And Blaze (Taufan (USA) 119) **44** [2004 40: f8g* f8g⁴ f7g⁴ f8s³ f8s² f8g* f8g 8.1d⁵ 8v f8g 8.1d⁴ f8g⁵ p9.5g* Dec 22] leggy **a54** mare: modest performer: won banded races at Southwell in January and March and

Wolverhampton in December: stays 1m: acts on fibresand and good to soft ground: tried in cheekpieces: none too consistent. *J. R. Norton*

PRIORS DALE 4 b.g. Lahib (USA) 129 – Mathaayl (USA) 79 (Shadeed (USA) 135) **71** [2004 82: p10g² p8g⁶ p8g⁶ 8g⁴ 8g 8g Oct 10] leggy, good-topped gelding: fair maiden: stays easy 1¼m: acts on polytrack, raced only on good ground or softer on turf: tried tongue tied: fairly useful hurdler. *K. Bell*

PRITHEE 2 b.f. (Mar 3) Barathea (IRE) 127 – Bina Ridge 90 (Indian Ridge 123) **67 p** [2004 7d Oct 30] lengthy, good-topped filly: first foal: dam, 9f winner from 2 starts, half-sister to smart 1½m winner Bequeath: 8/1 and better for race, seventh to Songthrush in maiden at Newmarket, green and not knocked about when no extra: will do better. *J. H. M. Gosden*

PRIVATE BENJAMIN 4 gr.g. Ridgewood Ben 113 – Jilly Woo 60 (Environment **62** Friend 128) [2004 64: p13g p12g* p12g p12g⁶ 11.9m³ 10m 12m* 12g 11.9f⁵ 12d 11.6g 11g⁵ p16g³ p12g² p12m⁵ p13g Dec 29] angular gelding: has a round action: modest performer: won maiden at Lingfield in February and handicap at Salisbury in June: stays 2m: acts on polytrack, firm and soft going: sometimes looks difficult ride. *Jamie Poulton*

PRIVATE CHARTER 4 b.c. Singspiel (IRE) 133 – By Charter 104 (Shirley Heights **109** 130) [2004 113: p10g 10g² 12g 10.5m⁶ 12f 12g* Oct 1] strong, lengthy colt: not a good walker: useful performer: ran creditably in 2004 only when length second to Bandari in minor event at Newmarket and when winning listed event there by head from Fantastic Love (wore cheekpieces, made all, racing alone on far rail in straight): stays 1½m: acts on firm going, probably on good to soft and polytrack: sold 80,000 gns, sent to Saudi Arabia. *B. W. Hills*

Sheikh Mohammed's "Privy Seal"

PRIVATE JESSICA   3 ch.f. Cadeaux Genereux 131 – Rose Bay 64 (Shareef Dancer (USA) 135) [2004 7g 6.1s 7m⁴ f8s 8g Sep 22] 35,000Y: lengthy, angular filly: first foal: dam, maiden, who should have proved best at 1½m, out of half-sister to top-class 1m and 1¼m winner Cormorant Wood: seemingly modest maiden: tailed off in handicaps last 2 starts: best effort at 6f on soft going: sold 4,000 gns. *J. R. Fanshawe*   **50 ?**

PRIVATE SEAL   9 b.g. King's Signet (USA) 110 – Slender 79 (Aragon 118) [2004 50§: p10g⁶ p10g³ p12g² p10g² p12g p12g² p12g p10g⁵ 10m 10m 10.9m 10f³ p10g² 10m⁶ 10.1m³ 10s⁴ 9.7f p13m p13.9g p10m⁶ Dec 15] workmanlike gelding: modest performer: stays easy 1½m: acts on polytrack, firm and soft going: tried blinkered/in cheekpieces: tongue tied: has carried head awkwardly/flashed tail: one to treat with caution. *Julian Poulton*   **50 §**

PRIVY SEAL (IRE)   3 b.g. Cape Cross (IRE) 129 – Lady Joshua (IRE) 88 (Royal Academy (USA) 130) [2004 103: 8d³ 10d² 12.3d² 12m³ 10m 10g⁴ 9.9g² Sep 22] tall, quite attractive gelding: has a quick action: smart performer: won listed race at Kempton in April by a length from Mutahayya: at least respectable placed efforts after in Classic Trial at Sandown (3½ lengths second to African Dream), Chester Vase (went down by 5 lengths to Red Lancer), Derby Italiano at Rome (5½ lengths third to Groom Tesse) and listed race at Goodwood (beaten 3½ lengths by Alkaadhem): probably stays 1½m: acts on firm and good to soft going: visored fourth to sixth starts: sometimes bandaged fore joints at 2 yrs: has worn crossed noseband: pulled hard fifth appearance. *J. H. M. Gosden*   **110**

PRIZE FIGHTER (IRE)   2 b.g. (Mar 10) Desert Sun 120 – Papal (Selkirk (USA) 129) [2004 7g² f7m* f7m² Jul 26] €17,000Y: second foal: dam unraced: won maiden at Southwell in July: best effort when head second to Caitlin in nursery there final start: should stay 1m. *P. W. Chapple-Hyam*   **88**

PRIZEMAN (USA)   6 b.g. Prized (USA) – Shuttle (USA) (Conquistador Cielo (USA)) [2004 8g 8.1d² Jun 5] strong, lengthy gelding: useful performer, missed 2002/3: creditable 1½ lengths second to Bishopric in handicap at Haydock: barely stays 2m: acts on firm and soft going. *G. B. Balding*   **100**

PRIZE RING   5 ch.g. Bering 136 – Spot Prize (USA) 108 (Seattle Dancer (USA) 119) [2004 65: 12m⁶ 14d² 14.1f⁶ 14g Aug 6] tall gelding: modest performer: stays 1¾m: acts on firm and good to soft going: tried in cheekpieces: sometimes races freely/finds little: held up. *G. M. Moore*   **60**

PROCLAMATION (IRE)   2 gr.c. (May 1) King's Best (USA) 132 – Shamarra (FR) (Zayyani 119) [2004 8d* Oct 15] 84,000Y: tall, lengthy colt: good walker: fifth foal: half-brother to 4-y-o No Refuge and 2001 2-y-o 6f winner Denmark (by Danehill): dam unraced: 12/1 from 20/1, won maiden at Newmarket by 3½ lengths from Unfurled, travelling strongly before quickening clear final 1f despite drifting left: will be suited by 1¼m/1½m: smart prospect, likely to make his mark in stronger company. *J. Noseda*   **100 p**

PROCRASTINATE (IRE)   2 ch.g. (Apr 19) Rossini (USA) 118 – May Hinton 82 (Main Reef 126) [2004 5v³ 5g 6s⁶ 6m⁵ 5g³ 5d 6f⁵ 5g² 7m 5g³ 5g p6g⁶ p6g⁵ Dec 27] quite good-topped gelding: modest maiden: best at 5f/6f: acts on heavy going: wore cheekpieces (ran poorly) sixth start. *R. F. Fisher*   **62**

PROCREATE (IRE)   4 b.g. Among Men (USA) 124 – Woodbury Princess (Never So Bold 135) [2004 –: 7.2m 10f 10d 7.1f 6.5d 6s⁶ Oct 30] poor maiden: left Miss A. Winters in Ireland after fifth start. *Miss L. A. Perratt*   **35**

PROFIT'S REALITY (IRE)   2 br.c. (Mar 21) Key of Luck (USA) 126 – Teacher Preacher (IRE) 37 (Taufan (USA) 119) [2004 6s 6m⁵ 6d⁵ 6d⁴ 6d³ 7.1g⁴ 6d³ 8d Oct 18] €10,500Y, 25,000 2-y-o: big, useful-looking colt: has scope: third foal: brother to 3-y-o Key Partners: dam Irish 7f winner: fairly useful performer: won maiden at Musselburgh in September: creditable third in nursery at Hamilton next time: stays 7f: acts on good to soft ground. *P. A. Blockley*   **85**

PROMENADE   3 b.f. Primo Dominie 121 – Hamsah (IRE) 86 (Green Desert (USA) 127) [2004 87: 6.1d⁵ 5f 5m Jun 19] smallish, sturdy filly: found to be lame behind after final 2-y-o start: just fair performer in 2004: should stay 6f: acts on good to firm ground: moved poorly to post third start at 2 yrs. *M. L. W. Bell*   **68**

PROMOTE   8 gr.g. Linamix (FR) 127 – Rive (USA) (Riverman (USA) 131) [2004 –: p10g 14.1m⁶ 19.1f⁶ 16m 16m Jul 26] poor nowadays: barely stays 19f: acts on fibresand, firm and soft going: sometimes tongue tied. *Ms A. E. Embiricos*   **44**

PROMOTED DEPUTY (USA)   2 b.f. (Apr 6) Deputy Minister (CAN) – Shouldnt Say Never (USA) (Meadowlake (USA)) [2004 p7g* Sep 7] sixth foal: sister to a winner,   **79 p**

closely related to a winner by Dehere and half-sister to a winner by Storm Cat, all in USA: dam, won 8.5f minor stakes in USA, half-sister to US Grade 3 2-y-o 6f winner Crafty But Sweet: 15/8 on, won maiden at Lingfield by length from Improvise, getting on top final 1f: sure to improve. *Saeed bin Suroor*

PROMOTER 4 ch.g. Selkirk (USA) 129 – Poplina (USA) (Roberto (USA) 131) [2004 **99** 100: 16g 13.9s 20f² 16.1s 16.2g⁴ 21g 14.8d² Aug 27] tall, leggy gelding: useful handicapper: good efforts when in frame in 2004, including 5 lengths second to Double Obsession in Ascot Stakes third start: stays 2½m: acts on firm and good to soft going: has worn crossed noseband: raced freely and dropped out tamely penultimate start: tends to carry head high. *J. Noseda*

PROMOTION 4 b.g. Sadler's Wells (USA) 132 – Tempting Prospect 95 (Shirley **111** Heights 130) [2004 90: 10g* 10m² 10.4g² Jul 10] lengthy, attractive gelding: smart performer, lightly raced: won handicap at Newmarket in May by 2½ lengths from Tizzy May: good second in similar events at Royal Ascot (free to post, beaten 8 lengths by Red Fort) and York (John Smith's Cup, beaten head by Arcalis) after: reported in early-August to have suffered a setback: better form at 1¼m than 1½m: yet to race on ground softer than good. *Sir Michael Stoute*

PROPELLOR (IRE) 2 ch.c. (Mar 27) Pivotal 124 – Clunie 84 (Inchinor 119) [2004 **90** 6s³ 6g* 6f³ 6s⁴ 6d⁴ Oct 11] 19,000Y: strong colt: second foal: half-brother to 3-y-o Poker: dam 6f winner, including at 2 yrs: fairly useful performer: won maiden at Hamilton in July: creditable efforts after, especially in nursery at Ayr final start (short of room): should stay 7f: acts on firm and good to soft going. *A. Dickman*

PROPHET'S CALLING (IRE) 2 b.g. (Apr 18) Brave Act 119 – Arbitration (IRE) **52** (Bigstone (IRE) 126) [2004 7m 8g p6g Oct 2] leggy gelding: modest form in maidens: best effort at 6f. *Miss D. A. McHale*

PROPINQUITY 2 b.c. (Apr 16) Primo Dominie 121 – Lydia Maria 70 (Dancing **103** Brave (USA) 140) [2004 7g* 7g³ 7.1d² 8g⁵ Sep 2] robust colt: brother to useful 6f (at 2 yrs) and 10.4f winner Premier Bay and half-brother to several winners, including 5-y-o Barolo and 4-y-o Albavilla: dam, maiden who stayed 1¼m, sister to dam of smart sprinter Primo Valentino (by Primo Dominie): useful performer: won maiden at Salisbury in June: good third in minor event at Ascot and Solario Stakes at Sandown (beaten 2¾ lengths by Windsor Knot): hung right and possibly amiss final start: should stay 1m: acts on good to soft ground. *P. W. Harris*

PROPRIOCEPTION (IRE) 2 ch.f. (May 14) Danehill Dancer (IRE) 117 – Pepper – And Salt (IRE) (Double Schwartz 128) [2004 8s Aug 28] €20,000Y: leggy filly: fourth foal: half-sister to 5-y-o Unshakable: dam unraced: slowly away and always rear in maiden at Goodwood (reportedly lame behind). *M. R. Channon*

PROPRIUS 4 b.g. Perpendicular 119 – Pretty Pollyanna (General Assembly (USA)) – [2004 –: f7g⁵ f8g Jan 20] little form. *B. Smart*

PROSPECT COURT 4 ch.g. (Apr 11) Pivotal 124 – Scierpan (USA) 86 (Sharpen Up **80 d** 127) [2004 5s 5g³ 5f 6m* 6f 6g 6m 6g 6g Oct 8] 14,000F, 42,000Y: close-coupled gelding: half-brother to several winners, including French 1m winner Pan Galactic (by Lear Fan) and 6f (including at 2 yrs) winner Specified (by Known Fact), both useful: dam placed at 5f/6f at 2 yrs: fairly useful performer: won nursery at Pontefract in July: below form in similar events after, especially when blinkered final start (gelded after): likely to stay 7f: acts on good to firm ground. *J. D. Bethell*

PROSPECT HILL (IRE) 6 ch.g. Nucleon (USA) 94 – Ann Hill (IRE) 58 (Bob Back – (USA) 124) [2004 –: 7f p6g f6g Dec 28] lightly-raced maiden: left Miss A. Winters in Ireland after reappearance: tried tongue tied. *K. A. Morgan*

PROSPECT PARK 3 b.c. Sadler's Wells (USA) 132 – Brooklyn's Dance (FR) 119 **118** (Shirley Heights 130) [2004 104: 10.5d* 10.5g* 12d² 12g² 12g* 12d² 12m Oct 3] tall, close-coupled colt: half-brother to several winners in France, including useful winners around 1¼m Out of Control (by Gulch) and Brooklyn's Gold (by Seeking The Gold): dam won Prix Cleopatre and stayed 12.5f: smart performer: won minor event at Saint-Cloud in March, listed race at Longchamp (by a head from Millemix) in April and Prix du Lys on latter course (by 1½ lengths from Lord Darnley) in June: best efforts when second to Blue Canari in Prix du Jockey Club at Chantilly fourth outing (beaten a head) and to Valixir in Prix Niel at Longchamp (just unable to hang on and beaten a nose): surprise favourite, only sixteenth of 19 in Prix de l'Arc de Triomphe at Longchamp (took too strong a hold) final start: stays 1½m: acts on good to soft ground: has worn crossed noseband/been bandaged hind joints. *C. Laffon-Parias, France*

PROSPECT POINT   2 ch.f. (Apr 26) Cayman Kai (IRE) 114 – Sassy Lady (IRE) 63   **30**
(Brief Truce (USA) 126) [2004 p7.1g⁴ p6d f6g Nov 9] second foal: dam, maiden, form
only at 6f at 2 yrs: poor maiden: in cheekpieces last 2 starts. *C. A. Dwyer*

PROTECTING HEIGHTS (IRE)   3 br.g. Hector Protector (USA) 124 – Height of   **62**
Fantasy (IRE) 101 (Shirley Heights 130) [2004 8g 10g⁶ p10g Nov 16] close-coupled
gelding: first foal: dam, 1¾m/2m winner, half-sister to 5-y-o Persian Lightning: modest
form: best effort when sixth in maiden at Windsor (slowly away): off nearly 7 months
after: should stay 1½m. *J. L. Dunlop*

PROTECTIVE   3 ch.c. Hector Protector (USA) 124 – You Make Me Real (USA)   **93**
(Give Me Strength (USA)) [2004 9g⁴ 10.5m 11.9d* 11.9s⁴ 12g 11.9g 13d³ 12s 12s Nov
6] quite good-topped colt: half-brother to several winners, including useful Irish 1998
2-y-o 5f/6f winner Camargo (by Brief Truce), later successful in USA, and Irish 9f and
1¾m winner Real Guest (by Be My Guest): dam minor winner in USA: fairly useful
performer: won maiden at Haydock in June: good efforts after only when in frame in
listed event Haydock (to Frank Sonata) and handicap at Hamilton (behind Zeitgeist):
stays 13f: form only on going softer than good: none too consistent. *J. G. Given*

PRO TEMPORE   2 b.f. (Jan 18) Fraam 114 – Record Time 69 (Clantime 101) [2004   **64**
5m⁴ 5f* 5m⁶ 5.1g⁶ 5.9g³ 7m 6g 7d⁶ Oct 15] 21,000Y: sturdy filly: first foal: dam, 5f
winner, sister to useful sprinter Lago di Varano: modest performer: won maiden at
Carlisle in July: creditable efforts in nurseries next 3 starts: needs to settle to stay 7f: acts
on firm ground: sold 15,000 gns. *Mrs J. R. Ramsden*

PROTOCOL (IRE)   10 b.g. Taufan (USA) 119 – Ukraine's Affair (USA) (The Minstrel (CAN) 135) [2004 33, a–: 12v 21.6v f12g Jun 11] rather leggy gelding: little form in
2004: tried visored/in cheekpieces: usually tongue tied. *Mrs S. Lamyman*

PROUD BOAST   6 b.m. Komaite (USA) – Red Rosein 97 (Red Sunset 120) [2004   **97**
103: 5.1g 5d* 5.1g 6d 5d 5g² 5m³ 5m 6m 6g⁶ 5.8g⁵ 5g Sep 30] rather leggy, angular mare:
useful performer: won minor event at Beverley in April by ¾ length from Caribbean
Coral: seemingly good fifth in Taby Open Sprint Championship penultimate outing:
effective at 5f/6f: acts on firm and good to soft going: usually held up. *D. Nicholls*

PROUD NATIVE (IRE)   10 b.g. Imp Society (USA) – Karamana (Habitat 134) [2004   **76**
90: 5s 6m 5g 5m³ 5g Jun 24] sturdy gelding: poor walker/mover: smart performer at best,
winner of 18 races, including Ballyogan Stakes at Leopardstown in 1999: just fair form
in 2004: best at 5f: acted on firm and soft ground: tried blinkered: edgy sort: usually
early to post: usually waited with: retired (reportedly suffered heart and wind problems).
D. Nicholls

PROUD SCHOLAR (USA)   2 br. or b.f. (Feb 3) Royal Academy (USA) 130 – Proud   **80**
Fact (USA) 108 (Known Fact (USA) 135) [2004 7m² 7g⁶ Sep 2] leggy filly: fifth foal:
half-sister to winner in USA by Kris S: dam, French 7f/1m winner, half-sister to Poule
d'Essai des Pouliches winner Houseproud: much better effort in maidens when second at
Newbury, slowly away: should stay 1m. *Mrs A. J. Perrett*

PROUD TRADITION (USA)   3 b.f. Seeking The Gold (USA) – Family Tradition   **–**
(IRE) 107 (Sadler's Wells (USA) 132) [2004 78p: 11.4d 10m⁶ Jun 10] leggy, quite good-
topped filly: won maiden at Newmarket only run at 2 yrs: well beaten in 2004: sold
125,000 gns in November. *J. H. M. Gosden*

PROUD VICTOR (IRE)   4 b.g. Victory Note (USA) 120 – Alberjas (IRE) (Sure Blade   **46**
(USA) 130) [2004 60d: f8.5g⁴ f8.5g⁵ f8g⁶ f12g⁶ f8g⁵ Feb 9] poor performer: barely stays
1m: acts on all-weather: usually visored: has looked wayward. *D. Shaw*

PROUD WESTERN (USA)   6 b.g. Gone West (USA) – Proud Lou (Proud   **40**
Clarion) [2004 62: 5v 5d 5m 7.1f 7.6g⁵ f6g Dec 12] good-topped gelding: poor performer:
effective at 5f to 1m: acts on fibresand, soft and good to firm ground: tried blinkered/in
cheekpieces, sometimes tongue tied: sometimes slowly away. *B. Ellison*

PSYCHIATRIST   3 ch.g. Dr Devious (IRE) 127 – Zahwa 72 (Cadeaux Genereux 131)   **99**
[2004 104: 8d³ 9g² 8m⁴ 7f 7m⁶ 8m Sep 26] tall, angular, useful-looking gelding: useful
performer: creditable efforts in 2004 only when ¾-length second to Gold History in listed
race and 4½ lengths fourth to Almuraad in minor event, both at Newmarket: barely stays
9f: acts on good to firm and good to soft going. *R. Hannon*

PTARMIGAN RIDGE   8 b.h. Sea Raven (IRE) 75 – Panayr (Faraway Times (USA)   **94 §**
123) [2004 90: 5g 5.1d* 5m 5m 5d⁶ 5d⁵ 5g⁵ 5.6m³ 5s 5d Oct 17] quite good-
topped horse: fairly useful handicapper: won at Chester (by head from Simianna) in May
and Ayr (by length from Proud Boast) in July: best around 5f: acts on any going: effective
ridden prominently or held up: unreliable. *Miss L. A. Perratt*

Tattersalls Musidora Stakes, York—
Punctilious draws right away to land the odds from Glen Innes (left) and Bay Tree (right)

PUBLIC FORUM   2 b.c. (Jan 10) Rainbow Quest (USA) 134 – Valentine Girl 109   **84 p**
(Alzao (USA) 117) [2004 8.2v* Oct 20] first foal: dam 7f (at 2 yrs) and 11.4f winner: 9/4,
won 5-runner minor event at Nottingham by neck from Miss L'Augeval, never far away
and leading near finish: will be well suited by 1¼m/1½m: useful prospect. *Sir Michael
Stoute*

PUGIN (IRE)   6 b.h. Darshaan 133 – Gothic Dream (IRE) 113 (Nashwan (USA) 135)   **107**
[2004 117d: p10g⁵ 12g⁵ 12g 22.2f Jun 19] strong horse: has stringhalt: only useful in
2004: best effort when 6 lengths fifth to Dubai Success in John Porter Stakes at Newbury
second start: should stay at least 2m: acts on polytrack and good to firm going (won on
soft on debut): has worn crossed noseband/been bandaged in front: has awkward head
carriage: joined A. Al Raihe in UAE. *D. R. Loder*

PUKKA (IRE)   3 b.c. Sadler's Wells (USA) 132 – Puce 112 (Darshaan 133) [2004   **112 p**
80p: 11m* 12m 11.9s² 11.9d⁵ Aug 17] strong, neat colt: improved into a smart performer:
won handicap at Newbury in May by 1¼ lengths from Maraahel: beaten just under 10
lengths when ninth to North Light in Derby at Epsom, then a neck when second to Frank
Sonata in listed race at Haydock (finished strongly despite edging left) and 7¾ lengths
when fifth to Rule of Law in Great Voltigeur Stakes at York: should stay 1¾m: acts on
polytrack, soft and good to firm going: should do better still. *L. M. Cumani*

PULSE   6 b.g. Salse (USA) 128 – French Gift 99 (Cadeaux Genereux 131) [2004 70: 5d   **72 d**
f6g 5.3m² 5v³ 5.1d⁶ 5g⁶ 5m⁴ 5f⁵ 5m³ 5.3g 5g 5m⁵ 5.7m⁵ 5d⁴ 5.3d 5g 5.7f⁶ 5.1m 5.7g⁵ 5m²
5.3s³ p6d p6g⁶ Nov 15] fair handicapper: below form after third start: best at 5f/6f: acts
on all-weather and any turf going: usually wears cheekpieces. *J. M. Bradley*

Ribblesdale Stakes, Royal Ascot—Punctilious has to work harder this time;
Sahool is second and Quiff (right) overhauls New Morning to take third

Godolphin's "Punctilious"

PUNCTILIOUS   3 b.f. Danehill (USA) 126 – Robertet (USA) 118 (Roberto (USA)   **116**
131) [2004 107p: 10.4s* 12m³ 12m* 12f² 11.9s⁴ 10g² Oct 24] big, good-topped filly:
smart performer: trained by M. Jarvis at 2 yrs: won Tattersalls Musidora Stakes at York
(by 6 lengths from Glen Innes) in May and Ribblesdale Stakes at Royal Ascot (beat
Sahool by 1½ lengths) in June: ran well when second in Irish Oaks at the Curragh (beaten
a length by Ouija Board, giving flash of tail under whip) and E. P. Taylor Stakes at
Woodbine (went down by ½ length to Commercante): below form otherwise in Oaks at
Epsom (10½ lengths third to Ouija Board) and Yorkshire Oaks at York (soon labouring in
straight when well-held fourth to Quiff): stays 1½m: acts on firm and soft going: usually
tongue tied: often makes running. *Saeed bin Suroor*

PUP'S PRIDE   7 b.g. Efisio 120 – Moogie 103 (Young Generation 129) [2004 –, a66:   –
f9.4g⁶ f8.5s f8d f8g Nov 23] good-topped gelding: fair performer at best: no form in
2004: usually wears headgear. *Mrs N. Macauley*

PURDEY   4 ch.f. Double Trigger (IRE) 123 – Euphorie (GER) (Feenpark (GER) 115)   **51**
[2004 –: 11.7s 14.1m⁵ 17.2f⁴ 17.2g⁵ Jul 3] modest handicapper: stays 17.2f: form only on
good ground or firmer. *H. Morrison*

PURE EMOTION   3 b.f. Primo Dominie 121 – Yasalam (IRE) (Fairy King (USA))   **48 ?**
[2004 –p: p7g⁵ p6g p7g f8.5g Mar 17] poor maiden: should prove best short of 1m: raced
only on all-weather. *W. R. Muir*

827

PURE FOLLY (IRE) 3 b.f. Machiavellian (USA) 123 – Spirit Willing (IRE) 99 (Fairy **58**
King (USA)) [2004 54p: p5g³ p5g⁴ p6g⁴ 6.9m f5f Aug 20] angular filly: modest maiden:
should stay 7f. *Sir Mark Prescott*

PURE IMAGINATION (IRE) 3 ch.g. Royal Academy (USA) 130 – Ivory Bride 86 **72**
(Domynsky 110) [2004 7g⁶ 7m³ 7.1m 6d⁶ 6m 6.1d⁴ 6m 5.7g 6s* 6d Oct 4] 31,000Y,
10,000 2-y-o: eighth foal: half-brother to several winners, including 5-y-o Funfair Wane
and 6-y-o Parkside Pursuit: dam 2-y-o 6f winner: fair handicapper: won at Hamilton in
September: better at 6f than 7f: acts on soft and good to firm going: reared leaving stall
and saddle slipped fifth outing. *J. M. Bradley*

PURE MISCHIEF (IRE) 5 b.g. Alhaarth (IRE) 126 – Bellissi (IRE) 77 (Bluebird **78**
(USA) 125) [2004 f9.4g³ 10.1v* 10s* 10.1s⁵ f11d* 10.1s³ 10.5s² 10.5s⁴ 10g⁶ 10.1d⁵ p8g⁵
8.2v p8g³ p8g³ p9.5g⁴ f8g Dec 11] good-topped gelding: fair performer: won handicaps
at Newcastle in April and Nottingham in May and claimer at Southwell (left W. M. Brisbourne) in June: stays 11f: acts on all-weather, goes particularly well on soft/heavy: held
up. *C. R. Dore*

PURE SPECULATION 4 b.f. Salse (USA) 128 – Just Speculation (IRE) 86 (Aho- **62**
noora 122) [2004 79: f12g p10g 9.7s⁶ 8v⁴ 8.1v May 4] workmanlike filly: only modest
nowadays: stays 9f: acts on soft and good to firm going: tends to race freely: sold 10,000
gns. *M. L. W. Bell*

PURE VINTAGE (IRE) 3 b.g. Fasliyev (USA) 120 – Tootling (IRE) (Pennine Walk **54**
120) [2004 7m 8.1d⁶ 7m 10.1d 7.1g⁶ Aug 26] tall, lengthy gelding: unimpressive mover:
modest maiden: should stay 1m. *R. A. Fahey*

PURI 5 b.g. Mujadil (USA) 119 – Prosperous Lady (Prince Tenderfoot (USA) 126) [2004 **50**
–: f8.5g⁴ 7g f7g 10.9m 7.2g⁴ 8m Aug 16] tall, good-topped gelding: modest maiden: stays
8.5f: acts on fibresand: tried blinkered/visored: usually races prominently. *J. G. Given*

PURPLE DOOR 2 b.f. (Feb 8) Daggers Drawn (USA) 114 – Carreamia 62 (Weldnaas **56**
(USA) 112) [2004 5.7m⁶ 7.1g 6m⁶ 6d Oct 14] 4,800Y: second foal: dam, maiden, should
have stayed 1m: modest maiden: should stay 7f: ran wide bend at Musselburgh second
start. *R. M. Beckett*

PURPLE RAIN (IRE) 3 b.f. Celtic Swing 138 – Calypso Grant (IRE) 98 (Danehill **46**
(USA) 126) [2004 8.1s 8g 8.2s⁶ f8g5 8g Jun 17] 20,000Y: leggy filly: second foal: sister
to 4-y-o Calypso Dancer: dam, 1m (including at 2 yrs) winner who stayed 1¼m, sister to
4-y-o Leporello: poor maiden: difficult ride. *M. L. W. Bell*

PURR 3 b.g. Pursuit of Love 124 – Catawba 98 (Mill Reef (USA) 141) [2004 –p: 10g **–**
11g⁶ 10.2f 17.1d 9.7g 9.9s 12f 14.1s⁴ Oct 27] smallish, good-bodied gelding: little form.
T. T. Clement

PUSHKIN (IRE) 6 b.h. Caerleon (USA) 132 – Palmeraie (USA) (Lear Fan (USA) **97**
130) [2004 a10f³ 14g 18f² 13d⁵ 18s Oct 16] leggy horse: smart performer when trained
by E. Lellouche in France at 4 yrs: left K. McAuliffe in Saudi Arabia after reappearance:
only useful form at best in 2004: effective at 1½m to 2½m: acts on soft going, probably
on firm: has had tongue tied: sold 14,000 gns. *M. Johnston*

PUSSY CAT 2 b.f. (Mar 10) Josr Algarhoud (IRE) 118 – Swan Lake (FR) 56 (Lyphard **–**
(USA) 132) [2004 6g 6d⁶ 7g 7m⁵ 8s Oct 19] first foal: dam, maiden, seemed to stay 1¼m:
little form in minor event/maidens. *K. O. Cunningham-Brown*

PUTRA KUANTAN 4 b.c. Grand Lodge (USA) 125 – Fade (Persepolis (FR) 127) **106**
[2004 100: 10d⁶ 10g³ 8.1f* 8f 7.9d⁶ 8m 9g 8d Oct 15] angular, quite attractive colt:
useful performer: best effort when winning handicap at Sandown in May by 2 lengths
from Impeller: better at 1m than 1¼m: acts on firm and good to soft ground: usually races
prominently. *M. A. Jarvis*

PUTRA PEKAN 6 b.h. Grand Lodge (USA) 125 – Mazarine Blue 65 (Bellypha 130) **114**
[2004 115§: 8s* 8.3s* 8g 8.1g 8s² 8.5d³ 8d Oct 30] good-topped horse: good walker:
smart performer: won 4-runner listed events at Ascot (by 4 lengths from New Seeker) in
April and Windsor (by 2½ lengths from Ancient World) in May: ran creditably otherwise
in 2004 when neck second to Eagle Rise in Grosse Europa-Meile at Cologne and 2¼
lengths third to Peppercorn in Grosser Preis der Landeshauptstadt Dusseldorf: stays easy
9f: acts on soft and good to firm going: often blinkered, including for all wins: free-going
sort (pulled too hard third/fourth starts): gave temperamental display fifth 5-y-o start:
often races prominently: none too reliable. *M. A. Jarvis*

PUTRA SANDHURST (IRE) 6 b.h. Royal Academy (USA) 130 – Kharimata (IRE) **108**
(Kahyasi 130) [2004 108: 12.3d* 10g 12m 12g 10m Jul 24] big, lengthy, good sort: smart
performer at 3 yrs, just useful since: won minor event at Ripon in April by length from

Grampian: ran creditably otherwise in 2004 only when seventh to Eastern Breeze in similar event at Newmarket penultimate start: effective at 1½m/1¾m: acted on firm and good to soft going: wore cheekpieces (below form) once as 5-y-o: often heavily bandaged in front: to stand at New Hill Farm Stud, Worsley, Lancashire, fee £750. *M. A. Jarvis*

PUTRA SAS (IRE) 3 b.c. Sri Pekan (USA) 117 – Puteri Wentworth 88 (Sadler's Wells (USA) 132) [2004 89p: 8.1d² 10.3d² 12m⁶ May 30] strong, lengthy colt: useful performer, lightly raced: second in minor event at Sandown (beaten 2 lengths by Thajja) and in 3-runner Dee Stakes at Chester (beaten ¾ length by African Dream) before creditable 8¾ lengths sixth to Groom Tesse in Derby Italiano at Rome: stays 1½m: acts on firm and good to soft ground: has raced freely: has worn crossed noseband. *P. F. I. Cole*   **102**

PUYA 2 b.f. (May 14) Kris 135 – Pervenche (Latest Model 115) [2004 6d² 6s² Oct 29] tall, rangy filly: has scope: closely related to smart 6f winner (including at 2 yrs) Gorse (by Sharpo): dam unplaced in Britain/USA: green, fair form in maidens won by Hanseatic League at Windsor (slowly away) and by Maggie Jordan at Newmarket (beaten 2 lengths, leading briefly over 1f out): will probably stay 7f: should progress. *H. Candy*   **77 p**

PYRRHIC 5 b.g. Salse (USA) 128 – Bint Lariaaf (USA) (Diesis 133) [2004 54: p10g³ p10g p10g² p12g p10g⁶ p10g⁵ p12g p10g⁶ p10g p10g⁶ p10g⁶ Apr 15] smallish gelding: modest maiden: stays 1¼m: acts on polytrack, good to firm and good to soft going: has worn cheekpieces, blinkered nowadays. *R. M. Flower*   **56**

Q

QABAS (USA) 4 b.g. Swain (IRE) 134 – Classical Dance (CAN) (Regal Classic (CAN)) [2004 78d: 10g⁵ 10f 10m⁶ Jun 11] lengthy, good-topped gelding: has a round action: fair maiden: stays 11.7f: acts on any going: very slowly away final outing: none too genuine: sold 4,800 gns, joined P. Bowen: fair hurdler. *P. R. Webber*   **73**

QADAR (IRE) 2 b.c. (Mar 8) Xaar 132 – Iktidar 80 (Green Desert (USA) 127) [2004 6g² 6g³ p7m* Oct 6] 250,000Y: strong, good sort: fourth foal: half-brother to 3 winners, including 4-y-o Ikan and 3-y-o Valjarv: dam, maiden who stayed 1m, out of half-sister to Sheikh Albadou: useful form at Goodwood first 2 starts in maidens: odds on, won comfortably at Lingfield by 2½ lengths from Balkan Leader: likely to stay 1m: tongue tied all outings: should progress. *M. P. Tregoning*   **96 p**

QASIRAH (IRE) 3 b.f. Machiavellian (USA) 123 – Altaweelah (IRE) 104 (Fairy King (USA)) [2004 97p: 7g 11.4d⁵ 8.5m³ 8f⁶ 8g 8m Sep 4] tall, good-topped filly: fairly useful performer: best effort in 2004 when 3½ lengths third to Gonfilia in Princess Elizabeth Stakes at Epsom: stays 8.5f: acts on firm ground: blinkered last 5 starts. *M. A. Jarvis*   **92**

QAWAAFIL (USA) 2 b. or br.f. (Feb 13) Intidab (USA) 115 – Indihash (USA) 81 (Gulch (USA)) [2004 6m⁵ 6g 6.1m 7v* 7s Nov 6] tall, leggy filly: half-sister to useful 7f (at 2 yrs)/1m winner Emran (by Silver Hawk) and German 7f winner Munqith (by Bahri): dam, 2-y-o 7f winner, out of smart 6f/7f winner Lluna's Magic: fair performer: easily best effort when winning maiden at Catterick in October by ¾ length from Fine Lady: should stay 1m: acts on heavy going. *E. A. L. Dunlop*   **72**

QOBTAAN (USA) 5 b.g. Capote (USA) – Queen's Gallery (USA) 98 (Forty Niner (USA)) [2004 52: f9.4g⁶ f8.5g* f8g* f8f f8g f8.5g f8m 8.1g p8.6g⁴ p8.6d* p8.6g² p8.6g Dec 27] big, strong gelding: fair performer on all-weather: won banded race at Wolverhampton and handicap at Southwell in January and minor event at Wolverhampton (hung left and idled) in November: barely stays 9.4f: acts on all-weather, little form on turf: tried blinkered/visored, not in 2004: held up. *M. R. Bosley*   **– a68**

QUALITAIR WINGS 5 b.g. Colonel Collins (USA) 122 – Semperflorens (Don 128) [2004 81, a68: 7d³ 8.1m 7.9g 7m 8.5d² 7.5g 8m² 8m 8.3d⁶ 8g³ 10d 8.3d⁵ 7v p8.6g Nov 13] lengthy, quite good-topped gelding: fairly useful performer: stays easy 8.5f: acts on polytrack, firm and soft ground: tried in cheekpieces/blinkers: tends to wander: sometimes slowly away. *J. Hetherton*   **80 a?**

QUANTICA (IRE) 5 b.g. Sri Pekan (USA) 117 – Touche-A-Tout (IRE) (Royal Academy (USA) 130) [2004 77: 6s⁶ 5d 6d 6m 6m 6g Sep 16] very tall, workmanlike gelding: only modest in 2004: effective at 5f/6f: best on good going or softer (acts on heavy): tongue tied. *N. Tinkler*   **58**

QUANTUM LEAP 7 b.g. Efisio 120 – Prejudice 83 (Young Generation 129) [2004 76: p10g p10g⁶ p8g³ p8g p7g³ 8m 8g³ 7m* 7g⁶ 7g⁶ 7.6g⁴ 7g² 6d⁴ 7m 7m 7g⁶ p7g p6m²   **79**

p7g* Dec 30] quite good-topped gelding: fair handicapper: won at Lingfield in May and December: effective at 6f to easy 1¼m: acts on polytrack, good to firm and good to soft going: usually visored: often races prominently. *S. Dow*

QUARRY ISLAND (IRE) 3 b.f. Turtle Island (IRE) 123 – Last Quarry 52 (Handsome **50** Sailor 125) [2004 40: p10g⁵ f8s² f8g f7s p10g 12.1d² 10.2s 11.9f* May 24] modest performer: won 4-runner claimer at Carlisle, dictating pace: stays 1½m: acts on all-weather, firm and soft ground: tried visored/blinkered: none too genuine. *P. D. Evans*

QUARRYMOUNT 3 b.g. Polar Falcon (USA) 126 – Quilt 53 (Terimon 124) [2004 **88** –p: 6m 8.5g² p10g* 10.9g² 11.9s* 12.4s² 11.6m² 14g* 11.6d² 14.6s⁵ Oct 22] lengthy, quite good-topped gelding: fairly useful handicapper: won at Lingfield in July, Brighton in August and Newmarket (beat Fort Churchill by 6 lengths) in October: stays 1¾m: acts on polytrack, soft and good to firm ground: often races prominently: consistent: sold 67,000 gns, joined J. Old. *Sir Mark Prescott*

QUARTER TO 5 gr.m. Chocolat de Meguro (USA) 98 – Miss Lakeland (Pongee 106) **–** [2004 p7g Mar 9] no sign of ability. *W. de Best-Turner*

QUARTINO 3 b.c. Dynaformer (USA) – Qirmazi (USA) 113 (Riverman (USA) 131) **77** [2004 90: 10m 12d 11g 16m 10s² Oct 15] close-coupled, useful-looking colt: fairly useful at 2 yrs: form in 2004 only when second in minor event at Brighton: stays 1¼m: acts on soft and good to firm going: tried blinkered: sold 25,000 gns. *J. H. M. Gosden*

QUATRE SAISONS 2 ch.c. (Mar 30) Bering 136 – Inseparable 90 (Insan (USA) **–** 119) [2004 6s Oct 29] big, workmanlike colt: third foal: closely related to French 7.5f/1m winner Saint-Saens (by Pennekamp): dam, French 11f winner, sister to smart 1¼m winner Maidment: 66/1 and backward, behind in maiden at Newmarket, slowly away. *J. M. Bradley*

QUAY WALLOPER 3 b.g. In Command (IRE) 114 – Myrrh (Salse (USA) 128) [2004 **–** –: 9g 14.1m f12d 14g 12m 9.9d Aug 28] good-bodied gelding: little form: tried visored. *J. R. Norton*

QUDRAAT (IRE) 3 b.c. In The Wings 128 – Urgent Liaison (IRE) (High Estate 127) **92** [2004 10g⁵ 12g 12.3d* 11g² 11.8g 12s Oct 23] 230,000Y: smallish, close-coupled colt: third foal: half-brother to 1¼m winner Imoya (by Desert King): dam unraced half-sister to very smart performer up to 1¼m Great Dane from family of Croco Rouge and Sleepytime: fairly useful performer: trained by A. Stewart first 2 starts: won maiden at Ripon in August: good efforts in handicaps at Goodwood (second to Nordwind) and Leicester next 2 outings: stays 1½m: acts on good to soft going, well held on soft. *E. F. Vaughan*

QUDRAH (IRE) 4 b.f. Darshaan 133 – Alwiyda (USA) (Trempolino (USA) 135) **88** [2004 p10g f12g p10g⁵ 14.1g⁴ 12g 12m⁵ 10.1s 14.1d Sep 17] IR 130,000Y: first foal: dam, French 1½m winner, half-sister to smart 1½m and 1¾m winner Artillery (by Darshaan), out of half-sister to disqualified Oaks winner Aliysa (also by Darshaan): fairly useful performer: trained at 3 yrs by F. Head in France: creditable fourth in listed race at Nottingham in March: tailed off all starts after: stays 1¾m: acts on polytrack, raced mainly on good ground or softer on turf: tried blinkered *E. J. O'Neill*

QUEDEX 8 b.g. Deploy 131 – Alwal (Pharly (FR) 130) [2004 –: 16m* 18g⁵ 16.1v² 14d* **86** 16.2s* 21g p12.2g 18s⁴ Oct 16] neat gelding: has a round action: fairly useful handicapper: won at Kempton in May and Sandown (by 7 lengths) and Haydock in July: 5 lb out of weights, very good fourth to Contact Dancer in Cesarewitch at Newmarket final start: effective at 1¾m to 2¼m: acts on heavy and good to firm going: tried in cheekpieces: game. *R. J. Price*

QUEEN CHARLOTTE (IRE) 5 ch.m. Tagula (IRE) 116 – Tisima (FR) 61 (Selkirk **72** (USA) 129) [2004 77: 8g² 7m 8m 8m 7.9m⁵ 8g⁶ 7m f8g Nov 9] strong mare: fair handicapper: stays 1m: acts on good to firm ground: usually races prominently. *Mrs K. Walton*

QUEEN EXCALIBUR 5 ch.m. Sabrehill (USA) 120 – Blue Room 70 (Gorytus **43** (USA) 132) [2004 69d: p7g f8.5g p8g p8g 12g 10.9d⁶ 10.9g³ f12m⁵ May 6] rather leggy mare: poor performer: trained by J. M. Bradley first 2 starts, left C. Roberts prior to final one: effective at 7f to 11f: acts on soft and good to firm going: tried in cheekpieces/blinkers. *A. G. Juckes*

QUEEN LOUISA 4 b.f. Piccolo 121 – Queen of Scotland (IRE) 75 (Mujadil (USA) **–** 119) [2004 –: f6s 10s Nov 1] no sign of ability: tried tongue tied. *F. Watson*

QUEEN LUCIA (IRE) 3 b.f. Pursuit of Love 124 – Inquirendo (USA) 81 (Roberto **59** (USA) 131) [2004 8g⁴ 9g⁴ 7.2f⁴ 10m⁵ 9.9g⁴ p10g 9s² 8d³ p8.6g p8.6g Dec 15] smallish, leggy filly: sixth living foal: half-sister to 3 winners abroad: dam 1½m winner: modest maiden handicapper: stays 1¼m: acts on soft going, below form on polytrack. *J. G. Given*

QUEEN NEFITARI   2 b.f. (Jan 27) Celtic Swing 138 – Opalette 75 (Sharrood (USA) 124) [2004 7.9g Oct 9] 2,500Y: third foal: dam 1¼m winner: 100/1, green and edgy, tenth in maiden at York, not knocked about. *M. W. Easterby*   **57**

QUEEN OF BULGARIA (IRE)   3 b.f. Imperial Ballet (IRE) 110 – Sofia Aurora (USA) (Chief Honcho (USA)) [2004 63: f5s 6d 6.1s 6m 6.1m 6m 6d 6d Oct 16] small, compact filly: modest at 2 yrs: well held in 2004. *J. Pearce*   **–**

QUEEN OF ICENI   2 b.f. (Apr 14) Erhaab (USA) 127 – Princess Genista 108 (Ile de Bourbon (USA) 133) [2004 7g 7g² 7d Oct 30] workmanlike filly: half-sister to several winners, including smart 1¾m to 2½m winner Give Notice (by Warning), 3-y-o Race The Ace and 4-y-o Stoop To Conquer: dam, 1m (including at 2 yrs) winner, stayed 15f: clearly best effort in maidens when second to Saywaan at Leicester: should be suited by at least 1½m. *J. L. Dunlop*   **76**

QUEEN OF NIGHT   4 b.f. Piccolo 121 – Cardinal Press (Sharrood (USA) 124) [2004 81: f6g f6g⁴ 5v f7m⁴ 6m 6d f5g* f5m* 5m² 5f 5g⁵ 5.1g⁶ 5d⁶ f5m p5.1g⁶ f6g* p5.1g* f7g³ Dec 14] tall filly: fair performer: left T. D. Barron after reappearance: won 3 sellers at Southwell and handicap at Wolverhampton between June and December: stays 6f: acts on all-weather, soft and good to firm going: refused to race fifth outing. *D. W. Chapman*   **72**

QUEEN OF POLAND   2 b.f. (Feb 28) Halling (USA) 133 – Polska (USA) 103 (Danzig (USA)) [2004 7m* 7.1m* 8m² 8m⁶ Oct 3] rather leggy filly: fifth foal: half-sister to 3-y-o White Hawk and fairly useful 2001 2-y-o 5f/6f winner Grizel (by Lion Cavern): dam, 2-y-o 6f winner, closely related to useful 5f performer Millstream: useful performer: **109**

Sheikh Mohammed's "Queen of Poland"

won maiden at Yarmouth and listed race at Sandown (by head from Maids Causeway) in July: creditable efforts in May Hill Stakes at Doncaster (¾-length second to Playful Act) and Prix Marcel Boussac at Longchamp (about 3 lengths behind Divine Proportions): stays 1m: joined Godolphin. *D. R. Loder*

QUEENSBERRY 5 b.g. Up And At 'em 109 – Princess Poquito (Hard Fought 125) – § [2004 67§: p16g p12.2g Oct 9] heavy-topped gelding: fair performer on all-weather (no form on turf) at 4 yrs: well held in 2004: often wears headgear: ungenuine. *Mrs L. J. Mongan*

QUEEN'S DANCER 2 b.f. (Apr 17) Groom Dancer (USA) 128 – Special Beat 65 71 (Bustino 136) [2004 8m 8v⁵ 8.2v² p8.6g⁵ Nov 26] lengthy filly: third foal: half-sister to 5-y-o Samba Beat and winner in Greece by Efisio: dam 17f winner (also successful over hurdles): fair maiden: staying-on second at Nottingham, best effort: will be suited by 1¼m/1½m: acts on heavy ground. *M. R. Channon*

QUEEN'S ECHO 3 b.f. Wizard King 122 – Sunday News'n'echo (USA) 78 (Trempo- 55 lino (USA) 135) [2004 54: 7v² 8g⁵ 10s p8.6d Nov 3] modest maiden: should stay 1¼m: acts on heavy going. *M. Dods*

QUEENS FANTASY 3 ch.f. Grand Lodge (USA) 125 – Alcalali (USA) 96 (Septieme 66 Ciel (USA) 123) [2004 –: f9.4g 11.8d⁴ 10g 10m² f12g* f14g⁶ 10g⁶ Jul 24] strong filly: fair performer: won handicap at Wolverhampton in June: stays 1½m: tried blinkered, visored last 4 starts. *D. Haydn Jones*

QUEEN'S GLORY (IRE) 2 b.f. (Mar 10) Mujadil (USA) 119 – Karenaragon (Ara- 66 d gon 118) [2004 5v⁶ 6m² 5.3f⁵ 5.3f⁵ 6m f6d p6g⁶ 6.1d⁶ 5.3m³ Sep 23] €10,000Y, 5,000 2-y-o: second foal: dam, of little account, sister to useful sprinter in Britain/USA Evening Promise: fair maiden: well below form, including in sellers, last 4 starts: stays 6f: acts on good to firm going: visored eighth outing. *W. R. Muir*

QUEENS HAND (IRE) 2 b.f. (May 2) Lend A Hand 124 – Winchester Queen (IRE) – (Persian Bold 123) [2004 7d p6d Oct 30] close-coupled filly: fourth living foal: half-sister to 1999 2-y-o 5f seller winner Firepower (by Hamas): dam unraced: well held in claimer at Redcar (hung right) and maiden at Wolverhampton. *G. A. Swinbank*

QUEENSLANDER (IRE) 3 b.f. Inchinor 119 – Royal Subject (USA) 53 (King- – mambo (USA) 125) [2004 –: 9g Apr 8] no sign of ability in maidens at Leicester (pulled up) and Musselburgh. *G. A. Swinbank*

QUEENS RHAPSODY 4 gr.g. Baryshnikov (AUS) – Digamist Girl (IRE) (Digamist 87 (USA) 110) [2004 92: p6g² p7g f6g² f7s⁴ p7g 7.1d⁴ 8d 7.6d 7m 6d⁵ 7d³ 7s³ p8g⁵ Dec 18] a95 tall gelding: fairly useful performer: in frame 6 times in 2004: effective at 6f to easy 1m: acts on all-weather and soft ground: reliable. *A. Bailey*

QUEENS SQUARE 3 b.f. Forzando 122 – Queens Check 69 (Komaite (USA)) [2004 36 52: 5s f6d 8.5m 6m Jun 1] quite good-topped filly: just poor maiden in 2004. *N. Tinkler*

QUEENSTOWN 3 b.g. Desert Style (IRE) 121 – Fanciful (IRE) (Mujtahid 59 (USA) 118) [2004 89: 8g p8g³ 8g⁵ 8g 7m 7.1d⁴ p7m p6g Dec 30] long-backed gelding: a71 fair performer on all-weather, modest on turf: left B. Meehan before penultimate start: stays 1m: acts on all-weather, good to firm and good to soft going: usually wears blinkers/cheekpieces: has ungainly action (often changes legs under pressure): usually races prominently. *B. A. Pearce*

QUEEN TOMYRA (IRE) 2 b.f. (May 15) Montjeu (IRE) 137 – Kama Tashoof 72 75 p (Mtoto 134) [2004 8m 7g p7.1g³ p8.6g* Nov 29] 25,000Y: strong, close-coupled filly: sixth foal: closely related to ungenuine 1¼m winner Alchemystic (by In The Wings) and half-sister to useful 7f/1m winner Judicious (by Fairy King): dam maiden who stayed 1½m: won nursery at Wolverhampton by ¾ length from Tomobel: should be suited by 1¼m/1½m: open to improvement. *L. M. Cumani*

QUERIDO (USA) 2 b.c. (Mar 11) Spectrum (IRE) 126 – Polent (Polish Precedent 88 p (USA) 131) [2004 6g⁴ 7m* Aug 5] quite attractive colt: fifth foal: closely related to useful Irish 1¾m winner Tentpole (by Rainbow Quest) and half-brother to 1½m winner Choral Chimes (by Sunday Silence): dam, French 13f and 15.5f winner, half-sister to Oaks winner Snow Bride (dam of Lammtarra): confirmed promise when landing odds in maiden at Folkestone easily by 4 lengths from Mansiya: will stay 1m: useful prospect. *Saeed bin Suroor*

QUEST ON AIR 5 b.g. Star Quest 79 – Stormy Heights 62 (Golden Heights 82) [2004 42 53: p12g² 14.1m 11.5f⁶ p12m Dec 15] poor performer nowadays: stays 11.5f: acts on polytrack and firm going. *J. R. Jenkins*

QUEUE UP 2 b.g. (Feb 12) Royal Applause 124 – Faraway Lass 94 (Distant Relative **71** 128) [2004 6m³ 6g 6.1d Sep 17] lengthy gelding: second foal: half-brother to 3-y-o Harry Up: dam 6f winner: third in maiden at Doncaster: ran as if amiss in similar events after: bred to be best at 5f/6f. *J. G. Given*

QUIBBLE 7 ch.g. Lammtarra (USA) 134 – Bloudan (USA) (Damascus (USA)) [2004 – f11g f11g Dec 16] maiden: off 2 years, well beaten both 7-y-o starts: usually blinkered. *A. Bailey*

QUICK 4 b.g. Kahyasi 130 – Prompt (Old Vic 136) [2004 –: 19.1f 15m Jul 2] useful – winning hurdler up to 25f: lightly-raced maiden on Flat: well held only completed start in 2004: usually visored. *M. C. Pipe*

QUICKFIRE 2 b.f. (Feb 22) Dubai Millennium 140 – Daring Miss 113 (Sadler's Wells **88 p** (USA) 132) [2004 6m² 7g* Sep 20] well-made filly: first foal: dam, French 1½m/14.5f winner, out of Oaks runner-up Bourbon Girl: confirmed promise when landing odds in maiden at Kempton by 1¾ lengths from Love Always, leading 2f out then hanging badly left: should stay at least 1m: useful prospect. *Sir Michael Stoute*

QUICK GRAND (IRE) 2 br.f. (Mar 19) Raise A Grand (IRE) 114 – Rose 'n Reason – (IRE) (Reasonable (FR) 119) [2004 6g⁶ 5f⁶ 6g⁶ Aug 7] €5,000F: sturdy filly: seventh foal: half-sister to 2002 2-y-o 6f winner All Night Thing (by General Monash) and 2 winners in Italy by Mukaddamah: dam unraced: well held in maidens. *Miss L. A. Perratt*

QUICKS THE WORD 4 b.g. Sri Pekan (USA) 117 – Fast Tempo (IRE) 74 (Statoblest **62 §** 120) [2004 78§: 6s 6s 5v⁴ 5m 5.9f 8d 8m² 8g² 8.1g⁶ 7.2s² f8s f8g⁶ p9.5g Dec 3] rather leggy gelding: modest handicapper: effective at 7f/1m: acts on heavy and good to firm going: sometimes blinkered: unreliable. *C. W. Thornton*

QUICKSTYX 3 b.f. Night Shift (USA) – Red Bouquet (Reference Point 139) [2004 **72** p8g⁴ 8.2g⁴ 7.5d⁵ 10d⁴ 10.2m⁴ 12.1m⁶ 16.1m 12g⁶ 12d⁶ Oct 10] 100,000Y: close-coupled filly: fourth foal: half-sister to useful 1m to 1½m winner Red Carnation (by Polar Falcon), 5-y-o Red Wine and 4-y-o Red Fort: dam, 1½m/13f winner in Germany, half-sister to smart filly up to 1m Red Camellia: fair performer: won maiden at Lingfield in January: several creditable efforts in handicaps after: stays 1¼m: acts on polytrack and good to firm going, probably on good to soft: visored (tailed off) final appearance: slowly away 3 of first 4 outings. *M. R. Channon*

QUIET READING (USA) 7 b.g. Northern Flagship (USA) 96 – Forlis Key (USA) – (Forli (ARG)) [2004 –, a76: f8g³ 8.5g⁴ f8.5g⁶ f8.5s³ f8g² f8.5g² 8.1v p8g f8d⁴ f8g p8.6g⁶ **a74** f8g⁴ f8g² f8g Dec 28] big, lengthy gelding: fair on all-weather, poor on turf: best recent efforts at 7f to 8.5f: acts on fibresand and any turf going: wears headgear (usually visor): usually waited with: tough. *M. R. Bosley*

QUIET STORM (IRE) 4 b.f. Desert Prince (IRE) 130 – Hertford Castle (Reference **99** Point 139) [2004 99: 10g 8g 8f³ 7m⁶ Jul 29] workmanlike filly: useful performer: creditable seventh to Bandari in minor event at Newmarket on reappearance: just respectable efforts after: best form around 1¼m: acts on polytrack, good to firm and good to soft ground. *G. Wragg*

QUIET TIMES (IRE) 5 ch.g. Dolphin Street (FR) 125 – Super Times (Sayf El Arab **67** (USA) 127) [2004 76, a85: f6g* f5g⁴ f6g f6g⁴ f6s* 6s⁵ 6v⁵ 6d 6d p6g² f5s* p6g f5g³ Dec **a102** 7] strong gelding: useful handicapper on all-weather, fair on turf: won at Southwell in January, Wolverhampton in March and again at Southwell (beat Moayed by length) in November: effective at 5f/6f: acts on all-weather, heavy and good to firm going: usually blinkered/visored: often slowly away: refused to race once at 4yrs. *K. A. Ryan*

QUIFF 3 b.f. Sadler's Wells (USA) 132 – Wince 117 (Selkirk (USA) 129) [2004 **124** 68P: 9.9g* 12m³ 11.9s* 14.6f² Sep 11]

The Dickensian character Mr Micawber habitually believed that something would 'turn up' to solve his and his family's difficulties, and eventually it did, albeit several thousand miles from the initial point of expectation. Sir Michael Stoute might be excused for echoing the sentiment with regard to the St Leger, since the trainer remains without a win in the final classic after twenty attempts spread over twenty-five years beginning with the filly Reprocolor. Stoute has run some first-class horses, notably Shergar in 1981, but the closest he has come to success is second with Hellenic in 1990, Air Marshall in 2000, Highest in 2002 and Quiff in the latest renewal. Quiff came closer than the other three, going down only by a head to Rule of Law. While Stoute—and stable jockey Kieren Fallon, who had finished ahead of only three horses in three previous rides in the race—must have

*Aston Upthorpe Yorkshire Oaks, York—a most striking performance from Quiff,
who provides Sir Michael Stoute with a fourth win in the race in five years;
Pongee (left) and Hazarista are the only others in the picture*

been disappointed, the trainer could still draw great satisfaction from the filly's
campaign, since her improvement through the season surpassed that of any other
leading horse in the land.

Quiff ran only once as a juvenile, when green and fifth of eight in a maiden
at Newmarket at the height of summer, though there was no hiding her promise. As
Timeform Perspective noted: 'A fine, big, strapping filly, with bundles of scope,
(she) shouldn't in any way be judged on what she showed here as, given her physique, connections and pedigree, it will come as a big surprise if she doesn't leave
this form well behind.' The form was indeed left behind when Quiff reappeared in
a ten-runner maiden event at Salisbury in mid-May, as she stayed on really well
once her rider got serious with her a couple of furlongs out, leading near the finish
to beat the favourite Dawn Surprise a shade cosily by a length. Pattern company
and a longer trip beckoned and Quiff's lack of experience proved crucial when
she came third to Punctilious in the Ribblesdale Stakes at Royal Ascot after racing
freely, losing her place and having only one rival behind when hampered on the
home turn, eventually finishing best of all to be beaten three lengths. Quiff was
clearly going the right way, but she still looked to have a lot on her plate in the
Aston Upthorpe Yorkshire Oaks when seen again in August. The withdrawal of
warm favourite Ouija Board on account of the going led to Quiff's starting second
favourite behind Punctilious, second to Ouija Board in the Irish Oaks on her last
start, and ahead of the third in that race Hazarista and Ribblesdale runner-up
Sahool. Fillies aged four and up have done pretty well since the Yorkshire Oaks was
opened to them in 1991, winning five times, but there was only one older candidate
in the latest edition, Lancashire Oaks winner Pongee. The three other runners were
all 33/1-shots, and in the final two furlongs it was 33/1 any runner besides Quiff,
who had travelled strongly throughout, taken up the running from Punctilious and
Danelissima early in the straight and proceeded to forge clear after seeing off a
challenge by Hazarista. Pongee made late headway, but Quiff passed the post full
of running, officially eleven lengths clear, one of the widest winning margins in the
race's history, though the testing conditions exaggerated that verdict by a couple of
lengths. For the record, Hazarista was outstayed in third place and Punctilious
finished a tired fourth, but the Yorkshire Oaks was about one horse and one horse
only. Quiff's performance was breathtaking, one of the best by a filly over middle
distances all year and little if anything behind what Ouija Board had accomplished
and went on to accomplish.

The soft going at York clearly placed an emphasis on stamina and the St
Leger, for which Quiff was quoted as low as 5/2 favourite after her victory, looked
a realistic target, not least because the colts entered in that classic had generally
impressed less in their trials than she had in the Yorkshire Oaks. Stoute had run
two Yorkshire Oaks winners in the St Leger, Untold, third in 1986, and Hellenic,
mentioned earlier; they both started favourite. Running for only the fifth time,
Quiff started 3/1 joint favourite with Rule of Law, but only after connections had
agonised for much of the preceding week over whether to chance her on the prevailing firm going, conditions perceived to be against her. The Yorkshire Oaks had
provided a glowing report in every respect except one—with an eye to the future,

Quiff still had not gained the valuable experience of engaging in a set-to with a good, battle-hardened opponent. Rule of Law was exactly that and he proved an impossible nut to crack, hard though Quiff tried. She raced a shade freely early on in a good position off the pace set by Rule of Law, but got into a pocket on the inside with three furlongs to go. Perhaps crucially, a bit of momentum was lost as Quiff was angled outside to get a run but, once clear, she made up ground strongly and briefly looked like getting up, only for Rule of Law to pull out a bit more in the final fifty yards. The St Leger was the last we saw of Quiff. The Prix de l'Arc de Triomphe was a possible target but the prevailing firmish ground discouraged Stoute from supplementing her, and she was put by until her four-year-old campaign, which reportedly will involve races at a mile and a half, including the Yorkshire Oaks again. It will take a good filly to beat Quiff at any distance—she will stay two miles, though is unlikely to be required to do so. Whether she will be up to defeating the colts remains to be seen. Given her performance in the St Leger, it is impossible to argue that Quiff is not fully effective on firm, since the form was almost as good as she showed at York. However, given her connections' repeated misgivings about firm conditions, it will come as no surprise if she is campaigned principally in races on good or softer.

		Northern Dancer (b 1961)	Nearctic
			Natalma
	Sadler's Wells (USA) (b 1981)	Fairy Bridge (b 1975)	Bold Reason
Quiff (b.f. 2001)			Special
		Selkirk (ch 1988)	Sharpen Up
	Wince (b 1996)		Annie Edge
		Flit (b 1988)	Lyphard
			Nimble Folly

The big, strong, lengthy Quiff is typical of her sire Sadler Wells' progeny in showing more stamina than speed, and she is as well bred as any filly in training. She is the first foal of Wince, who proceeded to abort in 2002 and slip in 2003

Mr K. Abdulla's "Quiff"

before producing a brother to Quiff in February 2004. Stamina was not Wince's strong suit but she was a smart filly, successful in four races from six furlongs to a mile, notably the One Thousand Guineas for which she started favourite; she ran only once after that classic. Wince is a half-sister to the very smart middle-distance performer Ulundi and useful French mile and a quarter winner Fleeting Glimpse, the latter dam of May Hill Stakes winner Half Glance and three-year-old Tycoon, who finished a place behind Quiff in the St Leger after coming third in the Irish Derby. Quiff's grandam Flit, a mile and a quarter winner, is a sister to Skimble, winner of two Grade 2 events and placed in two Grade 1 races after winning a maiden race over six furlongs at two and a minor event over a mile and a quarter at three. Skimble's son Skimming was a very smart performer on dirt in the States, winning the Pacific Classic twice. This is also the family of Eltish, successful in the Royal Lodge Stakes and runner-up in the Breeders' Cup Juvenile. *Sir Michael Stoute*

QUINCANNON (USA) 3 b.g. Kayrawan (USA) 91 – Sulalat 82§ (Hamas (IRE) 125§) [2004 57p: f6g6 f6s f6g* Dec 28] lengthy, good-topped gelding: modest performer: won maiden at Southwell in December: will be suited by 7f/1m: raced only on fibresand. *T. D. Barron* — **61**

QUINN 4 ch.g. First Trump 118 – Celestine 62 (Skyliner 117) [2004 44: f16s 12.1m May 24] lengthy gelding: maiden: well held both starts in 2004. *C. W. Fairhurst* — **–**

QUINTILLION 3 gr.g. Petong 126 – Lady Quinta (IRE) 59 (Gallic League 119) [2004 –: p6g 6m 8f 6g p7m Dec 8] heavy-topped gelding: no sign of ability. *T. J. Etherington* — **–**

QUINTOTO 4 b.g. Mtoto 134 – Ballet 61 (Sharrood (USA) 124) [2004 82d: 9g6 10.4m 10m 8.1d p9.5d p9.5d Nov 4] smallish, stocky gelding: just modest in 2004: stays 1¼m: acts on firm going: hung markedly right second start. *R. A. Fahey* — **58**

QUITO (IRE) 7 b.r. Machiavellian (USA) 123 – Qirmazi (USA) 113 (Riverman (USA) 131) [2004 106: f6g* f8.5s p7g6 8g2 p7g5 7.1d5 7.1g6 6d* 8m 7.1g6 6d5 8g* 7g6 6s5 6d3 7s3 8d5 6s* p7g p6g2 Nov 29] tall, leggy rig: smart performer: better than ever in 2004, winning handicaps at Wolverhampton in February and York in May, minor event at Haydock in July and listed race at Doncaster (beat Millennium Force by 1¼ lengths) in November: very good second to Moayed in handicap at Wolverhampton final start: best effort (in 4 attempts) in pattern races when 2 lengths third to Royal Millennium in Bentinck Stakes at Newmarket fifteenth outing: effective at 5f (given test) to 1m: acts on all-weather, soft and good to firm ground, below form on firm: blinkered: tried tongue tied at 5 yrs: has been early to post: sometimes starts slowly: held up, and suited by well-run race: very tough and reliable. *D. W. Chapman* — **115**

QUIZZENE (USA) 2 gr.c. (Mar 13) Cozzene (USA) – Company Binness (USA) (Seattle Dancer (USA) 119) [2004 8s5 10.1d* Nov 5] $65,000: fifth foal: half-brother to useful 2002 2-y-o 1m winner (stayed 14.6f) Itemise (by Kris S) and a winner in USA by Pleasant Colony: dam unraced out of US Grade 3 8.5f winner Summer Secretary: still green, better effort in maidens when winning at Yarmouth by short head from Cordage, staying on to lead close home: will be suited by 1½m+: should progress. *M. Johnston* — **78 p**

totescoop6 Wentworth Stakes, Doncaster—Quito (blinkers) quickens well to beat Millennium Force (left), Ruby Rocket (right) and Royal Storm (stars)

R

RAAKAAN 3 b.c. Halling (USA) 133 – Glimpse 77 (Night Shift (USA)) [2004 8.3d³ **83 p**
10m* Jul 15] 72,000Y: fifth foal: closely related to a winner in Italy by Elmaamul and
half-brother to 1998 2-y-o 6f winner Focus (later successful in USA) and 2002 2-y-o 1m
winner Shenley Charm (both by First Trump): dam 2-y-o 6f winner: better effort in
maidens (fairly useful form) when winning at Leicester by 2 lengths from Antigiotto:
should stay 1½m: joined D. Selvaratnam in UAE: looks open to further improvement.
A. C. Stewart

RABBIT 3 b.f. Muhtarram (USA) 125 – Ninia (USA) 102 (Affirmed (USA)) [2004 **49**
8.3g 8.2m 6d⁵ Oct 10] 6,800Y: fourth foal: half-sister to French 8.3f winner Milord Jones
(by Emperor Jones): dam 7.5f to 1¼m winner: poor maiden: refused to enter stall second
intended outing. *Mrs A. L. M. King*

RABITATIT (IRE) 3 b.f. Robellino (USA) 127 – Coupled 64 (Wolfhound (USA) **66**
126) [2004 62: 8g² 9.3f⁴ 8.5m 9.2m² 8.3g⁵ 9.7g⁵ 8g⁶ 10d² 10.2m 9.2s⁴ 10f Sep 23] leggy
filly: has a long stride: fair performer: probably stays 1¼m: acts on firm and good to soft
going: tried in cheekpieces: usually makes running. *J. G. M. O'Shea*

RACCOON (IRE) 4 b.g. Raphane (USA) 102 – Kunucu (IRE) 94 (Bluebird (USA) **96**
125) [2004 79p: 5m⁴ 5m* 5m* 5m 6m 5g 5.6m 6s Sep 18] strong, good-quartered gelding: useful handicapper: won at Haydock (by 3 lengths from Connect) and Musselburgh
(quite valuable event, by ¾ length from Corridor Creeper) in May: below form in Portland at Doncaster (sweating and edgy) and Ayr Gold Cup last 2 outings: best at 5f: acts on
good to firm ground: visored second to seventh starts, tongue tied final one: tends to edge
right: races up with pace. *T. D. Barron*

RACE THE ACE 3 b.g. First Trump 118 – Princess Genista 108 (Ile de Bourbon **94 p**
(USA) 133) [2004 10d⁴ 10m⁵ 12m² 14.1d³ 16.4m³ 16s* 16m² 16s* Oct 29] leggy gelding: half-brother to several winners, including smart 1¾m to 2½m winner Give Notice
(by Warning) and 4-y-o Stoop To Conquer: dam, 1m (including at 2 yrs) winner, stayed
15f: progressive handicapper: won at Goodwood in August and Newmarket in October,
beating Laggan Bay impressively by 7 lengths in latter: stays 2m: acts on soft and good to
firm going: should make a useful 4-y-o. *J. L. Dunlop*

RACHEL'S VERDICT 3 b.f. Royal Applause 124 – Shady Street (USA) (Shadeed **75**
(USA) 135) [2004 6g⁴ 6f⁵ 6d⁵ Aug 20] 12,500F, €35,000Y: half-sister to several winners
abroad: dam unraced: fair form in maidens: won at Salisbury by head from Zwadi, strong
burst to lead close home: will stay 7f: sold 18,000 gns, sent to USA. *J. R. Fanshawe*

RACING NIGHT (USA) 4 b.g. Lear Fan (USA) 130 – Broom Dance (USA) (Dance **54 ?**
Spell (USA)) [2004 80: p8g 8.1d Apr 24] heavy-topped gelding: fairly useful performer
at 3 yrs: just modest form in 2004: should stay 1¼m: acts on good to firm ground.
J. R. Best

RADIANT BRIDE 4 ch.f. Groom Dancer (USA) 128 – Radiancy (IRE) 77 (Mujtahid **53 §**
(USA) 118) [2004 52§: p13g p16g² p13g⁶ f16g* f12g² p13g p13g* f16.2s⁴ f12d* Dec 21]
modest performer: won banded race at Southwell in February and claimers at Lingfield in
March and Southwell (flashed tail) in December: stays 2m: acts on all-weather and good
to firm ground: often wears blinkers/cheekpieces: ungenuine. *K. R. Burke*

RADISH (IRE) 3 b.f. Alhaarth (IRE) 126 – Nichodoula 65 (Doulab (USA) 115) [2004 **75 p**
63p: 8g 10.2s* Oct 19] tall, leggy filly: fair form: off 3 months, best effort when winning
maiden at Bath by 5 lengths from Santa Caterina: stays 1¼m: acts on soft ground: withdrawn after refusing to enter stall third intended outing: sold 25,000 gns: capable of
further improvement. *E. F. Vaughan*

RADLETT LADY 3 ch.f. Wolfhound (USA) 126 – Royal Dream 81 (Ardkinglass **50**
114) [2004 p6g 5s 6m 6m 5d f6g* f5g² f6g Dec 12] 5,000Y: leggy filly: second foal: dam
5f/6f winner (including at 2 yrs): modest performer: won banded race at Southwell in
November: effective at 5f/6f: acts on fibresand. *D. K. Ivory*

RADMORE SPIRIT 4 b.f. Whittingham (IRE) 104 – Ruda (FR) (Free Round (USA)) **–**
[2004 f9.4s 5.1g p5.1g p8.6g Dec 27] deep-girthed filly: sister to 9.4f and 1½m winner
Dunkirk Spirit and half-sister to 2 winners, including 8.3f and 1½m winner Wings
Awarded (by Shareef Dancer): dam unraced: no form: left G. Ham after debut. *J. W. Unett*

RAETIHI 3 b.f. Wizard King 122 – Foreno (Formidable (USA) 125) [2004 6m 5s⁴ 5g **32**
p6g Oct 18] half-sister to 3 winners, including 1999 2-y-o 5f winner Turtle Surprise (by
Turtle Island) and 1½m seller winner Early To Rise (by Don't Forget Me): dam lightly
raced: well held in maidens. *A. Senior*

RAFFERTY (IRE)   5 ch.g. Lion Cavern (USA) 117 – Badawi (USA) 103 (Diesis   **89**
133) [2004 95, a103: 8m 7m⁵ 8.3m³ 8.3g⁴ 8g 8m p7g p8.6g⁵ Dec 10] angular gelding:
fairly useful handicapper: left C. Brittain 22,000 gns after sixth start: stays 8.5f: acts on
all-weather, firm and good to soft ground: often blinkered: free-going sort: sometimes
early to post. *T. D. Barron*

RAFFISH   2 ch.g. (Feb 20) Atraf 116 – Valadon 72 (High Line 125) [2004 7m 7.1g⁴ p8g*   **72**
6d Oct 14] 2,000F, 10,000Y: close-coupled gelding: half-brother to numerous winners,
including smart 7f (at 2 yrs) to 1½m winner Sandmoor Chambray (by Most Welcome):
dam 1½m winner: fair performer: won maiden at Lingfield in September: well held in
sales race at Newmarket final start: stays easy 1m: acts on polytrack, best turf effort on
good going. *J. M. P. Eustace*

RAFTERS MUSIC (IRE)   9 b.g. Thatching 131 – Princess Dixieland (USA) (Dixie-   **64**
land Band (USA)) [2004 74, a80: f6s³ f6s f6g² 7d 6g⁵ 5.1d⁵ f6g⁴ p7.1g² Dec 14] good-   **a74**
bodied gelding: fair handicapper: stays easy 7f: acts on all-weather and any turf going:
tried blinkered/in cheekpieces/tongue tied, not in 2004: usually held up: sometimes
hangs. *Julian Poulton*

RAGAMUFFIN   6 ch.g. Prince Sabo 123 – Valldemosa 81 (Music Boy 124) [2004 79:   **75 d**
6g 6m 6m⁵ 6g Jun 2] sturdy gelding: fair handicapper: below form in 2004 after reappearance: effective at 5f/6f: acts on soft and good to firm ground: often blinkered earlier in
career: held up. *T. D. Easterby*

RAGASAH (IRE)   4 b.m. Glory of Dancer 121 – Slight Risk 72 (Risk Me (FR) 127) [2004 –:   **47**
p10g p8g⁴ p10m⁴ p10m Dec 15] sparely-made mare: poor performer: stays 11f: acts on
all-weather. *E. R. Oertel*

RAGAZZI (IRE)   3 ch.g. Raphane (USA) 102 – Zalotti (IRE) 84 (Polish Patriot (USA)   **?**
128) [2004 6s 6m 7g f6g³ f8g⁵ 6.9m Sep 11] lengthy, angular gelding: modest maiden: **a60**
easily best effort at Southwell on fourth start: stays 6f: acts on fibresand: sold 1,200 gns.
T. D. Barron

RAGGED GLORY (IRE)   2 br.c. (Feb 11) Foxhound (USA) 103 – Resurgence (Polar   **70**
Falcon (USA) 126) [2004 5g⁵ 5g⁶ 7m² 8d p8g² p8.6g⁶ Oct 9] 22,000F, 25,000Y: quite
good-topped colt: first foal: dam unraced sister to very smart sprinter Pivotal: fair
maiden: second twice at Lingfield: stays easy 1m: acts on polytrack and good to firm
going: visored last 2 starts. *R. Hannon*

RAGGED JACK (IRE)   3 b.g. Cape Cross (IRE) 129 – Isticanna (USA) 96 (Far North   **70**
(CAN) 120) [2004 76p: 6g² 6.1m³ 5g* p7g⁵ p6g⁶ 10m⁶ 7d Aug 27] leggy gelding: fair
performer: won maiden at Hamilton in July: stays 7f: acts on good to firm going and
polytrack: tried in blinkers/cheekpieces: sold 4,500 gns. *G. A. Butler*

RAHEED (IRE)   3 b.g. Daggers Drawn (USA) 114 – In Due Course (USA) (A P Indy   **57**
(USA) 131) [2004 63: p8g⁶ 9.9s 10m 7m 6g⁴ Sep 14] good-topped gelding: modest
maiden: left E. Dunlop 2,000 gns after third start: should stay 1¼m: tried visored.
Mrs C. A. Dunnett

RAHEEL (IRE)   4 ch.g. Barathea (IRE) 127 – Tajawuz 82 (Kris 135) [2004 66: p13g⁵   **67 §**
p10g⁴ p8g p12g⁶ p10g* p10g⁴ p10g³ p8d 8.3m 10d p8g p12g p12m 10.1d Oct 16]
big, workmanlike gelding: fair handicapper: won at Lingfield in February: effective at
1¼m/1½m: acts on polytrack, no recent form on turf: tried blinkered, usually tongue tied:
often slowly away, and virtually refused to race tenth outing: difficult ride: ungenuine.
P. Mitchell

RAHJEL SULTAN   6 b.g. Puissance 110 – Dalby Dancer 71 (Bustiki) [2004 –: f12g³   **68 §**
f8.5g⁶ 8g* 8v⁶ 8m f8d⁶ f8g Dec 28] big, heavy-topped gelding: 100/1, only form when
winning maiden at Bath in April: stays 1m: tried blinkered/tongue tied/in cheekpieces:
unreliable. *B. A. McMahon*

RAHWAAN (IRE)   5 b.g. Darshaan 133 – Fawaakeh (USA) 84 (Lyphard (USA) 132)   **90**
[2004 95: 18g* 18.7d May 5] lengthy gelding: fairly useful handicapper: made all at Doncaster in March by ¾ length from Vicars Destiny: ran as if amiss in Chester Cup: stayed
18.7f: acted on firm and good to soft going: probably best up with pace: dead. *C. W. Fairhurst*

RAINBOW COLOURS (IRE)   3 br.f. Linamix (FR) 127 – Mill Rainbow (FR) (Rain-   **–**
bow Quest (USA) 134) [2004 –p: 9.9g 8.2g Jun 21] useful-looking filly: little form: tried
tongue tied: sold 6,000 gns, sent to France. *J. R. Fanshawe*

RAINBOW IRIS   2 b. or br.f. (Feb 24) Mister Baileys 123 – Kastaway 91 (Distant   **69**
Relative 128) [2004 5m⁴ 6d⁵ 6d² 6f 6d⁶ 6g⁵ p6g 6s⁴ Nov 2] 14,000Y: sturdy filly: second
foal: half-sister to 3-y-o Oro Verde: dam 2-y-o 5f winner: fair maiden: barely stays 6f:
acts on good to soft going. *B. Smart*

RAINBOW QUEEN   4 b.f. Rainbow Quest (USA) 134 – Dazzle 116 (Gone West – (USA)) [2004 10.4f³ 10.4s 10.1g Sep 15] good-topped filly: won maiden in 2002: missed 2003 and well held in 2004: sold 32,000 gns. *Sir Michael Stoute*

RAINBOW RISING (IRE)   2 b. or br.g. (Mar 8) Desert King (IRE) 129 – Fantastic   93 Bid (USA) (Auction Ring (USA) 123) [2004 5.9f⁴ 6s² 6m Sep 8] 36,000Y: useful-looking gelding: half-brother to 7f winner Fantastic Dance (by Imperial Ballet): dam, French 1m winner, half-sister to smart middle-distance performer Germano: fairly useful maiden: made most when second to Dario Gee Gee in minor event at Ripon: first home far side when ninth in sales race at Doncaster (gelded after): will stay at least 1m. *J. Howard Johnson*

RAINBOW SKY   2 b.f. (Apr 1) Rainbow Quest (USA) 134 – Safayn (USA) 82   – (Lyphard (USA) 132) [2004 7g Oct 1] £85,000Y: compact filly: fourth foal: half-sister to winner in Spain by Mujtahid: dam, Irish 7f winner, out of US Grade 1 1¼m winner Mountain Bear, herself half-sister to very smart miler Efisio: 66/1, well held in maiden at Newmarket. *B. W. Hills*

RAINBOW TREASURE (IRE)   2 ch.f. (Mar 2) Rainbow Quest (USA) 134 – Gaily   57 Royal (IRE) (Royal Academy (USA) 130) [2004 7g 7.2d⁶ 6d Oct 15] 65,000Y: leggy filly: third foal: dam, Japanese 1m/9f winner, half-sister to smart French winner up to 15f New Frontier: modest form in maidens: best effort when sixth at Ayr: should be suited by 1¼m/1½m. *J. S. Goldie*

RAINBOW WORLD (IRE)   4 b.c. Rainbow Quest (USA) 134 – Far Fetched (IRE)   65 92 (Distant Relative 128) [2004 83: f8.5s p12g³ p12g 11.6d 11.6m³ 12g 10f³ 9g 10f 10f Jul 26] first foal: dam, 6f (at 2 yrs) and 1m (in USA) winner, half-sister to smart dam of Pilsudski: fairly useful performer for J. Oxx in Ireland in 2003, winning maiden at Gowran: just fair form in 2004: should stay 1½m: acts on polytrack, firm and soft going: tried tongue tied, wore cheekpieces last 6 starts. *Andrew Reid*

RAINSBOROUGH HILL   3 b.g. Groom Dancer (USA) 128 – Ellebanna 69 (Tina's   – Pet 121) [2004 –: 9.7s 12.1m Aug 5] rather leggy, close-coupled gelding: no form. *A. King*

RAIN STOPS PLAY (IRE)   2 b.c. (Mar 20) Desert Prince (IRE) 130 – Pinta (IRE)   82 (Ahonoora 122) [2004 7m³ 7g 8g² 8s* Oct 19] €110,000Y: useful-looking colt: sixth foal: brother to 8.5f winner Prince Dmitri and half-brother to 2 winners, including fairly useful 1999 2-y-o 6f winner Teodora (by Fairy King): dam 5f to 7.5f winner in Ireland/Italy, including at 2 yrs: fairly useful performer: won maiden at Bath by head from Jaamid: should stay at least 1¼m: acts on soft and good to firm ground. *M. R. Channon*

RAINSTORM   9 b.g. Rainbow Quest (USA) 134 – Katsina (USA) 98 (Cox's Ridge   48 (USA)) [2004 54: f8.5g⁶ 10.2f⁵ 9g⁶ 12.3g 9g 10m 7m 9.9m² 7.9m 8.1m⁵ Aug 5] stocky gelding: poor handicapper: effective at 1m to 11f: acts on fibresand and firm going, probably on soft: tried visored earlier in career: sometimes slowly away. *W. M. Brisbourne*

RAISE A TUNE (IRE)   2 ch.c. (Apr 14) Raise A Grand (IRE) 114 – Magic Melody   76 p 62 (Petong 126) [2004 8m p8g* Sep 22] €19,000F, €34,000Y: fourth foal: half-brother to 6f winner Molly Ellen (by Fayruz): dam, maiden best at 6f at 2 yrs, half-sister to 3 useful sprinters: still green, better effort in maidens when winning at Lingfield by neck from Watchmyeyes, dictating pace: not sure to stay much beyond 1m: likely to progress. *J. A. Osborne*

RAISON DETRE   2 b.c. (May 2) Mtoto 134 – Kelimutu 58 (Top Ville 129) [2004 7d   – p8.6g Dec 17] rather leggy colt: sixth foal: half-brother to 3 winners, including useful 1m (at 2 yrs) and 1¼m winner Whitefoot (by Be My Chief) and fairly useful 1¼m winner Ark Admiral (by Inchinor): dam 1¼m/1½m winner: signs of a little ability in maidens. *J. Pearce*

RAJAM   6 b.g. Sadler's Wells (USA) 132 – Rafif (USA) 68 (Riverman (USA) 131)   83 [2004 82: 12g 13.8g⁶ 18v 12m* 13.1f³ 14m 12.3g⁶ 11.9g⁵ 12g² 11.9f² 12g⁴ 11.7m 15.9s 12g Aug 30] stocky gelding: fairly useful handicapper: won at Musselburgh in May: effective at 1½m/1¾m: acts on firm and soft going: usually visored, tried blinkered/tongue tied in 2002. *D. Nicholls*

RAJAYOGA   3 ch.g. Kris 135 – Optimistic 90 (Reprimand 122) [2004 62: f8g 8.3m   57 10m⁴ 10f 10.1d p10m⁶ f12g Dec 1] modest maiden: stays 1¼m: acts on polytrack and firm going. *M. H. Tompkins*

RAJWA (USA)   2 ch.c. (Jan 13) Dubai Millennium 140 – Zelanda (IRE) 108 (Night   97 Shift (USA)) [2004 6g² 6s² 6f² Sep 11] sturdy, close-coupled colt: fluent mover: third foal: closely related to 4-y-o Silver Seeker and half-brother to 3-y-o Pearl Grey: dam, 5f/

6f winner, out of smart Irish 9f and 11f winner (also third in Irish St Leger) Zafadola: favourite, second in maidens at Goodwood and York and minor event at Doncaster (2 lengths behind Galeota in 4-runner contest), tending to find little: needs to settle to stay beyond 6f: tongue tied all starts. *Saeed bin Suroor*

RAKTI 5 b.h. Polish Precedent (USA) 131 – Ragera (IRE) (Rainbow Quest (USA) **129** 134) [2004 126: 10f* 10d 10m⁵ 8m* 8f 10m Dec 12]

'Nobody takes an Italian Group 1 performer seriously until he has shown he is capable of attaining that level outside Italy.' The remark of Rakti's owner, Gary Tanaka, is borne out by the fact that, despite becoming—in 2002—the first home-trained winner of the Derby Italiano for fourteen years and then winning the Group 1 Premio Presidente della Repubblica at Rome as a four-year-old, Rakti started at 50/1 in the Prince of Wales's Stakes at Royal Ascot in 2003. He had been transferred to Michael Jarvis after his three-year-old campaign—Jarvis saddled him in the Premio Presidente—and he finished a good second to Nayef at Royal Ascot, returning with a small crack in his near-hind fetlock. Off the course for the rest of the summer, Rakti won the Champion Stakes at Newmarket on his return (he had refused to enter the stalls in the race as a three-year-old). The Champion Stakes victory and a creditable second after a sluggish start to another notable ex-Italian, Falbrav, in the Hong Kong Cup established Rakti at the top. When he reappeared as a five-year-old in the latest Prince of Wales's Stakes, he was 3/1 second favourite, behind Godolphin's most successful turf performer of 2003 Sulamani.

Rakti had clearly thrived physically since last seen on a racecourse and, in particularly fine shape at Royal Ascot, stood out as a most imposing individual. He gave a performance to match his appearance, one of the most striking seen all season. Full of himself beforehand and taking a strong hold under restraint on the way to post, the handily-placed Rakti was pulling double as the field reached the home turn and soon took command when eased out early in the straight. Powerscourt and Ikhtyar, both held up in a race run at a fairly steady gallop early on, stayed on strongly to finish second and third, beaten two lengths and half a length, with Sulamani only fourth. Rakti's performance represented an improvement even on his Champion Stakes form and he looked set for a magnificent season, his first target the Coral-Eclipse Stakes at Sandown. Rakti's trainer expressed some concern that there was only two and a half weeks between the two races, and, on the day, there were reservations about the good to soft going, Rakti having shown his very best form on good or firmer. Whether either accounted for, or contributed to, Rakti's substandard performance—he came eighth, not knocked about when beaten —is debatable. Rakti threw his chance away after getting very much on edge on the way to the start and at the stalls. Tardily away and quickly chased along to track his pacemaker, he raced much too freely, his jockey looking at times in danger of being run away with, and had nothing left in the straight. Rakti's excitability and his problems at the stalls had led to connections employing expert horse handler Steve 'Yarmy' Dyble to school Rakti at Newmarket as a four-year-old. Dyble was regularly at the start for Rakti's races in the latest season but problems were again apparent in the Irish Champion Stakes in September, his next race after missing

Prince of Wales's Stakes, Royal Ascot—Rakti is better than ever on his return; Powerscourt, Ikhtyar (striped cap) and Sulamani (rail) are next to finish

Queen Elizabeth II Stakes (sponsored by NetJets), Ascot—Rakti has no problems dropped back to a mile; Lucky Story runs him close, the pair clear of Refuse To Bend

the International at York because of softish going. Given permission by the Leopardstown stewards to miss the parade and go straight to the start, Rakti refused to settle in the race, after once more missing the break. He performed much better than at Sandown, however, not discredited in finishing fifth behind Azamour, beaten around two lengths.

Rakti's display in the Prince of Wales's Stakes, under conditions which placed the emphasis firmly on speed, reaffirmed the impression, gained the previous season, that he might well prove just as effective back at a mile. His trainer seemed to rule out the idea when the subject of Rakti's tackling the Sussex Stakes came up in mid-July. Rakti had never raced over a distance as short as a mile, but two weeks after Leopardstown he was in the line-up for Britain's most prestigious Group 1 event over the trip, the Queen Elizabeth II Stakes, sponsored by NetJets, a race won the previous year by Falbrav who had not been inconvenienced by dropping back to a mile. The latest field was weakened by the late defection of three of the season's classic winners, Attraction (taken out at the final declaration stage because of worries about watering), Bachelor Duke (training setback) and Haafhd (because of the firmish going), the last-named withdrawn only an hour before the race. Dispensation was given for Rakti to be taken last to post and, wearing a rope halter for stalls entry and tried in a crossed noseband, he proved more tractable in the race, following Godolphin's pacemaker before being sent on soon after entering the home straight. Rakti quickened clear two furlongs out, stealing a march on his main rivals, and held off the three-year-old Lucky Story by half a length, with the Queen Anne and Coral-Eclipse winner Refuse To Bend a further two and a half lengths away third, the high-class Nayyir fourth and that gelding's narrow Sussex conqueror the filly Soviet Song, who started favourite, below form in sixth.

Rakti was clearly right back to his best and he became a possible for the Breeders' Cup Mile (the meeting had originally been ruled out because 'there is no turf race over ten furlongs, his best trip'). It would have cost 135,000 dollars to supplement Rakti for Lone Star Park and there was also the equally lucrative Mile Championship at Kyoto three weeks later to consider. A trip to Japan was also thought to fit better with Rakti's final assignment of the campaign, an attempt to go one better in the Hong Kong Cup at Sha Tin in December. But the season ended in anticlimax: Rakti ran a long way below form, beating only two home in a field of sixteen, a slow start again not helping; favourite at Sha Tin, he was able to keep on at only one pace for seventh of fourteen behind Alexander Goldrun, expending too much energy by fighting for his head in the first part of the race.

The strapping Rakti—a tall, good-topped individual who invariably impresses in appearance—is by the top-class miler Polish Precedent, whose stud career has fallen short of the highest expectations held for him. His fee was originally £35,000 and this had fallen to £20,000 when Rakti's dam Ragera visited him in 1998. It is down to £9,000 for 2005, despite the achievements of Rakti and Polish Summer's victory in the Dubai Sheema Classic. Polish Precedent's own record at stud—he has come up with the occasional major performer, most notably the redoubtable Pilsudski—affects the commercial stud appeal of Rakti and, at the time

Mr Gary A. Tanaka's "Rakti"

Rakti (b.h. 1999)	Polish Precedent (USA) (b 1986)	Danzig (b 1977)	Northern Dancer
			Pas de Nom
		Past Example (ch 1976)	Buckpasser
			Bold Example
	Ragera (IRE) (b 1992)	Rainbow Quest (b 1981)	Blushing Groom
			I Will Follow
		Smageta (b 1979)	High Top
			Christine

of writing, he is set to stay in training, good news for racegoers who will have another chance of seeing him. There should be no reservations among breeders about the distaff side of Rakti's pedigree. He comes from a good family, the third foal of the lightly-raced maiden Ragera (a daughter of excellent broodmare sire Rainbow Quest) whose first foal, the filly Riksha (by Zilzal), was a prolific winner in Italy. Rakti's grandam Smageta was a pattern winner in Italy and third in the Italian equivalents of the One Thousand Guineas and Oaks, the Premio Regina Elena and the Oaks d'Italia; Rakti's great grandam Christine, who was a useful racemare in England, produced another Italian classic performer in Svelt, winner of the Premio Parioli (Two Thousand Guineas). Smageta is also the dam of Rusoli, placed in the St Leger Italiano, and grandam (not dam as stated in *Racehorses of 2003*) of Risiat, beaten a nose in the Parioli. Rakti is almost certainly best at a mile to a mile and a quarter (he hasn't tackled a mile and a half since the Derby Italiano). He won on good to soft ground earlier in his career but his best efforts have been put up on good going or firmer (the ground was very firm when he won the Prince of Wales's Stakes). A hard puller, who is usually held up, he is often difficult to handle at the races, tending to play up and be reluctant at the start, and he sometimes races too freely for his own good. Though his idiosyncracies cast a shadow over him, making him none too reliable as a betting proposition, the volatile Rakti has still built up a fine record, winning five Group 1 races, and is a cracking horse on his day. *M. A. Jarvis*

RAMBO BLUE   4 b.g. Elmaamul (USA) 125 – Copper Trader 53 (Faustus (USA) 118) [2004 10g 10.2g⁶ p9.5d p8.6g p12.2g Nov 29] modest maiden: should stay 1½m. *A. W. Carroll*   **53**

RAMPAGE   3 ch.f. Pivotal 124 – Noor El Houdah (IRE) 61 (Fayruz 116) [2004 6d* Jun 25] 45,000Y: fourth foal: half-sister to useful 6f winner (including at 2 yrs) J M W Turner (by Forzando): dam, 5f to 7f winner (including at 2 yrs), half-sister to useful 1998 2-y-o 6f/7f winner Smittenby: favourite, won maiden at Newcastle by 2½ lengths from Brain Washed, quickening clear over 1f out: suffered back problem after, but stays in training, and looks sure to improve. *W. J. Haggas*   **76 p**

RAMSGILL (USA)   2 b.g. (Mar 25) Prized (USA) – Crazee Mental 107 (Magic Ring (IRE) 115) [2004 p8.6d p9.5g Nov 13] modest form in maidens, then gelded. *J. A. R. Toller*   **56**

RANCHO CUCAMONGA (IRE)   2 ch.f. (Apr 25) Raphane (USA) 102 – Kunucu (IRE) 94 (Bluebird (USA) 125) [2004 5m 5g 6.1s* 6m 6m 5.1g⁵ 5g⁵ 6.1d 6g² f6s* p6g² p6g² p7g⁶ Dec 29] good-topped filly: fourth foal: sister to 4-y-o Raccoon and half-sister to 2003 2-y-o 5f winner Hillside Girl (by Tagula): dam 5f winner, including at 2 yrs: fair performer: won maiden at Nottingham in July and claimer at Southwell in November: better at 6f than 5f: acts on all-weather and good to soft ground: visored last 5 starts: best efforts when held up: sometimes looks none too keen. *T. D. Barron*   **69**

RANDALLS TOUCH   2 b.g. (May 9) Mind Games 121 – L A Touch 58 (Tina's Pet 121) [2004 5g p6g p7.1g Oct 16] seems of little account. *B. D. Leavy*   **–**

RANDOM QUEST   6 b.g. Rainbow Quest (USA) 134 – Anne Bonny 105 (Ajdal (USA) 130) [2004 98: 16g 18.7d 16.2d 16.2g² 16.1f Aug 7] leggy, useful-looking gelding: fairly useful handicapper: best effort in 2004 when neck second to Dorothy's Friend in valuable event at Ascot: ran as if amiss final start: stays 21f: acts on good to firm and soft ground. *B. J. Llewellyn*   **92**

RANGOON (USA)   3 ch.c. Distant View (USA) 126 – Rustic (IRE) 99 (Grand Lodge (USA) 125) [2004 75P: 6s³ 7d² 7s⁵ 7g² 8.1m* Sep 6] good-topped colt: fair performer: won maiden at Warwick in September: stays 1m: acts on soft and good to firm going: hung markedly left penultimate start: sold 14,000 gns. *Mrs A. J. Perrett*   **76**

RANI TWO   5 b.m. Wolfhound (USA) 126 – Donya 74 (Mill Reef (USA) 141) [2004 80: 10.3g 10m 10m⁶ 10.3g⁵ 10.4f⁴ 10s⁴ 10.1g 10m² 9.9g² 10d Oct 18] strong mare: fair performer: left W. M. Brisbourne after sixth start: stays 1¼m: acts on polytrack, firm and soft ground. *W. R. Muir*   **75**

RANNY   4 b.f. Emperor Jones (USA) 119 – Defined Feature (IRE) 91 (Nabeel Dancer (USA) 120) [2004 57: p8g⁴ p7g² p7g² 7m 6g⁶ 7m⁴ 8m⁴ p7g⁵ 8m⁶ Aug 16] modest handicapper: effective at 7f/1m: acts on firm ground and polytrack. *Dr J. D. Scargill*   **52**
a59

RANSACKER   2 b.g. (Mar 6) Bahamian Bounty 116 – Hazy Heights 56 (Shirley Heights 130) [2004 6f⁵ 6m³ Jun 5] 25,000Y: sturdy gelding: first foal: dam, 1m winner, out of sister to smart 1m/1¼m performer Feminine Wiles: better effort in maidens when third at Doncaster, behind long way: should stay 7f: slowly away both outings. *C. E. Brittain*   **62**

RANVILLE   6 ch.g. Deploy 131 – Kibitka (FR) (Baby Turk 120) [2004 11.6m 13.9g 12d⁵ 14.8d Aug 27] heavy-bodied gelding: poor mover: missed 2003 and just fairly useful handicapper in 2004: stays 2¼m: acts on heavy and good to firm going: races prominently. *M. A. Jarvis*   **89**

RAPHAEL (IRE)   5 b.m. Perugino (USA) 84 – Danny's Miracle (Superlative 118) [2004 88: 7g 7d* 7.6d 8f³ 7s 7m⁴ 7g 7d² 7g² 8m² 8m Aug 7] leggy, quite good-topped mare: fairly useful handicapper: won at Thirsk in April: severed a tendon and put down at Redcar: effective at 7f to 8.5f: acted on firm and soft going: blinkered once at 3 yrs: usually raced handily: was tough and consistent. *T. D. Easterby*   **88**

RAPID FLOW   2 b.c. (Mar 24) Fasliyev (USA) 120 – Fleet River (USA) 93 (Riverman (USA) 131) [2004 7g 6g Aug 28] strong, lengthy colt: has a quick action: fourth foal: half-brother to fairly useful 9f winner Humber (by Bering) and useful 1m winner Delta (by Zafonic), both in France: dam, 2-y-o 7f winner, half-sister to very smart performer up   **67**

843

to 1½m Eltish and smart US sprinter Forest Gazelle: better effort when eighth in maidens at Newmarket on final start: should stay at least 7f. *Mrs A. J. Perrett*

RAPID RIVER   2 b.f. (Mar 17) Lahib (USA) 129 – Cast A Spell (Magic Ring (IRE) **52**
115) [2004 6m Sep 5] quite good-topped filly: second foal: dam, ran once, out of sister
to very modest 1m/1¼m performer Broken Hearted: 50/1, eighth in maiden at York.
Mrs L. Stubbs

RAPID ROMANCE (USA)   2 b.f. (May 15) Theatrical 128 – Fast Nellie (USA) (Ack **63**
Ack (USA)) [2004 6.1d⁵ 6.1g⁶ 6.1s⁴ Sep 20] half-sister to several winners, including
useful Irish 1996 2-y-o sprinter Raphane (by Rahy) and French 9f winner Where's Dave
(by Eagle Eyed): dam unraced sister to US Grade 1 8.5f winner Caline: modest form in
maidens: carried head bit awkwardly when fourth at Chepstow: should stay 1m: sold
20,000 gns, sent to USA. *E. A. L. Dunlop*

RAPPORT (IRE)   3 ch.f. Zafonic (USA) 130 – In The Groove 127 (Night Shift **68**
(USA)) [2004 7s 7m⁶ 8m 10g³ 11f p10g p9.5g Nov 13] sixth foal: half-sister to 3 winners,
including useful 1995 2-y-o 5f/6f winner Incarvillea (by Mr Prospector) and UAE
1m winner Incentive (by Rainbow Quest): dam won 4 Group 1s, including Irish 1000
Guineas and Coronation Cup: fair maiden: left J. Oxx in Ireland 28,000 gns, then well
held in 2 handicaps: stays 1¼m. *S. Kirk*

RARE COINCIDENCE   3 ch.g. Atraf 116 – Green Seed (IRE) 78 (Lead On Time **69**
(USA) 123) [2004 59: f8g* f8.5g* f8g³ f8.5g⁶ f8g 9.2d⁴ 8m⁴ 9.2g⁴ f8d 9.2g 8.1s³ 7.1g⁴ **a74**
7.2d 7.2s p9.5g⁵ f8g Dec 16] quite good-topped gelding: fair handicapper: won at Southwell (seller) in January and Wolverhampton in February: stays 1m: acts on all-weather,
soft and good to firm ground: usually wears cheekpieces: tried tongue tied: sometimes
hangs/finds little. *R. F. Fisher*

RAREFIED (IRE)   3 b.g. Danehill (USA) 126 – Tenuous 111 (Generous (IRE) 139) **82**
[2004 81: 10d 11.6g* 12.3d 12d 8d 8g 8g 10m⁴ 10d Oct 18] neat gelding: fairly useful
handicapper: below form after winning at Windsor in April: left R. Charlton 42,000 gns
after fourth outing: gelded after final start: stays 11.6f: unraced on extremes of going.
T. D. Easterby

RARE PRESENCE (IRE)   5 b.g. Sadler's Wells (USA) 132 – Celebrity Style (USA) **–**
96 (Seeking The Gold (USA)) [2004 –: 11.6m Jun 7] fair maiden: lightly raced and no
form since 2002: tried blinkered/visored: tongue tied final start. *C. P. Morlock*

RASA SAYANG (USA)   2 b. or br.c. (Mar 24) Salt Lake (USA) – Annie Ruth (USA) **63**
(Gulch (USA)) [2004 5.1g 5g² 6m² 6m⁶ Aug 8] $20,000Y: quite good-topped colt: fourth
foal: half-brother to winners in USA by Clever Trick and Regal Classic: dam winning
sprinter in USA: modest maiden: stayed 6f: dead. *T. D. Barron*

RASHIDA   2 b.f. (Jan 29) King's Best (USA) 132 – Nimble Lady (AUS) (Fairy King **67**
(USA)) [2004 6g³ 7.1m Sep 6] €150,000Y: rangy filly: first foal: dam unraced half-sister
to useful performer up to 2m Breyani, herself dam of Irish 1000 Guineas winner Tarascon: better effort when third of 5 to Satin Kiss in minor event at Haydock: should stay
1m. *J. Noseda*

RASID (USA)   6 b.g. Bahri (USA) 125 – Makadir (USA) (Woodman (USA) 126) **80**
[2004 75+: p10g* p12g p12g² 12s³ 10.1v* 12g 10m p10d⁵ 10m³ 10s* 10g 11g 10.4g
p12g 10v p10g³ p9.5g⁶ p9.5g³ p10g 10m p9.5g⁶ Dec 27] rangy gelding: fairly useful
performer: won handicap at Lingfield in January, minor event at Newcastle in April and
handicap at Nottingham in July: effective at 1¼m/easy 1½m: acts on polytrack, heavy
and good to firm ground: tried visored: sometimes slowly away. *C. A. Dwyer*

RASSEEM (IRE)   2 b.f. (Feb 8) Fasliyev (USA) 120 – Yorba Linda (IRE) 97 (Night **76 d**
Shift (USA)) [2004 5.1g² 5.1d 6f³ 6.1m⁶ f5g p6g Dec 27] 140,000Y: strong filly: first
foal: dam 5f (including at 2 yrs) and 7.5f winner: fair maiden: left Saeed bin Suroor 6,000
gns after fourth outing: stays 6f: acts on firm going. *M. D. Hammond*

RATHMULLAN   5 ch.g. Bluegrass Prince (IRE) 110 – National Time (USA) (Lord **45**
Avie (USA)) [2004 –: p6g f8g f6g³ 6m⁴ f7g³ f6g* p7g³ f8.5m⁵ 7m f6g 7m 6f⁴ p8g 8d³
f6g⁵ f7g⁶ p7m³ p7g Dec 20] workmanlike gelding: poor performer: won banded race at
Wolverhampton in May: effective at 6f to 1m: acts on all-weather, good to firm and good
to soft going: usually wears blinkers/cheekpieces. *E. A. Wheeler*

RATIO   6 ch.g. Pivotal 124 – Owdbetts (IRE) 69 (High Estate 127) [2004 112: 5d* 6g **114**
6f 5m 6s 6s² Nov 17] angular, good-bodied gelding: carries plenty of condition: smart
performer: won listed race at Deauville in July by a head from Miss Emma: not discredited when tenth in Sprint Cup at Haydock next time: creditable short-neck second to
Striking Ambition in listed race at Maisons-Laffitte final start: effective at 5f/6f: acts on

firm and soft going: effective blinkered/visored or not: has been tongue tied: reportedly had fibrillating heart final 5-y-o start. *J. E. Hammond, France*

RATUKIDUL (FR) 2 b.f. (Jan 2) Danehill (USA) 126 – Whakilyric (USA) 113 (Miswaki (USA) 124) [2004 7g* 8f⁵ 7d 7.5s³ Nov 16] compact filly: half-sister to several winners, notably high-class French 10.5f and 1½m winner Hernando (by Niniski) and very smart French 10.5f winner Johann Quatz (by Sadler's Wells): dam French 2-y-o 5.5f/7f winner: fair performer: won maiden at Folkestone in August: creditable efforts in nurseries/minor event after, leaving Sir Michael Stoute before final start: should stay 1¼m: acts on firm and soft ground. *D. Sepulchre, France*   **79**

RAVEL (IRE) 3 b.g. Fasliyev (USA) 120 – Lili Cup (FR) (Fabulous Dancer (USA) 124) [2004 –p: 7d 6m 10f Jun 8] big, strong, good sort: little form. *M. L. W. Bell*   **–**

RAVENGLASS (USA) 5 b.h. Miswaki (USA) 124 – Urus (USA) (Kris S (USA)) [2004 92: 12g 16g⁶ 12m⁵ 18g Jun 3] compact horse: fairly useful handicapper: ran as if amiss final start: stays 2m: acts on firm ground, probably on soft. *J. G. M. O'Shea*   **82**

RAVEN (IRE) 2 b.f. (Feb 13) Alzao (USA) 117 – Eman's Joy 68 (Lion Cavern (USA) 117) [2004 8.3g 6s⁶ Nov 6] 28,000Y: rather leggy filly: first foal: dam, 6f winner, half-sister to useful 1m/9f winner Eton Lad: seemingly much better effort (ran in seller for J. Osborne on debut) when never-dangerous sixth in maiden at Doncaster: should stay 1m. *M. E. Sowersby*   **66 ?**

RAVE REVIEWS (IRE) 3 b.f. Sadler's Wells (USA) 132 – Pieds de Plume (FR) (Seattle Slew (USA)) [2004 76p: 10m³ 10g* 12m 12.5d Aug 7] strong, sturdy filly: useful performer: 6½ lengths third to Ouija Board in listed race at Newmarket: won similar event at Newbury in May by ¾ length from Sahool: well held after in Ribblesdale Stakes at Royal Ascot and Prix de Pomone at Deauville: should stay 1½m: acts on good to firm ground. *J. L. Dunlop*   **104**

RAWAABET (IRE) 2 b.c. (Apr 30) Bahhare (USA) 122 – Haddeyah (USA) 68 (Dayjur (USA) 137) [2004 7g 7.1m Jul 21] good-topped colt: modest form in maidens at Salisbury and Sandown: sold 3,000 gns. *M. P. Tregoning*   **54**

RAWALPINDI 3 ch.g. Intikhab (USA) 135 – Just A Treat (IRE) 47 (Glenstal (USA) 118) [2004 –: 7s 7f 8m f12f² 13.1f⁵ 17.1g Oct 4] sturdy gelding: modest maiden: stays 1½m: acts on fibresand: none too consistent: sold 5,000 gns. *J. A. R. Toller*   **62**

RAWDON (IRE) 3 b.g. Singspiel (IRE) 133 – Rebecca Sharp 122 (Machiavellian (USA) 123) [2004 8g 10m⁵ Jun 12] tall, good-topped gelding: third foal: half-brother to useful 6f (at 2 yrs) and 1m winner Miss Pinkerton (by Danehill): dam 7f/1m (Coronation Stakes) winner: visored, better effort (fairly useful form) when 1¾ lengths fifth to Trew Class in maiden at Sandown (looked none too keen): gelded after: stays 1¼m. *J. H. M. Gosden*   **80**

RAWYAAN 5 b.h. Machiavellian (USA) 123 – Raheefa (USA) 75 (Riverman (USA) 131) [2004 117: 12f* 12m⁶ 12m 13.4d 12g May 19] close-coupled, quite attractive horse: has a round action: smart performer: won handicap at Nad Al Sheba in February by ¾ length from Kayseri: respectable eighth to Polish Summer in Dubai Sheema Classic there on third outing: well below form back in Britain after: stays 1½m: acts on firm and good to soft ground: blinkered/visored: has worn crossed noseband: sold 38,000 gns, sent to Saudi Arabia. *J. H. M. Gosden*   **117 d**

RAYBERS MAGIC 3 b.f. Magic Ring (IRE) 115 – Kirkadian (Norwick (USA) 125) [2004 10m 7.9g 7.5g 9.2f Jul 31] third foal: dam, no sign of ability, half-sister to high-class 1m/1¼m performer Bijou d'Inde: no sign of ability. *J. R. Weymes*   **–**

RAYMOND'S PRIDE 4 b.g. Mind Games 121 – Northern Sal 59 (Aragon 118) [2004 73: f6g f5g 6s⁵ 5v* 6s* 5d⁴ 5v⁵ 6g 7s Nov 2] tall gelding: fairly useful handicapper on turf, fair on all-weather: won twice at Newcastle in April: effective at 5f/6f: acts on heavy going and fibresand: tried in cheekpieces, usually blinkered: usually races prominently. *K. A. Ryan*   **86 a?**

RAYSHAN (IRE) 4 b.g. Darshaan 133 – Rayseka (IRE) 112 (Dancing Brave (USA) 140) [2004 107: 18.7d 11.9m 16.1s 13.9s Aug 18] quite good-topped gelding: useful performer in 2003, winning maiden at Limerick and third to Maharib in Curragh Cup: left J. Oxx 140,000 gns and won over hurdles before well beaten on Flat in 2004: stays 1¾m: acts on good to firm ground, probably on good to soft: tried blinkered. *J. Howard Johnson*   **–**

RAYSOOT (IRE) 3 b.c. Cape Cross (IRE) 129 – Mashkorah (USA) (Miswaki (USA) 124) [2004 –p: 6s f8.5g² 8.2g⁵ 7g 8m* Aug 10] big, good-bodied colt: fair handicapper: trained until after fourth start by A. Stewart: tongue tied, won at Bath in August, making all: stays 8.5f: acts on fibresand and good to firm going: joined D. Selvaratnam in UAE. *E. F. Vaughan*   **70**

RAY

RAYWARE BOY (IRE) 8 b.g. Scenic 128 – Amata (USA) (Nodouble (USA)) [2004 – §: p13g Mar 2] leggy, short-backed gelding: temperamental performer. *D. Shaw* **– §**

RAZA CAB (IRE) 2 b.g. (Mar 13) Intikhab (USA) 135 – Laraissa (Machiavellian (USA) 123) [2004 7m³ p7g⁸ 7d⁶ p7g² 8m Sep 9] 31,000Y: heavy-topped gelding: first foal: dam unraced out of useful French 1m winner Bint Lariaaf: useful performer: won maiden at Lingfield in July, then left C. Allen: creditable efforts in listed race/minor event next 2 starts: should stay 1m: acts on polytrack, probably on good to soft going. *G. A. Huffer* **95**

RAZE 2 ch.f. (Mar 1) Halling (USA) 133 – Rive (USA) (Riverman (USA) 131) [2004 7d Aug 27] tall, good-topped filly: sister to useful 2001 2-y-o 1m winner Revealing and half-sister to 3 winners, including useful 1½m winner Singleton (by Singspiel), who stayed 2m: dam, French 2-y-o 1¼m winner, half-sister to dam of very smart performer up to 1¾m Mons: 5/1 and very green, eighth to Playful Act in maiden at Newmarket: should do better. *Sir Michael Stoute* **– p**

RAZKALLA (USA) 6 b.g. Caerleon (USA) 132 – Larrocha (IRE) 116 (Sadler's Wells (USA) 132) [2004 118: 10m* 12m⁴ 12m⁴ 12g⁵ 16s Nov 2] lengthy gelding: smart performer: won handicap at Nad Al Sheba in February, and good 2 lengths fourth to Polish Summer in Dubai Sheema Classic there on third outing (left D. Loder and off 6 months after): last of 5 listed race at Newmarket before respectable ninth to Makybe Diva in Melbourne Cup (Handicap) at Flemington final start: stays 13.4f: acts on fibresand and good to firm going, probably on soft: genuine. *Saeed bin Suroor* **117**

REACHING OUT (IRE) 2 b.g. (Feb 3) Desert Prince (IRE) 130 – Alwiyda (USA) (Trempolino (USA) 135) [2004 f7g 7g p6g² p8g² Dec 18] €52,000Y: close-coupled gelding: third foal: half-brother to 4-y-o Qudrah: dam, French 1½m winner, half-sister to smart 1½m/1¾m winner Artillery, out of half-sister to disqualified Oaks winner Aliysa: fair maiden: trained on debut by G. Bravery: second twice at Lingfield: effective at 6f to easy 1m: acts on polytrack. *H. J. Collingridge* **71**

READ FEDERICA 2 ch.f. (Feb 8) Fusaichi Pegasus (USA) 130 – Reading Habit (USA) (Half A Year (USA) 130) [2004 7d* Oct 30] $140,000Y: strong filly: first foal: dam, 5f (at 2 yrs) to 6f (minor stakes) winner in USA, out of half-sister to dam of high-class US 1¼m performer Best Pal: 14/1 and green, won maiden at Newmarket by neck from Sharaby, held up and plenty to do but good headway to lead close home: will stay 1m: open to considerable improvement, and likely to prove useful. *Sir Michael Stoute* **77 P**

READY TEDDY GO 2 b.g. (Feb 8) Danzig Connection (USA) – Mariette 35 (Blushing Scribe (USA) 107) [2004 p7g Oct 28] 66/1, slowly away and always rear in maiden at Lingfield. *D. K. Ivory* **–**

REAL COOL CAT (USA) 2 gr.f. (Feb 26) Storm Cat (USA) – Hail Kris (USA) (Kris S (USA)) [2004 6g⁴ 7s Oct 22] leggy, good-topped filly: fourth foal: closely related to US Grade 2 2000 2-y-o 6f winner Give Praise (by Pioneering): dam 1m winner in USA: better effort in maidens when fourth at York: disputed lead long way at Doncaster: should stay 7f: type to do better. *M. Johnston* **66 p**

REAL ESTATE 10 b.g. High Estate 127 – Haitienne (FR) (Green Dancer (USA) 132) [2004 11.6m 15m 16.4g 17.2g Jul 11] strong gelding: missed 2003: just poor form in 2004. *J. S. King* **43**

REALISM (FR) 4 b.g. Machiavellian (USA) 123 – Kissing Cousin (IRE) 116 (Danehill (USA) 126) [2004 60: f8f⁴ f7g⁴ f8g* f8.5s 8.3d⁵ f8g 8.1g³ 8m⁶ 10m* 10.2m² 10.2m* 10m* 12m 10m* 10g⁵ 10.1m⁶ 10g Sep 29] strong, good-bodied gelding: fairly useful handicapper: won at Southwell, Nottingham, Chepstow, Pontefract and Leicester between February and July, 3 of them apprentice races: stays 1¼m: acts on fibresand, yet to race on extremes of going on turf: tough: sold 38,000 gns. *P. W. Hiatt* **86**

REAL QUALITY (USA) 2 br.g. (May 11) Elusive Quality (USA) – Pleasant Prize (USA) (Pleasant Colony (USA)) [2004 6d² 7m* Oct 10] $25,000Y: half-brother to several minor winners in USA: dam unraced: favourite, won maiden at Newcastle by ¾ length from Three Degrees, held up going well before leading final 1f: should stay 1m: useful prospect. *I. Semple* **90 p**

REAL TING 8 br.g. Forzando 122 – St Helena (Monsanto (FR) 121) [2004 f6m Apr 19] little form in 3 races since 1999: tried visored/tongue tied. *Ms Deborah J. Evans* **–**

REAP 6 b.g. Emperor Jones (USA) 119 – Corn Futures 78 (Nomination 125) [2004 79: p10g 8v³ 8.1g 8m⁶ 10g 10.1d⁴ Nov 5] leggy, good-topped gelding: fair handicapper: effective at 1m/1¼m: acts on all-weather, good to firm and heavy going: tried visored at 2 yrs: usually races up with pace. *J. Pearce* **73**

846

REBATE 4 b.g. Pursuit of Love 124 – Aigua Blava (USA) (Solford (USA) 127) [2004 **76 d**
81: p10g p10g⁵ 9.7d 8.1d 8g p8g³ 10f³ 10.2m⁶ 10.2f³ 10m⁵ 8g 10f⁵ 11g⁶ p10g⁵ 10d Sep
20] lengthy gelding: just fair handicapper in 2004: below form after sixth start: stays
1¼m: acts on polytrack, firm and good to soft ground: tongue tied last 5 starts: sometimes
races freely. *R. Hannon*

REBEL LEADER 7 br.g. Ezzoud (IRE) 126 – Haitienne (FR) (Green Dancer (USA) **?**
132) [2004 8m Jul 17] fairly useful performer in Hong Kong for G. Lane, winner of 5
races: off 18 months, well held in handicap at Newbury on British debut: stays 1¼m: acts
on soft and good to firm going: usually wore blinkers in Hong Kong. *W. R. Muir*

REBEL RAIDER (IRE) 5 b.g. Mujadil (USA) 119 – Emily's Pride (Shirley Heights **63**
130) [2004 p8.6g* p8.6g p12.2d² p12.2g² p12.2g Dec 11] modest handicapper: trained at
3 yrs by P. Flynn in Ireland: won at Wolverhampton in October: stays 1½m: acts on soft
going and polytrack. *B. N. Pollock*

REBEL REBEL (IRE) 2 b.c. (Mar 25) Revoque (IRE) 122 – French Quarter (Ile de **93**
Bourbon (USA) 133) [2004 6g 7g 8d⁵ 7m⁴ 8g* 7m* 7m² Sep 26] big, strong, lengthy colt:
has a quick action: half-brother to several winners, including 7f/1m winner Broughton's
Pride (by Superpower) and 4-y-o Montmartre: dam, French 1¼m to 11.5f winner, half-
sister to high-class performer up to 1¼m Executive Pride: fairly useful performer: won
20-runner nurseries at Yarmouth and Lingfield in September: very good second to Wise
Dennis in similar event at Ascot, staying on from rear under 7-lb claimer: stays 1m: acts
on good to firm going. *N. A. Callaghan*

REBEL ROUSER 3 b.g. Kris 135 – Nanouche (Dayjur (USA) 137) [2004 –: 8.1s⁵ **–**
f9.4g⁵ f12d Apr 29] good-topped gelding: little form. *W. R. Muir*

REBUTTAL (USA) 2 b.c. (Mar 12) Mr Greeley (USA) 122 – Reboot (USA) **118**
(Rubiano (USA)) [2004 6g² 6s* 6g³ 6g² Oct 1]
     Brian Meehan went close to becoming the first trainer since Geoffrey
Brooke in 1962 to complete the Cheveley Park and Middle Park Stakes double in
the same year, Brooke having won the former with My Goodness Me and the latter
with Crocket. Two days after his 40/1-shot Magical Romance had sprung a surprise
in the Cheveley Park, Meehan sent out Rebuttal to finish second in the Middle Park,
the colt going down by three quarters of a length to the unbeaten Ad Valorem.
Rebuttal, who started at 9/1, was asked to make his move on the outside and
responded so well that, for a few strides a furlong out, he looked likely to overhaul
Ad Valorem, but the latter proved just the stronger up the hill, Rebuttal nevertheless
running on well enough to pull two and a half lengths clear of third-placed Iceman.
It was a smart performance from Rebuttal and represented further significant
improvement from a colt having only his fourth race. A promising second behind
One Putra in a maiden at Windsor in August on his debut, Rebuttal then made all to
beat Tremar by a neck in a similar event at Kempton before being stepped up
markedly in class in the Mill Reef Stakes at Newbury. Rebuttal finished third to
Galeota in the Mill Reef, and might have won had the race panned out differently.
Whereas Galeota was able to dictate the pace, which in the early stages was no
more than steady as the runners bunched on the stand side, Rebuttal was restrained
in the rear. Still going well at the back of the field over two furlongs out, Rebuttal's
rider was forced to switch him for a run and found himself with a lot of ground to
make up. Rebuttal ran on well but never had a hope of getting there. The Horris Hill
Stakes and Breeders' Cup Juvenile were mentioned as possible targets for Rebuttal
after the Middle Park, but he missed both engagements, his trainer reportedly
saying that it would be in the colt's best interests to leave him until the next year,
when the Two Thousand Guineas is likely to be on the agenda.
     Rebuttal has raced only at six furlongs so far and, while he may well stay
seven, there has to be a big doubt about his getting a mile. Speed looks to be his
forte, as his pedigree suggested it would be. Rebuttal's sire Mr Greeley, a son of
Gone West, was runner-up in the Breeders' Cup Sprint, while his dam Reboot was
also a sprinter. Rebuttal is his dam's second foal after the US six-furlong winner
Courriel (by French Deputy). Reboot won three races in the States at three and one
at four, all of them over six furlongs. Four of her dam Launch Light Tek's six wins
came in non-graded stakes up to an extended mile. Easily the best of Mr Greeley's
European representatives prior to Rebuttal stayed a mile. That was the Sussex

Mr P. Minikes' "Rebuttal"

		Gone West	Mr Prospector
	Mr Greeley (USA)	(b 1984)	Secrettame
	(ch 1992)	Long Legend	Reviewer
Rebuttal (USA)		(ch 1978)	Lianga
(b.c. Mar 12, 2002)		Rubiano	Fappiano
	Reboot (USA)	(gr 1987)	Ruby Slippers
	(b or br 1995)	Launch Light Tek	Relaunch
		(b 1987)	Princess Leyte

Stakes winner Reel Buddy, but Reel Buddy was out of a mare who had won over that trip and plied his trade at six and seven furlongs for much of his career. Rebuttal, a 110,000-dollar yearling, who was resold for 400,000 dollars at two, has raced only on good ground apart from at Kempton, where he made hard work of landing the odds on soft. *B. J. Meehan*

RECKLESS FRED 5 ch.g. So Factual (USA) 120 – Winnie Reckless (Local Suitor – (USA) 128) [2004 p6g p8g p10g Feb 26] well held in maidens/seller. *Miss K. M. George*

RECKLESS MOMENT 3 b.f. Victory Note (USA) 120 – Blue Indigo (FR) (Pistolet – Bleu (IRE) 133) [2004 49: 8.1d Oct 9] poor maiden: well held only 3-y-o start. *Jane Southcombe*

RECOGNISE (IRE) 3 ch.g. Groom Dancer (USA) 128 – Broken Romance (IRE) 71 (Ela-Mana-Mou 132) [2004 12.1g² 11.1d⁴ 12.1g² 18m² Jun 27] €50,000Y: half-brother to several winners, including smart 7f (at 2 yrs) to 2m winner Romantic Affair and 5-y-o Gulf (both by Persian Bold): dam unraced: fair maiden: should stay 1¾m (below form over 2¼m). *M. Johnston*

RECOUNT (FR)　4 b.g. Sillery (USA) 122 – Dear Countess (FR) (Fabulous Dancer　**80**
(USA) 124) [2004 83: 10.1s 14m 7m⁶ 8g⁵ p8g 9g 10m² 10f³ 12m⁴ 10.1d³ 10g Sep 15]
good-topped gelding: fairly useful handicapper: stays 1½m: acts on firm and good to soft
ground: wayward (withdrawn after bolting to post intended second start). *J. R. Best*

RECTANGLE (IRE)　4 ch.g. Fayruz 116 – Moona (USA) 73 (Lear Fan (USA) 130)　**75**
[2004 89: 5g 5s 5m 5d 6g² 5m 5f 5.1g 5d Sep 16] strong gelding: fair handicapper: stays
6f: acts on good to firm and good to soft ground: races prominently. *D. Nicholls*

RED ACER (IRE)　3 ch.g. Shinko Forest (IRE) – Another Baileys 60 (Deploy 131)　**–**
[2004 –: p10g f9.4s 11.6m Jun 7] quite good-topped gelding: little form. *P. D. Evans*

RED ADMIRAL (USA)　2 b.c. (Feb 18) Red Ransom (USA) – Ausherra (USA) 106　**94 p**
(Diesis 133) [2004 7.1d 8g* Sep 16] tall, close-coupled colt: fluent mover: half-brother to
several winners, including smart 1m (at 2 yrs) to 2¼m winner Yorkshire (by Generous)
and 6-y-o Riyadh: dam, 6f (at 2 yrs) and 11.5f (Lingfield Oaks Trial) winner, sister to
Oaks winner Ramruma: much better effort in maidens when winning at Yarmouth comfortably by 2 lengths from Clasp, leading 3f out: will stay at least 1¼m: useful prospect,
should win more races. *Saeed bin Suroor*

RED AFFLECK (USA)　2 b.g. (Mar 28) Nicholas (USA) 111 – Lucie Mon Amour　**84**
(USA) (Meadowlake (USA)) [2004 5.2m³ 7d² 7.1d* 8d 7s⁴ 7s Nov 6] 15,000Y: sturdy,
compact gelding: second foal: dam 1m winner in USA: fairly useful performer: made all
in maiden at Warwick in September: fourth at Doncaster, only creditable effort in nurseries after: stays 7f: acts on soft going. *P. W. Chapple-Hyam*

RED APACHE (IRE)　2 b.c. (May 3) Namid 128 – Special Dissident (Dancing Dis-　**–**
sident (USA) 119) [2004 7m 6d Nov 5] leggy colt: well held in maidens at Leicester and
Yarmouth. *H. J. Collingridge*

REDBANK (IRE)　3 b.g. Night Shift (USA) – Bush Rose (Rainbow Quest (USA) 134)　**54**
[2004 69, a64: p8g² p7g p7g p8g p8.6g p8g Dec 20] close-coupled, good-topped gelding:
modest maiden: claimed from N. Callaghan on reappearance: barely stays 1¼m: acts on
all-weather, good to firm and good to soft going: tried tongue tied/blinkered. *S. Dow*

RED BIRR (IRE)　3 b.g. Bahhare (USA) 122 – Cappella (IRE) 75 (College Chapel　**87**
122) [2004 78p: 7g 9.9g² 9.9d* 10d 14m Jul 29] leggy, quite good-topped gelding: fairly
useful performer: best effort when winning minor event at Salisbury in June by 5 lengths
from Antigiotto: stays 1¼m: acts on good to firm and good to soft going. *A. M. Balding*

RED BLOOM　3 b.f. Selkirk (USA) 129 – Red Camellia 116 (Polar Falcon (USA)　**114**
126) [2004 110p: 8m⁴ 8m³ 8.9g* 10g⁴ Sep 19] tall, rather leggy filly: has a quick, rather
choppy action: smart performer: in frame behind Attraction in 1000 Guineas at Newmarket (2¼ lengths fourth) and Coronation Stakes at Royal Ascot (2¾ lengths third) prior
to winning 4-runner sportingoptions.co.uk Strensall Stakes at York in September by ½
length from Salselon: below-form fourth to Monturani in Blandford Stakes at the Curragh
final start: should stay 1¼m: raced only on good ground or firmer. *Sir Michael Stoute*

sportingoptions.co.uk (Betting Exchange) Strensall Stakes, York—
Kevin Darley takes over from Kieren Fallon on Red Bloom, who comes out on top
in a close finish with Salselon (virtually obscured), Imperial Dancer and Babodana (right)

Wolferton Rated Stakes (Handicap), Ascot—
Red Fort is well clear of Promotion and Blythe Knight (blaze)

RED CHAIRMAN 2 b. or br.g. (Apr 4) Red Ransom (USA) – Chine 100 (Inchinor **84**
119) [2004 7m 7m⁵ 6m⁴ 6f⁶ Jul 31] $150,000Y: good-topped, close-coupled gelding: first
foal: dam, French 1¼m winner, later successful in USA: fairly useful maiden: seemingly
best effort when last of 4 in minor race at Newmarket: should stay at least 1m: gelded
after final start. *D. R. Loder*

RED CONTACT (USA) 3 b.g. Sahm (USA) 112 – Basma (USA) 104 (Grey Dawn II **84**
132) [2004 72: 7m f8g² f8g² p10g f8g* Dec 28] fairly useful performer: left A. Charlton
and off 5½ months after reappearance: much improved for new stable, winning handicaps
at Southwell in November and December: stays 1m, possibly not 1¼m: acts on fibresand.
Julian Poulton

RED CRYSTAL 6 b.m. Presidium 124 – Crystallography (Primitive Rising (USA) **–**
113) [2004 f11g⁶ Jan 4] leggy, plain mare: no sign of ability: tried in cheekpieces.
C. R. Wilson

RED DAMSON (IRE) 3 b.g. Croco Rouge (IRE) 126 – Damascene (IRE) (Scenic **94**
128) [2004 81: 14m² p12g* 14.4m² Sep 4] good-bodied gelding: fairly useful performer:
won maiden at Lingfield in August: best effort when head second to Leg Spinner in
handicap at Kempton after, dictating pace: effective at 1½m/1¾m: acts on polytrack,
good to firm and good to soft ground (tailed off sole start on fibresand). *Sir Mark Prescott*

RED DELIRIUM 8 b.g. Robellino (USA) 127 – Made of Pearl (USA) 107 (Nureyev **– §**
(USA) 131) [2004 –§, a65d: f8.5g⁶ f11g⁴ f11g⁵ f8s² f8s⁵ f8g⁵ f11s² f12g⁵ 9.2g Apr 26] **a59 §**
small, sturdy gelding: modest performer: left R. Brotherton after third start: barely stays
1½m: acts on fibresand, lightly raced and no recent form on turf: usually blinkered, tried
visored/tongue tied: sometimes slowly away: unreliable. *P. A. Blockley*

RED DUCHESS 2 ch.f. (Jan 28) Halling (USA) 133 – Red Empress 88 (Nashwan **64 p**
(USA) 135) [2004 7g 8m Sep 21] rangy filly: has scope: first foal: dam, 1½m winner,
closely related to smart 1¼m/1½m performer Happy Valentine out of smart sister to
Salsabil: better effort when ninth in maidens at Salisbury on debut: slowly away and still
green next time: should be suited by 1¼m/1½m: likely to do better. *Sir Michael Stoute*

RED FEATHER (IRE) 3 b.f. Marju (IRE) 127 – Galyph (USA) 72 (Lyphard (USA) **110**
132) [2004 102: 7m² 7f* 7d³ 8m* 8m⁴ 8g Oct 1] €62,000Y: leggy, close-coupled filly:
fifth foal: half-sister to 3 winners, including smart 1¼m winner Frankies Dream (by
Grand Lodge) and fairly useful Irish 7f winner Echo Canyon (by Lahib): dam Irish 1¼m
winner: smart performer: won maiden at Limerick at 2 yrs when also length second to
Necklace in Moyglare Stud Stakes at the Curragh: successful in 2004 in 3-runner minor
event at Limerick in June and ladbrokes.com International Stakes at the Curragh (dictated
pace, beat Trefflich 2½ lengths) in July: below form last 2 starts, fourth to Soviet Song
in Matron Stakes at Leopardstown (very edgy) and ninth to Polar Ben in Joel Stakes at
Newmarket: stays 1m: acts on firm and good to soft ground: often tongue tied. *Edward
Lynam, Ireland*

RED FINESSE 2 b.f. (Mar 10) Soviet Star (USA) 128 – Jouet 71 (Reprimand 122) **60 p**
[2004 6m 6d Oct 14] 20,000Y: good-topped filly: second foal: half-sister to 3-y-o Rising
Shadow: dam, placed at 7f/1m, sister to useful sprinter Deep Finesse: modest form in
maidens at Windsor (favourite) and Newmarket (ninth to Tomoohat), travelling strongly
long way both times: will do better. *M. A. Jarvis*

RED FLYER (IRE) 5 br.g. Catrail (USA) 123 – Marostica (ITY) (Stone 124) [2004 46: **51**
f7g* Apr 16] close-coupled gelding: modest performer: won banded race at Southwell in
April: effective at 7f to 9f: acts on all-weather and any turf going: sometimes starts
slowly/carries head high. *P. C. Haslam*

RED FOREST (IRE)   5 b.g. Charnwood Forest (IRE) 125 – High Atlas 65 (Shirley   **78**
Heights 130) [2004 61d: f12g³ f12g² 11.7s⁶ 12m* 12m* 10m⁵ 11.9g f12m³ 13f³ 13.8m³
14g* 12.1s⁶ 14.1m* 14.6s Oct 22] medium-sized gelding: fair handicapper: won at Wolverhampton in April, Pontefract in May, Thirsk in June, Musselburgh (apprentices) in
August and Redcar in October: stays 1¾m: acts on soft ground, good to firm and
all-weather: tongue tied: tough. *J. Mackie*

RED FORT (IRE)   4 b.g. Green Desert (USA) 127 – Red Bouquet (Reference Point   **117**
139) [2004 95: 10.5d* 12m³ 10m* 10.4g⁴ 10.3f² Sep 10] useful-looking gelding: smart
performer: much improved in 2004, winning handicaps at Haydock in April and Royal
Ascot (listed event, beat Promotion by 8 lengths) in June: creditable efforts after, 2½
lengths fourth to Arcalis in John Smith's Cup (Handicap) at York and ¾-length second to
Big Bad Bob in minor event at Doncaster (might well have won had effort started sooner):
best around 1¼m: acts on firm and good to soft going: has been bandaged hind joints:
sent to USA. *M. A. Jarvis*

RED GALAXY (IRE)   4 b.f. Tagula (IRE) 116 – Dancing Season (Warrshan (USA)   **45**
117) [2004 85: 7d 8s 6g p8.6g f6g f6g³ f7g Dec 11] lengthy, well-made filly: poor performer: stays 6f: acts on fibresand and good to firm ground: tried tongue tied/in cheekpieces.
D. W. P. Arbuthnot

RED GENIE   6 ch.g. Primitive Rising (USA) 113 – Marsden Rock (Tina's Pet 121)   **–**
[2004 p8.6g Nov 27] maiden hurdler: well beaten in seller at Wolverhampton. *C. J. Gray*

RED HOT RUBY   3 ch.f. Komaite (USA) – Gleam of Gold (Crested Lark 78) [2004   **45**
6g 5d³ 5g³ 6g Sep 14] 4,000Y: third foal: sister to 4-y-o Newcorp Lad and 1998 2-y-o 5f
seller winner Ok Maite, later winner in Sweden: dam no form: poor maiden: should stay
6f. *R. A. Fahey*

REDI (ITY)   3 b.c. Danehill Dancer (IRE) 117 – Rossella (Shareef Dancer (USA) 135)   **77**
[2004 73p: p8g 10m* 8m⁶ 11.6m³ 12.1s* 14.1d p12m² Oct 6] tall, angular colt: has a
quick action: fair performer: won handicap at Chepstow in August, tending to edge left:
good second in handicap at Lingfield final start: stays 1½m: acts on polytrack, firm and
soft ground: sold 52,000 gns, joined A. Balding. *L. M. Cumani*

RED LANCER   3 ch.g. Deploy 131 – Miss Bussell 65 (Sabrehill (USA) 120) [2004   **109**
61: f8.5g⁶ f11g* f9.4s* f12g² 9s² 8.1s² 8g² 10d² 12.3d* 11g³ 16.2m⁶ 16.1s 11.9s⁶ 12g
11.9d⁶ Aug 17] smallish, stocky gelding: useful performer: claimed from S. Keightley
£5,500 final 2-y-o start: vastly improved in 2004, winning handicaps at Southwell and
Wolverhampton in February and MBNA Europe Bank Chester Vase (beat Privy Seal by 5
lengths) in May: respectable efforts after when 2¾ lengths third to Manyana in listed race
at Goodwood and sixth of 7 to Rule of Law in Great Voltigeur Stakes at York final start:
stays 1½m: acts on fibresand and soft going: tends to edge left: tough. *R. J. Price*

RED LANTERN   3 ch.g. Young Ern 120 – Croft Sally (Crofthall 110) [2004 p7g p7.1g   **–**
p7.1g Nov 19] well held in maidens. *R. M. H. Cowell*

RED LEICESTER   4 b.f. Magic Ring (IRE) 115 – Tonic Chord 49 (La Grange Music   **59 §**
111) [2004 52: 6g³ 6g 6m⁵ 5.1g* f5g⁶ 5g 5.5g⁵ 5d 5.1g 5d⁶ p5.1g³ Oct 25] smallish filly:
modest performer: won maiden at Nottingham in June: best at 5f: acts on good to firm
ground and polytrack: tried blinkered, usually visored: unreliable. *J. A. Glover*

MBNA Europe Bank Chester Vase, Chester—
the vastly improved Red Lancer makes a successful step up to pattern company;
Privy Seal (star on cap) takes second in front of Temple Place (rail) and Isidore Bonheur

RED

REDMARLEY (IRE)   3 b.g. Croco Rouge (IRE) 126 – Dazzling Fire (IRE) 78 (Blue- —
bird (USA) 125) [2004 59: 9g⁶ 12.1m Jun 2] workmanlike gelding: modest maiden at 2
yrs: well held in 2004. *J. G. Given*

RED MARTEENEY   2 ch.c. (May 15) Indian Lodge (IRE) 127 – Miss Rossi (Artaius   50
(USA) 129) [2004 6m 6.1m⁶ 6m f6s Nov 17] rather leggy colt: modest maiden: left
D. Elsworth after third start: sold 1,100 gns, sent to Denmark. *J. G. Given*

RED MELODICA (USA)   4 b.f. Red Ransom (USA) – Melodica 84 (Machiavellian   —
(USA) 123) [2004 –: 10m f7m f7d 7m 8d 8s Oct 26] second foal: dam 1¾m winner out
of Italian Oaks winner/Irish Oaks dead-heater Melodist: no form: trained by J. Quinn
second/third starts (on all-weather in Britain) only. *W. P. Browne, Ireland*

RED MONARCH (IRE)   3 ch.g. Woodborough (USA) 112 – Sans Ceriph (IRE) 75   69
(Thatching 131) [2004 f6g 6d 5.1m 8m⁶ 6f² 6d* 5d* 6g Aug 28] €8,000Y: angular, workmanlike gelding: brother to 5-y-o Next Flight and half-brother to 3 winners, including 1m
winner Lady Ward (by Mujadil): dam Irish 7f winner: fair performer: won handicap at
Ripon in July and minor event at Hamilton in August: effective at 5f/6f: acts on firm and
good to soft going. *P. A. Blockley*

RED MOOR (IRE)   4 gr.g. Eagle Eyed (USA) 111 – Faakirah (Dragonara Palace   53
(USA) 115) [2004 54: f11g² f9.4g⁶ f12g* f12g² f14.8m³ f12d Jun 10] leggy gelding:
modest performer: won handicap at Southwell in April: barely stays 14.8f: raced only on
fibresand and good/good to firm ground: tried in cheekpieces. *R. Hollinshead*

RED MOUNTAIN   3 b.g. Unfuwain (USA) 131 – Red Cascade (IRE) (Danehill (USA)   47
126) [2004 –: 10.5g 9d 12s p13.9g⁴ Nov 29] very big, long-backed gelding: form only
when fourth in amateur minor event at Wolverhampton: will stay 2m: acts on polytrack.
D. W. Barker

RED OPERA   2 ch.g. (Mar 10) Nashwan (USA) 135 – La Papagena (Habitat 134)   — p
[2004 8f 8m p7m p7g Oct 13] big, lengthy, good-topped gelding: half-brother to several
winners, notably high-class 1m/1¼m performer Grand Lodge (by Chief's Crown), Dewhurst winner at 2 yrs, useful Irish 1m (at 2 yrs) and 1½m winner Sorcerous (by Sadler's
Wells) and 3-y-o La Persiana: dam unraced: not knocked about when well held in
maidens, then gelded: will be suited by 1¼m/1½m: type to do fair bit better as 3-y-o. *Sir
Mark Prescott*

REDOUBTABLE (USA)   13 b.h. Grey Dawn II 132 – Seattle Rockette (USA) (Seattle   62 §
Slew (USA) 132) [2004 44d: f6g⁶ p6g* f6g⁴ p7g* p7g 6v 6g* 6.1s 7.2m 6.1g² 7.5g* 7.6g⁶   a53 §
6.9f 6m⁴ 7m 6d 6v⁴ 6g 7.1d f7g f5g Dec 11] small, sturdy horse: modest performer: won
banded events at Lingfield in February (amateurs) and March and at Ayr in April, and
selling handicap at Beverley in July: effective at 6f to 7.5f: acts on any turf going/all-
weather: occasionally blinkered: sometimes slowly away: unreliable. *D. W. Chapman*

RED PEONY   2 b.f. (Mar 25) Montjeu (IRE) 137 – Red Azalea 95 (Shirley Heights   93
130) [2004 7f* 7s³ 8m⁶ 7g² Oct 12] good-topped filly: fifth foal: half-sister to 3-y-o
Grandalea and winner up to 1¼m in Spain by Polar Falcon: dam, 7f (at 2 yrs) and 1¼m
winner, half-sister to smart 7f/1m performer Red Camellia (dam of 3-y-o Red Bloom):
fairly useful performer: made all in maiden at Epsom in July: staying-on 3½ lengths third
to Dubai Surprise in Prestige Stakes at Goodwood: bit below form in May Hill Stakes
at Doncaster and 3-runner minor event at Leicester: should stay at least 1m. *Sir Mark
Prescott*

RED RACKETEER (USA)   2 b.c. (May 1) Red Ransom (USA) – Furajet (USA)   77 p
101 (The Minstrel (CAN) 135) [2004 7s⁴ Oct 27] brother to very smart 6.5f (in France at
2 yrs) to 9f winner China Visit and half-brother to useful 1m winners Dubai Visit and Al
Saqaar (both by Quiet American): dam, best at 5f, closely related to 2000 Guineas winner
King of Kings: 16/1, 3½ lengths fourth to Zalongo in maiden at Yarmouth, briefly a threat
over 1f out then not knocked about: sure to improve. *E. A. L. Dunlop*

RED RACKHAM (IRE)   4 b.g. Groom Dancer (USA) 128 – Manarah 76 (Marju   59
(IRE) 127) [2004 76: p13g p12g p13.9g Dec 13] modest maiden, lightly raced: probably
stays 13f: raced only on polytrack: refused to enter stall intended reappearance. *J. Nicol*

RED RIOT (USA)   2 b.c. (Jan 31) Red Ransom (USA) – Musical Treat (IRE) 98 (Royal   65
Academy (USA) 130) [2004 7.5d⁵ 8.5g³ 10.2g Sep 27] $17,000F, €120,000Y: first foal:
dam 7f winner who stayed 1¼m, later successful in North America: fair form in maidens:
stays 1m: sold 10,000 gns. *D. R. Loder*

RED RIVER REBEL   6 b.g. Inchinor 119 – Bidweaya (USA) 45 (Lear Fan (USA)   63
130) [2004 68: 11.8m 12m⁴ 12.6f 12.1g² 12.6g² 12.1m⁴ Jul 27] tall, leggy gelding: modest handicapper: stays 1¾m: acts on good to firm and good to soft going (no show only
start on fibresand): tried visored, not in 2004: usually races up with pace. *J. R. Norton*

RED RIVER ROCK (IRE) 2 b.c. (Apr 25) Spectrum (IRE) 126 – Ann's Annie (IRE) **72**
78 (Alzao (USA) 117) [2004 7g³ 8.2d 8g p8.6d⁴ p8.6g⁵ p8.6g³ Dec 11] 24,000Y: compact
colt: first foal: dam, Irish 2-y-o 1m winner, half-sister to smart 6f to 1m winner Pipe
Major: fair maiden: stays 8.6f: acts on polytrack, best turf effort on good going. *C. Tinkler*

RED ROCKY 3 b.f. Danzero (AUS) – Post Mistress (IRE) 79 (Cyrano de Bergerac **50**
120) [2004 61: p6g 5.9f 8g⁵ 6.1m 7g² 6m 8f³ 7m⁵ 7g³ 10g³ p9.5d p9.5g Dec 22] sturdy
filly: modest maiden: stays 1¼m: acts on polytrack and firm ground: wears cheekpieces
nowadays: free-going sort. *R. Hollinshead*

RED ROMEO 3 ch.g. Case Law 113 – Enchanting Eve 67 (Risk Me (FR) 127) [2004 **97**
73: 6d² 6m⁴ 6g⁴ 6m* 6m* 6g* 6g² 6g³ Aug 28] good-topped gelding: useful performer:
won handicaps at Pontefract and Windsor in June and minor event at Kempton in July:
good third to Prince Aaron in listed race at Newmarket final start: best form around 6f:
acts on good to firm and good to soft going: usually races prominently. *G. A. Swinbank*

RED RUDY 2 ch.g. (Mar 22) Pivotal 124 – Piroshka (Soviet Star (USA) 128) [2004 **61**
6f⁶ 7d³ 7.5m 6v Oct 23] 23,000F, 14,000Y: tall, close-coupled gelding: third foal: half-
brother to winner in Italy by Case Law: dam unraced: modest maiden: barely stays 7.5f:
acts on firm and good to soft going. *R. M. Beckett*

RED SAHARA (IRE) 3 ch.f. Desert Sun 120 – Red Reema (IRE) (Red Sunset 120) **83**
[2004 73p: 7m* 8m⁶ 7m⁶ 8.3g² 8d⁴ 8.3d 8g 7m Sep 29] lengthy filly: fairly useful
performer: won handicap at Newbury in May: effective at 7f/1m: acts on good to firm
going and fibresand: blinkered (ran as if amiss) final start: sent to Oman. *W. J. Haggas*

RED SAIL 3 ch.f. Dr Fong (USA) 128 – Manhattan Sunset (USA) 76 (El Gran Senor **76**
(USA) 136) [2004 8m³ 9f³ 10g 10.1m⁵ Oct 10] 22,000Y: sixth foal: half-sister to 3 winners, including fairly useful 2001 2-y-o 7f/7.6f winner Tramonto (by Sri Pekan) and 4-y-o
Sun Hill: dam 2-y-o 7f winner who stayed 1½m: fair maiden: should stay at least 1¼m:
ran as if amiss third start. *J. R. Fanshawe*

RED SAM (IRE) 2 ch.g. (Mar 15) Desert King (IRE) 129 – Mustique Dream 87 (Don't **52**
Forget Me 127) [2004 p8.6g p8.6g Dec 6] modest form on first start in maidens at
Wolverhampton: will stay at least 1¼m. *M. L. W. Bell*

RED SANS 2 b.c. (Apr 13) Rainbow Quest (USA) 134 – Sarah Georgina 79 (Persian **57 p**
Bold 123) [2004 p8m³ Dec 21] 5,000 2-y-o: brother to smart French 1m to 10.5f winner
Audacieuse and half-brother to 3 winners, including useful 1½m/1¾m winner Lord Jim
(by Kahyasi) and 3-y-o Gironde: dam, 2-y-o 6f winner, half-sister to very smart French
performer up to 1m Danseuse du Soir: 14/1, 8½ lengths third to Humble Opinion in
maiden at Lingfield: will be suited by 1¼m/1½m: should improve. *P. Mitchell*

RED SCORPION (USA) 5 ch.g. Nureyev (USA) 131 – Pricket (USA) 111 (Diesis **70**
133) [2004 79: p16g* p16g⁶ p16g⁵ 16d 16f² 14.8m³ 14g 16.2m⁶ 16.1f⁵ 16g Sep 3] stocky **a76**
gelding: fair handicapper: won apprentice event at Lingfield in January: effective at 1¾m/
2m: acts on all-weather, firm and good to soft ground. *W. M. Brisbourne*

RED SILK 3 b.f. Polish Precedent (USA) 131 – Red Tulle (USA) 66 (A P Indy (USA) **–**
131) [2004 p10g 10d Apr 5] second foal: dam, third at 1¼m on debut from 3 starts, half-
sister to US Grade 3 8.5f winner Namaqualand: last in maidens. *Mrs A. J. Perrett*

RED SKELTON (IRE) 3 ch.g. Croco Rouge (IRE) 126 – Newala 61 (Royal Academy **70**
(USA) 130) [2004 82p: 10s 9.9g 11.8g 10.1m p12g³ 12m 11.9s 15.8g p12g p12.2d p13.9g
p9.5g* p9.5g p9.5g³ p8.6g⁶ p9.5g Dec 20] tall, leggy gelding: fair performer: claimed
from W. Haggas £6,000 fifth start: won handicap at Wolverhampton in November: stays
1¼m: acts on all-weather: tried in blinkers/cheekpieces/tongue strap: very slowly away
sixth outing: inconsistent. *Ms Deborah J. Evans*

RED SOVEREIGN 3 b.f. Danzig Connection (USA) – Ruby Princess (IRE) 70 **81**
(Mac's Imp (USA) 116) [2004 79: 6s 6g 5g* 5g 5g⁵ 5.7g p5.1g p6g² p6g⁶ p5g³ p6g⁴ Dec
30] leggy filly: fairly useful performer: won handicap at Kempton in July: effective at 5f/
6f: acts on polytrack, good to firm and good to soft going: races prominently. *I. A. Wood*

RED SPELL (IRE) 3 ch.c. Soviet Star (USA) 128 – A-To-Z (IRE) 101 (Ahonoora **94**
122) [2004 77p: 8.3d 8g⁵ 8m* 8m² 8d⁶ 8m³ p10g* p9.5g³ Dec 11] good-topped colt:
fairly useful performer: won handicaps at Newmarket in May and Lingfield (beat Northside Lodge a length) in November: stays 1¼m: acts on polytrack and good to firm going,
below form on good to soft. *R. Hannon*

REDSPIN (IRE) 4 ch.g. Spectrum (IRE) 126 – Trendy Indian (IRE) 71 (Indian Ridge **72**
123) [2004 82: p16g³ 10.3g 16g 20f⁴ 14.1g⁴ 14d⁴ 16.1m 21g 14.1m 14g³ 15.9g 16d Oct
10] leggy gelding: fair handicapper: effective at 1¾m to 2½m: acts on polytrack and firm

going: visored once in 2003: ran badly in cheekpieces third outing: sometimes hangs: none too reliable. *J. S. Moore*

RED STORM 5 ch.m. Dancing Spree (USA) – Dam Certain (IRE) 61 (Damister (USA) **56** 123) [2004 61: f9.4g f12g⁶ f9.4s* f9.4g⁵ p10g f9.4g⁶ Mar 29] modest performer: easily best effort in 2004 when winning banded event at Wolverhampton in February: stays 11f: acts on fibresand and any turf going: tried blinkered/visored/tongue tied. *J. R. Boyle*

RED SUN 7 b.g. Foxhound (USA) 103 – Superetta 65 (Superlative 118) [2004 53: **71** 16.1m* 16m² 17.1f⁶ 16.1v 14.1d⁶ 15.9g³ 17.2g p16.5g* f14g³ Dec 11] smallish gelding: fair handicapper: won at Newcastle in May and Wolverhampton in December: stays 17f: acts on all-weather and good to firm going: often makes running: tongue tied in 2004. *J. Mackie*

REDSWAN 9 ch.g. Risk Me (FR) 127 – Bocas Rose 106 (Jalmood (USA) 126) [2004 **69 §** 8.1g² Sep 3] big, workmanlike gelding: fair performer: missed 2003: unseated rider and ran loose to start before creditable second in minor event at Chepstow only outing in 2004: best at 7f/1m: acts on all-weather, firm and soft ground: occasionally blinkered/tongue tied: often races freely/finds little: has bled from nose: unreliable. *A. E. Jones*

RED TOP (IRE) 3 b.f. Fasliyev (USA) 120 – Petite Epaulette 80 (Night Shift (USA)) **85 +** [2004 76: 7g² 8s³ 7m² 8f 7d² 7.6g* 9f 8f* 8.5g² Nov 26] tall, good-topped filly: fairly useful performer: didn't need to be at best to land odds in maiden at Chester in July with plenty in hand on final start for R. Hannon: very stiff task on US debut when last of 7 in Del Mar Oaks: won allowance race at Santa Anita in October: stays 8.5f: acts on firm and soft going: usually waited with. *P. Gallagher, USA*

RED WINE 5 b.g. Hamas (IRE) 125§ – Red Bouquet (Reference Point 139) [2004 **90** 102: f12s⁵ 16d Apr 10] smallish, leggy gelding: handicapper: just fairly useful form in 2 runs in 2004: effective at 1½m to 2m: acts on any turf going/all-weather: blinkered (well beaten) once in 2002. *J. A. Osborne*

REDWOOD ROCKS (IRE) 3 b.g. Blush Rambler (USA) 119 – Crisp And Cool **83** (USA) (Ogygian (USA)) [2004 82: 7g 7.1g* 7s 8g⁶ 7.1g p7g Nov 16] rather leggy gelding: fluent mover: fairly useful handicapper: made all at Musselburgh in April: better at 7f than 1m: acts on good to firm going: sweating (found little) final 2-y-o start: head-strong front runner. *B. Smart*

REDWOOD STAR 4 b.f. Piccolo 121 – Thewaari (USA) 68 (Eskimo (USA)) [2004 **66** 60: 5g⁴ 5m 6m 5.3f³ 5g 5.3f⁴ 5.3d³ 5.1m² Sep 9] fair handicapper: best at 5f: acts on firm and good to soft going: tried tongue tied/blinkered. *P. L. Gilligan*

REEDSMAN (IRE) 3 ch.g. Fayruz 116 – The Way She Moves (North Stoke 130) **–** [2004 44: p6g² 8s 8m 6m 12m Jun 28] modest maiden: form only when second in seller at **a52** Lingfield (final outing for M. Tompkins) in January: stays 6f: acts on polytrack: often wears headgear. *R. C. Guest*

REEM ONE (IRE) 3 b.f. Rainbow Quest (USA) 134 – Felona 92 (Caerleon (USA) **79** 132) [2004 9.2d* 10s² 12s² f12s⁵ Nov 17] leggy, angular filly: first foal: dam, 9f/1¼m winner from 3 starts, out of smart 1¼m winner Felawnah: fair performer: won maiden at Hamilton in September: good second in handicaps at Ayr and Newmarket: tried to run out final bend when below form in similar event at Southwell final outing: stays 1½m: acts on soft going. *M. A. Jarvis*

REEM TWO 3 b.f. Mtoto 134 – Jamrat Samya (IRE) 79 (Sadler's Wells (USA) 132) **62 ?** [2004 7.6g⁶ 9.2f³ 12.3s² 9.3g Sep 2] 1,300 2-y-o: third foal: dam, ran once, out of sister to Flame of Tara, herself dam of Salsabil and Marju: seemingly best effort in maidens when 8 lengths second of 5 to Daze at Chester: stays 1½m: acts on soft ground. *D. McCain*

REFERENCE (IRE) 2 b.g. (Apr 1) Almutawakel 126 – Uffizi (IRE) (Royal Academy **–** (USA) 130) [2004 7f 6g 8g Oct 10] well beaten in maidens. *R. Hannon*

REFLEX BLUE 7 b.g. Ezzoud (IRE) 126 – Briggsmaid 70 (Elegant Air 119) [2004 **?** f16.2g* f16g⁴ Feb 12] lengthy, angular gelding: modest handicapper: unraced on Flat **a59** in 2003: won seller at Wolverhampton in February: stays 2m: acts on fibresand, firm and good to soft going: often blinkered/visored: none too reliable. *R. J. Price*

REFUSE TO BEND (IRE) 4 b.c. Sadler's Wells (USA) 132 – Market Slide **128** (USA) 94 (Gulch (USA)) [2004 124: 8.9m 8m 8f* 10d* 8g 8m³ 10s⁵ Oct 16]
      The decision to keep Refuse To Bend in training—one that is the norm rather than the exception with top three-year-olds owned by Sheikh Mohammed or Godolphin—proved the right one, since the colt added two Group 1 victories to his

tally in the space of eighteen days in early-summer. The wins restored a reputation that had become somewhat tarnished, a situation providing an excellent reason to keep a horse of his ilk in training, and gave a much needed boost to his appeal as a stallion for the Darley operation, which had suffered two notable losses during the year with the deaths of In The Wings in April and Machiavellian in June. On the debit side, just as had happened the previous season, Refuse To Bend let himself down at least as often as he did himself justice, and, while lacking nothing in courage in a finish, he can hardly be called a model of consistency.

On the face of it, by mid-June the purchase of Refuse To Bend part-way through his three-year-old campaign, after he had won the Two Thousand Guineas and Desmond Stakes but been soundly beaten in the Derby and Prix du Moulin, looked almost as wise, in hindsight, as investing in GEC/Marconi after the depart-ure of Lord Weinstock. The colt had run below par in the Breeders' Cup Mile and, following a break of five months, in the Dubai Duty Free in March and the Lockinge Stakes in May. At both Nad Al Sheba and Newbury, he was prominent early on before dropping back, though it is worth noting that he was clearly the stable's second string behind Crimson Palace in Dubai, where he reportedly came back from the race running a temperature, and at Newbury he still looked as though the outing would bring him on. Refuse To Bend's position in the betting for the Queen Anne Stakes at Royal Ascot reflected his status as virtually a forgotten horse, though he was backed from 16/1 to 12/1. The five ahead of him in the bet-ting in the sixteen-runner field were the fillies Six Perfections, Soviet Song and Nebraska Tornado and the colts Alkaadhem and Norse Dancer, none of whom had shown form in the current season to suggest they would be able to beat Refuse To Bend if he returned to his best. That was precisely what he did, taking a good hold as usual while tracking the pace set by stable-companion Lateen Sails, follow-ing Soviet Song through a furlong out and responding well to pressure to catch her near the line for a neck victory. Salselon finished strongly to be three quarters of a length away third; Nebraska Tornado in fourth and Six Perfections in sixth were not in the same form as in 2003.

Refuse To Bend's naturally free-running style inhibited his prospects of being effective over a mile and a half, a trip which ought to have suited him judged on breeding alone, but the way he finished at Royal Ascot indicated he was well worth trying over a mile and a quarter. The Coral-Eclipse Stakes at Sandown offered a perfect opportunity but Refuse To Bend was only third favourite of the twelve runners behind Prince of Wales's Stakes winner Rakti and the runner-up in that race, Powerscourt. Just two of the classic generation, the smart pair Salford City and African Dream, lined up, for once undermining the race's claims to pro-vide the first major clash over middle distances in Britain between the generations.

Queen Anne Stakes, Royal Ascot—Refuse To Bend (No.12) re-establishes himself
as one of the best milers around as he catches Soviet Song close home,
the pair followed by Salselon and Nebraska Tornado (No.15)

Coral-Eclipse Stakes, Sandown—Refuse To Bend (left) and Warrsan pull clear

The other older horses in the latest edition included Coronation Cup winner Warrsan, Norse Dancer again and Kalaman, successful in a listed race at Goodwood. The finish was one of the season's best, fulfilling the criterion often quoted as typifying such an event by having two runners drawing clear of their rivals while engaged in a ding-dong tussle. After breaking sharply, Refuse To Bend pulled pretty hard through the early stages and his rider did well to settle him back in mid-division. Easing into contention after the three-furlong marker, Refuse To Bend challenged Warrsan a furlong and a half out and took a length advantage. The move proved crucial as Refuse To Bend battled on gamely to hold the equally determined runner-up by a head. Kalaman, badly hampered as they turned for home, was four lengths further back. Refuse To Bend's reputation was at a peak now, but he lost his three remaining starts. It is possible that two hard races temporarily knocked the stuffing out of him. That certainly might explain his dismal display in the Sussex Stakes at Goodwood, where he started favourite but soon dropped back, after leading three furlongs out, and finished last of eleven, hampered a furlong out when no longer in contention. Refuse To Bend did better in the Queen Elizabeth II Stakes at Ascot nearly two months later, running on in the straight for third after being forced to race wide early on, but he posed no threat to Rakti or Lucky Story, being beaten three lengths by the winner. Then in the Champion Stakes at Newmarket he did better than the stable's first string Doyen but could make no impression on the principals, coming home ten lengths fifth to Haafhd. This was Refuse To Bend's only outing on soft ground, which might not have suited him. He proved at Sandown that he acted on good to soft, though, and he also acted on firm.

			Northern Dancer	Nearctic
Refuse To Bend (IRE) (b.c. 2000)	Sadler's Wells (USA) (b 1981)		(b 1961)	Natalma
		Fairy Bridge	Bold Reason
			(b 1975)	Special
	Market Slide (USA) (ch 1991)	Gulch	Mr Prospector
		(b 1984)	Jameela
		Grenzen	Grenfall
		(ch 1975)	My Poly

Unlike Northern Dancer, Sadler's Wells' record as a sire of sires is more miss than hit, with In the Wings his only unqualified success in Europe and a list of ultimately disappointing sons including Carnegie, King's Theatre and Old Vic. The middle-distance performers who are most typical of the sire's progeny also include Montjeu, who has made a distinctly promising start, while two other top-notchers, Galileo and High Chaparral, have yet to have runners, so there is still time for a star to emerge. Among the sire's untypical milers, fifteen-year-old El Prado is making a huge success of his career in Kentucky, where he has sired winners of more than 40,000,000 dollars including a high-class pair in Medaglia d'Oro and Kitten's Joy, winning the champion sire title in 2002 and finishing runner-up both years since. Sadler's Wells' son Barathea has sired several Group 1 winners without quite living

Godolphin's "Refuse To Bend"

up to the expectations invested in him on his retirement—his average earnings index is 1.21, which compares unfavourably with El Prado's 2.24 and In the Wings' 2.10. Against that, King of Kings and Entrepreneur (notwithstanding that he is the sire of Damson and Irish Oaks winner Vintage Tipple) have indifferent records and will be standing in Switzerland and Russia respectively in 2005. Refuse To Bend is to stand at Kildangan Stud in County Kildare, where he replaces In the Wings at a fee of €20,000. The distaff family was covered in detail in previous annuals, one update being that the grandam Grenzen died at the ripe old age of twenty-nine in July. Refuse To Bend's three-year-old sister Genuine Charm appeared in the latest season, showing fair form in maidens at up to a mile and a half in Ireland. Refuse To Bend, who was effective at a mile and a mile and a quarter, is a medium-sized, quite attractive individual with a round action. *Saeed bin Suroor*

REGAL ALI (IRE) 5 ch.g. Ali-Royal (IRE) 127 – Depeche (FR) (Kings Lake (USA) – 133) [2004 –: f9.4g Mar 27] smallish, close-coupled gelding: maiden: no form since 2002: tried blinkered. *G. A. Ham*

REGAL ATTIRE (USA) 2 ch.c. (May 16) Kingmambo (USA) 125 – Style Setter – **p** (USA) (Manila (USA)) [2004 7m⁶ Jul 23] tall, close-coupled colt: closely related to useful French 2003 2-y-o 5.5f/6f winner Saville Row (by Gone West) and half-brother to several winners, notably 1m (at 2 yrs) and 1½m (Oaks) winner Casual Look and French 1¼m winner Shabby Chic (both smart, by Red Ransom): dam, US 1m (including at 2 yrs)/8.5f winner, out of US Grade 1 2-y-o 1m winner Charleston Rag: 14/1 and in need of run, last in maiden at Ascot, racing freely: should do better. *A. M. Balding*

REGAL DREAM (IRE) 2 b.c. (May 8) Namid 128 – Lovely Me (IRE) 70 (Vision **72** (USA)) [2004 5f 6g³ 5.7g³ p5g Nov 10] €40,000F: fifth foal: half-brother to useful 5f winner (including at 2 yrs) Red Millennium (by Tagula): dam maiden who stayed 7f: fair form in maidens: third at Epsom and Bath: will probably prove best at 5f/6f. *J. W. Hills*

REGAL FANTASY (IRE) 4 b.f. King's Theatre (IRE) 128 – Threesome (USA) 79 **40** (Seattle Dancer (USA) 119) [2004 35: 10.9m 12m 16f* 16s⁵ Aug 9] IR 3,500Y: third foal: half-sister to a winner in Turkey by Lake Coniston: dam, maiden, should have been suited by 1m+: poor performer: left F. J. Bowles in Ireland after final start in 2003: won amateur handicap at Musselburgh in July: stays 2m: acts on firm going. *P. A. Blockley*

REGAL FLIGHT (IRE) 3 b.g. King's Theatre (IRE) 128 – Green Belt (FR) (Tirol **42** 127) [2004 55: 7m⁶ 10m 8g⁶ 7m 6.1g Sep 3] close-coupled gelding: poor maiden: stays 7f: raced only on good going or firmer. *J. M. Bradley*

REGAL GALLERY (IRE) 6 b.m. Royal Academy (USA) 130 – Polistatic 53 (Free **?** State 125) [2004 ?, a65: p10g* p12g* p10g³ p10g⁴ p12g² p12m⁴ p13.9g⁶ p12g Oct **a76** 28] lengthy mare: fair performer: won at Lingfield in January (minor event) and February (handicap): stays 1½m: acts on polytrack, little form on turf: tried tongue tied. *C. A. Horgan*

REGAL LUSTRE 2 b.f. (Feb 2) Averti (IRE) 117 – Noble Lustre (USA) 71 (Lyphard's **50** Wish (FR) 124) [2004 5m³ 6d⁵ 5g² 7m⁶ 6f⁶ Jul 31] 11,500Y: sister to 4-y-o Caerphilly Gal and half-sister to 3 winners, including 7-y-o Doctor Dennis and useful 7f and (in USA) 1m winner Royal Rebuke (by Reprimand): dam, 6f winner, stayed 1m: modest maiden: stays 6f: acts on good to soft going. *J. R. Weymes*

REGAL PERFORMER (IRE) 3 b.g. Ali-Royal (IRE) 127 – Khatiynza (Nishapour **60** (FR) 125) [2004 –: 10s 10.2g 11.5m² 10.9f² 11.9f³ 12g⁴ 12m⁵ 11.9f⁶ 12.1d⁶ Aug 19] modest maiden: stays 1½m: acts on firm going: tried blinkered. *S. Kirk*

REGAL REPOSE 4 b.f. Classic Cliche (IRE) 128 – Ideal Candidate 80 (Celestial **–** Storm (USA) 132) [2004 52: p16g f11g f14.8g⁶ 16.2m Jul 23] modest winner at 3yrs: well beaten in 2004. *A. J. Chamberlain*

REGAL SETTING 3 br.g. King's Theatre (IRE) 128 – Cartier Bijoux 96 **98 p** (Ahonoora 122) [2004 75p: 12g⁶ 14.1d* 14s* Sep 25] quite good-topped gelding: useful performer, lightly raced (off 11 months before reappearance): won handicaps at Nottingham and Haydock in September, still looking green (went in snatches) when beating Big Moment ¾ length in latter: will stay 2m: acts on fibresand, raced only on good or softer ground on turf: sold 215,000 gns, joined J. Howard Johnson, won over hurdles in December: remains open to improvement on Flat. *Sir Mark Prescott*

REGAL SONG (IRE) 8 b.g. Anita's Prince 126 – Song Beam 84 (Song 132) [2004 **65 §** 76§: p6g p6g 5s 5d 5d 5d p6d* p5.1g p6g Nov 30] useful-looking gelding: fair performer: won banded race at Wolverhampton in October: best at 5f/6f: acts on all-weather, probably best on softer than good on turf: usually blinkered: often races prominently: weak finisher: unreliable. *T. J. Etherington*

REGAL VINTAGE (USA) 4 ch.g. Kingmambo (USA) 125 – Grapevine (IRE) 88 **–** (Sadler's Wells (USA) 132) [2004 –: 12.4v 21.6v⁵ Apr 19] big, good-bodied gelding: little form: tried tongue tied/visored. *C. Grant*

REGENCY MALAYA 3 b.f. Sri Pekan (USA) 117 – Paola (FR) (Fabulous Dancer **49** (USA) 124) [2004 57d: f8g f11g⁵ p8g² f8.5g p8g p10g³ p8g² f9.4g⁵ p10g⁶ p10m² p9.5g p10g Dec 30] poor maiden: stays 1¼m: acts on polytrack: tongue tied/blinkered. *M. F. Harris*

REGENCY RED (IRE) 6 ch.g. Dolphin Street (FR) 125 – Future Romance (Distant **53** Relative 128) [2004 14.1f⁴ 15.9g 12.1m* 12m 15.8g 14.1d⁴ p12.2g f11g* Dec 12] lengthy gelding: modest performer: off nearly 2 years before reappearance: won seller at Beverley in September and banded race at Southwell in December: effective at 11f to 2m: acts on all-weather and firm going. *W. M. Brisbourne*

REGENT'S SECRET (USA) 4 br.g. Cryptoclearance (USA) – Misty Regent (CAN) **70** (Vice Regent (CAN)) [2004 74: 8g⁴ 7.1d 7.2f 8g² 9.2d⁴ 8g 7.1f³ 8.1g³ 9.2d 7.9m⁶ 8g 8m³ 8m³ p9.5d* p12.2g⁵ p9.5g³ Dec 1] leggy, useful-looking gelding: fair performer: won handicap at Wolverhampton in October: stays 9.5f: acts on polytrack, soft and firm going: tried visored/in cheekpieces. *J. S. Goldie*

REGINA 2 b.f. (Mar 8) Green Desert (USA) 127 – Dazzle 116 (Gone West (USA)) **93** [2004 5.1g³ 5.2m* 6g⁶ 5s* Oct 16] sturdy filly: fourth foal: closely related to 2001 2-y-o 6f winner Wish (by Danehill) and half-sister to 4-y-o Rainbow Queen and 3-y-o Dubois:

dam best at 2 yrs when 5f/6f winner, later 7f winner and third in 1000 Guineas: fairly useful performer: won maiden at Yarmouth in August and minor event at Catterick (made all, beat Bond City a length) in October: needs to settle to stay 6f: acts on soft and good to firm going: sometimes early to post. *Sir Michael Stoute*

REGIS FLIGHT   2 b.c. (Apr 24) Piccolo 121 – Anthem Flight (USA) (Fly So Free   **61** (USA) 122) [2004 6g 6g⁶ Jul 10] good-topped colt: second foal: dam no form: modest form in maidens at Thirsk and York: will stay 7f. *R. Hollinshead*

REGISTRAR   2 ch.c. (Apr 16) Machiavellian (USA) 123 – Confidante (USA) 95   **79** (Dayjur (USA) 137) [2004 7m⁵ 8g² p8g Oct 31] lengthy, good-topped colt: third foal: brother to fairly useful 7f winner Crown Counsel: dam, 7f winner, half-sister to smart 6f/ 7f performer Wind Cheetah out of close relative to Affirmed: best effort in maidens when second to River Alhaarth at Leicester: eased once held final start: not sure to stay beyond 1m. *R. Charlton*

REGULATED (IRE)   3 b.g. Alzao (USA) 117 – Royal Hostess (IRE) (Be My Guest   **63 d** (USA) 126) [2004 72: f7g² f9.4s p10g* f8g⁵ 10.1g⁵ 10m* 11.6m⁶ 10f p10g⁵ p12d 11.7d 9m 10m Sep 27] leggy, useful-looking gelding: good mover: modest performer: won claimer at Lingfield in March and seller at Leicester (first start after leaving J. Osborne) in May: stays 1¼m: acts on good to firm ground and all-weather: tried blinkered: sold £1,600. *D. B. Feek*

REHEARSAL   3 b.g. Singspiel (IRE) 133 – Daralaka (IRE) (The Minstrel (CAN) 135)   **95** [2004 8g² 8m* 10m⁵ 8g⁶ 11.9g Sep 1] 47,000Y: lengthy, good-topped gelding: fourth foal: half-brother to useful French 1½m winner Darghar (by Kahyasi), later useful winner in Singapore, and a 1½m winner in Sweden by Darshaan: dam unraced: useful performer: won 24-runner maiden at Newmarket in May: good fifth of 6 to Hazyview in listed race at Newmarket there third start: well held final outing: gelded after: stays 1¼m: raced only on good/good to firm ground: free-going sort. *C. G. Cox*

REHIA   3 b.f. Desert Style (IRE) 121 – Goes A Treat (IRE) 82 (Common Grounds 118)   **57** [2004 61: p5g p6g⁶ p5g⁵ p6g⁴ f5s⁴ 5.1g 5.3m³ 5.1f⁵ 5.3f 5.1m³ 5g* 5m p6d Oct 23]   **a47** smallish filly: modest handicapper on turf, poor on all-weather: won seller at Ripon in August: best at 5f: acts on firm ground and all-weather: sold 2,000 gns, sent to Belgium. *J. W. Hills*

REIDIES CHOICE   3 b.g. Royal Applause 124 – Fairy Ring (IRE) 69 (Fairy King   **78 §** (USA)) [2004 79§: 6d 7m² 8m 7g⁴ 7m² 7f 7f³ 7.1d⁵ 7m² Sep 29] lengthy, quite attractive gelding: fair performer: stays 7f: acts on firm going, probably on good to soft: wore cheekpieces last 2 starts at 2 yrs: often slowly away: ungenuine: sent to Bahrain. *J. G. Given*

REIGN OF FIRE (IRE)   3 b.f. Perugino (USA) 84 – White Heat 67 (Last Tycoon 131)   **–** [2004 69: 8.3s 10.2m p8g 10f 10g Sep 29] rather sparely-made filly: maiden: soundly beaten in 2004, leaving B. Meehan after second start: tried visored. *J. W. Hills*

REJOYCE (IRE)   3 ch.f. Dancing Spree (USA) – Zoyce (Zilzal (USA) 137) [2004   **–** f8.5g Jan 12] 1,000Y: first foal: dam unraced: tailed off in seller at Wolverhampton. *J. Jay*

RELATIVE HERO (IRE)   4 ch.g. Entrepreneur 123 – Aunty (FR) 114 (Riverman   **55** (USA) 131) [2004 70: 8m 10m 11.8m² 10.2m³ 12.1d⁶ 11.7d⁴ p12.2g p12.2g⁶ Nov 26] smallish gelding: modest performer: stays 1½m: acts on polytrack, firm and good to soft going: usually wears headgear. *Miss S. J. Wilton*

RELAXED GESTURE (IRE)   3 ch.c. Indian Ridge 123 – Token Gesture (IRE) 113   **112** (Alzao (USA) 117) [2004 107: 10d² May 9] smart performer: neck second to Azamour in Beresford Stakes at the Curragh at 2 yrs: good 1½ lengths second of 4 to Yeats in Derrinstown Stud Derby Trial Stakes at Leopardstown on only outing in 2004, keeping on without threatening: stays 1¼m: tongue tied (won maiden) once: sent to USA. *D. K. Weld, Ireland*

RELAXED (USA)   3 b.f. Royal Academy (USA) 130 – Sleep Easy (USA) 116 (Seattle   **94** Slew (USA)) [2004 80p: 7g* 8m a7f⁶ Oct 22] strong, lengthy filly: fairly useful form: won maiden at Newmarket in April by ½ length from Red Top: far from discredited when never-dangerous eighth to Attraction in Coronation Stakes at Royal Ascot, then left Sir Michael Stoute: off 4 months, well held in allowance race at Belmont: probably stays 1m. *R. J. Frankel, USA*

RELEASED (USA)   2 b.f. (Apr 3) Red Ransom (USA) – Ispirata (IRE) (Lure (USA)   **– p** 131) [2004 8m Sep 7] $130,000F, €220,000Y: tall filly: second foal: half-sister to French 7.5f winner Trainer Choice (by Woodman): dam unraced half-sister to smart French performer up to 10.5f Cloudings: 16/1 and backward, always rear in maiden at Leicester, slowly away: type to do better. *J. H. M. Gosden*

RELEASE (USA) 4 b.f. Benny The Dip (USA) 127 – Lemhi Go (USA) (Lemhi Gold (USA) 123) [2004 61d: 11g 14f 16g⁶ f12g Dec 1] 2,600 2-y-o: sixth foal: sister to 5-y-o Unleash and half-sister to 2 winners, including useful 1¼m winner Abscond (by Unbridled): dam won 12 times in USA, including Grade 2 1½m event: modest maiden: no form in 2004, in banded race at Southwell final start: tried blinkered. *John Joseph Murphy, Ireland* —

RELLIM 5 b.m. Rudimentary (USA) 118 – Tycoon Girl (IRE) 74 (Last Tycoon 131) [2004 56, a61: p5g⁵ f5g f5g 5d p5.1g Oct 25] tall, angular mare: poor performer: left P. Blockley after third start: best at 5f: acts on all-weather and good to firm ground: tried in cheekpieces/blinkers: has reportedly broken blood vessels: front runner/often finds little. *J. Balding* — a46

REMAADD (USA) 3 gr. or ro.c. Daylami (IRE) 138 – Bint Albaadiya (USA) 108 (Woodman (USA) 126) [2004 10g* 12g³ 12g² Aug 14] strong, good-bodied colt: good walker: has a fluent, round action: second foal: half-brother to 4-y-o Almizan: dam, 6f (including at 2 yrs) winner who probably stayed 7f, out of smart miler Pixie Erin: smart form: made impressive winning debut in maiden at Newbury in May, beating Massif Centrale 1¾ lengths: best effort when 3 lengths third to Maraahel in ABN Amro Stakes (Gordon) at Goodwood, green but staying on well: odds on, 6 lengths second of 4 to Orange Touch in minor event at Newmarket final start: should stay 1¾m: joined D. Selvaratnam in UAE: sort to improve further at 4 yrs. *M. P. Tregoning* 112 p

Sheikh Ahmed Al Maktoum's "Remaadd"

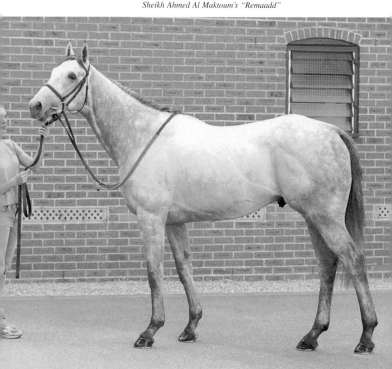

REMEMBRANCE   4 b.g. Sabrehill (USA) 120 – Perfect Poppy 73 (Shareef Dancer   – §
(USA) 135) [2004 74§: p10g Feb 7] good-topped gelding ungenuine maiden: well held
only outing in 2004: tried in cheekpieces/blinkers/tongue tie: dead. *M. J. Gingell*

REMINISCENT (IRE)   5 b.g. Kahyasi 130 – Eliza Orzeszkowa (IRE) 69 (Polish   **61**
Patriot (USA) 128) [2004 62, a75: f16s⁴ 11.8m² p12g⁴ 12m⁵ 13.3g 11.7g Jul 11]   **a72**
rather leggy gelding: fair handicapper on all-weather, modest on turf: stays 2m: acts on
all-weather and firm going: usually blinkered/visored: sometimes slowly away.
R. F. Johnson Houghton

REMONSTRATE (IRE)   3 b.g. Alhaarth (IRE) 126 – Truffa (IRE) (Selkirk (USA)   **56**
129) [2004 7.5g⁶ 8.1d Jun 4] rather leggy, lengthy gelding: modest form when sixth in
maiden at Beverley: well held in similar event at Haydock. *T. D. Easterby*

REMUS LUPIN   3 b.g. Wolfhound (USA) 126 – Incharder (IRE) 86 (Slip Anchor 136)   –
[2004 p7.1g p10g p8.6g Dec 27] well held in maidens: visored final start. *W. R. Swinburn*

RENDEZVOUS POINT (USA)   3 ch.f. Kingmambo (USA) 125 – Reggie V (USA)   **90**
(Vanlandingham (USA)) [2004 78p: 10m 10.3m p10g* a10f Dec 18] big, good-topped
filly: has a round, unimpressive action: fairly useful performer, lightly raced: won handicap at Lingfield in November: not discredited when last of 8 in Grade 3 Ladies Handicap
at Aqueduct final outing: stays 1¼m: acts on polytrack. *J. H. M. Gosden*

RENE BARBIER (IRE)   3 b.g. Desert Style (IRE) 121 – Sweet Decision (IRE) 70   **66**
(Common Grounds 118) [2004 6.1s 6.1s⁴ 5m* 6m⁵ 5g⁶ 6g 7g 6.1m 7d Oct 15] good-
topped gelding: fair performer: won maiden at Doncaster in June: stays 5f: acts on good
to firm going: tried visored: sold 2,500 gns, sent to Spain. *J. A. Glover*

RENO'S MAGIC   3 b.f. Hello Mister 106 – Mountain Magic 58 (Magic Ring (IRE)   –
115) [2004 –: 5s Apr 17] strong filly: little form. *W. G. M. Turner*

REN'S MAGIC   6 gr.g. Petong 126 – Bath 76 (Runnett 125) [2004 42, a50: 14.1d Oct   –
16] maiden handicapper: well held only 6-y-o start: tried in visor/cheekpieces/tongue tie.
J. R. Jenkins

REPEAT (IRE)   4 ch.g. Night Shift (USA) – Identical (IRE) (Machiavellian (USA)   **45**
123) [2004 59: f7g* f7s² f7g f8s⁴ f8g⁴ f8.5s f7s 5g 8.1m⁶ 6.1d 7m f6g p7.1g Nov 15] tall,   **a57**
close-coupled gelding: poor performer: won seller at Wolverhampton in January: left Gay
Kelleway after eleventh start: stays 8.5f: acts on all-weather and good to firm going: has
worn cheekpieces/tongue tie. *J. W. Unett*

REPENT AT LEISURE   4 b.g. Bishop of Cashel 122 – Sutosky 78 (Great Nephew   –
126) [2004 11.5m 14.1d 12f Sep 4] little form. *Julian Poulton*

REPERTORY   11 b.g. Anshan 119 – Susie's Baby (Balidar 133) [2004 112: 5.2g 5g   **103 d**
5g 5m 6m⁶ 5d Jul 2] tall, angular gelding: smart performer at best, successful in Prix du
Petit Couvert at Longchamp 3 times, equalling record for oldest British-trained horse
to win a pattern race on last occasion in 2003: very much on downgrade in 2004: front
runner, best at 5f: acted on any going: retired. *M. S. Saunders*

REPETOIRE (FR)   4 ch.f. Zafonic (USA) 130 – Lady Kate (USA) (Trempolino (USA)   –
135) [2004 –: f9.4g f16.2g⁶ Jan 14] little form: tried in blinkers. *K. O. Cunningham-
Brown*

REPULSE BAY (IRE)   6 b.g. Barathea (IRE) 127 – Bourbon Topsy 108 (Ile de Bour-   **53 §**
bon (USA) 133) [2004 67§: 8g⁶ 13g 16m³ 14m 12g⁵ 10.9d 12m 10g 16f 10s 14g 10.9s
Sep 16] big gelding: modest handicapper: stays easy 2m: acts on firm and soft ground:
tried visored/blinkered: sometimes starts slowly: ungenuine. *J. S. Goldie*

REQQA   2 b.c. (Feb 14) Royal Applause 124 – Kangra Valley 56 (Indian Ridge 123)   **95**
[2004 6g⁶ 6g* 6d⁴ 6f⁴ Sep 11] 18,000F, 160,000Y: tall, rather leggy colt: sixth foal: half-
brother to several sprint winners, notably 4-y-o Airwave: dam 2-y-o 5f winner: useful
performer: won maiden at Pontefract in August by 5 lengths: much better effort after
when 1¼ lengths fourth to Space Shuttle in listed race at Ripon: bred to have proved best
at 5f/6f: acted on good to soft ground: dead. *M. Johnston*

RESCIND (IRE)   4 b.f. Revoque (IRE) 122 – Sunlit Ride (Ahonoora 122) [2004 –:   –
p9.5g Oct 25] leggy filly: lightly raced and no form on Flat since 2 yrs. *Jedd O'Keeffe*

RESERVOIR (IRE)   3 b.g. Green Desert (USA) 127 – Spout 115 (Salse (USA) 128)   **84**
[2004 79: 9.2d² 11g* 10f 12d⁵ 13.9s 11.9g² Sep 3] well-made gelding: fairly useful performer: won maiden at Goodwood in June: good second to Sendintank in handicap at
Haydock final start: stays 1½m: acts on soft ground: sold 30,000 gns. *W. J. Haggas*

RESIDENTIAL 3 ch.g. Zilzal (USA) 137 – House Hunting (Zafonic (USA) 130) [2004 **63** 75p: 7m⁴ 8g⁶ 10d⁴ Oct 4] modest maiden: stays 1m: unraced on extremes of ground: sold 12,000 gns. *Mrs A. J. Perrett*

RESISTANCE HEROINE 2 b.f. (Mar 2) Dr Fong (USA) 128 – Odette 72 (Pursuit **75** of Love 124) [2004 6.1d 7m 7m³ 8.1s 7m⁴ Sep 22] 125,000Y: lengthy filly: third foal: half-sister to 3-y-o Silca's Gift and 5f winner On Point (by Kris): dam, 5f/5.7f winner, half-sister to useful 6f/7f winner Caballero out of Queen Mary winner On Tiptoes: fair maiden: stays 7f: acts on good to firm ground: sold 26,000 gns. *E. A. L. Dunlop*

RESONANCE 3 b.f. Slip Anchor 136 – Music In My Life (IRE) 59 (Law Society **67** (USA) 130) [2004 71p: p12g² p10g 12d³ 14.1d Aug 12] useful-looking filly: fair maiden: stays 1½m: raced only on polytrack/good to soft going: often slowly away. *N. A. Twiston-Davies*

RESONATE (IRE) 6 b.h. Erins Isle 121 – Petronelli (USA) (Sir Ivor (USA) 135) **83** [2004 82, a65+: 7g⁴ 9g 10.1m* p12.2g² p8.6g⁴ p10g* p10g² Dec 29] useful-looking **a75** horse: fairly useful handicapper on turf, fair on all-weather: won at Epsom in September and Lingfield in December: effective at 7f to 1¼m: acts on polytrack, firm and soft going: often held up. *A. G. Newcombe*

RESPLENDENT CEE (IRE) 5 ch.h. Polar Falcon (USA) 126 – Western Friend **–** (USA) (Gone West (USA)) [2004 108: 6s Aug 14] rangy, quite attractive horse: fluent mover: useful 6f performer at best: well held in valuable handicap at Ripon only 5-y-o start. *P. W. Harris*

RESPLENDENT KING (USA) 3 b.g. King of Kings (IRE) 125 – Sister Fromseattle **73** (USA) (Seattle Slew (USA)) [2004 73: p7g³ p8g³ p8g⁵ p7g⁵ 8.5s³ 9m² 11.9f³ 10g³ 8.5g Jul 15] tall, close-coupled gelding: fair maiden on Flat: barely stays 1¼m: acts on polytrack and firm ground, probably on soft: tried blinkered and in cheekpieces: races up with pace: won juvenile hurdle in August. *T. G. Mills*

RESPLENDENT ONE (IRE) 3 b.g. Marju (IRE) 127 – Licentious 45 (Reprimand **101** 122) [2004 87p: 8m⁶ 8m 8g⁴ 8m⁴ 8.1s Sep 24] close-coupled gelding: useful performer: best efforts when fourth to Kehaar in handicap at Newmarket and to Fong's Thong in listed race at Goodwood (beaten 5 lengths): races freely, and not sure to stay beyond 1m: acts on good to firm ground, well held on soft: gelded after final start. *T. G. Mills*

RESPLENDENT PRINCE 2 ch.c. (Apr 27) Primo Dominie 121 – Last Result **76** (Northern Park (USA) 107) [2004 p7g p7.1g² p7m* Dec 22] 18,000F, 17,000Y: second foal: half-brother to 3-y-o Lasting Delight: dam, Italian 2-y-o 5.5f to 9.5f winner, half-sister to 6-y-o Foreign Affairs: fair performer: trained on debut by P. Harris: won maiden at Lingfield by 1¼ lengths from Bluff: needs to settle to stay 1m. *T. G. Mills*

RESSOURCE (FR) 5 b.g. Broadway Flyer (USA) 121 – Rayonne (Sadler's Wells **44** (USA) 132) [2004 –: p13g⁵ Apr 6] blinkered, only Flat form when fifth in banded race at Lingfield: stays 13f: acts on polytrack. *G. L. Moore*

RESTART (IRE) 3 b.g. Revoque (IRE) 122 – Stargard (Polish Precedent (USA) 131) **67** [2004 62: 8m 14g 14.1g* 14.1f 16.1m² 17.1g Oct 4] lengthy gelding: fair handicapper: won at Redcar in August: stays 2m: acts on fibresand, raced only on good ground or firmer on turf. *P. C. Haslam*

RESTORATION (FR) 2 gr.c. (Mar 3) Zafonic (USA) 130 – Restless Mixa (IRE) **70 p** (Linamix (FR) 127) [2004 7s² Nov 1] €110,000Y: third foal: half-brother to useful French 6f (at 2 yrs) and 1m winner Mes Bleus Yeux (by Exit To Nowhere) and fairly useful French 1¼m winner Noble Request (by Highest Honor): dam, French 1½m/13f winner, half-sister to Prix de Diane winner Resless Kara: 9/2 from 3/1, 2 lengths second to Game Lad in maiden at Redcar, no extra only late on: sure to do better. *J. H. M. Gosden*

RETAIL THERAPY (IRE) 4 b.f. Bahhare (USA) 122 – Elect (USA) 113 (Vaguely **50** Noble 140) [2004 45: f12g² f12g⁶ 14.1g 12f Sep 4] strong, close-coupled filly: modest maiden: should stay 1¾m: acts on fibresand: tried blinkered/visored: none too consistent. *M. A. Buckley*

RETIREMENT 5 b.g. Zilzal (USA) 137 – Adeptation (USA) (Exceller (USA) 129) **80** [2004 85: 8s* 7.6d³ 8m 7.9d 8.1d 8d 7s Nov 6] leggy, good-topped gelding: unimpressive mover: fairly useful handicapper: won at Ascot in April: mainly well below form after next start: effective at 1m/1¼m: acts on all-weather, soft and good to firm going: sometimes edges left. *M. H. Tompkins*

REVEILLEZ 5 gr.g. First Trump 118 – Amalancher (USA) 85 (Alleged (USA) 138) **99** [2004 100: 16d⁶ 14g⁵ May 20] tall, angular gelding: useful handicapper: better effort in

2004 when creditable fifth to Barolo at Goodwood, flashing tail: effective at 1½m to 15f: acts on firm and good to soft going: consistent. *J. R. Fanshawe*

REVELINO (IRE) 5 b.g. Revoque (IRE) 122 – Forelino (USA) 62§ (Trempolino (USA) 135) [2004 12.3s⁶ Aug 20] useful-looking gelding: fairly useful in 2002: well held only Flat outing since. *Miss S. J. Wilton* –

REVENIR (IRE) 3 ch.g. Spectrum (IRE) 126 – Petite Liqueurelle (IRE) (Shernazar 131) [2004 7m 8.1g² p8g² 7g² 10.1g⁴ p10g⁸ 10.3s Oct 22] good-bodied gelding: half-brother to several winners, including useful 5f (at 2 yrs) and 1m winner Caviar Royale (by Royal Academy) and 1½m winner Typhoon Todd (by Entrepreneur): dam unraced: fair performer: trained until after third start by A. Stewart: won handicap at Lingfield in October, starting slowly: stays 1¼m: acts on polytrack and good to firm ground, tailed off on soft: sometimes wanders: sold 18,000 gns. *E. F. Vaughan* **74**

REVERSIONARY 3 b.g. Poyle George 113 – Harold's Girl (FR) (Northfields (USA)) [2004 49: 5g 8.2g 7s⁵ 6m 6m 6s 7.9g⁸ 8.5g f8m³ 9.1s² 10s² f8g* f7g f8g Dec 28] workmanlike gelding: modest performer: won seller at Carlisle in July and banded race at Southwell in November: effective at 1m/1¼m: acts on fibresand and soft going: usually blinkered. *M. W. Easterby* **60**

REVIEN (IRE) 2 b.g. (Mar 18) Rossini (USA) 118 – Kazimiera (IRE) 77 (Polish Patriot (USA) 128) [2004 5g³ p6g³ p5g⁴ Nov 10] €18,000Y, 25,000 2-y-o: well-made gelding: third foal: dam, placed up to 1m, half-sister to useful 1994 2-y-o 5f/6f winner Fallow: fair maiden: should prove best at 5f/6f. *G. A. Huffer* **69**

REVIEWER (IRE) 6 b.g. Sadler's Wells (USA) 132 – Clandestina (USA) 98 (Secretariat (USA)) [2004 p12g 12f 13.3m 12d⁵ 12d⁵ Jul 10] rangy gelding: fair handicapper: stays 1½m: acts on soft and good to firm going: tried blinkered: held up: carries head awkwardly. *C. M. Meade* **68**

REVIVALIST 2 b.f. (Feb 24) Benny The Dip (USA) 127 – Brave Revival 93 (Dancing Brave (USA) 140) [2004 7f a6.8g³ 5.8g² a6g⁴ a6.8g* Nov 14] sixth foal: half-sister to fairly useful 2000 2-y-o 6f winner Bravado (by Zafonic) and 1999 2-y-o 7f winner Vigour (by Lion Cavern): dam, 1m winner (including at 2 yrs) who stayed 1¼m, half-sister to very smart sprinter Pivotal: sold from M. Bell 8,000 gns after well held on debut: won maiden at Yabb: stays 7f. *M. Kahn, Sweden* **?**

REWAYAAT 3 b.f. Bahhare (USA) 122 – Alumisiyah (USA) 93 (Danzig (USA)) [2004 80: 5m May 24] strong, sturdy filly: fairly useful 5f performer: well held only 3-y-o start: headstrong: sold 3,200 gns. *B. Hanbury* –

REX ROMELIO (IRE) 5 ch.g. Priolo (USA) 127 – Romelia (USA) (Woodman (USA) 126) [2004 –: f8g f11g² p10g Feb 4] poor performer nowadays: stays 11f: acts on fibresand: visored last 2 outings. *K. R. Burke* **48**

RHAPSODY IN SILVER (FR) 2 gr.c. (Feb 20) Medaaly 114 – Concert (Polar Falcon (USA) 126) [2004 7g Jul 8] 66/1, well held in maiden at Folkestone. *J. Jay* –

RHETORICAL 3 b.g. Unfuwain (USA) 131 – Miswaki Belle (USA) 73 (Miswaki (USA) 124) [2004 –p: 10m⁵ 10d 14g⁶ 15.8m 12m p13m Nov 22] tall gelding: poor maiden: well held in 2004, leaving Sir Mark Prescott after fifth start: tried blinkered/tongue tied. *P. Butler* –

RHETORIC (IRE) 5 b.g. Desert King (IRE) 129 – Squaw Talk (USA) (Gulch (USA)) [2004 –: f16s f12m⁴ f11m* 10v f14g⁶ May 19] quite attractive gelding: poor performer: won banded race at Southwell in April: stays 1½m: acts on fibresand: tried blinkered/in cheekpieces. *D. G. Bridgwater* **48**

RHINEFIELD BOY 3 ch.g. Wolfhound (USA) 126 – Rhinefield Beauty (IRE) 52 (Shalford (IRE) 124§) [2004 –: 5m 5g Jun 3] little sign of ability. *J. S. Goldie* –

RHOSLAN (IRE) 2 b.c. (Mar 1) Trans Island 119 – Flimmering (Dancing Brave (USA) 140) [2004 7g 7.6m 7g Aug 22] good-topped colt: has a markedly round action: signs of just a little ability in maidens. *C. A. Dwyer* –

RHUM 4 ch.g. Bahamian Bounty 116 – Rynavey 67 (Rousillon (USA) 133) [2004 8d 10.1s⁵ 10s Oct 12] lengthy gelding: little form in maidens. *I. Semple* –

RIBBONS AND BOWS (IRE) 4 gr.f. Dr Devious (IRE) 127 – Nichodoula 65 (Doulab (USA) 115) [2004 79: 11.6d 12g⁶ p12g 12m⁴ 12g p16d 10.2s⁴ 10.9d⁵ 14.1d⁵ p9.5d* p9.5g Nov 6] leggy, angular filly: fair performer: won minor event at Wolverhampton in November: stays 1½m: acts on polytrack, soft and good to firm going: sometimes blinkered/visored: none too consistent. *C. A. Cyzer* **74**

RIBBONS OF GOLD 2 b.f. (Feb 17) Primo Dominie 121 – In Love Again (IRE) 86 **59**
(Prince Rupert (FR) 121) [2004 5s⁶ 5.7m Aug 10] 17,000Y: fifth foal: half-sister to 6-y-o
Forever My Lord: dam, 2-y-o 5f winner, half-sister to high-class sprinter Hallgate: sixth
in maiden at Warwick: reportedly scoped poorly after final start. *J. A. Osborne*

RICH ALBI 2 b.g. (Feb 16) Mind Games 121 – Bollin Sophie (Efisio 120) [2004 5m⁶ **65**
5m 6g⁴ 6d 8d Oct 18] 24,000Y: leggy, quite good-topped gelding: fifth foal: half-brother
to 4 winners, including 4-y-o Go Tech and 5-y-o Travelling Times: dam, little sign of
ability, half-sister to St Leger winner Bollin Eric and smart sprinter Bollin Joanne: fair
maiden: needs to settle to stay beyond 6f: visored (best effort) third start: blinkered
(looked difficult ride) next time. *T. D. Easterby*

RICH CHIC (IRE) 3 b. or br.f. Sri Pekan (USA) 117 – Ring Side (IRE) (Alzao (USA) **36**
117) [2004 8.1d 8s⁴ 8g f12g Dec 11] sturdy filly: fourth foal: half-sister to 6-y-o Border
Terrier: dam unraced: poor form in maidens. *M. D. Hammond*

RICHEMAUR (IRE) 4 b.f. Alhaarth (IRE) 126 – Lady President (IRE) 72 (Dominion **85 d**
123) [2004 85?: 8m⁴ 8.1d 8.3d 12g⁴ 12g 11m Jul 1] leggy, workmanlike filly: fairly useful
handicapper: below form after reappearance: stays 1¼m: acts on soft and good to firm
going: tried blinkered: sold 17,000 gns. *M. H. Tompkins*

RICHIE BOY 3 b.c. Dr Fong (USA) 128 – Alathezal (USA) (Zilzal (USA) 137) [2004 **71**
–p: 7m 8.3f⁶ p10g 8.1s 12.6d* 10g 8.2v* 10s* p12.2g p12g p8.6g Nov 20] smallish, leggy **a54**
colt: fair performer on turf, modest on all weather: claimed from M. Jarvis £12,000 third
start: won claimer at Warwick (claimed from V. Smith £5,000) and apprentice handicap
at Nottingham, both in October, and seller at Redcar in November: effective at 1m (given
a test) to 12.6f: acts on any turf ground: wore cheekpieces (well held, only outing for
G. L. Moore) fourth start: sometimes starts slowly/races freely. *P. A. Blockley*

RICHMOND LODGE (IRE) 4 br.g. Sesaro (USA) 81 – Richmond Lillie (Fairbairn) **59**
[2004 60: 9.9g 10s⁵ p12g p10g⁴ Dec 30] modest performer: won handicap at Tramore for
D. Wachman in Ireland in 2003: stays 1½m: acts on polytrack and firm going: visored
final start. *M. Madgwick*

RICHTEE (IRE) 3 ch.f. Desert Sun 120 – Santarene (IRE) 46 (Scenic 128) [2004 54: **76**
10f* 9g² 11d⁵ 12m* 10.9g³ 12.1d* 12.4s⁴ 16m⁶ Sep 28] strong filly: fair handicapper:
won at Redcar in June, Thirsk in July and Hamilton in August: reportedly choked final
start: stays 1½m: acts on firm and good to soft going. *R. A. Fahey*

RICKY MARTAN 3 ch.c. Foxhound (USA) 103 – Cyrillic 88 (Rock City 120) [2004 **41**
66: p8g p8g p6g p7g 5.7s 7f⁶ 7.9f p10g⁶ 12m p12.2d Oct 23] small, close-coupled colt:
poor maiden: should stay at least 1m: acts on good to firm ground: tried blinkered/
visored. *G. C. Bravery*

RIDAPOUR (IRE) 5 b.g. Kahyasi 130 – Ridiyara (IRE) 94 (Persian Bold 123) [2004 **–**
–: 18g Mar 26] sturdy, close-coupled gelding: lightly-raced maiden: dead. *D. J. Wintle*

RIDDER 2 b.c. (Jan 5) Dr Fong (USA) 128 – Frond 85 (Alzao (USA) 117) [2004 6g⁴ **93**
5.7f⁵ 6d 6m² 6d² 6m* 7d³ Sep 29] 20,000Y: rather leggy colt: third foal: half-brother to
fairly useful Scandinavian 1m/1¼m winner Azolla (by Cadeaux Genereux): dam, 7f
winner (ran only at 2 yrs), out of useful 1½m winner Fern: fairly useful performer: won
maiden at York in September: excellent ½-length third to Gaff in listed race at Fairyhouse: stays 7f: acts on good to firm and good to soft going: joined C. Yip in Hong Kong.
D. J. Coakley

RIDE SAFARI 2 b.g. (Apr 2) Fraam 114 – Vocation (IRE) 74 (Royal Academy (USA) **70**
130) [2004 5m⁶ 5.3f³ 7f⁴ p7m Dec 22] 11,000Y: second foal: half-brother to 3-y-o Divine
Spirit: dam, 2-y-o 7f winner, sister to useful performer up to 1m Caviar Royale: fair
maiden: stays 7f: acts on firm going: slowly away first 3 outings. *P. Winkworth*

RIDGEBACK 4 ch.g. Indian Ridge 123 – Valbra (Dancing Brave (USA) 140) [2004 **–**
81: 6g Mar 25] small, sturdy gelding: fairly useful performer in 2003: well held only
4-y-o outing: dead. *I. Semple*

RIDGE BOY (IRE) 3 b.c. Indian Ridge 123 – Bold Tina (IRE) 72 (Persian Bold 123) **81**
[2004 8g⁵ 8.1g⁶ 6m 8.3f* 9g 10m³ 8g² 8.5g* 8v Oct 23] second foal: dam, 7f winner, out
of half-sister to dam of high-class miler Ridgewood Pearl (by Indian Ridge): fairly useful performer: won handicaps at Windsor in July and Epsom in October: effective at 1m
to easy 1¼m: acts on firm ground, well beaten on heavy: usually races up with pace.
R. Hannon

RIDICULE 5 b.g. Piccolo 121 – Mockingbird 64 (Sharpo 132) [2004 78: f6g 5.7g 6d **46**
6.1v 5.7m 5m 6.1s 5.7m p7m Dec 15] tall, lengthy gelding: fair performer in 2003: well
held in 2004: usually visored/blinkered: tried tongue tied. *J. G. Portman*

RIFLEMAN (IRE) 4 ch.g. Starborough 126 – En Garde (USA) 82 (Irish River (FR) – 131) [2004 91: 7g 10g 9.2g 9d Jul 4] compact gelding: fairly useful handicapper in 2003: well beaten in 2004: tried in visor/cheekpieces: joined P. Bowen 25,000 gns. *Mrs A. Duffield*

RIGHT ANSWER 2 b.f. (Mar 3) Lujain (USA) 119 – Quiz Show 82 (Primo Dominie 95 121) [2004 5g⁴ 5d* 5f² 5g² 6m⁵ 5.2g³ 6m 5s Oct 16] 25,000Y: tall, attractive filly: second foal: dam, 7f winner, half-sister to very smart sprinter Mind Games: useful performer: won maiden at Salisbury in June: good placed efforts in minor event at Windsor, nursery at York and listed event (2¼ lengths third to Sumora) at Newbury: poor efforts last 2 starts: barely stays 6f: acts on firm and good to soft going: sold 40,000 gns. *A. P. Jarvis*

RIGHT APPROACH 5 b.h. Machiavellian (USA) 123 – Abbey Strand (USA) 78 118 (Shadeed (USA) 135) [2004 117: 8.9m* 8.9m* 10m⁵ Apr 25] leggy, useful-looking horse: fluent mover: reportedly suffered hairline fracture of vertebra at 3 yrs: smart performer: sold from Sir Michael Stoute after final 4-y-o start: successful at Nad Al Sheba in listed race (by neck form Surveyor) in February and Dubai Duty Free (dead-heated with Paolini) in March, finishing well both times: creditable 2¼ lengths fifth to River Dancer in Queen Elizabeth II Cup at Sha Tin final start: stays 1¼m: acts on firm and good to soft going: has had tongue tied: held up: often takes strong hold, and suited by strongly-run race. *M. F. de Kock, South Africa*

RIGHTFUL RULER 2 b.c. (Mar 21) Montjoy (USA) 122 – Lady of The Realm 80 (Prince Daniel (USA)) [2004 8g⁴ 8g⁴ 8s Oct 27] fourth foal: half-brother to 11.6f winner Haile Selassie (by Awesome): dam ran 3 times: fairly useful form on first 2 starts in maidens: should stay 1¼m. *B. W. Hills*

RIGHTPRICE PREMIER (IRE) 2 b.f. (Feb 15) Cape Cross (IRE) 129 – Machudi 77 (Bluebird (USA) 125) [2004 5g³ 5d² f5m* 5f⁵ Jun 14] 8,000Y: first foal: dam, maiden, stayed 7f: fair performer: won maiden at Wolverhampton in May, easily best effort: needed to settle to stay beyond 5f: dead. *K. A. Ryan*

RIGHT TO ROAM (IRE) 2 b.g. (Mar 1) Namid 128 – Lloc 79 (Absalom 128) [2004 56 p 6f⁴ 6m p6g⁵ Oct 1] 35,000F, 50,000Y: fourth foal: half-brother to 4-y-o Aimee's Delight: dam, 5f (including at 2 yrs), half-sister to July Cup winner Compton Place: modest form in minor event/maidens: best effort in blinkers second start: not knocked about final one (gelded after): likely to prove best at 5f/6f: should do better. *J. A. R. Toller*

RIGHTY HO 10 b.g. Reprimand 122 – Challanging 95 (Mill Reef (USA) 141) [2004 53 50: 13.1g* 11m³ 9.9m³ 12m 12m⁶ 14.1m* 14.1f 12.1m³ Sep 21] tall, leggy gelding: modest performer: won banded race at Ayr in April and claimer at Redcar in August: effective at 1¼m to 2m: acts on any going: often visored earlier in career: usually races prominently. *W. H. Tinning*

RIGONZA 3 ch.g. Vettori (IRE) 119 – Desert Nomad 56 (Green Desert (USA) 127) 68 [2004 72: 7.5d 10s 9g⁵ 11d 9d³ 9d⁴ 12s² Aug 13] good-bodied gelding: fair maiden: seemed to stay 1½m: acted on good to firm going, probably on soft: tried visored: dead. *T. D. Easterby*

RILEY BOYS (IRE) 3 ch.g. Most Welcome 131 – Scarlett Holly 81 (Red Sunset 85 120) [2004 63: f7g* 7.5d² 8.2s* 8.5v² 8.5m* 7m² 8.5s² 8.2d² 8d⁶ Aug 15] close-coupled gelding: fairly useful performer: won maiden at Wolverhampton in March and handicaps at Nottingham in April and Beverley in June: runner-up on 6 other occasions: effective at 7f to 8.5f: acts on fibresand, heavy and good to firm ground: ran creditably only try in cheekpieces: usually races up with pace: tough and reliable. *J. G. Given*

RILEYS DREAM 5 b.m. Rudimentary (USA) 118 – Dorazine 77 (Kalaglow 132) 53 § [2004 67§: 6v 7s⁵ 5.7s 6g 6m* 7.1m 6.1s 7m⁵ 6f* 7s² 6.1g Sep 3] modest performer: won sellers at Leicester in May and Brighton (handicap) in August: effective at 6f/7f: acts on firm and soft ground: wore cheekpieces last 4 starts: unreliable. *B. J. Llewellyn*

RILEYS ROCKET 5 b.m. Makbul 104 – Star of Flanders (Puissance 110) [2004 – 51: f9.4s 9.9m 10g f7g Jun 11] leggy, angular mare: maiden: well held in 2004, trained reappearance only by J. Pickering. *R. Hollinshead*

RILL 2 ch.f. (Apr 21) Unfuwain (USA) 131 – River Cara (USA) 86 (Irish River (FR) 71 p 131) [2004 8.2m⁴] well-made filly: fourth foal: closely related to 2001 2-y-o 9.4f winner Araglin (by Sadler's Wells) and half-sister to 2002 2-y-o 1m winner Ciel (by Rainbow Quest): dam French 2-y-o 1m winner: 33/1 and green, fourth to Sharaiji Blossom in maiden at Nottingham, not knocked about: will be well suited by 1¼m/1½m: will do better. *J. H. M. Gosden*

*King George Stakes, Goodwood—Ringmoor Down (near side) catches Boogie Street on the line,
with The Tatling third and Avonbridge fourth*

RINGAROOMA 2 b.f. (Mar 16) Erhaab (USA) 127 – Tatouma (USA) 79 (The Mins- **61**
trel (CAN) 135) [2004 6g⁵ 7m 7g⁴ 6g² 6g Sep 20] 10,000Y: quite good-topped filly:
half-sister to fairly useful 1994 2-y-o 7f winner Trimming (by Thatching) and winner up
to 1m in Germany by Dowsing: dam 2-y-o 5f/6f winner: modest maiden: free-going sort,
barely stays 7f. *M. H. Tompkins*

RINGMOOR DOWN 5 b.m. Pivotal 124 – Floppie (FR) (Law Society (USA) 130) **113**
[2004 100: 5.2g⁶ 5.1g* 6m³ 5f⁴ 5d² 6d⁴ 5m* 5m* 6f 5m 6d² Oct 14] smallish, strong
mare: smart performer: better than ever in 2004, winning listed race at Bath in April,
King George Stakes at Goodwood (beat Boogie Street) in July and Nolan & Brophy
Auctioneers Flying Five at the Curragh (beat Benbaun) in September, last 2 by a head:
good 1½ lengths second to Ruby Rocket in listed race at Newmarket final start: effective
at 5f/6f: acts on firm and good to soft going: sometimes bandaged behind: usually held
up: tough and consistent. *D. W. P. Arbuthnot*

RING OF DESTINY 5 b.g. Magic Ring (IRE) 115 – Canna (Caerleon (USA) 132) **86**
[2004 102: 12g 11.9s 12m Jun 5] quite attractive gelding: just fairly useful form at best in
2004: stays 1½m: acts on firm and good to soft going: often races prominently: none too
consistent: sold 30,000 gns. *P. W. Harris*

RINGSIDE JACK 8 b.g. Batshoof 122 – Celestine 62 (Skyliner 117) [2004 54+: 18v³ **52**
14s 16.2v May 8] quite good-topped gelding: modest handicapper: barely stays 2¼m:
acts on any going, though all 4 wins on softer than good: effective visored or not.
C. W. Fairhurst

RINGSIDER (IRE) 3 ch.g. Docksider (USA) 124 – Red Comes Up (USA) (Blushing **93**
Groom (FR) 131) [2004 81p: 7.6d 10.1m 8g² 9m* 9.9d 11.6m* Sep 27] close-coupled
gelding: fairly useful handicapper: won at Goodwood (apprentices) in July and Windsor
(by ¾ length from Quarrymount) in September: stays 11.6f: acts on good to firm going:
sometimes bandaged/early to post: held up. *G. A. Butler*

RINJANI (USA) 3 b.c. Gone West (USA) – Ringshaan (FR) (Darshaan 133) [2004 91p: **–**
10f 9.7g Aug 13] quite attractive colt: fairly useful winner at 2 yrs for D. Loder: tongue
tied, well held in 2004, looking difficult ride: sold 18,000 gns, sent to Bahrain. *Saeed bin
Suroor*

RINNEEN (IRE) 3 b.f. Bien Bien (USA) 125 – Sparky's Song 63 (Electric 126) [2004 **56**
67d: 10.2g 11.6s 11.5m⁵ 12g³ 12m⁴ 16.2s⁵ 10s f16s⁶ p12.2g Nov 19] modest maiden
handicapper: left R. Hannon after sixth start: stays 1½m: acts on good to firm going,
probably on polytrack: tried visored/in cheekpieces/tongue tied. *T. Hogan, Ireland*

RIO BRANCO 3 b.f. Efisio 120 – Los Alamos 73 (Keen 116) [2004 66p: f7g* a6f a7f⁶ **71 d**
a6.5f Dec 29] medium-sized filly: made all in maiden at Wolverhampton in January:

866

left B. Hills, beaten long way after in allowance race and 2 claimers in US, leaving S. Margolis and off 7½ months before final one: should stay at least 1m. *N. J. Rennekamp, USA*

RIO DE JANEIRO (IRE) 3 b.g. Sadler's Wells (USA) 132 – Alleged Devotion (USA) (Alleged (USA) 138) [2004 10m 10m² 10f* 11.9d Aug 17] sturdy gelding: brother to useful Irish 1¼m and 1½m winner Royal Devotion, closely related to useful 1999 2-y-o 7f winner Thady Quill (by Nureyev) and fairly useful 1998 Irish 2-y-o 6f winner April Starlight (by Storm Bird) and half-brother to 2 winners in USA: dam unraced half-sister to Oaks/Irish Derby winner Balanchine: fairly useful form: first past post in maidens at the Curragh (beat Eldorado a head, demoted) and Fairyhouse (by ¾ length from Freud Bacon) in July: visored, tailed-off last in Great Voltigeur Stakes at York final start: should stay 1½m: wandered and hung markedly left second/third starts: sold 60,000 gns, then gelded. *A. P. O'Brien, Ireland* **82**

RIO DE JUMEIRAH 3 b.f. Seeking The Gold (USA) – Tegwen (USA) 79 (Nijinsky (CAN) 138) [2004 71: 11.5s³ 10m⁶ 10d 8g⁵ 10.3d* 10g² Aug 2] leggy filly: fairly useful handicapper: won at Doncaster in July: good ½-length second to Double Vodka at Ripon final start: effective at 1¼m/11.5f: acts on soft and good to firm going. *C. E. Brittain* **92**

RIO RIVA 2 b.c. (Mar 30) Pivotal 124 – Dixie Favor (USA) 82 (Dixieland Band (USA)) [2004 6s² p6g² Nov 8] tall colt: half-brother to several winners, including 2003 2-y-o 6f winner River Belle (by Lahib), later smart Grade 2 8.5f winner in USA: dam Irish 6f (at 2 yrs) to 1m winner: fairly useful form when second in maidens at Haydock and Wolverhampton, still green when beaten neck by Petite Spectre in latter: should stay 7f. *Miss J. A. Camacho* **81**

RIPCORD (IRE) 6 b.g. Diesis 133 – Native Twine 114 (Be My Native (USA) 122) [2004 –§: p12g⁵ p12g⁶ 12f Jun 25] big gelding: poor maiden: left Lady Herries after reappearance: stays 1½m: acts on polytrack, firm and soft going: unreliable. *B. R. Johnson* **38 §**

RIPPLE EFFECT 4 ch.f. Elmaamul (USA) 125 – Sharp Chief 71 (Chief Singer 131) [2004 79: p6g² p7g* p7g² p6g p7g⁵ p7g* p6g⁵ f7g⁶ 6g May 3] leggy filly: fairly useful performer: won claimer in January and handicap in March, both at Lingfield: stays easy 7f: acts on firm ground and polytrack (below form both starts on fibresand): often tongue tied. *C. A. Dwyer* **85**

RIQUEWIHR 4 ch.f. Compton Place 125 – Juvenilia (IRE) 55 (Masterclass (USA) 116) [2004 62+: 6g⁴ 6.1d³ 6g⁴ p7.1g p5.1g p6g Dec 30] quite good-topped filly: fair handicapper, lightly raced: left D. Loder after third start: should stay 7f: acts on good to soft going. *P. Howling* **67**

Nolan & Brophy Auctioneers Flying Five, the Curragh—a British-trained 1,2 as Ringmoor Down again leaves it late; Benbaun (near side) and the other blinkered runner Osterhase fill the minor placings

RISE 3 b.f. Polar Falcon (USA) 126 – Splice 114 (Sharpo 132) [2004 84: p6g 6s 6s⁶ 7m **78**
6m 6d* 6m² 6s 6g* 6m² 6.1g Sep 11] fair performer: won handicaps at Salisbury in June
and Yarmouth in August: effective at 6f/easy 7f: acts on all-weather, good to firm and
good to soft going: wears blinkers: usually races prominently. *Andrew Reid*

RISING SHADOW (IRE) 3 b.g. Efisio 120 – Jouet 71 (Reprimand 122) [2004 86: **88**
6m⁶ 6s² 7f⁴ 7m⁶ 6.1g 6d Sep 17] compact gelding: fairly useful handicapper: well below
form last 3 starts: stays 7f: acts on good to firm and soft going. *R. A. Fahey*

RISKA KING 4 b.g. Forzando 122 – Artistic Licence (High Top 131) [2004 83: f8g **80**
f7s 7.6d 7m 7.1m 8.5g⁴ 8.3d³ 6.9g³ 7.5g⁶ 7.5d* 7.9g⁵ 8d⁴ p8.6g* p8g p8.6g Nov 13] **a74**
smallish, good-bodied gelding: fairly useful handicapper on turf, fair on all-weather: won
at Beverley in August and Wolverhampton in October: stays 8.6f: acts on polytrack, good
to firm and heavy ground: tried blinkered/visored at 2 yrs. *R. A. Fahey*

RISK FREE 7 ch.g. Risk Me (FR) 127 – Princess Lily 65 (Blakeney 126) [2004 68, **57**
a78: 7.6g 5m⁶ 7.1f 7s 7g p7.1g p8.6g⁴ p7.1g p8.6g⁶ p8g⁶ p8.6g⁴ p9.5g³ p10g³ Dec 30] **a60**
lengthy gelding: modest performer: stays easy 1¼m: acts on all-weather, firm and good
to soft ground: wears blinkers/visor: sometimes tongue tied: sometimes looks reluctant.
P. D. Evans

RISK SEEKER 4 b.c. Elmaamul (USA) 125 – Robertet (USA) 118 (Roberto (USA) **118 ?**
131) [2004 111: 15.5s² 16.2s* 16.4f⁴ 15d⁴ Jul 17] rather leggy, quite good-topped
colt: seventh foal: half-brother to several winners, including 3-y-o Punctilious: dam won
Grand Prix de Deauville and stayed 15.5f: smart performer: won 3 times at 3 yrs, including Prix Berteux at Deauville and Prix de Lutece at Longchamp: seemingly best effort
when winning Bovis Homes Sagaro Stakes at Ascot in April by 18 lengths from Dusky
Warbler with rest well strung out, readily going clear over 1f out in gruelling conditions:
creditable efforts on balance of form afterwards when 3¾ lengths fourth to Papineau
in Henry II Stakes at Sandown and 3½ lengths last of 4 to Forestier in Prix Maurice de
Nieuil at Maisons-Laffitte: stays 2m: goes particularly well on soft going: usually wears
ear plugs (rider fined for removing them during race both outings in Britain): held up.
E. Lellouche, France

RISKY WAY 8 b.g. Risk Me (FR) 127 – Hot Sunday Sport 42 (Star Appeal 133) [2004 **–**
f12s Feb 29] winning hurdler/chaser: wearing cheekpieces, well held only Flat outing
since 1999. *B. S. Rothwell*

RIVAL (IRE) 5 b.g. Desert Style (IRE) 121 – Arab Scimetar (IRE) (Sure Blade (USA) **– §**
130) [2004 –§: f12s f8.5s Mar 5] no form since 2002: tried blinkered/in cheekpieces.
S. T. Lewis

RIVA ROYALE 4 b.f. Royal Applause 124 – Regatta (Mtoto 134) [2004 93: 7d 7s 6g **84**
7m⁴ 7g⁶ 7m Jul 22] close-coupled, useful-looking filly: fairly useful handicapper: stays
7f: acts on firm and soft going: tried in cheekpieces: often races up with pace. *I. A. Wood*

RIVELLI (IRE) 5 b.m. Lure (USA) 131 – Kama Tashoof 72 (Mtoto 134) [2004 –: **–**
f8.5s Mar 1] strong mare: maiden: well held since 2002: tried blinkered/tongue tied.
B. R. Foster

RIVENDELL 8 b.m. Saddlers' Hall (IRE) 126 – Fairy Kingdom (Prince Sabo 123) **–**
[2004 –: f6g⁶ f7g f8.5s Feb 17] of little account. *M. Wigham*

RIVER ALHAARTH (IRE) 2 b.c. (May 1) Alhaarth (IRE) 126 – Sudden Interest **81 p**
(FR) (Highest Honor (FR) 124) [2004 7.1m⁵ 8g* Oct 12] €35,000Y, 25,000 2-y-o:
close-coupled colt: sixth foal: brother to fairly useful 1½m winner Curlew River and
half-brother to 3 winners, including fairly useful 1¼m/1½m winner After The Blue (by
Last Tycoon): dam, French 9f/10.5f winner, half-sister to very smart 1¼m winner/Oaks
second Sudden Love: better effort in maidens when winning at Leicester by ¾ length
from Registrar, rallying to lead close home: will be suited by 1¼m/1½m: should make a
useful handicapper. *P. W. Chapple-Hyam*

RIVER BISCUIT (USA) 2 ch.c. (Feb 2) Diesis 133 – Elle Est Revenue (IRE) 91 **70**
(Night Shift (USA)) [2004 7m 7m⁵ 8d 7d² p7g p7g* p8.6g⁴ p8g⁶ Dec 18] €90,000Y: **a77**
strong, close-coupled colt: fourth foal: half-brother to 3 winners abroad, including useful Italian winner (including at 7.5f) Scalino (by Benny The Dip): dam French 2-y-o 6f
winner who stayed 1m: fair performer: won claimer at Lingfield in November: barely
stays 8.6f: acts on polytrack, good to firm and good to soft going. *R. Hannon*

RIVER CANYON (IRE) 8 b.g. College Chapel 122 – Na-Ammah (IRE) 90 (Ela- **–**
Mana-Mou 132) [2004 –: f7g Feb 15] workmanlike gelding: lightly raced: little form
since 2001: tried blinkered. *W. Storey*

RIVER CARD 2 ch.f. (Feb 20) Zaha (CAN) 106 – Light Hand 80 (Star Appeal 133) **55**
[2004 8g 7.1d Oct 17] close-coupled filly: seventh foal: half-sister to fairly useful 1998
2-y-o 5f and 7f winner Light Fingered (by Soviet Lad): dam 1¼m winner: better effort
when seventh in maiden at Yarmouth on debut: handled turn poorly in seller at Musselburgh final start. *M. H. Tompkins*

RIVER DAYS (IRE) 6 b.m. Tagula (IRE) 116 – Straw Boater 89 (Thatch (USA) 136) **?**
[2004 60, a72: p6g f5g² f5s f6s⁶ p6g⁵ f5g² f5g⁴ Apr 17] modest performer: effective at 5f/ **a54**
6f: acts on firm going and all-weather: blinkered/visored: tongue tied: usually races up
with pace. *Miss Gay Kelleway*

RIVER FALCON 4 b.g. Pivotal 124 – Pearly River 72 (Elegant Air 119) [2004 85: **92**
5g⁵ 5g 5s* 5m 6m 6d³ 6f 6g* 5g 6s 5s⁴ 6g⁵ 5d 6s Nov 1] useful-looking gelding: fairly
useful performer: won handicap at York (by ½ length from Watching) in May and minor
event at Haydock (by head from Compton's Eleven) in August: effective at 5f/6f: acts on
firm and soft ground: none too consistent. *J. S. Goldie*

RIVER GYPSY 3 b.c. In The Wings 128 – River Erne (USA) (Irish River (FR) 131) **76**
[2004 72p: 12s² May 2] twice-raced maiden, fair form: best work late on when 6 lengths
second to Day Flight at Salisbury only 3-y-o start: will stay 1¾m. *D. R. C. Elsworth*

RIVER LARK (USA) 5 b.m. Miswaki (USA) 124 – Gold Blossom (USA) (Blushing **54**
John (USA) 120) [2004 48: f6g⁶ f5g⁴ f5g⁴ f5g⁶ 5d 6g⁶ 5v⁵ 5d 5f5g³ 6.1d Jul 10] modest
performer: ran as if amiss final start: effective at 5f/6f: acts on fibresand, good to firm and
good to soft ground: tried in cheekpieces/blinkers. *M. A. Buckley*

RIVER LIFFEY 2 b.c. (Apr 29) Forzando 122 – Rion River (IRE) (Taufan (USA) **83**
119) [2004 6d 7s² 8.5s² Aug 29] 8,000F, 15,000Y, 43,000 2-y-o: good-topped colt: half-
brother to 3 winners, including 6-y-o Monica Geller: dam Irish 1¼m winner: fairly useful
form when second in claimer at Chester and maiden at Beverley (looked unwilling): stays
8.5f: joined M. Al Kurdi in UAE. *M. L. W. Bell*

RIVER LINE (USA) 3 b.g. Keos (USA) 120 – Portio (USA) (Riva Ridge (USA)) **–**
[2004 50: 10m⁴ 9m 9.9g 16.1d 14.1f Sep 2] tall, lengthy gelding: little form at 3yrs.
C. W. Fairhurst

RIVER NUREY (IRE) 3 gr.c. Fasliyev (USA) 120 – Dundel (IRE) 82 (Machiavellian **77**
(USA) 123) [2004 72: 7f³ 7.1f² 8g⁵ 8m² 8.1s² 8g⁴ Sep 6] angular, good-topped colt: fair
maiden: stays 1m: acts on firm ground: sometimes makes running: sold 17,000 gns.
B. W. Hills

RIVER OF BABYLON 3 b.f. Marju (IRE) 127 – Isle of Flame (Shirley Heights 130) **91 ?**
[2004 62: 7.1d² 7g⁶ 8g⁵ 7g* p8g⁴ 7s Oct 15] lengthy filly: fairly useful performer: won
maiden at Catterick and handicap at Lingfield in September: seemed to run very well
when seventh to Dalna in listed race at Maisons-Laffitte final start: effective at 7f/easy
1m: acts on polytrack, soft and good to firm ground. *M. L. W. Bell*

RIVER OF DIAMONDS 3 b.g. Muhtarram (USA) 125 – City Gambler 74 (Rock **60**
City 120) [2004 8g 10d 11.9s² 11.5d* Nov 5] modest performer: won seller at Yarmouth
in November: stays 11.5f: acts on good to soft going. *R. Guest*

RIVER OF FIRE 6 ch.g. Dilum (USA) 115 – Bracey Brook (Gay Fandango (USA) **43**
132) [2004 52: 15g f14.8g³ f16g 10m⁴ 11.5f 17.2f 12f 16.4g* 15g⁵ 16m⁶ Jul 26] poor
handicapper: won at Folkestone (for second successive year) in July: effective at 1¼m to
2m: acts on fibresand, soft and good to firm ground: usually visored: often races up with
pace: none too consistent. *C. N. Kellett*

RIVER ROYALE 2 b.c. (Feb 10) Royal Applause 124 – Trundley Wood 66 (Wassl **93**
125) [2004 6g³ 6d³ 7d³ Oct 30] 36,000Y, 31,000 2-y-o: well-made colt: fluent mover:
fourth foal: half-brother to 2 winners abroad, including German 1m (at 2 yrs)/1¼m
winner Flaviatore (by Deploy): dam 2-y-o 7f winner: best effort in maidens at Newmarket
behind Tomoohat second start: respectable effort behind Centaurus final one: barely stays
7f. *P. W. Chapple-Hyam*

RIVER TREAT (FR) 3 ch.g. Irish River (FR) 131 – Dance Treat (USA) 115 (Nureyev **85**
(USA) 131) [2004 88: 7.1d* 7.1g⁶ 6m⁵ 6m 7m⁴ 10.1g² 10m Oct 2] angular gelding: has a
quick action: fairly useful performer: won maiden at Warwick in April: good length
second to Tata Naka in handicap at Yarmouth sixth start: stays 1¼m: acts on good to firm
and good to soft going: sold 12,000 gns. *G. Wragg*

RIVERWELD 2 ch.g. (Apr 4) Weldnaas (USA) 112 – Riverain 65 (Bustino 136) [2004 **52**
6g⁶ 7f⁴ 7g² 7.5d⁵ 7.5m 7d Oct 15] sparely-made gelding: modest maiden: stays 7.5f: acts
on good to soft ground. *G. M. Moore*

RIVIERA RED (IRE) 4 b.g. Rainbow Quest (USA) 134 – Banquise (IRE) (Last – Tycoon 131) [2004 12f p13g p12g f12g⁶ Dec 11] well held in maidens. *L. Montague Hall*

RIYADH 6 ch.g. Caerleon (USA) 132 – Ausherra (USA) 106 (Diesis 133) [2004 92: **74 §** 18g 16g 16g 16d 16d³ 14m 17.1f³ 20f 16.2d 16.2m² 21g 16.1d² 16s⁶ 16g 16m⁴ 17.2g⁶ 17.1g⁴ 18d³ Oct 18] lengthy, angular gelding: poor mover: fair handicapper: effective at 2m to 2½m: acts on firm and good to soft ground: often blinkered/visored: held up: often starts slowly/hangs: ungenuine. *M. Johnston*

RIYMA (IRE) 2 b.f. (Mar 14) Dr Fong (USA) 128 – Riyafa (IRE) 112 (Kahyasi 130) **55** [2004 7m 7.5d Aug 28] leggy filly: first foal: dam 1½m winner: modest form in maidens at Yarmouth and Beverley. *Sir Michael Stoute*

ROAD RAGE (IRE) 2 b.f. (Jan 18) Giant's Causeway (USA) 132 – Endorsement **78 p** 107 (Warning 136) [2004 7g³ 7f* 8m Sep 9] sturdy filly: first foal: dam 1½m and 2m winner: won maiden at Newmarket in July by short head from Elizabethan Age: tailed off in May Hill Stakes at Doncaster: will be suited by 1¼m/1½m: likely to do better. *E. A. L. Dunlop*

ROAD TO HEAVEN (USA) 2 ch.c. (Mar 7) Southern Halo (USA) – Glory Way **63** (USA) (Woodman (USA) 126) [2004 7.1d³ 7.1m 7m 8d Oct 18] $110,000Y: strong, stocky colt: has a fluent, round action: first foal: dam unraced close relation to US Grade 2 2-y-o 1m winner Supremo: modest maiden: third at Sandown, best effort: should stay 1m: tongue tied final start: sold 15,000 gns, sent to Sweden. *E. A. L. Dunlop*

ROAMING VAGABOND (IRE) 3 ch.g. Spectrum (IRE) 126 – Fiveofive (IRE) – 61 (Fairy King (USA)) [2004 –p: 11.1d⁶ 11.6m 8f Jun 29] rangy gelding: little form. *N. A. Callaghan*

ROAN RAIDER (USA) 4 gr. or ro.g. El Prado (IRE) 119 – Flirtacious Wonder **61** (USA) (Wolf Power (SAF)) [2004 54, a48: p7g f6g 7m 5d³ 5m⁴ 6m 6.1m⁵ 5m³ 6m⁵ 6.1g **a–** 5d² 5g 5d² 6m⁵ 5f 5m 6g Oct 5] workmanlike gelding: modest maiden: left M. Polglase after fourteenth start: best form at 5f: acts on fibresand, good to firm and good to soft ground: usually wears headgear: tried tongue tied. *Miss V. Haigh*

ROBBIE CAN CAN 5 b.g. Robellino (USA) 127 – Can Can Lady 82 (Anshan 119) **70** [2004 59: f12g* f12s³ p12g* 12g² Mar 25] leggy, unlucky-looking gelding: fair handicapper: won amateur events at Wolverhampton and Lingfield in February: short-headed at Doncaster (apprentices) final start: effective at 1½m to 2¼m: acts on all-weather and good to firm going: sometimes carries head high/drifts left: usually held up. *A. W. Carroll*

ROBBO 10 b.g. Robellino (USA) 127 – Basha (USA) (Chief's Crown (USA)) [2004 **54** 18d Oct 18] small gelding: very lightly raced on Flat nowadays, modest form in handicap at Pontefract only 10-y-o start: best at 15f+: acts on fibresand and heavy ground: usually blinkered earlier in career. *K. G. Reveley*

ROBESON 2 br.g. (Feb 2) Primo Dominie 121 – Montserrat 81 (Aragon 118) [2004 **72** 7m 8m⁵ p8g⁶ Nov 13] strong, close-coupled gelding: fifth foal: half-brother to 2002 2-y-o 6f winner Sarayat (by Polar Falcon) and 6f (at 2 yrs) to 1m winner Terfel (by Lion Cavern), both useful: dam 5f (at 2 yrs) and 6f winner: best effort in maidens (fair form) when fifth at Newmarket: not sure to stay beyond 1m. *D. M. Simcock*

ROBIN SHARP 6 ch.h. First Trump 118 – Mo Stopher 47 (Sharpo 132) [2004 –, a64: – f8f² f8s⁶ p7g p7g⁵ f7g f7m p8g⁴ 7v p8g² p7m p8g Dec 20] strong horse: modest **a55** performer: stays easy 1m: acts on all-weather, no form on turf since 2000: usually wears visor/cheekpieces: tried tongue tied: inconsistent. *J. Akehurst*

ROBINZAL 2 b.g. (Apr 15) Zilzal (USA) 137 – Sulitelma (USA) 63 (The Minstrel **65** (CAN) 135) [2004 7g 7d³ 7d² 7m⁶ 8s Oct 12] 15,000F, 12,500Y: tall, close-coupled gelding: seventh foal: half-brother to several winners, including 2000 2-y-o 1m winner Min Mirri (by Selkirk) and Irish 5f winner Neeze (by Cadeaux Genereux), both fairly useful: dam, 5f winner (ran only at 2 yrs), out of half-sister to Petoski: fair maiden: needs to settle to stay 1m: best efforts on good to soft going. *T. D. Easterby*

ROBMANTRA 2 b.c. (Feb 5) Mistertopogigo (IRE) **60 §** 118) [2004 7.1f⁶ 6f⁵ 5.1g³ 5g⁶ 7.1m 5.1s⁴ 5.1g 5.1v p7.1g f6s f7g f5f³ Dec 28] good- **a52 §** topped colt: modest maiden: should stay 6f: acts on heavy ground: often wears cheekpieces/blinkers: wandered penultimate start: unreliable. *B. J. Llewellyn*

ROB ROY (USA) 2 b. or br.c. (Mar 27) Lear Fan (USA) 130 – Camanoe (USA) **94 P** 63 (Gone West (USA)) [2004 7g* Oct 1]

'Riding a proper racehorse is awesome, the ground covered, the stride, the power, the speed—at the start, they could be anything, raw lumps of meat Sir Michael turns into athletes.' The task of turning a raw recruit into a top-class race-

Beech House Stud EBF Maiden Stakes, Newmarket—
Rob Roy looks a colt of considerable potential on his debut; Fortunate Isle (No. 10) is second

horse, hinted at in an interview in the *Racing Post* in the spring with Stuart Messenger, Sir Michael Stoute's head groom, can sometimes turn into a race against time in the top yards preparing a horse for the Two Thousand Guineas, the first classic. Not surprisingly, maturity plays its part at Newmarket in the cut-and-thrust of what is nearly always the most competitive event the runners have encountered, but, among those successful of late, maturity hasn't necessarily manifested itself in racecourse experience. Half of the Guineas winners in the last ten years had no more than three runs behind them, and arguably a stronger pointer to those able to beat the clock in that period has come from foaling dates, each of the last ten winners foaled in January, February or March, when only approximately thirty-eight per cent of the overall horse population is foaled in those months. Interestingly, all bar one of those winners gave a further demonstration of sorts of their maturity by making their debut no later than August as a two-year-old, though only six of the ten contested a pattern race as juveniles.

Sir Michael Stoute has shown a greater ability then most to knock the rough edges off horses in time for the Guineas, without the need to give them much race-course experience. Among Stoute's five Guineas winners—a modern-day record—only King's Best, successful in 2000, had as many as four runs beforehand and he was also the only one to contest a pattern race as a juvenile, finishing down the field in the Dewhurst. Stoute was also responsible for 2001 winner Golan, the only horse successful in the Guineas in the last ten years to have made his debut as a two-year-old later than August, winning a maiden at Chepstow in September. The imposing Rob Roy made a similarly impressive start on his only outing as a two-year-old in the Beech House Stud EBF Maiden over seven furlongs at Newmarket in October. Rumoured to have been taking the eye on the gallops, Rob Roy went off favourite at 4/1 in a field of twenty-three, and outclassed his opponents in the paddock and in the race. A big, rangy, good sort, he travelled strongly in the main behind the leaders, on and off the bridle occasionally only through greenness, and stormed away in the Dip, not needing to be touched with the whip as he beat Fortunate Isle by two and a half lengths. The bare form received a few knocks subsequently, but Rob Roy's timefigure was encouraging, given the gallop hadn't seemed strong, and he could hardly have made a bigger impression. There were few more promising debuts made all season.

Rob Roy was purchased at the Keeneland September Yearling Sale, where he made 300,000 dollars, the top price in 2003 for any of the progeny of his sire Lear Fan, who was retired from stud duties in the latest season. Lear Fan was a top-class miler who ran away with the Prix Jacques le Marois after finishing third

871

ROB

	Lear Fan (USA) (b 1981)	Roberto (b 1969)	Hail To Reason
Rob Roy (USA)			Bramalea
(b. or br.c. Mar 27, 2002)		Wac (b 1969)	Lt Stevens
			Belthazar
	Camanoe (USA) (br 1996)	Gone West (b 1984)	Mr Prospector
			Secrettame
		Prodigious (ch 1979)	Pharly
			Vichy

to El Gran Senor in the Two Thousand Guineas. The average distance of races won by the progeny of Lear Fan is around a mile and a quarter, but few of his best performers have shown their form over further. Rob Roy's dam is the twice-raced Camanoe, a half-sister to Public Purse, a very smart performer at up to a mile and a half in France/America, also third in the Dubai World Cup, and to the Grade 1 Yellow Ribbon Stakes winner Super Staff over a mile and a quarter. Rob Roy's grandam Prodigious was useful at a mile and a mile and a quarter in France. Rob Roy will be well suited by a step up to a mile and should stay a mile and a quarter, though he's far from sure to stay a mile and a half. Quoted at 20/1 with one firm for the Guineas at the time of writing, he should make up into a smart colt at least, especially given his physical scope. Among his trainer's Guineas winners, Doyoun, Shadeed and King's Best all tackled the Craven Stakes at three beforehand, Doyoun and Shadeed running out impressive winners, while Entrepreneur and Golan (who won the Guineas on only his second start) made their reappearance as three-year-olds in the Guineas. It will be interesting to see which approach Stoute opts for with Rob Roy. *Sir Michael Stoute*

ROBURY 2 b.g. (Apr 25) Robellino (USA) 127 – Youdontsay 85 (Most Welcome 131) – [2004 5s 6m 5g Jul 3] strong, lengthy gelding: well held in maidens. *E. J. Alston*

ROBWILLCALL 4 b.f. Timeless Times (USA) 99 – Lavernock Lady (Don't Forget **54** Me 127) [2004 61: 5d 5m⁵ 5m* 5f⁵ 5f⁵ 5d 5m⁵ 5d 6d 5d 5s² f5g Dec 1] modest performer: won claimer at Hamilton in June: best at 5f: acts on firm and soft ground: tried in cheek-pieces/blinkers: often races prominently. *A. Berry*

ROCAMADOUR 2 b.c. (Feb 10) Celtic Swing 138 – Watch Me (IRE) 106 (Green **85** Desert (USA) 127) [2004 7d⁵ 8.5s* 8d² 8.5g² Oct 2] rangy colt: fourth foal: half-brother to fairly useful Irish 2001 2-y-o 5f winner Church Cross (by Cadeaux Genereux) and winner abroad by Key of Luck: dam 6f winner: fairly useful performer: won maiden at Beverley in August: creditable second in minor events at Ayr and Epsom: will stay 1¼m: acts on soft going. *M. R. Channon*

ROCINANTE (IRE) 4 b.g. Desert Story (IRE) 115 – Antapoura (IRE) 82 (Bustino **57 §** 136) [2004 65: f9.4s p8g f8s f7g³ 10.9s 8s* 8v* f9.4m 8m f8m⁶ 9d 8.2v f7g p8.6g Dec 22] sturdy gelding: modest handicapper: won at Pontefract in April and Redcar in May: stays 8.5f: acts on fibresand, heavy and good to firm going: tried blinkered/visored: unreliable. *J. J. Quinn*

ROCKBURST 2 b.f. (Mar 9) Xaar 132 – Topwinder (USA) (Topsider (USA)) [2004 **83** 5v⁵ 6m² 6g* 6g³ 7s 6.1g* 6d Oct 14] quite good-topped filly: seventh living foal: half-sister to 3 winners, including 5f winner Piper's Clan (by Aragon) and fairly useful 1¼m winner (stayed 1¾m) Master George (by Mtoto): dam ran twice in France: fairly useful performer: won maiden at Hamilton in June and minor event at Nottingham (by 1½ lengths from Sam's Secret) in September: needs to settle to stay 7f: acts on good to firm ground: races prominently. *K. R. Burke*

ROCK CHICK 2 ch.f. (May 11) Halling (USA) 133 – Band (USA) (Northern Dancer) **55** [2004 6m May 29] half-sister to several winners, including 1995 2-y-o 5f/6f winner Applaud (by Rahy), 1¼m winner Glam Rock (by Nashwan), both useful, and 3-y-o Abington Angel: dam maiden out of high-class sprinter Swingtime: 9/1, ninth in maiden at Lingfield, very green. *J. H. M. Gosden*

ROCK CONCERT 6 b.m. Bishop of Cashel 122 – Summer Pageant 81 (Chief's – Crown (USA)) [2004 56, a69: f9.4g* f8.5s² f9.4g³ p8.6g f8s⁵ p7.1g p10m Dec 21] deep- **a71** girthed mare: fair handicapper on all-weather, modest on turf: won at Wolverhampton in January: effective at 1m/1¼m: acts on fibresand, firm and good to soft going: effective visored and off. *I. W. McInnes*

ROCK DOVE (IRE) 2 b.f. (Mar 26) Danehill (USA) 126 – Littlefeather (IRE) 107 **73 p** (Indian Ridge 123) [2004 5.1g* Sep 29] first foal: dam, 5f/6f winner (including at 2 yrs), half-sister to very smart miler Marling out of top-class sprinter Marwell: 11/4, won maiden at Nottingham by short head from Disguise, getting up close home: likely to prove best at 5f/6f: sure to improve. *Sir Mark Prescott*

ROCKERFELLA LAD (IRE)   4 b.g. Danetime (IRE) 121 – Soucaro (Rusticaro   –
(FR) 124) [2004 75: 9.9d 8d Apr 24] good-topped gelding: fair performer: well held in 2004: tried visored/blinkered. *M. Todhunter*

ROCKET FORCE (USA)   4 ch.g. Spinning World (USA) 130 – Pat Us (USA)   –
(Caucasus (USA) 127) [2004 103: 10g 10g 10.1m Jun 4] well-made gelding: useful performer: at 3 yrs: well held in 2004, including in visor: sold 35,000 gns, gelded and joined S. Gollings. *E. A. L. Dunlop*

ROCKET (IRE)   3 ch.g. Cadeaux Genereux 131 – Prends Ca (IRE) 98 (Reprimand   64
122) [2004 7.1d p7g⁴ 5.7s³ 7g 6m³ Aug 16] modest maiden: should stay 7f: acts on soft and good to firm ground. *R. Hannon*

ROCKETS 'N ROLLERS (IRE)   4 b.c. Victory Note (USA) 120 – Holly Bird   105
(Runnett 125) [2004 104: f7s³ 8g³ 7s³ 7.1d² 7d³ 7.1g* 8.3s⁴ 7d⁵ 7m⁴ 7s 8f 7g Sep 30] leggy, good-topped colt: useful performer: won listed race at Haydock in May by short head from Polar Ben, dictating steady pace: best effort after when creditable fifth to Puppeteer in Prix du Palais-Royal at Longchamp: effective at 7f/1m: acts on firm and soft ground: races prominently: sold 37,000 gns, joined M. Al Muhairi in UAE. *R. Hannon*

ROCK FEVER (IRE)   2 ch.f. (May 5) Desert Sun 120 – Icefern 88 (Moorestyle 137   52
[2004 6m 6g 7s 6d Nov 5] €25,000Y: tall filly: half-sister to several winners, including useful 1m winner Iamus (by Most Welcome) and 3-y-o Mac The Knife: dam sprinter: modest maiden: should stay 7f: acts on good to firm going. *M. J. Wallace*

ROCK HAVEN (IRE)   2 b.c. (May 8) Danehill Dancer (IRE) 117 – Mahabba (USA)   –
74 (Elocutionist (USA)) [2004 6g Aug 4] €23,000F, €25,000Y: closely related to 7f winner in Hong Kong by Danehill and half-brother to numerous winners, including Irish 1m to 1¼m winner Radomsko (by Polish Precendent) and 11.5f winner Finance Director (by Shareef Dancer), both useful: dam 1½m winner: 40/1 and green, always outpaced in maiden at Pontefract. *P. W. Harris*

ROCKLEY BAY (IRE)   3 b.g. Mujadil (USA) 119 – Kilkee Bay (IRE) 61 (Case Law   59
113) [2004 65: 6s 7m 6m 8.1g 6g² 6.1g p8m f8g Nov 22] lengthy, quite good-topped   a?
gelding: modest maiden: left P. Makin after seventh start: stays 6f: acts on polytrack and good to soft ground: tried blinkered/tongue tied: inconsistent. *Mrs L. C. Jewell*

ROCK LOBSTER   3 b.g. Desert Sun 120 – Distant Music (Darshaan 133) [2004 76:   72
10s 11.8d⁵ 10v⁶ f12g³ f12g⁶ 10g* 10.1d⁴ 10g⁶ Aug 16] leggy gelding: fair performer: won handicap at Nottingham in July: stays 1½m: acts on fibresand and good to soft ground. *J. G. Given*

ROCKPILER   2 b.g. (Feb 16) Halling (USA) 133 – Emma Peel 113 (Emarati (USA)   –
74) [2004 6g⁴ 8m Sep 4] 60,000F, €300,000Y: first foal: dam 5f and (including at 2 yrs) 6f winner: virtually pulled up in minor event at Ripon and maiden at Thirsk. *J. Howard Johnson*

ROCKY RAMBO   3 b.g. Sayaarr (USA) – Kingston Girl (Formidable (USA) 125)   –
[2004 –: 12d f8g Jun 11] no sign of ability: tried blinkered. *R. D. E. Woodhouse*

ROCKY REPPIN   4 b.g. Rock City 120 – Tino Reppin 46 (Neltino 97) [2004 57: 10g   51
8s 8.2d 7m f7g³ f8m⁴ f8m 8.1d 8d f7g f8g Dec 16] leggy, close-coupled gelding: modest maiden: effective at 7f/1m: acts on fibresand and good to firm ground: tried blinkered. *J. Balding*

ROCKYS GIRL   2 b.f. (Mar 9) Piccolo 121 – Lady Rockstar 90 (Rock Hopper 124)   –
[2004 6g p7g 7g 7s 6d Nov 5] first foal: dam 1m/1¼m winner: signs of only a little ability in maidens. *M. J. Ryan*

RODIAK   5 b.g. Distant Relative 128 – Misty Silks 81 (Scottish Reel 123) [2004 f14g   –
p10g Feb 3] good-topped gelding: missed 2003, and well held in banded races in 2004: tried visored/blinkered. *P. R. Hedger*

ROEHAMPTON   3 b.c. Machiavellian (USA) 123 – Come On Rosi 77 (Valiyar 129)   103
[2004 83P: 9g⁶ 12.3d⁵ 10.3f³ 12m 10v Oct 20] tall, angular colt: useful performer: little impact in listed race at Newmarket on first 2 starts: best effort when 1½ lengths third to Colisay in handicap at Doncaster: tailed off final outing: stays 1¼m: acts on firm and soft ground: tried tongue tied: blinkered/visored last 3 appearances: inconsistent: sold 28,000 gns, joined M. de Kock in UAE. *Sir Michael Stoute*

RO ERIDANI 4 b.f. Binary Star (USA) – Hat Hill (Roan Rocket 128) [2004 54: p8g p10g p10g Feb 16] maiden: well held in 2004: tried blinkered. *T. J. Etherington* –

ROJABAA 5 b.g. Anabaa (USA) 130 – Slava (USA) (Diesis 133) [2004 60: 10.1f⁶ 10g⁵ 10f⁵ 10.2m⁵ 10m Sep 25] lengthy gelding: poor performer: stays easy 1½m: acts on firm going: tried in cheekpieces. *W. G. M. Turner* **49**

ROKO 2 b.g. (Apr 22) Komaite (USA) – Robert's Daughter (Robellino (USA) 127) [2004 f5g 6m 6g 5g⁴ 5g³ 5s³ f6s* 7m 5.1s 5.1v f6s f5g f5g p6g Dec 27] plain gelding: modest performer: won claimer at Southwell in August, then left M. Easterby: below form after: stays 6f: acts on fibresand and soft ground: usually wears headgear: ungenuine. *D. Shaw* **55 §**

ROLEX FREE (ARG) 6 ch.g. Friul (ARG) – Karolera (ARG) (Kaljerry (ARG)) [2004 79: p12g f16s⁶ 10f p10g 10.2m³ f12m* 11.9f⁴ p12d* 15.9s 11.5d⁴ 12.1g³ 17.2g p12g p12.2g³ f16g⁵ p13.9g f11g⁵ p10m Dec 22] fair performer on all-weather, modest on turf: left Mrs L. Taylor after second outing: won handicap at Southwell in July and seller at Lingfield in August: stays 1½m: acts on all-weather, dirt and firm ground: usually wears headgear: front runner: inconsistent. *D. Flood* **54 a71**

ROLLERBIRD 2 b.f. (Apr 12) Sinndar (IRE) 134 – Speedybird (IRE) 71 (Danehill (USA) 126) [2004 p8g² Oct 31] 32,000F, 60,000Y: sixth foal: half-sister to winner in USA by Rahy: dam, 7f winner, out of half-sister to Mill Reef: joint-favourite, 3 lengths second to Marhoon in maiden at Lingfield, leading 2f out until close home: will probably be suited by 1¼m/1½m: should improve. *A. M. Balding* **67 p**

ROLLSWOOD (USA) 4 ch.g. Diesis 133 – Spit Curl (USA) (Northern Dancer) [2004 p10g⁵ 10.5g⁶ p12g⁶ 9.9g p12m Oct 6] modest maiden: stays 1½m: raced only on polytrack/good ground: tried in cheekpieces/tongue strap. *P. R. Hedger* **62**

ROMAN ARMY (IRE) 2 b.c. (May 22) Trans Island 119 – Contravene (IRE) 64 (Contract Law (USA) 108) [2004 8.2v⁵ Nov 4] €9,000F, €18,000Y: third foal: half-brother to Italian 7.5f and 9f winner by Mujadil: dam 2-y-o 5f to 7f winner: 16/1, fifth to Tawqeet in maiden at Nottingham, slowly away: should improve. *A. M. Balding* **65 p**

ROMAN EMPIRE 4 b.g. Efisio 120 – Gena Ivor (USA) (Sir Ivor (USA) 135) [2004 59: p8g p6g⁴ f6g* f7g³ f6d³ f7m⁵ 7s⁴ 6d 6g* p6g f7g² f6g* p7g Nov 27] lengthy, good-bodied gelding: fair handicapper: won at Southwell in May, Newcastle in September and Southwell in November: effective at 6f/7f: acts on all-weather and soft going: usually blinkered/visored, but effective without: sometimes starts slowly. *K. A. Ryan* **71**

ROMAN FORUM 3 b.c. Selkirk (USA) 129 – Flit (USA) 72 (Lyphard (USA) 132) [2004 10m⁶ 12g⁵ Jun 30] quite attractive colt: brother to smart 6f (at 2 yrs) and 1m (1000 Guineas) winner Wince (dam of 3-y-o Quiff), and half-brother to 3 winners, including very smart 8.5f to 1½m winner Ulundi (by Rainbow Quest): dam, 1¼m winner, sister to smart performer up to 1¼m Skimble: fair form at best in maidens: sold 2,500 gns. *H. R. A. Cecil* **72**

ROMAN KING (IRE) 9 b.g. Sadler's Wells (USA) 132 – Romantic Feeling 88 (Shirley Heights 130) [2004 12d Apr 5] sturdy gelding: fairly useful handicapper in 2001: lightly raced and well held since. *B. D. Leavy* –

ROMAN LOVE (IRE) 3 ch.f. Perugino (USA) 84 – Bordighera (USA) (Alysheba (USA)) [2004 f7s⁴ Aug 23] sixth foal: half-sister to high-class but untrustworthy 7f (at 2 yrs) to 11f winner Grandera (by Grand Lodge) and a winner in France by Lake Coniston: dam useful 13f French winner: 11/4, 9¼ lengths fourth to Oh Golly Gosh in maiden at Southwell, not knocked about: should improve. *J. R. Fanshawe* **– p**

ROMAN MAZE 4 ch.g. Lycius (USA) 124 – Maze Garden (USA) (Riverman (USA) 131) [2004 75: 7.1m 7.2f⁵ 7.6g 7g 7m 7m⁴ 7.6m² 7s⁴ 7m² 7.2d p6d³ p6g* p6g⁵ p7.1g⁴ p7.1g⁶ p6g* Dec 27] fairly useful on all-weather, fair on turf: won minor event in November and amateur handicap in December, both at Wolverhampton: effective at 6f to 7.6f: acts on all-weather and firm going. *W. M. Brisbourne* **72 a86**

ROMAN MISTRESS (IRE) 4 ch.f. Titus Livius (FR) 115 – Repique (USA) 88 (Sharpen Up 127) [2004 79: 6d 5m⁴ 5m⁶ 6m³ 5g 5.1d⁵ 6m 5f⁴ 5.1g* 5d 5d 5g Oct 8] smallish, angular filly: fair handicapper: won at Nottingham in August: effective at 5f/6f: acts on soft and firm going: often blinkered: sometimes slowly away: races prominently: withdrawn after unseating rider and bolting intended fifth outing. *T. D. Easterby* **73**

ROMANOVA (IRE) 2 b.f. (Feb 21) Grand Lodge (USA) 125 – Millitrix 82 (Doyoun 124) [2004 6d 7.1m⁴ 7g Oct 11] 60,000Y: tall, leggy filly: on weak side at 2 yrs: second foal: dam, ran 4 times (second at 7f at 2 yrs), half-sister to 6-y-o Royal Millennium out of **68**

half-sister to Croco Rouge: best effort in maidens when fourth at Warwick: should stay 1m. *D. R. Loder*

ROMAN QUINTET (IRE) 4 ch.g. Titus Livius (FR) 115 – Quintellina 83 (Robellino **74** (USA) 127) [2004 72: f5g p6g 5s 5.2g³ 5.7g² 6d² 6g² p7g² p7.1g² p7g* p7.1g⁴ Dec 20] fair performer: won handicap at Lingfield in December: stays 7f: acts on all-weather, firm and good to soft going: tried in cheekpieces/tongue tie: races freely/prominently: consistent. *D. W. P. Arbuthnot*

ROMAN THE PARK (IRE) 3 b.f. Titus Livius (FR) 115 – Missfortuna 71 (Priolo **46** (USA) 127) [2004 –: f8s³ f8g* f7m² f8m³ 8.5m* 8f³ 9m⁴ 7.9f³ 7.9m² 8.1d Oct 9] leggy, quite attractive filly: poor performer: won banded races at Southwell in April and Beverley in May: stays 9f: acts on fibresand and firm going. *T. D. Easterby*

ROMANTIC DRAMA (IRE) 3 b.f. Primo Dominie 121 – Antonia's Choice 73 **–** (Music Boy 124) [2004 65: 6.1g 8g 7.1d Oct 9] well-made filly: modest maiden at 2 yrs: tailed off in 2004: tried blinkered/tongue tied. *Mrs A. L. M. King*

ROMANTIC GIFT 2 b.f. (Feb 12) Cadeaux Genereux 131 – Last Romance (IRE) **59** (Last Tycoon 131) [2004 5g 6m 7m 7g 6d Oct 11] 13,000F: rather leggy filly: first foal: dam, French maiden, out of smart French performer up to 1½m Fleur d'Oranger: modest maiden: probably stays 7f: acts on good to firm going. *J. M. P. Eustace*

ROMANY NIGHTS (IRE) 4 b.g. Night Shift (USA) – Gipsy Moth 99 (Efisio 120) **87** [2004 88: f6s⁵ f6s f7g⁴ 6d³ 6m⁴ 6m² 6d² 5.1g² 5g⁴ 5.1d⁶ 6m 5.7g² 5m 6m⁵ 6g³ 6s p5.1g p6g f5g⁶ f5g⁵ Dec 14] strong gelding: fairly useful handicapper: in frame 9 times in 2004: left J. Unett and off 3 months after fifteenth start: effective at 5f to easy 7f: acts on all-weather, firm and good to soft going: usually visored/blinkered. *Miss Gay Kelleway*

ROMANY PRINCE 5 b.g. Robellino (USA) 127 – Vicki Romara 83 (Old Vic 136) **109** [2004 107: 14g³ 22.2f³ 16.4d² 16m⁵ 15.9d⁵ 18m Sep 9] rangy gelding: usually impresses in appearance: useful performer: first past post in listed race at Sandown in July by short head from Silver Gilt, drifting right (placings reversed on appeal): creditable fifth in Goodwood Cup (to Darasim) and Lonsdale Cup at York (to First Charter): not disgraced when seventh in Doncaster Cup final outing: best form around 2m: unraced on heavy going, acts on any other: usually waited with: sold 60,000 gns, joined S. Gollings. *D. R. C. Elsworth*

ROMARIC (USA) 3 b.g. Red Ransom (USA) – Eternal Reve (USA) 116 (Diesis 133) **–** [2004 87: 7.1g⁴ 8g 7s f11g f7g p9.5g Dec 20] close-coupled gelding: fairly useful performer at 2 yrs: well held in 2004: often blinkered/visored. *J. R. Norton*

ROMA VALLEY (FR) 2 gr.f. (Mar 23) Sagamix (FR) 129 – Lois (IRE) (Be My Guest **–** (USA) 126) [2004 7g 7g Oct 11] €28,000Y: small filly: first foal: dam unraced half-sister to smart German middle-distance stayer Levirat: well held in maidens. *R. Guest*

ROME (IRE) 5 b.g. Singspiel (IRE) 133 – Ela Romara 124 (Ela-Mana-Mou 132) **79** [2004 68: p12g³ 14.4v 14g³ 14m⁵ 12g⁵ 14m⁴ 16g 12f p12g* p13g⁶ Dec 4] fair handicapper: won amateur event at Lingfield in November: stays 1¾m: acts on polytrack and good to firm ground: tried in blinkers/cheekpieces. *G. P. Enright*

ROMEO'S DAY 3 ch.g. Pursuit of Love 124 – Daarat Alayaam (IRE) (Reference **58** Point 139) [2004 –: 10s 10.1g² 12.3g⁴ 11.5m³ 14.1m 16.2g 16g 12g 11.7d⁵ 10.1g⁴ 10m 10d* p12.2g* Oct 9] tall gelding: modest performer: won banded race at Brighton and selling handicap at Wolverhampton in October: stays 1½m: acts on polytrack, good to firm and good to soft ground: effective visored: sold 17,000 gns. *M. R. Channon*

ROMIL STAR (GER) 7 b.g. Chief's Crown (USA) – Romelia (USA) (Woodman **57** (USA) 126) [2004 64?, a75: 14.1g 16s 16d² f11g* 11.9f⁴ f14.8g* f12g* f11d³ 12.4v⁵ **a73** f12g² 12s* 14g 11.9g⁶ f12g* p13.9g³ p13.9g⁴ f14g Dec 7] workmanlike gelding: fair performer on all-weather, modest on turf: won seller at Southwell in May, claimer at Wolverhampton and amateur seller at Southwell in June, amateur handicap at Catterick in August and claimer at Southwell in November: stays 14.8f: acts on heavy going and all-weather: usually visored/blinkered. *K. R. Burke*

RONDELET (IRE) 3 b.g. Bering 136 – Triomphale (USA) (Nureyev (USA) 131) **86** [2004 73: 8.3s² 7.9d 8.1g² 9m³ 10.3d² 10.1g* 10.3g 10.1g⁴ 10g⁵ 8.9g⁵ Oct 9] sturdy gelding: fairly useful performer: won minor event at Epsom in July: good efforts in handicaps all 4 starts after: stays 1¼m: acts on soft and good to firm going: usually held up: consistent: sold 41,000 gns, sent to Bahrain. *R. M. Beckett*

RONNIE FROM DONNY (IRE) 4 b.g. Eagle Eyed (USA) 111 – New Rochelle **73 d** (IRE) 65 (Lafontaine (USA) 117) [2004 87: f7g⁴ f6g f8.5s 6s 7g⁵ 7s⁵ 6v 6m 7m⁵ 7.5d⁵

7m⁵ 6m 6m 6f p6g p7.1g Oct 9] sturdy, useful-looking gelding: fair handicapper: well below form last 5 starts: stays 7f, probably not 8.5f: acts on fibresand, firm and soft ground: tried in cheekpieces, not in 2004. *B. Ellison*

RONNIES LAD 2 b.g. (Mar 23) Lake Coniston (IRE) 131 – Lycius Touch 50 (Lycius (USA) 124) [2004 f5g5 f5d 6m* 6f² 6f² 7m 6m⁴ p7.1g p7m p7g Dec 29] modest performer: won claimer at Newcastle in May for J. Norton: left G. L. Moore after next start: stays 7f: acts on polytrack and firm going: often wears cheekpieces. *Andrew Reid* **53**

ROOD BOY (IRE) 3 b.g. Great Commotion (USA) 123 – Cnocma (IRE) 58 (Tender King 123) [2004 61: f7g⁴ 8g⁵ 8.3s⁵ 8.1g 8.3g⁵ 9s Oct 22] modest maiden: effective at 6f to 8.5f: acts on fibresand: gelded after final start. *J. S. King* **58**

ROODEYE 2 b.f. (Feb 13) Inchinor 119 – Roo 97 (Rudimentary (USA) 118) [2004 5.1f² 5m* 5g⁵ 5.2g⁶ 6g³ 6g⁴ 6m Oct 2] leggy filly: first foal: dam 2-y-o 5f/6f winner: fairly useful performer: made all in maiden at Windsor in June: good 3½ lengths third to Suez in listed race at Salisbury: badly hampered next start: will prove best at 5f/6f: acts on firm going: sometimes sweating/edgy. *R. F. Johnson Houghton* **94**

ROOFTOP PROTEST (IRE) 7 b.g. Thatching 131 – Seattle Siren (USA) 101 (Seattle Slew (USA)) [2004 47: 12d⁴ 16f² 16s³ 17d* 16m* 16m⁶ 16f* 15.9g* 16g 14d⁵ Oct 2] tall gelding: fair handicapper: won at Killarney and Galway in July, Tramore in August and Chester by 8 lengths from Irish Blade) in September: stays 17f: acts on firm and good to soft going: blinkered (reluctant to post and failed to apply himself) once in 2000: usually tongue tied. *T. Hogan, Ireland* **78**

ROOKS BRIDGE (IRE) 2 ch.g. (Apr 26) General Monash (USA) 107 – Lisa's Pride (IRE) 68 (Pips Pride (117) [2004 6.1m p7g p7.1g p5.1d f7g⁶ Dec 12] modest maiden: easily best effort final start: stays 7f: acts on fibresand. *G. A. Ham* **57**

ROOSTER RELLIK 2 ch.c. (Apr 14) Mark of Esteem (IRE) 137 – Amaretto Flame (IRE) 69 (First Trump 118) [2004 p10g p9.5g Dec 20] well held in maidens. *T. D. McCarthy* **–**

ROPPONGI DANCER 5 b.m. Mtoto 134 – Ice Chocolate (USA) 77 (Icecapade (USA)) [2004 32: f14.8g⁵ f12g³ p16g f16.2g⁵ 11.5m Jul 1] small, quite good-topped mare: poor maiden: stays 1½m: acts on fibresand and good to firm ground: tried visored/blinkered/tongue tied. *Mrs N. Macauley* **32**

ROSABLANCA (IRE) 2 b.f. (May 15) Sinndar (IRE) 134 – Elegant Bloom (IRE) 84 (Be My Guest (USA) 126) [2004 p7g Oct 28] €55,000Y: closely related to 3-y-o Summer Sunset and half-sister to several winners, including smart Irish/Scandinavian performer up to 7f Rolo Tomasi (by Mujtahid) and 6-y-o Eastern Breeze: dam Irish 2-y-o 6f winner: 50/1, last in maiden at Lingfield. *J. G. Given* **–**

ROSACARA 3 b.f. Green Desert (USA) 127 – Rambling Rose 111 (Cadeaux Genereux 131) [2004 61: 7.2g² 8.3f² 8.5g 7m Sep 18] strong, close-coupled filly: has no off-side eye: fair maiden: ran poorly last 2 starts: stays 1m: acts on firm going: tongue tied. *D. J. Daly* **71 ?**

ROSAPENNA (IRE) 2 b.f. (Jan 20) Spectrum (IRE) 126 – Blaine (USA) (Lyphard's Wish (FR) 124) [2004 6m⁵ 6.1d p6d⁵ 7g⁶ 8d Oct 14] €40,000Y: workmanlike filly: sister to 1m winner Radiant Energy and half-sister to several winners, including fairly useful 1m winner St Blaine (by St Jovite), later successful in USA: dam, ran 4 times in North America, half-sister to dam of Croco Rouge: fair maiden: easily best effort at 7f on good going. *C. F. Wall* **68**

ROSEANNA (FR) 3 b.f. Anabaa (USA) 130 – Dancing Rose (FR) (Dancing Spree (USA)) [2004 7g³ 8s 8d 7d Jul 8] €95,000Y: sturdy filly: third foal: dam, French 7.5f/1m winner, out of half-sister to French Group 1 winners Vert Amande, Indian Rose and Le Nain Jaune: useful performer: made all in listed newcomers race at Deauville at 2 yrs: creditable 4 lengths third to Silca's Gift in Nell Gwyn Stakes at Newmarket on reappearance, best effort in 2004: stays 1m: acts on soft going: blinkered final start. *Mme C. Head-Maarek, France* **95**

ROSE BIEN 2 b. or br.f. (Mar 17) Bien Bien (USA) 125 – Madame Bovary 82 (Ile de Bourbon (USA) 133) [2004 8d Oct 16] 1,000Y: half-sister to several winners, including fairly useful 1994 2-y-o 7f winner La Contessa (by Robellino), later successful in USA, and 6-y-o Tomthevic: dam 1m/1¼m winner: 100/1, well held in maiden at Yarmouth. *P. J. McBride* **–**

ROSECLIFF 2 b.c. (May 4) Montjeu (IRE) 137 – Dance Clear (IRE) 99 (Marju (IRE) 127) [2004 8d⁴ 10.1d⁴ Nov 5] 150,000Y: quite good-topped colt: first living foal: dam **71 p**

Irish 6f (at 2 yrs)/7f winner (later successful in USA up to 9f): fair form in maidens at Newmarket and Yarmouth (behind Quizzene, not knocked about): likely to stay 1½m: capable of better. *A. M. Balding*

ROSEIN   2 b.f. (Apr 22) Komaite (USA) – Red Rosein 97 (Red Sunset 120) [2004 f5g*   **74** 5m 6d6 Aug 31] 20,000Y: big, heavy-topped filly: seventh foal: sister to 6-y-o Proud Boast and 3-y-o Buy On The Red and half-sister to 2 winners: dam, tough sprinter, won Wokingham: fair performer: won maiden at Southwell in May: best effort when sixth in nursery at Ripon, wandering: likely to prove best at 5f/6f. *Mrs G. S. Rees*

ROSENCRANS (USA)   3 b.c. Forest Wildcat (USA) 120 – General's Mistress (USA)   **105** (General Meeting (USA)) [2004 a8f3 a7.5f* p7g* p8g4 7.1g6 Jun 31] $200,000Y: sturdy colt: third foal: half-brother to winner in USA by Announce: dam, US maiden, half-sister to US Grade 2 6f winner Diablo: useful performer: successful in maiden at Arlington for E. Harty in USA only 2-y-o start: won minor event at Nad Al Sheba in February and listed race at Lingfield (beat Fokine by ½ length) in March: creditable efforts when in frame in UAE 2000 Guineas at Nad Al Sheba (3 lengths third to Little Jim) and listed race at Lingfield (2¼ lengths fourth to Leitrim House): well beaten on turf debut in listed event at Sandown final outing: stays 1m: acts on dirt/polytrack: blinkered/visored: tongue tied in 2004: races prominently. *Saeed bin Suroor*

ROSE OF YORK (IRE)   4 b.f. Emarati (USA) 74 – True Ring (High Top 131) [2004   **56** –: 6g4 6d f8s2 p9.5g f8g6 Dec 16] lengthy filly: modest maiden: stays 1m: acts on fibresand. *T. D. Walford*

ROSES IN MAY (USA)   4 b. or br.c. Devil His Due (USA) 126 – Tell A Secret (USA)   **131** (Speak John) [2004 a8.5f* a8.5f* a9f* a9f* a9f* a10f2 Oct 30] $19,000Y, $115,000 2-y-o: half-brother to several winners in USA: dam US 6f to 8.5f winner, placed in Grade 3 7f events: top-class performer: much improved in 2004, and won first 5 starts, allowance race at Keeneland in April, optional claimer at Churchill Downs in May, Grade 3 handicap at Prairie Meadows in July, Whitney Handicap at Saratoga (beat Perfect Drift by a nose) in August and Grade 2 Kentucky Cup Classic Handicap at Turfway Park (landed odds by 4 lengths from Pie N Burger) in September: ran very well when 3 lengths second to Ghostzapper in Breeders' Cup Classic at Lone Star Park final outing, tracking winner throughout, unable to get past him, but maintaining clear advantage over remainder in straight: stays 1¼m: acts on sloppy going: usually makes running: stays in training. *D. L. Romans, USA*

ROSES OF SPRING   6 gr.m. Shareef Dancer (USA) 135 – Couleur de Rose (Kala-   **86** glow 132) [2004 93: 5s 5g3 5m 5m 5g 5g6 5.3f 6g Aug 14] lengthy mare: fairly useful handicapper: best at 5f/easy 6f: acts on firm ground and all-weather: visored once, usually wears cheekpieces: tried tongue tied: sometimes slowly away, usually races prominently otherwise: reportedly in foal to Kyllachy. *R. M. H. Cowell*

ROSE TEA (IRE)   5 ro.m. Alhaarth (IRE) 126 – Shakamiyn (Nishapour (FR) 125)   **–** [2004 –: 15g Apr 23] plain mare: maiden: little form since 2002: tried in cheekpieces, blinkered only 5-y-o start. *N. A. Graham*

ROSIELLA   2 b.f. (Jan 28) Tagula (IRE) 116 – Queen of Silk (IRE) 93 (Brief Truce   **72** (USA) 126) [2004 6m 6m5 5.7m* 5.7d3 5g4 6.1d6 Sep 27] 5,000Y: leggy filly: second foal: half-sister to 4-y-o Brief Goodbye: dam, Irish 2-y-o 1m winner, half-sister to smart Irish 7f/1m performer Tarry Flynn: fair performer: won maiden at Bath in August: creditable efforts next 2 starts: will prove best at 5f/easy 6f: acts on good to firm and good to soft going. *M. Blanshard*

ROSIE MAC   3 ch.f. First Trump 118 – Carol Again 48 (Kind of Hush 118) [2004 7f6   **56** 7d3 7g4 7m6 10g6 7.9g 10.1m4 Oct 10] 8,000Y, 500 3-y-o: compact filly: dam 11f to 1¾m winner: modest maiden: effective at 7f to 1¼m: acts on good to firm and good to soft ground. *N. Bycroft*

ROSIE MALONEY (IRE)   3 b.f. Docksider (USA) 124 – Magic Lady (IRE) (Big-   **–** stone (IRE) 126) [2004 –: 7.1d Apr 12] well beaten in maidens/claimer. *N. P. Littmoden*

ROSIE MUIR   2 br.f. (Feb 14) Mind Games 121 – Step On Degas 69 (Superpower   **–** 113) [2004 5.7g 6g p6g Nov 8] first foal: dam 5f to 7f winner: signs of just a little ability in maidens. *Mrs A. L. M. King*

ROSIE'S RESULT   4 ch.g. Case Law 113 – Precious Girl 76 (Precious Metal 106)   **53 §** [2004 65: 5v 5m 5g 5d* 5m 5m 5d6 6v 5m Sep 11] sparely-made gelding: modest handicapper: won apprentice event at Doncaster in July: raced mainly at 5f: acts on firm and good to soft going: visored (below form) once: unreliable. *M. Todhunter*

ROSINGS 3 ch.f. Grand Lodge (USA) 125 – Hajat 64 (Mujtahid (USA) 118) [2004 – 8.3f 9f Sep 2] 20,000Y: second foal: half-sister to 2001 2-y-o 7f winner Desert Royal (by Ali-Royal): dam 5f winner: always behind in maidens. *P. W. Harris*

ROSKILDE (IRE) 4 br.g. Danehill (USA) 126 – Melisendra (FR) (Highest Honor (FR) 124) [2004 100: 8m 8f Sep 11] good-bodied gelding: useful performer at best: well held in handicaps in 2004. *M. R. Channon*

ROSSALL POINT 3 b.g. Fleetwood (IRE) 107 – Loch Clair (IRE) 53 (Lomond (USA) 128) [2004 10.2g⁴ 11.6f⁵ 10f 14.1m⁴ 16.2g 16d³ 17.2s³ Oct 19] 4,500Y: sixth foal: half-brother to fairly useful 1¼m winner Agony Aunt (by Formidable) and 6-y-o Magic Charm: dam, lightly-raced maiden, half-sister to smart middle-distance performer Wind In Her Hair: fair maiden: should stay beyond 2m: acts on good to firm and good to soft going: sold 22,000 gns. *J. L. Dunlop* **72**

ROSSBEIGH (IRE) 2 b.c. (Jan 16) Alhaarth (IRE) 126 – Ring of Kerry (IRE) 67 (Kenmare (FR) 125) [2004 7d Aug 27] €65,000F, €240,000Y: rather leggy colt: second foal: half-brother to 4-y-o Honeystreet: dam Irish maiden who stayed 1¼m: 8/1, tenth in maiden at Newmarket, not knocked about: should do better. *D. R. Loder* **60 p**

ROSSELLI (USA) 8 b.g. Puissance 110 – Miss Rossi (Artaius (USA) 129) [2004 60d: 6g 5v 6d 8d 7.1m 6g 7.2g Jul 20] tall, good-topped gelding: one-time useful performer: became unreliable, and little form in 2004: tried in headgear/tongue tie: unreliable: put down after fracturing a hind leg in fall at Ayr. *A. Berry* **– §**

ROSSIN GOLD (IRE) 2 b.g. (Apr 13) Rossini (USA) 118 – Sacred Heart (IRE) 45 (Catrail (USA) 123) [2004 p6d⁶ p6g* p8.6g Dec 1] €10,500F, 15,000Y, 21,000 2-y-o: first foal: dam little sign of ability: modest form: won seller at Wolverhampton in November: pulled too hard in nursery final start: should stay 7f: blinkered: signs of waywardness. *P. A. Blockley* **62**

ROSS IS BOSS 2 gr.g. (Feb 4) Paris House 123 – Billie Grey 72 (Chilibang 120) [2004 6g 6m Oct 2] tall, unfurnished gelding: last in maiden at Newcastle and listed race at Redcar. *C. J. Teague* **–**

ROSS MOOR 2 b.c. (Apr 26) Dansili 127 – Snipe Hall 93 (Crofthall 110) [2004 8m Sep 21] 31,000Y, 60,000 2-y-o: big, strong colt: fourth foal: half-brother to 3-y-o Spliff: dam, 2-y-o 5f/6f winner, half-sister to dam of smart sprinter Atraf: 9/1 and backward, always behind in maiden at Newmarket: should do better. *Mrs A. J. Perrett* **– p**

ROSTI 4 b.g. Whittingham (IRE) 104 – Uae Flame (IRE) (Polish Precedent (USA) 131) [2004 55+: f7g* f8g* p8g³ f8s f8s⁶ 7.2g Apr 29] big, workmanlike gelding: modest performer: won 2 banded races at Southwell in January: effective at 7f/1m: acts on fibresand, raced only on good/good to firm ground on turf. *P. C. Haslam* **55**

ROTUMA (IRE) 5 b.g. Tagula (IRE) 116 – Cross Question (USA) 84 (Alleged (USA) 138) [2004 74: 10.1v 10v⁵ 9.2g 10.5m³ 10.1g* 10.3g⁶ 9.9g* 10s² 10d⁵ 10m* 10g 10d 10s 10s Nov 1] smallish, useful-looking gelding: fairly useful handicapper: improved and won at Newcastle and Beverley in June and at Leicester in August: best around 1¼m: acts on any going: usually blinkered: carries head awkwardly: tough. *M. Dods* **81**

ROUGE BLANC (USA) 4 b.f. King of Kings (IRE) 125 – Style N' Elegance (USA) (Alysheba (USA)) [2004 65: 16d 16m 13.9m May 28] tall, leggy filly: fair handicapper at 3yrs, well beaten in 2004: tried in headgear/tongue strap. *G. A. Harker* **–**

ROUGE ET NOIR 6 b.g. Hernando (FR) 127 – Bayrouge (IRE) (Gorytus (USA) 132) [2004 8g 8.3f 10g⁴ 14.1f³ 15.8m p12.2g⁵ p12.2g Nov 19] lengthy gelding: runner-up 3 of 4 starts in bumpers but looked ungenuine: modest maiden on Flat: should stay 2m: acts on polytrack and firm ground: tongue tied last 4 starts. *K. G. Reveley* **55**

ROUSING THUNDER 7 b.g. Theatrical 128 – Moss (USA) (Woodman (USA) 126) [2004 49: f16g f11g Jan 20] leggy gelding: poor performer: well beaten in 2004: usually wore headgear/tongue strap: dead. *W. Storey* **–**

ROUTE SIXTY SIX (IRE) 8 b.m. Brief Truce (USA) 126 – Lyphards Goddess (IRE) (Lyphard's Special (USA) 122) [2004 55: f9.4g 8.1v⁶ 9.3g² 7m 8.1g 10s⁶ Aug 14] strong, close-coupled mare: modest handicapper: stays 1¼m: acts on any going: tried blinkered/in cheekpieces: held up. *Jedd O'Keeffe* **55**

ROVELLA 3 b.f. Robellino (USA) 127 – Spring Flyer (IRE) 66 (Waajib 121) [2004 –: 12s 10s f8.5m 12.1m May 28] leggy filly: little form: sold 1,600 gns. *Mrs H. Dalton* **–**

ROVING VIXEN (IRE) 3 b.f. Foxhound (USA) 103 – Rend Rover (FR) (Monseigneur (USA) 127) [2004 –: p7g 7.1d f7g⁴ 10v f8.5m³ f8.5m³ 8f⁴ 8m 8m 7d⁵ 8.1d⁶ 7d⁵ p7.1g **43**

f8g³ f8g p9.5g Dec 22] poor maiden: stays 8.5f: acts on all-weather, firm and good to soft going: usually wears cheekpieces/blinkers. *J. L. Spearing*

ROWANBERRY 2 b.f. (Apr 30) Bishop of Cashel 122 – Raintree Venture (Good **37** Times (ITY)) [2004 p6g f7g Dec 12] half-sister to 2 winners abroad, including French 11f/11.5f winner Cambaco (by Muhtarram): dam ran twice: poor form in maidens. *R. M. H. Cowell*

ROWAN LODGE (IRE) 2 ch.c. (Apr 30) Indian Lodge (IRE) 127 – Tirol Hope **84** (IRE) 100 (Tirol 127) [2004 6m 6g³ 6m* 7m² 6s* 6g 7g² 6m 6g⁴ Oct 8] 3,000F: sturdy colt: third foal: dam 7f (at 2 yrs in Ireland) to 8.5f (in USA) winner: fairly useful performer: won maiden at Brighton in July and nursery at Catterick in August: mostly creditable efforts in nurseries after: stays 7f: acts on soft and good to firm going. *M. H. Tompkins*

ROWAN PURSUIT 3 b.f. Pursuit of Love 124 – Golden Seattle (IRE) (Seattle Dancer **68** (USA) 119) [2004 63: p7g* p7g³ p7g⁵ p8g 8m 7s p8g p7m⁵ Dec 21] small filly: fair performer: won handicap at Lingfield in January: effective at 7f/1m: acts on polytrack and good to firm going: best in blinkers: sometimes carries head awkwardly. *J. Akehurst*

ROWAN TREE 2 b.c. (Mar 17) Singspiel (IRE) 133 – Dashing Water 87 (Dashing **98** Blade 117) [2004 6m* 7g 7g 7g Sep 19] 200,000Y: rather leggy colt: fifth foal: half-brother to 1¼m/1½m winner Night Diamond (by Night Shift): dam, 2-y-o 7f winner, half-sister to Nunthorpe winners Lochsong and Lochangel: useful performer: won maiden at the Curragh in June: highly tried after, seeming to run well when seventh in Vintage Stakes at Goodwood penultimate start: blinkered final one: should stay 1m: joined D. Hall in Hong Kong. *A. P. O'Brien, Ireland*

ROWAN WARNING 2 b.c. (May 11) Diktat 126 – Golden Seattle (IRE) (Seattle **– p** Dancer (USA) 119) [2004 6.1g⁵ Jun 21] 40,000Y: close-coupled, quite good-topped colt: second foal: half-brother to 3-y-o Rowan Pursuit: dam Italian 2-y-o 5f/6f winner: very green, fifth of 7 in maiden at Nottingham, speed 3f then edging left: suffered foot injury after: probably capable of better. *W. J. Haggas*

ROXANNE MILL 6 b.m. Cyrano de Bergerac 120 – It Must Be Millie 66 (Reprimand **82** 122) [2004 86, a61: 5s³ 5s² 5d⁶ 5m³ 5m² 5f³ 5m⁵ 5.1d⁶ 5m* 5f² 5s 5g² 5g Aug 26] sturdy **a–** mare: fairly useful performer: won claimer at Catterick (claimed from J. M. Bradley £12,000) in July: best at 5f: acts on fibresand, firm and soft ground: wore cheekpieces last 7 starts: races prominently/travels strongly: sometimes hangs left. *P. A. Blockley*

ROYAL ABIGAIL (IRE) 2 b.f. (Feb 10) Inchinor 119 – Lady Abigail (IRE) (Royal **–** Academy (USA) 130) [2004 6.1s 7m a8g Sep 21] €15,000F, €13,000Y: useful-looking filly: first foal: dam unraced half-sister to smart 6f performer Lionhearted: well held in maidens: sold from E. Dunlop 1,000 gns after second start. *M. Kahn, Sweden*

ROYAL ACCOLADE 2 b.f. (Jan 18) Royal Applause 124 – Zafaaf 105 (Kris 135) **–** [2004 5s 5g 5m Jun 26] 4,500F, €25,000Y: sixth foal: half-sister to 3 winners, including 3-y-o Fun To Ride and fairly useful 5f (at 2 yrs) to 9.4f winner Queens Bench (by Wolf-hound): dam 7f/1m winner: little sign of ability in maidens: tongue tied penultimate start: blinkered final one: sold 1,200 gns. *B. Hanbury*

ROYAL ADVOCATE 4 b.g. Royal Applause 124 – Kept Waiting 75 (Tanfirion 110) **68** [2004 63: p8g⁴ p8d⁵ 6f⁶ Jul 5] lengthy gelding: fair maiden: needs further than 6f, and stays 1m: acts on good to firm going and polytrack. *J. W. Hills*

ROYAL ALCHEMIST 2 b.f. (Feb 22) Kingsinger (IRE) 94 – Pure Gold 88 (Dilum **96** (USA) 115) [2004 6.1s* 6m² 7f 7s 6g⁵ 7g Oct 2] good-topped filly: second foal: half-sister to 4-y-o Swift Alchemist: dam, 2-y-o 7f winner (only season to race), out of half-sister to 2000 Guineas winner Don't Forget Me: useful performer: won maiden at Nottingham in May: good ¾-length second to Slip Dance in listed race at Newmarket: respectable efforts in pattern company third and fifth starts: probably stays 7f: acts on firm and soft going. *M. D. I. Usher*

ROYAL APPROACH 3 b.f. Royal Applause 124 – Passionelle 56 (Nashwan (USA) **60** 135) [2004 61: 10.5g⁵ f12g 10d Sep 17] rather leggy filly: modest maiden: stays 10.5f. *M. Blanshard*

ROYAL ATALZA (FR) 7 gr.g. Saint Preuil (FR) – Crystalza (FR) (Crystal Palace **62** (FR) 132) [2004 f12s* f16s Feb 26] ran 3 times on Flat in France at 3/4 yrs: useful chaser/fairly useful hurdler: wearing cheekpieces, modest form when winning maiden at Wol-verhampton in February: raced freely in blinkers when well held next time: should stay 2m: acts on fibresand. *C. N. Allen*

ROYAL AWAKENING (IRE)   3 b.g. Ali-Royal (IRE) 127 – Morning Surprise 58   **57 ?**
(Tragic Role (USA)) [2004 61: p6g 5d 7m⁴ 5.9m⁵ 6m 7g⁴ Sep 7] neat gelding: modest
maiden: left A. Jarvis and off 5 months after reappearance: barely stays 7f: acts on firm
ground. *R. E. Barr*

ROYAL AXMINSTER   9 b.g. Alzao (USA) 117 – Number One Spot 71 (Reference   **50**
Point 139) [2004 52, a48: f11g p12g⁵ 12f² 12.3m 11m 12.1m* p12m Dec 15] useful-   **a38**
looking gelding: modest handicapper on turf, poor on all-weather: made all at Chepstow
in August: stays 1½m: acts on all-weather, firm and good to soft going: blinkered (well
held) once: makes running/races prominently. *Mrs P. N. Dutfield*

ROYAL BATHWICK (IRE)   4 b.f. King's Theatre (IRE) 128 – Ring of Light   **77**
(Auction Ring (USA) 123) [2004 83: 10m³ 12g² 12s⁴ 11.6d⁶ 11.7s Oct 19] small filly: fair
performer: stays 1½m: acts on firm ground, probably on soft: sometimes slowly away:
sold 14,000 gns. *B. R. Millman*

ROYAL CASTLE (IRE)   10 b.g. Caerleon (USA) 132 – Sun Princess 130 (English   **–**
Prince 129) [2004 60: 16.1m⁶ 16f⁶ Jun 8] sturdy, lengthy gelding: poor performer: tried
visored. *Mrs K. Walton*

ROYAL CAVALIER   7 b.g. Prince of Birds (USA) 121 – Gold Belt (IRE) 61 (Bellypha   **104**
130) [2004 107, a–: p12g 12g* 13.4d⁴ 11.9g⁵ 13.9s Aug 18] sturdy gelding: useful   **a–**
performer: won minor event at Doncaster (beat Dunhill Star by length) in March: good
fifth to Alkaased in valuable handicap at Haydock: effective at 1½m/1¾m: acts on any
turf going, below form on all-weather since 2000: usually waited with: tough. *R. Hollinshead*

ROYAL CHALLENGE   3 b.g. Royal Applause 124 – Anotheranniversary 95 (Ema-   **85**
rati (USA) 74) [2004 61p: 5.2m² 5d* 5m* 5m⁶ 5.1d³ 6g Sep 20] well-made gelding:
fairly useful performer: won maiden at Beverley and handicap at Sandown in July: should
stay 6f: acts on good to firm and good to soft ground: waited with: sold 54,000 gns, then
gelded. *G. A. Butler*

ROYAL COZYFIRE (IRE)   2 b.g. (Mar 14) Revoque (IRE) 122 – Mystic Thoughts   **57**
(IRE) (Shernazar 131) [2004 6.1g⁵ 5.1m* Jun 21] better effort in sellers (slowly away on
debut) when winning at Chepstow: should stay 6f. *B. Palling*

ROYAL DIGNITARY (USA)   4 b. or br.g. Saint Ballado (CAN) – Star Actress (USA)   **99**
(Star de Naskra (USA)) [2004 111: a7f³ a8f⁶ 7.5f⁵ p7g Mar 20] useful-looking gelding:
useful handicapper: ran at Nad Al Sheba first 3 starts, best effort on first occasion: well
held at Lingfield on return to Britain: stays 1m: acts on dirt, raced only on good going or
firmer on turf: often visored/blinkered: sold 38,000 gns. *D. R. Loder*

ROYAL DISTANT (USA)   3 ch.f. Distant View (USA) 126 – Encoreous (USA)   **72**
(Diesis 133) [2004 81: 8.1s⁶ 7.5s 11.9d 10.3m 10f 9g 9.9g 10m² 12m 7.9g 12.1m 13.9g
10s Nov 1] sturdy, workmanlike filly: fair handicapper: better than bare result most
starts towards end of year: stays 1½m: acts on good to firm and good to soft ground.
M. W. Easterby

ROYALE PEARL   4 gr.f. Cloudings (IRE) 112 – Ivy Edith (Blakeney 126) [2004 –:   **49**
p8g p10g p12g⁴ p13g* 14.1m⁴ p12g⁵ 16m⁵ p16d Aug 9] poor performer: won handicap
race at Lingfield in April: effective at 1½m to 2m: acts on polytrack and firm going.
R. Ingram

ROYAL EXPOSURE (IRE)   7 b.g. Emperor Jones (USA) 119 – Blue Garter 70   **–**
(Targowice (USA) 130) [2004 f9.4m⁴ May 17] workmanlike gelding: trained at 3 yrs by
W. Musson: raced in Holland/Germany 2001-2003, winning 3 times at 4 yrs: showed
nothing on return to Britain. *M. Wigham*

ROYAL FASHION (IRE)   4 b.f. Ali-Royal (IRE) 127 – Fun Fashion (IRE) 64   **50**
(Polish Patriot (USA) 128) [2004 68: p10g⁶ p8g p8.6g Nov 13] neat filly: fair performer:
well held in 2004, leaving Miss S. West after second start: refused to enter stall intended
fourth outing. *I. W. McInnes*

ROYAL FLIGHT   3 b.c. Royal Applause 124 – Duende 75 (High Top 131) [2004 –p: **–**
7g 8.2d 8g Sep 27] big, strong, lengthy colt: little form. *P. W. Harris*

ROYAL FLYNN   2 b.g. (Mar 26) Royal Applause 124 – Shamriyna (IRE) (Darshaan   **60**
133) [2004 6f⁶ 7.5g⁴ 6g 7.1g⁶ 8g⁵ Sep 11] close-coupled gelding: modest maiden: stays
7.5f. *M. Dods*

ROYAL GAME   2 b.g. (May 2) Vettori (IRE) 119 – Ground Game 95 (Gildoran 123)   **–**
[2004 p8g Sep 22] 16,000Y: second foal: half-brother to fairly useful 1¼m/11f winner
Magic Sting (by Magic Ring): dam 1m (at 2 yrs) and 1¼m winner: 10/1, well held in
maiden at Lingfield: gelded after. *D. R. Loder*

ROYAL GRAND   4 ch.c. Prince Sabo 123 – Hemline 77 (Sharpo 132) [2004 72: f6g³   **75**
f6g f7s 7g Mar 31] small, leggy colt: fair performer: well below form after reappearance:
stays 6f: acts on fibresand and good to firm going: tried visored. *T. D. Barron*

ROYAL INDULGENCE   4 b.g. Royal Applause 124 – Silent Indulgence (USA)   **54**
(Woodman (USA) 126) [2004 53§: 9.1g* 9.7f⁴ 10f⁴ Sep 16] sturdy gelding: modest
performer: won handicap at Ayr in August: stays 1¼m: acts on firm ground: tried in
cheekpieces/blinkers, not in 2004. *W. M. Brisbourne*

ROYAL ISLAND (IRE)   2 b.c. (Apr 29) Trans Island 119 – Royal House (FR) 104   **93**
(Royal Academy (USA) 130) [2004 5v⁵ 5m⁵ 6m² 5f 5g 6s Aug 18] €17,000F, 14,000Y:
sturdy colt: has a round action: third foal: half-brother to fairly useful Italian 2002 2-y-o
7.5f winner Lips Plane (by Ashkalani) and fairly useful Irish 7f/1m winner Sugarhoneybaby (by Docksider): dam, Irish 6f (at 2 yrs)/1m winner, half-sister to smart French/US
9f/1¼m performer Ranger: fairly useful performer: won maiden at Beverley (by 8
lengths) and minor event at Newcastle in May: good neck second to Screwdriver in listed
race at Epsom, only form after: should stay 7f: acts on heavy and good to firm ground.
M. Johnston

ROYAL JELLY   2 b.f. (Mar 5) King's Best (USA) 132 – Baked Alaska 93 (Green   **82**
Desert (USA) 127) [2004 7g 7g p7g* p8g Nov 16] useful-looking filly: fourth foal: half-
sister to 4-y-o Aleutian and a winner in Italy by Machiavellian: dam very useful winner:
fairly useful performer: won maiden at Lingfield in October by ¾ length from Archeology, leading freely but ran respectably final start: probably stays 1m:
acts on polytrack. *J. H. M. Gosden*

ROYAL JET   2 b.g. (May 3) Royal Applause 124 – Red Bouquet (Reference Point   **85**
139) [2004 8m³ 8m⁶ 10g² 10v⁵ Oct 20] 58,000Y: leggy gelding: fifth foal: half-brother to
several winners, including 4-y-o Red Fort and useful 1m to 1½m winner Red Carnation
(by Polar Falcon): dam, German 1½m/13f winner, half-sister to smart filly up to 1m Red
Camellia, herself dam of 3-y-o Red Bloom: fairly useful maiden: second at Pontefract,
best effort: stays 1¼m: acts on good to firm going: visored last 2 starts. *M. R. Channon*

ROYAL LOGIC   3 b.f. Royal Applause 124 – Lucie Edward (Puissance 110) [2004   **–**
6m 9g 8m⁶ 7d p7m p8m Dec 15] 51,000Y: rather leggy filly: second foal: dam unraced
sister to very smart 5f performer Mind Games: little form. *M. R. Channon*

ROYAL LUSTRE   3 b.c. Deputy Minister (CAN) – Snow Bride (USA) 121 (Blushing   **68**
Groom (FR) 131) [2004 8g 8g³ 10g 9.9m² 9.9g⁵ Sep 30] good-topped colt: half-brother
to several winners, notably top-class 1½m (Derby, King George and Arc) winner Lammtarra (by Nijinsky): dam, awarded Oaks, out of top-class 1½m performer Awaasif: fair
maiden: found little final start: stays 1¼m: races prominently: sold 5,500 gns.
J. H. M. Gosden

ROYAL MASTER   2 b.c. (Apr 28) Royal Applause 124 – High Sevens 90 (Master   **65**
Willie 129) [2004 6f⁶ 6m⁶ 6d p6g³ p7.1g³ Dec 31] 7,000F, €35,000Y: half-brother to 2
winners, including 7f (including at 2 yrs)/1m winner Impulsif (by Diesis): dam 2-y-o 6f
winner: fair maiden: visored, creditable third at Lingfield (minor event) and Wolverhampton: stays 7f: acts on polytrack and firm ground. *E. Tyrrell, Ireland*

ROYAL MELBOURNE (IRE)   4 ch.g. Among Men (USA) 124 – Calachuchi 74   **58**
(Martinmas 128) [2004 –: 12.4s* 12.3m⁶ 10.9d 12.1g p12.2g⁶ Dec 11] lengthy, workmanlike gelding: modest performer: won handicap at Newcastle in May: stays 1½m: acts on
polytrack and soft going: inconsistent. *Miss J. A. Camacho*

ROYAL MILLENNIUM (IRE)   6 b.g. Royal Academy (USA) 130 – Galatrix   **123**
72 (Be My Guest (USA) 126) [2004 118: 6d* 6.5g 6g⁴ 6d* 5m³ 6d* 5m⁴ Dec 12]
  In the circus ring of sprinting, with its colourful acts and performers, many
with their own peculiar characteristics, Royal Millennium should perhaps have
drawn more applause for his efforts as the show rolled on around Britain and the
rest of Europe in 2004. The sprinters as a whole typically provide value for money
for followers of the sport and it can be easy to overlook the contribution of a
performer like Royal Millennium. All three of his wins came in Group 3 company,
but in terms of form he achieved more in the season as a whole than some of those
successful in more prestigious events, and he ended the year behind only Somnus,
Tante Rose and Var among the best sprinters in Europe.
  At the age of six, a whole season spent racing exclusively at sprint distances
was a new departure for Royal Millennium, who had raced at up to nine furlongs as
a three-year-old and, though winning over six furlongs, had put up his best effort in

Foster's Lager Chipchase Stakes, Newcastle—
Royal Millennium has a neck to spare over Somnus (rail) on his belated return

2003 when runner-up in the Prix de la Foret over seven furlongs in testing conditions. As his record in 2004 suggests, Royal Millennium coped well all the same and showed himself better than ever, ridden in customary style for each of his wins. After being sent to Dubai in the winter, only to return without running, he had a setback in the spring and wasn't seen out until late-June, when making a successful return in the Foster's Lager Chipchase Stakes at Newcastle, where he had merely to be nudged along to get on top near the finish, beating Somnus by a neck in receipt of 8 lb. Ridden by Richard Quinn at Newcastle, Royal Millennium was partnered for the rest of the season by Ted Durcan, including for his two other wins, in the Ballygallon Stud Renaissance Stakes at the Curragh in September and the Igloos Bentinck Stakes at Newmarket in October. He got the better of the three-year-old Moss Vale each time, putting up a particularly good effort when scoring by a short head under a penalty at Newmarket. Royal Millennium reached the frame in two of his three runs in Group 1 company in Europe. After a rare below-par effort in the Prix Maurice de Gheest at Deauville in August, he ran an excellent race in the Haydock Sprint Cup in September, beaten little over two lengths in fourth behind close-finishers Tante Rose and Somnus in a field of nineteen, despite still being in

Igloos Bentinck Stakes, Newmarket—Royal Millennium (nearest camera) edges ahead of Moss Vale;
Quito (blinkers) is about to take third place off Country Reel (dark colours)

rear two furlongs out and needing to be switched as he finished strongly. Royal Millennium added a new trick to his act in the Prix de l'Abbaye at Longchamp in October. Dropped to five furlongs for the first time in his career, he was taken off his feet early on before coming with a wet sail to be beaten half a length and a length behind all-the-way winner Var and The Tatling. Royal Millennium's only other run over five furlongs came in the very valuable Hong Kong Sprint in December, in which he finished fourth, again taken off his feet early on. He was beaten four lengths behind Silent Witness, doing much the best of the five British- and Irish-trained runners.

Royal Millennium (IRE) (b.g. 1998)	Royal Academy (USA) (b 1987)	Nijinsky (b 1967)	Northern Dancer Flaming Page
		Crimson Saint (ch 1969)	Crimson Satan Bolero Rose
	Galatrix (b 1986)	Be My Guest (ch 1974)	Northern Dancer What A Treat
		Alligatrix (b 1980)	Alleged Shore

Royal Millennium, whose pedigree was dealt with in *Racehorses of 2003*, has had a reputation for being difficult to win with, but he put that behind him in 2004, doubling his tally of wins for the three previous seasons put together. Held up, Royal Millennium probably still needs his run timing more precisely than most, given his tendency to idle, but his toughness and consistency is hard to fault. A lengthy, angular gelding, he has yet to race on heavy ground, but acts on any other and has run well when sweating. With the King's Stand being run at York instead of Ascot in 2005, his best chance of a big win may come at six furlongs or seven, at least away from softish ground, perhaps in the Golden Jubilee Stakes. However he fares in that event, Royal Millennium should hold his own in most of the races chosen for him. *M. R. Channon*

ROYAL MOUGINS 2 br.c. (Jan 25) Daylami (IRE) 138 – Miss Riviera Golf 106 (Hernando (FR) 127) [2004 6g 7.1d⁵ 8g⁵ 8d³ 7s⁵ Oct 22] close-coupled colt: first foal: dam, 1m winner, sister to useful 1¼m performer Miss Corniche: will stay 1¼m: acts on soft going: sold 40,000 gns. *G. Wragg* — **78**

ROYAL NITE OWL 3 b.g. Royal Applause 124 – Nite-Owl Dancer 75 (Robellino (USA) 127) [2004 –: f8.5s 8.1s f7m⁴ 6m⁴ 5.9m³ 6d f5g⁴ f6s p5.1g Dec 20] leggy gelding: poor maiden: left J. O'Reilly after fifth start: best form at 5f: acts on fibresand and good to firm ground: races up with pace. *J. Balding* — **46**

ROYAL ORISSA 2 b.c. (Apr 21) Royal Applause 124 – Ling Lane (Slip Anchor 136) [2004 6m⁴ 7g⁵ 6g³ 6m 6f² 6g⁵ 7s² Nov 6] 20,000F, 9,000Y, 21,000 2-y-o: leggy colt: sixth foal: half-brother to 3 winners, including 5-y-o Vicious Warrior: dam unraced out of close relation to Irish Oaks winner Bolas: fairly useful maiden: second at Doncaster in sales race and nursery: stays 7f: acts on firm and soft ground: tongue tied last 3 starts. *D. Haydn Jones* — **85**

ROYAL OVATION 5 b.g. Royal Applause 124 – Thevetia 65 (Mummy's Pet 125) [2004 –: f8.5g Jan 5] maiden: no form since 2002: tried blinkered. *N. P. Littmoden* — **–**

ROYAL PARDON 2 b.f. (Feb 11) Royal Applause 124 – Miss Mercy (IRE) 62 (Law Society (USA) 130) [2004 6f 6.1d 6m⁴ 5.9g⁴ 7m⁵ Sep 22] half-sister to several winners, including useful 2001 2-y-o 5f winner Pachara (by Mind Games), later successful in USA, and 3-y-o Shrink: dam 2-y-o 6f winner: modest maiden: stays 7f: acts on good to firm going. *M. L. W. Bell* — **56**

ROYAL PAVILLION (IRE) 3 b.g. Cape Cross (IRE) 129 – Regal Scintilla 103 (King of Spain 121) [2004 6¹p: p6g³ f6s* 6d⁴ 6d Apr 10] strong, well-made gelding: fair performer: won maiden at Wolverhampton in February: unfavoured by draw in handicaps next 2 starts: subsequently gelded: stays 6f: acts on fibresand, unraced on extremes of going on turf. *W. J. Musson* — **70**

ROYAL PRINCE 3 gr.c. Royal Applause 124 – Onefortheditch (USA) 79 (With Approval (CAN)) [2004 78p: 7d⁴ 7f* 7m* 7m³ 8.1g³ 8m⁴ 8g* Oct 1] leggy, lengthy colt: useful performer: won maiden at Yarmouth and handicap at Leicester in June and minor event at Newmarket in October: improved form when beating Dawn Surprise by ½ length for final success: stays 1m: acts on firm ground: tongue tied (ran creditably) sixth start: free-going sort. *J. R. Fanshawe* — **105**

ROY

ROYAL PRODIGY (USA) 5 ch.g. Royal Academy (USA) 130 – Prospector's Queen — (USA) (Mr Prospector (USA)) [2004 78: p13g p13g⁴ f12g² 17.2g Sep 27] close-coupled **a71** gelding: fair performer on all-weather, lightly raced and little recent form on turf: stays 13f: acts on all-weather and good to soft going: visored (well held) once. *R. J. Hodges*

ROYAL RACER (FR) 6 b.g. Danehill (USA) 126 – Green Rosy (USA) (Green **58** Dancer (USA) 132) [2004 –: 9.7d⁴ 9.7s³ 9.7s⁶ 7g 8g 9.7m⁶ 9.9m⁶ 9d p10g Nov 13] rangy gelding: modest handicapper: won at Folkestone in April and August: stays 1½m: acts on polytrack, good to firm and soft ground: visored/blinkered last 5 starts. *J. R. Best*

ROYAL REBEL 8 b.g. Robellino (USA) 127 – Greenvera (USA) (Riverman (USA) **112 §** 131) [2004 16.2s⁵ 16.4f 20m⁴ 16.4d⁴ 16m² 15.9d Aug 17] good-topped gelding: off 22 months (reportedly due to leg problem) and just smart form in 2004, best effort when 9 lengths fourth to Papineau in Gold Cup at Royal Ascot (had won race in 2001 and 2002) third start and 2½ lengths second to Darasim in Goodwood Cup: turned in moody display when well held in Lonsdale Cup at York final start: stays 2½m: acts on firm and good to soft going: effective with or without blinkers/visor: often soon off bridle. *M. Johnston*

ROYAL SAILOR (IRE) 2 b.g. (Mar 2) Bahhare (USA) 122 – Old Tradition (IRE) **66** 76 (Royal Academy (USA) 130) [2004 8m 7.9g p7g 8.2v Nov 4] 5,000F: tall gelding: third foal: half-brother to 2 winners, including fairly useful 5f (including at 2 yrs)/6f winner Litewska (by Mujadil): dam ran twice: fair maiden: best effort at 1m on good going. *J. M. P. Eustace*

ROYAL SAPPHIRE (USA) 2 b.c. (Jan 18) Kingmambo (USA) 125 – Amethyst **63 p** (IRE) 111 (Sadler's Wells (USA) 132) [2004 7s Oct 22] $80,000Y: smallish, well-made colt: first foal: dam, Irish 6f (at 2 yrs) and 7f winner (also second in Irish 1000 Guineas), sister to 2000 Guineas winner King of Kings: 20/1, raced alone when ninth to Tasdeed in maiden at Doncaster: sure to do better. *M. Johnston*

ROYAL SESSION (IRE) 4 b.f. Accordion – Mrs Keppel 67 (Castle Keep 121) — [2004 –: 8s 7d f12g Nov 9] fifth foal: half-sister to Irish 5f winner Rossmore Rosie (by Elbio): dam 1¼m winner in Ireland: well beaten in maidens, and in claimer at Wolverhampton final start. *D. P. Kelly, Ireland*

ROYAL SHEPLEY 3 b.f. Royal Applause 124 – Dekelsmary 61 (Komaite (USA)) — [2004 f6g f6g f6s Mar 14] first foal: dam 5f to 7f winner: soundly beaten in maidens/seller. *J. Balding*

ROYAL STARLET 3 b.f. Royal Applause 124 – Legend 74 (Belmez (USA) 131) **50** [2004 –: 8g 11.7f 11.5f⁴ 12g⁵ 10m 16s 11.5g Sep 14] well-made filly: modest maiden: barely stays 11.5f: raced mainly on good going or firmer: tried visored: sold 2,000 gns. *Mrs A. J. Perrett*

ROYAL STORM (IRE) 5 b.h. Royal Applause 124 – Wakayi 87 (Persian Bold 123) **110** [2004 102, a90: 7d 6m* 6f⁴ 7g⁶ 7m 6m 7f² 7m 7m 7g* 7m 7g 6s⁴ p7g⁵ p6g⁴ Dec 4] tall, **a97** lengthy horse: smart performer on turf, useful on all-weather: won handicap at Newmarket in May and listed event at Newbury (beat Meshaheer by ½ length) in September: creditable 2 lengths fourth to Quito in listed race at Doncaster, best effort after: effective at 6f/7f: acts on polytrack, firm and soft ground: usually races up with pace: tough and consistent. *Mrs A. J. Perrett*

ROYAL SUPREMACY (IRE) 3 ch.f. Desert Prince (IRE) 130 – Saucy Maid (IRE) — 69 (Sure Blade (USA) 130) [2004 55: 5.7s 5.7m 5.1m Aug 10] modest maiden at 2 yrs: last in handicaps in 2004: tried tongue tied. *J. M. Bradley*

ROYALTEA 3 ch.f. Desert King (IRE) 129 – Come To Tea (IRE) (Be My Guest (USA) **56 ?** 126) [2004 f7g⁶ f7g⁶ f8.5g⁴ f8.5s f9.4m 9.3g 7m Sep 25] sixth living foal: dam, Irish 2-y-o 7f winner, half-sister to very smart 1m/1¼m performer Hawkeye: signs of some ability. *Ms Deborah J. Evans*

ROYAL TIGRESS (USA) 3 b.f. Storm Cat (USA) – Warm Mood (USA) (Alydar **98** (USA)) [2004 80p: 8v³ 7s* 8g 8m 7d⁵ 12f 11.9s Aug 18] tall, close-coupled filly: fifth foal: half-sister to 3 winners, including 1999 2-y-o 5f (Norfolk Stakes) winner Warm Heart (by Diesis) and useful Irish 2002 2-y-o 5f/6f winner Miguel Cervantes (by Danzig): dam, unbeaten in 4 starts from 6f to 1m in Ireland, out of champion Canadian sprinter Summer Mood: useful performer: won listed race at Leopardstown in April by short head from Takrice: highly tried and below form after, including in Coronation Stakes at Royal Ascot (seventh to Attraction) and Yorkshire Oaks at York fourth/final outings: effective at 7f/1m: best efforts on soft/heavy going: blinkered/visored last 2 starts: has worn crossed noseband: sent to USA. *A. P. O'Brien, Ireland*

884

ROYAL TRIGGER 4 b.g. Double Trigger (IRE) 123 – Jeronime (USA) 81 (Sauce –
Boat (USA)) [2004 84: 11.6d 10g 13.3g 17.2g 12.1m 13.1d Aug 27] leggy, lightly-made
gelding: fairly useful handicapper at 3 yrs: well held in 2004: tried blinkered/tongue tied.
Ian Williams

ROYAL UPSTART 3 b.g. Up And At 'em 109 – Tycoon Tina 61 (Tina's Pet 121) 41
[2004 54: 10d f9.4g³ f9.4g² 14.1m⁶ 11.5f⁵ 12m 12.1m Jul 27] quite good-topped gelding:
poor maiden: stays 9.4f: acts on fibresand and good to firm going: usually blinkered.
W. M. Brisbourne

ROYAL WARRANT 3 b.c. Royal Applause 124 – Brand (Shareef Dancer (USA) 135) 102
[2004 81: p8g³ p7g⁶ p8g* p8g³ 9g⁴ 10.1m² 10f² 10m² 9.9m⁶ Jul 29] smallish, close-
coupled colt: useful handicapper: won at Lingfield in February: good second after at
Epsom, Windsor and Newmarket (best effort, beaten short head by Woodcracker): stays
1¼m: acts on polytrack and firm going: races up with pace: genuine: sent to Singapore.
A. M. Balding

ROYAL WEDDING 2 b.g. (Mar 7) King's Best (USA) 132 – Liaison (USA) (Blush- 76
ing Groom (FR) 131) [2004 6f 6s 7g Sep 14] good-topped gelding: half-
brother to several winners, including smart 7f (at 2 yrs) and 1¼m winner Lagudin (by
Eagle Eyed) and 1m winner Medfee (by Alzao): dam, French 1¼m listed winner, sister
to Prince of Wales's Stakes winner Two Timing: best effort in maidens on debut at
Yarmouth: bred to stay 1m: finished weakly all starts: gelded after final one. *D. R. Loder*

ROYAL WINDMILL (IRE) 5 b.g. Ali-Royal (IRE) 127 – Salarya (FR) (Darshaan 55
133) [2004 57: 7g 8.5d 8g⁵ 8d² 7.1f 8d⁶ 8m⁶ 6m³ 5m f7g² f6g Dec 7] leggy gelding:
modest performer: races freely, and at least as effective at 6f/7f as 1m: acts on fibresand,
firm and soft going: often wears cheekpieces: sometimes slowly away. *M. D. Hammond*

ROYAL ZEPHYR (USA) 3 b.f. Royal Academy (USA) 130 – Cassation (USA) (Lear –
Fan (USA) 130) [2004 62: 8g Sep 13] leggy, unfurnished filly: modest form in maidens
in 2003: well held in handicap at Bath only 3-y-o start. *Sir Mark Prescott*

ROY MCAVOY (IRE) 6 b.g. Danehill (USA) 126 – Decadence (Vaigly Great 127) –
[2004 77d: f8.5s p6g p8g p10g⁴ 7m May 18] one-time fair performer: well held in 2004:
tried in cheekpieces. *Mrs G. Harvey*

ROZANEE 4 ch.f. Nashwan (USA) 135 – Belle Genius (USA) 111 (Beau Genius 62
(CAN)) [2004 64: p12g⁶ 10.9d 9.9s Aug 29] big, lengthy filly: modest maiden: stays
1¼m: acts on polytrack and good to firm ground. *J. W. Payne*

RUBAIYAT (IRE) 3 b.g. Desert Story (IRE) 115 – Lovers' Parlour 83 (Beldale 71
Flutter (USA) 130) [2004 –p: 8v 8f f12d⁴ p12d³ p10g² p10g⁵ 8.1m³ p9.5g³ p8m² Oct 6]
fair maiden: effective at 1m, and probably stays easy 1½m: acts on all-weather, soft and
good to firm ground: sold 24,000 gns. *G. Wragg*

RUBIES 2 ch.f. (Feb 5) Inchinor 119 – Fur Will Fly 66 (Petong 126) [2004 5.1d² 5g⁶ 75
5.7g² 7g⁴ p7g⁶ Nov 10] 6,000F: second living foal: sister to 3-y-o So Will I: dam second
at 6f from 4 starts: fair maiden: stays 7f: acts on polytrack and good to soft going: free-
going sort. *R. F. Johnson Houghton*

RUBYANNE (IRE) 2 b.f. (May 24) Fasliyev (USA) 120 – Phyliel (USA) 82 (Lyphard 83
(USA) 132) [2004 5m⁶ 5.2m* 5.2g Aug 14] 45,000 2-y-o: lengthy filly: eighth foal: dam,
2-y-o 6f winner, out of half-sister to Royal Academy and to dam of Storm Cat: odds on,
won maiden at Yarmouth in July by 4 lengths from Danehill Willy: eighth in listed race at
Newbury, tending to hang: should prove best at 5f/easy 6f: joined M. Al Kurdi in UAE.
M. J. Wallace

RUBY MUJA 2 b.f. (Feb 22) Mujahid (USA) 125 – Ruby Julie (Clantime 101) [2004 62
5d 5g 5.1m³ 5d* 6m Oct 1] 5,000Y: quite good-topped filly: second foal: dam unraced
sister to smart sprinter Yorkies Boy: modest performer: won seller at Windsor in August,
then left R. Hannon: likely to prove best at 5f: acts on good to soft going. *Miss
E. C. Lavelle*

RUBY MURRAY 2 b.f. (Jan 14) Zafonic (USA) 130 – Poppadam 87 (Salse (USA) 56
128) [2004 6g 6g 6g 7g p7.1g Dec 15] 45,000Y: sturdy, close-coupled filly: first foal:
dam, 1m winner, half-sister to Irish 1000 Guineas winner Classic Park: modest maiden:
should stay 1m. *B. J. Meehan*

RUBY REBEL 2 ch.f. (Apr 14) Tomba 119 – Miss Chiquita (IRE) 64 (Waajib 121) –
[2004 5d 5g 6m 6f Jun 15] 800Y: leggy filly: third foal: half-sister to a winner in Hungary
by Bijou d'Inde: dam Irish 1½m winner: seems of little account. *P. T. Midgley*

RUBY ROCKET (IRE)   3 b.f. Indian Rocket 115 – Geht Schnell (Fairy King (USA))   **113**
[2004 100: 7g⁵ 6d² 6d³ 6d² 6m³ 6m² 6d 6d* 6s³ Nov 6] good-bodied filly: smart performer: won listed race at Newmarket in October by 1½ lengths from Ringmoor Down: also
ran well in similar event at Haydock (beaten a neck by Tante Rose), Chipchase Stakes at
Newcastle (¾-length third to Royal Millennium) and Summer Stakes at York (went down
by 2½ lengths to Tante Rose) second to fourth starts and in listed event at Doncaster (1¼
lengths third to Quito) final one: stays 6f: acts on firm and soft ground. *H. Morrison*

RUBY'S DREAM   2 b.f. (Apr 16) Tipsy Creek (USA) 115 – Sure Flyer (IRE) (Sure   **65 d**
Blade (USA) 130) [2004 5s⁴ 5v² 5g³ 5.1m⁴ 5.3f³ 5.7g⁵ 5d⁴ 6m 5m 5.1g p6g Oct 19]
1,800Y: workmanlike filly: half-sister to several winners, including useful Irish 2000
2-y-o 5f winner Sure Mark (by Goldmark), later 9f winner in Hong Kong: dam Irish
maiden half-sister to dam of smart stayer Jardines Lookout: fair maiden: below form last
4 starts: likely to prove best at 5f/easy 6f: acts on any turf going. *J. M. Bradley*

RUBY WINE   2 b.f. (Apr 17) Kayf Tara 130 – Cribella (USA) 71 (Robellino (USA)   **76 p**
127) [2004 6d² Aug 13] big, close-coupled filly: second reported foal: dam 1½m winner:
12/1, 4 lengths second to Shanghai Lily in maiden at Newbury, green before running on
well: bred to stay at least 1½m: should do better. *J. M. P. Eustace*

RUDAKI   2 ch.g. (Mar 26) Opening Verse (USA) 126 – Persian Fountain (IRE) 67   **61**
(Persian Heights 129) [2004 7m 6d⁴ 7m³ 6d Oct 14] 10,500Y: close-coupled gelding:
half-brother to 3 winners, including fairly useful Irish 2002 2-y-o 5f winner Annamoe
Boy (by Presidium): dam 2-y-o 7.5f winner who stayed 1¼m: modest maiden: should
stay 1m: acts on good to firm and good to soft going. *M. G. Quinlan*

RUDOOD (USA)   4 b.g. Theatrical 128 – Kardashina (FR) (Darshaan 133) [2004 78:   **81**
p8g⁵ 8m May 29] smallish, rather leggy gelding: fairly useful performer, lightly raced:
ran as if amiss final start: stays 1¼m: acts on polytrack, unraced on extremes of going on
turf. *Lady Herries*

RUE DE PARIS   4 br.g. Paris House 123 – Innocent Abroad (DEN) 53 (Viking (USA))   **42**
[2004 57d: 6d 7m⁵ f6f 7m Sep 4] leggy, good-topped gelding: poor maiden: stays 6f:
acts on firm and soft going: tried in tongue tie/cheekpieces: sometimes gives trouble in
preliminaries (withdrawn once). *John A. Harris*

RUGGTAH   3 gr.f. Daylami (IRE) 138 – Raneen Alwatar 80 (Sadler's Wells (USA)   **70**
132) [2004 9g 11.7f³ p13g⁵ 14d Oct 10] quite good-topped filly: seventh foal: half-sister
to fairly useful 1998 2-y-o 1m winner Raneen Nashwan (by Nashwan): dam, 1½m
winner, out of sister to Coronation Stakes winner Flame of Tara (dam of Marju and Salsabil): fair maiden: ran as though amiss final outing: should stay 1¾m: acts on firm ground
and polytrack: sold 10,500 gns. *M. R. Channon*

RULE OF LAW (USA)   3 b.c. Kingmambo (USA) 125 – Crystal Crossing (IRE)   **125**
99 (Royal Academy (USA) 130) [2004 109: 10.4s² 12m² 12f⁴ 11.9d* 14.6f*
Sep 11]
In one important respect, the St Leger is usually a show without Punch nowadays. Come to that, it is often a show without Judy as well, but, despite the rarity
of Derby and Oaks winners in the line-up at Doncaster of late, the final classic
has maintained a good standard, clashes of the sexes continuing to be central to
the entertainment provided. No Derby winner has contested the St Leger since
Reference Point won at Doncaster in 1987, and just three Oaks winners have taken
part in the meantime—only User Friendly in 1992 completing the double—but
some of the best finishes have continued to be between colts and fillies. In 1988,
Minster Son had a length to spare over Oaks winner Diminuendo, and in 1990
Snurge held off Yorkshire Oaks winner Hellenic by three quarters of a length. In
1998, Nedawi beat Yorkshire Oaks runner-up High And Low by half a length and
the following year Mutafaweq put up the best St Leger performance in recent years
to beat Oaks winner Ramruma by two lengths in a titanic struggle.
The market on the latest renewal of the St Leger—sponsored by betfair.com
and again worth £240,000 to the winner—was headed by Rule of Law and Quiff.
Both horses had been successful at York in August on their most recent start. Derby
runner-up Rule of Law had shown his well-being by winning the Great Voltigeur
Stakes, traditionally a key St Leger trial, by two and a half lengths from Derby third
Let The Lion Roar in a field of seven. Quiff, unraced outside maiden company until
third in the Ribblesdale Stakes at Royal Ascot, had shown much improved form
when scoring by eleven lengths in the Yorkshire Oaks, appearing to revel in the soft

ground. On the day at Doncaster, the market couldn't separate them at 3/1. Among seven opponents, Let The Lion Roar was at 9/2, with Aidan O'Brien's Irish Derby third Tycoon at 6/1. The first two in the Gordon Stakes at Goodwood, Maraahel, a stable-companion of Quiff, and Go For Gold, the second of Aidan O'Brien's three runners, were at 8/1 and 12/1 respectively, Frank Sonata was at 16/1, with Mikado, O'Brien's third runner, at 25/1 and Slovak-trained Darsalam (a half-brother to the 1994 Leger winner Moonax, and winner of the Czech version of the race) at 33/1. Not unusually in the Leger nowadays, few in the field had raced beyond a mile and a half, and, with no pacemakers involved, Rule of Law was soon in front under Kerrin McEvoy (Dettori was at Leopardstown for the Irish Champion Stakes). Rule of Law had made all at York and was asked to dictate a slow early pace at Doncaster, making the race far less of a test of stamina than it was designed to be, particularly given the firm ground. Turning for home, virtually all the runners were still on the bridle, but, as the race finally built to a crescendo, Rule of Law's main challenger was Quiff, who had needed to be switched to make her effort. Well inside the last furlong, Rule of Law looked in danger of being caught, as Quiff got upsides, but he found extra under pressure to hold on by a head, with Tycoon coming from the rear to be a length and a half further away, a length in front of Maraahel in fourth. Predictably, given the gallop, the timefigure for the race was slow, but, conceding the runner-up 3 lb, Rule of Law put up a high-class effort, a shade better, on form, than his second to North Light at Epsom.

Rule of Law ended a barren spell in the classics for Godolphin, as well as a frustrating one, giving them their first classic winner in Britain since Kazzia's success in the 2002 Oaks, though Godolphin runners had reached a place in all four classics earlier in 2004. Rule of Law was a fourth St Leger winner for Saeed bin Suroor and Godolphin, following Classic Cliche in 1995, Nedawi in 1998 and Mutafaweq in 1999, making Suroor the most successful trainer in the race currently holding a licence, two behind Cecil Boyd-Rochfort and Dick Hern, the most successful St Leger trainers of the twentieth century. Godolphin's trainer has even further still to go to catch the most successful St Leger trainer, Malton-based John Scott, who saddled sixteen winners of the race between 1827 and 1862, including the first triple crown winner West Australian in 1853. Rule of Law was a first British classic winner for Australian rider Kerrin McEvoy, who drew widespread praise for his effort, and capped a fine first season for him in his role as second jockey to Frankie Dettori at Godolphin. McEvoy, who turned twenty-four in October, was adding to a long tradition of success for Australian jockeys in the St Leger, Brownie Carslake (1919, 1924 and 1938), Edgar Britt (1947 and 1948), 'Rae' Johnstone (1950 and 1951), Garnie Bougoure (1963) and Ron Hutchinson (1969) all partnering at least one winner of the race in the previous century. Johnstone, based in France, where he was known as 'Le Crocodile' because of his knack of snapping up rivals late on, was one who was largely European in his style

Daily Telegraph Great Voltigeur Stakes, York—Rule of Law is impressive under Frankie Dettori; Let The Lion Roar, Go For Gold and Always First follow him home

in the saddle, as is McEvoy, though McEvoy is from a family of Australian jockeys,
including his father Tony, now a leading trainer at home, where Kerrin rode Brew
to victory in the Melbourne Cup in 2000.

With Dettori on Guineas runner-up Snow Ridge, McEvoy had also partnered Rule of Law in the Derby. After wintering in Dubai, Rule of Law had shown
improved form under Dettori on his reappearance at three in the Dante Stakes at
York, finishing a clear second of ten, though a little flattered by his proximity to the
eased-down winner North Light, who beat him by half a length, with Let The Lion
Roar third. Starting at 20/1, Rule of Law gave McEvoy a far better experience in
the Derby than second favourite Sundrop had twenty-four hours earlier on his first
ride on the course when tailed off in the Oaks. Held up, Rule of Law was still last
but one of the fourteen runners turning for home, and wandered noticeably once
switched wide in the straight, but he ran on strongly without reaching the length-
and-a-half winner North Light, edging second place by a head from Let The Lion
Roar, who also finished well. The knives were out afterwards for McEvoy in some
quarters, but he had ridden Rule of Law no differently than Dettori had at York.
Missing the King Edward VII Stakes at Royal Ascot after being diagnosed with a
'low-grade infection' in the week of the race, Rule of Law was supplemented for
the Irish Derby at a cost of €95,000. Partnered by Dettori and starting at 13/2, Rule
of Law was ridden differently this time and led briefly around two furlongs out,
but could still only keep on for fourth behind Grey Swallow, finishing a length
and a half and a neck behind runner-up North Light, marginally further behind him
than at Epsom.

Rule of Law is a third British classic winner for his highly-successful sire
Kingmambo, following King's Best in the Two Thousand Guineas in 2000 and

Russian Rhythm in the One Thousand Guineas in 2003. Kingmambo also has a good classic prospect in Prix Marcel Boussac winner Divine Proportions for 2005, when his fee at stud in America will be 300,000 dollars, making him second in the pecking order there only to Storm Cat, whose fee is 500,000 dollars. A son of the brilliant filly Miesque, Kingmambo was also responsible for 2003 Queen Anne winner Dubai Destination, but he has started to become a fair influence for stamina with the distances of races won by his three-year-olds averaging nearly a mile and a quarter. Kingmambo's best performer has been the top-class, Japanese-trained colt El Condor Pasa, runner-up in the Arc, while he has also been responsible for Lemon Drop Kid, winner of the Belmont Stakes, and King Kamehameha, successful in the latest Japanese Derby.

				Mr Prospector		Raise A Native
Rule of Law (USA) (b.c. 2001)		Kingmambo (USA) (b 1990)		(b 1970)		Gold Digger
				Miesque		Nureyev
				(b 1984)		Pasadoble
		Crystal Crossing (IRE) (b 1994)		Royal Academy		Nijinsky
				(b 1987)		Crimson Saint
				Never So Fair		Never So Bold
				(b 1987)		Favoletta

Rule of Law's dam, Crystal Crossing, traces back to one of the best families belonging to the Moller racing empire, her grandam being the Irish Guineas winner Favoletta, dam of the smart two-year-old five-furlong performer Amaranda and Favoridge, a very smart performer at up to one mile who was promoted to second after finishing third to Ma Biche in the One Thousand Guineas. Rule of Law's grandam the lightly-raced maiden Never So Fair has also produced Circle of Gold, winner of the Group 3 Prestige Stakes over seven furlongs as a two-year-old and

Godolphin's "Rule of Law"

third in a Grade 2 race over eight and a half furlongs on turf in America at three. Circle of Gold was trained in Britain for Robert Sangster by Peter Chapple-Hyam, as was Rule of Law's dam Crystal Crossing, a winner of a listed event over six furlongs at two before being sent to race in America. Crystal Crossing's first foal Crossbreeze (by Red Ransom) failed to progress after showing fairly useful form when third on her debut over six furlongs, also being sent to America, where Crystal Crossing's second foal Crystal Class, a colt by Kingmambo's sire Mr Prospector, was also only placed. Crystal Crossing's first foal since Rule of Law, a colt by Rahy, fetched 1,050,000 dollars as a yearling at Keeneland in September, a matter of days after Rule of Law's St Leger win—a timely one as it turned out!

Bred by Robert Sangster and his son Ben, Rule of Law never changed hands publicly before making his debut in Sheikh Mohammed's colours for David Loder as a two-year-old, being visored, after an inauspicious first outing, then winning a maiden and the listed Acomb Stakes over seven furlongs at York before finishing third in the Royal Lodge Stakes at Ascot over a mile. Rule of Law, who also wore a crossed noseband as a juvenile, wore a tongue strap on each outing at three, as did many of Godolphin's runners in 2004. A leggy, attractive colt with a quick action, Rule of Law's form in testing conditions over an extended mile and a quarter in the Dante is only a little behind his subsequent efforts over further, though it is likely he will do much of his racing at a mile and a half at four. Untried on heavy going, though proven on any other, his consistency and tactical versatility should see him pick up another good prize or two in 2005, when he will almost certainly become another Godolphin flagbearer on the world stage. *Saeed bin Suroor*

RULES FOR JOKERS (IRE) 3 b.g. Mujadil (USA) 119 – Exciting (Mill Reef – (USA) 141) [2004 80: 7g f7g6 Apr 17] rather leggy, useful-looking gelding: fairly useful performer in 2003: ran as if amiss both 3-y-o starts. *J. A. Osborne*

RULING REEF 2 b.f. (Apr 2) Diktat 126 – Horseshoe Reef 88 (Mill Reef (USA) 141) 39 [2004 p7m Dec 22] 11,000Y, 6,200 2-y-o: close-coupled filly: closely related to 1½m winner Warning Reef (by Warning) and half-sister to several winners, including useful 6f (at 2 yrs)/7f winner Reefs Sis (by Muhtarram): dam 1¼m winner: 66/1, tenth in maiden at Lingfield: refused to enter stall intended debut. *M. D. I. Usher*

RUMAN (IRE) 2 b.g. (Apr 11) Fayruz 116 – Starway To Heaven (ITY) (Nordance 59 (USA)) [2004 6s 6g Oct 8] lengthy gelding: better effort in maidens when seventh at York on final start. *M. J. Attwater*

RUMBALARA 2 b.f. (Feb 15) Intikhab (USA) 135 – Bint Zamayem (IRE) 95 (Rain- 79 bow Quest (USA) 134) [2004 7m 7g2 8g* Sep 13] 6,500F, 70,000Y: attractive filly: sixth foal: half-sister to useful Irish 6f (at 2 yrs)/7f winner Sweet Deimos (by Green Desert) and fairly useful 7.6f winner Queenie (by Indian Ridge): dam, 1¼m winner, half-sister to smart French miler Rouquette: won maiden at Bath by neck from Silver Highlight, making all: should stay 1¼m: tail flasher. *J. H. M. Gosden*

RUMBLING BRIDGE 3 ch.g. Air Express (IRE) 125 – Rushing River (USA) (Irish 58 River (FR) 131) [2004 56: 8g 9.9g 11.9s2 11.9s3 Oct 15] modest handicapper: stays 1½m: acts on soft and good to firm going. *J. L. Dunlop*

RUM CREEK 2 ch.c. (Apr 10) Tipsy Creek (USA) 115 – Carnbrea Belle (IRE) 76 53 (Kefaah (USA) 124) [2004 7d 6f 7s 5.7g Sep 27] modest maiden: best effort at 6f on firm going: dead. *S. Kirk*

RUM DESTINY (IRE) 5 b.g. Mujadil (USA) 119 – Ruby River (Red God 128§) 40 [2004 65: 6m 5g 5g 5d 5m f6g Nov 8] small gelding: just poor form in 2004: wears head-gear. *J. S. Wainwright*

RUMOUR 4 b.f. Lion Cavern (USA) 117 – Thea (USA) 95 (Marju (IRE) 127) [2004 83 65: f8m* Jul 6] fairly useful form: having only second outing when winning maiden at Southwell by 5 lengths from Telefonica: suffered an injury after: dead. *J. R. Fanshawe*

RUMOUR MILL (IRE) 3 b.g. Entrepreneur 123 – Pursuit of Truth (USA) 69 (Irish – River (FR) 131) [2004 67?: f9.4s5 10g 10.2m f8.5g 11.6f 8f 10.2m 8s 9.7f 8f 8.1m f12d Dec 21] maiden: little form at 3yrs: tried in cheekpieces/blinkers: left N. Berry before final start. *R. A. Harris*

RUM SHOT 3 b.c. Efisio 120 – Glass (Bering 136) [2004 104p: 6g4 6m 6.1m* 7g3 6v6 113 7g Sep 17] sturdy, close-coupled colt: smart performer: won listed race at Chester (by ½ length from Talbot Avenue) in August: best effort when 2½ lengths third to Chic in

Mr H. R. Mould's "Rum Shot"

Hungerford Stakes at Newbury: well held in Prix de Meautry at Deauville and listed race at Newbury after: effective at 6f/7f: acts on good to firm ground: has worn crossed noseband: sent to Hong Kong. *H. Candy*

RUN ON   6 b.h. Runnett 125 – Polar Storm (IRE) 76 (Law Society (USA) 130) [2004 **45** 58: 6.1s 5.7m 6f 6g 5.1g⁵ 5.3f⁵ 6d p5.1g Oct 25] robust horse: just a poor performer in 2004: stays 6f: acts on fibresand, firm and good to soft going: tried tongue tied/blinkered. *D. G. Bridgwater*

RUSKY DUSKY (USA)   2 b.c. (Apr 29) Stravinsky (USA) 133 – Celtic Shade **74** § (Lomond (USA) 128) [2004 6m 5.7f³ 6f² 6g⁵ 5d⁵ 6f⁶ 5.7g⁶ 5m⁴ Oct 1] 38,000Y: strong, good-quartered colt: sixth foal: half-brother to 3 winners, including 6f winner Iroquois Chief (by Known Fact) and Irish 2m winner Celtic Fame (by Quest For Fame): dam, third at 1m/10.5f in France, half-sister to very smart performer up to 1½m Urgent Request: fair maiden: effective at 5f/6f: acts on firm going: visored/blinkered last 3 starts, running creditably on first occasion only (hung right): ungenuine. *R. Hannon*

RUSSALKA   3 b.f. Opening Verse (USA) 126 – Philarmonique (FR) (Trempolino **54** § (USA) 135) [2004 65: p10g 8g f8.5g⁵ 12.6s 10f² 10m⁶ 10m 10.1g⁶ 10g 10f 7g⁵ 8m Sep 25] workmanlike filly: modest maiden: stays 1¼m: acts on fibresand, good to firm and good to soft ground: tried visored/in cheekpieces: unreliable. *Julian Poulton*

RUSSIAN APPLAUSE   4 b.g. Royal Applause 124 – Zeffirella 88 (Known Fact **64** (USA) 135) [2004 8.3g 9.7g 7.1g⁴ 8.3g⁵ f8g p7m⁶ Dec 21] modest maiden: should stay 1m: acts on polytrack. *P. R. Chamings*

RUSSIAN BLUE (IRE)   2 b.c. (Mar 15) Danehill (USA) 126 – Soviet Artic (FR) 84§ **112** (Bering 136) [2004 5v* 5m* 5m* 6f² 6m³ 6s³ 7g³ 6g⁵ Oct 1] good-topped colt: has a markedly round action: second foal: dam, French 1¼m winner who looked thoroughly mulish on second of 2 starts in Britain, out of half-sister to very smart middle-distance performer Antheus: smart performer: won maiden in March and minor event and listed race in May, all at the Curragh: placed in Railway Stakes, Phoenix Stakes (1¼ lengths third to Damson) and National Stakes (4½ lengths third to Dubawi) on same course and in Prix Morny (on sixth start, beaten 3 lengths by Divine Proportions) at Deauville: respectable fifth in Middle Park Stakes at Newmarket: barely stays 7f: acts on any turf ground: usually races close up: consistent. *A. P. O'Brien, Ireland*

RUSSIAN CAFE (IRE) 3 b.f. Stravinsky (USA) 133 – Bistro (USA) (Strawberry **64** Road (AUS) 128) [2004 6d³ 6d² Oct 15] 50,000F, 50,000Y: tall, leggy filly: first foal: dam unraced daughter of useful Irish 2-y-o sprinter Phils Fancy: tongue tied, fair form in maidens at Goodwood and Redcar: raced only at 6f: sold 17,000 gns. *M. A. Magnusson*

RUSSIAN COMRADE (IRE) 8 b.g. Polish Patriot (USA) 128 – Tikarna (FR) (Tar- **– §** gowice (USA) 130) [2004 71§: 8.1s Aug 12] ex-Irish gelding: looked reluctant and soon pulled up only 8-y-o outing: tried blinkered: has refused to race: one to leave alone. *J. C. Tuck*

RUSSIAN CONSORT (IRE) 2 ch.c. (Jan 18) Groom Dancer (USA) 128 – Ukraine **98** Venture 96 (Slip Anchor 136) [2004 p7g² p8d* 7s p7g* Nov 10] 52,000Y: lengthy colt: third foal: half-brother to 4-y-o Tricky Venture and 5-y-o Indian Steppes: dam 1¼m winner: useful performer: won maiden at Lingfield in August and nursery on same course (by 2 lengths from Asharon) in November: well held in Horris Hill Stakes at Newbury in between: stays 1m: acts on polytrack: twice slowly away. *A. King*

RUSSIAN DANCE (USA) 3 br.f. Nureyev (USA) 131 – Population (General **–** Assembly (USA)) [2004 93: 8m Jun 20] sturdy, attractive filly: fairly useful winner at 2 yrs: ran as though amiss only outing in 2004. *Sir Michael Stoute*

RUSSIAN GENERAL (IRE) 2 b.c. (Feb 11) Soviet Star (USA) 128 – Azra (IRE) **60** 102 (Danehill (USA) 126) [2004 5.1m* May 17] €55,000Y: second foal: half-brother to Irish 1m winner Spectacular (by Spectrum): dam Irish 2-y-o 5f to 7f winner: odds-on, won minor event at Bath by 1½ lengths from Dreamer's Lass: bred to stay 1m. *P. F. I. Cole*

RUSSIAN ICON 3 b.f. Wace (USA) 82 – Lady Millennium (IRE) (Prince Rupert (FR) **–** 121) [2004 –: p10g 14m Aug 6] no form. *L. A. Dace*

RUSSIANNIGHTINGALE 2 b.g. (Feb 24) Fraam 114 – Nightingale Song 66 **–** (Tina's Pet 121) [2004 6g 7v p8.6g Dec 31] close-coupled gelding: well beaten in maidens/seller. *J. O'Reilly*

RUSSIAN REVOLUTION 2 b.f. (Feb 14) Dubai Millennium 140 – Russian Snows **83 p** (IRE) 113 (Sadler's Wells (USA) 132) [2004 8m³ 8s* Oct 11] quite good-topped filly: fourth foal: half-sister to useful 1¼m winner Russian Society (by Darshaan): dam, 1¼m to 12.5f (Prix de Royallieu) winner who was second in Irish Oaks, out of Irish 1000 Guineas winner Arctique Royale: odds on, won maiden at Ayr by short head from Squaw Dance, leading 1f out: should be suited by 1¼m/1½m: tongue tied: likely to progress. *Saeed bin Suroor*

RUSSIAN RHYTHM (USA) 4 ch.f. Kingmambo (USA) 125 – Balistroika **122** (USA) (Nijinsky (CAN) 138) [2004 123: 8m* May 15]

Injury restricted Russian Rhythm to just one appearance in her third and final season and put paid to any chance of a meeting between herself and Attraction, the last two winners of the One Thousand Guineas, as well as to a rematch with her old adversary Soviet Song, who, in Russian Rhythm's absence, went on to prove herself the best miler of her sex in Europe in 2004. A race involving all three would have been one to savour, but it was not to be. While two of them were seemingly continually adding to their reputations, Russian Rhythm was stuck on the sidelines. Found to have a bit of a temperature after making a successful reappearance in the Lockinge Stakes at Newbury in May, Russian Rhythm then suffered a strain to her off-fore suspensory ligament and in September it was announced that she had been retired. Russian Rhythm ran almost right up to her best in the Lockinge and, while more would have been required from her if she had come up against Attraction and Soviet Song, there are sound reasons for thinking she might have made the necessary improvement had she been able to complete a full season. As it is, Russian Rhythm ends her career rated inferior to Soviet Song, whom she beat on the three occasions they met in 2003.

Juddmonte Lockinge Stakes, Newbury—
Russian Rhythm (centre) outbattles Salselon (right) and Norse Dancer

Russian Rhythm won three races as a two-year-old, including the Lowther Stakes, and the first three of her five starts the following season, her Guineas victory followed by those in the Coronation Stakes and Nassau Stakes, while she also distinguished herself when chasing home Falbrav in the Queen Elizabeth II Stakes. A big, good-topped individual with just nine appearances under her belt, Russian Rhythm promised to be at least as good at four as she was at three, and her performance in the Juddmonte Lockinge did nothing to make anyone think otherwise. It was only an average renewal of the Lockinge, despite the fact that it attracted the largest-ever field for a race first run in 1958. That edition was won by that year's Two Thousand Guineas winner Pall Mall, but the Lockinge was upgraded to Group 1 and restricted to four-year-olds and upwards in 1995. The 2003 Two Thousand Guineas winner Refuse To Bend was one of fourteen who lined up against Russian Rhythm, who looked extremely well and was sent off favourite. Russian Rhythm was held up as Gateman and Desert Deer set the pace, the field racing in the centre of the course. When asked for her effort, Russian Rhythm showed her customary speed to come to the fore over a furlong out. Pressed on one side by Salselon and on the other by Norse Dancer, Russian Rhythm proved much too tenacious for that reluctant-looking pair when it came to the crunch. At the line Russian Rhythm had half a length to spare over the former, with Norse Dancer a further neck away in third. In becoming the first filly to win the Lockinge since Cormorant Wood dead-heated with Wassl in 1984, Russian Rhythm had fully justified her connections' decision to keep her in training. What more might she have achieved had she stayed sound?

Russian Rhythm (USA) (ch.f. 2000)	Kingmambo (USA) (b 1990)	Mr Prospector (b 1970)	Raise A Native / Gold Digger
		Miesque (b 1984)	Nureyev / Pasadoble
	Balistroika (USA) (ch 1988)	Nijinsky (b 1967)	Northern Dancer / Flaming Page
		Balidaress (gr 1973)	Balidar / Innocence

It's the paddocks for Russian Rhythm now, with a visit to Pivotal, and what a fine broodmare she should make. Along with her ability and looks, she has a pedigree out of the top drawer, one which was discussed in detail in *Racehorses of 2003*. Suffice to say here that her dam Balistroika, an unraced half-sister to the Cheveley Park winners Park Appeal and Desirable and to the Irish Oaks winner Alydaress, is also responsible for winners in France, Japan and the States, as well as the 2004 Royal Lodge Stakes winner Perfectperformance (by Rahy). Russian Rhythm, who had a powerful, round action, sometimes got on edge before her races, though it never affected her performance. She also tended to race freely and usually wore a crossed noseband. While Russian Rhythm's very best efforts came at a mile, she did show her effectiveness at a mile and a quarter in the Nassau Stakes. On her only other attempt at the latter trip she was possibly past her best for the season when finishing fifth in the Champion Stakes at Newmarket. A thoroughly genuine and consistent sort with a good turn of foot, Russian Rhythm was an admirable filly. *Sir Michael Stoute*

RUSSIAN RIO (IRE) 2 b.g. (Mar 10) Imperial Ballet (IRE) 110 – L'Harmonie (USA) **66** (Bering 136) [2004 f5g 5g^5 5m^5 Sep 15] €11,000F, €16,000Y: fourth foal: half-brother to

Italian 2001 2-y-o 5f winner by Woodborough: dam, French maiden, stayed 1m: best effort in maidens at Carlisle second start: likely to prove best at 5f. *P. C. Haslam*

RUSSIAN ROCKET (IRE) 2 b.g. (Apr 27) Indian Rocket 115 – Soviet Girl (IRE) **86** (Soviet Star (USA) 128) [2004 5v 5m⁵ 5.3f² p5g* 5m² p5g⁵ 6m 5.2s* p6g Nov 8] 4,100Y: small, leggy gelding: second foal: dam, ran 3 times, granddaughter of Yorkshire Oaks winner Untold: fairly useful performer: won maiden at Lingfield in June and nursery at Yarmouth in October: likely to prove best at 5f: acts on polytrack, firm and soft ground. *Mrs C. A. Dunnett*

RUSSIAN RUBY (FR) 3 b.f. Vettori (IRE) 119 – Pink Sovietstaia (FR) (Soviet Star **77** (USA) 128) [2004 85: 8f⁵ Aug 7] good-bodied filly: fairly useful performer in 2003: took strong hold when respectable fifth in handicap at Newmarket only 3-y-o start: stays 7f: acts on good to firm going: has twice refused to enter stall: held up. *N. A. Callaghan*

RUSSIAN SERVANA (IRE) 2 b.f. (Apr 8) Rossini (USA) 118 – Ring of Light (Auc- **51** tion Ring (USA) 123) [2004 5.7f 5m² 5m⁵ 6g⁵ Aug 11] €3,000F, €3,200Y: sixth foal: half-sister to 3 winners, including 4-y-o Royal Bathwick: dam Irish 2-y-o 5f/6f winner: modest maiden: best effort when second in seller at Leicester, then left M. Attwater: should stay 6f. *J. Pearce*

RUSSIAN SYMPHONY (USA) 3 ch.g. Stravinsky (USA) 133 – Backwoods Teach- **91** er (USA) (Woodman (USA) 126) [2004 71p: 7d 7s⁶ 6m 6g p7.1g² p7.1g* p7.1g⁶ p7.1g* p7.1g⁴ Dec 31] fairly useful performer: won maiden at Wolverhampton in November and handicap on same course (best effort, by 5 lengths from Merdiff) in December: effective at 6f/easy 7f: acts on polytrack and good to firm going: usually blinkered: free-going sort. *C. R. Egerton*

RUSSIAN VALOUR (IRE) 3 b.c. Fasliyev (USA) 120 – Vert Val (USA) 103 (Sept- **–** ieme Ciel (USA) 123) [2004 115: 7g 6s⁶ 5m 6g Sep 14] big, good-bodied colt: not the best of movers in slower paces: smart form at 2 yrs: subsequently underwent surgery on knees to remove chips: well below best in 2004, including in blinkers. *M. Johnston*

RUST EN VREDE 5 b.g. Royal Applause 124 – Souveniers (Relko 136) [2004 51: **70** f8s* f8g* Apr 2] tall gelding: modest performer: won at Southwell in February and April, latter amateur handicap: stays 1m: acts on fibresand and good to firm ground: tried visor-ed. *D. Carroll*

RUSTIC CHARM (IRE) 4 b.f. Charnwood Forest (IRE) 125 – Kabayil 75 (Dancing **–** Brave (USA) 140) [2004 72: 10d Sep 20] tall, good-topped filly: fair maiden at 3 yrs: won over hurdles in May and June for C. Egerton: pulled up in claimer on return to Flat. *Miss K. Marks*

RUSTLER 2 b.c. (Apr 22) Green Desert (USA) 127 – Borgia 91 (Machiavellian (USA) **58 p** 123) [2004 p8.6d Nov 5] second foal: half-brother to 3-y-o Worcester Lodge: dam 1½m/ 1¾m winner: 10/1, seventh in maiden at Wolverhampton, slowly away: will stay 1¼m: should improve. *R. Charlton*

RUSTY BOY 3 b.g. Defacto (USA) – Berl's Gift 44 (Prince Sabo 123) [2004 –: 7m **–** 11.9f 5g Aug 2] of no account. *A. Crook*

RUTLAND CHANTRY (USA) 10 b.g. Dixieland Band (USA) – Christchurch (FR) **44** 88 (So Blessed 130) [2004 –: 10.9s⁵ 14.1g Apr 17] robust gelding: poor handicapper: stays 1½m: best recent form on good ground or softer: blinkered once. *S. Gollings*

RUTTERS REBEL (IRE) 3 b.g. Entrepreneur 123 – No Quest (IRE) (Rainbow Quest **76** (USA) 134) [2004 75: 12s⁵ 12.3d 11m⁴ 12.1m 11.8g² 12.3g⁴ 12.3d 10.9g* 12m 12g⁶ 11.6m Sep 22] smallish, sturdy gelding: fair handicapper: won at Ayr in August: left G. A. Swinbank before final start: effective at 11f/1½m: acts on good to firm ground, possibly unsuited by softer than good. *N. Tinkler*

RYAN'S BLISS (IRE) 4 b.f. Danetime (IRE) 121 – Raja Moulana 75 (Raja Baba **44** (USA)) [2004 –: p8g p8g p10g² p10g⁵ p10g³ p10g² 10.9m 10.9 p10d 10m⁵ 9.7g⁶ p10g* **a64** p8g³ Oct 13] modest performer on all-weather, poor on turf: won claimer at Lingfield in September: stays 1¼m: acts on polytrack. *T. D. McCarthy*

RYAN'S FUTURE (IRE) 4 b.c. Danetime (IRE) 121 – Era 70 (Dalsaan 125) [2004 **84** 88: p10g⁵ p10g 10.1g 8m⁵ 9d² 10d 10.1m⁴ 10g⁵ 10.4g 10v* p10g Nov 27] leggy, useful-looking colt: fairly useful handicapper: won at Nottingham in November by 4 lengths from McQueen: stays 1¼m: acts on polytrack, good to firm and heavy going: sometimes slowly away, markedly so final outing: consistent. *J. Akehurst*

RYANS LIL OL GAL 2 b.f. (May 2) Namaqualand (USA) – Kirby's Princess (Indian **–** King (USA) 128) [2004 5g f5d 6g May 16] leggy filly: ninth foal: half-sister to 2 winners, including Saladar (up to 1½m in Germany, by Deploy): dam poor maiden: seems of little account. *A. B. Coogan*

RYAN'S QUEST (IRE) 5 b.m. Mukaddamah (USA) 125 – Preponderance (IRE) 85 **49 §** (Cyrano de Bergerac 120) [2004 57: p5g 5m 5.3f 5m³ Dec 15] neat mare: poor maiden: best at 5f: acts on firm ground and polytrack: irresolute. *T. D. McCarthy*

RYDAL (USA) 3 ch.g. Gilded Time (USA) – Tennis Partner (USA) (Northern Dancer) **93** [2004 88: p7g 7.1g⁴ 6m 5m⁶ 5d² 6s⁴ 5m 5d⁴ 5s⁴ 5d⁵ 6.5f 5d p6g³ Dec 18] good-topped gelding: fairly useful handicapper: won at Sandown in August: effective at stiff 5f to easy 1m: acts on polytrack, good to firm and good to soft going: usually blinkered/visored: tongue tied (ran well) final start. *G. A. Butler*

RYEDANE (IRE) 2 b.c. (Apr 16) Danetime (IRE) 121 – Miss Valediction (IRE) (Petar- **70** dia 113) [2004 6s 5m³ 5g 6m⁵ 5g³ 5g 5.9g p5.1g² p6g⁵ p6g* p5.1g* Dec 14] 9,000Y: tall, **a86** leggy colt: second foal: dam unraced: fairly useful on all-weather, fair on turf: won nurseries at Wolverhampton in December, beating Turn On The Style by 1½ lengths on second occasion: effective at 5f/6f: acts on polytrack and good to firm ground: races up with pace. *T. D. Easterby*

RYE (IRE) 3 b.f. Charnwood Forest (IRE) 125 – Silver Hut (USA) 80 (Silver Hawk **69** (USA) 123) [2004 75p: p8g* p12g⁶ 12d 12.1d⁴ Apr 23] fair performer: off 8 months (reportedly underwent treatment for small chip in knee): lucky short-head winner (from Ballinger Ridge, whose jockey had stopped pushing him out briefly) of maiden at Lingfield in March: probably stays 1½m: acts on polytrack, firm and good to soft going. *J. A. Osborne*

RYMER'S RASCAL 12 b.g. Rymer 121 – City Sound 63 (On Your Mark 125) [2004 **57** 54§, a–§: 8s³ 8m² 7.9f 8d 8.1g² 8.1g 8d⁶ 8m* 8f² 9.1s³ Oct 12] sturdy gelding: modest **a–** performer: won seller at Thirsk in September: best at 7f/1m: acts on any going: takes good hold/sometimes finds little, and usually held up. *E. J. Alston*

S

SAADIGG (IRE) 2 b.g. (Apr 8) Indian Danehill (IRE) 124 – White Caps 71 (Shirley **87** Heights 130) [2004 p7g³ p8d⁴ 8.1g* 10g⁶ Oct 11] 27,000F, 105,000Y: good-topped geld- ing: half-brother to several winners, including Irish 11f and 2m winner Shampooed (by Law Society): dam, third at 7f at 2 yrs (only season to race), closely related to Yorkshire Oaks winner Hellenic, herself dam of Greek Dance and Islington: fairly useful performer: improved to win maiden at Haydock in September by 1½ lengths from Glen Ida, making all: found little final start (gelded after): should stay 1¼m. *M. A. Jarvis*

SAAMEQ (IRE) 3 b.g. Bahhare (USA) 122 – Tajawuz 82 (Kris 135) [2004 –: 10.3g⁶ **52** 10v 9.1g 12m³ 11.1g⁴ 10.9g⁴ Aug 7] strong gelding: modest maiden: should stay 1¾m: acts on good to firm going. *I. Semple*

SABALARA (IRE) 4 b.f. Mujadil (USA) 119 – Sabaniya (FR) (Lashkari 128) [2004 **58** 61: 7d 8.1d 7v 8f Jun 2] sturdy filly: modest maiden: stays 7f. *P. W. Harris*

SABANA (IRE) 6 b.g. Sri Pekan (USA) 117 – Atyaaf (USA) 48 (Irish River (FR) 131) **57 §** [2004 58: f6g⁴ f6g³ p6g² f7g f6s* f6s³ p6g f6g⁶ 6s 6v 6g 6.1s 6.1d* 6m⁶ 6m f6g p6g Dec 20] quite attractive gelding: modest performer: won sellers at Wolverhampton in February and Nottingham in July: stays 6f: acts on all-weather, firm and good to soft going: often wears blinkers/cheekpieces. *J. M. Bradley*

SABANDER BAY (USA) 3 b.f. Lear Fan (USA) 130 – Sambac (USA) 96 (Mr Pros- **51 ?** pector (USA)) [2004 6d 8s Sep 14] leggy filly: second foal: half-sister to fairly useful French 2002 2-y-o 6f winner Spinning Globe (by Spinning World): dam, 2-y-o 6f winner, closely related to smart 6f/7f performer Welcome Friend and half-sister to Poule d'Essai des Poulains second Rainbow Corner: 8/1, never-dangerous eighth of 10 in maiden at Salisbury: slowly away/tailed off following month. *J. H. M. Gosden*

SABBAAG (USA) 3 ch.c. Mark of Esteem (IRE) 137 – Saabga (USA) 83 (Woodman **83** (USA) 126) [2004 f7g² f8f* p10g Feb 7] third foal: half-brother to fairly useful 7f (at 2 yrs) and 8.5f winner Jazmeer (by Sabrehill): dam, second at 7f at 2 yrs (only outing), half- sister to smart middle-distance performers Close Conflict and Newton's Law out of sister to Secreto: fairly useful form: landed odds in maiden at Southwell in January: tongue tied, ran as if amiss at Lingfield subsequent start: sold 4,000 gns in July, sent to Holland. *D. R. Loder*

SABBEEH (USA) 3 b.c. Red Ransom (USA) – Capistrano Day (USA) 110 (Diesis 133) [2004 107: 7g 8s* Oct 11] well-made, quite attractive colt: useful performer: left M. Jarvis and off 11 months before reappearance: better effort in 2004 when winning 5-runner minor event at Ayr by short head from Jazz Scene: barely stays testing 1m: acts on soft ground (returned with sore shins after disappointing on firm at 2 yrs): tongue tied in 2004: free-going sort, and has been taken steadily to post: races prominently. *Saeed bin Suroor* **101 ?**

SABBIOSA (IRE) 2 b.f. (Mar 7) Desert Prince (IRE) 130 – Alla Marcia (IRE) 64 (Marju (IRE) 127) [2004 6m 7m 7g 8s Aug 28] 22,000Y: quite good-topped filly: first foal: dam, Irish maiden who stayed 1½m, half-sister to St Leger winner Snurge: modest maiden: should stay at least 1m: best effort on good going. *J. L. Dunlop* **60**

SABLE 'N SILK 3 b.f. Prince Sabo 123 – Sibilant (Selkirk (USA) 129) [2004 57: f7g f7g⁶ Feb 13] modest performer at 2 yrs: no form in 2004, looking moody in blinkers final start. *D. Haydn Jones* **–**

SABO PRINCE 2 ch.g. (May 4) Atraf 116 – Moving Princess 71 (Prince Sabo 123) [2004 6g 6m⁵ 5.3f 5.1m Jun 21] good-bodied gelding: bad maiden. *J. M. Bradley* **27**

SABRELINE 5 ch.m. Sabrehill (USA) 120 – Story Line 98 (In The Wings 128) [2004 53: f9.4g Feb 2] sturdy mare: maiden: well held only outing in 2004: tried blinkered. *B. R. Foster* **–**

SABRINA BROWN 3 br.f. Polar Falcon (USA) 126 – So True 116 (So Blessed 130) [2004 56: 6d² 8.1g² 7m 8.1s⁶ 6.1d⁸ 7s² 7g Sep 30] good-topped filly: has scope: fairly useful handicapper: won at Chepstow (maiden event) in August: reportedly lame final start: effective at 6f to 1m: acts on polytrack and soft going: tongue tied fifth/sixth starts: flashes tail. *G. B. Balding* **80**

SACCHARINE 3 b.f. Whittingham (IRE) 104 – Sweet And Lucky (Lucky Wednesday 124) [2004 –: 8m 5m⁶ 7s f6g p6g f6g Dec 28] poor maiden: left N. Littmoden after reappearance. *M. J. Polglase* **44**

SACHIN 3 b.g. Bijou d'Inde 127 – Dark Kristal (IRE) 66 (Gorytus (USA) 132) [2004 72: p6g p7g⁶ 7m 8.5m⁴ 8g* 8d³ 8s p8.6d p10g⁶ Dec 29] good-bodied gelding: fair on turf, modest on all-weather: won handicap at Bath in September: stays 8.5f: acts on polytrack, good to firm and good to soft going: blinkered final 2-y-o start. *J. R. Boyle* **72 a61**

SACHSENWALZER (GER) 6 ch.g. Top Waltz (FR) 119 – Stairway To Heaven (GER) (Nebos (GER) 129) [2004 10g Jun 11] ex-German gelding: has won 4 races, including handicap at Bremen in 2003: well held in handicap at Leicester on only Flat run in 2004: stays 1m: all wins on good going or softer: winning hurdler. *C. Grant* **–**

SACRANUN 2 ch.c. (Feb 10) Pivotal 124 – Spanish Craft (IRE) 50 (Jareer (USA) 115) [2004 6g² 6s³ 6g 6s⁴ Sep 24] 30,000F, 50,000Y: sturdy, close-coupled colt: third foal: half-brother to fairly useful 9f winner Dennis El Menace (by College Chapel), later successful abroad: dam second at 8.5f in Ireland: fair maiden: ran at Milan on debut: will probably stay 7f: acts on soft going. *L. M. Cumani* **76**

SACRED NUTS (IRE) 2 b.c. (Mar 7) Sri Pekan (USA) 117 – Sagrada (GER) (Primo Dominie 121) [2004 6m⁵ 6m* 6g* 7m³ 6f⁵ 6s⁴ Aug 18] 28,000Y: strong, lengthy colt: third foal: brother to fairly useful French 2002 2-y-o 1m winner Arikaria and half-brother to a winner in Turkey by Mukaddamah: dam German 7f winner: useful performer: won maiden at Hamilton in June and nursery at Ascot in July: should stay 7f: acts on firm and soft going: joined J. Moore in Hong Kong, where renamed Sunny Sing. *M. L. W. Bell* **102**

SACSAYHUAMAN 5 b.m. Halling (USA) 133 – La Dolce Vita 76 (Mazilier (USA) 107) [2004 –: f12s Feb 10] lengthy mare: maiden: lightly raced and well held since 2002: tried in cheekpieces. *D. W. Thompson* **–**

SADDLER'S QUEST 7 b.g. Saddlers' Hall (IRE) 126 – Seren Quest 90 (Rainbow Quest (USA) 134) [2004 67: 10.5s 11.6m 12.3s 11.9g Sep 2] rather leggy gelding: one-time smart performer: no form in 2004: tried in cheekpieces. *B. P. J. Baugh* **–**

SADIE'S STAR (IRE) 2 b.f. (Apr 23) Indian Lodge (IRE) 127 – Nishiki (USA) (Brogan (USA) 110) [2004 7m 7m⁵ p8.6d Oct 30] 5,000Y, 10,000 2-y-o: leggy filly: half-sister to several winners, 3 by Case Law, including fairly useful 2000 2-y-o 7f winner **45**

Monte Mayor Golf and 6f (at 2 yrs) and 2m winner Cashiki: dam, lightly raced on Flat, winning hurdler: poor form in maidens. *M. Dods*

SADIE THOMPSON (IRE)   2 b.f. (Feb 2) King's Best (USA) 132 – Femme Fatale   **79**
102 (Fairy King (USA)) [2004 7m 7.1m* Sep 6] 130,000Y: tall, rather unfurnished filly: first foal: dam, 6f winner (including at 2 yrs), half-sister to smart performer up to 1¼m Foodbroker Fancy: much better effort in maidens when winning at Warwick by head from Heat of The Night, leading 1f out: should stay 1m. *M. R. Channon*

SADLER'S COVE (FR)   6 b.g. King's Theatre (IRE) 128 – Mine d'Or (FR) (Posse   **57**
(USA) 130) [2004 64: p13.9g p12m Dec 22] modest performer: stays 2m: acts on poly-track, good to firm and good to soft going: tongue tied. *Mrs L. C. Jewell*

SADLER'S PRIDE (IRE)   4 b.g. Sadler's Wells (USA) 132 – Gentle Thoughts 73   **61**
(Darshaan 133) [2004 58?: 11.1g² 14.1s² 14d⁴ 12.1m 18d 11.9g 12m⁵ Sep 18] heavy-topped gelding: modest maiden: stays 1¾m: acts on soft going, probably on good to firm: tried tongue tied: gelded. *Andrew Turnell*

SADLER'S ROCK (IRE)   6 b.g. Sadler's Wells (USA) 132 – Triple Couronne (USA)   **53**
(Riverman (USA) 131) [2004 p12g 11.6d Aug 28] maiden hurdler: modest form on Flat debut when ninth of 15 in maiden at Lingfield (started slowly): well out of depth subse-quent outing: should stay 1¾m. *G. L. Moore*

SADLERS SWING (USA)   8 b.g. Red Ransom (USA) – Noblissima (IRE) 77 (Sad-   **44**
ler's Wells (USA) 132) [2004 –: f8.5s² f9.4s⁴ 8.1g Apr 23] leggy gelding: poor maiden: stays 9.4f: acts on fibresand, good to firm and good to soft going. *J. J. Sheehan*

SAFA PARK   3 ch.g. Machiavellian (USA) 123 – Ozone Friendly (USA) 107 (Green   **64**
Forest (USA) 134) [2004 9m 10g Jul 14] half-brother to several winners, including smart 1m winner (including at 2 yrs) who stayed 1¼m Musalsal and useful French 1¼m winner Amusing Time (both by Sadler's Wells): dam won Prix Robert Papin: better effort in maidens on second outing (tongue tied): gelded, then left Godolphin. *Saeed bin Suroor*

SAFARI SUNSET (IRE)   2 b.g. (Mar 25) Fayruz 116 – Umlani (IRE) (Great Commo-   **95**
tion (USA) 123) [2004 5m* 5f* 5.1g⁴⁰ 5g³ 6m 5f Sep 11] €10,500F, €25,000Y: strong, close-coupled gelding: first foal: dam unraced: useful performer: won maiden at Leic-ester in May: good third in Windsor Castle Stakes at Royal Ascot and Molecomb Stakes (beaten 2¼ lengths by Tournedos) at Goodwood: just respectable efforts last 2 starts: likely to prove best at 5f: acts on firm going: sometimes gives trouble in preliminaries (gelded after final start): races up with pace. *P. Winkworth*

SAFENDONSEABISCUIT   2 b.c. (Mar 14) Danzig Connection (USA) – The Fuga-   **83**
tive 94 (Nicholas (USA) 111) [2004 6g⁵ 6m³ 7f³ 7g⁴ 6m² 6f 6.1g 6m³ 6g* 6d p7g⁵ p6g⁴ p6g⁶ Dec 30] 13,000Y: strong, close-coupled colt: first foal: dam 5f/6f winner: fairly useful performer: won nursery at Pontefract in October by 4 lengths, making all: resp-ectable efforts at best after: barely stays 7f: acts on firm going, probably on polytrack: blinkered (raced freely and ran poorly) sixth start. *S. Kirk*

SAFFA GARDEN (IRE)   2 b.f. (Feb 16) King's Best (USA) 132 – Allegheny River   **49**
(USA) (Lear Fan (USA) 130) [2004 5m 6g 6g Sep 2] 46,000F, 40,000Y: small, strong filly: half-sister to several winners, including very smart 6f winner (including at 2 yrs) Danetime and useful Irish performer up to 7f Dane River (both by Danehill): dam Irish 7f winner: poor form in maidens/listed race. *C. E. Brittain*

SAFFRON FOX   3 ch.f. Safawan 118 – Fox Oa (FR) (French Friend (USA) 125)   **84**
[2004 89: 8.1s⁴ 10d 8.1d⁴ 8g² 10f 10s 8g⁵ 10.3s Oct 22] sturdy, workmanlike filly: fairly useful performer: should stay at least 1¼m: acts on soft going, well below form on firm: wore cheekpieces (below form) last 2 starts. *J. G. Portman*

SAFFRON RIVER   3 b.c. Polar Prince (IRE) 117 – Cloudy Reef 57 (Cragador 110)   **59**
[2004 57: p6g⁵ f6g f6g* f6g⁶ Dec 7] modest performer: won claimer at Southwell in Dec-ember: raced only at 5f/6f on all-weather: wore cheekpieces last 2 starts. *R. Hollinshead*

SAFIRAH   3 b.f. Singspiel (IRE) 133 – Princess Haifa (USA) 69 (Mr Prospector   **78**
(USA)) [2004 10g³ 10g⁵ 10m⁵ 10.5s 10.2g² 10s* p10g⁵ Nov 10] lengthy filly: fifth foal: closely related to 11.5f winner Zeyaarah (by Rahy) and half-sister to UAE 7f winner Kon-doty (by Mtoto), both fairly useful: dam, 1m winner (later successful up to 9f in USA), out of sister to Storm Bird: fair performer: won maiden at Redcar in November: will stay 1½m: acts on polytrack, soft and good to firm ground: sold 27,000 gns. *M. A. Jarvis*

SAF

SAFRANINE (IRE) 7 b.m. Dolphin Street (FR) 125 – Webbiana (African Sky 124) **64**
[2004 83, a54: p6g f5g f5g 6g 7m 6f 5m 6g 5f 8.3g⁶ 5.5m 5m 6m 6g⁶ p5m² p5m² Dec 15] **a52**
rather leggy mare: modest performer: effective at 5f/6f: acts on fibresand, firm and soft
going: tried blinkered/visored: often wears cheekpieces: sometimes slowly away: usually
races prominently. *Miss A. Stokell*

SAFSOOF (USA) 2 b.c. (Feb 11) Gilded Time (USA) – Halcyon Bird (IRE) (Storm **91**
Bird (CAN) 134) [2004 5g² 5f f5m* 5m³ Sep 21] $48,000F, $30,000Y, $275,000 2-y-o:
smallish, strong colt: second foal: dam unraced half-sister to 3-y-o Pearl of Love: fairly
useful performer: won maiden at Southwell in July by 8 lengths from Sister Gee: respectable third in minor event at Beverley: likely to prove best at 5f/6f: acts on fibresand,
probably on good to firm going. *Saeed bin Suroor*

SAHAAT 6 b. or br.g. Machiavellian (USA) 123 – Tawaaded (IRE) 91 (Nashwan **74**
(USA) 135) [2004 106d: f8.5s 8g 11.6d 14.1d 10.2m⁵ 8.2s f8d² 11.6g⁵ 8.2g 10g⁴ 12.1g⁶
10m 10.1m⁴ 10d* p9.5g p12m Dec 22] leggy gelding: just fair performer nowadays: left
J. Osborne after sixth start, M. Polglase after eleventh: won handicap at Pontefract in
October: probably best up to 1¼m: acts on fibresand, heavy and good to firm ground:
tried blinkered: usually waited with. *C. R. Dore*

SAHARA MIST (IRE) 2 b.f. (Apr 16) Desert Style (IRE) 121 – Tereed Elhawa **44**
75 (Cadeaux Genereux 131) [2004 5g f5g⁶ 5.1s⁵ 5.1g 8f p6g Dec 17] 3,000F, 8,000Y:
useful-looking filly: first foal: dam, 6f winner (ran only at 2 yrs), granddaughter of
US Grade 1 9f/1¼m winner Reloy: poor maiden: probably stays 1m: tried visored.
D. Shaw

SAHARAN SONG (IRE) 3 ch.f. Singspiel (IRE) 133 – Sahara Baladee (USA) 79 **55**
(Shadeed (USA) 135) [2004 64p: 8g 9g 10m 10d p8.6g Oct 9] rather leggy filly: modest
maiden: probably stays 1m. *B. W. Hills*

SAHARA PRINCE (IRE) 4 b.g. Desert King (IRE) 129 – Chehana 78 (Posse **90**
(USA) 130) [2004 78: 7s 8m² 8m 7g⁵ 7m² 7f³ 7m² 6s* 6g² 8m 7s⁵ Sep 24] fairly useful
handicapper: won at Haydock in August: effective at 6f to 1m: acts on firm and soft
going: effective with or without cheekpieces. *Michael Cunningham, Ireland*

SAHARA SCIROCCO (IRE) 3 b.g. Spectrum (IRE) 126 – St Bride's Bay (Caerleon **–**
(USA) 132) [2004 62?: p7g p8.6g Oct 16] leggy gelding: modest maiden at 2 yrs: no form
in 2004. *I. A. Wood*

SAHARA SILK (IRE) 3 b.f. Desert Style (IRE) 121 – Buddy And Soda (IRE) 75 **52**
(Imperial Frontier (USA) 112) [2004 61, a71: f5s f5g f6s⁶ f5g* p6g³ p5g⁴ f6s* f5g² f6d **a72**
f5g³ 5d 5m 6m p6g Nov 27] well-made filly: fair handicapper on all-weather, modest on
turf: won at Southwell in February and March: effective at 5f/6f: acts on all-weather and
good to firm ground: visored: races prominently: tends to edge left. *D. Shaw*

SAHARA STORM (IRE) 3 b.f. Desert Prince (IRE) 130 – Deluge (Rainbow Quest **62 ?**
(USA) 134) [2004 73: p7g 7g Jun 2] strong, well-made filly: has a quick action: just
modest form in handicaps in 2004: barely stays 1m: raced only on good ground or firmer
on turf: usually races up with pace. *L. M. Cumani*

SAHEM (IRE) 7 b.g. Sadler's Wells (USA) 132 – Sumava (IRE) (Sure Blade (USA) **87**
130) [2004 89: 18g⁵ 12.1g 13g⁴ 13.9s 14.1f* 13.1d² 16.2g 12g³ 12d³ 13d* 14g 12g³ 13d⁶
Sep 27] well-made gelding: fairly useful handicapper: won at Carlisle in June and (having
left D. Eddy) Hamilton in August: effective at 1½m to 2¼m: acts on firm and good to soft
going. *C. J. Teague*

SAHOOL 3 b.f. Unfuwain (USA) 131 – Mathaayl (USA) 79 (Shadeed (USA) 135) **109**
[2004 84p: 10m² 10g² 12m² 11.9g² 12f* 11.9s⁵ Aug 18] tall, good-topped filly: had a
quick action: useful performer: landed odds in listed event at Newbury in August by neck
from Polar Jem: runner-up previous 4 starts, including in Ribblesdale Stakes at Royal
Ascot (beaten 1½ lengths by Punctilious) and Lancashire Oaks at Haydock (beaten length
by Pongee): well held in Yorkshire Oaks at York final outing: stayed 1½m: acted on firm
and good to soft going, probably not on soft: usually raced prominently: visits Dalakhani.
M. P. Tregoning

SAIDA LENASERA (FR) 3 b.f. Fasliyev (USA) 120 – Lanasara (Generous (IRE) **66**
139) [2004 76: 11.9d 10.3m⁶ 12m⁶ 9.9d 10.2m⁵ 12g⁵ p12g p10g³ p16g² Nov 30] tall,
leggy filly: fair performer: stays easy 2m: acts on polytrack and good to firm going: races
prominently. *Mrs P. Sly*

SAIF SAREEA 4 b.g. Atraf 116 – Slipperose 72 (Persepolis (FR) 127) [2004 6m 6g 8d Jul 4] leggy gelding: modest maiden at 3 yrs: well held on Flat in 2004: tried blinkered: winning hurdler. *K. W. Hogg, Isle of Man*

SAILING THROUGH 4 b.g. Bahhare (USA) 122 – Hopesay 84 (Warning 136) [2004 88 101: 10f p8g⁶ p9.5g Dec 31] rangy gelding: just fairly useful in 2004: stays 1¼m: acts on polytrack and good to firm ground: has been mulish in preliminaries/slowly away, and refused to enter stall once at 3 yrs: has hung right: free-going sort. *R. Dickin*

SAILMAKER (IRE) 3 ch.g. Peintre Celebre (USA) 137 – Princess Amalie (USA) 76 (Rahy (USA) 115) [2004 66p: 8g² 8v³ 10.2m 9.9g³ 9.9d⁴ Jun 23] leggy, quite good-topped gelding: fair maiden: stayed 1¼m: unraced on firm going, seemed to act on any other turf: tongue tied last 2 starts: sold 26,000 gns in July, joined Venetia Williams: dead. *R. Charlton*

SAILORMAN 3 b.g. Alzao (USA) 117 – Sweet Pea 94 (Persian Bold 123) [2004 p10g – May 29] 10/1, ninth in maiden at Lingfield, unruly in preliminaries and slowly away. *G. A. Butler*

SAINT CLEMENTS (USA) 2 b.g. (Mar 15) Lemon Drop Kid (USA) 131 – Sophisti- 40 cated Lynn (USA) (Clever Trick (USA)) [2004 6m 6m 8v⁴ Aug 27] lengthy gelding: poor maiden. *M. Johnston*

SAINTE JUST (IRE) 5 b.g. Polish Precedent (USA) 131 – Charlotte Corday 105 (Kris – 135) [2004 p10m Dec 22] big, lengthy gelding: fair winner in 2001: well held only start since. *W. J. Musson*

SAINT ETIENNE (IRE) 3 b.f. Robellino (USA) 127 – Stop Out 89 (Rudimentary 87 + (USA) 118) [2004 p7g* 7m⁵ 7m Jul 30] tall, leggy filly: second foal: half-sister to useful 6f (in UAE)/7f (in Ireland) winner Hazelhatch (by Mukaddamah): dam, 2-y-o 5f winner, half-sister to 5-y-o Firebreak: fairly useful performer: favourite, won maiden at Lingfield in February, making all: much stiffer tasks after, fifth to Fokine in listed race at Newmarket and tenth to Phantom Wind in Oak Tree Stakes at Goodwood: will probably stay 1m. *A. M. Balding*

SAINT LAZARE (IRE) 3 b.c. Peintre Celebre (USA) 137 – Height of Passion (Shir- – ley Heights 130) [2004 61p: 10d Apr 1] quite good-topped colt: lightly-raced maiden: no form since debut. *J. G. Given*

SAINTLY PLACE 3 ch.g. Compton Place 125 – Always On A Sunday 101 (Star 56 d Appeal 133) [2004 57: 6d 6d 6.1d 8f⁵ 7g² 7.1d p7.1g f7g p7m f6d Dec 21] modest maiden: well below form after leaving M. Channon fifth start: seems best at 7f: acts on firm ground: tried visored. *C. Smith*

SAINTLY SCHOLAR (USA) 3 b.f. Danzig (USA) – Tres Facile (USA) (Easy Goer 56 (USA)) [2004 p7g p7g p7g⁵ Mar 31] $260,000Y: second foal: dam twice-raced half-sister to Grand Criterium winner Treizieme and Gold Cup runner-up Eastern Mystic: modest form in maidens: will stay 1m: sold 6,500 gns in November, sent to USA. *E. A. L. Dunlop*

SAINTLY THOUGHTS (USA) 9 b. or br.g. St Jovite (USA) 135 – Free Thinker – (USA) 100 (Shadeed (USA) 135) [2004 67: 14.1s p16.5g⁶ f16g⁶ Dec 14] good-bodied gelding: fair performer at best: well beaten in 2004: often wears headgear. *R. J. Hodges*

SAINT ZITA (IRE) 3 b.f. Desert Sun 120 – Chatelsong (USA) (Seattle Song (USA) – 130) [2004 p8g p10g 10.9g Jul 8] 8,500Y: fifth foal: half-sister to 3 winners, including French 1m winner Green Song (by Green Tune) and 4-y-o Tripti: dam won up to 1¼m in France: little form: blinkered (very slowly away) final outing. *B. J. Meehan*

SAKE (IRE) 2 b.g. (May 4) Shinko Forest (IRE) – Drosera (IRE) (Thatching 131) [2004 – 8m 7.9g Oct 9] sturdy gelding: well held in maidens at Newcastle (tongue tied) and York. *N. Tinkler*

SALAGAMA (IRE) 4 br.f. Alzao (USA) 117 – Waffle On 89 (Chief Singer 131) [2004 87 89: 8.3d⁴ 9g³ 8m 8m Jul 6] sturdy, angular filly: fairly useful performer, lightly raced: ran as if amiss last 2 starts (blinkered final one): stays 9f: acts on good to firm and good to soft ground. *P. F. I. Cole*

SALAMANCA 2 ch.f. (Feb 6) Pivotal 124 – Salanka (IRE) 68 (Persian Heights 129) 96 [2004 6d* 6.5g* 7g⁶ Oct 2] 35,000F, 28,000Y: rather leggy, attractive filly: half-sister to several winners, including Irish 7f/1m winner Set Barabbas Free (by Bishop of Cashel) and 4-y-o Salinor: dam 1¼m winner: won maiden in August and Watership Down Stud

Watership Down Stud Sales Race, Newbury—a new venue for this event as strong-finishing Salamanca (check cap) gets up from Arabian Dancer and Umniya (No.13) in one of the most thrilling finishes of the season; Bibury Flyer (nearest camera), Love Thirty and Alta Petens (far side) are just behind them

Sales Race in September (led on line when beating Arabian Dancer in 26-runner event), both at Newbury: just respectable sixth to Penkenna Princess in listed race at Newmarket: should stay 7f: useful. *S. Kirk*

SALAMBA　　3 ch.g. Indian Ridge 123 – Towaahi (IRE) (Caerleon (USA) 132) [2004　**68** 75: 9g⁵ 14m 14g 13.9g⁵ 14.1d 18d Oct 18] good-bodied gelding: fair maiden: barely stays 2¼m: yet to race on extremes of going: sold 9,000 gns. *M. H. Tompkins*

SALEEN (IRE)　　4 b.f. Kahyasi 130 – Sabrata (IRE) (Zino 127) [2004 p8g Jan 14]　**–** fourth foal: half-sister to fairly useful 2001 2-y-o 7f/7.5f winner Receivedwiththanx (by Celtic Swing), later 1m/1¼m winner in Spain, and to 7f seller winner Head Scratcher (by Alhijaz): dam French 2-y-o 4.5f winner: well beaten in bumper, and in maiden at Lingfield. *P. D. Cundell*

SALERNO　　5 ch.g. Mark of Esteem (IRE) 137 – Shamwari (USA) 63 (Shahrastani　**–** (USA) 135) [2004 66d: f5g f5g Jan 6] fair performer at best: on the downgrade: tried in headgear/tongue tied: tail flasher. *Miss Gay Kelleway*

SALFORD CITY (IRE)　　3 b.c. Desert Sun 120 – Summer Fashion 84 (Moorestyle　**118** 137) [2004 100P: 7g* 8g⁶ 12m⁵ 10d 10f³ 8f⁴ Dec 26] tall, imposing colt: impresses in appearance: has scope: smart performer: won Lane's End Greenham Stakes at Newbury in April by 1¾ lengths from Fokine: good efforts in 2000 Guineas at Newmarket (4½

Lane's End Greenham Stakes, Newbury—Salford City bursts clear of Fokine (left) and So Will I

lengths sixth to Haafhd, flashing tail) and Derby at Epsom (4¾ lengths fifth to North Light, edging left and no extra after promising headway): never dangerous when ninth to Refuse To Bend in Coral-Eclipse Stakes at Sandown (final one for D. Elsworth): off 4½ months, below form when in frame in allowance optional claimer at Hollywood and non-graded stakes at Santa Anita: may prove best around 1¼m: raced only on good/good to firm going: slowly into stride/raced lazily first 3 outings. *P. L. Biancone, USA*

SALFORD FLYER 8 b.g. Pharly (FR) 130 – Edge of Darkness 62 (Vaigly Great 127) **51** [2004 p13g p12g⁶ 10.2g 10.2g³ 11.7s³ 11.6m May 24] rather sparely-made gelding: only modest nowadays: stays 2m: acts on good to firm and good to soft going (has run poorly on fibresand and soft ground): blinkered last 5 starts: held up: none too genuine. *Jane Southcombe*

SALFORD ROCKET 4 b.g. Slip Anchor 136 – Mysterious Maid (USA) 76 – (L'Emigrant (USA) 129) [2004 –: f9.4g 9.7s 11.9m⁶ 13m f14g⁶ 14.1d Aug 29] no form: left G. Chung after fourth outing. *W. J. Musson*

SALINJA (USA) 2 b.c. (Mar 6) Boundary (USA) 117 – Lasha (USA) (Rahy (USA) **90** 115) [2004 6g³ 7s³ 8g² Sep 30] $85,000F, $90,000Y: well-made colt: fourth foal: half-brother to winner in North America by Thunder Gulch: dam 3.5f (at 2 yrs) to 8.5f winner in USA: best effort in maidens when neck second to Pevensey at Newmarket, finishing strongly: likely to stay 1¼m: should win a race. *Mrs A. J. Perrett*

SALINOR 4 ch.g. Inchinor 119 – Salanka (IRE) 68 (Persian Heights 129) [2004 85p: **86** 8.3g* 8g* 7.9g 8g⁶ 8g Sep 30] sturdy gelding: fairly useful performer: trained first 3 starts by A. Stewart: won handicap at Windsor in April and minor event at Kempton in May: stays 1m: acts on firm and soft ground: usually waited with: sold 10,000 gns. *E. F. Vaughan*

SALISBURY PLAIN 3 b.c. Mark of Esteem (IRE) 137 – Wild Pavane (Dancing – Brave (USA) 140) [2004 73p: 9v 9g May 18] smallish colt: lightly raced: soundly beaten in handicaps in 2004: sold 4,000 gns in July. *D. R. Loder*

SALLY TRAFFIC 5 b.m. River Falls 113 – Yankeedoodledancer (Mashhor Dancer – (USA)) [2004 –: f6g Jan 12] small, sturdy mare: modest winner at 3 yrs: little form since: tried in cheekpieces. *R. M. Whitaker*

SALONIKA SKY 3 ch.f. Pursuit of Love 124 – Willisa 67 (Polar Falcon (USA) 126) – [2004 40: f6g f5g⁶ f6g 5m⁶ 6m Jul 14] workmanlike filly: of little account nowadays. *C. W. Thornton*

SALON PRIVE 4 b.g. Green Desert (USA) 127 – Shot At Love (IRE) 79 (Last Tycoon **62** 131) [2004 73: p6g 8m p6g² 6m⁶ 6.1g² 6g p6g⁵ p7g² Dec 4] leggy gelding: fair maiden: **a72** effective at 6f/7f: acts on polytrack and firm going: blinkered (well held) second start. *C. A. Cyzer*

SALSA BRAVA (IRE) 2 b.f. (Feb 6) Almutawakel 126 – Ridotto (Salse (USA) 128) **106** [2004 5g* 6m³ 6m² 6s² 6g⁴ Sep 18] €16,000Y, 26,000 2-y-o: quite good-topped filly: first foal: dam, French maiden (best effort at 7.5f), granddaughter of Oaks d'Italia winner Carnauba: useful performer: won maiden at Windsor in May: good second in Cherry Hinton Stakes at Newmarket (beaten head by Jewel In The Sand) and Lowther Stakes at York (1½ lengths behind Soar): just respectable 3½ lengths fourth to Galeota in Mill Reef Stakes at Newbury: will probably stay 1m: acts on soft and good to firm going: sent to USA. *N. P. Littmoden*

SALSALINO 4 ch.g. Salse (USA) 128 – Alicedale (USA) (Trempolino (USA) 135) **104** [2004 115p: 12g⁶ 13.9d 12g 13.9s 14.6f Sep 10] rather leggy, quite attractive gelding: smart performer at 3 yrs: form in 2004 only when sixth to Dubai Success in John Porter Stakes at Newbury on reappearance: stayed 1¾m: acted on good to firm going: held up: won over hurdles in October, broke down following month: dead. *A. King*

SALSELON 5 b.h. Salse (USA) 128 – Heady (Rousillon (USA) 133) [2004 118: **124 §** 8.1d 8m² 8f³ 8g 8d⁵ 8.9g² 9.9m³ 8g² 10s⁶ 8d³ Nov 7]

So it's goodbye to Salselon, who is to return to Italy to continue his racing career with his former trainer Mario Ciciarelli after one season with Luca Cumani. Some would say good riddance. Salselon won't be missed by those punters who supported him in any of the eight races he contested in Britain, or by the jockeys who partnered him in them, Messrs Dettori, Dwyer, Fallon, Holland and Murtagh all having failed to persuade him to put his head in front where it mattered; and, given his antics at the start on occasions, they will probably be joined by the stalls handlers, one of whom was injured when kicked by Salselon at Royal Ascot. Salselon undoubtedly has a good deal of ability. Unfortunately, he has a temperamental streak to match.

Salselon had won seven races before coming to Britain, including the Premio Chiusura at Milan three years in a row (the first as a two-year-old) and another Group 3 event, the Prix Edmond Blanc at Saint-Cloud, on his only appearance outside Italy during that period. Blinkered on five occasions in his three-year-old season, including in the Chiusura, Salselon raced without headgear in 2003. It had been the intention to fit blinkers in the Edmond Blanc but Salselon had other ideas, and he ran without after reportedly trying to bite those attempting to put them on. Following a most unsatisfactory display when well held at Sandown on his reappearance in the latest season—he was mulish throughout the preliminaries and seemed reluctant to race in the early stages—Salselon wore blinkers or a visor on all his subsequent starts. They had an immediate effect. On his first outing after Sandown, Salselon showed improved form to finish a half-length second to Russian Rhythm in the Lockinge Stakes at Newbury; and he matched that next time when third behind Refuse To Bend and Soviet Song in the Queen Anne Stakes at Royal Ascot. In the former, Salselon improved to dispute the lead in the final furlong only to find little under pressure, wandering and carrying his head awkwardly; in the latter he did remarkably well to finish within a length of the winner, still having plenty to do when switched wide over a furlong out and making up ground hand over fist late on. Salselon had now shown that he had the ability to win races at the highest level, but he remained without a victory in 2004 despite being given opportunities in lesser contests. His performance when three quarters of a length second to Polar Ben in the Group 3 Joel Stakes at Newmarket on his eighth outing underlined just what an exasperating customer Salselon had become. He looked sure to end his losing run when sweeping through wide to lead approaching the final furlong and going a good three lengths up, only to be caught near the finish after deciding he had done enough. Salselon did make a couple of appearances abroad in the latest season, including on his final start when a very close third to Eagle Rise, finishing strongly under his former regular jockey Alessandro Parravani, in the Premio Ribot at Rome, for which he started a short-priced favourite. It is unlikely he would have been so well supported had the race taken place in Britain.

		Topsider	Northern Dancer
Salselon (b.h. 1999)	Salse (USA) (b 1985)	(b 1974)	Drum Top
		Carnival Princess	Prince John
		(ch 1974)	Carnival Queen
	Heady (b 1991)	Rousillon	Riverman
		(b 1981)	Belle Dorine
		Ghislaine	Icecapade
		(b 1981)	Cambretta

Salselon, a 33,000-guinea yearling, is the third foal of Heady, an unraced half-sister to the top-class miler Markofdistinction. Heady's first two foals are also winners, the useful Tipsy (by Kris) at up to a mile and a half and Tipsy Topsy (by Ashkalani) over a mile and a quarter in France. Salselon's grandam Ghislaine won at a mile and a quarter from only two starts. Her dam, Cambretta, a full sister to the Cumberland Lodge and Hardwicke winner Critique (another quirky type in this family), won in Ireland at nine furlongs. Salselon, a tall, quite attractive individual, has done all of his winning between seven furlongs and a mile, showing his best form at the latter trip. He acts on firm and soft going, and is held up. *L. M. Cumani*

SALTANGO (GER) 5 br.g. Acatenango (GER) 127 – Salde (GER) (Alkalde (GER)) **79** [2004 p10d 11.9g³ 14m⁵ Jul 21] won maiden at Dortmund at 2 yrs and (having missed 3-y-o season) minor event at Hanover in 2003: left P. Rau in Germany, fair form in handicaps in Britain: effective at 1½m to 1¾m: acts on soft and good to firm ground. *A. M. Hales*

SALTBURN LAD (IRE) 2 b.c. (Feb 13) Sadler's Wells (USA) 132 – Highest Accolade 71 (Shirley Heights 130) [2004 p8.6g⁵ Dec 17] third foal: brother to 4-y-o Urowells: **62 p** dam, 1¼m winner from 3 starts, out of half-sister to Yorkshire Oaks winner Awaasif, herself dam of Snow Bride and grandam of Lammtarra: 14/1, fifth to Pocketwood in maiden at Wolverhampton, not knocked about: should improve. *J. W. Hills*

SALUTE (IRE) 5 b.g. Muhtarram (USA) 125 – Alasib 93 (Siberian Express (USA) **88** 125) [2004 100: p9.5g p10m³ Dec 22] lengthy, quite attractive gelding: useful handicapper at 4 yrs: better effort on return to Flat when third at Lingfield: best form at 9f/1¼m: acts on polytrack, firm and soft going: effective visored or not: edgy sort. *P. J. Hobbs*

Prix de Royallieu Hotel du Golf Barriere, Longchamp—
Samando (far side) just beats Russian Hill; Behkara (noseband) comes third

SALUT SAINT CLOUD 3 b.g. Primo Dominie 121 – Tiriana (Common Grounds **66**
118) [2004 62d: 8s⁶ 7m f7g⁵ 10g* 11.9f³ f12m³ 11.9f³ f14g* f12f⁴ 16.2s* 16.2m Sep 6]
close-coupled gelding: fair performer: won claimer at Redcar (left Miss V. Haigh) in June
and handicaps at Southwell (apprentices) and Chepstow in August: stays 2m: acts on
fibresand, firm and soft going: tried blinkered/visored, wore cheekpieces last 4 starts:
fairly useful juvenile hurdler. *G. L. Moore*

SALVIATI (USA) 7 b.g. Lahib (USA) 129 – Mother Courage 67 (Busted 134) [2004 **88**
100: 5s 5m 5m 6f 5d 5m 5.7g 5g 5m⁴ 5g⁵ 5.2f* 5g 5.2g 5.1d 5.2g Sep 14] sturdy gelding:
fairly useful handicapper: won at Newbury in July: best at 5f: acts on firm and good to
soft ground: sometimes wears cheekpieces: often slowly away: travels strongly, and
usually held up. *J. M. Bradley*

SAMALAN 2 b.g. (Apr 18) Grey Desire 115 – Shalari (IRE) 50 (Shalford (IRE) 124§) **–**
[2004 6m 5g Jul 2] always behind in claimer/maiden. *J. Parkes*

SAMANDO (FR) 4 ch.f. Hernando (FR) 127 – Samshu (Nashwan (USA) 135) [2004 **116**
109: 10d³ 10g⁶ 10d³ 10.5g 10d⁶ 10s⁶ 12g⁴ 12.5m* 10g⁴ Oct 24] 250,000 francs Y: first
foal: dam unraced daughter of useful 1m winner Samsova: smart performer: improved at
4 yrs, best effort when winning Prix de Royallieu Hotel du Golf Barriere at Longchamp
in October by short neck from Russian Hill: respectable efforts when in frame otherwise,
including when fourth to Commercante in E. P. Taylor Stakes at Woodbine final start:
stays 12.5f: acts on soft and good to firm ground. *F. Doumen, France*

SAMARA SOUND 3 b.c. Savahra Sound 111 – Hosting (Thatching 131) [2004 –: f6s **43**
p6g⁶ 5.1g p6g p7m⁶ p6g Dec 20] smallish, close-coupled colt: poor maiden: stays 6f: best
effort on polytrack: sometimes slowly away. *A. G. Newcombe*

SAMARIA (GER) 3 b. or br.f. Acatenango (GER) 127 – Suanita (GER) (Big Shuffle **76**
(USA) 122) [2004 11.6f 10m⁴ 11.5m² 12.3d⁴ p13g³ 14.1s p12g² p12g p12.2g³ Dec 4]
second foal: dam, German 2-y-o 5.5f/6f winner, half-sister to smart German performer up
to 1½m Surako: fair maiden: stays 13f: acts on polytrack and good to firm going, probably on soft: visored 4 of last 5 starts: possibly none too genuine. *C. F. Wall*

SAMAR QAND 5 b.m. Selkirk (USA) 129 – Sit Alkul (USA) 73 (Mr Prospector **42**
(USA)) [2004 59d: f9.4g⁵ f11g³ f11s³ f11g⁴ 12d Apr 5] leggy, quite good-topped mare:
poor maiden: barely stays 1½m: acts on fibresand, firm and good to soft ground: has worn
cheekpieces: tongue tied last 3 starts. *Julian Poulton*

SAMBA BEAT 5 ch.m. Efisio 120 – Special Beat 65 (Bustino 136) [2004 –: f8s f8g **–**
f11g f7g May 19] no longer of much account. *R. F. Marvin*

SAMBARINA (IRE) 2 b.f. (Feb 26) Victory Note (USA) 120 – Brazilia 63 (Forzando **70**
122) [2004 6g³ 6m⁵ Jul 28] €46,000Y: smallish filly: fifth foal: closely related to useful
Italian miler Meanya (by Revoque) and half-sister to fairly useful winner around 7f

SAM

(including at 2 yrs) Santisima Trinidad (by Definite Article): dam, maiden who stayed 7f, half-sister to smart 5f performer Dominica: better effort in maidens when third at Haydock: should stay 7f. *C. G. Cox*

SAMMAGEFROMTENESSE (IRE) 7 b.g. Petardia 113 – Canoora (Ahonoora 39
122) [2004 48: 11d⁶ 8.5d⁵ p10g² Sep 18] one-time fairly useful performer (only win in handicap at Cork at 3 yrs): only poor nowadays: left N. Glynn in Ireland after second start: stays 1½m: acts on polytrack and soft going: tried blinkered/in cheekpieces/tongue tied. *A. E. Jones*

SAMMY'S SHUFFLE 9 b.g. Touch of Grey 90 – Cabinet Shuffle (Thatching 131) 52
[2004 60?: p10g p10g⁴ p10g 11.9m 10m 10.1f⁴ p10g 10.1m⁵ Jul 1] modest handicapper: best at 1¼m: acts on polytrack, firm and soft going: blinkered: held up. *Jamie Poulton*

SAMSON QUEST 2 b.c. (Apr 25) Cyrano de Bergerac 120 – Zenita (IRE) (Zieten 68
(USA) 118) [2004 p7g⁵ 7s Sep 14] sturdy colt: first foal: dam unraced half-sister to smart performer up to 1¼m Polar Prince: better effort in maidens when fifth at Lingfield: made early running at Salisbury: likely to stay 1m. *A. M. Balding*

SAM'S SECRET 2 b.f. (Apr 30) Josr Algarhoud (IRE) 118 – Twilight Time (Aragon 76
118) [2004 6m² 5f³ 6.1g² 7s p7.1g³ p7.1g Nov 20] 13,000Y: quite good-topped filly: half-sister to several winners, including 3-y-o Dispol Katie and fairly useful 5f winner Paradise Eve (by Bahamian Bounty): dam unraced: fair maiden: stays easy 7f: acts on polytrack and firm ground: wandered fourth/fifth outings: visored (pulled hard) final start. *J. A. Glover*

SAM THE SORCERER 3 b.g. Wizard King 122 – Awham (USA) (Lear Fan (USA) 47
130) [2004 –: 6.1s f6m* f7g 6s³ 6v 6d f6g Dec 12] quite good-topped gelding: poor performer: won banded race at Wolverhampton in May: stays 6f: acts on fibresand and soft going. *J. R. Norton*

SAMUEL CHARLES 6 b.g. Green Desert (USA) 127 – Hejraan (USA) 73 (Alydar 83
(USA)) [2004 64?: p8g* f8.5g² 8m³ 8m* 7.2f² 7f² 7g³ 8d³ 7.2d⁴ 7m² 7m 7f* 7f⁶ 7.1g p7.1g* p7.1g⁴ p7.1d³ p7.1g⁶ Nov 12] fairly useful performer: won handicap at Lingfield in March, minor events at Redcar in May and Brighton in August and claimer at Wolverhampton in October: effective at 7f/1m: acts on all-weather, firm and good to soft going: tried visored/in cheekpieces: races up with pace: sometimes carries head awkwardly. *W. M. Brisbourne*

SAN ANTONIO 4 b.g. Efisio 120 – Winnebago 63 (Kris 135) [2004 90: 7.1s 10m⁶ –
8m Aug 8] strong, well-made gelding: has a round action: fairly useful performer at 3 yrs: well held in 2004, leaving B. Hills after reappearance. *Mrs P. Sly*

SANBONAH (USA) 3 b.f. King of Kings (IRE) 125 – Oh Nellie (USA) 113 (Tilt The –
Stars (CAN)) [2004 75: 8m May 22] big, good sort: fair performer at 2 yrs: tailed off in handicap at Newmarket only run in 2004: stays 1m: acts on firm going. *N. A. Callaghan*

SANCHI (IRE) 2 b.c. (Apr 19) Darshaan 133 – Samara (IRE) 108 (Polish Patriot 81 p
(USA) 128) [2004 8m³ Sep 8] sturdy, attractive colt: fourth foal: half-brother to useful 1¼m/1½m winner Santa Sophia (by Linamix): dam, 1m winner, half-sister to smart middle-distance stayer Lille Hammer: 25/1, 2¾ lengths third to Monsoon Rain in maiden at Doncaster, slowly away and staying on: will be suited by 1¼m/1½m: joined Godolphin: sure to do better. *J. H. M. Gosden*

SAND AND STARS (IRE) 3 ch.f. Dr Devious (IRE) 127 – Charm The Stars (Roi 86
Danzig (USA)) [2004 68: 11m³ 10m⁵ 12d² 12.3g* 12g² 13.9s 12g³ 12d² Oct 10] sturdy filly: fairly useful handicapper: won at Ripon in July: stays 1½m: acts on good to soft ground, probably on good to firm: blinkered last 2 starts at 2 yrs: has flashed tail: usually races prominently. *M. H. Tompkins*

SAN DENG 2 gr.g. (Apr 6) Averti (IRE) 117 – Miss Mirror 77 (Magic Mirror 105) 51
[2004 6m 6m³ 6.1d 6m p6m Oct 6] tall gelding: modest maiden: likely to stay 7f: acts on good to firm going: gelded after final start. *W. R. Muir*

SAND FAIRY (IRE) 2 b.f. Desert King (IRE) 129 – Kinetic Force (USA) 73 p
(Holy Bull (USA) 134) [2004 p8g* p8g⁵ Nov 30] 9,000Y: first foal: dam, fairly useful French maiden who stayed 7.5f, half-sister to very smart French/US 7f to 1¼m performer Mizzen Mast: won maiden at Lingfield in November: similar form when fifth in nursery there, still green and not knocked about: likely to be suited by 1¼m/1½m: should progress. *M. A. Jarvis*

SANDGATE CYGNET 4 ch.f. Fleetwood (IRE) 107 – Dance of The Swans (IRE) 75
69 (Try My Best (USA) 130) [2004 69: f6g* Jan 2] workmanlike filly: fair handicapper:

won at Wolverhampton in January: best at 5f/6f: acts on fibresand, heavy and good to firm ground: has worn cheekpieces 4 of last 5 starts. *I. Semple*

SAN DIMAS (USA) 7 gr.g. Distant View (USA) 126 – Chrystophard (USA) (Lypheor 118) [2004 16f Jul 19] strong gelding: winning hurdler: poor maiden on Flat, well held both outings since 2001: tried blinkered/visored. *R. Allan* —

SAND IRON (IRE) 2 b.f. (Apr 28) Desert Style (IRE) 121 – Mettlesome (Lomond (USA) 128) [2004 p7g⁶ 6s⁴ p7.1g Oct 19] €8,500Y: quite good-topped filly: half-sister to several winners, including 8-y-o Sea Mark and Irish 10.5f to 1¾m winner Lily Shing Shang (by Spectrum): dam, French 1m (at 2 yrs) and 9f winner, half-sister to very smart performer up to 1½m Urgent Request: modest form in maidens: needs to settle to stay 7f. *S. L. Keightley* — **60**

SAND N SEA (IRE) 3 b.f. Desert Story (IRE) 115 – Poscimur (IRE) (Prince Rupert (FR) 121) [2004 82: 7v 9g 10m* 9.5m³ 8f 12f 8.5m 10m 8v 9.5d Aug 29] €1,000Y: rather leggy filly: sixth foal: half-sister to 5f (at 2 yrs) to 9.4f winner Dust To Dust (by College Chapel): dam ran 3 times in Ireland: useful performer: won handicap at the Curragh in May: good 1½ lengths third to Misty Heights in listed race at Gowran, but below form after, including in listed handicap at Royal Ascot fifth start: stays 1¼m: acts on good to firm and good to soft ground: tried tongue tied. *T. Hogan, Ireland* — **95**

SANDOKAN (GER) 3 b.g. Tiger Hill (IRE) 127 – Suivez (FR) (Fioravanti (USA) 115) [2004 9.7g 8.3g 10v 12s Nov 2] poor form in maidens: should stay 1½m: has carried head high. *B. J. Curley* — **46**

SANDORRA 6 b.m. Emperor Jones (USA) 119 – Oribi 59 (Top Ville 129) [2004 54: f7g³ f7g* f8f⁶ f8.5g f8s f7m* 7v⁶ f7d f7m 7.2s⁵ f7g f7g Dec 1] big, leggy mare: modest performer: won banded races at Southwell in January and May: best form at 7f: acts on fibresand, heavy and good to firm going: usually races prominently. *M. Brittain* — **55**

SAND REPEAL (IRE) 2 b.g. (Mar 7) Revoque (IRE) 122 – Columbian Sand (IRE) (Salmon Leap (USA) 131) [2004 7g 8s³ 10v² Oct 20] seventh foal: half-brother to fairly useful 7f to 9.4f winner Arc (by Archway): dam unraced: fair form in maidens: staying-on second to Louise Rayner at Nottingham: will stay 1½m. *Miss J. Feilden* — **74**

SANDY BAY (IRE) 5 b.g. Spectrum (IRE) 126 – Karinski (USA) (Palace Music (USA) 129) [2004 –: f12g 9g 7.2g 12m 9.2d⁴ 10.1g 12g³ 12d⁵ Oct 17] poor maiden: left R. Allan after second start: stays 1½m: acts on good to firm and good to soft ground: tried blinkered/in cheekpieces. *A. R. Dicken* — **45**

SANDY'S LEGEND (USA) 2 ch.g. (Jun 3) Tale of The Cat (USA) 113 – Avasand (USA) (Avatar (USA)) [2004 8g p8.6g⁵ p8.6d² p10g² Nov 27] leggy, useful-looking gelding: half-brother to several winners, notably 4-y-o Makhlab and very smart US Grade 1 9f/1¼m winner Possibly Perfect (by Northern Baby): dam US 6f and 9f winner: modest maiden: second at Wolverhampton and Lingfield: stays 1¼m: visored last 2 starts: races up with pace. *J. H. M. Gosden* — **63**

SANGIOVESE 5 b.g. Piccolo 121 – Kaprisky (IRE) (Red Sunset 120) [2004 91: p10g f7g³ f8.5s³ 7s⁵ 8.1g² 8m³ 10m* 12d² 12g 11.7m⁵ 10m 10g⁵ 8v* Oct 23] strong gelding: fairly useful handicapper: won at Newbury (amateurs) and Kempton in June, and Newbury (ladies) in October: free-going sort, effective at 1m (given test) to 1½m: acts on fibresand, heavy and good to firm going. *H. Morrison* — **90**

SAN HERNANDO 4 b.g. Hernando (FR) 127 – Sandrella (IRE) (Darshaan 133) [2004 79: 14.4s⁶ 16g⁴ 14.1s 16.2m 13.3m⁴ 14.1g 16m⁴ 14.1g² 16.4m 16g 14.1g 16d* 16s³ Oct 29] leggy, workmanlike gelding: shows knee action: fair handicapper: won NH jockeys race at Goodwood in October: effective at 1½m to 2m: acts on firm and soft ground: tried visored/in cheekpieces at 3 yrs: has been slowly away/carried head high. *D. R. C. Elsworth* — **77**

SAN LORENZO (UAE) 3 ch.f. Machiavellian (USA) 123 – Sanchez 77 (Wolfhound (USA) 126) [2004 7g 6g³ 6m² Jun 16] close-coupled, attractive filly: first foal: dam, Irish maiden who stayed 9f, closely related to high-class miler Starborough: fair maiden: placed at Haydock and Ripon: should stay 7f: sold 10,000 gns in November. *M. R. Channon* — **66**

SAN MARCO (IRE) 6 b.g. Brief Truce (USA) 126 – Nuit Des Temps (Sadler's Wells (USA) 132) [2004 54: f14g f12s Feb 17] modest performer in 2003: well held in 2004: tried blinkered: usually wears cheekpieces nowadays: sold 6,200 gns, joined M. Sheppard and won over hurdles. *Mrs P. Sly* —

SANTA CATALINA (IRE)   5 br.m. Tagula (IRE) 116 – Bui-Doi (IRE) 58 (Dance of   –
Life (USA)) [2004 –, a53: f8g p8g f8g⁵ f8s⁴ f12g p10g p8m f7g Dec 16] poor maiden: **a45 ?**
left Gay Kelleway after reappearance, C. Dwyer after sixth start: stays 1m: acts on all-
weather, little form on turf since 2 yrs: has worn cheekpieces/visor/tongue tie. *R. J. Price*

SANTA CATERINA (IRE)   3 b.f. Daylami (IRE) 138 – Samara (IRE) 108 (Polish   **74**
Patriot (USA) 128) [2004 64p: 9.9g⁴ 11.8g⁵ 10d² 10.5g 10.5g 8.1s³ 10.2s² 10v Nov 4]
angular filly: fair maiden: stays 1¼m: acts on heavy and good to firm going. *J. L. Dunlop*

SANTA FE (IRE)   2 b.c. (Mar 25) Green Desert (USA) 127 – Shimna 62 (Mr Prospec-   **102 p**
tor (USA)) [2004 6f⁵ 7m* 7g⁴ Sep 30] 210,000Y: good-topped colt: second living foal:
dam, ran once in Ireland, half-sister to St Leger winner Shantou out of smart daughter of
Oh So Sharp: won maiden at Leicester in September by head from Silent Jo: improved
plenty when ¾-length fourth to Diktatorial in Somerville Tattersall Stakes at Newmarket,
still green but running on well despite short of room: will stay at least 1m: already useful,
and capable of better as 3-y-o. *Sir Michael Stoute*

SANTANDO   4 b.g. Hernando (FR) 127 – Santarem (USA) 71 (El Gran Senor (USA)   **102**
136) [2004 107: p12g⁵ p10g³ a10f 12f⁵ 11.9g 13.9g 14g⁴ 16.2g 13.9s 14.6f 12s Oct 23]
tall, useful-looking gelding: useful handicapper: best efforts at 4 yrs when in frame at
Lingfield (third to Eastern Breeze) and Goodwood (1½ lengths fourth behind Mephisto):
stays 1¾m: acts on all-weather, good to firm and good to soft going: tried in cheekpieces,
usually visored nowadays: has run well when sweating: lazy sort, often soon off bridle:
held up. *C. E. Brittain*

SANTIBURI LAD (IRE)   7 b.g. Namaqualand (USA) – Suggia (Alzao (USA) 117)   **73**
[2004 64: 9.9v³ 12.3m² 10.5d* 9.9d* 10.5d² 9.9m 7.9m 10.5s 10.1m Oct 10] leggy
gelding: fair handicapper: won at Haydock (ladies) in June and Beverley in July: stays
10.5f: acts on fibresand and any turf going: usually races prominently. *N. Wilson*

SANT JORDI   2 b.c. (Mar 4) Cape Cross (IRE) 129 – Foresta Verde 46 (Green   **97**
Forest (USA) 134) [2004 p6g³ 6m* 7g² 8d³ Oct 10] 5,200F, 25,000Y: sixth foal: dam,
sprint maiden, half-sister to smart performer up to 1m Tanouma out of very smart French
2-y-o Diffusion: useful performer: won maiden at Windsor in August, making most: good
efforts in minor event at Salisbury and Beresford Stakes at the Curragh (rallying 5 lengths
third to Albert Hall) after: stays 1m: acts on good to firm and good to soft going, promise
on polytrack: sent to UAE. *B. J. Meehan*

SAORSIE   6 b.g. Emperor Jones (USA) 119 – Exclusive Lottery (Presidium 124) [2004   **– §**
p16d Aug 9] tall, close-coupled gelding: modest and temperamental handicapper in 2002:
well held only outing on Flat since: tried blinkered: won twice over hurdles in October.
J. C. Fox

SAPOSCAT (IRE)   4 b.g. Groom Dancer (USA) 128 – Dance of Joy 59 (Shareef   **–**
Dancer (USA) 135) [2004 10.2m Jul 22] seemed to show fair form at 7.5f from 2 starts in
Ireland in 2002 for Miss I. Oakes: well held in novice hurdles/Flat seller: tongue tied.
W. G. M. Turner

SAPPHIRE DREAM   2 b.f. (Mar 8) Mind Games 121 – Bombay Sapphire (Be My   **77**
Chief (USA) 122) [2004 5v² 5.1d² 6m* 5m⁶ 6m 6g⁴ 5.1g⁴ 6f Sep 10] 7,500Y: close-
coupled, quite good-topped filly: fourth foal: sister to 3-y-o Mind Alert: dam, lightly
raced, out of smart Italian sprinter Ginny Binny: fair performer: won maiden at Haydock
in May: good fourth in minor event at Haydock and nursery at Chester: effective at 5f/6f:
acts on heavy and good to firm ground: wears bandages behind. *A. Bailey*

SAPPHIRE PRINCESS   2 b.f. (Apr 20) Namaqualand (USA) – Breakfast Creek 63   **44**
(Hallgate 127) [2004 5m⁴ 5.1m⁵ 5.1f⁵ 6m⁶ p6g* 5.1m⁵ 6m 7m Sep 7] 2,000Y: fourth foal: **a53**
half-sister to 3-y-o Game Flora and 2002 2-y-o 5f winner Donny Bowling (by Sesaro):
dam 2-y-o 5f winner: modest on all-weather, poor on turf: won seller at Lingfield in
August: stays 6f: acts on polytrack and firm going. *I. A. Wood*

SAPPHIRE SKY   3 b. or br.f. Compton Place 125 – Jewel (IRE) 64 (Cyrano de Berge-   **–**
rac 120) [2004 p6g 5s 5.1g Jun 2] 2,500 2-y-o: sturdy filly: third foal: dam, sprint maiden,
half-sister to smart 1996 2-y-o 5f/6.5f winner Deadly Dudley: well held in maidens.
D. K. Ivory

SARAH BROWN (IRE)   2 b.f. (Apr 4) Benny The Dip (USA) 127 – Lalique (IRE)   **–**
(Lahib (USA) 129) [2004 5.7f 7f 8d 8.1s Aug 30] second foal: half-sister to 3-y-o Mister
Marmaduke: dam unraced half-sister to smart French 7f to 1¼m performer Goofalik:
little form in maidens: visored second start, wore cheekpieces last 2: looks difficult ride.
I. A. Wood

SARATOGA SPLENDOUR (USA) 3 b.f. Diesis 133 – Saratoga One (USA) (Saratoga Six (USA)) [2004 –: 8v⁶ 6m 9m Jul 5] quite good-topped filly: little form. *Jedd O'Keeffe* –

SAREM (USA) 2 b. or br.c. (Jan 19) Kingmambo (USA) 125 – Storm Beauty (USA) (Storm Cat (USA)) [2004 7g 7g⁴ Oct 1] $600,000Y: well-made colt: good mover: third foal: half-brother to winner in USA by A P Indy: dam, minor 6f stakes winner in USA, half-sister to US Grade 2 6f/7f winner Gold Beauty, herself dam of Dayjur: sweating, much better effort in maidens when fourth to Rob Roy at Newmarket, held up and staying on: should stay 1m: likely to progress. *M. P. Tregoning* 75 p

SARENNE 3 b.f. Desert Sun 120 – Fabulous Pet (Somethingfabulous (USA)) [2004 9.2d⁶ 9.3g⁶ 11.9s⁵ Oct 15] €15,000Y: half-sister to several winners, notably smart 1½m to 1¾m winner Murghem (by Common Grounds): dam Irish 1½m winner: little form in maidens. *M. Johnston* –

SARGENTS DREAM 4 b.f. Regal Embers (IRE) – Dance Lady (Cosmonaut) [2004 –: f6g Jan 12] no form. *J. A. Gilbert* –

SARIBA 5 b.m. Persian Bold 123 – En Vacances (IRE) 90 (Old Vic 136) [2004 51: f16.2s p13g⁶ p16g* 17.2f⁵ 17.2f⁶ Jun 12] poor performer: won seller at Lingfield in April: stays 2¼m: acts on polytrack and firm ground: races up with pace. *A. Charlton* 47

SARISTAR 3 b.f. Starborough 126 – Sari 83 (Faustus (USA) 118) [2004 82: 6d* 6m 7m 7s⁵ 6f* 6.5f 6m⁶ 6s Oct 22] close-coupled, useful-looking filly: fairly useful handicapper: won at Newmarket in April and Pontefract in September: probably better at 6f than 7f: acts on fibresand, firm and soft going: tried tongue tied: usually races prominently. *P. F. I. Cole* 93

SARN 5 b.g. Atraf 116 – Covent Garden Girl 67 (Sizzling Melody 117) [2004 63, a–: f8.5g f8m⁴ 7d 13.9m 10.5d⁴ 12.3g 12.3m³ 13g² 14g 15.9g⁴ 12.1m 16f⁴ Jul 29] smallish gelding: only poor nowadays: barely stays 2m: acts on any turf going, well beaten on fibresand: tried in cheekpieces. *M. Mullineaux* 49 a–

SAROS (IRE) 3 b. or br.g. Desert Sun 120 – Fight Right (FR) (Crystal Glitters (USA) 127) [2004 51: 8s f7m* f8m* f8g⁶ f7g 7.1m² 7m 7m³ 6.9m 7.1g* 7g p7.1g p8.6d³ Nov 4] smallish, workmanlike gelding: fair performer: won banded events at Southwell in April/May and handicap at Musselburgh in August: effective at 7f to 8.6f: acts on all-weather and good to firm ground: sometimes carries head awkwardly/edges right. *B. Smart* 69 a65

SARRAAF (IRE) 8 ch.g. Perugino (USA) 84 – Blue Vista (IRE) (Pennine Walk 120) [2004 82§, a78§: f7s⁴ 7g² 8g³ 7.1g² 8s⁵ 8g 8.3d⁵ 7m³ 8m³ 7.2d³ 7s⁵ 8m 8f⁵ 7.2g² 9.2d 9g³ 7.9m⁴ 9g⁶ 9.1d 8m⁴ 7v p9.5d p8.6g⁶ p7.1g Nov 20] smallish, strong gelding: fair performer: trained by J. Goldie eighth to twentieth starts before returning to former stable: effective at 7f to 1¼m: acts on fibresand and any turf going: tried in blinkers/visor: effective ridden prominently or held up: tough but unreliable. *I. Semple* 78 § a71 §

SARTAENA (IRE) 2 b.f. (Apr 12) Imperial Ballet (IRE) 110 – Joza 90 (Marju (IRE) 127) [2004 5.1m 5.1s 5.3m Sep 23] third foal: half-sister to 3-y-o Sweetest Revenge: dam, 5f winner (ran only at 2 yrs), out of half-sister to 2000 Guineas winner Don't Forget Me: poor form in maidens/seller: blinkered final start. *R. M. Beckett* 36

SASHAY 6 b.m. Bishop of Cashel 122 – St James's Antigua (IRE) 79 (Law Society (USA) 130) [2004 55, a72: f16.2s⁵ p16g² 16s 13.1m³ 17.2f⁶ 16.2g Aug 30] close-coupled mare: modest performer: effective at 1½m to 17f: acts on all-weather and good to firm ground. *R. Hollinshead* 49 a60

SASPYS LAD 7 b.g. Faustus (USA) 118 – Legendary Lady (Reprimand 122) [2004 12s⁶ 11.1g⁵ 11.6g Aug 9] good-bodied gelding: lightly-raced maiden: should stay 1½m: raced only on good ground or softer: fair jumper. *W. M. Brisbourne* 61

SASTRE (IRE) 2 b.f. (Mar 23) Bluebird (USA) 125 – No Rehearsal (FR) (Baillamont (USA) 124) [2004 5m 6d⁴ p7g 6d Aug 20] 20,000Y: sister to useful French sprinter Lever To Heaven and half-sister to 2 winners, including 5-y-o Jelani: dam, French 8.5f and 1¼m winner, out of half-sister to Miesque: modest maiden: form only when fourth at Epsom: should stay 7f: wore cheekpieces final start. *P. M. Phelan* 61

SATAN'S SISTER 3 ch.f. Tout Ensemble – Winter Greeting (Hello Gorgeous (USA) 128) [2004 8g Jun 4] second reported foal: dam never ran: 50/1, always behind when tailed off in maiden at Goodwood. *A. W. Carroll* –

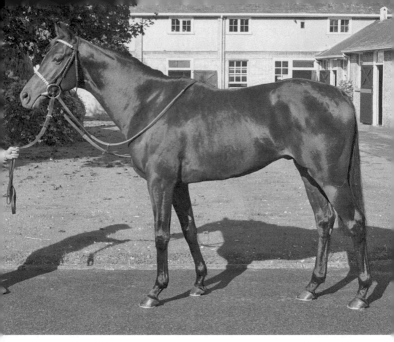

Sheikh Hamdan bin Mohammed Al Maktoum's "Satchem"

SATCHEM (IRE) 2 br.c. (Feb 11) Inchinor 119 – Mohican Princess (Shirley Heights **114**
130) [2004 6m² 6f* 7g* 6m* 6g⁴ Oct 1] 42,000F, 100,000Y: smallish, unfurnished colt:
first foal: dam once-raced daughter of smart 1¼m performer Mohican Girl, herself half-
sister to Yorkshire Oaks winners Untold and Sally Brown: smart performer: won minor
event at Yarmouth in June, nursery at Newmarket (then left D. Loder) in July and Pentax
Sirenia Stakes at Kempton (beat Council Member by 1½ lengths) in September: respectable 3½ lengths fourth to Ad Valorem in Middle Park Stakes at Newmarket: will stay 1m:
acts on firm going: joined Godolphin. *C. E. Brittain*

SATIN FINISH (IRE) 2 b.f. (Feb 11) Kingmambo (USA) 125 – Shimaal 95 (Sadler's **92**
Wells (USA) 132) [2004 6g⁴ 5d* 6m⁴ 5.2g 6d⁶ Aug 30] workmanlike filly: second report-
ed foal: dam, 1m winner who stayed 11.5f, closely related to top-class 1½m performer
Belmez: fairly useful performer: won maiden at Ripon in July: good 3½ lengths fourth to
Soar in Princess Margaret Stakes at Ascot: ran poorly in listed races last 2 starts: stays 6f:
acts on good to firm and good to soft ground. *M. R. Channon*

SATIN KISS (USA) 2 b.f. (Apr 7) Seeking The Gold (USA) – Satin Flower (USA) **93**
115 (Shadeed (USA) 135) [2004 6m* 6m 6g* 6g⁴ Sep 2] rather leggy filly: sister to smart
1998 2-y-o 6f (Middle Park) winner Lujain and 3-y-o Botanical, closely related to fairly
useful 2001 2-y-o 5f winner Deceptor (by Machiavellian), and half-sister to smart 7f (at 2
yrs) and 1½m winner Lilium (by Nashwan): dam won Jersey Stakes and second in US
Grade 1 9f event: fairly useful performer: won maiden at Leicester in June and minor
event at Haydock in August (last in Cherry Hinton Stakes in between): best effort when
3¾ lengths fourth to Suez in listed event at Salisbury, racing freely: needs to settle to stay
7f: acts on good to firm going. *Saeed bin Suroor*

SATIN ROSE 2 b.f. (Apr 18) Lujain (USA) 119 – Shamwari (USA) 63 (Shahrastani **52**
(USA) 135) [2004 6m⁵ f7g⁶ 7d 7.5m⁶ 6m Oct 10] 11,000Y: fifth foal: half-sister to 2 win-
ners, including 5-y-o Salerno: dam, maiden (stayed 2m), closely related to Derby winner
Golden Fleece: modest maiden: best effort at 7.5f on good to firm going. *T. D. Easterby*

908

SATSU (IRE) 3 ch.f. Shinko Forest (IRE) – Cap And Gown (IRE) 81 (Royal Academy **50**
(USA) 130) [2004 53: 8.2g 10s 8s⁶ f7m May 28] tall, useful-looking filly: modest
maiden: likely to prove best short of 1m: acts on good to firm ground. *J. G. Given*

SATTAM 5 b.g. Danehill (USA) 126 – Mayaasa (USA) 70 (Lyphard (USA) 132) [2004 **87**
86: 7.1g² 8g³ 8g Sep 30] smallish, stocky gelding: fairly useful handicapper, lightly raced:
effective at 7f to 8.5f: acts on good to firm ground: visored/blinkered nowadays: has been
slowly away/raced freely: held up, and tends to hang: sold 21,000 gns. *M. P. Tregoning*

SATURDAY'S CHILD (FR) 2 ch.f. (Mar 9) Hamas (IRE) 125§ – Pleasant Whisper **44**
(FR) (Marignan (USA) 117) [2004 5.7g p7.1g Nov 27] first foal: dam won up to 12.5f in
France: poor form in maidens at Bath (slowly away) and Wolverhampton. *M. S. Saunders*

SAUCEPOT 2 ch.f. (Feb 14) Bold Edge 123 – Apple Sauce 70 (Prince Sabo 123) [2004 **63**
5g 5m⁵ 5m² 5g 5.1m³ 5.1f⁶ 5.7g p5.1g f5g² f5g³ Dec 16] 6,500Y: sturdy filly: half-sister **a66**
to 3-y-o Cut And Dried: dam, 5f winner, half-sister to smart sprinter Sizzling Melody:
fair maiden on all-weather, modest on turf: likely to prove best at 5f/easy 6f: acts on
fibresand and firm going: often races prominently. *M. D. I. Usher*

SAUCY 3 b.f. Muhtarram (USA) 125 – So Saucy 59 (Teenoso (USA) 135) [2004 –: 9.7s⁶ **49**
8.1s⁶ 11.5m p10g⁵ 10.2f³ 9m⁵ 10.2s p10m Dec 15] poor maiden: stays 1¼m: acts on
polytrack and firm ground: sometimes blinkered: races freely. *B. J. Meehan*

SAUCY PICKLE 3 b.f. Makbul 104 – Bewails (IRE) 53 (Caerleon (USA) 132) [2004 **–**
–: p8g p7g Feb 3] well held in minor event/maidens at Lingfield. *Miss Z. C. Davison*

SAVANNAH BAY 5 ch.g. In The Wings 128 – High Savannah 77 (Rousillon (USA) **105**
133) [2004 113: 16.2s 13.3m⁴ 16.4f 22.2f Jun 19] good-topped gelding: only useful in
2004, best effort when fourth to The Whistling Teal in listed event at Newbury: stays
2½m: acts on firm going: tried blinkered/tongue tied: has worn crossed noseband: carries
head awkwardly: usually waited with: joined P. Hobbs. *B. J. Meehan*

SAVANNAH RIVER (IRE) 3 b.f. Desert King (IRE) 129 – Hayward 81 (Indian **49**
Ridge 123) [2004 47: 6v 10g³ 12.6s² 14.1m⁵ 12.1d⁴ 12m³ 16.2g² 12f 14.1g⁴ 10d Aug 30]
good-topped filly: poor maiden: stays 1¾m: acts on soft and good to firm ground: tongue
tied. *C. W. Thornton*

SAVANNAH SUE 3 b.f. Emarati (USA) 74 – Bidweaya (USA) 45 (Lear Fan (USA) **–**
130) [2004 –: 6v f7d f6g 5d Jul 4] no form: dead. *J. R. Norton*

SAVERNAKE BRAVE (IRE) 3 b.g. Charnwood Forest (IRE) 125 – Jordinda (IRE) **60 §**
64 (Indian Ridge 123) [2004 55§: f7g⁵ f6g² 5.3m 6f⁴ 5.3f 6m f5g 7m* 7m p7.1d⁴ f7g
f7g² p7m* f7g³ p7g⁵ Dec 30] compact gelding: modest performer: left K. Burke after
reappearance: won banded races at Folkestone (apprentices) in September and Lingfield
in December: stays 7f: acts on all-weather and firm going: often slowly away, reluctant to
race final 2-y-o outing: tried blinkered: temperamental. *Mrs H. Sweeting*

SAVILE'S DELIGHT (IRE) 5 b.g. Cadeaux Genereux 131 – Across The Ice (USA) **84**
(General Holme (USA) 128) [2004 72, a62: p6g³ f6g² f5g⁴ 6s³ 6.1v* 5.1d² 6m 6g* 7.1d⁴ **a73**
7.1m⁴ 7s³ 6m p5.1d⁴ p6g Nov 20] fairly useful handicapper on turf, fair on all-weather:
won at Warwick in May and twice at Haydock in July: best form at 6f/7f: acts on all-
weather, heavy and good to firm going: effective with or without blinkers/in cheekpieces:
tried tongue tied. *R. Brotherton*

SAVIOURS SPIRIT 3 ch.g. Komaite (USA) – Greenway Lady (Prince Daniel (USA)) **69**
[2004 70: p6g² p6g² p6g* 7g 7d p6m² p6g³ p6g³ p5g⁵ Dec 18] fairly useful on all- **a82**
weather, fair on turf: won maiden at Lingfield in February and handicap there in
December: effective at 5f/6f: acts on polytrack, good to firm and good to soft going: hung
right fifth outing. *T. G. Mills*

SAVOIE 2 ch.f. (Apr 1) Grand Lodge (USA) 125 – Spry 84 (Suave Dancer (USA) 136) **– p**
[2004 7d Oct 30] leggy filly: second foal: dam, 1½m winner from 2 starts, half-sister to
very smart 1½m winner Sandmason (by Grand Lodge) out of Lancashire Oaks winner
Sandy Island, herself close relation to Slip Anchor: 9/1, behind in maiden at Newmarket,
finding little: should do better. *H. R. A. Cecil*

SAVOY CHAPEL 2 br.c. (Jan 20) Xaar 132 – Royal Gift (Cadeaux Genereux 131) **55**
[2004 p6g 7.1m 7.1d 8.3m f8g⁶ p8g⁵ p8.6g⁴ f7g² p7m⁵ Dec 21] lengthy colt: modest
maiden: best efforts at 7f: acts on all-weather, some promise on turf: blinkered 2 starts
prior to final one. *A. W. Carroll*

SAWAH 4 br.g. Linamix (FR) 127 – Tarhhib 95 (Danzig (USA)) [2004 –: f6g⁵ f7g Mar **34**
23] poor maiden: best at 6f: raced only on all-weather. *D. Shaw*

SAWWAAH (IRE) 7 ch.g. Marju (IRE) 127 – Just A Mirage 76 (Green Desert (USA) **92** 127) [2004 93: 8g 8g 7m* 7m³ 8.5m⁴ 7m 7s 7g 7m³ 8m 8.1g² 7g* 7.6s 7m⁴ 7g Oct 2] big, useful-looking gelding: fairly useful handicapper: won at Redcar in May and Newbury in August: effective at 7f/1m: successful on soft going earlier in career, best recent form on good or firmer: held up, and no easy ride (often hangs/finds little). *D. Nicholls*

SAXE-COBURG (IRE) 7 b.g. Warning 136 – Saxon Maid 108 (Sadler's Wells **70 §** (USA) 132) [2004 66: f8.5g⁵ 10.2s* 10d 10.2f³ 14.1m³ 12m 12.6m³ 12.6m⁵ 14.4g³ 12m⁴ 12.1d 12s⁴ 13.1d⁶ 14.1g p12g f12g p12.2g Nov 26] fair handicapper: won at Bath in May: moody efforts last 4 starts: stays 14.4f: acts on all-weather, dirt, firm and soft going: tried in headgear: sometimes slowly away, and usually held up: ungenuine: sold £1,000. *G. A. Ham*

SAXON LIL (IRE) 2 b.f. (Mar 6) Second Empire (IRE) 124 – Salva 73 (Grand Lodge **60** (USA) 125) [2004 7.1g p7.1g⁴ Dec 31] 1,600Y: first foal: dam maiden who probably stayed 8.5f: much better effort in maidens 4 months apart when fourth to Play The Ball at Wolverhampton, still green and staying on: slowly away on debut. *J. L. Spearing*

SAYADAW (FR) 4 b.c. Darshaan 133 – Vingt Et Une (FR) (Sadler's Wells (USA) 132) **116** [2004 103: 12g⁴ Apr 17] strong, good-bodied, imposing colt: smart performer, lightly raced: tongue tied, easily best effort when 3½ lengths fourth to Dubai Success in John Porter Stakes at Newbury: will stay at least 1¾m: raced on good/good to firm going: tends to wander: reported in May to have jarred a suspensory. *H. R. A. Cecil*

SAYRIANNA 3 br.f. Sayaarr (USA) – Arianna Aldini (Habitat 134) [2004 8.3d 10g **46** 9.7m⁴ 12g p8.6g p10m p8m Dec 15] closely related to 6f winner John Bowdler Music (by Soviet Star) and half-sister to several winners, including 6-y-o Armagnac: dam unraced: poor maiden: seems to stay 9.7f. *T. J. Fitzgerald*

SAYWAAN (USA) 2 ch.f. (Apr 5) Fusaichi Pegasus (USA) 130 – Sharp Cat (USA) **90 P** 125 (Storm Cat (USA)) [2004 7g* Oct 11] $1,500,000Y: tall, leggy filly: second living foal: dam, won 7 US Grade 1 events from 1m (champion at 2 yrs) in Storm, half-sister to top-class 1¼m/1½m performer Royal Anthem: favourite, won maiden at Leicester by 3½ lengths from Queen of Iceni, briefly hanging right before leading over 1f out and quickening clear: will be suited by 1m/1¼m: open to considerable improvement, and will make her mark in stronger company. *Saeed bin Suroor*

SAY WHAT YOU SEE (IRE) 4 b.c. Charnwood Forest (IRE) 125 – Aster Aweke **81** (IRE) 87 (Alzao (USA) 117) [2004 77: f9.4g p10g⁴ p10g² p10g* 10.2g⁵ 10m⁴ 10m² 10m² 10g 10g⁴ 9m Jul 31] workmanlike colt: fairly useful handicapper: won at Lingfield in March: stays 1¼m: acts on polytrack and firm going: sometimes visored: usually makes running: joined M. Pipe and won over hurdles. *J. W. Hills*

SCALE THE HEIGHTS (IRE) 2 b.g. (Jan 15) Spectrum (IRE) 126 – Decrescendo **53** (IRE) (Polish Precedent (USA) 131) [2004 7m 7.1g 8.1s 8.1m Sep 9] smallish gelding: modest maiden: form only on debut: should be suited by 1¼m/1½m. *B. W. Hills*

SCALLOWAY (IRE) 4 b.g. Marju (IRE) 127 – Zany (Junius (USA) 124) [2004 74: **–** 8.1d p12g Oct 28] strong, compact gelding: fair handicapper at best: well held on Flat in 2004: effective blinkered or not. *D. J. Wintle*

SCANDINAVIA (USA) 2 b.c. (May 8) Fusaichi Pegasus (USA) 130 – Party Cited **108** (USA) 110 (Alleged (USA) 138) [2004 7.5f² 7g² 8.5m* 8f² a8.5f Oct 30] $725,000F: quite attractive colt: seventh foal: closely related to French winner up to 9.5f Palatial Affaire (by Kingmambo) and half-brother to 2 winners, notably very smart US Grade 1 1m/8.5f winner Composure (by Touch Gold): dam 1m/1¼m winner, later US Grade 3 11f winner: useful performer: odds-on in maidens first 3 starts, winning at Galway in July: much improved when 1½ lengths second to Perfectperformance in Royal Lodge Stakes at Ascot, tending to hang right and no extra near finish: last in Breeders' Cup Juvenile at Lone Star Park, bit slowly away: will stay 1¼m: acts on firm going. *A. P. O'Brien, Ireland*

SCARBOROUGH FLYER 2 b.c. (Apr 14) Almaty (IRE) 113§ – Calamanco 71 **–** (Clantime 101) [2004 6d p6d p6g Nov 27] 14,500Y: strong, close-coupled colt: sixth foal: half-brother to 5-y-o Artie and 6-y-o Kingscross: dam 5f winner: well held in maidens. *J. Balding*

SCARLET EMPRESS 3 b.f. Second Empire (IRE) 124 – Daltak (Night Shift (USA)) **–** [2004 79: 6d 6f Sep 16] strong filly: fair performer at 2 yrs: last in handicaps in 2004: blinkered last 4 outings in 2003. *R. Hannon*

SCARLET INVADER (IRE) 2 b.g. (Feb 1) Indian Ridge 123 – Scarlet Plume 103 **76** (Warning 136) [2004 6g⁴ 7f 7d² 8s⁶ 8d Oct 14] 27,000Y: sturdy gelding: fourth foal: half-brother to 2001 2-y-o 6f winner Scarlet Ribbons (by Anabaa): dam, 2-y-o 1m (including Italian Group 3) winner, out of Oaks winner Circus Plume: fair maiden: second at Salisbury, easily best effort: should stay 1m: acts on good to soft going: tends to get on toes. *J. L. Dunlop*

SCARLETT BREEZE 3 b.f. Shinko Forest (IRE) – La Suquet 72 (Puissance 110) **50** [2004 55: 6g 6m 6f 5.2m⁵ 5g 5m⁴ f5g 6g⁴ 5.7f 6d 6d Oct 16] leggy filly: modest maiden: stays easy 6f: acts on polytrack, good to firm and good to soft going. *J. W. Hills*

SCARLETT ROSE 3 b.f. Royal Applause 124 – Billie Blue 63 (Ballad Rock 122) **69** [2004 72: 6s⁶ 7m 7f³ 7f³ 7s 7m p7g Oct 31] neat filly: fair maiden: should stay 1m: acts on firm going, below form on soft. *Dr J. D. Scargill*

SCARPIA 4 ch.g. Rudimentary (USA) 118 – Floria Tosca § (Petong 126) [2004 –: 7.1m **42** 7.1m p10d⁵ p10m p10m Dec 15] poor maiden: left J. Fox after third start: stays 1¼m: acts on polytrack, raced only on good/good to firm ground on turf: sometimes slowly away. *J. S. Moore*

SCARP (USA) 2 b. or br.c. (Mar 29) Gulch (USA) – Rhetorical Lass (USA) (Capote **62 p** (USA)) [2004 7d 7d 8m Sep 21] fourth foal: closely related to fairly useful 2001 2-y-o 6f winner Ristra (by Kingmambo), later successful in USA, and half-brother to useful 1m winner Requite (by Red Ransom): dam, maiden in USA, half-sister to US Grade 1 9f/1¼m winner Reloy: modest form, burly and not knocked about, in maidens at Newmarket: sent to USA: type to do better. *J. Noseda*

SCARRABUS (IRE) 3 b.g. Charnwood Forest (IRE) 125 – Errazuriz (IRE) 94 **74** (Classic Music (USA)) [2004 66?: 11.1g⁴ 11.9d 9.9g⁶ 9.7m³ 12f⁴ p12g³ p12g⁵ 16g Sep 30] angular, good-topped gelding: fair maiden: stays easy 1½m: acts on polytrack and firm ground: usually held up: gelded after final outing. *B. G. Powell*

Godolphin's "Saywaan"

SCARROTTOO 6 ch.g. Zilzal (USA) 137 – Bold And Beautiful 105 (Bold Lad (IRE) **64** 133) [2004 64: p7g p6g³ f7g⁵ p7g p7g p7g p7g⁵ 6s⁵ 7m* 7d⁴ 7f 7g³ 7f* 7.6f⁵ 8m 7m³ 7g p8.6d **a58** p7.1g⁵ Oct 25] strong gelding: modest performer: won handicap at Yarmouth in April and claimer at Epsom in July: best at 7f: acts on all-weather, firm and soft going: tried in head-gear/tongue tie: usually waited with. *S. C. Williams*

SCARY NIGHT (IRE) 4 b.g. Night Shift (USA) – Private Bucks (USA) (Spend A **59** Buck (USA)) [2004 75: f6g f6g f5g* f5g⁶ f6g f6g f6g⁶ f5g f5g² 5d f5g p6d f5m* f5f Dec 28] tall, good-topped gelding: modest performer: won claimer at Southwell in March and handicap there in November: effective at 5f to easy 7f: acts on fibresand, best turf run on good going: usually wears cheekpieces: often races prominently. *J. Balding*

SCENIC FLIGHT 3 b.f. Distant View (USA) 126 – Bird of Time (IRE) 75 (Persian **–** Bold 123) [2004 57d: 7.1s p7g 6v May 10] no form at 3 yrs. *Mrs A. J. Bowlby*

SCENIC LADY (IRE) 8 b.m. Scenic 128 – Tu Tu Maori (IRE) (Kings Lake (USA) **58** 133) [2004 68: 9.7f⁵ 12g Jul 1] smallish mare: only modest nowadays: effective at 9f to 1½m: acts on firm and soft going: blinkered twice as 4-y-o: tried in cheekpieces: sometimes slowly away: none too reliable. *L. A. Dace*

SCENT 2 b.f. (May 13) Groom Dancer (USA) 128 – Sweet Pea 94 (Persian Bold 123) **63** [2004 6d⁵ 7g 7.1s³ 8d⁵ Oct 18] neat filly: second foal: dam 1m winner: modest maiden: likely to stay 1¼m: best efforts on good to soft going. *J. L. Dunlop*

SCENT AHEAD (USA) 5 b.g. Foxhound (USA) 103 – Sonseri 95 (Prince Tenderfoot **–** (USA) 126) [2004 44: f5g Nov 9] maiden: tailed off only 5-y-o outing: tried blinkered/tongue tied/in cheekpieces. *Mrs G. S. Rees*

SCHAPIRO (USA) 3 b.g. Nureyev (USA) 131 – Konvincha (USA) (Cormorant (USA)) **86** [2004 77: 9v 11.6g³ 12g⁴ 12m* Jun 20] strong, good sort: impresses in appearance: fairly useful performer: won maiden at Pontefract in June easily: stays 1½m: acts on good to firm ground, below form on softer than good: blinkered last 2 starts: sold 130,000 gns, joined Jonjo O'Neill and fair form over hurdles. *J. H. M. Gosden*

SCHINKEN OTTO (IRE) 3 ch.c. Shinko Forest (IRE) – Athassel Rose (IRE) **–** (Reasonable (FR) 119) [2004 –: 8.1d 7.1m⁶ 8.5g 9.3g⁵ 6g Sep 14] strong colt: little form: awkward leaving stall penultimate outing. *J. M. Jefferson*

SCHOLARSHIP (IRE) 3 b.g. College Chapel 122 – Royal Bracelet (IRE) (Night **72 §** Shift (USA)) [2004 85§: 7g p8g³ Jul 14] compact gelding: fair maiden: stays easy 1m: raced only on all-weather and good ground or softer on turf: tried blinkered: ungenuine. *C. F. Wall*

SCIENCE ACADEMY (USA) 3 ch.f. Silver Hawk (USA) 123 – Dance Design **72** (IRE) 119 (Sadler's Wells (USA) 132) [2004 62: 11.6s 11.8m⁵ 11.7f⁶ 12m² 11.5f* 12g* 11.9s⁶ p10g p13g Nov 10] smallish filly: fair handicapper: won at Yarmouth (maiden event) and Folkestone in August: stays 1½m: acts on firm going, weakened tamely on soft: *P. F. I. Cole*

SCIENTIST 3 ch.g. Dr Fong (USA) 128 – Green Bonnet (IRE) (Green Desert (USA) **76** 127) [2004 85p: 7d 6d 7m³ 8m 8.5f⁶ 8.2g 7d* 8.2v Nov 4] well-made gelding: fluent mover: fair performer: made all to win handicap at Redcar in October despite starting slowly/carrying head high: left J. Gosden before final outing: stayed 7f: acted on good to firm and good to soft ground: inconsistent: dead. *D. Burchell*

SCISSORS (IRE) 2 ch.f. (May 16) Desert King (IRE) 129 – Clipping 76 (Kris 135) **–** [2004 6m 7g Jul 8] leggy filly: half-sister to 6f and 1m winner French Fancy (by Paris House) and Irish 17f winner Big Bojangles (by Bigstone): dam 1m winner: signs of just a little ability in maidens. *Miss J. Feilden*

SCOOBY DOOBY DO 3 b.f. Atraf 116 – Redgrave Design 77 (Nebbiolo 125) [2004 **42** 62: 5s⁵ 6d⁶ 6d 5g⁶ 6d 7g Sep 20] lengthy filly: poor maiden: stays 6f: acts on good to firm and good to soft going: wore cheekpieces last 3 outings: sometimes slowly away/looks wayward. *R. M. Whitaker*

SCORCH 3 b.g. Mark of Esteem (IRE) 137 – Red Hot Dancer (USA) (Seattle Dancer **45** (USA) 119) [2004 62: 10g⁶ 7m³ p8g 10.1m² Apr 12] poor maiden, lightly raced: left H. Collingridge after second start: seems to stay easy 1¼m. *V. Smith*

SCORCHIO (IRE) 3 b.g. Desert Sun 120 – White-Wash 94 (Final Straw 127) [2004 **48** 45: f9.4g⁶ p10g² f12g⁵ 10.9f⁴ 12m⁶ Jun 28] poor maiden: stays 11f: acts on polytrack and firm ground. *M. F. Harris*

SCORPIO SALLY (IRE) 2 b.f. (Mar 6) Mujadil (USA) 119 – Clear Procedure (USA) **59**
(The Minstrel (CAN) 135) [2004 6f 6g⁵ 7g⁶ 7.5d⁵ 7.1g⁵ 10m Sep 28] €20,000F, 8,000Y:
close-coupled, heavy-topped filly: fifth foal: dam, Irish 1m winner, closely related to
smart Irish 7f to 1¼m performer Two-Twenty-Two: modest maiden: stays 7.5f: acts on
good to soft ground. *M. D. Hammond*

SCOTLAND THE BRAVE 4 ch.f. Zilzal (USA) 137 – Hunters of Brora (IRE) 102 **76**
(Sharpo 132) [2004 75: 8.3d 7.2f³ 8f⁵ 8f 7m⁴ 7d* 8f⁴ 8s² 7.2d 7.2s Oct 12] leggy, lengthy
filly: fair handicapper: won at Doncaster in July, edging right: raced only at 7f/1m: acts
on firm and soft ground: wore cheekpieces 4 of last 5 starts. *J. D. Bethell*

SCOTT 3 gr.g. Polar Falcon (USA) 126 – Circled (USA) 83 (Cozzene (USA)) [2004 **70**
7.5d 8.5g 10g⁶ 12m 11.5f³ f12f* p12g⁴ 11.9g* 11.9s² 13.8s³ Nov 2] 26,000Y: third foal:
half-brother to winners abroad by Inchinor and Efisio: dam 2-y-o 7f winner who stayed
1½m: fair handicapper: won at Southwell in August and York (apprentices) in October:
barely stays 13.8f: acts on fibresand, firm and soft ground. *J. Jay*

SCOTTISH EXILE (IRE) 3 b.f. Ashkalani (IRE) 128 – Royal Jade 82 (Last Tycoon **75**
131) [2004 63, a73: f6g⁶ f5g⁴ 5.1g⁴ f5g³ 5g* 5g 5.1g 5f² 5f* 5m 5f³ 5.3f⁴ 6d 5m Oct 2]
strong, angular filly: fair handicapper: won at Hamilton in May and Windsor in June:
raced mainly at 5f: acts on all-weather and firm ground: visored: sometimes finds little.
K. R. Burke

SCOTTISH RIVER (USA) 5 b.g. Thunder Gulch (USA) 129 – Overbrook 95 **89**
(Storm Cat (USA)) [2004 74: f9.4g³ p10g f9.4g* p10g⁵ f8.5s* f9.4s* f8.5s f8.5g⁵ 10.1s⁶ **a78**
10s* 8g⁴ 10.2g⁶ 8.3m⁶ 10.1d* 10.1g² 10.1g⁴ 10.5g 12g⁴ 10.1m 12f⁶ p9.5g⁶ p10g Dec 18]
strong gelding: fairly useful performer: won handicap in January and claimer and
handicap in February, all amateur events at Wolverhampton, and minor event at Windsor
in May and handicap at Epsom in July: stays 1½m: acts on all-weather, soft and good to
firm going: tried visored: often slowly away. *M. D. I. Usher*

SCOTT'S VIEW 5 b.g. Selkirk (USA) 129 – Milly of The Vally 93 (Caerleon (USA) **119**
132) [2004 116: 10m⁴ 12f* 12m 12m* 12m³ 10g* 10m³ 11g³ 12m 10f⁵ 10m⁵ 10m⁴
Aug 1] small, rather leggy gelding: smart performer: won handicaps at Nad Al Sheba in
February/March and listed race at Kempton (by 3 lengths from Bustan) in April: mostly
at least creditable efforts otherwise, including when third in Dubai Sheema Classic
(beaten 1¼ lengths by Polish Summer) at Nad Al Sheba fifth outing, ¾-length third to
River Dancer in Queen Elizabeth II Cup at Sha Tin seventh start, fifth to Rakti in Prince
of Wales's Stakes at Royal Ascot tenth start and 3¾ lengths fourth to Intendant in Grosser
Dallmayr-Preis at Munich (reportedly injured a tendon) final outing: effective at 1¼m to
1¾m: acts on polytrack, firm and good to soft going: sweated first 2 starts in 2003: has
been early to post: usually waited with (sometimes idles): tough. *M. Johnston*

SCOTTY'S FUTURE (IRE) 6 b.g. Namaqualand (USA) – Persian Empress (IRE) **83**
51 (Persian Bold 123) [2004 94: p10g p10g* f8.5s p10g* p10g 10g⁶ 8.9m⁵ 9g⁴ 9.1d Sep
16] close-coupled, quite good-topped gelding: just fairly useful nowadays: won 2 sellers
at Lingfield in February: left D. Loder to rejoin former trainer after fifth start: effective at
stiff 7f to easy 1¼m: acts on polytrack, firm and soft going: has been bandaged in front:
edgy sort: held up. *D. Nicholls*

SCRAMBLE (USA) 6 ch.g. Gulch (USA) – Syzygy (ARG) (Big Play (USA)) [2004 **50**
60: 7d⁶ 8m 8f 8f⁶ Jul 29] long-backed gelding: modest performer: best form at 1m to
1¼m: acts on fibresand, firm and good to soft going: tried blinkered, often wears cheekpieces: tongue tied. *B. Ellison*

SCREENPLAY 3 ch.g. In The Wings 128 – Erudite 114 (Generous (IRE) 139) [2004 **74**
76: 10g p12g p12g⁶ p10g² p10g⁶ p12m⁴ p13g³ p10g² Dec 30] smallish, sturdy gelding:
has a rather round action: fair maiden: left Michael Stoute after reappearance: stays
13f: acts on polytrack and good to firm going: ran creditably in cheekpieces last 2 starts:
has swished tail in paddock and hinted at temperament. *Miss S. West*

SCREWDRIVER 2 b.c. (May 4) Entrepreneur 123 – Lust (Pursuit of Love 124) **91**
[2004 6m² 6m* Jun 5] 30,000Y: stocky colt: fifth foal: half-brother to useful 7f (at 2 yrs)
to 1¾m winner Wavertree Boy (by Hector Protector): dam unraced half-sister to Classic
Cliche (won St Leger and Gold Cup) and My Emma (won Prix Vermeille and Yorkshire
Oaks): confirmed maiden promise when winning listed race at Epsom by neck from
Royal Island: jarred up after: should stay 7f. *R. Hannon*

SCRIPTED 2 b.g. (May 8) Diktat 126 – Krameria 72 (Kris 135) [2004 p6g⁴ 7m⁴ Oct **67**
10] 26,000Y: half-brother to 3 winners, including 8-y-o Palawan: dam, 2-y-o 5f winner,

half-sister to Nunthorpe winner So Factual: fair form in maidens at Lingfield and Newcastle: not sure to stay much beyond 7f: sold 23,000 gns. *Sir Mark Prescott*

SCRIPTORIUM 3 b.g. Singspiel (IRE) 133 – Annie Albright (USA) (Verbatim **70** (USA)) [2004 –p: p10g⁶ 10d 9f² 10f⁴ 10g² 10.1g 8g 7g Oct 11] fair maiden: will probably stay 1½m: acts on polytrack and firm going: sometimes finds little, including in visor final outing: sold 11,000 gns. *L. M. Cumani*

SCRIPTWRITER (IRE) 2 b.c. (Mar 31) Sadler's Wells (USA) 132 – Dayanata **86** (Shirley Heights 130) [2004 7.2s⁵ 8s² Oct 27] closely related to 3-y-o Portmanteau and half-brother to several winners, including smart 1m (at 2 yrs) to 12.5f winner Courteous (by Generous): dam unraced sister to Darshaan: better effort in maidens when head second to Very Wise at Yarmouth, leading over 1f out then veering left and idling: slowly away/flashed tail on debut: should be suited by 1¼m/1½m. *Saeed bin Suroor*

SCROOBY BABY 2 b.f. (Mar 13) Mind Games 121 – Lunar Music 67 (Komaite **66 d** (USA)) [2004 5.7g² 6.1g p6d² 6m⁴ p7g 6f p7.1g p6g Nov 20] 100,000Y: rather leggy filly: third foal: half-sister to 3-y-o Milk It Mick: dam 5f winner, including at 2 yrs: fair maiden: below form after third start: stays 6f: acts on polytrack, best turf effort on good going: blinkered (soon off bridle) final outing. *J. A. Osborne*

SCRUNCH 3 b.f. Royal Applause 124 – Antonia's Folly 64 (Music Boy 124) [2004 **71** 6s⁶ 7g 7d⁴ f6g³ Jul 9] 26,000Y: good-bodied filly: half-sister to several winners, including 5-y-o Bond Domingo and 4-y-o Coranglais: dam 2-y-o 5f winner: fair maiden: should be as effective at 6f as 7f: virtually unrideable in closing stages on second outing. *B. J. Meehan*

SCURRA 5 b.g. Spectrum (IRE) 126 – Tamnia 106 (Green Desert (USA) 127) [2004 **62** 52§: 12.4v⁶ 10.1v 8g³ 10.9d* 10.1s² 13g⁴ 10.5g⁶ 10s⁵ 11.9g² 13.8v⁴ 12d Nov 3] leggy gelding: modest handicapper: won at Ayr in June: stays 13f: acts on heavy and good to firm going, below form on fibresand. *A. C. Whillans*

SEA COVE 4 b.f. Terimon 124 – Regal Pursuit (IRE) 61 (Roi Danzig (USA)) [2004 –: **50** f12g⁴ 16m⁵ f12d⁵ 12d⁵ f14g⁴ Jul 9] workmanlike filly: modest maiden: stays easy 1½m: acts on fibresand and good to firm ground. *J. M. Jefferson*

SEA FERN 3 b.g. Petong 126 – Duxyana (IRE) (Cyrano de Bergerac 120) [2004 55: **45** 5d⁵ 5f 5m 5f 6g⁶ 6g Sep 25] small, good-bodied gelding: poor maiden: stays 6f. *D. Eddy*

SEAFIELD TOWERS 4 ch.g. Compton Place 125 – Midnight Spell 79 (Night Shift **82** (USA)) [2004 82: 5g 6m 5m³ 5m 5m 6g 5g 6f 6m 6f Jul 24] good-bodied gelding: fairly useful handicapper: well held after third start: effective at 5f/6f: acts on firm and good to soft ground: wears cheekpieces: looks difficult ride: none too consistent. *Miss L. A. Perratt*

SEAGOLD 3 b.f. Shahrastani (USA) 135 – Raeleen (Jupiter Island 126) [2004 –: 10g **–** 8f p12d p10g Sep 18] little form: left C. Wall after third start: blinkered final outing. *A. E. Jones*

SEA HOLLY (IRE) 4 b.g. Barathea (IRE) 127 – Mountain Holly 69 (Shirley Heights **68** 130) [2004 82: p10g p13g Dec 4] big gelding: has a round action: fairly useful at 3 yrs, just fair form in 2004: stays 13f: acts on all-weather, best turf efforts on good ground: has started slowly: carries head high. *G. G. Margarson*

SEA HUNTER 2 b.c. (Feb 10) Lend A Hand 124 – Ocean Grove (IRE) 84 (Fairy King **87** (USA)) [2004 5.1g 5g* 5g⁴ 7g² 7m³ 7s⁵ 8m 8d⁴ Oct 14] 110,000Y: well-made colt: fourth foal: half-brother to 3 winners, including 3-y-o Blue Tomato and fairly useful 2002 2-y-o 5f winner On The Brink (by Mind Games): dam 2-y-o 6f winner who stayed 1m: fairly useful performer: won maiden at Hamilton in May: good efforts in nurseries when placed at Newmarket fourth, fifth and final starts: stays 1m: acts on good to firm and good to soft ground. *M. R. Channon*

SEA JADE (IRE) 5 b.m. Mujadil (USA) 119 – Mirabiliary (USA) 74 (Crow (FR) **46** 134) [2004 51: 8.1g⁴ 8g² p7g² 5.7f May 27] workmanlike mare: poor maiden: effective at 7f to 8.5f: acts on polytrack, firm and soft going: sometimes flashes tail. *J. W. Payne*

SEA LARK 2 b.g. (Jan 27) Green Horizon – Fiora (IRE) (Sri Pekan (USA) 117) [2004 **61** p7.1d p8.6g p10g⁵ p9.5g Dec 20] first foal: dam last both starts: easily best effort when fifth in maiden at Wolverhampton. *W. J. Haggas*

SEAL OF OFFICE 5 ch.g. Mark of Esteem (IRE) 137 – Minskip (USA) 64 (The **–** Minstrel (CAN) 135) [2004 82?: 8.3g 10g May 22] workmanlike gelding: fairly useful performer at best: no form in 2004 (reportedly bled final outing): free-going sort. *A. M. Hales*

SEA MAP 2 ch.c. (Mar 24) Fraam 114 – Shehana (USA) 86 (The Minstrel (CAN) 135) **61**
[2004 7.1m 7f 8.3m 8g 8.2v⁶ p7.1g³ p9.5g Dec 20] 12,000Y: tall colt: half-brother to
several winners, including useful 1995 2-y-o 6f winner React (by Reprimand), later
successful in USA: dam 2-y-o 9f winner: modest maiden: will stay 1¼m: acts on polytrack and heavy ground. *S. Kirk*

SEA MARK 8 gr.g. Warning 136 – Mettlesome (Lomond (USA) 128) [2004 7d³ 7.1m⁵ **65**
8m May 26] big, rangy gelding: has a round action: just fair nowadays: finds 7f a minimum, probably stays 1¼m: acts on firm and good to soft going: blinkered once in 2002:
usually held up. *B. Ellison*

SEAMLESS 2 b.c. (Mar 23) Gold Away (IRE) 125 – Fallara (FR) (Tropular) [2004 6g⁵ **77 p**
p6d⁵ p6g² p6g* Dec 29] 7,000Y, 40,000 2-y-o: rather leggy colt: first foal: dam, French
15f winner, half-sister to useful French winner up to 1½m Home Alone: won maiden at
Lingfield readily by 3 lengths from Flying Dancer: will stay at least 7f: capable of better.
W. J. Haggas

SEAMUS SHINDIG 2 b.g. (Apr 26) Aragon 118 – Sheesha (USA) (Shadeed (USA) **87 p**
135) [2004 5f* 6s⁴ Oct 22] 2,800Y: small, sturdy gelding: sixth foal: brother to 3-y-o
Shielaligh and fairly useful 7f winner Shebeen: dam, ran once, closely related to smart
stayer Samraan: won maiden at Pontefract in September: respectable fourth to Pivotal
Flame in sales race at Doncaster: likely to prove best at 5f/6f: useful prospect. *H. Candy*

SEAN'S MEMORY (USA) 4 b.g. Theatrical 128 – Memories (IRE) 95 (Don't **52**
Forget Me 127) [2004 –: f12g f12g² p16g⁶ f14g Apr 2] modest maiden: barely stayed 2m:
raced only on all-weather: dead. *Mrs C. A. Dunnett*

SEA NYMPH (IRE) 3 b.f. Spectrum (IRE) 126 – Sea Picture (IRE) 82 (Royal **85**
Academy (USA) 130) [2004 8g⁵ 8.3f² 8.3g* 8.3d² 8.1g Sep/15] first foal: dam,
maiden who stayed 1¼m, half-sister to Yorkshire Oaks winner/St Leger second Hellenic,
herself dam of Greek Dance and Islington: fairly useful form: won maiden at Windsor in
August: good second in handicap there penultimate start: ran as if amiss final outing: bred
to stay at least 1¼m: acts on firm and good to soft ground. *Sir Michael Stoute*

SEA OF GOLD 3 b.f. Docksider (USA) 124 – Shadow Bird 70 (Martinmas 128) **71**
[2004 7g 8.3g⁶ 10f² 8.3f⁶ p10g⁴ 8g p8m Oct 6] 10,500Y: unfurnished filly: half-sister to
several winners, including useful 1996 2-y-o 6f winner Shadow Lead (by Midyan), later
successful in Hong Kong, and 8-y-o Air of Esteem: dam 13f winner: fair maiden: below
form last 3 starts, including in visor: likely to prove best up to 1¼m: sold 3,500 gns.
H. J. Cyzer

SEA OF HAPPINESS 4 b.g. Pivotal 124 – Ella Lamees 61 (Statoblest 120) [2004 **–**
33: 12.1m 16f 12m Jun 30] of little account. *C. Grant*

SEA PLUME 5 b.m. Slip Anchor 136 – Fine Quill (Unfuwain (USA) 131) [2004 80, **74**
a64: 12s⁵ 14m 14.1g 14m Jul 21] leggy mare: fair maiden on turf: stays 2m: acts on soft **a?**
and good to firm ground, best all-weather run on polytrack: tried blinkered: has hung left/
carried head high/flashed tail: often races prominently. *Lady Herries*

SEARCH MISSION (USA) 3 b.f. Red Ransom (USA) – Skimble (USA) 116 **84**
(Lyphard (USA) 132) [2004 82: 7m² 7g Jul 24] well-made filly: fairly useful performer,
lightly raced: all but pulled up final outing: stayed 7f: raced only on good ground or
firmer: stud. *Mrs A. J. Perrett*

SEASONS ESTATES 2 b.f. (Apr 26) Mark of Esteem (IRE) 137 – La Fazenda **68**
(Warning 136) [2004 5s⁴ 5.1g 7d⁴ 7m³ 7m* Oct 1] 20,000Y: third foal: dam unraced out
of smart Spanish filly (won Spanish 1000 Guineas/Oaks) Teresa: fair performer: won
nursery at Lingfield: should stay 1m: acts on good to firm going. *B. R. Millman*

SEASON TICKET (GER) 2 b.f. (Apr 20) Kornado 120 – Second Game (GER) **44**
(Second Set (IRE) 127) [2004 5.1g 6g 6m 7m Sep 29] €7,500Y: quite good-topped filly:
first foal: dam unraced out of useful German performer up to 1½m Secret Energy: poor
maiden: form only on second start: sold 800 gns. *W. J. Haggas*

SEA STORM (IRE) 6 b.g. Dolphin Street (FR) 125 – Prime Interest (IRE) (Kings **89**
Lake (USA) 133) [2004 96, a?: 7g 7.1g² 8d 7.2f¹³ 7.2f 8m* 8.9m 8m 8m⁶ 7g⁵ 8m⁶ 7m⁴
7.6s³ 7m 7.2s² 7.1g* 7.1d p8.6g⁵ Nov 8] big, strong gelding: fairly useful performer: won
minor event at Musselburgh in May and handicap there in September: best at 7f/1m: acts
on polytrack, firm and soft going: sometimes wears cheekpieces: blinkered once (forced
strong pace): has got past post: consistent. *D. R. MacLeod*

SEA TERN 4 b.f. Emarati (USA) 74 – Great Tern 59 (Simply Great (FR) 122) [2004 –: **–**
f7g 10m May 25] leggy filly: no sign of ability. *D. G. Bridgwater*

SEA THE WORLD (IRE)   4 b.g. Inzar (USA) 112 – Annie's Travels (IRE) (Mac's   –
Imp (USA) 116) [2004 –, a71: f5s⁵ f5g* f5g³ f5g² p5g⁶ f5d 6s p5.1g p5.1g p6m Dec 22]   **a68**
tall, leggy gelding: fair on all-weather, little form on turf: won minor event at Southwell
in February: reportedly finished lame final outing: should stay 6f: acts on all-weather:
usually visored: often slowly away: tends to hang. *D. Shaw*

SEATTLE ART (USA)   10 b.g. Seattle Slew (USA) – Artiste 95 (Artaius (USA) 129)   –
[2004 10m Jun 10] big gelding: very lightly raced on Flat nowadays: showed nothing
only run in 2004. *Dr P. Pritchard*

SEATTLE PRINCE (USA)   6 gr.g. Cozzene (USA) – Chicken Slew (USA) (Seattle   –
Slew (USA)) [2004 58: 16s 15.8g Oct 5] strong, quite attractive gelding: lightly raced on
Flat nowadays: well held in handicaps in 2004: tried visored/blinkered. *S. Gollings*

SEATTLE ROBBER   2 b.g. (Apr 1) Robellino (USA) 127 – Seattle Ribbon (USA) 70   **64**
(Seattle Dancer (USA) 119) [2004 7g p6g⁴ p6g⁵ p8.6g³ p8.6g² Dec 31] smallish, strong
gelding: third foal: brother to fairly useful 2003 2-y-o 6f winner Robocop and half-
brother to ungenuine 7f and 1¼m winner Seattle Express (by Salse): dam, maiden who
probably stayed 1¼m, sister to Racing Post Trophy winner Seattle Rhyme: modest
maiden: stays 8.6f: acts on polytrack: joined Gay Kelleway. *S. Kirk*

SEA YA MAITE   10 b.g. Komaite (USA) – Marina Plata (Julio Mariner 127) [2004 ?:   – §
f12g f12g⁵ f8g² f11g³ f9.4g⁵ f11g⁴ f14g⁵ f11s f8g² f8g⁴ 8.5m f8g f8m Jul 6] tall, rangy   **a45 §**
gelding: poor performer: stays 1¼m: acts on fibresand and firm going: tried blinkered,
usually tongue tied: sometimes slowly away/races lazily: not one to rely on. *S. R. Bowring*

SECAM (POL)   5 gr.g. Alywar (USA) – Scytia (POL) (Euro Star) [2004 p12g f8g³ 6d   **47 +**
7.6m f8m p7m³ p8g Dec 18] successful 3 times over 1m in Poland: poor form in Britain:
stays 1m: sometimes blinkered/in cheekpieces. *Mrs P. Townsley*

SECLUDED   4 b.g. Compton Place 125 – Secret Dance (Sadler's Wells (USA) 132)   **76**
[2004 72p: 10m⁵ 10m 8g 10s* 10.3g⁵ 10d Oct 18] fair performer: trained by A. Stewart
first 3 starts in 2004: won 5-runner handicap at Brighton in August: should stay 1½m:
acts on all-weather, soft and good to firm going: blinkered last 3 outings (found little last
2): sold 13,000 gns, joined T. McCourt in Ireland. *E. F. Vaughan*

SECOND GENERATION (IRE)   7 ch.g. Cadeaux Genereux 131 – Title Roll (IRE)   **35**
107 (Tate Gallery (USA) 117) [2004 –: f5g⁵ p5g⁵ p6g³ f6g⁴ f9.4m⁵ May 17] poor maiden:
stays 6f: acts on polytrack: tried blinkered. *R. J. Hodges*

SECOND MINISTER   5 ch.g. Lion Cavern (USA) 117 – Crime of Passion 115 (Dra-   **a61 d**
gonara Palace (USA) 115) [2004 –, a72: p5g³ f6s f6g⁶ 6g 6g p6g f6m Jul 26] big, leggy
gelding: fair performer at best: ran badly after reappearance: effective at 5f/6f: acts on
polytrack and good to firm ground: blinkered nowadays, sometimes tongue tied: often
races prominently. *D. Flood*

SECOND OF MAY   4 ch.f. Lion Cavern (USA) 117 – Giant Nipper (Nashwan (USA)   –
135) [2004 72: 10f Aug 4] sturdy filly: fair performer at best: well beaten only run in
2004. *P. R. Chamings*

SECOND PAIGE (IRE)   7 b.g. Nicolotte 118 – My First Paige (IRE) 53 (Runnett   **45**
125) [2004 56: p16g⁴ Feb 16] tall gelding: poor performer: stays 2m: acts on polytrack,
good to firm and good to soft going: usually blinkered: sometimes finds little: fairly
useful hurdler. *N. A. Graham*

SECOND REEF   2 b.c. (Apr 4) Second Empire (IRE) 124 – Vax Lady 98 (Millfontaine   **62 p**
114) [2004 f5g³ 6m Oct 2] 5,000Y: good-topped colt: has scope: half-brother to several
winners, including useful 1996 2-y-o 5f winner Vax Star (by Petong) and Irish 1¼m/1½m
winner Grand Madam (by Grand Lodge): dam sprinter: staying-on third in maiden at
Southwell: well held in listed event at Redcar: should stay at least 6f: capable of better.
R. A. Fahey

SECOND USER   3 b.g. Zilzal (USA) 137 – Glossary (Reference Point 139) [2004 p8g   –
p10g 10s 10m May 24] well beaten in maidens. *J. R. Jenkins*

SECOND VENTURE (IRE)   6 b.g. Petardia 113 – Hilton Gateway (Hello Gorgeous   **44**
(USA) 128) [2004 55d, a41: f8.5g f8g³ f7g Feb 2] good-topped gelding: poor performer:
stays 8.5f: acts on fibresand, soft and good to firm going. *P. Howling*

SECOND WARNING   3 ch.c. Piccolo 121 – St Helena (Monsanto (FR) 121) [2004   **53**
59: 8.5s⁵ p8d 8.3g⁵ 10g⁶ Aug 18] tall, workmanlike colt: modest maiden: will prove best
up to 1m. *D. J. Daly*

SECOND WIND   9 ch.g. Kris 135 – Rimosa's Pet 109 (Petingo 135) [2004 §§: 6d 8s Oct 30] lengthy, workmanlike gelding: of no account nowadays: sometimes refuses to race: one to leave alone. *D. A. Nolan* **§§**

SECRET AFFAIR   2 b.c. (Apr 10) Piccolo 121 – Secret Circle (Magic Ring (IRE) 115) [2004 p6g 7m 8s Oct 19] 34,000Y: good-topped colt: third foal: half-brother to 3-y-o Secret Place: dam unraced half-sister to high-class 1m/1¼m performer Bijou d'Inde: easily best effort in maidens when eighth at Leicester on second start: should stay 1m. *A. King* **66**

SECRETARY GENERAL (IRE)   3 b.c. Fasliyev (USA) 120 – Katie McLain (USA) 85 (Java Gold (USA)) [2004 88p: 8m 8.2s² 8.1m 8m⁵ 8g 8.2g* 9.7g² 11.9g² 12g 11.8g Oct 11] big, good-topped colt: has a quick action: useful handicapper: won at Nottingham in July: stays 1½m: acts on soft and good to firm going: reliable. *P. F. I. Cole* **99**

SECRET BLOOM   3 b.g. My Best Valentine 122 – Rose Elegance 83 (Bairn (USA) 126) [2004 –: f7g⁴ f8.5g⁴ f7g f11g⁵ f8.5g⁴ f8s² f8g⁴ f9.4g* f9.4g³ p9.5d f11g⁶ Nov 8] sturdy gelding: poor performer: won banded race at Wolverhampton in April: stays 9.4f: acts on fibresand: wears blinkers/visor. *J. R. Norton* **45**

SECRET CAVERN (USA)   2 b.g. (Apr 24) Lion Cavern (USA) 117 – River Dyna (USA) (Dynaformer (USA)) [2004 6g⁶ 7m 7s⁴ Oct 21] $5,000F, €4,000Y, 22,000 2-y-o: tall gelding: on weak side at 2 yrs: first foal: dam 1m winner in USA: fair form in maidens: needs to settle to stay beyond 7f: gelded after final start: type to do better as 3-y-o. *J. A. Osborne* **69 p**

SECRET CHARM (IRE)   3 b.f. Green Desert (USA) 127 – Viz (USA) (Kris S (USA)) [2004 105p: 8m⁵ 8m⁵ 8m 8f* 8g⁵ Oct 1] heavy-bodied filly: useful performer: won minor event at Doncaster in September by ½ length from Milk It Mick: fifth to Attraction in both 1000 Guineas at Newmarket (beaten 2¾ lengths) and Irish 1000 Guineas at the Curragh (beaten 4½ lengths) and to Polar Ben in Joel Stakes at Newmarket (beaten 4¾ lengths): stays 1m: acts on firm going: sweating/edgy in preliminaries in 2004: sent to USA. *B. W. Hills* **109**

SECRET CONNECTION   4 b.f. Danzig Connection (USA) – Red Secret (IRE) 49 (Valiyar 129) [2004 f9.4s Feb 17] sixth foal: half-sister to winners abroad by Siberian Express and Primo Dominie: dam 1½m winner: 14/1, soundly beaten in maiden at Wolverhampton. *M. Wigham* **–**

Centex Fairclough Homes Trophy (Conditions Stakes), Doncaster—
Secret Charm (right) makes virtually all and holds on gamely from Milk It Mick

SECRET DIVA (IRE)   2 ch.f. (Feb 7) Dr Devious (IRE) 127 – Deerussa (IRE) (Jareer   **29**
(USA) 115) [2004 5g 6m 5.1m 7g 6m p8g Sep 22] €2,000Y, resold €6,000Y: fifth foal:
half-sister to fairly useful 2000 2-y-o 5f winner Secret Index (by Nicolotte) and winner in
Italy by Archway: dam unraced: bad maiden. *Mrs P. N. Dutfield*

SECRET FLAME   3 b.f. Machiavellian (USA) 123 – Secret Obsession (USA) 89 (Sec-   **78**
retariat (USA)) [2004 74p: 8m³ 10m³ 9.2g* 8.1m 10g⁶ p10g⁵ Sep 22] leggy, unfurnished
filly: fair performer: won 4-runner maiden at Hamilton in June: stays 1¼m: raced only on
good/good to firm ground on turf, respectable effort on polytrack. *W. J. Haggas*

SECRET FORMULA   4 b.f. So Factual (USA) 120 – Ancient Secret (Warrshan   **–**
(USA) 117) [2004 92: 7d 7g May 13] tall filly: fairly useful handicapper at best: well
beaten in 2004. *S. Kirk*

SECRET HISTORY (USA)   2 b.f. (Mar 27) Bahri (USA) 125 – Ravnina (USA)   **79**
(Nureyev (USA) 131) [2004 6m² 6g³ 6m⁵ 7f4* 7f 8.3d² 7s³ Oct 22] 25,000Y: tall filly:
fourth foal: half-sister to winner in USA by Lear Fan: dam unraced close relative to useful
Irish sprinter Rhine Valley: fair performer: won maiden at Thirsk in August: good efforts
in nurseries after when placed: stays 1m: acts on soft going. *M. Johnston*

SECRET JEWEL (FR)   4 b.f. Hernando (FR) 127 – Opalette 75 (Sharrood (USA)   **62 §**
124) [2004 66: 10d⁶ 11.6f 12d⁵ 12s 9.9g 11.8g² 14.1s² p13.9g Nov 12] useful-looking
filly: modest maiden: should stay 1¾m: acts on firm and good to soft ground: tried in
cheekpieces/blinkers: ungenuine: sold £2,500. *Lady Herries*

SECRET OF SECRETS   3 b.g. Timeless Times (USA) 99 – Sophisticated Baby 39   **–**
(Bairn (USA) 126) [2004 5g 6g Sep 25] tailed off in maidens. *L. R. James*

SECRET PACT (IRE)   2 br.g. (Mar 4) Lend A Hand 124 – Schust Madame (IRE) 46   **89**
(Second Set (IRE) 127) [2004 5g⁴ 6s² 7g³ 6s 6.9m* 7m* 8g² 8s³ Oct 22] 30,000F,
100,000Y: leggy, useful-looking gelding: second foal: half-brother to fairly useful 2003
Irish 2-y-o 6f/7f winner Little Whisper (by Be My Guest): dam, Irish 1½m winner, half-
sister to smart Italian sprinter Late Parade: fairly useful performer: won maiden at
Carlisle and nursery at Catterick in September: good placed efforts in nurseries after:
should stay 1¼m: acts on soft and good to firm going: races prominently: gelded after
final start. *M. Johnston*

SECRET PLACE   3 ch.g. Compton Place 125 – Secret Circle (Magic Ring (IRE) 115)   **103**
[2004 71p: f7g* p7g* p8g³ 7g 7g* 7m 7g p7g³ p6g³ p6g³ p7.1g* Dec 31] good-bodied
gelding: useful performer: won maiden at Wolverhampton and handicap at Lingfield in
January, and handicaps at Goodwood in May and Wolverhampton (visored, beat Stage
Secret readily by 2 lengths) in December: effective at 6f to 1m: acts on all-weather, raced
only on good ground or firmer on turf. *E. A. L. Dunlop*

SECRET VISION (USA)   3 ch.f. Distant View (USA) 126 – Secret Angel (Halo   **–**
(USA)) [2004 83p: p8.6g Dec 27] promising second only run at 2 yrs: off 16 months, well
held on return for new trainer: should stay 1m. *R. M. H. Cowell*

SEDGE (USA)   4 b.g. Lure (USA) 131 – First Flyer (USA) (Riverman (USA) 131)   **56**
[2004 7m* 8d 8g 8.5m 8.5m 9d⁴ Oct 15] modest performer: won seller at Redcar in May:
seems to stay 9f: acts on good to firm and good to soft ground: raced freely fourth outing,
found little final one. *P. T. Midgley*

SEEJAY   4 b.f. Bahamian Bounty 116 – Grand Splendour 79 (Shirley Heights 130)   **?**
[2004 –: p8g³ 10.2s 8.2m 10.2m f8g p13m⁶ p12m² p12m⁵ Dec 15] modest maiden: left   **a53**
M. Allen after fourth start: stays 1½m: acts on polytrack. *J. Pearce*

SEEKING AN ALIBI (USA)   2 ch.c. (May 9) Storm Cat (USA) – Seeking Regina   **58**
(USA) 114 (Seeking The Gold (USA)) [2004 8g p8g Oct 31] $500,000F, $1,600,000Y:
leggy colt: sixth foal: brother to US Grade 3 6f winner Seeking The Sky and half-brother
to 3 winners in USA: dam US Grade 2 2-y-o 6.5f winner: modest form in maidens at
Leicester and Lingfield (tongue tied): not sure to stay much beyond 1m. *Saeed bin Suroor*

SEEKING A WAY (USA)   3 b.f. Seeking The Gold (USA) – Seattle Way (USA)   **75**
(Seattle Slew (USA)) [2004 78p: 11.7f² 10g³ 14d 13.1f⁶ p13g² 11.9s³ p12g⁶ Nov 10] big,
good-bodied filly: has a quick action: fair performer: stays easy 13f: acts on polytrack and
firm going. *J. H. M. Gosden*

SEEKING THE DIA (USA)   3 b.c. Storm Cat (USA) – Seeking The Pearl (USA)   **108**
121 (Seeking The Gold (USA)) [2004 7f* 8f* 8f* 8f 6g 6.5g a7s³ a7g* Dec 28] strong,
lengthy colt: first foal: dam, sprinter/miler, first Japanese Group 1 winner in Europe when
winning Prix Maurice de Gheest: useful performer: won maiden at Hanshin at 2 yrs,
minor stakes at Tokyo in January, Group 3 Arlington Cup at Hanshin in February, Group

2 New Zealand Trophy at Nakayama in April and Group 3 Hyogo Gold Trophy at Sonoda in December: well held both starts in Europe (July Cup at Newmarket and Prix Maurice de Gheest at Deauville) fifth/sixth outings: stays 1m: acts on firm ground and dirt: bandaged all round both starts in Europe. *H. Mori, Japan*

SEEL OF APPROVAL   5 br.g. Polar Falcon (USA) 126 – Petit Point (IRE) 78 (Petorius 117) [2004 113: 6m² May 2] strong gelding: smart performer: excellent head second to Royal Storm in handicap at Newmarket only run in 2004: stays 6f: acts on firm ground: reliable. *R. Charlton*   **115**

SEEYAAJ   4 b.g. Darshaan 133 – Subya 107 (Night Shift (USA)) [2004 90: 11.8m⁵ 11g 16 Oct 22] good-bodied gelding: fairly useful performer: stays 1½m: raced only on good ground or firmer until final start (beaten long way out): edgy (ran poorly) fourth 3-y-o outing: has worn blanket to stall entry: sold 10,000 gns. *Jonjo O'Neill*   **83**

SEGUIDILLA (IRE)   3 b.f. Mujadil (USA) 119 – Alzeam (IRE) 61 (Alzao (USA) 117) [2004 82: 6d 5d⁶ a5.5f⁴ a6f² 7.5f⁶ a5.5f² Dec 26] rather leggy, quite attractive filly: fairly useful maiden at 2 yrs: well held first 2 starts in 2004, then left G. Bravery: off 5 months, in frame 3 times at Turf Paradise, including in maiden optional claimers: stays 5.5f: acts on dirt and firm going. *R. Odom, snr, USA*   **?**

SEKWANA (POL)   5 b.m. Duke Valentino 86 – Surmia (POL) (Demon Club (POL)) [2004 p10g p13g 7f Jun 10] won over 5f/6f at 2/3 yrs in Poland: no sign of ability in Britain: tried in cheekpieces/blinkers/tongue tie. *Miss A. M. Newton-Smith*   **–**

SELDEMOSA   3 br.f. Selkirk (USA) 129 – Baldemosa (FR) (Lead On Time (USA) 123) [2004 p9.5g² f8g⁶ Dec 7] 4,000 3-y-o: fourth foal: half-sister to useful 6f winner (including at 2 yrs) Caustic Wit (by Cadeaux Genereux): dam, French 1m winner, half-sister to very smart French sprinter Balbonella, herself dam of top-class sprinter Anabaa: second in maiden at Wolverhampton on debut, slowly away: badly hampered 3f out next time. *M. S. Saunders*   **56**

SELEBELA   3 ch.f. Grand Lodge (USA) 125 – Risarshana (FR) (Darshaan 133) [2004 63p: 8.2s 11.8m* 11.8g* 12m* 12d² 12g² 12f³ 11.9s² 14.6m Sep 8] deep-girthed filly: useful performer: won handicaps at Leicester (2) and Salisbury in May/June: creditable efforts when placed in handicap/listed events after, including when 4 lengths second to Tarakala at York penultimate outing: should be suited by 1¾m+: acts on firm and soft ground: unusually on edge before running as if amiss final start: game and consistent. *L. M. Cumani*   **100**

SELECTIVE   5 b.g. Selkirk (USA) 129 – Portelet 91 (Night Shift (USA)) [2004 116: 8s⁴ 7m 7m p8g⁴ 8g 7s⁴ 10f⁶ 7.9g⁵ 8d⁵ Oct 15] good-bodied gelding: just useful form in 2004, trained first 4 starts by A. Stewart: effective at 7f/1m: acts on polytrack, good to firm and good to soft ground: respectable effort in cheekpieces final outing: carries head awkwardly: has run creditably when sweating: waited with: sold 48,000 gns. *E. F. Vaughan*   **95**

SELF BELIEF   3 b.f. Easycall 115 – Princess of Spain (King of Spain 121) [2004 67: 5m 5g 5m f5m Nov 22] close-coupled filly: lightly-raced maiden: well held in 2004. *M. C. Chapman*   **–**

SELF DEFENSE   7 b.g. Warning 136 – Dansara (Dancing Brave (USA) 140) [2004 16.1s 16.2g⁶ 14g⁵ 13.9s⁵ 12m² 12v³ p10g⁴ Nov 20] ex-French gelding: smart performer: left M. Zilber after final start in 2002: useful hurdler for Miss E. Lavelle prior to reappearance: ran well when neck second to High Accolade in Cumberland Lodge Stakes at Ascot fifth start: fifth to Mephisto in Ebor Handicap at York previous outing: probably best at 1½m/1¾m: acts on polytrack, heavy and good to firm going. *P. R. Chamings*   **114**

SELF RESPECT (USA)   2 b.c. (Jan 24) Lear Fan (USA) 130 – Cap of Dignity (Shirley Heights 130) [2004 10.1d Nov 5] $85,000Y: fourth foal: half-brother to winners in USA by Fairy King and Royal Academy: dam unraced out of Washington International runner-up Persian Tiara: 3/1, seventh to Quizzene in maiden at Yarmouth, green under pressure and short of room: will do better. *J. Noseda*   **63 p**

SELIKA (IRE)   2 ch.g. (Apr 12) Daggers Drawn (USA) 114 – Hint-Of-Romance (IRE) 86 (Treasure Kay 114) [2004 6g 7g 7.9g⁴ 8d Oct 18] 7,000F, €18,000Y: good-topped gelding: fourth foal: dam Irish 6f/7f winner: fair maiden: best efforts in blinkers (raced freely) last 2 outings, then gelded: stays 1m. *M. H. Tompkins*   **69**

SELKIRK GRACE   4 b.g. Selkirk (USA) 129 – Polina 69 (Polish Precedent (USA) 131) [2004 10d⁵ 12s² Nov 2] tall, angular gelding: lightly-raced maiden: fairly useful form only run at 2 yrs (got upset in stall): missed 2003, fair form on first of 2 starts on return: should stay 1¼m: pulled hard on reappearance. *K. A. Morgan*   **67**

SELKIRK STORM (IRE) 2 b.g. (Feb 12) Trans Island 119 – Force Divine (FR) **79 §**
(L'Emigrant (USA) 129) [2004 6s* 5m² 6g⁵ 5f 6d 7m 6s 6d³ 6s Oct 22] 16,000Y: leggy,
quite good-topped gelding: second foal: dam French 6f (at 2 yrs) to 1¼m winner: fair
performer: won maiden at Newcastle in May: not so good in second half of year, though
third in nursery at Ayr: stays 6f: acts on soft and good to firm going: sometimes edgy/
slowly away/hangs: unreliable: gelded after final start. *M. W. Easterby*

SELMA 2 ch.f. (Apr 15) Selkirk (USA) 129 – Mish Mish (Groom Dancer (USA) 128) **62 p**
[2004 p8g⁵ Dec 18] fourth living foal: half-sister to German 1m winner Morcotto (by
Zilzal) and to winner in Norway by Hernando: dam, French 1m/9f winner, out of half-
sister to Petoski: 10/1, swished tail throughout when 2½ lengths fifth to Nanton in minor
event at Lingfield, closing up late: open to improvement. *D. R. C. Elsworth*

SEMELLE DE VENT (USA) 3 b.f. Sadler's Wells (USA) 132 – Heeremandi (IRE) **64**
105 (Royal Academy (USA) 130) [2004 64p: f12g³ 12.1d³ 11.6s p12d p10d² 10m p8.6g³
p9.5d* Nov 5] strong filly: modest performer: won minor event at Wolverhampton in
November: effective at 8.6f to 1½m: acts on polytrack and good to soft ground: blinkered/
visored last 5 starts: has looked weak finisher. *J. H. M. Gosden*

SEMENOVSKII 4 b.g. Fraam 114 – Country Spirit (Sayf El Arab (USA) 127) [2004 **79**
84: p6g³ 5m⁶ 6m 6m* 6d 6m 6g 7v 7s⁵ Oct 27] strong gelding: fair handicapper: won at
Newmarket in August: left P. D'Arcy after seventh outing: effective at 5f/6f: acts on firm
and good to soft going: tried visored (below form): usually races prominently: none too
reliable. *R. Bastiman*

SEMPER PARATUS (USA) 5 b.g. Foxhound (USA) 103 – Bletcha Lass (AUS) **61 §**
(Bletchingly (AUS)) [2004 67§: f6f⁴ f7g 8s 6.1s² f8d f6g³ 6m 7g 6.1g 7.1s* f7g Dec 11]
close-coupled gelding: unimpressive mover: modest performer: left H. Collingridge after
second start: won minor event at Chepstow in September: effective at 6f/7f: acts on
fibresand, soft and firm going: tried in cheekpieces/visor, usually blinkered: unreliable.
V. Smith

SENDEED (USA) 2 br.c. (Feb 20) Gulch (USA) – Aghsaan (USA) (Wild Again **–**
(USA)) [2004 7.1m 7d Aug 13] strong, close-coupled colt: first foal: dam unraced sister
to very smart US Grade 1 7f/1m winner Wild Rush: tongue tied, well held in maidens at
Sandown and Newmarket: joined J. Hammond in France. *Saeed bin Suroor*

SENDINTANK 4 ch.g. Halling (USA) 133 – Colleville 97 (Pharly (FR) 130) [2004 **101**
–p: f12g* f12g* f12f* f12g* 12v³ 16s* 14.8d* 14.4s* 11.9g* 14g³ 16d* 16.5s* p12g³
p12.2g³ Dec 17] leggy gelding: progressed very well in 2004 and made into a useful
handicapper, winning 10 of 14 starts: successful at Wolverhampton (twice) and Southwell

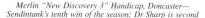

Merlin "New Discovery 3" Handicap, Doncaster—
Sendintank's tenth win of the season; Dr Sharp is second

(twice, including amateurs) in January, at Yarmouth, Newmarket and Newcastle in August, Haydock in September, then Musselburgh and Doncaster (beat Dr Sharp by ½ length) in November: good third behind Hello It's Me at Lingfield and Wolverhampton last 2 outings: effective at 1½m to 2m: acts on all-weather and heavy ground: usually held up, but made running penultimate start: sometimes carries head awkwardly: tough and reliable. *S. C. Williams*

SENESCHAL 3 b.g. Polar Falcon (USA) 126 – Broughton Singer (IRE) 61 (Common   **90 ?**
Grounds 118) [2004 97p: 8g 9.9s 9.9m 10.3s 7g 7g 7d⁵ 7m* 7.2s⁶ 7d² 7v⁶ 7s* Oct 23] big, leggy gelding: fairly useful handicapper: won at Newcastle and Doncaster (apprentices, by 11 lengths) in October: stays 7f: acts on soft and good to firm ground: often edges left: usually claimer ridden: sold 22,000 gns. *M. R. Channon*

SENEX (GER) 4 b.c. Pelder (IRE) 125 – Septima (GER) (Touching Wood (USA)   **121**
127) [2004 112: 11s³ 12d³ 11g⁵ 12m* 12d 12f* Sep 11] fifth foal: half-brother to several winners in Germany, including useful winner up to 11f Shredder (by Al Hareb): dam German 1m winner: very smart performer: best efforts in 2004 when winning Gran Premio di Milano in June by 2½ lengths from Maktub and when beating same rival ½ length in Bosphorus Cup at Veliefendi in September: stays 1½m: best form on good or firmer going (acts on firm). *H. Blume, Germany*

SENIOR MINISTER 6 b.g. Lion Cavern (USA) 117 – Crime Ofthecentury 80   **63 §**
(Pharly (FR) 130) [2004 68§: 10.2f 8f* 7.5g 8g 10f 8m 8.1g 7m p8.6g Oct 7] good-topped gelding: modest performer: won seller at Brighton in June: no form after: effective at 5f to 1m: acts on firm ground: tried blinkered: unreliable. *P. W. Hiatt*

SENIOR WHIM 2 b.c. (Mar 28) Lahib (USA) 129 – Euphorie (GER) (Feenpark   **–**
(GER) 115) [2004 10v Oct 20] 33/1, well held in maiden at Nottingham. *P. R. Webber*

SENNA (IRE) 4 b.g. Petardia 113 – Saborinie 56 (Prince Sabo 123) [2004 –: p8g Jan   **–**
14] leggy gelding: no form. *P. D. Cundell*

SENNEN COVE 5 ch.g. Bering 136 – Dame Laura (IRE) 100 (Royal Academy (USA)   **50**
130) [2004 54d: f6g f7g f7g⁶ p10g³ p8g⁶ 8g⁶ 8.5m* 7.1f* 8m 7.9m f8g f8g Dec 28]   **a36**
close-coupled gelding: modest performer on turf, poor on all-weather: won banded race at Beverley in May and handicap at Musselburgh in June: stays 9f: acts on firm and good to soft going: tried in cheekpieces/blinkers, usually tongue tied. *R. Bastiman*

SENOR BENNY (USA) 5 br.h. Benny The Dip (USA) 127 – Senora Tippy (USA)   **110**
(El Gran Senor (USA) 136) [2004 7.5v⁵ 7m 9g 9f⁶ 6f 7.5g 8.5m 7m 8v 6d* 6m² a6g* 6v²
6s* 5d* 6d³ 5s* 7v Oct 31] smart performer on turf, poor on all-weather: ran once for J. Gosden at 3 yrs and missed 2003: vastly improved switched to sprinting in 2004, winning handicaps at Ballinrobe in August, Laytown and Listowel in September and the Curragh in October, and listed race at Cork (best effort, beat Moon Unit 2½ lengths) in October: well held back over 7f final outing: best at 5f/6f: acts on heavy ground and sand: blinkered sixth start. *M. McDonagh, Ireland*

SENOR BOND (USA) 3 ch.g. Hennessy (USA) 122 – Troppa Freska (USA) (Silver   **66**
Hawk (USA) 123) [2004 79: f8g⁶ 6.1s³ 7.5d 6m⁶ f7m f6f Aug 20] smallish, good-bodied   **a55**
gelding: fair performer on turf, modest on fibresand: probably stays 7f: acts on good to firm going, probably on soft: sometimes reluctant to post. *B. Smart*

SENOR EDUARDO 7 gr.g. Terimon 124 – Jasmin Path (Warpath 113) [2004 63: 7s   **60**
7m 8d³ 8.1m⁵ 10.1m* 10.1m⁶ 9.2d² 11.9g³ 8.5m 9.9m³ 12g 9d Oct 15] good-topped gelding: modest performer: won seller at Yarmouth in July: stays around 1¼m: acts on good to firm and good to soft ground: sold 4,000 gns. *S. Gollings*

SENOR MIRO 6 b.g. Be My Guest (USA) 126 – Classic Moonlight (IRE) (Machia-   **–**
vellian (USA) 123) [2004 59: f7s Jan 8] leggy, useful-looking gelding: modest maiden: probably best at 7f: acted on polytrack, unraced on extremes of going on turf: tried tongue tied: dead. *J. Akehurst*

SENOR SET (GER) 3 b.g. Second Set (IRE) 127 – Shine Share (IRE) (El Gran Senor   **68**
(USA) 136) [2004 f8g² Jun 11] €10,000Y: sixth foal: half-brother to 3 winners in Germany, including 11f winner Sharea (by Shirley Heights): dam useful German 1m (at 2 yrs) and 1½m winner: 66/1 and very green, 6 lengths second to Pass The Port in maiden at Southwell, staying on despite hanging left. *P. A. Blockley*

SENOR TORAN (USA) 4 b.g. Barathea (IRE) 127 – Applaud (USA) 105 (Rahy   **55**
(USA) 115) [2004 –: p10g³ p10g⁴ p10g³ 9.9d p10g² 11.9m⁵ May 12] big, strong gelding: modest maiden: stays 1¼m: acts on all-weather and soft ground: tried blinkered/in cheek-pieces. *P. Burgoyne*

SENTIERO ROSSO (USA) 2 b.c. (Jan 28) Intidab (USA) 115 – Kheyrah (USA) 100 (Dayjur (USA) 137) [2004 5g⁴ 5d² 5v* 6d³ 5d 6m 6g 7s Oct 23] $21,000Y, resold €30,000Y, 92,000 2-y-o: strong, compact colt: second foal: dam, 6f (at 2 yrs) and 7f winner, out of half-sister to William Hill Futurity winner Dunbeath: useful performer: won minor event at Newcastle in August: easily best effort when ¾-length third of 6 to Space Shuttle in listed race at Ripon: well held in nursery final start: stays 6f: acts on heavy ground. *B. Ellison* — **97 d**

SENTRY (IRE) 4 b.g. In Command (IRE) 114 – Keep Bobbin Up (IRE) 76 (Bob Back (USA) [2004 88: 12g* 12.1g⁴ 14.1s³ 16.2d³ 20f 16.2g Jul 10] strong, leggy gelding: has a quick action: fairly useful handicapper: won at Newmarket in April by head from Prins Willem: stays 2m: acts on polytrack, soft and good to firm ground: consistent. *J. H. M. Gosden* — **92**

SENZA SCRUPOLI 4 ch.g. Inchinor 119 – Gravette 79 (Kris 135) [2004 61?: 10d³ Apr 24] good-bodied gelding: poor maiden: stays 1¼m: acts on good to firm and good to soft ground: blinkered (ran respectably) only run in 2004. *M. D. Hammond* — **49**

SERAPH 4 ch.g. Vettori (IRE) 119 – Dahlawise (IRE) 76 (Caerleon (USA) 132) [2004 48: f9.4g³ f11g* f12g f12s³ f12s³ f12g² p12g* p13g f14g³ 12.3m f12m Jul 26] leggy, workmanlike gelding: poor performer: won banded races at Southwell in January and Lingfield in April: stays 1¾m: acts on fibresand and good to firm ground: has been blinkered, wears cheekpieces nowadays. *John A. Harris* — **48**

SERBELLONI 4 b.g. Spectrum (IRE) 126 – Rose Vibert (Caerleon (USA) 132) [2004 74: 10m⁵ p9.5g² p12m* Dec 22] lengthy, useful-looking gelding: fair handicapper, lightly raced: won at Lingfield: stays 1½m: acts on polytrack, firm and good to soft ground. *W. R. Swinburn* — **78**

SERENE PEARL (IRE) 2 b.f. (Apr 20) Night Shift (USA) – Shanjah (Darshaan 133) [2004 5g 5m 5f⁶ 5m⁶ f5m⁴ f7g 5g Oct 5] 15,000F, 16,000Y: smallish filly: third foal: sister to 4-y-o Dark Shah and half-sister to winning sprinter in Austria by Perugino: dam, French 1¼m winner, sister to smart stayer And Beyond: modest maiden: likely to prove best at 5f/6f: acts on fibresand and good to firm going: tongue tied last 4 starts. *G. M. Moore* — **55**

SERENGETI SKY (USA) 3 br.c. Southern Halo (USA) – Genovefa (USA) 107 (Woodman (USA) 126) [2004 10v 12.1s⁴ 9.7s⁶ May 6] strong colt: no form in maidens. *D. R. Loder* — **–**

SERGEANT CECIL 5 ch.g. King's Signet (USA) 110 – Jadidh 64 (Touching Wood (USA) 127) [2004 95: 12s 12g³ 14d⁵ 12g* 14g² 14g² 14.6f² 12m³ Sep 26] workmanlike gelding: useful handicapper: won at Ascot in July by short head from Cutting Crew: good placed efforts after at Goodwood (to Mephisto), Haydock (behind Defining), Doncaster (1¼ lengths second to Lost Soldier Three in Mallard Stakes) and Ascot (to Fort): effective at 1½m/1¾m: seems best on good going or firmer (some promise on polytrack): ran badly in cheekpieces once in 2003: sometimes races freely/carries head awkwardly: held up: tough and consistent. *B. R. Millman* — **100**

SERGEANT LEWIS 2 gr.c. (Feb 12) Mind Games 121 – Silver Blessings (Statoblest 120) [2004 7m⁶ 6m Oct 1] well beaten in maiden at Brighton and claimer at Lingfield. *J. A. Osborne* — **–**

SERGEANT SHINKO (IRE) 2 ch.g. (May 3) Shinko Forest (IRE) – Sea Modena (IRE) (Mac's Imp (USA) 116) [2004 7m p8.6g 10v Oct 20] well held in maidens: blinkered last 2 starts. *M. Dods* — **–**

SERGEANT'S INN 7 b.g. Sabrehill (USA) 120 – Pink Brief (IRE) 71 (Ela-Mana-Mou 132) [2004 f14g Feb 24] strong gelding: probably of little account. *T. T. Clement* — **–**

SERGEANT SLIPPER 7 ch.g. Never So Bold 135 – Pretty Scarce (Handsome Sailor 125) [2004 –§, a51§: f6s f5g³ f6g f5s³ f5g* f6s² f7s f6g* 6v⁵ 6f 6.1g p5.1g f5m f6g Dec 7] workmanlike gelding: modest on all-weather, poor on turf: won banded race at Southwell in February and claimer there in April: raced mainly at 5f/6f: acts on fibresand, heavy and good to firm going: tried blinkered, visored nowadays: usually slowly away, often markedly so: untrustworthy. *C. Smith* — **45 §** / **a57 §**

SERGEANT SMALL (IRE) 2 b.g. (Mar 29) Dr Devious (IRE) 127 – Yavarro 44 (Raga Navarro (ITY) 119) [2004 6g 6m Sep 5] lengthy gelding: soundly beaten in maidens at Lingfield and York. *John Berry* — **–**

SERIEUX 5 b.g. Cadeaux Genereux 131 – Seranda (IRE) (Petoski 135) [2004 106§: p8g 8g 10d 8g² 8m 8m 8m 8.3g 7m 7m⁴ 8m 8g⁵ Sep 30] strong, lengthy, useful-looking gelding: useful handicapper: better at 1m than 1¼m, and should prove effective at 7f: acts on soft and good to firm going: has worn cheekpieces last 5 starts: free-going sort: effective making running or held up: ungenuine: sold 24,000 gns, then gelded. *Mrs A. J. Perrett*

SERRAMANNA 3 ch.f. Grand Lodge (USA) 125 – Spry 84 (Suave Dancer (USA) **75** 136) [2004 85p: 10g⁶ 10.3d⁵ 10g³ 12.3d³ 14.1d Sep 17] leggy, unfurnished filly: fair maiden: should stay 1¾m: raced only on good/good to soft ground: sold 6,500 gns. *H. R. A. Cecil*

SERRAVAL (FR) 6 ch.m. Sanglamore (USA) 126 – Saone (USA) (Bering 136) [2004 **64** 9.7m² 11g³ 11.9s⁵ 9.9s³ Aug 29] modest handicapper: missed 2003: should stay 1½m: acts on soft and good to firm ground: tried visored. *G. B. Balding*

SERRE CHEVALIER (IRE) 3 b.g. Marju (IRE) 127 – Ski Lodge (IRE) 78 (Persian **79** Bold 123) [2004 8m² 8.1m* 7.1g 7d Oct 30] IR 80,000Y: useful-looking gelding: first foal: dam, 2-y-o 7f winner, half-sister to smart German miler Sinyar: fair form: won maiden at Sandown in July: better effort in handicaps after when creditable eighth there next time: not sure to stay beyond 1m: acts on good to firm ground. *P. W. Harris*

SESSAY 3 b.g. Cyrano de Bergerac 120 – Green Supreme (Primo Dominie 121) [2004 **72** 67: 7d⁴ 6.1d³ 7m⁵ 5m 6d⁶ 7m 5d⁶ 6g* 5d Oct 11] leggy gelding: fair performer: dead-heated in maiden at Catterick in October: best at 5f/6f: acts on good to soft and good to firm ground: sold 6,500 gns. *D. Nicholls*

SES SELINE 3 b.f. Salse (USA) 128 – Absentee 66 (Slip Anchor 136) [2004 8g⁴ 8.2s⁵ **–** 11.8m 14.1g 10g Oct 11] tall, lengthy filly: first foal: dam, 1¾m winner, one to treat with caution: of little account: tried in cheekpieces/blinkers. *John A. Harris*

SET ALIGHT 3 b.f. Forzando 122 – Me Spede (Valiyar 129) [2004 7g 7f⁴ 7f³ f6f 7d **57** p8g p7.1g² Dec 22] big filly: seventh living foal: half-sister to 3 winners, including 2000 2-y-o 5f winner Reeds Rains (by Mind Games) and 7f/1m winner Sign of The Tiger (by Beveled): dam ran twice at 2 yrs: modest maiden: left Miss K. Boutflower after third start: stays 7f: best effort on polytrack. *Mrs C. A. Dunnett*

SETTLEMENT CRAIC (IRE) 3 b.g. Ela-Mana-Mou 132 – Medway (IRE) 60 **93** (Shernazar 131) [2004 79p: p12g* 12.3g⁴ 10d³ 12m 11.6g* 12g 11.8g Oct 11] leggy, close-coupled gelding: fairly useful performer: won maiden at Lingfield in March and handicap at Windsor in July: will stay at least 1¾m: acts on polytrack, yet to race on extremes of going on turf: held up: edgy sort: gelded after final start. *T. G. Mills*

SEVEN MAGICIANS (USA) 2 b.f. (Mar 10) Silver Hawk (USA) 123 – Mambo **79 P** Jambo (USA) (Kingmambo (USA) 125) [2004 7g⁴ Sep 20] rather leggy, attractive filly: third foal: closely related to smart 8.5f (in USA)/1¼m winner (stayed 1½m) Ocean Silk (by Dynaformer): dam, French 1½m winner, sister to 2-y-o Divine Proportions and closely related to 3-y-o Whipper: 25/1, fourth to Quickfire in maiden at Kempton, hampered and finishing strongly, not knocked about: will stay at least 1m: open to considerable improvement, and should win races. *Sir Michael Stoute*

SEVEN NO TRUMPS 7 ch.g. Pips Pride 117 – Classic Ring (IRE) 50 (Auction Ring **83** (USA) 123) [2004 88: 5s² 6g⁵ 6s 5d 5s 5g³ 6m⁶ 5m 5m⁴ 5g 5m 5d² 5m 5d 5.2g⁴ 5.1d p5.1d **a76** p5.1g⁵ p5.1g p5.1g⁶ p6g Dec 11] rangy, good-topped gelding: fairly useful handicapper: effective at 5f/6f: acts on polytrack and any turf going: blinkered once at 3 yrs, sometimes wears cheekpieces: edgy sort: tends to carry head high: inconsistent. *J. M. Bradley*

SEVEN SHIRT 3 b.g. Great Dane (IRE) 122 – Bride's Answer 81 (Anshan 119) [2004 **45** 65: 8.1d 8.1s 8.5m 7.1s⁶ 8.1d Oct 9] tall gelding: just poor maiden at 3 yrs: probably stays 1m: acts on soft going: tends to carry head awkwardly. *E. G. Bevan*

SEVEN YEAR ITCH (IRE) 4 b.g. Danehill (USA) 126 – Itching (IRE) (Thatching **82** 131) [2004 75p: 10s² 10m² May 26] strong gelding: fairly useful maiden: runner-up all 3 starts, including at Lingfield and Ripon (blinkered, carried head high) in 2004: suffered from lameness in near-hind after: not sure to stay beyond 1¼m: acts on polytrack, soft and good to firm going. *M. P. Tregoning*

SEVERELY (FR) 2 b.f. (Mar 10) Cape Cross (IRE) 129 – Sevres (USA) (Lyphard's **– p** Wish (FR) 124) [2004 6f Jul 17] 34,000Y: fourth foal: half-sister to French 11f winner Sterling Silver (by Bigstone): dam unraced daughter of Champion Stakes winner Swiss Maid: 5/1, behind in maiden at Windsor, not knocked about: suffered problem after: should do better. *B. W. Hills*

SEVILLANO 3 b.g. Nicolotte 118 – Nashville Blues (IRE) 94 (Try My Best (USA) **106**
130) [2004 95: 6d* 5g* 6g a6g Dec 10] big, lengthy gelding: useful performer: won
minor events at Leicester (by 10 lengths from Harry Up) and Hamilton (long odds on) in
April: subsequently below form in listed race at Newbury (left P. Cundell, off 7 months
after) and minor event at Jebel Ali: best form at 6f: unraced on extremes of going:
sweating (ran well) final 2-y-o start: free-going sort, and usually races prominently. *M. Al
Kurdi, UAE*

SEWMORE CHARACTER 4 b.c. Hector Protector (USA) 124 – Kyle Rhea 104 **81 d**
(In The Wings 128) [2004 84: p8g4 p10g6 p8g2 p8g5 8.2g 7.5d p10g2 p12m p12g p8.6g
p9.5g Dec 6] angular colt: fairly useful performer: below form after reappearance: stays
easy 1¼m: acts on polytrack and heavy ground: possibly none too resolute. *M. Blanshard*

SEWMUCH CHARACTER 5 b.g. Magic Ring (IRE) 115 – Diplomatist 69 (Dom- **75**
inion 123) [2004 82: 6d4 6.1s 7m6 6.1m4 6f2 6g 6g* 6g 5.7g6 p6g3 p7.1d p6g6 Nov 20]
big gelding: fair performer: won minor event at Folkestone in August: best at 6f/7f:
acts on polytrack, firm and soft going: usually races prominently: none too reliable.
M. Blanshard

SEW'N'SO CHARACTER (IRE) 3 b.g. Imperial Ballet (IRE) 110 – Hope And **98**
Glory (USA) 87 (Well Decorated (USA)) [2004 97: 7.6d4 9g 10.4m3 8.1g4 8g4 7m 9.7g4
9.9d6 8.1g 10.5s2 10v4 Oct 20] good-topped gelding: useful handicapper: mostly creditable efforts in 2004, including when third to Etmaam at York and second to Straw Bear at
Haydock: stays 10.4f: acts on soft and good to firm going: blinkered (respectable effort)
sixth start: usually held up: beaten after final outing. *M. Blanshard*

SEYAADI 2 b.g. (Jan 20) Intikhab (USA) 135 – Sioux Chef 78 (Be My Chief (USA) **76**
122) [2004 7m5 7d2 p7g5 Jul 21] 55,000Y: strong, well-made gelding: has markedly
round action: first foal: dam 2-y-o 5.7f winner: fair form in maidens: second at York: will
probably stay 1m. *E. A. L. Dunlop*

SEYED (IRE) 4 b.g. Desert Prince (IRE) 130 – Royal Bounty (IRE) 80 (Generous **49**
(IRE) 139) [2004 7.5m3 May 24] leggy, useful-looking gelding: trained by D. Loder only
start in 2002: off 24 months, poor form only 4-y-o outing. *V. Smith*

SFORZANDO 3 b.f. Robellino (USA) 127 – Mory Kante (Icecapade (USA)) **73**
[2004 68: 7g* 7m5 7g 8.3g Jul 12] well-made filly: fair performer: won minor event at
Yarmouth in May: stays 7f: acts on good to firm going. *J. A. R. Toller*

SGT PEPPER (IRE) 3 b.c. Fasliyev (USA) 120 – Amandine (IRE) (Darshaan 133) **94 ?**
[2004 100: 7m 7f 7d4 8m6 9d5 10g Oct 2] compact colt: just fairly useful at best in 2004:
stays 1m: acts on good to firm and good to soft going. *R. Hannon*

SHAABAN (IRE) 3 b.g. Woodman (USA) 126 – Ashbilya (USA) (Nureyev (USA) **63 ?**
131) [2004 8m 8m 8g 10.3d5 8d Aug 13] good-bodied gelding: second foal: closely related to fairly useful 1m/9f winner Najaaba (by Bahhare): dam unraced: modest maiden: left
M. Channon 10,000 gns and gelded prior to poor effort final start: likely to stay 1¼m: acts
on good to firm going. *Miss J. Feilden*

SHAAMIT'S ALL OVER 5 b.m. Shaamit (IRE) 127 – First Time Over (Derrylin **32**
115) [2004 –: p12g p10g f8m3 7d6 8.3g Oct 11] poor maiden: tried blinkered/in cheekpieces: sometimes slowly away. *B. A. Pearce*

SHADES OF GREEN 2 b.f. (May 20) Loup Sauvage (USA) 125 – Green Light (FR) **57**
(Green Dancer (USA) 132) [2004 8m p7g6 p9.5g p8.6g f7g4 Dec 14] leggy filly: half-
sister to several winners, notably smart French 1¼m (at 2 yrs) to 1½m winner Another
Dancer (by Groom Dancer): dam French 1¼m winner: modest maiden: should stay at
least 1m: acts on polytrack. *N. A. Callaghan*

SHADOWFAX 4 b.g. Anabaa (USA) 130 – Prends Ca (IRE) 98 (Reprimand 122) **64**
[2004 60: f6g4 f6g f6g f8.5s f6s2 f7.6s Feb 10] useful-looking gelding: modest maiden:
pulled up amiss final start: effective at 6f/7f: acts on fibresand, firm and soft ground: tried
in tongue tie: wears headgear: has carried head high/pulled hard. *Miss Gay Kelleway*

SHADY DEAL 8 b.g. No Big Deal – Taskalady 47 (Touching Wood (USA) 127) **50 §**
[2004 60: f5s f5s 5d 6s 6v3 5.7m 6.1m 6.1s3 5.1f 6.1d Jul 10] angular gelding: modest **a– §**
performer: best at 5f/6f nowadays: acts on any turf going: tried blinkered: usually races
prominently: unreliable. *J. M. Bradley*

SHADY REFLECTION (USA) 3 b.f. Sultry Song (USA) – Woodland Melody **88**
(USA) 108 (Woodman (USA) 126) [2004 74p: 8s* 9.9g5 May 19] strong filly: fairly

useful performer: won listed race at Ascot (beat Glen Innes short head) in April: not discredited when fifth to Halicardia in similar event at Goodwood after: stayed 1m: acted on soft going: stud. *J. H. M. Gosden*

SHAHAMA (IRE) 2 gr.c. (Feb 18) Daylami (IRE) 138 – Albertville (USA) 108 (Polish Precedent (USA) 131) [2004 7.1m 8d Aug 20] green, seemingly modest form in maidens at Sandown and Salisbury: sold 6,500 gns, sent to Denmark. *M. P. Tregoning* **53 ?**

SHAHEER (IRE) 2 b.g. (Feb 18) Shahrastani (USA) 135 – Atmospheric Blues (IRE) 91 (Double Schwartz 128) [2004 6m⁶ 6g² 6.1g 7m⁶ 10m p8.6g p9.5g⁵ Dec 20] 14,000Y: sturdy gelding: fluent mover: sixth foal: half-brother to 2002 2-y-o 6f winner Isolde's Idol (by Night Shift), later won at 1m in Germany, and Irish 7f winner Bear Camp (by Charnwood Forest): dam 2-y-o 5f winner, later 1m winner in Italy: fair maiden: stays 7f: acts on good to firm going, some promise on all-weather. *B. J. Meehan* **71**

SHAHM (IRE) 5 b.g. Marju (IRE) 127 – Istibshar (USA) 78 (Mr Prospector (USA)) [2004 60: f6s p8g Mar 8] good-topped gelding: modest handicapper: below form both starts in 2004: stays 1m: acts on fibresand, good to firm and good to soft going: tried visored/blinkered/tongue tied: sometimes carries head high/looks none too genuine. *B. J. Curley* **?**

SHAHZAN HOUSE (IRE) 5 b.h. Sri Pekan (USA) 117 – Nsx 74 (Roi Danzig (USA)) [2004 98: 10.1s³ 10.4d² 10.1m³ 10d³ 10.5g³ 10.4s³ 10v⁶ Oct 23] sturdy horse: fluent mover: useful handicapper: placed 6 times in 2004, best efforts when third in valuable events at Epsom (2 lengths behind Persian Lightning) and Haydock (1½ lengths behind Dunaskin in totesport Stakes) third/fifth starts: best around 1¼m: acts on soft and good to firm going: wore cheekpieces last 5 outings: races prominently: game. *M. A. Jarvis* **104**

SHALATI PRINCESS 3 b.f. Bluegrass Prince (IRE) 110 – Shalati (FR) (High Line 125) [2004 p8g p8g p8g⁶ p7g p10g⁴ 12s p10g³ p12d p10d⁵ Aug 7] £8,200Y: half-sister to several winners, including 1¼m winner Kewarra (by Distant Relative) and 7f (at 2 yrs)/ 1m winner Shalad'or (by Golden Heights), both useful: dam French 1m winner: poor maiden: probably stays 1½m: acts on polytrack, well held only start on turf. *J. C. Fox* **46**

SHALAYA (IRE) 3 b.f. Marju (IRE) 127 – Shalama (IRE) 91 (Kahyasi 130) [2004 87p: 10m⁵ 9m Jun 12] smallish, close-coupled filly: fairly useful performer: good fifth to Mudawin in handicap at Ascot on reappearance: better than result in similar event at Sandown only other 3-y-o start, hampered over 1f out: should stay 1½m: raced only on good/good to firm going: sold €30,000 in November. *Sir Michael Stoute* **89**

SHALBEBLUE (IRE) 7 b.g. Shalford (IRE) 124§ – Alberjas (IRE) (Sure Blade (USA) 130) [2004 59: 12f 12.3g 12f 9.9m 12s Aug 13] smallish gelding: poor handicapper in 2004: stays 1½m: acts on fibresand, firm and soft going: blinkered (tried in cheekpieces/visor): tends to hang. *B. Ellison* **47**

SHAMAN 7 b.g. Fraam 114 – Magic Maggie 38 (Beveled (USA)) [2004 64, a54: p10g⁵ p12g 9.7s⁴ May 6] fluent mover: modest handicapper: stays 1½m: acts on all-weather and any turf going: none too consistent. *G. L. Moore* **55**

SHAMARA (IRE) 4 b.f. Spectrum (IRE) 126 – Hamara (FR) (Akarad (FR) 130) [2004 85+: 10g² 9g² 10.1s⁴ 10.2g 10.1g² 10d⁶ Oct 14] lengthy, quite attractive filly: useful performer: best effort when ½-length second to Polar Jem in listed event at Yarmouth penultimate start (carried head high): effective at 9f to 1½m: acts on soft and good to firm going. *C. F. Wall* **99**

SHAMARDAL (USA) 2 b.c. (Mar 27) Giant's Causeway (USA) 132 – Helsinki (Machiavellian (USA) 123) [2004 6g* 7g* 7s* Oct 16] **126 p**
The tale of Shamardal may not have quite so many strands as *The Mousetrap*, and is unlikely to run anywhere near so long, but there are a number of twists and turns already in the background of the colt who was unquestionably the best of his age in Europe. First, the form. Shamardal's emphatic victory in the Darley Dewhurst Stakes at Newmarket in October marked him down as a worthy favourite for the Two Thousand Guineas. Indeed, such was his superiority in the best field assembled for a juvenile race all season that it was hard to see what might beat him in that classic, especially as fellow Godolphin inmate Dubawi had the Derby on his agenda and was not a guaranteed runner in the Guineas. However, the situation is different, at the time of writing, with Shamardal being talked of as a possible runner in the Kentucky Derby, a race which Godolphin has yet to win ('It's at the top of our

Veuve Clicquot Vintage Stakes, Goodwood—Shamardal has it well sewn up; Wilko is his nearest pursuer

shopping list'). The UAE Derby in March is pencilled in as Shamardal's 'trial', after which a final decision will be taken on the rest of his classic campaign.

The Dewhurst brought together seven pattern winners, the favourite Etlaala having beaten another contender, Coventry Stakes winner Iceman, in the Champagne Stakes. Also there were: Oratorio, successful a fortnight earlier in the Prix Jean-Luc Lagardere; Perfectperformance, a convincing winner of the Royal Lodge Stakes; Tremar (Prix Eclipse); Montgomery's Arch (Richmond Stakes); and Shamardal, having his first run for over two months after a slight setback. In conditions as testing as any seen at Newmarket at the time of year since 1980, when Storm Bird won the Dewhurst, Shamardal started second favourite on the strength of a stylish win in the Veuve Clicquot Vintage Stakes at Goodwood. Odds on at Goodwood after a facile all-the-way eight-length victory in a seven-runner maiden at Ayr in the second week of July, Shamardal dictated the pace and sealed matters quickly after being the only one still on the bridle over two furlongs out, winning smoothly by two and a half lengths from second favourite Wilko. This was the best performance by a juvenile up to that point and it led to Shamardal's being cut from 16/1 to 10/1 favourite in early ante-post betting on the Two Thousand Guineas. Shamardal was still around the same odds for the classic before the Dewhurst, but his odds were as short as 3/1 afterwards.

Shamardal performed at Newmarket exactly as he had done at Goodwood, leaving the stalls quickly and making the running by the stand rail. Shaken up with more than two furlongs left, at which point Etlaala was already in trouble, Shamardal was soon in command, as dual winner Librettist dropped away, and had no difficulty holding the challenges of Oratorio and Montgomery's Arch. Shamardal won by two and a half lengths from Oratorio, with Montgomery's Arch, Iceman and Librettist next. It is conceivable that racing by the rail provided Shamardal with marginally better going than that for his opponents who raced further outside—they certainly kicked up more divots—but, despite Oratorio also reportedly finishing with a pulled muscle, there was no denying the quality of the winner's performance. Apart from the form being first rate, Shamardal's timefigure of 0.93 fast equates to a timerating of 123, the best put up by a juvenile in 2004 and one which goes a long way towards providing confirmation of the Timeform rating. Shamardal's impressive victory was the highlight of a topsy-turvy day for trainer Mark Johnston, who also won the Cesarewitch with Contact Dancer but had the misfortune to lose his very promising three-year-old Mister Monet with a broken leg in the Champion Stakes.

Shamardal carried colours in the Dewhurst different from those on his two previous appearances, and he will be sporting yet a third outfit as he sets out on the classic trail in the spring for Godolphin, along with other acquisitions such as Berenson, Birthstone, Dubai Surprise, Henrik, Last Rhapsody, Layman, Queen of Poland, Satchem, Suez and Windsor Knot. Changing from Sheikh Maktoum Al Maktoum's Gainsborough Stud to Godolphin is not exactly newsworthy, but the same cannot be said about how the colt (and Lucky Story among others) switched ownership from Abdulla Buhaleeba to Gainsborough in early-October. There were plenty of rumours—one of them outlined in the essay on Lucky Story—but no substantive facts were forthcoming, not even from Michael Goodbody, managing director of Gainsborough Stud. In Delphic fashion, he said: 'I just got instructions that they were to be transferred into the colours of Gainsborough Stud, which I did. They are all owned by Gainsborough Stud and are leased out to the nominees—that's part of the company structure we have. They have always been the property of Gainsborough Stud . . .' Proof, at least as regards ownership, that you cannot always believe what you see on the racecourse with horses connected to one of racing's big battalions.

If Shamardal's change of ownership counts as one twist in his story, another lies in the fact that he was lucky even to make it to the racecourse. Like two other recent top performers, the sprinter Anabaa and St Leger winner Shantou, Shamardal was diagnosed as a 'wobbler'. Details of the complaint were given in the essay on Anabaa in *Racehorses of 1996*, but a reprise is worthwhile. 'Wobblers' are usually young colts who fall victim to a progressive illness involving ataxia, or lack of balance and co-ordination. The causes of the illness are not known, but hypotheses include genetic predisposition, nutritional imbalance, excessively fast growth, or physical trauma, notably injury to the spinal chord. Methods of assisting the horse include therapy with diuretic drugs, surgery to fuse and immobilise the affected vertebrae, and a substantial reduction in nutrient intake, along with a limitation in exercise, none of which provides a certain cure. It follows that a thoroughbred with the syndrome is far from certain to reach the track, even after considerable time and expense. Shamardal was diagnosed as a grade three sufferer (the most severe being grade five) after being knocked down for 485,000 dollars as a foal at the Keeneland November Sale. The sale was made null and void, and insurers paid up. Like Anabaa and Shantou, however, Shamardal came back. Depending on which story you believe, his recovery was the outcome of extensive but unspecified rehabilitation at a stud in Kentucky, or of 'reconnective therapy', an esoteric healing treatment used primarily on humans to connect functional areas of the body with dysfunctional ones, allowing the latter to begin working effectively. Reconnective therapy had apparently worked with the insurance loss adjuster's wife, which was why it was tried on Shamardal. Whatever the reason, Shamardal became a fully-functioning yearling and reappeared at the Houghton Yearling Sales without any reference to what had gone before. Shamardal fetched 50,000 guineas there to the bid of Goodbody, ironically bidding against the man to whom the colt was sent into training, Mark Johnston. Neither bidder had any knowledge of the previous insurance claim, as Johnston later admitted: 'Michael and I were completely unaware of the colt's condition. I didn't know until after he won his first race. I have to say that if we'd known his history we wouldn't have bought him.'

Judged on the way he looked as a two-year-old—he is a big, strong colt with scope, the type to train on—Shamardal was well bought even before he ran. He was one of the cheapest of the fifteen yearlings by Giant's Causeway to go through the ring at Newmarket, out of a total of more than seventy sold worldwide; the top lot went for 1,250,000 guineas and the average price was around 130,000 guineas. Giant's Causeway is one of a splendid band of first-crop sires, including two others responsible for Group 1 winners, Dubai Millennium and Montjeu. Giant's Causeway was a few pounds below the other two in merit, but he was a match in consistency and toughness for any horse in the last twenty years, winning nine of his thirteen races at up to a mile and a quarter—he never raced over a mile and a

Darley Dewhurst Stakes, Newmarket—
a high-class performance from Shamardal; Oratorio (third left), Montgomery's Arch (rail),
Iceman (left) and Librettist battle it out for the minor placings

half—including the Coral-Eclipse Stakes, Sussex Stakes and Juddmonte International. He finished second in the races he did not win, including in the Breeders' Cup Classic on dirt. Giant's Causeway covered one hundred and eighty-one mares in his first and only season at Coolmore in Ireland, being represented eventually by one hundred and thirty-seven foals, of whom eighteen have won, with Footsteps-inthesand and Maids Causeway also landing pattern races. As a point of interest, Giant's Causeway's brother Tiger Dance, also trained by Aidan O'Brien, showed great promise in winning his only start as a juvenile, a maiden race at Leopardstown in September, and looks one to follow. Giant's Causeway was transferred to Coolmore's Ashford Stud in Kentucky in 2002, where his fee for 2005 is 150,000 dollars, up from 75,000 dollars in 2004. He had more yearlings on offer than any other sire at Keeneland in September with seventy-six (his book was two hundred and thirteen), three of these fetching at least a million dollars.

Shamardal (USA) (b.c. Mar 27, 2002)	Giant's Causeway (USA) (ch 1997)	Storm Cat (b or br 1983)	Storm Bird	
			Terlingua	
		Mariah's Storm (b 1991)	Rahy	
			Immense	
	Helsinki (b 1993)	Machiavellian (b 1987)	Mr Prospector	
			Coup de Folie	
		Helen Street (b 1982)	Troy	
			Waterway	

There is stamina on the distaff side of Shamardal's pedigree, Shamardal completing a rather bizarre circle by joining Godolphin. His dam Helsinki raced for Sheikh Mohammed in France, winning a newcomers race over a mile and a quarter and finishing third in a listed event at Evry. She was sold for just 27,000 guineas at the end of her racing career, a far cry from the 3,900,000 dollars she fetched in foal to Cherokee Run at Keeneland in November. Almost inevitably, and as yet another

Gainsborough Stud's "Shamardal"

indication of the extent to which European racing at the top level revolves around the Maktoums and Coolmore, Helsinki was bought by John Magnier and returns to Giant's Causeway. The mare's foal by Unbridled's Song went for 1,150,000 dollars, though not to Magnier. Helsinki's family is well known to the Godolphin operation as they raced her brother Street Cry, who, interestingly, excelled on dirt, being successful in the Dubai World Cup then the Stephen Foster Handicap in the States. One of Helsinki's half-sisters Grecian Slipper is dam of two Group 3 winners in France and their dam Helen Street landed the Irish Oaks. The third dam Waterway was third in the Poule d'Essai des Pouliches and came from top miler Sun Prince's family. Shamardal is the third of Helsinki's foals to hit the target. The first, Lushs Lad (by Wolfhound), picked up a seven-furlong maiden race on the all-weather at Lingfield and Helsinka (by Pennekamp) won small races over ten and a half and eleven furlongs in France in the season under review. Shamardal, who will stay a mile and should get at least a mile and a quarter, has raced only on good or soft going. He looks capable of even more improvement and there is every reason to anticipate his 2005 campaign with relish, wherever it takes him. *M. Johnston*

SHAMBAR (IRE) 5 ro.g. Linamix (FR) 127 – Shamawna (IRE) (Darshaan 133) [2004 10d³ 10m⁵ 10.1d³ Jul 8] tall gelding: fourth in newcomers race at Longchamp for A. de Royer Dupre early in 2002: off over 2 years, appeared to run well when third to Fruhlingssturm in minor event at Epsom final start: stays 1¼m: acts on good to soft going. *P. R. Chamings* — **97 ?**

SHAMDIAN (IRE) 4 b.g. Indian Ridge 123 – Shamadara (IRE) 114 (Kahyasi 130) [2004 10g p7g Oct 25] lightly-raced maiden: fairly useful form at 3 yrs when trained in France by A. de Royer Dupre: just fair form on first of 2 starts in 2004: stays 9f: raced only on good ground or softer on turf: tried tongue tied: sold 9,500 gns: fair hurdler. *N. J. Henderson* — **78**

SHAMELESS 7 ch.g. Prince Daniel (USA) – Level Edge 55 (Beveled (USA)) [2004 f12g 9.9s 12.1m 12v Oct 16] no sign of ability: tongue tied. *H. Alexander* — **–**

SHAMROCK BAY 2 b.f. (Apr 9) Celtic Swing 138 – Kabayil 75 (Dancing Brave (USA) 140) [2004 6.1g 7.5m⁴ 7g Oct 11] close-coupled filly: sixth foal: half-sister to 7-y-o Dancing Bay and fairly useful 2001 2-y-o 7f winner Kasamba (by Salse): dam 1¼m winner and fairly useful hurdler: easily best effort in maidens when fourth at Beverley: should be suited by 1¼m+. *J. G. Given* — **66**

SHAMROCK CITY (IRE) 7 b.g. Rock City 120 – Actualite (Polish Precedent (USA) 131) [2004 95: 10.3g⁶ 8f 9g Jun 30] rather leggy, workmanlike gelding: one-time smart performer: well held in 2004. *P. Howling* — **–**

SHAMROCK TEA 3 b.g. Imperial Ballet (IRE) 110 – Yellow Ribbon (IRE) 72 (Hamas (IRE) 125§) [2004 77d: 6m 5m⁵ 6s* 6g⁴ 6g 6.1m 7g Oct 11] small gelding: modest handicapper: won at Newcastle in June: below form last 3 starts, struck into on first occasion: stays 6f: acts on soft ground: slowly away fourth outing. *R. A. Fahey* — **64**

SHAMWARI FIRE (IRE) 4 ch.g. Idris (IRE) 118 – Bobby's Dream 53 (Reference Point 139) [2004 65, a49: f9.4g⁴ p7g⁶ p7g 8.2d 7.5m* 7.5d⁶ 8.1m 8.1f 7.5g³ 8g³ 8f 8d 9.7f* 7.9m³ 10.1g⁶ 9.9m 8d³ Oct 2] modest on turf, poor on all-weather: won claimer at Beverley in May and banded race at Folkestone in September: stays 1¼m: acts on all-weather, good to firm and good to soft ground: unreliable. *I. W. McInnes* — **55 §**
a41 §

SHANGHAI LILY (IRE) 2 b.f. (Mar 2) King's Best (USA) 132 – Marlene-D 57 (Selkirk (USA) 129) [2004 6d* 7g* Sep 17] €300,000Y: rather leggy, lengthy filly: has scope: second foal: half-sister to fairly useful 2003 2-y-o 7f winner Eden Rock (by Danehill): dam, Irish 9f winner, half-sister to useful French sprinter Kerulen and smart stayer Arden: favourite, won maiden in August and minor event in September (4-runner contest, quickening well, by 2½ lengths from Sharp As A Tack), both at Newbury: missed Rockfel Stakes at Newmarket in October due to soft going: will stay 1m: potentially smart, and worth her place in stronger company. *Sir Michael Stoute* — **98 P**

SHANGHAI SURPRISE 3 b.g. Komaite (USA) – Shanghai Lil 57 (Petong 126) [2004 49: f8d³ 8.2s 5m 5m f5m Jul 12] close-coupled gelding: little form at 3 yrs: usually blinkered/in cheekpieces. *J. Balding* — **–**

SHANKLY BOND (IRE) 2 ch.g. (Apr 16) Danehill Dancer (IRE) 117 – Fanellan 76 (Try My Best (USA) 130) [2004 7d 6g 7g⁶ Sep 14] €27,000F, 28,000Y: sturdy gelding: — **60**

sixth foal: dam 2-y-o 6f winner who stayed 1m: modest form in maidens: not sure to stay beyond 7f. *B. Smart*

SHANNKARA'S QUEST (USA) 3 b. or br.c. Coronado's Quest (USA) 130 – – Shannkara (IRE) (Akarad (FR) 130) [2004 p8g p8g 6s f6g f6g Dec 28] no form: left P. Cole after second start. *C. N. Kellett*

SHANNON ARMS (USA) 3 b.g. Wolf Power (SAF) – Cresta's Best (USA) (Cresta 70 Rider (USA) 124) [2004 a6f⁶ a8f² 7s² p7.1g² f8g² p7g³ Dec 29] $4,000F, $32,000Y: half-brother to several minor winners in USA: dam winning sprinter in USA: fair maiden: left W. Jacot in USA after second start and trained next start only (short-headed in minor event at Limerick) by E. O'Grady in Ireland: stays 1m: acts on polytrack and soft ground: well below form in blinkers final start: hung right on bend and carried head high fourth outing. *J. S. Moore*

SHANNON'S DREAM 8 b.m. Anshan 119 – Jenny's Call (Petong 126) [2004 12.1m – 11.9m⁴ Aug 16] little form. *P. W. Hiatt*

SHANNON SPRINGS (IRE) 2 b.c. (Mar 14) Darshaan 133 – Our Queen of Kings 101 (Arazi (USA) 135) [2004 7g² 7d³ 8m² 8d Oct 17] 30,000Y: smallish, well-made colt: second foal: half-brother to 5f winner in Italy by Royal Academy: dam unraced half-sister to Fanmore (high class) and Labeeb (very smart), both best up to 1¼m: placed in maidens at Newmarket and Doncaster and listed race at York (best effort when ¾-length third to Elliots World): only seventh in Gran Criterium at Milan: should stay 1¼m. *B. W. Hills*

SHANTY STAR (IRE) 4 gr.g. Hector Protector (USA) 124 – Shawanni 105 (Shareef 108 Dancer (USA) 135) [2004 109: 13.9d 16.4f 12g³ 16s Oct 16] big, lengthy, good-bodied gelding: useful performer, lightly raced: gelded, good ½-length third to Private Charter in listed event at Newmarket: ran poorly in Yorkshire Cup at York and Jockey Club Cup at Newmarket other completed starts in 2004 (pulled up in Henry II Stakes at Sandown second one): stays 2m: acts on firm going: slowly away/ran in snatches final outing: sold 32,000 gns. *M. Johnston*

SHAPE UP (IRE) 4 b.g. Octagonal (NZ) 126 – Bint Kaldoun (IRE) 82 (Kaldoun (FR) 73 122) [2004 71: f12g³ 9.7s² 11.6m⁴ 12f* 12.3g* 12d* f12s² Nov 17] close-coupled, quite good-topped gelding: fair handicapper: won at Newmarket in May and Chester in June, both ladies events, and (having left T. Keddy) Musselburgh in November: stays 1½m: acts on polytrack, firm and soft ground: blinkered. *R. Craggs*

SHARAAB (USA) 3 b. or br.g. Erhaab (USA) 127 – Ghashtah (USA) (Nijinsky (CAN) 77 138) [2004 72: 10d⁶ 9.9g 7f⁵ 7.9m² 10g 10m 8g Sep 14] tall, rather leggy gelding: has a quick action: fair maiden: effective at 1m/1¼m: acts on good to firm and good to soft going: usually tongue tied: sold 17,000 gns, then gelded. *B. Hanbury*

SHARABAD (FR) 6 b.g. Ela-Mana-Mou 132 – Sharbada (FR) (Kahyasi 130) [2004 – 10m⁵ 10.5m 10m 8f 11.9g Sep 2] little form. *Mrs L. B. Normile*

SHARABY (IRE) 2 b.f. (Mar 26) Cadeaux Genereux 131 – Shawanni 105 (Shareef 76 Dancer (USA) 135) [2004 7g³ 7m 7.5d 7d² Oct 30] leggy filly: fifth foal: sister to 6-y-o Mystic Man and half-sister to 2 winners, including 4-y-o Shanty Star: dam, 2-y-o 7f winner, out of Rockfel Stakes winner Negligent: fair maiden: best effort when neck second to Read Federica at Newmarket, making most: edgy sort, needs to settle to stay 1m: tends to look tricky ride. *E. A. L. Dunlop*

SHARADI (IRE) 3 b.g. Desert Sun 120 – Sharadiya (IRE) 93 (Akarad (FR) 130) [2004 82 + 77: 11g 11d 12f 14d² 16s² 14g² 16g* 14g³ 17.2s* Oct 19] quite good-topped gelding: fifth foal: half-brother to French 7f winner Sharadpour (by Hamas): dam, won at 9f in Ireland, out of Prix Vermeille winner Sharaya: fairly useful handicapper: progressed well: won at Musselburgh in September and at Bath (beat Port Sodrick by 6 lengths, wandering) in October: stays 17f well: acts on soft going. *V. Smith*

SHARAIJI BLOSSOM (USA) 2 b.f. (May 20) Saint Ballado (CAN) – Lilac Garden 80 p (USA) (Roberto (USA) 131) [2004 7.5m³ 8.2m* Sep 28] $575,000Y: tall, good-topped filly: half-sister to several winners abroad, notably high-class Hong Kong 6f to 9f winner Electronic Unicorn (by Housebuster) and very smart US performer up to 9f Blushing K D (by Blushing John): dam 7f to 8.5f winner in USA: better effort in maidens when winning at Nottingham comfortably by 1½ lengths from Zayn Zen, making most: will stay at least 1¼m: should progress. *Saeed bin Suroor*

SHARDDA 4 b.f. Barathea (IRE) 127 – Kronengold (USA) (Golden Act (USA)) [2004 64 d 70?: 8v³ 8.3d 9v 8g 8m 10s⁵ f8g Nov 8] tall filly: modest maiden: ran poorly after reappearance: probably stays 9f: probably acts on any ground: tried tongue tied/visored. *F. Watson*

SHAREB (USA) 2 b.c. (Feb 14) El Prado (IRE) 119 – My Hansel (USA) 98 (Hansel (USA)) [2004 6d Oct 14] big, strong colt: has plenty of scope: first foal: dam, 7f (at 2 yrs)/1m winner, half-sister to smart 7f/1m winner Ramooz: 50/1, green and bandaged hind-joints, eleventh to Tomoohat in maiden at Newmarket, some late headway: will stay 1m: should improve. *B. W. Hills* — **59 p**

SHARED DREAMS 2 b.f. (Apr 29) Seeking The Gold (USA) – Coretta (IRE) 118 (Caerleon (USA) 132) [2004 7d³ Oct 30] close-coupled filly: second foal: dam, 1¼m/1½m winner (including Grade 2 in USA), out of smart half-sister to Barathea and Gossamer: 16/1 and green, 3½ lengths third to Songthrush in maiden at Newmarket, finishing strongly from rear without being knocked about: likely to be suited by 1m/1¼m: should improve considerably and win races. *L. M. Cumani* — **78 P**

SHARES (IRE) 4 b.g. Turtle Island (IRE) 123 – Glendora (Glenstal (USA) 118) [2004 60: 10.1v² 10s⁴ Oct 12] good-bodied gelding: fair maiden: should stay 1½m: acts on any going: tried tongue tied: blinkered (found little) final 3-y-o start. *P. Monteith* — **65**

SHARMY (IRE) 8 b.g. Caerleon (USA) 132 – Petticoat Lane (Ela-Mana-Mou 132) [2004 –, a109: 10f 12d Oct 14] close-coupled, quite attractive gelding: useful in 2003: well held both 8-y-o starts: sometimes slowly away. *Ian Williams* — **–**

SHAROURA 8 ch.m. Inchinor 119 – Kinkajoo 53 (Precocious 126) [2004 70, a59: 5m⁵ 6m 6m* 6m 6g³ 6m⁴ 6m² 6.9f⁴ 7g 6f 7.2d³ 6g p7g p7g f7g* p7.1g⁵ p7.1g⁵ p6g Dec 27] angular mare: poor mover: fair on turf, modest on all-weather: won handicap at Pontefract in June and minor event at Southwell in November: effective at 6f/7f: acts on all-weather, firm and soft going: tried visored/tongue tied/in cheekpieces. *R. A. Fahey* — **73 a62**

SHARP AS A TACK (IRE) 2 b.f. (Jan 29) Zafonic (USA) 130 – Pretty Sharp 64 (Interrex (CAN)) [2004 6f 6.1g² 7d* 7s 7g² 7v⁶ Oct 23] 35,000Y: neat filly: fourth foal: half-sister to 5-y-o Twilight Blues and 3-y-o Incise: dam maiden (best at 7f at 2 yrs) who became temperamental: fairly useful performer: made all in maiden at Salisbury in August: form after only when 2½ lengths second of 4 to Shanghai Lily in minor event at Newbury: stays 7f: acts on good to soft ground: blinkered last 2 starts: usually races up with pace: tail flasher: sold 25,000 gns. *B. J. Meehan* — **86**

SHARP DIVERSION (USA) 2 ch.f. (Apr 17) Diesis 133 – Jamie de Vil (USA) (Digression (USA) 116) [2004 5f⁶ Sep 2] $10,000Y, 25,000 2-y-o: fourth foal: dam, maiden in USA, half-sister to dam of smart sprinter Pharaoh's Delight: 28/1 and green, sixth in maiden at Redcar, slowly away: should do better. *J. G. Given* — **42 p**

SHARP HAT 10 ch.g. Shavian 125 – Madam Trilby (Grundy 137) [2004 83, a76: f5g⁵ f6g² f6g f6g f6s⁵ f5g⁵ f5g 6g p6g 5v 6m 6d 5m³ 5g 5m² 5d⁴ 5d⁵ 6g 5g 6d p5.1g⁴ p5.1g⁴ f6g⁵ p6g f6g⁴ f5f Dec 28] leggy, angular gelding: fair performer nowadays: well below form last 4 starts: effective at 5f to 7f: acts on any turf going/all-weather: well held in blinkers: sometimes goes freely. *D. W. Chapman* — **68 a70 d**

SHARPINCH 6 b.g. Beveled (USA) – Giant Nipper (Nashwan (USA) 135) [2004 80d: p7g Jan 6] one-time fairly useful handicapper on all-weather: last on only 6-y-o outing: has pulled hard. *P. R. Chamings* — **–**

SHARPLAW DESTINY (IRE) 3 br.f. Petardia 113 – Coolrain Lady (IRE) 74 (Common Grounds 118) [2004 55p: f7g⁵ p10g 7m 8f Jun 29] close-coupled, unfurnished filly: maiden: well held in 2004: blinkered (slowly away) third outing. *W. J. Haggas* — **–**

SHARPLAW STAR 2 b.f. (Apr 2) Xaar 132 – Hamsah (IRE) 86 (Green Desert (USA) 127) [2004 5g* 5f³ 5m* p5g³ Oct 28] 92,000Y: quite good-topped filly: sixth foal: half-sister to fairly useful 1998 Irish 2-y-o 5f winner Sparkling Outlook (by College Chapel) and 3-y-o Promenade: dam, 2-y-o 5f winner, half-sister to Irish 2000 Guineas winner Wassl: useful performer: won maiden at Leicester in June and minor event at Beverley (beat Cutlass Gaudy 2 lengths) in September: best effort when 4¼ lengths third to Damson in Queen Mary Stakes at Royal Ascot: well below form in minor event at Lingfield final start: will stay 6f: acts on firm going. *W. J. Haggas* — **97**

SHARPLAW VENTURE 4 b.f. Polar Falcon (USA) 126 – Breakaway 98 (Song 132) [2004 95: 8.3g³ p8g 8m Aug 4] lengthy, angular filly: just fairly useful in 2004: stays 1m: acts on firm going. *W. J. Haggas* — **82**

SHARP NEEDLE 3 b.f. Mark of Esteem (IRE) 137 – Blushing Sunrise (USA) (Cox's Ridge (USA)) [2004 7g 9g² 8.3g⁵ 9.2m* 8m* 8m⁴ p8g* Oct 25] well-made filly: second living foal: dam 6.5f winner in USA: fairly useful performer: won handicap at Hamilton — **84**

in June, minor event at Redcar in August and handicap at Lingfield in October: stays 9f: acts on polytrack and good to firm going: sold 17,000 gns, sent to USA. *J. Noseda*

SHARP N FROSTY 2 b.g. (Mar 12) Somayda (IRE) 98 – Wily Miss (Teenoso (USA) 135) [2004 5.1g⁴ 5.1d 7.1f⁴ 7m⁴ 8s 8g 10v⁵ Oct 20] good-bodied gelding: modest maiden: stays 1¼m: acts on heavy and good to firm going. *W. M. Brisbourne* **55**

SHARP RALLY (IRE) 3 ch.g. Night Shift (USA) – La Pointe (Sharpo 132) [2004 10.5s³ 9.5v 10.5s⁴ 9.5g⁵ 9.5g p9.5g Dec 1] fair performer: won maiden at Nort-sur-Erdre at 2 yrs: left H. Pantall in France and tongue tied, well beaten on British debut final 3-y-o outing: stays 10.5f: acts on soft going. *A. J. Wilson* **74**

SHARP REPLY (USA) 2 b.c. (Apr 30) Diesis 133 – Questonia 107 (Rainbow Quest (USA) 134) [2004 7s⁴ Oct 22] leggy colt: fourth foal: half-brother to 3 winners abroad, including fairly useful French 1¼m winner Common Request (by Lear Fan): dam, 1m winner, out of half-sister to champion 1997 2-y-o Xaar: 12/1, 3¾ lengths fourth to Tasdeed in maiden at Doncaster, squeezed out early and never nearer, not knocked about: sure to improve. *Sir Michael Stoute* **75 p**

SHARP RIGGING (IRE) 4 b.g. Son of Sharp Shot (IRE) 105 – In The Rigging (USA) 78 (Topsider (USA)) [2004 67: 10g Oct 12] leggy gelding: fair maiden at 3 yrs for E. Dunlop: well held only 4-y-o outing. *A. M. Hales* **–**

SHARP SECRET (IRE) 6 b.m. College Chapel 122 – State Treasure (USA) (Secretariat (USA)) [2004 65: 8m⁵ 8m* 8m 8m p8.6g Oct 7] smallish, workmanlike mare: modest handicapper: won at Pontefract in June: stays 1m: acts on firm and soft going: usually held up: sometimes carries head high/edges left. *J. A. R. Toller* **62**

SHARP SPICE 8 b.m. Lugana Beach 116 – Ewar Empress (IRE) 57 (Persian Bold 123) [2004 –, a50: p12g⁶ Apr 15] angular mare: poor performer: best around 1½m: acts on all-weather and any turf going: usually visored: sometimes slowly away, including only 8-y-o start: has carried head awkwardly/found little: held up. *D. L. Williams* **a33**

SHARVIE 7 b.g. Rock Hopper 124 – Heresheis 69 (Free State 125) [2004 p16g f16.2s⁵ Mar 8] poor handicapper in 2002: well held both starts since: tried visored/in cheekpieces: takes good hold. *M. R. Bosley* **–**

SHASTYE (IRE) 3 b.f. Danehill (USA) 126 – Saganeca (USA) 120 (Sagace (FR) 135) [2004 10m 12m³ 10g⁴ p13g* 14.1s Oct 27] useful-looking filly: half-sister to several winners, notably 1½m winner (including Arc) Sagamix (by Linamix) and 2000 2-y-o 9f/1¼m winner who stayed 1½m Sagacity (by Highest Honor), both high class in France: dam over 12.5f Prix de Royallieu: fair performer: won maiden at Lingfield (by 7 lengths) in October: stays easy 13f: acts on polytrack, best effort on good going (well held on soft in listed event at Yarmouth final outing). *J. H. M. Gosden* **77**

SHATIN LEADER 2 b.f. (Jan 27) Atraf 116 – Star Dancer (Groom Dancer (USA) 128) [2004 5m 5f⁶ 5f³ 5m⁴ 5g 6d 6m Oct 10] 1,000Y: fourth foal: half-sister to winner abroad by Dolphin Street: dam tailed off only start: poor maiden: should stay 6f: acts on firm going: tends to hang right: ungenuine. *Miss L. A. Perratt* **47 §**

SHATIN SPECIAL 4 ch.f. Titus Livius (FR) 115 – Lawn Order 51 (Efisio 120) [2004 57d: f11g⁵ f12g² f11g f12g⁴ f12s* f11s⁶ f12s⁶ 10.1g⁶ 11.6m 12.3m f12d³ f12g a11g Nov 21] modest performer: won banded race at Wolverhampton in February: left G. Chung before final start: stays 1½m: yet to race on firm going, acts on any other turf and fibresand: wears cheekpieces. *J. Guerra, Spain* **50**

SHATIN STAR 2 b. or br.c. (May 31) Killer Instinct 111 – Anetta 56 (Aragon 118) – [2004 7m Sep 21] close-coupled colt: 50/1, last in maiden at Newmarket, very slowly away. *G. C. H. Chung* **–**

SHAVA 4 b.g. Atraf 116 – Anita Marie (IRE) (Anita's Prince 126) [2004 58: p8g⁵ Dec 20] modest performer: stays 7f: acts on polytrack and good to firm going: tried blinkered/in cheekpieces. *Mrs Barbara Waring* **52**

SHAYADI (IRE) 7 b.g. Kahyasi 130 – Shayrdia (IRE) 57 (Storm Bird (CAN) 134) [2004 86: 10.3d⁵ May 6] leggy gelding: handicapper: just fair form only outing on Flat in 2004 (wore cheekpieces and tongue strap): was effective at 1¼m (ridden positively) to 2m: acted on firm and soft going: blinkered last five 6-y-o starts: fairly useful hurdler/chaser: dead. *B. Ellison* **78**

SHAYMEE'S GIRL 3 b.f. Wizard King 122 – Mouchez Le Nez (IRE) 41 (Cyrano de Bergerac 120) [2004 –: f6s⁵ f6g³ f6g³ 5g 6g³ p5.1g p5.1g² f5g* f5m³ p5.1g Nov 29] modest performer: won maiden at Southwell in November: best at 5f: acts on all-weather, **59**

raced only on good ground on turf: races up with pace: sometimes finishes weakly. *Ms Deborah J. Evans*

SHAZANA   3 gr.f. Key of Luck (USA) 126 – Shawanni 105 (Shareef Dancer (USA) 135) [2004 7g⁶ 10g p10d⁶ Jun 26] smallish, good-bodied filly: fourth foal: half-sister to 3 winners, including 4-y-o Shanty Star and 6-y-o Mystic Man: dam, 2-y-o 7f winner, out of Rockfel Stakes winner Negligent: modest maiden: raced freely second outing. *B. W. Hills*   **62**

SHEAPYS LASS   3 b.f. Perugino (USA) 84 – Nilu (IRE) 58 (Ballad Rock 122) [2004 50: f5s f6g f8g f5g Feb 24] good-bodied filly: maiden: well beaten in 2004: tried visored. *A. Crook*   **–**

SHEBAAN   3 b.f. Compton Place 125 – Chairmans Daughter 68 (Unfuwain (USA) 131) [2004 59: 7g 8m 6m 7f 7d 7d p8m Dec 15] leggy, unfurnished filly: no form at 3 yrs: possibly none too genuine. *P. S. McEntee*   **–**

SHEBOYGAN (IRE)   2 ch.f. (Feb 21) Grand Lodge (USA) 125 – White Satin (IRE) 83 (Fairy King (USA)) [2004 6g³ 7m* 7v³ Oct 23] leggy, quite good-topped filly: fifth foal: dam, Irish 2-y-o 7f winner, out of half-sister to Prix de la Foret winner Brocade, herself dam of Barathea and Gossamer: won maiden at Redcar in October by ¾ length from Her Own Kind, making most: creditable 4 lengths third to Bibury Flyer in listed event at Newbury final start, tiring late on: should stay 1m. *J. G. Given*   **90**

SHEER FOCUS (IRE)   6 b.g. Eagle Eyed (USA) 111 – Persian Danser (IRE) 69 (Persian Bold 123) [2004 57: 9.9m 8d p9.5g f8g⁵ f8g p7g Dec 20] leggy, angular gelding: modest at 5 yrs: well held in 2004: usually wears headgear: tried tongue tied: races freely. *I. W. McInnes*   **37**

SHEER TENBY (IRE)   7 b.g. Tenby 125 – Take My Pledge (IRE) (Ahonoora 122) [2004 91: 6m⁵ 5m⁴ 6f 6.3f 7m Aug 1] strong, quite attractive gelding: useful handicapper: better than ever when winning at Cork in May by 3½ lengths from Danecare: creditable fourth to Osterhase in listed race at Naas: below form last 3 starts, including in Wokingham at Royal Ascot: effective at 6f, won at 1¼m earlier in career: acts on fibresand, firm and soft ground: blinkered/tongue tied. *Paul A. Roche, Ireland*   **102**

SHEKAN STAR   2 b.f. (Feb 23) Sri Pekan (USA) 117 – Celestial Welcome 96 (Most Welcome 131) [2004 6g 6d 6s 6d Oct 15] 22,000Y: smallish, close-coupled filly: first foal: dam, 7f to 1½m winner, half-sister to smart middle-distance performer Snowstorm: modest maiden: seemingly best effort final start: should stay 1m. *K. G. Reveley*   **51 ?**

SHERBOURNE   2 b.f. (Mar 17) Tipsy Creek (USA) 115 – Margarets First (Puissance 110) [2004 5v 5.1m 5.2m⁶ 7m 7d 7m 8g p8.6g Oct 9] 1,200Y: lengthy filly: second foal: dam ran twice: poor maiden: stays 7f. *M. G. Quinlan*   **41**

SHERIFF'S DEPUTY   4 b.g. Atraf 116 – Forest Fantasy 61 (Rambo Dancer (CAN) 107) [2004 81: 8.1m 8.2s 8g³ 10.5s 8m p7.1g p9.5g p9.5g p8.6g⁵ Dec 27] strong gelding: fair performer: stays 9.4f: acts on all-weather, firm and good to soft going: tried tongue tied. *J. W. Unett*   **71**

SHERWOOD FOREST   4 ch.g. Fleetwood (IRE) 107 – Jay Gee Ell 78 (Vaigly Great 127) [2004 56: 8d 9m³ 10.9g⁶ 11.1g 10g⁵ 16f² 14g⁶ 11.9g 11.9g Sep 2] strong gelding: poor handicapper: stayed 2m: acted on firm ground: wore headgear: held up: none too consistent: dead. *Miss L. A. Perratt*   **49**

SHERZABAD (IRE)   7 b. or br.g. Doyoun 124 – Sheriya (USA) (Green Dancer (USA) 132) [2004 52: 11.8m May 31] sturdy, lengthy gelding: handicapper: well held only 7-y-o start: tried tongue tied. *Miss I. E. Craig*   **–**

SHE'S A DIAMOND   7 b.m. Mystiko (USA) 124 – Fairy Kingdom (Prince Sabo 123) [2004 –: f8g Jan 20] little sign of ability. *T. T. Clement*   **–**

SHE'S A FOX   3 b.f. Wizard King 122 – Foxie Lady 77 (Wolfhound (USA) 126) [2004 –: 8s 8.2m Sep 28] neat filly: little form: refused to enter stall on intended reappearance. *A. W. Carroll*   **–**

SHESHALAN (IRE)   3 ch.c. Indian Ridge 123 – Sheshara (IRE) 107 (Kahyasi 130) [2004 10v⁴ Oct 23] strong, lengthy colt: second living foal: half-brother to French 11.5f/ 1½m winner Sheshawa (by Doyoun): dam, French 1½m/15f winner, half-sister to Prix de Diane winner Shemaka: 9/2, coltish and green, 22 lengths fourth to Jolizero in maiden at Newbury: sold 25,000 gns later in month. *Sir Michael Stoute*   **–**

SHE'S MY DREAM (IRE)   2 ch.f. (Feb 5) General Monash (USA) 107 – She's My Love 80 (Most Welcome 131) [2004 p5g 5.2m p5g 6.1g May 31] €1,800Y: second living   **35**

foal: dam, 2-y-o 6f winner, sister to useful performer up to 1½m Naked Welcome: poor maiden: should stay 6f. *J. S. Moore*

SHE'S MY OUTSIDER   2 b.f. (Feb 21) Docksider (USA) 124 – Solar Flare (IRE)   **79**
(Danehill (USA) 126) [2004 7g 7m³ 8.1m* 7s Oct 16] useful-looking filly: first foal: plan tailed off only start (injured in process): fair performer: won maiden at Chepstow in September: very stiff task final start: stays 1m: acts on good to firm going: free-going sort. *I. A. Wood*

SHE'S OUR LASS (IRE)   3 b.f. Orpen (USA) 116 – Sharadja (IRE) (Doyoun 124)   **84**
[2004 57: p7g 7g 7.1s* 8.2g³ 7.2f* 7.2g* 8m* 8s* 8s² 8d p10g p8g Nov 20] sturdy filly: fairly useful performer: won handicap at Warwick in April, minor events at Ayr in May and June, and handicaps at Leicester in July and Thirsk (beat Cottingham by 1½ lengths) in August: stays 1m: acts on fibresand, firm and soft going: tough and reliable. *D. Carroll*

SHIBUMI   3 ch.f. Cigar 68 – Hurricane Rose (Windjammer (USA)) [2004 –p: 5m⁵ 6g⁵   **56**
7m⁴ 7.9f⁴ Jul 29] tall, rather unfurnished filly: modest maiden: should prove best around 7f: acts on firm going. *H. Morrison*

SHIELALIGH   3 ch.f. Aragon 118 – Sheesha (USA) (Shadeed (USA) 135) [2004 83:   **68 §**
p5g 6d 5.1f³ 6.1g 6m⁶ 5s⁶ 5d⁵ 5.7g⁵ p6g⁶ f7s³ p7.1g⁶ f6g p6g³ Dec 17] leggy, close-coupled filly: just fair performer at 3 yrs: stays 6f: acts on good to firm and good to soft ground, probably on polytrack: wore cheekpieces/visor last 9 starts: tried tongue tied: often slowly away: ungenuine. *Miss Gay Kelleway*

SHIFTY   5 b.g. Night Shift (USA) – Crodelle (IRE) (Formidable (USA) 125) [2004 66:   **56**
f12g⁵ p10g 8v 8v 7.1g⁴ 7.1d 8v⁵ 7.9f² f7g⁴ 7.5g⁴ 6.9g 8g 8f p9.5g² p12m Dec 8] well-made gelding: has a round action: modest performer: stays 1m: acts on all-weather and any turf going: sometimes blinkered/visored: has given trouble in preliminaries: sometimes slowly away: difficult ride. *D. Carroll*

SHIFTY NIGHT (IRE)   3 b.f. Night Shift (USA) – Bean Island (USA) (Afleet (CAN))   **46**
[2004 –: 6m 5m f6g⁴ f6g* 6m 7m⁶ 6g 7m f6f⁴ 6d f7g⁴ p6g⁶ p6g⁶ Dec 20] workmanlike   **a54**
filly: modest on all-weather, poor on turf: won handicap at Southwell in July: stays 7f: acts on all-weather and good to firm going: tried in cheekpieces. *Mrs C. A. Dunnett*

SHINGLE STREET (IRE)   2 b.g. (Feb 1) Bahhare (USA) 122 – Sandystones 60   **75**
(Selkirk (USA) 129) [2004 6m 6m 7.9g 8s² 7s⁵ Oct 21] €7,000F, €21,000Y: leggy gelding: third foal: half-brother to fairly useful 2001 2-y-o 5f winner Sighting (by Eagle Eyed), later successful abroad, and 4-y-o Tatweer: dam, maiden, best effort at 9f: fair maiden: form only when second at Brighton: stays 1m: acts on soft ground: sometimes looks none too genuine. *M. H. Tompkins*

SHINKO FEMME (IRE)   3 b.f. Shinko Forest (IRE) – Kilshanny 70 (Groom Dancer   **58**
(USA) 128) [2004 60: 7s 5.9f 6m 8g⁵ 7.1m* 7m 7m 7m* 7.5s³ 7g Sep 14] tall filly: modest performer: won handicap at Musselburgh in June and seller at Leicester in August: stays 7.5f: acts on firm and soft ground: often slowly away, virtually refused to race second outing: none too reliable. *N. Tinkler*

SHINY THING (USA)   2 br.f. (Mar 14) Lear Fan (USA) 130 – Juliet's Jewel (USA)   **70**
(Houston (USA)) [2004 7g⁵ 8g Oct 10] $12,000F, 30,000Y: big filly: second foal: dam unraced: much better effort in maidens when fifth at Kempton: raced freely at Bath: should stay 1m. *A. King*

SHIRLEY NOT   8 gr.g. Paris House 123 – Hollia 72 (Touch Boy 109) [2004 –: 5g 7s   **–**
Apr 20] big, lengthy gelding: of little account nowadays: often blinkered/visored earlier in career. *D. Nicholls*

SHIRLEY OAKS (IRE)   6 b.m. Sri Pekan (USA) 117 – Duly Elected (Persian Bold   **56**
123) [2004 40: p7g p6g⁵ p7g p6g² p7g³ p6g* 7v⁶ f7m³ 7m* 7g² 8.1f 7m 7g⁶ 7.6f p6g⁶ Nov 30] small, sparely-made mare: modest performer: won banded race at Lingfield in April and amateur claimer at Salisbury in June: stays easy 1m: acts on dirt, polytrack, good to firm and good to soft going: has been blinkered/visored/tongue tied. *Miss Z. C. Davison*

SHIROCCO (GER)   3 b.c. Monsun (GER) 124 – So Sedulous (USA) 102 (The   **125**
Minstrel (CAN) 135) [2004 11s² 11g* 11d³ 12v* 12d³ 12d* Oct 17]

How long will it be before a German horse wins the Derby? Although the image of racing in Germany is changing a little, with stallions that are an influence for speed becoming more fashionable, middle-distance horses nearly always dominate the three-year-old ranks. The racing programme very much reflects the breeding for stamina—at present all seven Group 1 races are run at between a mile and a quarter and a mile and a half—and the pick of the three-year-olds each season are little inferior to some of those capable of making an impact at Epsom. Since 1993 when the Deutsches Derby was opened up fully to horses bred elsewhere, six winners of the race have shown form on the day at Hamburg good enough to have reached a place at Epsom in the same year. In winning by four lengths in 2004, Shirocco put up just about the best performance by any of those six winners, one which suggests he would have been as stiff an opponent for North Light on Derby Day as any in the field at Epsom. Though denied a chance against the best in the Arc, Shirocco confirmed himself among the best three-year-olds in Europe with a second Group 1 victory in the autumn.

Shirocco was still among the possibles for Epsom in the spring, but, along with the two other German-trained Derby entries, Birkspiel and Gentle Tiger, was withdrawn in late-April. After making his debut in an eleven-furlong maiden at Krefeld only in March, finishing second, Shirocco ran out a seven-length winner of a listed event at Mulheim in May. As a result, he started at 5/2-on for the Oppenheim-Union-Rennen at Cologne in June, a traditional stepping stone to the Deutsches Derby, only to finish third to Malinas, beaten three and a half lengths. Shirocco was only third favourite at 5/1 behind his stable-companion Fight Club and Malinas in a field of eighteen for the BMW Deutsches Derby at Hamburg on the first Sunday in July, but he proved a different proposition this time. In heavy ground churned up by regular racing at the course, Shirocco showed much improved form, soon to the fore and going easily as he took it up off the turn, winning virtually unchallenged by four lengths from Malinas with Omikron, who was also ahead of him at Cologne, six lengths further away. Shirocco's success was a first in the race for leading rider Andreas Suborics, and a fifth in seven years for his trainer Andreas Schutz since taking over the licence from his father Bruno, responsible for four German Derby winners of his own.

Shirocco did all his racing in his first season on good ground or softer. He ran well after Hamburg in two all-aged races under less testing conditions than he had encountered in the Derby. After a break of two months, he finished a close third in Germany's most valuable race, the Grosser Preis von Baden at Baden-Baden in September, going down by three quarters of a length and a neck to Warrsan and another home-trained three-year-old Egerton (who'd been well held at Hamburg), beaten when the winner edged across him close home. Shirocco's next outing was due to be in the Arc, but, after being backed down to around 10/1 with British bookmakers, he was withdrawn after the final declarations were made due to the firmish ground. Shirocco was also considered for the Canadian International, but, in the end, he had his final run of the year in Italy, starting fractionally odds-on for the Group 1 Gran Premio del Jockey Club Italiano at Milan. A field of nine also included Derby fourth Percussionist, but Shirocco's biggest danger proved to be the unbeaten home-trained three-year-old Electrocutionist. Again ridden prominently, Shirocco was asked to stretch the field from over two furlongs out and, though Electrocutionist quickened to challenge as they came clear, Shirocco held on under pressure by a short head, with the subsequently-demoted Imperial Dancer five lengths back in third, and Prix Vermeille winner Sweet Stream fourth. Percussionist was sixth and two other British challengers, Dubai Success and Bandari, finished eighth and ninth.

Although his sire and dam's sire were mile-and-a-half winners, Shirocco isn't especially stoutly bred by German standards. His dam So Sedulous, a useful performer, successful in a maiden at seven furlongs and a minor event at a mile as a

BMW Deutsches Derby, Hamburg—Shirocco wins decisively from Malinas in testing conditions

Gran Premio del Jockey Club Italiano, Milan—Shirocco (left) inflicts a first defeat on Electrocutionist; Imperial Dancer, Sweet Stream (rail) and the grey Fair Mix are next

three-year-old in Britain for Geoff Wragg, was out of another useful filly Sedulous, a winner at five furlongs to a mile at two in Ireland, later successful in the States. Among So Sedulous' previous foals, Shirocco's brother Storm Trooper is a smart performer at up to a mile and a half, while Subiaco, another brother, showed similar ability at up to two miles. Storm Trooper and Subiaco were both placed in the Deutsches Derby, as was the sire Monsun, who has made a big impact at stud in Germany. His first crop included Samum, a five-length winner of the Deutsches Derby in 2000, and he has also sired Salve Regina and Amarette, winners of the Preis der Diana, the German Oaks, the latter unbeaten in 2004. Monsun stands at the historic Gestut Schlenderhan near Cologne, where his fee for 2005 will be double that of 2004 at €40,000. The Schlenderhan is run by Shirocco's owners, the Von Ullman family, whose yellow and blue colours, best remembered in Britain for the July Cup winner Owington, have been carried by seventeen winners of the Deutsches Derby in all, the last before Shirocco being Stuyvesant back in 1976.

		Konigsstuhl	Dschingis Khan
	Monsun (GER)	(br 1976)	Konigskronung
	(br 1990)	Mosella	Surumu
Shirocco (GER)		(b 1985)	Monasia
(b.c. 2001)		The Minstrel	Northern Dancer
	So Sedulous (USA)	(ch 1974)	Fleur
	(b 1991)	Sedulous	Tap On Wood
		(b 1986)	Pendulina

Shirocco has already shown himself to be a shade better as a racehorse than his sire Monsun, who raced until five, showing very smart form at around a mile and a half, including when runner-up in the Prix du Conseil de Paris at Longchamp on his final start at four, when he was also sixth in the Coronation Cup at Epsom. Opportunities to see Shirocco outside Germany may well depend on the ground, but he shouldn't be underestimated in any company. A genuine sort, still lightly raced, there may yet be a bit more improvement in him. *A. Schutz, Germany*

936

SHISH (IRE)   2 b.f. (Mar 10) Rossini (USA) 118 – Kebabs (IRE) 86 (Catrail (USA)   **43**
123) [2004 f5m⁶ f6g⁶ p5g⁴ 5m³ 6m Jun 14] €3,500Y: leggy filly: first foal: dam Irish
2-y-o 6f winner: poor maiden: should stay 6f. *J. A. Osborne*

SHIVAREE   2 ch.f. (Apr 13) Rahy (USA) 115 – Shmoose (IRE) 106 (Caerleon (USA)   **88**
132) [2004 6g³ 6g* 6m⁴ 7.1m 6s³ 8m 7s Oct 16] lengthy filly: third foal: half-sister to 5f
(in UAE)/6f (at 2 yrs) winner Semigold (by Seeking The Gold): dam, 2-y-o 6f winner,
half-sister to smart French miler Firth of Lorne out of smart sprinter/1000 Guineas second Kerrera: fairly useful performer: won maiden at Hamilton in June: good efforts
in Cherry Hinton Stakes at Newmarket (fourth to Jewel In The Sand) and listed race at
Sandown next 2 starts: probably stays 7f: acts on good to firm ground: sold 80,000 gns.
M. R. Channon

SHOHRAH (IRE)   2 ch.f. (Feb 1) Giant's Causeway (USA) 132 – Taqreem (IRE) 73   **103 p**
(Nashwan (USA) 135) [2004 6m* 8f⁵ Sep 25] strong, lengthy filly: sixth foal: half-sister
to useful 7f winner (stayed 1¼m) Ma-Arif (by Alzao) and 3-y-o Haadef: dam, middle-
distance maiden, half-sister to Ibn Bey and Roseate Tern: won maiden at Ascot in July:
still green, useful form when 3¾ lengths fifth to Playful Act in Fillies' Mile at same track,
taking good hold and bumped 2f out: missed Rockfel Stakes at Newmarket in October
due to soft going: will probably stay 1¼m: no hind shoes both starts (also lost one of front
shoes during debut): should progress. *M. P. Tregoning*

SHOLAY (IRE)   5 b.g. Bluebird (USA) 125 – Splicing 82 (Sharpo 132) [2004 65:   **–**
p13g p8g p12g 10m 12.1g⁴ 11g Aug 14] lightly-made gelding: fair performer in 2003:
showed little in 2004: tried visored/blinkered. *P. Mitchell*

SHOLTO   6 b.g. Tragic Role (USA) – Rose Mill (Puissance 110) [2004 71: 5v 5f² 5f   **68**
p6d f5m p5.1g⁵ p5.1g⁶ Dec 31] close-coupled gelding: fair on turf, modest on all-   **a61**
weather: best at 5f: acts on polytrack, firm and soft going: blinkered: tried tongue tied:
often hangs. *J. O'Reilly*

SHONGWENI (IRE)   3 gr.g. Desert King (IRE) 129 – Spend A Rubble (USA)   **73**
(Spend A Buck (USA)) [2004 11.5g⁴ p12d³ 11.6f³ 14m 16.1d⁵ Aug 4] 34,000Y: fourth
foal: half-brother to Italian 1m (including at 2 yrs) to 11f winner by Pennekamp: dam,
French 1¼m winner, half-sister to very smart French 5f/6f winner Kistena: fair maiden:
stays 1½m: acts on polytrack and firm going: blinkered (raced freely) penultimate start:
stays 1½m: acts on firm going and polytrack: joined Venetia Williams. *P. J. McBride*

SHOOTING LODGE (IRE)   3 b.f. Grand Lodge (USA) 125 – Sidama (FR) (Top   **63**
Ville 129) [2004 –p: 10d⁵ Jun 1] rangy filly: modest form when fifth in maiden at Sandown on only second outing: would have been suited by 1½m: stud. *Sir Michael Stoute*

SHORTBREAD   2 ch.c. (Apr 24) Selkirk (USA) 129 – Breadcrumb 111 (Final Straw   **63 p**
127) [2004 7g 8v Oct 23] 15,000Y: plain colt: half-brother to numerous winners, including German sprinter Barrow Creek (by Cadeaux Genereux) and 7f winner Last Resort (by
Lahib), both smart, and to dam of smart 7f/1m performer Trans Island (by Selkirk): dam
6f/7f winner, never dangerous, in maidens at Leicester and Newbury: not
sure to stay beyond 1m: will probably do better. *J. L. Dunlop*

SHORT CHANGE (IRE)   5 b.g. Revoque (IRE) 122 – Maafi Esm (Polish Precedent   **53**
(USA) 131) [2004 63: 11.9m 11.7s⁴ 10f⁵ 10.9m* Jun 14] big, lengthy gelding: modest
handicapper: won apprentice event at Warwick in June: stays 1½m: acts on firm and good
to soft ground: tried blinkered/in cheekpieces: often races prominently. *A. W. Carroll*

SHORT CHORUS   3 ch.f. Inchinor 119 – Strawberry Song 87 (Final Straw 127)   **62**
[2004 52: 5.1g 5s⁴ f6g 5d* 5m⁴ 5g² 5d⁴ 5m 5d³ Oct 11] small filly: modest handicapper: won at Hamilton in May: acts on good to firm and good to soft
going: wore cheekpieces after reappearance. *J. Balding*

SHOSOLOSA (IRE)   2 br.f. (Feb 17) Dansili 127 – Hajat 64 (Mujtahid (USA) 118)   **71**
[2004 6m 6g² 6.1s² 5.7m³ 6.5g 7g⁵ 7s Nov 6] close-coupled filly: third foal: half-sister to
2001 2-y-o 7f winner Desert Royal (by Ali-Royal): dam 5f winner: fair maiden: barely
stays 7f: acts on soft and good to firm ground. *B. J. Meehan*

SHOTLEY DANCER   5 ch.m. Danehill Dancer (IRE) 117 – Hayhurst (Sandhurst   **55**
Prince 128) [2004 53: f8g⁴ f7s 8.5d f7d⁴ 8g³ f8m⁵ 12g³ 12.1m* 12.3g⁴ 16.2d² 9.9s*
15.8m Sep 18] leggy mare: fluent mover: modest handicapper: won at Beverley in
July and August: effective at 1¼m to 2m: acts on firm and soft ground: tried blinkered.
N. Bycroft

Michael Page International Silver Trophy Stakes, Ascot—the improved Shot To Fame (No.9) holds the rallying Gateman, with Hurricane Alan (right) and Pentecost (No.8) next

SHOT TO FAME (USA) 5 b.g. Quest For Fame 127 – Exocet (USA) (Deposit **114** Ticket (USA)) [2004 104: 8v⁵ 8g 8v* 8.2g* 8.3m² 8g* 8d⁵ 8.1g⁵ 8g Oct 1] angular, lightly-made gelding: smart performer: better than ever in 2004, winning handicap at Kempton (by 11 lengths) in May, minor event at Nottingham in June and Michael Page International Silver Trophy at Ascot (beat Gateman a head) in July: good fifth to Norse Dancer in Sovereign Stakes at Salisbury, then ran poorly last 2 starts: best at 1m/9f: acts on heavy and good to firm going: usually races prominently. *P. W. Harris*

SHOWDANCE (USA) 2 b.c. (Feb 19) Kingmambo (USA) 125 – Island Jamboree **97 p** (USA) (Explodent (USA)) [2004 7m² 6f* Jun 12] $475,000Y: eighth foal: half-brother to 3 winners, notably high-class winner up to 1¼m in Britain and USA Fiji (by Rainbow Quest) and smart 1½m winner Capri (by Generous): dam won 10 times in USA from 6f to 8.5f, also second in 9f Grade 1 event: confirmed promise when winning 4-runner maiden at Cork by 4½ lengths from Aragorn, making all: should stay at least 1m: likely to do fair bit better if all is well. *A. P. O'Brien, Ireland*

SHOW ME HEAVEN 7 b.m. Rock City 120 – Tufty Lady 91 (Riboboy (USA) 124) **–** [2004 p10g Jan 7] no sign of ability in 3 appearances, off 4½ years prior to only 7-y-o start. *T. T. Clement*

SHOW NO FEAR 3 b.c. Groom Dancer (USA) 128 – La Piaf (FR) (Fabulous Dancer **74** (USA) 124) [2004 69: 9g* 9v 8m 10m⁶ May 24] good-topped colt: fair handicapper: won at Kempton in April: found little when below form after: stays 1¼m: acts on good to firm going: visored (ran to form) once at 2 yrs: joined G. M. Moore, won juvenile hurdle in September. *H. R. A. Cecil*

SHOWTIME ANNIE 3 b.f. Wizard King 122 – Rebel County (IRE) 97 (Maelstrom **61** Lake 118) [2004 63: f8.5s⁶ f6g* 6.1g f7g⁴ 8m* 7g⁵ 7.1g 7m 8d² 8m 7.2s f7g f8g⁵ Dec 16] good-bodied filly: modest performer: won maiden at Wolverhampton in March and minor event at Ayr in May: stays 1m: acts on fibresand, good to firm and good to soft going. *A. Bailey*

SHOWTIME FAYE 2 b.f. (Jan 22) Overbury (IRE) 116 – Rebel County (IRE) 97 **46** (Maelstrom Lake 118) [2004 7m 7.2s p7.1g f7g³ p8.6g Dec 17] 1,800Y: second foal: half-sister to 3-y-o Showtime Annie: dam 6f (at 2 yrs) to 1¼m winner: poor maiden: should stay 1m: acts on fibresand: looks none too easy ride. *A. Bailey*

SHREDDED (USA) 4 b.g. Diesis 133 – Shiitake (USA) (Green Dancer (USA) 132) **85** [2004 73+: 10s 10g² 14g* 11.6m 13.3d⁶ 13.1s³ 12s Nov 6] fairly useful handicapper: won at Sandown in June: below form subsequently, finding little last 2 starts: stays 1¾m: acts on good to soft ground: carried head awkwardly final 3-y-o start: tongue tied last 3 outings: gelded after final start. *J. H. M. Gosden*

SHRINE MOUNTAIN (USA) 2 b.c. (Mar 15) Distorted Humor (USA) 117 – Fancy **85** Ruler (USA) (Half A Year (USA) 130) [2004 6g 7m² 7d 8m Sep 9] good-topped colt: third foal: half-brother to smart 7f (at 2 yrs) and 10.3f winner Sohaib (by Kingmambo): dam, ran twice in USA, out of half-sister to Breeders' Cup Juvenile winner Success Express: fairly useful maiden: ½-length second of 4 to Wilko in minor event at Yarmouth:

938

seemed to run creditably in listed race at York next time also: stays 7f: free-going sort. *C. E. Brittain*

SHRINK 3 b.f. Mind Games 121 – Miss Mercy (IRE) 62 (Law Society (USA) 130) **67** [2004 71: p5g² p5g* 6d⁴ 6f⁴ 6m 5.1g 6g³ Aug 11] rather leggy filly: fair performer: won maiden at Lingfield in April: will prove best at 5f/6f: acts on polytrack, firm and good to soft ground: poor effort in blinkers fifth start, ran creditably in tongue strap final one: sometimes slowly away/races freely: sold 5,000 gns. *M. L. W. Bell*

SHUCHBAA 2 b.f. (Mar 21) Zaha (CAN) 106 – Little Miss Rocker 65 (Rock Hopper **38** 124) [2004 6m³ 6m 7.5d 6d Aug 30] 8,000Y: leggy filly: second foal: dam 1½m winner: poor maiden: form only on debut: very slowly away first 2 outings. *K. A. Ryan*

SHUHEB 3 ch.f. Nashwan (USA) 135 – Shimna 62 (Mr Prospector (USA)) [2004 9m⁵ **93 ?** 10m⁴ Jun 10] smallish, close-coupled filly: first living foal: dam, ran once in Ireland, half-sister to St Leger winner Shantou out of smart daughter of Oh So Sharp: better effort (though possibly bit flattered) when 3½ lengths fourth to Incheni in listed race at Newbury: stays 1¼m. *C. E. Brittain*

SHUJUNE AL HAWAA (IRE) 2 ch.f. (Feb 16) Grand Lodge (USA) 125 – Bank On **63** Her (USA) 76 (Rahy (USA) 115) [2004 5g⁵ 6g⁶ 7.2m³ 7f 7s 7m 8g⁶ 8s Oct 12] 35,000Y: smallish, lengthy filly: second foal: half-sister to a 5f to 7f winner in Hong Kong by Marju: dam, 7f winner from 3 starts, half-sister to smart 7f performer Weldnaas: modest maiden: stays 1m: acts on good to firm ground: visored (ran creditably on first occasion only) last 2 starts: none too reliable. *M. R. Channon*

SHUSH 6 b.g. Shambo 113 – Abuzz 101 (Absalom 128) [2004 70: 14.1g 11.9s Oct 15] **–** quite attractive gelding: fair handicapper at 5 yrs: well beaten in 2004: tried blinkered. *C. E. Brittain*

SHYSHIYRA (IRE) 3 b.f. Kahyasi 130 – Shiyra (Darshaan 133) [2004 10m Jul 6] **–** leggy filly: half-sister to 3 winners including useful German 2000 2-y-o 6f/7f winner Tagshira and fairly useful 2001 2-y-o 5f winner Triple Play (both by Tagula): dam Irish 1m/1¼m winner: 50/1 and backward, well beaten in maiden at Pontefract. *K. A. Ryan*

SIAN THOMAS 3 ch.f. Magic Ring (IRE) 115 – Midnight Break 78 (Night Shift **68** (USA)) [2004 8.5m³ 8.2d 10.2g⁵ p12g p10g³ Nov 16] sturdy filly: fourth foal: half-sister to 4-y-o Mac and fairly useful 2m winner Bobby Kennard (by Bobinski): dam 5f/6f winner: fair maiden: stays 1¼m: acts on polytrack and good to firm going. *M. P. Tregoning*

SIDESHOW 2 ch.f. (Jan 2) In The Wings 128 – Sheer Harmony (USA) 78 (Woodman **55** (USA) 126) [2004 8.2g 8.1s⁴ Sep 25] rather leggy filly: second foal: dam, 1m winner, out of US Grade 3 8.5f winner Memories of Pam: modest form in maidens at Nottingham and Haydock (visored, looked none too keen): sold 7,000 gns, sent to Kazakhstan. *D. R. Loder*

SIEGFRIEDS NIGHT (IRE) 3 ch.g. Night Shift (USA) – Shelbiana (USA) **69** (Chieftain) [2004 68§: f6g* f5g⁴ f6s³ f11g² f12g³ 10.3g³ 12g³ 11.6s⁶ 14.6g² 12.3g* 11.8g³ 14.1f³ 12.3m⁵ f12g⁵ 12.3g³ 12m 12f 14.1m² 13.8g⁵ 16.1m Sep 29] quite good-topped gelding: fair handicapper: won at Southwell in January and Ripon in May: mostly creditable efforts otherwise in 2004: stays 14.6f: acts on fibresand and firm ground: sometimes looks wayward. *M. C. Chapman*

SIENA GOLD 2 br. or b.f. (Feb 21) Key of Luck (USA) 126 – Corn Futures 78 **97** (Nomination 125) [2004 5g* 5.2g* 5f 5.2m³ 5g 5v⁴ 5.5m 6s³ 6s⁴ Nov 16] 12,000Y: sturdy filly: closely related to 6f (at 2 yrs)/7f winner Trading Aces (by Be My Chief) and half-sister to several winners, including useful 1998 2-y-o 6f winner Crazee Mental (by Magic Ring): dam 2-y-o 6f winner: useful performer: made all at Newmarket in April, minor event at Newbury in May and Weatherbys Super Sprint at Newbury (beat Don't Tell Mum ¾ length) in July: creditable efforts in frame in listed races at Deauville, Newmarket (under a length third to Bahia Breeze) and Saint-Cloud: stays 6f: acts on heavy and good to firm going: consistent: sold 46,000 gns. *B. J. Meehan*

SIENA STAR (IRE) 6 b.g. Brief Truce (USA) 126 – Gooseberry Pie 63 (Green **81** Desert (USA) 127) [2004 88: p10g² 10s Nov 23] close-coupled gelding: has a quick action: fairly useful performer: creditable second in handicap at Lingfield only 6-y-o start: stays easy 1½m: acts on polytrack, firm and soft going: held up: consistent. *P. F. I. Cole*

SIENNA SUNSET (IRE) 5 ch.m. Spectrum (IRE) 126 – Wasabi (IRE) (Polar Falcon **66** (USA) 126) [2004 68: 8.1d 10s⁶ 9.7f⁶ 10.2m² 10f⁴ 10s* 9.9s³ 10m 10d 9s p9.5d³ **a60** p9.5g² p9.5g p9.5g⁶ Dec 15] tall mare: fair handicapper: left Mrs H. Dalton after second start: won at Ripon in August: stays 1¼m: acts on polytrack, firm and soft going. *W. M. Brisbourne*

*Dubai Duty Free Arc Trial, Newbury—Sights On Gold shows himself as good as ever;
Imperial Dancer (left), Compton Bolter and Day Flight give chase*

SIERA SPIRIT (IRE) 3 b.f. Desert Sun 120 – Jay And-A (IRE) 98 (Elbio 125) [2004 **60**
p6g⁴ p6g³ p7g 6s² 7.1s³ Apr 7] 8,500Y: first foal: dam Irish 5f/6f winner: modest maiden:
barely stays 7f: best form on soft going. *M. G. Quinlan*

SIERRA 3 ch.f. Dr Fong (USA) 128 – Warning Belle (Warning 136) [2004 –: 10m⁵ **65**
10g⁶ 8g⁶ 7.9g⁶ 10.2m Sep 9] workmanlike filly: fair maiden: stays 1¼m: acts on good to
firm ground: looked none too keen third start. *C. E. Brittain*

SIERRA VISTA 4 ch.f. Atraf 116 – Park Vista (Taufan (USA) 119) [2004 91: 5g 5g³ **86**
5d 5s 6g⁵ 6d* 6g⁶ 7g 6s 6g⁵ 6d 5s Oct 16] leggy filly: fairly useful performer: won
handicap at Newcastle in June: effective at 5f/6f: acts on firm and good to soft going: tried
in cheekpieces: often races up with pace. *D. W. Barker*

SIGHTS ON GOLD (IRE) 5 ch.h. Indian Ridge 123 – Summer Trysting (USA) 83 **119**
(Alleged (USA) 138) [2004 119: 10.1g* 11m* 9.8m 9s² 12m² Dec 12] strong, angular
horse: smart performer: suffered injury final 4-y-o start: won minor event at Epsom in
August and Dubai Duty Free Arc Trial at Newbury (beat Imperial Dancer by length) in
September: runner-up last 2 starts, to Autumn Glory in Darley Stakes at Newmarket
(beaten 2 lengths) and to Phoenix Reach in Hong Kong Vase at Sha Tin (good effort,
beaten ½ length): effective at 9f to 1½m: acts on soft and good to firm going: usually
tongue tied, reportedly choked without in Prix Dollar third appearance: has been bandaged in front: reliable. *Saeed bin Suroor*

SIGN OF LUCK (IRE) 2 ch.f. (Apr 22) Daylami (IRE) 138 – Ascot Cyclone (USA) **71**
93 (Rahy (USA) 115) [2004 7g p7g⁴ Oct 28] smallish filly: third foal: half-sister to useful
2002 2-y-o 6f winner Fancy Lady (by Cadeaux Genereux) and 3-y-o Asia Winds: dam,
5.7f (at 2 yrs) and 7f winner, half-sister to smart performer at up to 1¼m Magellan out
of 1000 Guineas runner-up Dabaweyaa: better effort in maidens when close fourth at
Lingfield: will stay at least 1m. *C. E. Brittain*

SIGN OF PROMISE 2 b.f. (Apr 15) Groom Dancer (USA) 128 – Happy Omen **–**
(Warning 136) [2004 8d Oct 16] 4,000Y: first foal: dam once-raced half-sister to Middle
Park winner First Trump: 25/1, tailed off in maiden at Yarmouth. *S. C. Williams*

SIGNORA PANETTIERA (FR) 3 ch.f. Lord of Men 116 – Karaferya (USA) 101 **56 d**
(Green Dancer (USA) 132) [2004 54: 12.1d⁶ 12v p12g⁶ 11.5f 11.7f 12s 13.8m⁴ 14.1s⁶
Oct 27] leggy filly: modest maiden: well below form after reappearance: stays 1½m: acts
on good to soft going: ungenuine. *M. R. Channon*

SIGNOR PANETTIERE 3 b.c. Night Shift (USA) – Christmas Kiss 82 (Taufan **73 §**
(USA) 119) [2004 76§: 6g 5.7f² 5m⁶ 5f 5.1m² a5g a6g Nov 28] well-made colt: reportedly
had wind operation: fair performer: below form after second start and left R. Hannon after
fifth outing: headstrong, and will prove best at 5f/easy 6f: acts on firm going: hard ride:
untrustworthy. *R. J. Smith, Spain*

SIGN WRITER (USA) 2 b.c. (Mar 14) Quiet American (USA) – Mata Cara 98 **76**
(Storm Bird (CAN) 134) [2004 6m⁶ 6g² p5d⁴ 6d³ 8.3g Oct 11] tall, strong colt: sixth
living foal: half-brother to 2 winners, including fairly useful 1½m winner Liefling (by
Alleged): dam, 7f winner, out of Musidora winner Fatah Flare: fair maiden: second at
Newmarket: needs to settle to stay beyond 6f: best effort on good going: edgy sort: joined
D. Watson in UAE. *J. Noseda*

SILBER MOND 2 gr.g. (Feb 15) Monsun (GER) 124 – Salinova (FR) (Linamix (FR) **54 p**
127) [2004 8s 10.1d Nov 5] third living foal: half-brother to smart 1½m to 2m winner
Shabernak (by Akarad) and 3-y-o Silver Sash: dam unraced sister to useful French 1½m
winner Six Zero: green, modest form in maidens at Yarmouth, not knocked about
on second occasion (unruly beforehand): will stay at least 1½m: likely to do better.
M. L. W. Bell

SILCA'S GIFT 3 b.f. Cadeaux Genereux 131 – Odette 72 (Pursuit of Love 124) [2004 **107**
104: 7g⁸ 8m 6.1d⁵ 7f 6d Jul 9] rangy filly: useful performer: 25/1, won Shadwell Stud
Nell Gwyn Stakes at Newmarket (beat Incheni by 3 lengths) in April: failed to stay when
respectable eighth to Attraction in 1000 Guineas at Newmarket next time: below form
after: stays 7f: acts on firm going, won on soft on debut: sold 180,000 gns in November.
M. R. Channon

SILENCE IS GOLDEN 5 ch.m. Danehill Dancer (IRE) 117 – Silent Girl 75 (Kray- **120**
yan 117) [2004 103: 10d⁴ 9m² 10.5g 10d² 9.9m² Jul 31] rather leggy, angular mare: very
smart performer: won Coral Rosebery Handicap at Kempton in April by ¾ length from
Duraman: runner-up in Dahlia Stakes at Newmarket, listed race at Sandown (beaten a
neck by Crocodile Dundee) and Nassau Stakes at Goodwood (best effort, failed by only
short head to catch Favourable Terms): best form around 1¼m: unraced on heavy going,
acted on any other turf: blinkered once at 2 yrs: seemed best held up, and sometimes
wandered: tough and consistent: in foal to Medicean, and retired. *B. J. Meehan*

SILENCIO (IRE) 3 b.g. Sillery (USA) 122 – Flabbergasted (IRE) (Sadler's Wells **60**
(USA) 132) [2004 10g 10s 10m 10.2g 12.6m⁵ 11.7f Jul 5] modest maiden: should stay
1½m: best efforts on good ground: fairly useful juvenile hurdler, completed 4-timer in
October. *A. King*

SILENT ANGEL 4 b.f. Petong 126 – Valls d'Andorra 75 (Free State 125) [2004 –: **–**
f5g f5s Mar 1] smallish, compact filly: no form: tried in cheekpieces/visor. *Mrs Lucinda
Featherstone*

SILENT HAWK (IRE) 3 b.c. Halling (USA) 133 – Nightbird (IRE) 108 (Night Shift **89**
(USA)) [2004 86p: 8m⁴ 10m* 10.1m 10m⁴ 10d 10.3m 10.1s⁵ Oct 27] smallish, good-
topped colt: fairly useful performer: won maiden at Newmarket in May: off bridle long
way out, ran respectably final start: stays 1¼m: acts on soft and good to firm going:
sometimes visored: tongue tied in 2004. *Saeed bin Suroor*

SILENT JO (JPN) 2 b.c. (Feb 12) Sunday Silence (USA) – Jo Knows (USA) (The **86**
Minstrel (CAN) 135) [2004 7m³ 7m² 7g³ Oct 12] 70,000,000 yen F: close-coupled, quite
good-topped colt: fifth foal: dam, useful 1½m winner in France, later US Grade 3 9f
winner: fairly useful form in maidens at Goodwood and Leicester (carried head awkwardly) and minor event on latter course: should stay 1m. *Saeed bin Suroor*

SILENT SPRING (USA) 2 b.f. (Apr 12) Honour And Glory (USA) 122 – Polar Bird **51 p**
111 (Thatching 131) [2004 6g Jul 8] good-topped filly: half-sister to several winners,
including smart performer up to 1m Ocean Ridge (by Storm Bird), Prix Robert Papin
winner at 2 yrs, and 3-y-o Fokine: dam sprinter: 9/2, eighth to Vondova in maiden at
Newmarket, not knocked about (unimpressive to post): should do better. *B. W. Hills*

SILENT STORM 4 ch.c. Zafonic (USA) 130 – Nanda 83 (Nashwan (USA) 135) [2004 **81**
f6g³ 8.1m³ 8.1g p7d f6f² p6g³ p6g* p6g⁴ p7g⁵ p7.1g² Dec 11] sturdy colt: fairly useful
handicapper: won at Wolverhampton in October, then left H. Cyzer: good second there
final outing: effective at 6f to 1m: acts on all-weather and good to firm ground: visored
(ran poorly) fourth start. *C. A. Cyzer*

Shadwell Stud Nell Gwyn Stakes, Newmarket—
Silca's Gift is supplemented for the 1000 Guineas following this three-length success;
Incheni (noseband) takes second ahead of Roseanna (blaze) and Malvern Light (star on dark cap)

SILENT WITNESS (AUS) 5 b.g. El Moxie (USA) – Jade Tiara (AUS) (Bureaucracy **128** (NZ)) [2004 126: 5m*⸱5m*⸱6m* 5m* 5m* Dec 12] high-class performer: unbeaten in 13 races, all at Sha Tin, including Bauhinia Sprint Trophy, Centenary Sprint Cup, Chairman's Sprint Prize (all Group 1 events between February and April), Group 2 Cathay Pacific International Sprint Trial in November and Cathay Pacific Hong Kong Sprint in December: won last-named race for second year running when beating Cape of Good Hope by easy 1¾ lengths, not at all hard pressed in closing stages: stays 6f: acts on good to firm and good to soft going. *A. S. Cruz, Hong Kong*

SILISTRA 5 gr.g. Sadler's Wells (USA) 132 – Dundel (IRE) 82 (Machiavellian (USA) **44 §** 123) [2004 –§: p12g p10g 12m 7m 9.7m⁵ 8m 7m⁵ Sep 4] big, good-topped gelding: poor maiden: best recent effort at 1¼m: tried blinkered/visored, usually wears cheekpieces: tends to hang: ungenuine. *Mrs L. C. Jewell*

SILK AND SCARLET 2 b.f. (Mar 20) Sadler's Wells (USA) 132 – Danilova (USA) **108** (Lyphard (USA) 132) [2004 7m² 6d* 7m* 7m Sep 5] seventh foal: half-sister to smart 5.5f to 7f winner (including in France) Danger Over (by Warning) and 9-y-o Danakil: dam unraced half-sister to Prix du Jockey Club winner Sanglamore: useful performer: won listed race at Leopardstown (by 1½ lengths from Alexander Icequeen) in July and Robert H. Griffin Debutante Stakes at the Curragh (beat Luas Line comfortably by ½ length) in August: favourite, only seventh in Moyglare Stud Stakes on latter course: likely to be suited by 1¼m/1½m. *A. P. O'Brien, Ireland*

SILK CRAVAT (IRE) 3 ch.g. Dr Devious (IRE) 127 – Dances With Dreams 109 (Be **–** My Chief (USA) 122) [2004 –p: 8m Jun 19] close-coupled, good-bodied gelding: well held in maidens at Newmarket 9 months apart. *G. Wragg*

SILKEN BRIEF (IRE) 5 b.m. Ali-Royal (IRE) 127 – Tiffany's Case (IRE) 65 **78** (Thatching 131) [2004 81: p10g⁶ p8g Feb 24] sturdy mare: fair performer, lightly raced: barely stays 1¼m: acts on polytrack, good to soft and probably good to firm going: tried tongue tied (including last 3 starts): ran as if something amiss last outing. *D. J. Daly*

SILKEN JOHN (IRE) 3 ch.g. Grand Lodge (USA) 125 – Lady Ela (IRE) (Ela-Mana- **44** Mou 132) [2004 10.2m 12s⁵ 14d Oct 10] leggy gelding: form only when fifth in claimer at Salisbury. *J. G. Portman*

SILK FAN (IRE) 3 b.f. Unfuwain (USA) 131 – Alikhlas 81 (Lahib (USA) 129) [2004 **100** 98p: 7.1d* 7m⁶ 8.1d⁴ 7g⁴ 10.1g⁴ 8g⁴ Oct 12] good-bodied filly: has quick action: useful performer: won handicap at Sandown (beat Jazz Scene by ¾ length, idling) in July: creditable effort after only when fourth to Attune in similar event at Salisbury fourth outing: probably stays 1¼m: acts on firm and good to soft going. *P. W. Harris*

SILLOTH SPIRIT 4 b.g. Atraf 116 – Gaelic Air 65 (Ballad Rock 122) [2004 8g 10f⁴ **–** 8.2m Sep 28] well beaten in maidens. *Mrs A. M. Naughton*

SILSONG (USA) 2 ch.f. (Feb 23) Stephen Got Even (USA) 125 – Silver Trainor **62 ?** (USA) (Silver Hawk (USA) 123) [2004 7d⁵ 7.1g 8.2d 10m Sep 28] $25,000F, 9,000Y: leggy filly: seventh foal: half-sister to 3 winners in USA: dam, winner in USA, half-sister to US Grade 1 8.5f winner By Land By Sea: modest maiden: seemingly best effort at 1m. *B. R. Millman*

SILVALINE 5 gr.g. Linamix (FR) 127 – Upend 120 (Main Reef 126) [2004 83: p10g⁶ **89** p10g p10g⁴ 10g⁵ 10.1s⁵ 10g 10m⁶ 8.1d p10d* 10d* 12g 10f³ 10.5g 10d² 10g⁶ p10g Sep **a72** 22] close-coupled gelding: fairly useful handicapper on turf, fair on all-weather: won at Lingfield in June and Sandown in July: good second on latter course in August: best form at 1¼m: acts on polytrack, firm and good to soft going. *T. Keddy*

SILVER BARK 2 b.f. (Jan 26) Royal Applause 124 – Argent du Bois (USA) (Silver **68** Hawk (USA) 123) [2004 6m 6g⁵ 6g6³ p7m* Dec 22] smallish filly: second foal: sister to smart US Grade 1 9f/1¼m winner Ticker Tape, 6.5f/7f winner in Britain at 2 yrs: dam French maiden who stayed 1m: fair performer: won maiden at Lingfield readily by ¾ length from Lady Hen: should stay 1m: acts on polytrack. *E. A. L. Dunlop*

SILVER CACHE (USA) 3 b.f. Silver Hawk (USA) 123 – Nina Ashley (USA) (Crim- **59** inal Type (USA)) [2004 p8g f9.4g p8g⁵ 10m⁴ Apr 25] second foal: half-sister to Peruvian 2000 Guineas winner Maeto (by Spend One Dolar): dam, winner in Peru, half-sister to dam of Breeders' Cup Juvenile runner-up Chief Seattle: modest maiden: stays 1¼m: slowly away first 2 outings: soon off bridle last 3 appearances. *J. Noseda*

SILVER CHIME 4 gr.f. Robellino (USA) 127 – Silver Charm (Dashing Blade 117) **74** [2004 74: p6g 6.1s 6m⁴ 6f* 6m⁵ 6m⁶ 6g⁶ 6m 6g 6f 7m 6.1d p6g Oct 18] rather leggy filly: fair handicapper: won at Newmarket in May: stays 6f: acts on polytrack and firm ground: often races prominently: tried blinkered: reportedly bled final start. *D. M. Simcock*

SILVER CITY 4 ro.g. Unfuwain (USA) 131 – Madiyla 73 (Darshaan 133) [2004 85: **86 d**
10.1g² 11m 9.9g 10.1m 12g 11.8g⁴ Oct 12] big gelding: fairly useful performer: good
neck second to Woody Valentine in minor event at Epsom on reappearance: well below
form after: stays 1½m: acts on firm and soft ground: usually front runner: sold 20,000
gns. *Mrs A. J. Perrett*

SILVER COURT 2 b.c. (May 19) Silver Patriarch (IRE) 125 – Double Stake (USA) **–**
(Kokand (USA)) [2004 7g⁶ 8g 10v Oct 20] well beaten in minor event/maidens.
R. J. Price

SILVER CREEK 2 gr.c. (Mar 17) Tipsy Creek (USA) 115 – Silver Wedding (Warning **47**
136) [2004 5.1m 7g 7.1g p7g Sep 18] poor maiden: form only on second start. *I. A. Wood*

SILVER CRYSTAL (IRE) 4 b.f. Among Men (USA) 124 – Silver Moon (Environ- **–**
ment Friend 128) [2004 53: f11g f8g p10g Mar 9] lengthy filly: maiden: well beaten in
2004: tried in cheekpieces/visor. *Mrs N. Macauley*

SILVER DANE (IRE) 2 b.g. (Apr 14) Danetime (IRE) 121 – Silver Prairie (IRE) **–**
(Common Grounds 118) [2004 p6g Dec 29] 33/1, always behind in maiden at Lingfield.
Mrs C. A. Dunnett

SILVER DREAMER (IRE) 2 b.f. (Mar 28) Brave Act 119 – Heads We Called **–**
(IRE) (Bluebird (USA) 125) [2004 8.1s 7.1m Sep 6] leggy filly: half-sister to 6f winner
Seeking Destiny (by Two Timing) and French 1m (at 2 yrs) and 1½m winner Riofrio (by
Thatching): dam unraced: well held in maidens at Chepstow (slowly away) and Warwick.
H. S. Howe

SILVER EMPEROR (IRE) 3 gr.g. Lil's Boy (USA) 109 – Just Possible (Kalaglow **–**
132) [2004 f7g f8f Jan 22] well held in maidens at Wolverhampton (slowly away) and
Southwell. *P. A. Blockley*

SILVER GILT 4 b.g. Silver Hawk (USA) 123 – Memory's Gold (USA) 68 (Java Gold **111**
(USA)) [2004 104: 12.3d³ 10.3g³ 16.4d* 16m⁶ 15.9d 18m 12s Dec 5] strong, lengthy,
slightly dipped-backed gelding: smart performer, lightly raced: awarded latest race at
Sandown (short-headed by Romany Prince, placings reversed on appeal) in July: sweating, creditable sixth of 9 to Darasim in Goodwood Cup next time, racing freely: below
form last 3 starts, sold from J. Gosden 20,000 gns prior to final one: stays 2m: yet to race
on extremes of going: has worn crossed noseband: races prominently: flashes tail.
T. Clout, France

SILVERHAY 3 b.g. Inchinor 119 – Moon Spin 83 (Night Shift (USA)) [2004 73: 8.5v⁴ **78**
11m² 11.1m⁴ 8.1d* 8g* 8d⁴ 8d³ Sep 16] neat gelding: fair handicapper: won at Haydock
in July and Pontefract (drifted right) in August: has form at 11f, but best efforts around
1m: acts on heavy and good to firm going: races up with pace. *T. D. Barron*

SILVER HIGHLIGHT (CAN) 2 gr. or ro.f. (Feb 6) Silver Charm (USA) 132 – Rare **78**
Opportunity (USA) (Danzig Connection (USA)) [2004 7m 8f² 8g² Sep 13] $50,000Y:
good-topped filly: fourth foal: half-sister to 2 minor winners in USA: dam, North
American 5f (at 2 yrs)/6f winner, half-sister to useful French performer up to 10.5f
Sensitivity: fair form in maidens when second at Yarmouth and Bath: should stay 1¼m.
A. M. Balding

SILVER ISLAND 3 ch.g. Silver Patriarch (IRE) 125 – Island Maid (Forzando 122) **44**
[2004 –: f8g f6g 10.2s 7m⁶ 7d f8g⁴ p7m⁵ Dec 8] sturdy, compact gelding: poor maiden:
stays 7f: acts on all-weather and good to firm ground: tongue tied fifth start, visored on
last 2. *R. M. H. Cowell*

SILVERLEAF 2 b.c. (Apr 27) Lujain (USA) 119 – Lovely Millie (IRE) 108 (Bluebird **68**
(USA) 125) [2004 7m⁶ 7m⁵ 7.1d⁵ 8g 8g Sep 16] tall colt: fifth foal: half-brother to 3
winners abroad, including French winners Lovelyst (9.5f) and Millefiori (6.5f/1m),
both by Machiavellian: dam 2-y-o 6f/7f (Solario Stakes) winner: fair maiden: ran as if
amiss final start: seems barely to stay 7f: acts on good to firm and good to soft going.
M. R. Channon

SILVER LOUIE (IRE) 4 gr.f. Titus Livius (FR) 115 – Shakamiyn (Nishapour (FR) **§§**
125) [2004 §§: p10g p8g 9g Jun 2] leggy filly: very temperamental maiden. *G. B. Balding*

SILVER MASCOT 5 gr.g. Mukaddamah (USA) 125 – Always Lucky 71 (Absalom **65 §**
128) [2004 f6g⁴ p6g f7g² f7g² f7s⁵ f7s* f7g⁴ f6g² 7s³ 7.2m 6m 5.9f* 6g² f7m 5m 6g
5d Sep 16] sturdy, good-quartered gelding: fair performer: won seller at Wolverhampton
in March and (having left R. Hollinshead after ninth outing) handicap at Carlisle in June:
winner at 7f, probably best at 5f/6f: acts on fibresand and any turf going: edgy sort, tends

to sweat, and bolted to post last 2 outings: sometimes slowly away/hangs: races prominently: temperamental: sold 2,200 gns. *I. Semple*

SILVER MISTRESS 5 gr.m. Syrtos 106 – Galava (CAN) (Graustark) [2004 12v – May 10] tall, workmanlike mare: no sign of ability. *B. N. Doran*

SILVER PALACE (IRE) 3 b.g. Night Shift (USA) – French Quartet (IRE) (Lycius 72 p (USA) 124) [2004 p10g* Dec 30] 10,000Y, 7,000 2-y-o: first foal: dam, no form in Ireland, half-sister to smart dam of Luso, Needle Gun, Cloud Castle and 6-y-o Warrsan: 50/1, won 12-runner maiden at Lingfield by a neck from Screenplay, travelling well then running green before leading close home: sure to improve. *D. Mullarkey*

SILVER PHANTOM (IRE) 2 b.g. (Feb 14) Spectrum (IRE) 126 – Beat It (USA) – (Diesis 133) [2004 5d Apr 14] €32,000Y: sturdy gelding: first foal: dam once-raced half-sister to Kentucky Derby runner-up Proud Citizen: well held in maiden at Beverley. *D. R. Loder*

SILVER PRELUDE 3 b.g. Prince Sabo 123 – Silver Blessings (Statoblest 120) [2004 83 95: 6.1d 5f 5m 5m³ 5m* 5d 5m 5m 5f 5g 5g Sep 30] good-bodied gelding: fairly useful handicapper: won at Newmarket in July: best at bare 5f: acts on firm going: usually races up with pace: gelded after final start. *D. K. Ivory*

SILVERPRO 3 ch.f. Hector Protector (USA) 124 – Silver Gyre (IRE) 65 (Silver Hawk – (USA) 123) [2004 f11g Dec 16] first foal: dam, 17f winner, half-sister to dam of smart performer up to 1½m Housemaster: 25/1, well beaten in maiden at Southwell, slowly away. *D. J. Wintle*

SILVER PROPHET (IRE) 5 gr.g. Idris (IRE) 118 – Silver Heart (Yankee Gold 115) 74 [2004 84, a70: 10g 10s⁵ 12g⁵ 13.3m⁵ 14.1g 12.1m 12s* 12.6g⁵ 14.1g⁶ 11.7s³ p12.2g³ **a63** p12.2g² p12.2g⁵ Dec 20] rather leggy gelding: fair handicapper on turf, modest on all-weather: won at Kempton in August: best at 1¼m/1½m: acts on polytrack, soft and good to firm going: tried visored/in cheekpieces/tongue tied: sometimes slowly away. *M. R. Bosley*

SILVER REIGN 3 gr.g. Prince Sabo 123 – Primo Donna Magna (Primo Dominie 42 121) [2004 6s⁵ 6d⁶ 6s 5.7s Oct 19] poor form. *G. B. Balding*

SILVER RHYTHM 3 gr.f. Silver Patriarch (IRE) 125 – Party Treat (IRE) 69 (Mill- 53 fontaine 114) [2004 –p: 10.1v³ 11.1d⁵ 11.1m 12m f12f 12v⁵ Oct 16] strong filly: modest maiden: stays 1½m: acts on good to firm going, probably on good to soft (well held only outing on fibresand). *K. R. Burke*

SILVER SASH (GER) 3 gr.f. Mark of Esteem (IRE) 137 – Salinova (FR) (Linamix 83 (FR) 127) [2004 10m⁶ 10d³ 13.8m* 11.9s⁵ 14.4m 12s Sep 26] leggy filly: second living foal: half-sister to smart 1½m to 2m winner Shabernak (by Akarad): dam unraced sister to useful French 1½m winner Six Zero: fairly useful performer: landed odds in maiden at Catterick in July by 15 lengths: good fifth to Tarakala in listed race at York next time: well beaten in similar event at Cologne final start: may prove best short of 1¾m: acts on soft and good to firm going: raced freely fourth outing. *M. L. W. Bell*

SILVER SEEKER (USA) 4 gr. or ro.g. Seeking The Gold (USA) – Zelanda (IRE) 55 108 (Night Shift (USA)) [2004 74+: f7s⁵ 7v 7m 7m² 7.1m 6.9f⁶ 7.1f 6d 6g 8g Sep 26] smallish, good-bodied gelding: modest performer nowadays: left I. Semple after fourth start: stays 7f: acts on good to firm ground, probably on fibresand: tried in visor/cheekpieces: none too consistent. *A. R. Dicken*

SILVER SILENCE (JPN) 3 b. or br.g. Sunday Silence (USA) – Island of Silver 93 (USA) 107 (Forty Niner (USA)) [2004 8s 10m* 12g⁴d 12m⁵ 12g p12.2g⁴ p12.2g Dec 17] fourth foal: half-brother to fairly useful UAE 1m to 1½m winner Borneo Boy (by Danzig): dam winner up to 1¼m in Britain/UAE/USA: fairly useful performer: won maiden at Naas in June: left J. Bolger in Ireland 16,000 gns, better effort in Britain when good fourth to Blaze of Colour in handicap at Wolverhampton penultimate start: stays 1½m: acts on polytrack and good to firm ground: blinkered on debut. *V. Smith*

SILVERSKAYA (USA) 3 b. or br.f. Silver Hawk (USA) 123 – Boubskaia (Niniski 116 (USA) 125) [2004 10s* 12g* 10v* 12g* 12d 12.5v* 12d⁶ 12m Oct 3] €150,000Y: angular filly: half-sister to several winners, including smart French miler Daneskaya (by Dane-hill) and useful 6f/7f winner Ludynosa (by Cadeaux Genereux): dam French 1m winner: smart performer: won newcomers race at Toulouse, minor event at Saint-Cloud, listed race at Toulouse, Prix de Royaumont at Chantilly (by length from Kalatuna) and Prix Minerve at Deauville (by length from Reverie Solitaire) between March and August: good efforts at Longchamp in autumn, close sixth to Sweet Stream in Prix Vermeille (met trouble in running and finished well) and 6¾ lengths eighth of 19 behind Bago in Prix de l'Arc de Triomphe (ran on strongly from last place): stays 12.5f: acts on heavy and good to firm going: reportedly in season when running poorly fifth outing. *J-C. Rouget, France*

SILVER SONG 2 gr.c. (Feb 20) Silver Patriarch (IRE) 125 – Singing The Blues (Bonny Scot (IRE) 119) [2004 8g 8g 10.1d Nov 5] good-bodied colt: modest form in maidens: will be suited by 1½m+. *J. L. Dunlop* **52**

SILVERSTEIN (USA) 3 b. or br.c. Seeking The Gold (USA) – Salchow (USA) (Nijinsky (CAN) 138) [2004 8m³ May 15] $400,000Y: sixth foal: closely related to smart French 1998 2-y-o 6.5f and 1m (Grand Criterium) winner Way of Light (by Woodman) who stayed 1½m and French 1¼m winner Simadartha (by Gone West): dam unraced half-sister to Machiavellian and Exit To Nowhere, an excellent family: 5/1, ¾-length third to Credit in maiden at Newbury, only outing. *J. H. M. Gosden* **87**

SILVER SWING 2 gr.c. (Feb 11) Celtic Swing 138 – Poetry In Motion (IRE) 76 (Ballad Rock 122) [2004 6g 6d 6d⁶ Oct 18] poor form in maidens. *W. J. Haggas* **40**

SILVERTOWN 9 b.g. Danehill (USA) 126 – Docklands (USA) (Theatrical 128) [2004 81: 10.1v 10.1g 11.9g 10.1m 14.1d⁴ Oct 15] lengthy gelding: has reportedly had wind operation: just fair form in 2004: stays 1¾m: acts on all-weather, firm and good to soft going: raced freely second/final starts: tail flasher. *L. Lungo* **70**

SILVER VISAGE (IRE) 2 b.g. (Mar 25) Lujain (USA) 119 – About Face (Midyan (USA) 124) [2004 5.2m⁵ 6g⁵ 7g⁵ 8g p8g⁵ p7.1g⁵ p6g p6g Dec 4] unfurnished gelding: modest maiden: barely stays 1m: acts on polytrack: wore cheekpieces last 4 starts, blinkered previous one. *Miss J. Feilden* **62**

SILVER WRAITH (IRE) 2 b.c. (Mar 19) Danehill Dancer (IRE) 117 – Alpine Lady (IRE) (Tirol 127) [2004 6g⁴ 6f² 5.3f* 5.1f* 7g³ 7m* 6m³ 7.1d⁵ Aug 21] €41,000F, €180,000Y: quite good-topped colt: third foal: half-brother to 3-y-o Lady Piste: dam tailed off both starts: useful performer: won maiden at Brighton and minor event at Bath in June and nursery at Newmarket (under 9-7) in July: good 2¼ lengths third to Montgomery's Arch in Richmond Stakes at Goodwood penultimate start: stays 7f: acts on firm going: usually held up: sometimes hangs left: sold 110,000 gns, joined C. Yip in Hong Kong. *N. A. Callaghan* **101**

SIMIANNA 5 b.m. Bluegrass Prince (IRE) 110 – Lowrianna (IRE) 50 (Cyrano de Bergerac 120) [2004 99: 5d⁵ 5.1g⁵ 5.1d² 6g 5m⁶ 6d 6f² 6f 6d 6f⁴ 6f⁶ 6m 6m 6d³ 5d² 6.1g* 5d⁵ 6f 7m Oct 2] tall mare: useful performer: won listed race at Chester (beat Blue Dream ½ length) in September: several other good efforts, including 1½ lengths second to Golden Nun in Ballyogan Stakes at Cork seventh start: effective at 5f/6f: acts on polytrack and any turf going: blinkered once at 2 yrs: usually wears cheekpieces: consistent. *A. Berry* **101**

SIMLET 9 b.g. Forzando 122 – Besito 79 (Wassl 125) [2004 42: 15.8g⁵ Oct 5] angular gelding: poor handicapper: stays 2m: acts on fibresand, firm and soft going: has flashed tail/wandered: often blinkered/visored earlier in career. *E. W. Tuer* **47**

SIMONAS (IRE) 5 ro.g. Sternkoenig (IRE) 122 – Sistadari 84 (Shardari 134) [2004 110: 12g* 14s* 14m⁶ 12m⁶ 12g⁴ 12d⁴ 12g² 12m Dec 12] half-brother to smart German 1¼m performer Sir Warren (by Warning) and useful German 1¼m/1½m performer Syrakus (by Kris): dam, maiden who stayed 1¼m, out of sister to Bella Colora and half-sister to Colorspin: very smart performer: unraced prior to 2003 when successful in maiden and 4 handicaps: improved in 2004, winning minor events at Milan (2) and Premio Carlo d'Alessio at Rome (by 3½ lengths from Darrel) in April/May: best efforts when 3 lengths fourth to Warrsan in Grosser Preis von Baden and 1½ lengths second to Sulamani in Canadian International at Woodbine sixth/seventh starts: only tenth in Hong Kong Vase at Sha Tin final outing: stays 1¾m: acts on soft and good to firm ground. *A. Wohler, Germany* **121**

SIMONDA 3 ch.f. Singspiel (IRE) 133 – Jetbeeah (IRE) 95 (Lomond (USA) 128) [2004 8.3m² 11.7f* Sep 6] half-sister to several winners, including useful 7f/1m performer Dazilyn Lady (by Zilzal), 6f winner at 2 yrs, and 4-y-o Miss Grace: dam 1m winner: fairly useful form: confirmed debut promise when winning maiden at Bath readily by 8 lengths from Tashreefat, edging left when coming through to lead 2f out: stays 11.7f: should do better still. *Mrs A. J. Perrett* **84 p**

SIMONOVSKI (USA) 3 b.g. Miswaki (USA) 124 – Eartha (USA) (Rahy (USA) 115) [2004 69: p7g 10.2g 10m³ 16.2m² 16g 14.1g Sep 29] fair maiden: left J. Osborne after fourth start: stays 2m: acts on polytrack and good to firm ground: often slowly away: tended to hang third outing: free-going sort: gelded after final start. *S. C. Burrough* **66**

SIMON'S SEAT (USA) 5 ch.g. Woodman (USA) 126 – Spire (USA) (Topsider (USA)) [2004 75: 16g⁶ 14.8m⁶ 12f⁶ 16s p13g p16.5g⁶ p16.5g Dec 4] leggy, useful- **66**

looking gelding: fair maiden handicapper: left C. Drew after second start: stays 2m: acts on polytrack and firm ground: sometimes slowly away/looks none too keen: none too reliable. *P. Howling*

SIMPLE EXCHANGE (IRE) 3 b.c. Danehill (USA) 126 – Summer Trysting (USA) **110** 83 (Alleged (USA) 138) [2004 103: 10m⁴ 9.5f* 10f⁴ 9.8m⁶ Oct 2] good-topped colt: fifth foal: half-brother to 3 winners, including 5-y-o Sights On Gold and 6-y-o Beat The Heat: dam, Irish maiden (stayed 1½m), half-sister to smart winner up to 1¼m Smooth Perform- ance: smart performer: won Grade 2 American Derby at Arlington (beat Cool Conductor gamely by neck) in July: creditable efforts otherwise in 2004 when fourth in listed race at Ascot (beaten 3 lengths by Moscow Ballet) and Secretariat Stakes at Arlington (5½ lengths behind Kitten's Joy) and sixth in Prix Dollar at Longchamp (behind Touch of Land): stays 1¼m: acts on firm ground. *D. K. Weld, Ireland*

SIMPLE IDEALS (USA) 10 b. or br.g. Woodman (USA) 126 – Comfort And Style **40** 95 (Be My Guest (USA) 126) [2004 44, a–: 16.1v⁵ 16d⁴ f14m 16.1d⁶ 16s 16g⁵ Aug 31] **a–** smallish, workmanlike gelding: has a round action: poor handicapper: races mainly at 1¾m/2m: acts on any turf going, well held on all-weather: tried blinkered: sometimes races freely/carries head high: usually held up. *Don Enrico Incisa*

SIMPLIFY 2 b.c. (Feb 2) Fasliyev (USA) 120 – Simplicity 93 (Polish Precedent **77 §** (USA) 131) [2004 5.2g⁴ 6f⁵ 7.1f³ 6m² 6m⁵ 7f 6.1g⁶ 6m 7d Oct 10] 280,000Y: sturdy colt: first foal: dam, Irish 1½m winner, half-sister to Safawan (stayed 1m) out of French performer up to 1¼m Safita, both smart: fair maiden: won nursery at Warwick in August: well below form after: seems best at 6f: acts on firm going: blinkered last 6 starts: sometimes starts slowly: irresolute: sold 11,000 gns. *D. R. Loder*

SIMPLY HONEST (IRE) 9 ch.g. Simply Great (FR) 122 – Susans Glory (Billion **61** (USA) 120) [2004 63: 16m⁴ 16.2m 16g⁵ 16g⁴ 12g 14m Aug 15] useful bumper winner in 2001: modest handicapper: unraced on Flat prior to 2003: stays 2m: acts on soft and good to firm ground: wore cheekpieces fourth start and tongue tie fifth one: carried head high when well held at Ascot second outing. *A. J. Martin, Ireland*

SIMPLY RED 3 ch.g. Vettori (IRE) 119 – Amidst 86 (Midyan (USA) 124) [2004 –: 7g **–** 8.1s f6g 6m May 24] lengthy, rather sparely-made gelding: little sign of ability: tried in visor. *R. Brotherton*

SIMPLY ST LUCIA 2 b.f. (Mar 22) Charnwood Forest (IRE) 125 – Mubadara (IRE) **71** 80 (Lahib (USA) 129) [2004 f7g* 8.1d³ 8v³ 8.1g⁶ Sep 4] 1,400Y: third foal: dam, Irish 2-y-o 6f winner, out of half-sister to high-class miler Montekin: fair performer: won maiden at Southwell in June: stays 1m: acts on fibresand, probably on good to soft going. *J. R. Weymes*

SIMPLY THE GUEST (IRE) 5 b.g. Mujadil (USA) 119 – Ned's Contessa (IRE) 48 **–** (Persian Heights 129) [2004 44: f8g² f8g² f8f* f8s* f7g⁴ f8g 6f 7g f8s⁴ p9.5g² f8g³ Dec **a68** 16] lengthy gelding: fair handicapper: won at Southwell in January and February: stays 1m: acts on fibresand and firm ground: visored once at 3 yrs, tongue tied nowadays: has been slowly away. *Don Enrico Incisa*

SIMPSONS MOUNT (IRE) 3 ch.g. Tagula (IRE) 116 – Brunswick (Warning 136) **76** [2004 p5g⁶ p6g⁵ p5g³ 6g 5.1m⁵ 6g 6m* 5m⁵ 5m 6m p6m* p6m⁴ Dec 21] €1,200Y: compact gelding: second foal: dam unraced out of close relation to Poule d'Essai des Pouliches winner Houseproud: fair handicapper: won at Folkestone in June and Lingfield (apprentices) in October: effective at 5f/6f: acts on polytrack and good to firm ground: sometimes slowly away. *R. M. Flower*

SINAMAY (USA) 3 b.f. Saint Ballado (CAN) – Chenille (IRE) 95 (Tenby 125) [2004 **–** 8d Aug 15] $100,000F: good-topped filly: first foal: dam, 1m winner in Ireland (at 2 yrs) and USA, out of half-sister to Prix de la Foret winner Brocade, herself dam of Barathea and Gossamer: 50/1, well beaten in maiden at Pontefract. *J. J. Quinn*

SINGHALESE 2 ch.f. (Mar 3) Singspiel (IRE) 133 – Baize 95 (Efisio 120) [2004 7g⁴ **92** 8.2g³ 7d³ 8m⁶ Sep 9] €60,000Y: tall, leggy filly: fluent mover: fourth foal: half-sister to 3 winners, including fairly useful 6f (at 2 yrs) to 1m winner Masterpoint (by Mark of Esteem) and 3-y-o Patterdale: dam 2-y-o 5f winner (later 5f/6f winner in USA): fairly useful performer: improved to win nursery at Doncaster by 2 lengths from Mighty Empire, staying on to lead final 1f: shapes as if will stay 1¼m: acts on good to firm ground. *J. A. Osborne*

SINGHALONGTASVEER 2 b.g. (May 14) Namaqualand (USA) – Felinwen (White **49** Mill 76) [2004 6g 7f⁵ 6d³ 7m 7d 6.9m⁵ 6m 7d Oct 15] compact gelding: poor maiden: stays 7f: acts on good to firm and good to soft going. *W. Storey*

SINGITTA 3 b.f. Singspiel (IRE) 133 – Ferber's Follies (USA) (Saratoga Six (USA)) – [2004 10s 12.1m 10.2s Oct 19] 40,000Y: seventh foal: half-sister to 3 winners, including useful 6f (including at 2 yrs)/7f winner Injaaz (by Sheikh Albadou): dam 2-y-o 5.5f winner in USA: well held in maidens. *B. Palling*

SINGLET 3 ch.c. Singspiel (IRE) 133 – Ball Gown 98 (Jalmood (USA) 126) [2004 –: **65** 10.3m 10g Jul 14] leggy colt: second foal: half-brother to fairly useful 7f winner Leoballero (by Lion Cavern): dam 1m to 1½m winner: fair maiden: stays 1¼m: took strong hold final start. *D. J. Daly*

SINGLE TRACK MIND 6 b.g. Mind Games 121 – Compact Disc (IRE) 48 (Royal **52** Academy (USA) 130) [2004 –: f7g p7g² p8g⁵ p7g⁴ p7g⁵ p7g p8g² p7g³ p8g⁵ 7v 7f 7g⁶ 8m⁴ 10g 8.5g p8.6g p10m p10m p7g* Dec 20] neat gelding: modest performer: won banded race at Lingfield in December: stays 1m: acts on all-weather, soft and good to firm going: tried visored/tongue tied, often wears cheekpieces. *J. R. Boyle*

SINGULARITY 4 b.g. Rudimentary (USA) 118 – Lyrical Bid (USA) 77 (Lyphard – (USA) 132) [2004 63d: f12g p8g p8g p8g Sep 18] angular gelding: no longer seems of much account, refusing to race final outing. *K. F. Clutterbuck*

SINISTRA 3 br.f. Dracula (AUS) 121 – Sardegna 111 (Pharly (FR) 130) [2004 10g May – 14] rangy, angular filly: has a quick action: sixth foal: half-sister to smart 1¼m winner Samoa (by Rainbow Quest) and useful 1¼m winner Sardonic (by Kris): dam, 7f (at 2 yrs) and 1¼m winner, half-sister to very smart winner up to 1½m Sandmason: 14/1, well held in maiden at Newbury: sold 11,000 gns in December. *H. R. A. Cecil*

SINJAREE 6 b.g. Mark of Esteem (IRE) 137 – Forthwith 104 (Midyan (USA) 124) **51** [2004 68d: f8g f9.4s⁵ f9.4s* f9.4g 10v⁶ 10g 10.5g 8.2g 8.1d p9.5g⁴ 8d⁶ p9.5g⁶ Nov 15] leggy gelding: modest performer: won apprentice banded race at Wolverhampton in March: stays 1¼m: acts on all-weather, heavy and good to firm going: tried in visor/ cheekpieces. *Mrs S. Lamyman*

SINK OR SWIM (IRE) 6 b.m. Big Sink Hope (USA) – Cragreagh VII (Damsire – Unregistered) [2004 p12g p8g p10g⁵ 12v May 10] non-thoroughbred mare: in frame all 4 starts in bumpers in Ireland in 2003: little form on Flat. *J. J. Bridger*

SINNOMORE (IRE) 2 ch.g. (Mar 12) Sinndar (IRE) 134 – Demure (Machiavellian **73** (USA) 123) [2004 p8.6g p8.6g² Dec 17] €100,000Y: third foal: half-brother to 3-y-o Coy and 4-y-o Presumptive: dam unraced half-sister to very smart 6f/7f performer Diffident: better effort in maidens at Wolverhampton when second to Pocketwood, forcing strong pace and headed close home: will probably stay 1¼m. *M. A. Magnusson*

SION HILL (IRE) 3 b.g. Desert Prince (IRE) 130 – Mobilia 67 (Last Tycoon 131) **63** [2004 75: 5g 5m 7f 8.5m 8d p7.1d p9.5g f6g f8g Dec 28] well-made gelding: just modest performer in 2004: left Sir Michael Stoute after second start, J. O'Reilly after penultimate one: bred to be suited by at least 7f, but races freely: tried visored/blinkered. *Mrs N. Macauley*

SIRAJ 5 b.g. Piccolo 121 – Masuri Kabisa (USA) 48 (Ascot Knight (CAN) 130) [2004 **62** 72: f7g f6g* 5d 6d p7.1g p6g⁴ p7g p7.1g⁵ f6g p6g⁶ Dec 1] good-bodied gelding: modest performer: left N. Graham after reappearance: won seller at Southwell (left Mrs J. Candlish) in August: stays 6f: acts on all-weather, good to firm and good to soft going: tried blinkered/tongue tied. *P. S. McEntee*

SIR ALFRED 5 b.g. Royal Academy (USA) 130 – Magnificent Star (USA) 122 (Silver **56 §** Hawk (USA) 123) [2004 74§: 12g 14.1g⁴ 11.6g p8.6g Oct 19] modest handicapper: stays easy 1¾m: acts on firm and good to soft ground: visored final start: edgy sort, has been mounted on track/early to post: very slowly away second outing: tends to hang/flash tail: unreliable: sold 5,000 gns. *A. King*

SIR ANTHONY (IRE) 2 b.c. (Apr 4) Danehill Dancer (IRE) 117 – Brief Fairy (IRE) **90** (Brief Truce (USA) 126) [2004 6g* 6d³ 7d² 7s⁶ 7g² 8m³ Sep 9] €11,000F, €25,000Y, 39,000 2-y-o: rather leggy, close-coupled colt: first foal: dam Italian 5f (at 2 yrs) and 7f winner: fairly useful performer: won maiden at Thirsk in June: good efforts in nurseries at Newcastle and Doncaster third and final starts: stays 1m: acts on good to firm and good to soft going: sometimes slowly away/soon off bridle: joined J. Moore in Hong Kong. *B. Smart*

SIR BLUEBIRD (IRE) 2 ch.c. (Apr 12) Bluebird (USA) 125 – Persian Tapestry 70 **63** (Tap On Wood 130) [2004 5g 6g 6g⁶ p6m Oct 6] 25,000F, 38,000Y: sturdy colt: brother to useful 2000 2-y-o 5f/6f winner Triple Blue and 1¼m winner Authority and half-brother to 2 winners: dam, 1¼m winner, half-sister to top-class sprinter Lake Coniston (by Bluebird): modest maiden: likely to stay 7f: ran poorly on polytrack. *R. Hannon*

SIR

SIR BOND (IRE) 3 ch.g. Desert Sun 120 – In Tranquility (IRE) (Shalford (IRE) — 124§) [2004 –: 10.3g 12s⁴ 10g⁵ Apr 29] lengthy, heavy-bodied gelding: well held in maidens and banded stakes. *B. Smart*

SIRCE (IRE) 2 b.f. (Apr 19) Josr Algarhoud (IRE) 118 – Trading Aces 71 (Be My **67** Chief (USA) 122) [2004 6m 6f⁶ 5.7g 8f 8d⁴ p8.6g* p8.6g Nov 29] 2,600F, 3,500Y: strong filly: third foal: half-sister to 3-y-o Spring Breeze: dam, 6f (at 2 yrs)/7f winner, half-sister to useful 1997 2-y-o 6f winner Crazee Mental: fair performer: won claimer at Wolverhampton in November (looked less than keen final one). *D. J. Coakley*

SIR DESMOND 6 gr.g. Petong 126 – I'm Your Lady 77 (Risk Me (FR) 127) [2004 **91** 89: p6g³ f6g 6d 5g³ 5g⁵ 6g⁶ 6s⁴ 6d 5s⁴ 6s* p6g⁵ p6g* Dec 13] workmanlike gelding: fairly useful handicapper: won at Redcar in November and Wolverhampton (best effort, beat Jayanjay by ½ length) in December: effective at 5f/6f: acts on any turf going/all-weather: blinkered (ran poorly) once, wears cheekpieces nowadays: tends to edge left. *R. Guest*

SIR DON (IRE) 5 b.g. Lake Coniston (IRE) 131 – New Sensitive (Wattiefield 117) **72 §** [2004 77: 7g 7s 6g 6m 6m* 6m 7m³ 6m⁵ 6m 6m 6g 7s 5.1g 7.2d Sep 16] sparely-made gelding: fair handicapper: won at Hamilton in June: effective at 6f (very best form) to easy 1m: acts on polytrack, raced mainly on good going or firmer on turf: usually wears visor/blinkers: started very slowly penultimate outing: often races prominently: unreliable. *D. Nicholls*

SIR EDWARD BURROW (IRE) 6 b.g. Distinctly North (USA) 115 – Alalja (IRE) **49** 95 (Entitled 126) [2004 13.8v 13.1s² Oct 30] poor maiden: stays 2m: acts on firm and soft going (no show both starts on fibresand): none too consistent. *W. Storey*

SIR EDWIN LANDSEER (USA) 4 gr.c. Lit de Justice (USA) 125 – Wildcat Blue **78** (USA) (Cure The Blues (USA)) [2004 107d: a8f 7m 6m 5g 5.2f 5.2g a5.5f⁶ a6g* a6f⁶ Dec 30] good-quartered colt: one-time useful performer: mostly disappointing since early 2003 (ran in Britain second to sixth starts at 4 yrs), but won handicap at Nad Al Sheba in December: stays 7f: acts on dirt, yet to race on soft/heavy ground, acts on any other turf going: tried blinkered: sometimes slowly away/edges left. *C. Wroe, UAE*

SIR ERNEST (IRE) 3 b.g. Daggers Drawn (USA) 114 – Kyra Crown (IRE) (Astronef **78 §** 116) [2004 84: 5g 5.1d⁶ 5f 5d² 5d 6.1m⁴ 5.1g² 5g 5s 5g 5.1g⁶ Sep 11] rather leggy gelding: fair handicapper: effective at 5f/easy 6f: acts on all-weather, firm and good to soft going: wore cheekpieces tenth outing: unreliable. *M. J. Polglase*

SIR FRANCIS (IRE) 6 b.g. Common Grounds 118 – Red Note (Rusticaro (FR) 124) **70** [2004 84: p8g p7g p7g p7g 7.1v⁵ May 4] useful-looking gelding: has a round action: fair handicapper: stays easy 7f: acts on polytrack and soft ground: visored (tailed off) once: has wandered under pressure: sold 1,500 gns. *J. Noseda*

SIR FRANK GIBSON 3 b.g. Primo Dominie 121 – Serotina (IRE) 73 (Mtoto 134) **46** [2004 52: f8.5g f8g⁴ f11g² f11g³ f12g f12g⁵ f12m⁵ 11.6g⁵ p10g Jul 17] poor maiden: left M. Johnston after fifth start: stays 11f: acts on fibresand and good to firm going. *Mrs Jane Galpin*

SIR GALAHAD 3 ch.g. Hector Protector (USA) 124 – Sharpening 72 (Sharpo 132) **50** [2004 59p: f6g f6s 10s⁵ 8s³ 8s⁴ May 12] lengthy gelding: modest maiden: stays 1m: acts on soft and good to firm going. *T. D. Easterby*

SIR GEORGE TURNER 5 ch.g. Nashwan (USA) 135 – Ingozi 91 (Warning 136) **101** [2004 10d 10.4d 10m 10.1m 10m 9.9g 12g 7m 8s³ Sep 18] big, close-coupled gelding: smart performer at 3 yrs: missed 2003: just useful at 5 yrs, best efforts when mid-division at Redcar (Zetland Gold Cup) third outing and Goodwood (behind Coat of Honour) sixth one: effective at 1m given a test, and stays 1½m: acts on firm and soft going: tried blinkered/visored: has run well in tongue tie/cheekpieces: has looked none too keen: sold 12,000 gns. *M. Johnston*

SIR HAYDN 4 ch.g. Definite Article 121 – Snowscape (Niniski (USA) 125) [2004 78: **78** 10g³ 10d⁶ 10s 12m⁶ 12m 10s⁵ 10f³ 11.6f 10d 9.9m 10m p10m² Dec 21] big, leggy gelding: fair performer: stays 1¼m: acts on polytrack, firm and soft going: usually blinkered/visored: possibly ungenuine. *J. R. Jenkins*

SIR JASPER (IRE) 3 b.g. Sri Pekan (USA) 117 – Ashover Amber 81 (Green Desert **72 ?** (USA) 127) [2004 58: f7g* f6g f8.5g³ f7g⁴ f7g a10.5g a10.5g Dec 12] workmanlike gelding: seemingly easily best effort when winning claimer at Southwell in January by 10 lengths (claimed from T. D. Barron £6,000): sold from M. Harris after fifth start: stays 7f: raced only on fibresand/sand: usually visored in Britain. *R. J. Smith, Spain*

SIR LAUGHALOT   4 b.g. Alzao (USA) 117 – Funny Hilarious (USA) 76 (Sir Ivor **79**
(USA) 135) [2004 77: p7g² p7g p7g³ p8g² p8g³ 8.1d² 11g Sep 17] strong gelding: fair
maiden handicapper: stays 1m: acts on polytrack, good to firm and good to soft going.
Miss E. C. Lavelle

SIR LOIN   3 ch.g. Compton Place 125 – Charnwood Queen 61 (Cadeaux Genereux **69**
131) [2004 63: 5d 5d 5d⁵ 5m² 6m⁶ 5d 5d² 5m² 5d² Oct 11] leggy gelding: fair maiden:
runner-up 4 times in 2004: should stay 6f: acts on good to firm and good to soft going:
visored last 2 starts: races prominently. *N. Tinkler*

SIR MONTY (USA)   2 ch.g. (Apr 16) Cat's Career (USA) – Lady of Meadowlane **69**
(USA) (Pancho Jay (USA)) [2004 7.6m⁵ 7d⁶ 8s⁴ 8s Sep 14] $6,200Y, 27,000 2-y-o: leggy,
workmanlike gelding: half-brother to 3 winners, including 1½m/1¾m winner Access
Cruise (by Wajima): dam winner in USA: fair maiden: sweating, fourth at Goodwood,
best effort: stays 1m. *Mrs A. J. Perrett*

SIR NIGHT (IRE)   4 b.g. Night Shift (USA) – Highly Respected (IRE) 57 (High Estate **56**
127) [2004 67: 10m⁴ 10.5m 12f Jun 15] quite good-topped gelding: modest performer
nowadays: stays 1¼m: acts on fibresand, good to firm and good to soft going: tried in
headgear. *Jedd O'Keeffe*

SIR NINJA (IRE)   7 b.g. Turtle Island (IRE) 123 – The Poachers Lady (IRE) (Salmon **69**
Leap (USA) 131) [2004 –: 12d² 11s⁴ 10d May 15] heavy-bodied gelding: fair handicapper: barely stays 1½m: acts on polytrack, best turf form on ground softer than good:
visored once in 2000: difficult ride (tends to hang left): none too consistent. *S. Kirk*

SIR NOD   2 b.g. (Apr 22) Tagula (IRE) 116 – Nordan Raider 81 (Domynsky 110) [2004 **77 p**
p7.1g⁴ p7.1g* Dec 31] half-brother to 7.5f to 1¼m winner Nod's Nephew (by Efisio):
dam, 6f winner, half-sister to useful 7f/1m performer Hi Nod: won maiden at Wolverhampton comfortably by 1¾ lengths from Castanza: slowly away on debut: should stay
1m: capable of better. *Miss J. A. Camacho*

SIR SANDROVITCH (IRE)   8 b.g. Polish Patriot (USA) 128 – Old Downie (Be **64**
My Guest (USA) 126) [2004 78: 5v 5m 5g⁶ 5g 5m⁵ 5g f5m⁵ p5.1g² f6g² p5.1g⁴ Dec 31] tall
gelding: handicapper: just modest form in 2004: best at 5f: acts on all-weather, firm and
good to soft going: tried blinkered, usually wears cheekpieces: sometimes early to post/
slowly away: tends to pull hard, and best covered up. *R. A. Fahey*

SI SI AMIGA (IRE)   3 b.f. Desert Style (IRE) 121 – No Hard Feelings (IRE) 86 **92**
(Alzao (USA) 117) [2004 79p: 11.4d⁴ 10m⁴ 10m⁵ 11.9g 13.9s 8d⁶ Nov 6] neat filly: fairly
useful performer: good efforts in listed events at Chester, Newmarket (5 lengths fourth to
Hazyview) and Newbury (fifth to Incheni) first 3 starts: left B. Hills and off 2½ months,
respectable sixth in non-graded event at Woodbine (blinkered): stays 1¼m: acts on good
to firm and good to soft going. *R. Baker, Canada*

SI SI SI   2 b.f. (Mar 13) Lomitas 129 – Notturna (Diu Star) [2004 7m Aug 3] 21,000F: **–**
rather lengthy filly: half-sister to several winners abroad, notably smart German performer up to 1½m Narrabeth (by Shaadi): dam German 9f/1¼m winner: 25/1, last in maiden
at Catterick, unseating to post and very slowly away. *J. G. Given*

SISTER GEE (IRE)   2 b.f. (Apr 12) Desert Story (IRE) 115 – My Gloria (IRE) (Saint **60**
Estephe (FR) 123) [2004 f7g⁴ f6m³ f5m² 6.1d f6g² f5g Dec 16] €5,000Y: sturdy filly:
second foal: dam unraced: modest maiden: stays 6f: acts on fibresand, some promise on
good to soft going. *R. Hollinshead*

SISTER MOONSHINE (FR)   3 ch.f. Piccolo 121 – Cootamundra (FR) (Double **99**
Bed (FR) 121) [2004 97: 5.5d³ 5.5d* 5d⁵ 5d 5g⁶ 5d Sep 19] first foal: dam, French 1m
and (at 2 yrs) 9f winner, half-sister to high-class French performer up to 9f Big John:
useful performer: won minor event at Maisons-Laffitte (by ½ length fron Leila) in May:
good sixth to Pivotal Point in Prix du Petit Couvert at Longchamp: below form in listed
race at Hamilton final start: best around 5f: acts on good to soft ground: blinkered last 2
starts. *R. Pritchard-Gordon, France*

SISTER SOPHIA (USA)   4 b. or br.f. Deputy Commander (USA) 124 – Sophia's **68**
Choice (USA) (Clev Er Tell (USA)) [2004 71: 8m 7g 7m³ 8f⁶ 7d 8.1d p8g p9.5g p8m⁴
p8g⁴ Dec 20] lengthy, attractive filly: fair maiden: stays 1m: acts on polytrack and good
to firm going: tried in cheekpieces: tongue tied last 4 starts: sometimes slowly away: none
too consistent. *W. J. Musson*

SIX PACK (IRE)   6 ch.g. Royal Abjar (USA) 121 – Regal Entrance (Be My Guest **51**
(USA) 126) [2004 42: f8.5g² p10g² f9.4g⁴ p10g May 13] tall, good-topped gelding: modest performer: stays easy 1¼m: acts on all-weather, firm and soft ground: tried blinkered:
sometimes slowly away. *Andrew Turnell*

SIX PERFECTIONS (FR)   4 br. or bl.f. Celtic Swing 138 – Yogya (USA) (River-   **120**
man (USA) 131) [2004 124: 9.3g² 8f⁶ 8d² 8d³ Oct 30] close-coupled filly: very smart
performer: successful in 2003 in Prix Jacques le Marois at Deauville and Breeders' Cup
Mile at Santa Anita: not quite in same form in 2004, though placed in Prix d'Ispahan
at Longchamp (½-length second to Prince Kirk), Prix Jacques le Marois at Deauville
(beaten length by Whipper) and Breeders' Cup Mile at Lone Star Park (2 lengths third to
Singletary, staying on strongly after being hampered before home turn): only sixth behind
Refuse To Bend in Queen Anne Stakes at Royal Ascot on other start, tending to hang: best
at 1m: unraced on heavy going, acted on any other: had proved awkward at stall: tended
to race freely, and ideally needed covering up: had fine turn of foot: retired, and to visit
Storm Cat. *P. Bary, France*

SIXTILSIX (IRE)   3 ch.g. Night Shift (USA) – Assafiyah (IRE) 62 (Kris 135) [2004   **45**
–: 7g 10f p10g³ 10f p9.5d⁶ p10g Dec 20] sturdy gelding: poor maiden: left W. Jarvis after
third start: stays 1¼m: acts on polytrack: edgy sort. *H. Alexander*

SKATER BOY   3 b.g. Wizard King 122 – Makalu 79 (Godswalk (USA) 130) [2004 –:   **–**
10f Jun 22] small gelding: little form. *Miss S. West*

SKELLIGS ROCK (IRE)   4 b.c. Key of Luck (USA) 126 – Drew (IRE) (Double   **69**
Schwartz 128) [2004 74: 11.6d⁵ 14.4v May 3] fair maiden: should stay 1½m: acts on firm
and good to soft ground. *B. W. Duke*

SKELTHWAITE   3 b.g. Desert Story (IRE) 115 – Skip To Somerfield 79 (Shavian   **–**
125) [2004 –: 7.5g f7s 9.7f³ 11.5g p10g p9.5g p8m Dec 15] little form. *Miss D. A. McHale*

SKIBEREEN (IRE)   4 b.g. Ashkalani (IRE) 128 – Your Village (IRE) 64 (Be My   **66**
Guest (USA) 126) [2004 80, a70: p10g⁵ p12g⁶ 10g⁴ 9g⁵ f8.5g 8.2d³ 8m⁵ 10.3g 8.2g   **a50**
7.9m 10.1g² 10g² 12g Oct 2] leggy gelding: fair maiden: left I. McInnes after eleventh
start: stays 1½m: acts on polytrack, good to firm and good to soft going: tried tongue
tied/blinkered/in cheekpieces: sometimes races freely/carries head awkwardly: none too
genuine. *Mrs A. M. Thorpe*

SKIDDAW JONES   4 b.g. Emperor Jones (USA) 119 – Woodrising 64 (Nomination   **54 §**
125) [2004 67: 8.3g 10f⁵ 10.1g 9.2g⁶ 9.1g² 10f⁶ 7.9m Sep 11] good-topped gelding:
modest handicapper: stays 10.5f: acts on firm ground, below form all runs on softer than
good: sometimes slowly away: unreliable. *Miss L. A. Perratt*

SKIDDAW WOLF   2 ch.f. (Mar 18) Wolfhound (USA) 126 – Stealthy 73 (Kind of   **65**
Hush 118) [2004 5m 5.9g³ 5g⁶ 5g⁵ 5g⁴ 6d² 5.1v p6g f5g² Dec 16] 2,200Y: quite good-
topped filly: half-sister to 1999 2-y-o 6f winner Stealthy Times (by Timeless Times) and
winner up to 7.5f in Italy by Presidium: dam 1m winner: best maiden: second at Pontefract
and Southwell (nursery): likely to prove best at 5f/easy 6f: acts on fibresand and good to
soft going: edgy sort: often races up with pace. *B. Smart*

SKIDMARK   3 b.g. Pennekamp (USA) 130 – Flourishing (IRE) 85 (Trojan Fen 118)   **108**
[2004 79P: p8g² p10g* p10g* p8g³ 10.1s⁴ 10.4s 9.9g⁶ Sep 22] lengthy, useful-looking
gelding: useful performer: won handicap and minor event at Lingfield in February: best
effort when 1¼ lengths third to Leitrim House in listed race there: respectable sixth to
Alkaadhem in similar event at Goodwood final outing, racing freely (gelded after): stays
1¼m: acts on polytrack and good ground, well below form on soft in minor event at
Epsom and Dante Stakes at York (sweating). *D. R. C. Elsworth*

SKIDROW   2 b.c. (May 1) Bachir (IRE) 118 – Flourishing (IRE) 85 (Trojan Fen 118)   **91**
[2004 7.1m 7g* 7.6g² 8v² 8d³ Oct 15] 14,000Y: quite attractive colt: half-brother to
several winners, including 3-y-o Skidmark and fairly useful 1998 3-y-o 5f winner Kastaway (by Distant Relative): dam 2-y-o 7f winner: fairly useful performer: won maiden at
Newcastle in July: creditable placed efforts in minor events: stays 1m: acts on heavy
ground. *M. L. W. Bell*

SKI JUMP (USA)   4 gr.g. El Prado (IRE) 119 – Skiable (IRE) (Niniski (USA) 125)   **85**
[2004 85: 10.2g* 12d⁶ 10.5g 11.9d⁶ 14g 12g 14.1d 10.4g⁴ 16d⁴ Nov 3] good-bodied
gelding: fairly useful performer: won minor event at Chepstow in June: left R. Charlton
prior to third start: stays 1¾m: acts on firm and good to soft going: wears headgear:
effective making the running or held up. *R. A. Fahey*

SKIP OF COLOUR   4 b.g. Rainbow Quest (USA) 134 – Minskip (USA) 64 (The   **81**
Minstrel (CAN) 135) [2004 p8g⁴ f9.4g⁵ f6g* f6s² p6g 6g⁶ 5.1d⁵ 6d Sep 17] fairly useful
performer: trained in France at 3 yrs by P. Bary: won maiden at Southwell in February:
will prove best at 5f/6f: acts on fibresand and good to soft ground: races up with pace.
P. A. Blockley

SKIPPIT JOHN 2 b.g. (Mar 21) Abou Zouz (USA) 109 – Lady Quinta (IRE) 59 (Gallic **69 d**
League 119) [2004 5v² 5m⁶ 6m⁶ 7d 6s f6s Aug 23] workmanlike gelding: fair maiden:
best effort on debut: should stay beyond 5f: acts on heavy ground. *Ronald Thompson*

SKY COVE 3 b.g. Spectrum (IRE) 126 – Aurora Bay (IRE) (Night Shift (USA)) [2004 **–**
–: f8g Jan 20] leggy gelding: well held in maidens/banded event. *M. W. Easterby*

SKY CRUSADER 2 b.c. (May 9) Mujahid (USA) 125 – Red Cloud (IRE) 61 (Taufan **84**
(USA) 119) [2004 7f* 7g⁶ p7d⁵ 7m³ Sep 26] 8,500F: tall, leggy colt: sixth foal: dam,
maiden who stayed 7f (sometimes looked none too keen), half-sister to smart 1m/1¼m
performer Cape Town: fairly useful performer: won maiden at Folkestone in June: creditable third in nursery at Ascot: will probably stay 1m: acts on firm going. *R. Ingram*

SKY DOME (IRE) 11 ch.g. Bluebird (USA) 125 – God Speed Her (Pas de Seul 133) **58**
[2004 73+: 7m⁵ Apr 12] lengthy, leggy gelding: poor mover: fair handicapper in
2003, just modest form only 11-y-o start: stays easy 1¼m: acts on all-weather, firm and
soft going: often blinkered/visored: sometimes carries head awkwardly/finds little.
M. H. Tompkins

SKYE'S FOLLY (USA) 4 b.g. Kris S (USA) – Bittersweet Hour (USA) (Seattle **81**
Slew (USA)) [2004 86: 16d 16.2m 16.2d 14.8g³ 16m³ 13.9m³ 14.1d⁴ 13.9g⁴ p13.9g²
p16.5g³ Nov 8] good-topped gelding: fairly useful handicapper: mostly creditable efforts
in 2004: stays 16.5f: acts on polytrack, firm and good to soft ground: blinkered last 6
starts. *J. G. Given*

SKY GALAXY (USA) 3 ch.f. Sky Classic (CAN) – Fly To The Moon (USA) 90 **67**
(Blushing Groom (FR) 131) [2004 84: 7m 8.2m 8m⁶ Jul 13] stocky filly: type to carry
plenty of condition: just fair performer in 2004: races freely and barely stays 7f: acts on
good to firm and good to soft going: visored final start: sold 3,500 gns. *E. A. L. Dunlop*

SKYHARBOR 3 b.g. Cyrano de Bergerac 120 – Pea Green 98 (Try My Best (USA) **82**
130) [2004 87: 7.6d 6m⁵ 6g 5m⁵ 5m² 5s³ 5g⁴ 6g 6g p5.1d Nov 3] leggy, quite good-topped
gelding: fairly useful handicapper: left D. Nicholls after fourth start: below form last 3
appearances: probably best at 5f: acts on firm and soft ground: visored 3 outings prior to
final one: sold 20,000 gns. *A. M. Balding*

SKYLARK 7 ch.m. Polar Falcon (USA) 126 – Boozy 111 (Absalom 128) [2004 65: **–**
f7d 7m f8m Jul 12] leggy mare: fair performer at best: well held in 2004: often slowly
away/looks hard ride. *Don Enrico Incisa*

SKYLARKER (USA) 6 b.g. Sky Classic (CAN) – O My Darling (USA) 76 (Mr Pros- **89**
pector (USA)) [2004 83: f9.4g² f9.4g³ f8.5s³ p10g 8.1d 10s 10.2f⁴ 10.2m⁴ 12.6m*
11.6m⁵ 12g⁵ 12f* 11.7s² Oct 19] tall, rather leggy gelding: fairly useful handicapper: won
amateur events at Warwick in July and Ascot in September: effective at 8.5f to 1½m: acts
on all-weather, firm and soft going: tried in cheekpieces/visor: has been early to post.
W. S. Kittow

SKY QUEST (IRE) 6 b.g. Spectrum (IRE) 126 – Rose Vibert (Caerleon (USA) 132) **94**
[2004 94: 10m* 9.9g* 10d p12g⁵ p10g⁵ Nov 30] smallish, quite good-topped gelding:
fairly useful handicapper: won at Sandown in July and Goodwood (best effort, beat
Prime Powered by 2 lengths) in August: effective at 1¼m/easy 1½m: acts on polytrack,
firm and good to soft going: usually wears tongue tie/cheekpieces: suited by waiting
tactics: consistent. *W. R. Swinburn*

SKYSCAPE 2 b.f. (Mar 3) Zafonic (USA) 130 – Aquarelle (Kenmare (FR) 125) [2004 **59 p**
8g³ Oct 10] fourth foal: half-sister to fairly useful French 6f to 1m (including at 2 yrs)
winner Coastline (by Night Shift) and 3-y-o Aqualung: dam, useful French 2-y-o 1m
winner, out of close relative to St Leger winner Toulon: 10/1, 2 lengths third to Mayadeen
in maiden at Bath: will stay 1¼m: sure to improve. *A. J. Perrett*

SKYWARDS 2 b.c. (Jan 31) Machiavellian (USA) 123 – Nawaiet (USA) (Zilzal **105**
(USA) 137) [2004 5s⁵ 5f* 5m³ 5g 5f Sep 11] strong, attractive colt: has a fluent, round
action: sixth foal: brother to very smart 7f (at 2 yrs)/1m winner No Excuse Needed and
fairly useful 1¼m winner Nawadi: dam, French 6f winner, half-sister to high-class French
middle-distance filly Fitnah out of very smart sprinter Greenland Park: useful performer:
made all in maiden at Newmarket in May: good 1¼ lengths third to Blue Dakota in
Norfolk Stakes at Royal Ascot: found little when running poorly in Molecomb Stakes at
Goodwood and Flying Childers Stakes at Doncaster (tongue tied) after: likely to prove
best at 5f: acts on firm ground: races prominently. *Saeed bin Suroor*

SLALOM (IRE) 4 b.g. Royal Applause 124 – Skisette (Malinowski (USA) 123) [2004 **78**
78: f9.4g* 10g p8g 8.2d⁵ 8g 10.5s⁵ 10d p8g² Oct 25] well-made gelding: fair performer:
won maiden at Wolverhampton in May: left Gay Kelleway after sixth start: best form at

1m: acts on all-weather and soft ground: sometimes wears cheekpieces: often slowly away: sold 15,000 gns. *Julian Poulton*

SLATE GREY   2 gr.g. (Apr 24) Paris House 123 – Slipperose 72 (Persepolis (FR) 127)   **50** [2004 6m 6m 5f 5g 6d 6s Oct 22] tall, lengthy gelding: modest maiden: best effort at 5f on good going: visored last 2 starts: sometimes carries head awkwardly. *K. R. Burke*

SLAVONIC (USA)   3 ch.g. Royal Academy (USA) 130 – Cyrillic (USA) 106 (Irish   **73** River (FR) 131) [2004 80p: 9s⁵ 8g⁴ 10m⁴ 10.2m⁶ 9.9g⁴ 8g 10.3s 12d Nov 3] strong, close-coupled gelding: fair maiden: left J. Gosden 27,000 gns after fifth start: below form after: stays 1¼m: acts on good to firm ground: often blinkered/visored/in cheekpieces. *K. A. Ryan*

SLEEPING INDIAN   3 b.c. Indian Ridge 123 – Las Flores (IRE) 102 (Sadler's   **116 p** Wells (USA) 132) [2004 8.3g* 8d* Oct 30]

In response to a question about whether he rued 'ruining' Percussionist's handicap mark of 88 by running him in the Lingfield Derby Trial, which he won by a wide margin, John Gosden was reported in the *Observer* as saying: 'I think that if you have a mature three-year-old that stays a mile and a half well, then you are a bit of a wanker if you worry about a handicap mark. I prefer in life to throw the big dice.' Percussionist did enough to justify Gosden's approach when beaten less than two lengths into fourth in the Derby but was disappointing afterwards. Gosden does have a reputation for exploiting the handicap marks of his horses if they have been let in lightly, particularly at Royal Ascot, where he has saddled four winners of the Britannia Stakes in the last nine years. Halling provided another notable example, winning three handicaps when trained by Gosden as a three-year-old in 1994, including the Cambridgeshire, before, transferred to Godolphin, he won the Eclipse and the International at four. Judged on Gosden's placing of Sleeping Indian, who did not make his debut until October, it is clear that pattern races are going to be on the agenda for him in 2005.

Sleeping Indian could hardly have been found a much easier opportunity to make a winning debut than in a maiden at Windsor, and he took care of his rivals with the minimum of fuss, winning by six lengths. Just nineteen days later, faced with ten opponents, all of whom had shown at least useful form, in a listed race at Newmarket, Sleeping Indian was a well-backed joint-second favourite behind Babodana and went down by only a short head to the market leader. Badly hampered in the penultimate furlong, Sleeping Indian ran on well when switched and made up ground, but was then carried right by Babodana throughout the final furlong. Disqualifications are much rarer nowadays, but the Newmarket stewards deemed that the interference had cost Sleeping Indian the race and reversed the placings. Whatever the rights and wrongs of the stewards' decision, Sleeping Indian was manifestly the best horse in the race on the day and would have won anyway but for the interference in the penultimate furlong. The race attracted much publicity, not least because the stewards' decision cost seventy-five-year-old punter Jack Lee close to a million pounds on his Scoop6 bet and an accumulator, but the Newmarket stewards' ruling was upheld at an appeal. For Sleeping Indian, such a performance on just his second start marks him out as a very smart prospect. We should hear much more of him in the years to come, but not of Mr Lee, who sadly died less than three weeks later.

Sleeping Indian (b.c. 2001)	Indian Ridge (ch 1985)	Ahonoora (ch 1975)	Lorenzaccio / Helen Nichols
		Hillbrow (ch 1975)	Swing Easy / Golden City
	Las Flores (IRE) (b 1991)	Sadler's Wells (b 1981)	Northern Dancer / Fairy Bridge
		Producer (br 1976)	Nashua / Marion

The strong, good-topped Sleeping Indian is the best of Las Flores' six foals of racing age, all of which were owned and bred by George Strawbridge and have been trained by John Gosden. Apart from the once-raced two-year-old colt of 2004 Sun And Showers (by Rainbow Quest), all have won. The next best is Sleeping Indian's year-older half-sister Felicity (by Selkirk), who showed herself better than ever in 2004, winning the Group 3 Golden Daffodil Stakes at Chepstow. La Paz (by

Nashwan) was a useful performer at around a mile and a half as a three-year-old in 2002 and, coincidentally, was also awarded a listed race after finishing second, though connections had to wait longer for that success, at Maisons-Laffitte, than they did for Sleeping Indian's as the first past the post failed a drugs test. Sleeping Indian is also a half-brother to the useful mile-and-a-quarter winner Jalisco (by Machiavellian) and a full brother to the fairly useful mile winner Spanish Spur. Las Flores raced in the colours of Fahd Salman for Paul Cole and was useful herself, winning a maiden at Salisbury before finishing in the frame in listed and pattern races on her four subsequent runs, including when second in the Lingfield Oaks Trial and third in the Oaks d'Italia. Las Flores is by Sadler's Wells out of the top-class racemare Producer, winner of the Prix de la Foret and the Prix de l'Opera and runner-up over a distance beyond her best in the Irish Oaks. The pick of Producer's offspring is Bach, who was placed in top races when trained by Aidan O'Brien and is now at stud under the Coolmore banner. Sleeping Indian's sire Indian Ridge, whose other notable progeny in 2004 were Nayyir, Sights On Gold and Snow Ridge, is primarily an influence for speed—the average distance of races won by his three-year-olds and above is a mile—but Sleeping Indian is likely to stay a mile and a quarter. *J. H. M. Gosden*

SLING BACK (IRE) 3 b.f. Desert Style (IRE) 121 – Arabian Princess (Taufan **63** (USA) 119) [2004 6m² 7d 7g 6d p7.1g⁴ p7g³ Dec 30] €1,500Y: half-sister to several winners, including fairly useful 1¼m/1½m winner Master Cooper (by Kahyasi): dam Irish 2-y-o 7f winner: modest maiden: good efforts in handicaps last 2 starts: will stay 1m: acts on polytrack and good to firm going. *E. Tyrrell, Ireland*

SLIP CATCH (IRE) 2 b.f. (Apr 27) Intikhab (USA) 135 – Buckle (IRE) 77 (Common **60** Grounds 118) [2004 6g 7.1m⁶ p8.6g⁵ p9.5g² Dec 20] 7,000Y: big, good-topped filly: second foal: half-sister to winner in Spain by Cadeaux Genereux: dam, 1m winner, out of half-sister to Oh So Sharp: fair maiden: stays 9.5f: acts on polytrack. *W. Jarvis*

SLIP DANCE (IRE) 2 br.f. (Feb 8) Celtic Swing 138 – Hawala (IRE) 97 (Warning **106** 136) [2004 6d³ 6g* 6m⁴ 6m* 6.3f⁶ 7f² 7m⁶ 6.3g* 6g⁵ Sep 30] €8,000Y: lengthy filly: second foal: half-sister to French 8.5f winner Hawazi (by Ashkalani): dam 1m winner: useful performer: won maiden at Ballinrobe in May, listed race at Newmarket (by ¾ length from Royal Alchemist) in June and valuable contest at the Curragh (by 2 lengths from All Night Dancer) in September: good fifth to Magical Romance in Cheveley Park Stakes at Newmarket: should stay 1m: acts on firm going: genuine and consistent. *E. Tyrrell, Ireland*

SLITE 2 gr.f. (Feb 2) Mind Games 121 – Sapphire Mill (Petong 126) [2004 5.7m 7g² **55** 5d⁵ 7m⁵ 8d⁵ f8g Nov 9] 3,200Y: leggy, quite good-topped filly: first foal: dam, ran twice, half-sister to 4-y-o Golden Nun: modest maiden: trained first 2 starts by J. Osborne, next 2 by R. Hodges: probably stays 1m: acts on good to firm and good to soft going: reportedly finished lame final outing. *Miss D. Mountain*

SMALL STAKES (IRE) 2 b.c. (Mar 17) Pennekamp (USA) 130 – Poker Chip 106 **66** (Bluebird (USA) 125) [2004 5g p6g⁵ p5g² p6g⁴ Dec 3] 11,000F, 20,000Y: fifth foal: brother to German 7f/1m winner Pennechip and half-brother to 1999 2-y-o 5f winner Poker Polka (by Salse): dam 5f (including Flying Childers Stakes)/6f winner: fair maiden: likely to stay 7f: acts on polytrack. *P. J. Makin*

SMALL TIME BLUES (IRE) 2 b.f. (May 4) Danetime (IRE) 121 – Barinia (Cor- **–** varo (USA) 124) [2004 6.1g Sep 29] 9,800Y: half-sister to several winners, including 9-y-o King Priam and fairly useful Irish 1½m winner Oumaladia (by Waajib): dam French maiden: 100/1, tailed off in minor event at Nottingham. *M. J. Polglase*

SMART BOY PRINCE (IRE) 3 b.g. Princely Heir (IRE) 111 – Miss Mulaz (FR) **60** 114 (Luthier 126) [2004 61: f7f* f8g* p8g f7s⁵ 10.9d f8g³ 8f 10d 10.5g⁶ 8g 10g² 10g² **a66** f12g f16s Nov 17] workmanlike gelding: fair performer: made all in seller and selling handicap at Southwell in January: left P. Blockley after sixth start, F. Jordan after seventh and M. Attwater after twelfth: stays 1¼m: acts on all-weather and good to firm ground: usually races prominently. *C. Smith*

SMART DANNY 3 gr.g. Danzero (AUS) – She's Smart 88 (Absalom 128) [2004 –p: **45** f6g 5.1g⁵ f6g⁵ 5m 6s 5d 6g⁵ 6g Aug 5] good-topped gelding: poor maiden: likely to prove best at 5f/6f: none too reliable. *J. J. Quinn*

SMART DAWN 2 ch.f. (Apr 1) Cadeaux Genereux 131 – Blugem (FR) (Bluebird **56 ?** (USA) 125) [2004 6g 7g 8g Sep 29] 18,000Y: smallish filly: second foal: dam unraced: modest form in maidens on second start only. *C. Tinkler*

SMARTER CHARTER 11 br.g. Master Willie 129 – Irene's Charter 72 (Persian **45**
Bold 123) [2004 –: p12g⁵ p12g 10g² 10v 13.9m⁶ 11.8m⁵ 10.9d 12f⁴ 14.1m⁵ 12d⁶ 13f⁴
p10g³ 14.1d 13.1s⁵ Oct 30] leggy, lengthy gelding: poor performer nowadays: stays 1¾m:
acts on polytrack and any turf going. *Mrs L. Stubbs*

SMART HOSTESS 5 gr.m. Most Welcome 131 – She's Smart 88 (Absalom 128) **98**
[2004 101+: 5g 6g 5d 6g³ 6g 5s f5s³ p6g⁶ Nov 29] heavy-bodied mare: useful handicapper: good efforts in 2004 when third at Ripon (to Pic Up Sticks) and Southwell (to
Quiet Times): best at 5f/6f: acts on fibresand, soft and good to firm going: reportedly
broke blood vessel on reappearance: has been bandaged in front: usually waited with.
J. J. Quinn

SMART JOHN 4 b.g. Bin Ajwaad (IRE) 119 – Katy-Q (IRE) 58 (Taufan (USA) 119) **77**
[2004 68: 10s⁴ 10.5m* 10.2m⁴ 10m² 11.9g* 14d³ 11.9g⁵ 12d⁴ 12.6g* 12m³ 12f 11.9g⁶
Oct 8] good-topped gelding: fair handicapper: won at Haydock in May and July and
Warwick in August: stays 1½m: acts on soft and good to firm going. *W. M. Brisbourne*

SMART MINISTER 4 gr.g. Muhtarram (USA) 125 – She's Smart 88 (Absalom 128) **71**
[2004 63: f8.5g 8v 7.5m 6m* 7m 6g⁶ Jul 16] workmanlike gelding: fair performer: won
maiden at Ripon in June: well below form otherwise in 2004: best effort at 6f: acts on firm
and good to soft ground: slowly away penultimate outing. *J. J. Quinn*

SMART SCOT 5 ch.g. Selkirk (USA) 129 – Amazing Bay 100 (Mazilier (USA) 107) **62**
[2004 41: f8g* f7g* f7s* f7s* f8g² f8g p8.6g⁵ p7.1d p8.6g f8g² p8.6g Dec 15] modest
performer: won 4 banded races at Southwell between January and March (including amateur and apprentice events): free-going sort, best up to 1m: acts on all-weather: usually
wears cheekpieces. *B. P. J. Baugh*

SMART STARPRINCESS (IRE) 3 b.f. Soviet Star (USA) 128 – Takeshi (IRE) 67 **59**
(Cadeaux Genereux 131) [2004 56, a69: p5g* p5g* f5g² f5g³ p5g⁵ 6m 6m 5g 5.3s⁴ 5d **a70**
p5.1g p5.1g Nov 29] fair on all-weather, modest on turf: won handicap/seller at Lingfield
in January: left P. Blockley after fifth start: best at 5f: acts on all-weather, soft and good to
firm going: usually wears headgear: usually front runner. *M. J. Attwater*

SMARTY JONES (USA) 3 ch.c. Elusive Quality (USA) – I'll Get Along (USA) **134**
(Smile (USA)) [2004 a8.3f* a8f* a8.5f* a9s* a10s* a9.5f* a12f² Jun 5] second foal:
half-brother to winner in USA by Formal Gold: dam US 5.5f to 8.3f winner, including
minor stakes: reportedly suffered multiple fractures to skull in stall accident in summer
2003: subsequently developed into a top-class performer, and won first 8 races, including
non-graded stakes at Aqueduct and Oaklawn (2), Grade 2 Arkansas Derby at Oaklawn,
Kentucky Derby at Churchill Downs and Preakness Stakes at Pimlico in 2004: collected
$5m bonus for winning third to fifth starts, culminating in 2¾-length defeat of Lion Heart
at Churchill Downs, ridden to lead over 1f out after being only one to challenge leader:
beat Rock Hard Ten by record-winning margin for race of 11½ lengths at Pimlico, drawing right away without being asked a serious question: suffered only defeat when length
second to Birdstone in Belmont Stakes, clear approaching straight, but weakening markedly and caught in last 50 yards: would have proved best at 8.5f to 1¼m: acted well in wet
conditions: reported in early-August to have been retired due to chronic bruising in all
4 fetlock joints: to stand at Three Chimneys Farm, Kentucky, fee $100,000, live foal.
J. C. Servis, USA

*William Hill Great St Wilfrid Stakes (Handicap), Ripon—Smokin Beau's eighteen opponents
are unable to get anywhere near him; Pieter Brueghel is clear of the near-side runners in second*

SMEORACH 3 ch.f. My Generation 111 – Mohican 75 (Great Nephew 126) [2004 8g – 11.1m 15.8m Aug 3] half-sister to 6f (at 2 yrs) to 1½m winner Colonel Custer (by Komaite): dam 1½m winner at 5 yrs: well beaten sellers/claimer. *James Moffatt*

SMIDDY HILL 2 b.f. (Apr 13) Factual (USA) 108 – Hello Hobson's (IRE) 67 **85** (Fayruz 116) [2004 5g³ 5g² 5d⁴ 5m* 5m⁴ 5m⁵ 5.2m* 5g 5g² 5m³ 5d⁶ Oct 17] lengthy filly: fifth foal: half-sister to 3-y-o Hello Roberto: dam 5f/6f winner, including at 2 yrs: fairly useful performer: won maiden at York in May and minor event at Yarmouth in July: creditable efforts after only when placed in nurseries: will prove best at bare 5f: acts on good to firm ground: usually races up with pace. *R. Bastiman*

SMILING STARDUSTER (IRE) 2 b.c. (May 23) Danehill Dancer (IRE) 117 – Evriza (IRE) 81 (Kahyasi 130) [2004 7d f6s 7.1g Sep 11] useful-looking colt: well held in maidens/claimer. *D. Carroll*

SMIRFYS DANCE HALL (IRE) 4 b.f. Halling (USA) 133 – Bigger Dances (USA) **55** (Moscow Ballet (USA)) [2004 –: 8m⁴ 12m p8.6g Oct 9] tall, leggy filly: modest maiden: stays 1m: acts on good to firm going: tends to be slowly away/look none too keen. *W. M. Brisbourne*

SMIRFYS NIGHT 5 b.g. Tina's Pet 121 – Nightmare Lady 29 (Celestial Storm (USA) **57** 132) [2004 5.1d 5f 5g 6g⁵ 5d⁴ 5m Oct 2] quite good-topped gelding: modest performer nowadays: missed 2003: effective at 5f/6f: acts on firm and good to soft going. *D. Nicholls*

SMIRFYS PARTY 6 ch.g. Clantime 101 – Party Scenes (Most Welcome 131) [2004 **54** 65: 6g 6f 6g 6g³ 5d⁵ 6g 5m Oct 2] rather leggy gelding: modest performer: has form at 1m, raced solely at 5f/6f in 2004: acts on fibresand, firm and good to soft going: often visored: usually races prominently. *D. Nicholls*

SMIRFYS SYSTEMS 5 b.g. Safawan 118 – Saint Systems 68 (Uncle Pokey 116) **82** [2004 94: 6s 7.6d 6m⁵ 6d 6g 6m² 7.2s p6d p5.1g Nov 13] close-coupled, workmanlike gelding: fairly useful handicapper: creditable effort in 2004 only when second at Thirsk: best form at 6f: acts on firm and good to soft going, well held on soft: blinkered final outing: free-going sort. *W. M. Brisbourne*

SMITH N ALLAN OILS 5 b.g. Bahamian Bounty 116 – Grand Splendour 79 **59** (Shirley Heights 130) [2004 68: p7g* p7g 7.1d 7.1m 8m 7.5d 7.9f 7f 7.5g⁵ 7m² 7m² 6.9f⁴ **a67** 7m⁶ 7m p7.1g⁵ p8.6g p7.1g⁶ p7g⁶ Dec 30] sparely-made gelding: fair handicapper: won at Lingfield in January: effective at 7f/1m: acts on polytrack, firm and good to soft going, well below form only run on fibresand: tried blinkered, wears cheekpieces. *M. Dods*

SMOKIN BEAU 7 b.g. Cigar 68 – Beau Dada (IRE) 66 (Pine Circle (USA)) [2004 **118** 112: 6g⁶ 6g² 5g 5.1d 5f 6m⁴ 5m 6m 5g* 6s* 5s* Aug 21] smallish, robust gelding: smart performer: better than ever in 2004 and won last 3 starts, handicaps under big weights at Haydock (by ½ length from Devise), Ripon (William Hill Great St Wilfrid, beat Pieter Brueghel 5 lengths, soon across to lead far-side group and going clear final 2f) and Sandown (beat Mutawaqed by head) in August: effective at 5f/6f: acts on fibresand and any turf going: tried in headgear, better form without: sometimes gets upset in stall/starts slowly/edges right: usually front runner: game. *N. P. Littmoden*

SMOKINCANON 2 ch.c. (Apr 21) Fumo di Londra (IRE) 108 – Secret Miss 55 **70** (Beveled (USA)) [2004 5s³ p5g* 5d⁶ p5g⁵ May 26] third foal: half-brother to 6-y-o Molly's Secret: dam 5f winner: fair performer: made all in maiden at Lingfield in April: only fifth in seller there: likely to prove best at 5f/easy 6f. *W. G. M. Turner*

SMOKIN JOE 3 b.g. Cigar 68 – Beau Dada (IRE) 66 (Pine Circle (USA)) [2004 74: **91** p6g⁴ f5g p6g⁵ 6s 10g 6m p6g 6m 5m p7.1g⁵ p7g³ p7.1g² p6g* p7g* p6m* p10m² p7.1g Dec 31] small, quite attractive gelding: fairly useful performer: much improved late in year, winning minor event in November and 2 handicaps in December, all at Lingfield, beating Million Percent by length for final success: effective at 6f to easy 1¼m: acts on all-weather, best effort on turf on good to soft going: visored/blinkered nowadays. *J. R. Best*

SMOOTHIE (IRE) 6 gr.g. Definite Article 121 – Limpopo 49 (Green Desert (USA) **66** 127) [2004 67, a72: 11.6f 11.9g⁶ 12g 10m* 9.9g p12g³ p12.2g* Nov 8] close-coupled gelding: fair performer: won apprentice handicap at Leicester in September and minor event at Wolverhampton in November: stays 1½m: acts on all-weather, firm and soft going: tried blinkered, wore cheekpieces last 4 starts: none too consistent. *Ian Williams*

SMOOTHLY DOES IT 3 b.g. Efisio 120 – Exotic Forest 66 (Dominion 123) [2004 **77** 69: 10.2g 8.3s² 9g 10m⁶ 8.3m 8.1m⁴ 8m 8.1s* 8.1s² 10d⁶ 8g p10g Dec 18] leggy gelding: fair handicapper: won at Chepstow in August: stays 1m: has form on polytrack and good to firm going, but goes well on soft: raced freely and failed to handle bends at Windsor tenth start. *Mrs A. J. Bowlby*

SNAP 3 ch.g. Dr Fong (USA) 128 – Reactress (USA) (Sharpen Up 127) [2004 6.1s² 6d* **84** 7.5m³ 7d* 7g³ Jul 24] leggy, quite good-topped gelding: eighth foal: half-brother to useful 7f (at 2 yrs) and 1½m winner Shemozzle (by Shirley Heights) and 7f (at 2 yrs)/1m winner Realize (by Al Nasr): dam 2-y-o 6f winner in USA: fairly useful and progressive form: won maiden in May and handicap (beat Commando Scott by neck) in June, both at Thirsk: good close third to True Night in handicap at Newcastle final start: gelded after: should stay 1m: acts on soft and good to firm going. *M. Johnston*

SNEEM'S ROCK 3 br.c. Daylami (IRE) 138 – Urchin (IRE) (Fairy King (USA)) **–** [2004 p10g p10g Dec 30] signs of ability in maidens at Lingfield: slowly away on debut/ backed at long odds next time. *P. R. Hedger*

SNINFIA (IRE) 4 b.f. Hector Protector (USA) 124 – Christmas Kiss 82 (Taufan (USA) **55** 119) [2004 78: 10.2g 11.7g 8s 14.1m⁴ 17.2g 14.1g 14.1f f14g 11.7d Aug 27] rangy, unfurnished filly: just modest maiden in 2004: barely stays 17f: acts on good to firm going: sometimes slowly away: wore cheekpieces final start. *G. A. Ham*

SNOOKERED AGAIN 2 b.g. (Mar 8) Lujain (USA) 119 – Highest Bid (FR) (Highest **52 +** Honor (FR) 124) [2004 5d⁵ f6d* 6m f7m³ 7s 7f Sep 2] 2,700F: tall, leggy gelding: fourth **a72** foal: dam, French 7.5f (at 2 yrs) to 1¼m winner, half-sister to US Grade 1 9f/1¼m winner Janet: fair on all-weather, modest on turf: won maiden at Southwell in June: good third in nursery there: will stay at least 1m: acts on fibresand, firm and good to soft going. *M. W. Easterby*

SNOW BUNTING 6 ch.g. Polar Falcon (USA) 126 – Marl 94 (Lycius (USA) 124) **69** [2004 70: 7d 7m 6m³ 5f 6g² 7m 6g⁵ 2d³ 6m⁴ 6m⁴ 6f 6f⁶ 7g* Oct 11] leggy gelding: fair handicapper: won apprentice event at Leicester in October: effective at 6f/7f: raced mainly on good going or firmer, well held on heavy/fibresand: sometimes races freely: suited by waiting tactics. *Jedd O'Keeffe*

SNOW CHANCE (IRE) 3 ch.f. Compton Place 125 – Snowscape (Niniski (USA) **–** 125) [2004 43: 10f f8g 16g Jul 30] workmanlike filly: maiden: no form in 2004. *W. M. Brisbourne*

SNOWDRIFT 2 b.f. (Apr 8) Desert Prince (IRE) 130 – Snowing 88 (Tate Gallery **–** (USA) 117) [2004 6.1m p5g⁵ p5g Nov 20] 38,000Y: sturdy filly: fifth foal: half-sister to 6-y-o The Trader and 3-y-o Molly Moon: dam Irish 5f winner: last in maidens/minor event: blinkered second start. *D. J. Daly*

SNOWED UNDER 3 gr.g. Most Welcome 131 – Snowy Mantle 54 (Siberian Express **65** (USA) 125) [2004 –: 8.5s⁵ 9g⁵ 12.1d⁵ 10d 10g 9.9d* 10m⁶ 10f³ 10.3s Oct 22] good-topped gelding: fair handicapper: won apprentice event at Beverley in August: stays 1¼m: acts on firm and good to soft going. *J. D. Bethell*

SNOW GOOSE 3 b.f. Polar Falcon (USA) 126 – Bronzewing 103 (Beldale Flutter **111** (USA) 130) [2004 102p: 7g 7.1f⁴ 8.1d² 8m³ 9.9g³ 8s² 8d* 8d⁴ Nov 7] unfurnished filly: has a quick, fluent action: smart performer: won Premio Sergio Cumani at Milan (beat Kitcat by ¾ length) in October: mostly creditable efforts elsewhere in 2004, notably when short-head second to Secret Melody in Oppenheim-Stuten-Meile at Cologne sixth start and 2½ lengths fourth to Eagle Rise in Premio Ribot at Rome final outing: was ideally suited by 1m: acted on firm and soft going: usually raced up with pace (took time to settle under patient ride fifth appearance): sometimes wandered, but was game: stud. *J. L. Dunlop*

SNOW JOKE (IRE) 3 b.f. Desert Sun 120 – Snowcap (IRE) (Snow Chief (USA)) **59** [2004 57: 7.1d 7g⁴ 7g 10m 8.1g 8.3f 7d⁵ 7.1g Sep 3] sturdy filly: modest maiden: should stay 1m: acts on good to firm and good to soft going. *Mrs P. N. Dutfield*

SNOW LYNX (USA) 2 ch.f. (Mar 18) Lemon Drop Kid (USA) 131 – Snow Forest **– p** (USA) 97 (Woodman (USA) 126) [2004 7d Oct 30] $1,800,000Y: useful-looking filly: seventh foal: half-sister to 2 winners, including smart US performer at 6f/7f Snow Ridge (by Tabasco Cat): dam, 2-y-o 7f winner and later sprint winner in USA, half-sister to US Grade 3 8.5f winner Fighting Fantasy: 8/1, last in maiden at Newmarket, possibly amiss: likely to do better. *Saeed bin Suroor*

SNOW RIDGE (IRE) 3 b.c. Indian Ridge 123 – Snow Princess (IRE) 111 (Ela- **124 +** Mana-Mou 132) [2004 111p: 8g² 12m Jun 5]

    From the beginning of the twentieth century, Lester Piggott won nine, Steve Donoghue six, and Charlie Smirke and Willie Carson four each. Kieren Fallon has now won three, but a first success in the Derby continues to elude Frankie Dettori.

In 2004, 'renewed hunger' saw Dettori take the version of the jockeys' championship recognised by the Jockeys' Association for the first time since 1995, but, despite partnering the joint favourite, another year slipped by in Dettori's quest to win the Derby, reportedly the race he prizes above all others. At thirty-four, time may still appear to be on Dettori's side, but, given the annual schedules of top riders nowadays, it remains to be seen whether their careers will last as long as some of those in the past. The last of Piggott's thirty-six mounts in the Derby came forty years after his first win in the race as an eighteen-year-old on Never Say Die in 1954. Dettori hasn't enjoyed the freedom of choice in Derby mounts which played such a key role in Piggott's unprecedented success in the race. Since his Derby debut in 1992, all bar one of Dettori's twelve Derby rides have been in the maroon of Sheikh Mohammed or the blue of Godolphin—the exception the Michael Dickinson-trained Wolf Prince in 1993, a horse based in America. Dettori came closest to Derby success on the Gosden-trained Tamure, beaten a length into second by Lammtarra in 1995, and since 1997 Dettori has ridden exclusively in the race for Lammtarra's trainer, Saeed bin Suroor.

Dettori's latest Derby mount, Snow Ridge, was his shortest-priced ride in the race with the exception of Cape Verdi, 11/4 joint favourite in 1998. Snow Ridge started at 7/2, heading the market with North Light after his good second in the Two Thousand Guineas. Bought privately out of Marcus Tregoning's stable after winning the Royal Lodge Stakes and finishing down the field in the Dewhurst as a two-year-old, Snow Ridge's Guineas odds had tumbled from 25/1 after he made short work of the opposition in the best of the traditional round of trials held by Godolphin at Nad Al Sheba in the spring. Starting at 8/1 at Newmarket in a field of fourteen, which included Godolphin's Golden Sahara as pacemaker, Snow Ridge was kept well off the pace early on, though travelling comfortably from the start. He improved in the Dip but could never quite get to Haafhd, going down by a length

Godolphin's "Snow Ridge"

and three quarters, a length in front of Azamour with Grey Swallow fourth. Snow Ridge's pedigree gave some encouragement that he would stay a mile and a half, and Dettori was in optimistic mood before the Derby. Again ridden conservatively, Snow Ridge travelled comfortably towards the rear and began to improve smoothly early in the straight, but he got no closer to North Light than three or four lengths before fading to finish seventh of fourteen, beaten eight lengths by the winner, five places behind his stable-companion Rule of Law who held off Let The Lion Roar by a head.

Snow Ridge (IRE) (b.c. 2001)	Indian Ridge (ch 1985)	Ahoonora (ch 1975)	Lorenzaccio
			Helen Nichols
		Hillbrow (ch 1975)	Swing Easy
			Golden City
	Snow Princess (IRE) (b 1992)	Ela-Mana-Mou (b 1976)	Pitcairn
			Rose Bertin
		Karelia (b 1977)	Sir Ivor
			Karelina

If the Derby again failed to live up to expectations for Dettori, it was a red-letter day for Snow Ridge's breeders Ballymacoll Stud, which also owned and bred North Light and had bred Ballerina, the dam of Let The Lion Roar. Snow Ridge's dam Snow Princess was sold in 2002, fetching 150,000 guineas at the Tattersalls December Sales, where Ballerina had been sold for 130,000 guineas in 1994. Snow Princess had produced a brother to Snow Ridge, the two-year-old Snow Plough, before she was sold to her new owners the Newsells Park Stud, and she has since produced a filly by Green Desert, sold for 120,000 guineas at Newmarket Sales in October. As a racehorse, Snow Princess stayed two miles and Snow Ridge should have been effective over at least a mile and a quarter, but the Derby proved his last race. Reported to have had a respiratory problem following Epsom, he was put down in early-September due to severe laminitis, an inflammation around the base of the foot. A lengthy, angular colt and an easy mover, he showed very smart form in a career spanning only five races and raced only on good ground or firmer. He was usually held up. *Saeed bin Suroor*

SNOW'S RIDE   4 gr.g. Hernando (FR) 127 – Crodelle (IRE) (Formidable (USA) 125)   **67**
[2004 103: 18g 16d 13.9s 16m 14m 16g⁶ 16.2g⁴ 14.1g 16d⁴ 13.8v² Oct 16] leggy, good-topped gelding: useful handicapper at 3 yrs, just fair in 2004: stays 2m: acts on all-weather, heavy and good to firm going: tried blinkered: none too consistent: sold 21,000 gns. *W. R. Muir*

Jaguar Lowther Stakes, York—Soar is confidently ridden to account for Salsa Brava and Spirit of Chester

SNOW TEMPEST (USA) 2 b.g. (May 1) Theatrical 128 – January's Storm (USA) **60 ?**
(Hennessy (USA) 122) [2004 7g 7d 7m 8.1g⁶ Sep 15] close-coupled gelding: modest
maiden: best effort at 1m. *T. G. Mills*

SNOW WOLF 3 ch.g. Wolfhound (USA) 126 – Christmas Rose (Absalom 128) [2004 **85 d**
80: 5g 6m* 6m² 6m 6g 5m⁴ 5g 5s p5.1d p5.1g Nov 26] smallish, quite attractive gelding:
fairly useful performer: won maiden at Redcar in May: well below form last 4 starts,
including on polytrack: effective at 5f/6f: raced mainly on good ground or firmer on turf
(acts on firm): none too consistent. *J. M. Bradley*

SNUKI 5 b.g. Pivotal 124 – Kennedys Prima 65 (Primo Dominie 121) [2004 –, a77: **–**
p10g p10g p10g Feb 25] modest handicapper: stays 1¼m: acts on polytrack: tried blink- **a50**
ered. *G. L. Moore*

SOAKED 11 b.g. Dowsing (USA) 124 – Water Well 96 (Sadler's Wells (USA) 132) **71 §**
[2004 70§, a62§: f5g² p5g⁶ p6g f5g f5g⁴ f6s f5g² f5g³ f5g⁴ 5v 5f⁴ 5g* 5m² 5d* 5f⁵ 5m² **a55 §**
5f³ 5g 5s³ 5d 5m Sep 15] workmanlike gelding: fair on turf, modest on all-weather: won
claimer and handicap at Newcastle in June: best at 5f: acts on fibresand, firm and soft
going: visored once, blinkered nowadays: sometimes early/led to post: has reportedly
bled from nose/finished lame: usually front runner. *D. W. Chapman*

SOAR 2 b.f. (Feb 4) Danzero (AUS) – Splice 114 (Sharpo 132) [2004 5g* 5f² 6m* 6s* **110**
6g⁶ Sep 30] good-topped filly: has a fluent, round action: sixth foal: half-sister to 3
winners, including 3-y-o Rise and 5-y-o Feet So Fast: dam 5f (at 2 yrs)/6f winner: smart
performer: won maiden at Kempton in June, Princess Margaret Stakes at Ascot (by 1¾
lengths from Valentin) in July and Jaguar Lowther Stakes at York (quickened well to beat
Salsa Brava by 1½ lengths) in August: had interrupted preparation before only sixth in
Cheveley Park Stakes at Newmarket (sweating, attended by 2 handlers, unruly in stall):
will probably prove best at 5f/6f: acts on firm and soft ground. *J. R. Fanshawe*

Cheveley Park Stud's "Soar"

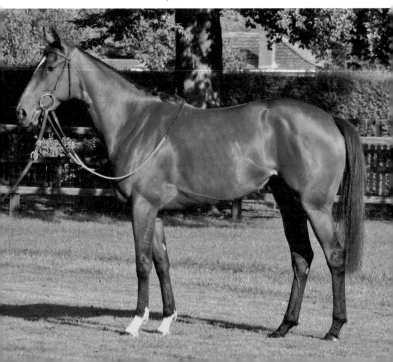

SOB

SOBA JONES 7 b.g. Emperor Jones (USA) 119 – Soba 127 (Most Secret 119) [2004 **84** 83: f6s* f6g² f5s⁴ f6g³ f6g² f6g⁵ 6s⁶ 6m⁵ 5.9g⁴ 5g² 6g⁵ 5d 5.1g⁵ p6g f5f⁶ Dec 28] tall gelding: fairly useful handicapper: won at Wolverhampton in January: best at 5f/6f: acts on fibresand and any turf going: effective blinkered or not, tried in cheekpieces: usually races prominently. *J. Balding*

SOBER AS A JUDGE 7 b.g. Mon Tresor 113 – Flicker Toa Flame (USA) 85 (Empery **–** (USA) 128) [2004 p10g Dec 20] poor maiden at 3 yrs: well held both outings since (latest after 3-year absence): tried visored. *C. A. Dwyer*

SOCIAL CONTRACT 7 b.g. Emarati (USA) 74 – Just Buy Baileys 69 (Formidable **48 §** (USA) 125) [2004 68§: p7g f7g f7g p8g⁶ p7g p7g⁶ p7g² p7g p7g f7g 6d 7m 7g 7s 6g⁶ Aug 30] strong, useful-looking gelding: poor performer nowadays: effective at 6f to easy 1m: acts on all-weather, firm and soft going: sometimes wears headgear: tried tongue tied: unreliable. *S. Dow*

SOCIETY MUSIC (IRE) 2 b.f. (Feb 24) Almutawakel 126 – Society Fair (FR) **79** (Always Fair (USA) 121) [2004 5v⁴ 6m³ 7.1f* 7m³ 7d⁶ 6g 7m⁵ 7m 6d Oct 11] €16,000Y: leggy filly: third foal: dam French 2-y-o 5.5f winner, later useful up to 1m: fair performer: won maiden at Pontefract in April and minor event at Musselburgh in June: will stay 1m: acts on any turf going: blinkered last 2 starts (respectable effort on first start only): tends to wander. *M. Dods*

SOCIETY PET 5 b.m. Runnett 125 – Polar Storm (IRE) 76 (Law Society (USA) 130) **– §** [2004 –§: 6d 6m Sep 25] ungenuine maiden. *D. G. Bridgwater*

SOCIETY TIMES (USA) 11 b.g. Imp Society (USA) – Mauna Loa (USA) (Hawaii) **–** [2004 8f 9.1g 9.2d 9g 10.9s⁵ Sep 18] little form: tried tongue tied. *D. A. Nolan*

SO DETERMINED (IRE) 3 b.g. Soviet Star (USA) – Memory Green (USA) **59** (Green Forest (USA) 134) [2004 –: 7m 10f² p12g Aug 21] well-grown gelding: modest maiden: stays 1¼m: acts on firm going: tried tongue tied: joined J. Lambe in Ireland. *G. A. Butler*

SO ELEGANT (IRE) 2 b.f. (Apr 29) Bahhare (USA) 122 – Soignee (Night Shift **42** (USA)) [2004 7.1d p7.1g⁵ p7m Nov 22] €3,000F, €3,500Y: half-sister to 3 winners, including fairly useful 1m (at 2 yrs) and 9f winner Radar (by Petardia): dam unraced: poor form in maidens. *J. Jay*

SOFISTICATION (IRE) 3 b.f. Dayjur (USA) 137 – Cieladeed (USA) (Shadeed **68** (USA) 135) [2004 p7g p7g* Jan 24] IR 7,000F, €55,000Y: first foal: dam unraced out of useful Irish 1m to 1½m performer Cielamour: better effort in maidens when winning at Lingfield by ½ length: sold 1,200 gns in December. *T. G. Mills*

SOFT FOCUS (IRE) 2 b.f. (May 16) Spectrum (IRE) 126 – Creme Caramel (USA) **47** 88 (Septieme Ciel (USA) 123) [2004 p8g p8.6g p8g 6.1v Nov 4] 6,000Y: leggy filly: second foal: half-sister to 2003 2-y-o 7f winner Monte Bianco (by King of Kings): dam, 2-y-o 7f winner, half-sister to smart performer up to 1m Robellation: poor maiden: form only on debut. *J. A. Osborne*

SOFT MIST (IRE) 4 gr.f. Up And At 'em 109 – Morgiana (Godswalk (USA) 130) **–** [2004 67: f8g⁶ f9.4g 8d 9.9v 8m 8.1m Jun 14] IR 2,000Y: half-sister to several winners, including 5f (at 2 yrs) to 7f winner Ochos Rios (by Horage): dam maiden: fair handi-capper for G. M. Lyons in 2003: little form in Britain at 4 yrs. *J. J. Quinn*

SO INDEPENDENT 2 b.f. (Feb 18) Tipsy Creek (USA) 115 – So Bold (Never So **–** Bold 135) [2004 6m 5.9f Jul 29] 1,500F, 1,100Y: sturdy filly: half-sister to useful 5f (at 2 yrs) to 8.5f winner Stoppes Brow (by Primo Dominie): dam lightly-raced maiden: always behind in maidens. *C. R. Wilson*

SOKOKE 3 ch.g. Compton Place 125 – Sally Green (IRE) 79 (Common Grounds 118) **64** [2004 5m² 5f³ 6s 5.7f p6g f6s Nov 17] workmanlike gelding: second foal: dam, 5f/6f (latter at 2 yrs) winner, half-sister to smart miler Soviet Bureau: modest maiden: well below form after second start: best efforts at 5f: acts on firm ground: sold 1,400 gns. *R. M. Beckett*

SOLANICH 2 ch.g. (May 4) Inchinor 119 – Gussy Marlowe 118 (Final Straw 127) **70** [2004 p6g p7.1g³ Dec 10] 40,000Y: seventh foal: half-brother to 7f winner Sloane and 5-y-o Alchemist Master (both fairly useful, by Machiavellian): dam won Falmouth Stakes and Musidora Stakes: better effort in maidens at Wolverhampton when third to Croon. *R. Hannon*

960

SOLAR FALCON   2 ch.f. (Apr 1) Polar Falcon (USA) 126 – Beryl 77 (Bering 136)   – [2004 8.3m 8g Oct 10] 3,200Y: second foal: dam, 1½m winner, out of half-sister to dam of 9-y-o Bahamian Pirate: well held in maidens at Windsor and Bath. *A. G. Newcombe*

SOLARIAS QUEST   2 b.g. (Feb 10) Pursuit of Love 124 – Persuasion 79 (Batshoof   **79** 122) [2004 8.1m³ 8.1s³ 10v² Oct 20] 16,000Y: sturdy gelding: third foal: half-brother to 7f/1m winner Nellie Melba (by Hurricane Sky) and 1m winner So Tempting (by So Factual), both fairly useful: dam 1¼m/1½m winner: fair form in maidens: second at Nottingham: shapes as if will stay at least 1½m. *A. King*

SOLAR POWER (IRE)   3 b.f. Marju (IRE) 127 – Next Round (IRE) 83 (Common   **101** Grounds 118) [2004 77p: 8m² 8s⁴ 8m⁴ 7m⁴ 7d³ 6g* 6s² 6m² Sep 30] smallish, compact filly: useful performer: won minor event at Haydock in September: good efforts after when runner-up in handicaps at same course (beaten ½ length by Eisteddfod) and Newmarket (beaten some distance by Paradise Isle, finishing strongly): better form at 6f than 7f: acts on soft and good to firm going: usually waited with. *J. R. Fanshawe*

SOLAR PRINCE (IRE)   3 b.g. Desert Prince (IRE) 130 – Quiche 83 (Formidable   – (USA) 125) [2004 57d: 5m 8v 6s Sep 19] lengthy gelding: no form since early-2003: left Joseph Quinn in Ireland prior to final start: tried tongue tied/blinkered. *H. Alexander*

SOLDERA (USA)   4 b.f. Polish Numbers (USA) – La Pepite (USA) (Mr Prospector   **108** (USA)) [2004 107: 8f³ 10m⁴ 10s 8m⁴ 9s Oct 16] lengthy filly: fluent mover: useful performer: good fourth to Tarfah in listed handicap at Ascot penultimate start: best efforts at 1m: acts on firm and good to soft going, well held on soft, including in Darley Stakes at Newmarket final outing: sent to USA. *J. R. Fanshawe*

SOLDIER HOLLOW   4 br.c. In The Wings 128 – Island Race 93 (Common Grounds   **119** 118) [2004 111: 10.5g⁴ 8.5d² 11g 10g² 10g* 10d* 10g* 10d* 10m Dec 12] 75,000Y: first foal: dam 6f winner: smart performer: ran only twice in 2003 (reportedly suffered severely inflamed intestine and off over 10 months): better than ever on return, winning Lotto Hessen-Pokal at Frankfurt (by 2½ lengths from Anolitas) in July, Preis der Sparkassen-Finanzgruppe at Baden-Baden (by ¾ length from Longridge) in August, Merrill Lynch Euro-Cup at Frankfurt (beat Fight Club by 1¼ lengths) in September and Premio Roma SIS (by 1½ lengths from Imperial Dancer) in November: below form in Hong Kong Cup at Sha Tin final start: stays 1¼m: acts on good to soft ground. *P. Schiergen, Germany*

SOLDIER'S TALE (USA)   3 ch.c. Stravinsky (USA) 133 – Myrtle 96 (Batshoof   **101** 122) [2004 6g² 7s* May 12] strong, good-bodied colt: type to carry condition: second foal: dam, 2-y-o 7.5f winner, later successful in USA: useful form: promising head second to Fun To Ride in maiden at Newmarket prior to winning similar event at York following month by 5 lengths from Capestar: reportedly suffered setback later in May: stays 7f: looked capable of better. *J. Noseda*

SOLE AGENT (IRE)   2 b.g. (Apr 20) Trans Island 119 – Seattle Siren (USA) 101   **66** (Seattle Slew (USA)) [2004 8m 8s³ 7s Oct 21] 5,000F: half-brother to numerous winners, including fairly useful 6f winner Focused Attraction (by Eagle Eyed) and 7-y-o Rooftop Protest: dam 2-y-o 6f winner: clearly best effort in maidens when third at Brighton: slowly away and never dangerous other outings: will stay 1¼m. *G. L. Moore*

SOLEIL D'HIVER   3 b.f. Bahamian Bounty 116 – Catriona 75 (Bustino 136) [2004   – 43: f9.4g f8g⁵ 7.5m May 24] sturdy, lengthy filly: maiden: little form on Flat at 3 yrs: won over hurdles in November. *P. C. Haslam*

SOLENT (IRE)   2 b.c. (Mar 18) Montjeu (IRE) 137 – Stylish (Anshan 119) [2004 7m*   **92** 7g 8g³ Sep 2] 60,000Y: big, good-topped colt: second foal: half-brother to fairly useful 7f (including at 2 yrs)/1m winner Due Respect (by Danehill): dam unraced half-sister to very smart sprinter Eveningperformance out of half-sister to 2000 Guineas winner Tirol: won maiden at Newmarket in June: length third of 5 to Liakoura in minor event at Salisbury: stays 1m: pulled hard second start. *R. Hannon*

SOLINIKI   3 b.g. Danzero (AUS) – Pride of My Heart 74 (Lion Cavern (USA) 117)   – [2004 84p: 7d 6g 7d p6g f7s Nov 17] lengthy, unfurnished gelding: fairly useful effort only 2-y-o start: little form in 2004: blinkered last 2 starts: sold 2,300 gns. *J. A. Osborne*

SOLIPSIST (IRE)   3 ch.c. Grand Lodge (USA) 125 – Mijouter (IRE) (Coquelin (USA)   – 121) [2004 8m 7m p8.6g Nov 20] little form in maidens: trained by R. Hannon first 2 starts. *N. I. M. Rossiter*

SOLLER BAY   7 b.g. Contract Law (USA) 108 – Bichette 66 (Lidhame 109) [2004   **82** 86, a–: 8.3d² 7.6d 8.1g 8s⁴ 8g 9.1d 11.6d Oct 4] quite good-topped gelding: fairly useful   **a–** performer: below form after reappearance: stays 1m: acts on fibresand, heavy and good to firm going: races freely/up with pace. *K. R. Burke*

SOLMORIN 6 b.m. Fraam 114 – Reclusive (Sunley Builds 102) [2004 p10g⁵ Jan 15] third foal: sister to 8.5f winner Sheerness Essity and half-sister to 7f winner Solianna (by Beveled): dam unraced: 20/1, well held in maiden at Lingfield. *R. J. Baker*

SOLO FLIGHT 7 gr.g. Mtoto 134 – Silver Singer 65 (Pharly (FR) 130) [2004 97: **96** 10m² 12g⁶ 10.3g 10m² 10g 11g* 12g³ 12d Oct 14] angular gelding: useful handicapper: won at Newbury (beat Tip The Dip by neck) in September: good third at Newmarket next start: effective at 1¼m/1½m: acts on firm and good to soft going, possibly not on soft/ heavy: edgy sort: best held up in truly-run race: sometimes finds little. *H. Morrison*

SOLOR 3 b.c. Spectrum (IRE) 126 – Bayadere (USA) 61 (Green Dancer (USA) 132) **85** [2004 p8g⁴ 10.2g* 10v Oct 23] 16,000Y: neat colt: half-brother to useful 1m to 1½m winner Bryony Brind (by Kris) and 7f (at 2 yrs) to 1½m winner Azur (by Brief Truce): dam staying maiden: fairly useful performer: won maiden at Bath in April: tailed off in handicap at Newbury next time (said to have finished lame): dead. *D. J. Coakley*

SOLO SOLE (ITY) 3 b.g. Grand Lodge (USA) 125 – Storm Flash 65 (Green Desert **–** (USA) 127) [2004 72: 10.2g 8.3s 8.2g Jun 21] fair maiden at 2 yrs: well held in handicaps in 2004: sold 5,500 gns, sent to Belgium. *L. M. Cumani*

SOL ROJO 2 b.g. (Feb 18) Efisio 120 – Shining Cloud 73 (Indian Ridge 123) [2004 **67** 6g p7.1g p8g p8.6d⁵ p8.6g³ p8.6g Nov 20] 12,000Y: third foal: half-brother to 2002 2-y-o 7f winner Dmitri (by Emperor Jones) and 3-y-o Vengerov: dam fair maiden: fair maiden: stays 8.6f: acts on polytrack: blinkered (ran poorly) final start. *J. A. Osborne*

SOLSKJAER (IRE) 4 b.c. Danehill (USA) 126 – Lyndonville (IRE) (Top Ville 129) **112** [2004 95: 7m* 8f² 10m² 10m* 10.4d Aug 17] well-made colt: sixth living foal: brother to smart Japanese performer up to 1½m Tsukuba Symphony and half-brother to 3-y-o Yeats: dam, Irish 1¾m winner, half-sister to Fillies' Mile winner Ivanka: smart per- former: behind in Irish 2000 Guineas at the Curragh only outing prior to 2004: won 4-runner minor event at Naas in June and Royal Whip Stakes at the Curragh (made all, beat Tropical Lady by a head) in August: good second in between to Grand Passion in listed race at the Curragh and to Latino Magic in Meld Stakes at Leopardstown (short- headed on line): below form when eighth behind Sulamani in International Stakes at York final start: stays 1¼m: acts on firm going, below form on good to soft: has worn crossed noseband. *A. P. O'Brien, Ireland*

SOLVED (USA) 3 b.f. Hennessy (USA) 122 – Claradane (IRE) 93 (Danehill (USA) **–** 126) [2004 80: 5.1f May 21] $35,000Y: fourth foal: dam Irish 2-y-o 6f winner who stayed 1m: fairly useful maiden for P. Doyle in Ireland in 2003: well below form only 3-y-o start: raced only at 5f. *P. A. Blockley*

SOMAYDA (IRE) 9 b.g. Last Tycoon 131 – Flame of Tara 124 (Artaius (USA) 129) **45 §** [2004 59: 9g 10m 9g 6d³ 12.1m 11.6m⁶ 8s⁵ p13g p7g Dec 20] poor handicapper: seems effective at 6f to 1½m: acts on heavy and good to firm going: tried in headgear: unreli- able. *Miss Jacqueline S. Doyle*

SOME NIGHT (IRE) 2 b.f. (Mar 24) Night Shift (USA) – Some Merit (Midyan **49** (USA) 124) [2004 6g⁵ 5.1d Oct 15] €15,000F, €15,000Y, resold €70,000Y: compact filly: fourth foal: half-sister to 5f to 7.5f winner in Italy by Hamas: dam unraced half- sister to Prix de la Foret winner Procida: poor form in maidens: sold 3,000 gns, sent to Sweden. *J. H. M. Gosden*

SOMEONE'S ANGEL (USA) 3 gr.f. Runaway Groom (CAN) – Yazeanhaa (USA) 68 **–** (Zilzal (USA) 137) [2004 –p: 6s Apr 28] leggy filly: well held in maidens. *E. A. L. Dunlop*

SOMERSET WEST (IRE) 4 b.g. Catrail (USA) 123 – Pizzazz 47 (Unfuwain (USA) **78** 131) [2004 64: p5g⁶ p6g p6g p7g* 7s* 7f 6g 5g* 6d 5.7g f8g p6g⁴ f6g p6g⁶ p5.1g² Dec **a63** 31] workmanlike gelding: fair on turf, modest on all-weather: won seller (sold from Mrs L. Stubbs) at Lingfield in April, and ladies handicaps at Lingfield (dead-heat) in May and Leicester in June: stays 7f: acts on polytrack, firm and soft going: tried tongue tied. *J. R. Best*

SOMETHINGABOUTHER 4 b.f. Whittingham (IRE) 104 – Paula's Joy 75 (Dane- **49** hill (USA) 126) [2004 64, a40: p6g⁴ f5s⁵ f5g p5g³ p6g p5g⁵ 5.1m 5g² 5.3f 5g 5.1f Jul 5] **a44** smallish, sturdy filly: poor maiden: best at 5f: acts on polytrack, firm and good to soft ground: none too consistent. *P. W. Hiatt*

SOMETHING EXCITING 2 ch.f. (Mar 7) Halling (USA) 133 – Faraway Waters **105** 102 (Pharly (FR) 130) [2004 7m⁴ 7m 7g 8s* 8g* 8d* 8d² Oct 30] 20,000Y: smallish, close-coupled filly: fourth foal: dam, 2-y-o 6f winner who probably stayed 1½m, out of sister to smart performer up to 14.6f Shining Water, herself dam of Tenby: useful performer: won nurseries at Salisbury and Goodwood in September and minor event at

Newmarket (came from off strong pace to beat Embossed by 3 lengths) in October: respectable 1½ lengths second to Squaw Dance in listed event at Newmarket, hanging right: will be suited by 1¼m/1½m: acts on soft going. *D. R. C. Elsworth*

SOMETHING (IRE)   2 b.c. (Mar 13) Trans Island 119 – Persian Polly 99 (Persian   **85**
Bold 123) [2004 6m² 6g⁶ Sep 29] €100,000Y: half-brother to numerous winners, notably top-class sprinter Lake Coniston (by Bluebird): dam Irish 2-y-o 7f winner: much better effort when head second to Sant Jordi in maiden at Windsor: hung right when last in minor event at Salisbury: should stay 7f. *T. G. Mills*

SOMEWHERE MY LOVE   3 br.f. Pursuit of Love 124 – Grand Coronet 66 (Grand   **68**
Lodge (USA) 125) [2004 63: p8g* p7g p8g f8.5m³ 6g p7.1g Nov 27] useful-looking filly: fair performer: won maiden at Lingfield in January: stays 8.5f: acts on all-weather, raced only on good/good to firm ground on turf. *T. G. Mills*

SOMEWIN (IRE)   4 b.f. Goldmark (USA) 113 – Janet Oliphant 49 (Red Sunset 120)   **–**
[2004 16.2m Jul 23] IR 3,000Y: fourth living foal: half-sister to a Scandinavian 5.5f (at 2 yrs) to 8.5f winner by Mujadil: dam, maiden, half-sister to high-class 1¼m/1½m performer Amyndas: bumper winner for R. Fahey: well beaten in claimer at Chepstow on Flat debut (wore cheekpieces). *Miss K. Marks*

SOMNUS   4 b.g. Pivotal 124 – Midnight's Reward 84 (Night Shift (USA)) [2004   **126**
125: 6s 6d² 6g⁵ 6.5g* 6g² 7d* Oct 9]
With some owners prepared to invest millions, rags to riches stories at the very top level, epitomised by the victory of 3,200-dollar yearling Singletary, in the Breeders' Cup Mile in October, tend to come along about as regularly as blue moons. Hitting the jackpot for a relatively small outlay is a bit more commonplace in the slightly less prestigious world of sprinting, especially in years lacking an outstanding champion. Sprinting in Britain certainly had its share of comparative shoestring successes in 2004. Fayr Jag, an 8,000-guinea yearling, won the Golden Jubilee Stakes at Royal Ascot, and Frizzante, bred by her owners out of a modest mare purchased for 2,100 guineas as a yearling, won the July Cup at Newmarket. Somnus, a stable-companion of Fayr Jag, bought back at the sales as a yearling by a partnership including his breeder for 13,500 guineas, failed narrowly to take the category's only other Group 1 event of the year over six furlongs in Britain, the Stanleybet Sprint Cup at Haydock, but he won two Group 1 prizes in France, and his short-head defeat by Tante Rose at Haydock, attempting to follow up his previous year's success in the race, was enough to give him a share of the title of champion sprinter for 2004.

The first of Somnus' Group 1 successes in 2004 came in the Prix Maurice de Gheest over six and a half furlongs at Deauville in August. Favourite at 33/10 in a field of eighteen was the home-trained Whipper, fifth in the Two Thousand Guineas at Newmarket in May. A strong British-trained contingent included July Cup winner Frizzante at 9/2, and The Trader, already successful in the Prix de Saint-Georges at Longchamp in May and the Prix de Ris-Orangis at Deauville in July, at 7/1. Below form in the Duke of York Stakes on his reappearance in May, Somnus had shown much of his old ability when a neck second to Royal Millennium, conceding him 8 lb, in the Chipchase Stakes at Newcastle, before finishing strongly into fifth in the July Cup, beaten under three lengths. Although officially good to soft, the ground was less testing than Somnus' connections might have hoped for at Deauville and he was sent off at 15/1. He travelled smoothly in a group of three led by Dolma on the stand side. Allowed to drift right to join the main group in the centre around halfway, Somnus was flanked by Whipper and July Cup runner-up Ashdown Express as he took a definite advantage approaching the

Prix Maurice de Gheest, Deauville—Somnus (No.5) holds on
in a very close finish with Whipper (hooped cap), Dolma (rail) and Ashdown Express (star on cap)

*Prix de la Foret, Longchamp—Somnus gains the third Group 1 success of his career
as he beats Denebola, Le Vie dei Colori (right) and Monsieur Bond*

final furlong, and he ran on tenaciously to hold Whipper by a neck. Dolma, who
had stuck to the stand side, edged Ashdown Express out of third by the same
margin, with The Trader clear of the remainder in fifth. Somnus' rider, American
Gary Stevens, made light afterwards of a difficult season overall in France in 2004,
details of which are included in the essay on Grey Lilas, commenting: 'I needed an
English-speaking horse to win my first Group 1 in France.'

With Stevens back in America, Somnus was partnered for the remainder of
the season by Michael Kinane. In a field of nineteen, Somnus started at 7/1 in the
Sprint Cup in September in what was probably the strongest sprint of the season.
Somnus had reportedly returned from France with a 'mucky nose', but looked in
magnificent shape at Haydock and could hardly have gone closer to emulating 1966
and 1967 winner Be Friendly, the only horse to take successive renewals of the
race. Soon prominent as the pace took a while to pick up, Somnus got the better of
Patavellian well inside the final furlong, only to find himself pipped on the line by
the flourish of Tante Rose, with Patavellian three quarters of a length away third.
On form, this was the sprinting performance of the season, conceding the winner
3 lb, though Tante Rose did well to prevail the way the race unfolded.

Somnus had finished only seventh when dropped to five furlongs in the Prix
de l'Abbaye for his only outing after Haydock in 2003, and, in a change of tack, he
was stepped back up to seven furlongs for the first time since tackling the Jersey
Stakes at Royal Ascot as a three-year-old for his final outing at Longchamp in
October in the Prix de la Foret, a race which is to become part of Arc weekend in
2005. In a field of seven, Somnus started favourite at 26/10, the three-year-old filly
Denebola and the five-year-old Charming Groom the only home-trained runners.
On softish going, Somnus threatened to spoil his chance by taking a strong hold
early on, but he soon settled towards the rear, as Monsieur Bond began to string
the field out. With the ground churned up on the inside, Somnus was kept wide from
the turn and was still last over two furlongs out, a good five lengths off the clear
leader, but he responded well to lead inside the last furlong, and, though tired, held
Denebola by three quarters of a length, with Le Vie dei Colori a length further away
in third and Monsieur Bond fourth. Pastoral Pursuits was fifth, with Nayyir well
below par in sixth.

		Pivotal (ch 1993)	Polar Falcon (b or br 1987)	Nureyev
Somnus (b.g. 2000)				Marie d'Argonne
			Fearless Revival (ch 1987)	Cozzene
				Stufida
		Midnight's Reward (b 1986)	Night Shift (b 1980)	Northern Dancer
				Ciboulette
			Margaret's Ruby (b 1968)	Tesco Boy
				Pixie Jet

'Dam winning sprinter' is often a good starting point for purchasing a future
winner at a modest price, at least bringing some likelihood of speed, and Somnus,
whose pedigree has been dealt with more fully in previous editions of *Racehorses*,
carried that statement in the catalogue when offered for sale as a yearling, as did

Fayr Jag and Frizzante. In sprinting at least, it often doesn't take a champion to produce a champion either. Somnus' dam Midnight's Reward was the best of the above-named trio's dams on the racecourse, though she showed only fairly useful form, winning over five furlongs. Somnus' sire Pivotal was a very smart sprinter, winning the King's Stand Stakes and the Nunthorpe as a three-year-old, and he has been a roaring success at stud. Among his other representatives in 2004 were Pivotal Point and Ringmoor Down. Pivotal, also responsible for the leading sprinter Kyllachy in 2002, still has plenty to do to match Danzig in terms of champions— Danzig was responsible for the best sprinter in Europe four times in the 'nineties —but Pivotal, though essentially a strong influence for speed, has had good horses over a variety of distances, including Champion Stakes runner-up Chorist in 2004. Somnus is effective at six and seven furlongs and, though a winner on good to firm ground, he goes particularly well on good/good to soft (his only runs on soft ground came at the end of one season and the beginning of another). A good-topped gelding, successful on nine of his nineteen runs so far, Somnus is genuine and reliable, and, still relatively lightly raced, should continue to be a tough opponent for some time to come. *T. D. Easterby*

SON AND HEIR (IRE)   3 b.c. Princely Heir (IRE) 111 – Margarets Memory (IRE)   –
83 (Imperial Frontier (USA) 112) [2004 p8m Oct 6] 50/1, well beaten in maiden at Lingfield. *N. J. Hawke*

SONDERBORG   3 b.f. Great Dane (IRE) 122 – Nordico Princess 71 (Nordico (USA))   58
[2004 55: p7g⁶ p8g⁴ p7g⁵ f8g³ f7s² p7g² p7g² p7g 10d 8m² 7m⁶ f8g 10m 8.3m 9s⁶ p10g⁶ p12g⁶ 8m³ 8d Oct 16] workmanlike filly: modest maiden: left G. L. Moore after eighth start: effective at 7f to easy 1¼m: acts on all-weather, firm and good to soft going: usually wears headgear. *Miss A. M. Newton-Smith*

SONEARSOFAR (IRE)   4 b.g. General Monash (USA) 107 – Not Too Near (IRE)   –
(Nashamaa 113) [2004 7.5d 6.9f⁶ 8d 9.9d p7.1d Oct 23] no sign of ability. *J. Parkes*

SONGERIE   2 b.f. (Mar 6) Hernando (FR) 127 – Summer Night 94 (Nashwan (USA)   105
135) [2004 7.1s* 7d 8d* Oct 19] second foal: half-sister to Italian 6.5f to 8.5f (including at 2 yrs) winner by Selkirk: dam, 6f winner who ran twice, out of half-sister to Petoski: won maiden at Chepstow (by 5 lengths) in September and Prix des Reservoirs at Deauville (by ½ length from Soignee) in October: favourite, ran poorly in C. L. Weld Park Stakes at the Curragh in between: will be suited by 1¼m/1½m: useful. *Sir Mark Prescott*

SONGGARIA   2 b.f. (Feb 3) Kingsinger (IRE) 94 – Paula's Joy 75 (Danehill (USA)   48
126) [2004 5m² 6m³ 5f 7.5d² Jul 3] £700Y: smallish: third foal: dam 2-y-o 5f winner (only season to race): poor maiden: trained debut by B. Palling, next start by J. Best: stays 7.5f: acts on good to firm and good to soft ground. *J. S. Wainwright*

SONG KOI   3 b.f. Sri Pekan (USA) 117 – Eastern Lyric 93 (Petong 126) [2004 57: 6g   49
5g² 5m p6g⁴ f5g p5m⁴ p6g³ Dec 22] smallish, lengthy filly: poor maiden: stays easy 6f: acts on polytrack and good to firm ground. *J. G. Given*

SONGLARK   4 br.c. Singspiel (IRE) 133 – Negligent 118 (Ahonoora 122) [2004 111,   115
a115: 10g⁵ 12g² 12f⁴ Jun 19] big, useful-looking colt: smart performer: back to best when 2½ lengths second to Papineau in well-contested minor event at Goodwood and when 8½ lengths fourth to Doyen in Hardwicke Stakes at Royal Ascot, in latter keeping on bravely after helping force strong pace: stays 1½m: acts on dirt and firm going: usually tongue tied, visored last 3 starts. *Saeed bin Suroor*

SONG OF THE SEA   3 ch.f. Bering 136 – Calypso Run (Lycius (USA) 124) [2004   60
–p: 10d 10d 12m⁴ 16.4m 18d p12g Sep 1] modest maiden: tried tongue tied: sold 5,500 gns. *J. W. Hills*

SONG OF VALA   3 ch.g. Peintre Celebre (USA) 137 – Yanka (USA) (Blushing John   77
(USA) 120) [2004 82: 9s 12.1g⁵ 10g 8.1m⁶ 8g³ p8m⁴ p8.6g² f8g* Dec 7] good-topped gelding: fair performer: won maiden at Southwell in December: effective at 1m to 1½m: acts on all-weather, good to firm and good to soft going: often tongue tied: blinkered last 2 starts. *R. Charlton*

SONG SPARROW   2 b.f. (Apr 1) Vettori (IRE) 119 – Fanfare 89 (Deploy 131) [2004   – p
p7m p7g⁶ p6g Nov 8] first foal: dam, 1¼m to 1¾m winner, out of close relative to very smart miler Mukaddamah: signs of ability in maidens on polytrack: should be suited by 1¼m/1½m: should do better. *G. A. Butler*

SONGTHRUSH (USA)   2 gr.f. (Mar 2) Unbridled's Song (USA) 125 – Virgin Michael   87 p
(USA) (Green Dancer (USA) 132) [2004 7d* Oct 30] $120,000Y: half-sister to several

winners in USA: dam, US 1m winner (including minor stakes), half-sister to US Grade 1 7f winner Virginia Rapids: 20/1, won maiden at Newmarket by 2½ lengths from Ladeena, racing alone and making all: will stay 1m: should progress. *P. F. I. Cole*

SONIC ANTHEM (USA) 2 b.g. (Apr 6) Royal Anthem (USA) 135 – Whisperifyou- –
dare (USA) (Red Ransom (USA)) [2004 6d Sep 16] 50/1, slowly away and always rear in maiden at Ayr. *D. Nicholls*

SONNTAG BLUE (IRE) 2 b.g. (Mar 17) Bluebird (USA) 125 – Laura Margaret **63**
(Persian Bold 123) [2004 6f 6g p6d 6.1d f8g³ p8.6g* f8g⁶ Dec 11] 25,000F, 28,000Y: leggy gelding: half-brother to several winners, including 3-y-o Yankeedoodledandy and useful Scandinavian winner up to 2m Account Express (by Roi Danzig): dam Italian 2-y-o 9.5f winner: modest performer: won seller at Wolverhampton in December: stays 8.6f: acts on polytrack: blinkered last 3 starts. *J. A. Osborne*

SONO 7 b.g. Robellino (USA) 127 – Sweet Holland (USA) (Alydar (USA)) [2004 85: **72**
16g 16d⁵ 16m⁴ May 26] close-coupled gelding: fair handicapper nowadays: stays 2m: acts on soft and good to firm ground: in cheekpieces last 2 starts: usually held up. *P. D. Niven*

SON OF REMBRANDT (IRE) 3 b.g. Titus Livius (FR) 115 – Avidal Park 68 **53 d**
(Horage 124) [2004 66: p6g f5g p5g⁵ f7s³ 6d⁶ f7g³ 6m f8.5g 7m Jun 8] smallish gelding: modest maiden: below form last 5 starts: stays 7f: acts on all-weather and good to firm going: tried blinkered. *D. K. Ivory*

SON OF THUNDER (IRE) 3 ch.g. Dr Fong (USA) 128 – Sakura Queen (IRE) 52 **70**
(Woodman (USA) 126) [2004 –: 7.1d⁶ 8m* 9.1g⁶ 8f² 8.1g 8f* 7.1g p8.6d Nov 4] leggy, close-coupled gelding: fair handicapper: won at Musselburgh in May and July: stays 1m: acts on firm going: raced freely/found little fifth start: usually held up. *M. Dods*

SONOMA (IRE) 4 ch.f. Dr Devious (IRE) 127 – Mazarine Blue (USA) (Chief's **73**
Crown (USA)) [2004 78: 16g⁵ 16g 14.4v⁶ 14.1d 14.1m 16g* 14.1d⁴ 16m⁴ 16s⁴ 16g³ Sep 13] sturdy filly: fair performer: won minor event at Nottingham in June: stays 2m: acts on good to firm and good to soft ground, seemingly not on soft: races prominently: sold 6,000 gns. *M. L. W. Bell*

SOOYOU SIR (IRE) 2 b. or br.g. (Mar 9) Orpen (USA) 116 – Naivement (IRE) –
(Doyoun 124) [2004 7g 10g 7s Nov 2] workmanlike gelding: no form in maidens. *Mrs A. Duffield*

SOPHOMORE 10 b.g. Sanglamore (USA) 126 – Livry (USA) (Lyphard (USA) 132) **34**
[2004 –: f8.5g f11g⁶ f9.4s³ f11s Mar 14] workmanlike gelding: poor performer nowadays: stays 9.4f: acts on fibresand: tried in cheekpieces. *John A. Harris*

SOPHRANO (IRE) 4 b.g. Spectrum (IRE) 126 – Sophrana (IRE) (Polar Falcon **58**
(USA) 126) [2004 68: 8.2g⁵ 7.1m³ 6g 6d³ 8.3d³ 7.1s 6.9m⁴ 7.1d Oct 9] leggy, angular gelding: modest maiden: effective at 6f to 1m: acts on polytrack and good to soft going: visored (only final 3-y-o outing) final 3-y-o outing: has carried head awkwardly. *P. A. Blockley*

SORBIESHARRY (IRE) 5 gr.g. Sorbie Tower (IRE) 120 – Silver Moon (Environ- –
ment Friend 128) [2004 –, a64: f9.4g⁵ f8g² f8f³ f9.4g⁵ f8.5g* f11s⁵ f8g f9.4g* f8g⁴ f9.4g **a61**
f8g⁵ f8s p8.6d f11g³ f8s* p9.5g f8g* p9.5g⁴ f7g⁵ f8g³ f8g² Dec 28] leggy gelding: poor mover: modest performer: won handicaps at Wolverhampton in February and March and Southwell in November, and apprentice banded race at Southwell in December: stays 9.5f: acts on all-weather, raced only on good going or firmer on turf: visored once, usually wears cheekpieces: often slowly away: has looked none too keen. *Mrs N. Macauley*

SORCERESS 2 b.f. (Apr 18) Wizard King 122 – Aonia 97 (Mummy's Pet 125) [2004 –
6f 6g p7.1g Dec 31] 800Y: half-sister to 3 winners, including 6f winner Suleyman (by Alhijaz): dam, 2-y-o 5f winner, half-sister to very smart performer up to 9f in Britain/USA Forzando: well held in maidens. *J. Gallagher*

SORRENTO KING 7 ch.g. First Trump 118 – Star Face (African Sky 124) [2004 f14g –
May 19] workmanlike gelding: poor maiden: well held only outing since 2002: usually blinkered. *C. N. Kellett*

SO SOBER (IRE) 6 b.g. Common Grounds 118 – Femme Savante 89 (Glenstal (USA) **49**
118) [2004 47, a53: f5g* f5g⁵ f5s⁴ p6g f5s f5g⁴ 5.3g³ 5m 5d 5.1m 5s⁵ f5g⁶ Aug 19] compact gelding: poor performer: won banded race at Wolverhampton in January: effective at 5f/6f: acts on all-weather, firm and soft going. *D. Shaw*

SO SURE (IRE) 4 b.g. Definite Article 121 – Zorilla (Belmez (USA) 131) [2004 67, **50**
a–: f11s⁴ p10g⁶ 10.2g Jul 11] sparely-made gelding: modest performer nowadays: stays 1¼m: acts on fibresand and firm going: blinkered (below form) final start. *J. G. M. O'Shea*

SOTONIAN (HOL) 11 br.g. Statoblest 120 – Visage 75 (Vision (USA)) [2004 48§, **40 §**
a53§: f5g⁵ f5g³ f6s³ f5s p6g⁵ p5g³ p6g³ p6g⁴ f5m⁵ 6.1m* f6m 6m 6d Oct 16] rather **a45 §**
sparely-made gelding: poor performer nowadays: won banded race at Nottingham in
May: best at 5f/easy 6f: acts on all-weather, firm and soft going: tried blinkered in 1996:
unreliable. *P. S. Felgate*

SOULACROIX 3 b.c. Kylian (USA) – California Dreamin (Slip Anchor 136) [2004 **97**
87p: 12m² 13.3d* 13.9s 12d³ 12s Oct 23] sturdy colt: useful handicapper, lightly raced:
won at Newbury (beat unlucky Lost Soldier Three by ¾ length) in August: good 2 lengths
third to Flamboyant Lad at Newmarket: stays 13f: acts on good to firm and good to soft
going. *Mrs A. J. Perrett*

SOUL DANCE 3 b.f. Imperial Ballet (IRE) 110 – Piccante (Wolfhound (USA) 126) **67 p**
[2004 6m² Sep 27] first foal: dam unraced out of sister to very smart middle-distance colt
Millkom: 15/2 and tongue tied, ½-length second to Pine Bay in maiden at Windsor,
running on well: will improve. *P. J. Makin*

SOUL PROVIDER (IRE) 3 ch.f. Danehill Dancer (IRE) 117 – Wing And A Prayer **54 d**
(IRE) 63 (Shalford (IRE) 124§) [2004 62: f6g⁵ f6s³ f6g⁴ p8g³ 6d² 7.1d⁴ 8f 7m⁵ 7.5g p7g
7d p7g Sep 18] leggy filly: modest maiden: left P. Blockley prior to seventh outing: below
form after: effective at 6f to easy 1m: acts on all-weather, good to firm and good to soft
ground: blinkered/in cheekpieces last 3 starts: wandered eighth outing. *M. J. Attwater*

SOUMILLON 2 br.f. (Mar 17) Benny The Dip (USA) 127 – Kembla 59 (Known Fact **46**
(USA) 135) [2004 p8.6g f6g p9.5g f7g f8d⁴ Dec 21] fifth foal: half-sister to 3 winners
abroad, including useful French performer up to 1¼m Quit Rent (by Fairy King): dam,
2-y-o 5.7f winner who later won in Italy, half-sister to very smart performer up to 1½m
Urgent Request: poor maiden: probably stays 9.5f: visored (ran respectably) final outing.
Ms Deborah J. Evans

SOUND AND VISION (IRE) 2 b.g. (Apr 23) Fayruz 116 – Lyrical Vision (IRE) **57**
(Vision (USA)) [2004 6m⁵ 6m⁶ 7.5g⁵ 6s⁶ 6g⁵ 6g Oct 4] leggy gelding: modest maiden:
barely stays 7.5f: acts on soft and good to firm going: blinkered last 2 starts. *M. Dods*

SOUND BLASTER (IRE) 3 ch.g. Zafonic (USA) 130 – Blasted Heath 105 (Thatch- **73**
ing 131) [2004 74p: 10m⁵ 8.1m Jun 11] tall gelding: has scope: fair performer: stays 1m:
acts on firm going: free-going sort: carried head awkwardly final start: sold 9,000 gns,
joined Liam McAteer in Ireland. *A. M. Balding*

SOUND BREEZE 2 ch.c. (Mar 23) Giant's Causeway (USA) 132 – Madame Est Sortie **68 p**
(FR) (Longleat (USA) 109) [2004 6s⁴ Oct 29] 54,000 2-y-o: close-coupled colt: half-
brother to several winners, including smart French performer up to 1½m Mousse Glacee
(by Mtoto) and useful French performer up to 11f Majoune (by Take Risks), both 1m
winners at 2 yrs: dam French 9f (at 2 yrs) to 10.5f (Prix Penelope) winner: 12/1, fourth to
Maggie Jordan in maiden at Newmarket, tiring late on: should do better. *M. Johnston*

SOUND OF FLEET (USA) 3 ch.c. Cozzene (USA) – Tempo (USA) (Gone West **92**
(USA)) [2004 82p: 10g⁴ 8m⁶ 10m* 10.4m⁵ 10f 13f² 13.9m 14.4m 14.1d Sep 17] big,
angular, good-bodied colt: has a powerful, round action: fairly useful handicapper: won
at Leicester in May: good second to Elusive Dream at Hamilton, despite hanging left: ran
poorly after: stays 13f: acts on firm ground. *P. F. I. Cole*

SOUNDS LUCKY 8 b.g. Savahra Sound 111 – Sweet And Lucky (Lucky Wednesday **–**
124) [2004 51, a76: p6g p6g⁵ p6g p5g* p6g² p6g⁶ p6g p6g⁴ f5d f6g 6.1s p6d Oct 23] leggy **a63 d**
gelding: has a round action: modest performer: won claimer at Lingfield in February:
left N. Littmoden after fifth start, then gradually lost form: effective at 5f/6f: acts on all-
weather and good to firm going: wears headgear: sometimes slowly away/swishes tail/
edges left: sold £700. *Andrew Reid*

SOUND THAT ALARM 2 b.g. (Jan 23) Groom Dancer (USA) 128 – Warning Star **69**
104 (Warning 136) [2004 5.1g² 5m⁶ Jul 22] 29,000Y: fifth foal: brother to a 9f/1¼m
winner in Italy and half-brother to 2 winners abroad: dam 5f (including at 2 yrs)/6f
winner: much better effort in maidens when second at Chester, slowly away: will stay at
least 6f. *G. A. Butler*

SOUND THE DRUM (USA) 2 b.c. (Mar 3) Stravinsky (USA) 133 – Uhavethebeat **82**
(USA) (Unbridled (USA) 128) [2004 6g³ 6.1d² a6g* Dec 9] $200,000Y: tall colt: has
scope: second foal: dam unraced out of US Grade 1 7f winner Feel The Beat: placed in
maidens at Salisbury and Nottingham for J. Gosden: won similar event at Nad Al Sheba
in December by ½ length from Nasseem Dubai: not sure to stay much beyond 6f: acts on
dirt and good to soft going. *M. Al Kurdi, UAE*

SOUTHAMPTON JOE (USA) 4 ch.g. Just A Cat (USA) – Maple Hill Jill (USA) –
(Executive Pride 127) [2004 –: 8.1g 10.2m⁶ Jul 22] quite good-topped gelding: fair
winner at 2 yrs: no form since: tried in cheekpieces/visor. *J. G. M. O'Shea*

SOUTHBURGH (IRE) 3 b.g. Spectrum (IRE) 126 – College Night (IRE) 54 (Night –
Shift (USA)) [2004 8g Jul 16] tall, good-topped gelding: 100/1 and very green, last in
maiden at Newmarket. *Mrs C. A. Dunnett*

SOUTHERN AFRICA (USA) 2 b. or br.c. (Feb 9) Cape Town (USA) 125 – Al Fahda 114
93 (Be My Chief (USA) 122) [2004 5.2m* 5d² 7m* a7f⁴ a8.5f⁴ Dec 18] 52,000Y: tall,
attractive colt: second foal: dam 6f (at 2 yrs) to 1m winner: smart performer: won maiden
at Newbury in June and minor event at Ascot (beat Group Captain a length, racing freely)
in July: left G. Butler, much improved when fourth behind Declan's Moon in Grade 3
Hollywood Prevue Stakes (beaten 4 lengths) and Grade 1 Hollywood Futurity (beaten 3
lengths): stays 8.5f: acts on dirt and good to firm going. *M. Puhich, USA*

SOUTHERN BAZAAR (USA) 3 ch.c. Southern Halo (USA) – Sunday Bazaar 83
(USA) (Nureyev (USA) 131) [2004 78p: 8f2 8m* p6g p7.1g Dec 20] good-bodied colt:
fluent mover: fairly useful performer, lightly raced: won maiden at Brighton (beat
Olivander by length, idling) in September: left B. Hills 8,000 gns after: should stay 1¼m:
acts on polytrack and good to firm going: tongue tied at Brighton and on final start.
C. A. Dwyer

SOUTHERN STAR (GER) 4 gr.g. Sternkoenig (IRE) 122 – Sun Mate (IRE) 59
(Miller's Mate 116) [2004 12.4v⁴ Apr 3] leggy gelding: in frame in maidens at Munich in
first half of 2003: left P. Schiergen in Germany, well-held fourth in maiden at Newcastle:
won over hurdles in September. *R. C. Guest*

SOUTHERN TIDE (USA) 2 b.c. (Apr 29) Southern Halo (USA) – My Own Lovely 58
Lee (USA) (Bucksplasher (USA)) [2004 7f 6g 7.1s 8g Sep 30] useful-looking colt:
modest maiden: form only at 6f. *J. J. Sheehan*

SOUTH FACE 3 ch.g. Hector Protector (USA) 124 – Crystal Cavern (USA) 89 (Be 84
My Guest (USA) 126) [2004 7g² Mar 26] 20,000Y: quite good-topped gelding: third foal:
half-brother to useful 2002 2-y-o 7f winner Crystal Star (by Mark of Esteem) and fairly
useful Irish 7f/8.5f winner Christavelli (by Machiavellian): dam, 2-y-o 7f winner (later
won in Canada), half-sister to Poule d'Essai des Pouliches winner Rose Gypsy: 33/1, 2½
lengths second to Zonus in maiden at Doncaster, missing break: dead. *R. M. Beckett*

SOUTH O'THE BORDER 2 b.g. (Apr 3) Wolfhound (USA) 126 – Abbey's Gal 55
100 (Efisio 120) [2004 7.1m 7m 7.1d 8g Sep 29] modest maiden: needs to settle to stay
1m: gelded after final start. *T. G. Mills*

SOVEREIGN DREAMER (USA) 4 b.c. Kingmambo (USA) 125 – Spend A Dream 79 d
(USA) (Spend A Buck (USA)) [2004 90: 11.9s 12m⁶ 12g 14.8m 11.5m 12m 13.9g Oct 9]
tall colt: fair handicapper at best in 2004 (reportedly had breathing problem penultimate
start): stays 1½m: acts on soft and good to firm going: tried blinkered, often tongue tied.
P. F. I. Cole

SOVEREIGN GIRL 3 b.f. Sovereign Water (FR) – The Quaker (Oats 126) [2004 –
10.2m 11.8m⁶ May 24] second foal: dam poor novice hurdler: no sign of ability in 2
maidens. *B. N. Doran*

SOVEREIGN SPIRIT (IRE) 2 b.g. (Feb 21) Desert Prince (IRE) 130 – Sheer Spirit 51
(IRE) 86 (Caerleon (USA) 132) [2004 7.1d 7.1m 8f⁶ Sep 23] leggy gelding: modest form
in maidens: likely to be suited by 1¼m/1½m. *P. W. Harris*

SOVEREIGN STATE (IRE) 7 b.g. Soviet Lad (USA) – Portree 82 (Slip Anchor 55
136) [2004 12m* 12.6g⁴ 12m⁵ 13f² 16s 14.1f² 12g Sep 14] small, well-made gelding:
modest handicapper: unraced on Flat in 2003: won at Catterick in June: stays 1¾m: acts
on firm and good to soft going: tried visored, wore cheekpieces in 2004. *D. W. Thompson*

SOVEREIGNTY (JPN) 2 b.g. (Apr 10) King's Best (USA) 132 – Calando (USA) 79
110 (Storm Cat (USA)) [2004 6m² 6g⁴ Jul 12] second foal: dam, 2-y-o 7f/1m (May Hill
Stakes) winner, out of Oaks winner and St Leger runner-up Diminuendo: fair form in
maidens at Yarmouth and Windsor: needs to settle to stay beyond 6f. *D. R. Loder*

SOVIET SCEPTRE (IRE) 3 ch.c. Soviet Star (USA) 128 – Princess Sceptre (Cade- 69
aux Genereux 131) [2004 75: 6.1s³ 6m 8.1g⁴ 7m⁶ 7d 10.1g 10m* 11d⁵ p9.5g Oct 18]
lengthy colt: fair performer: left G. Butler after second start: won seller at Windsor in
September: barely stays 11f: acts on soft and good to firm going: tried tongue tied.
Miss D. Mountain

SOVIET SONG (IRE)   4 b.f. Marju (IRE) 127 – Kalinka (IRE) 88 (Soviet Star   **126**
(USA) 128) [2004 118: 8d² 8.1d³ 8m* 8f² 8m* 8g* 8m* 8m⁶ Sep 25]

With a high proportion of the best three-year-old milers among the European fillies of 2003 staying in training, there were great expectations of some
memorable competition, particularly with the elevation of several races to Group 1
status. In the event, *Great Expectations* turned into *Bleak House* for Six Perfections
and Nebraska Tornado, who failed to win in nine starts between them, while
Russian Rhythm did not reach the racecourse again after a victory against the colts
in the Lockinge Stakes. One four-year-old, in particular, did shine—Soviet Song,
who, in a full and very tough campaign, showed the best form of her life to lift three
Group 1 races including the Cantor Odds Sussex Stakes. Hopes that she might
prove capable of adding to her laurels as a five-year-old are in the balance, however,
because she injured a fetlock on her final appearance.

Soviet Song's unbeaten run of three races as a juvenile, culminating in the
Fillies' Mile at Ascot, appeared to bode well for her classic season, but the closest
she came to winning at three was when runner-up to Russian Rhythm in the Coronation Stakes at Royal Ascot. There seemed no excuses apart from the obvious
one—she simply was not up to beating the best. Soviet Song's starting price of
11/4-on for the Snowdrop Fillies Stakes, on her reappearance at Kempton in April,
reflected the perfect opportunity for her to get back on the winning trail. Things
didn't go to plan, however, Beneventa beating Soviet Song by a head at level
weights. Soviet Song might have needed the run, and almost certainly needed a
more even gallop than at Kempton, since she takes a good hold and is invariably
waited with. She got a stronger and more consistent gallop later in the month in
the betfred.com Mile at Sandown but failed to get the run of the race, finishing best
of all in third behind Hurricane Alan. Soviet Song duly got off the mark for the
year a month later in the Group 2 Ridgewood Pearl Stakes at the Curragh, one of
the new pattern races inaugurated under the European-wide scheme to create extra
opportunities for older fillies and mares. Only four opposed Soviet Song, led by
Echoes In Eternity, and the confidently-ridden favourite crushed them, quickening
impressively off a sound gallop to lead over a furlong out and account for
eight-year-old Livadiya by six lengths.

Ridgewood Pearl Stakes, the Curragh—
Soviet Song quickens impressively to take this newly-created Group 2 contest from Livadiya,
Hanami (right) and Echoes In Eternity (noseband)

UAE Equestrian and Racing Federation Falmouth Stakes, Newmarket—
Soviet Song ends Attraction's unbeaten run; Baqah (rail) and Monturani also make the frame

Another new Group 2 for fillies and mares, the Windsor Forest Stakes, was an option at Royal Ascot but Soviet Song's connections seized the bull by the horns and took on the colts instead in the Group 1 Queen Anne Stakes. No filly had won since Kandy Sauce in 1956, but the boldness nearly paid off as Soviet Song travelled well close to the pace, led a furlong out and only just failed to hold on, going down by a neck to Refuse To Bend. Nebraska Tornado and Six Perfections were further back. The form was at least as good as anything Soviet Song had achieved before and, with the upgrading of the Falmouth Stakes, Prix d'Astarte, Matron Stakes and Sun Chariot Stakes to Group 1, options against her own sex through to the end of the season were plentiful. Wasting no time, Soviet Song was sent to Newmarket three weeks after the Queen Anne to contest the seven-runner UAE Equestrian and Racing Federation Falmouth Stakes. In the interim, Refuse To Bend had won the Eclipse Stakes but, regardless of this, and despite the enforced absence of Russian Rhythm through injury, Soviet Song started only second favourite behind the unbeaten three-year-old Attraction. The latter was odds on, with Soviet Song at 11/4; Favourable Terms, successful in the Windsor Forest Stakes, came next in the betting, while none of the remainder, including French Group 2 winner Baqah, appeared to have much prospect of bustling up the principals. Patiently ridden as Attraction attempted to make all, albeit not setting quite so strong a gallop as usual, Soviet Song made ground smoothly, wide of the leader, with a quarter of a mile to go, edged in when driven but was soon on top and drew away to score by two and a half lengths. Attraction might not have been in

Cantor Odds Sussex Stakes, Goodwood—Soviet Song gets first run on Nayyir;
Le Vie dei Colori (partially obscured by the winner) is third and Norse Dancer (second right) fourth

quite the form she had shown when winning three Group 1 races earlier, but she wasn't far off it and lowering her colours in such style was a major achievement.

Clearly Soviet Song was now going to take a deal of beating whatever the company, and she started second favourite behind Refuse To Bend in the Sussex Stakes at Goodwood later in the month, a race in which fillies and mares have produced six winners in the last fifty years (Petite Etoile, Humble Duty, On The House, Sonic Lady, Marling and Sayyedati). Next in the betting after Refuse To Bend and Soviet Song was Two Thousand Guineas winner Haafhd, trying to restore his reputation after defeat at Royal Ascot where another Sussex contender, Antonius Pius, had finished just ahead of him. All the others, notably Hurricane Alan again, the durable Nayyir and Norse Dancer, were at 12/1 or longer. Not an outstanding renewal, but not a weak one either, and Soviet Song had to run to almost the same level of form she had shown at Newmarket to gain the day. After travelling strongly from the start as the pace was set first by Passing Glance, then by Refuse To Bend and ex-Italian Le Vie dei Colori, Soviet Song produced her customary turn of foot to go two lengths clear a furlong out, where there was considerable bunching behind. She held on by a neck as Nayyir launched a resolute challenge, with Le Vie dei Colori two lengths away third, ahead of Norse Dancer. There were one or two hard-luck stories further back and, in occupying two of the last three places, Haafhd and Refuse To Bend ran way below form. None of this should be allowed to detract from Soviet Song's achievement, her form being at least on a par with that shown by some of the fillies mentioned above—Petite Etoile ended her season rated 134, Sonic Lady 129, Humble Duty 127, On The House 125, Marling 124 and Sayyedati 122.

Striking while the iron is hot is usually wise practice and next up for Soviet Song was another of the upgraded races for fillies, the Coolmore Fusaichi Pegasus Matron Stakes at Leopardstown in September, when the opposition again included Attraction, below form at Deauville on her last start. Unsurprisingly, Soviet Song was a hot favourite for the Matron at 13/8-on, with Attraction at 7/2. The field was made up by four-year-old Yesterday, making a belated reappearance, three-year-old Group 3 winners Phantom Wind and Red Feather, and Livadiya. The result was the same as at Newmarket and, although the margin of victory was less, half a length to be precise, Soviet Song was just as impressive, arguably even more so. All of eight lengths off the lead early in the straight, she made ground readily and needed just a few smacks in the final hundred yards to assert.

Drawing hard-and-fast conclusions from the evidence of one season is rarely sensible but, on the face of it, upgrading the four Group 2s already mention-

Coolmore Fusaichi Pegasus Matron Stakes, Leopardstown—
Soviet Song (left) is about to overhaul Attraction again and win her third successive Group 1

Elite Racing Club's "Soviet Song"

ed, plus the Pretty Polly Stakes and Premio Lydia Tesio over a mile and a quarter, and opening the Group 1 Prix Vermeille to four-year-olds, did what it was supposed to do by attracting a significant number of older fillies. Each race had at least two of them and the Pretty Polly and Vermeille had five apiece, with a tally of five victories out of seven, though this does not necessarily mean that all the events had strength in depth, either in numbers or quality. There were fewer runners than average in all of the races except the Lydia Tesio and the Vermeille, which were the only races to attract fields in double figures. Judged on quality, the three races over a mile in Britain and Ireland, plus the Pretty Polly, were virtual matches between high-class runners, and there is no guarantee that there will be performers every year of the mettle of Alexander Goldrun, Attraction, Chic, Chorist and Soviet Song. Judgement is best reserved, but one encouraging element is that the owners of the fillies just named, plus connections of Russian Rhythm, did not hesitate to compete with the colts. Besides Soviet Song's success at Goodwood, Russian Rhythm won the Lockinge Stakes, Chic the Celebration Mile and Alexander Goldrun the Hong Kong Cup, while Chorist was the only one to make a race of it with Haafhd in the Champion Stakes. The number of fillies contesting open Group 1 events was twenty out of a total of one hundred and ninety-five runners, which is on a par with the average over the five previous years. Sprints have the greatest drawing power, probably owing to a lack of opportunities. There is only one sprint pattern race confined to fillies and mares in Britain, the Summer Stakes at York, and the Golden Jubilee Stakes, July Cup, Nunthorpe Stakes and Haydock Sprint Cup attracted

972

fifty-seven fillies and mares from 1999 to 2004, compared with a combined total of forty-seven for all the eleven other open Group 1s. This scale of competition by fillies is nothing new and is much better than what happens in North America, where fillies and mares are usually notable by their almost total absence from the top open events. The European season perhaps afforded confirmation of the words written in the essay on Russian Rhythm in *Racehorses* a year ago: 'Some top owners are likely to continue running their fillies in open Group 1s. It has to be more satisfying to take on the opposite sex and beat them than to compete solely in restricted events.'

With her Group 1 hat-trick completed, the redoubtable Soviet Song, with her good turn of foot, should have given the colts plenty to think about in the Queen Elizabeth II Stakes at Ascot a fortnight later. Soviet Song started favourite but fell short, perhaps owing to her sustaining that leg injury, in finishing a never-dangerous sixth to an in-form Rakti whom, truth to tell, she would have found a tough nut to crack on this particular day even at her best. Suffice to say that if Soviet Song comes back for more as a five-year-old—at the time of writing she was reportedly responding to treatment—the races she contests will be enriched, and racegoers will be happy, since she has developed into one of the most popular horses in training.

Soviet Song (IRE) (b.f. 2000)	Marju (IRE) (br 1988)	Last Tycoon (b 1983)	Try My Best
			Mill Princess
		Flame of Tara (b 1980)	Artaius
			Welsh Flame
	Kalinka (IRE) (b 1994)	Soviet Star (b 1984)	Nureyev
			Veruschka
		Tralthee (ch 1983)	Tromos
			Swalthee

Coincidentally, Soviet Song's sire Marju was also responsible for the Prix d'Astarte winner Marbye, thereby boosting his reputation as a sire principally of good fillies. All his four Group 1 winners are female and so are three of his six Group 2 winners. Details of Soviet Song's dam Kalinka were given in *Racehorses of 2002*. She has had another winner with her 2001 foal, the Pennekamp gelding Penzance, successful over a mile and a mile and a quarter. The two-year-old, Kazatzka (by Groom Dancer), like Penzance and Soviet Song, was in training with Fanshawe but has not yet run and Kalinka produced a filly foal sister to Soviet Song in March before visiting Red Ransom. Soviet Song is a good advert for her sire and dam in looks as well as ability—she is a sturdy, lengthy filly who is thoroughly genuine and consistent—and her success is a good advert for her trainer, who planned her campaign skilfully, keeping her in form for a long time. Soviet Song may get a shade further than a mile, and she acts on firm and soft going.
J. R. Fanshawe

SOVIET SPIRIT 3 ch.f. Soviet Star (USA) 128 – Kristina 92 (Kris 135) [2004 8.2s[5] **51** 10s 7.5d[5] 8m[3] 8.3f[5] 7m 10.1g[4] 8s 10.1g p8m Oct 6] workmanlike filly: first foal: dam, 2-y-o 1m winner who stayed 1¾m, out of half-sister to very smart sprinter/miler Pursuit of Love: modest maiden: trained by J. Fanshawe prior to fifth start: may prove best around 1m: acts on firm going: blinkered (ran as if amiss) final outing. *C. A. Dwyer*

SOVIETTA (IRE) 3 b.f. Soviet Star (USA) 128 – La Riveraine (USA) 90 (Riverman **66** (USA) 131) [2004 10g[4] 11.7m[3] 11.7f 11.8g[*] Oct 12] fifth foal: half-sister to 1m winner Riparian (by Last Tycoon) and 6f (at 2 yrs) to 9.4f winner Riverblue (by Bluebird): dam won around 1½m: fair performer: won claimer at Leicester: stays 1½m: acts on good to firm going. *R. M. Beckett*

SOVIET TREAT (IRE) 3 b.f. Ashkalani (IRE) 128 – Mystery Treat (Plugged Nickle **86** (USA)) [2004 85: 8m[5] 8v[6] 7m[3] 5d Oct 2] lengthy, hollow-backed filly: has quick action: half-sister to several winners, including useful Irish 7f (at 2 yrs)/1m winner Apache Twist (by Digamist): dam ran twice: fairly useful maiden: trained by T. Doyle in Ireland at 2 yrs and M. Johnston on reappearance only: stays 7f: acts on good to firm going. *J. S. Bolger, Ireland*

SO VITAL 4 b.c. Pivotal 124 – Sumoto 101 (Mtoto 134) [2004 74: p12g[*] f14g p12g[3] **76** 12g 12g 17.1f Jun 7] fair performer, lightly raced: won maiden at Lingfield in January: stays 1½m: acts on polytrack (went with little fluency on fibresand): tried in cheekpieces: sold 8,500 gns. *J. Pearce*

SOWERBY 2 b.g. (Mar 25) Grey Desire 115 – Brief Star (IRE) 49 (Brief Truce (USA) **58**
126) [2004 6s 6m⁶ 5g⁴ 5g 5s p6g Dec 1] quite good-topped gelding: modest maiden: best
effort when fourth at Beverley: should stay 6f. *M. Brittain*

SO WILL I 3 ch.c. Inchinor 119 – Fur Will Fly 66 (Petong 126) [2004 95p: 7g³ 6g* 6d **111**
6m⁴ 7g 7g⁵ 6m³ 7g⁴ Sep 30] sturdy colt: smart performer: won listed race at Newbury
(beat Mac Love by length) in May: good efforts in listed race (2 lengths third to Var) and
Supreme Stakes (in cheekpieces, 3 lengths fourth behind Mac Love), both at Goodwood,
last 2 starts: effective at 6f/7f: acts on good to firm going: has worn crossed noseband:
joined D. Watson in UAE. *M. P. Tregoning*

SOYUZ (IRE) 4 ch.g. Cadeaux Genereux 131 – Welsh Mist 102 (Damister (USA) **95**
123) [2004 92: 8.3d² 8.1d³ 7.6s* 7g⁵ 7s 7.1g 7g p7.1g⁵ 7s* p7g² p9.5g Nov 27] smallish, good-topped gelding: useful performer: won minor event at Lingfield in May and
(having left M. Jarvis 10,000 gns after eighth outing) apprentice handicap at Doncaster in
November: beat Kirkby's Treasure by 3 lengths in latter: effective from 6f to 1m: acts on
polytrack, heavy and good to firm going: well held only try in blinkers. *K. A. Ryan*

SPACE COWBOY (IRE) 4 b.c. Anabaa (USA) 130 – Lady Moranbon (USA) (Trem- **–**
polino (USA) 135) [2004 84: 10g Oct 11] fairly useful at 3 yrs: well beaten only run on
Flat in 2004. *G. L. Moore*

SPACED (IRE) 2 b.c. (Apr 4) Indian Rocket 115 – Tolomena 61 (Tolomeo 127) [2004 **91**
6g 7g⁶ 7g* 7s³ 8.1g* Sep 4] 20,000Y: quite good-topped colt: sixth foal: half-brother to
fairly useful 1994 2-y-o 7f/1m winner Menas Gold (by Heights of Gold) and a winning
sprinter in Italy by Danetime: dam ungenuine maiden who stayed 2m: fairly useful
performer: won maiden at Folkestone in July and nursery at Haydock (by short head from
Hallhoo) in September: stays 1m: acts on soft ground. *R. Hannon*

SPACE MAKER 2 b.c. (Feb 21) Almutawakel 126 – Into Orbit 63 (Safawan 118) **84**
[2004 6m⁴ 5g 5m* Sep 15] 1,000F, 23,000 2-y-o: second foal: half-brother to 3-y-o
Camberwell: dam ran once at 2 yrs: won maiden at Beverley by 6 lengths from Waggledance, making all and clear over 1f out: should stay 6f: hung left (reportedly lame) second
start, edged left for win. *M. L. W. Bell*

SPACE SHUTTLE 2 b.c. (Mar 22) Makbul 104 – Sky Music 85 (Absalom 128) **99**
[2004 5g³ 5m² 6m* 5g³ 6f³ 6m³ 6d* 6d* 6s Oct 22] 7,500Y: strong colt: sixth foal:
half-brother to 7-y-o Polar Haze: dam 6f/7f winner: useful performer: won maiden at
Doncaster in June and nursery at York and listed race at Ripon (by ½ length from Abraxas
Antelope) in August: well held in sales race at Doncaster final start: stays 6f: acts on firm
and good to soft ground: blinkered third to fifth starts. *T. D. Easterby*

SPACE TO RUN 2 ch.f. (Mar 22) Dancing Spree (USA) – Approved Quality (IRE) **–**
66 (Persian Heights 129) [2004 p6g f7g p8.6g Dec 31] second foal: dam maiden who
probably stayed 1½m: no form, including in sellers. *R. P. Elliott*

SPAINKRIS 5 b.g. Kris 135 – Pennycairn 84 (Last Tycoon 131) [2004 –: f12g Jan 23] **–**
useful performer at best when trained in France by X. Nakkachdji: tailed off only 5-y-o
outing: stays 1½m. *A. Crook*

SPANISH ACE 3 b.g. First Trump 118 – Spanish Heart 86 (King of Spain 121) [2004 **97**
99: p7g 7g 8.1m 7m 6m⁵ 6m⁵ 5m 5s⁴ 5.1d* 5.6m Sep 8] rather leggy, close-coupled
gelding: useful performer: won minor event at Bath (beat Devise by a head) in August:
effective at 5f/6f: acts on good to firm and good to soft going: often races up with pace:
wore blinkers and hood last 2 starts, visored on previous 5. *A. M. Balding*

SPANISH DON 6 b.g. Zafonic (USA) 130 – Spanish Wells (IRE) (Sadler's Wells **113**
(USA) 132) [2004 100: 8g 8g 8m⁵ 9g* 10g* 9.9g⁵ 10d 9g* 10s* p10g Nov 20] tall
gelding: smart performer: better than ever in 2004, winning handicaps at Kempton in
June and July, and totesport Cambridgeshire (100/1, beat Take A Bow by neck) and listed
race (by ¾ length from Menokee, making most) at Newmarket in October: effective at
1m/1¼m: acts on firm and soft going, below form on polytrack final start: blinkered (well
held) once: usually waited with. *D. R. C. Elsworth*

SPANISH GOLD 4 b.f. Vettori (IRE) 119 – Spanish Heart 86 (King of Spain 121) **–**
[2004 82: f9.4g Jan 12] big, useful-looking filly: has a quick action: fairly useful performer at 3 yrs: well held only 4-y-o start. *A. M. Balding*

SPANISH LAW 2 b.g. (Feb 17) Zaha (CAN) 106 – Misty Moon (Polar Falcon (USA) **–**
126) [2004 7.2d Jun 19] 25/1, last in maiden at Ayr. *M. Dods*

SPANISH RIDGE (IRE) 2 b.c. (Mar 18) Indian Ridge 123 – Spanish Lady (IRE) 61 **71**
(Bering 136) [2004 7g⁵ 7m⁴ 7g Oct 12] big, good-topped colt: second foal: dam, maiden
who stayed 1½m, half-sister to useful 1¼m winner Berenice: fair form first 2 starts in
maidens: should stay 1m. *J. L. Dunlop*

SPANISH STAR 7 b.g. Hernando (FR) 127 – Desert Girl (Green Desert (USA) 127) [2004 –, a58: f11g⁴ f12f⁶ f12g* f11g³ f12s³ f12s f12g f12m f12m p12.2d⁴ p13.9g⁶ f11g f12d⁴ Dec 21] compact gelding: modest performer: won claimer at Southwell in February: effective at 9.4f to 1½m: acts on fibresand, probably on polytrack, unraced on turf since 2002: tried visored. *Mrs N. Macauley* — a55

SPARKFORD (USA) 2 b.c. (Jun 5) Red Ransom (USA) – Arsaan (USA) 106 (Nureyev (USA) 131) [2004 8g Sep 30] good-bodied colt: 8/1, always rear, carrying head awkwardly, in maiden at Newmarket: joined M. Al Kurdi in UAE. *J. H. M. Gosden* —

SPARKLING CLEAR 3 b.f. Efisio 120 – Shoot Clear 111 (Bay Express 132) [2004 48: f6s 6s f6g⁶ 7g May 4] small filly: poor maiden at 2 yrs: well held in 2004: tried in cheekpieces/visor. *R. M. H. Cowell* —

SPARKLING JEWEL 4 b.f. Bijou d'Inde 127 – Jobiska (Dunbeath (USA) 127) [2004 75: 6f 6m⁶ 5.7f² 6g Jun 30] good-topped filly: fair performer: effective at 5f/6f: acts on polytrack and good to firm going: blinkered (not discredited) third start. *R. Hannon* — 77

SPARKLING WATER (USA) 5 br. or b.h. Woodman (USA) 126 – Shirley Valentine 104 (Shirley Heights 130) [2004 –§: 6f] quite attractive horse: useful but unreliable performer at 3 yrs: well held on Flat since. *D. L. Williams* — §

SPARK UP 4 b.f. Lahib (USA) 129 – Catch The Flame (USA) (Storm Bird (CAN) 134) [2004 71: f7g f8f f7s⁶ f8.5g² f8.5g⁴ f8.5g⁴ f8.5g* 10s 8m⁶ 7m 7m 8m⁶ p8.6g f7g p8.6g Dec 17] smallish, quite attractive filly: fair handicapper: won at Wolverhampton in April: stays 8.5f: acts on fibresand, good to firm and good to soft ground: often blinkered/visored. *J. W. Unett* — 65

SPARKWELL 2 b.c. (Mar 8) Dansili 127 – West Devon (USA) (Gone West (USA)) [2004 7g⁵ Sep 18] good-topped colt: fourth foal: half-brother to smart 2002 2-y-o 6f winner (stays 1¼m) Salcombe (by Elmaamul) and 3-y-o Moors Myth: dam unraced sister to smart 5f performer Western Approach and half-sister to very smart performer up to 1¼m Tinners Way: 8/1 and burly, fifth to Esquire in maiden at Newbury, travelling well long way: sure to do better. *B. W. Hills* — 79 p

SPARTAN ODYSSEY 3 b.g. Overbury (IRE) 116 – Spartan Native (Native Bazaar 122) [2004 –: f7g Mar 22] close-coupled, plain gelding: no sign of ability. *A. Senior* —

SPARTAN PRINCIPLE 4 b.f. Spartan Monarch – Altar Point (Persian Bold 123) [2004 –: f9.4g Mar 27] well held in 2 maidens. *R. Guest* —

SPARTAN SPEAR 3 b.g. Sure Blade (USA) 130 – Confection (Formidable (USA) 125) [2004 74: 6.1s 7m 8g Jul 22] strong, lengthy gelding: fair maiden at 2 yrs: well beaten in 2004: tried in cheekpieces. *J. Balding* —

SPEAGLE (IRE) 2 ch.c. (Apr 5) Desert Sun 120 – Pohutakawa (FR) (Affirmed (USA)) [2004 6f 7.2d⁵ 7g⁶ 8g Sep 11] modest maiden: needs to settle to stay 1m: acts on good to soft going. *E. J. O'Neill* — 57

SPEARIOUS (IRE) 3 b.g. Tagula (IRE) 116 – Gloria Crown (IRE) (Waajib 121) [2004 74: 5.1m⁴ May 17] strong gelding: maiden: tongue tied, modest form only 3-y-o start: will prove best at 5f/easy 6f: acts on fibresand, good to firm and good to soft going. *B. R. Millman* — 58

totesport Cambridgeshire (Handicap), Newmarket—a big upset as Spanish Don (near side), Take A Bow and Fine Silver, all drawn low, occupy the first three places at odds of 100/1 and 25/1 twice respectively

SPEAR (IRE) 2 b.c. (Jan 22) Almutawakel 126 – Les Hurlants (IRE) (Barathea (IRE) **81**
127) [2004 7m² 7.2s³ 9f* Sep 13] 70,000Y: close-coupled colt: second foal: half-brother
to 3-y-o Happy Crusader: dam French 1½m winner: made all in maiden at Redcar, holding Haatmey by short head: will be suited by 1¼m/1½m: acts on firm going, possibly not
on soft. *D. R. Loder*

SPEAR THISTLE 2 ch.g. (Mar 18) Selkirk (USA) 129 – Ardisia (USA) 87 (Affirmed **90 p**
(USA)) [2004 8m⁴ 8g⁴ 8v* Oct 23] tall, close-coupled gelding: seventh foal: brother to
3-y-o Thistle and half-brother to 3 winners, including smart 1¾m winner Ashgar (by Bien
Bien) and fairly useful 11.5f winner Halcyon Daze (by Halling): dam, winner around
1¼m, half-sister to Oaks winner Ramruma: favourite, won maiden at Newbury by neck
from General Jumbo, making all: gelded after: will be suited by 1¼m/1½m: acts on heavy
going: useful prospect. *J. H. M. Gosden*

SPECIAL BRANCH 4 ch.g. Woodborough (USA) 112 – Sixslip (USA) 94 (Diesis **–**
133) [2004 66: 17.1d 11.9g Sep 2] maiden handicapper: ran as though amiss both starts in
2004: free-going sort. *Jedd O'Keeffe*

SPECIAL DELIVERY (IRE) 4 b.f. Danehill (USA) 126 – Seconde Bleue (Glint of **104**
Gold 128) [2004 10.5d* 10g⁴ 9m³ May 2] leggy filly: sixth foal: closely related to French
2000 2-y-o 8.5f/9.5f winner Schema (by Anabaa) and half-sister to 2 winners in France,
including 1¾m winner/smart jumper Scout Master (by Marignan): dam, French 10.5f/
12.5f winner, half-sister to Breeders' Cup Mile winner Steinlen: useful performer, lightly
raced: won minor events at Saint-Cloud at 3 yrs and on reappearance in March, latter
by ¾ length from Russian Hill: creditable efforts afterwards in frame in listed race at
Longchamp and Dahlia Stakes at Newmarket (2¾ lengths third to Benveneta): stayed
10.5f: acted on good to firm and good to soft ground (well beaten on heavy): stud.
E. Lellouche, France

SPECIAL GOLD 2 b.c. (Mar 22) Josr Algarhoud (IRE) 118 – Inya Lake 101 (Whit- **65**
tingham (IRE) 104) [2004 5s⁵ 5d⁴ May 1] 26,000Y: rather leggy colt: second foal: dam 5f
(including Molecomb Stakes at 2 yrs) winner: fair form in maiden/minor event: likely to
prove best at 5f/6f. *T. D. Easterby*

SPECIALISE 2 b.f. (Apr 2) Atraf 116 – Summerhill Special (IRE) 80 (Roi Danzig **–**
(USA)) [2004 7m 7m 6.9m Sep 11] quite good-topped filly: third foal: sister to 3-y-o
Summerise: dam 1½m/13f winner, also won over hurdles: no form, including in seller.
D. W. Barker

SPECIAL KALDOUN (IRE) 5 b.h. Alzao (USA) 117 – Special Lady (FR) (Kaldoun **116**
(FR) 122) [2004 124: 8d 8d 8d³ 10s* 10g³ 9.8m³ 8d Nov 7] reportedly had back problems
in spring 2004 and just smart form at 5 yrs: won Prix Gontaut-Biron Le Royal Palm Hotel
at Deauville (by a length from Demon Dancer) in August: creditable third to Fair Mix in
La Coupe de Maisons-Laffitte and Touch of Land in Prix Dollar at Longchamp after:
bridle reportedly broke final start: stays 1¼m: acts on heavy and good to firm ground:
held up, and suited by well-run race. *D. Smaga, France*

SPECTACULAR HOPE 4 b.f. Marju (IRE) 127 – Distant Music (Darshaan 133) **–**
[2004 55: f16.2s Feb 20] modest maiden at 3 yrs: tailed off only 4-y-o start. *J. W. Mullins*

SPECTAIT 2 b.g. (Mar 12) Spectrum (IRE) 126 – Shanghai Girl 102 (Distant Relative **71**
128) [2004 7.1s² p6g p8.6g³ Oct 16] fourth foal: dam, 5f/6f winner, sister to very smart
7f/1m performer Bin Rosie: best effort in maidens when promising second to Karlu at
Chepstow: reportedly banged head on stall next start: looked hard ride final one: should
stay 1m. *Sir Mark Prescott*

SPECTESTED (IRE) 3 ch.g. Spectrum (IRE) 126 – Nisibis (In The Wings 128) **61**
[2004 52: 10.9d 14.1s f12m²¹ 10.9m⁵ 11.6g 10g⁴ 16.2s² p13.9g p12.2g³ Dec 15] modest
maiden: left B. Meehan after third start: seems to stay 2m: acts on soft and good to firm
going: blinkered final 2-y-o start, usually wears cheekpieces: carries head high: none too
genuine. *A. W. Carroll*

SPECTOR (IRE) 4 gr.g. Spectrum (IRE) 126 – Safkana (IRE) 78 (Doyoun 124) **51 ?**
[2004 8m 7s 8.1g May 31] poor form in maidens: should stay 1¼m: gelded after final
outing. *J. J. Sheehan*

SPECTROMETER 7 ch.g. Rainbow Quest (USA) 134 – Selection Board 75 (Welsh **–**
Pageant 132) [2004 93: 12.1g 16.1s 11.9d Aug 17] close-coupled, leggy gelding: fairly
useful performer at best: last on all starts in 2004. *R. C. Guest*

SPECTRUM OF LIGHT 2 b.f. (Feb 2) Spectrum (IRE) 126 – Empress of Light 47 **–**
(Emperor Jones (USA) 119) [2004 6f 5m⁵ Jun 16] 2,700Y: first foal: dam, ran 3 times,
half-sister to smart performer up to 1½m Medaille Militaire: only a little sign of ability in
maiden/minor event. *C. W. Fairhurst*

SPECTRUM STAR   4 b.g. Spectrum (IRE) 126 – Persia (IRE) (Persian Bold 123)   –
[2004 –: 10s 13.1s Oct 30] quite good-topped gelding: little form: tried blinkered.
F. P. Murtagh

SPEEDBIRD (USA)   3 ch.f. Sky Classic (CAN) – Egoli (USA) 93 (Seeking The Gold   75
(USA)) [2004 76: 7g 7g² 8.2m Jun 2] strong filly: fair maiden: runner-up in minor event
at Yarmouth: should stay 1m: best efforts on good going. *G. Wragg*

SPEED COP   4 ch.f. Cadeaux Genereux 131 – Blue Siren 113 (Bluebird (USA) 125)   99
[2004 104: p5g² 5.1g³ 5m 5f 6g⁴ 5s⁶ 5g 5m Sep 7] rather leggy, useful-looking filly:
has a quick action: useful performer: creditable efforts in 2004 when third to Ringmoor
Down in listed race at Bath and fourth to Tychy in handicap at Ascot: best at 5f: acts on
polytrack, firm and good to soft ground: visored (below par) last 2 outings: sometimes
bandaged behind: races prominently (lost all chance when slowly away from tape start in
Temple Stakes at Epsom third outing). *A. M. Balding*

SPEED DIAL HARRY (IRE)   2 b.g. (Apr 30) General Monash (USA) 107 – Jaco-   78
bina 71 (Magic Ring (IRE) 115) [2004 p5g⁵ 5s² 5g³ f6g* 6f³ 5.1d² 5g* 6m 6f⁴ p6g f5g³
p6g³ Dec 17] 3,800F, 2,500Y: sturdy gelding: first foal: dam 7f winner: fair performer:
won seller at Southwell in May and minor event at Hamilton (by 7 lengths) in July:
barely stays 6f: acts on fibresand, firm and good to soft going: often visored/blinkered.
K. R. Burke

SPEEDFIT FREE (IRE)   7 b.g. Night Shift (USA) – Dedicated Lady (IRE) 101 (Pen-   47 §
nine Walk 120) [2004 68§, a58§: f6g² f6g⁵ f6s⁶ f6s² 6s⁴ 7g 6v f6g³ f5d 8.3g f6g⁴ 7.2f 7.2f   a59 §
6m⁶ 6d 6.1f 6.1g 7.1m f6m 6g 6d f6g p7.1g p13.9g Nov 27] smallish, well-made gelding:
modest performer: claimed from I. Semple after eighth outing: effective at 6f to easy 1m:
acts on fibresand and any turf going: usually wears headgear: unreliable. *Miss A. Stokell*

SPEEDIE ROSSINI (IRE)   2 b.g. (May 13) Rossini (USA) 118 – Skatt (Caerleon   41
(USA) 132) [2004 7.6m 7m 7g 8m Sep 21] strong gelding: poor maiden: best effort in
blinkers final start. *S. C. Williams*

SPEED OF SOUND   2 ch.f. (Apr 10) Zafonic (USA) 130 – Blue Siren 113 (Bluebird   69
(USA) 125) [2004 5s³ 5g³ 5.1g⁴ p6g Nov 30] tall, good-topped filly: fourth foal: half-
sister to 4-y-o Speed Cop and 3-y-o Indiana Blues: dam, 5f (at 2 yrs) to 7f winner, first
past post in Nunthorpe Stakes: fair maiden: best effort when third in minor event at
Windsor: should stay 6f. *A. M. Balding*

SPEED ON   11 b.g. Sharpo 132 – Pretty Poppy 67 (Song 132) [2004 51§: 6.1s f5g Jun   41 §
4] small, strong gelding: poor handicapper nowadays: barely stays 6f: acts on polytrack,
firm and soft going: tried visored: often apprentice ridden: unreliable. *H. Candy*

SPEED RACER   3 b.f. Zieten (USA) 118 – Sharenara (USA) (Vaguely Noble 140)   52 ?
[2004 62: 7f 6d⁵ 6m 8m³ 7v⁶ 7f³ 8.2m 8.1d f7g f8g Nov 23] maiden: seemed to show
modest form on occasions in 2004: probably stays 1m: acts on good to firm and good to
soft going. *Don Enrico Incisa*

SPEEDY JAMES (IRE)   8 ch.g. Fayruz 116 – Haraabah (USA) 99 (Topsider (USA))   50
[2004 –: f6g f6s 6s² 6v Apr 6] strong gelding: good mover: one-time useful performer:
only modest nowadays: best at 5f: acts on soft and good to firm going: tried visored: often
slowly away. *D. Nicholls*

SPEEDY SPIRIT   2 ch.f. (Mar 5) Wolfhound (USA) 126 – Ansellady 67 (Absalom   –
128) [2004 6g 8g 6s Oct 22] 2,000F: sturdy filly: sixth foal: half-sister to 2000 2-y-o 5f
winner Miss Verity (by Factual): dam 6f winner: well held in maidens. *M. Salaman*

SPEIGHTSTOWN   2 gr.c. (Jan 25) Grand Lodge (USA) 125 – Farfala (FR) 106 (Lina-   78 p
mix (FR) 127) [2004 7.1d 8.2d³ 8.3m* 8.3g Oct 11] good-bodied colt: first foal: dam,
10.5f and 1½m winner in France, sister to very smart French middle-distance performer
Fragrant Mix: won maiden at Windsor in September: only seventh in nursery final start:
will be suited by 1¼m/1½m: type to improve and win more races at 3 yrs. *P. F. I. Cole*

SPENCE APPEAL (IRE)   2 b.g. (Mar 11) Nicolotte 118 – It's All Academic (IRE) 91   62
(Mazaad 106) [2004 6g 8f 7s p8g* f8g Dec 11] €11,000F, 21,000Y: good-bodied gelding:
fifth living foal: half-brother to 7f winner Warrior King (by Fairy King): dam 2-y-o 5f
winner: modest performer: in cheekpieces, won seller at Lingfield in November: stays
1m: best effort on polytrack: blinkered final start. *K. A. Ryan*

SPERRIN VALLEY (IRE)   2 ch.f. (Mar 27) Rossini (USA) 118 – Astra (IRE)   –
(Glenstal (USA) 118) [2004 p7g Sep 18] €3,000Y: eighth foal: half-sister to 3 winners,
including 1998 2-y-o 6f winner Montague Tigg (by Common Grounds) and 3-y-o City
General: dam Irish middle-distance maiden: 66/1, well held in maiden at Lingfield.
J. S. Moore

SPES BONA (USA) 3 b.g. Rakeen (USA) 99 – Novelette (Darshaan 133) [2004 8m **49** 8g⁴ 8.3g 8.5m p12.2g Oct 9] strong gelding: poor maiden: bred to stay beyond 1m, raced too freely over 1½m final start: gelded after. *W. J. Haggas*

SPIDERS WEB 4 gr.g. Linamix (FR) 127 – Cattermole (USA) (Roberto (USA) 131) **40 §** [2004 p7g p8g p12g p10g p10g f8.5s² f11g³ p8g p10g f8m 10f Jul 19] poor maiden: trained by Mme C. Head-Maarek in France only outing prior to 2004: stays 8.5f: usually blinkered: unreliable: sold 4,000 gns. *T. Keddy*

SPILL A LITTLE 2 b.c. (Mar 9) Zafonic (USA) 130 – Lypharitissima (FR) (Lightning **80** (FR) 129) [2004 7.1d⁶ 8g⁵ 8g f8g² p8g Nov 16] good-topped colt: half-brother to several winners, including fairly useful 9f/1¼m winner Generous Diana (by Generous) and 4-y-o Claradotnet: dam unraced sister to Prix de Diane winner Lypharita: fairly useful maiden: second in nursery at Southwell: needs to settle to stay beyond 1m. *M. R. Channon*

SPINDOR (USA) 5 ch.g. Spinning World (USA) 130 – Doree (USA) 110 (Stop The **70** Music (USA)) [2004 73, a62: f7g² f6f⁵ f7g³ f7s⁴ p6g² p7g* f6g f7g³ 8.3g³ 8m⁶ 8m p8g f7m⁴ Jul 6] fair performer: won handicap at Lingfield in March: effective at 6f to 1m: acts on all-weather, good to firm and good to soft going: blinkered: tried in cheekpieces: sometimes races slowly away/looks none too keen. *J. A. Osborne*

SPINETAIL RUFOUS (IRE) 6 b.g. Prince of Birds (USA) 121 – Miss Kinabalu 50 **63** (Shirley Heights 130) [2004 55§: p7g 6m* 6d* 5.3s 5.7s Oct 19] modest performer: won banded races at Kempton in September and Brighton in October: best at 5f/6f: acts on all-weather, soft and good to firm going: blinkered: tried tongue tied/in cheekpieces. *D. Flood*

SPIN KING (IRE) 3 b.g. Intikhab (USA) 135 – Special Dissident (Dancing Dissident **79** (USA) 119) [2004 79: 10g 8m⁴ 7m 7m³ 8m⁴ 7g 7f⁶ 7d Aug 27] strong, lengthy gelding: fair performer: well below form last 2 starts: likely to prove best up to 1m: acts on good to firm going: visored penultimate outing: sold 7,000 gns, then gelded. *M. L. W. Bell*

SPINNAKERS GIRL 2 b.f. (Mar 2) Bluegrass Prince (IRE) 110 – Brac Princess **69 d** (IRE) (Nicolotte 118) [2004 6g 7.1f³ 7g² 7d⁴ f7g 7.1d 8s⁴ 7s Nov 2] 800F, 1,500Y: first foal: dam unraced: fair maiden: below form after fourth start, including in seller: should stay 1m: acts on firm and good to soft going: blinkered final start. *J. R. Weymes*

SPINNING COIN 2 b.f. (Mar 10) Mujahid (USA) 125 – Cointosser (IRE) 66 (Nordico **59** (USA)) [2004 6m 7g⁶ 7m 8s 8f Sep 6] 4,600F, 6,500Y: quite good-topped filly: third foal: half-sister to 5f (at 2 yrs)/6f winner Primrose And Rose (by Primo Dominie): dam 7f/1m winner, also won over hurdles: modest maiden: possibly amiss final start: should stay 1m: acts on good to firm going. *J. G. Portman*

SPINNING DOVE 4 ch.f. Vettori (IRE) 119 – Northern Bird 86 (Interrex (CAN)) **68 §** [2004 68: p7g³ p8g² p8g p8g⁵ 7.5m May 24] big, workmanlike filly: fair maiden: refused to race on 2 of last 3 outings: stays easy 1m: acts on polytrack, good to firm and good to soft going: tried in cheekpieces: ungenuine: sold 3,200 gns. *N. A. Graham*

SPINNING JENNI 4 b.f. Mind Games 121 – Giddy 60 (Polar Falcon (USA) 126) **–** [2004 –: p6g Feb 4] close-coupled filly: fair at 3 yrs: well beaten only 4-y-o start: visored and tongue tied final 3-y-o outing. *J. M. Bradley*

SPIRIT OF CHESTER (IRE) 2 b.f. (Apr 12) Lend A Hand 124 – It Takes Two (IRE) **95** (Alzao (USA) 117) [2004 5.2g⁴ 6m² 6.3g 6s³ Aug 19] €30,000Y: tall, quite good-topped filly: has a round action: fifth living foal: half-sister to 3 winners, including smart Irish 5f/ 6f (latter including at 2 yrs) winner Final Exam (by College Chapel) and fairly useful Irish 13f winner Final Opinion (by King's Theatre): dam ran 3 times at 2 yrs in Ireland: useful maiden: best efforts when placed in listed race at Royal Ascot (second to Jewel In The Sand) and Lowther Stakes at York (3 lengths third to Soar, reportedly bled from nose): stays 6f: acts on soft and good to firm ground: raced up with pace last 2 starts. *Mrs P. N. Dutfield*

SPIRIT OF FRANCE (IRE) 2 b.g. (Apr 12) Anabaa (USA) 130 – Les Planches **93** (Tropular) [2004 5v² 5g² 6m* 6m² 7g⁵ 8m⁶ Sep 21] €60,000Y: tall gelding: has scope: first foal: dam, fairly useful French 1½m winner, half-sister to smart French performer up to 1½m Mousse Glacee: fairly useful performer: won maiden at Ripon in June: creditable efforts in nurseries/minor event after: stays 1m: acts on good to firm ground: races prominently: gelded after final start. *M. Johnston*

SPIRIT'S AWAKENING 5 b.g. Danzig Connection (USA) – Mo Stopher 47 (Sharpo **69** 132) [2004 69: 8.3g 8g⁶ 8.1d³ 8m² 7m⁴ 7.1d² 8.1d⁶ 8m 8.2g* 8.2v 7s Oct 27] good-topped gelding: fair handicapper: won at Nottingham in September: stays 9f: acts on any ground: sometimes races freely. *J. Akehurst*

SPITFIRE BOB (USA)   5 b.g. Mister Baileys 123 – Gulf Cyclone (USA) (Sheikh   –
Albadou 128) [2004 71, a76: f9.4g 12m Sep 18] sturdy gelding: fair handicapper at 4 yrs:
well held both starts in 2004, leaving T. D. Barron in between. *M. E. Sowersby*

SPITTING IMAGE (IRE)   4 ch.f. Spectrum (IRE) 126 – Decrescendo (IRE) (Polish   66
Precedent (USA) 131) [2004 68: 13.8g 14g³ 13g 11.9f² 14.1m⁴ 16f* 16g² 16d³ 16m*
16g⁶ 14.1m Oct 2] close-coupled, quite attractive filly: fair performer: won claimer in
June and handicap in August, both at Redcar: will stay beyond 2m: acts on firm and good
to soft going, ran poorly on soft and fibresand: tends to edge right. *K. G. Reveley*

SPLENDID TOUCH   4 b.f. Distinctly North (USA) 115 – Soft Touch (GER) (Horst-   –
Herbert) [2004 –: f11g 11.5d Aug 26] well held in Britain. *J. R. Jenkins*

SPLIFF   3 b.c. Royal Applause 124 – Snipe Hall 93 (Crofthall 110) [2004 89p: 6s* 6m   92
6m 5g 6g 6m⁵ 6s Sep 25] leggy, useful-looking colt: fairly useful handicapper: won
at Salisbury (beat Star Pupil by 1¼ lengths) in May: creditable fifth to Texas Gold at
Goodwood penultimate start: best at 5f/6f: acts on soft and good to firm going: blinkered
fourth start: sold 15,000 gns. *H. Candy*

SPLODGER MAC (IRE)   5 b.g. Lahib (USA) 129 – Little Love (Warrshan (USA)   59
117) [2004 47: 7.5g 8g 8.5m* 7m² 8.2g⁶ 8g 8m² 8.5m⁴ 8m Oct 2] sturdy gelding: modest
performer: won handicap at Beverley in July: stays 8.5f: acts on good to firm ground:
free-going sort, and usually races prominently. *N. Bycroft*

SPORTING GESTURE   7 ch.g. Safawan 118 – Polly Packer 81 (Reform 132) [2004   82
86: 11.9s 12m⁵ 11.9m⁴ 11.9g⁴ 12.3d⁴ 11.9f³ 12.3m⁶ 11.9d 12m² 14.1d⁵ Sep 17] rather
leggy, close-coupled gelding: has a round action: fairly useful handicapper: stays 1½m:
acts on firm and good to soft going: tried blinkered in 2002: usually waited with: tough
and reliable. *M. W. Easterby*

SPORTSMAN (IRE)   5 b.g. Sri Pekan (USA) 117 – Ardent Range (IRE) (Archway   36
(IRE) 115) [2004 44: f16.2s⁴ f16g⁴ 12.3m May 26] poor maiden: stays 1½m: blinkered:
sometimes slowly away. *M. W. Easterby*

SPOT IN TIME   4 b.f. Mtoto 134 – Kelimutu 58 (Top Ville 129) [2004 f12s 9.9g 10.3m   –
6.9f 11.9s Aug 24] strong, lengthy filly: fifth foal: half-sister to 3 winners, including
useful 1m (at 2 yrs) and 1¼m winner Whitefoot (by Be My Chief) and 5-y-o Ark
Admiral: dam 1¼m/1½m winner: third in bumper: well held on Flat (left J. Pearce after
second outing, P. Wood after fourth). *I. W. McInnes*

SPOTLIGHT   3 ch.f. Dr Fong (USA) 128 – Dust Dancer 116 (Suave Dancer (USA)   110
136) [2004 104p: 7g⁴ 8m 9.9g² 9s* 9g* 9f² 9g⁴ Oct 23] rather leggy, quite good-topped
filly: smart performer: good neck second to Halicardia in listed Lupe Stakes at Goodwood in May (final outing for J. Dunlop): won allowance race at Belmont in July and
Grade 2 Lake Placid Handicap at Saratoga (beat Mambo Slew 3½ lengths) in August:
creditable 2¾ lengths second to Ticker Tape in Grade 3 Pucker Up Stakes at Arlington
next time: odds on, only fourth to Hopelessly Devoted in non-graded Calder Oaks final
outing: should stay 1½m: acts on firm going, successful on soft: got very worked up
beforehand when last in 1000 Guineas at Newmarket second outing. *C. Clement, USA*

SPREE (IRE)   2 gr.f. (Feb 3) Dansili 127 – Ibiza (GER) (Linamix (FR) 127) [2004 5s⁶   93 §
5m* 5m 5g 6.1g Sep 29] €30,000Y: rather leggy, good-topped filly: first foal: dam,
German 10.5f winner, half-sister to useful German performer up to 1½m Iberus: fairly
useful performer: won maiden at Sandown in June by 6 lengths, soon in front: no other
form in minor events/pattern races: should stay 6f: acts on good to firm ground: unreliable. *R. Hannon*

SPREE VISION   8 b.g. Suave Dancer (USA) 136 – Regent's Folly (IRE) 101 (Touch-   57
ing Wood (USA) 127) [2004 10.1v⁶ 12.1g 11.9g⁴ 10.9g² 11.9f² 12.1f⁴ 12.1s⁵ 9.1d⁶ 10s⁴
Oct 30] smallish, good-topped gelding: modest performer: stays 13f: acts on any going:
often visored: sometimes looks none too keen. *P. Monteith*

SPRING ADIEU   3 b.f. Green Desert (USA) 127 – Nanda 83 (Nashwan (USA) 135)   60
[2004 60: 9g⁴ 9.9g 10m 11.9s⁴ 13.1f Sep 6] modest maiden: stays 1½m: acts on soft
and good to firm going: blinkered (looked wayward) final start: sold 3,000 gns. *Mrs
A. J. Perrett*

SPRINGALONG (USA)   4 ch.g. Gone West (USA) – Seven Springs (USA) 114   71 d
(Irish River (FR) 131) [2004 75d: p10g p10g⁴ p10g⁵ 10.2g 8.2d 10f p12g 10.1m⁶ Jul 22]
smallish, sturdy gelding: fair maiden: creditable effort in 2004 only on third start: stays
easy 1¼m: acts on polytrack and good to firm going. *P. D. Evans*

SPRING BREEZE   3 ch.g. Dr Fong (USA) 128 – Trading Aces 71 (Be My Chief   69
(USA) 122) [2004 55: 10s⁶ 12.1g 14.1m² 16.2g³ 16g² 14.1g⁵ 16g² 15.8m* 16.1m⁶ 15s³

f16s² p16.5g² Dec 4] workmanlike gelding: fair handicapper: won at Catterick in September: stays 16.5f: acts on all-weather, firm and soft going: wore headgear after reappearance. *M. Dods*

SPRING DANCER 3 b.f. Imperial Ballet (IRE) 110 – Roxy Music (IRE) 63 (Song 132) [2004 78d: p7g 6d 7g 11g⁵ f8.5g³ 6.9f⁶ 8d 7m⁶ p7.1d Oct 23] quite good-topped filly: just modest performer in 2004: left A. Jarvis after second start, B. Powell after fifth: stays 7f: acts on firm going: tried in visor/cheekpieces, tongue tied last 4 outings: unreliable. *T. J. Fitzgerald* — **50 §**

SPRING DEW (FR) 3 b.f. Starborough 126 – Penniless (IRE) 74 (Common Grounds 118) [2004 p7.1g⁵ p7g⁶ Dec 29] £3,000Y: second foal: half-sister to 2002 2-y-o 5f seller winner Buster Brown (by Presidium): dam 5f winner (including at 2 yrs): better effort in maidens on debut: pulled too hard after slow start next time. *J. A. Geake* — **53**

SPRING GIFT 7 b.m. Slip Anchor 136 – Belmez Melody 73 (Belmez (USA) 131) [2004 f11g Jan 29] lightly-raced maiden: well held only 7-y-o start. *D. W. Thompson* — **–**

SPRING GODDESS (IRE) 3 b.f. Daggers Drawn (USA) 114 – Easter Girl (Efisio 120) [2004 82: 10m³ 10.1m 10.4m⁴ 10g³ 9g³ Jul 28] good-topped filly: fairly useful handicapper: third at Ascot (2) and Goodwood (to Diamond Lodge): stays 1¼m: acts on good to firm going. *A. P. Jarvis* — **88**

SPRING JIM 3 b.g. First Trump 118 – Spring Sixpence 60 (Dowsing (USA) 124) [2004 71: 7m⁴ 8.2g* 9g² 10g⁴ 10g² Sep 10] close-coupled gelding: fairly useful handicapper: won at Nottingham in June: creditable efforts after, particularly when second to Top Spec at Sandown final start: stays 1¼m: raced only on good/good to firm ground: held up. *J. R. Fanshawe* — **88**

SPRING PURSUIT 8 b.g. Rudimentary (USA) 118 – Pursuit of Truth (USA) 69 (Irish River (FR) 131) [2004 –: 13.1d⁴ Aug 27] close-coupled gelding: modest handicapper nowadays: stays 13f: goes well on ground softer than good: usually held up: fair hurdler. *E. G. Bevan* — **52**

SPRING SURPRISE 3 b.f. Hector Protector (USA) 124 – Tender Moment (IRE) 78 (Caerleon (USA) 132) [2004 82p: 8d⁶ p8.6g Dec 6] strong, lengthy filly: fairly useful winner at 2 yrs: well beaten in listed race at Kempton (flashed tail) and handicap at Wolverhampton (blinkered) in 2004, leaving B. Hills prior to latter. *B. R. Johnson* — **–**

SPRING TIME GIRL 2 b.f. (May 8) Timeless Times (USA) 99 – Daira 72 (Daring March 116) [2004 5m Sep 15] second foal: dam 1½m winner: 33/1, slowly away and always behind in maiden at Beverley. *B. Ellison* — **–**

SPRINGTIME ROMANCE (USA) 3 br.f. Kris S (USA) – Khamsin (USA) (Mr Prospector (USA)) [2004 10d³ 12d⁶ 9g* 9.9g⁶ 9d⁴ 8.3g Jul 12] tall, leggy filly: fifth foal: half-sister to 3 winners, including 1998 2-y-o 6f winner Subeen (by Caerleon) and 1m winner Khalkissa (by Diesis), both useful: dam, second at 11f in France, half-sister to US Grade 1 1¼m winner Storm Trooper: fairly useful performer: won maiden at Goodwood in May: good fourth to Unsuited in handicap at Kempton: should stay 1½m: acts on good to soft going: hung/got unbalanced at Newmarket second outing. *E. A. L. Dunlop* — **80**

SPRING WHISPER (IRE) 3 b.f. Halling (USA) 133 – Light Fresh Air (USA) (Rahy (USA) 115) [2004 49: p10g p7g 12m 10d Oct 2] poor maiden: left E. Dunlop after reappearance: best efforts at 1¼m: often visored/blinkered: hung right final 2-y-o start. *C. A. Dwyer* — **43**

SPURADICH (IRE) 4 b.c. Barathea (IRE) 127 – Svanzega (USA) (Sharpen Up 127) [2004 106+: 8.5g 10m⁶ 10m⁶ 10d* Sep 18] strong colt: useful handicapper: won John Smith's Stakes at Newbury by ¾ length from Jabaar, hanging left after leading over 1f out: stays 1¼m: acts on good to firm and good to soft going: tends to race freely/carry head high: reportedly finished lame final 3-y-o outing: sold 82,000 gns. *L. M. Cumani* — **100**

SPY GUN (USA) 4 ch.g. Mt Livermore (USA) – Takeover Target (USA) (Nodouble (USA)) [2004 68: f8.5s³ f8g⁵ f8.5g f7s f8.5s⁵ f8g f7g⁴ 10.9s 7s⁶ f8g² 7m 8m p8.6g p8.6g Dec 17] angular, useful-looking gelding: just modest handicapper on dirt: stays 8.5f (raced too freely at 11f): acts on fibresand and good to firm ground: has been slowly away. *T. Wall* — **52 a60**

SPY KING (USA) 2 ch.c. (Feb 28) Distant View (USA) 126 – Regal Princess (USA) (Royal And Regal (USA)) [2004 6g² 6d* 6d* 6g³ Aug 28] $35,000Y: good-topped colt: half-brother to several winners in USA, including minor stakes winners by With Approval and Southern Halo: dam US 5f (at 2 yrs) to 8.5f (minor stakes) winner: fairly useful performer: won maiden at Newcastle and minor event at Hamilton in August: good third in nursery at Newmarket: will stay 7f: acts on good to soft going: sold 50,000 gns, sent to Hong Kong. *M. Johnston* — **88**

SPY MASTER 6 b.g. Green Desert (USA) 127 – Obsessive (USA) 102 (Seeking The **36**
Gold (USA)) [2004 –: f5g³ f6g² f6s⁵ f6s f5s⁶ f6m⁵ f6g 6.1d f6m 5d Sep 16] small, strong
gelding: poor performer: stays 6f: acts on fibresand, heavy and good to firm ground:
wears headgear/tongue strap. *J. Parkes*

SQUARE DANCER 8 b.g. Then Again 126 – Cubist (IRE) 71 (Tate Gallery (USA) **–**
117) [2004 –: 6g 6d 7.2m May 21] tall, good-bodied gelding: of no account nowadays.
D. A. Nolan

SQUAW DANCE 2 ch.f. (Feb 9) Indian Ridge 123 – Likely Story (IRE) 94 (Night Shift **100 p**
(USA)) [2004 6m⁶ 6s³ 8s² 8d* Oct 30] 68,000Y: good-topped filly: third foal: half-sister
to 4-y-o Border Tale and 3-y-o Poule de Luxe: dam 6f winner (including at 2 yrs): placed
in maidens before winning listed race at Newmarket by 1½ lengths from Something
Exciting, dictating pace and finding plenty: should stay 1¼m: already useful, and probably capable of better. *W. J. Haggas*

SQUEAKY 7 ch.m. Infantry 122 – Steady Saunter VII (Damsire Unregistered) [2004 **–**
72: p7g Jan 21] lengthy mare: fair handicapper: well held over unsuitable trip only 7-y-o
start: stays 12.6f: acts on firm and soft going. *Miss K. M. George*

SQUIRTLE TURTLE 4 ch.g. Peintre Celebre (USA) 137 – Hatton Gardens 96 **75 d**
(Auction Ring (USA) 123) [2004 79: f11g* f12g 12g 12m⁴ 11.9f⁵ 16g⁴ Jun 21] tall, quite
good-topped gelding: fair handicapper: won amateur event at Southwell in January:
below form after: stays 1½m: acts on fibresand and firm going: tried blinkered/tongue
tied: has been slowly away/hung left. *P. F. I. Cole*

SRI DIAMOND 4 b.g. Sri Pekan (USA) 117 – Hana Marie 101§ (Formidable (USA) **85**
125) [2004 92: 8v 8g 8.1d⁶ 8m² p8g⁶ Dec 30] good-topped gelding: fairly useful handicapper, lightly raced: at least as effective at 7f as 1m: acts on polytrack and good to firm
ground. *S. Kirk*

SRI LIPIS 2 ch.c. (Jan 29) Cadeaux Genereux 131 – Katrina (IRE) (Ela-Mana-Mou **77**
132) [2004 7m⁴ 7m⁴ Jul 6] 200,000Y: workmanlike colt: first foal: dam unraced half-
sister to smart middle-distance stayer Kithanga, herself dam of St Leger winner Milan:
fair form in maidens at Newmarket, hanging left final start: will stay at least 1m.
P. F. I. Cole

SRIOLOGY (IRE) 3 b.g. Sri Pekan (USA) 117 – Sinology (Rainbow Quest (USA) **59 +**
134) [2004 –: 8s⁴ f8d² Dec 21] modest maiden, lightly raced: left M. Holden in Ireland,
good second in banded race at Southwell: stays 1m: acts on fibresand and soft going:
tongue tied. *G. Prodromou*

STAFF NURSE (IRE) 4 b.f. Night Shift (USA) – Akebia (USA) (Trempolino (USA) **45**
135) [2004 53: 12.4v f12g f14g⁴ f14g 12g⁵ f14g³ f12s³ 12.1m² 13.1s⁴ f11g³ f16g Dec 14]
well-made filly: poor performer: stays 1¾m: acts on fibresand, firm and soft going:
visored (ran poorly) once. *Don Enrico Incisa*

John Smith's Stakes (Handicap) Newbury—
Spuradich makes amends after going lame in the equivalent race the previous year;
he wins from stable-companions Jabaar (grey) and Blue Spinnaker (right)

STAFFORD KING (IRE) 7 b.h. Nicolotte 118 – Opening Day (Day Is Done 115) –
[2004 12.1m 10.2s 18d Aug 19] lengthy, workmanlike horse: maiden: well beaten in
2004: tried visored. *J. G. M. O'Shea*

STAGBURY HILL (USA) 2 ch.c. (Mar 12) Woodman (USA) 126 – Shalabia 84 (Fast **101**
Topaze (USA) 128) [2004 6m⁵ 7g⁶ 7.6g³ 6m⁶ Sep 4] $45,000Y: sturdy colt: half-brother
to winner in USA by Sadler's Wells: dam, 7f winner, half-sister to very smart performer
around 1m Allied Forces: useful performer: dead-heated for first with St Andrews Storm
in maiden at Newmarket in June: good sixth in Vintage Stakes at Goodwood and Sirenia
Stakes at Kempton: stays 7f: acts on good to firm going. *J. W. Hills*

STAGECOACH RUBY 3 b.f. Bijou d'Inde 127 – Forum Girl (USA) 79 (Sheikh **48**
Albadou 128) [2004 58d: p10g p8g p10g⁵ p8g⁴ p8g³ 7g³ 7f 6f 7m⁵ p10g* 7m p10m
p10m³ Dec 15] tall, plain filly: blind in one eye: poor performer: won banded race at
Lingfield in September: stays easy 1¼m: acts on polytrack and good to firm going: tried
in eyeshields: has wandered. *Mrs L. C. Jewell*

STAGE DIRECTION (USA) 7 b.g. Theatrical 128 – Carya (USA) (Northern Dan- –
cer) [2004 –: 12.1g Jul 9] modest performer at 5 yrs: well beaten both starts since: tried
tongue tied. *J. D. Frost*

STAGE LEFT 3 ch.f. Nashwan (USA) 135 – Interval 122 (Habitat 134) [2004 10v² **57**
Oct 20] half-sister to several winners, including smart French 1m to 1½m winner Short
Pause (by Sadler's Wells) and to dam of 7-y-o Continent: dam 5f (at 2 yrs) to 1m winner:
4/1 and green, ¾-length second to Lomapamar in maiden at Nottingham, running on
again having lost position 2f out, only outing: stud. *H. R. A. Cecil*

STAGE RIGHT 3 b.c. In The Wings 128 – Spot Prize (USA) 108 (Seattle Dancer **92**
(USA) 119) [2004 p7g⁴ 8.3d⁶ 12g* 12g⁵ 13.3d⁴ 12d⁶ 14s³ Aug 28] big, strong colt: fifth
foal: half-brother to several winners, including useful 7f (at 2 yrs) and 1¼m winner
Premier Prize (by Selkirk) and 4-y-o Gold Medallist: dam, 2-y-o 5f winner, fourth in
Oaks: fairly useful performer: won maiden at Kempton in June: mainly creditable efforts
after, stiff task when third to impressive Orange Touch in minor event at Goodwood final
start: stays 1¾m: acts on soft going: sold 24,000 gns. *D. R. C. Elsworth*

STAGE SCHOOL (USA) 2 b. or br.f. (Apr 19) Sunday Silence (USA) – Danseur **64 p**
Fabuleux (USA) 106 (Northern Dancer) [2004 6d² Nov 5] half-sister to several winners,
notably outstanding 1991 2-y-o Arazi (by Blushing Groom), successful up to 1m, and
high-class 5f (at 2 yrs) to 1m winner Noverre (by Rahy): dam, French maiden who stayed
1½m, out of very smart French middle-distance filly Fabuleux Jane: 10/1 and green, 3
lengths second to Westland in maiden at Yarmouth, running on not knocked about: will
stay 1m: sure to improve. *M. Johnston*

STAGE SECRET (IRE) 3 ch.c. Zilzal (USA) 137 – Tuxford Hideaway 102 (Caws- **88**
ton's Clown 113) [2004 10m p7.1g* p8.6g⁴ p7.1g² p7.1g² Dec 31] 100,000Y, 27,000
3-y-o: half-brother to numerous winners, including smart 5f (at 2 yrs) to 7f winner Branston Abby (by Risk Me) and 6-y-o Desert Deer: dam sprinter: fairly useful performer,
lightly raced: won maiden at Wolverhampton in November: good efforts in handicaps
there after: stays 8.6f: acts on polytrack. *Miss E. C. Lavelle*

STAGE TWO (IRE) 3 b.g. Sadler's Wells (USA) 132 – Meteor Stage (USA) (Stage **47**
Door Johnny (USA)) [2004 p12g f12g 12g⁴ 12.6s 12v 12.1m² 14.1m Jun 1] poor
maiden: stays 1½m: acts on good to firm ground: visored final start: sold 3,500 gns.
M. Johnston

STAGNITE 4 ch.g. Compton Place 125 – Superspring (Superlative 118) [2004 65: **65**
6.1m 6m² 6m² 5.1m* 5g 5.3f 5g⁶ 5.7f⁵ 5.7g 5f p6d Nov 5] fair handicapper: won at
Chepstow in July: effective at 5f/easy 7f: acts on polytrack and firm going: often races
prominently: wore cheekpieces after second start. *Mrs H. Sweeting*

STAKHANOV 2 b.g. (May 22) Dr Fong (USA) 128 – Russian Grace (IRE) (Soviet –
Star (USA) 128) [2004 7d Aug 13] 50/1, well held in maiden at Newmarket: sold 4,000
gns. *W. J. Haggas*

STAKHANOVITE (IRE) 4 b.c. Darshaan 133 – Homage (Ajdal (USA) 130) [2004 **55**
84: 8g 10m Sep 5] rather leggy colt: shaped well in maiden only start prior to 2004 (struck
into on hind leg): well below form in similar events at Bath (took strong hold) and the
Curragh, leaving D. Loder 17,000 gns in between. *James Leavy, Ireland*

STALLONE 7 ch.g. Brief Truce (USA) 126 – Bering Honneur (USA) (Bering 136) **80**
[2004 79: 10.3g 10g³ 10m⁴ 11.9m³ 12.3d⁶ 11.9f 12m 12m⁶ 10m⁶ 11.9g³ 12d⁵ p13.9g²
Dec 31] good-bodied gelding: fairly useful handicapper: creditable efforts when in frame

in 2004: effective at 1¼m/1½m: acts on polytrack, firm and soft going: tried tongue tied: tends to start slowly (refused to race once at 5 yrs): usually held up. *N. Wilson*

STAMFORD BLUE 3 b.g. Bluegrass Prince (IRE) 110 – Fayre Holly (IRE) 57 (Fayruz 116) [2004 58: p6g² p5g⁴ p6g⁶ p6g² p7g p5g⁶ p7g 6d* 6d² p6g p6g p6m⁵ Dec 22] workmanlike gelding: fair on turf, modest on all-weather: won seller at Leicester in April: best efforts at 6f: acts on polytrack and good to soft going, well held on fibresand: tried in cheekpieces, usually blinkered. *J. S. Moore* **69 a61**

STANBURY (USA) 2 ch.g. (Jan 7) Zamindar (USA) 116 – Staffin 93 (Salse (USA) 128) [2004 5s² Mar 29] $75,000F, 130,000Y: well-made gelding: third foal: dam, 2-y-o 7f winner (later successful in USA), out of half-sister to Jersey Stakes winner Ardkinglass: favourite, second in maiden at Newcastle: gelded after: bred to stay 7f. *M. R. Channon* **73**

STANCE 5 b.g. Salse (USA) 128 – De Stael (USA) 93 (Nijinsky (CAN) 138) [2004 ?: 20f 21g² 16.2m 18s Oct 16] strong, well-made, attractive gelding: type to carry condition: has a quick, fluent action: useful at 3 yrs, fairly useful nowadays: creditable effort in 2004 only when second in handicap at Goodwood: stays 21f: acts on sand, firm and good to soft going: wore cheekpieces last 3 starts: fairly useful hurdler. *G. L. Moore* **83**

STANCOMB WILLS (IRE) 2 b.c. (Feb 17) Trans Island 119 – First Nadia (Auction Ring (USA) 123) [2004 7d 7d 7.5m² 8s² Oct 12] €12,000Y: strong, workmanlike colt: half-brother to several winners, including useful but unreliable 5f (at 2 yrs) and 7m winner My Lucy Locket (by Mujadil): dam well beaten: fair maiden: second at Beverley (edged left) and Ayr (nursery): stays 1m: acts on soft and good to firm going. *M. H. Tompkins* **79**

ST ANDREWS (IRE) 4 b.c. Celtic Swing 138 – Viola Royale (IRE) 90 (Royal Academy (USA) 130) [2004 7m² 7m⁶ 8.1d² 7m⁵ 8g 8.1s* 9g 8.2v* 8s⁶ Nov 23] lengthy, quite attractive colt: smart performer: missed 2003 due to fracture of hind fetlock: won handicap at Haydock (beat Excelsius by 7 lengths) in September and minor event at Nottingham (by 3½ lengths from Fine Silver) in November: below form in Cambridgeshire at Newmarket (raced too freely) in between and in listed race at Saint-Cloud final outing: effective at 7f/1m: acts on good to firm going, best efforts on softer than good (acts on heavy): swished tail third start. *M. A. Jarvis* **110**

ST ANDREWS STORM (USA) 2 b.c. (Feb 4) Storm Creek (USA) – L'Amour Toujours (USA) (Blushing Groom (FR) 131) [2004 6m* 6m⁴ 6m⁴ 7s Oct 22] 160,000 2-y-o: quite attractive colt: closely related to winner in USA by Mountain Cat and half-brother to 3 winners there, including Grade 2 7f winner C'Est L'Amour (by Thunder Gulch): dam French 1¼m/10.5f winner, later successful in USA: useful performer: dead-heated for first with Stagbury Hill in maiden at Newmarket in June: 2¾ lengths fourth to Captain Hurricane in July Stakes there next start, easily best effort: off 3 months before final outing: should stay 7f. *R. Hannon* **101**

STANHOPE FORBES (IRE) 3 b.c. Danehill Dancer (IRE) 117 – Hinari Disk Deck 75 (Indian King (USA) 128) [2004 66, a54: p6g³ p6g⁵ Jan 28] sturdy colt: modest maiden at 2yrs: poor form in 2004: will prove best at 6f/7f: acts on polytrack and firm ground: tried in cheekpieces: sold 7,500 gns. *N. P. Littmoden* **41**

STANLEY ARTHUR 2 b.g. (Jan 29) Mind Games 121 – Midnight Orchid (IRE) 74 (Petardia 113) [2004 6d 7m Oct 10] well held in maidens at Ayr and Newcastle. *D. Nicholls* **–**

STANLEY CRANE (USA) 3 br.g. Bahri (USA) 125 – Grey Starling 70 (Pharly (FR) 130) [2004 79: 10m 7f⁵ 9.3f⁴ p8g⁵ 8m⁴ 10m³ 10g Aug 18] good-topped gelding: just modest maiden at 3 yrs: stays 1m: acts on polytrack and good to firm going: wears tongue tie: sold 6,500 gns. *B. Hanbury* **56**

STAN'S GIRL 2 b.f. (Mar 14) Fraam 114 – Gigetta (IRE) (Brief Truce (USA) 126) [2004 5d 5d³ 6g² 6d 6.1v p5.1g Dec 13] 14,500Y: neat filly: second foal: half-sister to a winner in Greece by Fayruz: dam well beaten only start: modest maiden: left M. Channon after second in seller at Ripon: ran poorly after: should prove best at 5f/6f. *I. A. Wood* **54**

STAR APPLAUSE 4 b.f. Royal Applause 124 – Cominna (Dominion 123) [2004 54d: f5g f6g 5f⁶ 5g 5m 5f 6g⁴ Aug 7] good-topped filly: poor performer: left J. Balding after second start: raced only at 5f/6f: acts on fibresand and good to firm ground: tried in cheekpieces/visor. *J. S. Goldie* **44**

STARBECK (IRE) 6 b.m. Spectrum (IRE) 126 – Tide of Fortune (Soviet Star (USA) 128) [2004 94, a?: 7d 7s 8g⁵ 7m⁴ 8f 8.1g 6.5g⁵ 7d⁴ 6m 7f 7d⁴ 7m p8g 7m 7d Oct 15] lengthy mare: fairly useful handicapper,: mostly creditable efforts in 2004: form up to 7f: **87 a?**

acts on all-weather, soft and good to firm ground: tried tongue tied: has been bandaged/early to post: often slowly away. *P. Howling*

STARBRIGHT 3 b.g. Polar Falcon (USA) 126 – Treasure Hunt (Hadeer 118) [2004 –: 9.3g Sep 2] soundly beaten in maidens at Catterick and Carlisle (took good hold) 12 months apart. *Miss S. E. Hall*

STARCHY 2 b.f. (Jan 16) Cadeaux Genereux 131 – Sahara Star 95 (Green Desert (USA) 127) [2004 6.1v* Nov 4] lengthy filly: sister to smart sprinter Land of Dreams, and half-sister to 3 winners, including useful 1½m winner Edraak (by Shirley Heights): dam 2-y-o 5f (including Molecomb Stakes) winner: 12/1, won maiden at Nottingham by 6 lengths from Allegretto, travelling strongly and pushed clear final 1f: shapes as if will stay 7f: useful prospect. *M. Johnston*   **84 p**

STARCROSS MAID 2 ch.f. (Apr 6) Zaha (CAN) 106 – Maculatus (USA) (Sharpen Up 127) [2004 p8.6g p9.5g³ Dec 20] 6,000Y: eighth foal: half-sister to 3 winners, including 7f winner Nordic Doll (by Royal Academy) and useful 1998 2-y-o 5f winner Chomper (by Mujtahid, later successful in USA): dam ran twice: better effort in maidens at Wolverhampton when third to Blue Bajan: slowly away on debut. *P. W. D'Arcy*   **59**

STARCROSS VENTURE 3 b.f. Orpen (USA) 116 – Maculatus (USA) (Sharpen Up 127) [2004 63: f6g p6g Jan 21] modest form only 2-y-o start: poor form in 2004: raced only at 6f on all-weather. *R. A. Fahey*   **43**

STAR DUSTER 2 gr.f. (May 2) Paris House 123 – To The Stars (IRE) (Zieten (USA) 118) [2004 5.1m 5.1g² 5.1f 5m² 5m² 5.1g² Oct 10] first foal: dam, well beaten in 3 starts, out of smart 6f/7f winner Rocket Alert: fair maiden: second in nurseries last 3 starts: will prove best at 5f/easy 6f: acts on good to firm going. *B. R. Millman*   **69**

STAR FERN 3 br.g. Young Ern 120 – Christening (IRE) (Lahib (USA) 129) [2004 63p: p8g⁵ p7g⁵ p7g 7s 7m 6g p6g⁴ f7g f7g p7m f6g* p6g⁶ Dec 22] big, close-coupled gelding: modest performer: left J. Akehurst after fifth start: won banded race at Southwell in December: stays 7f: acts on all-weather: unreliable. *R. M. H. Cowell*   **54 §**

STARGEM 3 b.f. Compton Place 125 – Holy Smoke 83 (Statoblest 120) [2004 81: 6m² f6g² 6m 6s² 6g² Sep 14] rather leggy filly: fair maiden: runner-up on 4 of 5 starts in 2004: will probably prove best at 5f/6f: acts on soft and good to firm going: races prominently. *J. Pearce*   **67**

STARJESTIC 3 b.f. Bijou d'Inde 127 – Risalah (Marju (IRE) 127) [2004 10.2s p8.6g f6g Dec 7] 1,100Y: half-sister to 7-y-o Atlantic Ace and 6-y-o Lockstock: dam ran once: well held in maiden/sellers. *M. S. Saunders*   **–**

STAR LAD (IRE) 4 ch.g. Lake Coniston (IRE) 131 – Simply Special (IRE) (Petit Loup (USA) 123) [2004 62: f7g³ f7s* f7g f6g f6s* f6s⁴ f5g⁵ 6.1s f5g³ 6g f6g f6g f6g⁴ f6d Dec 21] modest performer: won seller at Wolverhampton in January and banded race at Southwell in February: stays 7f: acts on fibresand and good to firm going: wears blinkers/visor: usually races up with pace. *R. Brotherton*   **57**

STARLIGHT RIVER (IRE) 2 b.f. (Feb 16) Spectrum (IRE) 126 – Prosaic Star (IRE) 81 (Common Grounds 118) [2004 5.1s 6g 5.1s³ 5g 7m⁴ p8g p7.1g Dec 15] €42,000Y: leggy filly: half-sister to several winners, including 5f winner Lupine (including at 2 yrs, by Lake Coniston) and 3-y-o Blue Crush: dam Irish 2-y-o 1m winner: modest maiden: left W. Muir prior to final start: barely stays 7f: acts on soft and good to firm going: signs of temperament. *J. Parkes*   **62**

STAR MAGNITUDE (USA) 3 ch.g. Distant View (USA) 126 – Stellaria (USA) 98 (Roberto (USA) 131) [2004 8m 7g² 7.5g² 10.2g⁵ Oct 10] good-bodied gelding: brother to top-class 6f (at 2 yrs) to 9.3f winner Observatory and half-brother to several winners, including smart 7f (at 2 yrs) to 1½m (Prix de Malleret) winner High Praise (by Quest For Fame): dam 5f (at 2 yrs) to 8.5f (in USA) winner: fairly useful maiden: runner-up at Doncaster and Beverley: should stay 1m: sold 34,000 gns, then gelded. *J. H. M. Gosden*   **80**

STAR MEMBER (IRE) 5 b.g. Hernando (FR) 127 – Constellation (IRE) (Kaldoun (FR) 122) [2004 87: 14.4v⁵ 13.9s* 16.2m⁴ 13.9m* 13.9g² 13.9s⁶ 14.6f⁶ 12d Oct 14] leggy, quite good-topped, close-coupled gelding: useful handicapper: better than ever in 2004, winning at York in May and June (beat Escavola by 4 lengths): also ran well on same course next 2 starts, when second to Distinction in listed rated stakes and sixth to Mephisto in Ebor: sometimes races freely, but stays 2m: acts on all-weather, firm and soft going: usually waited with: joined I. Williams. *A. P. Jarvis*   **104**

STARMIX 3 br.g. Linamix (FR) 127 – Danlu (USA) (Danzig (USA)) [2004 p12g 10s 8g⁴ 11.6g 8g 10.1g Aug 11] sturdy gelding: half-brother to several winners, notably very   **70**

smart 1¼m to 1¾m winner Strategic Choice (by Alleged) and useful 1m/1¼m winner Sure Dancer (by Affirmed): dam, Irish 1m (at 2 yrs)/8.5f winner, sister to smart 6f/7f performer Nicholas: fair maiden: should stay at least 1¼m: tried blinkered: gelded after final start. *P. F. I. Cole*

STAR OF KILDARE (IRE) 2 b.f. (May 23) Raphane (USA) 102 – Lady Fleetsin **41** (IRE) (Double Schwartz 128) [2004 5m 5g 5m 5d f5s Aug 23] €2,000Y: workmanlike filly: third foal: sister to 3-y-o Barras and half-sister to 6f (including at 2 yrs) to 1m (in UAE) winner Cable Media Boy (by Great Commotion): dam unraced: poor maiden: form only at 5f on good going. *N. Tinkler*

STAR OF LIGHT 3 b.g. Mtoto 134 – Star Entry 67 (In The Wings 128) [2004 77: 7m³ **85** 10g⁴ Sep 10] good-bodied gelding: fairly useful handicapper: good efforts at Newbury and Sandown (fourth to Top Spec, racing freely and staying on after being short of room 3f out): stays 1¼m: acts on polytrack and good to firm going. *B. J. Meehan*

STAR OF NORMANDIE (USA) 5 b.m. Gulch (USA) – Depaze (USA) (Deputy **93** Minister (CAN)) [2004 91: p10g p10g 10g 10d p8g 10.3s² p8g³ p10g p10g Nov 30] tall mare: fairly useful performer: good efforts in listed race at Doncaster (second to Mango Mischief) and handicap at Lingfield (third to Tawoos) sixth/seventh starts: effective at 1m/1¼m: acts on all-weather, firm and soft going: tried blinkered/in cheekpieces earlier in career. *G. G. Margarson*

STAR OVATION (IRE) 7 ch.g. Fourstars Allstar (USA) 122 – Standing Ovation **–** (Godswalk (USA) 130) [2004 65?: 7m Aug 3] good-bodied gelding: maiden: well held at Catterick only 7-y-o start. *Miss R. Bowden, Ireland*

STAR PUPIL 3 ch.g. Selkirk (USA) 129 – Lochangel 119 (Night Shift (USA)) [2004 **81** 86p: 7d⁴ 6s² 6s 8.1m 8.3f⁵ 7d⁵ 7.1s⁵ 7d⁴ 7g* Oct 11] strong, good-topped gelding: fairly useful performer: made all in maiden at Leicester (beat Barons Spy by 1½ lengths) in October: stays 7f: acts on soft ground: tried blinkered/visored, including last 2 starts: took strong hold sixth start: sold 22,000 gns, sent to USA. *A. M. Balding*

STARRY LODGE (IRE) 4 b.c. Grand Lodge (USA) 125 – Stara (Star Appeal 133) **107** [2004 104: 12m* 10.4g³ 12g⁵ 12f⁵ Sep 10] useful-looking colt: useful handicapper: won at Epsom (beat Swift Tango by head) in June: at least creditable efforts after, running particularly well when 2¾ lengths third to Arcalis in John Smith's Cup at York: effective at 1¼m to 13f: acts on polytrack and firm going: usually held up: game and reliable: sold 205,000 gns, sent to Saudi Arabia. *L. M. Cumani*

STARRY MARY 6 b.m. Deploy 131 – Darling Splodge (Elegant Air 119) [2004 64, **61** a50: 12d² 16s² 14.1s 16g⁵ 10.2g Sep 3] close-coupled mare: modest handicapper: left **a?** R. Beckett prior to final start: stays 2m: acts on all-weather, heavy and good to firm going: sometimes slowly away: usually held up. *R. J. Price*

STARS AT MIDNIGHT 4 b.f. Magic Ring (IRE) 115 – Boughtbyphone 62 (Warning **38** 136) [2004 54+: 10.1f 8.1d 7.1g⁶ f7g f8g Dec 1] poor form in 2004 only on third start: stays 1m. *J. M. Bradley*

STAR SENSATION (IRE) 4 b. or br.f. Sri Pekan (USA) 117 – Dancing Sensation **85** (USA) 72 (Faliraki 125) [2004 98: 8g⁶ 8.5g⁵ 8m⁶ 8d 7m 8s⁴ 8g 7g Sep 30] smallish, good-topped filly: fairly useful handicapper: stays 1m: acts on soft and good to firm going: tried in cheekpieces: slowly away last 3 outings: sold 11,000 gns. *P. W. Harris*

STAR SEVENTEEN 6 ch.m. Rock City 120 – Westminster Waltz (Dance In Time **–** (CAN)) [2004 –: f12s⁵ p12g f14g Apr 2] angular mare: fair performer in 2002: well held all 4 starts since. *Mrs N. S. Sharpe*

STAR SIDE (IRE) 2 b.c. (Mar 6) Ashkalani (IRE) 128 – Rachel Pringle (IRE) (Doulab **54** (USA) 115) [2004 7g⁶ Aug 22] 33/1, sixth in maiden at Folkestone. *C. Tinkler*

STARTLED 5 ch.m. Zilzal (USA) 137 – Zelda (USA) (Sharpen Up 127) [2004 –: f7g **–** Jan 8] maiden: no form since 2002. *J. Jay*

START OF AUTHORITY 3 ch.g. Muhtarram (USA) 125 – Heiden's Delight (USA) **48 ?** (Shadeed (USA) 135) [2004 10f 8.1s⁵ 8.1m Sep 6] poor form in maidens: raced freely last 2 starts. *J. Gallagher*

STAR VALLEY (FR) 4 b.c. Starborough 126 – Valleyrose (IRE) (Royal Academy **119** (USA) 130) [2004 115: 7g⁵ 7d⁴ 8g³ 8d³ 6v* 6s Oct 29] €50,000 2-y-o: first foal: dam French 1m/9f winner: smart performer: winner of listed races at Toulouse at 2 yrs and Deauville at 3 yrs: dropped in trip, better than ever when winning Prix de Meautry Royal Barriere at Deauville in August by 2 lengths from Swedish Shave, well on top inside final

1f: well beaten in Prix de Seine-et-Oise at Maisons-Laffitte final start: effective at 6f, at least under testing conditions, and stays 1m: acts on heavy ground. *J-C. Rouget, France*

STAR WELCOME 3 ch.f. Most Welcome 131 – My Greatest Star 93 (Great Nephew 126) [2004 –p: f7g p8g³ Mar 2] rather leggy, close-coupled filly: modest maiden: stays 1m: acts on polytrack: slowly away first 2 outings. *W. J. Musson* — **51**

STAR WONDER 4 b.f. Syrtos 106 – Galava (CAN) (Graustark) [2004 –: f7s Feb 17] lengthy, workmanlike filly: no form: tried blinkered. *B. N. Doran* — —

STATE CITY (USA) 5 ch.h. Carson City (USA) – Wajna (USA) 108 (Nureyev (USA) 131) [2004 117: a6f 7g⁴ May 18] robust horse: left T. Albertrani in USA prior to reappearance and just useful form in 2004 (tongue tied), better effort when fourth to Naahy in minor event at Goodwood: has won at 1m, but probably best at shorter (effective at 5f): acts on dirt (below form in sloppy conditions): left Godolphin. *Saeed bin Suroor* — **102**

STATE DILEMMA (IRE) 3 b.c. Green Desert (USA) 127 – Nuriva (USA) 100 (Woodman (USA) 126) [2004 91p: 8m⁵ 7s* 8m 8g 7.9s 8m⁴ 8g p7.1g Dec 31] good-bodied colt: has a quick, fluent action: useful handicapper: won at York (beat Key Partners by 1¼ lengths) in May: left B. Hills 37,000 gns after penultimate start: effective at 7f/1m: acts on soft and good to firm going, some promise on polytrack at Wolverhampton final start: usually waited with. *D. Shaw* — **95**

STATE OF BALANCE 6 ch.m. Mizoram (USA) 105 – Equilibrium 67 (Statoblest 120) [2004 65: p10g f9.4g⁴ p10g* p8g⁶ p12g p9.5g p9.5g⁵ Dec 6] modest handicapper: won at Lingfield in May: stays 1¼m: acts on polytrack (unraced on turf): tongue tied final start: sometimes slowly away/races freely. *K. Bell* — **63**

STATEROOM (USA) 6 ch.g. Affirmed (USA) – Sleet (USA) (Summer Squall (USA)) [2004 83: p10g⁵ 10m³ 9g Jul 7] close-coupled gelding: fair performer: stays 1¼m: acts on firm going, probably on polytrack: blinkered: sometimes tongue tied: sold 800 gns in October, sent to Germany. *J. A. R. Toller* — **78**

STATOYORK 11 b.g. Statoblest 120 – Ultimate Dream 74 (Kafu 120) [2004 55: f5g⁴ f6g Feb 9] strong gelding: poor performer nowadays: best at 5f: acts on polytrack, firm and soft going: tried visored/blinkered: usually slowly away: has reportedly bled from nose on several occasions. *D. Shaw* — **43**

ST AUSTELL 4 b.g. Compton Place 125 – Paris Joelle (IRE) (Fairy King (USA)) [2004 76: 6d 5d 5.7f 6.1m p6d⁵ p5.1g³ p5.1g³ p5g Dec 18] sturdy gelding: modest performer nowadays: probably best at 5f/easy 6f: acts on polytrack and firm going: has carried head high. *J. A. R. Toller* — **60**

STAVROS (IRE) 4 b.g. General Monash (USA) 107 – Rivers Rainbow (Primo Dominie 121) [2004 49: 6s 5d 5s⁵ 5m f7g f6d Dec 21] rather leggy, lengthy gelding: poor maiden: effective at 5f/6f: acts on firm and soft going: tried in blinkers/cheekpieces: sometimes slowly away: none too consistent. *J. S. Wainwright* — **42**

STAY CLOSE 2 b.g. (Jan 30) Belong To Me (USA) – Cymbala (FR) (Assert 134) [2004 p7m³ Dec 22] fourth foal: half-brother to fairly useful 1m (at 2 yrs) and 1½m winner Editor In Chief (by Kingmambo): dam 5.5f (in France) to 1½m (US Grade 3 event) winner: 12/1, 1¼ lengths third to Resplendent Prince in maiden at Lingfield: should improve. *A. M. Balding* — **66 p**

ST BARCHAN (IRE) 3 ch.g. Grand Lodge (USA) 125 – Moon Tango (IRE) 81 (Last Tycoon 131) [2004 10g⁴ 9d² 9.9s³ 11d* Oct 10] 40,000Y: second foal: dam, 6f winner, half-sister to useful 1996 2-y-o 6f winner Elegant Warning: fair performer: won claimer at Goodwood (claimed by J. O'Shea for £18,000), tending to carry head high: stays 11f: slowly away on debut: drifted left penultimate start. *W. Jarvis* — **71**

STEALING BEAUTY (IRE) 4 b.f. Sadler's Wells (USA) 132 – Imitation (Darshaan 133) [2004 80p: 12m⁴ 12.1g 11.9g⁵ Jul 4] leggy filly: fairly useful performer: well below form after reappearance: stays 1½m: acts on firm going. *L. M. Cumani* — **81**

STEAL THE THUNDER 2 br.g. (Feb 7) Timeless Times (USA) 99 – Lavernock Lady (Don't Forget Me 127) [2004 5g 5g⁵ 6g⁵ 5m 5d 5d 5d⁵ 7s⁶ Nov 2] quite good-topped gelding: modest maiden: likely to prove best at 5f/6f: acts on good to soft going: blinkered (well held) fifth start. *A. Berry* — **53**

STEDFAST MCSTAUNCH (IRE) 2 gr.g. (Feb 15) Desert Style (IRE) 121 – Aneydia (IRE) (Kenmare (FR) 125) [2004 5v⁴ 6.1s² 6f³ 7f* Jun 15] €39,000F, €32,000Y: strong gelding: second foal: dam, second at 10.5f in France, half-sister to useful French 1m/9f performer Aneysar: fairly useful performer: won maiden at Thirsk, making most comfortably: should stay 1m: acts on firm and soft going. *B. J. Meehan* — **85**

STEEL BLUE   4 b.g. Atraf 116 – Something Blue (Petong 126) [2004 91, a83: 6g* 6g 6g 6m* 6d² 6m⁵ 5d³ Jun 25] leggy, quite good-topped gelding: useful handicapper: won at Doncaster in March and Ripon (beat Johnston's Diamond by 1½ lengths) in May: good efforts when second to Traytonic in minor event at Haydock and third to Caribbean Coral in Gosforth Park Cup at Newcastle: effective at 5f/6f: acts on dirt, soft and good to firm going: tried visored/in cheekpieces: usually races prominently. *R. M. Whitaker*   **100 a?**

STEELY DAN   5 b.g. Danzig Connection (USA) – No Comebacks 70 (Last Tycoon 131) [2004 –: p6g p7g p7g p8g² p10g² p7g* p8g³ p10g* p10g* p12g² p12g* p8g* 11.5m⁶ 8.1d 8m⁴ 8g 7m p7g p8m⁵ p7g⁵ p8g³ Dec 30] strong gelding: fairly useful on all-weather, fair on turf: won 3 handicaps and 2 minor events at Lingfield in first half of 2004, beating Katiypour by short head in minor event for final success: effective at 7f to easy 1½m: acts on all-weather, firm and good to soft going: sometimes carries head high/hangs right: best with waiting tactics. *J. R. Best*   **71 a91**

STEENBERG (IRE)   5 ch.g. Flying Spur (AUS) – Kip's Sister (Cawston's Clown 113) [2004 111: 7s² 6g* 6s² 6f 6g 6f Sep 25] big, lengthy gelding: smart performer: won minor event at Haydock (beat Bahamian Pirate 3½ lengths) in May: good 1½ lengths second to Monsieur Bond in Duke of York Stakes next time: well held in Golden Jubilee Stakes at Royal Ascot, July Cup at Newmarket and Diadem Stakes at Ascot after: best at 6f/7f: acts on soft and good to firm going, below form recent starts on firm: blinkered (well below form) twice: tends to carry head awkwardly/hang right: usually held up. *M. H. Tompkins*   **115**

STELLA MARAIS (IRE)   3 b.f. Second Empire (IRE) 124 – Karakapa (FR) (Subotica (FR) 131) [2004 63: 8f⁶ f8g p7g Dec 30] rather sparely-made filly: maiden: well beaten in 2004. *P. R. Chamings*   **–**

STELLITE   4 ch.g. Pivotal 124 – Donation (Generous (IRE) 139) [2004 –: 10.1v 7.2g* 8v 7d 7.2s 6s² f7g* f7g Dec 11] workmanlike gelding: modest performer: won banded races at Ayr in April and Southwell in December: best efforts around 7f: acts on fibresand and good to soft going. *J. S. Goldie*   **61**

STEPASTRAY   7 gr.g. Alhijaz 122 – Wandering Stranger 69 (Petong 126) [2004 56: 10m⁵ 9f 12m 10m 9.2g⁵ 12m 8.5d 10g 9.3m Sep 11] tall gelding: poor performer: stays 1½m: acts on fibresand and firm ground, probably on soft: tried in headgear. *R. E. Barr*   **50 d**

STEPHANIE'S MIND   2 b.f. (Feb 12) Mind Games 121 – Adorable Cherub (USA) 58 (Halo (USA)) [2004 5g 6m³ 6m⁴ 5.2m⁴ 5.1d Aug 27] 15,000Y: tall filly: sister to 4-y-o Dazzling Bay and half-sister to 5.5f to 7.5f winner in Italy by Warrshan: dam, maiden, bred to stay at least 1m: fair maiden: left C. Allen, well below form last 2 starts, in cheekpieces on final one: likely to prove best at 5f/6f. *G. A. Huffer*   **73**

STEPHANO   3 ch.g. Efisio 120 – Polo 83 (Warning 136) [2004 79: 7g 8.5g⁵ 8.1s 10f* 10.5g* 10.2m² 10g Oct 12] workmanlike gelding: fair handicapper: won at Redcar and Haydock within 3 days in September: ran as though amiss final start: will be suited by 1½m+: acts on firm ground: sold 26,000 gns, sent to Bahrain. *B. W. Hills*   **76**

STEPPENWOLF   3 gr.g. Sesaro (USA) 81 – Lozzie (Siberian Express (USA) 125) [2004 –: p8g⁶ p10g p10g 11.9m 10s 10.2m p10d 8g 14.1m⁵ 16m⁶ Aug 8] close-coupled gelding: poor maiden: stayed 1¼m: tried in cheekpieces: dead. *W. de Best-Turner*   **45**

STERLING GUARANTEE (USA)   6 b.g. Silver Hawk (USA) 123 – Sterling Pound (USA) (Seeking The Gold (USA)) [2004 65: p10g² p12g⁴ p12g p12g⁴ Mar 14] close-coupled gelding: modest maiden, lightly raced: trained by D. Nicholls on reappearance: stays easy 1½m: acts on polytrack, unraced on extremes of going on turf: visored final start: refused to enter stall intended final outing. *Andrew Reid*   **58**

STERLING SUPPORTER   2 b.f. (Apr 4) Josr Algarhoud (IRE) 118 – Riyoom (USA) 83 (Vaguely Noble 140) [2004 6f p8.6g Dec 3] seventh foal: half-sister to 3 winners, including 3-y-o Wing Collar: dam, Irish 2-y-o 1m winner, half-sister to US Grade 3 8.5f/ 9f winner Lt Lao: well held in maidens at Redcar and Wolverhampton. *D. W. Thompson*   **–**

STETCHWORTH PRINCE   2 b.c. (Jan 23) Cadeaux Genereux 131 – Elfin Laughter 76 (Alzao (USA) 117) [2004 6m* 6m⁴ 6s⁶ Aug 18] 120,000Y: quite attractive colt: sixth foal: brother to UAE 6f winner Joyous Gift and half-brother to 2 winners, including smart 7f/1m winner Smirk (by Selkirk): dam 2-y-o 7.5f/1m winner: won minor event at Newmarket in July: 3¾ lengths fourth to Montgomery's Arch in Richmond Stakes at Goodwood, much better effort in pattern company after: will stay 7f: acts on good to firm going. *D. R. Loder*   **97**

STEVEDORE (IRE)   3 ch.c. Docksider (USA) 124 – La Belle Katherine (USA) (Lyphard (USA) 132) [2004 80: 8m 8.1d 7m f8g⁴ 7m* 8m⁵ 7g⁵ 8s⁵ 7d 7g⁵ p7.1d⁶ p8.6g Nov 11] good-topped colt: fair performer: left B. Meehan after fourth start: won claimer at Leicester (left J. Harris) in July and handicap at Lingfield in August: stays 1m: acts on firm and good to soft ground: blinkered (below form) once: usually races up with pace. *B. R. Millman*

STEVE'S CHAMP (CHI) 4 b.c. Foxhound (USA) 103 – Emigracion (CHI) (Semenenko (USA) 111) [2004 a6f 5.8g⁶ 6g² 6d* 5.1g 6.8g⁶ a6g⁶ 4.5s* 5.8g* 5g² 5s⁶ Oct 22] big, strong, close-coupled Chilean-bred colt: smart performer: winner of 3 races in native country: successful in listed race at Ovrevoll in July, minor event there in August and Taby Open Sprint Championship (by length from Waquaas) in September: contested listed races at Chester and Newmarket fifth/tenth starts, much better effort when ½-length second to Nights Cross in latter, collared only close home: effective at 4.5f to 7.5f: acts on dirt and soft ground: has worn tongue tie: blinkered last 4 starts. *R. Haugen, Norway*   **111**

STEVMARIE STAR 2 b.f. (Apr 23) Muhtarram (USA) 125 – Cabaret Artiste (Shareef Dancer (USA) 135) [2004 6s 7s⁶ p6d p8.6g Dec 11] 5,700Y: sturdy filly: seventh foal: half-sister to 3 winners, including 1997 2-y-o 7f winner Misalliance (by Elmaamul) and 7.5f/1m winner Cabaret Quest (by Pursuit of Love): dam unraced: poor maiden: visored final start. *J. A. Glover*   **41**

ST FRANCIS WOOD (USA) 3 ch.f. Irish River (FR) 131 – Francisco Road (USA) (Strawberry Road (AUS) 128) [2004 95p: 7g p10g² 8f* 8f 8.5f⁴ 6.5f 5.5f Nov 21] leggy filly: fairly useful performer: won 4-runner maiden at Brighton in June: well beaten in listed rated stakes at Royal Ascot next time, then left J. Noseda: respectable fourth in optional claimer at Del Mar, but well held in allowance races last 2 starts, in blinkers final one: probably stays 8.5f: acts on firm going, probably on polytrack: tends to pull hard/wander. *Kathy Walsh, USA*   **80**

ST GEORGE'S GIRL 3 b.f. Muthahb (IRE) – Nickelodeon (Nickel King 116) [2004 –: 8.3s 6v f6g 7m Jun 30] of little account. *J. R. Jenkins*   **–**

STILETTO LADY (IRE) 3 b.f. Daggers Drawn (USA) 114 – Nordic Pride (Horage 124) [2004 64: f8.5m⁴ 8.3m 8.1d 9m Jul 5] lengthy filly: modest maiden: below form after reappearance: probably stays 8.5f: tried blinkered. *J. G. Given*   **62 d**

STING LIKE A BEE (IRE) 5 b.g. Ali-Royal (IRE) 127 – Hidden Agenda (FR) 55 (Machiavellian (USA) 123) [2004 63: f9.4g* f8.5g f11s² f8.5s⁴ 10.3g⁴ 9.2g⁶ 10f⁶ 9.1d* 10.9g⁵ Jul 12] rather unfurnished gelding: fair handicapper on all-weather, modest on turf: won at Wolverhampton (amateurs) in January and Ayr in June: best form at 9f to 11f: acts on fibresand, heavy and good to firm going: tried tongue tied: usually held up. *J. S. Goldie*   **59**
a68

ST IVIAN 4 b.g. Inchinor 119 – Lamarita 92§ (Emarati (USA) 74) [2004 77§: f6s⁴ f5s⁶ p6g f6g² f5g f6s f7g² 7d 5d f6m 7f 5g f7m f6m 6m p5.1g³ p7.1g⁶ f6g² p5.1g⁶ f6g² f7g Dec 14] leggy gelding: fair on all-weather, modest on turf: effective at 5f to easy 7f: acts on all-weather, soft and good to firm going: usually wears headgear: sometimes slowly away: tends to hang, and looked set to win when swerving violently right and unseating rider fifth 3-y-o start: unreliable. *Mrs N. Macauley*   **57 §**
a74 §

ST JEROME 4 ch.g. Danzig Connection (USA) – Indigo Dawn 78 (Rainbow Quest (USA) 134) [2004 63: 14.1s 11.8m 14.1m Jun 2] big, rather angular gelding: modest winner at 3 yrs: well beaten in handicaps in 2004. *N. P. Littmoden*   **–**

ST JUDE 4 b.c. Deploy 131 – Little Nutmeg 38 (Gabitat 119) [2004 –: 8m 9.9s 8.1d Oct 9] small colt: little form. *J. Balding*   **–**

STOCKING ISLAND 3 ch.f. Desert King (IRE) 129 – Rawya (USA) 80 (Woodman (USA) 126) [2004 7g 10d² 11.9m³ 10m 14.1d 12.3s³ p12g Sep 7] 43,000F: good-topped filly: fifth foal: sister to fairly useful French 2001 2-y-o 7f/1m winner Erimos and half-sister to 3 winners, including fairly useful 1¼m winner Calling Dot Com (by Halling): dam, 2-y-o 7f winner, stayed 1¼m: fair maiden: pulled up early final outing: stays 1¾m: acts on good to firm and good to soft going. *B. Hanbury*   **74**

STOIC LEADER (IRE) 4 b.g. Danehill Dancer (IRE) 117 – Starlust 79 (Sallust 134) [2004 76: f5s⁴ f7g f7g* f7g* 6s⁴ 7d 8.1g* 7.1d* 6d* 7g 8g 8d² 7.9g⁴ 7.1m² 6.9g⁶ 10.3g⁵ 8g² 8m⁵ 7s⁶ 8.1g⁴ 7m 8f⁴ 8.3s⁴ 7.1g p6g⁶ p8.6g p7.1g* p7.1g p8.6g⁴ Dec 27] sturdy gelding: fairly useful handicapper: won at Wolverhampton and Lingfield in March, Haydock, Musselburgh and Hamilton in May, and Wolverhampton in December: effective at 6f to easy 8.6f: acts on all-weather, firm and soft ground: sometimes races freely: has edged left: tough. *R. F. Fisher*   **88**
a78 +

STOKESIES WISH 4 ch.f. Fumo di Londra (IRE) 108 – Jess Rebec 63 (Kala Shikari 125) [2004 67: 5d 6s 6g 6g² 6m 6f⁵ 6m⁴ 6m 6f⁶ 6f³ 6g³ 7s 5.1m 6.1d⁴ 6d⁵ p6g Nov 13] strong filly: fair handicapper: won at Nottingham in September: effective at 5f/6f: acts on firm and soft ground: usually races up with pace. *J. L. Spearing*   **72**

STOLEN 2 b.c. (May 9) Groom Dancer (USA) 128 – Jezyah (USA) 80 (Chief's Crown (USA)) [2004 7.1g 8.1m p8.6g 8s Oct 19] poor maiden: should stay 1¼m: acts on soft and good to firm going. *W. R. Muir* **44**

STOLEN HOURS (USA) 4 b. or br.c. Silver Deputy (CAN) – Fasta (USA) (Seattle Song (USA) 130) [2004 74: 12s 14.1s 12g 10m 13.3g² 12g² 12d³ 12m* 12d³ 10.2g Sep 3] good-topped colt: fair handicapper: won at Newmarket in July: effective at 1½m/1¾m: acts on firm and soft ground: visored (carried head awkwardly) final 3-y-o start. *J. Akehurst* **71**

STOLEN SONG 4 b.g. Sheikh Albadou 128 – Sparky's Song 63 (Electric 126) [2004 67, a64: p10g⁴ f16g* f12s³ 16g 14.1d 10f⁶ 11.6f³ 11.6m² 11.6g⁶ Aug 9] good-topped gelding: fair handicapper on all-weather, modest on turf: won at Southwell in January: effective at 1½m to easy 2m: acts on all-weather and firm ground: sometimes wears headgear. *M. J. Ryan* **62 a67**

STONEACRE 4 ch.f. Gothenberg (IRE) 117 – Musical Star 54 (Music Boy 124) [2004 6g Mar 31] 4,000Y: third foal: dam maiden (form only at 6f at 2 yrs): 14/1 and backward, tailed off in maiden at Catterick. *D. Nicholls* **–**

STONE CREST (IRE) 6 b.m. Bigstone (IRE) 126 – Hillcrest (IRE) 76 (Thatching 131) [2004 7m f8g 8d Jun 24] little form. *T. H. Caldwell* **–**

STONOR LADY (USA) 3 b. or br.f. French Deputy (USA) 118 – Blush With Love (USA) (Mt Livermore (USA)) [2004 57: p8g p7g p7g f8.5g* 10d 8f Aug 5] smallish filly: poor performer: won seller at Wolverhampton (edged left) in March: stays 8.5f: acts on all-weather: tried visored. *P. W. D'Arcy* **45**

STOOP TO CONQUER 4 b.g. Polar Falcon (USA) 126 – Princess Genista 108 (Ile de Bourbon (USA) 133) [2004 78: 14.1s 16.2m 17.1f* 18m⁴ 14s* 16m 16s* Oct 22] leggy, lengthy gelding: fairly useful handicapper: won at Pontefract in June, Goodwood in August and Newbury (best effort, beat Teresa by 3½ lengths) in October: stays 17f: acts on firm and soft going: sometimes races freely: sold 58,000 gns, joined A. Carroll. *J. L. Dunlop* **86**

STOP THE NONSENSE (IRE) 3 b.g. Orpen (USA) 116 – Skip The Nonsense (IRE) (Astronef 116) [2004 –: p8g⁵ 10g 8.2d 7m Jun 4] leggy gelding: modest form only on reappearance: tried tongue tied/blinkered: sold 2,000 gns, and gelded. *E. J. O'Neill* **64 ?**

STOPWATCH (IRE) 9 b.g. Lead On Time (USA) 123 – Rose Bonbon (FR) (High Top 131) [2004 –: p10g p12g p16g⁵ 16.4g Jul 8] well held since 2002: tried in cheekpieces. *Mrs L. C. Jewell* **–**

STORM CHASE (USA) 2 b. or br.g. (Apr 19) Awad (USA) 124 – Night Duja (USA) (Dayjur (USA) 137) [2004 p6g 5m Sep 15] poor form in maidens, then gelded. *A. P. Jarvis* **36**

STORM CLEAR (IRE) 5 b.g. Mujadil (USA) 119 – Escape Path (Wolver Hollow 126) [2004 61: p10g Mar 4] tall, good sort: maiden handicapper: well held only 5-y-o start on Flat: gelded after: sometimes finds little. *D. J. Wintle* **43**

STORM CLOUDS 3 gr.g. Cloudings (IRE) 112 – Khalsheva 55 (Shirley Heights 130) [2004 –: 7d 10m May 25] strong, workmanlike filly: little form. *T. D. Easterby* **–**

STORM FURY (USA) 2 b.g. (Feb 9) Storm Creek (USA) – Danseuse du Nord (IRE) 106 (Kahyasi 130) [2004 7d 6m³ 7g 6.1g 6m 7m Oct 1] close-coupled gelding: modest maiden: third at Leicester, best effort: should stay at least 7f. *P. W. Chapple-Hyam* **63**

STORMONT (IRE) 4 gr.c. Marju (IRE) 127 – Legal Steps (IRE) (Law Society (USA) 130) [2004 116: a6f⁴ 6.5m 6m 5f 5d 7m 6m Jul 31] leggy, good-topped colt: just useful in 2004, best effort when twelfth in King's Stand Stakes at Royal Ascot fourth outing: stays 6f: acts on polytrack and firm going, probably on good to soft: tried visored: sent to USA. *H. J. Collingridge* **106**

STORM SHOWER (IRE) 6 b.g. Catrail (USA) 123 – Crimson Shower 61 (Dowsing (USA) 124) [2004 –§, a51§: f7g⁴ Jan 4] good-topped gelding: poor performer nowadays: stays 9.4f: acts on fibresand: visored: ungenuine. *Mrs N. Macauley* **– § a45 §**

STORM SILK (CAN) 2 b. or br.c. (Feb 28) Stormin Fever (USA) 116 – Carpenter's Lace (USA) (Woodman (USA) 126) [2004 6g⁴ 7m* Sep 4] $100,000Y, $500,000 2-y-o: tall, attractive colt: has scope: half-brother to several winners in USA/Japan: dam lightly-raced US maiden: fourth in maiden at Goodwood: favourite, much improved to win minor event at Kempton comfortably by 3½ lengths from Peruvian Prince, going clear final 2f: will stay 1m: smart prospect, should make his mark in stronger company. *Saeed bin Suroor* **106 p**

STORMVILLE (IRE)   7 b.g. Catrail (USA) 123 – Haut Volee (Top Ville 129) [2004   **61**
–: 6s 7g 7d² 7.2s 6.9g p9.5g³ p8.6g Dec 22] sparely-made gelding: modest performer: **a50**
stays 1m: acts on polytrack, good to firm and good to soft ground, no form on soft/heavy:
often races prominently. *M. Brittain*

STORMY DAY   4 b.f. Rainbow Quest (USA) 134 – Broken Peace (USA) (Devil's Bag   **73**
(USA)) [2004 –: 11.7f⁶ p12g* p12.2g⁵ p12g* Nov 13] tall, good-topped filly: fair performer, lightly raced: won minor event and handicap at Lingfield in October/November:
stays 1½m: acts on polytrack: usually held up: sold 11,000 gns. *Mrs A. J. Perrett*

STORMY NATURE (IRE)   3 b. or br.f. Mujadil (USA) 119 – Ossana (USA) (Tejano   **81**
(USA)) [2004 74: 6d³ 6s 6m 6g 6.1d p7.1g* p7.1d² p7.1g³ p8.6g⁶ Dec 6] rather leggy,
lengthy filly: fairly useful handicapper: won at Wolverhampton in October: creditable
efforts after: barely stays 8.6f: acts on polytrack, good to firm and good to soft going.
W. R. Swinburn

STORY OF ONE (IRE)   2 b.g. (Apr 27) Desert Story (IRE) 115 – One O One (IRE)   **56 +**
58 (Wolfhound (USA) 126) [2004 5s² 5v p5g* 6f³ 6f⁵ 5m⁵ 8g⁴ a6.8d³ a6.8d* a8d⁶ Dec 28]
good-topped gelding: modest performer: left Ronald Thompson after debut: won seller at
Lingfield in May and, having left N. Littmoden after sixth start, minor event at Taby in
December: stays 6.8f: acts on polytrack, dirt, firm and soft going. *M. Kahn, Sweden*

STORYVILLE   2 br.g. (Mar 1) Lujain (USA) 119 – Slow Jazz (USA) 106 (Chief's   **– p**
Crown (USA)) [2004 6m Sep 7] 47,000F: seventh foal: half-brother to useful Italian 5f
(at 2 yrs) to 1m winner Mister Cavern (by Lion Cavern) and fairly useful 6f (at 2 yrs) and
1m winner Mellow Jazz (by Lycius): dam, French 6f (at 2 yrs) to 1m winner, closely
related to smart 6f/7f performers Zieten and Blue Duster: 5/1, behind in maiden at
Lingfield, disputing lead long way: gelded after: should do better. *D. R. Loder*

ST PANCRAS (IRE)   4 b.c. Danehill Dancer (IRE) 117 – Lauretta Blue (IRE) (Blue-   **91**
bird (USA) 125) [2004 –: 7d 10g 10.4d 8f² 10.1m 8f* 8m⁵ 7m³ 7d² 10g 7s Nov 6] big,
good-topped colt: fairly useful performer nowadays: won handicap at Bath in June by
neck from Voice Mail: left N. Callaghan 30,000 gns before final start: effective at 7f,
probably stays 1¼m: acts on firm and good to soft going: blinkered (ran in snatches) fifth
start. *D. W. Chapman*

ST PETERSBURG   4 ch.g. Polar Falcon (USA) 126 – First Law 57 (Primo Dominie   **107**
121) [2004 96: 8g² 8v* 8g 8v² 7.9d* 7.9s³ 8.1g⁶ Sep 4] strong, lengthy gelding: useful
performer: progressed in handicaps in 2004, winning at Pontefract in April and York (beat
Flighty Fellow by 1½ lengths) in July: good close third to Audience at York, racing freely:
below form in listed race at Haydock final start: stays 1m: acts on all-weather, raced only
on good ground or softer on turf (goes well on heavy). *M. H. Tompkins*

STRAFFAN (IRE)   2 b. or br.f. (Jan 17) Shinko Forest (IRE) – Katherine Gorge   **59**
(USA) (Hansel (USA)) [2004 5d⁶ 5s³ f5m³ 6m² 5g⁵ 6f⁴ 5.1f* 5m² 5f² 5g Aug 6] lengthy
filly: fourth foal: half-sister to 4-y-o Miss Champers and winner in Spain by Petardia:
dam unraced daughter of useful sprinter Katies First: modest performer: won seller at
Bath in July: creditable efforts next 2 starts (left E. O'Neill in between): barely stays 6f:
acts on fibresand and firm going: usually races prominently: sometimes looks less than
keen. *D. Nicholls*

STRANGELY BROWN (IRE)   3 b.g. Second Empire (IRE) 124 – Damerela (IRE)   **78**
(Alzao (USA) 117) [2004 –p: f9.4s 6g 10s³ 10m f12d 16.2g² 16g* 16.4m* 17.5d* 16g³
14g⁵ 17.2s⁴ Oct 19] sturdy gelding: fair handicapper: won at Nottingham in July, Sandown in August and Ayr in September: stays 17.5f: acts on soft and good to firm going:
sold 11,000 gns. *S. C. Williams*

STRATEGIC QUEST   2 b.f. (Apr 28) Rainbow Quest (USA) 134 – Danlu (USA)   **57 p**
(Danzig (USA)) [2004 p10g³ Nov 27] half-sister to several winners, notably very smart
1¼m to 1¾m winner Strategic Choice (by Alleged) and useful 1m/1¼m winner Sure
Dancer (by Affirmed): dam, Irish 1m (at 2 yrs)/8.5f winner, sister to smart 6f/7f performer
Nicholas: 8/1, 3 lengths third to Kinrande in maiden at Lingfield, taking while to settle
and keeping on: should improve. *P. F. I. Cole*

STRATEGY   4 br.f. Machiavellian (USA) 123 – Island Story 88 (Shirley Heights 130)   **79 +**
[2004 92: 8m 10m⁶ 10m 8.5g² 11f⁶ 8f Oct 8] quite good-topped filly: fairly useful performer at 3 yrs: just fair form in handicaps in Britain first 3 starts in 2004: left P. Webber,
beaten a head in allowance race at Monmouth in August: not discredited in Grade 3
handicap at Saratoga and restricted event at Belmont last 2 outings: probably stays 11f:
acts on good to firm going, probably on firm: visored/blinkered last 4 appearances.
P. L. Biancone, USA

STRATHCLYDE (IRE)   5 b.g. Petong 126 – It's Academic 73 (Royal Academy **63**
(USA) 130) [2004 91: p5g 5m 6m 5.1g p5g Dec 18] good-topped gelding: fairly useful
sprint handicapper in 2003: only modest form in 2004, trained by J. Best on reappearance:
effective at 5f/6f: acts on firm ground, good to soft and polytrack: free-going sort.
A. M. Hales

STRATHSPEY   5 ch.m. Dancing Spree (USA) – Diebiedale 58 (Dominion 123) [2004 **72**
76: p12m⁵ 10s⁵ 8d⁴ Nov 5] sturdy mare: fair handicapper: below form after reappearance:
stays easy 1½m: acts on polytrack and firm going. *P. J. McBride*

STRATHTAY   2 ch.f. (Mar 23) Pivotal 124 – Cressida (Polish Precedent (USA) 131) **60**
[2004 5m³ 6g 6m⁵ 6s⁶ 7.1g 7m 6m² 7.1d* 8s⁴ Nov 1] 20,000Y: neat filly: first foal: dam
well beaten both starts: modest performer: left P. Haslam, won seller at Musselburgh in
October: creditable fourth in nursery at Redcar: stays 1m: acts on soft and good to firm
ground: wore cheekpieces fifth start, visored last 3. *A. Berry*

STRAVMOUR   8 ch.h. Seymour Hicks (FR) 125 – La Stravaganza 74 (Slip Anchor **55**
136) [2004 54: f12g f12g⁵ f12s³ f16.2s³ f14s* f16s* f12g* f14g f14g⁴ Dec 11] big,
lengthy horse: modest performer: won 3 banded races at Southwell in March/April: stays
2m: acts on fibresand. *R. Hollinshead*

STRAVONIAN   4 b.g. Luso 124 – In The Evening (IRE) 73 (Distinctly North (USA) **– §**
115) [2004 12g 9.2d 10s⁵ 12d⁶ p9.5g Dec 13] poor maiden: probably stays 1¼m: acts on
soft ground: ungenuine. *D. A. Nolan*

STRAW BEAR (USA)   3 ch.c. Diesis 133 – Highland Ceilidh (IRE) 100 (Scottish **100**
Reel 123) [2004 83: 8.1m² 9d³ 8.3d⁵ 10d* 10.5s* 10g³ Sep 29] good-bodied colt: useful
performer: upped in trip, won handicaps at Ayr and Haydock (beat Sew'n'so Character
easily by 5 lengths) in September: creditable third to Honorine at Nottingham final start:
will stay 1½m: acts on fibresand, soft and good to firm going. *Sir Mark Prescott*

STRAWBERRY DALE (IRE)   2 b.f. (Mar 23) Bering 136 – Manchaca (FR) (Highest **91**
Honor (FR) 124) [2004 5g* 7m* 7f 6.5m Sep 8] 20,000Y: tall, close-coupled filly: has
a fluent action: third foal: half-sister to 2 winners by Sillery, including French 1¼m
winner Marguerita: dam, French 9f winner, half-sister to useful French miler Marethea
(by Bering): fairly useful performer: won maiden at Carlisle and minor event at Thirsk in
July: no luck in running next start, and first home far side in nursery at Doncaster final
one: free-going sort, not sure to stay much further than 7f. *J. D. Bethell*

STRAWBERRY FAIR   3 b.f. Kingmambo (USA) 125 – Storm Song (USA) 123 (Sum- **69**
mer Squall (USA)) [2004 75p: 8.1m⁴ 8.3f 8.1m 7m⁶ Sep 20] compact, attractive filly: fair
maiden: stays 1m: acts on good to firm going: tongue tied last 3 starts: left Godolphin.
Saeed bin Suroor

STRAWBERRY PATCH (IRE)   5 b.g. Woodborough (USA) 112 – Okino (USA) **66**
(Strawberry Road (AUS) 128) [2004 71: 6g 5g 5g⁵ 5f 6g² 5.2g* 5d 6f⁶ 5d² 5f 6d Oct 12]
strong, good-topped gelding: fair handicapper: won at Newbury in August: effective at
5f/6f: acts on firm and good to soft going: wears cheekpieces. *Miss L. A. Perratt*

STREAM OF GOLD (IRE)   3 b.c. Rainbow Quest (USA) 134 – River Dancer 118 **107 p**
(Irish River (FR) 131) [2004 10m⁵ 8d* 8.1g* 7d⁶ Oct 15] tall, leggy, quite attractive colt:
brother to 2 winners, notably high-class 1m (Irish 2000 Guineas, also successful at 2 yrs)
and 1¼m (Champion Stakes) winner Spectrum, and half-brother to 2 winners, including
useful 1m winner who stayed 1½m Nash House (by Nashwan): dam, French 5f (at 2 yrs)
and 1m winner, half-sister to dam of Millenary and Let The Lion Roar: useful form: won
maiden at Pontefract in August and handicap at Newmarket (improved form, beat King's
Caprice by 3½ lengths) in October: bred to stay 1¼m, but not short of speed: smart performer in the making. *Sir Michael Stoute*

STREET BALLAD (IRE)   2 b.f. (Mar 23) Fasliyev (USA) 120 – Nancy Maloney **59**
(IRE) 53 (Persian Bold 123) [2004 6g⁴ 7.5d 6g³ 8f 7g 7.1d Oct 17] 22,000F, 22,000Y:
lengthy filly: third foal: half-sister to winning sprinter in Norway by Bluebird: dam,
maiden (should have stayed further than 1m), half-sister to Cherry Hinton winner Torgau:
modest maiden: ran poorly in seller final start: seems to stay 1m: acts on firm going.
Mrs J. R. Ramsden

STREET CRED   2 ch.g. (Feb 18) Bold Edge 123 – Trump Street 77 (First Trump **76**
118) [2004 6f* 6m 7g 6d Aug 20] 18,000Y: leggy gelding: first foal: dam 6f winner:
fair performer: won maiden at Windsor in July: best effort at 6f on firm going: dead.
A. M. Balding

STREET DANCER (IRE)   2 b.g. (Apr 26) Imperial Ballet (IRE) 110 – Life On The   **57**
Street 62 (Statoblest 120) [2004 6s 7m 6g 6.1v⁵ Nov 4] tall, quite good-topped gelding:
modest maiden: should stay 7f: best effort on heavy ground. *J. J. Quinn*

STREET GAMES   5 b.g. Mind Games 121 – Pusey Street 96 (Native Bazaar 122)   **30**
[2004 –: 10.2s⁵ p10g⁶ Sep 18] poor maiden: stays 1¼m: acts on polytrack: tried tongue
tied. *D. G. Bridgwater*

STREET LIFE (IRE)   6 ch.g. Dolphin Street (FR) 125 – Wolf Cleugh (IRE) 65 (Last   **82**
Tycoon 131) [2004 76: f11g² f9.4g⁵ 10g² 10d³ 10s³ 10m⁴ 10m³ 10m⁵ 12g⁴ 10m⁴ 10g⁴
10.1d* Nov 5] tall gelding: fairly useful handicapper: won at Yarmouth (ridden by 7-lb
claimer) in November: effective at 1¼m/1½m: acts on all-weather and good to firm
ground, very best turf form on good or softer: held up: sometimes edges left: consistent.
W. J. Musson

STRENGTH 'N HONOUR   4 b.g. Hernando (FR) 127 – Seasonal Splendour (IRE)   **99**
95 (Prince Rupert (FR) 121) [2004 104: p10g Nov 20] strong, workmanlike gelding:
useful performer: gelded, not disgraced when held to Grand Passion in listed race at
Lingfield only 4-y-o start: bred to be suited by 1¾m+ (pulled hard when tried): acts on
polytrack, raced only on firm/good to firm going on turf: has worn crossed noseband.
C. A. Cyzer

STRENSALL   7 b.g. Beveled (USA) – Payvashooz 78 (Ballacashtal (CAN)) [2004 86,   **83**
a67: 5m 5m² 5m 5m 5g³ 5g⁴ 5g 5m⁵ 5g 5.1g⁵ 5.1s⁵ 5g² 5.1g 5m 5s 5d Nov 3] leggy geld-   **a–**
ing: fairly useful handicapper: best at 5f: acts on fibresand, firm and soft going: sometimes slowly away: often races prominently. *R. E. Barr*

STRETFORD END (IRE)   2 b.g. (May 13) Zieten (USA) 118 – Creese (USA) (Diesis   **85**
133) [2004 6g 6d² 6d⁴ Aug 27] €8,000Y, 41,000 2-y-o: lengthy gelding: third foal:
half-brother to useful 7f winner Weavers Pride (by Barathea): dam, placed at 11f/1½m in
France, out of half-sister to dam of Oh So Sharp: ran out early on debut: fairly useful form
in maidens at Newcastle and Thirsk (first on far side but fourth overall): should stay 7f:
joined M. Al Kurdi in UAE. *B. Smart*

STRETTON (IRE)   6 br.g. Doyoun 124 – Awayil (USA) 82 (Woodman (USA) 126)   **86**
[2004 88: 10.3d 8.5g⁶ 10m 8.9m 10g³ 10d⁴ 10m⁴ 10f 10g* 10.1g 10.4g³ Oct 8] leggy,
close-coupled gelding: fairly useful handicapper: won at Ripon in August: good third to
Go Tech at York final start: unraced on heavy going, acts on any
other turf: wore cheekpieces (not discredited) once: has run respectably when sweating:
held up: consistent. *J. D. Bethell*

STRIDER   3 ch.g. Pivotal 124 – Sahara Belle (USA) (Sanglamore (USA) 126) [2004   **80**
70p: f9.4g² 10.3m⁴ 10d⁴ 9d* 10g p8m Dec 21] good-topped gelding: good mover: fairly
useful performer: won minor event at Sandown (beat Ryan's Future by neck, racing
freely) in August: left Sir Michael Stoute 20,000 gns and gelded prior to final start: stays
1¼m: acts on fibresand, good to firm and good to soft going: visored (ran poorly) penultimate start: tends to edge left. *P. D. Evans*

STRIDES OF FIRE (IRE)   3 b.g. General Monash (USA) 107 – Lagrion (USA) 68   **–**
(Diesis 133) [2004 6s 6.1s May 7] well beaten in maidens at Salisbury and Nottingham
(blinkered), slowly away both times: gelded, sold 6,000 gns and joined John Codd in
Ireland. *J. H. M. Gosden*

STRIKE   3 b.c. Silver Hawk (USA) 123 – Shemozzle (IRE) 108 (Shirley Heights 130)   **86**
[2004 11g² 12s⁶ 11.9m* 16.2m⁵ Jun 18] angular, useful-looking colt: first foal: dam 7f (at
2 yrs) and 1½m winner in Britain (later US Grade 3 11f winner): fairly useful performer:
won maiden at Haydock in May: visored, creditable fifth to Duke of Venice in Queen's
Vase at Royal Ascot final start, though seemed to find stamina stretched: should stay
1¾m: acts on good to firm going: sold 10,000 gns. *J. H. M. Gosden*

STRIKE GOLD   2 b.c. (Mar 9) Mujahid (USA) 125 – Gracious Beauty (USA) 67   **75**
(Nijinsky (CAN) 138) [2004 7.1d 7.1m³ 7.1s Sep 20] half-brother to 3 winners, including
useful 1¼m/1½m winner Jazil (by Nashwan) and 11.5f winner Labeed (by Riverman):
dam, maiden who stayed 1¼m, sister to US Grade 1 9f/1¼m winner Maplejinsky and
closely related to Dayjur: easily best effort in maidens when close third at Chepstow: will
stay 1m. *S. Kirk*

STRIKE LUCKY   4 ch.g. Millkom 124 – Lucky Flinders 77 (Free State 125) [2004   **57**
64?: f6g* f6g 6m p6d Oct 23] good-topped gelding: modest performer: won maiden at
Wolverhampton in January: stays 7f: acts on fibresand and good to firm going: tried in
cheekpieces. *P. J. Makin*

STRIKING AMBITION   4 b. or br.c. Makbul 104 – Lady Roxanne 65 (Cyrano de   **117**
Bergerac 120) [2004 114: p5g 6g 6v³ 6d* 6s² 6s* Nov 17] rather unfurnished, useful-

looking colt: smart performer: left G. Bravery after second start: won listed races at the Curragh (beat Grand Reward by 3½ lengths) in October and Maisons-Laffitte (by short neck from Ratio) in November: good ½-length second to Miss Emma in Prix de Seine-et-Oise at latter course in between: stays 6f: acts on heavy and good to firm going, probably on polytrack: usually races prominently. *R. Charlton*

STRIKING ENDEAVOUR   2 b.c. (Mar 7) Makbul 104 – Nineteenth of May 86   **72** (Homing 130) [2004 5s* 6f⁶ 6f 6d Oct 11] 16,000Y: quite good-topped colt: half-brother to several winners, including smart 1m/1¼m winner Zanay (by Forzando) and useful 11f/1½m winner Quintrell Downs (by Efisio): dam 1m winner: fair performer: won maiden at Folkestone in May: left G. Bravery, well below form last 2 starts (reportedly broke blood vessel on first of them): likely to stay 6f: sold only 800 gns. *N. P. Littmoden*

STRONG HAND   4 b.f. First Trump 118 – Better Still (IRE) (Glenstal (USA) 118)   **82** [2004 85, a99: 8g⁶ 8v³ 7d 7.6s 8d 10d⁶ 8.3d² 7v⁴ p8.6g⁴ p9.5g p9.5g Dec 11] big, lengthy,   **a91** heavy-topped filly: fairly useful performer: several creditable efforts in 2004: stays 9.4f: acts on all-weather, good to firm and good to soft going, probably on heavy: tried tongue tied, blinkered (below form) final start. *M. W. Easterby*

ST SAVARIN (FR)   3 ch.g. Highest Honor (FR) 124 – Sacara (GER) (Monsagem   **79** (USA) 117) [2004 72: p7g² p8g⁵ p6g³ p7g* 7f.6d 7m 7.5g³ 7.5g³ 7.1f* p7d p7g 7g 8d⁵ 10m² p9.5g⁵ Oct 18] workmanlike gelding: fair handicapper: won at Lingfield in February and Musselburgh in July: effective at 7f to 1¼m: acts on polytrack, firm and good to soft ground: usually races up with pace: sold 22,000 gns. *J. R. Best*

ST TROPEZ (IRE)   3 b.f. Revoque (IRE) 122 – Kaziranga (USA) 69 (Lear Fan (USA)   **–** 130) [2004 –: 8.3s 10s 7.1m 8m Sep 25] sturdy filly: little form: left B. Powell after third start: tried blinkered. *Mrs A. J. Hamilton-Fairley*

STUNNING MAGIC   4 b.g. Magic Ring (IRE) 115 – Absolutelystunning 63 (Aragon   **–** 118) [2004 –: p10g p12g Jan 15] of little account: tried blinkered. *Mrs Barbara Waring*

STUNNING SPARK   2 b.f. (Mar 13) Fraam 114 – Lady Jo 74 (Phountzi (USA) 104)   **–** [2004 8.3m 8.3g Oct 11] first foal: dam 1¼m/11.5f winner: well held in maiden/seller (slowly away) at Windsor. *T. D. McCarthy*

STYLISH DANCER   3 b.f. Muhtarram (USA) 125 – Iltimas (USA) 95 (Dayjur (USA)   **–** 137) [2004 10m 11g⁵ 12m p10g⁶ p12g 10.2s Sep 20] leggy filly: fourth foal: half-sister to 4-y-o Zoom Zoom and 1999 2-y-o 5f winner Cautionary (by Warning): dam 5f and (including at 2 yrs) 6f winner: little form. *M. Blanshard*

STYLISH PRINCE   4 b.g. Polar Prince (IRE) 117 – Simply Style (Bairn (USA) 126)   **–** [2004 –: f11g Feb 8] lightly raced and no form since 2002: tried visored. *J. G. M. O'Shea*

STYLISH SUNRISE (IRE)   3 b.g. Desert Style (IRE) 121 – Anita At Dawn (IRE)   **52** 77 (Anita's Prince 126) [2004 76: p8g 10.1g¹ 10m³ 11.1m⁵ 12.6m p10g³ 10g p16g⁵ Sep 1] lengthy gelding: modest maiden: left M. Bell after fourth start: stays easy 2m: acts on polytrack, firm and good to soft going: tongue tied last 6 outings, visored final one. *I. A. Wood*

SUALDA (IRE)   5 b.g. Idris (IRE) 118 – Winning Heart 98 (Horage 124) [2004 75:   **83** 12.3g⁵ 12.3m² 12.1g* 13g² 11.1g³ 12.3m* 16.1f⁴ 11.9d* 13.9m Sep 5] tall gelding: fairly useful handicapper: won at Beverley, Chester and York (best effort, beat Court of Appeal by neck) in summer: stays 2m: acts on firm and good to soft going: tried in blinkers/cheekpieces/tongue tie: usually held up. *R. A. Fahey*

SUAVE QUARTET (USA)   3 b.g. Slew City Slew (USA) – Leallah M (USA) (Big   **–** Spruce (USA)) [2004 75: 8f⁵ Jun 22] attractive gelding: maiden: blinkered, pulled hard then ran as though amiss only start at 3 yrs. *G. A. Butler*

SUBADAR MAJOR   7 b.g. Komaite (USA) – Rather Gorgeous 37§ (Billion (USA)   **–** 120) [2004 –: 16g 15.9g 15.8m Sep 18] big gelding: no longer of any account. *Mrs G. S. Rees*

SUBLIMITY (FR)   4 b.g. Selkirk (USA) 129 – Fig Tree Drive (USA) 94 (Miswaki   **114** (USA) 124) [2004 109p: 8g* 8.1d 9.9g⁴ 8.5m 8f³ 8d Aug 12] big, strong gelding: smart performer: won listed race at Doncaster in March by 1¼ lengths from Gateman: 1½ lengths fourth to Alkaadhem in similar event at Goodwood in May, best effort after: effective at 1m/1¼m: acts on good to firm going: sometimes wears crossed noseband: tongue tied since debut: often taken steadily to post: sometimes sweats, did so markedly second/fourth starts: usually waited with: temperament under suspicion: gelded, then sold 32,000 gns. *Sir Michael Stoute*

SUBMISSIVE   3 ch.c. Young Ern 120 – Sublime (Conquering Hero (USA) 116) [2004   **75** 7d f8.5g* 8.3d Aug 28] strong, well-made colt: third foal: dam unraced half-sister to smart 1m/1¼m performer Penny Drops: fair form: won maiden at Wolverhampton in April: stays 8.5f: sold 11,000 gns. *B. W. Hills*

SUBPOENA 2 b.c. (May 8) Diktat 126 – Trefoil 111 (Kris 135) [2004 7g* 7g Sep 30] **93 p** strong, lengthy colt: eighth foal: half-brother to 4-y-o Three Graces and useful French 1¼m (at 2 yrs) to 1½m winner Trefula (by Rainbow Quest): dam, French 10.5f/11f winner, half-sister to 3 very smart middle-distance performers: won maiden at York in September comfortably by 2 lengths from Paper Talk, leading 1f out: favourite, only seventh in Somerville Tattersall Stakes at Newmarket, in trouble long way out: should stay 1m: joined Godolphin: likely to make a useful 3-y-o at least. *M. A. Jarvis*

SUBTLE AFFAIR (IRE) 2 b.f. (Apr 26) Barathea (IRE) 127 – Uncertain Affair **68 p** (IRE) 79 (Darshaan 133) [2004 8m 10.1d³ Nov 5] €60,000Y: rather unfurnished filly: half-sister to several winners, including 3-y-o Lochbuie and useful Irish stayer Direct Bearing (by Polish Precedent): dam, Irish 1¾m winner, out of half-sister to dam of Slip Anchor: better effort in maidens (raced freely both times) when third to Quizzene at Yarmouth, held up and staying on: should stay 1½m: capable of better. *M. G. Quinlan*

SUBTLE BREEZE (USA) 3 ch.f. Storm Cat (USA) – Morning Devotion (USA) **67** 102 (Affirmed (USA)) [2004 7m³ 8.2d p8m⁶ a6f Dec 8] lengthy filly: sister to useful Irish 2002 2-y-o 7f winner Some Kind of Tiger, closely related to 2 winners by Storm Bird, notably top-class Oaks/Irish Derby winner Balanchine (also 7f winner at 2 yrs), and half-sister to 3 winners, including smart winner up to 1½m Romanov (by Nureyev): dam, 2-y-o 6f winner, stayed 1½m: best effort in maidens when third at Lingfield on debut in September: left J. Gosden before final outing: stayed 7f: stud. *P. B. Byrne, USA*

SUBTLE MOVE (USA) 4 b.f. Known Fact (USA) 135 – Substance (USA) (Diesis – 133) [2004 60d: f5g Jan 12] angular, quite good-topped filly: no longer of any account. *D. Shaw*

SUBYAN DREAMS 2 b.f. (Feb 17) Spectrum (IRE) 126 – Subya 107 (Night Shift **93 ?** (USA)) [2004 6g⁵ 6m³ 7d³ 7s 8g⁵ Sep 29] 45,000Y: sturdy filly: sixth foal: closely related to smart 1¼m/1½m winner Villa Carlotta (by Rainbow Quest) and half-sister to 4-y-o Seeyaaj: dam 5f (at 2 yrs) to 1¼m winner: seemingly fairly useful form when third to Kings Quay in listed contest at Newbury third start: some way below that level otherwise, mostly in maidens: should stay at least 1m: edged right/found little final start. *P. W. Chapple-Hyam*

SUCCESSION 2 ch.f. (Mar 16) Groom Dancer (USA) 128 – Pitcroy 99 (Unfuwain **86** (USA) 131) [2004 6m 6d 7d 8.5s⁶ 8g* 7g* 8g* 8g³ Sep 30] workmanlike, rather leggy filly: fourth living foal: half-sister to useful 1¼m winner Succinct (by Hector Protector): dam, 1¼m winner, half-sister to smart 7f/1m performer Ardkinglass: fairly useful performer: won nurseries at Musselburgh (2) and Yarmouth in September: creditable third in similar event at Goodwood: should stay 1¼m: best efforts on good ground: sometimes wanders/flashes tail: usually races up with pace. *Sir Mark Prescott*

SUCCESSOR 4 ch.g. Entrepreneur 123 – Petralona (USA) (Alleged (USA) 138) **58** [2004 8.1d 8.2g⁶ Jun 21] lengthy gelding: lightly-raced maiden: fairly useful form only 2-y-o start: missed 2003 (reportedly injured a pastern): better effort (modest form) at 4 yrs when sixth at Nottingham: sold 10,000 gns and gelded. *B. W. Hills*

SUCHWOT (IRE) 3 b.g. Intikhab (USA) 135 – Fairy Water 88 (Warning 136) [2004 **59** 56: 8.2g 10.9d⁶ 8.1v² 8.1s 12g Oct 5] workmanlike gelding: modest maiden: barely stays 11f: acts on heavy going. *F. Jordan*

SUDDEN 9 ch.g. off in. Positive Statement (USA) – Tala 'a Ranee (Layal 94) [2004 p10g⁶ – Mar 29] 50/1, tailed off in claimer at Lingfield. *J. J. Bridger*

SUDDEN DISMISSAL (IRE) 2 b.c. (Apr 4) Inchinor 119 – Suddenly 86 (Puissance **95** 110) [2004 6g⁴ 6g* 6m 7g* 7s Oct 22] €26,000Y: leggy, useful-looking colt: second foal: half-brother to fairly useful Irish 1m winner Sudden Silence (by Kris): dam 2-y-o 7f winner: useful performer: won maiden at Lingfield in August and minor event at Salisbury (beat Sant Jordi by 1¾ lengths) in September: ran in pattern company in between (ran creditably) and final start: should stay 1m: acts on good to firm going. *G. A. Butler*

SUDDEN FLIGHT (IRE) 7 b.g. In The Wings 128 – Ma Petite Cherie (USA) 93 **74** (Caro 133) [2004 78+, a87: p12g p12g p12g f12s³ 12.3d 10s 16m⁴ 14g³ 15.9g* 16m⁶ 12m⁵ 14.4m 12s³ 11.9s Sep 24] close-coupled gelding: fair handicapper: left R. Ingram after third start: won at Chester in July: stays 2m: acts on all-weather and any turf going: tried visored: effective held up or making running. *P. D. Evans*

SUDDEN IMPULSE 3 b.f. Silver Patriarch (IRE) 125 – Sanshang (FR) (Astronef **63** 116) [2004 8m⁶ p10d Jun 26] first foal: dam placed in Belgium at 2 yrs: better effort in maidens when sixth at Salisbury: should stay at least 1¼m. *A. Charlton*

994

SUDRA 7 b.g. Indian Ridge 123 – Bunting 102 (Shaadi (USA) 126) [2004 –, a72: f8.5g³ f8.5g³ f7g⁴ f7g⁴ f7g³ f7g* f8.5s⁴ f8g³ f8s Aug 23] smallish gelding: modest performer: won seller at Southwell in February: left J. O'Reilly after next start: stays 8.5f: raced mainly on all-weather since 2001: usually wears cheekpieces/blinkers: carries head high: none too trustworthy. *D. J. Daly* — **a59**

SUERTE 4 b.f. Halling (USA) 133 – Play With Me (IRE) 73 (Alzao (USA) 117) [2004 55: f9.4g 8.2d f9.4m 9.7f f8g Jul 9] rather leggy filly: poor maiden: left J. Given after reappearance: stays 1¼m: acts on fibresand and soft going: tried in cheekpieces. *R. M. H. Cowell* — **44**

SUEZ 2 b.f. (Feb 21) Green Desert (USA) 127 – Repeat Warning 72 (Warning 136) [2004 6g* 6g* 6g² Sep 30] 480,000Y: sturdy filly: second foal: dam, third at 1m from 2 starts, half-sister to very smart winner around 1¼m Cezanne and Irish Oaks winner Colorspin, herself dam of Kayf Tara and Opera House: won maiden at Goodwood in July and listed race at Salisbury (by 2½ lengths from Castelletto, dictating pace) in September: free to post, good neck second to Magical Romance in Cheveley Park Stakes at Newmarket, caught close home: likely to stay 7f, not necessarily 1m: withdrawn from Lowther Stakes second intended start due to soft going: races up with pace: joined Godolphin: type to train on well from 2 to 3 yrs. *M. A. Jarvis* — **109**

SUFFOLK HOUSE 2 b.g. (Mar 8) Paris House 123 – Suffolk Girl (Statoblest 120) [2004 p7.1g⁵ f7g* Dec 12] second foal: dam won bumper: better effort in maidens when winning at Southwell (beat Waterloo Dancer by short head): needs to settle to stay 1m: probably capable of better. *K. A. Ryan* — **69 p**

Sheikh Mohammed's "Suez"

SUGAR CUBE TREAT   8 b.m. Lugana Beach 116 – Fair Eleanor (Saritamer (USA) – 130) [2004 –: f6g f6s 6v 6d⁵ 6.1s 5f 5g⁶ 7.6m 6g Aug 6] small, close-coupled mare: little form since 2001. *M. Mullineaux*

SUGAR SNAP   4 b.f. Sesaro (USA) 81 – Cuddle Bunny (IRE) (Statoblest 120) [2004 – –: f12f f6d Jun 17] no longer of any account. *C. Drew*

SUGGESTIVE   6 b.g. Reprimand 122 – Pleasuring 68 (Good Times (ITY)) [2004 114:   **117**
8g⁴ 6g⁵ 7g² 7.1g* 7g⁴ 8g 7g² 7g² 7m⁶ 7g Sep 30] big, good sort: smart performer: won listed race at Haydock in June by ½ length from Makhlab, leading close home: best efforts when runner-up, including in Betfair Cup (Lennox) at Goodwood (beaten ¾ length by Byron) and Hungerford Stakes at Newbury (beaten 1¾ lengths by Chic) seventh/eighth starts: probably best at 7f: acts on soft and good to firm going: visored/blinkered: has had 2 handlers: carries head high: best waited with. *W. J. Haggas*

SUGITANI (USA)   2 b.c. (Apr 5) Kingmambo (USA) 125 – Lady Reiko (IRE) (Sadler's Wells (USA) 132) [2004 7g 7g Oct 1] sturdy colt: tongue tied, only a little sign of ability in maidens at York and Newmarket. *Saeed bin Suroor*

SUITCASE MURPHY (IRE)   3 b.g. Petardia 113 – Noble Rocket (Reprimand 122)   **48**
[2004 49: f6g 5m⁶ 6g³ 6m 8.1d Oct 9] tall gelding: poor maiden: stays 6f. *Ms Deborah J. Evans*

SUIVEZ MOI (IRE)   2 ch.c. (May 31) Daggers Drawn (USA) 114 – Pamiers (Hunter-   **70**
combe 133) [2004 6d p8.6g² p8.6g⁴ Dec 6] €5,500Y: half-brother to 1996 2-y-o 6f winner Key Largo (by Priolo), later successful in Hong Kong, and 2000 2-y-o 7f winner Carnot (by General Monash): dam Italian 7.5f and 9.5f winner: best effort in maidens when second to Bridegroom at Wolverhampton: will stay 1¼m. *P. W. Chapple-Hyam*

SUJOSISE   3 b.c. Prince Sabo 123 – Statuette 57 (Statoblest 120) [2004 48: 6d 5g 6m   –
6d Jul 17] well-grown colt: maiden: little form in 2004, including in visor. *J. J. Quinn*

SUKUMA (IRE)   2 ch.f. (Mar 27) Highest Honor (FR) 124 – Selva (IRE) 70 (Darshaan   **43**
133) [2004 6m f7g 6f p6g Dec 4] well grown, leggy filly: fifth foal: half-sister to 2 winners in Germany, including 11.5f winner Schnipp Schnapp (by Acatenango): dam Irish maiden: poor form in maidens. *A. M. Balding*

SULAMANI (IRE)   5 b.h. Hernando (FR) 127 – Soul Dream (USA) 78 (Alleged   **128**
(USA) 138) [2004 128: 10f⁴ 12m² 12m³ 10.4d* 12g* Oct 24]
'Geography is history.' The changes that have taken place over the years in the travelling and preparation of horses for international races has made the racing world much smaller. Most of the top stables are equipped nowadays to take up a challenge virtually anywhere where there are worthwhile events to aim at. The United States, Canada, Hong Kong, Japan, Australia and Singapore have become regular stopping-off points for European-trained horses, while Dubai was boosted as a destination in the latest season by its International Racing Carnival in the early part of the year (according to figures prepared by the International Racing Bureau, there were one hundred and thirty-two European-trained runners in Dubai in 2004, compared to sixteen the previous year). The nine-week carnival, incidentally, also attracted runners from Brazil, Hong Kong, India, Japan, Macau, South Africa and the United States, a case of the mountain coming to Mohammed, it could be said.

Sheikh Mohammed, architect of Godolphin, has done as much as anyone to push back the frontiers of international racing. Widely-travelled, inter-continental performers such as Daylami, Fantastic Light and Grandera became 'the equine manifestation of the Godolphin ethos.' All three were sent in pursuit of the World Series Championship which initially provided further valuable momentum to international racing and helped to bring wider recognition for racing as a global sport. The series is decided by points achieved in a dozen or so (thirteen in 2004) of the world's top middle-distance races in ten different countries and on four continents. Daylami won the inaugural series in 1999, Fantastic Light was successful in 2000 and 2001, before the 2002 series was won by Grandera, who did even more travelling than his predecessors in contesting eight races—not all of them in the series—in six different countries, visiting three continents, in a campaign beginning in February and ending in December.

The concept of the World Series—which was inaugurated with a million-dollar bonus for the winner—has not been supported so wholeheartedly by Godolphin since Emirates stopped its sponsorship. The withdrawal from the series of the world's richest race, the Dubai World Cup, was another blow and in 2003 and 2004 the series was run, in the words of the organisers, 'solely for prestige', a search for another sponsor having proved fruitless. The concept looks in danger of turning into something of a non-event. The winner in 2004, whose connections received the World Series trophy at the Hong Kong international meeting in December, was German-trained Epalo, who not only lost out to Soldier Hollow for Germany's Horse of the Year title but wasn't even the best horse in his own stable (that was Shirocco), let alone a world champion. Epalo won the series with points and prize money collected with a victory in the second leg, the Singapore Airlines International Cup in May, and a third place (promoted from fourth) in the fourth leg, the Arlington Million in August. He wasn't seen out after September, missing an intended start in the eighth leg, the Cox Plate in Australia in October, after coming down with a bug just before going into quarantine. Epalo stays in training with events in the World Series, assuming it survives, again on the agenda.

Though not targeted at the World Series, Sulamani finished level with Epalo at the top of the points table. Epalo took the title by virtue of winning more prize money in his two races than Sulamani did by finishing third in the third leg, the King George VI and Queen Elizabeth Stakes, and winning the ninth leg, the Canadian International at Woodbine in October. Some of the courses which stage the races, and now foot the promotional bill for the series, may be less enthusiastic—there is talk of the Prix de l'Arc following the Dubai World Cup out—and French racing supremo Louis Romanet, president of the International Federation of Horseracing Authorities, claims that 'the personal feeling of many members is that a points system to establish a world champion is not working well enough.' The World Thoroughbred Racehorse Rankings, which replaced the International Classifications when published for the first time in January 2005 and are due to be updated four times a year, are seen by the International Federation as the latest vehicle for promoting racing globally. Similar rankings or orders of merit are published regularly in sports such as golf and tennis.

In its ten-year existence, Godolphin has had Group/Grade 1 successes in eleven different countries. In 2004, Godolphin-owned horses won eleven Group/Grade 1 races in six different countries, Britain, the United States, Ireland, Italy, Canada and Hong Kong. Notable by its absence was a Group 1 success in Dubai, where Sulamani's victory in the Dubai Sheema Classic and Moon Ballad's in the Dubai World Cup had given the operation a flying start the previous year. Godolphin had won four of the last five runnings of the Dubai World Cup but fielded a considerably weaker team at the meeting in 2004. It was thought that Sulamani, Godolphin's most successful performer on turf in 2003, when he also won the

Juddmonte International Stakes, York—
Sulamani (right) wears down Norse Dancer as Bago (left) closes in third

Pattison Canadian International Stakes, Woodbine—
Sulamani wins his sixth (gained in five different countries) Group/Grade 1 from the roan Simonas;
Brian Boru (left) and Mubtaker (rail) make it a clean sweep for European stables

Arlington Million (on a disqualification) and the Turf Classic Invitational, would be a candidate for one of the big races at the Dubai World Cup meeting. Godolphin said, however, that it was 'feeling the way' with some of its top horses, Sulamani's reappearance being pencilled in for the Tattersalls Gold Cup at the Curragh in May. A minor infection in a pastern caused Sulamani to miss that engagement and he began his latest campaign in the Prince of Wales's Stakes at Royal Ascot, where firm ground and a fairly steady early pace put the emphasis very much on speed. Starting favourite, Sulamani couldn't quite get into contention in the home straight and finished fourth behind the impressive Rakti. Returned to a mile and a half on his next start—after talk of a possible tilt at the Coral-Eclipse—Sulamani failed only narrowly to get the better of Bandari, to whom he conceded 5 lb, in the Princess of Wales's Stakes at Newmarket. This was a high-class performance and, despite Godolphin's also having the hot favourite Doyen, Sulamani fully deserved his place in the line-up for the King George VI and Queen Elizabeth Stakes, Britain's most prestigious weight-for-age event for three-year-olds and upwards. Sulamani chased home Alamshar in the race in 2003 and should probably have finished second again in the latest edition. Waited with, he lost ground when the pace quickened, after a steady first six furlongs, and was still towards the rear, with plenty to do, as the field straightened for home. Kerrin McEvoy was noticeably less free with his whip than Godolphin's number-one jockey Dettori tended to be on Sulamani, but the colt ran on well in the last furlong and a half to finish a head behind runner-up Hard Buck, the pair three lengths adrift of the impressive Doyen.

The Grosser Preis von Baden, Germany's most valuable race and the fifth leg of the World Series, was mentioned as a possible next target for Sulamani (Godolphin had won the two previous runnings with Mamool and Marienbard). In the event, Sulamani was dropped back in trip once again for the Juddmonte International at York. Persistent rain turned the going good to soft and resulted in a number of absentees, notably Rakti and the St James's Palace Stakes winner Azamour, the latter taken out on the morning of the race. The unbeaten French-trained three-year-old Bago started favourite at 13/8, with Sulamani next best at 3/1 in a nine-runner renewal that seemed a little weaker than usual on the day. With Sulamani's stable-companion Millstreet in the race to ensure a good gallop, the field was well strung out turning for home. Patiently and confidently ridden by Dettori, Sulamani was produced with a strong run in the last two furlongs to get the better of Norse Dancer by three quarters of a length, winning with a little in hand, though Dettori picked up a one-day ban for using his whip with excessive frequency. Bago finished a further three quarters of a length behind Norse Dancer in third, with another French-trained three-year-old Cacique fourth.

As well as providing Sulamani with his first victory in Britain, the International also gave him ten points in the BHB's Middle Distance Championship, which enabled him to overhaul Doyen and Warrsan in the table, securing the

998

£100,000 prize—reduced from £250,000 in 2003—for the owners. The championship and the Summer Triple Crown lasted only for two years, both axed for 2005 in cutbacks announced in December. The Summer Grand Slam—involving success in four events—had been dropped after the first year 'because trainers felt it put too much pressure on horses.' With Sulamani reportedly 'a little bit quiet' after York, he eventually bypassed the Arc, for which he was promoted to ante-post favouritism for a time after Doyen's defeat in the Irish Champion Stakes. Sheikh Mohammed had spoken after the International about an autumn campaign possibly involving the Breeders' Cup, the Japan Cup and/or one of the big events at Hong Kong's international meeting in December. But Sulamani was seen out only once more after York, over two months later in the Pattison Canadian International at Woodbine, the week before the Breeders' Cup. Starting at odds on, he led home a one, two, three, four for European-trained runners, winning by a length and a half, two lengths and three quarters of a length from German-trained Simonas, Brian Boru (third for the second year running) and Mubtaker. It was a sixth Group/Grade 1 win for Sulamani, the victories gained in five different countries and with four different jockeys—France (where he won the Prix du Jockey Club, ridden by Thierry Thulliez, for his breeders the Niarchos Family) and—after his purchase by Godolphin—in Dubai, the United States (twice, once ridden by Jerry Bailey and once by David Flores), Britain and Canada.

Sulamani (IRE) (b.h. 1999)	Hernando (FR) (b 1990)	Niniski (b 1976)	Nijinsky Virginia Hills
		Whakilyric (b 1984)	Miswaki Lyrism
	Soul Dream (USA) (br 1990)	Alleged (b 1974)	Hoist The Flag Princess Pout
		Normia (gr 1981)	Northfields Mia Pola

Godolphin's "Sulamani"

Sulamani is a lightly-made, close-coupled, attractive horse, but he didn't always fill the eye in the paddock and showed a short, unimpressive action in his faster paces. Sulamani's pedigree has been dealt with fully in the last two editions of *Racehorses* and there is nothing significant to add. He emulated both his sire Hernando and half-brother Dream Well (by Sadler's Wells) when winning the Prix du Jockey Club. Dream Well also won the Irish Derby, though the dam Soul Dream's own racing record was modest, her best effort when trained in Britain by Julie Cecil a third in a Pontefract maiden over a mile and a quarter; Soul Dream subsequently won over eleven furlongs at Clairefontaine, in the Provinces, after being sent to France. Sulamani's sire—who has another Prix du Jockey Club winner, Holding Court, to his credit—has proved an influence for stamina, but Sulamani was effective at a mile and a quarter and a mile and a half. He acted on firm and good to soft going, and was unraced on soft and heavy. Tongue tied in his races from the Princess of Wales's Stakes onwards and usually bandaged on his fore joints as a five-year-old, he was held up and had a good turn of foot. Though looking a tricky ride, often hanging and carrying his head awkwardly when let down, sometimes flashing his tail, Sulamani rarely ran a bad race and finished out of the first four only twice in seventeen starts, on his racecourse debut and in the 2003 Breeders' Cup Turf. He begins his stud career at Dalham Hall, Newmarket, in 2005 at a fee of £7,000. *Saeed bin Suroor*

SUMMER BOUNTY 8 b.g. Lugana Beach 116 – Tender Moment (IRE) 78 (Caerleon (USA) 132) [2004 73, a48: 10.9d 8.1v* 10d* 10m 10.3g³ 10.1v² 10.3g 10m⁵ Jul 28] leggy, close-coupled gelding: fairly useful performer: back to best in 2004, winning handicaps at Warwick and Nottingham in May: effective at 1m to 1½m: acts on fibresand and any turf going: tried blinkered/tongue tied: sometimes starts slowly (has virtually refused to race): often held up. *F. Jordan* — **83 a?**

SUMMER CHARM 2 b.f. (May 17) Dansili 127 – Regent's Folly (IRE) 101 (Touching Wood (USA) 127) [2004 6g 7.1g 6.1m p7g f8d* Dec 21] 4,500Y: sturdy filly: half-sister to several winners, including 8-y-o Spree Vision and 3-y-o Our Emmy Lou: dam 2-y-o 7f winner who stayed 14.6f: modest performer: improved to win maiden at Southwell by 2½ lengths from Fantasy Defender: stays 1m. *W. Jarvis* — **57**

SUMMER CHERRY (USA) 7 b.g. Summer Squall (USA) – Cherryrob (USA) (Roberto (USA) 131) [2004 54: 11.9m 12m² 12m⁵ 12f 11.9f 10m Jul 13] leggy gelding: poor handicapper: stays 1½m: unraced on heavy going, acts on polytrack, firm and soft going: tried blinkered: tongue tied: sometimes slowly away. *Jamie Poulton* — **49**

SUMMERISE 3 b.f. Atraf 116 – Summerhill Special (IRE) 80 (Roi Danzig (USA)) [2004 55: p8g 10s⁶ 8.1s³ 10s 8g⁶ p10m³ f12g p10m* p10m* Dec 15] fair performer: left H. Collingridge after fifth start: won 2 banded races at Lingfield in December: stays 1¼m: acts on polytrack, soft and good to firm going: sometimes slowly away. *C. N. Allen* — **60**

SUMMER JOY 3 b.f. Myfontaine 74 – Marycee (IRE) (King's Ride 88) [2004 8.1s 7m Jun 8] first foal: dam unraced: tailed off in maidens. *D. K. Ivory* — **–**

SUMMER RECLUSE (USA) 5 gr.g. Cozzene (USA) – Summer Retreat (USA) 78 (Gone West (USA)) [2004 87+: p8g p7g p8g⁶ p8g⁴ p7.1g p9.5g³ p8m Dec 21] useful performer: left B. Johnson after fourth start: stays 1m: acts on polytrack, probaby on soft and good to firm going: tried in cheekpieces: sometimes races freely. *J. M. Bradley* — **84**

SUMMER SERENADE 3 b.f. Sadler's Wells (USA) 132 – Summer Sonnet (Baillamont (USA) 124) [2004 10m² 10g³ p12g p9.5g⁴ p10g⁶ p9.5g Dec 13] smallish, quite good-topped filly: fifth foal: closely related to very smart French 1m (at 2 yrs) and 10.5f winner who stayed 1½m Act One (by In The Wings) and half-sister to 2 useful performers by Caerleon, including 2000 2-y-o 7f winner Summer Symphony: dam French 1½m winner on turf: fair maiden on turf, modest on all-weather: should stay at least 1½m: acts on good to firm going. *L. M. Cumani* — **75 a54**

SUMMER SHADES 6 b.m. Green Desert (USA) 127 – Sally Slade 80 (Dowsing (USA) 124) [2004 79: f8.5g⁶ 8g⁵ 8m² 8f⁴ 8f⁴ 8m³ 9d⁵ 8.2g⁶ 8.2g* 8f² 8.3m⁵ 8g² p8.6g p8.6g p8.6g⁶ p7.1g Nov 27] small mare: fair on turf, modest on all-weather: won handicap at Nottingham in July: stays 9.4f: acts on all-weather and firm going: sometimes blinkered at 3 yrs. *W. M. Brisbourne* — **79 a58**

SUMMER SILKS 2 ch.f. (Mar 31) Bahamian Bounty 116 – Sadler's Song 54 (Sadlers' Hall (IRE) 126) [2004 5g 7g⁴ 7d 7f 7g Oct 5] 500Y: sturdy filly: first foal: dam maiden who stayed 1½m: modest maiden: form only when fourth at Newcastle: stays 7f. *R. A. Fahey* — **54**

SUMMER SPECIAL 4 b.g. Mind Games 121 – Summerhill Special (IRE) 80 (Roi **54**
Danzig (USA)) [2004 70d: 6d⁵ 10.1v⁵ 9.2g³ 12.4s 11.6m⁵ 12.3g 8g³ 8d³ 8m 7g 8d 8s⁴ 8f
Sep 16] close-coupled gelding: modest maiden: stays 9f: acts on any going: sometimes
wears cheekpieces: often looks less than keen. *D. W. Barker*

SUMMER STOCK (USA) 6 b.g. Theatrical 128 – Lake Placid (IRE) (Royal **?**
Academy (USA) 130) [2004 64, a59+: p10g p9.5g Oct 25] poor maiden: stays 11f: acts **a45**
on fibresand, firm and good to soft going: tried blinkered/in cheekpieces: tongue tied.
J. A. Supple

SUMMER SUNSET (IRE) 3 ch.f. Grand Lodge (USA) 125 – Elegant Bloom (IRE) **90 ?**
84 (Be My Guest (USA) 126) [2004 87: 7d⁵ 7m⁵ 8f 7m 7d 7.5s Aug 19] €60,000Y: leggy
filly: half-sister to several winners, including smart sprinter in Ireland/Scandinavia Rolo
Tomasi (by Mujtahid) and 6-y-o Eastern Breeze: dam Irish 2-y-o 6f winner: fairly useful
performer: won maiden at Tralee in 2003: creditable fifth in 1000 Guineas Trial and
Ballycorus Stakes at Leopardstown first 2 starts at 3 yrs: below form after, including in
listed handicap at Royal Ascot third outing: stays 1m: acts on firm and soft going: tried
blinkered. *D. K. Weld, Ireland*

SUMMER WINE 5 b.m. Desert King (IRE) 129 – Generous Lady 98 (Generous **–**
(IRE) 139) [2004 –: 10s Apr 30] good-topped mare: fairly useful at 3 yrs: well held since.
C. F. Wall

SUMMITVILLE 4 b.f. Grand Lodge (USA) 125 – Tina Heights 79 (Shirley Heights **106**
130) [2004 114: 10.4s³ 12m² 11.9g⁶ 14m³ 11g⁶ 12f⁴ Sep 24] tall, close-coupled filly:
useful performer: mostly at least respectable efforts in pattern company in 2004, ½-length
second to Danelissima in Noblesse Stakes at Naas in June: stays 1½m: acts on firm and
soft going: takes strong hold, and often wears crossed noseband. *J. G. Given*

SUMORA (IRE) 2 b.f. (Feb 23) Danehill (USA) 126 – Rain Flower (IRE) (Indian **105**
Ridge 123) [2004 p5d⁷ 5.2g⁴ 5f⁶ 5s Oct 16] 75,000Y: stocky filly: first foal: dam unraced
close relative to Derby winner Dr Devious and half-sister to smart performer up to 1½m
Hill Country (by Danehill): useful performer: won maiden at Lingfield in July and listed
race at Newbury (comfortably, by 1½ lengths from Castelletto) in August: below form
in Flying Childers Stakes at Doncaster (ran too fast in front) and
Cornwallis Stakes at Newmarket (pulled too hard held up): needs to settle to stay beyond
5f. *G. A. Butler*

SUN AND SHOWERS (IRE) 2 b.c. (Apr 18) Rainbow Quest (USA) 134 – Las **60 p**
Flores (IRE) 102 (Sadler's Wells (USA) 132) [2004 8s Oct 27] closely related to useful
1½m winner La Paz (by Nashwan) and half-brother to several winners, including 3-y-o
Sleeping Indian and 4-y-o Felicity: dam, 1¼m winner, half-sister to very smart Irish 1m/
1¼m performer Bach: 33/1 and green, ninth in maiden at Yarmouth, late headway: will
be suited by 1¼m/1½m: should do better. *J. H. M. Gosden*

SUN BIRD (IRE) 6 ch.g. Prince of Birds (USA) 121 – Summer Fashion 84 (Moorestyle **93**
137) [2004 112: 12.1d⁵ May 14] well-made gelding: useful handicapper at 5 yrs: shaped
well only start in 2004: stays 18.7f: acts on any going: ran well in blinkers/visor earlier in
career. *R. Allan*

SUNCLIFF 2 b.g. (May 2) Most Welcome 131 – Marjorie's Orchid 49 (Petong 126) **–**
[2004 p8.6d Oct 30] 66/1 and blinkered, tailed off in maiden at Wolverhampton. *Mrs
A. Duffield*

SUNDANCE (IRE) 2 ch.c. (Apr 19) Namid 128 – Titchwell Lass 57 (Lead On Time **94**
(USA) 123) [2004 5g* p5g² 5d* 5d⁶ 6g Oct 9] €10,000F, €17,500Y, 30,000 2-y-o: strong,
lengthy colt: has a round action: fifth foal: half-brother to 3 winners, including 3-y-o
Louisiade and 6-y-o Denise Best: dam 1¼m winner: fairly useful performer: won maiden
at Windsor in July and minor event at Ripon (beat Bond City by length) in August: not
run of things in listed races last 2 starts: needs to settle to stay 6f: acts on polytrack and
good to soft going. *H. J. Collingridge*

SUNDAY CITY (JPN) 3 ch.c. Sunday Silence (USA) – Diamond City (USA) 104 **81**
(Mr Prospector (USA)) [2004 12m³ 12m³ 10.2f⁵ 14.1m⁵ 13.1f² 16.1m Sep 29] leggy colt:
fifth foal: half-brother to several winners, including 7f (at 2 yrs)/1m winner Catienus (by
Storm Cat), later smart performer up to 1¼m in USA: dam, 7f to 1¼m winner in Britain,
later successful in USA: fairly useful maiden: best effort on debut: stays easy 1¾m: acts
on firm going: visored second/third starts: sold 20,000 gns. *D. R. Loder*

SUNDAY SYMPHONY 2 br.c. (Mar 10) Sunday Silence (USA) – Darrery 98 (Dars- **92**
haan 133) [2004 8d² 8m* 10g* 10d⁵ Oct 30] 250,000F: big, useful-looking colt: half-
brother to 3 winners, including useful 1998 2-y-o 7f winner Al Waffi (by Fairy King) and

fairly useful 2002 2-y-o 1m winner (later Triumph Hurdle winner) Made In Japan (by Barathea): dam, 1¼m/1½m winner, out of smart performer up to 1m Flamenco: fairly useful performer: won maiden at Thirsk (flashed tail) in September and minor event at Leicester (beat Bayeux de Moi ½ length) in October: creditable fifth to Ayam Zaman in listed event at Newmarket, fading: stays 1¼m: acts on good to firm and good to soft going. *Saeed bin Suroor*

SUNDRIED TOMATO   5 b.g. Lugana Beach 116 – Little Scarlett 54 (Mazilier **70** (USA) 107) [2004 88, a99: f6g f7g⁶ f6g⁴ f6g⁶ f6s f6s⁶ 5.7g 7s 6d⁵ 6d 6g f6g⁵ p7.1g p6g **a84** p6g Dec 27] good-topped gelding: fairly useful on all-weather, fair on turf: stays easy 7f: acts on all-weather, heavy and good to firm going: blinkered penultimate outing: often races prominently. *P. W. Hiatt*

SUNDROP (JPN)   3 b.f. Sunday Silence (USA) – Oenothera (IRE) 106 (Night Shift **115** (USA)) [2004 107p: 8m² 12m⁶ 10d* Oct 14] neat, strong filly: has a round action: smart performer: excellent ½-length second to Attraction in 1000 Guineas at Newmarket, isolated early and running on strongly from rear: ran as if amiss in Oaks at Epsom next time (reportedly returned home with soft-tissue injury): off 4½ months, didn't need to be at best to win listed race at Newmarket in October by ½ length from I Had A Dream, jinking left before asserting: should stay 1½m: acts on polytrack, firm and good to soft ground. *Saeed bin Suroor*

SUNGIO   6 b.g. Halling (USA) 133 – Time Or Never (FR) (Dowsing (USA) 124) [2004 **62** 59: p16g* p13g³ f12s* f13g² f16.2g³ p13g³ p16g⁵ 16d p16.5g* p16g³ p13.9g Dec 10] modest performer: won sellers at Lingfield in January and Wolverhampton in February and handicap at Wolverhampton in November: stays 16.5f: acts on all-weather, soft and good to firm going: tried visored, often blinkered: sometimes slowly away/wanders. *B. G. Powell*

Godolphin's "Sundrop"

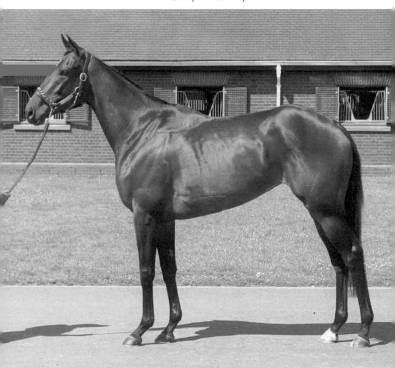

SUN HILL 4 b.g. Robellino (USA) 127 – Manhattan Sunset (USA) 76 (El Gran Senor **74** (USA) 136) [2004 –: f14g* f16.2s* f16.2s* 18g 15s 14.1s⁵ 14.1d 11.9s 16d 16s p16.5g **a85** p16.5g³ p13.9g* Dec 31] sturdy, close-coupled gelding: fairly useful handicapper on all-weather, fair on turf: won at Southwell in February and at Wolverhampton in March (twice) and December: stays 16.5f: acts on all-weather and soft going. *M. Blanshard*

SUNISA (IRE) 3 b.f. Daggers Drawn (USA) 114 – Winged Victory (IRE) 93 (Dancing **85** Brave (USA) 140) [2004 73: p8g² f8.5g* 10.3m³ 9m 9d² 10m 10.3s⁵ Oct 22] robust, close-coupled filly: fairly useful performer: won maiden at Wolverhampton in April: best efforts in handicaps after when placed at Doncaster and Kempton: stays 1¼m: acts on all-weather, soft and good to firm going: sold 14,000 gns, joined J. Mackie. *B. W. Hills*

SUN KISSED (JPN) 2 ch.c. (Mar 6) Sunday Silence (USA) – Flying Kiss (IRE) **93** (Sadler's Wells (USA) 132) [2004 6m* 8g² 8d Oct 15] strong, well-made colt: has a quick action: second foal: dam, ran twice in France, sister to Racing Post Trophy winner Commander Collins, and closely related to Breeders' Cup Sprint winner Lit de Justice and Derby third Colonel Collins: won maiden at Newmarket in July: creditable length second, weakening late on, to Liakoura at Salisbury, much better effort in minor events: seems barely to stay 1m: acts on good to firm going. *Saeed bin Suroor*

SUNLEY SENSE 8 b.g. Komaite (USA) – Brown Velvet 68 (Mansingh (USA) 120) **83 d** [2004 5m³ 5m 5g 5d 5m⁶ Jul 27] sturdy, workmanlike gelding: unraced in 2003: fairly useful at best at 8 yrs: effective at 5f/6f: acts on firm and soft going: ran poorly both starts in visor. *M. R. Channon*

SUNNY GLENN 6 ch.h. Rock Hopper 124 – La Ballerine 62 (Lafontaine (USA) 117) **87** [2004 71+: 12m 12g⁶ 12m 10.5s Sep 24] lengthy horse: unimpressive mover: just fairly useful performer in 2004: left Mrs P. N. Dutfield before running poorly final outing: stays 1½m: acts on firm and soft going. *Simon Earle*

SUNNY LADY (FR) 3 ch.f. Nashwan (USA) 135 – Like The Sun (USA) 74 (Wood- **80** man (USA) 126) [2004 56: 11.1g² 12m² 11.9m² 14g² 11.9f* 11.9g⁴ 11.6m⁴ p12g⁶ Oct 25] sparely-made filly: fairly useful handicapper: won at Brighton in June by ½ length from Crocolat: creditable 3½ lengths fourth to Ringsider at Windsor penultimate start: stays 1¾m: acts on good to firm going: sold 16,000 gns. *E. A. L. Dunlop*

SUNNY NATURE 2 b.f. (Apr 23) Sadler's Wells (USA) 132 – Bright Spells (USA) **– p** (Alleged (USA) 138) [2004 7d Oct 30] leggy, useful-looking filly: fifth foal: half-sister to 7f winners (including at 2 yrs) Clearing (smart, also second in Poule d'Essai des Poulains) and Blazing Thunder (useful), both by Zafonic: dam, fairly useful French 1½m winner, sister to smart performer up to 15.5f Non Partisan: 7/1, last in maiden at Newmarket, possibly amiss: joined H-A. Pantall in France: should do better. *J. H. M. Gosden*

SUNNYSIDE ROYALE (IRE) 5 b.g. Ali-Royal (IRE) 127 – Kuwah (IRE) 77 (Be **54** My Guest (USA) 126) [2004 56: 14.1g f14m* f11m³ f16g May 15] leggy gelding: modest performer: won banded event at Southwell in April: stays 1¾m: acts on fibresand and good to firm going: tried blinkered/tongue tied. *R. Bastiman*

SUNNY TIMES (IRE) 2 b.f. (Apr 24) Raise A Grand (IRE) 114 – Dragon Star 54 **59** (Rudimentary (USA) 118) [2004 6m⁵ 5m 6m 8m⁵ 8d² 8d p7m⁶ Nov 22] first foal: dam, maiden, best effort at 5f at 2 yrs: modest maiden: stays 1m: acts on good to firm and good to soft going. *J. W. Payne*

SUN ON THE SEA (IRE) 4 ch.f. Bering 136 – Shimmer (FR) (Green Dancer (USA) **–** 132) [2004 109: 10.4s⁶ May 12] good-bodied filly: useful at 3 yrs: bandaged in front, well held only start in 2004: free-going front runner. *B. J. Meehan*

SUNRIDGE FAIRY (IRE) 5 b.m. Definite Article 121 – Foxy Fairy (IRE) (Fairy **–** King (USA)) [2004 –: f8g 9.9m⁶ May 24] smallish, lengthy mare: modest at best: lightly raced and little form since 2002. *A. J. Lockwood*

SUNSET BLUES (FR) 4 ch.g. Green Tune (USA) 125 – Sunset Reef (Mill Reef **48** (USA) 141) [2004 f8.5s⁵ p8g f9.4g p8g³ f8g May 19] poor maiden: stays 1m: blinkered. *K. O. Cunningham-Brown*

SUNSET DREAMER (USA) 3 ch.f. Boundary (USA) 117 – Quaff (USA) 115 **39** (Raise A Cup (USA)) [2004 p8g⁶ p7g 7g p10g 10m 8d Oct 16] $2,500F, 12,000Y: quite good-topped filly: half-sister to several winners, including unreliable 9f to 2m winner Sconced (by Affirmed): dam won at 1m/8.5f (2 yrs to 5 yrs) in France/USA: poor maiden. *P. Mitchell*

SUNSET KING (USA) 4 b.c. King of Kings (IRE) 125 – Sunset River (USA) (North- **–** ern Flagship (USA) 96) [2004 66: p8g Mar 31] close-coupled colt: maiden: well held only start in 2004: tried blinkered. *J. C. Fox*

SUNSET MIRAGE (USA) 3 br.f. Swain (IRE) 134 – Yafill (USA) 80 (Nureyev **76** (USA) 131) [2004 63p: 10d² 11.5g⁶ 9.3f* 8.1m 8.1m⁶ 9.7g 10.1m⁴ 10f² 9.7g³ 9.2d² Aug 23] rather leggy filly: fair handicapper: won at Carlisle in May: creditable efforts in frame in visor/blinkers last 4 starts: stays 1¼m: acts on firm and good to soft going: sometimes finds little: held up. *E. A. L. Dunlop*

SUNSET STRIP 2 b.g. (Apr 9) Josr Algarhoud (IRE) 118 – Shady Street (USA) (Sha- **76** deed (USA) 135) [2004 6f² 7g² 6g³ 6d⁶ Aug 4] 52,000F: tall gelding: half-brother to several winners, including 3-y-o Rachel's Verdict: dam unraced: fair maiden: stays 7f: acts on firm ground: carried head high penultimate start: gelded after final outing. *M. R. Channon*

SUNSHINE ON ME 3 ch.f. Kris 135 – Degannwy 52 (Caerleon (USA) 132) [2004 **53** 9f p12g⁵ p13g p12g Oct 31] closely related to smart performer up to 1¼m in Hong Kong Keen Winner (by Selkirk) and half-sister to winning sprinter in Italy by Lion Cavern: dam 1½m winner who probably stayed 15f: modest maiden: seems to stay 13f: slowly away first 2 outings. *C. F. Wall*

SUNSTRACH (IRE) 6 b.h. Polar Falcon (USA) 126 – Lorne Lady (Local Suitor **116** (USA) 128) [2004 119: 10d³ 9.3g⁴ 10d³ 10d³ Jul 2] big, lengthy horse: smart performer: at least respectable efforts in frame in Gordon Richards Stakes at Sandown (2 lengths third to Chancellor), Prix d'Ispahan at Longchamp (4½ lengths fourth to Prince Kirk), and Brigadier Gerard Stakes (third behind Bandari) and listed race (reportedly fractured cannon bone and operated on after finishing third to Crocodile Dundee) at Sandown in 2004: stays 1¼m: acts on soft and good to firm going: tried tongue tied: often takes strong hold. *L. M. Cumani*

SUPAMACH (IRE) 3 b.f. Machiavellian (USA) 123 – Supamova (USA) 88 (Seattle **69 d** Slew (USA)) [2004 p10g³ 7.9m⁴ 8.3f⁴ 8m 10.5g 8s p8.6g Oct 16] strong, lengthy filly: fourth foal: half-sister to 5-y-o Swellmova: dam, 8.5f winner, sister to very smart French 7f to 9f performer Septieme Ciel: fair maiden: below form after third start, often folding tamely: stays 1¼m: acts on polytrack and firm going: tried in cheekpieces: sold 20,000 gns. *P. F. I. Cole*

SUPER BOSTON 4 b.g. Saddlers' Hall (IRE) 126 – Nasowas (IRE) (Cardinal Flower – 101) [2004 8.2g 10.1s⁶ Aug 30] tall, leggy gelding: tailed off in maidens at Nottingham (for R. Woodhouse) and Newcastle. *Miss L. C. Siddall*

SUPER CANYON 6 ch.g. Gulch (USA) – Marina Park 112 (Local Suitor (USA) 128) **69 d** [2004 73: f6s⁴ f7g² p7g 7m 6.1g f7m p8g p7.1g Dec 20] fair performer: below form after second start: stays 7f: acts on fibresand and firm going: effective with or without visor, often tongue tied. *J. Pearce*

SUPERCHIEF 9 b.g. Precocious 126 – Rome Express (Siberian Express (USA) 125) – [2004 –, a74: p7g p7g⁶ p6g⁴ p7g³ p7g⁵ p6g⁵ p7g² p8g⁵ p8g 6m p7g p7g p7g p6m Dec 22] **a74 d** smallish, sturdy gelding: fair handicapper: below form after seventh start: effective at 6f to 1m: acts on polytrack, little form on turf since 6 yrs: tried visored, usually blinkered/ tongue tied. *Miss B. Sanders*

SUPERCLEAN 4 ch.f. Environment Friend 128 – Star Mover 48 (Move Off 112) – [2004 –: p8g p12g 10.2d⁶ p12g May 13] leggy, plain filly: little form: visored last 2 starts. *A. W. Carroll*

SUPER DOMINION 7 ch.g. Superpower 113 – Smartie Lee 66 (Dominion 123) [2004 **53 §** 58: f9.4g⁵ f8.5m* f9.4m⁴ f7g f8g* f8m f8m 8d f8f⁵ 8f⁴ f8g f7g³ f7g Dec 12] sturdy geld- ing: modest performer: won banded race at Wolverhampton in May and amateur handi- cap at Southwell in June: stays 1¼m: acts on fibresand, firm and soft going: often tongue tied prior to 2004: wore cheekpieces after reappearance: unreliable. *R. Hollinshead*

SUPER FELLOW (IRE) 10 b.g. Shy Groom (USA) – Killough (Lord Gayle (USA) **55** 124) [2004 16m³ 16s* 17.1d* 15.8m⁵ 17.1g⁵ Oct 4] big, workmanlike ex-Irish gelding: fair chaser: modest form in handicaps back on Flat in 2004, winning at Thirsk and Ponte- fract in August: will stay beyond 17f: acts on soft and good to firm going: tried tongue tied: held up: started slowly last 2 outings (ran well second occasion). *C. N. Kellett*

SUPERFLING 3 ch.g. Superpower 113 – Jobiska (Dunbeath (USA) 127) [2004 7d **58** 5.7f⁴ 6m p7g p7.1g Nov 20] lengthy gelding: modest maiden: stays 6f: acts on firm going. *R. Hannon*

SUPER KING 3 b.g. Kingsinger (IRE) 94 – Super Sisters (AUS) (Call Report (USA)) **69** [2004 76: 8m 7.9m f8m 7.5g 9.9g⁵ 9.9d² 10.1s³ 11.9s 10.1m Oct 10] leggy gelding: fair maiden: stays 1¼m: acts on soft and good to firm going. *N. Bycroft*

SUPERPRIDETWO 4 b.g. Superpower 113 – Lindrake's Pride (Mandrake Major – 122) [2004 –: p7g Apr 15] lengthy gelding: of little account. *P. D. Niven*

SUPER SONG 4 b.g. Desert Prince (IRE) 130 – Highland Rhapsody (IRE) 78 (Kris 135) [2004 85: p8g 8.3d 8s 6m 6f 7g⁶ 5g 7.1m 7.1s p7.1g p7m⁴ p6g Dec 30] quite good-topped gelding: modest handicapper: stays 7f: acts on good to firm and good to soft going: tongue tied after reappearance, visored last 4 starts. *P. D. Evans* **58**

SUPERSTITIOUS (IRE) 2 b.c. (Feb 25) Bluebird (USA) 125 – Stellar Empress (USA) (Star de Naskra (USA)) [2004 6g 6g 7g⁶ 6f 7s Nov 6] 47,000F, 75,000Y: good-topped colt: closely related to useful 1999 2-y-o 6f winner Delphinius (by Dolphin Street) and half-brother to 2 winners: dam Irish 2-y-o 5f/6f winner: modest maiden: form only on first and third starts: not sure to stay beyond 7f. *B. A. McMahon* **61**

SUPREMACY 5 ch.g. Vettori (IRE) 119 – High Tern 93 (High Line 125) [2004 110: 16.2s 12g⁴ 16m 14s⁴ 14.6f 16.2m³ Sep 26] sturdy gelding: useful performer: some respectable efforts in 2004, including when 2¼ lengths fourth to Eastern Breeze in minor event at Newmarket second start and 5 lengths third to Defining in listed race at Ascot: stays 2m: acts on firm going: often races prominently: sold 36,000 gns, sent to Saudi Arabia. *Sir Michael Stoute* **109**

SUPREME SALUTATION 8 ch.g. Most Welcome 131 – Cardinal Press (Sharrood (USA) 124) [2004 81§, a72§: f7g f8s* p7g* 8.3g 8.1v* p8g⁴ 10d* 8.3g 8.3d⁴ 10g 8g Sep 20] leggy, sparely-made gelding: fairly useful performer: better than ever in 2004, winning claimers at Southwell and Lingfield (left D. Chapman) in March and handicaps at Warwick and Nottingham in May: effective at 7f to 11f: acts on all-weather and any turf going: tried blinkered: sometimes slowly away. *D. K. Ivory* **90 a79**

SURDOUE 4 b.g. Bishop of Cashel 122 – Chatter's Princess (Cadeaux Genereux 131) [2004 75: f12g f11g² f12s⁴ f12g² f9.4s 8v 8.3g p12m p9.5d p10g p12.2g⁴ p12.2g⁶ f8g³ Dec 28] leggy gelding: fair handicapper: below form after fourth start: stays easy 1½m: acts on fibresand and good to firm going: tried in cheekpieces. *P. Howling* **70 d**

SURE FUTURE 8 b.g. Kylian (USA) – Lady Ever-So-Sure 80 (Malicious) [2004 12v³ May 10] short-backed gelding: maiden: poor form on only start on Flat since 2000: stays 1½m: acts on soft and good to firm going: blinkered at 4 yrs: modest chaser/fair hurdler. *R. M. Stronge* **33**

SURFACE TO AIR 3 b.g. Samraan (USA) 117 – Travelling Lady (Almoojid 69) [2004 p10g 10m 10f 10m p16g⁵ Oct 13] modest maiden: stays 2m: slowly away first/third outings. *Mrs P. N. Dutfield* **57**

SURF THE NET 3 b.f. Cape Cross (IRE) 129 – On The Tide 72 (Slip Anchor 136) [2004 91p: 7g³ 8f 7d 7m³ 8.3m⁴ 8m 7d 7d Oct 30] rather leggy, close-coupled filly: fairly useful performer: below form in cheekpieces/visor last 3 starts: stays 1m: acts on good to firm going. *R. Hannon* **83**

SURREPTITIOUS 3 ch.f. Machiavellian (USA) 123 – Nadma (USA) 82 (Northern Dancer) [2004 7g⁸ 8d³ 7s Aug 29] close-coupled filly: has a moderate, quick action: half-sister to several winners, including UAE 1m to 2m winner Nadeem (by Zafonic) and 7f/1m winner Noisette (by Nashwan), both useful: dam, 1¼m winner, closely related to top-class American filly Sabin and half-sister to Musidora winner Fatah Flare: modest form: won maiden at Newmarket in July: tailed off in handicap final start: stays 1m: acts on good to soft going: sent to Australia. *D. R. Loder* **70**

SURREY DOWNS GIRL 2 ch.f. (May 8) Lake Coniston (IRE) 131 – Kingston Girl (Formidable (USA) 125) [2004 f5g Jun 17] 900Y: third foal: dam unraced: 33/1, last in maiden at Southwell. *T. T. Clement* **–**

SURWAKI (USA) 2 b.c. (Apr 5) Miswaki (USA) 124 – Quinella (Generous (IRE) 139) [2004 7.1m³ 7.1d² 7f Sep 10] €90,000Y: close-coupled colt: fourth foal: dam, ran twice, half-sister to very smart Princess Royal Stakes winner Banket and Ribblesdale Stakes winner Gull Nook, herself dam of top-class 1¼m/1½m performer Pentire: fairly useful form in maidens at Sandown first 2 starts: stiff task in Champagne Stakes at Doncaster (sweating, tended to hang/carry head awkwardly): will stay at least 1m. *C. G. Cox* **83**

SUSIEDIL (IRE) 3 b.f. Mujadil (USA) 119 – Don't Take Me (IRE) (Don't Forget Me 127) [2004 65: 8d 8.3s 8.2m⁶ 8f⁶ 7m 7m 8d p8.6g Oct 25] close-coupled filly: poor performer: stays 1m: acts on firm going: tried visored: sometimes hangs. *P. W. Harris* **49**

SUSPICIOUS MINDS 3 b.f. Anabaa (USA) 130 – Paloma Bay (IRE) 92 (Alzao (USA) 117) [2004 p8g 8m 8m 10d Jun 23] 30,000Y: leggy filly: fourth foal: half-sister to 11f/1½m winner Spectroscope (by Spectrum): dam 2-y-o 6f winner who stayed 1m: little form in maidens: sold 10,000 gns and joined J. Mullins. *G. C. Bravery* **–**

SUSSEX STYLE (IRE) 3 b.g. Desert Style (IRE) 121 – Anita's Love (IRE) 53 (Anita's Prince 126) [2004 –: p6g p8g p6g⁶ p6g 5.3m⁶ 6m 6m 6f⁵ Jun 14] poor maiden: stays 6f: tongue tied last 2 starts. *R. M. Flower* **49**

SUSTAINABLE STYLE (FR) 3 gr.f. Formal Gold (CAN) 132 – Spectacular Face –
(USA) (Spectacular Bid (USA)) [2004 8s 10d 8.3g 8d Nov 5] €40,000Y: half-sister to
several winners abroad, including useful French 9f (at 2 yrs) to 13f winner Polities (by
Atticus): dam, French 2-y-o 6f winner, later useful at 1m/successful in USA: no form:
trained first 2 starts by X. Thomas Demeaulte in France: tried blinkered. *L. A. Dace*

SUTURIA 2 b.f. (Jan 17) Cadeaux Genereux 131 – Cream Tease 99 (Pursuit of Love 55
124) [2004 p7g p8.6g p6g p6g⁶ Dec 29] 31,000F, 40,000Y, 27,000 2-y-o: first foal: dam,
7f winner (including at 2 yrs), half-sister to smart milers Enharmonic and Soprano:
modest maiden: left N. Chance before final outing: best effort at 8.6f. *W. R. Muir*

SUVARI 3 b.f. Indian Ridge 123 – Falconera (IRE) (Tirol 127) [2004 p7g⁶ 8m Apr 12] 49
40,000F: second foal: dam French 1¼m winner: better effort in maidens on debut.
G. C. Bravery

SVENSON 3 ch.c. Dancing Spree (USA) – Bella Bambola (IRE) 42 (Tate Gallery –
(USA) 117) [2004 –: f6g f7g 10m 8m 8g 7.9m 6g⁶ 6d Oct 15] strong, workmanlike colt:
little form: left A. Berry after reappearance. *J. S. Wainwright*

SWAGGER STICK (USA) 3 gr. or ro.c. Cozzene (USA) – Regal State (USA) 122 95
(Affirmed (USA)) [2004 73: 10d* 11.8d* 12m⁶ 11.9g 10g 10.3s⁶ 10.3m 10d 12d⁵ Oct 14]
tall, leggy colt: useful handicapper: won twice at Leicester in April: some creditable
efforts after, sixth to Admiral in King George V Stakes at Royal Ascot next time: should
stay beyond 1½m: acts on soft and good to firm going: often on toes: blinkered (seemed
not to apply himself) last 2 outings: sold 220,000 gns, sent to USA. *J. L. Dunlop*

SWAHILI DANCER (USA) 3 b.c. Swain (IRE) 134 – Bella Ballerina 90 (Sadler's –
Wells (USA) 132) [2004 10m⁵ Jun 1] 7/1 and green, well-held fifth in maiden at Redcar:
sold 10,000 gns. *L. M. Cumani*

SWAIN DAVIS 4 b.f. Swain (IRE) 134 – Exclusive Davis (USA) (Our Native (USA)) –
[2004 72: f14g Jun 16] tall, leggy, quite good-topped filly: fair handicapper: tailed off
only start at 4 yrs. *D. J. S. ffrench Davis*

SWAINSON (USA) 3 br.c. Swain (IRE) 134 – Lyphard's Delta (USA) 112 (Lyphard 86
(USA) 132) [2004 p10g³ 10s⁴ p10g* 9.9g² 10d 12m⁵ 12g Jul 28] $42,000Y, resold
38,000Y: sturdy colt: half-brother to several winners in USA, notably smart Grade 1 9f
winner Indy Five Hundred (by A P Indy): dam 1m to 11f winner, including Nassau
Stakes: fairly useful performer: won maiden at Lingfield in May: good short-head second
to Gavroche in handicap at Goodwood: below form after, running as if amiss next 2
starts: should stay 1½m: acts on polytrack. *P. Mitchell*

SWAINSWORLD (USA) 3 b. or br.g. Swain (IRE) 134 – Highest Dream (IRE) 77
(Highest Honor (FR) 124) [2004 7m⁴ 7f⁴ 8.5g* 8.5d Jul 3] €3,000Y: rather leggy gelding:
second foal: dam, French 2-y-o 1m winner (later successful in USA), half-sister to very
smart French/US 1m/9f performer Special Ring: fair form: won maiden at Beverley in
June: ran as if amiss final start: stays 8.5f. *T. D. Easterby*

SWALLOW FALLS (IRE) 2 b.f. (Feb 5) Lake Coniston (IRE) 131 – Common Cause 52
87 (Polish Patriot (USA) 128) [2004 5.1g 7m⁵ 6s Sep 24] €2,200Y: compact filly: first
foal: dam, 11.5f/1½m winner, out of half-sister to smart French/US performer up to 1¼m
Kirkwall: form in maidens only when fifth at Chester: needs to settle to stay 1m.
D. McCain

SWALLOW SENORA (IRE) 2 b.f. (Jan 25) Entrepreneur 123 – Sangra (USA) 69 58 p
(El Gran Senor (USA) 136) [2004 7d Oct 30] lightly-made filly: first foal: dam, maiden,
might have proved best up to 7f: 33/1, eleventh in maiden at Newmarket, showing up well
for long way: sure to do better. *P. W. Chapple-Hyam*

SWAN NEBULA (USA) 2 b. or br.f. (Feb 15) Seeking The Gold (USA) – Bright 92
Tiara (USA) (Chief's Crown (USA)) [2004 6m³ 7m⁵ 6f* 6.5m* 6s Sep 18] angular filly:
fifth foal: sister to Japanese 6f to 9f stakes winner Gold Tiara and half-sister to winners in
USA by Relaunch and Storm Boot: dam, 2-y-o 6f winner in USA, sister to US Grade 1
winner Chief Honcho: fairly useful performer: won maiden at Newbury in August and
nursery at Doncaster (beat Indiena by 1¾ lengths) in September: stays 6.5f: acts on firm
going, ran no sort of race on soft: tongue tied. *Saeed bin Suroor*

SWEENEY TODD (IRE) 2 ch.g. (Apr 7) Raise A Grand (IRE) 114 – Optional 74 43
(Prince Sabo 123) [2004 7f⁶ 7g Aug 11] poor form in maiden at Brighton (slowly away)
and claimer at Salisbury. *J. G. Portman*

SWEEP THE BOARD (IRE) 3 b.g. Fasliyev (USA) 120 – Fun Board (FR) (Sau- 53
marez 132) [2004 –: 9f 8.3g⁶ 12.1m Sep 15] modest maiden: barely stays 1m: carried
head awkwardly penultimate start. *A. P. Jarvis*

SWEET AT HEART (IRE) 3 b.f. Catrail (USA) 123 – Lost Shadow (First Trump –
118) [2004 f8g 12.3d 12g⁵ Sep 7] IR 900F, €11,000Y: sturdy filly: first foal: dam unraced:
well held in maidens. *P. A. Blockley*

SWEET AZ 4 b.f. Averti (IRE) 117 – Yen Haven (USA) (Lear Fan (USA) 130) [2004 –
–: 8.1g 6.1m 10.2g Jul 11] of little account nowadays. *S. C. Burrough*

SWEET CANDO (IRE) 3 b. or br.f. Royal Applause 124 – Fizzygig 71 (Efisio 120) 72 §
[2004 66: 6d⁶ 7f 5d² 5g 5d⁵ 6g 5.2g 5d³ 5d 6s 5d⁶ Oct 11] fair handicapper: effective at 5f/
6f: acts on fibresand, good to firm and good to soft going: wore cheekpieces after second
start: sometimes slowly away: unreliable. *Miss L. A. Perratt*

SWEET COINCIDENCE 2 b.f. (Mar 1) Mujahid (USA) 125 – Sibilant (Selkirk 69
(USA) 129) [2004 6g³ 6.1s 6.1m* Jul 23] third foal: half-sister to 3-y-o Sable 'N Silk:
dam, ran 3 times in France, out of half-sister to very smart 7f to 1¼m performer in Britain/
USA Tinners Way: some improvement to win maiden at Chepstow: will stay 7f: acts on
good to firm going. *I. A. Wood*

SWEET CORAL (FR) 4 b.f. Pennekamp (USA) 130 – Sweet Contralto 89 (Danehill 45
(USA) 126) [2004 –: f7g f8g⁴ f8s f6s f7s Feb 29] good-topped filly: poor maiden: stays
1m: raced only on fibresand/going firmer than good: tried blinkered/in cheekpieces.
B. S. Rothwell

SWEETEST REVENGE (IRE) 3 ch.f. Daggers Drawn (USA) 114 – Joza 90 65
(Marju (IRE) 127) [2004 69, a78: 6m p6g⁶ 5g p7g³ p6g³ 5.7m p5.1g p6g p6g p6g p6g⁶ a75
Dec 27] leggy filly: fair performer: probably stays easy 7f: acts on polytrack and firm
going: tried in cheekpieces: usually races up with pace. *M. D. I. Usher*

SWEET INDULGENCE (IRE) 3 ch.c. Inchinor 119 – Silent Indulgence (USA) 86
(Woodman (USA) 126) [2004 84p: 8m 8g 8g⁵ 8m³ 8g⁴ 9.9d Aug 28] strong, lengthy colt:
has scope: fairly useful performer: best effort in 2004 when 5¼ lengths third to Welcome
Stranger in minor event at Kempton in July, racing freely/carrying head awkwardly:
stays 1m: acts on good to firm going, probably on good to soft: sold 27,000 gns.
Dr J. D. Scargill

SWEET LORRAINE 2 b.f. (Mar 31) Dashing Blade 117 – Royal Future (IRE) 67
(Royal Academy (USA) 130) [2004 7m² 7g Aug 13] 3,000Y: fifth foal: sister to a winner
in Slovakia and half-sister to 2 winners in Germany, including useful 9f/10.5f winner
Royal Fire (by Bin Ajwaad): dam unraced half-sister to very smart miler Where Or
When: fair form in maidens at Folkestone: should stay 1m. *T. G. Mills*

SWEET MARGUERITE 2 b.f. (Feb 21) Diktat 126 – Margaret's Gift 101 (Beveled 54
(USA)) [2004 6m⁵ 6f⁴ 5g⁴ 6.1s⁶ 7f 6d 5g 6m Oct 10] 10,000Y: quite good-topped
filly: sixth foal: half-sister to 2 winners, including 2000 2-y-o 5f winner Game N Gifted
(by Mind Games), later 7f/1m winner in Italy: dam 5f (at 2 yrs)/6f winner: modest
maiden: better at 6f than 5f: acts on firm and soft ground: sold 2,600 gns, sent to Sweden.
T. D. Easterby

SWEET NAMIBIA (IRE) 2 ch.f. (Apr 1) Namid 128 – Almond Flower (IRE) (Alzao 64
(USA) 117) [2004 p6g³ p6d³ Oct 30] 130,000Y: half-sister to several winners, including
useful 7f winner Macaroon and fairly useful 2002 2-y-o 7f/7.5f winner Bakewell Tart
(both by Tagula): dam Irish 2-y-o 5f winner: third in maidens at Wolverhampton, slowly
away on final occasion: likely to prove best at 5f/6f. *J. W. Hills*

SWEET PICKLE 3 b.f. Piccolo 121 – Sweet Wilhelmina 87 (Indian Ridge 123) [2004 68
75: 6f² 6.1f⁴ 6f⁶ 6m 7.1d 6.1m⁶ p5.1g p7m² p6g Dec 20] leggy filly: fair performer: stays
7f: acts on polytrack and firm going. *D. J. Coakley*

SWEET POTATO (IRE) 2 b.f. (Mar 25) Monashee Mountain (USA) 115 – Villa- 53
franca (IRE) (In The Wings 128) [2004 6g⁵ 7m 7d Oct 15] rather unfurnished filly:
second foal: dam, French 1¼m winner, out of half-sister to Arlington Million winner Mill
Native and high-class 1m/9f performer French Stress: modest form in maidens/claimer at
Redcar: stays 7f: acts on good to firm going. *T. D. Barron*

SWEET REFLECTION (IRE) 4 b.f. Victory Note (USA) 120 – Shining Creek –
(CAN) (Bering 136) [2004 –: p10g p10g p12g⁵ 9g Jun 4] little form: tried tongue tied.
W. J. Musson

SWEET REPLY 3 ch.f. Opening Verse (USA) 126 – Sweet Revival 41 (Claude Monet 70
(USA) 121) [2004 84: 7g 8m⁵ 7f* 7.1f 7.5g 7g⁵ 7g 7d p10g Oct 31] tall, angular filly: fair
performer: won minor event at Brighton in June: stays 7f: acts on firm going: tried in
cheekpieces. *I. A. Wood*

SWEET REPOSE (USA) 3 b.f. Gulch (USA) – Bint Baladee 101 (Nashwan (USA) –
135) [2004 –p: 8g 9.9g May 18] soundly beaten in maidens. *E. A. L. Dunlop*

Prix Vermeille Fouquet's Barriere, Longchamp—in a race opened up to four-year-olds for the first time, Sweet Stream enjoys a clear run up the rail and wins from Royal Fantasy (No.4), Pride (No.3) and Vallera (No.9), all the principals returned at odds of more than 25/1

SWEET ROYALE 2 b.f. (Jan 29) Royal Applause 124 – Sorara (Aragon 118) [2004 **79**
5m² 5g* 5g⁵ 5.2g Aug 14] 15,000Y: third foal: dam once-raced half-sister to dam of very
smart miler Revoque: fair performer: won maiden at Ayr in June by 6 lengths: ran as if
amiss after: needs to settle to stay 6f. *Miss L. A. Perratt*

SWEET SIOUX 2 ch.f. (Feb 5) Halling (USA) 133 – Mohican Girl 112 (Dancing Brave **–**
(USA) 140) [2004 p7.1d Nov 3] 40,000Y: fifth foal: half-sister to 3 winners, including 1m
winner Estimation and 10-y-o The Prince: dam, 1¼m/11.4f winner, half-sister to Yorkshire Oaks winners Untold and Sally Brown: 10/1, slowly away when well held in maiden
at Wolverhampton. *P. W. Harris*

SWEET STREAM (ITY) 4 b.f. Shantou (USA) 125 – Snug Dinner (IRE) (Jareer **117**
(USA) 115) [2004 105: 10d 12.5d³ 12d* 12d³ 12m⁴ Dec 12] tall filly: third foal: half-
sister to winners in Italy by College Chapel and Petardia: dam Italian 9f/1¼m winner:
smart performer: trained by F. Contu in Italy at 2 yrs, winning maiden and minor event
at Milan: progressed well in 2003, winning handicap at Saint-Cloud and listed race at
Maisons-Laffitte: improved good deal further to win Prix Vermeille Fouquet's Barriere at
Longchamp in September by ½ length from Royal Fantasy, staying on strongly to lead
close home: respectable fourth (promoted to third) behind Shirocco in Gran Premio del
Jockey Club Italiano at Milan and to Phoenix Reach in Hong Kong Vase at Sha Tin
(beaten 2¾ lengths) last 2 starts: stays 1½m: has won on heavy ground, ran respectably
on good to firm: blinkered on reappearance: has worn tongue tie. *J. E. Hammond, France*

SWEET TALKING GIRL 4 b.f. Bin Ajwaad (IRE) 119 – Arabellajill 97 (Aragon **–**
118) [2004 –: 6.1g 6.1s 6m 6g 5.3d Aug 24] small filly: of little account. *J. M. Bradley*

SWEETWATER (GER) 4 b.f. Goofalik (USA) 118 – Safrane (GER) (Mister Rock's **75 d**
(GER)) [2004 10.5d³ 10s 15g⁶ 12.5s⁶ 12g² p12.2g⁶ 12d p16.5g p12.2g p12.2g³ p12m
p13.9g² p12.2g³ Dec 27] second foal: sister to German 8.5f winner Sunday Kid: dam
German 1m to 9.5f winner: fair form before leaving left M. Rolland in France after fifth
start at 4 yrs, then showed more temperament than ability over hurdles for M. Pipe: just
modest form back on Flat later in 2004: stays 15f: acts on polytrack, heavy and good to
firm going: visored/blinkered last 4 starts. *Mrs Stef Liddiard*

SWELL LAD 2 b.g. (Feb 1) Sadler's Wells (USA) 132 – Lydara (USA) (Alydar **70 §**
(USA)) [2004 7f 7.1m 7g⁶ 8f² 8m 8.3d Oct 4] big, strong, rangy gelding: has scope: sixth
foal: closely related to 2 winners around 7f by Danzig, including useful Sporting Lad:
dam winning sprinter in USA: fair maiden: second in nursery at Bath, best effort: stays
1m: acts on firm going: blinkered at Bath and final start (gelded after latter): unreliable.
P. F. I. Cole

SWELLMOVA 5 b.g. Sadler's Wells (USA) 132 – Supamova (USA) 88 (Seattle Slew **70**
(USA)) [2004 10g² 12m* 12g⁶ Jul 8] fair handicapper: missed 2003: won handicap at
Newmarket in June: stays 1½m: acts on soft and good to firm going. *J. R. Boyle*

SWIFT ALCHEMIST 4 b.f. Fleetwood (IRE) 107 – Pure Gold 88 (Dilum (USA) **65**
115) [2004 78: 8.1d 8.1g 7.1v³ p8d 7g 10.3g 11.6g 12s 10g* 10m 11.7g p12g Nov 13] tall,
rather angular filly: fair handicapper: won at Redcar in August: ran as if amiss all starts

after (reportedly broke blood vessel final one): stays 1¼m: acts on polytrack, soft and good to firm going: wore cheekpieces last 6 outings. *Mrs H. Sweeting*

SWIFT DAME (IRE)   2 b.f. (Feb 14) Montjeu (IRE) 137 – Velvet Appeal (IRE) 101   **60**
(Petorius 117) [2004 7g p7g⁵ 6.1m 5.1s Oct 19] 27,000F, 45,000Y: strong, well-made filly: fourth foal: half-sister to 5-y-o Craiova and 3-y-o Nephetriti Way: dam Irish 1m winner: modest maiden: stays 7f: best effort on polytrack: tends to hang left. *R. Hannon*

SWIFT OSCAR   2 b.c. (Mar 11) Mark of Esteem (IRE) 137 – Surf Bird (Shareef   **73**
Dancer (USA) 135) [2004 6f⁶ 7d p6g⁴ p7.1g³ p8.6g* Dec 17] 6,000Y: close-coupled, useful-looking colt: has a quick action: half-brother to several winners, including useful 1m (at 2 yrs) and 1¾m winner Baffin Bay (by Bustino) and fairly useful 1m (at 2 yrs)/9f winner Epic Stand (by Presidium): dam, ran 3 times, out of Oaks third Britannia's Rule: fair performer: won maiden at Wolverhampton by 1½ lengths from Missella: stays 8.6f: acts on polytrack. *J. W. Hills*

SWIFT SAILING (USA)   3 b.c. Storm Cat (USA) – Saytarra (USA) 111 (Seeking   **72**
The Gold (USA)) [2004 84: 7.9d 7m 7m 10g² 10f⁴ Jun 29] rather leggy colt: fair handicapper: stays 1¼m: acts on firm and good to soft going: tried blinkered: sold 12,500 gns. *B. W. Hills*

SWIFT SAILOR   3 gr.g. Slip Anchor 136 – New Wind (GER) (Windwurf (GER))   **91 p**
[2004 10.2g³ 12d* Oct 17] 13,000 3-y-o: third foal: half-brother to useful 8.5f (at 2 yrs) and 1½m winner Stunning Force (by Ezzoud): dam, German 6f (at 2 yrs) and 1m winner, half-sister to useful German 1¼m performer No Dancer: fairly useful form in maidens in October, winning at Musselburgh by 7 lengths from Day One, leading 3f out and still looking green (gelded after): will stay 1¾m: type to progress further at 4 yrs. *M. Johnston*

Team Valor's "Sweet Stream"

*Blue Square Chester Rated Stakes (Handicap), Chester—Swift Tango quickens past pacesetter Midas Way,
with Hambleden (No.6), Albanov (checks), Desert Quest (No.8) and Delsarte completing the field*

SWIFT TANGO (IRE) 4 b.g. Desert Prince (IRE) 130 – Ballet Society (FR) **114**
(Sadler's Wells (USA) 132) [2004 94: p10g* a10f 10m² 8g³ 10v⁴ 12m* 12m² 12f³ 11.9g⁶
10m⁴ 12g³ 13.4s* 14s² 12f³ 16.2m² Sep 26] good-topped gelding: smart performer: progressed well in 2004, winning handicaps at Lingfield in January, Newbury in May and
Chester (listed rated stakes, by 1½ lengths from Midas Way) in August: placed in listed
races after, 2¼ lengths third to Distinction at Doncaster and 2½ lengths second to Defining at Ascot last 2 starts: barely stays 2m: acts on polytrack, firm and soft going: has worn
cheekpieces/visor: held up: reliable. *E. A. L. Dunlop*

SWINBROOK (USA) 3 ch.g. Stravinsky (USA) 133 – Dance Diane (USA) (Affirmed **84**
(USA)) [2004 88p: 6g 6m 6g² 5f* 6g 6g Sep 29] workmanlike gelding: fairly useful
performer: landed odds in maiden at Folkestone in June: easily best effort at 3 yrs when
head second to Kind in minor event at Kempton: will stay 7f: raced only on good going or
firmer. *J. A. R. Toller*

SWINDON (USA) 2 b.f. (Mar 18) Kingmambo (USA) 125 – Dance Design (IRE) 119 **49 p**
(Sadler's Wells (USA) 132) [2004 f8g⁶ Nov 22] third foal: half-sister to 1½m winner
Sindy (by A P Indy) and 11.5f/1½m winner Science Academy (by Silver Hawk): dam
Irish 7f (at 2 yrs) to 1½m (Irish Oaks) winner: 12/1, sixth in minor event at Southwell:
will stay at least 1¼m: should improve. *P. F. I. Cole*

SWING WEST (USA) 10 b.g. Gone West (USA) – Danlu (USA) (Danzig (USA)) **–**
[2004 –: f16.2g⁴ f14g Apr 2] quite good-topped gelding: modest in 1998: ran without
success in Ireland next 5 seasons: well held on return to Britain. *A. E. Jones*

SWING WING 5 b.g. In The Wings 128 – Swift Spring (FR) 56 (Bluebird (USA) 125) **114**
[2004 113: 15.5g⁵ 18.7d 15m* 16.1s² 15.9d⁴ 12.5v⁴ Aug 29] good-topped gelding: has a
quick, fluent action: smart performer: won listed race at Milan in May: in frame after in
Northumberland Plate (Handicap) at Newcastle (head second to Mirjan), Lonsdale Cup
at York (fourth behind First Charter) and Grand Prix de Deauville (7 lengths fourth to
Cherry Mix): stays 2m: acts on heavy and good to firm going: tried blinkered at 4 yrs:
races prominently. *P. F. I. Cole*

SWINTON 3 gr.g. Grey Desire 115 – Portite Sophie 54 (Doulab (USA) 115) [2004 7v **–**
8g Sep 6] well held in maidens at Newcastle: gelded after final start. *M. Brittain*

SWORDS 2 b.c. (Jan 29) Vettori (IRE) 119 – Pomorie (IRE) 67§ (Be My Guest (USA) **73**
126) [2004 8m 8g 10g⁵ 8d Nov 5] 3,500Y: sturdy colt: sixth foal: half-brother to German
6.5f and 1¼m winner My Little Princess (by Celtic Swing) and 1¼m and 15f winner
Habitual Dancer (by Groom Dancer): dam, 1¼m winner (also successful over hurdles),
became untrustworthy: fair maiden: best effort when fifth in minor event at Leicester:
will be suited by at least 1½m. *D. J. Daly*

SWORDS AT DAWN (IRE) 3 ch.f. Daggers Drawn (USA) 114 – Caraway 53 (Shadeed (USA) 135) [2004 9.2d Aug 23] €10,000Y, 800 3-y-o: second foal: dam, Irish
maiden who stayed 1½m, half-sister to 5-y-o Vanderlin: 33/1, tailed off in maiden at
Hamilton. *J. Barclay*

SWORN TO SECRECY 3 ch.f. Prince Sabo 123 – Polly's Teahouse 68 (Shack (USA) **63 ?** 118) [2004 62: p6g 6.1g f8.5g 8.3m 7.1f 6m⁶ 5g 7m 7m Aug 8] modest maiden: should stay 7f: acts on good to firm going: tried blinkered. *S. Kirk*

SWYNFORD PLEASURE 8 b.m. Reprimand 122 – Pleasuring 68 (Good Times **57** (ITY)) [2004 68, a–: 12m² 12m⁵ 12m⁴ 11.9g³ Jul 1] strong mare: modest handicapper: stays 1¾m: acts on firm and soft going: tried blinkered earlier in career: has given trouble at start (refused to enter stall on 3 occasions) and banned from racing from stalls on Flat until mid-Jan 2005. *J. Hetherton*

SYBILL 4 b.f. Danzig Connection (USA) – Stock Pile 39 (Galveston 114) [2004 f7g⁵ **–** f7g Apr 15] third reported foal: dam maiden who stayed 1m: well held in maidens. *J. W. Unett*

SYDNEYROUGHDIAMOND 2 b.g. (Mar 3) Whittingham (IRE) 104 – November **62** Song (Scorpio (FR) 127) [2004 6s 7.2s⁵ 6g 6s 6d p6g⁵ p7.1g⁶ Dec 31] big, workmanlike gelding: fifth foal: dam unraced: modest maiden: needs to settle to stay beyond 6f: acts on polytrack and soft going. *M. Mullineaux*

SYDNEY STAR 3 b.f. Machiavellian (USA) 123 – Sena Desert 89 (Green Desert **82** (USA) 127) [2004 91p: 7d* 8m 7d p8g Nov 20] neat filly: fairly useful performer, lightly raced: won maiden at Chester in May: creditable efforts last 2 starts: stays easy 1m: acts on polytrack and good to soft going. *B. W. Hills*

SYLVAN TWISTER 5 br.g. First Trump 118 – Storm Party (IRE) (Bluebird (USA) **43** 125) [2004 –: p10g⁵ p10g⁵ p13g⁵ p12g³ May 13] poor maiden: stays 13f: raced mainly on polytrack. *P. Mitchell*

SYLVA ROYAL (IRE) 3 gr.f. Royal Applause 124 – Trim Star (Terimon 124) [2004 **62** p7g⁴ 6m⁴ 6g⁶ f6s p7g* 8s⁴ p8g³ p8.6g Nov 27] €24,000Y, resold 37,000Y: first foal: dam lightly-raced close relative to smart performer up to 14.6f Startino: modest performer: won banded race at Lingfield in September: stays easy 1m: best efforts on polytrack: withdrawn after bolting to start intended second outing. *C. E. Brittain*

SYLVATICUS (IRE) 3 b.g. Shinko Forest (IRE) – Calamity Kate (IRE) 67 (Fairy **–** King (USA)) [2004 7g 8.3f Jul 26] 66/1, tailed off in maidens: gelded after. *R. Hannon*

SYSTEMATIC 5 b.h. Rainbow Quest (USA) 134 – Sensation 114 (Soviet Star (USA) **118** 128) [2004 118: 12g³ 12m² 13.4d* 12m 12f⁵ 12m⁶ Jul 7] leggy, good-topped horse: smart performer: good 1¼ lengths second to Gamut in Jockey Club Stakes at Newmarket prior to winning Betdaq Ormonde Stakes at Chester in May by 1¾ lengths from The Whistling Teal: respectable fifth behind Doyen in Hardwicke Stakes at Royal Ascot, best effort after: stayed 13.4f: acted on soft and good to firm going: visored (folded tamely) final 4-y-o outing: sometimes difficult at start: to stand at East Burrow Farm, Devon, fee £2,500, Oct 1st. *M. Johnston*

Betdaq Ormonde Stakes, Chester—Systematic keeps on too strongly for The Whistling Teal

SZEROKI BOR (POL) 5 b.g. In Camera (IRE) 110 – Szuana (POL) (Five Star Camp – (USA)) [2004 f16.2s Mar 13] Polish-bred gelding: successful 6 times from 6f to 2m in Poland: tailed off in Wolverhampton handicap in March: won over hurdles in June. *M. Pitman*

T

TAAKEED 2 b.c. (May 9) Mark of Esteem (IRE) 137 – Walimu (IRE) 82 (Top Ville – p 129) [2004 7d Oct 30] sturdy colt: seventh foal: brother to 1000 Guineas winner Ameerat, 7f winner at 2 yrs, and half-brother to 2 winners, including smart miler in UAE Walmooh (by In The Wings): dam 1m to 1½m winner: 20/1, well held in maiden at Newmarket: likely to do better. *M. A. Jarvis*

TAAQAAH 3 ch.g. Grand Lodge (USA) 125 – Belle Ile (USA) 67 (Diesis 133) [2004 88 72: 7f² 8m² 6g 7.1m² a6.5f Dec 18] sturdy gelding: has a quick action: fairly useful maiden: well below form last 3 starts: left M. Tregoning before final outing: should prove at least as effective at 7f as 1m: raced only on good going or firmer on turf. *D. J. Selva-ratnam, UAE*

TABARKA (GER) 3 b.f. Big Shuffle (USA) 122 – Tirana (GER) (Esclavo (FR)) [2004 ? 61: f5s⁵ f6g 8.5g 7g 7g⁵ 8.5d³ 8.5g 9s 9v³ 9s³ 8v a7.5g³ a9.5g² Dec 31] modest maiden: sold from P. Blockley after second start: stays 9.5f: acts on heavy and good to firm ground, and on sand: blinkered final 2-y-o start. *J. H. Smith, Holland*

TABLEAU (USA) 3 ch.c. Marquetry (USA) 121 – Model Bride (USA) (Blushing 92 Groom (FR) 131) [2004 68p: 7g³ 8m* 8g* 10.3s 8d Aug 30] tall, quite good-topped colt: fairly useful performer: won maiden at Leicester in May and handicap at Newmarket in July: probably best up to 1m: acts on good to firm ground: sold 42,000 gns. *B. W. Hills*

TABOOR (IRE) 6 b.g. Mujadil (USA) 119 – Christoph's Girl 50 (Efisio 120) [2004 64 65, a76: p5g p6g p5g f5g⁵ f5s 5d 5.3m⁵ 5v 5g² 5m 5.3g⁶ 5m 5.3f* 5d² 5.7g 5.3s⁵ p6g² a69 p5.1g⁴ f6g p6m Dec 22] heavy-topped gelding: fair handicapper: won at Brighton in August: best at 5f/easy 6f: acts on all-weather, firm and good to soft ground: wears blinkers/hood nowadays: often tongue tied. *J. W. Payne*

TACA D'OLI (FR) 5 br.m. Octagonal (NZ) 126 – Marie de Fontenoy (FR) (Lightning – (FR) 129) [2004 p10g Feb 28] sparely-made mare: modest form in 3 maidens in 2002: well held in handicap at Lingfield on return. *E. J. O'Neill*

TADAWUL (USA) 3 b.f. Diesis 133 – Barakat 93 (Bustino 136) [2004 8g 8.5m* 8d⁶ 73 10s Oct 15] well-made filly: half-sister to several winners, including useful 1¼m performer Ta Awun (by Housebuster) and fairly useful 1½m winner Mumaris (by Capote): dam, winner around 1¾m, half-sister to Ibn Bey and Roseate Tern: fair performer: trained by A. Stewart on debut: won maiden at Epsom in September: should stay 1¼m (raced freely at trip final start): sold 34,000 gns. *E. F. Vaughan*

TAFAAHUM (USA) 3 b.g. Erhaab (USA) 127 – Makadir (USA) (Woodman (USA) – 126) [2004 88: 8m 8m⁶ Jun 17] good-bodied gelding: poor mover: fairly useful performer at 2 yrs: tailed off both starts in 2004: sold 2,500 gns, joined B. Llewellyn and gelded. *M. Johnston*

TAFFRAIL 6 b.g. Slip Anchor 136 – Tizona (Pharly (FR) 130) [2004 –: 14.1g⁵ 11.8m – Aug 8] lengthy, good sort: useful performer at best: mostly well held since 2002: has worn cheekpieces. *D. Burchell*

TAG TEAM (IRE) 3 ch.g. Tagula (IRE) 116 – Okay Baby (IRE) 67 (Treasure Kay 78 114) [2004 –p: p5g* p6g* p5g³ 6d 5g⁵ 5.7f* 6m³ p6g² 5s p6g f5g² p5g p6g³ Dec 30] tall a89 gelding: fairly useful performer: won maiden and handicap at Lingfield in February and handicap at Bath in May: left A. Balding after ninth start: best at 5f: acts on all-weather and firm going: races up with pace. *D. Flood*

TAGULA BAY (IRE) 2 b.f. (Feb 16) Tagula (IRE) 116 – Nezool Almatar (IRE) (Last 63 Tycoon 131) [2004 5v² 6m³ 5m⁵ May 28] €8,500Y: quite good-topped filly: fourth foal: half-sister to winners in Scandinavia by Eagle Eyed and Titus Livius: dam, ran twice, out of half-sister to Oh So Sharp: modest form in maidens: likely to prove best at 5f/6f. *T. D. Easterby*

TAGULA BLUE (IRE) 4 b.g. Tagula (IRE) 116 – Palace Blue (IRE) (Dara Monarch 80 § 128) [2004 94: 8v 7.1s 8m 10.5g³ 8g⁶ 8.2g⁵ 9v⁴ 7.9m 8.1d* 8g³ 10v⁵ p8.6g Dec 27] good-bodied gelding: has a round action: fairly useful handicapper: won at Warwick in September: best form around 1m: acts on heavy ground: tried visored/blinkered, often tongue tied: usually slowly away (unseated leaving stall on reappearance, refused to race third outing): not one to trust. *J. A. Glover*

TAGULA SUNRISE (IRE)   2 ch.f. (Feb 22) Tagula (IRE) 116 – Lady From Limerick (IRE) 61 (Rainbows For Life (CAN)) [2004 5f² 5m² 5m² 5.2m 6d³ 5f² 6f* 6s* Sep 24] 35,000Y: good-topped filly: fluent mover: third foal: sister to fairly useful 2002 2-y-o 7f/1m winner Pacific Paddy and half-sister to 3-y-o Lord Links: dam sprint maiden: fairly useful performer: won sales race at Doncaster and nursery at Haydock in September: should stay 7f: acts on firm and soft ground: usually held up. *R. A. Fahey*   **88**

TAHIRAH   4 b.f. Green Desert (USA) 127 – Kismah 111 (Machiavellian (USA) 123) [2004 99: 6m 7m 7m 7f 8m 7m 7m³ 7s p8g² p10g p8g² Dec 18] smallish, close-coupled filly: useful performer: placed in listed races at Ascot (to Badminton) and Lingfield (length second to Miss George) and minor event on latter course (unlucky neck second to Lygeton Lad): stays easy 1¼m: acts on polytrack, good to firm and good to soft ground, possibly not on soft: often gets behind. *R. Guest*   **96**

TAHLAL (IRE)   2 b.c. (Mar 31) Dr Fong (USA) 128 – Chatterberry 67 (Aragon 118) [2004 5f⁵ 6d 7.1g 7m⁴ p8g Oct 25] workmanlike colt: modest maiden: stays 7f: acts on good to firm going: in cheekpieces final start. *Mrs A. Duffield*   **54**

TAHREEB (FR)   3 ch.c. Indian Ridge 123 – Native Twine 114 (Be My Native (USA) 122) [2004 108: 7g⁴ 10g² 8m* 8.8m* 8.1d⁴ 8g³ Aug 1] compact, attractive colt: smart performer: won listed race at Kempton (by a neck from Leicester Square) in May and Grosser Preis der Wirtschaft at Dortmund (by 1¼ lengths from Anolitas) in June: good third to Pepperstorm in Globetrotter-Meile at Cologne final outing: barely stays 1¼m: acts on good to soft ground, probably on firm: usually races prominently: joined D. Selvaratnam in UAE. *M. P. Tregoning*   **112**

Sheikh Ahmed Al Maktoum's "Tahreeb"

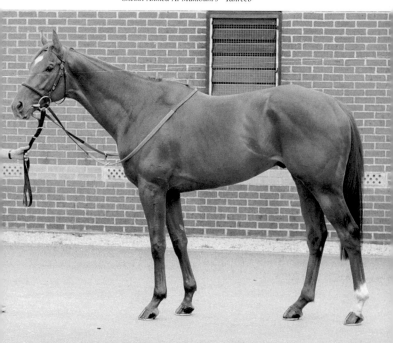

TAHRIR (IRE) 2 gr.f. (May 13) Linamix (FR) 127 – Miss Sacha (IRE) 107 (Last **83** Tycoon 131) [2004 7g² 7g³ Sep 17] 350,000Y: rather leggy, lengthy filly: fifth foal: sister to 2 winners in France, including useful 6.5f (at 2 yrs) to 7.5f winner Mister Charm (later successful in Hong Kong) and half-sister to smart French 1m/9f winner Mister Sacha (by Tiger Hill): dam Irish 5f winner who stayed 1m: fairly useful form in minor events at Kempton and Newbury: will stay at least 1m. *B. W. Hills*

TAHTHEEB (IRE) 3 b.f. Muhtarram (USA) 125 – Mihnah (IRE) 87 (Lahib (USA) **105 p** 129) [2004 9f* 9.9g² 10d⁴ Oct 14] tall, good sort: second foal: dam, 6f (at 2 yrs) and 1m winner, half-sister to smart performer up to 14.6f Ranin: won maiden at Newbury in August, edging left: best effort when 1¾ lengths second to New Morning in listed race at Salisbury later in month: not discredited when fourth to Sundrop in steadily-run similar event at Newmarket: will be suited by 1½m+: smart performer in the making. *M. P. Tregoning*

TAILI 3 b.f. Taipan (IRE) 124 – Doubtfire 71 (Jalmood (USA) 126) [2004 –: 8m 12g⁶ **–** 12d Oct 17] deep-girthed filly: no sign of ability: tried blinkered. *D. A. Nolan*

TAIPAN TOMMY (IRE) 2 ch.g. (Feb 11) Shinko Forest (IRE) – Adieu Cherie (IRE) **56** (Bustino 136) [2004 5s⁶ 6m⁶ 6g 5g⁶ 6m⁶ p6g⁶ p6g⁶ p7g Dec 29] modest maiden: stays 6f: acts on polytrack. *S. Dow*

TAIYO 4 b.f. Tagula (IRE) 116 – Tharwa (IRE) 63 (Last Tycoon 131) [2004 59: p7g⁶ **57** p8g⁵ f9.4g⁴ f9.4s⁴ f8.5s p8g 8.2m 8f 8m* 8m⁵ 7g⁶ p7g Sep 18] well-made filly: modest performer: won selling handicap at Yarmouth in August: has form at 9.4f, but probably best up to 1m: raced only on all-weather and good ground or firmer: tried visored (below form). *J. W. Payne*

TAJAATHUB (USA) 2 ch.f. (Apr 22) Aljabr (USA) 125 – Tajannub (USA) 104 **78 p** (Dixieland Band (USA)) [2004 7g⁴ Oct 11] sturdy filly: half-sister to 7-y-o Nashaab and winner in USA by Thunder Gulch: dam 6f (Princess Margaret Stakes at 2 yrs)/7f winner: 14/1, length fourth to Corcoran in maiden at Leicester, no extra late on: should do better. *E. F. Vaughan*

TAJ INDIA (USA) 2 b. or br.c. (Apr 7) Gone West (USA) – Circle of Gold (IRE) 110 **69** (Royal Academy (USA) 130) [2004 6m⁵ 7.1m Sep 6] $175,000Y: compact colt: second foal: dam, 2-y-o 6f/7f (Prestige Stakes) winner who stayed 8.5f, sister to useful dam of 3-y-o Rule of Law: fair form in newcomers race at Ascot and maiden at Warwick: should stay 1m: sold 5,500 gns. *M. Johnston*

TAKE A BOW 3 b.c. Royal Applause 124 – Giant Nipper (Nashwan (USA) 135) [2004 **113** 83: 8.3d* 8d* 7m⁴ 7.1m* 7.9s² 8.1g² 9g² 8d³ Oct 30] rather leggy, lengthy colt: progressed into a smart performer: won maiden at Windsor in June and handicaps at Salisbury in July and Sandown in August: good efforts after, including when beaten neck by Spanish Don in Cambridgeshire at Newmarket and third to demoted Babodana in listed race there last 2 starts: stays 9f: acts on soft and good to firm going: genuine and consistent. *P. R. Chamings*

TAKE A MILE (IRE) 2 ch.c. (Mar 16) Inchinor 119 – Bu Hagab (IRE) (Royal Acad- **72** emy (USA) 130) [2004 p8.6g³ p8g Dec 18] €28,000F, 32,000Y: fifth foal: half-brother to winners up to 1¼m abroad by In The Wings and Robellino: dam unraced: better effort when 2½ lengths third of 11 to Linda's Colin in maiden at Wolverhampton: should stay at least 1¼m. *B. J. Meehan*

TAKE GOOD TIME (IRE) 4 ch.g. Among Men (USA) 124 – Bold Motion (Anshan **42** 119) [2004 46: 5s⁴ 6m Aug 2] poor maiden: left John Berry after reappearance: should be suited by 7f+. *T. Cooper, Ireland*

TAKE IT THERE 2 ch.f. (Jan 24) Cadeaux Genereux 131 – Feel Free (IRE) 86 (Gen- **57** erous (IRE) 139) [2004 7g 7m Jul 16] lengthy filly: second foal: half-sister to winner in Sweden by Highest Honor: dam, 9f/1¼m winner, half-sister to smart but untrustworthy performer up to 1¼m Intimate Guest: modest form in maidens at Kempton and Newbury: should stay 1m. *R. Hannon*

TAKEMETOYOURHEART 2 ch.f. (Mar 16) Zaha (CAN) 106 – Mother Molly **–** (USA) 78 (Irish River (FR) 131) [2004 p6g 8.3m Sep 27] first foal: dam temperamental maiden: well held in maidens at Lingfield and Windsor. *I. A. Wood*

TAKES TUTU (USA) 5 b.g. Afternoon Deelites (USA) 122 – Lady Affirmed (USA) **83** (Affirmed (USA)) [2004 94§: 7.1d 8d 10g 8m² 9.2g² 8.3m⁵ 7.9g⁵ 7m 7m² 7m 8m 8f³ 9g⁵ 8.5g p7g⁴ Oct 13] tall, useful-looking gelding: fairly useful performer: effective at 7f to easy 10.5f: acts on all-weather and firm going, possibly not on softer than good: usually wears headgear: sometimes races freely/idles: sold 5,200 gns. *K. R. Burke*

TAKE THE PLUNGE 2 br.f. (Apr 19) Benny The Dip (USA) 127 – Pearly River 72 **46 p** (Elegant Air 119) [2004 p7.1g p7.1g Dec 31] half-sister to several winners, including useful 2003 2-y-o 5f winner Ballykeating (by Danzero) and 4-y-o River Falcon: dam, 7f (at 2 yrs) and 1½m winner, out of half-sister to Roseate Tern and Ibn Bey: poor form in maidens at Wolverhampton: should stay at least 1m: should do better. *L. G. Cottrell*

TAKHLEED (USA) 2 b.c. (Jan 29) Stravinsky (USA) 133 – Bold Threat (CAN) **80** (Bold Ruckus (USA)) [2004 p7g5 8g5 Sep 17] $220,000Y: lengthy colt: sixth foal: half-brother to winner in Canada by Regal Classic: dam Canadian 2-y-o 5.5f winner: fifth in minor events at Lingfield and Newbury, fairly useful form behind Merchant in latter: not sure to stay beyond 1m. *M. P. Tregoning*

TAKHMIN (IRE) 2 b.c. (Apr 17) Almutawakel 126 – Magdalene (FR) (College **86** Chapel 122) [2004 6f 6g2 7m3 8s6 Sep 18] 46,000F, 60,000Y: second foal: half-brother to French 2003 2-y-o 5f winner Nasaria (by Starborough): dam, French maiden, half-sister to 7-y-o Cut Quartz: fairly useful maiden: placed at Thirsk and Ascot: stays 7f: acts on good to firm going. *M. Johnston*

TAK'S GIRL 2 ch.f. (Apr 15) Takhlid (USA) 91 – Sans Rivale 57 (Elmaamul (USA) **–** 125) [2004 5d 5g 6g 7m Jul 21] neat filly: first foal: dam 5f winner, including seller at 2 yrs: probably of little account. *P. T. Midgley*

TALBOT AVENUE 6 b.g. Puissance 110 – Dancing Daughter 79 (Dance In Time **111** (CAN)) [2004 99: 5.1d 5m5 6m5 5m 5d2 5.1g2 6f 6.1m2 5s 5m2 5m2 5.2g 6g2 Oct 9] compact gelding: smart performer: improved in 2004, running particularly well at York when eighth to Bahamian Pirate in Nunthorpe on ninth start and ½-length second to Jonny Ebeneezer in valuable handicap final one: effective at 5f/easy 6f: acts on firm and soft ground: sometimes bandaged on joints: often wanders (would have probably won a Leicester tenth start but for edging right). *M. Mullineaux*

TALCEN GWYN (IRE) 2 b.g. (May 2) Fayruz 116 – Cheerful Knight (IRE) (Mac's **82** Imp (USA) 116) [2004 5.3f4 5.3f* 5.1g4 5m 6m4 5s5 6m 5g4 5g* 5m 5d4 5.2s Oct 27] €4,500Y, 8,000 2-y-o: workmanlike gelding: fourth living foal: brother to 4-y-o Arabian Knight: dam Irish maiden: fairly useful performer: won maiden at Brighton in June and nursery at Ripon in September: well below form last 3 starts: barely stays easy 6f: acts on firm going: usually races prominently: sometimes hangs right. *M. F. Harris*

TALE OF DUBAI (USA) 2 ch.f. (Feb 27) Tale of The Cat (USA) 113 – Jamaican Me **–** Smile (USA) (Sovereign Dancer (USA)) [2004 8m Sep 21] $75,000Y: third foal: dam unraced: 33/1, well held in maiden at Newmarket: sent to USA. *Saeed bin Suroor*

TALE OF THE TIGER 3 ch.g. Bijou d'Inde 127 – La Belle Dominique 76 (Domin- **–** ion 132) [2004 –: p6g f8s5 Jan 29] soundly beaten in maidens: visored in 2004. *Julian Poulton*

TALK TO MOJO 7 ch.g. Deploy 131 – Balnaha 67 (Lomond (USA) 128) [2004 12g **–** Mar 25] big, lengthy gelding: fair form to win 1½m maiden on only outing at 3 yrs (suffered injury afterwards and gelded): well held from starts since. *J. H. M. Gosden*

TALLDARK'N'ANDSOME 5 b.g. Efisio 120 – Fleur du Val (Valiyar 129) [2004 **–** 84: 10.4g 12s Nov 6] workmanlike gelding: fairly useful handicapper at 4 yrs: well held in 2004: blinkered last 5 starts. *N. P. Littmoden*

TALLY (IRE) 4 ch.g. Tagula (IRE) 116 – Sally Chase 101 (Sallust 134) [2004 68: f7g **71** p6g f6g 10.2g 8.1v6 7.1m 5f3 6g* 6m2 6m 5g 5g2 5.1d4 5d4 5d3 5f 6g f6m* 5.1g4 6g 6d f6f6 5m 6g p6g 5g f8g6 Dec 11] close-coupled gelding: fair handicapper: left A. Berry after second outing: won at Newcastle in June and Southwell in July: effective at 5f/6f: acts on all-weather, firm and good to soft going. *M. J. Polglase*

TALWANDI (IRE) 3 b.c. Alhaarth (IRE) 126 – Talwara (USA) (Diesis 133) [2004 **85** 10d6 11.5g3 11.9m* May 23] compact colt: sixth foal: half-brother to French/US 1m/1¼m winner Tavildaran (by Darshaan): dam lightly-raced maiden half-sister to Dante winner Torjoun out of sister to Prix du Jockey Club winner Top Ville: fairly useful form: won maiden at Brighton in May by head from Sunny Lady, flashing tail repeatedly: stays 1½m: sold 15,000 gns in July, sent to Sweden. *Sir Michael Stoute*

TAMALAIN (USA) 2 b.f. (Mar 12) Royal Academy (USA) 130 – Woodland Orchid **80** (IRE) 64 (Woodman (USA) 126) [2004 7g5 8m4 Sep 21] 200,000Y: tall filly: fourth foal: sister to 6-y-o Cd Europe and half-sister to French 1m winner Cedar Sea (by Persian

Bold): dam, lightly raced in Ireland, half-sister to 7-y-o D'Anjou: much better effort in maidens (edgy and very green on debut) when fourth to Titian Time at Newmarket: not sure to stay beyond 1m. *Mrs A. J. Perrett*

TAMARELLA (IRE) 4 b.f. Tamarisk (IRE) 127 – Miss Siham (IRE) 59 (Green **52 d** Forest (USA) 134) [2004 75d, a–: p6g p6g p6g 5g⁵ 5m 5m 6m 6.1g 5.1f⁵ 5.3f 6m 6d p5.1g Oct 25] smallish filly: modest performer: on the downgrade: effective at 5f/6f: acts on polytrack and firm going: usually visored/blinkered after fifth start. *G. G. Margarson*

TAMARILLO 3 gr.f. Daylami (IRE) 138 – Up And About 77 (Barathea (IRE) 127) **105** [2004 98: a8f⁵ a8.5f² a9f* a9f⁶ 11m⁵ 16.2m 10.2g a10g Dec 9] compact filly: useful performer: won UAE Oaks at Nad Al Sheba in March by 1½ lengths from Festive Style: not discredited in UAE Derby and Oaks d'Italia next 2 outings: well below form after (trained by M. Bell in Europe fifth to seventh outings): should stay 1½m (failed to stay 2m in Queen's Vase at Royal Ascot): acts on dirt and firm going: tongue tied first 2 outings in 2004. *M. Al Kurdi, UAE*

TAMARINA (IRE) 3 ch.f. Foxhound (USA) 103 – Tamasriya (IRE) (Doyoun 124) **–** [2004 56: f9.4g f7f p12g 9.9g 8f 10.2m⁵ 10s⁵ 8.1m Sep 9] leggy, angular filly: maiden: well held at 3 yrs: tried in cheekpieces/blinkers (looked reluctant). *N. E. Berry*

TAMATAVE (IRE) 2 b.c. (Apr 2) Darshaan 133 – Manuetti (IRE) 86 (Sadler's Wells **81** (USA) 132) [2004 8d⁶ 8m⁴ 8m² 8s⁴ Oct 19] quite attractive colt: has a quick action: fourth foal: half-brother to useful 1¼m/1½m winner Manoubi (by Doyoun): dam, maiden who would have been suited by 1½m, out of Prix Saint-Alary winner Rosefinch: fairly useful maiden: best efforts at Goodwood and Newcastle second and third starts: bred to be suited by 1¼m/1½m: acts on good to firm ground: tongue tied. *Saeed bin Suroor*

TAMINOULA (IRE) 3 b.f. Tagula (IRE) 116 – Taormina (IRE) (Ela-Mana-Mou **79** 132) [2004 82: 9g 8s 8.1g⁶ 8f 10g p9.5g p10g⁶ p8g⁶ p10g⁴ p13g⁴ Dec 29] strong filly: **a74** fair handicapper: stays 13f: acts on polytrack and firm going, well beaten on soft: tried blinkered. *Mrs A. J. Perrett*

TAMORA 2 ch.f. (Apr 9) Dr Fong (USA) 128 – Tahara (IRE) (Caerleon (USA) 132) **61** [2004 6g⁶ 6f 7.5m p8.6g³ 8d Oct 18] 10,000Y: fourth foal: half-sister to winning sprinters abroad by Pennekamp and Zamindar: dam ran twice: modest maiden: barely stays 8.6f: acts on polytrack, probably on good to firm going. *A. P. Jarvis*

TANAFFUS 4 ch.g. Cadeaux Genereux 131 – El Rabab (USA) 70 (Roberto (USA) **–** 131) [2004 –: p6g f8g f7g 6d 6d Jul 17] strong, well-made gelding: fair maiden at 2 yrs: no form since: blinkered final start. *D. W. Chapman*

TANAJI 5 b.m. Marju (IRE) 127 – Hamsaat (IRE) 80 (Sadler's Wells (USA) 132) **–** [2004 76: p10g Jan 21] strong, lengthy mare: fair performer at best: well beaten only run on Flat in 2004: effective blinkered or not: sold 5,500 gns. *P. R. Webber*

TANCRED ARMS 8 b.m. Clantime 101 – Mischievous Miss 73 (Niniski (USA) 125) **45 §** [2004 51§, a–§: 7g 7.2g⁴ 7.2g 7g 7d⁴ 8f Sep 16] lengthy mare: poor performer: best **a– §** around 7f: acts on fibresand and probably any turf going: sometimes visored: unreliable. *D. W. Barker*

TANCRED IMP 3 b.f. Atraf 116 – Tancred Mischief 44 (Northern State (USA) 91) **44** [2004 49: 8s 8s⁵ 9.2g³ 12.3g 12.1m 10d³ 10.9m Sep 6] sturdy filly: poor maiden: stays 1¼m: acts on good to firm and good to soft going. *D. W. Barker*

TANCRED MISS 5 b.m. Presidium 124 – Mischievous Miss 73 (Niniski (USA) 125) **45** [2004 50d: f7g* 7.2g f8m² 7d 8s Aug 30] smallish, leggy mare: poor handicapper: won at Southwell in June: stays easy 1m: acts on fibresand, no recent form on turf: usually races prominently. *D. W. Barker*

TANCRED TIMES 9 ch.m. Clantime 101 – Mischievous Miss 73 (Niniski (USA) **70** 125) [2004 70: f5g 6g⁴ 6g2 5m 6m³ 5g³ 6m* 6m⁴ 6f* 6m³ 6g² 6.1d Sep 17] small mare: fair performer: won seller at Catterick and claimer at York (left D. Barker) in July: best at 5f/easy 6f: acts on fibresand, firm and soft going: tried blinkered: usually races up with pace: tough and consistent. *C. F. Wall*

TANDAVA (IRE) 6 ch.g. Indian Ridge 123 – Kashka (USA) (The Minstrel (CAN) **77** 135) [2004 84: 14g* 13g 14m⁵ 13g⁴ 16.1v 13f⁵ Jul 16] lengthy gelding: fair handicapper: won at Musselburgh in April: stays 17f: acts on firm and soft going, below form on heavy: tried visored, wore cheekpieces last 4 starts: sometimes slowly away: has taken good hold: none too consistent. *I. Semple*

TANFORAN 2 b.g. (Mar 9) Mujahid (USA) 125 – Florentynna Bay 61 (Aragon 118) **71** [2004 f7g p7.1g³ Dec 31] 8,000Y: half-brother to several winners, including smart 1m winner Sunstreak (by Primo Dominie) and 3-y-o Carry On Doc: dam, 2-y-o 5f winner, half-sister to smart sprinter Superpower: much better effort in maidens (jockey received 14-day ban for failing to obtain best possible placing on debut) when 2¼ lengths third to Sir Nod at Wolverhampton, making much of running: needs to settle to stay 1m. *Mrs J. R. Ramsden*

TANGIBLE   2 b.f. (Feb 23) Hernando (FR) 127 – Trinity Reef 80 (Bustino 136) [2004   **59 p** 8s p7g⁵ p8.6d Nov 5] 40,000F: third foal: dam, 1½m winner, sister to smart 1¼m/1½m performer Talented: modest form in maidens: favourite, not knocked about final start: should do better at 1¼m/1½m. *Sir Mark Prescott*

TANGO STEP (IRE)   4 b.c. Sesaro (USA) 81 – Leitrim Lodge (IRE) 64 (Classic   **51** Music (USA)) [2004 57: 8v 8.5d 9f³ 8m 9d 8g 8m a6g² 5s² p7m* Dec 15] modest performer: won banded race at Lingfield in December: effective at 5f to 1m: acts on polytrack, firm and soft going: tried blinkered/in cheekpieces. *Bernard Lawlor, Ireland*

TANIA DI SCEPTRE (ITY)   4 b.f. King's Theatre (IRE) 128 – Timarete (ITY) – (Green Dancer (USA) 132) [2004 14g 9.5d 16v⁴ 14d p16.5g Nov 6] half-sister to several winners abroad, notably smart French performer up to 1½m Thompson Rouge (by Machiavellian): dam Italian maiden half-sister to Derby Italiano winner Tisserand: trained by P. Bary at 3 yrs, best effort when second in 11f maiden in French Provinces: little form since, including in cheekpieces. *Ms Caroline Hutchinson, Ireland*

TANK (IRE)   3 ch.g. Woodborough (USA) 112 – Fiddes (IRE) 52 (Alzao (USA) 117) – [2004 9.9g Sep 30] 33/1, well held after slow start in maiden at Goodwood. *Miss S. West*

TANMEYA   3 gr.f. Linamix (FR) 127 – Ta Awun (USA) 99 (Housebuster (USA)) – [2004 10d Jun 23] fourth foal: half-sister to fairly useful 7.5f (in UAE) to 1¼m winner Shafeeq (by Halling): dam, 1¼m winner, out of half-sister to Ibn Bey and Roseate Tern: 16/1, well held in maiden at Kempton: sold 18,000 gns in December. *A. C. Stewart*

TANNE BLIXEN   3 b.f. Great Dane (IRE) 122 – Night Transaction 59 (Tina's Pet 121) – [2004 f6g 7.1g 6m p6g Oct 18] seventh living foal: half-sister to 3 winners, including fairly useful 6f winner (including at 2 yrs) Silca Key Silca (by Polar Falcon) and 7-y-o Prime Recreation: dam 1m winner: soundly beaten in maidens. *P. S. Felgate*

TANNING   2 b.f. (Jan 29) Atraf 116 – Gerundive (USA) (Twilight Agenda (USA) 126)   **60** [2004 5.1m⁶ 5.1m² 6m³ 7m p7.1g⁵ Dec 15] 2,200Y: first foal: dam unraced out of half-sister to Derby winner Benny The Dip: modest maiden: placed at Bath and Folkestone: should stay 7f. *H. Morrison*

TANNOOR (USA)   3 b.c. Miswaki (USA) 124 – Iolani 59 (Alzao (USA) 117) [2004   **74** 79p: 11.1g³ 10m* 10f⁵ 9g 9.7m⁶ 8d⁴ a7g⁵ Dec 10] well-made colt: fair performer: landed odds in maiden at Ayr in May: left M. Jarvis and off 4 months before final outing: likely to prove best at 1m/1¼m: acts on firm and soft going: ran respectably in cheekpieces penultimate start (also sweating/on edge): usually races freely up with pace. *D. J. Selvaratnam, UAE*

TANTE ROSE (IRE)   4 b.f. Barathea (IRE) 127 – My Branch 111 (Distant Rela-   **126** tive 128) [2004 111: 6d* 6d* 6g* Sep 4]

In the wake of the upgraded programme of races for older fillies and mares, instituted in 2004 and aimed at encouraging more fillies to remain in training beyond three, the so-called 'weaker sex' experienced an upturn in fortunes in open competition at the top level in Britain. The victories of Russian Rhythm in the Lockinge Stakes at Newbury, Frizzante in the July Cup at Newmarket, Soviet Song in the Sussex Stakes at Goodwood and Tante Rose in the Sprint Cup at Haydock doubled the number of successes achieved by fillies in Group 1 races open to all-comers in the five previous seasons combined. Their successes also added to the season as a whole, though the narrow margin of victory for the four fillies, in each case receiving weight from colts or geldings in second, re-opened the debate on the validity of the sex allowance in championship events—on paper, neither Russian Rhythm, Frizzante, Soviet Song nor Tante Rose was the best horse at the weights on the day.

Rather than fillies and mares being at an unfair advantage, however, there is plenty of evidence to suggest that the standard 3-lb allowance is less than they deserve, making the performances of Russian Rhythm, Frizzante, Soviet Song and Tante Rose look all the better. Looking at the two-year-old horse population as a whole, about forty-five percent of which in the last ten years have been fillies, the median Timeform ratings in that period suggest a difference of 8 lb between colts and fillies. Among the three-year-olds, at the top end of the scale, in the last ten years, the average Oaks winner has been similarly inferior to the average Derby winner, as has the average winner of the One Thousand Guineas to the average winner of the Two Thousand, and, on average as well, the tenth-best three-year-old filly of the year has been around 6 lb inferior to the tenth-best colt. Whether or not, for some reason, the divisions become less marked among the cream of the older horses is an interesting debate, but, for her part, Tante Rose's short-head victory over Somnus in the Stanleybet Sprint Cup at Haydock showed her to be the best sprinting filly since Lochsong won a second consecutive Prix de l'Abbaye at Long-champ in 1994, the style of her success enough to make her the equal of any sprinter in Europe in 2004, albeit in an ordinary year.

It is unlikely that the upgraded programme of fillies' and mares' events at pattern level was uppermost in the minds of Tante Rose's new connections in keeping her in training at four. No provision was made for a Group 1 or Group 2 event restricted to fillies at short of a mile in 2004, when the Group 3 Cuisine de France Summer Stakes over six furlongs at York in July remained the only pattern race restricted to fillies and mares over sprint distances in Britain. Tante Rose started favourite in a field of nine at York after a comfortable success in June on her first outing for Roger Charlton in a listed event for fillies over the same trip at Haydock, where she had beaten the three-year-old Ruby Rocket by a neck under a confident ride, despite looking as though the run would do her good. With the outing behind her, Tante Rose looked in magnificent shape at York and showed improved form, sailing through inside the final furlong to beat Ruby Rocket again, this time by two and a half lengths, with Lochridge third and Ringmoor Down fourth.

Tante Rose was among the five-day entries for the Prix Maurice de Gheest at Deauville in August, but wasn't seen out again before Haydock in September. The title of champion sprinter has often been a foregone conclusion by September, but, with the July Cup and the Nunthorpe having taken less winning than usual in 2004, no dominant performer had emerged by the time of Haydock's Stanleybet Sprint Cup, which attracted its largest field since the race was inaugurated in 1966. Among nineteen runners, Nunthorpe third One Cool Cat started favourite at 6/4, with Frizzante at 13/2 and Somnus, the winner twelve months earlier, at 7/1 after his success in the Prix Maurice de Gheest. Tante Rose was next best at 10/1. With Steve Drowne on stable-companion Patavellian, Richard Hughes took over on Tante Rose from Michael Hills, who had substituted for Drowne at York. Again patiently ridden, Tante Rose travelled strongly in mid-field but was shuffled back a couple of places over two furlongs out. She still had plenty to do as Somnus and Patavellian went on together over a furlong from home, but Tante Rose stormed

Cuisine de France Summer Stakes, York—
Tante Rose is clear of Ruby Rocket and fourth-placed Ringmoor Down

*Stanleybet Sprint Cup, Haydock—Tante Rose improves again
and gains easily her biggest win, quickening really well to get up and beat Somnus (near side);
the winner's stable-companion Patavellian (virtually obscured) is third*

through to deny Somnus on the line with Patavellian three quarters of a length away, the winner value more than the bare result and rated accordingly. By all accounts, Tante Rose and Patavellian had spent the two previous weeks in isolation due to coughing in the yard, and the race was a triumph for their trainer, who has had few peers with his handling of sprinters of late. Tante Rose was his second Sprint Cup winner after Tamarisk in 1998, since when, among other races, he has also won the Cork And Orrery Stakes (now the Golden Jubilee) with Harmonic Way and the Prix de l'Abbaye with Patavellian, both also successful in the Stewards' Cup.

Tante Rose changed hands as part of the dispersal sale which followed the withdrawal of her owner/breeder Wafic Said from racing in 2003, making 350,000 guineas at the Newmarket December Sales, where her purchase was managed by renowned bloodstock agent Joss Collins, who died in 2004, the same year another of his buys, Bachelor Duke, won the Irish Two Thousand Guineas. Wafic Said, who sponsored the Guineas meeting for several years through his company Sagitta, raised over 4,000,000 guineas from his bloodstock interests sold at Newmarket alone, including 1,050,000 guineas for Oaks winner Lady Carla. Said sold his other British classic winner, the outstanding filly Bosra Sham, successful in the One Thousand Guineas, privately in America. The Newmarket draft also yielded 450,000 guineas for Tante Rose's half-sister Bay Tree (by Daylami), a two-year-old winner over six and seven furlongs who enhanced her value by finishing third in the Musidora Stakes at York in May. Their dam My Branch's two previous foals to race were winners, Future Flight (by Polar Falcon) over seven furlongs and Rosie's Posy (by Suave Dancer) over an extended five furlongs at two. Trained by Barry Hills, My Branch won at five to six and a half furlongs as a two-year-old, when she was also second in the Cheveley Park Stakes, and she reached the frame in the One Thousand Guineas at Newmarket and the Curragh as a three-year-old, also winning a listed race over seven furlongs.

Mr B. E. Nielsen's "Tante Rose"

Tante Rose (IRE) (b.f. 2000)	Barathea (IRE) (b 1990)	Sadler's Wells (b 1981)	Northern Dancer Fairy Bridge
		Brocade (b 1981)	Habitat Canton Silk
	My Branch (b 1993)	Distant Relative (b 1986)	Habitat Royal Sister II
		Pay The Bank (b 1987)	High Top Zebra Grass

Tante Rose was also trained by Barry Hills at two and three, winning a maiden over six furlongs as a juvenile and the Dubai Duty Free Stakes (Fred Darling) at Newbury over seven furlongs on her reappearance at three. A free-going sort, best held up and with a good turn of foot, she was never tried at a mile again after finishing down the field in the Guineas at Newmarket. Indeed, Tante Rose showed so much speed at four that she would probably have been as effective at five furlongs as six, the trip at which she showed her best form. Unraced on extremes of ground, her tendency to be on her toes and slowly away was much less in evidence in the latest season when she was a credit to those who worked with her at Beckhampton. A big, good-bodied filly, the type to carry some condition, she took the eye with her well-being each time she ran. She is reportedly to be covered by Daylami. *R. Charlton*

TANTIEN 2 b.f. (Apr 5) Diktat 126 – Tahilla 112 (Moorestyle 137) [2004 5d^5 6s^4 5m **53** 6m^5 7f 7g Sep 14] rather leggy filly: closely related to winners abroad by Warning and Bishop of Cashel, and half-sister to 3 winners, including fairly useful 6f (including at 2 yrs) winner Pluck (by Never So Bold): dam, 6f (at 2 yrs) and 1m winner, half-sister to very smart sprinter Piccolo: modest maiden: well held in nurseries last 2 starts: seems to stay 6f. *John A. Harris*

TANTRIC 5 br.g. Greensmith 121 – Petunia (GER) (Chief Singer 131) [2004 75: f7s **66** f7g 7m³ 6.9g 7m 6g³ 5m³ 5d⁴ 5d³ Aug 17] quite attractive gelding: fair performer: effective at 5f to 9.4f: acts on fibresand, firm and good to soft going: blinkered twice in 2003: has raced freely/found little: usually races prominently. *J. O'Reilly*

TANZANITE (IRE) 2 b.f. (Jan 30) Revoque (IRE) 122 – Resume (IRE) 69 (Lahib **77** (USA) 129) [2004 6d 6.1g⁶ 8v³ Oct 23] €4,500Y, resold 11,000Y: close-coupled, quite good-topped filly: second foal: sister to 1m/9f winner Rookwith: dam Irish 1½m and 2m winner: easily best effort when third to Spear Thistle in maiden at Newbury, travelling smoothly long way: stays 1m: acts on heavy going. *D. W. P. Arbuthnot*

TANZANI (USA) 2 b.c. (Feb 13) Giant's Causeway (USA) 132 – Aunt Pearl (USA) **79** (Seattle Slew (USA)) [2004 6m⁴ 6m Jul 16] good-topped colt: half-brother to several winners, including 3-y-o Pearl of Love and useful 1998 2-y-o 7f winner Kalidasa (by Nureyev): dam won up to 7f at 4 yrs in USA: fair form in maiden at Yarmouth and listed race at Newbury: should stay 1m. *C. E. Brittain*

TAP 7 b.g. Emarati (USA) 74 – Pubby 73 (Doctor Wall 107) [2004 63: 7.1g* 7d* 7m⁵ **64** 7.5d Aug 28] angular gelding: modest handicapper: won at Musselburgh in April and Thirsk in May: best around 7f nowadays: acts on fibresand, soft and good to firm ground: tried blinkered/visored/tongue tied, wore cheekpieces in 2004. *Ian Emmerson*

TAPA 2 b.f. (Jan 14) Tagula (IRE) 116 – Tweed Mill 88 (Selkirk (USA) 129) [2004 6g⁶ **50** 6d Oct 14] sturdy filly: first foal: dam 8.5f winner: never dangerous in maiden at Goodwood (modest form) and sales race at Newmarket. *A. M. Balding*

TAPAU (IRE) 6 b.m. Nicolotte 118 – Urtica (IRE) (Cyrano de Bergerac 120) [2004 **–** 82: 5s⁵ 6m 6m 7m 7m 7.1g Jul 9] lengthy mare: fairly useful at 5 yrs: well held in 2004: wore cheekpieces last 3 starts: races freely. *J. M. Bradley*

TAP DANCE CITY (USA) 7 b.h. Pleasant Tap (USA) – All Dance (USA) (Northern **125** Dancer) [2004 125: 10f* 11f* 12m 12.5f² Dec 26] big, strong horse: has a fluent, quick action: half-brother to several winners, including 7f winner Shake Town (by Caro) and very smart hurdler Ruling (by Alleged): dam, French 1m winner, half-sister to Kentucky Derby winner Winning Colors: high-class performer: winner of 11 races in Japan, notably 2003 Japan Cup at Tokyo by 9 lengths from That's The Plenty, allowed clear lead from early stage: successful in 2004 in Group 2 Kinko Sho at Chukyo (for second year running) in May and Group 1 Takarazuka Kinen at Hanshin (by 2 lengths from Silk Famous) in June: behind in Prix de l'Arc de Triomphe at Longchamp penultimate start, racing freely up with pace until straight: good ½-length second to Zenno Rob Roy in Arima Kinen at Nakayama final outing: stays 12.5f: acts on firm and good to soft going: races prominently. *S. Sasaki, Japan*

TAP DANCER (IRE) 6 b.g. Sadler's Wells (USA) 132 – Watch Out (USA) (Mr Prospector (USA)) [2004 p8g 10d Oct 2] modest winner in 2002, well beaten both starts since: blinkered once at 3 yrs: often slowly away/refuses to settle. *B. G. Powell*

TAPIOKA CITY (USA) 3 b.f. Danehill (USA) 126 – Taroob (IRE) 72 (Roberto **–** (USA) 131) [2004 10g Jul 4] €120,000Y: half-sister to 1½m winner Iffah (by Halling), later successful in USA, and 1999 2-y-o 1m winner Maraha (by Lammtarra) who stayed 1¾m, both fairly useful: dam, 2-y-o 9f winner who stayed 1¾m, sister to Celestial Storm and half-sister to dam of Sakhee: last of 7 in minor event at Milan. *L. M. Cumani*

TAPLEON 3 br.f. Danzig Connection (USA) – Reem El Fala (FR) (Fabulous Dancer **–** (USA) 124) [2004 –: 5s⁶ 6g f7g May 19] well beaten all starts. *C. J. Teague*

TAPPIT (IRE) 5 b.g. Mujadil (USA) 119 – Green Life 63 (Green Desert (USA) 127) **55** [2004 79: 6s 5.7g 5.3m 7.1v 6m³ 5g 5.7f⁵ 5.1f 6m 6f 6d⁶ 5.1m 6d⁵ 6d* 5.7s⁵ p6d⁶ f5g Dec 21] neat gelding: modest performer: left J. M. Bradley after seventh start: won banded race at Yarmouth in October: effective at 5f to 7f: acts on all-weather, firm and soft going: tried in cheekpieces/blinkers. *R. A. Harris*

TARABUT 2 b.f. (Feb 19) Green Desert (USA) 127 – Nabadhaat (USA) 72 (Mr Pros- **59 p** pector (USA)) [2004 7.1m 7g Oct 11] tall filly: first foal: dam, maiden who should have stayed at least 1¼m, out of Yorkshire Oaks winner Roseate Tern: better effort in maidens when seventh at Leicester on final start: should stay 1m: likely to make better 3-y-o. *E. A. L. Dunlop*

TARAGAN 2 b.f. (Apr 30) Kayf Tara 130 – Morgannwg (IRE) 86 (Simply Great (FR) **39** 122) [2004 6s 7s p7.1g Nov 13] 10,000Y: compact filly: half-sister to several winners, including 3-y-o Incursion and 7-y-o Welsh Dream: dam 7f winner: poor form in maidens: likely to stay at least 1½m. *J. J. Quinn*

TARAKALA (IRE)   3 ch.f. Dr Fong (USA) 128 – Tarakana (USA) 101 (Shahrastani   **103**
(USA) 135) [2004 100: 7v 8.7d* 12m* 12f³ 12m³ 12f² 11.9s* 14.6m⁴ 12d³ Oct 10] good-
topped filly: sixth foal: half-sister to 3 winners, including useful Irish 7f/1m winner
Tarakan (by Doyoun) and 9f winner Tarabaya (by Warning): dam Irish 9f winner who
stayed 1½m: useful performer: won minor events at Cork in April and Gowran in May
and listed race at York (by 4 lengths from Selebela) in August: creditable efforts after
when fourth to Echoes In Eternity in Park Hill Stakes at Doncaster (though looked none
too keen) and length third to Tipperary All Star in listed race at the Curragh: stays 14.6f:
acts on firm and soft going: blinkered last 4 starts: sometimes looks quirky (tended to idle
at York). *J. Oxx, Ireland*

TARANAI (IRE)   3 ch.f. Russian Revival (USA) 125 – Miss Flite (IRE) (Law Society   **53 d**
(USA) 130) [2004 55: p7g⁴ p10g p7g p8g 7.1s 7g⁴ 6v⁶ May 10] close-coupled filly: poor
maiden: stays 7f: acts on polytrack and firm ground: tried blinkered: won juvenile hurdle
in July. *B. W. Duke*

TARANAKI   6 b.h. Delta Dancer – Miss Ticklepenny (Distant Relative) 128) [2004   **91**
89: p6g 7s⁴ 7d* 6g⁴ 7s 7g* 7f⁵ 7g 7m p7d 7g³ 7s⁶ p7g⁵ 6g 7g⁴ 7d p7.1g⁶ f8g⁵ Nov 23]   **a76**
rather leggy horse: fairly useful handicapper on turf, fair on all-weather: successful in
large fields at Leicester in April and Goodwood in May: best at 6f/7f: acts on all-weather,
firm and good to soft going: blinkered (raced freely) once: tends to edge right: tough.
P. D. Cundell

TARANDOT (IRE)   3 b.f. Singspiel (IRE) 133 – Rifada 103 (Ela-Mana-Mou 132)   **81**
[2004 –: 9.9g² 11.9m* 16.2m 10m Jul 7] fairly useful performer: won maiden at York in
May: ran as if amiss final outing: should stay beyond 1½m (raced freely, but wasn't
discredited when seventh in Queen's Vase at Royal Ascot at 2m): yet to race on ground
softer than good. *G. G. Margarson*

TARAS TREASURE (IRE)   2 b.f. (Feb 19) Desert King (IRE) 129 – Oklahoma   **69**
(Shareef Dancer (USA) 135) [2004 6m² 6f⁶ 6m⁴ 7m³ 6m⁵ 6g* 7s⁵ Oct 23] €48,000Y:
stocky filly: second foal: half-sister to useful 2003 2-y-o 5f/6f winner Soonest (by Intikhab): dam unraced: fair performer: won maiden at Thirsk in September: barely stayed 7f:
acted on good to firm going: dead. *J. J. Quinn*

TARA TARA (IRE)   2 b.f. (Apr 2) Fayruz 116 – Gobolino (Don 128) [2004 5s* 5.1d   **69 +**
5f 5.1g Aug 16] €20,000Y: rather leggy filly: sister to 7.5f (at 2 yrs in Italy) and 1m
winner Don Fayruz and half-sister to 3 winners, including useful Irish performer up to
2m Bolino Star (by Stalker): dam Irish 2-y-o 7f winner: fair performer: won maiden at
Newcastle in March despite meeting trouble: respectable effort after on next start only:
should stay at least 6f: acts on soft going. *J. J. Quinn*

TARAWAN   8 ch.g. Nashwan (USA) 135 – Soluce 98 (Junius (USA) 124) [2004 80,   **–**
a74: 10.9s 9.9g Sep 29] strong, long-backed gelding: fairly useful handicapper at 7 yrs:
well held both starts in 2004: tried blinkered, usually visored. *A. M. Balding*

TARDIS   3 ch.f. Vettori (IRE) 119 – Time Lapse 62 (The Noble Player (USA) 126) [2004   **–**
63: 10f 8f 10m 8m 8f⁶ 7g 7d Oct 16] smallish, angular filly: little form in 2004: visored
final start. *M. L. W. Bell*

TARFAH (USA)   3 b.f. Kingmambo (USA) 125 – Fickle 95 (Danehill (USA) 126)   **102 p**
[2004 8m* 8.3g* 10.3s² 8m* Sep 25] first foal: dam, 1m/1¼m winner, half-sister to
useful French winner up to 13.5f Faru: useful performer: successful in maiden at Ascot in
July, minor event at Windsor (by 5 lengths) in August and listed handicap at Ascot (idled
when holding Golden Island by a head) in September: best form at 1m (raced freely at
1¼m): capable of better still. *G. A. Butler*

TARJMAN   4 b.c. Cadeaux Genereux 131 – Dodo (IRE) 90 (Alzao (USA) 117) [2004   **101 ?**
118: 8.3m 8f⁵ Jul 31] neat colt: smart performer at 3 yrs (ran as though amiss final start):
well below form in listed events in 2004: should prove at least as effective at 1m as 7f: yet
to race on extremes of going: carries head awkwardly: held up: joined D. Selvaratnam in
UAE. *A. C. Stewart*

TARKEEZ (USA)   3 b.g. Lear Fan (USA) 130 – Mt Morna (USA) (Mt Livermore   **75**
(USA)) [2004 79: 7d³ 10d 9.5g 10m³ 8g f8g Aug 19] $115,000Y: fifth foal: brother to
French 1997 2-y-o 1m winner Chateau Country and half-brother to winners in USA and
South Africa: dam, minor winner in USA, half-sister to Kentucky Derby runner-up
Casual Lies (by Lear Fan): fair maiden: left D. Weld in Ireland 25,000 gns, well beaten in
maiden at Southwell final outing: gelded after: stays 1¼m: acts on firm and good to soft
going: blinkered (well beaten) third and fifth starts. *R. M. H. Cowell*

TARKWA   5 gr.m. Doyoun 124 – Shining Fire (Kalaglow 132) [2004 51: f9.4g⁶ p10g   **47**
p8g* 9.9m 9g 8f⁵ Jun 14] strong, sturdy mare: poor performer: won banded race at

Lingfield in May: stays 1½m: acts on polytrack and firm going: none too consistent. *R. M. H. Cowell*

TAROT CARD 3 b.f. Fasliyev (USA) 120 – Well Beyond (IRE) 101 (Don't Forget Me 127) [2004 100: 8f Sep 10] lengthy filly: useful form at 2 yrs: ran poorly only outing in 2004: stud. *B. W. Hills*   –

TARRAMAN (USA) 2 b.c. (Apr 9) Fusaichi Pegasus (USA) 130 – Gerri N Jo Go (USA) (Top Command (USA)) [2004 7.9g² Oct 9] $150,000Y: big, lengthy colt: closely related/half-brother to several winners, including smart US sprinter Kamsack (by Crafty Prospector) and useful 2000 2-y-o 5f to 7f winner Freefourracing (by French Deputy), later successful in USA: dam, minor US 6f/7f stakes winner, sister to US Grade 1 9f winner Five Star Flight: 7/2, 1¼ lengths second to Daring Ransom in maiden at York, disputing lead 2f out then hanging left: not sure to stay much beyond 1m: should improve and win races. *M. Johnston*   93 p

TARTAN SPECIAL 2 b.g. (Apr 20) Fasliyev (USA) 120 – Colchica (Machiavellian (USA) 123) [2004 6g⁴ 6s⁶ 6.1m⁵ Sep 6] 27,000Y: leggy gelding: second foal: brother to winner abroad: dam French 1¼m and 11.5f winner: modest form in maidens: will probably stay 7f: best effort on soft going: gelded after final start. *K. R. Burke*   64

TARTATARTUFATA 2 b.f. (May 2) Tagula (IRE) 116 – It's So Easy 63 (Shaadi (USA) 126) [2004 5d 5s⁴ p5g 5.1g f5g² 5s 6s Oct 22] 11,000Y: good-bodied filly: fourth foal: sister to 5f (at 2 yrs)/6f winner Gemtastic: dam 7f winner: modest maiden: should stay 6f: acts on fibresand and soft going. *D. Shaw*   62

TARTIRUGA (IRE) 3 b.g. Turtle Island (IRE) 123 – Palio Flyer (Slip Anchor 136) [2004 –: 7m 9.9g 12.1g 8.3f 7.1s⁵ 8.1m⁶ 10.2s² 10d⁴ p8.6g⁵ Nov 15] workmanlike gelding: modest maiden: stays 1¼m: acts on polytrack and soft ground, probably on firm. *L. G. Cottrell*   57

TARTOUCHE 3 b.f. Pursuit of Love 124 – Megan's Flight 74 (Welsh Pageant 132) [2004 10d* 10g* 10.3m* 10.5s² Sep 25] leggy, quite good-topped filly: half-sister to 1m winner Magic Flute (by Magic Ring) and 1½m winner Capricious (by Primo Dominie): dam 1¾m/2m winner, also 2¾m winner over hurdles: useful form: won maiden at Kempton in June, handicap at Ascot in July and minor event at Doncaster (beat Mocca ½ length) in September: good ¾-length second to La Sylphide in handicap at Haydock final start, rallying: will prove at least as effective at 1½m as 1¼m: remains capable of better. *Lady Herries*   100 p

TARUSKIN (IRE) 3 b.g. Danehill Dancer (IRE) 117 – Jungle Jezebel 107 (Thatching 131) [2004 85: 7g³ 8m* 6s³ 7m 8g 8g Sep 30] tall, useful-looking gelding: fairly useful handicapper: landed odds at Brighton in April: effective at 6f (given test) to 1m: acts on firm and soft ground: sold 15,500 gns. *N. A. Callaghan*   91

TASDEED 2 ch.c. (Apr 10) Cadeaux Genereux 131 – Miss Universe (IRE) 99 (Warning 136) [2004 7s* Oct 22] 100,000Y: good-topped colt: has scope: second foal: half-brother to 3-y-o Day To Remember: dam 2-y-o 6f winner: 12/1, won maiden at Doncaster by 2½ lengths from Daniel Thomas, storming clear having been short of room and had plenty to do 2f out: will stay 1m: joined Godolphin: open to considerable improvement, and should make his mark in stronger company. *E. F. Vaughan*   93 P

TASHKIL (IRE) 3 b.g. Royal Applause 124 – Surprise Visitor (IRE) (Be My Guest (USA) 126) [2004 104: 7f 6g⁵ 7s Aug 20] lengthy, good-topped gelding: has scope: lightly raced: useful performer at 2 yrs: below form in 2004: needs to settle to stay beyond 7f: acts on good to firm ground: tongue tied final outing: has had 2 handlers/hung right: joined M. Al Muhairi in UAE. *J. H. M. Gosden*   89

TASHREEFAT (IRE) 3 b.f. Danehill (USA) 126 – Aigue 96 (High Top 131) [2004 10m³ 10g⁴ 11.7f² 14d⁴ Oct 10] 325,000F: half-sister to 3 winners, including 7f (at 2 yrs) and 1¼m winner Mezzogiorno (also third in Oaks, by Unfuwain) and winner around Rainbow Top (by Rainbow Quest), both useful: dam, 1m winner, sister to smart 1½m/13f performer Torchon: fair maiden: trained first 2 outings by A. Stewart: should prove best around 1½m: acts on firm ground, probably on good to soft: tongue tied (probably failed to stay) final start: sold 37,000 gns. *E. F. Vaughan*   70

TASHYRA (IRE) 2 b.f. (Apr 3) Tagula (IRE) 116 – Shiyra (Darshaan 133) [2004 5.7m⁴ 5.1s⁴ 6g 5.7g p6g p6g⁵ Dec 10] leggy filly: sister to useful German 2000 2-y-o 6f/7f winner Tagshira and fairly useful 2001 2-y-o 5f winner Triple Play, and half-sister to 5f/6f winner in Italy by Mac's Imp: dam Irish 1m/1¼m winner: modest maiden: stays 5.7f: acts on soft and good to firm going: blinkered (ran respectably) final start. *A. M. Balding*   59

TASK'S MUPPET (IRE) 2 ch.f. (Mar 29) Raise A Grand (IRE) 114 – Highland **56**
Crumpet 46 (First Trump 118) [2004 5.7m⁵ 5.1s⁵ 6m⁵ 5.7g 5.1v⁴ f6g f6s Nov 17]
€6,500Y: leggy filly: third foal: half-sister to 2002 2-y-o 5f winner Highness (by Titus
Livius): dam, sprint maiden (ran only at 2 yrs), half-sister to Middle Park winner Stalker:
modest maiden: stays 5.7f: acts on heavy and good to firm ground: in cheekpieces final
start. *J. A. Osborne*

TASNEEF (USA) 5 b.g. Gulch (USA) – Min Alhawa (USA) 108 (Riverman (USA) **63**
131) [2004 72: 12m 12.6f⁶ 11m⁶ 11.6f 12.6d⁴ 12m⁴ 10.1d⁵ p12m p10m* p10g* Dec 20]
lengthy, workmanlike gelding: fair performer: won 2 banded races at Lingfield in December: effective at 1¼m to 1¾m: acts on polytrack, firm and good to soft ground: tried in
blinkers, visored last 3 starts: races up with pace. *T. D. McCarthy*

TASS HEEL (IRE) 5 b.g. Danehill (USA) 126 – Mamouna (USA) 113 (Vaguely Noble **58 +**
140) [2004 72: 12g f12g⁴ Dec 16] strong, lengthy gelding: just modest performer in 2004:
stays 2m: acts on all-weather, raced mainly on good going or firmer on turf (acts on firm):
effective making running/held up. *W. Jarvis*

TATA NAKA 4 ch.f. Nashwan (USA) 135 – Overcast (IRE) 72 (Caerleon (USA) 132) **74 ?**
[2004 54?: p10g 7g 7g⁵ 6f f8g 10.1m² 11.5f² 11.9s³ 12f⁴ 10.1g* 10f 10d 10.1d Nov 5]
workmanlike filly: seemingly fair performer: 100/1, won handicap at Yarmouth in September: no comparable form: stays 1½m: acts on firm and soft going: tried tongue tied/
visored/in cheekpieces. *Mrs C. A. Dunnett*

TATWEER (IRE) 4 b.g. Among Men (USA) 124 – Sandystones 60 (Selkirk (USA) **62 §**
129) [2004 63d: 6s⁵ 5s* 5f 5d 6d 8.2g 12.1m 8.3d² f8s⁵ p8g Dec 20] good-bodied gelding: **a49 §**
has a round action: modest performer on turf, poor on all-weather: won maiden at Newcastle in May: effective at 5f to 1m: acts on all-weather and soft going: usually visored:
blinkered penultimate start: has been slowly away/looked wayward. *D. Shaw*

TAVALU (USA) 2 b.c. (Apr 9) Kingmambo (USA) 125 – Larrocha (IRE) 116 (Sadler's **45**
Wells (USA) 132) [2004 7g⁶ 8g Sep 29] fifth foal: closely related to fairly useful 1½m
winner Golden Lariat (by Mr Prospector) and half-brother to smart 9f to 1½m winner
Razkalla (by Caerleon): dam, 1¼m/1½m (latter Galtres Stakes) winner and third in Prix
Vermeille, half-sister to Ardross: easy to back, poor form in maidens at Chester and Salis-
bury (slowly away). *Saeed bin Suroor*

TAWNY WAY 4 b.f. Polar Falcon (USA) 126 – Ma Petite Anglaise 81 (Reprimand 122) **95**
[2004 92+: 10.5s⁵ 10g* 12g² 13.1d⁶ 12g 12f* 12d* 12m 12d Oct 14] tall, good-topped
filly: has a powerful, round action: useful performer: won minor events at Windsor in
April and Newmarket in July and handicap (best effort, beat Fling 1¾ lengths) at latter
track in August: stays 1½m: acts on firm and soft ground: usually races prominently.
W. Jarvis

TAWOOS (FR) 5 b.m. Rainbow Quest (USA) 134 – Queen of Dance (IRE) (Sadler's **104**
Wells (USA) 132) [2004 8g 8.8g³ 8g² 8d* a8.7g³ 12s 9.8g² 9s* 8g* 10.3s p8g* p10g⁶
p9.5g Dec 31] lengthy, angular mare: useful performer: had another good year in 2004,
winning listed races at Ovrevoll in July and September and Taby in October and handicap
at Lingfield (by head from Crafty Fancy) in November (final run for A. Lund, Norway):
effective at 1m to 1½m: acts on dirt/polytrack, soft and good to firm going: usually blinkered: held up. *R. Guest*

TAWQEET (USA) 2 ch.c. (Apr 30) Kingmambo (USA) 125 – Caerless (IRE) 77 (Caer- **78 p**
leon (USA) 132) [2004 8d 8.2v* Nov 4] 100,000Y: big, strong colt: second foal: dam,
1½m winner, half-sister to smart performers Baya (around 1¼m in France) and 6-y-o
Narrative out of sister to Triptych: much better effort in maidens when winning at
Nottingham by length from Queen's Dancer, leading 2f out: will be suited by 1¼m/1½m:
sure to progress. *J. L. Dunlop*

TAXMAN (IRE) 2 ch.g. (Apr 23) Singspiel (IRE) 133 – Love of Silver (USA) 110 **62**
(Arctic Tern (USA) 126) [2004 7s p8.6d⁴ Nov 5] 50,000F: eighth foal: half-brother to
fairly useful 1m winner Silver Bracelet (by Machiavellian): dam, 2-y-o 6f/7f (including
Prestige Stakes) winner, third in Prix Marcel Boussac: better effort in maidens when
fourth at Wolverhampton: should stay at least 1¼m. *C. E. Brittain*

TAYIF 8 gr.g. Taufan (USA) 119 – Rich Lass (Broxted 120) [2004 80: p6g² p6g* p6g* **77**
p6g² p6g⁶ p7g p6g² p6g 6s⁵ 6s³ 6m* p6d p7g⁴ p7.1g² p6g* Dec 30] quite good-topped
gelding: fair performer: won claimer and handicap at Lingfield in January, handicap
at Thirsk in June and claimer at Lingfield in December: effective at 6f/easy 7f: acts on
polytrack, soft and good to firm ground: tongue tied: sometimes slowly away: held up.
Andrew Reid

TAYLOR MAID   2 b.f. (Feb 10) First Trump 118 – Island Maid (Forzando 122) [2004 **56** p6g f7g⁵ p7g⁴ Dec 20] second foal: dam unraced: modest form in maidens: should stay at least 1m. *R. M. H. Cowell*

TBM CAN   5 b.g. Rock City 120 – Fire Sprite 83 (Mummy's Game 120) [2004 74: 14g⁶ **67** 13g⁵ 12m⁶ May 17] quite good-topped gelding: fair handicapper: effective at 1½m/1¾m: acts on firm going: held up. *W. M. Brisbourne*

TCHERINA (IRE)   2 b.f. (Jan 27) Danehill Dancer (IRE) 117 – Forget Paris (IRE) **77** (Broken Hearted 124) [2004 6m 6m 7m² 8.5s³ 8m 8.1s* Sep 25] €7,500F, 54,000Y: useful-looking filly: second foal: half-sister to Austrian 7f/1m winner by General Monash: dam no form: fair performer: slight improvement to win maiden at Haydock: will stay 1¼m: acts on soft and good to firm ground. *T. D. Easterby*

TEA FOR TEXAS   7 ch.m. Weldnaas (USA) 112 – Polly's Teahouse 68 (Shack (USA) **– §** 118) [2004 f6m Apr 19] lengthy mare: temperamental handicapper: tried visored. *I. W. McInnes*

TEAM-MATE (IRE)   6 b.g. Nashwan (USA) 135 – Ustka 60 (Lomond (USA) 128) **78** [2004 84: p12g 12m⁵ 12g⁵ Jul 8] leggy gelding: fair handicapper: should stay 1¾m: acts on firm going, probably on soft: tried tongue tied at 3 yrs: below form in cheekpieces: occasionally slowly away: has hinted at temperament. *Miss J. Feilden*

TEAM PLAYER   3 b.c. Mark of Esteem (IRE) 137 – Colorspin (FR) 118 (High Top **74** 131) [2004 7.9m 9.8d Sep 18] 200,000Y: strong, lengthy colt: half-brother to several winners, notably top-class performers Opera House (up to 1½m) and Kayf Tara (up to 2½m), both by Sadler's Wells: dam won Irish Oaks: sold from L. Cumani 17,000 gns after debut (very green in maiden at York): some improvement when eighth of 15 in minor event at Longchamp 3 months later: should stay 1¼m. *F. Poulsen, France*

TEAM TACTICS (IRE)   3 b.f. Son of Sharp Shot (IRE) 105 – Sportin' Notion (USA) **–** (Sportin' Life (USA)) [2004 62: 11.5g p7g Aug 6] €600Y: sixth foal: half-sister to 1¼m/ 1½m winner Coalminersdaughter (by Dynaformer): dam, placed in USA, out of half-sister to Cacoethes: modest maiden: left G. Lyons in Ireland after 2 yrs: well held in 2004: tongue tied final 2-y-o outing. *L. A. Dace*

TE ANAU   7 b.m. Reprimand 122 – Neenah 107 (Bold Lad (IRE) 133) [2004 f8g f8g⁶ **–** p10g⁶ f11g May 19] no form since 2 yrs. *W. J. Musson*

TECHNICIAN (IRE)   9 ch.g. Archway (IRE) 115 – How It Works (Commanche Run **–** 133) [2004 69d: p6g⁵ Apr 15] good-bodied gelding: well held only outing in 2004: usually blinkered/visored, tried in cheekpieces. *Miss K. M. George*

TEDBURROW   12 b.g. Dowsing (USA) 124 – Gwiffina 87 (Welsh Saint 126) [2004 **93** 105d: 5v⁵ 6d³ 6g⁴ Jul 31] sturdy, workmanlike gelding: smart performer at best, winner of 21 races, including 3 Group 3 events: became oldest horse to win a pattern race in Britain when successful in Chipchase Stakes at Newcastle as 10-y-o (record since equalled): only fairly useful in 2004: effective at 5f/6f: acted on firm and soft going, probably not on heavy: had won when sweating: reportedly retired. *E. J. Alston*

TEDSDALE MAC   5 ch.g. Presidium 124 – Stilvella (Camden Town 125) [2004 68: **72** 7m 5.9f⁴ 7.5g² 8.5g⁵ 7.9d² 10d³ 8.5m² 10.3g² 12.1s⁵ 7.9m² 12m 8m 8m* 10d 10.3s⁴ Oct 22] close-coupled, quite good-topped gelding: fair performer: won minor event at Newcastle in October, idling: effective at 6f to 1¼m: yet to race on heavy going, acts on any other turf: tried blinkered/in cheekpieces. *N. Bycroft*

TEDSTALE (USA)   6 ch.g. Irish River (FR) 131 – Carefree Kate (USA) (Lyphard **87** (USA) 132) [2004 94: 7d 8d 8m⁵ 8.9m 7.9g³ 8.5g⁶ 8.3g⁴ 8.5m⁵ 8m³ 8.2g 10g⁴ 9g 8.9g Oct 9] smallish, sturdy, close-coupled gelding: unimpressive mover: fairly useful performer: best around 1m/9f: acts on firm and good to soft going: often blinkered: sometimes slowly away: usually waited with: sometimes finds little: sold 9,500 gns. *T. D. Easterby*

TEDZAR (IRE)   4 b.g. Inzar (USA) 112 – Chesham Lady (IRE) (Fayruz 116) [2004 –: **–** p8g Jan 15] little form: tried blinkered. *B. R. Johnson*

TEEBA (USA)   2 ch.f. (Apr 27) Seeking The Gold (USA) – Shadayid (USA) 122 **83 P** (Shadeed (USA) 135) [2004 6d⁴ Oct 14] big, good-looking filly: closely related to 5-y-o Imtiyaz and useful 7f winner Shawaf (by Mr Prospector) and half-sister to several winners, including useful 1995 2-y-o 6f/7f winner (stayed 1¼m) Bint Shadayid (by Nashwan): dam won Prix Marcel Boussac and 1000 Guineas: 16/1 and green, 3½ lengths fourth to Tomoohat in maiden at Newmarket, slowly away and very green but good late headway: should stay at least 1m: sure to improve considerably and win races. *J. L. Dunlop*

TEEHEE (IRE)   6 b.g. Anita's Prince 126 – Regal Charmer (Royal And Regal (USA))   **–**
[2004 –, a76: f7s⁴ f7g⁶ f6m f8d f7g² f7m³ f7m⁴ 8.1g f7g⁴ p7.1g⁵ Nov 19] tall, useful-   **a68**
looking gelding: fair performer: stays 7f: acts on fibresand, lightly raced recently on turf
but seems best on going softer than good: has been visored, blinkered nowadays: tongue
tied final start: free-going sort: sometimes carries head awkwardly/finds little. *B. Palling*

TEE JAY KASSIDY   4 b.g. Petong 126 – Priceless Fantasy (Dunbeath (USA) 127)   **74**
[2004 –: f7g* f8.5m² 7.1d⁵ f7m² 7v f8g⁴ 7f² 7f⁵ 7f f8g* f8g* p8g* f8g⁶ Dec 28]
smallish gelding: fair performer: won 3 banded races and handicap at Southwell and
banded race at Lingfield in 2004, completing 4-timer in December: stays 8.5f: acts on all-
weather: tried blinkered/visored at 3 yrs. *Julian Poulton*

TEFI   6 ch.g. Efisio 120 – Masuri Kabisa (USA) 48 (Ascot Knight (CAN) 130) [2004 –,   **–**
a50: f7g f7s³ f7g⁵ Jan 12] smallish gelding: has a round action: poor performer: best form   **a40**
at 6f to 1m: acts on firm going and all-weather: visored once, usually blinkered: often
tongue tied: usually races up with pace. *J. Balding*

TELEFONICA (USA)   3 b.f. Distant View (USA) 126 – Call Account (USA) (Private   **66**
Account (USA)) [2004 74p: 8m⁴ 7m f8m² Jul 6] tall filly: fair maiden: stays 1m: raced
only on good/good to firm going and fibresand: sold 18,000 gns in December. *Sir Michael
Stoute*

TELEGRAM SAM (IRE)   2 b.c. (Mar 14) Soviet Star (USA) 128 – She's The Tops   **58**
83 (Shernazar 131) [2004 6g 7s p7.1g⁵ Dec 1] quite good-topped colt: modest form in
maidens: will be suited by at least 1m: acts on polytrack. *R. A. Fahey*

TELEMACHUS   4 b.g. Bishop of Cashel 122 – Indian Imp (Indian Ridge 123) [2004   **95**
97: 10.5d⁶ 10.3g* 10.4d 10m 10g 11.9d 9.9g 10.5g 10d* 10g⁵ 10d Sep 18] workmanlike
gelding: useful handicapper: won at Doncaster (by length from Briareus) in May and Sandown (by 1½ lengths from Silvaline) in August: stays 1¼m: acts on fibresand, soft and
good to firm going: blinkered last 5 starts: usually races prominently: sold 45,000 gns.
J. G. Given

TELEPATHIC (IRE)   4 b.g. Mind Games 121 – Madrina 70 (Waajib 121) [2004 82:   **65 d**
f6s f5s f5g 6g⁶ 6d 5m 6d 7.1m⁴ 8d⁶ 7.1m 7g⁵ 8g⁶ 8.3g⁵ 7.2g⁴ 6g 6g 6g 6d⁵ 5d 5d f5g Dec
21] big, good-bodied gelding: only fair at best nowadays: stays 6f: acts on firm and good
to soft ground: has reared leaving stall/been slowly away: tried tongue tied/blinkered.
A. Berry

TELL THE TREES   3 br.f. Tamure (IRE) 125 – Bluebell Copse (Formidable (USA)   **55**
125) [2004 –: 9m 10.2f⁵ 16.2g⁵ 15.8m* Aug 3] close-coupled, quite good-topped filly:
modest performer: won seller at Catterick in August: stays 2m: raced only on good
ground or firmer: joined M. Pipe, won juvenile hurdle in September. *R. M. Beckett*

TEMPER TANTRUM   6 b.g. Pursuit of Love 124 – Queenbird 90 (Warning 136)   **71**
[2004 71: p7g⁵ p7g⁵ p6g² p7g 7m⁴ 7d 7g⁵ 8m⁴ 7s⁶ 7.1m⁵ 7g p8.6g³ p8.6g* p8.6g³
p8.6g⁵ p7g Dec 30] strong, good-bodied gelding: fair performer: left Andrew Reid after
eighth start: won minor event at Wolverhampton in October: effective at 7f to 8.6f: acts
on all-weather, firm and good to soft ground: tried visored/blinkered/tongue tied, wears
cheekpieces nowadays: held up. *J. R. Best*

TEMPESTAD (IRE)   2 b.f. (Apr 15) Giant's Causeway (USA) 132 – Arutua (USA)   **83 p**
(Riverman (USA) 131) [2004 7g³ 8d⁵ Oct 30] 240,000Y: close-coupled filly: fifth foal:
half-sister to 3 winners, including Irish 7f (at 2 yrs) and 1½m winner Juliette (by Sadler's
Wells) and Irish 6f (at 2 yrs) and 1m winner Plato (by Lure), both useful: dam unraced out
of top-class middle-distance mare All Along: third in maiden at Leicester and fifth in
listed race (raced freely, slightly better effort) at Newmarket: bred to be suited by 1¼m/
1½m: should progress. *H. R. A. Cecil*

TEMPLE BELLE XPRES   2 b.f. (Mar 29) Overbury (IRE) 116 – Kustom Kit Xpres   **36**
69 (Absalom 128) [2004 6.1d 6.1m 8.6g f7g Dec 12] close-coupled filly: fourth foal:
half-sister to 3-y-o Xpres Digital and a winner in Greece by Samim: dam maiden, form
only at 2 yrs (best effort at 6f): poor maiden: blinkered penultimate start. *S. R. Bowring*

TEMPLE PLACE (IRE)   3 b.c. Sadler's Wells (USA) 132 – Puzzled Look (USA)   **99**
(Gulch (USA)) [2004 97p: 9g³ 12.3d³ May 6] good-topped, attractive colt: useful performer: creditable third in listed race at Newmarket (1¼ lengths behind Gold History)
and Chester Vase (some extra after travelling well, 6¾ lengths behind Red Lancer): will
prove best up to 1½m: wears crossed noseband: reported later in May to have undergone
surgery after fracturing off-fore cannon bone on gallops: said to have fully recovered.
M. L. W. Bell

TEMPLET (USA) 4 b.g. Souvenir Copy (USA) 113 – Two Step Trudy (USA) **80**
(Capote (USA)) [2004 70p: 12.4v² 11.1g³ 11.1g⁴ 10.3m⁵ 10.9g³ 10g 11.9g 9.2d²
9.2d* 7.9g⁴ 10.5s p7.1d⁴ p8.6g² p8.6g² p9.5g² p8.6g⁵ f8g⁴ Dec 28] stocky gelding: fairly
useful performer: won maiden at Hamilton in August: has form at 1½m, best at 1m/1¼m:
acts on all-weather and heavy ground: tried visored/in cheekpieces, usually blinkered:
has found little, but is consistent. *I. Semple*

TEMPSFORD (USA) 4 b.g. Bering 136 – Nadra (IRE) 61 (Sadler's Wells (USA) 132) **95**
[2004 98: f12g⁵ 13.9s 16.2m⁵ 18s 12s* 12s Nov 6] sturdy gelding: useful handicapper:
won by 1¼ lengths from Millville at Doncaster in October: effective at 1½m, barely stays
2m: acts on all-weather, soft and good to firm going: usually races prominently. *Sir Mark
Prescott*

TEMPTATION ISLAND (IRE) 5 b.m. Spectrum (IRE) 126 – Kiya (USA) 85 **48**
(Dominion 123) [2004 51: f8.5s f8s 12v 5d 5.8m 5m 7f 10g 10f 10.5f*ᵈⁱˢ 5s Oct 20] **a–**
20,000Y: sixth foal: half-sister to winners abroad by Night Shift and Sharrood: dam, best
at 1m, half-sister to smart 1993 2-y-o Lemon Souffle: poor performer: disqualified (failed
dope test) after winning apprentice handicap at Down Royal in September: well held on
all-weather in Britain first 2 starts: needs further than 5f, stays 10.5f: acts on firm and soft
going: tried blinkered/in cheekpieces/tongue tied. *John A. Quinn, Ireland*

TEN CARAT 4 b.g. Grand Lodge (USA) 125 – Emerald (USA) (El Gran Senor (USA) **97**
136) [2004 106: 16.1m³ 21g 14.8d Aug 27] big, strong gelding: useful performer, lightly
raced: easily best effort of 2004 when third in handicap at Newmarket on reappearance:
stays 2m: best efforts on good to firm going: gelded after final start. *Mrs A. J. Perrett*

TEN CENTS 2 b.f. (May 22) Dansili 127 – Daylight Dreams 77 (Indian Ridge 123) **70**
[2004 6d⁴ 6g⁴ 6g⁴ p7g p8g⁶ p8.6g² Dec 6] close-coupled filly: third foal: half-sister to
5-y-o Dixie Dreaming: dam 2-y-o 5f winner who probably stayed 1m: fair maiden:
second at Wolverhampton: stays 8.6f: acts on polytrack, best turf efforts on good going.
C. A. Cyzer

TENDER FALCON 4 br.g. Polar Falcon (USA) 126 – Tendresse (IRE) 60 (Tender **87**
King 123) [2004 73: 10f⁵ 11.8g* 12g 11.8f² 11.7m* 12g* 12f³ 12s Nov 6] tall, good-
topped gelding: fairly useful performer: won minor event at Leicester in June and
amateur handicaps at Bath (ladies) and Epsom in August: effective at 1¼m/1½m: acts on
firm and good to soft going: tough. *R. J. Hodges*

TENDER (IRE) 4 b.f. Zieten (USA) 118 – Jayess Elle 55 (Sabrehill (USA) 120) **62**
[2004 71, a66: 5g³ 6g⁵ 7m 5.3f 6f⁵ 6g 6.1g 6f 5.5g⁴ p5g⁴ 5m 5.1m 5.1g³ 5g⁶ 5g⁶ Sep 15] **a55**
angular filly: modest handicapper: left D. Daly after second start: won at Lingfield in
July: effective at 5f to easy 7f: acts on polytrack, firm and soft going: wore cheekpieces/
visor after fifth start. *Mrs Stef Liddiard*

TENNY'S GOLD (IRE) 3 b.f. Marju (IRE) 127 – Itatinga (USA) 66 (Riverman **71**
(USA) 131) [2004 74p: 8.3g⁴ 8g³ 10.2g⁵ 8.1s⁴ 7g³ p7.1d* p8.6g Nov 6] rather leggy filly:
fair performer: won minor event at Wolverhampton in November: best at 7f/1m: acts on
polytrack and soft ground. *B. W. Hills*

TEN PAST SIX 12 ch.g. Kris 135 – Tashinsky (USA) (Nijinsky (CAN) 138) [2004 –: **–**
f12g Jan 4] lengthy, good-quartered gelding: of little account. *R. C. Guest*

TENSILE (IRE) 9 b.g. Tenby 125 – Bonnie Isle 115 (Pitcairn 126) [2004 p16.5g **–**
Dec 3] small, sturdy gelding: has a quick action: fairly useful at best: well held only Flat
run since 2001: visored (raced too freely) once: tricky ride. *R. J. Hodges*

TENTATIVE (USA) 3 ch.f. Distant View (USA) 126 – Danzante (USA) 107 (Danzig **–**
(USA)) [2004 93: 5.1g 6m⁶ Jun 25] sturdy, quite attractive filly: fairly useful at 2 yrs: well
held in listed/minor event in 2004: barely stayed 6f: acted on firm going: usually raced
prominently/freely: stud. *R. Charlton*

TEORBAN (POL) 5 b.g. Don Corleone 115 – Tabaka (POL) (Pyjama Hunt 126) **64**
[2004 ?, a76: f16.2s⁶ 16.2m²* 16.4m 16.2g 15.9g 17.2g² Sep 27] modest performer: won
claimer at Chepstow (left M. Pitman) in July: should stay further than 17f: acts on fibresand and good to firm going. *D. J. S. ffrench Davis*

TE QUIERO 6 gr.g. Bering 136 – Ma Lumiere (FR) (Niniski (USA) 125) [2004 ?, **73**
a101: f7g p12g p10g f8.5s² f8.5s² 8.3d a8.7f 10m 8m 7g 6g p7g p7g Nov 20] good-topped **a110**
gelding: smart on all-weather, fair on turf: best efforts when second in handicaps at
Wolverhampton in February (beaten neck by Consonant) and March (short-headed by
stable-companion Vortex): stays 9.4f, probably not 1½m: acts on fibresand (below form
on polytrack), soft and good to firm going: tongue tied, tried in cheekpieces: usually
makes running. *Miss Gay Kelleway*

TEQUILA SHEILA (IRE) 2 ch.f. (Apr 19) Raise A Grand (IRE) 114 – Hever Rosina 83
63 (Efisio 120) [2004 6f 6g* 6f⁶ 6g* 6.1g⁶ 6d 7g⁴ Oct 5] €13,000Y: quite attractive filly:
second foal: half-sister to fairly useful 2003 2-y-o 5f winner Shank On Fourteen (by
Fayruz): dam 6f winner: fairly useful performer: won minor event at Hamilton in June
and nursery at Windsor in August: good fourth in nursery at Catterick: stays 7f: best
efforts on good going: sometimes wanders. *K. R. Burke*

TERDAD (USA) 11 ch.g. Lomond (USA) 128 – Istiska (FR) (Irish River (FR) 131) –
[2004 f16g Jan 27] big, rangy gelding: fair handicapper in 1998: well beaten only Flat
start since (untrustworthy hurdler): has high head carriage: tried tongue tied. *J. G. Given*

TERENURE GIRL 3 br.f. Averti (IRE) 117 – Royal Fontaine (IRE) 84 (Royal Acad- –
emy (USA) 130) [2004 6g⁶ 6m p7g Oct 25] first foal: dam 1¼m winner: last in maidens.
P. S. Felgate

TERESA 4 b.f. Darshaan 133 – Morina (USA) (Lyphard (USA) 132) [2004 85: 16d² 83
14.8s⁶ 20f⁶ 16.1m 21g 15.9s 14.1d 16s² 16s Oct 29] leggy filly: fairly useful handicapper:
stays 2½m: unraced on heavy going, acts on any other turf: sold 50,000 gns. *J. L. Dunlop*

TERMINATE (GER) 2 ch.g. (Mar 28) Acatenango (GER) 127 – Taghareed (USA) 65
93 (Shadeed (USA) 135) [2004 7.5m p8d 8s⁵ 8g p10g p7m Dec 21] €90,000Y: sturdy
gelding: half-brother to 3 winners, including useful Irish 2001 2-y-o 8.5f winner (stayed
1½m) Rahn (by Elmaamul) and fairly useful 6.5f (in Ireland at 2 yrs) and 9f (in USA)
winner Matanah (by Machiavellian): dam, 2-y-o 6f winner, half-sister to very smart 1m/
1¼m performer Zaahi: fair maiden: left Sir Mark Prescott after fourth start: should be
suited by 1¼m/1½m: acts on soft going, promise on polytrack. *N. A. Callaghan*

TERMONFECKIN 6 b.g. Runnett 125 – Crimson Sol (Crimson Beau 124) [2004 57: – §
16g 14.1g 10.9g Apr 23] plain gelding: temperamental maiden. *P. W. Hiatt*

TERN INTERN (IRE) 5 b. or br.g. Dr Devious (IRE) 127 – Arctic Bird (USA) –
(Storm Bird (CAN) 134) [2004 –: f8.5s p7g f8g f8g Apr 2] workmanlike gelding: of little
account nowadays. *Miss J. Feilden*

TERRAQUIN (IRE) 4 b.g. Turtle Island (IRE) 123 – Play The Queen (IRE) (King of 80 §
Clubs 124) [2004 84: p8g p8g⁴ 7s 6g 8s⁵ 7g 7g⁵ 7d⁵ 7m 9g 8g 8d 7g³ 8g⁶ 7s Sep 14]
good-bodied gelding: fairly useful performer: stays 9f: acts on polytrack and good to
firm going: sometimes races freely: sometimes wears cheekpieces/visor: unreliable.
J. J. Bridger

TESARY 2 b.f. (Apr 9) Danehill (USA) 126 – Baldemara (FR) (Sanglamore (USA) 80
126) [2004 5d⁵ 6m² 5m* 6m⁴ 5m³ 6.1g³ 6m 6.1d² Sep 17] compact filly: fourth foal:
closely related to fairly useful 7f/1m winner Baldour (by Green Desert) and half-sister to
3-y-o Music Mix: dam unraced half-sister to very smart French filly up to 1m Balbonella,
herself dam of top-class sprinter Anabaa: fairly useful performer: won maiden at Lingfield in June: in frame in nurseries after: stays 6f: acts on good to firm and good to soft
going. *E. A. L. Dunlop*

TETCHY 4 b.f. Robellino (USA) 127 – Putout 69 (Dowsing (USA) 124) [2004 8.1s –
8.1d Jun 4] sixth foal: half-sister to 3 winning sprinters, including useful 2001 2-y-o 6f
winner Rajab (by Selkirk): dam, 5f winner, half-sister to useful 7f/1m winner Danceabout
and smart sprinter Pole Position: well held in maidens at Warwick and Haydock: sent to
New Zealand. *J. G. Given*

TETCOTT (IRE) 3 ch.f. Definite Article 121 – Charlene Lacy (IRE) 77 (Pips Pride 64
117) [2004 7d⁵ 7d³ 6d⁴ 7.1d³ p10g p8.6g⁶ Dec 27] 20,000Y: smallish filly: first foal: dam,
5f winner at 2 yrs, out of sister to smart sprinter Fayruz: modest maiden: left M. Tregoning after fourth start: stays 7f. *A. G. Newcombe*

TETOU (IRE) 4 ch.f. Peintre Celebre (USA) 137 – Place of Honour (Be My Guest –
(USA) 126) [2004 70: p10g 10m May 18] lengthy filly: lightly-raced filly: fair winner at
3 yrs: well held in handicaps in 2004: covered by Cadeaux Genereux. *B. J. Meehan*

TETRA SING (IRE) 2 b.f. (Mar 31) Sinndar (IRE) 134 – Tetralogy (USA) (Mt Liver- 60 ?
more (USA)) [2004 7s 7.5m 8m f8g Nov 23] €65,000Y: leggy filly: on weak side at 2 yrs:
second foal: half-sister to winner in USA by Dehere: dam, lightly-raced French maiden,
closely related to Prince of Wales's Stakes winner Two Timing: modest form at best in
maidens/claimer. *P. C. Haslam*

TEWITFIELD LASS 2 b.f. (Mar 21) Bluegrass Prince (IRE) 110 – Madam Marash 27
(IRE) 51 (Astronef 116) [2004 7.5d 7m⁵ 7m 7s f5f Dec 28] leggy filly: second foal: dam,
maiden, should have stayed further than 1m: bad maiden. *A. Berry*

TEXAS GOLD 6 ch.g. Cadeaux Genereux 131 – Star Tulip 99 (Night Shift (USA)) **110**
[2004 99: 5g² 5m⁴ 6f 5g⁶ 5g⁶ 6m 5g² 5.6m² 6m* 5.2g⁴ 5g⁴ 6s p5g* p6g Nov 29] sturdy,
close-coupled gelding: developed into smart performer in 2004: won handicaps at Goodwood (by 1¾ lengths from Cd Europe) in September and Lingfield (by length from Who's
Winning) in November: very good fourth to The Tatling in World Trophy at Newbury
tenth start: effective at 5f/easy 6f: acts on polytrack (well beaten on fibresand), firm and
good to soft going: has been early to post: usually waited with: tough and consistent.
W. R. Muir

TEXT 3 b.g. Atraf 116 – Idle Chat (USA) 93 (Assert 134) [2004 61: 8.1g 7m² 7g³ 6s⁵ **68**
7m⁶ 8g p8.6g Oct 2] fair maiden: stays 7f: acts on polytrack and good to firm going,
below form on soft: tried in headgear. *Mrs Stef Liddiard*

TEYAAR 8 b.g. Polar Falcon (USA) 126 – Music In My Life (IRE) 59 (Law Society –
(USA) 130) [2004 –, a79: p6g p5g f6g⁶ p6g f6s p6g⁵ 6d f5g² f6g⁴ p5.1g p6g p6g Dec 20] **a59**
strong gelding: modest performer: left Mrs N. Macauley after ninth start: best at 5f/6f:
acts on all-weather, best turf form on good going or softer: has been blinkered/visored:
sometimes hangs: none too reliable. *M. Wellings*

THADEA (IRE) 3 b. or br.f. Grand Lodge (USA) 125 – Kama Tashoof 72 (Mtoto 134) –
[2004 64: 8.2g 7.1s 7m May 18] close-coupled filly: maiden: little form in 2004 (pulled
up final outing). *J. G. Given*

THAJJA (IRE) 3 b.c. Daylami (IRE) 138 – Jawlaat (USA) 91 (Dayjur (USA) 137) **109**
[2004 80p: 8.1d* 8f 8m² 8d Oct 15] sturdy colt: useful performer, lightly raced: won
4-runner minor event at Sandown in April by 2 lengths from Putra Sas: best effort when 2
lengths second to Welcome Stranger in handicap at Ascot: likely to prove best at 7f/1m:
acts on good to firm and good to soft going: joined D. Watson in UAE. *J. L. Dunlop*

THAKAFAAT (IRE) 2 b.f. (Feb 11) Unfuwain (USA) 131 – Frappe (IRE) 93 (Inch- **80 p**
inor 119) [2004 7f⁵ 7d* 8d⁶ Oct 14] 160,000Y: good-topped filly: has a round action:
second foal: dam, 2-y-o 6f winner, out of Prestige Stakes winner Glatisant: won maiden
at Newmarket in August, hanging left: only sixth in nursery there: should stay at least 1m:
type to make a better 3-y-o. *J. L. Dunlop*

THAMINAH (USA) 3 b.f. Danzig (USA) – Bashayer (USA) 103 (Mr Prospector **91**
(USA)) [2004 84p: 7m⁵ 6d Oct 14] sturdy filly: fairly useful performer, lightly raced:
reportedly suffered from an allergy early in year: best effort when fifth to Badminton in
listed race at Ascot: effective at 6f/7f: visits Rahy. *M. P. Tregoning*

THARA'A (IRE) 3 b.f. Desert Prince (IRE) 130 – Tycoon's Drama (IRE) (Last Tycoon **69**
131) [2004 –: 8g² 8.2s 7g⁵ 7g⁷ Jul 21] leggy filly: poor mover: fair maiden, lightly raced:
stays 1m: well held both starts on all-weather, yet to race on ground firmer than good on
turf: sold 35,000 gns in October. *E. A. L. Dunlop*

THARUA (IRE) 2 b.f. (Mar 2) Indian Danehill (IRE) 124 – Peig Sayers (IRE) 58 **72**
(Royal Academy (USA) 130) [2004 7g³ 8d³ p7m⁴ Nov 22] €8,500F, 5,000Y: leggy,
lengthy filly: fourth foal: dam, Irish maiden (best at 1m at 2 yrs), closely related to very
smart stayer Assessor: easily best effort in maidens behind Rob Roy at Newmarket on
debut: hung right second start: should stay 1m. *E. A. L. Dunlop*

THATS ALL JAZZ 6 b.m. Prince Sabo 123 – Gate of Heaven 43 (Starry Night (USA)) – §
[2004 46§, a–§: f7g p7g p10g p10g p10g Mar 9] workmanlike mare: unreliable handicapper: tried visored. *C. R. Dore*

THAT'S RACING 4 ch.g. Classic Cliche (IRE) 128 – All On 68 (Dunbeath (USA) **41**
127) [2004 62d: f11g² 12v⁶ 21.6v f14g 10g Aug 28] rather lengthy, good-topped gelding:
poor maiden: bred to be suited by at least 1¾m. *J. Hetherton*

THE ABBESS 2 gr.f. (Apr 22) Bishop of Cashel 122 – Nisha (Nishapour (FR) 125) **81 p**
[2004 6.1d* Sep 17] rather leggy filly: seventh foal: sister to 4-y-o Bishopric and half-
sister to 1m winner Snow And Ice (by Chilibang): dam, lightly-raced maiden, out of half-
sister to high-class sprinter New Model: 10/1, won maiden at Nottingham comfortably by
1½ lengths from Sound The Drum, green before leading final 1f: should stay 1m: sure to
improve. *H. Candy*

THEAS DANCE 2 b.f. (Apr 6) Danzig (USA) – Teggiano (IRE) 108 (Mujtahid **66**
(USA) 118) [2004 7m⁵ 6g 6s³ 7g Sep 14] smallish, sturdy filly: first foal: dam 2-y-o 6f
and 1m (Fillies' Mile) winner who stayed 1½m: fair maiden: form only on first and third
starts: gave trouble at start other appearances: should stay 1m. *D. R. Loder*

THEATRE BELLE 3 b.f. King's Theatre (IRE) 128 – Cumbrian Rhapsody 79 (Shar- **51**
rood (USA) 124) [2004 57: 8g 7d f12d 12d⁶ 12m⁵ 14.1f 15.8m Sep 18] rather leggy filly:
modest maiden: bred to be suited by 1¼m+: pulled hard in visor fifth start. *T. D. Easterby*

THEATRE LADY (IRE) 6 b.m. King's Theatre (IRE) 128 – Littlepace (Indian King **56** (USA) 128) [2004 59, a–: p10g* p8g² p8g p8g³ p10g⁶ p10g³ p8g 10.9s⁴ p8g³ 10m⁵ 7.9f⁶ **a48** 10.9m⁶ 11.5m 11.7g* 10m⁵ 12.1m* 9.9m 14.1m⁶ 12m* Sep 25] sturdy mare: modest performer: won banded race at Lingfield in February, ladies handicap at Bath and amateur handicap at Chepstow in July and banded race at Kempton in September: stays 1½m: acts on polytrack (no form in 4 runs on fibresand) and any turf going: tried visored: usually held up: tough. *P. D. Evans*

THEATRE OF DREAMS 2 b.g. (Mar 2) Averti (IRE) 117 – Loch Fyne 70 (Ardkin- **83** glass 114) [2004 5g⁵ 5.1d⁴ 5m* 5g 5d⁶ 5d Sep 17] 8,000Y: smallish gelding: second foal: dam, sprint maiden, half-sister to useful sprinter Lennox Lewis: fairly useful performer: won seller at Musselburgh in May: good tenth (despite being hampered) in Molecomb Stakes at Goodwood next start, only form after: will prove best at bare 5f: acts on good to firm ground: races up with pace: gelded after final start. *D. Nicholls*

THEATRE TIME (USA) 4 b.g. Theatrical 128 – Kyka (USA) (Blushing John (USA) **–** 120) [2004 82: 10m⁶ 11.9g Sep 3] lengthy, well-made gelding: fairly useful performer at best (lightly raced): well held in 2 handicaps in 2004. *Ian Williams*

THEATRE TINKA (IRE) 5 b.g. King's Theatre (IRE) 128 – Orange Grouse (IRE) **62** 105 (Taufan (USA) 119) [2004 69: f11g⁵ f12g⁵ f12g² 13.8g⁴ 11s f12g⁵ 12.6f² 15m 13.8m⁴ 12g³ 11.7g p12.2g⁶ p12.2g* p12.2g³ p12.2g Dec 15] close-coupled gelding: modest handicapper: won at Wolverhampton in November: stays 1¾m: acts on all-weather, firm and good to soft ground: wears cheekpieces. *R. Hollinshead*

THEATRE (USA) 5 b.g. Theatrical 128 – Fasta (USA) (Seattle Song (USA) 130) **88** [2004 91: 14.1s 14g 16m² 14.8m² 14d³ 16.2g 14.8d 16m 16.2m 18s Oct 16] close-coupled gelding: fairly useful handicapper: effective at 1¾m/2m: acts on polytrack, firm and soft going: blinkered (ran to form) twice at 3 yrs: usually held up. *Jamie Poulton*

THE BARONESS (IRE) 4 b.f. Blues Traveller (IRE) 119 – Wicken Wonder (IRE) **?** 71 (Distant Relative 128) [2004 65, a57: p6g f5g 5m f5g p5m* p5.1g Dec 31] modest **a56** performer: won banded race at Lingfield in December: best at 5f/6f: acts on all-weather and good to firm ground. *E. R. Oertel*

THE BEDUTH NAVI 4 b.g. Forzando 122 – Sweets (IRE) (Persian Heights 129) **52** [2004 –: f12s² p16g² f12s* f11s² f14g³ 16s⁴ f14.8m f16s Nov 17] angular, heavy-topped gelding: modest performer: won maiden at Wolverhampton in March: stays easy 2m: acts on all-weather and soft going: blinkered once (looked wayward) at 3 yrs. *D. G. Bridgwater*

THE BEST YET 6 ch.h. King's Signet (USA) 110 – Miss Klew (Never So Bold 135) **82** [2004 84: p7g⁴ p8g 6m Jun 8] compact horse: fairly useful performer: below form after reappearance: best at 6f/7f: acts on all-weather and firm ground: has been slowly away: sometimes races freely/looks wayward: held up. *A. G. Newcombe*

THE BLOCK MONSTER (IRE) 5 b.m. Petorius 117 – Balgren (IRE) (Ballad **–** Rock 122) [2004 75d: f6g f8s f8.5g Feb 9] IR 600Y: second foal: dam unraced: one-time fairly useful performer in Ireland: no longer of much account. *P. A. Blockley*

THE BONUS KING 4 b.g. Royal Applause 124 – Selvi (Mummy's Pet 125) [2004 **89 d** 94?: f8.5s⁴ p7g⁵ 8v² 10.5s 10g 8.1s 8.5g 7.2f² 8.1g⁴ 7.2d 7m f7f⁵ 8d p8.6g⁶ Oct 2] strong, angular, good-topped gelding: has a fluent action: just fairly useful at best in 2004: left M. Johnston after tenth start: stays 1m, not 10.5f: acts on any turf going, probably on all-weather: tried blinkered: usually races prominently. *J. Jay*

THE BUTTERFLY BOY 3 ch.c. Inchinor 119 – Crime of Passion 115 (Dragonara **42** Palace (USA) 115) [2004 67p: 7.1d f5g³ 6.1m 5g Jul 7] poor maiden: stays 6f. *P. F. I. Cole*

THE CAT'S WHISKERS (NZ) 4 b.f. Tale of The Cat (USA) 113 – Good Faith (NZ) **91 ?** (Straight Strike) [2004 8g³ 8g* 8d 8f² 7g* 8g 7d² 7m 5g⁶ Sep 30] neat ex-New Zealand filly: third foal: half-sister to Australian Group 3 5.5f winner Tully Dane (by Danehill): dam champion 2-y-o filly in New Zealand (Group 1 7f winner): won 2 of 11 starts in native country for R. James, namely maiden at Te Rapa and intermediate event at Arawa Park: fairly useful form in Britain last 2 starts, in listed events at Doncaster and Newmarket (sweating): raced mainly at 7f/1m: acts on firm and good to soft going. *P. W. Chapple-Hyam*

THE CHEQUERED LADY 2 b.f. (Feb 23) Benny The Dip (USA) 127 – Hymne **–** d'Amour (USA) 58 (Dixieland Band (USA)) [2004 7g Aug 13] 7,500Y: seventh foal: half-sister to 3 winners, including smart performer up to 1¾m in Britain/USA Chelsea Barracks (by Deploy), 1m winner at 2 yrs: dam, lightly raced on Flat and winning hurdler, out of half-sister to Alzao: 66/1 and green, last in maiden at Folkestone. *T. D. McCarthy*

THE COIRES (IRE)   2 b.c. (Mar 18) Green Desert (USA) 127 – Purple Heather   **86**
(USA) 93 (Rahy (USA) 115) [2004 7g 7m 7d* 8m⁶ 7m Sep 26] strong, compact colt:
good mover: first foal: dam, 1¼m winner, out of half-sister to dam of Nashwan, Unfuwain and Nayef: fairly useful performer: won maiden at Newmarket in August: creditable
sixth at Doncaster, better effort in nurseries after (not clear run final start): stays 1m: acts
on good to firm and good to soft going. *R. Hannon*

THE COMPOSER   2 b.c. (Mar 16) Royal Applause 124 – Superspring (Superlative   **83 p**
118) [2004 8g⁴ 8g* Sep 29] 26,000Y: well-made colt: half-brother to 6-y-o Our Destiny
and 4-y-o Stagnite: dam unraced sister to smart sprinter Superpower: favourite, won
maiden at Salisbury by ½ length from Wotchalike, getting up close home: will stay 1¼m:
should progress. *M. Blanshard*

THE COPT   5 b.g. Charmer 123 – Coptic Dancer (Sayf El Arab (USA) 127) [2004 –:   **–**
f8g f6m Jul 6] leggy gelding: maiden handicapper: no form since 3 yrs: tongue tied in
2004. *Mrs S. Lamyman*

THE COUNT (FR)   5 b.g. Sillery (USA) 122 – Dear Countess (FR) (Fabulous Dancer   **–**
(USA) 124) [2004 8s⁵ Oct 30] leggy gelding: maiden: well held only outing since 2002:
tried blinkered. *F. P. Murtagh*

THE CROOKED RING   2 b.g. (Mar 13) Magic Ring (IRE) 115 – My Bonus 79   **95**
(Cyrano de Bergerac 120) [2004 5g⁵ 5.1g² 5.1d³ 6.1s² 5f* 6g³ 5.1g⁴ 6m* 6m* 6m² 6d³
6g⁶ 6s⁵ Oct 22] 9,000Y: workmanlike gelding: fourth foal: half-brother to fairly useful
2000 2-y-o 5f winner My Lovely (by Dolphin Street): dam 5f (including at 2 yrs) winner:
useful performer: won maiden at Warwick in June and nurseries at Ayr and Kempton in
July: good placed efforts in nurseries after: will prove best at 5f/6f: acts on firm and soft
ground: visored for first win: tough and consistent. *P. D. Evans*

THE CROSS FOX   2 gr.g. (Apr 20) Wizard King 122 – Megs Pearl 56 (Petong 126)   **–**
[2004 p7.1g p9.5g Dec 20] well held in maidens at Wolverhampton. *P. D. Evans*

THE DUKE OF DIXIE (USA)   2 b.c. (Mar 20) Dixieland Band (USA) – Money   **77**
Madam (USA) (A P Indy (USA) 131) [2004 6m³ 7d³ 10.2g⁶ Sep 27] $150,000Y: heavy-
topped colt: has markedly round action: fourth foal: half-brother to winner in USA by
Langfuhr: dam, won in USA, half-sister to US Grade 2 6f winner Funistrada: fair form
at York and Newmarket first 2 starts in maidens: should stay 1m: sent to South Africa.
P. F. I. Cole

THE FAIRY FLAG (IRE)   6 ch.m. Inchinor 119 – Good Reference (IRE) 84 (Refer-   **62**
ence Point 139) [2004 70: 9.9v⁴ 10d 10.9s 13.8s p13.9g* f12g Dec 1] angular mare:
modest nowadays: won amateur minor event at Wolverhampton in November: stays
easy 1¾m: acts on all-weather and any turf going: wears cheekpieces: often front runner.
A. Bailey

THE FISIO   4 b.g. Efisio 120 – Misellina (FR) 57 (Polish Precedent (USA) 131) [2004   **81**
80: p5g* f5s* p5g⁵ f5g⁶ p5g³ p6g 5s 5.7g² 5g 5s⁴ 5d* 5g 6m² 5m 5m 5.1s 5g Sep 20]
smallish, strong gelding: fairly useful performer: won handicaps at Lingfield and Southwell (dead-heated) in January and minor event at Hamilton in May: left A. Balding after
thirteenth start: best at 5f/easy 6f: acts on all-weather, soft and good to firm going: often
visored: unruly in stall (ran poorly) final outing: usually races prominently. *S. Gollings*

THEFLYINGSCOTTIE   2 gr.g. (Mar 22) Paris House 123 – Miss Flossa (FR) (Big   **–**
John (FR) 125) [2004 5.7m 5.1m Aug 5] well held in maidens at Bath and Chepstow.
J. D. Frost

THE FOOTBALLRESULT   3 b.f. The West (USA) 107 – Bunny Gee (Last Tycoon   **37**
131) [2004 59: p7g p8g 7g⁵ 7m 10.2f Jun 23] rather leggy filly: poor maiden: seems to
stay 1¼m. *Mrs G. Harvey*

THE FOX'S HEAD (IRE)   3 b.f. Imperial Ballet (IRE) 110 – Lovely Leitrim (IRE)   **–**
(Erin's Hope 117) [2004 9.2g⁵ 11.1m Jun 9] fifth foal: dam Irish maiden hurdler: well
held in claimers at Hamilton. *B. Mactaggart*

THE FUN MERCHANT   3 b.g. Mind Games 121 – Sinking (Midyan (USA) 124)   **71**
[2004 55: 7.1d 8g* 8m* 8m² 8m 8g⁵ p10g p9.5g 8s³ Oct 29] close-coupled, workmanlike
gelding: fair performer: won maiden claimer at Ayr (left W. Jarvis) and claimer at Newmarket (left D. Carroll) in June: stays 1m: acts on polytrack, firm and soft going: ran
creditably in cheekpieces final outing. *J. Pearce*

THE GAIKWAR (IRE)   5 b.h. Indian Ridge 123 – Broadmara (IRE) 91 (Thatching   **69**
131) [2004 76: p7g⁶ p7g⁴ p8g² p7g⁵ p10g p8g* 8.5s² 8.1v 8m 9g 7.1g 7.1m⁴ 8m³ 8m²   **a73**
8.1s³ 8d⁶ p8g Nov 10] lengthy horse: fair performer: left N. Berry after third start: won
claimer at Lingfield (left N. Littmoden) in March: stays 1m: acts on polytrack, firm and
soft going: blinkered: has raced freely: often slowly away. *N. E. Berry*

THE GAMBLER   4 ch.g. First Trump 118 – Future Options 71 (Lomond (USA) 128)   **55**
[2004 71: 7.1g 10.1v 6s 7.1d² f6g 8.1f 7.1f 6m 6v⁶ 8m⁵ f7g p7g Dec 20] good-bodied
gelding: just modest at best nowadays: effective at 6f/7f: acts on firm and good to soft
ground, lightly raced on all-weather: tried blinkered/tongue tied, usually wears cheekpieces. *Paul Johnson*

THE GAY FOX   10 gr.g. Never So Bold 135 – School Concert 80 (Music Boy 124)   **52 d**
[2004 56d: p7g² f6g⁴ p6g² p6g³ p7g p7g f7s³ p7g p7g p7g⁶ Mar 29] good-topped gelding:
unimpressive mover: modest at best nowadays: stays 7f: acts on all-weather/any turf
going: usually blinkered/visored, has worn cheekpieces: tongue tied: often slowly away.
B. G. Powell

THE GEEZER   2 ch.c. (Mar 4) Halling (USA) 133 – Polygueza (FR) 78 (Be My Guest   **72**
(USA) 126) [2004 p8g⁴ p10g² Nov 27] 21,000Y: fifth foal: half-brother to 3-y-o Doctored
and winner in Italy by Barathea: dam Irish 7f winner: still green, better effort in maidens
at Lingfield when short-headed by Chocolate Caramel, finishing strongly: will stay at
least 1½m. *D. R. C. Elsworth*

THE GREAT GATSBY (IRE)   4 b.c. Sadler's Wells (USA) 132 – Ionian Sea (Slip   **115**
Anchor 136) [2004 120: 12m³ 12m 13.3g⁴ 15s Aug 22] compact, quite attractive ex-Irish
colt: had a short, choppy action: very smart performer for A. O'Brien at 3 yrs, runner-up
in Derby at Epsom: off 12 months, smart form when 3½ lengths third to Senex in Gran
Premio di Milano on reappearance: dropped away tamely all 3 starts after, blinkered on
last 2: stayed 1½m: acted on heavy and good to firm ground: sold to stand at stud in
Russia. *J. H. M. Gosden*

THE JOB   3 ch.c. Dancing Spree (USA) – Bay Bianca (IRE) (Law Society (USA) 130)   **60**
[2004 61: p7g⁶ p7g² 8.2g⁵ 8.3s p7.1d⁵ p7.1g p9.5g⁴ p10m Dec 21] workmanlike colt:
modest performer: stays 9.5f: acts on all-weather: poor efforts on ground softer than
good. *A. D. Smith*

THE JOBBER (IRE)   3 b.g. Foxhound (USA) 103 – Clairification (IRE) 57 (Sherna-   **86**
zar 131) [2004 70: 6d⁴ 5m 6g⁶ p6g² 6d² 6.1g 6g⁵ Sep 20] strong gelding: fairly useful
handicapper: second at Lingfield and Newbury: stays 6f: acts on polytrack, unraced on
extremes of going on turf. *M. Blanshard*

THE KEEP   2 ch.f. (Apr 24) Shinko Forest (IRE) – Poyle Amber 55 (Sharrood (USA)   **48**
124) [2004 6m 6f 7.1g 6.1m⁴ 6g p8.6g p8g p6g⁶ Dec 27] 7,800Y: leggy filly: sixth foal:
half-sister to 6f (at 2 yrs) to 1½m winner Wilton (by Sharpo) and 6f winner Railroader
(by Piccolo), later successful in USA, both fairly useful: dam sprint maiden: poor maiden:
may prove best at 5f/easy 6f: blinkered last 2 starts. *R. Hannon*

THE KELT (IRE)   7 b.g. Leading Counsel (USA) 122 – Casheral (Le Soleil 96) [2004   **45**
16s³ 17.2g* f14g Jul 9] winning hurdler: poor handicapper: won at Carlisle in July: pulled
up lame subsequent start: stays 17.2f: raced only on good/soft going on turf: tongue tied
in 2004. *Eoin Doyle, Ireland*

THE KHAMSIN (DEN)   5 b.h. Kateb (IRE) 68 – Medinova (Mas Media) [2004 11g³   **109**
12g² 11d⁶ 13g³ 12m⁵ 8s 9m² 12m Sep 26] Danish-bred horse: useful performer: has won
6 races, including Dansk Derby at 3 yrs and handicap at Ovrevoll in 2003: best effort
when 3 lengths fifth to Crocodile Dundee in Scandinavian Open Championship at Copenhagen fifth start: not discredited when seventh in Cumberland Lodge Stakes at Ascot final
outing: stays 1½m: acts on soft and good to firm ground. *Ms C. Erichsen, Norway*

THE KIDDYKID (IRE)   4 b.g. Danetime (IRE) 121 – Mezzanine (Sadler's Wells   **114**
(USA) 132) [2004 111: 6g³ 6g 6m⁶* 6d⁴ 5d⁶ 6m 6m² 6v Aug 29] tall, lengthy gelding:
smart performer: won Weatherbys Ireland Greenlands Stakes at the Curragh in May by
head from Arakan: creditable efforts after when 1¾ lengths fourth to Royal Millennium
in Chipchase Stakes at Newcastle and length second to One Cool Cat in Phoenix Sprint
Stakes at the Curragh: best form at 6f: acts on any turf going: usually races up with pace.
P. D. Evans

THE KING OF ROCK   3 b.c. Nicolotte 118 – Lv Girl (IRE) 67 (Mukaddamah (USA)   **59**
125) [2004 61: 6g 10.9d⁵ 9.9s⁴ 12.3g f12d² 11.7g 6m 10g⁵ Aug 18] rather leggy colt:
modest maiden handicapper: stays 1½m: acts on fibresand, firm and soft going: tried
visored (ran creditably)/blinkered: usually held up. *A. G. Newcombe*

THE KING'S BISHOP   3 b.g. Bishop of Cashel 122 – Kennedys Prima 65 (Primo   **69**
Dominie 121) [2004 p8g⁴ p7g 7d³ Apr 7] 1,500F, 4,000Y: sixth foal: half-brother to 5-y-o
Snuki: dam, sprint maiden, half-sister to high-class sprinter Mr Brooks: best effort in
maidens when close third to Wistman at Folkestone, hanging left and just caught having
led under 1f out: stays 7f: raced freely second start. *S. C. Williams*

THE LADY WOULD (IRE) 5 ch.m. Woodborough (USA) 112 – Kealbra Lady – (Petong 126) [2004 40: f5g p6g f6m Apr 19] little form in 2004: tried in cheekpieces/blinkers. *D. G. Bridgwater*

THE LAST CAST 5 ch.g. Prince of Birds (USA) 121 – Atan's Gem (USA) (Sharpen **81** Up 127) [2004 14.1s* 18s Oct 16] sturdy, close-coupled gelding: fairly useful handicapper: missed 2003: won at Salisbury in May: similar form when eleventh in Cesarewitch at Newmarket subsequent outing: barely stays 2¼m: acts on heavy and good to firm ground (well beaten only run on polytrack): useful jumper. *H. Morrison*

THE LAST MOHICAN 5 b.g. Common Grounds 118 – Arndilly 75 (Robellino **47** (USA) 127) [2004 40: f14.8g⁴ f16.2g² p13g³ f16.2g² p13g⁴ p12g p13g p12g³ f14.8g² f12m* p12g f12g f14g Aug 19] small, workmanlike gelding: bad mover: poor performer: won banded race at Southwell in May: stays 2m: acts on all-weather and firm ground: usually wears cheekpieces: fair hurdler. *P. Howling*

THE LAST SABO 2 b.g. (Mar 11) Prince Sabo 123 – Classic Fan (USA) (Lear Fan – (USA) 130) [2004 p9.5g Dec 20] 16/1, well held in maiden at Wolverhampton. *P. W. D'Arcy*

THE LAVERTON LAD 3 ch.g. Keen 116 – Wyse Folly (Colmore Row 111) [2004 41: – f9.4g Jan 3] smallish gelding: poor form only on second outing at 2 yrs. *C. W. Thornton*

THE LEATHER WEDGE (IRE) 5 b.h. Hamas (IRE) 125§ – Wallflower (Polar **41** Falcon (USA) 126) [2004 46, a57: f5g⁶ f5g f5g⁴ f5s f5g⁵ f5g² f5d⁵ f5g⁵ 5m f5g³ p5.1g 5s⁴ **a55** Nov 2] tall horse: modest on all-weather, poor on turf: best at 5f: acts on fibresand, firm and good to soft going: tried blinkered/in cheekpieces: usually races up with pace: none too consistent. *A. Berry*

THE LOOSE SCREW (IRE) 6 b.g. Bigstone (IRE) 126 – Princess of Dance (IRE) **50** (Dancing Dissident (USA) 119) [2004 53: 10.9s 10.1v 10m 13.9m 8.1g 9d⁵ 8.1s⁵ 8.1d⁶ 7.2s² Oct 30] good-bodied gelding: modest maiden: effective at 7f to 1¼m: acts on heavy and good to firm going: tried blinkered, wore cheekpieces last 5 starts. *G. M. Moore*

Weatherbys Ireland Greenlands Stakes, the Curragh—a British-trained domination
as The Kiddykid (noseband) holds off Arakan with Ringmoor Down (left) third

THE LORD 4 b.g. Averti (IRE) 117 – Lady Longmead (Crimson Beau 124) [2004 **85** 97d: 6m³ 5.2f 6s⁶ 5.2g 5.1s⁶ Aug 21] close-coupled, quite good-topped gelding: has a quick action: fairly useful handicapper: effective at 5f/6f: acts on firm and soft ground: tried in cheekpieces: often races prominently: inconsistent. *W. G. M. Turner*

THEME PARK 4 b.g. Classic Cliche (IRE) 128 – Arcady 69 (Slip Anchor 136) [2004 **–** –: f14g f12g Feb 9] lightly-raced maiden: last both starts in 2004: tried tongue tied. *John A. Harris*

THEMESOFGREEN 3 ch.g. Botanic (USA) – Harmonia (Glint of Gold 128) [2004 **52 ?** –: 5.1g 6m 6g 7.1m⁵ Jun 28] tall, leggy, unfurnished gelding: lightly-raced maiden, seemingly modest at best: raced only on good/good to firm ground. *M. R. Channon*

THEME SONG (IRE) 5 b.g. Singspiel (IRE) 133 – Glatisant 104 (Rainbow Quest **95** (USA) 134) [2004 93: 12m 12.9m³ 12f* 13.9g Jul 10] useful performer: won maiden at Clonmel and minor event at Thurles in 2003, and handicap at the Curragh in June: raced too freely in listed rated stakes at York final outing: effective at 1½m to 2m: raced mainly on good going or firmer: wore cheekpieces last 2 starts. *Anthony Mullins, Ireland*

THE MOG 5 b.g. Atraf 116 – Safe Secret 50 (Seclude (USA)) [2004 –§, a47§: f8s **– §** Mar 11] close-coupled gelding: ungenuine performer: sometimes tongue tied: has been blinkered (including for only win). *Miss M. E. Rowland*

THE NIBBLER 3 b.g. General Monash (USA) 107 – Spoilt Again 91 (Mummy's Pet **48 ?** 125) [2004 8m⁴ p8g⁶ p10d 8g⁶ 8s Oct 15] poor maiden. *G. C. H. Chung*

THE NUMBER 3 gr.g. Silver Wizard (USA) 117 – Elite Number (USA) 56 (Elmaamul **68** (USA) 125) [2004 70: 8m³ 8s³ 7.1g⁵ 8g² 8m⁶ p8.6g Oct 16] rather leggy gelding: fair maiden: stays 1m: acts on soft and good to firm going: tried in cheekpieces: wandered fourth start. *I. Semple*

THE OLD SOLDIER 6 b.g. Magic Ring (IRE) 115 – Grecian Belle 53 (Ilium 121) **60** [2004 64: 6d 6v 7.1f² 6g 7.1d² 5d⁵ p7.1g² Oct 25] tall gelding: modest performer: stays 7f: acts on polytrack, firm and good to soft going. *A. Dickman*

THE PALLETMAN 4 ch.g. Lion Cavern (USA) 117 – Aquarela (Shirley Heights 130) **–** [2004 p8g Jul 14] well beaten in maiden at Lingfield on Flat debut. *M. F. Harris*

THE PEN 2 ch.f. (Apr 2) Lake Coniston (IRE) 131 – Come To The Point (Pursuit of **65** Love 124) [2004 6m 6m* 7f² 8s* f8g⁶ p8.6g⁶ Nov 20] workmanlike filly: third foal: dam unraced half-sister to useful Irish sprinter Sharp Point: fair performer: won seller at Redcar in August and nursery there in November: stays 1m: acts on firm and soft ground, respectable efforts on all-weather: found little final start. *P. C. Haslam*

THE PERSUADER (IRE) 4 b.g. Sadler's Wells (USA) 132 – Sister Dot (USA) (Sec- **–** retariat (USA)) [2004 88+: 13.8g 12g 16.2v 13.3m Jun 9] good-topped, quite attractive gelding: fairly useful handicapper at best: well beaten in 2004. *M. Johnston*

THE PHEASANT FLYER 2 ch.g. (Mar 17) Prince Sabo 123 – Don't Jump (IRE) **91** 71 (Entitled 126) [2004 6d³ 6.1m* 6m* 7s Oct 22] 6,000F, 18,500Y: tall, lengthy gelding: fifth foal: half-brother to 3-y-o Head Boy: dam 1m winner: fairly useful performer: won maiden at Warwick and nursery at Newmarket (by 1¼ lengths from Elgin Marbles) in September: well held in Horris Hill Stakes at Newbury: should stay 7f: acts on good to firm and good to soft going: races up with pace: sold 70,000 gns, sent to USA. *B. J. Meehan*

THE PLAINSMAN 2 b.g. (Mar 10) Atraf 116 – Mylania 70 (Midyan (USA) 124) **60 ?** [2004 6m⁶ p7m p8.6g p7g⁵ Dec 20] 1,000Y, resold 1,600Y: leggy gelding: first foal: dam maiden who stayed 1m: modest maiden: easily best effort when fifth at Lingfield, making running: stays 7f. *P. W. Hiatt*

THE PLAYER 5 b.g. Octagonal (NZ) 126 – Patria (USA) 76 (Mr Prospector (USA)) **–** [2004 82p: 8.5g Aug 30] angular gelding: fairly useful winner, lightly raced: well held in handicap only outing in 2004. *A. M. Balding*

THE PRINCE 10 b.g. Machiavellian (USA) 123 – Mohican Girl 112 (Dancing Brave **99** (USA) 140) [2004 93: 8m³ 9.2d* a7.5g² 9s* 9g* 9.1d* 8.9g* 8d³ p9.5g⁵ p10g³ Nov 30] well-made gelding: has a quick action: useful performer: had an excellent season, winning claimers at Yarmouth in June, Hamilton and Goodwood in August and Musselburgh and Ayr in September, and handicap at York (beat Khanjar 5 lengths) in October: best at 7.5f to easy 1¼m: acts on all-weather and soft going, probably on firm: tried visored/blinkered: effective with/without tongue tie: sometimes slowly away: held up: tough and consistent. *Ian Williams*

THE QUIET WOMAN (IRE)   2 b.f. (Feb 15) Barathea (IRE) 127 – Tajawuz 82   **74**
(Kris 135) [2004 5v³ 5d² 6d⁵ 6.3g⁴ 5.2m 6.5v⁶ Aug 18] €18,000Y: third foal: sister to
4-y-o Raheel: dam 1¼m winner: fair maiden: below form last 2 starts, in sales race at
Newbury on penultimate: should stay at least 7f: acts on heavy ground: tongue tied final
appearance. *Francis Ennis, Ireland*

THE RECRUITER   4 gr.g. Danzig Connection (USA) – Tabeeba (Diesis 133) [2004   **–**
–: f11g Jan 12] little form: tried visored. *J. G. M. O'Shea*

THE RING (IRE)   4 b.g. Definite Article 121 – Renata's Ring (IRE) (Auction Ring   **78**
(USA) 123) [2004 79: 16g 16d² 16.2v³ 16.1v 16.1m⁵ 13f 14.8g⁵ 14g⁵ Sep 11] big, rangy
gelding: fair handicapper: stays 2m: acts on fibresand, heavy and good to firm ground:
visored final start (had found little penultimate one). *K. G. Reveley*

THE RIP   3 ch.g. Definite Article 121 – Polgwynne 48 (Forzando 122) [2004 68p: 9.3f   **56**
8g³ 12g Oct 5] strong gelding: lightly-raced maiden: modest at best at 3 yrs: stays 1m:
acts on good to firm ground. *T. D. Easterby*

THE ROUNDSILLS   10 ch.g. Handsome Sailor 125 – Eye Sight 67 (Roscoe Blake   **–**
120) [2004 10.5s 12g⁶ Aug 4] modest handicapper at best: well held both Flat runs after
1997: best form at 1¼m: acted on good to soft going: dead. *M. Mullineaux*

THE SPOOK   4 b.g. Bin Ajwaad (IRE) 119 – Rose Mill (Puissance 110) [2004 41: 9m   **44 §**
7.9m 7.2g 9.1s⁵ 10s Nov 1] poor and temperamental maiden: left W. M. Brisbourne after
third start. *Miss L. A. Perratt*

THE STICK   3 b.f. Singspiel (IRE) 133 – Fatah Flare (USA) 121 (Alydar (USA)) [2004   **54**
61: p7g 12g 8.1v 8m 10f 8.1g p7m⁴ Nov 22] rather leggy filly: modest maiden: should
stay 1¼m: acts on polytrack and good to firm going. *M. R. Channon*

THE TATLING (IRE)   7 b.g. Perugino (USA) 84 – Aunty Eileen (Ahonoora   **123**
122) [2004 120: 5g² 5m³ 5g⁴ 5f* 5d 5m³ 5s² 5g² 5.2g* 6f³ 5m² 5m Dec 12]
    Cross-continental competition among sprinters is to have a new, more
visible, structure in 2005 with the inauguration of the Global Sprint Challenge, a
series of six races, beginning in Australia with the Lightning Stakes at Flemington
and the Australia Stakes at Moonee Valley in February, and ending in Japan with
the Centaur Stakes at Hanshin and the Sprinters Stakes at Nakayama in October. In
between, the King's Stand Stakes and the Golden Jubilee Stakes at Royal Ascot
(York in 2005) will form the middle legs of the series, the winner determined by
points, ranging in each race from ten for the winner to two for fifth, with double
points awarded for horses competing outside their own country. The winner,
though, has to have accumulated at least thirty points. As The Tatling is a gelding
approaching the veteran stage, it remains to be seen how attractive the series proves
to connections, one of the main aims being to promote potential stallions, and the
only prize announced being an all-expenses paid trip to the King George, the
Melbourne Cup and the Japan Cup in 2006 for the owners of the winning horse. Be
that as it may, if the title of champion sprinter at home had been decided by points
in 2004, The Tatling would have run away with it. Better than ever at seven, he was

King's Stand Stakes, Royal Ascot—The Tatling is in command
as Hong Kong raider Cape of Good Hope (visor) and Frizzante (rail) capture the minor placings

Dubai International Airport World Trophy, Newbury—
The Tatling (rail) and Var have drawn clear of Airwave

almost an ever-present in the top sprints. He reached the frame in ten of his eleven starts in Europe and gained reward for his remarkable consistency with victory in the King's Stand Stakes at Royal Ascot and the Dubai International Airport World Trophy at Newbury.

By Royal Ascot, The Tatling had already made two trips abroad, finishing a two-length second to The Trader, conceding him 4 lb, in the Prix de Saint-Georges at Longchamp on his reappearance in May and fourth of eight behind Avonbridge, beaten about the same distance, in the Prix du Gros-Chene at Chantilly in June, in between finishing third to Boogie Street in a listed event at Kempton. In a field of nineteen, The Tatling started fifth favourite for the Group 2 King's Stand Stakes, going off at 8/1 in an open market, headed by Palace House Stakes winner Frizzante at 9/2. Majestic Missile, winner of the Cornwallis Stakes over course and distance on his final outing as a two-year-old, was second favourite at 5/1, followed at 13/2 by Cape of Good Hope, in the absence of ill-fated South African-trained National Currency representing the form from Hong Kong, where the pair had been placed behind Silent Witness the previous December. Few horses travel more strongly in sprints than The Tatling and, as Boogie Street set a strong pace from a wide draw at Ascot, he cruised along, held up by Darryll Holland. The Tatling improved more or less on the bridle as he picked his way between runners to take command inside the final furlong, and his rider was able to wave his whip in celebration at the line, The Tatling holding Cape of Good Hope by a length and a half, with Frizzante finishing well, after meeting trouble, to be a neck further behind, Ringmoor Down also closing up late in fourth.

As a result of his win in the King's Stand, The Tatling had to carry a penalty in minor pattern races subsequently, and he ran very well in defeat in the King George Stakes at Goodwood in July and the Prix du Petit Couvert at Longchamp in September. He conceded 11 lb to the winner Ringmoor Down and was beaten less than a length into third when bidding to repeat his success of twelve months earlier at Goodwood, and went down by a length to Pivotal Point at Longchamp, conceding him 5 lb. The Tatling started joint second favourite behind Pivotal Point when gaining his second success of the year in the Dubai International Airport World Trophy at Newbury in September, but, with the favourite not at his best, was run closest by Var, The Tatling coming through to beat him a head, conceding him 5 lb.

The Tatling also performed well in his two outings in Group 1 company in Europe in 2004. In August, he finished runner-up in the Nunthorpe Stakes at York for the second year running, getting much closer to the winner than he had when beaten by Oasis Dream in the race twelve months earlier, going down by a neck this time to Bahamian Pirate. The Tatling's second chance in Group 1 company in 2004 came in the Prix de l'Abbaye at Longchamp in October. After a respectable third behind Pivotal Point in the Diadem Stakes over six furlongs at Ascot following Newbury, The Tatling ran one of his best races back over five at Longchamp, finishing strongly to go down by half a length to the improved Var in a field of fifteen, improving a place on his third in the race the previous year. On his final start, The Tatling was given the chance to improve on his seventh behind Silent Witness in the Hong Kong Sprint at Sha Tin in 2003, but he trailed in a well-beaten twelfth after having an interrupted preparation.

			Northern Dancer
	Perugino (USA)	Danzig	Pas de Nom
	(b 1991)	(b 1977)	Bold Reason
The Tatling (IRE)		Fairy Bridge	Special
(b.g. 1997)		(b 1975)	Lorenzaccio
	Aunty Eileen	Ahonoora	Helen Nichols
	(b 1983)	(ch 1975)	Blakeney
		Safe Haven	Amazer
		(b 1974)	

The Tatling's win in the King's Stand was the biggest in the career of veteran trainer Milton Bradley, who plucked The Tatling out of a claimer at Catterick in 2002. The Tatling, whose pedigree details were discussed in last year's annual, has run nearly forty times for Bradley in two and a half seasons, winning six races.

Dab Hand Racing's "The Tatling"

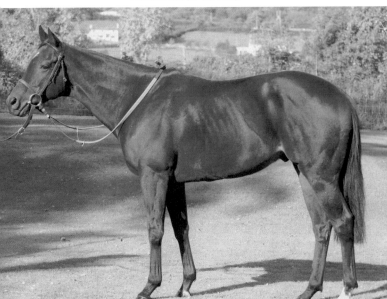

Successful over six furlongs, he has done most of his racing at five with Bradley, and acts on firm and soft ground. Usually waited with, The Tatling has been slowly away and edged off a true line on occasions, but there is little doubting his gameness or his toughness and reliability. A Group 1 victory still eludes him and his trainer, but there is inspiration for 2005 in the achievement of Bahamian Pirate in 2004, successful in the Nunthorpe at the age of nine for The Tatling's former trainer David Nicholls. *J. M. Bradley*

THE TERMINATOR (IRE) 2 b.g. (May 10) Night Shift (USA) – Surmise (USA) **46** 75 (Alleged (USA) 138) [2004 5.1d 6d 6s 6g 5d 7g⁴ 9d Oct 17] good-topped gelding: poor maiden: stays 9f: in cheekpieces fourth start. *A. Berry*

THE TRADER (IRE) 6 ch.g. Selkirk (USA) 129 – Snowing 88 (Tate Gallery **123** (USA) 117) [2004 120: 5g* 5g³ 5f 6d* 6.5g⁵ 6g 5m Oct 3]

On the ferries docking at Dover from Calais, white vans loaded up from moneyspinning 'booze cruises' were, in 2004, bumper to bumper with horseboxes carrying British-trained sprinters returning from lucrative trips of their own. Britain's sprinters met with almost unprecedented success in the top races in France, where they won six of the eight pattern events, including all four at five furlongs. Prize money levels hardly encourage sprinters in France, where the Prix Maurice de Gheest and the Prix de l'Abbaye, the country's Group 1 events, were worth substantially less than their counterparts in Britain in 2004, and the home-trained runners found themselves swamped by British horses almost throughout the latest season. Only Star Valley in the Prix de Meautry and the ex-Irish filly Miss Emma in the Prix Seine-et-Oise were able to turn back the tide, as The Trader won the Prix de Saint-Georges and the Prix de Ris-Orangis, Avonbridge the Prix du Gros-Chene, Somnus the Prix Maurice de Gheest, Pivotal Point the Prix du Petit Couvert and Var the Prix de l'Abbaye, in which Britain provided ten of the fifteen runners, Ireland and Germany two each and France only one.

At six, The Trader has something of the stereotypical white van about him. A poor mover in his slower paces, inclined to be sluggish early on, he has an awkward head carriage, but is capable of a surprising burst of speed when the mood takes him. The Trader's turn of foot was very much in evidence when he set the tone for the season on his reappearance in the Group 3 Prix de Saint-Georges at Longchamp in May. Favoured by the weights after winning only in minor company as a five-year-old, he started fourth favourite in a field of twelve and won most

Prix de Saint-Georges, Longchamp—The Trader wins his first pattern race; The Tatling and Patavellian help make it a 1,2,3 for British-trained runners

decisively, soon off the bridle but storming through to beat The Tatling by two lengths in receipt of 4 lb, with favourite Patavellian completing a clean sweep of the places for British-trained runners. After finding his stride too late from a slow start when a close third to Avonbridge in the Prix du Gros-Chene at Chantilly in June, The Trader lost his chance when stumbling leaving the stalls in the King's Stand at Royal Ascot, finishing only tenth, but he soon bounced back, gaining the second pattern success of his career at Deauville in July. For once the only British-trained runner, The Trader started favourite in a field of nine for the Prix de Ris-Orangis, another Group 3, and his turn of foot again proved decisive on a rare outing beyond five furlongs. Forced to make his challenge wide, despite being drawn on the rail, The Trader quickened to take command late on, beating Swedish Shave by two lengths. Next time out, The Trader ran a highly respectable race, stepped up to Group 1 company in the Prix Maurice de Gheest over six and a half furlongs at Deauville in August, though spoiling his effort by hanging left as he went down only by around a length and a half in fifth to Somnus. The Trader's final two outings were an anti-climax, as he trailed home last in the Sprint Cup at Haydock, where he was reportedly struck into, and beat only one rival in the Prix de l'Abbaye.

The Trader (IRE) (ch.g. 1998)	Selkirk (USA) (ch 1988)	Sharpen Up (ch 1969)	Atan
			Rochetta
		Annie Edge (ch 1980)	Nebbiolo
			Friendly Court
	Snowing (gr 1991)	Tate Gallery (b 1983)	Northern Dancer
			Fairy Bridge
		Biding (ro 1977)	Habat
			Pelting

The average distance of races won by the progeny of The Trader's sire Selkirk is around a mile, but The Trader is nearly all speed on the distaff side of his pedigree, going back several generations. His great grandam Pelting was a useful five-furlong winner and appears in the pedigree of numerous pattern winners, including the Prix de l'Abbaye winner Keen Hunter, whose grandam Splashing is half-sister to Biding, the grandam of The Trader. Biding also showed useful form at five furlongs, winning two of her three starts as a two-year-old, and her daughter Snowing, dam of The Trader, was fairly useful over the minimum trip in Ireland. Snowing has produced only one winner apart from The Trader, Molly Moon (by Primo Dominie), a winner twice over five furlongs as a two-year-old in 2003, also for Michael Blanshard. The trainer had to go to 100,000 guineas to secure a yearling brother to The Trader at the latest October Sales. The Trader cost 23,000 guineas as a yearling and showed a deal of speed from early in his career, finishing fourth in the Flying Childers Stakes as a two-year-old, but his form took a step forward when he was tried in blinkers halfway through his three-year-old season, and he has worn them ever since. A sturdy, close-coupled gelding, who usually impresses in appearance, he seems equally effective over six and a half furlongs as five nowadays, and acts on firm and soft going. He stays in training. *M. Blanshard*

THE VARLET 4 b.g. Groom Dancer (USA) 128 – Valagalore 91 (Generous (IRE) 139) **76** [2004 74: 14g 12m³ 12g⁶ 14.1g* 16.1f 13.1d 16g Sep 3] leggy gelding: fair handicapper: won at Salisbury in July: should stay 2m: acts on good to firm ground: effective visored/ in cheekpieces or not: tried tongue tied: sometimes slowly away, markedly so final outing: sold 1,200 gns. *B. I. Case*

THEVENIS 3 ch.c. Dr Fong (USA) 128 – Pigeon Hole (Green Desert (USA) 127) [2004 **–** 60: f12g Mar 3] sturdy colt: modest maiden at 2 yrs: well held only run in 2004. *J. S. King*

THE VIOLIN PLAYER (USA) 3 b.g. King of Kings (IRE) 125 – Silk Masque **70** (USA) 91 (Woodman (USA) 126) [2004 81: 8.1s 8m 10s 11.5m⁵ 12g p10g² p10g* **a78** p10g⁶ p9.5g p10g² Dec 18] stocky gelding: fair handicapper: left W. Jarvis after fourth start: won at Lingfield in October: stays 1¼m: acts on polytrack and firm ground, probably on soft. *H. J. Collingridge*

THE WARLEY WARRIOR 3 b.g. Primo Dominie 121 – Brief Glimpse (IRE) 108 **45** (Taufan (USA) 119) [2004 54: 6s⁶ 6d 6m May 26] tall, quite good-topped gelding: poor maiden: slowly away last 2 outings: often proves troublesome at stall (has been withdrawn). *M. W. Easterby*

THE WAY WE WERE 3 ch.g. Vettori (IRE) 119 – Pandrop (Sharrood (USA) 124) **75**
[2004 74P: 8.3s⁶ 9g⁵ 8.1m 8g³ 8g Sep 27] fair performer: bred to stay 1¼m: best efforts on
polytrack/good ground: edged right penultimate start: gelded after final one. *T. G. Mills*

THEWHIRLINGDERVISH (IRE) 6 ch.g. Definite Article 121 – Nomadic Dancer **89**
(IRE) 52 (Nabeel Dancer (USA) 120) [2004 87: 14s³ 16d⁴ 16d 13.9m³ 18m* 16.2g³
18.7m² 16.1f⁶ 16g 16.2m Sep 25] leggy, lengthy gelding: fairly useful handicapper: won
at Pontefract in June: stays 2¼m (though probably not 2½m): acts on firm and soft
ground: sometimes finds little. *T. D. Easterby*

THE WHISTLING TEAL 8 b.g. Rudimentary (USA) 118 – Lonely Shore (Blakeney **116**
126) [2004 110: 12g 13.4d² 13.3m* 14m⁵ 12v⁴ Oct 23] strong gelding: carries condition:
smart performer: 1¾ lengths second to Systematic in Ormonde Stakes at Chester prior to
winning listed race at Newbury in May by 4 lengths from Delsarte: off 4 months, well
below form on heavy ground in St Simon Stakes at Newbury final outing: stays 13.4f:
acts on fibresand, firm and soft going: held up: genuine and reliable. *G. Wragg*

THE WIZARD MUL 4 br.g. Wizard King 122 – Longden Pride (Superpower 113) **55**
[2004 74: 6s 8d 7d 6d 6.9g 6g 9d³ 10s⁵ Oct 30] leggy gelding: only modest nowadays:
stays 9f: acts on firm and good to soft going: tried blinkered: none too consistent.
W. Storey

THIHN (IRE) 9 ch.g. Machiavellian (USA) 123 – Hasana (USA) (Private Account **101**
(USA)) [2004 101: 8g 7d* 8g 9g Oct 2] sturdy gelding: useful handicapper: won at Newmarket in April by ½ length from Chappel Cresent: below form otherwise, including in
Cambridgeshire after 5½-month absence final outing: acts on 7f/1m: acts on any going:
sometimes starts slowly/hangs right: free-going sort, and usually travels strongly: held
up. *J. L. Spearing*

THINGMEBOB 4 b.f. Bob Back (USA) 124 – Kip's Sister (Cawston's Clown 113) **92**
[2004 106: 10.4s⁵ 11.9m⁵ May 22] leggy, rather unfurnished filly: useful performer at
3 yrs: below form both runs in 2004: should stay 1¾m: acts on firm going, possibly
unsuited by other than good. *M. H. Tompkins*

THINK IT OVER (IRE) 5 ch.m. Bijou d'Inde 127 – Good News (IRE) 61 (Ajraas **–**
(USA) 88) [2004 p7g p6g p8g Feb 18] first foal: dam 7f winner: no form. *A. P. Jones*

THINK QUICK (IRE) 4 b.f. Goldmark (USA) 113 – Crimson Ring (Persian Bold **41**
123) [2004 50: f11g f12s⁵ f9.4g⁶ f12s⁶ f12s³ f12s⁴ f12s f11s f11g f11s⁶ f12m² 14.1g
12m⁴ f14g Aug 19] workmanlike filly: poor maiden: stays 1½m: acts on fibresand, good
to firm and good to soft going: tried tongue tied: has raced freely. *R. Hollinshead*

THIRD EMPIRE 3 b.g. Second Empire (IRE) 124 – Tahnee (Cadeaux Genereux 131) **69**
[2004 61: 10s³ 10v 8s⁵ 9.3f² 10m⁴ 9v Aug 27] robust gelding: has a round action: fair
maiden handicapper: stays 1¼m: acts on firm and soft ground. *C. Grant*

THIRTEEN TRICKS (USA) 3 b.f. Grand Slam (USA) 120 – Talltalelady (USA) **77**
(Naskra (USA)) [2004 76: 9v 9d³ 10m⁴ 10f* 10d Aug 26] strong, lengthy filly: fair performer: landed odds in 4-runner maiden at Brighton in August: stays 1¼m: acts on firm
and good to soft going. *Mrs A. J. Perrett*

THIS IS MY SONG 2 b.f. (Mar 20) Polish Precedent (USA) 131 – Narva (Nashwan **74**
(USA) 135) [2004 6d 7d³ Aug 27] good-topped filly: fourth foal: closely related to useful
1m winner Pretence (by Danehill): dam unraced half-sister to high-class performer up to
1½m Predappio (by Polish Precedent): better effort in maidens when third to Playful Act
at Newmarket: should stay 1m. *Mrs A. J. Perrett*

THISTLE 3 ch.c. Selkirk (USA) 129 – Ardisia (USA) 87 (Affirmed (USA)) [2004 8d **80**
8g² 8g² 8.2m² 8.3g* Oct 11] good-topped colt: sixth foal: half-brother to 3 winners, including smart 1¾m winner Ashgar (by Bien Bien) and fairly useful 11.5f winner Halcyon
Daze (by Halling): dam, winner around 1¼m, half-sister to Oaks winner Ramrama: fairly
useful performer: landing odds readily in maiden at Windsor in October, making all: will
stay 1¼m: acts on good to firm ground: sold 90,000 gns, joined J. Howard Johnson.
J. H. M. Gosden

THIS WAY THAT WAY 3 b.g. Dr Devious (IRE) 127 – Ellway Dancer (IRE) 56 **–**
(Mujadil (USA) 119) [2004 f8g Feb 5] 25/1, always behind in maiden at Southwell.
G. C. Bravery

THOMAS LAWRENCE (USA) 3 ch.g. Horse Chestnut (SAF) 119 – Olatha (USA) **70 §**
(Miswaki (USA) 124) [2004 94: 6m⁶ 6s³ 6m Sep 4] well-made gelding: has scope:
lightly-raced maiden: ran as if amiss first/third starts in 2004, blinkered on latter: should
stay 7f: carries head awkwardly: one to treat with caution: sold 5,500 gns. *P. F. I. Cole*

THORNABY GREEN 3 ch.g. Whittingham (IRE) 104 – Dona Filipa 51 (Precocious **69** 126) [2004 67: 5f⁴ 6m⁴ 6g* 7m 6g⁵ 6d⁴ 7.1g 6s² 6d Oct 12] tall, quite good-topped gelding: fair handicapper: won at Hamilton in July: effective at 5f/6f: yet to race on heavy going, acts on any other. *T. D. Barron*

THORNBER COURT (IRE) 2 b.f. (Jan 24) Desert Sun 120 – Goldfinch 61 (Zilzal **65** (USA) 137) [2004 6m 6d⁴ 5g 5g² 5g³ 5s⁵ f5g⁶ p5.1g⁵ Dec 20] €10,500Y: smallish, stocky filly: first foal: dam, maiden, stayed 1m: fair maiden: should stay at least 6f: best efforts on good going. *A. Berry*

THORNTOUN PICCOLO 2 ch.f. (Jan 26) Groom Dancer (USA) 128 – Massorah **64** (FR) 108 (Habitat 134) [2004 7.2s 7.2d⁵ Sep 17] 9,000F: sister to winner in Greece and half-sister to several winners, including 5-y-o Vanderlin and fairly useful 6f winner Massiba (by Shareef Dancer): dam French sprinter: modest form in maidens at Ayr: not sure to stay much beyond 7f. *J. S. Goldie*

THORNY MANDATE 2 b.g. (Jan 26) Diktat 126 – Rosa Canina 91 (Bustino 136) **–** [2004 7d 7s Sep 14] smallish, sturdy gelding: well held in maidens at Salisbury, then gelded. *R. F. Johnson Houghton*

THREAT 8 br.g. Zafonic (USA) 130 – Prophecy (IRE) 109 (Warning 136) [2004 57, **47 ?** a–: f6g f6g⁴ f5g f7g p6g³ 5.1d⁴ 5.3g⁴ 5v⁶ 6g 7m⁵ 6.1m⁴ May 25] well-made gelding: poor **a38** performer: effective at 5f to easy 7f: acts on fibresand and any turf going: occasionally wears headgear: usually tongue tied away from 2002: sometimes slowly away. *J. M. Bradley*

THREE ACES (IRE) 2 ch.f. (Apr 28) Raise A Grand (IRE) 114 – Fallacy (Selkirk **55 §** (USA) 129) [2004 5d 5.1s⁵ 5.3m⁶ 7m 7m 8s 8s Nov 1] 8,500Y: close-coupled filly: half-sister to 2 winners by Victory Note, including 4-y-o Bad Intentions: dam unraced: modest maiden: stays 7f: acts on soft and good to firm going: blinkered last 4 starts: often slowly away: unreliable. *R. M. Beckett*

THREE BOARS 2 ch.g. (May 8) Most Welcome 131 – Precious Poppy 70 (Polish **47** Precedent (USA) 131) [2004 6g 8m 10g Oct 4] quite good-topped gelding: poor form in maidens. *W. Jarvis*

THREE DEGREES (IRE) 2 gr.f. (Feb 9) Singspiel (IRE) 133 – Miss University **81 p** (USA) (Beau Genius (CAN)) [2004 6.1d³ 7m² Oct 10] quite good-topped filly: second foal: dam well beaten both starts: better effort in maidens when ¾-length second to Real Quality at Newcastle: will stay at least 1m: sent to USA: should progress. *R. M. Beckett*

THREE DEUCES (USA) 2 gr. or ro.f. (Feb 22) Two Punch (USA) – Too Fast To Catch **68** (USA) (Nice Catch (USA)) [2004 5g⁵ p7g⁴ p6g⁶ p6g⁵ Nov 30] $110,000Y, $210,000 2-y-o: sister to useful American sprinter Storm Punch, and half-sister to 3 minor winners: dam minor winner in USA: fair maiden: likely to prove best at 5f/6f: wore cheekpieces final start: wore cheekpieces final start: joined R. Barbara in USA. *B. J. Meehan*

THREE EAGLES (USA) 7 ch.g. Eagle Eyed (USA) 111 – Tertiary (USA) (Vaguely **– §** Noble 140) [2004 16.2g⁶ Jul 8] angular gelding: modest handicapper at 4 yrs: well held both Flat starts since (refused to race once over hurdles in between): tried blinkered: temperamental. *M. Scudamore*

THREE GRACES (GER) 4 ch.g. Peintre Celebre (USA) 137 – Trefoil 111 (Kris 135) **114** [2004 109: 7.5f* 6.5m 7.1g³ Jun 3] good-bodied gelding: smart performer: career-best effort when winning handicap at Nad Al Sheba in February by 3½ lengths from One More Round: gelded, not discredited when ½-length third to Suggestive in listed race at Haydock final outing, settting good pace: races freely, and probably better at 7f/1m than further: best efforts on good ground or firmer: effective visored or not: tongue tied in 2004. *Saeed bin Suroor*

THREE PENNIES 2 b.f. (Mar 12) Pennekamp (USA) 130 – Triple Zee (USA) (Zilzal **72 d** (USA) 137) [2004 6m 7.5g* 7.5d³ 7f 7f 6g p8.6g⁵ Oct 9] 25,000Y: rather leggy filly: fourth foal: half-sister to useful 2000 2-y-o 7f winner Cauvery (by Exit To Nowhere): dam unraced: fair performer: won maiden at Beverley in June: respectable efforts at best after: stays 7.5f. *M. Dods*

THREE SECRETS (IRE) 3 b.f. Danehill (USA) 126 – Castilian Queen (USA) 82 **92 ?** (Diesis 133) [2004 82: 6g 7.1m* 7m² 8.1d³ 8m Sep 25] close-coupled, workmanlike filly: fairly useful performer: won maiden at Warwick in July: seemingly best effort when close third of 5 to Zietory in listed race at Sandown, dictating pace: stays 1m: acts on good to firm and good to soft going. *P. W. Chapple-Hyam*

THREE SHIPS 3 ch.g. Dr Fong (USA) 128 – River Lullaby (USA) (Riverman (USA) **63** 131) [2004 67p: 8m 7f⁵ p7.1g p12g p9.5g³ p8.6g Dec 17] leggy, quite good-topped gelding: modest maiden: left B. Hills after second start: stays 9.5f: acts on polytrack: wore cheekpieces last 2 outings. *Miss J. Feilden*

THREE STRIKES (IRE) 2 b.f. (Apr 14) Selkirk (USA) 129 – Special Oasis (Green **57** Desert (USA) 127) [2004 5m 5.1s⁵ f8g Dec 11] 85,000Y: leggy filly: second foal: sister to 5-y-o Golden Chalice: dam unraced half-sister to smart/very smart 1¼m performers Alnasr Alwasheek and One So Wonderful: trained on debut by J. Fanshawe: best effort in maidens when fifth at Bath, only run for S. Williams: should stay at least 7f (refused to settle at 1m). *N. Tinkler*

THREE VALLEYS (USA) 3 ch.c. Diesis 133 – Skiable (IRE) (Niniski (USA) 125) **117** [2004 119: 8g² 8g 8.5f³ Nov 27] strong, close-coupled colt: has a powerful, fluent action: smart performer: first past post 3 times at 2 yrs, including in Coventry Stakes at Royal Ascot (by 8 lengths) and Middle Park Stakes at Newmarket (failed dope test and disqualified): below best behind Haafhd on last-named course first 2 starts in 2004 in Craven Stakes (5 lengths second, refusing to settle) and 2000 Guineas (well-beaten eleventh, pushed along early): left R. Charlton and off nearly 7 months, creditable 1½ lengths third to Leroidesanimaux in Citation Handicap at Hollywood (not clear run early in straight): stays 8.5f: acts on firm going, winner on good to soft on debut. *R. J. Frankel, USA*

THREE WELSHMEN 3 b.g. Muhtarram (USA) 125 – Merch Rhyd-Y-Grug (Sabrehill **62** (USA) 120) [2004 64d: p7g f8.5g 8.2g⁵ 8.1s* 7s³ 11.8g 8m 10g 8.1g² Jul 8] unfurnished gelding: modest handicapper: won at Warwick in May: stays 1m: acts on polytrack and soft ground: sometimes slowly away: sometimes blinkered/in cheekpieces. *B. R. Millman*

THREE WRENS (IRE) 2 b.f. (Apr 2) Second Empire (IRE) 124 – Three Terns (USA) **62** (Arctic Tern (USA) 126) [2004 8d³ 8s* Oct 30] 26,000F: tall, sparely-made filly: closely related to 1m winner Celerity (by Fairy King) and half-sister to several winners, including smart French 1m/1¼m performer Thames (by Fabulous Dancer): dam, French 9f winner, out of Arc winner Three Troikas: joint favourite, won maiden at Ayr by neck from Jeffslottery: should stay 1¼m. *D. J. Daly*

THREEZEDZZ 6 ch.g. Emarati (USA) 74 – Exotic Forest 66 (Dominion 123) [2004 **88** 7g 7.1g 6g 7.1m* 6m 7m* p7d 8.1s* 8.2g³ 8.1d³ 7.1s* 7m 8.9g 10g 8s Oct 19] tall, useful-looking gelding: fairly useful performer: missed 2003: left Mrs P. N. Dutfield after reappearance: won handicaps at Chepstow (2) and Yarmouth and minor event at Chepstow in July/August: stays 1m: acts on firm and soft going: tried blinkered: usually tongue tied: edgy type: best forcing pace. *P. D. Evans*

THROUGH THE SLIPS (USA) 3 ch.f. Boundary (USA) 117 – Fast Selection **46** (USA) (Talinum (USA)) [2004 10m 8.2g f7s³ 7m Sep 18] fifth foal: half-sister to winners in USA/Puerto Rico by Fly So Free and Rhythm: dam unraced half-sister to very smart 1¼m performer Montjoy: poor maiden: should be suited by 1m: sold 1,000 gns, sent to Belgium. *J. G. Given*

THROWMEUPSOMETHING (IRE) 3 b.g. Cape Cross (IRE) 129 – Hawksbill **–** Special (IRE) (Taufan (USA) 119) [2004 12d Oct 17] 66/1: tailed off in maiden at Musselburgh. *A. Berry*

THROW THE DICE 2 b.c. (Mar 26) Lujain (USA) 119 – Euridice (IRE) 66 (Wood- **85 p** man (USA) 126) [2004 6s² 6g* 6s⁴ Sep 24] 5,500F, 13,000Y: strong, lengthy colt: half-brother to several winners, including 3-y-o Hazyview and 6-y-o Dusty Carpet: dam 1¼m winner who probably stayed 15f: favourite, won maiden at Haydock in August: good fourth to Tagula Sunrise in nursery there, still green but looking big danger 2f out: free-going sort, but should stay at least 7f: heavily bandaged and hung left on debut: type to make a useful handicapper at 3 yrs. *K. A. Ryan*

THUMAMAH (IRE) 5 b.m. Charnwood Forest (IRE) 125 – Anam 79 (Persian Bold **–** 123) [2004 64: p8g p8g 8.1d 8m⁶ f7d 8d Aug 9] lengthy mare: has a short action: little form in 2004: usually tongue tied: tried visored. *B. P. J. Baugh*

THUNDER CALLING (USA) 2 b.f. (May 9) Thunder Gulch (USA) 129 – Glori- **66** ous Calling (USA) (Nijinsky (CAN) 138) [2004 6m⁴ May 21] big filly: half-sister to several winners, including 4-y-o Crafty Calling and US Grade 2 11f winner Mr Bluebird (by Crafty Prospector): dam, won up to 9f in USA, out of half-sister to Japan Cup winner Mairzy Doates: favourite, fourth to Heres The Plan in maiden at Newmarket. *P. F. I. Cole*

THUNDERCLAP 5 b. or br.g. Royal Applause 124 – Gloriana 78 (Formidable (USA) **61** 125) [2004 67: f8g* f8.5s² p8g f8.5g 8v 7s Aug 13] quite good-topped gelding: modest handicapper: won apprentice event at Southwell in March: best at 7f/1m: acts on all-weather, firm and good to soft going: tried in headgear: often slowly away: usually held up. *J. J. Quinn*

THUNDERING SURF   7 b.g. Lugana Beach 116 – Thunder Bug (USA) 66 (Secreto   –
(USA) 128) [2004 12m 12m Jun 5] big, lengthy gelding: has a round action: useful performer at best: missed 2003: well beaten in 2004. *J. R. Jenkins*

THUNDERWING (IRE)   2 b. or br.c. (May 2) Indian Danehill (IRE) 124 – Scandisk   97
(IRE) 88 (Kenmare (FR) 125) [2004 7m³ 7d* 8v* 8d* 8s⁵ Oct 13] €12,000Y, 18,000
2-y-o: good-bodied colt: third foal: closely related to a winner in Italy by Desert King:
dam 7f winner in Italy at 2 yrs: useful performer: won maiden at Thirsk in August and
minor events at Newcastle in August and Ayr (comfortably, by 2½ lengths from Rocamadour in 4-runner event) in September: respectable fifth in listed race at Bordeaux: likely
to prove best at 7f/1m: acts on heavy going. *K. R. Burke*

THURLESTONE ROCK   4 ch.g. Sheikh Albadou 128 – Don't Smile 76 (Sizzling   86
Melody 117) [2004 83: 6m 6m⁵ 6m 6m* 6g p7g⁵ p6g³ p6g⁴ Dec 30] compact gelding:
fairly useful handicapper: won at Kempton in September: probably better at 6f than 7f:
acts on all-weather, raced only on good/good to firm going on turf: effective blinkered or
not: has hung left. *B. J. Meehan*

THWAAB   12 b.g. Dominion 123 – Velvet Habit 89 (Habitat 134) [2004 8d 7.9m 8m 8d   –
Oct 2] strong gelding: no longer of much account. *F. Watson*

THYOLO (IRE)   3 ch.g. Bering 136 – Topline (GER) (Acatenango (GER) 127) [2004   103
91p: 8m² 10.4s 8m³ 8.1d 8m 10d 11.8g Oct 11] big, useful-looking gelding: useful performer: best effort when 1½ lengths third of 27 to Mandobi in Britannia Handicap at Royal
Ascot: seems to stay 1½m: acts on good to firm ground, seems unsuited by softer than
good: edgy sort: usually races freely: gelded after final outing. *C. G. Cox*

TI ADORA (IRE)   2 b.f. (Mar 2) Montjeu (IRE) 137 – Wavy Up (IRE) (Brustolon 117)   61
[2004 7g 7g 10.1d Nov 5] 62,000Y: second foal: dam, French 8.5f winner, half-sister to
smart performer up to 1m Wavy Run: modest form in maidens: best effort on debut: not
knocked about final start. *P. W. Chapple-Hyam*

TIAMO   2 ch.c. (Mar 16) Vettori (IRE) 119 – Speed To Lead (IRE) 90 (Darshaan 133)   70
[2004 7d 8m⁶ 7.9g Oct 9] 8,000F, 26,000Y: quite good-topped colt: half-brother to 4-y-o
Decelerate and 2001 2-y-o 7f winner Elucidate (by Elmaamul): dam 2m winner who
stayed 2¾m: best effort in maidens when sixth at Goodwood: should stay at least 1½m.
M. H. Tompkins

TIBER TIGER (IRE)   4 b.g. Titus Livius (FR) 115 – Genetta (Green Desert (USA)   86 d
127) [2004 86: 8.3d⁴ 8m* 8f 8.1f² 7.9g 8m 8m⁵ 8m⁵ 7m⁵ 8s⁶ 8.5g 8g 8.3m 10.1d p7g
p8.6g Dec 17] rather angular gelding: fairly useful handicapper: won at Newmarket in
May: below form last 7 starts: effective at 7f/1m: acts on firm and good to soft going,
some encouragement on polytrack (well held on fibresand): usually wears headgear:
found little third start. *N. P. Littmoden*

TICERO   3 ch.g. First Trump 118 – Lucky Flinders 77 (Free State 125) [2004 79p: 8g   73
6.1d 7m p6g 7m⁴ 8g p8m p10m* Dec 22] close-coupled gelding: fair performer: left
C. Brittain, won claimer at Lingfield (claimed by K. Ryan 8,000 gns): stays easy 1¼m:
acts on polytrack and good to firm going: blinkered last 5 starts. *G. L. Moore*

TICKI TORI (IRE)   2 b.f. (May 5) Vettori (IRE) 119 – Lamees (USA) (Lomond   80
(USA) 128) [2004 7.9g³ 7s³ Oct 27] tall, quite good-topped filly: has scope: half-sister to
several winners, including smart 7f (at 2 yrs) and 1¼m winner Francesco Guardi and
useful 7f (at 2 yrs) and 1¼m winner Lomberto, both by Robellino, and 3-y-o Dumnoni:
dam unraced: third in maidens at York and Yarmouth (better effort, beaten ½ length by
Zalongo): likely to be suited by 1¼m/1½m. *Julian Poulton*

TICKLE   6 b.m. Primo Dominie 121 – Funny Choice (IRE) 68 (Commanche Run 133)   46
[2004 67: p5g⁴ p6g p6g³ 6v⁶ 5s⁶ 6g f5g Jun 28] good-topped mare: poor nowadays: best
up to 7f: acts on polytrack and soft ground, below form on good to firm: sometimes
visored/tongue tied/blinkered: inconsistent. *P. J. Makin*

TICKLEPENNY LOCK (IRE)   3 b.c. Mujadil (USA) 119 – Barncogue (Monseig-   –
neur (USA) 127) [2004 –: f7f f8g f11g Feb 17] smallish, compact colt: little form.
C. Smith

TICTACTOE   3 b.f. Komaite (USA) – White Valley (IRE) 54 (Tirol 127) [2004 64: f7g⁶   55
5s⁶ 7f 7.1d p5.1g⁵ p7.1g⁴ f6g⁵ Dec 12] modest performer: stays 7f: acts on all-weather
and good to firm going: tried visored: tends to start slowly: inconsistent. *D. J. Daly*

TIDAL   5 br.m. Bin Ajwaad (IRE) 119 – So Saucy 59 (Teenoso (USA) 135) [2004 –:   94
10.2s⁶ 12.1g* 10.2m* 12g 10.2g³ 10.1g⁴ 12f 10m* 10.1g Sep 15] lengthy, angular mare:
fairly useful handicapper: won at Chepstow in May and June and Kempton in September:
best around 1¼m: acts on firm going: tried blinkered: often races prominently: genuine.
A. W. Carroll

TIDAL FURY (IRE)   2 b.c. (Mar 2) Night Shift (USA) – Tidal Reach (USA) 68   **63**
(Kris S (USA)) [2004 6g 7d⁴ Aug 27] €48,000F, 28,000Y: big, strong colt: fifth foal:
half-brother to 3 winners, including 3-y-o Arfinnit and useful 2000 2-y-o 5f to 1m winner
Innit (by Distinctly North), later US Grade 2 1¼m winner: dam 2-y-o 1m winner who
stayed 10.5f: modest form in maidens at Pontefract and Thirsk: should stay 1m. *J. Jay*

TIDES   3 b.f. Bahamian Bounty 116 – Petriece 64 (Mummy's Pet 125) [2004 7g 6f⁶ 6g   **–**
Aug 11] 36,000Y: sister to fairly useful 6f winner The Privateer and half-sister to several
winners, including useful 1995 2-y-o 5f/6f winner Amazing Bay (by Mazilier): dam, 7f
winner, half-sister to dam of Lochsong and Lochangel: little sign of ability. *W. J. Musson*

TIDY (IRE)   4 b.c. Mujadil (USA) 119 – Neat Shilling (IRE) (Bob Back (USA) 124)   **86**
[2004 80: f6s 7v* 6v⁵ 6d 7.2d 7s³ 6.9g 7g 7g⁴ 8v⁴ 7d⁵ 7s Nov 6] smallish colt: fairly
useful handicapper: won at Newcastle in April: best at 7f: acts on fibresand and heavy
ground: none too consistent. *M. D. Hammond*

TIEGS (IRE)   2 ch.f. (Feb 22) Desert Prince (IRE) 130 – Helianthus (Groom Dancer   **–**
(USA) 128) [2004 7.1m Sep 6] 38,000Y: third foal: dam, French 1¾m winner, closely
related to high-class performer up to 1½m Wagon Master: 100/1, slowly away and always
behind in maiden at Warwick. *Mrs A. L. M. King*

TIFFIN BROWN   2 br.g. (Mar 1) Erhaab (USA) 127 – Cockatrice 61 (Petong 126)   **–**
[2004 6g f7g Nov 23] well held in maidens at York and Southwell. *P. C. Haslam*

TIFFIN DEANO (IRE)   2 b.g. (Mar 28) Mujadil (USA) 119 – Xania 32 (Mujtahid   **60**
(USA) 118) [2004 5d⁵ 5g 6g 7f 5g⁴ p6g f7g⁵ Dec 14] good-topped gelding: modest
maiden: should stay 7f: acts on good to soft going. *P. C. Haslam*

TIGER BOND   2 br.g. (Feb 23) Diktat 126 – Blackpool Belle 70 (The Brianstan 128)   **49**
[2004 5g 5f⁵ p7.1g Dec 31] poor form in maidens: off nearly 4 months before final start.
B. Smart

TIGER DANCE (USA)   2 b.c. (May 16) Storm Cat (USA) – Mariah's Storm   **95 P**
(USA) 116 (Rahy (USA) 115) [2004 7m* Sep 11]
    The job of advertising and public relations has been described as making
'flower arrangements of the facts, placing them so that the wilted and less attractive
petals are hidden by sturdy blooms.' The marketing teams employed by racing's
biggest battalions in Britain and Ireland have few peers in the peculiarly creative art
of promoting stallions, but the team at Walmac Farm in Kentucky could evidently
teach them a thing or two, judged by the advertising that appeared for new stallion
Tumblebrutus. Proclaimed as 'One of the *FAST CATS*' the full brother to Giant's
Causeway was trumpeted as having 'defeated champions Three Valleys and One
Cool Cat in the Group 1 Classic Two Thousand Guineas.' Starting at 200/1 and
evidently in the race to ensure a sound gallop for stable-companion One Cool Cat,
Tumblebrutus finished ninth of fourteen at Newmarket (beaten more than seventeen lengths behind the winner) and did indeed beat both Three Valleys and One
Cool Cat, well below form in eleventh and thirteenth respectively. The same claim,
of course, could also be made on behalf of the eight who finished ahead of Tumblebrutus, and also for tenth-placed Glaramara, another 200/1-shot who didn't win in
twelve starts in 2004 and reached a place only twice. Tumblebrutus was a useful

*Irish Stallion Farms EBF Maiden, Leopardstown—Giant's Causeway's brother Tiger Dance looks a very
good prospect in landing the odds on his debut*

performer, second in pattern company at two, but, seen out once more after the Guineas, he was retired to stud successful only in maiden company.

Tumblebrutus is one of five winning brothers, all by the most sought-after American sire Storm Cat out of Mariah's Storm, that have been trained at Ballydoyle. The Magnier/Tabor team bought Mariah's Storm, carrying her first foal Giant's Causeway, for 2,600,000 dollars, the top price paid for a broodmare in North America in 1996. Her second and third foals the smart sprinter-miler Freud and Roar of The Tiger, winner of a maiden on the first of four starts for O'Brien and later successful in the States, are also now at stud in North America. Mariah's Storm's fifth winner is the very promising two-year-old Tiger Dance who is her sixth foal (O'Brien also trained her fourth foal the Deputy Minister colt Wordsworth who failed to win in four starts for Ballydoyle). Tiger Dance created a big impression on his only start, running away with the seven-furlong maiden which opened proceedings on Irish Champion Stakes day at Leopardstown in September. Sent off at odds on, and with his tongue tied, Tiger Dance travelled strongly from the start, soon reached the leaders when shaken up and stretched out very well to win with plenty in hand by four and a half lengths from the filly Irish Question. The form was nothing to write home about but Tiger Dance won in the style of a very good prospect. He held entries in all the top two-year-old events in the autumn and is a best-priced 25/1 for the Two Thousand Guineas at the time of writing. He is one to watch out for in races at a mile and mile and a quarter.

			Storm Bird	Northern Dancer
	Storm Cat (USA)		(b 1978)	South Ocean
	(b or br 1983)		Terlingua	Secretariat
Tiger Dance (USA)			(ch 1976)	Crimson Saint
(b.c. May 16, 2002)			Rahy	Blushing Groom
	Mariah's Storm (USA)		(ch 1985)	Glorious Song
	(b 1991)		Immense	Roberto
			(b 1979)	Imsodear

Tiger Dance has the physique to go with his pedigree, being a strong, well-made individual who looks the type to train on. His dam Mariah's Storm won ten races from sixteen starts, two of them Grade 2 events, the Arlington-Washington Lassie Stakes at two and the Turfway Park Breeders' Cup Handicap at four. She won at up to nine furlongs but her very smart French-trained close relative Panoramic, by Blushing Groom's son Rainbow Quest out of Grade 3 Little Silver Handicap winner Immense, was effective at a mile and a quarter and a mile and a half. Giant's Causeway never ran beyond the extended mile and a quarter of the International at York, which he won, along with the St James's Palace, the Coral-Eclipse, the Sussex and the Irish Champion in a magnificent three-year-old campaign in the memorable 'millennium season' which also featured, among others, top-class performers Dubai Millennium, Montjeu and King's Best, all of whom, along with Giant's Causeway, were among the leading first-season sires in the latest season. *A. P. O'Brien, Ireland*

TIGER DAWN (IRE) 2 b.g. (Apr 24) Anabaa (USA) 130 – Armorique (IRE) (Top **63** Ville 129) [2004 8g p7.1g* p7g² p8g³ p7.1g Dec 6] €20,000Y, €65,000 2-y-o: eighth foal: closely related to useful 6f (at 2 yrs) to 7.5f (in Italy) winner Darwin and fairly useful 7f winner Camaret (both by Danehill) and half-brother to 1¼m winner Crozon (by Peintre Celebre): dam French 1½m winner: modest performer: won seller at Wolverhampton in October: ran creditably in nurseries after when placed at Lingfield: stays easy 1m: blinkered on debut. *W. J. Haggas*

TIGER FROG (USA) 5 b.g. French Deputy (USA) 118 – Woodyoubelieveit (USA) **68** (Woodman (USA) 126) [2004 11.1g* 11.8f⁵ 12.3g³ Aug 2] strong, lengthy gelding: fair handicapper: won at Hamilton in July: stays 1½m: acts on polytrack and firm going (form on soft over hurdles): blinkered last 4 starts: winning hurdler/chaser. *J. Mackie*

TIGER HUNTER 2 b.g. (May 17) Lake Coniston (IRE) 131 – Daynabee 61 (Common **41** Grounds) [2004 6m 6m 8m p7.1g³ p7m f5f Dec 28] poor maiden: stays 7f: acts on polytrack. *P. Howling*

TIGER TIGER (FR) 3 b.c. Tiger Hill (IRE) 127 – Adorable Emilie (FR) (Iron Duke **96** (FR) 122) [2004 –: p8g* p8g³ 8.5s* 9.9s² 9g 10.1m 12d⁴ 8m² 10v* 10.1s⁴ 10s Nov 29] close-coupled colt: useful performer: won maiden at Lingfield in February, minor event at Epsom (by 12 lengths) in April and handicap at Newbury in October: probably best around 1¼m: acts on polytrack, heavy and good to firm ground: usually held up: reliable. *Jamie Poulton*

TIGER TOPS 5 ch.g. Sabrehill (USA) 120 – Rose Chime (IRE) 58 (Tirol 127) [2004 71, a77: p7g⁵ p8g Feb 24] good-topped gelding: fair handicapper: had form at 1¼m, seemed best at 1m: acted on polytrack, good to firm and good to soft going: free-going sort: dead. *J. A. Supple* — a69

TIGGERS TOUCH 2 b.f. (Mar 23) Fraam 114 – Beacon Silver 75 (Belmez (USA) 131) [2004 6g⁴ 7g 7s⁶ 6g Oct 11] neat filly: second foal: dam, maiden on Flat who stayed 10.5f, winning hurdler: modest maiden: needs to settle to stay beyond 7f: acts on soft going. *B. R. Millman* 64

TIGHT CIRCLE 2 b.f. (Apr 22) Danzero (AUS) – Tight Spin (High Top 131) [2004 5g 5g⁵ 5.1d⁶ 5.7m* Jul 22] 800Y, 7,000 2-y-o: half-sister to several winners, notably smart 1¼m to 1¾m winner Vicious Circle (by Lahib): dam ran once: fair performer: made all in maiden at Bath: should stay 7f: acts on good to firm and good to soft going: sold 7,500 gns, sent to USA. *Mrs G. Harvey* 69

TIGHT SQUEEZE 7 br.m. Petoski 135 – Snowline (Bay Express 132) [2004 85+: p12g⁶ p12g⁵ p12g³ p10g p10g p10g* p13g p10g* 12g 10m 10m⁶ 9.9g³ Jun 22] big, plain mare: fairly useful handicapper: won at Lingfield in February and April, latter apprentice event: effective at 1¼m/easy 1½m: acts on firm and soft going: usually waited with: game. *P. W. Hiatt* 88

TIGRESS (IRE) 5 b.m. Desert Style (IRE) 121 – Ervedya (IRE) (Doyoun 124) [2004 –, a72: f6g⁶ f6g⁵ f5g² f5s⁶ f5s² f5g f5g Mar 29] tall mare: fair performer: 6 of 7 career wins at Wolverhampton: best at 5f/easy 6f: acts on fibresand and soft going: tried visored, blinkered nowadays: has been slowly away/wandered. *J. W. Unett* — a66

TIKITANO (IRE) 3 b.f. Dr Fong (USA) 128 – Asterita 103 (Rainbow Quest (USA) 134) [2004 55: 6m 7f 5f p5g Jul 21] modest form only 2-y-o start: no form in 2004. *D. K. Ivory* —

TILLA 4 b.f. Bin Ajwaad (IRE) 119 – Tosca (Be My Guest (USA) 126) [2004 78: 14g⁵ 18m⁶ 14m 14g² 14.1d² 14.8d⁶ 13.9m⁵ 14.1g Sep 29] workmanlike filly: fair handicapper: effective at 1½m to 2m: unraced on extremes of going: held up, and probably best produced late: consistent, though none too straightforward: sold 8,500 gns. *H. Morrison* 78

TILLERMAN 8 b.h. In The Wings 128 – Autumn Tint (USA) (Roberto (USA) 131) [2004 122: 8f⁵ 8g⁶ 7m Sep 9] big, strong, good sort: usually impressed in appearance: very smart performer: won 7 races, including Tote International Handicap at Ascot in 2000 and Celebration Mile at Goodwood in 2002: best effort at 8 yrs when 3¼ lengths fifth behind Refuse To Bend in Queen Anne Stakes at Royal Ascot, despite being short of room 2f out: race not run to suit when sixth to Soviet Song in Sussex Stakes at Goodwood, but disappointing in Park Stakes at Doncaster final outing: best at 7f/1m on good going or firmer: wore crossed noseband: usually taken steadily to post: sometimes slowly away: held up: to stand at Tally-Ho Stud, Co Westmeath, Ireland, fee €3,500. *Mrs A. J. Perrett* 119

TILLINGBORN DANCER (IRE) 2 b.g. (Mar 25) Imperial Ballet (IRE) 110 – Exhibit Air (IRE) 77 (Exhibitioner 111) [2004 5f 6d 7m 7g 6s Aug 14] close-coupled gelding: poor maiden: should stay 1m. *M. D. Hammond* 45

TILL THERE WAS YOU 3 b.f. Vettori (IRE) 119 – Fleur Rouge 71 (Pharly (FR) 130) [2004 p8g 7g 5.1m 7d Oct 12] half-sister to several winners, including smart 6f winner (including at 2 yrs) Red Carpet (by Pivotal): dam 2-y-o 6f winner: little sign of ability (left B. Meehan after debut). *W. G. M. Turner* —

TILLY FLOSS 2 ch.f. (Apr 27) Piccolo 121 – Lv Girl (IRE) 67 (Mukaddamah (USA) 125) [2004 p6g Dec 29] close-coupled filly: second foal: dam maiden who stayed 1m: 40/1, always behind in maiden at Lingfield: refused to enter stall intended debut in June (also very worked up in paddock). *J. A. Geake* —

TILT 2 b.g. (Apr 30) Daylami (IRE) 138 – Tromond 94 (Lomond (USA) 128) [2004 8g Oct 12] useful-looking gelding: half-brother to several winners (3 at least useful), including very smart 1m (at 2 yrs) to 1½m winner Nowhere To Exit (by Exit To Nowhere): dam, 9f winner who stayed 1½m, out of half-sister to Yorkshire Oaks and St Leger second Hellenic: 16/1 from 25/1 but very green, eighth in maiden at Leicester, travelling strongly just off pace long way and not knocked about (gelded after): should be well suited by 1¼m/1½m: type to do considerably better at 3 yrs. *J. R. Fanshawe* 61 P

TIMBER ICE (USA) 4 b.f. Woodman (USA) 126 – Salchow (USA) (Nijinsky (CAN) **63**
138) [2004 76: 11.9f 11.5m⁵ 10m⁵ 11.3m 13d* Nov 14] big, good-topped filly: just modest form at best in 2004, leaving H. Cecil after third start: won minor event at Maure-
de-Bretagne in November: stays 13f: acts on good to firm and good to soft ground.
D. Sepulchre, France

TIMBER SCORPION (UAE) 2 b.c. (Mar 5) Timber Country (USA) 124 – Aqraba **66**
69 (Polish Precedent (USA) 131) [2004 9f⁵ 10.2g Sep 27] first foal: dam, ran twice, closely related to useful sprinter Millstream: better effort in maidens when fifth at Redcar: led
long way at Bath: should stay 1¼m: sold 13,000 gns. *M. Johnston*

TIMBUKTU 3 b.g. Efisio 120 – Sirene Bleu Marine (USA) (Secreto (USA) 128) [2004 **45**
–: f9.4g 10d 10g 13.1g² 11.9g 14g Jul 2] stocky gelding: poor maiden: stays 13f: raced
only on fibresand and good/good to soft going. *C. W. Thornton*

TIME FLYER 4 b.g. My Best Valentine 122 – Sally's Trust (IRE) 51 (Classic Secret **–**
(USA) 91) [2004 –: p7g p8g p12g p10g 8m 6.1g⁶ p6g Dec 13] sturdy gelding: poor
maiden: tried blinkered. *W. de Best-Turner*

TIME FOR MEE 2 ch.f. (May 21) Timeless Times (USA) 99 – Heemee 81 (On Your **–**
Mark 125) [2004 5g 6d Oct 18] 2,000Y: half-sister to 1995 2-y-o 5f winner Dancing Rainbow (by Rambo Dancer) and 1m winner Picture Mee (by Aragon): dam 2-y-o 5f winner:
well held in maidens at Ripon and Pontefract. *R. A. Fahey*

TIME FOR YOU 2 b.f. (Mar 4) Vettori (IRE) 119 – La Fija (USA) 49 (Dixieland Band **64**
(USA)) [2004 6m 7g⁴ 6m* 7m 6.1d⁴ p7g 6d Oct 14] 1,700Y: workmanlike filly: third
foal: dam ran 3 times: modest performer: won maiden at Lingfield in July: well below
form last 2 starts, leaving P. McBride in between: should stay 7f: acts on good to firm and
good to soft ground. *J. M. Bradley*

TIMELY TWIST 3 b.f. Kirkwall 118 – Timely Raise (USA) (Raise A Man (USA)) **–**
[2004 54: p10g Jan 3] lengthy filly: maiden: well held only outing at 3 yrs. *S. Kirk*

TIME MARCHES ON 6 b.g. Timeless Times (USA) 99 – Tees Gazette Girl 44 (Kala- **54**
glow 132) [2004 42: f9.4s⁴ f12s 10f* 10f Sep 23] leggy gelding: modest performer: won
apprentice handicap at Pontefract in September: stays 1½m: acts on firm and soft going:
sometimes looks none too keen. *K. G. Reveley*

TIME N TIME AGAIN 6 b.g. Timeless Times (USA) 99 – Primum Tempus 49 **77**
(Primo Dominie 121) [2004 76: f6s⁵ f5s* f5g f6g* f6g³ f5g³ f6s³ f6s* f6s⁵ 6g 7.6d 6.1s⁶ **a88**
6m³ 6m 5.1d³ 6g² 5.9g² 6d³ 6m⁶ f5s p6g p5.1g f5g p6g⁴ Dec 13] leggy, useful-looking
gelding: fairly useful handicapper on all-weather, fair on turf: won at Southwell in January and February and Wolverhampton (dead-heat) in March: best at 5f/6f: acts on fibresand, firm and good to soft going: tried blinkered, usually wears cheekpieces: usually
races up with pace: has quirky side, but is tough. *E. J. Alston*

TIMES REVIEW (USA) 3 b.c. Crafty Prospector (USA) – Previewed (USA) (Ogy- **82**
gian (USA)) [2004 81: 6g² 7m⁵ 6g* 6m 6g 6g 6.1g Aug 19] quite good-topped colt: fairly
useful performer: won minor event at Leicester in June: below form in handicaps after:
stays 6f, probably not 7f: acts on firm and good to soft going, probably on fibresand:
usually races prominently. *T. D. Easterby*

TIME'S THE MASTER (IRE) 3 b.g. Danetime (IRE) 121 – Travel Tricks (IRE) **–**
(Presidium 124) [2004 40: f6g Mar 3] leggy gelding: poor maiden: will prove best at 5f/
6f: below form on fibresand: proved almost unrideable on debut. *M. F. Harris*

TIME TO REGRET 4 b.g. Presidium 124 – Scoffera 63 (Scottish Reel 123) [2004 **64**
57: f9.4g⁶ 7.5m² 7m⁴ 7.9f 8g* 7.5g 8f 7.9g 8.5m² 9.9m⁵ 9d* p8.6d⁶ 8.2v⁴ Nov 4] tall
gelding: modest handicapper: left J. Quinn after fourth outing: won at Pontefract in July
and Redcar in October: stays 1¼m: acts on polytrack and any turf going. *J. S. Wainwright*

TIME TO RELAX (IRE) 3 b.f. Orpen (USA) 116 – Lassalia (Sallust 134) [2004 63: **68**
f6g² f6s⁴ 8g* 9.9s 9.2d² 8m³ May 20] smallish, sturdy filly: fair performer: won handicap
at Bath in April: stays 9.2f: acts on fibresand, good to firm going and good to soft going:
wandered once at 2 yrs. *J. J. Quinn*

TIME TO REMEMBER (IRE) 6 b.g. Pennekamp (USA) 130 – Bequeath (USA) **63 §**
(Lyphard (USA) 132) [2004 82: 7d 6d 5m 7.2f⁶ 6m 6m 6.9f 5g² 6m 7m 8g 6g p8.6d⁶ p6g⁵
Nov 15] big gelding: fluent mover: only modest in 2004, leaving D. Nicholls after tenth
start: effective at 5f to 7f: acts on firm ground: usually wears crossed noseband/early to
post: has got upset in stall: often races freely: has hung left: unreliable: sold 2,600 gns.
R. A. Fahey

TIME TO SUCCEED 2 b.g. (Apr 5) Pennekamp (USA) 130 – Ivory League 47 (Last –
Tycoon 131) [2004 8.5s 6m Sep 5] tailed off in maidens. *J. S. Wainwright*

TIME TRAVELLER 2 b.g. (Apr 5) Timeless Times (USA) 99 – Belltina 41 (Belfort –
(FR) 89) [2004 p6d 6m Sep 1] tailed off, signs of temperament, in maiden and seller
(blinkered) at Lingfield. *T. M. Jones*

TIMMY 2 b.c. (Mar 17) Timeless Times (USA) 99 – Ohnonotagain 45 (Kind of Hush **41**
118) [2004 5v 6g 5d 7.5d 6d⁵ 6m f6s Aug 23] small colt: poor maiden: blinkered fifth (ran
creditably) and sixth starts. *M. E. Sowersby*

TINIAN 6 b.g. Mtoto 134 – Housefull 81 (Habitat 134) [2004 55: p8g⁵ f8g³ f8.5g f8g³ **55**
f8s 7g⁴ 8.5d 8g⁴ f7m⁵ f8.5g⁴ 8m³ 10.1f² 8d⁴ 10.1s f12m³ f8g⁴ f11d⁶ Dec 21] short-backed **a46**
gelding: modest performer: stays 1¼m: acts on all-weather and any turf going: tried in
headgear: none too reliable. *K. R. Burke*

TINKER'S FIRST 2 b.f. (Jan 28) First Trump 118 – Tinker Osmaston 79 (Dunbeath –
(USA) 127) [2004 5.1m 6m p7g Sep 7] first foal: dam 5f (including at 2 yrs) to 6f winner:
no form in sellers/maiden: in cheekpieces final start. *W. G. M. Turner*

TINTA 4 b.f. Robellino (USA) 127 – Albahaca (USA) (Green Dancer (USA) 132) [2004 –
f16g May 15] first foal: dam, French 10.5f winner, out of half-sister to Caerleon: ex-
French maiden: tailed off in Southwell handicap on British debut: best effort at 12.5f.
P. A. Blockley

TINTAWN GOLD (IRE) 4 b.f. Rudimentary (USA) 118 – Clear Ahead (Primo **54**
Dominie 121) [2004 62: p10g 9g 12f⁴ 10.9m² 9.7m 12f² 12m Sep 25] sturdy filly: modest
maiden: effective at 1¼m/1½m: unraced on soft/heavy going, acts on any other turf: wore
cheekpieces last 2 starts. *S. Woodman*

TINY TIM (IRE) 6 b.g. Brief Truce (USA) 126 – Nonnita 71 (Welsh Saint 126) [2004 **44**
p6g⁴ p8g⁴ p7g² p8g³ p7g⁵ p8g² p6g² 7g* f6g⁵ p6g² f7g² 7m p7g Dec 20] leggy, sparely-
made gelding: poor performer: won banded race at Brighton in May: stays 1m: acts on
all-weather, form only on good going or firmer on turf: tried blinkered/tongue tied.
A. M. Balding

TIOGA GOLD (IRE) 5 b.g. Goldmark (USA) 113 – Coffee Bean (Doulab (USA) –
115) [2004 58: f11m⁵ 14.1m f14g 13.8v Oct 16] leggy gelding: little form in 2004: tried
blinkered/in cheekpieces. *L. R. James*

TIPO (GER) 3 ch.c. Big Shuffle (USA) 122 – Triple Transe (USA) (Trempolino **87 d**
(USA) 135) [2004 6s⁵ 6s⁵ 7g³ 6g⁶ 7g 7d* p6g p6g Dec 4] second foal: dam German 7f
winner: fairly useful performer at best: winner of 2 races in Germany, namely maiden at
Dresden at 2 yrs and handicap at Hoppegarten in 2004: left A. Trybuhl, well held both
British starts: stays 7f: acts on good to soft going. *D. Flood*

TIPSY LAD 2 b.g. (Apr 3) Tipsy Creek (USA) 115 – Perfidy (FR) (Persian Bold 123) –
[2004 p7g Dec 20] 28/1, well held in maiden at Lingfield. *D. J. S. ffrench Davis*

TIPSY LADY 3 b.f. Intikhab (USA) 135 – Creme de Menthe (IRE) (Green Desert **64 ?**
(USA) 127) [2004 6s 7g 8m 9f 8.1m⁵ 8.1d⁵ 7s Sep 14] 38,000Y: big, workmanlike filly:
fourth foal: half-sister to 3 winners, including 6-y-o Piccled and 1½m winner Sticky
Green (by Lion Cavern): dam unraced half-sister to high-class 1m to 1½m performer In
The Groove: modest maiden: seems to act on firm going, well held on soft: should stay
1¼m: sold 3,000 gns. *D. R. C. Elsworth*

TIPSY LILLIE 2 ch.f. (Apr 26) Tipsy Creek (USA) 115 – Belle de Nuit (IRE) 85 **59**
(Statoblest 120) [2004 5v⁵ 6f 6m f6d 5m* 5m⁴ 6m* 6m⁴ 6.1v⁴ p6g Dec 1] third foal: dam,
2-y-o 6f/7f winner who stayed 1¼m, out of half-sister to very smart 1¼m performer Ruby
Tiger: modest performer: won sellers at Leicester and Yarmouth in July: stays 6f: acts on
heavy and good to firm ground. *Julian Poulton*

TIP THE DIP (USA) 4 ch.c. Benny The Dip (USA) 127 – Senora Tippy (USA) (El **92**
Gran Senor (USA) 136) [2004 90p: 11g² 12g 10.1s³ 12s Nov 6] sturdy, compact colt: has
a quick action: fairly useful performer: stays 1½m: acts on soft and good to firm going:
tongue tied last 2 starts: has worn crossed noseband: sold 20,000 gns. *J. H. M. Gosden*

TIP TOES (IRE) 2 b.f. (Mar 15) Bianconi (USA) 123 – Tip Tap Toe (USA) (Pleasant **47**
Tap (USA)) [2004 5m 5.1f⁶ 6m 6d⁴ 6m⁵ 7m 7s⁶ 8g⁴ 8d p8g⁴ f8g² p8.6g⁴ Dec 11] €2,000Y:
close-coupled, plain filly: third foal: half-sister to minor winner in USA by Halory Hunter: dam unraced out of sister to Derby winner Secreto: modest maiden: left M. Channon
after eleventh start: stays 1m: acts on all-weather, firm and good to soft ground. *Mrs
C. A. Dunnett*

TIRAILLEUR (IRE) 4 b.f. Eagle Eyed (USA) 111 – Tiralle (IRE) 71 (Tirol 127) **51**
[2004 56: p13.9g p10m⁵ p10g⁵ Dec 30] sturdy filly: modest performer: best up to 1¼m:
acts on all-weather, good to firm and good to soft going: tried blinkered. *Mrs P. Townsley*

TIT FOR TAT 2 b.f. (Feb 1) Diktat 126 – Wenda (IRE) 93 (Priolo (USA) 127) [2004 **54**
5m 7f⁵ 7d⁴ 8g 6m a6.8d² a8d³ Dec 28] 22,000F, €47,000Y: good-topped filly: third foal:
dam, 2-y-o 6f winner (stayed 11.5f), sister to useful Irish 1½m performer Carnelly: modest maiden: trained first 2 starts by M. Johnston, next 2 by J. Given: stays 1m: acts on dirt
and good to soft going: blinkered fifth outing. *J-E. Pettersson, Sweden*

TITIAN FLAME (IRE) 4 ch.f. Titus Livius (FR) 115 – Golden Choice (Midyan –
(USA) 124) [2004 69: 9g f8d Jul 23] unfurnished filly: fair at best: well held on Flat in
2004. *Mrs P. N. Dutfield*

TITIAN LASS 5 ch.m. Bijou d'Inde 127 – Liebside Lass (IRE) (Be My Guest (USA) **55**
126) [2004 58: f9.4g⁴ p8g* p7g⁵ p8g² p8g⁵ 8f Jun 2] quite attractive mare: modest performer: won banded race at Lingfield in January: stays 1¼m: acts on all-weather, raced
mainly on good/good to firm going on turf: blinkered. *C. E. Brittain*

TITIAN TIME (USA) 2 b.f. (Feb 5) Red Ransom (USA) – Timely 104 (Kings Lake **107**
(USA) 133) [2004 7g² 7g³ 8m* 8m² Oct 3] tall, leggy filly: sister to useful 1999 2-y-o 5f
(Queen Mary)/5.7f winner Shining Hour, closely related to a winner in USA by Dynaformer, and half-sister to 3 winners: dam 1m winner: useful performer: won maiden at
Newmarket in September by 1¼ lengths from Hallowed Dream: on toes, much improved
when 2 lengths second to Divine Proportions in Prix Marcel Boussac at Longchamp,
rallying: stays 1m: acts on good to firm going: races up with pace. *J. H. M. Gosden*

TITO GOFIRST 2 b.c. (Feb 12) Gone West (USA) – Torgau (IRE) 109 (Zieten (USA) –
118) [2004 6s p7.1g Nov 11] quite good-topped colt: behind in maidens at Newmarket
and Wolverhampton. *J. Pearce*

Lady Bamford & The Sangster Family's "Titian Time"

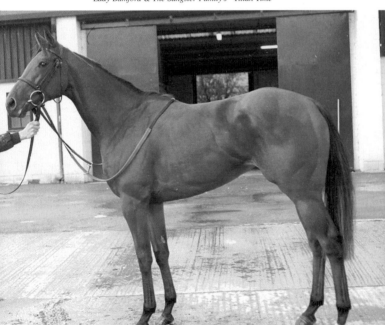

TITUS ROCK (IRE) 2 b.f. (Apr 26) Titus Livius (FR) 115 – Cossack Princess (IRE) — 72 (Lomond (USA) 128) [2004 5g Jul 3] €1,500Y: sixth foal: half-sister to fairly useful 1m winner My Very Own (by Persian Bold): dam fourth at 1¼m in Ireland: well held in maiden at Carlisle, slowly away. *D. McCain*

TITUS SALT (USA) 3 ch.g. Gentlemen (ARG) 136 – Farewell Partner (USA) (North- 80 ern Dancer) [2004 80: f7g³ 7g f8g Dec 11] sturdy gelding: fairly useful performer: below form after reappearance, leaving T. D. Barron and off over 8 months before final start: should stay 1m: acts on fibresand: blinkered last 4 starts. *M. D. Hammond*

TIVISKI (IRE) 2 b.f. (Feb 16) Desert Style (IRE) 121 – Mummys Best (Bustino 136) 75 d [2004 5g³ 5g⁴ 5.1d* 5m 6m⁴ 5.1g⁵ 6.1m 6m 7m 6s Sep 24] €14,500F, €14,000Y, resold 9,000Y: leggy filly: has quick action: sixth foal: half-sister to smart Irish 7f to 9f winner Rush Brook (by Pips Pride): dam, Irish 1¼m winner, half-sister to useful Irish 6f/7f winner Quintiliani: fair performer: won maiden at Chester in May: respectable efforts at best after: likely to prove best at 5f/6f: acts on good to firm and good to soft going. *E. J. Alston*

TIYOUN (IRE) 6 b.g. Kahyasi 130 – Taysala (IRE) (Akarad (FR) 130) [2004 82: 90 13.8g² 13g⁶ 16m* 13.9m 15.8m² 21g Jul 28] leggy, lengthy gelding: fairly useful handi- capper: won at Ripon in May: stays 2m, had excuse at 21f: acts on firm and soft going: tried visored. *Jedd O'Keeffe*

TIZDUBAI (USA) 3 b.f. Cee's Tizzy (USA) – Cee's Song (USA) (Seattle Song — (USA) 130) [2004 114: 8.5m⁶ 8m Jul 6] $950,000F: leggy, quite attractive filly: sister to several winners in US, notably top-class 8.5f to 1¼m (latter including Breeders' Cup Classic) winner Tiznow and very smart performer up to 1¼m Budroyale, and half-sister to winner in US by Moscow Ballet: dam winner up to 9f in USA: won both 2-y-o starts in USA for E. Harty, namely maiden at Hollywood and Grade 2 Sorrento Stakes at Del Mar: subsequently sustained condylar fracture to a bone in off-fore: well below best in Britain, in Princess Elizabeth Stakes at Epsom (sixth to Gonfilia, tiring) and Falmouth Stakes at Newmarket (edgy, folded tamely): likely to have proved best short of 1m: tongue tied in 2004: reportedly retired after sustaining hairline fracture of near hock, and sent to USA. *Saeed bin Suroor*

TIZI OUZOU (IRE) 3 ch.f. Desert Prince (IRE) 130 – Tresor (USA) (Pleasant Tap 57 (USA)) [2004 –: 10g⁶ 10m² Sep 27] good-bodied filly: modest maiden, lightly raced: stays 1¼m: acts on good to firm going: jinked and unseated rider on debut: joined M. Pipe, won juvenile hurdle in October. *J. L. Dunlop*

TIZ MOLLY (IRE) 3 ch.f. Definite Article 121 – Almadaniyah (Dunbeath (USA) — 127) [2004 54: 9.7m Jul 22] angular filly: lightly-raced maiden: pulled up only outing in 2004. *M. R. Channon*

TIZ WIZ 3 b.f. Wizard King 122 – Dannistar 57 (Puissance 110) [2004 44: 8s 6g² 5.9m 39 7.5s 8s Oct 30] poor maiden: stays 6f. *W. Storey*

TIZZY MAY (FR) 4 ch.c. Highest Honor (FR) 124 – Forentia 89 (Formidable (USA) 107 d 125) [2004 106: 10d 10g² 12g⁵ 12m 12m⁴ 16.4d 12m 10m⁵ 11.6d⁵ 12g 10v Oct 23] close- coupled colt: has a quick action: useful performer: hasn't won since early at 2 yrs: ran well in 2004 only when second to Promotion in handicap and when 3¼ lengths fourth to First Charter in listed event, both at Newmarket: stays easy 1½m: acts on soft and good to firm going: tends to sweat: usually held up: sold 30,000 gns. *R. Hannon*

TIZZY'S LAW 3 b.f. Case Law 113 – Bo' Babbity 75 (Strong Gale 116) [2004 –p: 5s* 71 6d⁶ 6m⁴ 5d⁵ 5m 5d 5g* 5s⁵ 5m⁵ Sep 11] sturdy filly: fair performer: won maiden at Thirsk in April and handicap at Folkestone in August: at least as effective at 5f as 6f: acts on soft and good to firm going. *M. A. Buckley*

T K O GYM 5 b.g. Atraf 116 – Pearl Pet 56 (Mummy's Pet 125) [2004 46: f7g f8.5s⁵ 39 Jan 8] smallish, close-coupled gelding: poor maiden: probably stays 1½m: acts on fibre- sand and firm ground. *D. Nicholls*

TOBEROE COMMOTION (IRE) 6 b.g. Great Commotion (USA) 123 – Fionn — Varragh (IRE) (Tender King 123) [2004 57, a62: f12g 8f May 27] maiden: well held in 2004: tried blinkered. *B. J. Llewellyn*

TOBEROGAN (IRE) 3 b.g. Docksider (USA) 124 – Beltisaal (FR) (Belmez (USA) 61 131) [2004 68: 6v⁶ 6s 7.5v 6m 7f 6f⁵ 6m⁴ 7g 6s³ 6d p7.1g Dec 11] third foal: half-brother to 7.5f (including at 2 yrs)/1m winner in Italy by Eagle Eyed: dam French maiden: modest maiden: best at 6f: probably acts on any turf going: none too consistent. *W. A. Murphy, Ireland*

TOBY'S DREAM (IRE)   2 b.c. (Apr 30) Mujadil (USA) 119 – Islandagore (IRE) 97   **73**
(Indian Ridge 123) [2004 6g 5.9f* 6d 6m⁶ 6g Sep 30] €30,000F, 24,000Y: sturdy colt:
first foal: dam, Irish 7f winner, out of smart Irish middle-distance performer Dancing
Sunset: fair performer: won maiden at Carlisle in July: respectable sixth at Epsom, only
form in nurseries after: should stay 7f: acts on firm ground. *M. Johnston*

TOCCATA ARIA   6 b.m. Unfuwain (USA) 131 – Distant Music (Darshaan 133) [2004   **58**
51: 10.9m* 9.7g* 12g 8.1m Aug 5] big mare: modest handicapper, lightly raced: won at
Warwick (maiden event) and Folkestone in July: stays 11f: acts on firm and good to soft
ground. *J. M. Bradley*

TODDEANO   8 b.g. Perpendicular 119 – Phisus 48 (Henbit (USA) 130) [2004 –: f7g   **–**
7m May 18] no form: tried in cheekpieces/tongue tie. *G. Fierro*

TODLEA (IRE)   4 b.g. Desert Prince (IRE) 130 – Imelda (USA) (Manila (USA)) [2004   **84**
81, a72: p10g⁶ 8.1d⁴ 10g⁴ 10m³ 10m⁶ 9g² 10.2f² 9g³ 8m* 8f 8g³ 9g³ 8g p8g Nov 10]   **a67**
smallish, quite good-topped gelding: has reportedly had wind operation: fairly useful
handicapper on turf, fair on all-weather: won at Kempton in July: effective at 1m/1¼m:
acts on polytrack, firm and good to soft going: tried tongue tied. *J. A. Osborne*

TOFFEE VODKA (IRE)   2 b.f. (Apr 12) Danehill Dancer (IRE) 117 – Vieux Carre   **73**
(Pas de Seul 133) [2004 6g⁶ 6g³ p6g* 6f 7g Oct 2] €9,000F, 12,000Y: tall filly: sister to
2001 2-y-o 6f winner Bond Jovi and half-sister to several winners, including 1996 2-y-o
5f to 7f winner Contravene (by Contract Law): dam, poor maiden, sometimes appeared
reluctant: fair performer: won maiden at Lingfield in August: should stay 7f: acts on
polytrack, probably on firm going. *J. W. Hills*

TOHAMA   2 b.f. (Jan 31) In The Wings 128 – Tanouma (USA) 114 (Miswaki (USA)   **73**
124) [2004 7f⁶ 7.5d 7s⁵ 8g Sep 30] good-bodied filly: unimpressive mover: half-sister to
several winners, including 1m (at 2 yrs) to 13f winner Azzilfi (by Ardross) and 1¼m to
15f winner Khamaseen (by Slip Anchor), both smart: dam 6f (at 2 yrs)/7f winner: fair
maiden: should be suited by 1¼m/1½m: best effort on good going: sold 13,000 gns.
J. L. Dunlop

TOILE   3 ch.f. Zafonic (USA) 130 – Princess Sadie 86 (Shavian 125) [2004 14.1g⁶   **–**
Sep 2] leggy, lengthy filly: fourth living foal: half-sister to 6-y-o Attorney: dam 2-y-o 5f
winner: 200/1, well held in minor event at Salisbury. *J. G. Given*

TOJONESKI   5 b.g. Emperor Jones (USA) 119 – Sampower Lady 55 (Rock City 120)   **55**
[2004 67d: p12g p8g p7g³ p8g⁴ f9.4m² 8.1g² 7v² 8.2m³ 8.1m³ 7.1f⁴ 8.5g² 8.1g 8f³ 7.6f
7s p7.1g⁵ p8m³ f8g p7g Dec 20] compact gelding: modest performer: effective at 7f to
easy 1½m: acts on all-weather and any turf going: tried visored/blinkered, usually wears
cheekpieces. *I. W. McInnes*

TOKEWANNA   4 b.f. Danehill (USA) 126 – High Atlas 65 (Shirley Heights 130)   **65**
[2004 63: f7g 7m 7.6g³ 7.1f p7g⁴ 8m⁵ 7.9m⁴ 7m³ 8m⁵ 8d p7.1d* p8.6g* p8.6g p8.6g²
p8.6g³ p8.6g² p8.6g² f8g Dec 28] good-bodied filly: fair performer: won 2 banded races
at Wolverhampton within 3 days in October: effective at 7f to 8.6f: acts on polytrack and
firm ground: tried visored/in cheekpieces (found little): usually tongue tied: races freely.
W. M. Brisbourne

TOLAGA BAY   6 ch.m. Dr Devious (IRE) 127 – Swordlestown Miss (USA) (Apala-   **–**
chee (USA) 137) [2004 f12g⁴ Apr 23] no form. *T. J. Fitzgerald*

TOLDO (IRE)   2 gr.g. (May 2) Tagula (IRE) 116 – Mystic Belle (IRE) 88 (Thatching   **76**
131) [2004 5d 5.9g 5g 5g⁴ 5.9f 7s² 7.1g* 8v* 8d* 7s Oct 23] €21,500F, €19,000Y, 10,000
2-y-o: strong, close-coupled gelding: second foal: half-brother to 2003 Spanish 2-y-o 1m
winner by Mukaddamah: dam 7f winner: fair performer: won seller at Musselburgh and
claimer at Newcastle on consecutive days in August for A. Berry, and nursery at Pontefract in October: stays 1m: acts on heavy going: blinkered and looked none too genuine
fourth/fifth starts. *G. M. Moore*

TOLEDO SUN   4 b.g. Zamindar (USA) 116 – Shafir (IRE) 68 (Shaadi (USA) 126)   **58**
[2004 62: f11s³ 11.5m⁵ f14.8m* 14.1m² May 25] compact gelding: modest handicapper:
left H. Collingridge after reappearance: won at Wolverhampton in May: stays easy 14.8f:
acts on all-weather, soft and good to firm going: tried visored/blinkered. *V. Smith*

TOMASINO   6 br.g. Celtic Swing 138 – Bustinetta 89 (Bustino 136) [2004 –: 10.4m⁴   **75**
12.4v⁶ 10g 11.9f* 11.9f 16d³ 13.1s Sep 18] good-topped gelding: just fair nowadays: won
claimer at Carlisle in July: barely stays 2m: acts on any going: tongue tied last 5 starts:
often races prominently. *K. G. Reveley*

TOM BELL (IRE) 4 b.g. King's Theatre (IRE) 128 – Nordic Display (IRE) 77 (Nordico (USA)) [2004 –: 12v² 14.1g 11.8m⁴ 13m⁴ 17.2g² 16.4g⁴ 12.1m 11.9m* p13.9g Nov 12] leggy gelding: modest handicapper: won amateur event at Brighton in September: effective at 1½m to 17.2f: acts on heavy and good to firm ground: tried visored, better form when not. *J. G. M. O'Shea* **61**

TOMBOLA (FR) 2 b.g. (Apr 12) Trempolino (USA) 135 – Green Charter 77 (Green Desert (USA) 127) [2004 7g⁴ 7m 7.1m Sep 6] strong, close-coupled gelding: half-brother to 2001 2-y-o 7f winner Safe Trip (by Hector Protector): dam, 2-y-o 7f winner, closely related to 5-y-o First Charter and half-sister to 4-y-o Private Charter: best effort in maidens when fourth at Salisbury: gelded after final start: likely to be suited by 1¼m/1½m: sent to Sweden. *J. L. Dunlop* **62**

TOM FOREST 2 b.c. (Mar 21) Forest Wildcat (USA) 120 – Silk Masque (USA) 91 (Woodman (USA) 126) [2004 6m⁶ 6m² 6m² 7.2m⁵ 7s 7s p7.1g p8.6g Nov 29] $135,000F, $57,000Y, 60,000 2-y-o: smallish, lengthy colt: half-brother to several winners, including 3-y-o The Violin Player and 8.5f (at 2 yrs) and 1½m winner Forum Finale (by Silver Hawk): dam, 2-y-o 6f winner (later won in USA), out of Fillies' Mile winner Silk Slippers: fair maiden: below form after third start, leaving A. Crook after fifth: should stay 1m: acts on good to firm ground. *J. R. Fanshawe* **74 d**

TOM FROM BOUNTY 4 ch.g. Opera Ghost 91 – Tempus Fugit 85 (Timeless Times (USA) 99) [2004 –: 6d p7m⁶ p7g⁵ Dec 20] poor maiden: should stay 1m: tried tongue tied. *W. de Best-Turner* **46**

TOMINA 4 b.g. Deploy 131 – Cavina 64 (Ardross 134) [2004 82: 16g² 16s Oct 22] workmanlike gelding: fairly useful handicapper, lightly raced: left N. Graham after reappearance: stays 2m: acts on polytrack and good to firm ground. *Miss E. C. Lavelle* **80**

TOMMY CARSON 9 b.g. Last Tycoon 131 – Ivory Palm 93 (Sir Ivor (USA) 135) [2004 –: f16g³ 11.5m p16d* 16d⁶ Oct 10] sturdy gelding: modest handicapper: won at Lingfield in August: stays easy 2m: acts on all-weather and any turf going: usually blinkered earlier in career: fair chaser. *Jamie Poulton* **54**

TOMMY SMITH 6 ch.g. Timeless Times (USA) 99 – Superstream (Superpower 113) [2004 90§: 5s 5d 5m 5m 5f* 5m 5g 5m 5d 5m Sep 15] smallish, sturdy gelding: fair performer: won minor event at Pontefract in June: best at 5f: goes well on going firmer than good: visored/blinkered: often starts slowly/hangs: front runner: untrustworthy. *J. S. Wainwright* **75 §**

TOMMYTYLER (IRE) 5 b.g. Goldmark (USA) 113 – John's Ballad (IRE) (Ballad Rock 122) [2004 p7.1g⁵ f6g Dec 28] well beaten in bumper in Ireland: poor form in maidens at Wolverhampton and Southwell. *D. Carroll* **47**

TOMOBEL 2 b.f. (Mar 19) Josr Algarhoud (IRE) 118 – Eileen's Lady 50 (Mtoto 134) [2004 5m 7g 7.1g⁵ 8g² p7m* p8.6g² Nov 29] 800Y: good-topped filly: second foal: dam, maiden who stayed 1¼m, out of half-sister to smart middle-distance fillies Braiswick and Percy's Lass: fair performer: won maiden at Lingfield in November: good second in nurseries: should stay 1¼m: acts on polytrack. *M. H. Tompkins* **70**

TOMOKIM (IRE) 3 b.c. Mujadil (USA) 119 – Snowtop (Thatching 131) [2004 –: p8g Mar 2] good-bodied colt: no form: tried visored: sold 1,500 gns in July, sent to Italy. *M. Quinn* **–**

TOMOOHAT (USA) 2 b.f. (Feb 17) Danzig (USA) – Crystal Downs (USA) 105 (Alleged (USA) 138) [2004 6d* Oct 14] $650,000Y: angular, useful-looking filly: second foal: dam, Irish 2-y-o 7f winner, half-sister to 7-y-o Mubtaker: 12/1 and green, won maiden at Newmarket by 1¼ lengths from Kenmore, travelling strongly behind leaders and asserting from over 1f out: should stay 1m: smart prospect, sure to go on to better things. *Sir Michael Stoute* **96 P**

TOMSK (IRE) 4 b.g. Definite Article 121 – Merry Twinkle (Martinmas 128) [2004 –: f8.5m⁶ 10.2s³ p10g Sep 18] poor maiden: left A. Berry after reappearance. *Miss K. M. George* **38**

TOMTHEVIC 6 ch.g. Emarati (USA) 74 – Madame Bovary 82 (Ile de Bourbon (USA) 133) [2004 67: 5g 5m 5g 5.1f 5m⁴ 5d 5g⁵ 5.1m 6g 5d f5g Nov 8] strong-quartered gelding: modest performer: left Mrs P. Sly after fifth start: probably best at 5f on good going or firmer: tried tongue tied/visored/in cheekpieces: sometimes slowly away: usually races prominently. *J. M. Bradley* **55**

TOM TUN 9 b.g. Bold Arrangement 127 – B Grade 59 (Lucky Wednesday 124) [2004 103: 6g 6d² 6d 6g⁴ 6f² 6s 6d³ 6g⁵ 6s 6g 5s³ 6s Nov 6] workmanlike gelding: has a round action: useful performer: several creditable efforts in 2004, including when placed in **103**

handicaps at York (behind Quito), Hamilton (to Blackheath), York again and Doncaster: effective at 6f/easy 7f: acts on all-weather and any turf going: blinkered: tongue tied earlier in career. *J. Balding*

TON-CHEE   5 b.g. Vettori (IRE) 119 – Najariya (Northfields (USA)) [2004 31+: f16.2s⁶ f16.2m 17.2g⁶ 16m Jul 5] poor maiden: stays 2m: acts on good to soft ground: raced freely third start: won over hurdles in September. *K. W. Hogg, Isle of Man*   –

TONG ICE   5 gr.g. Petong 126 – Efficacious (IRE) 49 (Efisio 120) [2004 –: p8g p6g⁶ p6g⁵ Apr 29] maiden: no form since 2002: usually wears headgear: sometimes carries head awkwardly. *B. A. Pearce*   –

TONI ALCALA   5 b.g. Ezzoud (IRE) 126 – Etourdie (USA) (Arctic Tern (USA) 126) [2004 75: f12s³ f16.2g⁵ 16.1v⁴ 12.4v 14g² 21.6v³ 14g⁴ 16d⁶ 13.1f* 14m³ 13g⁵ 17.1f² 14.1f⁴ 18m⁵ 16m* 16.1d* 16m⁵ 15.9s⁵ 14.4s⁶ 17.5d 16g⁴ 17.1g 18d Oct 18] close-coupled gelding: fair handicapper: won at Musselburgh in April, Ayr in May, Musselburgh in June and Newcastle in August: effective at 13f to 17f: acts on any turf going and fibresand: edgy sort: sometimes slowly away/races freely, and is usually held up: tough. *R. F. Fisher*   79

TONIGHT (IRE)   2 b.g. (Mar 30) Imperial Ballet (IRE) 110 – No Tomorrow (IRE) (Night Shift (USA)) [2004 6f³ 6g⁴ 7f³ 7m⁶ 8v 7m 8g Sep 16] stocky gelding: poor maiden: stays 7f: acts on firm going: blinkered (ran creditably) sixth start. *W. M. Brisbourne*   49

TONTO (FR)   3 gr.g. Second Empire (IRE) 124 – Malabarista (FR) (Assert 134) [2004 82§: p6g f7g⁴ f8g³ f8g p8g⁶ p10g 8.1g Jul 8] leggy gelding: modest maiden: seemed to stay 1m: acted on all-weather, raced only on good ground or firmer on turf: tried in cheekpieces: was ungenuine: dead. *Miss D. Mountain*   52 §

TONY JAMES (IRE)   2 b.c. (Feb 20) Xaar 132 – Sunset Ridge (FR) (Green Tune (USA) 125) [2004 6m* 6f⁴ 6m⁵ 6s* 7m⁶ 6s Oct 29] €22,000Y: tall, close-coupled colt: somewhat unfurnished at 2 yrs: has a quick action: first foal: dam, French maiden, half-   110

Scottish Equitable Gimcrack Stakes, York—
Tony James runs on strongly ahead of Andronikos (left) and Abraxas Antelope

Mr A. J. Richards' "Tony James"

sister to smart French performer up to 13f Ben Ewar: smart performer: won minor event at Pontefract in May and Scottish Equitable Gimcrack Stakes at York (led over 1f out to beat Andronikos by 1¼ lengths) in August: last in Prix Jean-Luc Lagardere at Longchamp and Criterium de Maisons-Laffitte last 2 starts: should stay 1m: acts on firm and soft ground. *C. E. Brittain*

TONY THE TAP   3 b.g. Most Welcome 131 – Laleston 73 (Junius (USA) 124) [2004   **92** 69p: p5g* 5m² 5m² 5m² 7g⁵ 6m² 6f* 6m 6d 6g⁵ 5.2g² 6.5f Sep 24] smallish gelding: fairly useful performer: won maiden at Lingfield in February and handicap at Epsom in July: stays 6f: acts on polytrack and firm going: usually waited with: genuine and consistent. *N. A. Callaghan*

TONY TIE   8 b.g. Ardkinglass 114 – Queen of The Quorn 53 (Governor General 116)   **90** [2004 84: 10.1v⁶ 9.9d² 8g² 10m⁵ 10m 8.3m² 8d* 7s⁶ 8g* 8m 9.2d⁶ 8.3d 8s⁵ 8.3d 8.9g 7.1d Oct 17] leggy, angular gelding: unimpressive mover: fairly useful performer: won minor events at Ayr in June/July: below form after: effective at 1m/1¼m: acts on any going: tried in cheekpieces/visor: has idled in front. *J. S. Goldie*

TOO KEEN   3 ch.f. Keen 116 – Janie-O 62 (Hittite Glory 125) [2004 f7d⁵ 7d f8m Jul   **–** 6] ninth foal: dam, best at 7f/1m on Flat, winning selling hurdler: little sign of ability in maidens. *J. R. Fanshawe*

TOOTSY   2 b.f. (May 2) Dansili 127 – Totom 80 (Mtoto 134) [2004 p7m Dec 22] first   **54 p** foal: dam 1¼m and 11.5f winner: 20/1, seventh in maiden at Lingfield, slowly away and not knocked about: should do better. *J. M. Jefferson*

TOP ACHIEVER (IRE)   3 ch.g. Intikhab (USA) 135 – Nancy Maloney (IRE) 53 (Per-   **64** sian Bold 123) [2004 –: 8.1s 8.5s 8.2d 8g⁶ 12g² Aug 13] heavy-bodied gelding: modest maiden: stays 1½m: blinkered penultimate start: hung in behind winner final start. *Mrs L. Stubbs*

TOPARUDI 3 b.g. Rudimentary (USA) 118 – Topatori (IRE) 89 (Topanoora 118) [2004   **77**
72: 8g 8d* 8m 8g³ Jul 9] big, good-topped gelding: fair performer: won handicap at Leicester in April: stays 1m: acts on good to firm and good to soft ground. *M. H. Tompkins*

TOPATOO 2 ch.f. (Apr 10) Bahamian Bounty 116 – Topatori (IRE) 89 (Topanoora   **68 p**
118) [2004 6s³ Oct 29] angular filly: second foal: half-sister to 3-y-o Toparudi: dam 7f to
10.5f winner: 50/1, 5 lengths third to Maggie Jordan in maiden at Newmarket, slowly
away and green but running on well: will stay at least 7f: should do better. *M. H. Tompkins*

TOP DIRHAM 6 ch.g. Night Shift (USA) – Miller's Melody 86 (Chief Singer 131)   **79**
[2004 82: 8v² 8s³ 8g² 8.9m 7.9g 8m* 7g⁶ 8g⁶ Sep 26] good-topped gelding: fair handicapper: won at Ayr in July: stays 1m: acts on heavy and good to firm ground: tried tongue
tied, not in 2004: consistent. *M. W. Easterby*

TOP FORM (IRE) 2 b.f. (Mar 27) Almutawakel 126 – Top of The Form (IRE) 79   **77**
(Masterclass (USA) 116) [2004 6m 6m⁵ 6m* 6.1m⁵ 6.5g 5m Oct 2] 40,000Y: leggy, good-
topped filly: third foal: half-sister to 3-y-o Glencalvie: dam, 5f (at 2 yrs)/6f winner, half-
sister to useful 5f performer Double Quick: fair performer: won maiden at Thirsk in July:
respectable effort next time, best effort after: likely to prove best at 5f/6f: acts on good to
firm going: often races prominently: sent to Oman. *E. A. L. Dunlop*

TOP GEAR 2 b.c. (Mar 12) Robellino (USA) 127 – Bundle (Cadeaux Genereux 131)   **85 p**
[2004 8g² Sep 29] 30,000Y: first foal: dam unraced out of half-sister to Japan Cup winner
Jupiter Island and high-class 1983 2-y-o Precocious: 10/1, 1½ lengths second to Night
Hour in maiden at Salisbury, slowly away and staying on well: will be suited by 1¼m/
1½m: sure to improve. *D. R. C. Elsworth*

TOPKAMP 4 b.f. Pennekamp (USA) 130 – Victoria Regia (IRE) 90 (Lomond (USA)   **104**
128) [2004 104: 6g² 6f³ 6m³ 6d⁶ Jul 9] small, strong, lengthy filly: useful performer: best
effort in 2004 when 2 lengths second to Lucky Strike in Benazet-Rennen at Baden-Baden
on reappearance: effective at 6f/easy 7f: acts on firm going, probably on soft: sometimes
starts slowly: raced freely last 2 outings: reportedly in foal to Cadeaux Genereux.
M. L. W. Bell

TOPKAT (IRE) 3 b.g. Simply Great (FR) 122 – Kitty's Sister (Bustino 136) [2004 9.9g   **81**
9.7m² 9f⁵ 12d* 14.4m Sep 4] €58,000Y: quite good-topped gelding: brother to several
winners, including useful Irish 1¼m to 1¾m winner General Cloney and fairly useful 7f
winner Morgannwg: dam, Irish maiden, sister to Lowther winner Kittyhawk: fairly useful
performer: won handicap at Salisbury in August: should stay 1¾m: acts on firm and good
to soft ground: usually waited with. *D. R. C. Elsworth*

TOP LINE DANCER (IRE) 3 b.c. Fasliyev (USA) 120 – Twafeaj (USA) 110 (Top-   **63**
sider (USA)) [2004 72: 6g⁴ 7s 7f 8g Sep 14] well-made colt: lightly-raced maiden:
only modest in 2004, leaving M. Johnston after third start: stays 7f: acts on firm ground:
tongue tied (reportedly had breathing problem) final start. *M. D. Hammond*

TOP MARK 2 b.c. (Apr 7) Mark of Esteem (IRE) 137 – Red White And Blue (Zafonic   **74**
(USA) 130) [2004 8v p8g³ p8.6g⁴ Dec 3] first foal: dam no sign of ability: in frame in
maidens at Lingfield and Wolverhampton: should stay 1¼m. *H. Morrison*

TOP OF THE CLASS (IRE) 7 b.m. Rudimentary (USA) 118 – School Mum (Repri-   **63**
mand 122) [2004 66, a53: f9.4g f9.4g⁶ f12g³ f9.4g³ p12g⁴ p12g p10g p12g p10g³ f12s⁵   **a50**
f12g 10.9d⁴ 11s 10.2f p12g 12.1g May 31] modest handicapper: barely stays 1½m: acts
on all-weather and any turf going: tried blinkered, visored nowadays: has been slowly
away/raced freely. *P. D. Evans*

TOP PLACE 3 b.f. Compton Place 125 – Double Top (IRE) (Thatching 131) [2004   **46 ?**
47: p5g p6g p6g p6g⁵ 6.1g⁵ 5.3g 7.1f⁶ 6d p5.1g p7g⁵ Dec 29] had a foal in 2003: poor
maiden: left C. Dwyer after sixth start: probably stays 7f: wore cheekpieces first 6 starts,
blinkered penultimate outing. *B. A. Pearce*

TOPPLE 3 b.f. Master Willie 129 – Top Cover (High Top 131) [2004 9g May 20] com-   **–**
pact filly: eighth foal: half-sister to 7f to 9.4f winner Marowins (by Sweet Monday): dam
ran twice: 25/1, well held in maiden at Goodwood, slowly away. *H. Candy*

TOPPLING 6 b.g. Cadeaux Genereux 131 – Topicality (USA) (Topsider (USA)) [2004   **59**
71, a–: p6g 6m 6m 6g 6.1g⁴ 6m 6m 7m 7.6f 7.1g Sep 3] smallish, good-bodied gelding: **a–**
modest handicapper: free-going sort, and probably best at 6f/7f: acts on good to firm
going: tried in cheekpieces/blinkers. *J. M. Bradley*

TOP PURSUIT 2 b.g. (Apr 26) Pursuit of Love 124 – Top of The Parkes 60 (Mister-   **–**
topogigo (IRE) 118) [2004 7g Jul 4] first foal: dam, maiden sprinter, out of half-sister to

useful sprinter Lucky Parkes: behind in maiden at Brighton: gave trouble at stall and withdrawn later in July. *J. L. Spearing*

TOP ROMANCE (IRE) 3 ch.f. Entrepreneur 123 – Heart's Harmony (Blushing Groom (FR) 131) [2004 105p: 7g 8.5m⁴ 9.9g Aug 11] close-coupled filly: just fairly useful form in 2004, best effort when fourth to Gonfilia in Princess Elizabeth Stakes at Epsom (again hung): should stay 1¼m: raced only on good/good to firm going. *Sir Michael Stoute* **90**

TOP SEED (IRE) 3 b.c. Cadeaux Genereux 131 – Midnight Heights 104 (Persian Heights 129) [2004 109: 10g² 10.4s⁴ 12g 16.2m³ 14.8m² 13.9s 12m 12v 12s p12g⁶ Nov 20] quite good-topped colt: smart performer: can well when ½-length second to Let The Lion Roar in minor event at Newbury in April and 4 lengths fourth to North Light in Dante Stakes at York in May: mostly disappointing after, pulled up eighth/ninth outings: probably stays 1½m: acts on soft and good to firm going, some promise on polytrack: tried tongue tied: sometimes edgy: one to treat with caution. *M. R. Channon* **112 d**

TOP SPEC (IRE) 3 b.g. Spectrum (IRE) 126 – Pearl Marine (IRE) (Bluebird (USA) 125) [2004 88: 10.4s 10m 10.2g⁵ 10d 8g² 10g 10d* 10m² 10d 10f 12d⁴ 10.3s Oct 22] leggy, close-coupled gelding: has a quick action: fairly useful performer: won claimer in August and handicap in September, both at Sandown: effective at 1m/1¼m: acts on firm and good to soft ground: often slowly away: held up. *R. Hannon* **88**

TOP STYLE (IRE) 6 ch.g. Topanoora 118 – Kept In Style 49 (Castle Keep 121) [2004 f11g p7g² p10g² 10s* Oct 30] modest performer: missed 2003: left M. Wallace and off 6 months, won banded race at Ayr in October: seems to stay 1½m: acts on soft going. *J. Howard Johnson* **59**

TOP TENOR (IRE) 4 b.g. Sadler's Wells (USA) 132 – Posta Vecchia (USA) (Rainbow Quest (USA) 134) [2004 80: p16g p12g p12g⁶ p12g³ Mar 24] strong, compact gelding: fairly useful handicapper at 3 yrs: just modest form tried on polytrack in 2004: stays 2m: raced only on good ground or firmer on turf: has shown reluctance at stall. *B. R. Johnson* **50**

TOP THE CHARTS 2 b.c. (Apr 21) Singspiel (IRE) 133 – On The Tide 72 (Slip Anchor 136) [2004 7d⁴ 7g⁴ 8g³ 7s² Oct 23] 90,000F, 80,000Y: tall, lengthy, good-topped colt: good walker: half-brother to several winners, including useful 1m/1¼m winner Tier Worker (by Tenby) and 3-y-o Surf The Net: dam, 1m winner, half-sister to very smart winner up to 1m Rock City: in frame in maidens and nursery (best effort when second to Crosspeace at Doncaster): should stay 1¼m: acts on soft ground: sometimes gives trouble stall (refused to enter once)/slowly away: has scope to make a useful 3-y-o and should win a race or 2. *R. Hannon* **91 p**

TOPTON (IRE) 10 b.g. Royal Academy (USA) 130 – Circo 77 (High Top 131) [2004 89, a78: p10g⁴ f8s³ p8g⁸ 8.3d 8s 8m 8f⁴ 8m⁶ 8m² 8m⁶ 8d⁵ 8m⁴ 8m 8.1s⁵ 7s p8.6g³ p8.6g⁴ p9.5g f8g⁵ p8.6g³ Dec 27] tall, angular gelding: fairly useful handicapper: won at Lingfield in February: best at 7f/1m: acts on all-weather/dirt, firm and soft going: has won in visor, blinkered nowadays: sometimes slowly away: has run well sweating: usually held up: tough. *P. Howling* **84 a80**

TOP TREES 6 b.g. Charnwood Forest (IRE) 125 – Low Line 66 (High Line 125) [2004 52§: 12m 17.2g⁶ 14m* 16.4m⁵ 13.1d 12.6d⁵ Sep 18] modest handicapper: won at Sandown in July: stays 16.4f: acts on fibresand and firm ground: has been slowly away/reluctant to race: unreliable. *W. S. Kittow* **56 §**

TOQUE 2 ch.f. (Mar 5) King's Best (USA) 132 – Barboukh 95 (Night Shift (USA)) [2004 7g p8g p8g³ p8.6g Dec 1] seventh foal: half-sister to smart French 1¼m performer Barbola (by Diesis) and fairly useful 1m/1¼m winner Tarboush (by Polish Precedent): dam, 1m winner, out of half-sister to Old Vic: fair maiden: best effort when third at Lingfield: should stay 1¼m. *H. Morrison* **67**

TORCELLO (IRE) 6 b.g. Royal Academy (USA) 130 – Vanya (Busted 134) [2004 10f⁵ 10v⁴ Oct 23] rangy, attractive gelding: has a quick action: useful winner at best: missed 2003: fairly useful form in 2 handicaps on belated return: stays 1½m: acts on any going: blinkered (ran creditably) once: formerly looked no easy ride: sold 18,000 gns. *G. Wragg* **91**

TORCHLIGHT (USA) 4 b. or br.f. Seeking The Gold (USA) – Cap Beino (USA) (Lyphard (USA) 132) [2004 66: 8.3g 8.2g a6s* a6f Nov 3] tall, useful-looking filly: well held first 2 starts in 2004, then left J. Gosden: off 3½ months, won maiden at Penn National in October: stays 7f: acts on dirt and good to firm going: edgy in blinkers/tongue tie second outing. *M. Zwiesler, USA* **?**

TORICELLA (USA) 3 gr.f. Tactical Cat (USA) 116 – Harlan Honey (USA) (Silver **81**
Hawk (USA) 123) [2004 8.3s⁴ 8g⁶ 9s* 8v⁶ 8.5g 7v⁵ 12.5d 6d 8s* 8s* 8v p10g Nov 27]
$115,000F, $90,000Y: ex-French filly: sixth foal: half-sister to 3 winners in USA: dam
8.5f/9f minor stakes winner in USA: fairly useful performer: won claimer at Dieppe in
July (final start for A. de Royer-Dupre) and handicaps at Cork and Leopardstown in
October: well held in handicap at Lingfield final start: stays 9f: raced only on good going
or softer on turf: usually blinkered, has worn cheekpieces. *K. J. Condon, Ireland*

TORINMOOR (USA) 3 ch.g. Intikhab (USA) 135 – Tochar Ban (USA) 83 (Assert **100**
134) [2004 93p: 9.9s⁵ 10f³ 10m³ 11.9d⁵ 10g⁴ Aug 28] good-bodied gelding: useful
handicapper: mostly ran creditably in 2004, best effort when third to La Persiana at
Windsor on second outing: free-going sort, and probably better at 1¼m than 1½m: acts
on firm and good to soft going: hung left penultimate start: gelded after final appearance.
Mrs A. J. Perrett

TORNADO BAY (IRE) 3 b.f. Desert Style (IRE) 121 – Dromoland (Cadeaux Gen- –
ereux 131) [2004 9g f12m May 28] rather leggy filly: third foal: half-sister to Belgian
winner around 1m In Xanadu (by Persian Bold): dam unraced: well held in maiden at
Ripon and claimer at Wolverhampton. *I. A. Wood*

TORO BRAVO (IRE) 4 b.g. Alhaarth (IRE) 126 – Set Trail (IRE) 76 (Second Set **43**
(IRE) 127) [2004 –: f8.5g⁵ f9.4g³ Jan 16] small, lengthy gelding: poor nowadays: seems
to stay 9.4f: acts on all-weather, raced only on good/good to soft ground on turf: tried in
cheekpieces/tongue tie/blinkers. *R. M. Beckett*

TORONTO HEIGHTS (USA) 3 ch.g. King of Kings (IRE) 125 – Revoltosa (IRE) **81**
(Catrail (USA) 123) [2004 81: f6g² p6g* p6g* p7g 7g p6g 6g p6g⁵ p6g⁴ Nov 27] smallish,
compact, attractive gelding: has a quick action: fairly useful performer: won maiden
and handicap at Lingfield in February: effective at 6f/7f: acts on all-weather, unraced on
extremes of going on turf: tried in cheekpieces/blinkers: raced freely/carried head high on
reappearance. *P. W. Chapple-Hyam*

TORQUEMADA (IRE) 3 ch.c. Desert Sun 120 – Gaelic's Fantasy (IRE) (Statoblest **76**
120) [2004 68: p6g³ 6d 6s 7m p6g³ p6g 6d 7m* 6m⁵ p7g³ p7g² Nov 27] compact colt: fair
handicapper: won at Leicester in September: stays 7f: acts on polytrack and good to firm
going: races freely: sometimes looks none too keen. *W. Jarvis*

TORRENS (IRE) 2 b.c. (Jan 28) Royal Anthem (USA) 135 – Azure Lake (USA) (Lac **73**
Ouimet (USA)) [2004 7.1d⁴ 8.1s* 8s 8d 8s³ 7s p8.6g⁵ Nov 29] €100,000F, €100,000Y:
good-bodied colt: first foal: dam, minor winner in USA, out of Italian Group 1 1¼m
winner Azzurrina: fair performer: won maiden at Chepstow in August: left M. Johnston
after fourth start: should stay 1¼m: acts on soft going, probably on polytrack: found little
fourth start, tongue tied on sixth: usually races prominently. *S. P. Griffiths*

TORRENT 9 ch.g. Prince Sabo 123 – Maiden Pool 85 (Sharpen Up 127) [2004 62§, **63 §**
a49§: f5g² p6g⁶ f6s³ f5g* f5s⁵ f5g³ f6s f5g f5g* f5g 5g 5d 5m* 5g² 5g 6m 5m 5m² 6g 5s **a57 §**
f5g⁶ f5m f5g² f5g⁶ Dec 21] strong, lengthy gelding: modest performer: won banded races
at Wolverhampton in February and March and handicap at Ripon in June: best at 5f/6f:
acts on all-weather and any turf going: wears headgear (blinkers in 2004): tried tongue
tied: has broken blood vessels, and reportedly can't be subjected to strong pressure:
carries head high: unreliable. *D. W. Chapman*

TORRESTRELLA (IRE) 3 b.f. Orpen (USA) 116 – Sea Ring (FR) (Bering 136) **117**
[2004 8d⁴ 9g* 8g* 10.5g 9g⁶ 8f⁵ Oct 28]
    A most progressive filly when unbeaten in three starts in the spring, Torre-
strella regressed just as quickly and didn't even make the frame in three subsequent
appearances, the last two of which came after she had left Francois Rohaut's stable
to continue her career in the States. Torrestrella, runner-up on both her outings at
two, won a minor event at Maisons-Laffitte on her reappearance and followed up in
a listed race at Longchamp, which led to her connections deciding to supplement
her for the Gainsborough Poule d'Essai des Pouliches, also run at Longchamp.
With neither the Prix Marcel Boussac winner Denebola nor the Prix Imprudence
winner Onda Nova in the line-up, it looked just an average running of the Pouliches,
even though it attracted a field of thirteen (and a crowd of 17,764, three times the
2003 figure, as the day was part of a series of free entry Sundays in the spring). The
Andre Fabre-trained Grey Lilas, who on her previous start had won the Prix de la
Grotte over the same course and distance, headed the market, coupled with
Nyramba, runner-up in the Fred Darling Stakes. Next in the betting were the

Godolphin pair Carry On Katie and Cairns, sixth and tenth respectively in the One Thousand Guineas at Newmarket. Carry On Katie set the pace, tracked by Torrestrella, and when the former began to tire approaching two furlongs out it was the latter who took over, pressed by Grey Lilas. From that point the race really only concerned Torrestrella and Grey Lilas, Torrestrella staying on the better to win by a length and a half. According to her Pau-based trainer, who in 2002 sent out Pearly Shells to win the Prix Vermeille, Torrestrella hadn't been entered for the Pouliches originally as she was backward as a two-year-old. Torrestrella's winning time equalled the fastest recorded for the race. She was then stepped up to ten and a half furlongs in the Prix de Diane at Chantilly, where she raced freely and didn't get home, finishing eleventh of seventeen behind Latice. Torrestrella was subsequently transferred to Christophe Clement in the States, but she was well below her best on both her starts there. She pulled hard on her first outing for three months in the Garden City Breeders' Cup Handicap at Belmont in September, finishing a well-beaten sixth of seven, and then beat only two home in an allowance race at Aqueduct, for which she started at odds on. It was a most disappointing end to the season.

Torrestrella (IRE) (b.f. 2001)	Orpen (USA) (b 1996)	Lure (b 1989)	Danzig Endear
		Bonita Francita (b 1987)	Devil's Bag Raise The Standard
	Sea Ring (FR) (b 1990)	Bering (ch 1983)	Arcic Tern Beaune
		Blue River (b 1980)	Riverman Azurella

Torrestrella, bought for €30,000 as a yearling, is from the first crop of the Prix Morny winner and Irish Two Thousand Guineas third Orpen, who never raced beyond a mile. There is more stamina on the dam's side of her pedigree, Sea Ring having won in France over eight and a half furlongs as a three-year-old and ten and a half furlongs at four. Torrestrella is the fifth foal of Sea Ring, and all are winners. The first, the useful French mare Torrealta (by In The Wings), showed her form over as far as fifteen and a half furlongs; the second, the fair French hurdler Comandante (by Apple Tree), won a juvenile event at Kempton in 2001; the third, Lingo (by Poliglote), is a smart performer at up to a mile and a quarter who made a very promising start as a hurdler before that career was interrupted by a series of setbacks; and the fourth, Campo Charro (by Alhaarth), is a fairly useful French mile-and-a-quarter to mile-and-a-half winner. Torrestrella's grandam Blue River, a seven-furlong winner in France at two who went on to finish third in the Prix d'Aumale, is a half-sister to the Prix de Minerve winner Anitra's Dance, whose successful produce include Solveig, a Group 3 winner over ten and a half furlongs. The great grandam of Torrestrella, Azurella, is also the third dam of the 1999 Criterium de Saint-Cloud winner and Prix de Diane third Goldamix. Azurella was a smart middle-distance filly, winner of the Prix de Malleret and Prix de Royaumont. Torrestrella's last race was the only occasion she encountered ground firmer than good, and she acts on good to soft. *C. Clement, USA*

1058

TORRID KENTAVR (USA) 7 b.g. Trempolino (USA) 135 – Torrid Tango (USA) **79**
(Green Dancer (USA) 132) [2004 73: 8v 8v* 8.5g² Jul 2] close-coupled gelding: fairly
useful performer: won minor event at Pontefract in April: effective at 1m/1¼m: acts on
fibresand and any turf ground: tried blinkered (not since 2000): free-going sort, usually
held up: has hung: useful jumper. *B. Ellison*

TORTUETTE 3 b.f. Turtle Island (IRE) 123 – Allmosa 66 (Alleging (USA) 120) [2004 **–**
–: f9.4s p8g f8s Feb 10] smallish filly: little form: tried visored/in cheekpieces. *Jean-Rene
Auvray*

TORZAL 4 br.g. Hector Protector (USA) 124 – Alathezal (USA) (Zilzal (USA) 137) **–**
[2004 –: 11.8g Oct 12] tall, leggy gelding: little sign of ability. *Miss M. E. Rowland*

TOSCO (GER) 4 b.c. Second Set (IRE) 127 – Tosca Rhea (Song 132) [2004 a7.5g² **?**
a5.5g² 7.5d² 8s⁴ 7g³ 7s* 8v⁵ 6.5g⁶ 7s f7g Dec 14] €40,000 2-y-o: brother to useful
German performer up to 7f Twin Set and half-brother to several winners, including useful
German performer up to 7f Takin (by Formidable): dam German 2-y-o 5f winner: fairly
useful form at best in Germany, winning twice including in handicap at Hamburg in June:
left A. Schutz, well held on British debut in handicap at Southwell final start: stays 7.5f:
acts on dirt and good to soft going: often blinkered in Germany. *D. Flood*

TOSHI (USA) 2 b.g. (May 10) Kingmambo (USA) 125 – Majestic Role (FR) 107 **50 p**
(Theatrical 128) [2004 6g 7s Aug 21] 200,000Y: tall gelding: sixth foal: half-brother to
useful French performer up to 1½m Aiglonne (by Silver Hawk) and winner in Japan by
Caerleon: dam, Irish 2-y-o 7f winner who stayed 1½m, half-sister to smart dam of White
Muzzle/grandam of Almutawakel: modest form in maidens at Goodwood and Chester,
tiring late on both times: sold 8,000 gns, then gelded: likely to do better. *M. Johnston*

TOSS THE CABER (IRE) 2 ch.g. (Apr 10) Dr Devious (IRE) 127 – Celtic Fling 77 **–**
(Lion Cavern (USA) 117) [2004 6m 6m Jun 12] tall, useful-looking gelding: has quick,
fluent action: last in maidens at Ayr and York (fractious), hanging left both times: gelded
after. *M. R. Channon*

TOTAL FORCE (IRE) 3 b.c. Night Shift (USA) – Capegulch (USA) (Gulch (USA)) **52**
[2004 59: 8.1g 7g Jun 22] tall colt: modest maiden: sold 5,500 gns, sent to Germany.
R. Hannon

TOTALLY SCOTTISH 8 b.g. Mtoto 134 – Glenfinlass (Lomond (USA) 128) [2004 **54**
51: 16s³ 15.8g³ Oct 5] smallish, quite attractive gelding: modest maiden handicapper on
Flat: finds 13f a minimum, and stays 2m well: acts on soft and good to firm going: tried
blinkered/tongue tied: held up: fair but moody hurdler. *K. G. Reveley*

TOTALLY YOURS (IRE) 3 b.f. Desert Sun 120 – Total Aloof 72 (Groom Dancer **90**
(USA) 128) [2004 90: 7g 7g⁴ 8f 7d⁵ 9g 6g 6g 6g² 6s 6s Oct 29] tall filly: fairly useful
performer: effective at 6f/7f: acts on good to firm and good to soft ground (well held on
firm): below form in cheekpieces final start: tends to flash tail. *W. R. Muir*

TOTAL TURTLE (IRE) 5 b.g. Turtle Island (IRE) 123 – Chagrin d'Amour (IRE) **88**
(Last Tycoon 131) [2004 12f⁶ 16.2m⁵ Sep 26] big, strong gelding: vastly improved in
2002, making into a smart handicapper: missed 2003: fairly useful form when sixth
at Doncaster on belated return: virtually pulled up in listed race at Ascot later in month:
should stay 2m: acts on firm and soft going: has been slowly away: waited with.
P. F. I. Cole

TOUCH OF EBONY (IRE) 5 b.g. Darshaan 133 – Cormorant Wood 130 (Home **55**
Guard (USA) 129) [2004 66?: 7.9m 12g 14.1d² 13.1s³ Oct 30] sparely-made gelding:
modest maiden: stays 1¾m: acts on fibresand, soft and good to firm going: blinkered
(well beaten) once at 4 yrs, wore cheekpieces third start: sometimes slowly away: held
up. *C. Roberts*

TOUCH OF LAND (FR) 4 b.c. Lando (GER) 128 – Touch of Class (GER) (Be My **122**
Guest (USA) 126) [2004 111: 12g² 10.5d⁶ 11g* 12d 12f³ 9.8m* 10m³ Dec 12] 90,000
francs Y: third foal: dam, German maiden, out of half-sister to very smart German performer up to 1½m Turfkonig: very smart performer: successful in minor events at Saint-
Cloud and Fontainebleau at 3 yrs when also second in Prix Hocquart at Longchamp and
fourth to Dalakhani in Prix du Jockey Club at Chantilly: improved form in 2004, winning
Grosser Mercedes-Benz-Preis at Baden-Baden (by ¾ length from Rotteck) in May and
Prix Dollar Casino Barriere de Montreux at Longchamp (by neck from Gateman, staying
on strongly from rear) in October: ran well when ¾-length third to Alexander Goldrun in
Hong Kong Cup at Sha Tin final start: effective at 9.8f to 1½m: acts on firm and soft
going. *H-A. Pantall, France*

TOUCH OF SILK (IRE) 2 ch.f. (Apr 1) Night Shift (USA) – Blew Her Top (USA) **70**
(Blushing John (USA) 120) [2004 5g⁵ 5f² 6m 6g Sep 4] €110,000Y: strong, close-
coupled filly: third foal: half-sister to useful French/US performer up to 1¼m Arabic
Song (by Alhaarth): dam unraced half-sister to US Grade 1 9f/1¼m winner Life At The
Top: fair maiden: second at Sandown, best effort: should stay 6f. *B. W. Hills*

TOUCH OF SPICE 2 ch.g. (Feb 26) Lake Coniston (IRE) 131 – Soft Touch (GER) **–**
(Horst-Herbert) [2004 6m p7g 8m Sep 25] well beaten in maidens. *J. R. Jenkins*

TOUCH OF SPIRIT 5 b.m. Dancing Spree (USA) – Soft Touch (GER) (Horst- **–**
Herbert) [2004 f8g Jan 12] poor maiden. *J. R. Jenkins*

TOUGH LOVE 5 ch.g. Pursuit of Love 124 – Food of Love 109 (Music Boy 124) **87**
[2004 102: 8g 7v 7d 8d 8m 8.1g⁵ 7.6s 7m Sep 9] strong, lengthy gelding: only fairly
useful handicapper in 2004: effective at 7f to 8.5f: acts on firm and soft ground: waited
with. *T. D. Easterby*

TOURNEDOS (IRE) 2 b.c. (Mar 9) Rossini (USA) 118 – Don't Care (IRE) 93 (Nor- **104**
dico (USA)) [2004 5.2g* 5m² 5f² 5.2m 5g* 6s 6d³ 5f² 6.3g⁵ 5v² 5s⁶ Oct 16] €23,000F,
€30,000Y: useful-looking colt: good walker: has a quick action: third foal: dam, Irish 5f/
6f winner, out of half-sister to Irish Derby winner Malacate: useful performer: won
maiden at Newbury in April and Betfair Molecomb Stakes at Goodwood (burst through
late on to beat Mary Read by neck) in July: creditable placed efforts in Maurice Lacroix-
Trophy at Baden-Baden, Flying Childers Stakes at Doncaster (2 lengths second to
Chateau Istana) and listed race at Tipperary after: barely stays 6f: acts on any turf going:
sometimes sweats: sold 80,000 gns. *M. R. Channon*

TOUT LES SOUS 3 ch.g. Tout Ensemble – Suzie Sue (IRE) (Ore 116) [2004 –: 11.8m **–**
12g Jun 30] tailed off in 3 maidens. *Jean-Rene Auvray*

TOUT SEUL (IRE) 4 b.c. Ali-Royal (IRE) 127 – Total Aloof 72 (Groom Dancer **112**
(USA) 128) [2004 115: 7d⁵ 8m 7.1g 7f⁶ 8d 8g⁴ 8d⁴ Oct 30] smallish, leggy, quite good-
topped colt: smart performer: best at 2 yrs when winner of Dewhurst Stakes: won listed
event at Leicester in April by 1¾ lengths from Polar Ben: good efforts when fourth at
Newmarket last 2 starts, behind Polar Ben in Joel Stakes, and behind demoted Babodana
in listed race: stayed 1m: acted on heavy and good to firm going: tried blinkered: to stand
at Tenuta della Calandrina, Italy, fee €4,500. *R. F. Johnson Houghton*

TO WIT TO WOO 4 b.g. Efisio 120 – Sioux 76 (Kris 135) [2004 70: f9.4g² f9.4s **69 d**
9.7d 8.1v⁵ May 4] good-bodied gelding: fair performer: well held after reappearance:
stays easy 1½m: acts on fibresand and good to firm going: wore cheekpieces last 2 starts.
B. W. Hills

TOWN END TOM 2 b.g. (Apr 18) Entrepreneur 123 – Prima Silk 82 (Primo Dominie **59**
121) [2004 5f⁵ 6.1g⁶ 5m⁶ 7f 5.1g p6g⁴ p6g² p7g p8.6g Dec 31] useful-looking gelding:
modest maiden: left D. Simcock after seventh start: best form at 6f: acts on polytrack,
probably on firm going: blinkered fifth start. *P. A. Blockley*

TOWN HOUSE 2 gr.f. (Mar 29) Paris House 123 – Avondale Girl (IRE) 73 (Case **68 d**
Law 113) [2004 5.1g⁵ 5d 5.1d² 5.1m* 5.1d 5s 5m p5.1g Oct 7] close-coupled filly: first
foal: dam 5f (including at 2 yrs)/6f winner: fair performer: won maiden at Nottingham in
May: well below form last 3 starts: will prove best at 5f: acts on good to firm and good to
soft going: usually races prominently. *B. P. J. Baugh*

TRACE CLIP 6 b.g. Zafonic (USA) 130 – Illusory 81 (Kings Lake (USA) 133) [2004 **68**
–: p5.1g⁶ p6g p6m p5.1g² Dec 31] neat, quite attractive gelding: only fair in 2004: stays
6f: acts on polytrack and firm going: has been tongue tied: headstrong: has found little.
N. I. M. Rossiter

TRACKATTACK 2 ch.g. (May 10) Atraf 116 – Verbena (IRE) (Don't Forget Me 127) **69 d**
[2004 6m³ f6m⁵ 5.7m 7f 6m f7g⁵ p6g⁵ p7.1g Dec 31] 15,000Y: third foal: half-brother to
3-y-o La Puce: dam French 11f winner: fair maiden: best effort on debut: left J. Osborne
after fifth outing: should stay 7f: tried blinkered: sometimes slowly away/looks temperamental. *P. D. Evans*

TRACTOR BOY 2 b.c. (Mar 25) Mind Games 121 – Day Star 77 (Dayjur (USA) 137) **87 p**
[2004 5g 6g* Oct 11] 30,000Y: second foal: dam, 6f winner, closely related to Poule
d'Essai des Pouliches winner Rose Gypsy: 33/1, much better effort in maidens (very
green on debut) when winning at Windsor by ½ length from Holly Springs, ridden to lead
close home: not sure to stay 7f: sold 60,000 gns, sent to USA: likely to make useful 3-y-o.
W. J. Haggas

TRADE FAIR 4 b.c. Zafonic (USA) 130 – Danefair 109 (Danehill (USA) 126) [2004 **116**
124: 6s 7m³ 7f* 7g⁶ Jul 27] strong, good-bodied, attractive colt: very smart performer at
3 yrs: not quite so good in 2004, though won Emirates Airline Minstrel Stakes at the
Curragh in July shade comfortably by 1½ lengths from One More Round: only sixth to
Byron in Betfair Cup (Lennox) at Goodwood 9 days later: stays 7f: acts on firm going,
well below form on softer than good: sometimes edgy and taken last/steadily to post:
sometimes races freely: joined R. Frankel in USA. *R. Charlton*

TRAFALGAR SQUARE 2 b.c. (Apr 7) King's Best (USA) 132 – Pat Or Else 72 **– p**
(Alzao (USA) 117) [2004 7m Sep 21] stocky colt: fifth foal: half-brother to 3 winners,
including 3-y-o Dumfries and fairly useful 1½m winner Saluem (by Salse): dam, staying
maiden, half-sister to St Leger/Gold Cup winner Classic Cliche and Yorkshire Oaks/Prix
Vermeille winner My Emma: 25/1 and in need of race, never dangerous in maiden at
Newmarket: should do better. *R. Guest*

TRAGEDIAN (USA) 2 ch.c. (Apr 4) Theatrical 128 – Foreign Courier (USA) (Sir Ivor **79 p**
(USA) 135) [2004 7g³ Oct 12] tall, rather unfurnished colt: fluent mover: half-brother to
several winners, notably high-class sprinter/miler Green Desert (by Danzig) and useful
French 1m (at 2 yrs) and 1½m winner Latarmiss (by Sadler's Wells): dam unraced half-
sister to top-class US filly Althea: 16/1 and green, close third to Eqdaam in maiden at
Leicester, always prominent: sure to do better. *J. H. M. Gosden*

TRAGIC DANCER 8 b.g. Tragic Role (USA) – Chantallee's Pride (Mansooj 118) **–**
[2004 12s Mar 30] workmanlike gelding: fair handicapper at best: unraced on Flat in
2003: well held only Flat run in 2004. *D. J. Wintle*

TRAIANOS (USA) 2 b. or br.c. (May 21) Mt Livermore (USA) – Shiitake (USA) **74**
(Green Dancer (USA) 132) [2004 6m⁵ 7g⁶ 7m⁵ 8.1g Sep 4] $95,000Y: tall, rather leggy
colt: half-brother to several winners, including US Grade 1 8.5f winner Taking Risks
(by Two Punch) and 4-y-o Shredded: dam, 1m winner in US, half-sister to very smart
performer up to 1¾m Per Quod out of half-sister to Alleged: fair maiden: needs to settle
to stay 1m: acts on good to firm going. *P. F. I. Cole*

TRANCE (IRE) 4 ch.g. Bahhare (USA) 122 – Lady of Dreams (IRE) 84 (Prince Rupert **93**
(FR) 121) [2004 82: 10m 10.1g⁴ 12g*⁴ 13.1d* 12d 14g 14.1d 14s³ 18s 16.5s⁵ f14g⁴ Dec 7]
lengthy gelding: fairly useful handicapper: won at Doncaster and Ayr in June: stays 2¼m:
acts on fibresand and soft going: blinkered (well held) twice at 3 yrs. *T. D. Barron*

TRANQUILIZER 2 b.f. (Feb 12) Dr Fong (USA) 128 – Tranquillity 70 (Night Shift **61**
(USA)) [2004 8.3m⁶ 8s 8m 8g² p8.6d³ p8g Nov 16] 4,000Y: big, good-bodied filly: fifth
foal: half-sister to 3 winners, including 3-y-o Tranquil Sky: dam 1m winner: modest
maiden: will probably stay 1¼m: acts on polytrack, best turf run on good going: tongue
tied all starts. *D. J. Coakley*

TRANQUIL SKY 3 b.f. Intikhab (USA) 135 – Tranquillity 70 (Night Shift (USA)) **91**
[2004 87: 7g 8m 9g⁵ 8m² 8m 8g⁴ 8m 7.1g⁵ 8d⁵ p10g³ Nov 10] strong, lengthy filly: fairly
useful handicapper: stays easy 1¼m: acts on polytrack and firm going. *N. A. Callaghan*

TRANSACTION (IRE) 2 ch.g. (Mar 13) Trans Island 119 – Meranie Girl (IRE) 52 **88**
(Mujadil (USA) 119) [2004 p5g³ 6g² 6g* 6f* 6d⁶ 6m 6s Sep 24] 19,000Y: good-topped
gelding: second foal: half-brother to 3-y-o Cheverak Forest: dam, maiden best at 5f at 2
yrs, out of sister to very smart sprinter Hever Golf Rose: fairly useful performer: won
maiden at York and nursery at Newmarket in July: respectable effort penultimate start:
will probably stay 7f: acts on firm ground: genuine. *J. M. P. Eustace*

TRANSCENDANTALE (FR) 6 b. or br.m. Apple Tree (FR) 126 – Kataba (FR) **43**
(Shardari 134) [2004 54, a37: 11.5m² 9.9s³ 10s⁵ 11.9m⁶ 10m 8f 9.9g⁴ 8m 11.9g⁴ 8.3g⁵ **a37**
11.9g 8m 8f Sep 16] smallish mare: poor nowadays: stays 11.5f: acts on fibresand, firm
and soft going. *Mrs S. Lamyman*

TRANSGRESS (IRE) 2 b.c. (Feb 11) Trans Island 119 – Ned's Contessa (IRE) 48 **65**
(Persian Heights 129) [2004 7m³ 7d 6g⁶ 7m⁵ Sep 9] 26,000F, 35,000Y: strong colt: fourth
foal: half-brother to 5-y-o Simply The Guest and 4-y-o Brandywine Bay: dam, 7f winner,
half-sister to useful 5f winner Connemara: fair maiden: stays 7f: acts on good to firm
ground: races up with pace: sometimes wanders. *R. Hannon*

TRANSIT 5 b.g. Lion Cavern (USA) 117 – Black Fighter (USA) 79 (Secretariat (USA)) **–**
[2004 72: 12.4v⁵ Apr 3] tall, leggy gelding: has a fluent, round action: fair maiden: well
held only Flat run in 2004: tried in cheekpieces: fair hurdler/chaser. *B. Ellison*

TRANSKEI 3 b.f. Sesaro (USA) 81 – In The Sky (IRE) 70 (Imp Society (USA)) [2004 **–**
8g 12s⁴ 9.3g 7.2s Oct 30] second foal: dam, maiden, stayed 8.5f: no form, including in a
claimer. *Mrs L. Stubbs*

TRANSVESTITE (IRE) 2 b.g. (Mar 29) Trans Island 119 – Christoph's Girl 50 **76** (Efisio 120) [2004 5g⁵ 6m⁴ 5.1s³ 7g⁶ 7m p6m³ p7g p7.1g* Nov 26] 25,000F, 27,000Y: sixth foal: half-brother to 3 winners, including fairly useful Irish 5f winner Eveam (by Mujadil) and 6-y-o Taboor: dam, Belgian 6f/7f winner, sister to very smart 5f/6f performer Hever Golf Rose: fair performer: won nursery at Wolverhampton: stays 7f: acts on polytrack, soft and good to firm going: visored 3 of last 4 starts: gelded after final outing. *J. W. Hills*

TRAPPETO (IRE) 2 b.c. (Feb 9) Barathea (IRE) 127 – Campiglia (IRE) (Fairy King **57** (USA)) [2004 7.1g f8g p7.1g Dec 1] modest form in maidens/minor event: likely to be suited by 1¼m/1½m. *W. R. Muir*

TRAVELLERS JOY 4 b.f. The West (USA) 107 – Persian Fortune 53 (Forzando **36** 122) [2004 53: p6g 5.1d f5g³ f5m 6m 6.1m⁶ 6.1m 5g⁶ 5.5g Jul 8] poor maiden: best at 5f/6f: acted on firm ground: dead. *R. J. Hodges*

TRAVELLER'S TALE 5 b.g. Selkirk (USA) 129 – Chere Amie (USA) 75 (Mr **69** Prospector (USA)) [2004 79: p10g 10g 10.2g⁶ 10g 12m 11.8g⁶ 10.2f 11.6f⁶ 11g² 12s² 13.1d p12.2g³ p12.2d⁴ p12.2g p12.2g Nov 19] leggy, useful-looking gelding: fair performer: stayed 1½m: acted on polytrack, firm and soft going: sometimes hung: dead. *P. G. Murphy*

TRAVELLING BAND (IRE) 6 b.g. Blues Traveller (IRE) 119 – Kind of Cute 52 **74** (Prince Sabo 123) [2004 85: p10g 8.1g 10.1g⁶ 10d 9s² 9.1d 8g Oct 10] leggy, quite attractive gelding: just fair performer nowadays: stays 1¼m: raced only on good going or softer on turf (acts on heavy): visored/blinkered last 3 starts: sold 7,500 gns. *A. M. Balding*

TRAVELLING TIMES 5 ch.g. Timeless Times (USA) 99 – Bollin Sophie (Efisio **53 §** 120) [2004 63: f6g⁵ f6g⁶ 6.1m 5.9f 5g⁴ 6g f6m² f6s⁶ p5.1g⁶ f7g f6g Dec 12] strong, lengthy gelding: modest performer: best at 6f: acts on fibresand and firm going, possibly not on softer than good: blinkered/visored: unreliable. *J. S. Wainwright*

TRAVEL TARDIA (IRE) 6 br.h. Petardia 113 – Annie's Travels (IRE) (Mac's Imp **58 §** (USA) 116) [2004 –: p10g p8g f7s⁴ f7g* f11s 7g Mar 31] sturdy horse: just modest in 2004, winning claimer at Wolverhampton (left I. Wood) in March: stays 7f: acts on fibresand and heavy ground: tongue tied last 3 starts: unreliable. *P. A. Blockley*

TRAVEL TIP (USA) 2 ch.c. (Mar 2) Gone West (USA) – Cap Beino (USA) (Lyphard **59** (USA) 132) [2004 8f⁴ 8g Oct 12] good-bodied colt: green, fourth in maiden at Pontefract, slowly away: pulled up lame at Leicester. *J. H. M. Gosden*

TRAYTONIC 3 b.c. Botanic (USA) – Lady Parker (IRE) (Nordico (USA)) [2004 101: **109** 5m⁵ 6m 6d* 6m³ 6m 6g 7m⁴ 7s⁶ Oct 23] tall, useful-looking colt: useful performer: left H. Cyzer after second outing: won minor event at Haydock in June by 2½ lengths from Steel Blue: ran well when third to Two Step Kid in William Hill Trophy (Handicap) at York and fourth to Kehaar in valuable handicap at Ascot: stays 7f: acts on firm and good to soft ground: reliable. *J. R. Fanshawe*

TREASON TRIAL 3 b.g. Peintre Celebre (USA) 137 – Pampabella (IRE) (High **68** Estate 127) [2004 70p: 8.1g 8.5g⁶ 8f⁴ 8.1g³ 10.1g* 10d³ 11.9s³ 16g⁴ 13.9g* p13.9g p16.5g⁵ p13.9g³ Dec 13] fair performer: won claimer at Yarmouth (left N. Tinkler) in August and handicap at York in October: stays 2m: acts on good to soft going. *Mrs Stef Liddiard*

TREASURE CAY 3 ch.c. Bahamian Bounty 116 – Madame Sisu 47 (Emarati (USA) **94** 74) [2004 78p: p5g⁵ 6d³ 6m⁵ 5m³ 5g* 5d 5m³ 5m² 5d⁶ p5.1g² p6g⁶ Dec 18] strong colt: fairly useful handicapper, generally progressive: won at Carlisle in June: effective at 5f/ 6f: acts on polytrack and good to firm going, yet to race on extremes of going on turf: has run creditably blinkered/tongue tied. *P. W. D'Arcy*

TREASURE HOUSE (IRE) 3 b.g. Grand Lodge (USA) 125 – Royal Wolff (Prince **82 +** Tenderfoot (USA) 126) [2004 100: p7g 8g 6s⁵ 7g 6m 5g 5d p6g* Nov 27] well-made gelding: only fairly useful nowadays: left B. Meehan after fourth start: won minor event at Wolverhampton in November: stays best at 5f/6f: acts on polytrack, raced mainly on good or firmer ground on turf: races prominently. *J. Jay*

TREASURE THE LADY (IRE) 3 b.f. Indian Ridge 123 – Kasora (IRE) (Darshaan **95** 133) [2004 91p: 7s⁴ 9f⁵ 9.5d⁴ 8m 8d⁶ Oct 17] workmanlike filly: has round, unimpressive action: fourth foal: half-sister to 2 winners, notably top-class 1¼m/1½m performer High Chaparral (by Sadler's Wells): dam unraced daughter of high-class French 1m/1¼m winner and Arc third Kozana: useful performer: won minor event at the Curragh at 2 yrs: below form in listed handicap at Ascot (tongue tied) penultimate start: ran at least creditably in listed events otherwise in 2004: stays 9.5f: acts on firm and soft ground: blinkered final start. *J. Oxx, Ireland*

TREASURE TRAIL   5 b.g. Millkom 124 – Forever Shineing 62 (Glint of Gold 128)   **73**
[2004 85: p16g⁵ 14.4v 14.1d 17.2f* 16m⁶ May 29] good-bodied gelding: fair handicapper: won at Bath in May: effective at 1½m to 17f: acts on firm and good to soft going. *S. Kirk*

TREASURY (IRE)   2 b.f. (Apr 19) King's Best (USA) 132 – Copious (IRE) (Generous   –
(IRE) 139) [2004 8.2m Sep 28] 25,000Y, 20,000 2-y-o: leggy filly: third foal: half-sister to fairly useful Irish 2002 2-y-o 7f winner Fluirseach (by In The Wings) who stayed 1½m: dam unraced half-sister to dam of high-class miler Landseer and 4-y-o Ikhtyar: 66/1, well held in maiden at Nottingham. *C. E. Brittain*

TREAT ME WILD (IRE)   2 ch.f. (Apr 3) Loup Sauvage (USA) 125 – Goes A Treat   **72 d**
(IRE) 82 (Common Grounds 118) [2004 5.1g* 7.1g⁶ 7m⁵ 6m* 6d⁴ 7f 6d p7.1g p6g p6g⁵ Dec 18] 2,000Y: leggy filly: second foal: half-sister to 3-y-o Rehia: dam 7f winner: fair performer: won claimer at Bath in April and nursery at Kempton in August: well below form last 5 starts: should stay 7f: acts on good to firm going, probably on good to soft. *R. Hannon*

TREBELLO   3 b.c. Robellino (USA) 127 – Trempkate (USA) (Trempolino (USA)   –
135) [2004 9.2d Sep 27] 9/2, last in maiden at Hamilton. *M. Johnston*

TREBLE SEVEN (USA)   2 b. or br.f. (Feb 24) Fusaichi Pegasus (USA) 130 – Nemea   **58**
(USA) 97 (The Minstrel (CAN) 135) [2004 7g⁶ 6g Oct 2] $60,000Y: rather leggy filly: fifth foal: half-sister to 4-y-o Foodbroker Founder and smart 7f/1m winner Lovers Knot (by Groom Dancer): dam 1¼m winner who probably stayed 2m: better effort in maidens when sixth at Yarmouth (edgy, led briefly 2f out): bred to stay at least 1m. *C. E. Brittain*

TRE COLLINE   5 b.g. Efisio 120 – Triple Joy 70 (Most Welcome 131) [2004 82: 6s   **69 +**
7s 6s 7m 7m f8d* f7g⁵ f8d* p8g⁴ 8.2d⁶ p8g* 7g p7d⁶ p7g p7.1g⁴ Oct 2] robust gelding: **a84**
fairly useful performer: won 2 handicaps at Southwell in June and claimer at Lingfield in July: stays 1m: acts on all-weather and good to firm ground: tried visored: sold 30,000 gns. *N. Tinkler*

TREE CHOPPER (USA)   3 ch.f. Woodman (USA) 126 – Gazayil (USA) 80 (Irish   –
River (FR) 131) [2004 79p: 10m Jul 17] lengthy filly: tongue tied, won maiden at Bath only start at 2 yrs: tailed-off last in listed race at Newbury on return: should stay 1¼m: sent to USA. *M. P. Tregoning*

TREE ROOFER   5 b.g. King's Signet (USA) 110 – Armaiti 78 (Sayf El Arab (USA)   –
127) [2004 50, a57: p7g p5g p6g p6g² p6g Dec 20] modest maiden: best at 5f/6f: acts on   **a52**
all-weather and good to firm ground: tried in headgear. *N. P. Littmoden*

TREE TOPS   3 b.f. Grand Lodge (USA) 125 – The Faraway Tree 113 (Suave Dancer   **77 d**
(USA) 136) [2004 7g⁵ 8.2s² 9.9g³ 10m³ 10f⁶ 10g 10d 10.2s p12g Nov 27] useful-looking filly: second foal: dam, 6f (at 2 yrs) and 1¾m winner, half-sister to very smart 9f/1¼m performer Sasuru: fair maiden: ran poorly last 4 starts: stays 1¼m: acts on soft and good to firm ground: sold 20,000 gns. *J. H. M. Gosden*

TREETOPS HOTEL (IRE)   5 ch.g. Grand Lodge (USA) 125 – Rousinette (Rousil-   **66**
lon (USA) 133) [2004 86d: p10g² 8m 7m 7g 8.1m² 11.9m⁴ 7m² 11g 6g p8g⁴ p9.5g⁴ Dec 6] quite attractive gelding: fair performer: probably best at 7f to 1¼m: acts on polytrack, firm and good to soft going: sometimes visored/in cheekpieces/tongue tied: has carried head awkwardly. *B. R. Johnson*

TREGARRON   3 br.g. Efisio 120 – Language of Love 63 (Rock City 120) [2004 68:   **77**
5.2m* 5m⁴ 6f² 5s 6d³ 5g 6g 7d Oct 30] leggy, quite good-topped gelding: fair performer: won maiden at Newbury in June: well below form last 3 starts: stays 6f: acts on firm and good to soft going: gelded after final start. *R. Hannon*

TREGENNA   3 b.f. Forzando 122 – Nineteenth of May 86 (Homing 130) [2004 7m⁴   –
7g⁵ 8g 10m Sep 25] 16,500Y: sister to smart 1m/1¼m winner Zanay, closely related to 2 winners, including useful 11f/1½m winner Quintrell Downs (by Efisio) and half-sister to a winner in Italy by Sharpo: dam 1m winner: little form. *R. M. H. Cowell*

TREMANE FLYER (IRE)   4 gr.f. Lycius (USA) 124 – Burishki 49 (Chilibang 120)   –
[2004 p8.6g Dec 27] fifth living foal: half-sister to 3 winners, including 5-y-o Climate: dam 6f winner, including at 2 yrs: 66/1, very slowly away and tailed off in maiden at Wolverhampton. *K. G. Wingrove*

TREMAR   2 b.c. (Mar 14) Royal Applause 124 – Sabina 87 (Prince Sabo 123) [2004   **110**
5s⁴ 5d³ 6s² p6g* 6m⁴ 6g* 7s⁶ Oct 16] 22,000F, 26,000Y: smallish colt: second living foal:

half-brother to 2002 2-y-o 5f seller winner Zafine (by Zafonic): dam, 2-y-o 5.7f winner, half-sister to smart performer up to 1½m Lady In Waiting and 5-y-o Savannah Bay: smart performer: won maiden at Lingfield in August and Prix Eclipse at Chantilly (beat Crossover 1½ lengths) in October: only sixth in Dewhurst Stakes at Newmarket, though disputed lead until halfway: stays 6f, possibly not 7f: acts on polytrack, best turf effort on good going: races up with pace. *T. G. Mills*

TREMPJANE 2 b.f. (Apr 30) Lujain (USA) 119 – Trempkate (USA) (Trempolino (USA) 135) [2004 6g* 5f⁵ 6m⁵ 7m 6m Sep 12] leggy, close-coupled filly: third foal: half-sister to 2002 2-y-o 5.7f winner Katdogawn (by Bahhare), later Grade 2 1m/9f winner in USA: dam, French 2-y-o 9f winner, out of smart performer up to 7f Glen Kate: fair performer: won maiden at Goodwood in June: well held in nurseries there last 2 starts: should stay 7f. *R. Hannon* **71**

TRENCH COAT (USA) 3 ch.c. Gulch (USA) – Glamor Queen (USA) (Prized (USA)) [2004 72: p7g² 7.1d 7m f8d Jun 17] workmanlike colt: fair maiden: stays 7f: acts on polytrack: sold 9,000 gns in July. *A. M. Balding* **70**

TRESOR SECRET (FR) 4 b.g. Green Desert (USA) 127 – Tresor (USA) (Pleasant Tap (USA)) [2004 10g 10m⁵ 8.1g p12g² p12d² Jun 26] close-coupled gelding: fairly useful performer at best: won handicaps at Chantilly and Compiegne in 2003 for M. Zilber in France: only fair form at best in Britain, leaving N. Callaghan after fourth start: stays 1½m: acts on extremes of going on turf: tried blinkered: flashes tail: ungenuine. *P. Butler* **74 §**

TREVIAN 3 ch.g. Atraf 116 – Ascend (IRE) (Glint of Gold 128) [2004 70p: p7g p8g* p10g⁶ p8g⁶ p8g⁵ 8m p7g p9.5g⁶ Dec 13] big gelding: fair handicapper: won apprentice event at Lingfield in January: should stay 1¼m: raced only on polytrack/good to firm ground: hung right third start. *S. C. Williams* **68**

TREW CLASS 3 ch.f. Inchinor 119 – Inimitable 66 (Polish Precedent (USA) 131) [2004 8.1s 10s 10m* 10m* 10.3d³ 10.1g 11.6m⁶ Sep 27] 10,000F, €26,000Y: lengthy filly: third foal: sister to fairly useful 1m winner Inverness and half-sister to 1m (at 2 yrs)/1¼m winner Royal Approval (by Royal Applause): dam, 1¼m winner, out of half-sister to Melbourne Cup winner Jeune: fairly useful performer: won maiden at Sandown in June and minor event at Pontefract in July: barely stays 11.6f: acts on good to firm and good to soft going. *M. H. Tompkins* **81**

TREW FLIGHT (USA) 2 b.g. (Mar 25) Rahy (USA) 115 – Magdala (IRE) (Sadler's Wells (USA) 132) [2004 8d 7s⁵ p7g Nov 27] 20,000F, 35,000Y: fourth foal: dam unraced half-sister to smart performer up to 2½m Heron Island out of half-sister to Darshaan: best effort when eighth of 13 to Chief Exec in minor event at Lingfield final start: bred to stay at least 1m. *M. H. Tompkins* **65**

TREW STYLE 2 ch.c. (Feb 12) Desert King (IRE) 129 – Southern Psychic (USA) (Alwasmi (USA) 115) [2004 8d 7d⁴ Oct 30] 26,000Y: big, workmanlike colt: fifth foal: half-brother to several winners, including 5-y-o Wing Commander and useful 6f (at 2 yrs) and 1m winner Rumpold (by Mister Baileys): dam sprint winner in USA: clearly better effort in maidens at Newmarket when patiently-ridden fourth to Centaurus: should stay at least 1m. *M. H. Tompkins* **72**

TRIAGE (IRE) 3 b.f. Mujadil (USA) 119 – Trebles (IRE) (Kenmare (FR) 125) [2004 6s Mar 27] 7,500Y: third foal: half-sister to winner in Greece by Titus Livius: dam French 1¼m winner: 14/1 and green, well held in maiden at Kempton. *M. R. Channon* **–**

TRIBUTE (IRE) 3 b.g. Green Desert (USA) 127 – Zooming (IRE) (Indian Ridge 123) [2004 87: 5.1d 5m 6m⁵ 5m⁵ 6.1g⁵ 7m 5d f6g p6g Nov 27] quite attractive gelding: only fair in 2004: left D. Loder after fourth start: ran poorly last 4 outings: effective at 5f/6f: unraced on extremes of going: tried visored: sometimes early to post. *K. A. Ryan* **76**

TRICK CYCLIST 3 b.g. Mind Games 121 – Sabonis (USA) 68 (The Minstrel (CAN) 135) [2004 81: p5g² p5g⁴ 6s 5.1f⁶ 6m 5m² 5.3f* 5.7m³ 5s⁵ 5f 5.7g⁴ 5d Nov 3] leggy gelding: fairly useful performer: made all in minor event at Brighton in August: left A. Balding before final outing: effective at 5f/6f: acts on polytrack, firm and good to soft going: visored (ran creditably) once at 2 yrs: sometimes slowly away. *M. W. Easterby* **84**

TRICKSHOT 2 ch.f. (Mar 15) Mister Baileys 123 – Zizi (IRE) 87 (Imp Society (USA)) [2004 6d² 6f 7g Jul 24] 4,200Y: workmanlike filly: has a markedly round action: second foal: dam 2-y-o 5f winner: form in maidens only when second at Hamilton (detached long way): should stay 7f. *T. D. Easterby* **60**

TRICKSTEP 3 b.g. Imperial Ballet (IRE) 110 – Trick of Ace (USA) (Clever Trick (USA)) [2004 –: 7s 8s 12d 9f 13g² 12g⁶ 10s* p12.2d⁵ p9.5g⁴ p12.2g f11g² Dec 14] **63**

16,000F, 27,000Y: second foal: dam, US 1m/8.5f winner, half-sister to US Grade 2 1½m winner Prospectress: modest performer: left D. Gillespie in Ireland, won claimer at Ayr in October, despite tending to run in snatches: stays 13f: acts on all-weather and soft ground: usually in cheekpieces/blinkers (not for win). *I. Semple*

TRICKY VENTURE   4 gr.g. Linamix (FR) 127 – Ukraine Venture 96 (Slip Anchor 136) [2004 71: 9.9s² 10d⁴ f12s p10g² p10g* Dec 30] leggy gelding: fair performer: left P. Hiatt prior to winning seller at Lingfield: should stay 1½m: acts on polytrack, soft and good to firm ground. *P. A. Blockley*   **71**

TRIFFID   2 b.g. (Apr 17) Dracula (AUS) 121 – Rockfest (USA) 104 (Stage Door Johnny (USA)) [2004 p5.1g⁵ f7g³ Dec 12] 15,000 2-y-o: half-brother to several winners, including smart 1¼m/1½m (Lancashire Oaks) winner Rainbow Lake (dam of 4-y-o Powerscourt) and useful but untrustworthy 7f/1m performer Rock Falcon (by Polar Falcon): dam 2-y-o 7f/1m winner who stayed 1½m: better effort in maidens when 2 lengths third to Suffolk House at Southwell: should stay at least 1m. *R. A. Fahey*   **64**

TRIFTI   3 b.g. Vettori (IRE) 119 – Time For Tea (IRE) 73 (Imperial Frontier (USA) 112) [2004 p8g⁴ 10d 6g p6g p8g⁴ 7m² 8g 8m p8.6g* p8.6g Dec 10] £2,600Y: medium-sized gelding: third foal: half-brother to fairly useful 7f/1m winner Frazzled (by Greensmith): dam, maiden who stayed 1¼m, out of useful half-sister to Kalaglow: fair on all-weather, modest on turf: won maiden at Wolverhampton in November, racing freely: stays easy 8.6f: acts on polytrack and good to firm going. *C. A. Cyzer*   **60 a73**

TRIGGER MEAD   4 b.f. Double Trigger (IRE) 123 – Normead Lass 36 (Norwick (USA) 125) [2004 50: p10g Sep 18] workmanlike filly: lightly-raced maiden: sold £3,000. *Mrs Stef Liddiard*   **–**

TRIGGERS DOUBLE   3 ch.g. Double Trigger (IRE) 123 – Princess Alaska (Northern State (USA) 91) [2004 p12d Jun 12] 33/1, tailed off in maiden at Lingfield: gelded after. *K. Bell*   **–**

TRIGONY (IRE)   2 b.g. (Jan 30) Brave Act 119 – Lulu Island (Zafonic (USA) 130) [2004 7g 7d 9f⁶ Sep 13] 13,000Y: angular gelding: first foal: dam unraced out of smart 6f performer Twafeaj: form in maidens only when sixth at Redcar: shapes as if will stay at least 1¼m. *T. D. Easterby*   **60**

TRILEMMA   3 b.f. Slip Anchor 136 – Thracian 92 (Green Desert (USA) 127) [2004 59p: 10.1s 10d 12f⁶ 16g* 16.1g* 16m* 16s Oct 22] fairly useful handicapper: won at Ripon, Newcastle and Nottingham in August/September: stays 2m: should be as effective at 1¾m: acts on firm and good to soft going: blinkered (tailed off) on reappearance. *Sir Mark Prescott*   **84**

TRIM IMAGE   2 br.f. (Apr 4) Averti (IRE) 117 – Altizar 66 (Zafonic (USA) 130) [2004 5d² 5m³ 5g³ 5g³ 5.1s* 5g Sep 13] 12,000F, €25,000Y: second foal: dam, ran twice around 1¼m, out of half-sister to disqualified Oaks winner Aliysa: fair performer: left Ms J. Morgan in Ireland after third start: made all in maiden at Chepstow in August, then left W. Jarvis: below form in nursery final start: likely to prove best at 5f/6f: acts on soft and good to firm ground. *H. Alexander*   **71**

TRINAREE (IRE)   3 b.g. Revoque (IRE) 122 – Ball Cat (FR) (Cricket Ball (USA) 124) [2004 –: 5m 6m 7g 8m Jul 23] of little account. *S. Gollings*   **–**

TRINCULO (IRE)   7 b.g. Anita's Prince 126 – Fandangerina (USA) (Grey Dawn II 132) [2004 99: f6g f5g p5g p5g 5g² 5.1g⁵ 5d 5.2g 6g⁶ 5s 5.2d 5g 5d⁵ 5s* f5s Nov 17] tall, rather leggy gelding: has a long, raking action: fairly useful performer: left N. Littmoden and no headgear, won claimer at Catterick (by 8 lengths) in November: effective at 5f/6f: acts on fibresand, firm and soft going: tried blinkered, usually wears cheekpieces: has been early to post: often forces pace: sometimes finds little: none too reliable. *D. Nicholls*   **94**

TRINITY FAIR   3 b.f. Polish Precedent (USA) 131 – Chita Rivera 61 (Chief Singer 131) [2004 7.9m 10g 8m 11.5m Aug 16] 11,000F, 32,000Y: small, sparely-made filly: half-sister to useful but untrustworthy performer up to 1½m Sunstone (by Caerleon): dam, staying maiden, half-sister to Oaks winner Lady Carla: soundly beaten in maidens. *J. G. Given*   **–**

TRINITY (IRE)   8 b.h. College Chapel 122 – Kaskazi (Dancing Brave (USA) 140) [2004 57: 6s 7d 5g 6g Aug 7] close-coupled horse: modest handicapper: effective at 5f/6f: acts on firm and good to soft going. *M. Brittain*   **50**

TRIPHENIA (IRE)   6 b.g. Ashkalani (IRE) 128 – Atsuko (IRE) (Mtoto 134) [2004 12m May 29] strong, lengthy gelding: fairly useful handicapper at best: suffered tendon injury final start at 4 yrs: well held only outing since (took strong hold to post). *M. L. W. Bell*

TRIPLE JUMP 3 ch.g. Inchinor 119 – Meteoric 102 (High Line 125) [2004 –: 8g2 **81** 8m* 10.3s3 10.5s Sep 24] angular, useful-looking gelding: fairly useful performer, lightly raced: won maiden at Thirsk in July: stays 1¼m: acts on soft and good to firm ground: tongue tied only run at 2 yrs. *T. D. Easterby*

TRIPLE TWO 2 ch.f. (Feb 2) Pivotal 124 – Tara's Girl (IRE) 95 (Fayruz 116) [2004 **78 p** p7.1g* p6g* Dec 10] 12,000F, 12,000Y: first foal: dam 2-y-o 5f winner: won maiden in November and nursery (beat Rancho Cucamonga by ¾ length) in December, both at Wolverhampton: not sure to stay beyond 7f: open to improvement. *E. A. L. Dunlop*

TRIPLE ZERO (IRE) 2 b.f. (Feb 10) Raise A Grand (IRE) 114 – Locorotondo (IRE) **70** 83 (Broken Hearted 124) [2004 6g 7g 7.6m* Jul 31] 36,000Y: fourth foal: half-sister to Irish 7f winner Good Day Too (by Danetime): dam, 1¼m/11f winner, half-sister to useful 6f/7f performer Pepperdine: easily best effort in maidens when winning at Lingfield by ½ length from Keynes, leading over 1f out: should stay 1m. *A. P. Jarvis*

TRIPTI (IRE) 4 b.f. Sesaro (USA) 81 – Chatelsong (USA) (Seattle Song (USA) 130) **52** [2004 72d: p6g2 p6g p6g p6g p6g p6g p6g 5.3m 5m 5g4 6g5 Aug 30] angular filly: modest performer: best at 5f/easy 6f: acts on polytrack and firm going: has worn cheekpieces/ blinkers. *J. J. Bridger*

TRISHAY 3 gr.f. Petong 126 – Marjorie's Memory (IRE) 76 (Fairy King (USA)) [2004 **–** 56: p7g p10g p8.6g p10m Dec 21] maiden: no form in 2004, leaving A. Jarvis after second start: has started slowly/carried head high. *J. R. Boyle*

TRITONVILLE LODGE (IRE) 2 b.g. (Mar 28) Grand Lodge (USA) 125 – Olean **60 p** (Sadler's Wells (USA) 132) [2004 8v Oct 23] €10,500Y, 26,000 2-y-o: brother to 3 winners, including useful 10.5f winner Architect and 4-y-o Gran Dana, and half-brother to several winners: dam ran twice: 50/1, seventh to Spear Thistle in maiden at Newbury, travelling well long way: should do better. *Miss E. C. Lavelle*

TRIVIAL PURSUIT 3 b.c. Mind Games 121 – Chushan Venture (Pursuit of Love **?** 124) [2004 7m 7g a7.5g2 Dec 31] left W. Jarvis after debut: first form when second in maiden at Neuss. *N. Minner, Belgium*

TROFANA FALCON 4 b.g. Polar Falcon (USA) 126 – Silk St James (Pas de Seul **42** 133) [2004 –: 11.9d 10.3m p10g4 Dec 20] workmanlike gelding: poor maiden: form only in tongue tie final start. *H. J. Collingridge*

TROIS ETOILES (IRE) 3 ch.f. Grand Lodge (USA) 125 – Stardance (USA) (Rahy **62** (USA) 115) [2004 –: 6g5 7g 8m5 10m5 8.1m3 8g6 9.5g p8.6d6 Nov 3] workmanlike filly: modest maiden handicapper: takes good hold, and probably better at 7f/1m than 1¼m: raced only on polytrack and good/good to firm ground: visored penultimate start: sold 11,000 gns after final start. *J. W. Hills*

TROJAN FLIGHT 3 ch.g. Hector Protector (USA) 124 – Fairywings 85 (Kris 135) **77** [2004 70: 6s4 8.5v5 7s4 7.5m6 8.2g 9.3f6 6m4 6g3 5d2 5d* 6d2 6f* 5d 6s4 5f2 5d4 6d Oct 12] good-topped gelding: fair handicapper: won at Beverley in August and Redcar in September: effective at 5f/6f: acts on any going: has worn cheekpieces, better form without: usually waited with: tough. *Mrs J. R. Ramsden*

TROJAN WOLF 9 ch.g. Wolfhound (USA) 126 – Trojan Lady (USA) (Irish River **– §** (FR) 131) [2004 –§, a56d: f11g f14g4 f11s f11g5 Mar 23] strong gelding: only poor nowa- **a41 §** days: best at 1m to 1½m: acts on fibresand, firm and soft going: tried visored/tongue tied earlier in career: usually races up with pace: moody and unreliable. *P. Howling*

TROMP 3 ch.c. Zilzal (USA) 137 – Sulitelma (USA) 63 (The Minstrel (CAN) 135) **66** [2004 7m5 7f6 p9.5d2 p10g2 p9.5g2 Dec 17] 10,500F, 52,000Y: sixth foal: half-brother to several winners, including fairly useful 2000 2-y-o 1m winner Min Mirri (by Selkirk) and untrustworthy 9.4f winner Semiramis (by Darshaan): dam 5f winner (ran only at 2 yrs): fair maiden: stays 1¼m: acts on polytrack. *D. J. Coakley*

TROMPE L'OEIL (IRE) 3 b.f. Distant View (USA) 126 – Milly Ha Ha 106 (Dancing **51** Brave (USA) 140) [2004 63: p10g p10g p10g6 p7g 8g 8.1s May 3] leggy filly: modest maiden: left E. Dunlop after reappearance: stays 1¼m: acts on all-weather, probably on firm ground: wore cheekpieces last 3 starts: none too reliable: sold 3,500 gns later in May. *Andrew Reid*

TROODOS JET 3 b.g. Atraf 116 – Costa Verde 77 (King of Spain 121) [2004 64: 6m4 **62** 6.1m4 f6g4 f6g4 5s* 6g 6s 5d Oct 11] big, good-topped gelding: modest performer: made all in 4-runner maiden at Ripon in August: stays 6f: acts on polytrack, soft and good to firm going. *A. Berry*

TROPICAL CORAL (IRE) 4 ch.f. Pennekamp (USA) 130 – Tropical Dance (USA) 93 (Thorn Dance (USA) 107) [2004 82: f9.4g⁶ Jan 12] sturdy filly: fairly useful performer: stays 1¼m: acts on all-weather and firm going: has raced freely/hung left. *C. Tinkler*   **81**

TROPICAL LADY (IRE) 4 b.f. Sri Pekan (USA) 117 – Tropical Lake (IRE) 100 (Lomond (USA) 128) [2004 84: 7g* 8m* 8f* 7d* 9f* 10m² 8m⁵ 10g⁵ 10d Oct 2] third foal: dam Irish 1m to 1¾m winner and useful hurdler: smart performer: won handicaps at Gowran and the Curragh (2), Irish Stallion Farms EBF Brownstown Stakes at Leopardstown (by neck from Majestic Desert) and listed race at the Curragh (by 1½ lengths from Noahs Ark) between May and July: persistently short of room when neck second to Solskjaer in Royal Whip Stakes at the Curragh: below form last 3 starts: stays 1¼m: acts on firm and good to soft ground, well beaten on soft. *J. S. Bolger, Ireland*   **114**

TROPICAL SON 5 b.g. Distant Relative 128 – Douce Maison (IRE) 67 (Fools Holme (USA)) [2004 52: f9.4g² f8g⁵ p10g* f9.4g p13g² f12s⁵ p10g p12g⁵ p12.2d p13m² p16.5g p13.9g³ p12m³ p13.9g⁶ Dec 22] well-made gelding: modest performer: won banded race at Lingfield in January: stays 13f: acts on all-weather, little recent form on turf: blinkered/ visored. *D. Shaw*   **?** **a57**

TROPICAL STORM (IRE) 3 ch.g. Alhaarth (IRE) 126 – Rainstone 57 (Rainbow Quest (USA) 134) [2004 70: 7g³ 7d 6f⁴ 6g² 7v* Aug 27] rather leggy gelding: fair performer: landed odds in maiden at Newcastle (unimpressively) in August: effective at 6f/7f: acts on any ground: carries head awkwardly: sold 7,200 gns. *J. Noseda*   **77**

TROTTERS BOTTOM 3 b.g. Mind Games 121 – Fleeting Affair 98 (Hotfoot 126) [2004 82: p5g 6g⁵ Jun 2] quite good-topped gelding: just fair form in 2004: best at 5f/6f: acts on polytrack and good to firm going: has been unruly at start (withdrawn second intended outing and failed 2 stall tests in 2004): banned from Flat racing from stalls until late-Jan 2005. *Andrew Reid*   **67 §**

Mr George J. Kent's "Tropical Lady"

TROUBADOUR (IRE)   3 b.c. Danehill (USA) 126 – Taking Liberties (IRE) 57   **113**
(Royal Academy (USA) 130) [2004 114: 8f³ 8.1g² 8g* 8g Oct 1] big, rangy colt: has
badly scarred near hip/quarter/knee: smart performer: easy winner of 3-runner minor
event at Naas on reappearance in July and made all in listed race at the Curragh (held on
gamely by ½ length from Miss Mambo) in September: good length second to With
Reason in listed event at Haydock in between: well below form in Joel Stakes at Newmarket final outing: should stay 1¼m: raced only on good ground or firmer: joined
D. Hayes in Hong Kong, where renamed Stable Mail. *A. P. O'Brien, Ireland*

TROUBLEINPARADISE (IRE)   3 b.f. Pursuit of Love 124 – Sweet Holland (USA)   **–**
(Alydar (USA)) [2004 59: 10d 10.9d p12d 8d Sep 11] rangy filly: lightly-raced maiden:
well beaten in 2004, including in blinkers: left J. Given 4,700 gns before final start.
R. Pritchard-Gordon, France

TROUBLE MOUNTAIN (USA)   7 br.g. Mt Livermore (USA) – Trouble Free (USA)   **80**
(Nodouble (USA)) [2004 80: f11g³ 9.9d³ 11s³ 12.3d⁵ 10m² 12.3m⁴ 10.3g⁴ 10m 10.5g²
10.5s* 8d⁴ 10d² 10.5s³ 10s⁵ Oct 11] small, sparely-made gelding: fairly useful handicapper: won at Haydock in August: effective at 1m to 1½m: acts on fibresand, firm and soft
going: effective blinkered or not: sometimes soon off bridle: consistent. *M. W. Easterby*

TROUBLE NEXT DOOR (IRE)   6 b.g. Persian Bold 123 – Adjacent (IRE) 82   **54**
(Doulab (USA) 115) [2004 p12g³ p12g² Jan 15] big, strong, workmanlike gelding: has
markedly round action: modest maiden: missed 2002/2003: stays 1½m: acts on polytrack
and good to firm ground. *N. P. Littmoden*

TROUBLESOME GERRI   2 b.f. (May 7) Thowra (FR) – Sid's Pretence (Southern   **49 ?**
Music 104) [2004 5.1s⁶ 5.1m³ 6.1m⁵ Jun 11] first foal: dam poor maiden hurdler: poor
form in maiden/minor events: bred to stay 1½m+. *S. C. Burrough*

TROUSERS   5 b.g. Pivotal 124 – Palo Blanco 82 (Precocious 126) [2004: p8g 8v*   **67**
8.2s³ 8d⁴ Jul 15] fair handicapper: won at Newcastle in April: effective at 7f/1m: acts on
polytrack and heavy ground: usually races prominently: sold 13,000 gns in October.
Andrew Reid

TROUVILLE (IRE)   5 b.m. Mukaddamah (USA) 125 – Trouville Lass (IRE) 77 (Be   **60**
My Native (USA) 122) [2004 66: 7s 8d 7f 7f⁵ 7.5g 8g⁶ 10m 12g 13g* 13d p12.2g⁵ Nov 8]
first foal: dam, 1½m winner, also successful over hurdles: modest performer: won handicap at Downpatrick in September: ran creditably in minor event at Wolverhampton final
start: stays 13f: acts on polytrack and firm going. *G. O'Leary, Ireland*

TRUCKLE   2 b.c. (Mar 3) Vettori (IRE) 119 – Proud Titania (IRE) 103 (Fairy King   **69**
(USA)) [2004 6.1s 8m⁶ 7.9g⁴ f8g⁵ p9.5g* Dec 20] lengthy, angular colt: fifth foal: half-
brother to 1½m winner Fraternize (by Spectrum) and 3-y-o Daze: dam Irish 7f winner
(including at 2 yrs) who stayed 1m: fair performer: left M. Johnston after third start: won
maiden at Wolverhampton, wandering/carrying head awkwardly: stays 9.5f: acts on
polytrack, best turf effort on good going: races up with pace. *C. W. Fairhurst*

TRUE COMPANION   5 b.g. Brief Truce (USA) 126 – Comanche Companion 88   **80**
(Commanche Run 133) [2004 72: p10g p10g* p10g³ p10g p10g³ 10.9d* 12.3d⁴ 10f² p10d
p10g p13g³ p10g³ Dec 18] fairly useful handicapper: won at Lingfield in January and
Warwick in April: stays 13f: acts on polytrack, firm and soft going: free-going sort: has
wandered markedly: usually held up: reliable. *N. P. Littmoden*

TRUE HOLLY   4 b.f. Bishop of Cashel 122 – Polly's Teahouse 68 (Shack (USA) 118)   **39**
[2004 –: p6g p6g f7s⁵ Mar 14] good-topped filly: poor maiden: probably stays 7f: tried
blinkered/visored. *S. Kirk*

TRUE (IRE)   3 ch.f. Barathea (IRE) 127 – Bibliotheque (USA) 79 (Woodman (USA)   **66**
126) [2004 72: 8.3s 7m 7m² 7m 7m³ 7.5g⁴ 7f 8d⁶ 7.5d 8g² 8.5m 8g⁵ 8s Oct 29] lengthy
filly: fair maiden: left M. Tregoning after third start: stays 1m: acts on good to firm and
good to soft going: has carried head awkwardly. *Mrs S. Lamyman*

TRUE LOVER (GER)   7 b.g. Winged Love (IRE) 121 – Truneba (GER) (Nebos   **109**
(GER) 129) [2004 16s³ Oct 16] useful performer in Scandinavia for W. Neuroth at 3/4
yrs, winning 6 of his 14 starts: progressive form over hurdles for current year prior to
very good 5¼ lengths third to Millenary in Jockey Club Cup at Newmarket on Flat return:
stays 2m: acts on soft ground and dirt. *J. W. Mullins*

TRUE MAGIC   3 b.f. Magic Ring (IRE) 115 – True Precision 84 (Presidium 124)   **80**
[2004 59: 5s⁵ 6m⁶ 5f² 5g² 5f* 5d* 5g 5f 5d Oct 18] compact filly: fairly useful performer:
won maiden at Leicester in July and handicap at Thirsk in August: effective at 5f/6f:
unraced on heavy going, acts on any other. *J. D. Bethell*

TRUE NIGHT 7 b.g. Night Shift (USA) – Dead Certain 123§ (Absalom 128) [2004 93: 7.1g 6d 7d 6m 7.2f⁴ 6m² 7g³ 7m³ 7.9g 8m³ 7g* 7g* 7.6m³ 8m 7.6s 8.9m² 7.2s 7g Oct 2] smallish, attractive gelding: fairly useful handicapper: won at Ascot and Newcastle in July: effective at 6f to 1m: acts on firm and good to soft going, below form all starts on soft: sometimes races freely: effective held up or ridden prominently: tough. *D. Nicholls* **91**

TRUENO (IRE) 5 b.g. Desert King (IRE) 129 – Stitching (IRE) 50 (High Estate 127) [2004 89: 10m* 10.2g² 10g 10f⁵ 10m⁵ 12g 10.4g⁶ Oct 8] leggy, quite good-topped gelding: fairly useful performer: won minor event at Newmarket in May: effective at 1¼m to 15f: acted on firm and good to soft going: often raced prominently/freely: sold 31,000 gns, joined N. Gifford, fell fatally over hurdles in December. *L. M. Cumani* **87**

TRUE PATRIOT 3 b.g. Rainbow Quest (USA) 134 – High Standard 83 (Kris 135) [2004 –: 10g 11g May 26] lengthy, good-topped gelding: looks of little account. *P. Mitchell* **–**

TRUE TO YOURSELF (USA) 3 b.g. Royal Academy (USA) 130 – Romilly (Machiavellian (USA) 123) [2004 –: 8.1s f9.4g² f12g* 11.8g f12d⁶ f12g* p12m p13.9g³ Dec 22] tall gelding: modest performer: won banded races at Wolverhampton in May and Southwell in December: stays 1¾m: acts on all-weather. *J. G. Given* **57**

TRULLITTI (IRE) 3 b.f. Bahri (USA) 125 – Penza 79 (Soviet Star (USA) 128) [2004 71p: 10d³ 10s⁵ 11.9g 11s* 12s³ 14.1s Oct 27] quite attractive filly: fairly useful performer: won maiden at Goodwood in August: good third to Aviane in listed race at Cologne next time: stayed 1½m: acted on firm and soft going: blinkered last 3 starts: pulled up lame third outing: hung persistently right final appearance: stud. *J. L. Dunlop* **91**

TRUMAN 3 b.g. Entrepreneur 123 – Sabria (USA) (Miswaki (USA) 124) [2004 –p: 6m 6m³ 7f⁵ 7d p8.6g² p10g⁶ Nov 16] quite attractive gelding: fair maiden: stays 8.6f: acts on polytrack and good to firm ground: gelded after final start. *J. A. R. Toller* **74**

TRUSTED INSTINCT (IRE) 4 b.c. Polish Precedent (USA) 131 – Trust In Luck (IRE) 83 (Nashwan (USA) 135) [2004 75: p12g p8g 8.3d 12f 8f 6s⁵ 7.9m Sep 11] fair performer in Ireland for D. Weld, winning 1¼m maiden at Fairyhouse at 3 yrs: no form in Britain: tried blinkered/in cheekpieces/tongue tied: best treated with caution. *C. A. Dwyer* **–**

TRUSTED MOLE (IRE) 6 b.g. Eagle Eyed (USA) 111 – Orient Air 74 (Prince Sabo 123) [2004 61: 11.8m⁵ 11.8m⁵ 13g⁶ 10.9m² 12.6m⁴ 12.6m 12.3g 12m p12.2g Oct 16] deep-girthed gelding: modest handicapper: won apprentice events at Leicester in May and Warwick in June: stays easy 1¾m: acts on polytrack (no form on fibresand), firm and good to soft going: often blinkered prior to 2003. *W. M. Brisbourne* **61**

TRUST RULE 4 b.c. Selkirk (USA) 129 – Hagwah (USA) 109 (Dancing Brave (USA) 140) [2004 108p: 10d 12g⁶ 12m⁵ 12f 11.9g 13.9s 14g 14.6f⁴ 12m Sep 26] big, good-topped colt: useful handicapper: respectable efforts at best in 2004: stays 1¾m: acts on good to firm and good to soft ground: wore tongue tie/cheekpieces last 2 starts: usually held up: sometimes carries head high/wanders: sold 20,000 gns. *B. W. Hills* **102**

TRYLKO (USA) 2 ch.f. (Apr 12) Diesis 133 – Gossamer (USA) (Seattle Slew (USA)) [2004 6m² Jun 26] smallish, quite good-topped filly: fifth foal: half-sister to 3 winners, notably 3-y-o Bachelor Duke and useful 10.5f/1½m winner in USA/Germany Translucid (by Woodman): dam, won at around 1m in USA, from excellent family: second to Deeday Bay in maiden at Doncaster, starting slowly but making most: should stay at least 1m: likely to do better. *J. G. Given* **77 p**

TRYMORE (IRE) 2 ch.c. (Mar 15) Tagula (IRE) 116 – Marimar (IRE) (Grand Lodge (USA) 125) [2004 p8m³ Dec 21] €8,000Y: first foal: dam Italian 1¼m/11f winner: 8/1 and green, 3½ lengths third of 11 to Alessano in maiden at Lingfield: should do better. *A. M. Balding* **70 p**

TRYSTING GROVE (IRE) 3 b.f. Cape Cross (IRE) 129 – Elton Grove (IRE) (Astronef 116) [2004 8g 7d 7f 7.5g⁵ 7.9f 12.1d* f11g* Nov 8] leggy, unfurnished filly: third foal: half-sister to 4-y-o La Muette: dam French 9f and 10.5f winner: modest performer: won selling handicap at Chepstow in August (left K. Ryan) and banded race at Southwell in November: stays 1½m: acts on fibresand and good to soft ground. *E. G. Bevan* **58**

TRY THE AIR (IRE) 3 ch.f. Foxhound (USA) 103 – Try To Catch Me (USA) (Shareef Dancer (USA) 135) [2004 –: p8g Jan 14] smallish, close-coupled filly: little form. *C. Tinkler* **–**

TSARBUCK 3 b.g. Perugino (USA) 84 – Form At Last (Formidable (USA) 125) [2004 –: 8m 8.5s 8v f7g* 8.5m⁵ f7g² 7d⁵ f6g² f7m³ f6m³ 6g 6g 7d⁶ p6g⁴ p7.1d f6g³ Nov 23] **48 a63**

compact gelding: modest on all-weather, poor on turf: won banded race at Southwell in May: probably better at 6f than 7f: acts on all-weather: sometimes visored/in cheekpieces: carries head awkwardly. *R. M. H. Cowell*

TSAROXY (IRE)   2 b.g. (Feb 27) Xaar 132 – Belsay 68 (Belmez (USA) 131) [2004   **79**
6d³ 6g³ 6g* 6d⁵ 6s Nov 2] €420,000Y: rather leggy gelding: fourth foal: half-brother to fairly useful 2002 2-y-o 6f winner Lady's Mantle (by Sri Pekan): dam, ran twice in Ireland, closely related to smart performer up to 1m Crystal Gazing: fair performer: won maiden at Redcar in August: creditable fifth at Ayr, much better effort in nurseries after: likely to prove best at 5f/6f: acts on good to soft going: blinkered final start (gelded after): races up with pace. *J. Howard Johnson*

TSHUKUDU   3 ch.f. Fleetwood (IRE) 107 – Pab's Choice 61 (Telsmoss 91) [2004 46:   **45**
f7g p12d p8g 8f 10.1g³ p10g 10s² 9.7f p10g 10d Oct 2] poor maiden: stays 1¼m: acts on soft going. *M. Blanshard*

TUCKER   2 b.c. (Apr 9) Inchinor 119 – Tender Moment (IRE) 78 (Caerleon (USA)   **87 p**
132) [2004 6d 6s* Oct 29] well-made colt: has a round action: closely related to fairly useful 1m winner Spring Fever (by Indian Ridge) and half-brother to several winners, including 8-y-o Summer Bounty: dam 7f winner: favourite, won maiden at Newmarket by 1¾ lengths from Lake Chini, green but leading over 1f out then idling: should stay 1m: useful prospect, should do well in handicaps in 2005. *D. R. C. Elsworth*

TUDOR BELL (IRE)   3 b.c. Definite Article 121 – Late Night Lady (IRE) 65 (Mujadil   **87**
(USA) 119) [2004 65p: 8g 10v³ 10g³ 11.1d* 11.6g* 12.1m⁶ 14.1m² 14.1g* 15.8m³ 16g 16m⁴ 16d⁵ Nov 3] useful-looking colt: fairly useful performer: won maiden at Hamilton and handicaps at Windsor and Salisbury in May/June: stays 1¾m: acts on heavy and good to firm ground: usually races prominently: game. *J. G. M. O'Shea*

TUMBAGA (USA)   3 b.c. Seeking The Gold (USA) – Didina 115 (Nashwan (USA)   **66**
135) [2004 8g 10g 8m⁵ May 29] good-topped colt: third foal: closely related to smart 7f winner Tantina (by Distant View) and fairly useful 1¼m winner Trekking (by Gone West): dam, 6f (at 2 yrs) to 8.5f (US Grade 2 event) winner, out of half-sister to Xaar: tongue tied, form only when fifth in maiden at Kempton: joined R. Frankel in USA. *R. Charlton*

TUMBLEBRUTUS (USA)   3 br.c. Storm Cat (USA) – Mariah's Storm (USA) 116   **?**
(Rahy (USA) 115) [2004 102: 8g 7g³ Sep 7] close-coupled colt: useful performer at 2 yrs (reportedly lame after final start, in US): well below best in 2004 in 2000 Guineas at Newmarket and minor event at Galway (tongue tied) 4 months later: stayed 7f: acted on good to firm and good to soft going: to stand at Walmac International, USA, fee $6,000. *A. P. O'Brien, Ireland*

TUMBLEWEED GALORE (IRE)   2 b.g. (Feb 27) Bluebird (USA) 125 – Mary   **77**
Hinge 100 (Dowsing (USA) 124) [2004 7.1d 7f³ 7.5m³ 8d³ 8d⁶ 7m² p8.6g³ 7s⁵ Oct 22] 30,000Y: small, strong gelding: fifth foal: half-brother to 7-y-o Compton Banker: dam 5f/6f winner, including at 2 yrs: fair maiden: stays 8.6f: acts on polytrack, firm and good to soft going: blinkered penultimate start: sold 22,000 gns. *B. J. Meehan*

TUNGSTEN STRIKE (USA)   3 ch.g. Smart Strike (CAN) 121 – Bathilde (IRE)   **107**
102 (Generous (IRE) 139) [2004 70?: 11.6d 14.4g* 16m* 14m³ 16.1f² 14g* 18s Oct 16] good-bodied gelding: made into a useful performer in 2004, winning handicaps at Kempton and Lingfield in July and listed race at Newmarket (beat Carte Diamond by 2 lengths) in September: should stay beyond 2m: acts on firm going, well beaten both outings on softer than good: usually races prominently. *Mrs A. J. Perrett*

TUNING FORK   4 b.g. Alzao (USA) 117 – Tuning 114 (Rainbow Quest (USA) 134)   **97**
[2004 113d: 10g 12g 11g 10m 8.1d 8m³ 7g 10d 9m 8m Sep 26] strong, lengthy, attractive gelding: just useful for new trainer at 4 yrs, third to Ancient World in William Hill Mile (Handicap) at Goodwood: poor efforts after: effective at 1m/1¼m: acts on good to firm going: tried visored/tongue tied/in cheekpieces: has raced freely/hung left/found little: often makes running: temperament under suspicion: gelded after final outing. *J. Akehurst*

TURBO (IRE)   5 b.g. Piccolo 121 – By Arrangement (IRE) 60 (Bold Arrangement   **96**
127) [2004 103: p10g 10d 12m⁴ 11.9g 11.9d 12f 10d 10v² 12s Nov 6] close-coupled gelding: useful handicapper: favourite, well held when attempting repeat win in November Handicap at Doncaster final outing: effective at 1¼m/1½m: acts on any going: tried visored, wears cheekpieces nowadays. *G. B. Balding*

TURF PRINCESS   3 b.f. Wizard King 122 – Turf Moor (IRE) 53 (Mac's Imp (USA)   **58 d**
116) [2004 60: f7g* f7g² f7g⁴ f7g⁵ 7s³ 7m 7.5g⁴ f8g 6v 6g f7g f7s⁵ f6g⁵ Dec 7] lengthy

filly: modest performer: won claimer at Wolverhampton in January: below form last 8 starts: barely stays 1m: acts on fibresand, firm and soft going: visored last 2 starts. *Ian Emmerson*

TURFTANZER (GER) 5 b.g. Lomitas 129 – Tower Bridge (GER) (Big Shuffle (USA) 122) [2004 –: f12g⁵ f14g f11g⁴ f8s⁶ 12v 10s 11m 12.3m 10g⁴ 12.1g⁵ 12.3g 8s 10f⁵ 10f 10s⁶ f12d⁵ Dec 21] sparely-made gelding: poor maiden: stays 11f: best efforts on fibresand: tongue tied. *Don Enrico Incisa* **39**

TURIBIUS 5 b.g. Puissance 110 – Compact Disc (IRE) 48 (Royal Academy (USA) 130) [2004 83: p5g⁶ p5g* p5g³ 5g 6m 5m 5m 6m 5g 6g⁴ p5g³ p5.1g Dec 4] compact gelding: fairly useful handicapper on all-weather, fair on turf: won at Lingfield in February: effective at 5f/easy 6f: acts on polytrack and firm ground, below form on softer than good: sometimes visored: sometimes slowly away: effective held up or ridden up with pace. *T. E. Powell* **78 a86**

TURKANA GIRL 2 ch.f. (Feb 27) Hernando (FR) 127 – Miss Penton 66 (Primo Dominie 121) [2004 6.1m⁶ Sep 28] strong filly: second live foal: half-sister to useful Italian 7.5f (at 2 yrs) to 1¼m winner Balkenhol (by Polar Falcon): dam, maiden who stayed 7f, out of 1000 Guineas winner On The House: 18/1, sixth in maiden at Nottingham, getting hang of things late on: likely to be suited by 1¼m/1½m: will improve. *G. Wragg* **52 p**

TURKISH DELIGHT 3 b.f. Prince Sabo 123 – Delicious 51 (Dominion 123) [2004 67: f6d⁵ 6m⁶ 6m 6m 6g³ 6g 6g 6m 6g 5m Sep 22] modest maiden: likely to prove best at 5f/6f: acts on fibresand, good to firm and good to soft going: tried in cheekpieces. *J. Balding* **62**

TURKS AND CAICOS (IRE) 3 b. or br.g. Turtle Island (IRE) 123 – Need You Badly 59 (Robellino (USA) 127) [2004 60: f8g² f8.5g² f11g* 11.1g p9.5g⁶ p12.2d⁶ f16s Nov 17] modest handicapper: won at Southwell in February: stays 11f: acts on fibresand. *P. C. Haslam* **61**

TURKS WOOD (IRE) 2 b.g. (Mar 2) Charnwood Forest (IRE) 125 – Nairasha (IRE) (Niniski (USA) 125) [2004 5m⁴ 6g⁵ 6g⁵ 8.1g 8s 6d Oct 18] €15,000Y: good-topped gelding: half-brother to winners in Sweden by Brief Truce and Fourstars Allstar: dam placed in Sweden: fair maiden: well below form last 2 starts (blinkered on first occasion, gelded after final one): should stay 1m: acts on good to firm going. *M. H. Tompkins* **65**

TURN AROUND 4 b.g. Pivotal 124 – Bemuse 89 (Forzando 122) [2004 –: f6s 8.3d f8.5g² f7m* f7g⁵ f7d* f6g Jun 25] well-made gelding: fairly useful at 2 yrs, fair nowadays: won seller at Wolverhampton in May and selling handicap at Southwell (left B. Hills) in June: stays easy 8.5f: acts on all-weather, good to firm and good to soft going: has been slowly away/carried head high: upset in stall/pulled too hard final outing. *P. A. Blockley* **– a75**

TURNAROUND (GER) 2 gr.g. (Jan 28) Highest Honor (FR) 124 – Tamacana (Windwurf (GER)) [2004 5d³ 6d² 5m* 6d 7f² 6g Sep 30] €40,000Y: tall gelding: half-brother to several winners, including useful German miler Turning Leaf (by Last Tycoon): dam German 7f (at 2 yrs) to 9f winner: fairly useful performer: landed odds in maiden at Thirsk in July: creditable effort in nurseries after only when second at Doncaster: hampered final start (gelded after): stays 7f: acts on firm and good to soft going: tested positive for tranquilliser when running badly fourth appearance. *Mrs J. R. Ramsden* **81**

TURNBERRY (IRE) 3 b.c. Petardia 113 – Sunrise (IRE) 58 (Sri Pekan (USA) 117) [2004 60: p7g⁴ f7g³ f8g⁶ 8.1s² 7m² 7f⁵ Jun 14] modest maiden: barely stays 1m: acts on all-weather, good to firm going: blinkered/visored. *J. W. Hills* **61**

TURNER 3 gr.g. El Prado (IRE) 119 – Gaily Royal (IRE) (Royal Academy (USA) 130) [2004 73§: 11.9m⁶ 10.3g³ 10.3d³ 10m 10f 10.5g Sep 4] compact gelding: fair maiden: stays 1¼m: acts on good to firm going: visored (tailed off) final outing: weak finisher, and sometimes hangs: not to be trusted. *W. M. Brisbourne* **76 §**

TURNKEY 2 br.c. (Feb 14) Pivotal 124 – Persian Air (Persian Bold 123) [2004 5g² 5v* 6f⁵ 6.3f⁴ 6s Aug 18] 60,000F, 130,000Y: rather leggy, close-coupled colt: has a quick action: half-brother to several winners, including fairly useful 1½m and 2m winner Forzair and unreliable 1997 2-y-o 5f winner Persian Fortune (both by Forzando): dam well beaten: useful performer: won maiden at Kempton in May by 11 lengths: creditable efforts in Coventry Stakes at Royal Ascot and Anglesey Stakes at the Curragh (2¾ lengths fourth to Oratorio) next 2 starts: ran as if amiss final one: will stay 7f: seems to act on any turf going. *M. R. Channon* **104**

TURN 'N BURN 3 b.g. Unfuwain (USA) 131 – Seasonal Splendour (IRE) 95 (Prince **83** Rupert (FR) 121) [2004 69p: 12d 10g³ 11.7m² p12g⁴ Sep 1] sturdy gelding: fairly useful maiden: should be suited by 1½m+: acts on polytrack, yet to race on extremes of going on turf: tried to run out first bend Lingfield final outing. *C. A. Cyzer*

TURN OF PHRASE (IRE) 5 b.g. Cadeaux Genereux 131 – Token Gesture (IRE) 113 **67** (Alzao (USA) 117) [2004 70: p16g 12.1m 14g² 11.9g* 14g⁴ p12.2g p12.2g² p13.9g Dec 31] fair handicapper: won at Carlisle in September: stays 1¾m: acts on polytrack and firm ground: blinkered/visored. *R. A. Fahey*

TURN ON THE STYLE 2 ch.g. (May 8) Pivotal 124 – Elegant Rose 72 (Noalto 120) **76** [2004 6g 6g 5g² 5g* p5.1g f5g⁶ p5.1g² p5.1g* Dec 20] 26,000Y, 5,000 2-y-o: good-topped gelding: seventh living foal: half-brother to 2 winners, including useful 5f/6f (latter including at 2 yrs) winner Bowden Rose (by Dashing Blade): dam 6f winner: fair performer: won maiden at Catterick (veered left in front) in October and nursery at Wolverhampton in December: best at 5f: acts on polytrack: blinkered last 3 starts: sometimes slowly away. *R. P. Elliott*

TURNOVER 2 ch.f. (Feb 18) Gold Away (IRE) 125 – Turn To Vodka (FR) (Polish **–** Precedent (USA) 131) [2004 7.1s⁵ 8g p8g Nov 20] sturdy filly: first foal: dam unraced half-sister to smart French performer up to 12.5f Fabulous Hostess: well held in maidens/ seller. *M. J. Wallace*

TURNSTILE 3 gr.c. Linamix (FR) 127 – Kissing Gate (USA) 62 (Easy Goer (USA)) **83** [2004 73p: 11g⁴ 12m² 14d 12d³ 12f² 12d 14.4m⁶ 14d* Oct 10] tall, good-topped colt: has plenty of scope: fairly useful performer: won maiden at Goodwood in October: stays 1¾m: acts on firm and good to soft going: free-going sort. *R. Hannon*

TURTLE BAY 2 ch.f. (Feb 18) Dr Fong (USA) 128 – My Valentina 84 (Royal Academy **–** (USA) 130) [2004 p7g Aug 26] €75,000Y: fourth foal: dam, 2-y-o 7f winner who stayed 1¼m, half-sister to smart sprinter Averti: 66/1, last in minor event at Lingfield. *A. P. Jarvis*

TURTLE DANCER (IRE) 6 b.g. Turtle Island (IRE) 123 – Love Me Please (IRE) **74** 64 (Darshaan 133) [2004 10.1s² f14g Jun 16] fairly useful maiden at best: left D. Weld in Ireland after final start at 3 yrs: easily better effort on Flat since when second in minor event at Newcastle: stays 12.5f: raced mainly on ground softer than good: has been blinkered: sold 3,500 gns in August. *B. Ellison*

TURTLE MAGIC (IRE) 2 b.f. (Apr 17) Turtle Island (IRE) 123 – Theda 61 **67 d** (Mummy's Pet 125) [2004 p5g 5d² 5g³ 5.1g⁶ f5m⁶ 6m⁴ 6g 5m³ p6g⁴ 5.1m⁶ 5d⁴ 6m Sep 4] €4,000Y: half-sister to several winners, including fairly useful 1994 2-y-o 6f winner I Should Cocoa (by Magical Strike): dam maiden who stayed 7f: fair maiden: not so good in second half of season as first: probably stays 6f: acts on good to firm and good to soft going: in headgear last 5 starts: weak finisher. *W. G. M. Turner*

TURTLE PATRIARCH (IRE) 3 b.c. Turtle Island (IRE) 123 – La Doyenne (IRE) **78** 65 (Masterclass (USA) 116) [2004 62+: 6d 8.5g 8g 9.7g⁴ 12g² 10.5g⁶ p12g 10s² p12.2g* **a61** p13.9g Dec 10] angular, quite good-topped colt: fair on turf, modest on all-weather: won handicap at Wolverhampton in November: stays 1½m: acts on polytrack and soft going: sometimes wanders/carries head high. *Mrs A. J. Perrett*

TURTLE VALLEY (IRE) 8 b.g. Turtle Island (IRE) 123 – Primrose Valley 99 (Mill **78** Reef (USA) 141) [2004 75, a–: p13g⁵ p16g 14.4s³ 15s* 14s 14.1s May 2] small, strong **a60** gelding: unimpressive mover: fair handicapper: won at Warwick in April: stays 2m: has form on firm going, very best efforts on good or softer: blinkered once at 2 yrs: sometimes hangs left. *S. Dow*

TUSCAN DREAM 9 b.g. Clantime 101 – Excavator Lady 65 (Most Secret (119) [2004 **47** 47: f5g f5g f5g f5s f5g² f5s² f5g⁵ f5g* f5m⁵ f5g⁵ f5m May 17] smallish, sturdy gelding: poor performer: won banded race at Wolverhampton in April: best at bare 5f: acts on all-weather, raced mainly on good ground or firmer on turf: below form in blinkers: has bolted to post: sometimes rears as stall opens: usually races prominently. *A. Berry*

TUSCAN FLYER 6 b.g. Clantime 101 – Excavator Lady 65 (Most Secret 119) [2004 **68** 73: 6d 6m 7f³ 6m 5g⁴ 5d 5f⁴ 6g 5.2d 5m 5f³ Sep 23] deep-bodied gelding: fair handicapper: effective at 5f/6f: acts on polytrack, firm and good to soft going: often blinkered: races up with pace. *R. Bastiman*

TUSCAN TREATY 4 b.f. Brief Truce (USA) 126 – Fiorenz (USA) (Chromite (USA)) **52** [2004 60: p7g 8s 7g⁴ 6f 6m⁶ 6.1g 8g 6d⁴ Oct 2] quite good-topped filly: modest performer: effective at 6f/7f: acts on firm going, some promise on fibresand: visored 4 of last 5 starts: sometimes slowly away. *T. T. Clement*

TUSCARORA (IRE) 5 b.m. Revoque (IRE) 122 – Fresh Look (IRE) 64 (Alzao (USA) 117) [2004 71: 6.1s 8m 8.1m⁵ 8g² 7.1g⁶ 8.3g* 7m 9g⁵ 8.1m* 7g³ 8.3d³ 8g⁴ 6.1m p7.1g* p7.1g² p7.1g⁴ Dec 20] smallish mare: fairly useful handicapper: won at Windsor in July, Chepstow in August and Wolverhampton in November: effective at 7f to 9f: acts on polytrack and firm going: often slowly away: sometimes races freely: consistent. *A. W. Carroll* **80**

TUVALU (GER) 2 ch.c. (Apr 8) Dashing Blade 117 – Tepana (GER) (Polish Precedent (USA) 131) [2004 7.1m 7g⁵ 7.1g⁶ 8.3g⁴ p7g p8.6g⁶ Dec 1] €30,000Y: second foal: dam, German performer who stayed 11f, half-sister to smart German performer up to 11f Twen out of sister to Deutsches Derby winner Temporal: fair maiden: fourth in nursery at Windsor: sometimes races freely. *A. M. Balding* **68 a65**

TWEED 7 ch.g. Barathea (IRE) 127 – In Perpetuity 90 (Great Nephew 126) [2004 55, a63: 12.1g Sep 3] good-bodied gelding: modest performer: showed nothing only Flat run in 2004: tried in headgear. *C. Roberts* **–**

TWELVE BAR BLUES 3 ch.f. Nashwan (USA) 135 – Throw Away Line (USA) (Assert 134) [2004 10g 9.9g 11.9m⁵ 10.2m 13s 9s⁶ Nov 29] 37,000Y: quite good-topped filly: half-sister to several winners, including useful French 1½m winner Rebuff and fairly useful 7.5f (at 2 yrs in Britain) and 1¼m (in France) winner Wavey (both by Kris): dam, minor winner at 4 yrs in USA, half-sister to champion US filly Go For Wand: modest maiden: left J. Gosden after fourth start: bred to be suited by 1½m. *E. Lellouche, France* **61**

TWENTYTWOSILVER (IRE) 4 ro.g. Emarati (USA) 74 – St Louis Lady 71 (Absalom 128) [2004 73d: p10g Jan 17] fair performer at best: well held only Flat run in 2004: blinkered (went too freely) last 2 starts in 2003. *O. Sherwood* **–**

TWICE NIGHTLY 2 b.g. (Apr 29) Wolfhound (USA) 126 – Dusty's Darling (Doyoun 124) [2004 5d³ 6g³ 5g⁶ 7m⁵ 7d 7.1g 6.1d p7.1g Dec 15] 10,000Y: neat gelding: half-brother to 3 winners, including fairly useful 1997 2-y-o 5f winner Filey Brigg (by Weldnaas): dam no sign of ability: modest maiden: should stay 7f: acts on good to soft going: carried head awkwardly/hung left final start. *J. D. Bethell* **63**

TWICE UPON A TIME 5 ch.m. Primo Dominie 121 – Opuntia (Rousillon (USA) 133) [2004 79: 5d⁴ 6g⁴ 5m 6g 5.5m 5.1d⁴ 5g 5.1g 5g⁶ 5m Sep 15] good-topped mare: has a quick action: fair handicapper: best at 5f/6f: acts on firm and soft ground: often loses chance at start. *B. Smart* **73**

TWILIGHT BLUES (IRE) 5 ch.h. Bluebird (USA) 125 – Pretty Sharp 64 (Interrex (CAN)) [2004 118: 6m⁵ 6f 5d⁵ 7m² 6d Oct 15] good-topped horse: smart performer in 2003: only useful in 2004 (left B. Meehan after third start), best effort when 1¾ lengths second to Gonfilia in listed event at Redcar penultimate outing: probably best at 6f/7f: acts on firm and soft going: wore cheekpieces third start: has been mulish at stall and equipped with rope halter final start entry. *J. Noseda* **104**

TWILIGHT YEARS 3 b.g. Silver Patriarch (IRE) 125 – Adjusting (IRE) (Busted 134) [2004 10.5m 12.1g 13.8m⁴ 16g⁶ 14.1g Aug 28] tall, good-topped gelding: poor maiden: raced freely at 2m, but seemed to stay. *T. D. Easterby* **43**

TWOFAN (USA) 3 b.c. Lear Fan (USA) 130 – Double Wedge (USA) (Northern Baby (CAN) 127) [2004 10.1v² 10.5g² 14.1s* 14d⁶ 14.8g⁴ 14m⁵ Jul 29] $13,000F, €55,000Y: big, strong colt: ninth foal: half-brother to 3 winners in USA: dam US Grade 1 9f winner, also successful at 1m in France at 2 yrs: fairly useful performer: won maiden at Nottingham in May: should prove as effective at 1½m as 1¾m: acts on soft and good to firm ground: usually makes running: sold 13,000 gns in October. *M. Johnston* **83**

TWO MILES WEST (IRE) 3 b.c. Sadler's Wells (USA) 132 – User Friendly 128 (Slip Anchor 136) [2004 12m* 16.2m² 14d² 12m⁴ 14g⁶ Sep 18] smallish, strong colt: sixth foal: half-brother to 3 winners abroad, including French 1½m winner Dream Merchant (by Deputy Minister): dam won 5 Group 1 events, including Oaks and St Leger: smart performer: won maiden at Leopardstown in June: 6 lengths second to Duke of Venice in Queen's Vase at Royal Ascot next outing: progressed further after, best effort when 6 lengths sixth to Vinnie Roe in Irish St Leger at the Curragh (tongue tied): reportedly sold privately following month: stays 2m. *A. P. O'Brien, Ireland* **115**

TWO OF A KIND (IRE) 4 ch.g. Ashkalani (IRE) 128 – Dulcinea 73 (Selkirk (USA) 129) [2004 58: p12g* Jan 6] modest performer: won maiden at Lingfield in January, **57**

despite wandering: stays 1½m, not 15f: raced only on all-weather/ground firmer than good: sometimes slowly away: carries head high: sold 10,500 gns in February. *J. W. Hills*

TWO OF CLUBS 3 b.g. First Trump 118 – Sulaka (Owington 123) [2004 71: f7g³ **67** f8g³ f7s* 7.5s⁵ p7.1g* p9.5g⁵ Dec 15] lengthy, good-topped gelding: fair performer: won maiden at Wolverhampton in March and seller there (left P. Haslam) in October: stays 7f: acts on all-weather, raced mainly on good ground or softer on turf: wore cheekpieces last 4 starts. *Miss S. J. Wilton*

TWO STEP KID (USA) 3 ch.c. Gone West (USA) – Marsha's Dancer (USA) (North- **109** ern Dancer) [2004 94p: 7d⁶ 5m⁴ 6m* 6m³ 6f⁴ 6m⁴ 6m⁴ Sep 12] smallish, strong, stocky colt: useful handicapper: won William Hill Trophy at York in June by neck from Delphie Queen: ran well after, fourth to Pivotal Point in Stewards' Cup at Goodwood and to Texas Gold there last 2 starts: best at 5f/6f: acts on good to firm going: races up with pace: genuine and consistent: sent to USA. *J. Noseda*

TWO STEPS TO GO (USA) 5 b.g. Rhythm (USA) – Lyonushka (CAN) (Private **39 §** Account (USA)) [2004 44§: f12g⁴ f11g⁴ f9.4g⁵ Jan 26] smallish, sturdy gelding: poor performer: seems to stay 11f: acts on fibresand and good to firm going, probably on good to soft: sometimes blinkered/visored: temperamental. *Ian Emmerson*

TWYLA THARP (IRE) 2 b.f. (Mar 4) Sadler's Wells (USA) 132 – Sumoto 101 **83 p** (Mtoto 134) [2004 8.2g 8s² Oct 22] half-sister to several winners, including very smart 7f (at 2 yrs) to 1¼m winner Compton Admiral (by Suave Dancer) and smart 1m (including at 2 yrs)/1¼m winner Summoner (by Inchinor): dam 6f (at 2 yrs)/7f winner: much better effort in maidens when 3 lengths second to Her Own Kind at Doncaster: should be suited by 1¼m/1½m: likely to progress. *J. H. M. Gosden*

TYBALT 2 b.c. (Mar 26) Polar Falcon (USA) 126 – Once Removed 65 (Distant **64** Relative 128) [2004 6m² 6g⁵ 6g 7f 7m³ 8d Nov 5] 14,000F, 5,500Y: useful-looking colt: first foal: dam maiden who stayed 7f: modest maiden: stays 7f, probably not 1m: acts on good to firm ground: visored last 2 starts: signs of temperament. *P. W. Harris*

TYCHEROS 2 b.g. (May 12) Polar Falcon (USA) 126 – Marie de Flandre (FR) 109 **– p** (Crystal Palace (FR) 132) [2004 6g Oct 11] 7,500Y: half-brother to numerous winners, including very smart 1¼m to 2m winner Solo Mio (by Sadler's Wells) and fairly useful 1¼m winner Count of Flanders (by Green Desert): dam, French 1¼m winner, half-sister to Prix Morny winner Sakura Reiko: 33/1, well held in maiden at Windsor: likely to do better in due course. *S. C. Williams*

William Hill Trophy (Handicap), York—Two Step Kid wins the principal race on the 34th Timeform Charity Day from Delphie Queen (left) and Traytonic (right); £239,904 was raised, the highest total in the history of this popular day's racing

Prince's Trust Shergar Cup Distaff (Rated Handicap), Ascot—Tychy, ridden by Gerald Mosse,
wins the first race on Shergar Cup day, which attracted a crowd of 22,489;
the trophy was won by The Rest of The World with 138 points to Great Britain and Ireland's 102

TYCHY   5 ch.m. Suave Dancer (USA) 136 – Touch of White 77 (Song 132) [2004 97:   **102**
6g⁵ 5m³ 6f 5m 5m⁵ 6g* 6d 5g⁴ 6g 6.1g 6d Oct 14] good-topped mare: useful performer: won handicap at Ascot in August by length from Fruit of Glory: good 2¼ lengths
fifth to Ringmoor Down in King George Stakes at Goodwood previous outing: best
efforts at 5f/6f: yet to race on heavy going, acts on any other: usually races up with pace.
S. C. Williams

TYCOON   3 b.c. Sadler's Wells (USA) 132 – Fleeting Glimpse 109 (Rainbow   **123**
Quest (USA) 134) [2004 101: 12f³ 12m⁶ 10.4d 14.6f³ 12d³ Oct 2]
   'We are the champions my friends . . .' Even the most powerful and wealthy
don't have a monopoly on success. Manchester United, champions seven times in
the first nine seasons of football's Premier League, have added only one title in
three campaigns since, and they have drawn a blank in five attempts at repeating
their win in the European Champions' League in 1998/9. After winning twenty-
three Group 1 races in 2001 from his Ballydoyle stable, owned by Coolmore
supremo and Manchester United shareholder John Magnier, trainer Aidan O'Brien
has seen his own success rate dwindle, saddling the winners of nineteen Group 1
races in 2002, nine in 2003 and three—Powerscourt, Ad Valorem and Oratorio—in
2004. After winning five British classics—the Two Thousand Guineas, the Oaks,
the Derby twice and the St Leger—in 2001 and 2002, O'Brien has added only the
2003 St Leger to his haul in Britain since. Classic success, of course, is far from
routine for any trainer. Mark Johnston's victory with Attraction in 2004 ended a
wait since Mister Baileys in 1994 for a second British classic winner. Sir Michael
Stoute had waited since 1986 for a third Derby winner before Kris Kin came along
in 2003, to be followed by North Light, and Rule of Law's St Leger success in
2004 was Saeed bin Suroor's first British classic winner since Kazzia won the One
Thousand Guineas and Oaks in 2002. O'Brien's early classic hopes in Britain in
2004 foundered on the failure of favourite One Cool Cat in the Two Thousand
Guineas and, though All Too Beautiful was second in the Oaks, O'Brien had
Magritte and, more notably, ante-post favourite Yeats sidelined for the Derby. Undeterred, O'Brien turned to the substitute's bench and gave a reminder of his skills
with Tycoon, who showed very smart form in finishing placed in three Group 1
events, including the St Leger, a record which could have been even better had
things gone more his way.
   After seeming to have his limitations exposed somewhat when fourth past
the post in the Prix Jean-Luc Lagardere over seven furlongs at Longchamp on the
last of four starts at two, Tycoon benefited greatly from a step up in distance in

2004, when he tackled one Group 1 race a month from June until October. The rank outsider under Colm O'Donoghue at 150/1 in the Irish Derby, he did best of his stable's five runners at the Curragh all the same, showing much improved form to be a never-nearer third of ten to Grey Swallow and North Light, beaten half a length and a length and a half, with Rule of Law a neck away fourth. On the strength of that run, Tycoon got the nod ahead of the four-year-old Powerscourt for the King George VI and Queen Elizabeth Stakes at Ascot in July. The only three-year-old in a field of eleven, he went off at 16/1, and ran another fine race to be sixth, a position he would have improved upon had he not become pocketed as Spencer went for a run up the inside in the straight. Running on, but with too much to do once switched, Tycoon was beaten only three and a half lengths for second behind the three-length winner Doyen.

Tycoon's one poor performance of the season came when tailed off in the International at York in August, but he put that run behind him in the St Leger the following month. With Spencer at Leopardstown for the Irish Champion Stakes, Tycoon was partnered at Doncaster by Darryll Holland and started fourth favourite of nine at 6/1. Tried in a tongue strap, Tycoon didn't help his rider by going a bit in snatches early on, but, in hindsight, he would have gone very close asked for his effort sooner in a slowly-run race. Tycoon was travelling strongly in rear two furlongs out and finished just about best of all in third, a length and a half behind close finishers Rule of Law and Quiff. Tycoon's final run of the year came in America in the Joe Hirsch Turf Classic Invitational at Belmont Park. Starting only fifth favourite in a field of seven, he ran as well as he had ever done, reunited with Spencer, again nearest at the finish in a steadily-run race, going down by two and a half lengths and three quarters of a length to American three-year-old Kitten's Joy and the former British-trained four-year-old Magistretti.

Although he raced in the colours of Mrs John Magnier at two and three, Tycoon was bred by Juddmonte Farms out of Fleeting Glimpse, who showed useful form at three, winning a newcomers event at Longchamp over a mile and a quarter and finishing second in the Prix Saint-Alary over the same course and distance for Andre Fabre on her only starts. Tycoon is the second and last live foal out of Fleeting Glimpse, a half-sister to One Thousand Guineas winner Wince, dam of Quiff, and a sister to the very smart middle-distance performer Ulundi. Fleeting Glimpse's first foal was Half Glance (by Danehill), winner of the May Hill Stakes at two.

		Northern Dancer (b 1966)	Nearctic
	Sadler's Wells (USA) (b 1981)		Natalma
Tycoon		Fairy Bridge (b 1975)	Bold Reason
(b.c. 2001)			Special
		Rainbow Quest (b 1981)	Blushing Groom
	Fleeting Glimpse (b 1994)		I Will Follow
		Flit (b 1988)	Lyphard
			Nimble Folly

A small, sturdy colt, Tycoon was bought at the end of his three-year-old season by Sheikh Mohammed's son, Sheikh Rashid, and will reportedly be aimed at the Dubai Sheema Classic in March by his new trainer Mazin Al Kurdi, though he could return to Europe afterwards. Effective at a mile and a half and a mile and three quarters, Tycoon acts on firm and good to soft going. There is the possibility that Tycoon has his share of temperament. He sweated and was reluctant to post at Longchamp as a two-year-old and reportedly reared over in the preliminaries at three at Ascot, clearly shaken when coming into the paddock. *A. P. O'Brien, Ireland*

TYCOON HALL (IRE) 4 ch.c. Halling (USA) 133 – Tycooness (IRE) 80§ (Last Tycoon 131) [2004 96: 10d Apr 10] good-topped colt: useful performer at best, lightly raced: showed nothing only outing in 2004: joined Mrs J. Harrington, Ireland. *R. Hannon* —

TYNE 3 b.g. Komaite (USA) – High Typha 61 (Dowsing (USA) 124) [2004 88: 5s 5f⁶ 6g⁴ 5g Jul 5] tall, quite good-topped gelding: fairly useful performer: will prove best at 5f/6f: probably acts on firm going. *T. D. Barron* **80**

TYNEHAM 4 b.c. Robellino (USA) 127 – Diamond Wedding (USA) 65 (Diamond Shoal 130) [2004 –: p8.6g* 8d f8g p8.6g⁵ p9.5g⁴ p10g Dec 30] well-made colt: modest performer: left M. Pimbonnet in France before winning claimer at Wolverhampton in October: stays 8.6f: acts on polytrack and soft going: wore cheekpieces in 2004. *W. G. M. Turner* **58**

TYPE ONE (IRE) 6 b.g. Bigstone (IRE) 126 – Isca 66 (Caerleon (USA) 132) [2004 **72**
87: p6g p5g* f6g p5g 6g 6s 6g² 6m 6d 6d⁴ Jun 25] well-made gelding: fairly useful on **a80**
all-weather, fair on turf: won claimer at Lingfield (left T. Mills) in January: best at 5f/6f:
acts on polytrack, firm and good to soft going: tried visored: ran creditably in cheekpieces
seventh start: often races up with pace. *J. J. Quinn*

TYPHOON GINGER (IRE) 9 ch.m. Archway (IRE) 115 – Pallas Viking (Viking –
(USA)) [2004 7s Oct 23] close-coupled mare: fairly useful handicapper in 2001: well
beaten only outing since. *G. Woodward*

TYPHOON TILLY 7 b.g. Hernando (FR) 127 – Meavy 86 (Kalaglow 132) [2004 87: **80**
p12g⁶ p16g⁴ p16g³ p12g⁶ 14.4s⁴ 16d 14.1d³ 13.1d² 16g* 16g⁶ 16d p16.5g⁶ p13.9g*
p13.9g Dec 31] quite good-topped gelding: fairly useful performer: won handicap at
Kempton in September and claimer at Wolverhampton in November: effective at 1½m to
2½m: acts on polytrack, very best turf efforts on good ground or firmer: blinkered twice
at 4 yrs: races freely: sometimes finds little. *C. R. Egerton*

TYRONE SAM 2 b.g. (Apr 5) Mind Games 121 – Crystal Sand (GER) (Forzando **71**
122) [2004 5m 5f 7.1d f6g* p7.1g⁵ p8.6g f7g* Dec 14] 34,000Y: fourth foal: brother to
useful 2002 2-y-o 6f winner Cumbrian Venture: dam unraced: fair performer: won seller
in November and nursery in December, both at Southwell: stays 7f: form only on all-
weather: blinkered last 4 starts: sometimes looks none too keen. *K. A. Ryan*

TYRRELLSPASS (IRE) 7 b.g. Alzao (USA) 117 – Alpine Chime (IRE) 72 (Tirol –
127) [2004 f7s 10.2d⁵ Apr 23] poor maiden in Ireland (stayed 1¼m, acted on good to soft
going, blinkered once): tongue tied, little form on return to Flat in 2004. *J. D. Frost*

TYSON RETURNS 2 b.g. (Feb 16) Mujahid (USA) 125 – Mabrookah 73 (Deploy –
131) [2004 6.1s f6d Jun 10] sturdy gelding: only a little sign of ability in maidens.
P. A. Blockley

TYTHEKNOT 3 b.g. Pursuit of Love 124 – Bundled Up (USA) (Sharpen Up 127) **76**
[2004 76: 8.1s² 10s³ 8s⁶ 10s⁴ 10m³ 10.1s* 8d⁵ 10s 10.3s Oct 22] tall, leggy gelding: fair
performer: won maiden at Newcastle in August: barely stays 1¼m: acts on soft and good
to firm ground: tried in cheekpieces: sold 20,000 gns. *Jedd O'Keeffe*

TYTHERLEY 3 b.f. Man Among Men (IRE) – Sharp Thistle 87 (Sharpo 132) [2004 –
8.3g May 17] sister to 1m winner Sharp Monkey and half-sister to winner abroad by
Kalaglow: dam, 7f winner, stayed 1½m: 100/1, unsteerable and eventually pulled up in
maiden at Windsor. *J. R. Boyle*

TYUP POMPEY (IRE) 3 ch.g. Docksider (USA) 124 – Cindy's Baby 36 (Bairn –
(USA) 126) [2004 58p: 9.9m⁴ 10.2g 10v⁵ Oct 23] strong, close-coupled gelding: lightly-
raced maiden: well held in 2004. *D. R. C. Elsworth*

TYZACK (IRE) 3 b.g. Fasliyev (USA) 120 – Rabea (USA) 61 (Devil's Bag (USA)) **53 §**
[2004 79§: 6.1s⁵ 7m 8g 7m 10f Sep 16] good-topped gelding: disappointing maiden: left
J. Given after second start: barely stays 1m: acts on good to firm ground: sometimes
troublesome to post: tends to find little/hang: not to be trusted. *J. Balding*

U

UGLY SISTER (USA) 2 gr.f. (Feb 14) Aljabr (USA) 125 – Cinderella Ball (USA) **33**
(Nureyev (USA) 131) [2004 6g f7g 7s⁶ 7m Sep 7] 6,500Y: lengthy filly: second foal:
dam unraced half-sister to US Grade 3 1m/9f winner El Amante: poor maiden: somewhat
headstrong. *G. C. Bravery*

UHOOMAGOO 6 b.g. Namaqualand (USA) – Point of Law (Law Society (USA) **101**
130) [2004 90, a77: f7s* 8g 8d 8.1m 7m* 8.5m* 8f 7m 7m³ 8m 7m 7m p7g Oct 28] leggy **a90**
gelding: useful on turf, fairly useful on all-weather: better than ever at 6 yrs, winning
minor event at Southwell in February and handicaps at Doncaster in May and Epsom
(beat Alrafid by 3 lengths) in June: good third to Court Masterpiece in valuable handicap
at Ascot ninth start: effective at 7f/1m: acts on all-weather and any turf going: usually
blinkered, also tried in cheekpieces/visor: sometimes takes long time to warm up: held
up: tends to wander: tough. *K. A. Ryan*

UHURU PEAK 3 ch.c. Bal Harbour 113 – Catherines Well 99 (Junius (USA) 124) **60**
[2004 f5s³ f6s 6g⁵ 6m 7f 6m³ 6d² 6m 8s⁶ 6g 7d³ Oct 15] modest maiden handicapper:
stays 7f: acts on fibresand, good to firm and good to soft going: blinkered last 2 outings.
M. W. Easterby

UIG 3 ch.f. Bien Bien (USA) 125 – Madam Zando 51 (Forzando 122) [2004 10.2g 9.9g **80** 10m³ 10m² 11.9s 8.3d⁴ 10.2g² 10.5s 10.1g² Oct 2] 2,800 2-y-o: small filly: third foal: dam maiden who stayed 1m: fair maiden: stays 1¼m: acts on good to firm and good to soft going: races up with pace. *H. S. Howe*

ULSHAW 7 ch.g. Salse (USA) 128 – Kintail 76 (Kris 135) [2004 63, a59: 21.6v 19.1f 17.2g 16.2m Jul 23] quite good-topped gelding: modest handicapper in 2003: well beaten in 2004: tried visored. *B. J. Llewellyn*

ULTIMATA 4 ch.f. Unfuwain (USA) 131 – Last Look (Rainbow Quest (USA) 134) **88** [2004 81: 10m 8.3m² 8.3m² 10.1s 8.9g 10d* 10.1s⁶ Oct 27] leggy filly: fairly useful performer: won 3-runner Newmarket Challenge Whip (Handicap) in October by 1¼ lengths from Vamp, dictating pace: stays 1¼m: acts on good to firm and good to soft going: sold 17,000 gns. *J. R. Fanshawe*

ULTRA MARINE (IRE) 4 b.c. Blues Traveller (IRE) 119 – The Aspecto Girl (IRE) **–** 53 (Alzao (USA) 117) [2004 56: 10g 12m 12.6g Jul 8] leggy, useful-looking colt: modest maiden: well beaten in 2004: tried in cheekpieces/blinkers. *J. S. Wainwright*

ULUNDI 9 b.g. Rainbow Quest (USA) 134 – Flit (USA) 72 (Lyphard (USA) 132) [2004 **–** 99: p10g 12g 10m 10m Jun 18] rangy gelding: very smart performer at 7 yrs: lightly raced and mostly well held since. *P. R. Webber*

ULYSEES (IRE) 5 b.g. Turtle Island (IRE) 123 – Tamasriya (IRE) (Doyoun 124) **79** [2004 83d: 6g* 6g 6g³ 6g* 7s 5.9g⁵ 6g 6d 6s⁴ 7.2s 6d 6d⁵ 7s Nov 2] quite good-topped gelding: fair handicapper: won at Hamilton in April and Ayr in June: best form at 6f/7f: raced mainly on good going or softer: tried in cheekpieces/visor: carries head high: none too reliable. *I. Semple*

UMNIYA (IRE) 2 b.f. (Mar 22) Bluebird (USA) 125 – Sparky's Song 63 (Electric **95** 126) [2004 5s³ 6s² 6m* 6m³ 6m³ 6m⁴ 6m⁵ 6s⁶ 7s⁶ 7m⁴ 6.5g³ 7g⁵ 8m³ 8d⁶ 8s Oct 31] 40,000Y: leggy, quite good-topped filly: fifth foal: half-sister to useful 6f (including at 2 yrs) winner Lady Links (by Bahamian Bounty) and 4-y-o Stolen Song: dam, 1¼m/1½m winner, half-sister to very smart sprinter Bold Edge: useful performer: won maiden at Redcar in May: mostly creditable efforts after, including in Moyglare Stud Stakes at the Curragh tenth start and Premio Dormello at Milan on thirteenth: stays 1m: acts on soft and good to firm going: visored last 2 outings: tough and consistent. *M. R. Channon*

UMOJA (FR) 4 b. or br.f. Anabaa (USA) 130 – Frustration 108 (Salse (USA) 128) **71** [2004 76: 12d 10s 10s³ 12v p12.2g² p12.2g Dec 14] well-made filly: fair maiden: ran at Wolverhampton last 2 starts: stays easy 1½m: acts on polytrack, soft and good to firm going. *Miss S. Cox, Ireland*

UN AUTRE ESPERE 5 b.g. Golden Heights 82 – Drummer's Dream (IRE) 48 **46 §** (Drumalis 125) [2004 –: f9.4s f8.5s⁶ f8.5g f9.4g p7g f7g⁵ 7.1d* f8m⁵ 11.7s p10m Dec 15] leggy gelding: poor performer: won banded race at Chepstow in April: little other form, leaving T. Wall before final start: stays 7f: acts on good to soft going: tried in cheekpieces, often blinkered: unreliable. *M. Wellings*

UNBRIDLED'S DREAM (USA) 3 gr. or ro.g. Unbridled's Song (USA) 125 – Diamond Dream (FR) (Diamond Prospect (USA) 126) [2004 8m May 2] leggy gelding: well held in maiden at Newmarket: sold 2,200 gns, then gelded. *H. J. Cyzer*

UNCLE BATTY 4 b.g. Bob Back (USA) 124 – Aunt Sadie 71 (Pursuit of Love 124) **45** [2004 10m⁴ 12.1m⁵ Jun 21] unfurnished gelding: modest form in bumpers: poor form when fourth in seller at Leicester (claimed from G. Harker £6,000), better effort on Flat: should stay 1¼m. *G. J. Smith*

UNCLE BULGARIA (IRE) 2 b.c. (May 3) Alhaarth (IRE) 126 – Istibshar (USA) **62** 78 (Mr Prospector (USA)) [2004 f7m³ 7g 8g 8g⁵ 8d⁶ Nov 5] 7,500Y: leggy colt: brother to 3-y-o Iktitaf, closely related to fairly useful 7f (in UAE) and 1½m winner Mostabshir (by Unfuwain) and half-brother to 2 winners: dam 6f winner: modest maiden: should stay 1¼m: acts on good to soft going, probably on fibresand. *G. C. Bravery*

UNCLE JOHN 3 b.g. Atraf 116 – Bit O' May 71 (Mummy's Pet 125) [2004 67: 9g **72** 9.9g 10g⁴ 11.9m² 12m⁴ 10d 10.2m 10.2s p12g² p12.2g² p12.2g³ p12.2g² p12m p13.9g⁵ Dec 31] fair performer: stays 1½m: acts on all-weather and good to firm going: blinkered last 6 starts. *S. Kirk*

UNDERGRADUATE (IRE) 2 b.g. (Apr 19) Unfuwain (USA) 131 – Starlet 119 **69 p** (Teenoso (USA) 135) [2004 8s⁵ Oct 19] closely related to useful 1m (at 2 yrs) and 13.5f winner Interlude (by Sadler's Wells) and half-brother to several winners, including useful 1¼m winner Border Comet (by Selkirk): dam, best at 1¼m/1½m at 4 yrs, second in

Nassau and Sun Chariot Stakes: 10/1 and green, fifth to Rain Stops Play in maiden at Bath, late headway having been slowly away and soon off bridle (gelded after): will be suited by 1¼m/1½m: sure to improve. *Sir Michael Stoute*

UNDER MY SKIN (IRE) 3 ch.f. Mark of Esteem (IRE) 137 – Convenience (IRE) **40** (Ela-Mana-Mou 132) [2004 10g 7d Aug 13] 130,000Y: leggy, lengthy filly: second foal: half-sister to useful performer up to 1¼m Dust Cover (by Desert Story): dam unraced half-sister to smart sprinter Fire Dome: poor form in maidens: tried tongue tied. *T. G. Mills*

UNDER MY SPELL 3 b.f. Wizard King 122 – Gagajulu 75 (Al Hareb (USA) 123) **79** [2004 80: 7g 6.1g 6.1s² 6.1g² 6.1g² 6m⁵ 6m* 6g 6m 6f 8.1s Aug 12] leggy filly: fair handicapper: won at Leicester in June: stays 6f: acts on firm and soft ground. *P. D. Evans*

UNDERTHEMISTLETOE (IRE) 2 b.f. (Mar 10) Lujain (USA) 119 – Christmas **49** Kiss 82 (Taufan (USA) 119) [2004 6m⁶ 5g³ 6f 5g⁶ Oct 5] 9,200Y: compact filly: fifth foal: half-sister to 3 winners, including fairly useful 5f/6f winner Night Runner (by Polar Falcon) and 3-y-o Signor Panettiere: dam 5f/6f winner: poor maiden: likely to prove best at 5f/6f: acts on good to firm going: sometimes flashes tail. *B. Smart*

UNDETERRED 8 ch.g. Zafonic (USA) 130 – Mint Crisp (IRE) 108 (Green Desert **79** (USA) 127) [2004 90: 6s 6m⁵ 6m 6m 6m⁴ 6g⁴ 6m⁴ 6m* 6m 6g Sep 22] lengthy, deepgirthed gelding: has a quick action: fair handicapper: won at Pontefract in July: best form at 6f: acts on firm going, probably on soft: tried blinkered/visored: edgy sort: sometimes early/reluctant to post: often slowly away. *T. D. Barron*

UNFURLED (IRE) 2 ch.c. (Apr 5) Unfuwain (USA) 131 – Peony 108 (Lion Cavern **90 p** (USA) 117) [2004 8g⁶ 8d² Oct 15] 85,000Y: angular colt: first foal: dam, French 7f and (including at 2 yrs) 1m winner, second in Poule d'Essai des Pouliches: much better effort in maidens when 3½ lengths second to Proclamation at Newmarket: likely to stay 1¼m: useful prospect, should win a race or 2. *J. L. Dunlop*

UNICORN REWARD (IRE) 4 b.c. Turtle Island (IRE) 123 – Kingdom Pearl 57 **64 ?** (Statoblest 120) [2004 91: 8g 8v⁴ 8m May 26] neat colt: fairly useful handicapper at 3 yrs: well held in 2004. *M. D. Hammond*

UNINTENTIONAL 3 b.f. Dr Devious (IRE) 127 – Tamnia 106 (Green Desert (USA) **–** 127) [2004 60: f8.5g⁶ f8.5g 10s⁶ 11.5m 12.1s 10.2s p7.1g f12g Nov 22] sturdy filly: maiden: little form at 3 yrs: tried visored/blinkered. *R. Brotherton*

UNION JACK JACKSON (IRE) 2 b.c. (Jan 18) Daggers Drawn (USA) 114 – **65** Beechwood Quest (IRE) 65 (River Falls 113) [2004 6d⁴ 6g 6d f7g⁶ 8g⁴ 8d⁴ p8.6g* f8g² **a72** p8g³ f8g² Dec 28] 17,000Y: good-topped colt: second foal: dam 2-y-o 5f seller winner: fair performer: won nursery at Wolverhampton in December: creditable efforts after: should stay 1¼m: acts on all-weather and good to soft going: reliable. *J. G. Given*

UNITED NATIONS 3 ch.g. Halling (USA) 133 – Congress (IRE) 86 (Dancing Brave **96** (USA) 140) [2004 8g* 8.1d³ 8g⁴ 8g Oct 1] 140,000F: sturdy gelding: sixth foal: halfbrother to fairly useful 7.7f winner Serra Negra (by Kris) and 6f winner Promessa (by Reprimand): dam, 2-y-o 1m winner, sister to very smart 6f/7f performer Cherokee Rose: useful performer: won newcomers event at Newmarket in April by 2½ lengths from Denounce: off 5 months, creditable fourth to Flipando in handicap at Musselburgh third start: ran poorly next time: should stay 1¼m: raced only on good/good to soft ground: visored last 2 outings: sold 13,500 gns, then gelded. *D. R. Loder*

UNITED SPIRIT (IRE) 3 b.f. Fasliyev (USA) 120 – Atlantic Desire (IRE) 100 **76** (Ela-Mana-Mou 132) [2004 55p: 7g 7.2g⁶ 7m³ 6m* p7g* 7g⁴ 6m⁵ 6.1d p9.5g* p9.5g Dec 27] rather leggy, lengthy filly: fair handicapper: won at Lingfield in July and August and at Wolverhampton (first start after leaving M. Magnusson) in December: stays 9.5f: acts on polytrack and good to firm going: tried in cheekpieces, effective blinkered or not. *Jedd O'Keeffe*

UNITED UNION (IRE) 3 b. or br.g. Imperial Ballet (IRE) 110 – Madagascar 43 **54** (Puissance 110) [2004 62: 6d⁴ 5.1g Apr 8] leggy, quite good-topped gelding: modest maiden: should stay 7f: acts on good to soft ground: tried blinkered. *D. Haydn Jones*

UNLEADED 4 ch.f. Danzig Connection (USA) – Mo Stopher 47 (Sharpo 132) [2004 **48** –: f14.8g² f16.2g* f16g² p16g⁵ 14.4s f16.2m⁴ f16.2m⁵ May 17] small, stocky filly: poor performer: won banded race at Wolverhampton in January: stays 2m: acts on fibresand. *J. Akehurst*

UNLIMITED 2 b.g. (Apr 1) Bold Edge 123 – Cabcharge Blue 81 (Midyan (USA) **66** 124) [2004 f5g² f5d* 5m² 5m⁵ 7m 6g³ 6.1g⁵ 6d f6g p5.1g⁴ Nov 19] 7,000Y: big, leggy gelding: first foal: dam 5f (at 2 yrs) to 1½m winner: fair performer: won maiden at South-well in April: stays 6f: acts on fibresand and good to firm going: blinkered last 2 starts (ran creditably on second occasion): often races prominently: none too consistent. *Mrs A. Duffield*

UNO MENTE   5 b.m. Mind Games 121 – One Half Silver (CAN) (Plugged Nickle   **58** (USA)) [2004 70: 9.9s 8.3d 10m 8f⁶ 8m³ 8m 8g 9.9m 8.2g 9.9m Sep 21] sturdy mare: modest handicapper: stays 1¼m: acts on polytrack and firm ground: tried in visor/cheek-pieces. *Don Enrico Incisa*

UNPRECEDENTED (IRE)   3 br.g. Primo Dominie 121 – Misellina (FR) 57 (Polish   **–** Precedent (USA) 131) [2004 –: f8g 7d 9g⁴ 8m 8g 8.3g p7m Dec 8] quite good-topped gelding: little form: tried blinkered/visored: inconsistent. *T. T. Clement*

UNREAL   2 b.f. (Feb 14) Dansili 127 – Illusory 81 (Kings Lake (USA) 133) [2004   **79** 5.2g⁶ 6g² 6g⁶ 6.1g² 5g* Sep 10] strong, well-made filly: half-sister to several winners, including 1m/9f winner Phantom Quest (by Rainbow Quest) and 1¼m winner Illustrator (by Sadler's Wells), both smart: dam, 6f winner, sister to Lowther winner Kingscote: fair performer: won maiden at Sandown by ½ length from Park Approach: second in nursery at Warwick previous outing: likely to prove best at 5f/6f. *B. W. Hills*

UNSCRUPULOUS   5 ch.g. Machiavellian (USA) 123 – Footlight Fantasy (USA) 68   **109** (Nureyev (USA) 131) [2004 91p: 8f³ 7m* Jun 18] angular gelding: useful performer, lightly raced: improved form when winning valuable 28-runner handicap at Royal Ascot in very good style by 5 lengths from Maghanim, producing good turn of foot to lead inside final 1f: reported in mid-July to have injured a joint: effective at 7f/1m: raced on good going or firmer: held up. *J. R. Fanshawe*

UNSHAKABLE (IRE)   5 b.g. Eagle Eyed (USA) 111 – Pepper And Salt (IRE)   **103** (Double Schwartz 128) [2004 106: 8g 10d 8.1d* 8.1d³ 8m 8g⁵ 7.9s⁴ 9g⁵ 8d 8d Oct 30] good-bodied gelding: useful handicapper: won at Sandown in April by ¾ length from Always Esteemed: held his form well, good fifth of 32 to Spanish Don in Cambridgeshire at Newmarket eighth start: effective at 1m/9f: acts on soft and good to firm ground. *Bob Jones*

UNSHAKEN   10 b.h. Environment Friend 128 – Reel Foyle (USA) 77 (Irish River   **–** (FR) 131) [2004 65, a–: 6m 8d Jun 18] strong, sturdy horse: fairly useful performer in his prime: tailed off in 2004: dead. *D. A. Nolan*

UNSHOODA   3 ch.f. Machiavellian (USA) 123 – Rawaabe (USA) 87 (Nureyev (USA)   **89** 131) [2004 96: 7g 6d Jun 5] sturdy, lengthy filly: has a quick action: seventh of 8 in Fred Darling Stakes at Newbury, then well held in listed race at Haydock in 2004: best form at 6f: acts on good to firm going. *B. W. Hills*

UNSUITED   5 b.m. Revoque (IRE) 122 – Nagnagnag (IRE) 103 (Red Sunset 120) [2004   **73** –: p10g f9.4s³ f9.4s² f9.4s⁶ 8.1d⁴ 10v* 9g* 9d* 11m³ 10g 9.9g Sep 29] fair performer: won banded race, apprentice handicap and handicap, all at Kempton in May/June: ran as if amiss final start: stays 11f: acts on all-weather, good to firm and heavy going. *J. E. Long*

UNTIDY DAUGHTER   5 b.m. Sabrehill (USA) 120 – Branitska (Mummy's Pet 125)   **57** [2004 –: 9.9s⁵ 12m 10m³ 10.1s Jun 25] lengthy mare: modest maiden: stays 1¼m: acts on soft and good to firm going: wore cheekpieces/blinkers last 5 starts. *B. Ellison*

Buckingham Palace Stakes (Handicap), Royal Ascot—Unscrupulous runs away with what beforehand had looked a very competitive race; Maghanim (striped cap) and True Night follow him home, while top weight and favourite New Seeker (right) is first home on the other side

UNTIMELY 2 ch.f. (May 18) Inchinor 119 – All The Time 59 (Dancing Brave (USA) **54**
140) [2004 f8g4 p7m Dec 22] fifth foal: half-sister to 9.4f winner Garden of Eden (by
Green Desert) and a winner in Greece by Mark of Esteem: dam, maiden, half-sister to
very smart performers Reprimand and Wiorno: better effort in maidens when fourth at
Southwell: disputed lead long way at Lingfield. *H. Morrison*

UP TEMPO (IRE) 6 b.g. Flying Spur (AUS) – Musical Essence 65 (Song 132) [2004 **89**
76: f7g2 f6f* f7s3 f6s* 6s* 7s* 7s4 6d2 7m 7m 7g5 6m p7.1d* p7.1g2 f8g3 p8.6g Dec 27]
useful-looking gelding: fairly useful performer: won minor event at Southwell in January, handicap there in February, handicap at Newcastle in March, minor event at Redcar
in April and handicap at Wolverhampton in October: effective at 6f to 1m: acts on all-
weather and any turf going: usually wears headgear: carried head high final start: often
soon off bridle. *K. A. Ryan*

UP THE AISLE 7 b.g. Rambo Dancer (CAN) 107 – Mardessa 74 (Ardross 134) [2004 **–**
10m 10f5 Sep 16] quite good-topped gelding: tailed off in maidens. *M. Mullineaux*

UPTHEDALE (IRE) 3 b.g. General Monash (USA) 107 – Pimpinella (IRE) (Repri- **39**
mand 122) [2004 49: 7.1s f9.4g4 9.2d3 10v 12.1m5 14.1m 12.1g6 Jun 17] sturdy gelding:
poor maiden: seems to stay 1½m: tried in cheekpieces. *J. R. Weymes*

UP THE ORDER 2 b.f. (Apr 2) Forzando 122 – Art Deco Lady 51 (Master Willie 129) **–**
[2004 f6g p6g Nov 19] 1,000Y: fourth foal: half-sister to 3-y-o Aperitif: dam, maiden,
stayed 1¾m: well beaten in maiden/seller (blinkered). *P. J. McBride*

URABANDE 2 b.f. (Apr 23) Tipsy Creek (USA) 115 – La Belle Mystere 48 (Lycius **57 d**
(USA) 124) [2004 5g f5d2 f5g 5d6 6f4 6m p6g Dec 13] 2,600Y: sturdy filly: second foal:
dam, ran twice, out of sister to smart French sprinter Monde Bleu: modest maiden: easily
best effort second start: likely to prove best at 5f/6f: acts on fibresand: tried in cheekpieces. *Julian Poulton*

URBAN CALM 3 b.f. Cadeaux Genereux 131 – Silver Sun 83 (Green Desert (USA) **61 d**
127) [2004 5s4 5s2 5m2 6g 5g4 p5.1g p5.1g5 f6g p5.1g Dec 31] 42,000F, 15,000 2-y-o:
compact filly: second foal: dam, 9f winner at 4 yrs, half-sister to smart stayer Tioman
Island: modest maiden: below form after second start, leaving R. Cowell after fifth: best
efforts at 5f on soft going. *J. W. Unett*

URBAN ROSE 3 b.f. Piccolo 121 – Blue Lamp (USA) 68 (Shadeed (USA) 135) [2004 **66**
69: 6.1g 7.1s 6.1g3 6m 6g4 6g 5m4 5g Sep 22] leggy, close-coupled filly: fair handicapper:
left J. Unett after fourth outing: stays 6f: acts on firm ground: tongue tied last 4 starts, and
wore cheekpieces last 2. *R. M. H. Cowell*

UREDALE (IRE) 2 b.c. (Mar 14) Bahhare (USA) 122 – Baileys First (IRE) 74 (Alzao **60**
(USA) 117) [2004 5s5 f5g 5m6 7m5 7m* 7d 8g Sep 11] strong, close-coupled colt: modest
performer: made all in seller at Catterick in July: last in nurseries after: stays 7f: acts on
good to firm ground. *Mrs A. Duffield*

UROWELLS (IRE) 4 b.g. Sadler's Wells (USA) 132 – Highest Accolade 71 (Shirley **86**
Heights 130) [2004 94+: 12m 11.9d 12d 10d 8.3d Sep 27] small, good-bodied gelding:
fairly useful performer: visored, well beaten last 2 starts: should stay 1½m: acts on good
to firm ground, probably on good to soft: sold 11,000 gns. *E. A. L. Dunlop*

URSA MAJOR 10 b.g. Warning 136 – Double Entendre 81 (Dominion 123) [2004 **47**
10m 10.1f 14.4g6 10g 9.7m p9.5g Dec 13] small gelding: poor handicapper: stays easy
1½m: acts on all-weather, firm and soft ground: tried blinkered earlier in career: often
races up with pace. *T. Keddy*

USHINDI (IRE) 2 b.f. (May 1) Montjeu (IRE) 137 – Fern 100 (Shirley Heights 130) **73**
[2004 7m 8.2g 7.1m4 7g3 Oct 5] €130,000Y: leggy filly: closely related to fairly useful
1¼m winner Dimple Chad and 1½m winner Frangy (both by Sadler's Wells) and half-
sister to several winners, including 3-y-o Aurelia and 4-y-o Fernery: dam, 1½m winner,
half-sister to Oaks second Shamshir: fair maiden: best effort when second in nursery at
Catterick (wandered and demoted a place): bred to be well suited by 1¼m/1½m: races up
with pace. *M. L. W. Bell*

USTAD (IRE) 2 br.c. (Feb 28) Giant's Causeway (USA) 132 – Winsa (USA) 80 (River- **60**
man) 131) [2004 7d 8.1g Sep 15] heavy-bodied colt: third foal: half-brother to
3-y-o Mutahayya and fairly useful 1½m winner Majhud (by Machiavellian): dam, 1½m
winner, sister to high-class miler Bahri and half-sister to very smart 1996 2-y-o 7f winner
Bahhare: modest form in maidens at Newmarket (burly) and Sandown: should be suited
by 1¼m/1½m. *J. L. Dunlop*

UTAH FLATS (IRE) 3 ch.g. Bluebird (USA) 125 – Desert Rose (Green Desert — (USA) 127) [2004 f7s f6g Feb 17] well beaten in maidens, looking ungenuine second start: sold 1,000 gns. *Mrs J. R. Ramsden*

V

VADEMECUM 3 br.g. Shinko Forest (IRE) – Sunshine Coast 86 (Posse (USA) 130) — [2004 7.5s⁶ 6d 7f 7f 6s 7m p7.1d Nov 3] good-topped gelding: fairly useful performer at 2 yrs: well held in 2004. *B. Smart*

VAGUE STAR (ITY) 2 b.c. (Apr 30) Soviet Star (USA) 128 – Simova (USA) (Vagu- **72** ely Noble 140) [2004 6.1m 5.1g³ p6g³ p7g p6g* p6g⁶ p6g Dec 30] 8,000Y, 26,000 2-y-o: closely related to winner in Italy by Zilzal and half-brother to several winners, including smart 1992 2-y-o 7f winner Semillon (by Rousillon), later successful in USA: dam French maiden: fair performer: won maiden at Wolverhampton in December: below form in nurseries after, including in tongue tie: effective at 5f/6f: acts on polytrack, better turf effort on good going. *R. Ingram*

VALANCE (IRE) 4 br.g. Bahhare (USA) 122 – Glowlamp (IRE) 93 (Glow (USA)) **87** [2004 89: 12m³ 14.1g⁵ 16.1m* 16.2m⁴ 21g 13.9m² 16.2m Sep 25] lengthy gelding: fairly useful handicapper: won at Newmarket in July: also ran well when in frame at Ascot and York after: stays 2m: acts on polytrack, raced only on good going or firmer on turf: consistent. *C. R. Egerton*

VALAZAR (USA) 5 b.g. Nicholas (USA) 111 – Valor's Minion (USA) (Turkey Shoot **51** (USA)) [2004 63: f5g f5s f5g f5g² f6m³ 6.1m² 5g³ f5g⁴ 5m Aug 3] sturdy gelding: modest performer: effective at 5f/6f: acts on fibresand, raced only on good ground or firmer on turf: blinkered (below form) once. *D. W. Chapman*

VALDASHO 5 b.m. Classic Cliche (IRE) 128 – Ma Rivale (Last Tycoon 131) [2004 –: — p10g Feb 26] sturdy mare: lightly raced and no form since 2002. *Miss K. M. George*

VAL DE FLEURIE (GER) 9 b.m. Mondrian (GER) 125 – Valbonne (Master Willie **56** 129) [2004 64: 12s⁶ Mar 30] modest performer: stays 1½m: acts on firm ground, probably on soft: often races prominently. *J. G. M. O'Shea*

VAL DE MAAL (IRE) 4 ch.g. Eagle Eyed (USA) 111 – Miss Bojangles (Gay Fan- **72** dango (USA) 132) [2004 79: f6g³ 7s 6m⁴ 7g 6g⁴ 6.1g⁶ 6g p6g p6d⁶ p8.6g⁵ Nov 11] quite good-topped gelding: fair performer: effective at 6f/7f: acts on all-weather and good to firm going, no form on softer than good: tried in visor/cheekpieces: usually races up with pace. *G. C. H. Chung*

VALDESCO (IRE) 6 ch.g. Bluebird (USA) 125 – Allegheny River (USA) (Lear Fan **66** (USA) 130) [2004 11.9g 10.5d 17.1d Aug 15] leggy, quite good-topped gelding: fairly useful performer in 2002: missed 2003 and just fair form in 2004: stays 1¾m: acts on fibresand and any turf going: usually wears headgear. *Mrs S. J. Smith*

VAL D'ISERE 2 ch.c. (Feb 21) Tomba 119 – Dancing Diana 82 (Raga Navarro (ITY) **48** 119) [2004 p6g p7g f7g⁴ Dec 14] poor maiden: blinkered last 2 starts. *B. J. Meehan*

VALE DE LOBO 2 b.f. (Mar 29) Loup Sauvage (USA) 125 – Frog 84 (Akarad (FR) **72** 130) [2004 p6g⁵ f7d* 8d³ Aug 27] sturdy, close-coupled filly: fourth foal: half-sister to fairly useful 2m/17f winner Froglet (by Shaamit) and 2000 2-y-o 7f seller winner Sel (by Salse): dam 1¼m/1½m winner: landed odds in seller at Southwell (sold from Sir Mark Prescott 20,000 gns) in July by 6 lengths, making most: best effort when third to Merchant in nursery at Newmarket: will stay 1¼m. *A. W. Carroll*

VALENTIA (IRE) 3 b.f. Perugino (USA) 84 – Teide (Sabrehill (USA) 120) [2004 61: — p5g Mar 4] modest maiden: well held only 3-y-o start: sold 2,500 gns, sent to Holland. *M. H. Tompkins*

VALENTIN (IRE) 2 ch.f. (Apr 30) King of Kings (IRE) 125 – Slip Ashore (IRE) **97** (Slip Anchor 136) [2004 6g* 6m² 7f 6g Sep 2] €20,000Y: well-made filly: half-sister to several winners, including useful Irish 7f winner Storm Ashore (by Storm Cat) and fairly useful Irish 1m winner (stayed 1½m) Crest of A Wave (by Woodman): dam unraced half-sister to dam of high-class Japanese sprinter/miler Taiki Shuttle: useful performer: won maiden at Ascot in July: good 1¾ lengths second to Soar in Princess Margaret Stakes there, best effort after: should stay 1m. *R. Hannon*

VALENTINO (FR) 5 b.h. Valanour (IRE) 125 – Rotina (FR) (Crystal Glitters (USA) **117**
127) [2004 115: 8g² a7.5g* 10d* 10m² 9.8m⁴ 9.5s* 8s* 8m Dec 12] sixth foal: half-
brother to several winners, including 4-y-o Whortleberry: dam placed at 10.5f in France:
smart performer: gradually returned to best, winning 2 minor events at Deauville in July
and Prix Andre Baboin at Bordeaux (readily, by 3 lengths from Marshall) and Prix Perth
at Saint-Cloud (by neck from Svedov) in October: respectable tenth to Firebreak in Hong
Kong Mile at Sha Tin final start: effective at 1m to 10.5f: acts on soft and good to firm
ground, has won on all-weather at Deauville: held up. *A. de Royer Dupre, France*

VALET 2 b.c. (May 18) Kayf Tara 130 – Val de Fleurie (GER) 64 (Mondrian (GER) 125) **–**
[2004 7g 8d Nov 3] good-topped colt: slowly away when last in maidens. *J. G. M. O'Shea*

VALEUREUX 6 ch.g. Cadeaux Genereux 131 – La Strada (Niniski (USA) 125) [2004 **62**
64: 10m³ 10m² 12d⁴ 12m Jul 21] big gelding: modest handicapper: stays 1½m: acts on
good to firm and heavy ground: tried visored/in cheekpieces: usually waited with.
J. Hetherton

VALIANT ACT (IRE) 2 b.f. (Mar 2) Brave Act 119 – Jungle Story (IRE) 74 (Alzao **60**
(USA) 117) [2004 7.1s⁶ 7.1d³ p8.6g⁶ f8g Dec 11] €18,000Y: second foal: dam, 2-y-o 7f
winner, half-sister to useful 7f/1m performer Lady Lindsay: modest maiden: should stay
1m: ran as if amiss final start. *D. M. Simcock*

VALIANT AIR (IRE) 3 b.g. Spectrum (IRE) 126 – Shining Desert (IRE) 82 (Green **53**
Desert (USA) 127) [2004 –: f12g⁴ 12g⁵ 12v² f12d⁴ 14.1s 14.1m 12m⁴ 10g⁵ 10g 12v
p12.2d³ f11g f12d Dec 21] good-bodied gelding: modest maiden: stays 1½m: acts on
polytrack, heavy and good to firm going: often visored/blinkered. *J. R. Weymes*

VALIANT EFFORT 5 b. or br.g. In The Wings 128 – Viz (USA) (Kris S (USA)) [2004 **–**
12m May 15] big, lengthy gelding: fairly useful winner in 2002, well held only outing
since. *C. M. Meade*

VALIANT ROMEO 4 b.g. Primo Dominie 121 – Desert Lynx (IRE) 79 (Green Desert **63**
(USA) 127) [2004 –: 5g⁵ 5d² 5m² 5g⁴ 5m 5g⁵ 5f² 5g 5.2d³ 5m³ 5d³ p6d Nov 5] sturdy
gelding: modest handicapper: best at 5f: acts on firm and good to soft ground: often wears
visor/cheekpieces: usually races prominently. *R. Bastiman*

VALIOS (IRE) 2 b.c. (Mar 30) Royal Applause 124 – Swing And Brave (IRE) 70 **–**
(Arctic Tern (USA) 126) [2004 6g 6m 9s 6.5d Oct 26] well held in maidens (for
L. Cumani first 2 starts) and claimers. *C. Laffon-Parias, France*

VALIXIR (IRE) 3 b.c. Trempolino (USA) 135 – Vadlamixa (FR) 114 (Linamix (FR) **118**
127) [2004 107: 9s* 10.5g³ 12g³ 10d* 12d* 12m Oct 3] big, good-topped colt: has an
unimpressive action: fifth foal: half-brother to useful French 1¼m winner Vadaza (by

Prix Niel Casino Barriere d'Enghien Les Bains, Longchamp—
Valixir reverses Prix du Jockey Club form with Prospect Park as Bago manages only third

Zafonic) and French 10.5f winner Vadlaviria (by Bering): dam, French 1m winner (including at 2 yrs) who stayed 10.5f, half-sister to Breeders' Cup Mile winner Val Royal: smart performer: successful at Maisons-Laffitte in listed race in April and Prix Eugene Adam (made all, beat Delfos easily by 3 lengths) in July, and at Longchamp in Prix Niel Casino Barriere d'Enghien Les Bains (by nose from Prospect Park) in September: good third earlier, behind Voix du Nord in Prix Lupin at Longchamp (beaten 2 lengths) and Blue Canari (beaten ¾ length) in Prix du Jockey Club at Chantilly: creditable 7 lengths tenth behind Bago in Prix de l'Arc de Triomphe at Longchamp final start (sweating/on toes, raced freely and tended to wander): stays 1½m: acts on soft and good to firm going: tends to carry head awkwardly. *A. Fabre, France*

VALJARV (IRE) 3 b.f. Bluebird (USA) 125 – Iktidar 80 (Green Desert (USA) 127) **97 §**
[2004 94: p7g 7g 8m 6m 7.1f 6m⁴ 6m⁴ 6g² 6g 6g 6m⁵ 6g 6d⁴ 6s⁴ p8g Oct 31] sturdy filly: useful performer: some creditable efforts in 2004, including when short-head second to Kind in handicap at Newmarket and fourth to Ruby Rocket in listed race at Newmarket eighth/thirteenth starts: stays 6.5f: acts on firm and good to soft going: effective blinkered/visored or not: usually held up: often slowly away: ungenuine. *N. P. Littmoden*

VALLEE ENCHANTEE (IRE) 4 b.f. Peintre Celebre (USA) 137 – Verveine (USA) **120**
120 (Lear Fan (USA) 130) [2004 115: 10.5d⁴ 12m³ 12m⁵ 12m⁶ 12m³ Dec 12] leggy, sparely-made filly: not the best of movers in slower paces: very smart performer: unlucky 1¾ lengths third to Warrsan in Coronation Cup at Epsom on second outing, finishing best having been hemmed in: creditable efforts next 2 starts, 6 lengths fifth to Doyen in King George VI and Queen Elizabeth Stakes at Ascot and 4 lengths sixth to Bago in Prix de l'Arc de Triomphe at Longchamp: below best when third to Phoenix Reach in Hong Kong Vase at Sha Tin final outing (had won race year before): stays 13.5f: acts on heavy and good to firm going: wears special noseband: held up: consistent. *E. Lellouche, France*

VALUABLE GIFT 7 ch.g. Cadeaux Genereux 131 – Valbra (Dancing Brave (USA) **–**
140) [2004 59d: f6g f6g f6s 6v 6m Jun 1] strong gelding: maiden: well held in 2004: tried in headgear: none too genuine. *R. C. Guest*

VALUE PLUS (IRE) 2 b.f. (Feb 11) Mujadil (USA) 119 – Brittas Blues (IRE) 52 **76**
(Blues Traveller (IRE) 119) [2004 5m² 6d² 6f² 6g² 5.7g Jul 11] €18,000Y: first foal: dam maiden who stayed 9f: fair maiden: in cheekpieces, ran well at Hamilton penultimate start, then left Ms J. Morgan: brought down early final one: stays 6f: acts on firm and good to soft going. *Joseph Quinn, Ireland*

VAMOSE (IRE) 3 ro.g. Victory Note (USA) 120 – Narrow Band (IRE) (Standaan (FR) **71**
118) [2004 69+: 8m⁴ 11.5g 9d⁴ p7.1g⁴ p9.5g* Dec 17] workmanlike gelding: fair performer: made all in maiden at Wolverhampton in December: stays 9.5f: acts on polytrack, good to firm and good to soft ground: races up with pace. *Miss Gay Kelleway*

VAMP 3 b.f. Dracula (AUS) 121 – Circe 73 (Main Reef 126) [2004 7g 8f² 9.7m³ 10.2f* **80**
10m⁵ 10m 10.1g⁴ 11.6m³ 10d² Oct 15] lightly-made filly: half-sister to several winners, including fairly useful 9f to 1½m winner My Learned Friend (by Broken Hearted) and 4-y-o Cantrip: dam 1m winner who stayed 1¼m: fairly useful performer: won maiden at Bath in June: in frame in handicaps last 3 starts: stays 11.6f: acts on firm and good to soft going: reliable. *R. M. Beckett*

VAMPIRE QUEEN (IRE) 3 b.f. General Monash (USA) 107 – Taniokey (Grundy **54**
137) [2004 54: f6g* f6s⁴ f6g p7g Mar 8] modest handicapper: won at Wolverhampton in January: better form at 6f than 7f: acts on fibresand. *R. P. Elliott*

VANBRUGH (FR) 4 ch.g. Starborough 126 – Renovate (Generous (IRE) 139) **49**
[2004 ?, a74: f16g* p16g f14g⁶ 16d 14.1d 14m 14.1m 17.1f 17.2f f14g 16m 16s 14.1d **a82 d**
16.2m⁶ 14.1d p13.9g p16.5g f16g² Dec 14] leggy gelding: fairly useful handicapper on all-weather, poor on turf: won at Southwell in January: well below form after: stays 2m: acts on fibresand and firm ground: usually visored/tongue tied. *Miss D. A. McHale*

VANCOUVER GOLD (IRE) 2 b.f. (Apr 24) Monashee Mountain (USA) 115 – **63**
Forest Berries (IRE) (Thatching 131) [2004 7m³ 7m⁵ Sep 29] €14,000Y: sparely-made filly: half-sister to several winners, including 3-y-o Orpenberry and fairly useful 6f (including at 2 yrs) and 1m winner Forest Dancer (by Charnwood Forest): dam unraced: better effort in maidens when third at Thirsk: favourite when only fifth at Newcastle: not sure to stay much beyond 7f. *K. R. Burke*

VANDENBERGHE 5 b.g. Millkom 124 – Child Star (FR) 58 (Bellypha 130) [2004 **54**
57: f9.4m* 10m⁵ f9.4m³ 12m⁴ 10.9m³ 10g⁵ 11.7g⁶ 12.1m³ 14.1f³ p16d³ p16g⁴ 12f 12m **a66**
p16g* p13.9g* f14g Nov 22] deep-girthed gelding: fair handicapper on all-weather, modest on turf: won at Wolverhampton (apprentices) in May, Lingfield in October and

Wolverhampton (apprentices) in November: stays 2m: acts on all-weather and firm going: usually held up: reliable. *J. A. Osborne*

VANDERLIN 5 ch.g. Halling (USA) 133 – Massorah (FR) 108 (Habitat 134) [2004 **112** 114: p7g³ 8g³ 8.5m⁵ 8.3m³ 7g* 7g 7s³ 7m³ 7g² 7s Oct 16] strong gelding: usually impresses in appearance: smart performer: won minor event at Chester in July by 1¾ lengths from Makhlab: subsequently creditable third in listed races at Epsom (behind Mac Love) and York (behind Polar Bear), and good 2 lengths second to Mac Love in Supreme Stakes at Goodwood: best at 6f/7f: acts on polytrack, soft and good to firm ground: tried visored earlier in career: consistent. *A. M. Balding*

VANGELIS (USA) 5 gr.h. Highest Honor (FR) 124 – Capades Dancer (USA) (Gate **119** Dancer (USA)) [2004 116: 10g* 10.5d 10f⁴ 9f⁶ 10f⁵ 10f³ Oct 3] ex-French-trained horse: smart performer: won Prix d'Harcourt at Longchamp in April by ¾ length from Execute: just respectable efforts subsequently, including when 3¼ lengths fourth to Sabiango in Charles Whittingham Memorial Handicap at Hollywood (left A. de Royer Dupre afterwards), 4½ lengths fifth to demoted Powerscourt in Arlington Million and 1½ lengths third to Star Over The Bay in Clement L. Hirsch Memorial Turf Championship at Santa Anita: seems best around 1¼m: acts on soft going, probably on firm: blinkered last 2 starts: has worn crossed noseband: held up. *R. J. Frankel, USA*

VANILLA MOON 4 b.f. Emperor Jones (USA) 119 – Daarat Alayaam (IRE) (Refer- **54** ence Point 139) [2004 61: p12g⁵ p10g² p13g⁴ 11.6m³ 11.6m⁶ 11.5m⁴ 11.5f⁶ p16g⁴ Sep 18] tall, leggy filly: modest maiden: probably stays easy 2m: acts on polytrack and firm ground: usually blinkered/visored. *J. R. Jenkins*

VANISHED (IRE) 4 b.f. Fayruz 116 – Where's The Money 87 (Lochnager 132) [2004 – 62: f5g f5g f5g Mar 3] modest handicapper: well held in 2004: tried in blinkers/ cheekpieces. *M. J. Polglase*

VANTAGE (IRE) 3 b.g. Marju (IRE) 127 – Anna Comnena (IRE) 71 (Shareef Dancer **86** (USA) 135) [2004 79: p10g² p10g² 12d³ 12.1s* 11.8d⁴ 11.6g⁵ 10.1m 9s⁴ 10.1g⁶ 11.6m Sep 27] big, lengthy gelding: fairly useful performer: won maiden at Beverley in April: effective at 1¼m/1½m: acted on polytrack, soft and good to firm going: blinkered/wore cheekpieces last 4 outings. *N. P. Littmoden*

VARENKA (IRE) 2 b.f. (Feb 8) Fasliyev (USA) 120 – Castara Beach (IRE) 74 **91** (Danehill (USA) 126) [2004 7m⁵ 7.5d* 7.5m² Sep 5] 52,000F: lengthy filly: second foal: dam lightly-raced sister to useful 6f/7f winner Hill Hopper and half-sister to smart 1½m performer Water Boatman: won maiden at Beverley in August by 5 lengths from Brahminy Kite: similar form when second in listed race at Rome: will stay 1m: races up with pace. *Sir Mark Prescott*

VARIETY CLUB 3 b.g. Royal Applause 124 – Starfida (Soviet Star (USA) 128) [2004 – 63: 7.1m 8.1g 8f Aug 5] leggy gelding: modest maiden: well beaten in 2004, including in blinkers/visor. *A. M. Balding*

VARNAY 3 b.f. Machiavellian (USA) 123 – Valleria 76 (Sadler's Wells (USA) 132) – [2004 91: 7s May 11] quite attractive filly: fairly useful performer in 2003: well held only 3-y-o start: stays 7f: usually acts on good to firm and good to soft ground: usually visored: sold 26,000 gns in November. *D. R. Loder*

VARUNI (IRE) 3 b.f. Ali-Royal (IRE) 127 – Sauvignon (IRE) 63 (Alzao (USA) 117) **66 d** [2004 –: p10g* p10g 12.1d² 11.6s 10m 12g⁵ 12s⁴ p12.2g p12.2g Dec 15] quite good-topped filly: fair performer: won claimer at Lingfield in February: below form after third start: stays 1½m: acts on polytrack and good to soft ground. *J. G. Portman*

VAR (USA) 5 b. or br.h. Forest Wildcat (USA) 120 – Loma Preata (USA) (Zilzal **124** (USA) 137) [2004 5f* 6m* 5.2g² 5m* 5m Dec 12]

Sarava, Dessert, Ticker Tape. Who? Each season seems to be peppered with ex-British-trained horses making good in America, often flying in the face of their relative anonymity during their time here. Sarava won the Belmont Stakes in 2002 and Dessert another Grade 1, the Del Mar Oaks, in 2003, the pair doing so after leaving Britain as maidens. In 2004, Ticker Tape won the American Oaks and the Queen Elizabeth II Cup, also Grade 1s, after showing little better than fairly useful form in Britain the previous year. Given such transformations, one possible interpretation might be that British trainers aren't a patch on their counterparts in the States. However, the improvement horses can make from one country to another, or from one stable to another, is often as much a reflection of circumstances as anything. In 2004, Clive Brittain took charge of the five-year-old Var, winner of an optional claimer at Calder in Florida in January, and transformed him rapidly into one of the fastest horses in Europe, winning the Prix de l'Abbaye at Longchamp in October.

Var's British debut was delayed when he was kicked by another horse on the gallops, resulting in his needing a piece of bone removed from his shoulder, and then kicked again in the same place three months later, on this occasion requiring forty stitches. Var quickly began to make up for lost time once on the course. Starting at 16/1, the outsider in a field of seven for a listed race over six furlongs at Goodwood in September, he made all to beat the smart Ruby Rocket by a length and a half. Because of his setbacks, Var had reportedly done only two bits of work before Goodwood, and he showed even better form when turned out a week later in the Group 3 Dubai International Airport World Trophy over five furlongs at Newbury, leading over a furlong out before going down by a head to The Tatling. Var received 5 lb from The Tatling at Newbury but, with Frankie Dettori taking over at Longchamp, he started favourite in the Prix de l'Abbaye de Longchamp Majestic Barriere, going off at 29/10. In a field of fifteen, ten of which were pattern winners in the current season, Prix du Gros-Chene winner Avonbridge was coupled as second favourite at 32/10 with his stable-companion and half-brother Pata-vellian, successful in the race twelve months earlier. The Tatling, also successful in the King's Stand Stakes, was at 45/10, with The Trader, winner of two pattern races in France in 2004, at 77/10. Among those at longer odds were Continent, winner of the Abbaye in 2002, his stable-companion Bahamian Pirate, winner of the Nun-thorpe Stakes from The Tatling in August, and Ratio, the only French-trained runner. Var, supplemented for the race at €12,000, was drawn two from the out-side in stall thirteen, but he soon set the race alight under Dettori. Racing wide, he was rather isolated early on as Irish-trained Osterhase, Avonbridge and Orientor towards the rail tried to keep up with him, but Var shot clear when shaken up vigorously over a furlong out, going a good two lengths up before holding on by half a length from The Tatling. Royal Millennium ran on to finish a length further away, with Osterhase fourth, Avonbridge fifth and Orientor sixth.

With conditions at Longchamp firmer than the official good, Var's time of 55.00sec was marginally the closest any winner has got to Habibti's course record of 54.30sec, set in the race on firm ground in 1983, but Var's performance was only about average among those successful in recent runnings of the race, in which Namid and Lochsong have been the best winners in the last twelve years. All the same, Var's win at Longchamp was remarkable for a horse that had made his first appearance in Britain only twenty-two days earlier. Hopes were high that Var would prove a threat to the previous year's winner, and still unbeaten, Silent Witness in the Hong Kong Sprint at Sha Tin in December. For Clive Brittain, a Group 1-winning sprinter was a new departure, even in his colourful and highly successful career around the world. He was dubbed by the *South China Morning Post* as the 'fearless traveller' and Var went off third favourite at Sha Tin, starting at 14/1, much the shortest odds of four British-trained challengers in a market dominated by Silent Witness at around 3/1-on. The race proved a let-down for Brittain, Var,

Prix de l'Abbaye de Longchamp Majestic Barriere, Longchamp—the very speedy Var makes all; The Tatling, Royal Millennium (No.10) and Osterhase (rail) are next to finish in a race completely dominated by overseas challengers

again isolated early on, trailing in tenth of fourteen behind the favourite, Dettori reporting he felt something might have been amiss. Royal Millennium did best of the British-trained challengers in fourth, with The Tatling twelfth and Pivotal Point last but one.

Var is the only foal of his dam Loma Preata, who died in foal to Gulch in 2001. Loma Preata, out of a five-furlong winner herself, won twice over six furlongs as a two-year-old in France, when she was also placed at up to a mile in listed company. Var's sire Forest Wildcat has had few representatives in Europe, but he has made quite a promising start at stud in North America, where Forest Secrets won the Grade 1 Acorn Stakes over a mile in 2001 and D'Wildcat was also a Grade 1 winner on dirt in the Frank J. De Francis Memorial Dash over six furlongs, the same race won in 2004 by another of his sons, Wildcat Heir.

		Storm Cat	Storm Bird
	Forest Wildcat (USA)	(br 1983)	Terlingua
	(b or br 1991)	Victoria Beauty	Bold Native
Var (USA)		(ch 1972)	Abifaith
(b. or br.h. 1999)		Zilzal	Nureyev
	Loma Preata (USA)	(ch 1986)	French Charmer
	(b or br 1994)	Halley's Comeback	Key To The Kingdom
		(br 1984)	Promised Princess

As a racehorse, Forest Wildcat recorded his most important successes at five, showing smart form in winning in Grade 3 company over six furlongs on dirt. Var was purchased by agent Dick O'Gorman for 120,000 dollars at Keeneland as a yearling and made his debut for Bill Mott in America as a three-year-old in the colours of his present owner. At four, he won a maiden and a claimer on dirt and an allowance race on turf before adding an optional claimer on turf in the colours of Darley Stud, for whom he also gained his final success in America in January, his third in seven starts there on turf. Var was unplaced in two races over seven furlongs in America, where his dirt wins were gained at six furlongs and his turf successes at five. His best form in Europe has come at five furlongs, though it is not out of the question that he will end up in the Breeders' Cup Sprint over six in 2005. Twenty years on from Pebbles' win in the Breeders' Cup Turf, his trainer would probably quite enjoy giving America a further reminder of his skills. *C. E. Brittain*

VAS Y CARLA (USA) 3 ch.f. Gone West (USA) – Lady Carla 122 (Caerleon (USA) **64 +**
132) [2004 80: 8m 7.5m² 8.1m Jun 21] close-coupled filly: maiden: just modest form at 3 yrs: should be suited by 1¼m+: raced only on good/good to firm going. *D. R. Loder*

VAUDEVIRE 3 b.g. Dancing Spree (USA) – Approved Quality (IRE) 66 (Persian **36**
Heights 129) [2004 –: f7g⁶ f8s f5g³ f6g 6g⁴ 5m⁴ 5g Aug 2] tall gelding: poor maiden: form only at 5f: blinkered last 5 outings. *R. P. Elliott*

VAUGHAN 3 b.c. Machiavellian (USA) 123 – Labibeh (USA) 109 (Lyphard (USA) **95**
132) [2004 94p: 9m 12g⁴ 12g Oct 1] big, good-topped colt: useful performer: best effort when fourth to Camrose in minor event at Kempton, carrying head high: stays 1½m: acts on good to soft going: has worn crossed noseband. *Mrs A. J. Perrett*

VELOCITAS 3 b.g. Magic Ring (IRE) 115 – Folly Finnesse 80 (Joligeneration 111) **64**
[2004 –: 6g⁴ 6s 7m 8.1d 8.1m⁵ p9.5g² p9.5d² p12.2g³ p12.2g⁶ Nov 29] leggy gelding: modest maiden: stays 1½m: acts on good to firm going and polytrack: visored last 3 starts. *H. J. Collingridge*

VELOCITYS IMAGE (IRE) 4 b.f. Tagula (IRE) 116 – Pike Creek (USA) 86 **–**
(Alwasmi (USA) 115) [2004 –: f5s f7g Feb 8] lengthy filly: little form. *E. J. Alston*

VELVETEEN RABBIT 2 b.f. (Jan 17) Singspiel (IRE) 133 – Velvet Lady 102 **71**
(Nashwan (USA) 135) [2004 6g 7m³ 7g² 7g 8s p7.1g³ p7.1g⁶ Nov 26] well-made filly: first foal: dam, 1m winner, half-sister to Moon Ballad (by Singspiel) out of half-sister to very smart performer up to 2m Central Park: fair maiden: left Saeed bin Suroor after fifth start: should stay at least 1m: acts on polytrack. *J. H. M. Gosden*

VELVET HEIGHTS (IRE) 2 b.c. (Mar 21) Barathea (IRE) 127 – Height of Fantasy **78**
(IRE) 101 (Shirley Heights 130) [2004 7m 7.1m 8.1d* 8s 8m Sep 21] sturdy, close-coupled colt: second foal: dam, 1¾m/2m winner, half-sister to 5-y-o Persian Lightning: fair performer: won maiden at Sandown in August: respectable effort in nursery next start: should be suited by 1¼m/1½m: acts on good to soft going. *J. L. Dunlop*

VELVET JONES 11 gr.g. Sharrood (USA) 124 – Cradle of Love (USA) 87 (Roberto   –
(USA) 131) [2004 7.1d Aug 19] angular gelding: of little account. *G. F. H. Charles-Jones*

VELVET RHYTHM 4 b.f. Forzando 122 – Bold Gayle 57 (Never So Bold 135)   –
[2004 –: f7g f7g f11g Feb 15] no sign of ability. *K. R. Burke*

VELVET SHADOW (IRE) 2 b.c. (Mar 3) Soviet Star (USA) 128 – Tajanama (IRE)   70 +
52 (Gorytus (USA) 132) [2004 p7g⁴ p7.1g Dec 10] €9,500Y, 40,000 2-y-o: sixth
foal: half-brother to 2 winners in Italy by Mukaddamah: dam Irish 6.5f winner: shaped
well when fourth in minor event at Lingfield: odds on, broke down at Wolverhampton.
Noel T. Chance

VELVET TOUCH 3 b.f. Danzig Connection (USA) – Soft Touch (GER) (Horst-   53 d
Herbert) [2004 66: f6g² p6g⁶ 6s f6d⁶ 5s⁵ f5g f6g p6g 6d p5.1g⁶ Dec 20] workmanlike
filly: disappointing maiden: effective at 5f/6f: acts on fibresand: tried visored: unreliable.
J. R. Jenkins

VELVET WATERS 3 b.f. Unfuwain (USA) 131 – Gleaming Water 81 (Kalaglow   77
132) [2004 60: 10.2m³ 10f⁶ 14.1f⁴ 11.7f* 11.5g² 12m² 11.7m* 12d³ 14.4m³ 12g Sep 22]
leggy filly: progressed into a fair performer, winning handicaps at Bath in July and
August: effective at 1½m/1¾m: acts on firm and good to soft going: usually races prominently: tough and reliable. *R. F. Johnson Houghton*

VENABLES (USA) 3 ch.c. Stravinsky (USA) 133 – Hope For A Breeze (CAN) (Bri-   100
artic (CAN)) [2004 100: p7g⁵ 7g 6g May 14] rangy colt: useful performer: creditable 2
lengths fifth to Rosencrans in listed event at Lingfield: tongue tied, tailed off in similar
events after: stays easy 7f: acts on firm going and polytrack. *R. Hannon*

VENDORS MISTAKE (IRE) 3 b.f. Danehill (USA) 126 – Sunspangled (IRE) 111   52
(Caerleon (USA) 132) [2004 61?: p7g f6g⁶ 6g³ 5m³ 5.3f⁶ 6d⁶ p7m² p7m p6g² Dec 20]
modest maiden: effective at 6f/easy 7f: acts on polytrack, good to firm and good to soft
going. *Andrew Reid*

VENEER (IRE) 2 b.g. (May 9) Woodborough (USA) 112 – Sweet Lass (Belmez (USA)   70
131) [2004 5s⁴ 5s 6.1g 7.1d⁵ p8.6g p8.6g* p8g⁴ Dec 18] €7,000F, 12,500Y: lengthy
gelding: second foal: dam French 1¼m/11f winner: fair performer: much improved when
winning claimer at Wolverhampton (for R. Hannon) in December: ran well final start:
stays 8.6f: acts on polytrack: blinkered last 2 outings. *Miss Gay Kelleway*

VENERDI TREDICI (IRE) 3 b.f. Desert Style (IRE) 121 – Stifen (Burslem 123)   –
[2004 55: 9g 7.1m 10s Aug 24] rather leggy filly: modest maiden at 2 yrs: well held in
2004. *P. A. Blockley*

VENETIAN KING (USA) 2 b.g. (Feb 11) King of Kings (IRE) 125 – Vena (IRE)   68
97 (Danehill (USA) 126) [2004 6m⁵ 7.2m² Jul 19] $85,000F, €19,000Y: useful-looking
gelding: rather unfurnished at 2 yrs: has a quick action: third foal: half-brother to winner
in Japan by Wild Rush: dam, 9f winner, half-sister to smart performer up to 1½m Cicerao:
fair form in maidens at York and Ayr (raced freely when second to Ballycroy Girl): bred
to stay 1m. *J. Howard Johnson*

VENETIAN ROMANCE (IRE) 3 ch.f. Desert Story (IRE) 115 – Cipriani 102   43
(Habitat 134) [2004 54: f7g⁵ 8.1s 10m 8m 8.1g 12m 12g³ 14.1g 10g 14.1d Oct 16] smallish filly: poor maiden handicapper: stays 1½m: acts on good to soft ground: tried in
headgear. *A. P. Jones*

VENEZIANA 3 ch.f. Vettori (IRE) 119 – Fairy Story (IRE) 80 (Persian Bold 123) [2004   –
67: 11.6f 8.1g Aug 5] tall, leggy filly: maiden: well beaten in 2004: sent to Saudi Arabia.
P. F. I. Cole

VENGEANCE 4 b.g. Fleetwood (IRE) 107 – Lady Isabell 62 (Rambo Dancer (CAN)   104
107) [2004 95: 10d 12s³ 11.6m* 11.9d⁵ 10m⁵ Jul 25] tall gelding: useful performer: won
handicap at Windsor (by 1¼ lengths from Nawamees) in June: creditable fifth after in
similar race at York (behind Carte Diamond) and minor event at Ascot (behind Wunderwood): stays 1½m: acts on soft and good to firm ground: consistent. *Mrs A. J. Perrett*

VENGEROV 3 b.g. Piccolo 121 – Shining Cloud 73 (Indian Ridge 123) [2004 64:   65
f8g* f8.5s⁶ 11.7f³ 10s a12g⁵ a8.3g Nov 14] useful-looking gelding: fair performer: won   a72
maiden at Southwell in February: left M. Bell 10,000 gns after fourth start: stays 1m:
acts on fibresand and firm ground: refused to enter stall on intended debut. *J. Bidgood,
Spain*

VERASI 3 b.g. Kahyasi 130 – Fair Verona (USA) (Alleged (USA) 138) [2004 –: 8v⁴   67 ?
11.8g 10.9f p13g 14d Oct 10] leggy gelding: fair maiden: clearly best effort on reappear-

ance: left R. Charlton after third start: should stay beyond 1m: acts on heavy going: tried blinkered. *G. L. Moore*

VERBIER (USA) 2 b. or br.f. (Jan 29) Fusaichi Pegasus (USA) 130 – Oh Nellie (USA) 113 (Tilt The Stars (CAN)) [2004 6g⁶ 7.5m* 8g⁵ p7g⁴ Nov 10] lengthy filly: has scope: second foal: half-sister to 3-y-o Sanbonah: dam 5.5f (at 2 yrs) to 1m (Grade 3 event) winner in USA and second in 1000 Guineas: fairly useful performer: won maiden at Beverley in September: good fourth in nursery at Lingfield: stays 1m: acts on polytrack and good to firm going. *N. A. Callaghan* **80**

VERITABLE 2 br.f. (Mar 11) So Factual (USA) 120 – Madam Trilby (Grundy 137) [2004 5g⁴ 6m 6g Sep 3] leggy filly: half-sister to several winners, including 10-y-o Sharp Hat: dam ran once: best effort in maidens when fourth at Salisbury: should stay 6f. *S. Kirk* **64**

VERKHOTINA 3 b.f. Barathea (IRE) 127 – Alusha 88 (Soviet Star (USA) 128) [2004 75: 7.1d⁶ 6.1g* 6m 7m³ 8g Jul 10] close-coupled, good-topped filly: fairly useful performer: won handicap at Chepstow in May: effective at 6f/7f: acts on good to firm ground, well held on good to soft: sold 12,000 gns in November. *R. Charlton* **83**

VERMILION CREEK 5 b.m. Makbul 104 – Cloudy Reef 57 (Cragador 110) [2004 68, a54: f7g⁵ f11g f12s⁶ f9.4s⁶ 8.5d⁶ 8.1d² 8m 8.2s⁶ 8.1g 8f* Sep 16] close-coupled mare: modest on turf, poor on all-weather: won selling handicap at Pontefract in September: effective at 1m to easy 1½m: acts on all-weather, firm and good to soft ground: sometimes wears cheekpieces: usually held up. *R. Hollinshead* **60 a38**

VERMILLIANN (IRE) 3 b.f. Mujadil (USA) 119 – Refined (IRE) 95 (Statoblest 120) [2004 98: 5.1g 6.1d 5m Jun 12] angular filly: useful performer at 2 yrs: well held in listed events/handicap in 2004. *R. Hannon* **–**

VERSTONE (IRE) 2 b.f. (Mar 27) Brave Act 119 – Golden Charm (IRE) 63 (Common Grounds 118) [2004 5s f5g 5v f7g Dec 16] 12,000Y: leggy filly: second foal: half-sister to 3-y-o English Rocket: dam 2-y-o 6f winner: poor maiden. *R. F. Fisher* **32**

VERTEDANZ (IRE) 4 b.f. Sesaro (USA) 81 – Blade of Grass 78 (Kris 135) [2004 57: 7.1m 8m 7m Sep 4] good-topped filly: maiden: well beaten in 2004: tried visored/tongue tied. *Miss I. E. Craig* **–**

VERY WISE 2 b.c. (May 2) Pursuit of Love 124 – With Care 78 (Warning 136) [2004 8s* Oct 27] fourth foal: half-brother to 4-y-o Forever Phoenix and 6-y-o On Guard: dam 7f winner: 50/1, won maiden at Yarmouth by head from Scriptwriter, travelling well and leading close home under hands and heels: should progress. *W. J. Haggas* **86 p**

VESPONE (IRE) 4 ch.c. Llandaff (USA) – Vanishing Prairie (USA) 93 (Alysheba (USA)) [2004 125: 8.9m² 10.5d² 10g² 8.5m 10m² 10f 9.9m⁵ Sep 12] rather unfurnished colt: smart performer: runner-up in Jebel Hatta at Nad Al Sheba (beaten short head by Surveyor), Prix Ganay at Longchamp (went down by 1½ lengths to Execute), Premio Presidente della Repubblica at Rome (beaten 3 lengths by Altieri, wandering) and listed event at Newbury (beaten ¾ length by Muqbil) in 2004: well below form in Arlington Million and Select Stakes at Goodwood last 2 starts: stays 10.5f: acts on soft and good to firm ground: effective visored or not: usually tongue tied: often races freely/makes running: stumbled badly leaving stall fourth outing: none too reliable. *Saeed bin Suroor* **119**

VESTA FLAME 3 b.f. Vettori (IRE) 119 – Ciel de Feu (USA) (Blushing John (USA) 120) [2004 –: f9.4g³ f8.5g³ 12g Mar 31] rather sparely-made filly: poor maiden: left M. Johnston after second start: should be suited by 1¼m+: acts on fibresand. *P. A. Blockley* **38**

VETTORIOUS 2 ch.c. (Feb 28) Vettori (IRE) 119 – Sleepless 92 (Night Shift (USA)) [2004 7s Oct 22] rangy colt: 40/1, backward and very green, tailed off in maiden at Doncaster. *J. G. Given* **–**

VIABLE 2 b.g. (Apr 25) Vettori (IRE) 119 – Danseuse Davis (FR) (Glow (USA)) [2004 7.5d Aug 11] 50/1, slowly away and always behind in maiden at Beverley. *Mrs P. Sly* **–**

VIAGRAH (IRE) 3 b.g. Danetime (IRE) 121 – Classic Choice (Patch 129) [2004 f9.4s Feb 20] always behind in maiden at Wolverhampton. *M. J. Polglase* **–**

VIBE 3 gr.g. Danzero (AUS) – Courting 108 (Pursuit of Love 124) [2004 8g 8v 7g 7.5g⁴ 10f 9.9g⁶ Jun 22] 70,000Y: leggy, useful-looking gelding: first foal: dam 7f (at 2 yrs) to 1¼m winner: fair maiden: should stay 1¼m: sold 11,000 gns in July. *M. Johnston* **66**

VICARIO 3 gr.g. Vettori (IRE) 119 – Arantxa 77§ (Sharpo 132) [2004 –: 9.7s⁵ 11.5m* 12.1m³ 12.3m³ 12g² 12m⁶ 14d⁵ 16g⁴ 16.1m³ Sep 29] close-coupled gelding: fair handi- **66**

capper: won at Lingfield in May: stays 2m: acts on good to firm ground, probably on soft: usually waited with: joined D. McCain 12,000 gns. *M. L. W. Bell*

VICARS DESTINY 6 b.m. Sir Harry Lewis (USA) 127 – Church Leap (Pollerton 115) [2004 73: 18g² 18v² 16d 14m 17.1f 15.8m⁶ 16.2g⁴ 16.2d³ 17.1d³ 16d² 18f³ 17.1g³ 18d f14g Dec 7] leggy mare: fair maiden handicapper: stays 2¼m: acts on any going: tried in cheekpieces once: usually held up. *Mrs S. Lamyman* **73**

VICAT COLE 3 ch.g. Hector Protector (USA) 124 – Dancing Spirit (IRE) 72 (Ahonoora 122) [2004 8m p12d⁵ 12g 10.1f Jul 29] 21,000Y: strong, workmanlike gelding: has a moderate, round action: half-brother to several winners, including 6f (including at 2 yrs) and 1m (in Spain) winner Beware (by Warning): dam, 6f winner, out of half-sister to Irish Derby winner Law Society: fair maiden: left H. Cyzer after third start: ran as if amiss final one: likely to prove best short of 1½m. *Mrs L. J. Mongan* **71**

VICIOUS KNIGHT 6 b.g. Night Shift (USA) – Myth 89 (Troy 137) [2004 106§: 8.9m 8f 7g 7m 7m 7.9s⁵ 8d³ 7.9g 8v Oct 23] robust, good sort: good walker: just fairly useful handicapper in 2004: best at 7f/1m: acts on soft and good to firm ground: sometimes finds little: unreliable. *D. Nicholls* **93 §**

VICIOUS PRINCE (IRE) 5 b.g. Sadler's Wells (USA) 132 – Sunny Flower (FR) (Dom Racine (FR) 121) [2004 –: 12s⁴ 10.5d 11.9g 16d⁵ Jul 4] strong, lengthy gelding: has a fluent, round action: fair handicapper: stays 1½m: best efforts on good ground or softer. *R. M. Whitaker* **74**

VICIOUS WARRIOR 5 b.g. Elmaamul (USA) 125 – Ling Lane (Slip Anchor 136) [2004 93, a83: 8d² 8.5g 10m⁵ 8.9m³ 10.4g 8m² 8d³ 9g 7.9g⁶ p8g* p8.6g³ p8g³ Dec 18] good sort: fairly useful handicapper: won at Lingfield in November: effective at 1m/ 1¼m: acts on polytrack, good to firm and good to soft ground: free-going sort: reliable. *R. M. Whitaker* **94**

VICTIMISED (IRE) 2 b.g. (Apr 18) Victory Note (USA) 120 – Eurolink Virago (Charmer 123) [2004 5d 7g 6m⁵ Jul 13] tall gelding: on weak side at 2 yrs: poor form in maidens/seller: best effort at 6f. *P. Burgoyne* **46**

VICTOR BUCKWELL 2 br.c. (May 26) Pivotal 124 – Lonely Shore (Blakeney 126) [2004 7.2d 7m 8v Oct 23] close-coupled colt: unfurnished at 2 yrs: only a little sign of ability in maidens: slowly away first 2 outings. *B. Ellison*

VICTORIANA 3 b.f. Wolfhound (USA) 126 – Silk St James (Pas de Seul 133) [2004 6.1s⁶ 6s⁴ 5d⁵ 6.1m 6d Oct 10] neat filly: half-sister to several winners, including useful 1m winner Silk St John (by Damister) and fairly useful 1m to 1¼m winner Lady Rockstar (by Rock Hopper): dam unraced: modest maiden: should stay 7f: acts on soft ground. *H. J. Collingridge* **53**

VICTORIAN DANCER (IRE) 3 b.f. Groom Dancer (USA) 128 – Victoria Regia (IRE) 90 (Lomond (USA) 128) [2004 60: 7s May 12] smallish filly: modest maiden: well held only 3-y-o start. *K. A. Ryan* **–**

VICTORIA PEEK (IRE) 2 b.f. (Feb 27) Cape Cross (IRE) 129 – Night Spirit (IRE) 78 (Night Shift (USA)) [2004 5.1d⁴ 6m 5g Jun 17] €14,500F, 20,000Y: smallish filly: third foal: half-sister to Italian 2002 2-y-o 5f winner Night Spectr (by Spectrum): dam 6f winner: form only when fourth in maiden at Chester: ran as if amiss final start: likely to prove best at 5f. *D. Nicholls* **61**

VICTORY DESIGN (IRE) 2 b.c. (Apr 10) Danehill (USA) 126 – Sun Silk (USA) 64 (Gone West (USA)) [2004 6g⁶ Aug 28] 250,000Y: quite attractive colt: good walker and mover: first foal: dam, lightly-raced maiden (might have proved best up to 1¼m), out of Fillies' Mile winner Silk Slippers: 4/1, sixth in maiden at Newmarket, looking and running as if in need of race: should stay 1m: will improve. *J. Noseda* **69 p**

VICTORY FLIP (IRE) 4 b.f. Victory Note (USA) 120 – Two Magpies 43 (Doulab (USA) 115) [2004 58: f6g f8.5g⁶ f7g⁵ f8g³ Mar 3] lengthy filly: poor maiden: stays 8.5f: acts on fibresand: often wears cheekpieces: sometimes slowly away. *R. Hollinshead* **41**

VICTORY HYMN (IRE) 2 b.f. (Apr 28) Victory Note (USA) 120 – Nordic Union (IRE) 67 (Nordico (USA)) [2004 6g 7.1m⁵ 7m Jul 28] €1,500F, €12,000Y: half-sister to several winners, including useful Irish/US 1m winner Union Project (by Project Manager) and fairly useful Irish 1¼m/1½m winner Consalvo (by Erins Isle): dam, Irish middle-distance maiden, half-sister to smart Irish 1¼m winner Project Manager: poor form in maidens: should stay 1m. *M. R. Channon* **48**

VICTORY LAP (GER) 3 ch.f. Grand Lodge (USA) 125 – Vicenca (USA) (Sky Classic (CAN)) [2004 67p: 12s 12m⁶ 12.1m⁵ 18m Jun 27] tall, sparely-made filly: fair **66**

maiden: stays 1½m, probably not 2¼m: acts on fibresand, soft and good to firm ground: sold 3,000 gns. *M. R. Channon*

VICTORY MOON (SAF) 5 b.h. Al Mufti (USA) 112 – Dancing Flower (SAF) **120** (Dancing Champ (USA)) [2004 120: a8f³ a9f* a10f* a10f³ Mar 27] tall, rather leggy South African-bred horse: very smart performer: won Rounds 2 and 3 of Maktoum Challenge at Nad Al Sheba in February/March, former by 3¼ lengths from Inamorato, latter by 2¼ lengths from Dinyeper: good 5¾ lengths third to Pleasantly Perfect in Dubai World Cup on same course final start: stayed 1¼m: acted on dirt, best turf run on good ground: sweated up last 2 outings in 2003: free-going sort: joined A. Balding, but reported in August to have sustained an injury: sold R5m (around £462,000) in January 2005. *M. F. de Kock, South Africa*

VICTORY QUEST (IRE) 4 b.g. Victory Note (USA) 120 – Marade (USA) (Dahar **91** (USA) 125) [2004 82: p12g f12g f14g* f16s* f16.2s⁴ Mar 13] fairly useful handicapper: won twice at Southwell in February, improved form when beating Northern Nymph by 2 lengths in latter: will stay beyond 2m: acts on fibresand and good to firm ground: usually visored: game. *Mrs S. Lamyman*

VICTORY VEE 4 ch.g. Vettori (IRE) 119 – Aldevonie 75 (Green Desert (USA) 127) – [2004 –, a66: f7s f8.5s⁶ f12g f7g Apr 23] well-made gelding: modest performer: well beaten in 2004. *M. Blanshard*

VICTORY VENTURE (IRE) 4 b.g. Victory Note (USA) 120 – Shirley Venture 74 – (Be My Chief (USA) 122) [2004 87: 10m 11m 10f 11.6g Aug 9] leggy, quite good-topped gelding: fairly useful performer at 3 yrs: well held in 2004: sold 2,700 gns in October, sent to France. *Ian Williams*

VIENNA'S BOY (IRE) 3 b.g. Victory Note (USA) 120 – Shinkoh Rose (FR) 67 **87** (Warning 136) [2004 93: 6d⁴ 6s⁴ 6m⁶ 6g⁴ 5m⁶ 5m 6d⁵ 6m² 6g⁵ 8m⁴ 7d⁴ 7d* 7d Oct 30] tall, leggy gelding: fairly useful performer: won claimer at Newmarket (claimed from R. Hannon £20,000) in August: effective at 5f to easy 1m: unraced on heavy going, acts on any other: tends to hang: gelded after final start. *W. J. Musson*

VIEWFORTH 6 b.g. Emarati (USA) 74 – Miriam 59 (Forzando 122) [2004 91: 5g⁴ **83 d** 5v⁴ 6g 6m 6m 6m 5d 5g⁴ 5g³ 5g 5f 5g 6g 6g 5d 6d³ Sep 27] good-bodied gelding: fairly useful handicapper: regressed after second outing, leaving I. Semple after fourth: best at 5f/6f: acts on any going: usually blinkered/visored: none too consistent. *J. S. Goldie*

VIEW THE FACTS 5 b.m. So Factual (USA) 120 – Scenic View (IRE) (Scenic 128) – [2004 –: f5g p10g Feb 16] no form: tried in tongue tie. *P. L. Gilligan*

VIGOROUS (IRE) 4 b.f. Danetime (IRE) 121 – Merrily 73 (Sharrood (USA) 124) **71** [2004 82: 6g 5d⁵ 5m 5m 5g⁶ 6g² 5m⁵ Sep 29] leggy, quite good-topped filly: fair handicapper: left D. Nicholls after fourth start: effective at 5f/6f: acts on firm and good to soft ground: has run well when sweating: often slowly away. *M. Todhunter*

VIJAY (IRE) 5 ch.g. Eagle Eyed (USA) 111 – Foolish Fun (Fools Holme (USA)) **60 d** [2004 65: f5s f5s³ f6s 5g⁶ 6g 5m² 5f 5m 5m⁶ 6g 5m 5.9f² 7.2g⁶ Aug 7] modest performer: effective at 5f to 7f: acts on fibresand, firm and good to soft going: often wears headgear: unreliable. *I. Semple*

VIKING SPIRIT 2 b.c. (Feb 12) Mind Games 121 – Dane Dancing (IRE) 68 (Danehill **96** (USA) 126) [2004 6g 6f² 6.1d² 6.1m* 6.1d* 6g Sep 30] 15,000Y: tall, quite attractive colt: first foal: dam, 9.4f winner, sister to useful performer up to 1¼m Sundari: useful performer: won nurseries at Warwick and Nottingham in September in good style: gone in coat when running poorly final start: likely to stay 7f: acts on good to firm and good to soft ground. *P. W. Harris*

VILLA CHIGI (IRE) 2 ch.g. (May 12) Pistolet Bleu (IRE) 133 – Musical Refrain – (IRE) (Dancing Dissident (USA) 119) [2004 7m p7.1g Nov 11] well held in maidens. *B. Smart*

VILLAROSI (IRE) 2 b.f. (Apr 20) Rossini (USA) 118 – Trinida (Jaazeiro (USA) **71** 127) [2004 7d⁵ p7m Dec 22] €3,500Y: workmanlike filly: half-sister to several winners abroad, including Brazilian Group 1 winner Davsoyan (by Gorytus): dam Irish 1¼m to 13.5f winner: much better effort in maidens when fifth at Newmarket. *P. W. Chapple-Hyam*

VILLARRICA (USA) 2 ch.f. (Feb 24) Selkirk (USA) 129 – Melikah (IRE) 116 **78 p** (Lammtarra (USA) 134) [2004 7s⁴ 7m³ Oct 2] rangy, unfurnished filly: has scope: first foal: dam, 1¼m winner who was second in Oaks, half-sister to 3-y-o All Too Beautiful, Galileo and Black Sam Bellamy out of Arc winner Urban Sea: fair form in maidens at

Salisbury and Redcar (third to Sheboygan): likely to be suited by 1¼m/1½m: type to do better. *Sir Michael Stoute*

VINANDO   3 ch.c. Hernando (FR) 127 – Sirena (GER) (Tejano (USA)) [2004 76p: **108 p**
10s* 11m 12m* 12g⁵ 12g* Oct 1] tall, close-coupled colt: quickly made into a useful performer, winning maiden at Windsor in April and handicaps at Ascot in July and Newmarket in October: best effort when beating Manorson by neck in last-named: should stay 1¾m: acts on soft and good to firm ground: tongue tied last 3 starts: capable of better still. *C. R. Egerton*

VINCENT   9 b.g. Anshan 119 – Top-Anna (IRE) 71 (Ela-Mana-Mou 132) [2004 54:   **53**
f16g⁴ f16.2g³ f14.8g* f16g⁶ f16g³ Feb 12] tall gelding: modest performer: won seller at Wolverhampton in January: stays 17f: acts on any turf going and fibresand: tried visored/blinkered earlier in career: tends to hang/carry head high: best with waiting tactics. *John A. Harris*

VINDICATION   4 ch.g. Compton Place 125 – Prince's Feather (IRE) 77 (Cadeaux   **91**
Genereux 131) [2004 102: 7m 7f⁶ 7m⁶ 7.1m 7m 7g p7.1g 7s Nov 6] well-made gelding: fairly useful handicapper: left J. Fanshawe after sixth start: stays 7f: acts on polytrack and firm going, probably on soft: visored (slowly away) once: usually tongue tied. *R. M. H. Cowell*

VIN DU PAYS   4 b.g. Alzao (USA) 117 – Royale Rose (FR) 75 (Bering 136) [2004   **–**
54+, a78: 15s 11m 14.1d 12g 16.2g p12.2g p13.9g Oct 18] fair on all-weather, modest on turf at 3 yrs: well beaten in 2004. *M. Blanshard*

VINNIE ROE (IRE)   6 b.h. Definite Article 121 – Kayu (Tap On Wood 130)   **128**
[2004 125: 14m² 12m² 14g* 16s² Nov 2]
If the Irish Derby victory of Grey Swallow made the summer for the team at Rosewell House, the performances of stable stalwart Vinnie Roe provided the autumn highlights. He won his fourth consecutive Irish St Leger and then travelled 12,000 miles to run the race of his life under top weight in Australia's most prestigious race, the Melbourne Cup over two miles, denied the £1,142,858 first prize only by the previous year's winner Makybe Diva. Vinnie Roe was having only his third run of the year in the Irish St Leger, having missed a number of summer targets earmarked for him, most notably the Gold Cup at Royal Ascot (a race in which he was beaten narrowly in 2002) where concerns over a muscular injury and the prevailing firm ground ruled him out at the eleventh hour. He finished second in his Royal Ascot warm-up, the Saval Beg Stakes at Leopardstown in May, and also in the mile-and-a-half Ballyroan Stakes, which he had won in the two previous years, over the same course in August. British-trained Foreign Affairs got the better of Vinnie Roe by a neck in the Ballyroan but the patiently-ridden Vinnie Roe was reducing the winner's advantage hand over fist in the closing stages and looked firmly on course for his fourth Irish Leger.
Ireland's fifth 'classic' has been open to four-year-olds and upwards since 1983 when the filly Mountain Lodge made history by becoming the first horse above the age of three to win a classic in Britain or Ireland, 'at least with the blessing of the turf authorities', as *Racehorses of 1983* pointed out, since the ineligible four-year-old Maccabaeus had been disqualified after winning the 1844 Derby as Running Rein. The standard of the older horses that contest the Irish St Leger nowadays is high and the St Leger at Doncaster—the two races were a week apart in 2004—is a very strong counter-attraction for the classic generation. Vinnie Roe is the only horse to have won the Irish St Leger as a three-year-old since the 'eighties, his performance in 2001 (when he won from older horses Millenary, Marienbard and Persian Punch) bettered in the race in recent times only by the form of Kayf Tara's eight-length romp when he won for the second time in 1999. Vinnie Roe became the fourth to win the Irish St Leger twice, when successful as a four-year-old, the others being Vintage Crop (also trained by Dermot Weld) in 1993 and 1994 and Oscar Schindler in 1996 and 1997, and Vinnie Roe's third victory (over Gamut, the three-year-old Powerscourt and Bollin Eric in 2003) put him out on his own. There was no shortage of rivals standing in the way of a fourth success, the thirteen-strong line-up for the latest Irish Field St Leger the biggest since the same number went to post in 1988. The previous year's St Leger winner Brian Boru was the only other in the field with a European Group 1 victory to his name, though Vinnie Roe's stable-companion Media Puzzle had won the Melbourne Cup, a

Group 1 event notwithstanding that it is a handicap (disparagingly nicknamed in some quarters the 'Australian Cesarewitch'). Vinnie Roe and Brian Boru started joint favourites at the Curragh at 7/2, with the smart British-trained pair Orange Touch (9/2) and Lonsdale Cup winner First Charter (5/1) the only others at shorter than 10/1. Orange Touch set a true gallop, heading a group of four including Vinnie Roe and First Charter, who were clear of the remainder for much of the race. Travelling smoothly all the way, Vinnie Roe was sent to the front over a furlong out and won comfortably by two and a half lengths from the staying-on Brian Boru, who never looked like troubling him. Vinnie Roe's jockey Pat Smullen, who has partnered him in all his races except one, picked up his whip only to wave it in celebration in the last fifty yards. First Charter finished a further half length behind Brian Boru in third, Orange Touch weakening into eighth. Sagaro won three Gold Cups at Royal Ascot in the 'seventies, but Vinnie Roe is the only horse to win the same European Group 1 event four years running since a European-wide pattern system came into existence in 1971 (Marsyas won four successive Prix du Cadrans between 1944 and 1947).

More than a hundred European-trained horses were entered in Australia's top autumn races, the Caulfield Cup, the Melbourne Cup and the Cox Plate. Despite its big prize, the last-named suffers from clashing with the Breeders' Cup though it is a mile-and-a-quarter weight-for-age race on turf, an event the Breeders' Cup doesn't have. Vinnie Roe was one of six entered by his stable alone in the Melbourne Cup, in which Godolphin also had nine entries. Vinnie Roe was joined in the maximum twenty-four-runner line-up by Media Puzzle, having only his third outing since winning the race in 2002, and three British-trained challengers, Mamool and Razkalla for Godolphin and Distinction (who had missed the Caulfield Cup because of a low blood count) from the Stoute stable. Makybe Diva was a hot favourite to become the first since Think Big in 1975 to win successive Melbourne Cups, but, with the prevailing soft going thought likely to be in his favour, Vinnie Roe was a well-supported 5/1-shot, Distinction, third favourite at

Irish Field St Leger, the Curragh—Pat Smullen celebrates as the remarkable Vinnie Roe becomes the first horse in pattern-race history to win the same Group 1 event four years in succession

12/1, and 20/1-shot Media Puzzle being the only other European challengers shorter than 25/1. Vinnie Roe had finished fourth on firm going in Media Puzzle's year,
when he also carried top weight, and he made the frame for the second time, keeping on well after travelling strongly early in the straight, but proving no match at the
weights for Makybe Diva, in receipt of 6 lb, who beat him by a length and a quarter
after quickening through on the inside to lead a furlong out. Distinction, Mamool
(whose rider Dettori received a month's ban for causing interference), Razkalla and
Media Puzzle all finished in the first half of the field, coming sixth, seventh, ninth
and twelfth respectively. Smullen was criticised by some in the Australian media
for coming wide on the home bend, but Vinnie Roe's performance was the best of
his career, as well as being the best of the year by a European-trained horse over a
distance beyond a mile and a half.

			Indian Ridge	Ahonoora
	Definite Article		(ch 1985)	Hillbrow
	(b 1992)		Summer Fashion	Moorestyle
Vinnie Roe (IRE)			(b 1985)	My Candy
(b.h. 1998)			Tap On Wood	Sallust
	Kayu		(ch 1976)	Cat O'Mountaine
	(ch 1985)		Ladytown	English Prince
			(ch 1980)	Supreme Lady

The leggy, useful-looking Vinnie Roe, a game, genuine and consistent stayer who acts on any going, is set to remain in training as a seven-year-old, with a
fifth Irish St Leger and possibly a third appearance in the Melbourne Cup among
his objectives. Vinnie Roe, who has been tried visored but is usually blinkered, is
easily the best racehorse sired by Irish Derby runner-up Definite Article, whose
representatives in Britain in 2004 included the smart stayer Defining. Vinnie Roe's
dam Kayu was unraced, but she was out of the staying-bred mile-and-a-quarter
winner Ladytown, a half-sister to the 1978 Irish St Leger winner M-Lolshan.
Kayu's other winners include the useful Rich Victim (by Lapierre), who twice won
the Queen Mother's Cup in Hong Kong under the name of Mazal. Vinnie Roe's
great grandam Supreme Lady also appears in the extended pedigree of Arc fourth
Acropolis. *D. K. Weld, Ireland*

VINO VENUS   2 b.f. (May 8) Tipsy Creek (USA) 115 – Galaxy Glow (Kalaglow 132)   **33**
[2004 6m 6d⁵ Oct 2] 800F, 1,300Y: second foal: half-sister to Italian 2003 2-y-o 6f winner
by Woodborough: dam no form: poor form in maidens at Brighton. *Miss S. West*

VINTAGE PREMIUM   7 b.g. Forzando 122 – Julia Domna (Dominion 123) [2004   **112**
104: p10g f8.5s⁶ p10g 10.4d* 12.1d² May 14] tall, leggy gelding: smart performer: won
handicap at York by neck from Shahzan House) in May: very good neck second to
Collier Hill in listed handicap at Hamilton following day, rallying gamely: stayed 1¼m:
acted on fibresand, heavy and good to firm ground: visored once in 2001: usually raced
prominently: died on gallops in June. *R. A. Fahey*

VINTAGE STYLE   5 ch.g. Piccolo 121 – Gibaltarik (IRE) 68 (Jareer (USA) 115)   **–**
[2004 61, a49+: 6.1g 6.1s Jul 3] lengthy gelding: modest performer: well held in 2004:
usually wears headgear: sold 900 gns, sent to Denmark. *J. R. Weymes*

VIOLA DA BRACCIO (IRE)   3 ch.f. Vettori (IRE) 119 – Push A Button (Bold Lad   **58**
(IRE) 133) [2004 –: 8.1s 8m⁵ 11.1m⁵ f8m⁶ 12.5d² 12.5s 10s a11.5g a17g Dec 31] lengthy,
quite good-topped filly: modest maiden: left D. Daly after fourth start: acts 12.5f: acts
on good to firm and good to soft ground, below form on all-weather: reluctant and led to
post final outing in Britain. *Mme M. Bollack-Badel, France*

VIOLET AVENUE   3 ch.f. Muhtarram (USA) 125 – Ivoronica 89 (Targowice (USA)   **59**
130) [2004 61: 8m 8.2g⁶ 8.1g⁴ 7.6m 7m⁵ 8d 10.9d Sep 18] tall filly: modest maiden:
barely stays 1m: acts on good to firm going: well beaten in blinkers. *J. G. Given*

VIOLET PARK   3 b.f. Pivotal 124 – Petonellajill 73 (Petong 126) [2004 7g² 7g² 8.3f³   **80**
7.1m* 7d* 7d Sep 18] half-sister to 6-y-o Piquet: dam 7f winner: fairly useful performer:
won maiden at Chepstow and handicap at Newmarket in August: mid-field in 25-runner
handicap at Newbury final start: probably better at 7f than 1m: acts on firm and good to
soft going. *B. J. Meehan*

VIP   2 ch.c. (Mar 24) Dubai Millennium 140 – Danish (IRE) 117 (Danehill (USA) 126)   **71 p**
[2004 7s⁴ Oct 27] fifth foal: half-brother to fairly useful Irish 2000 2-y-o 6f winner Blixen
and to French 1½m winner Wester Skeld (both by Gone West): dam, 6f (at 2 yrs in Ire-

land) to 9f (US Grade 1) winner, sister to very smart 1m/1¼m performer Hawkeye: weak 11/2, fourth to Plea Bargain in maiden at Yarmouth, taking strong hold up with pace and carrying head bit awkwardly late on: bred to stay at least 1m: likely to do better. *Saeed bin Suroor*

VIRGIN'S TEARS 2 b.f. (Apr 23) Bishop of Cashel 122 – Lola Mora (Nearly A — Hand 115) [2004 7.9g 6s Oct 22] workmanlike filly: first foal: dam unraced: behind in maidens at York (showed signs of ability) and Newbury. *P. W. Chapple-Hyam*

VISIONIST (IRE) 2 b.c. (Apr 7) Orpen (USA) 116 – Lady Taufan (IRE) (Taufan **103** (USA) 119) [2004 6g* 7m⁴ 6m³ 6m³ Sep 4] €4,200F, €52,000Y: big, good-topped colt: has scope: good walker: has a quick action: seventh foal: brother to useful 2003 2-y-o 6f/7f (Prestige Stakes) winner Gracefully and half-brother to 2 winners, including useful 1996 2-y-o 6f winner Speedball (by Waajib): dam, Irish maiden, stayed 9f: useful performer: won maiden at York in July: good third to Beaver Patrol in sales race at the Curragh and to Satchem (beaten 3 lengths) in Sirenia Stakes at Kempton: should stay 7f: flashed tail second start. *J. A. Osborne*

VISION VICTORY (GER) 2 b.g. (Apr 7) Dashing Blade 117 – Val d'Isere (GER) **49** (Surumu (GER)) [2004 5v⁴ 5v 6f 7f 8s Nov 1] compact gelding: poor maiden: best effort on debut: should stay 1m. *T. P. Tate*

VITA SPERICOLATA (IRE) 7 b.m. Prince Sabo 123 – Ahonita 90 (Ahonoora 122) **88 §** [2004 100: 5d 5.1d 5v³ 5m⁵ 6m 5d 6d 5m⁵ 6.1m⁵ 6d⁶ 5d Aug 28] lengthy, rather plain mare: fairly useful performer: best at 5f/6f: acts on any going: occasionally blinkered/visored: often races prominently: sometimes edges left: unreliable: sold 38,000 gns in November. *J. S. Wainwright*

VITELUCY 5 b.m. Vettori (IRE) 119 – Classic Line 71 (Last Tycoon 131) [2004 54: **45** f12s⁵ f12g⁵ f16s³ f12g⁵ p12.2d⁵ Oct 23] lengthy mare: poor performer: stays 2m: acts on all-weather: tried in visor/cheekpieces. *Miss S. J. Wilton*

VITTORIOSO (IRE) 3 b.g. Victory Note (USA) 120 – Miss Anita (IRE) 70 (Anita's **54** Prince 126) [2004 55: f7g⁵ p5g³ p5g³ f5s² p5g 5f 5m⁵ 6g 7g 10m⁶ 10g⁵ p8.6g p9.5g⁵ Dec 22] modest maiden: stays 9.5f: acts on all-weather: tried in headgear. *Miss Gay Kelleway*

VIVA ATLAS ESPANA 4 b.f. Piccolo 121 – Bay Risk (Risk Me (FR) 127) [2004 39: — p7g 9.7s May 6] poor maiden: often slowly away. *Miss B. Sanders*

VIVRE SA VIE 3 ch.f. Nashwan (USA) 135 – La Strada (Niniski (USA) 125) [2004 **55** f9.4g⁴ f8s³ f12s² f12s⁵ 13.8v Oct 16] fifth foal: closely related to 7-y-o Bow Strada and half-sister to 6-y-o Valeureux: dam, champion 2-y-o filly in Spain, sister to smart German/New Zealand middle-distance horse Vialli: modest maiden: ran wide and folded tamely at Catterick final start: stays 1½m: acts on fibresand. *Sir Mark Prescott*

VIZULIZE 5 b.m. Robellino (USA) 127 – Euridice (IRE) 66 (Woodman (USA) 126) **54** [2004 66: p7g p8g⁶ f7g⁵ p7g p8g p7g⁴ p8g 8d 8.1d³ p9.5g f8g⁶ p10m² Dec 15] good-topped mare: modest maiden: stays 1¼m: acts on all-weather, firm and good to soft ground: tried blinkered/visored. *A. W. Carroll*

VLASTA WEINER 4 b.g. Magic Ring (IRE) 115 – Armaiti 78 (Sayf El Arab (USA) **41** 127) [2004 –: f6g f7g² p8g⁵ f8g f7g⁴ f8g⁶ p8g⁴ p8g⁶ 6.1m 6.1m Jun 11] poor maiden: stays easy 1m: acts on all-weather and good to firm ground: usually blinkered. *J. M. Bradley*

VOCATIVE (GER) 2 gr.f. (Jan 25) Acatenango (GER) 127 – Vadinaxa (FR) (Linamix **60** (FR) 127) [2004 8m p9.5g⁶ p9.5g⁴ Dec 20] 19,000Y: tall filly: second foal: dam, French 1¼m winner, half-sister to dams of Breeders' Cup Mile winner Val Royal and very smart French miler Vahorimix: modest form in maidens: will stay at least 1¼m. *P. C. Haslam*

VOICE MAIL 5 b.g. So Factual (USA) 120 – Wizardry 83 (Shirley Heights 130) **83** [2004 81: 9.7s 8.5s 8m* 10.2f* 10.2f³ 8.5m 8f² 9g 10.3g³ 9m⁴ 8f 11.7m³ 10m p8g Oct 13] **a78** useful-looking gelding: fairly useful handicapper: won twice at Bath in May: seems to stay 11.7f: acts on polytrack and firm going: probably on soft: sometimes visored: held up. *A. M. Balding*

VOICE OF AN ANGEL (IRE) 2 b.f. (Mar 4) Desert Style (IRE) 121 – Madame **36** Curie (Polish Precedent (USA) 131) [2004 f5g⁵ 5d f5m⁵ 6m 5f⁵ Jun 21] €4,000Y: third **a51** foal: dam ran once: modest maiden on all-weather, poor on turf: should stay 6f: acts on fibresand and firm going. *A. Berry*

VOILE (IRE) 3 b.f. Barathea (IRE) 127 – Samriah (IRE) (Wassl 125) [2004 100: 7m **90** 6d p8g Oct 31] quite good-topped filly: fairly useful performer: mid-field in listed races in 2004: stays 7f: acts on good to firm going, probably on good to soft. *R. Hannon*

VOIR DIRE   2 b.c. (May 11) Vettori (IRE) 119 – Bobbie Dee 93 (Blakeney 126) [2004   **60**
7m 7m 8d 8g 10v³ Oct 20] fourth foal: dam, maiden, should have stayed 1½m: modest
maiden: will stay at least 1½m: acts on heavy going, probably on good to firm. *Mrs
P. N. Dutfield*

VOIX DU NORD (FR)   3 b.c. Valanour (IRE) 125 – Dame Edith (FR) (Top Ville 129)   **119**
[2004 113: 11g* 10.5g* May 16] smart performer: won Criterium de Saint-Cloud at 2
yrs: successful at Longchamp on return in Prix Noailles (by 3 lengths from Cherry Mix)
in April and Prix Lupin (by nose from Millemix after good duel) in May: reportedly
fractured off-fore pastern on eve of Prix du Jockey Club in early-June: will stay 1½m:
raced only on good/good to soft ground: held up: reliable. *D. Smaga, France*

VOLATICUS (IRE)   3 b.c. Desert Story (IRE) 115 – Haysel (IRE) (Petorius 117) [2004   **60**
–: 6g² 6s 6m⁴ 5d⁴ 6m a10.5g a10.5g Oct 10] close-coupled colt: modest maiden: sold
from D. Nicholls 7,500 gns after fifth start: effective at 5f/6f: acts on good to firm and
good to soft ground: visored (raced freely) last 2 starts in Britain. *R. J. Smith, Spain*

VOLITIO   2 b.c. (Mar 23) Mind Games 121 – Millie's Lady (IRE) (Common Grounds   **64**
118) [2004 7d 8.1m 8g 8d p7.1g⁶ p6g* Dec 1] 15,000Y: good-topped colt: brother to 3
winners, including 2000 2-y-o 5f winner Milly's Lass and 3-y-o Willjojo: dam unraced:
modest performer: blinkered, won nursery at Wolverhampton: likely to prove best at 6f/
7f: acts on polytrack. *S. Kirk*

VONADAISY   3 b.f. Averti (IRE) 117 – Vavona 60 (Ballad Rock 122) [2004 72: 7.1g*   **70 ?**
7d p8g⁵ p8.6g p7.1g⁴ Oct 19] rather leggy filly: fair performer: won maiden at Warwick
in August: well below form last 2 starts: stays easy 1m: acts on polytrack, good to firm
and good to soft going: tried blinkered: sold 4,000 gns. *W. J. Haggas*

VONDOVA   2 b.f. (Mar 16) Efisio 120 – Well Proud (IRE) (Sadler's Wells (USA) 132)   **88**
[2004 5m³ 7d 6g⁴ 7.1m 6.1g² 6g Sep 2] 29,000Y: tall, leggy filly: half-sister to fairly
useful 7f winner Michael Maher (by Indian Ridge): dam unraced half-sister to middle-
distance fillies Ghaiya (smart) and Fiesta Gal (high class in USA): fairly useful performer: won maiden at Newmarket in July: good efforts in listed race at Sandown (raced
freely) and minor event at Chester (second) next 2 starts: barely stays 7f: acts on good to
firm ground: signs of temperament second start. *R. Hannon*

VON WESSEX   2 b.g. (Apr 2) Wizard King 122 – Gay Da Cheen (IRE) (Tenby 125)   **63 §**
[2004 5g⁶ p5g⁵ 5.2m* 5s⁶ 5d³ 5m³ 5d* 5g⁴ 5s⁶ 5d⁶ 5.3m² Sep 23] €2,000Y: compact
gelding: modest performer: won maiden at Yarmouth in April and claimer at Beverley
in June: likely to prove best at 5f/easy 6f: acts on good to firm and good to soft ground:
tongue tied ninth start, in cheekpieces (ran well) final one: tends to race up with pace/
hang right: unreliable. *W. G. M. Turner*

VOOM   2 b.f. (Apr 4) Fraam 114 – Natalie Jay 88 (Ballacashtal (CAN)) [2004 5.7f 6m⁴   **55 d**
5.1f³ p8g p5.1g f5f Dec 28] first foal: dam, 7f/1m winner, half-sister to useful 1m/1¼m
performer You Know The Rules: modest maiden: seemingly best effort on debut: should
stay 7f. *M. R. Channon*

*Prix Lupin, Longchamp—a good duel between Voix du Nord (No.5) and Millemix,
neither of whom was seen out again; Valixir is third in an event which is to be scrapped in 2005*

Littlewoods Bet Direct Lincoln Trial Stakes (Handicap), Wolverhampton—a fifth win in a row for Vortex, who battles it out with stable-companion Te Quiero (grey)

VORTEX 5 b.g. Danehill (USA) 126 – Roupala (USA) 75 (Vaguely Noble 140) [2004 **111** 82, a88: f8.5g* p8g* f8.5s* f8.5s* f8.5s* p10g 8g a8.7f* 7m³ 8f 8m² 7m⁴ 8g² a8g* 7m⁴ a10.5g Nov 28] big, good-bodied gelding: smart performer: much improved at 5 yrs, winning handicaps at Wolverhampton (4) and Lingfield between January and March and listed races at Jagersro (by head from Mandrake El Mago) in May and Taby (by head from Hovman) in September: also ran well when second in handicaps at Newbury (beaten short head by Everest) and Ascot (beaten 1¼ lengths by Pentecost): reportedly pulled muscles in back when virtually pulled up final outing (Japan Cup Dirt): effective at 7f to 8.7f: acts on all-weather/dirt and good to firm going: usually tongue tied: visored once at 4 yrs, and usually wears eyeshields: often wears bandages: travels strongly, and tends to idle: tough and genuine. *Miss Gay Kelleway*

VRISAKI (IRE) 3 b.g. Docksider (USA) 124 – Kingdom Queen (IRE) 65 (Night Shift **52** (USA)) [2004 61: f7g² f7g 7s⁴ 8m 11.5m 11.5f³ 10.2f⁶ 11.5m³ 12m 12f 11.5f f12g p12g Nov 27] modest maiden: stays 11.5f: acts on all-weather and firm going: tried in cheekpieces/visor: sometimes slowly away: inconsistent. *Miss D. Mountain*

VRUBEL (IRE) 5 ch.g. Entrepreneur 123 – Renzola (Dragonara Palace (USA) 115) **52** [2004 53: p9.5g² f11g p9.5g⁵ p12m f12d⁶ Dec 21] well-made gelding: modest performer: stays 1¼m: acts on all-weather, firm and soft going: tried in headgear/tongue tie. *V. Smith*

W

WAAEDAH (USA) 3 ch.f. Halling (USA) 133 – Agama (USA) 44 (Nureyev (USA) **–** 131) [2004 81: 7m 8f 7.5s Aug 19] rangy, rather unfurnished filly: no form in handicaps in 2004, leaving M. Channon after reappearance: blinkered final start. *D. J. Barry, Ireland*

WAATHEB (IRE) 2 b.c. (Apr 1) Barathea (IRE) 127 – Bally Souza (IRE) 87 (Alzao **79** (USA) 117) [2004 6m 6d p8g Oct 25] 45,000Y: sturdy colt: third foal: half-brother to smart Irish 2003 2-y-o 6f winner Wathab (by Cadeaux Genereux): dam, 11f/1½m winner, half-sister to useful miler A La Carte: best effort in maidens when seventh to Tomoohat at Newmarket second start: should stay 1m. *R. Hannon*

WAFANI 5 b.g. Mtoto 134 – Wafa (IRE) (Kefaah (USA) 124) [2004 –: 10m May 31] – leggy gelding: no form: tried blinkered. *W. J. Musson*

WAGGLEDANCE (IRE) 2 b.g. (Apr 22) Mujadil (USA) 119 – Assertive Lass (USA) (Assert 134) [2004 5m⁵ 5g 5m 5g 5m² 5g Sep 26] €16,000Y: lengthy, quite good-topped gelding: half-brother to several winners in Italy, including useful performer up to 9f Golden Kabubby (by Green Forest): dam Italian 7f winner, including at 2 yrs: fair maiden: second at Beverley, best effort: should stay 6f: acts on good to firm going: wore cheek-pieces last 2 outings: usually races prominently. *J. S. Wainwright* **65**

WAHCHI (IRE) 5 ch.g. Nashwan (USA) 135 – Nafhaat (USA) 91 (Roberto (USA) 131) [2004 –: 10v 12g 11.9s 10.1g 10g⁶ Jun 19] strong, lengthy gelding: useful at best: form since 2002 only when sixth in handicap at Redcar final start: stays 1¼m: acts on good to firm going. *G. P. Kelly* **57**

WAHOO SAM (USA) 4 ch.g. Sandpit (BRZ) 129 – Good Reputation (USA) (Gran Zar (MEX)) [2004 –: 7s 8g 7.9f³ 9.2d* 9.2g* 10g 9.2f* 9.2d² 9.2d f8g* f8g Dec 28] good-topped gelding: fairly useful handicapper: won at Hamilton in June and July (twice) and at Southwell in December: stays 9f: acts on fibresand, firm and good to soft going: blinkered (well held) on reappearance: effective waited with or making running. *T. D. Barron* **87**

WAINWRIGHT (IRE) 4 b.g. Victory Note (USA) 120 – Double Opus (IRE) (Petorius 117) [2004 69: f6s* p6g 6s 5.1d 6m 7m⁶ May 31] quite attractive gelding: fair performer: reportedly underwent throat surgery in 2003: won handicap at Wolverhampton in January: below form after: stays 7f: acts on fibresand, soft and good to firm going: tried tongue tied/blinkered/in cheekpieces. *P. A. Blockley* **73 d**

WAIT FOR SPRING (USA) 3 b.f. Seeking The Gold (USA) – Polish Spring (IRE) 104 (Polish Precedent (USA) 131) [2004 10g⁵ 10d² 8g 10.2g p10g Nov 16] first foal: dam, 6f (at 2 yrs) to 1m (in USA) winner, half-sister to useful French 1¼m/1½m performer Go Boldly: fair maiden: stays 1¼m: acts on good to soft going: hinted at temperament second start, folded tamely last 3 outings, in blinkers final one. *J. H. M. Gosden* **70**

WAIT FOR THE WILL (USA) 8 ch.g. Seeking The Gold (USA) – You'd Be Surprised (USA) 117 (Blushing Groom (FR) 131) [2004 97: 12g 12g 14g 12g* 12m* 12f² 14s⁵ 12g Sep 20] tall gelding: fairly useful performer: won handicaps at Goodwood and Newmarket in June: best other effort when head second to Tawny Way in minor event at Newmarket: stays 1¾m: acts on polytrack, firm and good to soft going: tongue tied/visored once, usually blinkered: held up: sometimes finds little. *G. L. Moore* **93**

WAKE UP HENRY 3 ch.g. Nashwan (USA) 135 – River Saint (USA) 73§ (Irish River (FR) 131) [2004 56p: 8.1v 10m³ 11.9f⁴ 10f Sep 16] good-bodied gelding: modest maiden: should stay 1½m: acts on all-weather and good to firm going: visored (ran poorly) final start: sold 9,000 gns. *R. Charlton* **56**

WAKE (USA) 4 b.c. Storm Cat (USA) – Ladies Cruise (USA) (Fappiano (USA)) [2004 p8g* 9g⁶ 9.9g 8d⁶ p8.6g² Nov 8] lengthy, angular colt: useful performer: missed 2003: won maiden at Lingfield in March: left B. Meehan after third start: improved effort when 2 lengths second to Del Mar Sunset in handicap at Wolverhampton: stays 8.6f: acts on polytrack and good to soft going. *M. L. W. Bell* **99**

WALKER BAY (IRE) 6 ch.m. Efisio 120 – Lalandria (FR) (Highest Honor (FR) 124) [2004 57, a–: p10g⁵ p13g Feb 3] poor maiden: probably stays 1¼m: acts on polytrack and good to firm going: tried blinkered. *J. C. Fox* **? a40**

WALK IN THE PARK (IRE) 2 b.c. (Jan 20) Montjeu (IRE) 137 – Classic Park 115 (Robellino (USA) 127) [2004 7d³ 7g³ 8g² 8s* 8s³ Oct 31] €130,000Y, 270,000 2-y-o: fourth foal: half-brother to fairly useful Irish 6f/7f winner Mufradat (by Desert Prince): dam Irish 5f (at 2 yrs) to 1m (Irish 1000 Guineas) winner: smart performer: won minor event at Saint-Cloud in October: much improved when 1¾ lengths third to Helios Quercus in Criterium International at same course, staying on well despite having pulled hard in rear early: will stay at least 1¼m: acts on soft ground. *J. E. Hammond, France* **114**

WALKONTHEWILDSIDE 2 b.c. (Jan 28) Giant's Causeway (USA) 132 – Wannabe Grand (IRE) 116 (Danehill (USA) 126) [2004 6m⁵ 7m⁴ 7.1m* 7g Sep 30] 160,000Y: well-made colt: second foal: half-brother to useful 2003 2-y-o 5f winner Bachelor of Arts (by Stravinsky): dam Cherry Hinton/Cheveley Park winner and runner-up in 1000 Guineas: visored and edgy, won maiden at Warwick in September, making all: tailed off in Somerville Tattersall Stakes at Newmarket final start: should stay 1m. *D. R. Loder* **85**

WALL STREET RUNNER 3 ch.f. Kirkwall 118 – Running Tycoon (IRE) 62 (Last **63 d**
Tycoon 131) [2004 64: a7g a6g² a8g* a6g* a5g* a6g a6g⁶ a6g⁵ a6g² 6.1d p7g p8.6g p7g
p7.1d f8g Nov 23] close-coupled filly: modest performer: ran in Spain for P. Haley first 9
starts in 2004, winning a maiden at Seville and minor events at Mijas and Seville: well
below form last 3 starts: effective at 5f, barely at 8.6f: acts on sand, polytrack and firm
going: visored final outing. *C. A. Dwyer*

WALTONS GROVE (IRE) 3 b.f. Machiavellian (USA) 123 – Priory Belle (IRE) **56**
104 (Priolo (USA) 127) [2004 60: 6m 7.5m⁶ p10g Nov 16] fourth foal: half-sister to Irish
1½m winners Kiltubber (useful, by Sadler's Wells) and Seeking Bellissimo (fairly useful,
by Rainbow Quest): dam, Irish 2-y-o 6f/7f (Moyglare Stud Stakes) winner, later stayed
1m: modest maiden: left J. Bolger in Ireland after second start: should stay at least 1m:
raced only on polytrack and good going or firmer: tried in blinkers. *M. J. Wallace*

WALTZING BEAU 3 ch.g. Dancing Spree (USA) – Blushing Belle 74 (Local Suitor **57**
(USA) 128) [2004 –p: f9.4g² p10g 11.8g 14g 10.2f 10.9g² 10m³ 10m⁶ p16g⁶ 11.9m Sep
23] tall, leggy gelding: modest maiden: left I. Wood after second outing: stays easy 2m:
acts on all-weather and firm going: tried visored: usually races prominently: won juvenile
hurdle in October. *B. G. Powell*

WALTZING WIZARD 5 b.g. Magic Ring (IRE) 115 – Legendary Dancer 90 (Shareef **59**
Dancer (USA) 135) [2004 60: f7g³ f8f⁵ f7g⁴ f7f⁵ 6g⁵ 7.1g⁵ 7d 7.2m⁵ 7.2f⁴ 7.9f 7.1f⁶ 7m³
6.9g⁴ 6.9f 6.9m⁶ 6.9g f7g⁵ f7g f7g³ f8g* f8d³ f8g² Dec 28] tall, leggy gelding: modest
performer: won handicap at Southwell in December: stays 1m: acts on all-weather and
any turf going: tried tongue tied: wore cheekpieces last 4 starts. *A. Berry*

WANCHAI LAD 3 b.c. Danzero (AUS) – Frisson (Slip Anchor 136) [2004 89: 5.1d³ **87**
6m 5m⁵ 5.1d 5f 5d 7.2s Sep 18] good-topped colt: fairly useful handicapper: ran as if
amiss 2 of last 4 starts: barely stays 6f: acts on firm and good to soft going. *D. Nicholls*

WANDERING ACT (IRE) 2 b.g. (May 2) Brave Act 119 – Cwm Deri (IRE) (Alzao **48**
(USA) 117) [2004 7f 8s p7.1g Dec 31] poor form in maidens: left M. Wallace after second
start. *Miss Gay Kelleway*

WANNA SHOUT 6 b.m. Missed Flight 123 – Lulu (Polar Falcon (USA) 126) [2004 **52**
48§: p8g² p8g* p10g² p8g* p8g² p10g 10.2f⁵ 8m p12g⁶ p10g³ p7g⁶ p9.5g³ p8.6g Dec 15] **a64**
modest performer: won banded event in February and handicap in March, both at Lingfield: stays 1¼m: acts on all-weather, firm and soft going: tried tongue tied/blinkered/
visored. *R. Dickin*

WANSDYKE LASS 2 b.f. (May 13) Josr Algarhoud (IRE) 118 – Silankka 70 (Slip **51**
Anchor 136) [2004 7m⁵ Jul 11] 4,200Y: leggy filly: fourth foal: half-sister to 2001 2-y-o
5.7f winner Piccolo Party, later successful up to 1¾m abroad, and 6f winner Potwash
(both by Piccolo): dam, 1½m/13f winner, out of half-sister to Ibn Bey and Roseate Tern:
33/1, fifth to Grand Marque in maiden at Newbury, late headway. *M. R. Channon*

WANT (USA) 3 ch.c. Miswaki (USA) 124 – Substance (USA) (Diesis 133) [2004 67p: **61**
8m 8m May 15] quite attractive colt: has a fluent, quick action: modest maiden: should
stay 1m: sold 16,000 gns. *J. H. M. Gosden*

WARAQA (USA) 5 b.m. Red Ransom (USA) – Jafn 104 (Sharpo 132) [2004 –: p6g **–**
Jan 6] smallish, good-topped mare: no longer of any account. *T. M. Jones*

WAR AT SEA (IRE) 2 b.c. (Feb 15) Bering 136 – Naval Affair (IRE) 101 (Last Tycoon **71 p**
131) [2004 7d⁵ Aug 27] well-made colt: first foal: dam, 2-y-o 7f winner who should have
stayed 1½m, half-sister to smart 1m/1¼m winner King Adam: 7/1 and green, fifth to
Chief Scout in maiden at Newmarket, slowly away but some late headway: likely to
improve. *M. P. Tregoning*

WARBRECK 3 ch.g. Selkirk (USA) 129 – Wigging 96 (Warning 136) [2004 7d 8.1g **58**
8.1s p8m⁵ p12g f12g* Dec 11] strong, compact gelding: modest performer: won maiden
at Southwell: stays 1½m: acts on all-weather: blinkered after second start. *C. R. Egerton*

WARDEN COMPLEX 3 b.g. Compton Place 125 – Miss Rimex (IRE) 84 (Ezzoud **96**
(IRE) 126) [2004 75p: p7g³ 6d² 7m* 7m* 7g 7.1m⁵ p7g² Sep 7] smallish, quite good-
topped gelding: useful handicapper: won at Leicester in May and Doncaster (beat Flipando by short head) in June: stays 7f: acts on polytrack, good to firm and good to soft
going: joined C. Shum in Hong Kong. *J. R. Fanshawe*

WARDEN WARREN 6 b.g. Petong 126 – Silver Spell 54 (Aragon 118) [2004 81§: **81 §**
f7g³ f7g⁴ f7g⁶ f7s* f7s f7g f7g* 7.6d 6g 7m⁴ 7f* 7m 7m 7g² 7s 7s p7g p8.6g p7.1g f7g* **a86 §**
p7.1g Dec 31] sparely-made gelding: fairly useful performer: won handicaps at Wolverhampton in February and Southwell in April, minor event at Redcar in June and handicap

at Southwell in December: best around 7f: acts on fibresand, firm and soft going: wears headgear: sometimes slowly away: often races alone (reportedly unsuited by being crowded): unreliable. *Mrs C. A. Dunnett*

WARES HOME (IRE)   3 b.g. Indian Rocket 115 – Pepilin (Coquelin (USA) 121)   **55**
[2004 78: p7g f8g⁶ 8.3s 6m³ 7m⁴ 6g³ 7m³ 6m² 7.2g³ 8f 6f³ 6v f7g f7g² f8g⁵ f7g⁶ Dec 16] tall, close-coupled gelding: modest performer: effective at 6f/7f: acts on fibresand, probably on any turf going: effective visored or not, tried in cheekpieces: sometimes slowly away: has shown signs of temperament. *K. R. Burke*

WARIF (USA)   3 ch.c. Diesis 133 – Alshoowg (USA) (Riverman (USA) 131) [2004   **–**
59?: 9.9v⁵ 10.1g p12g p9.5d Oct 23] compact colt: maiden: well held in 2004, leaving E. O'Neill after third start (blinkered). *M. E. Sowersby*

WARLINGHAM (IRE)   6 b.g. Catrail (USA) 123 – Tadjnama (USA) (Exceller (USA)   **61**
129) [2004 ?, a60: f6g p7g f7g* f7g* f7s⁵ f7s 7g* 7m 7f⁵ 6m 7f⁵ 6m 7m 6m 6g p7.1g p6g   **a68**
p7g f6g⁵ f7g⁴ f8g f8g⁶ Dec 28] strong gelding: fair on all-weather, modest on turf: won seller and handicap at Wolverhampton and minor event at Yarmouth in first half of 2004: stays 7f: acts on all-weather, firm and good to soft going: tried blinkered: tends to carry head awkwardly. *P. Howling*

WARNINGCAMP (GER)   3 b.g. Lando (GER) 128 – Wilette (GER) (Top Ville 129)   **77**
[2004 10g⁴ 9.9g⁶ 10m³ 8.2g Aug 18] €45,000Y, resold 34,000Y: leggy gelding: half-brother to several winners in Germany, including 1m/9f winner Winning Great (by Great Lakes): dam German 2-y-o 6f winner: fair maiden: tailed off in handicap final start: stays 1¼m. *Lady Herries*

WAR OWL (USA)   7 gr.g. Linamix (FR) 127 – Ganasheba (USA) (Alysheba (USA))   **77**
[2004 59: f8g² p10g p10g* 10.2g* 10.9d³ 10.5d⁵ 10s 10m* 10.3g 10.3g 9.2d⁴ 10g Sep 15] lengthy gelding: fair handicapper: won at Lingfield, Bath and Windsor in first half of 2004: effective at 1m to 11f: acts on all-weather, heavy and good to firm going: often tongue tied in 2002: often slowly away: takes strong hold, and usually held up. *Ian Williams*

WAR PENNANT   2 b.g. (Apr 9) Selkirk (USA) 129 – Bunting 102 (Shaadi (USA)   **–**
126) [2004 8.3m⁶ p8.6g Oct 16] well held in maidens at Windsor (carried head high) and Wolverhampton. *M. R. Channon*

WARRAD (USA)   3 b.c. Kingmambo (USA) 125 – Shalimar Garden (IRE) 89 (Caer-   **93**
leon (USA) 132) [2004 90p: 8.1d⁴ p8g³ 9.9m⁵ 9s³ Aug 27] close-coupled colt: fairly useful performer: good efforts last 3 starts, 6½ lengths third to Exterior in handicap at Goodwood final one: stays easy 1¼m: acts on polytrack, soft and good to firm going: sent to Bahrain. *G. A. Butler*

WARREN PLACE   4 ch.g. Presidium 124 – Coney Hills 35 (Beverley Boy 99) [2004   **–**
–: f8m 6m 5d 5g f7g Dec 1] leggy, sparely-made gelding: maiden: little form at 4 yrs: tried blinkered/visored. *J. Hetherton*

WARRSAN (IRE)   6 b.h. Caerleon (USA) 132 – Lucayan Princess 111 (High   **127**
Line 125) [2004 121: 12m⁵ 12m³ 12m* 10d² 12m 12d* 12m 12f 12m Dec 12]
Compared with their forebears, racehorses have a pretty straightforward time of it travelling to international meetings. In a celebrated case a hundred years ago, well before thoroughbreds could be transported by air, outstanding three-year-old filly Pretty Polly lost her unbeaten record in the Prix du Conseil Municipal at Longchamp, her sixteenth career start. Her journey from England was first delayed at Folkestone by a storm, after which she still had a bad cross-Channel boat trip, followed by spending much longer than necessary in a private train on the way to Paris, repeatedly shunted into sidings to let other trains through. Nowadays, some challengers for Longchamp's big races from Newmarket are put on to a plane at Cambridge Airport, for example, as were Warrsan and stable-companion Var on Arc weekend. Modern methods of transport do not mean that thoroughbreds necessarily race more often than their predecessors, but it does lead to some covering distances unimaginable to trainers of an earlier era. Warrsan provides a good example of the way the modern-day thoroughbred can flit from continent to continent to contest Group 1 events. In a campaign running from March to December, he contested eight Group 1s in six countries (Dubai, Britain, Germany, France, Japan and Hong Kong) and notched up air miles that would be the envy of some businessmen, over 28,000 on the clock during the year to be precise. Warrsan did not reproduce his best form on every occasion, particularly on his last three starts, but when he was at the top of his game—in mid-season—he won two major

races, the Coronation Cup and Grosser Preis von Baden, and finished a close second in another, the Coral-Eclipse. Warrsan has improved every year he has raced and his earnings now stand at over £1m, so all credit to his connections, particularly to his veteran trainer, for pursuing such an adventurous policy.

Warrsan's form as a five-year-old, highlighted by a victory in the Coronation Cup, gave him a reasonable chance on his reappearance in the Dubai Sheema Classic at Nad Al Sheba where he ran creditably to be fifth to Polish Summer, making the running and keeping on. Another defeat followed in the Jockey Club Stakes at Newmarket in May, when he had to give weight all round and battled on stoutly for third to Gamut, after again attempting to make all. Clive Brittain's horses were not in top form at this stage of the season, and things were not going much better a month later when Warrsan started joint-fourth favourite at 7/1 to win a second successive Vodafone Coronation Cup at Epsom, a feat last achieved by Triptych in 1988. In a stronger renewal than in 2003, the favourite was High Accolade from another four-year-old Doyen, and French-trained filly Vallee Enchantee. Neither Doyen nor Vallee Enchantee enjoyed a clear passage, but Warrsan still had to put up an improved performance to gain the day. After losing his place five furlongs out, he was being scrubbed along with plenty to do at Tattenham Corner but, switched to the outside, made relentless progress to forge ahead inside the final furlong, keeping on tenaciously to hold Doyen by a length and three quarters.

Never one to let his horses rest on their laurels, Brittain next sent Warrsan for the Coral-Eclipse Stakes at Sandown. Throughout his career Warrsan had looked as though a mile and a half was a minimum for him; he had not been raced over a mile and a quarter since his debut in May 2001, and he had contested the Gold Cup over two and a half miles in 2002. Taking on horses such as Rakti, Powerscourt, Ikhtyar and Refuse To Bend, was a tall order but Warrsan proved well up to the task, coming from some way back to challenge Refuse To Bend in the final furlong and losing out only after a tremendous battle. The margin was only a head, with the first two four lengths clear. Warrsan's rider Darryll Holland was suspended for a day for causing interference to Salford City, who in turn badly hampered third-placed Kalaman. Some observers doubted the value of the form, due to Warrsan's proximity to the winner, but the performance represented the best run of Warrsan's life, one repeated in the Grosser Volkswagen Preis von Baden in September after a below-form effort in the King George VI and Queen Elizabeth Stakes at Ascot (it may be significant that Refuse To Bend also ran below form in the Sussex Stakes on his next start after the Eclipse). Mubtaker, winner of the Geof-

Vodafone Coronation Cup, Epsom—
Warrsan becomes the first since Triptych to win the race for the second year in succession;
Doyen (No.2), Vallee Enchantee, finishing best of all, and High Accolade (No.4) are next

Grosser Volkswagen Preis von Baden, Baden-Baden—Warrsan beats the home-trained pair Egerton (right) and Shirocco, giving Australian rider Kerrin McEvoy his first Group 1 success in Europe

frey Freer Stakes on his comeback, was odds on in a field of eleven at Baden-Baden ahead of Deutsches Derby winner Shirocco, Grand Prix de Saint-Cloud winner Gamut, Malinas, placed in the Deutsches Derby and Rheinland-Pokal, and Warrsan. Not all of the market leaders ran to form, but Warrsan still had to be at his best to win by a neck from Egerton. Staying on under pressure after being forced wide on the home turn, Warrsan led a furlong out before edging left close home; Shirocco was third, Gamut fifth and Mubtaker seventh. This victory suggested Warrsan would play a prominent role in international races in the autumn but he fluffed his lines in the Prix de l'Arc de Triomphe (ninth to Bago, though hampered in the early stages) and was then down the field in the Japan Cup (last but one to Zenno Rob Roy) and the Hong Kong Vase (ninth to Phoenix Reach), in hindsight almost certainly past his best for the season on the last two occasions.

Warrsan (IRE) (b.h. 1998)	Caerleon (USA) (b 1980)	Nijinsky (b 1967)	Northern Dancer
			Flaming Page
		Foreseer (b or br 1969)	Round Table
			Regal Gleam
	Lucayan Princess (b 1983)	High Line (ch 1966)	High Cat
			Time Call
		Gay France (b 1976)	Sir Gaylord
			Sweet And Lovely II

Warrsan's pedigree was dealt with in *Racehorses of 2003*, but it is worth singing the praises again of his dam Lucayan Princess. Her record is arguably as good as that of any broodmare in the last thirty years, with a smart filly in Cloud Castle (dam of pattern-placed French three-year-old Reverie Solitaire) and three colts—Needle Gun, Luso and Warrsan—who have earned more than £3m between them. Warrsan is now the best of the bunch, just ahead of Luso. The records of the three colts indicate a degree of toughness rare in modern racehorses, with respective tallies of thirty-six starts, thirty-five starts and thirty-five starts again. The final figure is set to increase with Warrsan staying in training, presumably with the aim in the first part of the season of landing a third Coronation Cup, something which has not been achieved before—besides the aforementioned Triptych, the only other dual winners of the race, instituted in 1902, have been Pretty Polly in 1905 and 1906, The White Knight in the next two years and Petite Etoile in 1960 and 1961. Provided Warrsan regains his form after a winter's rest, he will not be easy to beat at Epsom, or anywhere else for that matter, given his reliability and gameness, not to mention tactical adaptability. He is effective on firm and soft going, and he has not encountered heavy. It is to be supposed that he will eventually find a place at stud, although given modern fashions in bloodstock circles there is no certainty that the neat Warrsan will attract enough attention to find a better role than either Needle Gun or Luso, both of whom are jumps sires. That, though, is at least one season ahead. In the meantime, the racing public should make the most of a horse who represents so much that is admirable in the thoroughbred. *C. E. Brittain*

WASALAT (USA)   2 b.f. (Jan 27) Bahri (USA) 125 – Saabga (USA) 83 (Woodman (USA) 126) [2004 6m⁴ 6d² 6m³ 7m² 7f 7s⁶ Aug 20] smallish, strong filly: fourth foal: half-sister to 7f (at 2 yrs) and 8.5f winner Jazmeer (by Sabrehill) and 3-y-o Sabbaag: dam, second at 7f at 2 yrs (only outing), half-sister to smart middle-distance performers Close Conflict and Newton's Law out of unraced sister to Secreto: fair maiden: well below form last 2 outings, starting very slowly on first occasion: will stay 1m: acts on good to firm going. *M. R. Channon*   **76**

WASHBROOK   3 b.g. Royal Applause 124 – Alacrity 62 (Alzao (USA) 117) [2004 64: 8.2s 8.3m 7f³ 7g 8m 7.2s Oct 12] good-topped gelding: modest maiden: stays 7f: acts on firm going: tongue tied (ran poorly) final outing: refused to enter stall intended fourth start: sold 1,600 gns, joined M. Hammond. *Andrew Turnell*   **60**

WASHINGTON PINK (IRE)   5 b.g. Tagula (IRE) 116 – Little Red Rose (Precocious 126) [2004 –: 12v 9.9d 14.4v⁴ 12d 13.9m 16m Jul 5] strong, close-coupled gelding: poor performer: stays 14.4f: acts on heavy and good to firm going: tried in cheekpieces. *C. Grant*   **42**

WASTED TALENT (IRE)   4 b.f. Sesaro (USA) 81 – Miss Garuda 94 (Persian Bold 123) [2004 81, a66: 11.7g* 12.1g² 20f 12g 12g⁴ Sep 22] angular filly: fairly useful on turf, fair when last seen on all-weather: dead-heated in handicap at Bath in April: good second in similar event at Chester following month, best effort after: stays 1½m: acts on all-weather and firm going: usually wears cheekpieces/visor: front runner. *J. G. Portman*   **84 a?**

WATAMU (IRE)   3 b.c. Groom Dancer (USA) 128 – Miss Golden Sands 80 (Kris 135) [2004 84p: 8g 9v 11g* 12g² 12d⁶ 9.9m³ 9.9g⁵ Aug 14] strong, lengthy colt: fairly useful handicapper: won at Goodwood in May by 1¼ lengths from Mystical Girl: at least respectable efforts after, in visor last 2 starts: stays 1½m: acts on good to firm and good to soft going: has runs in snatches. *P. J. Makin*   **92**

WATCHFUL WITNESS   4 ch.c. In The Wings 128 – Eternal (Kris 135) [2004 14.1s³ 11.9m⁴ 11.6f p16g Jul 24] 8,500 3-y-o: sixth foal: half-brother to 3 winners, including 1¼m to 1½m winner Wadi (by Green Desert) and 2000 2-y-o 7f winner Never End (by Alzao), both fairly useful: dam, ran once, half-sister to Derby winner Quest For Fame: winning hurdler: lightly-raced maiden on Flat: stays 1¾m: visored final start. *Dr J. R. J. Naylor*   **60**

WATCHING   7 ch.g. Indian Ridge 123 – Sweeping 104 (Indian King (USA) 128) [2004 101d: 7g³ 6g 5s² 5m⁵ 5m⁵ 6m 5d 5d 7f 6d² 6s³ 7.2s³ 7g Oct 9] neat gelding: fairly useful handicapper: left D. Nicholls after eighth start: creditable efforts after when placed at York, Goodwood and Ayr: effective at 5f to 7f: acts on heavy and good to firm going: tried in cheekpieces/visor at 6 yrs: sometimes early to post. *R. A. Fahey*   **90**

WATCHMYEYES (IRE)   2 ch.g. (Feb 4) Bold Fact (USA) 116 – Shadow Smile (IRE) 74 (Slip Anchor 136) [2004 5.7m⁶ 7m⁴ 6.1d⁴ 7m² p8.6g* p8.6g* Oct 9] €8,000F, €11,000Y, 21,000 2-y-o: third foal: dam second at 1¼m in Ireland from 3 starts: fairly useful performer: won maiden (hung right) and minor event (cheekpieces, produced late) at Wolverhampton in October: likely to stay 1¼m: acts on polytrack and good to firm going: tends to take good hold/carry head bit high. *N. P. Littmoden*   **85**

WATERFRONT DANCER   2 b.g. (Mar 2) Groom Dancer (USA) 128 – Azula 80 (Bluebird (USA) 125) [2004 5.1g 5m p5.1g 6g Oct 11] little sign of ability in maidens/minor event. *J. R. Best*   **–**

WATERLINE BLUE (IRE) 3 b.g. Mujadil (USA) 119 – Blues Queen 85 (Lahib   –
(USA) 129) [2004 86: 7m⁵ p6g May 26] workmanlike gelding: fairly useful at 2 yrs:
tongue tied, well below that form in 2004: tried visored. *P. D. Evans*

WATERLINE DANCER (IRE) 4 b. or br.f. Danehill Dancer (IRE) 117 – Thrill   39
Seeker (IRE) (Treasure Kay 114) [2004 59: p10g p8g p7g f8.5s f7g⁴ 7v May 10] leggy
filly: poor performer: stays easy 1m: acts on all-weather, firm and good to soft going:
tongue tied: usually visored. *P. D. Evans*

WATERLINE LOVER 2 ch.f. (Apr 11) Efisio 120 – Food of Love 109 (Music Boy   53
124) [2004 5g⁶ 5g 5s 6g⁴ 6g 6.1m⁶ 5g⁴ 5.1g Oct 10] 18,000Y: close-coupled filly: half-
sister to 3 winners, including 5-y-o Tough Love and fairly useful 5f winner (including at
2 yrs) Price of Passion (by Dolphin Street): dam 5f winner, including at 2 yrs: modest
maiden: stays 6f: acts on good to firm going: visored (ran poorly) final start. *P. D. Evans*

WATERLINE SPIRIT 4 b.g. Piccolo 121 – Gina of Hithermoor (Reprimand 122)   §§
[2004 §§: 11.7g 16f Jul 29] ungenuine maiden. *P. D. Evans*

WATERLOO CORNER 2 b.g. (Mar 27) Cayman Kai (IRE) 114 – Rasin Luck   69
(Primitive Rising 113) [2004 7s p8.6g⁶ f7g² Dec 12] first reported foal: dam poor
maiden hurdler: fair form in maidens: stays 8.6f: acts on all-weather. *R. Craggs*

WATER OF LIFE (IRE) 5 b.m. Dr Devious (IRE) 127 – Simulcast (Generous (IRE)   43
139) [2004 63d: p10g p10g Jan 28] well-made mare: poor performer nowadays: stays
easy 1½m: acts on soft going, good to firm and all-weather: tried tongue tied: none too
genuine. *J. R. Boyle*

WATERPARK 6 b.m. Namaqualand (USA) – Willisa 67 (Polar Falcon (USA) 126)   70
[2004 54: 6.1s 7v* f8g 8f² Jun 15] leggy mare: fair handicapper: won at Redcar in May:
effective at 7f/1m: acts on fibresand and any turf going: tried visored at 3 yrs: usually
races prominently. *R. Craggs*

WATER PISTOL 2 b.g. (Feb 22) Double Trigger (IRE) 123 – Water Flower 79   69
(Environment Friend 128) [2004 7g 8.1g 8g⁶ 7s Oct 22] 24,000Y: leggy gelding: first
foal: dam, 1½m winner (also successful over hurdles), half-sister to smart 1m winner who
seemed to stay 14.6f Eco Friendly: fair maiden: will be suited by 1½m+. *Mrs A. J. Perrett*

WATERSHIP CRYSTAL (IRE) 3 b.f. Sadler's Wells (USA) 132 – Crystal Spray 75   –
(Beldale Flutter (USA) 130) [2004 –p: 10m Jun 10] rather lengthy, good-topped filly: has
a round action: soundly beaten in maidens 7 months apart: sent to USA. *J. H. M. Gosden*

WATERSHIP DOWN (IRE) 7 b.g. Dolphin Street – Persian Myth (Persian   –
Bold 123) [2004 14.1m 12f Jun 25] lightly raced and little sign of ability on Flat: tried
blinkered: modest chaser. *B. G. Powell*

WATERSIDE (IRE) 5 b.g. Lake Coniston (IRE) 131 – Classic Ring (IRE) 50 (Auction   90
Ring (USA) 123) [2004 79+, a92: 6s 5.7g 6.1v³ 6.1s p6g³ 7m* 7.1m* 7d² 6g⁴ 7.6m⁶ 7f
7d³ 7s* 7.1g 7g Sep 30] strong gelding: has a round action: fairly useful performer: won
minor event at Folkestone (first start since leaving J. Hills) and handicap at Sandown in
June and minor event at Goodwood (beat Idle Power by 7 lengths) in August: stays 7f:
acts on polytrack, heavy and good to firm going: tried tongue tied: sometimes slowly
away: races up with pace. *G. L. Moore*

WATER TAXI 3 ch.g. Zafonic (USA) 130 – Trellis Bay 100 (Sadler's Wells (USA)   77
132) [2004 12s⁴ 12m³ 12.6m³ Jun 14] first foal: dam, 1½m winner who stayed 2m, half-
sister to Irish Oaks winner Wemyss Bight: fair form in maidens: should stay 1¾m: sold
28,000 gns, then gelded. *R. Charlton*

WAVERLEY ROAD 7 ch.g. Pelder (IRE) 125 – Lillicara (FR) (Caracolero (USA)   ?
131) [2004 55, a53: p12g p16g⁴ Apr 27] leggy gelding: poor maiden: stays 2m: acts on   a39
soft going, good to firm and polytrack: tried visored. *M. Madgwick*

WAVERTREE GIRL (IRE) 3 b.f. Marju (IRE) 127 – Lust (Pursuit of Love 124)   71
[2004 93: p7g³ p8g 7.5s⁵ 7m 6f⁴ 6d³ p7g 6g Aug 11] tall, leggy filly: just fair maiden at 3
yrs: should stay 1m: acts on polytrack, good to firm and good to soft going: blinkered last
3 starts: sometimes slowly away: has shown signs of temperament: sold 42,000 gns in
December. *N. P. Littmoden*

WAVERTREE SPIRIT 3 ch.g. Hector Protector (USA) 124 – Miss Clarinet (Pharly   –
(FR) 130) [2004 –p: 10m⁶ May 21] compact gelding: well held in maidens 8½ months
apart. *N. P. Littmoden*

WAVERTREE WARRIOR (IRE) 2 br.c. (May 15) Indian Lodge (IRE) 127 –   78
Karamana (Habitat 134) [2004 6m 6g³ 6g² 6.3g 7d³ 8s Oct 22] 30,000Y: leggy colt: half-

brother to several winners, including 10-y-o Proud Native and useful Irish performer up to 1½m Karikata (by Doyoun): dam unraced: fair maiden: should stay 1m: acts on good to soft ground: in cheekpieces final start. *N. P. Littmoden*

WAVET   4 b.f. Pursuit of Love 124 – Ballerina Bay 75 (Myjinski (USA)) [2004 53: p10g   **50** f8g² p8.6g Nov 15] lengthy filly: modest maiden, lightly raced: probably stays 1½m: acts on fibresand. *J. Pearce*

WAY OUT   3 b.f. Robellino (USA) 127 – Exit 82 (Exbourne (USA) 125) [2004 8.1m   **–** 8.1g Jul 1] smallish filly: first foal: dam, 8.5f winner, half-sister to dam of smart 1998 2-y-o 7f winner Auction House: well held in maidens. *B. P. J. Baugh*

WAYWARD MELODY   4 b.f. Merdon Melody 98 – Dubitable 59 (Formidable (USA)   **–** 125) [2004 –: p12g⁴ Apr 27] lightly-raced maiden: tried visored/blinkered: modest hurdler, successful in May. *G. L. Moore*

WAYWARD SHOT (IRE)   2 b.g. (Mar 26) Desert Prince (IRE) 130 – Style Parade   **60** (USA) 78 (Diesis 133) [2004 5g⁵ 5m 5d 7m⁵ 7s⁴ Oct 16] lengthy gelding: modest maiden: stays 7f: acts on soft and good to firm going. *M. W. Easterby*

WAZIRI (IRE)   3 b.g. Mtoto 134 – Euphorie (GER) (Feenpark (GER) 115) [2004 71:   **78** 9.9g* 10.1g 14m 9d³ 10d 8.1s 10g Oct 12] close-coupled gelding: fair handicapper: won at Goodwood in June: stays 1¼m: acts on polytrack and good to soft going: visored final start: sometimes races freely: none too consistent. *H. Morrison*

WAZIR (USA)   2 b. or br.c. (Feb 21) Pulpit (USA) 117 – Top Order (USA) 94 (Dayjur   **90** (USA) 137) [2004 p6g² 6m* Sep 12] first foal: dam, 5f (at 2 yrs) and 6.5f (in USA) winner, closely related to top-class sprinter Mozart: 5 lengths second to Afrashad in maiden at Lingfield, slowly away: didn't need to run to that form to land odds in similar event at Goodwood, rallying to lead again near line: will stay 7f. *J. H. M. Gosden*

WEAKEST LINK   3 b.g. Mind Games 121 – Sky Music 85 (Absalom 128) [2004 –p: **50** f7g² f6g³ f7g³ p7g 6g 8.5m 6g⁴ f7g⁴ Dec 11] useful-looking gelding: modest maiden: left   **a57** W. Jarvis after fourth start: stays 7f: best form on fibresand. *E. J. Alston*

WEAVER OF DREAMS (IRE)   4 b.g. Victory Note (USA) 120 – Daziyra (IRE)   **–** (Doyoun 124) [2004 –: 12.4v Apr 3] good-topped gelding: little form. *G. A. Swinbank*

WEAVER SPELL   3 b.g. Wizard King 122 – Impy Fox (IRE) 53 (Imp Society (USA))   **32** [2004 37: f6g⁵ f7m⁶ 8.2s⁴ 12m 13.8m 10g Oct 11] leggy gelding: poor maiden: probably stays 1m: visored last 2 starts. *J. R. Norton*

WEBBINGTON LASS (IRE)   3 b.f. Petardia 113 – Richardstown Lass (IRE) (Mus-   **–** catite 122) [2004 –: p10g 7.1s 6.1d Aug 19] lengthy filly: little form: tried visored. *Dr J. R. J. Naylor*

WEBBSWOOD LAD (IRE)   3 b.g. Robellino (USA) 127 – Poleaxe (Selkirk (USA)   **71** 129) [2004 p8g³ p8g² Jan 28] 4,000Y: third foal: dam, ran twice, out of half-sister to Kris and Diesis: fair form in maidens at Lingfield: gelded after. *Mrs Stef Liddiard*

WEB RACER (IRE)   2 b.f. (Apr 19) Bold Fact (USA) 116 – Sky Lover (Ela-Mana-   **38** Mou 132) [2004 6f⁵ 7f f7d Jul 23] €2,200M, 3,000Y: lightly-made filly: seventh foal: half-sister to several winners, including useful 1999 2-y-o 6f winner (later won at 5.5f in USA) Royal Highlander (by Foxhound) and fairly useful Irish 11f/1½m winner Rainbow Warrior (by Imperial Frontier): dam Irish 2-y-o 5f winner: poor form in maidens/seller: blinkered final start. *J. R. Weymes*

WEBSTER   2 b.g. (Mar 4) Kingsinger (IRE) 94 – Worsted 70 (Whittingham (IRE) 104)   **63 p** [2004 p7m⁵ Dec 22] first foal: dam, sprint maiden, sister to 5-y-o Artie: 50/1, fifth to Resplendent Prince in maiden at Lingfield: should improve. *M. Blanshard*

WEDDING CAKE (IRE)   3 ch.f. Groom Dancer (USA) 128 – Greektown (Ela-   **71** Mana-Mou 132) [2004 8.3d 10.2f³ 11.5g⁴ p12g* 11g Sep 22] sister to useful 7f (at 2 yrs)/ 1¼m winner Athens Belle, closely related to 2 winners by Rainbow Quest, notably smart 1¼m/13f winner Multicoloured, and half-sister to 5-y-o Gamut: dam, French 1¼m/1½m winner, half-sister to Prix du Cadran winner Sought Out (dam of Derby winner North Light) and to grandam of Golan: fair performer: won maiden at Lingfield in September: should stay 1¾m: acts on polytrack and firm going. *Sir Michael Stoute*

WEDDING PARTY   2 ch.f. (Mar 18) Groom Dancer (USA) 128 – Ceanothus (IRE)   **91** 61 (Bluebird (USA) 125) [2004 6g³ p6d* p7g⁴ 7g* 7v² Oct 23] strong, lengthy filly: fourth foal: half-sister to 5-y-o Prince Hector and 3-y-o Competitor: dam, maiden who stayed 1½m, half-sister to smart performers Golden Wells (9f/1¼m winner) and Golden Pond (US Grade 2 1½m winner): fairly useful performer: won maiden at Lingfield in

August and nursery at Newmarket (beat Love Affair by 1¼ lengths) in October: good 2 lengths second to Bibury Flyer in listed event at Newbury: will stay 1m: acts on polytrack and heavy going. *Mrs A. J. Perrett*

WEDLOCK 2 b.c. (Mar 21) Pursuit of Love 124 – Promise Fulfilled (USA) 90 (Bet **57** Twice (USA)) [2004 6d⁴ 6m 6g Jun 24] best effort in maidens when fourth at Haydock: should stay 1m. *T. D. Easterby*

WEDOWANNAGIVEUTHAT (IRE) 3 b.f. Desert Prince (IRE) 130 – Mimansa **–** (USA) (El Gran Senor (USA) 136) [2004 8g 7g 7.5m⁶ 9.9g f8g 8m Jul 23] IR 9,500F, €10,000Y: lengthy, quite good-topped filly: fourth foal: dam French 13f winner: little form. *T. D. Easterby*

WEECANDOO (IRE) 6 b.m. Turtle Island (IRE) 123 – Romantic Air 62 (He Loves **82** Me 120) [2004 97?, a72: 10d 10m 10.3f⁵ 10.1g 12m 10d 10s⁶ p9.5g² p10g p9.5g* p9.5g² **a86** Dec 15] workmanlike mare: fairly useful performer: won handicap at Wolverhampton in December: stays 1¼m: acts on all-weather and firm going: sometimes sweating and edgy. *C. N. Allen*

WEE DINNS (IRE) 3 b.f. Marju (IRE) 127 – Tir-An-Oir (IRE) (Law Society (USA) **92** 130) [2004 67: 10g 8.2s⁵ 10f² 10m² 10m* 9g² 9.9g⁶ 10.1s⁶ Aug 24] strong, close-coupled filly: fairly useful handicapper: won at Newbury in July: ½-length second to Diamond Lodge at Goodwood, best effort after: stays 1¼m: acts on firm going: waited with. *S. Kirk*

WEET A HEAD (IRE) 3 b.c. Foxhound (USA) 103 – Morale (Bluebird (USA) 125) **81** [2004 87: f9.4s⁵ 10.5s³ 10s⁵ 10.4s⁶ 8m³ 8m⁴ 10.3g⁶ 8.1g 8d 11.8g³ Oct 12] quite good-topped colt: fairly useful performer: best effort at 3 yrs when third to Mystic Man in minor event at Doncaster fifth start: stays 10.6f: acts on fibresand, firm and soft going. *R. Hollinshead*

WEET AN HAUL 3 b.g. Danzero (AUS) – Island Ruler 79 (Ile de Bourbon (USA) **53** 133) [2004 58: 6m f8.5g 8m³ p8.6d f8g⁵ f7g Dec 14] sturdy gelding: modest performer: stays 1m: acts on fibresand and good to firm going: visored last 4 starts. *P. A. Blockley*

WEET AN STORE (IRE) 3 gr.c. Spectrum (IRE) 126 – Karmisymixa (FR) (Linamix **–** (FR) 127) [2004 –: 12.1g Jun 17] tailed off in maidens: tongue tied last 2 starts. *R. Hollinshead*

WEET FOR ME 8 b.g. Warning 136 – Naswara (USA) 88 (Al Nasr (FR) 126) [2004 **83** 13.9s 16m 15.9g² 14.8g⁶ 14g⁵ 13.9m⁶ 14.1d 14.1d p13.9g² p13.9g² p16.5g Dec 3] big gelding: fairly useful handicapper: missed 2002/3: reportedly finished lame final outing: stays 2m: acts on all-weather, firm and soft going: wore cheekpieces last 3 starts: front runner. *R. Hollinshead*

WEET N MEASURES 2 b.c. (May 8) Weet-A-Minute (IRE) 106 – Weet Ees Girl **55** (IRE) 75 (Common Grounds 118) [2004 5s⁵ f6s⁵ p6g Nov 8] modest form in claimers/ maiden: not sure to stay much beyond 6f. *R. Hollinshead*

WEET WATCHERS 4 b.g. Polar Prince (IRE) 117 – Weet Ees Girl (IRE) 75 (Com- **69** mon Grounds 118) [2004 75: f7g* f7g⁶ f7s⁴ 8.5d³ 7m 7m⁵ 6m* 7.5g 7g p6d f5m Nov 22] rather leggy, workmanlike gelding: fair performer: won sellers at Southwell in February and, having left P. Blockley after fourth start, Ripon in June: stays 7f: acts on fibresand, soft and good to firm going: wore cheekpieces final start: usually races prominently. *P. A. Blockley*

WEET YER TERN (IRE) 2 b.c. (Apr 3) Brave Act 119 – Maxime (IRE) 60 (Mac's **68** Imp (USA) 116) [2004 5.1g⁴ 5.3m² f6g⁴ Jun 11] €35,000Y: tall colt: on weak side at 2 yrs: second foal: dam, sprint maiden, half-sister to useful winner up to 1½m Weet-A-Minute: fair form in maidens: best effort on debut: likely to prove best at 5f/6f. *P. A. Blockley*

WEIR'S ANNIE 3 b.f. Puissance 110 – Hyde Princess 75 (Touch Paper 113) [2004 **–** 6.1s 5.1m 5.1g Jun 2] 17,000Y: neat filly: sister to fairly useful 5f winner (including at 2 yrs) Angie Baby and half-sister to 3 winners, including 5f winner Pop The Cork (by Clan-time): dam sprinter: well held in maidens, weakening each time. *H. Candy*

WEKIWA SPRINGS (FR) 7 gr.g. Kendor (FR) 122 – Ti Mamaille (FR) (Dom Racine **–** (FR) 121) [2004 f8.5g⁶ Jan 19] big, good-topped gelding: lightly raced and little form since 2001, well held in claimer at Wolverhampton (tongue tied) only start at 7 yrs: tried visored. *Thomas Carberry, Ireland*

WELCOME ARCHIE 4 ch.g. Most Welcome 131 – Indefinite Article (IRE) (Indian **29** Ridge 123) [2004 8g 6v 7.5m 8m Jul 5] well beaten in bumper: poor form in sellers/ claimers. *J. S. Haldane*

WELCOME BACK   7 ch.g. Most Welcome 131 – Villavina 59 (Top Ville 129) [2004   **36**
38: f14.8g³ Jan 3] leggy gelding: poor performer: stayed 2m: acted on fibresand, firm and
good to soft going: dead. *K. A. Ryan*

WELCOME DREAM   2 ch.f. (Feb 14) Most Welcome 131 – Sweet Dreams 85 (Sel-   **45**
kirk (USA) 129) [2004 5d f7m Jul 6] strong filly: third foal: dam 1m winner: poor form in
maidens. *Mrs A. Duffield*

WELCOME SIGNAL   4 ch.g. Most Welcome 131 – Glenfinlass (Lomond (USA)   **81**
128) [2004 72+: p10d 8m⁵ 10g⁵ 10f 7s³ 7m² 8g² Oct 10] fairly useful maiden: good
second in handicaps at Leicester and Bath last 2 starts: effective at 7f to 1¼m: acts on
polytrack, soft and good to firm going: wore cheekpieces last 5 starts: sold 17,000 gns,
joined M. Al Kurdi in UAE. *J. R. Fanshawe*

WELCOME STRANGER   4 b.g. Most Welcome 131 – Just Julia (Natroun (FR)   **108**
128) [2004 86: 8.3d 8g 10f 7.6g² 8m* 8m² 8m* 8m² 8f 8m* 7.9g Oct 8] leggy gelding:
useful performer: won handicap at Yarmouth in June, minor event at Kempton in July and
handicap at Ascot (best effort, beat Thajja by 2 lengths) in September: stays 1m: acts on
polytrack and good to firm going: sometimes slowly away (reared leaving stall eighth
outing). *J. M. P. Eustace*

WELKINO'S BOY   3 ch.g. Most Welcome 131 – Khadino (Relkino 131) [2004 10.3m   **67**
12m⁵ 10m⁶ 14.1m³ 14.4s³ 13.9g Oct 9] good-topped gelding: brother to 5-y-o Duelling
Banjos and winner up to 1½m in Norway, and half-brother to 3 winners by Komaite,
including fairly useful 7.6f to 1¼m winner Mr Teigh: dam no form: fair maiden: stays
14.4f: acts on good to soft and good to firm going: raced too freely final start. *J. Mackie*

WELL CONNECTED (IRE)   4 b.g. Among Men (USA) 124 – Wire To Wire (Welsh   **–**
Saint 126) [2004 57: 9.3g 7.9m Sep 11] tall gelding: headstrong maiden: well held in
2004. *B. Smart*

WELL ESTABLISHED (IRE)   2 b.c. (Feb 22) Sadler's Wells (USA) 132 – Riveryev   **73 p**
(USA) Irish River (FR) 131) [2004 8d⁶ Oct 15] 210,000Y: sturdy colt: brother to French
11.5f winner Lady Wells, closely related to useful French 1m (at 2 yrs) to 13f winner
Okabango (by Unfuwain), and half-brother to several winners, including useful French
1996 2-y-o 5.5f and 7f (Prix du Calvados) winner Shigeru Summit (by Be My Chief):
dam French maiden: 16/1, sixth to Proclamation in maiden at Newmarket, slowly away
and some late headway: will be suited by 1¼m/1½m: should improve. *M. A. Jarvis*

WELLINGTON HALL (GER)   6 b.g. Halling (USA) 133 – Wells Whisper (FR) 71   **80**
(Sadler's Wells (USA) 132) [2004 55: 11.5m* 11.9m 10f* 12.6g³ 11.5g⁵ 10.3s* Oct 22]
fairly useful handicapper: won at Yarmouth in April, Newmarket in August and Doncaster (apprentices), in October: effective at 1¼m to 1¾m: acts on any going: usually wore
headgear before 2004. *P. W. Chapple-Hyam*

WELL KNIT   3 b.f. Robellino (USA) 127 – Wydah (Suave Dancer (USA) 136) [2004   **?**
p8g p7g 8g 7d 10s 11.5m 7g³ 12g 8g⁴ 12g⁴ 8g 8g Oct 17] 3,500Y: small, quite good-
topped filly: first foal: dam unraced daughter of Pretty Polly Stakes winner Calandra,
herself half-sister to Oaks winner Intrepidity: winner in Czech Republic at 2 yrs, and
returned there after well held for P. D'Arcy first 6 starts in 2004. *V. Chaloupka, Czech
Republic*

WELL KNOWN   3 b.f. Sadler's Wells (USA) 132 – Danefair 109 (Danehill (USA)   **80**
126) [2004 86P: 9.9g* 12f 9.9g Aug 11] compact filly: very promising second in minor
event at Kempton only 2-y-o outing: fairly useful form when winning maiden at Salisbury (reluctant to post, beat Anna Pallida eased by a head) in May: pulled hard and
dropped away quickly in listed events last 2 starts: not sure to stay much further than
1¼m: raced only on good going or firmer: sold 82,000 gns in December. *R. Charlton*

WE'LL MEET AGAIN   4 ch.g. Bin Ajwaad (IRE) 119 – Tantalizing Song (CAN)   **60**
(The Minstrel (CAN) 135) [2004 61: 7.9f³ 7.5d 8.1f⁴ 10m⁵ f8g⁴ Nov 22] well-grown
gelding: has round action: modest handicapper: should stay 1¼m: acts on fibresand, firm
and good to soft going. *M. W. Easterby*

WELSH AND WYLDE (IRE)   4 b.g. Anita's Prince 126 – Waikiki (GER) (Zampano   **–**
(GER)) [2004 56: f12g f16g⁶ Jul 23] maiden: no form in 2004: tried blinkered/in cheekpieces. *B. Palling*

WELSH DREAM   7 b.g. Mtoto 134 – Morgannwg (IRE) 86 (Simply Great (FR) 122)   **41**
[2004 16m⁶ 16f⁶ Jul 29] useful-looking gelding: handicapper: showed little at 7 yrs.
Miss S. E. Forster

WELSH EMPEROR (IRE) 5 b.g. Emperor Jones (USA) 119 – Simply Times **114** (USA) 64 (Dodge (USA)) [2004 113: 6s* 6s⁴ 6d⁶ 6v⁵ 7s² 6g 6d* 6s Oct 29] tall gelding: smart performer: won minor events at Thirsk (by length from Halmahera) in April and Hamilton (beat Cartography 1¾ lengths) in September: mostly creditable efforts in between, particularly when short-head second to Polar Bear in listed event at York and eighth to Tante Rose in Sprint Cup at Haydock: ran poorly in Prix de Seine-et-Oise at Maisons-Laffitte final outing: effective at 6f/7f: raced mainly on good going or softer (acts on heavy) since 2 yrs: blinkered: races up with pace. *T. P. Tate*

WELSH EMPRESS 3 b.f. Bahamian Bounty 116 – Azola (IRE) 63 (Alzao (USA) **51** 117) [2004 53: 8.2g 8m³ 8f 8d 7.1g 7m Sep 25] rather sparely-made filly: modest maiden: stays 1m: acts on good to firm going: sometimes slowly away. *P. L. Gilligan*

WELSH GALAXY (IRE) 2 b.f. Pennekamp (USA) 130 – Jamaiel (IRE) 64 **40** (Polish Precedent (USA) 131) [2004 p7g 8.2g 7.9g 8.1m 6m p8g⁶ Nov 20] €22,000F, 8,000Y: close-coupled filly: first foal: dam, maiden who stayed 1½m, granddaughter of Breeders' Cup Juvenile Fillies' winner Outstandingly: poor maiden: needs to settle to stay beyond 1m: hung badly right third start: blinkered final outing. *P. L. Gilligan*

WELSH MAIN 7 br.g. Zafonic (USA) 130 – Welsh Daylight (Welsh Pageant 132) **–** [2004 14.1d Jul 10] good-topped gelding: useful at best: well below form only start on Flat since 2002: tried visored: fair hurdler. *F. Jordan*

WELSH WHISPER 5 b.m. Overbury (IRE) 116 – Grugiar (Red Sunset 120) [2004 **48** –: f8.5g f8.5g f8.5g⁴ f9.4s f8.5s f7g⁵ f6m⁶ f7g⁶ f6g* f7g³ 6m f6g p7.1g Dec 14] poor performer: won banded race at Wolverhampton in May: best at 6f/7f: acts on fibresand. *S. A. Brookshaw*

WELSH WIND (IRE) 8 b.g. Tenby 125 – Bavaria 80 (Top Ville 129) [2004 82d: **69** p10g³ p10g² f8.5g p10g³ p8g* p12g p10g⁴ 10d p8.6g* Dec 17] strong, lengthy gelding: fair handicapper: won at Lingfield in February: stays easy 1¼m: acts on polytrack, firm and soft going: wore cheekpieces last 5 starts: tongue tied: consistent. *M. Wigham*

WEMBURY POINT (IRE) 2 gr.c. (Apr 16) Monashee Mountain (USA) 115 – Lady **52** Celina (FR) (Crystal Palace (FR) 132) [2004 6g 7g 7.1m 6.9m⁶ 7m 8s p8g⁵ p9.5g² Nov **a62** 15] modest maiden: stays 9.4f: acts on all-weather, soft and good to firm going: visored (looked ungenuine)/blinkered last 2 starts. *B. G. Powell*

WENDY'S GIRL (IRE) 3 b.f. Ashkalani (IRE) 128 – Mrs Evans (IRE) 97 (College **66** Chapel 122) [2004 64: f5s p7g 6d⁵ f7g² f6g f6g 5d⁴ 5g 6.1m* 6s 6m* 5m⁶ 5f⁵ 5d⁵ f5f³ 5.3s³ f5m f6g p5.1g Dec 31] strong, compact filly: fair handicapper: won at Warwick in June and Catterick in July: best at 5f/6f: acts on fibresand, soft and good to firm going: blinkered after seventh start: often races prominently: none too reliable. *R. P. Elliott*

WE'RE STONYBROKE (IRE) 5 b.g. College Chapel 122 – Mokaite 55 (Komaite **59** (USA)) [2004 63: 7s 6f 8g 8v 7g 6d³ 6s⁵ 7v p7g p6m⁴ Dec 22] workmanlike gelding: modest handicapper: ran at Lingfield last 2 starts: stays 6f: acts on polytrack, good to firm and good to soft going: tried blinkered/tongue tied/in cheekpieces. *T. Cooper, Ireland*

WESSEX (USA) 4 ch.g. Gone West (USA) – Satin Velvet (USA) 103 (El Gran Senor **76** (USA) 136) [2004 90: 7d 7m⁶ 8.3m 7.2d 8g⁵ 9.3f 8g 6g p6g³ f7g* Dec 16] big, rather leggy gelding: fair performer: won seller at Southwell (first start since leaving J. Moffatt) in December: stays 1m: acts on all-weather and firm going: tried visored. *P. A. Blockley*

WESTBOROUGH (IRE) 3 ch.g. Woodborough (USA) 112 – Filey Brigg 80 (Weld- **69** naas (USA) 112) [2004 59: 5s² 5f⁵ f7d 6s⁵ 5g² 5f f5d* 5g 6g² 6m 6g* 5d* Oct 11] good-topped gelding: fair performer: won maiden at Catterick and handicap at Ayr in October: best at 5f/6f: acts on firm and soft going: visored (raced too freely) ninth start, tongue tied after. *N. Tinkler*

WESTBROOK BLUE 2 b.c. (Apr 26) Kingsinger (IRE) 94 – Gold And Blue (IRE) **74** (Bluebird (USA) 125) [2004 5g³ f5g* 5.1m³ p5g⁴ 5.1g⁶ Aug 19] 4,000Y: half-brother to several winners, including 6f to 9f winner Blue Star (by Whittingham) and 5f winner Jodeeka (by Fraam), both useful: dam lightly-raced Irish maiden: fair performer: won maiden at Southwell in April: creditable efforts in minor events/nursery after: should stay 6f: acts on all-weather and good to firm going: races prominently. *W. G. M. Turner*

WEST COUNTRY (UAE) 3 br.c. Gone West (USA) – Crystal Gazing (USA) 114 **72 d** (El Gran Senor (USA) 136) [2004 85: a7.5f⁴ a8f³ 7g 6g 11.7f⁴ a6f a7.5f a7.5f Dec 30] leggy, close-coupled colt: fair maiden at best: respectable third at Nad Al Sheba second start: well held after, in Britain (3 times) and back at Nad Al Sheba (off 4½ months, having left M. Johnston): seems to stay 1m: raced only on good ground or firmer on turf. *D. Watson, UAE*

WESTCOURT DREAM 4 ch.f. Bal Harbour 113 – Katie's Kitty 42 (Noble Patri- 57
arch 115) [2004 53: 8f³ 9.9g* 12d 10.4m⁶ 12g 9d Oct 15] workmanlike filly: modest
handicapper: won apprentice event at Beverley in June: stays 1¼m: acts on firm and good
to soft going: none too reliable. *M. W. Easterby*

WEST END WONDER (IRE) 5 b.g. Idris (IRE) 118 – Miss Plum 86 (Ardross 134) –
[2004 10.3m 10f⁴ 11.5m Aug 16] big, good-topped gelding: soundly beaten in maidens.
M. J. Wallace

WESTER LODGE (IRE) 2 ch.c. (Feb 24) Fraam 114 – Reamzafonic 46 (Grand 76
Lodge (USA) 125) [2004 7m 7m² 7s Oct 27] 23,000F, 25,000Y: big, strong colt:
second foal: dam, lightly-raced maiden, half-sister to useful Irish performer up to 9f
Hasanat: best effort in maidens when staying-on second at Newcastle: will stay 1m.
J. M. P. Eustace

WESTERN BLUEBIRD (IRE) 6 b.g. Bluebird (USA) 125 – Arrastra 79 (Bustino 47
136) [2004 16d⁶ 16m⁴ 13.9m 16m² 16m Jul 5] leggy gelding: poor handicapper: unraced
on Flat in 2003: stays easy 2m: acts on fibresand, good to firm and good to soft going:
tried visored, blinkered last 4 starts. *Miss Kate Milligan*

WESTERN COMMAND (GER) 8 b.g. Saddlers' Hall (IRE) 126 – Western Friend –
(USA) (Gone West (USA)) [2004 –, a33: f8g f11g f8g⁴ f12f⁵ f9.4g⁶ f12g⁶ f11g f9.4s⁵ f11s **a45**
f12s f16s⁵ f14g⁵ f14g³ f12g³ f12g⁵ f9.4g f14g⁵ f12g² f12g⁶ f14g f12m f12m⁶ p13.9g f11g⁶
Dec 14] quite good-topped gelding: poor performer: stays 1¾m: acts on fibresand: tried
in headgear: none too reliable. *Mrs N. Macauley*

WESTERNER 5 b.h. Danehill (USA) 126 – Walensee 126 (Troy 137) [2004 121: **123**
15.5g* 15.5g² 20m² 12d 15.5d* 20m* 15.5s* Oct 24]
    For the second year running, Westerner was the top stayer in France. He
won four of Longchamp's important long distance events, including completing a
Group 1 double for the second year running in the Prix du Cadran and the Prix
Royal-Oak in the autumn. These last two performances underlined Westerner's
superiority over the rest of the French stayers—he was always going well and won
easily on both occasions—and a top-form Westerner would have a first-rate chance
if sent over again for the Gold Cup, which will be run at York in 2005. Westerner
went down by a length and a half to Papineau at Royal Ascot in the latest season, on
his only outing so far outside France, but the form of that run is a little below his
best efforts in France and he is well worth another chance.
    Westerner was seen out twice at Longchamp in the latest season before
Royal Ascot, successfully conceding weight all round in the Prix de Barbeville in
April just unable to catch the Barbeville runner-up Forestier in a very muddling
Prix Vicomtesse Vigier the following month. Westerner was sent off third choice
for the Gold Cup, behind hot favourite Mr Dinos and Papineau. Westerner had
every chance on the day and momentarily looked like winning before Papineau
got the better of him in the final furlong. Unfortunately, the merit of Westerner's
performance tended to be overshadowed in the aftermath. Westerner wears ear
plugs, which are said to keep him calm and help his rider to settle him in his races.
In the previous season's Prix du Cadran, Westerner's ear plugs had been pulled out
by the owners' retained rider Dominique Boeuf in the closing stages, an action said
by some exponents to be effective in spurring a horse to greater efforts. The rules in
Britain do not permit ear plugs to be removed in the course of a race, but Wester-

Prix du Cadran Casino Les Princes Barriere de Cannes, Longchamp—
Westerner is clear of Cut Quartz, Le Carre (grey) and Dancing Bay

Prix Royal-Oak, Longchamp—Westerner completes the Cadran/Royal-Oak double for the second year running; Behkara (No.7) and Alcazar change places from the previous year, while Le Carre is fourth

ner's jockey at Royal Ascot, reportedly under instructions, pulled them out as Papineau drew alongside. Dominique Boeuf, since fired as stable jockey to Ecurie Wildenstein, had flouted the same rule on the owners' Risk Seeker earlier in the season in both the Sagaro Stakes and the Henry II Stakes (fined £250 and £500 respectively). The Royal Ascot stewards elected to impose a £1,000 fine on Westerner's Gold Cup rider, Gerald Mosse, which seemed bizarre since it was his first transgression. Astonishingly, the stewards did not look into the involvement of either owner or trainer. Shenanigans in the unsaddling enclosure, which included Alec Wildenstein's telling the media 'I don't mind breaking the rules' and aiming a graceless 'the dope-testing machine must be broken' at Papineau's entourage, gave the Press in Britain a field day, the incidents given much more prominence than they deserved.

When the ear plugs were left in (as they also were in the Cadran) during the Prix Gladiateur Royal Thalasso Barriere at Longchamp in September, Westerner's trainer quipped 'We're teaching our horses to run with them in, just in case we go over to England again.' Westerner conceded weight all round and held on gamely by a short neck from Cut Quartz after quickening impressively from off the pace. Westerner did not have to carry a penalty in the Prix du Cadran Casino Les Princes Barriere de Cannes on Arc day and he was even more impressive in winning by three lengths, Cut Quartz again his closest pursuer. Westerner followed up in equally good style in the Prix Royal-Oak at the end of October, accelerating to beat Behkara by two and a half lengths, with British-trained Alcazar third (second and third picking up place money in the race for the second year). The reliable Westerner is usually held up and has a fine turn of foot for such a thorough stayer. He is suited by further than a mile and a half and never landed a blow in the latest Grand Prix de Saint-Cloud, though connections thought the race might have come too soon after the Gold Cup. The Grand Prix de Saint-Cloud is the only occasion in Westerner's last twelve outings—the others all between a mile and three quarters and two and a half miles—that he has finished out of the first two. He acts on soft going but doesn't need the mud; the going was good to firm for the Prix du Cadran—in which Westerner put up as good a performance as any in his career—as well as for the Gold Cup. Ear plugs do not have to be declared in Britain but York racegoers might note that, although Westerner's ear plugs were pulled out again in the Prix Royal-Oak, he had seemed just as effective when they stayed in for the Gladiateur and Cadran!

Westerner (b.h. 1999)	Danehill (USA) (b 1986)	Danzig (b 1977)	Northern Dancer
			Pas de Nom
		Razyana (b 1981)	His Majesty
			Spring Adieu
	Walensee (b 1982)	Troy (b 1976)	Petingo
			La Milo
		Warsaw (b 1972)	Bon Mot
			War Path

Home-bred Westerner, a good-topped horse who has a short, choppy action in his slower paces, is the product of a mating between the sprinter Danehill and Prix Vermeille winner Walensee. Walensee is also the dam of War Game (by Caerleon), the winner of the Prix Maurice de Nieuil over twelve and a half furlongs, and was fairly stoutly bred herself, by Derby winner Troy out of thirteen-furlong listed winner Warsaw, a winning half-sister to middle-distance performer Waya, the champion older mare in North America in 1979. Warsaw was by Arc winner Bon Mot, who was also second in the Prix Royal-Oak, out of a daughter of the 1955 Gold Cup runner-up Blue Prince. Walensee's visit to Danehill was clearly designed to introduce more speed and Westerner spent the early part of his career racing over much shorter distances, only belatedly being switched to staying events as a four-year-old. The now-deceased Danehill, who broke a leg in a paddock at Coolmore in May 2003, had another exceptional year, siring the winners of twenty-five European pattern races, four more than Sadler's Wells, the pair head and shoulders above the rest in the list. Danehill sired the Derby winner North Light, the Prix du Moulin winner Grey Lilas and, in addition to Westerner's Prix du Cadran, also enjoyed pattern success at the two-day Arc meeting with Cacique and Oratorio. Those winners alone illustrate the wide range of distances at which Danehill's progeny have been successful. As stated in Westerner's essay in *Racehorses of 2003*, Danehill is one of only three sires in modern times—the others being Warning and Machiavellian—to be represented by Group 1 winners aged three and upwards at five furlongs (Mozart) and two and a half miles. *E. Lellouche, France*

WESTERN (IRE) 4 ch.g. Gone West (USA) – Madame Est Sortie (FR) (Longleat (USA) 109) [2004 80: p16g² p12g f16s 12d 14.4m 12s 14.1g 11.7g p12g p13.9g Nov 11] close-coupled gelding: fairly useful handicapper: below form after reappearance: stays easy 2m: acts on polytrack and good to firm going: tried in cheekpieces. *J. Akehurst* — **a80 d**

WESTERNMOST 6 b.g. Most Welcome 131 – Dakota Girl 55 (Northern State (USA) 91) [2004 17.2g Jul 3] sturdy gelding: modest handicapper at best: well held only start on Flat since 2002. *M. Todhunter* —

WESTERN RIDGE (FR) 7 b.g. Darshaan 133 – Helvellyn (USA) 83 (Gone West (USA)) [2004 –: 11.7s 15m Jul 2] close-coupled gelding: handicapper: no form in 2004 (reportedly lame final start): tried in cheekpieces. *B. J. Llewellyn* —

WESTERN ROOTS 3 ch.g. Dr Fong (USA) 128 – Chrysalis 66 (Soviet Star (USA) 128) [2004 81: p7g² p8g⁴ p10g 8.1s 7m⁶ 8g* 8d⁵ 8m⁵ 8.2g p10g p8.6g p7g² 8s f7s p7.1g² p7g Dec 30] lengthy gelding: fairly useful performer: won claimer at Leicester (left P. Cole) in June: left K. Morgan after fourteenth start: stays 1m: acts on polytrack. *I. W. McInnes* — **80**

WESTFIELD BOY 2 b.g. (Apr 9) Unfuwain (USA) 131 – Pick of The Pops 109 (High Top 131) [2004 8d 10.1d Nov 5] 20,000Y: big, heavy-topped gelding: has a round action: brother to 1¼m/1½m winner Migwar (useful at best, later temperamental) and half-brother to 3 winners, including 1996 2-y-o 1m winner Fascinating Rhythm (by Slip Anchor): dam 2-y-o 7f winner and second in Fillies' Mile: well held in maidens at Newmarket (burly) and Yarmouth (raced freely, gelded after): likely to do better. *N. P. Littmoden* — **p**

WEST HIGHLAND WAY (IRE) 3 b.g. Foxhound (USA) 103 – Gilding The Lily (IRE) 58 (High Estate 127) [2004 58: 7.2f* 8m⁵ 8d p7.1d⁵ Oct 30] good-bodied gelding: fairly useful performer: won 4-runner maiden at Ayr in May: stays 1m: acts on firm going, probably on polytrack. *I. Semple* — **81**

WESTLAKE BOND (IRE) 2 b.f. (Feb 28) Josr Algarhoud (IRE) 118 – Rania (Aragon 118) [2004 6d⁵ 6s² Nov 6] €29,000Y: workmanlike filly: first foal: dam unraced half-sister to useful sprinter Deep Finesse: better effort in maidens when 1¾ lengths second to Bow Wave at Doncaster, leading over 3f out until final 1f: likely to prove best at 5f/6f. *B. Smart* — **68**

WESTLAND (USA) 2 gr.c. (Feb 3) Cozzene (USA) – Cherie Yvonne (USA) (Vice Regent (CAN)) [2004 6s² 6d* Nov 5] $180,000Y: sturdy colt: first foal: dam US 6f to 8.5f winner, including minor stakes: favourite, won maiden at Yarmouth comfortably by 3 lengths from Stage School, leading over 1f out: should stay 1m: should progress. *Mrs A. J. Perrett* — **81 p**

WESTMEAD ETOILE 4 b.f. Unfuwain (USA) 131 – Glossary (Reference Point 139) [2004 53: p8g 8s³ p8g f7g 7v f7g³ May 19] leggy filly: poor maiden: stays 1m: acts on fibresand, good to firm and good to soft going: tried visored/blinkered/tongue tied. *J. R. Jenkins* — **41**

WESTMEAD TANGO   4 b.f. Pursuit of Love 124 – Tango Teaser (Shareef Dancer **39**
(USA) 135) [2004 57: p6g⁶ p5g⁶ p6g p6g Apr 6] poor performer: effective at 5f/easy
6f: acts on polytrack, good to firm and good to soft going: often visored: has given plenty
of trouble at start, and at 3yrs was temporarily banned from Flat races with stalls.
J. R. Jenkins

WESTMORELAND ROAD (USA)   4 b.g. Diesis 133 – Tia Gigi (USA) (Assert **112**
134) [2004 117: 12m² 12g² 14.1g⁴ 11m Sep 17] rangy, good-topped gelding: smart
performer: creditable second in listed race (beaten ½ length by First Charter) and minor
event (beaten ¾ length by Eastern Breeze) at Newmarket: below form after (looked less
than keen penultimate start, hung final outing): should stay 1¾m: raced only on good
going or firmer: gelded after final outing.. *Mrs A. J. Perrett*

WETHAAB (USA)   7 b.g. Pleasant Colony (USA) – Binntastic (USA) (Lyphard's Wish   **–**
(FR) 124) [2004 –, a45: f11g f11s f9.4m⁵ f12g⁶ 15g Apr 23] sturdy gelding: no form at 7
yrs: usually wears headgear/tongue tie. *Miss A. Stokell*

WET LIPS (AUS)   6 ch.g. Grand Lodge (USA) 125 – Kissing (AUS) (Somalia (AUS))
[2004 11.9d Aug 17] ex-Australian gelding: won twice around 1m (placed at 1¼m) from
16 starts in native country: blinkered/tongue tied, soundly beaten only start on Flat in
Britain: fair hurdler. *R. C. Guest*

WHALEEF   6 b.g. Darshaan 133 – Wilayif (USA) 75 (Danzig (USA)) [2004 80: 10g² **80**
Aug 23] fairly useful performer: good second in claimer at Windsor (wore cheekpieces/
tongue strap) only start in 2004: stays 1½m: acts on polytrack and firm going: fair hurdler.
B. J. Llewellyn

WHAT-A-DANCER (IRE)   7 b.g. Dancing Dissident (USA) 119 – Cool Gales 85 **81**
(Lord Gayle (USA) 124) [2004 93: p7g⁴ p7g³ p7g⁶* 7.1g⁴ 7m 7m⁴ 7g⁴ 7m 7m⁶ 8g⁵ 7f⁴ 7m⁶ **a93**
p8.6g p7g³ p6g* Dec 30] sparely-made gelding: fairly useful performer: won handicap at
Lingfield in March and claimer there in December: effective at 6f to 1m: acts on polytrack
and firm going: held up: sometimes races freely/finds little. *G. A. Swinbank*

WHATATODO   2 b.f. (Apr 6) Compton Place 125 – Emerald Dream (IRE) 47 (Vision **72**
(USA)) [2004 6g 6f³ 6d 7m* 7m² 6g 7g⁴ 6d Oct 14] 500Y, resold 5,500Y: angular, quite
good-topped filly: fourth foal: half-sister to 3-y-o Cotosol: dam maiden who stayed 1¼m:
fair performer: won nursery at Brighton in July: good efforts in frame in similar events
after: stays 7f: acts on good to firm going: usually races up with pace. *M. L. W. Bell*

WHATSHEWORTH   2 b.g. (May 10) Pyramus (USA) 78 – Princess Aurora 58   **–**
(Prince Sabo 123) [2004 5f 5m⁶ Jun 7] leggy gelding: tailed off in maiden and seller.
P. S. McEntee

WHAT'S UP DOC (IRE)   3 b.c. Dr Massini (IRE) 117 – Surprise Treat (IRE) 75 **80**
(Shalford (IRE) 124§) [2004 76: 10.1m* 12g²¹ 8s Oct 23] first foal: dam Irish 2-y-o 7f
winner: fairly useful performer: trained by S. Treacy in Ireland at 2 yrs: won maiden at
Newcastle in May: left M. Johnston after next start: stays 1½m: acts on heavy and good
to firm going: tongue tied final outing: hangs left. *J. S. Bolger, Ireland*

WHAZZAT   2 b.f. (Feb 2) Daylami (IRE) 138 – Wosaita 70 (Generous (IRE) 139) **105 p**
[2004 6m* 7f* Jun 19] 30,000Y: good-topped filly: third foal: half-sister to 2002 2-y-o
1m winner Special Envoy (by Barathea), later winner in Switzerland: dam, third at 1½m
from 3 starts, half-sister to Prix de Diane winner Rafha, herself dam of very smart sprinter
Invincible Spirit: won maiden at Newbury (by neck from Maids Causeway) and listed
race at Royal Ascot (by 3½ lengths from Brecon Beacon, quickening well) in June: bred
to be suited by 1¼m/1½m: reportedly had setback but will be back in training at all 3 yrs:
smart prospect if all is well. *B. W. Hills*

WHENWILLITWIN   3 b.g. Bluegrass Prince (IRE) 110 – Madam Marash (IRE) 51 **44**
(Astronef 116) [2004 10.2f⁶ 11.6g⁶ 10.1m Jul 22] poor form in maiden/sellers: probably
stay 11.6f. *J. S. Moore*

WHERE WITH ALL (IRE)   2 b.c. (Jan 14) Montjeu (IRE) 137 – Zelding (IRE) 108 **101**
(Warning 136) [2004 6d* 7f 7.5g* Jul 19] close-coupled, quite attractive colt: easy
mover, with a quick action: third foal: half-brother to French 6f (including at 2 yrs)
winner Deziring (by Desert Prince): dam, French 5f winner (including at 2 yrs), half-
sister to smart French sprinter Zipping: won maiden at Haydock in June and minor event
at Beverley (by 6 lengths from Blue Prince) in July: subsequently suffered condylar
fracture to near-hind: should stay 1m: acts on good to soft going: useful. *Saeed bin Suroor*

WHINHILL HOUSE   4 ch.g. Paris House 123 – Darussalam 78 (Tina's Pet 121)   **64**
[2004 56: 5.9f 5g 5d 5d³ 6d f5g³ p6g f5g³ f5g* Dec 21] strong gelding: modest performer:
won banded race at Southwell: stays 6f: acts on fibresand, good to firm and good to soft
going: tried in cheekpieces: usually races prominently. *D. W. Barker*

WHIPLASH (IRE)   3 b.g. Orpen (USA) 116 – La Colombari (ITY) (Lomond (USA)   **56 d**
128) [2004 54: 8.3d 7d⁴ 8.3s 7g* 7g p8g⁶ p10g 7.6f 7.1s⁶ 8d 7m f8g p7m p7m Dec 15]
lengthy gelding: modest performer: won claimer at Salisbury (left R. Hannon) in May:
below form after: probably stays 1m: acts on polytrack, good to firm and good to soft
going: tried blinkered/visored. *K. O. Cunningham-Brown*

WHIPPASNAPPER   4 b.g. Cayman Kai (IRE) 114 – Give Us A Treat (Cree Song 99)   **72**
[2004 68d, a74: f7g p6g* p5g² p6g* p7g³ p7g 6s² 6d* 5.3m 6d³ 7m² 7.2f² 7.1m 7.1f p7d   **a77**
7g⁴ 7m 6d p6g⁶ Oct 7] leggy gelding: fair performer: won amateur handicap and minor
event at Lingfield in January and handicap at Leicester in April: acts on 6f/7f: acts on
polytrack, firm and soft going: sometimes slowly away/wanders. *J. R. Best*

WHIPPER (USA)   3 b.c. Miesque's Son (USA) 117 – Myth To Reality (FR)   **125**
(Sadler's Wells (USA) 132) [2004 118: 7s* 8g⁵ 6.5g² 8d* 8g⁵ 8d Oct 30]
   The essay on Ouija Board outlines the incalculable contribution made to
the modern thoroughbred by the 17th Earl of Derby whose stud produced the likes
of Phalaris, Pharos, Colorado, Fairway, Hyperion and Alycidon, who through their
sons, grandsons and other descendants have exerted worldwide influence. Some of
the matings in the Derby studs, which also practiced inbreeding, were repeated
year after year, including the matings of Phalaris with Scapa Flow, which produced
Pharos and Fairway, and with Selene, which produced Hyperion, Sickle and
Pharamond. All those mentioned were raced in the Derby colours and all went on
to become outstanding sires. While any number of other examples could be chosen,
the pedigree of the Prix Jacques le Marois winner Whipper provides a good illustration of the impact of the Derby studs. Sickle heads the line, through Native Dancer,
that leads to Mr Prospector, paternal grandsire of Whipper; the Pharos line through
Nearctic and Northern Dancer played its part in producing Whipper's paternal
grandam Miesque and was also responsible for Whipper's maternal grandsire
Sadler's Wells; while Whipper's maternal grandam Millieme is by Mill Reef, also a
descendant, through his grandsire Nasrullah and his sire Never Bend, of Pharos.
   Whipper himself is a product of the Niarchos studs which bred both his
sire the six- and seven-furlong performer Miesque's Son, who gained his only win
in Group 3 company, and his dam the useful French middle-distance performer
Myth To Reality. Both Miesque's Son and Myth To Reality were impeccably bred,
Miesque's Son out of the brilliant Miesque, one of the best milers of her sex in
modern times, and Myth To Reality out of Millieme, a placed sister to Derby winner
Shirley Heights. Being blue-blooded guaranteed nothing, though, and neither
Miesque's Son nor Myth To Reality looked like making a lasting impact at first
when they were retired to stud. The reflected glory from his older brother
Kingmambo ensured a place for Miesque's Son, but he has been moved on twice,
first to California and then to France, since beginning his stallion career a few miles
down the road from Kingmambo at Three Chimneys Farm in Kentucky. Myth To
Reality was also rather slow to make her mark and, though all her foals to reach the
racecourse have won, was probably being regarded as something of a disappointment at stud when she was sent to Miesque's Son in 1997, producing a colt who
fetched 20,000 dollars as a foal and, named Meteorite Sun, has so far won only
once, and was still racing at the age of six in the latest season when he finished third
in a handicap at Pontefract. In the two years after Meteorite Sun, Myth To Reality
was barren and then slipped her foal. She then produced her eighth foal (and eighth
winner), another colt to Miesque's Son who realised only 4,000 dollars at the
Keeneland November Sale as a foal, reflecting both his sire's unfashionable status
and his dam's unexceptional record as a broodmare. The colt failed to reach his
reserve when re-offered as a yearling at Deauville (though he was reportedly
bought privately for €30,000). That colt was Whipper whose victory in the Prix
Jacques le Marois at Deauville gave him a second Group 1 victory, following his
victory in the Prix Morny at two over the same course.
   Whipper failed to do himself justice on his only outing in Britain as a
two-year-old, finishing strongly for fifth (eventually promoted to fourth), after

being dropped out nearly last, in the Middle Park Stakes, a race in which none of those held up got into the race. Whipper was returned to Newmarket for the Two Thousand Guineas, booking his place with an eight-length win in the listed Prix Djebel at Maisons-Laffitte in April. He wasn't discredited in the Guineas, coming fifth to Haafhd, looking a big threat in the penultimate furlong, after being attended by two handlers in the paddock where he was sweating and became increasingly on edge. Given a three-month break, Whipper was brought back for the Deauville meeting in August. He ran Somnus to a neck, held up and keeping on well, in the Prix Maurice de Gheest over six and a half furlongs and a week later landed the Prix du Haras de Fresnay-Le-Buffard-Jacques le Marois, one of Europe's top races at a mile. The field included the top three-year-old filly at the trip, British-trained Attraction, and the four-year-old filly Six Perfections who had been the top miler of her sex the previous year when she had won the Jacques le Marois and the Breeders' Cup Mile. The Niarchos family, owner and breeder of Six Perfections (who is out of a half-sister to Miesque), sponsors the Jacques le Marois through its French stud. The race was the main European target for Six Perfections in the latest season. Whipper, somewhat surprisingly on previous evidence, saw the mile out well, leading a furlong out when switched towards the centre of the course after being waited with. He held on by a length from Six Perfections, who never quite matched the best of her three-year-old form at four; My Risk and British-trained Majestic Desert were third and fourth, with Attraction completely failing to give her running on the good to soft going. Whipper's season was an anticlimax after Deauville. He failed to repeat his Jacques le Marois form in either the Prix du Moulin at Longchamp (fifth to Grey Lilas, beaten around two lengths) or in the Breeders' Cup Mile at Lone Star Park (tenth of fourteen after being in a good position on the home turn). Whipper's connections—his present owner purchased him after the Prix Morny—won the Breeders' Cup Mile with Last Tycoon in 1986.

			Mr Prospector (b 1970)	Raise A Native
		Miesque's Son (USA) (b or br 1992)		Gold Digger
			Miesque (b 1984)	Nureyev
Whipper (USA) (b.c. 2001)				Pasadoble
		Myth To Reality (FR) (b 1986)	Sadler's Wells (b 1981)	Northern Dancer
				Fairy Bridge
			Millieme (b 1977)	Mill Reef
				Hardiemma

Whipper's triumph in the Jacques le Marois added another chapter to the success in the race for horses with Niarchos connections. Miesque won in 1987 and 1988 and another of her produce, East of The Moon, was victorious in 1994, while success narrowly eluded Kingmambo, beaten a head and a neck in 1993 when he won the Poule d'Essai des Poulains, the St James's Palace Stakes and the Prix du Moulin. The latest season continued the transformation in the fortunes of Whipper's dam Myth To Reality, though not before she had been sold out of

Niarchos ownership early in 2003 (in foal to Mt Livermore) for 125,000 dollars at Keeneland. Previous matings with Kingmambo had produced a minor winner at a mile and a half in Mambo Jambo (who became the dam of 2003 Yorkshire Oaks runner-up Ocean Silk, also the winner of two allowance races in the States in 2004) and Indigo Myth, a mile-and-a-quarter winner in France, also successful in North America, who was placed in stakes company. With Indigo Myth's racing career turning out better than Mambo Jambo's, another valuable Kingmambo nomination was allotted to Myth To Reality in 2001 and persistence paid off when the result of that mating produced Divine Proportions, the best two-year-old filly in Europe in the latest season when she was unbeaten in five races, including the Prix Morny and the Prix Marcel Boussac. Myth To Reality's covering by Mt Livermore produced a filly—now named Anse Victorin—and she has a colt foal by the King-mambo stallion Lemon Drop Kid. The matings that eventually produced Whipper and Divine Proportions illustrate the rewards of persevering with convictions, and also illustrates success with inbreeding. There are a number of patterns in the pedigrees of Whipper and Divine Proportions, among them the fact that Nureyev, the sire of Miesque, and Sadler's Wells, the sire of Myth To Reality, are three parts brothers, by Northern Dancer out of Special and her daughter Fairy Bridge respectively. At the time of writing, Whipper seems set to stay in training at four, with good prospects that he will cross swords with his close relative Divine Proportions at some point. Whipper is probably effective at six furlongs to a mile. Tall and leggy with a round action, he has shown his form on good going and softer (acts on soft), the Middle Park being the only occasion he has encountered firmish going. *R. Collet, France*

WHIRLING 2 ch.f. (Feb 20) Groom Dancer (USA) 128 – Supersonic 80 (Shirley Heights 130) [2004 8s p8.6d p9.5g p8.6g Nov 26] 4,000Y: first foal: dam, maiden who stayed 10.5f, sister to useful winner up to 2m Upper Strata: modest form in maidens at Ayr and Wolverhampton: will stay at least 1¼m. *J. G. Given* — **53**

WHIRLY BIRD 3 b.f. Nashwan (USA) 135 – Inchyre 102 (Shirley Heights 130) [2004 10.2s³ p9.5d* p10g* Nov 13] third living foal: half-sister to useful 1¼m/1½m winner Inchiri (by Sadler's Wells) and to Oaks fourth Inchberry (by Barathea): dam, 1m winner who stayed 1½m, half-sister to smart performer up to 1m Inchinor: fair form: won maiden at Wolverhampton in October and minor event at Lingfield in November: should stay 1½m: slowly away first 2 outings: should progress further at 4 yrs. *Mrs A. J. Perrett* — **74 p**

WHISPERED PROMISES (USA) 3 b.g. Real Quiet (USA) 131 – Anna's Honor (USA) (Alleged (USA) 138) [2004 83: 10.4s 12d³ 12g 10m⁵ Jul 25] strong gelding: fairly useful handicapper: stays 1½m: acts on good to firm and good to soft going: blinkered (folded tamely) final start. *M. Johnston* — **84**

WHISPERING DEATH 2 br.g. (Feb 5) Pivotal 124 – Lucky Arrow 60 (Indian Ridge 123) [2004 6d 7s 7s p7.1g Dec 10] tall, good-topped gelding: well beaten in maidens. *W. J. Haggas* — **–**

WHISPERING VALLEY 4 ch.f. The West (USA) 107 – Taciturn (USA) 32 (Tasso (USA)) [2004 –: 11.5g 14m 9.7g 10.9d 8g Sep 27] no form in maidens/handicaps. *Mrs A. J. Perrett* — **–**

WHIST DRIVE 4 ch.g. First Trump 118 – Fine Quill (Unfuwain (USA) 131) [2004 65: 15s⁶ Apr 7] big, lengthy gelding: modest maiden, lightly raced: probably stays 15f: acts on soft and good to firm going: tried blinkered: fair hurdler. *Mrs N. Smith* — **60**

WHISTFUL (IRE) 3 b.f. First Trump 118 – Atmospheric Blues (IRE) 91 (Double Schwartz 128) [2004 68: 6.1g³ 6s 6m³ 6m⁵ 5.5g 6g⁴ 6m 6g⁴ Oct 5] quite good-topped filly: fair maiden: stays 6f: acts on good to firm going: found little final start. *C. F. Wall* — **71**

WHISTLER 7 ch.g. Selkirk (USA) 129 – French Gift 99 (Cadeaux Genereux 131) [2004 88: 5s 5d 5m 5m³ 5m 5g* 5.1g 5m³ 5g* 5.5m 5d* 5g⁴ 5m 5.2f³ 5g⁴ 5g 5.6m⁴ 5s² 5d⁶ 5d⁵ Oct 17] angular, workmanlike gelding: has a quick action: useful handicapper: won at Sandown and Salisbury in June and Sandown again in July: mostly good efforts otherwise in 2004, notably when 2 lengths second to Jonny Ebeneezer at Haydock in September: best at 5f: acts on any turf going: tried blinkered, wore cheekpieces at 6/7 yrs: sometimes hangs left: travels strongly, and best covered up. *J. M. Bradley* — **100**

WHISTLING ALONG 2 b.c. (Apr 25) Atraf 116 – Forest Song 60 (Forzando 122) [2004 5s 5.1s⁶ 6g 5f Jul 26] rather leggy colt: little sign of ability in maidens/minor event. *J. M. Bradley* — **–**

WHITBARROW (IRE)   5 b.g. Royal Abjar (USA) 121 – Danccini (IRE) 78 (Danc-   **101**
ing Dissident (USA) 119) [2004 90?: 5.2g⁵ 5.1d 5s 5g* 5m 5m 6f 5d 5g 5m 6m 5g 5g
5.6m⁵ 6g⁴ 5s 5m 5d³ 5s² f5s⁶ p6g f5g⁵ Dec 7] strong, good sort: useful handicapper: won
at Goodwood in May by ¾ length from Texas Gold: best at 5f/6f: acts on fibresand, firm
and soft going: tried in cheekpieces and blinkers: usually races prominently: none too
consistent. *J. M. Bradley*

WHITE HAWK   3 b.c. Silver Hawk (USA) 123 – Polska (USA) 103 (Danzig (USA))   **–**
[2004 98: 10g⁴ 7.6d 8.1m May 22] good-topped colt: useful at 2 yrs: soundly beaten in
2004: sold 3,500 gns. *D. R. Loder*

WHITE LEDGER (IRE)   5 ch.g. Ali-Royal (IRE) 127 – Boranwood (IRE) (Exhibi-   **69**
tioner 111) [2004 –: f6d f7m 6g³ 5s* 5d* 5.2d 5.3s⁶ p5.1g² Oct 18] useful-looking gelding: fair performer: won claimer at Catterick and handicap at Sandown in August: best at
5f/6f: acts on all-weather, firm and soft going: often visored: sold £1,400. *R. A. Fahey*

WHITE O' MORN   5 gr.m. Petong 126 – I'm Your Lady 77 (Risk Me (FR) 127)   **47**
[2004 –: f7g f5g⁴ f5g² f5s⁴ f5s* f5g f5g² f5m 5m⁴ 5d 5.1g Aug 18] poor performer: won
banded race at Wolverhampton in March: left B. McMahon after next start: should
prove best at 5f/6f: acts on fibresand and good to firm going: sometimes tongue tied: wore
cheekpieces after third outing. *J. W. Unett*

WHITE PARK BAY (IRE)   4 b.f. Blues Traveller (IRE) 119 – Valiant Friend (USA)   **49**
(Shahrastani (USA) 135) [2004 62, a72: f11g⁵ 11.6g² f12m 11.5d⁶ Aug 26] quite good-   **a–**
topped filly: poor maiden: left J. Gallagher after reappearance: stays 1½m: acts on fibresand, good to firm and good to soft going. *Miss Suzy Smith*

WHITE SAIL   3 b.f. Polar Falcon (USA) 126 – Felucca 94 (Green Desert (USA) 127)   **–**
[2004 7f Jun 2] fifth foal: half-sister to 2 winners, notably 4-y-o Lateen Sails: dam, 2-y-o
6f winner, half-sister to very smart French performer up to 1½m Radevore: 8/1 and green,
well held in maiden at Yarmouth. *H. R. A. Cecil*

WHITE STAR MAGIC   2 ch.c. (Apr 10) Bluegrass Prince (IRE) 110 – Bless 58   **61**
(Beveled (USA)) [2004 7.2s 8v 6g⁶ p7.1g⁴ Oct 18] first foal: dam 1½m winner: modest
maiden: should stay 1m: acts on soft going, probably on polytrack. *J. R. Weymes*

WHITGIFT ROCK   3 b.g. Piccolo 121 – Fly South (Polar Falcon (USA) 126) [2004   **79**
72: p8g* p8g² 7.5d 7.1f 8.1m 8g³ 10s² 10.1g p7g 8.5g p10g Sep 22] good-topped gelding:
fair performer: won handicap at Lingfield in January: stays 1¼m: acts on polytrack, firm
and soft going: tried visored: sold 16,000 gns, then gelded. *S. Dow*

WHITKIRK STAR (IRE)   3 b.g. Alhaarth (IRE) 126 – Three Stars 93 (Star Appeal   **–**
133) [2004 –: 8.1s⁶ 10s Nov 1] close-coupled gelding: tailed off in maidens. *S. P. Griffiths*

WHITLAND   2 b.g. (Mar 8) Namaqualand (USA) – Whittle Rock 91 (Rock City 120)   **56**
[2004 7d 7s 8m Sep 25] stocky gelding: tongue tied, modest form in maidens: stays 1m.
Mrs P. N. Dutfield

WHITSBURY CROSS   3 b.c. Cape Cross (IRE) 129 – Vallauris 94 (Faustus (USA)   **86**
118) [2004 –: 8g⁵ 8m⁵ 9.7m* 10m 10d⁴ 10m³ 10g⁵ Aug 14] tall, good sort: has a quick
action: fairly useful performer: won maiden at Folkestone in June: good efforts in
handicaps last 3 starts: will stay 1½m: acts on good to firm and good to soft going.
D. R. C. Elsworth

WHITTINGHAMVILLAGE   3 b.f. Whittingham (IRE) 104 – Shaa Spin 63 (Shaadi   **–**
(USA) 126) [2004 58: f7g⁶ Jan 2] leggy, workmanlike filly: maiden: last in claimer only
3-y-o start. *A. Berry*

WHITTLE WARRIOR   4 b.g. Averti (IRE) 117 – Polish Descent (IRE) (Danehill   **–**
(USA) 126) [2004 58: 6f f7g Nov 9] leggy gelding: no form in 2004: tried blinkered.
C. W. Fairhurst

WHO CARES WINS   8 ch.g. Kris 135 – Anne Bonny 105 (Ajdal (USA) 130) [2004   **–**
–: 14.1d Oct 16] rather leggy, quite good-topped gelding: no form on Flat since 2001:
tried visored/blinkered at 4 yrs. *J. R. Jenkins*

WHOLE GRAIN   3 b.f. Polish Precedent (USA) 131 – Mill Line 71 (Mill Reef (USA)   **72**
141) [2004 –p: 10d⁴ Jun 23] rangy filly: better effort in maidens over 8 months apart when
fourth at Kempton in June: will stay 1½m: sent to France. *Sir Michael Stoute*

WHOOPSIE   2 b.f. (May 13) Unfuwain (USA) 131 – Oops Pettie 93 (Machiavellian   **–**
(USA) 123) [2004 8m 8.2m 8s Oct 22] stocky filly: fourth foal: half-sister to 3 winners,

including useful Irish 1½m winner Orpington (by Hernando): dam 1¼m winner: well held in maidens. *J. A. Glover*

WHORTLEBERRY (FR)   4 ch.f. Starborough 126 – Rotina (FR) (Crystal Glitters   **118**
(USA) 127) [2004 111: 12s⁴ 10.5g⁴ 12g* 12.5d⁶ 10s* 12d 10m⁶ 11f Nov 14] 70,000
francs Y: strong, medium-sized filly: seventh foal: half-sister to several winners, notably
5-y-o Valentino: dam placed at 10.5f in France: smart performer: successful at 3 yrs in
Prix Minerve at Deauville and Premio Lydia Tesio at Rome: unlucky not to win Prix de
Royallieu at Longchamp in between, beaten a nose after rider misjudged winning post:
won minor event at La Teste in July and Prix Jean Romanet at Deauville (by 2 lengths
from Pride) in August: below form last 3 starts, in Prix Vermeille and Prix de l'Opera at
Longchamp and Queen Elizabeth II Commemorative Cup at Kyoto: stays 12.5f: acts on
heavy and good to firm going: blinkered 3 of last 4 starts. *F. Rohaut, France*

WHO'S WINNING (IRE)   3 ch.g. Docksider (USA) 124 – Quintellina 83 (Robellino   **93**
(USA) 127) [2004 75: 6d 5m 6m⁶ 7m 6.1m² 6f* 5g² 5m* 6g* p6g p5g² Nov 13] sturdy
gelding: fairly useful handicapper: left C. Dwyer after fifth start: won at Brighton in
August and Goodwood and Kempton in September: good second to Texas Gold at
Lingfield final outing: effective at 5f/6f: acts on polytrack and firm ground: tried in
blinkers/cheekpieces: free-going sort. *B. G. Powell*

WHY DUBAI (USA)   3 br.f. Kris S (USA) – Highest Goal (USA) (Slew O' Gold   **87**
(USA)) [2004 93: 8d 9g⁶ 8m⁶ 7m Sep 19] quite good-topped filly: has a fluent, quick
action: fairly useful performer: stiff tasks in 2004 (mostly in listed races), not discredited
last 3 starts: stays 9f: acts on good to firm going: joined D. Watson in UAE. *R. Hannon*

WHY HARRY   2 b.g. (Apr 5) Cyrano de Bergerac 120 – Golden Ciel (USA) (Septieme   **55**
Ciel (USA) 123) [2004 f5g³ 5g 5s* 5d⁶ 5g⁶ May 18] 2,500F, 5,000Y: sturdy gelding: third   **a62**
foal: half-brother to 2 winners, including 3-y-o Bold Blade: dam 2-y-o sprint winner in
Italy: modest performer: won claimer at Beverley in April: likely to prove best at 5f/6f:
acts on fibresand and soft going. *J. J. Quinn*

WICKED UNCLE   5 b.g. Distant Relative 128 – The Kings Daughter 79 (Indian King   **93**
(USA) 128) [2004 82: 5g 5.1g 5m* Jun 30] smallish, sturdy gelding: impresses in appearance: fairly useful handicapper: better than ever when winning at Catterick in June by 4
lengths from Brigadier Monty, making virtually all: best at 5f: acts on firm going: wears
headgear. *S. Gollings*

WIGGY SMITH   5 ch.g. Master Willie 129 – Monsoon 66 (Royal Palace 131) [2004   **91**
88p: 10g⁵ 12m 10.1g* 10.1s² Oct 27] angular gelding: fairly useful performer, lightly
raced: won handicap at Epsom in August by 1½ lengths from Camrose: good second to
Ofaraby in minor event at Yarmouth final start: stays 1½m: acts on soft and good to firm
going. *H. Candy*

WIGMO PRINCESS   5 ch.m. Factual (USA) 108 – Queen of Shannon (IRE) 76   **–**
(Nordico (USA)) [2004 50d: f12s Feb 14] handicapper: blinkered, well held only start in
2004. *S. C. Burrough*

WIGWAM WILLIE (IRE)   2 b.g. (Feb 25) Indian Rocket 115 – Sweet Nature (IRE)   **75**
71 (Classic Secret (USA) 91) [2004 6f⁴ 5.1g⁵ 6g² 6f Sep 10] €12,500F, 20,000Y: unfurnished gelding: fourth foal: half-brother to 2 winners abroad, including Ivans Bride (by
Inzar), also 5.7f winner in Britain at 2 yrs: dam, 2-y-o 6f winner, half-sister to useful 1994
2-y-o sprinter Princely Hush: fair maiden: second at Redcar, best effort: should stay 7f.
M. J. Wallace

WILD PITCH   3 ch.g. Piccolo 121 – Western Horizon (USA) 58 (Gone West (USA))   **65**
[2004 –: p10g 10s 9g³ 11.6d 10g⁶ p10g Dec 18] fair maiden: stays 9f: blinkered final start.
P. Mitchell

WILD POWER (GER)   6 br.g. Turtle Island (IRE) 123 – White On Red (GER)   **62**
(Konigsstuhl (GER)) [2004 10.2g⁴ 12g² 9.9m⁴ Sep 21] ex-German gelding: won maiden
at Cologne at 3 yrs for A. Wohler: modest form in handicaps in 2004: stays 1½m: modest
chaser, successful in November. *J. G. M. O'Shea*

WILD TIDE   5 b.m. Runnett 125 – Polly Two (Reesh 117) [2004 8g 5.9f 6g 8.3d 8m   **–**
Sep 4] leggy mare: modest foal: dam maiden hurdler: poor maiden. *D. W. Thompson*

WILD WILD WES   4 ch.g. The West (USA) 107 – Dam Certain (IRE) 61 (Damister   **–**
(USA) 123) [2004 p12g p10g Feb 24] tailed off in maidens. *R. Ingram*

WILFORD MAVERICK (IRE)   2 b.c. (Apr 10) Fasliyev (USA) 120 – Lioness 74   **53 ?**
(Lion Cavern (USA) 117) [2004 6m f6m 6g p5.1g Oct 2] close-coupled colt: modest
maiden: seemingly best effort at 6f on good to firm going. *M. J. Attwater*

WILFRED (IRE)   3 b.g. Desert King (IRE) 129 – Kharaliya (FR) (Doyoun 124)   –
[2004 70: 11.6s 11.6g May 17] close-coupled gelding: maiden handicapper: well below
form in 2004: fair juvenile hurdler, successful twice in September. *Jonjo O'Neill*

WILHEHECKASLIKE   3 b.g. Wizard King 122 – La Ciotat (IRE) 40 (Gallic League   –
119) [2004 51: f8s 6s f5m 6m^6 6m 14.1m^6 Aug 7] no longer of any account. *W. Storey*

WILKO (USA)   2 ch.c. (Jan 13) Awesome Again (CAN) 133 – Native Roots   **107**
(IRE) (Indian Ridge 123) [2004 5v^3 6s 6f* 7f^3 7g^3 7g^2 7m* 7d^2 7f^4 8f^3 a8.5f* a8.5f^3 **a118**
Dec 18]
    'If your selection finishes second, beaten by a Frankie Dettori-ridden horse,
we will refund your losing win stake.' The offer made by one bookmaking firm
advertising prices on the Breeders' Cup races at Lone Star Park gave some
indication of what was thought of the chances of the four horses Dettori was due to
ride, none of whom went on to start at odds shorter than 10/1. In the event, those
customers who backed Afleet Alex, one of the favourites for the Bessemer Trust
Breeders' Cup Juvenile, benefited from the concession, as that colt took second
place behind the Dettori-ridden Wilko. With Ouija Board having won the previous
race on the card, Wilko's victory made it an even more memorable night for British
racing, this pair being the only challengers from Britain. Two shies, two coconuts,
as they say.
    Whereas Ouija Board was a hot favourite for the Filly & Mare Turf, only
one of the eight runners in the Breeders' Cup Juvenile started at odds longer than
Wilko, who in ten outings on turf, at distances ranging from five furlongs through
to a mile, had seemed fully exposed as no more than useful. Wilko had proved himself a genuine and consistent performer in Britain, if nothing else, winning minor
events at Yarmouth in June and August and finishing in the frame in all but one of
his other starts, including in four pattern races. He was third to Dubawi and Henrik
in the Superlative Stakes at Newmarket, runner-up to Shamardal in the Vintage
Stakes at Goodwood, fourth to Etlaala in the Champagne Stakes at Doncaster and,
on his final outing before the Breeders' Cup Juvenile, third to Perfectperformance
in the Royal Lodge Stakes at Ascot, after which a reported three-quarter share in

Bessemer Trust Breeders' Cup Juvenile, Lone Star Park—Wilko (nearest camera) improves
for the switch from turf to dirt and collars Afleet Alex (centre) and Sun King late on,
giving Britain only its second Breeders' Cup victory on the surface

the colt was purchased by Paul Reddam. The Breeders' Cup Juvenile provided Wilko and the other European challenger Scandinavia, both of whom were bred in the States, with the opportunity to race on dirt for the first time. Whereas Scandinavia, who had finished one place and just over a length ahead of Wilko in the Royal Lodge, didn't take to the surface and trailed home in last place, Wilko left his turf form well behind to account for three Grade 1 winners among the home-trained juveniles. Drawn widest of all in what was the smallest field for the race in its twenty-one year history, Wilko was soon racing in third, dropped back to fourth when a bit outpaced before the home turn, then stayed on strongly down the outer to overhaul Afleet Alex, Sun King and Consolidator, hitting the front around half a furlong out to win going away by three quarters of a length. Wilko is only the second British-trained runner to win a race on dirt at the Breeders' Cup, following Sheikh Albadou in the 1991 Sprint. Wilko remained in the States to be trained by Craig Dollase and ran once more before the end of the year, finishing third to Declan's Moon, beaten a length, in the Hollywood Futurity at Hollywood Park, a creditable effort considering that he had suffered a quarter crack on the inside of his near-fore the day before. Despite this defeat, Wilko was awarded joint-top weight, alongside Declan's Moon, in the Experimental Free Handicap.

			Vice Regent
	Awesome Again (CAN)	Deputy Minister	Mint Copy
	(b 1994)	(b or br 1979)	Blushing Groom
Wilko (USA)		Primal Force	Prime Prospect
(ch.c. Jan 13, 2002)		(b 1987)	Ahonoora
	Native Roots (IRE)	Indian Ridge	Hillbrow
	(ch 1997)	(ch 1985)	Tap On Wood
		Phazania	Contrail
		(ro 1986)	

Wilko, a 35,000-dollar foal and 75,000-dollar yearling, is the first produce of Native Roots, a winner over six and a half furlongs in the States at three years, who was herself sold for 1,100,000 dollars, in foal to Street Cry, at Keeneland in January 2005. Native Root's dam Phazania, who won at six furlongs and a mile in Ireland as a two-year-old, has bred several other winners, including the fairly useful performers Future Prospect and Il Caravaggio. The next dam, Contrail, a maiden half-sister to the Oaks and Irish Oaks winner Blue Wind and the very good sire of jumpers Callernish, is also the great grandam of the high-class Japanese colt Taiki Shuttle, winner of the 1998 Prix Jacques le Marois. Wilko's sire Awesome Again was responsible for another winner at the Breeders' Cup meeting (becoming only the second sire after Kris S to have achieved a double on the same Breeders' Cup card) in the shape of Ghoztzapper, successful in the Classic, a race which Awesome Again also won, accounting for Silver Charm and the Dettori-ridden Swain in the 1998 running. Awesome Again, whose fee was set at 50,000 dollars when he began his stud career the following year, was available at 75,000 dollars in 2004 but, unsurprisingly, it will require 125,000 dollars to secure his services in 2005. A well-made, attractive individual with a quick action, Wilko will probably be doing all of his racing on dirt from now on, but it is worth pointing out that he has shown his form on turf on ground ranging from firm to good to soft. He will stay a mile and a quarter, the distance of the Kentucky Derby, which could well be his first major target in 2005. *C. Dollase, USA*

WILLHECONQUERTOO 4 ch.g. Primo Dominie 121 – Sure Care 62 (Caerleon (USA) 132) [2004 87: p8g 7f 6g³ 6g⁵ 6f* 5g 6g 6m⁵ 5.7f⁴ p6g⁴ p6g p6d⁴ p5.1g² p5.1g⁵ p6g³ p5g* Dec 18] sturdy gelding: fairly useful performer: won handicaps at Windsor in July and Lingfield in December: effective at 5f to easy 7f: acts on polytrack and firm going: tongue tied: often wears cheekpieces: sometimes slowly away: none too consistent. *Andrew Reid* **80**

WILLHEGO 3 ch.g. Pivotal 124 – Woodrising 64 (Nomination 125) [2004 53: 5s 7.9f p10g² p10g³ 10d* p12g⁵ 8d p12g p10g⁴ f8g Nov 22] plain gelding: fair performer: won handicap at Lingfield in August: stays 1¼m: acts on polytrack and good to soft going. *J. R. Best* **67**

WILL HE WISH 8 b.g. Winning Gallery 94 – More To Life (Northern Tempest (USA) 120) [2004 103: 6g p7g 6g⁵ 7d⁶ 7.1g 7m 6m 7m 7g 7m* 8m³ 7.1d⁶ 8d² 8f 8.1s Sep 24] good-bodied gelding: useful performer: won handicap at Yarmouth in July by 1½ lengths **97**

from And Toto Too: several creditable efforts otherwise at 8 yrs, sixth to Tout Seul in listed race at Leicester in April: dropped away tamely last 2 outings: stays 1m: acts on firm and good to soft going: effective blinkered or not. *S. Gollings*

WILLHEWIZ 4 b.g. Wizard King 122 – Leave It To Lib 66 (Tender King 123) [2004 **85** 100: 5g 5s⁵ 6g⁶ 6m 5m* 6m* 6m 6m 5g 7g 5.1d⁴ 6m 5g p6g² p6d p6g Nov 27] good-topped gelding: fairly useful performer: won claimer at Sandown (left C. Dwyer) and minor event at Newmarket in June: creditable efforts after only when in frame: effective at 5f/6f: acts on all-weather, firm and good to soft going: tried blinkered, effective visored or not: usually races up with pace. *R. M. Stronge*

WILLIAM JAMES 2 b.g. (Mar 23) Mujahid (USA) 125 – Pain Perdu (IRE) (Waajib **48** 121) [2004 5.2m⁵ 7g p5.1g⁶ Oct 2] poor form in maidens/seller: visored second start: looked difficult ride final one. *M. J. Wallace*

WILLIAM'S WELL 10 ch.g. Superpower 113 – Catherines Well 99 (Junius (USA) **63** 124) [2004 69: 6v 6d 6g 6g⁵ 6g 6g⁶ 6g³ 6g³ 5d 6g⁵ Oct 5] useful-looking gelding: modest handicapper: effective at 6f to 7.5f: acts on firm and soft going: blinkered. *M. W. Easterby*

WILLIAM TELL (IRE) 2 b.c. (Apr 25) Rossini (USA) 118 – Livry (USA) (Lyphard **78** (USA) 132) [2004 7m⁶ 8.1d⁴ 8.1g⁵ 8s² 7.9g² 8d² p8.6g⁴ p8g Nov 30] €20,000Y (twice), resold again 40,000Y: leggy, angular colt: half-brother to several winners, including 6f winner Deliver (by Rousillon) and 7f (at 2 yrs)/1m winner Sophomore (by Sanglamore): dam French 11f winner: fair maiden: should stay 1¼m: acts on polytrack and soft going: consistent. *M. R. Channon*

WILLJOJO 3 b.f. Mind Games 121 – Millie's Lady (IRE) (Common Grounds 118) **61** [2004 55: 5g³ 5.9f⁵ f6g⁴ 7g* 7m* 7.2g⁵ Jul 12] quite good-topped filly: modest performer: won seller at Leicester in June and handicap at Catterick in July: stayed 7f: acted on fibresand, good to firm and good to soft going: visored 5 of last 7 starts: dead. *R. A. Fahey*

WILLOFCOURSE 3 b.g. Aragon 118 – Willyet (Nicholas Bill 125) [2004 85: 6m **–** May 18] lightly-raced maiden: below form only 3-y-o start. *H. Candy*

WILL THE TILL 2 b.g. (Mar 1) Fraam 114 – Prim Ajwaad (Bin Ajwaad (IRE) 119) **54 ?** [2004 5.1m 5.7g 7g Oct 12] 5,000Y: leggy, good-topped gelding: seemingly modest form in maidens: likely to prove best up to 7f. *J. M. Bradley*

WILLYEVER 10 b.g. Merdon Melody 98 – Stonebroker 59 (Morston (FR) 125) **51** [2004 64: f7g 5.8m 7f 6f⁶ 6.5d³ 8g 8.5d 6g 6.5v a7g Sep 9] fairly useful at best: won handicap at Roscommon in 2003: just modest in 2004: probably stays 9f: acts on any turf going, well beaten both outings on fibresand (including at Southwell on reappearance): tried tongue tied/visored/in cheekpieces, usually blinkered. *Frederick John Bowles, Ireland*

WILOM (GER) 6 ch.g. Lomitas 129 – Whispering Willows (Mansingh (USA) 120) **44** [2004 48: p8g² p8g⁵ p8g⁴ p8g⁵ p10g p10g p8g 8g⁶ p10g Dec 20] poor performer: stays 10.5f: acts on polytrack, heavy and good to firm going: tried blinkered. *M. R. Hoad*

WILSON BLUEBOTTLE (IRE) 5 ch.g. Priolo (USA) 127 – Mauras Pride (IRE) **53** (Cadeaux Genereux 131) [2004 52: f8.5g⁶ f9.4s* f8s f9.4g² f8g² f9.4g f8g 9f 10g f6m⁶ f8f⁶ Aug 20] smallish, strong, lengthy gelding: modest performer: won banded event at Wolverhampton in February: stays 9.4f: acts on fibresand and good to firm going: blinkered: often makes running. *M. W. Easterby*

WILTSHIRE (IRE) 2 br.g. (Apr 3) Spectrum (IRE) 126 – Mary Magdalene 78 (Night **59** Shift (USA)) [2004 7.1d 7.1g 8m 8.1g 5.3m* 6m 6m³ f7g p7m Dec 21] leggy gelding: modest performer: won seller at Brighton in September: left M. Channon after seventh start: should stay 7f: acts on good to firm going: blinkered last 2 outings: none too consistent. *D. Flood*

WIN ALOT 6 b.g. Aragon 118 – Having Fun (Hard Fought 125) [2004 52: 13.8s f12g **–** f14g f11d Dec 21] sturdy gelding: no form in 2004: tried blinkered/tongue tied. *M. C. Chapman*

WIND CHIME (IRE) 7 ch.h. Arazi (USA) 135 – Shamisen 86 (Diesis 133) [2004 **72** 76, a58: p10g p8g² p8g 8.1f* 7g³ 9m 9m p8.6g Nov 6] smallish horse: fair handicapper **a60** on turf, modest on all-weather: won at Warwick in June: best at 7f to easy 9f: acts on all-weather, firm and good to soft going. *A. G. Newcombe*

WINDERMERE (IRE) 5 b.h. Lear Fan (USA) 130 – Madame L'Enjoleur (USA) **113** (L'Enjoleur (CAN)) [2004 113: 14m* 22.2f Jun 19] tall, lengthy, good sort: smart performer: won listed race at Leopardstown in May by 4½ lengths from Vinnie Roe, soon establishing huge advantage: tailed off in Queen Alexandra Stakes at Royal Ascot: stays 15f: acts on firm and good to soft going: front runner. *T. M. Walsh, Ireland*

WINDERMERE ISLAND 2 b.f. (Feb 8) Cadeaux Genereux 131 – Corndavon (USA) 95 (Sheikh Albadou 128) [2004 6f⁴ Aug 5] second foal: half-sister to smart 2003 2-y-o 5f/6f winner Nevisian Lad (by Royal Applause): dam 6f winner: 20/1 and green, fourth to Ghurra in maiden at Yarmouth, slowly away and not knocked about: should improve. *M. L. W. Bell* — **78 p**

WINDSCREAMER 2 b.f. (Apr 20) Josr Algarhoud (IRE) 118 – St James's Antigua (IRE) 79 (Law Society (USA) 130) [2004 7m* 7f⁶ 8m Sep 9] 10,000Y: sturdy filly: half-sister to several winners, including 1¼m winner Ibin St James (by Salse) and 6-y-o Sashay: dam 1m winner: won maiden at Newbury in July: more highly tried after, creditable sixth in Sweet Solera Stakes at Newmarket: should have stayed 1m: dead. *J. W. Hills* — **88**

WINDS OF MARCH (IRE) 3 b.f. Sadler's Wells (USA) 132 – Alidiva 105 (Chief Singer 131) [2004 10g* 10g⁴ May 14] big, strong, lengthy filly: has a fluent, rather round action: sister to useful 1¼m winner Curtain Time, closely related to 2 winners by Fairy King, and half-sister to 1000 Guineas winner Sleepytime and high-class miler Ali-Royal (both by Royal Academy) and very smart performer up to 12.5f Taipan (by Last Tycoon): dam, 6f (at 2 yrs) to 1m winner, half-sister to high-class French middle-distance colt Croco Rouge: fairly useful form: won maiden at Newbury in April by short head from Crystal: reportedly in season when 5¼ lengths fourth to Rave Reviews in listed race there following month: likely to stay 1½m. *J. H. M. Gosden* — **94**

WINDS OF TIME (IRE) 2 b.f. (Mar 18) Danehill (USA) 126 – Windmill 71 (Ezzoud (IRE) 126) [2004 6g* Jul 8] 350,000Y: smallish, close-coupled filly: first foal: dam, 1¾m winner, half-sister to very smart Princess Royal Stakes winner Banket and Ribblesdale Stakes winner Gull Nook, herself dam of Pentire: won maiden at Newmarket by neck from Unreal, slowly away but staying on to lead line: will stay at least 1m: should improve if all is well. *Mrs A. J. Perrett* — **80 p**

WINDSOR BEAUTY (IRE) 6 b. or br.g. Woods of Windsor (USA) – Tumble Dale 88§ (Tumble Wind) [2004 15.4s Apr 20] ex-Irish gelding: fair performer in 2001/2 for K. Prendergast: well held only start on Flat since. *R. Rowe* — **–**

Saval Beg Stakes, Leopardstown—
Windermere, under a most enterprising ride from Johnny Murtagh, is in an unassailable lead

Sheikh Mohammed's "Windsor Knot"

WINDSOR KNOT (IRE)   2 ch.c. (Mar 3) Pivotal 124 – Triple Tie (USA) 81 (The   **110 p**
Minstrel (CAN) 135) [2004 7.1m⁴ 7m* 7.1d* Aug 21] €260,000Y: big, rangy colt: has
scope: fluent mover: fourth living foal: half-brother to winner in Hungary by Bin Ajwaad:
dam 1¾m winner: made all in maiden at Newmarket (beat Monsoon Rain by 2 lengths)
and Iveco Daily Solario Stakes at Sandown (by 2½ lengths from Embossed) in August:
will stay 1¼m: acts on good to firm and good to soft going: joined Godolphin: smart
already, and likely to progress. *J. H. M. Gosden*

WINDWOOD (IRE)   2 b.g. (Apr 6) Piccolo 121 – Presently 48 (Cadeaux Genereux   **60**
131) [2004 5g 5.7g p6g⁵ Oct 7] 60,000Y: sixth foal: half-brother to 3 winners, including
3-y-o Ace Club and 4-y-o Brioso: dam, 5f winner, half-sister to smart sprinter Sizzling
Melody: modest form in maidens/claimer: should prove best at 5f/6f: gelded after final
start. *J. W. Hills*

WINDY BRITAIN   5 b.m. Mark of Esteem (IRE) 137 – For My Love (Kahyasi 130)   **106**
[2004 100: 10m 10m⁴ 10g² 9.9g⁶ 10.5g 10.1s 10d* 10m* 10g 10d⁴ Nov 7] compact mare:
useful performer: mostly creditable efforts in handicaps in Britain before winning minor
event at Milan in September (final outing for L. Cumani) and listed race at Rome (by 3½
lengths from Quetena) in October: effective at 1¼m/1½m: acts on polytrack, soft and
good to firm going: held up: consistent but no easy ride. *V. Valiani, Italy*

WINDY PROSPECT   2 ch.c. (Apr 8) Intikhab (USA) 135 – Yellow Ribbon (IRE) 72   **96**
(Hamas (IRE) 125§) [2004 p5g³ 5g⁵ 5d² f6m* 5m 7.1f³ 6f² 6m² f7g* 6d* Sep 19] 8,500F,
€30,000Y: rather leggy colt: second foal: half-brother to 3-y-o Shamrock Tea: dam 7f
winner: useful performer: won maiden at Wolverhampton in May and nurseries at
Southwell in August and Hamilton (under 9-6, held Gifted Gamble by short head) in
September: effective at 6f/7f: acts on fibresand, firm and good to soft going: races up with
pace: game. *P. A. Blockley*

WING COLLAR 3 b.g. In The Wings 128 – Riyoom (USA) 83 (Vaguely Noble 140) **79**
[2004 66: 12.3g 10v³ 10m³ 12.1d² 11d 16.2d⁴ 10f³ 12.1m* 14.1d² Oct 15] tall, quite
good-topped gelding: fair handicapper: won at Beverley in September: effective at 1¼m,
barely at 2m: acts on any going: sometimes races freely: consistent. *T. D. Easterby*

WING COMMANDER 5 b.g. Royal Applause 124 – Southern Psychic (USA) **100**
(Alwasmi (USA) 115) [2004 98: 8g⁴ 10v³ 7f 8f 10.4g 8m* 8m 8g³ 10.4s 10.1g⁵ 8s 9g Oct
2] strong, lengthy gelding: useful handicapper: won at Pontefract (readily by 3 lengths
from Vicious Warrior) in July: creditable effort after only when third to Pentecost at Ascot
in August: probably best at 1m/1¼m on good going or firmer: tried visored: has been
bandaged: usually held up. *R. A. Fahey*

WINGED D'ARGENT (IRE) 3 b.c. In The Wings 128 – Petite-D-Argent 91 **103 p**
(Noalto 120) [2004 10v* 10d⁵ 13.1s* 14.6s* 16d² Nov 3] sturdy colt: fourth foal:
half-brother to 3 winners, including 8.5f (at 2 yrs) to 1½m winner Greta d'Argent (by
Great Commotion) and 7-y-o Mana d'Argent, both useful: dam 6f (at 2 yrs) and 7f
winner: progressive form: won maiden at Pontefract in April and handicaps at Ayr (after
5½-month lay-off) and Doncaster (beat Jeepstar by 8 lengths) in October: 5 lengths
second to Alcazar in listed race at Musselburgh final start: stays 2m: raced only on going
softer than good: should make a smart 4-y-o. *M. Johnston*

WINGMAN (IRE) 2 b.c. (May 18) In The Wings 128 – Precedence (IRE) 88 (Polish **93**
Precedent (USA) 131) [2004 7m 7g⁵ 8g* 9s³ Oct 17] €26,000Y: sturdy, useful-looking
colt: second foal: half-brother to 3-y-o Charlie Tango: dam, Irish maiden who stayed 9f,
out of smart 1¼m performer Braiswick: fairly useful performer: won maiden at
Goodwood in September comfortably by neck from Foxhaven: creditable 10 lengths third
of 4 to Musketier in Prix de Conde at Longchamp: should be suited by 1¼m/1½m: acts
on soft going. *J. W. Hills*

WINGS OF MORNING (IRE) 3 ch.g. Fumo di Londra (IRE) 108 – Hay Knot **68**
(Main Reef 126) [2004 58+: f7g* f7g⁵ f7s⁶ 7.5d³ 8m f7g 9.2d³ f6g⁴ 7g p7.1d f7g Nov 9]
sturdy gelding: fair performer: won maiden at Southwell in January: below form after
fourth start, leaving P. Blockley when eighth: stays 7.5f: acts on fibresand and good to soft
ground: tried blinkered/visored: races prominently. *D. Carroll*

WINGSPEED (IRE) 2 b.g. (Feb 19) Bluebird (USA) 125 – Aneeda (Rainbow Quest **82**
(USA) 134) [2004 7g⁵ 7m² 7m⁴ Sep 23] 28,000F: sturdy gelding: seventh foal: closely
related to fairly useful 7f and (in Italy at 2 yrs) 8.5f winner Pride of Dingle (by Dolphin
Street) and half-brother to 2 winners, including useful 1999 2-y-o 7f winner Issey Rose
(by Bigstone): dam unraced: easily best effort in maidens when second at Epsom: will
stay 1m: tends to carry head high: gelded after final start. *Mrs A. J. Perrett*

WINNERS DELIGHT 3 ch.g. First Trump 118 – Real Popcorn (IRE) 52 (Jareer **86**
(USA) 115) [2004 82: 9s 9g 8.1d⁵ 12g⁵ 10d³ 10g 10g 10.1g³ 14g⁶ p12g* p10g Nov 27]
compact gelding: fairly useful handicapper: banned under non-triers rule second start:
improved form after, winning at Lingfield in October by neck from King of Diamonds:
stays 1½m: acts on polytrack, firm and good to soft going: held up. *A. P. Jarvis*

WINNING PLEASURE (IRE) 6 b.g. Ashkalani (IRE) 128 – Karamana (Habitat **–**
134) [2004 68, a82: f6g⁶ Jan 13] leggy, sparely-made gelding: handicapper: just fair form **a71**
only 6-y-o start: probably best at 6f: acts on fibresand, best runs on turf on good/ good to
firm ground: tried visored/in cheekpieces, often blinkered. *J. Balding*

WINNING VENTURE 7 b.g. Owington 123 – Push A Button (Bold Lad (IRE) 133) **90**
[2004 97: 6g⁶ 6g 8m³ 7.2g² 8g 7.6s 7.1s² 7m p7.1g 7d Oct 30] lengthy, good-topped
gelding: unimpressive mover: fairly useful performer: idled having looked likely winner
when beaten neck in minor events at Ayr and Chepstow in summer: stays 1m: acts on firm
and soft going: tried in blinkers/cheekpieces: often tongue tied at 4 yrs: usually races
prominently: flashed tail third outing: none too consistent. *A. W. Carroll*

WINSLOW BOY (USA) 3 b. or br.g. Expelled (USA) 116 – Acusteal (USA) **68**
(Acaroid (USA)) [2004 55: 10g 12.1g⁴ 11.5m⁶ 11.5f* 14g² 14.1g⁶ 14d³ 14.1d⁶ 12g⁶ 15s²
Oct 11] fair handicapper: won at Yarmouth in June: left C. Wall after eighth outing:
should stay 2m: acts on firm and soft going: sometimes gives trouble at start: held up.
P. Monteith

WINSLOW HOMER (FR) 3 b.c. Peintre Celebre (USA) 137 – Armorique (IRE) **–**
(Top Ville 129) [2004 10g Aug 23] 33/1, well held in maiden at Windsor: sold 6,000 gns.
J. H. M. Gosden

WINTER MIST 2 gr.f. (Feb 19) Tomba 119 – Misty Goddess (IRE) 63 (Godswalk **–**
(USA) 130) [2004 6g p6d 7.1m 10.1d p8.6g Nov 12] sturdy filly: seventh foal: half-sister

to 3 winners, including 1m/1¼m winner Imari (by Rock City): dam 7f (at 2 yrs) to 11f winner: no form in claimers/maidens: signs of temperament. *N. P. Littmoden*

WINTER MOON 2 b.f. (Mar 19) Mujadil (USA) 119 – Crofters Ceilidh 101 (Scottish –
Reel 123) [2004 6f Jul 19] 29,000Y: fourth foal: half-sister to useful 2003 2-y-o 5f/6f winner Cop Hill Lad (by Atraf): dam, 5f winner (including at 2 yrs), half-sister to 9-y-o Lord Kintyre: 16/1, well held in maiden at Windsor. *B. R. Millman*

WINTHORPE (IRE) 4 b.g. Tagula (IRE) 116 – Zazu 58 (Cure The Blues (USA)) **76**
[2004 85: f6g f6g 6g 6s 6g 6m⁴ 6m 5d³ 5d² 5m 5g⁵ 5g⁴ 5m⁴ 6f³ 6g 5g⁶ Oct 8] leggy gelding: fair handicapper: effective at 5f/6f: acts on fibresand, firm and good to soft going: ran creditably in cheekpieces final start: sometimes carries head high: none too consistent. *J. J. Quinn*

WISE DENNIS 2 b.g. (Apr 11) Polar Falcon (USA) 126 – Bowden Rose 100 (Dashing **102**
Blade 117) [2004 6g 7g 6f³ p7g³ 8.1g³ 7m* 8d² Oct 18] well-grown, leggy gelding: third foal: dam 5f and (including at 2 yrs) 6f winner: useful performer: won nursery at Ascot in October by 1¾ lengths from Rebel Rebel: good 3½ lengths second to Comic Strip in listed event at Pontefract, leading briefly over 1f out: stays 1m: acts on good to firm and good to soft going (promise only run on polytrack): usually held up. *A. P. Jarvis*

WISE OWL 2 b.g. (Mar 22) Danehill (USA) 126 – Mistle Thrush (USA) 90 (Storm **87**
Bird (CAN) 134) [2004 6m² 6g⁴ 6f* 6g Oct 8] 200,000Y: angular, good-topped gelding: fifth foal: half-brother to 4-y-o Estimate and smart 1¼m to 14.6f (Park Hill Stakes) winner Mistle Song (by Nashwan): dam 1¼m winner: fairly useful performer: odds on, won maiden at Pontefract in September by 4 lengths from Circumspect: ran poorly in nursery final start (gelded after): will stay at least 1m: acts on firm going. *M. Johnston*

WISE WAGER (IRE) 2 b.f. (Mar 17) Titus Livius (FR) 115 – Londubh (Tumble **75**
Wind) [2004 f5m² 5f³ 5g³ 5f³ 5m* 5g² 5.1g² 5g Sep 13] €3,500Y: unfurnished, rather plain filly: fifth foal: half-sister to dam unraced in Sweden by Goldmark: dam unraced: fair performer: made all in nursery at Thirsk in July: creditable efforts in similar events after: likely to prove best at 5f: acts on fibresand and firm going: usually races prominently/carries head awkwardly: consistent. *R. A. Fahey*

WISTMAN (UAE) 3 br.g. Woodman (USA) 126 – Saik (USA) (Riverman (USA) 131) **86**
[2004 7d* 7.5s³ Apr 22] first foal: dam unraced half-sister to smart 1¼m/1½m winner Husyan and to dam of 7-y-o Mubtaker: fairly useful form: won maiden at Folkestone in April: better effort when 1¾ lengths third to Imperialistic in handicap at Beverley: will stay 1m: sold 8,000 gns in October, then gelded. *D. R. Loder*

WITCHCRAFT 3 b.g. Zilzal (USA) 137 – Witch of Fife (USA) 91 (Lear Fan (USA) –
130) [2004 p8.6g Dec 27] 40/1, eighth of 13 in maiden at Wolverhampton, slowly away. *D. Shaw*

*Stanleybet Robert Sangster Superior Mile, Haydock—the six-year-old With Reason
makes his contribution to Godolphin's tally of winners with an all-the-way success from Troubadour,
who is carrying the Sangster colours, and Audience*

WITCHELLE   3 br.f. Wizard King 122 – Tachelle (IRE) (Elbio 125) [2004 f8g Dec 7]   **45**
1,300Y, 2,000 3-y-o: first foal: dam tailed off only start: 50/1, seventh in maiden at Southwell, weakening. *R. Craggs*

WITCHES BROOM   3 b.f. Fraam 114 – Carte Blanche 67 (Cadeaux Genereux 131)   **59**
[2004 p8g 7m³ 8.1m⁶ 6m p6g⁵ p8.6g Dec 15] £2,000Y: leggy filly: fifth foal: dam 1m
winner: modest maiden: stays 7f: raced freely second/third starts. *C. A. Cyzer*

WITCHING   3 b.f. Hector Protector (USA) 124 – Charming Life 88 (Habitat 134)   –
[2004 9.7m⁶ Jul 22] half-sister to several winners, including smart French 5f (at 2 yrs)
to 1m winner Run And Gun (by Lomond) and useful 1¼m and (in France) 11f winner
Caerau (by Nashwan): dam 7f winner: 7/2, well beaten in maiden at Folkestone.
D. J. Daly

WITCHRY   2 gr.g. (Jan 29) Green Desert (USA) 127 – Indian Skimmer (USA) 132   **87**
(Storm Bird (CAN) 134) [2004 6m⁴ 5f³ 5m* 5g Aug 14] seventh known foal: dam won 5
Group 1s from 9f to 10.5f, including Prix de Diane and Champion Stakes: fairly useful
performer: odds on, won maiden at Pontefract in July by 4 lengths from Graze On:
favourite, got no sort of run in nursery final start: shapes as if will prove best at 5f/6f.
M. A. Jarvis

WITCHY VIBES   2 ch.f. (Mar 15) Tomba 119 – Risk The Witch (Risk Me (FR) 127)   –
[2004 6s 7.1d Oct 9] 1,500Y: sturdy filly: sixth foal: half-sister to winner in Greece
by Most Welcome: dam of little account: last in maidens at Haydock and Warwick.
M. Appleby

WITHERING LADY (IRE)   2 b.f. (Jan 28) Tagula (IRE) 116 – Princess Oberon   **76**
(IRE) 91 (Fairy King (USA)) [2004 5d³ 5.1g⁴ 5g⁶ 5d² 5.2m 5m* 6g 5.7d⁵ 5m⁴ p5.1g
p5.1g Dec 20] 1,800F, 8,000Y: big, good-topped filly: fourth living foal: half-sister to
6-y-o Midnight Arrow: dam 5f winner (including at 2 yrs): fair performer: landed odds in
maiden at Beverley in July: fourth in nursery at Windsor, only creditable effort after:
seems best at 5f: acts on good to firm and good to soft going. *Mrs P. N. Dutfield*

WITH HONOURS   2 b.f. (Feb 4) Bien Bien (USA) 125 – Fair Test 95 (Fair Season   **44**
120) [2004 7s p8.6g p8.6g f7g Dec 16] 2,500Y: half-sister to several winners, including
4-y-o Nawow and 5-y-o Flaming Spirt: dam 5f winner, including at 2 yrs: poor form in
maidens: should stay 1¼m: best efforts on polytrack. *T. J. Fitzgerald*

WITHORWITHOUTYOU (IRE)   3 b.f. Danehill (USA) 126 – Morningsurprice   **71**
(USA) (Future Storm (USA)) [2004 91: 5.1g⁶ 6g⁵ 5.1g 7.1f 7m Jul 6] tall, good-topped
filly: fair performer: raced only on good going or firmer: stays 7f. *B. A. McMahon*

WITH REASON (USA)   6 ch.g. Nashwan (USA) 135 – Just Cause (Law Society   **114**
(USA) 130) [2004 117: 8m 8.1g* Sep 4] sturdy, lengthy gelding: smart performer: off 3½
months, won listed event at Haydock in September by length from Troubadour, well
ridden from front: best at 7f/1m: acts on all-weather, good to firm and good to soft going:
tongue tied at 6 yrs: wears crossed noseband: usually races prominently: reliable. *Saeed
bin Suroor*

WITTILY   4 ch.f. Whittingham (IRE) 104 – Lucky Dip 68 (Tirol 127) [2004 48: f5g   –
Jan 12] strong, lengthy filly: well held only start in 2004: tried in cheekpieces/blinkers.
A. Berry

WITTY GIRL   2 b.f. (Feb 15) Whittingham (IRE) 104 – Zando's Charm 60 (Forzando   **52**
122) [2004 5.1m³ 6f⁴ 6m p5.1g Dec 14] small filly: first foal: dam 2-y-o 7f winner:
modest maiden: trained debut by M. Usher, next start by C. Dwyer: should stay 7f.
M. J. Polglase

WITWATERSRAND (IRE)   2 b.f. (Apr 22) Unfuwain (USA) 131 – Valley of Gold   **71 p**
(FR) 117 (Shirley Heights 130) [2004 7g⁴ Sep 20] tall filly: fourth foal: closely related to
17f winner Honest Obsession (by Sadler's Wells) and half-sister to smart 7f (at 2 yrs) and
1m winner Splendid Era (by Green Desert) and 5-y-o Hills of Gold: dam 1¼m/11f (Oaks
d'Italia) winner: 16/1, fourth to Fen Shui in maiden at Kempton, late headway when not
clear run: likely to be suited by 1¼m/1½m: sure to improve. *B. W. Hills*

WIZARD LOOKING   3 b.g. Wizard King 122 – High Stepping (IRE) (Taufan (USA)   **68 d**
119) [2004 73: 8g⁶ 7.1f 7m 8m⁶ p8g 8f Jul 21] tall, close-coupled gelding: fair maiden:
below form after reappearance, in seller final start: stays 1m: acts on polytrack and good
to firm going: tried blinkered, usually tongue tied. *R. Hannon*

WIZARDMICKTEE (IRE)   2 b.c. (Mar 3) Monashee Mountain (USA) 115 – Epsilon   **73**
62 (Environment Friend 128) [2004 6s 7m² 6s² 6.1s⁴ 5g 5.1v p7.1g³ p6g Dec 10]
€6,000F, 8,000Y, 11,000 2-y-o: leggy colt: first foal: dam ran twice (better effort at 7f at 2

yrs): fair maiden: probably stays 7f: acts on soft going, probably on good to firm and polytrack: often races up with pace. *A. Bailey*

WIZARD OF EDGE   4 b.g. Wizard King 122 – Forever Shineing 62 (Glint of Gold 128) [2004 66+: p10g⁶ 12.1m 9d⁴ Aug 13] modest maiden, lightly raced: left G. Balding after reappearance: stays 1½m: acts on fibresand, soft and good to firm going: fairly useful hurdler. *R. J. Hodges*   **64**

WIZARD OF NOZ   4 b.g. Inchinor 119 – Winning Girl (Green Desert (USA) 127) [2004 111: 8m² 7.5f⁶ 8f 7.9d⁵ 7m⁵ 7f⁵ 8d⁵ 7g* 7d Oct 15] workmanlike gelding: useful handicapper: won at Newmarket in October by length from Leoballero: found little final start: stays 1m: acts on firm and soft going: visored/blinkered last 4 outings: sold 38,000 gns, joined M. Al Kurdi in UAE. *J. Noseda*   **107**

WIZARD OF THE WEST   4 b.g. Wizard King 122 – Rose Burton 42 (Lucky Wednesday 124) [2004 ?, a65: 12f 12f 12f 16.4g Jul 8] maiden handicapper on Flat: mostly well held in 2004: tried blinkered: won claiming hurdle in August. *Miss S. West*   **–**

WIZARD OF US   4 b.g. Wizard King 122 – Sian's Girl (Mystiko (USA) 124) [2004 –: 7.2s* p8.6d 8.2v² p13.9g f8g⁵ Dec 1] smallish, workmanlike gelding: fair on turf, modest on all-weather: much improved when winning handicap at Ayr in October: stays 1m: acts on fibresand and heavy going. *M. Mullineaux*   **66 a46**

WIZARDS PRINCESS   4 b.f. Wizard King 122 – Chalice 69 (Governor General 116) [2004 12s⁵ 9f Sep 2] first foal: dam 5f winner: well held in bumper/maidens. *D. W. Thompson*   **–**

WIZ IN   2 gr.g. (Mar 29) Wizard King 122 – Great Intent (Aragon 118) [2004 p6g p8g Oct 31] well held in maidens at Lingfield. *T. Keddy*   **–**

WIZZSKILAD   2 b.c. (Feb 28) Wizard King 122 – Sure Babe (Sure Blade (USA) 130) [2004 p5g 5d⁴ 5g⁶ 5v³ 5.1m 5.1m⁵ 5.1g 5d³ Aug 28] modest maiden: will prove best at 5f/easy 6f: acts on heavy and good to firm ground: sold 500 gns, sent to Denmark. *Mrs P. N. Dutfield*   **56**

WODHILL BE   4 b.f. Danzig Connection (USA) – Muarij (Star Appeal 133) [2004 –: f7g⁵ p7g⁶ p8g⁵ 7m 8s 7m³ 7m 8m 7m 8m 8.1m 7d² 6d Oct 16] poor maiden: stays 1m: acts on polytrack, good to firm and good to soft going. *D. Morris*   **49 d**

WODHILL FOLLY   7 ch.m. Faustus (USA) 118 – Muarij (Star Appeal 133) [2004 52: f9.4g⁴ f9.4g⁶ f9.4g Feb 13] angular, workmanlike mare: modest handicapper: best up to 1¼m: acts on all-weather and good to firm going: visored. *D. Morris*   **50**

WODHILL GOLD   3 ch.g. Dancing Spree (USA) – Golden Filigree 48 (Faustus (USA) 118) [2004 8m p7.1g p9.5g Nov 26] sturdy gelding: little form in maidens. *D. Morris*   **–**

WODHILL HOPE   4 b.f. Distinctly North (USA) 115 – Golden Filigree 48 (Faustus (USA) 118) [2004 14.1s⁴ 11.5m³ 12f 14.1m 12.6d 11.8g Oct 12] lengthy filly: second foal: dam, ran 3 times, showed signs of ability: poor form. *D. Morris*   **48**

WOLDS DANCER   2 b.f. (Apr 6) Fraam 114 – Dancing Em 60 (Rambo Dancer (CAN) 107) [2004 6g⁶ 6f 7.5g Jun 17] 8,000Y: angular, unfurnished filly: second foal: dam, 7f/1m winner, half-sister to smart performer up to 8.5f Jo Mell: best effort in maidens when seventh at Redcar on second start: should stay 7f. *T. D. Easterby*   **57**

WOLF CUB   3 ch.g. Wolfhound (USA) 126 – Ansellady 67 (Absalom 128) [2004 7s May 7] 33/1, ran as if amiss in maiden at Lingfield. *Miss Gay Kelleway*   **–**

WOLF HAMMER (USA)   2 ch.g. (May 6) Diesis 133 – Polly's Link (USA) (Phone Trick (USA)) [2004 7d 6g² 5v² Aug 27] $35,000Y, 90,000 2-y-o: second foal: dam, French 1m winner, half-sister to smart French middle-distance performer Solid Illusion: fair form when second in minor events in small fields at Thirsk and Newcastle: bred to stay at least 7f. *J. Howard Johnson*   **70**

WOMAN IN WHITE (FR)   3 gr.f. Daylami (IRE) 138 – Nicer (IRE) 113 (Pennine Walk 120) [2004 7g 9g² 10g⁶ 11.5g³ Aug 11] lengthy filly: fifth living foal: half-sister to 4-y-o Night Wolf: dam 6f (at 2 yrs) and Irish 1000 Guineas winner: barely stays 11.5f: raced freely third/fourth starts. *J. H. M. Gosden*   **71**

WONDERFUL MIND   2 b.c. (Feb 12) Mind Games 121 – Signs And Wonders 75§ (Danehill (USA) 126) [2004 5g 5d⁵ 5g² 5g* 5g⁵ 5f⁶ 5.1g³ 5g 5g⁵ 5m Oct 2] 25,000Y: tall, lengthy colt: first foal: dam, 1¼m winner, sister to dam of Queen Mary winners Romantic Liason and Romantic Myth: fair performer: won maiden at Beverley in July: creditable efforts when placed in nurseries after: will prove best at 5f: acts on firm and   **73**

good to soft going: blinkered 4 of last 5 starts: races up with pace: occasionally looks none too genuine. *T. D. Easterby*

WONDER WOLF 3 b.f. Wolfhound (USA) 126 – Wrangbrook (Shirley Heights 130) **40** [2004 –: 6m 9m⁵ 8f Sep 16] poor maiden. *R. A. Fahey*

WONKY DONKEY 3 b.g. Piccolo 121 – Salinas 65 (Bay Express 132) [2004 –: f8.5s³ **55** f8.5s⁴ f6g³ 6m f5g⁵ 7m Jul 7] modest maiden: should prove best at 5f/6f: acts on fibresand: tongue tied (reportedly lost action) fourth start: reportedly bled from nose when tailed off final outing. *S. C. Williams*

WON OF A FEW 4 b.g. Danzig Connection (USA) – Wonderful Day 71 (Niniski **–** (USA) 125) [2004 p9.5d p5.1g p8.6g p10g Dec 4] little form in maidens. *M. Wigham*

WOODBURY 5 b.m. Woodborough (USA) 112 – Jeewan 82 (Touching Wood (USA) **68** 127) [2004 70: p6g p6g⁴ p6g* 6m 6g⁴ 5.7f* 5.7g 6.1d⁶ p6g² p6g⁵ p5.1g⁵ p6g Nov 30] small mare: fair handicapper: left K. Burke after second start: won at Lingfield in July and Bath in September: stays 6f: acts on polytrack, firm and good to soft going: often races prominently: sometimes edges right. *Mrs H. Sweeting*

WOODBURY LANE (USA) 2 b. or br.f. (Jan 24) Wild Wonder (USA) 117 – Maxi- **59 p** mum Blue (USA) (Blue Ensign (USA)) [2004 8d⁵ Oct 15] $10,000F: tall, leggy filly: third foal: dam unraced: 9/2, fifth to Duroob in maiden at Redcar: likely to do better. *Saeed bin Suroor*

WOODCOTE (IRE) 2 b.c. (Apr 4) Monashee Mountain (USA) 115 – Tootle (Main **97 p** Reef 126) [2004 5g* 6g³ Oct 9] €11,000Y, 15,000 2-y-o: big, strong, lengthy colt: half-brother to several winners, including fairly useful 1993 2-y-o 7f winner Suaad (by Fools Holme) and 3-y-o Malibu: dam French 5.5f winner: won maiden at Windsor in August: still green, useful form when 3¾ lengths third to Moth Ball in listed event at York: not sure to stay much beyond 6f: type to make a better 3-y-o. *C. G. Cox*

WOODCRACKER 3 ch.g. Docksider (USA) 124 – Hen Harrier 94 (Polar Falcon **104** (USA) 126) [2004 69p: 10g* 10.4s² 12m 10m* Jul 7] lengthy, good-topped gelding: has a quick action: useful performer: won maiden at Nottingham in April and handicap at Newmarket (by short head from Royal Warrant) in July: injured hind leg after, but stays in training: should 1½m: acts on soft and good to firm going. *M. L. W. Bell*

WOOD DALLING (USA) 6 b.g. Woodman (USA) 126 – Cloelia (USA) (Lyphard **60 §** (USA) 132) [2004 78d: 7.2f 7.9f 9.2d⁶ 6.9f* 8g⁶ 9.1g⁶ 7.2s 6.9g⁶ 8g Sep 13] small, sturdy gelding: modest handicapper: left R. Allan after reappearance: won at Carlisle in July: probably best at 7f/1m: acts on all-weather, firm and good to soft going: tried in visor/cheekpieces at 5 yrs: ungenuine. *I. Semple*

WOOD FERN (UAE) 4 b.g. Green Desert (USA) 127 – Woodsia 97 (Woodman **52 §** (USA) 126) [2004 80: p7g 7s 8.3d 8.1v 7m⁵ 7.6g 8g 7m 7.6f 8.3d⁶ 7s* 7.1g 7g 7.1s⁴ 8m 8d 8d³ Oct 16] strong, close-coupled gelding: modest performer: won seller at Brighton in August: stays 1m: acts on polytrack, soft and good to firm going: effective visored or not: temperamental: sold 7,000 gns. *M. R. Channon*

WOODFORD CONSULT 2 b.f. (Mar 6) Benny The Dip (USA) 127 – Chicodove **46** 91 (In The Wings 128) [2004 7.9g p7.1g 8s³ Oct 30] 3,500F, 3,000Y: second foal: dam 11f/1½m winner: poor form in maidens: should be suited by 1¼m/1½m. *M. W. Easterby*

WOODFORD WONDER (IRE) 2 b.f. (Mar 17) Xaar 132 – Unscathed (Warning **–** 136) [2004 6m 5g 7m Oct 10] 3,200Y: leggy filly: second foal: half-sister to 3-y-o Grand But One: dam unraced: well held in maidens: unruly and withdrawn final intended start. *M. W. Easterby*

WOODLAND GLADE 3 b.f. Mark of Esteem (IRE) 137 – Incendio (Siberian Express **72** (USA) 125) [2004 7d² 8s² 7g⁵ Oct 11] quite good-topped filly: fifth foal: half-sister to 4-y-o Baron's Pit and winner abroad by Be My Chief: dam winning sprinter in Italy: fair form in maidens when runner-up: stays 1m: acts on soft going. *R. Hannon*

WOODSLEY HOUSE (IRE) 2 b.c. (Mar 31) Orpen (USA) 116 – Flame And Sha- **92** dow (IRE) (Turtle Island (IRE) 123) [2004 7d² 7.1m² 7.9g² 7s⁵ Oct 22] €9,500F, 7,000Y: tall, lengthy colt: first living foal: dam unraced half-sister to useful French performer up to 1¼m Blasket Island: fairly useful maiden: second at Salisbury, Sandown and York: best effort when fifth to Cupid's Glory in Horris Hill Stakes at Newbury: not sure to stay beyond 1m: usually races up with pace. *Mrs P. N. Dutfield*

WOOD SPIRIT (IRE) 2 b.f. (Apr 17) Woodborough (USA) 112 – Windomen (IRE) **62** (Forest Wind (USA) 111) [2004 5g⁶ 6s⁶ 8d⁴ p7.1g Nov 12] €4,500Y: quite good-topped filly: first foal: dam unraced out of half-sister to smart 7f to 9f performer Lapierre: modest maiden: best effort when fourth at Redcar: stays 1m: twice slowly away. *Mrs P. N. Dut-field*

WOOD SPRITE 2 b.f. (Apr 2) Mister Baileys 123 – Woodbeck 90 (Terimon 124) – p [2004 8s Oct 22] third foal: half-sister to 4-y-o Franklins Gardens and 5-y-o Polar Ben: dam, 7f winner, out of half-sister to Prix de Diane winner Madam Gay: 40/1, well held in maiden at Doncaster: likely to do better. *J. G. Given*

WOODSTOCK EXPRESS 4 b.g. Alflora (IRE) 120 – Young Tess 56 (Teenoso – (USA) 135) [2004 –: 17.2f Jun 12] tailed off in maidens/handicap. *P. Bowen*

WOOD STREET (IRE) 5 b.g. Eagle Eyed (USA) 111 – San-Catrinia (IRE) (Knesset – (USA) 105) [2004 59: 10.2f May 27] big, strong gelding: handicapper: well held only 5-y-o start: refused to enter stall in June. *R. J. Baker*

WOODUDANCE (USA) 2 br.f. (Mar 11) You And I (USA) 118 – Lina Cavalieri 53 (Star Appeal 133) [2004 6m⁵ 6g 6d 5s p6g p7m Dec 22] $22,000F, 16,000Y: sister to winner in USA, closely related to US Grade 3 8.5f winner Princess Kali (by Kris S), and half-sister to several winners in USA: dam Group 3 1m winner in Italy, also successful in USA: modest maiden: ran at Lingfield last 2 starts, creditable effort final one: stays easy 7f: acts on polytrack, best turf effort on good to firm going. *E. Tyrrell, Ireland*

WOODWIND DOWN 7 b.m. Piccolo 121 – Bint El Oumara (Al Nasr (FR) 126) [2004 52 12m* 15g 12g Sep 14] sturdy mare: modest handicapper, unraced on Flat in 2002/3: won at Musselburgh in July, dictating pace: stays easy 1½m: acts on firm going: tried blinkered. *M. Todhunter*

WOODY VALENTINE (USA) 3 ch.g. Woodman (USA) 126 – Mudslinger (USA) 92 (El Gran Senor (USA) 136) [2004 79: 12g⁴ 10s² 10s* 9g⁶ 9m⁶ 10.1g* 8.3g² 9.9m 8m 10.1m⁵ 8g² 10.3s⁴ Oct 22] rather leggy gelding: has a round action: fairly useful performer: won handicap at Pontefract in April and minor event at Epsom in July: good efforts last 2 starts, 2 lengths second to Desert Cristal in minor event at Goodwood penultimate one: effective at 1m to 1½m: acts on soft and good to firm going: sometimes on toes: usually races up with pace: consistent: sold 30,000 gns, joined Venetia Williams, successful in juvenile hurdle in December. *M. Johnston*

WOOLFALL JOANNA 2 gr.f. (Feb 8) Petong 126 – Real Princess 78 (Aragon 118) 44 [2004 6d 7d p6g p8.6g p8.6g Dec 6] 7,000F: workmanlike filly: sister to winner in USA and half-sister to 2 winners, including 6f and 1m winner Prince Caspian (by Mystiko): dam 7f winner: poor maiden: best effort when blinkered final start. *G. G. Margarson*

WOOLLY BACK (IRE) 3 b.g. Alzao (USA) 117 – Hopping Higgins (IRE) 103 80 (Brief Truce (USA) 126) [2004 11.9d² 11.9m² 11.9d⁶ 12d Oct 15] sturdy gelding: second foal: dam, Irish 5f winner, best at 2 yrs: fairly useful maiden: runner-up at Haydock first 2 starts: off over 4 months, pulled hard when tailed off in claimer final outing: sold 4,800 gns. *R. Hollinshead*

WOOLSACK (USA) 2 ch.c. (May 3) Spinning World (USA) 130 – Rich And Famous 73 p (FR) 111 (Deep Roots 124) [2004 7s⁵ 7.1d⁶ Nov 3] $40,000F: good-topped colt: brother to a winner in Italy and half-brother to 3 winners abroad, including German 1996 2-y-o 7f winner Ranghiroah (by Woodman): dam French 2-y-o 5f (Prix du Bois) winner: better effort in maidens when fifth to Tasdeed at Doncaster: favourite, travelled strongly long way at Musselburgh: has scope to do better as 3-y-o. *H. Morrison*

WOOLSTONE BOY (USA) 3 ch.g. Will's Way (USA) 125 – My Pleasure (USA) 54 (Marfa (USA)) [2004 10.2g 10v⁵ f12g⁴ p12m⁶ f11d⁴ Dec 21] modest maiden: stays 1¼m: has carried head high. *J. Jay*

WORCESTER LODGE 3 ch.g. Grand Lodge (USA) 125 – Borgia 91 (Machiavellian 76 (USA) 123) [2004 58p: 12f* 12s Aug 18] strong, good sort: fair handicapper, lightly raced: won at Newmarket in July: weakened quickly final start: should stay 1¾m: acts on firm going: sold 5,200 gns. *R. Charlton*

WORD PERFECT 2 b.f. (Apr 27) Diktat 126 – Better Still (IRE) (Glenstal (USA) 87 118) [2004 5s³ 5g* 5d* 6s⁵ 6d 6d⁵ 6m 6g³ 6s² Oct 29] tall, useful-looking filly: seventh foal: half-sister to 4-y-o Strong Hand and 6f winner Snappy (by First Trump): dam little form: fairly useful performer: won maiden at Ripon in April and minor event at Doncaster in July: creditable efforts in nursery/minor event last 2 starts: stays 6f: acts on soft and good to firm ground. *M. W. Easterby*

WOR KID 2 br.f. (Mar 25) Charnwood Forest (IRE) 125 – Patience Please 59 (King of 39 Spain 121) [2004 5.9g 7d Jul 4] first reported foal: dam 7f winner: poor form in maidens at Carlisle (slowly away) and Redcar (wandered). *R. P. Elliott*

WORLABY DALE 8 b.g. Terimon 124 – Restandbethankful (Random Shot 116) [2004 55: f16g⁴ f14g⁴ f16g f16g⁶ Feb 12] workmanlike gelding: poor maiden: stays 2m: acts on fibresand and good to firm going. *Mrs S. Lamyman* **?** **a42**

WORLD AT MY FEET 2 b.f. (Mar 16) Wolfhound (USA) 126 – Rehaab 72 (Mtoto 134) [2004 5s² 5d* 5m³ 5g 5d⁴ 6s 6m 5s⁴ 6s Oct 22] 1,400F, 1,600Y: small filly: has a short action: third foal: dam 1¼m/1½m winner: fairly useful performer: won minor event at Thirsk in May: poor efforts last 4 starts, including in blinkers: should stay 6f: acts on good to firm and good to soft ground. *N. Bycroft* **81 d**

WORLD MUSIC (USA) 2 b.f. (Apr 29) Dixieland Band (USA) – Headline (Machiavellian (USA) 123) [2004 5.1d³ p6g⁶ Oct 1] fifth foal: half-sister to smart US 1m and (Grade 1) 1½m winner Jilbab (by A P Indy) and 4-y-o Ancient World: dam unraced half-sister to US Grade 1 2-y-o 1m winner Saratoga Six and William Hill Futurity winner Dunbeath: much better effort in maidens when third at Bath: possibly failed to handle course at Lingfield (raced freely): bred to stay at least 7f. *Saeed bin Suroor* **70**

WORLD REPORT (USA) 2 b. or br.c. (Mar 22) Spinning World (USA) 130 – Miss Woodchuck (USA) (Woodman (USA) 126) [2004 6s⁴ 7.1m⁶ 7g⁴ 6s⁵ 6g Dec 29] €70,000Y: leggy, quite good-topped colt: half-brother to winner in USA by Lord Carson: dam 6f (including at 2 yrs) to 1m winner in USA: fair maiden: needs to settle to stay beyond 7f: acts on soft going: none too reliable. *R. Hannon* **79**

WORTH ABBEY 2 b.g. (May 7) Mujadil (USA) 119 – Housefull 81 (Habitat 134) [2004 7m 6f 6m 6g Sep 17] modest maiden: not sure to stay beyond 7f. *R. Hannon* **54**

WORTH A GAMBLE 6 ch.g. So Factual (USA) 120 – The Strid (IRE) 53 (Persian Bold 123) [2004 f11d Jun 17] good-topped gelding: maiden: missed 2003: well held only 6-y-o start. *H. E. Haynes* **–**

WORTH A GRAND (IRE) 2 br.g. (Mar 21) Raise A Grand (IRE) 114 – Ballykett Pride (IRE) 68 (Indian Ridge 123) [2004 7g 6d⁵ 6f⁵ 6s 5.1s⁶ p7.1g⁵ p6g p6g Dec 13] leggy gelding: moderate on turf, poor on all-weather: left J. Mullins after fifth start: best efforts at 6f/7f: acts on polytrack and good to soft going. *J. J. Bridger* **61** **a45**

WOTCHALIKE (IRE) 2 ch.c. (Feb 28) Spectrum (IRE) 126 – Juno Madonna (IRE) (Sadler's Wells (USA) 132) [2004 7m⁵ 6m 7s² 8g² 8s* 10d⁶ p8g⁵ Nov 16] €24,000F, 13,000Y: good-topped colt: fourth foal: closely related to fairly useful Irish 1½m and 17f winner Coquette Rouge (by Croco Rouge): dam, ran twice in France, closely related to useful sprinters Title Roll and Northern Express: fairly useful performer: landed odds in maiden at Bath in October, then left D. Elsworth: creditable efforts in listed race/nursery last 2 starts: stays 1¼m: acts on polytrack, soft and good to firm going. *R. J. Price* **82**

WOU OODD 3 ch.f. Barathea (IRE) 127 – Abyaan (IRE) 106 (Ela-Mana-Mou 132) [2004 –p: 9.9g⁴ 10m³ 9.9g⁵ 12.3d⁴ 10d Jul 10] lengthy filly: fair maiden: stays 1½m: acts on good to soft going: sold 15,000 gns in December. *M. R. Channon* **78**

WRENLANE 3 ch.g. Fraam 114 – Hi Hoh (IRE) (Fayruz 116) [2004 67: 6m² 6g⁶ 7.5g⁵ 8.5m 8s⁴ 7.9g 10d³ 8m⁴ 8d* p9.5d³ p8.6d* p9.5g f8g Dec 11] compact gelding: fair performer: won minor events at Pontefract in October and Wolverhampton in November: ran as if amiss final start: stays 1¼m: acts on polytrack, good to firm and good to soft going: tends to edge left. *R. A. Fahey* **76**

WUB CUB 4 b.f. Averti (IRE) 117 – Ray of Hope 53 (Rainbow Quest (USA) 134) [2004 53?: f6s⁶ f6g f5m Apr 27] sturdy filly: maiden: poor form in banded races in 2004. *A. Dickman* **35**

WUJOOD 2 b.g. (Mar 9) Alzao (USA) 117 – Rahayeb 79 (Arazi (USA) 135) [2004 7g 7m 7.1m 8s² Oct 19] small, good-topped gelding: first foal: dam, 1½m winner, out of useful close relative to Nayef and half-sister to Nashwan and Unfuwain: fair maiden: second to Wotchalike at Bath, best effort: will be suited by 1¼m/1½m: acts on soft ground: sold 18,000 gns, joined H. Morrison, then gelded. *J. L. Dunlop* **74**

WUNDERBRA (IRE) 3 b.f. Second Empire (IRE) 124 – Supportive (IRE) (Nashamaa 113) [2004 6d³ 7d⁴ f6g⁵ 6f* 5m³ 5m* f5f* 5.3s* 5s² 5d⁵ Sep 27] €52,000Y: deep-girthed filly: half-sister to several winners, including useful sprinters Galloway Boy, Grand Lad (both by Mujtahid) and La Stellina (by Marju): dam fairly useful Irish 5f performer: fairly useful performer: won handicaps at Windsor (2) and Southwell and minor event at Brighton in July/August: creditable ¾-length second to La Vie Est Belle in handicap at Goodwood penultimate start: effective at 5f/6f: acts on fibresand, firm and soft going: tongue tied last 7 outings: travels strongly. *M. L. W. Bell* **80**

Duke of Edinburgh Stakes (Handicap), Royal Ascot—Wunderwood produces a fine burst of speed to go clear of Pagan Dance (cheekpieces), Swift Tango and Hambleden (stars on sleeves)

WUNDERWOOD (USA)   5 b.g. Faltaat (USA) – Jasoorah (IRE) 98 (Sadler's Wells   **111**
(USA) 132) [2004 100: 12g 12m 12m* 12f* 10m* 12f³ 9.5s Oct 13] well-made gelding:
useful performer: won minor event at Newmarket (dictated pace) and Duke of Edinburgh
Handicap at Royal Ascot (beat Pagan Dance by 3½ lengths) in June and minor event at
Ascot (by ¾ length from Mutasallil, wandered) in July: ran respectably in handicap at
Doncaster and Prix Andre Baboin at Bordeaux after: effective at 1¼m/1½m: acts on
polytrack, firm and good to soft going: genuine and reliable. *Lady Herries*

WUXI VENTURE   9 b.g. Wolfhound (USA) 126 – Push A Button (Bold Lad (IRE)   **64**
133) [2004 73: 9.9v 8.3d⁶ 8.5g 9.9m 10.4m Sep 5] sturdy gelding: has a fluent, round
action: modest handicapper: stays 1¼m: acts on fibresand, heavy and good to firm going:
tried blinkered/visored at 2 yrs: fair chaser. *R. A. Fahey*

WYATT EARP (IRE)   3 b.g. Piccolo 121 – Tribal Lady 80 (Absalom 128) [2004 75:   **85**
6d 6g* 5.7g 6g 6m 6g² p7g³ Oct 1] smallish gelding: fairly useful handicapper: won at
Newbury in May: good placed efforts last 2 starts: stays easy 7f: acts on polytrack and
good to firm going: sold 38,000 gns. *J. A. R. Toller*

WYCHBURY (USA)   3 ch.g. Swain (IRE) 134 – Garden Rose (IRE) 115 (Caerleon   **74**
(USA) 132) [2004 79: 6m⁵ 7m² 7f² 8.1m 7m* 7m⁵ 10g 8.5g Oct 2] neat gelding: has a
quick action: fair performer: landed odds in maiden at Thirsk in July: stays 1m: acts on
firm going: sold 9,000 gns. *M. J. Wallace*

WYOMING   3 ch.f. Inchinor 119 – Shoshone (Be My Chief (USA) 122) [2004 –: 7s³   **62**
10m 10g 12g 12g³ 16s 12g³ Oct 4] smallish filly: modest maiden: stays 1½m: acts on soft
going: sold 7,500 gns. *J. A. R. Toller*

WYVERN (GER)   3 b.c. Unfuwain (USA) 131 – Wladinova (GER) (Aspros (GER))   **–**
[2004 10m Sep 7] good-topped colt: 11/2 and coltish, well held in maiden at Leicester:
sold 6,000 gns. *W. J. Haggas*

X

XAARA DOON (IRE)   2 b.f. (Mar 25) Xaar 132 – Hill of Doon (IRE) (Fairy King   **–**
(USA)) [2004 p7g p8g Nov 13] 12,500Y: first foal: dam unraced sister to smart miler
Prince Arthur: well held in maidens at Lingfield. *M. J. Attwater*

XAARIST (IRE)   2 b.c. (May 2) Xaar 132 – Can Can Lady 82 (Anshan 119) [2004 6s   **–**
7g Jul 24] leggy colt: well held in maidens at Newcastle. *T. P. Tate*

XALOC BAY (IRE)   6 br.g. Charnwood Forest (IRE) 125 – Royal Jade 82 (Last   **46**
Tycoon 131) [2004 61, a65: f7g² f7g f6s f8g* p8g* p8g² p8g³ f7g⁶ 7g f8.5g³ f8g f8.5m⁶   **a61**
6d p7.1g p8.6g Dec 15] sturdy gelding: modest performer: won sellers at Southwell and
Lingfield in February: stays 8.5f: acts on all-weather, soft and good to firm going: tried in
headgear: usually races prominently. *B. P. J. Baugh*

XANADU   8 ch.g. Casteddu 111 – Bellatrix 45 (Persian Bold 123) [2004 59§: 7.1g 6g²   **58 §**
7.1m 6m 5f 6m⁶ 5.9f² 5g 6g 5f⁶ 6m⁵ 6g Sep 6] big gelding: modest handicapper: best at
5f/6f on good going or firmer: usually wears cheekpieces nowadays: sometimes slowly
away, usually races prominently otherwise: carries head awkwardly: unreliable. *Miss
L. A. Perratt*

XEBEC (IRE)   2 b.c. (Feb 20) Xaar 132 – Via Camp 88 (Kris 135) [2004 6g 8s Oct 19]   **59**
good-topped colt: better effort in maidens when eighth at York on debut: should stay 1m.
P. F. I. Cole

XEERAN 2 b.f. (Mar 20) Xaar 132 – Cyclone Flyer 67 (College Chapel 122) [2004 5f⁵ **63**
5m⁵ 6g⁵ 6g⁴ 6g³ 6.1v Nov 4] 60,000Y: big, lengthy filly: has scope: second foal: half-
sister to 3-y-o Autumn Pearl: dam, 5f winner, half-sister to very smart sprinter Bolshoi:
modest maiden: stays 6f: best efforts on good ground. *M. A. Jarvis*

XEIGHT EXPRESS (IRE) 2 b.f. (Mar 7) Ashkalani (IRE) 128 – Believing 74 (Bel- **31**
mez (USA) 131) [2004 6f 6g 5.1g 7d Aug 27] 2,500F, 5,500Y: angular filly: first foal:
dam, 2-y-o 5f winner, half-sister to smart performer up to 7f Double Blue: poor maiden:
stays 7f. *M. A. Buckley*

XELLANCE (IRE) 7 b.g. Be My Guest (USA) 126 – Excellent Alibi (USA) (Exceller **–**
(USA) 129) [2004 20f Jun 15] leggy gelding: one-time fairly useful handicapper: missed
2003: ran as if amiss in Ascot Stakes only 7-y-o start: has found little: fairly useful
hurdler/fair chaser. *P. J. Hobbs*

XIXITA 4 ch.f. Fleetwood (IRE) 107 – Conquista 87 (Aragon 118) [2004 42: f12g⁶ **42**
f14g⁴ f16g Feb 8] poor maiden: raced only on fibresand. *Dr J. D. Scargill*

XPRES DIGITAL 3 b.g. Komaite (USA) – Kustom Kit Xpres 69 (Absalom 128) [2004 **72**
77: 7s 6d⁴ 7.1s f6m³ 6g f6f p6g Nov 27] good-topped gelding: fair performer: stays 7f:
acts on fibresand, good to firm and good to soft going: usually tongue tied: sometimes
slowly away. *S. R. Bowring*

XPRESSIONS 3 b.g. Turtle Island (IRE) 123 – Make Ready 76 (Beveled (USA)) [2004 **48**
58: 12.1g⁶ 12.1m⁶ Jun 2] close-coupled gelding: has round action: poor handicapper at 3
yrs: should stay 1½m: acts on good to firm going. *R. A. Fahey*

XSYNNA 8 b.g. Cyrano de Bergerac 120 – Rose Ciel (IRE) 80 (Red Sunset 120) [2004 **40 §**
55§: p6g³ p6g⁶ p7g p6g⁶ f7s 6.1g³ 5.1f 6m Jul 28] tall gelding: poor mover: poor performer: **a48 §**
left P. McEntee after reappearance, T. Clement after fifth outing: stays easy 1m: acts on
fibresand, firm and good to soft going: tried in headgear: has reportedly bled from nose:
unreliable. *Miss M. E. Rowland*

XTRA TORRENTIAL (USA) 2 b.c. (Feb 28) Torrential (USA) 117 – Offering **93**
(USA) (Majestic Light (USA)) [2004 7.9g* 8d⁴ Oct 15] $1,700Y, 14,000 2-y-o: tall,
leggy colt: half-brother to several minor winners in USA: dam, US maiden, half-sister to
US Grade 3 7f winner Basket Weave: green, won maiden at York in September by neck
from Woodsley House, slowly away but getting up close home: creditable fourth to
Something Exciting in minor event at Newmarket, taking good hold to post and tiring late
on: not sure to stay beyond 1m. *D. M. Simcock*

Y

YAAHOMM 3 ch.c. Unfuwain (USA) 131 – Walesiana (GER) (Star Appeal 133) **79**
[2004 11g³ 9g* 10.3g 10m a7.5g Dec 9] strong, compact colt: seventh living foal: brother
to smart winner around 1¼m Zahrat Dubai and half-brother to 2 winners, including 1½m
winner Warluskee (by Dancing Brave): dam German 6f (at 2 yrs) to 1m (Group 2) winner:
fairly useful form when third in maiden at Newbury and when winning similar event at
Ripon (went left at start) in May: well beaten after, leaving D. Loder before final start:
likely to prove better at 1¼m/1½m than shorter: visored fourth outing. *D. J. Selvaratnam,
UAE*

YAHESKA (IRE) 7 b.m. Prince of Birds (USA) 121 – How Ya Been (IRE) (Last **–**
Tycoon 131) [2004 45: 14.1d Oct 16] sparely-made mare: poor in 2003, tailed off only
7-y-o start: tried blinkered. *N. E. Berry*

YAJBILL (IRE) 2 b.c. (Feb 23) Royal Applause 124 – Tee Cee 77 (Lion Cavern **103**
(USA) 117) [2004 6g² 6m³ 6g² 6g² 6d* 6m* 6g* 6g⁵ Oct 9] 47,000F, 140,000Y: sturdy
colt: first foal: dam, 7f winner, granddaughter of Nell Gwyn winner Ghariba: useful
performer: won maiden at Brighton in August and nursery at Epsom (under 9-7, by 5
lengths) and minor event at Salisbury (by neck from Claret And Amber) in September:
respectable fifth to Moth Ball in listed event at York: will prove best at 5f/6f: acts on good
to firm and good to soft going: visored last 4 starts: makes running. *M. R. Channon*

YAKIMOV (USA) 5 ch.g. Affirmed (USA) – Ballet Troupe (USA) (Nureyev (USA) **–**
131) [2004 102: p7g 8g 8v 7g Jun 2] strong, lengthy gelding: useful handicapper at best:
well held for new trainer in 2004. *D. J. Wintle*

YALLAMBIE 5 b.m. Revoque (IRE) 122 – Tahnee (Cadeaux Genereux 131) [2004 **–**
10.9g⁶ f8.5g⁶ May 11] lightly-raced maiden: tried tongue tied. *K. A. Morgan*

YAMATO PINK 3 ch.f. Bijou d'Inde 127 – Time Or Never (FR) (Dowsing (USA) 124) **56**
[2004 51: p7g p6g* 6m² 7m⁵ 6.1m³ 6.1g 6g⁴ 6d⁶ p6g³ p6g Dec 30] modest performer: left
K. Burke after reappearance: won banded race at Lingfield in April: stays 6f: acts on
polytrack and firm going. *Mrs H. Sweeting*

YANKEEDOODLEDANDY (IRE) 3 b.g. Orpen (USA) 116 – Laura Margaret **84**
(Persian Bold 123) [2004 43: f9.4s* p8g² f8g* f11g² f12g²⁹ 12g² 11.9g³ 10m² 14g³ 12.3s²
13d² Aug 23] compact gelding: fairly useful handicapper: much improved in 2004,
winning at Wolverhampton and Southwell in January and Southwell (beat Red Lancer by
¾ length) in March: creditable placed efforts other 8 starts: may prove best around 1½m:
acts on fibresand (probably on polytrack), soft and good to firm going: effective in
cheekpieces or not: has raced lazily: consistent: useful juvenile hurdler, successful all 3
starts. *P. C. Haslam*

YANKEY 2 b.c. (Mar 6) Amfortas (IRE) 115 – Key 70 (Midyan (USA) 124) [2004 8s **–**
8.5g⁵ 7.5m 8d Oct 16] well-made colt: no form in maidens: reportedly had breathing
problem final start. *C. E. Brittain*

YARDSTICK 2 ch.c. (May 15) Inchinor 119 – Fair Verona (USA) (Alleged (USA) **54**
138) [2004 7g 8.1m⁶ p8g 10g 8d p6g⁴ p7g Dec 29] close-coupled colt: modest maiden:
stays 1m: acts on polytrack and good to firm going: looks difficult ride. *S. Kirk*

YASHIN (IRE) 3 b.g. Soviet Star (USA) 128 – My Mariam 79 (Salse (USA) 128) [2004 **70**
62: 7m f6d 8m³ 7g² 7m 7m⁴ 7d 7g³ 10g* p12.2g⁴ p7.1d² p8.6g Nov 11] sturdy gelding:
fair performer: won seller at Leicester (left M. Tompkins) in October by 8 lengths: stays
1¼m: acts on polytrack and good to firm going: has pulled hard to post. *P. A. Blockley*

YAWMI 4 ch.c. Zafonic (USA) 130 – Reine Wells (IRE) 107 (Sadler's Wells (USA) **–**
132) [2004 109: 10d 13.3m May 15] angular, good-topped colt: useful performer at 3 yrs:
tailed off in Gordon Richards Stakes at Sandown and listed race at Newbury in 2004: sold
15,000 gns in November. *B. W. Hills*

YDRAVLIS 6 ch.m. Alflora (IRE) 120 – Levantine Rose (Levanter 121) [2004 p12g **–**
Jun 19] £2,000 5-y-o: fifth foal: dam winning hurdler: 50/1, tailed off in seller at Lingfield. *D. J. S. ffrench Davis*

YEATS (IRE) 3 b.c. Sadler's Wells (USA) 132 – Lyndonville (IRE) (Top Ville **117**
129) [2004 95P: 10s* 10d* May 9]
   For those connected with one-time Derby favourite Yeats, some of the
bulletins regarding his condition were no laughing matter. Phrases such as 'a shade
stiff' and 'recurring stiffness' meant that the colt was still troubled by a muscular
problem between his near-side hip and backbone, a problem which not only
resulted in his missing the Derby but also the remainder of the season. Yeats had
been promoted to the head of the Derby betting after an impressive win in a maiden
at the Curragh on his only outing as a two-year-old. At the time of Yeats's withdrawal from the Derby, three days beforehand, the Two Thousand Guineas second
Snow Ridge was disputing favouritism as doubts about the latter's participation

*Derrinstown Stud Derby Trial Stakes, Leopardstown—Yeats maintains his position at the head of the
Derby betting with a workmanlike victory over Relaxed Gesture (left), Medicinal and Barati (rail)*

increased. According to trainer Aidan O'Brien, Yeats had been responding well to physiotherapy treatment but then stopped doing so. O'Brien's Derby winners Galileo and High Chaparral had both taken Leopardstown's Ballysax Stakes and Derrinstown Stud Derby Trial Stakes before Epsom, and Yeats followed in their footsteps. He couldn't have been more impressive in landing the odds in the three-runner P. W. McGrath Memorial Ballysax Stakes, making the running and quickening before the turn to win as his rider pleased by ten lengths from Dabiroun, who had shown useful form when a close second in a listed event on his previous start. More of the same was expected in the four-runner Derrinstown, for which Yeats started 5/1-on, but he was made to work harder by stronger opposition this time, winning by a length and a half and a length from the Dermot Weld-trained pair Relaxed Gesture and Medicinal. Once again Yeats made the running, his rider just having to wave the whip rather than use it as Yeats kept up the gallop from the home turn, never seriously threatened.

		Sadler's Wells (USA)		Northern Dancer (b 1961)		Nearctic
		(b 1981)		Fairy Bridge (b 1975)		Natalma
Yeats (IRE)						Bold Reason
(b.c. 2001)						Special
		Lyndonville (IRE)		Top Ville (b 1976)		High Top
		(b 1988)				Sega Ville
				Diamond Land (br 1978)		Sparkler
						Canaan

Both the Ballysax and Derrinstown are run over a mile and a quarter, a distance which is likely to prove a bare minimum for Yeats when, as expected, he returns to action in 2005. A step up to a mile and a half will suit him very well, and he should stay even further. By the same sire, Sadler's Wells, as Galileo and High Chaparral, Yeats is the seventh living foal of Lyndonville, who won a mile-and-a-quarter maiden at Galway on the second of her three starts. Lyndonville has produced two other winners, both of them by Danehill. Tsukuba Symphony was a smart performer at up to a mile and a half in Japan, where he won the Group 3 Epsom Cup and was beaten less than three lengths when seventh to Pilsudski in the 1997 Japan Cup, while Yeats's year-older stable-companion Solskjaer showed smart form at up to a mile and a quarter in the latest season, winning two races including the Royal Whip Stakes at the Curragh. Yeats, a good-topped colt and a good walker, wears a crossed noseband. In his three races to date, he has raced on good to firm, good to soft and soft ground. Yeats has always worked like a champion, according to his trainer, and it is to be hoped the colt has plenty of opportunities to try to prove himself one as a four-year-old. *A. P. O'Brien, Ireland*

YEHUDI (IRE)   2 b.c. (May 7) Sadler's Wells (USA) 132 – Bella Vitessa (IRE) (That-   **108 p**
ching 131) [2004 8s⁵ 9v* 10s² Nov 6] €160,000Y: sixth foal: half-brother to 3 winners, including 1999 2-y-o 6f winner Bella Bellisimo (by Alzao) and 7f/1m winner Ros The Boss (by Danehill), both fairly useful: dam, no form, half-sister to smart 1½m performer Wind In Her Hair: won maiden at Navan and listed race at Leopardstown (by 3 lengths from Imperial Brief) in October: further improvement when ¾-length second to Paita in Criterium de Saint-Cloud: will stay at least 1½m: races prominently: should make smart 3-y-o. *A. P. O'Brien, Ireland*

YELDHAM LADY   2 b.f. (Apr 9) Mujahid (USA) 125 – Future Options 71 (Lomond   **52**
(USA) 128) [2004 6g 7f p6g² 6s 6m 8g³ p8g f7g Dec 14] 2,000Y, resold 3,500Y, 4,000
2-y-o: quite attractive filly: half-sister to 4-y-o The Gambler and 3 winners abroad: dam maiden who stayed 1m: modest maiden: stays 1m: acts on polytrack, best turf efforts on good going: tried in cheekpieces/blinkers: tends to be slowly away/look none too keen. *J. Pearce*

YELLOW RIVER (IRE)   4 b.g. Sesaro (USA) 81 – Amtico (Bairn (USA) 126) [2004   **–**
–, a68: f9.4g⁴ f9.4g f7s 7s 6.1m May 25] strong gelding: modest performer: barely stays   **a59**
9.4f: acts on all-weather, no form on turf: tried tongue tied/blinkered/in cheekpieces. *R. Curtis*

YENALED   7 gr.g. Rambo Dancer (CAN) 107 – Fancy Flight (FR) 74 (Arctic Tern   **78**
(USA) 126) [2004 74, a78: f8f³ f7g f7g⁵ f9.4s 10.3g f8g⁴ 8.3g⁵ 9.9v* f8g* 12.3g² 10.3g²   **a86**
9.9m⁴ 9.2d² 9g* 9g 9.1d⁴ 12g* 12v* p13g³ f12s* f11g³ Nov 23] leggy, sparely-made gelding: fairly useful performer: won handicaps at Beverley (amateurs) and Southwell

in May, claimers at Musselburgh in August and September and (having left K. Ryan after seventeenth start) Catterick in October, and handicap at Southwell in November: effective at 1m to easy 13f: acts on all-weather and any turf going: tried visored/in cheekpieces: sometimes slowly away: best held up. *N. Wilson*

YEOMAN LAD 4 b.g. Groom Dancer (USA) 128 – First Amendment (IRE) 78 **74** (Caerleon (USA) 132) [2004 86: 7g 10m 8.3m⁴ 9.9g⁵ p10g Jul 7] angular gelding: fair handicapper: creditable effort in 2004 only on third start: stays 9f: acts on firm and good to soft ground: visored last 4 starts: has hung left: sold 2,800 gns. *A. M. Balding*

YESTERDAY (IRE) 4 b.f. Sadler's Wells (USA) 132 – Jude 53 (Darshaan 133) **111** [2004 119: 8m⁵ 10m⁴ 11d⁵ Oct 30] good-topped filly: had a short, choppy action: smart performer: won Irish 1000 Guineas at the Curragh in 2003: reportedly suffered bout of colitis in spring and not so good at 4 yrs: 4 lengths fourth to Alexander Goldrun in Prix de l'Opera at Longchamp and 5¾ lengths fifth to Ouija Board in Breeders' Cup Filly & Mare Turf at Lone Star Park (visored, slowly away) last 2 outings: stayed 1½m: acted on any going: waited with: stud. *A. P. O'Brien, Ireland*

YLANG YLANG (IRE) 3 ch.f. Hennessy (USA) 122 – Princess Alydar (USA) (Aly-**68** dar (USA)) [2004 74: f8f⁴ f9.4s* f12g⁶ Mar 3] sister to 2 winners in USA, closely related to US Grade 1 7f/1¼m winner November Snow and US Grade 3 7f winner Scatmandu (both by Storm Cat) and half-sister to several winners in USA: dam maiden in USA: fair performer: left A. O'Brien in Ireland 100,000 gns after 2 yrs: won maiden at Wolverhampton (carried head awkwardly) in February: stays 9.4f: acts on fibresand and good to firm going. *W. Jarvis*

YNYS 3 b.g. Turtle Island (IRE) 123 – Kiss Me Goodknight 86 (First Trump 118) [2004 **–** 39: f8g f9.4s Feb 17] maiden: well held both starts in 2004. *B. Palling*

YOMALO (IRE) 4 ch.f. Woodborough (USA) 112 – Alkariyh (USA) 79 (Alydar **92 +** (USA)) [2004 77: 5g 5.7s 5.7f⁵ 6m⁶ 6m² 6g⁵ 6m⁶ 6.1d² 6g* f6g³ p6g² p6g* Dec 13] angular filly: progressed into fairly useful handicapper: won at Windsor in October and Wolverhampton (beat Kostar readily by ¾ length) in December: should stay 7f: acts on all-weather, firm and good to soft going: sometimes slowly away. *R. Guest*

YORK CLIFF 6 b.g. Marju (IRE) 127 – Azm (Unfuwain (USA) 131) [2004 91: f7g **76** p10g⁵ f12s⁴ p12g⁵ 9.1d 10s 8.2v p10g p8.6g⁴ p9.5g⁵ p8.6g* p9.5g Dec 27] good-bodied gelding: fair handicapper: won at Wolverhampton in December: stays easy 1½m: acts on all-weather and heavy going: not straightforward. *W. M. Brisbourne*

YORKER (USA) 6 b.g. Boundary (USA) 117 – Shallows (USA) (Cox's Ridge (USA)) **77** [2004 77: f7g² f8.5g⁵ f7g³ f8.5s⁴ f7s² f12s² f8.5s f7s 8.1g f8d³ f7g⁶ 7.5d 6d* 7m³ p7.1g p9.5d 8.2v Nov 4] strong, lengthy gelding: fair handicapper: won apprentice event at Hamilton in September, edging right: effective at 6f, barely at 1½m: acts on all-weather, firm and soft ground: tried visored, blinkered last 5 starts: often races up with pace. *Ms Deborah J. Evans*

YORKE'S FOLLY (USA) 3 b.f. Stravinsky (USA) 133 – Tommelise (USA) (Dayjur **45** (USA) 137) [2004 50: 6m 6.9g 6g 5.9m 6m³ 6g⁵ 6d Oct 15] big, lengthy filly: poor maiden: stays 6f: acts on fibresand and good to firm ground: visored last 3 outings. *C. W. Fairhurst*

YORKIE 5 b.g. Aragon 118 – Light The Way 72 (Nicholas Bill 125) [2004 71: p6g* **64** f5g p6g 5.3m 5.3f² 5.3f² 5m 5.7m⁴ 5.3d Aug 24] tall, quite good-topped gelding: modest performer: won seller at Lingfield (sold from D. Carroll) in March: has form at easy 1m, but races freely and effective at 5f: acts on polytrack, firm and soft going: tried blinkered/tongue tied. *P. A. Blockley*

YORKIES BOY 9 gr.g. Clantime 101 – Slipperose 72 (Persepolis (FR) 127) [2004 **62** 78d: 5g⁵ 5m⁴ 6g 5f 6m 5.1m 5m⁴ 6m 6g³ 6.1g* 6m* 7.1m 6g 5m⁵ 6g⁶ 5.7s Oct 19] good-bodied gelding: modest performer nowadays: left J. M. Bradley after fourth outing: won handicap at Chepstow and banded race at Folkestone on consecutive days in September: probably stays 7f: acts on firm and soft going: tried blinkered, usually wears cheekpieces. *N. E. Berry*

YORKSHIRE BLUE 5 b.g. Atraf 116 – Something Blue (Petong 126) [2004 64d: **67** 7.1g 7.2m 7.2f* 7m* 7f 7m⁵ 7m* 7m 7.2d Sep 16] close-coupled gelding: fair handicapper: won at Ayr in May, Doncaster in June and Redcar in August: stays 1m: acts on fibresand and firm ground: blinkered (below form) last two 4-y-o starts. *J. S. Goldie*

YORKSHIRE LAD (IRE) 2 b.c. (Apr 16) Second Empire (IRE) 124 – Villaminta **61** (IRE) (Grand Lodge (USA) 125) [2004 5g 6g⁶ 6s⁵ p6g² Dec 13] €10,000Y: well-grown, lengthy colt: second foal: dam ran once at 2 yrs: modest maiden: left D. Carroll prior to final start: should stay 7f: signs of temperament. *J. A. Osborne*

YORKSHIRE SPIRIT   3 b.g. Imperial Ballet (IRE) 110 – Barnacla (IRE) 83 (Blue-bird (USA) 125) [2004 –: 8v Apr 20] smallish gelding: well held in maidens at York (tongue tied) and Newcastle. *N. Tinkler*

YOSHKA   3 ch.c. Grand Lodge (USA) 125 – Greenvera (USA) (Riverman (USA) 131) **99** [2004 78p: 11.8d³ 12.3m* 15.8m* 14m² 14.6f Sep 10] good-topped colt: progressed into a useful handicapper: won at Ripon in June and Catterick (edged right and idled in front) in July: good ¾-length second to Lochbuie at Goodwood, but then well held in Mallard Stakes at Doncaster: will prove better at 2m+ than shorter: acts on firm and good to soft going. *M. Johnston*

YOU FOUND ME   2 b.f. (Mar 10) Robellino (USA) 127 – Hana Marie 101§ (Formid- **62** able (USA) 125) [2004 6m 7f⁶ 8.1s³ 10m 8d⁶ f8g p8.6g Dec 1] 25,000F, €36,000Y: smal-lish, sturdy filly: eighth foal: half-sister to 3 winners, including fairly useful 6f winner Naughty Nell (by Danehill Dancer) and 4-y-o Sri Diamond: dam, 2-y-o 5f/6f winner, became unreliable: modest maiden: should stay 1¼m: acts on soft going. *C. Tinkler*

YOUNG ALEX (IRE)   6 ch.g. Midhish 109 – Snipe Hunt (IRE) (Stalker 121) [2004 **77** 80, a?: 8g⁵ 7s² 7g p7.1g p7.1g Dec 6] leggy, workmanlike gelding: fair performer: left **a–** M. Pipe after third start: stays easy 1m: better form on polytrack than fibresand, acts on firm and soft going: usually wears headgear: sometimes carries head awkwardly: held up. *N. M. Babbage*

YOUNG BOLDRIC   2 b.g. (Mar 12) Faustus (USA) 118 – Bold Byzantium (Bold **–** Arrangement 127) [2004 6g 6m 7.1s p9.5g Nov 15] no form in maidens: slowly away first 2 starts. *K. Bell*

YOUNG DYNASTY   4 ch.g. Young Ern 120 – Miss Michelle 38 (Jalmood (USA) 126) **–** [2004 p8g p8g⁵ p10g⁵ 7s f7m⁵ 9g 8.1g Jul 9] little form: tried blinkered. *E. A. Wheeler*

YOUNG KATE   3 b.f. Desert King (IRE) 129 – Stardyn (Star Appeal 133) [2004 6d⁶ **50** p7g p5.1g p7m⁵ p9.5g Dec 22] sturdy filly: half-sister to several winners, notably very smart 6f (at 2 yrs)/7f winner Young Ern (by Efisio): dam maiden who stayed 1½m: modest maiden: best effort on debut: should stay at least 7f. *J. R. Best*

YOUNG LOVE   3 ch.f. Pursuit of Love 124 – Polar Fair 62 (Polar Falcon (USA) 126) **54** [2004 –: 10s 9m⁶ 8.1m⁴ 7m 8.1m⁶ 7s⁴ 8f⁴ p10g⁴ f7g p12m Dec 8] lengthy filly: modest **a39** maiden on turf, poor on all-weather: left Miss E. Lavelle after eighth start: stays 1¼m: acts on polytrack, firm and soft going: tried blinkered/visored. *A. B. Haynes*

YOUNG MICK   2 br.g. (Feb 14) King's Theatre (IRE) 128 – Just Warning (Warning **69** 136) [2004 7m 7.6m³ 8.5s⁴ Sep 16] useful-looking gelding: first foal: dam, well beaten only start, half-sister to very smart 6f to 1m performer Young Ern: fair maiden: barely stays testing 8.5f: acts on soft and good to firm going. *G. G. Margarson*

YOUNG MR GRACE (IRE)   4 b.c. Danetime (IRE) 121 – Maid of Mourne (Fairy **90** King (USA)) [2004 86: 6g 7s³ 7d⁴ 8.1m² 8m⁵ 6.9g* 8d⁶ 7.5g² 8.1g* 8.3d³ 8d 8s* 8.1s⁵ 7g 7s⁵ Nov 2] quite good-topped colt: fairly useful handicapper: won at Carlisle in July, Haydock in August and Ayr (beat Jazz Scene by 1¼ lengths) in September: stays 1m: acts on firm and soft ground, well held on heavy/fibresand: usually races prominently: tough. *T. D. Easterby*

YOUNG OWEN   6 b.g. Balnibarbi 95 – Polly Potter (Pollerton 115) [2004 69: f12s⁵ **–** f12g Jan 9] fair maiden at 5 yrs: well held in 2004: joined A. Juckes, and won over fences in October. *Mrs L. B. Normile*

YOUNG PATRIARCH   3 b.g. Silver Patriarch (IRE) 125 – Mortify (Prince Sabo **–** 123) [2004 61: 10d 11.9m 8.1d Jun 5] well-made gelding: maiden: well held in 2004. *B. J. Meehan*

YOUNG ROONEY   4 b.g. Danzig Connection (USA) – Lady Broker 54 (Petorius **75 +** 117) [2004 74: 10m⁴ 11.9m 10s³ 9.3g² 10.3g² 8.1s⁶ 10m³ 10s² 10s⁶ 12s³ Nov 6] fair maiden: mostly creditable efforts in 2004 (flattered final outing): seems to stay 1½m: acts on fibresand, soft and good to firm going: tried in cheekpieces/blinkers: usually makes running. *M. Mullineaux*

YOUNGS FORTH   4 b.f. Most Welcome 131 – Pegs 60 (Mandrake Major 122) [2004 **37** 50: f7g p6g p7g⁵ f8.5g⁵ p8g Apr 15] close-coupled filly: poor maiden: stays 8.5f: acts on all-weather and soft going: tried visored/tongue tied: sometimes slowly away: broke blood vessel final start. *A. W. Carroll*

YOUNG THOMAS (IRE)   2 ch.g. (Apr 29) Inchinor 119 – Splicing 82 (Sharpo 132)   **67**
[2004 6g 7.1m⁴ 7.1g⁴ 7s³ 8s³ 8s⁵ 8d Oct 18] 10,000Y: strong, lengthy gelding: fifth foal:
half-brother to 6-y-o Pairing and 5-y-o Sholay: dam, 5f/6f winner, sister to smart sprinter
Splice: fair maiden: ran badly final start: stays 1m: acts on soft ground. *M. L. W. Bell*

YOUNG VALENTINO   2 ch.g. (Feb 14) Komaite (USA) – Caprice (Mystiko (USA)
124) [2004 6s Oct 22] sturdy gelding: 50/1 and better for race, well held in maiden at
Newbury, slowly away. *A. W. Carroll*

YOUNG WARRIOR (IRE)   3 b.g. Desert Style (IRE) 121 – Arctic Splendour (USA)
66 (Arctic Tern (USA) 126) [2004 7s 8m⁵ 9.3f⁶ Jun 14] good-topped gelding: well held in
maidens: troublesome at start first 2 outings. *D. Nicholls*

YOUR JUST LOVELY (IRE)   3 b.f. Second Empire (IRE) 124 – Nawaji (USA) 45
(Trempolino (USA) 135) [2004 61: p7g 6d Apr 1] sturdy filly: modest maiden at 2 yrs:
poor efforts in 2004. *A. M. Balding*

YOURS SINCERELY (IRE)   2 ch.c. (Mar 16) Mark of Esteem (IRE) 137 – Evrobi
(IRE) 84 (Grand Lodge (USA) 125) [2004 6m⁴ May 24] 40/1, well-beaten fourth in
maiden at Leicester. *P. A. Blockley*

Z

ZABADANI   2 ch.f. (Apr 25) Zafonic (USA) 130 – Bloudan (USA) (Damascus (USA))   **52 p**
[2004 p8g Oct 31] half-sister to several winners, including very smart French/US winner
up to 1½m Radevore (by Generous): dam unraced half-sister to Irish 1000 Guineas
winner Al Bahathri, herself dam of 3-y-o Haafhd: 33/1, ninth in maiden at Lingfield, very
green until some late headway: sure to do better. *Mrs A. J. Perrett*

ZABADOU   3 b.g. Abou Zouz (USA) 109 – Strapped 57 (Reprimand 122) [2004 –:   **—**
8.1s 10d⁶ f6m May 6] no sign of ability. *C. B. B. Booth*

ZABEEL PALACE   2 b.g. (Feb 25) Grand Lodge (USA) 125 – Applecross 117 (Glint   **77**
of Gold 128) [2004 7g 7m⁵ 7m⁴ Aug 4] useful-looking gelding: half-brother to several
winners, notably stayer Invermark (by Machiavellian) and 1½m/1¾m performer Craigsteel (by Suave Dancer), both very smart: dam, 1¼m to 13f winner, second in Park Hill
Stakes: fair form in minor events: should be suited by 1¼m/1½m: gelded after final start.
D. R. Loder

ZACHY BOY   2 b.g. (Feb 3) Inchinor 119 – Ellway Dancer (IRE) 56 (Mujadil (USA)   **49**
119) [2004 p5g⁶ 5.2m 5g⁵ 5v 6.1g 6m⁶ 5.1m⁶ 6m⁵ 5.1f⁴ 5.1m⁶ Aug 10] sturdy gelding:
poor maiden: stays 6f: acts on polytrack and firm ground: in cheekpieces/blinkers last 4
starts. *J. S. Moore*

ZADALRAKIB   2 ch.c. (Feb 28) Machiavellian (USA) 123 – Party Doll 108 (Be My   **68 p**
Guest (USA) 126) [2004 7d⁵ Oct 30] 240,000Y: strong, compact colt: brother to 3
winners, including French sprinters Titus Livius (smart) and Bahama Dream (useful), and
half-brother to 3 winners: dam French 5f (at 2 yrs) to 1m winner: 12/1, 9½ lengths fifth to
Centaurus in maiden at Newmarket, slowly away and green but some late headway:
joined D. Watson in UAE: sure to improve. *Sir Michael Stoute*

ZAFARSHAH (IRE)   5 b.g. Danehill (USA) 126 – Zafarana (FR) (Shernazar 131)   **72**
[2004 70: p7g* p7g⁴ p7g* p7g⁴ p7g⁶ 8m² p8g 7g³ 8.1f 7.1g 8m⁴ 8.2g 8.1g* 8.2g⁵ p8.6g
p7.1g Nov 19] good-bodied gelding: fair performer: won minor event in January and
apprentice handicap in February, both at Lingfield, and minor event at Chepstow in September: best form at 7f to 8.5f: acts on all-weather, firm and soft going: tried visored/
tongue tied. *P. D. Evans*

ZAFFEU   3 ch.g. Zafonic (USA) 130 – Leaping Flame (USA) (Trempolino (USA) 135)   **78 d**
[2004 p10g p10g⁶ p12g⁶ 10.9d² 12s⁴ 10.3m⁵ 11.7f* 12d 10g⁶ 11.7m 10.5g 11.5g 11.7g
11.5d² p12.2g⁵ p12.2g p12m Dec 22] 32,000Y: leggy, useful-looking gelding: has no left
eye: first foal: dam, French 7f winner, half-sister to smart performers up to/around 1m
Apple of Kent and War Zone: fair performer: won 4-runner minor event at Bath in June:
stays 1½m: acts on polytrack, firm and soft ground: blinkered (well held) eleventh/
twelfth starts. *N. P. Littmoden*

ZAGALA   4 b.f. Polar Falcon (USA) 126 – Whittle Woods Girl 80 (Emarati (USA) 74)   **70 d**
[2004 70: f6g² f6g f6g² f7g f7m p6g p6g⁶ Oct 18] fair performer: well below form after
third start: stays 7f: raced only on all-weather: tongue tied. *S. L. Keightley*

ZAGREUS (GER) 2 gr.g. (Apr 7) Fasliyev (USA) 120 – Zephyrine (IRE) (Highest **70 p**
Honor (FR) 124) [2004 7.5m³ Sep 15] 30,000Y: half-brother to 3 winners abroad, including Swedish Derby winner Zenato (by Acatenango): dam unraced half-sister to very
smart 1½m performer Mutamam: 50/1, third in maiden at Beverley, not unduly knocked
about: likely to improve. *M. W. Easterby*

ZAHUNDA (IRE) 5 b.m. Spectrum (IRE) 126 – Gift of Glory (FR) (Niniski (USA) **50 §**
125) [2004 55§: p8g⁶ f7g f8.5g² f9.4g f8.5s⁴ f8.5s⁶ f8.5g³ f8.5g³ 8.1g⁶ 8.1d⁴ 8.1g
7.2g² 7.1f⁴ 7.2g⁵ 7.2s 8s Oct 30] modest performer: best recent form around 1m: acts on
fibresand and heavy going: tried blinkered/in cheekpieces: usually races up with pace:
unreliable. *W. M. Brisbourne*

ZAK ATTACK 3 ch.g. Young Ern 120 – Premiere Moon 80 (Bold Owl 101) [2004 8g **–**
Jul 16] good-topped gelding: 40/1, well beaten in maiden at Newmarket. *D. J. Daly*

ZAK FACTA (IRE) 4 b.g. Danetime (IRE) 121 – Alexander Goddess (IRE) (Alzao **60 d**
(USA) 117) [2004 72d: f6g⁵ p7g⁵ f6g² p7g⁴ f6s⁶ f6g 6.1s 7d 7m f9.4m f6g f6g p7m
Dec 15] leggy gelding: modest maiden: well below form after fifth start: stays 8.5f:
acts on all-weather and firm going: tried blinkered/tongue tied: usually visored. *Miss
D. A. McHale*

ZAKFREE (IRE) 3 b.g. Danetime (IRE) 121 – Clipper Queen 66 (Balidar 133) [2004 **69**
67: p10g² 10.1s² 10d² 10s⁶ Oct 11] rather leggy gelding: fair maiden: stays 1¼m: acts on
polytrack, soft and probably good to firm ground: blinkered: has looked no easy ride: sold
15,000 gns. *N. P. Littmoden*

ZALAAL (USA) 2 b.c. (Apr 6) A P Indy (USA) 131 – Scoot Yer Boots (USA) (Seek- **81**
ing The Gold (USA)) [2004 7m⁶ p8d² 8s Aug 24] second foal: dam, 6f to 7f winner in
USA, half-sister to US Grade 1 1m winner Furiously: easily best effort in maidens when
second to Russian Consort at Lingfield: will probably stay 1¼m. *Saeed bin Suroor*

ZALAM (IRE) 4 b.g. Alzao (USA) 117 – Zarlana (IRE) (Darshaan 133) [2004 80: **–**
10g 10g p8.6g f11g Dec 16] ex-Irish gelding: fairly useful maiden at 3 yrs for J. Oxx: well
held in 2004, leaving T. O'Mara in Ireland after reappearance. *P. A. Blockley*

ZALDA 3 ch.f. Zilzal (USA) 137 – Gold Luck (USA) (Slew O' Gold (USA)) [2004 59p: **72**
12.1m* 12.3m⁶ 14g⁵ 14.1g 14.1d* Aug 12] big, close-coupled filly: fair handicapper:
won at Beverley in June and Salisbury (visored) in August: stays 1¾m: acts on good to
firm and good to soft going: sold 28,000 gns. *R. Charlton*

ZALEBE 3 b.f. Bahamian Bounty 116 – Alo Ez 100 (Alzao (USA) 117) [2004 8m 7.1g **52**
7g* 7g Oct 12] sparely-made filly: half-sister to several winners, including fairly useful
5f/6f winner Mousehole (by Statoblest) and 1¾m/2m winner Pleasant Mount (by First
Trump): dam 5f (at 2 yrs)/6f winner: modest performer: won seller at Yarmouth in
September: should stay 1m. *J. Pearce*

ZALIMAR (IRE) 2 b.f. (Apr 3) Montjeu (IRE) 137 – Zanella (IRE) 87 (Nordico **63**
(USA)) [2004 p7.1g⁵ p7.1g⁴ p9.5g² Dec 20] fourth living foal: half-sister to 3 winners,
including 4-y-o Zan Lo and 5-y-o Monsal Dale: dam Irish 2-y-o 7.7f winner who stayed
1¼m: modest form in maidens at Wolverhampton: should stay 1½m: slowly away on
debut: upset in stall second outing. *L. M. Cumani*

ZALKANI (IRE) 4 ch.g. Cadeaux Genereux 131 – Zallaka (IRE) (Shardari 134) [2004 **75**
–: p10g³ p10g³ p8g 9.7d 8.2d 10.1f⁵ 10.9m 8.1g 10.2s⁴ p10g 10.2s p10g² p12g p10g*
p10m* p10g⁴ Dec 29] fair performer on all-weather, poor on turf: won claimer and
handicap on successive days at Lingfield in December: stays 1¼m: acts on polytrack and
firm going, probably on soft. *B. G. Powell*

ZALONGO 2 ch.c. (Feb 7) Zafonic (USA) 130 – Tamasos 67 (Dance In Time (CAN)) **87 p**
[2004 7s* Oct 27] half-brother to several winners, notably middle-distance performers
Posidonas (very smart, by Slip Anchor) and Carry The Flag (smart, by Tenby): dam, 1¼m
winner, half-sister to Ile de Chypre: 20/1 from 12/1, won maiden at Yarmouth by ½ length
from Paradise Mill, green but running on well to lead close home: likely to be suited by
1¼m/1½m: useful prospect. *Sir Michael Stoute*

ZAMBEZI RIVER 5 ch.g. Zamindar (USA) 116 – Double River (USA) (Irish River **47 §**
(FR) 131) [2004 8g f8.5g 7s 6m⁶ 6.1m 7.1d 5.1m 6m Sep 25] has only one eye: poor
maiden: not raced on Flat until 2004, having twice failed stall test: stays 6f: temperamental. *J. M. Bradley*

ZAMBOOZLE (IRE) 2 ch.c. (Feb 28) Halling (USA) 133 – Blue Sirocco (Bluebird **70**
(USA) 125) [2004 7m⁴ 8d Aug 20] 35,000 2-y-o: strong colt: second foal: dam, ran
once, half-sister to smart middle-distance stayers Khamaseen and Azzilfi: fair form in

maidens at Goodwood (better effort) and Salisbury: should be suited by 1¼m/1½m. *D. R. C. Elsworth*

ZAMEEL (IRE)   3 b.g. Marju (IRE) 127 – Impatiente (USA) (Vaguely Noble 140)   – [2004 –: 12m May 15] quite good-topped gelding: no form. *Jedd O'Keeffe*

ZAMEYLA (IRE)   3 b.f. Cape Cross (IRE) 129 – Angelic Sounds (IRE) (The Noble   **86** Player (USA) 126) [2004 6m 7f² 7f² 8s* 8d* 8.3d 8s Oct 19] €150,000Y: tall, leggy filly: half-sister to several winners, including Irish 5f winner Alegranza (by Lake Coniston) and 1999 2-y-o 5f winner Seraphina (by Pips Pride), both useful: dam, Irish 2-y-o 5f winner, half-sister to smart 6f/7f performer Mount Abu: fairly useful performer: won maiden at Salisbury and minor event at Leicester (by length from Honest Injun) in September: stays 1m: acts on firm and soft going. *M. A. Jarvis*

ZAMIR   5 ch.g. Zamindar (USA) 116 – Fairy Flax (IRE) 97 (Dancing Brave (USA)   – 140) [2004 –: 12v Oct 16] sturdy gelding: no sign of ability: tried visored. *W. Storey*

ZAMYATINA (IRE)   5 br.m. Danehill Dancer (IRE) 117 – Miss Pickpocket (IRE) 64   **40 §** (Petorius 117) [2004 64: 7s 7d 8m 8.1m 7m⁵ 7.6g 6m 8m Sep 4] angular mare: poor performer nowadays: stays easy 7f: acts on polytrack, soft and good to firm ground: unreliable. *P. L. Clinton*

ZANDEED (IRE)   6 b.g. Inchinor 119 – Persian Song 45 (Persian Bold 123) [2004   **65** 9.1g 7.2s³ 8g* 10.1g⁴ 8g 10.9s⁵ 10.3s Oct 22] fair performer nowadays: left J. Goldie and off nearly 2 years prior to reappearance: won handicap at Redcar in August: looked none too keen when below form last 3 starts: effective at 1m/1¼m: acts on soft and good to firm going: usually visored at 3/4 yrs. *Miss L. A. Perratt*

ZANDERIDO   2 b.g. (Mar 18) Forzando 122 – Triple Concerto (Grand Lodge (USA)   **48 ?** 125) [2004 5g⁴ 6g 6m⁶ 7.5m Sep 15] sturdy gelding: poor maiden: stays 6f. *B. S. Rothwell*

ZANDO   2 b.g. (Feb 9) Forzando 122 – Rockin' Rosie 59 (Song 132) [2004 f6m 5m   **62** 7g⁶ 7f f8g* p8.6g Nov 29] big, good-topped gelding: modest performer: won nursery at Southwell in November: stays 1m: acts on fibresand. *P. C. Haslam*

ZANGEAL   3 ch.g. Selkirk (USA) 129 – Generous Lady 98 (Generous (IRE) 139) [2004   **80** p10g⁴ 10g³ 12m⁴ 10f⁴ 8g⁴ Aug 14] 40,000Y: strong, rangy gelding: third living foal: half-brother to 4-y-o High Accolade and 1½m winner Summer Wine (by Desert King): dam Irish 1½m/1¾m winner: fairly useful maiden: best effort when third at Sandown: should stay 1½m: tongue tied fourth outing (hung badly right): reportedly suffered sore throat after debut: gelded after final start. *C. F. Wall*

ZANJEER   4 b.g. Averti (IRE) 117 – Cloudslea (USA) (Chief's Crown (USA)) [2004   **78** –: f7g 8g* 8d⁶ 6.9f³ 7.5g* 7.6m 8s⁵ p7.1d Oct 30] good-topped gelding: fair performer: left D. Nicholls after reappearance: won amateur maiden event at Redcar in June and handicap at Beverley in July: effective at 7f/1m: acts on good to firm and good to soft going. *N. Wilson*

ZAN LO (IRE)   4 ch.f. Grand Lodge (USA) 125 – Zanella (IRE) 87 (Nordico (USA))   **54** [2004 12s 10.1s 10m⁶ 12m 12d 12.1m 12.3g 14g⁴ 14.1f* 15.8m 12g 13.9g 14.1d Oct 15] 48,000F, IR 210,000Y: rather leggy filly: third foal: half-sister to unreliable Irish 6.5f winner Paws (by Brief Truce) and 5-y-o Monsal Dale: dam Irish 2-y-o 7.7f winner who stayed 1¼m: modest performer: trained in France at 3 yrs by A. de Royer Dupre: won handicap at Redcar in September: stays 1¾m: acts on firm going: possibly ungenuine. *B. S. Rothwell*

ZANTERO   2 b.c. (Feb 28) Danzero (AUS) – Cruinn A Bhord 107 (Inchinor 119)   **53** [2004 f6m⁴ 7m⁶ f5g⁴ 5.9g⁶ 8g 7m⁶ 7s⁵ p6g p5.1g f5g⁵ Dec 16] modest maiden: stays 7f: acts on fibresand and good to firm going: blinkered penultimate start. *R. P. Elliott*

ZAP ATTACK   4 b.g. Zafonic (USA) 130 – Rappa Tap Tap (FR) 111 (Tap On Wood   **64** 130) [2004 74: 6m 7m 8m⁴ 7m 6.1m f7g³ f8s p8.6g p8.6g Dec 17] close-coupled gelding: modest performer: stays 7f: acts on fibresand and firm going: none too consistent. *J. Parkes*

ZAQRAH (USA)   3 b.f. Silver Hawk (USA) 123 – Istiqlal (USA) (Diesis 133) [2004   – 80p: 7g Apr 14] big, good-topped filly: fourth in maiden at Newmarket only outing at 2 yrs: odds on, only tenth to Relaxed in similar event there only start in 2004. *J. L. Dunlop*

ZARABAD (IRE)   2 b.c. (May 28) King's Best (USA) 132 – Zarannda (IRE) 112   **85 p** (Last Tycoon 131) [2004 p7.1g* Nov 11] fifth foal: half-brother to 9.6f winner Zarakash (by Darshaan), 1½m winner Zanara (by Kahyasi), both fairly useful, and 1m winner Zarad (by Selkirk), all in Ireland: dam French 7f/1m winner: 11/4, won maiden at Wolverhampton comfortably by length from Resplendent Prince, idling after quickening well: will stay at least 1m: useful prospect. *Sir Michael Stoute*

ZARA LOUISE 4 b.f. Mistertopogigo (IRE) 118 – Petonica (IRE) 77 (Petoski 135) **37**
[2004 52d: f6g⁴ f7g f6g Feb 15] leggy filly: maiden: poor form in banded races in 2004: stays 7f: acts on fibresand, good to firm and good to soft ground: tried visored. *R. P. Elliott*

ZARGUS 5 b.g. Zamindar (USA) 116 – My First Romance 61 (Danehill (USA) 126) **55**
[2004 83: p5g⁵ 5.7g 5.3m 5g 5g Jul 3] stocky, quite attractive gelding: fairly useful handicapper in 2003, only modest form in 2004: left W. Muir after third start: effective at 5f/6f: acts on firm and good to soft going: tried in cheekpieces/blinkers. *A. M. Balding*

ZARIANO 4 b.g. Emperor Jones (USA) 119 – Douce Maison (IRE) 67 (Fools Holme **78**
(USA)) [2004 87: p8g² p7d 10m 8g 8.3m p7.1d p8g p7m Dec 21] fair performer: trained by R. Stronge second to sixth starts: stays 1m: acts on polytrack, good to firm and good to soft going: often early to post. *S. L. Keightley*

ZARIN (IRE) 6 b.g. Inzar (USA) 112 – Non Dimenticar Me (IRE) 63 (Don't Forget **62**
Me 127) [2004 91d: f8s f7s³ f8d 8d f7m 7.2g⁶ 8d² f8f* 8g⁵ 7.9g 8m p9.5d f7s Nov 17] tall, leggy gelding: modest performer: made all in seller at Southwell in August: effective at 7f/1m: acts on all-weather and soft going: blinkered (below form) fifth start. *D. W. Chapman*

ZARNEETA 3 b.f. Tragic Role (USA) – Compton Amber 78 (Puissance 110) [2004 **46**
63d: 7m 10.2g 10m 12.1g 10.2g 10d 10d³ 10.1d p9.5d⁶ Nov 5] smallish, leggy filly: poor maiden: stays 1¼m: acts on good to firm and good to soft ground: tried blinkered. *W. de Best-Turner*

ZAROVA (IRE) 2 gr.c. (Mar 12) Zafonic (USA) 130 – Estarova (FR) (Saint Estephe **53**
(FR) 123) [2004 6m 5g⁶ 6g 5.9g Sep 2] leggy colt: modest maiden: form only at 5f on good going. *M. W. Easterby*

ZARZU 5 b.g. Magic Ring (IRE) 115 – Rivers Rhapsody 104 (Dominion 123) [2004 **86**
81, a92: f6g³ f5g⁵ p5g⁴ p5g³ 5g⁴ 5.7g³ 6m 5m 5d 5g* 5g⁶ 5g⁵ 5.2g 5s 5f⁵ 6g 5g p5g* **a94**
f5s p5.1g⁵ Dec 4] close-coupled, good-topped gelding: fairly useful handicapper: won at Musselburgh in July and Lingfield (beat Fruit of Glory by head) in November: effective at 5f to easy 7f: acts on all-weather, firm and good to soft going: tried in visor/cheekpieces. *C. R. Dore*

ZATHONIA 3 b.f. Zafonic (USA) 130 – Danthonia (USA) 80 (Northern Dancer) **68**
[2004 8.2g² 8.3f³ 8g² Aug 4] rather leggy, close-coupled filly: eighth foal: sister to useful 1m (including in USA) and 1¼m winner Zante and half-sister to 2 winners by Rainbow Quest, including stayer French/US performer up to 11f Requete: dam, 2-y-o 5f winner, half-sister to Xaar (by Zafonic): fair maiden: placed at Nottingham, Windsor and Pontefract: raced only around 1m: acted on firm going: stud. *R. Charlton*

ZAVILLE 2 gr.f. (Jan 22) Zafonic (USA) 130 – Colleville 97 (Pharly (FR) 130) [2004 **60**
7g 8g Oct 12] sturdy filly: second foal: half-sister to 4-y-o Sendintank: dam 7f (at 2 yrs) to 1½m winner: tenth in maidens at Kempton (better effort) and Leicester. *M. A. Jarvis*

ZAWRAK (IRE) 5 ch.g. Zafonic (USA) 130 – Gharam (USA) 108 (Green Dancer **68**
(USA) 132) [2004 69: p13g⁶ p10g³ p10g 7.9f* 8.1g 10.2g⁵ 8g² 9.2f 11.5g 7.5m p9.5d⁴ p9.5g p12.2g Nov 20] tall, close-coupled gelding: fair handicapper: won apprentice event at Carlisle in May: fell final start: stayed 1¼m: acted on polytrack and firm going: sometimes visored/in cheekpieces: none too consistent: dead. *I. W. McInnes*

ZAYN ZEN 2 ch.f. (Jan 30) Singspiel (IRE) 133 – Roshani (IRE) 79 (Kris 135) [2004 **76**
7d⁶ 8m⁴ 8.2m² 8s⁵ Oct 11] good-topped filly: first foal: dam, 1m/1¼m winner, out of half-sister to Oh So Sharp: fair maiden: second at Nottingham: should be suited by 1¼m/1½m: acts on good to firm going. *M. A. Jarvis*

ZAZOUS 3 b.c. Zafonic (USA) 130 – Confidentiality (USA) (Lyphard (USA) 132) **56**
[2004 73: 6m⁶ 7g³ 7.1m 8g 11.8g Oct 12] well-made colt: just modest maiden in 2004: raced only on good/good to firm going. *A. King*

ZEALAND 4 ch.g. Zamindar (USA) 116 – Risanda (Kris 135) [2004 p7.1g³ p8.6g⁴ **52 p**
Dec 27] modest form in 2 bumpers, and when in frame in 2 maidens at Wolverhampton, not knocked about in latter: will stay 1¼m: will probably still do better. *R. A. Fahey*

ZEENA 2 b.f. (Mar 31) Unfuwain (USA) 131 – Forest Fire (SWE) 88 (Never So Bold **61**
135) [2004 6s⁵ 7s⁴ 8.3m⁵ Sep 27] rather leggy filly: first foal: dam 1m to 1½m winner: modest form in maidens: should be suited by 1¼m/1½m: best effort on good to firm going. *M. P. Tregoning*

ZEIS (IRE) 4 ch.g. Bahhare (USA) 122 – Zoom Lens (IRE) 65 (Caerleon (USA) 132) **68** [2004 –: p8g p8g 10d 10f* 11.8m* 10m 11.5g p12.2g p12.2g p13.9g Oct 18] sturdy, **a56** good-bodied gelding: fair performer: won claimers at Brighton in June and Leicester (left H. Morrison) in July: stays 1½m: acts on firm and soft going, below form on polytrack: tongue tied after second outing. *Andrew Reid*

ZEITGEIST (IRE) 3 b.g. Singspiel (IRE) 133 – Diamond Quest (Rainbow Quest **96** (USA) 134) [2004 80p: 11.6g⁴ 11m* 12.1m² 12g⁵ 12g 13d* 11.8g² 14s Oct 31] useful-looking gelding: useful handicapper: won at Redcar in May and Hamilton (beat Albanov a short head) in September: good second to Massif Centrale at Leicester penultimate start: should stay at least 1¾m: acts on soft and good to firm going: seemed unsuited by course at Goodwood fifth outing: gelded after final start. *L. M. Cumani*

ZEITLOS 5 b.g. Timeless Times (USA) 99 – Petitesse 55 (Petong 126) [2004 44, a50: **–** p6g Jan 14] small gelding: poor at 4 yrs: well beaten only 5-y-o start: blinkered. *R. M. Flower*

ZELEA (IRE) 5 br.m. Be My Guest (USA) 126 – Ebony And Ivory (IRE) 95 (Bob **39** Back (USA) 124) [2004 f12g⁵ f11m⁴ f12m⁴ May 6] tall, sparely-made mare: maiden: missed 2003: only poor form in 2004: stays 1½m: acts on fibresand and good to firm ground: often tongue tied: sometimes slowly away. *J. Parkes*

ZELOSO 6 b.g. Alzao (USA) 117 – Silk Petal 105 (Petorius 117) [2004 p10g⁶ p10d² **56** p12.2g⁵ p12m* p12.2g p13.9g Dec 22] good-bodied gelding: fairly useful at 3 yrs: lightly raced on Flat since: modest form in 2004: won banded race at Lingfield in December: stays 1½m: acts on polytrack, soft and good to firm going: tried blinkered, visored in 2004. *M. F. Harris*

ZENDARO 2 b.g. (Apr 5) Danzero (AUS) – Countess Maud (Mtoto 134) [2004 f5d⁴ **49** 6g⁶ 6d 5.9g 6d⁶ Oct 18] poor maiden: should stay 7f: acts on fibresand and good to soft going. *W. M. Brisbourne*

ZENNO ROB ROY (JPN) 4 b.c. Sunday Silence (USA) – Roamin Rachel (USA) **126** 116 (Mining (USA)) [2004 117: 12.5f² 16f² 11f⁴ 12f² 10g* 12f* 12.5f* Dec 26] 90,000,000 yen F: half-brother to smart US performer around 1m Darling My Darling (by Deputy Minister) and useful UAE 1m winner Qawaqeb (by A P Indy): dam US Grade 1 7f winner: high-class performer: second in Tokyo Yushun (Japanese Derby) in 2003: improved in second half of 2004, winning 3 Group 1s in a row, namely Tenno Sho (Autumn) at Tokyo (by 1¼ lengths from Dance In The Mood) in October, Japan Cup on same course (beat Cosmo Bulk by 3 lengths) in November and Arima Kinen at Nakayama (by ½ length from Tap Dance City) in December: stays 2m: acts on firm going: reliable. *K. Fujisawa, Japan*

ZERLINA (USA) 3 b.f. Singspiel (IRE) 133 – Tass (Soviet Star (USA) 128) [2004 **90** 92p: 8d 8.2s 7d p7g⁴ 8.1g² 8g* p8g p10g⁴ Nov 10] small, quite good-topped filly: fairly useful performer: left R. Hannon after second start: won handicap at Pontefract (beat Little Jimbob by 2 lengths) in October: stays 1m: acts on polytrack and good to firm going. *W. J. Musson*

ZERO TOLERANCE (IRE) 4 ch.g. Nashwan (USA) 135 – Place de L'Opera 98 **107** (Sadler's Wells (USA) 132) [2004 94p: 10.5s* 10m⁴ 8f 10.4g 10g 10.4s² 10g² 8d* Oct 30] leggy, workmanlike gelding: useful performer: won minor event at Haydock in April and handicap at Newmarket (beat Impeller by ¾ length, dictating pace) in October: stays 1¼m: acts on fibresand, soft and good to firm ground: free-going sort: has carried head awkwardly. *T. D. Barron*

ZHITOMIR 6 ch.g. Lion Cavern (USA) 117 – Treasure Trove (USA) 62 (The Minstrel **67** (CAN) 135) [2004 67d: 7g* 8v⁶ 7.2m⁶ 7.2g* 7s⁶ 7.2s⁴ 6.9g 7.1s² 7.1d* p7.1g⁶ p7.1d² p7.1g³ p8.6g⁶ p8.6g⁶ Dec 17] strong gelding: fair performer: won sellers at Catterick in March and Ayr in July, banded race at Warwick in October, and apprentice minor event at Wolverhampton in December: stays 8.6f: acts on polytrack, soft and good to firm going: has run well when edgy/sweating: sometimes slowly away. *M. Dods*

ZIBELINE (IRE) 7 b.g. Cadeaux Genereux 131 – Zia (USA) 88 (Shareef Dancer **95** (USA) 135) [2004 97: 12m³ 16.1s 14.6f Sep 10] tall gelding: useful handicapper: fit from hurdling (useful winner), good third to Starry Lodge at Epsom on reappearance: below form after: effective at 1½m to 2¼m: acts on firm going, probably not on softer than good: tried in cheekpieces, blinkered in 2004: held up (sometimes pulls hard). *B. Ellison*

ZIET D'ALSACE (FR) 4 b.f. Zieten (USA) 118 – Providenc Mill (FR) (French **66** Stress (USA) 125) [2004 64: 8m 7m² 8f 8f 7f² 7g 7m* 7m 7f⁴ 7f⁶ 6.1m p8.6g² p8g p8.6g⁵ **a62**

p8.6d³ p8.6g⁴ p6g Dec 27] fair handicapper: won at Brighton in July: best around 7f to 8.6f: acts on polytrack and firm going: sometimes races freely. *A. W. Carroll*

ZIETORY 4 b.f. Zieten (USA) 118 – Fairy Story (IRE) 80 (Persian Bold 123) [2004 **95** 107: 9m⁵ 8g 8m³ 8.1d* 7g p8g³ p7g Nov 20] angular, workmanlike filly: useful performer: won listed race at Sandown (beat Bayberry by neck) in August: stays 1m: acts on polytrack, soft and good to firm going: looked none too keen second start. *P. F. I. Cole*

ZIETZIG (IRE) 7 b.g. Zieten (USA) 118 – Missing You 89 (Ahonoora 122) [2004 **54 §** 62§, a–§: 6g 7d f7d 5g 6.1s 6.1d⁵ 6m⁶ 6m* 6m Aug 7] shallow-girthed gelding: modest **a– §** performer: won ladies selling handicap at Thirsk in July: best at 6f/7f: acts on firm and soft going: free-going sort: usually races prominently: unreliable. *D. Nicholls*

ZIGGY DAN 4 b.g. Slip Anchor 136 – Nikatino 63 (Bustino 136) [2004 –: f12s⁵ Mar **–** 8] no sign of ability. *Ms Deborah J. Evans*

ZILCH 6 ch.g. Zilzal (USA) 137 – Bunty Boo 110 (Noalto 120) [2004 85: 7s* 7v² 6g² **104** 6v* 6m⁴ 7s 6m* 7g 6g 6s 6g Oct 9] leggy, close-coupled gelding: useful handicapper: won at Kempton in March, Pontefract in April and Windsor (beat Caustic Wit by ¾ length) in June: effective at 6f/7f: acts on polytrack, heavy and good to firm ground: tried blinkered at 4 yrs: slowly away eighth outing: effective held up or ridden prominently. *M. L. W. Bell*

ZILMY (IRE) 3 ch.g. Zilzal (USA) 137 – My Lewicia (IRE) 100 (Taufan (USA) 119) **59** [2004 8g May 18] strong gelding: third foal: dam, 1m winner who stayed 1¼m, half-sister to smart sprinter To The Roof: 4/1, seventh to Dubois in maiden at Goodwood, racing freely and not knocked about when fading. *P. W. Harris*

ZIMBALI 2 ch.f. (Mar 2) Lahib (USA) 129 – Dawn 70 (Owington 123) [2004 5.1g⁵ **59** 5d⁴ 5g* 5.1s³ 6m⁴ 6f² 6m² Jul 1] 1,000Y: small filly: first foal: dam maiden who stayed 6f: modest performer: won maiden at Warwick in April: second in sellers: will prove best at 5f/easy 6f: acts on good to firm and good to soft going: races up with pace. *J. M. Bradley*

ZINGING 5 b.g. Fraam 114 – Hi Hoh (IRE) (Fayruz 116) [2004 58§: p6g⁵ p10g p7g⁶ **40 §** p8g⁴ p8g p7g 7.1d⁶ 8g⁵ 7m⁵ 7f⁶ 7f p8g 7s⁴ 7m 6m⁶ 8d⁴ p5m⁵ p6g p7m Dec 15] small **a54 §** gelding: modest on all-weather, poor on turf: probably best at 1m: acts on all-weather, firm and soft going: tried visored/blinkered: ungenuine. *J. J. Bridger*

ZIPADEEDOODAH 2 b.c. (Mar 15) Bluebird (USA) 125 – River Divine (USA) 59 **60** (Irish River (FR) 131) [2004 p7.1g p6g⁵ Dec 4] 8,000Y: fifth foal: half-brother to 3-y-o Iron Temptress: dam ran once: modest form in maidens: not sure to stay beyond 7f. *P. J. Makin*

ZIZZLE 2 ch.c. (Mar 28) Zaha (CAN) 106 – Maria Cappuccini 70 (Siberian Express **63** (USA) 125) [2004 p8m Dec 21] half-brother to 3 winners, including 6-y-o Kumakawa: dam, 5f winner who stayed 7f, half-sister to smart performer up to 7f Marina Park: 66/1, eighth in maiden at Lingfield. *I. A. Wood*

ZOHAR (USA) 2 b.c. (Feb 1) Aljabr (USA) 125 – Dafnah (USA) (Housebuster **84** (USA)) [2004 6g* 7s Oct 22] $26,000Y: tall, lengthy colt: third foal: dam unraced out of sister to Dayjur and close relation of US Grade 1 9f/1¼m winner Maplejinsky: won maiden at Haydock in September by 1¼ lengths from Munaddam, green but leading over 1f out: last in Horris Hill Stakes at Newbury, soon in trouble: should stay 7f. *B. J. Meehan*

ZOLASH (IRE) 2 b.c. (Apr 11) General Monash (USA) 107 – Zolba (IRE) 56 (Classic **58** Secret (USA) 91) [2004 5.1m⁵ 6m 6m⁶ 7f 8f⁴ 7g⁴ 7.1g³ 8f⁶ 8g p8.6d p8g³ p8m⁶ p8.6g⁵ Dec 31] leggy colt: modest maiden: left J. S. Moore before final start: barely stays 1m: acts on polytrack and firm going: tried blinkered: signs of temperament. *Mrs Jane Galpin*

ZOLTANO (GER) 6 b.g. In The Wings 128 – Zarella (GER) (Anatas) [2004 16.1v³ **72** 16g* 16d Apr 24] tall gelding: fair handicapper: winner in Germany for P. Rau prior to 2004: won at Musselburgh in April: ran as if amiss final start: stays 2m: acts on heavy going. *M. Todhunter*

ZOLUSHKA (IRE) 3 ch.f. Russian Revival (USA) 125 – Persian Myth (Persian Bold **41** 123) [2004 –: p8g³ p8g p7g p7g Mar 4] smallish filly: form only when third in seller at Lingfield on reappearance: often slowly away. *B. W. Duke*

ZOMERLUST 2 b.g. (Jan 24) Josr Algarhoud (IRE) 118 – Passiflora 75 (Night Shift **86** (USA)) [2004 5m³ 6s* 6d² 7f⁴ 6g⁴ 6d² 7s³ Nov 6] 10,000Y: good-topped gelding: second foal: half-brother to 4-y-o Bond Royale: dam, 2-y-o 6f winner, half-sister to very smart 6f/7f performer Harmonic Way out of half-sister to In The Groove: fairly useful performer: won maiden at Ripon in August: creditable efforts in nurseries after, especially when third at Doncaster: stays 7f: acts on firm and soft going. *J. J. Quinn*

ZONERGEM   6 ch.g. Zafonic (USA) 130 – Anasazi (IRE) (Sadler's Wells (USA) 132)   **101**
[2004 102: p10g p12g⁶ 8f³ 10.1g³ 9g Oct 2] good-topped gelding: useful performer: good efforts in 2004 when third in Hunt Cup at Royal Ascot (beaten narrowly by Mine) and minor event at Epsom (behind Impeller, edging left persistently in straight): seemed to take little interest in Cambridgeshire at Newmarket final start: stays 1¼m: acts on poly-track and firm going: tried blinkered, usually wears cheekpieces: has been slowly away/carried head high/found little: usually held up: quirky: fairly useful hurdler. *Lady Herries*

ZONIC   2 b.f. (Mar 30) Zafonic (USA) 130 – Ferber's Follies (USA) (Saratoga Six   **59**
(USA)) [2004 6m p7g 6f³ Sep 23] 110,000Y: leggy filly: eighth foal: half-sister to 3 winners, including 6f winner Corndavon and 6f (including at 2 yrs)/7f winner Injaaz (both useful performers by Sheikh Albadou): dam 2-y-o 5.5f winner in USA: modest form in maidens: late headway when third at Pontefract: probably stays 7f. *Sir Michael Stoute*

ZONIC BOOM (FR)   4 ch.g. Zafonic (USA) 130 – Rosi Zambotti (IRE) 104 (Law   **67**
Society (USA) 130) [2004 61: 8g⁵ 8.3g³ 8.1d 10g³ 10g p12.2g⁶ Oct 16] fair maiden, lightly raced: stays 1¼m: best efforts on good going: sold 18,000 gns. *J. R. Fanshawe*

ZONNEBEKE   3 b.f. Orpen (USA) 116 – Canlubang (Mujtahid (USA) 118) [2004 64:   **53**
f7g⁴ f7f⁵ p8g² f8s p7g³ p7g 6.1m 7g³ 7m⁴ 8m* 8m² 8m 8s⁶ 7g 7d 6d f6g⁶ f7g⁴ p7m p8m   **a46**
Dec 15] smallish filly: modest performer: won selling handicap at Thirsk in July: claimed from K. Burke after next start: below form after: stays 1m: acts on all-weather and good to firm going: tried visored/in cheekpieces: sometimes finds little. *Mrs C. A. Dunnett*

ZONUS   3 b.c. Pivotal 124 – Jade Mistress 51 (Damister (USA) 123) [2004 87P: 7g*   **106**
8g⁴ 7.6d² 8.1m³ 8m 7.1d³ 8g 7.6s* 7g Sep 17] tall colt: useful performer: won maiden at Doncaster in March and handicap at Chester (beat Pango by 5 lengths) in August: below form in listed event at Newbury final outing: stays 1m: acts on soft and good to firm going: blinkered last 2 starts: below form after: sometimes hangs/carries head awk-wardly: joined T. Leung in Hong Kong. *B. W. Hills*

ZOOMIEZANDO   3 b.g. Forzando 122 – Zarah (Rudimentary (USA) 118) [2004   **–**
8.2g 9m 7.5s Aug 29] well held in maidens/claimer: refused to enter stalls intended fourth outing. *Mrs Lucinda Featherstone*

ZOOM ZOOM   4 b.c. Abou Zouz (USA) 109 – Iltimas (USA) 95 (Dayjur (USA) 137)   **80**
[2004 6d* 6m 5g⁵ 6d 7m⁴ 6d p7.1d* p7.1g³ Dec 20] fairly useful performer: won minor events at Haydock (first run for 18 months) in April and Wolverhampton in November: stays 7f: acts on polytrack and soft going: usually front runner. *Mrs L. Stubbs*

ZORIPP (IRE)   2 b.g. (Jan 16) Spectrum (IRE) 126 – Allspice (Alzao (USA) 117)   **47**
[2004 7d⁶ 7g 7.1d Sep 18] small, sturdy gelding: poor form in maidens: should stay at least 1¼m. *J. G. Given*

ZORN   5 br.h. Dilum (USA) 115 – Very Good (Noalto 120) [2004 –: 10d 8.3g f12s   **55**
p7.1g² p7g² Dec 29] modest maiden: stays 1½m, but probably better at shorter: form only on all-weather. *P. Howling*

ZOSIMA (USA)   3 b.f. Capote (USA) – Grafin (USA) 113 (Miswaki (USA) 124)   **113**
[2004 111: 8f³ 9.9m⁴ 7m Sep 9] big, leggy filly: second foal: half-sister to French 11f winner Violin Time (by Theatrical): dam, French 1m/1¼m (Prix de la Nonette) winner and later successful in USA, half-sister to useful dam of 5-y-o Mamool: smart performer: won maiden (blinkered), allowance race and Grade 3 Arlington Washington Lassie, all at Arlington, in 2003: left E. Harty in USA after fifth in Breeders' Cup Juvenile Fillies at Santa Anita: unlucky third to Celtic Heroine in listed handicap at Royal Ascot on British debut, persistently short of room before switched and staying on strongly: seemed unsuited by course when 7¼ lengths fourth to Favourable Terms in Nassau Stakes at Goodwood penultimate start: well below form in listed event at Doncaster final outing (didn't take eye): stays 1m: acts on dirt and firm ground: tongue tied last 3 starts. *Saeed bin Suroor*

ZOUAVE (IRE)   3 b.g. Spectrum (IRE) 126 – Lady Windley (Baillamont (USA) 124)   **–**
[2004 91: 11g 11.9d 14.1m⁵ 16.2m Jun 18] sturdy, angular gelding: fairly useful perfor-mer at 2 yrs: beat only 1 home in 4 races in 2004: blinkered last 2 starts: joined C. Mann. *B. J. Meehan*

ZOUCHE   4 b.g. Zamindar (USA) 116 – Al Corniche (IRE) 62 (Bluebird (USA) 125)   **– §**
[2004 65d: 7.9f 8d 10.9m Jul 2] close-coupled gelding: maiden: no form in 2004: tried blinkered/in cheekpieces: ungenuine. *W. M. Brisbourne*

ZUCCHERO   8 br.g. Dilum (USA) 115 – Legal Sound 85 (Legal Eagle 126) [2004 –: **77**
8d 8.2d³ 8m Jul 17] big, lengthy gelding: type to carry condition: just fair handicapper
nowadays: stays 1m: yet to race on heavy going, acts on any other: effective with or
without headgear. *D. W. P. Arbuthnot*

ZUHAIR   11 ch.g. Mujtahid (USA) 118 – Ghzaalh (USA) 87 (Northern Dancer) [2004 **68**
87: 5d 6d 6m 6m 5m 6d Jul 11] strong gelding: just fair handicapper in 2004: reported in
late-July to have suffered minor injury: effective at 5f/6f: unsuited by soft/heavy going,
acts on any other: well beaten both runs in blinkers: wears bandages: tends to sweat:
usually held up: successful 6 times at Goodwood. *D. Nicholls*

ZULETA   3 ch.f. Vettori (IRE) 119 – Victoria (Old Vic 136) [2004 57: 10.2m 10m 12g⁶ **52**
12.1d² 11.7d² 13.8m² 10g⁴ 12.6d² Oct 9] angular filly: modest maiden: claimed from
M. Blanshard after fifth start and by B. Leavy after final one: stays easy 1¾m: acts on
fibresand, good to firm and good to soft going: visored last 2 starts. *J. G. M. O'Shea*

ZULOAGO (USA)   3 b.f. Stravinsky (USA) 133 – Attitre (FR) 105 (Mtoto 134) [2004 **62 ?**
f7s⁵ f9.4s³ f8.5s² f8g f8.5g f8g p8.6g f8d Dec 21] 5,500Y: first foal: dam 2-y-o 1m winner
who stayed 1½m: modest maiden: second at Wolverhampton in March: no form after,
leaving S. Keightley after sixth start: stays 8.5f. *A. G. Newcombe*

ZUMA (IRE)   3 b.c. Grand Lodge (USA) 125 – Paradise Waters 73 (Celestial Storm **78**
(USA) 132) [2004 63: 8m 8m³ 10m 9.9g⁵ 10.3g⁵ 12m⁴ p12g⁴ 11d² 12d⁶ Oct 15] good-
bodied colt: fair maiden: probably stays 1½m: acts on good to firm going, probably on
good to soft: tried in headgear: has looked difficult ride: sold 13,500 gns. *R. Hannon*

ZURI (IRE)   3 b.f. Kris S (USA) – Amizette (USA) (Forty Niner (USA)) [2004 8m⁶ **65**
10m⁴ 8.3f 12m 9.9g 8g p8m Oct 6] fifth foal: half-sister to UAE 1m winner Rio Hondo
(by Storm Cat) and half-sister to a winner in USA by A P Indy: dam, placed in USA,
sister to US Grade 2 1m/9f winner Twining and half-sister to dam of Green Desert: fair
maiden: barely stays 1½m: acts on good to firm going: sold 20,000 gns. *L. M. Cumani*

ZWADI (IRE)   3 b.f. Docksider (USA) 124 – Local Custom (IRE) (Be My Native **70 d**
(USA) 122) [2004 74: 8m⁴ 8m 7m⁵ 6f 7f³ 6d² 6m⁴ 7m³ 8.3g⁴ p7.1g p6g⁶ Dec 14] leggy
filly: fair maiden: left H. Candy after ninth start: best at 6f/7f: acts on firm and good to
soft ground: free-going sort: usually races prominently. *J. A. Osborne*

ZWEIBRUCKEN (IRE)   3 b.f. Alhaarth (IRE) 126 – Solar Attraction (IRE) 60 (Salt **88**
Dome (USA)) [2004 83: 9g 9m 8d* 8.1g 8f 8s Oct 19] leggy filly: fairly useful handicapper: won at Salisbury (beat Nouveau Riche by 1½ lengths) in August: stays 1m: acts
on firm and good to soft going: often takes strong hold. *S. Kirk*

The following unraced horses appeared in ante-post lists for 2005 classics and
are included for information purposes.

AFRICANUS (IRE)   2 b.c. (Feb 5) Dubai Millennium 140 – Asfurah (USA) 108
(Dayjur (USA) 137) third foal: half-brother to fairly useful 1¼m winner Ijtihad (by
Darshaan): dam, 2-y-o 5f/6f (Cherry Hinton) winner, half-sister to smart US 6f/7f
performer Istintaj. *Saeed bin Suroor*

AIR COMMODORE (USA)   2 ch.c. (Jan 31) Diesis 133 – La Sky (IRE) 107 (Law
Society (USA) 130) brother to 2 winners, notably Oaks winner Love Divine, also
successful at 1¼m, and half-brother to 3 winners, including useful 1½m winner Floreeda
(by Linamix): dam, 1¼m winner (probably stayed 1¾m), closely related to Champion
Stakes winner Legal Case. *H. R. A. Cecil*

AVALON   2 b.c. (Mar 7) Kingmambo (USA) 125 – Lady Carla 122 (Caerleon (USA)
132) 1,000,000Y: fourth foal: dam 1m (at 2 yrs) to 1½m (Oaks) winner. *A. P. O'Brien,
Ireland*

DIAMOND REEF   2 b.f. (Feb 21) Alzao (USA) 117 – Caroline (Sadler's Wells
(USA) 132) fourth foal: half-sister to smart French performers up to 1¾m/15f Martaline,
Reefscape (both by Linamix) and Clear Thinking (by Rainbow Quest): dam, French 12.5f
winner, half-sister to Irish Oaks winner Wemyss Bight. *A. Fabre, France*

KALAMKAR (IRE)   2 gr.c. (Feb 19) Daylami (IRE) 138 – Kalamba (IRE) (Green
Dancer (USA) 132) sixth foal: closely related to top-class 7f to 1½m winner Kalanisi (by
Doyoun) and half-brother to 3 winners, notably very smart 1m/1¼m winner Kalaman (by
Desert Prince): dam third at 9f (at 2 yrs) and 1¼m in France . *Sir Michael Stoute*

KING'S ADMIRAL (USA)   2 b.c. (May 6) Danzig (USA) – Bubbles Darlene (USA) (Fappiano (USA)) $575,000Y: half-brother to a winner in USA by Ogygian and useful 5f/ 6f winner (including at 2 yrs) Elrafa Ah (by Storm Cat), herself dam of Dewhurst winner Mujahid (by Danzig): dam 6f and 1m winner in USA. *Sir Michael Stoute*

MORDOR (FR)   2 b.c. (Jan 25) Sadler's Wells (USA) 132 – Moon Driver (USA) 98 (Mr Prospector (USA)) first foal: dam, French 2-y-o 5.5f (Prix d'Arenberg) winner, out of very smart miler/Prix de Diane winner East of The Moon, herself half-sister to Kingmambo. *Sir Michael Stoute*

RAYDAN (IRE)   2 b.c. (Apr 4) Danehill (USA) 126 – Rayseka (IRE) 112 (Dancing Brave (USA) 140) sixth foal: half-brother to several winners (all at least useful), including Irish 9f/11f winner Raypour (by Barathea) and Irish 1½m winner Rayshan (by Darshaan) who stays 1¾m: dam Irish 11f/1½m winner and second in Irish St Leger. *J. Oxx, Ireland*

ERRATA & ADDENDA
'Racehorses of 1964'

p106/p107	The picture captions for the Prix de Diane and Prix Saint-Alary are transposed

'Racehorses of 1994'

p65 tabulated pedigree	Shirley Heights was foaled in 1975

'Racehorses of 2001'

p375 end of 1st paragraph	Saeed bin Suroor also achieved the Derby and Oaks double in 1995
Crossbreeze	dam is sister to smart performer up to 8.5f **Circle of Gold**

'Racehorses of 2002'

Beauvrai	disqualified from win at Wolverhampton after failing dope test (morphine); race awarded to Percy Douglas
La Paz	awarded listed race at Maisons-Laffitte after winner Moon Search failed dope test and was disqualified
Red Storm	disqualified from win at Wolverhampton after failing dope test (morphine); race awarded to Champain Sands
Supreme Salutation	disqualified from win at Wolverhampton in November after failing dope test (morphine); race awarded to Leonora Truce
Valazar	disqualified from win at Southwell after failing dope test (morphine); race awarded to Festive Affair

'Racehorses of 2003'

Absolute Utopia	disqualified from first win at Lingfield after failing dope test (morphine); race awarded to Hidden Surprise
Bago	in the photo caption on p98 it should read **Top Seed**
Dubai Success	disqualified from win at Doncaster after failing a dope test; race awarded to Wareed
Lobos	disqualified from last three races after failing dope tests; Bath race awarded to Cooden Beach, Lingfield race awarded to Sewmore Character

PROMISING HORSES

Selected British-trained horses (plus those trained by Aidan O'Brien) with either a p or P in *Racehorses of 2004* are listed under the trainer for whom they had their final start.

A. M. BALDING
Diktatorial 2 br.c   105p
Marajuana 2   b.f   82p

T. D. BARRON
Premier Fantasy 2   b.c   93p

R. M. BECKETT
Three Degrees (IRE) 2 gr.f   81p

M. L. W. BELL
Kahira (IRE) 2 ch.f   80p
Motivator 2   b.c   122p

M. BLANSHARD
The Composer 2   b.c   83p

C. E. BRITTAIN
Amalie (IRE) 2   b.f   89p

G. A. BUTLER
Forgery (IRE) 2 ch.c   85p
Tarfah (USA) 3   b.f   102p

H. CANDY
Bow Wave 2   b.c   81p
Seamus Shindig 2   b.g   87p
The Abbess 2 gr.f   81p

H. R. A. CECIL
Camacho 2   b.c   92p
Tempestad (IRE) 2   b.f   83p

P. W. CHAPPLE-HYAM
Clear Impression (IRE) 2   b.f   87P
Divinely Decadent (IRE) 2 br.f   85p
River Alhaarth (IRE) 2   b.c   81p

R. CHARLTON
Macaulay (IRE) 2 ch.c   81p
Pike Bishop (IRE) 2   b.c   103p
Piper's Ash (USA) 2   b.f   84p
Kind (IRE) 3   b.f   100p
Dorothy's Friend 4   b.g   101p

P. F. I. COLE
My Putra (USA) 2   b.c   82p
Nanton (USA) 2 gr.g   82p
Songthrush (USA) 2 gr.f   87p
Eisteddfod 3 ch.g   113p

C. G. COX
Woodcote (IRE) 2   b.c   97p

L. M. CUMANI
Dash To The Top 2   b.f   109p
Shared Dreams 2   b.f   78P
Mandatum 3   b.g   84p
One So Marvellous 3 ch.f   86p
Pukka (IRE) 3   b.c   112p
Literatim 4   b.g   95p
Mephisto (IRE) 5   b.g   111p

E. A. L. DUNLOP
Polish Eagle 2   b.c   83p
Gentleman's Deal (IRE) 3   b.c   88p

J. L. DUNLOP
Eva Soneva So Fast (IRE) 2 ch.c   87p
Kong (IRE) 2   b.c   81p

Ladeena (IRE) 2   b.f   80p
Muraabet 2   b.c   88p
Museeb (USA) 2   b.c   87p
Teeba (USA) 2 ch.f   83P
Thakafaat (IRE) 2   b.f   80p
Unfurled (IRE) 2 ch.c   90p
Race The Ace 3   b.g   94p

T. D. EASTERBY
Big Hassle (IRE) 2   b.c   92p

C. R. EGERTON
Vinando 3 ch.c   108p

D. R. C. ELSWORTH
Cape Columbine 2   b.f   99P
Nota Bene 2   b.c   94p
Top Gear 2   b.c   85p
Tucker 2   b.c   87p

J. R. FANSHAWE
Tilt 2   b.g   61p
High Reserve 3   b.f   80p
Musicanna 3   b.f   81p
Polar Magic 3 ch.g   91p

J. H. M. GOSDEN
Alhaadh (USA) 2   b.f   57P
Australian 2   b.c   80p
Bureaucrat 2   b.g   83p
Code Orange 2   b.f   91p
Glorious Step (USA) 2   b.f   91p
Jonquil (IRE) 2 ch.c   95p
Karen's Caper (USA) 2   b.f   80p
Paradise Mill (USA) 2   b.f   81p
Playful Act (IRE) 2   b.f   113p
Plea Bargain 2   b.c   100p
Sanchi (IRE) 2   b.c   81p
Spear Thistle 2 ch.g   90p
Twyla Tharp (IRE) 2   b.f   83p
Windsor Knot (IRE) 2 ch.c   110p
Maraakeb (FR) 3 gr.c   84p
Sleeping Indian 3   b.c   116p

W. J. HAGGAS
Clueless 2   b.c   87p
Squaw Dance 2 ch.f   100p
Tractor Boy 2   b.c   87p
Very Wise 2   b.c   86p
Choir Leader 3   b.g   93p

R. HANNON
Bailey Gate 2   b.f   85p
Forward Move (IRE) 2 ch.c   97p
Kamakiri (IRE) 2   b.c   100p
Top The Charts 2   b.c   91p

LADY HERRIES
Tartouche 3   b.f   100p

B. W. HILLS
Dhaular Dhar (IRE) 2   b.c   92p
Grigorovitch (IRE) 2   b.c   83p
Kenmore 2   b.c   95p

Whazzat 2 b.f 105p
Kamanda Laugh 3 ch.g 93p

A. P. JARVIS
For Life (IRE) 2 b.c 88p

M. A. JARVIS
Ayam Zaman (IRE) 2 b.f 106p
Donyana 2 b.f 89p
Subpoena 2 b.c 93p

M. JOHNSTON
Brahminy Kite (USA) 2 b.c 99p
Crosspeace (IRE) 2 b.c 94p
I'm So Lucky 2 b.g 90p
Mafaheem 2 b.c 91p
Shamardal (USA) 2 b.c 126p
Starchy 2 b.f 84p
Tarraman (USA) 2 b.c 93p
Swift Sailor 3 gr.g 91p
Winged d'Argent (IRE) 3 b.c 103p

D. R. LODER
Francis Cadell 2 b.c 84p
Fu Manchu 2 b.c 82p

M. A. MAGNUSSON
Kehaar 3 ch.c 108p

B. J. MEEHAN
David Junior (USA) 2 ch.c 89p
Fongtastic 2 ch.c 87p
General Jumbo 2 b.c 88p
Maggie Jordan (USA) 2 b.f 86p
Poker Player (IRE) 2 ch.g 80p

H. MORRISON
Postgraduate (IRE) 2 b.c 83p

J. NOSEDA
Daring Ransom (USA) 2 b.c 96p
Proclamation (IRE) 2 gr.c 100p
Ecomium (IRE) 3 b.c 118p
Majors Cast (IRE) 3 b.c 102p

A. P. O'BRIEN, IRELAND
Ad Valorem (USA) 2 b.c 121p
Albert Hall 2 b.c 113p
Almighty (USA) 2 b.c 98p
Cherokee (USA) 2 b.f 102p
Footstepsinthesand 2 b.c 114p
Grand Central (IRE) 2 b.c 97p
Hills of Aran 2 b.c 103p
Kitty O'Shea 2 b.f 87P
Showdance (USA) 2 b.c 97p
Tiger Dance (USA) 2 b.c 95P
Yehudi (IRE) 2 b.c 108p

J. A. OSBORNE
Cloonavery (IRE) 2 b.g 83p
Major Faux Pas (IRE) 2 b.g 85p

MRS A. J. PERRETT
Bayeux de Moi (IRE) 2 b.c 91p
Blue Torpedo (USA) 2 ch.g 82p
Corcoran (USA) 2 b.f 81p
Liakoura (GER) 2 b.g 95p
Westland (USA) 2 gr.c 81p
Winds of Time (IRE) 2 b.f 80p
Simonda 3 ch.f 84p

SIR MARK PRESCOTT
Comic Strip 2 b.g 110p
Intrigued 2 gr.f 105p

Kiswahili 2 ch.f 89p
Regal Setting (IRE) 3 br.g 98p

M. G. QUINLAN
Baradore (IRE) 2 ch.f 82p

K. A. RYAN
Throw The Dice 2 b.c 85p

I. SEMPLE
Mintlaw 2 b.f 80p
Real Quality (USA) 2 br.g 90p

SIR MICHAEL STOUTE
Asawer (IRE) 2 b.f 82p
Blue Train (IRE) 2 b.c 78P
Discuss (USA) 2 b.f 77P
Echelon 2 b.f 99P
Front Stage (IRE) 2 b.c 92p
Hard Top (IRE) 2 b.c 74P
Highland Diva (IRE) 2 ch.f 67P
Home Affairs 2 b.c 94p
Hornpipe 2 b.c 86p
Insinuation (IRE) 2 b.f 66P
King's Majesty (IRE) 2 b.c 89P
Linngari (IRE) 2 ch.c 93p
Master of The Race 2 ch.c 94p
Mutajammel (FR) 2 b.c 87P
Public Forum 2 b.c 84p
Quickfire 2 b.f 88p
Read Federica 2 ch.f 77P
Rob Roy (USA) 2 b.c 94P
Santa Fe (IRE) 2 b.c 102p
Seven Magicians (USA) 2 b.f 79P
Shanghai Lily (IRE) 2 b.f 98P
Tomoohat (USA) 2 b.f 96P
Zalongo 2 ch.c 87p
Zarabad (IRE) 2 b.c 85p
Antediluvian 3 b.f 106p
Day of Reckoning 3 b.f 82p
Menokee (USA) 3 b.c 111p
Notable Guest (USA) 3 b.c 95p
Peeress 3 ch.f 105p
Poise (IRE) 3 b.f 93p
Stream of Gold (IRE) 3 b.c 107p

SAEED BIN SUROOR
Afrashad (USA) 2 ch.c 107p
Army of Angels (IRE) 2 ch.c 103p
Atlantic Story (USA) 2 b.c 94p
Ballinteni 2 b.c 88p
Belenus (IRE) 2 ch.c 103p
Centaurus 2 br.c 97p
Classicism (USA) 2 b.f 82p
Descartes 2 b.c 90P
Desert Chief 2 b.c 81p
Desert Commander (IRE) 2 b.c 82p
Dubai Dreamer (USA) 2 gr.c 82p
Dubawi (IRE) 2 b.c 123p
Esquire 2 b.c 92p
Fen Shui (UAE) 2 b.f 96p
Financial Times (USA) 2 b.c 82p
Grosvenor Square (IRE) 2 b.c 97p
Halle Bop 2 b.f 85p
Happy As Larry (USA) 2 b.c 93p
Her Own Kind (JPN) 2 b.f 89p
Librettist (USA) 2 b.c 114p
Loyal Love (USA) 2 br.f 85p
Macabre 2 b.c 87p
Monsoon Rain (USA) 2 b.c 103p

Munaddam (USA) 2 ch.c   95p
Noble Duty (USA) 2 b.c   91p
Oude (USA) 2 b.c   105p
Potent Heir (USA) 2 b.c   90p
Querido (USA) 2 b.c   88p
Red Admiral (USA) 2 b.c   94p
Russian Revolution 2 b.f   83p
Saywaan (USA) 2 ch.f   90P
Sharaiji Blossom (USA) 2 b.f   80p
Storm Silk (CAN) 2 b.c   106p
Into The Dark 3 ch.c   119p

J. A. R. TOLLER

Peruvian Prince (USA) 2 b.c   86p

M. P. TREGONING

Emile Zola 2 b.c   81p
Night Hour (IRE) 2 b.c   89p
Qadar (IRE) 2 b.c   96p
Shohrah (IRE) 2 ch.f   103p
Deep Purple 3 b.g   89p
Oriental Warrior 3 b.c   106p
Remaadd (USA) 3 gr.c   112p
Tahtheeb (IRE) 3 b.f   105p

E. F. VAUGHAN

Tasdeed 2 ch.c   93P
Day To Remember 3 gr.c   93P
Namroc (IRE) 3 b.c   97p

S. C. WILLIAMS

Exponential (IRE) 2 b.g   82p
Dont Call Me Derek 3 b.g   84p

G. WRAGG

Bon Nuit (IRE) 2 b.f   81p

SELECTED BIG RACES 2004

Prize money for racing abroad has been converted to £ sterling at the exchange rate current at the time of the race. The figures are correct to the nearest £. The Timeform ratings (TR) recorded by the principals in each race appear on the last line.

NAD AL SHEBA Saturday, Mar 27   FAST

1   Dubai World Cup (Gr 1) (4yo+) £1,956,522   1¼m (Dirt)

PLEASANTLY PERFECT (USA) *REMandella,USA* 6-9-0 (b+t) ASolis (7) ..	5/2	1
MEDAGLIA D'ORO (USA) *RJFrankel,USA* 5-9-0 (t) JBailey (11)	2/1f	¾ 2
VICTORY MOON (SAF) *MFdeKock,SouthAfrica* 5-9-0 WCMarwing (9)	4/1	5 3
Grand Hombre (USA) *SaeedbinSuroor,UAE* 4-9-0 (v+t) LDettori (8)	12/1	7¾ 4
King's Boy (GER) *JBarton,SaudiArabia* 7-9-0 (b) MJKinane (2)	66/1	4 5
Domestic Dispute (USA) *PGallagher,USA* 4-9-0 (t) GaryStevens (1)	22/1	4 6
Fleetstreet Dancer (USA) *DO'Neill,USA* 6-9-0 (b+t) JKCourt (10)	16/1	nk 7
Admire Don (JPN) *HMatsuda,Japan* 5-9-0 (h) KAndo (3)	11/1	2¼ 8
Regent Bluff (JPN) *YOkubo,Japan* 8-9-0 YYoshida (5).................................	40/1	1¾ 9
Dinyeper *AKasar,Turkey* 5-9-0 (h) HKaratas (4).......................................	40/1	7¾ 10
State Shinto (USA) *MAlKurdi,UAE* 8-9-0 (b) TEDurcan (12)......................	66/1	3¼ 11
Silent Deal (JPN) *YIkee,Japan* 4-9-0 YTake (6)...	25/1	13 12

Diamond A Racing Corporation 12ran 2m00.24   TR: 130/129/120/108/101

NEWMARKET Thursday, Apr 15   GOOD (Rowley Mile Course)

2   Bet365 Craven Stks (Gr 3) (3yo c+g) £29,750   1m

HAAFHD *BWHills* 3-8-9 RHills (2)...	10/3	1
THREE VALLEYS (USA) *RCharlton* 3-8-9 RHughes (1)............................	2/1f	5 2
PEAK TO CREEK *JNoseda* 3-8-9 EAhern (4)...	6/1	1¼ 3
Imperial Stride *SirMichaelStoute* 3-8-9 KFallon (5)	7/1	2½ 4
Fantastic View (USA) *RHannon* 3-8-9 PJDobbs (3)	10/3	4 5

Mr Hamdan Al Maktoum 5ran 1m38.33   TR: 124/110/107/100

NEWMARKET Saturday, May 1   GOOD (Rowley Mile Course)

3   UltimateBet.com 2000 Guineas Stks (Gr 1) (3yo c+f) £174,000   1m

2 HAAFHD *BWHills* 3-9-0 RHills (4)...	11/2	1
SNOW RIDGE (IRE) *SaeedbinSuroor* 3-9-0 LDettori (14).........................	8/1	1¾ 2
AZAMOUR (IRE) *JOxx,Ireland* 3-9-0 MJKinane (1)................................	25/1	1 3
Grey Swallow (IRE) *DKWeld,Ireland* 3-9-0 PJSmullen (3).......................	10/1	1 4
Whipper (IRE) *RCollet,France* 3-9-0 CSoumillon (8)	9/1	hd 5
Salford City (IRE) *DRCElsworth* 3-9-0 JMurtagh (6)	11/2	½ 6
Bachelor Duke (USA) *JARToller* 3-9-0 SSanders (9)	20/1	1½ 7
Milk It Mick *JAOsborne* 3-9-0 DHolland (1)	12/1	3½ 8
Tumblebrutus (USA) *APO'Brien,Ireland* 3-9-0 PCosgrave (7)	200/1	8 9
Glaramara *ABailey* 3-9-0 TEDurcan (10)	200/1	2½ 10
2 Three Valleys (USA) *RCharlton* 3-9-0 KFallon (2)	20/1	½ 11
Barbajuan (IRE) *NACallaghan* 3-9-0 PRobinson (10)	150/1	sh 12
One Cool Cat (USA) *APO'Brien,Ireland* 3-9-0 JPSpencer (13)	15/8f	dist 13
Golden Sahara (IRE) *SaeedbinSuroor* 3-9-0 (v+t) JCarroll (5)..................	200/1	nk 14

Mr Hamdan Al Maktoum 14ran 1m36.64   TR: 129/124/121+/118/118/117

NEWMARKET Sunday, May 2   GOOD to FIRM (Rowley Mile Course)

4   UltimateBet.com 1000 Guineas Stks (Gr 1) (3yo f) £187,195   1m

ATTRACTION *MJohnston* 3-9-0 KDarley (8)...	11/2	1
SUNDROP (JPN) *SaeedbinSuroor* 3-9-0 KMcEvoy (1)............................	16/1	½ 2
HATHRAH (IRE) *JLDunlop* 3-9-0 RHills (16)...	6/1	½ 3
Red Bloom *SirMichaelStoute* 3-9-0 KFallon (7)	4/1f	1¼ 4
Secret Charm (IRE) *BWHills* 3-9-0 MHills (6)	14/1	½ 5
Carry On Katie (USA) *SaeedbinSuroor* 3-9-0 LDettori (10)	7/1	hd 6
Nataliya *JLDunlop* 3-9-0 SSanders (14)	20/1	1¼ 7
Silca's Gift *MRChannon* 3-9-0 TEDurcan (15).......................................	16/1	nk 8
Majestic Desert *MRChannon* 3-9-0 DHolland (4)	7/1	hd 9
Cairns (UAE) *SaeedbinSuroor* 3-9-0 JCarroll (12)	25/1	2½ 10
Kelucia (IRE) *JSGoldie* 3-9-0 JFEgan (4)	100/1	2 11
Necklace *APO'Brien,Ireland* 3-9-0 JMurtagh (13)...................................	8/1	¾ 12
Valjarv (IRE) *NPLittmoden* 3-9-0 TGMcLaughlin (5)	200/1	2½ 13
Incheni (IRE) *GWragg* 3-9-0 SDrowne (4)	25/1	3 14
Jath *JulianPoulton* 3-9-0 NCallan (11)	100/1	1½ 15
Spotlight *JLDunlop* 3-9-0 EAhern (2)	33/1	sh 16

Duke of Roxburghe 16ran 1m36.78   TR: 116/115/113/110/108+/108

LONGCHAMP Sunday, May 2   GOOD to SOFT

5   **Prix Ganay (Gr 1) (4yo+)** £67,114   1¼m110y

EXECUTE (FR) *JEHammond,France* 7-9-2 TGillet 219/10   1
VESPONE (IRE) *SaeedbinSuroor,GB* 4-9-2 C-PLemaire 42/10   1½ 2
FAIR MIX (IRE) *MRolland,France* 6-9-2 OPeslier .... 46/10   ½ 3
Vallee Enchantee (IRE) *ELellouche,France* 4-8-13 DBoeuf .... 56/10   ½ 4
Polish Summer *AFabre,France* 7-9-2 GaryStevens .... 11/10f   ½ 5
Touch of Land (FR) *H-APantall,France* 4-9-2 SPasquier .... 48/1   nk 6
Vangelis (USA) *AdeRoyerDupre,France* 5-9-2 CSoumillon 66/10   3 7
Chancellor (IRE) *JLDunlop,GB* 6-9-2 TJarnet .... 50/1   ¾ 8

Ecurie Chalhoub 8ran 2m14.60   TR: 121/119/117/114+/115/115

YORK Wednesday, May 12   SOFT

6   **Totesport Dante Stks (Gr 2) (3yo)** £84,100   1¼m88y

NORTH LIGHT (IRE) *SirMichaelStoute* 3-8-11 KFallon (1)......................... 6/1   1
RULE OF LAW (USA) *SaeedbinSuroor* 3-8-11 LDettori (3)..................... 8/1   ½ 2
LET THE LION ROAR *JLDunlop* 3-8-11 MJKinane (9)......................... 3/1f   2½ 3
Top Seed (IRE) *MRChannon* 3-8-11 TEDurcan (6)....................................... 8/1   1 4
Andean *DRLoder* 3-8-11 TPQueally (7).. 4/1   6 5
Moscow Ballet (IRE) *APO'Brien,Ireland* 3-8-11 JPSpencer (5) 5/1   3½ 6
Mutawaffer *BWHills* 3-8-11 RHills (8)... 33/1   5 7
3   Barbajuan (IRE) *NACallaghan* 3-8-11 PRobinson (4) 33/1   5 8
Skidmark *DRCElsworth* 3-8-11 RHughes (10)................................... 25/1   5 9
Oman Gulf (USA) *BWHills* 3-8-11 MHills (2)....................................... 25/1   1¼ 10

Ballymacoll Stud 10ran 2m15.69   TR: 120+/119/114/112/102

NEWBURY Saturday, May 15   GOOD to FIRM

7   **Juddmonte Lockinge Stks (Gr 1) (4yo+)** £116,000   1m

RUSSIAN RHYTHM (USA) *SirMichaelStoute* 4-8-11 KFallon (3) 3/1f   1
SALSELON *LMCumani* 5-9-0 (b) JMurtagh (8).................................. 66/1   ½ 2
NORSE DANCER (IRE) *DRCElsworth* 4-9-0 TQuinn (14) .... 10/1   nk 3
Firebreak *SaeedbinSuroor* 5-9-0 (b) KMcEvoy (10).......................... 16/1   1 4
Hurricane Alan (IRE) *RHannon* 4-9-0 PDobbs (15)............................ 14/1   1 5
Ikhtyar (IRE) *JHMGosden* 4-9-0 RHills (12)................................... 11/2   ¾ 6
Checkit (IRE) *MRChannon* 4-9-0 TEDurcan (6)................................ 25/1   ½ 7
Refuse To Bend (IRE) *SaeedbinSuroor* 4-9-0 (v) LDettori (9)................... 5/1   1½ 8
Indian Haven *PWD'Arcy* 4-9-0 DHolland (1)..................................... 20/1   ¾ 9
Quito (IRE) *DWChapman* 7-9-0 (b) ACulhane (4) .... 25/1   ¾ 10
Gateman *MJohnston* 7-9-0 KDalgleish (7).. 16/1   sh 11
Krataios (FR) *CLaffon-Parias,France* 4-9-0 OPeslier (11) .... 25/1   ½ 12
With Reason (USA) *SaeedbinSuroor* 6-9-0 (b) RHughes (13) 25/1   5 13
Desert Deer *JHMGosden* 6-9-0 KDarley (2)..................................... 16/1   15 14
Tout Seul (IRE) *RFJohnsonHoughton* 4-9-0 SCarson (5)............................ 12/1   6 15

Cheveley Park Stud 15ran 1m37.00   TR: 122/124/123/120/117/115

KRANJI Sunday, May 16   GOOD

8   **Singapore Airlines International Cup (Gr 1) (3yo+)** £523,026   1¼m

EPALO (GER) *ASchutz,Germany* 5-9-0 AStarke 64/10   1
SURVEYOR (SAF) *MFdeKock,SouthAfrica* 5-9-0 (b) BVorster 126/10   5 2
BOWMAN'S CROSSING (IRE) *DOughton,HongKong* 5-9-0 MJKinane .. 54/10   ¾ 3
Ain't Here (AUS) *DAHayes,HongKong* 5-9-0 GMosse 23/1   2½ 4
Moon Shadow (AUS) *DBaertschiger,Malaysia* 6-9-0 CCarmody .... 30/1   sh 5
Imperial Dancer *MRChannon,GB* 6-9-0 TEDurcan .... 3/1f   nk 6
Sarrasin (FR) *CLaffon-Parias,France* 5-9-0 MBlancpain 25/1   1 7
Superior Star (AUS) *LLaxon,Singapore* 4-8-10 JLTaylor .... 21/1   ¾ 8
Gruntled *JEHammond,France* 5-9-0 DBeadman.................................. 126/10   nk 9
Lord of The Pines (AUS) *JMeagher,Singapore* 9-9-0 KBSoo 50/1   4 10
Paolini (GER) *AWohler,Germany* 7-9-0 (b) EPedroza.............................. 96/10   nk 11
Blizz Bless (ARG) *PShaw,Malaysia* 5-9-0 JGeroudis............................ 66/1   hd 12
Exaggerate (NZ) *JMeagher,Singapore* 5-9-0 (b) JPatton 116/10   1½ 13
Physique (NZ) *LTreloar,Australia* 5-9-0 (b) NRawiller.............................. 116/10   ½ 14
Muscle Man (NZ) *CLeck,Singapore* 4-9-0 JSaimee .... 154/10   dist 15
Confluence (NZ) *FNathan,Malaysia* 8-8-10 OChavez................................ 166/10   pu

Mr Gary A. Tanaka 16ran 2m02.60   TR: 122/112/111/107/105/105

LONGCHAMP Sunday, May 16   GOOD

9   **Gainsborough Poule d'Essai des Pouliches (Gr 1) (3yo f)** £133,327   1m

TORRESTRELLA (IRE) *FRohaut,France* 3-9-0 OPeslier (5) 97/10   1
GREY LILAS (IRE) *AFabre,France* 3-9-0 GaryStevens (1)......................... 6/5f   1½ 2
MISS MAMBO (USA) *ELibaud,France* 3-9-0 CSoumillon (13)............... 38/10   2 3

Via Milano (FR) *MmeJLaurent-JoyeRossi,France* 3-9-0 TThulliez (11)....... 37/1   nk 4
Nyramba *JHMGosden,GB* 3-9-0 IMendizabal (4).. 6/5f   sn 5
4 Cairns (UAE) *SaeedbinSuroor,GB* 3-9-0 TGillet (12)................................... 7/2   sh 6
Dalna (FR) *MmeCHead-Maarek,France* 3-9-0 C-PLemaire (10) .... 19/1   hd 7
Cattiva Generosa *RGibson,France* 3-9-0 TJarnet (3) 25/1   1½ 8
4 Carry On Katie (USA) *SaeedbinSuroor,GB* 3-9-0 LDettori (2) 7/2   1 9
Rumba Loca (IRE) *BGrizzetti,Italy* 3-9-0 MDemuro (9) .... 27/1   nk 10
Tulipe Royale (FR) *MmeNRossio,France* 3-9-0 ELegrix (8)....................... 52/1   nk 11
Grandes Illusions (FR) *DSmaga,France* 3-9-0 DBoeuf (6) 33/1   2 12
Royal Tigress (USA) *APO'Brien,Ireland* 3-9-0 JPSpencer (7)..................... 25/1   1½ 13

Mr B. Bargues 13ran 1m35.70   TR: 117/113/108/107/107/107/107

10   **Gainsborough Poule d'Essai des Poulains (Gr 1) (3yo c) £133,327**   1m

AMERICAN POST *MmeCHead-Maarek,France* 3-9-2 RHughes (4).......... 4/10f   1
DIAMOND GREEN (FR) *AFabre,France* 3-9-2 GaryStevens (6)............. 34/10   ½ 2
BYRON *SaeedbinSuroor,GB* 3-9-2 LDettori (2)...................................... 82/10   nk 3
Ershaad (USA) *JEHammond,France* 3-9-2 TGillet (7).............................. 29/1   ½ 4
Antonius Pius (USA) *APO'Brien,Ireland* 3-9-2 JPSpencer (3).................... 15/1   nk 5
Newton (IRE) *APO'Brien,Ireland* 3-9-2 (b) PaulScallan (1) 15/1   1½ 6
Sunday Doubt (USA) *MmeCHead-Maarek,France,*3-9-2 OPeslier (5) 16/1   2½ 7

Mr K. Abdulla 7ran 1m36.50   TR: 119+/118+/117/115/115+/110?

11   **Prix de Saint-Georges (Gr 3) (3yo+) £24,333**   5f

THE TRADER (IRE) *MBlanshard,GB* 6-9-2 (b) JPSpencer (5) 56/10   1
THE TATLING (IRE) *JMBradley,GB* 7-9-6 LDettori (3)............................. 82/10   2 2
PATAVELLIAN (IRE) *RCharlton,GB* 6-9-11 (b) SDrowne (1)................. 23/10f   1½ 3
Chineur (FR) *MDelzangles,France* 3-8-8 ELegrix (8) 69/10   1 4
Rue La Fayette (SWE) *FReuterskiold,Sweden* 4-8-10 TGillet (10)............ 45/10   sn 5
Dobby Road (FR) *MlleVDissaux,France* 5-9-0 IMendizabal (4)................... 33/1   1 6
Much Faster (IRE) *PBary,France* 3-8-12 TThulliez (2) .... 73/10   nk 7
Melkior (FR) *TLallie,France* 7-9-2 C-PLemaire (12) .... 24/1   sn 8
Meliksah (IRE) *WBaltromei,Germany* 3-9-0 CSoumillon (7)...................... 24/1   sh 9
Sweet Salsa (FR) *YdeNicolay,France* 3-8-3 DBonilla (9).......................... 33/1   3 10
Swedish Shave (FR) *RGibson,France* 6-9-6 TJarnet (6)............................ 45/10   1½ 11
St Paul House *DCamuffo,Italy* 6-9-0 PAragoni (11)................................... 12/1   3 12

Mrs C. J. Ward 12ran 56.80secs   TR: 123/120/120/104

ROME Sunday, May 16   GOOD

12   **Premio Presidente della Repubblica SIS (Gr 1) (4yo+) £202,000**   1¼m

ALTIERI *VCaruso,Italy* 6-9-2 MEsposito 332/100   1
5 VESPONE (IRE) *SaeedbinSuroor,GB* 4-9-2 KMcEvoy 73/100f   3 2
NONNO CARLO (IRE) *MGrassi,Italy* 4-9-2 MBelli 22/1   2 3
Le Vie Dei Colori *RBrogi,Italy* 4-9-2 DVargiu.................................... 169/100   nk 4
Duca d'Atri (IRE) *ARenzoni,Italy* 5-9-2 GBietolini 25/1   2½ 5
Quel Del Giaz (IRE) *FCamici,Italy* 5-9-2 MPasquale 47/1   3 6
Blu For Life (IRE) *RMimmocchi,Italy* 7-9-2 MMimmocchi....................... 58/1   2 7

Scuderia Incolinx 7ran 1m58.70   TR: 122/117/112/112/105

CURRAGH Saturday, May 22   GOOD to FIRM

13   **Boylesports Irish 2000 Guineas (Gr 1) (3yo c+f) £157,568**   1m

3 BACHELOR DUKE (USA) *JARToller,GB* 3-9-0 SSanders (8) 12/1   1
3 AZAMOUR (IRE) *JOxx* 3-9-0 MJKinane (5).. 6/4f   1 2
3 GREY SWALLOW (IRE) *DKWeld* 3-9-0 PJSmullen (3).......................... 2/1   ½ 3
Leitrim House *BJMeehan,GB* 3-9-0 SJDrowne (2)................................... 5/1   1½ 4
Grand Reward (USA) *APO'Brien* 3-9-0 JPSpencer (6) 14/1   3 5
10 Newton (IRE) *APO'Brien* 3-9-0 (b) PaulScallan (4)............................... 50/1   1½ 6
Amarula Ridge (IRE) *KPrendergast* 3-9-0 DPMcDonogh (1)..................... 50/1   4½ 7
Hayburn Street (IRE) *DKWeld* 3-9-0 PShanahan (7)............................ 200/1   ¾ 8

Exors of the Late Duke of Devonshire 8ran 1m40.17   TR: 120+/117/116/112/104/100

CURRAGH Sunday, May 23   GOOD to FIRM

14   **Boylesports Irish 1000 Guineas (Gr 1) (3yo f) £152,162**   1m

4 ATTRACTION *MJohnston,GB* 3-9-0 KPDarley (5) 2/1f   1
ALEXANDER GOLDRUN (IRE) *JSBolger* 3-9-0 KJManning (12) 8/1   1 2
ILLUSTRIOUS MISS (USA) *DRLoder,GB* 3-9-0 KFallon (6) 9/2   2 3
Kinnaird (IRE) *PCHaslam,GB* 3-9-0 MJKinane (9) 16/1   1 4
4 Secret Charm *BWHills,GB* 3-9-0 MHills (15)... 4/1   ½ 5
4 Necklace *APO'Brien* 3-9-0 JAHeffernan (8).. 16/1   1½ 6
4 Majestic Desert *MRChannon,GB* 3-9-0 TEDurcan (7)............................ 12/1   1½ 7
Misty Heights *DKWeld* 3-9-0 (b) PJSmullen (13) 20/1   5 8
Last Love (IRE) *APO'Brien* 3-9-0 JPSpencer (1) 20/1   2 9

Kisses For Me (IRE) *APO'Brien* 3-9-0 PCosgrave (3) .... 100/1 ½ 10
Takrice *KPrendergast* 3-9-0 WJSupple (10) 66/1 2½ 11
Follow (USA) *APO'Brien* 3-9-0 CO'Donoghue (1) 100/1 2 12
Miss Childrey (IRE) *FrancisEnnis* 3-9-0 PShanahan (11) 3 13
Queen of Palms (IRE) *KPrendergast* 3-9-0 DPMcDonogh (4) 33/1 2 14
Lucky (IRE) *APO'Brien* 3-9-0 PaulScallan (2) 40/1 6 15

The Duke Of Roxburghe 15ran 1m37.82   TR: 122+/119/114+/111/109/105

LONGCHAMP Sunday, May 23   GOOD

15 **Prix d'Ispahan (Gr 1) (4yo+)** £77,216   1m1f55y

PRINCE KIRK (FR) *EBorromeo,Italy* 4-9-2 (b) MMonteiro 66/10   1
SIX PERFECTIONS (FR) *PBary,France* 4-8-13 TThulliez .... 1/2f   ½ 2
7 CHECKIT (IRE) *MRChannon,GB* 4-9-2 SHitchcott 21/1   2½ 3
Sunstrach (IRE) *LMCumani,GB* 6-9-2 JMurtagh 11/1   1½ 4
Nebraska Tornado (USA) *AFabre,France* 4-8-13 GaryStevens 7/4   4 5

Scuderia Pieffegi 5ran 1m52.00   TR: 120+/116/114/112

SANDOWN Tuesday, Jun 1   GOOD to SOFT

16 **Betfair.com Brigadier Gerard Stks (Gr 3) (4yo+)** £29,000   1¼m7y

BANDARI (IRE) *MJohnston* 5-8-10 WSupple (3) 7/2   1
7 IKHTYAR (IRE) *JHMGosden* 4-8-10 RHills (5) .... 7/2   nk 2
15 SUNSTRACH (IRE) *LMCumani* 6-8-10 JMurtagh (6) 10/1   7 3
Nysaean (IRE) *RHannon* 5-8-13 RHughes (2) 12/1   2½ 4
Comfy (USA) *SirMichaelStoute* 5-8-10 KFallon (1) 12/1 3½ 5
Kaieteur (USA) *BJMeehan* 5-8-10 DHolland (8) 7/1   1 6
Lateen Sails *SaeedbinSuroor* 4-8-13 (t) LDettori (7) 3/1f   6 7
Easter Ogil (IRE) *JaneSouthcombe* 9-8-10 NPollard (9) 200/1   21 8
5 Chancellor (IRE) *JLDunlop* 6-8-13 SSanders (4) 20/1   5 9

Mr Hamdan Al Maktoum 9ran 2m10.65   TR: 124/123/109/106

EPSOM DOWNS Friday, Jun 4   GOOD to FIRM

17 **Vodafone Coronation Cup (Gr 1) (4yo+)** £145,000   1½m10y

WARRSAN (IRE) *CEBrittain* 6-9-0 DHolland (5) 7/1   1
DOYEN (IRE) *SaeedbinSuroor* 4-9-0 LDettori (1) 9/2 1¾ 2
5 VALLEE ENCHANTEE (IRE) *ELellouche,France* 4-8-11 DBoeuf (3)........ sh 3
High Accolade *MPTregoning* 4-9-0 MartinDwyer (11) .... 4/1f sh 4
Brian Boru *APO'Brien,Ireland* 4-9-0 (t) JPSpencer (10) 9/1 1½ 5
Magistretti (USA) *NACallaghan* 4-9-0 JMurtagh (12) 7/1 1 6
Scott's View *MJohnston* 5-9-0 KFallon (4) .... 10/1 sh 7
Dubai Success *BWHills* 4-9-0 MHills (8) .... 25/1 ½ 8
8 Imperial Dancer *MRChannon* 6-9-0 TEDurcan (6) 11/1 3 9
Systematic *MJohnston* 5-9-0 KDarley (9) 10/1 1¼ 10
Sunny Glenn *MrsPNDutfield* 6-9-0 RHavlin (2) 100/1 6 11

Mr Saeed Manana 11ran 2m35.96   TR: 124/122+/119/122/120/118/117/117

18 **Vodafone Oaks (Gr 1) (3yo f)** £203,000   1½m10y

OUIJA BOARD *EALDunlop* 3-9-0 KFallon (3) 7/2   1
ALL TOO BEAUTIFUL (IRE) *APO'Brien,Ireland* 3-9-0 JPSpencer (6) 11/4f 7 2
PUNCTILIOUS *SaeedbinSuroor* 3-9-0 (t) LDettori (2) 10/3 3½ 3
14 Necklace *APO'Brien,Ireland* 3-9-0 JMurtagh (5) 10/1 1½ 4
Crystal (IRE) *BJMeehan* 3-9-0 MHills (7) 25/1 18 5
4 Sundrop (JPN) *SaeedbinSuroor* 3-9-0 KMcEvoy (4) 3/1   4 6
14 Kisses For Me (IRE) *APO'Brien,Ireland* 3-9-0 PaulScallan (1) .... 66/1 dist 7

Lord Derby 7ran 2m35.41   TR: 124/113/107/105

EPSOM DOWNS Saturday, Jun 5   GOOD to FIRM

19 **Vodafone Derby Stks (Gr 1) (3yo c+f)** £788,220   1½m10y

6 NORTH LIGHT (IRE) *SirMichaelStoute* 3-9-0 KFallon (6) 7/2jf   1
6 RULE OF LAW (USA) *SaeedbinSuroor* 3-9-0 (t) KMcEvoy (11) 20/1 1½ 2
6 LET THE LION ROAR *JLDunlop* 3-9-0 (v) MJKinane (3) .... 14/1 hd 3
Percussionist (IRE) *JHMGosden* 3-9-0 KDarley (5) .... 7/1 hd 4
3 Salford City (IRE) *DRCElsworth* 3-9-0 JMurtagh (8) 8/1 3 5
10 American Post *MmeCHead-Maarek,France* 3-9-0 RHughes (13) 13/2 1½ 6
3 Snow Ridge (IRE) *SaeedbinSuroor* 3-9-0 LDettori (7) 7/2jf 1¾ 7
Hazyview *NACallaghan* 3-9-0 EAhern (12) .... 40/1 hd 8
Pukka (IRE) *LMCumani* 3-9-0 DHolland (9) 10/1 1½ 9
Gatwick (IRE) *MRChannon* 3-9-0 TQuinn (2) 16/1 2½ 10
Massif Centrale *DRCElsworth* 3-9-0 DaneO'Neill (10) .... 100/1 nk 11
Coming Again (IRE) *BWHills* 3-9-0 MHills (14) 80/1 19 12
Elshadi (IRE) *MPTregoning* 3-9-0 (v) MartinDwyer (4) 25/1 1¼ 13

Meath (IRE) *APO'Brien,Ireland* 3-9-0 JPSpencer (1)..................................... 16/1   7 14
Ballymacoll Stud 14ran 2m33.72   TR: 125+/122/122/121/116+/114

CHANTILLY Sunday, Jun 6   GOOD

20 Prix du Jockey Club (Gr 1) (3yo c+f) £419,027   1½m

BLUE CANARI (FR) *PBary,France* 3-9-2 TThulliez (10) 332/10   1
PROSPECT PARK *CLaffon-Parias,France* 3-9-2 OPeslier (8).............. 28/10cpf   hd 2
VALIXIR (IRE) *AFabre,France* 3-9-2 ELegrix (1) .... 89/10   ½ 3
Day Flight *JHMGosden,GB* 3-9-2 RHughes (2)... 28/10cpf   ¾ 4
Ange Gardien (IRE) *RCollet,France* 3-9-2 CSoumillon (3) 81/10   2½ 5
Lord du Sud (FR) *J-CRouget,France* 3-9-2 IMendizabal (12) .... 9/2   sh 6
Reefscape *AFabre,France* 3-9-2 GaryStevens (7)................................... 28/10cpf   sh 7
Five Dynasties (USA) *APO'Brien,Ireland* 3-9-2 JPSpencer (9) .... 75/1   ¾ 8
Top of The Bill (USA) *AFabre,France* 3-9-2 TFarina (14) .... 54/1   hd 9
Day Or Night *JEPease,France* 3-9-2 TGillet (15).................................... 21/1   ¾ 10
Manyana (IRE) *MPTregoning,GB* 3-9-2 MartinDwyer (16)........................ 64/1   2 11
Delfos (IRE) *CLaffon-Parias,France* 3-9-2 LDettori (13)................... 59/10   1½ 12
6 Top Seed (IRE) *MRChannon,GB* 3-9-2 TEDurcan (5)............................ 42/1   8 13
King of Cry (FR) *RMartin-Sanchez,Spain* 3-9-2 CNora (17) 109/1   8 14
Yorik *CLaffon-Parias,France* 3-9-2 MBlancpain (6)......................... 28/10cpf   20 15
Ecurie Jean-Louis Bouchard 15ran 2m25.20   TR: 118/118/117/116/111/111/111

CHANTILLY Sunday, Jun 13   GOOD

21 Prix de Diane Hermes (Gr 1) (3yo f) £190,467   1¼m110y

LATICE (IRE) *J-MBeguigne,France* 3-9-0 CSoumillon (18)..................... 9/5f   1
MILLIONAIA (IRE) *ELellouche,France* 3-9-0 TThulliez (1)..................... 57/10   ¾ 2
9 GREY LILAS (IRE) *AFabre,France* 3-9-0 GaryStevens (14).................. 121/10   ½ 3
14 Alexander Goldrun (IRE) *JSBolger,Ireland* 3-9-0 KJManning (4) .... 165/10   ¾ 4
Agata (FR) *YdeNicolay,France* 3-9-0 DBoeuf (13)................................... 17/1   1½ 5
Barancella (FR) *FHead,France* 3-9-0 DBonilla (10).................................. 54/1   2½ 6
Ask For The Moon (FR) *J-CRouget,France* 3-9-0 IMendizabal (17) 51/10   1½ 7
Dreams Come True (FR) *RGibson,France* 3-9-0 (b) C-PLemaire (6).......... 17/1   ½ 8
Asti (IRE) *ELellouche,France* 3-9-0 KFallon (3).................................. 57/10   ¾ 9
Steel Princess (IRE) *RGibson,France* 3-9-0 TJarnet (16) .... 15/1   ½ 10
9 Torrestrella (IRE) *FRohaut,France* 3-9-0 GMosse (12)......................... 91/10   1½ 11
Love And Bubbles (USA) *RCollet,France* 3-9-0 SMaillot (11) 40/1   2½ 12
Menhoubah (USA) *CEBrittain,GB* 3-9-0 (s) DHolland (15) .... 18/1   ½ 13
Colony Band (USA) *MmeCHead-Maarek,France* 3-9-0 OPeslier (7)........... 16/1   2 14
Ometsz (IRE) *RodolpheCollet,France* 3-9-0 ELegrix (9) 30/1   5 15
Symphony of Psalms (USA) *JEHammond,France* 3-9-0 TGillet (5) 80/1   1½ 16
Prairie Flower (IRE) *ELellouche,France* 3-9-0 SCoffigny (8)................... 57/10   10 17
Mr E. Ciampi 17ran 2m07.00   TR: 121/119/118/117/114/110

ASCOT Tuesday, Jun 15   FIRM

22 St James's Palace Stks (Gr 1) (3yo c) £139,896   1m (Rnd)

13 AZAMOUR (IRE) *JOxx,Ireland* 3-9-0 MJKinane (1) 9/2   1
10 DIAMOND GREEN (FR) *AFabre,France* 3-9-0 (t) KFallon (2).................. 10/1   nk 2
10 ANTONIUS PIUS (USA) *APO'Brien,Ireland* 3-9-0 (t) JPSpencer (10) .... 7/1   ¾ 3
3 Haafhd *BWHills* 3-9-0 RHills (6).. 6/4f   nk 4
Brunel (IRE) *WJHaggas* 3-9-0 DHolland (4)....................................... 14/1   1½ 5
Castleton *HJCyzer* 3-9-0 KFallon (7) .... 66/1   sh 6
13 Bachelor Duke (USA) *JARToller* 3-9-0 SSanders (9) 6/1   1¼ 7
10 Byron *SaeedbinSuroor* 3-9-0 (t) LDettori (3) 20/1   1½ 8
Madid *JHMGosden* 3-9-0 WSupple (5)... 12/1   ½ 9
Pearl of Love (IRE) *MJohnston* 3-9-0 KDarley (2) 25/1   3 10
13 Newton (IRE) *APO'Brien,Ireland* 3-9-0 (v) PaulScallan (11) 100/1   20 11
H.H. Aga Khan 11ran 1m39.02   TR: 121+/120/118+/117/113/113

23 Queen Anne Stks (Gr 1) (4yo+) £145,000   1m (Str.)

7 REFUSE TO BEND (IRE) *SaeedbinSuroor* 4-9-0 (t) LDettori (1) 12/1   1
SOVIET SONG (IRE) *JRFanshawe* 4-8-11 JMurtagh (3).............................. 6/1   nk 2
7 SALSELON *LMCumani* 5-9-0 (b) DHolland (9) .... 12/1   ¾ 3
15 Nebraska Tornado (USA) *AFabre,France* 4-8-11 GaryStevens (4) 7/1   1 4
Tillerman *MrsAJPerrett* 8-9-0 RHughes (5)....................................... 20/1   1¼ 5
15 Six Perfections (FR) *PBary,France* 4-8-11 TThulliez (12)........................ 5/2f   ¾ 6
8 Bowman's Crossing (IRE) *DOughton,HongKong* 5-9-0 (v) MJKinane (6)... 33/1   hd 7
15 Checkit (IRE) *MRChannon* 4-9-0 TEDurcan (7)..................................... 66/1   1½ 8
Martillo (GER) *RSuerland,Germany* 4-9-0 WMongil (10) .... 14/1   nk 9
7 Hurricane Alan (IRE) *RHannon* 4-9-0 PDobbs (8)................................... 25/1   2½ 10
Alkaadhem *MPTregoning* 4-9-0 RHills (8) 9/1   1¾ 11
Arakan (USA) *SirMichaelStoute* 4-9-0 KFallon (17)............................. 16/1   5 12

Just James *JNoseda* 5-9-0 EAhern (16) 33/1 1½ 13

7 Norse Dancer (IRE) *DRCElsworth* 4-9-0 TQuinn (14)................................. 10/1 12 14

16 Lateen Sails *SaeedbinSuroor* 4-9-0 KMcEvoy (2) 33/1 7 15

Beauchamp Pilot *GAButler* 6-9-0 JPSpencer (15)....................................... 66/1 24 16

Godolphin 16ran 1m39.14   TR: 127+/123/124/119/119/114/117

ASCOT Wednesday, Jun 16   FIRM

24   **Prince of Wales's Stks (Gr 1) (4yo+) £203,000**   1¼m

RAKTI *MAJarvis* 5-9-0 PRobinson (10) 3/1 1

POWERSCOURT *APO'Brien,Ireland* 4-9-0 JPSpencer (5)........................... 9/2 2 2

16 IKHTYAR (IRE) *JHMGosden* 4-9-0 RHills (3).. 8/1 ½ 3

Sulamani (IRE) *SaeedbinSuroor* 5-9-0 LDettori (4)..................................... 11/4f 1½ 4

17 Scott's View *MJohnston* 5-9-0 SChin (2) .... 25/1 nk 5

Phoenix Reach (IRE) *AMBalding* 4-9-0 DHolland (7)................................ 16/1 ¾ 6

16 Comfy *SirMichaelStoute* 5-9-0 KFallon (11).. 16/1 2½ 7

16 Kaieteur (USA) *BJMeehan* 5-9-0 MJKinane (9).. 16/1 2½ 8

16 Bandari (IRE) *MJohnston* 5-9-0 WSupple (1).. 8/1 3 9

Lunar Sovereign (USA) *SaeedbinSuroor* 5-9-0 KMcEvoy (8) 66/1 1¼ 10

Mr Gary A. Tanaka 10ran 2m04.95   TR: 128+/124/123/120/119/118

ASCOT Thursday, Jun 17   GOOD to FIRM

25   **Gold Cup (Gr 1) (4yo+) £139,896**   2½m

PAPINEAU *SaeedbinSuroor* 4-9-0 (t) LDettori (4).. 5/1 1

WESTERNER *ELellouche,France* 5-9-2 GMosse (9) 13/2 1½ 2

DARASIM (IRE) *MJohnston* 6-9-2 (v) JFanning (1) 28/1 2½ 3

Royal Rebel *MJohnston* 8-9-2 JMurtagh (2) 10/1 5 4

17 Brian Boru *APO'Brien,Ireland* 4-9-0 (t) JPSpencer (11) .... 8/1 nk 5

Mr Dinos *PFICole* 5-9-2 KFallon (3) 5/4f 1¼ 6

Highest (IRE) *SaeedbinSuroor* 5-9-2 (t) TEDurcan (14) .... 25/1 nk 7

Misternando *MRChannon* 4-9-0 SHitchcott (6).. 25/1 1¼ 8

Ingrandire (JPN) *YShimizu,Japan* 5-9-2 NYokoyama (8)........................... 16/1 24 9

New South Wales *SaeedbinSuroor* 4-9-0 (t) KMcEvoy (13) 20/1 14 10

Chimes At Midnight (USA) *LukeComer,Ireland* 7-9-2 (b) JAHeffernan (7) 200/1 10 11

Dusky Warbler *MLWBell* 5-9-2 DHolland (10) 66/1 1¾ 12

Alcazar (IRE) *HMorrison* 9-9-2 MFenton (12) 33/1 9 13

Godolphin 13ran 4m20.90   TR: 123+/119/117/112/113/110

ASCOT Friday, Jun 18   GOOD to FIRM

26   **Coronation Stks (Gr 1) (3yo f) £139,823**   1m (Rnd)

14 ATTRACTION *MJohnston* 3-9-0 KDarley (10)... 6/4f 1

14 MAJESTIC DESERT *MRChannon* 3-9-0 TEDurcan (5) 25/1 2½ 2

4 RED BLOOM *SirMichaelStoute* 3-9-0 KFallon (12)................................... 10/3 hd 3

Moon Dazzle (USA) *WJHaggas* 3-9-0 RHills (6).. 25/1 3½ 4

14 Kinnaird (IRE) *PCHaslam* 3-9-0 MJKinane (1).. 12/1 3½ 5

4 Kelucia (IRE) *JSGoldie* 3-9-0 WSupple (8) 100/1 1 6

9 Royal Tigress (USA) *APO'Brien,Ireland* 3-9-0 JPSpencer (11) .... 40/1 nk 7

Relaxed (USA) *SirMichaelStoute* 3-9-0 RHughes (3).................................. 9/1 1½ 8

9 Cairns (UAE) *SaeedbinSuroor* 3-9-0 LDettori (7)....................................... 7/1 hd 9

Aricia (IRE) *JHMGosden* 3-9-0 JMurtagh (2) .... 20/1 nk 10

14 Secret Charm (IRE) *BWHills* 3-9-0 MHills (9) 14/1 5 11

Duke of Roxburghe 11ran 1m38.54   TR: 120+/113/112/104

ASCOT Saturday, Jun 19   FIRM

27   **Hardwicke Stks (Gr 2) (4yo+) £81,200**   1½m

17 DOYEN (IRE) *SaeedbinSuroor* 4-8-9 LDettori (7)...................................... 6/5f 1

17 HIGH ACCOLADE *MPTregoning* 4-8-9 WSupple (2)................................. 9/4 6 2

PERSIAN MAJESTY (IRE) *PWHarris* 4-8-9 JMurtagh (8) .... 6/1 ½ 3

Songlark *SaeedbinSuroor* 4-8-9 (v+t) KMcEvoy (6) 25/1 2 4

17 Systematic *MJohnston* 5-8-9 KDarley (3) .... 9/1 nk 5

Musanid (USA) *SirMichaelStoute* 4-8-9 RHills (4) 14/1 18 6

Godolphin 6ran 2m26.53   TR: 131+/120/119/115/114

CURRAGH Sunday, Jun 27   FIRM

28   **Budweiser Irish Derby (Gr 1) (3yo c+f) £484,605**   1½m

13 GREY SWALLOW (IRE) *DKWeld* 3-9-0 PJSmullen (6)............................. 10/1 1

19 NORTH LIGHT (IRE) *SirMichaelStoute,GB* 3-9-0 KFallon (10) .... 8/11f ½ 2

TYCOON *APO'Brien* 3-9-0 CO'Donoghue (4) 150/1 1½ 3

19 Rule of Law (USA) *SaeedbinSuroor,GB* 3-9-0 (t) LDettori (1).................... 13/2 nk 4

19 Let The Lion Roar *JLDunlop,GB* 3-9-0 (v) MJKinane (11) 11/2 2½ 5

Book of Kings (USA) *APO'Brien* 3-9-0 PCosgrave (9) 66/1 1½ 6

| | 6 | Moscow Ballet (IRE) *APO'Brien* 3-9-0 PJScallan (7) | 50/1 | 5 7 |

	6	Moscow Ballet (IRE) *APO'Brien* 3-9-0 PJScallan (7)	50/1	5 7
	20	Five Dynasties (USA) *APO'Brien* 3-9-0 JAHeffernan (3)	33/1	2½ 8
		Cobra (IRE) *APO'Brien* 3-9-0 JPSpencer (2)	25/1	25 9
	19	Percussionist (IRE) *JHMGosden,GB* 3-9-0 KPDarley (5)	10/1	dist 10

Mrs Rochelle Quinn 10ran 2m28.49   TR: 127/126/123/122/117/114

SANDOWN Saturday, Jul 3   GOOD to SOFT

29   **Coral-Eclipse Stks (Gr 1) (3yo+)** £237,220   1¼m7y

23	REFUSE TO BEND (IRE) *SaeedbinSuroor* 4-9-7 (t) LDettori (9)	15/2	1
17	WARRSAN (IRE) *CEBrittain* 6-9-7 DHolland (6)	12/1	hd 2
23	KALAMAN (IRE) *SirMichaelStoute* 4-9-7 KFallon (3)	12/1	4 3
23	Norse Dancer (IRE) *DRCElsworth* 4-9-7 (b) TQuinn (11)	20/1	½ 4
24	Powerscourt *APO'Brien,Ireland* 4-9-7 JPSpencer (10)	11/2	hd 5
24	Ikhtyar (IRE) *JHMGosden* 4-9-7 RHills (7)	8/1	1¾ 6
17	Imperial Dancer *MRChannon* 6-9-7 TEDurcan (4)	25/1	2 7
24	Rakti *MAJarvis* 5-9-7 PRobinson (12)	13/8f	nk 8
19	Salford City (IRE) *DRCElsworth* 3-8-10 JMurtagh (2)	8/1	nk 9
	African Dream *PWChapple-Hyam* 3-8-10 JQuinn (5)	16/1	2½ 10
	Maktub (ITY) *MAJarvis* 5-9-7 GCarter (1)	100/1	2½ 11
16	Chancellor (IRE) *JLDunlop* 6-9-7 SSanders (13)	66/1	30 12

Godolphin 12ran 2m08.31   TR: 128/127/119+/118/118/114

HAMBURG Sunday, Jul 4   HEAVY

30   **BMW Deutsches Derby (Gr 1) (3yo c+f)** £212,000   1½m

SHIROCCO (GER) *ASchutz,Germany* 3-9-2 ASuborics	5/1	1
MALINAS (GER) *PSchiergen,Germany* 3-9-2 WMongil	4/1	4 2
OMIKRON (IRE) *MHofer,Germany* 3-9-2 AdeVries	234/10	6 3
Saldentigerin (GER) *PSchiergen,Germany* 3-8-12 TQuinn	63/10	1½ 4
Gentle Tiger (GER) *PSchiergen,Germany* 3-9-2 THellier	17/1	¾ 5
El Tiger (GER) *PSchiergen,Germany* 3-9-2 FMinarik	27/1	hd 6
Salonhonor (GER) *ALowe,Germany* 3-9-2 JPalik	21/1	nk 7
Farouge (FR) *WNeuroth,Norway* 3-9-2 FJohansson	61/1	1 8
Apeiron (GER) *MHofer,Germany* 3-9-2 JPCarvalho	25/1	1¼ 9
Fight Club (GER) *ASchutz,Germany* 3-9-2 AStarke	37/10f	½ 10
Dayano (GER) *AWohler,Germany* 3-9-2 EPedroza	21/2	ns 11
Egerton (GER) *PRau,Germany* 3-9-2 AHelfenbein	27/1	2 12
Delsun (GER) *MHofer,Germany* 3-9-2 (b) ODoleuze	54/1	2½ 13
Classic Croco (GER) *CVonDerRecke,Germany* 3-9-2 MJKinane	33/2	12 14
Oakboy (GER) *HSteinmetz,Germany* 3-9-2 (b) JBojko	80/1	¾ 15
Intendant (GER) *FrauABertram,Germany* 3-9-2 ABoschert	45/1	8 16
Sweet Wake (GER) *MHofer,Germany* 3-9-2 LDettori	8/1	7 17
Golden Millenium (GER) *THHansen,Germany* 3-9-2 LHammer-Hansen	56/1	11 18

Baron G. von Ullmann 18ran 2m39.64   TR: 122/116/108/102/104/104/104

SAINT-CLOUD Sunday, Jul 4   GOOD to SOFT

31   **Grand Prix de Saint-Cloud (Gr 1) (3yo+)** £133,327   1½m

	GAMUT (IRE) *SirMichaelStoute,GB* 5-9-8 KFallon	22/10	1
	POLICY MAKER (IRE) *ELellouche,France* 4-9-8 TThulliez	18/10f	3 2
	VISORAMA (IRE) *AFabre,France* 4-9-5 ELegrix	22/1	½ 3
	Short Pause *AFabre,France* 5-9-8 TGillet	21/10	nk 4
	Pride (FR) *AdeRoyerDupre,France* 4-9-5 DBonilla	26/1	sh 5
24	Phoenix Reach (IRE) *AMBalding,GB* 4-9-8 MartinDwyer	87/10	¾ 6
5	Polish Summer *AFabre,France* 7-9-8 GaryStevens	21/10	1½ 7
5	Touch of Land (FR) *H-APantall,France* 4-9-8 C-PLemaire	23/1	½ 8
25	Westerner *ELellouche,France* 5-9-8 OPeslier	18/10f	¾ 9
	Poussin (IRE) *ELellouche,France* 6-9-8 SCoffigny	18/10f	20 10

Mrs G. Smith 10ran 2m36.10   TR: 122/118/114/116/113/115

NEWMARKET Tuesday, Jul 6   GOOD to FIRM (July Course)

32   **UAE Equestrian and Racing Federation Falmouth Stks (Gr 1) (3yo+ f+m)** £116,000   1m

23	SOVIET SONG (IRE) *JRFanshawe* 4-9-1 JMurtagh (3)	11/4	1
26	ATTRACTION *MJohnston* 3-8-6 KDarley (4)	4/5f	2½ 2
	BAQAH (IRE) *FHead,France* 3-8-6 (t) DBonilla (6)	33/1	2½ 3
	Monturani (IRE) *GWragg* 5-9-1 DHolland (5)	50/1	¾ 4
14	Illustrious Miss (USA) *DRLoder* 3-8-6 TPQueally (1)	14/1	7 5
	Favourable Terms *SirMichaelStoute* 4-9-1 KFallon (7)	6/1	1½ 6
	Tizdubai (USA) *SaeedbinSuroor* 3-8-6 (t) KMcEvoy (2)	100/1	3½ 7

Elite Racing Club 7ran 1m36.11   TR: 126/118/111/112

NEWMARKET Wednesday, Jul 7   GOOD to FIRM (July Course)

33   Princess of Wales's Cantorodds.com Stks (Gr 2) (3yo+) £58,000   1½m

24	BANDARI (IRE) *MJohnston* 5-9-2 RHills (8)	12/1	1
24	SULAMANI (IRE) *SaeedbinSuroor* 5-9-7 (t) LDettori (7)	11/8f	½ 2
27	HIGH ACCOLADE *MPTregoning* 4-9-2 MartinDwyer (2)	6/1	2½ 3
17	Magistretti (USA) *NACallaghan* 4-9-2 DHolland (5)	10/3	3½ 4
27	Persian Majesty (IRE) *PWHarris* 4-9-2 JMurtagh (6)	8/1	hd 5
27	Systematic *MJohnston* 5-9-2 KDarley (1)	20/1	3 6
	The Great Gatsby (IRE) *JHMGosden* 4-9-2 JFortune (4)	10/1	12 7
	Naheef (IRE) *SaeedbinSuroor* 3-9-2 (v+t) KMcEvoy (3)	66/1	dist 8

Mr Hamdan Al Maktoum 8ran 2m32.90   TR: 124/128/119/113/113

NEWMARKET Thursday, Jul 8   GOOD   (July Course)

34   Darley July Cup (Gr 1) (3yo+) £145,000   6f

	FRIZZANTE *JRFanshawe* 5-9-2 JMurtagh (18)	14/1	1
	ASHDOWN EXPRESS (IRE) *CFWall* 5-9-5 SSanders (11)	100/1	nk 2
	BALMONT (USA) *JNoseda* 3-8-13 JAhern (16)	25/1	2 3
	Cape of Good Hope *DOughton,HongKong* 6-9-5 (v+t) MJKinane (20)	20/1	nk 4
	Somnus *TDEasterby* 4-9-5 TEDurcan (17)	12/1	hd 5
	Monsieur Bond (IRE) *BSmart* 4-9-5 FLynch (14)	14/1	nk 6
22	Antonius Pius (USA) *APO'Brien,Ireland* 3-8-13 (t) JPSpencer (5)	5/1	nk 7
	Porlezza (FR) *YdeNicolay,France* 3-9-2 OPeslier (13)	33/1	hd 8
	Airwave *HCandy* 4-9-2 DaneO'Neill (15)	20/1	nk 9
11	Patavellian (IRE) *RCharlton* 6-9-5 (b) SDrowne (12)	7/1	sh 10
	Country Reel (USA) *SaeedbinSuroor* 4-9-5 (v+t) RHills (4)	25/1	1¼ 11
	Seeking The Dia (USA) *HMori,Japan* 3-8-13 YTake (1)	50/1	hd 12
	Fayr Jag (IRE) *TDEasterby* 5-9-5 WSupple (10)	25/1	sh 13
	Kheleyf (USA) *SaeedbinSuroor* 3-8-13 LDettori (8)	8/1	sh 14
	Continent *DNicholls* 7-9-5 JFortune (19)	50/1	nk 15
	Nayyir *GAButler* 6-9-5 RHughes (7)	12/1	nk 16
	Bahamian Pirate (USA) *DNicholls* 9-9-5 KDarley (9)	66/1	1 17
	Steenberg (IRE) *MHTompkins* 5-9-5 PRobinson (6)	22/1	¾ 18
	Exceed And Excel (AUS) *TimMartin,Australia* 4-9-5 (t) KMcEvoy (3)	4/1f	1 19
	Moss Vale (IRE) *BWHills* 3-8-13 MHills (2)	14/1	1 20

Mrs Jan Hopper & Mrs Elizabeth Grundy 20ran 1m11.51
                                    TR: 120+/122/114/115/114+/114

DEAUVILLE Saturday, Jul 10   GOOD to SOFT

35   Prix de Ris-Orangis (Gr 3) (3yo+) £24,497   6f

11	THE TRADER (IRE) *MBlanshard,GB* 6-9-4 (b) DSweeney	21/10f	1
11	SWEDISH SHAVE (FR) *RGibson,France* 6-9-0 TJarnet	7/1	2 2
	VASYWAIT (FR) *J-LGay,France* 5-9-0 DBoeuf	7/2	2 3
	The Wise Lady (FR) *MNigge,France* 4-8-10 GaryStevens	117/10	½ 4
	Blanche (FR) *JRossi,France* 5-9-1 DBonilla	20/1	½ 5
	Miss Emma (IRE) *JEHammond,France* 4-8-10 TGillet	11/2	1½ 6
	Malaica (FR) *RPritchard-Gordon,France* 3-8-5 C-PLemaire	119/10	¾ 7
	Art Moderne (FR) *ELellouche,France* 4-9-0 OPeslier	112/10	1½ 8
	Glad To Be Fast (IRE) *MHofer,Germany* 4-9-4 JPCarvalho	8/1	¾ 9

Mrs C. J. Ward 9ran 1m10.70   TR: 123/113/107/101/104

CURRAGH Sunday, Jul 18   FIRM

36   Darley Irish Oaks (Gr 1) (3yo f) £150,133   1½m

18	OUIJA BOARD *EALDunlop,GB* 3-9-0 KFallon (4)	4/7f	1
18	PUNCTILIOUS *SaeedbinSuroor,GB* 3-9-0 (t) LDettori (6)	5/1	1 2
	HAZARISTA (IRE) *JOxx* 3-9-0 MJKinane (5)	20/1	¾ 3
18	All Too Beautiful (IRE) *APO'Brien* 3-9-0 JPSpencer (7)	4/1	7 4
	Marinnette (IRE) *MPSunderland* 3-9-0 JAHeffernan (1)	200/1	4 5
	Danelissima (IRE) *JSBolger* 3-9-0 (b) KJManning (3)	16/1	4 6
26	Royal Tigress (USA) *APO'Brien* 3-9-0 (b) CO'Donoghue (2)	50/1	4 7

Lord Derby 7ran 2m27.92   TR: 117+/115/113/99

ASCOT Saturday, Jul 24   GOOD to FIRM

37   King George VI and Queen Elizabeth Diamond Stks (Gr 1) (3yo+) £435,000   1½m

27	DOYEN (IRE) *SaeedbinSuroor* 4-9-7 LDettori (5)	11/10f	1
	HARD BUCK (BRZ) *KGMcPeek,USA* 5-9-7 GaryStevens (6)	33/1	3 2
33	SULAMANI (IRE) *SaeedbinSuroor* 5-9-7 (t) JPSpencer (7)	7/1	hd 3
31	Gamut (IRE) *SirMichaelStoute* 5-9-7 (b) KFallon (11)	12/1	1¾ 4
17	Vallee Enchantee (IRE) *ELellouche,France* 4-9-4 OPeslier (4)	6/1	1 5
28	Tycoon *APO'Brien,Ireland* 3-8-9 JPSpencer (3)	16/1	¾ 6
33	Bandari (IRE) *MJohnston* 5-9-7 RHills (2)	12/1	nk 7

```
 33  High Accolade MPTregoning 4-9-7 JMurtagh (10).........................................  25/1    2  8
 29  Warrsan (IRE) CEBrittain 6-9-7 DHolland (9)............................................  13/2    1¼ 9
 31  Phoenix Reach (IRE) AMBalding 4-9-7 (v) MartinDwyer (1)......................  33/1    2½ 10
 24  Lunar Sovereign (USA) SaeedbinSuroor 5-9-7 (t) TEDurcan (8) ..............  100/1   dist 11
     Godolphin 11ran 2m33.18                              TR: 132/127/127+/124/119/121+/121
```

GOODWOOD Wednesday, Jul 28   GOOD

38   **Cantor Odds Sussex Stks (Gr 1) (3yo+) £174,000**   1m

```
 32  SOVIET SONG (IRE) JRFanshawe 4-9-4 JMurtagh (5).............................  3/1     1
 34  NAYYIR GAButler 6-9-7 MJKinane (11) ........................................................  12/1    nk  2
 12  LE VIE DEI COLORI LMCumani 4-9-7 DHolland (7)...................................  12/1    2  3
 29  Norse Dancer (IRE) DRCElsworth 4-9-7 (b) TQuinn (1).............................  20/1    2  4
 34  Antonius Pius (USA) APO'Brien,Ireland 3-8-13 (v+t) JPSpencer (10) ....... 8/1     nk  5
 23  Tillerman MrsAJPerrett 8-9-7 OPeslier (6) ................................................  20/1    sh  6
 23  Hurricane Alan (IRE) RHannon 4-9-7 KFallon (3)......................................  40/1    2  7
 23  Checkit (IRE) MRChannon 4-9-7 ACulhane (2) ........................................  100/1   2  8
 22  Haafhd BWHills 3-8-13 RHills (8)..............................................................  9/2     ¾ 9
     Passing Glance AMBalding 5-9-7 MartinDwyer (4) ...................................  16/1    2 10
 29  Refuse To Bend (IRE) SaeedbinSuroor 4-9-7 (t) LDettori (9)...................  11/4f   6 11
     Elite Racing Club 11ran 1m36.98                      TR: 124/126/121/116+/113+/115
```

MUNICH Sunday, Aug 1   GOOD to FIRM

39   **Grosser Dallmayr-Preis (Bayerisches Zuchtrennen) (Gr 1) (3yo+) £60,265**   1¼m

```
 30  INTENDANT (GER) FrauABertram,Germany 3-8-9 JPalik ...................  153/10    1
 29  POWERSCOURT APO'Brien,Ireland 4-9-6 JPSpencer .............................  3/5f    1½ 2
 29  IMPERIAL DANCER MRChannon,GB 6-9-6 SHitchcott............................  20/1    1  3
 24  Scott's View MJohnston,GB 5-9-6 SChin.................................................  87/10   1¼ 4
     Deva (GER) DRonge,Germany 5-9-2 JPCarvalho.....................................  8/1     2  5
 30  Gentle Tiger (GER) PSchiergen,Germany 3-8-9 ASuborics .................  46/10   5  6
     Serenus (GER) WFigge,Germany 6-9-6 (b) ThomasO'Sullivan..................  31/1    ½ 7
     Next Gina (GER) ASchutz,Germany 4-9-2 AStarke .................................  63/10   5  8
 30  Egerton (GER) PRau,Germany 3-8-9 AHelfenbein ................................  149/10  18 9
     Mr F. Leve 9ran 2m04.27                              TR: 120/120+/118/115/107
```

HAYDOCK Saturday, Aug 7   GOOD

40   **Petros Rose of Lancaster Stks (Gr 3) (3yo+) £37,700**   1¼m120y

```
     MISTER MONET (IRE) MJohnston 3-8-7 JFanning (6)..............................  1/1f    1
     MUQBIL (USA) JLDunlop 4-9-3 RHills (4) .................................................  5/2     1½ 2
 38  CHECKIT (IRE) MRChannon 4-9-3 ACulhane (2) ...................................  13/2    5  3
     Franklins Gardens MHTompkins 4-9-3 PRobinson (5)...........................  14/1    1¾ 4
 23  Lateen Sails SaeedbinSuroor 4-9-3 (t) KMcEvoy (3) .............................  12/1    1  5
 29  Chancellor (IRE) JLDunlop 6-9-7 JFortune (1).......................................  40/1    ¾ 6
     Syndicate 2002 6ran 2m10.40                          TR: 122+/120/110/107
```

CURRAGH Sunday, Aug 8   GOOD to FIRM

41   **Independent Waterford Wedgwood Phoenix Stks (Gr 1) (2yo c+f) £111,656**   6f

```
     DAMSON (IRE) DWachman 2-8-11 KFallon (1) .........................................  8/11f   1
     ORATORIO (IRE) APO'Brien 2-9-0 JAHeffernan (2) ...............................  15/2    ¾ 2
     RUSSIAN BLUE (IRE) APO'Brien 2-9-0 JPSpencer (4)............................  9/4     ½ 3
     Billet (IRE) AnthonyMullins 2-8-11 FMBerry (3)......................................  50/1    5  4
     Camouflage (FR) KPrendergast 2-9-0 DPMcDonogh (6)........................  10/1    9  5
     Premier Dane (IRE) KPrendergast 2-9-0 JHBowman (5)........................  20/1    1  6
     Mrs John Magnier 6ran 1m13.07                        TR: 113/114/112/93
```

42   **Patrick P. O'Leary Memorial Phoenix Sprint Stks (Gr 3) (3yo+)**   6f

```
  3  ONE COOL CAT (USA) APO'Brien 3-9-8 JPSpencer (7)..........................  3/1f    1
     THE KIDDYKID (IRE) PDEvans,GB 4-9-7 PJSmullen (6).........................  8/1     1  2
     NIGHTS CROSS (IRE) MRChannon,GB 3-9-0 (v) ACulhane (2)..............  10/1    ¾ 3
     Osterhase (IRE) JEMulhern 5-9-4 (b) FMBerry (3)...............................  10/3    1½ 4
     Ulfah (USA) KPrendergast 3-8-11 DPMcDonogh (3) ............................  9/1     hd 5
     Desert Fantasy (IRE) CRoche 5-9-4 (b+t) JAHeffernan (8).....................  4/1     hd 6
     Simianna ABerry,GB 5-9-1 (s) PShanahan (5) .......................................  20/1    1  7
     Hanabad (IRE) JOxx 4-9-4 (b) MJKinane (4) ........................................  10/1    hd 8
     Moon Unit (IRE) HRogers 3-8-11 DMGrant (9).....................................  20/1    2  9
 13  Grand Reward (USA) APO'Brien 3-9-0 CO'Donoghue (1) ...................          rtr
     Mrs John Magnier 10ran 1m12.56                       TR: 121+/114/107/103/99/102
```

DEAUVILLE Sunday, Aug 8   GOOD

43   **Prix Maurice de Gheest (Gr 1) (3yo+) £75,682**   6f110y

```
 34  SOMNUS TDEasterby,GB 4-9-2 GaryStevens (2)....................................  15/1    1
  3  WHIPPER (USA) RCollet,France 3-8-11 CSoumillon (10).........................  13/4    nk 2
```

	DOLMA (FR) *NClement,France* 3-8-8 C-PLemaire (4)	19/1	nk 3
34	Ashdown Express (IRE) *CFWall,GB* 5-9-2 SSanders (6)	21/1	hd 4
35	The Trader (IRE) *MBlanshard,GB* 6-9-2 (b) DSweeney (15)	7/1	1 5
	Lucky Strike *ATrybuhl,Germany* 6-9-2 AdeVries (5)	13/1	2 6
	Golden Nun *TDEasterby,GB* 4-8-13 (b) RWinston (8)	93/1	¾ 7
	Dexterity (USA) *H-APantall,France* 6-9-2 TJarnet (7)	36/1	hd 8
34	Monsieur Bond (IRE) *BSmart,GB* 4-9-2 FLynch (19)	55/1	sh 9
34	Frizzante *JRFanshawe,GB* 5-8-13 JMurtagh (18)	9/2	nk 10
22	Brunel (IRE) *WJHaggas,GB* 3-8-11 DHolland (12)	21/1	hd 11
	Royal Millennium (IRE) *MRChannon,GB* 6-9-2 TEDurcan (11)	34/1	nk 12
	Charming Groom (FR) *FHead,France* 5-9-2 OPeslier (20)	23/1	¾ 13
34	Porlezza (FR) *YdeNicolay,France* 5-8-13 DBoeuf (3)	11/1	3 14
34	Seeking The Dia (USA) *HMori,Japan* 3-8-11 YTake (9)	27/1	ns 15
35	Vasywait (FR) *J-LGay,France* 5-9-2 FSpanu (16)	43/1	6 16
	Crystal Castle (USA) *JEHammond,France* 6-9-2 TGillet (13)	33/4	nk 17
	Dorubako (IRE) *HMori,Japan* 3-8-11 NYokoyama (17)	47/1	2½ 18

Legard Sidebottom & Sykes 18ran 1m16.00   TR: 122/120/116/120+/118+/113

NEWBURY Saturday, Aug 14   GOOD

44   **Stan James Geoffrey Freer Stks (Gr 2) (3yo+) £62,000**   1m5f61y

	MUBTAKER (USA) *MPTregoning* 7-9-3 RHills (4)	3/10f	1
17	DUBAI SUCCESS *BWHills* 4-9-3 MHills (3)	9/2	2½ 2
	COMPTON BOLTER (IRE) *GAButler* 7-9-3 RHughes (2)	16/1	1¾ 3
33	The Great Gatsby (IRE) *JHMGosden* 4-9-3 (b) JFortune (1)	16/1	5 4

Mr Hamdan Al Maktoum 4ran 2m50.69   TR: 121+/117/114/107

ARLINGTON Saturday, Aug 14   FIRM

45   **Arlington Million Stks (Gr 1) (3yo+) £326,087**   1¼m

> Order as they passed the post: Powerscourt was demoted to fourth place for causing interference

39	POWERSCOURT *APO'Brien,Ireland* 4-9-0 (v) JPSpencer	46/10	1
	KICKEN KRIS (USA) *MRMatz,USA* 4-9-0 KDesormeaux	97/10	1½ 2
33	MAGISTRETTI (USA) *NACallaghan,GB* 4-9-0 (b) EPrado	24/1	1 3
8	Epalo (GER) *ASchutz,Germany* 5-9-0 AStarke	41/10f	½ 4
5	Vangelis (USA) *RJFrankel,USA* 5-9-0 (b) JValdivia	112/10	1½ 5
	Mr O'Brien (IRE) *RLGraham,USA* 5-9-0 PDay	47/10	¾ 6
	Senor Swinger (USA) *RBaffert,USA* 4-9-0 BBlanc	217/10	½ 7
	Sweet Return *RLMcAnally,USA* 4-9-0 JBailey	53/10	¾ 8
	Mobil (CAN) *MKeogh,Canada* 4-9-0 JonoJones	402/10	1¾ 9
	Mystery Giver (USA) *CMBlock,USA* 6-9-0 RDouglas	209/10	½ 10
	Sabiango (GER) *RBaffert,USA* 6-9-0 VEspinoza	15/1	2¾ 11
12	Vespone (GER) *SaeedbinSuroor,GB* 4-9-0 (v) LDettori	95/10	2 12
	Hatif (BRZ) *PHLobo,USA* 5-9-0 MESmith	568/10	7 13

Brushwood Stable 13ran 2m00.08   TR: 124/121+/118/117/114/112

COLOGNE Sunday, Aug 15   GOOD

46   **Rheinland-Pokal der Stadtsparkasse Koln (Gr 1) (3yo+) £63,333**   1½m

	ALBANOVA *SirMarkPrescott,GB* 5-9-2 THellier	57/10	1
37	HIGH ACCOLADE *MPTregoning* 4-9-6 (v) MartinDwyer	28/10	¾ 2
30	MALINAS (GER) *PSchiergen,Germany* 3-8-8 ASuborics	9/10f	3 3
	Simonas (IRE) *AWohler,Germany* 5-9-6 EPedroza	93/10	nk 4
30	Omikron (IRE) *MHofer,Germany* 5-9-6 AdeVries	10/1	nk 5
	Well Made (GER) *HBlume,Germany* 7-9-6 WMongil	135/10	1½ 6
	Rotteck (GER) *HSteguweit,Germany* 4-9-6 JPalik	69/10	20 7

Miss K. Rausing 7ran 2m31.30   TR: 119/122/116/116/116/113+

DEAUVILLE Sunday, Aug 15   GOOD to SOFT

47   **Prix du Haras de Fresnay-Le-Buffard Jacques le Marois (Gr 1) (3yo+ c+f)**   1m
     £209,513

43	WHIPPER (USA) *RCollet,France* 3-8-11 CSoumillon (5)	49/10	1
23	SIX PERFECTIONS (FR) *PBary,France* 4-9-1 TThulliez (3)	32/10	1 2
	MY RISK (FR) *J-MBeguigne,France* 5-9-4 OPeslier (10)	127/10	1½ 3
26	Majestic Desert *MRChannon,GB* 3-8-8 TEDurcan (6)	16/1	1½ 4
23	Salselon *LMCumani,GB* 5-9-4 (b) JMurtagh (7)	92/10	½ 5
34	Kheleyf (USA) *SaeedbinSuroor,GB* 3-8-11 LDettori (4)	123/10	3 6
32	Baqah (IRE) *FHead,France* 3-8-8 DBonilla (2)	99/10	2½ 7
	Fomalhaut (USA) *PBary,France* 5-9-4 C-PLemaire (8)	32/10	1 8
22	Byron *SaeedbinSuroor,GB* 3-8-11 KMcEvoy (9)	123/10	2 9
32	Attraction *MJohnston,GB* 3-8-8 KDarley (1)	7/5f	10 10

Mr R. C. Strauss 10ran 1m38.40   TR: 125/120/119/112/114

YORK Tuesday, Aug 17   GOOD to SOFT

48   Daily Telegraph Great Voltigeur Stks (Gr 2) (3yo c+g) £78,300   1m3f198y

28	RULE OF LAW (USA) *SaeedbinSuroor* 3-8-9 (t) LDettori (2)	11/8f	1
28	LET THE LION ROAR *JLDunlop* 3-8-9 (v) MJKinane (1)	11/4	2½ 2
	GO FOR GOLD (IRE) *APO'Brien,Ireland* 3-8-9 JPSpencer (8)	7/1	1½ 3
	Always First *SirMichaelStoute* 3-8-9 KFallon (4)	8/1	1¼ 4
19	Pukka (IRE) *LMCumani* 3-8-9 DHolland (5)	8/1	2½ 5
	Red Lancer *RJPrice* 3-8-9 MFenton (6)	33/1	2½ 6
	Rio de Janeiro (IRE) *APO'Brien,Ireland* 3-8-9 (v) JMurtagh (7)	40/1	12 7

Godolphin 7ran 2m37.10   TR: 124/120/118/116/112/108

49   Juddmonte International Stks (Gr 1) (3yo+) £266,800   1¼m88y

37	SULAMANI (IRE) *SaeedbinSuroor* 5-9-5 (t) LDettori (9)	3/1	1
38	NORSE DANCER (IRE) *DRCElsworth* 4-9-5 JFEgan (1)	16/1	¾ 2
	BAGO (FR) *JEPease,France* 3-8-11 TGillet (6)	13/8f	¾ 3
	Cacique (IRE) *AFabre,France* 3-8-11 GaryStevens (10)	10/1	5 4
	Millstreet *SaeedbinSuroor* 5-9-5 (t) KMcEvoy (4)	100/1	¾ 5
29	Kalaman (IRE) *SirMichaelStoute* 4-9-5 KFallon (2)	6/1	½ 6
39	Imperial Dancer *MRChannon* 6-9-5 TEDurcan (8)	33/1	½ 7
	Solskjaer (IRE) *APO'Brien,Ireland* 4-9-5 JMurtagh (5)	33/1	6 8
37	Tycoon *APO'Brien,Ireland* 3-8-11 JPSpencer (7)	7/1	dist 9

Godolphin 9ran 2m11.82   TR: 126+/125/122/113/112/111/110

YORK Wednesday, Aug 18   SOFT

50   Aston Upthorpe Yorkshire Oaks (Gr 1) (3yo+ f+m) £145,000   1m3f198y

	QUIFF *SirMichaelStoute* 3-8-8 KFallon (3)	7/2	1
	PONGEE *LMCumani* 4-9-4 JFortune (8)	10/1	11 2
36	HAZARISTA (IRE) *JOxx,Ireland* 3-8-8 MJKinane (9)	9/2	1½ 3
36	Punctilious *SaeedbinSuroor* 3-8-8 (t) LDettori (10)	6/4f	9 4
	Sahool *MPTregoning* 3-8-8 RHills (7)	7/1	8 5
36	Danelissima (IRE) *JSBolger,Ireland* 3-8-8 (v) WSupple (1)	33/1	4 6
36	Royal Tigress (USA) *APO'Brien,Ireland* 3-8-8 (v) JPSpencer (2)	33/1	21 7
21	Menhoubah (USA) *CEBrittain* 3-8-8 (s) SSanders (4)	33/1	5 8

Mr K. Abdulla 8ran 2m38.03   TR: 124/110/108+

YORK Thursday, Aug 19   SOFT

51   Victor Chandler Nunthorpe Stks (Gr 1) (2yo+) £116,000   5f

34	BAHAMIAN PIRATE (USA) *DNicholls* 9-9-11 SSanders (5)	16/1	1
11	THE TATLING (IRE) *JMBradley* 7-9-11 RLMoore (11)	13/2	nk 2
42	ONE COOL CAT (USA) *APO'Brien,Ireland* 3-9-9 JPSpencer (15)	3/1f	1 3
	Avonbridge *RCharlton* 4-9-11 (b) SDrowne (9)	8/1	hd 4
	Orientor *JSGoldie* 6-9-11 KFallon (14)	9/2	hd 5
34	Airwave *HCandy* 4-9-8 DHolland (3)	6/1	½ 6
34	Balmont (USA) *JNoseda* 3-9-9 EAhern (7)	13/2	½ 7
	Talbot Avenue *MMullineaux* 6-9-11 KMcEvoy (12)	100/1	½ 8
34	Moss Vale (IRE) *BWHills* 3-9-9 MHills (10)	14/1	½ 9
34	Fayr Jag (IRE) *TDEasterby* 5-9-11 WSupple (2)	25/1	2 10
	Fire Up The Band *DNicholls* 5-9-11 ANicholls (8)	33/1	2 11
	Night Prospector *JWPayne* 4-9-11 JMurtagh (6)	66/1	14 12

Lucayan Stud 12ran 59.89secs   TR: 118/117/114+/114/114+/110

DEAUVILLE Sunday, Aug 22   SOFT

52   Prix Morny Casinos Barriere (Gr 1) (2yo c+f) £95,872   6f

	DIVINE PROPORTIONS (USA) *PBary,France* 2-8-11 C-PLemaire (9)	33/10	1
	LAYMAN (USA) *AFabre,France* 2-9-0 GaryStevens (8)	1/1f	1½ 2
41	RUSSIAN BLUE (IRE) *APO'Brien,Ireland* 2-9-0 JPSpencer (6)	31/4	1½ 3
	Captain Hurricane *PWChapple-Hyam,GB* 2-9-0 JFortune (7)	14/1	3 4
	Mystical Land (IRE) *JHMGosden,GB* 2-9-0 LDettori (4)	11/1	5 5
	Salut Thomas (FR) *RCollet,France* 2-9-0 CSoumillon (3)	15/2	1½ 6
	Tournedos (IRE) *MRChannon,GB* 2-9-0 TEDurcan (2)	31/1	3 7
	Doctor's Cave *CEBrittain,GB* 2-9-0 OPeslier (5)	27/1	2½ 8
	Shifting Place *RMenichetti,Italy* 2-8-11 DVargiu (1)	13/1	5 9

Niarchos Family 9ran 1m12.80   TR: 119/117/112/102

GOODWOOD Saturday, Aug 28   SOFT

53   Totesport Celebration Mile (Gr 2) (3yo+) £58,000   1m

	CHIC *SirMichaelStoute* 4-8-12 KFallon (5)	4/1	1
38	NAYYIR *GAButler* 6-9-1 MJKinane (2)	5/4f	1¼ 2
38	HURRICANE ALAN (IRE) *RHannon* 4-9-4 PDobbs (3)	11/2	5 3
	Court Masterpiece *EALDunlop* 4-9-1 JFortune (4)	8/1	nk 4

38 Passing Glance *AMBalding* 5-9-4 MartinDwyer (6) 12/1   5 5
43 Brunel (IRE) *WJHaggas* 3-8-12 DHolland (7)... 12/1 2½ 6
    Naahy *MRChannon* 4-9-1 JMurtagh (1) 25/1 25 7
    Cheveley Park Stud 7ran 1m43.22   TR: 123/123+/114/111

DEAUVILLE Sunday, Aug 29   HEAVY

54   **Grand Prix de Deauville Lucien Barriere (Gr 2) (3yo+) £50,068**   1½m110y

    CHERRY MIX (FR) *AFabre,France* 3-8-8 TGillet 5/1   1
    MARTALINE *AFabre,France* 5-9-3 GaryStevens 13/4 4 2
    BAILADOR (IRE) *AFabre,France* 4-9-3 CSoumillon .... 11/2 sh 3
    Swing Wing *PFICole,GB* 5-9-3 SDrowne 13/2 3 4
    Kindjhal (FR) *ELellouche,France* 4-9-3 SPasquier.................................. 29/4 2½ 5
  5 Fair Mix (IRE) *MRolland,France* 6-9-3 OPeslier 9/4f 6 6
40 Franklins Gardens *MHTompkins,GB* 4-9-3 DBoeuf 10/1 3 7
    Famille Lagardere 7ran 2m55.10   TR: 122/115/115/111/107

HAYDOCK Saturday, Sep 4   GOOD

55   **Stanleybet Sprint Cup (Gr 1) (3yo+) £130,500**   6f

    TANTE ROSE (IRE) *RCharlton* 4-8-11 RHughes (14) 10/1   1
43 SOMNUS *TDEasterby* 4-9-0 MJKinane (5).. 7/1 sh 2
34 PATAVELLIAN (IRE) *RCharlton* 6-9-0 (b) SDrowne (4) .... 14/1 ¾ 3
43 Royal Millennium (IRE) *MRChannon* 6-9-0 TEDurcan (8) 50/1 1½ 4
43 Monsieur Bond (IRE) *BSmart* 4-9-0 (b) FLynch (19)................................ 33/1 hd 5
51 One Cool Cat (USA) *APO'Brien,Ireland* 3-8-12 JPSpencer (7).................... 6/4f 1 6
51 Orientor *JSGoldie* 6-9-0 WSupple (16) .... 25/1 ½ 7
    Welsh Emperor (IRE) *TPTate* 5-9-0 (b) RWinston (17) .... 66/1 hd 8
43 Ashdown Express (IRE) *CFWall* 5-9-0 RMullen (13) .... 16/1 ½ 9
    Ratio *JEHammond,France* 6-9-0 (t) PRobinson (1)................................... 18/1 hd 10
51 Airwave *HCandy* 4-8-11 KDarley (12).. 16/1 ¾ 11
51 Bahamian Pirate (USA) *DNicholls* 9-9-0 DHolland (9)............................. 40/1 nk 12
    Mac Love *JAkehurst* 3-8-12 JFEgan (6) 100/1 1 13
    Lochridge *AMBalding* 5-8-11 MartinDwyer (3).. 100/1 nk 14
    Tychy *SCWilliams* 5-8-11 PHanagan (10).. 200/1 hd 15
    Capricho (IRE) *JAkehurst* 7-9-0 JQuinn (2)... 150/1 nk 16
43 Frizzante *JRFanshawe* 5-8-11 JMurtagh (18).. 13/2 ¾ 17
    Cartography (IRE) *SaeedbinSuroor* 3-8-12 (t) KMcEvoy (11)..................... 50/1 nk 18
43 The Trader (IRE) *MBlanshard* 6-9-0 (b) DSweeney (15) 20/1 1 19
    Mr B. E. Nielsen 19ran 1m11.58   TR: 123+/126/123/119+/118/115/114/114

BADEN-BADEN Sunday, Sep 5   GOOD to SOFT

56   **Grosser Volkswagen Preis von Baden (Gr 1) (3yo+) £335,571**   1½m

37 WARRSAN (IRE) *CEBrittain,GB* 6-9-6 KMcEvoy 78/10   1
39 EGERTON (GER) *PRau,Germany* 3-8-9 AHelfenbein............................... 39/1 nk 2
30 SHIROCCO (GER) *ASchutz,Germany* 3-8-9 ASuborics.......................... 42/10 ¾ 3
46 Simonas (GER) *AWohler,Germany* 5-9-6 ABoschert 172/10 2 4
37 Gamut (IRE) *SirMichaelStoute,GB* 5-9-6 KFallon 47/10 2 5
    Malinas (GER) *PSchiergen,Germany* 3-8-9 AStarke .... 15/2 hd 6
44 Mubtaker (USA) *MPTregoning,GB* 7-9-6 RHills....................................... 9/10f 2 7
    Mohandas (FR) *WHefter,Germany* 3-8-9 JPCarvalho............................... 33/1 1¾ 8
46 Omikron (GER) *MHofer,Germany* 3-8-9 MartinDwyer............................. 33/1 nk 9
46 Well Made (GER) *HBlume,Germany* 7-9-6 AdeVries................................ 42/1 8 10
    Dano-Mast *FPoulsen,France* 8-9-6 FSanchez... 31/1 2 11
    Mr Saeed Manana 11ran 2m32.79   TR: 127/124/123/121/118/116

LONGCHAMP Sunday, Sep 5   GOOD

57   **NetJets Prix du Moulin de Longchamp (Gr 1) (3yo c+f) £115,047**   1m

21 GREY LILAS (IRE) *AFabre,France* 3-8-8 ELegrix................................... 5/1   1
22 DIAMOND GREEN (FR) *AFabre,France* 3-8-11 TGillet........................... 87/10 1 2
38 ANTONIUS PIUS (USA) *APO'Brien,Ireland* 3-8-11 JMurtagh .... 194/10 ns 3
    Denebola (USA) *PBary,France* 3-8-8 C-PLemaire .... 349/10 nk 4
47 Whipper (USA) *RCollet,France* 3-8-11 CSoumillon .... 23/10f ¾ 5
 8 Paolini (GER) *AWohler,Germany* 7-9-2 EPedroza.................................... 26/1 sn 6
    Lucky Story (USA) *MJohnston,GB* 3-8-11 DHolland................................ 96/10 nk 7
38 Le Vie Dei Colori *LMCumani,GB* 4-9-2 LDettori .... 54/10 ns 8
23 Martillo (GER) *RSuerland,Germany* 4-9-2 WMongil .... 191/10 ½ 9
19 American Post *MmeCHead-Maarek,France* 3-8-11 RHughes 44/10 1½ 10
    Actrice (IRE) *ELellouche,France* 4-8-13 OPeslier.................................... 196/10 11
    Gestut Ammerland 11ran 1m37.50   TR: 120/120+/120+/116/117+/117+

DONCASTER Thursday, Sep 9   GOOD to FIRM

58   **GNER Park Stks (Gr 2) (3yo+) £60,000**   7f

    PASTORAL PURSUITS *HMorrison* 3-8-10 SDrowne (7) 5/1   1

```
     7  FIREBREAK SaeedbinSuroor 5-9-4 (t) LDettori (1)...........................   5/2f   1¼ 2
    53  COURT MASTERPIECE EALDunlop 4-9-0 KFallon (3) ..................   13/2   1½ 3
    43  Golden Nun TDEasterby 4-8-11 (b) RWinston (4)..........................   33/1   1½ 4
        Fong's Thong (USA) BJMeehan 3-8-10 JFortune (8)....................   9/2   ½ 5
        Suggestive WJHaggas 6-9-0 (b) MHills (5)..................................   9/1   nk 6
    53  Naahy MRChannon 4-9-0 SHitchcott (2) ......................................   50/1   2½ 7
    38  Tillerman MrsJAPerrett 8-9-0 RHughes (6) ..................................   7/2    4 8
        The Pursuits Partnership 8ran 1m21.66        TR: 123/124/116/108/108/109
```

DONCASTER Friday, Sep 10   FIRM

59   **SGB Champagne Stks (Gr 2) (2yo c+g) £60,000**   7f

```
        ETLAALA BWHills 2-8-10 RHills (3)..............................................   6/1    1
        ICEMAN JHMGosden 2-9-1 KFallon (2) ........................................   5/2jf   ½ 2
        OUDE (USA) SaeedbinSuroor 2-8-10 LDettori (9) ........................   5/2jf   2½ 3
        Wilko (USA) JNoseda 2-8-10 EAhern (5).......................................   16/1   1¼ 4
        Grand Marque (IRE) RHannon 2-8-10 RLMoore (7) ..................   50/1   nk 5
        Elliots World (IRE) MJohnston 2-8-10 JFanning (1) ..................   11/2   1½ 6
        Mister Genepi WRMuir 2-8-10 SDrowne (10) .............................   100/1   nk 7
        Jonquil (IRE) JHMGosden 2-8-10 JFortune (12) .........................   11/1   2 8
        Surwaki (USA) CGCox 2-8-10 PRobinson (11).............................   100/1   5 9
        Leo's Lucky Star (USA) MJohnston 2-8-10 KDarley (6) ..........   16/1   1½ 10
        Mr Hamdan Al Maktoum 10ran 1m23.33          TR: 114+/117/104+/100/99
```

DONCASTER Saturday, Sep 11   FIRM

60   **Betfair.com St Leger Stks (Gr 1) (3yo c+f) £240,000**   1¾m132y

```
    48  RULE OF LAW (USA) SaeedbinSuroor 3-9-0 (t) KMcEvoy (9)................   3/1jf   1
    50  QUIFF SirMichaelStoute 3-8-11 KFallon (4) ...............................   3/1jf   hd 2
    49  TYCOON APO'Brien,Ireland 3-9-0 (t) DHolland (6) ..................   6/1   1½ 3
        Maraahel (IRE) SirMichaelStoute 3-9-0 RHills (5)....................   8/1   1 4
        Mikado APO'Brien,Ireland 3-9-0 JFortune (7) ..........................   25/1   hd 5
        Darsalam (IRE) ArslangireyShavuyev,CzechRepublic 3-9-0 SChin (10) .......   33/1   1½ 6
    48  Go For Gold (IRE) APO'Brien,Ireland 3-9-0 SSanders (1)..........   12/1   3 7
    48  Let The Lion Roar JLDunlop 3-9-0 (v) TQuinn (2).....................   9/2   6 8
        Frank Sonata MGQuinlan 3-9-0 RLMoore (3) ...........................   16/1   nk 9
        Godolphin 9ran 3m06.29                 TR: 125/122+/122+/121/121/118
```

LEOPARDSTOWN Saturday, Sep 11   GOOD to FIRM

61   **Baileys Irish Champion Stks (Gr 1) (3yo+) £393,878**   1¼m

```
    22  AZAMOUR (IRE) JOxx 3-8-11 MJKinane (8) ...............................   8/1   1
    49  NORSE DANCER (IRE) DRCElsworth,GB 4-9-4 JFEgan (1)............   20/1   ½ 2
    45  POWERSCOURT APO'Brien 4-9-4 (b) JPSpencer (2).................   11/1   nk 3
    28  Grey Swallow (IRE) DKWeld 3-8-11 PJSmullen (2) .................   9/2   ¾ 4
    29  Rakti MAJarvis,GB 5-9-4 PRobinson (4) ......................................   5/1   ½ 5
    49  Imperial Dancer MRChannon,GB 6-9-4 SHitchcott (7) .............   66/1   2 6
    37  Doyen (IRE) SaeedbinSuroor,GB 4-9-4 LDettori (3) ..................   4/5f   ¾ 7
    49  Millstreet SaeedbinSuroor,GB 5-9-4 (v) TEDurcan (5).............   100/1   15 8
        H. H. Aga Khan 8ran 2m01.45            TR: 126+/125/124/122/121/116/114
```

62   **Coolmore Fusaichi Pegasus Matron Stks (Gr 1) (3yo+ f+m) £114,966**   1m

```
    38  SOVIET SONG (IRE) JRFanshawe,GB 4-9-2 JMurtagh (7) .........   8/13f   1
    47  ATTRACTION MJohnston,GB 3-8-11 KPDarley (5) ...................   7/2   ½ 2
        PHANTOM WIND (USA) JHMGosden,GB 3-8-11 RHughes (3) ..............   9/1   5 3
        Red Feather (IRE) EdwardLynam 3-8-11 (t) NGMcCullagh (1)........   20/1   4½ 4
        Yesterday (IRE) APO'Brien 4-9-2 JPSpencer (8)........................   7/1   3½ 5
        Livadiya (IRE) HRogers 8-9-2 KJManning (4).............................   50/1   9 6
        Elite Racing Club 6ran 1m36.38            TR: 126/125/111
```

BELMONT PARK Saturday, Sep 11   GOOD to SOFT

63   **Man o'War Stks (Gr 1) (3yo+) £168,902**   1m3f

```
    45  MAGISTRETTI (USA) PLBiancone,USA 4-9-0 (b) EPrado ..................   315/100   1
    45  EPALO (GER) ASchutz,Germany 5-9-0 AStarke .........................   24/10cf   1¼ 2
        KING'S DRAMA (IRE) RJFrankel,USA 4-9-0 JChavez.......................   24/10cf   2 3
        Better Talk Now (USA) HGMotion,USA 5-9-0 (b) RADominguez...........   61/10   ¾ 4
        Request For Parole (USA) SMHough,USA 5-9-0 JCastellano ...................   64/10   ½ 5
        Ballingarry (IRE) LDeSeroux,USA 5-9-0 (b) RDouglas ..................   159/10   2½ 6
        Balto Star (USA) TAPletcher,USA 6-9-0 JVelazquez ....................   97/10   2¼ 7
        Greek Sun (USA) RJFrankel,USA 3-8-9 CVelasquez .....................   385/100   ¾ 8
        Mr M. Tabor 8ran 2m14.65               TR: 124/122/118/117/116
```

LONGCHAMP Sunday, Sep 12   GOOD to SOFT

64   **Prix Niel Casino Barriere d'Enghien Les Bains (Gr 2) (3yo c+f) £42,653**   1½m

```
    20  VALIXIR (IRE) AFabre,France 3-9-2 ELegrix (6) ......................   36/10   1
```

20	PROSPECT PARK *CLaffon-Parias,France* 3-9-2 OPeslier (2)	7/2	ns 2
49	BAGO (FR) *JEPease,France* 3-9-2 TGillet (3)	14/10cpf	1 3
20	Lord du Sud (FR) *J-CRouget,France* 3-9-2 IMendizabal (4)	84/10	nk 4
20	Blue Canari (FR) *PBary,France* 3-9-2 TThulliez (8)	49/10	6 5
	Mister Farmer (FR) *NBranchu,France* 3-9-2 CSoumillon (6)	166/10	10 6
	Primaxis (IRE) *CLaffon-Parias,France* 3-9-2 MBlancpain (1)	7/2	6 7
	Alnitak (USA) *JEPease,France* 3-9-2 (b) C-PLemaire (5)	14/10cpf	5 8

Lagardere Family 8ran 2m29.40 TR: 118/118/116/116/105

65 **Prix Vermeille Fouquet's Barriere (Gr 1) (3 and 4yo f)** £97,177 1½m

	SWEET STREAM (ITY) *JEHammond,France* 4-9-2 TGillet (6)	308/10	1
	ROYAL FANTASY (GER) *HSteinmetz,Germany* 4-9-2 EBotti (2)	44/1	½ 2
31	PRIDE (FR) *AdeRoyerDupre,France* 4-9-2 DBonilla (13)	40/1	½ 3
	Vallera (GER) *UOstmann,Germany* 3-8-7 ABoschert (11)	26/1	sn 4
	Diamond Tango (FR) *AFabre,France* 3-8-7 OPeslier (7)	87/10	hd 5
	Silverskaya (USA) *J-CRouget,France* 3-8-7 IMendizabal (3)	64/10	sn 6
31	Visorama (IRE) *AFabre,France* 4-9-2 ELegrix (12)	87/1	hd 7
21	Latice (IRE) *J-MBeguigne,France* 3-8-7 CSoumillon (4)	1/1f	sh 8
	Whortleberry (FR) *FRohaut,France* 4-9-2 (b) C-PLemaire (5)	133/10	2½ 9
	Lune d'Or (FR) *RGibson,France* 3-8-7 TJarnet (10)	3/1	6 10
	Anabaa Republic (FR) *FDoumen,France* 3-8-7 TThulliez (1)	46/1	1¾ 11
	Gloirez (FR) *PHDemercastel,France* 3-8-7 SPasquier (8)	41/1	nk 12
	Pilgrim of Grace (FR) *RGibson,France* 3-8-7 SMaillot (9)	3/1	13

Team Valor 13ran 2m29.50 TR: 117/116/115+/115/115/114+/114/114

CURRAGH Saturday, Sep 18 GOOD

66 **Irish Field St Leger (Gr 1) (3yo+)** £115,479 1¾m

	VINNIE ROE (IRE) *DKWeld* 6-9-8 (b) PJSmullen (5)	7/2jf	1
25	BRIAN BORU *APO'Brien* 4-9-8 (t) JPSpencer (14)	7/2jf	2½ 2
	FIRST CHARTER *SirMichaelStoute,GB* 5-9-8 KFallon (13)	5/1	½ 3
44	Dubai Success *BWHills,GB* 4-9-8 MHills (10)	10/1	¾ 4
25	Alcazar (IRE) *HMorrison,GB* 9-9-8 MFenton (9)	14/1	hd 5
	Two Miles West (IRE) *APO'Brien* 3-8-12 (t) JAHeffernan (7)	10/1	2 6
	Media Puzzle (USA) *DKWeld* 7-9-8 (b) PShanahan (11)	20/1	3½ 7
	Orange Touch (GER) *MrsAJPerrett,GB* 4-9-8 JMurtagh (4)	9/2	3 8
	Cruzspiel *JOxx* 4-9-8 (b) MJKinane (2)	33/1	¾ 9
	Blue Corrig (IRE) *JosephCrowley* 4-9-8 (b) PCosgrave (12)	100/1	2½ 10
	Jagger *GAButler,GB* 4-9-8 DPMcDonogh (3)	33/1	10 11
25	Chimes At Midnight (USA) *LukeComer* 7-9-8 (b) CatherineGannon (1)	100/1	25 12
	Napoleon (IRE) *APO'Brien* 3-8-12 (b+t) CO'Donoghue (6)	100/1	1 13

Mr Seamus Sheridan 13ran 3m03.14 TR: 123+/119/118/117/117/115

CURRAGH Sunday, Sep 19 GOOD

67 **Dunnes Stores National Stks (Gr 1) (2yo c+f)** £121,507 7f

	DUBAWI (IRE) *SaeedbinSuroor,GB* 2-9-0 LDettori (2)	8/13f	1
	BERENSON (IRE) *TStack* 2-9-0 WMLordan (1)	12/1	3 2
52	RUSSIAN BLUE (IRE) *APO'Brien* 2-9-0 JPSpencer (3)	5/1	1½ 3
	Democratic Deficit (IRE) *JSBolger* 2-9-0 KJManning (6)	9/2	3 4
	In Excelsis (USA) *APO'Brien* 2-9-0 JMurtagh (5)	16/1	2½ 5
	Elusive Double (IRE) *DKWeld* 2-9-0 PJSmullen (4)	12/1	nk 6
	Rowan Tree *APO'Brien* 2-9-0 (b) JAHeffernan (7)	16/1	sh 7

Godolphin 7ran 1m24.69 TR: 123/114/109/100

ASCOT Saturday, Sep 25 Race 68: FIRM; Race 69: GOOD to FIRM

68 **Meon Valley Stud Fillies' Mile (Gr 1) (2yo f)** £116,000 1m (Rnd)

	PLAYFUL ACT (IRE) *JHMGosden* 2-8-10 JFortune (2)	11/4	1
	MAIDS CAUSEWAY (IRE) *BWHills* 2-8-10 MHills (8)	7/1	1 2
	DASH TO THE TOP *LMCumani* 2-8-10 DHolland (6)	16/1	¾ 3
	Mona Lisa *APO'Brien,Ireland* 2-8-10 JPSpencer (4)	14/1	sh 4
	Shohrah (IRE) *MPTregoning* 2-8-10 RHills (1)	10/1	2 5
	Joint Aspiration *MRChannon* 2-8-10 TEDurcan (7)	20/1	sh 6
	Echelon *SirMichaelStoute* 2-8-10 KFallon (5)	15/8f	1¾ 7
	Dubai Surprise (IRE) *DRLoder* 2-8-10 LDettori (3)	7/1	3 8
	Ghasiba (IRE) *CEBrittain* 2-8-10 SSanders (9)	100/1	7 9

Sangster Family 9ran 1m42.22 TR: 113/109/108/103/103/99+

69 **Queen Elizabeth II Stks (Sponsored By NetJets) (Gr 1) (3yo+)** £145,000 1m (Rnd)

61	RAKTI *MAJarvis* 5-9-1 PRobinson (13)	9/2	1
57	LUCKY STORY (USA) *MJohnston* 3-8-11 DHolland (6)	16/1	½ 2
38	REFUSE TO BEND (IRE) *SaeedbinSuroor* 4-9-1 (t) LDettori (3)	4/1	2½ 3
53	Nayyir *GAButler* 6-9-1 JFortune (5)	11/1	1¼ 4

1161

Ace (IRE) *APO'Brien,Ireland* 3-8-11 JPSpencer (1).................................. 12/1   4 5
62 Soviet Song (IRE) *JRFanshawe* 4-8-12 JMurtagh (8) 5/2f   1¼ 6
58 Fong's Thong (USA) *BJMeehan* 3-8-11 (t) PJSmullen (4)........................... 50/1   1¼ 7
57 Diamond Green (FR) *AFabre,France* 3-8-11 CSoumillon (11) 8/1   4 8
57 Antonius Pius (USA) *APO'Brien,Ireland* 3-8-11 (t) KFallon (12) 14/1   2½ 9
61 Norse Dancer (IRE) *DRCElsworth* 4-9-1 JFEgan (14) 11/1   4 10
    Blatant *SaeedbinSuroor* 5-9-1 (v+t) KMcEvoy (7) 100/1   3 11
    Mr Gary A. Tanaka 11ran 1m39.82   TR: 129/128/121/118+/108

ASCOT Sunday, Sep 26   GOOD to FIRM

70 **Barnardo's Cumberland Lodge Stks (Gr 3) (3yo+)** £29,000   1½m
46 HIGH ACCOLADE *MPTregoning* 4-9-0 (v+t) MartinDwyer (8) 3/1   1
    SELF DEFENSE *PRChamings* 7-9-0 KFallon (9) .... 9/1   nk 2
37 BANDARI (IRE) *MJohnston* 5-9-5 RHills (5)... 7/4f   ¾ 3
44 Compton Bolter (IRE) *GAButler* 7-9-0 JFortune (6)............................... 11/1   4 4
40 Muqbil (USA) *JLDunlop* 4-9-0 WSupple (3).. 9/1   1¼ 5
54 Franklins Gardens *MHTompkins* 4-9-0 PRobinson (2) .... 33/1   nk 6
    The Khamsin (DEN) *MscErichsen,Norway* 5-9-0 EAhern (7).................. 100/1   1½ 7
    Alpino Chileno (ARG) *RHaugen,Norway* 5-9-0 (b) FernandoDiaz (4)......... 66/1   sh 8
33 Persian Majesty (IRE) *PWHarris* 4-9-0 (b) JMurtagh (1)............................ 6/1   1½ 9
    Lady Tennant 9ran 2m33.21   TR: 121/120/124/111

NEWMARKET Thursday, Sep 30   GOOD (Rowley Mile Course)

71 **Sky Bet Cheveley Park Stks (Gr 1) (2yo f)** £110,606   6f
    MAGICAL ROMANCE (IRE) *BJMeehan* 2-8-11 RWinston (4) 40/1   1
    SUEZ *MAJarvis* 2-8-11 PRobinson (7) .... 4/1   nk 2
41 DAMSON (IRE) *DWachman,Ireland* 2-8-11 KFallon (5)......................... 10/11f   nk 3
    Golden Legacy (IRE) *RAFahey* 2-8-11 PHanagan (2) .... 16/1   ½ 4
    Slip Dance (IRE) *ETyrrell,Ireland* 2-8-11 JFEgan (6)............................... 40/1   hd 5
    Soar *JRFanshawe* 2-8-11 JMurtagh (3) 4/1   3½ 6
    Jewel In The Sand (IRE) *RHannon* 2-8-11 RLMoore (1)............................ 12/1   3½ 7
    Mr F. C. T. Wilson 7ran 1m12.61   TR: 110/109/108/106+/106

NEWMARKET Friday, Oct 1   GOOD (Rowley Mile Course)

72 **Shadwell Stud Middle Park Stks (Gr 1) (2yo c)** £110,606   6f
    AD VALOREM (USA) *APO'Brien,Ireland* 2-8-11 JPSpencer (4) 9/2   1
    REBUTTAL (USA) *BJMeehan* 2-8-11 PJSmullen (1)................................ 9/1   ¾ 2
59 ICEMAN *JHMGosden* 2-8-11 KFallon (6) 9/4f   2½ 3
    Satchem (IRE) *CEBrittain* 2-8-11 LDettori (9) .... 9/2   nk 4
67 Russian Blue (IRE) *APO'Brien,Ireland* 2-8-11 JMurtagh (7).................... 9/1   ½ 5
    Josh *MAJarvis* 2-8-11 PRobinson (2) 33/1   1 6
    Dramaticus *DRLoder* 2-8-11 SSanders (3) 14/1   1 7
    Prince Charming *JHMGosden* 2-8-11 KMcEvoy (8) .... 14/1   sh 8
    Chateau Istana *NPLittmoden* 2-8-11 (t) KDarley (5)................................ 16/1   hd 9
    Mrs John Magnier 9ran 1m12.19   TR: 121/118/110/109/107/104

NEWMARKET Saturday, Oct 2   GOOD (Rowley Mile Course)

73 **Kingdom of Bahrain Sun Chariot Stks (Gr 1) (3yo+ f+m)** £116,000   1m
62 ATTRACTION *MJohnston* 3-8-11 KDarley (3).. 11/4   1
53 CHIC *SirMichaelStoute* 4-9-0 KFallon (1)... 9/4f   nk 2
23 NEBRASKA TORNADO (USA) *AFabre,France* 4-9-0 RHughes (5)........... 5/2   1½ 3
47 Majestic Desert *MRChannon* 3-8-11 DHolland (4) 11/2   5 4
9 Miss Mambo (USA) *DKWeld,Ireland* 3-8-11 JMurtagh (2) 14/1   14 5
    Duke of Roxburghe 5ran 1m36.27   TR: 125/123/119/107

BELMONT PARK Saturday, Oct 2   GOOD to SOFT

74 **Joe Hirsch Turf Classic Invitational Stks (Gr 1) (3yo+)** £250,000   1½m
    KITTEN'S JOY (USA) *DLRomans,USA* 3-8-9 JVelazquez...................... 24/10   1
63 MAGISTRETTI (USA) *PLBiancone,USA* 4-9-0 (b) EPrado 17/10f   2½ 2
60 TYCOON *APO'Brien,Ireland* 3-8-9 JPSpencer .... 92/10   ¾ 3
63 Request For Parole (USA) *SMHough,USA* 5-9-0 CVelasquez 145/10   3 4
31 Polish Summer (FR) *AFabre,France* 7-9-0 GaryStevens 84/10   2¼ 5
45 Kicken Kris (USA) *MRMatz,USA* 4-9-0 JCastellano 4/1   1½ 6
29 Maktub (ITY) *MAJarvis,GB* 5-9-0 JChavez.. 234/10   32 7
    Kenneth L. & Sarah K. Ramsey 7ran 2m29.97   TR: 128/121/123/115

LONGCHAMP Saturday, Oct 2   GOOD to FIRM

75 **Prix Dollar Casino Barriere de Montreux (Gr 2) (3yo+)** £40,714   1m1f165y
31 TOUCH OF LAND (FR) *H-APantall,France* 4-9-4 C-PLemaire (3)........ 232/10   1
7 GATEMAN *MJohnston,GB* 7-9-0 TJarnet (4)... 59/10   nk 2

SPECIAL KALDOUN (IRE) *DSmaga,France* 5-9-0 DBoeuf (1).................. 9/2   1 3
Valentino (FR) *AdeRoyerDupre,France* 5-9-0 IMendizabal (11)............... 134/10   1 4
Shakis (IRE) *JEHammond,France* 4-9-0 TGillet (2)................................ 145/10   2½ 5
Simple Exchange (IRE) *DKWeld,Ireland* 3-9-0 PJSmullen (5)................ 11/1   2 6
Sights On Gold (IRE) *SaeedbinSuroor,GB* 5-9-0 LDettori (7)............... 13/10f   ½ 7
54 Kindjhal (FR) *ELellouche,France* 4-9-0 SPasquier (10)........................ 24/1   ¾ 8
Weightless *PBary,France* 4-9-0 TThulliez (6)...................................... 153/10   1½ 9
Binary File (USA) *SJensen,Denmark* 6-9-0 ELegrix (8) .... 82/1   ¾ 10
Morning Eclipse *MmeCHead-Maarek,France* 4-9-0 OPeslier (9) 157/10   6 11
Maxwell (FR) *MmeCHead-Maarek,France* 4-9-0 CSoumillon (12)............. 33/1   nk 12
Mr Gary A. Tanaka 12ran 1m58.30   TR: 122/117/115/113/108/110

LONGCHAMP Sunday, Oct 3   GOOD to FIRM

76   **Prix du Cadran Casino Les Princes Barriere de Cannes (Gr 1) (4yo+)**   2½m
£68,027

31 WESTERNER *ELellouche,France* 5-9-2 OPeslier (3)................................ 3/5f   1
CUT QUARTZ (FR) *RGibson,France* 7-9-2 TJarnet (5).......................... 103/10   3 2
LE CARRE (USA) *AdeRoyerDupre,France* 6-9-2 IMendizabal (7)........ 128/10   1 3
Dancing Bay *NJHenderson,GB* 7-9-2 KFallon (6)................................. 73/10   2 4
Holy Orders (IRE) *WPMullins,Ireland* 7-9-2 (b) DJCondon (2) 244/10   3 5
25 Darasim (IRE) *MJohnston,GB* 6-9-2 (v) KDarley (1)............................ 52/10   2½ 6
Anak Pekan *MAJarvis,GB* 4-9-2 PRobinson (4)................................... 233/10   10 7
Clear Thinking *AFabre,France* 4-9-2 CSoumillon (4)............................ 119/10   10 8
Ecurie Wildenstein 8ran 4m19.80   TR: 121+/117/116/113/109

77   **Prix de l'Abbaye de Longchamp Majestic Barriere (Gr 1) (2yo+)** £77,741   5f

VAR (USA) *CEBrittain,GB* 5-9-11 (b) LDettori (13) 29/10f   1
51 THE TATLING (IRE) *JMBradley,GB* 7-9-11 RLMoore (14)...................... 9/2   ½ 2
55 ROYAL MILLENNIUM (IRE) *MRChannon,GB* 6-9-11 TEDurcan (4).... 113/10   1 3
42 Osterhase (IRE) *JEMulhern,Ireland* 5-9-11 (b) FMBerry (8) .... 24/1   nk 4
51 Avonbridge *RCharlton,GB* 4-9-11 (b) JFortune (9)................................ 32/10   1½ 5
55 Orientor *JSGoldie,GB* 6-9-11 JMurtagh (6)... 35/1   ns 6
55 Patavellian (IRE) *RCharlton,GB* 6-9-11 (b) SDrowne (10) .... 32/10   ½ 7
Ringmoor Down *DWPArbuthnot,GB* 5-9-8 TQuinn (1)..................... 28/1   hd 8
55 Bahamian Pirate (USA) *DNicholls,GB* 9-9-11 SSanders (7).................. 114/10   1 9
34 Continent *DNicholls,GB* 7-9-11 DHolland (5) .... 114/10   sn 10
Raffelberger (GER) *MHofer,Germany* 3-9-11 ASuborics (12)................ 40/1   2½ 11
55 Ratio *JEHammond,France* 6-9-11 (b) TGillet (11) 159/10   1½ 12
43 Lucky Strike *ATrybuhl,Germany* 6-9-11 AdeVries (15) .... 198/10   hd 13
55 The Trader (IRE) *MBlanshard,GB* 6-9-11 (b) KFallon (1) 77/10   1½ 14
42 Grand Reward (USA) *APO'Brien,Ireland* 3-9-11 JPSpencer (3)............. 30/1   3 15
Mr Mohammed Rashid 15ran 55.00secs   TR: 124/123/120+/119/114/114

78   **Prix de l'Opera Casino Barriere d'Enghien Les Bains (Gr 1) (3yo+ f+m)**   1¼m
£97,177

21 ALEXANDER GOLDRUN (IRE) *JSBolger,Ireland* 3-8-12 KJManning (3)   13/2   1
57 GREY LILAS (IRE) *AFabre,France* 3-8-12 ELegrix (10).......................... 4/5f   1 2
WALKAMIA (FR) *AFabre,France* 4-9-2 CSoumillon (7)......................... 13/1   1½ 3
62 Yesterday (IRE) *APO'Brien,Ireland* 4-9-2 JPSpencer (2) 47/10   1½ 4
57 Actrice (IRE) *ELellouche,France* 4-9-2 OPeslier (4)............................ 101/10   1½ 5
65 Whortleberry (FR) *FRohaut,France* 4-9-2 (b) C-PLemaire (1) .... 27/1   hd 6
Shapira (GER) *ALowe,Germany* 3-8-12 JPalik (5)............................... 179/10   2½ 7
50 Menhoubah (USA) *CEBrittain,GB* 3-8-12 (s) RLMoore (6) .... 66/1   nk 8
Green Noon (FR) *CLerner,France* 3-8-12 SDrowne (8)....................... 32/1   sh 9
65 Vallera (GER) *UOstmann,Germany* 3-8-12 TGillet (9) 164/10   2½ 10
Mrs N. O'Callaghan 10ran 2m02.30   TR: 121/119/114/111/108/108

79   **Prix Marcel Boussac-Criterium des Pouliches Royal Barriere de Deauville**   1m
(Gr 1) (2yo f) £97,177

52 DIVINE PROPORTIONS (USA) *PBary,France* 2-8-11 C-PLemaire (4)..... 9/10f   1
TITIAN TIME (USA) *JHMGosden,GB* 2-8-11 JFortune (5)................... 169/10   2 2
FRALOGA (IRE) *AFabre,France* 2-8-11 CSoumillon (10) .... 85/10   ns 3
Intrigued *SirMarkPrescott,GB* 2-8-11 SSanders (7) .... 97/10   ½ 4
Portrayal (USA) *AFabre,France* 2-8-11 OPeslier (9)............................ 39/10   sn 5
Queen of Poland *DRLoder,GB* 2-8-11 LDettori (8)............................ 39/10   nk 6
Gorella (FR) *JdeRoualle,France* 2-8-11 ELegrix (2)............................ 278/10   sn 7
New Largue *RCollet,France* 2-8-11 TJarnet (6).................................. 40/1   1½ 8
Mirabilis (USA) *AFabre,France* 2-8-11 RHughes (5)........................... 56/10   2½ 9
Cours de La Reine (IRE) *PWChapple-Hyam,GB* 2-8-11 KFallon (8) 21/1   3 10
Niarchos Family 10ran 1m36.70   TR: 113+/107/107/105/105/104/103

80   **Prix Jean-Luc Lagardere (Grand Criterium) (Gr 1) (2yo c+f)** £136,048   7f

41 ORATORIO (IRE) *APO'Brien,Ireland* 2-9-0 JPSpencer (1)........................... 3/1   1

1163

	EARLY MARCH *MmeCHead-Maarek,France* 2-9-0 OPeslier (6)	16/10f	sn 2
52	LAYMAN (USA) *AFabre,France* 2-9-0 CSoumillon (4)	18/10	ns 3
	Montgomery's Arch (USA) *PWChapple-Hyam,GB* 2-9-0 JFortune (3)	82/10	2½ 4
67	Democratic Deficit (IRE) *JSBolger,Ireland* 2-9-0 KJManning (5)	157/10	1 5
	Tony James (IRE) *CEBrittain,GB* 2-9-0 SSanders (2)	162/10	¾ 6

Mrs John Magnier & Mr M. Tabor 6ran 1m19.30　　　TR: 118+/117+/117/108/104/101

81　**Prix de l'Arc de Triomphe Lucien Barriere (Gr 1) (3yo+ c+f)** £621,932　　1½m

64	BAGO (FR) *JEPease,France* 3-8-11 TGillet (5)	77/10	1
54	CHERRY MIX (FR) *AFabre,France* 3-8-11 CSoumillon (1)	73/10	½ 2
36	OUIJA BOARD *EALDunlop,GB* 3-8-8 JMurtagh (9)	9/1	1 3
	Acropolis (IRE) *AP'Brien,Ireland* 3-8-11 JPSpencer (19)	84/1	2 4
28	North Light (IRE) *SirMichaelStoute,GB* 3-8-11 KFallon (12)	56/10	sh 5
37	Vallee Enchantee (IRE) *ELellouche,France* 4-9-2 SPasquier (16)	131/10	½ 6
65	Latice (IRE) *J-MBeguigne,France* 3-8-8 MJKinane (13)	40/1	sn 7
65	Silverskaya (USA) *J-CRouget,France* 3-8-8 IMendizabal (6)	64/1	2½ 8
56	Warrsan (IRE) *CEBrittain,GB* 6-9-5 KMcEvoy (8)	126/10	½ 9
64	Valixir (IRE) *AFabre,France* 3-8-11 ELegrix (20)	73/10	sh 10
5	Execute (FR) *JEHammond,France* 7-9-5 DBoeuf (17)	39/1	nk 11
64	Blue Canari (FR) *PBary,France* 3-8-11 C-PLemaire (3)	29/1	½ 12
65	Pride (FR) *AdeRoyerDupre,France* 4-9-2 TJarnet (10)	47/1	½ 13
61	Imperial Dancer *MRChannon,GB* 6-9-5 TEDurcan (15)	107/1	sn 14
	Mamool (IRE) *SaeedbinSuroor,GB* 5-9-5 LDettori (4)	139/10	hd 15
64	Prospect Park *CLaffon-Parias,France* 3-8-11 OPeslier (2)	5/1f	½ 16
	Tap Dance City (USA) *SSasaki,Japan* 7-9-5 TSato (18)	116/10	8 17
61	Grey Swallow (IRE) *DKWeld,Ireland* 3-8-11 PJSmullen (11)	69/10	1½ 18
31	Policy Maker (IRE) *ELellouche,France* 4-9-5 TThulliez (4)	131/10	10 19

Niarchos Family 19ran 2m25.00
　　　TR: 130/129/124+/124/124+/120/119+/116/118/118/117/117+

LONGCHAMP Saturday, Oct 9　GOOD to SOFT

82　**Prix de la Foret (Gr 1) (3yo+)** £78,814　　7f

55	SOMNUS *TDEasterby,GB* 4-9-2 MJKinane	26/10f	1
57	DENEBOLA (USA) *PBary,France* 3-8-10 C-PLemaire	41/10	¾ 2
57	LE VIE DEI COLORI *LMCumani,GB* 4-9-2 CSoumillon	64/10	1 3
55	Monsieur Bond (IRE) *BSmart,GB* 4-9-2 (b) FLynch	165/10	nk 4
58	Pastoral Pursuits *HMorrison,GB* 3-9-0 SDrowne	41/10	1 5
69	Nayyir *GAButler,GB* 6-9-2 JFortune	39/10	3 6
43	Charming Groom (FR) *FHead,France* 5-9-2 OPeslier	56/10	6 7

Legard Sidebottom & Sykes 7ran 1m22.30　　　TR: 124/119/119/118/117

NEWMARKET Saturday, Oct 16　SOFT (Rowley Mile Course)

83　**Victor Chandler Challenge Stks (Gr 2) (3yo+)** £58,000　　7f

58	FIREBREAK *SaeedbinSuroor,GB* 5-9-4 (t) LDettori (9)	11/2	1
	KELTOS (FR) *CLaffon-Parias,France* 6-9-0 OPeslier (13)	6/1	1 2
	POLAR BEAR *WJHaggas* 4-9-0 KFallon (7)	5/1f	nk 3
	Polar Way *MrsAJPerrett* 5-9-0 RHughes (14)	11/1	2½ 4
51	Balmont (USA) *JNoseda* 3-8-12 JPSpencer (8)	6/1	1¾ 5
	Caradak (IRE) *JOxx,Ireland* 3-8-12 MJKinane (2)	20/1	½ 6
	Vanderlin *AMBalding* 5-9-0 MartinDwyer (1)	20/1	3½ 7
	Badminton *SaeedbinSuroor* 3-8-9 (t) KMcEvoy (4)	10/1	3½ 8
	Polar Ben *JRFanshawe* 5-9-0 JMurtagh (10)	11/2	sh 9
	Cape Fear *BJMeehan* 3-8-12 JFortune (5)	33/1	1½ 10
58	Golden Nun *TDEasterby* 4-8-11 TQuinn (6)	25/1	18 11
	Tahirah *RGuest* 4-8-11 SSanders (3)	66/1	8 12

Godolphin 12ran 1m27.22　　　TR: 124+/118/117/111/108/106

84　**Emirates Airline Champion Stks (Gr 1) (3yo+)** £215,064　　1¼m

38	HAAFHD *BWHills* 3-8-11 RHills (9)	12/1	1
	CHORIST *WJHaggas* 5-8-13 KFallon (4)	20/1	2½ 2
61	AZAMOUR (IRE) *JOxx,Ireland* 3-8-11 MJKinane (10)	6/1	1 3
69	Norse Dancer (IRE) *DRCElsworth* 4-9-2 JFEgan (7)	12/1	6 4
69	Refuse To Bend (IRE) *SaeedbinSuroor* 4-9-2 (t) KMcEvoy (8)	7/1	½ 5
47	Salselon *LMCumani* 5-9-2 (b) JMurtagh (2)	16/1	nk 6
61	Doyen (IRE) *SaeedbinSuroor* 4-9-2 LDettori (5)	3/1f	1¾ 7
	Mingun (USA) *APO'Brien,Ireland* 4-9-2 JPSpencer (11)	33/1	6 8
69	Lucky Story (USA) *MJohnston* 3-8-11 DHolland (3)	9/2	dist 9
33	Naheef (IRE) *SaeedbinSuroor* 5-9-2 (v+t) TEDurcan (1)	100/1	dist 10
40	Mister Monet (IRE) *MJohnston* 3-8-11 KDarley (6)	5/1	pu

Mr Hamdan Al Maktoum 11ran 2m06.90　　　TR: 129/120/121/107/106/105

85　**Darley Dewhurst Stks (Gr 1) (1) (2yo c+f)** £152,772　　7f

| | SHAMARDAL (USA) *MJohnston* 2-9-0 KDarley (4) | 9/2 | 1 |

1164

80	ORATORIO (IRE) *APO'Brien,Ireland* 2-9-0 JPSpencer (10)	15/2	2½	2
80	MONTGOMERY'S ARCH (USA) *PWChapple-Hyam* 2-9-0 MJKinane (1)	10/1	nk	3
72	Iceman *JHMGosden* 2-9-0 JFortune (11)	7/1	½	4
	Librettist (USA) *SaeedbinSuroor* 2-9-0 KMcEvoy (9)	10/1	¾	5
	Tremar *TGMills* 2-9-0 GCarter (5)	33/1	8	6
	Perfectperformance (USA) *SaeedbinSuroor* 2-9-0 LDettori (8)	8/1	4	7
59	Etlaala *BWHills* 2-9-0 RHills (6)	9/4f	4	8
	Home Affairs *SirMichaelStoute* 2-9-0 KFallon (7)	12/1	1¼	9

Gainsborough Stud 9ran 1m27.16 TR: 126/119/118/117/114

MILAN Sunday, Oct 17 GOOD to SOFT

86 Gran Premio del Jockey Club Italiano (Gr 1) (3yo+) £147,931 1½m

Order as they passed the post: Imperial Dancer was demoted to fifth for causing interference

56	SHIROCCO (GER) *ASchutz,Germany* 3-8-13 ASuborics	9/10f		1
	ELECTROCUTIONIST (USA) *VValiani,Italy* 3-8-13 EBotti	38/10	sh	2
81	IMPERIAL DANCER *MRChannon,GB* 6-9-4 TEDurcan	29/1	5	3
65	Sweet Stream (ITY) *JEHammond,France* 4-9-1 TGillet	69/10	1¼	4
54	Fair Mix (IRE) *MRolland,France* 6-9-4 SPasquier	31/2	½	5
28	Percussionist (IRE) *JHMGosden,GB* 3-8-13 JFortune	96/10	sh	6
	Without Connexion (IRE) *MGuarnieri,Italy* 5-9-4 DVargiu	52/1	nk	7
66	Dubai Success *BWHills,GB* 4-9-4 MHills	96/10	5	8
70	Bandari (IRE) *MJohnston,GB* 5-9-4 WSupple	46/10	3	9

Baron G. von Ullmann 9ran 2m31.60 TR: 125/125/115/110/112/114/111+

DONCASTER Saturday, Oct 23 SOFT

87 Racing Post Trophy (Gr 1) (2yo c+f) £120,000 1m (Str.)

	MOTIVATOR *MLWBell* 2-9-0 KFallon (5)	6/4f		1
	ALBERT HALL *APO'Brien,Ireland* 2-9-0 JPSpencer (7)	5/2	2½	2
	HENRIK *MRChannon* 2-9-0 TEDurcan (2)	12/1	1	3
	Hills of Aran *APO'Brien,Ireland* 2-9-0 CO'Donoghue (1)	11/1	8	4
	Beaver Patrol (IRE) *RFJohnsonHoughton* 2-9-0 SCarson (6)	25/1	6	5
	Berkhamsted (IRE) *JAOsborne* 2-9-0 RLMoore (4)	20/1	6	6
59	Elliots World (IRE) *MJohnston* 2-9-0 KDarley (3)	13/2	17	7
	Frith (IRE) *BWHills* 2-9-0 SSanders (8)	18/1	sh	8

The Royal Ascot Racing Club 8ran 1m42.62 TR: 119+/113/111+/93

LONGCHAMP Sunday, Oct 24 SOFT

88 Prix Royal-Oak (Gr 1) (3yo+) £78,813 1m7f110y

76	WESTERNER *ELellouche,France* 5-9-4 SPasquier	2/5f		1
	BEHKARA (IRE) *AdeRoyerDupre,France* 4-9-1 CSoumillon	48/10	2½	2
66	ALCAZAR (IRE) *HMorrison,GB* 9-9-4 MFenton	21/1	½	3
76	Le Carre (USA) *AdeRoyerDupre,France* 6-9-4 DBoeuf	63/10	2	4
86	Percussionist (IRE) *JHMGosden,GB* 3-8-9 (b) JFortune	27/1	5	5
70	Franklins Gardens *MHTompkins,GB* 4-9-4 DHolland	25/1	2	6
76	Holy Orders (IRE) *WPMullins,Ireland* 7-9-4 (b) DJCondon	39/1	6	7
	Double Green (IRE) *FHead,France* 3-8-7 OPeslier	156/10	10	8

Ecurie Wildenstein 8ran 3m28.90 TR: 122+/116/118/116/112

WOODBINE Sunday, Oct 24 GOOD

89 Pattison Canadian International Stks (Gr 1) (3yo+) £497,238 1½m

49	SULAMANI (IRE) *SaeedbinSuroor,GB* 5-9-0 LDettori	85/100f		1
56	SIMONAS (IRE) *AWohler,Germany* 5-9-0 KFallon	2135/100	1½	2
66	BRIAN BORU *APO'Brien,Ireland* 4-9-0 JPSpencer	49/10	2	3
56	Mubtaker (USA) *MPTregoning,GB* 7-9-0 RHills	55/10	¾	4
63	King's Drama (IRE) *RJFrankel,USA* 4-9-0 JVelazquez	11/1	4¼	5
45	Senor Swinger (USA) *RBaffert,USA* 4-9-0 EPrado	92/10	3¾	6
	Burst of Fire (CAN) *MRFrostad,Canada* 3-8-7 (b) SCallaghan	35/1	7¼	7
	Colorful Judgement (CAN) *MRFrostad,Canada* 4-9-0 TKabel	32/1	2½	8
45	Sabiango (GER) *TYakteen,USA* 6-9-0 BBlanc	22/1	1	9
	Lenny The Lender (CAN) *RJukosky,Canada* 8-9-0 (b) ChantalSutherland...	38/1	1	10

Godolphin 19ran 2m28.64 TR: 124+/121/118/117/110

LONE STAR PARK Saturday, Oct 30 Turf course: GOOD to SOFT; Dirt track: FAST

90 NetJets Breeders' Cup Mile (Gr 1) (3yo+) £477,377 1m (Turf)

	SINGLETARY (USA) *DChatlos,jnr,USA* 4-9-0 DFlores (10)	165/10		1
69	ANTONIUS PIUS (USA) *APO'Brien,Ireland* 3-8-10 JPSpencer (7)	314/10	½	2
47	SIX PERFECTIONS (FR) *PBary,France* 4-8-11 JBailey (11)	59/10	1½	3
	Soaring Free (CAN) *MRFrostad,Canada* 5-9-0 TKabel (4)	109/10	nk	4
	Silver Tree (USA) *WIMott,USA* 4-9-0 EPrado (2)	22/1	¾	5

	Musical Chimes (USA) *NDDrysdale,USA* 4-8-11 KDesormeaux (9)	23/1	nk	6
	Blackdoun (FR) *JCCanani,USA* 3-8-10 (b) CNakatani (13)	106/10	nk	7
69	Diamond Green (FR) *AFabre,France* 3-8-10 LDettori (8)	197/10	nk	8
45	Mr O'Brien (IRE) *RLGraham,USA* 5-9-0 ECoa (14)	21/1	1	9
57	Whipper (USA) *RCollet,France* 3-8-10 CSoumillon (1)	71/10	ns	10
	Nothing To Lose (USA) *RJFrankel,USA* 4-9-0 (b) JVelazquez (12)	43/10	ns	11
	Artie Schiller (USA) *JAJerkens,USA* 3-8-10 RMigliore (6)	38/10f	½	12
	Special Ring (USA) *JCCanani,USA* 7-9-0 (b) VEspinoza (3)	86/10	3¾	13
1	Domestic Dispute (USA) *PGallagher,USA* 4-9-0 KJohn (5)	54/1	3½	14

Little Red Feather Racing 14ran 1m36.90 TR: 125/123/117+/120/118/114/115/115+

91 VO5 Breeders' Cup Filly & Mare Turf (Gr 1) (3yo+ f+m) £400,656 1m3f (Turf)

81	OUIJA BOARD *EALDunlop,GB* 3-8-6 KFallon (5)	9/10f		1
	FILM MAKER (USA) *HGMotion,USA* 4-8-11 (b) JVelazquez (3)	165/10	1½	2
	WONDER AGAIN (USA) *JJToner,USA* 5-8-11 EPrado (12)	107/10	nk	3
	Moscow Burning (USA) *JMCassidy,USA* 4-8-11 JValdivia (4)	19/1	2¾	4
78	Yesterday (IRE) *APO'Brien,Ireland* 4-8-11 (v) JPSpencer (11)	9/1	1¼	5
	Shaconage (USA) *MShirota,USA* 4-8-11 RBejarano (6)	62/1	1	6
	Light Jig *RJFrankel,USA* 4-8-11 RDouglas (7)	64/10	¾	7
	Riskaverse (USA) *PJKelly,USA* 5-8-11 CVelasquez (9)	137/10	½	8
	Super Brand (SAF) *KPMcLaughlin,USA* 5-8-10 PDay (1)	33/1	1	9
	Katdogawn *JMCassidy,USA* 4-8-11 KDesormeaux (2)	55/1	5½	10
	Megahertz *RJFrankel,USA* 5-8-11 CNakatani (10)	101/10	1	11
	Aubonne (GER) *ELibaud,France* 4-8-11 JBailey (8)	168/10	nk	12

Lord Derby 12ran 2m18.25 TR: 124/120/119/114/111/110

92 Bessemer Trust Breeders' Cup Juv (Gr 1) (2yo c+g) £426,230 1m110y (Dirt)

59	WILKO (USA) *JNoseda,GB* 2-8-10 LDettori (8)	283/10		1
	AFLEET ALEX (USA) *TFRitchey,USA* 2-8-10 JRose (3)	3/1	¾	2
	SUN KING (USA) *NPZito,USA* 2-8-10 EPrado (1)	69/10	nk	3
	Consolidator (USA) *DWLukas,USA* 2-8-10 RBejarano (4)	75/10	1¼	4
	Roman Ruler (USA) *RBaffert,USA* 2-8-10 CNakatani (2)	2/1f	1½	5
	Proud Accolade (USA) *TAPletcher,USA* 2-8-10 JVelazquez (6)	26/10	1¼	6
	Twice Unbridled (USA) *DMJensen,USA* 2-8-10 (b) VEspinoza (7)	33/1	9¾	7
	Scandinavia (USA) *APO'Brien,Ireland* 2-8-10 JPSpencer (5)	145/10	1¼	8

J. Paul Reddam & Susan Roy 8ran 1m42.09 TR: 118/116/116/113/110/107

93 John Deere Breeders' Cup Turf (Gr 1) (3yo+) £568,306 1½m (Turf)

63	BETTER TALK NOW (USA) *HGMotion,USA* 5-9-0 (b) RADominguez (5)	279/10		1
74	KITTEN'S JOY (USA) *DLRomans,USA* 3-8-9 JVelazquez (4)	7/10f	1¾	2
61	POWERSCOURT *APO'Brien,Ireland* 4-9-0 (v) JPSpencer (1)	29/10	1	3
74	Magistretti (USA) *PLBiancone,USA* 4-9-0 (b) EPrado (6)	61/10	2¼	4
	Mustanfar (USA) *KPMcLaughlin,USA* 3-8-9 (b) JSantos (8)	23/1	2¾	5
74	Request For Parole (USA) *SMHough,USA* 5-9-0 PDay (2)	22/1	nk	6
	Strut The Stage (USA) *MRFrostad,Canada* 6-9-0 (b) CNakatani (3)	27/1	4	7
	Star Over The Bay (USA) *MRMitchell,USA* 6-9-0 TBaze (7)	81/10	3¾	8

Bushwood Stable 8ran 2m29.70 TR: 126/125+/121/118+/116/113

94 Breeders' Cup Classic Powered By Dodge (Gr 1) (3yo+) £1,136,612 1¼m (Dirt)

	GHOSTZAPPER (USA) *RJFrankel,USA* 4-9-0 (b) JCastellano (1)	25/10jf		1
	ROSES IN MAY (USA) *DLRomans,USA* 4-9-0 JVelazquez (6)	87/10	3	2
1	PLEASANTLY PERFECT (USA) *REMandella,USA* 6-9-0 (v) JBailey (12)	25/10jf	4	3
	Perfect Drift (USA) *MWJohnson,USA* 5-9-0 KDesormeaux (4)	138/10	¾	4
	Azeri (USA) *DWLukas,USA* 6-8-11 PDay (3)	152/10	2	5
	Personal Rush (USA) *KYamauchi,Japan* 3-8-9 (s+h) LDettori (8)	25/1	2	6
	Birdstone (USA) *NPZito,USA* 3-8-9 EPrado (7)	65/10	¾	7
	Dynever (USA) *CClement,USA* 4-9-0 CNakatani (13)	153/10	nk	8
	Fantasticat (USA) *RCBarnett,USA* 3-8-9 (b) GMelancon (5)	60/1	¾	9
	Funny Cide (USA) *BTagg,USA* 4-9-0 JSantos (9)	77/10	¾	10
	Bowman's Band (USA) *HAJerkens,USA* 6-9-0 CVelasquez (11)	62/1	nk	11
	Newfoundland (USA) *TAPletcher,USA* 4-9-0 (b) ECoa (10)	39/1	3	12
	Freefourinternet (USA) *MJMaker,USA* 6-9-0 GretaKuntzweiler (2)	54/1	6	13

Stronach Stables 13ran 1m59.02 TR: 137/131/125/123/117/116

SAINT-CLOUD Sunday, Oct 31 SOFT

95 Criterium International (Gr 1) (2yo c+f) £98,517 1m

	HELIOS QUERCUS (FR) *CDiard,France* 2-9-0 ARoussel	51/10		1
68	DUBAI SURPRISE (IRE) *DRLoder,GB* 2-8-11 TJarnet	26/1	1½	2
	WALK IN THE PARK (IRE) *JEHammond,France* 2-9-0 TGillet	41/10	sn	3
	Cupid's Glory *SirMarkPrescott,GB* 2-9-0 SSanders	89/10	¾	4

80 Early March *MmeCHead-Maarek,France* 2-9-0 RHughes........................ 11/10f 2½ 6
    Merchant (IRE) *MLWBell,GB* 2-9-0 KDarley 19/10 2½ 7
    Umniya (IRE) *MRChannon,GB* 2-8-11 (v) ACulhane 50/1 3 8

Mr T. Maudet 8ran 1m45.30   TR: 118/112/114/113+/107

FLEMINGTON Tuesday, Nov 2   SOFT

96 **Emirates Melbourne Cup (Hcap) (Gr 1) (3yo+)** £1,142,858   2m

    MAKYBE DIVA *DLFreedman,Australia* 6-8-10 GBoss (7) 26/10f 1
66 VINNIE ROE (IRE) *DKWeld,Ireland* 6-9-2 (b) PJSmullen (10) 5/1 1¼ 2
    ZAZZMAN (AUS) *AJVasil,Australia* 7-8-4 (b) NRyan (6) 100/1 2½ 3
    ELVSTROEM (AUS) *AJVasil,Australia* 4-8-13 NRawiller (3) 15/1 1½ 4
    Hugs Dancer (FR) *TMcEvoy,Australia* 7-8-4 GChilds (4) .... 16/1 nk 5
    Distinction (IRE) *SirMichaelStoute,GB* 5-8-7 DBeadman (12) 12/1 1¾ 6
81 Mamool (IRE) *SaeedbinSuroor,GB* 5-9-0 LDettori (21) .... 25/1 sh 7
    Catchmeifyoucan (NZ) *MMoroney,NewZealand* 5-7-10 (b) BShinn (1)....... nk 8
    Razkalla (USA) *SaeedbinSuroor,GB* 6-8-9 KMcEvoy (16) .... 40/1 nk 9
    Strasbourg (AUS) *BCummings,Australia* 5-8-3 (b) MduPlessis (22)........... 40/1 1¼ 10
    On A Jeune (AUS) *PMontgomerie,Australia* 4-7-13 (b) JBowditch (18) ..... 60/1 nk 11
66 Media Puzzle (USA) *DKWeld,Ireland* 7-8-10 (b) DMOliver (11) .... 20/1 nk 12
    Grey Song (AUS) *THughes,Australia* 6-8-3 DBeasley (24) 20/1 2 13
    Roman Arch (AUS) *MWhittle,Australia* 6-8-4 LCurrie (5) 100/1 1¼ 14
    Upsetthym (NZ) *KarenFursdon,Australia* 6-8-0 RMcLeod (23) 70/1 3 15
    Another Warrior (AUS) *AlanBailey,Australia* 6-8-0 (b) JByrne (13) 40/1 1½ 16
    Winning Belle (NZ) *MsGWaterhouse,Australia* 4-7-11 CMunce (17)......... 40/1 1¼ 17
    Lashed (AUS) *GARogerson,Australia* 5-8-3 (b) JCassidy (20) 80/1 5 18
    Mummify (AUS) *DLFreedman,Australia* 5-8-11 DNikolic (15) 30/1 1¾ 19
    Don Raphael (AUS) *KParker,Australia* 5-7-13 SSeamer (19) 60/1 4 20
    Pacific Dancer (NZ) *SDwyer,Australia* 4-8-2 GGrylls (8) 17/1 1¼ 21
    Hard To Get (AUS) *MKavanagh,Australia* 4-8-0 LNolen (14) 100/1 1½ 22
    Delzao (AUS) *GKavanagh,Australia* 4-8-7 (b) SKing (2)............................ 40/1 25 23
    She's Archie (AUS) *DWeir,Australia* 6-8-2 (b) CBrown (9)...................... 14/1 15 24

Emily Krstina (Aus) Pty Ltd Syndicate 24ran 3m28.55
                         TR: 124+/128/113/120/110/111+/118

TOKYO Sunday, Nov 28   FIRM

97 **Japan Cup (Gr 1) (3yo+)** £1,308,901   1½m

    ZENNO ROB ROY (JPN) *KFujisawa,Japan* 4-9-0 OPeslier (9) 17/10f 1
    COSMO BULK (JPN) *KTabe,Japan* 3-8-10 C-PLemaire (10).................. 52/10 3 2
    DELTA BLUES (JPN) *KSumii,Japan* 3-8-10 KAndo (7) .... 124/10 nk 3
81 Policy Maker (IRE) *ELellouche,France* 4-9-0 SPasquier (1) .... 81/1 hd 4
    Narita Century (JPN) *NFujisawa,Japan* 5-9-0 YShibata (4).................... 101/10 ½ 5
37 Phoenix Reach (IRE) *AMBalding,GB* 4-9-0 (b) MartinDwyer (5) 467/10 1¼ 6
65 Lune d'Or (FR) *RGibson,France* 3-8-10 TJarnet (2) .... 219/10 ½ 7
    Er Nova (JPN) *KFujisawa,Japan* 5-8-10 SFujita (8) .... 74/1 ¾ 8
    Hishi Miracle (JPN) *MSayama,Japan* 5-9-0 KTsunoda (11)........................ 24/1 2 9
    Heart's Cry (JPN) *KHashiguchi,Japan* 3-8-10 YTake (3).......................... 55/10 ¾ 10
93 Powerscourt *APO'Brien,Ireland* 4-9-0 (b) JPSpencer (15) .... 128/10 dh 10
    Tosen Dandy (JPN) *HMori,Japan* 6-9-0 TEda (13)................................ 156/1 ns 12
    Higher Game (JPN) *YOkubo,Japan* 3-8-10 (b) MDemuro (12)................ 11/1 ¾ 13
    Magnaten (USA) *KFujisawa,Japan* 8-9-0 YOkabe (6)............................ 114/1 7 14
81 Warrsan (IRE) *CEBrittain,GB* 6-9-0 KFallon (16)................................ 197/10 3 15
    Hookipa Wave (JPN) *YNinomiya,Japan* 3-8-10 NYokoyama (14) 114/10 2½ 16

Shinobu Oosako 16ran 2m24.20   TR: 125/122/121/119/118/116/113

SHA TIN Sunday, Dec 12   GOOD to FIRM

98 **Cathay Pacific Hong Kong Vase (Gr 1) (3yo+)** £531,209   1½m

97 PHOENIX REACH (IRE) *AMBalding,GB* 4-9-0 MartinDwyer (5) 265/10 1
75 SIGHTS ON GOLD (IRE) *SaeedbinSuroor,GB* 5-9-0 (t) LDettori (7)........ 21/1 ½ 2
81 VALLEE ENCHANTEE (IRE) *ELellouche,France* 4-8-10 OPeslier (10) . 18/10f 1½ 3
86 Sweet Stream (ITY) *JEHammond,France* 4-8-11 (t) TGillet (6).................. 39/1 ¾ 4
    Super Kid (NZ) *JSize,HongKong* 5-9-0 DJWhyte (8)................................ 11/2 1½ 5
74 Polish Summer *AFabre,France* 7-9-0 CSoumillon (12)............................ 14/1 hd 6
    Beethoven (NZ) *DAHayes,HongKong* 5-9-0 (b) GMosse (1)...................... 31/1 1 7
86 Imperial Dancer *MRChannon,GB* 6-9-0 TEDurcan (2) .... 73/1 ¾ 8
97 Warrsan (IRE) *CEBrittain,GB* 6-9-0 SSanders (3) .... 15/1 ¾ 9
89 Simonas (IRE) *AWohler,Germany* 5-9-0 KFallon (11) .... 29/10 nk 10
    Roosevelt (IRE) *DOughton,HongKong* 4-9-0 MJKinane (9) .... 72/10 ¾ 11
89 Brian Boru *APO'Brien,Ireland* 4-9-0 (t) JPSpencer (4)........................ 18/1 1¾ 12

Winterbeck Manor Stud 12ran 2m29.80   TR: 120/119/112/111+/111/111

99   **Cathay Pacific Hong Kong Sprint (Gr 1) (3yo+)** £378,486   5f

           SILENT WITNESS (AUS) *ASCruz,HongKong* 5-9-0 FCoetzee (6) 3/10f   1
34   CAPE OF GOOD HOPE *DOughton,HongKong* 6-9-0 MJKinane (7) . 43/1   1¾ 2
           NATURAL BLITZ I (AUS) *MPThwaites,Macau* 4-9-0 (t) JDidham (10) 65/1   2¼ 3
77   Royal Millennium (IRE) *MRChannon,GB* 6-9-0 TEDurcan (8) .... 100/1   sh 4
           Able Prince (AUS) *JMoore,HongKong* 4-9-0 (b) ESoumillon (12) .... 35/1   ½ 5
           Multidandy (AUS) *ASCruz,HongKong* 6-9-0 (t) WMLai (14) 94/1   1¾ 6
           Sunningdale (JPN) *TSetoguchi,Japan* 5-9-0 YFukunaga (4) .... 38/1   ½ 7
           Battle Won (USA) *CSimon,USA* 4-9-0 KFallon (5) .... 96/1   sh 8
           Yell (AUS) *JHawkes,Australia* 5-9-0 (t) DJWhyte (3)...................... 28/1   1¾ 9
77   Var (USA) *CEBrittain,GB* 5-9-0 (b) LDettori (13) 14/1   2¾ 10
77   Osterhase (IRE) *JEMulhern,Ireland* 5-9-0 (b) FBerry (11)........................ 100/1   4 11
77   The Tatling (IRE) *JMBradley,GB* 7-9-0 RMoore (9) .... 48/1   ½ 12
           Pivotal Point *PJMakin,GB* 4-9-0 SSanders (2) 57/1   3 13
           Calstone Light O (JPN) *HOneda,Japan* 6-9-0 (h) NOnishi (2) 9/2   13¾ 14

           Mr A. A. Da Silva 14ran 56.80secs   TR: 123+/116/107/106+/104

100   **Cathay Pacific Hong Kong Cup (Gr 1) (3yo+)** £677,291   1¼m

78   ALEXANDER GOLDRUN (IRE) *JSBolger,Ireland* 3-8-7   1
           KJManning (12).. 215/10
           BULLISH LUCK (USA) *ASCruz,HongKong* 5-9-0 (b) FCoetzee (10)......... 20/1   sh 2
75   TOUCH OF LAND (FR) *H-APantall,France* 4-9-0 C-PLemaire (4)............. 55/1   ¾ 3
97   Powerscourt *APO'Brien,Ireland* 4-9-0 (v) JPSpencer (1) 64/10   1¼ 4
           Ancient World (USA) *SaeedbinSuroor,GB* 4-9-0 LDettori (3) .... 11/1   sh 5
           Elegant Fashion (AUS) *DAHayes,HongKong* 6-8-10 GMosse (11) .... 11/1   ns 6
69   Rakti *MAJarvis,GB* 5-9-0 PRobinson (7) .... 31/10f   hd 7
8   Ain't Here (AUS) *DAHayes,HongKong* 5-9-0 BPrebble (9) 8/1   1½ 8
78   Walkamia (FR) *AFabre,France* 4-8-10 ELegrix (14)................................ 100/1   1¼ 9
81   Latice (IRE) *J-MBeguigne,France* 3-8-7 ESoumillon (6).................... 73/10   ½ 10
           Soldier Hollow *PSchiergen,Germany* 4-9-0 WMongil (5)............................ 31/1   2¼ 11
           Fields of Omagh (AUS) *TMcEvoy,Australia* 7-9-0 (b) DNikolic (3)............ 22/1   1¼ 12
           Dance In The Mood (JPN) *KFujisawa,Japan* 3-8-7 OPeslier (8)............... 4/1   1 13
23   Bowman's Crossing (IRE) *DOughton,HongKong* 5-9-0 MJKinane (2) 16/1   1½ 14

           Mrs N. O'Callaghan 14ran 2m03.30   TR: 121/124/122/119+/119/115/119/115+

INDEX TO SELECTED BIG RACES

1169

1170

THE TIMEFORM 'TOP HORSES ABROAD'

This review of the year covers the major racing countries outside Britain. It includes Timeform Ratings for the top two-year-olds, three-year-olds and older horses. Horses not rated highly enough to be included in the main lists, but which finished in the first three in a European pattern race, or, in the sections on Japan and North America, won a Grade 1 during the season are included below the cut-off line. Fillies and mares are denoted by (f); * denotes the horse was trained for only a part of the season in the country concerned; † against a horse in the sections outside Europe and the UAE indicates the horse has a commentary in the main section of *Racehorses*. Overseas customers wishing to keep in touch with Timeform's coverage of racing through the year can subscribe to Computer Timeform, Timeform Perspective or our internet site (http://www.timeform.com) for reports on all the important races. It is now possible to obtain up-to-date Timeform commentaries (including many not published in the weekly Timeform Black Book), undertake progeny research and access daily form guides on the internet site. Race Cards for many Group 1 races in France and Ireland, plus major races in several other countries, including the Dubai Carnival, the Breeders' Cup and the Hong Kong International meeting, are also available.

IRELAND   Aidan O'Brien's total of three Group 1 winners in 2004—**Powerscourt**, Ad Valorem and Oratorio—was far removed from the outstanding twenty-three such successes he achieved in 2001 but, despite enduring a frustrating campaign at times, O'Brien was the champion trainer in Ireland for the sixth successive year and for the seventh time overall. This was due in no small part to the stable sending out the winners of fourteen of Ireland's forty-six pattern races (only fifteen more of those races were won by other Irish trainers). Powerscourt was O'Brien's sole Group 1 winner on home soil after his facile success in the Tattersalls Gold Cup. He did not win again, though he was first past the post in the Arlington Million before being demoted for causing interference. Powerscourt was just one of several horses to test O'Brien's patience. **Antonius Pius** had the Poule d'Essai des Poulains at his mercy in May before jinking and almost unseating his rider around fifty yards out, and temperamental shortcomings probably contributed to his defeat in the Breeders' Cup Mile, too. **One Cool Cat** was arguably the biggest cause for concern. He won only one race, the Phoenix Sprint Stakes, with his disappointments including a flop in the Two Thousand Guineas on his reappearance. All three showed very smart form, though, as did O'Brien's now-retired **Brian Boru** (second in Irish St Leger), **Tycoon** (third in the Irish Derby and St Leger), **Acropolis** (fourth in the Arc), and **Mikado** (fifth in the St Leger). O'Brien also trained the Oaks runner-up **All Too Beautiful** and the smart performers **Ace**, **Necklace** and **Yeats**. The unbeaten Yeats was not seen out after winning the Ballysax Stakes and the Derrinstown Stud Derby Trial, and it is to be hoped that the one-time Derby favourite will be able to fulfil as a four-year-old the undoubted potential he had shown.

Unlike the previous two seasons Ballydoyle did not house the highest-rated horse in Ireland. That honour was shared between the Dermot Weld-trained **Vinnie Roe** and John Oxx's **Azamour**. The admirable Vinnie Roe was better than ever at the age of six, becoming the first horse since the European pattern was instituted in 1971 to win the same Group 1 race four years running when successful in the Irish St Leger. He also came close to winning the Melbourne Cup, beaten only by the home-trained Makybe Diva. Meanwhile, the three-year-old Azamour showed himself a high-class performer, too, with decisive successes in the St James's Palace Stakes and the Irish Champion Stakes. Rated just behind this pair is Weld's second Irish Derby winner **Grey Swallow**. Like Vinnie Roe and Azamour, Grey Swallow is set to race on in 2005.

In general the Irish older horses did not make a huge impact. Only four achieved ratings of 120 or more, with Vinnie Roe, Powerscourt and Brian Boru being joined by the sprinter **Osterhase**. He did not win in pattern company, but his three wins included a fine weight-carrying performance in the Ladbrokes Rockingham Handicap, and he was not beaten far into fourth in the Prix de l'Abbaye. Several other older horses worthy of mention are: **Solskjaer**, who won the Royal Whip Stakes; **Mkuzi**, who won the Curragh Cup; **Tropical Lady**, whose five wins included the Brownstown Stakes; and the much improved **Senor Benny**, who won five races, the first a handicap off a mark of 60 and the last a listed race at Cork where he showed smart form. Besides the three-year-olds already noted, Jim Bolger's **Alexander Goldrun** was a model of consistency and gained just reward when winning the Prix de l'Opera and the Hong Kong Cup on her last two starts, while Oxx's **Hazarista** won the Blue Wind Stakes before finishing third in the Irish Oaks.

On the two-year-old front, **Ad Valorem** and **Oratorio** showed themselves to be amongst the best of their generation with their Group 1 successes. Ad Valorem gained his in the Middle Park Stakes, extending his unbeaten record to three, and seems sure to do well as a three-year-old. Oratorio had more racing than his stable companion and showed smart form to win the Prix Jean-Luc Lagardere at Longchamp and finish second in the Dewhurst Stakes. **Damson** won her first four starts, including the Queen Mary at Royal Ascot and the Phoenix Stakes at the Curragh, before running below form in the Cheveley Park. She deservedly remains prominent in the betting for the One Thousand Guineas though. Ten of the eleven juvenile pattern races in Ireland were won by the home team, including the last such contest of the year, the Killavullan Stakes at Leopardstown, which was won by **Footstepsinthesand**. O'Brien's colt recorded a good time when winning in fine style and he could well prove a very smart three-year-old. A few others to keep an eye out for are **Albert Hall** and **Merger**, first and second in the Beresford Stakes respectively; the National Stakes runner-up **Berenson**, who has left Tommy Stack and is now with Godolphin; and the Criterium de Saint-Cloud runner-up **Yehudi**. One exciting prospect in particular is the once-raced Leopardstown maiden winner **Tiger Dance**. A brother to Giant's Causeway, Tiger Dance looks open to considerable improvement.

Two-Year-Olds			
121p	Ad Valorem		
119	Oratorio		
114p	Berenson		
114p	Footstepsinthesand		
113p	Albert Hall		
113	Damson (f)		
112p	Merger		
112	Russian Blue		
109	Cougar Cat		
109	Dark Cheetah		
109	Democratic Deficit		
109	*Gaff		
108p	Jazz Princess (f)		
108p	Yehudi		
108	Indesatchel		
108	Mona Lisa (f)		
108	Scandinavia		
108	Silk And Scarlet (f)		
106	Slip Dance (f)		
104	Alexander Icequeen (f)		
104	Chelsea Rose (f)		
103p	Hills of Aran		
103	Kay Two		
103	L'Altro Mondo		
102p	Cherokee (f)		
102	Alayan		
102	Elusive Double		
102	Pictavia (f)		
101	Carnegie Hall		
100	*Fearless Flyer (f)		
100	Imperial Brief		
100	Lock And Key (f)		
99p	Allexina (f)		
99	Amsterdam		
99	Faint Heart (f)		
99	Saoire (f)		
98p	Almighty	111	Five Dynasties
98	Joyce	111	Moscow Ballet
98	*La Maitresse (f)	110	Fandango Dancer
98	Man O World	110	Medicinal
98	Rowan Tree	110	*Miss Mambo (f)
97p	Grand Central	110	Noah's Ark (f)
97p	Showdance	110	Red Feather (f)
96p	Forecourt	110	Simple Exchange
96	Crystal View (f)	109	Lord Admiral
96	Luas Line (f)	109	Trefflich
95P	Tiger Dance	108+	Cairdeas
95p	Adaala (f)	108	Esperanto
95p	Etijahaat	108	Meath
95	Virginia Waters (f)	107	Danelissima (f)
91	Clash of The Ash	107	*Grand Reward
		106	Baraka (f)
Three-Year-Olds		105	King Hesperus
128	Azamour	105	Misty Heights (f)
127	Grey Swallow	105	Moon Unit (f)
124	Acropolis	105	Orpington
123	One Cool Cat	105	Ulfah (f)
123	Tycoon	104	Barati
123§	Antonius Pius	104	Cobra
121	Alexander Goldrun (f)	104	Queen of Palms (f)
121	Mikado	103	Alexander Duchess (f)
118	Ace	103	Faasel
118	Go For Gold	103	Poetical (f)
117	Yeats	103	Tarakala (f)
115	Necklace (f)	102	Arch Rebel
115	Two Miles West	102	Bywayofthestars (f)
114	Book of Kings	102	Valentina Guest (f)
113	All Too Beautiful (f)	102?	Dangle (f)
113	Caradak	101	Amourallis (f)
113	Hazarista (f)	101	Inspector Powell
113	Troubadour	101	Mullins Bay
112	Hamairi	101	Wathab
112	Relaxed Gesture	101§	Newton

100	Dabiroun	113	Media Puzzle	102	Frosty Wind
100	Ocean Bounty	113	Windermere	102	Major Title
100	Palace Star (f)	112	Abunawwas	102	Mombassa
99	Balyan	112	Mkuzi	102	Sheer Tenby
99	I Like The Theatre	112	Solskjaer	101+	Excalibur
99	Kisses For Me (f)	111	Cruzspiel	101	Dashing Home
98	Amarula Ridge	111	Desert Fantasy	101	Jacks Estate
98	King Jock	111	Yesterday (f)	101	Pantarez
98	Royal Tigress (f)	111§	One More Round	101	Prize Time
98	Zarafsha (f)	110	Senor Benny	101	Royal Devotion (f)
97	Cupids Ray	109	Latino Magic	100	Blue Dream (f)
97	Desert Gold (f)	109	Mutakarrim	100	Twiggy's Sister (f)
97	Lamberto	109	My Renee (f)	99	Christavelli
97	Leonor Fini (f)	109	Tolpuddle	99	Danecare
97	Starrystarrynight (f)	109§	Holy Orders	99	Fit The Cove
97	Takrice (f)	108	Glocca Morra	99	Miss Trish (f)
97d	Miss Childrey (f)	108	Maharib	99	Senators Alibi
96	Empirical Power	108	Napper Tandy	99	Shersha (f)
96	Jemmy's Brother	108	Power Elite	98	Antrim Coast
96	Liss Ard	108	Tipperary All Star	98	Dawn Invasion
95	Favourite Nation	107	Eklim	98	High Priestess (f)
95	Little Whisper (f)	107	Hanabad	98	King Carew
95	Lucky (f)	106	Revenue	97	*Chappel Cresent
95	Rich Sense (f)	106d	Blue Reema (f)	97	Cloone River
95	Sand N Sea (f)	105	Jade Quest	97	Handel
95	Treasure The Lady (f)	104	Cache Creek (f)	97d	Imoya (f)
		104	Icklingham	96+	Al Eile
92	Megec Blis (f)	104	Ivowen (f)	96	Anna Frid (f)
		104	Peace Offering (f)	96	Edaliya (f)
		104	Pepperwood	96	Emmas Princess (f)
Older Horses		104	Tacitus	96	Former Senator
128	Vinnie Roe	104§	One Won One	96	High Country
124	Powerscourt	104d	Livadiya (f)	96	Solerina (f)
120	Brian Boru	104d	Tiger Royal	95	Desert Hill
120	Osterhase	103	Akshar	95	Sissy Slew (f)
117	Evolving Tactics	103	Fearn Royal (f)	95	Tender Cove
114	Mingun	103	Mr Houdini	95	Theme Song
114	Tropical Lady (f)	103	Multazem		
113	D'Anjou	103	Queen Astrid (f)		

FRANCE   For the second year running, the top French two-year-old from the previous season trained on into a top-class middle-distance performer, with **Bago** succeeding Dalakhani on the list of Prix de l'Arc de Triomphe winners. Despite making a delayed return, Bago carried on where he had left off at two with a couple more Group 1 wins in the Prix Jean Prat and Grand Prix de Paris. However, with his unbeaten record lost in the Juddmonte International and the Prix Niel—he finished third in both races—there were other three-year-olds ahead of him in the betting by the time of the Arc. The Arc runner-up **Cherry Mix**, who subsequently joined Godolphin, was a much later developer altogether. Placed in a couple of Prix du Jockey Club trials in the spring, it was not until the end of August that he burst onto the scene with a convincing defeat of older horses on heavy ground in the Grand Prix de Deauville. He showed he could handle very different conditions in the Arc which was run on unseasonably firmish ground. The surprise favourite for the Arc was **Prospect Park** who had run consistently all year but was tightly matched with other rivals after narrow defeats in both the Prix du Jockey Club and Prix Niel. At Chantilly he was headed in the last strides by outsider **Blue Canari**, with **Valixir** a close third, while in the Niel it was Valixir who came out on top ahead of Prospect Park, with Bago third, the Prix Hocquart winner **Lord du Sud** fourth and Blue Canari only fifth. Prospect Park, Valixir and Blue Canari all finished well down the field in the Arc, providing further evidence that the Chantilly form was only ordinary. The Prix du Jockey Club was notable for the absence of both colts who had dominated the main trial. **Voix du Nord** got the better of a tight finish with **Millemix** for the Prix Lupin, but Millemix was put down after breaking a leg a few weeks later and Voix du Nord sustained a leg injury on the eve of the Jockey Club. That proved to be the final running of the Prix Lupin after controversial plans to reform the three-year-old colts' programme were announced in the autumn; these are discussed in the essay on Blue Canari. **Reefscape** was seventh in the Prix du Jockey Club but proved himself the top three-year-old stayer in the autumn with a defeat of Lord du Sud (a place ahead of him at Chantilly) in the Prix Chaudenay at the Arc meeting.

Like Bago, both **Whipper** and **American Post** trained on well after already showing plenty of ability at two. Whipper ran his best races at Deauville in August, winning the Prix Jacques le Marois just a week after finishing second in the Prix Maurice de Gheest. An impressive reappearance in the Prix Djebel saw Whipper take his chance in the Two Thousand Guineas, in which he finished a creditable fifth. In Whipper's absence for the French equivalent, American Post won the Poule d'Essai des Poulains before failing to stay in the Derby, but he has to go down as one of the luckiest winners of a classic after Irish colt Antonius Pius had swerved away what would have been a certain win. The same race initiated a frustrating run of second places for another leading two-year-old from the year before, **Diamond Green**. He ran well when runner-up in the St James's Palace Stakes and Prix du Moulin but, like Whipper, finished down the field in the Breeders' Cup Mile. Diamond Green, as well as the aforementioned Cherry Mix and Valixir, gave the Lagardere family a strong hand of three-year-old colts. The future of the late Jean-Luc Lagardere's extensive bloodstock empire was in doubt for much of the year, with the Aga Khan reported to be a potential buyer. **Cacique** came off the worse in three meetings with Bago, notably when runner-up in the Prix Jean Prat and Grand Prix de Paris, but he also won the Prix Daphnis and Prix Daniel Wildenstein and looks a good four-year-old prospect.

Torrestrella improved rapidly in the spring, winning the Poule d'Essai des Pouliches, but proved disappointing subsequently and ended the year in the USA. Second in the Pouliches was **Grey Lilas**, who maintained her form all year, finishing third in the Prix de Diane and second in the Prix de l'Opera. She ran her best race when returned to a mile to win the Prix du Moulin in her only race so far against the colts. The Prix de Diane, which drew the largest field for twenty-one years, proved the highlight of **Latice**'s season with a defeat of the lightly-raced **Millionaia**, who was not seen out again. Latice lost her unbeaten record in the Prix Vermeille but ran creditably in the Arc when tried again at a mile and a half, finishing seventh. **Lune d'Or** enjoyed a good season in middle-distance fillies' races, winning the Prix de Malleret, Prix de Pomone and Premio Lydia Tesio at Rome. Jean-Claude Rouget's stable housed a couple of smart middle-distance fillies who between them won eleven races. **Silverskaya** won the Prix de Royaumont and Prix Minerve, though sixth place in the Vermeille and eighth in the Arc were at least as good performances form-wise. Stable-companion **Eleusis** was beaten only once in seven starts and can progress again at four after ending the season with a win across the Atlantic in the Grade 2 Long Island Handicap at Aqueduct. Back over shorter trips, the previous year's Marcel Boussac winner **Denebola** took longer to find her form but eventually did so at Longchamp in the autumn, finishing fourth in the Moulin and second in the Prix de la Foret.

The older horses who remained in training lacked a high-class performer among them, and only three of their number managed a Group 1 success in Europe. Top stayer **Westerner** dominated the long-distance races again, winning both the Prix du Cadran (from **Cut Quartz** and **Le Carre**) and the Prix Royal-Oak for the second year running, in the latter race beating the filly **Behkara** who was also placed in the race for the second time. **Forestier** inflicted a rare defeat on Westerner when getting weight in the Prix Vicomtesse Vigier but was not seen out again after following up in the Prix Maurice de Nieuil in the summer. Westerner was second in the Gold Cup, and is to be aimed at the race again, but stable-companion **Risk Seeker** had gone one better at Ascot earlier in the year with a wide-margin success in testing ground in the Sagaro Stakes.

Policy Maker represented the same Lellouche/Wildenstein stable in good company over a mile and a half, winning the Grand Prix de Chantilly and the Prix Foy, and running well in defeat when second in the Grand Prix de Saint-Cloud and fourth in the Japan Cup. After finishing second to **Vangelis** in the Prix d'Harcourt, **Execute** landed the Prix Ganay at the third attempt after twice finishing runner-up. Former Ganay winner **Fair Mix** had to settle for third place this time, but took La Coupe de Maisons-Laffitte for a second time later in the season, ahead of **Marshall**. Fair Mix's campaign had begun successfully in Dubai, where **Polish Summer**'s victory in the Dubai Sheema Classic signalled a bright start to the association between Andre Fabre and American jockey Gary Stevens, though it was a partnership which was to end prematurely in August. **Touch of Land** improved to be another of the leading older horses in France by the end of the year, with a Group 2 win at Baden-Baden and another in the Prix Dollar at Longchamp, before a good third in the Hong Kong Cup.

France can usually boast some good older milers, though in the latest season it was the three-year-olds who tended to dominate at that trip. Nevertheless, the genuine **My Risk** fared best of the older milers, winning the Prix Edmond Blanc and Prix du Chemin de Fer du Nord and finishing third in the Jacques le Marois. Former Lockinge winner **Keltos** returned from an unsuccessful spell at stud to be placed several times in pattern company, including in the Challenge Stakes at Newmarket and the Prix Perth at Saint-Cloud, the latter race won by **Valentino**.

Three leading fillies from the previous season remained in training as four-year-olds, but surprisingly **Six Perfections**, **Nebraska Tornado** and **Vallee Enchantee** failed to muster another win between them all year. Six Perfections ran her best races when placed in races she had won the year before, the Prix Jacques le Marois and the Breeders' Cup Mile, while the pick of Nebraska Tornado's efforts came on her two starts in Britain, making the frame in the Queen Anne and Sun Chariot Stakes. Unlike that pair, Vallee Enchantee did manage to improve from three to four and she too ran well in Britain, finishing an unlucky third in the Coronation Cup (a result that led to a split between owner Alec Wildenstein and rider Dominique Boeuf) before a fifth place in the King George at Ascot, a sixth in the Arc, and a third when seeking a repeat win in the Hong Kong Vase. The expanded programme of pattern races for older fillies enabled other names to come to the fore. The opening of the Prix Vermeille to four-year-olds for the first time saw success for the ex-Italian filly **Sweet Stream**, while the formerly British-trained **Pride** took third in the same race. Pride ran well all year, winning the new Prix Allez France at Chantilly in May as well as the Prix du Conseil de Paris in clear-cut fashion against the colts in the autumn. She was also second to **Whortleberry** in another new fillies' race, the Prix Jean Romanet at Deauville. **Bright Sky** made a brief return as a five-year-old before retiring to stud, her better effort coming when a close second to Polish Summer in the Prix Exbury as a prep for Dubai.

Before leaving the older horses, a brief mention of the sprinters who generally struggled against British-trained opposition all year. **Star Valley**, who had raced at further previously, put up the best effort by a French-trained horse in a sprint when beating **Swedish Shave** in testing conditions in the Prix de Meautry at Deauville. The mare **Porlezza** had beaten the same runner-up in a listed race before finishing second to the British-trained Avonbridge when attempting a hat-trick of wins in the Prix du Gros-Chene at Chantilly. The weakness of the French sprinting division was exemplified when **Ratio** was their sole representative in the country's top sprint, the Prix de l'Abbaye. The John Hammond-trained gelding finished down the field, but earlier in the year stable-companion **Crystal Castle** nearly struck a blow for the French sprinters when a close second in the Golden Jubilee Stakes at Royal Ascot.

Unbeaten filly **Divine Proportions** was the top French two-year-old, and her final win in the Prix Marcel Boussac was a third consecutive win in the race for trainer Pascal Bary and owner-breeders the Niarchos family after Six Perfections and Denebola. Divine Proportions also had the speed to win over sprint trips earlier in the year, taking the Prix du Bois, Prix Robert Papin and Prix Morny, emulating her close relative Whipper in the last-named contest. The Prix de Cabourg winner **Layman** was a good second in the Morny and confirmed himself one of the best colts of his age in France when coming off the worst in a tight finish with the Irish colt Oratorio and the Prix La Rochette winner **Early March** in the Prix Jean-Luc Lagardere. Early March was a short price to make amends in the Criterium International but disappointed behind **Helios Quercus**, who kept improving all season for his small stable after making his debut in March. His five wins included a defeat of **Musketier** and **Vatori** in the Prix des Chenes. Musketier, who went on to win the Prix de Conde, was another who failed to meet expectations on his final start, finishing only fifth in the Criterium de Saint-Cloud, which went to the German filly Paita. Vatori later edged out his stable-companion **Guillaume Tell** in the Prix Thomas Bryon. The other colt to show smart form was the Criterium International third **Walk In The Park** who represented the same connections, John Hammond and Michael Tabor, as his sire Montjeu. Robert Collet sent out the winner of the Criterium de Maisons-Laffitte for the second year running when **Centifolia** followed on from Whipper twelve months earlier. Beaten only once in five starts, and with her wins gained by an aggregate of sixteen lengths, Centifolia gives the impression that she will continue to prove best over sprint trips. A filly who looks a good prospect for longer distances, and a potential Prix de Diane type, is the Marcel Boussac third **Fraloga**, while as well as Layman, Godolphin acquired a couple of potentially smart fillies in Prix d'Aumale winner **Birthstone** (transferred from Alex Pantall) and **Last Rhapsody** who won a newcomers race at Longchamp in impressive fashion for Eric Libaud.

Two-Year-Olds

119	Divine Proportions (f)
118	Early March
118	Helios Quercus
117	Layman
114	Musketier
114	Walk In The Park
112	Centifolia (f)
110	Guillaume Tell
110	Vatori
109p	Birthstone (f)
108p	Last Rhapsody (f)
108	Campo Bueno
108	Salut Thomas
107p	Fraloga (f)
107p	Ozone Bere (f)
107p	Private Banking
107	Stop Making Sense
106	Laverock
106	Osidy
106	Stella Blue (f)
106	Toupie (f)
105p	Kendor Dine
105	Crossover (f)
105	Great Blood (f)
105	Green Girl (f)
105	*Louvain (f)
105	Portrayal (f)
105	Starpix
105	Witten (f)
104	Ysoldina (f)
103p	Silent Name
103	Birthplace (f)
103	Gorella (f)
103	Grand Bahama
103	Long Range
103	Medigating
103	Nipping (f)
103	*Royal Copenhagen (f)
102p	Zenon
102	Ascot Dream (f)
102	Doctor Dino
102	Eligibilis
102	Inhabitant
101p	King Kasyapa
101	Azay Le Rideau
101	Corsario
101	*Madame Topflight (f)
101	Michelucci
101	Mirabilis (f)
100p	Sablonne (f)
100	Arabian Spell (f)
100	Nanabanana (f)

Three-Year-Olds

130	Bago
129	Cherry Mix
125	Whipper
121	American Post
121	Diamond Green
121	Latice (f)
120	Grey Lilas (f)
119p	Cacique
119	Denebola (f)
119	Millemix
119	Millionaia (f)
119	Voix du Nord
118	Blue Canari
118	*Fast And Furious
118	Prospect Park
118	Valixir
117	*Torrestrella (f)
116	Dolma (f)
116	Lord du Sud
116	Lune d'Or (f)
116	Reefscape
116	Silverskaya (f)
115	*Blackdoun
115	Diamond Tango (f)
115	Mister Sacha
115	Onda Nova (f)
115?	Ershaad
114p	Eleusis (f)
114	*Agata (f)
114	Australie (f)
114	*Barancella (f)
114	Darkara (f)
114	Delfos
113	Chineur
113	Geordieland
113	Levitski
113	Night Chapter
113	Reverie Solitaire (f)
112	Art Master
112	Baqah (f)
112	Dream Play (f)
112	Love And Bubbles (f)
112	Svedov
111	Ange Gardien
111	Buoyant (f)
111	Etendard Indien
111	Ometsz (f)
111	Tiganello
111	*Tunduru
110	Artiste Royal
110	Ask For The Moon (f)
110	Dalna (f)
110	Islero Noir
110	*Martha Stewart (f)

110	Miss France (f)
110	*Miss Mambo (f)
110	Mister Farmer
110	Red Tune
110	Simplex
110?	*Top of The Bill
109p	Fracassant
109	Apsis
109	Asti (f)
109	Cattiva Generosa (f)
109	Coupe de Champe (f)
109	Ecole d'Art
109	Linda Regina (f)
109	Lord Darnley
108	Charmo
108	Day Or Night
108	Ostankino
108	Petit Calva (f)
108	Poly Dance
107	Advice
107	Colony Band (f)
107	Flip Flop (f)
107	Lougo
107	Miss Me (f)
107	Sunday Doubt
107	Via Milano (f)
107	Visanilla (f)
107	Young Tiger
107?	Alnitak
107?	Marnhac
107?	Ursis
106	Anabaa Republic (f)
106	*Belle Ange (f)
106	Cloon (f)
106	Dreams Come True (f)
106	High Flash
106	Kurm
106	Mardouk
106	Secret Melody (f)
106	Steel Princess (f)
106	Vassilievsky
105	A Little Dream
105	Amie de Mix (f)
105	Bright Abundance (f)
105	Confluence
105	*Green Swallow (f)
105	Hamriya
105	Highland Dancer
105	*King of Cry
105	Malevitch
105	Popee (f)
105	Squad
105	Staramix
104	Double Green (f)
104	*Joursanvault

1177

104 Polyfirst (f)
104 Super Lina (f)
104 Trinity Joy (f)
103 Kalatuna (f)
98 Roseanna (f)

Older Horses
123 Westerner
122 Touch of Land
121 Execute
121 Fair Mix
120 Polish Summer
120 Six Perfections (f)
120 Vallee Enchantee (f)
119 My Risk
119 Nebraska Tornado (f)
119 Policy Maker
119 Star Valley
119 *Vangelis
118 Keltos
118 *King's Drama
118 Whortleberry (f)
118? Risk Seeker
117 Bright Sky (f)
117 Cut Quartz
117 Forestier
117 Marshall
117 Porlezza (f)
117 Pride (f)
117 Sweet Stream (f)
117 Valentino
116 Aubonne (f)

116 Behkara (f)
116 *Crystal Castle
116 Le Carre
116 Look Honey
116 Russian Hill (f)
116 Samando (f)
116 Short Pause
116 Special Kaldoun
116? Charming Groom
115 Art Moderne
115 *Bailador
115 Kalabar
115 Martaline
114 Actrice (f)
114 Demon Dancer
114 Ratio
114 Swedish Shave
114 Visorama (f)
114 Walkamia (f)
113 *Puppeteer
113 Sarrasin
112+ Sarre (f)
112 Dano-Mast
112 Saratan
112 *Vasywait
112 *Without Connexion
112? Miss Emma (f)
111 Clear Thinking
111 Dexterity
111 *El Hurano
111 Kindjhal
111 Maxwell
111 Sasanuma (f)
110 Clety

110 Idaho Quest
110 Morning Eclipse
110 Pont d'Or
109 Almond Mousse (f)
109 Billy The Kid
109 Coroner
109 Krataios
109 Maredsous (f)
109 Prends Ton Temps
109? Streamix
108 Affirmative Action
108 Bouthan
108 Shakis
108 Top World
108? Comete (f)
107 Caesarion
107 Maia Eria (f)
107 Weightless
106 Allez Olive
106 Blanche (f)
106 Fomalhaut
106 Frosted Aclaim
106 Petite Speciale (f)
105 Amathia (f)
105 Dobby Road
105 Farazdaq
105 Millenium Mambo
105 Mocham Glen
105 Smala Tica (f)
105 Superman

104 Special Delivery (f)

GERMANY   The increasing success of German-trained horses beyond their own borders is showing no signs of slowing down. According to figures published in *Sport-Welt*, in 1997 German horses made 214 starts abroad and earned the equivalent of just over €2 million. Their number of foreign starts has increased every year since then, and by the end of 2004 new records had been set, with 1,479 starts abroad notched up and over €8 million earned in win and place money, flat and jumps combined. Italy remains the main foreign target for German trainers, and no less than seven of Italy's thirteen pattern races in the autumn were won by German stables, including the Gran Premio del Jockey Club, the Premio Roma and the Gran Criterium, all Group 1 events. France is becoming an increasingly attractive—or less daunting—destination as well, and German-trained runners in Britain are no longer that much of a rarity. German success abroad is by no means confined to her European neighbours. Both **Paolini**, who dead-heated in the Dubai Duty Free, and **Epalo**, who won the Singapore Airlines International Cup, brought back huge prizes from much further afield. Epalo's foreign campaign also clinched him the World Series championship at the end of the year. Neither of those horses contested any of Germany's top races in 2004 (the now-retired Paolini had not raced at home since 2001), and with some of their best horses being lured away by more valuable contests abroad, Germany's Group 1 events are potentially left more vulnerable to being won by foreign stables. That seemed to be the case in the latest season when the British-trained pair Warrsan and Albanova between them took four of Germany's five Group 1 events open to older horses, the Sir Mark Prescott-trained mare completing a hat-trick in the Deutschlandpreis at Dusseldorf and the Rheinland-Pokal and Preis von Europa at Cologne.

Once again, it was the Derby winner who was Germany's best horse. **Shirocco**, who was trainer Andreas Schutz's fifth winner of the race in the last seven runnings, ran out a really authoritative winner from the two colts who had inflicted a surprise defeat on him at Cologne in one of the main trials, **Malinas** and **Omikron**. Shirocco had the same colts behind him when a close third to Warrsan and the Deutsches Derby also-ran **Egerton** (who is, remarkably, still a maiden) in the Grosser Preis von Baden. By now a leading contender for the Arc, Shirocco was taken out of the race at a late stage because of the firm conditions and ended his season instead with a win in the Gran Premio del Jockey Club at Milan. He looks sure to do well again as a four-year-old when the Arc will be a likely target again, ground permitting. **Intendant** was the other leading three-year-old colt, though he gave little indication of that when trailing home in the Deutsches Derby. But dropped to a mile and a quarter on much firmer ground he put up a very smart effort to beat Powerscourt and Imperial Dancer in the Grosser Dallmayr-Preis at Munich. He was being prepared for the Champion Stakes but was not seen out again after requiring an operation for a bone chip, though he too remains in training in 2005. **Dayano** was another who failed to give his running in the mud at Hamburg but showed smart form otherwise, including when runner-up in the Derby Italiano and in the Deutschlandpreis behind Albanova.

Neither winner of Germany's fillies' classics, Henkel-Rennen (Guineas) winner **Shapira** and Preis der Diana (Oaks) winner **Amarette**, had the opportunity to prove themselves any better than useful after just three starts apiece, the latter retiring to stud unbeaten. **La Ina** finished runner-up in both those races, but it was **Saldentigerin** and **Vallera**, third and seventh respectively in the Preis der Diana who went on to show the best form among the three-year-old fillies, Saldentigerin when second in the Preis von Europa and Vallera when fourth in the Prix Vermeille. Epalo's half-sister **Elopa** looks a particularly promising type for older fillies' events in 2005 after a couple of smart performances at Saint-Cloud late in the year.

The exploits of two of the leading older horses, Paolini and Epalo, have already been touched upon. Epalo went on to pick up place money in the USA in both the Arlington Million (in which he was promoted to third) and Man o'War Stakes, starting favourite or joint-favourite for both races. His promotion in the Arlington Million turned out to be crucial in making him World Series champion. Paolini's stable-companion **Simonas** also earned good place money across the Atlantic when second to Sulamani in the Canadian International. Simonas had earlier won a weak Group 2 event at Rome and finished a good fourth in the Grosser Preis von Baden. **Senex** was an improved four-year-old and saved his best efforts for his travels abroad, winning the Gran Premio di Milano as well

pferdewetten.de Deutsches-Stuten Derby—Preis Der Diana, Hamburg—a new venue for the German Oaks, formerly run at Mulheim; Amarette (centre) wins from La Ina (left), with the favourite Saldentigerin a close third

*Grosser Dallmayr-Preis (Bayerisches Zuchtrennen), Munich—
locally-trained Intendant moves past front-running Powerscourt (blaze);
Imperial Dancer (left) and Scott's View (star on cap) take third and fourth*

as the Bosphorus Cup in Turkey. Peter Schiergen had his string in excellent form in the autumn, and after completing a domestic hat-trick in pattern races in the Euro-Cup at Frankfurt, **Soldier Hollow** (later elected as Germany's Horse of the Year) made it a four-timer by winning the Premio Roma. Two of the best efforts by older middle-distance performers on home turf came from **Rotteck** and Shirocco's elder brother **Storm Trooper** who fought out a tight finish to the Hansa-Preis at Hamburg in June. The previous year's Deutsches St Leger winner **Royal Fantasy** failed to add any further successes in the latest season but proved the best older filly with second places in France in the Prix Maurice de Nieuil and the Prix Vermeille.

Martillo's position as Germany's best miler looked safe in the first half of the season after wins in the Prix du Muguet at Saint-Cloud and the Berlin Brandenburg-Trophy, the latter for a second year. By the autumn, he had a serious rival in the form of improved four-year-old **Eagle Rise**, who won the Europa-Meile at Cologne before beating Martillo a short neck in the Premio Ribot at Rome. Seven-year-old **Peppercorn** was as good as ever when winning a Group 3 event at Dusseldorf in October for a third time, and both **Ryono** (another winner in France, taking the Prix Messidor at Deauville) and **Tiberius Caesar**, a wide-margin winner of a Group 3 contest at Bremen in October, also had some of the best form at a mile. Peppercorn's brother **Pepperstorm** was the best three-year-old at the trip. He beat Eagle Rise in the Globetrotter-Meile at Cologne and followed up in the Oettingen-Rennen at Baden-Baden before joining Godolphin. Three of Germany's leading sprinters dominated the country's most valuable sprint, the Goldene Peitsche at Baden-Baden, in which three-year-old **Raffelberger** got the better of his stable-companion **Key To Pleasure** and the Benazet-Rennen and Holsten-Trophy winner **Lucky Strike**. Raffelberger went on to win the Premio Omenoni at Milan over five furlongs, while Key To Pleasure was also second to **Areias** in the seven-furlong Baden Sprint-Cup at Baden-Baden's new October meeting.

German two-year-old racing has traditionally been a low-key affair, but there were some interesting performances from that age-group in the latest season, both at home and abroad. Chief among them was **Manduro**'s five-length victory over **Kahn** in the top colts' race, the Preis des Winterfavoriten, the best performance by a German-trained two-year-old for many a year. By Monsun, he looks a first-rate Deutsches Derby prospect. The Peter Schiergen stable had plenty of strength in depth, and on the same day as Manduro's win, two more of its youngsters, **Konigstiger** and **Idealist**, took the first two places in Italy's top two-year-old contest, the Gran Criterium. Germany's top two-year-old fillies' race, the Preis der Winterkonigin, also had a clear-cut winner in the form of **Sorrent**, another product of Monsun, and like Manduro, unbeaten in two starts. The Mario Hofer-trained **Paita** gained a rare Group 1 success for a German two-year-old filly when landing the Criterium de Saint-Cloud, while another good effort in France came from her stable-companion **Soignee** who was second in the Prix des Reservoirs at Deauville.

Two-Year-Olds

115p	Manduro
108p	Paita (f)
107p	Konigstiger
107p	Sorrent (f)
106p	Idealist
104	Soignee (f)
103	Kahn
102p	Auenweise (f)
101	Daring Love (f)
100	Bernard
100	Omasheriff
98	Beirut (f)
98	Gonbarda (f)
98	Nouvelle Noblesse (f)
97	Kahlua (f)
96p	Maya Enterprise
96	Lord Areion
96	Mandahush (f)
95p	Furstenberg
95	Early Wings
95	Fullmix

Three-Year-Olds

125	Shirocco
124	Egerton
120	Intendant
116	Dayano
116	Malinas
116	Omikron
116	Pepperstorm
115	Raffelberger
115	Saldentigerin (f)
115	Vallera (f)
113p	Elopa (f)
113	Salonhonor
112	Fight Club
111	Felicity (Ger) (f)
111	Give Me Five (f)
110	Assiun
110	El Tiger
110	Glad Lion
109	Apeiron
109	Lazio
109	Lyonels Glory
109	Quilanga (f)
109?	Mohandas
108	Tocopilla (f)

107	Amarette (f)
107	Daytona (f)
107	Near Dock
107	Shapira (f)
106	Aviane (f)
106	Champion's Day
106	Fulminant
106	La Ina (f)
106	Mamela (f)
106	Sweet Wake
105	At Once (f)
105	Genios
105	Starla (f)

104	Arc Bleu
104	Gentle Tiger
104	Kitcat (f)
104	Mensatiger
103	Fiepes Winged
103	Nightdance Forest (f)
103	Tarlac
102	Delsun
101	Siberion
101	Sword Roche (f)

Older Horses

122	Epalo
121	Senex
121	Simonas
119	Eagle Rise
119	Martillo
119	Soldier Hollow
118	Paolini
116	Rotteck
116	Royal Fantasy (f)
116	Ryono
116	Storm Trooper
116	Tiberius Caesar
115	Areias
115	Lucky Strike
115	Olaso
115	Peppercorn
114	Key To Pleasure
114	Well Made
113	Aolus
113	Bailamos
113	Flambo
112	Bear King

112	Fiepes Shuffle
112	Horeion Directa
111	*Anolitas
111	Sambaprinz
111	Winning Dash
110	Near Honor
110	Sacho
110?	Bodyguard of Spain
109	Anna Victoria (f)
109	Liquido
109	Madresal
109	Soterio
108	Deva (f)
108	Glad To Be Fast
108	Le Royal
108	Lindholm
108	Longridge
108	Tempelwachter
108	Toylsome
107	Fruhtau
107	Mity Dancer (f)
107	Serenus
107	Soave
107	Syrakus
107§	King of Boxmeer
106	Delightful Sofie (f)
106	Diable
106	El Dessert
106	Furioso Directa
106	Kastoria (f)
106	Minley
106	Next Gina (f)
106	Pappus
106	Salon Turtle
106	So Royal (f)
106	Up And Away
106	Western Devil
105	Cheirokratie
105	Gold Type
105	Grantley
105	Kastalia (f)
105	Kasus
105	Morbidezza (f)
105	Peppershot
105	Rajpute

103	Arlecchina (f)
102	Golden Rose (f)
100	One Little David

ITALY   The competitiveness of Italian racing at the top level has been weakened in recent seasons by the loss of several of their best horses to British stables. By the start of 2004, Italy's top three older horses from the year before, Sunstrach, Maktub and Salselon, had all departed, though the last-named has been returned to his former stable for 2005. They were joined in Britain halfway through the year by the previous season's top Italian three-year-old **Le Vie dei Colori**. That left a depleted stock of older horses for the top contests, and **Altieri** and **Prince Kirk**, both sons of Selkirk, stood out among those who remained, both winning Group 1 races. Altieri returned in good heart to win his first three starts, notably the Premio Presidente della Repubblica, though he then injured himself in the Gran Premio di Milano and was well beaten after an absence in the autumn. Prince

Premio Presidente della Repubblica SIS, Rome—
six-year-old Altieri wins this Group 1 race at the third attempt;
runner-up Vespone (rail) is the only foreign raider while fourth-placed Le Vie dei Colori (second right)
has his last run for an Italian stable

Kirk, who had finished second in the Prix Jean Prat in 2003, ran an even better race in France to win the Prix d'Ispahan at Longchamp in May, but unfortunately was not seen out again.

The filly **Marbye** also enjoyed Group 1 success in France when winning the Prix d'Astarte at Deauville after a Group 2 win at home in the Premio Emilio Turati. Another Italian horse to do well abroad was **Caluki** who took the European All-Weather Series, winning two legs of the five-race competition, notably the Winter Derby at Lingfield. Of the other smart older horses over a mile or more, **Nonno Carlo** finished third in the Presidente della Repubblica and fourth in the Premio Roma, **Scabiun** won a listed race at Milan before finishing fourth in the Premio Vittorio di Capua, and both **Duca d'Atri** and **Giovane Imperatore** finished a good second to Le Vie dei Colori in races at Rome in the spring, the latter when trying to give him 10 lb.

Italy's top sprinter was the six-year-old **St Paul House** who won five times at Rome, notably the Premio Tudini (from **Krisman**) in May and the Premio Umbria in November. The latter race, incidentally, was one of just two of Italy's thirteen pattern races in the autumn which did not go abroad, the majority of the remainder going to German stables.

Derby Italiano, Rome—the grey Groom Tesse becomes only the second Italian-trained winner
in sixteen years; German-trained Dayano comes second with John Gosden-trained
Privy Seal (star on cap) doing best of the British

Krisman ran his best races over five furlongs at Milan, winning a listed race in May and finishing second in the Premio Omenoni in the autumn. The other sprinter of note was **T E Lawrence** who won the Premio Citta di Napoli.

The top two-year-old of 2003, **Spirit of Desert**, trained on well to take an otherwise weak-looking Premio Parioli (2000 Guineas). Unfortunately, a hairline fracture sustained there caused him to miss the rest of the year. **Groom Tesse** briefly took over as the leading three-year-old when becoming only the second colt since 1988 (Rakti was the other) to keep the Derby Italiano at home, though he too was on the sidelines after finishing last in the Gran Premio di Milano next time out. But the best three-year-old, and by far Italy's main hope for big-race success in 2005, did not emerge until the autumn when **Electrocutionist** put up a high-class effort in going down narrowly to the German Derby winner Shirocco in the Gran Premio del Jockey Club, his first defeat after three wins at Milan. The best three-year-old fillies filled the first two places in the Premio Regina Elena (1000 Guineas). **Rumba Loca** gained a clear-cut win over **Super Bobbina** in that race, but it was the runner-up who fared the better of the pair later in the year, winning a listed race at Rome before finishing a good third against foreign rivals in the Premio Lydia Tesio, a race whose Group 1 status was restored in 2004.

The latest crop of Italian two-year-olds lacked any particularly promising types. **Becrux** started favourite for the Gran Criterium but finished well held, losing his unbeaten record in the process; he joined Mike de Kock to race in Dubai early in 2005. **Shifting Place** put up the best effort by an Italian youngster when second to Divine Proportions in the Prix Robert Papin, though that was well in advance of the rest of her form. She was awarded the Premio Primi Passi, and Italy's other juvenile pattern winner, **Le Giare**, was likewise given the Premio Guido Berardelli in the stewards' room.

Two-Year-Olds					
108?	Shifting Place (f)	108	Kaypen	112	Scabiun
101	Becrux	108	Rumba Loca (f)	111	Arrears
98p	Scartozz	108?	Sa Fem Zifulum	111	Giovane Imperatore
97	Le Giare	106	Cocktail (f)	111	Krisman
96	Chapel Tale	105	Ceprin	111	T E Lawrence
96	Kykuit (f)	105	Distant Way	110	Blu For Life
95	Golden Stravinsky	105	Step Danzer (f)	109	Caluki
		104	Bravo Tazio	108	Big Luciano
94	Tedo	101	Loriana (f)	108	*Landinium (f)
92	Gold Marie (f)	96	Dorr (f)	108	Regina Saura (f)
92	Tenderlit (f)			107	*Miss Nashwan (f)
		Older Horses		107	She Breeze (f)
Three-Year-Olds		122	Altieri	106	Darrel
125	Electrocutionist	122	Prince Kirk	106	Honey Bunny
117	Groom Tesse	121	*Le Vie dei Colori	106	Vale Mantovani (f)
112	*Whilly	115	St Paul House	106	*Windy Britain (f)
111	Spirit of Desert	114	Marbye (f)	105	Dasami
111	Super Bobbina (f)	114	Nonno Carlo	105	Sayuri (f)
109	Stoxx (f)	112	Duca d'Atri	105	Sunsu Desura

SCANDINAVIA   The 2004 season in Scandinavia was one of transition. As we pointed out here last year, many of the horses who dominated the top middle-distance races in recent years were getting long in the tooth, and in the latest season they were either no longer around or on the downgrade. It was no coincidence therefore that British-trained horses took the first two places in both of Scandinavia's mile and a half Group 3 contests, Crocodile Dundee beating Maktub in the Scandinavian Open Championship at Copenhagen and Collier Hill getting the better of Foreign Affairs in the Stockholm Cup at Taby. It was the first time since 1997 (when Harbour Dues won both races) that a British-trained horse had won either contest.

Scandinavia's best horse in both 2002 and 2003, Dano-Mast, was one of those who was no longer as good as he once was (and nor was he trained in Scandinavia any longer, his trainer Flemming Poulsen having moved from Denmark to France), though he was still capable of smart form (rated 112) and finished fourth in the Scandinavian Open. Fifth and sixth in the race were **The Khamsin** and **Alpino Chileno**, neither of whom were discredited in the face of stiff tasks when contesting the Cumberland Lodge Stakes at

Ascot. Alpino Chileno also finished fourth in the Marit Sveaas Minnelop (another Group 3 event) over nine furlongs and the Stockholm Cup. The Marit Sveaas Minnelop winner was **Mandrake El Mago** who had looked the type to enjoy a good season in 2004. As well as beating the versatile **Hovman** and the ex-British horse **Binary File** in the Marit Sveaas, he also defeated Binary File in a listed race at Taby, won a valuable and well-contested conditions event at Ovrevoll, and finished third in the Stockholm Cup for the second year running. Hovman has run well at a variety of trips, and as well as second place in the Marit Sveaas, he was also runner-up in the Polar Cup over an extended six furlongs after winning the listed Swedish Open Mile from **Magic Fact** and **Ecology**. **Royal Experiment** gave plenty of weight to most of the field when beating Binary File in a listed race at Copenhagen early in the year but failed to repeat the form. Another Norwegian horse, dirt specialist **Nicki Hill**, won a similar event at Taby for the second time in three years.

Musadif's defeat of Hovman in the Group 3 Polar Cup entitled him to be considered the top sprinter. **Steve's Champ** came off the worse in most clashes with Musadif but had that rival back in third when winning Scandinavia's other Group 3 sprint, the Taby Open Sprint Championship, before running well to finish second in a listed race at Newmarket. **Waquaas** was not quite as good as he once was but was thereabouts in the top sprints again, finishing fourth in the Polar Cup and second in the Taby Open Sprint; he also had Musadif and Steve's Champ behind him when winning a listed race at Taby in June. The Polar Cup third **Eyeq**, a Danish filly, gained a rare success for a Scandinavian-trained horse further afield when winning a Group 3 event over a mile at Hamburg. An even rarer win for a Scandinavian horse in Britain came when the then Norwegian-trained mare Tawoos (rated 104) added a Lingfield handicap to three listed successes earlier in the year.

Older Horses

114	Musadif	108	Alpino Chileno	106	Santiago Matias
111	Mandrake El Mago	108	Binary File	105	Buffalo Boy
111	Steve's Champ	108	Ecology	105	Damachida
110	Hovman	108	Waquaas	105	Hide And Seek
109	Magic Fact	107	Killaden	105	Jagodin
109	Nicki Hill	106	Eyeq (f)	105	Lores Joy
109	Royal Experiment	106	Hanzano	105	Pipoldchap
109	The Khamsin	106	Honeysuckle Player	105	Rex
		106	Rue La Fayette (f)	105	Shawdon

UNITED ARAB EMIRATES   Following on from the creation of the world's richest race, the Dubai World Cup in 1996, and then the progressive strengthening of the supporting card around it in the years which followed, 2004 saw the next major development in the growth of racing in the Emirates with the inaugural Dubai International Racing Carnival. Spread over nine weeks, with World Cup night as its finale, the Carnival was aimed at attracting foreign stables to compete throughout the most important period of the Dubai season. Much of the Carnival programme consists of rated stakes style handicaps, and it also incorporates the 'Super Saturday' meeting, three weeks before the World Cup, with trial races for each of the events on the World Cup card. The inaugural Carnival offered $21 million in prize money and attracted worldwide interest, not only from major racing countries (Mark Johnston, Mick Channon, Gerard Butler and Clive Brittain were some of the British trainers who sent teams), but from the likes of India, Turkey, Saudi Arabia and Macau.

But if any country had its international profile raised by success during the Carnival, it was South Africa thanks mainly to the performances of horses from the Mike de Kock stable. **Victory Moon** had already won the UAE 2000 Guineas and Derby the year before, and returned to win the last two rounds of the Maktoum Challenge series (from Godolphin's **Inamorato** and the Turkish horse **Dinyeper** respectively) before running a good third to the high-class American pair, Pleasantly Perfect and Medaglia d'Oro in the Dubai World Cup. The formerly British-trained **Right Approach** dead-heated with the German horse Paolini in a thrilling Dubai Duty Free, having earlier beaten stable-companion **Surveyor** in a listed race. Surveyor went on to win the trial for the Duty Free, the Jebel Hatta. De Kock's other winner on World Cup night was the Brazilian-bred **Lundy's Liability** who took the UAE Derby for the stable for the second year, turning the tables on the horse

Dubai Golden Shaheen, Nad Al Sheba—
Our New Recruit becomes the fourth North American-trained winner of the race in five years;
compatriot Alke makes it a 1, 2

who had beaten him in the main trial, the Saudi-trained **Petit Paris**, with the UAE 2000 Guineas winner **Little Jim** in third. The mare Crimson Palace began the Carnival with de Kock but joined Godolphin after an impressive win on the opening day and later finished fourth in the Duty Free.

South Africa was also represented by the Mike Azzie-trained sprinter **National Currency** who was an emphatic winner of a listed event early in the Carnival. Plans for National Currency included a visit to Britain in the summer, but unfortunately he was put down with suspected laminitis before contesting another race. In National Currency's absence, the Dubai Golden Shaheen was fought out by American sprinters Our New Recruit and Alke, ahead of **Conroy** who had won the main trial, the Mahab Al Shimaal, for the third year running. **Feet So Fast** was well held in the Golden Shaheen (on dirt) but had shown smart form in handicaps on turf earlier at the Carnival.

Although represented in all the races on World Cup night, Godolphin fielded a weaker team than in the past, and their only success came in the Godolphin Mile which **Firebreak** won for a second year. Runner-up **Tropical Star** had earlier been placed in the main trial (won by **Cherry Pickings**) as well as in the first two rounds of the Maktoum Challenge. Other good performances at a mile, this time in handicaps on turf, were put up by **Trademark**, **Walmooh** and the Irish-trained Evolving Tactics. Over a mile and a half on turf, the British-trained horses Scott's View, Razkalla and Rawyaan all put up smart efforts to win handicaps, with Scott's View faring best of the trio to take third in the Dubai Sheema Classic behind the French-trained Polish Summer and American horse Hard Buck.

UAE Derby, Nad Al Sheba—South African-trained Lundy's Liability wins from Petit Paris and Little Jim;
British challengers Jack Sullivan, Ascertain and Menhoubah are fourth, fifth and seventh

The fillies' classics in the UAE offer good money, but the form was no better than useful; Catstar (rated 104) took the 1000 Guineas from Menhoubah and Festive Style, while the placed horses finished the other way round behind **Tamarillo** in the Oaks.

The performances reviewed here are those that took place in the calendar year 2004. Horses which were trained and raced in the UAE but showed significantly better form elsewhere are not included in the list below.

Three-Year-Olds					
105	*Rosencrans	114	*Dinyeper	109	St Expedit
105	*Tamarillo (f)	114	*Little Jim	108	Al Maali
		114	*Three Graces	108	Grand Hombre
Older Horses		114	Winisk River	108	*Lodge Keeper
125	*Firebreak	112	Burnt Ember	108	*Northern Rock
124	*National Currency	112	Curule	108	Summoner
120	*Victory Moon	112	*Prince of War	107	*Dantana
119	*Vespone	112	Sleeping Weapon	107	Divine Task
118	Feet So Fast	111	Conflict	107	Emteyaz
118	*Right Approach	111	*El Hurano	106	Estimraar
118	*Surveyor	111	*Grand Ekinoks	106	Muthaaber
117	*Lundy's Liability	111	Kayseri	106	Saddad
117	Trademark	111	*Mubeen	106?	Magic Master
116	Cherry Pickings	111d	State Shinto	106§	Clodion
116	*Petit Paris	110	*Anani	105	Cat Belling (f)
116	Tropical Star	110	Deodatus	105	Dubai Honor
115	Conroy	110	*San Salvador	105	Mugharreb
115	Inamorato	110	Western Diplomat	105	Persuasivo Fitz
115	*Lunar Sovereign	109	Conceal	105	*Zirna (f)
115	Walmooh	109	*Gonfilia (f)		
		109	*Naheef		

NORTH AMERICA   For a horse to win the first two legs of the Triple Crown and then fail in the final race of the series, the Belmont Stakes, has become a regular occurrence in recent years. But that has not meant that American racing fans have lost their enthusiasm for yet another Triple Crown challenger. Quite the opposite in fact, as the expectation fuelled by so many near-misses in recent times seems to grow each year. A record crowd of over 120,000 turned up for the latest Belmont Stakes, many finally expecting to see the first Triple Crown winner since Affirmed in 1978, but instead they witnessed the sixth candidate since 1997 to fail in the final leg after Silver Charm, Real Quiet, Charismatic, War Emblem and Funny Cide. As well as recent history to make up for, the weight of expectation on **Smarty Jones** and his connections was all the greater after he'd won the Preakness Stakes by a record margin of eleven and a half lengths. Additionally, his unbeaten record was also still intact before the Belmont, making him potentially the first unbeaten Triple Crown winner since Seattle Slew in 1977.

The Kentucky Derby had looked an open race beforehand after none of the main trials had thrown up a decisive winner. As a result, Smarty Jones, who had come via a win in the non-graded Rebel Stakes and the Grade 2 Arkansas Derby, both at Oaklawn, started favourite on his Grade 1 debut and was in line for a $5 million bonus if successful. Sloppy conditions rendered the race much less competitive as things turned out, and he was one of only two horses who ever looked like winning. Smarty Jones's runaway win in the Preakness a fortnight later over **Rock Hard Ten** and **Eddington**, with the placed horses from Churchill Downs, **Lion Heart** and **Imperialism**, fourth and fifth respectively, was a top-class effort, but at Belmont he was worn down in the closing stages by a stouter stayer in 36/1-shot **Birdstone**. The Belmont turned out to be Smarty Jones's final race. The decision to retire him in the summer was a controversial one as it was felt in some quarters that bruised joints—the reason given for his retirement—did not constitute a career-ending injury.

Birdstone had won the Champagne Stakes at two but his long price at Belmont was a reflection of some poor recent efforts, including when only eighth in the Kentucky Derby. He went on to win the Travers Stakes in August against the best of the three-year-old colts still in training and was the only serious representative of his age-group when finishing seventh against older rivals in the Breeders' Cup Classic. The Travers turned out to be the final start for Lion Heart. After making the frame in the Kentucky Derby and Preakness Stakes, the front-running Lion Heart returned to Grade 1 company to win the Haskell Invitational Handicap under top weight (with Belmont third **Royal Assault** only fourth) but broke a bone in his off-fore when finishing last as favourite for the Travers. As well as Birdstone, Nick Zito had another leading colt in **The Cliff's Edge**. He had looked a major contender for the Kentucky Derby after a defeat of Lion Heart in the Blue Grass Stakes, but finished only fifth at Churchill Downs after losing both front shoes. Runner-up to his stable companion in the Travers, The Cliff's Edge was another to suffer a career-ending injury, when running a good third against older horses in the Jockey Club Gold Cup in the autumn.

A number of colts ran their best races before disappointing in the Kentucky Derby, among them Grade 1 winners **Castledale**, **Tapit** and **Friends Lake**. The ex-Irish colt Castledale beat Rock Hard Ten, who was demoted to third, and Imperialism in the Santa Anita Derby, Tapit got the better of **Master David** and Eddington in the Wood Memorial Stakes, and Friends Lake was a long-priced winner of the Florida Derby. As well as finishing third in the Preakness, Eddington was fourth in the Belmont Stakes and third again in the Travers. Of the colts who did not come to the fore until after the Triple Crown, **Purge** had the best form. After a Grade 2 success in the Peter Pan Stakes, he finished last in the Belmont, the only Triple Crown race he contested, but proved himself much better at Saratoga, beating The Cliff's Edge in the Grade 2 Jim Dandy Stakes and running fourth in the Travers. **Pomeroy** put up the best effort by a three-year-old colt over shorter trips to win the King's Bishop Stakes at Saratoga from **Weigelia**. **Bwana Charlie** was only fourth there, but had earlier beaten the winner in a Grade 2 event at the same track and went on to fare best of the three-year-olds to take fourth in the Breeders' Cup Sprint.

There was good competition among the leading three-year-old fillies on dirt, and in contrast to the colts, three of the top four were still around to contest their championship event at the Breeders' Cup meeting. The genuine and consistent **Ashado** (yet to finish out of the first three in fourteen starts) rounded off a fine season by justifying favouritism in the Breeders' Cup Distaff and remains in training at four. She had already won a strong

Preakness Stakes, Pimlico—a record winning margin for the race
as Smarty Jones draws eleven and a half lengths clear of Rock Hard Ten, with Eddington third

renewal of the Kentucky Oaks and gained a decisive win in the Coaching Club American Oaks. **Society Selection** was disappointing in the Distaff but she was at least the equal of Ashado on other form. She showed versatility too, with a wide-margin win over **Bending Strings** in a strongly-run Test Stakes over seven furlongs, but following up at the same track in the ten-furlong Alabama Stakes, with Ashado only third. Society Selection also ran a good second against older rivals in the Beldame Stakes. Kentucky Oaks runner-up **Island Sand** gained a deserved Grade 1 win over Society Selection in the Acorn Stakes but wasn't at her best afterwards, including when third in the Mother Goose Stakes and once on turf. **Stellar Jayne** took longer to come to hand than the other leading fillies (she was only seventh in the Kentucky Oaks) but gained a surprise win over Ashado in the Mother Goose and confirmed that improvement when runner-up in the CCA Oaks and the Alabama Stakes, and when third in the Distaff. She picked up a second Grade 1 win in the Gazelle Handicap in September, and joined Godolphin at the end of the year.

Inevitably, injury took its toll on the campaigns of some of the better fillies. **Madcap Escapade** fractured a hip after finishing third in the Kentucky Oaks, but that was her only defeat in five starts (she's due to return in 2005) and she had earlier beaten Ashado in the Ashland Stakes. **Silent Sighs** was not seen out after the Kentucky Oaks, though had beaten the previous year's Breeders' Cup Juvenile Fillies winner Halfbridled in the Santa Anita Oaks. Halfbridled had looked a really good prospect when beating Ashado at the Breeders' Cup the previous autumn but was restricted to just two starts in a troubled campaign and was eventually retired with a stress fracture. The other filly of note was **Friendly Michelle**. Her Grade 1 win came in a weak Prioress Stakes over six furlongs, though her best effort was when third to Island Sand in the Acorn over a mile.

America's best three-year-olds on turf generally fall well short of their dirt counterparts, but **Kitten's Joy** emerged as a rare high-class three-year-old on grass and the best in that sphere for many a year. His career record on turf stands at eight wins from ten starts, with his biggest wins coming in the Secretariat Stakes, and the Joe Hirsch Turf Classic Invitational which he took in great style against older horses. Kitten's Joy started odds on for the Breeders' Cup Turf and he did well to finish second after being kept in at a crucial stage. Assuming he recovers well from a bone chip operation, he could easily dominate the ten-to-twelve furlong turf races in 2005 and may be targeted at the Arc. **Artie Schiller** (by the same sire as Kitten's Joy, El Prado) finished second to that rival in the Grade 3 Virginia Derby over ten furlongs but had his attentions switched to shorter distances. He set a new track record at Belmont in the Grade 2 Jamaica Handicap over nine furlongs and surprisingly started favourite in the Breeders' Cup Mile, his Grade 1 debut, but didn't get the best of runs. **Good Reward** twice finished behind Artie Schiller in graded company and ended the year with a Grade 1 success over the ex-French colt **Fast And Furious** in the Hollywood Derby. By Storm Cat out of the high-class filly Heavenly Prize, Good Reward can win more good races. **Mustanfar** was another to find Artie Schiller too good when second in a Grade 2 at Saratoga but showed smart form and finished fifth in the Breeders' Cup Turf. **Three Valleys** ran well on his US debut to finish third against older horses in the Citation Handicap on his first outing since the Two Thousand Guineas. **Prince Arch** took the notable scalp of Kitten's Joy in a Grade 3 at Churchill Downs in June and beat Mustanfar in a similar event at Saratoga in September.

Ouija Board was the only three-year-old in the field when winning the Breeders' Cup Filly & Mare Turf. She was a good deal better than America's best three-year-old turf fillies, **Ticker Tape**, **Miss Vegas** and **Amorama**, who had started their careers in Britain, Italy and France respectively. Ticker Tape won the upgraded American Oaks (from the Japanese filly Dance In The Mood) and the Queen Elizabeth II Challenge Cup before running a good third against older fillies in the Matriarch Stakes. Between her Grade 1 wins she was beaten a nose by Amorama in the Del Mar Oaks. Miss Vegas had Ticker Tape and Amorama immediately behind her when winning the Grade 3 Senorita Stakes over a mile at Hollywood in May.

Whilst Smarty Jones's all-too-brief three-year-old career was a cause for regret, the fact that the horse who beat him to the Horse of the Year title, the four-year-old **Ghostzapper**, made only four appearances, was seen in some quarters as further proof of the frailty of modern racehorses. Bill Heller of the *Thoroughbred Times* contrasted

Ghostzapper's light campaign with the far busier schedule of the winners of the Horse of the Year title in the 1950s, who ran on average more than a dozen times in their championship seasons. Heller made a direct link between the widespread use of medication and the diminishing number of appearances made by the best horses. Ghostzapper had looked an exciting prospect after an impressive win in the Vosburgh Stakes over an extended six furlongs on his final outing at three. He did not return until July in the latest season and won all four of his starts, making into the best American-trained horse, in our view, since Cigar in 1996. The most notable aspect of Ghostzapper's campaign was that he was stepped up in trip from sprinting, and it culminated in an impressive front-running display in race-record time in the Breeders' Cup Classic. At least Ghostzapper, beaten only twice in ten starts, stays in training. His other Grade 1 win had been a battling neck success over the subsequent Grade 2 Clark Handicap winner **Saint Liam** in the Woodward Stakes, but his near eleven-length win in the Grade 3 Philip H. Iselin Breeders' Cup Handicap on sloppy going at Monmouth had been particularly impressive, earning him the highest 'Beyer' speed figure since they started being published in 1992.

The Breeders' Cup Classic runner-up **Roses In May** was a top-class colt in his own right, and he too was unbeaten for the year before going to Lone Star Park. Much improved, Roses In May gained his Grade 1 success narrowly over **Perfect Drift** in the Whitney Handicap and had the same rival (who made the frame in several top events without winning) a lot further behind him in fourth when they met again in the Classic. Roses In May also stays in training, and reportedly has the Dubai World Cup on his agenda. The winner of that race in the latest season was **Pleasantly Perfect** who took third place when attempting a repeat win in the Breeders' Cup Classic. The genuine and consistent Pleasantly Perfect became only the second horse after Cigar to win both of the world's richest races on dirt, and as in the Breeders' Cup the year before, it was **Medaglia d'Oro** who finished second at Nad Al Sheba, going down by three quarters of a length after a good duel. Pleasantly Perfect won another big race when taking the Pacific Classic at Del Mar in August from Perfect Drift, and when he retired at the end of the year, he did so as the third-highest all-time earner trained in North America behind Cigar and Skip Away. Smarty Jones had held that third spot briefly after his retirement earlier in the year. With Medaglia d'Oro retired after the Dubai World Cup (he had won the Donn Handicap under top weight beforehand), the chief absentee among the leading older horses from the Breeders' Cup Classic was **Southern Image**. He was much improved in the first half of the year, winning the Santa Anita Handicap and Pimlico Special (the latter from **Midway Road**) before going down by a nose to the lightly-weighted outsider **Colonial Colony** in the Stephen Foster Handicap at Churchill Downs. Southern Image was kept off the track by foot trouble for the rest of the year, but he has lost only twice in eight starts and is to be aimed at the Breeders' Cup in 2005. Conditions were probably against **Peace Rules** in the Stephen Foster and he put up a much better effort when winning a thrilling Suburban Handicap at Belmont under top weight in a tight finish from **Newfoundland** and **Funny**

Breeders' Cup Classic Powered By Dodge, Lone Star Park—front-running Ghostzapper puts up one of the best performances in recent years; runner-up Roses In May is beaten for the first time in six starts, as Dubai World Cup winner Pleasantly Perfect (centre) is only third

Vosburgh Stakes, Belmont Park—a terrific performance by Pico Central (sheepskin noseband) in a field including top sprinters Speightstown (second right) and Cajun Beat (right)

Cide. The placed horses fought out another stirring finish in the Jockey Club Gold Cup there later in the year, Funny Cide turning the tables on Newfoundland at level weights, but it was a substandard renewal of what is traditionally one of North America's most prestigious races. Funny Cide had been in Smarty Jones's position during the previous year's Triple Crown races, but he found success harder to come by as a four-year-old and was below form in the Breeders' Cup Classic for a second time, in which Newfoundland also trailed home.

Another prestigious race which was poorly contested by historical standards was the Hollywood Gold Cup. Its winner, the Chilean-bred **Total Impact**, later proved himself not far behind the best dirt horses when third in the Pacific Classic, and he ran fourth in the Japan Cup Dirt late in the year. A place behind him in the Pacific Classic was **Choctaw Nation**, who had been unbeaten in five previous starts, notably when defeating Pleasantly Perfect in the Grade 2 San Diego Handicap at Del Mar in August. **Ten Most Wanted**, the 2003 Travers Stakes winner, showed he'd retained plenty of ability with a wide-margin success in a Grade 3 at Hawthorne, but was retired due to injury in May. **Evening Attire**, a former Jockey Club Gold Cup winner, failed to show his best form in Grade 1 company in the latest season, but gained a five-length win over Funny Cide in the Grade 2 Saratoga Breeders' Cup Handicap at Saratoga and was in the frame on numerous other occasions.

Top sprinting honours lay between **Pico Central** and **Speightstown**, the Eclipse award going to the latter. Like most South American-bred horses, the former Brazilian Grade 1 winner Pico Central had not been nominated for the Breeders' Cup and was not supplemented at what would have been a cost of $200,000. In any case, Pico Central had already gained an impressive win over his main rival for divisional honours when beating an admittedly below-par Speightstown into third in the Vosburgh Stakes, in which the previous year's Breeders' Cup Sprint winner **Cajun Beat** (almost as good as ever early in the year) was only fourth. The Vosburgh was run over six furlongs for the first time, but Pico Central had already proved himself over further with wins in the Carter Handicap over seven furlongs and the Metropolitan Handicap over a mile. Nunthorpe winner Bahamian Pirate's half-brother **Strong Hope** was runner-up in the Carter and fared best of those who took on Pico Central again in the Metropolitan, finishing third behind runner-up **Bowman's Band**. Pico Central was a creditable third, back over a longer trip, behind **Lion Tamer** in the Cigar Mile on his final start but is to be aimed at the Dubai Golden Shaheen in 2005, the big sprint on the World Cup card.

The Vosburgh was Speightstown's only defeat in six starts all year. The six-year-old had been very lightly raced in previous seasons but won three times in Grade 2 company before the Vosburgh and ended his career with a defeat of another six-year-old, the Bing Crosby Breeders' Cup Handicap winner **Kela**, and rank outsider **My Cousin Matt**, in the Breeders' Cup Sprint. **Midas Eyes** started favourite for the Breeders' Cup Sprint after winning the Forego Handicap but finished down the field for the second year running. He returned to form later in the autumn when beaten a neck by **Wildcat Heir** in the Frank J. De Francis Memorial Dash. As usual, American sprinters dominated the Dubai Golden Shaheen early in the year. **Our New Recruit** beat **Alke** into second, with Cajun Beat only fourth, but the winner was well held at the Breeders' Cup.

For the second year running, the high-class mares **Azeri** and **Sightseek** dominated the races for older females on dirt. There was little between the pair on form, each added another three Grade 1 wins to their already excellent records, and on the two occasions their paths crossed, they shared the honours with a win apiece. Azeri reportedly bled when last of four behind Sightseek in the Ogden Phipps Handicap at Belmont (a track where Sightseek was unbeaten in six starts) but she gained her revenge in the Go For Wand Handicap at Saratoga, in the process breaking the record for the most prize money earned by a filly or mare in North America. Azeri had moved to Wayne Lukas' stable prior to the latest season, and while her air of invincibility had gone, her reputation was none the worse for being campaigned more boldly. Two of her defeats came against male rivals in the Metropolitan Handicap and Breeders' Cup Classic, finishing fifth in the latter event as only the third filly or mare ever to contest the race. She lost no caste in defeat when beaten narrowly by the lightly-weighted **Mayo On The Side** in the Humana Distaff Handicap at Churchill Downs, and in the other race she lost, she went off too quickly over a trip beyond her best in the Personal Ensign Handicap. As well as winning the Go For Wand, Azeri's other Grade 1 successes came in the Apple Blossom Handicap at Oaklawn (for the third year) and the Spinster Stakes at Keeneland. Azeri has been retired to stud, the winner of eleven Grade 1s in all, and she visits Storm Cat. Sightseek had already been retired by the time of the Breeders' Cup after continuing ankle problems. Nonetheless, after her two meetings with Azeri, she signed off with two more Grade 1 wins at Belmont, sweeping to a win by more than eleven lengths in the Ruffian Handicap and impressing again with a defeat of a stronger field (headed by three-year-old Society Selection) for a second successive win, and seventh Grade 1 win in all, in the Beldame Stakes.

The other leading older fillies were closely matched but **Storm Flag Flying** had the best record against the 'big two'. The 2002 Breeders' Cup Juvenile Fillies winner had

Breeders' Cup Nextel Distaff, Lone Star Park—a fourth Grade 1 for Ashado;
Storm Flag Flying squeezes between Stellar Jayne (blinkers) and Tamweel to take second

John Deere Breeders' Cup Turf, Lone Star Park—
outsider Better Talk Now wins from odds-on Kitten's Joy (left)
and the only European challenger Powerscourt

looked a good prospect but she was restricted to just two starts as a three-year-old. She was finally able to fulfil earlier promise in the latest season and was a most apt winner of the Personal Ensign Handicap, a race named in honour of her own grandam. That was the only time she managed to beat Azeri, but she was placed behind both her and Sightseek in the Go For Wand Handicap and behind Sightseek in the Ogden Phipps and the Beldame. She ended her career with a good second in the Breeders' Cup Distaff, a race Personal Ensign had won sixteen years earlier. The 2003 Distaff winner **Adoration** showed that that had been no flash in the pan by winning the Santa Margarita Handicap, turning the form round with the three fillies, headed by **Star Parade**, who had finished ahead of her in the Santa Maria. Subsequently beaten by **Victory Encounter** in the Vanity Handicap, Adoration was retired with an ankle injury before she was able to defend her Distaff title. **Wild Spirit** had looked an interesting prospect for the latest season but managed just one outing, finishing a good second nonetheless to Azeri in the Apple Blossom. The Santa Monica Handicap winner **Island Fashion** had a less conventional campaign than most of the other leading dirt fillies, running a good second against male rivals in the Santa Anita Handicap and even contesting the Yasuda Kinen on turf in Japan. She took fifth place in the Breeders' Cup Distaff, a place behind the ex-British filly **Tamweel** who had also finished second in the Spinster Stakes. **Lady Tak**, who put up the best performance by a three-year-old filly when winning the Test Stakes at Saratoga the year before, gained another Grade 1 win over seven furlongs in the Ballerina Handicap, from **My Trusty Cat** and the previous year's winner **Harmony Lodge**. Incidentally, Lady Tak's trainer, Steve Asmussen, set a new world record for the most number of winners trained in a year, with a final tally of 555 wins.

American-trained horses managed to keep both the Mile and Turf races at the Breeders' Cup at home, only the second time that they have done so in the same year since 1993, and that despite conditions on the turf course (good to soft) being more familiar to the European visitors than the hosts. Lone Star Park in Texas staged the Breeders' Cup for the first time, the first track to do so which does not host any Grade 1 contests during the rest of the year. American success in those turf races was more a reflection of the numerically-weak European challenge than the strength of the American turf performers. Britain fielded its smallest (but ironically, its most successful) team in the history of the meeting, and Irish-trained **Powerscourt** was, unusually, the sole European-trained representative in the Breeders' Cup Turf.

With hot favourite Kitten's Joy only second in the Turf, an unsatisfactory race went to the outsider of the field, **Better Talk Now**. The common belief in Europe that *all* American races are run at a furious pace is well wide of the mark when it comes to turf races over a mile and a quarter and more in particular, and the Turf was far from unusual in being steadily run. Better Talk Now's other Grade 1 success (he was the only older horse who managed to win more than one Grade 1 race on turf in the latest season) came in another slowly-run race, the Sword Dancer Invitational Handicap at Saratoga, in which he beat the consistent United Nations Stakes winner **Request For Parole**, later sixth in the Turf. Better Talk Now was turned out again after the Breeders' Cup but finished only sixth in the Hollywood Turf Cup behind two ex-South American performers in **Pellegrino** and **License To Run**, the latter making a promising US debut in third place. The best older turf horse, **Hard Buck**, had been retired by the time of the Breeders' Cup, though he had been in line for big prizes abroad in the autumn instead. Hard Buck had already earned place money abroad when runner-up in the Dubai Sheema Classic and, in what proved to be his final start, the King George VI and Queen Elizabeth Diamond Stakes at Ascot. Now at stud, he put up a career-best effort at Ascot, and had also won the Gulfstream Park Breeders' Cup Handicap early in the year from **Balto Star**.

For the second year running, the result of the Arlington Million was decided by the stewards. Powerscourt, first past the post, was demoted to fourth for causing interference, resulting in **Kicken Kris** (who had beaten Better Talk Now in the Grade 2 Bowling Green Handicap at Belmont the time before) being awarded the race. **Magistretti**, having his final run for Neville Callaghan, and the German colt **Epalo**, were promoted to second and third respectively, and the same pair took the first two places in the Man o' War Stakes the following month, by which time Magistretti was in the care of Patrick Biancone. After finishing second to Kitten's Joy in the Joe Hirsch Turf Classic (Kicken Kris only sixth), Magistretti went on to take fourth place in the Breeders' Cup Turf, a place behind Powerscourt, the ride on whom in that race was not without controversy either. **Star Over The Bay** began the year in claimers but earned his place in the Breeders' Cup Turf (in which he finished last) with a defeat of **Sarafan** and the ex-French horse **Vangelis** in the Clement L. Hirsch Memorial Turf Championship. The ex-German horse **Sabiango**, now owned by 'horse whisperer' Monty Roberts, put up another of the turf division's better efforts when winning the Charles Whittingham Memorial Handicap at Hollywood but was well held in Grade 1 company subsequently in the Arlington Million and the Canadian International. The latter race saw European horses take the first four places, led home by **Sulamani**.

Like the Turf, the Breeders' Cup Mile went to an outsider, **Singletary**. There was trouble in running too, with the placed horses, Irish-trained **Antonius Pius** and the French filly **Six Perfections**, the previous year's winner, both better than the bare result. Singletary had an admirably consistent record on turf, which included a second to **Designed For Luck** in the Shoemaker Breeders' Cup Mile at Hollywood, but not one that suggested he held a leading chance at the Breeders' Cup, where he put up an improved effort. **Nothing To Lose** ran one of the best trials for the Mile when an impressive winner of the Shadwell Turf Mile at Keeneland, but he cut little ice at Lone Star Park. Like Nothing To Lose, **Mr O'Brien** had been placed in the United Nations Stakes over eleven furlongs earlier in the year but took his chance in the Mile after a win over that trip in the Grade 2 Kelso Breeders' Cup Handicap, though he too finished down the field at Lone Star. Canada could lay claim to a couple of North America's best milers. Canada's Horse of the Year **Soaring Free** went one better than the year before when beating **Perfect Soul** in the Atto

NetJets Breeders' Cup Mile, Lone Star Park—
Singletary holds the quirky Antonius Pius to keep the prize at home

Mile at Woodbine and also improved a place on his effort the previous year to take fourth in the Breeders' Cup Mile. Several other South American imports did well in the latest season, including **Leroidesanimaux**, who completed a five-timer when taking the upgraded Citation Handicap at Hollywood in November. Nothing To Lose was below form again in the same race, and so was **Special Ring**, another also-ran in the Breeders' Cup Mile, who had won the Eddie Read Handicap at Del Mar in the summer for the second time. **Stroll** confirmed the promise he had shown at three when making a successful Grade 1 debut in the Woodford Reserve Turf Classic, but was retired to stud in the autumn without adding to that success.

The older females on turf were not a strong group, as Ouija Board proved when beating her elders at odds on in their championship event at the Breeders' Cup, the Filly & Mare Turf. Trainer Bobby Frankel and owner Juddmonte Farms had the two leading older fillies in **Intercontinental** and **Light Jig**. Intercontinental beat stable-companion **Etoile Montante** in the Matriarch Stakes, the second year running that a daughter of the excellent broodmare Hasili had won the race for connections, after Heat Haze the year before. Light Jig, who, like Intercontinental and Etoile Montante had started her career in France, won the Yellow Ribbon Stakes in clear-cut fashion, but disappointed at the Breeders' Cup. The Flower Bowl Invitational Stakes at Belmont brought together a number of the other leading fillies, though a slow pace resulted in a bunched finish and the form was turned upside down at the Breeders' Cup. Flower Bowl winner **Riskaverse** was well held in the Filly & Mare Turf, whilst **Film Maker**, **Wonder Again** and Moscow Burning (rated 116), who finished fourth, sixth and third respectively behind her at Belmont, all ran well to fill the frame in that order behind Ouija Board next time out. Riskaverse had earlier finished second in both the Diana Handicap at Saratoga, where Wonder Again beat her by almost six lengths, and the Beverly D Stakes at Arlington, where she went down by half a length to Godolphin's **Crimson Palace**. The Flower Bowl runner-up **Commercante** went on to win the E. P. Taylor Stakes at Woodbine, while Moscow Burning ended her season with an unlucky fourth against male rivals in the Hollywood Turf Cup, a race in which the mare Megahertz (rated 116) was beaten only narrowly in second. The former Poule d'Essai des Pouliches winner **Musical Chimes** took on the males several times, finishing sixth in the Breeders' Cup Mile after a narrow win over them (Singletary only third) in the Grade 2 Oak Tree Breeders' Cup Mile at Santa Anita. She also gained a Grade 1 win against her own sex when beating Moscow Burning in the John C. Mabee Handicap at Del Mar.

What had looked a good crop of American two-year-old colts were upstaged by the then British-trained outsider **Wilko** in the Breeders' Cup Juvenile. He joined Craig Dollase from Jeremy Noseda after the race, having become only the second British-trained Breeders' Cup winner on dirt after Sheikh Albadou in the 1991 Sprint. Wilko was making his dirt debut, and is a son of the 1998 Breeders' Cup Classic winner Awesome Again, also responsible for Ghostzapper. Wilko's claims to being top juvenile looked shaky however, and while he ran well subsequently in the Hollywood Futurity, it was only good enough to secure him third place behind **Declan's Moon** and **Giacomo**, with another ex-British trained colt, **Southern Africa**, in fourth. The winner, a gelding who had sidestepped the Breeders' Cup, kept his unbeaten record with an impressive win in the Futurity and clinched the champion two-year-old male title in the process, though unlike the runner-up he is not certain to be suited by ten furlongs as a three-year-old. Back at Lone Star Park, Wilko was chased home by **Afleet Alex** and **Sun King**, the colts who had filled the same places behind **Proud Accolade** (only sixth at the Breeders' Cup and fifth at Hollywood) in the Champagne Stakes. Afleet Alex lost his unbeaten record in the Champagne Stakes after a Grade 1 success in the Hopeful Stakes at Saratoga over **Devils Disciple**. **Consolidator** was only fourth in the Hopeful, but improved considerably over a longer trip to win the upgraded Lane's End Breeders' Futurity at Keeneland and then finished a creditable fourth in the Juvenile. The Bob Baffert-trained **Roman Ruler** was sent off favourite for the Juvenile after going down by a neck to Declan's Moon, who received 4 lb, in the Grade 2 Del Mar Futurity and then winning the Grade 2 Norfolk Stakes at Santa Anita, but he could finish only fifth at Lone Star Park. **Park Avenue Ball** won the Grade 2 Futurity Stakes, downgraded from 2003, at Belmont before finishing a well-held fifth in the Champagne Stakes. Among those who were not tested at Grade 1 level, **Rockport Harbor** kept his unbeaten record at the expense of another previously unbeaten colt, **Galloping Grocer**, in a good renewal of the Grade 2 Remsen Stakes over nine furlongs at Aqueduct. The winner hails from the same stable as Smarty Jones, that of John Servis. **Greater Good** was not tried in Grade 1 company either, but ended his season with a second graded stakes win in the Grade 2 Kentucky Jockey Club Stakes at Churchill Downs. The well-bred Harlington (by Unbridled out of champion filly Serena's Song) made a good impression, winning both his starts, and the Todd Pletcher-trained colt could be among the leading contenders by the time of the Kentucky Derby. An injury sustained early in 2005 ruled Fusaichi Samurai out of the Triple Crown races, but the son of Fusaichi Pegasus made an impressive debut at Hollywood in December for Neil Drysdale (who won the Kentucky Derby with his sire), having fetched a record $4.5 million at a breeze-up sale.

Whilst the Breeders' Cup Juvenile has tended to be won by long-shots in recent years, the Juvenile Fillies has been a favourite's race, and that was the case again when **Sweet Catomine** ran out an impressive winner, the best in our view since Countess Diana in 1997. Although checked on the far turn, she swept to her second Grade 1 win in a better time than the colts' race later on the card. Sweet Catomine had also won the Del Mar Debutante Stakes from **Souvenir Gift** and the Grade 2 Oak Leaf Stakes from the subsequent Hollywood Starlet Stakes winner **Splendid Blended**. The UAE-bred filly **Balletto** fared best of the remainder in the Juvenile Fillies and was subsequently transferred to Godolphin. She had earlier won the Frizette Stakes from **Ready's Gal** (who missed the Breeders' Cup through injury) and **Sis City**, the latter going on to finish fourth at Lone Star Park and then win the Grade 2 Demoiselle Stakes at Aqueduct. **Runway Model** had the busiest campaign among the leading fillies, running her best race in defeat when third in the Juvenile Fillies after being short of room in the straight. She also won in Grade 2 company either side of the Breeders' Cup, winning the Alcibiades Stakes at Keeneland and the Golden Rod Stakes (her tenth outing) at Churchill Downs. **Sense of Style** looked the main danger to Sweet Catomine in the Juvenile Fillies beforehand but ran well below form. Her best efforts had been a clear-cut win in the Grade 2 Spinaway

Stakes at Saratoga, and then a defeat of Balletto and **Play With Fire** in the Matron Stakes at Belmont.

European-trained horses who showed or reproduced their best form in North America are included in this list

Two-Year-Olds
122	Sweet Catomine (f)
120p	Declan's Moon
118	Giacomo
118	†Wilko
117	Proud Accolade
116	Afleet Alex
115	Balletto (f)
115	Devils Disciple
115	Roman Ruler
115	Sun King
114p	Rockport Harbor
114p	Splendid Blended (f)
114	Consolidator
114	†Southern Africa
113p	Galloping Grocer
113	Park Avenue Ball
113	Ready's Gal (f)
113	Runway Model (f)
113	Sense of Style (f)
113	Souvenir Gift (f)
113	Straight Line
112	Flamenco
112	Greater Good
112	Inspiring (f)
111	Chandtrue
111	Sis City (f)
111	Toll Taker (f)
110	Culinary (f)
110	Dance Away Capote (f)
110	In The Gold (f)
110	Patriot Act
110	Play With Fire (f)
110	Seize The Day
110	Sharp Lisa (f)

DIRT

Three-Year-Olds
134	†Smarty Jones
129	Birdstone
125	Ashado (f)
125	Society Selection (f)
124	Lion Heart
123	The Cliff's Edge
122	Island Sand (f)
121	Purge
121	Stellar Jayne (f)
120	Pomeroy
119	Castledale
119	Friendly Michelle (f)
119	Imperialism
119	Madcap Escapade (f)
118	Brass Hat
118	Bwana Charlie
118	Fantasticat
118	Love of Money
118	Friends Lake

118	Rock Hard Ten
118	Silent Sighs (f)
118	Tapit
117	Bending Strings (f)
117	Borrego
117	Eddington
117	Master David
117	Medallist
117	My Snookie's Boy
117	Royal Assault
117	Suave
117	Value Plus (USA)
117	Weigelia
115	Alphabet Kisses (f)
113	A. P. Adventure (f)
112	Pt's Grey Eagle

Older Horses
137	†Ghostzapper
131	†Roses In May
130	†Pleasantly Perfect
129	Medaglia d'Oro
129	Southern Image
127	Azeri (f)
126	Pico Central
126	Sightseek (f)
124	Peace Rules
124	Perfect Drift
124	Speightstown
123	Funny Cide
123	Our New Recruit
123	Saint Liam
123	Total Impact
122	Adoration (f)
122	Newfoundland
122	Ten Most Wanted
121	Cajun Beat
121	Choctaw Nation
121	Evening Attire
121	Island Fashion (f)
121	Kela
121	Lady Tak (f)
121	Midas Eyes
121	Storm Flag Flying (f)
120	Champali
120	Harmony Lodge (f)
120	Midway Road
120	Strong Hope
120	Victory Encounter (f)
120	Wild Spirit (f)
119	Ema Bovary (f)
119	Lion Tamer
119	My Cousin Matt
119	The Lady's Groom
118	Alke
118	Bare Necessities (f)
118	Bear Fan (f)
118	Board Elligible (f)
118	Colonial Colony
118	Elloluv (f)
118	Even The Score
118	Halory Leigh (f)
118	My Trusty Cat (f)

118	Pohave
118	Tamweel (f)
118	Wildcat Heir
117	Beau's Town
117	Bluesthestandard
117	Bowman's Band
117	Cat Genius
117	Domestic Dispute
117	Freefourinternet
117	Gators N Bears
117	*Lundy's Liability
117	Mayo On The Side (f)
117	Olmodavor
117	Publication
117	Randaroo (f)
117	Star Parade (f)
117	Voodoo

TURF

Three-Year-Olds
128	Kitten's Joy
125	†Ouija Board (f)
123	†Tycoon
123§	†Antonius Pius
121	Artie Schiller
119	Good Reward
119	Prince Arch
118	Amorama (f)
118	*Fast And Furious
118	Miss Vegas (f)
118	Ticker Tape (f)
117	Mustanfar
117	†Three Valleys
116	Lucifer's Stone (f)

Older Horses
128	†Sulamani
127	†Hard Buck
126	Better Talk Now
125	Singletary
124	†Magistretti
124	†Powerscourt
123	Kicken Kris
123	Nothing To Lose
122	†Epalo
122	Intercontinental (f)
122	Perfect Soul
122	Soaring Free
121	Light Jig (f)
121	†Simonas
120	†Brian Boru
120	Designed For Luck
120	Film Maker (f)
120	Leroidesanimaux
120	Mr O'Brien
120	Pellegrino
120	Request For Parole
120	Sabiango
120	†Six Perfections (f)
120	Star Over The Bay
119	Balto Star
119	Host

119	License To Run	118	Dreadnaught	117	Commercante (f)
119	Royal Regalia	118	Just Wonder	117	Etoile Montante (f)
119	Special Ring	118	*King's Drama	117	Musical Chimes (f)
119	Stroll	118	Meteor Storm	117	Senor Swinger
119	†Vangelis	118	Quantum Merit	117	Sweet Return
119	Wonder Again (f)	118	Riskaverse (f)		
118	Bayamo	118	Sarafan	111	Noches de Rosa (f)
118	Belleski (f)	118	Silver Tree		
118	†Crimson Palace (f)	117	A To The Z		

JAPAN   No sooner had one Japanese Horse of The Year been retired to stud—Symboli Kris S had earned the title in both 2002 and 2003—than his stable, that of champion trainer Kazuo Fujisawa, came up with his successor, **Zenno Rob Roy**. Runner-up in the previous year's Japanese Derby, it was not until the autumn of the latest season that Zenno Rob Roy began showing anything better than smart form, but he dominated the top middle-distance races once doing so, completing a hat-trick under Olivier Peslier in the Tenno Sho (Autumn), the Japan Cup and the Arima Kinen, breaking Symboli Kris S's track record in the last-named event. Connections are reportedly keen to race Zenno Rob Roy in Europe in 2005. The Arima Kinen runner-up, and previous year's Japan Cup winner, **Tap Dance City**, was himself seen out in Europe in the latest season, though failed to do himself justice when finishing well held in the Arc. He had won both his starts at home earlier in the year, a Group 2 event at Chukyo from **Blue Eleven** and the Takarazuka Kinen, in which Zenno Rob Roy finished only fourth. Another leading older horse to try his luck in Europe was **Ingrandire** who finished well beaten in the Gold Cup at Royal Ascot, though he too had won in Group 1 company in Japan at the expense of Zenno Rob Roy, giving him a seven-length beating into second in the two-mile Tenno Sho (Spring). **Silk Famous** won twice in Group 2 company early in the year before being placed behind the above-named horses in the Tenno Sho (Spring), Takarazuka Kinen and Arima Kinen, running his best race when third in the last-named race, ahead of **Daitaku Bertram** who ensured that older horses filled the frame. **Admire Groove** took the Queen Elizabeth II Commemorative Cup for the second year running and emulated her own dam, Air Groove, by being named champion older female.

Over shorter trips, **Durandal** was still a leading performer. He failed in his attempt to win the Sprinters Stakes for a second year when beaten four lengths by **Calstone Light O** in heavy ground, but managed to retain his Mile Championship title later in the autumn. He also lost out narrowly in the spring's big sprint when going down by a neck to **Sunningdale** in the Takamatsunomiya Kinen. Although campaigned mainly at longer trips, **Tsurumaru Boy** was dropped back successfully to land the Yasuda Kinen, the top open-aged mile event of the first half of the year, by a neck from **Telegnosis**, the latter going on to finish third in the Mile Championship in the autumn. Telegnosis, along with Durandal, Calstone Light O and Sunningdale seemed to give Japan a strong hand at the Hong Kong International meeting where Japanese horses have performed well in the past, but all ran well below par. **Time Paradox** put up the best performance on dirt when beating stable-companion and February Stakes winner **Admire Don** in the Japan Cup Dirt. The runner-up was one of three Japanese horses who had been well beaten in the Dubai World Cup.

Japan Cup, Tokyo—a 1, 2, 3 for home-trained runners
as Zenno Rob Roy, Cosmo Bulk (No.10) and Delta Blues are followed home
by French-trained Policy Maker (No.1); Phoenix Reach (No.5) runs well on his first start for four months

*Japan Cup Dirt, Tokyo—only three foreign challengers for this
and Time Paradox leads home another Japanese 1, 2, 3; the only British challenger Vortex
is right at the back, virtually pulled up in the end*

A good crop of three-year-olds was headed by the Tokyo Yushun (Derby) winner **King Kamehameha**, a Kingmambo half-brother to the formerly British-trained Santa Anita Derby winner The Deputy. Neither of the placed horses from the Derby, **Heart's Cry** and **Higher Game**, advertised the form that well against older rivals later on, and King Kamehameha had actually put up a better performance when running out a five-length winner of the NHK Mile Cup three weeks earlier. Although successful in Group 2 company in the autumn, a tendon injury caused King Kamehameha's premature retirement, and he was syndicated for around 19 million US dollars, a record for a Japanese-trained horse. Other three-year-olds did perform well against their elders later in the year. Both the Satsuki Sho (2000 Guineas) runner-up **Cosmo Bulk** and the Kikuka Sho (St Leger) winner **Delta Blues** went on to fill the places in the Japan Cup, with the latter also running a good fifth in the Arima Kinen. The 2000 Guineas went to **Daiwa Major** who failed to progress, while another three-year-old worthy of a mention is **Personal Rush** who was not at all discredited in finishing sixth in the Breeders' Cup Classic.

There was little to choose between the leading three-year-old fillies. **Daiwa El Cielo** came out on top in the Yushun Himba (Oaks), with the future Shuka Sho winner **Sweep Tosho** in second and **Dance In The Mood**, who had won the Oka Sho (1000 Guineas) in fourth. Dance In The Mood was campaigned the most boldly of the trio and to her credit finished second in the American Oaks at Hollywood, as well as finishing runner-up to leading older horses Zenno Rob Roy in the Tenno Sho (Autumn) and Durandal in the Mile Championship.

2005 will see the number of races opened to international competition more than double. Among them, all of the Japan Racing Association's Group 1 events on turf open to older horses (except the Arima Kinen which remains Japan's domestic end-of-year championship race) will now be open to foreign-trained horses. The main benefit to the Japanese racing and bloodstock industry will be that such races will now have internationally recognised Group 1 status, something they did not enjoy when restricted to Japanese-trained horses. Foreign trainers are already taking advantage of the growing opportunities to campaign their horses in pursuit of huge prizes in Japan. Rakti, Fayr Jag and Ashdown Express were among those to take their chance from Britain in the latest season in races other than the Japan Cup. For the first time ever in 2004, and to celebrate its fiftieth anniversary, the JRA held two Group 1 races on the same card, with the more recently-introduced Japan Cup Dirt (contested by horses from the USA and Germany, as well as Vortex from Britain) staged alongside the Japan Cup which has always been the main draw to foreign stables since its inception in 1981. To stimulate international competition even more, this is a meeting which the authorities could develop further in years to come. Either by moving existing races, or adding new ones, to the Japan Cup card, the potential is there to create an international meeting along the lines of those that have proved so successful in Dubai and Hong Kong. Recent years have shown that Japanese horses are well able to hold their own against international competition, be it abroad or at home.

1198

Three-year-olds		Older Horses			
125	King Kamehameha	126	†Zenno Rob Roy	118	Lincoln
122	Cosmo Bulk	125	Calstone Light O	118	Narita Century
122	Delta Blues	125	Durandal	118	Neo Universe
118	Daiwa Major	125	†Tap Dance City	117	Balance of Game
118	Heart's Cry	122	†Ingrandire	117	Osumi Haruka (f)
118	Higher Game	122	Silk Famous	117	Silent Deal
117	Adjudi Mitsuo	121	Daitaku Bertram	116	Fine Motion (f)
117	Daiwa El Cielo (f)	121	Tsurumaru Boy	116	Meiner Solomon
117	Keiai Guard	120	Blue Eleven	116	Sakura President
116	Dance In The Mood (f)	120	Sunningdale	116	Utopia
116	Gene Crisis	120	Telegnosis	115	Er Nova (f)
116	Hookipa Wave	120	Time Paradox	115	Gallant Arrow
116	Personal Rush	119	That's The Plenty	115	Keeneland Swan
116	Sweep Tosho (f)	119	Win Radius	115	Lohengrin
115	Black Tide	118	Admire Don	115	Mitsuaki Turbine
115	Opera City	118	Admire Groove (f)	115	Sterling Rose
115	Yamanin Sucre (f)	118	Golden Cast	115	Tosen Dandy
				115	Yukino Sun Royal

HONG KONG   With his unbeaten record still intact after thirteen career starts to the end of 2004, **Silent Witness** not only strengthened his position as Hong Kong's best horse but had good claims to being considered the best sprinter in the world. The acid test of his claims to being the best sprinter around ought to have been the Hong Kong Sprint in December, but for the second year running, Silent Witness gained a rather bloodless victory after his international rivals—from Europe, Japan and Australia—collectively failed to give anything like their running. Earlier in the year, Silent Witness was unextended in four outings against local opposition, notably when winning all three legs of the Champion Sprint Series (starting at 10/1-on each time), consisting of the Bauhinia Sprint Trophy, Centenary Sprint Cup and Chairman's Sprint Prize. Silent Witness has nothing more to prove domestically and is due to be campaigned beyond six furlongs later in 2005, after his effectiveness at beyond six furlongs has been tested. A visit to Britain looks to have been ruled out however, as being a gelding Silent Witness has no stud value to enhance and the prize money alone is not considered enough of an incentive to make the trip.

Silent Witness' domination of the sprints came at the chief expense of **Cape of Good Hope**, who was placed in all three Champion Sprint Series races and went one better than the year before when runner-up in the Hong Kong Sprint. He managed to avoid his chief rival by trying his luck abroad as well, and was rewarded by finishing in the frame in the King's Stand Stakes, Golden Jubilee Stakes and July Cup in Britain, and in the Sprinters Stakes in Japan. Cape of Good Hope was due to continue his travels in Australia in 2005. The front-running **Scintillation** was one of the most improved horses in 2004, completing a four-timer in seven-furlong handicaps for the now-retired trainer Ivan Allan in the first half of the year. He returned in the autumn to win the Sha Tin Sprint Trophy, but after finishing third to Silent Witness in the International Sprint Trial, ran in the Mile at the International meeting rather than taking on the champion again in the Sprint, finishing a close fourth.

In a bunched finish to the Hong Kong Mile won by Godolphin's Firebreak, **Perfect Partner** and **The Duke** took the places. The Duke had previously won the International Mile Trial, just one of several races during the autumn in which Perfect Partner had endured bad luck in running. Eight-year-old **Electronic Unicorn**, runner-up in the Hong

Cathay Pacific Hong Kong Sprint, Sha Tin—Silent Witness wins for a second successive year, extending his unbeaten run to thirteen; Cape of Good Hope chases him home with fourth-placed Royal Millennium (rail) best of the British challengers

Kong Mile in 2001 and 2002, returned from twelve months off the track with a foot injury and showed he retained plenty of ability in the first half of the year, winning the Queen's Silver Jubilee Cup and giving plenty of weight to the three-year-old Stay Young (ex-British Romancero) in the Sha Tin Mile Trophy.

As well as Silent Witness, the Tony Cruz stable had the next-best horse in Hong Kong as well, **Bullish Luck**, formerly known as Al Moughazel when trained by Pip Payne in Britain. He began the year with a defeat of the mare **Elegant Fashion** (later successful in the Chairman's Trophy) and ended it with a fine second to the Irish filly Alexander Goldrun in the Hong Kong Cup, in which Elegant Fashion ran well in sixth. Elegant Fashion also contested the Cox Plate in her native Australia (badly hampered when a close ninth) and ran well in Hong Kong's big international race of the first half of the year when second to **River Dancer** (the ex-Irish horse Diaghilev) in the Queen Elizabeth II Cup.

Ain't Here and **Bowman's Crossing** were the other local runners who contested the Hong Kong Cup, Ain't Here faring much the better of the pair in eighth. Ain't Here had got the better of their two previous exchanges as well, beating Bowman's Crossing narrowly in the Sha Tin Trophy when in receipt of weight but confirming the placings on level terms in the International Cup Trial. Bowman's Crossing failed to win during the year, but also ran a good fourth in the Queen Elizabeth II Cup, and ran twice at Ascot during the summer, finishing seventh in the Queen Anne Stakes.

As usual at the International meeting, it was in the mile and a half Vase in which the local horses found the foreign challengers at their strongest. The remarkably versatile Super Kid (rated 113) fared best in finishing fifth behind Phoenix Reach. His wins came in the Stewards' Cup over a mile, and the Champions & Chater Cup over a mile and a half, but he also ran creditably over six furlongs. With geldings making up most of the Hong Kong horse population, Lucky Owners (114) was a rarity in retiring to stud (shuttling between Australia and Britain) during the latest season. The New Zealand-bred son of Danehill (out of a close relative to the Melbourne Cup/Cox Plate winner Might And Power) won eight of his fourteen career starts in Hong Kong, adding the Hong Kong Derby to the Hong Kong Mile he had won in 2003.

128	†Silent Witness	117	†Bowman's Crossing	116	Scintillation
124	Bullish Luck	117	Electronic Unicorn	116	The Duke
120	River Dancer	116	†Cape of Good Hope	115	Elegant Fashion (f)
118	Ain't Here	116	Perfect Partner		

AUSTRALIA AND NEW ZEALAND   2004 was another absorbing year for racing enthusiasts, full of noteworthy performances, and importantly, it saw the emergence of likely successors to the high-class performers Lonhro and Northerly who were both retired. **Lonhro** raced fives times in 2004, winning at Group 1 level three times (C. F. Orr Stakes at Caulfield, Australian Cup at Flemington, George Ryder Stakes at Rosehill) and at Group 2 level in the St George Stakes at Caulfield. Lonhro's magnificent win in the Australian Cup at Flemington, his last appearance in Melbourne (before being beaten in the Queen Elizabeth Stakes at Randwick on his final start), was a memorable one. After being seriously blocked at the furlong-and-a-half mark, his chance of winning a tenth Group 1 looked forlorn, but once in the clear, he caught **Delzao**. Lonhro dropped back in distance to seven and a half furlongs in the George Ryder Stakes and again displayed his trademark acceleration to dispose of Grand Armee and Private Steer in race record time of 1m 27.24sec. Lonhro retires to stud as the sixth highest earner in Australian racing history ($5.8m) and the winner of twenty-six of his thirty-five starts, including eleven at Group 1 level. Meanwhile, Australia's best horse of 2002, Northerly, made a brief but unsuccessful return to the track following an injury he sustained in 2003.

With the retirement of these two high-class performers **Grand Armee** will go into 2005 as the highest-rated horse still racing in Australia and New Zealand. The Hennessy six-year-old gelding will be best remembered for beating Lonhro by six lengths in the Queen Elizabeth Stakes. He also won the George Main Stakes and MacKinnon Stakes and was also one of many unlucky runners behind Savabeel in the Cox Plate at Moonee Valley when a fast-finishing close-up fourth.

Carlton Draught Cox Plate, Moonee Valley—
in a rough race, Savabeel wins the Australian leg of the World Series;
the blinkered head of runner-up Fields of Omagh just gets into picture
with Starcraft a close third

Australia's most famous horse race the Melbourne Cup was an historic occasion, won for the second year running by Northern Hemisphere-bred mare **Makybe Diva**. The mare not only rewrote the record books but proved better than ever as she defeated high-class Irish stayer Vinnie Roe and the locally-trained **Zazzman**. Makybe Diva had also scored in the Sydney Cup earlier in the year, becoming the first horse in thirty-seven years to capture the Melbourne and Sydney Cups in the same season. After the decision of her trainer David Hall to take up an offer to train in Hong Kong, following her Sydney Cup win, Lee Freedman took over the training of the mare. Upon her return to racing in the second half of the year, her early runs indicated she had come back better than ever, a fact reinforced by her narrow defeat in the Caulfield Cup prior to the Melbourne Cup. As well as becoming the first mare to win the Cup twice, she also shouldered a mare's weight-carrying record of 8-10 and was the shortest-priced winner since Rising Fast at the same odds of 5/2 some fifty years earlier. Makybe Diva is scheduled to race overseas in 2005 with Dubai and Europe as possible venues.

The second highest-rated mare, **Private Steer**, had an outstanding year, winning the Group 2 Apollo Stakes, Group 1 Doncaster Handicap and Group 1 All Aged Stakes, all at Randwick. She also took the Group 2 Warwick Stakes in August but suffered an injury not long afterwards which ruled her out for the rest of the year. Later sold, she will now be trained in North America in 2005.

While there was a general lack of depth in the older horses in 2004, **Takeover Target** remains unbeaten in seven starts and with some excellent opportunities in 2005 could easily continue his winning streak. Purchased at a horses in training sale for £550 sterling, the son of Celtic Swing progressed from a Queanbeyan maiden to the Group 1 Salinger Stakes at Flemington on Victoria Derby day. Other sprinters in the older horses category who performed well were **Regal Roller** and **Super Elegant**. Regal Roller made rapid strides, winning at Group 1 level in the Dubai Racing Club Cup and Toorak Handicap. All his best performances have been at Caulfield where he has been victorious eight times.

1201

Emirates Melbourne Cup, Flemington—favourite Makybe Diva wins for the second year running, with top weight Vinnie Roe putting up a career-best effort in second

Super Elegant became the first horse to win the Group 1 double of the Goodwood Handicap at Morphettville in South Australia and the Doomben 10,000 at Doomben in Queensland.

Unlike the older horses, the four-year-olds were an above-average group with plenty of depth, headed in the ratings by **Exceed And Excel** who started just twice in Australia, winning the Group 2 Royal Sovereign Stakes at Kensington and the Group 1 Newmarket Handicap at Flemington. Exceed And Excel gave a brilliant exhibition in the Newmarket Handicap winning in 1m 8.72sec and breaking twelve seconds in four consecutive furlong intervals.

The second highest-rated four-year-olds were Reset, Starcraft and Spark of Life. **Reset** was unbeaten in five runs, his last two at Group 1 level in the Australian Guineas at Flemington and then against older horses in the Futurity Stakes at Caulfield. In the Australian Guineas he beat a good field including Starcraft, Delzao and Elvstroem. It was unfortunate Reset went amiss and had to be retired to stud (under the Darley banner, alongside Exceed And Excel), because he would almost certainly have been one of the stars of the second half of the year.

Starcraft had racegoers on the edge of their seats every time he raced. After being beaten narrowly by Reset in the Australian Guineas, Starcraft took on the older horses in the Chipping Norton Stakes over a mile at Warwick Farm in Sydney, winning easily. Twenty-eight days later, in the Group 2 Tulloch Stakes at Rosehill, he came from well back to win running away. The prestigious AJC Australian Derby over a mile and a half was next, and in typical fashion, Starcraft again claimed the prize right on the line. Connections immediately aimed the colt at the Cox Plate in October but took the unusual step of sending him to New Zealand in preparation, targeting New Zealand's richest weight-for-age race, the Kelt Stakes, along the way. Starcraft began his New Zealand campaign with wins in the Group 1 Mudgway Stakes and then in the Group 2 Stony Bridge Stakes at Hastings, both times defeating the New Zealand mare Miss Potential (rated 113). However on Kelt Stakes day, Starcraft led the field early before being run down to finish second to Balmuse. Starcraft returned to Australia where he subsequently finished third to Savabeel in the Cox Plate and is due to be based in Britain with Luca Cumani in 2005. Sydney-trained sprinter **Spark of Life** came of age in 2004, winning his last five starts, culminating in the Manikato Stakes at Moonee Valley in September, and should be a force in major sprints in 2005.

The Caulfield Cup was won by **Elvstroem**, winner of the 2003 Victoria Derby. Elvstroem became the first Victoria Derby winner since Manfred in 1926 to win the Caulfield Cup the following season. Elvstroem had an excellent year, also winning the Group 2 Shannons Classic at Caulfield, the Group 1 Underwood Stakes at Caulfield and the Group 2 Turnbull Stakes at Flemington. Early in the year, Elvstroem had also finished third to Lonhro in the Australian Cup. Lonhro's younger brother **Niello** also had a good year, winning the Canterbury Guineas and Rosehill Guineas before suffering an injury which ruled him out for the rest of the season. The highest-rated sprinting filly was Queensland-trained **Regimental Gal** who began the year impressively by winning the Lightning Stakes at Flemington. Two starts later Regimental Gal followed up with another Group 1 win, this time over six furlongs in the Australia Stakes at Moonee Valley. **Special Harmony** was the highest-rated filly over middle distances, winning the Group 2 Moonee Valley Oaks and the Group 1 Arrowfield Stud Stakes.

There looked to be considerable depth in the 2004 group of three-year-olds, with twelve of them rated 120 or higher, compared to ten in 2003, which augurs well for 2005. The year began with the emergence of exciting three-year-old gelding **Dance Hero**, who took all before him, becoming the first horse to win the Magic Millions Classic on the Gold Coast and the Golden Slipper Stakes at Rosehill. Dance Hero also became just the fifth horse to win the Juvenile Triple Crown of Group 1 races, consisting of the Golden Slipper Stakes, AJC Sires' Produce Stakes and AJC Champagne Stakes. Dance Hero set new race records in the Golden Slipper Stakes of 1m 8.6sec and in the AJC Champagne Stakes of 1m 34.75sec. These efforts made him the highest-rated three-year-old.

Fastnet Rock was a late-maturing colt who was second only to Dance Hero among the three-year-olds after some fine efforts later in the year. Trained by Paul Perry (of Choisir fame), Fastnet Rock gained four successes, all at six furlongs. After winning the Roman Consul Stakes and the Up And Coming Stakes at Warwick Farm in Sydney, Perry took the colt to Melbourne, aiming him at the Caulfield Guineas over a mile. However, Fastnet Rock was not as effective beyond six furlongs and was switched back in distance to win the Group 3 L'Oreal Paris Plate and the Group 2 Lexus Classic, races Choisir also contested before carrying all before him the following year.

One of the best performances among the three-year-olds was the win by **Savabeel** in Australia's premier weight-for-age race, the Cox Plate at Moonee Valley. After finishing third to Dance Hero in the AJC Champagne Stakes, Savabeel really blossomed in the second half of the year, winning another Group 1, the Spring Champion Stakes at Randwick, prior to the Cox Plate. Savabeel became the sixth of his age group to win the Cox Plate since 1970 and the first since Octagonal in 1995. On his final run of the year, Savabeel tackled the Victoria Derby but found West Australian three-year-old **Plastered** too strong. Plastered is a young stayer with a future who ended the year with seven wins from eight starts.

The leading three-year-old filly was **Alinghi**, who scored at Group 1 level in the Blue Diamond Stakes and Thousand Guineas, both at Caulfield. Alinghi was also beaten narrowly in the Golden Slipper Stakes behind Dance Hero and **Charge Forward**, and in the Empire Rose Stakes when runner-up to Miss Potential. Alinghi has won eight of her twelve starts and connections are considering an overseas campaign in 2005. Other promising three-year-olds to watch in 2005 include **Binding**, **Not A Single Doubt**, **Lotteria** and **Brannigan**. The lightly-raced Binding, went from restricted class to winning the Group 2 Sandown Guineas, showing dramatic improvement each time. Lotteria is an exciting prospect for 2005. She remains unbeaten from four appearances, becoming the first filly to win the Group 3 Spring Stakes over a mile at Newcastle in its twenty-one-year history. In her last run of the year she demolished the Group 1 Flight Stakes field over the Randwick mile by seven lengths and more.

The two-year-olds look to be above average at this stage, with impressive early-season displays coming from **Snitzel**, **Gonski**, **Mnemosyne**, **Blizzardly** and **Meriwether**. Snitzel won the Listed Breeders' Plate in impressive fashion before taking the Strawberry Hill Stud Slipper at Wyong also over five furlongs. Gonski, Mnemosyne and Blizzardly made outstanding debuts, beating their rivals easily.

Australia and New Zealand did not fare too well overseas in 2004. Top sprinter Exceed And Excel was set to follow in the footsteps of Choisir in 2003 but unfortunately became ill while in training at Newmarket for the Royal Ascot meeting. He finally took his place in the July Cup field but was soon beaten after leading early on, and was retired to stud shortly afterwards. Australia had two representatives at the Hong Kong International meeting in sprinter **Yell** and Cox Plate runner-up **Fields of Omagh** but both were well held. 2004 also brought up a milestone for leading trainer Lee Freedman who notched his hundredth Group 1 winner in his training career when 2003 Caulfield Cup winner **Mummify** won the Yalumba (Caulfield) Stakes.

Ratings and text for Australia and New Zealand are supplied courtesy of Gary Crispe (www.aapracingandsports.com.au). The ages listed below are as at 31st December 2004.

Two-Year-Olds

120p	Gonski
120	Snitzel
119p	Mnemosyne (f)
116	Al Samer
116	Jiang
116	Power of Destiny
116	Quarterman
115p	Blizzardly (f)
115	Meriwether (f)
115	Media (f)
115	Dr Green
115	The Rhine
115?	Rossa Glory
114	Fullazz (f)
114	Seidnazar
114?	Red Enzo
113	Junebug (f)
112	Banished
112	Come Undone
112	Danger Looms
112	Freestyle (f)

Three-Year-Olds

125	Dance Hero
124p	Fastnet Rock
123	Charge Forward
122p	Not A Single Doubt
122	Alinghi (f)
122	Savabeel
121p	Binding
121p	Brannigan
121	Alizes (f)
120	Outback Prince
120	Tirade
120	Wager (f)
119p	Lotteria (f)
119p	Plastered
119	Barely A Moment

119	Crimson Reign (f)
119	Dane Shadow
119	Econsul
118	Al Maher
118	Classiconi
118	Oratorio (Aus)
118?	Star Shiraz (f)
117	Commands Nothin' (f)
117	Count Ricardo
117	One World (f)
117	Prisoner of Love (f)
117	Squad
117	Zankel
117?	Golden Fox
117?	Segments (f)
116	Ballybleue (f)
116	Cedar Manor
116	Eltonjon
116	Gator
116	Our Sweet Moss (f)
116	Star Cat
116	Tahni Girl (f)
116	Wildly

Four-Year-Olds

126	†Exceed And Excel
124	Reset
124	Spark of Life
124	Starcraft
123	Grand Zulu
123	King's Chapel
122	Elvstroem
122	Regimental Gal (f)
121	Taikun
121d	*Ambulance
120	Delzao
120	Cross Current
120	Russian Pearl
120	Shamekha (f)
120	Sharp (f)
119	Niello
118	Dilly Dally (f)
118	Keep The Faith
118	Special Harmony (f)
117	Gallieni
117	Legally Bay (f)
117d	Scaredee Cat
116p	Desert War

116+	Falkirk
116+	Toulouse Lautrec
116	*Allgunadoit
116	Devastating
116	Only Words (f)
116	Picaday
116	Polar Success (f)
116?	Braeloch
115	Confectioner
115	Hinting (f)
115	Recapitalize
115	Timbourina (f)
115	Under The Bridge
115	Wild Iris (f)

Older Horses

128	Lonhro
126	Grand Armee
125	†Makybe Diva (f)
123	Fields of Omagh
123	Private Steer (f)
122	Mummify
121	Defier
121	Regal Roller
120p	Takeover Target
120	Star of Florida
120	Super Elegant
120	Thorn Park
120	Yell
119	Mistegic
119	Our Egyptian Raine (f)
119	Titanic Jack
118	Hugs Dancer
118	Make Mine Magic
118	Platinum Scissors
118	Sportsman
118	True Glo
116	County Tyrone
115	Bomber Bill
115	Pentastic
115	Scenic Peak
115	She's Archie (f)
115	Sound Action (f)
115	St Reims
115	Super Impressive
115	Zazzman

The following horses trained elsewhere also figured in races outside their own country:

Three-Year-Old		**Older Horse**	
118	Darsalam (Slovakia)	104	*Jacira (f) (Spain)

INDEX TO PHOTOGRAPHS

PORTRAITS & SNAPSHOTS

1205

RACE PHOTOGRAPHS

betfair.com St Leger Stakes (Doncaster)	*John Crofts*	888
betfair.com Two-Year-Old Trophy (Redcar)	*Alec Russell*	730
Betfair Cup (Lennox) (Goodwood)	*John Crofts*	182
betfred.com Mile (Sandown)	*Ed Byrne*	482
bet365 Craven Stakes (Newmarket)	*John Crofts*	445
bet365 Lancashire Oaks (Haydock)	*Alec Russell*	807
bet365 Old Newton Cup (Handicap) (Haydock)	*Alec Russell*	50
Blue Square Chester Rated Stakes (Handicap) (Chester)	*Alec Russell*	1010
BMW Deutsches Derby (Hamburg)	*Frank Sorge*	935
bonusprint.com Henry II Stakes (Sandown)	*John Crofts*	762
Boylesports Irish 1000 Guineas (the Curragh)	*Peter Mooney*	92
Boylesports Irish 2000 Guineas (the Curragh)	*Caroline Norris*	107
Britannia Stakes (Handicap) (Royal Ascot)	*Ed Byrne*	617
Buckingham Palace Stakes (Handicap) (Royal Ascot)	*Alec Russell*	1080
Budweiser Irish Derby (the Curragh)	*Bill Selwyn*	439
cantorodds.com Stakes (Handicap) (Goodwood)	*John Crofts*	257
cantorodds.com Steventon Stakes (Newbury)	*Bill Selwyn*	687
Cantor Odds Sussex Stakes (Goodwood)	*Ed Byrne*	970
Cathay Pacific Hong Kong Cup (Sha Tin)	*George Selwyn*	45
Cathay Pacific Hong Kong Mile (Sha Tin)	*Frank Sorge*	372
Cathay Pacific Hong Kong Vase (Sha Tin)	*George Selwyn*	787
Centex Fairclough Homes Trophy (Conditions Stakes) (Doncaster)	*Ed Byrne*	917
Champagne Laurent-Perrier Sprint Stakes (Sandown)	*Ed Byrne*	744
Chippenham Lodge Stud Cherry Hinton Stakes (Newmarket)	*Ed Byrne*	518
Coolmore Fusaichi Pegasus Matron Stakes (Leopardstown)	*Ed Byrne*	971
Coral-Eclipse Stakes (Sandown)	*John Crofts*	856
Coral Sprint Trophy (Handicap) (York)	*Alec Russell*	521
Coronation Stakes (Royal Ascot)	*Bill Selwyn*	93
Coventry Stakes (Royal Ascot)	*John Crofts*	485
Criterium International (Saint-Cloud)	*John Crofts*	466
Cuisine de France Summer Stakes (York)	*Alec Russell*	1018
Daily Record Scottish Derby (Ayr)	*Alec Russell*	527
Daily Telegraph Great Voltigeur Stakes (York)	*John Crofts*	887
Darley Dewhurst Stakes (Newmarket)	*Ed Byrne*	927
Darley Irish Oaks (the Curragh)	*John Crofts*	748
Darley July Cup (Newmarket)	*John Crofts*	394
Derrinstown Stud Derby Trial Stakes (Leopardstown)	*Peter Mooney*	1132
Dubai Duty Free (Nad Al Sheba)	*Frank Sorge*	761
Dubai Duty Free Arc Trial (Newbury)	*John Crofts*	940
Dubai Duty Free Mill Reef Stakes (Newbury)	*Ed Byrne*	400
Dubai Duty Free Stakes (Fred Darling) (Newbury)	*John Crofts*	611
Dubai International Airport World Trophy (Newbury)	*Ed Byrne*	1036
Dubai Sheema Classic (Nad Al Sheba)	*Frank Sorge*	806
Dubai World Cup (Nad Al Sheba)	*Bill Selwyn*	801
Duke of Edinburgh Stakes (Handicap) (Royal Ascot)	*John Crofts*	1130
Duke of York Hearthstead Homes Stakes (York)	*Alec Russell*	665
Dunnes Stores National Stakes (the Curragh)	*Caroline Norris*	318
Earth Mortgages Scarbrough Stakes (Doncaster)	*John Crofts*	203
Emirates Airline Champion Stakes (Newmarket)	*John Crofts*	447
Emirates Airline Yorkshire Cup (York)	*John Crofts*	645
Enter The £1 Million totetentofollow November Stakes (Handicap) (Doncaster)	*Alec Russell*	195
Foster's Lager Chipchase Stakes (Newcastle)	*Alec Russell*	882
Freephone Stanleybet Lincoln (Handicap) (Doncaster)	*Alec Russell*	106
Gainsborough Poule d'Essai des Poulains (Longchamp)	*John Crofts*	59
Gainsborough Poule d'Essai des Pouliches (Longchamp)	*John Crofts*	1058
Galileo EBF Futurity Stakes (the Curragh)	*Peter Mooney*	741
Gallagher Group Ltd Derby Trial Stakes (Lingfield)	*Ed Byrne*	777
GNER Diadem Stakes (Ascot)	*Ed Byrne*	793
GNER Doncaster Cup (Doncaster)	*John Crofts*	531
GNER Park Stakes (Doncaster)	*John Crofts*	769
Godolphin Mile (Nad Al Sheba)	*Bill Selwyn*	371
Golan EBF Mooresbridge Stakes (the Curragh)	*Caroline Norris*	725
Gold Cup (Royal Ascot)	*John Crofts*	762
Golden Jubilee Stakes (Royal Ascot)	*George Selwyn*	364
Grand Prix de Deauville Lucien Barriere (Deauville)	*Bertrand*	213
Grand Prix de Saint-Cloud (Saint-Cloud)	*John Crofts*	404

Gran Premio del Jockey Club Italiano (Milan)	*Enzo De Nardin*	936
Grosser Volkswagen Preis von Baden (Baden-Baden)	*George Selwyn*	1102
Hackney Empire Royal Lodge Stakes (Ascot)	*Ed Byrne*	778
Hardwicke Stakes (Royal Ascot)	*W. Everitt*	307
Haynes, Hanson and Clark Conditions Stakes (Newbury)	*Ed Byrne*	639
Hong Kong Jockey Club Sprint (Handicap) (Ascot)	*Bill Selwyn*	122
Igloos Bentinck Stakes (Newmarket)	*Ed Byrne*	882
Independent Waterford Wedgwood Phoenix Stakes (the Curragh)	*Caroline Norris*	261
Irish Field St Leger (the Curragh)	*Caroline Norris*	1093
Irish National Stud Blandford Stakes (the Curragh)	*Peter Mooney*	670
Irish Stallion Farms EBF Maiden (Leopardstown)	*Ed Byrne*	1044
Jaguar Lowther Stakes (York)	*Alec Russell*	958
Jardine Lloyd Thompson Dee Stakes (Chester)	*Ed Byrne*	33
Jersey Stakes (Royal Ascot)	*Alec Russell*	536
John Smith's Cup (Handicap) (York)	*Bill Selwyn*	77
John Smith's Northumberland Plate (Handicap) (Newcastle)	*Bill Selwyn*	651
John Smith's Stakes (Handicap) (Newbury)	*Ed Byrne*	981
Juddmonte Beresford Stakes (the Curragh)	*Peter Mooney*	41
Juddmonte Grand Prix de Paris (Longchamp)	*John Crofts*	112
Juddmonte International Stakes (York)	*Ed Byrne*	997
Juddmonte Lockinge Stakes (Newbury)	*Ed Byrne*	893
Killavullan Stakes (Leopardstown)	*Caroline Norris*	384
Kingdom of Bahrain Sun Chariot Stakes (Newmarket)	*Ed Byrne*	95
King Edward VII Stakes (Royal Ascot)	*John Crofts*	376
King George Stakes (Goodwood)	*George Selwyn*	866
King George V Stakes (Handicap) (Royal Ascot)	*Alec Russell*	29
King George VI and Queen Elizabeth Diamond Stakes (Ascot)	*George Selwyn*	308
King's Stand Stakes (Royal Ascot)	*Ed Byrne*	1035
Ladbrokes Bunbury Cup (Handicap) (Newmarket)	*John Crofts*	629
Ladbrokes Rockingham Handicap (the Curragh)	*Caroline Norris*	746
Lady O Goodwood Cup (Goodwood)	*George Selwyn*	270
Lane's End Greenham Stakes (Newbury)	*Ed Byrne*	900
Leopardstown 2000 Guineas Trial Stakes (Leopardstown)	*Caroline Norris*	438
Letheby & Christopher Cheshire Oaks (Chester)	*Ed Byrne*	471
Littlewoods Bet Direct Lincoln Trial Stakes (Handicap) (Wolverhampton)	*Alec Russell*	1097
Littlewoods Bet Direct Winter Derby (Lingfield)	*W. Everitt*	185
MBNA Europe Bank Chester Vase (Chester)	*George Selwyn*	851
McKeever St Lawrence Conditions Stakes (Doncaster)	*Alec Russell*	577
Mehl-Mulhens-Rennen (Cologne)	*Frank Nolting*	176
Meon Valley Stud Fillies' Mile (Ascot)	*John Crofts*	797
Merlin "New Discovery 3" Handicap (Doncaster)	*Alec Russell*	920
Michael Page International Silver Trophy Stakes (Ascot)	*Ed Byrne*	938
Moyglare Stud Stakes (the Curragh)	*Caroline Norris*	210
NetJets Prix du Moulin de Longchamp (Longchamp)	*Ed Byrne*	434
Nexus GSA Conditions Stakes (Chester)	*Alan Wright*	133
NGK Spark Plugs Abernant Stakes (Newmarket)	*John Crofts*	76
Nolan & Brophy Auctioneers Flying Five (the Curragh)	*Caroline Norris*	867
Oaks d'Italia (Milan)	*Enzo De Nardin*	636
Oak Tree Stakes (Goodwood)	*John Crofts*	785
£100000 Tattersalls Autumn Auction Stakes (Newmarket)	*John Crofts*	188
orderIT-online.com Troy Stakes (Doncaster)	*Ed Byrne*	294
O2 Kilternan Stakes (Leopardstown)	*Ed Byrne*	27
Owen Brown Rockfel Stakes (Newmarket)	*Ed Byrne*	610
Patrick P. O'Leary Memorial Phoenix Sprint Stakes (the Curragh)	*Caroline Norris*	735
Pattison Canadian International Stakes (Woodbine)	*Bill Selwyn*	998
Pentax UK September Stakes (Kempton)	*Bill Selwyn*	616
Persian Punch Jockey Club Cup (Newmarket)	*George Selwyn*	646
Petros Rose of Lancaster Stakes (Haydock)	*Alec Russell*	658
Polypipe Flying Childers Stakes (Doncaster)	*John Crofts*	208
Premio Vittorio di Capua (Milan)	*Enzo De Nardin*	65
Prince of Wales's Stakes (Royal Ascot)	*John Crofts*	840
Princess of Wales's cantorodds.com Stakes (Newmarket)	*John Crofts*	124
Prince's Trust Shergar Cup Distaff (Rated Handicap) (Ascot)	*W. Everitt*	1075
Prix Daniel Wildenstein Casino Barriere La Rochelle (Longchamp)	*John Crofts*	182

Prix d'Astarte (Deauville)	*John Crofts*	621
Prix de Cabourg (Deauville)	*Bertrand*	567
Prix de Conde (Longchamp)	*Bertrand*	689
Prix de Diane Hermes (Chantilly)	*John Crofts*	563
Prix de l'Abbaye de Longchamp Majestic Barriere (Longchamp)	*Bertrand*	1086
Prix de la Foret (Longchamp)	*John Crofts*	964
Prix de l'Arc de Triomphe Lucien Barriere (Longchamp)	*Bertrand*	113
Prix de l'Opera Casino Barriere d'Enghien Les Bains (Longchamp)	*Bertrand*	44
Prix de Royallieu Hotel du Golf Barriere (Longchamp)	*Bertrand*	903
Prix de Saint-Georges (Longchamp)	*Ed Byrne*	1038
Prix d'Ispahan (Longchamp)	*John Crofts*	819
Prix du Cadran Casino Les Princes Barriere de Cannes (Longchamp)	*John Crofts*	1109
Prix du Gros-Chene (Chantilly)	*Ed Byrne*	100
Prix du Haras de Fresnay-Le-Buffard Jacques le Marois (Deauville)	*Bertrand*	1114
Prix du Jockey Club (Chantilly)	*John Crofts*	152
Prix Ganay (Longchamp)	*Bertrand*	352
Prix Guillaume d'Ornano (Deauville)	*John Crofts*	659
Prix Jean-Luc Lagardere (Grand Criterium) (Longchamp)	*Bertrand*	742
Prix Jean Prat (Chantilly)	*Bertrand*	111
Prix Kergorlay (Deauville)	*John Crofts*	423
Prix La Rochette (Longchamp)	*Bertrand*	325
Prix Lupin (Longchamp)	*John Crofts*	1096
Prix Marcel Boussac-Criterium des Pouliches Royal Barriere de Deauville (Longchamp)	*George Selwyn*	296
Prix Maurice de Gheest (Deauville)	*Bertrand*	963
Prix Morny Casinos Barriere (Deauville)	*Bertrand*	295
Prix Niel Casino Barriere d'Enghien Les Bains (Longchamp)	*Bertrand*	1083
Prix Royal-Oak (Longchamp)	*John Crofts*	1110
Prix Saint-Alary (Longchamp)	*Bertrand*	85
Prix Vermeille Fouquet's Barriere (Longchamp)	*Bertrand*	1008
Queen Alexandra Stakes (Royal Ascot)	*Alec Russell*	240
Queen Anne Stakes (Royal Ascot)	*Alec Russell*	855
Queen Elizabeth II Stakes (sponsored by NetJets) (Ascot)	*John Crofts*	841
Queen Mary Stakes (Royal Ascot)	*Alec Russell*	261
Queen's Vase (Royal Ascot)	*John Crofts*	321
Racing Post Trophy (Doncaster)	*Alec Russell*	675
Rheinland-Pokal der Stadtsparkasse Koln (Cologne)	*Frank Sorge*	39
Ribblesdale Stakes (Royal Ascot)	*John Crofts*	826
Richmond Stakes (Goodwood)	*John Crofts*	667
Ridgewood Pearl Stakes (the Curragh)	*Bill Selwyn*	969
Rolls-Royce Motor Cars London Darley Stakes (Newmarket)	*George Selwyn*	99
Royal Hunt Cup (Handicap) (Royal Ascot)	*John Crofts*	648
Sandringham Rated Stakes (Handicap) (Royal Ascot)	*John Crofts*	202
Saval Beg Stakes (Leopardstown)	*Peter Mooney*	1121
Scottish Equitable Gimcrack Stakes (York)	*Alec Russell*	1053
SGB Champagne Stakes (Doncaster)	*Ed Byrne*	347
Shadwell Stud Middle Park Stakes (Newmarket)	*John Crofts*	31
Shadwell Stud Nell Gwyn Stakes (Newmarket)	*John Crofts*	941
Sky Bet Cheveley Park Stakes (Newmarket)	*Ed Byrne*	606
Slatch Farm Stud Flying Fillies' Stakes (Pontefract)	*Alec Russell*	422
sportingoptions.co.uk (Betting Exchange) Strensall Stakes (York)	*Alec Russell*	849
Stan James Geoffrey Freer Stakes (Newbury)	*John Crofts*	684
Stan James Horris Hill Stakes (Newbury)	*John Crofts*	254
stanleybet.com Old Borough Cup Stakes (Handicap) (Haydock)	*Alec Russell*	279
Stanleybet Diamond Stakes (the Curragh)	*Caroline Norris*	643
Stanleybet Robert Sangster Superior Mile (Haydock)	*Alec Russell*	1124
Stanleybet Sprint Cup (Haydock)	*Alec Russell*	1019
Sterling Insurance Summer Stakes (Handicap) (Goodwood)	*John Crofts*	228
St James Security Classified Stakes (Carlisle)	*John Grossick*	626
St James's Palace Stakes (Royal Ascot)	*Alec Russell*	102
Tatler Summer Season Stakes (Handicap) (Goodwood)	*John Crofts*	637
Tattersalls Gold Cup (the Curragh)	*Bill Selwyn*	811
Tattersalls Ireland Sale Stakes (the Curragh)	*Peter Mooney*	132
Tattersalls Musidora Stakes (York)	*Ed Byrne*	826

TNT July Stakes (Newmarket)	*John Crofts*	191
totejackpot On Saturday Stakes (Handicap) (Ascot)	*Ed Byrne*	532
totepool Mallard Stakes (Handicap) (Doncaster)	*John Crofts*	591
totescoop6 Stakes (Handicap) (Sandown)	*John Crofts*	776
totescoop6 Wentworth Stakes (Doncaster)	*Alec Russell*	836
totesport Ayr Gold Cup (Handicap) (Ayr)	*Alec Russell*	398
totesport Ayr Silver Cup (Handicap) (Ayr)	*Alec Russell*	332
totesport Cambridgeshire (Handicap) (Newmarket)	*Ed Byrne*	975
totesport Celebration Mile (Goodwood)	*George Selwyn*	216
totesport Cesarewitch (Handicap) (Newmarket)	*John Crofts*	237
totesport Chester Cup (Handicap) (Chester)	*Bill Selwyn*	63
totesport Dante Stakes (York)	*John Crofts*	717
totesport Ebor (Handicap) (York)	*George Selwyn*	638
totesport International Stakes (Handicap) (Ascot)	*John Crofts*	245
totesport Portland (Handicap) (Doncaster)	*John Crofts*	452
totesport Rated Stakes (Handicap) (Newmarket)	*George Selwyn*	42
totesport Silver Bowl (Handicap) (Haydock)	*Alec Russell*	409
totesport Sovereign Stakes (Salisbury)	*Mirrorpix*	714
totesport Stakes (Handicap) (Ascot)	*George Selwyn*	302
totesport Stakes (Handicap) (Haydock)	*Alec Russell*	322
totesport Zetland Gold Cup (Handicap) (Redcar)	*Alec Russell*	157
TSG Firth of Clyde Stakes (Ayr)	*Alec Russell*	420
£200000 St Leger Yearling Stakes (Doncaster)	*John Crofts*	183
UAE Equestrian and Racing Federation Falmouth Stakes (Newmarket)	*John Crofts*	970
UltimateBet.com 1000 Guineas Stakes (Newmarket)	*Ed Byrne*	91
UltimateBet.com 2000 Guineas Stakes (Newmarket)	*Ed Byrne*	446
Veuve Clicquot Vintage Stakes (Goodwood)	*John Crofts*	926
Victor Chandler Challenge Stakes (Newmarket)	*Alec Russell*	372
Victor Chandler Nunthorpe Stakes (York)	*Ed Byrne*	116
Vodafone Coronation Cup (Epsom)	*Alec Russell*	1101
Vodafone 'Dash' Stakes (Handicap) (Epsom)	*Bill Selwyn*	193
Vodafone Derby Stakes (Epsom)	*Ed Byrne*	719
Vodafone Derby Stakes (Epsom)	*John Crofts*	720
Vodafone Derby Stakes (Epsom)	*W. Everitt*	721
Vodafone Diomed Stakes (Epsom)	*Alec Russell*	768
Vodafone Live! Stakes (Handicap) (Epsom)	*Alec Russell*	590
Vodafone Nassau Stakes (Goodwood)	*Bill Selwyn*	362
Vodafone Oaks (Epsom)	*Ed Byrne*	747
Vodafone Stewards' Cup (Handicap) (Goodwood)	*John Crofts*	792
Vodafone Temple Stakes (Epsom)	*Bill Selwyn*	709
VO5 Breeders' Cup Filly & Mare Turf (Lone Star Park)	*George Selwyn*	750
Watership Down Stud Sales Race (Newbury)	*Ed Byrne*	900
Weatherbys Bank Stakes (Doonside Cup) (Ayr)	*Alec Russell*	501
Weatherbys Earl of Sefton Stakes (Newmarket)	*John Crofts*	407
Weatherbys Insurance Lonsdale Cup (York)	*John Crofts*	374
Weatherbys Ireland Greenlands Stakes (the Curragh)	*Caroline Norris*	1033
William Hill Great St Wilfrid Stakes (Handicap) (Ripon)	*Alec Russell*	954
William Hill Mile (Handicap) (Goodwood)	*John Crofts*	64
William Hill Trophy (Handicap) (York)	*Alec Russell*	1074
Windsor Forest Stakes (Royal Ascot)	*John Crofts*	361
Wokingham Stakes (Handicap) (Royal Ascot)	*Alec Russell*	556
Wolferton Rated Stakes (Handicap) (Ascot)	*Alec Russell*	850

grey 1999
by IN THE WINGS
- SUMMER SONNET
by Baillamont

ACT ONE

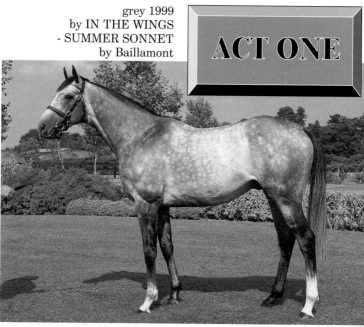

GROUP 1 WINNER AT 2 AND 3

RACE RECORD

WON	Gr.1	Criterium International, Saint-Cloud, 8f
WON	Gr.1	Prix Lupin, Longchamp, 10½f
WON	Gr.2	Prix Greffulhe, Longchamp, 10½f
WON	Gr.3	Prix Thomas Bryon, Saint-Cloud, 8f
WON		Prix du Val Profond, Chantilly, 8f
2nd	Gr.1	Prix du Jockey Club, Chantilly, 12f, beaten 1½l
		by SULAMANI, and *5l clear of the third*

Highest Rated French-trained Two Year Old   Timeform: **124**

FIRST YEARLINGS IN 2005

Standing at:

Nunnery Stud

Fee: £10,000 October 1st

The Nunnery Stud
Shadwell, Thetford
Norfolk IP24 2QE
Telephone: 01842 755913
Fax: 01842 755189

LTS

Enquiries to:
LONDON THOROUGHBRED
SERVICES LTD.,
Biddlesgate Farm, Nr Cranborne,
Dorset BH21 5RS.
Tele: 01725 - 517711.
Fax: 01725 - 517833.
email: lts@lts-uk.com
Website: www.lts-uk.com

chesnut 1994
by INDIAN RIDGE
- NOSEY by Nebbiolo

COMPTON PLACE

CHAMPION EUROPEAN 3-Y-O SPRINTER

LEADING BRITISH-BASED SIRE OF 2YO.S IN 2004
(winners / runners)

FREE OF NORTHERN DANCER BLOOD

Standing at:
Whitsbury Manor Stud
Fee: £5,000 October 1st
Limited to 90 Mares

C. Oakshott,
Whitsbury Manor Stud,
Fordingbridge, SP6 3QP
Telephone: 01725 - 518254
Fax: 01725 - 518503

LTS

Enquiries to:
LONDON THOROUGHBRED
SERVICES LTD.,
Biddlesgate Farm, Nr Cranborne,
Dorset BH21 5RS.
Telephone: 01725 - 517711.
Fax: 01725 - 517833.
email: lts@lts-uk.com
Website: www.lts-uk.com

bay 1998
by DARSHAAN
- GARAH by Ajdal

OLDEN TIMES

GR.1 WINNING SON OF DARSHAAN

defeated 3 Classic Winners and
13 other Gr.1 Winners

Performed consistently at the highest level from **8F - 10F**

Timeform Racehorses of 2002 - Rated 121

A SPEEDY SON OF DARSHAAN
FOR YOUR NORTHERN DANCER LINE MARES

FIRST FOALS 2005

bay 1989
by GROOM DANCER
- DANCE QUEST
by Green Dancer

PURSUIT OF LOVE

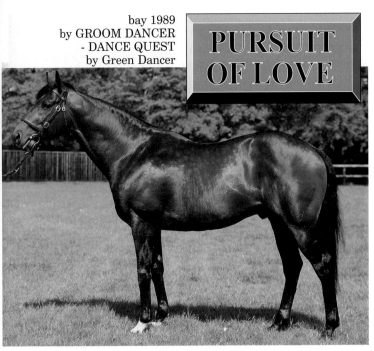

SIRE OF THE WINNERS OF
616 RACES and OVER £6.3 million
and 61% winners to runners

In 2004
TWO STAKES-WINNING 2-Y-O.s
CUPID'S GLORY (Horris Hill S, **Gr.3**) and **LASIKA**
and multiple winners **JUSTAQUESTION**
and **TARTOUCHE**

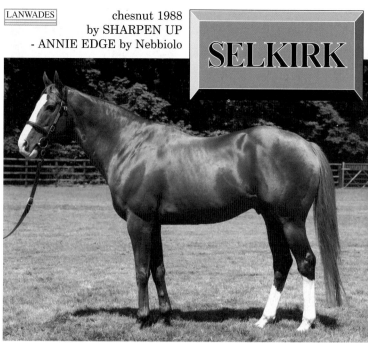

brown 1994
by FORZANDO
- DEVIL'S DIRGE by Song

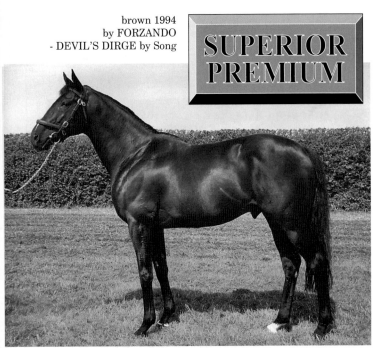

SUPERIOR PREMIUM

ROYAL ASCOT GR.2 WINNING SPRINTER

By **FORZANDO** - Prolific Sire of winners including
**EASYCALL (Sire), GREAT DEEDS, HIGH PREMIUM,
MISTERIOSO, PHILIDOR (Sire), POOL MUSIC,
PUNCH N'RUN, UP AND AT 'EM (Sire),
VINTAGE PREMIUM, ZANAY**

GROUP WINNING SON OF A LEADING 2-Y-O SIRE

FIRST 2.Y.O's IN 2005

Standing at:
Throckmorton Court Stud
Fee: £2,000 October 1st

Peter Balding,
Throckmorton Court Stud,
Throckmorton, Nr. Pershore,
Worcestershire WR10 2JX
Telephone: 01386 - 462559
Fax: 01386 - 462566

LTS

Enquiries to:
LONDON THOROUGHBRED
SERVICES LTD.,
Biddlesgate Farm, Nr Cranborne,
Dorset BH21 5RS.
Telephone: 01725 - 517711
Fax: 01725 - 517833
email: lts@lts-uk.com
Website: www.lts-uk.com

THE CHAMPIONS

Timeform's 'Racehorses' series stretches back to 1948 when the first prototype Annual—the 'Timeform Supplement'—was produced covering the 1947 season. The selecting of a 'horse of the year' began in the 'sixties.

Horse of the Year

The title has usually been awarded to the highest rated horse, except in 1969 (when Habitat was rated higher at 134), 1984 (El Gran Senor 136), 1985 (Slip Anchor 136) and 2003 (Hawk Wing 136).

1960	Charlottesville	**135**
	Floribunda	**135**
1961	Molvedo	**137**
1962	Match	**135**
1963	Exbury	**138**
1964	Relko	**136**
1965	Sea Bird	**145**
1966	Danseur	**134**
1967	Petingo	**135**
1968	Vaguely Noble	**140**
1969	Levmoss	**133**
1970	Nijinsky	**138**
1971	Brigadier Gerard	**141**
	Mill Reef	**141**
1972	Brigadier Gerard	**144**
1973	Apalachee	**137**
	Rheingold	**137**
1974	Allez France	**136**
1975	Grundy	**137**
1976	Youth	**135**
1977	Alleged	**137**
1978	Alleged	**138**
1979	Troy	**137**
1980	Moorestyle	**137**
1981	Shergar	**140**
1982	Ardross	**134**
1983	Habibti	**136**
1984	Provideo	**112**

1985	Pebbles	**135**
1986	Dancing Brave	**140**
1987	Reference Point	**139**
1988	Warning	**136**
1989	Zilzal	**137**
1990	Dayjur	**137**
1991	Generous	**139**
1992	St Jovite	**135**
1993	Opera House	**131**
1994	Celtic Swing	**138**
1995	Lammtarra	**134**
1996	Mark of Esteem	**137**
1997	Peintre Celebre	**137**
1998	Intikhab	**135**
1999	Daylami	**138**
2000	Dubai Millennium	**140**
2001	Sakhee	**136**
2002	Rock of Gibraltar	**133**
2003	Falbrav	**133**
2004	Doyen	**132**

Best Two-Year-Old Colt

1960	Floribunda	**135**	1982	Diesis	**133**
1961	Abdos	**134 p**	1983	El Gran Senor	**131**
1962	Le Mesnil	**131 ?**	1984	Kala Dancer	**129**
1963	Santa Claus	**133 +**	1985	Huntingdale	**132**
	Showdown	**133**	1986	Reference Point	**132**
1964	Grey Dawn	**132**	1987	Warning	**127 p**
1965	Soleil	**133**	1988	Prince of Dance	**128**
	Young Emperor	**133**		Scenic	**128**
1966	Bold Lad (Ire)	**133**	1989	Be My Chief	**123 p**
1967	Petingo	**135**	1990	Hector Protector	**122 p**
1968	Ribofilio	**130**	1991	Arazi	**135**
	Yelapa	**130**	1992	Armiger	**131 p**
1969	Nijinsky	**131**	1993	Grand Lodge	**120 p**
1970	My Swallow	**134**	1994	Celtic Swing	**138**
1971	Deep Diver	**134**	1995	Alhaarth	**126 p**
1972	Simbir	**130**	1996	Bahhare	**122 p**
	Targowice	**130**		Revoque	**122 p**
1973	Apalachee	**137**	1997	Xaar	**132**
1974	Grundy	**134**	1998	Mujahid	**125 p**
1975	Manado	**130**	1999	Distant Music	**121 p**
1976	Blushing Groom	**131**	2000	Nayef	**123 p**
1977	Try My Best	**130 p**	2001	Johannesburg	**127**
1978	Tromos	**134**	2002	Oasis Dream	**122**
1979	Monteverdi	**129**	2003	Bago	**121 p**
1980	Storm Bird	**134**	2004	Shamardal	**126p**
1981	Wind And Wuthering	**132**			

Best Two-Year-Old Filly

Year	Horse	Rating	Year	Horse	Rating
1960	Kathy Too	131	1984	Triptych	125
1961	La Tendresse	135	1985	Femme Elite	124
1962	Hula Dancer	133	1986	Forest Flower	127
1963	Texanita	128	1987	Ravinella	121 p
1964	Fall In Love	126	1988	Pass The Peace	116 p
1965	Soft Angels	124		Tessla	116 p
1966	Silver Cloud	125	1989	Negligent	118 p
1967	Sovereign	129	1990	Shadayid	117 p
1968	Saraca	125	1991	Midnight Air	111 p
1969	Mange Tout	125	1992	Sayyedati	116 p
1970	Cawston's Pride	131	1993	Lemon Souffle	115
1971	First Bloom	129	1994	Gay Gallanta	112
1972	Jacinth	133	1995	Blue Duster	116 p
1973	Hippodamia	130	1996	Dazzle	116 d
1974	Broadway Dancer	131		Red Camellia	116
1975	Theia	128	1997	Embassy	114
1976	Cloonlara	130	1998	Bint Allayl	114 p
1977	Cherry Hinton	125	1999	Morning Pride	113 p
1978	Sigy	132	2000	Superstar Leo	114
1979	Aryenne	120	2001	Queen's Logic	125
1980	Marwell	124	2002	Six Perfections	120 p
1981	Circus Ring	122	2003	Attraction	118
1982	Ma Biche	123	2004	Divine Proportions	119
1983	Treizieme	121			

Best Sprinter

Year	Horse	Rating	Year	Horse	Rating
1960	Bleep Bleep	134	1981	Marwell	133
1961	Floribunda	136	1982	Sharpo	130
1962	Gay Mairi	131	1983	Habibti	136
	Secret Step	131	1984	Chief Singer	131
1963	Matatina	132	1985	Never So Bold	135
1964	Althrey Don	130	1986	Last Tycoon	131
1965	Majority Blue	126	1987	Ajdal	130
	Port Merion	126	1988	Soviet Star	128
1966	Caterina	124	1989	Cadeaux Genereux	131
1967	Be Friendly	126	1990	Dayjur	137
1968	Be Friendly	130	1991	Polish Patriot	128
	So Blessed	130	1992	Sheikh Albadou	128
1969	Song	132	1993	Lochsong	129
1970	Amber Rama	133	1994	Lochsong	129
	Balidar	133	1995	Lake Coniston	131
	Huntercombe	133	1996	Anabaa	130
1971	Joshua	129	1997	Elnadim	126 p
1972	Deep Diver	134	1998	Elnadim	128
1973	Sandford Lad	133	1999	Stravinsky	133
1974	Saritamer	130	2000	Namid	128
1975	Flirting Around	134	2001	Mozart	131
1976	Lochnager	132	2002	Kyllachy	129
1977	Gentilhombre	131	2003	Oasis Dream	129
1978	Solinus	130	2004	Somnus	126
1979	Thatching	131		Tante Rose	126
1980	Moorestyle	137			

Best Miler

Year	Horse	Rating	Year	Horse	Rating
1960	Martial	131	1970	Nijinsky	138
1961	Petite Etoile	131	1971	Brigadier Gerard	141
1962	Romulus	129	1972	Brigadier Gerard	144
1963	Hula Dancer	133	1973	Thatch	136
1964	Baldric	131	1974	Nonoalco	131
1965	Carlemont	132	1975	Bolkonski	134
1966	Silver Shark	129	1976	Wollow	132
1967	Reform	132	1977	Blushing Groom	131
1968	Sir Ivor	135	1978	Homing	130
1969	Habitat	134	1979	Kris	135

Year	Horse	Rating		Year	Horse	Rating
1980	Known Fact	135		1993	Zafonic	130
1981	Northjet	136		1994	Barathea	127
1982	Green Forest	134		1995	Pennekamp	130
1983	Luth Enchantee	130		1996	Mark of Esteem	137
1984	El Gran Senor	136		1997	Spinning World	130
1985	Shadeed	135		1998	Intikhab	135
1986	Dancing Brave	140		1999	Dubai Millennium	132
1987	Miesque	131		2000	King's Best	132
1988	Warning	136		2001	Medicean	128
1989	Zilzal	137			Slickly	128
1990	Markofdistinction	130		2002	Rock of Gibraltar	133
	Royal Academy	130		2003	Hawk Wing	136
1991	Selkirk	129		2004	Haafhd	129
1992	Lahib	129			Rakti	129
	Selkirk	129				

Best Middle-Distance Horse

Year	Horse	Rating		Year	Horse	Rating
1960	Charlottesville	135			Teenoso	135
1961	Molvedo	137		1985	Slip Anchor	136
1962	Match	135		1986	Dancing Brave	140
1963	Exbury	138		1987	Reference Point	139
1964	Relko	136		1988	Mtoto	134
1965	Sea Bird	145			Tony Bin	134
1966	Nelcius	133		1989	Old Vic	136
1967	Busted	134		1990	Saumarez	132
1968	Vaguely Noble	140		1991	Generous	139
1969	Levmoss	133		1992	St Jovite	135
1970	Nijinsky	138		1993	Opera House	131
1971	Mill Reef	141		1994	Balanchine	131
1972	Mill Reef	141		1995	Lammtarra	134
1973	Rheingold	137		1996	Helissio	136
1974	Allez France	136		1997	Peintre Celebre	137
1975	Grundy	137		1998	Swain	132
1976	Youth	135		1999	Daylami	138
1977	Alleged	137		2000	Dubai Millennium	140
1978	Alleged	138		2001	Sakhee	136
1979	Troy	137		2002	High Chaparral	130
1980	Argument	133			Sulamani	130
1981	Shergar	140		2003	Alamshar	133
1982	Ardross	134			Dalakhani	133
	Assert	134			Falbrav	133
1983	Shareef Dancer	135		2004	Doyen	132
1984	Sagace	135				

Best Stayer/Best Performance In A Staying Race

Year	Horse	Rating		Year	Horse	Rating
1960	Charlottesville	135		1978	Buckskin	133
1961	Pandofell	132		1979	Buckskin	131
	St Paddy	132			Le Moss	131
1962	Hethersett	134		1980	Le Moss	135
1963	Ragusa	137		1981	Ardross	131
1964	Prince Royal	134		1982	Ardross	134
1965	Reliance	137		1983	Little Wolf	127
1966	Danseur	134		1984	Commanche Run	129
1967	Ribocco	129		1985	Lanfranco	123
1968	Dhaudevi	127			Phardante	123
	Samos	127		1986	Moon Madness	128
1969	Levmoss	133		1987	Reference Point	139
1970	Hallez	130		1988	Minster Son	130
	Roll of Honour	130		1989	Michelozzo	127 p
1971	Ramsin	130		1990	Snurge	130
1972	Rock Roi	127		1991	Toulon	125
1973	Parnell	130		1992	Mashaallah	123
1974	Sagaro	131		1993	Vintage Crop	125
1975	Bruni	132		1994	Moonax	121
1976	Crow	131 *			Vintage Crop	121
1977	Alleged	135 *		1995	Double Trigger	122

	Moonax	**122**	1999	Kayf Tara	**130**
	Strategic Choice	**122**	2000	Kayf Tara	**130**
1996	Classic Cliche	**124** *	2001	Milan	**129**
	Oscar Schindler	**124** *	2002	Vinnie Roe	**126**
	Shantou	**124**	2003	Vinnie Roe	**125**
1997	Classic Cliche	**126**	2004	Vinnie Roe	**128**
1998	Kayf Tara	**126**			

achieved higher rating at middle distances

Best Three-Year-Old Colt

1960	Charlottesville	**135**	1981	Shergar	**140**
1961	Molvedo	**137**	1982	Assert	**134**
1962	Arctic Storm	**134**		Green Forest	**134**
	Hethersett	**134**	1983	Shareef Dancer	**135**
1963	Ragusa	**137**	1984	El Gran Senor	**136**
1964	Prince Royal	**134**	1985	Slip Anchor	**136**
1965	Sea Bird	**145**	1986	Dancing Brave	**140**
1966	Danseur	**134**	1987	Reference Point	**139**
1967	Reform	**132**	1988	Warning	**136**
1968	Vaguely Noble	**140**	1989	Zilzal	**137**
1969	Habitat	**134**	1990	Dayjur	**137**
1970	Nijinsky	**138**	1991	Generous	**139**
1971	Brigadier Gerard	**141**	1992	St Jovite	**135**
	Mill Reef	**141**	1993	Zafonic	**130**
1972	Deep Diver	**134**	1994	Tikkanen	**130**
	Sallust	**134**	1995	Lammtarra	**134**
1973	Thatch	**136**	1996	Mark of Esteem	**137**
1974	Caracolero	**131**	1997	Peintre Celebre	**137**
	Dankaro	**131**	1998	Desert Prince	**130**
	Nonoalco	**131**		High-Rise	**130**
	Sagaro	**131**	1999	Montjeu	**137**
1975	Grundy	**137**	2000	Sinndar	**134**
1976	Youth	**135**	2001	Galileo	**134**
1977	Alleged	**137**	2002	Rock of Gibraltar	**133**
1978	Ile de Bourbon	**133**	2003	Alamshar	**133**
1979	Troy	**137**		Dalakhani	**133**
1980	Moorestyle	**137**	2004	Bago	**130**

Best Three-Year-Old Filly

1960	Marguerite Vernaut	**129**	1982	Akiyda	**131**
1961	Crisper	**127**		Time Charter	**131**
	Sweet Solera	**127**	1983	Habibti	**136**
1962	Gay Mairi	**131**	1984	Northern Trick	**131**
	Secret Step	**131**	1985	Oh So Sharp	**131**
1963	Hula Dancer	**133**	1986	Darara	**129**
	Noblesse	**133**		Sonic Lady	**129**
1964	La Bamba	**129**	1987	Indian Skimmer	**132**
1965	Aunt Edith	**128**	1988	Diminuendo	**126**
1966	Caterina	**124**	1989	Behera	**129**
1967	Casaque Grise	**126**		Sierra Roberta	**129**
1968	Roseliere	**127**	1990	Salsabil	**130**
1969	Flossy	**129**	1991	Magic Night	**128**
1970	Highest Hopes	**129**	1992	User Friendly	**128**
	Miss Dan	**129**	1993	Intrepidity	**124**
1971	Pistol Packer	**133**	1994	Balanchine	**131**
1972	San San	**133**	1995	Ridgewood Pearl	**125**
1973	Allez France	**132**	1996	Bosra Sham	**132**
	Dahlia	**132**	1997	Borgia	**124**
1974	Comtesse de Loir	**131**	1998	Cape Verdi	**126**
1975	Rose Bowl	**133**	1999	Ramruma	**123**
1976	Pawneese	**131**	2000	Egyptband	**128**
1977	Dunfermline	**133**	2001	Banks Hill	**128**
1978	Swiss Maid	**129**	2002	Bright Sky	**124**
1979	Three Troikas	**133**	2003	Six Perfections	**124**
1980	Detroit	**131**	2004	Attraction	**125**
1981	Marwell	**133**		Ouija Board	**125**

Best Older Male

Year	Horse	Rating	Year	Horse	Rating
1960	Bleep-Bleep	134	1983	Diamond Shoal	130
1961	Pandofell	132	1984	Sagace	134
	St Paddy	132		Teenoso	134
1962	Match	135	1985	Rainbow Quest	134
1963	Exbury	138		Sagace	134
1964	Relko	136	1986	Shardari	134
1965	Free Ride	129	1987	Mtoto	134
	Indiana	129	1988	Mtoto	134
1966	Diatome	132		Tony Bin	134
1967	Busted	134	1989	Carroll House	132
1968	Royal Palace	131	1990	Markofdistinction	130
1969	Levmoss	133		Old Vic	130
1970	Balidar	133	1991	Epervier Bleu	129
1971	Caro	133	1992	Pistolet Bleu	133
1972	Brigadier Gerard	144	1993	Opera House	131
1973	Rheingold	137	1994	Barathea	127
1974	Admetus	133		Hernando	127
	Margouillat	133	1995	Freedom Cry	132
1975	Bustino	136	1996	Halling	133
1976	Trepan	133 ?	1997	Pilsudski	134
	Lochnager	132		Swain	134
1977	Balmerino	133	1998	Intikhab	135
	Sagaro	133	1999	Daylami	138
1978	Alleged	138	2000	Dubai Millennium	140
1979	Ile de Bourbon	133	2001	Sakhee	136
1980	Le Moss	135	2002	Keltos	132
1981	Northjet	136	2003	Hawk Wing	136
1982	Ardross	134	2004	Doyen	132

Best Older Female

Year	Horse	Rating	Year	Horse	Rating
1960	Petite Etoile	134	1988	Indian Skimmer	133
1961	Petite Etoile	131		Miesque	133
1962	Crisper	126	1989	Gabina	121
1963	Secret Step	128		Indian Skimmer	121
1964	Matatina	124		Royal Touch	121
1965	Astaria	123	1990	Lady Winner	121
1966	Aunt Edith	126		Ode	121
1967	Parthian Glance	119	1991	Miss Alleged	125
1968	Bamboozle	114	1992	Kooyonga	125
	Park Top	114	1993	Lochsong	129
	Secret Ray	114	1994	Lochsong	129
1969	Park Top	131	1995	Hever Golf Rose	123
1970	Park Top	129	1996	Timarida	125
1971	Miss Dan	124	1997	Bosra Sham	130
1972	Abergwaun	128	1998	One So Wonderful	121
1973	Attica Meli	125		Seeking The Pearl	121
1974	Allez France	136	1999	Alborada	122
1975	Lianga	133		Susu	122
1976	Ivanjica	132	2000	Shiva	127
1977	Flying Water	132	2001	Pipalong	121
1978	Sanedtki	129	2002	Banks Hill	126
	Trillion	129	2003	Islington	124
1979	Trillion	124	2004	Soviet Song	126
1980	Three Troikas	128		Tante Rose	126
1981	Gold River	132			
1982	April Run	130			
1983	All Along	134			
1984	Cormorant Wood	130			
1985	Pebbles	135			
1986	Triptych	132			
1987	Triptych	133			

AGE, WEIGHT & DISTANCE TABLE

Timeform's scale of weight-for-age for the flat

Dist	Age	July 1-16	17-31	Aug 1-16	17-31	Sept 1-16	17-30	Oct 1-16	17-31	Nov 1-16	17-30	Dec 1-16	17-31
5f	4	10-0	10-0	10-0	10-0	10-0	10-0	10-0	10-0	10-0	10-0	10-0	10-0
	3	9-11	9-12	9-12	9-12	9-13	9-13	9-13	9-13	10-0	10-0	10-0	10-0
	2	8-8	8-9	8-10	8-11	8-12	8-13	9-0	9-1	9-2	9-2	9-3	9-4
6f	4	10-0	10-0	10-0	10-0	10-0	10-0	10-0	10-0	10-0	10-0	10-0	10-0
	3	9-10	9-10	9-11	9-11	9-12	9-12	9-12	9-13	9-13	9-13	9-13	10-0
	2	8-5	8-6	8-7	8-8	8-9	8-10	8-11	8-12	8-13	9-0	9-1	9-2
7f	4	10-0	10-0	10-0	10-0	10-0	10-0	10-0	10-0	10-0	10-0	10-0	10-0
	3	9-9	9-9	9-10	9-10	9-11	9-11	9-11	9-12	9-12	9-12	9-13	9-13
	2	8-2	8-3	8-4	8-5	8-6	8-7	8-9	8-10	8-11	8-12	8-13	9-0
1m	4	10-0	10-0	10-0	10-0	10-0	10-0	10-0	10-0	10-0	10-0	10-0	10-0
	3	9-7	9-8	9-8	9-9	9-9	9-10	9-10	9-11	9-11	9-12	9-12	9-12
	2			8-2	8-3	8-4	8-5	8-6	8-7	8-8	8-9	8-10	8-11
9f	4	10-0	10-0	10-0	10-0	10-0	10-0	10-0	10-0	10-0	10-0	10-0	10-0
	3	9-6	9-7	9-7	9-8	9-8	9-9	9-9	9-10	9-10	9-11	9-11	9-12
	2					8-1	8-3	8-4	8-5	8-6	8-7	8-8	8-9
1¼m	4	10-0	10-0	10-0	10-0	10-0	10-0	10-0	10-0	10-0	10-0	10-0	10-0
	3	9-5	9-5	9-6	9-7	9-7	9-8	9-8	9-9	9-9	9-10	9-10	9-11
	2					8-0		8-1	8-2	8-4	8-5	8-6	8-7
11f	4	10-0	10-0	10-0	10-0	10-0	10-0	10-0	10-0	10-0	10-0	10-0	10-0
	3	9-3	9-4	9-5	9-5	9-6	9-7	9-7	9-8	9-8	9-9	9-9	9-10
1½m	4	10-0	10-0	10-0	10-0	10-0	10-0	10-0	10-0	10-0	10-0	10-0	10-0
	3	9-2	9-2	9-3	9-4	9-5	9-5	9-6	9-7	9-7	9-8	9-9	9-9
13f	4	9-13	9-13	10-0	10-0	10-0	10-0	10-0	10-0	10-0	10-0	10-0	10-0
	3	9-0	9-1	9-2	9-3	9-4	9-4	9-5	9-6	9-6	9-7	9-8	9-8
1¾m	4	9-13	9-13	9-13	10-0	10-0	10-0	10-0	10-0	10-0	10-0	10-0	10-0
	3	8-13	9-0	9-1	9-2	9-3	9-3	9-4	9-5	9-5	9-6	9-7	9-7
15f	4	9-12	9-13	9-13	9-13	9-13	10-0	10-0	10-0	10-0	10-0	10-0	10-0
	3	8-12	8-13	9-0	9-1	9-1	9-2	9-3	9-4	9-4	9-5	9-6	9-6
2m	4	9-12	9-12	9-13	9-13	9-13	9-13	10-0	10-0	10-0	10-0	10-0	10-0
	3	8-10	8-11	8-12	8-13	9-0	9-1	9-2	9-3	9-3	9-4	9-5	9-5
2¼m	4	9-11	9-12	9-12	9-12	9-13	9-13	9-13	9-13	10-0	10-0	10-0	10-0
	3	8-8	8-9	8-10	8-11	8-12	8-13	9-0	9-1	9-2	9-2	9-3	9-4
2½m	4	9-10	9-11	9-11	9-12	9-12	9-12	9-13	9-13	9-13	9-13	10-0	10-0
	3	8-6	8-7	8-8	8-9	8-10	8-11	8-12	8-13	9-0	9-1	9-2	9-3

For 5-y-o's and older, use 10-0 in all cases
Race distances in the above tables are shown only at 1 furlong intervals.
For races over odd distances, the nearest distance shown in the table should be used:
thus for races of 1m to 1m 109 yards, use the table weights for 1m;
for 1m 110 yards to 1m 219 yards use the 9f table

**The age, weight and distance table covering January to June
appears on the end paper at the front of the book**

THE BEST SIRES IN THE BUSINESS!

FORTY-TWO STALLIONS WERE REPRESENTED BY PROGENY IN THE TWO-YEAR-OLD EUROPEAN CLASSIFICATIONS. THE FOLLOWING SIRED TWO OR MORE.

NUMBER OF HORSES IN RATINGS

STALLION	No.	TOP PERFORMER	RATING
GIANT'S CAUSEWAY	4	SHAMARDAL	123
DANEHILL	3	ORATORIO	117
MONTJEU	3	MOTIVATOR	117
DANZIG	2	AD VALOREM	122
ENTREPRENEUR	2	BERENSON	116
GRAND LODGE	2	FRALOGA	113
SADLER'S WELLS	2	PLAYFUL ACT	113

STATISTICS FROM EBN, JAN. 19TH 2005.

COOLMORE

Contact: **Coolmore Stud**, Fethard, Co. Tipperary, Ireland. Tel: 353-52-31298. Fax: 353-52-31382.
Christy Grassick, David O'Loughlin, Eddie Fitzpatrick, Tim Corballis, Kevin Buckley, Maurice Moloney or **Stuart Fitzgibbon. Tom Gaffney, David Magnier** or **Joe Hernon**: 353-25-31966/31689.
E-mail: **sales@coolmore.ie**   Web site: **www.coolmore.com**